KEY TO WORLD MAP PAG

66
64
O EUROPE AND
OUNTRY INDEX
AR ENDPAPER
68
144
88
65
74
70
96
91
72
103
92
106
76
90
98
94
69
86
80
PACIFIC
OCEAN
134
78
133
95
120
84
87
82
118
121
132
133
79
121
124
126
133
16
133
INDIAN
OCEAN
121
121
128
130
131

PHILIP'S

ATLAS OF THE WORLD

COMPREHENSIVE EDITION

IN ASSOCIATION WITH

THE ROYAL GEOGRAPHICAL SOCIETY

WITH THE INSTITUTE OF BRITISH GEOGRAPHERS

Foreword

Philip's have been mapping the world since 1834. The *Atlas of the World* is the flagship of the Philip's range, an authoritative and serious reference work and one of the finest atlases available anywhere in the world. The atlas incorporates computer-derived maps which have been produced using the very latest in digital cartographic techniques.

Philip's Atlas of the World has been revised and updated with the help of a panel of specialist geography consultants from the United Kingdom and the United States, whose specialities range from the history of cartography, urban and social geography, epidemiology and the European Union to biogeography and applied geomorphology. The result of their valuable input can be seen in the wealth of up-to-date maps and data contained in the '*Introduction to World Geography*' section of this atlas.

Specialist Geography Consultants

Philip's are grateful to the following people for acting as specialist geography consultants on the '*Introduction to World Geography*' front section:

Professor D. Brunsden Kings College, University of London, UK
Dr C. Clarke Oxford University, UK
Professor P. Haggett University of Bristol, UK
Professor M-L. Hsu University of Minnesota, Minnesota, USA
Professor K. McLachlan Geopolitical and International Boundaries Research Centre, School of Oriental and African Studies, University of London, UK
Professor M. Monmonier Syracuse University, New York, USA
Professor M. J. Tooley University of St Andrews, UK
Dr T. Unwin Royal Holloway, University of London, UK

Philip's would also like to thank
Keith Lye
Robin Scagell
Dr I. S. Evans Durham University, UK
Dr Andrew Tatham The Royal Geographical Society

Philip's is proud to announce that its World Atlases are published in association with The Royal Geographical Society (with The Institute of British Geographers).

The Society was founded in 1830 and given a Royal Charter in 1859 for 'the advancement of geographical science'. It holds historical collections of national and international importance, many of which relate to the Society's association with and support for scientific exploration and research from the 19th century onwards. It was pivotal in establishing geography as a teaching and research discipline in British universities close to the turn of the century, and has played a key role in geographical and environmental education ever since.

Today the Society is a leading world centre for geographical learning – supporting education, teaching, research and expeditions, and promoting public understanding of the subject. The Society welcomes those interested in geography as members. For further information, please visit the website at: **www.rgs.org**

Acknowledgements

Images of Earth (pages ix–xxiv)
All satellite images in this section courtesy of NPA Group Limited, Edenbridge, Kent (www.satmaps.com)

Introduction to World Geography
Picture Acknowledgements
Courtesy of NPA Group, Edenbridge, UK 9, 48
Science Photo Library /Earth Satellite Corporation 20, /NOAA 22 bottom left and bottom right

Illustrations
Stefan Chabluk, William Donohoe, Bernard Thornton Artists /Steve Seymour

Star Charts
John Cox and Richard Monkhouse

Cartography by Philip's

City Maps
Page 11, Dublin. Based on Ordnance Survey Ireland by permission of the Government Permit No. 7338.
© Government of Ireland

Page 15, London. Based upon the Ordnance Survey Maps with the permission of the Controller of Her Majesty's Stationery Office. © Crown copyright 2001.
All rights reserved. Licence No. 339817

Vector data: Courtesy of Gräfe and Unser Verlag GmbH, München, Germany (city centre maps of Bangkok, Beijing, Cape Town, Jerusalem, Mexico City, Moscow, Singapore, Sydney, Tokyo and Washington D.C.)

Published in Great Britain in 2001 by George Philip Ltd, a division of Octopus Publishing Group Ltd, 2–4 Heron Quays, London E14 4JP

ISBN 0-540-08024-1

A CIP catalogue record for this book is available from the British Library.

Printed in Spain

Details of other Philip's titles and services can be found on our website at:
www.philips-maps.co.uk

PHILIP'S WORLD MAPS

The reference maps which form the main body of this atlas have been prepared in accordance with the highest standards of international cartography to provide an accurate and detailed representation of the Earth. The scales and projections used have been carefully chosen to give balanced coverage of the world, while emphasizing the most densely populated and economically significant regions. A hallmark of Philip's mapping is the use of hill shading and relief colouring to create a graphic impression of landforms: this makes the maps exceptionally easy to read. However, knowledge of the key features employed in the construction and presentation of the maps will enable the reader to derive the fullest benefit from the atlas.

MAP SEQUENCE

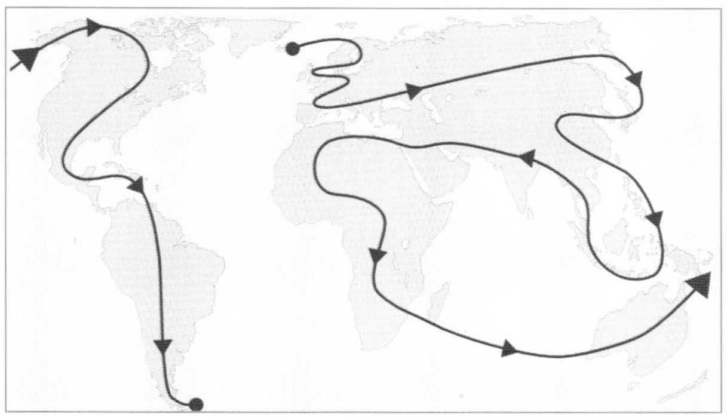

The atlas covers the Earth continent by continent: first Europe; then its land neighbour Asia (mapped north before south, in a clockwise sequence), then Africa, Australia and Oceania, North America and South America. This is the classic arrangement adopted by most cartographers since the 16th century. For each continent, there are maps at a variety of scales. First, physical relief and political maps of the whole continent; then a series of larger-scale maps of the regions within the continent, each followed, where required, by still larger-scale maps of the most important or densely populated areas. The governing principle is that by turning the pages of the atlas, the reader moves steadily from north to south through each continent, with each map overlapping its neighbours. A key map showing this sequence, and the area covered by each map, can be found on the endpapers of the atlas.

MAP PRESENTATION

With very few exceptions (e.g. for the Arctic and Antarctic), the maps are drawn with north at the top, regardless of whether they are presented upright or sideways on the page. In the borders will be found the map title; a locator diagram showing the area covered and the page numbers for maps of adjacent areas; the scale; the projection used; the degrees of latitude and longitude; and the letters and figures used in the index for locating place names and geographical features. Physical relief maps also have a height reference panel identifying the colours used for each layer of contouring.

MAP SYMBOLS

Each map contains a vast amount of detail which can only be conveyed clearly and accurately by the use of symbols. Points and circles of varying sizes locate and identify the relative importance of towns and cities; different styles of type are employed for administrative, geographical and regional place names to aid identification. A variety of pictorial symbols denote landforms such as glaciers, marshes and coral reefs, and man-made structures including roads, railways, airports and canals. International borders are shown by red lines. Where neighbouring countries are in dispute, for example in parts of the Middle East, the maps show the *de facto* boundary between nations, regardless of the legal or historical situation. The symbols are explained on the first page of the World Maps section of the atlas.

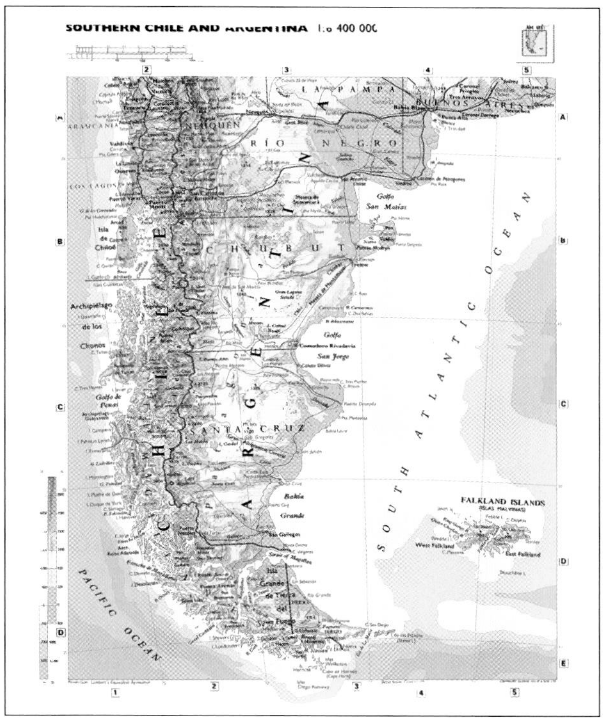

MAP SCALES

1:16 000 000
1 inch = 252 statute miles

The scale of each map is given in the numerical form known as the 'representative fraction'. The first figure is always one, signifying one unit of distance on the map; the second figure, usually in millions, is the number by which the map unit must be multiplied to give the equivalent distance on the Earth's surface. Calculations can easily be made in centimetres and kilometres, by dividing the Earth units figure by 100 000 (i.e. deleting the last five 0s). Thus 1:1 000 000 means 1 cm = 10 km. The calculation for inches and miles is more laborious, but 1 000 000 divided by 63 360 (the number of inches in a mile) shows that 1:1 000 000 means approximately 1 inch = 16 miles. The table below provides distance equivalents for scales down to 1:50 000 000.

LARGE SCALE		
1:1 000 000	1 cm = 10 km	1 inch = 16 miles
1:2 500 000	1 cm = 25 km	1 inch = 39.5 miles
1:5 000 000	1 cm = 50 km	1 inch = 79 miles
1:6 000 000	1 cm = 60 km	1 inch = 95 miles
1:8 000 000	1 cm = 80 km	1 inch = 126 miles
1:10 000 000	1 cm = 100 km	1 inch = 158 miles
1:15 000 000	1 cm = 150 km	1 inch = 237 miles
1:20 000 000	1 cm = 200 km	1 inch = 316 miles
1:50 000 000	1 cm = 500 km	1 inch = 790 miles
SMALL SCALE		

MEASURING DISTANCES

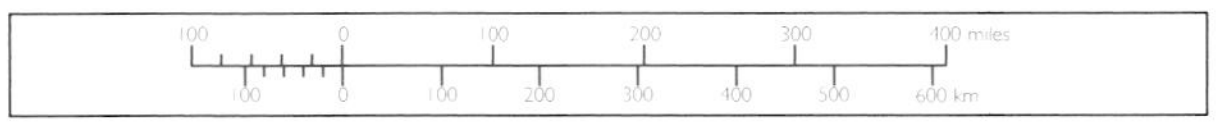

Although each map is accompanied by a scale bar, distances cannot always be measured with confidence because of the distortions involved in portraying the curved surface of the Earth on a flat page. As a general rule, the larger the map scale, the more accurate and reliable will be the distance measured. On small-scale maps such as those of the world and of entire continents, measurement may only be accurate along the 'standard parallels', or central axes, and should not be attempted without considering the map projection.

MAP PROJECTIONS

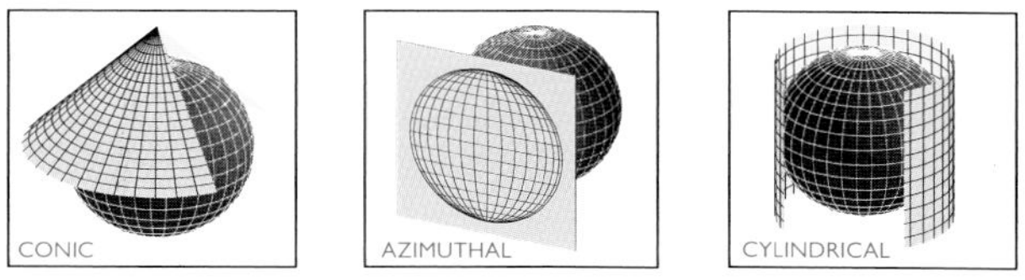

Unlike a globe, no flat map can give a true scale representation of the world in terms of area, shape and position of every region. Each of the numerous systems that have been devised for projecting the curved surface of the Earth on to a flat page involves the sacrifice of accuracy in one or more of these elements. The variations in shape and position of landmasses such as Alaska, Greenland and Australia, for example, can be quite dramatic when different projections are compared.

For this atlas, the guiding principle has been to select projections that involve the least distortion of size and distance. The projection used for each map is noted in the border. Most fall into one of three categories – conic, cylindrical or azimuthal – whose basic concepts are shown above. Each involves plotting the forms of the Earth's surface on a grid of latitude and longitude lines, which may be shown as parallels, curves or radiating spokes.

LATITUDE AND LONGITUDE

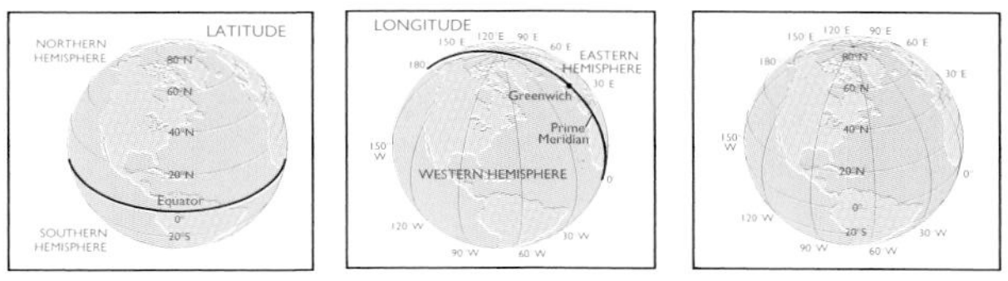

Accurate positioning of individual points on the Earth's surface is made possible by reference to the geometrical system of latitude and longitude. Latitude parallels are drawn west–east around the Earth and numbered by degrees north and south of the Equator, which is designated 0° of latitude. Longitude meridians are drawn north–south and numbered by degrees east and west of the prime meridian, 0° of longitude, which passes through Greenwich in England. By referring to these co-ordinates and their subdivisions of minutes (1/60th of a degree) and seconds (1/60th of a minute), any place on Earth can be located to within a few hundred metres. Latitude and longitude are indicated by blue lines on the maps; they are straight or curved according to the projection employed. Reference to these lines is the easiest way of determining the relative positions of places on different maps, and for plotting compass directions.

NAME FORMS

For ease of reference, both English and local name forms appear in the atlas. Oceans, seas and countries are shown in English throughout the atlas; country names may be abbreviated to their commonly accepted form (e.g. Germany, not The Federal Republic of Germany). Conventional English forms are also used for place names on the smaller-scale maps of the continents. However, local name forms are used on all large-scale and regional maps, with the English form given in brackets only for important cities – the large-scale map of Russia and Central Asia thus shows Moskva (Moscow). For countries which do not use a Roman script, place names have been transcribed according to the systems adopted by the British and US Geographic Names Authorities. For China, the Pin Yin system has been used, with some more widely known forms appearing in brackets, as with Beijing (Peking). Both English and local names appear in the index, the English form being cross-referenced to the local form.

Contents

World Statistics

Images of Earth

Introduction to World Geography

City Maps

Index to City Maps 33-39

World Maps

The World

Europe

Asia

Africa

Australia and Oceania

North America

South America

Index to World Maps

World Statistics: Countries

This alphabetical list includes all the countries and territories of the world. If a territory is not completely independent, then the country it is associated with is named. The area figures give the total area of land, inland water and ice. Units for areas and populations are thousands. The population figures are 2000 estimates. The annual income is the Gross National Product per capita in US dollars. The figures are the latest available, usually 1999 estimates.

Country/Territory	**Area** km² *Thousands*	**Area** miles² *Thousands*	**Population** *Thousands*	**Capital**	**Annual Income** US $
Afghanistan	652	252	26,511	Kabul	800
Albania	28.8	11.1	3,795	Tirana	870
Algeria	2,382	920	32,904	Algiers	1,550
American Samoa (US)	0.20	0.08	39	Pago Pago	2,600
Andorra	0.45	0.17	49	Andorra La Vella	18,000
Angola	1,247	481	13,295	Luanda	220
Anguilla (UK)	0.1	0.04	8	The Valley	6,800
Antigua & Barbuda	0.44	0.17	79	St John's	8,520
Argentina	2,767	1,068	36,238	Buenos Aires	7,600
Armenia	29.8	11.5	3,968	Yerevan	490
Aruba (Netherlands)	0.19	0.07	58	Oranjestad	22,000
Australia	7,687	2,968	18,855	Canberra	20,050
Austria	83.9	32.4	7,613	Vienna	25,970
Azerbaijan	86.6	33.4	8,324	Baku	550
Azores (Portugal)	2.2	0.87	238	Ponta Delgada	–
Bahamas	13.9	5.4	295	Nassau	20,100
Bahrain	0.68	0.26	683	Manama	7,640
Bangladesh	144	56	150,589	Dhaka	370
Barbados	0.43	0.17	265	Bridgetown	7,890
Belarus	207.6	80.1	10,697	Minsk	2,630
Belgium	30.5	11.8	9,832	Brussels	24,510
Belize	23	8.9	230	Belmopan	2,730
Benin	113	43	6,369	Porto-Novo	380
Bermuda (UK)	0.05	0.02	62	Hamilton	35,590
Bhutan	47	18.1	1,906	Thimphu	510
Bolivia	1,099	424	9,724	La Paz/Sucre	1,010
Bosnia-Herzegovina	51	20	4,601	Sarajevo	1,720
Botswana	582	225	1,822	Gaborone	3,240
Brazil	8,512	3,286	179,487	Brasilia	4,420
Brunei	5.8	2.2	333	Bandar Seri Begawan	24,630
Bulgaria	111	43	9,071	Sofia	1,380
Burkina Faso	274	106	12,092	Ouagadougou	240
Burma (= Myanmar)	677	261	51,129	Rangoon	1,200
Burundi	27.8	10.7	7,358	Bujumbura	120
Cambodia	181	70	10,046	Phnom Penh	260
Cameroon	475	184	16,701	Yaoundé	580
Canada	9,976	3,852	28,488	Ottawa	19,320
Canary Is. (Spain)	7.3	2.8	1,494	Las Palmas/Santa Cruz	–
Cape Verde Is.	4	1.6	515	Praia	1,330
Cayman Is. (UK)	0.26	0.10	35	George Town	20,000
Central African Republic	623	241	4,074	Bangui	290
Chad	1,284	496	7,337	Ndjaména	200
Chile	757	292	15,272	Santiago	4,740
China	9,597	3,705	1,299,180	Beijing	780
Colombia	1,139	440	39,397	Bogotá	2,250
Comoros	2.2	0.86	670	Moroni	350
Congo	342	132	3,167	Brazzaville	670
Congo (Dem. Rep. of the)	2,345	905	49,190	Kinshasa	110
Cook Is. (NZ)	0.24	0.09	17	Avarua	900
Costa Rica	51.1	19.7	3,711	San José	2,740
Croatia	56.5	21.8	4,960	Zagreb	4,580
Cuba	111	43	11,504	Havana	1,560
Cyprus	9.3	3.6	762	Nicosia	11,960
Czech Republic	78.9	30.4	10,500	Prague	5,060
Denmark	43.1	16.6	5,153	Copenhagen	32,030
Djibouti	23.2	9	552	Djibouti	790
Dominica	0.75	0.29	87	Roseau	3,170
Dominican Republic	48.7	18.8	8,621	Santo Domingo	1,910
Ecuador	284	109	13,319	Quito	1,310
Egypt	1,001	387	64,210	Cairo	1,400
El Salvador	21	8.1	6,739	San Salvador	1,900
Equatorial Guinea	28.1	10.8	455	Malabo	1,170
Eritrea	94	36	4,523	Asmara	200
Estonia	44.7	17.3	1,647	Tallinn	3,480
Ethiopia	1,128	436	61,841	Addis Ababa	100
Faroe Is. (Denmark)	1.4	0.54	49	Tórshavn	16,000
Fiji	18.3	7.1	883	Suva	2,210
Finland	338	131	5,077	Helsinki	23,780
France	552	213	58,145	Paris	23,480
French Guiana (France)	90	34.7	130	Cayenne	6,000
French Polynesia (France)	4	1.5	268	Papeete	18,050
Gabon	268	103	1,612	Libreville	3,350
Gambia, The	11.3	4.4	1,119	Banjul	340
Georgia	69.7	26.9	5,777	Tbilisi	620
Germany	357	138	76,962	Berlin	25,350
Ghana	239	92	20,564	Accra	390
Gibraltar (UK)	0.007	0.003	32	Gibraltar Town	5,000
Greece	132	51	10,193	Athens	11,770
Greenland (Denmark)	2,176	840	60	Nuuk (Godthåb)	16,100
Grenada	0.34	0.13	83	St George's	3,450
Guadeloupe (France)	1.7	0.66	365	Basse-Terre	9,200
Guam (US)	0.55	0.21	128	Agana	19,000
Guatemala	109	42	12,222	Guatemala City	1,660
Guinea	246	95	7,830	Conakry	510
Guinea-Bissau	36.1	13.9	1,197	Bissau	160
Guyana	215	83	891	Georgetown	760
Haiti	27.8	10.7	8,003	Port-au-Prince	460
Honduras	112	43	6,846	Tegucigalpa	760
Hong Kong (China)	1.1	0.40	6,336	–	23,520
Hungary	93	35.9	10,531	Budapest	4,650
Iceland	103	40	274	Reykjavik	29,280
India	3,288	1,269	1,041,543	New Delhi	450
Indonesia	1,905	735	218,661	Jakarta	580
Iran	1,648	636	68,759	Tehran	1,760
Iraq	438	169	26,339	Baghdad	2,400
Ireland	70.3	27.1	4,086	Dublin	19,160
Israel	27	10.3	5,321	Jerusalem	17,450
Italy	301	116	57,195	Rome	19,710
Ivory Coast (Côte d'Ivoire)	322	125	17,600	Yamoussoukro	710
Jamaica	11	4.2	2,735	Kingston	2,330
Japan	378	146	128,470	Tokyo	32,230
Jordan	89.2	34.4	5,558	Amman	1,500
Kazakstan	2,717	1,049	19,006	Astana	1,230
Kenya	580	224	35,060	Nairobi	360
Kiribati	0.72	0.28	72	Tarawa	910
Korea, North	121	47	26,117	Pyŏngyang	1,000
Korea, South	99	38.2	46,403	Seoul	8,490
Kuwait	17.8	6.9	2,639	Kuwait City	22,700
Kyrgyzstan	198.5	76.6	5,403	Bishkek	300
Laos	237	91	5,463	Vientiane	280
Latvia	65	25	2,768	Riga	2,470

Country/Territory	**Area** km² *Thousands*	**Area** miles² *Thousands*	**Population** *Thousands*	**Capital**	**Annual Income** US $
Lebanon	10.4	4	3,327	Beirut	3,700
Lesotho	30.4	11.7	2,370	Maseru	550
Liberia	111	43	3,575	Monrovia	1,000
Libya	1,760	679	6,500	Tripoli	6,700
Liechtenstein	0.16	0.06	28	Vaduz	50,000
Lithuania	65.2	25.2	3,935	Vilnius	2,620
Luxembourg	2.6	1	377	Luxembourg	44,640
Macau (China)	0.02	0.006	656	Macau	16,000
Macedonia	25.7	9.9	2,157	Skopje	1,690
Madagascar	587	227	16,627	Antananarivo	250
Madeira (Portugal)	0.81	0.31	253	Funchal	–
Malawi	118	46	12,458	Lilongwe	190
Malaysia	330	127	21,983	Kuala Lumpur	3,400
Maldives	0.30	0.12	283	Malé	1,160
Mali	1,240	479	12,685	Bamako	240
Malta	0.32	0.12	366	Valletta	9,210
Marshall Is.	0.18	0.07	70	Dalap-Uliga-Darrit	1,560
Martinique (France)	1.1	0.42	362	Fort-de-France	10,700
Mauritania	1,030	412	2,702	Nouakchott	380
Mauritius	2.0	0.72	1,201	Port Louis	3,590
Mayotte (France)	0.37	0.14	141	Mamoundzou	1,430
Mexico	1,958	756	107,233	Mexico City	4,400
Micronesia, Fed. States of	0.70	0.27	110	Palikir	1,810
Moldova	33.7	13	4,707	Chişinău	370
Monaco	0.002	0.0001	30	Monaco	25,000
Mongolia	1,567	605	2,847	Ulan Bator	350
Montserrat (UK)	0.10	0.04	13	Plymouth	4,500
Morocco	447	172	31,559	Rabat	1,200
Mozambique	802	309	20,493	Maputo	230
Namibia	825	318	2,437	Windhoek	1,890
Nauru	0.02	0.008	10	Yaren District	10,000
Nepal	141	54	24,084	Katmandu	220
Netherlands	41.5	16	15,829	Amsterdam/The Hague	24,320
Netherlands Antilles (Neths)	0.99	0.38	203	Willemstad	11,500
New Caledonia (France)	18.6	7.2	195	Nouméa	11,400
New Zealand	269	104	3,662	Wellington	13,780
Nicaragua	130	50	5,261	Managua	430
Niger	1,267	489	10,752	Niamey	190
Nigeria	924	357	105,000	Abuja	310
Northern Mariana Is. (US)	0.48	0.18	50	Saipan	11,500
Norway	324	125	4,331	Oslo	32,880
Oman	212	82	2,176	Muscat	7,900
Pakistan	796	307	162,409	Islamabad	470
Palau	0.46	0.18	18	Koror	5,000
Panama	77.1	29.8	2,893	Panama City	3,070
Papua New Guinea	463	179	4,845	Port Moresby	800
Paraguay	407	157	5,538	Asunción	1,580
Peru	1,285	496	26,276	Lima	2,390
Philippines	300	116	77,473	Manila	1,020
Poland	313	121	40,366	Warsaw	3,960
Portugal	92.4	35.7	10,587	Lisbon	10,600
Puerto Rico (US)	9	3.5	3,836	San Juan	8,200
Qatar	11	4.2	499	Doha	17,100
Réunion (France)	2.5	0.97	692	Saint-Denis	4,800
Romania	238	92	24,000	Bucharest	1,520
Russia	17,075	6,592	155,096	Moscow	2,270
Rwanda	26.3	10.2	10,200	Kigali	250
St Kitts & Nevis	0.36	0.14	44	Basseterre	6,420
St Lucia	0.62	0.24	177	Castries	3,770
St Vincent & Grenadines	0.39	0.15	128	Kingstown	2,700
Samoa	2.8	1.1	171	Apia	1,020
San Marino	0.06	0.02	25	San Marino	20,000
São Tomé & Príncipe	0.96	0.37	151	São Tomé	270
Saudi Arabia	2,150	830	20,697	Riyadh	6,910
Senegal	197	76	8,716	Dakar	510
Seychelles	0.46	0.18	75	Victoria	6,540
Sierra Leone	71.7	27.7	5,437	Freetown	130
Singapore	0.62	0.24	3,000	Singapore	29,610
Slovak Republic	49	18.9	5,500	Bratislava	3,590
Slovenia	20.3	7.8	2,055	Ljubljana	9,890
Solomon Is.	28.9	11.2	429	Honiara	750
Somalia	638	246	9,736	Mogadishu	600
South Africa	1,220	471	43,666	C. Town/Pretoria/Bloem.	3,160
Spain	505	195	40,667	Madrid	14,000
Sri Lanka	65.6	25.3	19,416	Colombo	820
Sudan	2,506	967	33,625	Khartoum	330
Surinam	163	63	497	Paramaribo	1,660
Swaziland	17.4	6.7	1,121	Mbabane	1,360
Sweden	450	174	8,560	Stockholm	25,040
Switzerland	41.3	15.9	6,762	Bern	38,350
Syria	185	71	17,826	Damascus	970
Taiwan	36	13.9	22,000	Taipei	12,400
Tajikistan	143.1	55.2	7,041	Dushanbe	290
Tanzania	945	365	39,639	Dodoma	240
Thailand	513	198	63,670	Bangkok	1,960
Togo	56.8	21.9	4,861	Lomé	320
Tonga	0.75	0.29	92	Nuku'alofa	1,720
Trinidad & Tobago	5.1	2	1,484	Port of Spain	4,390
Tunisia	164	63	9,924	Tunis	2,100
Turkey	779	301	66,789	Ankara	2,900
Turkmenistan	488.1	188.5	4,585	Ashkhabad	660
Turks & Caicos Is. (UK)	0.43	0.17	12	Cockburn Town	5,000
Tuvalu	0.03	0.01	11	Fongafale	600
Uganda	236	91	26,958	Kampala	320
Ukraine	603.7	233.1	52,558	Kiev	750
United Arab Emirates	83.6	32.3	1,951	Abu Dhabi	17,870
United Kingdom	243.3	94	58,393	London	22,640
United States of America	9,373	3,619	266,096	Washington, DC	30,600
Uruguay	177	68	3,274	Montevideo	5,900
Uzbekistan	447.4	172.7	26,044	Tashkent	720
Vanuatu	12.2	4.7	206	Port-Vila	1,170
Venezuela	912	352	24,715	Caracas	3,670
Vietnam	332	127	82,427	Hanoi	370
Virgin Is. (UK)	0.15	0.06	15	Road Town	–
Virgin Is. (US)	0.34	0.13	135	Charlotte Amalie	12,500
Wallis & Futuna Is. (France)	0.20	0.08	26	Mata-Utu	–
Western Sahara	266	103	228	El Aaiún	300
Yemen	528	204	13,219	Sana	350
Yugoslavia	102.3	39.5	10,761	Belgrade	2,300
Zambia	753	291	12,267	Lusaka	320
Zimbabwe	391	151	13,123	Harare	520

World Statistics: Physical Dimensions

Each topic list is divided into continents and within a continent the items are listed in order of size. The bottom part of many of the lists is selective in order to give examples from as many different countries as possible. The order of the continents is the same as in the atlas, beginning with Europe and ending with South America. The figures are rounded as appropriate.

World, Continents, Oceans

	km^2	miles^2	%
The World	509,450,000	196,672,000	–
Land	149,450,000	57,688,000	29.3
Water	360,000,000	138,984,000	70.7
Asia	44,500,000	17,177,000	29.8
Africa	30,302,000	11,697,000	20.3
North America	24,241,000	9,357,000	16.2
South America	17,793,000	6,868,000	11.9
Antarctica	14,100,000	5,443,000	9.4
Europe	9,957,000	3,843,000	6.7
Australia & Oceania	8,557,000	3,303,000	5.7
Pacific Ocean	179,679,000	69,356,000	49.9
Atlantic Ocean	92,373,000	35,657,000	25.7
Indian Ocean	73,917,000	28,532,000	20.5
Arctic Ocean	14,090,000	5,439,000	3.9

Ocean Depths

Atlantic Ocean	m	ft
Puerto Rico (Milwaukee) Deep	9,220	30,249
Cayman Trench	7,680	25,197
Gulf of Mexico	5,203	17,070
Mediterranean Sea	5,121	16,801
Black Sea	2,211	7,254
North Sea	660	2,165
Indian Ocean	**m**	**ft**
Java Trench	7,450	24,442
Red Sea	2,635	8,454
Pacific Ocean	**m**	**ft**
Mariana Trench	11,022	36,161
Tonga Trench	10,882	35,702
Japan Trench	10,554	34,626
Kuril Trench	10,542	34,587
Arctic Ocean	**m**	**ft**
Molloy Deep	5,608	18,399

Mountains

Europe		m	ft
Elbrus	*Russia*	5,642	18,510
Mont Blanc	*France/Italy*	4,807	15,771
Monte Rosa	*Italy/Switzerland*	4,634	15,203
Dom	*Switzerland*	4,545	14,911
Liskamm	*Switzerland*	4,527	14,852
Weisshorn	*Switzerland*	4,505	14,780
Taschorn	*Switzerland*	4,490	14,730
Matterhorn/Cervino	*Italy/Switzerland*	4,478	14,691
Mont Maudit	*France/Italy*	4,465	14,649
Dent Blanche	*Switzerland*	4,356	14,291
Nadelhorn	*Switzerland*	4,327	14,196
Grandes Jorasses	*France/Italy*	4,208	13,806
Jungfrau	*Switzerland*	4,158	13,642
Grossglockner	*Austria*	3,797	12,457
Mulhacén	*Spain*	3,478	11,411
Zugspitze	*Germany*	2,962	9,718
Olympus	*Greece*	2,917	9,570
Triglav	*Slovenia*	2,863	9,393
Gerlachovka	*Slovak Republic*	2,655	8,711
Galdhöpiggen	*Norway*	2,468	8,100
Kebnekaise	*Sweden*	2,117	6,946
Ben Nevis	*UK*	1,343	4,406
Asia		**m**	**ft**
Everest	*China/Nepal*	8,850	29,035
K2 (Godwin Austen)	*China/Kashmir*	8,611	28,251
Kanchenjunga	*India/Nepal*	8,598	28,208
Lhotse	*China/Nepal*	8,516	27,939
Makalu	*China/Nepal*	8,481	27,824
Cho Oyu	*China/Nepal*	8,201	26,906
Dhaulagiri	*Nepal*	8,172	26,811
Manaslu	*Nepal*	8,156	26,758
Nanga Parbat	*Kashmir*	8,126	26,660
Annapurna	*Nepal*	8,078	26,502
Gasherbrum	*China/Kashmir*	8,068	26,469
Broad Peak	*China/Kashmir*	8,051	26,414
Xixabangma	*China*	8,012	26,286
Kangbachen	*India/Nepal*	7,902	25,925
Trivor	*Pakistan*	7,720	25,328
Pik Kommunizma	*Tajikistan*	7,495	24,590
Demavend	*Iran*	5,604	18,386
Ararat	*Turkey*	5,165	16,945
Gunong Kinabalu	*Malaysia (Borneo)*	4,101	13,455
Fuji-San	*Japan*	3,776	12,388
Africa		**m**	**ft**
Kilimanjaro	*Tanzania*	5,895	19,340
Mt Kenya	*Kenya*	5,199	17,057
Ruwenzori (Margherita)	*Ug./Congo (D.R.)*	5,109	16,762
Ras Dashan	*Ethiopia*	4,620	15,157
Meru	*Tanzania*	4,565	14,977
Karisimbi	*Rwanda/Congo (D.R.)*	4,507	14,787
Mt Elgon	*Kenya/Uganda*	4,321	14,176
Batu	*Ethiopia*	4,307	14,130
Toubkal	*Morocco*	4,165	13,665
Mt Cameroon	*Cameroon*	4,070	13,353
Oceania		**m**	**ft**
Puncak Jaya	*Indonesia*	5,029	16,499
Puncak Trikora	*Indonesia*	4,750	15,584
Puncak Mandala	*Indonesia*	4,702	15,427
Mt Wilhelm	*Papua New Guinea*	4,508	14,790
Mauna Kea	*USA (Hawaii)*	4,205	13,796
Mauna Loa	*USA (Hawaii)*	4,169	13,681
Mt Cook (Aoraki)	*New Zealand*	3,753	12,313
Mt Kosciuszko	*Australia*	2,237	7,339
North America		**m**	**ft**
Mt McKinley (Denali)	*USA (Alaska)*	6,194	20,321
Mt Logan	*Canada*	5,959	19,551
Citlaltepetl	*Mexico*	5,700	18,701
Mt St Elias	*USA/Canada*	5,489	18,008
Popocatepetl	*Mexico*	5,452	17,887
Mt Foraker	*USA (Alaska)*	5,304	17,401
Ixtaccihuatl	*Mexico*	5,286	17,342
Lucania	*Canada*	5,227	17,149
Mt Steele	*Canada*	5,073	16,644
Mt Bona	*USA (Alaska)*	5,005	16,420
Mt Whitney	*USA*	4,418	14,495
Tajumulco	*Guatemala*	4,220	13,845
Chirripó Grande	*Costa Rica*	3,837	12,589
Pico Duarte	*Dominican Rep.*	3,175	10,417
South America		**m**	**ft**
Aconcagua	*Argentina*	6,960	22,834
Bonete	*Argentina*	6,872	22,546
Ojos del Salado	*Argentina/Chile*	6,863	22,516
Pissis	*Argentina*	6,779	22,241
Mercedario	*Argentina/Chile*	6,770	22,211
Huascaran	*Peru*	6,768	22,204
Llullaillaco	*Argentina/Chile*	6,723	22,057
Nudo de Cachi	*Argentina*	6,720	22,047
Yerupaja	*Peru*	6,632	21,758
Sajama	*Bolivia*	6,542	21,463
Chimborazo	*Ecuador*	6,267	20,561
Pico Colon	*Colombia*	5,800	19,029
Pico Bolivar	*Venezuela*	5,007	16,427
Antarctica		**m**	**ft**
Vinson Massif		4,897	16,066
Mt Kirkpatrick		4,528	14,855

Rivers

Europe		km	miles
Volga	*Caspian Sea*	3,700	2,300
Danube	*Black Sea*	2,850	1,770
Ural	*Caspian Sea*	2,535	1,575
Dnepr (Dnipro)	*Black Sea*	2,285	1,420
Kama	*Volga*	2,030	1,260
Don	*Black Sea*	1,990	1,240
Petchora	*Arctic Ocean*	1,790	1,110
Oka	*Volga*	1,480	920
Dnister (Dniester)	*Black Sea*	1,400	870
Vyatka	*Kama*	1,370	850
Rhine	*North Sea*	1,320	820
N. Dvina	*Arctic Ocean*	1,290	800
Elbe	*North Sea*	1,145	710
Asia		**km**	**miles**
Yangtze	*Pacific Ocean*	6,380	3,960
Yenisey–Angara	*Arctic Ocean*	5,550	3,445
Huang He	*Pacific Ocean*	5,464	3,395
Ob–Irtysh	*Arctic Ocean*	5,410	3,360
Mekong	*Pacific Ocean*	4,500	2,795
Amur	*Pacific Ocean*	4,400	2,730
Lena	*Arctic Ocean*	4,400	2,730
Irtysh	*Ob*	4,250	2,640
Yenisey	*Arctic Ocean*	4,090	2,540
Ob	*Arctic Ocean*	3,680	2,285
Indus	*Indian Ocean*	3,100	1,925
Brahmaputra	*Indian Ocean*	2,900	1,800
Syrdarya	*Aral Sea*	2,860	1,775
Salween	*Indian Ocean*	2,800	1,740
Euphrates	*Indian Ocean*	2,700	1,675
Amudarya	*Aral Sea*	2,540	1,575
Africa		**km**	**miles**
Nile	*Mediterranean*	6,670	4,140
Congo	*Atlantic Ocean*	4,670	2,900
Niger	*Atlantic Ocean*	4,180	2,595
Zambezi	*Indian Ocean*	3,540	2,200
Oubangi/Uele	*Congo (D.R.)*	2,250	1,400
Kasai	*Congo (D.R.)*	1,950	1,210
Shaballe	*Indian Ocean*	1,930	1,200
Orange	*Atlantic Ocean*	1,860	1,155
Cubango	*Okavango Swamps*	1,800	1,120
Limpopo	*Indian Ocean*	1,600	995
Senegal	*Atlantic Ocean*	1,600	995
Australia		**km**	**miles**
Murray–Darling	*Indian Ocean*	3,750	2,330
Darling	*Murray*	3,070	1,905
Murray	*Indian Ocean*	2,575	1,600
Murrumbidgee	*Murray*	1,690	1,050
North America		**km**	**miles**
Mississippi–Missouri	*Gulf of Mexico*	6,020	3,740
Mackenzie	*Arctic Ocean*	4,240	2,630
Mississippi	*Gulf of Mexico*	3,780	2,350
Missouri	*Mississippi*	3,780	2,350
Yukon	*Pacific Ocean*	3,185	1,980
Rio Grande	*Gulf of Mexico*	3,030	1,880
Arkansas	*Mississippi*	2,340	1,450
Colorado	*Pacific Ocean*	2,330	1,445
Red	*Mississippi*	2,040	1,270
Columbia	*Pacific Ocean*	1,950	1,210
Saskatchewan	*Lake Winnipeg*	1,940	1,205
South America		**km**	**miles**
Amazon	*Atlantic Ocean*	6,450	4,010
Paraná–Plate	*Atlantic Ocean*	4,500	2,800
Purus	*Amazon*	3,350	2,080
Madeira	*Amazon*	3,200	1,990
São Francisco	*Atlantic Ocean*	2,900	1,800
Paraná	*Plate*	2,800	1,740
Tocantins	*Atlantic Ocean*	2,750	1,710
Paraguay	*Paraná*	2,550	1,580
Orinoco	*Atlantic Ocean*	2,500	1,550
Pilcomayo	*Paraná*	2,500	1,550
Araguaia	*Tocantins*	2,250	1,400

Lakes

Europe		km^2	miles^2
Lake Ladoga	*Russia*	17,700	6,800
Lake Onega	*Russia*	9,700	3,700
Saimaa system	*Finland*	8,000	3,100
Vänern	*Sweden*	5,500	2,100
Asia		**km^2**	**miles^2**
Caspian Sea	*Asia*	371,800	143,550
Lake Baykal	*Russia*	30,500	11,780
Aral Sea	*Kazakstan/Uzbekistan*	28,687	11,086
Tonlé Sap	*Cambodia*	20,000	7,700
Lake Balqash	*Kazakstan*	18,500	7,100
Africa		**km^2**	**miles^2**
Lake Victoria	*East Africa*	68,000	26,000
Lake Tanganyika	*Central Africa*	33,000	13,000
Lake Malawi/Nyasa	*East Africa*	29,600	11,430
Lake Chad	*Central Africa*	25,000	9,700
Lake Turkana	*Ethiopia/Kenya*	8,500	3,300
Lake Volta	*Ghana*	8,500	3,300
Australia		**km^2**	**miles^2**
Lake Eyre	*Australia*	8,900	3,400
Lake Torrens	*Australia*	5,800	2,200
Lake Gairdner	*Australia*	4,800	1,900
North America		**km^2**	**miles^2**
Lake Superior	*Canada/USA*	82,350	31,800
Lake Huron	*Canada/USA*	59,600	23,010
Lake Michigan	*USA*	58,000	22,400
Great Bear Lake	*Canada*	31,800	12,280
Great Slave Lake	*Canada*	28,500	11,000
Lake Erie	*Canada/USA*	25,700	9,900
Lake Winnipeg	*Canada*	24,400	9,400
Lake Ontario	*Canada/USA*	19,500	7,500
Lake Nicaragua	*Nicaragua*	8,200	3,200
South America		**km^2**	**miles^2**
Lake Titicaca	*Bolivia/Peru*	8,300	3,200
Lake Poopo	*Bolivia*	2,800	1,100

Islands

Europe		km^2	miles^2
Great Britain	*UK*	229,880	88,700
Iceland	*Atlantic Ocean*	103,000	39,800
Ireland	*Ireland/UK*	84,400	32,600
Novaya Zemlya (N.)	*Russia*	48,200	18,600
Sicily	*Italy*	25,500	9,800
Corsica	*France*	8,700	3,400
Asia		**km^2**	**miles^2**
Borneo	*Southeast Asia*	744,360	287,400
Sumatra	*Indonesia*	473,600	182,860
Honshu	*Japan*	230,500	88,980
Sulawesi (Celebes)	*Indonesia*	189,000	73,000
Java	*Indonesia*	126,700	48,900
Luzon	*Philippines*	104,700	40,400
Hokkaido	*Japan*	78,400	30,300
Africa		**km^2**	**miles^2**
Madagascar	*Indian Ocean*	587,040	226,660
Socotra	*Indian Ocean*	3,600	1,400
Réunion	*Indian Ocean*	2,500	965
Oceania		**km^2**	**miles^2**
New Guinea	*Indonesia/Papua NG*	821,030	317,000
New Zealand (S.)	*Pacific Ocean*	150,500	58,100
New Zealand (N.)	*Pacific Ocean*	114,700	44,300
Tasmania	*Australia*	67,800	26,200
Hawaii	*Pacific Ocean*	10,450	4,000
North America		**km^2**	**miles^2**
Greenland	*Atlantic Ocean*	2,175,600	839,800
Baffin Is.	*Canada*	508,000	196,100
Victoria Is.	*Canada*	212,200	81,900
Ellesmere Is.	*Canada*	212,000	81,800
Cuba	*Caribbean Sea*	110,860	42,800
Hispaniola	*Dominican Rep./Haiti*	76,200	29,400
Jamaica	*Caribbean Sea*	11,400	4,400
Puerto Rico	*Atlantic Ocean*	8,900	3,400
South America		**km^2**	**miles^2**
Tierra del Fuego	*Argentina/Chile*	47,000	18,100
Falkland Is. (E.)	*Atlantic Ocean*	6,800	2,600

WORLD: REGIONS IN THE NEWS

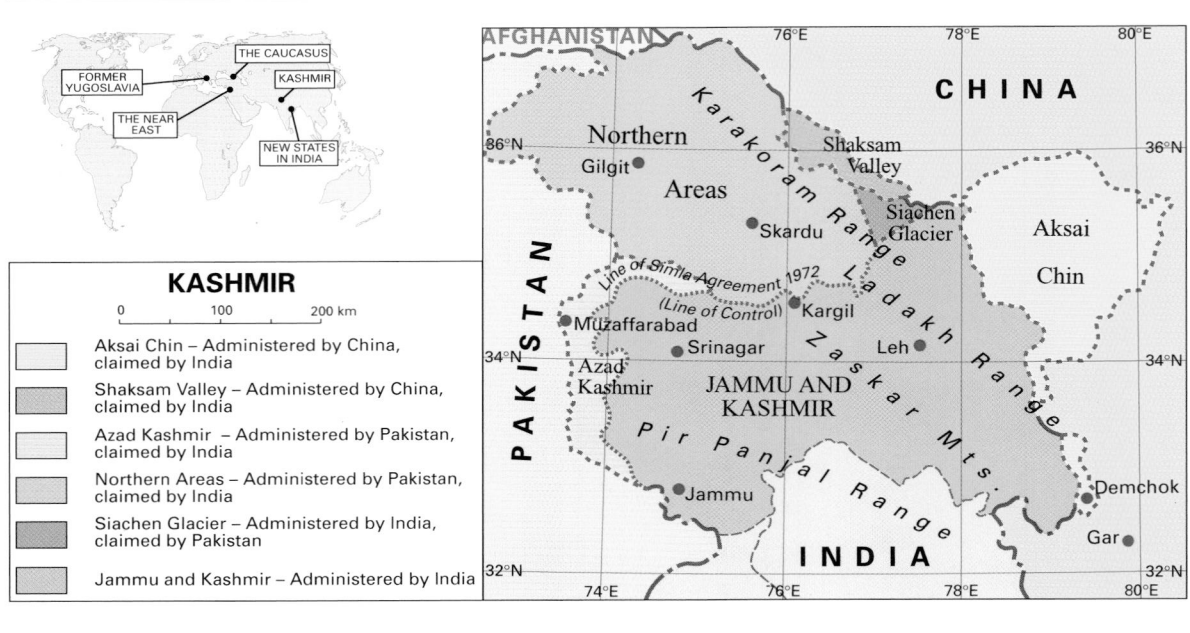

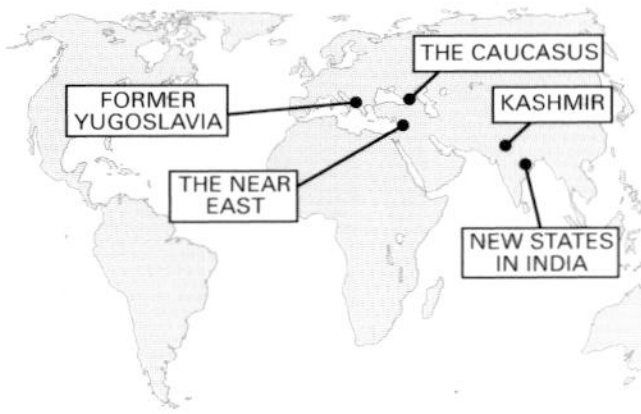

KASHMIR

0 100 200 km

- Aksai Chin – Administered by China, claimed by India
- Shaksam Valley – Administered by China, claimed by India
- Azad Kashmir – Administered by Pakistan, claimed by India
- Northern Areas – Administered by Pakistan, claimed by India
- Siachen Glacier – Administered by India, claimed by Pakistan
- Jammu and Kashmir – Administered by India

YUGOSLAVIA

Population 10,761,000 (Serb 62.6%, Albanian 16.5%, Montenegrin 5%, Hungarian 3.3%, Muslim 3.2%)

Serbia Population: 5,799,800 (Serb 87.7%, excluding the provinces of Kosovo and Vojvodina)

Kosovo Population: 2,084,4000 (Albanian 81.6%, Serb 9.9%)

Vojvodena Population: 1,980,800 (Serb 56.8%, Hungarian 16.9%)

Montenegro Population: 635,000 (Montenegrin 61.9%, Muslim 14.6%, Albanian 7%)

CROATIA
Population: 4,960,000 (Croat 78.1%, Serb 12.2%)

SLOVENIA
Population: 2,055,000 (Slovene 88%, Croat 3%, Serb 2%)

MACEDONIA (F. Y. R. O. M.)
Population: 2,157,000 (Macedonian 64%, Albanian 21.7%, Turkish 5%, Romanian 3%, Serb 2%)

BOSNIA-HERZEGOVINA
Population: 4,601,000 (Muslim 49%, Serb 31.2%, Croat 17.2%)

ISRAEL
Population: 5,321,000 (inc. East Jerusalem and Jewish settlers in the areas under Israeli administration. Jewish 82%, Arab Muslim 13.8%, Arab Christian 2.5%, Druze 1.7%)

West Bank
Population: 1,122,900 (Palestinian Arabs 97% [of whom Arab Muslim 85%, Jewish 7%, Christian 8%])

Gaza Strip
Population: 748,400 (Arab 98%)

JORDAN
Population: 5,558,000 (Arab 99% [of whom about 50% are Palestinian Arab])

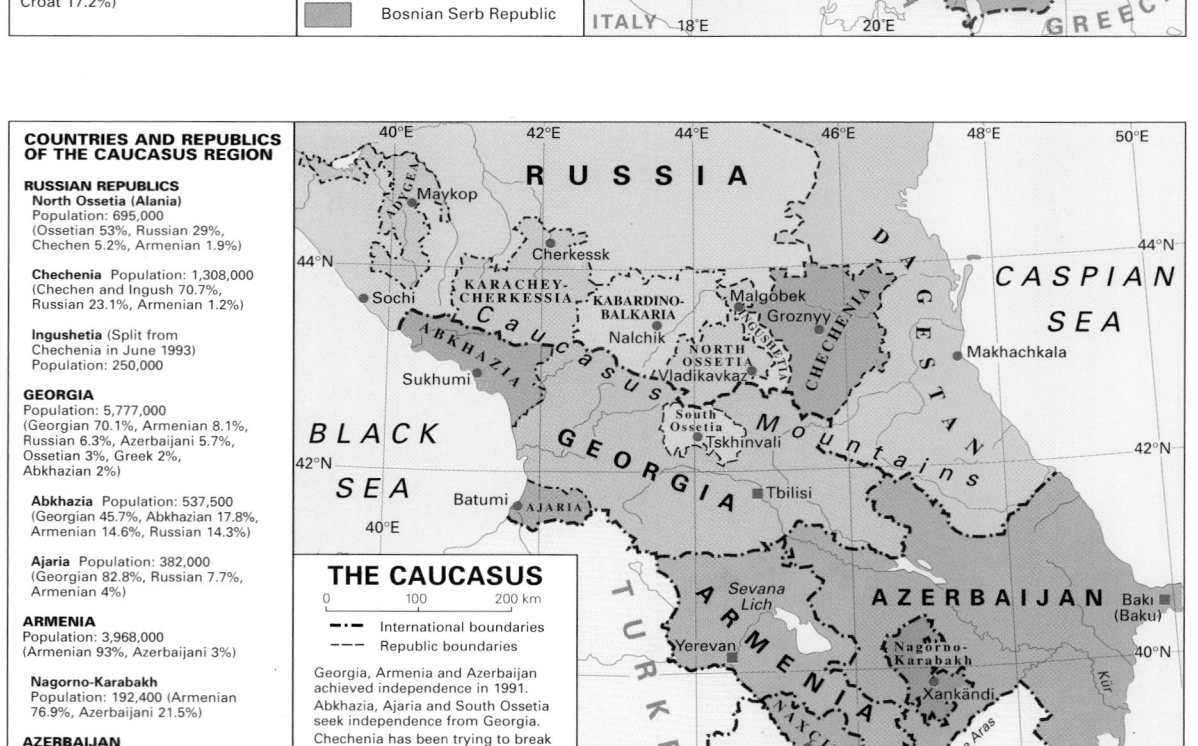

COUNTRIES AND REPUBLICS OF THE CAUCASUS REGION

RUSSIAN REPUBLICS

North Ossetia (Alania)
Population: 695,000 (Ossetian 53%, Russian 29%, Chechen 5.2%, Armenian 1.9%)

Chechenia Population: 1,308,000 (Chechen and Ingush 70.7%, Russian 23.1%, Armenian 1.2%)

Ingushetia (Split from Chechenia in June 1993) Population: 250,000

GEORGIA
Population: 5,777,000 (Georgian 70.1%, Armenian 8.1%, Russian 6.3%, Azerbaijani 5.7%, Ossetian 3%, Greek 2%, Abkhazian 2%)

Abkhazia Population: 537,500 (Georgian 45.7%, Abkhazian 17.8%, Armenian 14.6%, Russian 14.3%)

Ajaria Population: 382,000 (Georgian 82.8%, Russian 7.7%, Armenian 4%)

ARMENIA
Population: 3,968,000 (Armenian 93%, Azerbaijani 3%)

Nagorno-Karabakh
Population: 192,400 (Armenian 76.9%, Azerbaijani 21.5%)

AZERBAIJAN
Population: 8,324,000 (Azerbaijani 83%, Russian 6%, Armenian 6%, Lezgin 2%)

Naxçivan Population: 300,400

– Vancouver, Canada –

The city of Vancouver grew up around its fine, natural harbour on the north side of the Fraser River delta, developing as the western railhead of the Canadian Pacific Railroad. Just to the south of the delta runs the 49th parallel, the boundary between Canada and the USA. To the north of the city lie the Coast Mountains, and to the west, across the Strait of Georgia, is Vancouver Island with the town of Victoria visible at the bottom left of the image.

– Los Angeles, USA –

The sprawling urban area of Greater LA covers most of the area to the south of the San Gabriel Mountains, which run across the top of the image. The population of the whole area is over 14 million people. Jutting into the left-hand side of the image, just below centre, the darker colours of the eastern end of the Santa Monica range can be seen; the centre of the city proper is just to the south-east of the end of the range. On its southern slopes lie Beverly Hills and Hollywood, with the San Fernando Valley to the north.

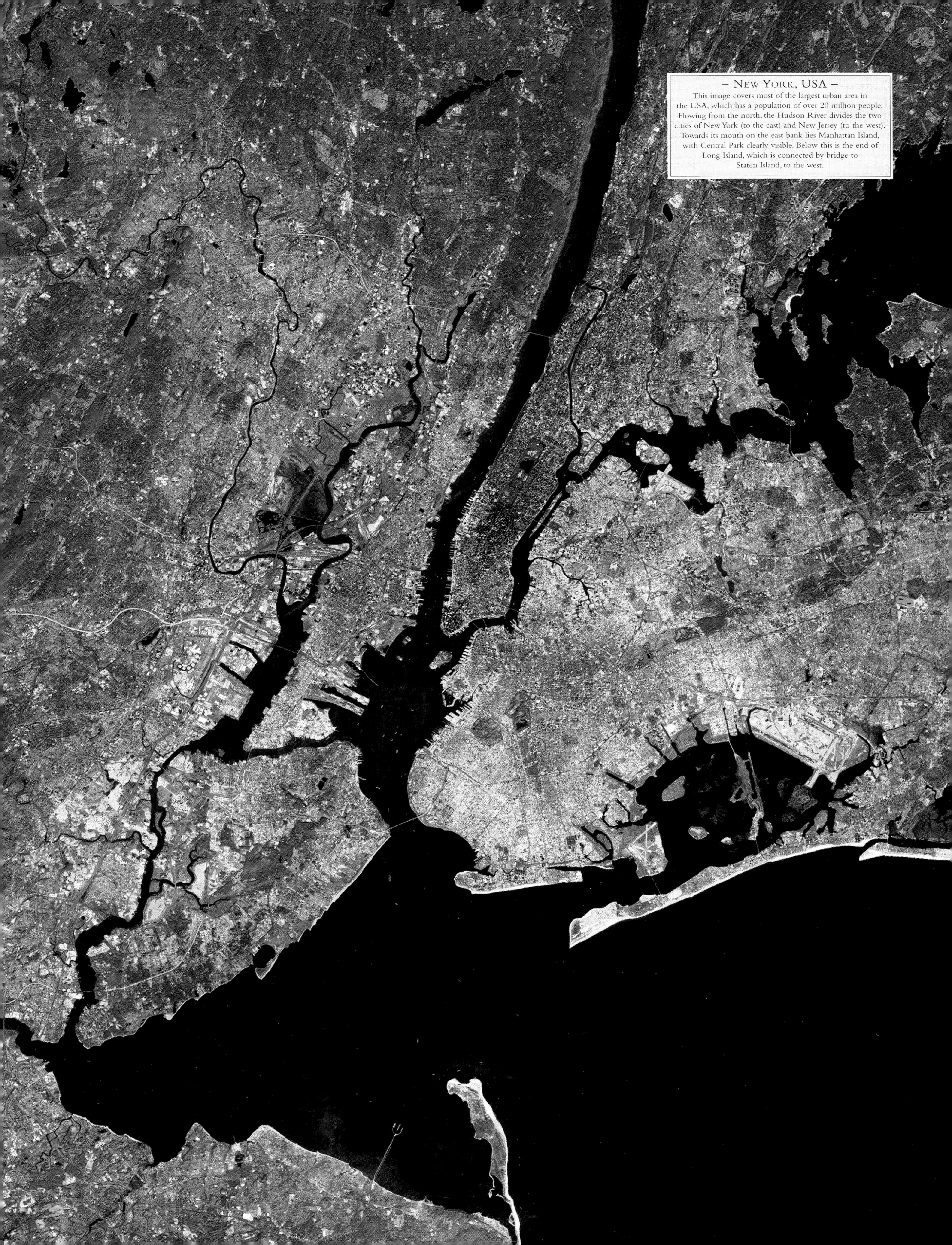

– New York, USA –

This image covers most of the largest urban area in the USA, which has a population of over 20 million people. Flowing from the north, the Hudson River divides the two cities of New York (to the east) and New Jersey (to the west). Towards its mouth on the east bank lies Manhattan Island, with Central Park clearly visible. Below this is the end of Long Island, which is connected by bridge to Staten Island, to the west.

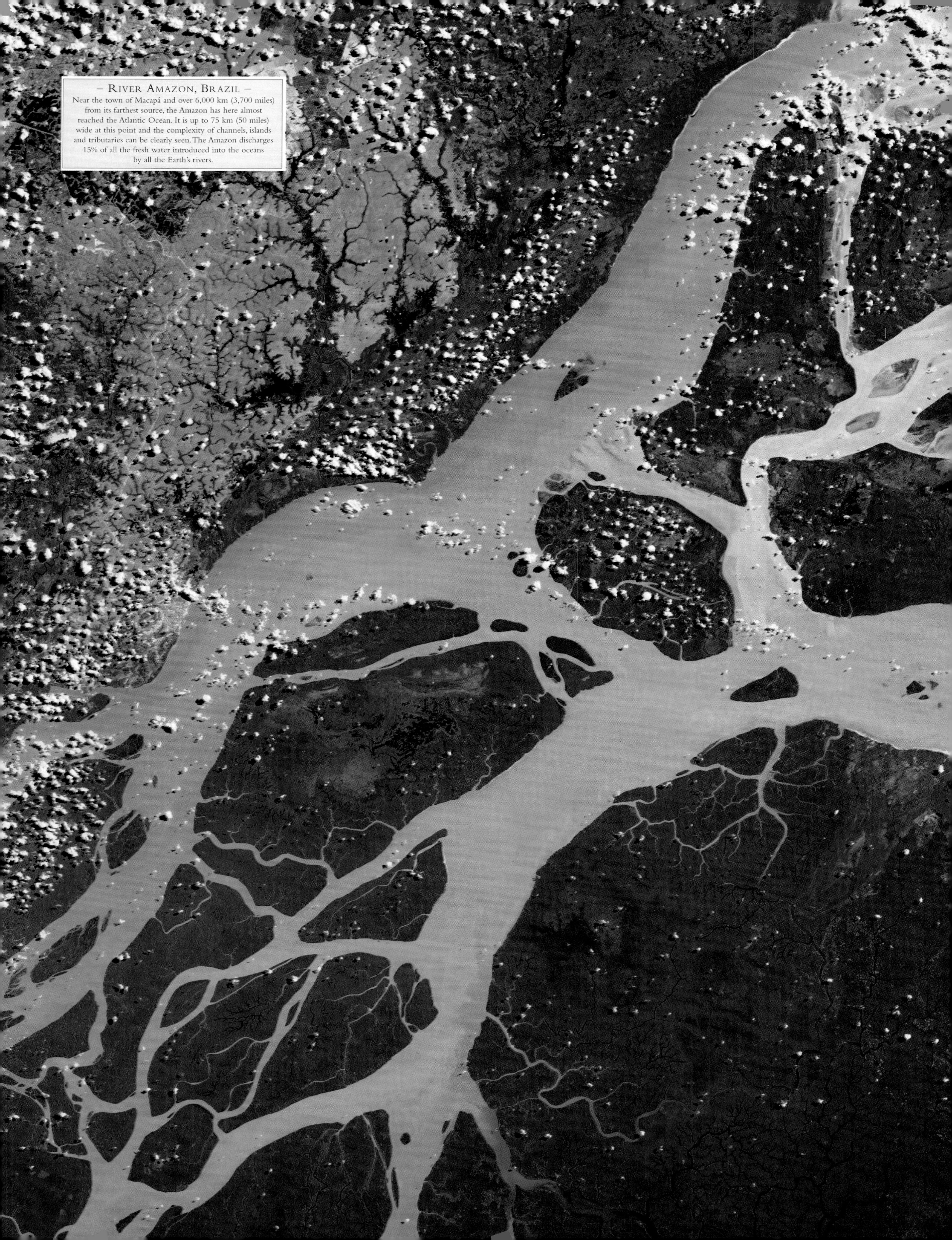

– River Amazon, Brazil –

Near the town of Macapá and over 6,000 km (3,700 miles) from its farthest source, the Amazon has here almost reached the Atlantic Ocean. It is up to 75 km (50 miles) wide at this point and the complexity of channels, islands and tributaries can be clearly seen. The Amazon discharges 15% of all the fresh water introduced into the oceans by all the Earth's rivers.

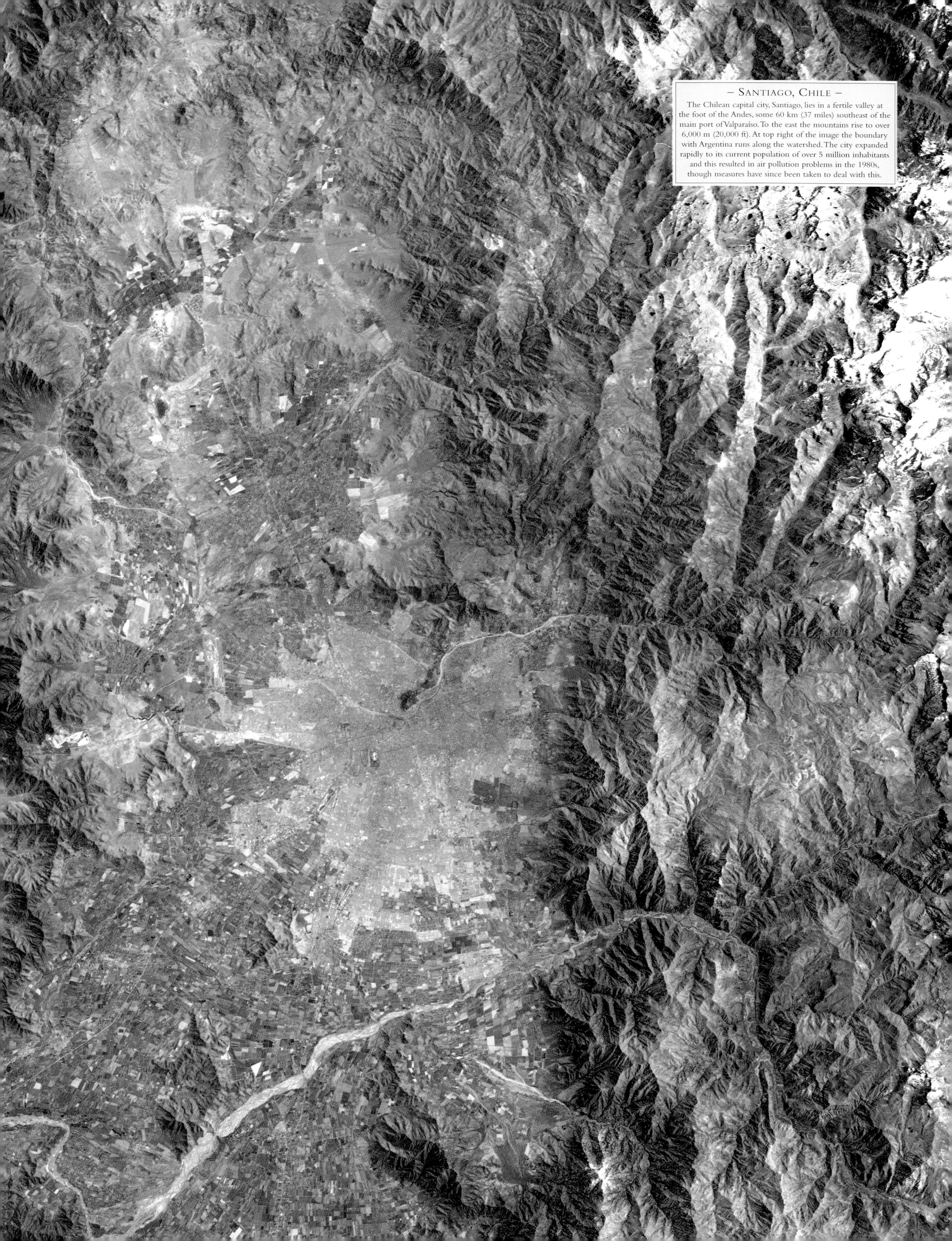

– Santiago, Chile –

The Chilean capital city, Santiago, lies in a fertile valley at the foot of the Andes, some 60 km (37 miles) southeast of the main port of Valparaíso. To the east the mountains rise to over 6,000 m (20,000 ft). At top right of the image the boundary with Argentina runs along the watershed. The city expanded rapidly to its current population of over 5 million inhabitants and this resulted in air pollution problems in the 1980s, though measures have since been taken to deal with this.

– London, United Kingdom –

The whole area of Greater London is shown here, including Heathrow Airport at far left. The River Thames stands out, as do the former London docks and the reservoirs in the River Lea valley to the north-east. Despite having a population in excess of 8 million people, there are still many open spaces and parks around the city centre.

– IJSSELMEER, NETHERLANDS –

This unique feature was created in the 13th century when the sea breached a protective sand bar, flooding all the low-lying land. The remnants of the bar can still be seen as the chain of Frisian Islands at the top of the image. Reclamation on a large scale started in 1932 with the completion of the causeway in the north. Since then four 'polders' have been drained and reclaimed. The city of Amsterdam is situated at bottom left.

– Naples, Italy –

The city, situated in the northeastern corner of the Bay of Naples, has a population in excess of 1 million inhabitants. The cone of the active volcano Vesuvius, 1,281 m (4,200 ft) high dominates the bay. Evidence of other volcanic activity can also be seen to the west of the town in the area known as the Phlegraean Fields. Pompei, once buried by it's lava, lies near the mountains to the southeast. On the southern peninsular is the town of Sorrento, and beyond, the island of Capri.

– STRAIT OF GIBRALTAR –

The strait separates the Mediterranean Sea (to the right) from the Atlantic Ocean, and the continent of Europe (above) from Africa. At its narrowest eastern end, shown in the image, the strait is only 13 km (8 miles) wide. On the Spanish side, the deep inlet of Algeciras Bay stands out, with the British naval base at Gibraltar on the tip of its eastern peninsula, beneath the Rock. The Moroccan port of Tangier is at the bottom left of the image.

– Cairo, Egypt –

The largest city in Africa with almost 10 million inhabitants, Cairo evolved on the eastern bank of the River Nile, near its delta. This image clearly shows the differences between the arid desert areas to the south-east and south-west, the fertile lands of the Nile flood plain, and the urban area itself. The shadows of the Pyramids on the Giza Plateau can be seen on the left-hand edge of the cultivated area, below where the road crosses it.

– Western Cape, South Africa –

Cape Town sits to the bottom left of this image, with the Cape Peninsula running south-east to the Cape of Good Hope. Inland from the fertile coastal plain, where most of South Africa's wine is produced, is the rugged interior of the Great Karoo where parallel mountain ranges are dissected by river valleys.

– Tehran, Iran –

On the sheltered southern slopes of the Elburz (Alborz) Mountains, the street layout of Tehran, the capital city of Iran, can be clearly seen towards the bottom left-hand side of this image. However, it is the dissected parallel ridges of the mountains and the spectacular snow-covered peak of Demavend which dominate this scene. At 5,604 m (18,386 ft), the peak is the highest in the Middle East and is an extinct volcanic cone with no recorded historic eruptions, although there are still active hot springs on its slopes.

– Karachi, Pakistan –

The largest city in Pakistan with over 9 million inhabitants, Karachi is the administrative headquarters of Sind province and is also the commercial and industrial capital of the whole country. To its south lie the mangrove swamps of the vast delta of the River Indus, 210 km (130 miles) wide where it flows into the Arabian Sea. To the north and east of the city are the dry, hot Sind plains, which are subject to a mean annual rainfall of only 125-250 mm (5-10 inches).

– Tokyo, Japan –

At the head of Tokyo Bay, the city, with its satellites of Kawasaki and Yokohama, forms one of the world's most densely populated areas with over 26 million people. Owing to the shortage of space, much development has taken place on areas reclaimed from the sea. One of these is Haneda International Airport, whose runway pattern is clearly visible at the mouth of the Tama River. The Tokyo Bay bridge/tunnel projects into the Bay from the eastern shore.

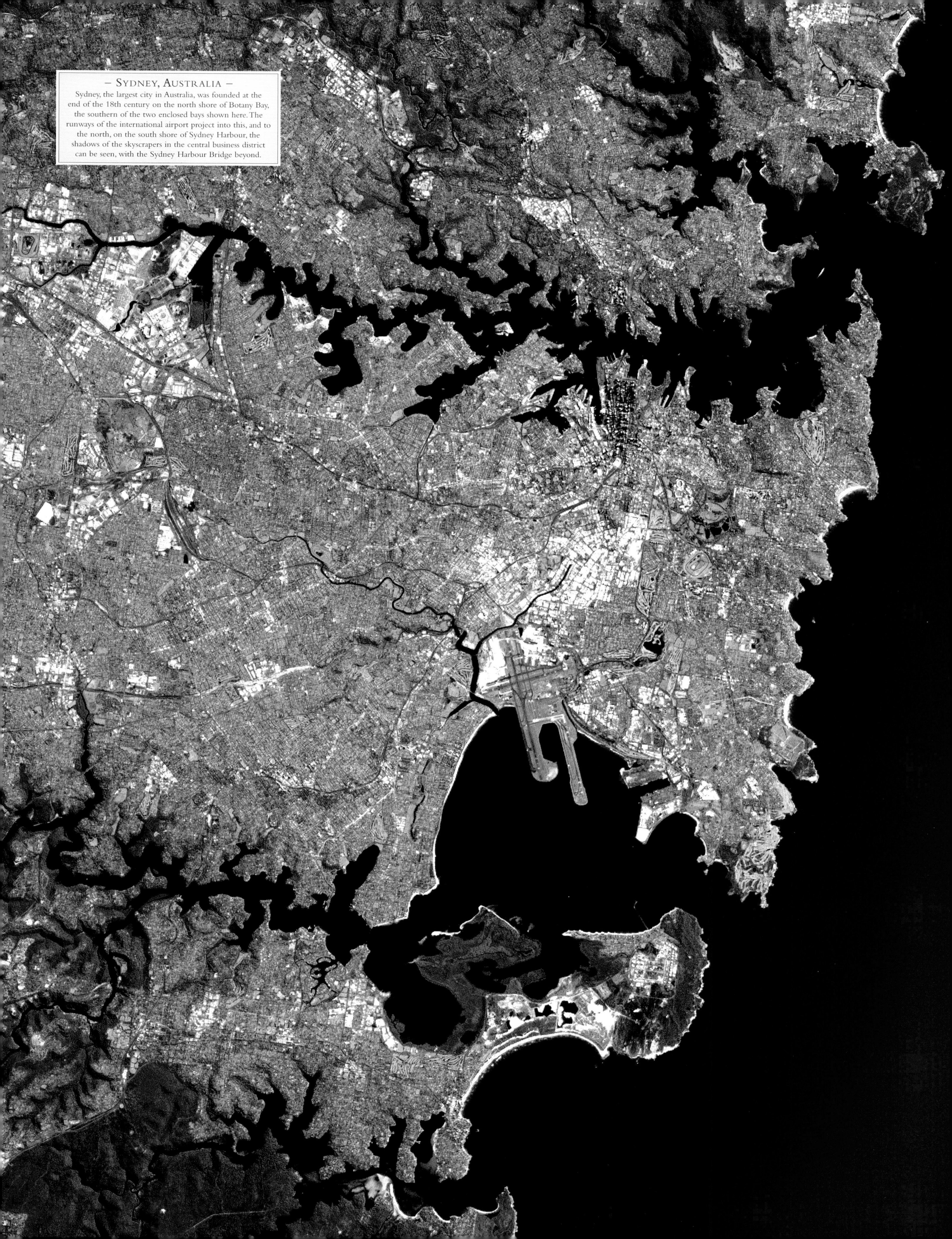

– Sydney, Australia –

Sydney, the largest city in Australia, was founded at the end of the 18th century on the north shore of Botany Bay, the southern of the two enclosed bays shown here. The runways of the international airport project into this, and to the north, on the south shore of Sydney Harbour, the shadows of the skyscrapers in the central business district can be seen, with the Sydney Harbour Bridge beyond.

– Christchurch, New Zealand –

Situated on the east coast of South Island, the city of Christchurch, with more than 300,000 inhabitants, lies between the braided River Waimakiriri and the spectacular Banks Peninsula. The latter was formed by the erosion of two ancient volcanic cones by glaciers and their subsequent inundation by the sea to create the two large harbours of Lyttleton to the north and Akaroa in the south, as well as numerous flooded valleys. Inland, to the west, lie the fertile Canterbury Plains, New Zealand's prime sheep-rearing area.

INTRODUCTION TO WORLD GEOGRAPHY

The Universe

For more information:
4 Orbits of the planets
Planetary data

About 15 billion years ago, time and space began with the most colossal explosion in cosmic history: the so-called 'Big Bang' that is believed to have initiated the universe. According to current theory, in the first millionth of a second of its existence it expanded from a dimensionless point of infinite mass and density into a fireball about 30 billion kilometres across; and it has been expanding ever since.

It took almost a million years for the primal fireball to cool enough for atoms to form. They were mostly hydrogen, still the most abundant material in the universe. But the new matter was not evenly distributed around the young universe, and a few billion years later atoms in relatively dense regions began to cling together under the influence of gravity, forming distinct masses of gas separated by vast expanses of empty space. To begin with, these first proto-galaxies were dark places: the universe had cooled. But gravitational attraction continued, condensing matter into coherent lumps inside the galactic gas clouds. About three billion years later, some of these masses had contracted so much that internal pressure produced the high temperatures necessary to bring about nuclear fusion: the first stars were born.

There were several generations of stars, each feeding on the wreckage of its extinct predecessors as well as the original galactic gas swirls. With each new generation, progressively larger atoms were forged in stellar furnaces and the galaxy's range of elements, once restricted to hydrogen, grew larger. About 10 billion years after the Big Bang, a star formed on the outskirts of our galaxy with enough matter left over to create a retinue of planets. Nearly five billion years after that human beings evolved.

The Sun is one of more than 100 billion stars in the home galaxy alone. Our galaxy, in turn, forms part of a local group of approximately 30 similar structures, some much larger than our own; there are at least 100 billion other galaxies in the universe as a whole. The most distant ever observed, a highly energetic galactic core known only as quasar PC 1247 +3406, lies about 12 billion light-years away.

Life of a Star

For most of its existence, a star produces energy by the nuclear fusion of hydrogen into helium at its core. The duration of this hydrogen-burning period – known as the main sequence – depends on the star's mass; the greater the mass, the higher the core temperatures and the sooner the star's supply of hydrogen is exhausted. Dim, dwarf stars consume their hydrogen slowly, eking it out over 1,000 billion years or more. The Sun, like other stars of its mass, should spend about 10 billion years on the main sequence; since it was formed less than five billion years ago, it still has half its life left.

Once all a star's core hydrogen has been fused into helium, nuclear activity moves outwards into layers of unconsumed hydrogen. For a time, energy production sharply increases: the star grows hotter and expands enormously, turning into a so-called red giant. Its energy output will increase a thousandfold, and it will swell to a hundred times its present diameter.

After a few hundred million years, helium in the core will become sufficiently compressed to initiate a new cycle of nuclear fusion: from helium to carbon. The star will contract somewhat, before beginning its last expansion, in the Sun's case engulfing the Earth and perhaps Mars. In this bloated condition, the Sun's outer layers will break off into space, leaving a tiny inner core, mainly of carbon, that shrinks progressively under the force of its own gravity: dwarf stars can attain a density more than 10,000 times that of normal matter, with crushing surface gravities to match. Gradually, the nuclear fires will die down, and the Sun will reach its terminal stage: a black dwarf, emitting insignificant amounts of energy.

However, stars more massive than the Sun may undergo another transformation. The additional mass allows gravitational collapse to continue indefinitely: eventually, all the star's remaining matter shrinks to a point, and its density approaches infinity – a state that will not permit even subatomic structures to survive.

The star has become a black hole: an anomalous 'singularity' in the fabric of space and time. Although vast coruscations of radiation will be emitted by any matter falling into its grasp, the singularity itself has an escape velocity that exceeds the speed of light, and nothing can ever be released from it. Within the boundaries of the black hole, the laws of physics are suspended, but no physicist can ever observe the extraordinary events that may occur.

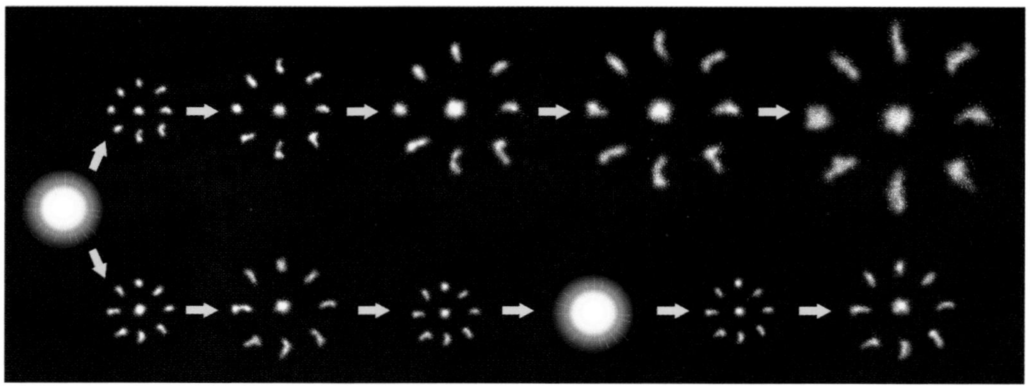

The End of the Universe

The likely fate of the universe is disputed. One theory (top left) dictates that the expansion begun at the time of the Big Bang will continue 'indefinitely', with ageing galaxies moving further and further apart in an immense, dark graveyard. Alternatively, gravity may overcome the expansion (bottom left). Galaxies will fall back together until everything is again concentrated at a single point, followed by a new Big Bang and a new expansion, in an endlessly repeated cycle.

The first theory is supported by the amount of visible matter in the universe; the second assumes there is enough dark material to bring about the gravitational collapse.

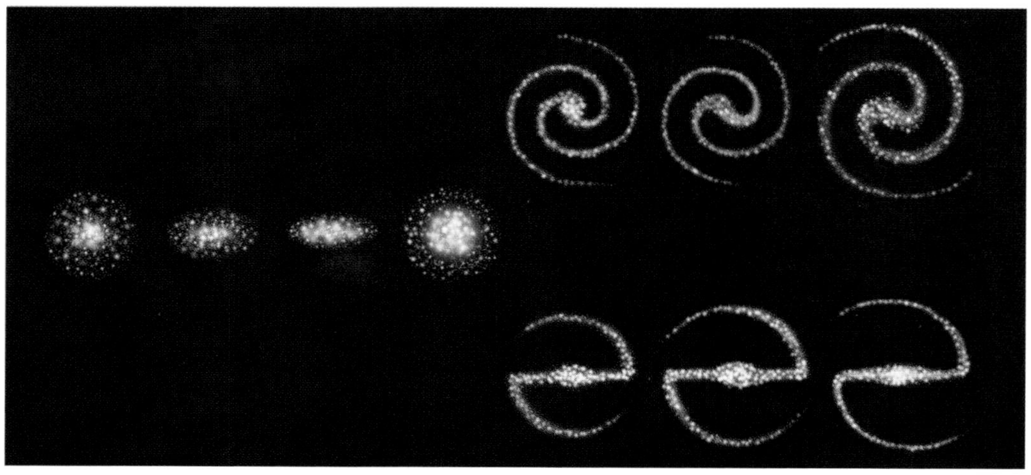

Galactic Structures

Many of the universe's 100 billion galaxies show clear structural patterns, originally classified by the American astronomer Edwin Hubble in 1925. Spiral galaxies like our own (top row) have a central, almost spherical bulge and a surrounding disk composed of spiral arms. Barred spirals (bottom row) have a central bar of stars across the nucleus, with spiral arms trailing from the ends of the bar. Elliptical galaxies (far left) have a uniform appearance, ranging from a flattened disk to a near sphere. So-called SO galaxies (left row, right) have a central bulge, but no spiral arms. Most galaxies, however, have no obvious structure at all.

Galaxies also vary enormously in size, from dwarfs only 2,000 light-years across to great assemblies of stars 80 or more times larger.

The Home Galaxy

The Sun and its planets are located in one of the spiral arms, a little less than 28,000 light-years from the galactic centre and orbiting around it in a period of 200 million years. The centre is invisible from the Earth, masked by vast, light-absorbing clouds of interstellar dust. The galaxy is probably around 12 billion years old and, like other spiral galaxies, has three distinct regions. The central bulge is about 30,000 light-years in diameter. The disk in which the Sun is located is not much more than 1,000 light-years thick but 100,000 light-years from end to end. Around the galaxy is the halo, a spherical zone 300,000 light-years across, studded with globular star-clusters and sprinkled with individual suns.

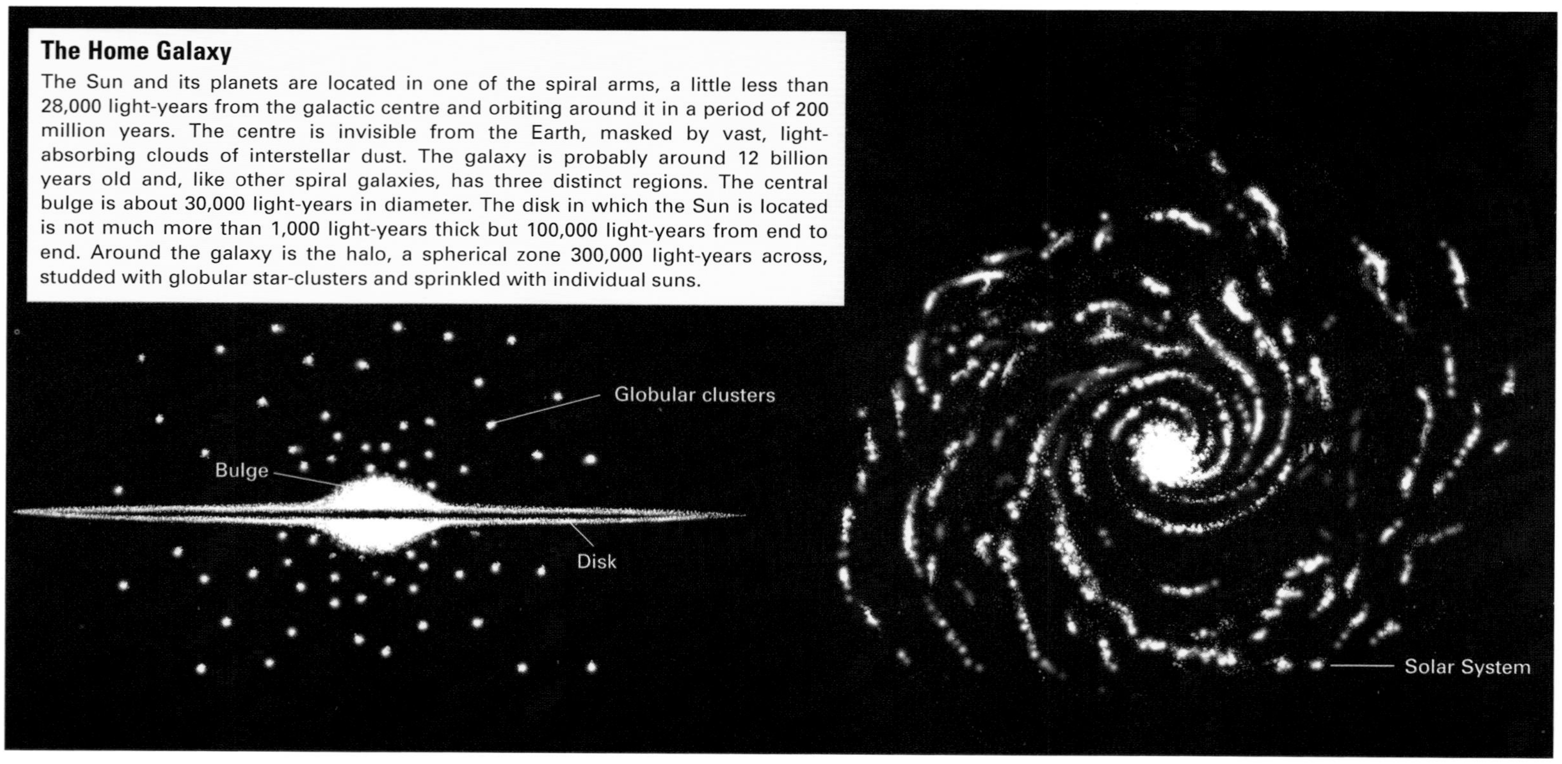
Globular clusters
Bulge
Disk
Solar System

Star Charts

Star charts are drawn as projections of a vast, hollow sphere with the observer in the middle. Each circle below represents slightly more than one hemisphere, centred on the north and south celestial poles respectively – projections of the Earth's poles in the heavens. At the present era, the north pole is marked by the star Polaris; the south pole has no such convenient reference point.

Astronomical co-ordinates are normally given in terms of 'Right Ascension' for longitude and 'Declination' for latitude or altitude. Since the stars appear to rotate around the Earth once every 24 hours, Right Ascension is measured eastwards – anticlockwise – in hours and minutes and is marked around the edge of the map. One hour is equivalent to 15 angular degrees; zero on the scale is the point at which the Sun crosses the celestial equator at the spring equinox, known to astronomers as the First Point in Aries. Unlike the Sun, stars always rise and set at the same point on the horizon. Declination measures (in degrees) a star's angular distance above or below the celestial equator and is marked on the vertical line.

To use the maps, first choose the one for your hemisphere and hold it with the month at the bottom. The stars in the lower part of the map are then due south (or north, in the southern hemisphere) at about 1 AM local time, not allowing for summer or daylight saving time. Their exact position above the horizon depends on your latitude. The closer to the Equator you live, the higher in the sky these stars will appear. Some additional stars from the map for the other hemisphere will be visible in the lower sky.

Stars near the top of the map will be below the opposite horizon at this date and time but will be visible at other times of the night and year. The sky appears to move anticlockwise around the celestial pole during the course of the day (clockwise in the southern hemisphere), so the same stars will be visible at 11 PM a month earlier.

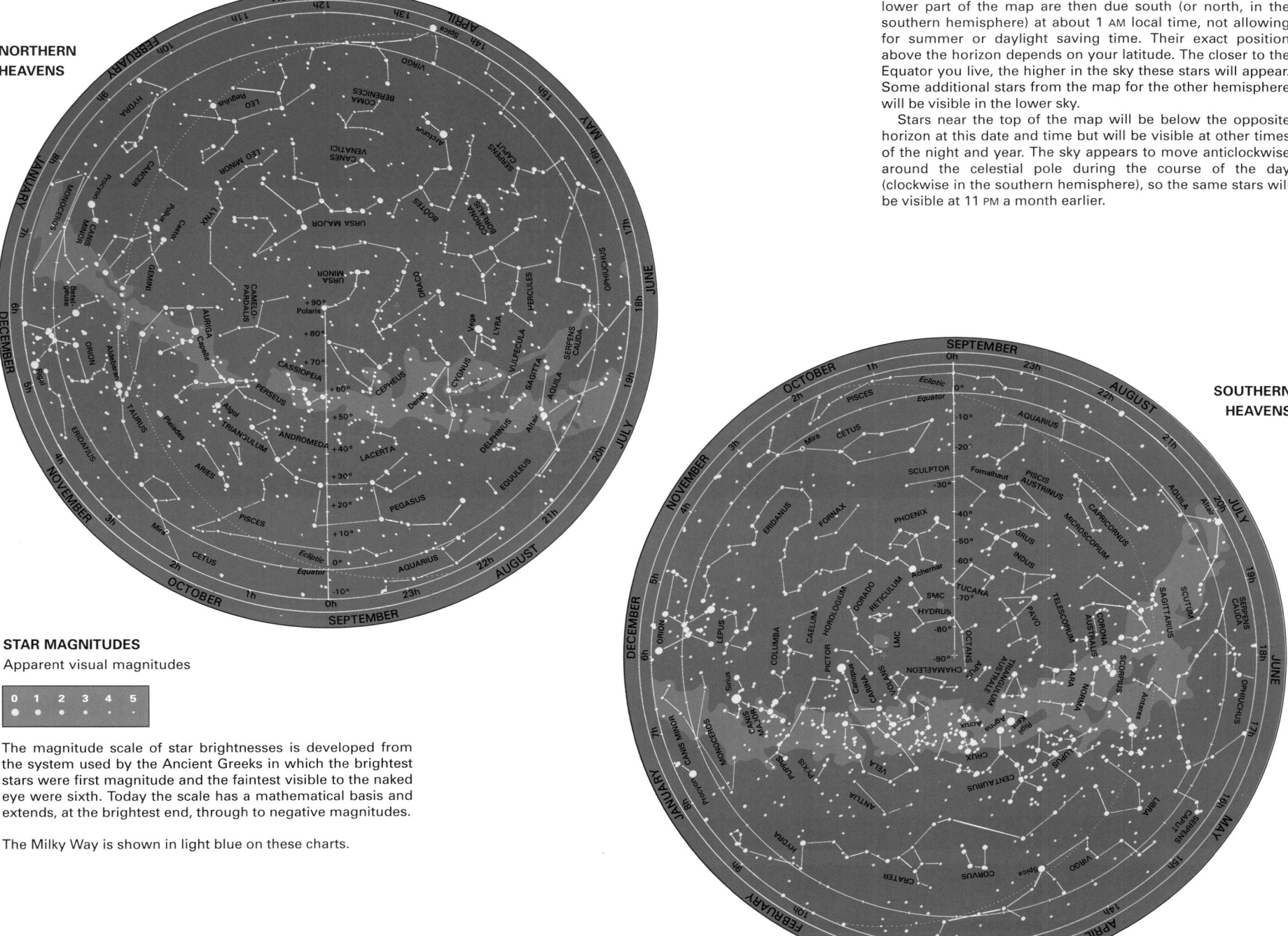

NORTHERN HEAVENS

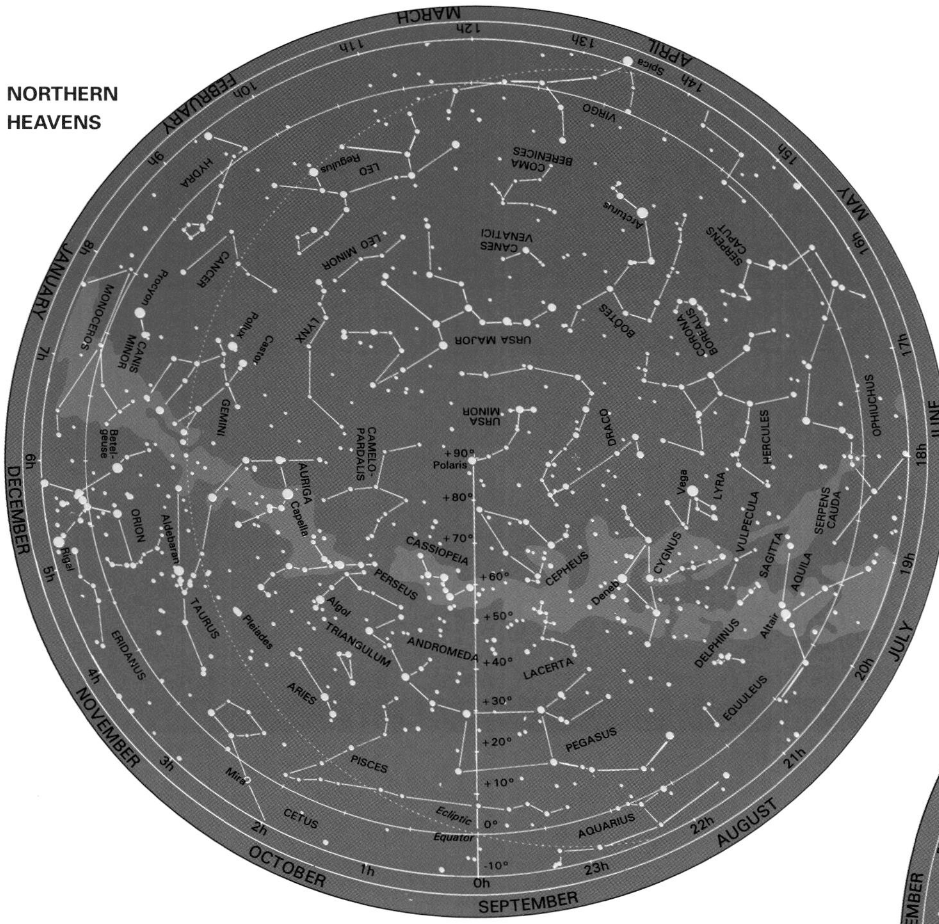

SOUTHERN HEAVENS

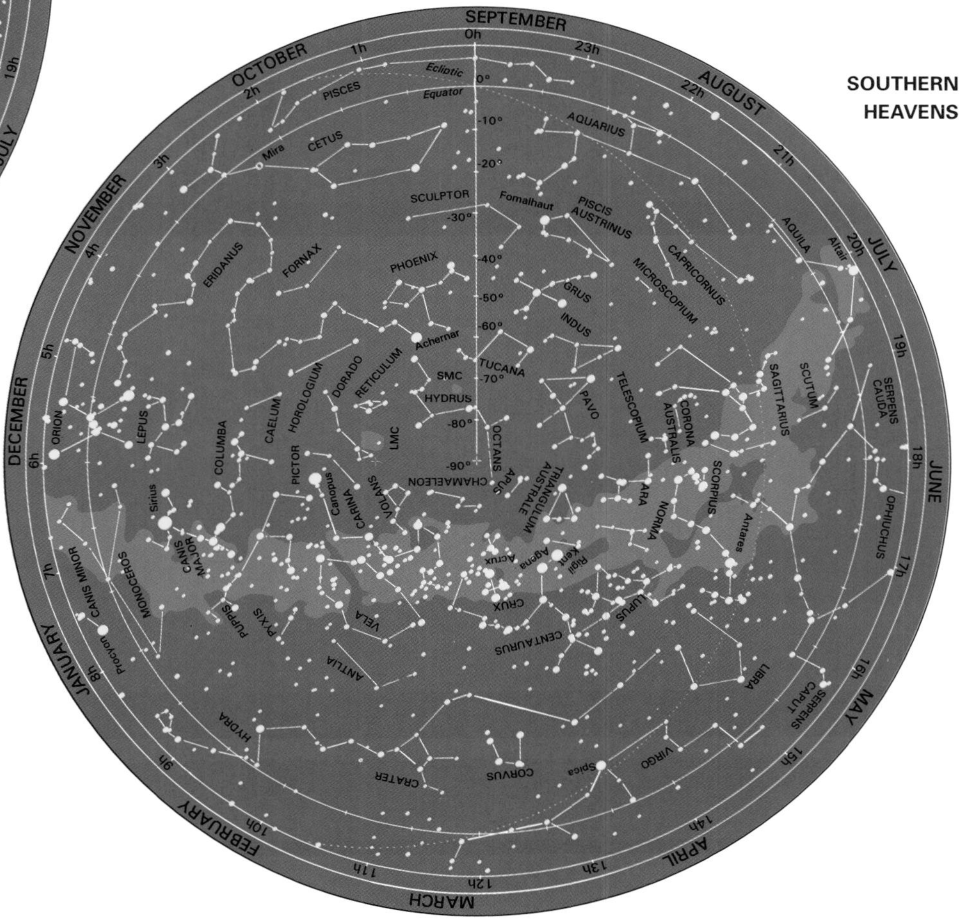

STAR MAGNITUDES

Apparent visual magnitudes

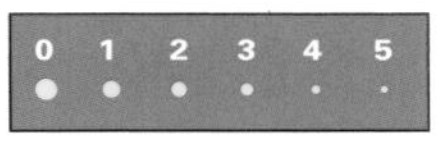

The magnitude scale of star brightnesses is developed from the system used by the Ancient Greeks in which the brightest stars were first magnitude and the faintest visible to the naked eye were sixth. Today the scale has a mathematical basis and extends, at the brightest end, through to negative magnitudes.

The Milky Way is shown in light blue on these charts.

THE NEAREST STARS

The 20 nearest stars, excluding the Sun, with their distance from Earth in light-years*

Proxima Centauri	4.25
Alpha Centauri A	4.3
Alpha Centauri B	4.3
Barnard's Star	6.0
Wolf 359	7.8
Lalande 21185	8.3
Sirius A	8.7
Sirius B	8.7
UV Ceti A	8.7
UV Ceti B	8.7
Ross 154	9.4
Ross 248	10.3
Epsilon Eridani	10.7
Ross 128	10.9
61 Cygni A	11.1
61 Cygni B	11.1
Epsilon Indi	11.2
Groombridge 34A	11.2
Groombridge 34B	11.2
L789-6	11.2
Procyon A	11.4
Procyon B	11.4

Many of the nearest stars, like Alpha Centauri A and B, are doubles, orbiting about the common centre of gravity and to all intents and purposes equidistant from Earth. Many of them are dim objects, with no name other than the designation given by the astronomers who investigated them. However, they include Sirius, the brightest star in the sky, and Procyon, the seventh brightest. Both are far larger than the Sun; of the nearest stars, only Epsilon Eridani is similar in size and luminosity.

* A light-year equals approx. 9,500,000,000,000 kilometres

THE CONSTELLATIONS

The constellations and their English names

Andromeda	Andromeda	Circinus	Compasses	Lacerta	Lizard	Piscis Austrinus	Southern Fish
Antlia	Air Pump	Columba	Dove	Leo	Lion	Puppis	Ship's Stern
Apus	Bird of Paradise	Coma Berenices	Berenice's Hair	Leo Minor	Little Lion	Pyxis	Mariner's Compass
Aquarius	Water Carrier	Corona Australis	Southern Crown	Lepus	Hare	Reticulum	Net
Aquila	Eagle	Corona Borealis	Northern Crown	Libra	Scales	Sagitta	Arrow
Ara	Altar	Corvus	Crow	Lupus	Wolf	Sagittarius	Archer
Aries	Ram	Crater	Cup	Lynx	Lynx	Scorpius	Scorpion
Auriga	Charioteer	Crux	Southern Cross	Lyra	Lyre	Sculptor	Sculptor
Boötes	Herdsman	Cygnus	Swan	Mensa	Table	Scutum	Shield
Caelum	Chisel	Delphinus	Dolphin	Microscopium	Microscope	Serpens	Serpent
Camelopardalis	Giraffe	Dorado	Swordfish	Monoceros	Unicorn	Sextans	Sextant
Cancer	Crab	Draco	Dragon	Musca	Fly	Taurus	Bull
Canes Venatici	Hunting Dogs	Equuleus	Little Horse	Norma	Level	Telescopium	Telescope
Canis Major	Great Dog	Eridanus	Eridanus	Octans	Octant	Triangulum	Triangle
Canis Minor	Little Dog	Fornax	Furnace	Ophiuchus	Serpent Bearer	Triangulum Australe	Southern Triangle
Capricornus	Goat	Gemini	Twins	Orion	Orion	Tucana	Toucan
Carina	Keel	Grus	Crane	Pavo	Peacock	Ursa Major	Great Bear
Cassiopeia	Cassiopeia	Hercules	Hercules	Pegasus	Winged Horse	Ursa Minor	Little Bear
Centaurus	Centaur	Horologium	Clock	Perseus	Perseus	Vela	Sails
Cepheus	Cepheus	Hydra	Water Snake	Phoenix	Phoenix	Virgo	Virgin
Cetus	Whale	Hydrus	Sea Serpent	Pictor	Easel	Volans	Flying Fish
Chamaeleon	Chameleon	Indus	Indian	Pisces	Fishes	Vulpecula	Fox

The Solar System

For more information:

2 The home galaxy
6 The seasons
Day and night
7 The Moon

Lying 28,000 light-years from the centre of one of billions of galaxies that comprise the observable universe, our Solar System contains nine planets and their moons, innumerable asteroids and comets, and a miscellany of dust and gas, all tethered by the immense gravitational field of the Sun, the middling-sized star whose thermonuclear furnaces provide them all with heat and light. The Solar System was formed about 4,600 million years ago, when a spinning cloud of gas, mostly hydrogen but seeded with other, heavier elements, condensed enough to ignite a nuclear reaction and create a star. The Sun still accounts for almost 99.9% of the system's total mass; one planet, Jupiter, contains most of the remainder.

By composition as well as distance, the planetary array divides quite neatly in two: an inner system of four small, solid planets, including the Earth, and an outer system, from Jupiter to Neptune, of four much larger planets composed of lighter materials, such as gas, liquid and ice. Between the two groups lies a scattering of rocky asteroids, perhaps as many as 400,000. They may be debris left over from the inner Solar System's formation. The outermost planet, Pluto, may simply be the largest of a number of bodies composed of rock and ice orbiting beyond Neptune, similarly left over from the formation of the outer Solar System.

By the 1990s, however, the Solar System also included some newer anomalies: several thousand spacecraft. Most were in orbit around the Earth, but some had probed far and wide around the system. The valuable information beamed back by these robotic investigators has transformed our knowledge of our celestial environment.

Much of the early history of science is the story of people trying to make sense of the errant points of light that were all they knew of the planets. Now, men have themselves stood on the Earth's Moon; probes have landed on Mars and Venus, and orbiting radars have mapped far distant landscapes with astonishing accuracy. In the 1980s, the US *Voyagers* skimmed all four major planets of the outer system, bringing new revelations with each close approach. Only Pluto, inscrutably distant in an orbit that takes it 50 times the Earth's distance from the Sun, remains unvisited by our messengers.

Orbits of the Planets

The solar planets and their orbits, showing the relative position of each planet at the vernal equinox of 1992.

Orbits are drawn to exact scale, but with the Sun and planets greatly enlarged for clarity. The Solar System is shown from the viewpoint of an observer a few light-hours distant in the direction of the constellation Hercules. Seen from such a position, above the plane of the ecliptic, all the planets revolve about the Sun in an anticlockwise direction. The perspective view exaggerates the elliptical form of all the planetary orbits: only Pluto and Mercury follow paths that deviate noticeably from circularity. Near perihelion – its closest approach to the Sun – Pluto actually passes inside the orbit of Neptune, an event that last occurred in 1983. Pluto did not regain its station as the Sun's outermost planet until February 1999.

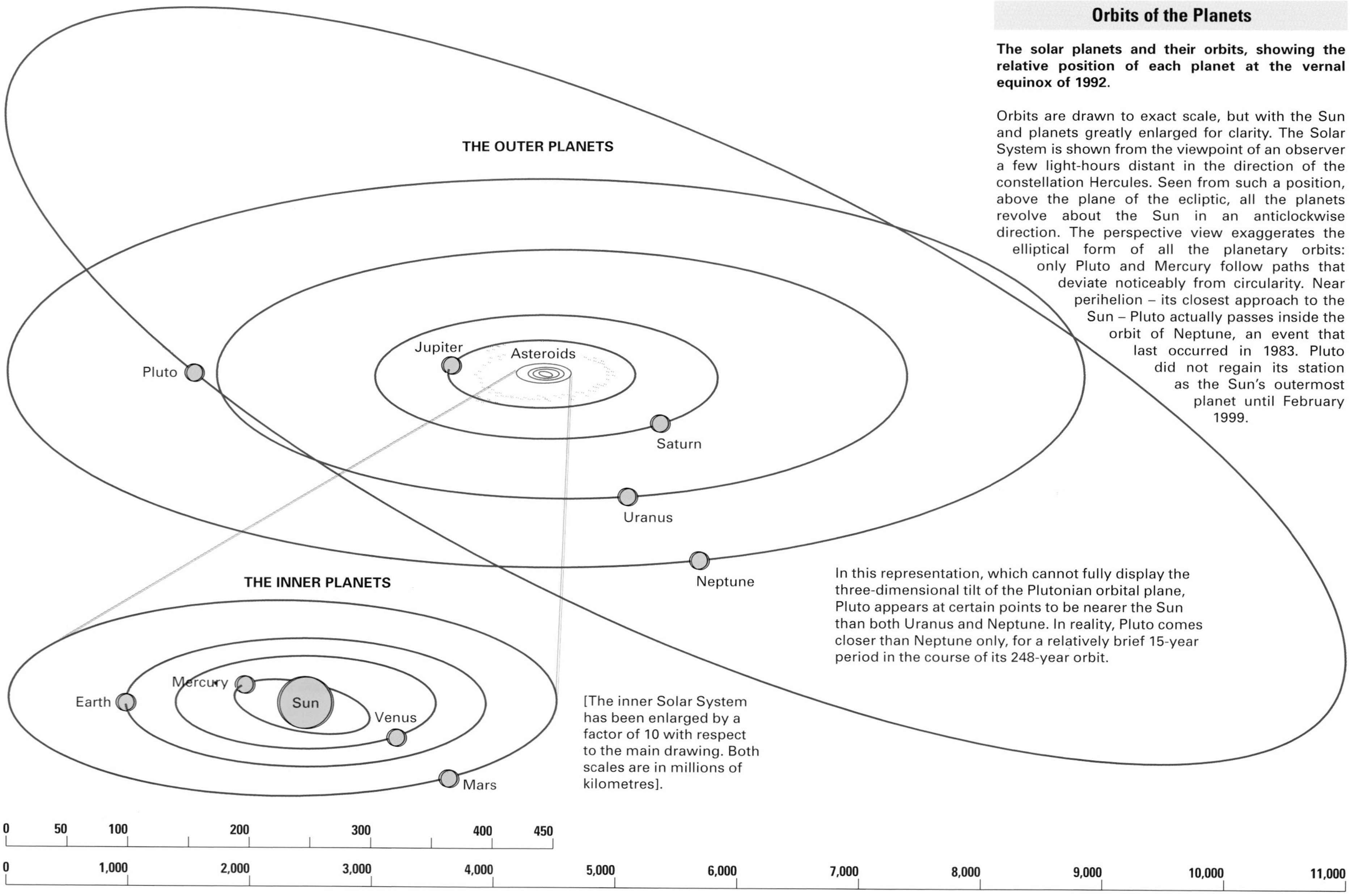

THE OUTER PLANETS
Jupiter
Asteroids
Pluto
Saturn
Uranus
Neptune
THE INNER PLANETS
Mercury
Earth
Sun
Venus
Mars
0
50
100
200
300
400
450
0
1,000
2,000
3,000
4,000
5,000
6,000
7,000
8,000
9,000
10,000
11,000

In this representation, which cannot fully display the three-dimensional tilt of the Plutonian orbital plane, Pluto appears at certain points to be nearer the Sun than both Uranus and Neptune. In reality, Pluto comes closer than Neptune only, for a relatively brief 15-year period in the course of its 248-year orbit.

[The inner Solar System has been enlarged by a factor of 10 with respect to the main drawing. Both scales are in millions of kilometres].

Planetary Data

	Mean distance from Sun (million km)	Mass (Earth = 1)	Period of orbit (Earth years)	Period of rotation (Earth days)	Equatorial diameter (km)	Average density (water = 1)	Surface gravity (Earth = 1)	Escape velocity (km/sec)	Number of known satellites
Sun	–	*332,946*	–	*25.38*	*1,392,000*	*1.41*	*27.9*	*617.5*	–
Mercury	57.9	0.06	0.241	58.67	4,878	5.43	0.38	4.25	0
Venus	108.2	0.8	0.615	243.00	12,100	5.24	0.90	10.36	0
Earth	149.6	1.0	1.00	1.00	12,756	5.52	1.00	11.18	1
Mars	227.9	0.1	1.88	1.02	6,794	3.93	0.38	5.03	2
Jupiter	778.3	317.8	11.86	0.41	142,800	1.33	2.69	59.60	28
Saturn	1,426.8	95.2	29.46	0.42	120,000	0.706	1.16	35.60	30
Uranus	2,869.4	14.5	84.01	0.45	52,400	1.25	0.93	21.10	21
Neptune	4,496.3	17.1	164.79	0.71	48,400	1.77	1.21	24.60	8
Pluto	5,900.1	0.002	247.7	6.39	2,445	1.40	0.05	1.20	1

Planetary days are given in sidereal time – that is, with respect to the stars rather than the Sun. Most of the information in the table was confirmed by spacecraft and often obtained from photographs and other data transmitted back to the Earth. In the case of Pluto, however, only earthbound observations have been made, and no spacecraft will encounter it until well into the 21st century. Given the planet's small size and great distance, figures for its diameter and rotation period have only recently been confirmed.

Pluto is not massive enough to account for the perturbations in the orbits of Uranus and Neptune that led to its 1930 discovery, but it is now widely believed that these perturbations can be explained away as observational errors made by the earlier observers.

The Planets

Mercury is the closest planet to the Sun and hence the fastest-moving. It is very hot with a cratered, wrinkled surface very similar to that of Earth's Moon. It is small and has no gravity, hence there is no significant atmosphere.

Venus has much the same physical dimensions as Earth. Its dense atmosphere is composed of 97% CO_2 resulting in a runaway greenhouse effect that makes the Venusian surface, at 475°C, the hottest of all the planets in the Solar System. Radar mapping shows relatively level land with volcanic regions whose sulphurous discharges explain the sulphuric acid rains reported by soft-landing space probes before they succumbed to Venus' fierce climate.

Earth seen from space is easily the most beautiful of the inner planets; it is also, and more objectively, the largest, as well as the only home of known life. Living things are the main reason why the Earth is able to retain a substantial proportion of corrosive and highly reactive oxygen in its atmosphere, a state of affairs that contradicts the laws of chemical equilibrium; the oxygen in turn supports the life that constantly regenerates it.

Mars, smaller and cooler than the Earth, is nevertheless the most likely planet other than Earth where life may have formed. Vast water channels show that it was once warmer and wetter; there may still be traces of former simple life forms, though whether life could thrive in its current cold, dry and thin atmosphere is doubtful. The ice caps are mainly frozen carbon dioxide, and whatever oxygen the planet once possessed is now locked up in the iron-bearing rock that covers its cratered surface and gives it its characteristic red hue. Mars is a dustbowl with occasional storms whirling the dust high into the air.

Jupiter masses almost three times as much as all the other planets combined; had it scooped up rather more matter during its formation, it might have evolved into a small companion star for the Sun. The planet is mostly gas, under intense pressure in the lower atmosphere above a core of fiercely compressed hydrogen and helium. The upper layers form strikingly-coloured rotating belts, the outward sign of the intense storms created by Jupiter's rapid diurnal rotation. Close approaches by spacecraft have shown an orbiting ring system and discovered several previously unknown moons: Jupiter has at least 28 moons.

Saturn is structurally similar to Jupiter, rotating fast enough to produce an obvious bulge at its equator. It is composed of 89% hydrogen and 11% helium, and has wind velocities in the outer atmosphere of 500 metres per second. Ever since the invention of the telescope, however, Saturn's rings have been the feature that has attracted most observers. *Voyager* probes in 1980 and 1981 sent back detailed pictures that showed them to be composed of thousands of separate ringlets, each in turn made up of tiny icy particles.

Uranus was unknown to the ancients. Although it is faintly visible to the naked eye, it was not discovered until 1781. Its interior is largely water, with an atmosphere of hydrogen, helium and some methane, which gives the planet its blue-green colour. Observations in 1977 suggested the presence of a faint ring system, amply confirmed when *Voyager 2* swung past the planet in 1986.

Neptune is always more than 4,000 million km from Earth, and despite its diameter of almost 50,000 km, it can only be seen by telescope. Its 1846 discovery was the result of mathematical predictions by astronomers seeking to explain irregularities in the orbit of Uranus, but until *Voyager 2* closed with the planet in 1989, little was known of it. Like Uranus, it has a ring system; *Voyager*'s photographs revealed a total of eight moons.

Pluto is the most mysterious of the solar planets, if only because even the most powerful telescopes can scarcely resolve it from a point of light to a disk. It was discovered as recently as 1930, like Neptune as the result of perturbations in the orbits of the two then outermost planets. Its small size, as well as its eccentric and highly tilted orbit, has led to suggestions that it is a former satellite of Neptune, somehow liberated from its primary. In 1978 Pluto was found to have a moon of its own, Charon, apparently half the size of Pluto itself.

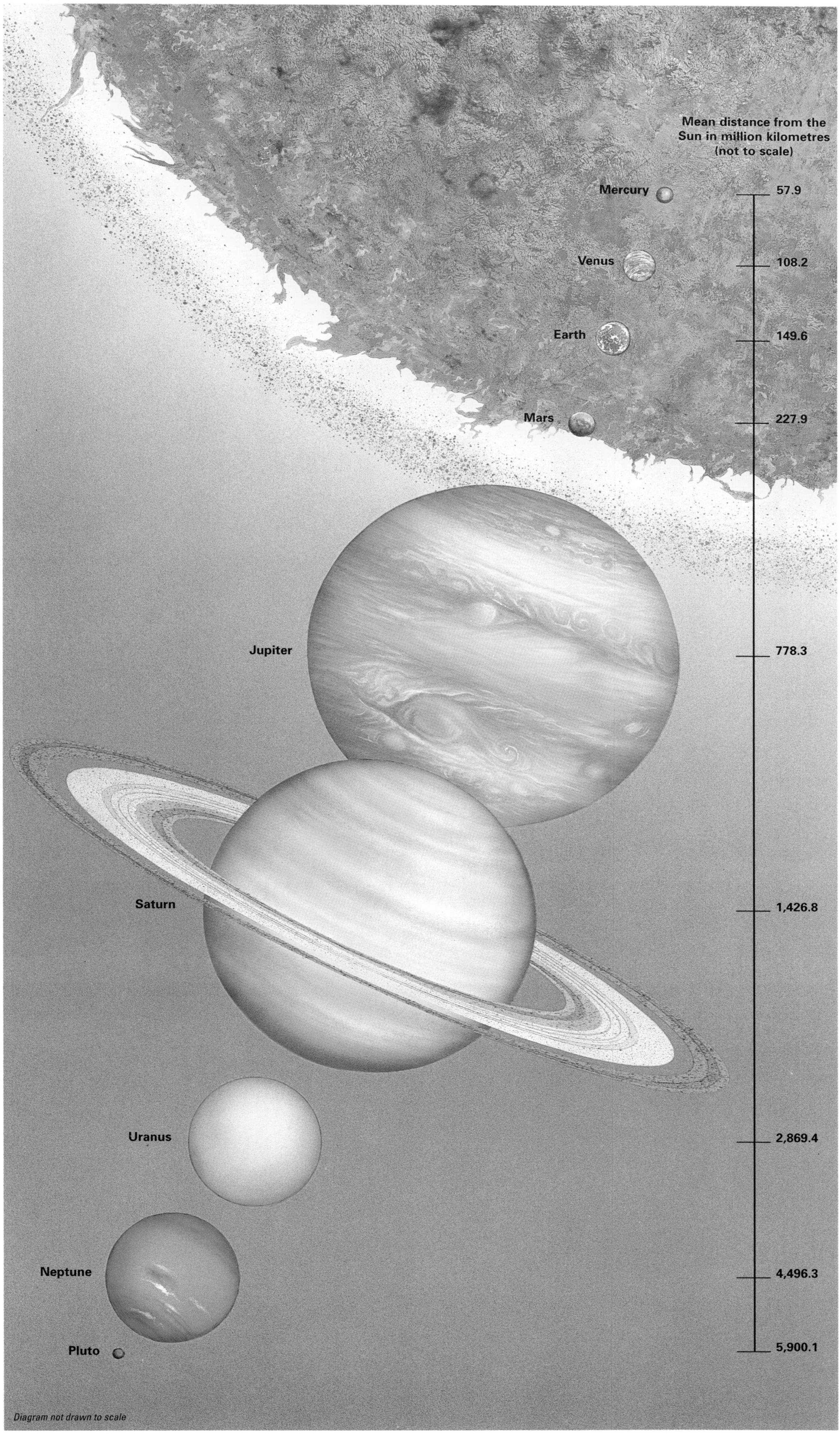

Mean distance from the Sun in million kilometres (not to scale)
Mercury
57.9
Venus
108.2
Earth
149.6
Mars
227.9
Jupiter
778.3
Saturn
1,426.8
Uranus
2,869.4
Neptune
4,496.3
Pluto
5,900.1
Diagram not drawn to scale

Time and Motion

For more information:

4 Orbits of the planets
9 Ocean currents
14 Circulation of the air
16 Climate

The basic unit of time measurement is the day, that is, one rotation of the Earth on its axis. Our present calendar is based on the solar year of 365.24 days, the time taken by the Earth to orbit the Sun.

Calendars based on the movements of the Sun and Moon have been used since ancient times. The average length of the year, according to the Julian Calendar introduced by Julius Caesar, was about 11 minutes too long. The cumulative error was rectified in 1582 by the Gregorian Calendar, when Pope Gregory XIII decreed that the day following 4 October was 15 October, and in that century years did not count as leap years unless they were divisible by 400. England finally adopted the reformed calendar in 1752, when it was 11 days behind the European mainland.

The rotation of the Earth on its axis causes day and night. Because the Earth rotates through 360° every 24 hours, the world is divided into 24 time zones centred on lines of longitude at 15° longitude.

The tilt of the Earth's axis, also called the obliquity of the ecliptic, accounts for the seasons which are so familiar in the middle latitudes. But geological evidence shows that, over long periods of time, climates change and the advances and retreats of the ice during the Pleistocene Ice Age may have been caused by regular variations in the Earth's tilt, its orbit around the Sun, and changes in the season when it is closest to the Sun (perihelion).

Earth Data

Aphelion (maximum distance from Sun): 152,007,016 km

Perihelion (minimum distance from Sun): 147,000,830 km

Angle of tilt (obliquity of the ecliptic): 23° 27′ 08″

Length of year – solar tropical (equinox to equinox): 365.24 days

Length of year: 365 days, 5 hours, 48 minutes, 46 seconds of mean solar time

Superficial area: 510,000,000 sq km

Land surface: 149,000,000 sq km (29.2%)

Water surface: 361,000,000 sq km (70.8%)

Equatorial circumference: 40,077 km

Polar circumference: 40,009 km

Equatorial diameter: 12,756.8 km

Polar diameter: 12,713.8 km

Equatorial radius: 6,378.4 km

Polar radius: 6,356.9 km

Volume of the Earth: 1,083,230 x 10^6 cu km

Mass of the Earth: 5.9 x 10^{21} tonnes

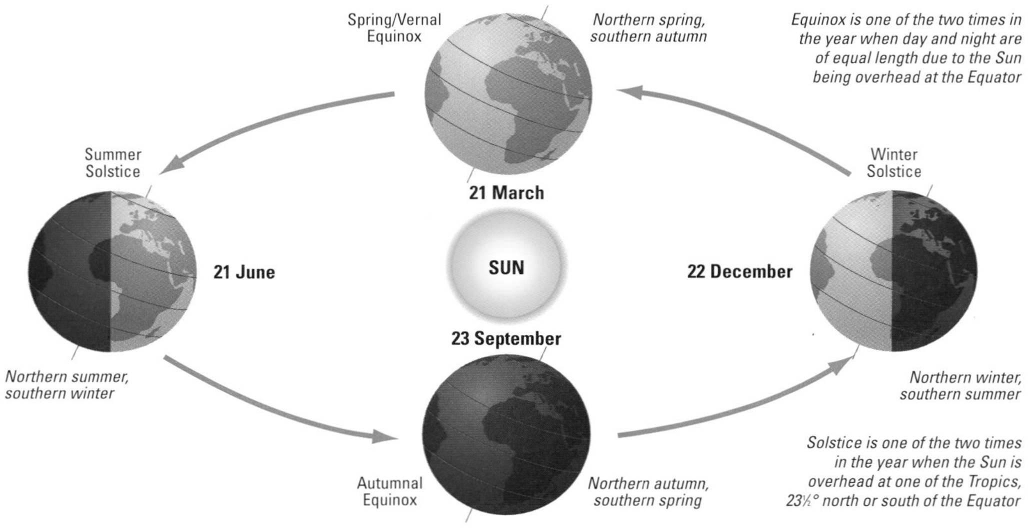

The Seasons

Seasons occur because the Earth's axis is tilted at a constant angle of 23½°. When the northern hemisphere is tilted to a maximum extent towards the Sun, on 21 June, the Sun is overhead at the Tropic of Cancer (latitude 23½° North). This is midsummer, or the summer solstice, in the northern hemisphere.

On 22 or 23 September, the Sun is overhead at the Equator, and day and night are of equal length throughout the world. This is the autumn equinox in the northern hemisphere. On 21 or 22 December, the Sun is overhead at the Tropic of Capricorn (23½° South), the winter solstice in the northern hemisphere. The overhead Sun then tracks north until, on 21 March, it is overhead at the Equator. This is the spring (vernal) equinox in the northern hemisphere.

In the southern hemisphere, the seasons are the reverse of those in the north.

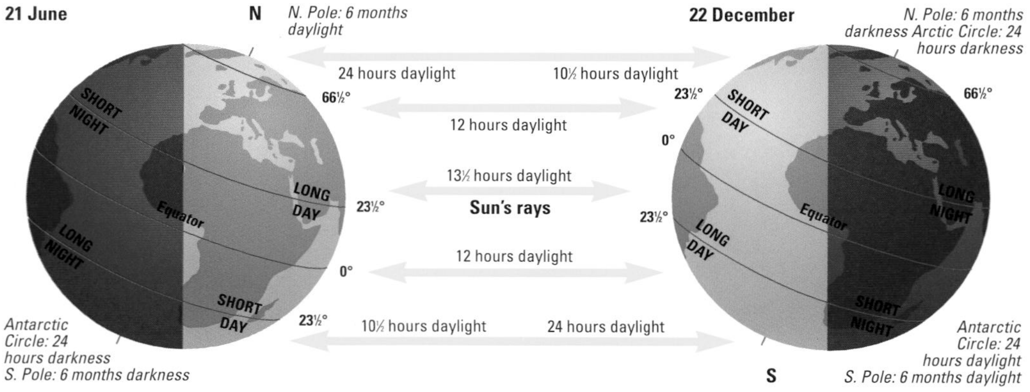

Day and Night

The Sun appears to rise in the east, reach its highest point at noon, and then set in the west, to be followed by night. In reality, it is not the Sun that is moving but the Earth rotating from west to east. The moment when the Sun's upper limb first appears above the horizon is termed sunrise; the moment when the Sun's upper limb disappears below the horizon is sunset.

At the summer solstice in the northern hemisphere (21 June), the Arctic has total daylight and the Antarctic total darkness. The opposite occurs at the winter solstice (21 or 22 December). At the Equator, the length of day and night are almost equal all year.

The Sun's Path

The diagrams on the right illustrate the apparent path of the Sun at (A) the Equator, (B) in mid-latitude (45°), (C) at the Arctic Circle (66½°), and (D) at the North Pole, where there are six months of continuous daylight and six months of continuous night.

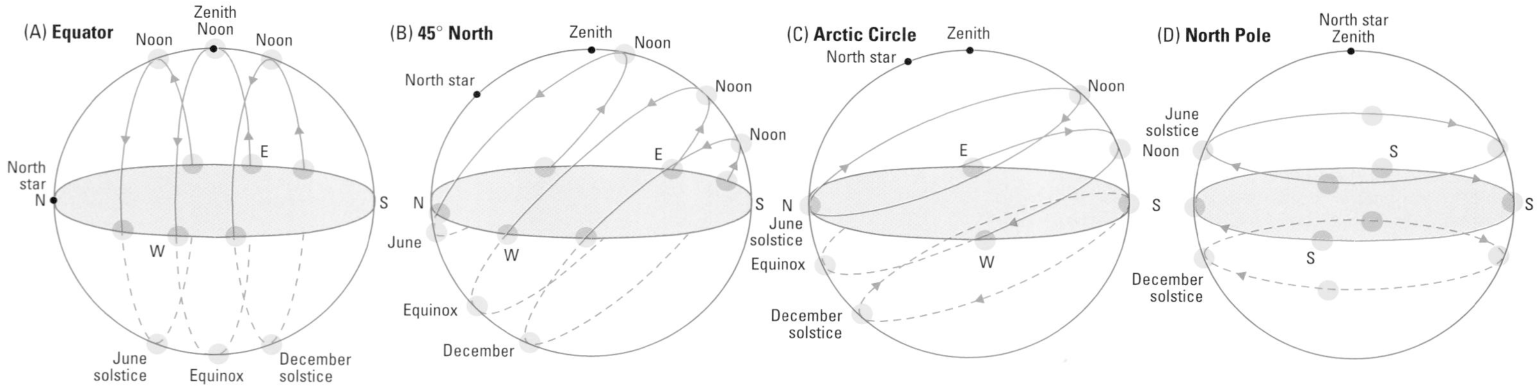

Sunrise and Sunset

The term equinox comes from two Latin words meaning 'equal night'. At the spring and autumn equinoxes, the Sun is vertically overhead at the Equator and all places on Earth have 12 hours of darkness and 12 of daylight. The graphs showing sunrise and sunset show that these occasions occur on 21 March and on 22 or 23 September. The graphs also show that, because the Sun remains high in the sky throughout the year, the length of the day and night at the Equator remain roughly the same throughout the year, with sunrise occurring around 6 AM and sunset at around 6 PM. The further north or south one travels, the greater the difference between the number of hours of daylight and darkness. For example, the graph, right, shows that at latitude 60°N, sunrise varies from just after 9 AM in midwinter (on 22 or 23 December) to about 2.30 AM in midsummer (around the summer solstice on 21 June). By contrast, the second graph, far right, shows that sunset at latitude 60°N occurs at about 2.45 PM in midwinter and 9.20 PM in midsummer.

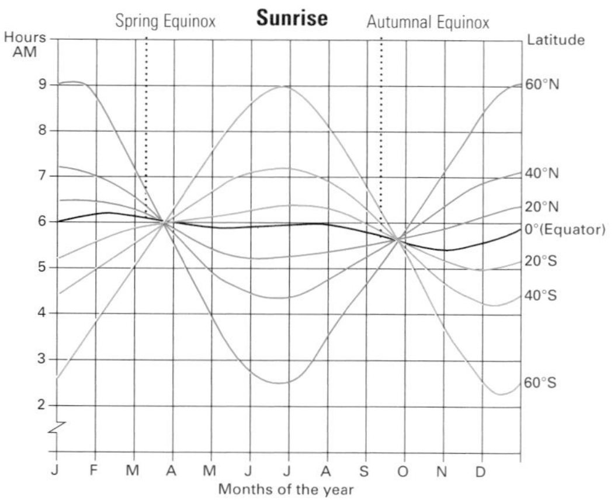

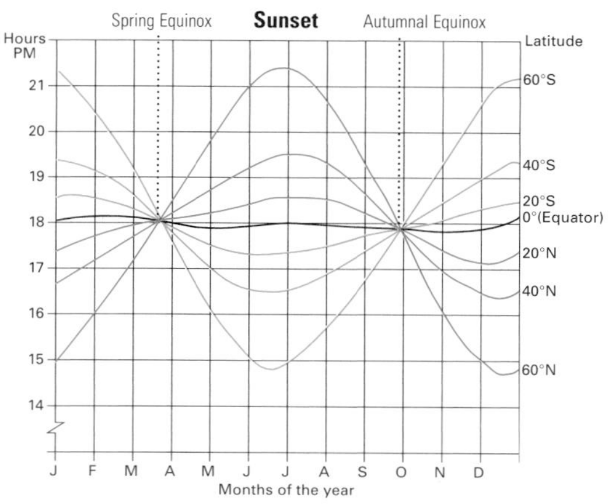

The Moon

The Moon rotates more slowly than the Earth, making one complete turn on its axis in just over 27 days. Since this corresponds to its period of revolution around the Earth, the Moon always presents the same hemisphere or face to us, and we never see 'the dark side'. The interval between one full Moon and the next (and between new Moons) is about 29½ days – a lunar month. The apparent changes in the shape of the Moon are caused by its changing position in relation to the Earth; like the planets, it produces no light of its own and shines only by reflecting the rays of the Sun.

Phases of the Moon

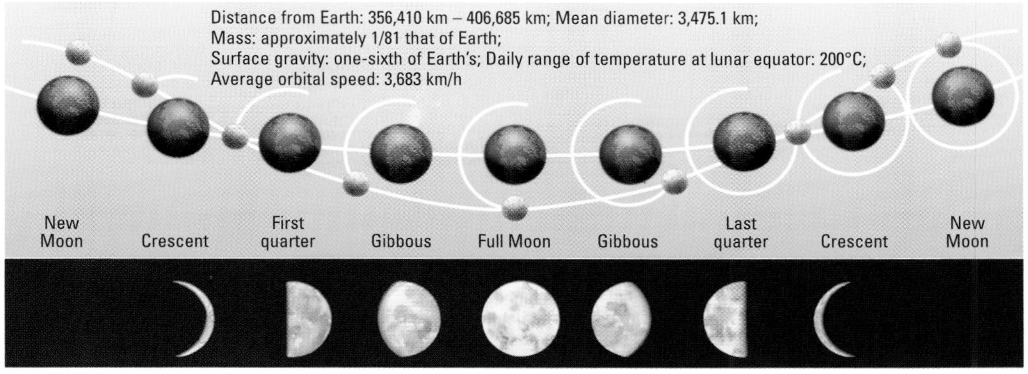

Moon Data

Distance from Earth
The Moon orbits at a mean distance of 384,199.1 km, at an average speed of 3,683 km/h in relation to the Earth.

Size and mass
The average diameter of the Moon is 3,475.1 km. It is 400 times smaller than the Sun but is about 400 times closer to the Earth, so we see them as the same size. The Moon has a mass of 7,348 x 10^{19} tonnes, with a density 3.344 times that of water.

Visibility
Only 59% of the Moon's surface is directly visible from Earth. Reflected light takes 1.25 seconds to reach Earth – compared to 8 minutes 27.3 seconds for light to reach us from the Sun.

Temperature
With the Sun overhead, the temperature on the lunar equator can reach 117.2°C [243°F]. At night it can sink to –162.7°C [–261°F].

Eclipses

When the Moon passes between the Sun and the Earth it causes a partial eclipse of the Sun (1) if the Earth passes through the Moon's outer shadow (P), or a total eclipse (2) if the inner cone shadow crosses the Earth's surface. In a lunar eclipse, the Earth's shadow crosses the Moon and, again, provides either a partial or total eclipse.

Eclipses of the Sun and the Moon do not occur every month because of the 5° difference between the plane of the Moon's orbit and the plane in which the Earth moves. In the 1990s only 14 lunar eclipses were possible, for example, seven partial and seven total; each was visible only from certain, and variable, parts of the world. The same period witnessed 13 solar eclipses – six partial (or annular) and seven total.

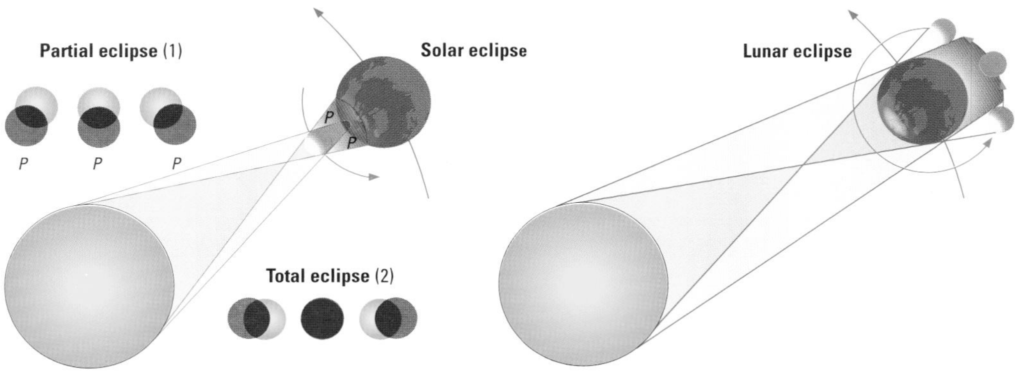

Tides

The daily rise and fall of the ocean's tides are the result of the gravitational pull of the Moon and that of the Sun, though the effect of the latter is only 46.6% as strong as that of the Moon. This effect is greatest on the hemisphere facing the Moon and causes a tidal 'bulge'. When the Sun, Earth and Moon are in line, tide-raising forces are at a maximum and Spring tides occur: high tide reaches the highest values, and low tide falls to low levels. When lunar and solar forces are least coincidental with the Sun and Moon at an angle (near the Moon's first and third quarters), Neap tides occur, which have a small tidal range.

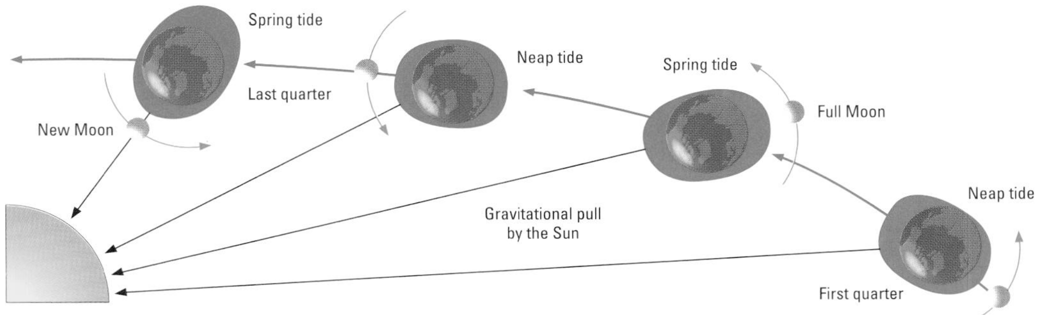

Time Zones

The Earth rotates through 360° in 24 hours, and so moves 15° every hour. The world is divided into 24 standard time zones, each centred on lines of longitude at 15° intervals. At the centre of the first zone is the Prime meridian or Greenwich meridian. All places to the west of Greenwich are one hour behind for every 15° of longitude; places to the east are ahead by one hour for every 15°. When it is 12 noon at the Greenwich meridian, 180° east it is midnight of the same day – while 180° west the day is just beginning. To overcome this, the International Date Line was established, approximately following the 180° meridian. Thus, if you travelled eastwards from Japan (140° East) to Samoa (170° West), you would pass from Sunday night into Sunday morning.

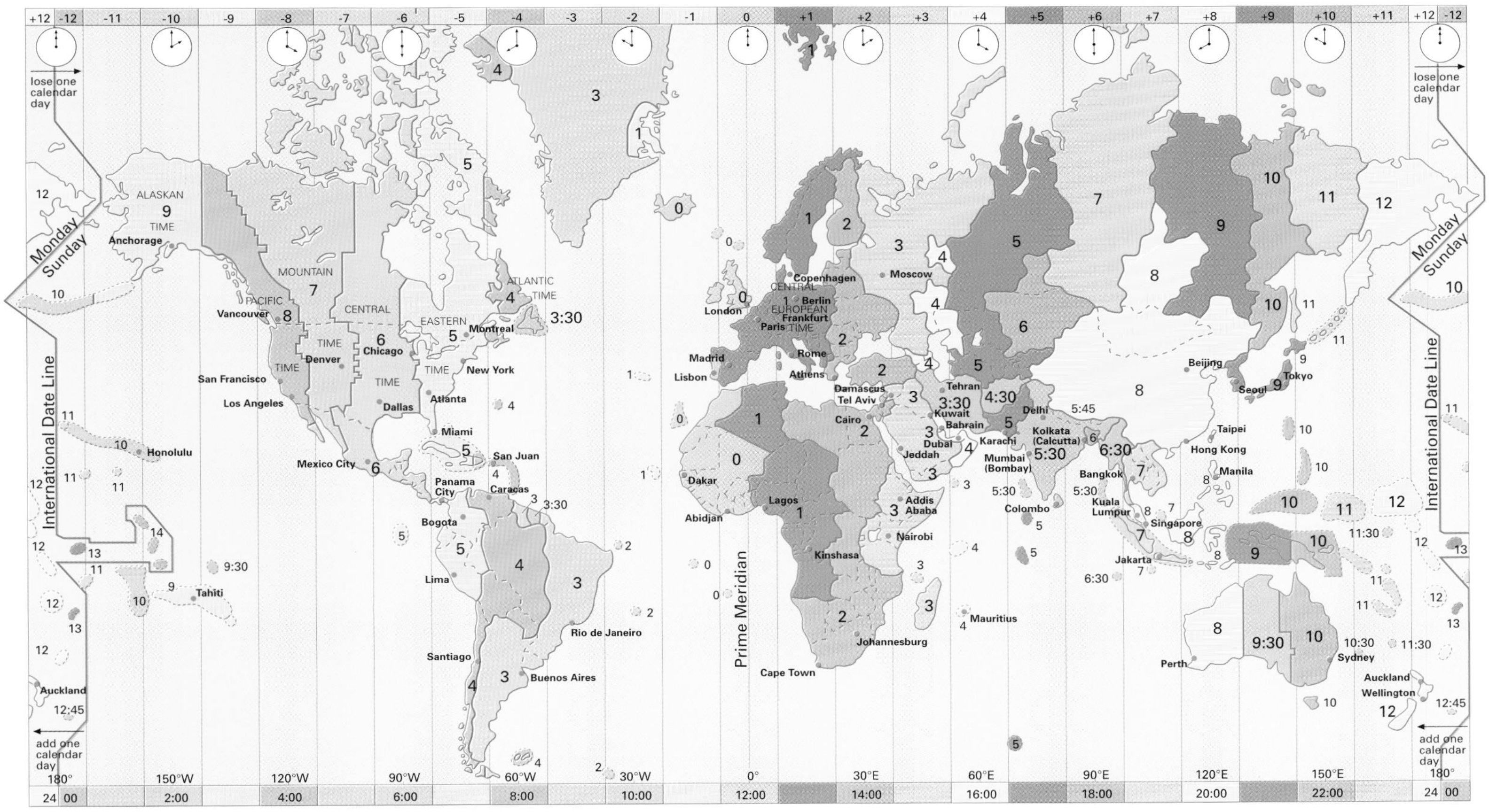

Projection: Mercator

- 10 — Hours slow or fast of UT or Co-ordinated Universal Time
- Zones using UT (GMT)
- Zones slow of UT (GMT)
- International boundaries
- Zones fast of UT (GMT)
- Half-hour zones
- Time zone boundaries
- International Date Line
- Actual Solar Time when time at Greenwich is 12:00 (noon)

Note: Certain of the above time zones are affected by the incidence of 'Summer Time' in countries where it is adopted.

Oceans

For more information:
7 Tides
10 The spreading Earth
14 Atmosphere
18 Hydrological cycle
Water distribution
19 Watersheds
23 Water pollution
41 Shipping

The last 40 years have been described as the 'Space Age', but another exciting and perhaps even more important area of discovery, proceeding at the same time, has been the exploration of 'inner space', namely the oceans which cover more than 70% of our planet. The study of the ocean floor and oceanic islands has revealed features that help to explain how continents move, and how the movements are related to earthquakes and volcanic activity.

Manned submersibles have established that life exists even in the deepest trenches, where the pressure reaches 1,000 atmospheres, the equivalent of the force of one tonne bearing down on every square centimetre. Further exploration in the pitch-black environment of the ocean ridges has revealed strange forms of marine life around scalding hot vents. The creatures include giant tubeworms, blind shrimps, and bacteria, some of which are genetically very different from any other known life forms. In 1996, an analysis of one micro-organism revealed that at least half of its 1,700 or so genes were hitherto unknown. This environment, which is based on chemicals, not sunlight, may resemble the places where life on Earth first began.

Another vital area of contemporary research concerns the interactions between the oceans and the atmosphere, as exemplified in the El Niño–Southern Oscillation (ENSO), and the bearing that these have on climatic change.

Most geographers divide the world's ocean waters into four areas: the Pacific, Atlantic, Indian and Arctic oceans. The most active zone in the oceans is the sunlit upper layer, where the water is moved around by wind-blown currents. It is the home of most sea life and acts as a membrane through which the ocean breathes, absorbing great quantities of carbon dioxide and partly exchanging it for oxygen.

As the depth increases, so light fades and temperatures fall until just before 1,000 metres where there is a marked temperature change at the thermocline, the boundary between the warm surface zone and the cold deep zone. Below the thermocline, slow currents are caused by density differences between bodies of water with varying temperatures and salinity.

Seawater

The chemical composition of the sea, by percentage, excluding the elements of water itself

Chloride (Cl)	55.04%
Sodium (Na)	30.61%
Sulphate (SO_4)	7.69%
Magnesium (Mg)	3.69%
Calcium (Ca)	1.16%
Potassium (K)	1.10%
Bicarbonate (HCO_3)	0.41%
Bromide (Br)	0.19%
Boric Acid (H_3BO_3)	0.07%
Strontium (Sr)	0.04%
Fluoride (Fl)	0.003%
Lithium (Li)	trace
Rubidium (Rb)	trace
Phosphorus (P)	trace
Iodine (I)	trace
Barium (Ba)	trace
Arsenic (As)	trace
Cesium (Cs)	trace

Eleven constituents account for over 99% of the salt content of seawater, but seawater also contains virtually every other element. In natural conditions, its composition is broadly consistent across the world's seas and oceans; but in coastal areas especially, variations are sometimes substantial. The oceans are about 35 parts water to one part salt.

Life in the Oceans

An imaginary profile of the typical coastal and oceanic zones is shown, with a selection of the life forms that might occur in the water off the Pacific Coast of Central America. The animals illustrated are not drawn to scale as the range of sizes is too great. Most marine life is confined to the first 200 metres, the upper sunlit (photic) zone, where sunlight can still penetrate. Plant and animal plankton, the basis of life in the ocean, occur in great quantities in all zones.

In the pelagic environment (open sea), vertical gradients, including those of light, temperature and salinity, determine the distribution of organisms. From the tidal zone at the coastline, the continental shelf, geologically still part of the continental landmass, drops gently to about 200 metres – the sunlit zone. At the end of the shelf, the seabed falls away in the steeper angle of the continental slope. The subsequent descent to the deep ocean floor, known as the continental rise, is more gentle, with gradients between 1 in 100 and 1 in 700 until the abyssal plains and hills between 2,500 and 6,000 metres below the surface.

The deep sea floor contains seamounts, some of which are capped by coral reefs, ocean ridges, the longest mountain chains on Earth, and deep ocean trenches, especially in the Pacific Ocean where six trenches reach depths of more than 10,000 metres, including the 11,022-metre deep Mariana Trench.

Each of these zones contains a distinctive community of species adapted to the different conditions of salinity, temperature and light intensity. Indeed, a few organisms have been found even in the abyssal darkness of the great ocean trenches.

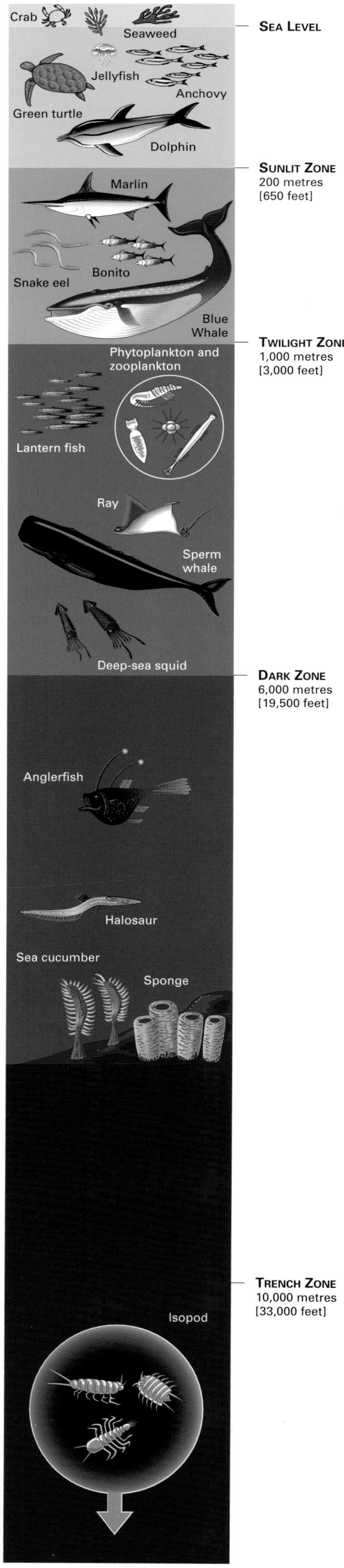
Crab
Seaweed
Jellyfish
Anchovy
Green turtle
Dolphin
Sea Level
Marlin
Bonito
Snake eel
Blue Whale
Sunlit Zone
200 metres
[650 feet]
Phytoplankton and zooplankton
Lantern fish
Twilight Zone
1,000 metres
[3,000 feet]
Ray
Sperm whale
Deep-sea squid
Dark Zone
6,000 metres
[19,500 feet]
Anglerfish
Halosaur
Sea cucumber
Sponge
Isopod
Trench Zone
10,000 metres
[33,000 feet]

Atoll Building

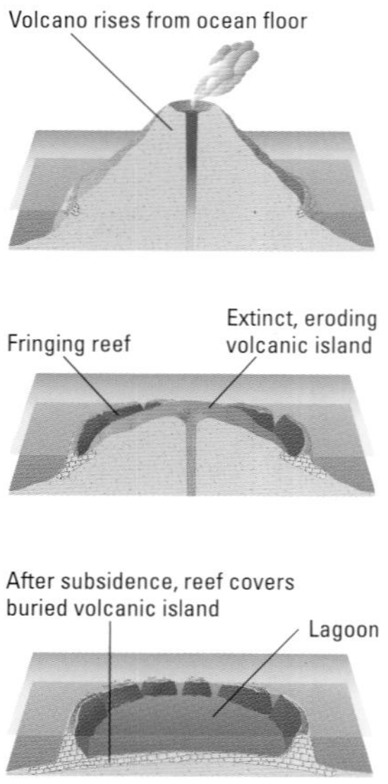
Volcano rises from ocean floor
Fringing reef
Extinct, eroding volcanic island
After subsidence, reef covers buried volcanic island
Lagoon

A coral atoll usually begins existence as a bare volcanic peak, thrusting above the surface of the ocean. A colony of coral – organisms with calcium carbonate skeletons – forms itself in the shallow water around the peak. The volcano is eroded and slowly sinks, leaving the coral forming a ring of hard limestone around its remnant. In time, the barrier reef of an atoll is all that remains.

The El Niño Phenomenon

The importance of the ocean–atmosphere interaction is nowhere more dramatically demonstrated than the El Niño phenomenon in the southern Pacific Ocean.

Under normal conditions, shown in the diagram, top right, surface water flows eastwards from South America under the influence of trade winds while, near the coast, cold, nutrient-rich water (dark blue) rises to the surface and spreads westwards. In the western Pacific, sea surface temperatures reach 28°C or more and warm air rises, creating a low pressure air system and causing heavy rains. The rising warm air spreads out and some of it descends over South America and the eastern Pacific creating a high pressure air system from which winds blow westwards. This rotating system is called a Walker Circulation Cell.

An El Niño event, also called an El Niño–Southern Oscillation cycle, or ENSO cycle, is characterized by a reversal of currents whereby the eastward-moving South Equatorial Current extends much further eastwards and the trade winds weaken. The upwelling of cold water off South America is greatly reduced and surface water temperatures rise, causing a drastic reduction in fish life. The heaviest rainfall is over the eastern Pacific, while South-east Asia is much drier than usual. Warm air rises in the east and spreads out, descending in the western Pacific, which then becomes a high pressure area, as shown on the second diagram, below right.

During an intense El Niño, such as in 1982–83 when sea temperatures in the eastern Pacific rose by 6°C, the effects of the current and wind reversals affect the weather around the world. In Australia and South-east Asia, the monsoon rainfall is reduced, while, in 1983–84, a severe drought occurred in the Sahel, south of the Sahara, and also in southern Africa. The south-east coast of the United States also suffered storms and heavy rainfall, and even Europe experienced changes in weather patterns, possibly as a result of consequent changes in the course of the jet stream.

Scientists have found evidence that the frequency of the El Niño event, which normally occurs every two to seven years, may have increased in recent years with warm conditions persisting in the eastern Pacific from 1990 until mid-1995, an unprecedented length of time during the 114 years for which data exist. Another intense El Niño occurred in 1997–98, with resultant freak weather conditions across the entire Pacific region. Scientists do not know the causes of the El Niño event, though some researchers are investigating possible connections between major volcanic eruptions in the tropical Pacific region, the ENSO cycle and atmospheric circulation.

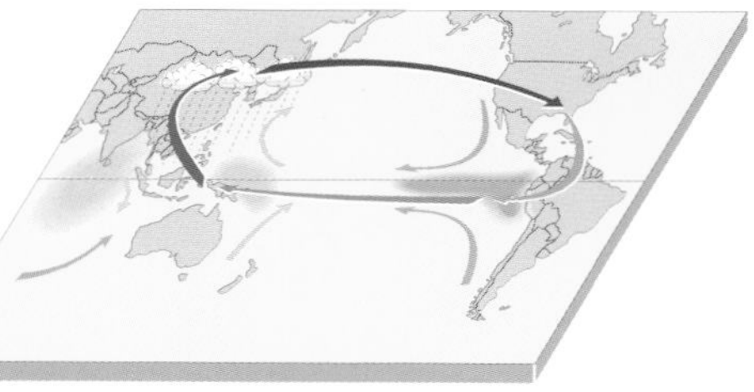

Normal year – Walker Circulation Cell

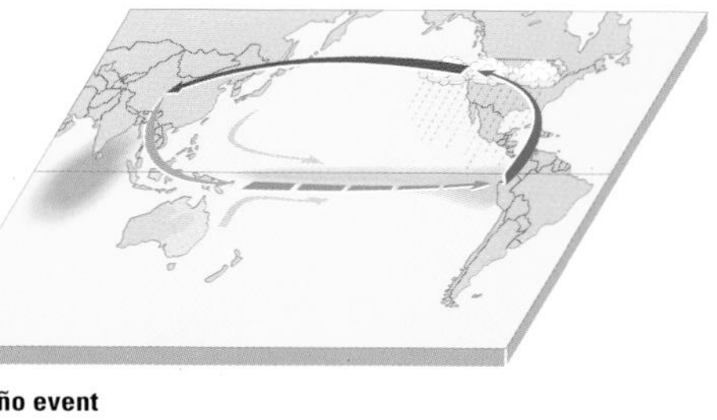

El Niño event

Ocean Currents

JANUARY CURRENTS AND TEMPERATURES
(Northern Hemisphere: winter)

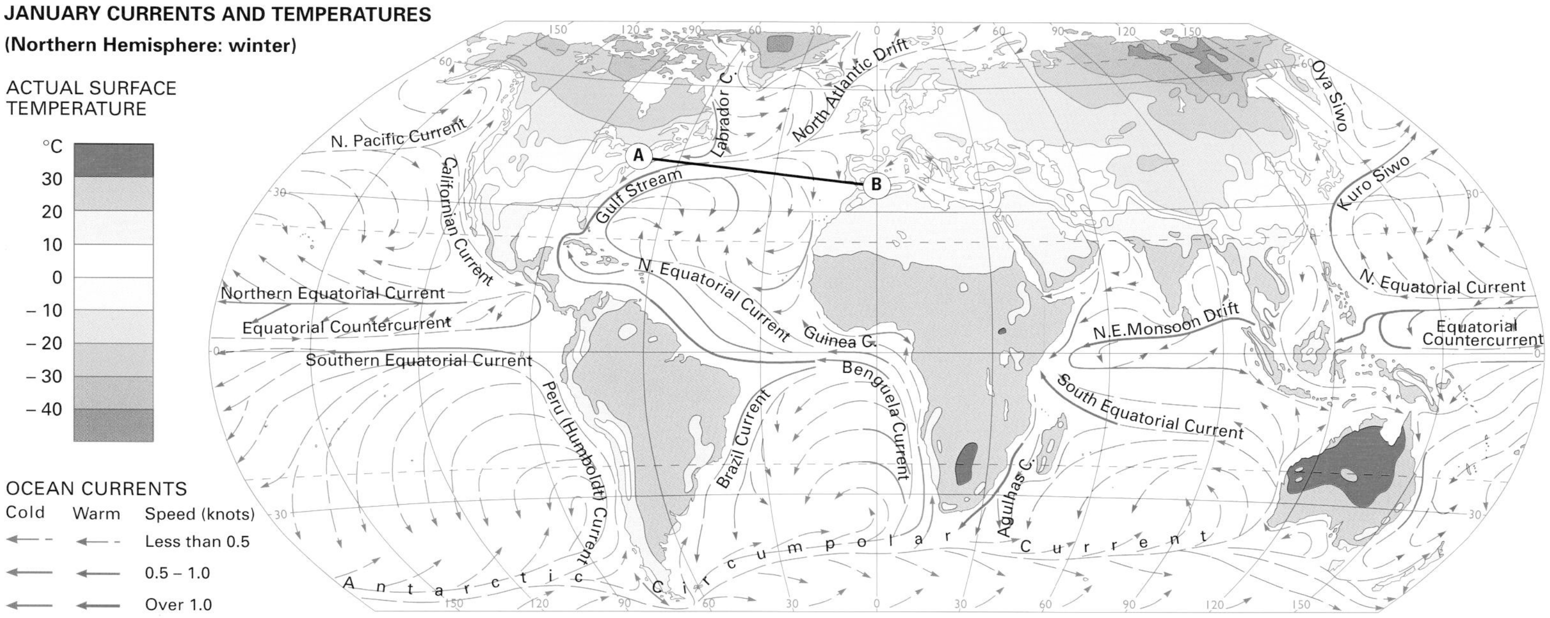

A ——— B Location of the Atlantic Ocean profile shown bottom left

JULY CURRENTS AND TEMPERATURES
(Northern Hemisphere: summer)

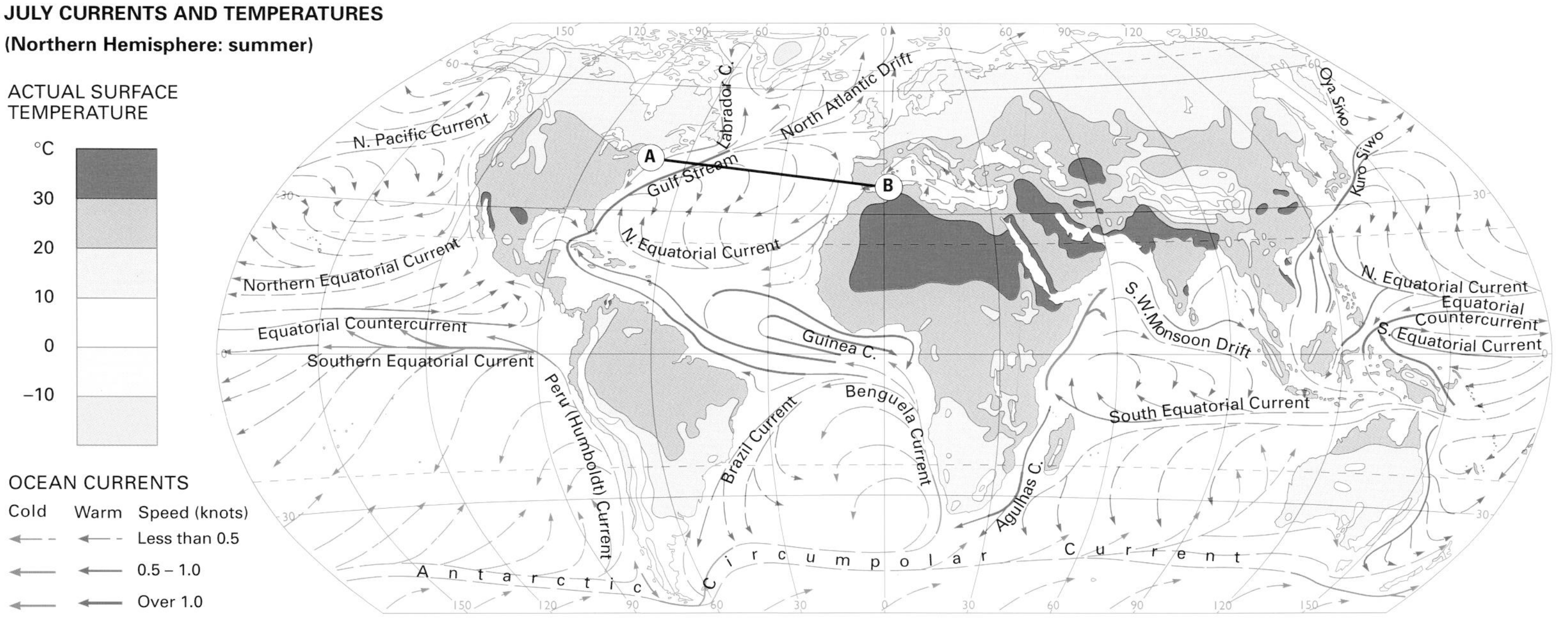

Moving immense quantities of energy as well as billions of tonnes of water every hour, the ocean currents are a vital part of the great heat engine that drives the Earth's climate. They themselves are produced by a twofold mechanism. At the surface, winds push huge masses of water before them; in the deep ocean, below an abrupt temperature gradient that separates the churning surface waters from the still depths, density variations cause slow vertical movements.

The pattern of circulation of the great surface currents is determined by the displacement known as the Coriolis effect. As the Earth turns beneath a moving object – whether it is a tennis ball or a vast mass of water – it appears to be deflected to one side. The deflection is most obvious near the Equator, where the Earth's surface is spinning eastwards at 1,700 km/h; currents moving polewards are curved clockwise in the northern hemisphere and anti-clockwise in the southern.

The result is a system of spinning circles known as gyres. Warm currents move constantly from the Equator towards the poles, while cold water moves in the reverse direction. In this way, ocean currents act like a thermostat, helping to regulate temperatures around the world.

Depending on the annual movements of the prevailing wind belts, some currents on or near the Equator may reverse their direction in the course of the year, a variation on which Asia's monsoon rains depend and whose occasional failure has brought disaster to millions of people.

Topography of the Ocean Floor

Profile of the Atlantic Ocean

The deep ocean floor was once believed to be flat, but maps compiled from readings made by sonar equipment show that it is no more uniform than the surface of the continents. The profile, below, shows some of the features on the Atlantic Ocean floor between Massachusetts in North America and Gibraltar (for location of profile, see maps above). Around the continents are shallow continental shelves composed of rocks which are less dense than the underlying oceanic crust. The continents end at the top of the steep continental slope, which descends to the abyss via the continental rise, made up of sediments washed down from the continental shelves. The abyss contains large plains overlain by oozes but the plains are broken by volcanic seamounts and guyots (flat-topped seamounts), a few of which reach the surface as islands. The other main feature is the Mid-Atlantic Ridge, through which runs a rift valley where new crustal rock is being formed as the plates on either side move apart.

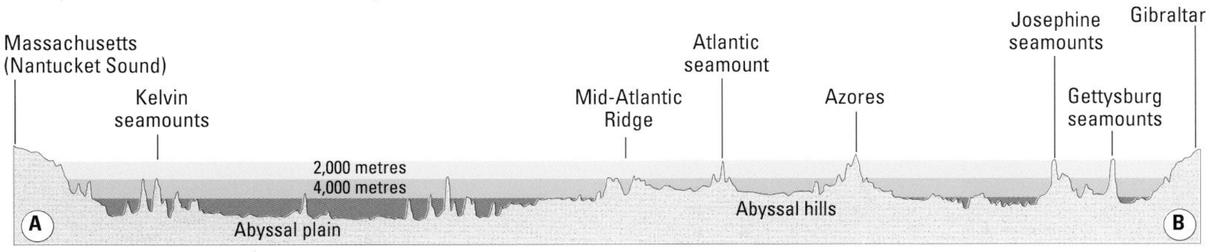

Topography of the ocean floor around Australia

In the image on the right, land areas are shown in grey, with shaded relief. The colours represent sea depth, with red representing the shallowest areas, through yellow and green to dark blue (the deepest). The data for the sea topography are from the Seasat radar satellite. The deep blue area in the upper left is the Java Trench which forms the boundary between the Indo-Australian plate and the Eurasian plate. In the top right, the New Guinea trench, which has a maximum depth of 9,103 metres, forms the border of the Indo-Australian and Pacific plates. Alongside the trenches are volcanic islands formed from magma, created as the edge of the Indo-Australian plate is subducted and melted.

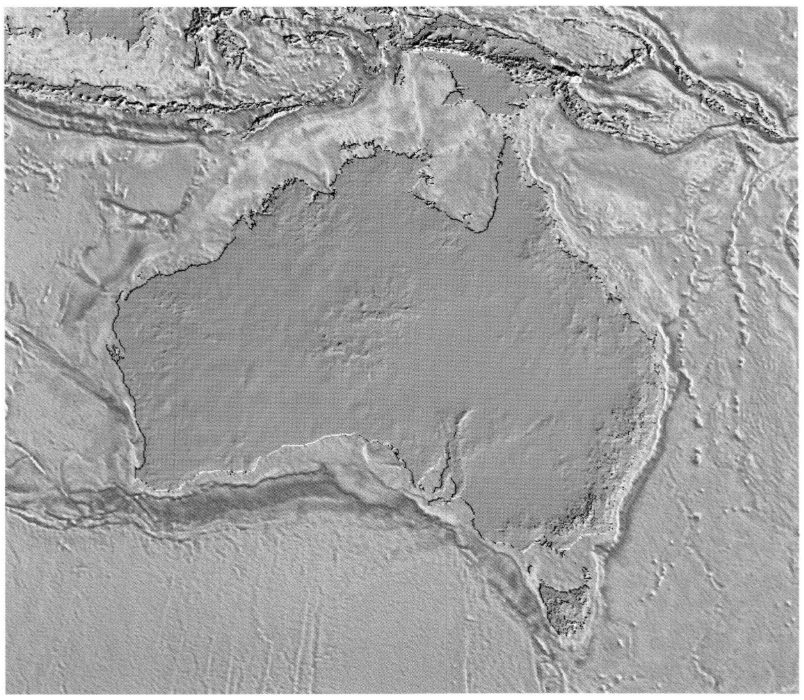

Geology of the Earth

For more information:

12 Types of rock
Mountain building
13 Surface processes
21 The carbon cycle
36 Minerals

Every year, earthquakes and volcanic eruptions cause much destruction throughout the world. Such phenomena were once thought to be unconnected but since the late 1960s, scientists have understood that these events are surface manifestations of the tremendous forces operating in the Earth's interior that are slowly but constantly changing the face of our planet.

The Earth is divided into three zones. The crust, a brittle, low-density zone, overlies the dense mantle. Separating the crust from the mantle is a distinct boundary called the Mohorovičić (or Moho) discontinuity. Enclosed by the mantle is the Earth's core, which consists mainly of iron and nickel.

Temperatures inside the Earth range from about 870°C in the upper mantle to perhaps 5,000°C in the core. Heat creates convection currents in a semi-molten part of the mantle called the asthenosphere. Above the asthenosphere is the lithosphere, a solid layer about 70 km thick, consisting of the crust and part of the mantle. The lithosphere is divided into rigid plates, moved around by the currents in the asthenosphere, a process named plate tectonics.

The Earth was formed around 4.6 billion years ago. Lighter elements floated towards the surface, where they formed crustal rocks. The oldest rocks so far discovered are nearly 4 billion years old, while the oldest fossils occur in rocks formed around 3.5 billion years ago. An explosion of life occurred at the start of the Cambrian period, 570 million years ago. The fossil record since the start of the Cambrian has enabled scientists to piece together the story of life on Earth.

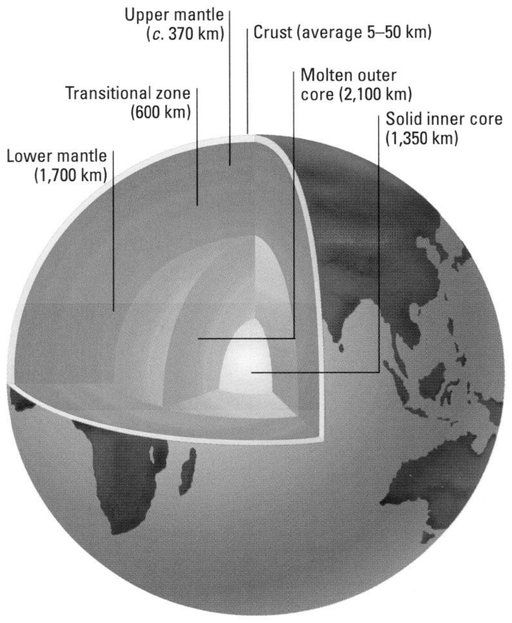

Upper mantle (*c.* 370 km)
Crust (average 5–50 km)
Molten outer core (2,100 km)
Transitional zone (600 km)
Solid inner core (1,350 km)
Lower mantle (1,700 km)

Plate Tectonics

In the early 20th century, the German scientist Alfred Wegener and others noticed similarities between the shapes of the continents. From a study of rocks and fossils in widely separated continents, they suggested that the continents had once been joined together and that somehow they had drifted apart. But no one knew of a mechanism that might cause continents to drift. However, in the 1950s and 1960s, evidence from studies of the ocean floor suggested that the low-density continents rest on huge slow-moving plates.

Sea-floor spreading in the Indian Ocean and continental plate collision

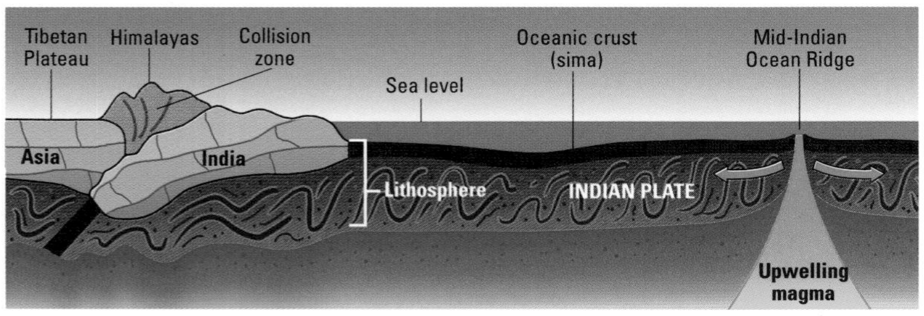

Tibetan Plateau
Himalayas
Collision zone
Oceanic crust (sima)
Mid-Indian Ocean Ridge
Sea level
Asia
India
Lithosphere
INDIAN PLATE
Upwelling magma

Sea-floor spreading in the Atlantic Ocean and plate collision

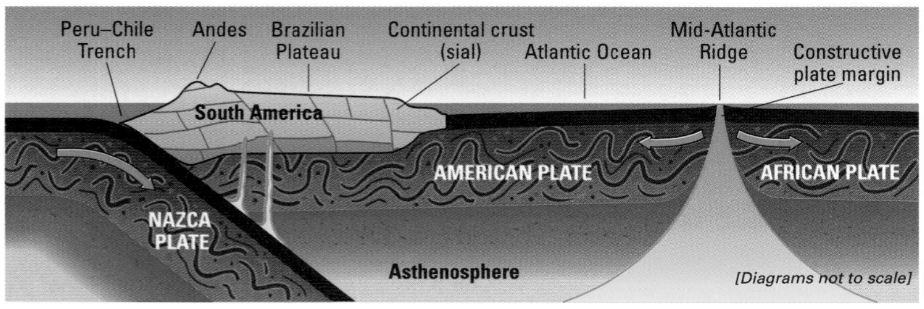

Peru–Chile Trench
Andes
Brazilian Plateau
Continental crust (sial)
Atlantic Ocean
Mid-Atlantic Ridge
Constructive plate margin
South America
AMERICAN PLATE
AFRICAN PLATE
NAZCA PLATE
Asthenosphere
[Diagrams not to scale]

The huge ridges that run through the oceans represent boundaries between plates. Here plates are diverging at rates of 20–41 mm a year. Molten magma from the mantle rises along a central rift valley to form new crustal rock. These ocean ridges, which are active zones where earthquakes and volcanic eruptions are common, are called constructive plate margins. Destructive plate margins, which occur when two plates converge, are marked by deep ocean trenches as one plate is forced under the other. The descending plate is melted to produce the magma that fuels volcanoes alongside the trenches. Movements of descending plates are often sudden and violent, triggering earthquakes in overlying continental areas. Where two continents collide, their margins are buckled up to form fold mountain ranges. A third type of plate margin, the transform fault, is not illustrated above. Along these plate margins, such as California's San Andreas fault, plates are moving parallel to each other.

The debate about plate tectonics is not over. Questions still arise as to why some active volcanoes lie far from plate margins, and why major earthquakes occur in mid-plate areas.

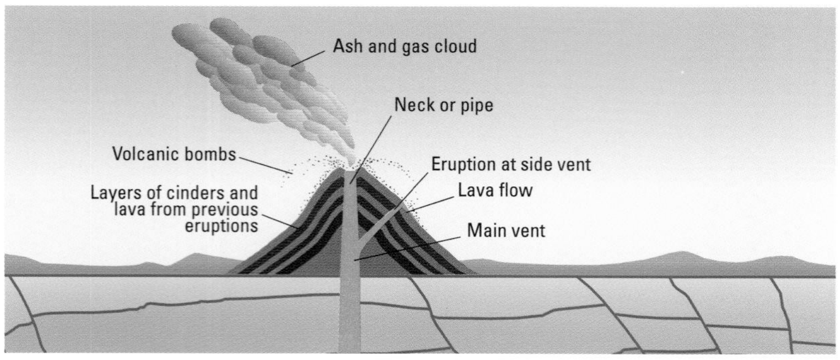

Ash and gas cloud
Neck or pipe
Volcanic bombs
Eruption at side vent
Layers of cinders and lava from previous eruptions
Lava flow
Main vent

Continental Drift

In 1915, Alfred Wegener produced a series of world maps proposing that, around 200 million years ago, the continents had been joined together in a supercontinent which he called Pangaea. This landmass started to break up about 180 million years ago and the parts drifted to their present positions. The arrows on the present day world map shows that the continents are still on the move.

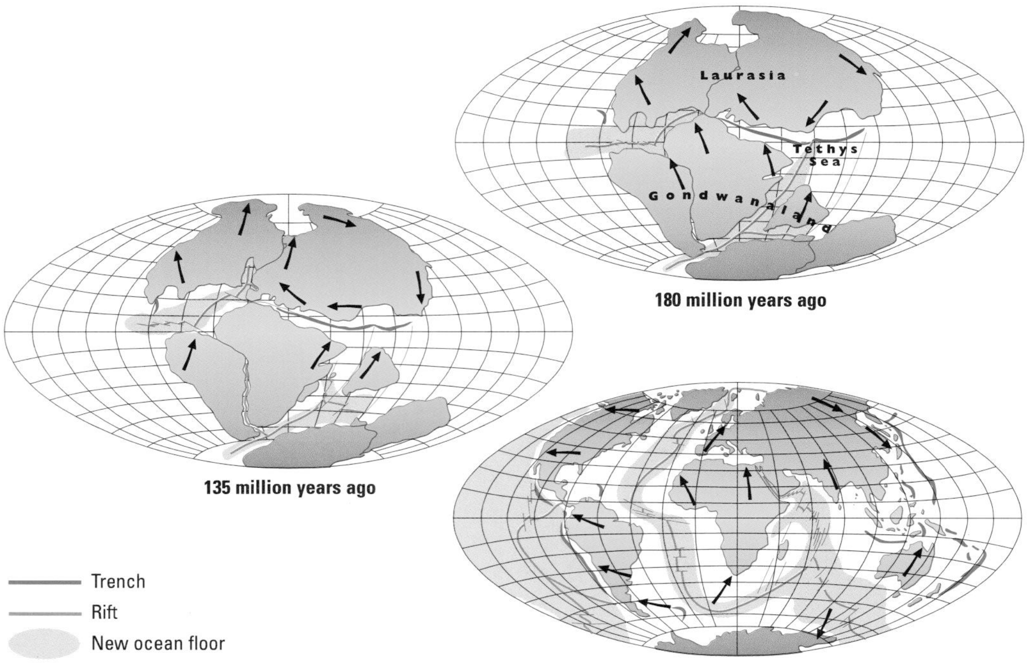

Laurasia
Tethys Sea
Gondwanaland
Trench
Rift
New ocean floor
Zones of slippage

180 million years ago

135 million years ago

Present day

Distribution of Volcanoes

Volcanoes occur when hot liquefied rock beneath the Earth's crust is pushed up by pressure to the surface as molten lava. There are some 550 known active volcanoes, around 20 of which are erupting at any one time.

- ▲ Land volcanoes active since 1700
- • Submarine volcanoes
- ↗ Direction of movement (cm/year)
- ◆ Geysers
- Boundaries of tectonic plates

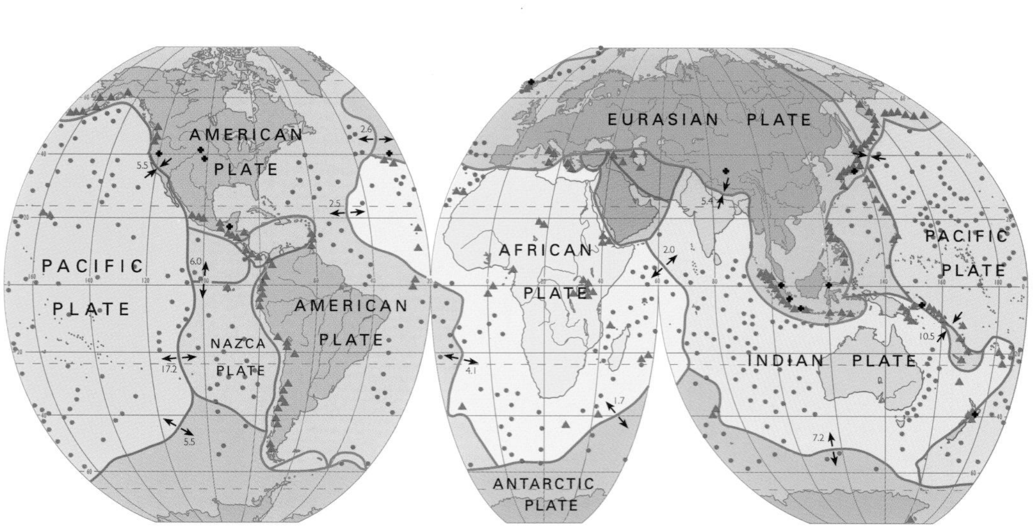

AMERICAN PLATE
PACIFIC PLATE
NAZCA PLATE
AMERICAN PLATE
EURASIAN PLATE
AFRICAN PLATE
PACIFIC PLATE
INDIAN PLATE
ANTARCTIC PLATE

Geological Time

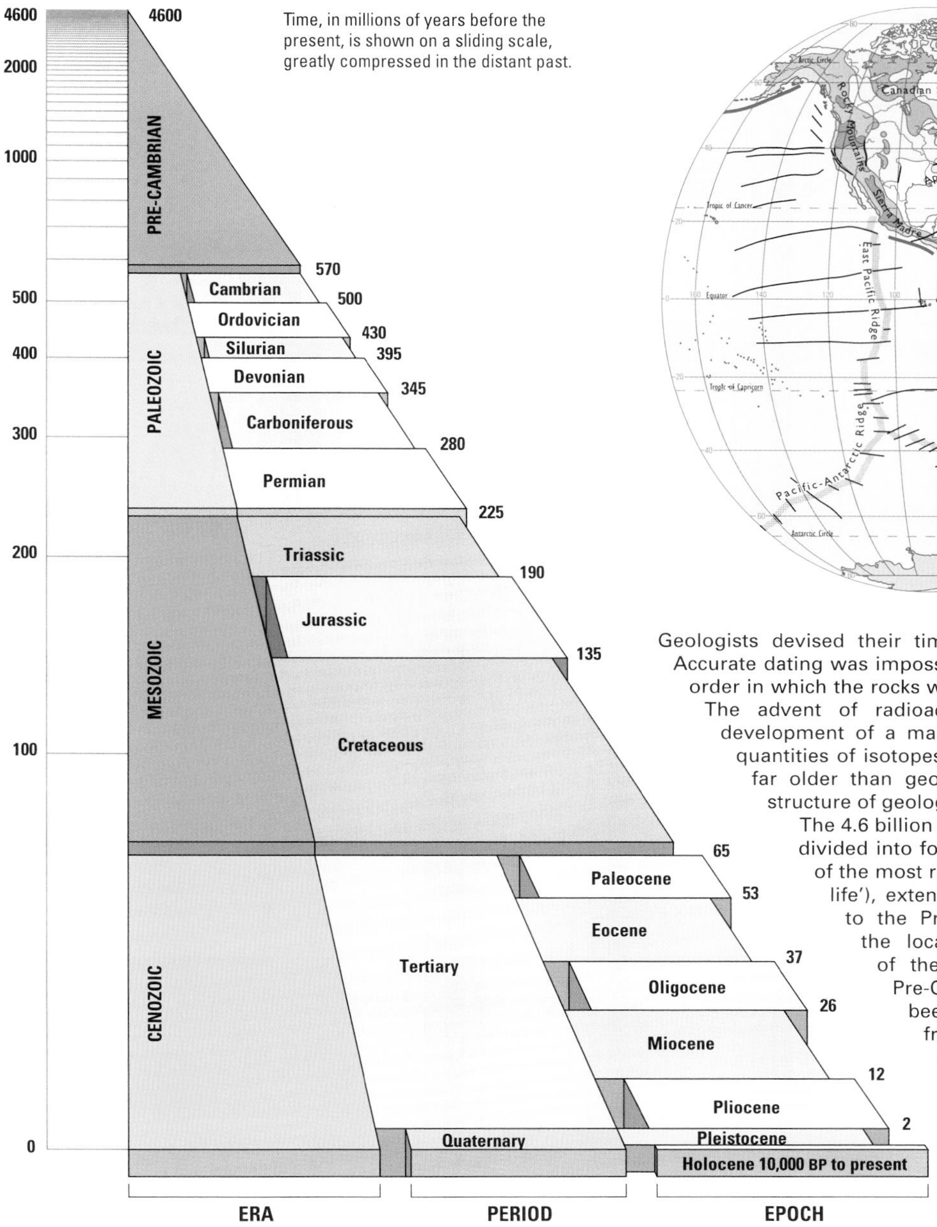

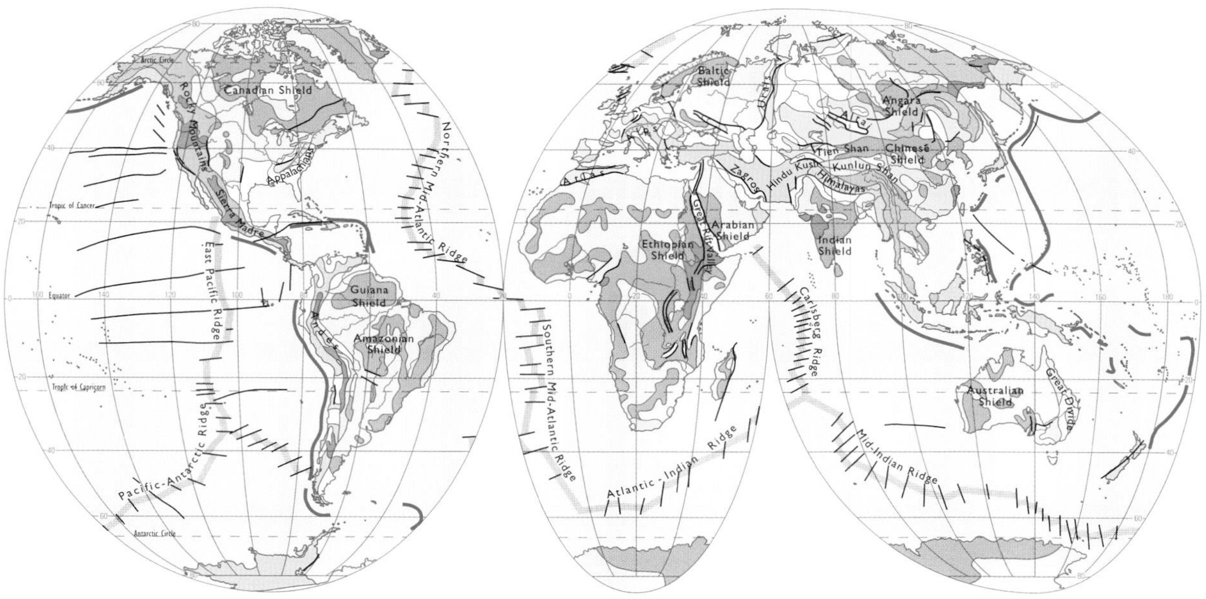

Geologists devised their timescale on the basis of relative, not calendar, ages. Accurate dating was impossible and estimates were often bitterly disputed, but the order in which the rocks were formed could be deduced from careful observation. The advent of radioactive dating – culminating in the 1950s with the development of a mass spectrometer capable of accurately measuring tiny quantities of isotopes – appears to have settled the arguments. The Earth is far older than geologists first imagined, but their painstakingly-created structure of geological time has withstood the advent of high technology.

The 4.6 billion (4,600 million) years since the formation of the Earth are divided into four great eras, further split into periods and, in the case of the most recent era, epochs. The present era is the Cenozoic ('new life'), extending backwards through 'middle life' and 'ancient life' to the Pre-Cambrian, named after the Latin word for Wales, the location of some of the earliest known fossils. Most of the Earth's geological history is encompassed by the Pre-Cambrian: though traces of ancient life have since been found, it was largely the proliferation of fossils from the beginning of the Paleozoic era onwards, some 570 million years ago, which first allowed precise subdivisions to be made.

Like the Cambrian, most are named after regions exemplifying a period's geology. Others – such as the Carboniferous ('coal-bearing') or the Cretaceous ('chalk-bearing') – are more directly descriptive.

- Pre-Cambrian shields
- Sedimentary cover on Pre-Cambrian shields
- Paleozoic (Caledonian and Hercynian) folding
- Sedimentary cover on Paleozoic folding
- Mesozoic folding
- Sedimentary cover on Mesozoic folding
- Cenozoic (Alpine) folding
- Sedimentary cover on Cenozoic folding
- Intensive Mesozoic and Cenozoic vulcanism
- Principal faults
- Oceanic marginal troughs
- Mid-oceanic ridges
- Overthrust faults

Earthquakes

Earthquake magnitude is usually rated according to either the Richter or the Modified Mercalli scale, both devised by seismologists in the 1930s. The Richter scale measures absolute earthquake power with mathematical precision: each step upwards represents a ten-fold increase in the amplitude of the shockwave. Theoretically, there is no upper limit, but the largest earthquakes measured have been rated at between 8.8 and 8.9. The 12-point Mercalli scale, based on observed effects, is often more meaningful, ranging from I (earthquakes noticed only by seismographs) to XII (total destruction); intermediate points include V (people awakened at night; unstable objects overturned), VII (collapse of ordinary buildings; chimneys and monuments fall) and IX (conspicuous cracks in ground; serious damage to reservoirs).

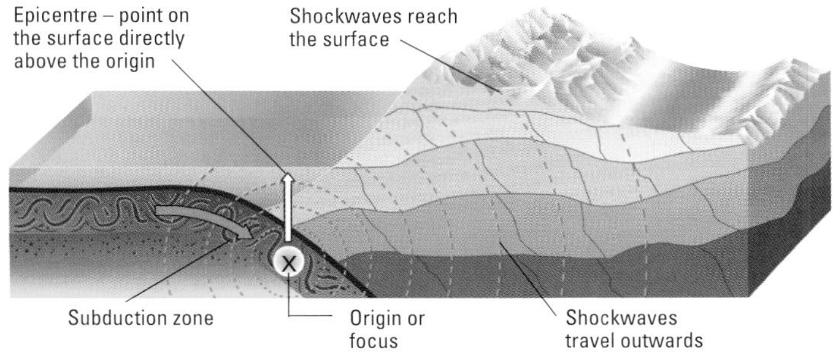

- Mobile land areas
- Submarine zones of mobile land areas
- Stable land platforms
- Submarine extensions of land platforms
- Mid-oceanic volcanic ridges
- Oceanic platforms
- 1976 Principal earthquakes and dates

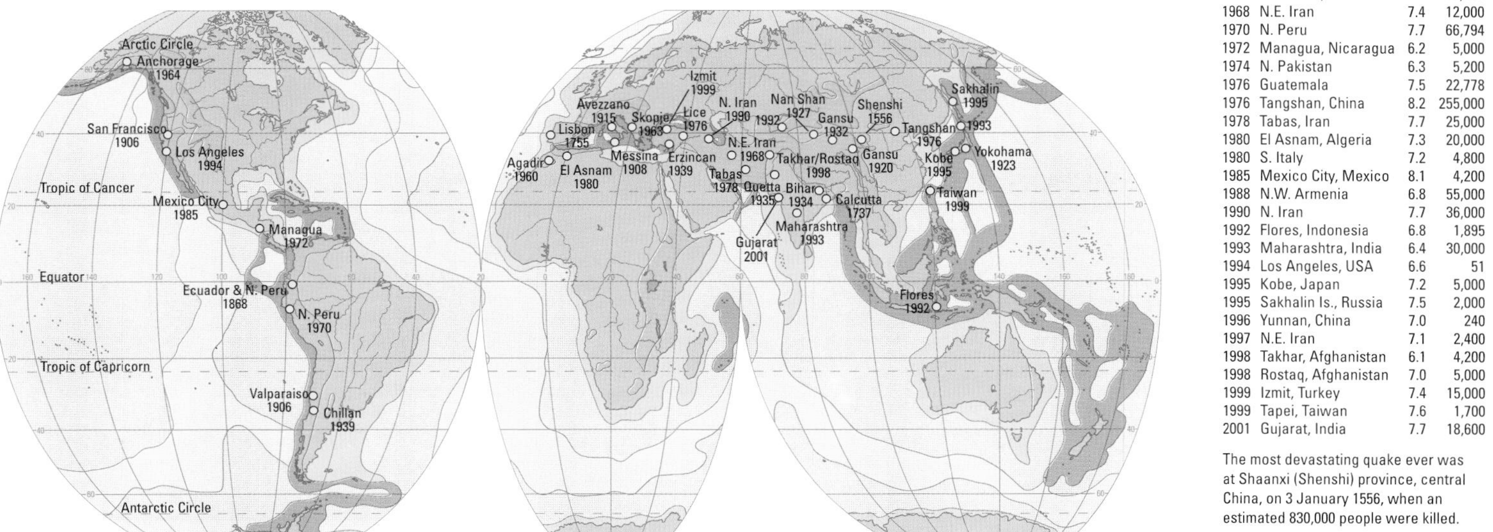

Earthquakes are a series of rapid vibrations originating from the slipping or faulting of parts of the Earth's crust when stresses within build up to breaking point. They usually happen at depths varying from 8 km to 30 km. Severe earthquakes cause extensive damage when they take place in populated areas, destroying structures and severing communications. Most initial loss of life occurs due to secondary causes such as falling masonry, fires and flooding.

Notable Earthquakes Since 1900

Year	Location	Mag.	Deaths
1906	San Francisco, USA	8.3	503
1906	Valparaiso, Chile	8.6	22,000
1908	Messina, Italy	7.5	83,000
1915	Avezzano, Italy	7.5	30,000
1920	Gansu (Kansu), China	8.6	180,000
1923	Yokohama, Japan	8.3	143,000
1927	Nan Shan, China	8.3	200,000
1932	Gansu (Kansu), China	7.6	70,000
1933	Sanriku, Japan	8.9	2,990
1934	Bihar, India/Nepal	8.4	10,700
1935	Quetta, India*	7.5	60,000
1939	Chillan, Chile	8.3	28,000
1939	Erzincan, Turkey	7.9	30,000
1960	Agadir, Morocco	5.8	12,000
1962	Khorasan, Iran	7.1	12,230
1968	N.E. Iran	7.4	12,000
1970	N. Peru	7.7	66,794
1972	Managua, Nicaragua	6.2	5,000
1974	N. Pakistan	6.3	5,200
1976	Guatemala	7.5	22,778
1976	Tangshan, China	8.2	255,000
1978	Tabas, Iran	7.7	25,000
1980	El Asnam, Algeria	7.3	20,000
1980	S. Italy	7.2	4,800
1985	Mexico City, Mexico	8.1	4,200
1988	N.W. Armenia	6.8	55,000
1990	N. Iran	7.7	36,000
1992	Flores, Indonesia	6.8	1,895
1993	Maharashtra, India	6.4	30,000
1994	Los Angeles, USA	6.6	51
1995	Kobe, Japan	7.2	5,000
1995	Sakhalin Is., Russia	7.5	2,000
1996	Yunnan, China	7.0	240
1997	N.E. Iran	7.1	2,400
1998	Takhar, Afghanistan	6.1	4,200
1998	Rostaq, Afghanistan	7.0	5,000
1999	Izmit, Turkey	7.4	15,000
1999	Tapei, Taiwan	7.6	1,700
2001	Gujarat, India	7.7	18,600

The most devastating quake ever was at Shaanxi (Shenshi) province, central China, on 3 January 1556, when an estimated 830,000 people were killed.

* now Pakistan

Landforms

For more information:

The theory of plate tectonics has offered new insights as to how the Earth works, elucidating mysteries concerning continental drift, volcanic eruptions and earthquakes. It has also contributed to our understanding of how plate collisions can squeeze up layers of sediments on seabeds into fold mountain ranges, such as the Himalayas.

Yet even as mountains rise, natural forces are wearing them away. In hot, dry climates, mechanical weathering, a result of rapid temperature changes, causes the outer layers of rocks to peel away, while, in cold mountain regions, boulders are prised apart when water freezes in cracks in rocks. Chemical weathering is responsible for hollowing out limestone caves and decomposing granites.

Climatic conditions have a great bearing on the principle agent of erosion in any particular area. Running water is most important in moist temperate regions. In cold regions, ice is the major agent of erosion, and in many mountain ranges, U-shaped valleys are evidence of the erosive power of valley glaciers. Ice sheets moulded much of the Earth's surface during the Ice Ages, the most recent of which, in the northern hemisphere, ended only 10,000 years ago. Polar climates also shape the scenery of the periglacial areas that border bodies of ice. Such areas are subject to constant freeze-thaw action, which creates such features as pingos (domed mounds).

Climatic change has also affected many of the landforms in hot deserts, which were shaped by running water at a time when the deserts enjoyed much wetter climates. However, the major agent of erosion in deserts today is wind-blown sand which erodes rock strata to form mushroom-shaped rocks and caves.

The surface of the Earth is under constant assault from tectonic processes and the agents of erosion. The products of erosion, fragments of rock such as sand, are deposited to form sedimentary rocks. Metamorphic rocks are created when igneous or sedimentary rocks are buried and metamorphosed by heat and pressure. Eventually the rocks are recycled to form magma, which rises upwards to start the rock cycle all over again.

The Rock Cycle

James Hutton first proposed the rock cycle in the late 1700s after he observed the slow but steady effects of erosion.

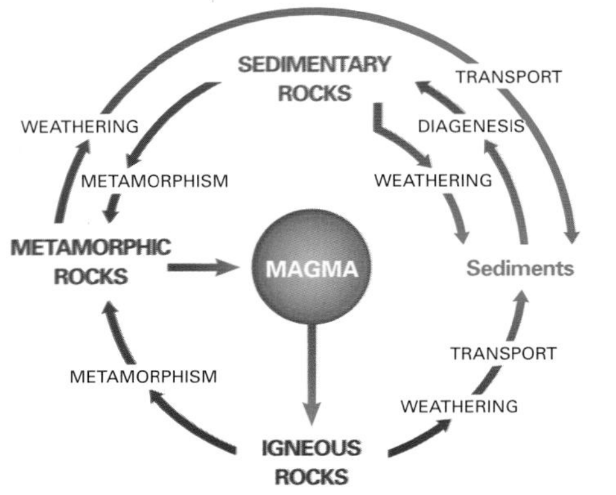

Rocks are divided into three types, according to the way in which they are formed:

Igneous rocks, including granite and basalt, are formed by the cooling of magma from within the Earth's crust.

Metamorphic rocks, such as slate, marble and quartzite, are formed below the Earth's surface by the compression or baking of existing rocks.

Sedimentary rocks, like sandstone and limestone, are formed on the surface of the Earth from the remains of living organisms and eroded fragments of older rocks.

Mountain Building

Mountains are formed when pressures on the Earth's crust caused by continental drift become so intense that the surface buckles or cracks. This happens where oceanic crust is subducted by continental crust or, more dramatically, where two tectonic plates collide: the Rockies, Andes, Alps, Urals and Himalayas resulted from such impacts. These are all known as fold mountains because they were formed by the compression of the rocks, forcing the surface to bend and fold like a crumpled rug. The Himalayas are formed from the folded former sediments of the Tethys Sea which was trapped in the collision zone between the Indian and Eurasian plates.

The other main mountain-building process occurs when the crust fractures to create faults, allowing rock to be forced upwards in large blocks; or when the pressure of magma within the crust forces the surface to bulge into a dome, or erupts to form a volcano. Large mountain ranges may reveal a combination of those features; the Alps, for example, have been compressed so violently that the folds are fragmented by numerous faults and intrusions of molten igneous rock.

Over millions of years, even the greatest mountain ranges can be reduced by the agents of erosion (especially rivers) to a low rugged landscape known as a peneplain.

Types of faults: Faults occur where the crust is being stretched or compressed so violently that the rock strata break in a horizontal or vertical movement. They are classified by the direction in which the blocks of rock have moved. A normal fault results when a vertical movement causes the surface to break apart; compression causes a reverse fault. Horizontal movement causes shearing, known as a strike-slip fault. When the rock breaks in two places, the central block may be pushed up in a horst fault, or sink (creating a rift valley) in a graben fault.

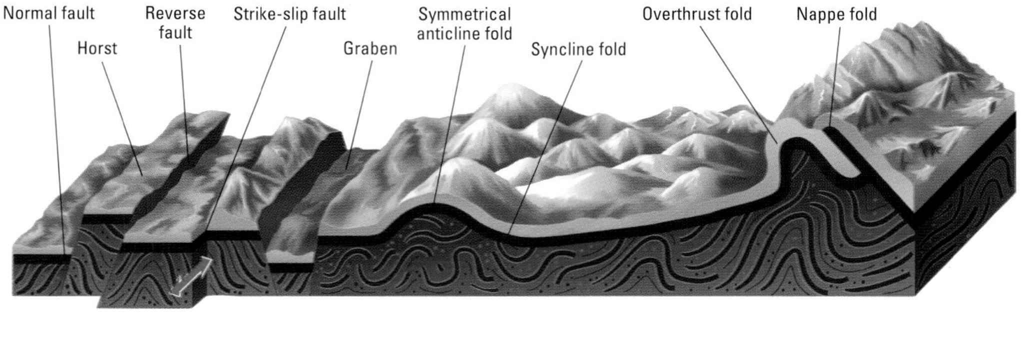

Types of fold: Folds occur when rock strata are squeezed and compressed. They are common, therefore, at destructive plate margins and where plates have collided, forcing the rocks to buckle into mountain ranges. Geographers give different names to the degrees of fold that result from continuing pressure on the rock. A simple fold may be symmetric, with even slopes on either side, but as the pressure builds up, one slope becomes steeper and the fold becomes asymmetric. Later, the ridge or 'anticline' at the top of the fold may slide over the lower ground or 'syncline' to form a recumbent fold. Eventually, the rock strata may break under the pressure to form an overthrust and finally a nappe fold.

Annual Fluctuations for Selected Glaciers

Glacier name and location	Change in mass balance 1970–90
Wolverine, USA	+2,320
Storglaciaren, Sweden	–120
Djankuat, Russia	–1,890
Grasubreen, Norway	–2,530
Ürümqi, China	–3,828
Golubin, Kyrgyzstan	–7,105
Gries, Switzerland	–10,600
Careser, Italy	–11,610
Abramov, Tajikistan	–13,700
Sarennes, France	–15,020
Place, Canada	–15,175

The mass balance is defined as the difference between glacier accumulation and ablation (melting), and is expressed as water equivalent in millimetres. A minus indicates a reduction in the depth or length of a glacier. As can be seen from this geographically diverse selection, glaciers are retreating in many areas worldwide. The most dramatic and serious example of this phenomenon is the continuing distintegration of several large Antarctic ice-shelves.

The extent to which glacial retreat is due to global warming, or to longer term climatic fluctuations, remains a matter for debate.

Continental Glaciation

Many landforms in the northern hemisphere were shaped by ice sheets and meltwater during the Pleistocene Ice Age, which began about two million years ago. During the Ice Age, the ice sheets periodically advanced and retreated. The first map shows the ice cover at its greatest extent about 200,000 years BP (before the present), when it covered about 30% of the land surface, as compared with 10% today. About 18,000 years BP, the ice covered most of Canada and as far south as the Bristol Channel in England. Around the ice sheets, land areas experienced periglacial conditions.

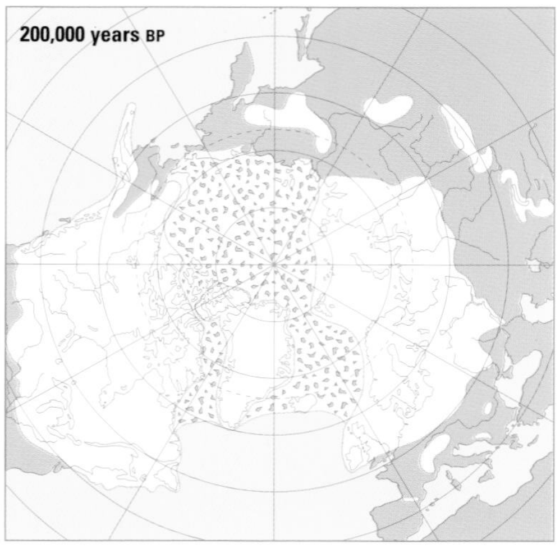

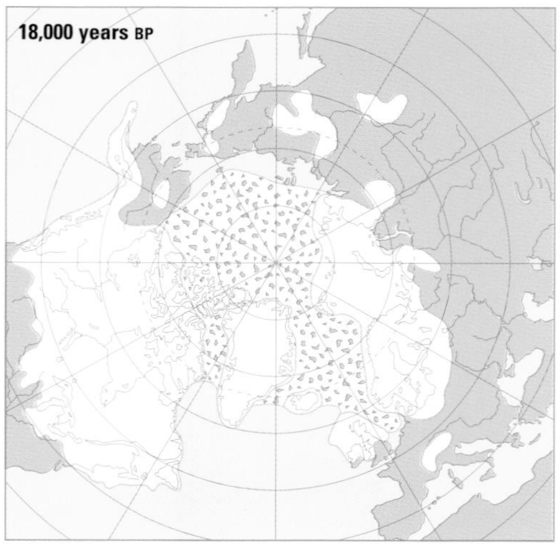

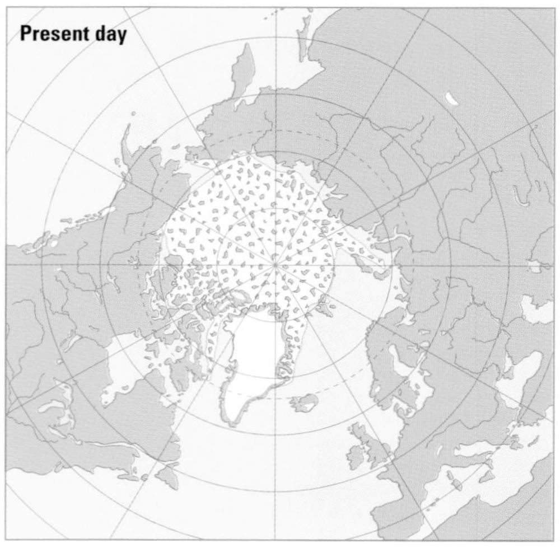

Natural Landforms

Natural landforms reflect the influence of plate tectonics through mountain-building and the generation of new rocks from the interior, together with the agents of erosion: running water, ice, winds and coastal waves. Over millions of years, mountains are gradually eroded, producing landforms that reflect the major forces that have been at work, as well as the underlying geology, the climatic conditions, which often vary over time, and the vegetation cover. The stylized diagram, below, shows some major natural landforms found in the mid-latitudes.

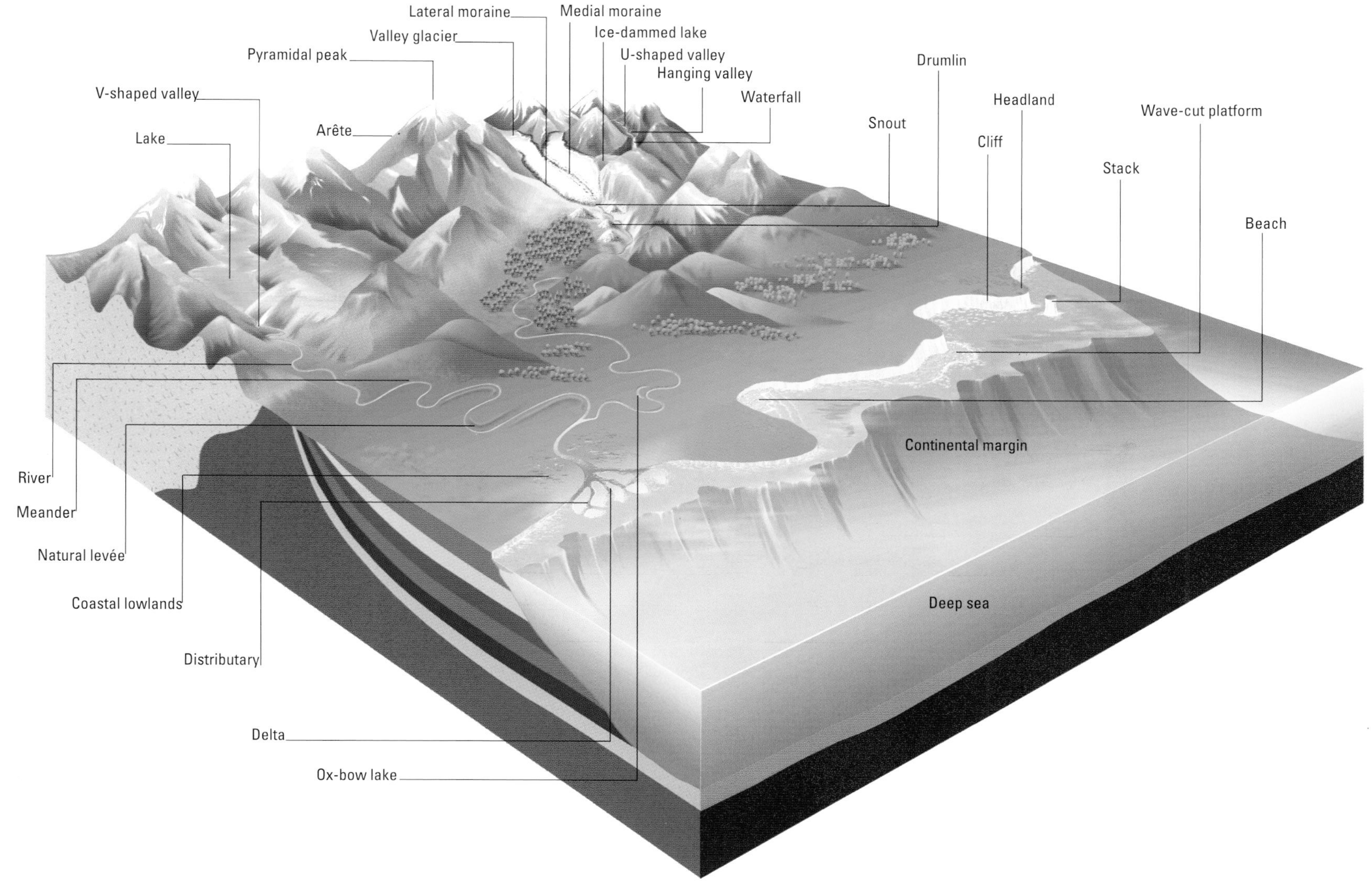

Desert Landforms

Deserts are defined as places with an average annual precipitation of 250 mm per year, though places with a higher rainfall and a high evaporation rate may also qualify as deserts. The three types of desert landforms are known by their Arabic names, a reflection of the fact that the Sahara in North Africa is the world's largest desert. Sand desert, called erg, covers about one-fifth of the world's deserts. The rest is divided between hammada (areas of bare rock) and reg (broad plains covered by loose gravel or pebbles).

The shapes of dunes in sand deserts reflect the character of local winds. Where winds are constant in direction, the sand often piles up in crescent-shaped dunes, called barchans. Barchans are constantly on the move and their forward march, unless halted by vegetation, may overwhelm settlements at oases. Seif dunes, named after the Arabic word for sword, are long ridges of sand which lie parallel to the direction of the wind, but where winds are variable, the sand sheets are often featureless.

Wind-blown sand is an effective agent of erosion but because of the weight of sand grains, this type of erosion is confined to within two metres of the land surface, creating caves and mushroom-shaped rocks.

In assessing desert landforms, it is important to remember that other processes were at work in the past when the climate was very different from today. For example, cave paintings suggest that the Sahara had a much wetter climate after the end of the Ice Age and only began to dry up after about 5000 BC. However, human action, including overgrazing and the cutting down of trees for firewood, can turn a grassland region into desert – a process known as desertification.

Surface Processes

Catastrophic changes to landforms are periodically caused by such phenomena as avalanches, landslides and volcanic eruptions, but most of the processes that shape the Earth's surface operate extremely slowly in human terms. One estimate, based on a study of landforms in the United States, suggests that, on average, one metre of land is removed from the entire surface of the country every 29,500 years. However, the terrain and the climate have a great effect on the erosion rate. For example, on cold plains, such as the Hudson Bay lowlands, the rate drops to around one metre for every 154,200 years, while in wet, tropical mountain areas, the rate may reach one metre for every 1,300 years.

Chemical weathering is at its greatest in warm, humid regions, while mechanical weathering, or the physical break-up of rocks, predominates in cold mountain or hot desert regions. The most familiar type of chemical weathering is caused by the reaction of rainwater containing dissolved carbon dioxide on limestone. This leads to the creation of labyrinthine cave networks dissolved by groundwater. Mechanical weathering includes frost action, while in hot deserts, rapid temperature changes cause the outer layers of rocks to expand and contract until they crack and peel away, a process called exfoliation.

The most important product of weathering is soil, which consists of rock fragments and humus, the decayed remains of plants and animals, together with living organisms, including vast numbers of micro-organisms. Soils vary in character according to the climate, ranging from the heavily leached, red laterite soils of wet tropical areas to the fertile, brown soils of dry grasslands. Soils are important because they support plants, which in turn anchor the soil and act as a protection against erosion. Soil erosion is greatest on sloping land because the steeper the slope, the greater the tendency for the soil to creep or flow downhill. The degree of movement of soil and rock downhill under the influence of gravity, called mass wasting, depends on a slope's stability. The stability may be disturbed by earthquakes or by heavy rain (water acts as a lubricant and increases the weight of the overlying material) which may trigger flows, slides or large falls of rock.

Running water is probably the world's leading agent of erosion and transportation. The energy of a river depends on several factors, including its velocity and volume, and its erosive power is at its peak when it is in full flood, sweeping soil, pebbles and even boulders along its course, cutting downwards into the bedrock or widening its valley. Sea waves also exert tremendous erosive power during storms when they hurl pebbles and large rocks against the shore, undercutting cliffs and hollowing out caves. Headlands are often attacked on both sides, forming caves, then a natural arch and eventually an isolated stack.

Glacier ice forms in mountain hollows, called cirques, and spills out to form valley glaciers, which transport rocks shattered by frost action. As a glacier moves, rocks embedded in the base and sides scrape away bedrock, eroding steep-sided, flat-bottomed, U-shaped valleys. Evidence of past glaciation in mountain regions includes cirques, knife-edged ridges, or arêtes, and pyramidal peaks, or horns.

Geologists once considered that landforms evolved from 'young', newly uplifted mountainous areas, through a 'mature' hilly stage, to an 'old age' stage when the land was reduced to an almost flat plain, or peneplain. This theory, called the 'cycle of erosion', fell into disuse when it became evident that so many factors, including the effects of plate tectonics and climatic change, constantly interrupt the cycle, which takes no account of the highly complex interactions that shape the surface of our planet.

The Atmosphere

For more information:

9 Ocean currents
17 Beaufort wind scale
Climate change
Monsoon
21 Solar energy
Greenhouse effect
22 Greenhouse power
23 Acid rain

The atmosphere is a meteor shield, a radiation deflector, a thermal blanket and a source of chemical energy for the Earth's diverse life forms. Five-sixths of its mass is in the lowest layer, the troposphere which ranges in thickness from 18 to 10 km between the Equator and the poles. Powered by the Sun, the air is always on the move, flowing generally from high- to low-pressure areas. The troposphere is the layer where virtually all weather phenomena, including clouds, precipitation and winds, occur. Above the troposphere is the stratosphere, which contains the important ozone layer and extends to about 50 km above the Earth's surface. Beyond 100 km, atmospheric density is lower than most laboratory vacuums.

Structure of the Atmosphere

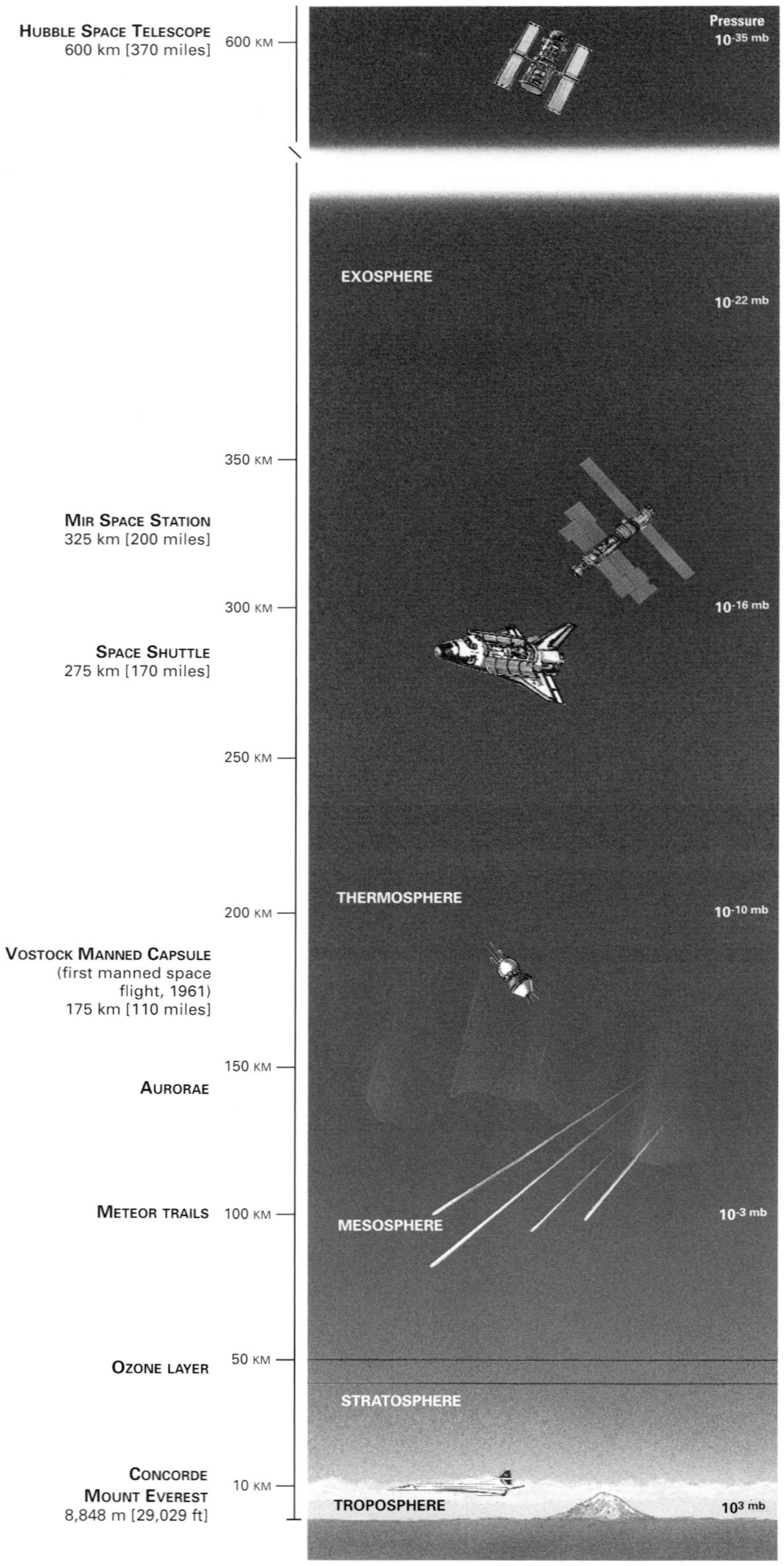

Hubble Space Telescope
600 km [370 miles]
600 km
Pressure
10^{-35} mb
Exosphere
10^{-22} mb
350 km
Mir Space Station
325 km [200 miles]
300 km
10^{-16} mb
Space Shuttle
275 km [170 miles]
250 km
Thermosphere
200 km
10^{-10} mb
Vostock Manned Capsule
(first manned space flight, 1961)
175 km [110 miles]
150 km
Aurorae
Meteor trails
100 km
Mesosphere
10^{-3} mb
Ozone layer
50 km
Stratosphere
Concorde
Mount Everest
8,848 m [29,029 ft]
10 km
Troposphere
10^{3} mb

Circulation of the Air

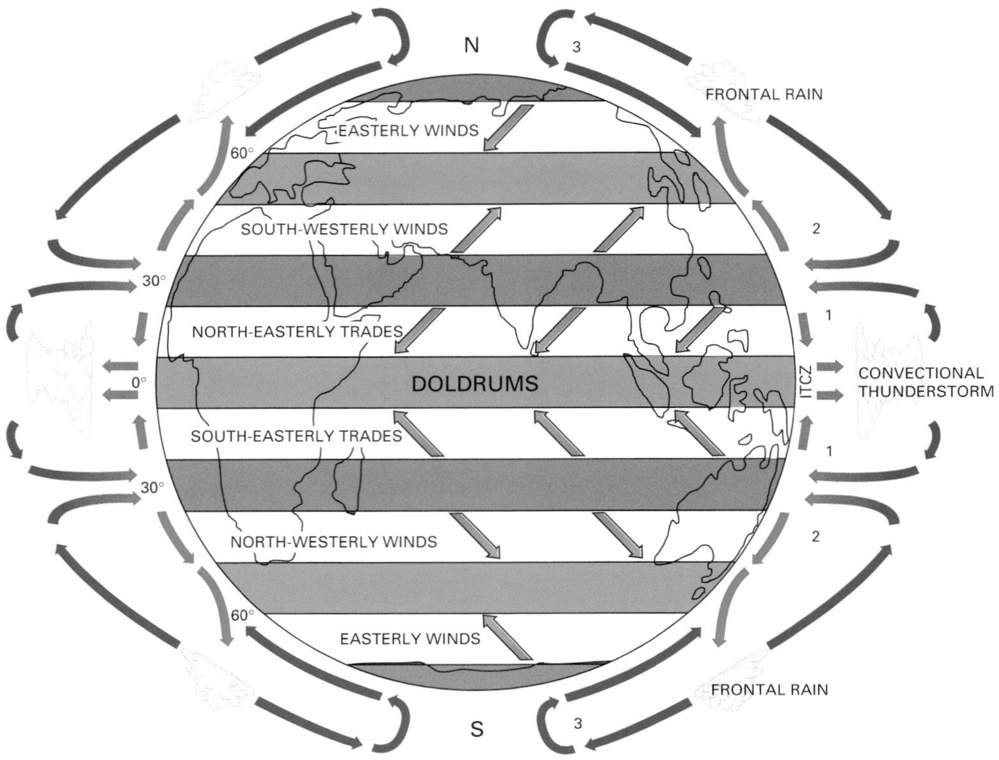

N
S
Frontal rain
Easterly winds
60°
South-westerly winds
30°
North-easterly trades
0°
Doldrums
ITCZ
Convectional thunderstorm
South-easterly trades
North-westerly winds
Easterly winds
1
2
3

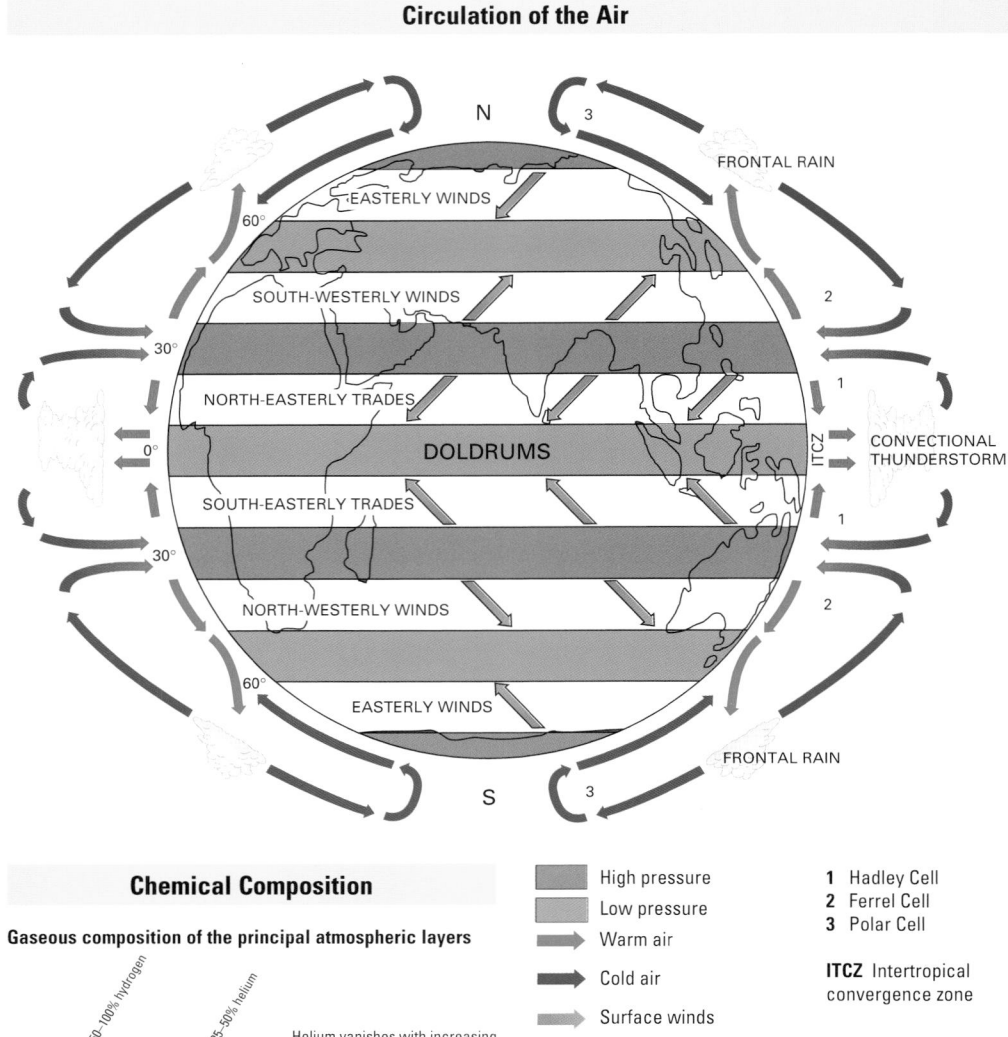

High pressure
Low pressure
Warm air
Cold air
Surface winds
Clouds

1 Hadley Cell
2 Ferrel Cell
3 Polar Cell

ITCZ Intertropical convergence zone

Chemical Composition

Gaseous composition of the principal atmospheric layers

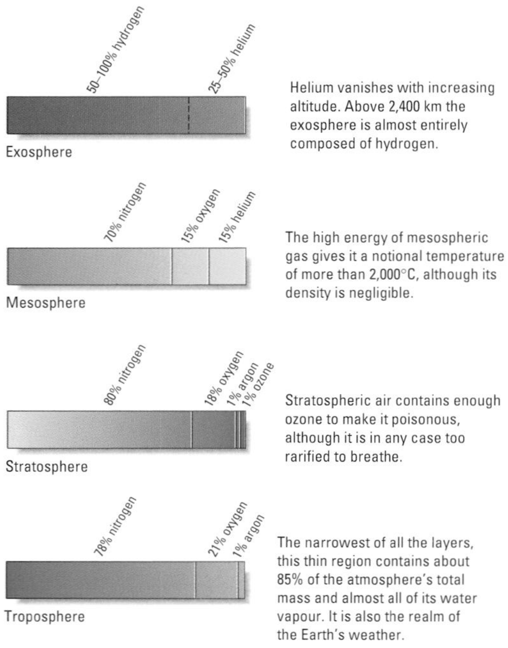

50–100% hydrogen
25–50% helium
Exosphere
Helium vanishes with increasing altitude. Above 2,400 km the exosphere is almost entirely composed of hydrogen.
70% nitrogen
15% oxygen
15% helium
Mesosphere
The high energy of mesospheric gas gives it a notional temperature of more than 2,000°C, although its density is negligible.
80% nitrogen
18% oxygen
1% argon
1% ozone
Stratosphere
Stratospheric air contains enough ozone to make it poisonous, although it is in any case too rarified to breathe.
78% nitrogen
21% oxygen
1% argon
Troposphere
The narrowest of all the layers, this thin region contains about 85% of the atmosphere's total mass and almost all of its water vapour. It is also the realm of the Earth's weather.

Frontal Systems

Depressions, or cyclones, form along the polar front where dense polar easterlies meet warm subtropical westerlies. Depressions occur when warm air flows into waves in the polar front, while cold air flows in behind it, creating rotating air systems that bring changeable weather. Along the warm front (the boundary on the ground between the warm and cold air), the warm air flows upwards over the cold air, producing a sequence of clouds which help forecasters to predict a depression's advance. Along the cold front, the advancing cold air forces warm air to rise steeply. Towering cumulonimbus clouds form in the rising air. When the cold front overtakes the warm front, the warm air is pushed above ground level to form an occluded front. Cloud and rain persist along occlusions until temperatures equalize, the air mixes, and the depression dies out.

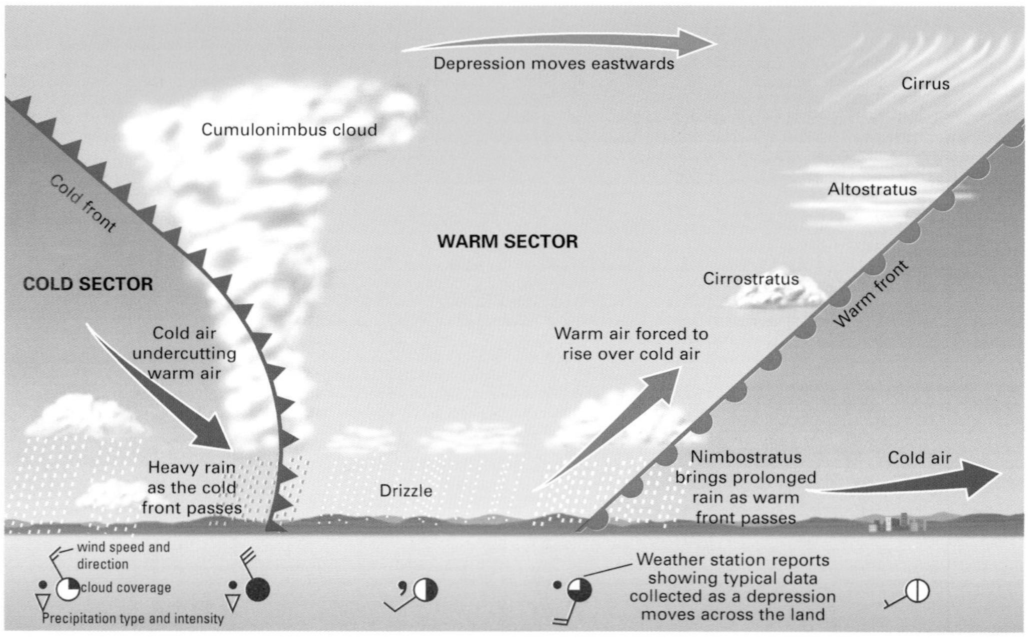

Depression moves eastwards
Cirrus
Cumulonimbus cloud
Cold front
Altostratus
Warm sector
Cold sector
Cirrostratus
Warm front
Cold air undercutting warm air
Warm air forced to rise over cold air
Heavy rain as the cold front passes
Drizzle
Nimbostratus brings prolonged rain as warm front passes
Cold air
wind speed and direction
cloud coverage
Precipitation type and intensity
Weather station reports showing typical data collected as a depression moves across the land

Air Masses

Air masses are bodies of air whose characteristics are broadly the same over a large area. Around the Equator, where the Sun's heat creates relatively high surface temperatures, warm air rises to create a zone of low pressure called the doldrums. The air cools and finally spreads out towards the poles. Around latitudes 30° north and south, the air sinks back to the surface, becoming warmer as it descends and creating zones of high pressure called the horse latitudes.

The high- and low-pressure zones are both areas of comparative calm, but between them lie the prevailing trade wind belts. Air also flows north and south from the high-pressure horse latitudes and these air flows meet up with cold, dense air flowing from the poles along the polar front. This basic circulatory system is complicated by the Coriolis effect, brought about by the spinning Earth. Because of the Coriolis effect, the prevailing winds do not flow directly north–south but are deflected to the right in the northern hemisphere and to the left in the southern. Along the polar front, depressions form where the polar easterlies meet the westerlies.

The first classification of clouds was developed by a London chemist, Luke Howard, in 1803, and it was later modified by the World Meteorological Organization. The main types are divided into three groups according to their altitude, and into subgroups according to their shape, which vary from hairlike filaments (cirrus), heaps or piles (cumulus), and layers (stratus). Each cloud carries some kind of message, though not always a clear one, to weather forecasters.

Classification of Clouds

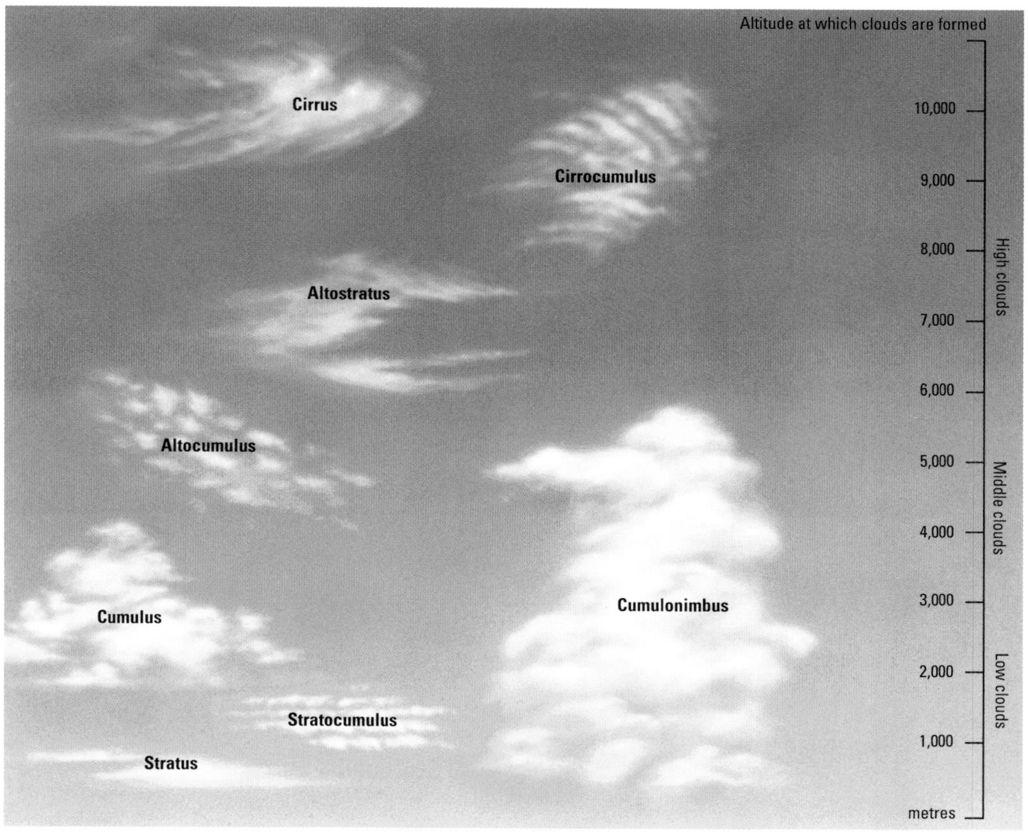

Clouds form when damp, usually rising, air is cooled. Thus they form when a wind rises to cross hills or mountains; when a mass of air rises over, or is pushed up by, another mass of denser air; or when local heating of the ground causes convection currents.

The types of clouds are classified according to altitude as high, middle or low. The high ones, composed of ice crystals, are cirrus, cirrostratus and cirrocumulus. The middle clouds are altostratus, a grey or bluish striated, fibrous or uniform sheet producing light drizzle, and altocumulus, a thicker and fluffier version of cirrocumulus.

Low clouds include nimbostratus, a dark grey layer that brings rain or snow; cumulus, a detached heap, dark at the base; stratus, which forms dull, overcast skies at low levels; and stratocumulus, which consists of fluffy greyish-white layers.

Cumulonimbus, associated with storms and rains, heavy and dense with a flat base and a high, fluffy outline, can be tall enough to occupy middle as well as low altitudes.

Pressure and Surface Winds

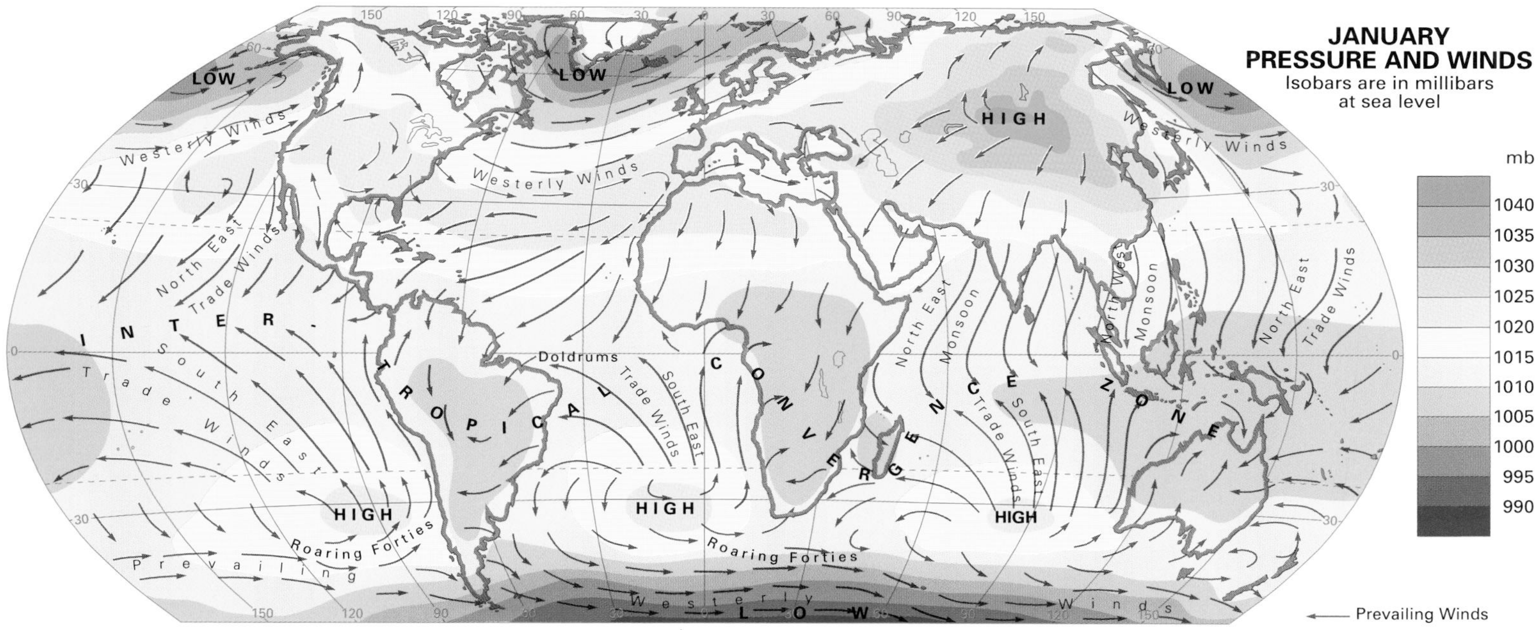

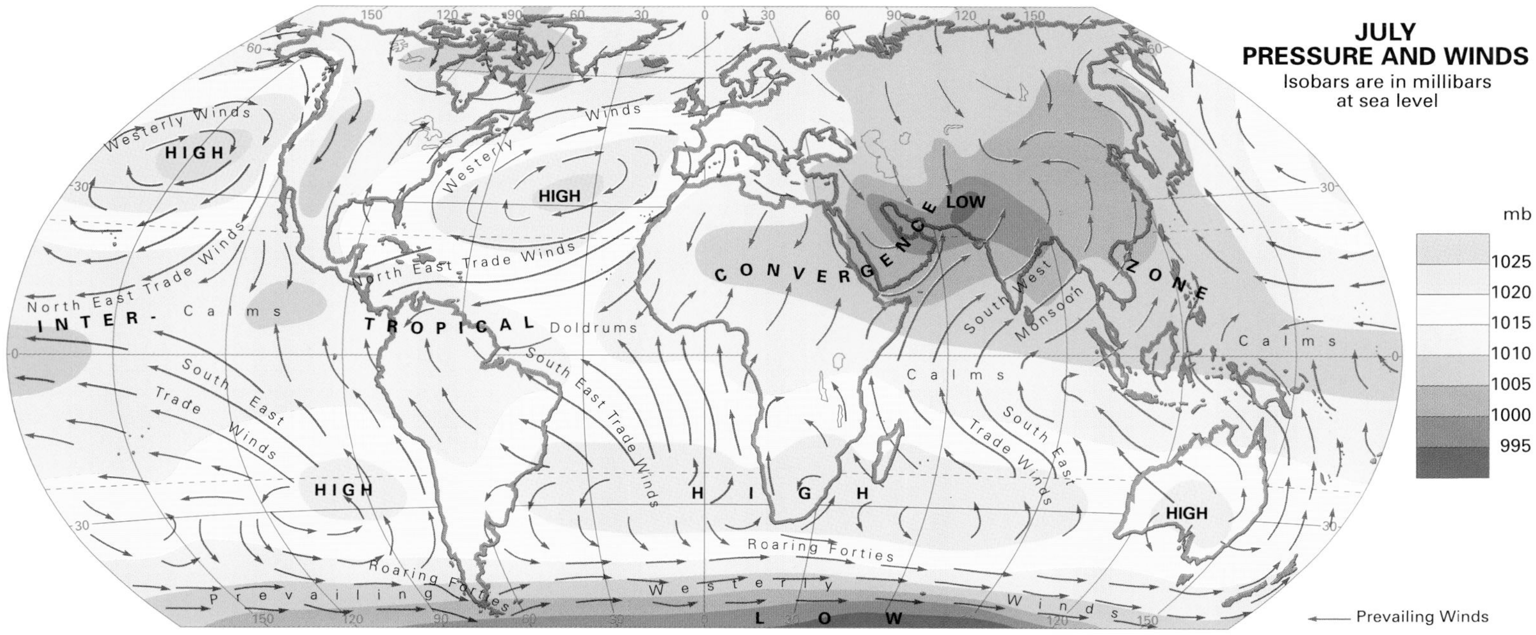

Climate Records

Pressure and winds

Highest barometric pressure: Agata, Siberia, 1,083.8 mb at altitude 262 m [862 ft], 31 December 1968.

Lowest barometric pressure: Typhoon Tip, 480 km [300 mls] west of Guam, Pacific Ocean, 870 mb, 12 October 1979.

Highest recorded wind speed: Mt Washington, New Hampshire, USA, 371 km/h [231 mph], 12 April 1934. This is three times as strong as hurricane force on the Beaufort Scale.

Windiest place: Commonwealth Bay, George V Coast, Antarctica, where gales frequently reach over 320 km/h [200 mph].

Worst recorded storm: Bangladesh (then East Pakistan) cyclone*, 13 November 1970 – over 300,000 dead or missing. The 1991 cyclone, Bangladesh's and the world's second worst in terms of loss of life, killed an estimated 138,000 people.

Worst recorded tornado: Missouri/Illinois/Indiana, USA, 18 March 1925 – 792 deaths. The tornado was only 275 m [300 yds] wide.

** Tropical cyclones are known as hurricanes in Central and North America, as typhoons in the Far East, and as willy-willies in northern Australia.*

CARTOGRAPHY BY PHILIP'S. COPYRIGHT GEORGE PHILIP LTD

Climate

For more information:

9 Ocean currents
14 Circulation of the air
15 Classification of clouds
Pressure and winds
18 Hydrological cycle
19 Natural vegetation
21 Greenhouse effect
22 Global warming

Weather is the day-to-day or hour-to-hour condition of the air, while climate is weather in the long term, the seasonal pattern of hot and cold, wet and dry, averaged over a long period. Most classifications of climate are based on a system developed by a Russian meteorologist, Vladimir Köppen, in the early 19th century. Using a code based on letters and a classification centred on two main features, temperature and precipitation, he identified five main climatic types: tropical (A), dry (B), warm temperate (C), cold temperate (D), and polar (E). A highland mountain climate (H), was added later to account for the variety of altitudinal climatic zones on high mountains. Each of these main regions was then further subdivided.

Latitude is a major factor in determining climate, but other factors add to the complexity. They include the differential heating of land and sea, the distance from the sea, the effect of mountains on winds, and the influence of ocean currents. For example, New York City, Naples and the Gobi Desert share almost the same latitude, but their climates are very different.

Climates are not indefinitely stable. During the last Ice Age, the Earth underwent alternating cold periods, called glacials, separated by warm interglacials. The Milankovich theory suggests such cycles may be caused by variations in the Earth's path around the Sun, changing from almost circular to elliptical every 95,000 years, and variations in the Earth's tilt from 21.5° to 24.5° every 42,000 years. Another factor is that the Earth is now closest to the Sun in the middle of winter in the northern hemisphere and furthest away in summer. But 12,000 years ago, at the height of the last glacial period, the northern winter fell with the Sun at its most distant.

Studies of these cycles suggest that we are now in an interglacial with a new glacial period on the way. However, many scientists believe that global warming, largely a result of burning fossil fuels and deforestation, may be occurring much faster than the great, slow cycles of the Solar System.

Tropical rainy climates
All mean monthly temperatures above 18°C.
- Af Rainforest climate
- Am Monsoon climate
- Aw Savanna climate

Dry climates
Low rainfall combined with a wide range of temperatures
- BS Steppe climate
- BW Desert climate

Warm temperate rainy climates
The mean temperature is below 18°C but above –3°C and that of the warmest month is over 10°C.
- Cw Dry winter climate
- Cs Dry summer climate
- Cf Climate with no dry season

Cold temperate rainy climates
The mean temperature of the coldest month is below –3°C but that of the warmest month is still over 10°C.
- Dw Dry winter climate
- Df Climate with no dry season

Polar climates
The mean temperature of the warmest month is below 10°C, giving permanently frozen subsoil.
- ET Tundra climate

The mean temperature of the warmest month is below 0°C, giving permanent ice and snow.
- EF Polar climate

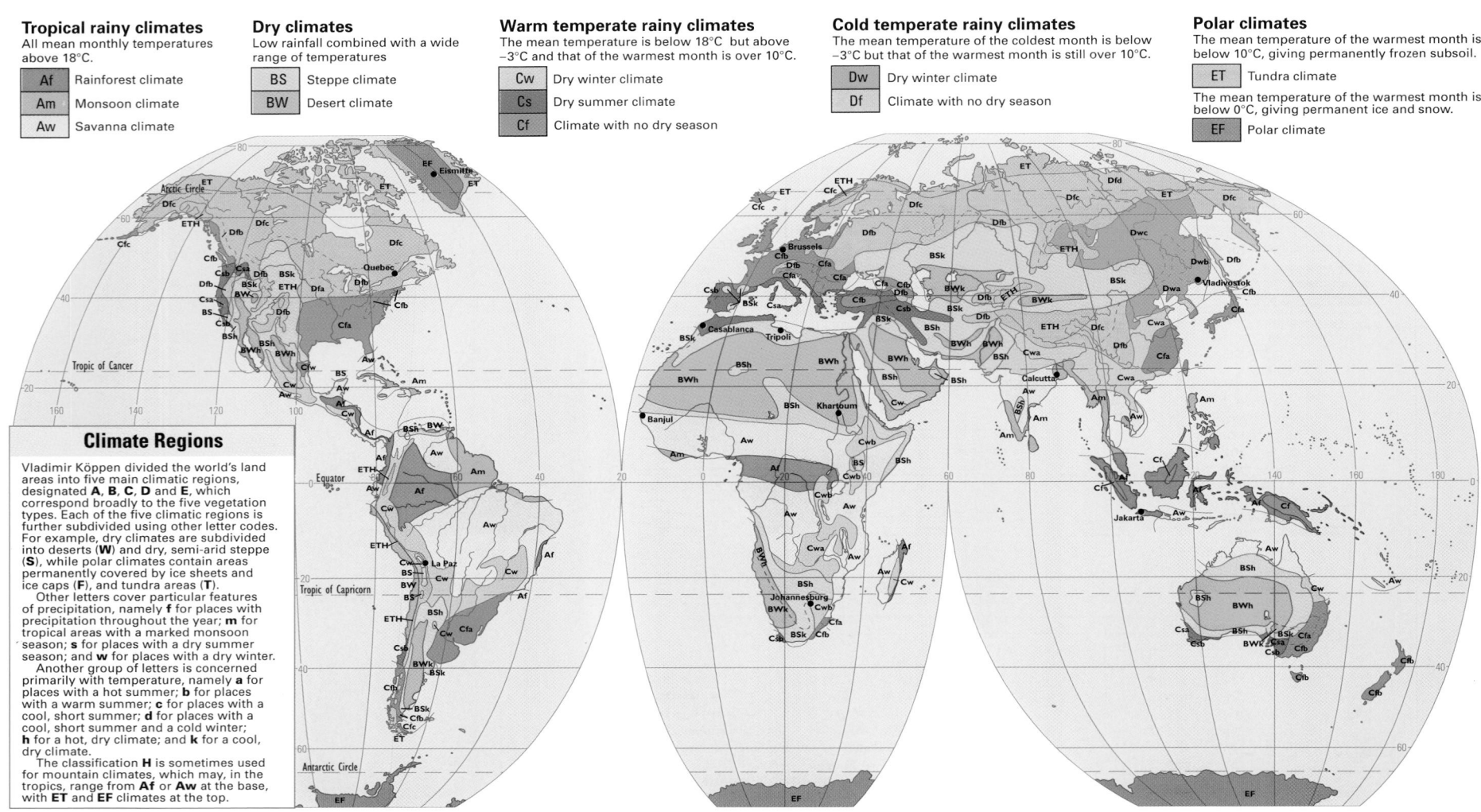

Climate Regions

Vladimir Köppen divided the world's land areas into five main climatic regions, designated **A**, **B**, **C**, **D** and **E**, which correspond broadly to the five vegetation types. Each of the five climatic regions is further subdivided using other letter codes. For example, dry climates are subdivided into deserts (**W**) and dry, semi-arid steppe (**S**), while polar climates contain areas permanently covered by ice sheets and ice caps (**F**), and tundra areas (**T**).

Other letters cover particular features of precipitation, namely **f** for places with precipitation throughout the year; **m** for tropical areas with a marked monsoon season; **s** for places with a dry summer season; and **w** for places with a dry winter.

Another group of letters is concerned primarily with temperature, namely **a** for places with a hot summer; **b** for places with a warm summer; **c** for places with a cool, short summer; **d** for places with a cool, short summer and a cold winter; **h** for a hot, dry climate; and **k** for a cool, dry climate.

The classification **H** is sometimes used for mountain climates, which may, in the tropics, range from **Af** or **Aw** at the base, with **ET** and **EF** climates at the top.

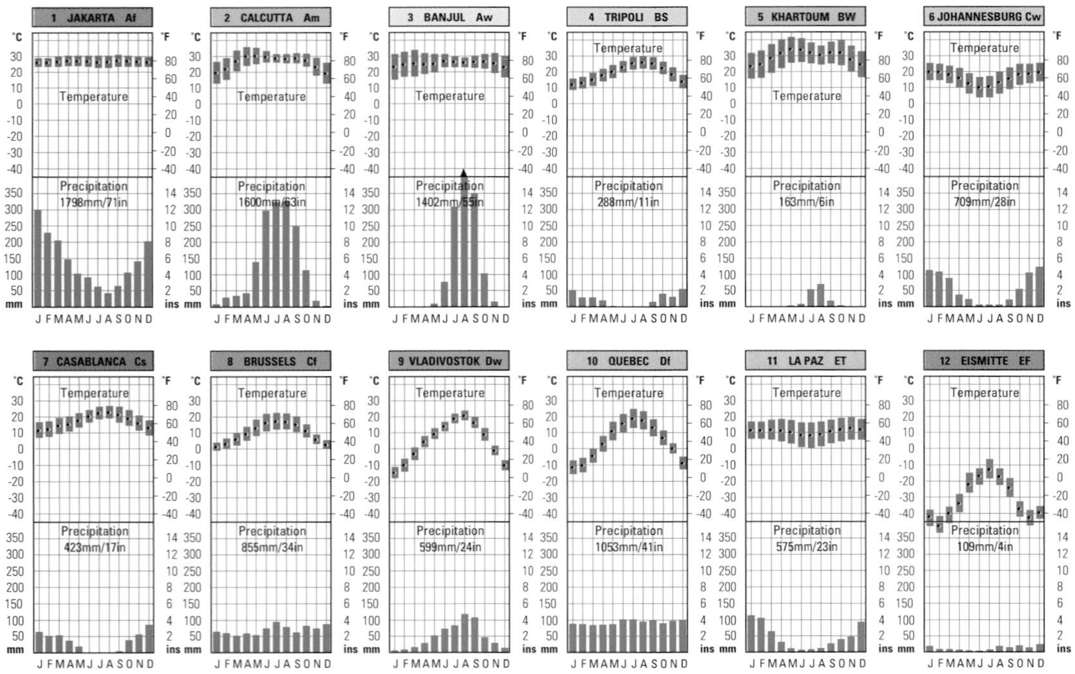

Climate and Weather Terms

Anticyclone: area of high pressure with light winds and generally quiet weather.
Absolute humidity: amount of water vapour contained in a given volume of air.
Cloud cover: amount of cloud in the sky; measured in oktas (from 1 – 8), with 0 clear, and 8 total cover.
Condensation: the conversion of water vapour, or moisture in the air, into liquid.
Cyclone: violent storm resulting from anticlockwise rotation of winds in the northern hemisphere and clockwise in the southern: called hurricane in N. America, typhoon in the Far East.
Depression: area of low pressure. The pressure gradient is towards the centre.
Dew: water droplets condensed out of the air after the ground has cooled at night.
Dew point: temperature at which air becomes saturated (reaches a relative humidity of 100%) at a constant pressure.
Drizzle: precipitation where drops are less than 0.5 mm [0.02 in] in diameter.
Evaporation: conversion of water from liquid into vapour, or moisture in the air.
Front: the dividing line between two air masses.
Frost: dew that has frozen when the air temperature falls below freezing point.
Hail: frozen rain; small balls of ice, often falling during thunderstorms.
Hoar frost: formed on objects when the dew point is below freezing point.
Humidity: amount of moisture in the air.
Isobar: cartographic line connecting places of equal atmospheric pressure.
Isotherm: cartographic line connecting places of equal temperature.
Lightning: massive electrical discharge released in thunderstorm from cloud to cloud or cloud to ground, the result of the tip becoming positively charged and the bottom negatively charged.
Precipitation: measurable rain, snow, sleet or hail.
Prevailing wind: most common direction of wind at a given location.
Rain: precipitation of liquid particles with diameter larger than 0.5 mm [0.02 in].
Relative humidity: amount of water vapour contained in a given volume of air at a given temperature.
Snow: formed when water vapour condenses below freezing point.
Thunder: sound produced by the rapid expansion of air heated by lightning.
Tornado: severe funnel-shaped storm that twists as hot air spins vertically (waterspout at sea).
Whirlwind: rapidly rotating column of air, only a few metres across, made visible by dust.

CARTOGRAPHY BY PHILIP'S. COPYRIGHT GEORGE PHILIP LTD

Climate Change

Human factors, such as the emission of greenhouse gases through the burning of fossil fuels and deforestation, have contributed to global warming. The histogram, below, shows in blue the average global temperatures from 1860 (when sufficient observations became available for global averages to be calculated) to 1996. The red line is a 10-year running average. Overall, there is an upward trend, particularly so since the 1970s, when global warming became a matter of concern in scientific circles. The large year-to-year changes indicate the Earth's natural climatic variability and the influence of such factors as major volcanic eruptions.

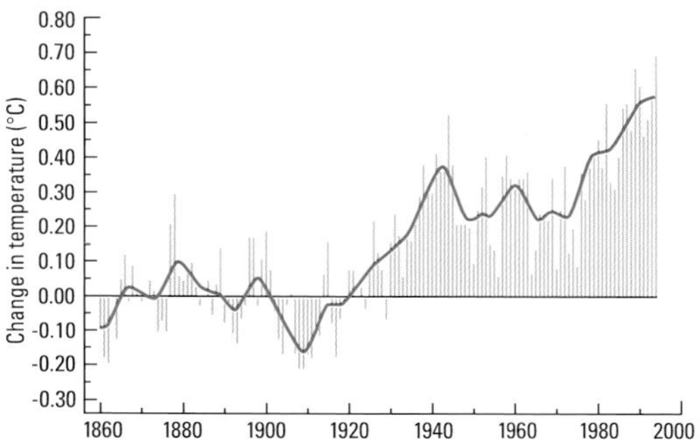

Change in temperature (°C)
0.80
0.70
0.60
0.50
0.40
0.30
0.20
0.10
0.00
-0.10
-0.20
-0.30
1860
1880
1900
1920
1940
1960
1980
2000

Data from the Hadley Centre for Climate Research and Prediction

Beaufort Wind Scale

Named after the 19th-century British naval officer who devised it, Admiral Beaufort, the Beaufort Scale assesses wind speed according to its effects. It was originally designed as an aid for sailors, but has since been adapted for use on the land. It is used internationally.

Scale	Wind speed km/h	mph	Effect
0	0–1	0–1	**Calm** Smoke rises vertically
1	1–5	1–3	**Light air** Wind direction shown only by smoke drift
2	6–11	4–7	**Light breeze** Wind felt on face; leaves rustle; vanes moved by wind
3	12–19	8–12	**Gentle breeze** Leaves and small twigs in constant motion; wind extends small flag
4	20–28	13–18	**Moderate** Raises dust and loose paper; small branches move
5	29–38	19–24	**Fresh** Small trees in leaf sway; crested wavelets on inland waters
6	39–49	25–31	**Strong** Large branches move; difficult to use umbrellas; overhead wires whistle
7	50–61	32–38	**Near gale** Whole trees in motion; difficult to walk against wind
8	62–74	39–46	**Gale** Twigs break from trees; walking very difficult
9	75–88	47–54	**Strong gale** Slight structural damage
10	89–102	55–63	**Storm** Trees uprooted; serious structural damage
11	103–117	64–72	**Violent storm** Widespread damage
12	118+	73+	**Hurricane**

The Monsoon

Monsoon is the term given to the seasonal reversal of wind direction, most noticeably in South-east Asia. It results from a combination of factors: the extreme heating and cooling of large landmasses in relation to the less marked changes in temperature of the adjacent seas; the northwards movement of the Intertropical Convergence Zone (ITCZ); and the effect of the Himalayas on the circulation of the air.

In early March, which normally marks the end of the sub-continent's cool season and the start of the hot season, winds blow outwards from the mainland. But as the overhead Sun and the ITCZ move northwards, the land is intensely heated, and a low-pressure system develops. The south-east trade winds, which are drawn across the Equator, change direction and are sucked into the interior to become south-westerly winds, bringing heavy rain. By November, the overhead Sun and the ITCZ have again moved southwards and the wind directions are again reversed. Cool winds blow from the Asian interior to the sea, losing any moisture on the Himalayas before descending to the coast.

Temperature

Average temperature in January

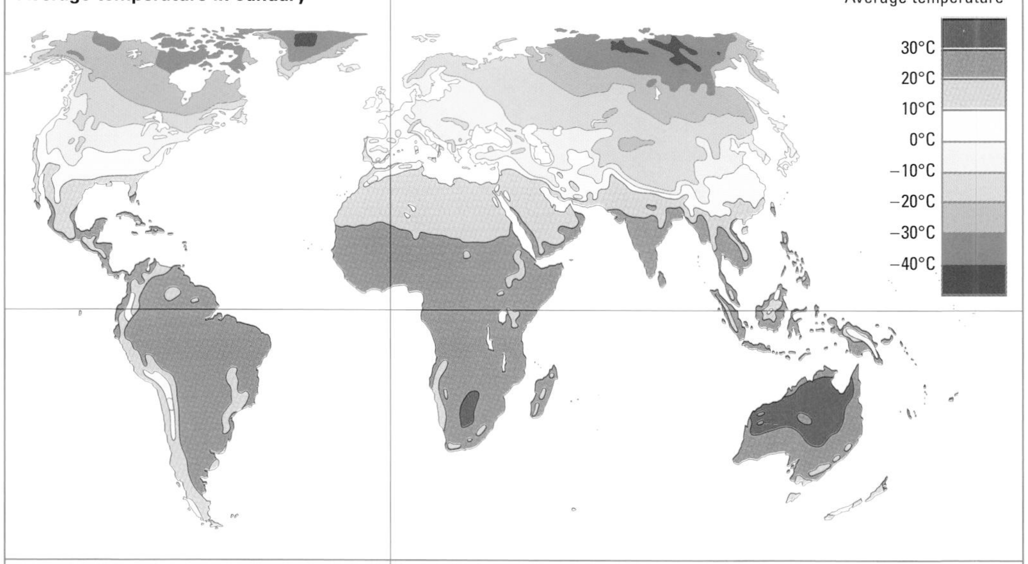

Average temperature
30°C
20°C
10°C
0°C
–10°C
–20°C
–30°C
–40°C

Average temperature in July

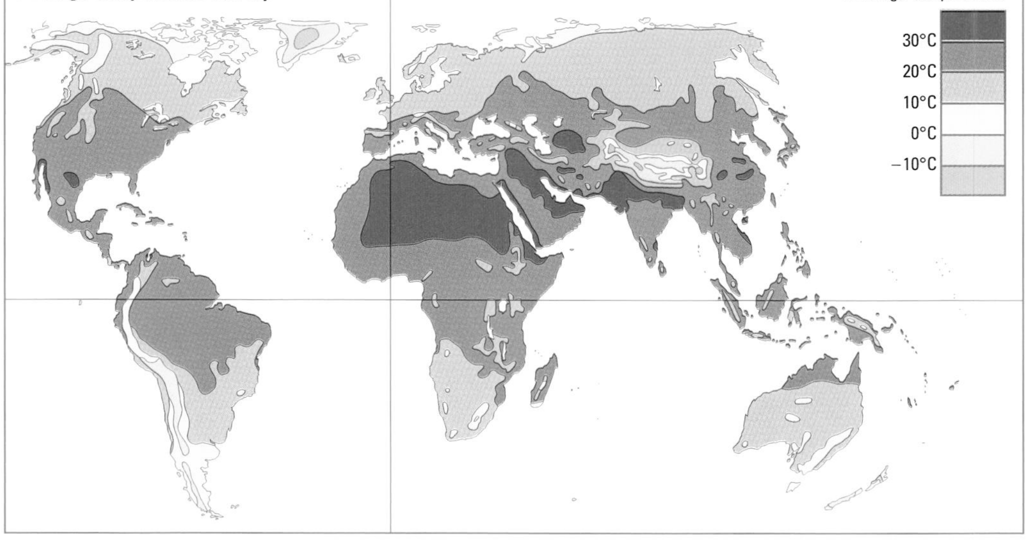

Average temperature
30°C
20°C
10°C
0°C
–10°C

Precipitation

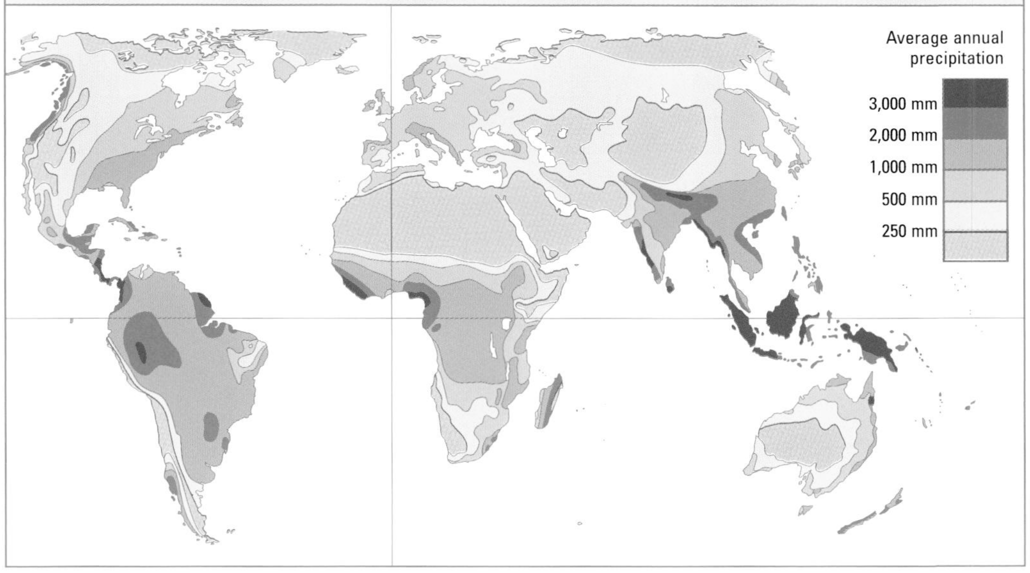

Average annual precipitation
3,000 mm
2,000 mm
1,000 mm
500 mm
250 mm

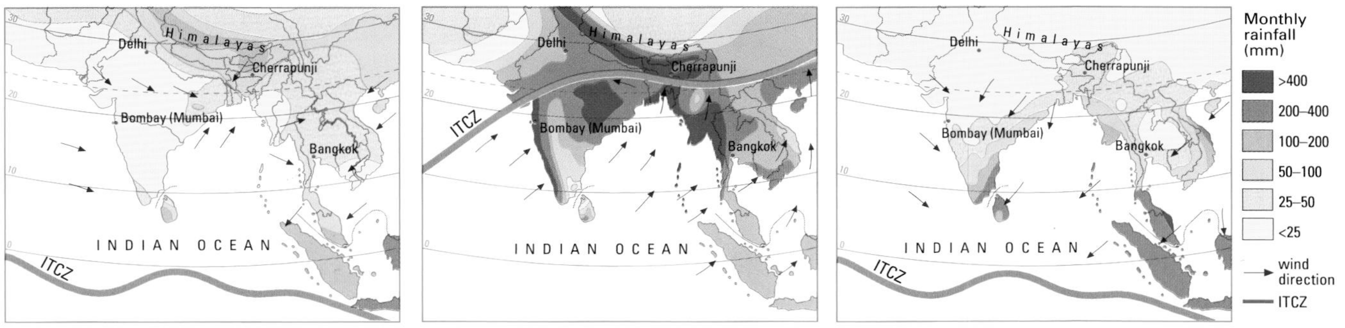

Delhi
Himalayas
Cherrapunji
Bombay (Mumbai)
Bangkok
INDIAN OCEAN
ITCZ
Monthly rainfall (mm)
>400
200–400
100–200
50–100
25–50
<25
wind direction
ITCZ

March – Start of the hot, dry season. The ITCZ is over the southern Indian Ocean.

July – The rainy season. The ITCZ has migrated northwards; winds blow onshore.

November – The ITCZ has returned south. The offshore winds are cool and dry.

Climate Records

Temperature

Highest recorded temperature: Al Aziziyah, Libya, 58°C [136.4°F], 13 September 1922.

Highest mean annual temperature: Dallol, Ethiopia, 34.4°C [94°F], 1960–66.

Longest heatwave: Marble Bar, W. Australia, 162 days over 38°C [100°F], 23 October 1923 to 7 April 1924.

Lowest recorded temperature (outside poles): Verkhoyansk, Siberia, –68°C [–90°F], 6 February 1933. Verkhoyansk also registered the greatest annual range of temperature: –70°C to 37°C [–94°F to 98°F].

Lowest mean annual temperature: Polus Nedostupnosti, Pole of Cold, Antarctica, –57.8°C [–72°F].

Precipitation

Driest place: Calama, N. Chile: no recorded rainfall in 400 years to 1971.

Wettest place (average): Tututendo, Colombia: mean annual rainfall 11,770 mm [463.4 in].

Wettest place (12 months): Cherrapunji, Meghalaya, N.E. India, 26,470 mm [1,040 in], August 1860 to August 1861. Cherrapunji also holds the record for rainfall in one month: 2,930 mm [115 in], July 1861. (See maps below.)

Wettest place (24 hours): Cilaos, Réunion, Indian Ocean, 1,870 mm [73.6 in], 15–16 March 1952.

Heaviest hailstones: Gopalganj, Bangladesh, up to 1.02 kg [2.25 lb], 14 April 1986 (killed 92 people).

Heaviest snowfall (continuous): Bessans, Savoie, France, 1,730 mm [68 in] in 19 hours, 5–6 April 1969.

Heaviest snowfall (season/year): Paradise Ranger Station, Mt Rainier, Washington, USA, 31,102 mm [1,224.5 in], 19 February 1971 to 18 February 1972.

CARTOGRAPHY BY PHILIP'S. COPYRIGHT GEORGE PHILIP LTD

Water and Vegetation

For more information:

12 Rivers and glaciers
14 Types of precipitation
20 Biodiversity

Without the hydrological cycle, whereby water is constantly recycled between the oceans, the atmosphere and the land, the continents would be barren. Precipitation enables plants to grow and soils to form, creating the world's natural vegetation regions and the ecosystems that support animal life. Running water also plays a major role in shaping landforms. Yet in many parts of the world, people do not have safe water to drink and suffer from diseases caused by water-borne organisms or pollution. In addition, the limited water supplies have to be shared with agriculture and industry.

In 1996, UN experts argued that the demand for water is increasing at about twice the rate of population growth. They predict that, by 2025, two-thirds of the world's population will face water shortages. This could lead to conflict and even boundary wars, especially because 300 major rivers cross national frontiers and access to their water is likely to be disputed.

The Hydrological Cycle

The world's water balance is regulated by the constant recycling of water between the oceans, atmosphere and land. The movement of water between these three reservoirs is known as the hydrological cycle. The oceans play a vital role in the hydrological cycle: 74% of the total precipitation falls over the oceans and 84% of the total evaporation comes from the oceans. Water vapour in the atmosphere circulates around the planet, transporting energy as well as the water itself. When the vapour cools, it falls as rain or snow. The whole cycle is driven by the Sun.

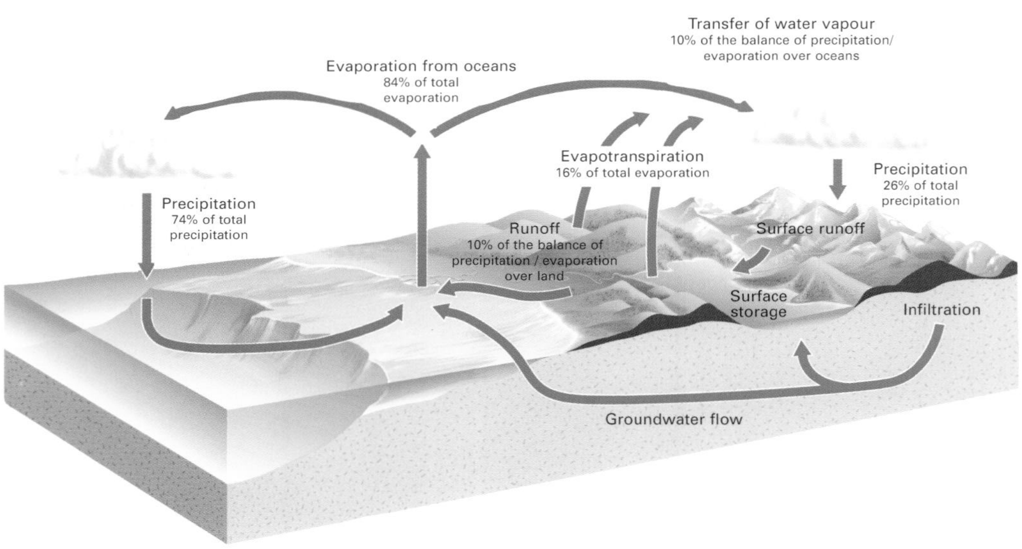

Water Distribution

The distribution of planetary water, by percentage. Oceans and ice caps together account for more than 99% of the total; the breakdown of the remainder is estimated.

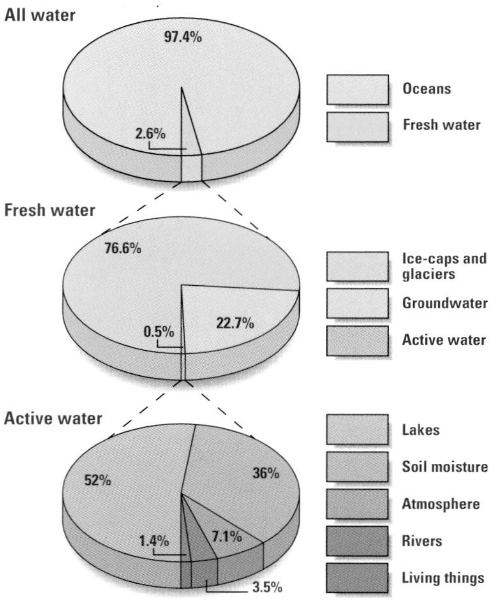

Almost all the world's water is 3,000 million years old, and all of it cycles endlessly through the hydrosphere, though at different rates. Water vapour circulates over days, even hours; deep ocean water circulates over millennia; and ice-cap water remains solid for millions of years.

Water Utilization

The percentage breakdown of water usage by sector, selected countries (1996)

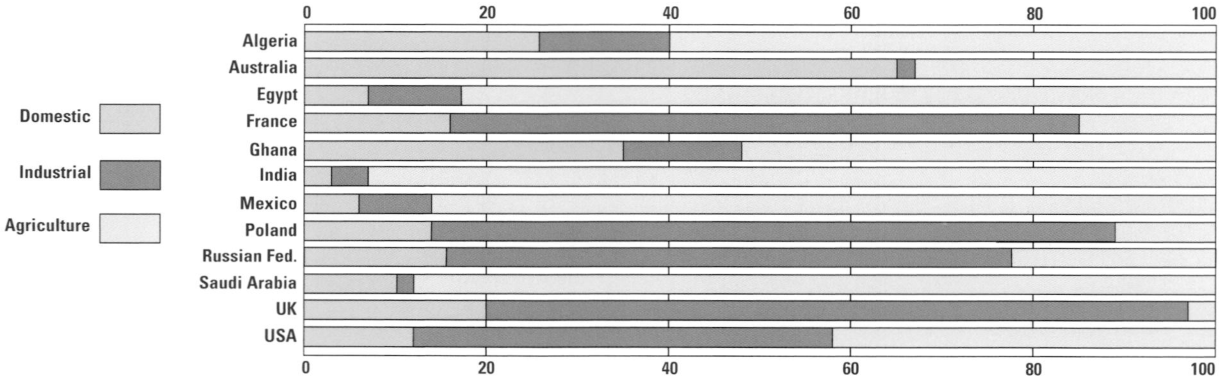

Water Runoff

Annual freshwater runoff by continent in cubic kilometres

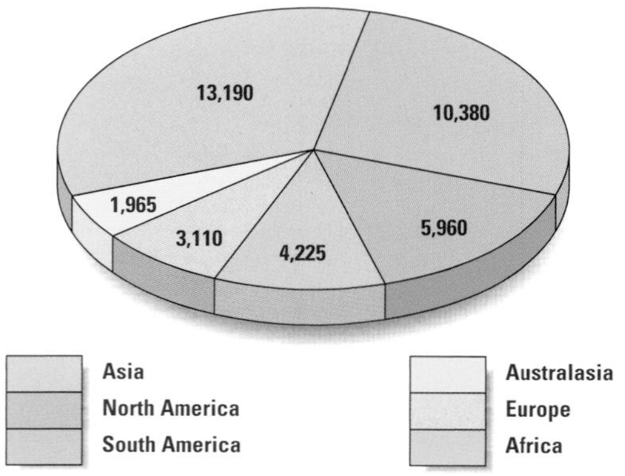

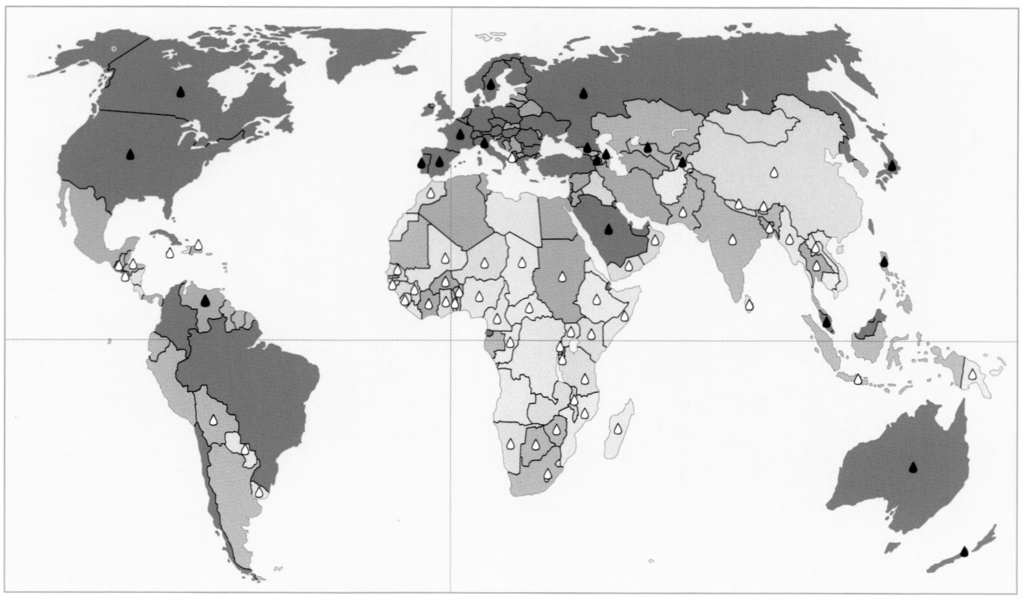

Water Supply

Percentage of total population with access to safe drinking water (1995)

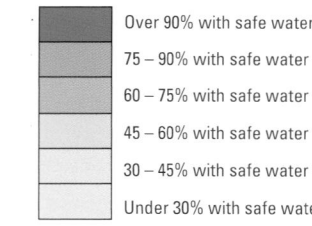

Over 90% with safe water
75 – 90% with safe water
60 – 75% with safe water
45 – 60% with safe water
30 – 45% with safe water
Under 30% with safe water

Under 80 litres average per capita daily water consumption
Over 320 litres average per capita daily water consumption

Least well-provided countries

Paraguay	8%	Central Afr. Rep.	18%
Afghanistan	10%	Bhutan	21%
Cambodia	13%	Congo (D. Rep.)	25%

Watersheds

The world's major rivers; the rank of the world's 20 longest is shown in square brackets, led by the Nile and the Amazon.

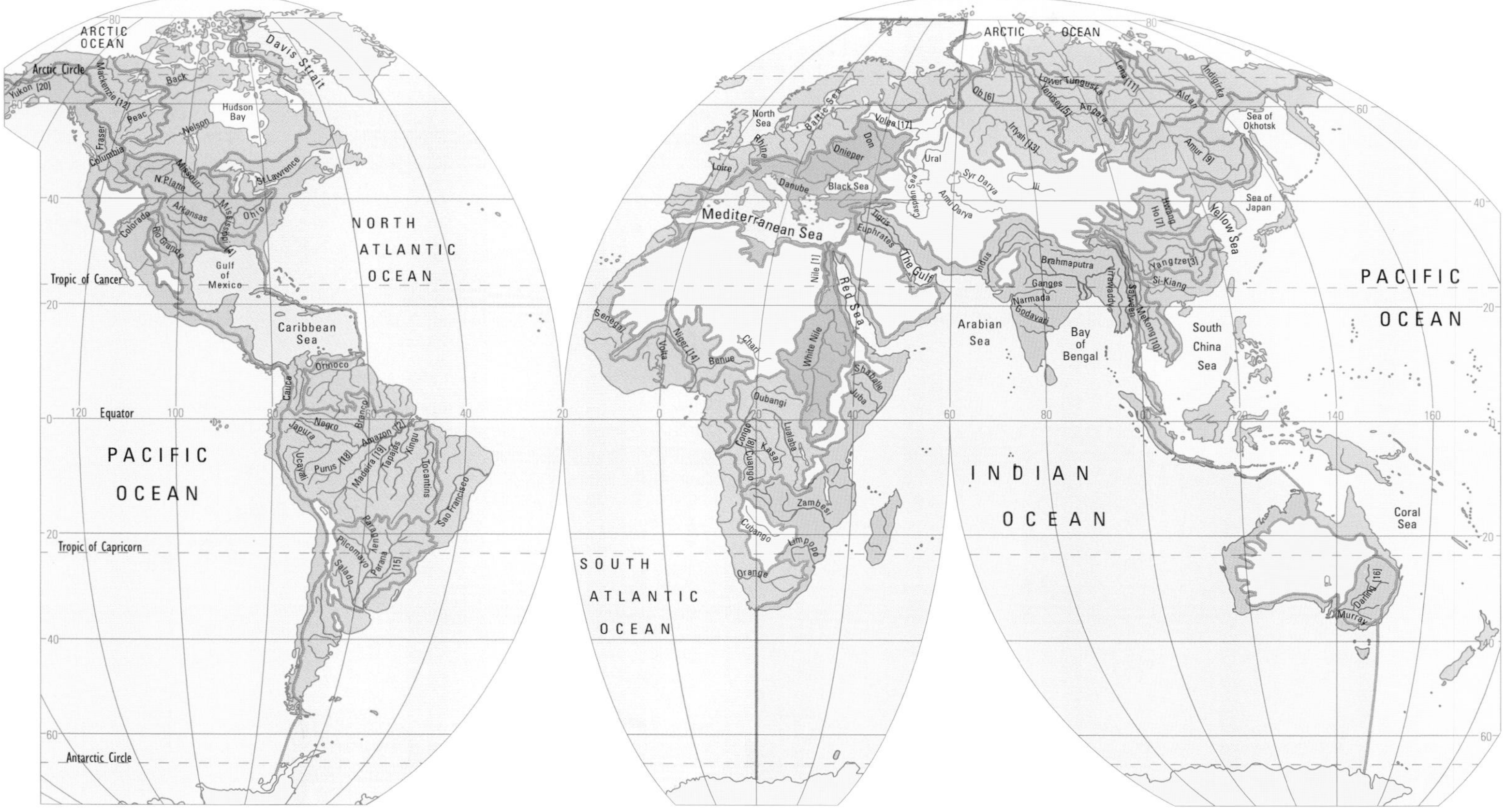

Where the rivers run

- Pacific Ocean
- Indian Ocean
- Arctic Ocean
- Atlantic Ocean
- Caribbean Sea–Gulf of Mexico
- Mediterranean Sea
- Inland basins, ice caps and deserts

The map shows the direction of freshwater flow on a continental scale; the water runoff chart on the facing page indicates the quantities involved. The rate of runoff varies seasonally and is affected by the surface vegetation. Most of the world's major rivers discharge into the Atlantic Ocean.

Annual Sediment Yield

Around 20% of all land-derived sediment is carried by three Asian rivers: the Brahmaputra, Huang He (Yellow River) and Ganges. Together these three rivers carry 3,206 million tonnes of sediment per year into the oceans. Sediment yield is affected by runoff and vegetation cover and is steadily increasing due to large-scale deforestation, most notably in South-east Asia and the Amazon basin. In these regions, deforesting the slopes allows the heavy tropical rains to wash away whatever thin and fragile soil there is, leading to severe erosion of the land.

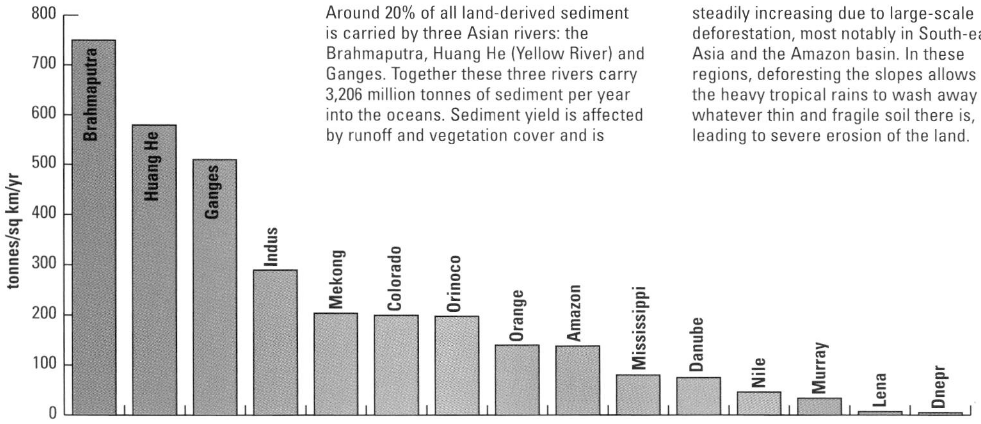

Land Use by Continent

The proportion of productive land has reached its upper limit in Europe, and in Asia more than 80% of potential cropland is already under cultivation.

- Forest
- Permanent pasture and rough grazing
- Permanent crops and plantations
- Arable
- Non-productive

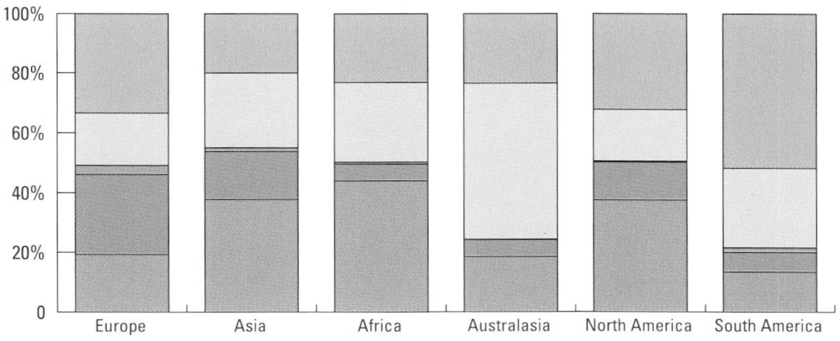

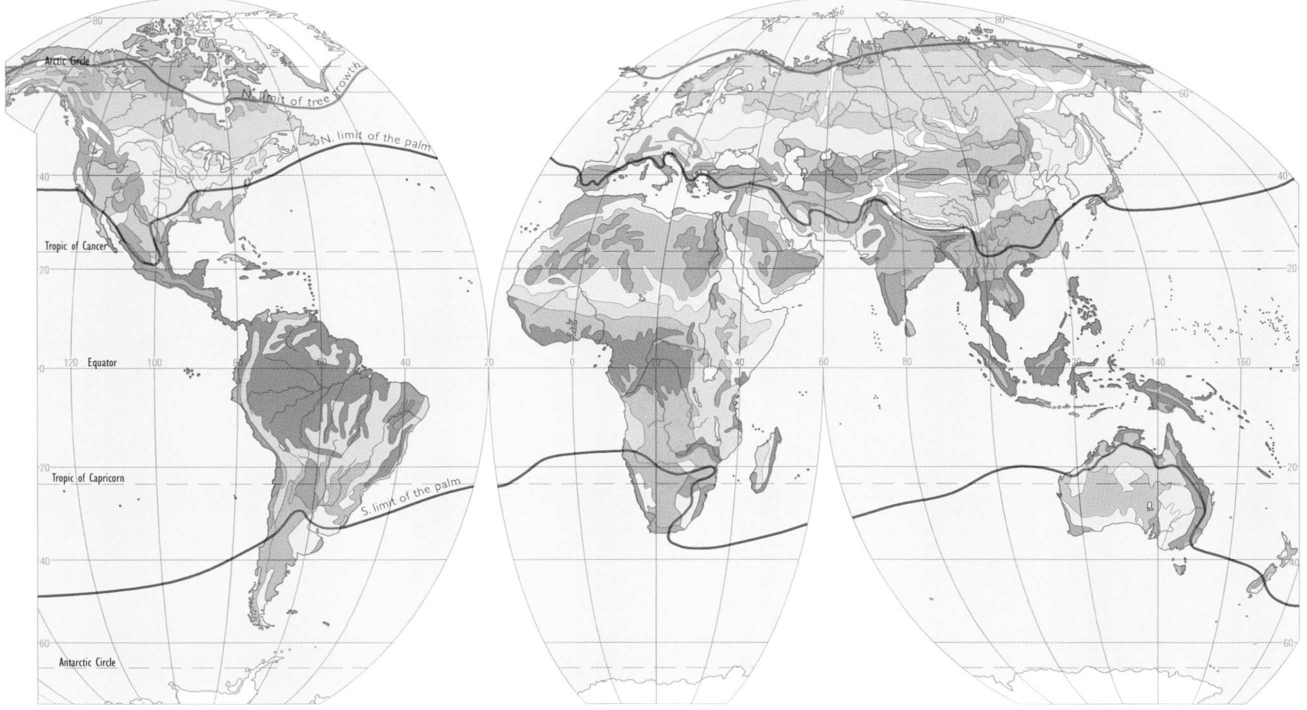

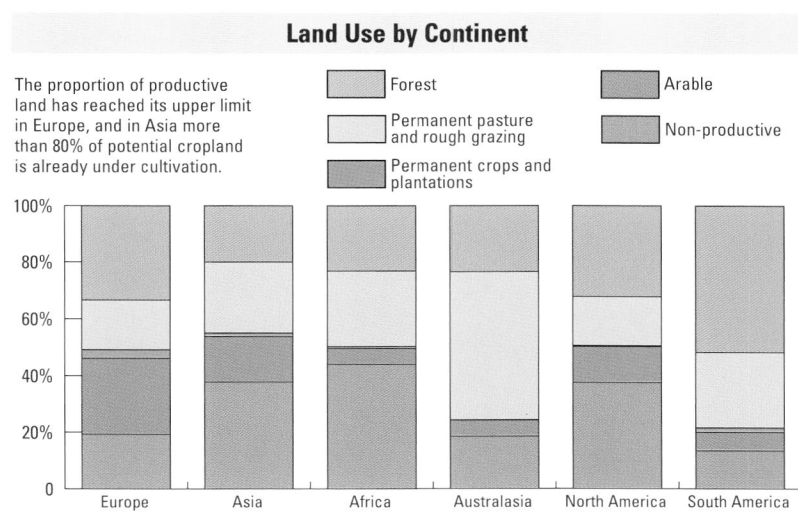

Natural Vegetation

- Tropical rainforest
- Subtropical and temperate rainforest
- Monsoon woodland and open jungle
- Subtropical and temperate woodland, scrub and bush
- Tropical savanna, with low trees and bush
- Tropical savanna and grasslands
- Dry semi-desert, with shrub and grass
- Desert shrub
- Desert
- Dry steppe and shrub
- Temperate grasslands, prairie and steppe
- Mediterranean hardwood forest and scrub
- Temperate deciduous forest and meadow
- Temperate deciduous and coniferous forest
- Northern coniferous forest (taïga)
- Mountainous forest, mainly coniferous
- High plateau steppe and tundra
- Arctic tundra
- Polar and mountainous ice desert

The map illustrates the natural 'climax vegetation' of a region, as dictated by its climate and topography. In most cases, human agricultural activity has drastically altered the vegetation pattern. Western Europe, for example, lost most of its broadleaf forest many centuries ago, while elsewhere irrigation has turned some natural semi-desert into productive land. The various vegetation regions support different kinds of animals and, in an undisturbed state, they are highly developed biological communities, or biomes.

The blue line on the map represents the northern limit of tree growth, and the red lines indicate the northern and southern limits of palm growth.

The Natural Environment

For more information:

Recent discoveries of life forms in some of the world's most hostile environments, such as around the black smokers along the ocean ridges, prepared the way for the announcement by NASA scientists in 1996 that they had found microfossils in a Martian meteorite. But other scientists were sceptical, believing them to be natural mineral structures and not evidence of extraterrestrial life.

Until further evidence is available, the Earth remains the only planet where we know for sure that life exists. According to the fossil record, life on Earth appeared at least 3,500 million years ago. Since then, it has evolved from its primitive beginnings to its modern biodiversity, including millions of plants, animals and micro-organisms. Living organisms have not only adapted to the environment but they have also changed their environment to suit themselves. For example, the Earth's early atmosphere contained little oxygen but the emergence of multi-celled, oxygen-producing algae, around 2,000 million years ago, led to the creation of an oxygen-rich atmosphere. This enabled land animals to populate the ancient continents.

The amount of the greenhouse gas carbon dioxide in the atmosphere would steadily increase from its present 0.03% were it not for plants. Without them, the Earth's atmosphere would, in a few million years, be similar to that of Venus, where surface temperatures reach 475°C. The Earth has evolved into a complex control system, sensing and reacting to changes and tending always to maintain the balance it has achieved.

Much discussion has centred on how that balance changes. Only recently, scientists were suggesting that we may be living in an interglacial stage of the Pleistocene Ice Age. From the 1980s, however, predictions of future climates have concentrated more on global warming, caused by pollution which has led to an increase in greenhouse gases in the atmosphere. Interference in the natural cycles that control the environment may have consequences that are hard to predict.

Furthermore, we are currently experiencing a period of mass extinction of species, causing a rapid reduction in our planet's biodiversity. A report by the World Conservation Union in 1996 stated that, of the 4,327 known mammal species, 1,096 were at risk and 169 'critically endangered'.

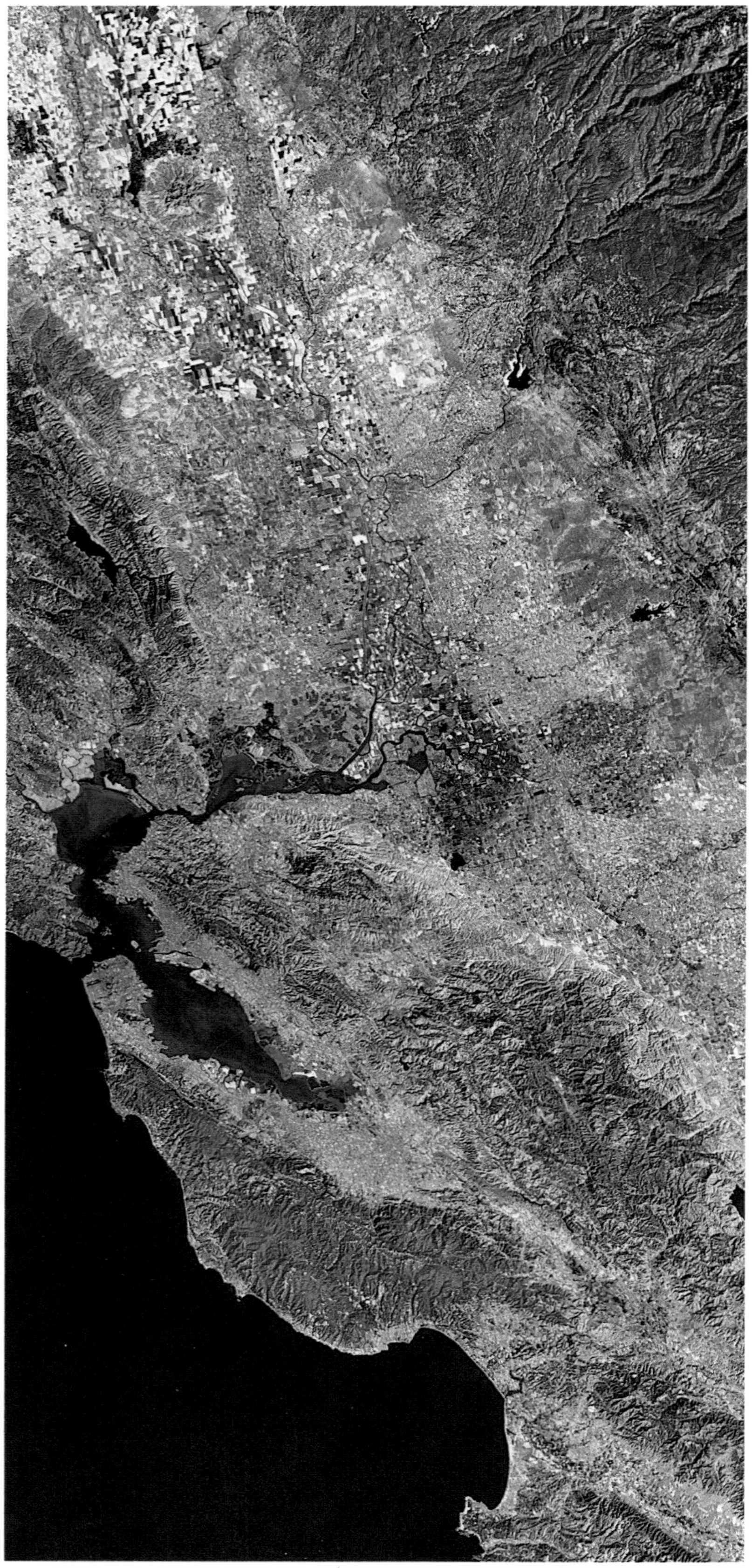

Biodiversity in California

The photograph, left, is a false-colour satellite image of central California in the south-western United States. The large inlet of the Pacific Ocean is San Francisco Bay. San Francisco lies just below the entrance to the bay, with Oakland on the far side and San Jose to the south-east. California, nicknamed the Golden State, is the third largest state in the United States and the most populous.

Because of its varied terrain and climate, California has a wide range of diverse habitats within a relatively small area. East of the forested Coast Ranges (the grey and red areas just inland from the bay) lies the fertile Central Valley, which appears as a red and blue chequerboard. The Sierra Nevada is the red area in the top right corner. In the north-west and south-west of the state, not shown here, lie parts of the Basin and Range region, much of which is desert. It includes Death Valley, which contains the country's lowest point on land at 86 m below sea level.

Forests cover about 40% of California and they include bristlecone pines, thought to be the oldest living things on Earth, together with coastal redwoods, the world's tallest trees. Wildlife is still abundant, though some species, such as the rare California condor, are on the endangered list.

The state has achieved much to protect its biodiversity. It contains eight of the 54 national parks in the United States. Two of them, Death Valley and Joshua Tree, were designated national parks as recently as 1994, as part of a conservation measure, including the protection of large areas of wilderness in the deserts.

California has vast resources and, were it a separate nation, it would rank among the world's ten most productive in terms of the total value of its goods and services. This means that, like the United States as a whole, it has resources, which many developing countries lack, to finance conservation measures. For example, the World Conservation Union reported in 1996 that 8% of mammals were threatened in the United States, as compared with 32% in the Philippines and 44% in Madagascar, two countries where habitat destruction has been on a large scale.

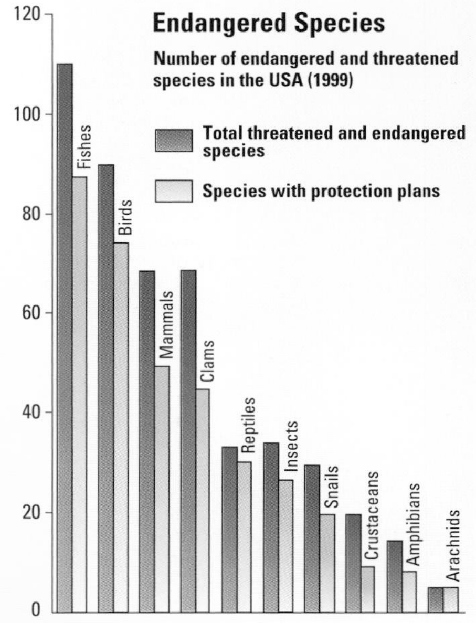

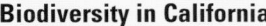

Endangered Species
Number of endangered and threatened species in the USA (1999)
Total threatened and endangered species
Species with protection plans
120
100
80
60
40
20
0
Fishes
Birds
Mammals
Clams
Reptiles
Insects
Snails
Crustaceans
Amphibians
Arachnids

Threatened Mammals

Percentage of mammal species classified as threatened (1996). Many scientists believe we are currently experiencing a period of mass extinction of species rivalling five other periods in the past half a billion years. Among the most threatened mammals are elephants, primates and rhinoceroses.

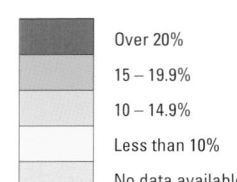

Over 20%
15 – 19.9%
10 – 14.9%
Less than 10%
No data available

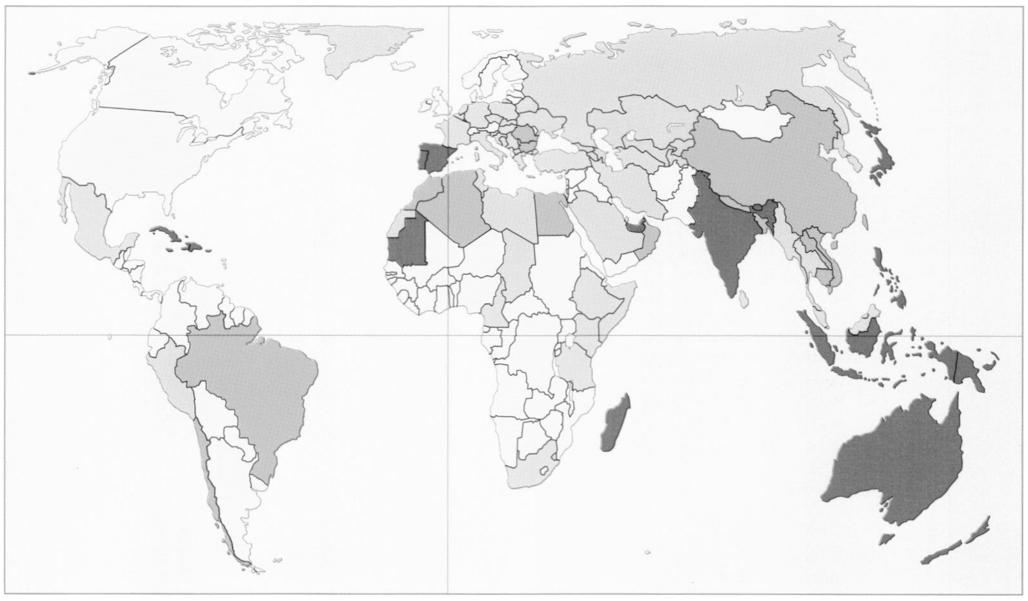

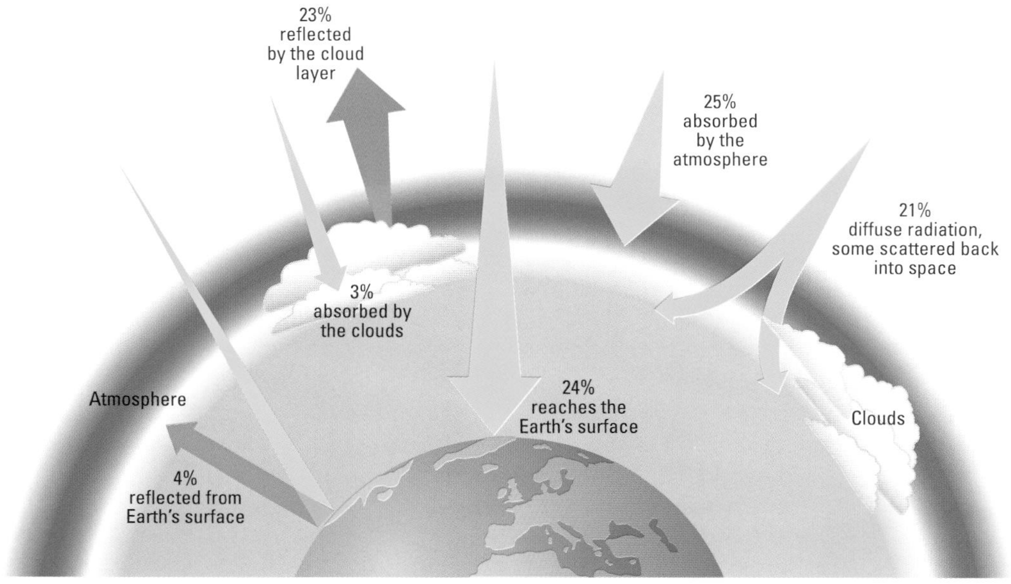

23%
reflected
by the cloud
layer
25%
absorbed
by the
atmosphere
21%
diffuse radiation,
some scattered back
into space
3%
absorbed by
the clouds
Atmosphere
24%
reaches the
Earth's surface
Clouds
4%
reflected from
Earth's surface

The Earth's Energy Balance

Apart from a modest quantity of internal heat from its molten core, the Earth receives all of its energy from the Sun. If the planet is to remain at a constant temperature, it must reradiate exactly as much energy as it receives. Even a minute surplus would lead to a warmer Earth, a deficit to a cooler one. The temperature at which thermal equilibrium is reached depends on a multitude of interconnected factors. Two of the most important are the relative brightness of the Earth – its index of reflectivity, called the 'albedo' – and the heat-trapping capacity of the atmosphere – the celebrated 'greenhouse effect' (see below).

Because the Sun is very hot, most of its energy arrives in the form of relatively short-wave radiation: the shorter the waves, the more energy they carry. Some of the incoming energy is reflected straight back into space, exactly as it arrived; some is absorbed by the atmosphere on its way towards the surface; some is absorbed by the Earth itself. Absorbed energy heats the Earth and its atmosphere alike. But since its temperature is very much lower than that of the Sun, the outgoing energy is emitted at much longer infra-red wavelengths. Some of the outgoing radiation escapes directly into outer space; some of it is reabsorbed by the atmosphere. Atmospheric energy eventually finds its way back into space, too, after a complex series of interactions. These include the air movements we call the weather and, almost incidentally, the maintenance of life on Earth.

This diagram does not attempt to illustrate the actual mechanisms of heat exchange, but gives a reasonable account (in percentages) of what happens to 100 energy 'units'. Short-wave radiation is shown in yellow, long-wave in orange.

The Carbon Cycle

Most of the constituents of the atmosphere are kept in constant balance by complex cycles in which life plays an essential and indeed a dominant part. The control of carbon dioxide, which if left to its own devices would be the dominant atmospheric gas, is possibly the most important, although since all the Earth's biological and geophysical cycles interact and interlock, it is hard to separate them even in theory and quite impossible in practice.

The Earth has a huge supply of carbon, only a small quantity of which is in the form of carbon dioxide. Of that, around 98% is dissolved in the sea; the fraction circulating in the air amounts to only 340 parts per million of the atmosphere, where its capacity as a greenhouse gas is the key regulator of the planetary temperature. In turn, life regulates the regulator, keeping carbon dioxide concentrations below danger level.

If all life were to vanish from the Earth tomorrow, the atmosphere would begin the process of change immediately, although it might take several million years to achieve a new, inorganic stability. First, the oxygen content would begin to fall away; with no more assistance than a little solar radiation, a few electrical storms and its own high chemical potential, oxygen would steadily combine with atmospheric nitrogen and volcanic outgassing. In doing so, it would yield sufficient acid to react with carbonaceous rocks such as limestone, releasing carbon dioxide. Once carbon dioxide levels exceeded about 1%, its greenhouse power would increase disproportionately. Rising temperatures – well above the boiling point of water – would speed chemical reactions; in time, the Earth's atmosphere would consist of little more than carbon dioxide and superheated water vapour.

Living things, however, circulate carbon. They do so first by simply existing: after all, the carbon atom is the basic building block of living matter.

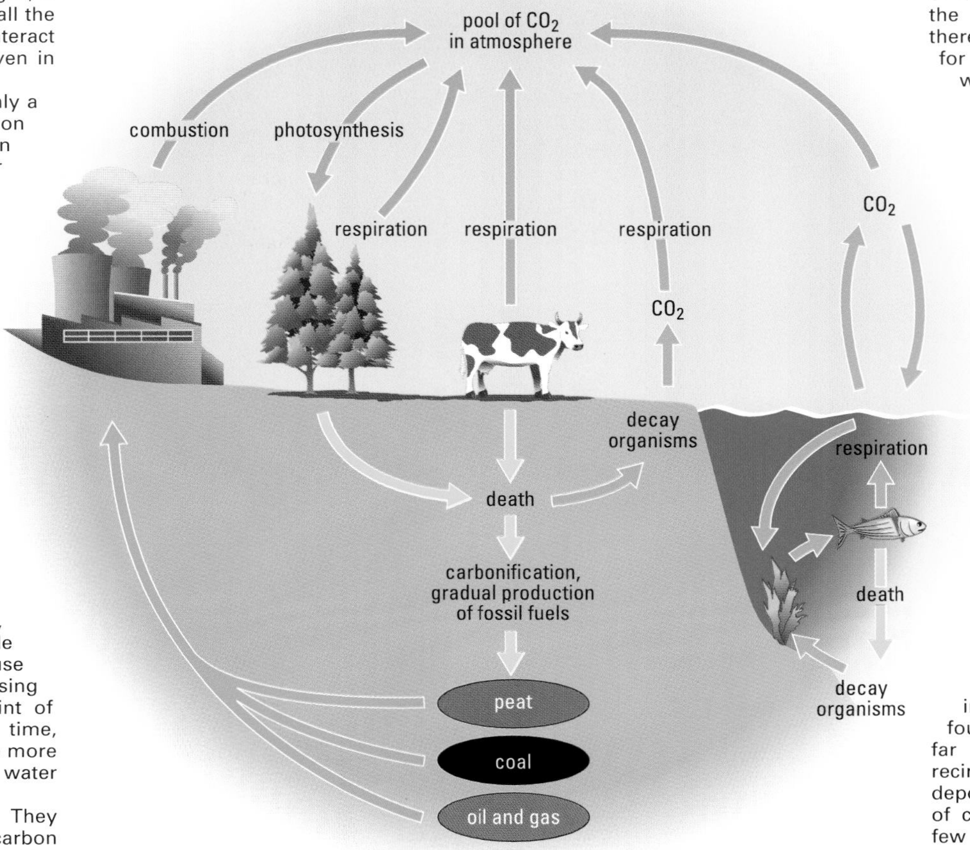

pool of CO_2
in atmosphere
combustion
photosynthesis
respiration
respiration
respiration
CO_2
CO_2
decay
organisms
death
respiration
death
carbonification,
gradual production
of fossil fuels
decay
organisms
peat
coal
oil and gas

During life, plants absorb carbon dioxide from the atmosphere and, along with various chemicals, as soluble salts from the soil, incorporating the carbon into their structure – leaves and trunks in the case of land plants, shells in the case of plankton and the tiny creatures that feed on it. The oxygen thereby freed is added to the atmosphere, at least for a time. The carbon is returned to circulation when the plants die or is passed up the food chain to the herbivores and then the carnivores that feed on them. As organisms at each of these trophic levels die, they decay, releasing the carbon which then combines once more with the oxygen released during life. However, a small proportion of carbon, about one part in 1,000, is removed almost permanently, buried beneath mud on land or at sea, sinking as dead matter to the ocean floor. In time, it is slowly compressed into sedimentary rocks such as limestone and chalk.

But in the evolution of the Earth, nothing is quite permanent. On an even longer timescale, the planet's crustal movements force new rock upwards in mid-ocean ridges. Limestone deposits are moved, and sea levels change; ancient carboniferous rocks are exposed to weathering, and a little of their carbon is released to be fixed in turn by the current generation of plants.

The carbon cycle has continued quietly for an immensely long time, and without gross disturbance there is no reason why it would not continue almost indefinitely in the future. However, human beings have found a way to release fixed carbon at a rate far faster than existing global systems can recirculate it. The fossil fuels, coal, oil, gas and peat deposits, represent the work of millions of years of carbon accumulation; but it has taken only a few human generations of high-energy scavenging to endanger the entire complex regulatory cycle.

The Greenhouse Effect

Constituting less than 1% of the atmosphere, the natural greenhouse gases (water vapour, carbon dioxide, methane, nitrous oxide and ozone) have a hugely disproportionate effect on the Earth's climate and even its habitability. Like the glass panes in a greenhouse, the gases are transparent to most incoming short-wave radiation, which passes freely to heat the planet beneath. But when the warmed Earth retransmits that energy, in the form of longer-wave infra-red radiation, the gases function as an opaque shield preventing some of it from escaping, so that the planetary surface (like the interior of a greenhouse) stays relatively hot.

Over the last 150 years, there has been a gradual increase in the levels of greenhouse gases (with the exception of water vapour which remains a constant in the system). These increases are causing alarm – global warming associated with a runaway greenhouse effect could bring disaster – and what is more, predictions suggest that there could be a further rise of 1.5–4.5°C by the year 2100. A serious reduction in the greenhouse gases would be just as damaging; a total absence of CO_2, for example, would leave the planet with a temperature roughly 33°C colder than at present.

N.B. The thickness of the Earth's atmosphere is proportionately much thinner than the peel of an apple.

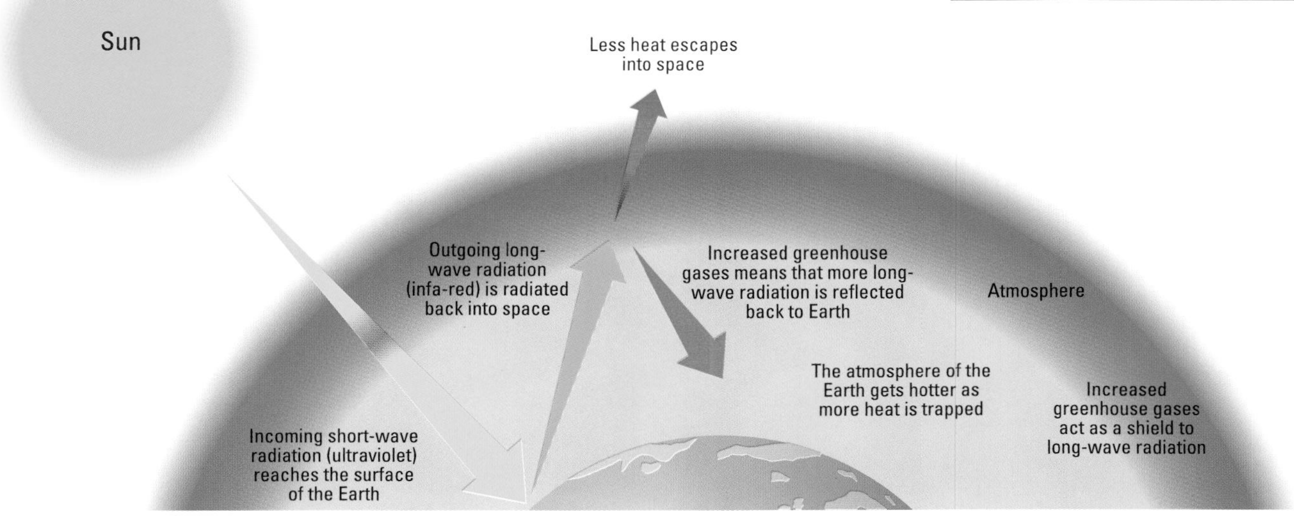

Sun
Less heat escapes
into space
Outgoing long-
wave radiation
(infa-red) is radiated
back into space
Increased greenhouse
gases means that more long-
wave radiation is reflected
back to Earth
Atmosphere
The atmosphere of the
Earth gets hotter as
more heat is trapped
Increased
greenhouse gases
act as a shield to
long-wave radiation
Incoming short-wave
radiation (ultraviolet)
reaches the surface
of the Earth

People and the Environment

For more information:

8 Oceans
14 Atmosphere
16 Climate
21 Greenhouse effect
27 Urban pollution

In 1996, the Intergovernmental Panel on Climate Change issued a report stating that 'The balance of evidence suggests a discernible human influence on global climate through emissions of carbon dioxide and other greenhouse gases.' The report acknowledged that average global temperatures have risen by about 0.5°C since the mid-19th century, but there were still reasons for caution, such as discrepancies between measurements of temperatures around the world. Furthermore, our knowledge about how climates change of their own accord is incomplete, as is our understanding of human interference, how this varies in different parts of the world and how it differs from natural climatic variability.

Human interference with nature is nothing new, at least since people turned from hunting and gathering to agriculture more than 10,000 years ago. At first, human actions seemed to have no ill effects because the systems that regulate the global environment were able to absorb damage. But from the late 18th century, the Industrial Revolution and the population explosion have caused pollution on a scale that threatens to overwhelm the Earth's ability to cope.

The 20th century experienced many disasters, including the dumping of industrial wastes in rivers and seas, accidents at nuclear power stations, and the creation of acid rain through the release of sulphur dioxides and nitrous oxides by the burning of fossil fuels. The release of greenhouse gases are held to be the main reason for global warming, while CFCs (chlorofluorocarbons) have damaged the ozone layer in the stratosphere, the planet's screen against ultraviolet radiation.

Global warming will lead to melting ice sheets and the flooding of fertile coastal plains. Computer models suggest that it might affect ocean currents so that northwestern Europe, which owes its mild climate to the Gulf Stream, could expect bitterly cold winters. Some models have suggested that cloud cover could increase, reflecting more solar energy back into space and so start a new Ice Age.

In many tropical areas, deforestation is making productive land barren, while in the dry grasslands bordering deserts, the removal of plant cover is causing desertification. But human ingenuity can respond to this crisis in planet management.

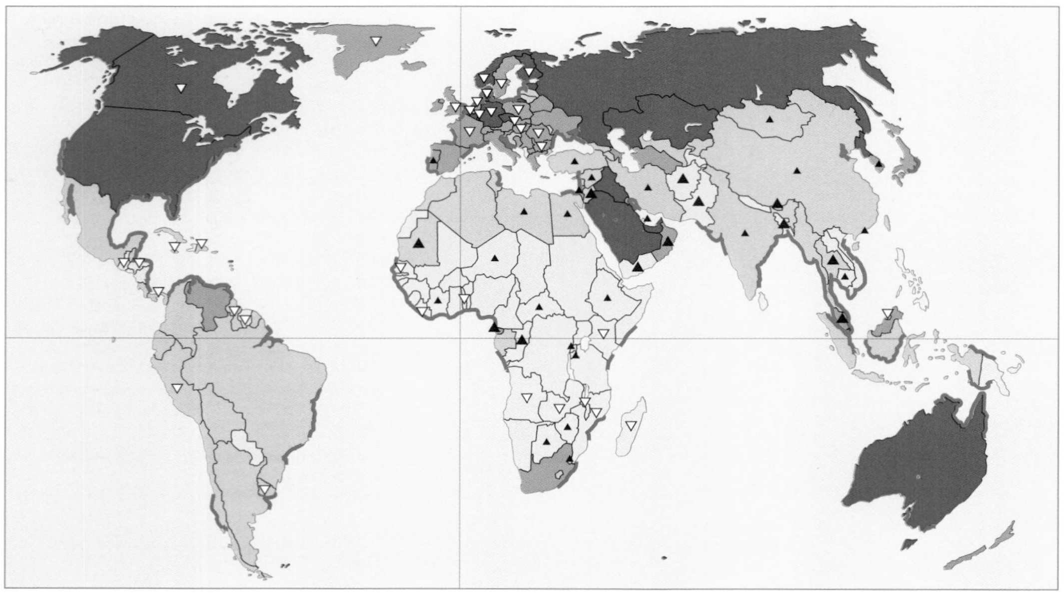

Global Warming

Carbon dioxide emissions in tonnes per person per year (1995)

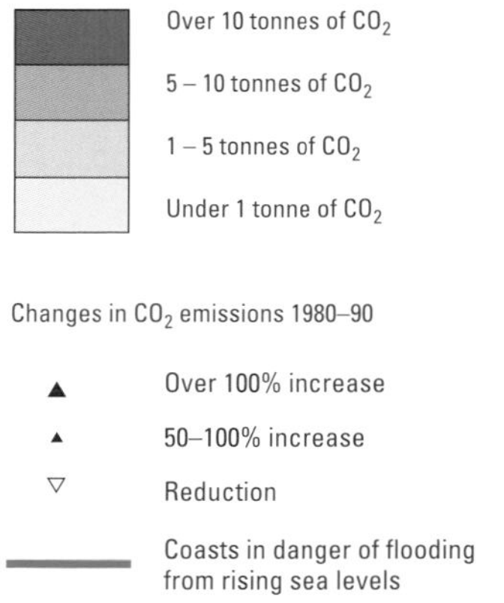

Over 10 tonnes of CO2
5 – 10 tonnes of CO2
1 – 5 tonnes of CO2
Under 1 tonne of CO2
Changes in CO2 emissions 1980–90
Over 100% increase
50–100% increase
Reduction
Coasts in danger of flooding from rising sea levels

Records of global mean surface temperatures from 1860 to the present show that 1995 was the warmest year and that nine of the ten warmest years have occurred since 1983. This evidence of global warming is attributed mainly to the Greenhouse Effect, caused by the emission of certain gases, notably carbon dioxide (CO_2), into the atmosphere since the start of the Industrial Revolution. At first, much of the CO_2 was absorbed by the oceans. However, the vast increase in fuel combustion since 1950 has led CO_2 content in the atmosphere to increase gradually from 280 parts per million to more than 350 parts per million. Despite international action to control the emissions of some greenhouse gases, CO_2 levels are still rising.

Greenhouse Power

Relative contributions to the Greenhouse Effect by the major heat-absorbing gases in the atmosphere

The chart combines greenhouse potency and volume. Carbon dioxide has a greenhouse potential of only 1, but its concentration of 350 parts per million makes it predominate. CFC 12, with 25,000 times the absorption capacity of CO_2, is present only as 0.00044 ppm.

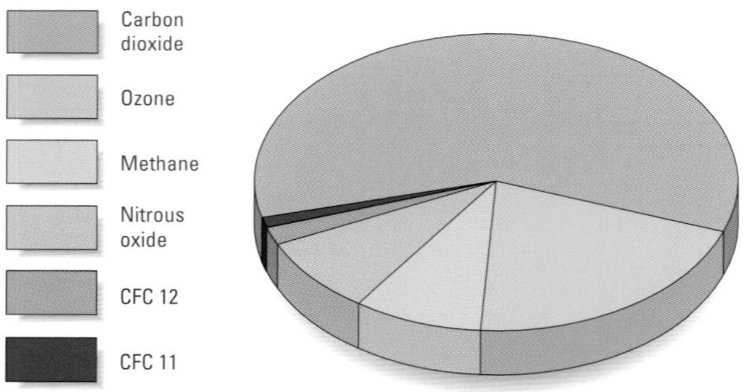

Carbon dioxide
Ozone
Methane
Nitrous oxide
CFC 12
CFC 11

Carbon Dioxide

Carbon dioxide released in millions of tonnes (latest available year)

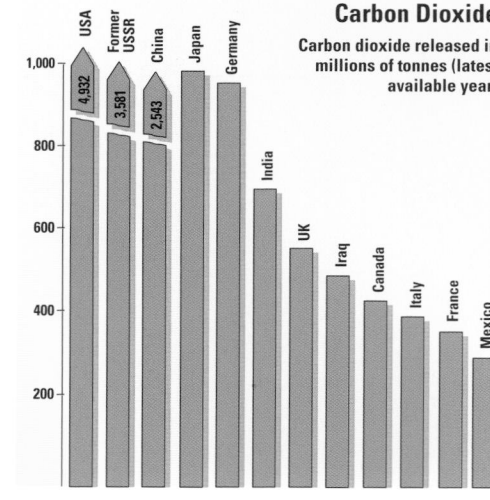

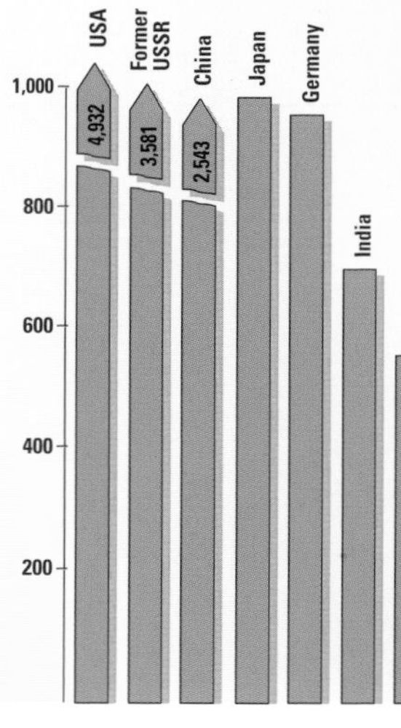

USA
Former USSR
China
Japan
Germany
India
UK
Iraq
Canada
Italy
France
Mexico
4,932
3,581
2,543
1,000
800
600
400
200

Temperature Rise

The rise in average temperatures caused by carbon dioxide and other greenhouse gases (1960–2020)

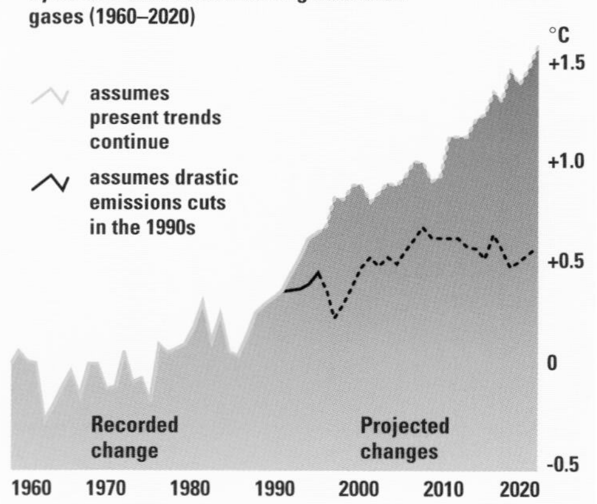

assumes present trends continue
assumes drastic emissions cuts in the 1990s
°C
+1.5
+1.0
+0.5
0
-0.5
Recorded change
Projected changes
1960
1970
1980
1990
2000
2010
2020

The Thinning Ozone Layer

Total atmospheric ozone concentration in the southern and northern hemispheres (Dobson units, 1995)

In 1985, scientists working in Antarctica discovered a thinning of the ozone layer, commonly known as an 'ozone hole'. This caused immediate alarm because the ozone layer absorbs most of the Sun's dangerous ultraviolet radiation, which is believed to cause an increase in skin cancer, cataracts and damage to the immune system. Since 1985, ozone depletion has increased and, by 1996, the ozone hole over the South Pole was estimated to be as large as North America. The false colour images, right, show the total atmospheric ozone concentration in the southern hemisphere (in October 1995) and the northern hemisphere (in March 1995) with the ozone hole clearly identifiable at the centre. The data are from the Tiros Ozone Vertical Sounder, an instrument on the American TIROS weather satellite. The colours represent the ozone concentration in Dobson Units (DU). Normal healthy values are around 280 DU but the lowest value in the northern hemisphere reached 98 DU. Scientists agree that ozone depletion is caused by CFCs, a group of manufactured chemicals used in air conditioning systems and refrigerators. In a 1987 treaty most industrial nations agreed to phase out CFCs and a complete ban on most CFCs was agreed after the end of 1995. However, scientists believe that the chemicals will remain in the atmosphere for 50 to 100 years. As a result, ozone depletion will continue for many years.

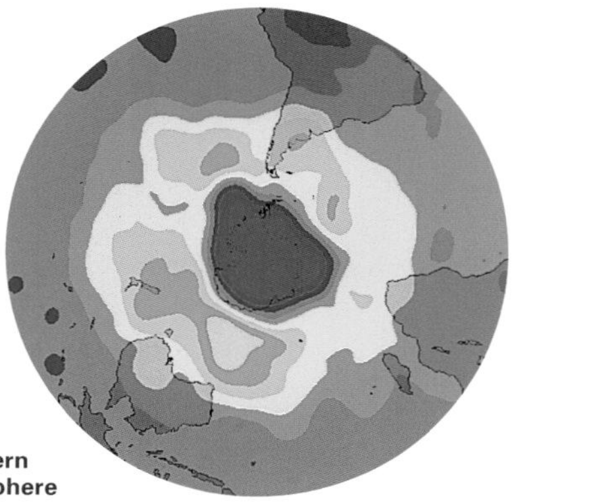

Southern hemisphere

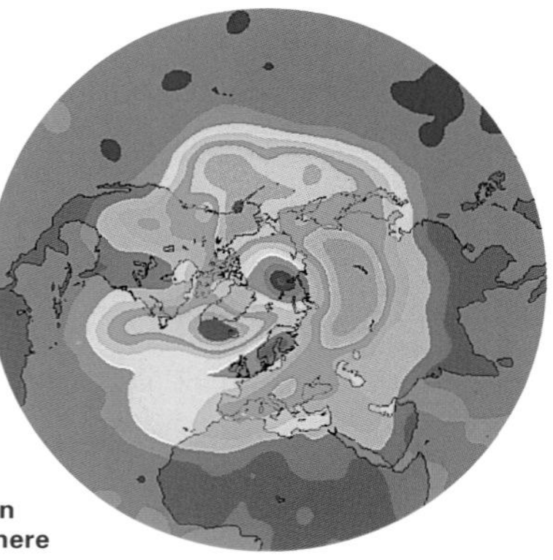

Northern hemisphere

World Pollution

Acid rain and sources of acidic emissions (latest available year)

Acid rain is caused by high levels of sulphur and nitrogen in the atmosphere. They combine with water vapour and oxygen to form acids (H_2SO_4 and HNO_3) which fall as precipitation.

Regions where sulphur and nitrogen oxides are released in high concentrations, mainly from fossil fuel combustion

Major cities with high levels of air pollution (including nitrogen and sulphur emissions)

Areas of heavy acid deposition

pH numbers indicate acidity, decreasing from a neutral 7. Normal rain, slightly acid from dissolved carbon dioxide, never exceeds a pH of 5.6.

pH less than 4.0 (most acidic)

pH 4.0 to 4.5

pH 4.5 to 5.0

Areas where acid rain is a potential problem

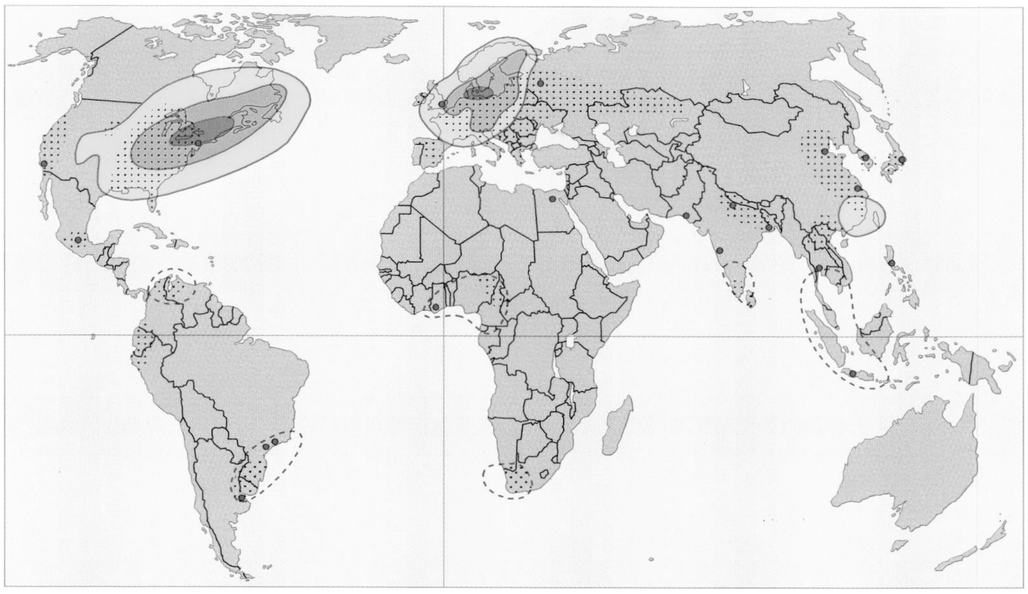

Desertification

Existing deserts

Areas with a high risk of desertification

Areas with a moderate risk of desertification

Former areas of rainforest

Existing rainforest

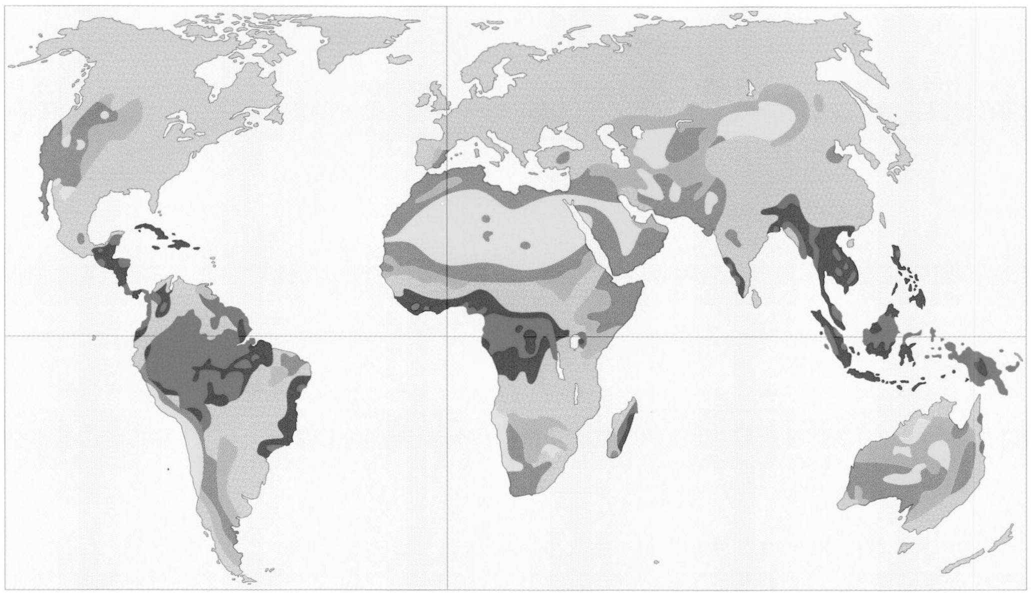

Deforestation

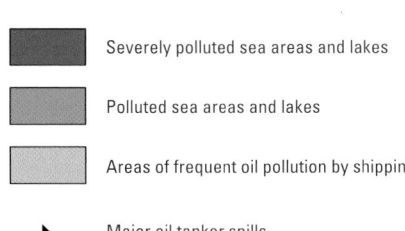

Thousands of hectares of forest cleared annually, tropical countries surveyed 1981–85 and 1987–90. Loss as a percentage of remaining stocks is shown in figures on each column.

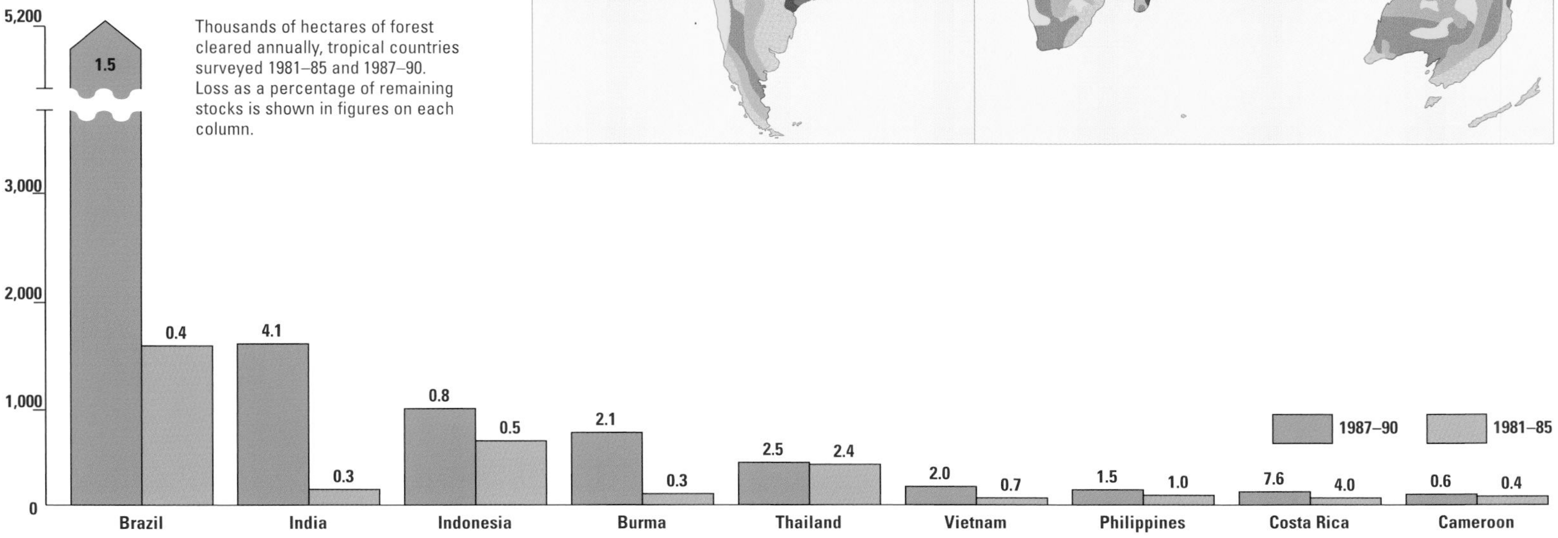
5,200
3,000
2,000
1,000
0
1.5
0.4
4.1
0.3
0.8
0.5
2.1
0.3
2.5
2.4
2.0
0.7
1.5
1.0
7.6
4.0
0.6
0.4
1987–90
1981–85
Brazil
India
Indonesia
Burma
Thailand
Vietnam
Philippines
Costa Rica
Cameroon

Antarctica

The vast Antarctic ice sheet, containing some 70% of the Earth's fresh water, plays a crucial role in the circulation of the atmosphere and oceans, and hence in determining the planetary climate. The frozen southern continent is also the last remaining wilderness – the largest area to remain free from human colonization.

Ever since Amundsen and Scott raced for the South Pole in 1911, various countries have pressed territorial claims over sections of Antarctica, spurred in recent years by its known and suspected mineral wealth: enough iron ore to supply the world at present levels for 200 years, large oil reserves and, probably, the biggest coal deposits on Earth.

However, the 1961 Antarctic Treaty set aside the area for peaceful uses only, guaranteeing freedom of scientific investigation, banning waste disposal and nuclear testing, and suspending the issue of territorial rights. By 1990, the original 12 signatories had grown to 25, with a further 15 nations granted observer status in subsequent deliberations. However, the Treaty itself was threatened by wrangles between different countries, government agencies and international pressure groups.

Finally, in July 1991, the belated agreement of the UK and the USA assured unanimity on a new accord to ban all mineral exploration for a further 50 years. The ban can only be rescinded if all the present signatories, plus a majority of any future adherents, agree. While the treaty has always lacked a formal mechanism for enforcement, it is firmly underwritten by public concern generated by the efforts of environmental pressure groups such as Greenpeace, which has been foremost in the campaign to have Antarctica declared a 'World Park'.

However, from the mid-1990s, the continent appeared to be under threat from global warming, which some scientists believe was the cause of the break-up of ice shelves along the Antarctic peninsula. Rising temperatures have also disturbed the breeding patterns of Adelie penguins.

Water Pollution

Severely polluted sea areas and lakes

Polluted sea areas and lakes

Areas of frequent oil pollution by shipping

Major oil tanker spills

Major oil rig blow-outs

Offshore dumpsites for industrial and municipal waste

Severely polluted rivers and estuaries

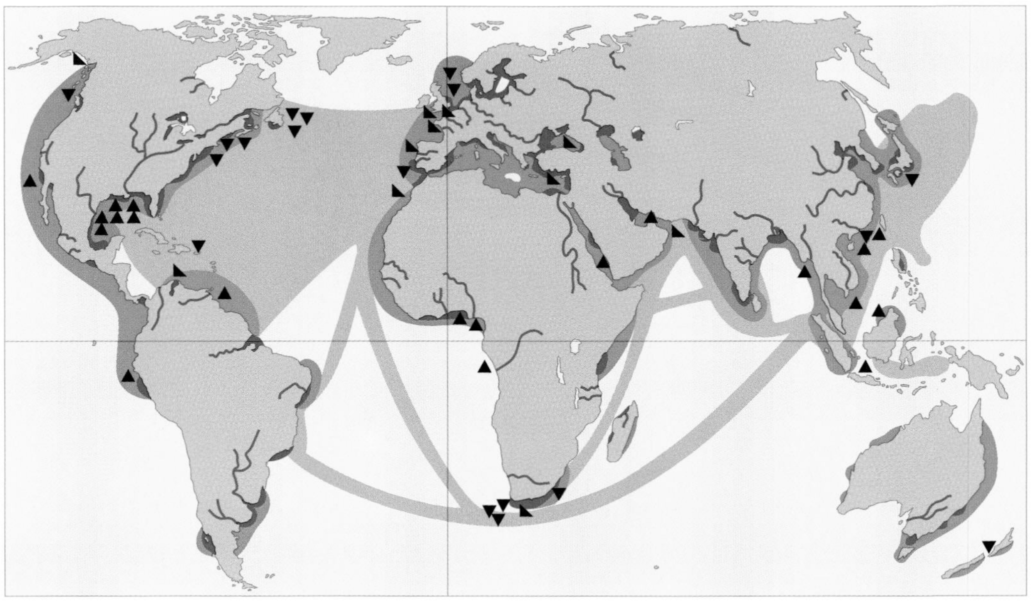

Poisoned rivers, domestic sewage and oil spillage have combined in recent years to reduce the world's oceans to a sorry state of contamination, notably near the crowded coasts of industrialized nations. Shipping routes, too, are constantly affected by tanker discharges. Oil spills of all kinds, however, declined significantly during the 1980s, from a peak of 750,000 tonnes in 1979 to under 50,000 tonnes in 1990. The most notorious tanker spill of that period – when the *Exxon Valdez* (94,999 grt) ran aground in Prince William Sound, Alaska, in March 1989 – released only 267,000 barrels, a relatively small amount compared to the results of blow-outs and war damage. Over 2,500,000 barrels were spilled during the Gulf War of 1991. The worst tanker accident in history occurred in July 1979, when the *Atlantic Empress* and the Aegean Captain collided off Trinidad, polluting the Caribbean with 1,890,000 barrels of crude oil.

Population

For more information:

26 Urbanization of the Earth
Urban population
27 Largest cities
33 Food and population
44 Wealth and population

In 8000 BC, following the development of agriculture, the world had an estimated population of 8 million and by AD 1000 it was about 300 million. The onset of the Industrial Revolution in the late 18th century led to a population explosion. The 1,000 million mark was passed by 1850, it doubled by the 1920s and doubled again to 4,000 million by 1975.

Most demographers agree that the world's population, which passed the 6 billion mark in October 1999, will reach 8.9 billion by 2050. It is not expected to level out until 2200, when it will peak at around 11 billion. After 2200, it is expected to level out or even decline a little. Rapid population growth is concentrated in the developing world; the populations of some developed countries, such as Belgium and Germany, are static or have even started to decline.

The developing world includes what the World Bank describes as low-income economies, with an average per capita GNP of US $380, and middle-income economies, with a per capita GNP of $2,520. Most developing countries are in Africa, Asia and Latin America. The developed world, made up of high-income, industrialized economies with an average per capita GNP of $23,420, contains Australasia, most of Europe and North America, and Japan in Asia.

In the poorer developing countries, a high proportion of the population is young, and they face high levels of expenditure on education and health until population growth rates start to decline. In developed countries, where the population pyramids are becoming increasingly top-heavy, expenditure on pensions and healthcare for the elderly is becoming a major social problem.

Crowded Nations

Population per square kilometre (1998), excluding nations of less than 1 million

1.	Monaco	32,894
2.	Macau	25,501
3.	Hong Kong	6,373
4.	Singapore	5,624
5.	Gibraltar	4,239
6.	Bermuda	1,199
7.	Malta	1,214
8.	Vatican City	1,090
9.	Maldives	909
10.	Bahrain	877
11.	Bangladesh	866
12.	Barbados	624
13.	Mauritius	559
14.	Nauru	529
15.	Armenia	487
16.	South Korea	466
17.	Puerto Rico	428
18.	Tuvalu	428
19.	San Marino	424
20.	Netherlands	384

Largest Nations

The world's most populous nations, in millions (2000 est.)

1.	China	1,299
2.	India	1,041
3.	USA	266
4.	Indonesia	218
5.	Brazil	179
6.	Pakistan	162
7.	Russia	155
8.	Bangladesh	150
9.	Japan	128
10.	Mexico	107
11.	Nigeria	105
12.	Vietnam	82
13.	Philippines	77
14.	Germany	76
15.	Iran	68
16.	Turkey	66
17.	Egypt	64
18.	Thailand	63
19.	Ethiopia	61
20.	France	58
21.	UK	58
22.	Italy	57
23.	Ukraine	52
24.	Burma (Myanmar)	51

Population Density

Inhabitants per square kilometre

Over 200
100 – 200
50 – 100
25 – 50
6 – 25
3 – 6
1 – 3
Under 1

Urban population

■ Over 10,000,000
● 5,000,000 – 10,000,000
• 1,000,000 – 5,000,000

Places marked are conurbations, not city limits; San Francisco itself, for example, has an official population of less than a million.

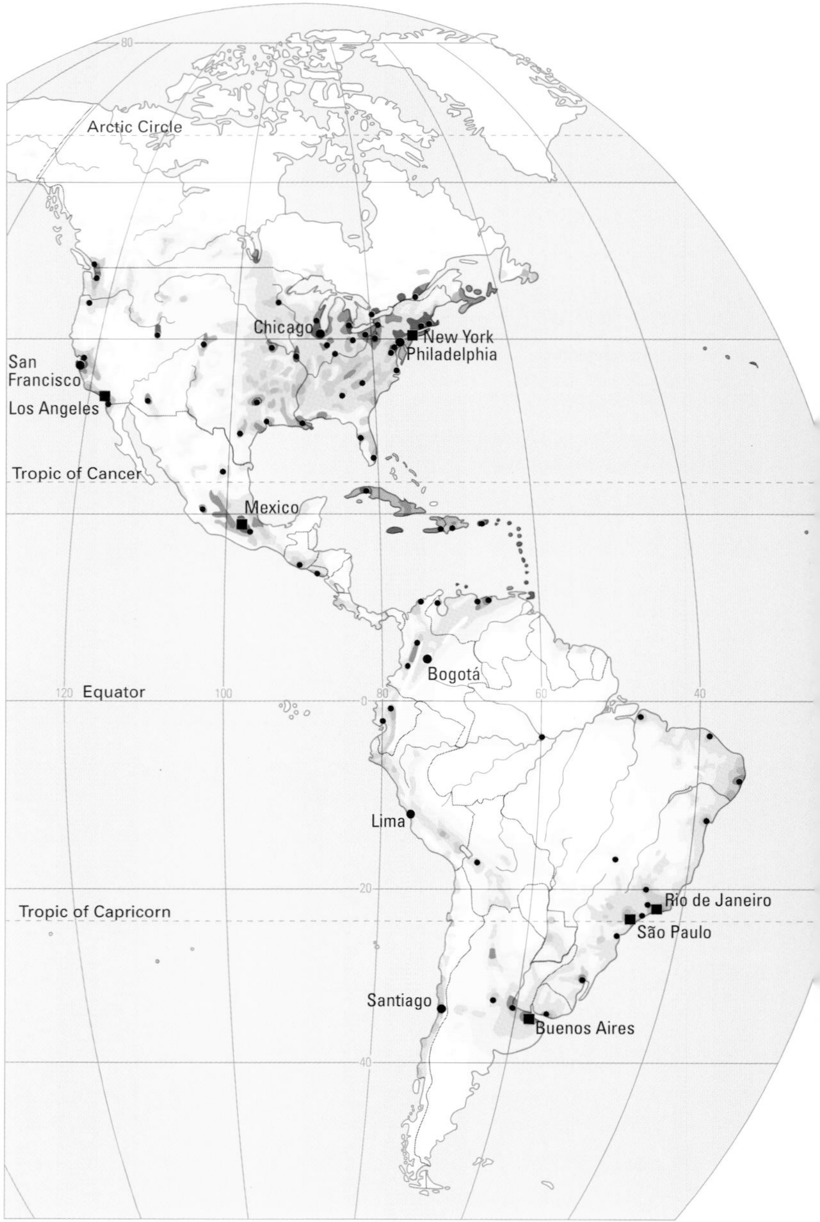

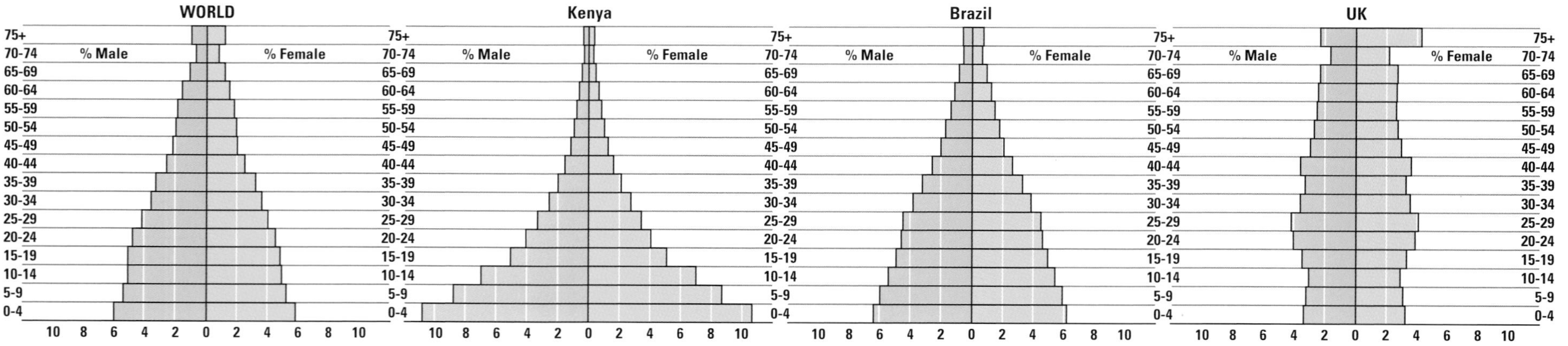

Rates of Growth

The world population doubled between 1950 and 1990. Small rates of population growth led to dramatic increases over two or three generations. The table below translates annual percentage growth into the number of years required to double a population.

% change	Doubling time
0.5	139.0
1.0	69.7
1.5	46.6
2.0	35.0
2.5	28.1
3.0	23.4
3.5	20.1
4.0	17.7

Population Change 1990–2000

The predicted population change for the years 1990–2000

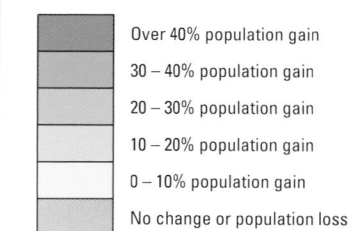

Over 40% population gain
30 – 40% population gain
20 – 30% population gain
10 – 20% population gain
0 – 10% population gain
No change or population loss

Top 5 countries		Bottom 5 countries	
Kuwait	+75.9%	Belgium	–0.1%
Namibia	+62.5%	Hungary	–0.2%
Afghanistan	+60.1%	Grenada	–2.4%
Mali	+55.5%	Germany	–3.2%
Tanzania	+54.6%	Tonga	–3.2%

CARTOGRAPHY BY PHILIP'S. COPYRIGHT GEORGE PHILIP LTD

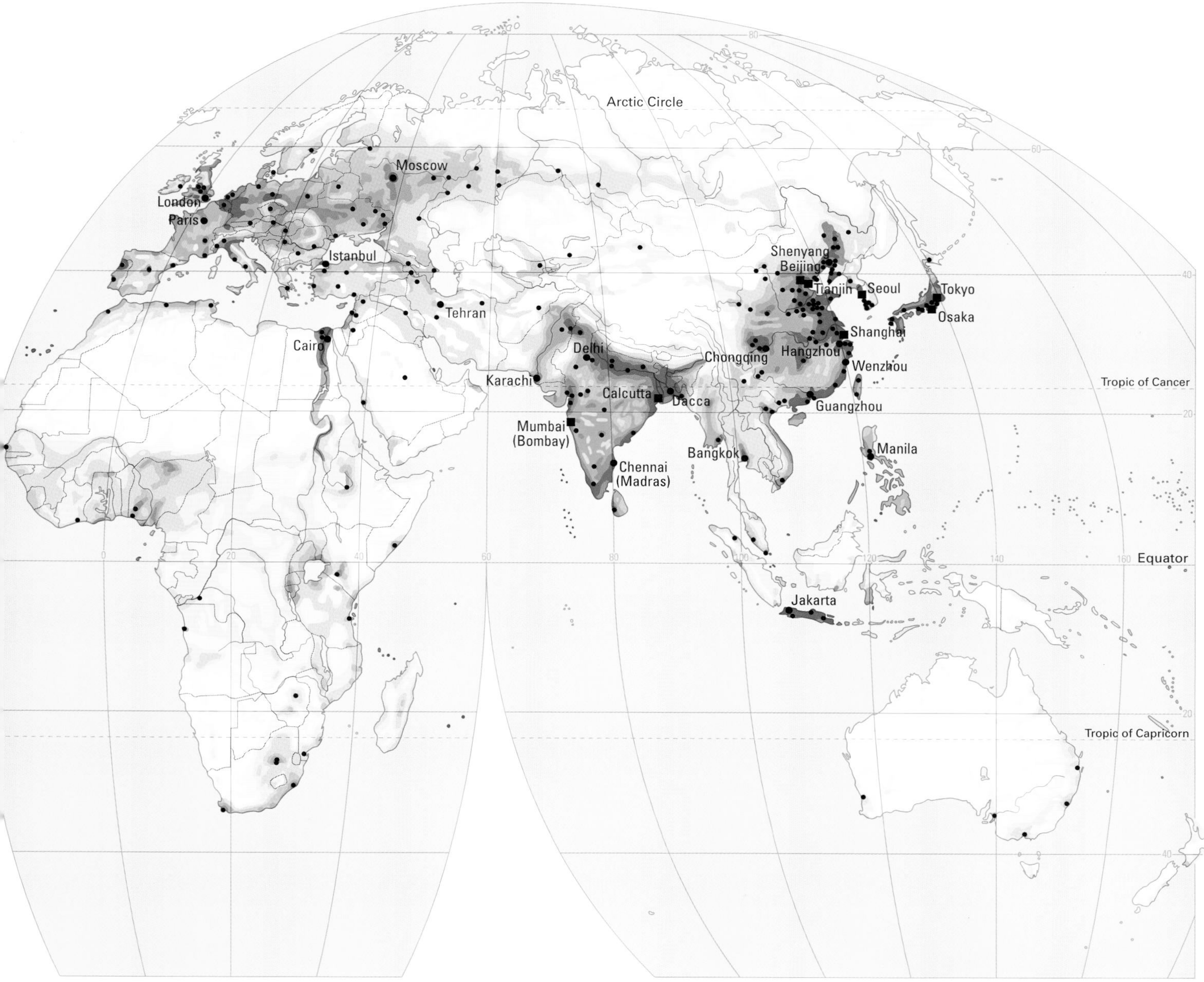

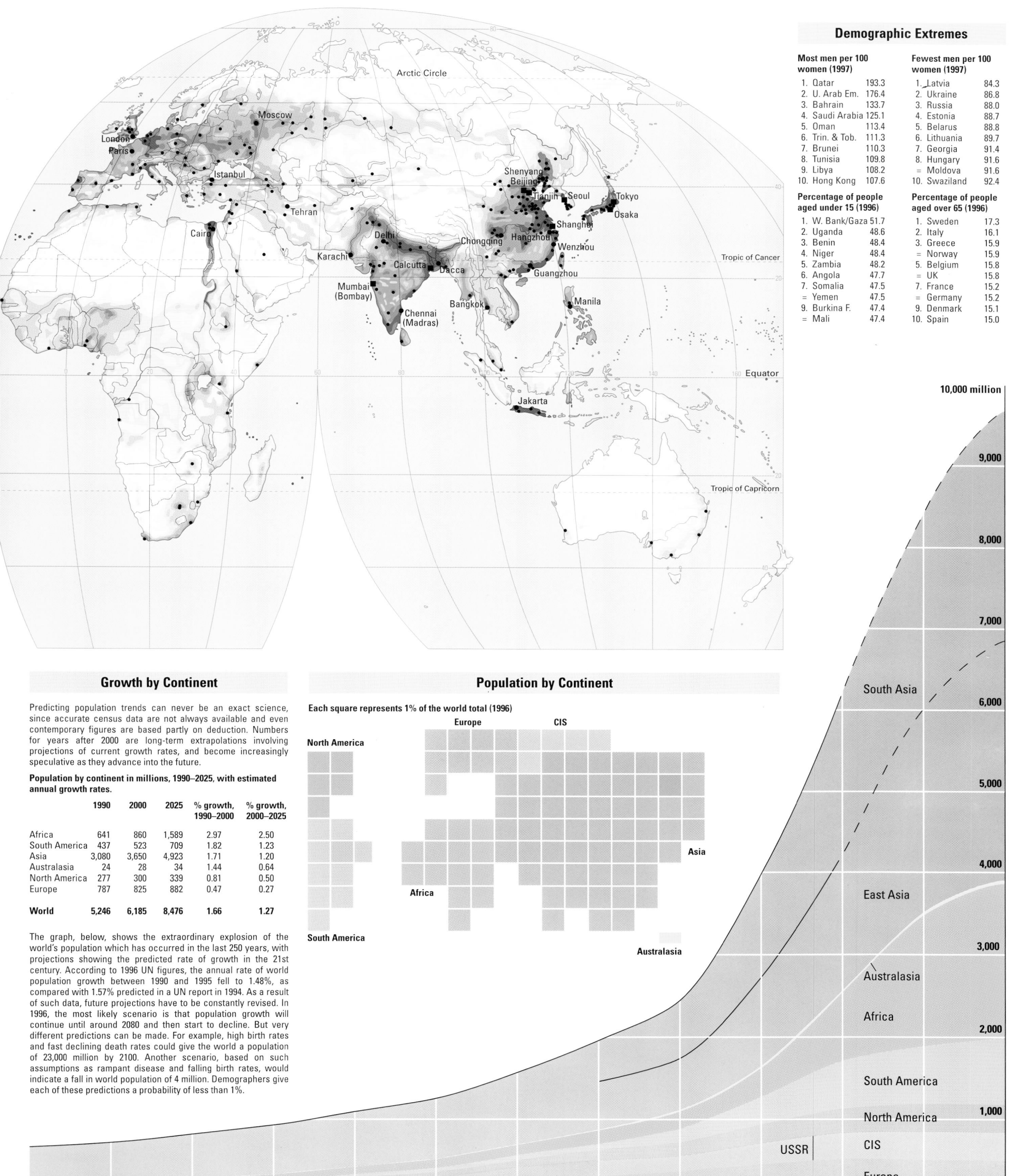

Demographic Extremes

Most men per 100 women (1997)

1.	Qatar	193.3
2.	U. Arab Em.	176.4
3.	Bahrain	133.7
4.	Saudi Arabia	125.1
5.	Oman	113.4
6.	Trin. & Tob.	111.3
7.	Brunei	110.3
8.	Tunisia	109.8
9.	Libya	108.2
10.	Hong Kong	107.6

Fewest men per 100 women (1997)

1.	Latvia	84.3
2.	Ukraine	86.8
3.	Russia	88.0
4.	Estonia	88.7
5.	Belarus	88.8
6.	Lithuania	89.7
7.	Georgia	91.4
8.	Hungary	91.6
=	Moldova	91.6
10.	Swaziland	92.4

Percentage of people aged under 15 (1996)

1.	W. Bank/Gaza	51.7
2.	Uganda	48.6
3.	Benin	48.4
4.	Niger	48.4
5.	Zambia	48.2
6.	Angola	47.7
7.	Somalia	47.5
=	Yemen	47.5
9.	Burkina F.	47.4
=	Mali	47.4

Percentage of people aged over 65 (1996)

1.	Sweden	17.3
2.	Italy	16.1
3.	Greece	15.9
=	Norway	15.9
5.	Belgium	15.8
=	UK	15.8
7.	France	15.2
=	Germany	15.2
9.	Denmark	15.1
10.	Spain	15.0

Growth by Continent

Predicting population trends can never be an exact science, since accurate census data are not always available and even contemporary figures are based partly on deduction. Numbers for years after 2000 are long-term extrapolations involving projections of current growth rates, and become increasingly speculative as they advance into the future.

Population by continent in millions, 1990–2025, with estimated annual growth rates.

	1990	2000	2025	% growth, 1990–2000	% growth, 2000–2025
Africa	641	860	1,589	2.97	2.50
South America	437	523	709	1.82	1.23
Asia	3,080	3,650	4,923	1.71	1.20
Australasia	24	28	34	1.44	0.64
North America	277	300	339	0.81	0.50
Europe	787	825	882	0.47	0.27
World	**5,246**	**6,185**	**8,476**	**1.66**	**1.27**

The graph, below, shows the extraordinary explosion of the world's population which has occurred in the last 250 years, with projections showing the predicted rate of growth in the 21st century. According to 1996 UN figures, the annual rate of world population growth between 1990 and 1995 fell to 1.48%, as compared with 1.57% predicted in a UN report in 1994. As a result of such data, future projections have to be constantly revised. In 1996, the most likely scenario is that population growth will continue until around 2080 and then start to decline. But very different predictions can be made. For example, high birth rates and fast declining death rates could give the world a population of 23,000 million by 2100. Another scenario, based on such assumptions as rampant disease and falling birth rates, would indicate a fall in world population of 4 million. Demographers give each of these predictions a probability of less than 1%.

Population by Continent

Each square represents 1% of the world total (1996)

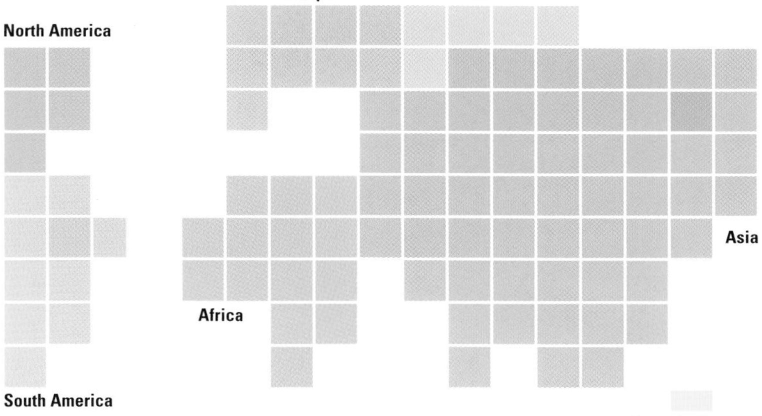

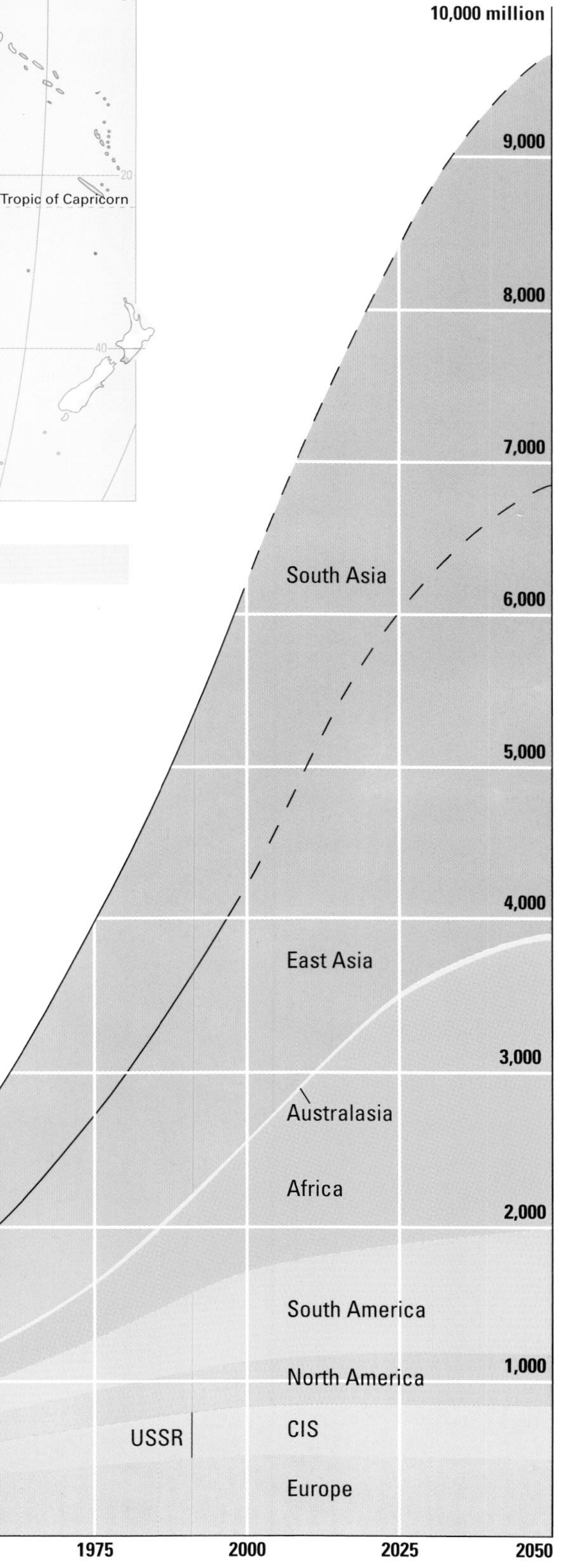

CARTOGRAPHY BY PHILIP'S. COPYRIGHT GEORGE PHILIP LTD

Cities

For more information:
18 Water supply
24 Population density
48 The great ports

Following the development of agriculture more than 10,000 years ago, people began to live in farming villages. Around 5,500 years ago, the world's first cities appeared in the lower Tigris and Euphrates valleys in Mesopotamia. Cities were founded in Ancient Egypt around 5,000 years ago and in China around 3,600 years ago. By contrast with the villages, most people in the early cities were not engaged in farming. Instead, they worked in craft industries, in government services, in religion and in trade. The cities became centres of early civilizations and, through trade, their influence spread far and wide. However, they were dependent on the surrounding farming communities for their food and other materials.

In 1750, prior to the start of the Industrial Revolution, barely 3% of the world's population lived in urban areas. By 1850, London and Paris had more than a million people, and, by 1900, 14% of the world's population lived in cities. By 1950, the world had 83 cities with more than a million people, and by 1996, there were 280. By 2015, experts predict that there will be more than 500. New York City was the only city with a population in excess of 10 million in 1950; by 2015 the experts predict 27 such cities worldwide, the majority located in the developing world.

By the end of the 20th century, more than half of the world's population was living in urban areas. Despite the rapid growth of cities in developing countries, urbanization is highest in industrialized countries. For example, 78% of the people in the United States live in urban areas, with the European Union not far behind with 77%. But in countries with low-income economies, which contained nearly 60% of the world's total population in 1996, only 28% lived in urban areas.

The rapid rate of urbanization has created problems, especially in cities which have not been able to provide enough jobs and services for the expanding population. Most new city dwellers are people from rural areas and because many of them are young there is a consequent acceleration in the rate of city population growth. In developed countries, with highly mechanized agriculture, it is population pressure that drives many people into urban areas. In developing countries, the grinding poverty of rural life and the lack of services leads to migration to urban areas.

A typical city in a developing country contains millions of people living, often illegally, in shanty towns (or 'informal settlements' in politically correct parlance), while thousands live on the streets. Yet many of these shanty towns are healthier than the industrial cities of 19th-century Europe and North America. Indeed, surveys have shown that the migrants to the cities in developing countries are less likely to face poverty than they are in rural areas, while benefiting from greater access to healthcare services and education.

Modern cities face many problems, including pollution, crime and unemployment. Yet, given competent central and local government, they are capable of generating the wealth they need to solve them, as well as making a major contribution to the economy.

The Urbanization of the Earth

City-building, 1850–2000; each white spot represents a city of at least 1 million inhabitants.

1850

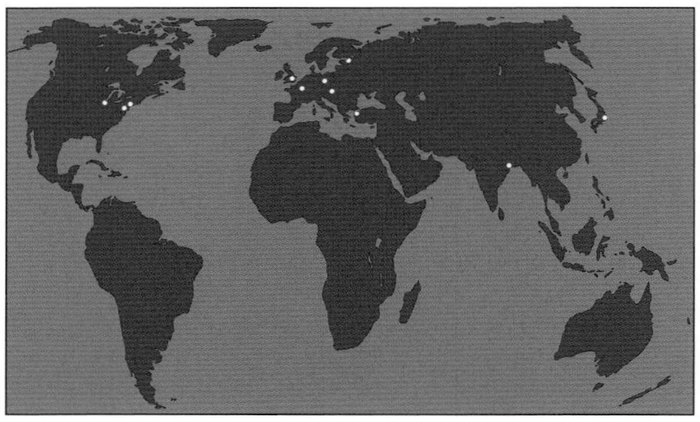

1900

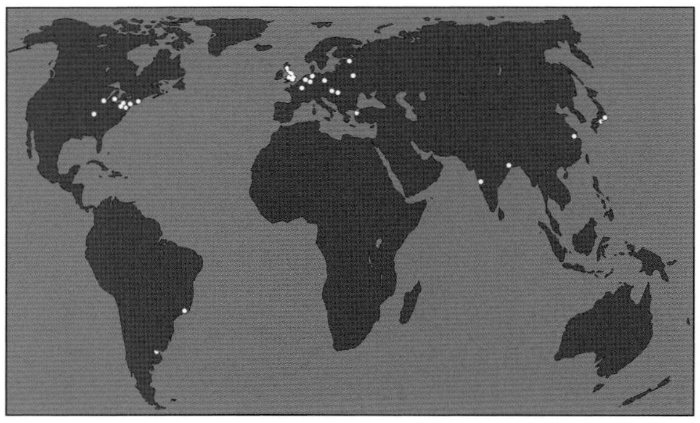

1925

1950

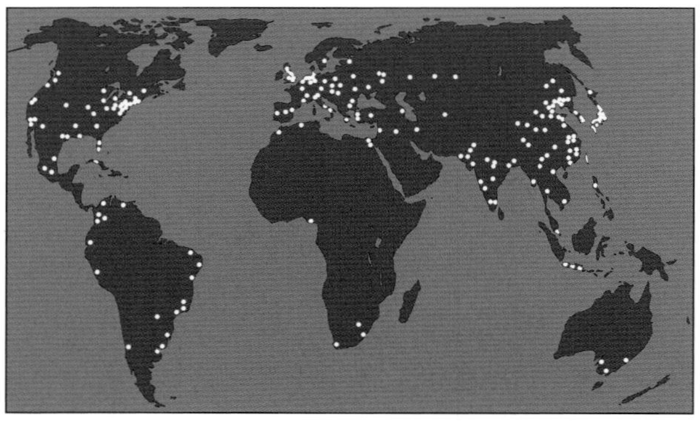

1975

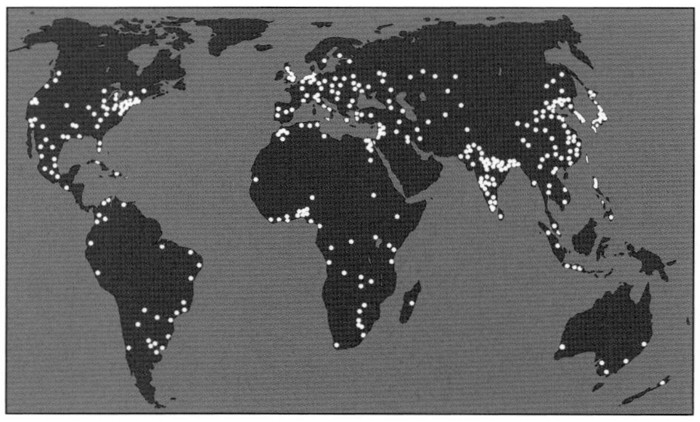

2000

Urban Population

Percentage of total population living in towns and cities (1997)

Most urbanized

Singapore	100%
Belgium	97%
Israel	91%
Uruguay	91%
Netherlands	89%

[UK 89%]

Least urbanized

Rwanda	6%
Bhutan	8%
Burundi	8%
Nepal	11%
Swaziland	12%

Over 75%
50 – 75%
25 – 50%
10 – 25%
Under 10%

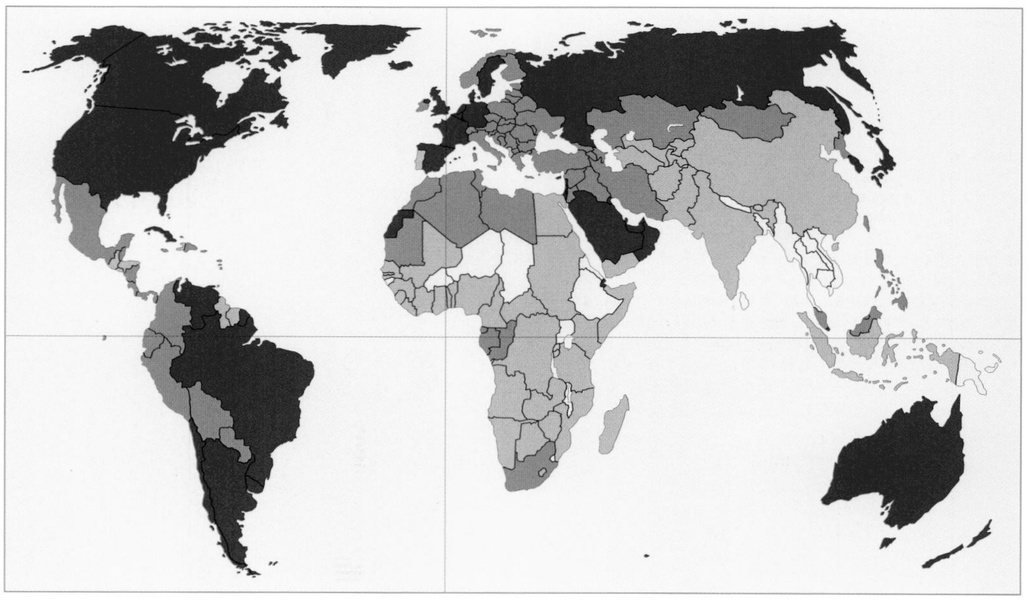

CARTOGRAPHY BY PHILIP'S. COPYRIGHT GEORGE PHILIP LTD

Expanding Cities

The growth of some of the world's largest cities in millions, 1950–2015.

Comparisons of city populations over time are problematic due to changes in the definition of the city limits. These figures attempt to take such changes into consideration. The figure for London is the metropolitan region.

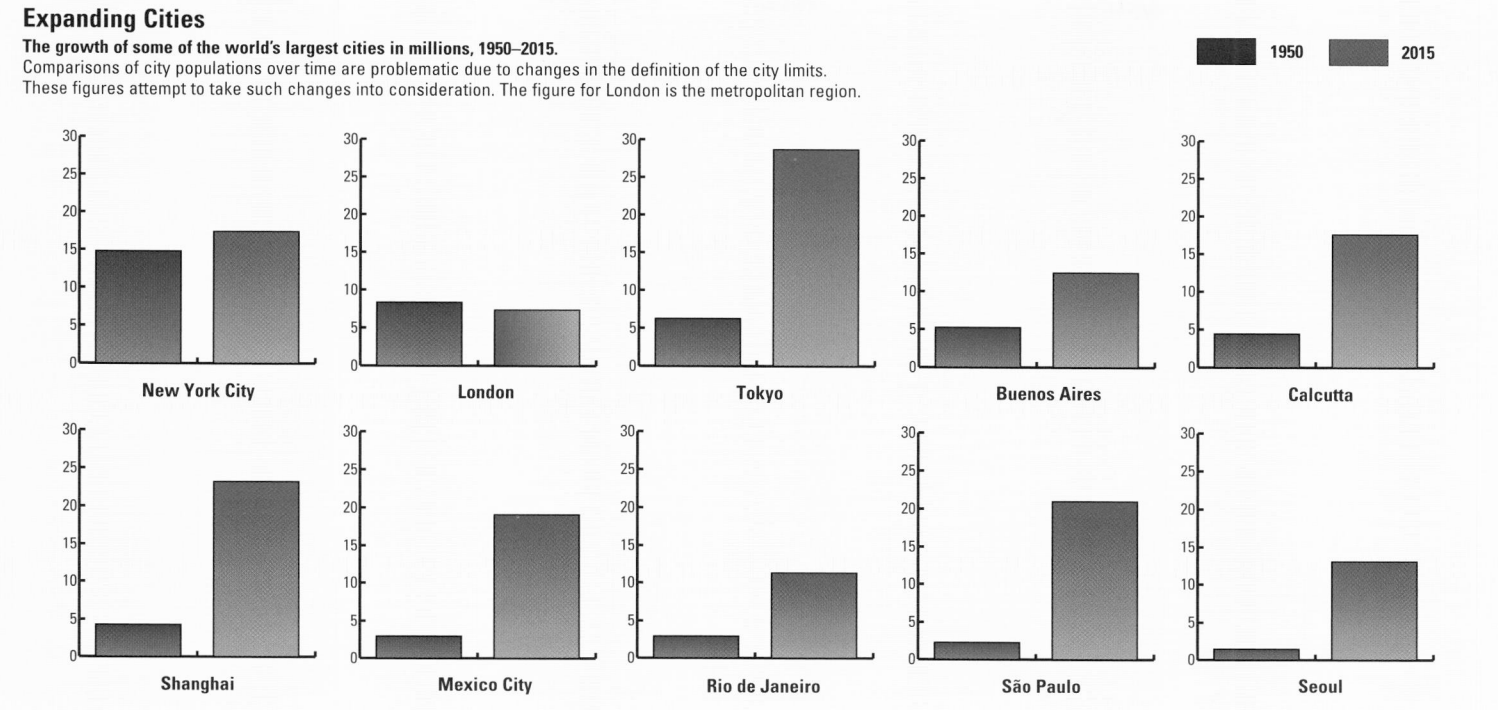

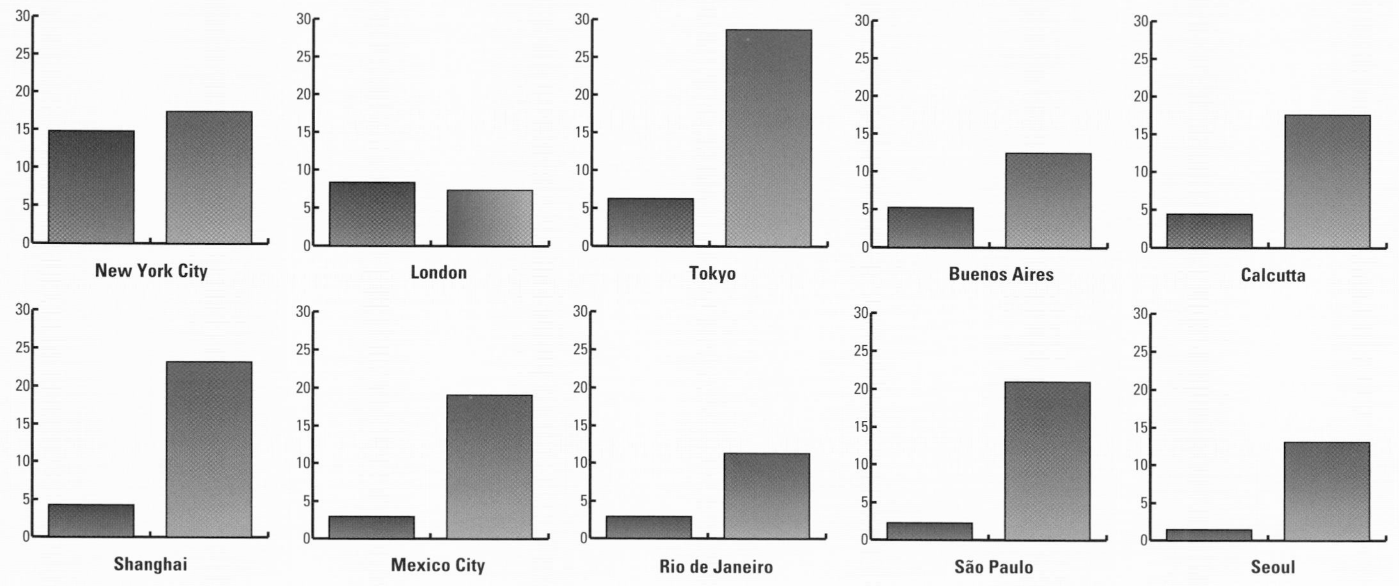

1950
2015
0
5
10
15
20
25
30
New York City
London
Tokyo
Buenos Aires
Calcutta
Shanghai
Mexico City
Rio de Janeiro
São Paulo
Seoul

The graphs show the projected growth of megacities between 1950 and 2015. New York City, the world's largest city in 1950, reached a peak in 1970, but it has experienced periods of negative growth. London's population also declined between 1970 and 1985, before resuming a modest rate of increase. In both cases, the divergence from world trends is explained in part by counting methods. Each lies at the centre of a great agglomeration, and definitions of the 'city limits' may vary over time. Also, in developing countries, many areas around the megacities which are counted as urban, are rural in character. The rates of city population growth in developing countries have also often been over-estimated. For example, it was once predicted that Calcutta would have a population of 40 million by the late 1990s. The reason why many estimates have proven incorrect is partly explained by a new trend, namely that rapid urban growth is now greatest, in some regions, in the smaller cities. For example, the main expansion in West Bengal is no longer in Calcutta, but in a rash of small cities across the state.

Cities in Danger

As the decade of the 1980s advanced, most industrial countries, alarmed by acid rain and urban smog, took significant steps to limit air pollution. Well into the 1990s, however, these controls proved expensive to install and difficult to enforce, and clean air remains a luxury most developed as well as developing cities must live without.

Those taking part in the United Nations' Global Environment Monitoring System (see right) frequently show dangerous levels of pollutants ranging from soot to sulphur dioxide and photo-chemical smog; air in the majority of cities without such sampling equipment is likely to be at least as bad. Traffic, a major source of air pollution worldwide, loses Thailand's workforce 44 working days each year.

Urban Air Pollution

The world's most polluted cities: number of days each year when sulphur dioxide levels exceeded the WHO threshold of 150 micrograms per cubic metre (averaged over 4 to 15 years, 1970s – 1980s)

Sulphur dioxide is the main pollutant associated with industrial cities. According to the World Health Organization, more than seven days in a year above 150 μg per cubic metre bring a serious risk of respiratory disease: at least 600 million people live in urban areas where SO_2 concentrations regularly reach damaging levels.

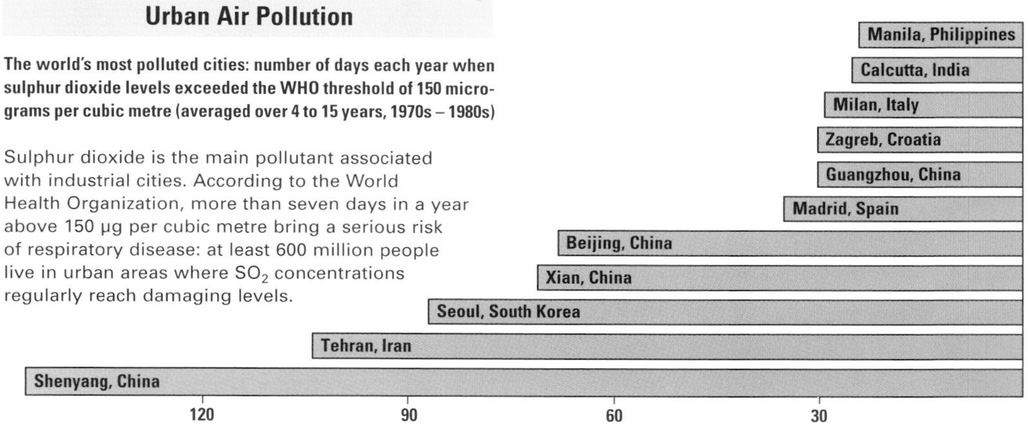

Manila, Philippines
Calcutta, India
Milan, Italy
Zagreb, Croatia
Guangzhou, China
Madrid, Spain
Beijing, China
Xian, China
Seoul, South Korea
Tehran, Iran
Shenyang, China
120
90
60
30

Urban Housing Needs

Proportion of the population living in squatter settlements and the number of homeless per thousand, for selected cities (1993)

Urbanization in most developing countries has been proceeding so rapidly that local governments have been unable to provide the necessary services and housing. In some cities, many people find their homes in squatter settlements, frequently without power, water and sanitation. Yet these communities are often a dynamic part of the city's economy, while their inhabitants sometimes take all kinds of initiatives, including the setting up of their own local government and self-help associations. Some of the world's richest cities also have a homeless underclass, although calculating the numbers of people involved is problematic. Yet it is the case that homelessness and unemployment are currently affecting an increasing number of people in the developed world.

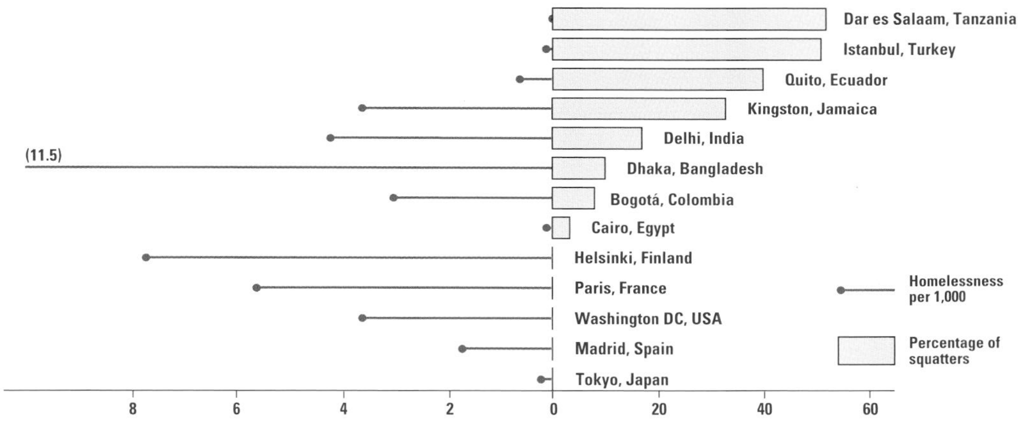

Dar es Salaam, Tanzania
Istanbul, Turkey
Quito, Ecuador
Kingston, Jamaica
Delhi, India
(11.5)
Dhaka, Bangladesh
Bogotá, Colombia
Cairo, Egypt
Helsinki, Finland
Paris, France
Washington DC, USA
Madrid, Spain
Tokyo, Japan
Homelessness per 1,000
Percentage of squatters
8
6
4
2
0
20
40
60

Largest Cities

Early in the 21st century, for the first time in history, the majority of the world's population will live in cities. Below is a list of all the cities with more than 10 million inhabitants, based on estimates for the year 2015.

1. Tokyo–Yokohama	28.7
2. Bombay	27.4
3. Lagos	24.1
4. Shanghai	23.2
5. Jakarta	21.5
6. São Paulo	21.0
7. Karachi	20.6
8. Beijing	19.6
9. Dhaka	19.2
10. Mexico City	19.1
11. Calcutta	17.6
12. Delhi	17.5
13. New York City	17.4
14. Tianjin	17.1
15. Manila	14.9
16. Cairo	14.7
17. Los Angeles	14.5
18. Seoul	13.1
19. Buenos Aires	12.5
20. Istanbul	12.1
21. Rio de Janeiro	11.3
22. Lahore	10.9
23. Hyderabad	10.6
24. Bangkok	10.4
25. Osaka	10.2
26. Lima	10.1
27. Tehran	10.0

City populations are based on urban agglomerations rather than legal city limits. In some cases where two adjacent cities have merged into one concentration, such as Tokyo–Yokohama, they have been regarded as a single unit.

Urban Advantages

Despite overcrowding and poor housing, living standards in the developing world's cities are almost invariably better than in the surrounding countryside. Resources – financial, material and administrative – are concentrated in the towns, which are usually also the centres of political activity and pressure. Governments – frequently unstable, and rarely established on a solid democratic base – are usually more responsive to urban discontent than rural misery.

In many countries, especially in Africa, food prices are kept artificially low, appeasing underemployed urban masses at the expense of agricultural development. The imbalance encourages further cityward migration, helping to account for the astonishing rate of post-1950 urbanization and putting great strain on the ability of many nations to provide even modest improvements for their people.

Relative Mortality

Infant deaths per 1,000 live births in rural and urban areas of selected developing countries (latest available year)

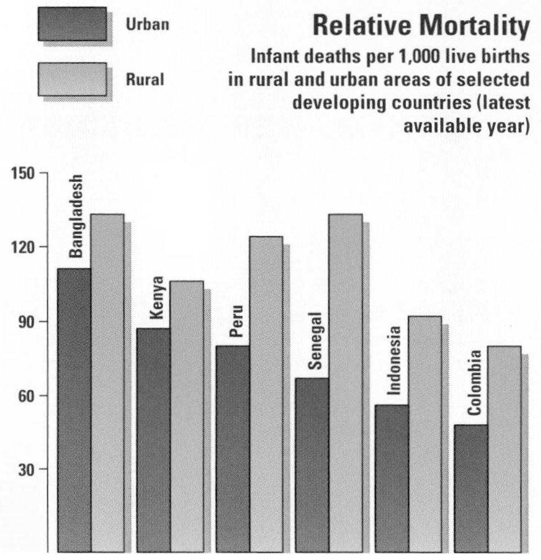

Urban
Rural
150
120
90
60
30
Bangladesh
Kenya
Peru
Senegal
Indonesia
Colombia

Relative Literacy

Adult literacy rates (%) in urban and rural areas of selected developing countries (latest available year)

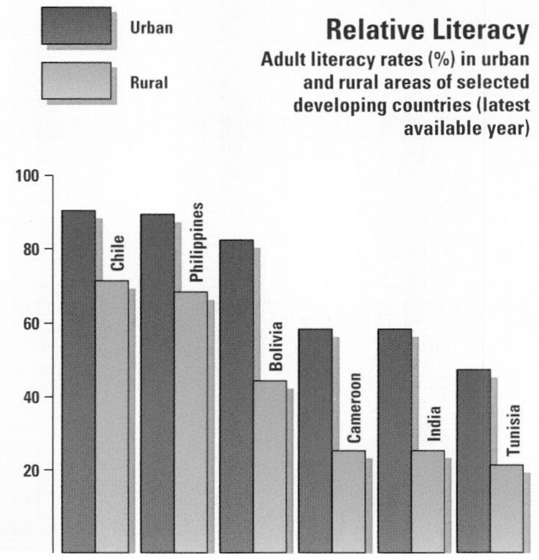

Urban
Rural
100
80
60
40
20
Chile
Philippines
Bolivia
Cameroon
India
Tunisia

The Human Family

For more information:

24 Population density
30 The world's refugees
War since 1945
31 United Nations
International organizations

Racial, language and religious differences have led to appalling acts of inhumanity throughout history. Yet strictly speaking, all human beings belong to one species, *Homo sapiens*, which has no subspecies. The differences between the three racial types which most people identify – namely Caucasoid, Mongoloid and Negroid – reflect not so much evolutionary differences as long periods of separation.

Migration has recently mingled the various groups to an unprecedented extent, and most nations now have some degree of racial mixing. For example, the United States has often been called a melting pot, because of the large numbers of people from various geographical locations which make up the population. The country has no official language but, until recently, English was spoken by the vast majority of the people. But in recent years, some of the immigrants from Mexico, Cuba and other parts of Latin America have not learned English and speak only Spanish. This development disturbs those Americans who believe that the use of English binds the nation together, and several states have passed laws stating that English is their only official language.

Language is fundamental to human culture and any particular language is almost the definition of that particular culture. Because definitions of languages vary, estimates of the total number range from 3,000 to 6,000, although most are spoken by only a few people. The world's languages are grouped into families, the largest of which are the Indo-European and Sino-Tibetan. Chinese, a Sino-Tibetan language, is spoken by more people as a first language than any other. English, an Indo-European tongue, ranks second, but it is the leading international language, because so many people speak it as their second tongue.

Like language, religion encourages cohesion in single human groups and it satisfies a deep human need by assigning people a place in a divinely ordered world. Religion is a way in which a culture can express its individuality. For example, the rise of Islamic fundamentalism in the late 20th century was partly an expression of resentment that secular Western values are being imposed on Muslims.

World Migration

The greatest voluntary migration was the colonization of North America by 30–35 million European settlers during the 19th century. The greatest forced migration involved 9–11 million Africans taken as slaves to America between 1550 and 1860. The migrations shown on the map below are mostly international, as population movements within borders are not usually recorded. Many of the statistics are necessarily estimates as so many refugees and migrant workers enter countries illegally and unrecorded. Emigrants may have a variety of motives for leaving, thus making it difficult to distinguish between voluntary and involuntary migrations.

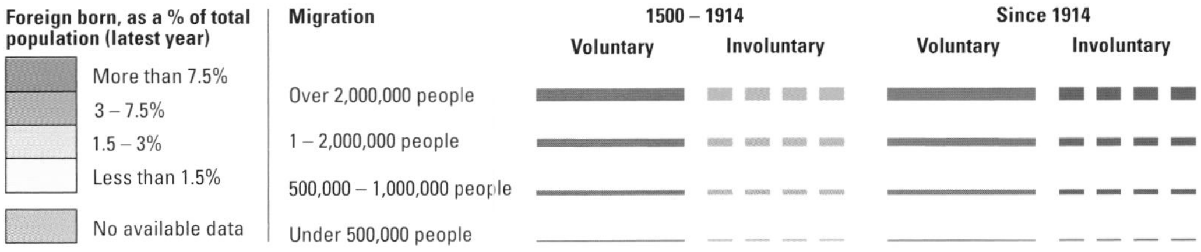

Foreign born, as a % of total population (latest year)
More than 7.5%
3 – 7.5%
1.5 – 3%
Less than 1.5%
No available data
Migration
1500 – 1914
Voluntary
Involuntary
Since 1914
Voluntary
Involuntary
Over 2,000,000 people
1 – 2,000,000 people
500,000 – 1,000,000 people
Under 500,000 people

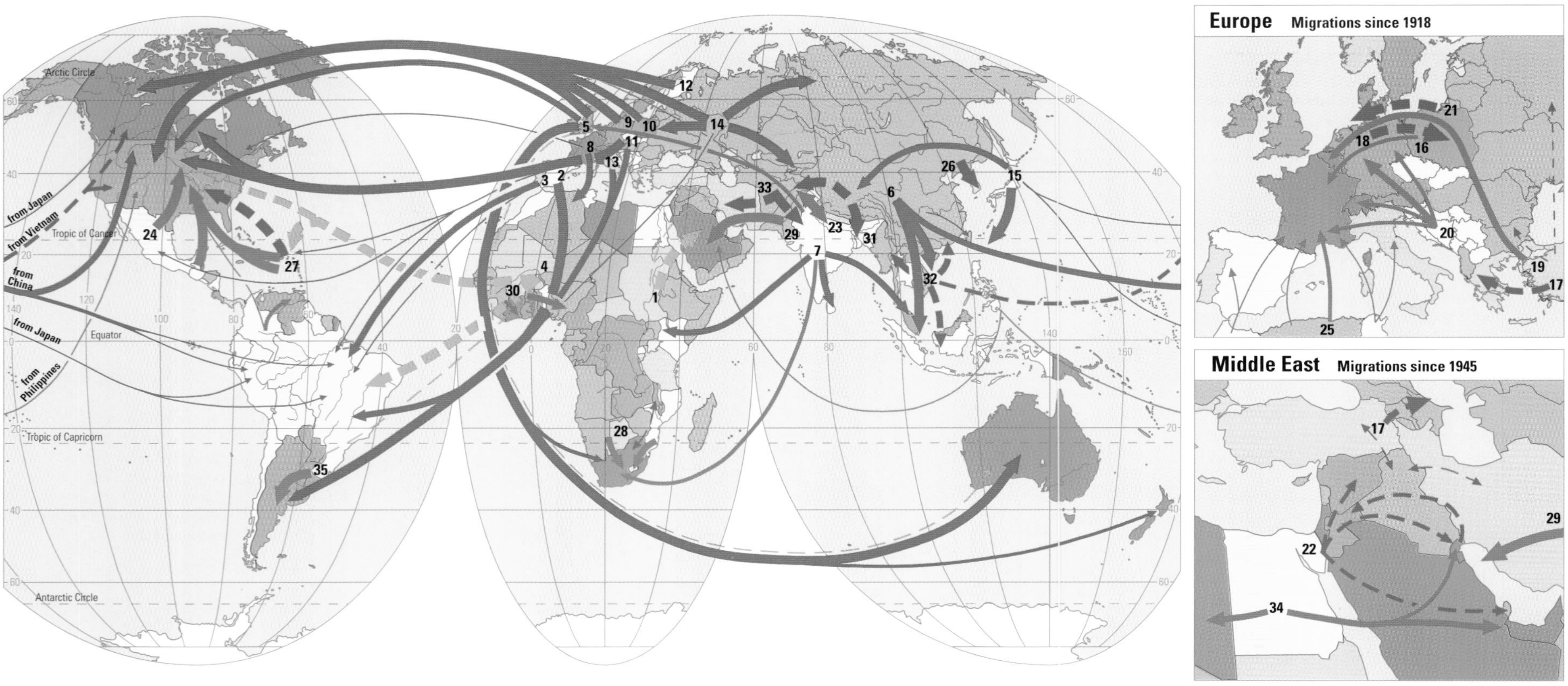

Arctic Circle
Tropic of Cancer
Equator
Tropic of Capricorn
Antarctic Circle
from Japan
from Vietnam
from China
from Japan
from Philippines
Europe Migrations since 1918
Middle East Migrations since 1945

Building the USA

US Immigration 1820–1990

'Give me your tired, your poor / Your huddled masses yearning to breathe free....'

So starts Emma Lazarus's poem 'The New Colossus', inscribed on the Statue of Liberty. For decades the USA was the magnet that attracted millions of immigrants, notably from Central and Eastern Europe, the flow peaking in the early years of the 20th century. By the mid-1990s the proportion of immigrants had increased again to pre-World War II rates. In 1993/4, net immigration accounted for 30% of US population growth. Of the 904,000 immigrants, 40% were from Asia and 31% from Central America and the Caribbean.

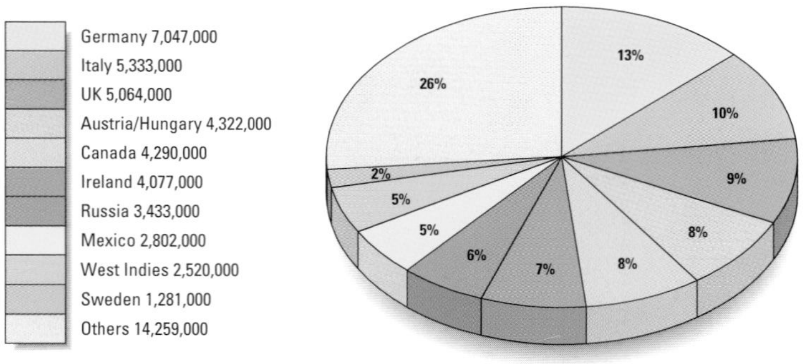

Germany 7,047,000
Italy 5,333,000
UK 5,064,000
Austria/Hungary 4,322,000
Canada 4,290,000
Ireland 4,077,000
Russia 3,433,000
Mexico 2,802,000
West Indies 2,520,000
Sweden 1,281,000
Others 14,259,000
13%
10%
9%
8%
8%
7%
6%
5%
5%
2%
26%

Major world migrations since 1500 (over 1,000,000 people)

1. North and East African slaves to Arabia (4.3m) 1500–1900
2. Spanish to South and Central America (2.3m) 1530–1914
3. Portuguese to Brazil (1.4m) 1530–1914
4. West African slaves to South America (4.6m) 1550–1860
   to Caribbean (4m) 1580–1860
   to North/Central America (1m) 1650–1820
5. British and Irish to North America (13.5m) 1620–1914
   to Australasia and South Africa (3m) 1790–1914
6. Chinese to South-east Asia (22m) 1820–1914
   to North America (1m) 1880–1914
7. Indian migrant workers (3m) 1850–1914
8. French to North Africa (1.5m) 1850–1914
9. Germans to North America (5m) 1850–1914
10. Poles to North America (3.6m) 1850–1914
11. Austro-Hungarians to North America (3.2m) 1850–1914
    to Western Europe (3.4m) 1850–1914
    to South America (1.8m) 1850–1914
12. Scandinavians to North America (2.7m) 1850–1914
13. Italians to North America (5m) 1860–1914
    to South America (3.7m) 1860–1914
14. Russians to North America (2.2m) 1880–1914
    to Western Europe (2.2m) 1880–1914
    to Siberia (6m) 1880–1914
    to Central Asia (4m) 1880–1914
15. Japanese to Eastern Asia, South-east Asia and America (8m) 1900–1914
16. Poles to Western Europe (1m) 1920–1940
17. Greeks and Armenians from Turkey (1.6m) 1922–1923
18. European Jews to extermination camps (5m) 1940–1944
19. Turks to Western Europe (1.9m) 1940–
20. Yugoslavs to Western Europe (2m) 1940–
21. Germans to Western Europe (9.8m) 1945–1947
22. Palestinian refugees (2m) 1947–
23. Indian and Pakistani refugees (15m) 1947
24. Mexicans to North America (9m) 1950–
25. North Africans to Western Europe (1.1m) 1950–
26. Korean refugees (5m) 1950–1954
27. Latin Americans and West Indians to North America (4.7m) 1960–
28. Migrant workers to South Africa (1.5m) 1960–
29. Indians and Pakistanis to The Gulf (2.4m) 1970–
30. Migrant workers to Nigeria and Ivory Coast (3m) 1970–
31. Bangladeshi and Pakistani refugees (2m) 1972
32. Vietnamese and Cambodian refugees (1.5m) 1975–
33. Afghan refugees (6.1m) 1979–
34. Egyptians to The Gulf and Libya (2.9m) 1980–
35. Migrant workers to Argentina (2m) 1980–
36. Mozambique refugees (1.7m) 1985–
37. Yugoslav/Balkan refugees (1.7m) 1992–
38. Rwanda/Burundi refugees (2.6m) 1994–

Predominant Languages

INDO-EUROPEAN FAMILY
- 1 Balto-Slavic group (incl. Russian, Ukrainian)
- 2 Germanic group (incl. English, German)
- 3 Celtic group
- 4 Greek
- 5 Albanian
- 6 Iranian group
- 7 Armenian
- 8 Romance group (incl. Spanish, Portuguese, French, Italian)
- 9 Indo-Aryan group (incl. Hindi, Bengali, Urdu, Punjabi, Marathi)
- 10 **CAUCASIAN FAMILY**

AFRO-ASIATIC FAMILY
- 11 Semitic group (incl. Arabic)
- 12 Kushitic group
- 13 Berber group
- 14 **KHOISAN FAMILY**
- 15 **NIGER-CONGO FAMILY**
- 16 **NILO-SAHARAN FAMILY**
- 17 **URALIC FAMILY**

ALTAIC FAMILY
- 18 Turkic group
- 19 Mongolian group
- 20 Tungus-Manchu group
- 21 Japanese and Korean

SINO-TIBETAN FAMILY
- 22 Sinitic (Chinese) languages
- 23 Tibetic-Burmic languages
- 24 **TAI FAMILY**

AUSTRO-ASIATIC FAMILY
- 25 Mon-Khmer group
- 26 Munda group
- 27 Vietnamese
- 28 **DRAVIDIAN FAMILY** (incl. Telugu, Tamil)
- 29 **AUSTRONESIAN FAMILY** (incl. Malay-Indonesian)
- 30 **OTHER LANGUAGES**

Official Languages

Language	Total population	World %
English	1,400m	27.0%
Chinese	1,070m	19.1%
Hindi	700m	13.5%
Spanish	280m	5.4%
Russian	270m	5.2%
French	220m	4.2%
Arabic	170m	3.3%
Portuguese	160m	3.0%
Malay	160m	3.0%
Bengali	150m	2.9%
Japanese	120m	2.3%

Languages form a kind of tree of development, splitting from a few ancient proto-tongues into branches that have grown apart and further divided with the passage of time. English and Hindi, for example, both belong to the great Indo-European family, although the relationship is only apparent after much analysis and comparison with non-Indo-European languages such as Chinese or Arabic; Hindi is part of the Indo-Aryan subgroup, whereas English is a member of Indo-European's Germanic branch; French, another Indo-European tongue, traces its descent through the Latin, or Romance, branch. A few languages – Basque is one example – have no apparent links with any other, living or dead. Most modern languages, of course, have acquired enormous quantities of vocabulary from each other.

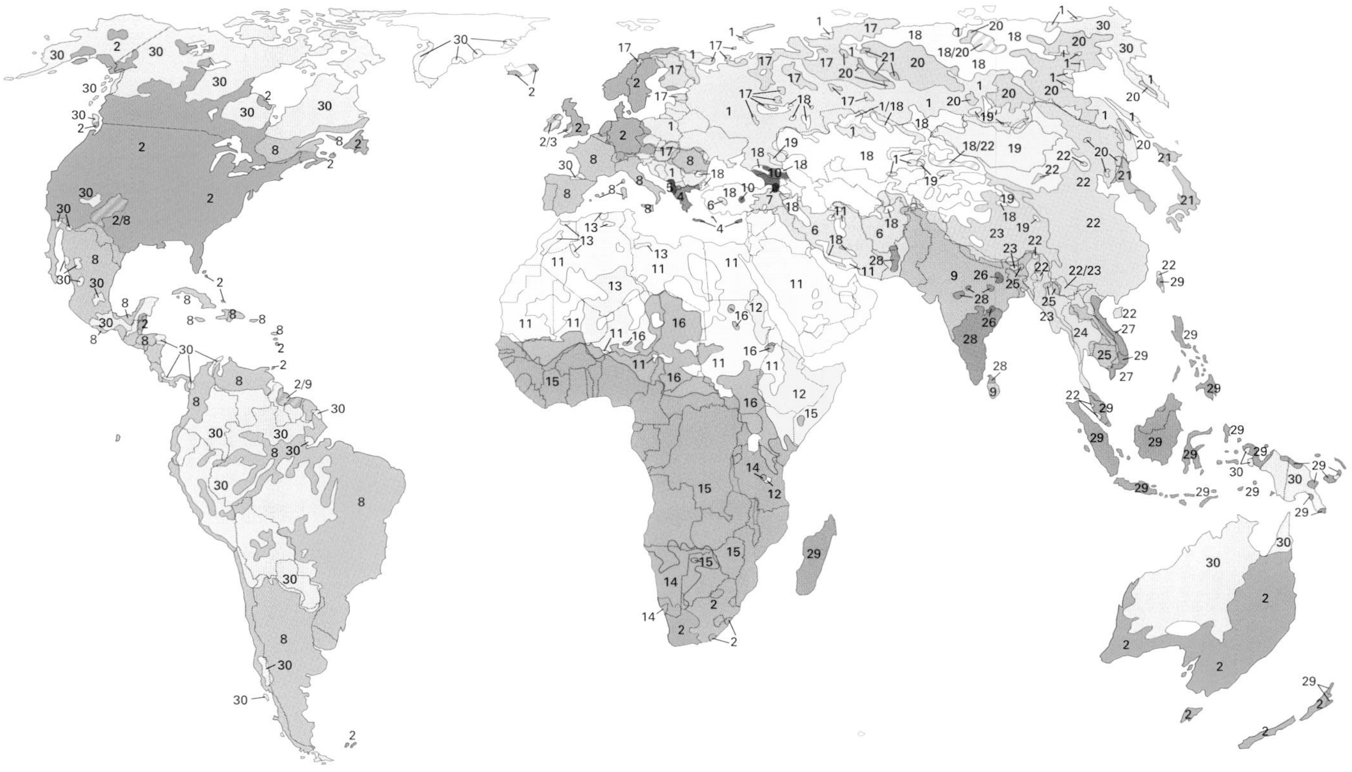

Distribution of Living Languages

The figures refer to the number of languages currently in use in the regions shown.

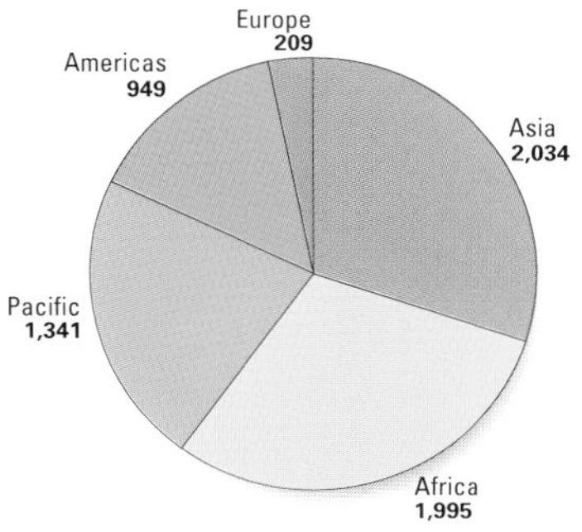

Europe 209
Asia 2,034
Africa 1,995
Pacific 1,341
Americas 949

Predominant Religions

- Roman Catholicism
- Orthodox and other Eastern Churches
- Protestantism
- Sunni Islam
- Shia Islam
- Buddhism
- Hinduism
- Confucianism
- Judaism
- Shintoism
- Tribal Religions

Religions are not as easily mapped as the physical contours of the land. Divisions are often blurred and frequently overlapping: most nations include people of many different faiths – or no faith at all. Some religions, like Islam and Christianity, have proselytes worldwide; others, like Hinduism and Confucianism, are restricted to a particular area, though modern migrations have taken some Indians and Chinese very far from their cultural origins. It is also difficult to show the degree to which religion controls daily life: Christian Western Europe, for example, is now far less dominated by its religion than are the Islamic nations of the Middle East. Similarly, figures for the major faiths' adherents make no distinction between nominal believers enrolled at birth and those for whom religion is a vital part of existence.

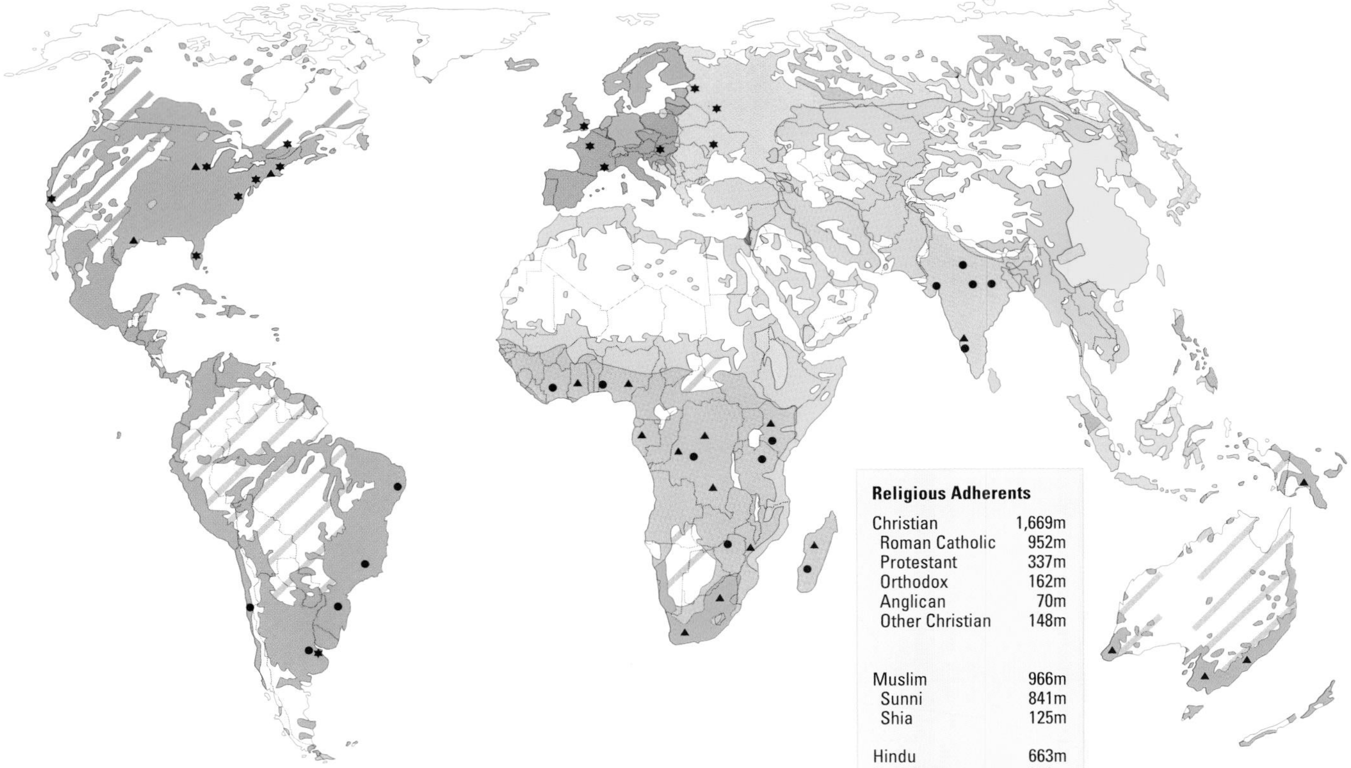

Religious Adherents

Christian	1,669m
Roman Catholic	952m
Protestant	337m
Orthodox	162m
Anglican	70m
Other Christian	148m
Muslim	966m
Sunni	841m
Shia	125m
Hindu	663m
Buddhist	312m
Chinese Folk	172m
Tribal	92m
Jewish	18m
Sikhs	17m

CARTOGRAPHY BY PHILIP'S. COPYRIGHT GEORGE PHILIP LTD

Conflict and Co-operation

For more information:
28 Migration
29 Religion

The 20th century witnessed two world wars, followed by a Cold War which several times threatened to erupt into a third world war, fought with nuclear weapons. The Cold War was marked by a great number of conflicts. Some were colonial wars, as the empires of the first half of the century fell apart, some were border wars, and some were civil wars. All the wars have caused great suffering among civilians, many of whom were forced to join the ranks of the world's refugees.

In the late 1980s, many people hoped that the end of the Cold War, following the collapse of Communist regimes in the former Soviet Union and Eastern Europe, would herald a new era of international stability. Instead, old ethnic and religious antagonisms surfaced in many areas, leading to civil war in such places as Chechenia, in Russia, and the former Yugoslavia. Nationalist rivalries, suppressed under Communist rule, replaced ideological factors as the major cause of conflict.

War is a very human activity, with no real equivalent in any other species. Yet humans also function well when they co-operate. Evolution has made this so. Hunter-gatherers in co-operative bands were far more effective than animals that prowled. Agriculture, urbanization and industrialization all depend on the ability of humans to co-operate.

The creation of the United Nations in 1945 held out hope that the world's nations, tired of war, would have the means to control humanity's aggressive instincts. Although the UN lacks the power to halt conflicts, it has often helped to achieve negotiation. Economic pressures have led to another kind of co-operation, the creation of common markets and economic unions, such as ASEAN in South-east Asia, the European Union and NAFTA in North America.

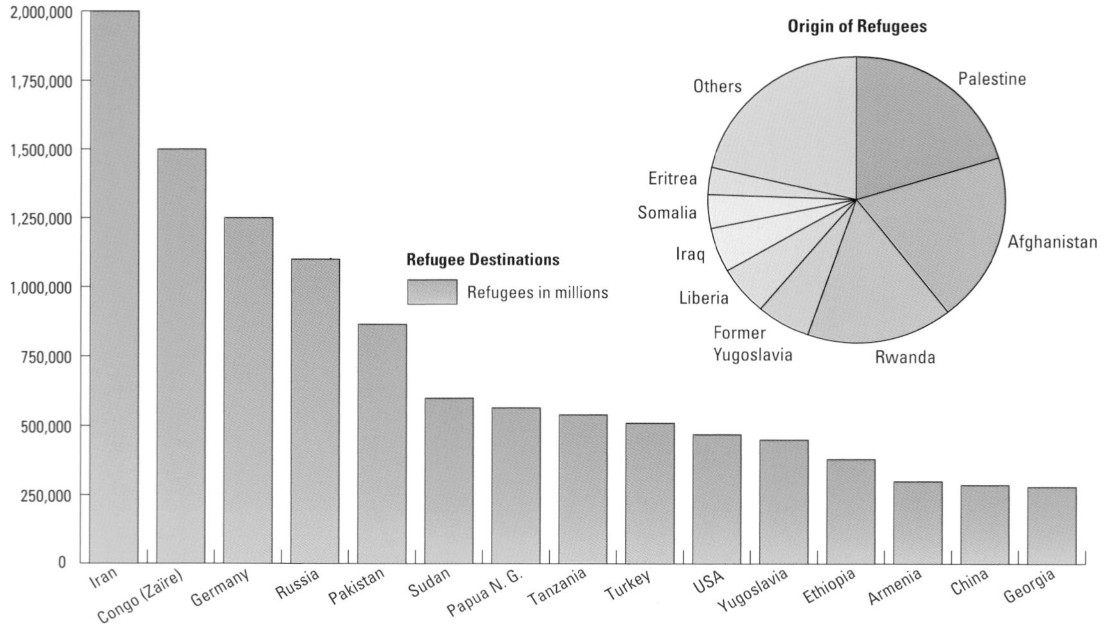

The World's Refugees

Refugees by host nation (bar-chart, left) and by nation of origin (pie-chart, left) (1995). The source is the United Nations High Commission for Refugees (UNHCR). The 3.2 million Palestinian refugees living in Jordan, Syria, Lebanon, Gaza and the West Bank fall under the mandate of United Nations Relief and Works Agency (UNRWA) and are not included on the bar-chart.

The pie-chart shows the origins of the world's refugees, while the bar-chart below shows their destinations. According to the United Nations High Commission for Refugees (UNHCR) in 1995 there were 14.5 million refugees. However, the UNHCR definition of a refugee, 'a person who has left or remains outside their own country because they have a well-founded fear of persecution, or because their safety is threatened by events seriously disturbing public order', does not include people who are in a refugee-like situation but who have not been formally recognized. In 1995, there were a further 3.5 million of these people worldwide and a further 4.5 million people who were internally displaced.

All but a few who cross international boundaries seek asylum in neighbouring countries, which are often the least equipped to deal with them. Lacking any rights or power, they frequently become an unwelcome burden to their hosts. Usually, the best any refugee can hope for is rudimentary food and shelter in temporary camps. Many Palestinians have been forced to live in camps since 1948.

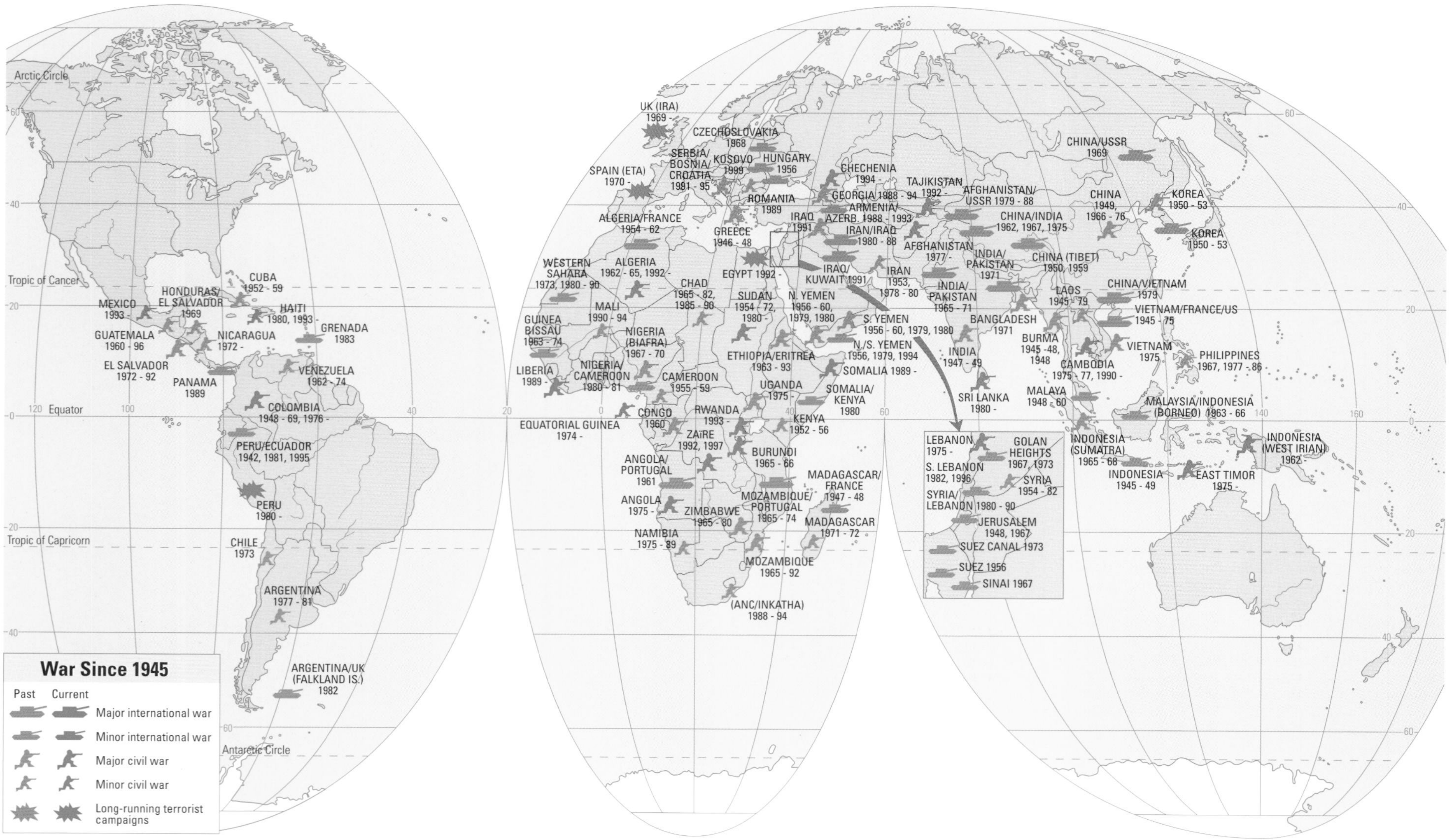

CARTOGRAPHY BY PHILIP'S. COPYRIGHT GEORGE PHILIP LTD

United Nations

The United Nations Organization was born as World War II drew to its conclusion. Six years of strife had strengthened the world's desire for peace, but an effective international organization was needed to help achieve it. That body would replace the League of Nations which, since its inception in 1920, had failed to curb the aggression of at least some of its member nations. At the United Nations Conference on International Organization held in San Francisco, the United Nations Charter was drawn up. Ratified by the Security Council and signed by the 51 original members, it came into effect on 24 October 1945.

The Charter set out the aims of the organization: to maintain peace and security, and develop friendly relations between nations; to achieve international co-operation in solving economic, social, cultural and humanitarian problems; to promote respect for human rights and fundamental freedoms; and to harmonize the activities of nations in order to achieve these common goals.

The United Nations has five principal organs :

The General Assembly
The forum at which member nations discuss moral and political issues affecting world development, peace and security meets annually in September, under a newly-elected President whose tenure lasts one year. Any member can bring business to the agenda, and each member nation has one vote.

The Security Council
A legislative and executive body, the Security Council is the primary instrument for establishing and maintaining international peace by attempting to settle disputes between nations. It has the power to dispatch UN forces, and member nations undertake to provide armed forces, assistance and facilities. The Security Council has ten temporary members elected by the General Assembly for two-year terms, and five permanent members – China, France, Russia, UK and USA.

The Economic and Social Council
By far the largest United Nations executive, the Council operates as a conduit between the General Assembly and the many United Nations agencies it instructs to implement Assembly decisions, and whose work it co-ordinates. The Council also commissions studies on economic conditions, collects data and makes recommendations to the Assembly.

The Secretariat
This is the staff of the United Nations, and its task is to administer the policies and programmes of the UN and its organs, and assist and advise the Head of the Secretariat, the Secretary-General – a full-time, non-political appointment made by the General Assembly.

The Trusteeship Council
This no longer administers any of the original 11 trust territories as they are all now independent.

The International Court of Justice (the World Court)
The World Court is the judicial organ of the United Nations. It deals only with United Nations disputes and all members are subject to its jurisdiction. There are 15 judges, elected for nine-year terms by the General Assembly and the Security Council.

The social and humanitarian operations of the UN include:
United Nations Development Programme (UNDP) Plans and funds projects to help developing countries make better use of their resources.
United Nations International Childrens' Fund (UNICEF) Created at the General Assembly's first session in 1945 to help children in the aftermath of World War II, it now provides basic health care and aid worldwide.
Food and Agriculture Organization (FAO) Aims to raise living standards and nutrition levels in rural areas by improving food production and distribution.
United Nations Educational, Scientific and Cultural Organization (UNESCO) Promotes international co-operation through broader and better education.
World Health Organization (WHO) Promotes and provides for better health care, public and environmental health and medical research.

United Nations agencies are involved in many aspects of international trade, safety and security:
International Maritime Organization (IMO) Promotes unity amongst merchant shipping, especially in regard to safety, marine pollution and standardization.
International Labour Organization (ILO) Seeks to improve labour conditions and promote productive employment to raise living standards.
World Meteorological Organization (WMO) Promotes co-operation in weather observation, reporting and forecasting.
World Trade Organization (WTO) On 1 January 1995 the WTO replaced GATT. It advocates a common code of conduct and its aim is the liberalization of world trade.
Disarmament Commission Considers and makes recommendations to the General Assembly on disarmament issues.
International Atomic Energy Agency (IAEA) Fosters development of peaceful uses for nuclear energy and establishes safety standards.

The World Bank comprises three United Nations agencies:
International Monetary Fund (IMF) Cultivates international monetary co-operation and expansion of trade.
International Bank for Reconstruction and Development (IBRD) Provides funds and technical assistance to developing countries.
International Finance Corporation (IFC) Encourages the growth of productive private enterprise in less developed countries.

Membership There are four independent states which are not members of the UN – Switzerland, Taiwan, Tuvalu and Vatican City. Official languages are Chinese, English, French, Russian, Spanish and Arabic.
Funding The UN budget for 1996–97 was US $2.6 billion. Contributions are assessed by the members' ability to pay, with the maximum 25% of the total, the minimum 0.01%.
Peacekeeping The UN has been involved in 43 peacekeeping operations worldwide since 1948. At the end of 1996 there were 16 areas of UN patrol and 25,649 'blue berets'.

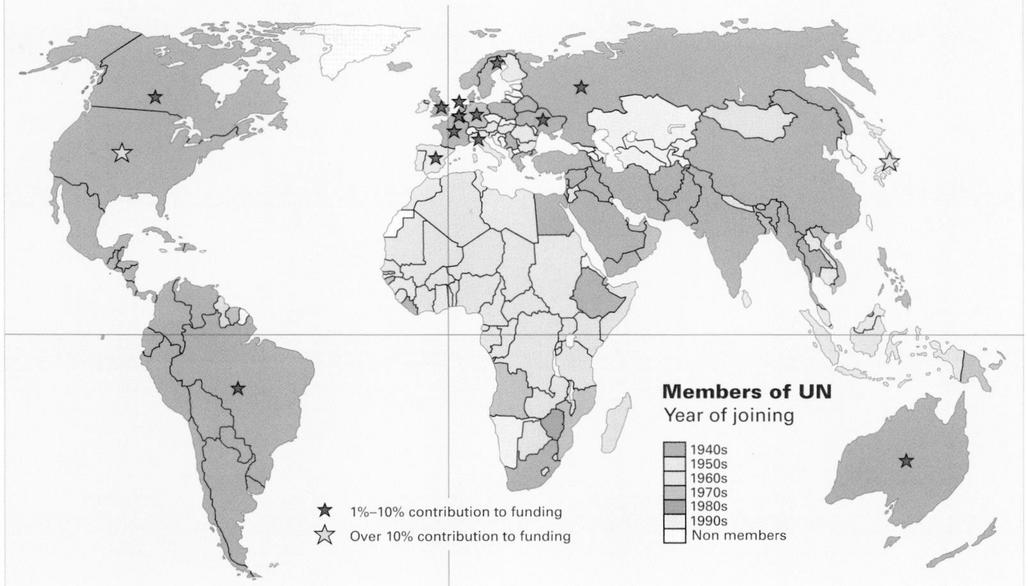

Military Spending

Military expenditure as a % of GNP or GDP, ranked selection of countries (1994)

1. Iraq	74.9%	14. Jordan	7.5%
2. North Korea	26.3%	15. Laos	7.4%
3. Angola	23.9%	16. Pakistan	6.0%
4. Oman	18.1%	17. UAE	5.7%
5. Syria	17.9%	18. Seychelles	5.6%
6. Sudan	17.1%	19. Sierra Leone	4.9%
7. Saudi Arabia	14.2%	20. Taiwan	4.8%
8. Yemen	14.1%	21. Liberia	4.8%
9. Russia	12.4%	22. Singapore	4.5%
10. Kuwait	11.1%	23. Sri Lanka	4.5%
11. Mozambique	8.7%	24. USA	4.3%
12. Israel	8.6%	25. Malaysia	4.2%
13. Rwanda	7.6%		

It is worth noting that the total amount of expenditure varies considerably depending on the size of the economy, so that although the percentages show the importance given to military spending within each country, they give no idea as to the total expenditure. In 1997, for example, the USA spent a total of US $271 billion, Russia US $70 billion, and the UK US $36 billion. In 1993, the USA also provided the most military assistance worldwide, providing US $3.4 billion, compared to a total of US $0.9 billion from Western Europe.

The period 1987–94 saw a decline in global military spending which generated what the United Nations Development Programme term a 'peace dividend' of US $935 billion. Unfortunately, there is no clear link between reduced military spending and enhanced expenditure on human development. Moreover, the poorest regions of the world (notably sub-Saharan Africa) failed to contain their military spending and, in some cases, it increased.

International Organizations

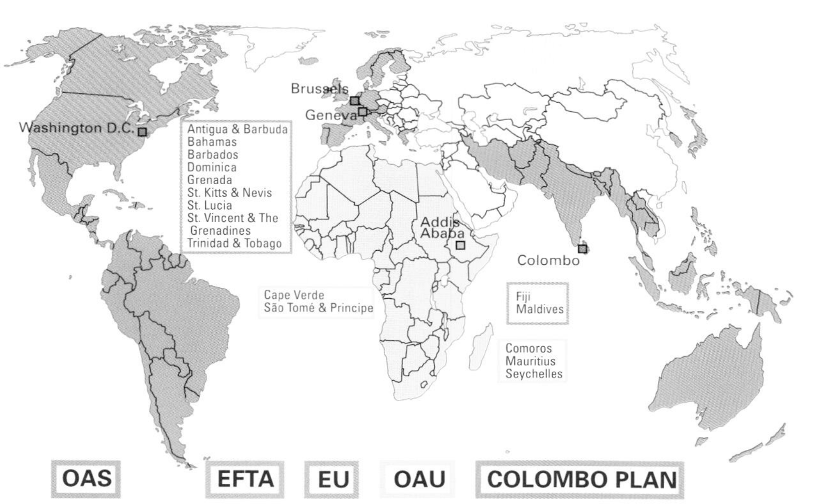

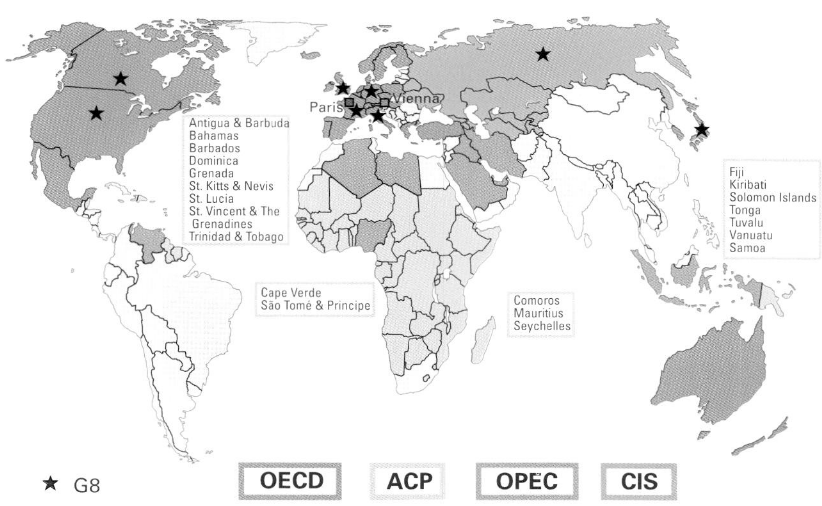

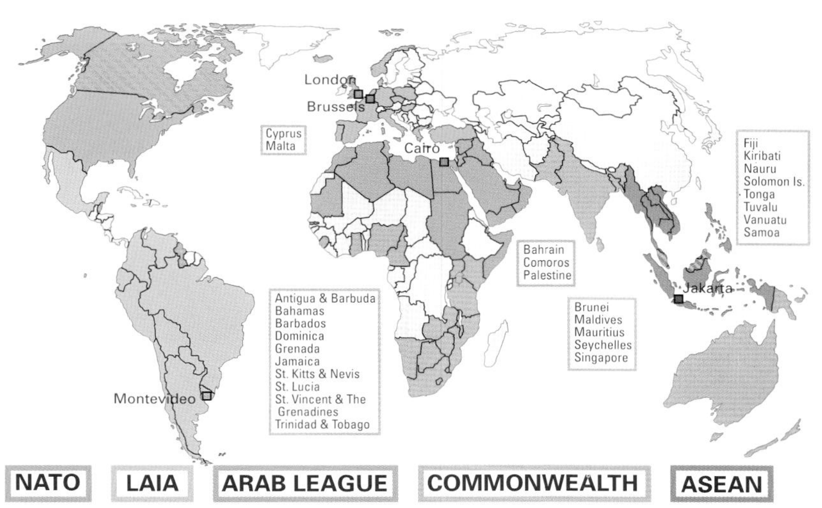

EU The European Union evolved from the European Community (EC) in 1993. The original body, the European Coal and Steel Community (ECSC), was created in 1951 following the signing of the Treaty of Paris. The 15 members of the EU – Austria, Belgium, Denmark, Finland, France, Germany, Greece, Ireland, Italy, Luxembourg, Netherlands, Portugal, Spain, Sweden and the UK – aim to integrate economies, co-ordinate social developments and bring about political union. These members, of what is now the world's biggest market, share agricultural and industrial policies and tariffs on trade.
EFTA European Free Trade Association (formed in 1960). Portugal left the original 'Seven' in 1989 to join what was then the EC, followed by Austria, Finland and Sweden in 1995. There are now only four members: Iceland, Liechtenstein, Norway and Switzerland.
ACP African-Caribbean-Pacific (formed in 1963). Members enjoy economic ties with the EU.
NATO North Atlantic Treaty Organization (formed in 1949). It continues despite the winding up of the Warsaw Pact in 1991. The Czech Rep., Hungary and Poland were the latest to join in 1999.
OAS Organization of American States (formed in 1948). It aims to promote social and economic co-operation between countries in the developed North America and developing Latin America.
ASEAN Association of South-east Asian Nations (formed in 1967). Cambodia joined in 1999.
OAU Organization of African Unity (1963). Its 53 members represent over 94% of Africa's population. Arabic, English, French and Portuguese are recognized as working languages.
LAIA The Latin American Integration Association (formed in 1980) superceded the Latin American Free Trade Association formed in 1961. Its aim is to promote freer regional trade.
OECD Organization for Economic Co-operation and Development (formed in 1961). It comprises 29 major free-market economies. The 'G8' is its 'inner group' of leading industrial nations, comprising Canada, France, Germany, Italy, Japan, Russia, UK and the USA.
COMMONWEALTH The Commonwealth of Nations evolved from the British Empire; it comprises 16 nations recognizing the British monarch as head of state, 32 republics and 5 indigenous monarchies, giving a total of 53. Nigeria was suspended in 1995.
CIS The Commonwealth of Independent States (formed in 1991) comprises the countries of the former Soviet Union except for Estonia, Latvia and Lithuania.
OPEC Organization of Petroleum Exporting Countries (formed in 1960). It controls about three-quarters of the world's oil supply. Gabon formally withdrew from OPEC in August 1996.
ARAB LEAGUE (1945) Aims to promote economic, social, political and military co-operation.
COLOMBO PLAN (formed in 1951) Its 26 members aim to promote economic and social development in Asia and the Pacific.

CARTOGRAPHY BY PHILIP'S. COPYRIGHT GEORGE PHILIP LTD

Agriculture

For more information:
14 Temperature and precipitation
16 Climate regions
18 Water utilization
19 Natural vegetation
Land use by continent
38 Division of employment

Bad harvests in 1995 caused a drop in world grain reserves to a 20-year low. This revived the ongoing debate as to whether the population explosion will cause major food crises in the 21st century.

Experts estimate that 3 billion tonnes of cereals will be needed to feed the world's population in 25 years' time, as compared with 1.9 billion tonnes at present. To expand food production to this extent, some argue, will place great strain on the environment. One suggestion to alleviate the situation is that people in developed countries should eat less meat. This would release more grain, which is used as cattle fodder, to feed people.

Other experts argue that there should be no food crises. World grain production tripled between 1950 and 1990, largely as a result of the Green Revolution, during which genetically improved, high-yield varieties of maize, rice and wheat, the world's three leading staple crops, were developed. These new varieties have helped many developing countries to achieve food surpluses and prevent widespread starvation.

The only region of the world which seems likely to suffer food shortages in the 21st century is sub-Saharan Africa, where in the late 1990s the average daily calorie intake was 6% less than what was needed and where the population is expected to double in 20 years. Improved land management and a huge increase in global trade, especially in food distribution, is necessary if sub-Saharan Africans are not to go hungry.

The development of agriculture more than 10,000 years ago transformed human existence more than any other major advance. By supporting larger populations, it led to the growth of early civilizations and later it sustained people in the industrial cities which sprang up in the 19th century.

Today, agricultural production varies a great deal between the developed world, where it is highly mechanized and employs few people, such as 3% of the workforce in the United States, and the developing world, such as sub-Saharan Africa, where it employs 66% of the workforce. Many Africans are engaged in subsistence farming, providing the basic needs of their families but not contributing to the national economy. Much of Africa also suffers from economic mismanagement, as well as civil war and banditry.

Political problems have also affected food production in other parts of the world. The former USSR had much excellent farmland, but the failure of the collectives and state farms to maintain sufficiently high levels of production helped to bring about the collapse of Communism.

Farmers are under great pressure not only to maintain high levels of production but to increase them. However, the cultivation of marginal areas is one of the prime causes of soil erosion and desertification.

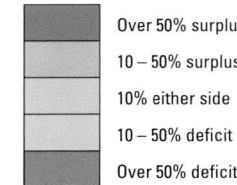

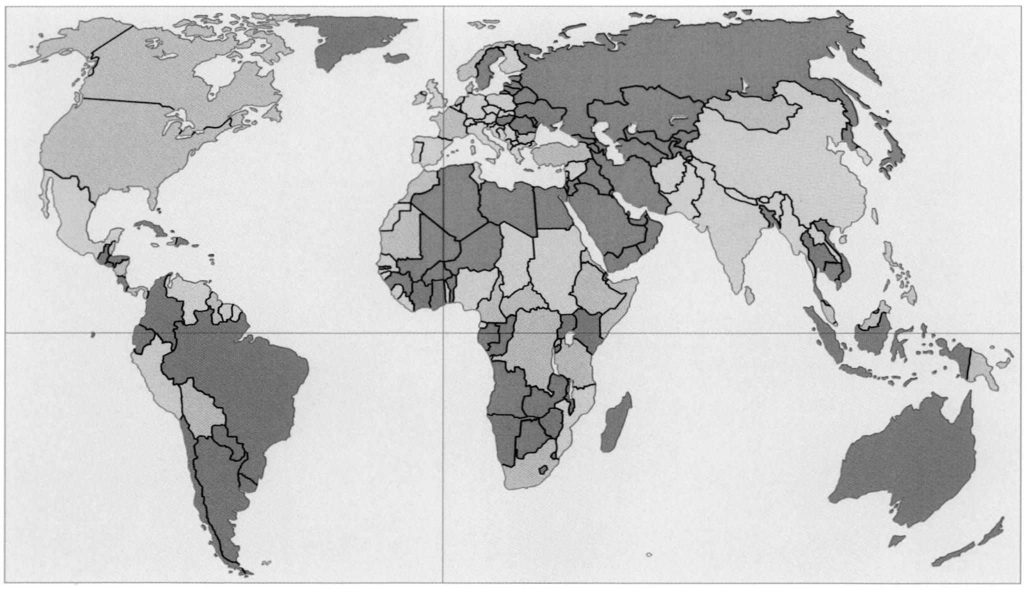

Self-sufficiency in Food

Balance of trade in food products as a percentage of total trade in food products – S.I.T.C. Classes 0, 1 and 4 (latest available year)

- Over 50% surplus
- 10 – 50% surplus
- 10% either side
- 10 – 50% deficit
- Over 50% deficit

Most self-sufficient		Least self-sufficient	
Argentina	95%	Algeria	–98%
Zimbabwe	87%	Djibouti	–97%
Honduras	81%	Yemen	–95%
Malawi	81%	Zambia	–95%
Costa Rica	79%	Japan	–91%
Iceland	78%	Gabon	–90%
Chile	75%	Kuwait	–90%
Uruguay	75%	Brunei	–89%
Ecuador	74%	Burkina Faso	–82%

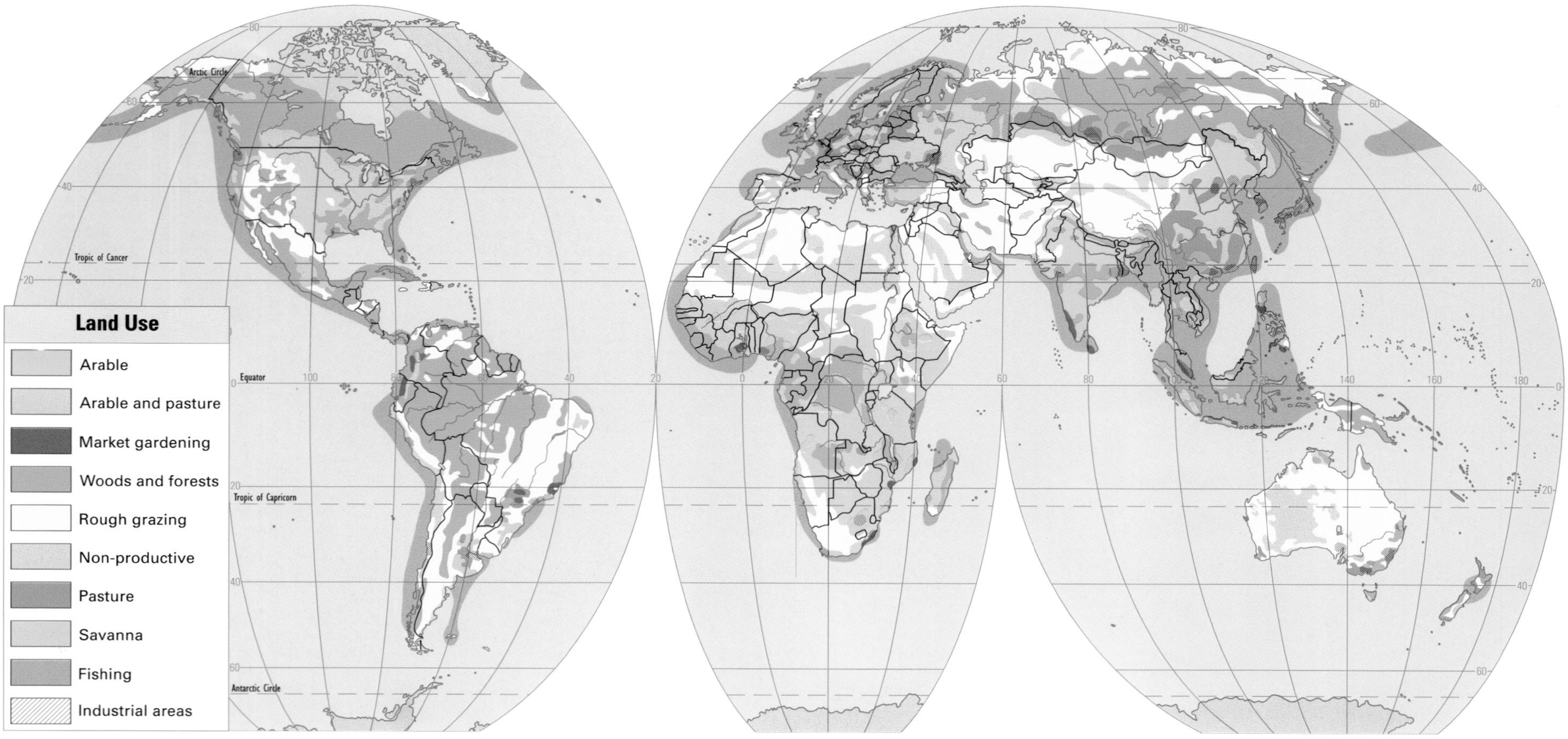
Land Use
Arable
Arable and pasture
Market gardening
Woods and forests
Rough grazing
Non-productive
Pasture
Savanna
Fishing
Industrial areas
Arctic Circle
Tropic of Cancer
Equator
Tropic of Capricorn
Antarctic Circle

Staple Crops

Wheat: Grown in a range of climates, with most varieties – including the highest-quality bread wheats – requiring temperate conditions. Mainly used in baking, it is also used for pasta and breakfast cereals.

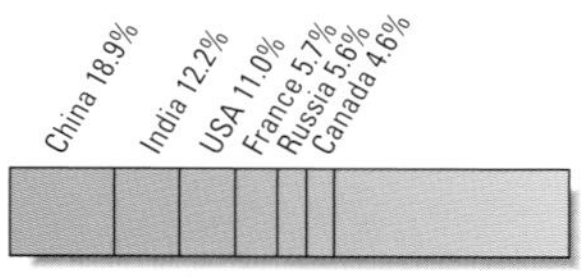

World total (1996): 584,874,000 tonnes

Maize: Originating in the New World and still an important human food in Africa and Latin America, in the developed world it is processed into breakfast cereals, oil, starches and adhesives. It is also used for animal feed.

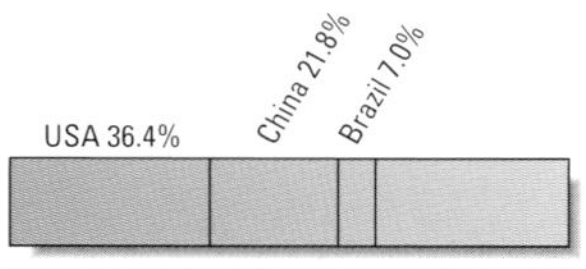

World total (1996): 576,821,000 tonnes

Oats: Most widely used to feed livestock, but eaten by humans as oatmeal or porridge. Oats have a beneficial effect on the cardiovascular system, and human consumption is likely to increase.

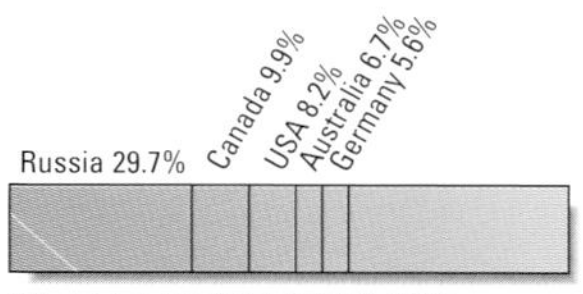

World total (1996): 28,794,000 tonnes

Millet: The name covers a number of small-grained cereals, members of the grass family with a short growing season. Used to produce flour, meal and animal feed, and fermented to make beer, especially in Africa.

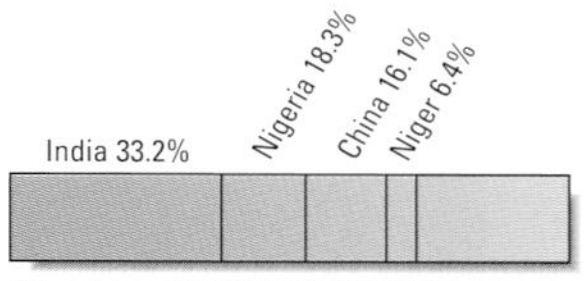

World total (1996): 29,563,000 tonnes

Rice: Thrives on the high humidity and temperatures of the Far East, where it is the traditional staple food of half the human race. Usually grown standing in water, rice responds well to continuous cultivation, with three or four crops annually.

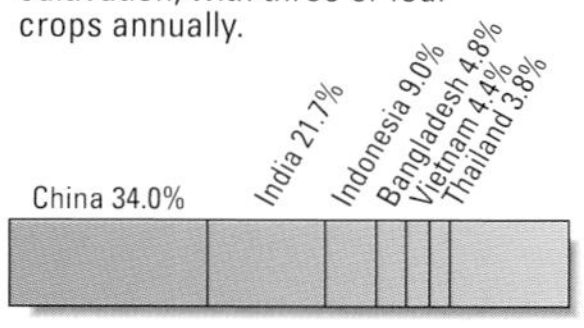

World total (1996): 562,259,000 tonnes

Potatoes: The most important of the edible tubers, potatoes grow in well-watered, temperate areas. Weight for weight less nutritious than grain, they are a human staple as well as an important animal feed.

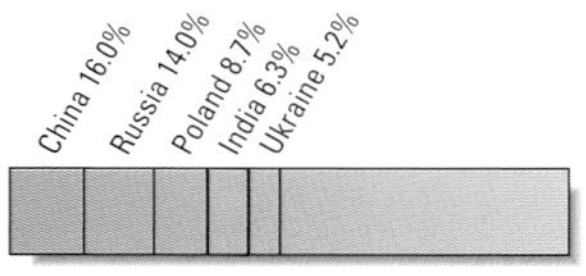

World total (1996): 294,834,000 tonnes

Soya: Beans from soya bushes are very high (30–40%) in protein. Most are processed into oil and proprietary protein foods. Consumption since 1950 has tripled, mainly due to the health-conscious developed world.

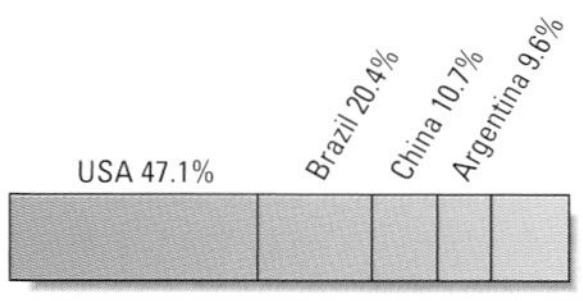

World total (1996): 130,302,000 tonnes

Cassava: A tropical shrub that needs high rainfall (over 1,000 mm annually) and a 10–30 month growing season to produce its large, edible tubers. Used as flour by humans, as cattle feed and in industrial starches.

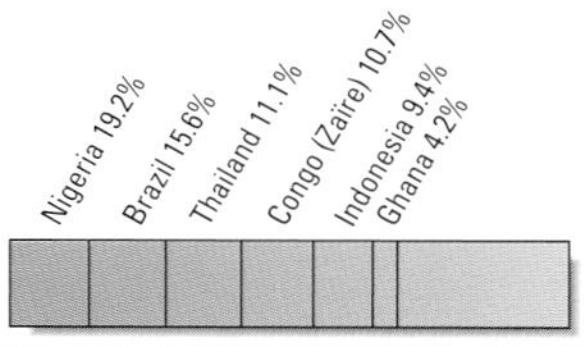

World total (1996): 162,942,000 tonnes

Sugars

Sugar cane: Confined to tropical regions, cane sugar accounts for the bulk of international trade in sugar. Most is produced as a foodstuff, but some countries, notably Brazil and South Africa, distill sugar cane to make motor fuels.

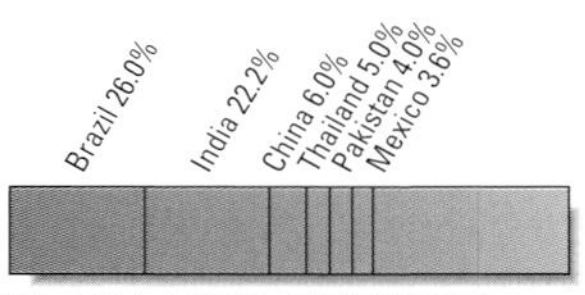

World total (1996): 1,192,555,000 tonnes

Sugar beet: Closely related to the beetroot, sugar beet's yield after processing is indistinguishable from cane sugar. It is replacing sugar-cane imports in Europe, to the detriment of the developing countries that rely on it as a major cash crop.

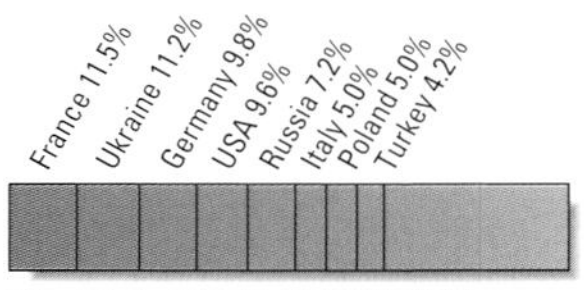

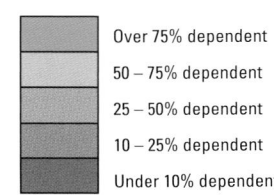

World total (1996): 255,500,000 tonnes

Cereals are grasses with starchy, edible seeds; every important civilization has depended on them as a source of food. The major cereal grains contain about 10% protein and 75% carbohydrate. Grain contributes more than any other group of foods to the energy and protein content of human diet. Starchy tuber crops or root crops are second in importance after cereals as staple foods; easily cultivated, they provide high yields for little effort.

Food and Population

Comparison of food production and population by continent.

The left column indicates the % of world food production and the right shows population in proportion.

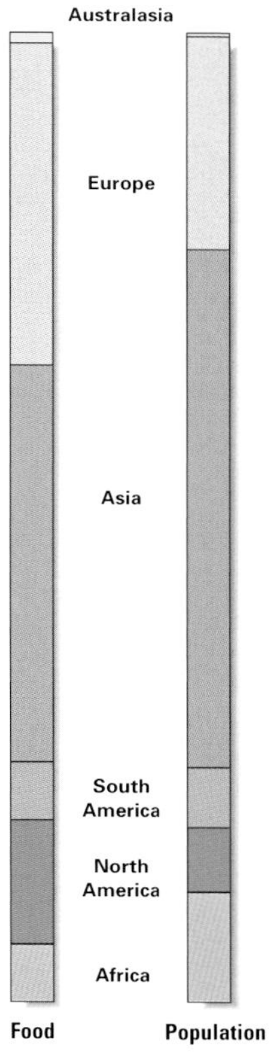

Agricultural Population

Percentage of the total population dependent on agriculture for their livelihood (1997)

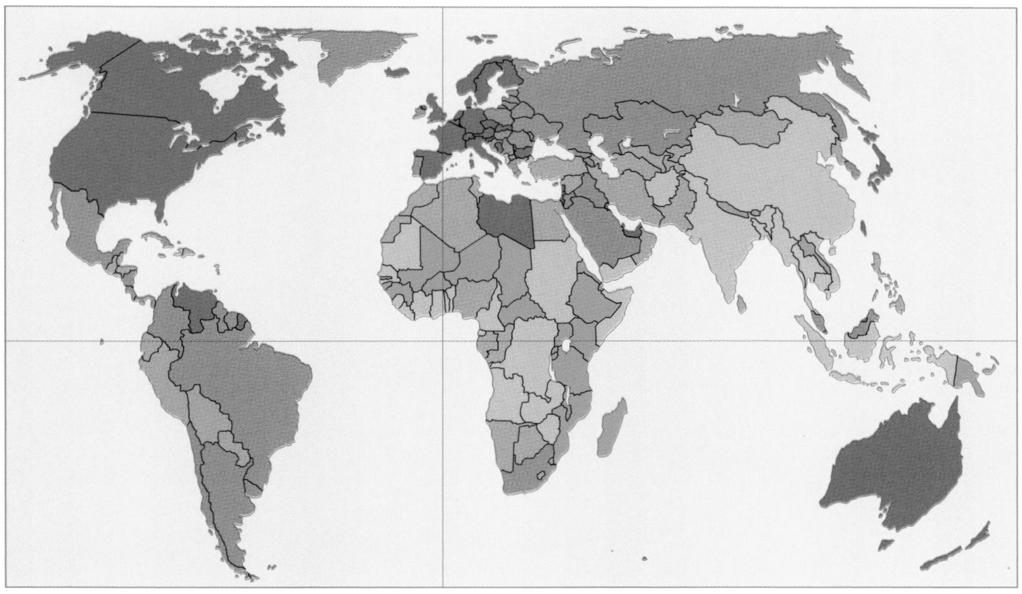

- Over 75% dependent
- 50 – 75% dependent
- 25 – 50% dependent
- 10 – 25% dependent
- Under 10% dependent

Top 5 countries (1997)	
Bhutan	94%
Nepal	93%
Burkina Faso	92%
Rwanda	91%
Burundi	91%

Bottom 5 countries (1997)	
Singapore	0.2%
Kuwait	1.0%
Brunei	1.0%
Bahrain	1.3%
Qatar	1.7%

Animal Products

Traditionally, food animals subsisted on land unsuitable for cultivation, supporting agricultural production with their fertilizing dung. But free-ranging animals grow slowly and yield less meat than those more intensively reared; the demands of urban markets in the developed world have encouraged the growth of factory-like production methods. A large proportion of staple crops, especially cereals, are fed to animals, an inefficient way to produce protein but one likely to continue as long as people value meat and dairy products in their diet.

Cheese: Least perishable of all dairy products, cheese is milk fermented with selected bacterial strains to produce a foodstuff with a potentially immense range of flavours and textures. The vast majority of cheeses are made from cow's milk, although sheep and goat cheeses are highly prized.

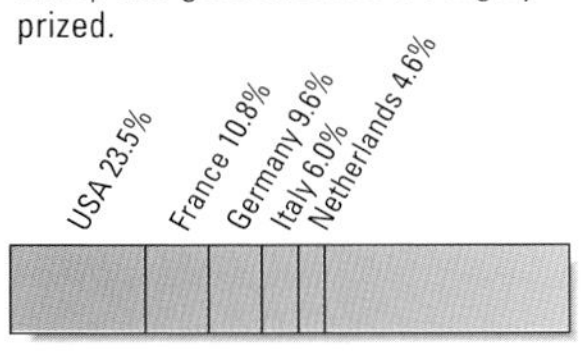

World total (1995): 14,754,000 tonnes

Beef and Veal: Most beef and veal is reared for home markets, and the top five producers are also the biggest consumers. The USA produces nearly a quarter of the world's beef and eats even more.

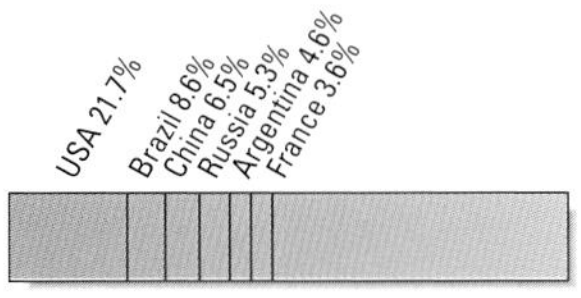

World total (1996): 53,965,000 tonnes

Milk: Many human groups, including most Asians, find raw milk indigestible after infancy, and it is often only the starting point for other dairy products such as butter, cheese and yoghurt. Most world production comes from cows, but sheep's milk and goats' milk are also important.

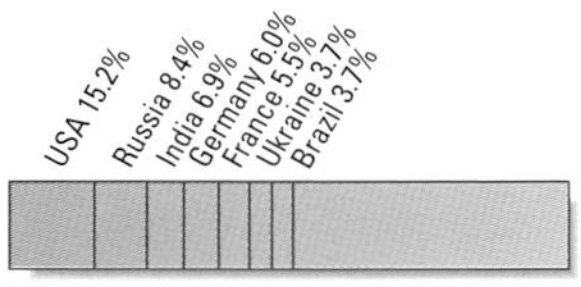

World total (1996): 466,317,000 tonnes

Butter: A traditional source of vitamin A as well as calories, butter has lost much popularity in the developed world for health reasons, although it remains a valuable food. Most butter from India, the world's largest producer, is clarified into ghee, which has religious as well as nutritional importance.

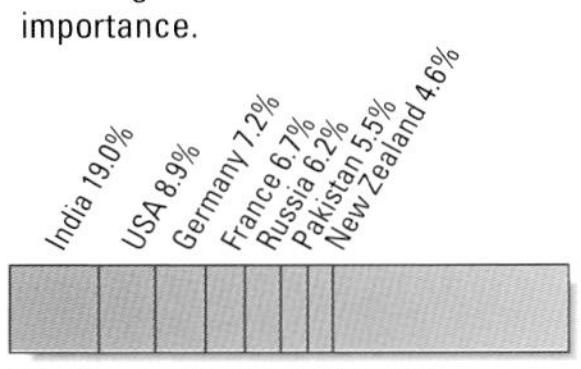

World total (1996): 6,565,000 tonnes

Pork: Although pork is forbidden to many millions, notably Muslims, on religious grounds, more is produced than any other meat in the world, mainly because it is the cheapest. It accounts for about 90% of China's meat output, although per capita meat consumption is relatively low.

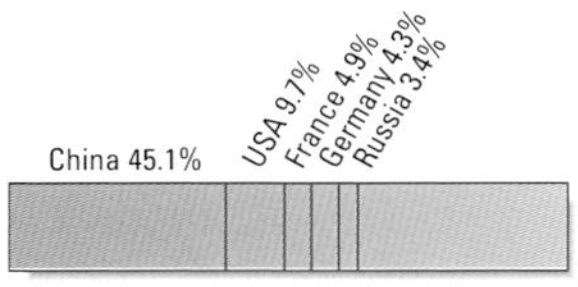

World total (1996): 85,761,000 tonnes

Crisis in Africa

Each year 40 million people, almost half of whom are children, die from starvation and related diseases. In 2000, 600 million people worldwide were estimated to be suffering from malnutrition. Africa suffers from more natural disasters than any other continent; pests such as locusts destroy crops, and tropical storms and flooding ruin harvests. Famines periodically affect parts of Africa causing widespread hardship, even though enough food is produced worldwide to feed everyone.

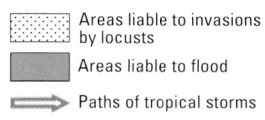

- Areas liable to invasions by locusts
- Areas liable to flood
- Paths of tropical storms
- Major famines since 1900 (with dates)

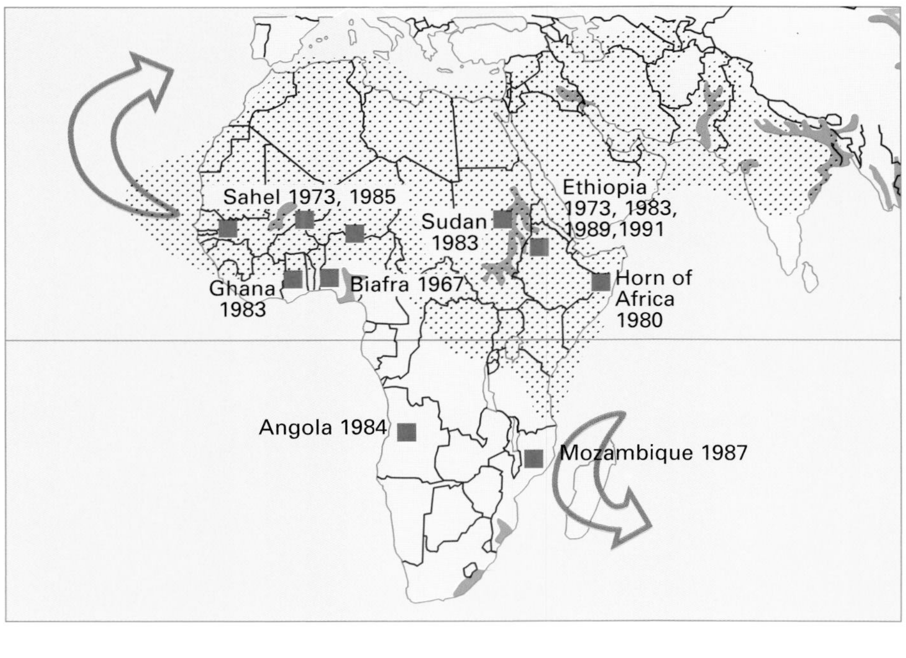

Energy

For more information:
22 Carbon dioxide
Greenhouse power
CO_2 producers
Global warming
23 Water pollution
39 World shipping

Every year, the world's energy consumption is about the equivalent of what would come from burning 8,000 million tonnes of oil (8,000 MtOe) – a 20-fold increase since 1850. Two-fifths of this total actually comes from burning oil and most of the rest comes from coal and natural gas.

The oil crises in the 1970s precipitated concern over dependence on finite fossil fuels as the primary source of energy, and growing environmental awareness has added impetus to the search for alternative energy resources. Fossil fuel combustion damages the environment through the release of gases and particulate matter but two other major sources of energy, hydroelectricity and nuclear power, are also controversial. For example, hydroelectricity production involves flooding large areas to create reservoirs, while nuclear power stations, which are costly to build, generate dangerous radioactive wastes, and can lead to disasters on an international scale.

Alternative energy resources may soon provide a much larger proportion of the world's energy consumption, especially in developing countries where millions of people currently have no access to electricity. Experts have predicted that solar and wind energy may have an important future in such countries as China and India, while other areas under development, such as tidal, wave and geothermal power, all have potential in appropriate areas. World Bank experts have calculated that solar power could, in theory, supply between five and ten times the present electricity supply of developing countries.

Conversions

For historical reasons, oil is still traded in barrels. The weight and volume equivalents shown below are all based on average density 'Arabian light' crude oil, and should be considered approximate.

The energy equivalents given for a tonne of oil are also somewhat imprecise: oil and coal of different qualities will have varying energy contents, a fact usually reflected in their price on world markets.

1 barrel:
0.136 tonnes
159 litres
35 Imperial gallons
42 US gallons

1 tonne:
7.33 barrels
1185 litres
256 Imperial gallons
261 US gallons

1 tonne oil:
1.5 tonnes hard coal
3.0 tonnes lignite
12,000 kWh

1 gallon (Imperial):
227,42 cubic inches
1.201 US gallons
4,546 litres

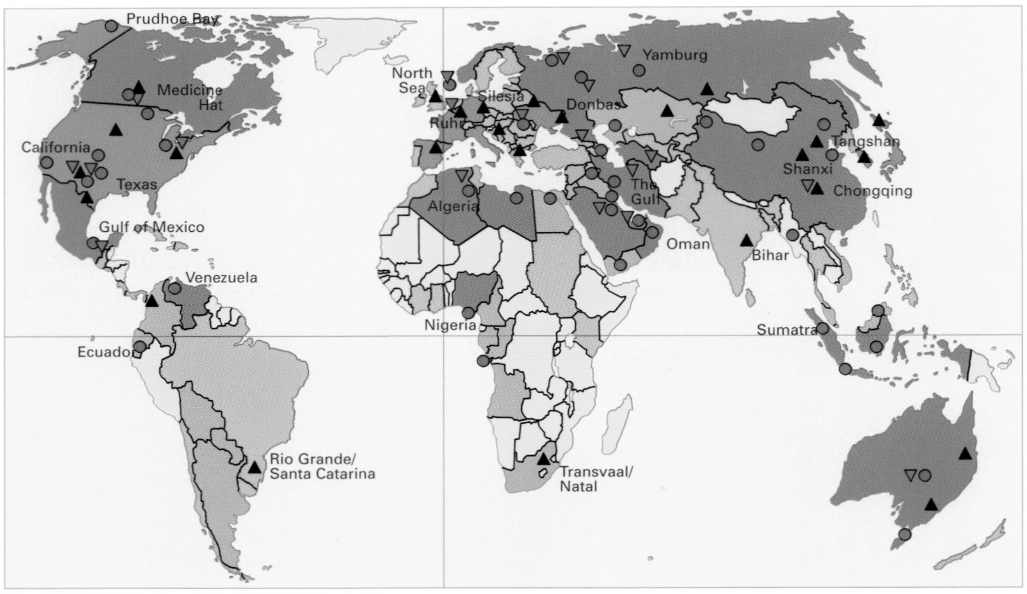

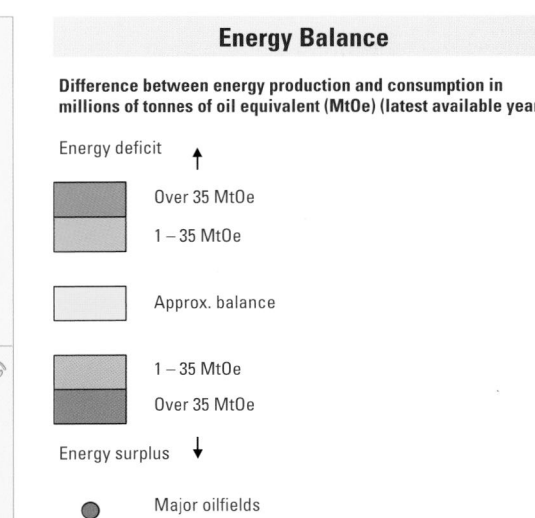

Energy Balance

Difference between energy production and consumption in millions of tonnes of oil equivalent (MtOe) (latest available year)

Energy deficit
Over 35 MtOe
1 – 35 MtOe
Approx. balance
1 – 35 MtOe
Over 35 MtOe
Energy surplus

Major oilfields
Major gasfields
Major coalfields

World Energy Consumption

Energy consumed by world regions, measured in million tonnes of oil equivalent in 1997. Total world consumption was 8,509 MtOe. Only energy from oil, gas, coal, nuclear and hydroelectric sources are included. Excluded are fuels such as wood, peat, animal waste, wind, solar and geothermal which, though important in some countries, are unreliably documented in terms of consumption statistics.

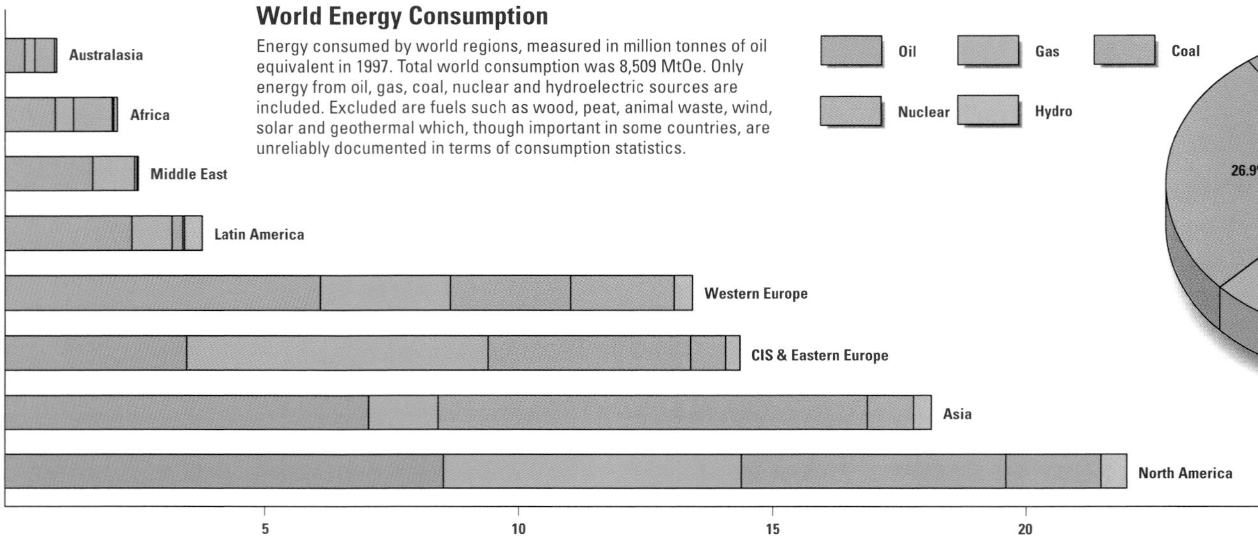

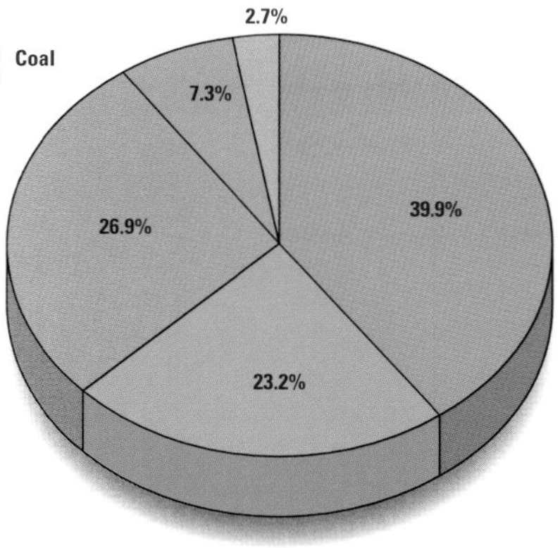

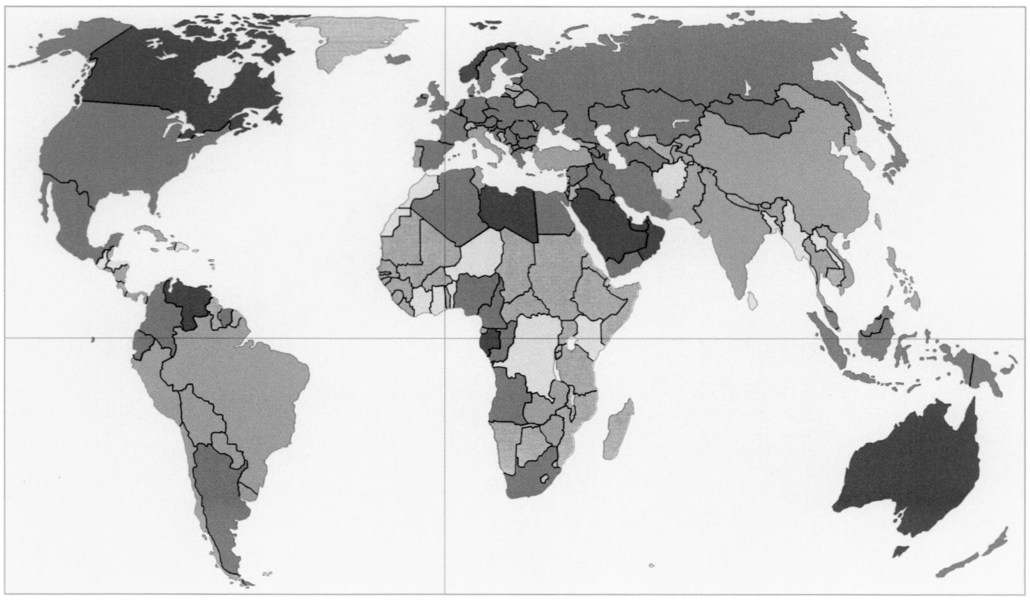

Energy Production

Primary energy production expressed in kilograms of coal equivalent per person (1994)

In developing countries traditional fuels are still very important. These so-called biomass fuels include wood, charcoal and dried dung. The pie-chart highlights the importance of biomass in terms of energy consumption in Nigeria. Collecting fuelwood can be a time-consuming task, sometimes taking all day.

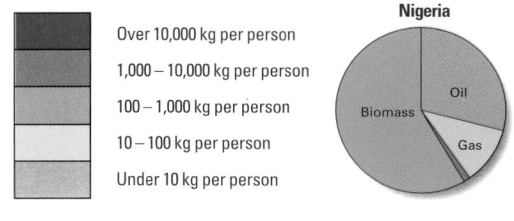

Over 10,000 kg per person
1,000 – 10,000 kg per person
100 – 1,000 kg per person
10 – 100 kg per person
Under 10 kg per person

Nigeria

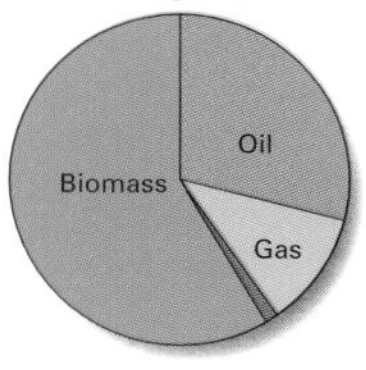

Oil Movements

Major world movements of oil in millions of tonnes (1997)

Middle East to Asia (not Japan)	294.4
Middle East to Japan	218.1
Middle East to Western Europe	187.9
South and Central America to USA	132.1
North Africa to Western Europe	97.9
CIS to Western Europe	90.8
Middle East to USA	86.9
Canada to USA	72.7
West Africa to USA	68.3
Mexico to USA	68.0
West Africa to Western Europe	40.1
Western Europe to USA	32.9
Middle East to Africa	32.0
CIS to Central Europe	31.8
Middle East to South and Central America	27.8
Middle East to Central Europe	19.3

Total world imports ....1,978,900,000 million tonnes

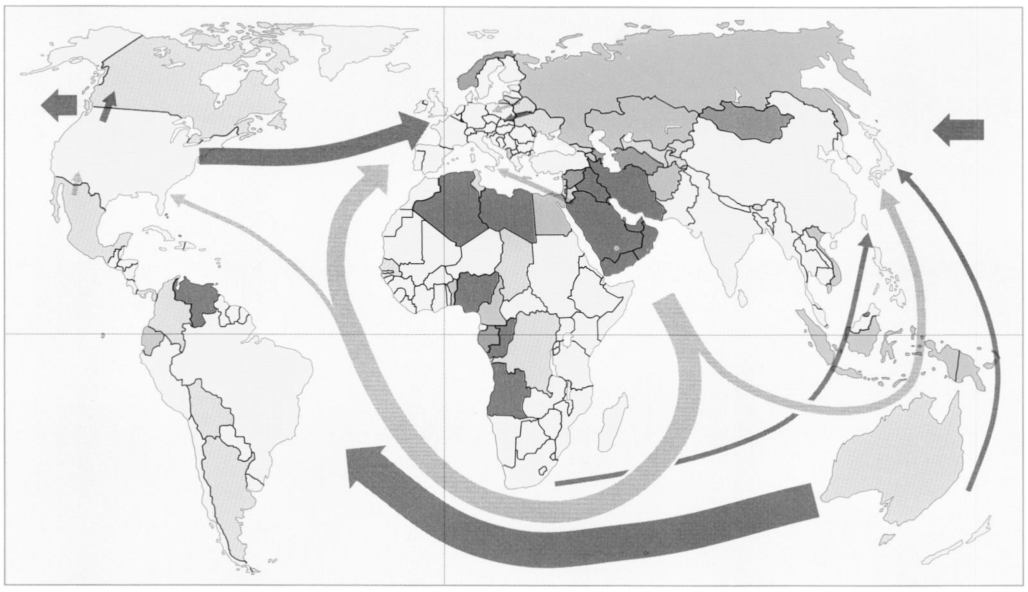

Fuel Exports

Fuels as a percentage of total value of exports (1996)

- Over 75%
- 50 – 75%
- 25 – 50%
- 10 – 25%
- Under 10%

Major movements of coal

Major movements of oil

In the 1970s, oil exports became a political issue when OPEC sought to increase the influence of developing countries in world affairs by raising oil prices and restricting production. But its power was short-lived, following a fall in demand for oil in the 1980s, due to an increase in energy efficiency and development of alternative resources.

Coal Reserves

Proved coal reserves in place by region and country, thousand million tonnes (1993)

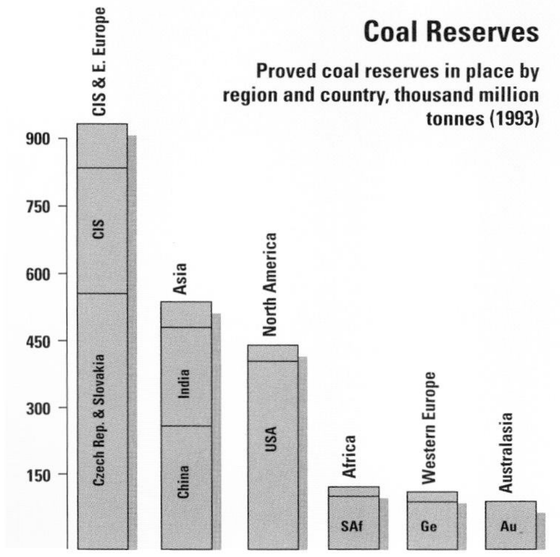

Gas Reserves

Proved recoverable natural gas reserves by region and country, thousand million tonnes (1993)

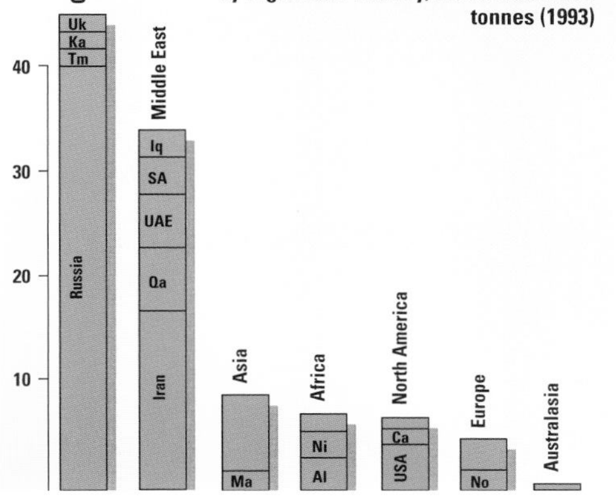

Oil Reserves

Crude oil reserves by region and country, thousand million tonnes (1993)

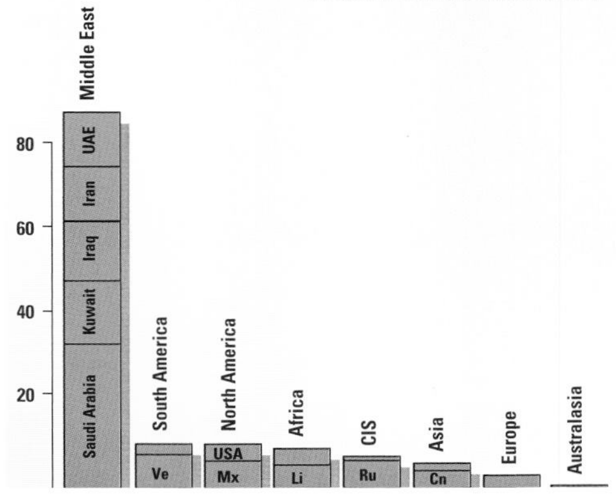

Al: Algeria
Au: Australia
Ca: Canada
Cn: China
Ge: Germany
Iq: Iraq
Ka: Kazakstan
Li: Libya
Ma: Malaysia
Mx: Mexico
Ni: Nigeria
No: Norway
Qa: Qatar
Ru: Russia
SA: Saudi Arabia
SAf: South Africa
Tm: Turkmenistan
Uk: Ukraine
Ve: Venezuela

Nuclear Power

Percentage of electricity generated by nuclear power stations, leading nations (1995)

1. Lithuania	85%	11. Spain	33%
2. France	77%	12. Finland	30%
3. Belgium	56%	13. Germany	29%
4. Slovak Rep.	49%	14. Japan	29%
5. Sweden	48%	15. UK	27%
6. Bulgaria	41%	16. Ukraine	27%
7. Hungary	41%	17. Czech Rep.	22%
8. Switzerland	39%	18. Canada	19%
9. Slovenia	38%	19. USA	18%
10. South Korea	33%	20. Russia	12%

Although the 1980s were a bad time for the nuclear power industry (major projects ran over budget and fears of long-term environmental damage were heavily reinforced by the 1986 disaster at Chernobyl), the industry picked up in the early 1990s. Whilst the number of reactors is still increasing, however, orders for new plants have shrunk. In 1997, the Swedish government began to decommission the country's 12 nuclear power plants; a bold environmental decision that could cost US $50 billion.

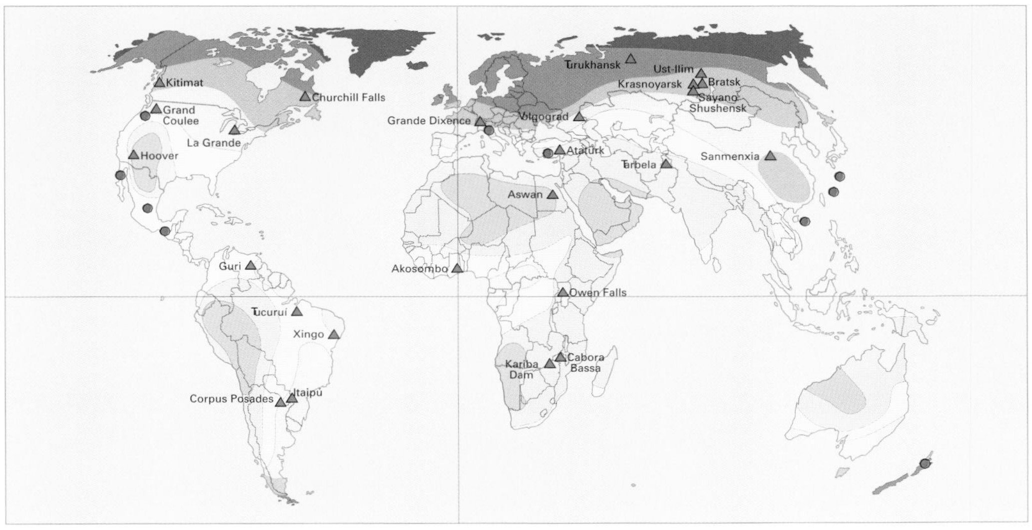

Renewable Energy

Average annual solar irradiance in kWh/m², with selected major hydroelectric and geothermal power stations

- Over 2,200
- 1,950 – 2,200
- 1,700 – 1,950
- 1,400 – 1,700
- 1,100 – 1,400
- 800 – 1,100
- Under 800

Hydroelectric plants

Geothermal plants

Hydroelectricity

Percentage of electricity generated by hydroelectric power stations, leading nations (1995)

1. Paraguay	99.9%	11. Rwanda	97.6%
2. Congo (Zaïre)	99.7%	12. Malawi	97.6%
3. Bhutan	99.6%	13. Cameroon	96.9%
4. Zambia	99.5%	14. Nepal	96.7%
5. Norway	99.4%	15. Laos	95.3%
6. Ghana	99.3%	16. Albania	95.2%
7. Congo	99.3%	17. Iceland	94.0%
8. Uganda	99.1%	18. Brazil	92.2%
9. Burundi	98.3%	19. Honduras	87.6%
10. Uruguay	98.0%	20. Tanzania	87.1%

Countries heavily reliant on hydroelectricity are usually small and non-industrial: a high proportion of hydroelectric power more often reflects a modest energy budget than vast hydroelectric resources. The USA, for instance, produces only 9% of power requirements from hydroelectricity; yet that 9% amounts to more than three times the hydropower generated by the whole of Africa.

Alternative Energy Resources

Solar: Each year the Sun bestows upon the Earth almost a million times as much energy as is locked up in all the planet's oil reserves, but only an insignificant fraction is trapped and used commercially. In a few installations around the world, mirrors focus the Sun's rays on to boilers, whose steam generates electricity by spinning turbines.

Wind: Caused by uneven heating of the Earth, winds are themselves a form of solar energy. Windmills have been used for centuries to turn wind power into mechanical work; recent models, often arranged in banks on wind-swept high ground, usually generate electricity. Figures for wind power worldwide are given in the table, right.

Tidal: The energy from tides is potentially enormous, although only a few installations have so far been built to exploit it. In theory at least, waves and currents could also provide almost unimaginable power, and the thermal differences in the ocean depths are another huge well of potential energy. But work on extracting it is still in the experimental stage.

Geothermal: The Earth's temperature rises by 1°C for every 30 metres descent, with much steeper temperature gradients in geologically active areas. El Salvador, for example, produces 39% of its electricity from geothermal power stations, whilst the USA, the world leader, produced 3,331 megawatts in 1993. Some of the oldest and most successful applications are in Iceland, where 86% of all households are heated by geothermal energy.

Biomass: The oldest of human fuels ranges from animal dung, still burned in cooking fires in much of North Africa and elsewhere, to sugar cane plantations feeding high-technology distilleries to produce ethanol for motor vehicle engines. In Brazil and South Africa, plant ethanol provides up to 25% of motor fuel. Throughout the developing world, most biomass energy comes from firewood: although accurate figures are impossible to obtain, it may yield as much as 10% of the world's total energy consumption.

Wind Power

World wind energy generating capacity, in megawatts

1980	10
1981	25
1982	90
1983	210
1984	600
1985	1,020
1986	1,270
1987	1,450
1988	1,580
1989	1,730
1990	1,930
1991	2,170
1992	2,510
1993	3,050
1994	3,710

Wind power is the fastest growing source of energy worldwide but still provides only 1% of the world's energy. Output grew by 33% in 1995.

CARTOGRAPHY BY PHILIP'S. COPYRIGHT GEORGE PHILIP LTD

Minerals

For more information:
10 Geology
39 Patterns of production
41 World shipping

The use of metals played a vital part in the evolving technologies of early peoples. Copper first came into use around 10,000 years ago, bronze about 5,000 years ago, and iron 3,300 years ago. In the early stages of the Industrial Revolution, the location of coal, iron ore and water power usually determined the location of new industries. But due to continuing improvements in transport, including oil pipelines, industries can now be located almost anywhere.

Minerals are distributed unevenly and some industrial countries, lacking their own mineral resources, import most of the raw materials they need. Some imports come from mineral-rich countries, such as Australia but others come from developing countries, especially in Africa and South America. Most of the developing countries export unprocessed ores, losing out on the much higher revenues gained from exporting metals.

Most minerals come from land deposits, because undersea deposits, with the exception of oil reserves under the continental shelves, have been regarded as inaccessible. But shortages of terrestrial minerals may one day encourage exploitation of the ocean floor.

Mineral Exports

Minerals and metals as a percentage of total exports (latest available year)

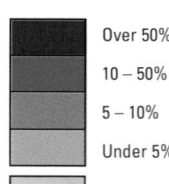

- Over 50%
- 10 – 50%
- 5 – 10%
- Under 5%
- No data available

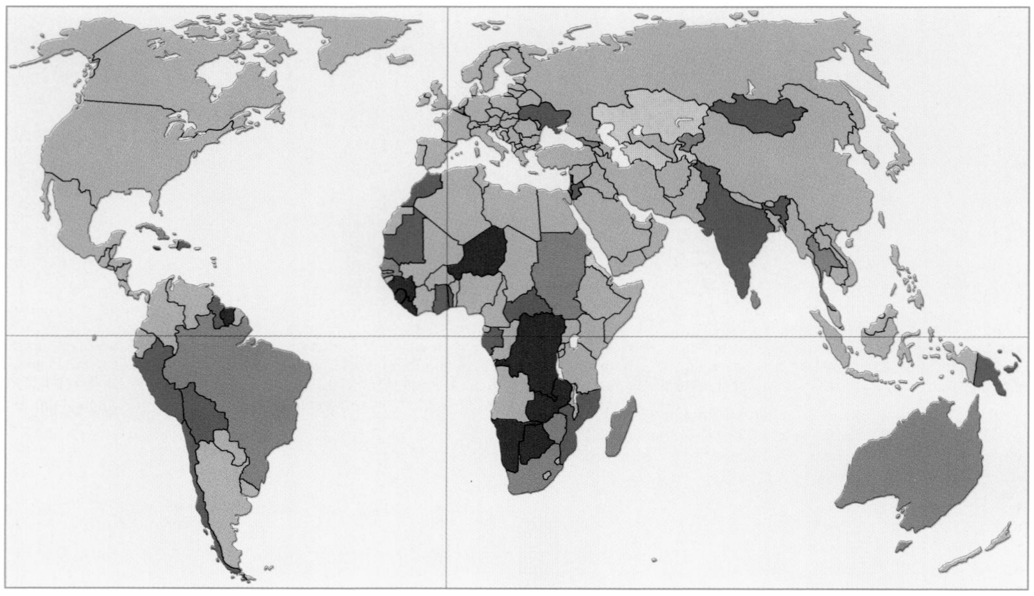

Uranium

In its pure state, uranium is an immensely heavy, white metal; but although spent uranium is employed as projectiles in anti-missile cannons, where its mass ensures a lethal punch, its main use is as a fuel in nuclear reactors, and in nuclear weaponry. Uranium is very scarce: the main source is the rare ore pitchblende, which itself contains only 0.2% uranium oxide. Only a minute fraction of that is the radioactive U^{235} isotope, though so-called breeder reactors can transmute the more common U^{238} into highly radioactive plutonium.

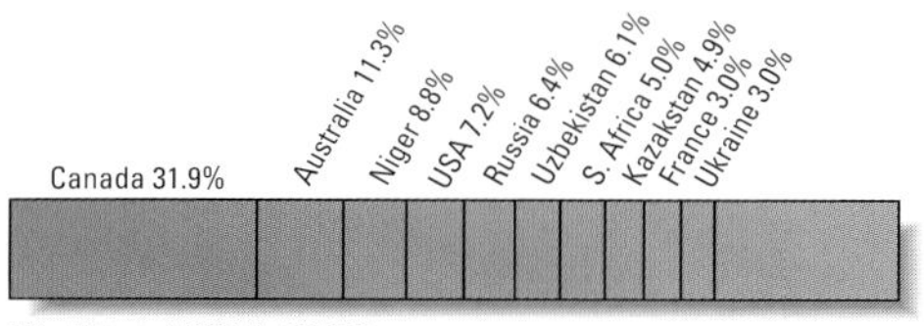
Canada 31.9%
Australia 11.3%
Niger 8.8%
USA 7.2%
Russia 6.4%
Uzbekistan 6.1%
S. Africa 5.0%
Kazakstan 4.9%
France 3.0%
Ukraine 3.0%

World total (1995): 32,976 tonnes

Metals

*** Figures for aluminium are for refined metal; all other figures refer to ore production.**

The world's leading producers of aluminium ore (bauxite) in 1995 were as follows:

1. Australia 41.9%
2. Papua New Guinea 14.3%
3. Jamaica 10.8%
4. Brazil 10.1%
5. Russia 6.7%
6. China 5.7%
7. India 5.0%
8. Surinam 2.8%
9. Venezuela 2.6%
10. Greece 1.9%

The figures shown above are in stark contrast to the figures showing aluminium production on the right. Australia, for example, produces 41.9% of the world's bauxite but only 5.9% of the aluminium metal. Papua New Guinea and Jamaica account for 25% of the bauxite mined but have no smelters and export virtually all of it to countries like the USA and Canada.

Aluminium: Produced mainly from its oxide, bauxite, which yields 25% of its weight in aluminium. The cost of refining and production is often too high for producer-countries to bear, so bauxite is largely exported. Lightweight and corrosion resistant, aluminium alloys are widely used in aircraft, vehicles, cans and packaging.

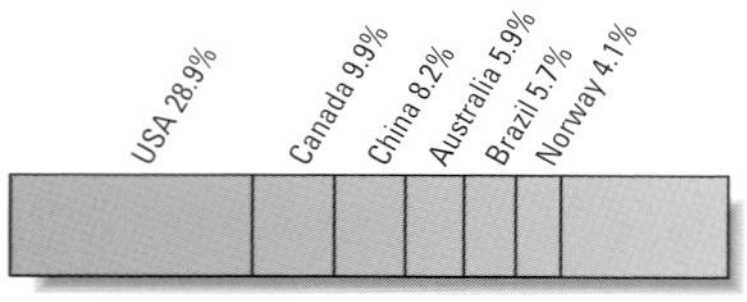
USA 28.9%
Canada 9.9%
China 8.2%
Australia 5.9%
Brazil 5.7%
Norway 4.1%

World total (1995): 22,706,000 tonnes *

Copper: Derived from low-yielding sulphide ores, copper is an important export for several developing countries. An excellent conductor of heat and electricity, it forms part of most electrical items, and is used in the manufacture of brass and bronze. Major importers include Japan and Germany.

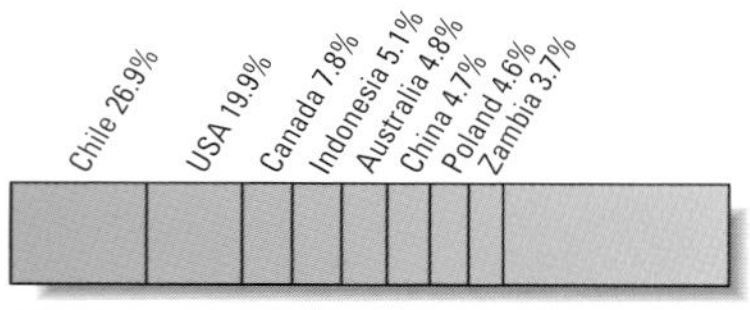
Chile 26.9%
USA 19.9%
Canada 7.8%
Indonesia 5.1%
Australia 4.8%
China 4.7%
Poland 4.6%
Zambia 3.7%

World total (1995): 9,311,000 tonnes *

Lead: A soft metal, obtained mainly from galena (lead sulphide), which occurs in veins associated with iron, zinc and silver sulphides. Its use in vehicle batteries accounts for the USA's prime consumer status; lead is also made into sheeting and piping. Its use as an additive to paints and petrol is decreasing.

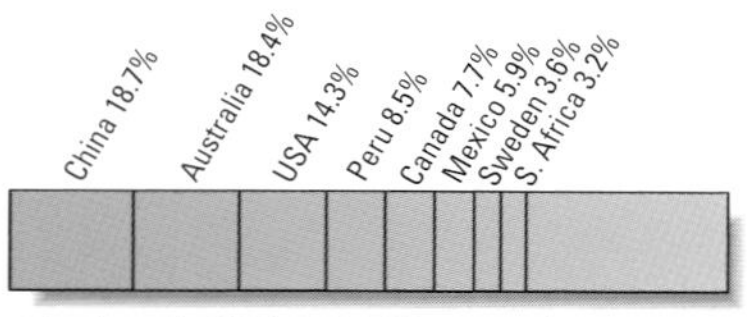
China 18.7%
Australia 18.4%
USA 14.3%
Peru 8.5%
Canada 7.7%
Mexico 5.9%
Sweden 3.6%
S. Africa 3.2%

World total (1995): 2,751,000 tonnes *

Mercury: The only metal that is liquid at normal temperatures, most is derived from its sulphide, cinnabar, found only in small quantities in volcanic areas. Apart from its value in thermometers and other instruments, most mercury production is used in anti-fungal and anti-fouling preparations, and to make detonators.

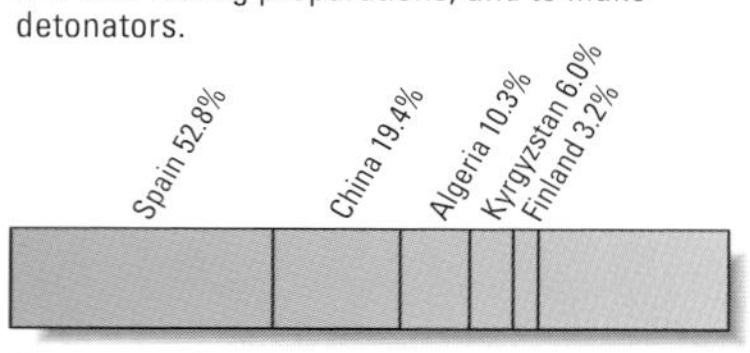
Spain 52.8%
China 19.4%
Algeria 10.3%
Kyrgyzstan 6.0%
Finland 3.2%

World total (1995): 2,837 tonnes *

Tin: Soft, pliable and non-toxic, used to coat 'tin' (tin-plated steel) cans, in the manufacture of foils and in alloys. The principal tin-bearing mineral is cassiterite (SnO_2), found in ore formed from molten rock. Producers and refiners were hit by a price collapse in 1991.

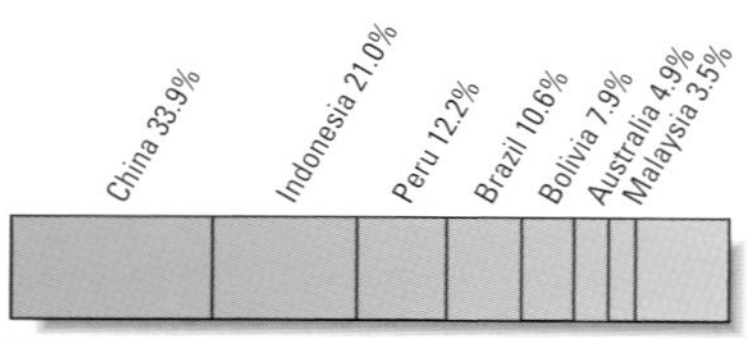
China 33.9%
Indonesia 21.0%
Peru 12.2%
Brazil 10.6%
Bolivia 7.9%
Australia 4.9%
Malaysia 3.5%

World total (1995): 182,518 tonnes *

Zinc: Often found in association with lead ores, zinc is highly resistant to corrosion, and about 40% of the refined metal is used to plate sheet steel, particularly vehicle bodies – a process known as galvanizing. Zinc is also used in dry batteries, paints and dyes.

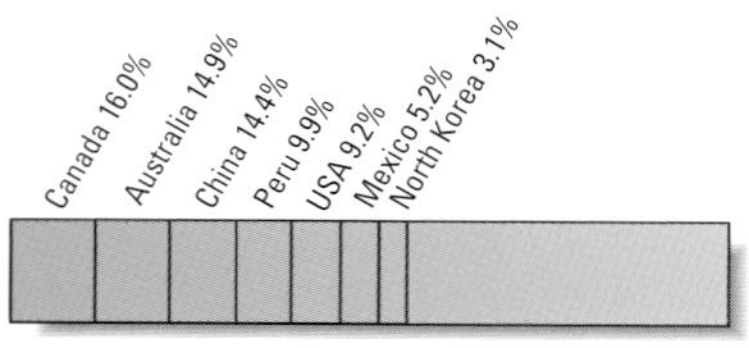
Canada 16.0%
Australia 14.9%
China 14.4%
Peru 9.9%
USA 9.2%
Mexico 5.2%
North Korea 3.1%

World total (1995): 6,953,000 tonnes *

Gold: Regarded for centuries as the most valuable metal in the world and used to make coins, gold is still recognized as the monetary standard. A soft metal, it is alloyed to make jewellery; the electronics industry values its corrosion resistance and conductivity.

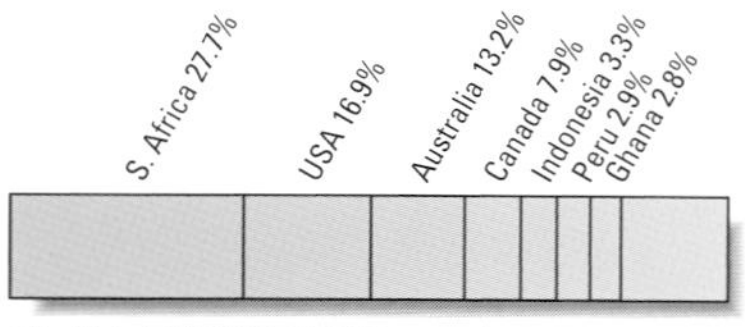
S. Africa 27.7%
USA 16.9%
Australia 13.2%
Canada 7.9%
Indonesia 3.3%
Peru 2.9%
Ghana 2.8%

World total (1995): 1,889 tonnes *

Silver: Most silver comes from ores mined and processed for other metals (including lead and copper). Pure or alloyed with harder metals, it is used for jewellery and ornaments. Industrial use includes dentistry, electronics, photography and as a chemical catalyst.

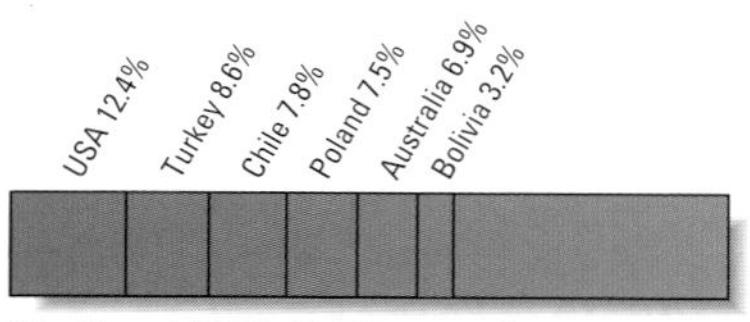
USA 12.4%
Turkey 8.6%
Chile 7.8%
Poland 7.5%
Australia 6.9%
Bolivia 3.2%

World total (1995): 13,266 tonnes *

Diamond

Most of the world's diamond is found in kimberlite, or 'blue ground', a basic peridotite rock; erosion may wash the diamond from its kimberlite matrix and deposit it with sand or gravel on river beds. Only a small proportion of the world's diamond, the most flawless, is cut into gemstones – 'diamonds'; most is used in industry, where the material's remarkable hardness and abrasion resistance finds a use in cutting tools, drills and dies, as well as in styluses. Australia, not among the top 12 producers at the beginning of the 1980s, had by 1986 become world leader and by 1993 was the source of 40.6% of world production. The other main producers were Congo (then Zaïre) (16.3%), Botswana (14.6%), Russia (11.4%) and South Africa (9.7%). Between them, these five nations accounted for over 82% of the world total of 100,850,000 carats.

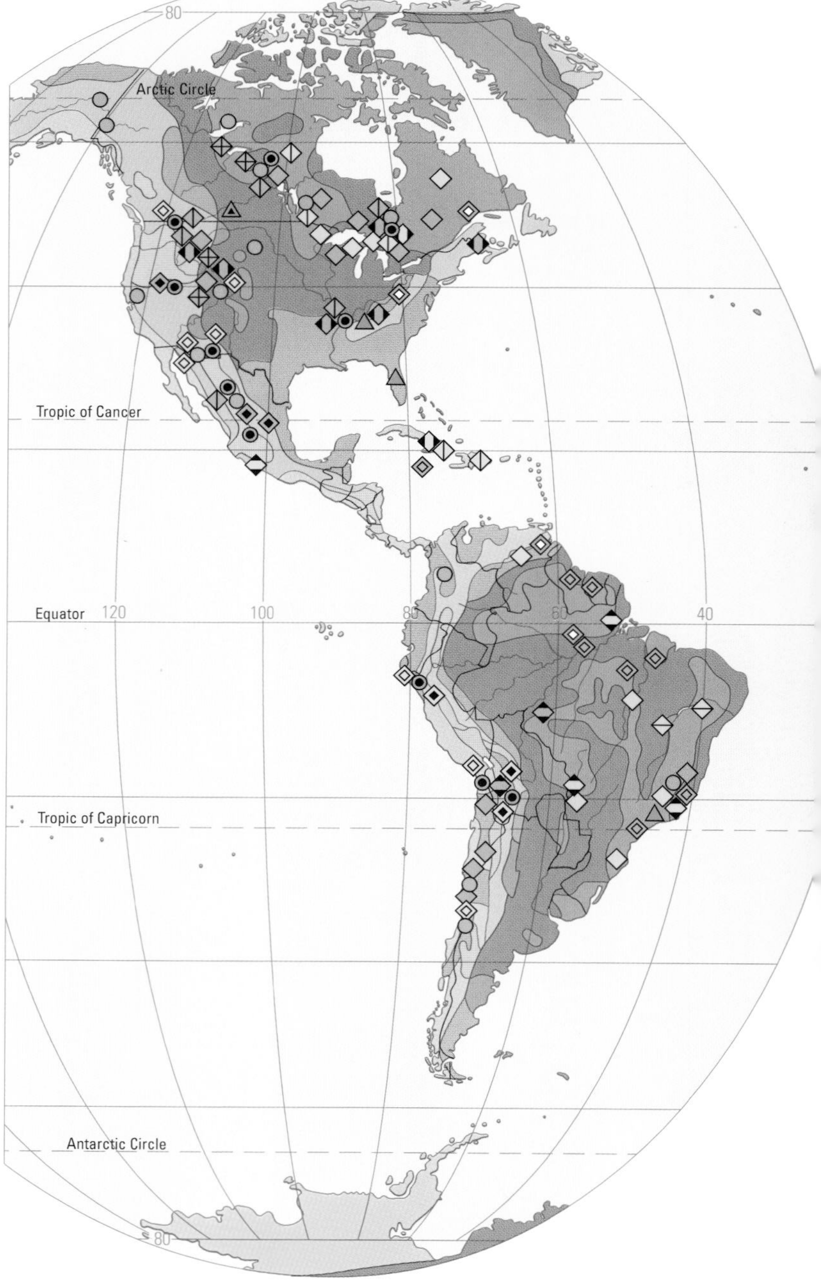
80
Arctic Circle
Tropic of Cancer
Equator
120
100
80
60
40
Tropic of Capricorn
Antarctic Circle
80

CARTOGRAPHY BY PHILIP'S. COPYRIGHT GEORGE PHILIP LTD

Strategic Minerals

Ever since the art of high-temperature smelting was discovered, some time in the second millennium BC, iron has been by far the most important metal known to man. The earliest iron ploughs transformed primitive agriculture and led to the first human population explosion, while iron weapons – or the lack of them – ensured the rise or fall of entire cultures.

Widely distributed around the world, iron ores usually contain 25–60% iron; blast furnaces process the raw product into pig-iron, which is then alloyed with carbon and other minerals to produce steels of various qualities. From the time of the Industrial Revolution, steel has been almost literally the backbone of modern civilization, the prime structural material on which all else is built.

Iron smelting usually developed close to the sources of ore and, later, to the coalfields that fuelled the furnaces. Today, most ore comes from a few richly-endowed locations where large-scale mining is possible. Iron and steel plants are generally built at coastal sites so that giant ore carriers, which account for a sizeable proportion of the world's merchant fleet, can easily discharge their cargoes.

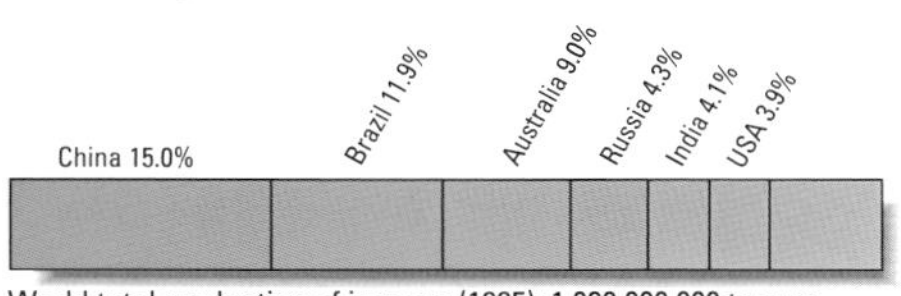

China 15.0%
Brazil 11.9%
Australia 9.0%
Russia 4.3%
India 4.1%
USA 3.9%

World total production of iron ore (1995): 1,020,000,000 tonnes

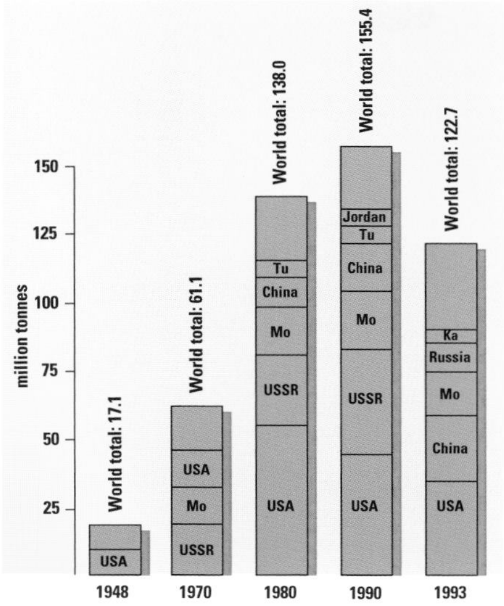

million tonnes
150
125
100
75
50
25
World total: 17.1
World total: 61.1
World total: 138.0
World total: 155.4
World total: 122.7
USA
USSR
Mo
USA
USA
USSR
Mo
China
Tu
USA
USSR
Mo
China
Tu
Jordan
USA
China
Mo
Russia
Ka
1948
1970
1980
1990
1993

World production of phosphates in millions of tonnes (1993). Phosphate production is vital to the economies of several small countries. Nauru, for example, is heavily dependent on phosphate exports – the island has one of the world's richest deposits. In 1994, 613,000 tonnes were mined, employing 1,000 people. In Togo, earnings from phosphate exports have superseded all agricultural exports.

Percentage of total world phosphate production (1994)

1. USA	32.4%	7. Israel	3.1%
2. China	20.2%	8. Brazil	2.6%
3. Morocco	15.4%	9. South Africa	2.0%
4. Russia	6.2%	10. Togo	1.7%
5. Tunisia	4.4%	11. Kazakstan	1.6%
6. Jordan	3.3%	12. Senegal	1.4%

World production of pig-iron and ferro-alloys (1995). All countries with an annual output of more than 1 million tonnes are shown

Total world production: 690 million tonnes

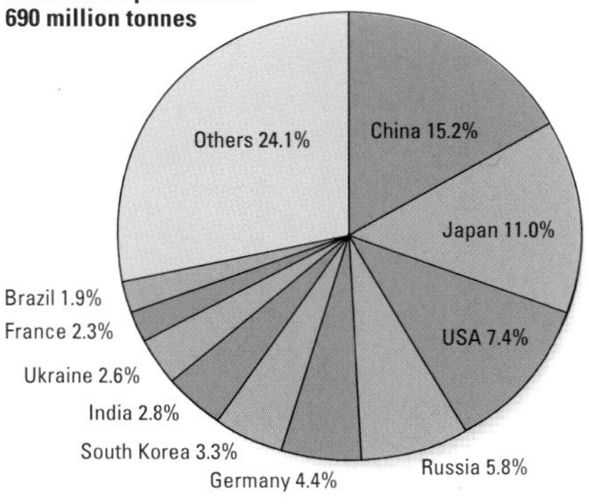

Others 24.1%
China 15.2%
Japan 11.0%
USA 7.4%
Russia 5.8%
Germany 4.4%
South Korea 3.3%
India 2.8%
Ukraine 2.6%
France 2.3%
Brazil 1.9%

Manganese: In its pure state, manganese is a hard, brittle metal. Alloyed with chrome, iron and nickel, it produces abrasion-resistant steels; manganese-aluminium alloys are light but tough. Found in batteries and inks, manganese is also used in glass production. Manganese ores are frequently found in the same location as sedimentary iron ores. Pyrolusite (MnO_2) and psilomelane are the main economically-exploitable sources.

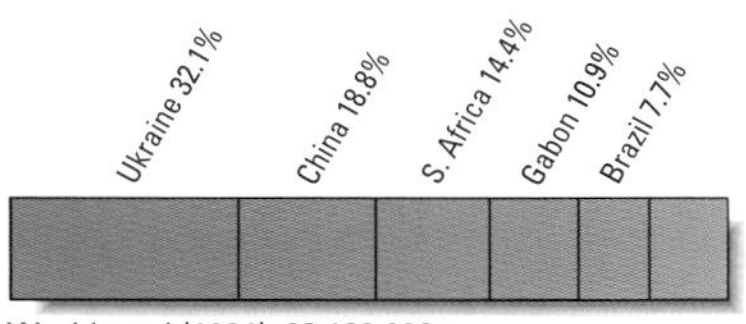

Ukraine 32.1%
China 18.8%
S. Africa 14.4%
Gabon 10.9%
Brazil 7.7%

World total (1994): 22,180,000 tonnes

Chromium: Most of the world's chromium production is alloyed with iron and other metals to produce steels with various different properties. Combined with iron, nickel, cobalt and tungsten, chromium produces an exceptionally hard steel, resistant to heat; chrome steels are used for many household items where utility must be matched with appearance – cutlery, for example. Chromium is also used in production of refractory bricks, and its salts for tanning and dyeing leather and cloth.

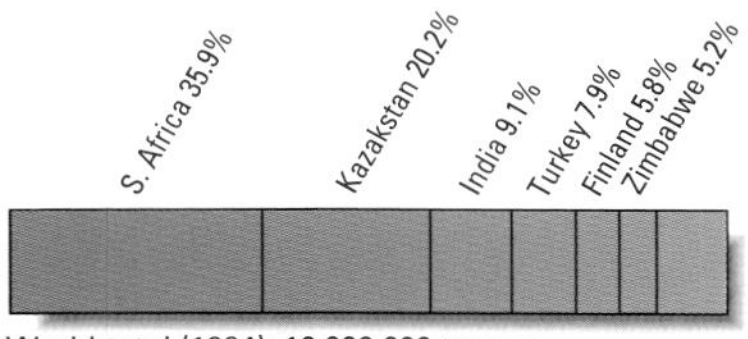

S. Africa 35.9%
Kazakstan 20.2%
India 9.1%
Turkey 7.9%
Finland 5.8%
Zimbabwe 5.2%

World total (1994): 10,000,000 tonnes

Nickel: Combined with chrome and iron, nickel produces stainless and high-strength steels; similar alloys go to make magnets and electrical heating elements. Nickel combined with copper is widely used to make coins; cupro-nickel alloy is very resistant to corrosion. Its ores yield only modest quantities of nickel – 0.5% to 3.0% – but also contain copper, iron and small amounts of precious metals. Japan, USA, UK, Germany and France are the principal importers.

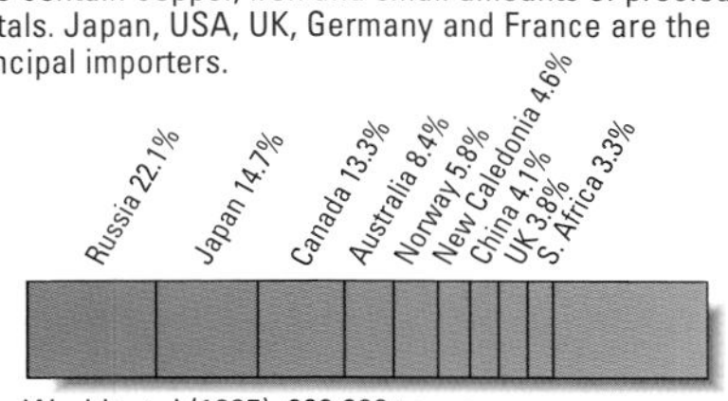

Russia 22.1%
Japan 14.7%
Canada 13.3%
Australia 8.4%
Norway 5.8%
New Caledonia 4.6%
China 4.1%
UK 3.8%
S. Africa 3.3%

World total (1995): 920,000 tonnes

Distribution of Minerals

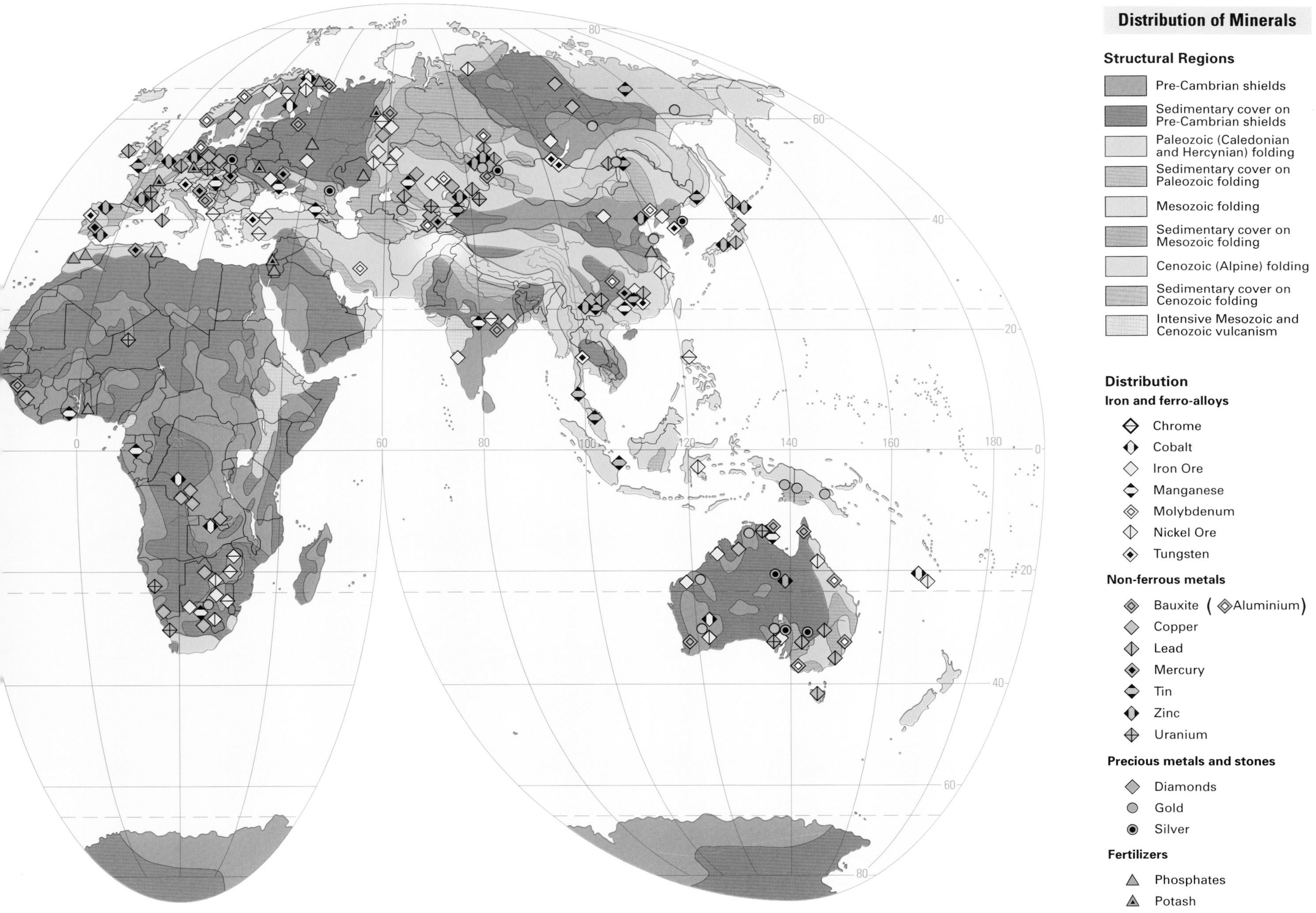

Structural Regions
Pre-Cambrian shields
Sedimentary cover on Pre-Cambrian shields
Paleozoic (Caledonian and Hercynian) folding
Sedimentary cover on Paleozoic folding
Mesozoic folding
Sedimentary cover on Mesozoic folding
Cenozoic (Alpine) folding
Sedimentary cover on Cenozoic folding
Intensive Mesozoic and Cenozoic vulcanism
Distribution
Iron and ferro-alloys
Chrome
Cobalt
Iron Ore
Manganese
Molybdenum
Nickel Ore
Tungsten
Non-ferrous metals
Bauxite (Aluminium)
Copper
Lead
Mercury
Tin
Zinc
Uranium
Precious metals and stones
Diamonds
Gold
Silver
Fertilizers
Phosphates
Potash

CARTOGRAPHY BY PHILIP'S. COPYRIGHT GEORGE PHILIP LTD

Manufacturing

For more information:

18 Water utilization
32 Land use and economy
36 Mineral production
37 Iron and ferro-alloys
40 Trading nations
Major exports
Traded products

The Industrial Revolution which began in Britain in the late 18th century, represented a major technological advance in the evolution of human society. It enabled a group of countries to become prosperous by replacing expensive human labour with increasingly sophisticated machinery. In economic terms, manufacturing is the transformation of raw materials, energy, labour and machines into finished goods, which have a higher value than the various elements used in production.

The economies of countries can be compared by reference to their per capita Gross National Products (or per capita GNPs), namely, the total value of goods and services produced in a country in a year, divided by the population.

The industrialized, or developed, countries accounted for 16% of the world's population in 1997 with an average per capita GNP of US $25,700. On the other hand, developing countries, with comparatively small industrial sectors and low-income economies, accounted for 35% of the world's population, with an average per capita GNP of just $350.

Kenya, with its low-income economy, had a per capita GNP in 1998 of $330. Agriculture employs 77% of the people, industry 8% and services 15%. The major industries are the processing of agricultural products and import substitution (the manufacture of such necessities as cement, footwear and textiles). Heavy industry plays a comparatively small part in the economy. By contrast, Germany, a major industrialized nation, had a per capita GNP in 1998 of $25,850. Agriculture employs only 1% of the population, with 32% in industry, and 67% in services. Germany's industrial sector differs greatly from Kenya's, with an emphasis on the manufacture of vehicles, machinery and chemicals.

Since the 1970s, some former developing countries in Asia have been transformed by rapid industrialization. These 'economic tigers', including China, Malaysia, South Korea, Singapore, Taiwan and Thailand, owe their success to low labour costs and substantial investment in education, together with advances in telecommunications, transport and computers, which have made technology more readily transferable around the world than ever before. They have also benefited from economic freedom and trade liberalization.

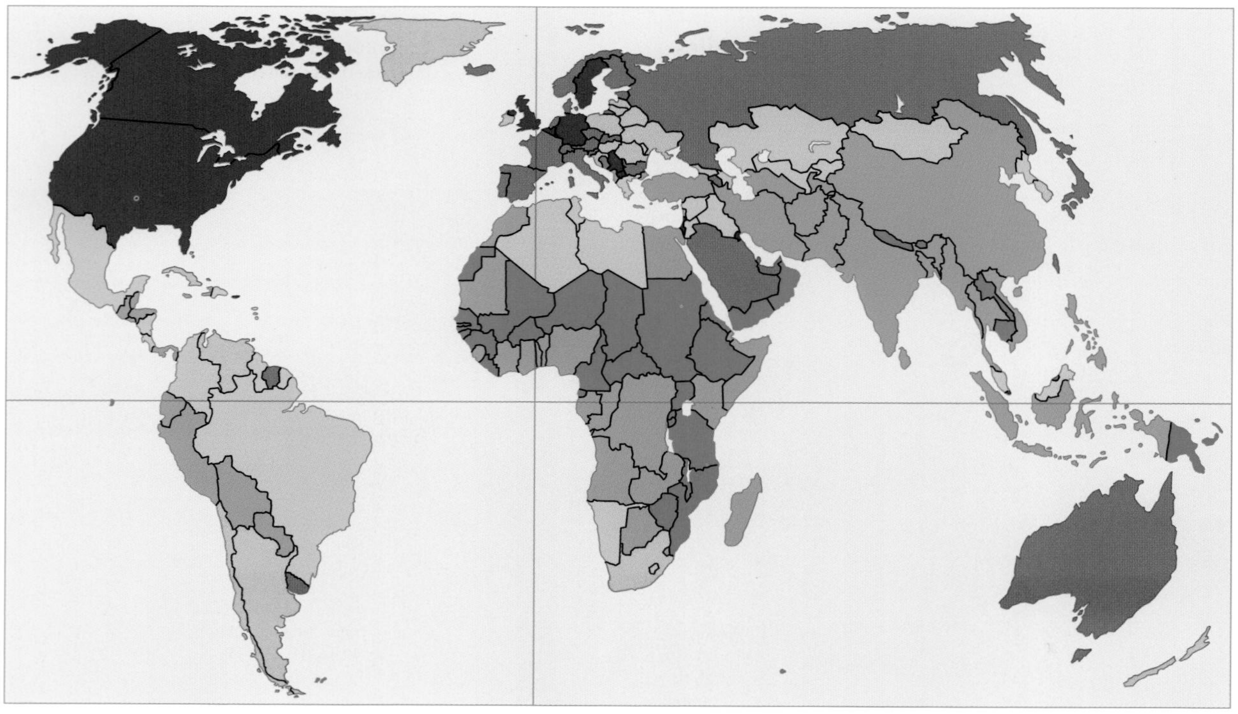

Employment

The number of workers employed in manufacturing for every 100 workers engaged in agriculture (latest available year)

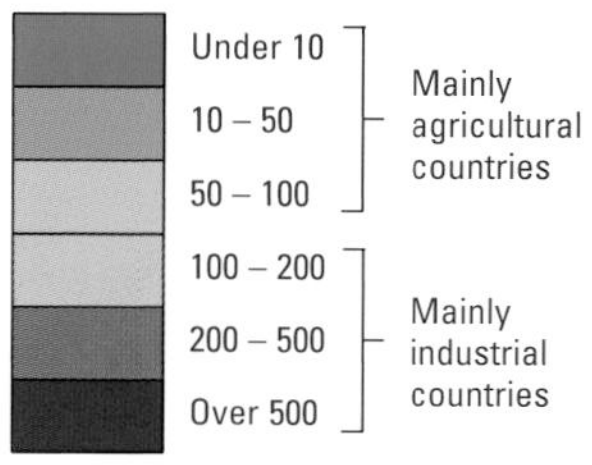
Under 10
10 – 50
50 – 100
Mainly agricultural countries
100 – 200
200 – 500
Over 500
Mainly industrial countries

Selected countries (latest available year)

Singapore	8,860
UK	1,270
Belgium	820
Germany	800
Kuwait	767
Bahrain	660
USA	657
Israel	633

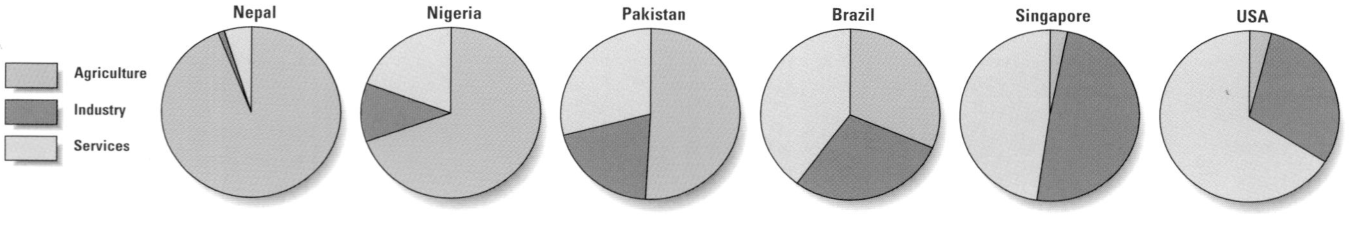
Agriculture
Industry
Services
Nepal
Nigeria
Pakistan
Brazil
Singapore
USA

Division of Employment

Distribution of workers between agriculture, industry and services, selected countries (latest available year)

The six countries selected illustrate the usual stages of economic development, from dependence on agriculture through industrial growth to the expansion of the service sector.

The Workforce

Percentages of men and women between 15 and 64 in employment, selected countries (latest available year)

The figures include employees and the self-employed, who in developing countries are often subsistence farmers. People in full-time education are excluded. Because of the population age structure in developing countries, the employed population has to support a far larger number of non-workers than its industrial equivalent. For example, more than 52% of Kenya's people are under 15, an age group that makes up less than a tenth of the UK population.

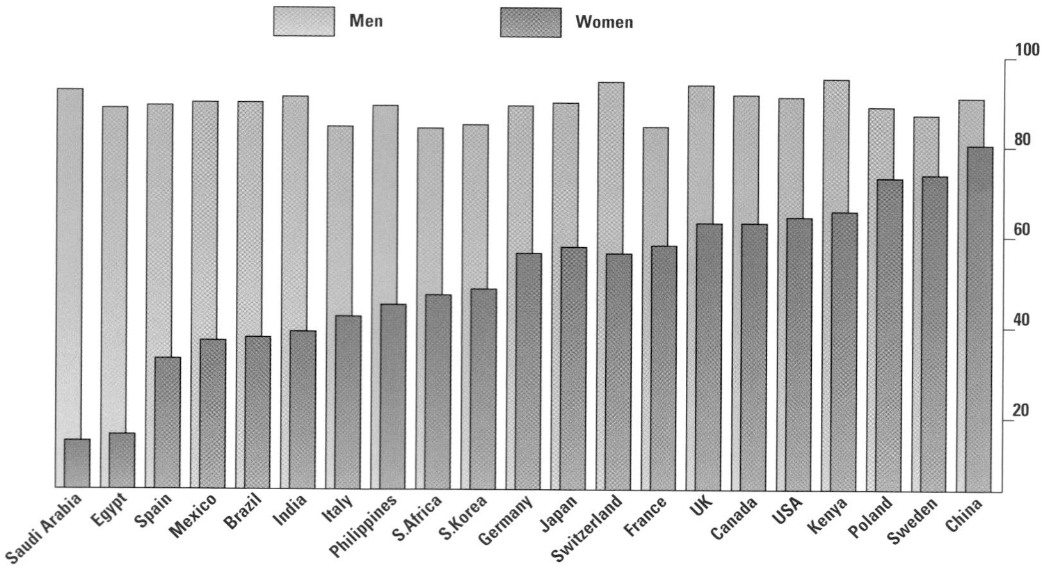
Men
Women
100
80
60
40
20
Saudi Arabia
Egypt
Spain
Mexico
Brazil
India
Italy
Philippines
S.Africa
S.Korea
Germany
Japan
Switzerland
France
UK
Canada
USA
Kenya
Poland
Sweden
China

Wealth Creation

The Gross National Product (GNP) of the world's largest economies, US $ million (1998)

1.	USA	7,922,651	21.	Austria	217,163
2.	Japan	4,089,910	22.	Turkey	200,505
3.	Germany	2,122,673	23.	Saudi Arabia	186,000
4.	Italy	1,666,178	24.	Denmark	176,374
5.	France	1,466,014	25.	Hong Kong	158,286
6.	UK	1,263,777	26.	Norway	152,082
7.	China	928,950	27.	Poland	150,798
8.	Botswana	758,043	28.	Indonesia	138,501
9.	Canada	612,332	29.	Thailand	134,433
10.	Spain	553,690	30.	Finland	124,293
11.	India	421,259	31.	Greece	122,880
12.	Netherlands	388,682	32.	South Africa	119,001
13.	Mexico	380,917	33.	Iran	109,645
14.	Australia	380,625	34.	Portugal	106,376
15.	South Korea	369,890	35.	Colombia	106,090
16.	Russia	337,914	36.	Israel	95,179
17.	Argentina	324,084	37.	Singapore	95,095
18.	Switzerland	284,808	38.	Venezuela	81,347
19.	Belgium	259,045	39.	Malaysia	79,848
20.	Sweden	226,861	40.	Egypt	79,208

Patterns of Production

Breakdown of industrial output by value, selected countries (latest available year)

	Food & agric. products	Textiles & clothing	Machinery & transport	Chemicals	Other
Algeria	26%	20%	11%	1%	41%
Argentina	24%	10%	16%	12%	37%
Australia	18%	7%	21%	8%	45%
Austria	17%	8%	25%	6%	43%
Belgium	19%	8%	23%	13%	36%
Brazil	15%	12%	24%	9%	40%
Burkina Faso	62%	18%	2%	1%	17%
Canada	15%	7%	25%	9%	44%
Denmark	22%	6%	23%	10%	39%
Egypt	20%	27%	13%	10%	31%
Finland	13%	6%	24%	7%	50%
France	18%	7%	33%	9%	33%
Germany	12%	5%	38%	10%	36%
Greece	20%	22%	14%	7%	38%
Hungary	6%	11%	37%	11%	35%
India	11%	16%	26%	15%	32%
Indonesia	23%	11%	10%	10%	47%
Iran	13%	22%	22%	7%	36%
Ireland	28%	7%	20%	15%	28%
Israel	13%	10%	28%	8%	42%
Italy	7%	13%	32%	10%	38%
Japan	10%	6%	38%	10%	37%
Kenya	35%	12%	14%	9%	29%
Malaysia	21%	5%	23%	14%	37%
Mexico	24%	12%	14%	12%	39%
Netherlands	19%	4%	28%	11%	38%
New Zealand	26%	10%	16%	6%	43%
Norway	21%	3%	26%	7%	44%
Pakistan	34%	21%	8%	12%	25%
Philippines	40%	7%	7%	10%	35%
Poland	15%	16%	30%	6%	33%
Portugal	17%	22%	16%	8%	38%
Singapore	6%	5%	46%	8%	36%
South Africa	14%	8%	17%	11%	49%
South Korea	15%	17%	24%	9%	35%
Spain	17%	9%	22%	9%	43%
Sweden	10%	2%	35%	8%	44%
Thailand	30%	17%	14%	6%	33%
Turkey	20%	14%	15%	8%	43%
UK	14%	6%	32%	11%	36%
USA	12%	5%	35%	10%	38%
Venezuela	23%	8%	9%	11%	49%

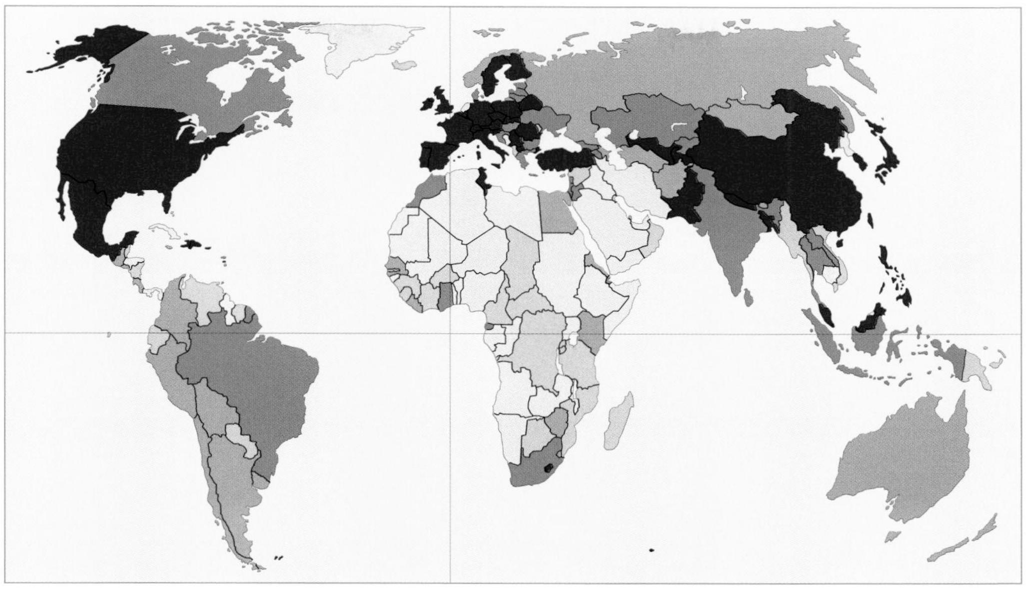

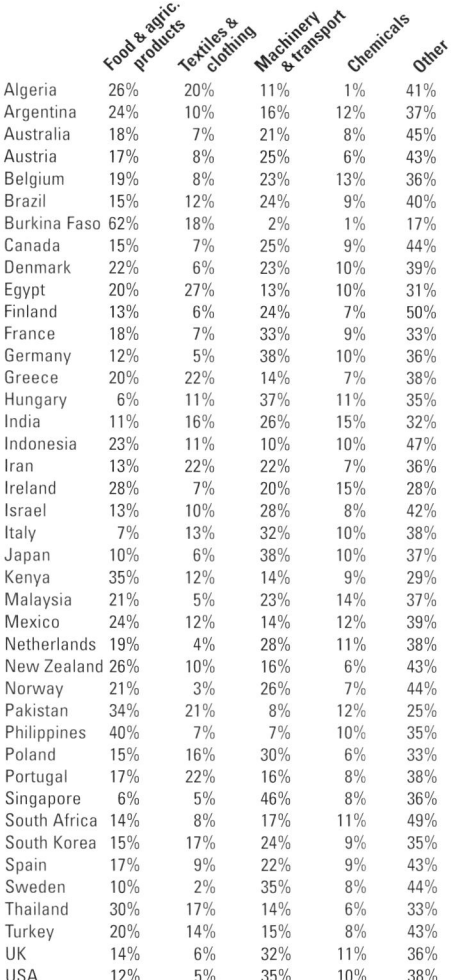

Industry and Trade

Manufactured goods (including machinery and transport) as a percentage of total exports (1996)

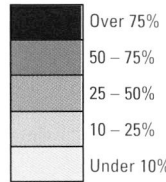

- Over 75%
- 50 – 75%
- 25 – 50%
- 10 – 25%
- Under 10%

The Far East and South-east Asia (Japan 98%, Macau 96%, Taiwan 95%, Hong Kong [now part of China] 94%, South Korea 94%) are most dominant, but many countries in Europe (e.g. Slovenia 93%) are also heavily dependent on manufactured goods.

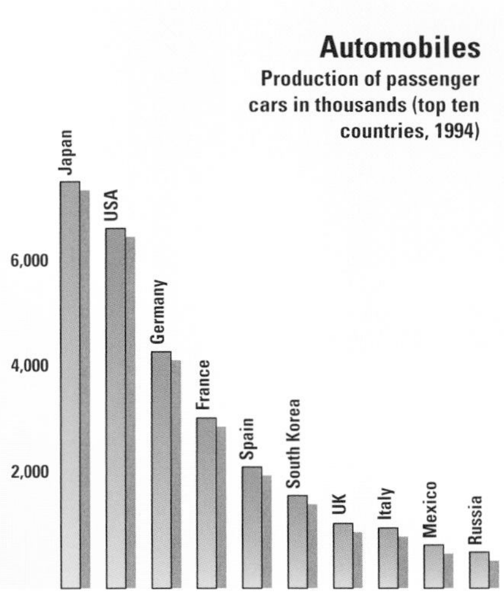

Automobiles

Production of passenger cars in thousands (top ten countries, 1994)

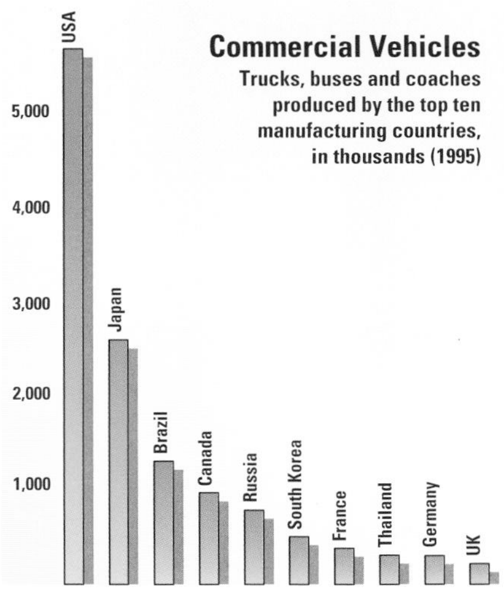

Commercial Vehicles

Trucks, buses and coaches produced by the top ten manufacturing countries, in thousands (1995)

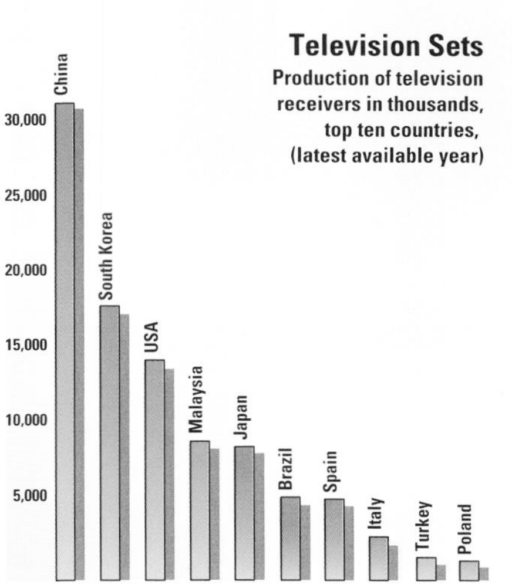

Television Sets

Production of television receivers in thousands, top ten countries, (latest available year)

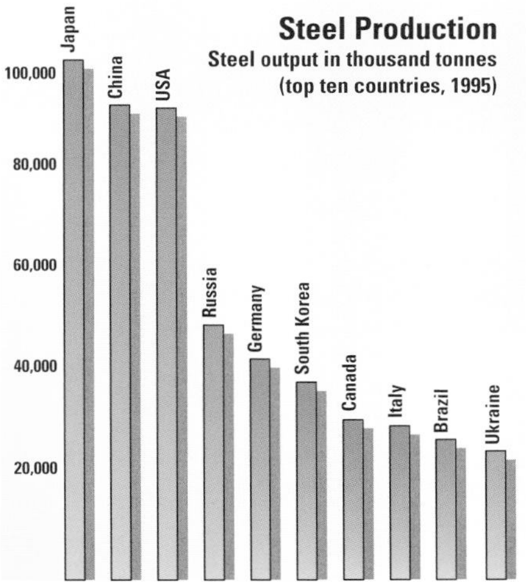

Steel Production

Steel output in thousand tonnes (top ten countries, 1995)

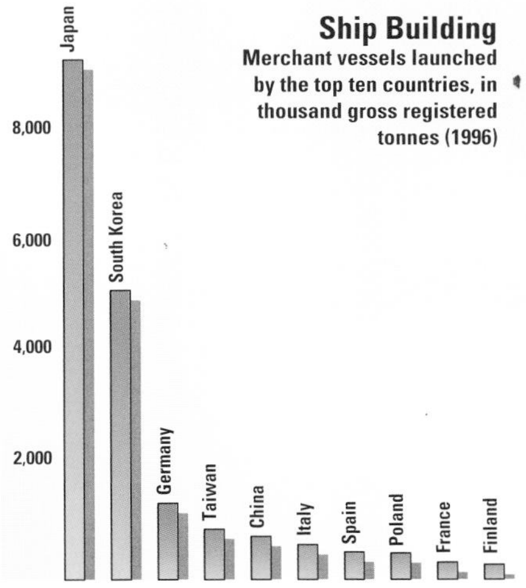

Ship Building

Merchant vessels launched by the top ten countries, in thousand gross registered tonnes (1996)

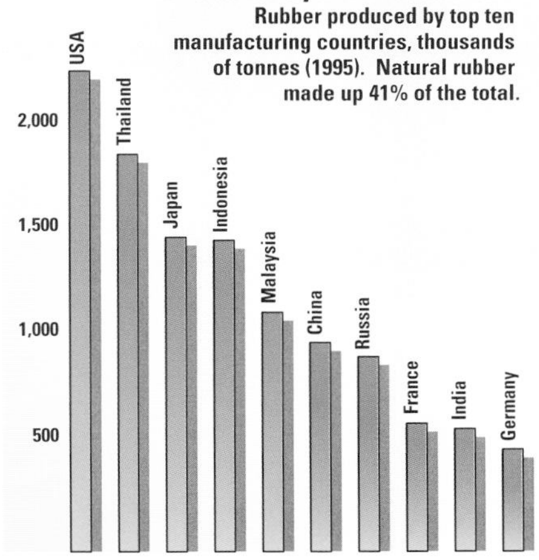

Natural & Synthetic Rubber

Rubber produced by top ten manufacturing countries, thousands of tonnes (1995). Natural rubber made up 41% of the total.

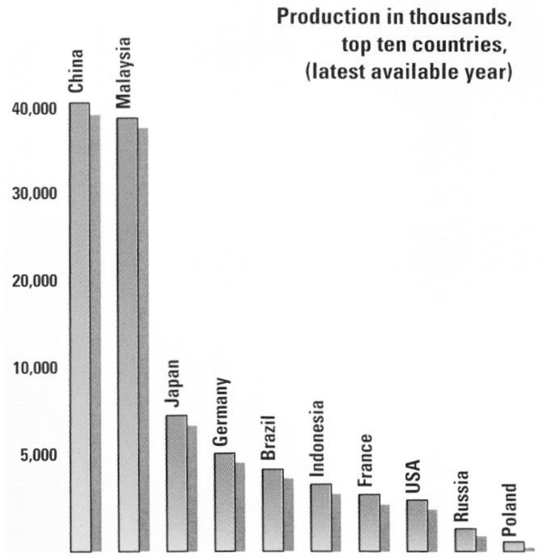

Radio Receivers

Production in thousands, top ten countries, (latest available year)

Industrial Output

Industrial output (mining, manufacturing, construction, energy and water production), US $ billion (1995)

1.	Japan	1,941	21.	Sweden	73
2.	USA	1,808	22.	Saudi Arabia	67
3.	Germany	780	=	Thailand	67
4.	France	415	24.	Mexico	65
5.	UK	354	25.	Turkey	51
6.	Italy	337	26.	Denmark	50
7.	China	335	27.	Finland	46
8.	Brazil	255	=	Poland	46
9.	South Korea	196	29.	Norway	44
10.	Spain	187	30.	Malaysia	37
11.	Canada	174	=	Portugal	37
12.	Russia	131	32.	Ukraine	34
13.	Netherlands	107	33.	Greece	33
14.	Australia	98	34.	Singapore	30
15.	Switzerland	96	35.	Venezuela	29
16.	India	94	=	Israel	29
17.	Argentina	87	37.	Chile	24
18.	Belgium	83	=	Colombia	24
=	Indonesia	83	=	Hong Kong	24
20.	Austria	79	=	Philippines	24

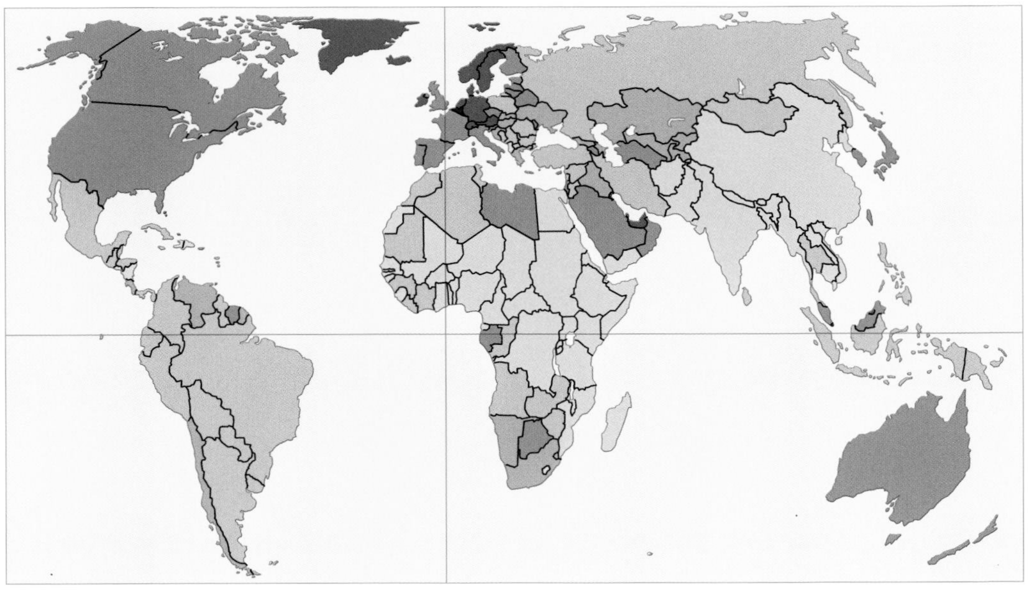

Exports Per Capita

Value of exports in US $, divided by total population (latest available year)

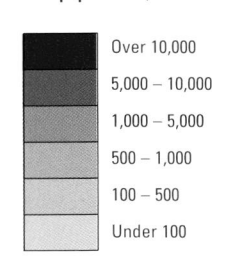

- Over 10,000
- 5,000 – 10,000
- 1,000 – 5,000
- 500 – 1,000
- 100 – 500
- Under 100

[UK 3,135] [USA 1,967]

Highest per capita exports (1993)

Singapore	25,787
Hong Kong	22,339
Benelux	12,295
Brunei	8,778
Netherlands	8,578
Switzerland	8,457

Trade

For more information:

31 International organizations
35 Fuel exports
Movements of oil
36 Mineral exports
39 Industry and trade
Exports per capita
46 Tourism

Trade played a vital role in the growth of early civilizations and it was later a spur to European exploration and colonization. The colonial powers grew rich by exporting cheap manufactures, such as clothing and footwear, while obtaining primary products from their colonies.

From the late 19th century to the early 1950s, as transport technology improved, primary products, especially oil in the later stages of this period, dominated world trade. However, since that time, manufactures have become the chief commodities in world trade, which is dominated by the industrialized countries. Nearly half of all world trade flows between the developed market economies of the European Union, the United States and Japan, although the Asian 'tiger economies', notably Singapore, South Korea, Taiwan, Malaysia and Thailand, have increased their share in recent years. Recent predictions suggest that the next 'tigers' might include Argentina and Chile in South America, Indonesia, the Philippines and Vietnam in Asia, and the Czech Republic and Poland in Europe.

There is little trade between developing countries, although some mineral- and oil-rich nations obtain a high proportion of their GNP from export sales. Growth in world trade is regarded as a sign of economic health, as is a favourable balance of trade (or trade surplus) in any country.

World Trade

Percentage share of total world exports by value (1996)

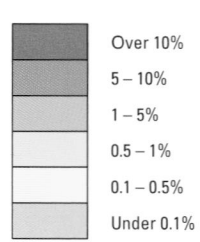

Over 10%
5 – 10%
1 – 5%
0.5 – 1%
0.1 – 0.5%
Under 0.1%

The Main Trading Nations

The imports and exports of the top ten trading nations as a percentage of world trade (1994). Each country's trade in manufactured goods is shown in dark blue. The graph shows that, in 1994, virtually all of Japan's imports and exports were manufactured goods.

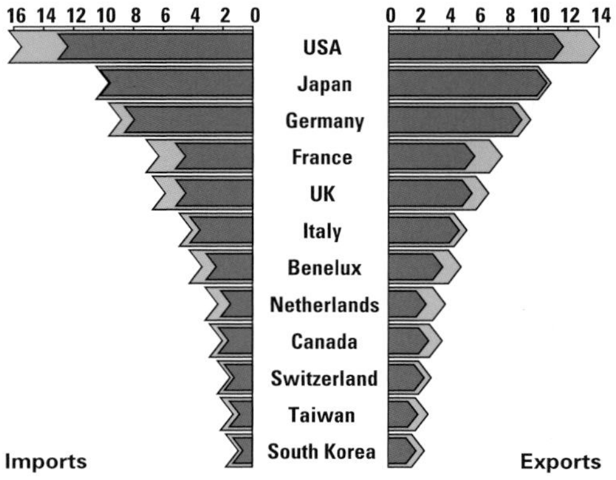
16 14 12 10 8 6 4 2 0
0 2 4 6 8 10 12 14
USA
Japan
Germany
France
UK
Italy
Benelux
Netherlands
Canada
Switzerland
Taiwan
South Korea
Imports
Exports

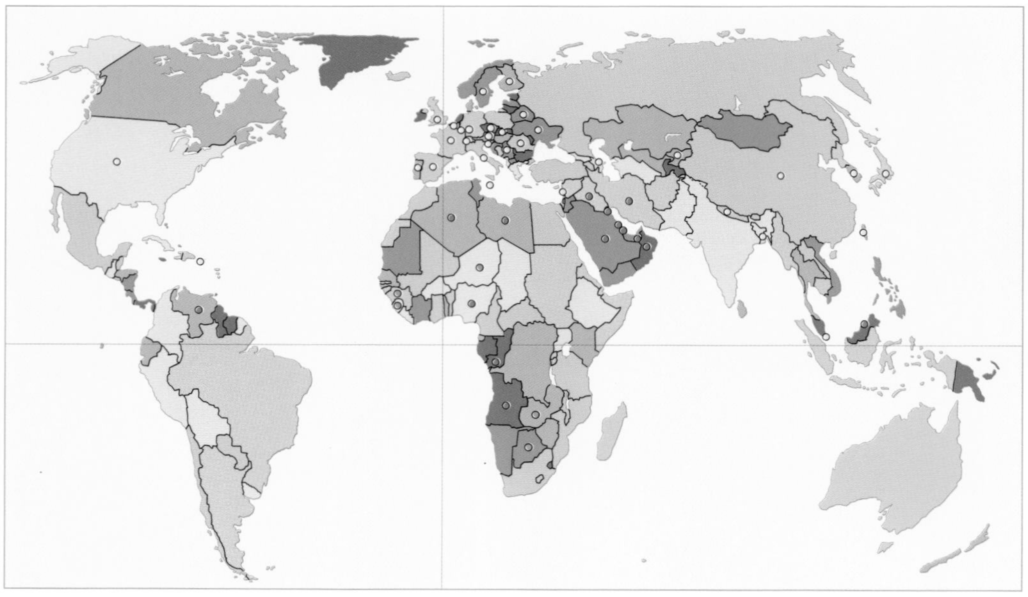

Dependence on Trade

Value of exports as a percentage of Gross Domestic Product (1997)

Over 50% GDP from exports
40 – 50% GDP from exports
30 – 40% GDP from exports
20 – 30% GDP from exports
10 – 20% GDP from exports
Under 10% GDP from exports

Most dependent on industrial exports (over 75% of total exports)
Most dependent on fuel exports (over 75% of total exports)
Most dependent on metal and mineral exports (over 75% of total exports)

Major Exports

Leading manufactured items and their exporters, by percentage of world total in US $ (latest available year)

Aircraft

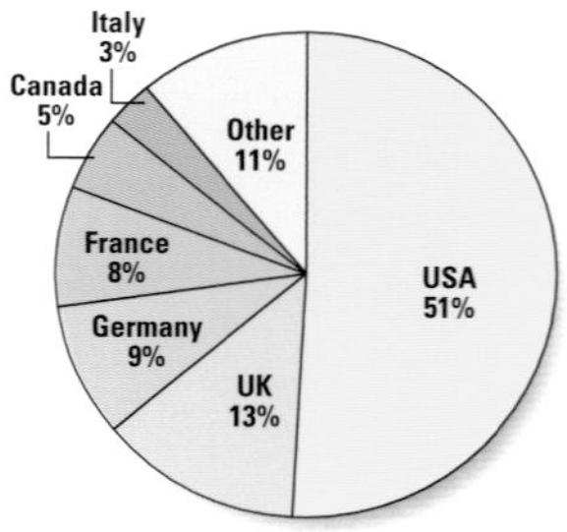
Italy 3%
Canada 5%
Other 11%
France 8%
Germany 9%
UK 13%
USA 51%

Telecommunications Gear

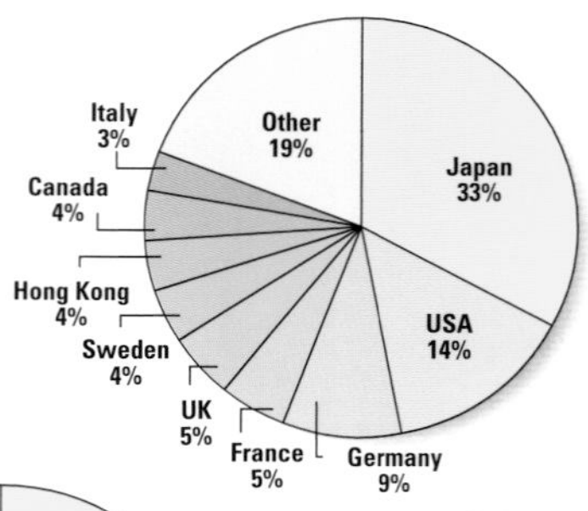
Italy 3%
Other 19%
Canada 4%
Japan 33%
Hong Kong 4%
Sweden 4%
USA 14%
UK 5%
France 5%
Germany 9%

Data Processing Equipment

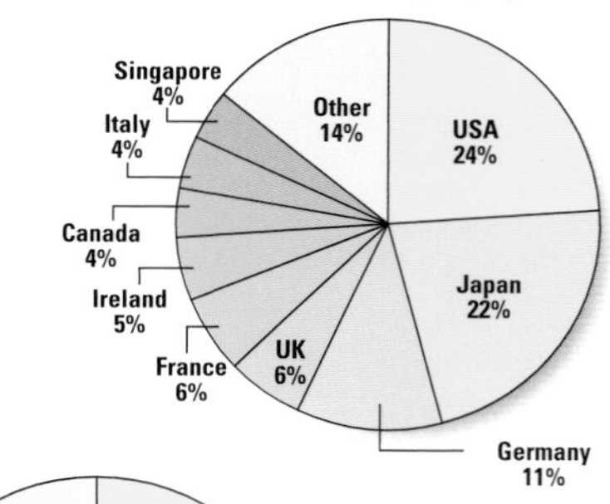
Singapore 4%
Italy 4%
Other 14%
USA 24%
Canada 4%
Ireland 5%
France 6%
UK 6%
Japan 22%
Germany 11%

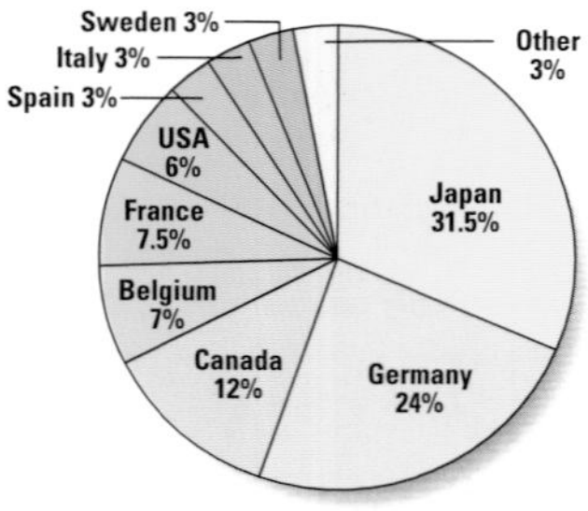
Sweden 3%
Italy 3%
Spain 3%
Other 3%
USA 6%
France 7.5%
Belgium 7%
Canada 12%
Germany 24%
Japan 31.5%

Automobiles

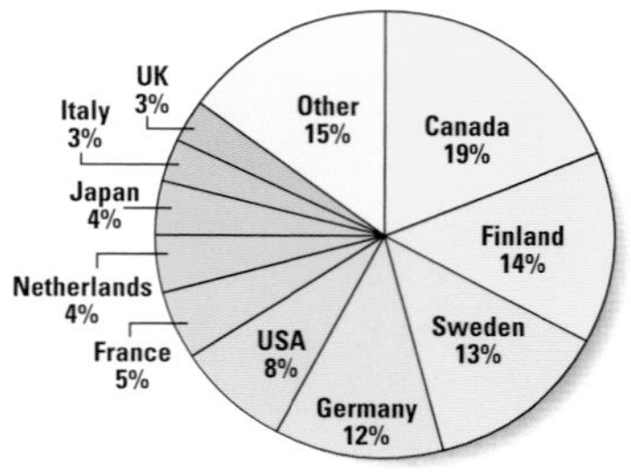
UK 3%
Italy 3%
Other 15%
Canada 19%
Japan 4%
Finland 14%
Netherlands 4%
France 5%
USA 8%
Sweden 13%
Germany 12%

Paper and Board

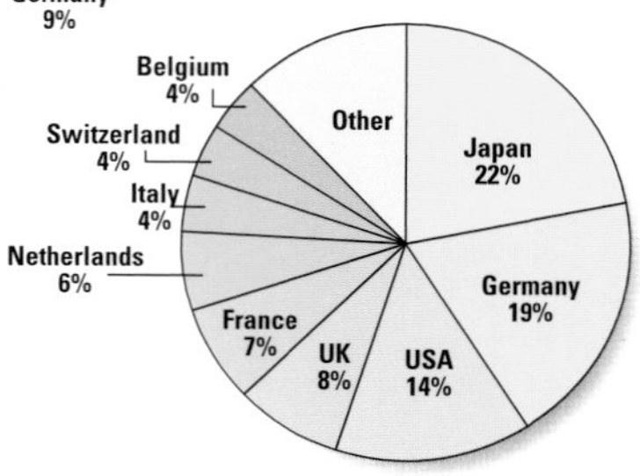
Belgium 4%
Switzerland 4%
Other
Italy 4%
Japan 22%
Netherlands 6%
Germany 19%
France 7%
UK 8%
USA 14%

Electrical Machinery

Traded Products

Top ten manufactures traded, by value in billions of US $ (latest available year)

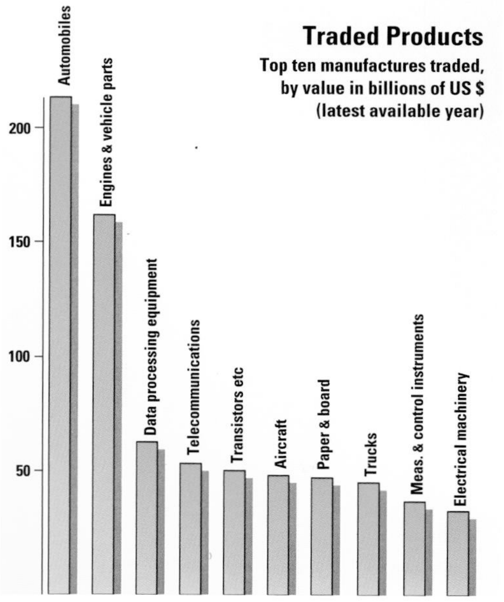
200
150
100
50
Automobiles
Engines & vehicle parts
Data processing equipment
Telecommunications
Transistors etc
Aircraft
Paper & board
Trucks
Meas. & control instruments
Electrical machinery

World Shipping

While ocean passenger traffic is nowadays relatively modest, sea transport still carries most of the world's trade. Oil and bulk carriers make up the majority of the world fleet, although the general cargo category is the fastest growing. Two innovations have revolutionized sea transport. The first is the development of the roll-on/roll-off (Ro-Ro) method where lorries or even trains loaded with freight are driven straight on to the ship, thus saving time. The second is containerization in which goods are packed into containers (the dimensions of which are fixed) at the factory, driven to the port and loaded on board by specialist machinery.

Almost 30% of world shipping sails under a 'flag of convenience', whereby owners take advantage of low taxes by registering their vessels in a foreign country the ships will never see, notably Panama and Liberia.

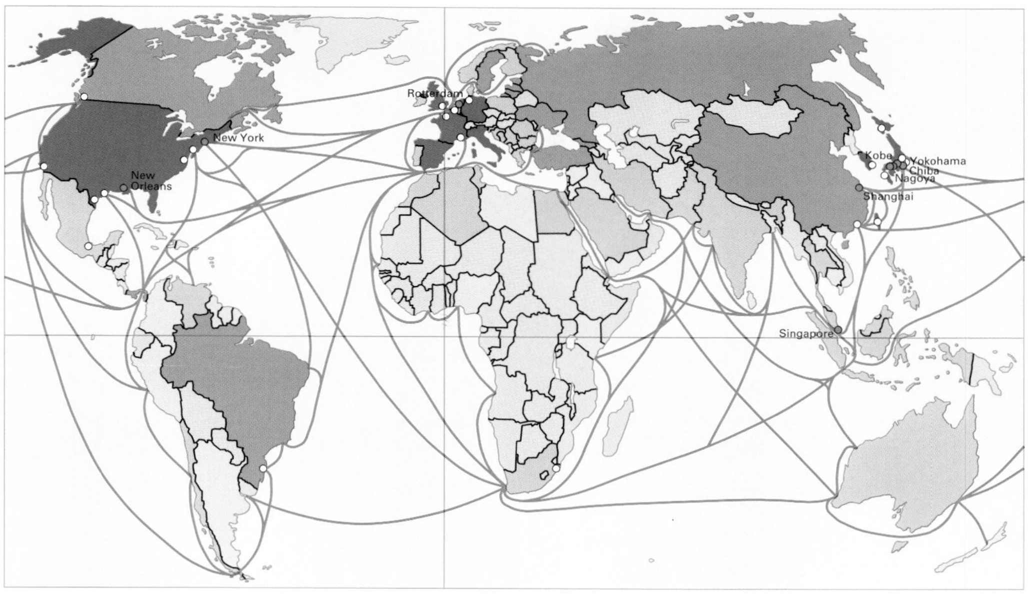

Rotterdam
New York
New Orleans
Kobe
Yokohama
Chiba
Nagoya
Shanghai
Singapore

Freight

Freight unloaded in millions of tonnes (latest available year)

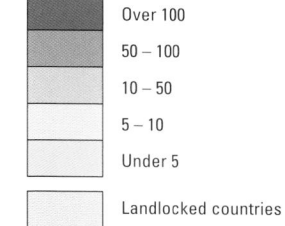

- Over 100
- 50 – 100
- 10 – 50
- 5 – 10
- Under 5
- Landlocked countries

Major seaports

- Over 100 million tonnes per year
- 50 – 100 million tonnes per year
- major shipping routes

Merchant Fleets

Merchant fleets in thousand gross tonnage (1996). A large number of vessels are registered in Liberia and Panama but they are not part of the national fleet.

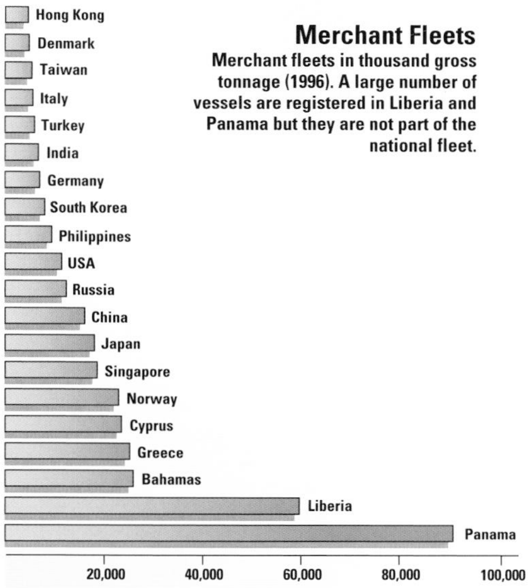

Hong Kong
Denmark
Taiwan
Italy
Turkey
India
Germany
South Korea
Philippines
USA
Russia
China
Japan
Singapore
Norway
Cyprus
Greece
Bahamas
Liberia
Panama
20,000
40,000
60,000
80,000
100,000

Types of Vessels

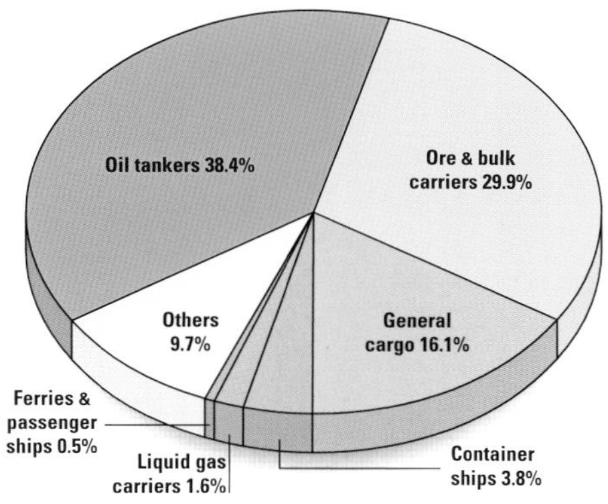

Oil tankers 38.4%
Ore & bulk carriers 29.9%
General cargo 16.1%
Others 9.7%
Ferries & passenger ships 0.5%
Liquid gas carriers 1.6%
Container ships 3.8%

The Great Ports

Total Cargo Traffic (1995) '000 tonnes

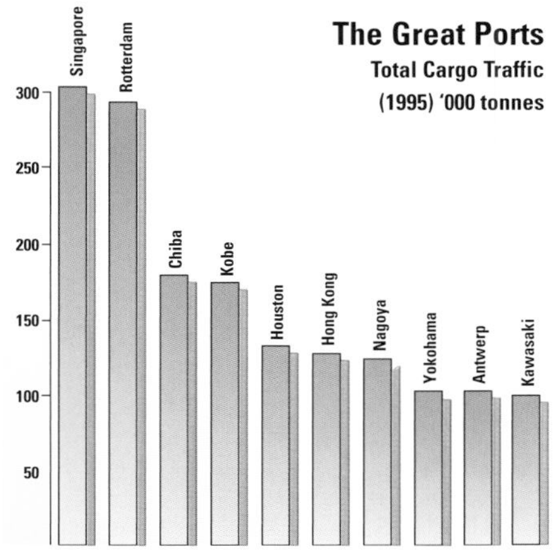

Singapore
Rotterdam
Chiba
Kobe
Houston
Hong Kong
Nagoya
Yokohama
Antwerp
Kawasaki
300
250
200
150
100
50

Trade in Primary Products

Primary products (excluding fuels, minerals and metals) as a percentage of total export value (latest available year)

- Over 75%
- 50 – 75%
- 25 – 50%
- 10 – 25%
- Under 10%

Primary products are raw materials or partly processed products which form the basis for manufacturing. They are the necessary requirements of industries and include agricultural products, minerals and timber, as well as many semi-manufactured goods such as cotton, which has been spun but not woven, wood pulp or flour. Many developed countries have few natural resources and rely on imports for the majority of their primary products. The countries of South-east Asia export hardwoods to the rest of the world, whilst many South American countries are heavily dependent on coffee exports.

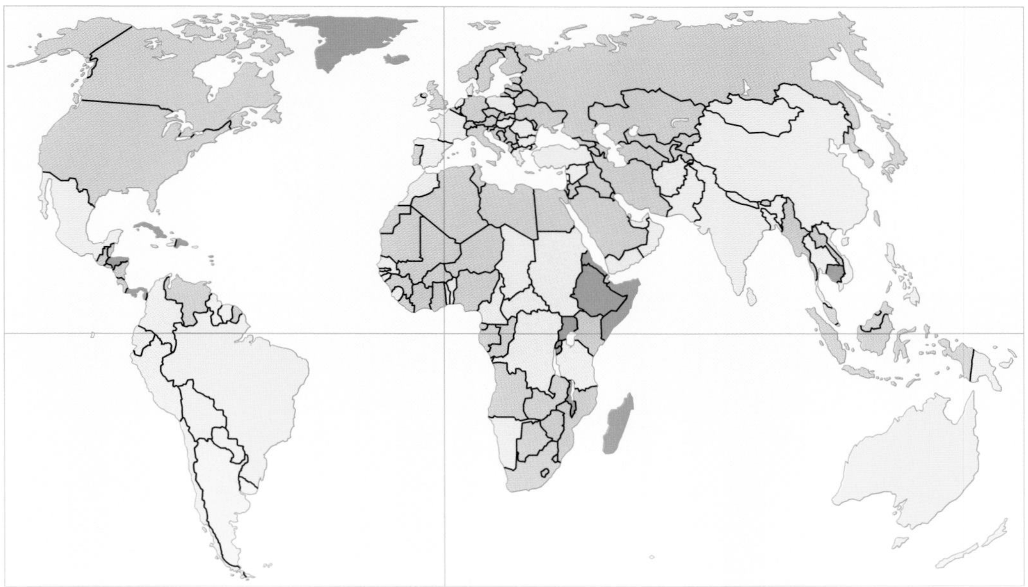

Air Freight

Trends in air freight in million tonne-km*, selected countries (1988–92)

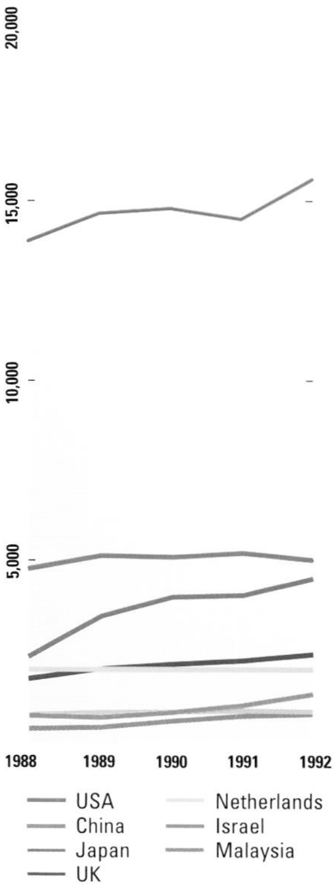

20,000
15,000
10,000
5,000
1988
1989
1990
1991
1992
USA
China
Japan
UK
Netherlands
Israel
Malaysia

* Equivalent to million tonnes of air freight flown over 1 million kilometres per year.

Air transport is important to countries of considerable size; where ground terrain is difficult; when crossing short stretches of sea; and where goods are of high value, light in weight or perishable. Recent deregulation of airlines (in the USA since 1978 and the EU in 1993) has led to increased competition and lower fares.

Balance of Trade

Value of exports in proportion to the value of imports (1995)

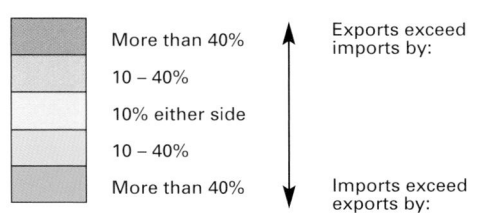

Exports exceed imports by:
- More than 40%
- 10 – 40%

- 10% either side

Imports exceed exports by:
- 10 – 40%
- More than 40%

The total world trade balance should amount to zero, since exports must equal imports on a global scale. In practice, at least $100 billion in exports go unrecorded, leaving the world with an apparent deficit and many countries in a better position than public accounting reveals. However, a favourable trade balance is not necessarily a sign of prosperity: many poorer countries must maintain a high surplus in order to service debts, and do so by restricting imports below the levels needed to sustain successful economies.

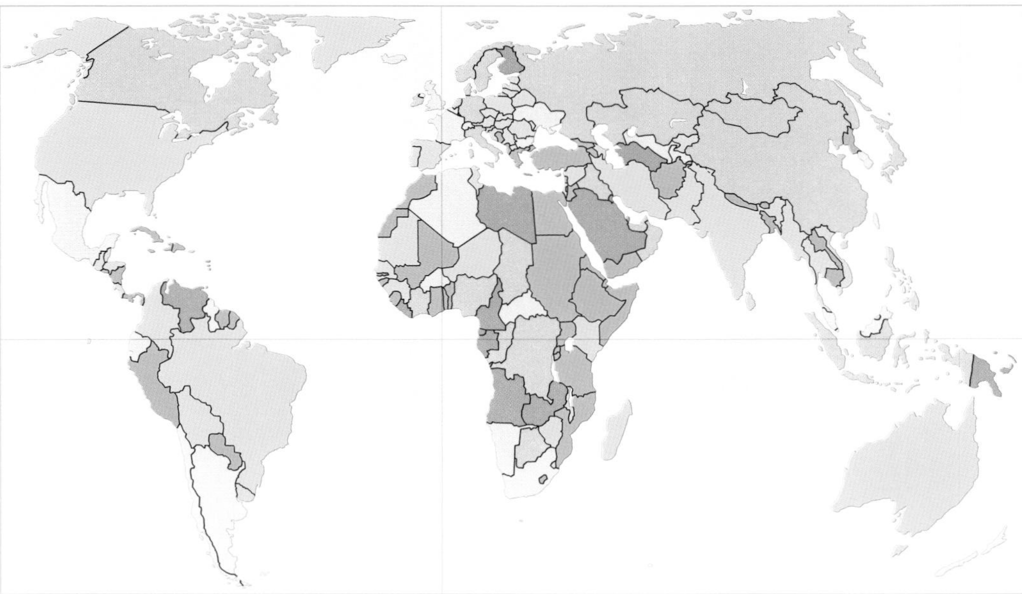

Health

For more information:

18 Water supply
27 Urban pollution
Urban advantages
33 Crisis in Africa
Food and population
47 Distribution of spending

Average life expectancies all over the world have never been higher. They range from an average of 77 years in high-income economies, to 67 years in middle-income economies and 63 in low-income economies. Even in poverty-stricken and strife-torn Burundi and Ethiopia, average life expectancies are around 50 years, as compared with less than 30 years for a citizen of Berlin in 1880.

In global terms, the radical improvements in health have much to do with improvements in agriculture and, hence, nutrition, as well as health education, an increase in sanitation and the quality of drinking water, together with advances in medicine. These radical changes have been responsible for falling death rates and rapid population growth, together with the expectation by most people that improvements in health will continue.

Health standards, life expectancies and causes of death vary considerably between the developed and developing world. The map on this page shows that in most of Africa, Asia and Latin America, the average daily calorie supply per person is so low as to cause malnutrition. (The daily requirement rated adequate by the World Health Organization is between 2,300 and 2,500 calories per person per day.) Malnutrition is a serious condition. For example, among pregnant women it causes high rates of child mortality.

Deficiency diseases occur when people do not have a balanced diet. Protein deficiency causes stunting and kwashiorkor, which can be fatal, especially among young children, while vitamin deficiencies cause such illnesses as beri beri, pellagra, scurvy and rickets. Iron deficiency causes anaemia, while a lack of iodine causes mental retardation. A UN report in the early 1990s reported that iodine deficiency affected 458 million women worldwide, as compared with 238 million men. Women's nutritional problems are especially acute in southern Asia. For example, the UN report stated that 88% of pregnant women in India were anaemic, as compared with 15% in developed countries.

Infectious diseases in association, directly or indirectly, with deficient diets, continue to affect people in developing countries, especially the 48 countries in the low human development category, where, in 1990–95, only 32% of the people had access to sanitation and 68% to safe water supplies.

A World Health report in 1996 stated that infectious diseases cause 17 million deaths per year. Most of the victims are young and otherwise fit people in developing countries. The major killers in 1995 were respiratory infections, including pneumonia (which caused 4.4 million deaths), cholera, typhoid, dysentery (3.1 million together), tuberculosis (almost 3 million), malaria (2.1 million), hepatitis B (1.1 million), AIDS and measles (more than 1 million each). Many of these diseases are preventable and, according to the United Nations Children's Fund, an investment of US $25,000 million per year, about half the money spent annually on cigarettes in Europe alone, would save the lives of all the children who currently die from avoidable diseases.

Infectious diseases are much less important as causes of death in developed countries, where cancer and circulatory diseases, such as atherosclerosis and hypertension, which cause strokes and heart attacks, are the most common causes of fatality. Because these diseases tend to kill older people, they are relatively less important in developing countries where people have shorter lifespans.

Harmful habits are also generally practised more by the rich than the poor. For example, smoking is an important cause of death in developed countries, though, curiously, the Japanese, with an average life expectancy of 79 years in 1996, are among the highest tobacco consumers. Similarly, high alcohol consumption, although it has bad effects on health, does not seem to affect longevity. The leading consumers, the French, had a life expectancy of 78 in 1996.

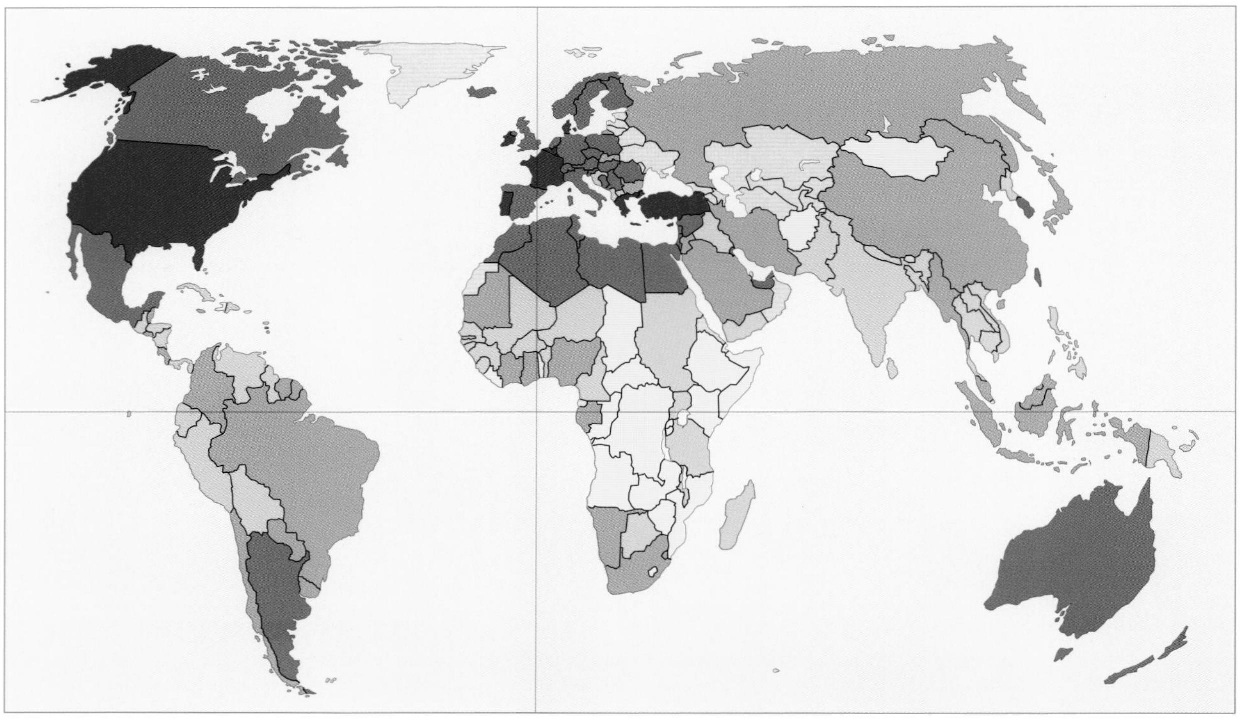

Food Consumption

Average daily food intake in calories per person (1995)

- Over 3,500 calories
- 3,000 – 3,500 calories
- 2,500 – 3,000 calories
- 2,000 – 2,500 calories
- Under 2,000 calories
- No available data

Top 5 countries

Cyprus	3,708 calories
Denmark	3,704 calories
Portugal	3,639 calories
Ireland	3,638 calories
USA	3,603 calories

Bottom 5 countries

Congo (D. Rep.)	1,879 calories
Djibouti	1,831 calories
Togo	1,754 calories
Burundi	1,749 calories
Mozambique	1,678 calories

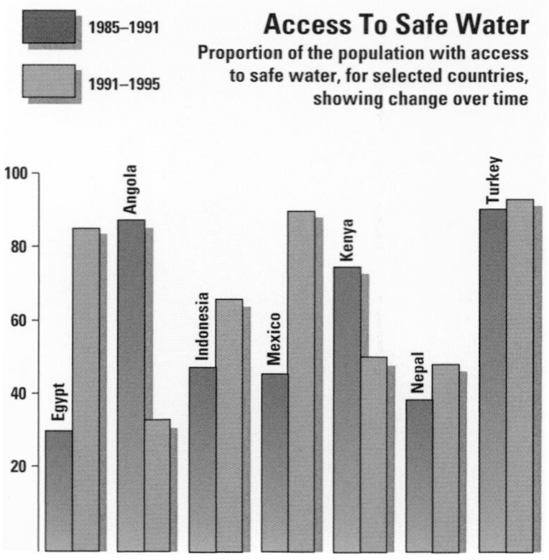

1985–1991
1991–1995
Access To Safe Water
Proportion of the population with access to safe water, for selected countries, showing change over time
100
80
60
40
20
Egypt
Angola
Indonesia
Mexico
Kenya
Nepal
Turkey

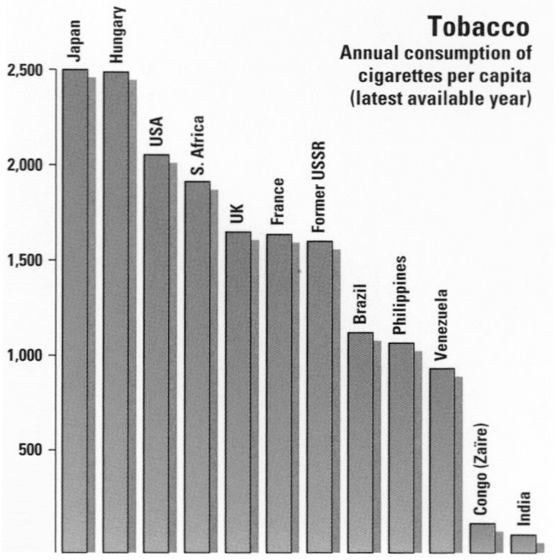

Tobacco
Annual consumption of cigarettes per capita (latest available year)
2,500
2,000
1,500
1,000
500
Japan
Hungary
USA
S. Africa
UK
France
Former USSR
Brazil
Philippines
Venezuela
Congo (Zaire)
India

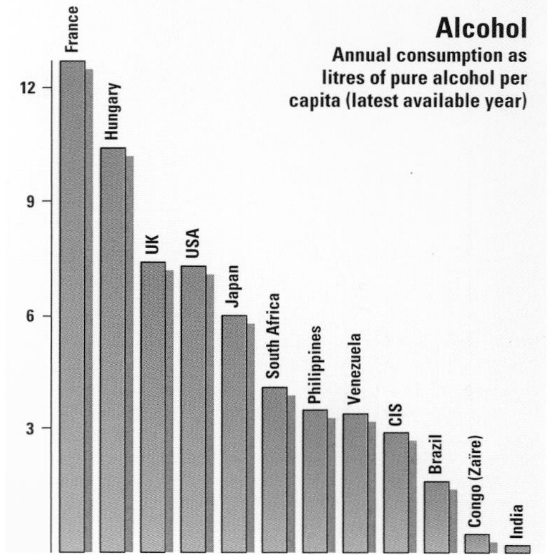

Alcohol
Annual consumption as litres of pure alcohol per capita (latest available year)
12
9
6
3
France
Hungary
UK
USA
Japan
South Africa
Philippines
Venezuela
CIS
Brazil
Congo (Zaire)
India

Life Expectancy

Years of life expectancy at birth, selected countries (1997)

The chart shows combined data for both sexes. On average, women live longer than men worldwide, even in developing countries with high maternal mortality rates. Overall, life expectancy is steadily rising, though the difference between rich and poor nations remains dramatic.

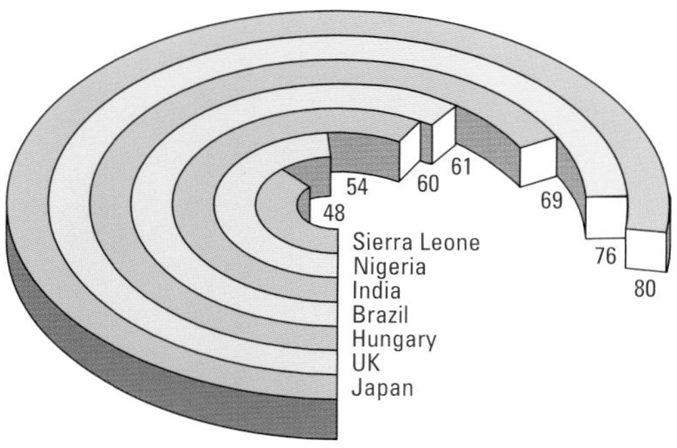

48
54
60
61
69
76
80
Sierra Leone
Nigeria
India
Brazil
Hungary
UK
Japan

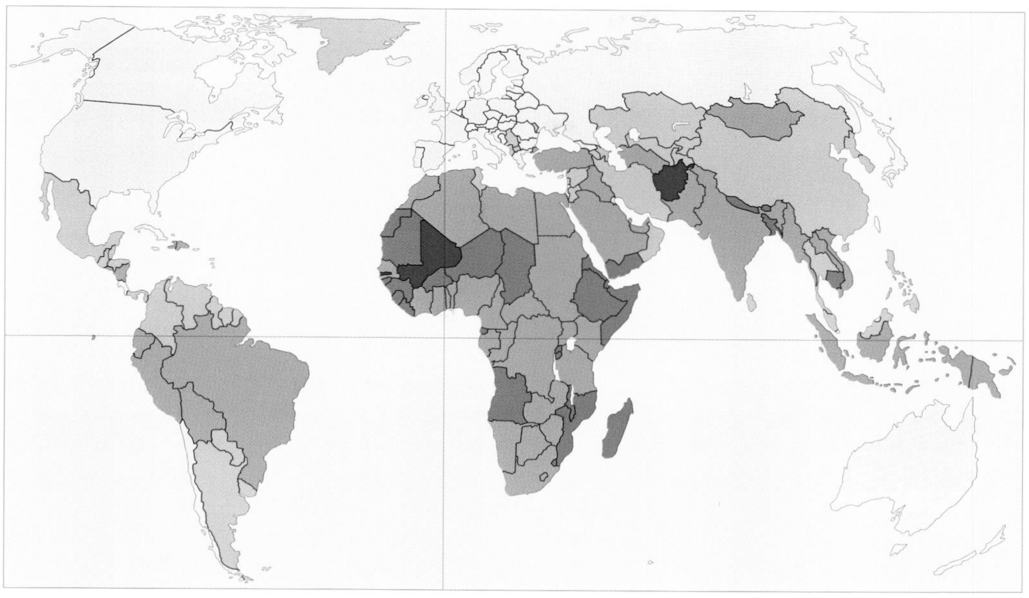

Child Mortality

Number of babies who will die under the age of one, per 1,000 births (average 1990–95)

- Over 150 deaths
- 100 – 150 deaths
- 50 – 100 deaths
- 20 – 50 deaths
- 10 – 20 deaths
- Under 10 deaths

Highest child mortality

Afghanistan	162 deaths
Mali	159 deaths

Lowest child mortality

Iceland	5 deaths
Finland	5 deaths

[UK 8 deaths] [USA 8 deaths]

Expenditure on Health

Public expenditure on health as a percentage of GDP (1996)

Countries with the highest spending		**Countries with the lowest spending**	
USA	14.2	Sudan	0.3
Argentina	10.6	Cameroon	1.4
Germany	10.4	Ghana	1.4
Croatia	10.1	Nigeria	1.4
Switzerland	10.0	Indonesia	1.8
France	9.9	Sri Lanka	1.9
Canada	9.6	Eritrea	2.0
Czech Rep.	9.6	Bangladesh	2.4
Australia	8.9	Kenya	2.5

The allocation of limited funds for health care in developing countries is rarely evenly spread – the quality of treatment can vary enormously from place to place within the same country. Urban dwellers tend to have much better access to health provisions than those living in rural areas.

Medical Provision

Doctors per 100,000 population, selected countries (latest available year, 1996)

Although the ratio of people to doctors gives a good approximation of a country's health provision, it is not an absolute indicator. Raw numbers may mask inefficiency and other weaknesses: the high proportion of physicians in Hungary, for example, has not prevented infant mortality rates more than twice as high as in the United Kingdom.

The definition of a doctor also varies from nation to nation. As well as registered medical practitioners, it may include trained medical assistants – an especially important category in developing countries, where they provide many of the same services as fully qualified physicians, including simple operations.

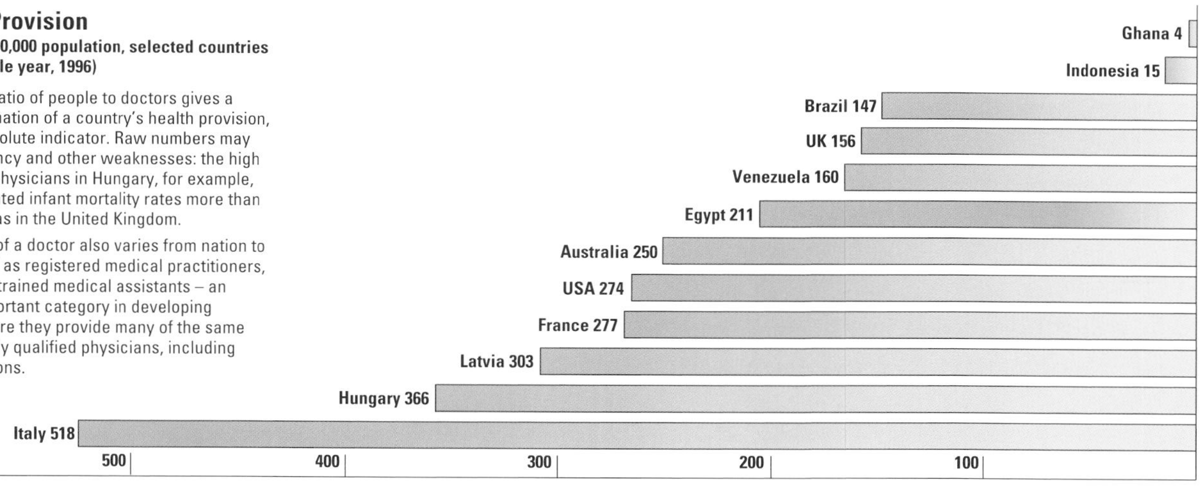

Ghana 4
Indonesia 15
Brazil 147
UK 156
Venezuela 160
Egypt 211
Australia 250
USA 274
France 277
Latvia 303
Hungary 366
Italy 518
500
400
300
200
100

The Aids Crisis

The Acquired Immune Deficiency Syndrome (AIDS) was first identified in 1981 when American doctors found otherwise healthy young men succumbing to rare infections. By 1984 the cause had been traced to the Human Immunodeficiency Virus (HIV) which can remain dormant for many years and perhaps indefinitely: only half of those known to carry the virus in 1981 had developed AIDS ten years later.

In Western countries in the mid-1990s, most AIDS deaths were among male homosexuals or needle-sharing drug-users. However, the disease is spreading fastest among heterosexual men and women, which is its usual vector in the developing world where most of its victims live.

The World Health Organization estimated that 1.3 million people died of AIDS in 1995 and that by the end of the same year 22 million people were HIV-positive. India has the largest number of HIV infections totalling more than 3 million, but two-thirds of all infections are in sub-Saharan Africa (where, unlike the rest of the world, more women are infected than men). It was estimated that two million African children would die of AIDS by the year 2000, and some 10 million would be orphaned.

Causes of Death

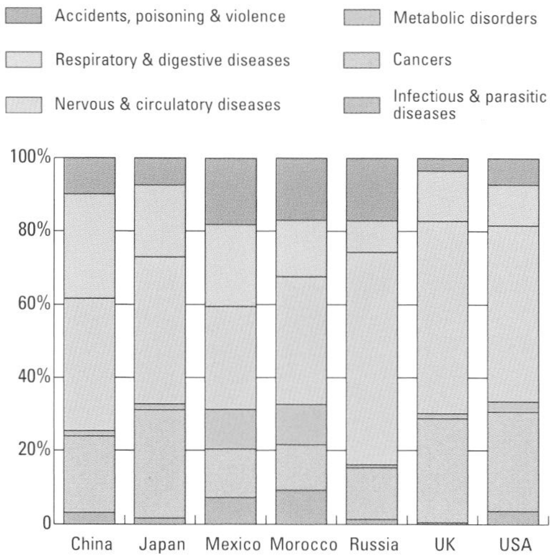

Accidents, poisoning & violence
Respiratory & digestive diseases
Nervous & circulatory diseases
Metabolic disorders
Cancers
Infectious & parasitic diseases
100%
80%
60%
40%
20%
0
China
Japan
Mexico
Morocco
Russia
UK
USA

Circulatory Disease in Europe

Diseases of the circulatory system per 100,000 people (latest available year 1992–95)

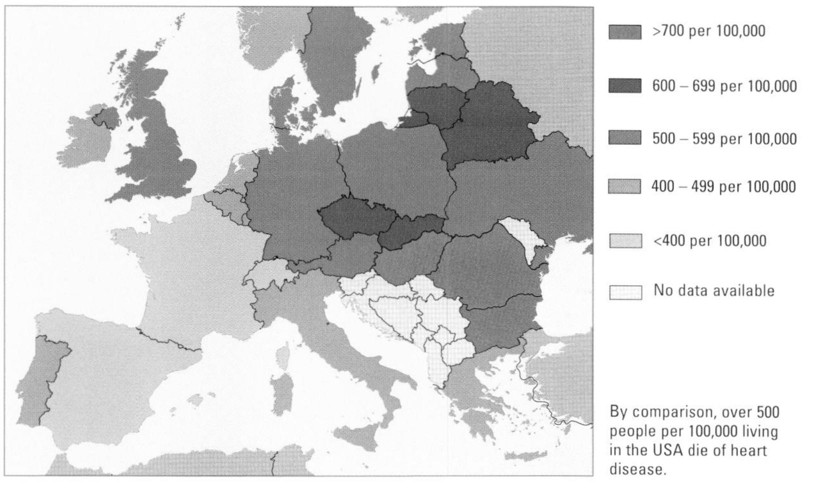

>700 per 100,000
600 – 699 per 100,000
500 – 599 per 100,000
400 – 499 per 100,000
<400 per 100,000
No data available

By comparison, over 500 people per 100,000 living in the USA die of heart disease.

Aids

Cases reported in 1997, per 100,000 population

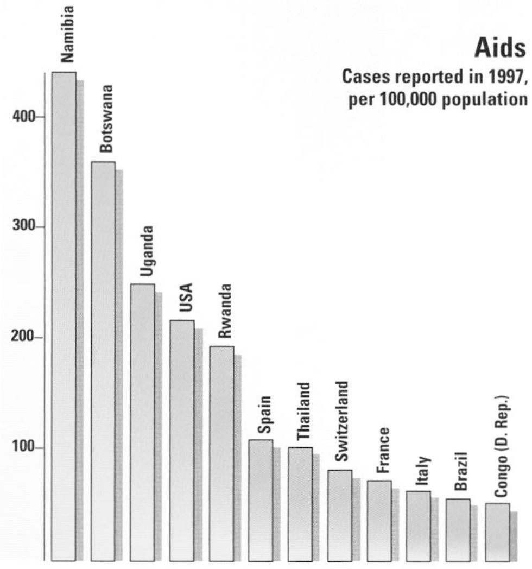

400
300
200
100
Namibia
Botswana
Uganda
USA
Rwanda
Spain
Thailand
Switzerland
France
Italy
Brazil
Congo (D. Rep.)

Sanitation

Percentage of the population with access to sanitation services, selected countries (latest available year)

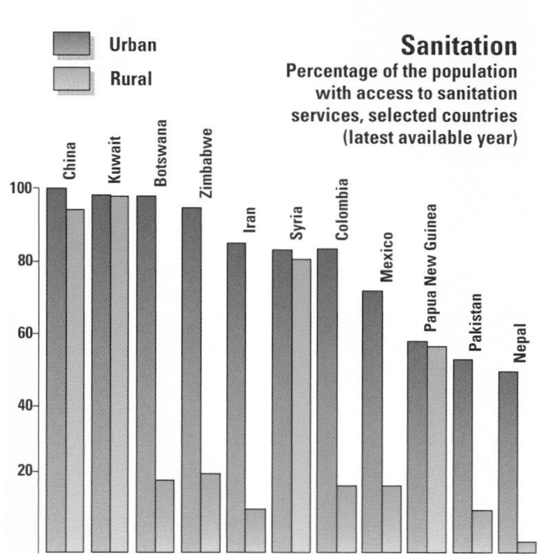

Urban
Rural
100
80
60
40
20
China
Kuwait
Botswana
Zimbabwe
Iran
Syria
Colombia
Mexico
Papua New Guinea
Pakistan
Nepal

Malaria

Cases of malaria per 100,000 people exposed to malaria-infected environments, selected countries* (latest available year)

* data are not available for Africa where 80% of malaria cases occur

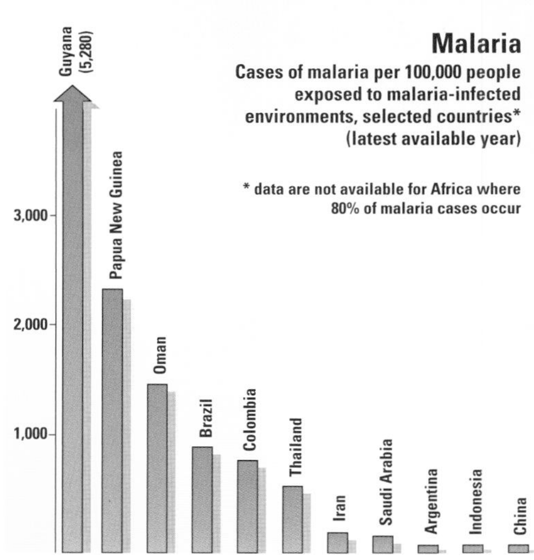

3,000
2,000
1,000
Guyana (5,280)
Papua New Guinea
Oman
Brazil
Colombia
Thailand
Iran
Saudi Arabia
Argentina
Indonesia
China

Infectious and parasitic diseases, such as malaria, which claimed 2.1 million lives in 1995, remain a scourge in the developing countries. Respiratory infections and injury also claim more lives in developing countries, which lack the drugs and the medical personnel to deal with them. Developing countries lack the basic services taken for granted in developed nations. For example, in sub-Saharan Africa in 1990–95, only 31% of the population had access to sanitation and 45% to safe water, with the situation being worse in rural areas. By contrast, circulatory diseases and cancer are the main causes of death in the rich, industrialized countries. For example, in the UK in the mid-1990s, circulatory diseases, which cause heart attacks and strokes, accounted for nearly half the deaths, with cancer accounting for nearly a quarter.

Wealth

For more information:

38 Wealth creation
39 Industrial power
Exports per capita
40 World trade
Major exports
41 Balance of trade
47 Distribution of spending
Distribution of income

Perhaps the most glaring differences in the world today are those between the rich and the poor. The World Bank divides countries into three main groups based on average economic production expressed in terms of per capita GNP (Gross National Product). They are the low-income economies, including most African countries and much of Asia; the middle-income economies, including most of Latin America and most of the former USSR; and the high-income economies of Canada, the United States, Western Europe, Japan and Australia.

Per capita GNPs are a measure of the total goods and services produced by a country divided by the population, and then converted into US dollars at official exchange rates. They are useful indicators of a country's prosperity, though, like all statistics, they must be treated with care. For example, the prices for goods and services in China are far cheaper than they are in the United States. China's per capita GNP in 1998 was $750 (as compared with $29,340 in the USA) but the PPP (Purchasing-Power Parity) estimate of China's per capita GNP was considerably higher at $3,570. Another problem with per capita GNPs is that they are averages, which often conceal wide internal variations.

The pattern of poverty varies from region to region. In Latin America, much progress has been made through industrialization, though startling inequalities still exist between rich and poor. In Asia, the 'tiger economies' have followed Japan's example in pursuing export-led industrial policies, while the success of China's Special Economic Zones, where foreign investment is encouraged, has led to a huge rise in China's per capita GNP, as shown on the map on page 45, bottom right.

Solutions to poverty in Africa are much harder to find because of its high population growth, civil wars, natural disasters and high inflation rates. Although Africa receives more aid than any other continent, aid is only a partial solution. Much aid has been wasted on overambitious projects, in the servicing of huge national debts, or lost by inexperienced or corrupt governments. One initiative in some African countries has been to improve the infrastructure and develop tourism, creating employment and providing much-needed foreign currency. But tourism alone cannot solve the problems of under-development.

The International Monetary Fund and the World Bank argue that real economic progress in Africa will be achieved only when African countries create market-friendly economies that encourage trade through export-led manufacturing, while at the same time strictly controlling public spending on welfare, the civil service and other areas.

Continental Shares

Shares of population and of wealth (GNP) by continent

These generalized continental figures show the startling difference between rich and poor but mask the successes or failures of individual countries. Japan, for example, with less than 4% of Asia's population, produces almost 70% of the continent's output. Within countries, the difference between rich and poor can also be startling. In Brazil, for example, the richest 20% of the population own 60% of the wealth.

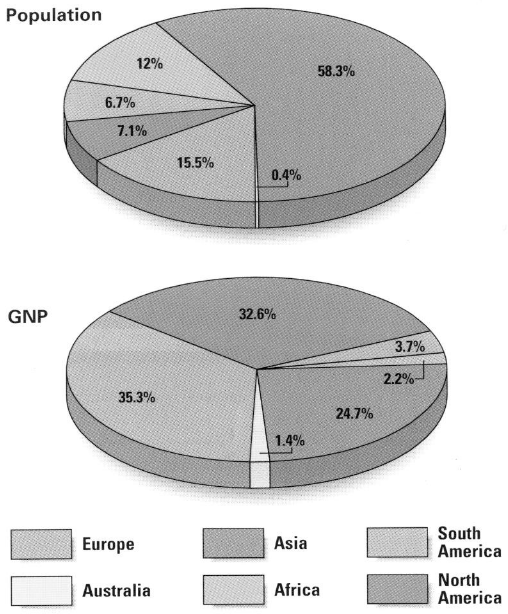

Currencies

Currency units of the world's most powerful economies

1. USA: US dollar ($, US $) = 100 cents
2. Japan: Yen (Y, ¥) = 100 sen
3. Germany: Euro; Deutsche Mark (DM)= 100 Pfennig
4. France: Euro; French franc (Fr) = 100 centimes
5. Italy: Euro; Italian lira (L, £, Lit)
6. UK: Pound sterling (£) = 100 pence
7. Canada: Canadian dollar (C$, Can$) = 100 cents
8. China: Renminbi yuan (RMBY, $, Y) = 10 jiao = 100 fen
9. Brazil: Cruzeiro real (BRC) = 100 centavos
10. Spain: Euro; Peseta (Pta, Pa) = 100 céntimos
11. India: Indian rupee (Re, Rs) = 100 paisa
12. Australia: Australian dollar ($A) = 100 cents
13. Netherlands: Euro; Guilder, florin (Gld, f) = 100 centimes
14. Switzerland: Swiss franc (SFr, SwF) = 100 centimes
15. South Korea: Won (W) = 100 chon
16. Sweden: Swedish krona (SKr) = 100 ore
17. Mexico: Mexican peso (Mex$) = 100 centavos
18. Belgium: Euro; Belgian franc (BFr) = 100 centimes
19. Austria: Euro; Schilling (S, Sch) = 100 Groschen
20. Finland: Euro; Markka (FMk) = 100 penniä
21. Denmark: Danish krone (DKr) = 100 øre
22. Norway: Norwegian krone (NKr) = 100 øre
23. Saudi Arabia: Riyal (SAR, SRI$) = 100 halalah
24. Indonesia: Rupiah (Rp) = 100 sen
25. South Africa: Rand (R) = 100 cents

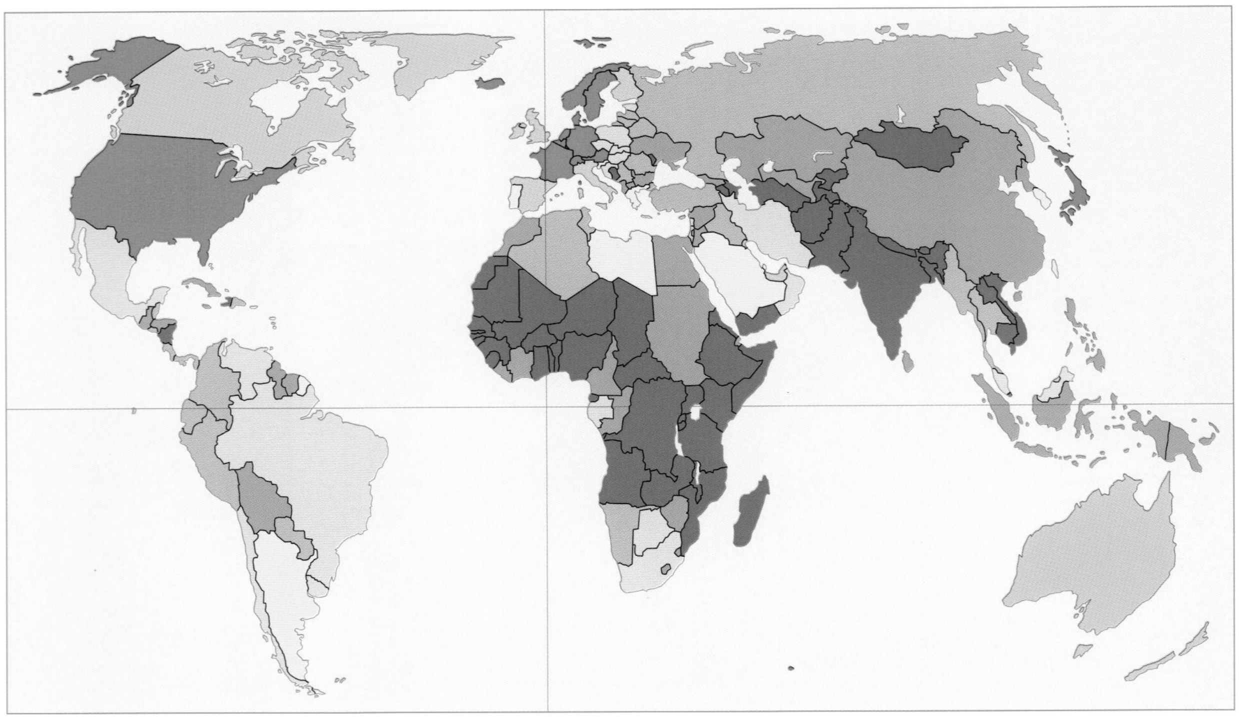

Levels of Income

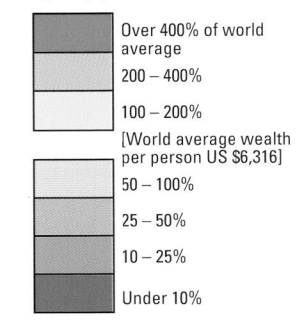

Gross National Product per capita: the value of total production divided by the population (1997)

- Over 400% of world average
- 200 – 400%
- 100 – 200%

[World average wealth per person US $6,316]

- 50 – 100%
- 25 – 50%
- 10 – 25%
- Under 10%

Top 5 countries

Luxembourg	$45,360
Switzerland	$44,220
Japan	$37,850
Norway	$36,090
Liechtenstein	$33,000

Bottom 5 countries

Mozambique	$90
Ethiopia	$110
Congo (Dem. Rep.)	$110
Burundi	$180
Sierra Leone	$200

Indicators

The gap between the world's rich and poor is now so great that it is difficult to illustrate on a single graph. Within each income group (as defined by the World Bank), however, comparisons have some meaning; the Chinese, perhaps because of propaganda value, have more TV sets than Indians, whereas Nigerians prefer to spend their money on radios. However, the wealth gap in many developing countries is wide, with a small, rich class and a large, impoverished majority, while many high-income countries contain an underclass of unemployed and homeless people.

High Income

Number of radios, televisions and mobile 'phones for each 10,000 people, selected high income countries (1996)

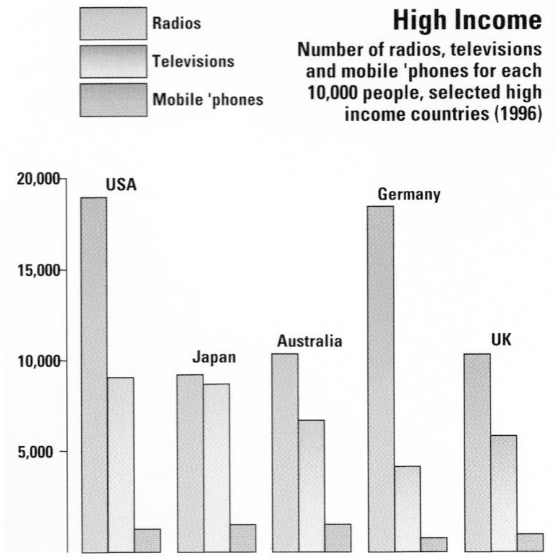

Middle Income

Number of radios, televisions and mobile 'phones for each 10,000 people, selected middle income countries (1996)

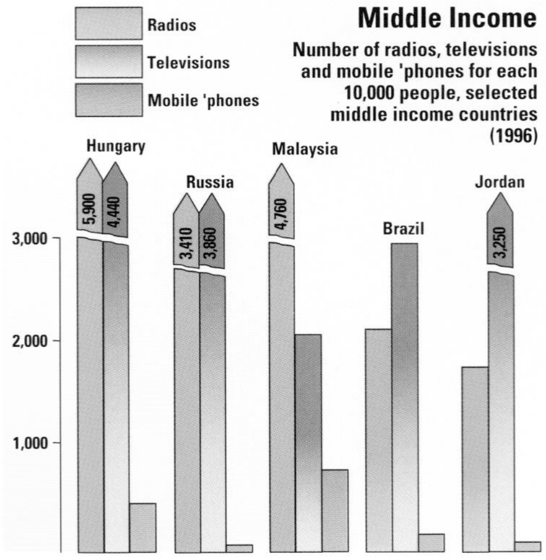

Low Income

Number of radios, televisions and mobile 'phones for each 10,000 people, selected low income countries (1996)

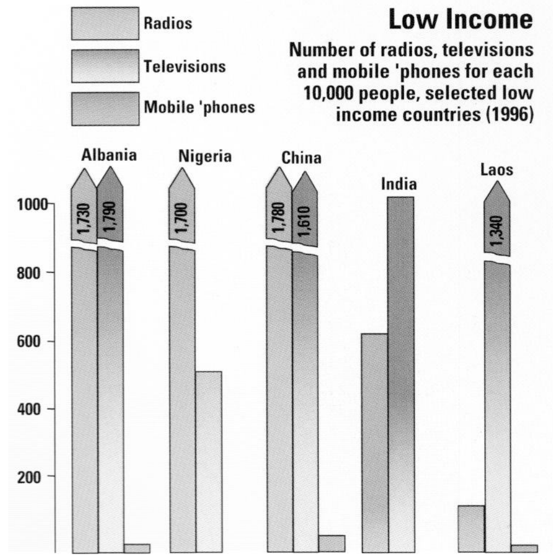

World Tourism

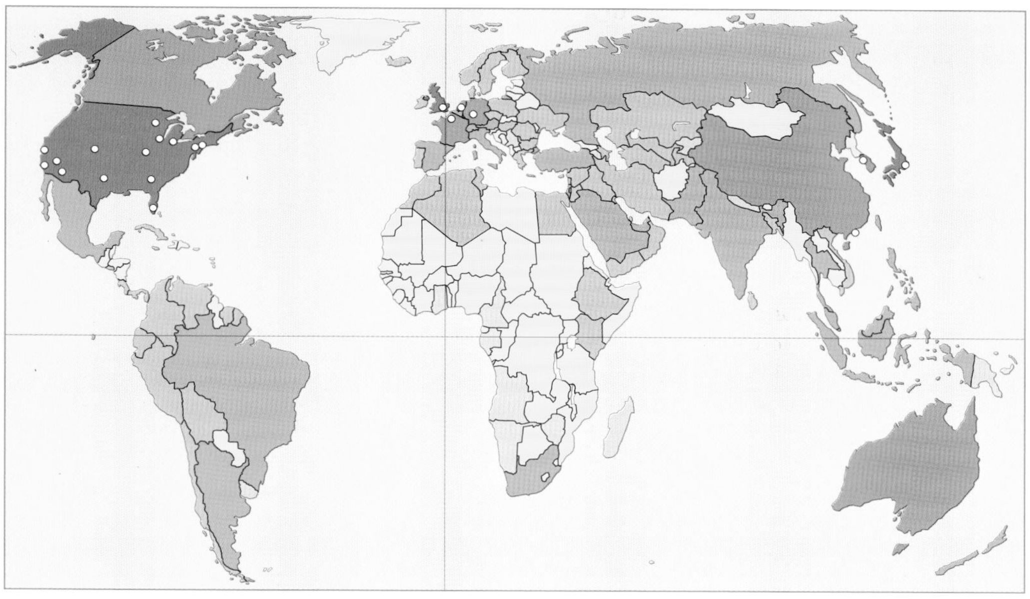

Passenger km flown (the number of passengers multiplied by the distance flown by each passenger from the airport of origin) (1997)

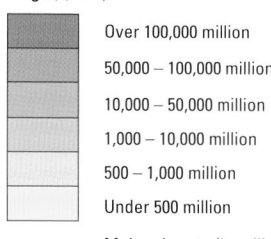

- Over 100,000 million
- 50,000 – 100,000 million
- 10,000 – 50,000 million
- 1,000 – 10,000 million
- 500 – 1,000 million
- Under 500 million
- ○ Major airports (handling over 25 million passengers in 2000)

Leisure and tourism is the world's second largest industry in terms of revenue generated. Small economies in attractive areas are often completely dominated by tourism: in some Caribbean islands, tourist spending provides over 90% of the total income and is the biggest foreign exchange earner. In cash terms the USA is the world leader: its 1999 earnings exceeded US $74 billion, though that sum amounted to approximately 0.9% of its total GDP. Of the 48 million visitors to the USA, 34% came from Canada and 25% from Mexico. Germany spends the most on overseas tourism; this amounts to over US $50,000 million. The next biggest spenders are the USA, Japan and the UK.

The world's busiest airport in terms of total number of passengers is Atlanta (78.1 million passengers in 1999); the busiest international airport is London's Heathrow.

Aid Donors

Development aid by donor country, in millions of US $ and as a percentage of donor's GNP (latest available year)

Not all aid is given in cash grants: much is delivered in the form of cheap loans or technical assistance. Since the 1970s, OECD countries belonging to the Development Assistance Committee (DAC) have agreed in principle to give 0.7% of their GNP. Most have failed to meet their commitment. In 1994, three countries exceeded this level. They were Norway (1.05%), the Netherlands (1.03%) and Sweden (0.96%). The countries with the largest aid budgets were Japan (US $13,239 million or 0.29% of GNP) and the United States (US $9,927 million or 0.15% of GNP).

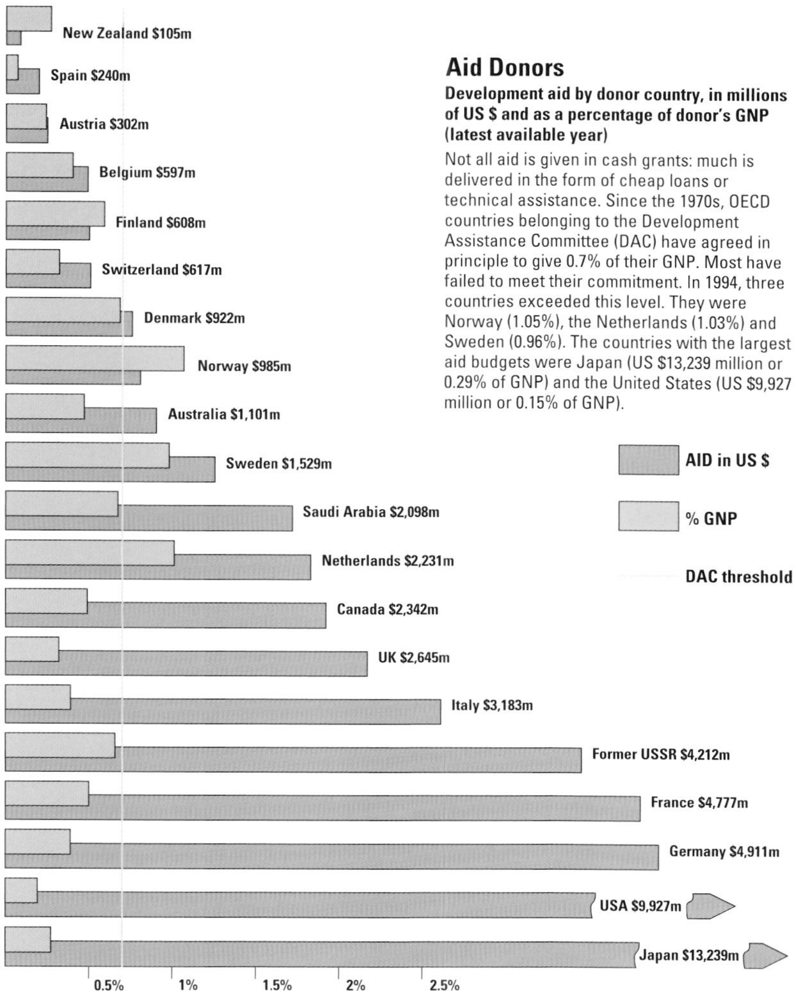

New Zealand $105m
Spain $240m
Austria $302m
Belgium $597m
Finland $608m
Switzerland $617m
Denmark $922m
Norway $985m
Australia $1,101m
Sweden $1,529m
Saudi Arabia $2,098m
Netherlands $2,231m
Canada $2,342m
UK $2,645m
Italy $3,183m
Former USSR $4,212m
France $4,777m
Germany $4,911m
USA $9,927m
Japan $13,239m
0.5%
1%
1.5%
2%
2.5%
AID in US $
% GNP
DAC threshold

State Finance

Inflation rates, shown on the map, right, are an index of a country's financial stability and usually of its prosperity. Annual inflation rates above 20% are usually marked by slow or even negative growth of the GNP. Above 50%, it becomes hyperinflation and an economy is reeling. In the late 1980s and early 1990s, many high-income countries had to contend with annual inflation rates of 10% or more, while Japan, the growth leader, had an average inflation rate of 1.3% between 1985 and 1994.

The per capita GNP figures listed below are useful indicators of economic success or failure, but they do not account for living costs. Nor do they reveal the gaps between the rich and poor within countries.

Market-friendly policies, including low taxes and state spending, liberal trade policies and a welcome for foreign investors, are major factors in countries which have enjoyed rapid economic growth since 1980. For example, the setting up of Special Economic Zones in eastern China has led to a spectacular rise in the per capita GNP. Other successful countries include the 'tiger economies' of South Korea, Thailand and Singapore, although an Asian market crash in 1997 temporarily halted the dramatic economic expansion in these countries.

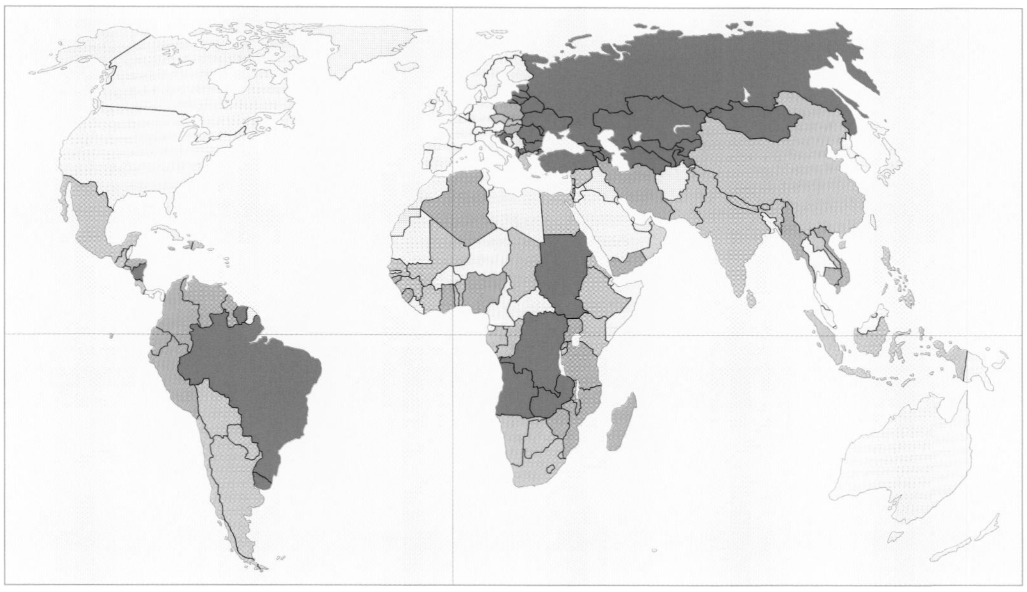

Inflation

Average annual rate of inflation (1990–96)

- Over 50%
- 20 – 50%
- 7.5 – 20%
- 1 – 7.5%
- Negative inflation
- No data available

Highest average inflation

Congo (Dem. R.) 2747%
Georgia 2279%
Angola 1103%

Lowest average inflation

Oman ...... –3.0%
Bahrain ...... –0.5%
Brunei ...... –0.0%

The Wealth Gap

The world's richest and poorest countries, by Gross National Product per capita in US $ (1999 estimates)

1. Liechtenstein	50,000	1. Ethiopia	100
2. Luxembourg	44,640	2. Congo (D. Rep.)	110
3. Switzerland	38,350	3. Burundi	120
4. Bermuda	35,590	4. Sierra Leone	130
5. Norway	32,880	5. Guinea-Bissau	160
6. Japan	32,230	6. Niger	190
7. Denmark	32,030	7. Malawi	190
8. USA	30,600	8. Eritrea	200
9. Singapore	29,610	9. Chad	200
10. Iceland	29,280	10. Nepal	220
11. Austria	25,970	11. Angola	220
12. Germany	25,350	12. Mozambique	230
13. Sweden	25,040	13. Tanzania	240
14. Monaco	25,000	14. Burkina Faso	240
15. Belgium	24,510	15. Mali	240
16. Brunei	24,630	16. Rwanda	250
17. Netherlands	24,320	17. Madagascar	250
18. Finland	23,780	18. Cambodia	260
19. Hong Kong	23,520	19. São Tomé & Príncipe	270
20. France	23,480	20. Laos	280

GNP per capita is calculated by dividing a country's Gross National Product by its total population.

Growth in GNP

GNP per capita annual growth rate (1985–95)

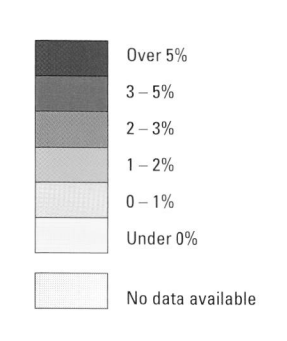

- Over 5%
- 3 – 5%
- 2 – 3%
- 1 – 2%
- 0 – 1%
- Under 0%
- No data available

Countries with highest growth rates

Maldives 9.9%
Thailand 9.7%
China 9.3%
Botswana 9.0%
South Korea 8.5%

Standards of Living

For more information:

18 Water supply
24 Population density
27 Urban pollution
Squatter settlements
Urban advantages
30 World's refugees
War since 1945
38 Employment
The workforce
46 The wealth gap
Aid donors
45 Life expectancy
Child mortality

Wealth is a basic factor in determining standards of living. Everywhere, the rich have more of everything, including higher average life expectancies, while the poor have to spend most of their income on basic human needs, such as food and clothing. Yet poverty and wealth are relative terms. Slum dwellers living on social security in an industrial society feel their poverty acutely, but they have far more resources than an average African living in a rural area.

In 1990 the United Nations Development Programme published its first Human Development Index (HDI), an attempt to construct a comparative scale by which a simplified form of well-being might be measured. The HDI, expressed as a value between 0 and 0.999, combines figures for life expectancy and literacy with a wealth scale, based on Purchasing-Power Parity. The world's countries are divided into three groups, those with a high HDI (0.800 and above); those with a medium HDI (0.500 to 0.799); and those with a low HDI (below 0.500).

National scores for 1993 ranged from 0.951 for Canada to a low of 0.204 in Niger. In fact, of the 48 countries with a low HDI, 37 were from Africa, 10 from Asia, plus Haiti from the Caribbean. Besides having low per capita GNPs, the average life expectancy in these countries was 56 years, while the adult literacy rate was 49%. By comparison, the average life expectancy at birth in countries in the high HDI group was 74 years, while the literacy rate was 97%.

Comparisons between countries with similar per capita GNPs reveal the effects of government actions. For example, the World Bank classifies both India and China as low-income economies, but India's HDI at 0.436 is much lower than that of China, at 0.609. This reflects not only China's economic progress in the 1980s and 1990s, but also differences in average life expectancies (61 years in India and 69 years in China), and adult literacy rates (51% in India and 80% in China).

Disparities in standards of living exist not only between countries but also between individuals, groups and regions within countries. For example, income distribution figures for 1995 show that, in the United States, the poorest 20% of households received less than 4% of the income.

Other contrasts exist in developing countries between rural communities, where incomes are low and basic services are often in short supply, and urban areas, where even those living in slums are generally better off than their rural neighbours. Other striking differences exist between men and women. For example, while adult literacy rates for men and women living in developed countries are more or less the same, large differences exist in many developing countries. In 1995, in countries in the lowest HDI category, only 37% of women were literate, as compared with 62% of men.

Female education is a factor in population control, especially as women's fertility rates appear to fall in direct proportion to the amount of secondary education they receive. This point was acknowledged in 1994 by the UN Population Fund, which defined four main objectives relating to women and population control. They were: the reduction of maternal, infant and child mortality; better education, especially for girls; universal access to reproductive health services; and gender equality.

Statistical analysis presents many problems of interpretation, especially when trying to define such intangible factors as a sense of well-being. For example, education helps create wealth; but are rich countries wealthy because their people are well-educated, or are they well-educated because they are rich?

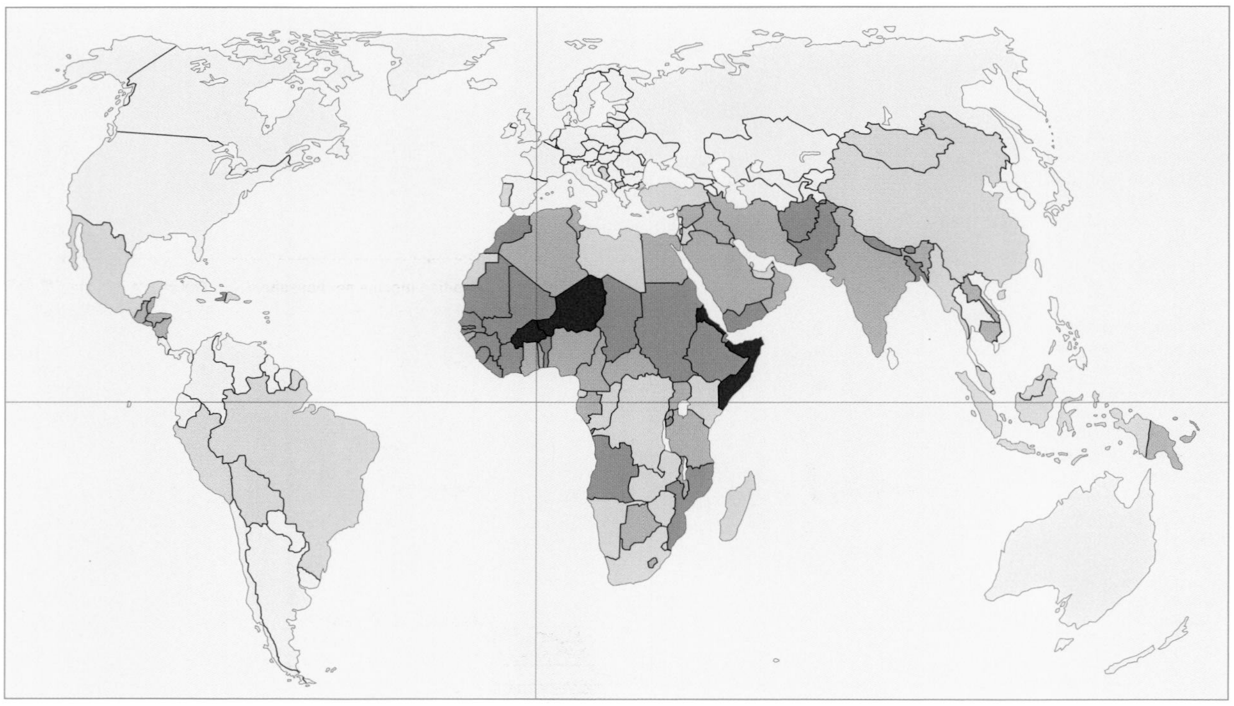

Illiteracy

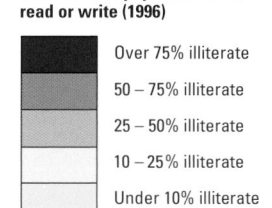

% of the total population unable to read or write (1996)

- Over 75% illiterate
- 50 – 75% illiterate
- 25 – 50% illiterate
- 10 – 25% illiterate
- Under 10% illiterate

Educational expenditure per person (latest available year)

Top 5 countries

Sweden	$997
Qatar	$989
Canada	$983
Norway	$971
Switzerland	$796

Bottom 5 countries

Chad	$2
Bangladesh	$3
Ethiopia	$3
Nepal	$4
Somalia	$4

[UK $447]

Education

The developing countries made great efforts in the 1970s and 1980s to bring at least a basic education to their people. Primary school enrolments rose above 60% in all but the poorest nations. Figures often include teenagers or young adults, however, and there are still an estimated 300 million children worldwide who receive no schooling at all. A lack of resources has restricted the development of secondary and higher education. Most primary education is free in the poorer countries, but fees are often paid for secondary and higher education, thus heightening the differences between rich and poor.

Primary
Percentage of age group in primary school, selected countries (latest available year)

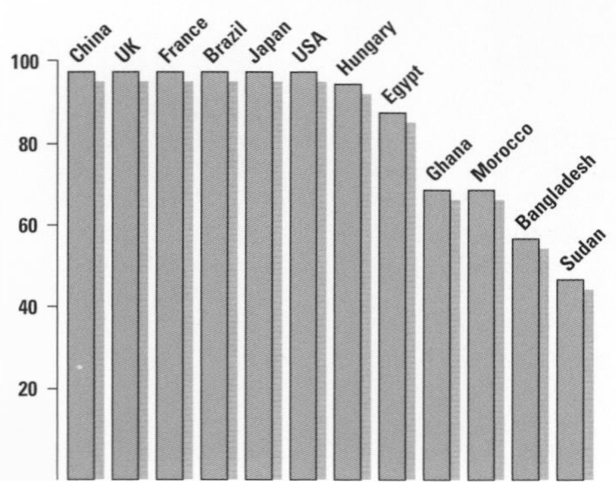

Secondary
Percentage of age group in secondary school, selected countries (latest available year)

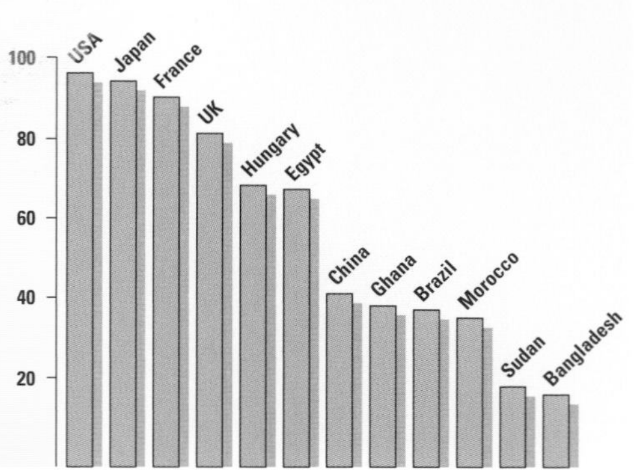

Higher
Percentage of age group in higher education, selected countries (latest available year)

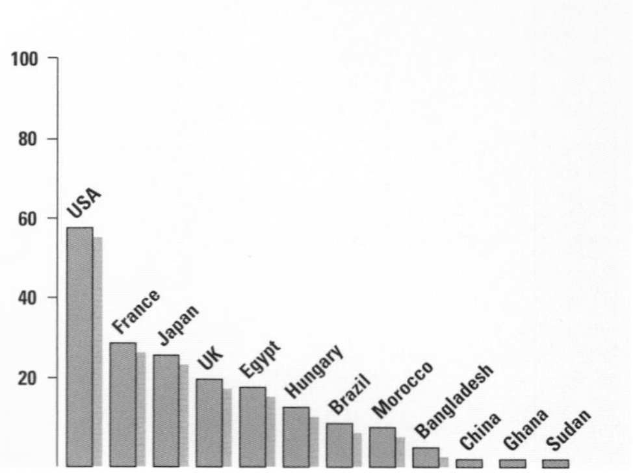

Distribution of Spending

Percentage share of household spending (latest available year)

A high proportion of the average income of households in developing nations is spent on basic needs such as food and clothing. In most Western countries food and clothing account for less than 25% of expenditure.

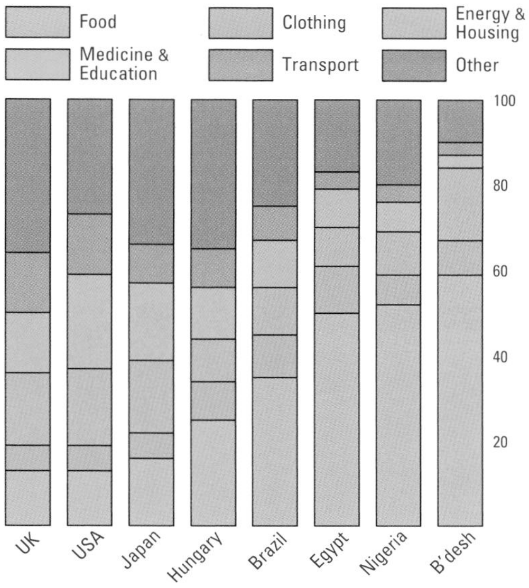

Food
Medicine & Education
Clothing
Transport
Energy & Housing
Other
100
80
60
40
20
UK
USA
Japan
Hungary
Brazil
Egypt
Nigeria
B'desh

Distribution of Income

Percentage share of household income from poorest fifth to richest fifth, selected countries (latest available year)

The graph below shows that wealth is not distributed evenly throughout the population of the six countries. In every country worldwide the richest 20% of the population have a disproportionately high percentage of the income. This disparity between rich and poor is nowhere more pronounced than in Brazil, where the richest 20% of the population have over 60% of the income. The poorest 20%, on the other hand, have less than 5%.

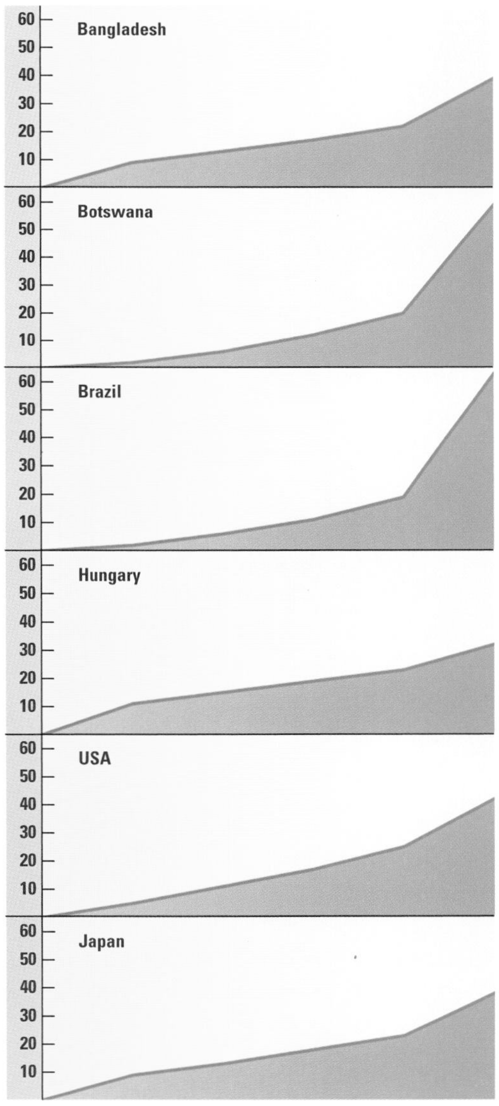

Bangladesh
Botswana
Brazil
Hungary
USA
Japan
60
50
40
30
20
10

Fertility and Education

Fertility rates compared with female education, selected countries (1992–95)

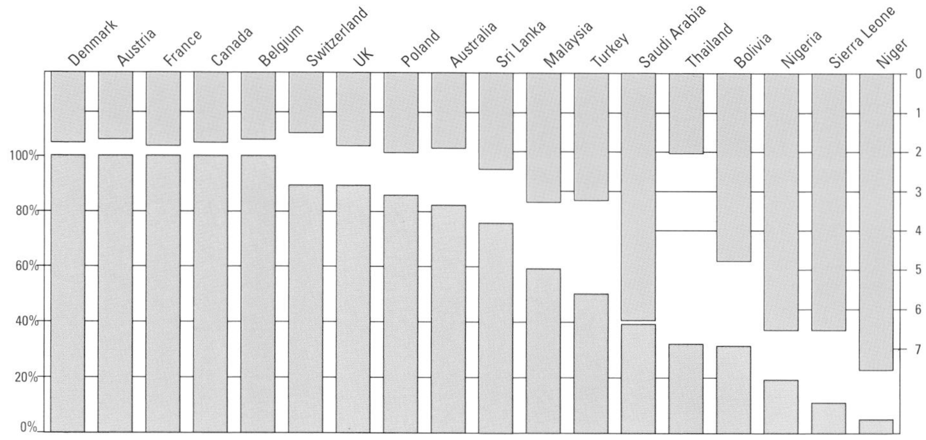

Denmark
Austria
France
Canada
Belgium
Switzerland
UK
Poland
Australia
Sri Lanka
Malaysia
Turkey
Saudi Arabia
Thailand
Bolivia
Nigeria
Sierra Leone
Niger
100%
80%
60%
40%
20%
0%
0
1
2
3
4
5
6
7

Percentage of females aged 12–17 in secondary education

Fertility rate: average number of children borne per woman

Access to secondary education is closely linked to low fertility rates in developed countries. By contrast, in many developing countries, women's lives are dominated by agriculture, or they lack access to secondary and higher education for cultural reasons, as in Muslim countries. Such disparities are reflected in women's parliamentary representation which is only one-seventh that of men, despite the emergence of such figures as Mrs Indira Gandhi, India's former prime minister. Female wages are also, on average, only two-thirds of those of men.

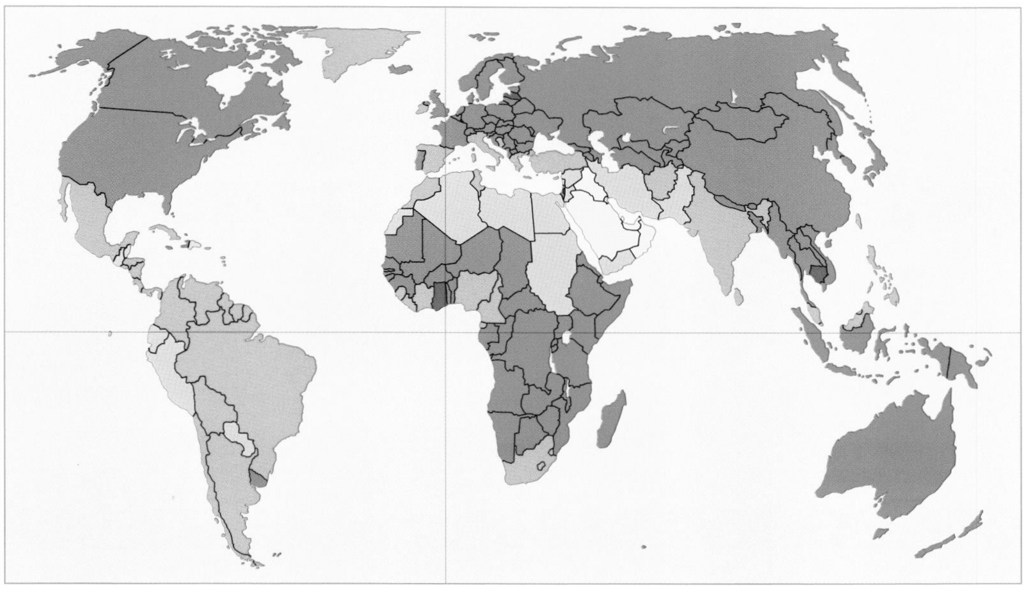

Women at Work

Women in paid employment as a percentage of the total workforce (1996)

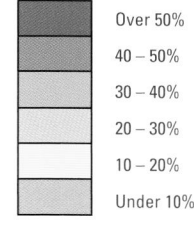

- Over 50%
- 40 – 50%
- 30 – 40%
- 20 – 30%
- 10 – 20%
- Under 10%

Most women in work

Cambodia	53%
Ghana	51%
Latvia	50%

Fewest women in work

Iraq	18%
Oman	15%
Saudi Arabia	14%

Car Ownership

Proportion of the world's vehicles, by region (1996)

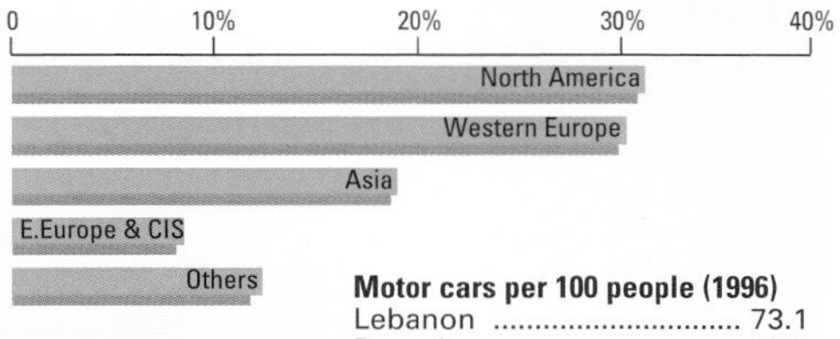

0
10%
20%
30%
40%
North America
Western Europe
Asia
E.Europe & CIS
Others

TOTAL = 312 million vehicles

Motor cars per 100 people (1996)

Lebanon	73.1
Brunei	57.5
Italy	56.8
Luxembourg	56.1
USA	51.8

Standards of Living in the USA by Race, Age and Region

A comparison of measures of income and education, by selected characteristics (1995)

Median income per household (US $), by age and region

15–24 years	20,979
25–34 years	34,701
35–44 years	43,465
45–54 years	48,058
55–64 years	38.077
65 years and over	19,096
North-east	36,111
Mid-west	35,839
South	30,942
West	35,979

Per capita income (US $), by race and Hispanic origin of householder

ALL RACES	17,227
White	18,304
Black	10,982
Asian & Pacific Is.	16,567
Hispanic (any race)	9,300

The poorest 20% of households received just 3.6% of the income, whereas the richest 20% received 48.2%.

Percentage of persons aged 25 and over who have completed High School, by race or origin

ALL RACES	1975	62.5
	1995	81.7
White	1975	64.5
	1995	83.0
Black	1975	42.5
	1995	73.8
Hispanic	1975	37.9
	1995	53.4

Regional Inequality in Italy

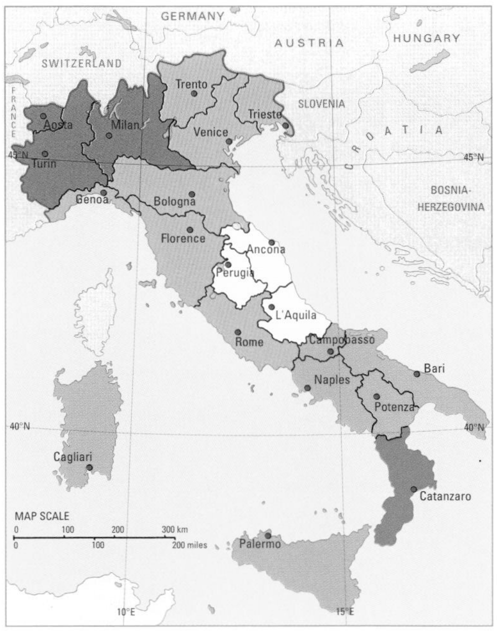

GERMANY
AUSTRIA
HUNGARY
SWITZERLAND
FRANCE
SLOVENIA
CROATIA
BOSNIA-HERZEGOVINA
Trento
Trieste
Aosta
Milan
Venice
Turin
Genoa
Bologna
Florence
Ancona
Perugia
L'Aquila
Rome
Campobasso
Naples
Bari
Potenza
Catanzaro
Cagliari
Palermo
45°N
40°N
10°E
15°E
MAP SCALE
0 100 200 300 km
0 100 200 miles

Gross Domestic Product (GDP) per capita in Italy, by region (1993)

- Over US $20,000
- $16,000 – $19,999
- $12,000 – $15,999
- $8,000 – $11,999
- Under $8,000

Average GDP per capita for Italy was $18,878. The per capita GDP, by comparison, for the UK was $17,920; for the USA $25,650; and for the EU $25,900.

The number of inhabitants per doctor, another social indicator, varies from less than 500 in the north-west of Italy to over 800 in the far south, with a national average of 607.

The southern part of Italy, known as the *Mezzogiorno* (or 'Land of the midday sun'), has been described as the poorest part of the European Union. It is identifiable on the map, left, as all the regions with a GDP per capita of less than $12,000 (including the two islands of Sicily and Sardinia), plus Abruzzi whose capital is L'Aquila.

The *Mezzogiorno* region suffers from a lack of mineral and energy resources, industry, commerce, services and skilled labour. As a result, standards of living in the region are well below the rest of Italy and Europe. Employment is predominantly agricultural and small-scale.

The north of Italy accounts for 60% of the population but 80% of the GDP, whereas the *Mezzogiorno* accounts for 40% of the population and only 20% of the GDP. Manpower surpluses in the south led to emigration to other parts of Europe and the Americas. It has also led, especially in the last 50 years, to inter-regional migration from the islands and the southern mainland to the north. The main regions attracting migrants were the north-west – the prosperous Liguria–Piedmont–Lombardy triangle with its great industrial cities of Genoa, Milan and Turin – and the Venetia region in the north-east. As a result, the north has experienced much higher population growth rates than the rest of Italy.

In 1996 the Northern League, one of Italy's political parties, exploited the regional differences by declaring the north to be the independent 'Republic of Padania'. However, only a small minority of northerners supports secession.

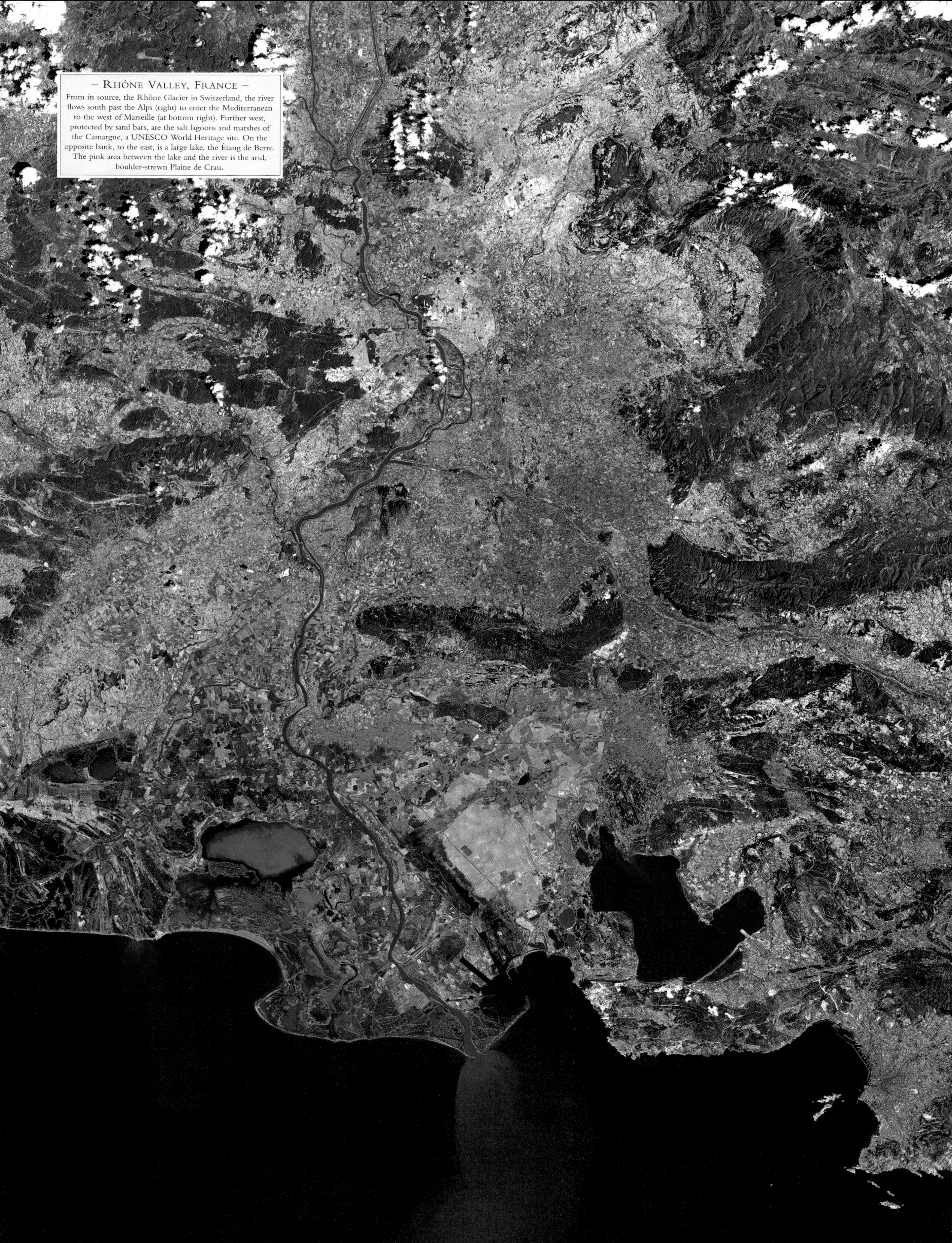

– Rhône Valley, France –

From its source, the Rhône Glacier in Switzerland, the river flows south past the Alps (right) to enter the Mediterranean to the west of Marseille (at bottom right). Further west, protected by sand bars, are the salt lagoons and marshes of the Camargue, a UNESCO World Heritage site. On the opposite bank, to the east, is a large lake, the Étang de Berre. The pink area between the lake and the river is the arid, boulder-strewn Plaine de Crau.

CITY MAPS

City Maps

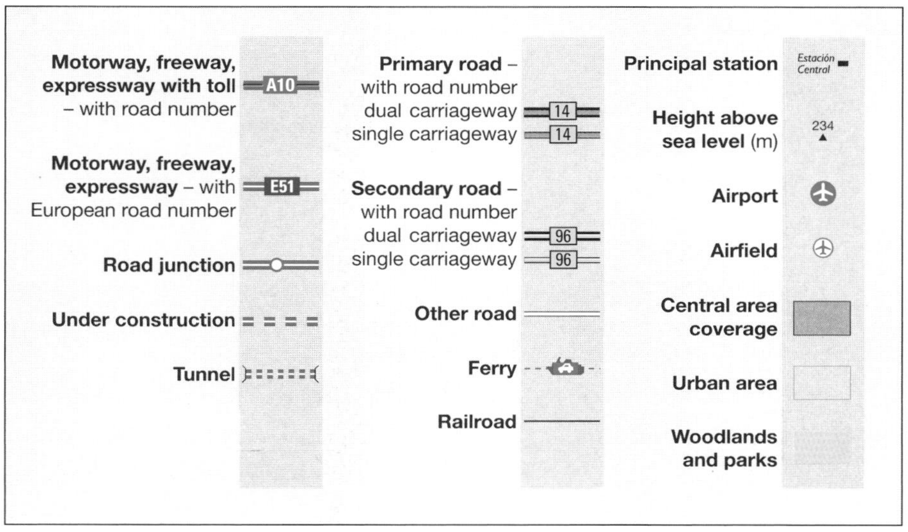

Central Area Maps

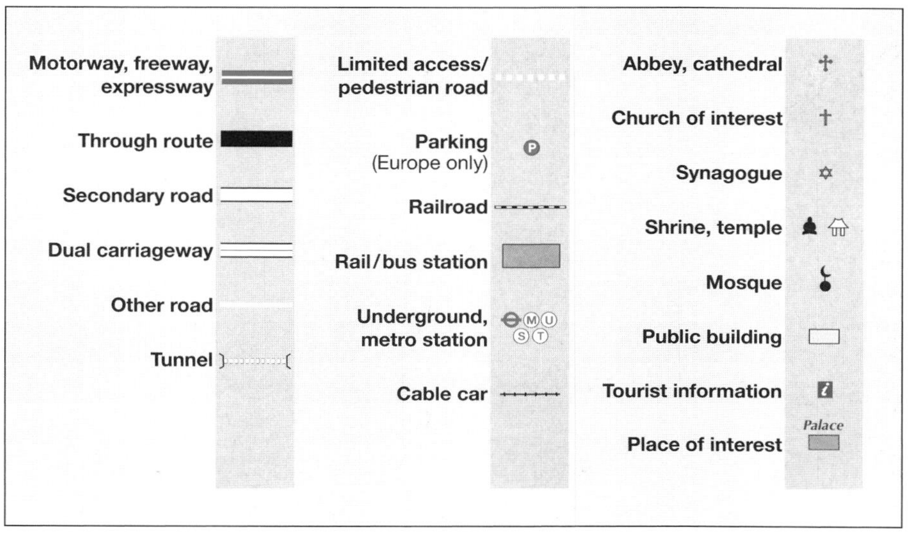

Amsterdam

0 km 5
0 miles 3

Central Amsterdam

0 km 2
0 miles 1

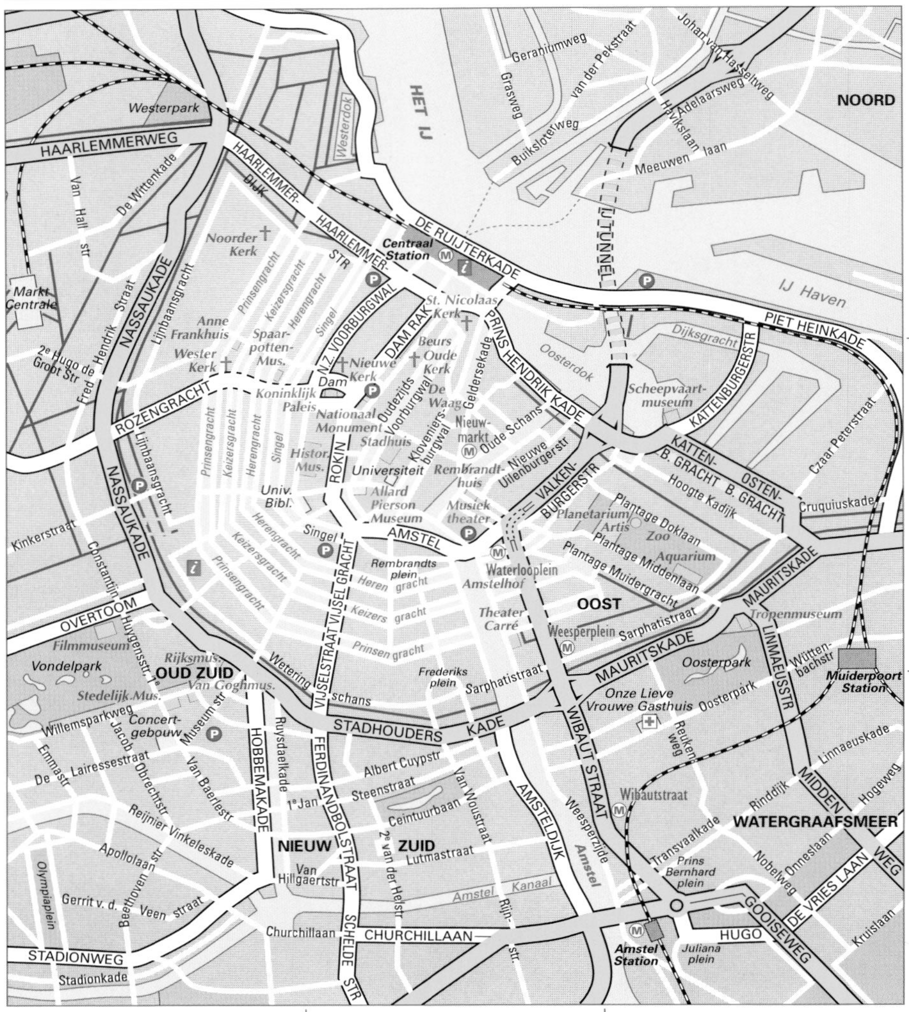

Athens

0 km 5
0 miles 3

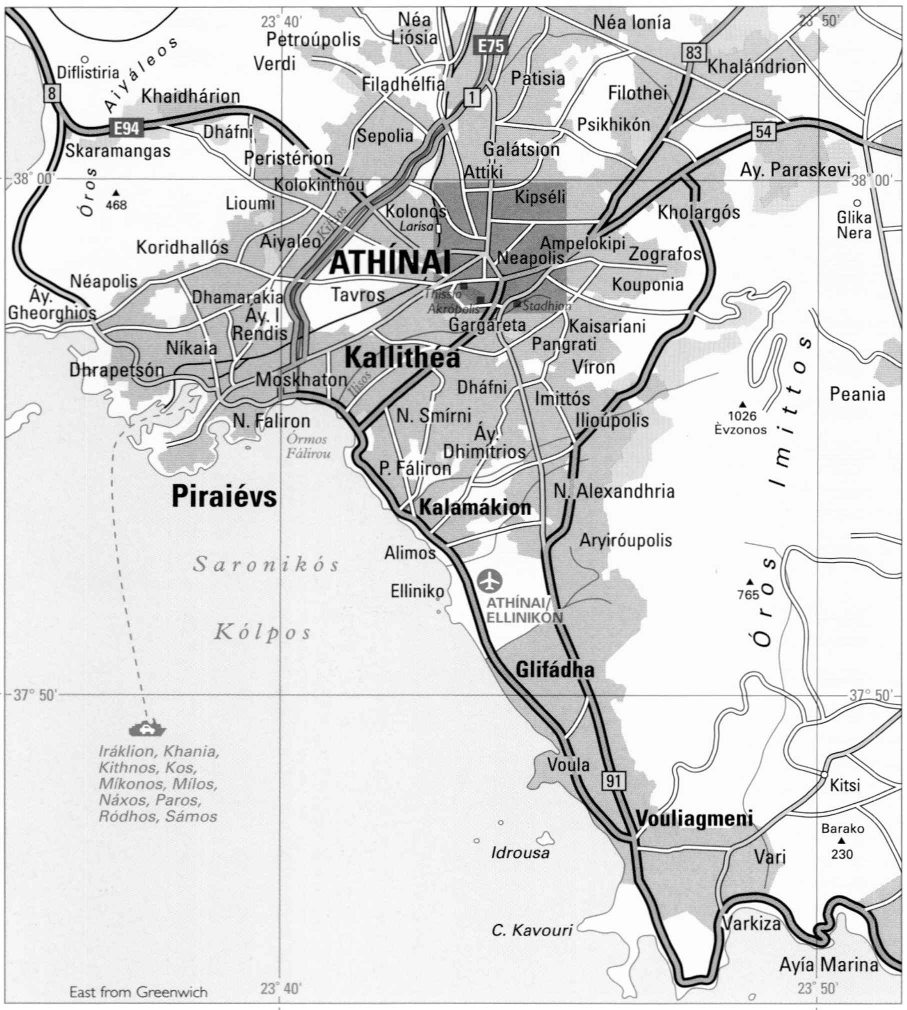

Central Athens

0 km 1
0 miles 0.5

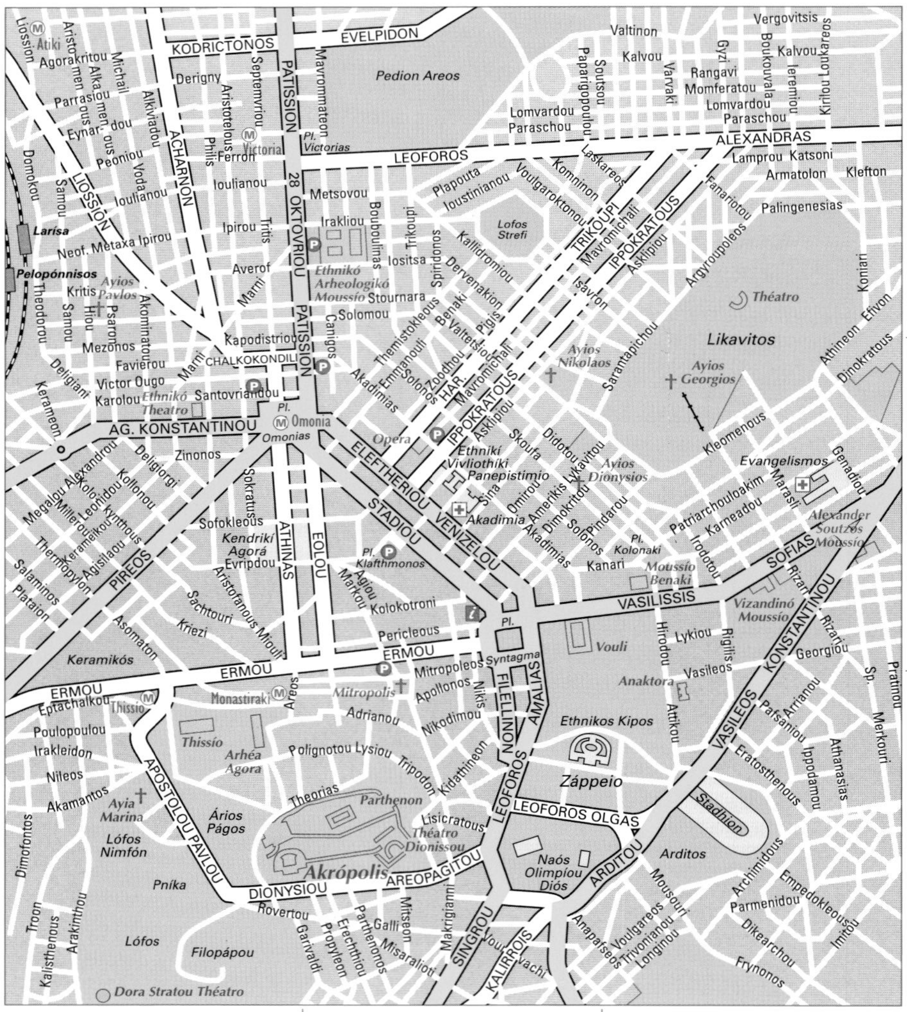

COPYRIGHT GEORGE PHILIP LTD

Atlanta

0 km 5
0 miles 3

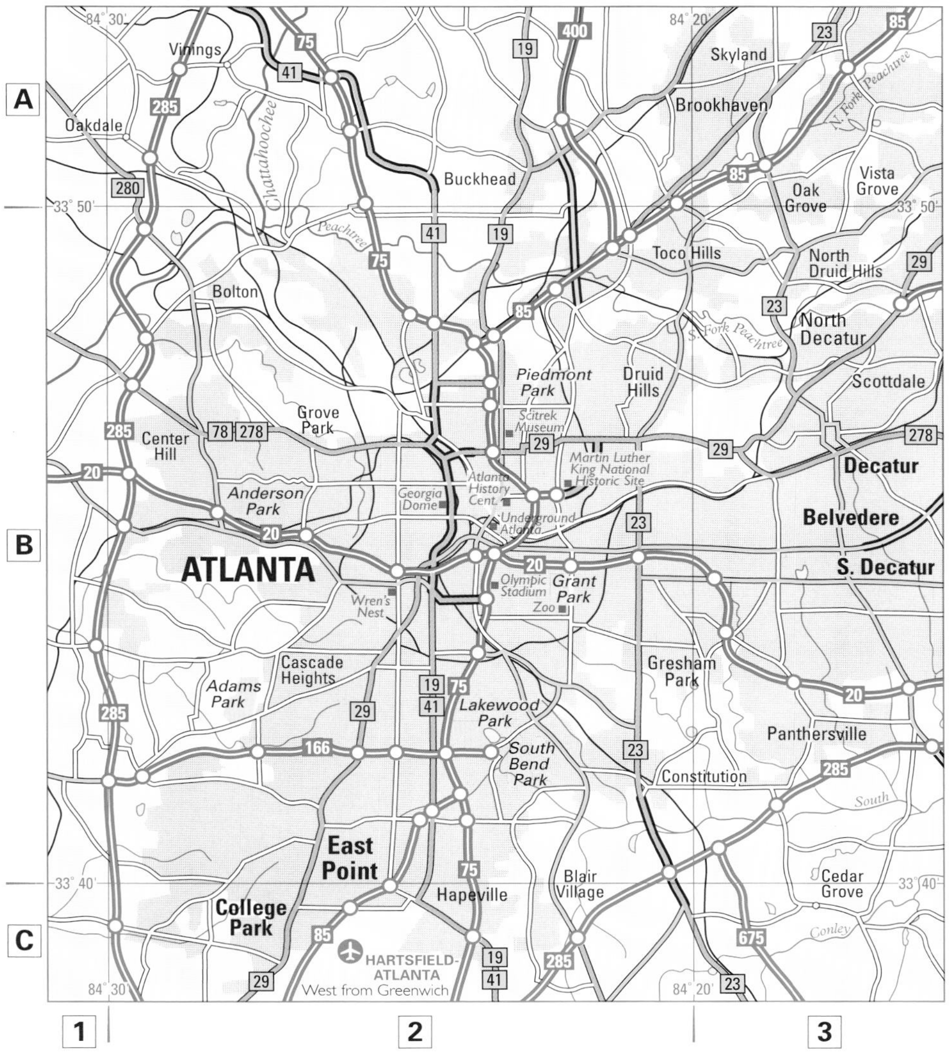

Vinings
Oakdale
Skyland
Brookhaven
Buckhead
Oak Grove
Vista Grove
Toco Hills
North Druid Hills
Bolton
North Decatur
Piedmont Park
Druid Hills
Scottdale
Grove Park
Center Hill
Sci-trek Museum
Martin Luther King National Historic Site
Decatur
Anderson Park
Georgia Dome
Atlanta History Cent.
Underground Atlanta
Belvedere
ATLANTA
Olympic Stadium
Grant Park
Zoo
S. Decatur
Wren's Nest
Adams Park
Cascade Heights
Gresham Park
Lakewood Park
Panthersville
South Bend Park
Constitution
East Point
Hapeville
Blair Village
Cedar Grove
College Park
HARTSFIELD-ATLANTA
West from Greenwich
Chattahoochee
Peachtree
Conley
South
A
B
C
1
2
3

Baghdad

0 km 5
0 miles 3

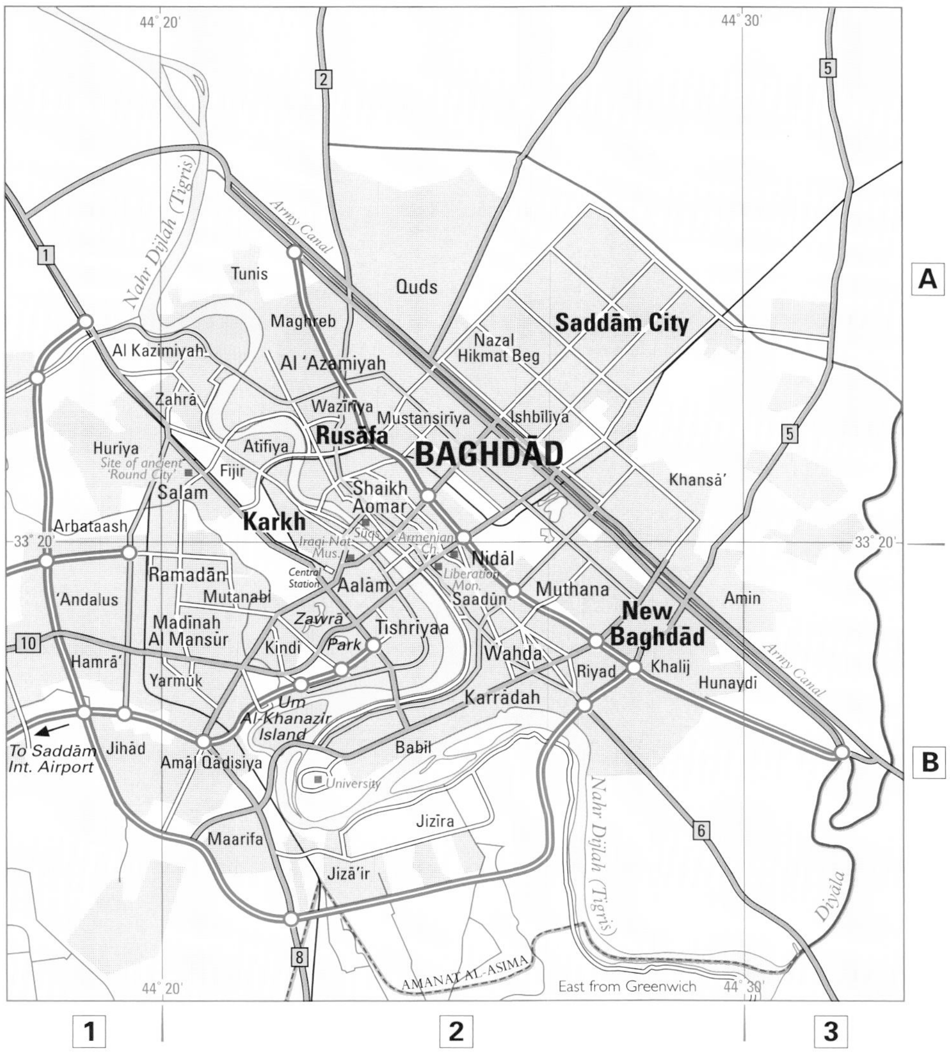

Army Canal
Nahr Dijlah (Tigris)
Tunis
Quds
Maghreb
Saddām City
Nazal Hikmat Beg
Al Kazimiyah
Al 'Azamiyah
Zahrā
Wazīriya
Mustansirīya
Ishbiliya
Hurīya
Site of ancient 'Round City'
Atifiya
Rusāfa
BAGHDĀD
Fijir
Salam
Khansā'
Shaikh Aomar
Arbataash
Karkh
Iraqi Nat. Mus.
Armenian City
Nidāl
Ramadān
Central Station
Liberation Mon.
'Andalus
Mutanabi
Aalām
Muthana
Amin
Madinah Al Mansūr
Saadūn
New Baghdād
Zawrā Park
Tishriyaa
Hamrā'
Kindi
Wahda
Riyad
Khalij
Hunaydi
Yarmūk
Karradah
Um Al-Khanazir Island
To Saddām Int. Airport
Jihād
Amāl Qādisiya
Babil
University
Jizīra
Maarifa
Jizā'ir
AMANAT AL ASIMA
East from Greenwich
Diyala
A
B
1
2
3

Bangkok

0 km 5
0 miles 3

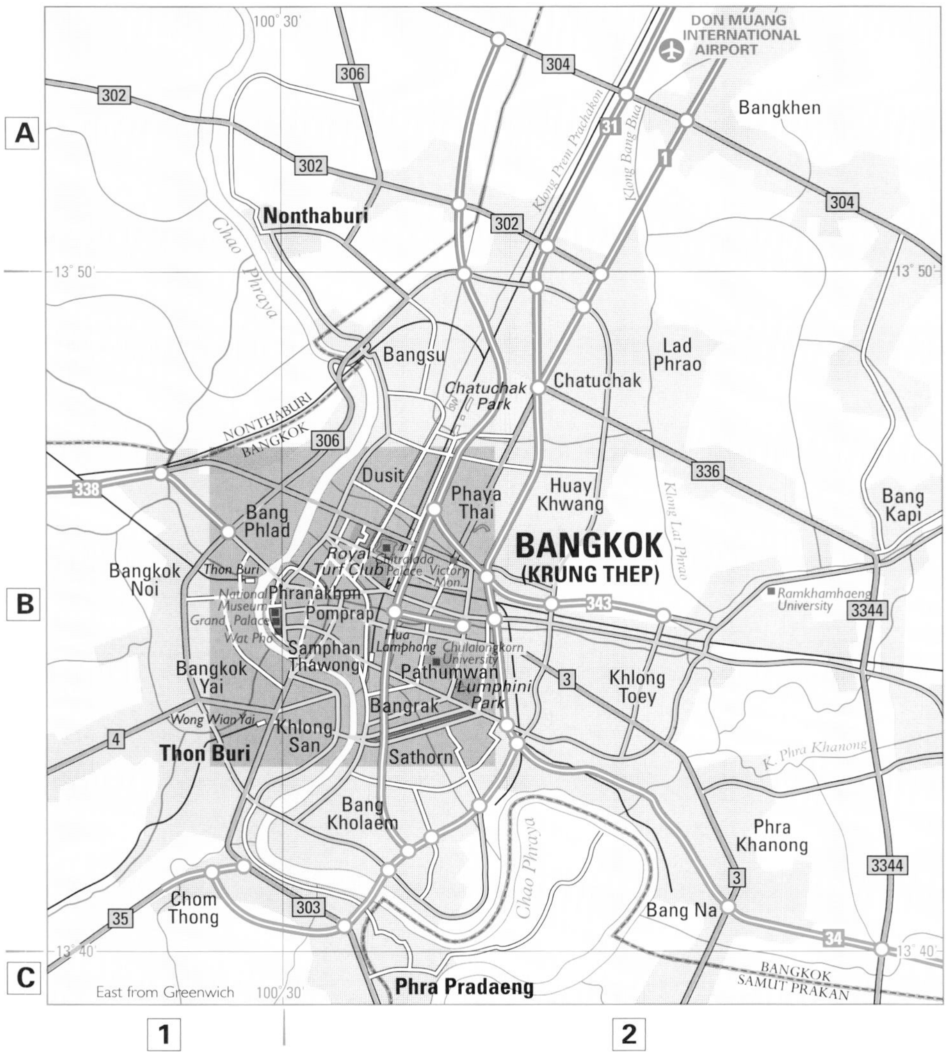

DON MUANG INTERNATIONAL AIRPORT
Bangkhen
Nonthaburi
Chao Phraya
Bangsu
Chatuchak Park
Chatuchak
Lad Phrao
NONTHABURI
BANGKOK
Dusit
Phaya Thai
Huay Khwang
Bang Kapi
Bang Phlad
BANGKOK (KRUNG THEP)
Bangkok Noi
Royal Turf Club
Phranakhon
Pomprap
Ramkhamhaeng University
Samphan Thawong
Hua Lamphong
Chulalongkorn University
Bangkok Yai
Pathumwan
Lumphini Park
Khlong Toey
Wong Wian Yai
Bangrak
Thon Buri
Khlong San
Sathorn
Bang Kholaem
Phra Khanong
Chom Thong
Bang Na
Phra Pradaeng
BANGKOK SAMUT PRAKAN
East from Greenwich
A
B
C
1
2

Central Bangkok

0 km 2
0 miles 1

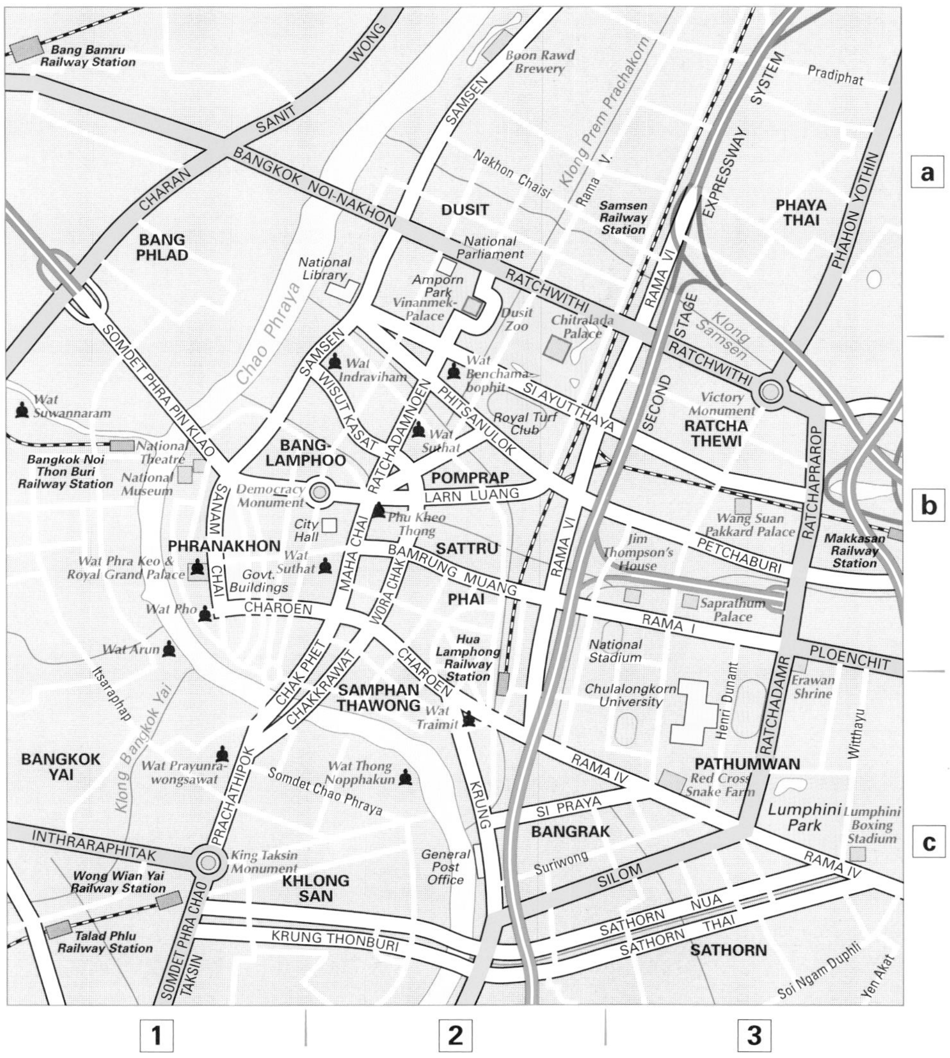

Bang Bamru Railway Station
Boon Rawd Brewery
Pradiphat
SANIT WONG
CHARAN
BANGKOK NOI-NAKHON
SAMSEN
Nakhon Chaisi
Klong Prem Prachakorn
Samsen Railway Station
EXPRESSWAY SYSTEM
PHAYA THAI
PHAHON YOTHIN
BANG PHLAD
DUSIT
National Parliament
National Library
Amporn Park
Vinanmek Palace
Dusit Zoo
RATCHWITHI
Chitralada Palace
Chao Phraya
SOMDET PHRA PIN KLAO
Wat Indraviham
Wat Benchamabophit
Wat Suwannaram
Royal Turf Club
Victory Monument
RATCHA THEWI
Bangkok Noi Thon Buri Railway Station
National Theatre
National Museum
BANG-LAMPHOO
POMPRAP
Democracy Monument
LARN LUANG
Wat Suthat
Phu Khao Thong
City Hall
PHRANAKHON
SATTRU
Wang Suan Pakkard Palace
Makkasan Railway Station
Wat Phra Keo & Royal Grand Palace
Govt. Buildings
BAMRUNG MUANG
PHAI
Jim Thompson's House
PETCHABURI
Wat Pho
CHAROEN
Saprathum Palace
RAMA I
PLOENCHIT
Wat Arun
Hua Lamphong Railway Station
National Stadium
Chulalongkorn University
Erawan Shrine
SAMPHAN THAWONG
Wat Traimit
Henri Dunant
RATCHADAMRI
Witthayu
BANGKOK YAI
Wat Prayunrawongsawat
Wat Thong Nopphakun
Somdet Chao Phraya
RAMA IV
PATHUMWAN
Red Cross Snake Farm
SI PRAYA
BANGRAK
Lumphini Park
Lumphini Boxing Stadium
INTHRAPHITAK
King Taksin Monument
General Post Office
Suriwong
SILOM
Wong Wian Yai Railway Station
KHLONG SAN
Talad Phlu Railway Station
KRUNG THONBURI
SATHORN NUA
SATHORN THAI
SATHORN
Soi Ngam Duphli
Yen Akat
a
b
c
1
2
3

COPYRIGHT GEORGE PHILIP LTD

Barcelona

0 km 5
0 miles 3

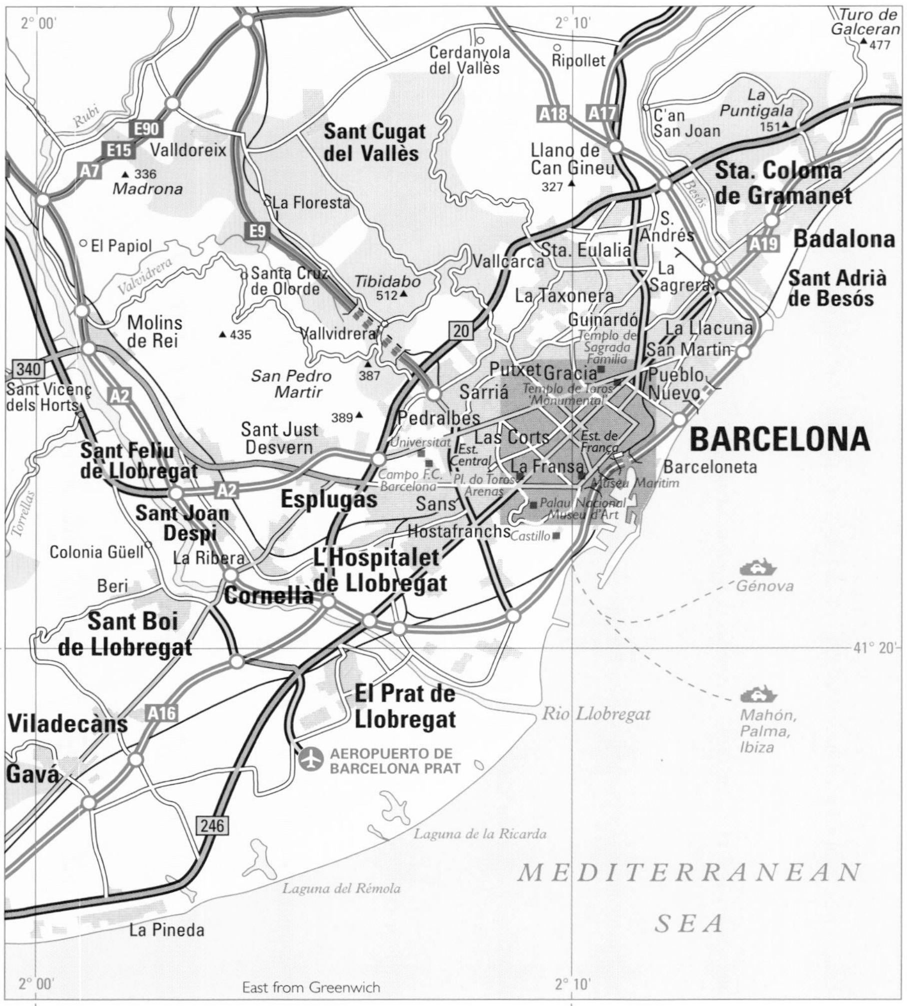

Cerdanyola del Vallès
Ripollet
Turo de Galceran 477
La Puntigala 151
C'an San Joan
Valldoreix
336 Madrona
Sant Cugat del Vallès
Llano de Can Gineu 327
Sta. Coloma de Gramanet
Badalona
La Floresta
El Papiol
Santa Cruz de Olorde
Tibidabo 512
S. Andrés
Sta. Eulalia
Vallcarca
La Sagrera
Sant Adrià de Besós
La Taxonera
Molins de Rei
435
Vallvidrera
Guinardó
La Llacuna
San Martin
San Pedro Martir
387
Putxet
Gracia
Sarrià
Pueblo Nuevo
Sant Vicenç dels Horts
389
Pedralbes
Sant Just Desvern
Las Corts
BARCELONA
Sant Feliu de Llobregat
La Fransa
Barceloneta
Sant Joan Despí
Esplugas
Sans
Hostafranchs
Colonia Güell
La Ribera
L'Hospitalet de Llobregat
Beri
Cornellà
Génova
Sant Boi de Llobregat
El Prat de Llobregat
Río Llobregat
Viladecans
Mahón, Palma, Ibiza
AEROPUERTO DE BARCELONA PRAT
Gavà
Laguna de la Ricarda
Laguna del Rèmola
MEDITERRANEAN SEA
La Pineda
East from Greenwich
2° 00'
2° 10'
41° 20'

Central Barcelona

0 km 1
0 miles 0.5

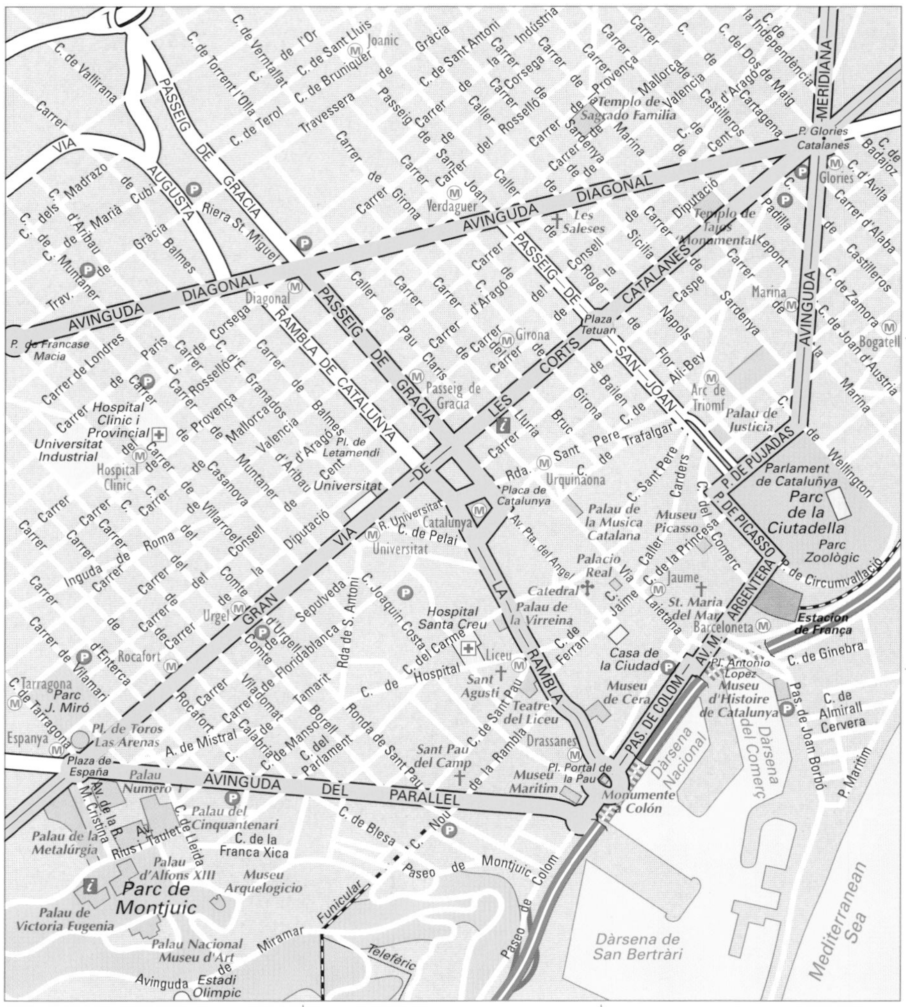

AVINGUDA DIAGONAL
PASSEIG DE GRACIA
RAMBLA DE CATALUNYA
GRAN VIA DE LES CORTS CATALANES
MERIDIANA
Templo de la Sagrada Familia
P. Glories Catalanes
Universitat Industrial
Hospital Clínic i Provincial
Pl. de Catalunya
Palau de la Música Catalana
Parlament de Catalunya
Parc de la Ciutadella
Parc Zoològic
Estación de França
Catedral
Palau de la Virreina
Hospital Santa Creu
Liceu
Museu Picasso
Palacio Real
Casa de la Ciudad
Museu d'Història de Catalunya
Parc J. Miró
Pl. de Toros Las Arenas
Plaza de España
AVINGUDA DEL PARALLEL
Drassanes
Museu Marítim
Monumento a Colón
Pl. Portal de la Pau
PAS. DE COLOM
Palau de la Metal·lúrgia
Palau del Cinquantenari
Museu Arqueològic
Parc de Montjuïc
Palau de Victoria Eugenia
Palau Nacional Museu d'Art de Catalunya
Estadi Olímpic
Miramar
Funicular
Teleféric
Dàrsena Nacional
Dàrsena del Comerç
Dàrsena de San Bertràn
Mediterranean Sea

Beijing

0 km 5
0 miles 3

Yiheyuan
Summer Palace
Qinghua University
Datun
Kunming Hu
Haidan
Qinghuayuan
Beijing International Airport
Ba He
Weigongcum
Beitaipingzhuang
Hepingli
Matihutong
Ditan Park
Beijing North Sta.
Beijing Zoo
Deshengmen
Andingmen
Xizhimen
Pinganli
Dongzhimen
Agricultural Exhibition Centre
Tiancun
Ganjiakou
Xicheng
Bei Hai
Dongcheng
Stadium
Yuyuantan Park
BEIJING (PEKING)
Imperial Palace Museum
Chaoyangmen
Ritan Park
Hongmiao
Yuyuan Tan
Military Museum
Sanlihe
Chaoyang
Shawocun
Fuxinglu
Xidan
Tian'anmen Square
Beijing Sta.
Jianguomen
Lianhua He
Xuanwu
Qianmen
Guangqumen
Lianhua Chi
Guang'anmen
Chongwen
Dajiaoting
Taoranting Park
Tiantan Park
Longtan Hu
You'anmen
Yongdingman
Puhuangyu
Fengtai
Yanghuayuan
Tiejiangyin
Huangtugang
Dahongmen
Liangshui He
East from Greenwich
116° 20'
40° 00'
39° 50'

Central Beijing

0 km 2
0 miles 1

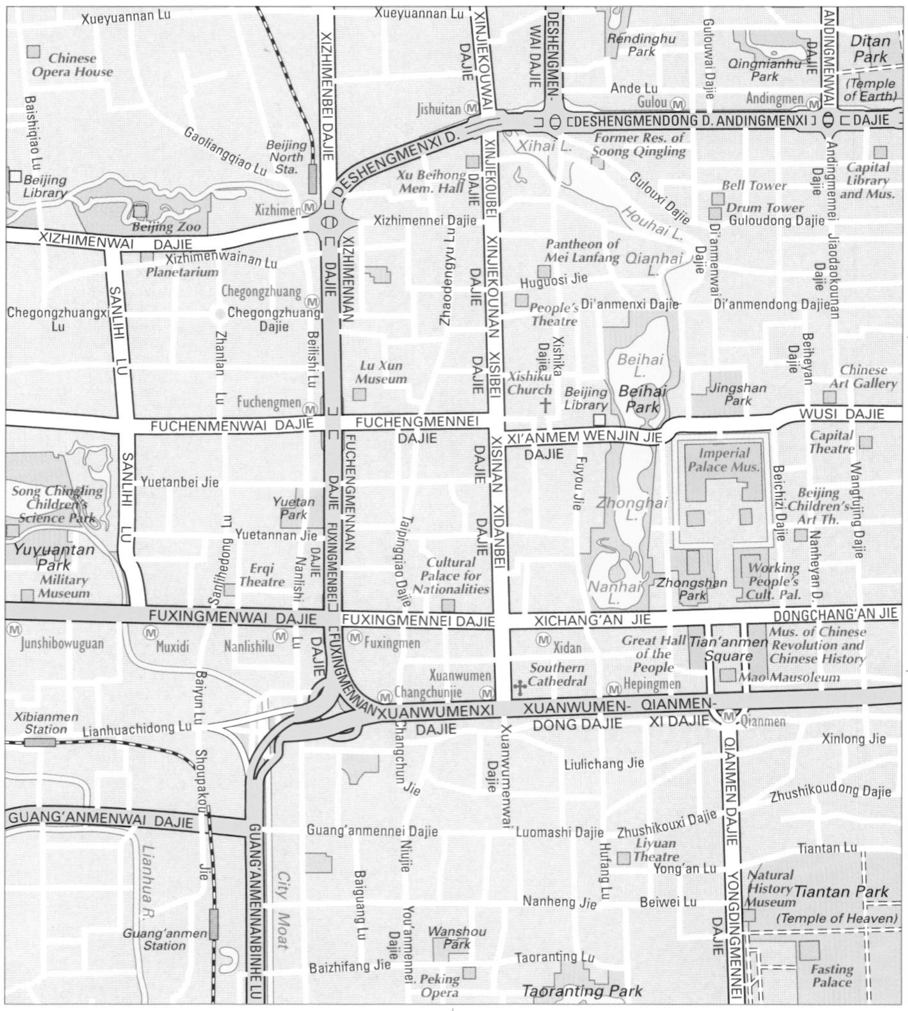

Xueyuannan Lu
Chinese Opera House
Rendinghu Park
Qingnianhu Park
Ditan Park (Temple of Earth)
Jishuitan
DESHENGMENDONG D.
ANDINGMENXI D.
Beijing North Sta.
Former Res. of Soong Qingling
Xihai L.
Beijing Library
Xu Beihong Mem. Hall
Bell Tower
Drum Tower
Capital Library and Mus.
Beijing Zoo
XIZHIMENWAI DAJIE
Xizhimen
Beijing Planetarium
Pantheon of Mei Lanfang
Qianhai L.
Chegongzhuang
People's Theatre
Lu Xun Museum
Xishiku Church
Beihai Park
Jingshan Park
Chinese Art Gallery
FUCHENGMENWAI DAJIE
FUCHENGMENNEI DAJIE
XI'ANMEN WENJIN JIE
WUSI DAJIE
Capital Theatre
Imperial Palace Mus.
Song Chingling Children's Science Park
Zhonghai L.
Beijing Children's Art Th.
Yuyuantan Park
Military Museum
Erqi Theatre
Cultural Palace for Nationalities
Nanhai L.
Zhongshan Park
Working People's Cult. Pal.
FUXINGMENWAI DAJIE
FUXINGMENNEI DAJIE
XICHANG'AN JIE
DONGCHANG'AN JIE
Muxidi
Xidan
Great Hall of the People
Tian'anmen Square
Mus. of Chinese Revolution and Chinese History
Mao Mausoleum
Southern Cathedral
XUANWUMENXI DAJIE
XUANWUMEN-DONG DAJIE
QIANMEN-XI DAJIE
Qianmen
Xibianmen Station
Liulichang Jie
Xinlong Jie
GUANG'ANMENWAI DAJIE
Guang'anmennei Dajie
Luomashi Dajie
Liyuan Theatre
Natural History Museum
Tiantan Park (Temple of Heaven)
City Moat
Guang'anmen Station
Wanshou Park
Taoranting Park
Peking Opera
Fasting Palace

COPYRIGHT GEORGE PHILIP LTD

Berlin

0 km 5
0 miles 3

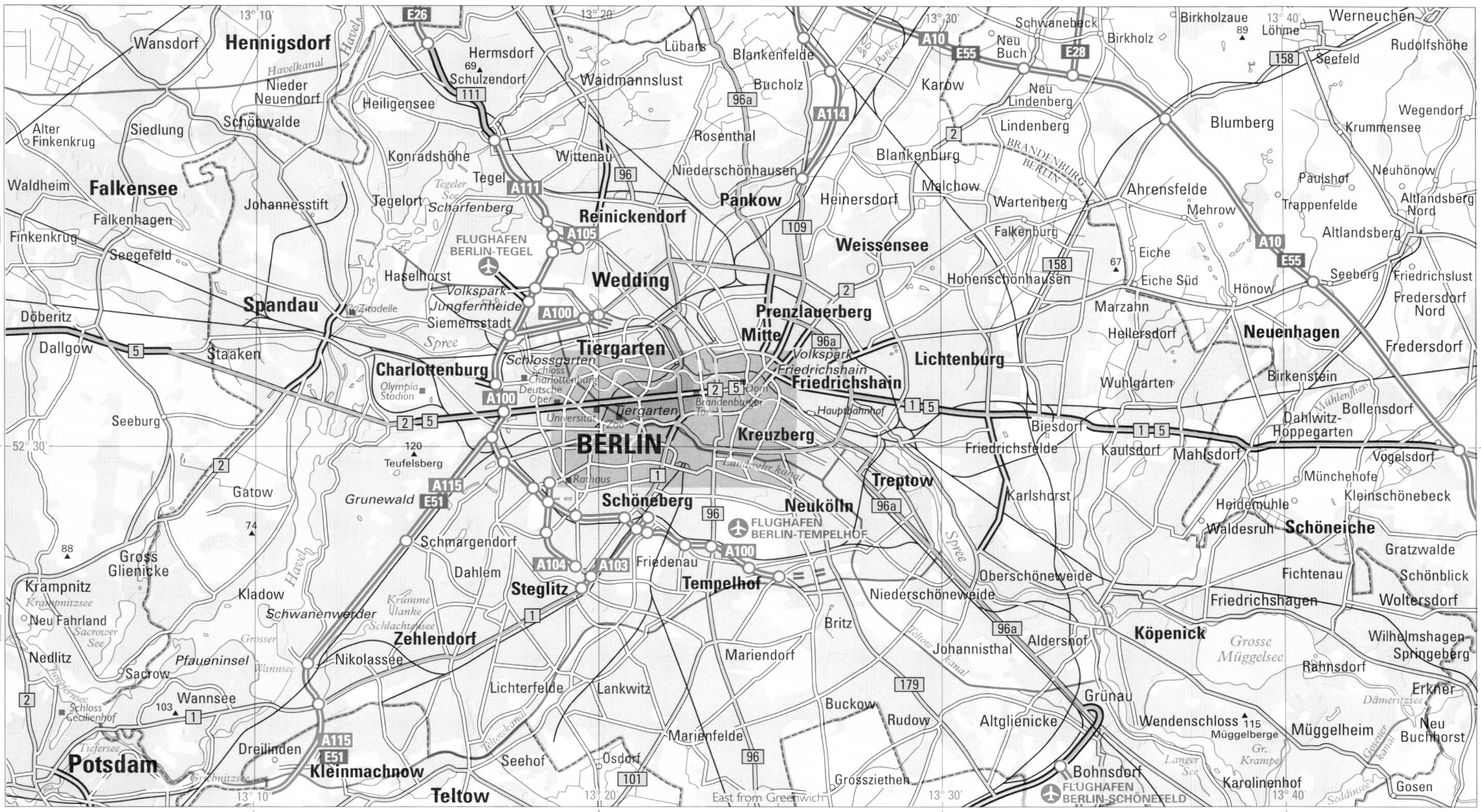
Hennigsdorf
Wansdorf
Hermsdorf
Schulzendorf
Waidmannslust
Lübars
Blankenfelde
Bucholz
Schwanebeck
Neu Buch
Birkholz
Birkholzaue
Löhme
Werneuchen
Rudolfshöhe
Seefeld
Nieder Neuendorf
Heiligensee
Schönwalde
Alter Finkenkrug
Siedlung
Konradshöhe
Tegel
Wittenau
Rosenthal
Niederschönhausen
Karow
Neu Lindenberg
Lindenberg
Blankenburg
Blumberg
Krummensee
Wegendorf
Waldheim
Falkensee
Falkenhagen
Finkenkrug
Seegefeld
Johannesstift
Tegelort
Scharfenberg
Reinickendorf
Pankow
Heinersdorf
Malchow
Wartenberg
Falkenburg
Ahrensfelde
Mehrow
Paulshof
Trappenfelde
Neuhönow
Altlandsberg Nord
Altlandsberg
FLUGHAFEN BERLIN-TEGEL
Weissensee
Eiche
Eiche Süd
Hönow
Seeberg
Friedrichslust
Fredersdorf Nord
Haselhorst
Spandau
Zitadelle
Volkspark Jungfernheide
Siemensstadt
Wedding
Hohenschönhausen
Prenzlauerberg
Marzahn
Hellersdorf
Neuenhagen
Döberitz
Dallgow
Staaken
Charlottenburg
Tiergarten
Mitte
Lichtenburg
Fredersdorf
Olympia Stadion
Schlossgarten
Schloss Charlottenburg
Deutsche Oper
Volkspark Friedrichshain
Friedrichshain
Wuhlgarten
Birkenstein
Seeburg
Universität
Tiergarten
Brandenburger Tor
Dom
Hauptbahnhof
Biesdorf
Dahlwitz-Hoppegarten
Bollensdorf
Teufelsberg
BERLIN
Kreuzberg
Friedrichsfelde
Kaulsdorf
Mahlsdorf
Vogelsdorf
Rathaus
Landwehr kanal
Treptow
Münchehofe
Gatow
Grunewald
Schöneberg
Neukölln
Karlshorst
Heidemühle
Kleinschönebeck
FLUGHAFEN BERLIN-TEMPELHOF
Waldesruh
Schöneiche
Schmargendorf
Gross Glienicke
Friedenau
Gratzwalde
Krampnitz
Dahlem
Steglitz
Tempelhof
Oberschöneweide
Fichtenau
Schönblick
Kladow
Niederschöneweide
Friedrichshagen
Woltersdorf
Neu Fahrland
Schwanenwerder
Zehlendorf
Britz
Aldershof
Köpenick
Grosse Müggelsee
Wilhelmshagen
Springeberg
Nedlitz
Nikolassee
Mariendorf
Johannisthal
Rahnsdorf
Sacrow
Pfaueninsel
Wannsee
Lichterfelde
Lankwitz
Buckow
Rudow
Grünau
Erkner
Schloss Cecilienhof
Altglienicke
Wendenschloss
Müggelberge
Müggelheim
Neu Buchhorst
Dreilinden
Marienfelde
Potsdam
Kleinmachnow
Seehof
Osdorf
Grossziethen
Bohnsdorf
Karolinenhof
Teltow
FLUGHAFEN BERLIN-SCHÖNEFELD
Gosen
East from Greenwich

Central Berlin

0 km 1
0 miles 0.5

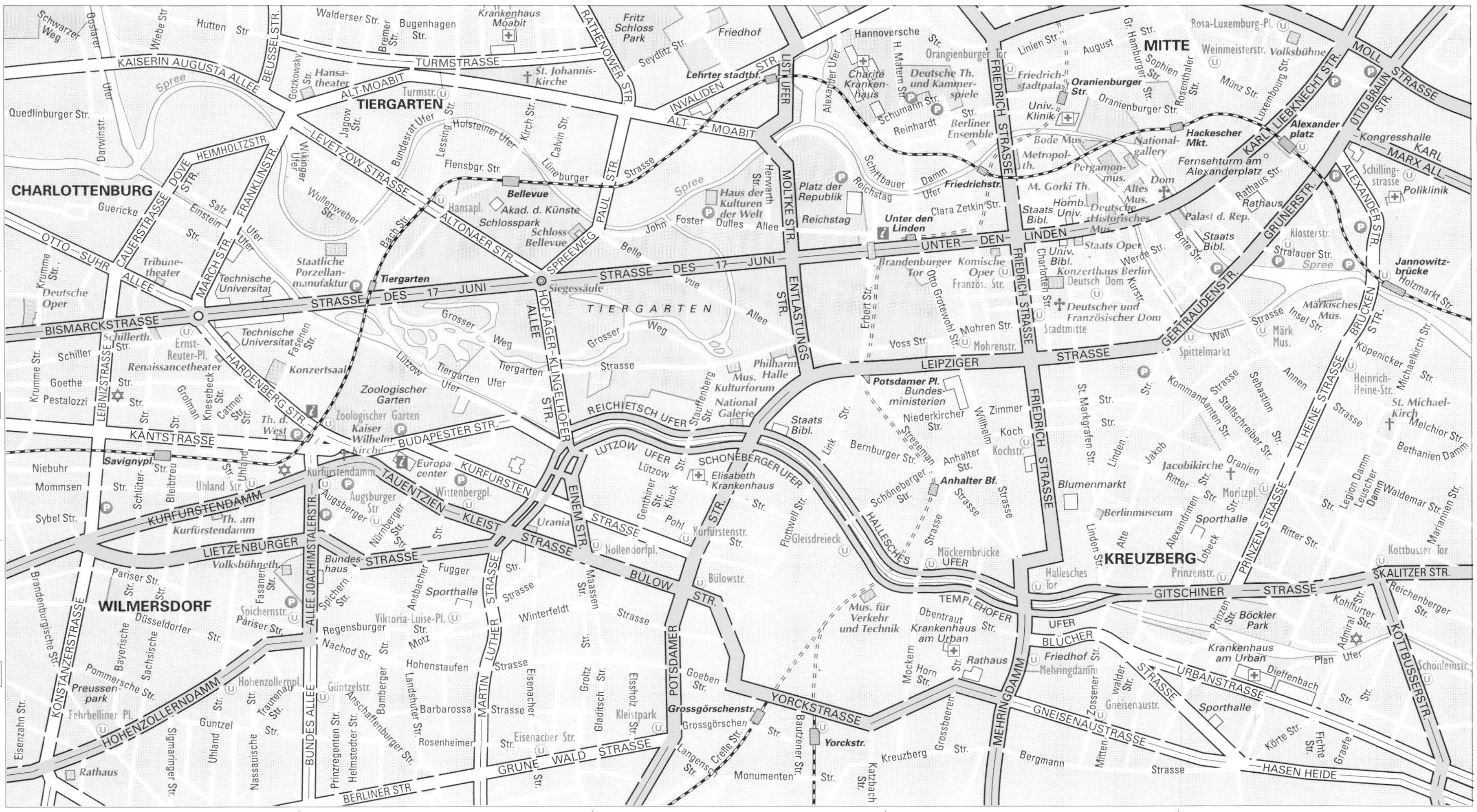
Hutten Str.
Walderser Str.
Bugenhagen Str.
Krankenhaus Moabit
Fritz Schloss Park
Friedhof
Hannoversche
Rosa-Luxemburg-Pl.
Volksbühne
MITTE
KAISERIN AUGUSTA ALLEE
TURMSTRASSE
Hansa-theater
ALT-MOABIT
St. Johannis-Kirche
Lehrter stadtbf.
Charité Kranken-haus
Deutsche Th. und Kammer-spiele
Oranienburger Str.
TIERGARTEN
INVALIDEN STR.
Friedrich-stadtpalast
Quedlinburger Str.
Univ. Klinik
Berliner Ensemble
Hackescher Mkt.
Alexander platz
Kongresshalle
Bode Mus.
Metropol-th.
National-gallery
Pergamon-mus.
Fernsehturm am Alexanderplatz
CHARLOTTENBURG
Bellevue
Haus der Kulturen der Welt
Platz der Republik
Reichstag
Friedrichstr.
M. Gorki Th.
Altes Mus.
Dom
Akad. d. Künste
Schlosspark
Schloss Bellevue
Unter den Linden
Staats Bibl.
Deutsche Historisches Mus.
Palast d. Rep.
Rathaus
Poliklinik
OTTO-SUHR ALLEE
Tribune-theater
Technische Universität
Staatliche Porzellan-manufaktur
Tiergarten
STRASSE DES 17 JUNI
Siegessäule
UNTER DEN LINDEN
Staats Oper
Univ.
Konzerthaus Berlin
Deutsch Dom
Französ. Str.
Deutscher und Französischer Dom
Märkisches Mus.
Jannowitz-brücke
Deutsche Oper
BISMARCKSTRASSE
TIERGARTEN
Brandenburger Tor
Komische Oper
Technische Universität
Ernst-Reuter-Pl.
Renaissancetheater
Schiller
Goethe
Pestalozzi
Konzertsaal
Zoologischer Garten
Philharm Halle
Mus. Kulturforum
National Galerie
Potsdamer Pl.
Bundes ministerien
LEIPZIGER STRASSE
Spittelmarkt
Märk Mus.
Heinrich-Heine-Str.
St. Michael-Kirch
KANTSTRASSE
Th. d. West
Kaiser Wilhelm Kirche
BUDAPESTER STR.
REICHPIETSCH UFER
Staats Bibl.
Savignypl.
Europa-center
KURFÜRSTEN
Elisabeth Krankenhaus
Anhalter Bf.
Blumenmarkt
Jacobikirche
Moritzpl.
Niebuhr
Mommsen
Sybel Str.
KURFÜRSTENDAMM
Th. am Kurfürstendamm
Augsburger Str.
Wittenbergpl.
Urania
TAUENTZIEN
KLEIST
Nollendorfpl.
Gleisdreieck
Berlinmuseum
Sporthalle
LIETZENBURGER STRASSE
Volksbühne
Bundes-haus
BÜLOW STR.
Bülowstr.
Möckernbrücke
Hallesches Tor
KREUZBERG
Prinzenstr.
Kottbusser Tor
SKALITZER STR.
WILMERSDORF
Fugger
Sporthalle
Mus. für Verkehr und Technik
TEMPELHOFER UFER
GITSCHINER STRASSE
Böckler Park
Viktoria-Luise-Pl.
Winterfeldt
Krankenhaus am Urban
Rathaus
BLUCHER
Friedhof
Mehringdamm
Krankenhaus am Urban
URBANSTRASSE
Dieffenbach
Hohenzollernpl.
Preussen park
Fehrbelliner Pl.
HOHENZOLLERNDAMM
Hohenstaufen
Barbarossa
Grossgörschenstr.
YORCKSTRASSE
Sporthalle
GNEISENAUSTRASSE
Rosenheimer
Eisenacher Str.
Kleistpark
Yorckstr.
Monumenten
Kreuzberg
Bergmann
HASEN HEIDE
Rathaus
GRUNE WALD STRASSE
BERLINER STR.

COPYRIGHT GEORGE PHILIP LTD

Boston

0 km 5
0 miles 3

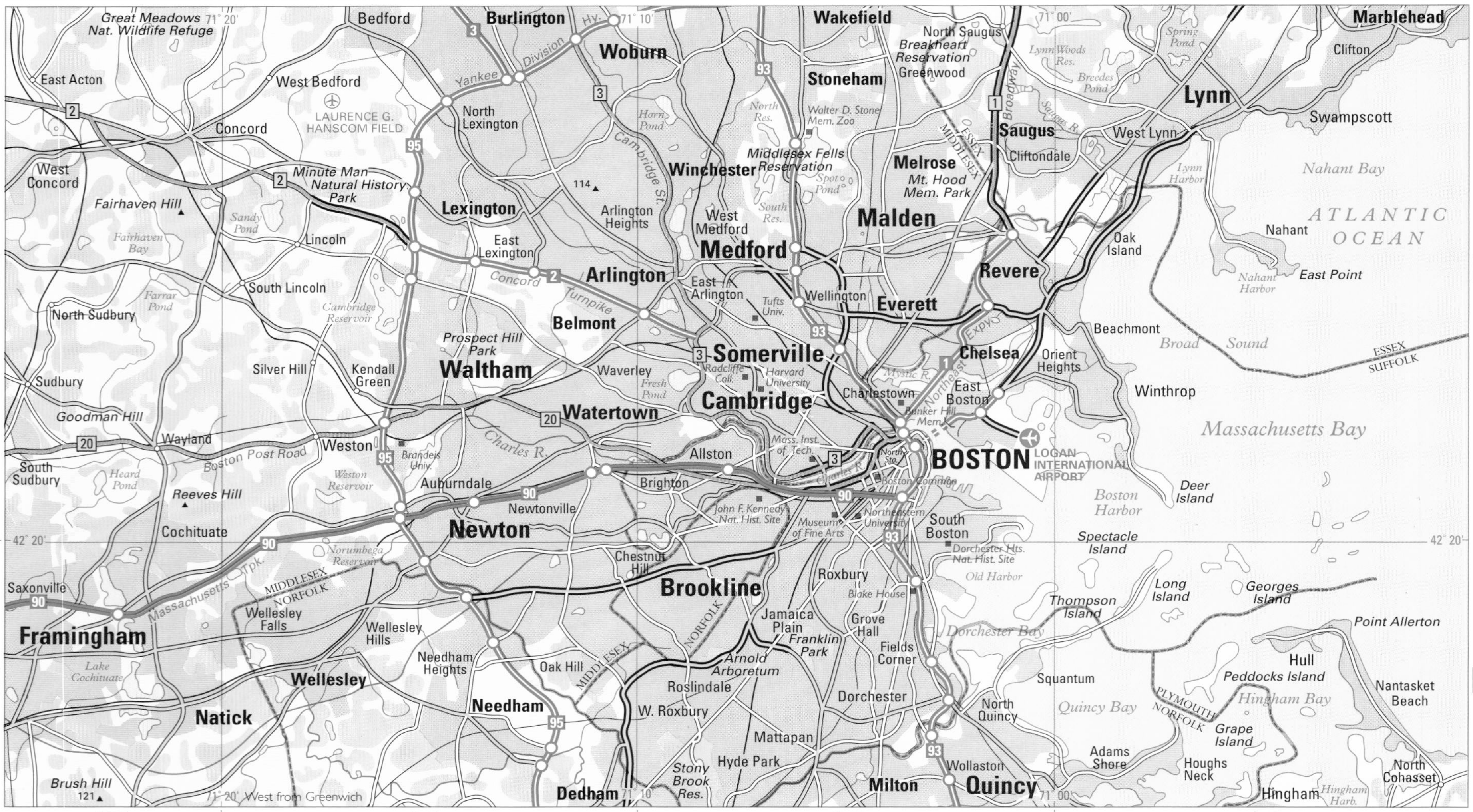

Brussels

0 km 5
0 miles 3

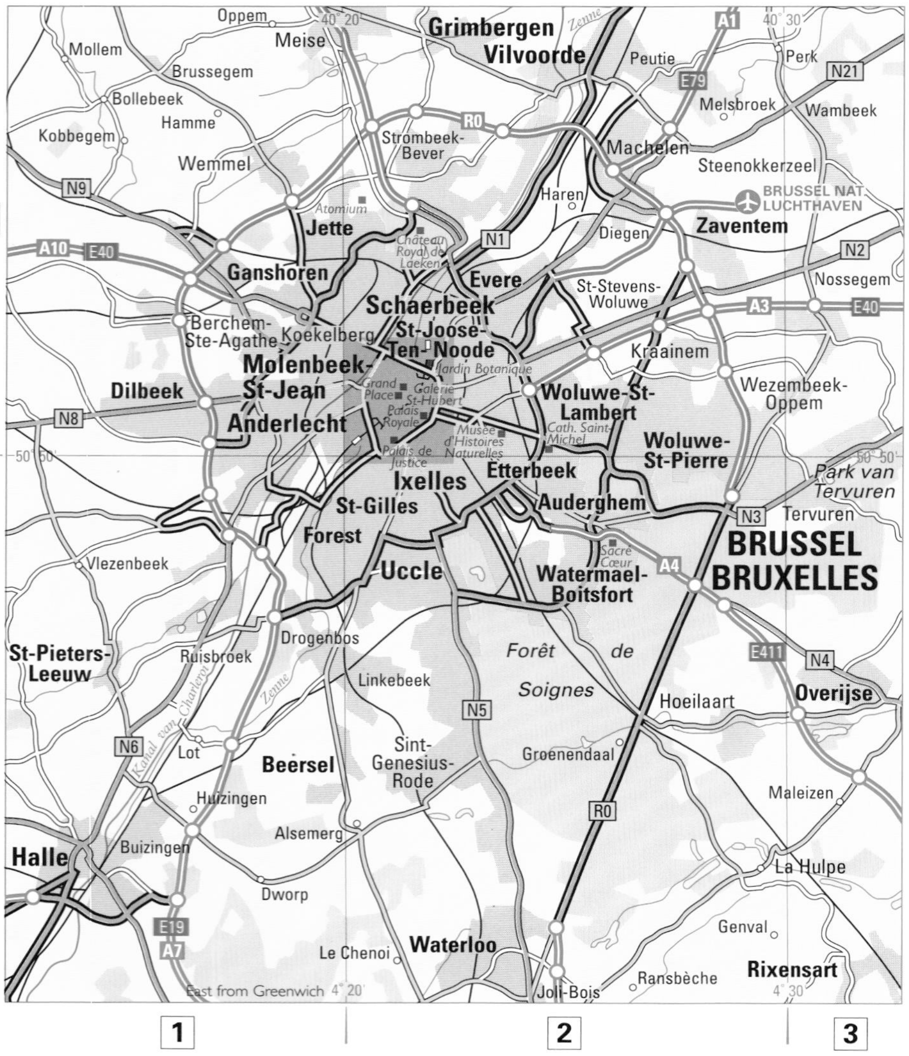

Central Brussels

0 km 1
0 miles 0.5

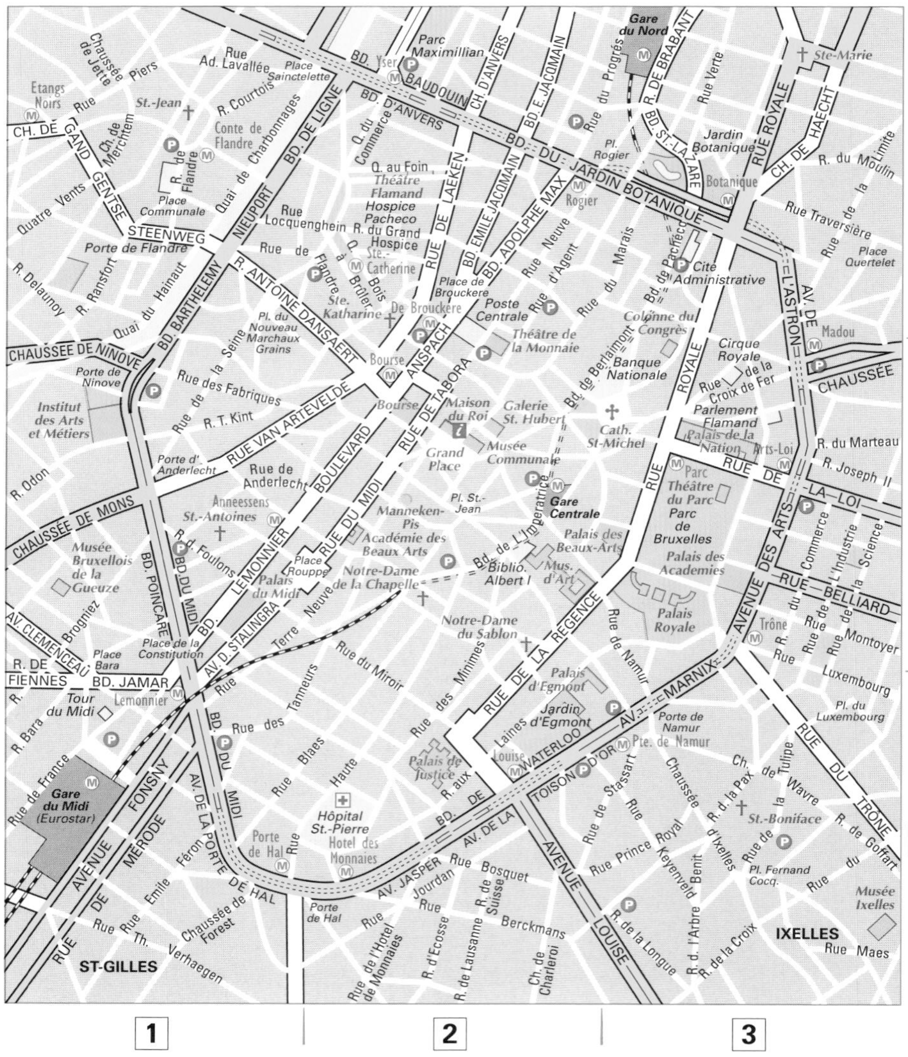

COPYRIGHT GEORGE PHILIP LTD

Budapest

0 km 5
0 miles 3

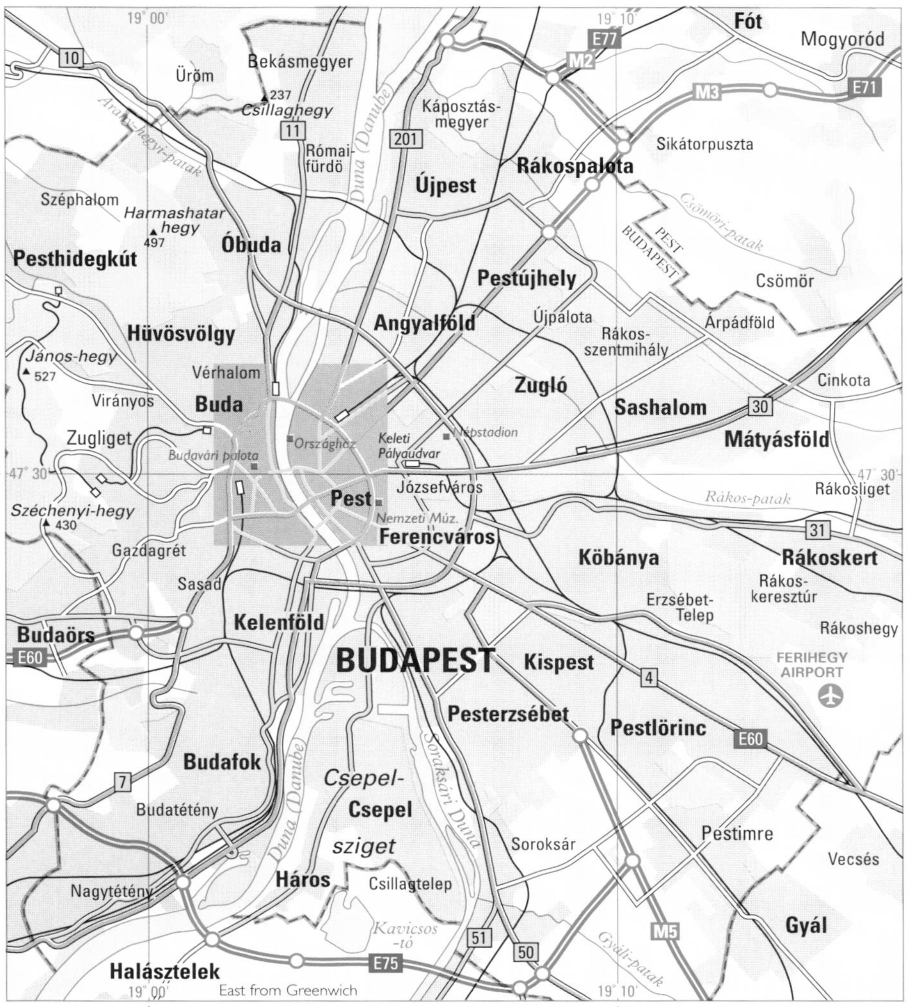

Central Budapest

0 km 1
0 miles 0.5

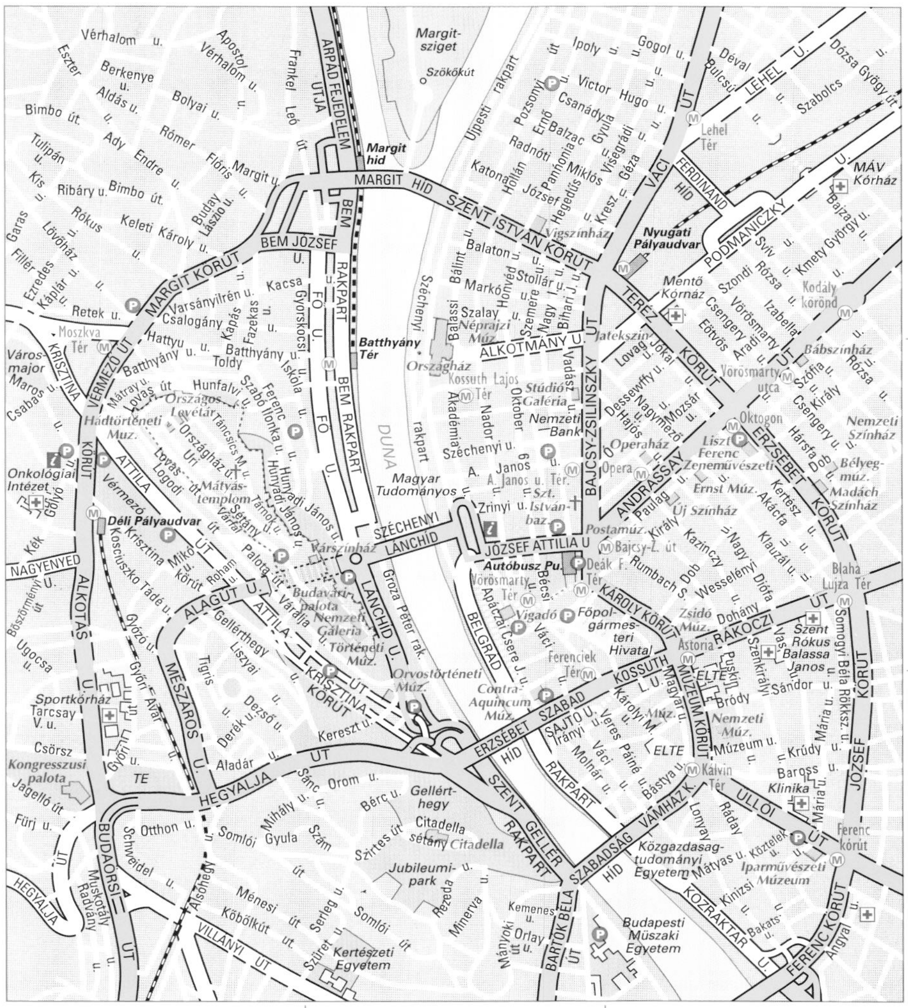

Buenos Aires

0 km 5
0 miles 3

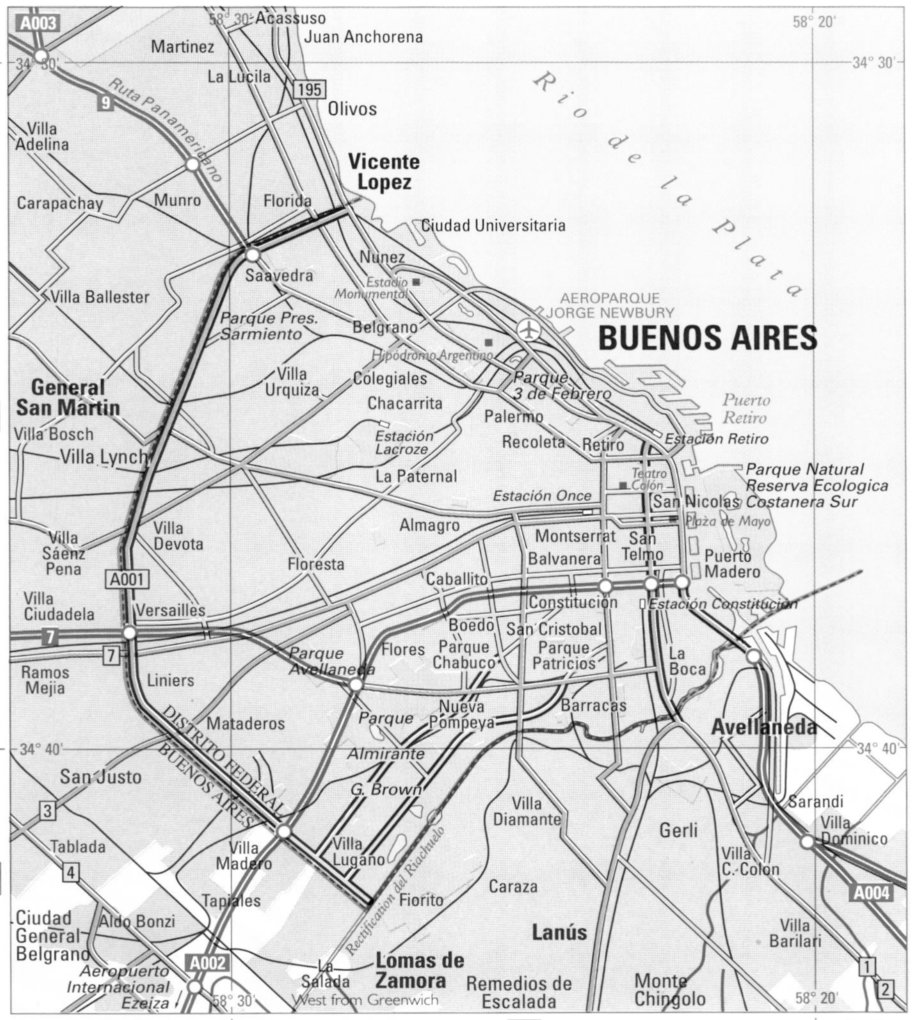

Cairo

0 km 5
0 miles 3

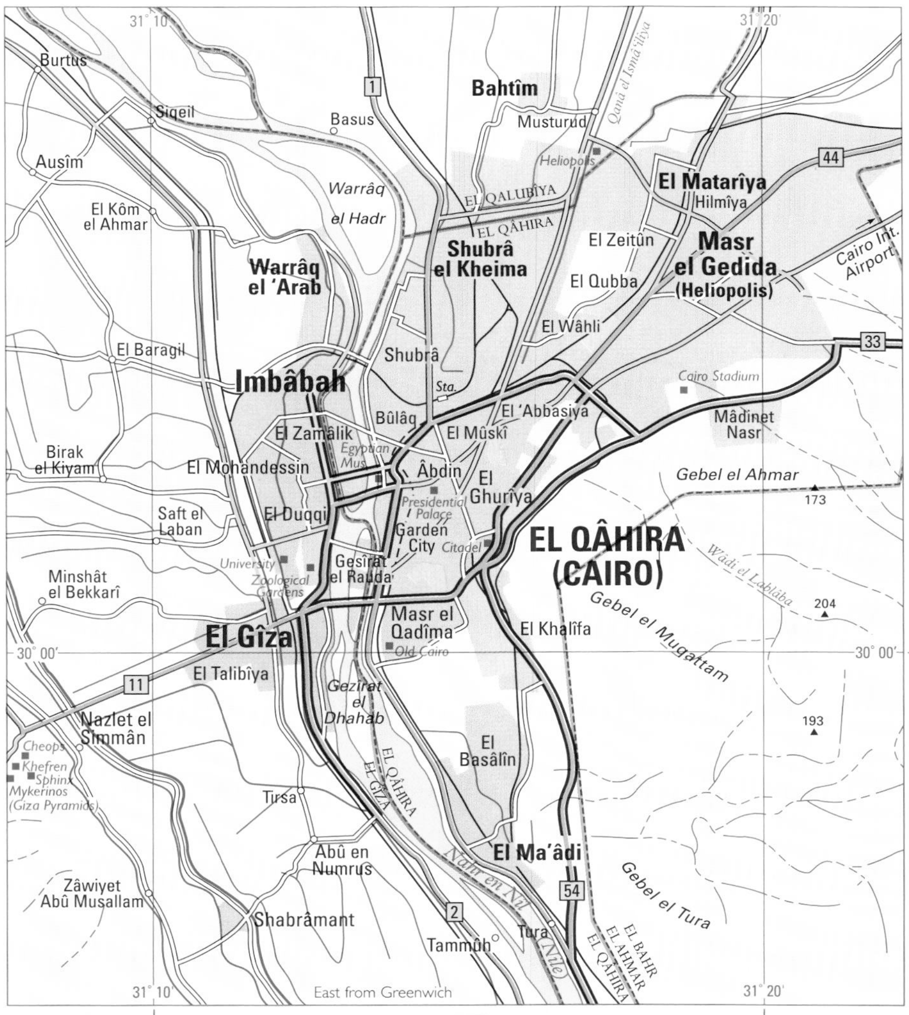

Calcutta

0 km 5
0 miles 3

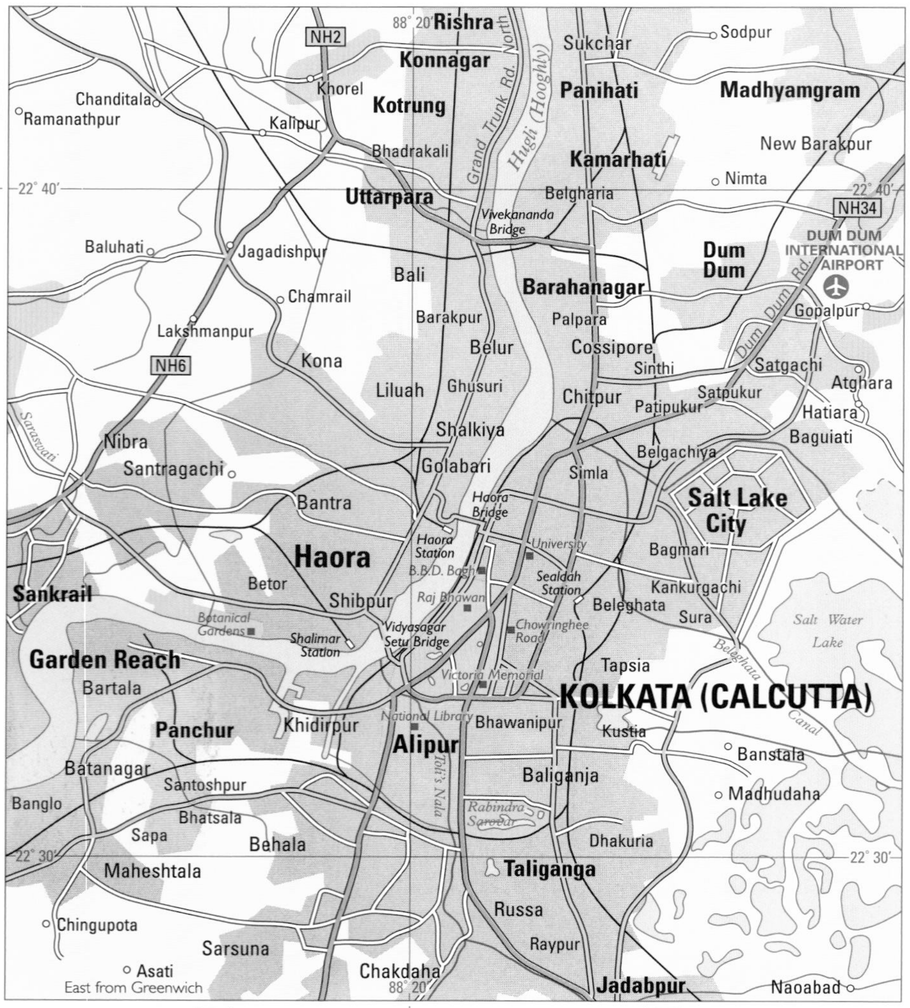
A
B
C
1
2
88° 20'
22° 40'
22° 30'
NH2
NH6
NH34
Rishra
Konnagar
Kotrung
Sukchar
Panihati
Sodpur
Madhyamgram
Chanditala
Ramanathpur
Khorel
Kalipur
Bhadrakali
Grand Trunk Rd.
Hugli (Hooghly)
Kamarhati
New Barakpur
Nimta
Uttarpara
Belgharia
Vivekananda Bridge
DUM DUM INTERNATIONAL AIRPORT
Dum Dum
Baluhati
Jagadishpur
Bali
Barahanagar
Chamrail
Barakpur
Palpara
Gopalpur
Lakshmanpur
Belur
Cossipore
Kona
Sinthi
Satgachi
Liluah
Ghusuri
Chitpur
Satpukur
Atghara
Patipukur
Hatiara
Shalkiya
Nibra
Baguiati
Santragachi
Golabari
Belgachiya
Simla
Salt Lake City
Bantra
Haora Bridge
Haora
Haora Station
University
Bagmari
Sealdah Station
Sankrail
Betor
B.B.D. Bagh
Raj Bhawan
Kankurgachi
Shibpur
Chowringhee Road
Beleghata
Sura
Salt Water Lake
Botanical Gardens
Shalimar Station
Vidyasagar Setu Bridge
Garden Reach
Victoria Memorial
Tapsia
Bartala
KOLKATA (CALCUTTA)
National Library
Panchur
Khidirpur
Bhawanipur
Alipur
Kustia
Canal
Banstala
Batanagar
Tolly's Nala
Santoshpur
Baliganja
Madhudaha
Banglo
Bhatsala
Rabindra Sarobar
Sapa
Behala
Dhakuria
Maheshtala
Taliganga
Chingupota
Russa
Sarsuna
Raypur
Asati
Chakdaha
Jadabpur
Naoabad
East from Greenwich

Canton

0 km 5
0 miles 3

A
B
1
2
3
113° 10'
113° 20'
23° 10'
Gangtou
Xiaoping
107
Yuanxiatian
Chienzui
Lishui
Chantian
BAIYUN AIRPORT
Zhushadi
Baiyun Hill Scenic Spot
205
106
Zhoucun
Shuikou
Hengsha
Shahe
Sanyuanli
Guangzhou Zhan (Railway Station)
Yongfucun
Xichang
Exhibition Hall
Huanghuagang Mausoleum of the 72 Martyrs
Guangzhou Zoo
Xiasha chong
Baisha
Datansha
Guangzhou Museum
Lieshi Lingyuan
Liurong Temple
Nongminyundong Jiangxisuo
Shipai
Beitsun
Haizhu
Guangchang
GUANGZHOU (CANTON)
Nan Zhan (Railway Station)
324
Shiweitang
Shamian
Dongshanhu Park
Ershatou
Zhu Jiang (Pearl)
Nandang
Xiaogang Park
Fangcun
Zhongshan University
Yanbu
Shayuan
Luojiang
Hedong
Gangwei
Dongjiao
Nanbiancun
Guanshuo
Lichiao
Zhu Jiang (Pearl)
Pingzhou
Dashi
Zhicun
105
East from Greenwich

Cape Town

0 km 5
0 miles 3

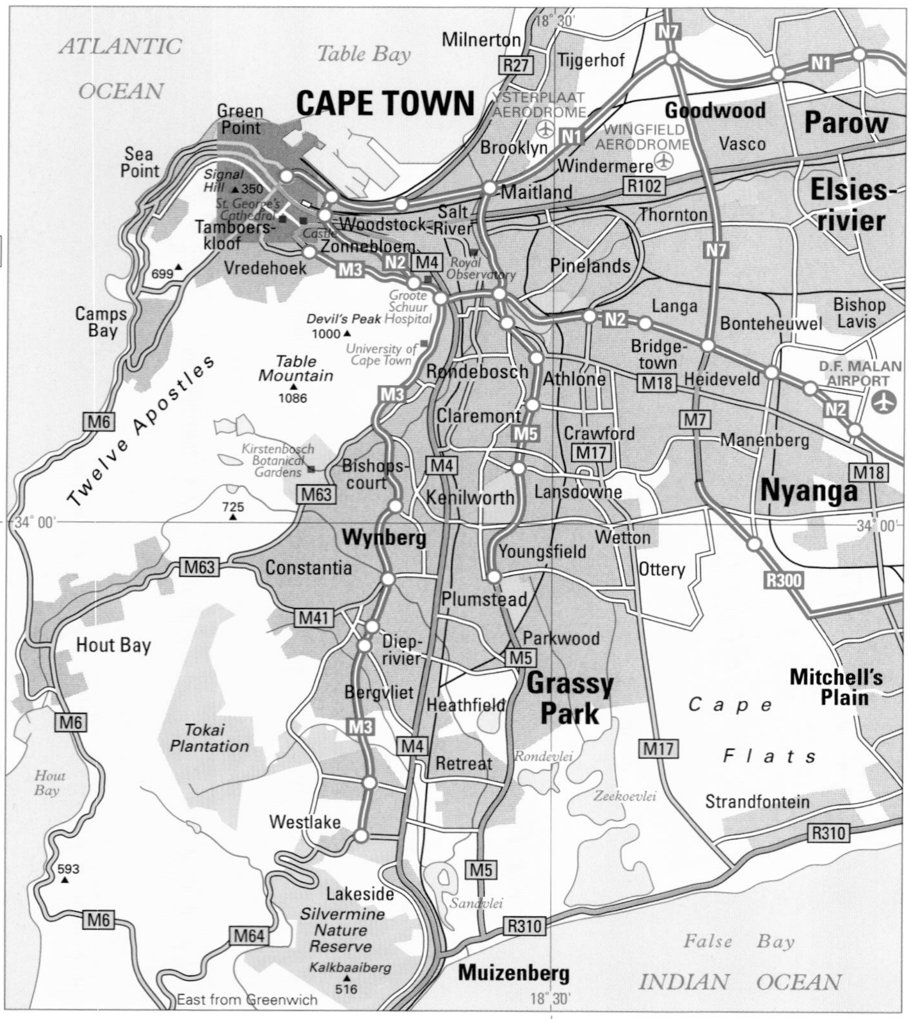
A
B
1
2
18° 30'
34° 00'
ATLANTIC OCEAN
Table Bay
Milnerton
R27
Tijgerhof
N7
N1
Green Point
CAPE TOWN
YSTERPLAAT AERODROME
WINGFIELD AERODROME
Goodwood
Parow
Sea Point
Brooklyn
Vasco
Signal Hill 350
Windermere
St. George's Cathedral
Maitland
R102
Elsies-rivier
Tamboers-kloof
Castle
Woodstock
Salt River
Thornton
Zonnebloem
699
Vredehoek
M3
N2
M4
Royal Observatory
Pinelands
N7
Camps Bay
Groote Schuur Hospital
Langa
Bishop Lavis
Devil's Peak 1000
N2
Bonteheuwel
University of Cape Town
Bridge-town
Table Mountain 1086
Rondebosch
Athlone
Heideveld
D.F. MALAN AIRPORT
M18
M3
Claremont
M6
M5
Crawford
M7
Manenberg
Twelve Apostles
M17
M18
Kirstenbosch Botanical Gardens
Bishops-court
M4
Lansdowne
Nyanga
725
M63
Kenilworth
Wetton
Wynberg
Youngsfield
Ottery
M63
Constantia
R300
Plumstead
M41
Parkwood
Hout Bay
Diep-rivier
M5
Grassy Park
Mitchell's Plain
M6
Bergvliet
Heathfield
Cape Flats
Tokai Plantation
M3
M4
Rondevlei
Hout Bay
Retreat
M17
Zeekoevlei
Strandfontein
Westlake
R310
593
M5
Lakeside
Sandvlei
M6
M64
Silvermine Nature Reserve
R310
False Bay
Kalkbaaiberg 516
Muizenberg
INDIAN OCEAN
East from Greenwich

Central Cape Town

0 km 1
0 miles 0.5

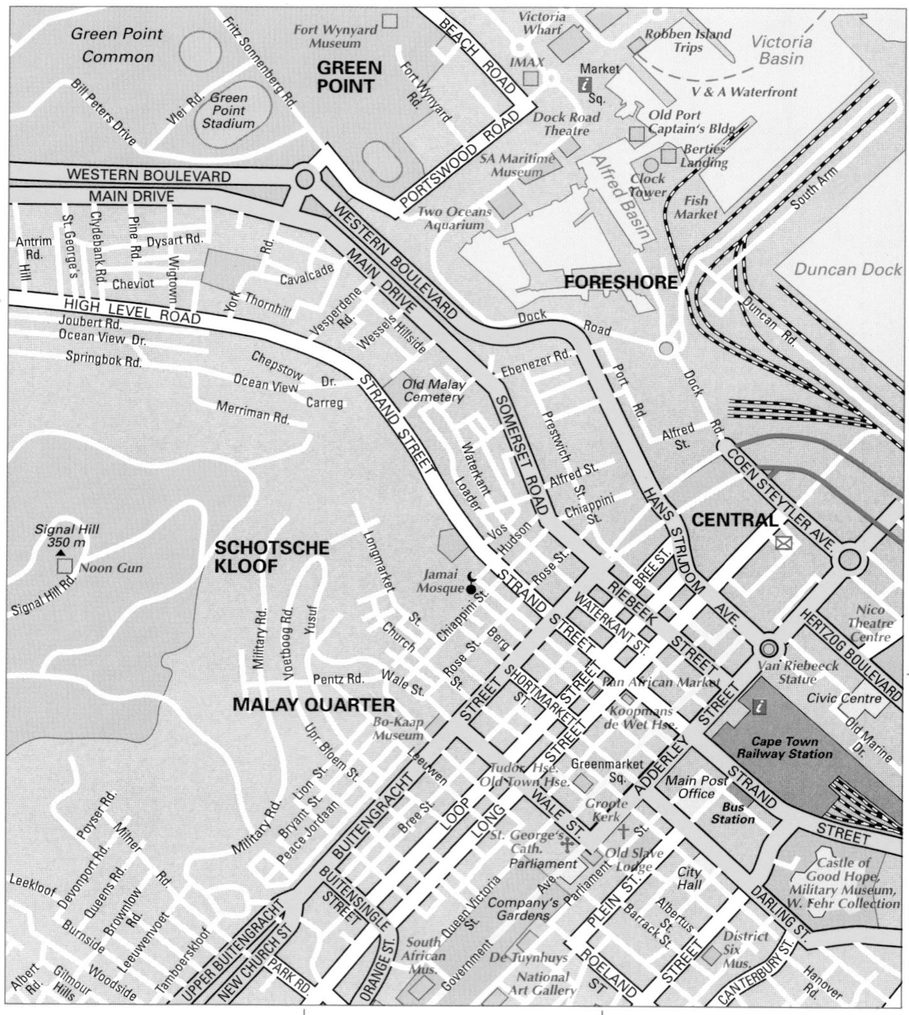
a
b
c
1
2
3
Green Point Common
Fritz Sonnenberg Rd.
Fort Wynyard Museum
BEACH ROAD
Victoria Wharf
Robben Island Trips
Victoria Basin
GREEN POINT
IMAX
Market Sq.
Bill Peters Drive
Vlei Rd.
Green Point Stadium
Fort Wynyard Rd.
V & A Waterfront
PORTSWOOD ROAD
Dock Road Theatre
Old Port Captain's Bldg.
SA Maritime Museum
Alfred Basin
Berties Landing
WESTERN BOULEVARD
MAIN DRIVE
Clock Tower
Fish Market
Two Oceans Aquarium
South Arm
Antrim Rd.
St. George's
Clydebank Rd.
Pine Rd.
Dysart Rd.
Wigtown
Hill
WESTERN BOULEVARD
MAIN DRIVE
Duncan Dock
Cheviot
Cavalcade
HIGH LEVEL ROAD
York
Thornhill
FORESHORE
Joubert Rd.
Ocean View Dr.
Vesperdene
Wessels
Hillside
Dock
Road
Duncan Rd.
Springbok Rd.
Chepstow
Ocean View
Dr.
Ebenezer Rd.
Port Rd.
Dock
Old Malay Cemetery
Carreg
STRAND STREET
SOMERSET ROAD
Prestwich
Merriman Rd.
Alfred St.
COEN STEYTLER AVE
Waterkant
Loader
Alfred St.
Chiappini St.
HANS STRIJDOM AVE
CENTRAL
Signal Hill 350 m
Noon Gun
SCHOTSCHE KLOOF
Vos
Hudson
Rose St.
BREE ST.
Signal Hill Rd.
Longmarket St.
Jamai Mosque
STRAND
WATERKANT ST.
HERTZOG BOULEVARD
Nico Theatre Centre
Military Rd.
Voetboog Rd.
Yusuf
Church
Chiappini St.
RIEBEEK STREET
Van Riebeeck Statue
Pentz Rd.
Wale St.
Rose St.
SHORTMARKET ST.
Pan African Market
Civic Centre
MALAY QUARTER
Bo-Kaap Museum
Berg
Koopmans de Wet Hse.
Old Marine Dr.
Cape Town Railway Station
Upr. Bloem St.
Leeuwen
Tudor Hse.
Old Town Hse.
Greenmarket Sq.
ADDERLEY
STRAND
Main Post Office
Bus Station
Lion St.
Bryant St.
Peace Jordan
Military Rd.
BUITENGRACHT
Bree St.
LOOP
LONG
WALE ST.
Groote Kerk
STREET
Poyser Rd.
Milner Rd.
St. George's Cath.
Parliament
Old Slave Lodge
City Hall
Castle of Good Hope Military Museum, W. Fehr Collection
Leekloof
Devonport Rd.
Queens Rd.
Browntow Rd.
Burnside
Leeuwvoet
Tamboerskloof
UPPER BUITENGRACHT
NEW CHURCH ST.
BUITENSINGLE STREET
Queen Victoria
Company's Gardens
Parliament
PLEIN ST.
Albertus St.
Barrack St.
DARLING ST.
District Six Mus.
Albert Rd.
Gilmour Hill
Woodside
PARK RD.
ORANGE ST.
South African Mus.
Government
De Tuynhuys
National Art Gallery
BOLAND
STREET
CANTERBURY ST.
Hanover

COPYRIGHT GEORGE PHILIP LTD

Chicago

0 km 5
0 miles 3

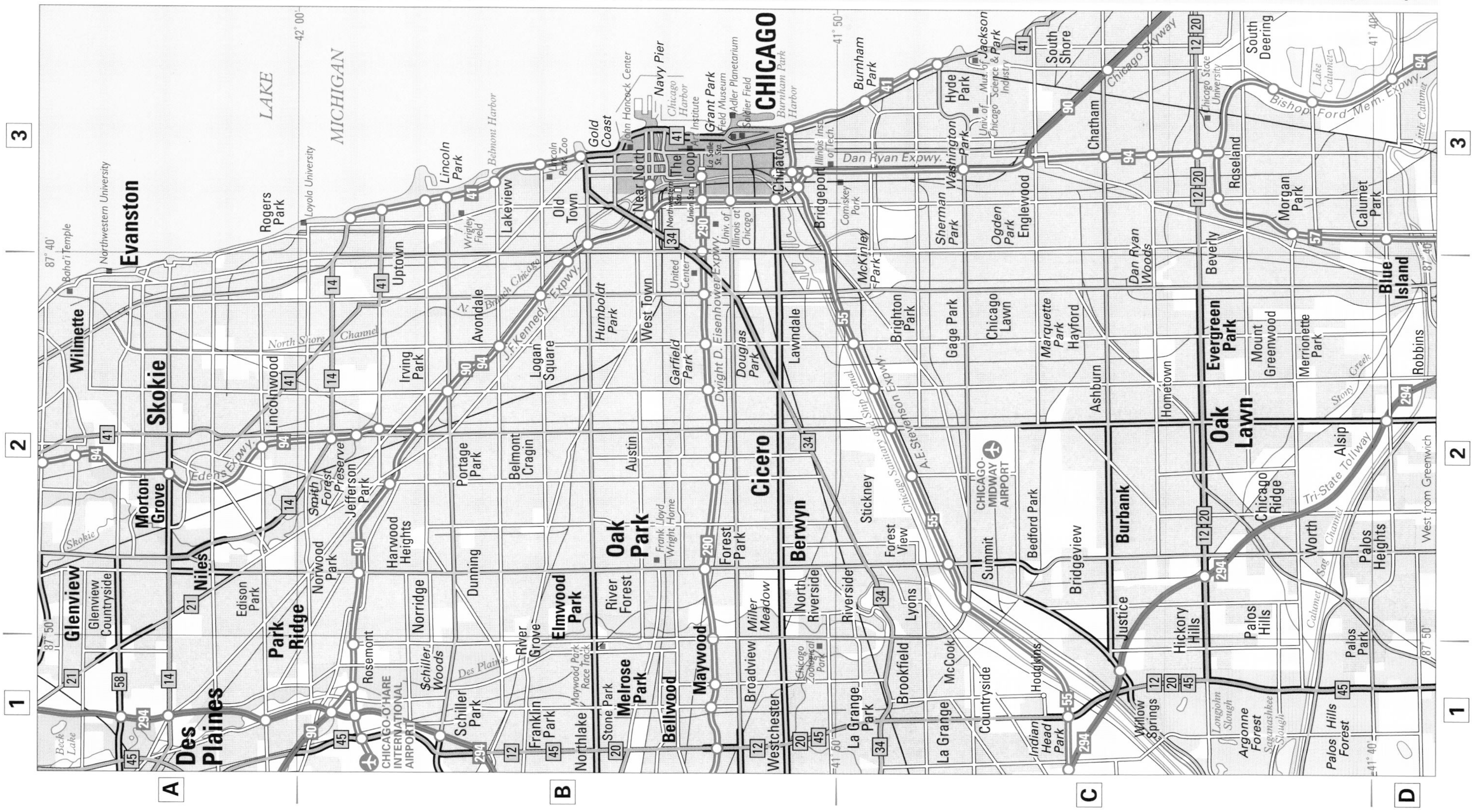
LAKE MICHIGAN
CHICAGO
Evanston
Wilmette
Skokie
Glenview
Morton Grove
Niles
Des Plaines
Park Ridge
Rosemont
CHICAGO O'HARE INTERNATIONAL AIRPORT
Norridge
Harwood Heights
Oak Park
Cicero
Berwyn
Maywood
Bellwood
Melrose Park
Elmwood Park
River Forest
Forest Park
Stickney
Lyons
Brookfield
La Grange
La Grange Park
McCook
Summit
Countryside
Hodgkins
Bridgeview
Burbank
Justice
Oak Lawn
Evergreen Park
Blue Island
Alsip
Chicago Ridge
Worth
Palos Heights
Palos Hills
Hickory Hills
CHICAGO MIDWAY AIRPORT
Dan Ryan Expwy.
A.E. Stevenson Expwy.
Dwight D. Eisenhower Expwy.
J.F. Kennedy Expwy.
Edens Expwy.
Bishop Ford Mem. Expwy.
Tri-State Tollway
Chicago Skyway
Navy Pier
The Loop
Chinatown
Hyde Park
Lincoln Park
Uptown
Lakeview
Old Town
Gold Coast
Near North
Bridgeport
Chatham
Roseland
Beverly
Morgan Park
Calumet Park
South Shore
South Deering
Englewood
Washington Park
Marquette Park
Chicago Lawn
Ashburn
Garfield Park
Douglas Park
Lawndale
Humboldt Park
Logan Square
Irving Park
Avondale
Portage Park
Belmont Cragin
Austin
Dunning
Edison Park
Jefferson Park
Norwood Park
Schiller Park
Franklin Park
Northlake
Stone Park
Westchester
Broadview
Hillside
North Riverside
Riverside
Forest View
A B C D
1 2 3

Central Chicago

0 km 1
0 miles 0.5

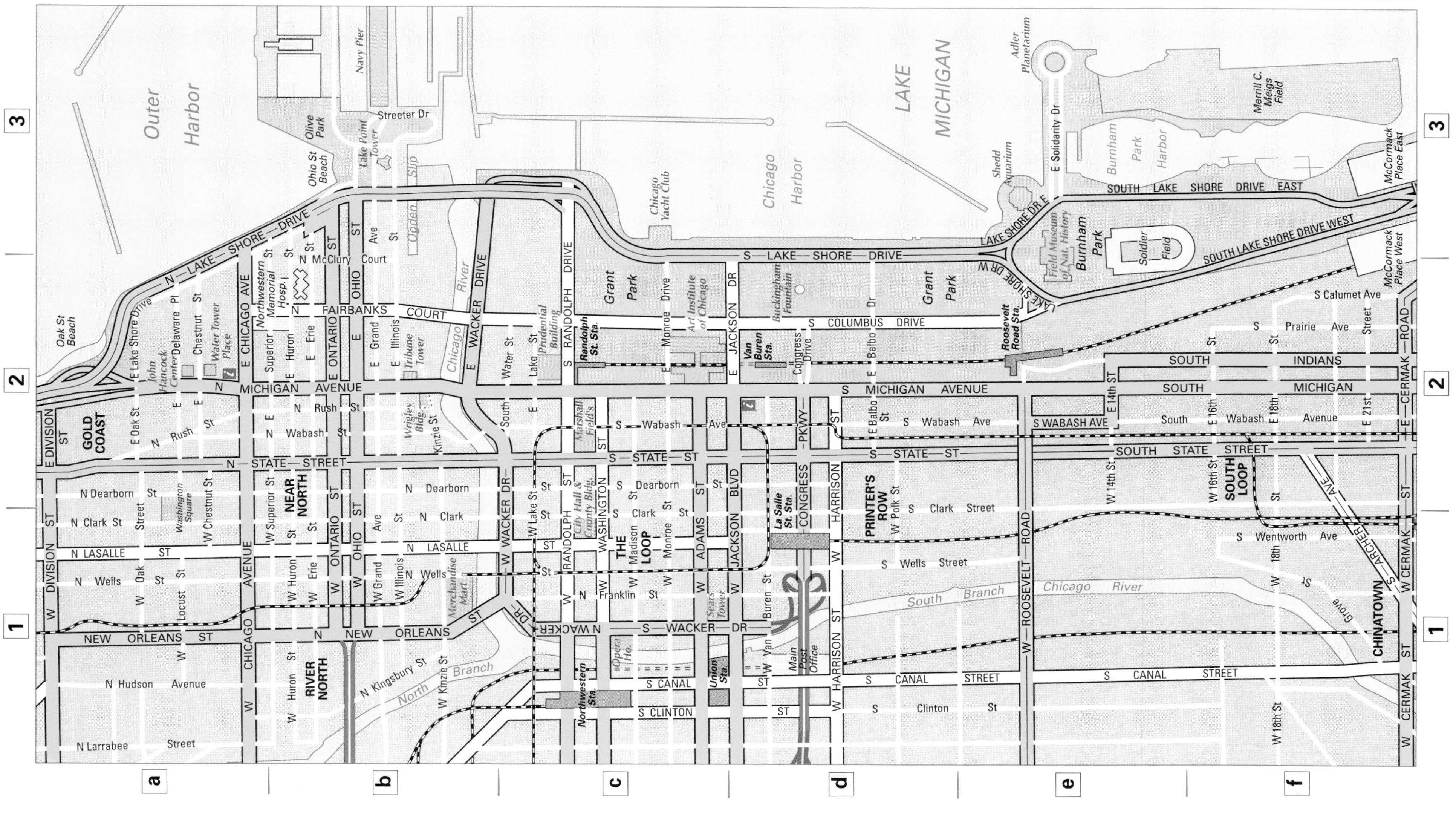
LAKE MICHIGAN
Outer Harbor
Chicago Harbor
Navy Pier
Olive Park
Ohio St Beach
Oak St Beach
Lake Point Tower
Streeter Dr
Ogden Slip
Chicago Yacht Club
Adler Planetarium
Shedd Aquarium
Field Museum of Nat. History
Burnham Park
Burnham Park Harbor
Soldier Field
Merrill C. Meigs Field
McCormack Place East
McCormack Place West
Grant Park
Buckingham Fountain
Art Institute of Chicago
Prudential Building
Randolph St. Sta.
Van Buren Sta.
Roosevelt Road Sta.
La Salle St. Sta.
Northwestern Sta.
Union Sta.
Sears Tower
Opera Ho.
Main Post Office
City Hall & County Bldg.
Marshall Field's
Merchandise Mart
Wrigley Bldg.
Tribune Tower
Water Tower Place
John Hancock Center
Northwestern Memorial Hosp.
Washington Square
GOLD COAST
NEAR NORTH
RIVER NORTH
THE LOOP
PRINTER'S ROW
SOUTH LOOP
CHINATOWN
N LAKE SHORE DRIVE
S LAKE SHORE DRIVE
SOUTH LAKE SHORE DRIVE EAST
SOUTH LAKE SHORE DRIVE WEST
MICHIGAN AVENUE
S MICHIGAN AVENUE
N STATE STREET
S STATE ST
SOUTH STATE STREET
S COLUMBUS DRIVE
FAIRBANKS COURT
E WACKER DRIVE
W WACKER DR
W ROOSEVELT ROAD
W CERMAK ROAD
S CANAL STREET
S CLINTON ST
N NEW ORLEANS ST
W DIVISION ST
CHICAGO AVENUE
E ONTARIO ST
W HARRISON ST
CONGRESS PKWY
SOUTH INDIANS
S ARCHER AVE
Chicago River
North Branch
South Branch
a b c d e f
1 2 3

COPYRIGHT GEORGE PHILIP LTD

Copenhagen

0 km 5
0 miles 3

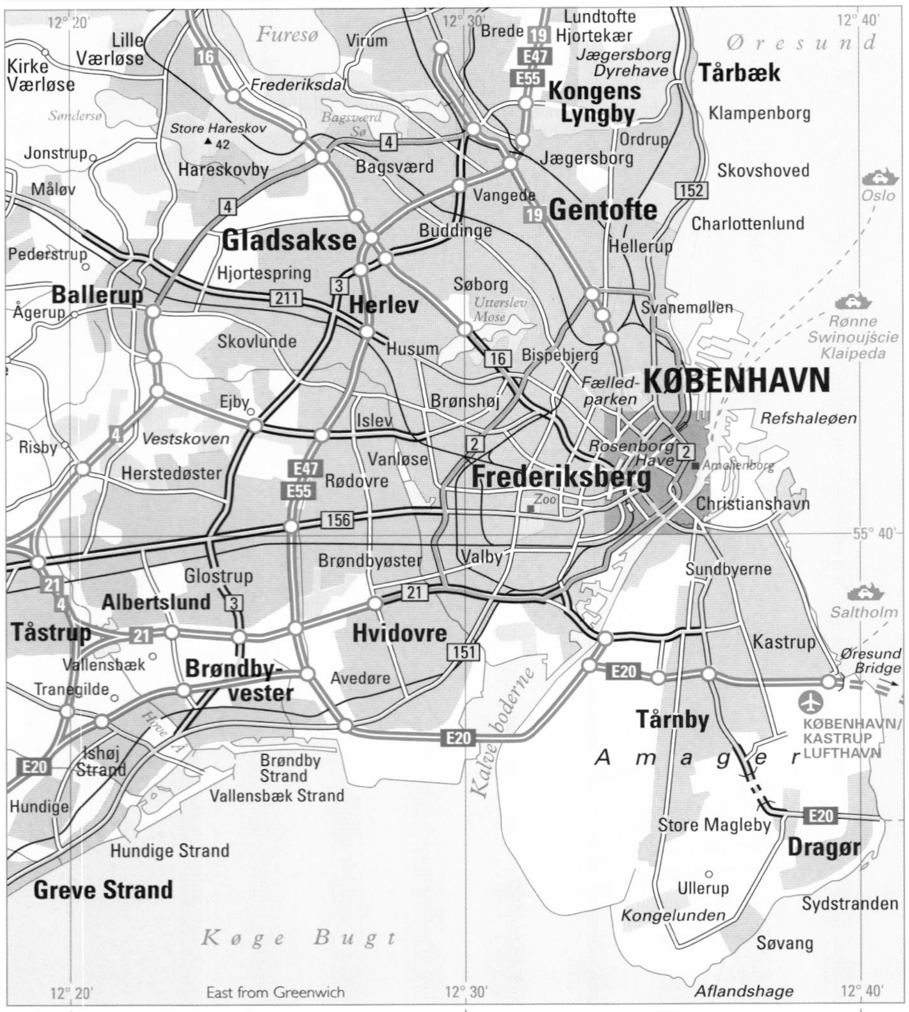

Furesø
Lille Værløse
Kirke Værløse
Virum
Brede
Lundtofte
Hjortekær
Jægersborg Dyrehave
Tårbæk
Øresund
Kongens Lyngby
Frederiksdal
Søndersø
Store Hareskov
Bagsværd Sø
Klampenborg
Ordrup
Jonstrup
Hareskovby
Bagsværd
Jægersborg
Skovshoved
Måløv
Vangede
Gentofte
Oslo
Charlottenlund
Buddinge
Gladsakse
Hellerup
Pederstrup
Hjortespring
Søborg
Ballerup
Herlev
Utterslev Mose
Svanemøllen
Ågerup
Skovlunde
Husum
Bispebjerg
Rønne Swinoujście Klaipeda
Fælled-parken
KØBENHAVN
Ejby
Brønshøj
Refshaleøen
Risby
Vestskoven
Islev
Herstedøster
Vanløse
Rosenborg Have
Amalienborg
Rødovre
Frederiksberg
Zoo
Christianshavn
Brøndbyøster
Valby
Glostrup
Sundbyerne
Albertslund
Saltholm
Tåstrup
Hvidovre
Kastrup
Vallensbæk
Brøndby-vester
Øresund Bridge
Tranegilde
Avedøre
Kalvebodeme
Tårnby
KØBENHAVN/KASTRUP LUFTHAVN
Ishøj Strand
Brøndby Strand
Amager
Vallensbæk Strand
Hundige
Store Magleby
Dragør
Hundige Strand
Greve Strand
Ullerup
Sydstranden
Kongelunden
Køge Bugt
Søvang
Aflandshage
East from Greenwich
12° 20'
12° 30'
12° 40'
55° 40'

Central Copenhagen

0 km 1
0 miles 0.5

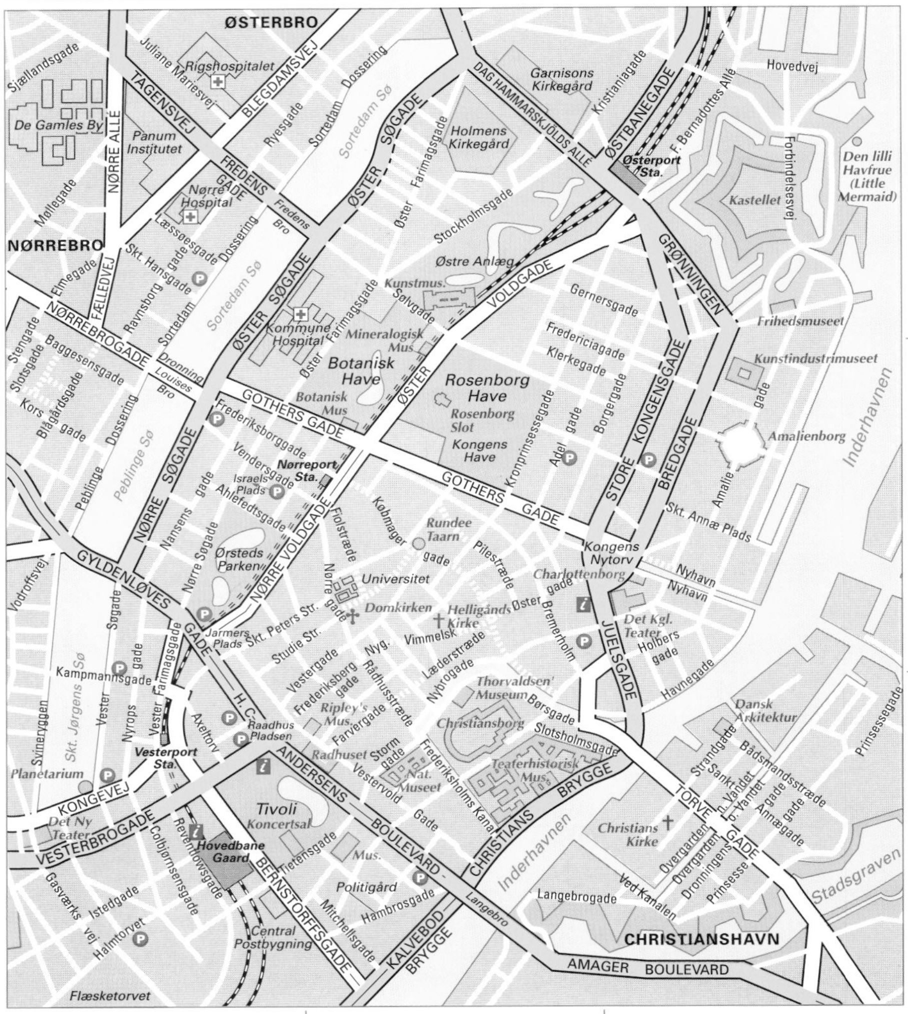

ØSTERBRO
Rigshospitalet
Garnisons Kirkegård
Hovedvej
De Gamles By
Panum Institutet
Holmens Kirkegård
Østerport Sta.
Den lilli Havfrue (Little Mermaid)
Kastellet
Nørre Hospital
Sortedam Sø
NØRREBRO
Østre Anlæg
Frihedsmuseet
Kunstmus.
Kunstindustrimuseet
Kommune Hospital
Mineralogisk Mus.
Botanisk Have
Botanisk Mus
Rosenborg Have
Rosenborg Slot
Kongens Have
Amalienborg
Inderhavnen
Peblinge Sø
Nørreport Sta.
Rundetaarn
Ørsteds Parken
Universitet
Kongens Nytorv
Charlottenborg
Nyhavn
Domkirken
Helligånds Kirke
Det Kgl. Teater
Thorvaldsen Museum
Christiansborg
Dansk Arkitektur
Raadhus Pladsen
Vesterport Sta.
Planetarium
Tivoli Koncertsal
Teaterhistorisk Mus.
Nat. Museet
Det Ny Teater
Hovedbane Gaard
Christians Kirke
Politigård
Central Postbygning
Christianshavn
Flæsketorvet
Stadsgraven
Langebrogade
AMAGER BOULEVARD
KALVEBOD BRYGGE
CHRISTIANS BRYGGE
VESTERBROGADE
H.C. ANDERSENS BOULEVARD
NØRRE SØGADE
ØSTER SØGADE
STORE KONGENSGADE
BREDGADE
GOTHERS GADE

Delhi

0 km 5
0 miles 3

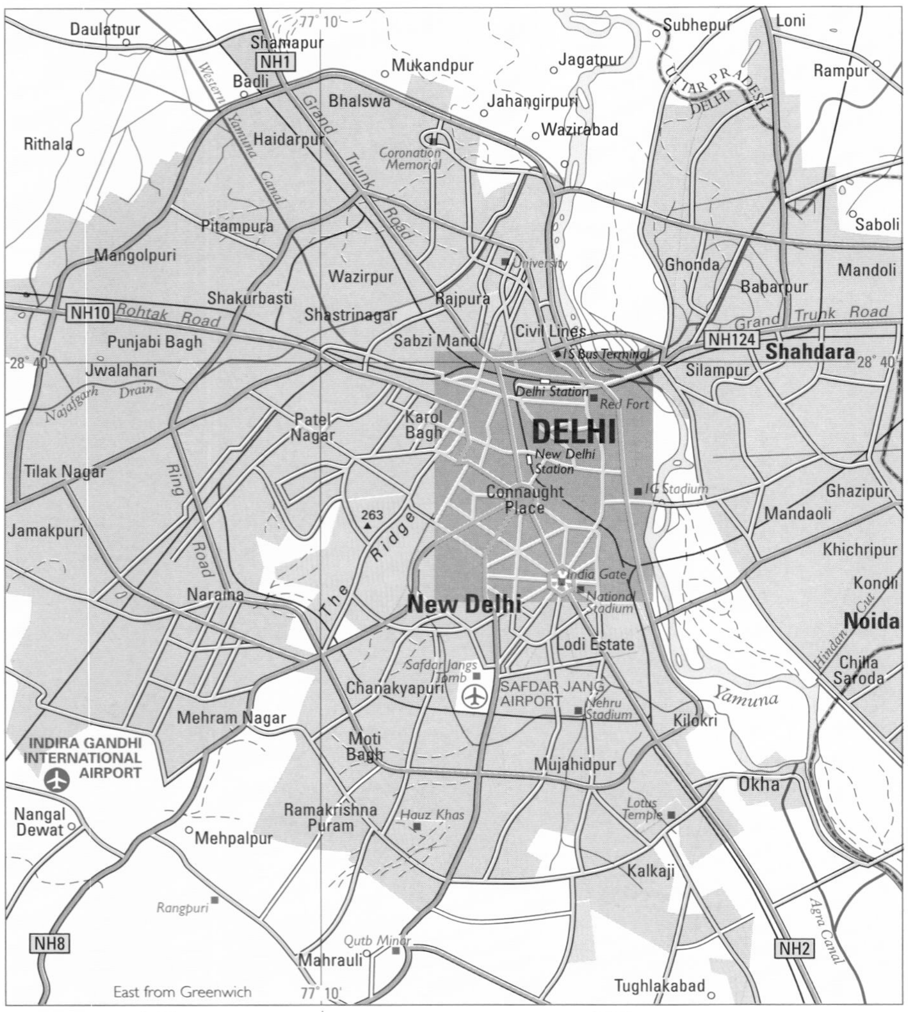

Daulatpur
Shamapur
Subhepur
Loni
Rampur
Mukandpur
Jagatpur
NH1
Badli
Bhalswa
Jahangirpuri
Rithala
Haidarpur
Wazirabad
Coronation Memorial
UTTAR PRADESH
DELHI
Saboli
Pitampura
Mangolpuri
University
Ghonda
Mandoli
Wazirpur
Babarpur
Shakurbasti
Rajpura
NH10
Rohtak Road
Shastrinagar
Grand Trunk Road
Punjabi Bagh
Sabzi Mandi
Civil Lines
NH124
Shahdara
Jwalahari
IS Bus Terminal
Silampur
Najafgarh Drain
Delhi Station
Red Fort
Patel Nagar
Karol Bagh
DELHI
New Delhi Station
Tilak Nagar
IG Stadium
Connaught Place
Ghazipur
263
Jamakpuri
Mandaoli
Khichripur
India Gate
Kondli
Narama
National Stadium
New Delhi
Noida
Lodi Estate
Chilla Saroda
Safdar Jang Tomb
Chanakyapuri
SAFDAR JANG AIRPORT
Yamuna
Nehru Stadium
Mehram Nagar
Kilokri
INDIRA GANDHI INTERNATIONAL AIRPORT
Moti Bagh
Mujahidpur
Okha
Nangal Dewat
Ramakrishna Puram
Hauz Khas
Lotus Temple
Mehpalpur
Kalkaji
Rangpuri
NH8
Qutb Minar
Mahrauli
NH2
Agra Canal
Tughlakabad
East from Greenwich
77° 10'
28° 40'

Central Delhi

0 km 2
0 miles 1

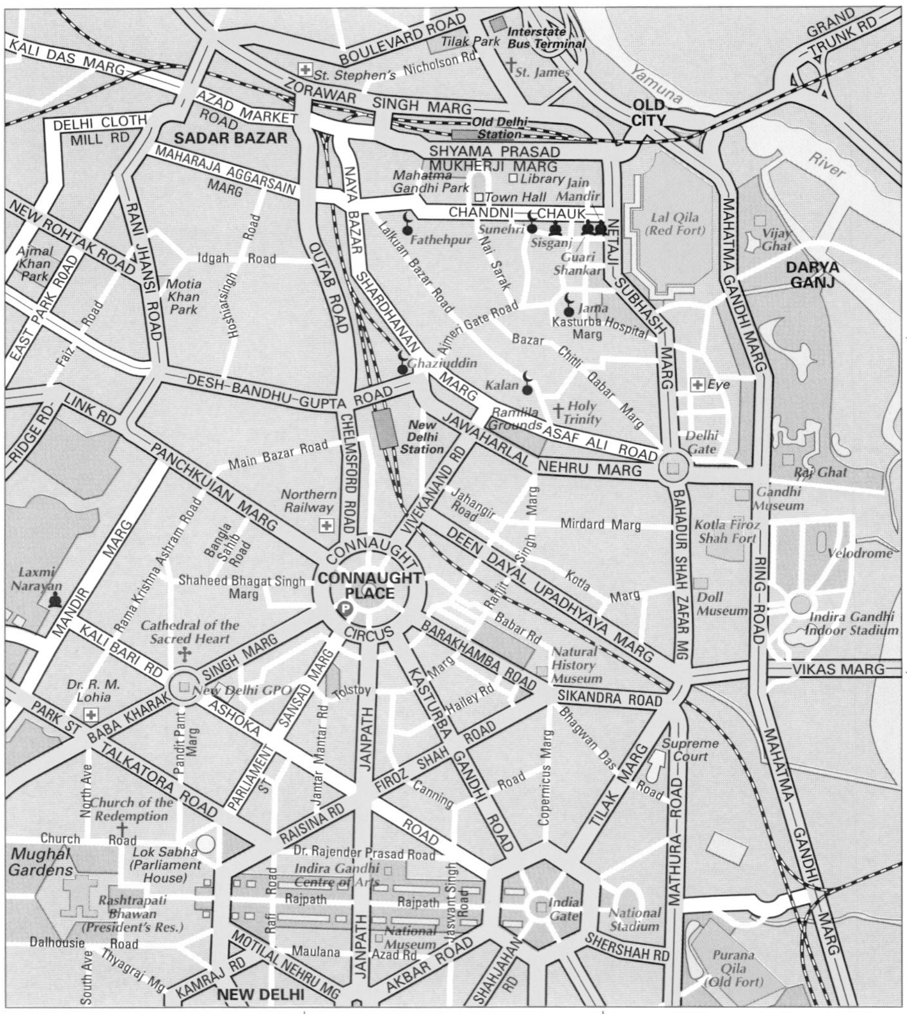

BOULEVARD ROAD
Interstate Bus Terminal
GRAND TRUNK RD
KALI DAS MARG
Tilak Park
St. Stephen's
Nicholson Rd
St. James
ZORAWAR SINGH MARG
AZAD MARKET ROAD
OLD CITY
Old Delhi Station
DELHI CLOTH MILL RD
SADAR BAZAR
SHYAMA PRASAD MUKHERJI MARG
Yamuna
MAHARAJA AGGARSAIN MARG
Mahatma Gandhi Park
Library
Jain Mandir
River
Town Hall
CHANDNI CHAUK
Lal Qila (Red Fort)
NEW ROHTAK ROAD
Fatehpur
Sunehri
Vijay Ghat
Sisganj
Gauri Shankar
DARYA GANJ
Ajmal Khan Park
Motia Khan Park
Jama Masjid
Kasturba Hospital
Ghaziuddin
Eye
DESH BANDHU GUPTA ROAD
Kalan
Holy Trinity
Ramlila Grounds
ASAF ALI ROAD
Delhi Gate
New Delhi Station
NEHRU MARG
Raj Ghat
RIDGE RD
Main Bazar Road
Northern Railway
Gandhi Museum
Mirdard Marg
Kotla Firoz Shah Fort
Velodrome
CONNAUGHT PLACE
Shaheed Bhagat Singh
Laxmi Narayan
Doll Museum
Cathedral of the Sacred Heart
Indira Gandhi Indoor Stadium
Natural History Museum
VIKAS MARG
New Delhi GPO
Dr. R. M. Lohia
SIKANDRA ROAD
PARK ST
BABA KHARAK SINGH MARG
Supreme Court
Church of the Redemption
Church
Mughal Gardens
Lok Sabha (Parliament House)
Dr. Rajendra Prasad Road
Indira Gandhi Centre of Arts
Rashtrapati Bhawan (President's Res.)
Rajpath
India Gate
National Stadium
Dalhousie Road
National Museum
Purana Qila (Old Fort)
Maulana Azad Rd
SHERSHAH RD
NEW DELHI
KAMRAJ RD
MOTILAL NEHRU MG
AKBAR ROAD
JANPATH
MATHURA ROAD
MAHATMA GANDHI MARG
RING ROAD
BAHADUR SHAH ZAFAR MG
DEEN DAYAL UPADHYAYA MARG
CHELMSFORD ROAD
PANCHKUIAN MARG
TALKATORA ROAD

COPYRIGHT GEORGE PHILIP LTD

Dublin

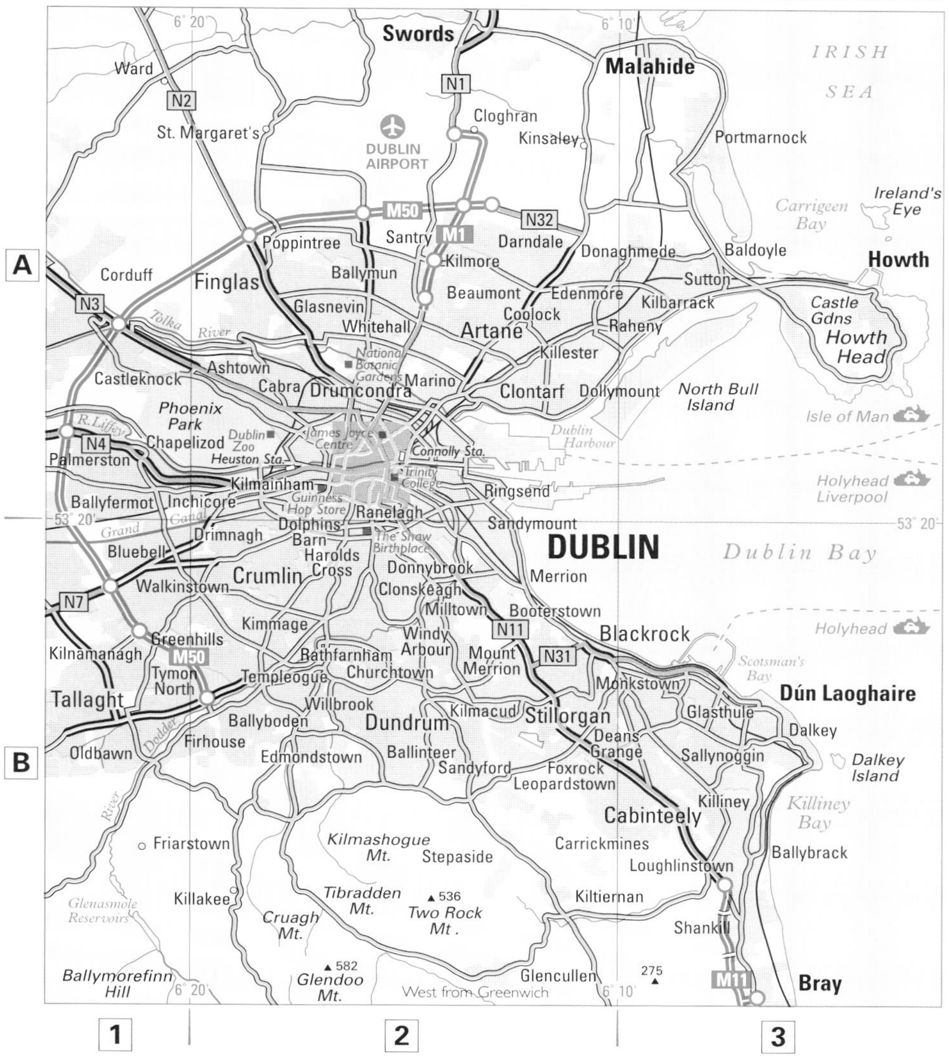
0 km 5
0 miles 3
Swords
Malahide
IRISH SEA
Ward
St. Margaret's
DUBLIN AIRPORT
Cloghran
Kinsaley
Portmarnock
Carrigeen Bay
Ireland's Eye
Poppintree
Santry
Darndale
Donaghmede
Baldoyle
Howth
Corduff
Finglas
Ballymun
Kilmore
Beaumont
Edenmore
Sutton
Kilbarrack
Castle Gdns
Howth Head
Glasnevin
Whitehall
Artane
Coolock
Raheny
Castleknock
Ashtown
Cabra
Drumcondra
Marino
Killester
Phoenix Park
Clontarf
Dollymount
North Bull Island
Chapelizod
Palmerston
Dublin Zoo
Heuston Sta.
Connolly Sta.
Isle of Man
Kilmainham
Ringsend
Holyhead
Liverpool
Ballyfermot
Inchicore
Guinness Hop Store
Ranelagh
Sandymount
Bluebell
Drimnagh
Dolphins Barn
DUBLIN
Dublin Bay
Walkinstown
Crumlin
Harolds Cross
Donnybrook
Merrion
Clonskeagh
Milltown
Booterstown
Kimmage
Kilnamanagh
Greenhills
Windy Arbour
Blackrock
Tymon North
Rathfarnham
Churchtown
Mount Merrion
Monkstown
Tallaght
Templeogue
Willbrook
Kilmacud
Stillorgan
Glasthule
Dún Laoghaire
Dalkey
Ballyboden
Dundrum
Deans Grange
Oldbawn
Firhouse
Edmondstown
Ballinteer
Sandyford
Foxrock
Leopardstown
Sallynoggin
Dalkey Island
Killiney
Killiney Bay
Cabinteely
Friarstown
Kilmashogue Mt.
Stepaside
Carrickmines
Loughlinstown
Ballybrack
Killakee
Tibradden Mt.
Two Rock Mt.
Kiltiernan
Glenasmole Reservoirs
Cruagh Mt.
Shankill
Ballymorefinn Hill
Glendoo Mt.
Glencullen
Bray
West from Greenwich
A
B
1
2
3

Central Dublin

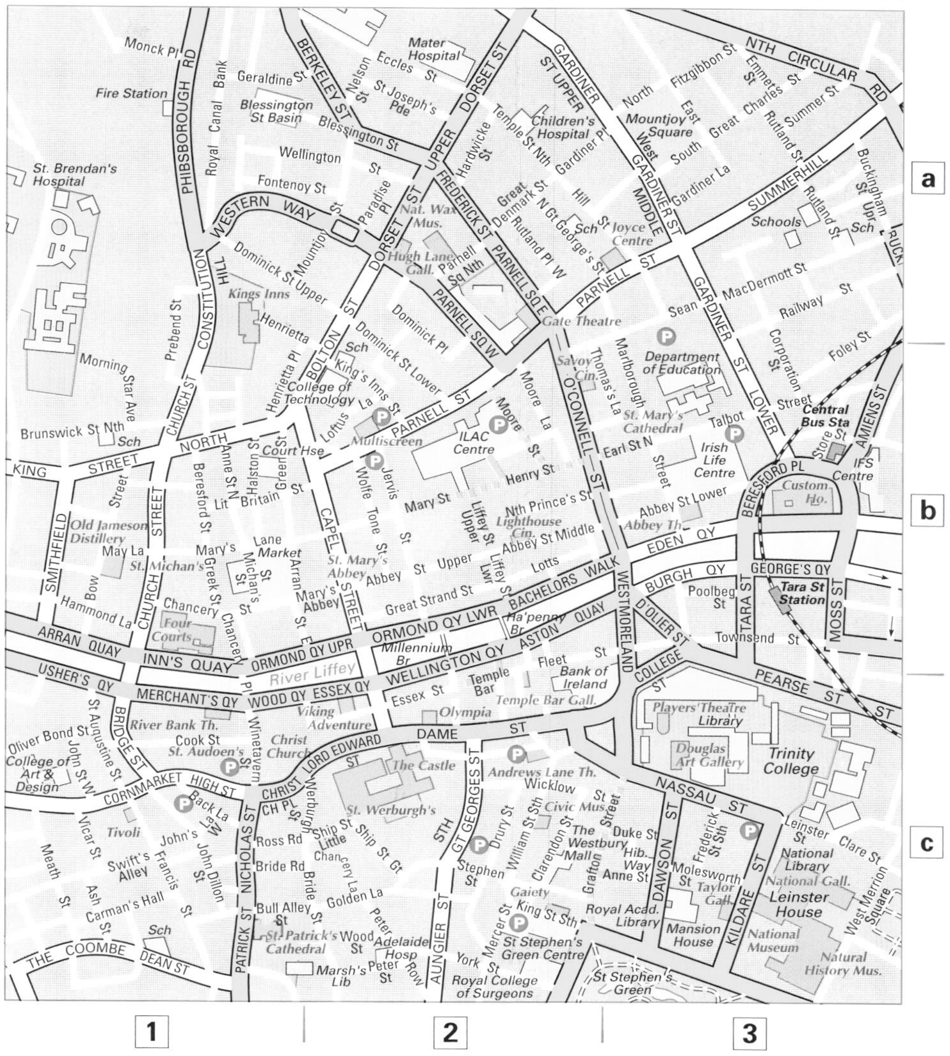
0 km 0.5
0 miles 0.25
Mater Hospital
Fire Station
St. Brendan's Hospital
Blessington St Basin
Children's Hospital
Mountjoy Square
Kings Inns
Hugh Lane Gall.
Gate Theatre
Department of Education
College of Technology
Custom Ho.
Central Bus Sta
ILAC Centre
St. Mary's Cathedral
Irish Life Centre
IFS Centre
Old Jameson Distillery
St. Michan's
Four Courts
Tara St Station
Abbey Th.
Lighthouse Cin.
River Liffey
Ha'penny Br.
Millennium Br.
Bank of Ireland
Temple Bar Gall.
Players' Theatre Library
Viking Adventure
Olympia
Trinity College
Douglas Hyde Art Gallery
Christ Church
The Castle
Andrews Lane Th.
St. Werburgh's
St. Audoen's
College of Art & Design
Tivoli
The Westbury Mall
National Library
National Gall.
Leinster House
National Museum
Natural History Mus.
Mansion House
Royal Acad. Library
Gaiety
St Stephen's Green Centre
St. Patrick's Cathedral
Marsh's Lib
Adelaide Hosp
Royal College of Surgeons
St Stephen's Green
a
b
c
1
2
3

Edinburgh

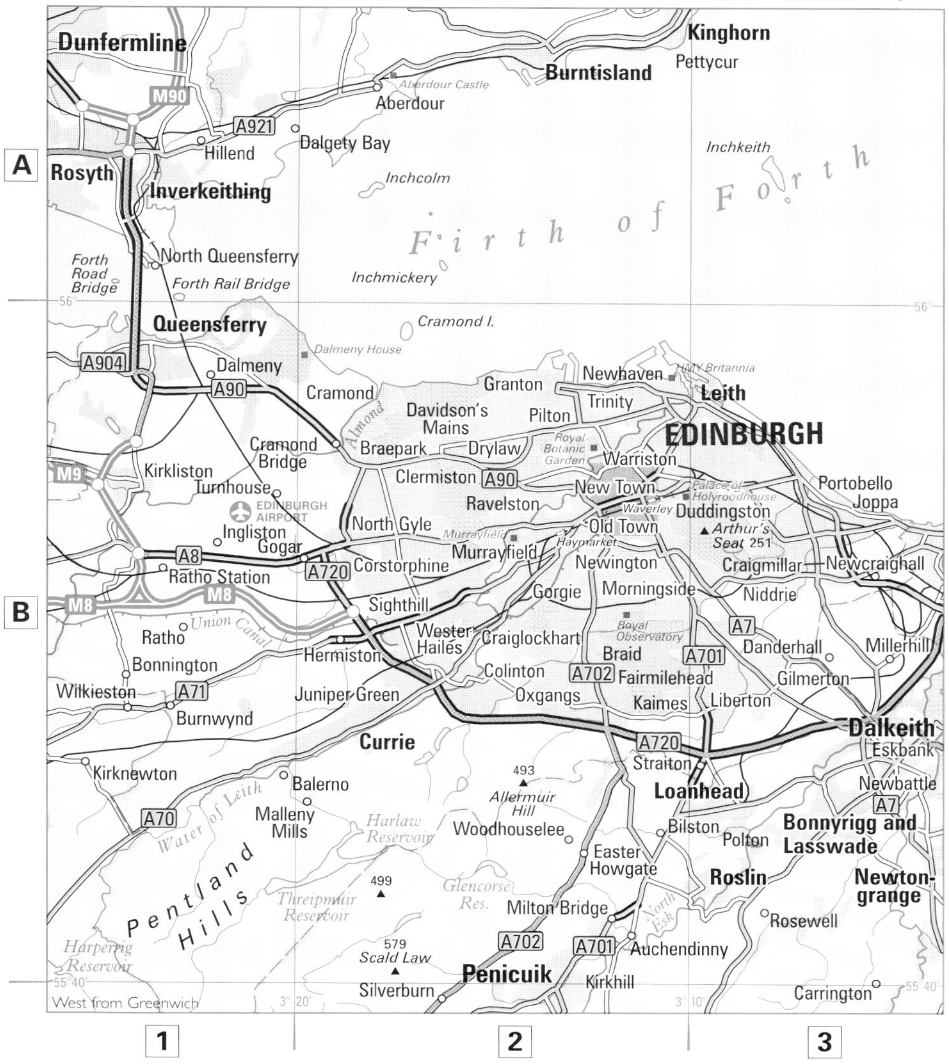
0 km 5
0 miles 3
Dunfermline
Kinghorn
Pettycur
Burntisland
Aberdour
Hillend
Dalgety Bay
Rosyth
Inverkeithing
Inchcolm
Inchkeith
Firth of Forth
North Queensferry
Forth Road Bridge
Forth Rail Bridge
Inchmickery
Queensferry
Cramond I.
Dalmeny House
Dalmeny
Cramond
Granton
Newhaven
Leith
Trinity
Davidson's Mains
Pilton
EDINBURGH
Cramond Bridge
Braepark
Drylaw
Royal Botanic Garden
Warriston
Kirkliston
Clermiston
Turnhouse
New Town
Portobello
Joppa
EDINBURGH AIRPORT
Ravelston
Duddingston
North Gyle
Old Town
Arthur's Seat 251
Ingliston
Gogar
Murrayfield
Ratho Station
Corstorphine
Newington
Craigmillar
Newcraighall
Gorgie
Morningside
Niddrie
Sighthill
Ratho
Union Canal
Bonnington
Wester Hailes
Craiglockhart
Braid
Royal Observatory
Danderhall
Millerhill
Hermiston
Colinton
Fairmilehead
Gilmerton
Wilkieston
Juniper Green
Oxgangs
Kaimes
Liberton
Burnwynd
Currie
Dalkeith
Eskbank
Straiton
Kirknewton
Balerno
Allermuir Hill
Loanhead
Newbattle
Malleny Mills
Harlaw Reservoir
Woodhouselee
Bilston
Polton
Bonnyrigg and Lasswade
Easter Howgate
Roslin
Newtongrange
Pentland Hills
Threipmuir Reservoir
Glencorse Res.
Milton Bridge
Rosewell
Harperrig Reservoir
Scald Law
Auchendinny
Penicuik
Silverburn
Kirkhill
Carrington
West from Greenwich
A
B
1
2
3

Central Edinburgh

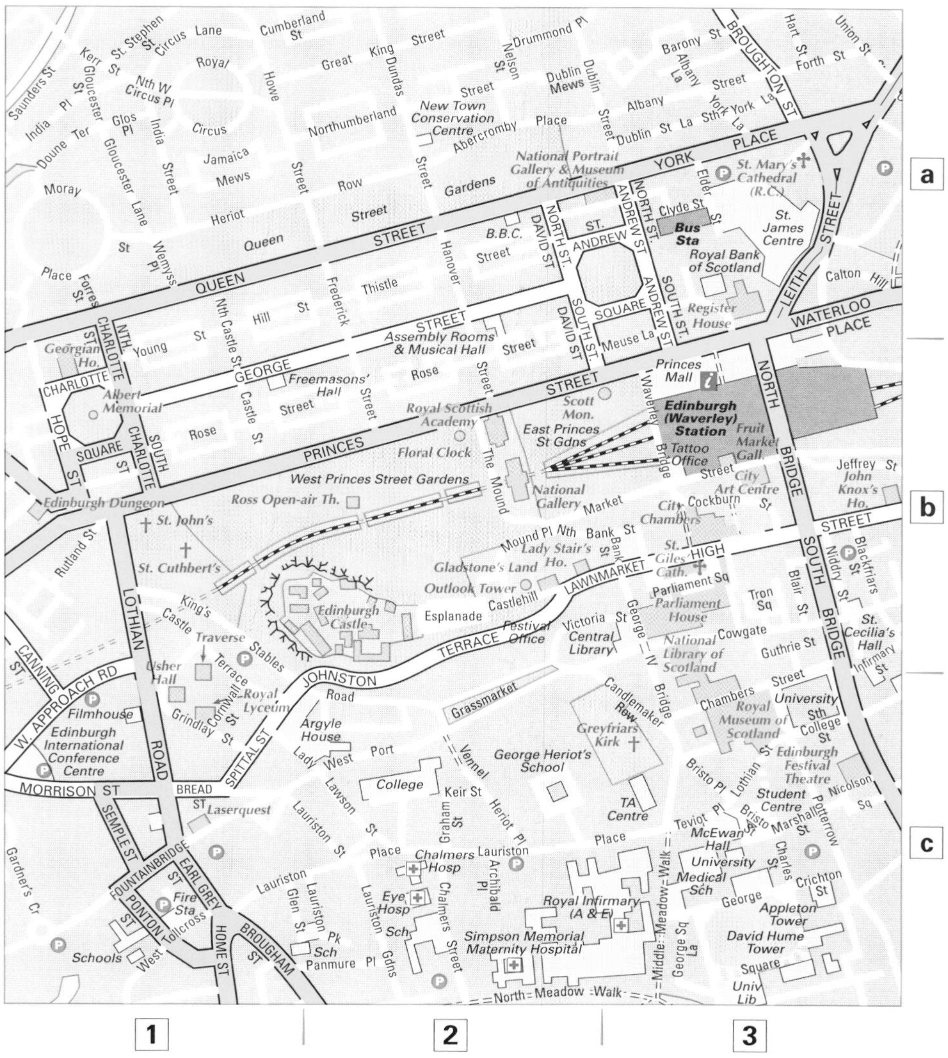
0 km 0.5
0 miles 0.25
Dublin Mews
New Town Conservation Centre
National Portrait Gallery & Museum of Antiquities
St. Mary's Cathedral (R.C.)
Bus Sta
St. James Centre
Royal Bank of Scotland
Register House
Assembly Rooms & Musical Hall
Georgian Ho.
Freemasons' Hall
Albert Memorial
Princes Mall
Royal Scottish Academy
Scott Mon.
East Princes St Gdns
Edinburgh (Waverley) Station
Fruit Market Gall.
Floral Clock
Tattoo Office
City Art Centre
John Knox's Ho.
West Princes Street Gardens
National Gallery
Edinburgh Dungeon
Ross Open-air Th.
St. John's
City Chambers
St. Cuthbert's
Gladstone's Land
Lady Stair's Ho.
St. Giles Cath.
Parliament House
Outlook Tower
Edinburgh Castle
Esplanade
Castlehill
Victoria St
Central Library
National Library of Scotland
Festival Office
Usher Hall
Traverse
Royal Lyceum
Chambers Royal Museum of Scotland
University
Filmhouse
Edinburgh International Conference Centre
Argyle House
Greyfriars Kirk
Edinburgh Festival Theatre
George Heriot's School
Student Centre
College
TA Centre
McEwan Hall
Laserquest
University Medical Sch
Chalmers Hosp
Eye Hosp
Royal Infirmary (A & E)
Simpson Memorial Maternity Hospital
Fire Sta
Schools
Appleton Tower
David Hume Tower
a
b
c
1
2
3

COPYRIGHT GEORGE PHILIP LTD

Helsinki

0 km 5
0 miles 3

Kongo
Ketunkorpi
Keimola
Linna
Seutula
Mäkiniitty
Maantiekylä
Hanala
Rekola
Lahnus
Vestra
Kivistö
Koivupää
HELSINKI-VANTAAN LENTOASEMA
Harjusuo
Röylä
Perusmaki
Gobbacka
Odilampi
Askisto
Niiperi
Petas
Vantaankoski
Vantaanpuisto
Vantaa
Ylästö
Hiekkaharju
Ita Hakkila
Tikkurila
Simonkylä
Martinkylä
Hämeenkylä
Friherrs
Haltiala
Tapanila
Puistola
Hakunila
Haltiavuori
Kaivoksela
Paloheinä
Malmi
TATTARISUO
Pukinmäki
Rastaala
Laaksolahti
Konala
Pakila
Rajakylä
Mellunmäki
Lintuvaara
Pirkkola
Pihlajamäki
Oulunkylä
Mellunkylä
Myllypuro
Vartiokylä
Kauniainen
Haaga
Käpylä
Viikki
Kilo
Leppävaara
Puotila
Pasila
Herttoniemi
Rastila
Tuomarila
Henttaa
Nuijala
Munkkiniemi
HELSINKI
Roihuvuori
Mankkaa
Otaniemi
Tammisalo
Vartiosaari
Olari
Tapiola
Lehtisaari
Kulosaari
Hietaniemi
Laajasalo
Jollas
Nöykkiö
Westend
Villinki
Nokkala
Lauttasaari
Suomenlinna
Miessaari
Pihlajasaari
Santahamina
Svinö
Melkki
Vallisaari
Stockholm, Lubeck, Travemund
Gulf of Finland
Harmaja
East from Greenwich

Istanbul

0 km 5
0 miles 3

Göktürk
Bahçeköy
Sarıyer
Anadolukavağı
Pirinççi
Kemerburgaz
Büyükdere
Yuşa Tepesi 197
Alibey Barajı
Beykoz
Cebecci
Tarabya
Yeniköy
Ayazağa
İstinye
Paşabahçe
Çubuklu
Kanlıca
Göz Tepe 285
Boyacıköy
Rumelihisarı
Levent
Bebek
Anadoluhisarı
Alibeyköy
Kâğıthane
Mecidiyeköy
Kandilli
Küçükköy
Gaziosmanpaşa
Şişli
Ortaköy
Vaniköy
Atışalen
Bayrampaşa
Besiktas
Çengelköy
Hasköy
Taksim
Beylerbeyi
Esenler
Eyüp
Dolmabahçe Sarayı
Bağcılar
Fener
Beyoğlu
Kuzguncuk
Güngören
Topkapı
Galata
Çamlıca
Eminönü
Üsküdar
Kısıklı
Ümraniye
Fatih
Istanbul Int. Airport (Atatürk)
Yenikapı
ISTANBUL
Selimiye Kışlası
Samatya
Yedikule
Kadıköy
Bakırköy
Zeytinburnu
Kızıltoprak
Fenerbahçe
Erenköy
İçerenköy
Marmara Denizi
(Sea of Marmara)
Bostancı
East from Greenwich
Izmir, Bandırma, Mudanya
Kızıl Adalar, Yalova

Hong Kong

0 km 5
0 miles 3

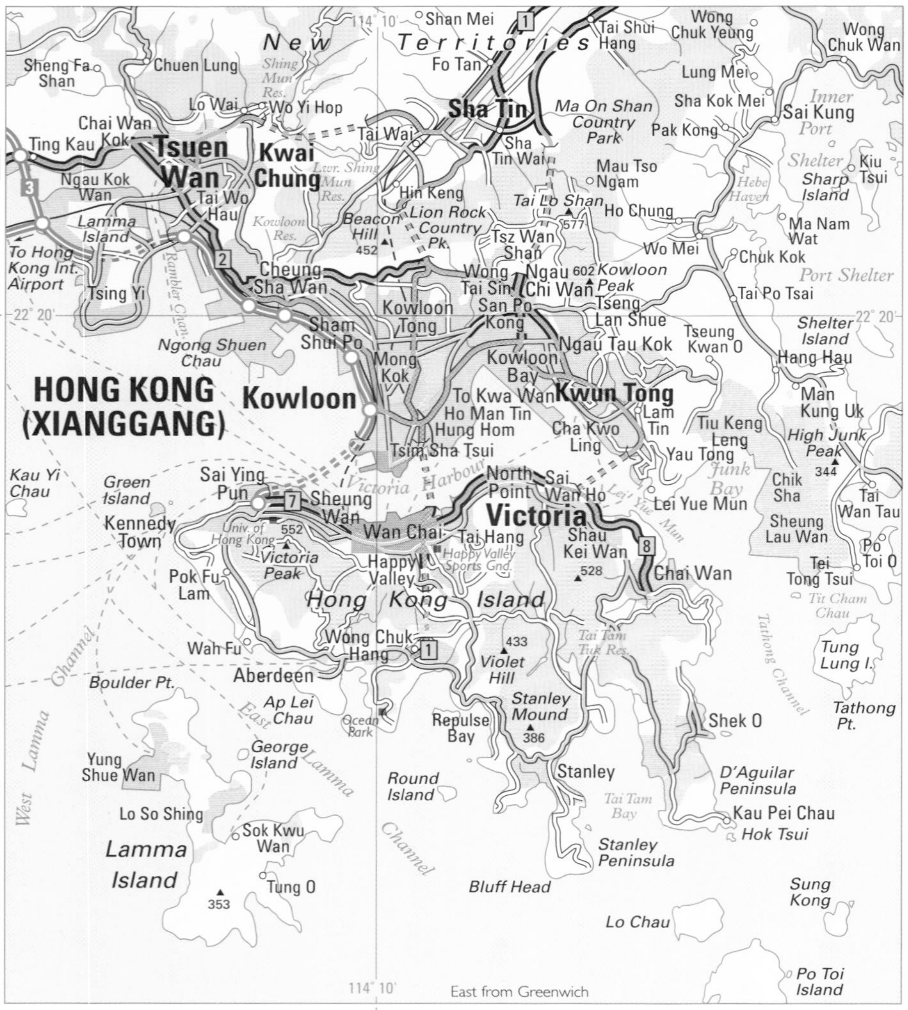
New Territories
Shan Mei
Wong Chuk Yeung
Wong Chuk Wan
Sheng Fa Shan
Chuen Lung
Fo Tan
Tai Shui Hang
Lung Mei
Lo Wai
Wo Yi Hop
Sha Tin
Ma On Shan Country Park
Sha Kok Mei
Sai Kung
Chai Wan Kok
Ting Kau
Tsuen Wan
Kwai Chung
Tai Wai
Pak Kong
Sha Tin Wai
Mau Tso Ngam
Kiu Tsui
Ngau Kok Wan
Tai Wo Hau
Hin Keng
Tai Lo Shan
Ho Chung
Sharp Island
Lamma Island
Lion Rock Country Pk.
Ma Nam Wat
To Hong Kong Int. Airport
Tsing Yi
Cheung Sha Wan
Tsz Wan Shan
Wo Mei
Chuk Kok
Wong Tai Sin
Ngau Chi Wan
Kowloon Peak
Port Shelter
Kowloon Tong
San Po Kong
Lan Shue
Tai Po Tsai
Ngong Shuen Chau
Sham Shui Po
Ngau Tau Kok
Tseung Kwan O
Shelter Island
Mong Kok
Kowloon Bay
Hang Hau
HONG KONG (XIANGGANG)
Kowloon
To Kwa Wan
Kwun Tong
Ho Man Tin
Hung Hom
Lam Tin
Man Kung Uk
Tsim Sha Tsui
Cha Kwo Ling
Yau Tong
Tiu Keng Leng
High Junk Peak 344
Kau Yi Chau
Green Island
Sai Ying Pun
Sheung Wan
North Point
Sai Wan Ho
Victoria Harbour
Victoria
Lei Yue Mun
Chik Sha
Tai Wan Tau
Kennedy Town
Wan Chai
Tai Hang
Shau Kei Wan
Sheung Lau Wan
Victoria Peak
Happy Valley
Chai Wan
Po Toi O
Pok Fu Lam
Tei Tong Tsui
Hong Kong Island
Wah Fu
Wong Chuk Hang
Tung Lung I.
Boulder Pt.
Aberdeen
Violet Hill
Ap Lei Chau
Stanley Mound 386
Tathong Pt.
Repulse Bay
Shek O
George Island
Yung Shue Wan
Round Island
Stanley
D'Aguilar Peninsula
Lo So Shing
Sok Kwu Wan
Kau Pei Chau
Hok Tsui
Lamma Island
Stanley Peninsula
Tung O
353
Bluff Head
Sung Kong
Lo Chau
Po Toi Island
East from Greenwich

Central Hong Kong

0 0.5
0 miles 0.25

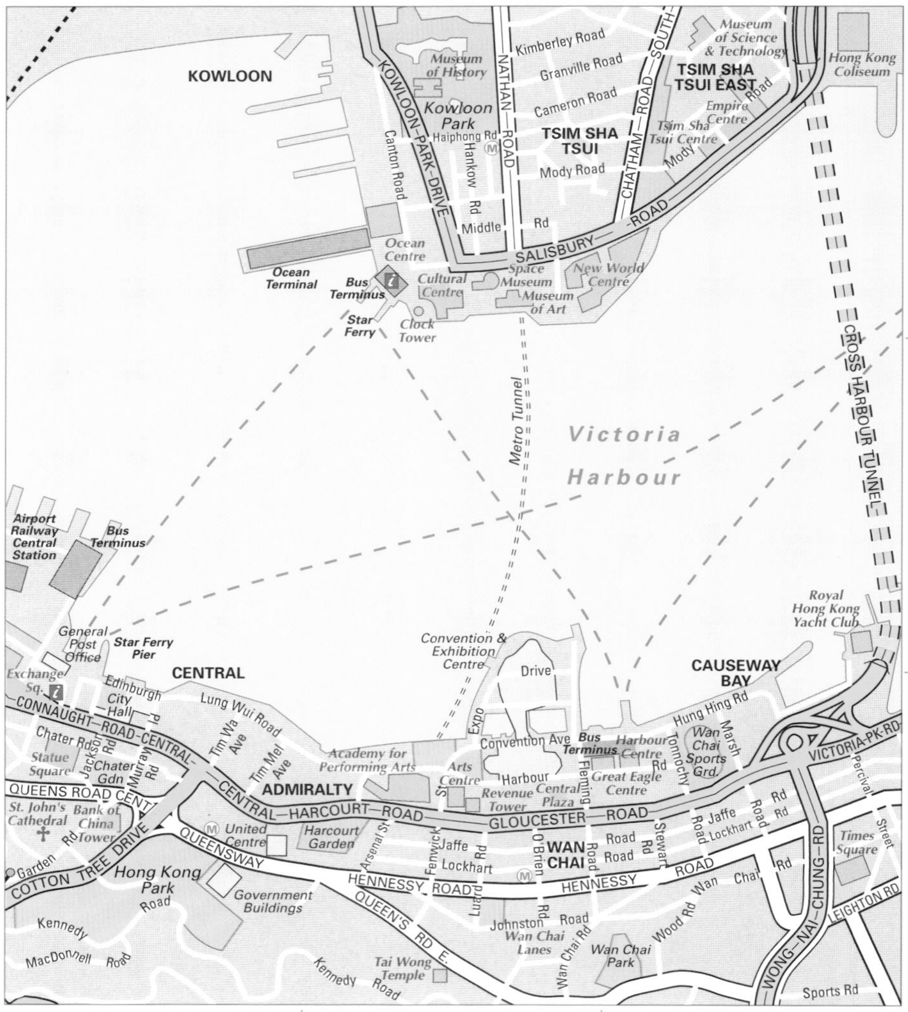
KOWLOON
Museum of History
Kowloon Park
Museum of Science & Technology
Hong Kong Coliseum
TSIM SHA TSUI EAST
TSIM SHA TSUI
Ocean Terminal
Ocean Centre
Cultural Centre
Space Museum
Museum of Art
New World Centre
Star Ferry
Clock Tower
Metro Tunnel
Victoria Harbour
CROSS HARBOUR TUNNEL
Airport Railway Central Station
Bus Terminus
Royal Hong Kong Yacht Club
General Post Office
Star Ferry Pier
CENTRAL
Convention & Exhibition Centre
CAUSEWAY BAY
Exchange Sq.
City Hall
Statue Square
ADMIRALTY
Academy for Performing Arts
Arts Centre
St. John's Cathedral
Bank of China Tower
Harbour Centre
Great Eagle Centre
Central Plaza
Revenue Tower
Harcourt Garden
WAN CHAI
Times Square
Hong Kong Park
Government Buildings
Tai Wong Temple
Johnston Road
Wan Chai Lanes
Wan Chai Park
CONNAUGHT ROAD CENTRAL
QUEENS ROAD CENTRAL
HARCOURT ROAD
GLOUCESTER ROAD
QUEENSWAY
COTTON TREE DRIVE
HENNESSY ROAD
VICTORIA PK RD
WONG NAI CHUNG RD
SALISBURY ROAD
NATHAN ROAD
KOWLOON PARK DRIVE
CHATHAM ROAD SOUTH

Jerusalem

0 km 5
0 miles 3

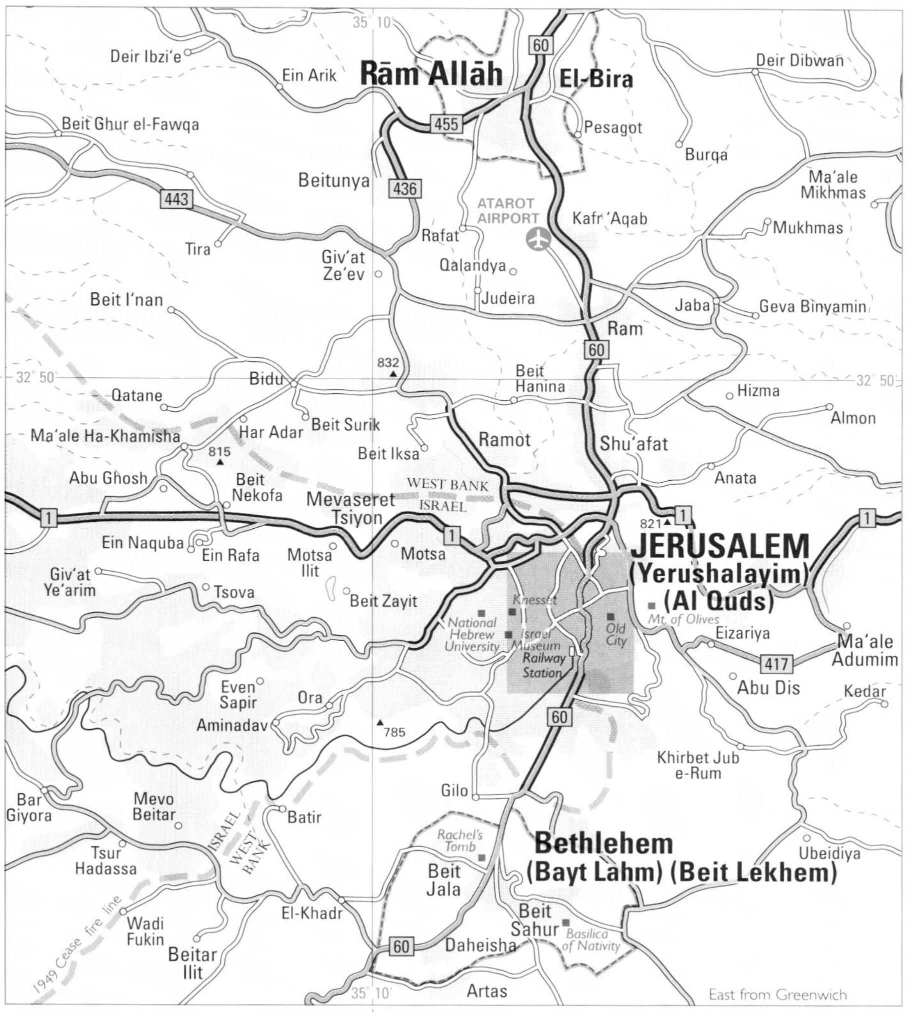

Central Jerusalem

0 km 1
0 miles 0.5

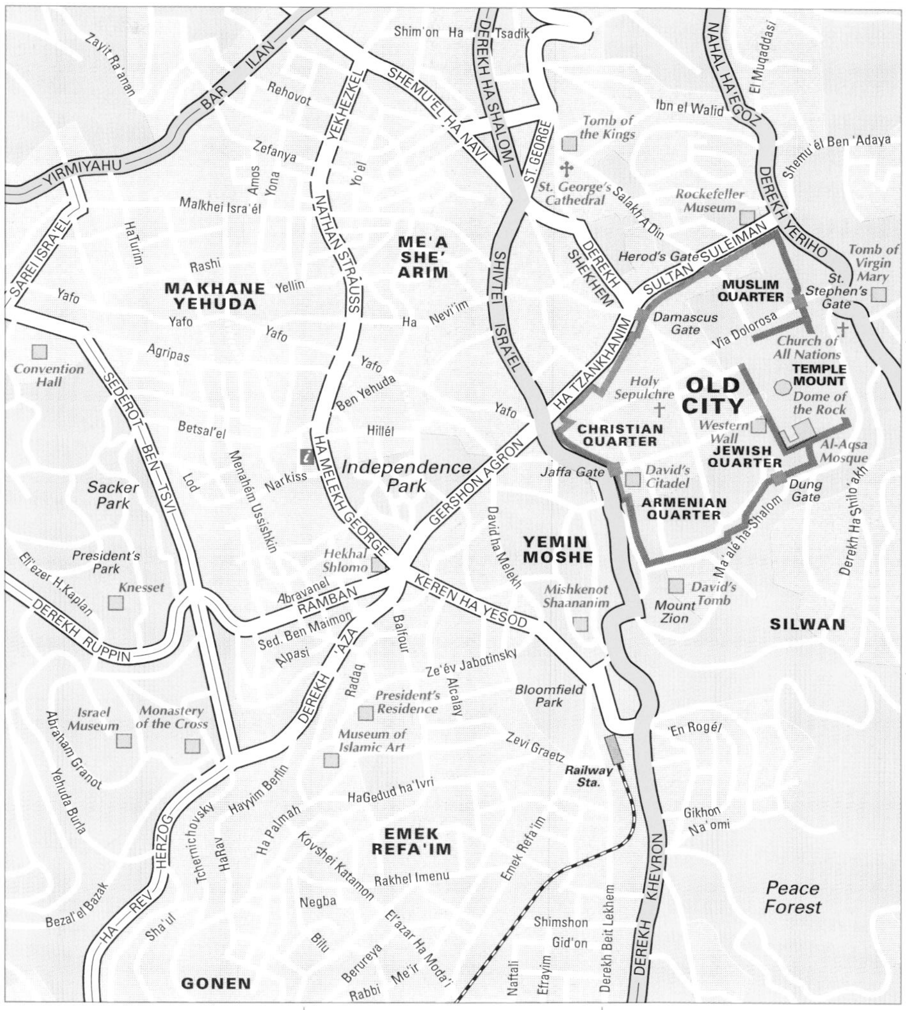

Jakarta

0 km 5
0 miles 3

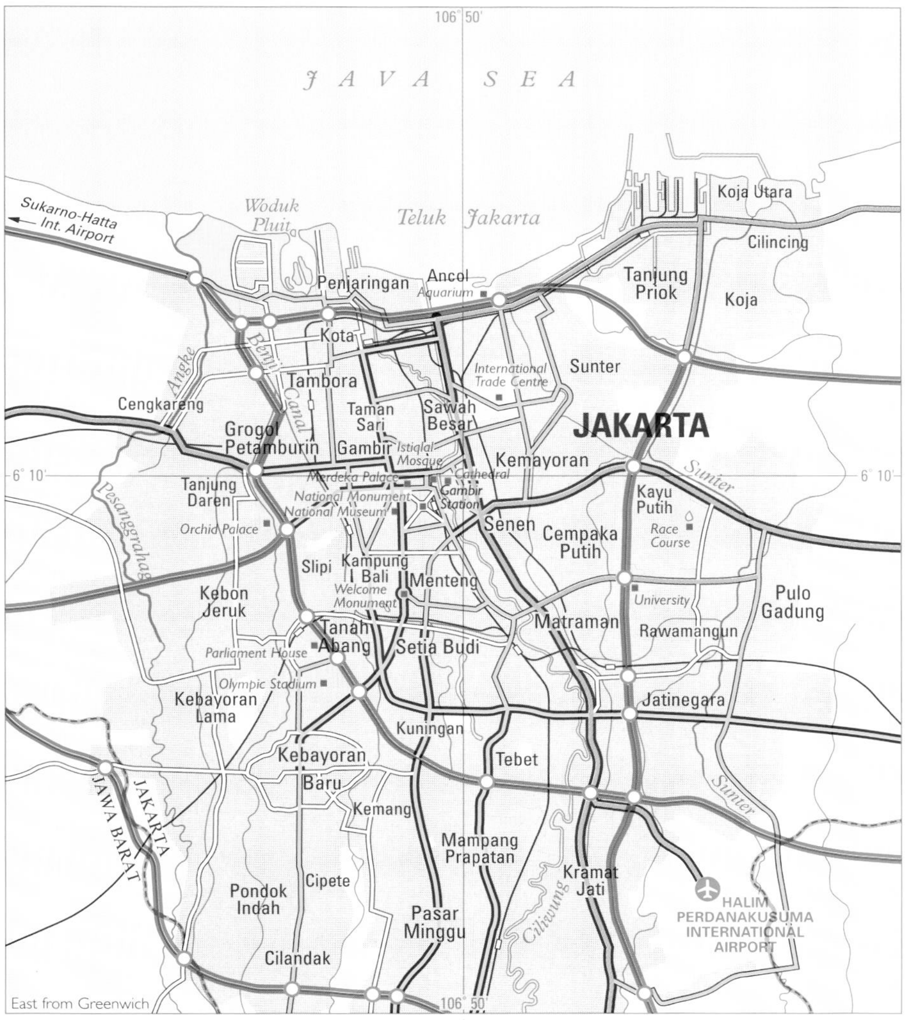

Johannesburg

0 km 5
0 miles 3

Karachi

0 km 5
0 miles 3

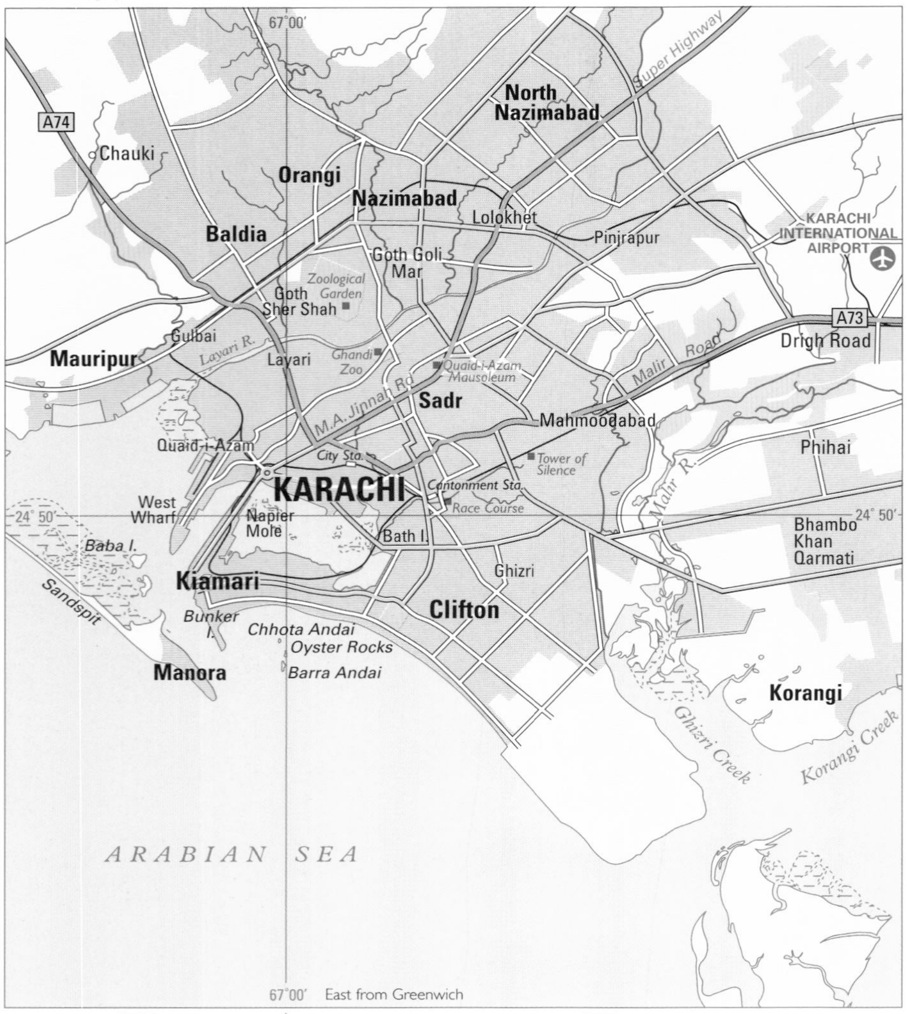

67°00'
Super Highway
North Nazimabad
A74
Chauki
Orangi
Nazimabad
Lolokhet
Pinjrapur
Baldia
Goth Goli Mar
KARACHI INTERNATIONAL AIRPORT
Zoological Garden
Goth Sher Shah
Gulbai
A73
Drigh Road
Mauripur
Layari R.
Layari
Ghandi Zoo
Quaid-i-Azam Mausoleum
Malir Road
M.A. Jinnah Rd.
Sadr
Mahmoodabad
Quaid-i-Azam
City Sta.
Tower of Silence
Phihai
KARACHI
Cantonment Sta.
Race Course
West Wharf
Napier Mole
24°50'
Baba I.
Bath I.
Malir R.
Bhambo Khan Qarmati
Sandspit
Kiamari
Ghizri
Bunker I.
Clifton
Chhota Andai
Oyster Rocks
Barra Andai
Manora
Korangi
Ghizri Creek
Korangi Creek
ARABIAN SEA
67°00' East from Greenwich
A
B
1
2

Lagos

0 km 5
0 miles 3

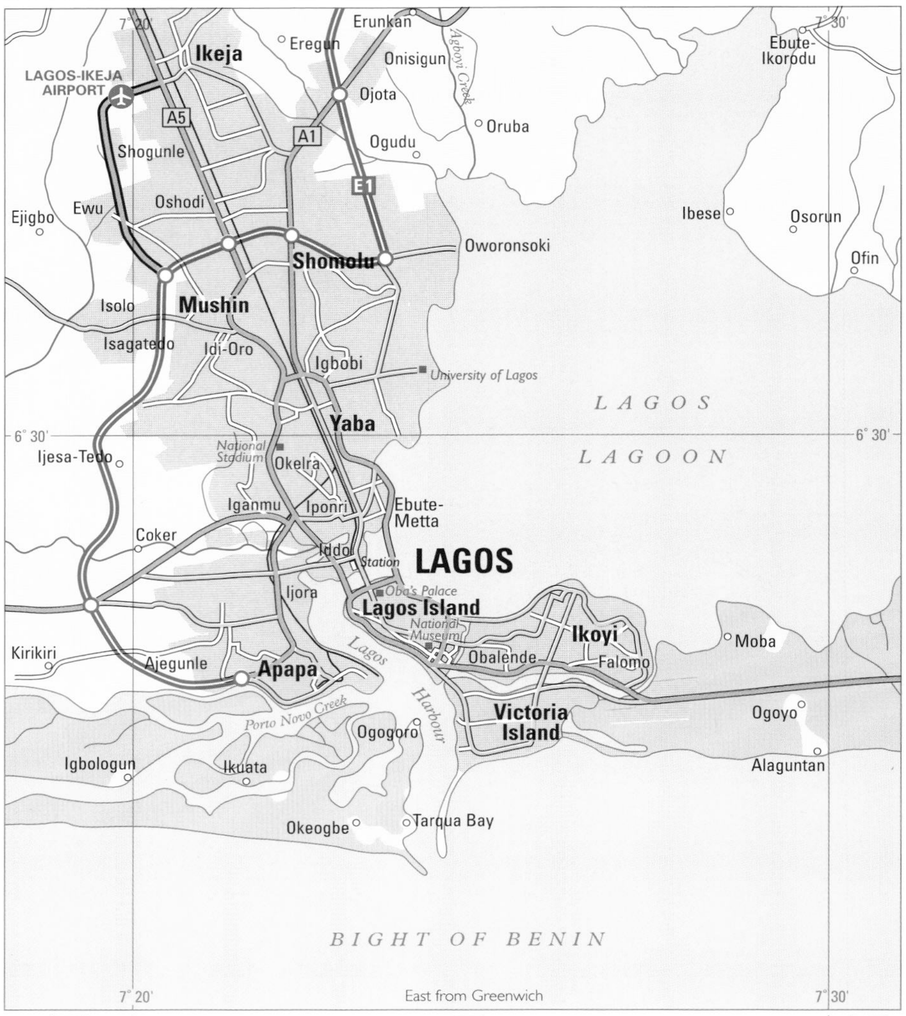

7°20'
7°30'
Erunkan
Ikeja
Eregun
Onisigun
Agboyi Creek
Ebute-Ikorodu
LAGOS-IKEJA AIRPORT
Ojota
A5
A1
Oruba
Ogudu
Shogunle
E1
Oshodi
Ejigbo
Ewu
Ibese
Osorun
Oworonsoki
Shomolu
Ofin
Mushin
Isolo
Isagatedo
Idi-Oro
Igbobi
University of Lagos
LAGOS
Yaba
6°30'
6°30'
National Stadium
LAGOON
Ijesa-Tedo
Okelra
Iganmu
Iponri
Ebute-Metta
Coker
Iddo
Station
LAGOS
Oba's Palace
Ijora
Lagos Island
National Museum
Ikoyi
Moba
Kirikiri
Lagos Harbour
Obalende
Falomo
Ajegunle
Apapa
Porto Novo Creek
Victoria Island
Ogoyo
Ogogoro
Igbologun
Ikuata
Alaguntan
Okeogbe
Tarqua Bay
BIGHT OF BENIN
7°20'
East from Greenwich
7°30'
A
B
1
2
3

Lisbon

0 km 5
0 miles 3

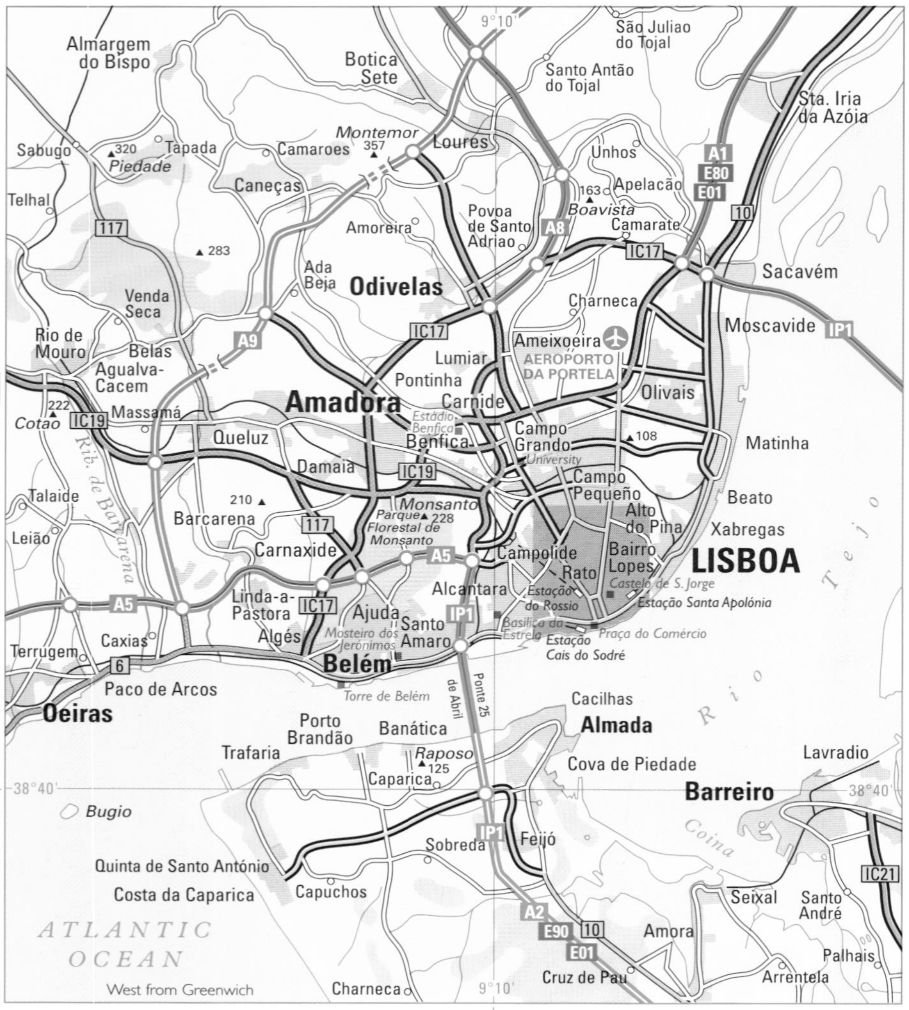

9°10'
São Juliao do Tojal
Almargem do Bispo
Botica Sete
Santo Antão do Tojal
Sta. Iria da Azóia
Montemor
Loures
Sabugo
320
Piedade
Tapada
Camaroes
357
Unhos
Caneças
Apelação
A1
E80
E01
Telhal
117
Povoa de Santo Adrião
163
Boavista
Camarate
Amoreira
A8
10
283
Ada Beja
Odivelas
IC17
Sacavém
Venda Seca
Charneca
A9
IC17
Moscavide
IP1
Rio de Mouro
Belas
Ameixoeira
AEROPORTO DA PORTELA
Lumiar
Agualva-Cacem
Pontinha
Olivais
Amadora
Carnide
222
Cotão
IC19
Massamá
Queluz
Estádio Benfica
Benfica
Campo Grande
108
Matinha
University
Damaia
IC19
Talaide
210
Monsanto
Campo Pequeño
Beato
Parque Florestal de Monsanto
228
Alto do Pina
Xabregas
Leião
Barcarena
117
Carnaxide
A5
Campolide
Bairro Lopes
LISBOA
Rato
A5
Linda-a-Pastora
IC17
Alcântara
Estação do Rossio
Castelo de S. Jorge
Estação Santa Apolónia
Caxias
Ajuda
IP1
Algés
Mosteiro dos Jerónimos
Santo Amaro
Basilica da Estrela
Praça do Comércio
Terrugem
6
Belém
Estação Cais do Sodré
Paco de Arcos
Torre de Belém
Ponte 25 de Abril
Oeiras
Porto Brandão
Cacilhas
Almada
Rio Tejo
Trafaria
Banática
Raposo
125
Cova de Piedade
Lavradio
38°40'
Caparica
Barreiro
Bugio
IP1
Sobreda
Feijó
Quinta de Santo António
Costa da Caparica
Capuchos
Coina
IC21
A2
E90
10
E01
Seixal
Santo André
ATLANTIC OCEAN
Amora
Palhais
West from Greenwich
Charneca
9°10'
Cruz de Pau
Arrentela
A
B
1
2

Central Lisbon

0 km 1
0 miles 0.5

Palácio de Justiça
Penitenciária
Hosp. Infantil
Maternidade
Praça Duque Saldanha
Instituto Superior Técnico
Rua Marquês da Fronteira
AV. ANTÓNIO AUGUSTO DE AGUIAR
AV. FONTES PEREIRA DE MELO
AV. CASAL RIBEIRO
Av. Cardeal Cerejeira
Parque
Forum Picoas
Praça do Chile
Eduardo VII
Pavilhão dos Desportos
RUA PASCOAL DE MELO
ESTEFÂNIA
Hospital D. Estefânia
ALMIRANTE REIS
Praça Marques de Pombal
R. JOAQUIM ANTONIO DE AGUIAR
R. Sousa Martins
RUA JACINTA MARTO
Hospital M. Bombarda
RUA ALEXANDRE HERCULANO
R. BRAAMCAMP
Hospital de Santa Marta
AVENIDA DA LIBERDADE
Hospital dos Capuchos
RATO
Academia das Ciências
Jardim Botanico
Hosp. do Desterro
Instituto de Medicina Legal
Hospital de S. José
BAIRRO LOPES
GRAÇA
Palácio de Assembleia Nacional
Praça dos Restauradores
Teatro Nacional
Estação do Rossio
Martim Moniz
BAIRRO ALTO
Hospital de Jesus
Museu de Arqueologia
Castelo de São Jorge
Museu de Arte Decorativas
Igreja Sta. Engrácia
Estação Santa Apolónia
ALFAMA
Museu Militar
Teatro San Carlos
Biblioteca Nacional
Museu d'Arte Contemporânea
Museu Antoniano
Sé Catedral
RUA DO ARSENAL
BAIXA
Praça do Comércio
AV. VINTE E QUATRO DE JULHO
AV. RIBEIRA DAS NAUS
Estação Cais do Sodré
Estação Fluvial
R. DA ALFÂNDEGA
AVENIDA INFANTE DOM HENRIQUE
Rio Tejo
RUA DO OURO
RUA DA PALMA
a
b
c
1
2
3

London

0 km 5
0 miles 3

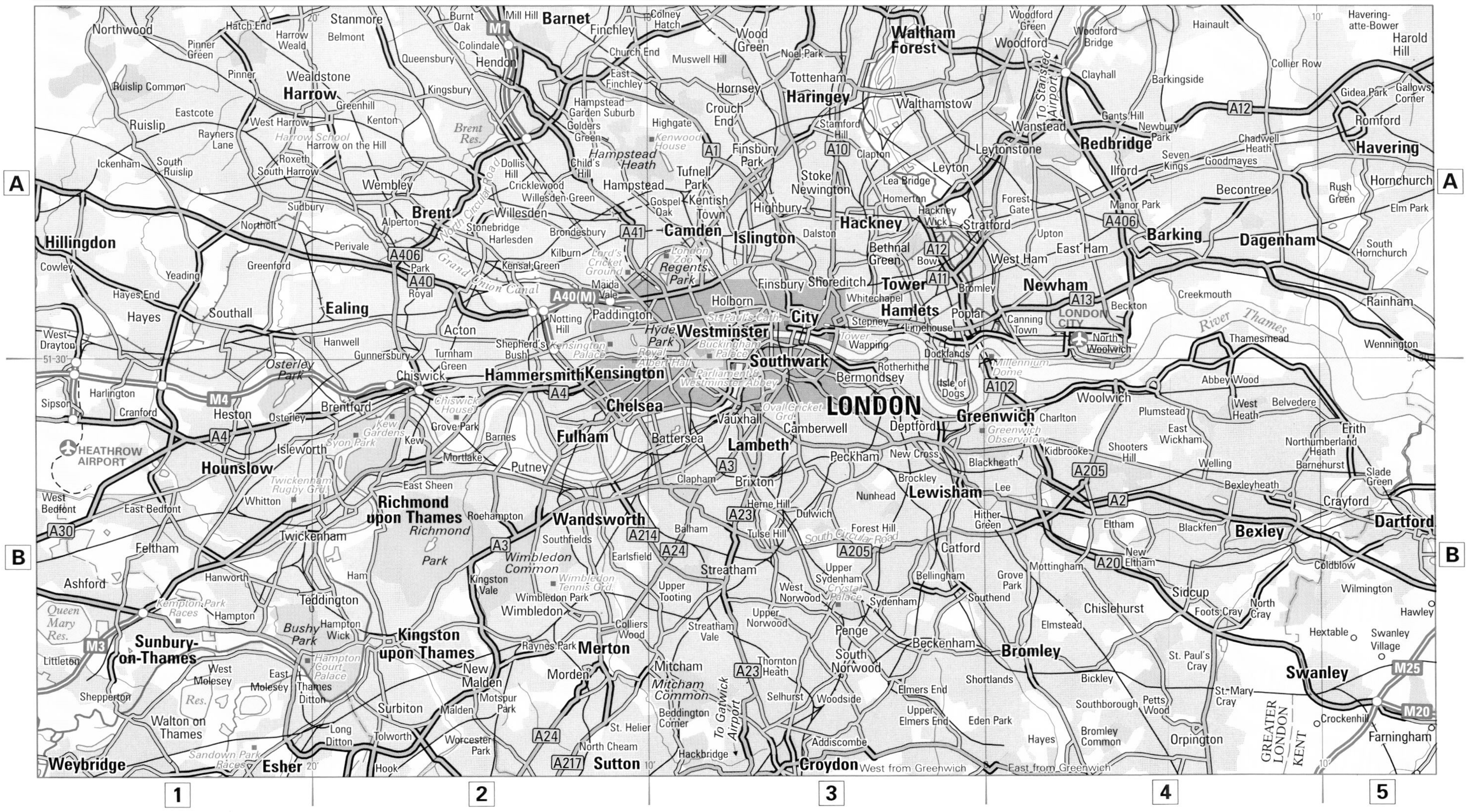

Central London

0 km 2
0 miles 1

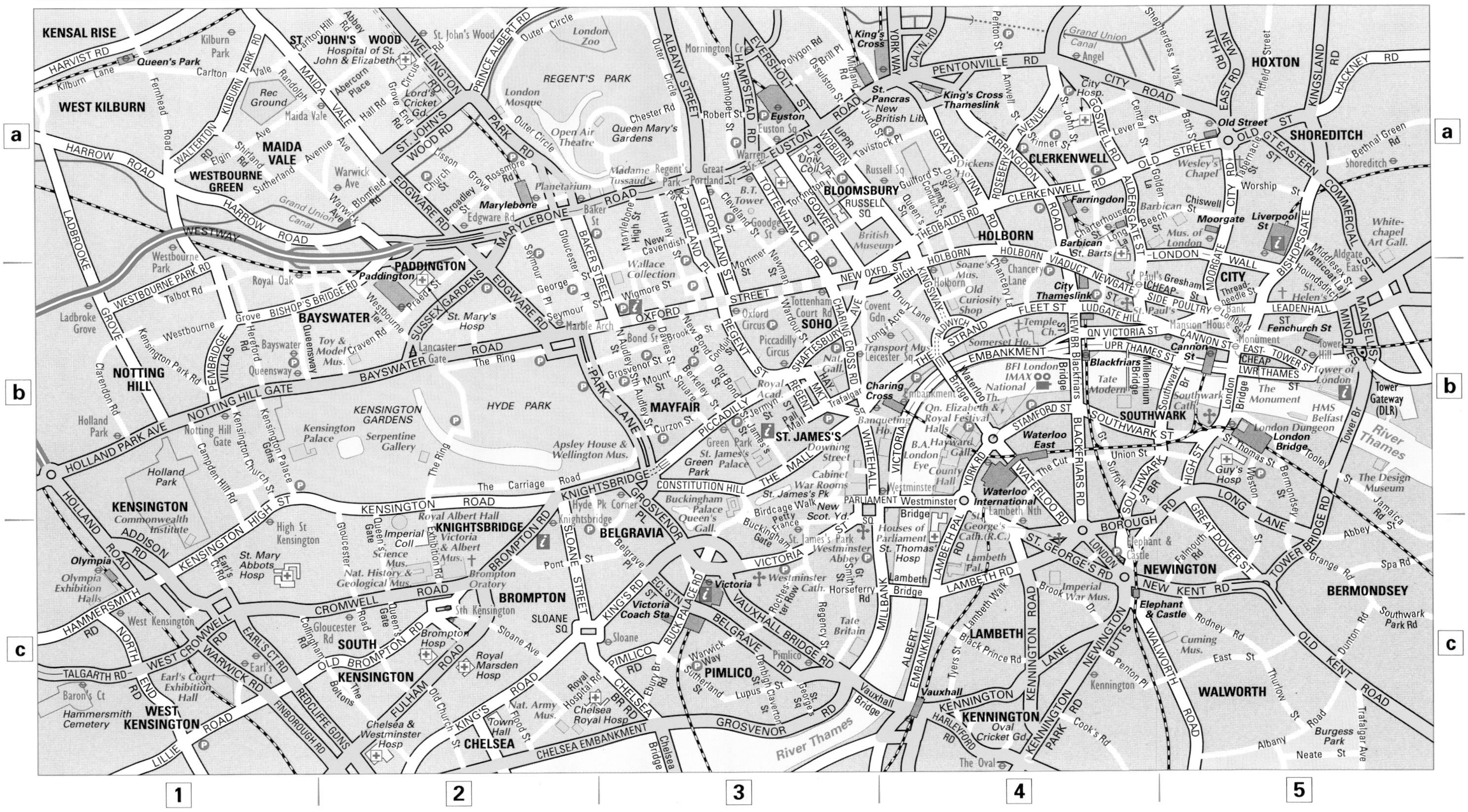

Los Angeles

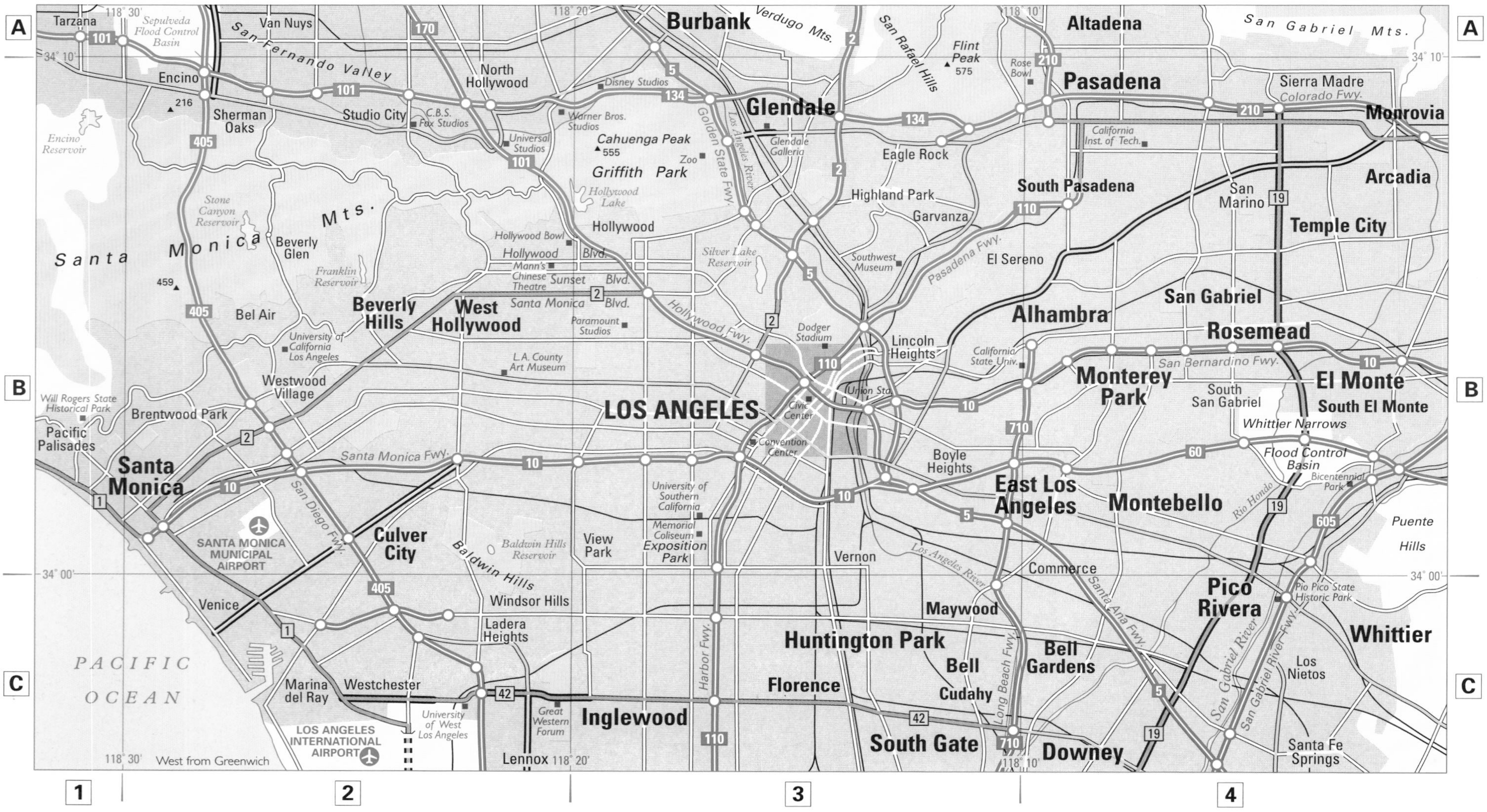
0 km 5
0 miles 3
Tarzana
Sepulveda Flood Control Basin
Van Nuys
San Fernando Valley
Burbank
Verdugo Mts.
San Rafael Hills
Flint Peak 575
Altadena
San Gabriel Mts.
Encino
216
Sherman Oaks
Studio City
C.B.S. Fox Studios
North Hollywood
Disney Studios
Warner Bros. Studios
Universal Studios
Glendale
Glendale Galleria
Rose Bowl
Pasadena
Sierra Madre
Colorado Fwy.
Monrovia
Encino Reservoir
Cahuenga Peak 555
Griffith Park
Zoo
Golden State Fwy.
Los Angeles River
Eagle Rock
California Inst. of Tech.
Arcadia
Stone Canyon Reservoir
Hollywood Lake
Highland Park
South Pasadena
San Marino
Temple City
Santa Monica Mts.
Beverly Glen
Hollywood
Garvanza
Franklin Reservoir
Hollywood Bowl
Hollywood Blvd.
Mann's Chinese Theatre
Sunset Blvd.
Silver Lake Reservoir
Southwest Museum
Pasadena Fwy.
El Sereno
459
Bel Air
Beverly Hills
West Hollywood
Santa Monica Blvd.
Paramount Studios
Hollywood Fwy.
Dodger Stadium
Alhambra
San Gabriel
Rosemead
University of California Los Angeles
L.A. County Art Museum
Lincoln Heights
California State Univ.
Monterey Park
San Bernardino Fwy.
El Monte
South El Monte
Will Rogers State Historical Park
Westwood Village
Union Sta.
Civic Center
South San Gabriel
Brentwood Park
LOS ANGELES
Whittier Narrows
Pacific Palisades
Convention Center
Boyle Heights
Flood Control Basin
Bicentennial Park
Santa Monica
Santa Monica Fwy.
East Los Angeles
Montebello
Rio Hondo
University of Southern California
Memorial Coliseum
Exposition Park
Puente Hills
SANTA MONICA MUNICIPAL AIRPORT
San Diego Fwy.
Culver City
Baldwin Hills Reservoir
View Park
Vernon
Los Angeles River
Commerce
Santa Ana Fwy.
Baldwin Hills
Pico Rivera
Pio Pico State Historic Park
Venice
Windsor Hills
Maywood
Ladera Heights
Huntington Park
Bell
Bell Gardens
Whittier
PACIFIC OCEAN
Harbor Fwy.
Long Beach Fwy.
Los Nietos
San Gabriel River
San Gabriel River Fwy.
Marina del Rey
Westchester
Florence
Cudahy
University of West Los Angeles
Great Western Forum
Inglewood
LOS ANGELES INTERNATIONAL AIRPORT
South Gate
Downey
Santa Fe Springs
Lennox
118° 30'
118° 20'
118° 10'
34° 10'
34° 00'
West from Greenwich
A
B
C
1
2
3
4

Lima

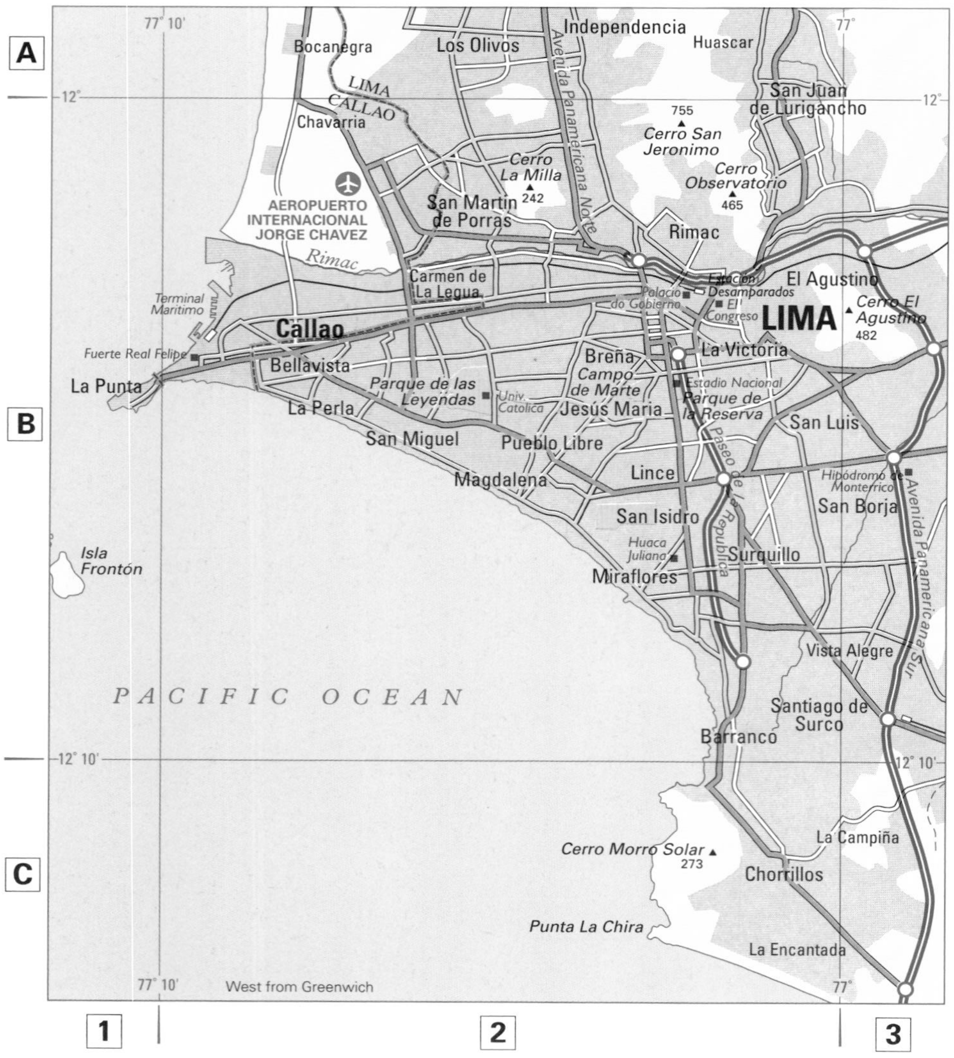
0 km 5
0 miles 3
77° 10'
77°
12°
12° 10'
Bocanegra
Los Olivos
Avenida Panamericana Norte
Independencia
Huascar
LIMA
CALLAO
Chavarria
San Juan de Lurigancho
755
Cerro San Jeronimo
Cerro La Milla 242
Cerro Observatorio 465
AEROPUERTO INTERNACIONAL JORGE CHAVEZ
San Martin de Porras
Rimac
Rimac
Terminal Maritimo
Carmen de La Legua
Palacio de Gobierno
Estación Desamparados
El Congreso
El Agustino
Cerro El Agustino 482
LIMA
Callao
Fuerte Real Felipe
La Punta
Bellavista
Breña
La Victoria
Campo de Marte
Parque de las Leyendas
Univ. Católica
Estadio Nacional
Parque de la Reserva
La Perla
Jesús Maria
San Luis
San Miguel
Pueblo Libre
Lince
Magdalena
Hipódromo de Monterrico
San Borja
San Isidro
Avenida Panamericana Sur
Paseo de la República
Isla Frontón
Huaca Juliana
Surquillo
Miraflores
Vista Alegre
PACIFIC OCEAN
Santiago de Surco
Barranco
La Campiña
Cerro Morro Solar 273
Chorrillos
Punta La Chira
La Encantada
West from Greenwich
A
B
C
1
2
3

Central Los Angeles

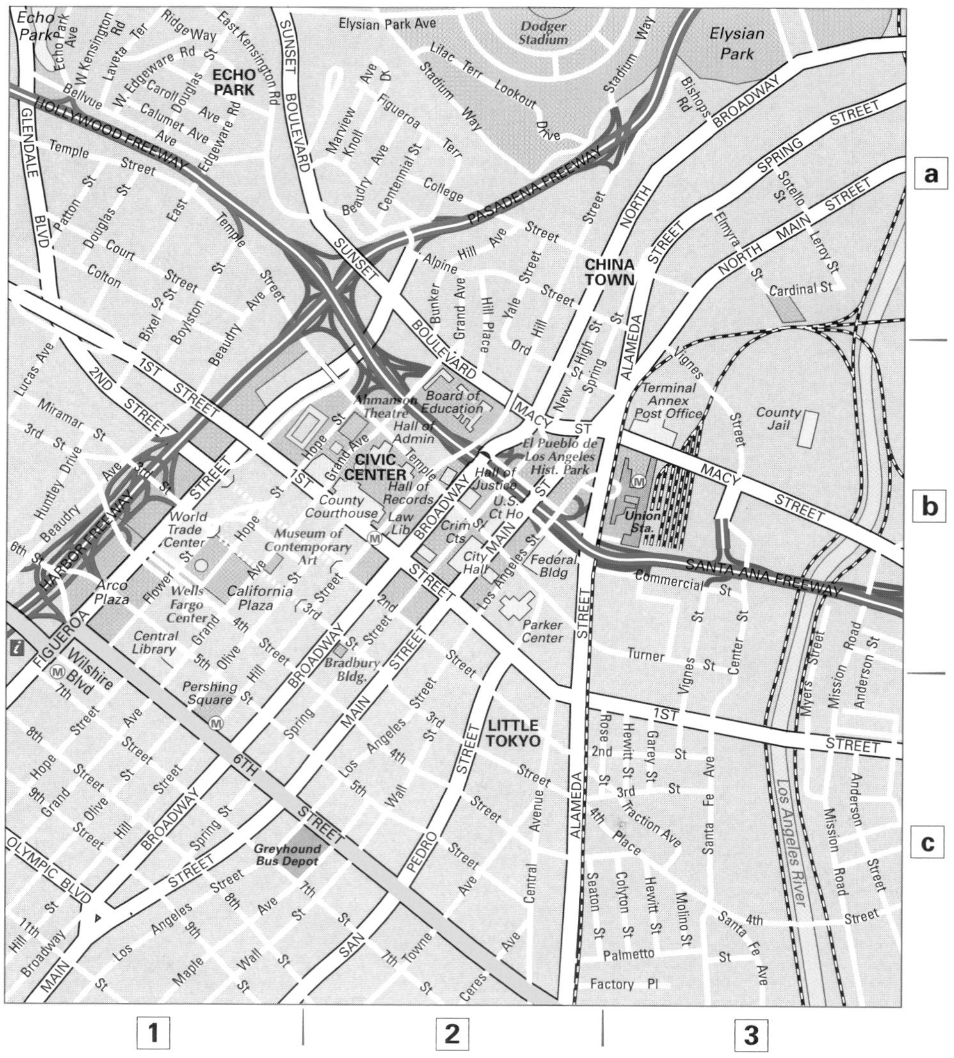
0 km 1
0 miles 0.5
Echo Park
Echo Park Ave
W Kensington Rd
Laveta Ter
Ridge Way
East Kensington Rd
SUNSET BOULEVARD
Elysian Park Ave
Dodger Stadium
Stadium Way
Elysian Park
ECHO PARK
Bellevue
W Edgeware Rd
Carroll
Douglas
Calumet Ave
Edgeware Rd
Marview
Knoll
Figueroa
Lilac Terr
Lookout
Stadium Way
Drive
Bishops Rd
BROADWAY
HOLLYWOOD FREEWAY
GLENDALE BLVD
Temple
Street
Centennial St
College
PASADENA FREEWAY
SPRING
Solano
STREET
a
Patton St
Douglas St
East
Temple
Beaudry
Alpine
Hill
Street
NORTH
Elmyra
NORTH MAIN
Leroy St
Court
Street
Bunker
Hill Place
Yale
Ord
CHINA TOWN
Cardinal St
Cotton
Bixel St
Boylston
Beaudry Ave
Hill
Lucas Ave
1ST STREET
2ND STREET
BOULEVARD
New High St
Spring
ALAMEDA
Vignes
Miramar
3rd
Ahmanson Theatre
Board of Education
MACY
Terminal Annex Post Office
County Jail
Huntley Drive
Hope
Grand
CIVIC CENTER
Hall of Records
Hall of Justice
El Pueblo de Los Angeles Hist. Park
MACY
STREET
World Trade Center
County Courthouse
Law Lib.
U.S. Ct Ho.
Union Sta.
b
Beaudry
Museum of Contemporary Art
Crim. Cts.
City Hall
Federal Bldg
SANTA ANA FREEWAY
HARBOR FREEWAY
California Plaza
Commercial
Arco Plaza
Wells Fargo Center
Parker Center
Central Library
Olive
Bradbury Bldg.
Turner
FIGUEROA
Wilshire Blvd
Pershing Square
BROADWAY
MAIN
STREET
LITTLE TOKYO
1ST
STREET
Vignes
Center
Mission Road
Anderson St
8th
Hope
Grand
6TH
Spring
Los Angeles
Rose
2nd
Hewitt St
Garey St
3rd
Traction Ave
4th Place
Santa Fe Ave
Los Angeles River
Myers Street
Mission Road
Anderson
9th
Olive
Hill
Street
BROADWAY
Greyhound Bus Depot
Central Avenue
ALAMEDA
c
OLYMPIC BLVD
11th
Broadway
MAIN
Los Angeles
Maple
Wall
SAN PEDRO
Towne
Ceres
Seaton St
Colyton St
Hewitt St
Molino St
Palmetto
Factory Pl
Santa Fe Ave
4th
1
2
3

Madrid

0 km 5
0 miles 3

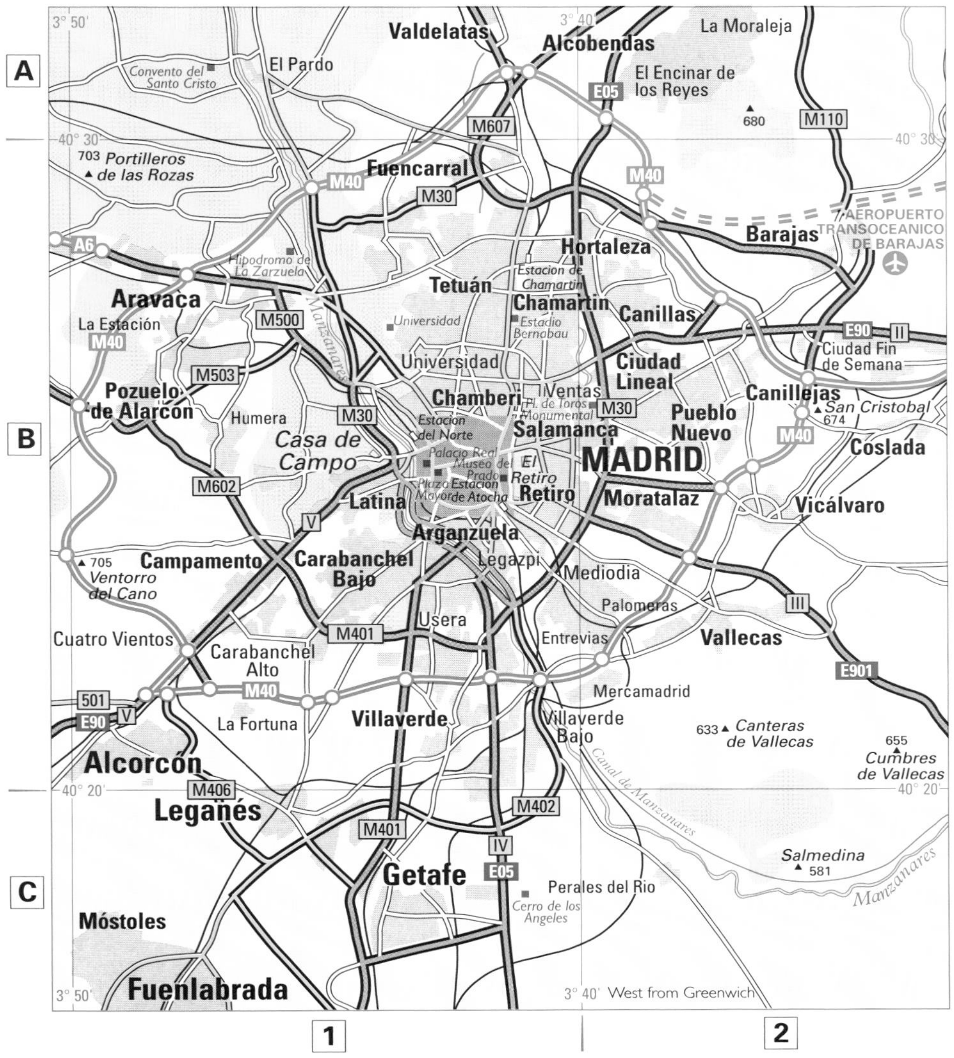

Central Madrid

0 km 1
0 miles 0.5

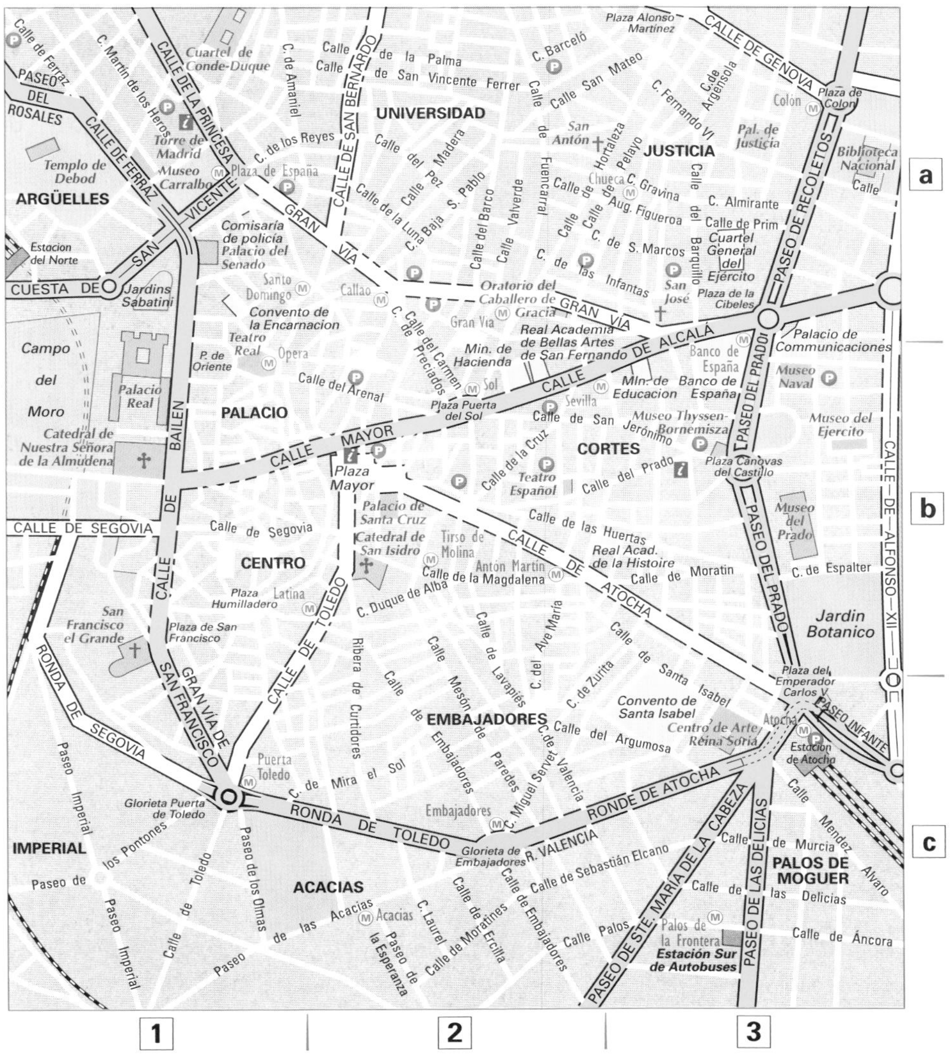

Manila

0 km 5
0 miles 3

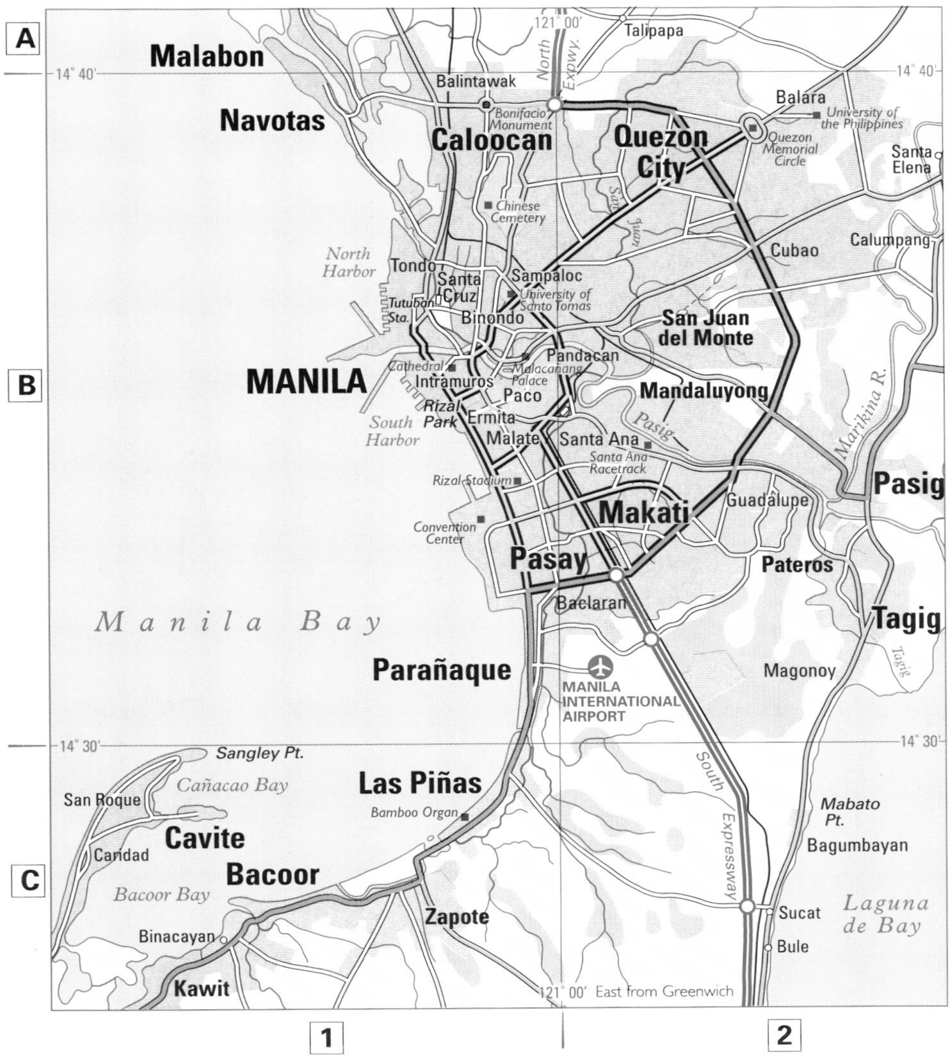

Melbourne

0 km 5
0 miles 3

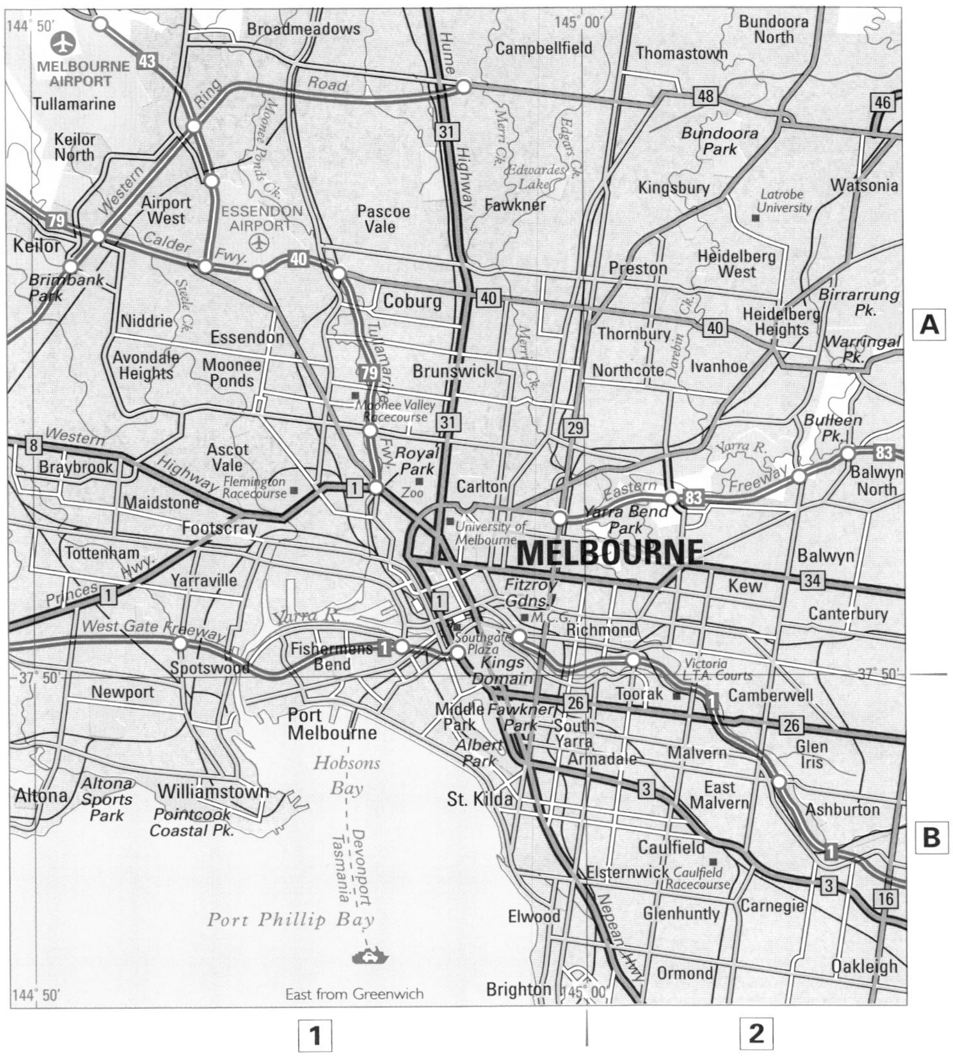

Mexico City

0 km 5
0 miles 3

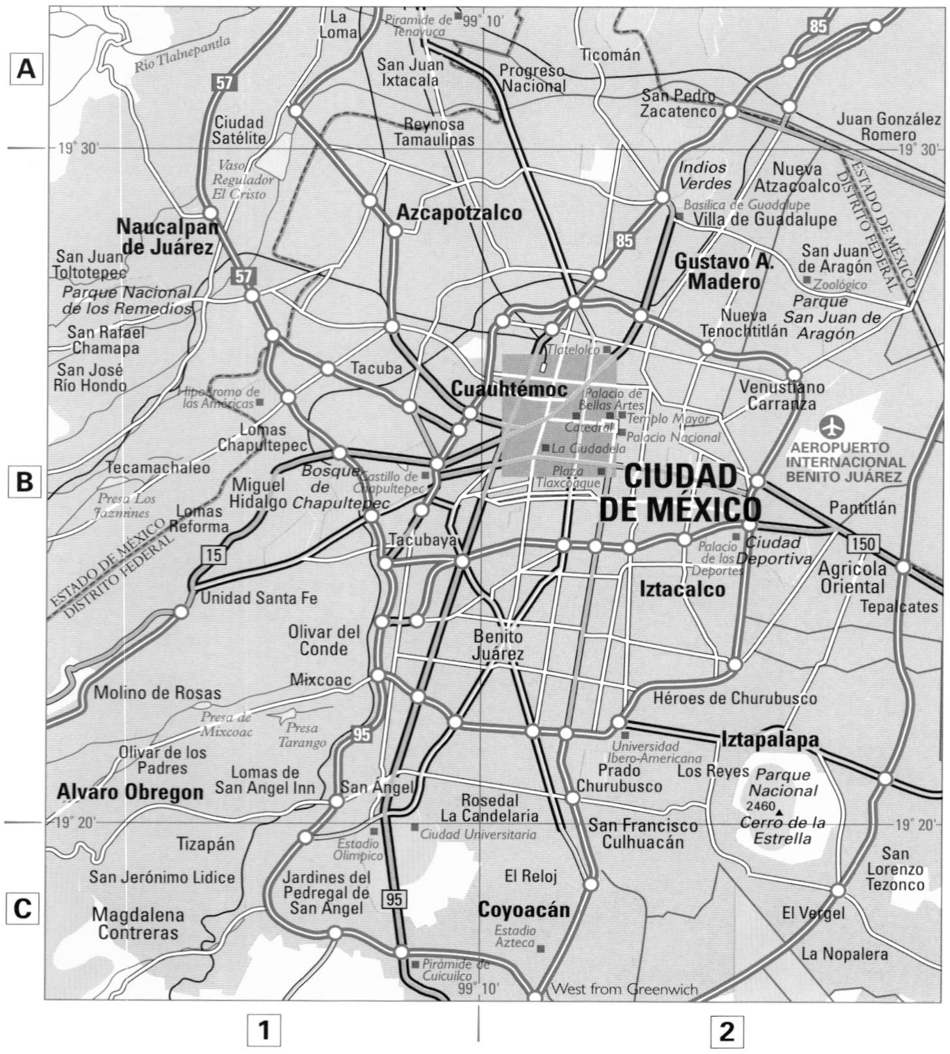

A
B
C
1
2
La Loma
Pirámide de Tenayuca
99° 10'
Río Tlalnepantla
San Juan Ixtacala
Progreso Nacional
Ticomán
San Pedro Zacatenco
Juan González Romero
Ciudad Satélite
Reynosa Tamaulipas
19° 30'
Vaso Regulador El Cristo
Indios Verdes
Nueva Atzacoalco
ESTADO DE MÉXICO
DISTRITO FEDERAL
Azcapotzalco
Basílica de Guadalupe
Villa de Guadalupe
Naucalpan de Juárez
San Juan Toltotepec
Gustavo A. Madero
San Juan de Aragón
Zoológico
Parque Nacional de los Remedios
Parque San Juan de Aragón
Nueva Tenochtitlán
San Rafael Chamapa
Tlatelolco
San José Río Hondo
Tacuba
Cuauhtémoc
Palacio de Bellas Artes
Templo Mayor
Venustiano Carranza
Hipódromo de las Américas
Catedral
Palacio Nacional
Lomas Chapultepec
La Cuidadela
AEROPUERTO INTERNACIONAL BENITO JUÁREZ
Tecamachalco
Bosque de Chapultepec
Castillo de Chapultepec
Plaza Tlaxcoaque
CIUDAD DE MÉXICO
Miguel Hidalgo
Presa Los Tazinnes
Lomas Reforma
Pantitlán
Tacubaya
Palacio de los Deportes
Ciudad Deportiva
Agrícola Oriental
Unidad Santa Fe
Iztacalco
Tepalcates
Olivar del Conde
Benito Juárez
Mixcoac
Molino de Rosas
Presa de Mixcoac
Presa Tarango
Héroes de Churubusco
Iztapalapa
Olivar de los Padres
Universidad Ibero-Americana
Alvaro Obregon
Lomas de San Angel Inn
Prado Churubusco
Los Reyes
Parque Nacional
San Angel
Rosedal
La Candelaria
2460
Cerro de la Estrella
Tizapán
Estadio Olímpico
Ciudad Universitaria
San Francisco Culhuacán
19° 20'
San Jerónimo Lidice
Jardines del Pedregal de San Angel
El Reloj
San Lorenzo Tezonco
Magdalena Contreras
Coyoacán
Estadio Azteca
El Vergel
La Nopalera
Pirámide de Cuicuilco
99° 10'
West from Greenwich
15
57
85
95
150

Central Mexico City

0 km 1
0 miles 0.5

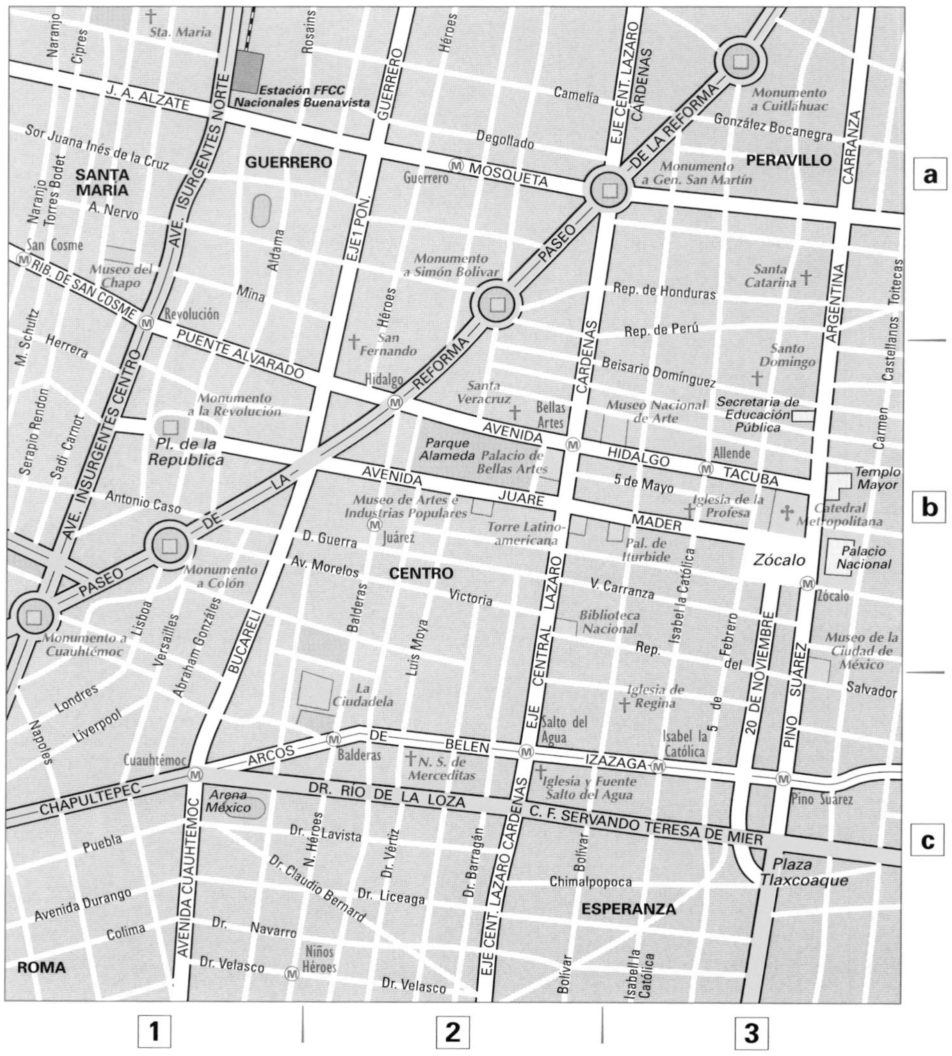

a
b
c
1
2
3
Naranjo
Ciprés
Sta. María
Rosains
Estación FFCC Nacionales Buenavista
Camelia
Monumento a Cuitlahuac
J. A. ALZATE
AVE. INSURGENTES NORTE
GUERRERO
Héroes
González Bocanegra
Sor Juana Inés de la Cruz
Degollado
CARRANZA
SANTA MARÍA
Torres Bodet
MOSQUETA
PERAVILLO
Guerrero
Monumento a Gen. San Martín
A. Nervo
Aldama
EJE 1 PON.
PASEO DE LA REFORMA
EJE CENT. LAZARO CÁRDENAS
San Cosme
Monumento a Simón Bolívar
Santa Catarina
Museo del Chopo
Mina
Rep. de Honduras
RIB. DE SAN COSME
Revolución
Rep. de Perú
San Fernando
Santo Domingo
M. Schultz
Herrera
PUENTE ALVARADO
Beisario Domínguez
ARGENTINA
Castellanos
Toltecas
Hidalgo
Santa Veracruz
Museo Nacional de Arte
Secretaria de Educación Pública
Bellas Artes
Serapio Rendón
Monumento a la Revolución
AVENIDA
Allende
Carmen
Sadi Carnot
Pl. de la República
Parque Alameda
Palacio de Bellas Artes
HIDALGO
TACUBA
5 de Mayo
Templo Mayor
AVE. INSURGENTES CENTRO
Antonio Caso
Museo de Artes e Industrias Populares
JUÁREZ
Iglesia de la Profesa
Catedral Metropolitana
Juárez
Torre Latino-americana
MADERO
Pal. de Iturbide
D. Guerra
Zócalo
Palacio Nacional
PASEO DE LA
Monumento a Colón
Av. Morelos
CENTRO
V. Carranza
Zócalo
Lisboa
Versalles
Abraham González
Balderas
Luis Moya
Victoria
Biblioteca Nacional
Museo de la Ciudad de México
Monumento a Cuahtémoc
BUCARELI
Rep.
Isabel la Católica
Febrero
20 DE NOVIEMBRE
PINO SUÁREZ
Salvador
Londres
La Ciudadela
Iglesia de Regina
Liverpool
EJE CENTRAL LAZARO
Salto del Agua
Isabel la Católica
Nápoles
Cuauhtémoc
ARCOS DE BELEN
Balderas
N. S. de Merced
IZAZAGA
Iglesia y Fuente Salto del Agua
CHAPULTEPEC
Arena México
DR. RÍO DE LA LOZA
Pino Suárez
C. F. SERVANDO TERESA DE MIER
Puebla
Dr. Lavista
Dr. Vértiz
Plaza Tlaxcoaque
Dr. Claudio Bernard
Dr. Barragán
Bolívar
Chimalpopoca
N. Héroes
Dr. Liceaga
ESPERANZA
Avenida Durango
Colima
AVENIDA CUAUHTÉMOC
Dr. Navarro
EJE CENT. LAZARO CÁRDENAS
Niños Héroes
ROMA
Dr. Velasco
Dr. Velasco
Bolívar
Isabel la Católica

Miami

0 km 5
0 miles 3

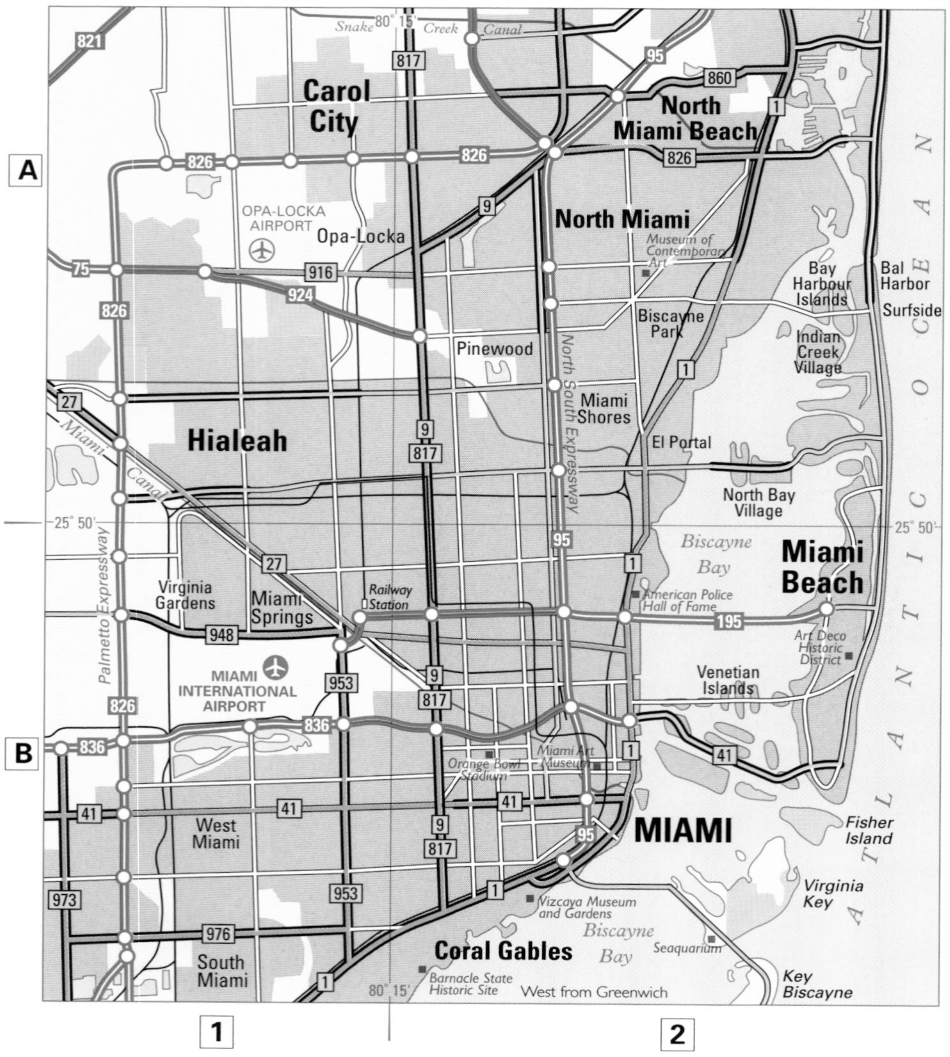

A
B
1
2
Snake
80° 15'
Creek
Canal
821
817
95
860
Carol City
North Miami Beach
826
826
826
OPA-LOCKA AIRPORT
Opa-Locka
North Miami
Museum of Contemporary Art
75
916
924
Bay Harbour Islands
Bal Harbor
Surfside
Pinewood
Biscayne Park
Indian Creek Village
North South Expressway
Miami Shores
Hialeah
El Portal
North Bay Village
25° 50'
Palmetto Expressway
Miami Canal
Biscayne Bay
Miami Beach
ATLANTIC OCEAN
Virginia Gardens
Miami Springs
Railway Station
American Police Hall of Fame
948
195
Art Deco Historic District
MIAMI INTERNATIONAL AIRPORT
953
Venetian Islands
836
Orange Bowl Stadium
Miami Art Museum
West Miami
MIAMI
Fisher Island
973
Vizcaya Museum and Gardens
Virginia Key
976
Biscayne Bay
Seaquarium
South Miami
Coral Gables
Barnacle State Historic Site
West from Greenwich
Key Biscayne
27
41
9
1

Milan

0 km 5
0 miles 3

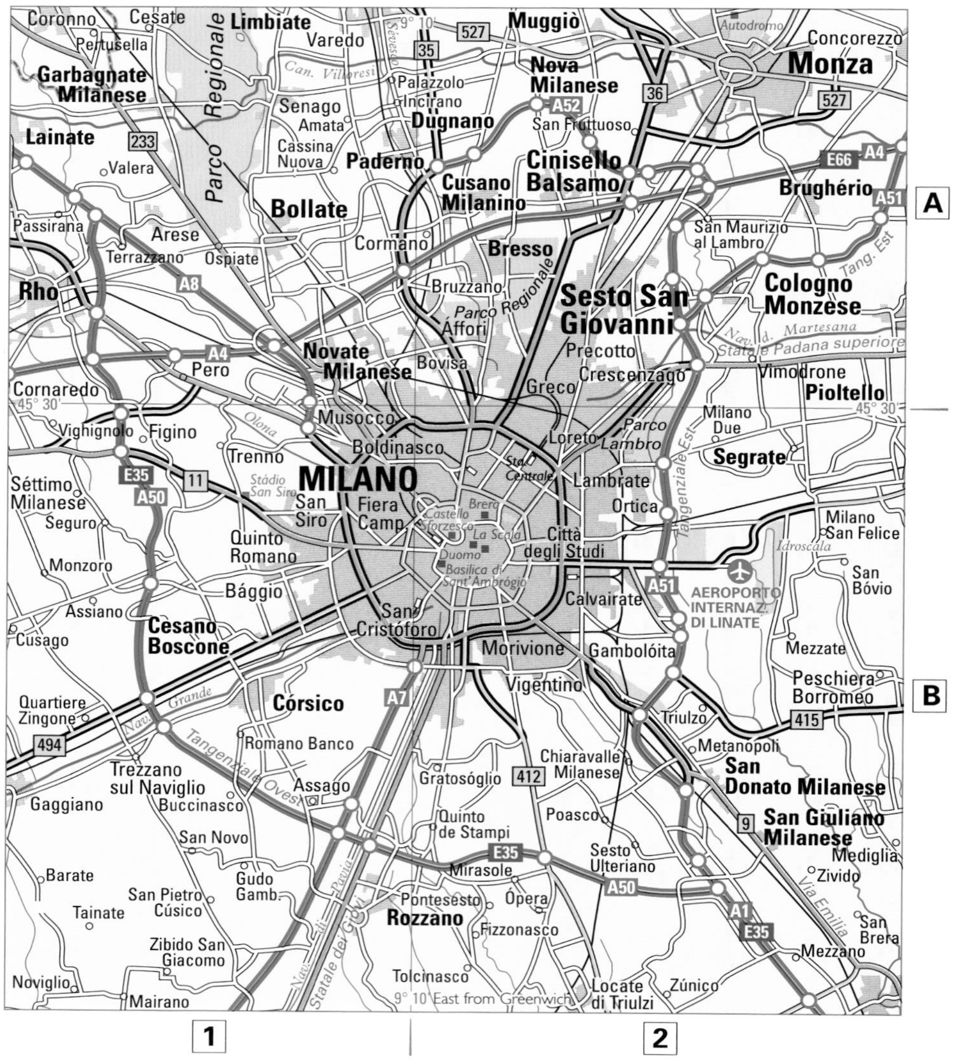

A
B
1
2
Coronno
Cesate
Pertusella
Limbiate
Varedo
9° 10'
527
Muggiò
Autodromo
Concorezzo
Garbagnate Milanese
Can. Villoresi
Palazzolo
Nova Milanese
Monza
Parco Regionale
Senago
Incirano
Amata
Dugnano
San Fruttuoso
Lainate
Cassina Nuova
Paderno
Cinisello Balsamo
Valera
Bollate
Cusano Milanino
Brughério
Passirana
Arese
San Maurizio al Lambro
Terrazzano
Ospiate
Cormano
Bresso
Tang. Est
Rho
Bruzzano
Parco Regionale
Sesto San Giovanni
Cologno Monzese
Affori
Novate Milanese
Precotto
Martesana
Pero
Bovisa
Strada Padana superiore
Cornaredo
Crescenzago
Vimodrone
45° 30'
Greco
Pioltello
Musocco
Vighignolo
Figino
Boldinasco
Loreto
Milano Due
Olona
Trenno
Stadio San Siro
Parco Lambro
Segrate
MILANO
Stazione Centrale
Lambrate
Séttimo Milanese
San Siro
Fiera Camp.
Brera
Ortica
Seguro
Castello Sforzesco
Tangenziale Est
Milano San Felice
Quinto Romano
La Scala
Città degli Studi
Duomo
Idroscala
Monzoro
Basilica di Sant'Ambrogio
Baggio
Calvairate
San Bovio
Assiano
AEROPORTO INTERNAZ. DI LINATE
San Cristoforo
Cesano Boscone
Cusago
Mezzate
Vigentino
Gamboloita
Peschiera Borromeo
Quartiere Zingone
Naviglio Grande
Corsico
Triulzo
Metanopoli
Tangenziale Ovest
Romano Banco
Chiaravalle Milanese
San Donato Milanese
Trezzano sul Naviglio
Assago
Gratosóglio
Gaggiano
Buccinasco
Quinto de Stampi
Poasco
San Giuliano Milanese
San Novo
Mediglia
Sesto Ulteriano
Zivido
Gudo Gamb.
Mirasole
Barate
San Pietro Cúsico
Pontesesto
Opera
Via Emilia
Tainate
Rozzano
San Brera
Zibido San Giacomo
Fizzonasco
Mezzano
Noviglio
Tolcinasco
Zúnico
Mairano
9° 10' East from Greenwich
Locate di Triulzi
Statale dei Giovi
Naviglio Pavese
35
36
233
412
415
494
11
9
A1
A4
A7
A8
A50
A51
A52
E35
E62
E66

Moscow

0 km 5
0 miles 3

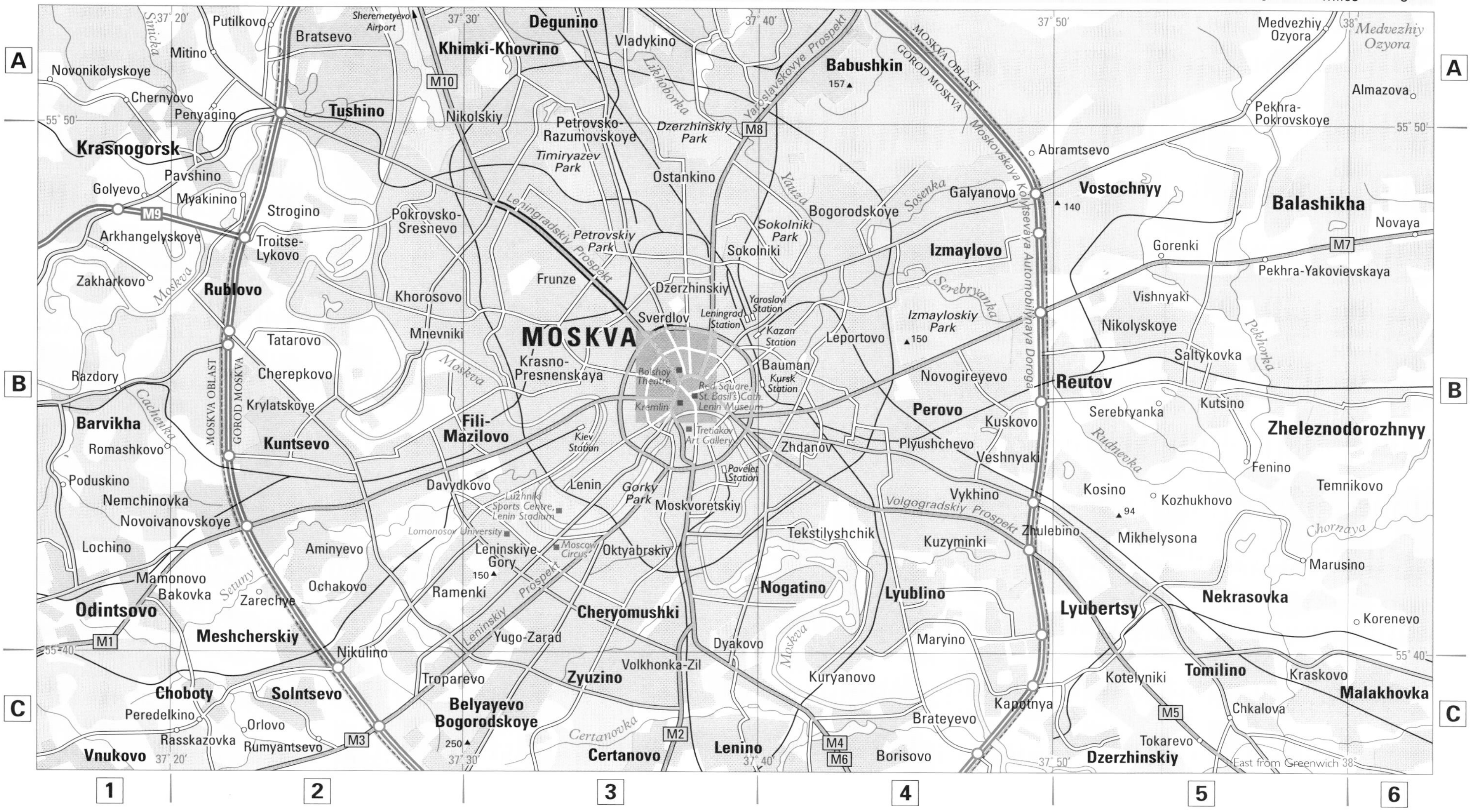

A
B
C
1
2
3
4
5
6
Novonikolyskoye
Putilkovo
Mitino
Bratsevo
Sheremetyevo Airport
Khimki-Khovrino
Degunino
Vladykino
Babushkin
Medvezhiy Ozyora
Chernyovo
Penyagino
Tushino
Nikolskiy
Petrovsko-Razumovskoye
Timiryazev Park
Dzerzhinskiy Park
Ostankino
Krasnogorsk
Pavshino
Golyevo
Myakinino
Strogino
Pokrovsko-Sresnevo
Leningradskiy Prospekt
Petrovskiy Park
Arkhangelyskoye
Troitse-Lykovo
Zakharkovo
Rublovo
Khorosovo
Frunze
Dzerzhinskiy
Sverdlov
Sokolniki
Sokolniki Park
Bogorodskoye
Izmaylovo
Izmayloskiy Park
Galyanovo
Vostochnyy
Balashikha
Abramtsevo
Pekhra-Pokrovskoye
Almazova
Novaya
Gorenki
Pekhra-Yakovievskaya
Vishnyaki
Nikolyskoye
Saltykovka
Tatarovo
Mnevniki
MOSKVA
Krasno-Presnenskaya
Bolshoy Theatre
Red Square
St. Basil's Cath.
Lenin Museum
Kremlin
Tretiakov Art Gallery
Leningrad Station
Yaroslavl Station
Kazan Station
Kursk Station
Bauman
Leportovo
Novogireyevo
Reutov
Razdory
Cherepkovo
Krylatskoye
Barvikha
Romashkovo
Kuntsevo
Fili-Mazilovo
Kiev Station
Pavelet Station
Zhdanov
Perovo
Kuskovo
Plyushchevo
Veshnyaki
Serebryanka
Kutsino
Zheleznodorozhnyy
Fenino
Poduskino
Nemchinovka
Novoivanovskoye
Davydkovo
Luzhniki Sports Centre Lenin Stadium
Lenin
Gorky Park
Moskvoretskiy
Vykhino
Volgogradskiy Prospekt
Kosino
Kozhukhovo
Temnikovo
Lochino
Lomonosov University
Leninskiye Gory
Moscow Circus
Oktyabrskiy
Tekstilyshchik
Zhulebino
Kuzyminki
Mikhelysona
Marusino
Mamonovo
Bakovka
Aminyevo
Ochakovo
Zarechye
Ramenki
Nogatino
Lyublino
Lyubertsy
Nekrasovka
Odintsovo
Cheryomushki
Korenevo
Meshcherskiy
Yugo-Zarad
Dyakovo
Maryino
Nikulino
Troparevo
Volkhonka-Zil
Kuryanovo
Kotelyniki
Tomilino
Kraskovo
Choboty
Solntsevo
Zyuzino
Kapotnya
Malakhovka
Peredelkino
Orlovo
Belyayevo Bogorodskoye
Certanovka
Brateyevo
Chkalova
Rasskazovka
Rumyantsevo
Tokarevo
Vnukovo
Certanovo
Lenino
Borisovo
Dzerzhinskiy
MOSKVA OBLAST
GOROD MOSKVA
Moskovskaya Kolytsevaya Automobilynaya Doroga
Yaroslavskoye Prospekt
Leninskiy Prospekt
Moskva
Yauza
M1
M2
M3
M4
M5
M6
M7
M8
M9
M10
East from Greenwich 38°

Montréal

0 km 5
0 miles 3

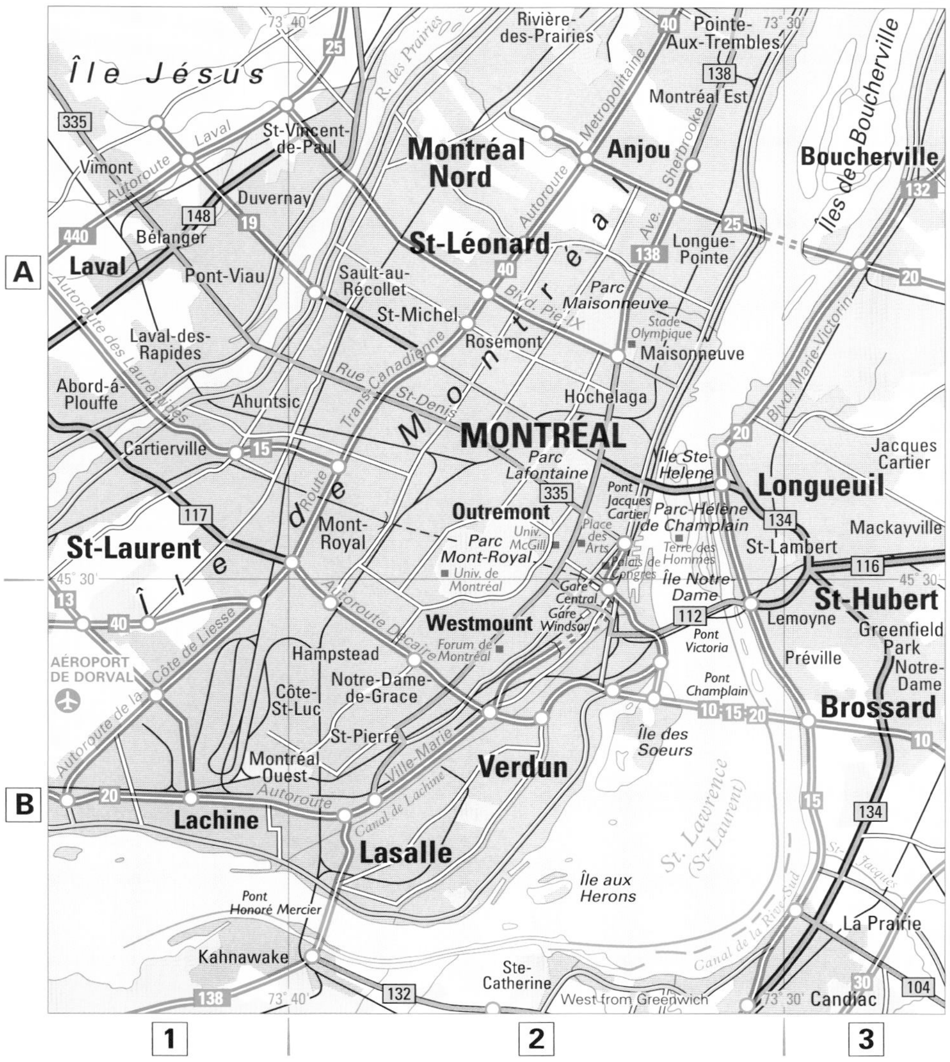

A
B
1
2
3
Île Jésus
Rivière-des-Prairies
Pointe-Aux-Trembles
Montréal Est
St-Vincent-de-Paul
Montréal Nord
Anjou
Boucherville
Vimont
Duvernay
Bélanger
Laval
St-Léonard
Longue-Pointe
Îles de Boucherville
Pont-Viau
Sault-au-Récollet
St-Michel
Parc Maisonneuve
Stade Olympique
Maisonneuve
Laval-des-Rapides
Rosemont
Abord-à-Plouffe
Ahuntsic
Hochelaga
Cartierville
MONTRÉAL
Parc Lafontaine
Île Ste-Hélène
Jacques Cartier
Longueuil
Outremont
Pont Jacques Cartier
Parc-Hélène Champlain
Mackayville
St-Laurent
Mont-Royal
Parc Mont-Royal
Univ. McGill
Place des Arts
Terre des Hommes
St-Lambert
Univ. de Montréal
Palais des Congrès
Île Notre-Dame
St-Hubert
Gare Central
Gare Windsor
Westmount
Lemoyne
Greenfield Park
Aéroport de Dorval
Hampstead
Forum de Montréal
Pont Victoria
Préville
Notre-Dame
Côte-St-Luc
Notre-Dame-de-Grace
Pont Champlain
Brossard
St-Pierre
Île des Soeurs
Montréal Ouest
Verdun
Lachine
Lasalle
Canal de Lachine
St. Lawrence (St-Laurent)
Île aux Herons
Pont Honoré Mercier
La Prairie
Kahnawake
Ste-Catherine
Candiac
West from Greenwich 73° 30'

Central Moscow

0 km 1
0 miles 0.5

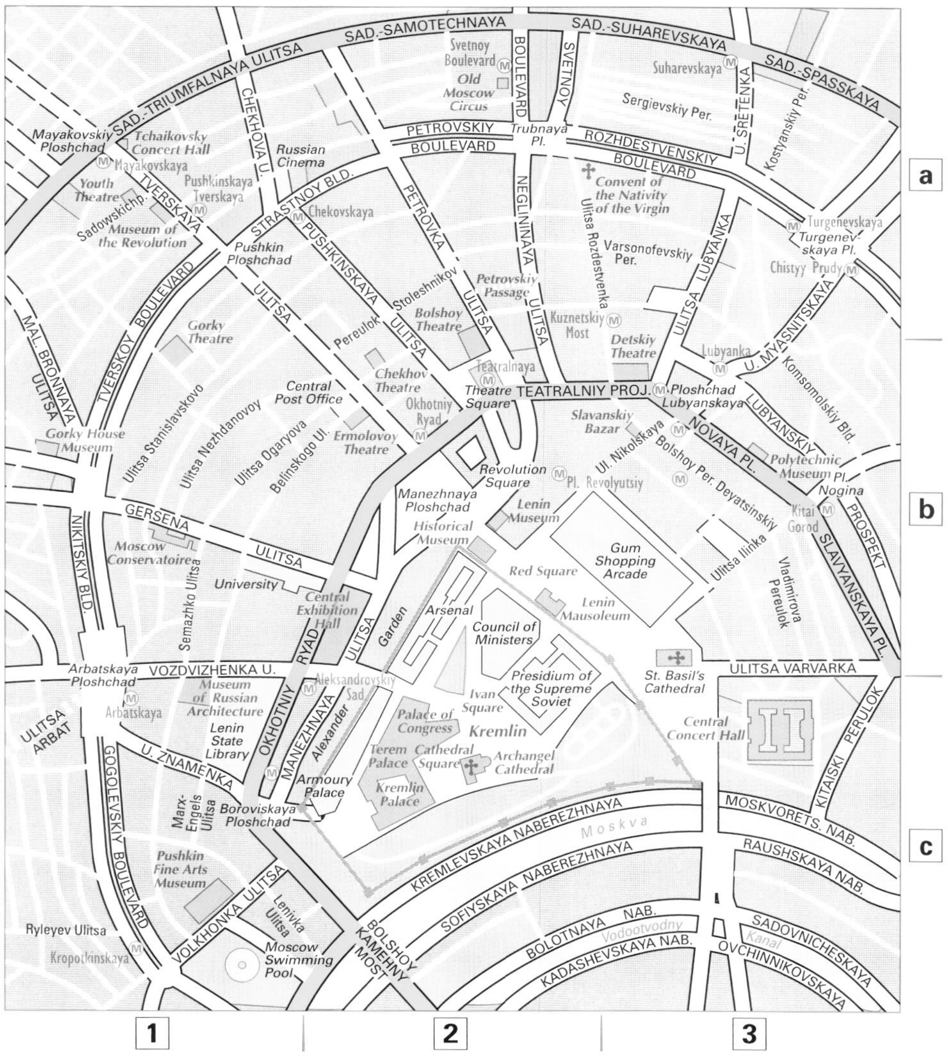

a
b
c
1
2
3
SAD.-SAMOTECHNAYA
SAD.-SUHAREVSKAYA
SAD.-SPASSKAYA
SAD.-TRIUMFALNAYA ULITSA
Svetnoy Boulevard
Old Moscow Circus
Suharevskaya
Sergievskiy Per.
Mayakovskiy Ploshchad
Tchaikovsky Concert Hall
Russian Cinema
PETROVSKIY BOULEVARD
Trubnaya Pl.
ROZHDESTVENSKIY BOULEVARD
Convent of the Nativity of the Virgin
Turgenevskaya
Youth Theatre
Pushkinskaya
Tverskaya
Chekovskaya
Sadowskichp
Museum of the Revolution
Pushkin Ploshchad
Varsonofevskiy Per.
Chistye Prudy
Petrovskiy Passage
Bolshoy Theatre
Kuznetskiy Most
Detskiy Theatre
Gorky Theatre
Stoleshnikov Pereulok
Teatralnaya
Lubyanka
Chekhov Theatre
Okhotniy Ryad
Theatre Square
TEATRALNIY PROJ.
Ploshchad Lubyanskaya
Central Post Office
Slavyanskiy Bazar
Ermolovoy Theatre
Polytechnic Museum
Gorky House Museum
Revolution Square
Pl. Revolyutsiy
Nogina
Kitai Gorod
Manezhnaya Ploshchad
Lenin Museum
Historical Museum
Moscow Conservatoire
Gum Shopping Arcade
Red Square
University
Central Exhibition Hall
Arsenal
Council of Ministers
Lenin Mausoleum
Presidium of the Supreme Soviet
St. Basil's Cathedral
ULITSA VARVARKA
Arbatskaya Ploshchad
VOZDVIZHENKA U.
Museum of Russian Architecture
Aleksandrovskiy Sad
Ivan Square
Kremlin
Palace of Congress
Central Concert Hall
Lenin State Library
Terem Palace
Cathedral Square
Archangel Cathedral
Armoury Palace
Kremlin Palace
Marx-Engels Ulitsa
Borovitskaya Ploshchad
MOSKVORETS. NAB.
KREMLEVSKAYA NABEREZHNAYA
RAUSHSKAYA NAB.
Pushkin Fine Arts Museum
SOFIYSKAYA NAB.
SADOVNICHESKAYA
BOLOTNAYA NAB.
KADASHEVSKAYA NAB.
OVCHINNIKOVSKAYA
Ryleyev Ulitsa
Kropotkinskaya
VOLKHONKA ULITSA
Moscow Swimming Pool
BOLSHOY KAMENNY MOST
GOGOLEVSKIY BOULEVARD
NIKITSKIY BLD.
TVERSKOY BOULEVARD
MAL. BRONNAYA ULITSA
GERSENA ULITSA
Moskva

Mumbai

0 km 5
0 miles 3

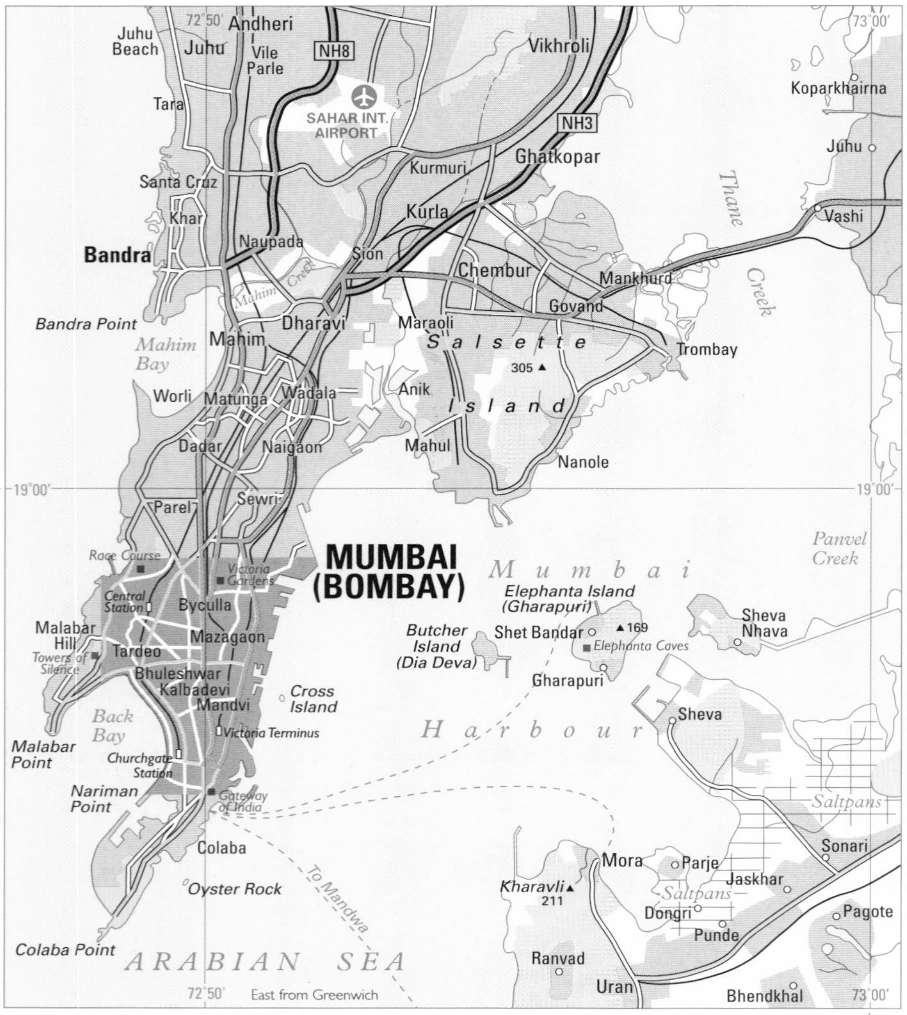

Central Mumbai

0 km 2
0 miles 1

Munich

0 km 5
0 miles 3

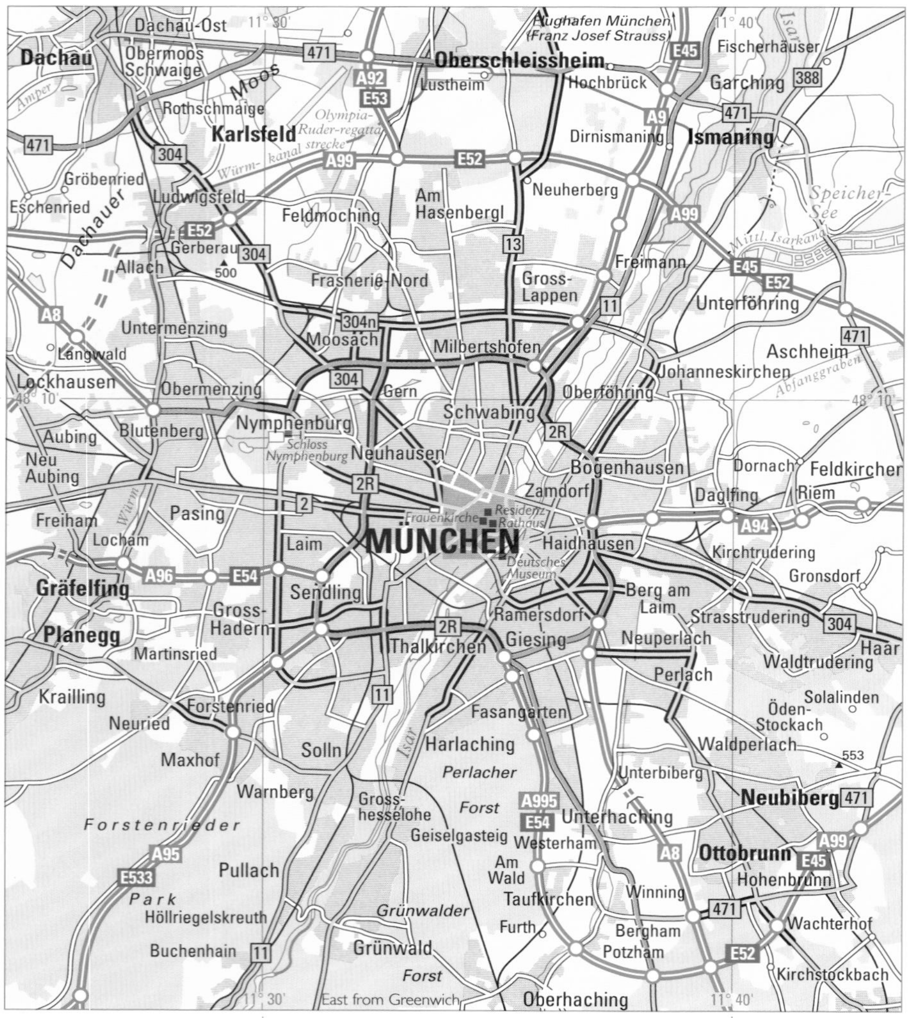

Central Munich

0 km 1
0 miles 0.5

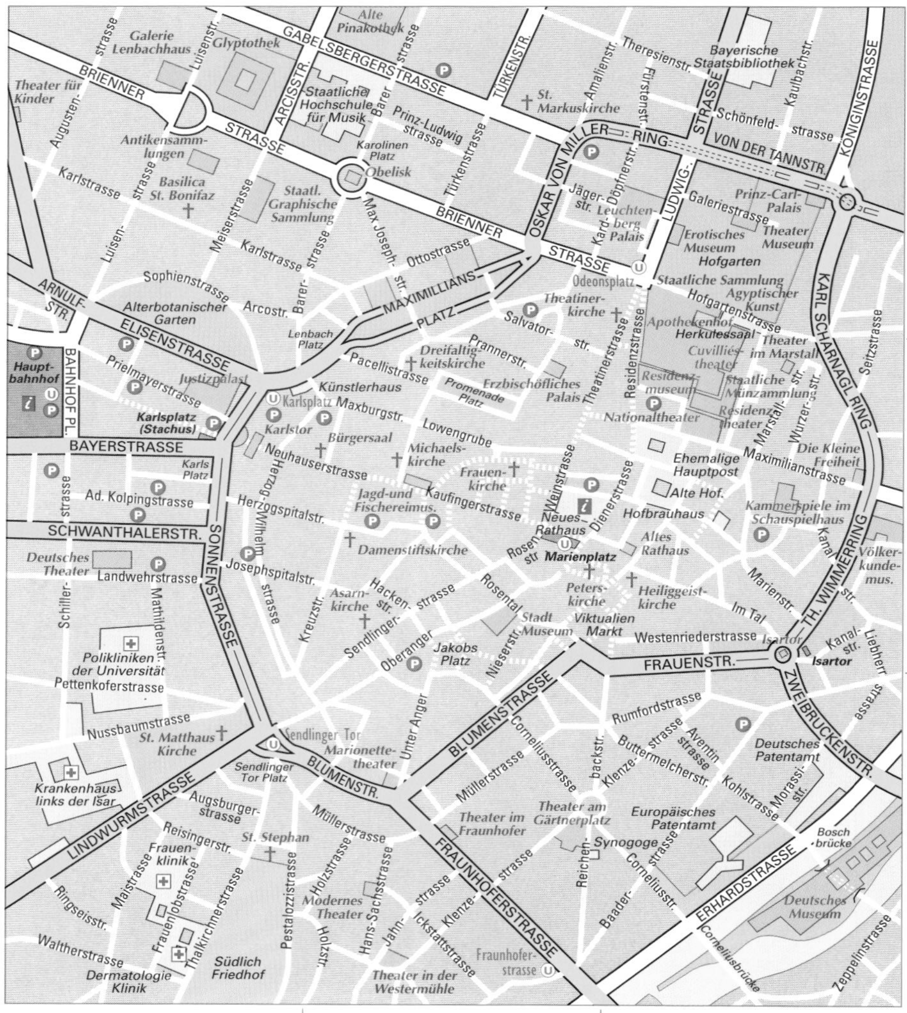

New York

0 km 5
0 miles 3

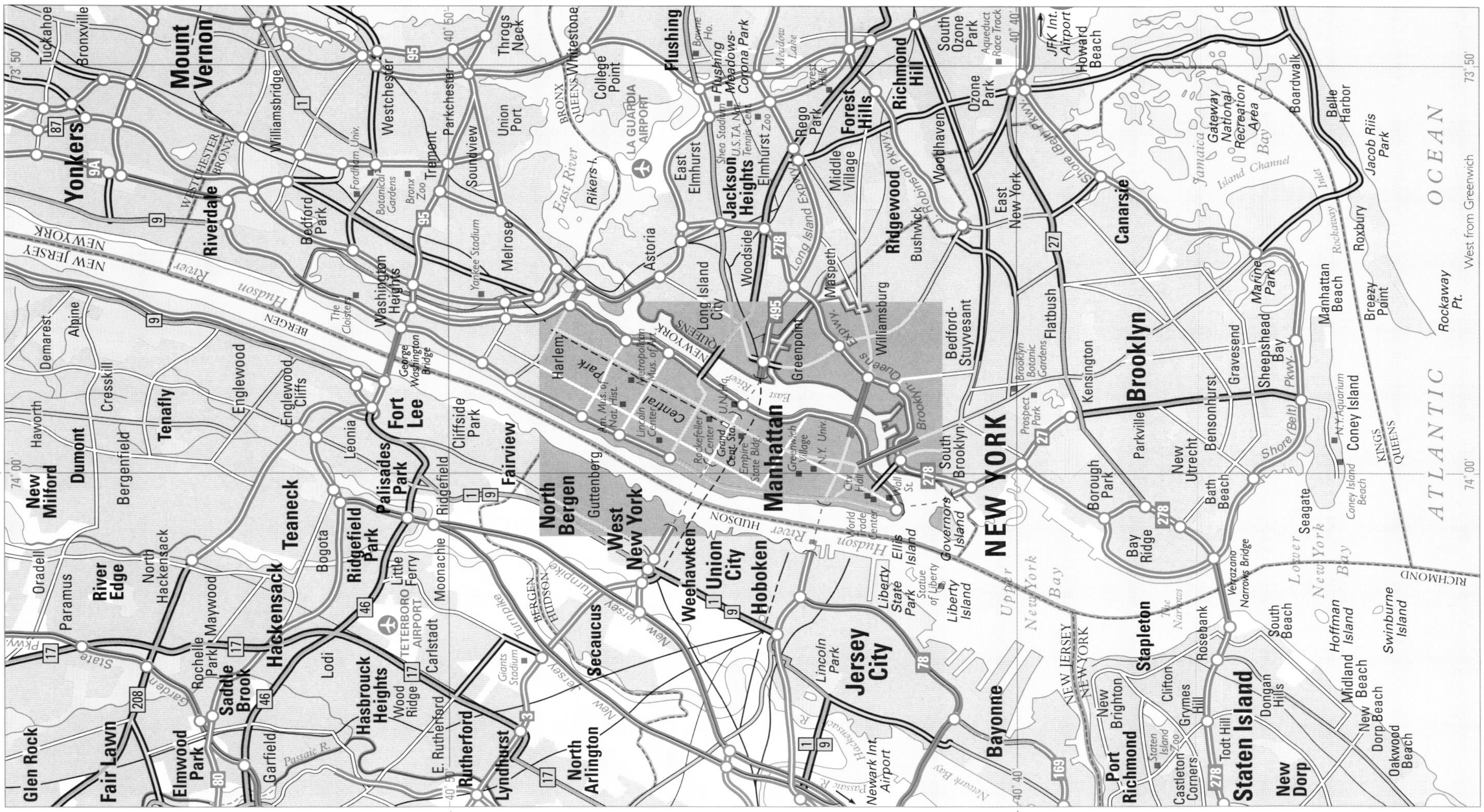

1 2 3
A B C

Central New York

0 km 2
0 miles 1

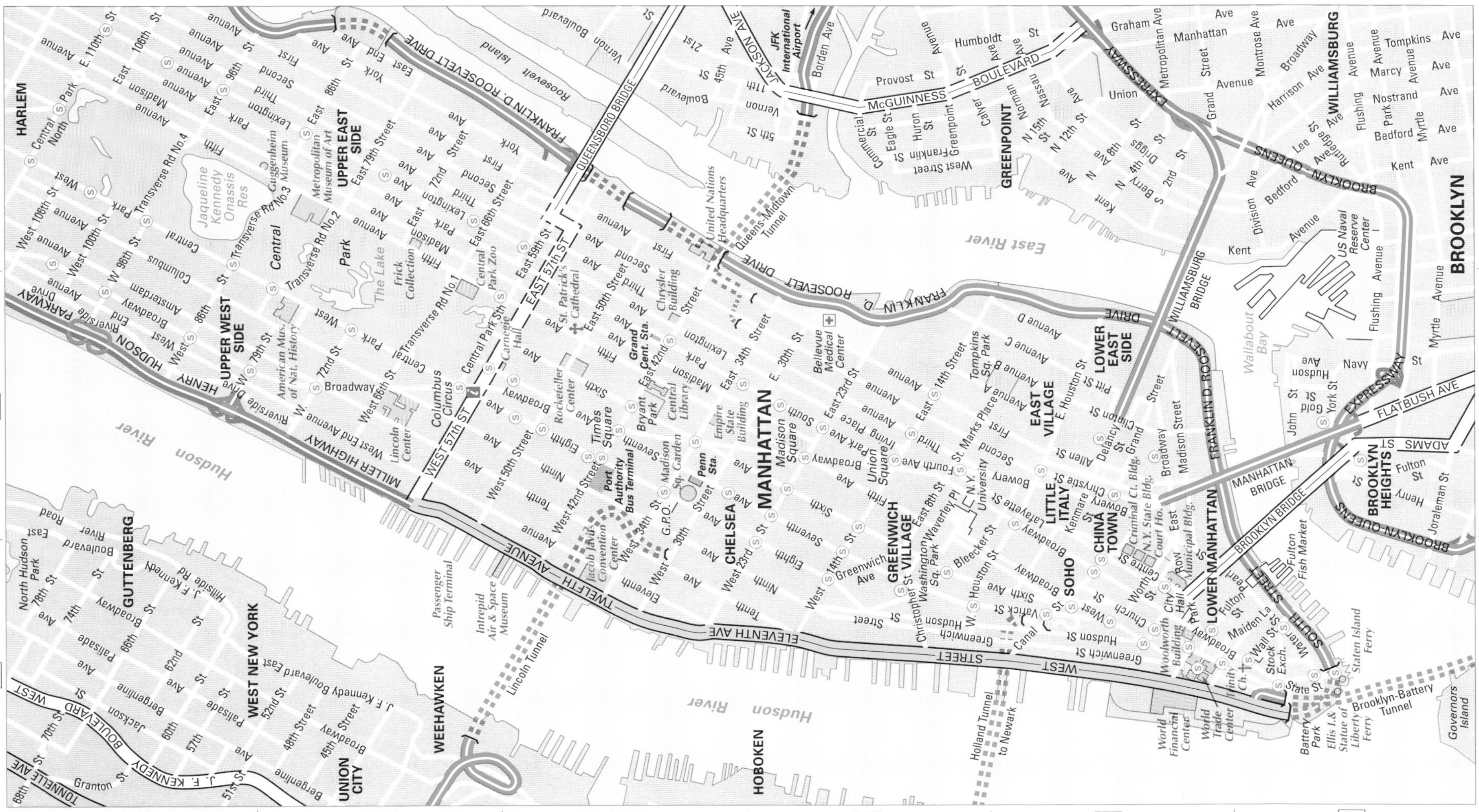

1 2 3
a b c d e f

Osaka

0 km 5
0 miles 3

Oslo

0 km 5
0 miles 3

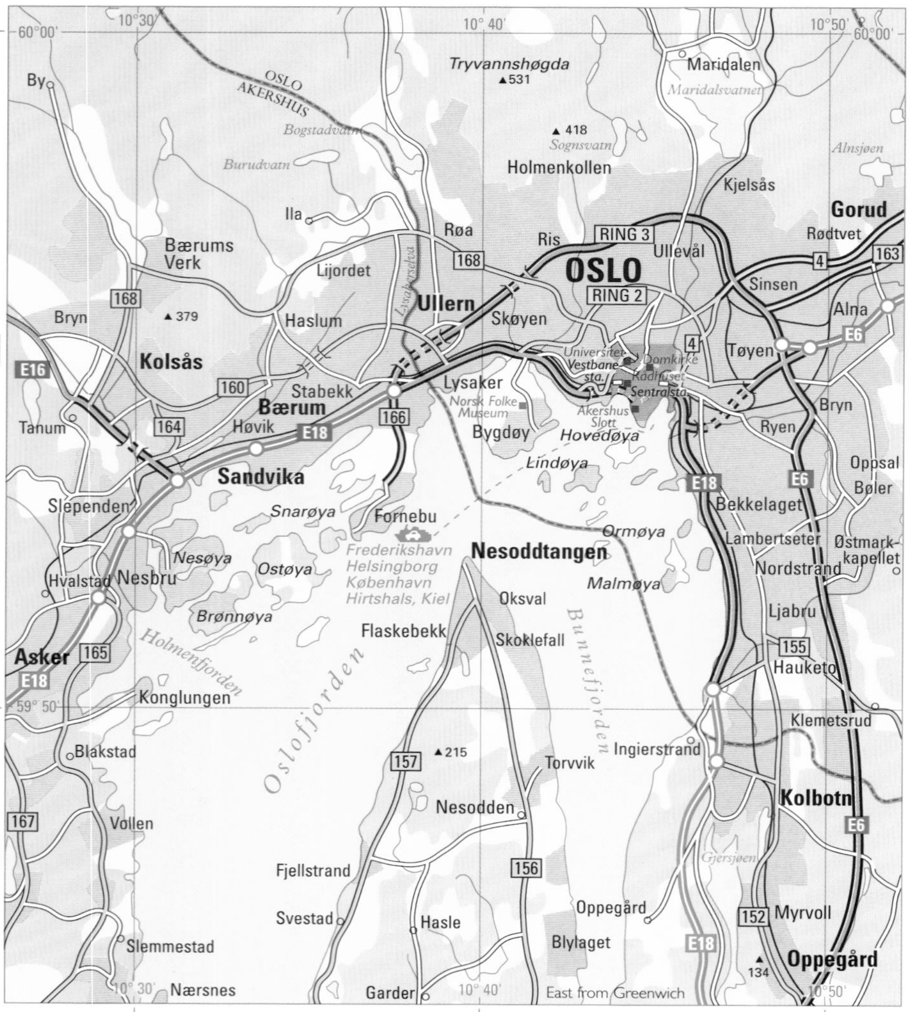

Central Oslo

0 km 0.5
0 miles 0.25

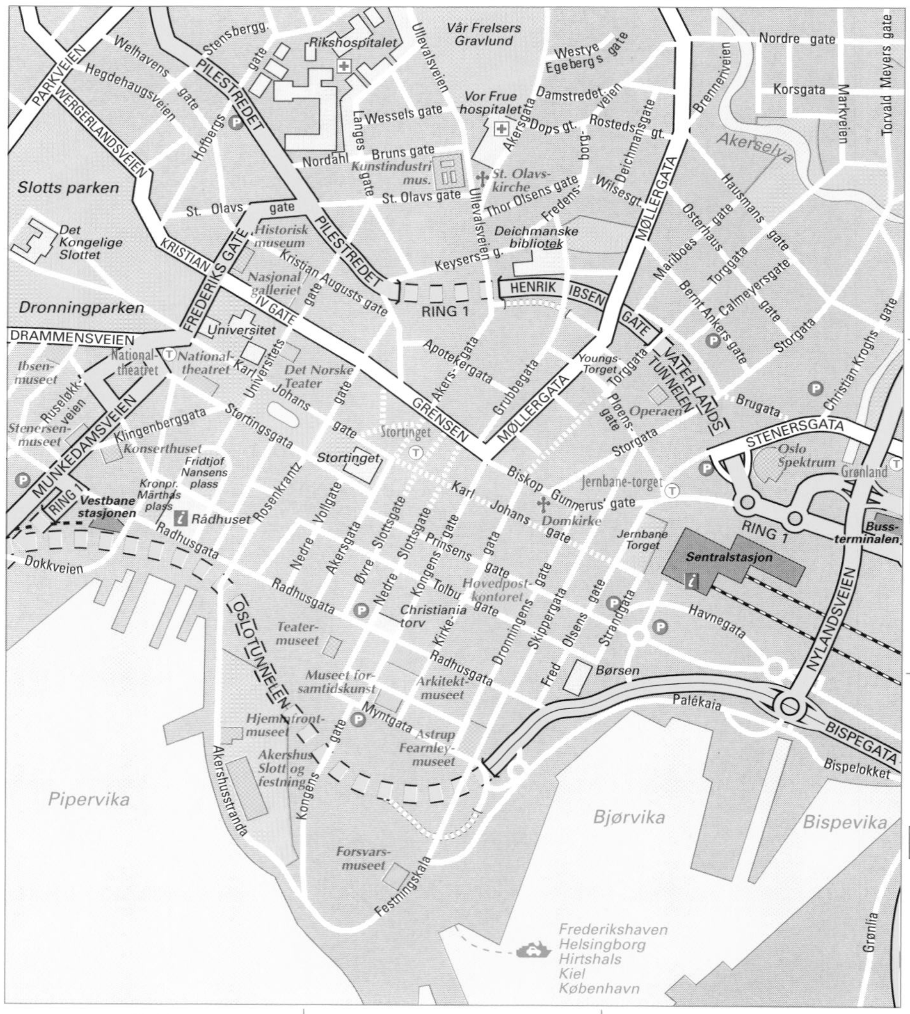

Paris

0 km 5
0 miles 3

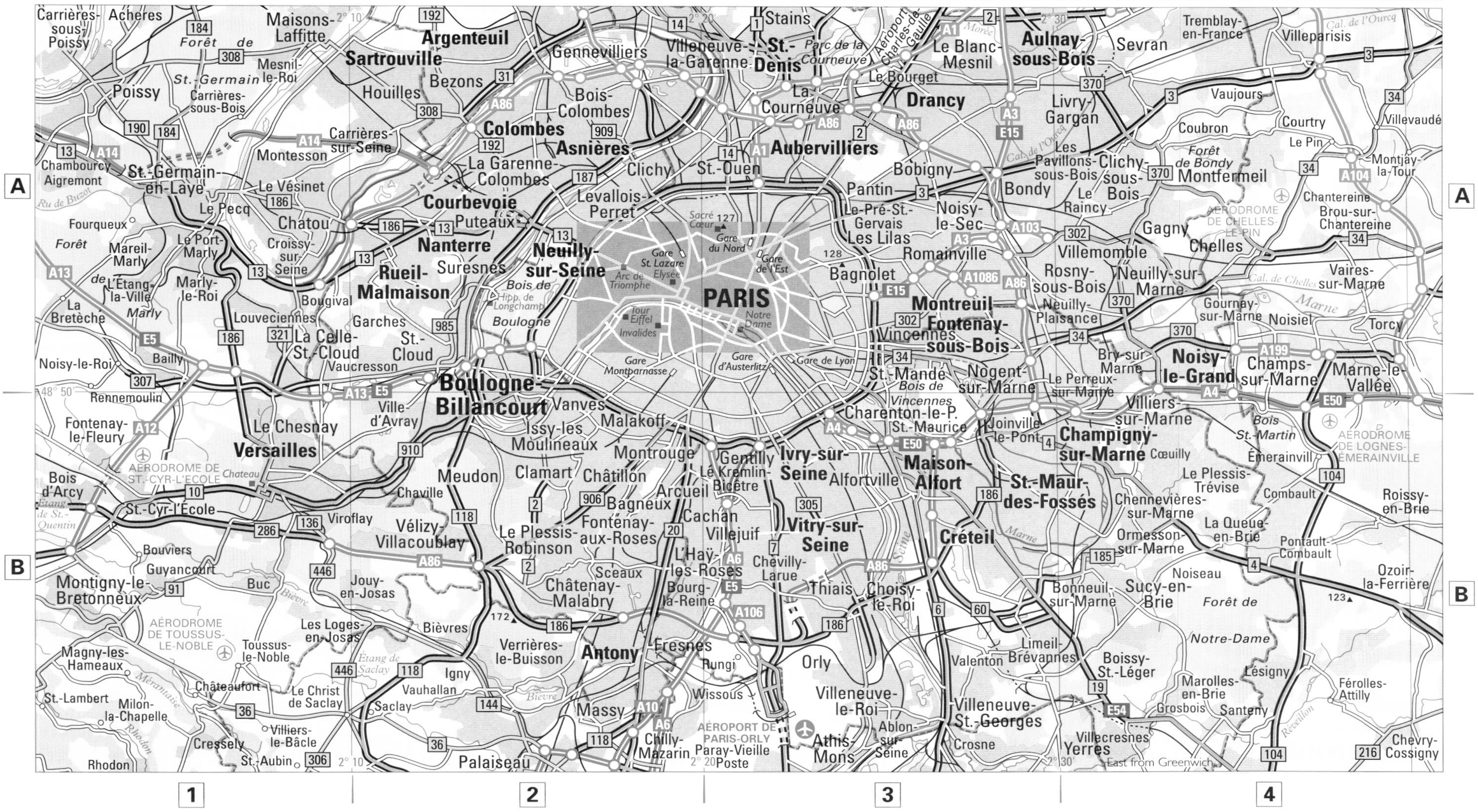

Central Paris

0 km 1
0 miles 0.5

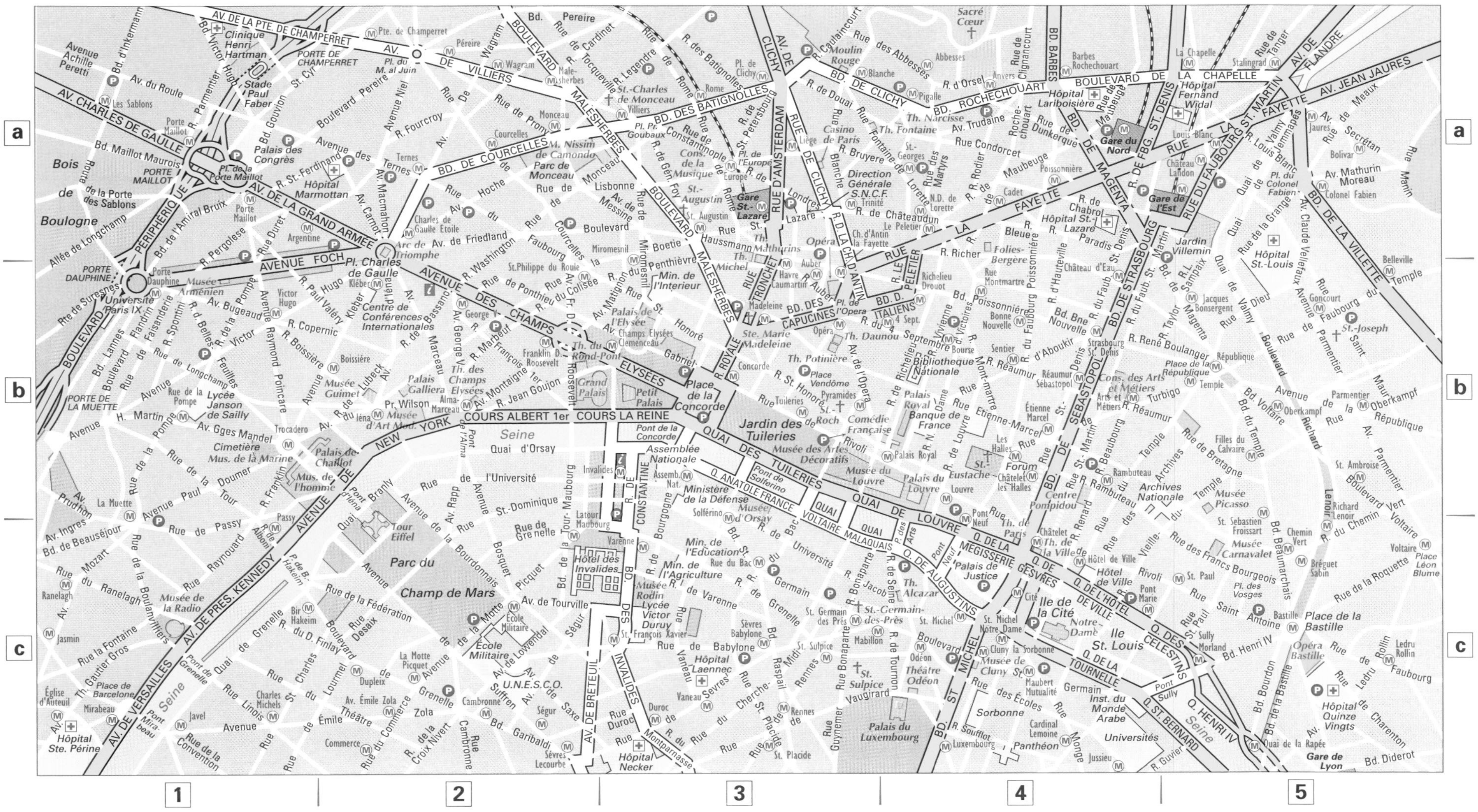

Prague

0 km 5
0 miles 3

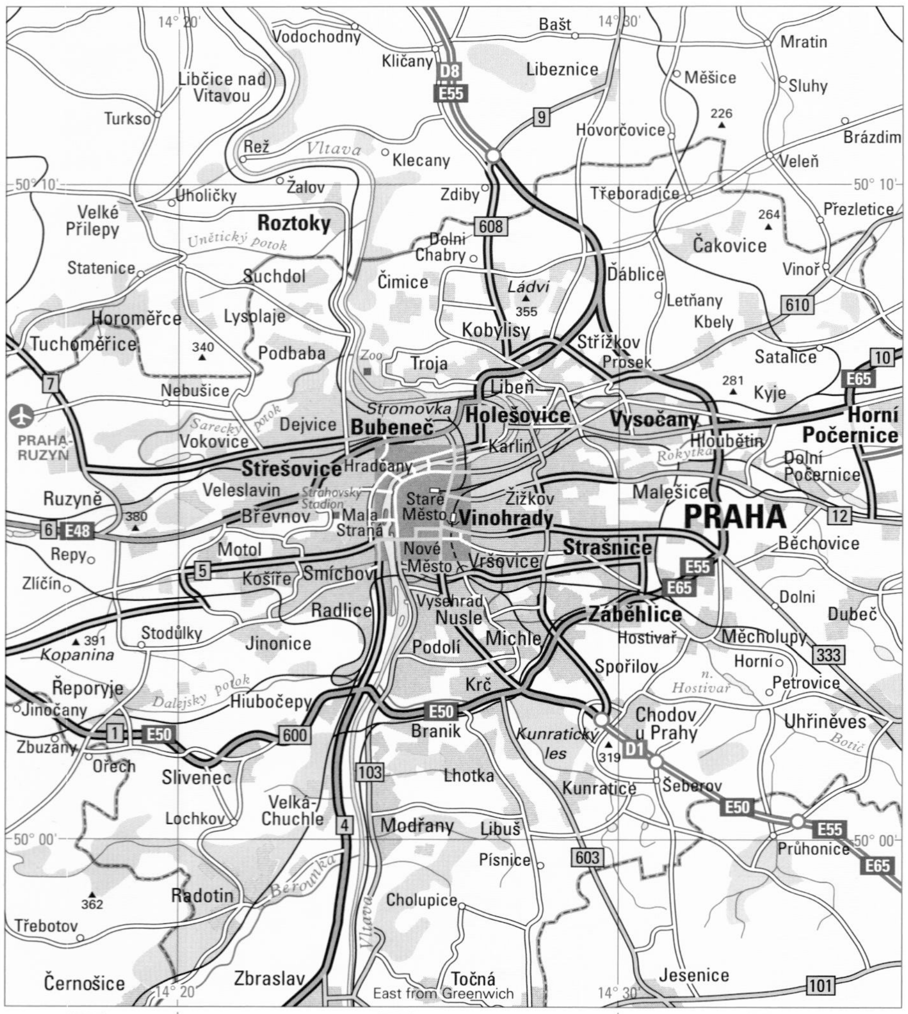

Central Prague

0 km 1
0 miles 0.5

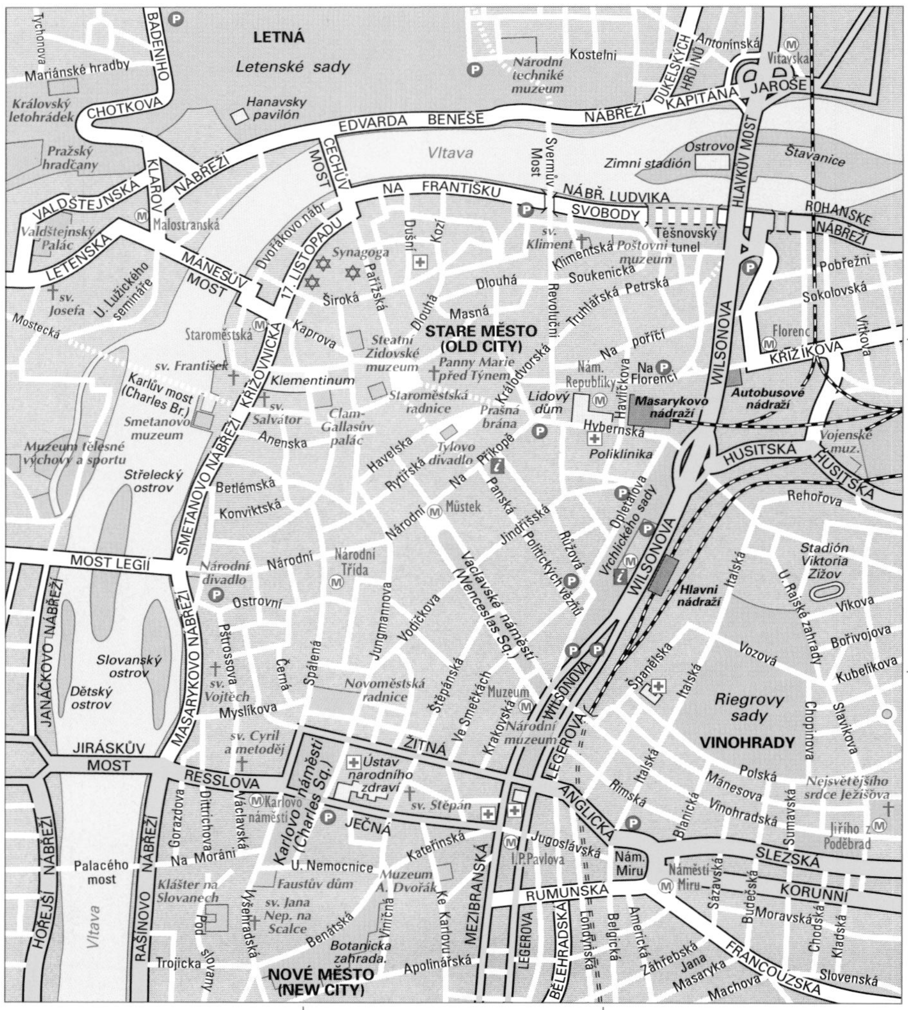

Rio de Janeiro

0 km 5
0 miles 3

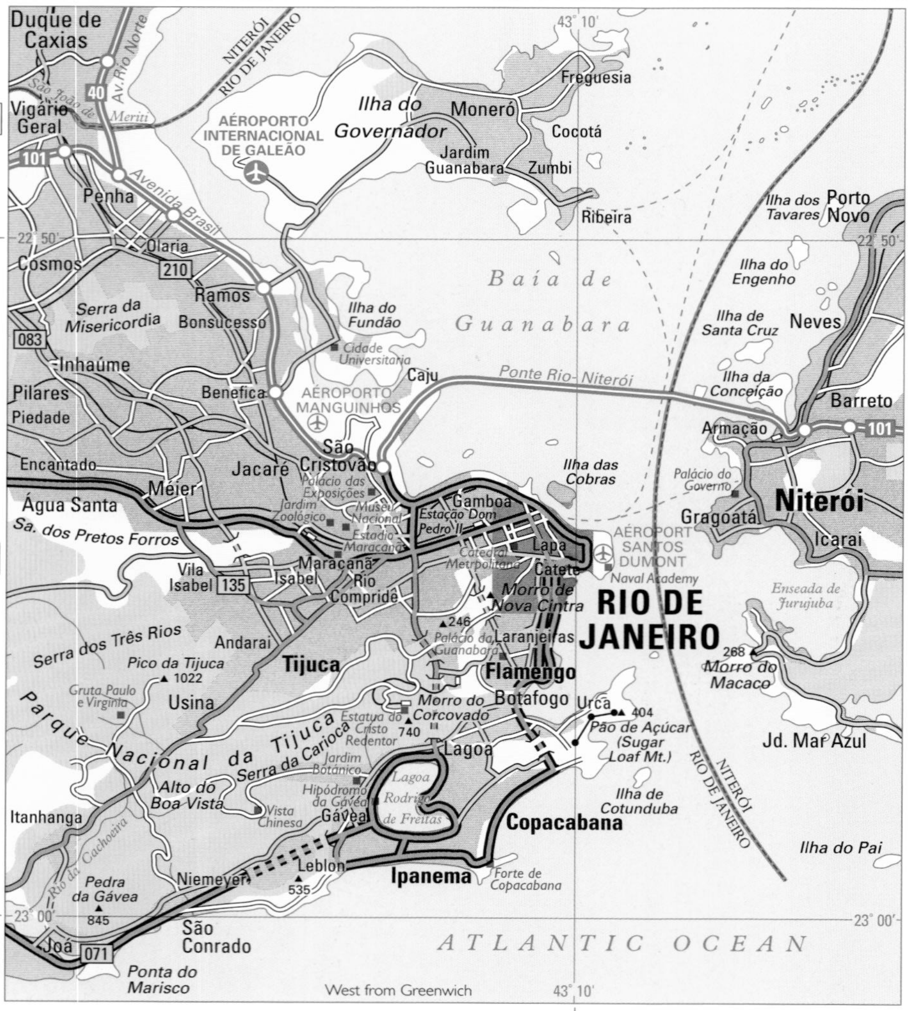

Central Rio de Janeiro

0 km 0.5
0 miles 0.25

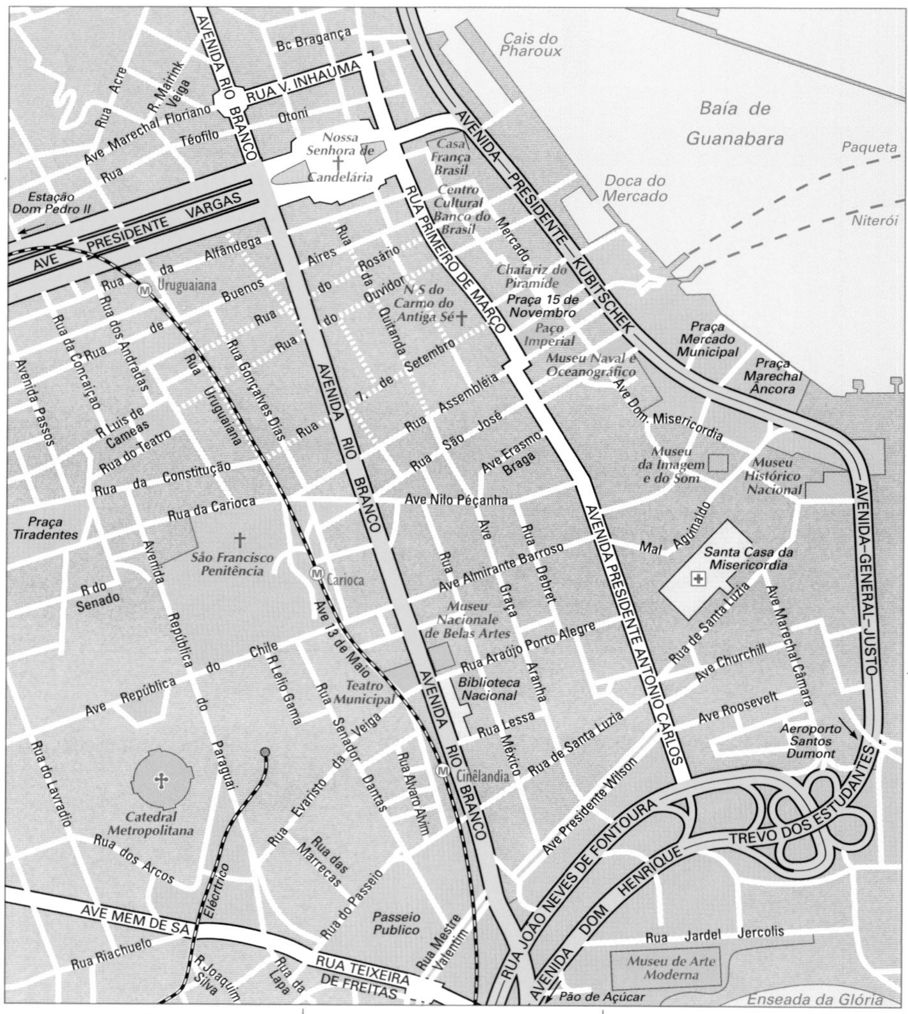

COPYRIGHT GEORGE PHILIP LTD

Rome

0 km 5
0 miles 3

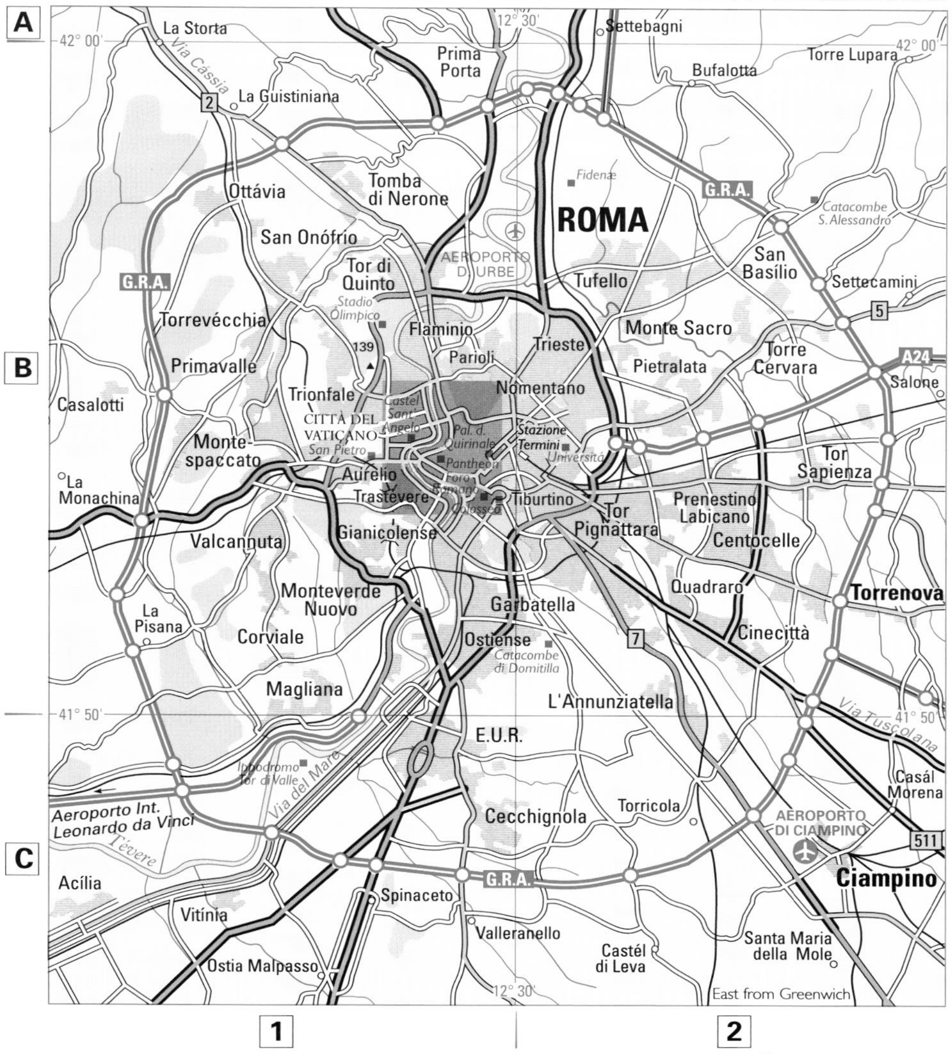
La Storta
Settebagni
Prima Porta
Bufalotta
Torre Lupara
La Giustiniana
Ottávia
Tomba di Nerone
ROMA
G.R.A.
San Onófrio
Tor di Quinto
AEROPORTO D'URBE
Tufello
San Basílio
Settecamini
Torrevécchia
Flaminio
Parioli
Trieste
Monte Sacro
Torre Cervara
Primavalle
Pietralata
Salone
Casalotti
Trionfale
Nomentano
CITTÀ DEL VATICANO
Monte-spaccato
Tor Sapienza
La Monachina
Aurélio
Trastevere
Tiburtino
Prenestino Labicano
Tor Pignattara
Valcannuta
Gianicolense
Centocelle
Quadraro
Torrenova
Monteverde Nuovo
La Pisana
Garbatella
Corviale
Ostiense
Cinecittà
Magliana
L'Annunziatella
E.U.R.
Via Tuscolana
Casál Morena
Aeroporto Int. Leonardo da Vinci
Cecchignola
Torricola
AEROPORTO DI CIAMPINO
Acília
Ciampino
Vitínia
Spinaceto
Valleranello
Castél di Leva
Santa Maria della Mole
Ostia Malpasso
East from Greenwich

Central Rome

0 km 1
0 miles 0.5

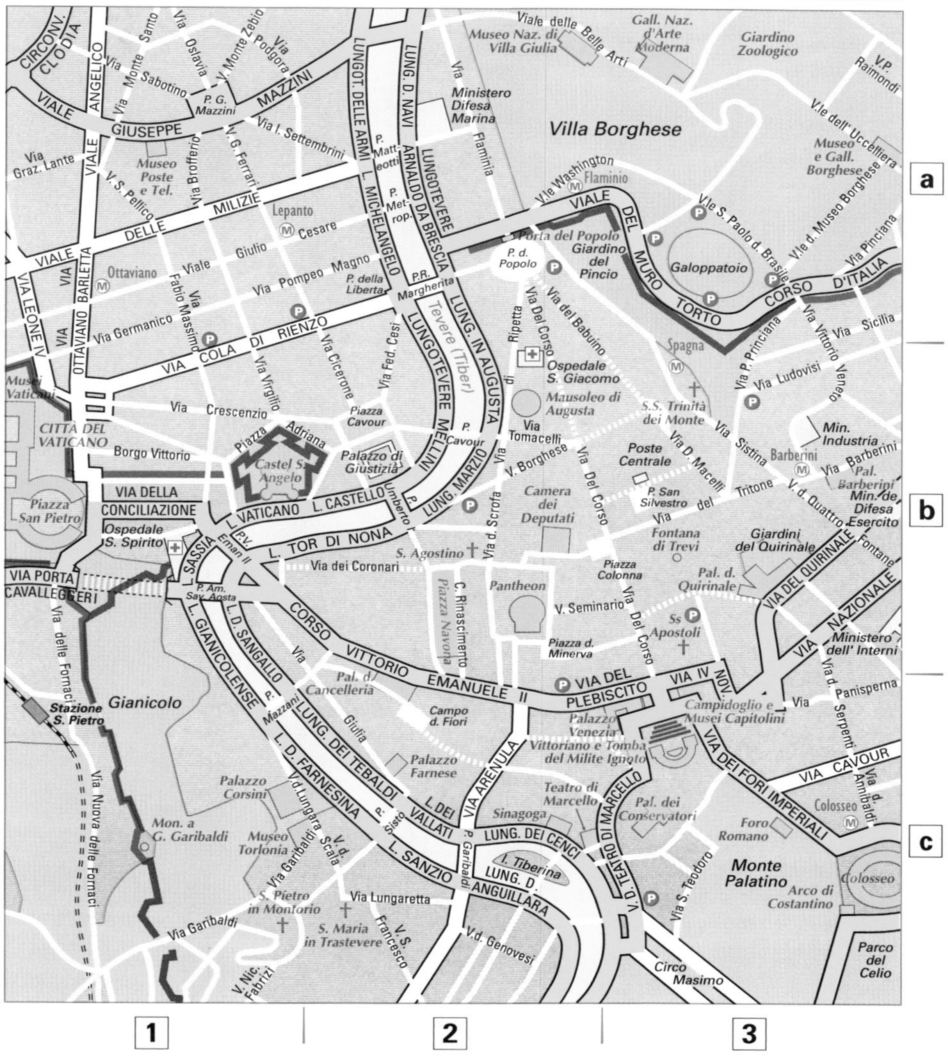
Villa Borghese
Museo Naz. di Villa Giulia
Gall. Naz. d'Arte Moderna
Giardino Zoologico
Ministero Difesa Marina
Museo e Gall. Borghese
Porta del Popolo
P. d. Popolo
Giardino del Pincio
Galoppatoio
CORSO D'ITALIA
VIALE GIUSEPPE MAZZINI
VIALE DELLE MILIZIE
Lepanto
Cesare
Ottaviano
VIA COLA DI RIENZO
Musei Vaticani
CITTÀ DEL VATICANO
Piazza San Pietro
VIA DELLA CONCILIAZIONE
Borgo Vittorio
Castel S. Angelo
Palazzo di Giustizia
Piazza Cavour
Ospedale S. Giacomo
Mausoleo di Augusta
Spagna
S.S. Trinità dei Monte
Barberini
Min. Industria
Poste Centrale
Camera dei Deputati
Fontana di Trevi
Giardini del Quirinale
Pal. d. Quirinale
Pantheon
Piazza Navona
Ospedale S. Spirito
Stazione S. Pietro
Gianicolo
CORSO VITTORIO EMANUELE II
Pal. d. Cancelleria
Campo d. Fiori
Palazzo Farnese
Palazzo Corsini
Palazzo Venezia
Vittoriano e Tomba del Milite Ignoto
Campidoglio e Musei Capitolini
VIA DEI FORI IMPERIALI
VIA CAVOUR
Colosseo
Teatro di Marcello
Pal. dei Conservatori
Foro Romano
Monte Palatino
Arco di Costantino
Mon. a G. Garibaldi
Museo Torlonia
Sinagoga
I. Tiberina
S. Pietro in Montorio
S. Maria in Trastevere
Circo Masimo
Parco del Celio

San Francisco

0 km 5
0 miles 3

Marin City
Tiburon
Belvedere
Angel Island
Angel Island State Park
Marin Pen.
Sausalito
Blunt Point
MARIN COUNTY
San Francisco Bay
Berkeley
Emeryville
Golden Gate Nat. Rec. Area
Alcatraz I.
Treasure Island
Golden Gate Bridge
Yerba Buena I.
Oakland
Presidio
Pacific Hts.
Lincoln Park
Point Lobos
Western Addition
South of Market
ALAMEDA NAVAL AIR STATION
Alameda
Richmond
Haight Ashbury
China Basin
Golden Gate Park
Sunset
Buena Vista
Twin Peaks
Potrero
Potrero Point
SAN FRANCISCO
Alameda Mem. State Beach Park
Forest Hill
Mission
Mt. Davidson
Bernal Heights
Bayview
Parkside
West of Twin Peaks
Hunters Point
PACIFIC OCEAN
Outer Mission
John McLaren Park
Visitacion Valley
SAN FRANCISCO COUNTY
SAN MATEO COUNTY
Daly City
Bayshore
Westlake
Sterling Park
Broadmoor
San Bruno Mountain
Brisbane
Colma
San Francisco Bay
South San Francisco
Edgemar
Serramonte
Point San Bruno
Pacifica
Pacific Manor
San Francisco Int. Airport
West from Greenwich

Central San Francisco

0 km 0.5
0 miles 0.25

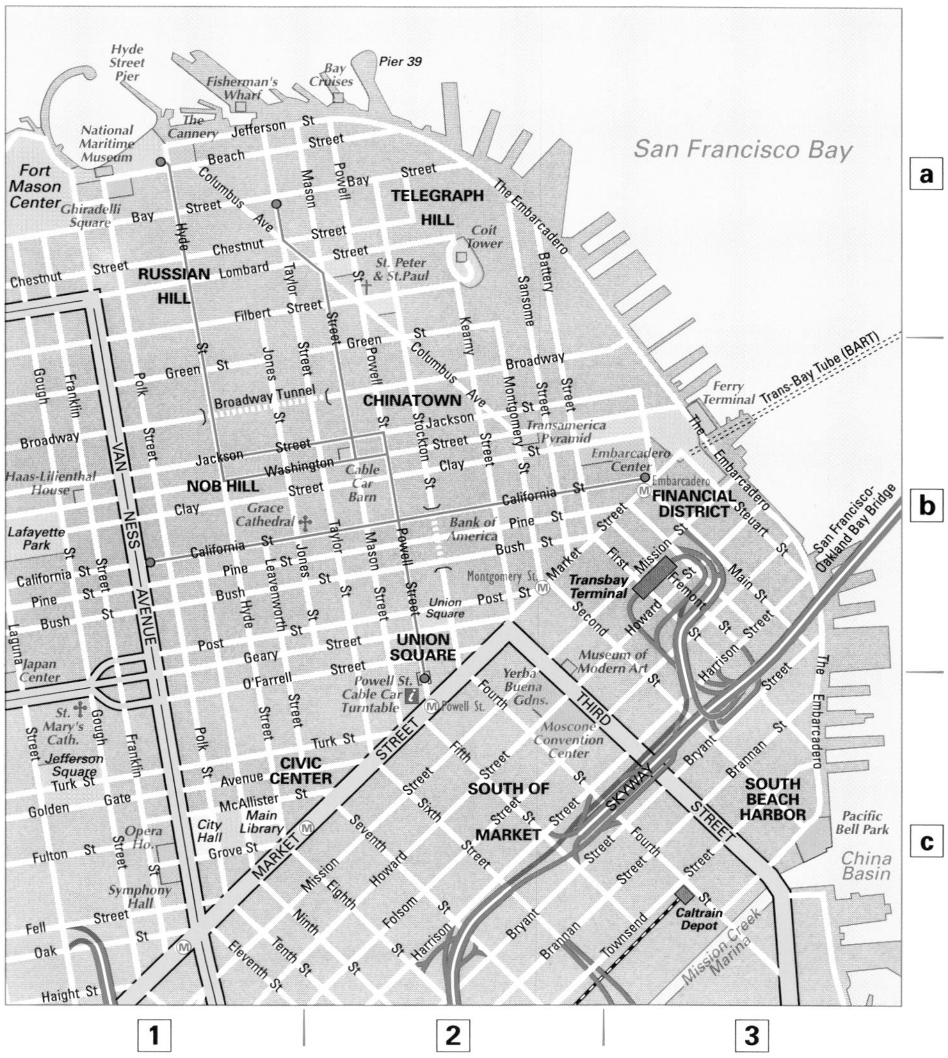
Hyde Street Pier
Fisherman's Wharf
Bay Cruises
Pier 39
National Maritime Museum
The Cannery
San Francisco Bay
Fort Mason Center
Ghiradelli Square
TELEGRAPH HILL
Coit Tower
RUSSIAN HILL
St. Peter & St.Paul
Ferry Terminal
Trans-Bay Tube (BART)
CHINATOWN
Transamerica Pyramid
Embarcadero Center
NOB HILL
Cable Car Barn
Grace Cathedral
Haas-Lilienthal House
FINANCIAL DISTRICT
Bank of America
Lafayette Park
Transbay Terminal
San Francisco-Oakland Bay Bridge
UNION SQUARE
Union Square
Japan Center
Powell St. Cable Car Turntable
Yerba Buena Gdns.
Museum of Modern Art
St. Mary's Cath.
Jefferson Square
Moscone Convention Center
CIVIC CENTER
SOUTH OF MARKET
SOUTH BEACH HARBOR
City Hall
Main Library
Opera Ho.
Symphony Hall
Pacific Bell Park
China Basin
Caltrain Depot
Mission Creek Marina

COPYRIGHT GEORGE PHILIP LTD

St. Petersburg

0 km 5
0 miles 3

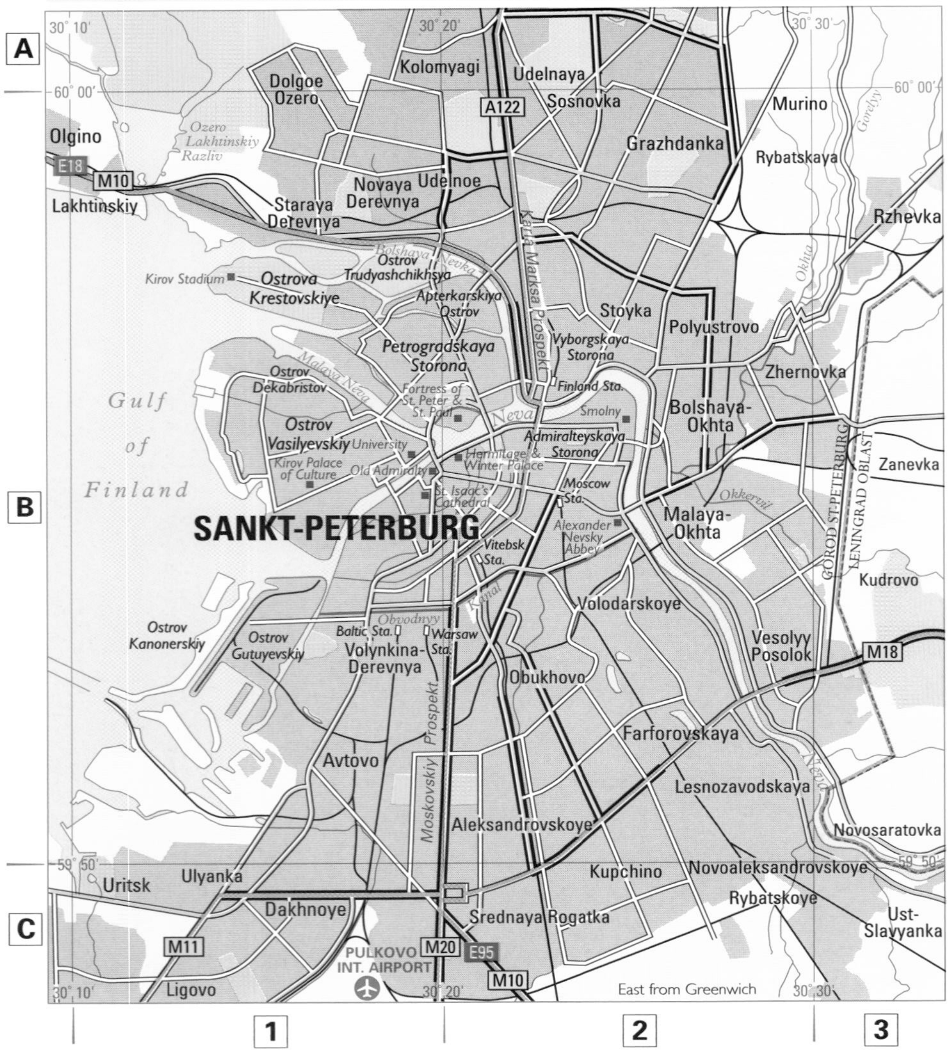

Santiago

0 km 5
0 miles 3

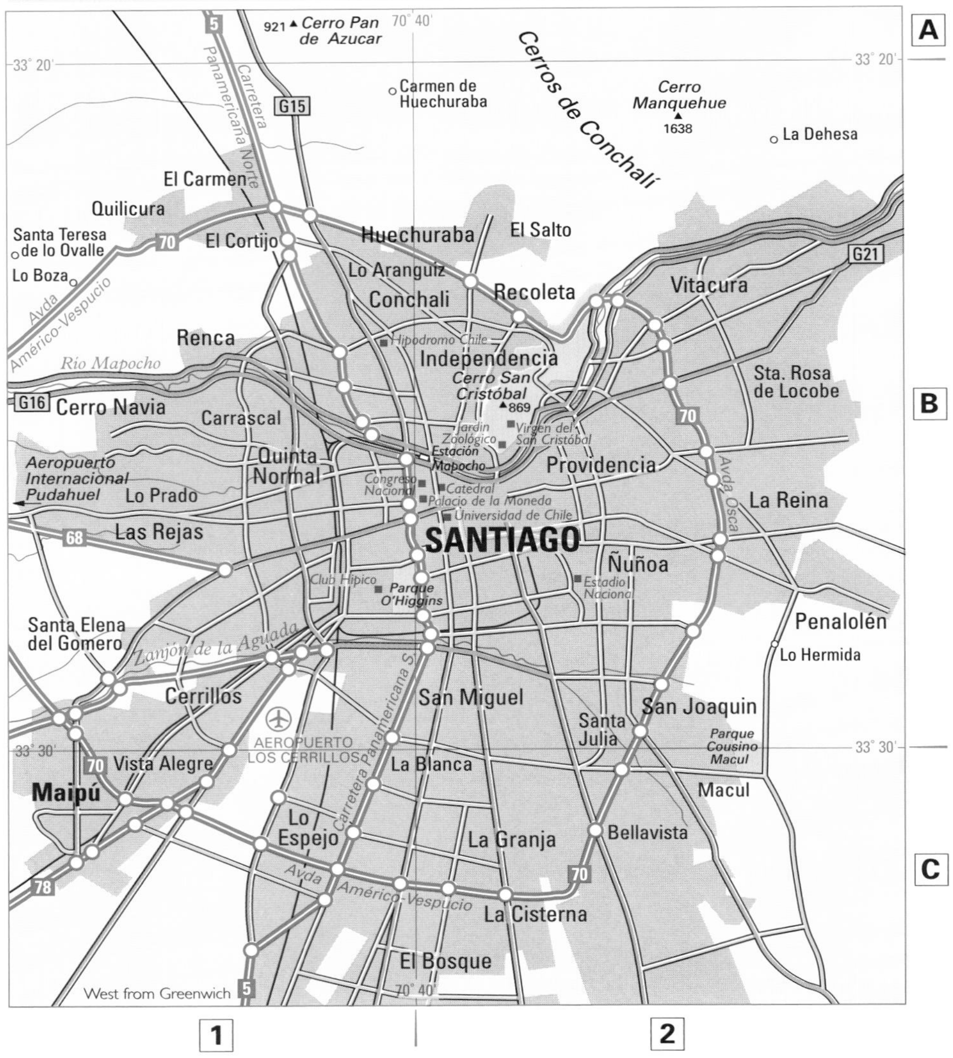

São Paulo

0 km 5
0 miles 3

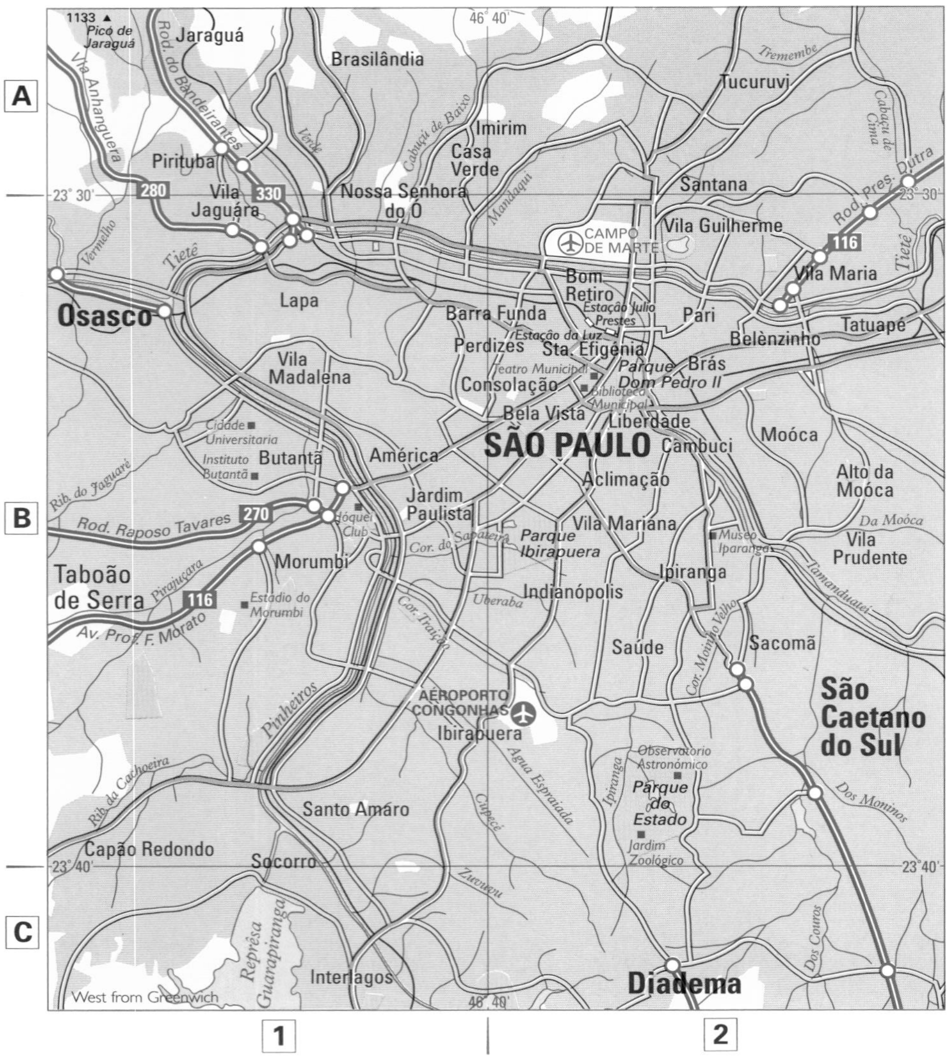

Seoul

0 km 5
0 miles 3

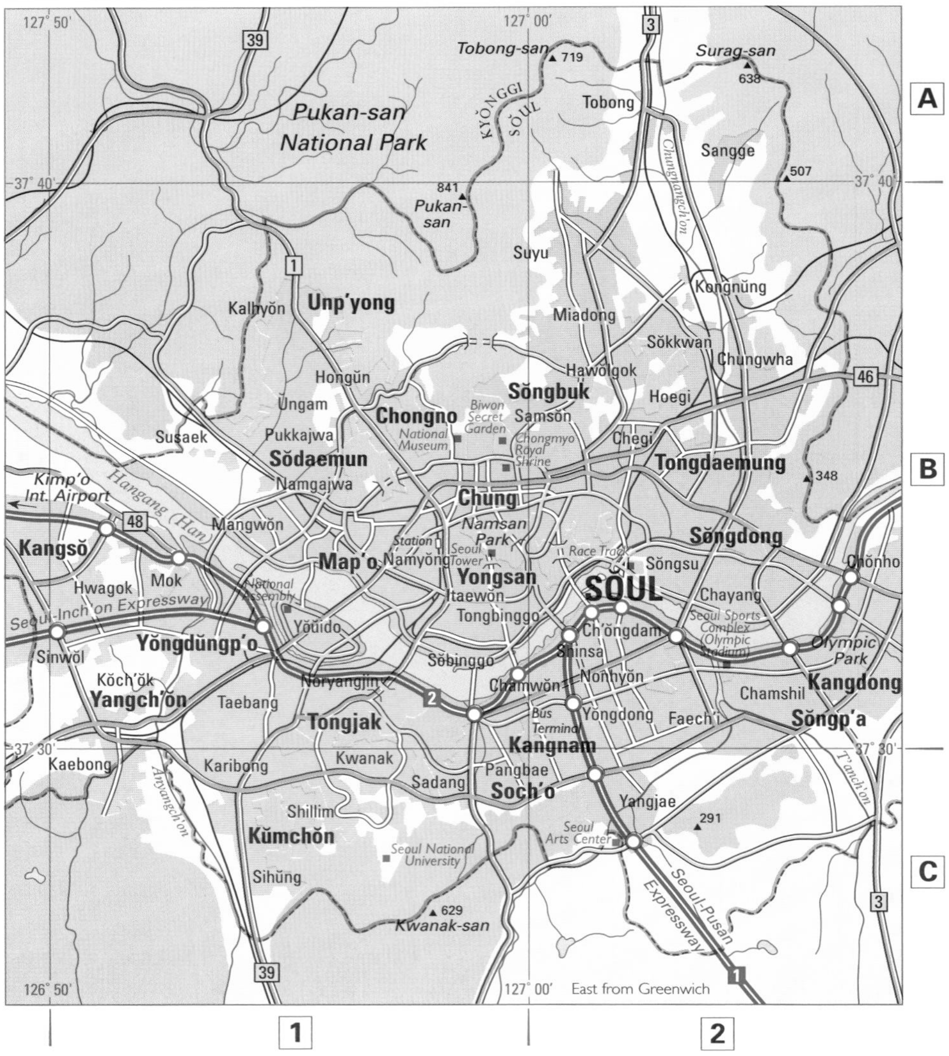

COPYRIGHT GEORGE PHILIP LTD

Shanghai

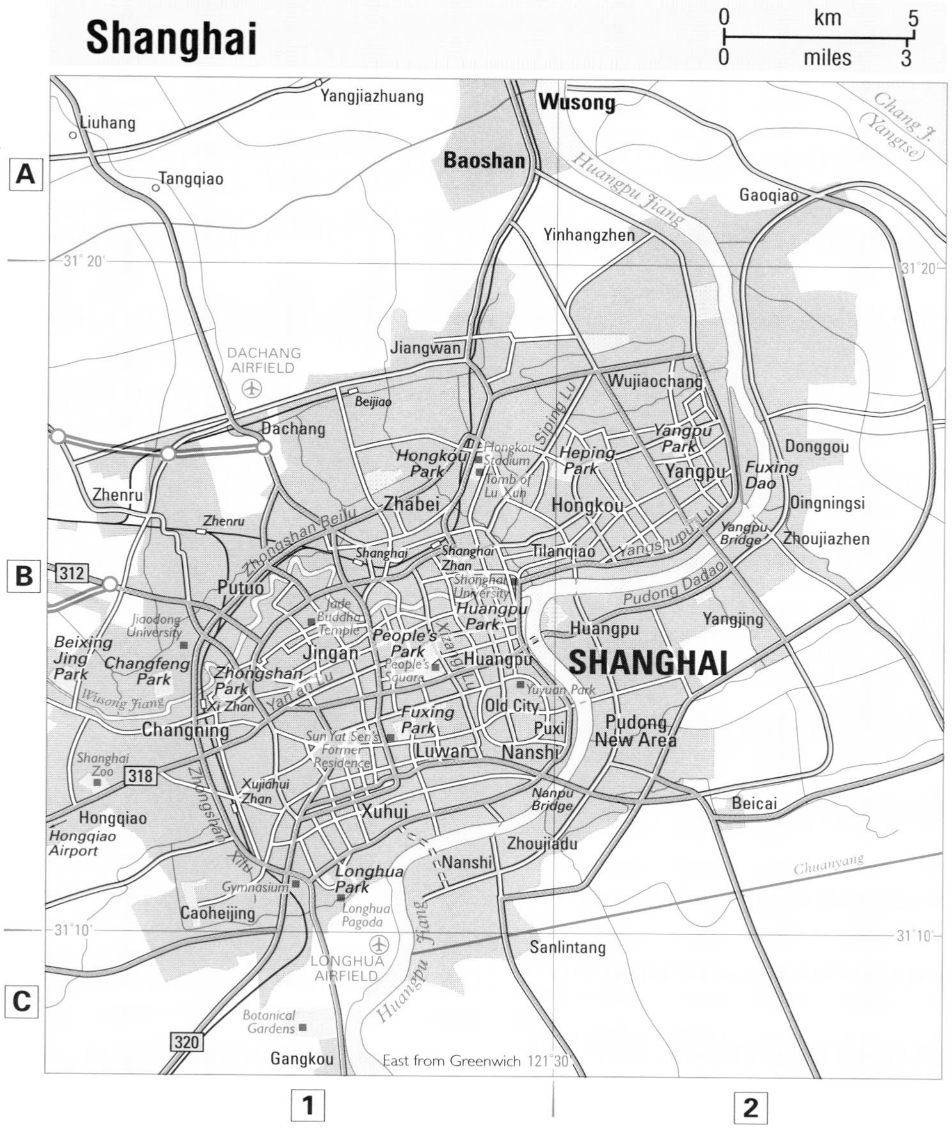
0 km 5
0 miles 3
A
B
C
1
2
Liuhang
Yangjiazhuang
Wusong
Chang Jiang (Yangtze)
Tangqiao
Baoshan
Huangpu Jiang
Gaoqiao
Yinhangzhen
31°20'
DACHANG AIRFIELD
Jiangwan
Wujiaochang
Beijiao
Dachang
Siping Lu
Yangpu Park
Donggou
Zhenru
Hongkou Park
Heping Park
Yangpu
Fuxing Dao
Zhenru
Zhabei
Hongkou
Oingningsi
Zhongshan Beilu
Yangshupu Lu
Yangpu Bridge
Zhoujiazhen
312
Shanghai
Shanghai Zhan
Tilanqiao
Putuo
Pudong Dadao
Jiaodong University
Jade Buddha Temple
Huangpu Park
Huangpu
Yangjing
Beixing Jing Park
Changfeng Park
Jingan
People's Park
Huangpu
SHANGHAI
Zhongshan Park
Yuyuan Park
Wusong Jiang
Yan'an Lu
Fuxing Park
Old City
Puxi
Changning
Pudong New Area
Shanghai Zoo
318
Sun Yat Sen's Former Residence
Luwan
Nanshi
Xujiahui Zhan
Xuhui
Beicai
Hongqiao
Hongqiao Airport
Nanpu Bridge
Longhua Park
Nanshi
Zhoujiadu
Chuanyang
Gymnasium
Caoheijing
Longhua Pagoda
31°10'
LONGHUA AIRFIELD
Sanlintang
Huangpu Jiang
Botanical Gardens
320
Gangkou
East from Greenwich 121°30'

Central Singapore

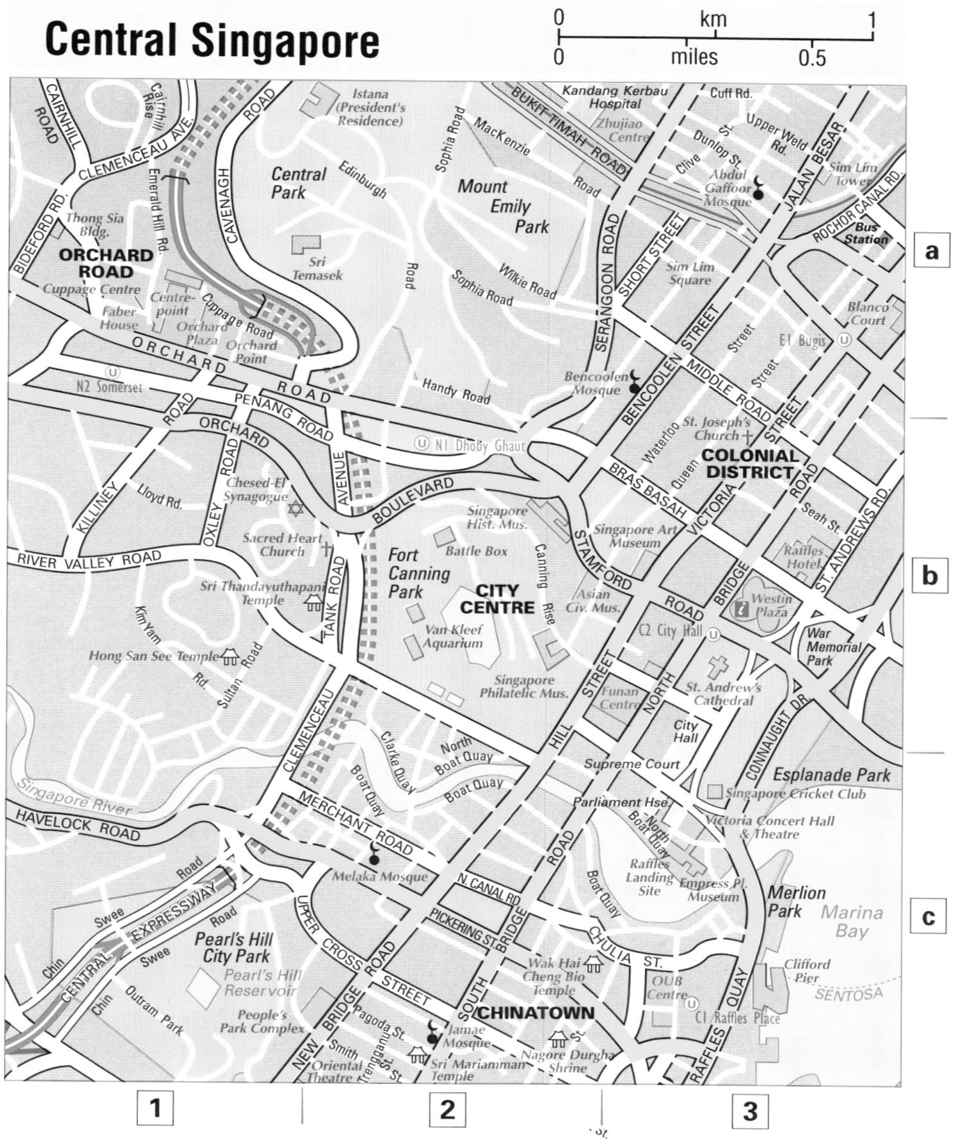
0 km 1
0 miles 0.5
a
b
c
1
2
3
CAIRNHILL ROAD
Cairnhill Rise
CLEMENCEAU AVE.
CAVENAGH ROAD
Istana (President's Residence)
BUKIT TIMAH ROAD
Kandang Kerbau Hospital
Cuff Rd.
Central Park
Edinburgh
Sophia Road
MacKenzie
Zhujiao Centre
Dunlop St.
Upper Weld Rd.
JALAN BESAR
Sim Lim Tower
Mount Emily Park
Abdul Gaffoor Mosque
ROCHOR CANAL RD.
Bus Station
BIDEFORD RD.
Thong Sia Bldg.
Emerald Hill Rd.
ORCHARD ROAD
Sri Temasek
Wilkie Road
Sophia Road
Sim Lim Square
Cuppage Centre
Faber House
Centre-point
Orchard Plaza
Cuppage Road
Orchard Point
SERANGOON ROAD
SHORT STREET
Blanco Court
ORCHARD ROAD
Handy Road
Bencoolen Mosque
BENCOOLEN STREET
MIDDLE ROAD
Bugis
N2 Somerset
PENANG ROAD
ORCHARD ROAD
N1 Dhoby Ghaut
St. Joseph's Church
COLONIAL DISTRICT
Waterloo
Queen
Chesed-El Synagogue
AVENUE
BOULEVARD
BRAS BASAH
VICTORIA
Seah St.
Lloyd Rd.
KILLINEY ROAD
OXLEY ROAD
Singapore Hist. Mus.
Singapore Art Museum
Raffles Hotel
RIVER VALLEY ROAD
Sacred Heart Church
Fort Canning Park
Battle Box
CITY CENTRE
STAMFORD
ROAD
BRIDGE
Westin Plaza
Sri Thandayuthapani Temple
Canning Rise
Asian Civ. Mus.
City Hall
War Memorial Park
Kim Yam Rd.
TANK ROAD
Van Kleef Aquarium
Hong San See Temple
Sultan Road
Singapore Philatelic Mus.
Funan Centre
St. Andrew's Cathedral
CONNAUGHT DR.
City Hall
HILL STREET
NORTH
Supreme Court
CLEMENCEAU
Clarke Quay
North Boat Quay
Esplanade Park
Singapore River
Boat Quay
Boat Quay
Parliament Hse.
Singapore Cricket Club
HAVELOCK ROAD
MERCHANT ROAD
North Boat Quay
Victoria Concert Hall & Theatre
Road
Melaka Mosque
N CANAL RD
Raffles Landing Site
Empress Pl. Museum
Merlion Park
Marina Bay
CENTRAL EXPRESSWAY
Swee
Road
PICKERING ST
SOUTH BRIDGE
Boat Quay
CHULIA ST.
Chin
Pearl's Hill City Park
Pearl's Hill Reservoir
UPPER CROSS ROAD
STREET
Wak Hai Cheng Bio Temple
OUB Centre
Clifford Pier
SENTOSA
Swee
Chin
Outram Park
People's Park Complex
CHINATOWN
C1 Raffles Place
NEW BRIDGE
Smith
Pagoda St.
Jamae Mosque
Oriental Theatre
Sri Mariamman Temple
Nagore Durgha Shrine
RAFFLES QUAY

Singapore

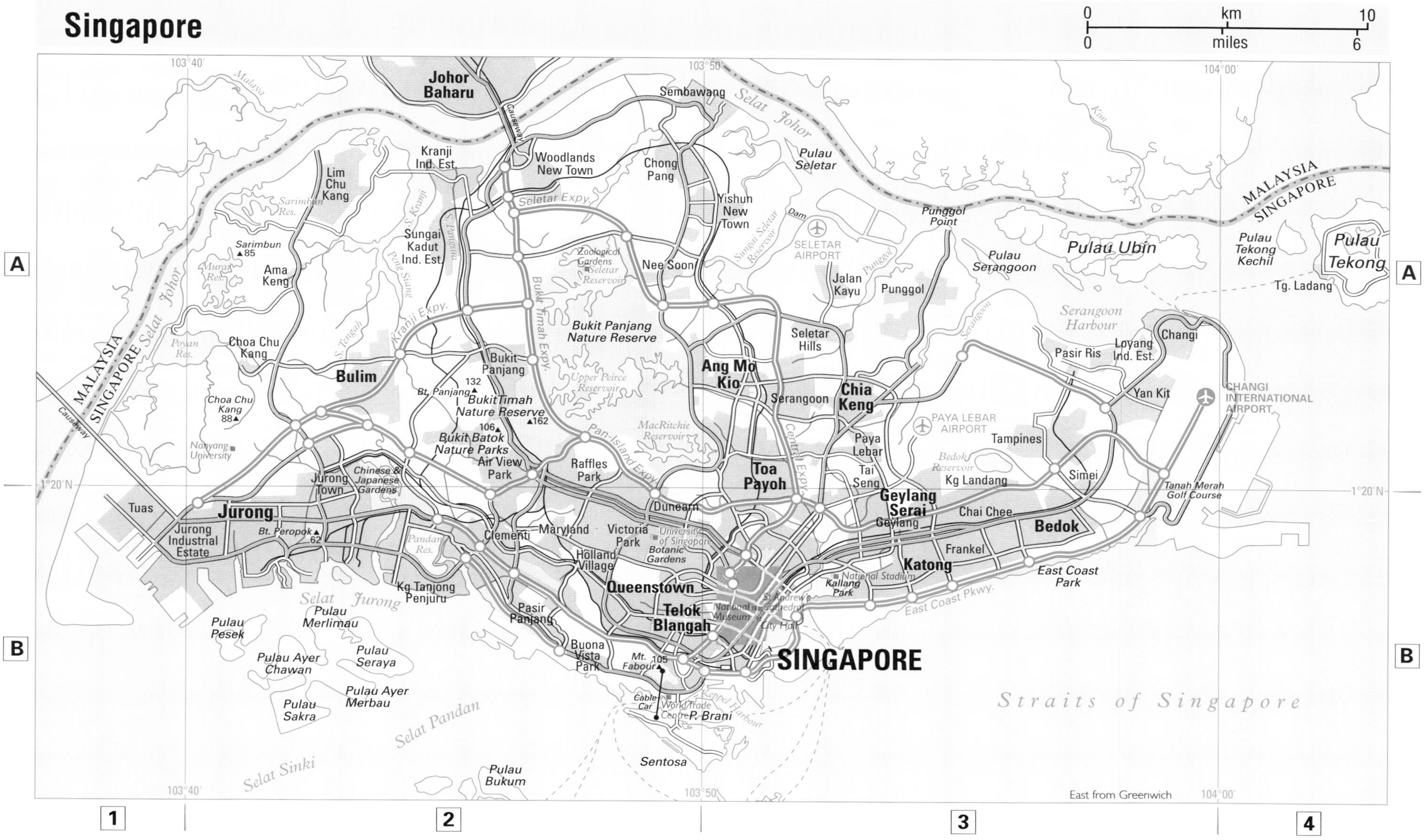
0 km 10
0 miles 6
A
B
1
2
3
4
103°40'
103°50'
104°00'
Malaysia
Johor Baharu
Causeway
Sembawang
Selat Johor
Kranji Ind. Est.
Woodlands New Town
Chong Pang
Pulau Seletar
Lim Chu Kang
Seletar Expy.
Yishun New Town
MALAYSIA
SINGAPORE
Sarimbun Res.
Sungai Kadut Ind. Est.
SELETAR AIRPORT
Punggol Point
Pulau Tekong Kechil
Pulau Tekong
Sarimbun 85
Zoological Gardens
Seletar Reservoir
Nee Soon
Pulau Serangoon
Pulau Ubin
Ama Keng
Murai Res.
Jalan Kayu
Punggol
Tg. Ladang
Kranji Expy.
Bukit Timah Expy.
Bukit Panjang Nature Reserve
Seletar Hills
Serangoon Harbour
Changi
MALAYSIA
SINGAPORE
Selat Johor
Choa Chu Kang
Poyan Res.
Bukit Panjang
Ang Mo Kio
Pasir Ris
Loyang Ind. Est.
Bulim
Upper Peirce Reservoir
Chia Keng
Yan Kit
CHANGI INTERNATIONAL AIRPORT
Choa Chu Kang 88
Bt. Panjang 132
Bukit Timah Nature Reserve 162
Serangoon
PAYA LEBAR AIRPORT
Causeway
Bukit Batok Nature Parks 106
MacRitchie Reservoir
Tampines
Nanyang University
Air View Park
Pan-Island Expy.
Paya Lebar
Raffles Park
Toa Payoh
Tai Seng
Bedok Reservoir
Kg Landang
Simei
1°20'N
Central Expy.
Jurong Town
Chinese & Japanese Gardens
Tanah Merah Golf Course
Tuas
Jurong
Dunearn
Geylang Serai
Chai Chee
Jurong Industrial Estate
Bt. Peropok 62
Clementi
Maryland
Victoria Park
University of Singapore
Geylang
Bedok
Pandan Res.
Botanic Gardens
Katong
Frankel
Holland Village
East Coast Park
National Stadium
Kg Tanjong Penjuru
Queenstown
Kallang Park
Selat Jurong
East Coast Pkwy.
Pulau Merlimau
Telok Blangah
St. Andrew's Cathedral
National Museum
City Hall
Pulau Pesek
Pasir Panjang
Pulau Ayer Chawan
Pulau Seraya
Buona Vista Park
Mt. Faber 105
SINGAPORE
Pulau Ayer Merbau
Straits of Singapore
Pulau Sakra
Selat Pandan
Cable Car
World Trade Centre
P. Brani
Keppel Harbour
Sentosa
Selat Sinki
Pulau Bukum
East from Greenwich

COPYRIGHT GEORGE PHILIP LTD

Stockholm

0 km 5
0 miles 3

Central Stockholm

0 km 1
0 miles 0.5

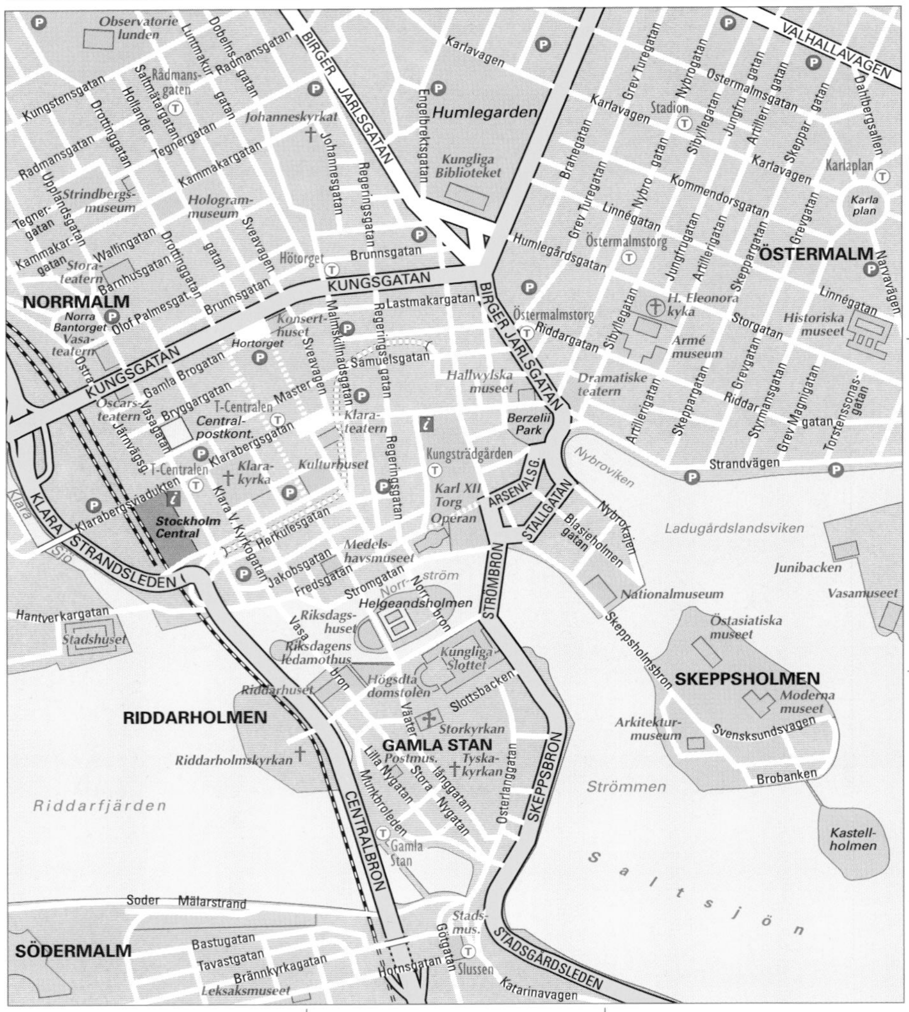

Sydney

0 km 5
0 miles 3

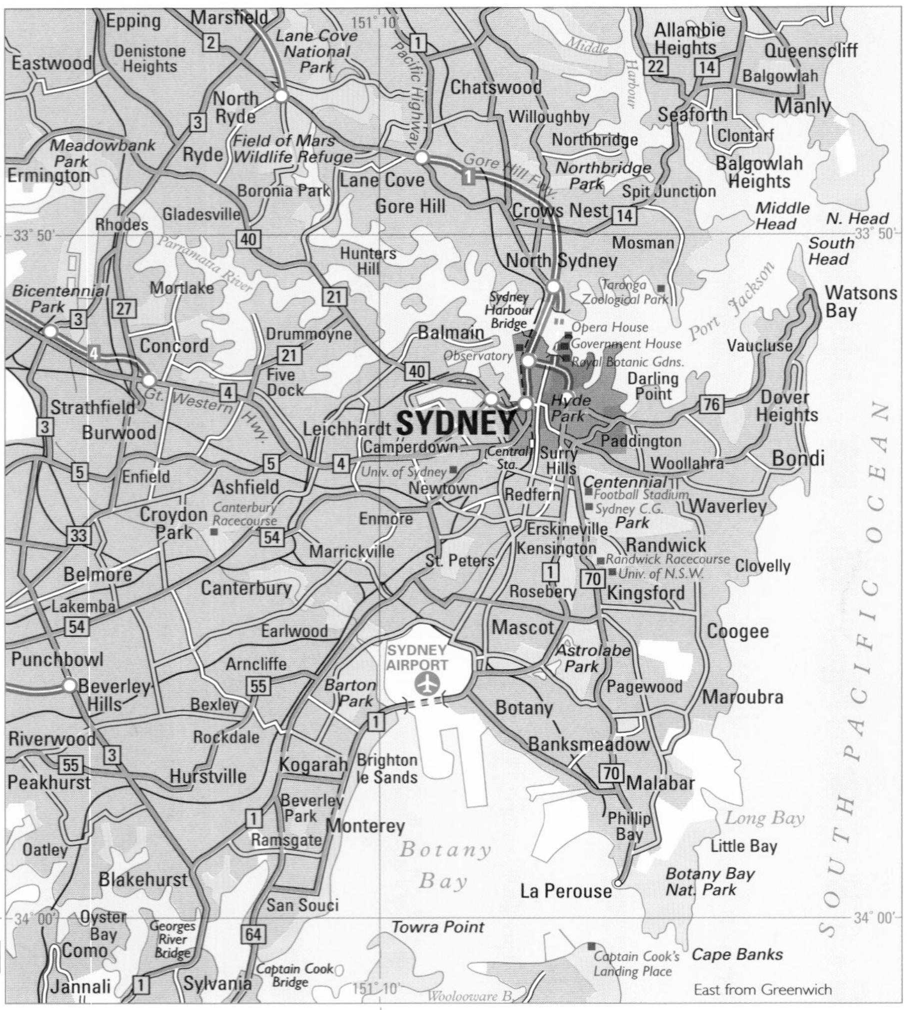

Central Sydney

0 km 2
0 miles 1

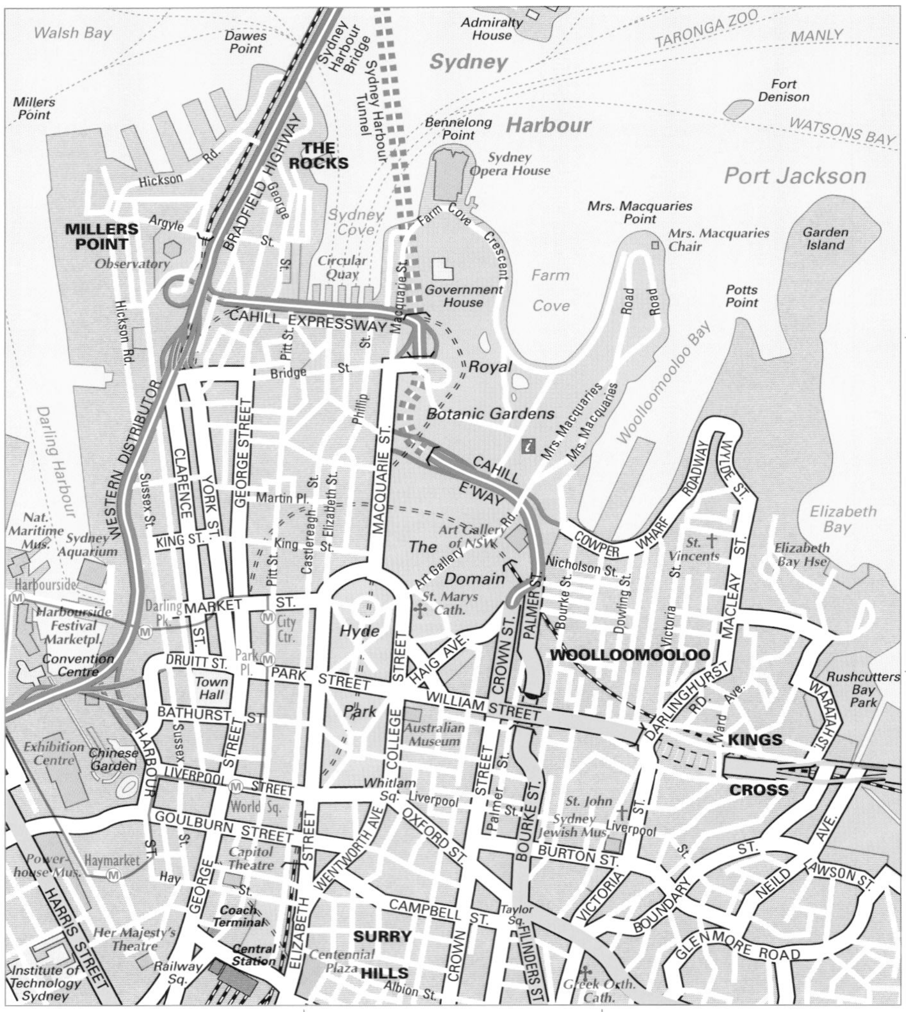

Tokyo

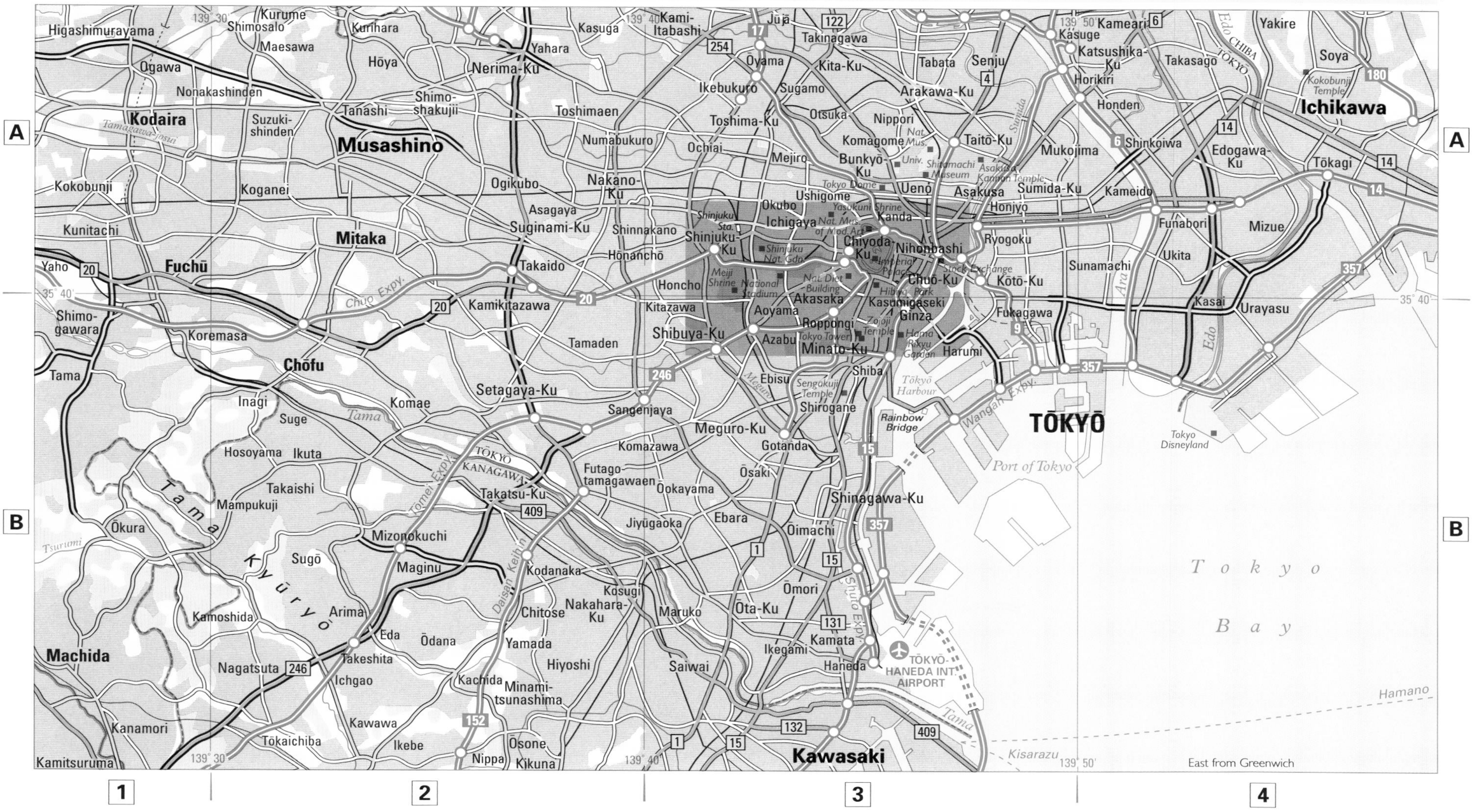

Central Tokyo

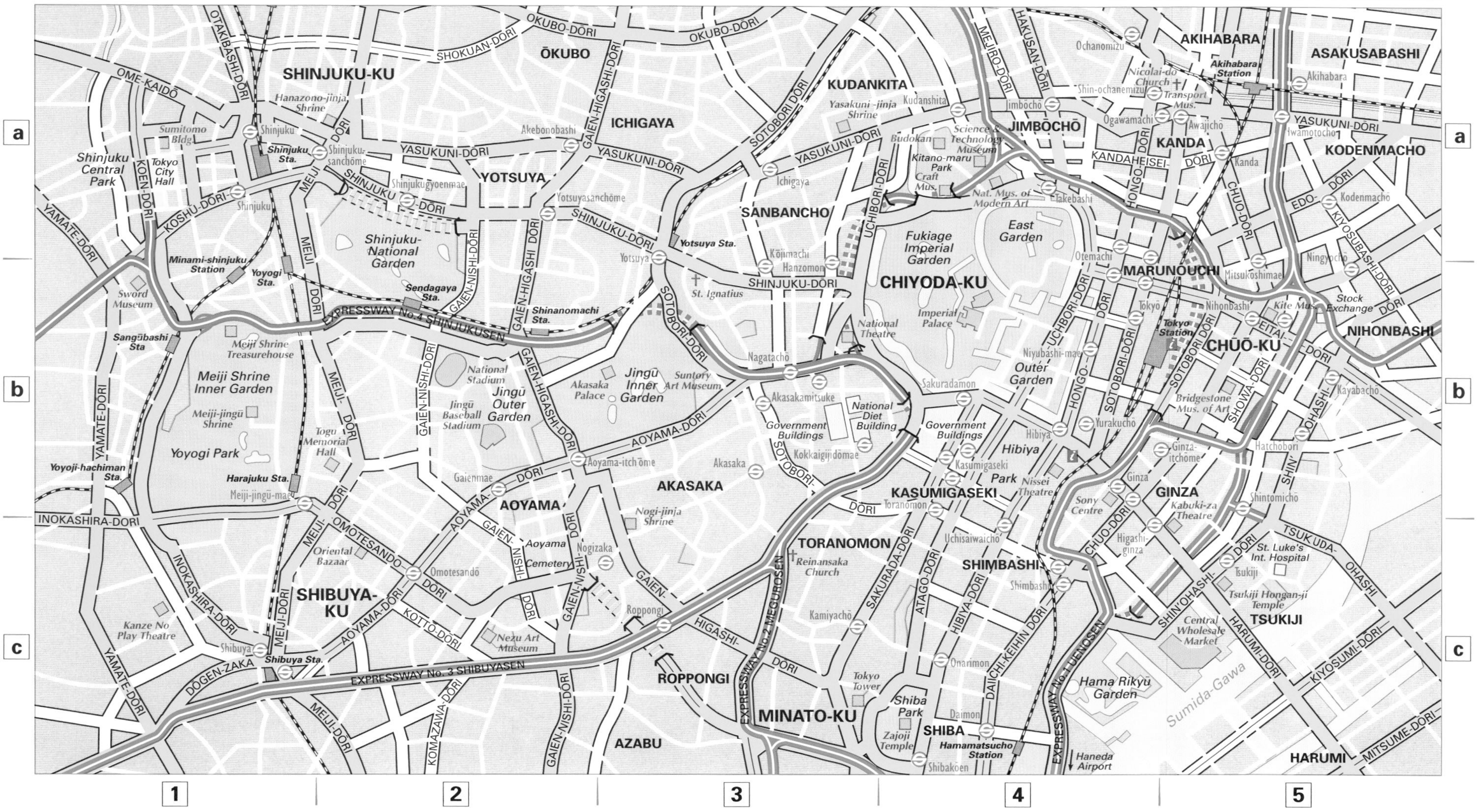

Tehran

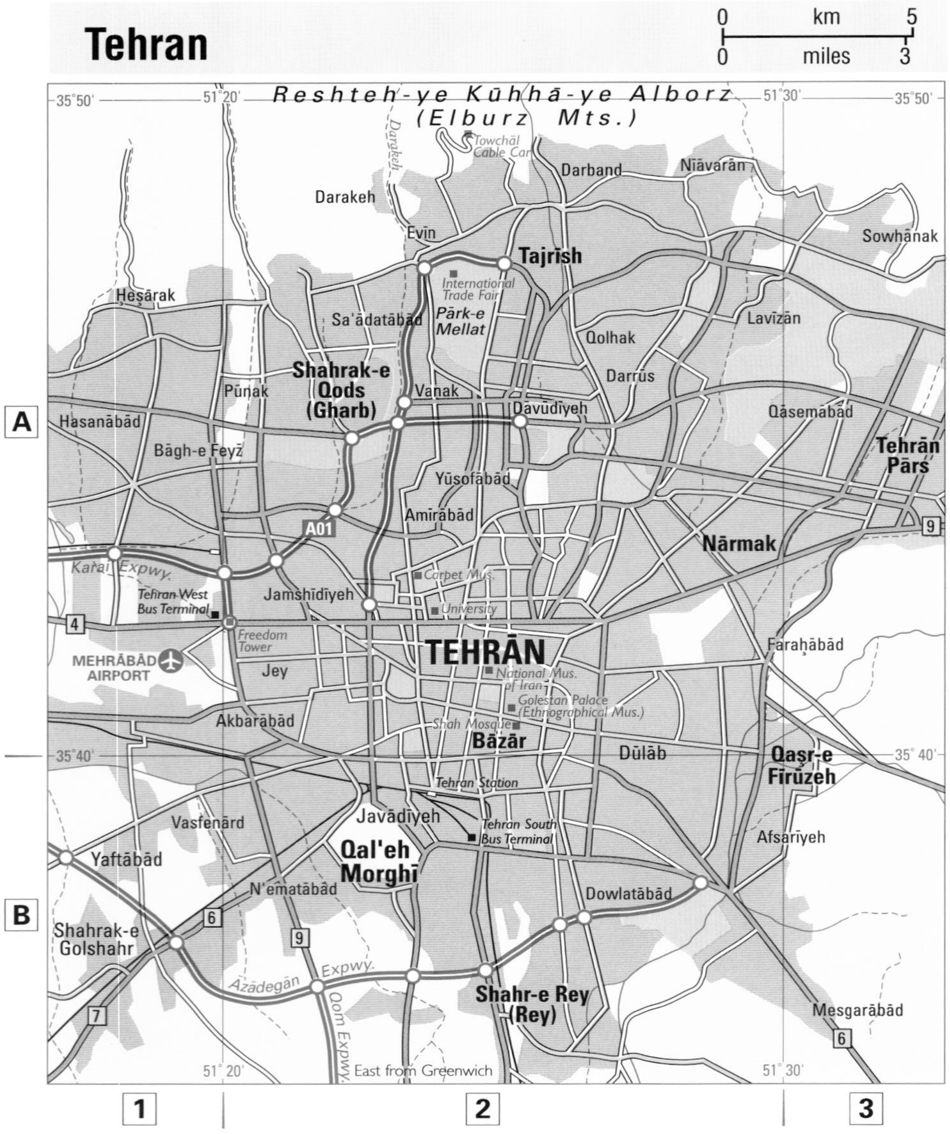
0 km 5
0 miles 3
Reshteh-ye Kūhhā-ye Alborz (Elburz Mts.)
35°50'
51°20'
51°30'
Towchāl Cable Car
Darband
Niāvarān
Darakeh
Evin
Sowhānak
Tajrīsh
International Trade Fair
Hesārak
Sa'ādatābād
Pārk-e Mellat
Lavīzān
Qolhak
Shahrak-e Qods (Gharb)
Pūnak
Darrūs
Vanak
Dāvūdīyeh
Hasanābād
Qāsemābād
Bāgh-e Feyz
Tehrān Pārs
Yūsofābād
Amīrābād
A01
Nārmak
Karaj Expwy.
Tehran West Bus Terminal
Jamshīdīyeh
Carpet Mus.
University
Freedom Tower
TEHRĀN
MEHRĀBĀD AIRPORT
Jey
National Mus. of Iran
Golestān Palace (Ethnographical Mus.)
Farahābād
Akbarābād
Shah Mosque
Bāzār
Dūlāb
Qasr-e Fīrūzeh
35°40'
Tehran Station
Javādīyeh
Vasfenārd
Tehran South Bus Terminal
Afsarīyeh
Yaftābād
Qal'eh Morghī
N'ematābād
Dowlatābād
Shahrak-e Golshahr
Āzādegān Expwy.
Qom Expwy.
Shahr-e Rey (Rey)
Mesgarābād
East from Greenwich
A
B
1
2
3

Tianjin

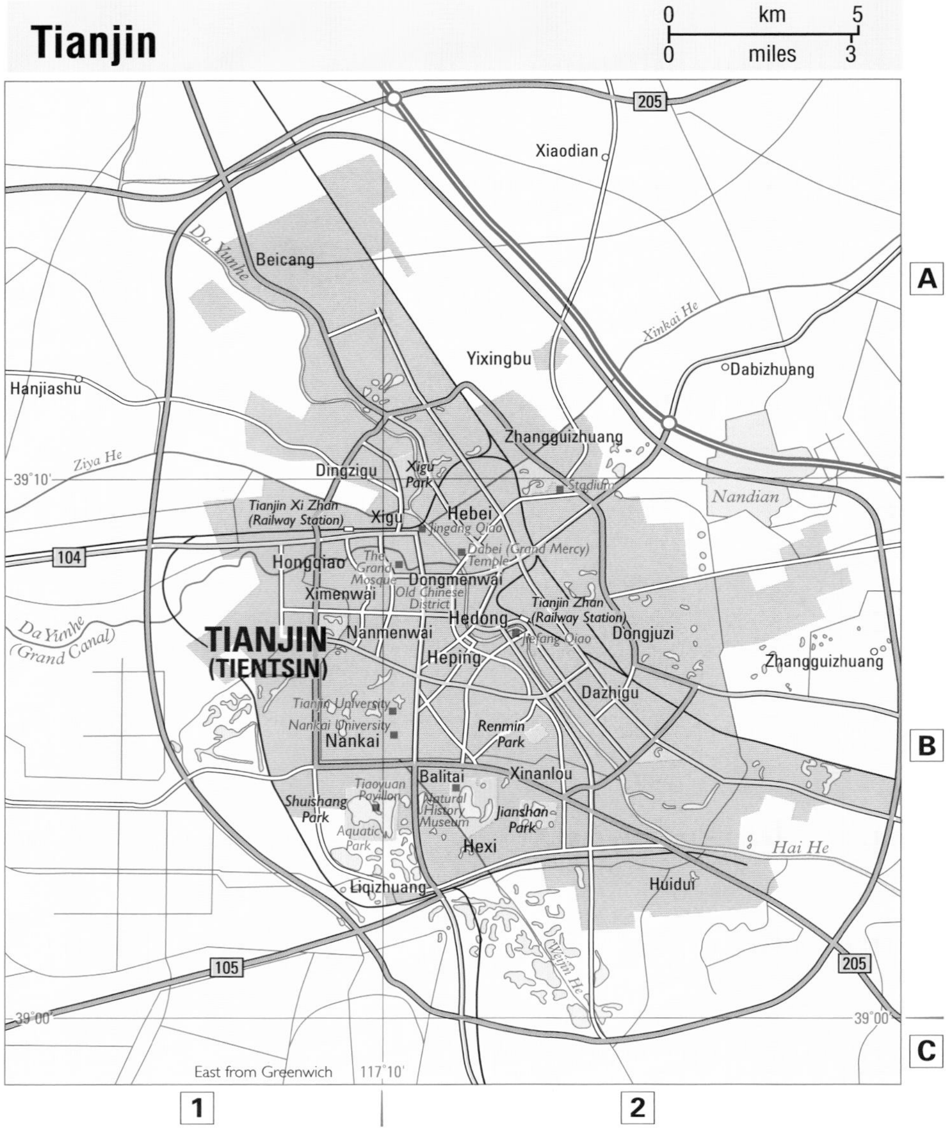
0 km 5
0 miles 3
205
Xiaodian
Beicang
Da Yunhe
A
Xinkai He
Yixingbu
Dabizhuang
Hanjiashu
Zhangguizhuang
Ziya He
Dingzigu
Xigu Park
Stadium
39°10'
Nandian
Tianjin Xi Zhan (Railway Station)
Xigu
Hebei
Jingang Qiao
104
Hongqiao
The Grand Mosque
Dabei (Grand Mercy) Temple
Ximenwai
Dongmenwai
Old Chinese District
Tianjin Zhan (Railway Station)
TIANJIN (TIENTSIN)
Nanmenwai
Hedong
Jiefang Qiao
Dongjuzi
Da Yunhe (Grand Canal)
Heping
Zhangguizhuang
Tianjin University
Dazhigu
Nankai University
Nankai
Renmin Park
B
Balitai
Xinanlou
Shuishang Park
Tiaoyuan Pavilion
Natural History Museum
Jianshan Park
Aquatic Park
Hexi
Hai He
Huidui
Liqizhuang
Weijin He
105
205
39°00'
C
East from Greenwich
117°10'
1
2

Toronto

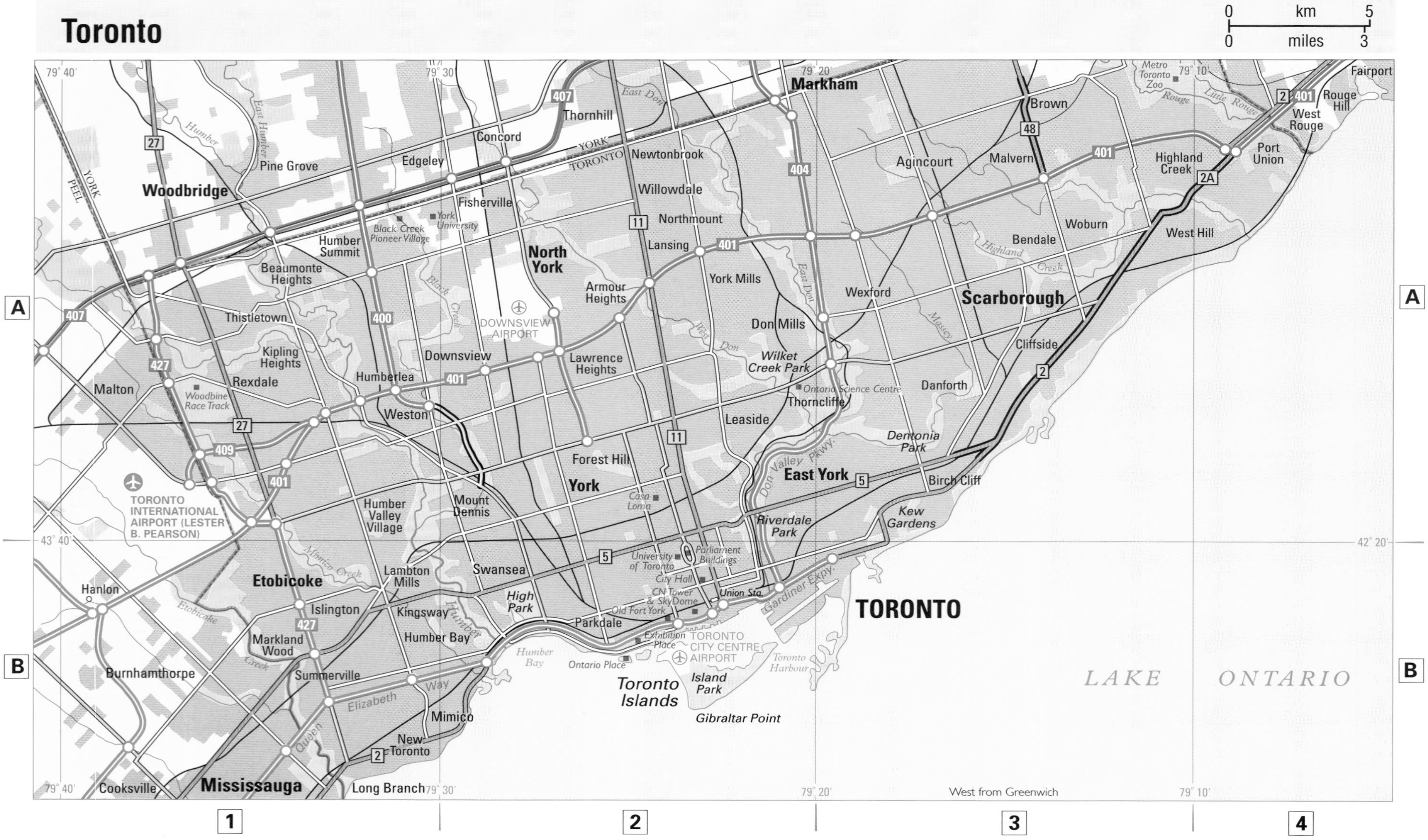
0 km 5
0 miles 3
79°40'
79°30'
79°20'
79°10'
Markham
407
Thornhill
East Don
Metro Toronto Zoo
Rouge
Little Rouge
Fairport
Rouge Hill
West Rouge
Brown
48
Concord
YORK TORONTO
Newtonbrook
27
Humber
East Humber
Pine Grove
Edgeley
Agincourt
Malvern
401
Highland Creek
Port Union
2A
YORK PEEL
Woodbridge
Fisherville
Willowdale
404
Black Creek Pioneer Village
York University
11
Northmount
Bendale
Woburn
West Hill
Humber Summit
Lansing
401
Highland Creek
Beaumonte Heights
North York
York Mills
A
407
Armour Heights
East Don
Wexford
Scarborough
Thistletown
400
Black Creek
Downsview Airport
West Don
Don Mills
Cliffside
Kipling Heights
Downsview
Lawrence Heights
Wilket Creek Park
427
Rexdale
Humberlea
401
Ontario Science Centre
Danforth
Malton
Woodbine Race Track
Weston
Thorncliffe
2
27
Leaside
Dentonia Park
409
Forest Hill
York
Don Valley Pkwy.
East York
5
Birch Cliff
TORONTO INTERNATIONAL AIRPORT (LESTER B. PEARSON)
401
Humber Valley Village
Mount Dennis
Casa Loma
Riverdale Park
Kew Gardens
43°40'
Mimico Creek
5
University of Toronto
Parliament Buildings
42°20'
Swansea
City Hall
Hanlon
Etobicoke
Lambton Mills
CN Tower & SkyDome
Union Sta.
Gardiner Expy.
Etobicoke
Islington
High Park
Old Fort York
TORONTO
Kingsway
Humber
427
Parkdale
Markland Wood
Humber Bay
Exhibition Place
TORONTO CITY CENTRE AIRPORT
Humber Bay
Ontario Place
Toronto Harbour
B
Burnhamthorpe
Creek
Toronto Islands
Island Park
LAKE ONTARIO
Summerville
Way
Elizabeth
Gibraltar Point
Mimico
Queen
New Toronto
2
Cooksville
Mississauga
Long Branch
West from Greenwich
1
2
3
4

COPYRIGHT GEORGE PHILIP LTD

Vienna

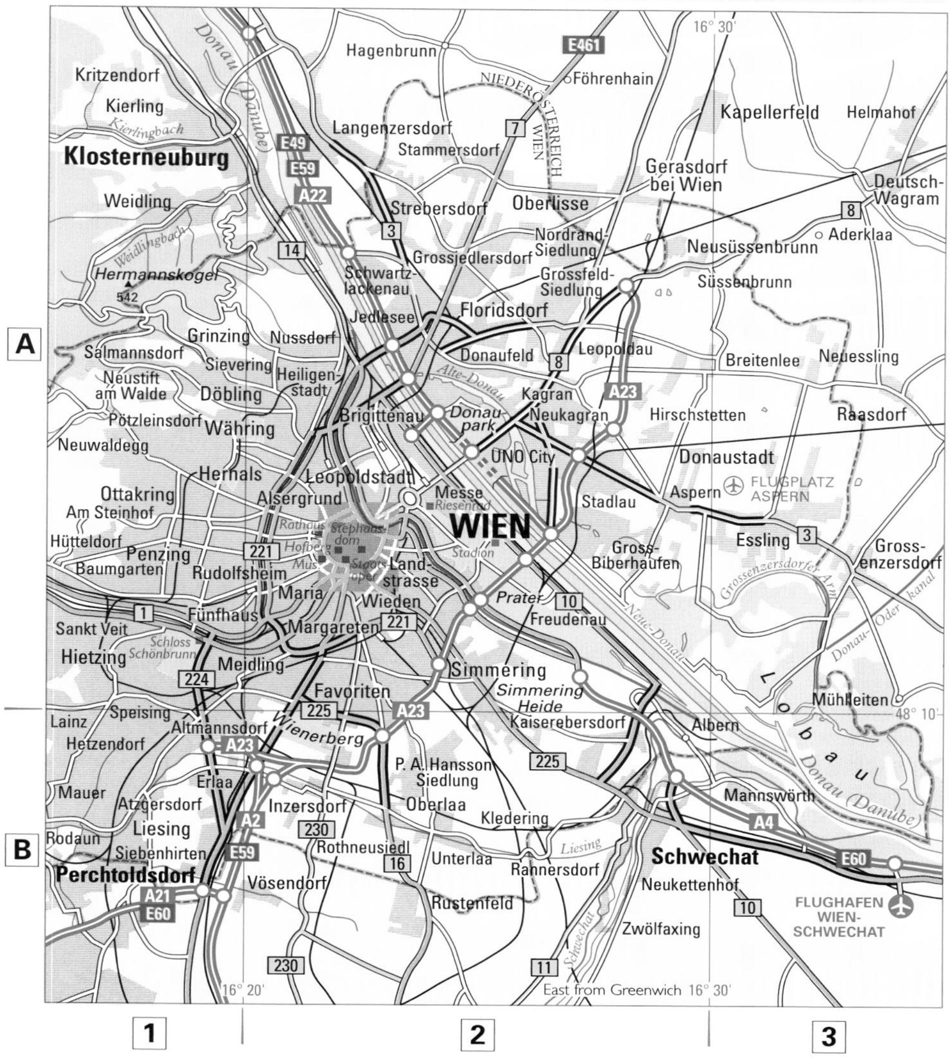
0 km 5
0 miles 3
Kritzendorf
Kierling
Klosterneuburg
Weidling
Hermannskogel
Hagenbrunn
Föhrenhain
Langenzersdorf
Stammersdorf
Kapellerfeld
Helmahof
Gerasdorf bei Wien
Deutsch-Wagram
Aderklaa
Strebersdorf
Oberlisse
Nordrand-Siedlung
Neusüssenbrunn
Süssenbrunn
Grossjedlersdorf
Schwartz-lackenau
Grossfeld-Siedlung
Jedlesee
Floridsdorf
Grinzing
Nussdorf
Salmannsdorf
Sievering
Heiligenstadt
Donaufeld
Leopoldau
Breitenlee
Neuessling
Neustift am Walde
Döbling
Pötzleinsdorf
Währing
Brigittenau
Donaupark
Kagran
Neukagran
Hirschstetten
Raasdorf
Neuwaldegg
Hernals
Leopoldstadt
UNO City
Donaustadt
Ottakring
Am Steinhof
Alsergrund
Messe
Stadlau
Aspern
FLUGPLATZ ASPERN
WIEN
Hütteldorf
Penzing
Baumgarten
Rudolfsheim
Landstrasse
Gross-Biberhaufen
Essling
Gross-enzersdorf
Maria
Wieden
Prater
Fünfhaus
Margareten
Freudenau
Sankt Veit
Hietzing
Schloss Schönbrunn
Meidling
Simmering
Simmering Heide
Favoriten
Kaiserebersdorf
Lainz
Speising
Altmannsdorf
Wienerberg
Albern
Mühlleiten
Hetzendorf
P. A. Hansson Siedlung
Mauer
Atzgersdorf
Erlaa
Inzersdorf
Oberlaa
Mannswörth
Liesing
Kledering
Rodaun
Siebenhirten
Rothneusiedl
Unterlaa
Rannersdorf
Schwechat
Perchtoldsdorf
Vösendorf
Neukettenhof
Rustenfeld
FLUGHAFEN WIEN-SCHWECHAT
Zwölfaxing
Donau (Danube)
Lobau
16° 20'
16° 30'
48° 10'
East from Greenwich 16° 30'
A
B
1
2
3

Central Vienna

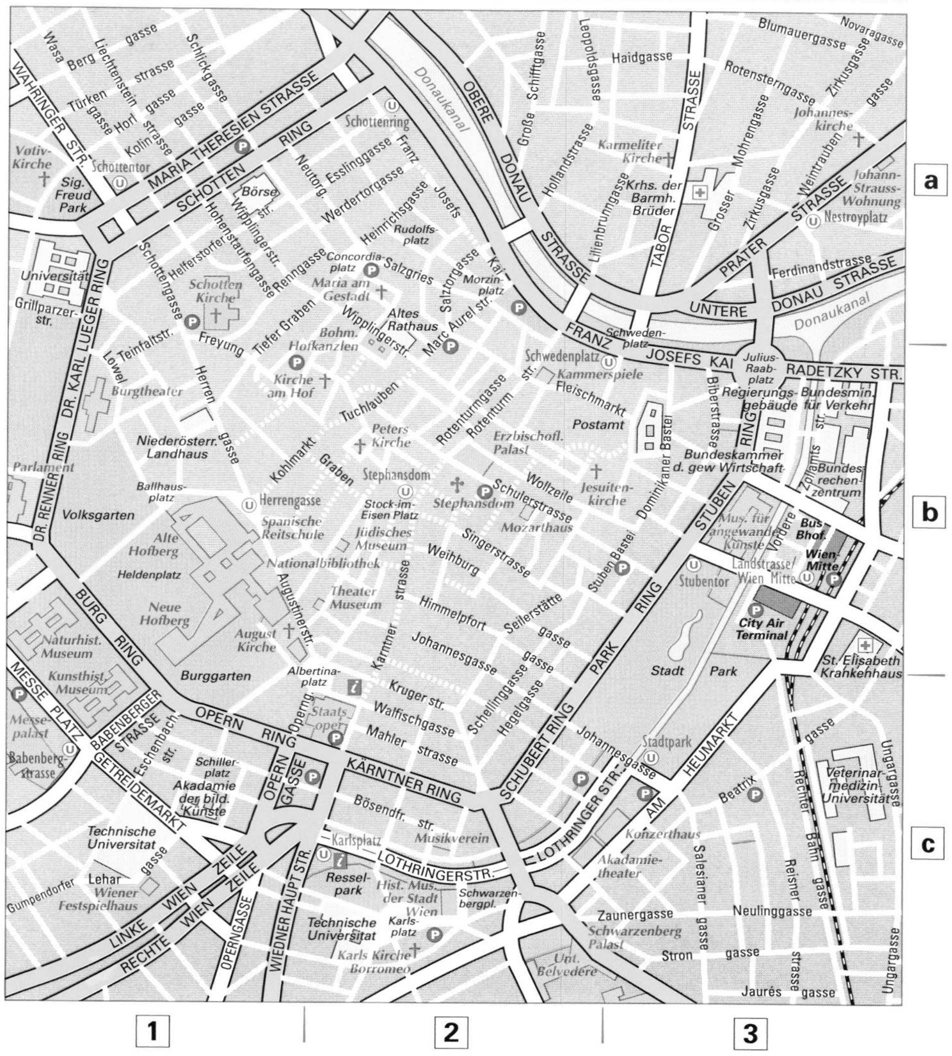
0 km 1
0 miles 0.5
Votiv-Kirche
Sig.-Freud Park
Universität
Grillparzer str.
Maria Theresien Strasse
Schotten Ring
Schottentor
Börse
Concordia-platz
Maria am Gestade
Schotten Kirche
Freyung
Tiefer Graben
Bohm. Hofkanzlei
Altes Rathaus
Kirche am Hof
Burgtheater
Niederösterr. Landhaus
Peters Kirche
Stephansdom
Dr. Karl Lueger Ring
Dr. Renner Ring
Parlament
Volksgarten
Ballhaus-platz
Heldenplatz
Alte Hofburg
Neue Hofburg
Spanische Reitschule
Nationalbibliothek
Augustinerstr.
August Kirche
Burggarten
Burg Ring
Naturhist. Museum
Kunsthist. Museum
Messe Platz
Messe-palast
Babenberger Strasse
Albertina-platz
Staats-oper
Opern Ring
Kärntner Ring
Schiller-platz
Akademie der bild. Künste
Getreidemarkt
Technische Universität
Lehar Wiener Festspielhaus
Linke Wien Zeile
Rechte Wien Zeile
Operngasse
Wiedner Haupt Str.
Karlsplatz
Ressel-park
Hist. Mus. der Stadt Wien
Technische Universität
Karls Kirche
Musikverein
Lothringerstr.
Schwarzenbergpl.
Schwarzenberg Palast
Akademie-theater
Konzerthaus
Zaunergasse
Unt. Belvedere
Heumarkt
Stadtpark
Schubert Ring
Park Ring
Stuben Ring
Stubentor
City Air Terminal
Wien Mitte
St. Elisabeth Krankenhaus
Veterinärmedizin. Universität
Neulinggasse
Jaurès gasse
Ungargasse
Donaukanal
Obere Donau Strasse
Franz Josefs Kai
Schwedenplatz
Kammerspiele
Fleischmarkt
Postamt
Erzbischöfl. Palast
Jesuitenkirche
Dominikaner Bastei
Bundeskammer d. gew Wirtschaft
Regierungsgebäude
Bundesministerium für Verkehr
Bundesrechenzentrum
Mus. für angewandte Kunst
Radetzky Str.
Untere Donau Strasse
Prater Strasse
Taborstrasse
Krhs. der Barmh. Brüder
Karmeliter Kirche
Johannes-kirche
Johann-Strauss-Wohnung
Nestroyplatz
Haidgasse
Blumauergasse
Novaragasse
Rotensterngasse
Ferdinandstrasse
Julius-Raab-platz
Mozarthaus
Himmelpfort
Johannesgasse
Singerstrasse
Weihburg
Kruger str.
Walfischgasse
Mahler strasse
Bösendf. str.
Graben
Kohlmarkt
Herrengasse
Rotenturmstrasse
Wollzeile
Schulerstrasse
Jüdisches Museum
Theater Museum
Stock-im-Eisen Platz
Salzgries
Rudolfs-platz
Morzin-platz
Hohenstaufengasse
Wipplinger str.
Tuchlauben
a
b
c
1
2
3

Warsaw

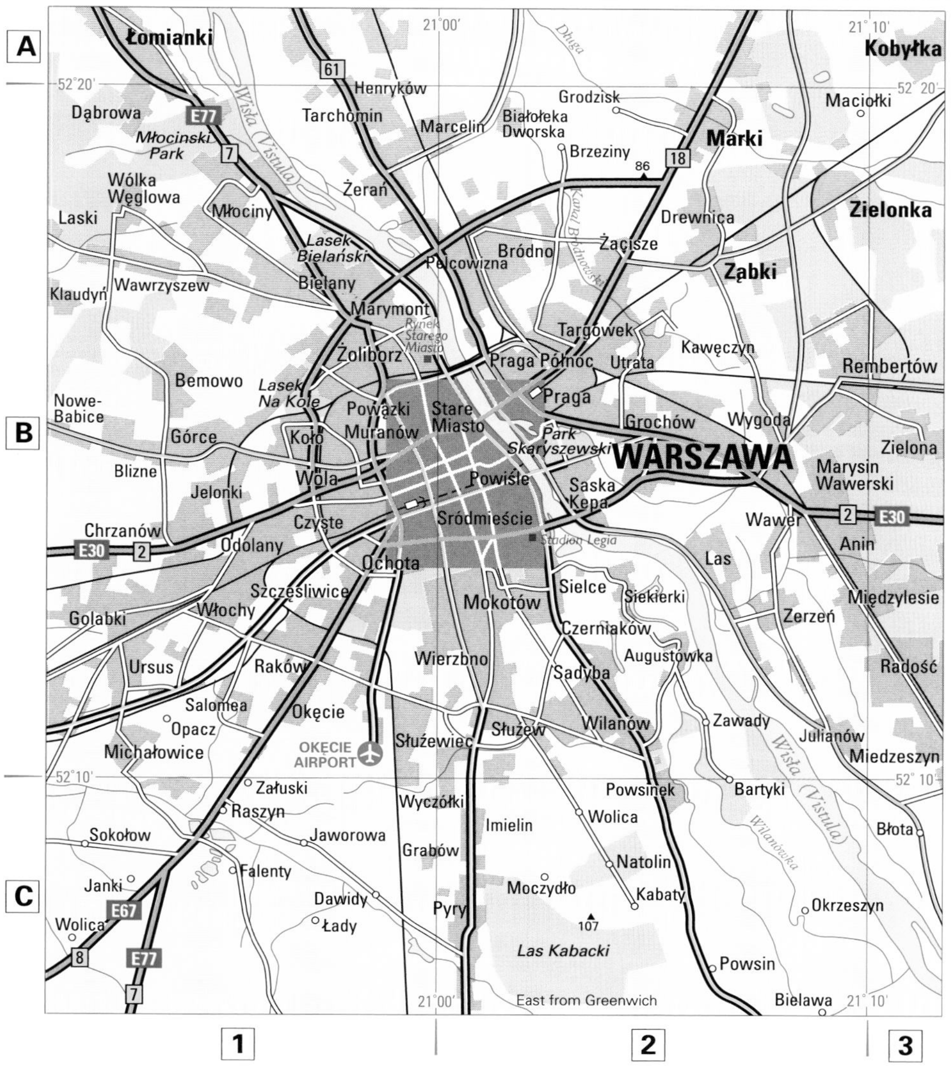
0 km 5
0 miles 3
Łomianki
Kobyłka
Dąbrowa
Henryków
Tarchomin
Marcelin
Białołęka Dworska
Grodzisk
Brzeziny
Marki
Maciołki
Młociński Park
Wólka Węglowa
Laski
Młociny
Żerań
Drewnica
Zielonka
Lasek Bielański
Bielany
Pelcowizna
Bródno
Żacisze
Ząbki
Klaudyń
Wawrzyszew
Marymont
Żoliborz
Targówek
Kawęczyn
Rembertów
Bemowo
Lasek Na Kole
Praga Północ
Utrata
Nowe-Babice
Powązki
Stare Miasto
Praga
Grochów
Wygoda
Górce
Koło
Muranów
Park Skaryszewski
WARSZAWA
Zielona
Blizne
Jelonki
Wola
Powiśle
Saska Kępa
Marysin Wawerski
Chrzanów
Czyste
Śródmieście
Wawer
Odolany
Ochota
Stadion Legia
Anin
Las
Szczęśliwice
Sielce
Siekierki
Międzylesie
Gołąbki
Włochy
Mokotów
Czerniaków
Zerzeń
Ursus
Rakow
Wierzbno
Augustówka
Radość
Salomea
Okęcie
Sadyba
Opacz
Służew
Wilanów
Zawady
Michałowice
OKĘCIE AIRPORT
Służewiec
Julianów
Miedzeszyn
Załuski
Wyczółki
Powsinek
Bartyki
Raszyn
Imielin
Wolica
Błota
Sokołów
Jaworowa
Grabów
Natolin
Falenty
Janki
Dawidy
Moczydło
Kabaty
Okrzeszyn
Wolica
Łady
Las Kabacki
Powsin
Bielawa
Wisła (Vistula)
21° 00'
21° 10'
52° 20'
52° 10'
East from Greenwich
A
B
C
1
2
3

Central Warsaw

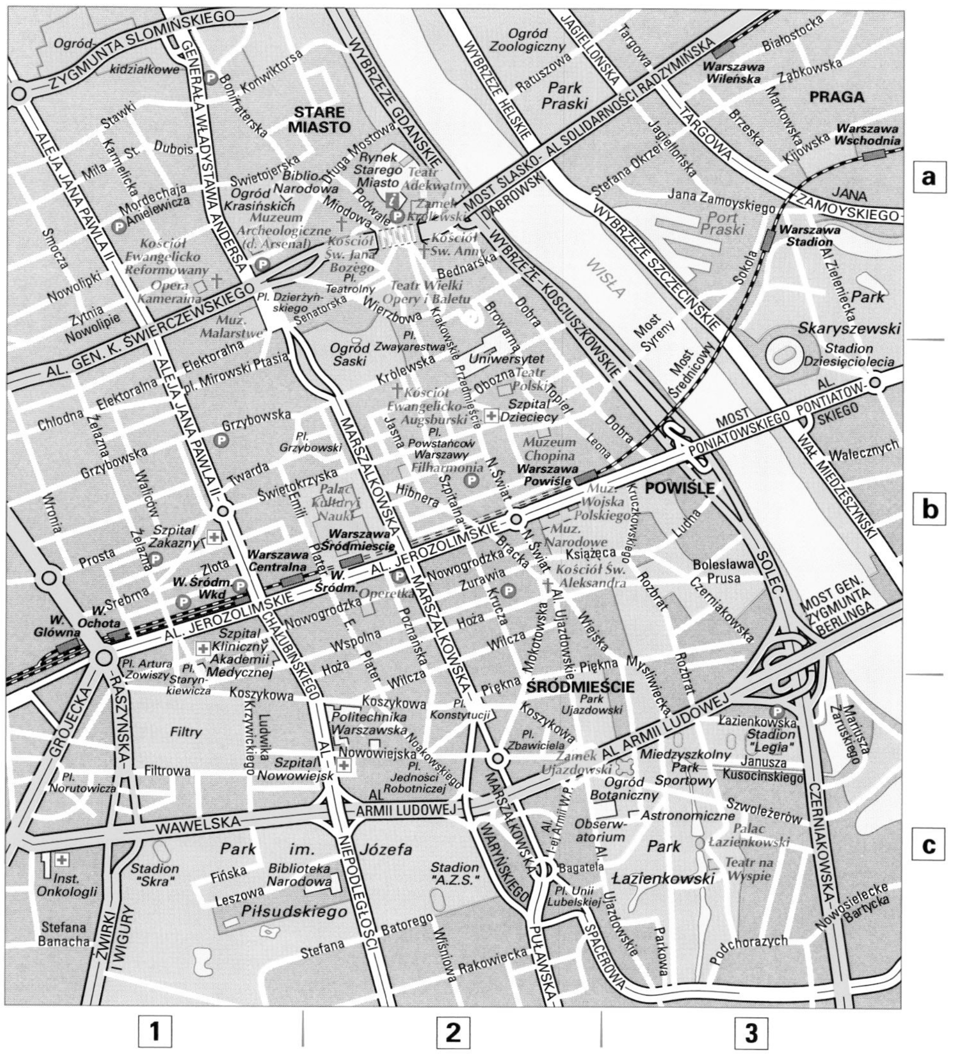
0 km 2
0 miles 1
Ogród Zoologiczny
Park Praski
Warszawa Wileńska
PRAGA
Warszawa Wschodnia
STARE MIASTO
Rynek Starego Miasta
Zamek Królewski
Kościół Sw. Anny
Teatr Wielki Opery i Baletu
Ogród Krasińskich
Muzeum Archeologiczne
Kościół Ewangelicko Reformowany
Opera Kameralna
Pl. Dzierżyńskiego
Pl. Bankowy
Muz. Malarstwa
Ogród Saski
Pl. Zwycięstwa
Pl. Mirowski
Uniwersytet
Kościół Ewangelicko Augsburski
Pl. Powstańców Warszawy
Filharmonia
Szpital Dziecięcy
Muzeum Chopina
Warszawa Powiśle
POWIŚLE
Pl. Grzybowski
Pałac Kultury i Nauki
Warszawa Śródmieście
Warszawa Centralna
W. Śródm.
W. Śródm. Wkd
Szpital Zakaźny
W. Ochota
W. Główna
Muz. Wojska Polskiego
Muz. Narodowe
Kościół Sw. Aleksandra
Szpital Kliniczny Akademii Medycznej
Politechnika Warszawska
Pl. Konstytucji
Szpital Nowowiejski
Filtry
Pl. Narutowicza
Inst. Onkologii
Stadion "Skra"
Park im. Józefa Piłsudskiego
Biblioteka Narodowa
Stadion "A.Z.S."
Pl. Unii Lubelskiej
Pl. Zbawiciela
Ogród Botaniczny
Obserwatorium
Astronomiczne
Park Łazienkowski
Teatr na Wyspie
Pałac Łazienkowski
Szwoleżerów
Stadion "Legia"
Międzyszkolny Park Sportowy
Łazienkowska
Park Skaryszewski
Stadion Dziesięciolecia
Warszawa Stadion
Most Śląsko-Dąbrowski
Most Poniatowskiego
Most Gen. Zygmunta Berlinga
Port Praski
Wisła
Al. Jerozolimskie
Al. Armii Ludowej
Al. Gen. K. Świerczewskiego
Al. Jana Pawła II
Marszałkowska
Niepodległości
Wybrzeże Gdańskie
Wybrzeże Kościuszkowskie
Wybrzeże Szczecińskie
Wybrzeże Helskie
Solidarności
Targowa
Jagiellońska
Zamoyskiego
Grójecka
Raszyńska
Żwirki i Wigury
Wawelska
Czerniakowska
Puławska
Nowy Świat
Stefana Banacha
Rakowiecka
Batorego
a
b
c
1
2
3

COPYRIGHT GEORGE PHILIP LTD

Washington

0 km 5
0 miles 3

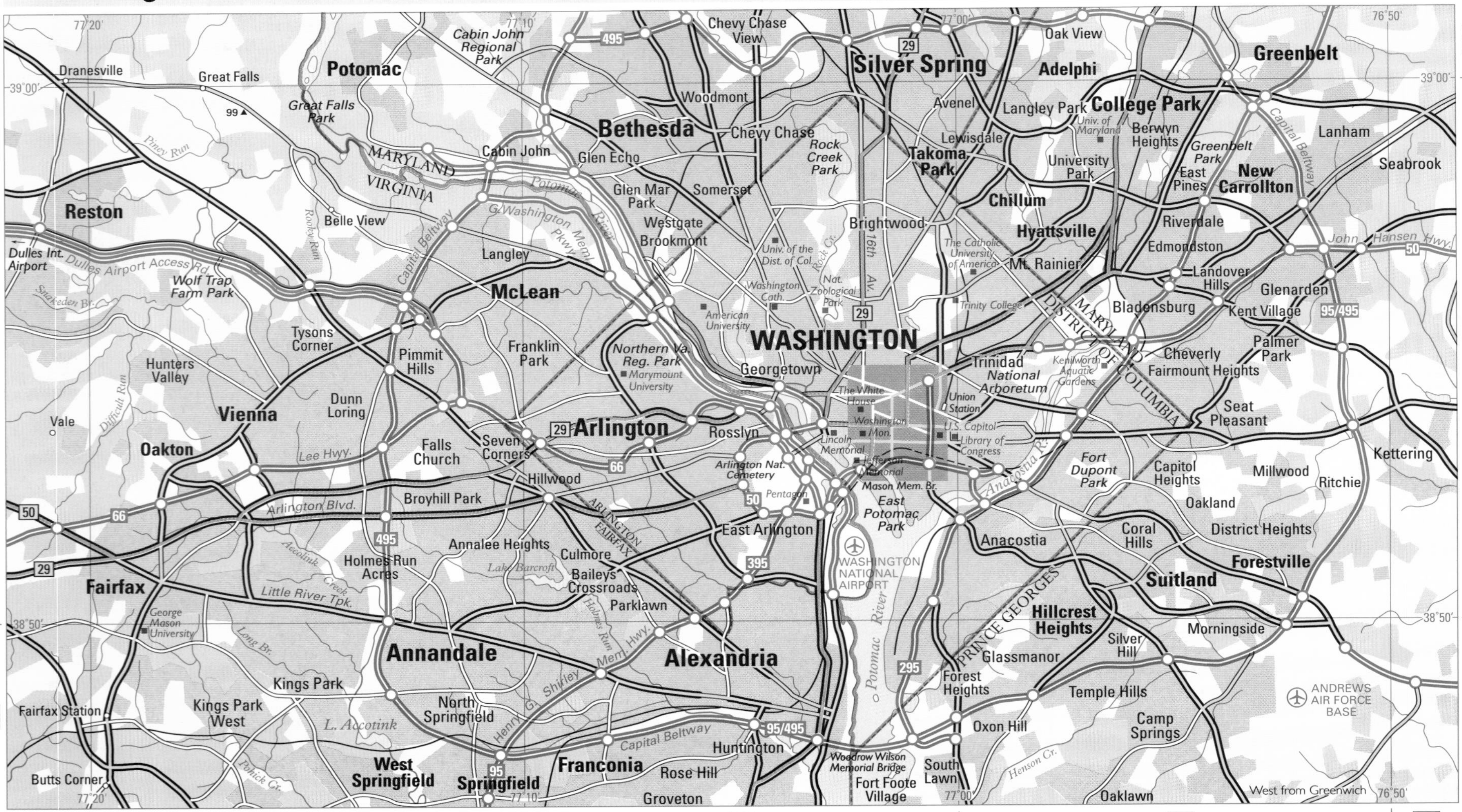

A
B
C
1
2
3
4
5
77°20'
77°10'
77°00'
76°50'
39°00'
38°50'
Dranesville
Great Falls
99
Great Falls Park
Potomac
Cabin John Regional Park
495
Chevy Chase View
Silver Spring
29
Oak View
Adelphi
Greenbelt
Woodmont
Bethesda
Chevy Chase
Avenel
Langley Park
College Park
Univ. of Maryland
Berwyn Heights
Lanham
Capital Beltway
Piney Run
MARYLAND
VIRGINIA
Cabin John
Glen Echo
Rock Creek Park
Lewisdale
Takoma Park
University Park
Greenbelt Park
East Pines
New Carrollton
Seabrook
Reston
Belle View
Glen Mar Park
Somerset
Chillum
Hyattsville
Riverdale
Westgate
Brookmont
Brightwood
Edmonston
Dulles Int. Airport
Dulles Airport Access Rd.
Wolf Trap Farm Park
Langley
Univ. of the Dist. of Col.
The Catholic University of America
Mt. Rainier
John Hansen Hwy.
50
Landover Hills
Glenarden
McLean
Washington Cath.
Nat. Zoological Park
16th Av.
Trinity College
Bladensburg
Kent Village
95/495
American University
WASHINGTON
DISTRICT OF COLUMBIA
MARYLAND
Tysons Corner
Pimmit Hills
Franklin Park
Northern Va. Reg. Park
Marymount University
Georgetown
Trinidad
Kenilworth Aquatic Gardens
Cheverly
Fairmount Heights
Palmer Park
Hunters Valley
Vienna
Dunn Loring
The White House
Union Station
National Arboretum
Seat Pleasant
Vale
Oakton
Lee Hwy.
Falls Church
Seven Corners
Arlington
Rosslyn
Washington Mon.
Lincoln Memorial
U.S. Capitol
Library of Congress
Jefferson Memorial
Fort Dupont Park
Capitol Heights
Millwood
Kettering
Hillwood
66
Arlington Nat. Cemetery
Mason Mem. Br.
Anacostia R.
Ritchie
Broyhill Park
Arlington Blvd.
Pentagon
East Potomac Park
Oakland
District Heights
ARLINGTON
FAIRFAX
East Arlington
WASHINGTON NATIONAL AIRPORT
Anacostia
Coral Hills
Forestville
Holmes Run Acres
Annalee Heights
Culmore
Lake Barcroft
Suitland
Fairfax
Baileys Crossroads
395
PRINCE GEORGES
Little River Tpk.
Parklawn
Hillcrest Heights
George Mason University
Morningside
Long Br.
Annandale
Alexandria
Potomac River
Silver Hill
Glassmanor
Forest Heights
295
Temple Hills
Kings Park
ANDREWS AIR FORCE BASE
Fairfax Station
Kings Park West
L. Accotink
North Springfield
Henry G. Shirley Mem. Hwy.
Huntington
Oxon Hill
Camp Springs
West Springfield
Springfield
Franconia
Rose Hill
Woodrow Wilson Memorial Bridge
South Lawn
Henson Cr.
Butts Corner
Pohick Cr.
Groveton
Fort Foote Village
Oaklawn
West from Greenwich

Central Washington

0 km 1
0 miles 0.5

a
b
c
1
2
3
P St.
16th St.
Logan Circle
NEW JERSEY AVE.
NORTH CAPITOL ST.
CONNECTICUT AVE.
RHODE ISLAND AVE.
Scott Circle
Thomas Circle
MASSACHUSETTS AVE.
VERMONT AVE.
13TH ST.
12th St.
11TH ST.
10th St.
9th St.
8th St.
7TH ST.
6TH
NORTH WEST
Mt. Vernon Sq.-UDC
NEW YORK AVE.
N St.
M St.
L St.
K St.
Farragut North
Mt. Vernon Square
1ST ST.
Farragut West
I St.
McPherson Sq.
Franklin Square
H St.
Convention Center
Lafayette Square
PENNSYLVANIA AVE.
Metro Center
Gallery Place
Union Station
World Bank
G St.
F St.
18th St.
17TH
15TH
14TH
The White House
National Place
Nat. Mus. of American Art
Judiciary Sq.
Fords Theater
Columbus Circle
E St.
Dept. of the Interior
Zero Milestone
Federal Triangle
LOUISIANA AVE.
D St.
C St.
The Ellipse
Nat. Museum of Natural History
Archives-Navy Memorial
Union Station Plaza
CONSTITUTION AVE.
Nat. Museum of American History
Supreme Court
Reflecting Pool
Washington Monument
Madison Dr.
National Gallery of Art
Grant Statue
U.S. Capitol
The Mall
National Air & Space Museum
D. C. War Memorial
Jefferson Dr.
Smithsonian
Smithsonian Institute
Botanic Gardens
Library of Congress
INDEPENDENCE AVE.
Hirshhorn Museum
US Holocaust Memorial Museum
Federal Center SW
Tidal Basin
L'Enfant Plaza
Capitol South
Jefferson Memorial
Outlet Bridge
14TH ST.
SOUTHWEST FREEWAY
MAINE AVE.
Francis Case Mem. Bridge
SOUTH WEST
Potomac R.
East Potomac Park
Washington Channel
SOUTH CAPITOL ST.
Waterfront
M ST.

Wellington

0 km 5
0 miles 3

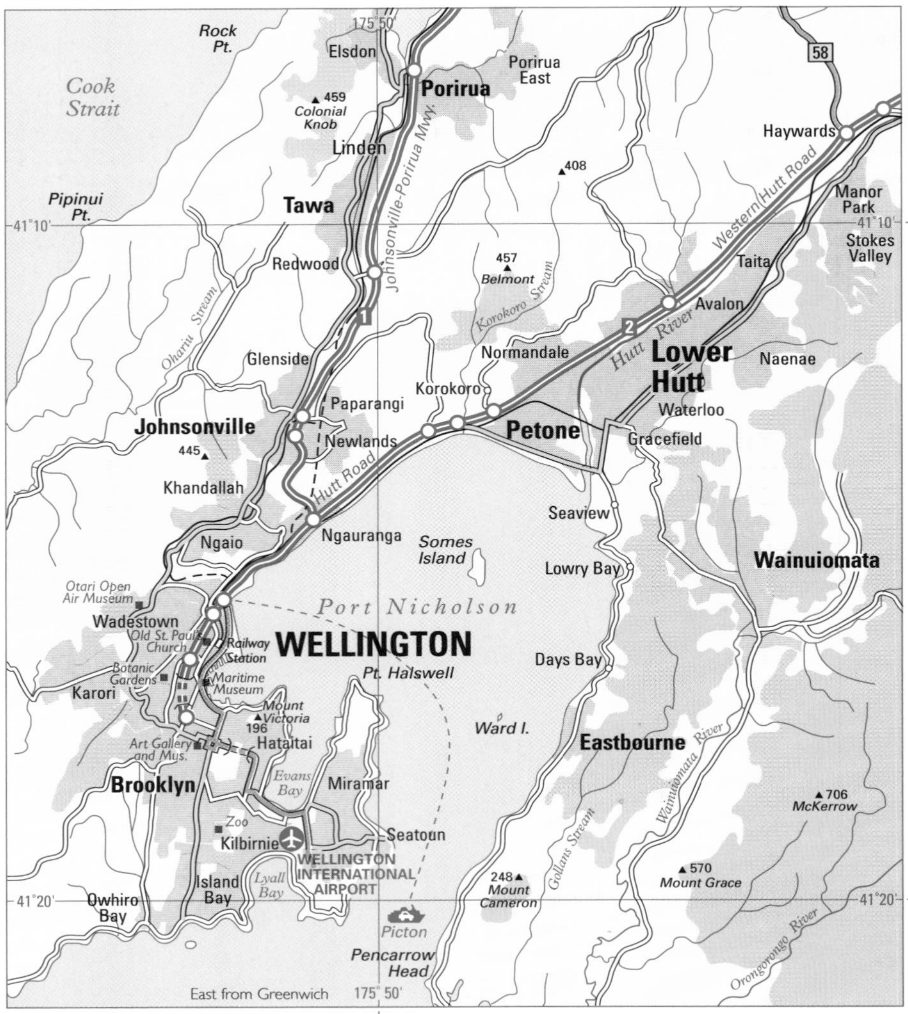

A
B
C
1
2
175°50'
41°10'
41°20'
Rock Pt.
Elsdon
Porirua
Porirua East
58
Cook Strait
459 Colonial Knob
Linden
Haywards
Johnsonville-Porirua Mwy.
408
Manor Park
Pipinui Pt.
Tawa
Western Hutt Road
Stokes Valley
Redwood
457 Belmont
Taita
Korokoro Stream
Ohariu Stream
Avalon
Normandale
Lower Hutt
Naenae
Glenside
Hutt River
Paparangi
Korokoro
Waterloo
Johnsonville
Newlands
Petone
Gracefield
445
Khandallah
Hutt Road
Ngaio
Ngauranga
Somes Island
Seaview
Wainuiomata
Lowry Bay
Otari Open Air Museum
Port Nicholson
Wadestown
Old St. Paul's Church
Railway Station
WELLINGTON
Botanic Gardens
Maritime Museum
Days Bay
Karori
Pt. Halswell
Mount Victoria
196
Ward I.
Art Gallery and Mus.
Hataitai
Eastbourne
Brooklyn
Evans Bay
Miramar
706 McKerrow
Zoo
Seatoun
Kilbirnie
WELLINGTON INTERNATIONAL AIRPORT
570 Mount Grace
248 Mount Cameron
Owhiro Bay
Island Bay
Lyall Bay
Picton
Pencarrow Head
East from Greenwich
Orongorongo River

COPYRIGHT GEORGE PHILIP LTD

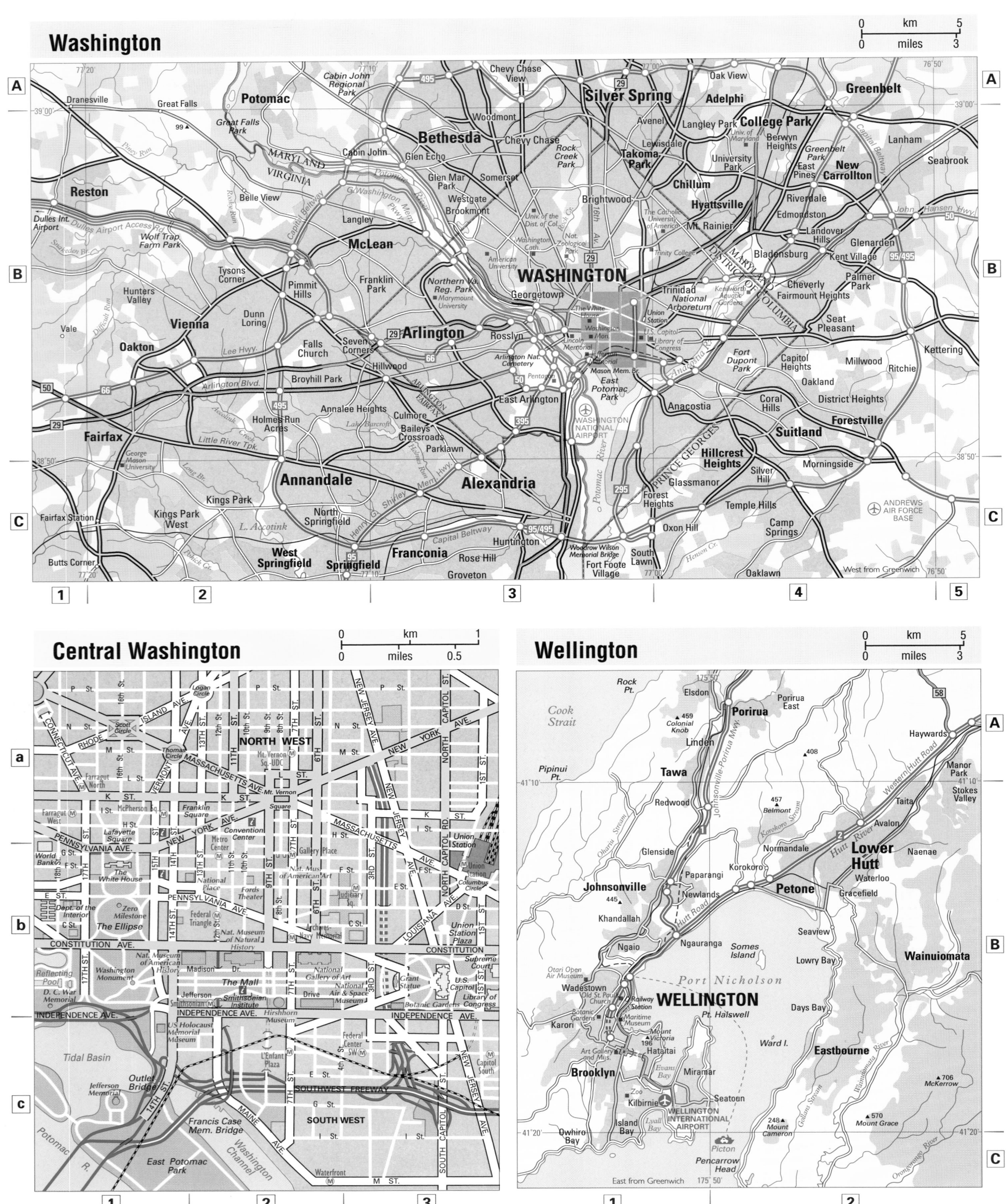

INDEX TO CITY MAPS

The index contains the names of all the principal places and features shown on the City Maps. Each name is followed by an additional entry in italics giving the name of the City Map within which it is located.

The number in bold type which follows each name refers to the number of the City Map page where that feature or place will be found.

The letter and figure which are immediately after the page number give the grid square on the map within which the feature or place is situated. The letter represents the latitude and the figure the longitude. Upper case letters refer to the City Maps, lower case letters to the Central Area Maps. The full geographic reference is provided in the border of the City Maps.

The location given is the centre of the city, suburb or feature and is not necessarily the name. Rivers, canals and roads are indexed to their name. Rivers carry the symbol → after their name.

An explanation of the alphabetical order rules and a list of the abbreviations used are to be found at the beginning of the World Map Index.

A

Aalām, *Baghdad* **3 B2**
Aalsmeer, *Amsterdam* **2 B1**
Abbey Wood, *London* **15 B4**
Abcoude, *Amsterdam* **2 B2**
Âbdin, *Cairo* **7 A2**
Abeno, *Osaka* **22 B4**
Aberdeen, *Hong Kong* **12 B2**
Aberdour, *Edinburgh* **11 A2**
Aberdour Castle, *Edinburgh* **11 A2**
Abfanggraben →, *Munich* **20 A3**
Ablon-sur-Seine, *Paris* **23 B3**
Abord-à-Plouffe, *Montreal* **19 A1**
Abramtsevo, *Moscow* **19 B4**
Abu Dis, *Jerusalem* **13 B2**
Abû en Numrus, *Cairo* **7 B2**
Abu Ghosh, *Jerusalem* **13 B1**
Acacias, *Madrid* **17 c2**
Acassuso, *Buenos Aires* **7 A1**
Accotink Cr. →, *Washington* **32 B2**
Acheres, *Paris* **23 A1**
Acília, *Rome* **25 C1**
Aclimação, *São Paulo* **26 B2**
Acton, *London* **15 A2**
Açúcar, Pão de, *Rio de Janeiro* **24 B2**
Ada Beja, *Lisbon* **14 A1**
Adams Park, *Atlanta* **3 B2**
Adams Shore, *Boston* **6 B4**
Addiscombe, *London* **15 B3**
Adelphi, *Washington* **32 A4**
Aderklaa, *Vienna* **31 A3**
Admiralteyskaya Storona, *St. Petersburg* **26 B2**
Áffori, *Milan* **18 A2**
Aflandshage, *Copenhagen* **10 B3**
Afsarīyeh, *Tehran* **30 B2**
Agboyi Cr. →, *Lagos* **14 A2**
Ågerup, *Copenhagen* **10 A1**
Ågesta, *Stockholm* **28 B2**
Agincourt, *Toronto* **30 A3**
Agora, Arhéa, *Athens* **2 c1**
Agra Canal, *Delhi* **10 B2**
Agricola Oriental, *Mexico City* **18 B2**
Agua Espraiada →, *São Paulo* **26 B2**
Agualva-Cacem, *Lisbon* **14 A1**
Agustino, Cerro El, *Lima* **16 B2**
Ahrensfelde, *Berlin* **5 A4**
Ahuntsic, *Montreal* **19 A1**
Ai →, *Osaka* **22 A4**
Aigremont, *Paris* **23 A1**
Air View Park, *Singapore* **27 A2**
Airport West, *Melbourne* **17 A1**
Aiyaleo, *Athens* **2 B2**
Aiyáleos, Óros, *Athens* **2 B1**
Ajegunle, *Lagos* **14 B2**
Aji, *Osaka* **22 A3**
Ajuda, *Lisbon* **14 A1**
Akalla, *Stockholm* **28 A1**
Akasaka, *Tokyo* **29 b3**
Akbarābād, *Tehran* **30 A2**
Akershus Slott, *Oslo* **22 A3**
Akihabara, *Tokyo* **29 a5**
Akrópolis, *Athens* **2 c2**
Al 'Azamiyah, *Baghdad* **3 A2**
Al Quds = Jerusalem, *Jerusalem* **13 B2**
Alaguntan, *Lagos* **14 B2**
Alameda, *San Francisco* **25 B3**
Alameda, Parque, *Mexico City* **18 b2**
Alameda Memorial State Beach Park, *San Francisco* **25 B3**
Albern, *Vienna* **31 B2**
Albert Park, *Melbourne* **17 B1**
Alberton, *Johannesburg* **13 B2**
Albertslund, *Copenhagen* **10 B2**
Albysjön, *Stockholm* **28 B1**
Alcantara, *Lisbon* **14 A1**
Alcatraz I., *San Francisco* **25 B2**
Alcobendas, *Madrid* **17 A2**
Alcorcón, *Madrid* **17 B1**
Aldershof, *Berlin* **5 B4**
Aldo Bonzi, *Buenos Aires* **7 C1**
Aleksandrovskoye, *St. Petersburg* **26 B2**
Alexander Nevsky Abbey, *St. Petersburg* **26 B2**
Alexander Soutzos Moussío, *Athens* **2 b3**
Alexandra, *Johannesburg* **13 A2**
Alexandra, *Singapore* **27 B2**
Alexandria, *Washington* **32 C3**
Alfama, *Lisbon* **14 c3**
Alfortville, *Paris* **23 B3**
Algés, *Lisbon* **14 A1**
Alhambra, *Los Angeles* **16 B4**
Alibey →, *Istanbul* **12 B1**
Alibey Barajı, *Istanbul* **12 B1**
Alibeyköy, *Istanbul* **12 B1**
Alimos, *Athens* **2 B2**
Alipur, *Calcutta* **8 B1**
Allach, *Munich* **20 A1**
Allambie Heights, *Sydney* **28 A2**
Allard Pierson Museum, *Amsterdam* **2 b2**
Allermuir Hill, *Edinburgh* **11 B2**
Allerton, Pt., *Boston* **6 B4**
Allston, *Boston* **6 A3**
Almada, *Lisbon* **14 A2**
Almagro, *Buenos Aires* **7 B2**
Almargem do Bispo, *Lisbon* **14 A1**
Almazovo, *Moscow* **19 A6**
Almirante G. Brown, Parque, *Buenos Aires* **7 C2**
Almon, *Jerusalem* **13 B2**
Almond →, *Edinburgh* **11 B2**
Alnabru, *Oslo* **22 A4**
Alnsjøen, *Oslo* **22 A4**
Alperton, *London* **15 A2**
Alpine, *New York* **21 A2**
Alrode, *Johannesburg* **13 B2**
Alsemerg, *Brussels* **6 B1**
Alsergrund, *Vienna* **31 A2**
Alsip, *Chicago* **9 C2**
Ålsten, *Stockholm* **28 B1**
Älta, *Stockholm* **28 B3**
Altadena, *Los Angeles* **16 A4**
Alte-Donau →, *Vienna* **31 A2**
Alte Hofburg, *Vienna* **31 b1**
Alter Finkenkrug, *Berlin* **5 A1**
Altes Rathaus, *Munich* **20 b3**
Altglienicke, *Berlin* **5 B4**
Altlandsberg, *Berlin* **5 A5**
Altlandsberg Nord, *Berlin* **5 A5**
Altmannsdorf, *Vienna* **31 B1**
Alto da Moóca, *São Paulo* **26 B2**
Alto do Pina, *Lisbon* **14 A2**
Altona, *Melbourne* **17 B1**
Alvaro Obregon, *Mexico City* **18 B1**
Alvik, *Stockholm* **28 B1**
Älvsjo, *Stockholm* **28 B2**
Älvvik, *Stockholm* **28 A3**
Am Hasenbergl, *Munich* **20 A2**
Am Steinhof, *Vienna* **31 A1**
Am Wald, *Munich* **20 B2**
Ama Keng, *Singapore* **27 A2**
Amadora, *Lisbon* **14 A1**
Amagasaki, *Osaka* **22 A3**
Amager, *Copenhagen* **10 B3**
Amāl Qādisiya, *Baghdad* **3 B2**
Amalienborg, *Copenhagen* **10 b3**
Amata, *Milan* **18 A1**
Ameixoeira, *Lisbon* **14 A2**
América, *São Paulo* **26 B1**
Amin, *Baghdad* **3 B2**
Aminadov, *Jerusalem* **13 B1**
Aminyevo, *Moscow* **19 B2**
Amīrābād, *Tehran* **30 A2**
Amora, *Lisbon* **14 B2**
Amoreira, *Lisbon* **14 A1**
Ampelokipi, *Athens* **2 B2**
Amper →, *Munich* **20 A1**
Amstel, *Amsterdam* **2 b2**
Amstel →, *Amsterdam* **2 c2**
Amstel-Drecht-Kanaal, *Amsterdam* **2 B2**
Amstel Station, *Amsterdam* **2 c3**
Amstelhof, *Amsterdam* **2 b2**
Amstelveen, *Amsterdam* **2 B2**
Amsterdam, *Amsterdam* **2 A2**
Amsterdam-Rijnkanaal, *Amsterdam* **2 B3**
Amsterdam Zoo, *Amsterdam* **2 b3**
Amsterdam Zuidoost, *Amsterdam* **2 B2**
Amsterdamse Bos, *Amsterdam* **2 B1**
Anacostia, *Washington* **32 B4**
Anadoluhisarı, *Istanbul* **12 B2**
Anadolukavağı, *Istanbul* **12 A2**
Anata, *Jerusalem* **13 B2**
Ancol, *Jakarta* **13 A1**
'Andalus, *Baghdad* **3 B1**
Andarai, *Rio de Janeiro* **24 B1**
Anderlecht, *Brussels* **6 A1**
Anderson Park, *Atlanta* **3 B2**
Andingmen, *Beijing* **4 B2**
Andrews Air Force Base, *Washington* **32 C4**
Ang Mo Kio, *Singapore* **27 A3**
Ängby, *Stockholm* **28 A1**
Angel I., *San Francisco* **25 A2**
Angel Island State Park, *San Francisco* **25 A2**
Angke, Kali →, *Jakarta* **13 A1**
Angyalföld, *Budapest* **7 A2**
Anik, *Mumbai* **20 A2**
Anin, *Warsaw* **31 B2**
Anjou, *Montreal* **19 A2**
Annalee Heights, *Washington* **32 B2**
Annandale, *Washington* **32 C2**
Anne Frankhuis, *Amsterdam* **2 a1**
Antony, *Paris* **23 B2**
Anyangch'on, *Seoul* **26 C1**
Aoyama, *Tokyo* **29 b2**
Ap Lei Chau, *Hong Kong* **12 B1**
Apapa, *Lagos* **14 B2**
Apelacão, *Lisbon* **14 A2**
Apterkarskiy Ostrov, *St. Petersburg* **26 B2**
Ar Kazimiyah, *Baghdad* **3 B1**
Ara →, *Tokyo* **29 A4**
Arakawa-Ku, *Tokyo* **29 A3**
Arany-hegyi-patak →, *Budapest* **7 A2**
Aravaca, *Madrid* **17 B1**
Arbataash, *Baghdad* **3 A1**
Arc de Triomphe, *Paris* **23 a2**
Arcadia, *Los Angeles* **16 B4**
Arceuil, *Paris* **23 B2**
Arco Plaza, *Los Angeles* **16 b1**
Arese, *Milan* **18 A1**
Arganzuela, *Madrid* **17 B1**
Argenteuil, *Paris* **23 A2**
Argonne Forest, *Chicago* **9 C1**
Argüelles, *Madrid* **17 a1**
Arima, *Osaka* **22 A2**
Arima, *Tokyo* **29 B2**
Ários Págos, *Athens* **2 c1**
Arkhangelyskoye, *Moscow* **19 B1**
Arlington, *Boston* **6 A2**
Arlington, *Washington* **32 B3**
Arlington Heights, *Boston* **6 A2**
Arlington Nat. Cemetery, *Washington* **32 B3**
Armação, *Rio de Janeiro* **24 B2**
Armadale, *Melbourne* **17 B2**
Armenian Quarter, *Jerusalem* **13 b3**
Armour Heights, *Toronto* **30 A2**
Arncliffe, *Sydney* **28 B1**
Arnold Arboretum, *Boston* **6 B3**
Árpádföld, *Budapest* **7 A3**
Arrentela, *Lisbon* **14 B2**
Årsta, *Stockholm* **28 B2**
Art Institute, *Chicago* **9 c2**
Artane, *Dublin* **11 A2**
Artas, *Jerusalem* **13 B2**
Arthur's Seat, *Edinburgh* **11 B3**
Aryiróupolis, *Athens* **2 B2**
Asagaya, *Tokyo* **29 A2**
Asahi, *Osaka* **22 A4**
Asakusa, *Tokyo* **29 A3**
Asakusabashi, *Tokyo* **29 a5**
Asati, *Calcutta* **8 C1**
Aschheim, *Munich* **20 A3**
Ascot Vale, *Melbourne* **17 A1**
Ashburn, *Chicago* **9 C2**
Ashburton, *Melbourne* **17 B2**
Ashfield, *Sydney* **28 B1**
Ashford, *London* **15 B1**
Ashiya, *Osaka* **22 A2**
Ashiya →, *Osaka* **22 A2**
Ashtown, *Dublin* **11 A2**
Askisto, *Helsinki* **12 B1**
Askrikefjärden, *Stockholm* **28 A3**
Asnières, *Paris* **23 A2**
Aspern, *Vienna* **31 A2**
Aspern, Flugplatz, *Vienna* **31 A3**
Assago, *Milan* **18 B1**
Assemblée Nationale, *Paris* **23 b3**
Assendelft, *Amsterdam* **2 A1**
Assiano, *Milan* **18 B1**
Astoria, *New York* **21 B2**
Astrolabe Park, *Sydney* **28 B2**
Atarot Airport, *Jerusalem* **13 A2**
Atghara, *Calcutta* **8 B2**
Athens = Athínai, *Athens* **2 B2**
Athínai, *Athens* **2 B2**
Athinai-Ellinikón Airport, *Athens* **2 B2**
Athis-Mons, *Paris* **23 B3**
Athlone, *Cape Town* **8 A2**
Atholl, *Johannesburg* **13 A2**
Atīfīya, *Baghdad* **3 A2**
Atişalen, *Istanbul* **12 B1**
Atlanta, *Atlanta* **3 B2**
Atlanta History Center, *Atlanta* **3 B2**
Atomium, *Brussels* **6 A2**
Attiki, *Athens* **2 A2**
Atzgersdorf, *Vienna* **31 B1**
Aubervilliers, *Paris* **23 A3**
Aubing, *Munich* **20 B1**
Auburndale, *Boston* **6 A2**
Aucherdinny, *Edinburgh* **11 B2**
Auckland Park, *Johannesburg* **13 B2**
Auderghem, *Brussels* **6 B2**
Augusta, Mausoleo di, *Rome* **25 b2**
Augustówka, *Warsaw* **31 B2**
Aulnay-sous-Bois, *Paris* **23 A3**
Aurelio, *Rome* **25 B1**
Ausîm, *Cairo* **7 A1**
Austerlitz, Gare d', *Paris* **23 A3**
Austin, *Chicago* **9 B2**
Avalon, *Wellington* **32 B2**
Avedøre, *Copenhagen* **10 B2**
Avellaneda, *Buenos Aires* **7 C2**
Avenel, *Washington* **32 B4**
Avondale, *Chicago* **9 B2**
Avondale Heights, *Melbourne* **17 A1**
Avtovo, *St. Petersburg* **26 B1**
Ayazağa, *Istanbul* **12 B1**
Ayer Chawan, P., *Singapore* **27 B2**
Ayer Merbau, P., *Singapore* **27 B2**
Ayía Marina, *Athens* **2 C3**
Ayía Paraskevi, *Athens* **2 A2**
Áyios Dhimitrios, *Athens* **2 B2**
Áyios Ioánnis Rendis, *Athens* **2 B1**
Azabu, *Tokyo* **29 c3**
Azcapotzalco, *Mexico City* **18 B1**
Azteca, Estadia, *Mexico City* **18 C2**
Azucar, Cerro Pan de, *Santiago* **26 A1**

B

Baambrugge, *Amsterdam* **2 B2**
Baba I., *Karachi* **14 B1**
Babarpur, *Delhi* **10 A2**
Babushkin, *Moscow* **19 A4**
Back B., *Mumbai* **20 B1**
Baclaran, *Manila* **17 B2**
Bacoor, *Manila* **17 C1**
Bacoor B., *Manila* **17 C1**
Badalona, *Barcelona* **4 A2**
Badhoevedorp, *Amsterdam* **2 A1**
Badli, *Delhi* **10 A1**
Bærum, *Oslo* **22 A2**
Bağcılar, *Istanbul* **12 B1**
Bággio, *Milan* **18 B1**
Bāgh-e-Feyz, *Tehran* **30 A1**
Baghdād, *Baghdad* **3 A2**
Bagmari, *Calcutta* **8 B2**
Bagneux, *Paris* **23 B2**
Bagnolet, *Paris* **23 A3**
Bagsværd, *Copenhagen* **10 A2**
Bagsværd Sø, *Copenhagen* **10 A2**
Baguiati, *Calcutta* **8 B2**
Bagumbayan, *Manila* **17 C2**
Bahçeköy, *Istanbul* **12 A1**
Bahtîm, *Cairo* **7 A2**
Baileys Crossroads, *Washington* **32 B3**
Bailly, *Paris* **23 A1**
Bairro Alto, *Lisbon* **14 c1**
Bairro Lopes, *Lisbon* **14 b3**
Baisha, *Canton* **8 B2**
Baisha →, *Canton* **8 B2**
Baixa, *Lisbon* **14 c2**
Baiyun Airport, *Canton* **8 A2**
Baiyun Hill Scenic Spot, *Canton* **8 B2**
Bakırköy, *Istanbul* **12 C1**
Bakovka, *Moscow* **19 B2**
Bal Harbor, *Miami* **18 A2**
Balara, *Manila* **17 B2**
Balashikha, *Moscow* **19 B5**
Baldia, *Karachi* **14 A1**
Baldoyle, *Dublin* **11 A3**
Baldwin Hills, *Los Angeles* **16 B2**
Baldwin Hills Res., *Los Angeles* **16 B2**
Balgowlah, *Sydney* **28 A2**
Balgowlah Heights, *Sydney* **28 A2**
Balham, *London* **15 B3**
Bali, *Calcutta* **8 B1**
Baliganja, *Calcutta* **8 B2**
Balingsnäs, *Stockholm* **28 B2**
Balingsta, *Stockholm* **28 B2**
Balintawak, *Manila* **17 B1**
Balitai, *Tianjin* **30 B2**
Ballerup, *Copenhagen* **10 A2**
Ballinteer, *Dublin* **11 B2**
Ballyboden, *Dublin* **11 B2**
Ballybrack, *Dublin* **11 B3**
Ballyfermot, *Dublin* **11 A1**
Ballymorefinn Hill, *Dublin* **11 B1**
Ballymun, *Dublin* **11 A2**
Balmain, *Sydney* **28 B2**
Baluhati, *Calcutta* **8 B1**
Balvanera, *Buenos Aires* **7 B2**
Balwyn, *Melbourne* **17 A2**
Balwyn North, *Melbourne* **17 A2**
Banática, *Lisbon* **14 A1**
Banco do Brasil, Centro Cultural, *Rio de Janeiro* **24 a2**
Bandra, *Mumbai* **20 A1**
Bandra Pt., *Mumbai* **20 A1**
Bang Kapi, *Bangkok* **3 B2**
Bang Kholaem, *Bangkok* **3 A2**
Bang Na, *Bangkok* **3 B2**
Bang Phlad, *Bangkok* **3 a1**
Bangkhen, *Bangkok* **3 A2**
Bangkok = Krung Thep, *Bangkok* **3 B2**
Bangkok Noi, *Bangkok* **3 B1**
Bangkok Yai, *Bangkok* **3 B1**
Banglamphoo, *Bangkok* **3 b2**
Banglo, *Calcutta* **8 B1**
Bangrak, *Bangkok* **3 B2**
Bangsu, *Bangkok* **3 B2**
Bank, *London* **15 b5**
Bank of America, *San Francisco* **25 b2**
Bank of China Tower, *Hong Kong* **12 c1**
Banks, C., *Sydney* **28 C2**
Banksmeadow, *Sydney* **28 B2**
Banstala, *Calcutta* **8 B2**
Bantra, *Calcutta* **8 B1**
Baoshan, *Shanghai* **27 A1**
Bar Giyora, *Jerusalem* **13 B1**
Barahanagar, *Calcutta* **8 B2**
Barajas, *Madrid* **17 B2**
Barajas, Aeropuerto Transoceanico de, *Madrid* **17 B2**
Barakpur, *Calcutta* **8 A2**
Barberini, Palazzo, *Rome* **25 b3**
Barbican, *London* **15 a4**
Barcarena, *Lisbon* **14 A1**
Barcarena, Rib. de →, *Lisbon* **14 A1**
Barcelona, *Barcelona* **4 A2**
Barcelona-Prat, Aeropuerta de, *Barcelona* **4 B1**
Barceloneta, *Barcelona* **4 A2**
Barking, *London* **15 A4**
Barkingside, *London* **15 A4**
Barnes, *London* **15 B2**
Barnet, *London* **15 A2**
Barra Andai, *Karachi* **14 B2**
Barra Funda, *São Paulo* **26 B2**
Barracas, *Buenos Aires* **7 B2**
Barranco, *Lima* **16 B2**
Barreiro, *Lisbon* **14 B2**
Barreto, *Rio de Janeiro* **24 B2**
Bartala, *Calcutta* **8 B1**
Barton Park, *Sydney* **28 B1**
Bartyki, *Warsaw* **31 C2**
Barvikha, *Moscow* **19 B1**
Bastille, Place de la, *Paris* **23 c5**
Basus, *Cairo* **7 A2**
Batanagar, *Calcutta* **8 B1**
Bath Beach, *New York* **21 C1**
Bath I., *Karachi* **14 B2**
Batir, *Jerusalem* **13 B1**
Batok, Bukit, *Singapore* **27 A2**
Battersea, *London* **15 B3**
Battery Park, *New York* **21 f1**
Bauman, *Moscow* **19 B4**
Baumgarten, *Vienna* **31 A1**
Bay Harbour Islands, *Miami* **18 A2**
Bay Ridge, *New York* **21 C1**
Bayonne, *New York* **21 B1**
Bayshore, *San Francisco* **25 B3**
Bayswater, *London* **15 b2**
Bayt Lahm = Bethlehem, *Jerusalem* **13 B2**
Bayview, *San Francisco* **25 B2**
Bāzār, *Tehran* **30 A2**
Beachmont, *Boston* **6 A4**
Beacon Hill, *Hong Kong* **12 A2**
Beato, *Lisbon* **14 A2**
Beaumont, *Dublin* **11 A2**
Beaumonte Heights, *Toronto* **30 A1**
Bebek, *Istanbul* **12 B2**
Běchovice, *Prague* **24 B3**
Beck L., *Chicago* **9 A1**
Beckenham, *London* **15 B3**
Beckton, *London* **15 A4**
Becontree, *London* **15 A4**
Beddington Corner, *London* **15 B3**
Bedford, *Boston* **6 A2**
Bedford Park, *Chicago* **9 C2**
Bedford Park, *New York* **21 A2**
Bedford Stuyvesant, *New York* **21 B2**
Bedford View, *Johannesburg* **13 B2**
Bedok, *Singapore* **27 B3**
Bedok, Res., *Singapore* **27 A3**
Beersel, *Brussels* **6 B1**
Behala, *Calcutta* **8 B1**
Bei Hai, *Beijing* **4 B2**
Beicai, *Shanghai* **27 B2**
Beicang, *Tianjin* **30 A1**
Beihai Park, *Beijing* **4 b2**
Beijing, *Beijing* **4 B1**
Beit Ghur el-Fawqa, *Jerusalem* **13 A1**
Beit Hanina, *Jerusalem* **13 B2**
Beit Iksa, *Jerusalem* **13 B2**
Beit I'nan, *Jerusalem* **13 A1**
Beit Jala, *Jerusalem* **13 B2**
Beit Lekhem = Bethlehem, *Jerusalem* **13 B2**
Beit Nekofa, *Jerusalem* **13 B1**
Beit Sahur, *Jerusalem* **13 B2**
Beit Surik, *Jerusalem* **13 B1**
Beit Zayit, *Jerusalem* **13 B1**
Beitaipingzhuan, *Beijing* **4 B1**
Beitar Ilit, *Jerusalem* **13 B1**
Beitsun, *Canton* **8 B2**
Beitunya, *Jerusalem* **13 A2**
Beixing Jing Park, *Shanghai* **27 B1**
Békásmegyer, *Budapest* **7 A2**
Bekkelaget, *Oslo* **22 A3**
Bel Air, *Los Angeles* **16 B2**
Bela Vista, *São Paulo* **26 B2**
Bélanger, *Montreal* **19 A1**
Belas, *Lisbon* **14 A1**
Belas Artes, Museu Nacionale de, *Rio de Janeiro* **24 b2**
Beleghata, *Calcutta* **8 B2**
Belém, *Lisbon* **14 A1**
Belém, Torre de, *Lisbon* **14 A1**
Belènzinho, *São Paulo* **26 B2**
Belgachiya, *Calcutta* **8 B2**
Belgharia, *Calcutta* **8 B2**
Belgrano, *Buenos Aires* **7 B2**
Belgravia, *London* **15 c3**
Bell, *Los Angeles* **16 C3**
Bell Gardens, *Los Angeles* **16 C4**
Bell Tower, *Beijing* **4 a2**
Bellavista, *Lima* **16 B2**
Bellavista, *Santiago* **26 C2**
Belle Harbor, *New York* **21 C2**
Belle View, *Washington* **32 B2**
Bellevue, Schloss, *Berlin* **5 a2**
Bellingham, *London* **15 B3**
Bellwood, *Chicago* **9 B1**
Belmont, *Boston* **6 A2**
Belmont, *London* **15 A2**
Belmont, *Wellington* **32 B2**
Belmont Harbor, *Chicago* **9 B3**
Belmore, *Sydney* **28 B1**
Belur, *Calcutta* **8 B2**
Belvedere, *Atlanta* **3 B3**
Belvedere, *London* **15 B4**
Belvedere, *San Francisco* **25 A2**
Belyayevo Bogorodskoye, *Moscow* **19 C3**
Bemowo, *Warsaw* **31 B1**
Benaki, Moussío, *Athens* **2 b3**
Bendale, *Toronto* **30 A3**
Bendkhal, *Mumbai* **20 B2**
Benefica, *Rio de Janeiro* **24 B1**
Benfica, *Lisbon* **14 A1**
Benito Juárez, *Mexico City* **18 B2**
Benito Juárez, Aeropuerto Int., *Mexico City* **18 B2**
Bensonhurst, *New York* **21 C2**
Berchem-Sainte-Agathe, *Brussels* **6 A1**
Berg am Laim, *Munich* **20 B2**
Bergenfield, *New York* **21 A2**
Bergham, *Munich* **20 B2**
Bergvliet, *Cape Town* **8 B1**
Beri, *Barcelona* **4 A1**
Berkeley, *San Francisco* **25 A3**
Berlin, *Berlin* **5 A3**
Bermondsey, *London* **15 B3**
Bernabeu, Estadio, *Madrid* **17 B1**
Bernal Heights, *San Francisco* **25 B2**
Berwyn, *Chicago* **9 B2**
Berwyn Heights, *Washington* **32 B4**
Besiktas, *Istanbul* **12 B2**
Besós →, *Barcelona* **4 A2**
Bethesda, *Washington* **32 B3**
Bethlehem, *Jerusalem* **13 B2**
Bethnal Green, *London* **15 A3**
Betor, *Calcutta* **8 B1**
Beurs, *Amsterdam* **2 b2**
Beverley Hills, *Sydney* **28 B1**
Beverley Park, *Sydney* **28 B1**
Beverly, *Chicago* **9 C3**
Beverly Glen, *Los Angeles* **16 B2**
Beverly Hills, *Los Angeles* **16 B2**
Bexley, *London* **15 B4**
Bexley, *Sydney* **28 B1**
Bexleyheath, *London* **15 B4**
Beykoz, *Istanbul* **12 B2**
Beylerbeyi, *Istanbul* **12 B2**
Beyoğlu, *Istanbul* **12 B1**
Bezons, *Paris* **23 A2**
Bezuidenhout Park, *Johannesburg* **13 B2**
Bhadrakali, *Calcutta* **8 A2**
Bhalswa, *Delhi* **10 A2**
Bhambo Khan Qarmati, *Karachi* **14 B2**
Bhatsala, *Calcutta* **8 B1**
Bhawanipur, *Calcutta* **8 B2**
Bhuleshwar, *Mumbai* **20 b2**
Białołeka Dworska, *Warsaw* **31 B2**
Biblioteca Nacional, *Rio de Janeiro* **24 c2**
Bicentennial Park, *Sydney* **28 B1**
Bickley, *London* **15 B4**
Bidu, *Jerusalem* **13 B1**
Bielany, *Warsaw* **31 B1**
Bielawa, *Warsaw* **31 C2**
Biesdorf, *Berlin* **5 A4**
Bièvre →, *Paris* **23 B1**
Bièvres, *Paris* **23 B2**
Bilston, *Edinburgh* **11 B2**
Binacayan, *Manila* **17 C1**
Binondo, *Manila* **17 B1**
Birak el Kiyam, *Cairo* **7 A1**
Birch Cliff, *Toronto* **30 A3**
Birkenstein, *Berlin* **5 A5**
Birkholz, *Berlin* **5 A4**
Birkholzaue, *Berlin* **5 A4**
Birrarrung Park, *Melbourne* **17 A2**
Biscayne Bay, *Miami* **18 B2**
Biscayne Park, *Miami* **18 A2**
Bishop Lavis, *Cape Town* **8 A2**
Bishopscourt, *Cape Town* **8 A1**
Bispebjerg, *Copenhagen* **10 A3**
Biwon Secret Garden, *Seoul* **26 B1**
Björknas, *Stockholm* **28 B3**
Black Cr. →, *Toronto* **30 A2**
Blackfen, *London* **15 B4**
Blackheath, *London* **15 B4**
Blackrock, *Dublin* **11 B2**
Bladensburg, *Washington* **32 B4**
Blair Village, *Atlanta* **3 C2**
Blairgowrie, *Johannesburg* **13 A2**
Blakehurst, *Sydney* **28 B1**
Blakstad, *Oslo* **22 B1**
Blankenburg, *Berlin* **5 A3**
Blankenfelde, *Berlin* **5 A3**
Blizne, *Warsaw* **31 B1**
Bloomsbury, *London* **15 a3**
Błota, *Warsaw* **31 C3**
Blue Island, *Chicago* **9 C2**
Bluebell, *Dublin* **11 B1**
Bluff Hd., *Hong Kong* **12 B2**
Blumberg, *Berlin* **5 A4**
Blunt Pt., *San Francisco* **25 A2**
Blutenberg, *Munich* **20 B1**
Blylaget, *Oslo* **22 B3**
Bo-Kaap Museum, *Cape Town* **8 c2**
Boa Vista, Alto do, *Rio de Janeiro* **24 B1**
Boardwalk, *New York* **21 C3**
Boavista, *Lisbon* **14 A2**
Bobigny, *Paris* **23 A3**
Bocanegra, *Lima* **16 A2**
Boedo, *Buenos Aires* **7 B2**
Bogenhausen, *Munich* **20 B2**
Bogorodskoye, *Moscow* **19 B4**
Bogota, *New York* **21 A1**
Bogstadvatnet, *Oslo* **22 A2**
Bohnsdorf, *Berlin* **5 B4**
Bois-Colombes, *Paris* **23 A2**
Bois-d'Arcy, *Paris* **23 B1**
Boissy-St.-Léger, *Paris* **23 B4**
Boldinasco, *Milan* **18 B1**
Bøler, *Oslo* **22 A4**
Bollate, *Milan* **18 A1**
Bollebeek, *Brussels* **6 A1**
Bollensdorf, *Berlin* **5 A5**
Bollmora, *Stockholm* **28 B3**
Bolshaya-Okhta, *St. Petersburg* **26 B2**
Bolton, *Atlanta* **3 B2**
Bom Retiro, *São Paulo* **26 B2**
Bombay = Mumbai, *Mumbai* **20 B2**
Bondi, *Sydney* **28 B2**
Bondy, *Paris* **23 A3**
Bondy, Forêt de, *Paris* **23 A4**
Bonifacio Monument, *Manila* **17 B1**
Bonneuil-sur-Marne, *Paris* **23 B4**
Bonnington, *Edinburgh* **11 B1**
Bonnyrig and Lasswade, *Edinburgh* **11 B3**
Bonsucesso, *Rio de Janeiro* **24 B1**
Bonteheuwel, *Cape Town* **8 A2**
Boo, *Stockholm* **28 A3**
Booterstown, *Dublin* **11 B2**
Borisovo, *Moscow* **19 C4**
Borle, *Mumbai* **20 A2**
Boronia Park, *Sydney* **28 A1**
Borough Park, *New York* **21 C2**
Bosmont, *Johannesburg* **13 B1**
Bosön, *Stockholm* **28 A3**
Bosporus = Istanbul Boğazi, *Istanbul* **12 B2**
Bostancı, *Istanbul* **12 C2**
Boston Harbor, *Boston* **6 A4**
Botafogo, *Rio de Janeiro* **24 B1**
Botanisk Have, *Copenhagen* **10 b2**
Botany, *Sydney* **28 B2**
Botany B., *Sydney* **28 B2**
Botany Bay Nat. Park, *Sydney* **28 B2**
Botič →, *Prague* **24 B3**
Botica Sete, *Lisbon* **14 A1**
Boucherville, *Montreal* **19 A3**
Boucherville, Îs. de, *Montreal* **19 A3**
Bougival, *Paris* **23 A1**
Boulder Pt., *Hong Kong* **12 B1**
Boulogne, Bois de, *Paris* **23 A2**
Boulogne-Billancourt, *Paris* **23 A2**
Bourg-la-Reine, *Paris* **23 B2**
Bouviers, *Paris* **23 B1**
Bovenkerk, *Amsterdam* **2 B2**
Bovenkerker Polder, *Amsterdam* **2 B2**
Bovisa, *Milan* **18 A2**
Bow, *London* **15 A3**
Bowery, *New York* **21 e2**
Boyacıköy, *Istanbul* **12 B2**
Boyle Heights, *Los Angeles* **16 B3**
Bradbury Building, *Los Angeles* **16 b2**
Braepark, *Edinburgh* **11 B2**
Braid, *Edinburgh* **11 B2**
Bramley, *Johannesburg* **13 A2**
Brandenburger Tor, *Berlin* **5 A3**
Brani, P., *Singapore* **27 B3**
Branik, *Prague* **24 B2**
Brännkyrka, *Stockholm* **28 B2**
Brás, *São Paulo* **26 B2**
Brasilândia, *São Paulo* **26 A1**
Brateyevo, *Moscow* **19 C4**
Bratsevo, *Moscow* **19 A2**
Bray, *Dublin* **11 B3**
Braybrook, *Melbourne* **17 A1**
Brázdim, *Prague* **24 A3**
Breach Candy, *Mumbai* **20 a1**
Breakheart Reservation, *Boston* **6 A3**
Brede, *Copenhagen* **10 A3**
Breeds Pond, *Boston* **6 A4**
Breezy Point, *New York* **21 C2**
Breitenlee, *Vienna* **31 A3**
Breña, *Lima* **16 B2**
Brent, *London* **15 A2**
Brent Res., *London* **15 A2**
Brentford, *London* **15 B2**
Brentwood Park, *Los Angeles* **16 B2**
Brera, *Milan* **18 B2**
Bresso, *Milan* **18 A2**
Brevik, *Stockholm* **28 A3**
Břevnov, *Prague* **24 B2**
Bridgeport, *Chicago* **9 B3**
Bridgetown, *Cape Town* **8 A2**
Bridgeview, *Chicago* **9 C2**
Brighton, *Boston* **6 A3**
Brighton, *Melbourne* **17 B1**
Brighton le Sands, *Sydney* **28 B1**
Brighton Park, *Chicago* **9 C2**
Brightwood, *Washington* **32 B3**
Brigittenau, *Vienna* **31 A2**
Brimbank Park, *Melbourne* **17 A1**
Brisbane, *San Francisco* **25 B2**
British Museum, *London* **15 a3**
Britz, *Berlin* **5 B3**
Brixton, *London* **15 B3**
Broad Sd., *Boston* **6 A4**
Broadmeadows, *Melbourne* **17 A1**
Broadmoor, *San Francisco* **25 B2**
Broadview, *Chicago* **9 B1**
Broadway, *New York* **21 e1**
Brockley, *London* **15 B3**
Bródno, *Warsaw* **31 B2**
Bródnowski, Kanal, *Warsaw* **31 B2**
Broek in Waterland, *Amsterdam* **2 A2**
Bromley, *London* **15 B4**
Bromley Common, *London* **15 B4**
Bromma, *Stockholm* **28 A1**
Bromma flygplats, *Stockholm* **28 A1**
Brompton, *London* **15 c2**
Brøndby Strand, *Copenhagen* **10 B2**
Brøndbyøster, *Copenhagen* **10 B2**
Brøndbyvester, *Copenhagen* **10 B2**
Brondesbury, *London* **15 A2**
Brønnøya, *Oslo* **22 A2**

Brønshøj, *Copenhagen* 10 A2
Bronxville, *New York* 21 A3
Brookfield, *Chicago* 9 C1
Brookhaven, *Atlanta* 3 A2
Brookline, *Boston* 6 B3
Brooklyn, *Cape Town* 8 A1
Brooklyn, *New York* 21 C2
Brooklyn, *Wellington* 32 B1
Brooklyn Bridge, *New York* 21 f2
Brookmont, *Washington* 32 B3
Brossard, *Montreal* 19 B3
Brou-sur-Chantereine, *Paris* 23 A4
Brown, *Toronto* 30 A3
Broyhill Park, *Washington* 32 B2
Brughério, *Milan* 18 A2
Brunswick, *Melbourne* 17 A1
Brush Hill, *Boston* 6 B1
Brussegem, *Brussels* 6 A1
Brussel Nat. Luchthaven, *Brussels* 6 A2
Brussels = Bruxelles, *Brussels* 6 A2
Bruxelles, *Brussels* 6 A2
Bruzzano, *Milan* 18 A2
Bry-sur-Marne, *Paris* 23 A4
Bryanston, *Johannesburg* 13 A1
Bryn, *Oslo* 22 A1
Brzeziny, *Warsaw* 31 B2
Bubeneč, *Prague* 24 B2
Buc, *Paris* 23 B1
Buchenhain, *Munich* 20 B1
Buchholz, *Berlin* 5 A3
Buckhead, *Atlanta* 3 A2
Buckingham Palace, *London* 15 b3
Buckow, *Berlin* 5 B3
Buda, *Budapest* 7 A2
Budafok, *Budapest* 7 B2
Budaörs, *Budapest* 7 B1
Budapest, *Budapest* 7 B2
Budatétény, *Budapest* 7 B2
Budavaripalota, *Budapest* 7 b2
Buddinge, *Copenhagen* 10 A3
Budokan, *Tokyo* 29 a4
Buena Vista, *San Francisco* 25 B2
Buenos Aires, *Buenos Aires* 7 B2
Bufalotta, *Rome* 25 B2
Bugio, *Lisbon* 14 B1
Buiksloot, *Amsterdam* 2 A2
Buitenveldert, *Amsterdam* 2 B2
Buizingen, *Brussels* 6 B1
Bukit Panjang Nature Reserve, *Singapore* 27 A2
Bukit Timah Nature Reserve, *Singapore* 27 A2
Bukum, P., *Singapore* 27 B2
Bûlâq, *Cairo* 7 A2
Bule, *Manila* 17 C2
Bulim, *Singapore* 27 A2
Bullen Park, *Melbourne* 17 A2
Bundoora North, *Melbourne* 17 A2
Bundoora Park, *Melbourne* 17 A2
Bunker I., *Karachi* 14 B1
Bunkyo-Ku, *Tokyo* 29 A3
Bunnefjorden, *Oslo* 22 A3
Buona Vista Park, *Singapore* 27 B2
Burbank, *Chicago* 9 C2
Burbank, *Los Angeles* 16 A3
Burlington, *Boston* 6 A2
Burnham Park, *Chicago* 9 c2
Burnham Park Harbor, *Chicago* 9 B3
Burnhamthorpe, *Toronto* 30 B1
Burnt Oak, *London* 15 A2
Burntisland, *Edinburgh* 11 A2
Burnwynd, *Edinburgh* 11 B1
Burqa, *Jerusalem* 13 A2
Burtus, *Cairo* 7 A1
Burudvatn, *Oslo* 22 A2
Burwood, *Sydney* 28 B1
Bushwick, *New York* 21 B2
Bushy Park, *London* 15 B1
Butantã, *São Paulo* 26 B1
Butcher I., *Mumbai* 20 B2
Butts Corner, *Washington* 32 C2
Büyükdere, *Istanbul* 12 B2
Byculla, *Mumbai* 20 B2
Bygdøy, *Oslo* 22 A3

C

C.N. Tower, *Toronto* 30 B2
Cabaçu de Cima →, *São Paulo* 26 A2
Caballito, *Buenos Aires* 7 B2
Cabin John, *Washington* 32 B2
Cabin John Regional Park, *Washington* 32 A2
Cabinteely, *Dublin* 11 B3
Cabra, *Dublin* 11 A2
Cabuçú de Baixo →, *São Paulo* 26 A1
Cachan, *Paris* 23 B2
Cachenka →, *Moscow* 19 B1
Cachoeira, Rib. da →, *São Paulo* 26 B1
Cacilhas, *Lisbon* 14 A2
Cahuenga Pk., *Los Angeles* 16 B3
Cairo = El Qâhira, *Cairo* 7 A2
Caju, *Rio de Janeiro* 24 B1
Čakovice, *Prague* 24 B3
Calcutta = Kolkata, *Calcutta* 8 B2
California Inst. of Tech., *Los Angeles* 16 B4
California Plaza, *Los Angeles* 16 b1
California State Univ., *Los Angeles* 16 B3
Callao, *Lima* 16 B2
Caloocan, *Manila* 17 B1
Calumet Park, *Chicago* 9 C3
Calumet Sag Channel →, *Chicago* 9 C2
Calumpang, *Manila* 17 B2
Calvairate, *Milan* 18 B2
Camarate, *Lisbon* 14 A2
Camaroes, *Lisbon* 14 A1
Camberwell, *London* 15 B3
Camberwell, *Melbourne* 17 B2
Cambridge, *Boston* 6 A3
Cambridge Res., *Boston* 6 A2
Cambuci, *São Paulo* 26 B2
Camden, *London* 15 A3
Cameron, Mt., *Wellington* 32 B2
Çamlıca, *Istanbul* 12 B2
Camp Springs, *Washington* 32 C4
Campamento, *Madrid* 17 B1
Campbellfield, *Melbourne* 17 A1
Camperdown, *Sydney* 28 B2
Campidoglio, *Rome* 25 c3
Campo, Casa de, *Madrid* 17 B1
Campo F.C. Barcelona, *Barcelona* 4 A1
Campo Grando, *Lisbon* 14 A2
Campo Pequeño, *Lisbon* 14 A2
Campolide, *Lisbon* 14 A2
Camps Bay, *Cape Town* 8 A1
C'an San Joan, *Barcelona* 4 A2
Cañacao B., *Manila* 17 C1
Canarsie, *New York* 21 C2
Cancelleria, Palazzo dei, *Rome* 25 c2
Candiac, *Montreal* 19 B3
Caneças, *Lisbon* 14 A1
Canillas, *Madrid* 17 B2
Canillejas, *Madrid* 17 B2
Canning Town, *London* 15 A4
Canteras de Vallecas, *Madrid* 17 B2
Canterbury, *Melbourne* 17 A2
Canterbury, *Sydney* 28 B1
Canton = Guangzhou, *Canton* 8 B2
Caoheijing, *Shanghai* 27 B1
Capão Redondo, *São Paulo* 26 B1
Caparica, *Lisbon* 14 A2
Caparica, Costa da, *Lisbon* 14 B1
Cape Flats, *Cape Town* 8 B2
Cape Town, *Cape Town* 8 A1
Capitol Heights, *Washington* 32 B4
Capitol Hill, *Washington* 32 B4
Capitolini, Musei, *Rome* 25 c3
Captain Cook Bridge, *Sydney* 28 C1
Captain Cook Landing Place Park, *Sydney* 28 C2
Capuchos, *Lisbon* 14 B1
Carabanchel Alto, *Madrid* 17 B1
Carabanchel Bajo, *Madrid* 17 B1
Carapachay, *Buenos Aires* 7 B1
Caraza, *Buenos Aires* 7 C2
Caridad, *Manila* 17 C1
Carioca, Sa. da, *Rio de Janeiro* 24 B1
Carlstadt, *New York* 21 A1
Carlton, *Melbourne* 17 A1
Carmen de Huechuraba, *Santiago* 26 B1
Carmen de la Legua, *Lima* 16 B2
Carnaxide, *Lisbon* 14 A1
Carnegie, *Melbourne* 17 B2
Carnegie Hall, *New York* 21 c2
Carnide, *Lisbon* 14 A1
Carol City, *Miami* 18 A1
Carrascal, *Santiago* 26 B1
Carrickmines, *Dublin* 11 B3
Carrières-sous-Bois, *Paris* 23 A1
Carrières-sous-Poissy, *Paris* 23 A1
Carrières-sur-Seine, *Paris* 23 A2
Carrigeen Bay, *Dublin* 11 A3
Cartierville, *Montreal* 19 A1
Casa Verde, *São Paulo* 26 A1
Casál Morena, *Rome* 25 C2
Casalotti, *Rome* 25 B1
Cascade Heights, *Atlanta* 3 B2
Castél di Leva, *Rome* 25 C2
Castel Sant'Angelo, *Rome* 25 B1
Castle, *Dublin* 11 c2
Castle, *Edinburgh* 11 b2
Castle of Good Hope, *Cape Town* 8 c3
Castleknock, *Dublin* 11 A1
Castleton Corners, *New York* 21 C1
Catedral Metropolitana, *Mexico City* 18 b3
Catedral Metropolitana, *Rio de Janeiro* 24 c1
Catete, *Rio de Janeiro* 24 B1
Catford, *London* 15 B3
Caulfield, *Melbourne* 17 B2
Causeway Bay, *Hong Kong* 12 c3
Cavite, *Manila* 17 C1
Caxias, *Lisbon* 14 A1
Cebeccı, *Istanbul* 12 B1
Cecchignola, *Rome* 25 C2
Cecilienhof, Schloss, *Berlin* 5 B1
Cedar Grove, *Atlanta* 3 C3
Cempaka Putih, *Jakarta* 13 B2
Çengelköy, *Istanbul* 12 B2
Cengkareng, *Jakarta* 13 A1
Centennial Park, *Sydney* 28 B2
Center Hill, *Atlanta* 3 B2
Centocelle, *Rome* 25 B2
Centraal Station, *Amsterdam* 2 a2
Central Park, *New York* 21 B2
Cerillos, *Santiago* 26 B1
Cerro de la Estrella, *Mexico City* 18 B2
Cerro de los Angeles, *Madrid* 17 C1
Cerro Navia, *Santiago* 26 B1
Certanovka →, *Moscow* 19 C3
Certanovo, *Moscow* 19 C3
Cesano Boscone, *Milan* 18 B1
Cesate, *Milan* 18 A1
Cha Kwo Ling, *Hong Kong* 12 B2
Chacarrita, *Buenos Aires* 7 B2
Chadwell Heath, *London* 15 A4
Chai Chee, *Singapore* 27 B3
Chai Wan, *Hong Kong* 12 B2
Chai Wan Kok, *Hong Kong* 12 A1
Chaillot, Palais de, *Paris* 23 b2
Chakdaha, *Calcutta* 8 C1
Chamartin, *Madrid* 17 B1
Chamberi, *Madrid* 17 B1
Chambourcy, *Paris* 23 A1
Champ de Mars, Parc du, *Paris* 23 c2
Champigny-sur-Marne, *Paris* 23 B4
Champlain, Pont, *Montreal* 19 B2
Champs Elysées, Avenue des, *Paris* 23 b2
Champs-sur-Marne, *Paris* 23 A4
Chamrail, *Calcutta* 8 B1
Chamshil, *Seoul* 26 B2
Chamwŏn, *Seoul* 26 B2
Chanakyapuri, *Delhi* 10 B2
Chanditala, *Calcutta* 8 A1
Changfeng Park, *Shanghai* 27 B1
Changi, *Singapore* 27 A3
Changi Int. Airport, *Singapore* 27 A3
Changning, *Shanghai* 27 B1
Chantereine, *Paris* 23 A4
Chantian, *Canton* 8 A2
Chao Phraya →, *Bangkok* 3 B2
Chaoyang, *Beijing* 4 B2
Chaoyangmen, *Beijing* 4 B2
Chapelizod, *Dublin* 11 A1
Chapultepec, Bosque de, *Mexico City* 18 B1
Chapultepec, Castillo de, *Mexico City* 18 B1
Charenton-le-Pont, *Paris* 23 B3
Charing Cross, *London* 15 b4
Charleroi, Kanal de →, *Brussels* 6 B1
Charles Bridge, *Prague* 24 b1
Charles Square, *Prague* 24 c1
Charlestown, *Boston* 6 A3
Charlottenburg, *Berlin* 5 A2
Charlottenburg, Schloss, *Berlin* 5 A2
Charlottenlund, *Copenhagen* 10 A3
Charlton, *London* 15 B4
Charneca, *Lisbon* 14 A2
Charneca, *Lisbon* 14 B1
Châteaufort, *Paris* 23 B1
Châtenay-Malabry, *Paris* 23 B2
Chatham, *Chicago* 9 C3
Châtillon, *Paris* 23 B2
Chatou, *Paris* 23 A1
Chatpur, *Calcutta* 8 B2
Chatswood, *Sydney* 28 A2
Chatuchak, *Bangkok* 3 B2
Chatuchak Park, *Bangkok* 3 B2
Chauki, *Karachi* 14 A1
Chavarria, *Lima* 16 B2
Chaville, *Paris* 23 B2
Chayang, *Seoul* 26 B2
Chegi, *Seoul* 26 B2
Chelles, *Paris* 23 A4
Chelles, Canal de, *Paris* 23 A4
Chells-le-Pin, Aérodrome, *Paris* 23 A4
Chelsea, *Boston* 6 A3
Chelsea, *London* 15 B2
Chelsea, *New York* 21 c1
Chembur, *Mumbai* 20 A2
Chennevières-sur-Marne, *Paris* 23 B4
Cheops, *Cairo* 7 B1
Cherepkovo, *Moscow* 19 B2
Chernyovo, *Moscow* 19 A1
Cheryomushki, *Moscow* 19 B3
Chestnut Hill, *Boston* 6 B2
Cheung Sha Wan, *Hong Kong* 12 A1
Cheverly, *Washington* 32 B4
Chevilly-Larue, *Paris* 23 B3
Chevry-Cossigny, *Paris* 23 B4
Chevy Chase, *Washington* 32 B3
Chevy Chase View, *Washington* 32 A3
Chia Keng, *Singapore* 27 A3
Chiaravalle Milanese, *Milan* 18 B2
Chicago, *Chicago* 9 B3
Chicago Harbor, *Chicago* 9 B3
Chicago Lawn, *Chicago* 9 C2
Chicago-Midway Airport, *Chicago* 9 C2
Chicago-O'Hare Int. Airport, *Chicago* 9 B1
Chicago Ridge, *Chicago* 9 C2
Chicago Sanitary and Ship Canal, *Chicago* 9 C2
Chienzui, *Canton* 8 A3
Chik Sha, *Hong Kong* 12 B2
Child's Hill, *London* 15 A2
Chilla Saroda, *Delhi* 10 B2
Chillum, *Washington* 32 B4
Chilly-Mazarin, *Paris* 23 B2
Chinatown, *Los Angeles* 16 a3
Chinatown, *New York* 21 e2
Chinatown, *San Francisco* 25 b2
Chinatown, *Singapore* 27 c2
Chingupota, *Calcutta* 8 C1
Chislehurst, *London* 15 B4
Chiswick, *London* 15 B2
Chiswick House, *London* 15 B2
Chitose, *Tokyo* 29 B2
Chitralada Palace, *Bangkok* 3 B2
Chiyoda-Ku, *Tokyo* 29 b4
Chkalova, *Moscow* 19 C5
Choa Chu Kang, *Singapore* 27 A2
Choboty, *Moscow* 19 C2
Chodov u Prahy, *Prague* 24 B3
Chōfu, *Tokyo* 29 B2
Choisy-le-Roi, *Paris* 23 B3
Cholupice, *Prague* 24 C2
Chom Thong, *Bangkok* 3 B1
Chong Pang, *Singapore* 27 A2
Ch'ŏngdam, *Seoul* 26 B2
Chongmyo Royal Shrine, *Seoul* 26 B1
Chongno, *Seoul* 26 B1
Chongwen, *Beijing* 4 B2
Chŏnho, *Seoul* 26 B2
Chopin, Muzeum, *Warsaw* 31 b2
Chornaya →, *Moscow* 19 B6
Chorrillos, *Lima* 16 C2
Chowpatty Beach, *Mumbai* 20 b1
Christian Quarter, *Jerusalem* 13 b3
Christiansborg, *Copenhagen* 10 c2
Christianshavn, *Copenhagen* 10 A3
Chrysler Building, *New York* 21 c2
Chrzanów, *Warsaw* 31 B1
Chuen Lung, *Hong Kong* 12 A1
Chuk Kok, *Hong Kong* 12 A2
Chulalongkom Univ., *Bangkok* 3 B2
Chung, *Seoul* 26 B1
Chunghwa, *Seoul* 26 B2
Chungnangch'on →, *Seoul* 26 B1
Chūō-Ku, *Tokyo* 29 b5
Church End, *London* 15 A2
Churchtown, *Dublin* 11 B2
Ciampino, *Rome* 25 C2
Ciampino, Aeroporto di, *Rome* 25 C2
Cicero, *Chicago* 9 B2
Cilandak, *Jakarta* 13 B1
Cilincing, *Jakarta* 13 A2
Ciliwung →, *Jakarta* 13 B2
Čimice, *Prague* 24 B2
Cinecittà, *Rome* 25 B2
Cinisello Bálsamo, *Milan* 18 A2
Cinkota, *Budapest* 7 A3
Cipete, *Jakarta* 13 B1
Citadella, *Budapest* 7 c2
Citta degli Studi, *Milan* 18 B2
Città del Vaticano, *Rome* 25 B1
City, *London* 15 A3
City Hall, *New York* 21 e1
Ciudad Deportiva, *Mexico City* 18 B2
Ciudad Fin de Semana, *Madrid* 17 B2
Ciudad General Belgrano, *Buenos Aires* 7 C1
Ciudad Lineál, *Madrid* 17 B2
Ciudad Satélite, *Mexico City* 18 A1
Ciudad Universitaria, *Buenos Aires* 7 B2
Ciudad Universitaria, *Mexico City* 18 C1
Ciutadella, Parc de la, *Barcelona* 4 b3
Civic Center, *Los Angeles* 16 b2
Clamart, *Paris* 23 B2
Clapham, *London* 15 B3
Clapton, *London* 15 A3
Claremont, *Cape Town* 8 A1
Clayhall, *London* 15 A4
Clerkenwell, *London* 15 a4
Clermiston, *Edinburgh* 11 B2
Clichy, *Paris* 23 A2
Clichy-sous-Bois, *Paris* 23 A4
Cliffside, *Toronto* 30 A3
Cliffside Park, *New York* 21 B2
Clifton, *Boston* 6 A4
Clifton, *Karachi* 14 B2
Clifton, *New York* 21 C1
Cliftondale, *Boston* 6 A3
Cloghran, *Dublin* 11 A2
Clonskeagh, *Dublin* 11 B2
Clontarf, *Dublin* 11 A2
Clontarf, *Sydney* 28 A2
Clovelly, *Sydney* 28 B2
Cobras, I. das, *Rio de Janeiro* 24 B2
Coburg, *Melbourne* 17 A1
Cochituate, *Boston* 6 A1
Cochituate, L., *Boston* 6 B1
Cocotá, *Rio de Janeiro* 24 A1
Cœuilly, *Paris* 23 B4
Coina, *Lisbon* 14 B2
Coit Tower, *San Francisco* 25 a2
Coker, *Lagos* 14 B2
Colaba, *Mumbai* 20 B1
Colaba Pt., *Mumbai* 20 B1
Colegiales, *Buenos Aires* 7 B2
Colindale, *London* 15 A2
Colinton, *Edinburgh* 11 B2
College Park, *Atlanta* 3 C2
College Park, *Washington* 32 B4
College Point, *New York* 21 B2
Collégien, *Paris* 23 A4
Collier Row, *London* 15 A4
Colliers Wood, *London* 15 B2
Colma, *San Francisco* 25 B2
Colney Hatch, *London* 15 A3
Cologno Monzese, *Milan* 18 A2
Colombes, *Paris* 23 A2
Colón, Monumente, *Barcelona* 4 c3
Colon, Plaza de, *Madrid* 17 a3
Colonia Güell, *Barcelona* 4 A1
Colonial Knob, *Wellington* 32 A1
Colosseo, *Rome* 25 c3
Columbus Circus, *New York* 21 b2
Combault, *Paris* 23 B4
Comércio, Praça do, *Lisbon* 14 A2
Commerce, *Los Angeles* 16 B4
Como, *Sydney* 28 C1
Company's Gardens, *Cape Town* 8 c2
Conceição, I. da, *Rio de Janeiro* 24 B2
Concertgebouw, *Amsterdam* 2 c1
Conchali, *Santiago* 26 B2
Concord, *Boston* 6 A1
Concord, *Sydney* 28 B1
Concord, *Toronto* 30 A2
Concorde, Place de la, *Paris* 23 b3
Concorezzo, *Milan* 18 A2
Coney Island, *New York* 21 C2
Congonhas, Aéroporto, *São Paulo* 26 B2
Connaught Place, *Delhi* 10 B2
Conservatori, Palazzo dei, *Rome* 25 c3
Consolação, *São Paulo* 26 B2
Constantia, *Cape Town* 8 B1
Constitución, *Buenos Aires* 7 B2
Constitution, *Atlanta* 3 B2
Convention and Exhibition Centre, *Hong Kong* 12 b2
Coogee, *Sydney* 28 B2
Cook Str., *Wellington* 32 A1
Cooksville, *Toronto* 30 B1
Coolock, *Dublin* 11 A2
Copacabana, *Rio de Janeiro* 24 B1
Copenhagen = København, *Copenhagen* 10 A2
Coral Gables, *Miami* 18 B2
Coral Hills, *Washington* 32 B4
Corcovado, Morro do, *Rio de Janeiro* 24 B1
Corduff, *Dublin* 11 A1
Cormano, *Milan* 18 A2
Cornaredo, *Milan* 18 A1
Córsico, *Milan* 18 B1
Corsini, Palazzo, *Rome* 25 c1
Corviale, *Rome* 25 B1
Coslada, *Madrid* 17 B2
Cossigny, *Paris* 23 B4
Cossipore, *Calcutta* 8 B2
Costantino, Arco di, *Rome* 25 c3
Costorphine, *Edinburgh* 11 B2
Cotao, *Lisbon* 14 A1
Côte St.-Luc, *Montreal* 19 B2
Cotunduba, I. de, *Rio de Janeiro* 24 B2
Coubron, *Paris* 23 A4
Countryside, *Chicago* 9 C1
Courbevoie, *Paris* 23 A2
Courtry, *Paris* 23 A4
Covent Garden, *London* 15 b4
Cowgate, *Edinburgh* 11 b3
Cowley, *London* 15 A1
Coyoacán, *Mexico City* 18 B2
Cragin, *Chicago* 9 B2
Craighall Park, *Johannesburg* 13 A2
Craiglockhart, *Edinburgh* 11 B2
Craigmillar, *Edinburgh* 11 B3
Cramond, *Edinburgh* 11 B2
Cramond Bridge, *Edinburgh* 11 B1
Cramond I., *Edinburgh* 11 B2
Cranford, *London* 15 B1
Crawford, *Cape Town* 8 A2
Crayford, *London* 15 B5
Creekmouth, *London* 15 A4
Crescenzago, *Milan* 18 A2
Cressely, *Paris* 23 B1
Cresskill, *New York* 21 A2
Creteil, *Paris* 23 B3
Cricklewood, *London* 15 A2
Cristo Redentor, Estatua do, *Rio de Janeiro* 24 B1
Crockenhill, *London* 15 B4
Croissy-Beaubourg, *Paris* 23 B4
Croissy-sur-Seine, *Paris* 23 A1
Crosby, *Johannesburg* 13 B1
Crosne, *Paris* 23 B3
Cross I., *Mumbai* 20 B2
Crouch End, *London* 15 A3
Crown Mine, *Johannesburg* 13 B1
Crows Nest, *Sydney* 28 A2
Croydon, *London* 15 B3
Croydon Park, *Sydney* 28 B1
Cruagh Mt., *Dublin* 11 B2
Crumlin, *Dublin* 11 B2
Cruz de Pau, *Lisbon* 14 B2
Crystal Palace, *London* 15 B3
Csepel, *Budapest* 7 B2
Csepelsziget, *Budapest* 7 B2
Csillaghegy, *Budapest* 7 A2
Csillagtelep, *Budapest* 7 B2
Csömör, *Budapest* 7 A3
Csömöri-patak →, *Budapest* 7 A3
Cuatro Vientos, *Madrid* 17 B1
Cuauhtémoc, *Mexico City* 18 B2
Cubao, *Manila* 17 B2
Çubuklu, *Istanbul* 12 B2
Cudahy, *Los Angeles* 16 C3
Cuicuilco, Pirámido de, *Mexico City* 18 C1
Culver City, *Los Angeles* 16 B2
Cumballa Hill, *Mumbai* 20 a1
Cumbres de Vallecas, *Madrid* 17 B2
Cupecé, *São Paulo* 26 B1
Currie, *Edinburgh* 11 B2
Cusago, *Milan* 18 B1
Cusano Milanino, *Milan* 18 A2
Custom House, *Dublin* 11 b3
Çuvuşabaşi →, *Istanbul* 12 B1
Czernriaków, *Warsaw* 31 B2
Czyste, *Warsaw* 31 B1

D

D.F. Malan Airport, *Cape Town* 8 A2
Da Moóca →, *São Paulo* 26 B2
Da Yunhe →, *Tianjin* 30 A1
Dabizhuang, *Tianjin* 30 A2
Ďablice, *Prague* 24 B2
Dąbrowa, *Warsaw* 31 B1
Dachang, *Shanghai* 27 B1
Dachang Airfield, *Shanghai* 27 B1
Dachau-Ost, *Munich* 20 A1
Dachauer Moos, *Munich* 20 A1
Dadar, *Mumbai* 20 A1
Dagenham, *London* 15 A4
Daglfing, *Munich* 20 B2
Daheisha, *Jerusalem* 13 B2
Dahlem, *Berlin* 5 B2
Dahlwitz-Hoppegarten, *Berlin* 5 A5
Dahongmen, *Beijing* 4 C2
Daitō, *Osaka* 22 A4
Dajiaoting, *Beijing* 4 B2
Dakhnoye, *St. Petersburg* 26 C1
Dalejsky potok →, *Prague* 24 B2
Dalgety Bay, *Edinburgh* 11 A1
Dalkeith, *Edinburgh* 11 B3
Dalkey, *Dublin* 11 B3
Dalkey Island, *Dublin* 11 B3
Dallgow, *Berlin* 5 A1
Dalmeny, *Edinburgh* 11 B1
Dalston, *London* 15 A3
Daly City, *San Francisco* 25 B2
Dam, *Amsterdam* 2 b2
Dam Rak, *Amsterdam* 2 a2
Damaia, *Lisbon* 14 A1
Dämeritzsee, *Berlin* 5 B5
Dan Ryan Woods, *Chicago* 9 C2
Danderhall, *Edinburgh* 11 B3
Danderyd, *Stockholm* 28 A2
Danforth, *Toronto* 30 A3
Darakeh, *Tehran* 30 A2
Darband, *Tehran* 30 A2
Darling Harbour, *Sydney* 28 b1
Darling Point, *Sydney* 28 B2
Darndale, *Dublin* 11 A2
Darrūs, *Tehran* 30 A2
Dartford, *London* 15 B5
Darya Ganj, *Delhi* 1 a3
Dashi, *Canton* 8 B2
Datansha, *Canton* 8 B2
Datun, *Beijing* 4 B2
Daulatpur, *Delhi* 10 A1
David's Citadel, *Jerusalem* 13 b3
David's Tomb, *Jerusalem* 13 b3
Davidson, Mt., *San Francisco* 25 B2
Davidson's Mains, *Edinburgh* 11 B2
Dāvūdiyeh, *Tehran* 30 A2
Davydkovo, *Moscow* 19 B2
Dawidy, *Warsaw* 31 C1
Days Bay, *Wellington* 32 B2
Dazhigu, *Tianjin* 30 B2
De Waag, *Amsterdam* 2 b2
Decatur, *Atlanta* 3 B3
Dedham, *Boston* 6 B2
Deer I., *Boston* 6 A4
Degunino, *Moscow* 19 A3
Deir Dibwan, *Jerusalem* 13 A2
Deir Ibzi'e, *Jerusalem* 13 A1
Dejvice, *Prague* 24 B2
Dekabristov, Ostrov, *St. Petersburg* 26 B1
Delhi, *Delhi* 10 B2
Delhi Gate, *Delhi* 1 b3
Demarest, *New York* 21 A2
Den Ilp, *Amsterdam* 2 A2
Denistone Heights, *Sydney* 28 A1
Dentonia Park, *Toronto* 30 A3
Deptford, *London* 15 B3
Deputati, Camera dei, *Rome* 25 b2
Des Plaines, *Chicago* 9 A1
Des Plaines →, *Chicago* 9 B1
Deshengmen, *Beijing* 4 B2
Deutsch-Wagram, *Vienna* 31 A3
Deutsche Oper, *Berlin* 5 A2
Deutscher Museum, *Munich* 20 B2
Devil's Peak, *Cape Town* 8 A1
Dháfni, *Athens* 2 B2
Dhakuria, *Calcutta* 8 B2
Dhamarakia, *Athens* 2 B1
Dharavi, *Mumbai* 20 A2
Dhrapersón, *Athens* 2 B1
Diadema, *São Paulo* 26 C2
Diegen, *Brussels* 6 A2
Diemen, *Amsterdam* 2 A2
Diepkloof, *Johannesburg* 13 B1
Dieprivier, *Cape Town* 8 B1
Difficult Run →, *Washington* 32 B2
Dilbeek, *Brussels* 6 A1
Dinzigu, *Tianjin* 30 A1
Dirnismaning, *Munich* 20 A2
District Heights, *Washington* 32 B4
Ditan Park, *Beijing* 4 a2
Diyāla →, *Baghdad* 3 B3
Djursholm, *Stockholm* 28 A2
Döberitz, *Berlin* 5 A1
Döbling, *Vienna* 31 A2
Docklands, *London* 15 A3
Dodder, R. →, *Dublin* 11 B1
Dodger Stadium, *Los Angeles* 16 B3
Dolgoe Ozero, *St. Petersburg* 26 A1
Doll Museum, *Delhi* 1 b3
Dollis Hill, *London* 15 A2
Dollymount, *Dublin* 11 A2
Dolni, *Prague* 24 B3
Dolni Chabry, *Prague* 24 B2
Dolni Počernice, *Prague* 24 B3
Dolphins Barn, *Dublin* 11 B2
Dom Pedro II, Parque, *São Paulo* 26 B2
Domain, The, *Sydney* 28 b2
Dome of the Rock, *Jerusalem* 13 b3
Don Mills, *Toronto* 30 A2
Don Muang Int. Airport, *Bangkok* 3 A2
Donaghmede, *Dublin* 11 A3
Donau-Oder Kanal, *Vienna* 31 A3
Donaufeld, *Vienna* 31 A2
Donaupark, *Vienna* 31 A2
Donaustadt, *Vienna* 31 A2
Dongan Hills, *New York* 21 C1
Dongcheng, *Beijing* 4 B2
Donggou, *Shanghai* 27 B2
Dongjiao, *Canton* 8 B2
Dongjuzi, *Tianjin* 30 B2
Dongmenwai, *Tianjin* 30 B2
Dongri, *Mumbai* 20 B2
Dongshanhu Park, *Canton* 8 B2
Dongzhimen, *Beijing* 4 B2
Donnybrook, *Dublin* 11 B2
Doornfontein, *Johannesburg* 13 B2
Dorchester, *Boston* 6 B3
Dorchester B., *Boston* 6 B3
Dornach, *Munich* 20 B3
Dorval, Aéroport de, *Montreal* 19 B1
Dos Couros →, *São Paulo* 26 C2
Dos Moninos →, *São Paulo* 26 C2
Douglas Park, *Chicago* 9 B2
Dover Heights, *Sydney* 28 B2
Dowlatābād, *Tehran* 30 B2
Downey, *Los Angeles* 16 C4
Downsview, *Toronto* 30 A1
Dragør, *Copenhagen* 10 B3
Drancy, *Paris* 23 A3
Dranesville, *Washington* 32 A1
Dreilinden, *Berlin* 5 B2
Drewnica, *Warsaw* 31 B2
Drigh Road, *Karachi* 14 A2
Drimnagh, *Dublin* 11 B2
Drogenbos, *Brussels* 6 B1
Druid Hills, *Atlanta* 3 B2
Drum Towwer, *Beijing* 4 a2
Drumcondra, *Dublin* 11 A2
Drummoyne, *Sydney* 28 B1
Drylaw, *Edinburgh* 11 B2
Dubeč, *Prague* 24 B3
Dublin, *Dublin* 11 A2
Dublin Airport, *Dublin* 11 A2
Dublin Bay, *Dublin* 11 B3
Dublin Harbour, *Dublin* 11 A2
Duddingston, *Edinburgh* 11 B3
Dugnano, *Milan* 18 A2
Dūlāb, *Tehran* 30 B2
Dulwich, *London* 15 B3
Dum Dum, *Calcutta* 8 B2
Dum Dum Int. Airport, *Calcutta* 8 B2
Dumont, *New York* 21 A2
Dún Laoghaire, *Dublin* 11 B3
Duna →, *Budapest* 7 A2
Duncan Dock, *Cape Town* 8 a3
Dundrum, *Dublin* 11 B2
Dunearn, *Singapore* 27 B2
Dunfermline, *Edinburgh* 11 A1
Dunn Loring, *Washington* 32 B2
Dunning, *Chicago* 9 B2
Dunvegan, *Johannesburg* 13 A2
Duomo, *Milan* 18 B2
Duque de Caxias, *Rio de Janeiro* 24 A1
Dusit, *Bangkok* 3 B2
Dusit Zoo, *Bangkok* 3 a2
Duvernay, *Montreal* 19 A1
Dworp, *Brussels* 6 B1
Dyakovo, *Moscow* 19 B3
Dzerzhinskiy, *Moscow* 19 C5
Dzerzhinskiy, *Moscow* 19 B3
Dzerzhinskiy Park, *Moscow* 19 B3

E

Eagle Rock, *Los Angeles* 16 B3
Ealing, *London* 15 A2
Earl's Court, *London* 15 c1
Earlsfield, *London* 15 B2
Earlwood, *Sydney* 28 B1
East Acton, *Boston* 6 A1
East Arlington, *Boston* 6 A3
East Arlington, *Washington* 32 B3
East Bedfont, *London* 15 B1
East Boston, *Boston* 6 A3
East Don →, *Toronto* 30 A2
East Elmhurst, *New York* 21 B2
East Finchley, *London* 15 A2
East Ham, *London* 15 A4
East Humber →, *Toronto* 30 A1
East Lamma Channel, *Hong Kong* 12 B1
East Lexington, *Boston* 6 A2
East Los Angeles, *Los Angeles* 16 B3
East Molesey, *London* 15 B1
East New York, *New York* 21 B2
East Pines, *Washington* 32 B4
East Point, *Atlanta* 3 B2
East Potomac Park, *Washington* 32 B3
East Pt., *Boston* 6 A4
East River →, *New York* 21 B2
East Rutherford, *New York* 21 A1
East Sheen, *London* 15 B2
East Village, *New York* 21 e2
East Wickham, *London* 15 B4
East York, *Toronto* 30 A2
Eastbourne, *Wellington* 32 B2
Eastcote, *London* 15 A1
Easter Howgate, *Edinburgh* 11 B2
Eastwood, *Sydney* 28 A1
Ebara, *Tokyo* 29 B3
Ebisu, *Tokyo* 29 B3
Ebute-Ikorodu, *Lagos* 14 A2
Ebute-Metta, *Lagos* 14 B2
Echo Park, *Los Angeles* 16 a1
Eda, *Tokyo* 29 B2
Edendale, *Johannesburg* 13 A2
Edenmore, *Dublin* 11 A2
Edgars Cr. →, *Melbourne* 17 A1
Edgeley, *Toronto* 30 A1
Edgemar, *San Francisco* 25 C2
Edinburgh, *Edinburgh* 11 B2
Edison Park, *Chicago* 9 A2
Edmondston, *Washington* 32 B4
Edmondstown, *Dublin* 11 B2
Edo →, *Tokyo* 29 B4
Edogawa-Ku, *Tokyo* 29 A4
Edsberg, *Stockholm* 28 A1
Edwards L., *Melbourne* 17 A1
Eiche, *Berlin* 5 A4
Eiche Sud, *Berlin* 5 A4
Eiffel, Tour, *Paris* 23 A2
Ein Arik, *Jerusalem* 13 A1
Ein Naquba, *Jerusalem* 13 B1
Ein Rafa, *Jerusalem* 13 B1
Eizariya, *Jerusalem* 13 B2
Ejby, *Copenhagen* 10 A2
Ejigbo, *Lagos* 14 A1
Ekeberg, *Oslo* 22 A3
Eknäs, *Stockholm* 28 B3
El 'Abbasiya, *Cairo* 7 A2
El Agustino, *Lima* 16 B2
El Baragil, *Cairo* 7 A1
El Basâlîn, *Cairo* 7 B2
El-Bira, *Jerusalem* 13 A2
El Bosque, *Santiago* 26 C2
El Carmen, *Santiago* 26 B1
El Cortijo, *Santiago* 26 B1
El Duqqi, *Cairo* 7 A2
El Encinar de los Reyes, *Madrid* 17 A2
El Ghurîya, *Cairo* 7 A2
El Gîza, *Cairo* 7 A2
El-Khadr, *Jerusalem* 13 B1
El Khalîfa, *Cairo* 7 A2
El Kôm el Ahmar, *Cairo* 7 A2
El Ma'âdi, *Cairo* 7 B2
El Matarîya, *Cairo* 7 A2
El Mohandessin, *Cairo* 7 A2
El Monte, *Los Angeles* 16 B4
El Mûskî, *Cairo* 7 A2
El Pardo, *Madrid* 17 A1
El Portal, *Miami* 18 A2
El Prat de Llobregat, *Barcelona* 4 B1
El Pueblo de L.A. Historic Park, *Los Angeles* 16 b2
El Qâhira, *Cairo* 7 A2
El Qubba, *Cairo* 7 A2
El Reloj, *Mexico City* 18 C2
El Retiro, *Madrid* 17 B1
El Salto, *Santiago* 26 B2
El Sereno, *Los Angeles* 16 B3
El Talibîya, *Cairo* 7 B2
El Vergel, *Mexico City* 18 C2
El Wâhli, *Cairo* 7 A2
El Zamâlik, *Cairo* 7 A2
El Zeitûn, *Cairo* 7 A2
Elephanta Caves, *Mumbai* 20 B2
Elephanta I., *Mumbai* 20 B2
Ellboda, *Stockholm* 28 A3
Ellinikón, *Athens* 2 B2
Ellis I., *New York* 21 B1
Elm Park, *London* 15 A5
Elmers End, *London* 15 B3
Elmhurst, *New York* 21 B2
Elmstead, *London* 15 B4
Elmwood Park, *Chicago* 9 B2
Elmwood Park, *New York* 21 A1
Elsdon, *Wellington* 32 A1
Elsiesrivier, *Cape Town* 8 A2
Elsternwick, *Melbourne* 17 B2
Eltham, *London* 15 B4
Elwood, *Melbourne* 17 B1
Élysée, *Paris* 23 A2
Elysian Park, *Los Angeles* 16 a3
Embajadores, *Madrid* 17 c2
Embarcadero Center, *San Francisco* 25 b3
Emek Refa'im, *Jerusalem* 13 c2
Émerainville, *Paris* 23 B4
Emeryville, *San Francisco* 25 A3
Eminönü, *Istanbul* 12 B1
Emmarentia, *Johannesburg* 13 A2
Empire State Building, *New York* 21 c2
Encantado, *Rio de Janeiro* 24 B1
Encino, *Los Angeles* 16 B2
Encino Res., *Los Angeles* 16 B1
Enebyberg, *Stockholm* 28 A1
Enfield, *Sydney* 28 B1
Engenho, I. do, *Rio de Janeiro* 24 B2
Englewood, *Chicago* 9 C3
Englewood, *New York* 21 A2
Englewood Cliffs, *New York* 21 A2
Enmore, *Sydney* 28 B2
Enskede, *Stockholm* 28 B2
Entrevias, *Madrid* 17 B1
Epping, *Sydney* 28 A1
Erawan Shrine, *Bangkok* 3 c3
Eregun, *Lagos* 14 A2
Erenköy, *Istanbul* 12 C2
Erith, *London* 15 B5
Erlaa, *Vienna* 31 B1
Ermington, *Sydney* 28 A1
Ermita, *Manila* 17 B1
Ershatou, *Canton* 8 B2
Erskineville, *Sydney* 28 B2
Erunkan, *Lagos* 14 A2
Erzsébet-Telep, *Budapest* 7 B3
Eschenried, *Munich* 20 A1
Esenler, *Istanbul* 12 B1
Esher, *London* 15 B1
Eskbank, *Edinburgh* 11 B3
Esperanza, *Mexico City* 18 c3
Esplanade Park, *Singapore* 27 c3
Esplugas, *Barcelona* 4 A1
Esposizione Univ. di Roma (E.U.R.), *Rome* 25 C1
Essendon, *Melbourne* 17 A1
Essendon Airport, *Melbourne* 17 A1
Essingen, *Stockholm* 28 B1
Essling, *Vienna* 31 A3
Est, Gare de l', *Paris* 23 a5
Estadio Maracanã, *Rio de Janeiro* 24 B1
Estado, Parque do, *São Paulo* 26 B2
Estefânia, *Lisbon* 14 a2
Estrela, Basilica da, *Lisbon* 14 A2
Ethnikó Arheologiko Moussío, *Athens* 2 a2
Etobicoke, *Toronto* 30 B1
Etobicoke Cr. →, *Toronto* 30 B1
Etterbeek, *Brussels* 6 B2
Euston, *London* 15 a3
Evanston, *Chicago* 9 A2
Even Sapir, *Jerusalem* 13 B1
Evere, *Brussels* 6 A2
Everett, *Boston* 6 A3
Evergreen Park, *Chicago* 9 C2
Evīn, *Tehran* 30 A2
Évzonos, *Athens* 2 B2
Ewu, *Lagos* 14 A1
Exchange Square, *Hong Kong* 12 c1
Exposições, Palácio das, *Rio de Janeiro* 24 B1
Eyüp, *Istanbul* 12 B1

F

Fabour, Mt., *Singapore* 27 B2
Faechi, *Seoul* 26 B2
Fælledparken, *Copenhagen* 10 A3
Fågelön, *Stockholm* 28 B1
Fagersjö, *Stockholm* 28 B2
Fair Lawn, *New York* 21 A1
Fairfax, *Washington* 32 B2
Fairfax Station, *Washington* 32 C2
Fairhaven Bay, *Boston* 6 A1
Fairhaven Hill, *Boston* 6 A1
Fairland, *Johannesburg* 13 A1
Fairmilehead, *Edinburgh* 11 B2
Fairmount Heights, *Washington* 32 B4
Fairport, *Toronto* 30 A4
Fairview, *New York* 21 B2
Falenty, *Warsaw* 31 C1
Fálirou, Órmos, *Athens* 2 B2
Falkenburg, *Berlin* 5 A4
Falkenhagen, *Berlin* 5 A1
Falkensee, *Berlin* 5 A1
Falls Church, *Washington* 32 B2
Falomo, *Lagos* 14 B2
False Bay, *Cape Town* 8 B2
Fangcun, *Canton* 8 B2
Faraḥābād, *Tehran* 30 A2
Farforovskaya, *St. Petersburg* 26 B2
Farningham, *London* 15 B5
Farrar Pond, *Boston* 6 A1
Farsta, *Stockholm* 28 B2
Fasanerie-Nord, *Munich* 20 A2
Fasangarten, *Munich* 20 B2
Fasting Palace, *Beijing* 4 c2
Fatih, *Istanbul* 12 B1
Favoriten, *Vienna* 31 B2

L

M

S

T

U

V

W

X

Y

Z

– Mt Everest, China/Nepal –

Part of the Himalaya range, Mt Everest – the highest mountain in the world at 8,850 m (29,035 ft) – lies just north of centre in this image. The two arms of the Rongbuk glacier flow away from the triangular shaded north wall, with the Kangshung glacier due east. The international boundary between China and Nepal bisects the peak, which was first climbed on 28 May 1953.

WORLD MAPS

SETTLEMENTS

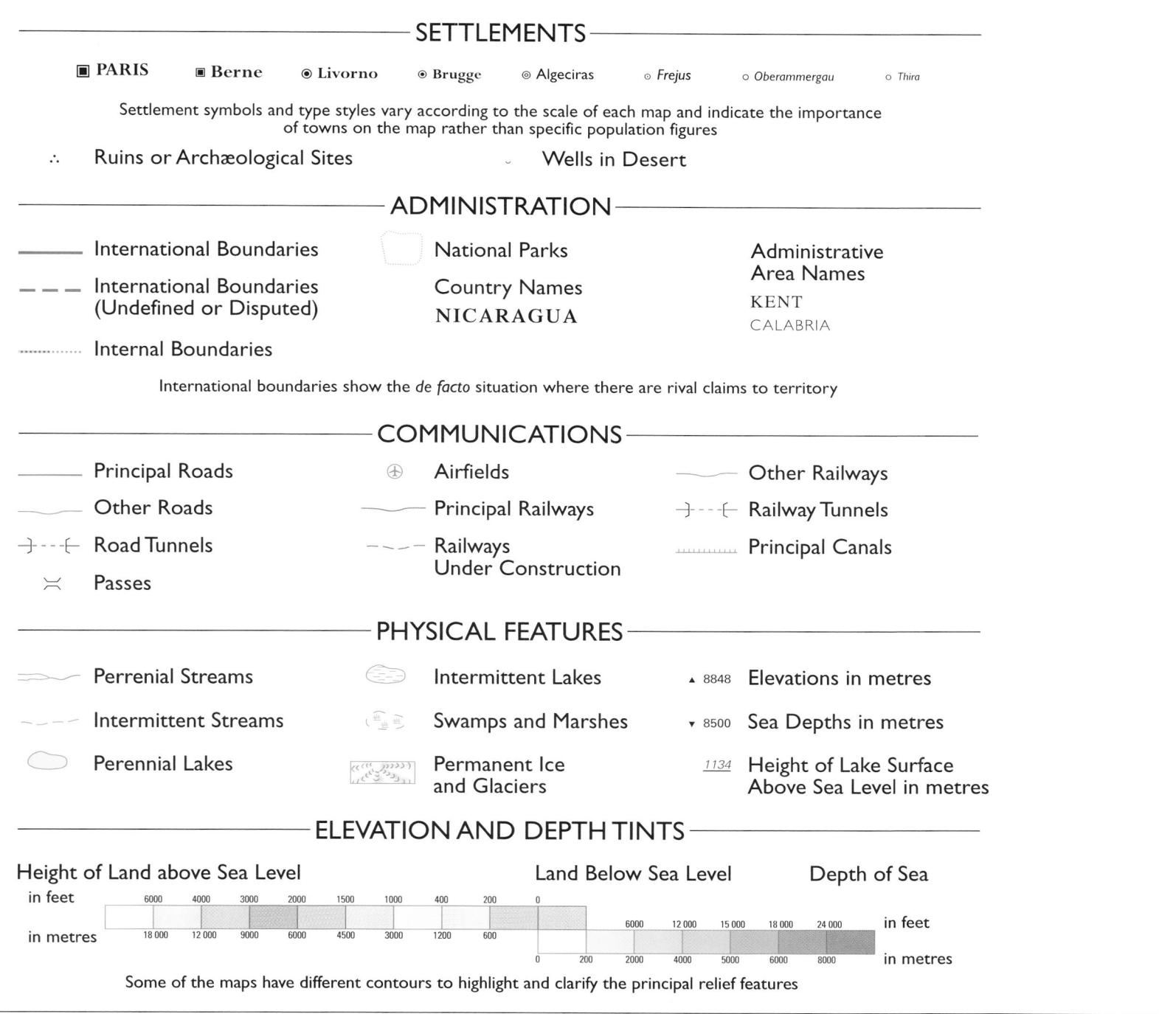

▣ **PARIS** ▪ **Berne** ⊙ **Livorno** ⊙ **Brugge** ◎ Algeciras ○ *Frejus* ○ *Oberammergau* ○ *Thira*

Settlement symbols and type styles vary according to the scale of each map and indicate the importance of towns on the map rather than specific population figures

∴ Ruins or Archæological Sites

Wells in Desert

ADMINISTRATION

International Boundaries

International Boundaries (Undefined or Disputed)

Internal Boundaries

National Parks

Country Names
NICARAGUA

Administrative Area Names
KENT
CALABRIA

International boundaries show the *de facto* situation where there are rival claims to territory

COMMUNICATIONS

Principal Roads

Other Roads

Road Tunnels

Passes

Airfields

Principal Railways

Railways Under Construction

Other Railways

Railway Tunnels

Principal Canals

PHYSICAL FEATURES

Perrenial Streams

Intermittent Streams

Perennial Lakes

Intermittent Lakes

Swamps and Marshes

Permanent Ice and Glaciers

▲ 8848 Elevations in metres

▼ 8500 Sea Depths in metres

1134 Height of Lake Surface Above Sea Level in metres

ELEVATION AND DEPTH TINTS

Height of Land above Sea Level

in feet	6000	4000	3000	2000	1500	1000	400	200	0
in metres	18 000	12 000	9000	6000	4500	3000	1200	600	

Land Below Sea Level

Depth of Sea

in feet		6000	12 000	15 000	18 000	24 000
in metres	0 · 200	2000	4000	5000	6000	8000

Some of the maps have different contours to highlight and clarify the principal relief features

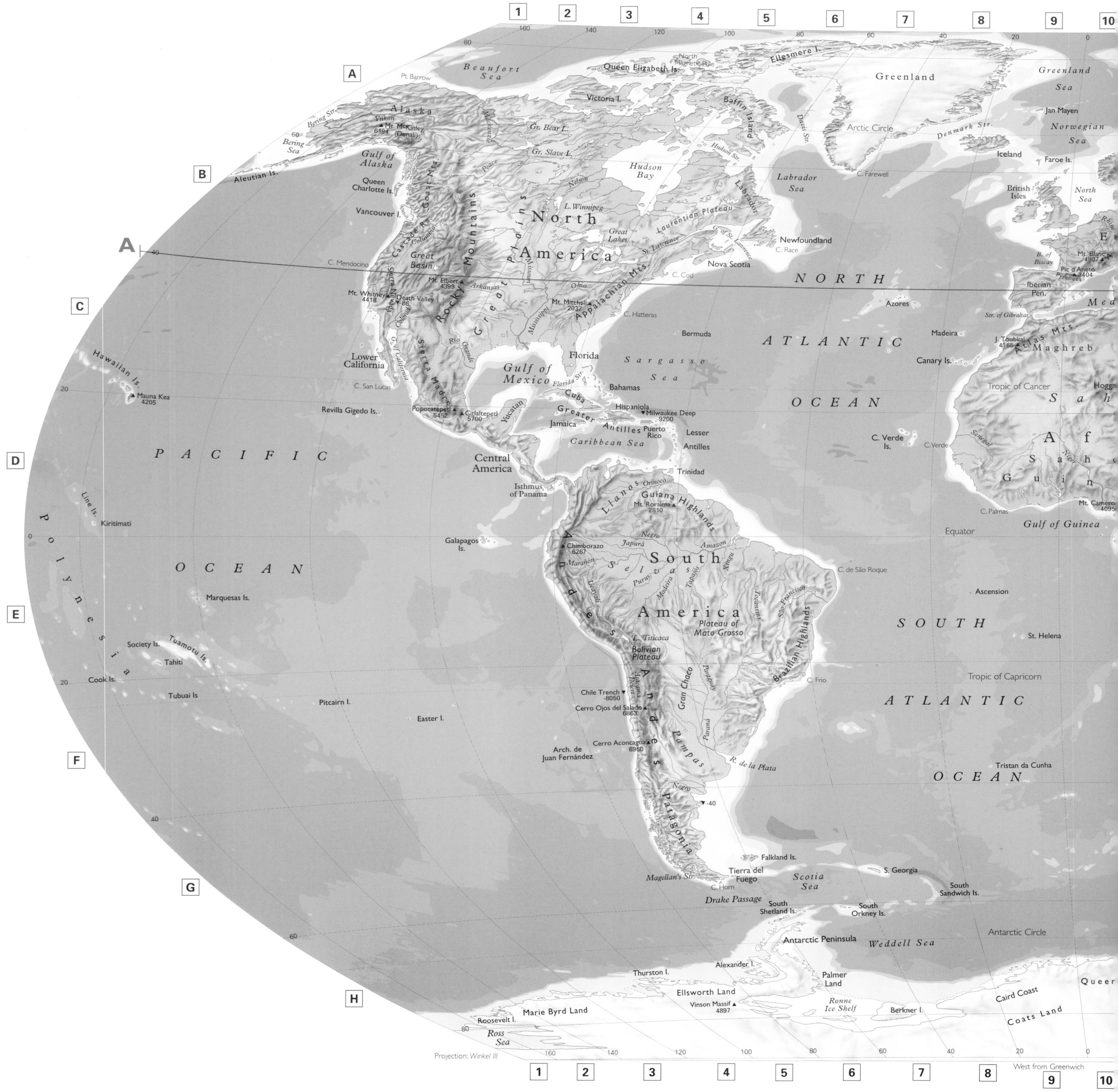
Beaufort Sea
Queen Elizabeth Is.
Ellesmere I.
Greenland
Greenland Sea
Alaska
Victoria I.
Baffin Island
Gulf of Alaska
Hudson Bay
Labrador Sea
Iceland
Aleutian Is.
North America
Rocky Mountains
Great Plains
Appalachian Mts.
Newfoundland
Nova Scotia
NORTH ATLANTIC OCEAN
Mt. McKinley (Denali) 6194
Mt. Whitney 4418
Mt. Elbert 4399
Mt. Mitchell 2037
Death Valley -86
Gulf of Mexico
Sargasso Sea
Bermuda
Azores
Madeira
Canary Is.
Hawaiian Is.
Mauna Kea 4205
PACIFIC OCEAN
Polynesia
Popocatepetl 5452
Citlaltepetl 5700
Caribbean Sea
Milwaukee Deep -9200
Central America
Isthmus of Panama
South America
Guiana Highlands
Mt. Roraima 2810
Chimborazo 6267
Galapagos Is.
Plateau of Mato Grosso
Brazilian Highlands
Bolivian Plateau
Gran Chaco
Pampas
Patagonia
Chile Trench -8050
Cerro Ojos del Salado 6863
Cerro Aconcagua 6960
SOUTH ATLANTIC OCEAN
Tropic of Cancer
Tropic of Capricorn
Equator
Gulf of Guinea
Ascension
St. Helena
Tristan da Cunha
Falkland Is.
Tierra del Fuego
S. Georgia
Scotia Sea
Drake Passage
South Shetland Is.
South Orkney Is.
South Sandwich Is.
Antarctic Peninsula
Weddell Sea
Antarctic Circle
Thurston I.
Alexander I.
Ellsworth Land
Palmer Land
Vinson Massif 4897
Ronne Ice Shelf
Berkner I.
Marie Byrd Land
Roosevelt I.
Ross Sea
Caird Coast
Coats Land
Projection: Winkel III
West from Greenwich

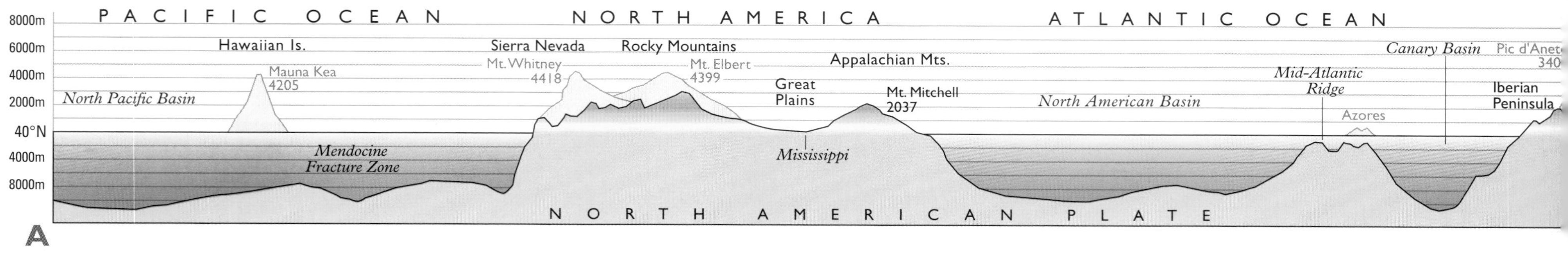
PACIFIC OCEAN
NORTH AMERICA
ATLANTIC OCEAN
Hawaiian Is.
Mauna Kea 4205
North Pacific Basin
Sierra Nevada
Mt. Whitney 4418
Rocky Mountains
Mt. Elbert 4399
Great Plains
Appalachian Mts.
Mt. Mitchell 2037
North American Basin
Mid-Atlantic Ridge
Azores
Canary Basin
Iberian Peninsula
Mendocine Fracture Zone
Mississippi
NORTH AMERICAN PLATE
8000m
6000m
4000m
2000m
40°N
A

ft
m
18 000
12 000
6000
3000
600
0
600
12 000
24 000
6000
4000
2000
1000
200
0
200
4000
8000
11
12
13
14
15
16
17
18
19
20
A
R C T I C O C E A N
Svalbard
N. Cape
Barents Sea
Novaya Zemlya
Kara Sea
Severnaya Zemlya
Taimyr Pen.
Laptev Sea
New Siberian Is.
Wrangel I.
C. Dezhneva
White Sea
L. Onega
L. Ladoga
G. of Bothnia
Baltic Sea
Narodnaya 1894
Ural Mts.
Ob
West Siberian Plain
S i b e r i a
Yenisey
Lower Tunguska
Lena
Verkhoyansk Ra.
Cherski Ra.
Kolyma Ra.
Aldan
Kamchatka
Klyuchevskaya 4750
Bering Sea
Sea of Okhotsk
Stanovoy Ra.
Aleutian Is.
-7822
Aleutian Trench
B
Central Russian Uplands
North European Plain
Volga
Don
A
Irtysh
Angara
L. Baikal
Sayan Mts.
Amur
Sakhalin
Kuril Is.
Kuril Trench
-10542
Hokkaido
B
Carpathians
Danube
Adriatic Sea
Black Sea
Elbrus 5642
Caucasus
-28
Caspian Sea
Aral Sea
Syrdarya
Amudarya
L. Balkhash
Altai
Gobi Desert
Manchuria
Tian Shan
Tarim Basin
Sea of Japan
Japan
Korea
Yellow Sea
Hwang-he
Anatolia
Mt. Ararat 5165
Elburz Mts.
5604
Pamirs
K2 8611
Karakoram
Kunlun Shan
Qilian Shan
Mt. Fuji 3776
Honshu
Shikoku
Kyushu
C
Mediterranean Sea
Middle East
Dead Sea
-411
Isthmus of Suez
Mesopotamia
Zagros
Euphrates
4548
Hindu Kush
Plateau of Tibet
C h i n a
Yangtze
Japan Trench
-10554
East China Sea
Ryukyu Is.
Libyan Desert
Nile
The Gulf
Indus
Thar Desert
Sulaiman Ra.
H i m a l a y a
Mt. Everest 8850
Gongga Shan 7556
Ganges
I n d i a
Arabia
Si
Taiwan
P A C I F I C
Tibesti
Red Sea
Rub' al Khali
Arabian Sea
Deccan
W. Ghats
E. Ghats
Bay of Bengal
Salween
Mekong
Hainan
Mariana Is.
Wake
Luzon
Philippine Is.
Indo-China
South China Sea
Guam
Mariana Trench
-11022
Marshall Is.
L. Chad
Blue Nile
White Nile
-156
G. of Aden
Socotra
C. Guardafui
Andaman Is.
Ethiopian Highlands
Somali Peninsula
Isthmus of Kra
G. of Thailand
Sulu Sea
Mindanao
Caroline Is.
M i c r o n e s i a
C. Comorin
Ceylon
Nicobar Is.
Belau
O C E A N
L. Turkana
Malay Pen.
Kinabalu 4101
Celebes Sea
Congo
Congo Basin
Ruwenzori 5109
Mt. Kenya 5199
Maldives
Str. of Malacca
Sumatra
Borneo
Moluccas
M e l a n e s i a
Gilbert Is.
Lake Victoria
5895
Kilimanjaro
Rift Valley
L. Tanganyika
Seychelles
I N D I A N
Celebes
Puncak Jaya 5029
New Guinea
Bismarck Arch.
Nauru
Phoenix Is.
Java Sea
Java
Sunda Is.
Banda Sea
-7450
Java Trench
New Britain
Solomon Is.
Ellice Is.
Kasai
L. Malawi
Comoros
Timor
Arafura Sea
Torres Str.
C. York
Tokelau Is.
Cocos Is.
E
Cubango
Zambezi
Mozambique Chan.
Madagascar
O C E A N
Timor Sea
Arnhem Land
Kimberley Plateau
Cape York Pen.
Great Barrier Reef
Coral Sea
New Hebrides
Samoa Is.
Namib Desert
Kalahari Desert
Limpopo
Pic Boby 2658
Réunion
Mauritius
Rodriguez
Tanami Desert
Fiji Is.
Hamersley Ra.
MacDonnell Ra.
Great Dividing Range
New Caledonia
Tonga Is.
Orange
Drakensberg
A u s t r a l i a
-10822
Great Victoria Desert
L. Eyre -16
Nullarbor Plain
Darling
Cape of Good Hope
C. Leeuwin
Great Australian Bight
Murray
Mt. Kosciuszko 2237
Kermadec Is.
-10047
F
Amsterdam I.
Bass Str.
Tasman Sea
North I.
Tasmania
Prince Edward Is.
Crozet Is.
South I.
3753
Aoraki-Mt. Cook
New Zealand
Chatham Is.
Kerguelen
Heard I.
Auckland Is.
S O U T H E R N O C E A N
Macquarie Is.
G
South Magnetic Pole
Amery Ice Shelf
Maud Land
Enderby Land
Queen Mary Coast
Wilkes Land
Balleny Is.
Victoria Land
H
Mt. Erebus 3743
Ross Sea
A n t a r c t i c a
East from Greenwich
11
12
13
14
15
16
17
18
19
20

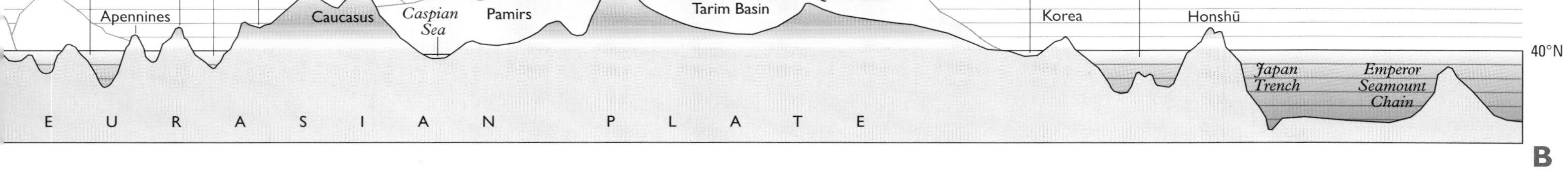
E U R O P E
A S I A
PACIFIC OCEAN
Mt. Blanc 4807
Tyrrhenian Sea
Ægean Sea
Elbrus 5642
K2 8611
Mt. Everest 8850
Gongga Shan 7556
Balkan Peninsula
Apennines
Anatolia
Caucasus
Caspian Sea
Pamirs
Tian Shan
Tarim Basin
Qilian Shan
Yellow Sea
Sea of Japan
Korea
Honshū
40°N
Japan Trench
Emperor Seamount Chain
E U R A S I A N P L A T E

B

Projection: *Hammer Equal Area*

Hanoi ◉ Capital Cities

COPYRIGHT GEORGE PHILIP LTD.

ARCTIC OCEAN 1:28 000 000

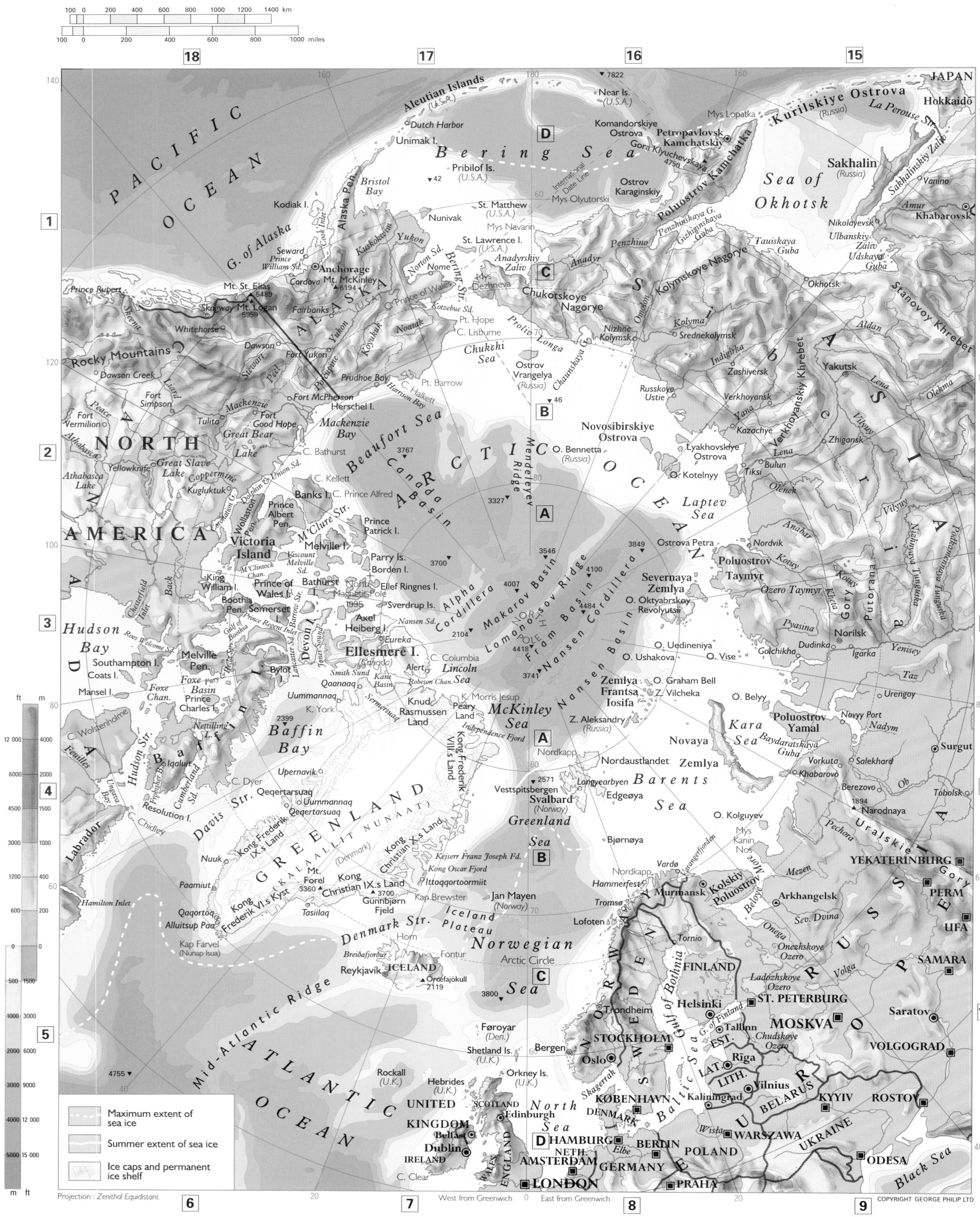
100 0 200 400 600 800 1000 1200 1400 km
100 0 200 400 600 800 1000 miles
PACIFIC OCEAN
Aleutian Islands (U.S.A.)
Dutch Harbor
Unimak I.
Bering Sea
Near Is. (U.S.A.)
Komandorskiye Ostrova
Petropavlovsk Kamchatskiy
Kurilskiye Ostrova (Russia)
JAPAN
Hokkaidō
La Perouse Str.
Sakhalin (Russia)
Sea of Okhotsk
Pribilof Is. (U.S.A.)
Bristol Bay
Kodiak I.
Alaska Pen.
G. of Alaska
Anchorage
Mt. McKinley 6194
Mt. St. Elias 5489
Mt. Logan 5959
ALASKA (U.S.A.)
St. Matthew (U.S.A.)
Nunivak
St. Lawrence I. (U.S.A.)
Anadyrskiy Zaliv
Chukotskoye Nagorye
Kolymskoye Nagorye
Chukchi Sea
Ostrov Vrangelya (Russia)
Pt. Barrow
Prudhoe Bay
Rocky Mountains
Beaufort Sea
Mackenzie Bay
Canada Basin
ARCTIC OCEAN
Mendeleyev Ridge
Novosibirskiye Ostrova
Laptev Sea
NORTH AMERICA
Great Bear Lake
Great Slave Lake
Athabasca Lake
Banks I.
Victoria Island
Melville I.
Prince Patrick I.
Alpha Cordillera
Makarov Basin
Lomonosov Ridge
Fram Basin
Nansen Cordillera
Nansen Basin
NORTH POLE
Severnaya Zemlya
Poluostrov Taymyr
Hudson Bay
Ellesmere I.
Lincoln Sea
Baffin Bay
Baffin I.
Devon I.
McKinley Sea
Zemlya Frantsa Iosifa
Kara Sea
Novaya Zemlya
Barents Sea
Svalbard (Norway)
Greenland Sea
GREENLAND (KALAALLIT NUNAAT) (Denmark)
Davis Str.
Labrador
Denmark Str.
Iceland Plateau
Norwegian Sea
Arctic Circle
Jan Mayen (Norway)
ICELAND
Reykjavík
Mid-Atlantic Ridge
ATLANTIC OCEAN
Føroyar (Den.)
Shetland Is. (U.K.)
North Sea
UNITED KINGDOM
IRELAND
Dublin
LONDON
NORWAY
SWEDEN
FINLAND
STOCKHOLM
Oslo
Helsinki
ST. PETERBURG
MOSKVA
RUSSIA
SIBERIA
Baltic Sea
Gulf of Bothnia
POLAND
WARSZAWA
BERLIN
GERMANY
UKRAINE
KYYIV
BELARUS
Black Sea
Maximum extent of sea ice
Summer extent of sea ice
Ice caps and permanent ice shelf
Projection : Zenithal Equidistant
West from Greenwich
East from Greenwich
COPYRIGHT GEORGE PHILIP LTD

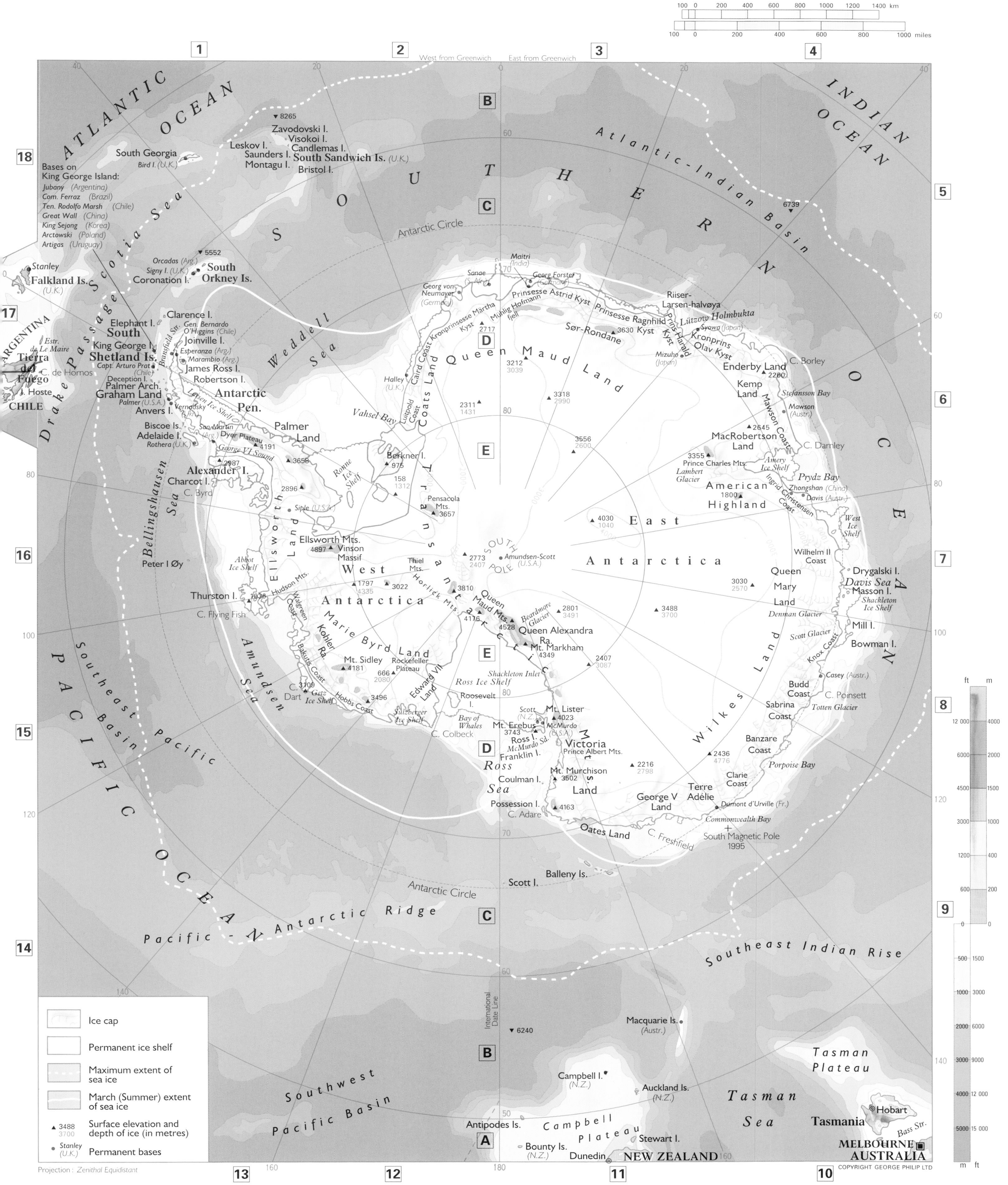

The Antarctic Treaty was signed in Washington in 1959 so that scientific and technical research could continue unhampered by international politics.

All territorial claims covering land areas south of latitude 60°S have been suspended. Those claims were:

Norwegian claim	45°E - 20°W	French claim	136°E - 142°E	British claim	80°W - 20°W
Australian claims	45°E - 136°E	New Zealand claim	160°E - 150°W	Argentine claim	74°W - 53°W
	142°E - 160°E	Chilean claim	90°W - 53°W		

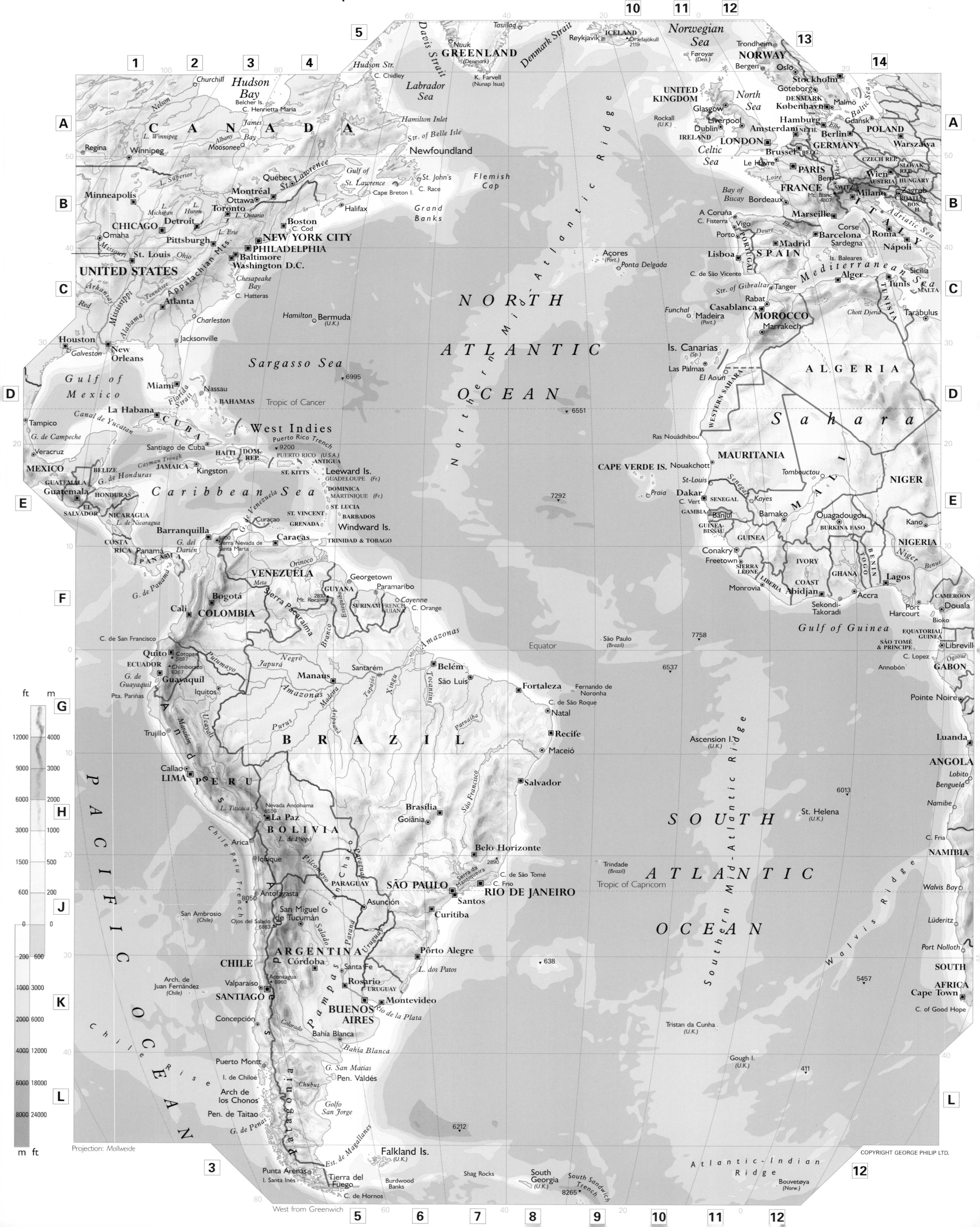
Norwegian Sea
GREENLAND (Denmark)
Nuuk
Tasiilaq
Denmark Strait
ICELAND
Reykjavík
Davis Strait
Hudson Str.
C. Chidley
Labrador Sea
K. Farvell (Nunap Isua)
Hudson Bay
Churchill
Belcher Is.
C. Henrietta Maria
James Bay
Moosonee
Albany
Nelson
L. Winnipeg
Winnipeg
Regina
C A N A D A
Hamilton Inlet
Str. of Belle Isle
Newfoundland
St. John's
C. Race
Gulf of St. Lawrence
Cape Breton I.
Halifax
Flemish Cap
Grand Banks
Québec
Montréal
Ottawa
St Lawrence
L. Superior
Minneapolis
L. Michigan
L. Huron
Toronto
L. Ontario
L. Erie
Detroit
CHICAGO
Omaha
Pittsburgh
Boston
C. Cod
NEW YORK CITY
PHILADELPHIA
Baltimore
Washington D.C.
Chesapeake Bay
C. Hatteras
St. Louis
Missouri
Ohio
Appalachian Mts.
UNITED STATES
Arkansas
Red
Mississippi
Tennessee
Alabama
Atlanta
Charleston
Jacksonville
Houston
Galveston
New Orleans
Gulf of Mexico
Miami
Florida Strait
Nassau
BAHAMAS
Tropic of Cancer
Hamilton
Bermuda (U.K.)
Sargasso Sea
6995
La Habana
CUBA
Canal de Yucatan
Tampico
G. de Campeche
Veracruz
MEXICO
BELIZE
GUATEMALA
Guatemala
HONDURAS
G. de Honduras
EL SALVADOR
NICARAGUA
L. de Nicaragua
COSTA RICA
Panamá
PANAMA
Santiago de Cuba
Cayman Trough
JAMAICA
Kingston
HAITI
DOM. REP.
West Indies
Puerto Rico Trench
9200
PUERTO RICO (U.S.A.)
ANTIGUA
ST. KITTS
Leeward Is.
GUADELOUPE (Fr.)
DOMINICA
MARTINIQUE (Fr.)
ST. LUCIA
BARBADOS
ST. VINCENT
GRENADA
Windward Is.
TRINIDAD & TOBAGO
Caribbean Sea
Curaçao
G. de Venezuela
Barranquilla
Caracas
G. del Darién
Sierra Nevada de Santa Marta
5800
Orinoco
VENEZUELA
Meta
Georgetown
GUYANA
Paramaribo
SURINAM
FRENCH GUIANA
Cayenne
C. Orange
2810
Mt. Roraima
Sierra Pacaraima
G. de Panamá
Bogotá
COLOMBIA
Cali
C. de San Francisco
Quito
Cotopaxi 5897
Chimborazo 6267
ECUADOR
G. de Guayaquil
Guayaquil
Pta. Pariñas
Putumayo
Japurá
Negro
Branco
Amazonas
Manaus
Santarém
Tapajós
Xingu
Tocantins
Belém
São Luís
Iquitos
Madeira
Aripuanã
Purus
Ucayali
Marañón
Trujillo
Parnaíba
Fortaleza
Fernando de Noronha
C. de São Roque
Natal
Recife
Maceió
Salvador
B R A Z I L
São Francisco
Callao
LIMA
PERU
Andes
L. Titicaca
Nevada Ancohuma 6550
La Paz
BOLIVIA
L. de Poopó
Brasília
Goiânia
Belo Horizonte
2890
Arica
Iquique
Pilcomayo
Gran Chaco
Paraguay
PARAGUAY
Paraná
SÃO PAULO
Serra da Mantiqueira
C. de São Tomé
C. Frio
RIO DE JANEIRO
Santos
Curitiba
Antofagasta
8050
Asunción
San Miguel de Tucumán
Ojos del Salado 6863
Salado
Uruguay
ARGENTINA
Córdoba
Santa Fe
Rosario
URUGUAY
Montevideo
Río de la Plata
BUENOS AIRES
Pampas
Pôrto Alegre
L. dos Patos
CHILE
Aconcagua 6960
Valparaíso
SANTIAGO
Concepción
Colorado
Bahía Blanca
Arch. de Juan Fernández (Chile)
San Ambrosio (Chile)
Chile Peru Trench
Chile Rise
PACIFIC OCEAN
Puerto Montt
I. de Chiloé
Arch de los Chonos
Pen. de Taitao
G. de Penas
Patagonia
Chubut
G. San Matías
Pen. Valdés
Golfo San Jorge
Est. de Magallanes
Punta Arenas
I. Santa Inés
Tierra del Fuego
C. de Hornos
Falkland Is. (U.K.)
Burdwood Banks
Shag Rocks
South Georgia (U.K.)
South Sandwich Trench
8265
6212
638
NORTH ATLANTIC OCEAN
Northern Mid-Atlantic Ridge
6551
7292
Açores (Port.)
Ponta Delgada
UNITED KINGDOM
Rockall (U.K.)
IRELAND
Glasgow
Liverpool
Dublin
LONDON
Celtic Sea
North Sea
Føroyar (Den.)
NORWAY
Trondheim
Bergen
Oslo
Stockholm
Göteborg
DENMARK
København
Malmö
Baltic Sea
Hamburg
Elbe
Gdańsk
POLAND
Warszawa
Amsterdam
NETH.
Berlin
GERMANY
Brussel
BELG.
Le Havre
PARIS
Loire
Rhein
FRANCE
Bern
SWITZ.
Mt. Blanc 4807
CZECH REP.
SLOVAK REP.
Wien
AUSTRIA
HUNGARY
Milano
Zagreb
CROATIA
BOS.-H.
Bay of Biscay
Bordeaux
Marseille
Adriatic Sea
ITALY
Corse
Roma
Nápoli
Sardegna
A Coruña
C. Fisterra
Vigo
Porto
Douro
Ebro
PORTUGAL
Madrid
Barcelona
SPAIN
Lisboa
Is. Baleares
C. de São Vicente
Mediterranean Sea
Alger
Tunis
TUNISIA
MALTA
Sicilia
Str. of Gibraltar
Tanger
Rabat
Casablanca
MOROCCO
Marrakech
Chott Djerid
Tarābulus
Funchal
Madeira (Port.)
Is. Canarias (Sp.)
Las Palmas
El Aaiún
WESTERN SAHARA
ALGERIA
Sahara
Ras Nouâdhibou
MAURITANIA
CAPE VERDE IS.
Nouakchott
Tombouctou
Praia
St-Louis
Sénégal
Dakar
C. Vert
SENEGAL
Kayes
MALI
NIGER
GAMBIA
Banjul
Bamako
GUINEA-BISSAU
GUINEA
Ouagadougou
BURKINA FASO
Kano
NIGERIA
Niger
Conakry
Freetown
SIERRA LEONE
LIBERIA
Monrovia
IVORY COAST
Abidjan
GHANA
TOGO
BENIN
Benue
Lagos
Accra
Sekondi-Takoradi
Port Harcourt
CAMEROON
Douala
Bioko
Gulf of Guinea
EQUATORIAL GUINEA
SÃO TOMÉ & PRINCIPE
Libreville
Ogooué
C. Lopez
GABON
Annobón
São Paulo (Brazil)
7758
Equator
6537
Pointe Noire
Ascension I. (U.K.)
Southern Mid-Atlantic Ridge
Luanda
ANGOLA
Lobito
Benguela
6013
St. Helena (U.K.)
Namibe
SOUTH ATLANTIC OCEAN
C. Fria
NAMIBIA
Trindade (Brazil)
Tropic of Capricorn
Walvis Bay
Walvis Ridge
Lüderitz
Port Nolloth
SOUTH AFRICA
5457
Cape Town
C. of Good Hope
Tristan da Cunha (U.K.)
Gough I. (U.K.)
411
Atlantic-Indian Ridge
Bouvetøya (Norw.)
Projection: Mollweide
West from Greenwich
COPYRIGHT GEORGE PHILIP LTD.
ft m
12000 4000
9000 3000
6000 2000
3000 1000
1500 500
600 200
0 0
200 600
1000 3000
2000 6000
4000 12000
6000 18000
8000 24000
m ft

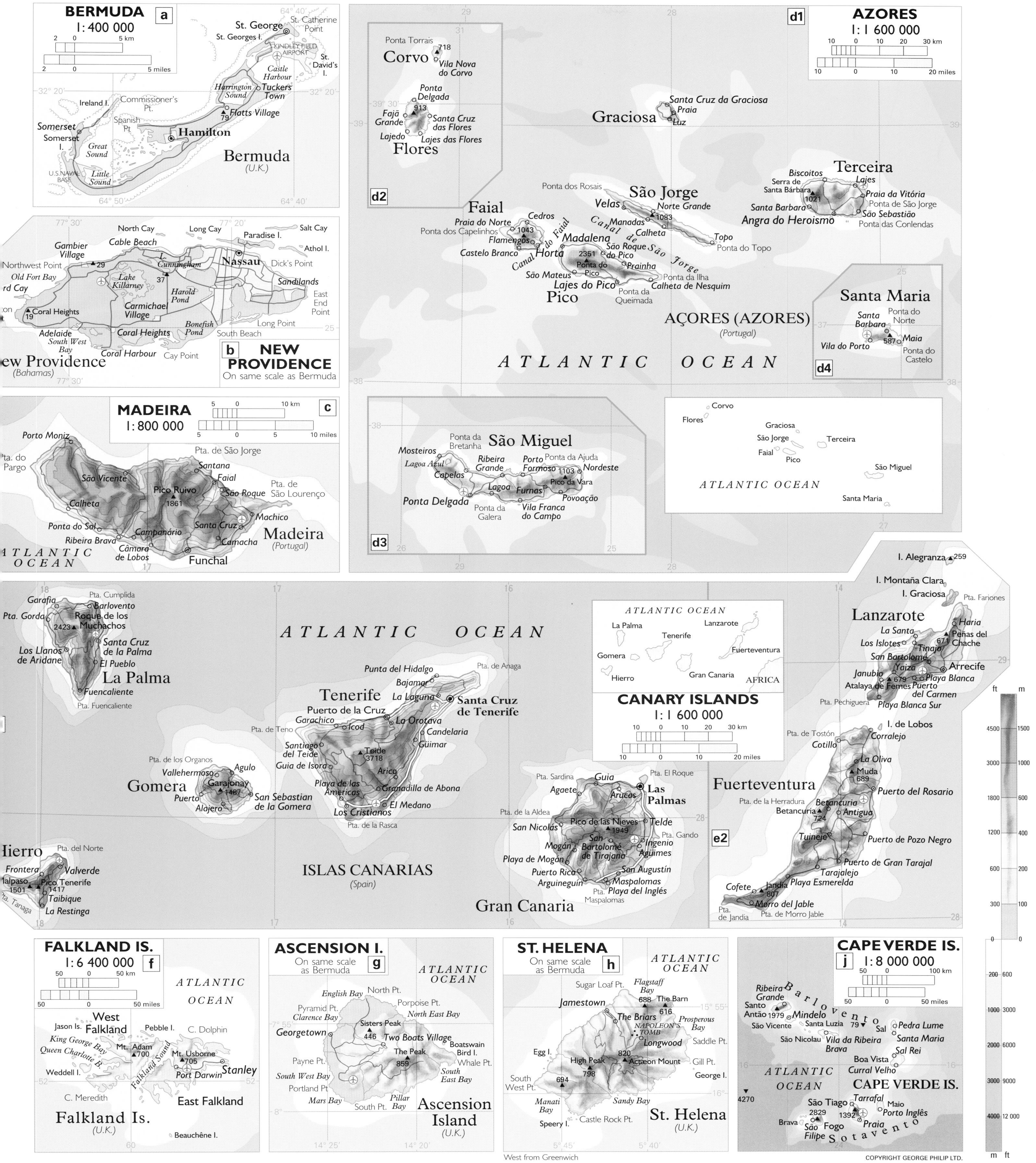
BERMUDA
a
1: 400 000
2 0 5 km
2 0 5 miles
St. George
St. Georges I.
St. Catherine Point
KINDLEY FIELD AIRPORT
St. David's I.
Castle Harbour
Harrington Sound
Tuckers Town
Ireland I.
Commissioner's Pt.
Spanish Pt
Flatts Village
79
Somerset
Somerset I.
Hamilton
Great Sound
Little Sound
U.S. NAVAL BASE
Bermuda
(U.K.)
32° 20'
64° 40'
64° 50'
North Cay
Long Cay
Salt Cay
Paradise I.
Athol I.
Gambier Village
Cable Beach
Nassau
Dick's Point
Northwest Point
L. Cunningham
Old Fort Bay
29
37
Sandilands
Lake Killarney
Harold Pond
East End Point
Carmichael Village
Coral Heights
19
Coral Heights
Bonefish Pond
Long Point
Adelaide
South West Bay
South Beach
Coral Harbour
Cay Point
b
NEW PROVIDENCE
On same scale as Bermuda
New Providence
(Bahamas)
77° 30'
77° 20'
25
MADEIRA
1: 800 000
5 0 10 km
5 0 5 10 miles
c
Porto Moniz
Pta. do Pargo
Pta. de São Jorge
Santana
São Vicente
Faial
Pta. de São Lourenço
Pico Ruivo
1861
São Roque
Calheta
Machico
Ponta do Sol
Santa Cruz
Campanário
Ribeira Brava
Camacha
Câmara de Lobos
Funchal
Madeira
(Portugal)
ATLANTIC OCEAN
17
AZORES
d1
1: 1 600 000
10 0 10 20 30 km
10 0 10 20 miles
Ponta Torrais
718
Corvo
Vila Nova do Corvo
Ponta Delgada
913
Fajã Grande
Santa Cruz das Flores
Lajedo
Lajes das Flores
Flores
d2
Santa Cruz da Graciosa
Praia
Graciosa
Luz
Biscoitos
Terceira
Serra de Santa Bárbara
1021
Lajes
Praia da Vitória
Ponta de São Jorge
Santa Barbara
São Sebastião
Angra do Heroismo
Ponta das Contendas
Ponta dos Rosais
São Jorge
Velas
Norte Grande
1083
Manadas
Calheta
Topo
Ponta do Topo
Faial
Cedros
Praia do Norte
1043
Ponta dos Capelinhos
Flamengos
Madalena
Castelo Branco
Horta
Canal do Faial
Canal de São Jorge
São Roque do Pico
2351
Ponta do Pico
Prainha
São Mateus
Ponta da Ilha
Lajes do Pico
Calheta de Nesquim
Ponta da Queimada
Pico
AÇORES (AZORES)
(Portugal)
Santa Maria
Santa Barbara
Ponta do Norte
587
Maia
Vila do Porto
Ponta do Castelo
d4
ATLANTIC OCEAN
Ponta da Bretanha
São Miguel
Mosteiros
Lagoa Azul
Ribeira Grande
Porto Formoso
Ponta da Ajuda
1103
Nordeste
Capelas
Pico da Vara
Lagoa
Furnas
Povoação
Ponta Delgada
Ponta da Galera
Vila Franca do Campo
d3
Corvo
Flores
Graciosa
São Jorge
Terceira
Faial
Pico
São Miguel
ATLANTIC OCEAN
Santa Maria
I. Alegranza
259
I. Montaña Clara
I. Graciosa
Pta. Fariones
Lanzarote
Haria
La Santa
Peñas del Chache
671
Los Islotes
Tinajo
San Bartolomé
Arrecife
Janubio
Yaiza
679
Playa Blanca
Atalaya de Femes
Puerto del Carmen
Pta. Pechiguera
Playa Blanca Sur
I. de Lobos
Corralejo
Pta. de Tostón
Cotillo
La Oliva
Muda
689
Fuerteventura
Puerto del Rosario
Pta. de la Herradura
Betancuria
Betancuria
724
Antigua
Tuineje
Puerto de Pozo Negro
Puerto de Gran Tarajal
Tarajalejo
Cofete
Jandía
807
Playa Esmeralda
Morro del Jable
Pta. de Jandía
Pta. de Morro Jable
e2
Garafía
Pta. Cumplida
Barlovento
Pta. Gorda
Roque de los Muchachos
2423
Santa Cruz de la Palma
Los Llanos de Aridane
El Pueblo
La Palma
Fuencaliente
Pta. Fuencaliente
ATLANTIC OCEAN
Punta del Hidalgo
Pta. de Anaga
Bajamar
Tenerife
La Laguna
Santa Cruz de Tenerife
Puerto de la Cruz
Garachico
La Orotava
Pta. de Teno
Icod
Candelaria
Güímar
Santiago del Teide
Teide
3718
Guía de Isora
Arico
Playa de las Américas
Granadilla de Abona
El Medano
Los Cristianos
Pta. de la Rasca
Pta. de los Organos
Agulo
Vallehermoso
Garajonay
1487
Gomera
Puerto
San Sebastian de la Gomera
Alajeró
ATLANTIC OCEAN
La Palma
Lanzarote
Tenerife
Fuerteventura
Gomera
Hierro
Gran Canaria
AFRICA
CANARY ISLANDS
1: 1 600 000
10 0 10 20 30 km
10 0 10 20 miles
Pta. Sardina
Guía
Pta. El Roque
Agaete
Arucas
Las Palmas
Pta. de la Aldea
Pico de las Nieves
1949
Telde
San Nicolás
Pta. Gando
Mogán
San Bartolomé de Tirajana
Ingenio
Agüimes
Playa de Mogán
San Augustín
Puerto Rico
Arguineguín
Maspalomas
Playa del Inglés
Pta. Maspalomas
Gran Canaria
ISLAS CANARIAS
(Spain)
Hierro
Pta. del Norte
Frontera
Valverde
Malpaso
1501
Pico Tenerife
1417
Taibique
Pta. Tanaga
La Restinga
18
17
16
14
28
29
ft m
4500 1500
3000 1000
1800 600
1200 400
600 200
300 100
0 0
200 600
1000 3000
2000 6000
3000 9000
4000 12 000
m ft
FALKLAND IS.
1: 6 400 000
50 0 50 km
50 0 50 miles
f
ATLANTIC OCEAN
West Falkland
Jason Is.
Pebble I.
C. Dolphin
King George Bay
Queen Charlotte B.
Mt. Adam
700
Mt. Usborne
705
Falkland Sound
Weddell I.
Port Darwin
Stanley
C. Meredith
East Falkland
Falkland Is.
(U.K.)
Beauchêne I.
60
52
ASCENSION I.
On same scale as Bermuda
g
ATLANTIC OCEAN
English Bay
North Pt.
Porpoise Pt.
Pyramid Pt.
Clarence Bay
North East Bay
Sisters Peak
Georgetown
446
Two Boats Village
Boatswain Bird I.
The Peak
859
Whale Pt.
Payne Pt.
South West Bay
South East Bay
Portland Pt
Mars Bay
South Pt.
Pillar Bay
Ascension Island
(U.K.)
7° 55'
8°
14° 25'
14° 20'
ST. HELENA
On same scale as Bermuda
h
ATLANTIC OCEAN
Sugar Loaf Pt.
Flagstaff Bay
Jamestown
688
The Barn
616
The Briars
NAPOLEON'S TOMB
Prosperous Bay
Longwood
Saddle Pt.
Egg I.
High Peak
820
Actæon Mount
798
Gill Pt.
South West Pt.
694
George I.
Sandy Bay
Manati Bay
Speery I.
Castle Rock Pt.
St. Helena
(U.K.)
15° 55'
16°
5° 45'
5° 40'
CAPE VERDE IS.
j
1: 8 000 000
50 0 100 km
50 0 50 miles
Barlovento
Ribeira Grande
Santo Antão
1979
Mindelo
São Vicente
Santa Luzia
79
Sal
Pedra Lume
São Nicolau
Vila da Ribeira Brava
Santa Maria
Sal Rei
Boa Vista
ATLANTIC OCEAN
Curral Velho
CAPE VERDE IS.
4270
São Tiago
Tarrafal
2829
1392
Maio
Porto Inglês
Brava
São Filipe
Fogo
Praia
Sotavento
16

GREENLAND 1:10 000 000

100 0 100 200 300 400 500 km
100 0 50 100 150 200 250 300 350 miles

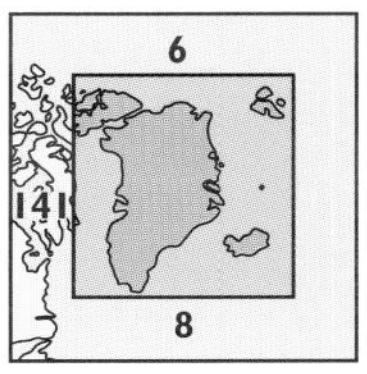
6
14
8

A
B
C
D
E
F
1
2
3
4
5
6
7
8
9
10
11
12
13
ARCTIC OCEAN
Lincoln Sea
McKinley Sea
GREENLAND SEA
Baffin Bay
Davis Strait
Labrador Sea
Denmark Strait
ATLANTIC OCEAN
Dohrne Banke
Melville Bugt
CANADA
Axel Heiberg I.
Ellesmere Island
Devon Island
Baffin I.
Clyde River
Jones Sd.
Alert
Robeson Chan.
Kennedy Kanal
Nares Str.
Smith Sund
Kane Basin
Nyeboe Land
Hall Land
Washington Land
Wulff Land
Warming Land
Nansen Land
J. P. Koch Fjord
Peary Land
Kap Morris Jesup
1920
Frederick E. Hyde Fjord
Jørgen Brønlund Fjord
Heilprin Land
Independence Fjord
Station Nord
Nordostrundingen
Mylius Erichsen Land
Danmark Fjord
Kronprins Christian Land
Ingolf Fjord
Mallemukfjeld
Kronprins Frederik Land
Knud Rasmussen Land
Inglefield Land
Siorapaluk
Qaanaaq (Thule)
Qeqertarsuaq
Kap Atholl
Uummannaq (Dundas)
Pituffik (Thule Air Base)
Kap York
Lauge Koch Kyst
2170
2000
AVANNAARSUA (NORDGRØNLAND)
Hovgaard Ø
Nioghalvfjerdsfjorden
Norske Øer
Lambert Land
Kong Frederik VIII.s Land
Franske Øer
Germania Land
Danmarkshavn
Store Koldewey
Dove Bugt
Hochstetter Forland
Shannon
Dronning Margrethe II Land
Steenstrup Gletscher
Nuussuaq (Kraulshavn)
Zackenberg
Wollaston Forland
Clavering Ø
Ole Rømer Land
Andrée Land
Kong Christian X.s Land
Nationalparken i Nord-og Østgrønland
2935
3220
2940
Petermann Bjerg
Kejser Franz Joseph Fd.
Traill Ø
Mestersvig
Kong Oscar Fjord
Stauning Alper
Jan Mayen (Norway)
Upernavik
Kangersuatsiaq
Upernavik Kujalleq
KITAA (VESTGRØNLAND)
TUNU (ØSTGRØNLAND)
Nunavik
Illorsuit
Uummannaq
Maarmorilik
2092
Ikerasak
Saqqaq
Renland
Jameson Land
Milne Land
Ittoqqortoormiit (Scoresbysund)
Ittaajimmiit
Uunarteq
Scoresby Sund
Kangikajik (Kap Brewster)
Qeqertarsuaq (Disko)
Kangerluk
Qeqertarsuaq (Godhavn)
Disko Bugt
Ilulissat (Jakobshavn)
Aasiaat (Egedesminde)
Ikamiut
Qasigiannguit (Christianshåb)
Kangaatsiaq
GREENLAND (KALAALLIT NUNAAT)
(Denmark)
Kap Dalton
Kong Christian IX.s Land
Gunnbjørn Fjeld
3700
Blosseville Kyst
Nordre Strømfjord
Kong Frederik IX.s Land
Sisimiut (Holsteinsborg)
Kangerlussuaq (Søndre Strømfjord)
Hilleq
Søndre Strømfjord
Kangaamiut
Maniitsoq (Sukkertoppen)
Kangerdlugssuaq
Arctic Circle
Mt. Forel
3360
Kap Gustav Holm
Ikkatteq
Kuummiut
Kulusuk
Isortoq
Tasiilaq (Ammassalik)
Dronning Ingrid Land
Nuuk (Godthåb)
Kapisillit
Kangerluarsoruseq (Færingehavn)
Qeqertarsuatsiaat (Fiskenæsset)
2850
Kong Frederik VI.s Kyst
Gyldenløve Fjord
Kap Møsting
Kap Moltke
Kap Skjold
Timmiarmiut
Mogens Heinesen Fjord
Paamiut (Frederikshåb)
Narsalik
Kangilinnguit (Grønnedal)
Arsuk
Ivittuut
Narsaq
Narsarsuaq
Qaqortoq (Julianehåb)
Alluitsup Paa (Sydprøven)
Nanortalik
Lindenow Fjord
Nunap Isua (Kap Farvel)
Prins Christian Sund
Nordkapp
Nordaustlandet
Olgastredet
Spitsbergen
Edgeøya
Longyearbyen
Storfjorden
Barentsburg
Svalbard (Norway)
Sørkapp
Horn
Ísafjörður
Húnaflói
Eyjafjörður
Akureyri
Neskaupstaður
Breiðafjörður
ICELAND
Vatnajökull
2119
Öræfajökull
Snæfellsnes
Faxaflói
Reykjavík
Vestmannaeyjar
Heimaey
Surtsey
80
75
70
65
60
100
90
50
40
30
20
10
0
West from Greenwich
Projection: Conic
ft m
3000 1000
1200 400
600 200
0 0
200 600
m ft
COPYRIGHT GEORGE PHILIP LTD.

Underlined towns give their name to the administrative area in which they stand.

1:2 000 000 **ICELAND** **II**

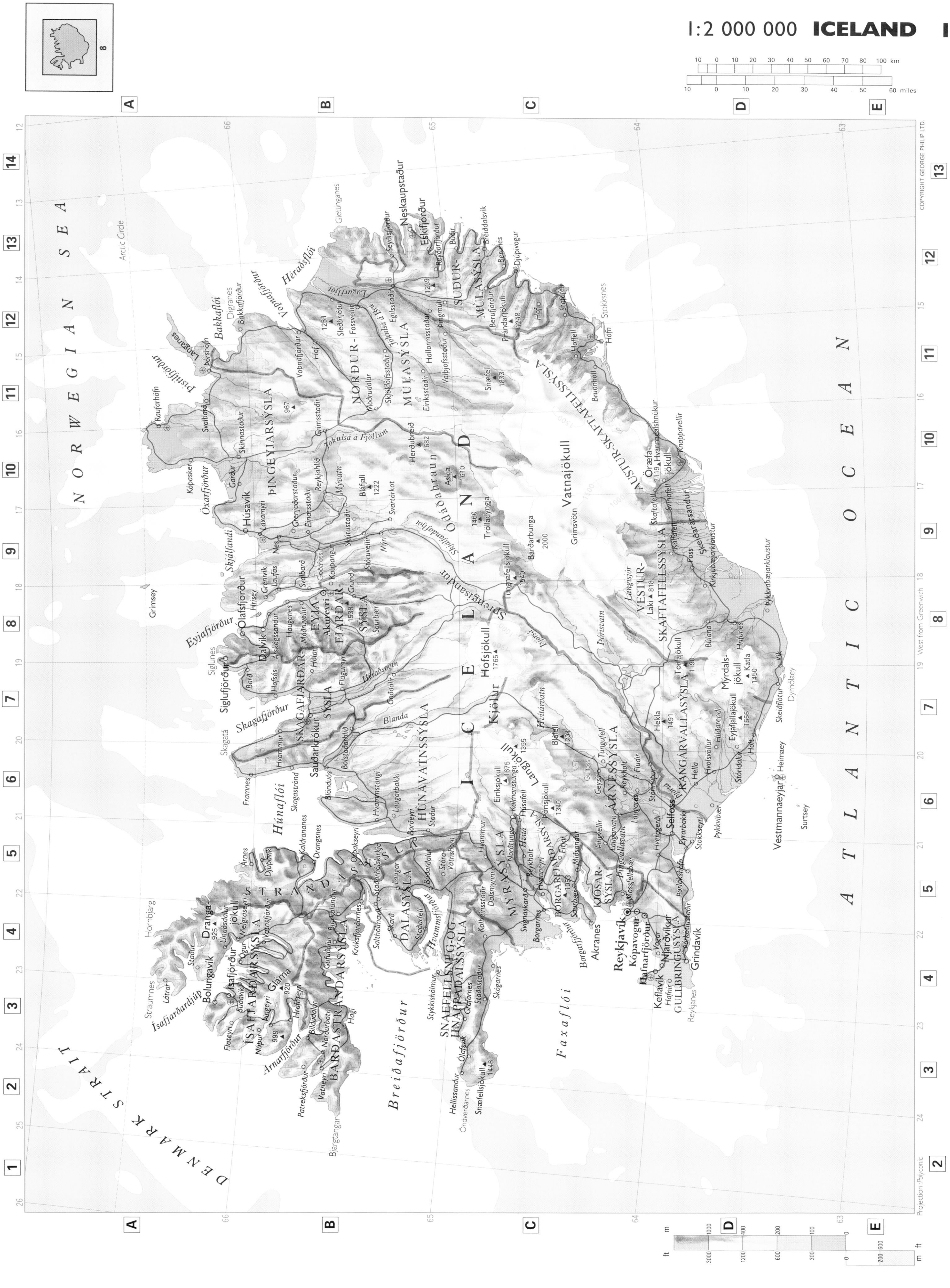

10 0 10 20 30 40 50 60 70 80 100 km
10 0 10 20 30 40 50 60 miles
NORWEGIAN SEA
ATLANTIC OCEAN
DENMARK STRAIT
ICELAND
Arctic Circle
Grímsey
Vatnajökull
Hofsjökull
Langjökull
Mýrdalsjökull
Eyjafjallajökull
Drangajökull
Snæfellsjökull
Ódáðahraun
Sprengisandur
Kjölur
Askja
Herðubreið
Hekla
Katla
Laki
Bárðarbunga
Grímsvötn
Öræfajökull
Hvannadalshnúkur
Reykjavík
Kópavogur
Hafnarfjörður
Keflavík
Njarðvík
Grindavík
Akranes
Borgarnes
Selfoss
Hella
Hvolsvöllur
Vík
Höfn
Akureyri
Húsavík
Dalvík
Ólafsfjörður
Siglufjörður
Sauðárkrókur
Blönduós
Ísafjörður
Bolungavík
Patreksfjörður
Ólafsvík
Stykkishólmur
Neskaupstaður
Eskifjörður
Seyðisfjörður
Egilsstaðir
Raufarhöfn
Þórshöfn
Vestmannaeyjar
Heimaey
Surtsey
Faxaflói
Breiðafjörður
Húnaflói
Skagafjörður
Eyjafjörður
Skjálfandi
Öxarfjörður
Þistilfjörður
Bakkaflói
Vopnafjörður
Héraðsflói
Ísafjarðardjúp
Mývatn
Þingvallavatn
Þórisvatn
Þjórsá
Blanda
Jökulsá á Fjöllum
Lagarfljót
Reykjanes
ÞINGEYJARSÝSLA
NORÐUR-MÚLASÝSLA
SUÐUR-MÚLASÝSLA
AUSTUR-SKAFTAFELLSSÝSLA
VESTUR-SKAFTAFELLSSÝSLA
RANGÁRVALLASÝSLA
ÁRNESSÝSLA
GULLBRINGUSÝSLA
KJÓSARSÝSLA
BORGARFJARÐARSÝSLA
MÝRASÝSLA
SNÆFELLSNES-OG-HNAPPADALSSÝSLA
DALASÝSLA
BARÐASTRANDARSÝSLA
ÍSAFJARÐARSÝSLA
STRANDASÝSLA
HÚNAVATNSSÝSLA
SKAGAFJARÐARSÝSLA
EYJAFJARÐARSÝSLA
West from Greenwich
Projection: Polyconic
COPYRIGHT GEORGE PHILIP LTD.
m ft
1000 3000
400 1200
200 600
100 300
0 0
200 600

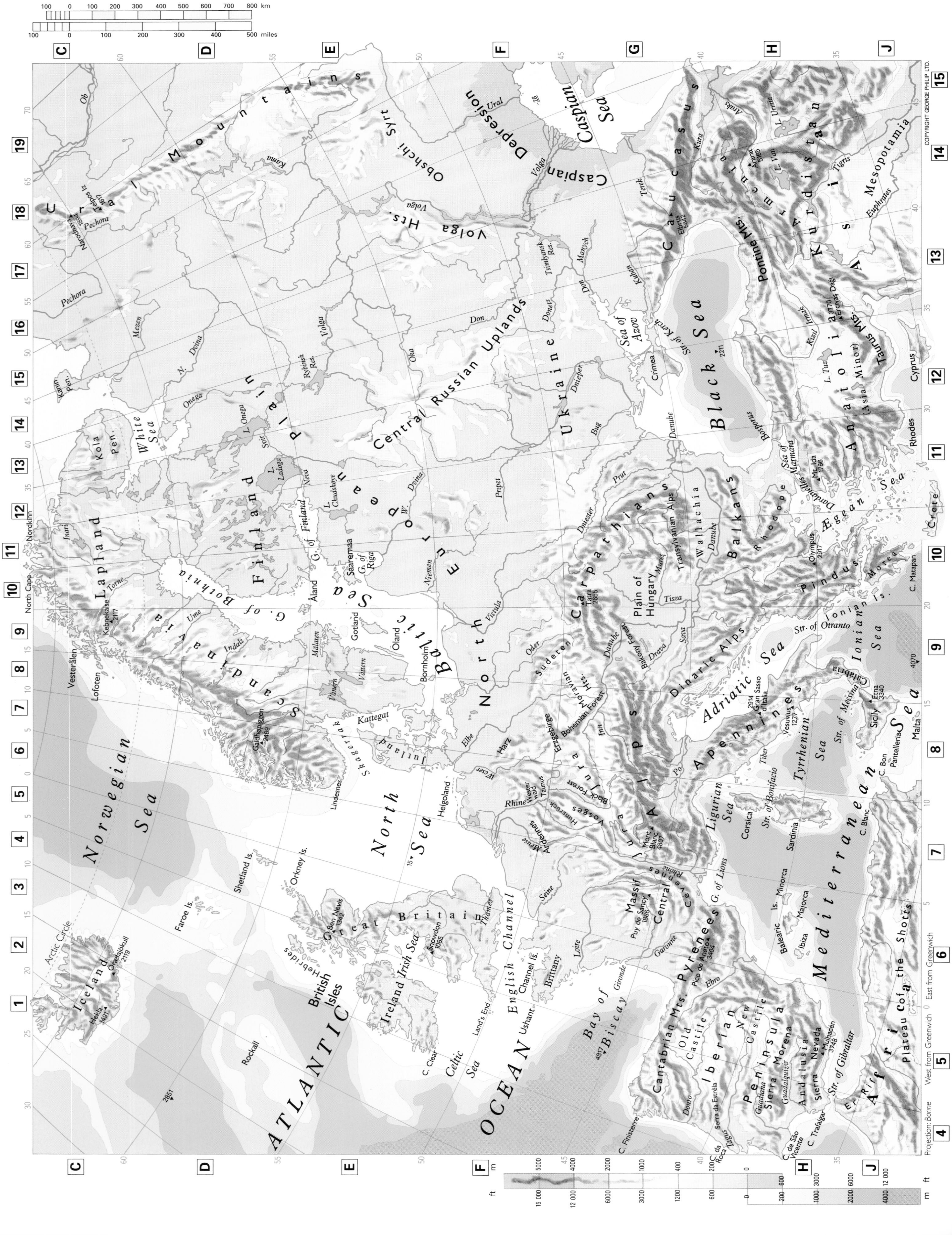

0 100 200 300 400 500 600 700 800 km
0 100 200 300 400 500 miles
Norwegian Sea
ATLANTIC OCEAN
North Sea
Baltic Sea
Black Sea
Caspian Sea
Mediterranean Sea
Adriatic Sea
Ionian Sea
Tyrrhenian Sea
Ligurian Sea
Ægean Sea
Bay of Biscay
English Channel
Celtic Sea
Irish Sea
White Sea
Sea of Azov
Sea of Marmara
G. of Bothnia
G. of Finland
G. of Riga
G. of Lions
Str. of Gibraltar
Str. of Otranto
Str. of Bonifacio
Str. of Messina
Str. of Kerch
Skagerrak
Kattegat
Iceland
Faroe Is.
Shetland Is.
Orkney Is.
Hebrides
British Isles
Great Britain
Ireland
Channel Is.
Brittany
Ushant
Land's End
C. Clear
Rockall
Lofoten
Vesterålen
North Cape
Nordkinn
Lindesnes
Jutland
Helgoland
Bornholm
Gotland
Öland
Saaremaa
Åland
Corsica
Sardinia
Sicily
Malta
Pantelleria
Balearic Is.
Majorca
Minorca
Ibiza
Crete
Rhodes
Cyprus
Crimea
Kola Pen.
Kanin Pen.
Scandinavia
Lapland
Finland
European Plain
Central Russian Uplands
Volga Hts.
Obshchi Syrt
Caspian Depression
Ural Mountains
Ukraine
Caucasus
Pontine Mts.
Armenia
Kurdistan
Mesopotamia
Anatolia (Asia Minor)
Taurus Mts.
Carpathians
Transylvanian Alps
Plain of Hungary
Wallachia
Balkans
Rhodope
Dinaric Alps
Pindus
Morea
Alps
Jura
Apennines
Massif Central
Cevennes
Pyrenees
Cantabrian Mts.
Iberian Peninsula
Old Castile
New Castile
Sierra Morena
Sierra Nevada
Andalusia
Africa
Plateau of the Shotts
Er Rif
Harz
Erzgebirge
Bohemian Forest
Black Forest
Vosges
Ardennes
Sudeten
Moravian Hts.
Bakony Forest
Westerwald
Taunus
Hunsrück
Volga
Don
Dnieper
Dniester
Danube
Rhine
Elbe
Oder
Vistula
Seine
Loire
Garonne
Rhone
Po
Tiber
Ebro
Douro
Tagus
Guadiana
Guadalquivir
Pechora
Mezen
N. Dvina
Onega
Kama
Oka
Ural
Terek
Kura
Manych
Kuban
Donets
Pripet
Bug
Prut
Mureș
Tisza
Sava
Drava
Niemen
W. Dvina
Neva
Torne
Ume
Indals
Weser
Meuse
Thames
Gironde
Euphrates
Tigris
L. Ladoga
L. Onega
L. Chudskoye
Vänern
Vättern
Mälaren
Inari
Rybinsk Res.
Tsimlyansk Res.
L. Van
L. Urmia
L. Tuz
Ben Nevis 1342
Snowdon 1085
Öræfajökull 2119
Hekla 1491
Galdhøpiggen 2469
Kebnekaise 2117
Narodnaya 1894
Mont Blanc 4807
Gran Sasso d'Italia 2914
Vesuvius 1277
Etna 3340
Olympus 2917
Tatra 2655
Elbrus 5642
Ararat 5165
Puy de Sancy 1886
Pico de Aneto 3404
Mulhacén 3478
Serra da Estrêla
Mt. Ida 1766
Erciyas Dağı 3916
C. Finisterre
C. da Roca
C. de São Vicente
C. Trafalgar
C. Matapan
C. Bon
C. Blanc
Bosporus
Dardanelles
Arctic Circle
Projection: Bonne
West from Greenwich
East from Greenwich
COPYRIGHT GEORGE PHILIP LTD.
m ft
5000 15 000
4000 12 000
2000 6000
1000 3000
400 1200
200 600
0
200 600
1000 3000
2000 6000
4000 12 000

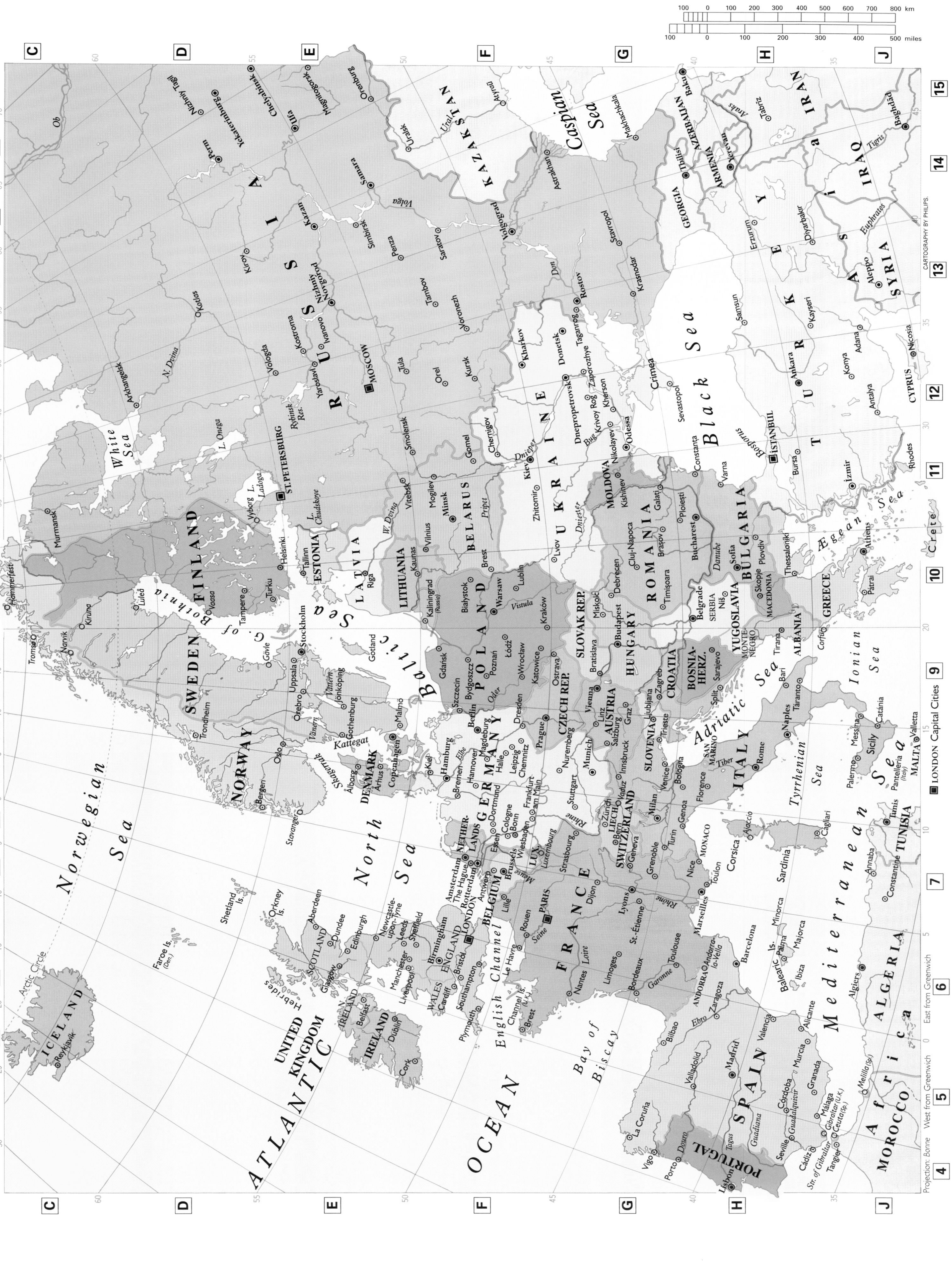
100 0 100 200 300 400 500 600 700 800 km
100 0 100 200 300 400 500 miles
Norwegian Sea
North Sea
Baltic Sea
G. of Bothnia
White Sea
Black Sea
Caspian Sea
Adriatic Sea
Tyrrhenian Sea
Ionian Sea
Ægean Sea
Mediterranean Sea
Bay of Biscay
English Channel
ATLANTIC OCEAN
Skagerrak
Kattegat
ICELAND
Reykjavik
Arctic Circle
Faroe Is. (Den.)
Shetland Is.
Orkney Is.
Hebrides
UNITED KINGDOM
SCOTLAND
ENGLAND
WALES
N. IRELAND
IRELAND
Dublin
LONDON
NORWAY
Oslo
SWEDEN
Stockholm
FINLAND
Helsinki
DENMARK
Copenhagen
ESTONIA
Tallinn
LATVIA
Riga
LITHUANIA
Vilnius
BELARUS
Minsk
POLAND
Warsaw
GERMANY
Berlin
NETHERLANDS
Amsterdam
BELGIUM
Brussels
LUX.
FRANCE
PARIS
SWITZERLAND
Bern
LIECH.
AUSTRIA
Vienna
CZECH REP.
Prague
SLOVAK REP.
Bratislava
HUNGARY
Budapest
SLOVENIA
Ljubljana
CROATIA
Zagreb
BOSNIA-HERZ.
Sarajevo
YUGOSLAVIA
SERBIA
MONTENEGRO
Belgrade
MACEDONIA
Skopje
ALBANIA
Tirana
GREECE
Athens
BULGARIA
Sofia
ROMANIA
Bucharest
MOLDOVA
Kishinev
UKRAINE
Kiev
RUSSIA
MOSCOW
ST. PETERSBURG
KAZAKSTAN
GEORGIA
Tbilisi
ARMENIA
Yerevan
AZERBAIJAN
Baku
TURKEY
Ankara
ISTANBUL
CYPRUS
Nicosia
SYRIA
IRAQ
IRAN
ITALY
Rome
SAN MARINO
MALTA
Valletta
Corsica
Sardinia
Sicily
Crete
SPAIN
Madrid
PORTUGAL
Lisbon
ANDORRA
MONACO
Balearic Is.
AFRICA
MOROCCO
ALGERIA
Algiers
TUNISIA
Tunis
■ LONDON Capital Cities
Projection: Bonne
West from Greenwich
East from Greenwich
CARTOGRAPHY BY PHILIPS.

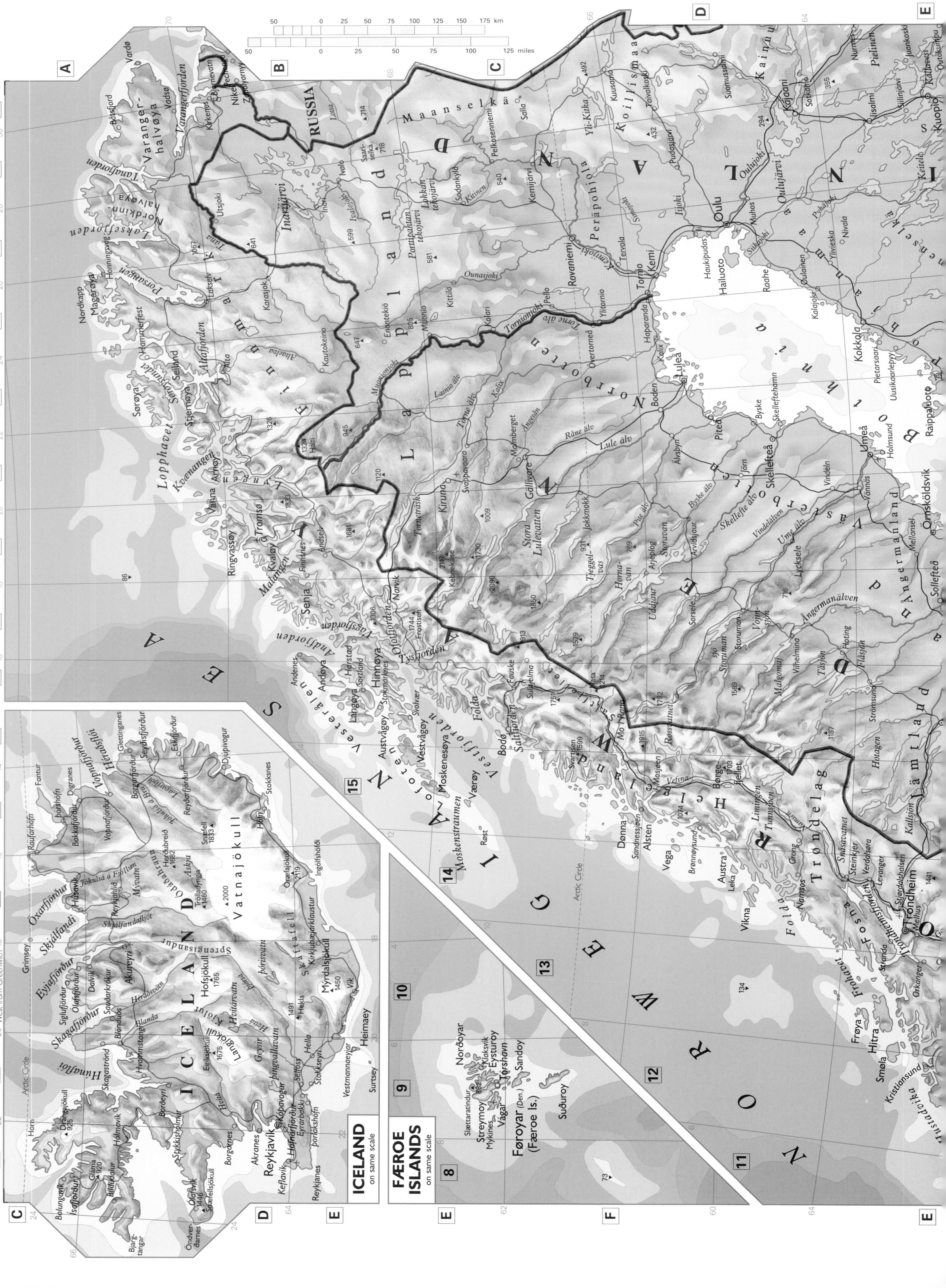

50 0 25 50 75 100 125 150 175 km
50 0 25 50 75 100 125 miles
RUSSIA
Lapland
Norrbotten
Västerbotten
Ångermanland
Jämtland
Trøndelag
Helgeland
Lofoten
Vesterålen
Vestfjorden
Lopphavet
Maanselkä
Koillismaa
Peräpohjola
Kainuu
Bothnia
NORWEGIAN SEA
Kirkenes
Vardø
Vadsø
Varangerfjorden
Varangerhalvøya
Tanafjorden
Nordkinnhalvøya
Laksefjorden
Porsangen
Nordkapp
Magerøya
Hammerfest
Altafjorden
Alta
Kautokeino
Karasjok
Utsjoki
Inarijärvi
Ivalo
Sodankylä
Kittilä
Muonio
Kolari
Pello
Rovaniemi
Kemijärvi
Salla
Kuusamo
Taivalkoski
Pudasjärvi
Oulu
Oulujärvi
Kajaani
Kuopio
Tornio
Kemi
Haparanda
Luleå
Boden
Piteå
Skellefteå
Umeå
Örnsköldsvik
Sollefteå
Kokkola
Pietarsaari
Raahe
Hailuoto
Kiruna
Gällivare
Jokkmokk
Arjeplog
Arvidsjaur
Lycksele
Vilhelmina
Storuman
Stora Lulevatten
Torneträsk
Kebnekaise 2117
Narvik
Tromsø
Senja
Kvaløya
Ringvassøy
Andøya
Hinnøya
Harstad
Svolvær
Austvågøy
Vestvågøy
Moskenesøya
Værøy
Røst
Bodø
Fauske
Saltfjorden
Mo i Rana
Mosjøen
Vefsna
Dønna
Vega
Vikna
Namsos
Grong
Steinkjer
Levanger
Stjørdalshalsen
Trondheim
Trondheimsfjorden
Hitra
Frøya
Smøla
Kristiansund
Orkanger
Östersund
Storsjön
Kallsjön
Arctic Circle
ICELAND on same scale
Reykjavík
Kópavogur
Hafnarfjördur
Keflavík
Akureyri
Húsavík
Ísafjördur
Vatnajökull
Hofsjökull
Langjökull
Mýrdalsjökull
Hekla
Askja
Mývatn
Þingvallavatn
Heimaey
Surtsey
Vestmannaeyjar
Grímsey
Snæfellsjökull
FÆROE ISLANDS on same scale
Føroyar (Den.) (Færoe Is.)
Tórshavn
Streymoy
Eysturoy
Vágar
Sandoy
Suðuroy
Norðoyar
Klaksvík
Mykines

Gulf of Finland
Gulf of Bothnia
Gulf of Riga
Ålands hav
BALTIC SEA
Skagerrak
Kattegat
ESTONIA
LATVIA
LITHUANIA
POLAND
GERMANY
DENMARK
NORWAY
SWEDEN
FINLAND
BELARUS
RUSSIA
Helsinki (Helsingfors)
STOCKHOLM
Oslo
KØBENHAVN (Copenhagen)
Tallinn
Riga
Vilnius
Kaunas
Kaliningrad (Russia)
Gdańsk
Gdynia
Göteborg (Gothenburg)
Malmö
Turku (Åbo)
Tampere
Uppsala
Västerås
Örebro
Norrköping
Linköping
Jönköping
Bergen
Stavanger
Kristiansand
Ålborg
Århus
Odense
Kiel
Lübeck
Rostock
Gotland
Öland
Bornholm
Saaremaa (Ösel)
Hiiumaa (Dagö)
Åland (Ahvenanmaa)
Sjælland
Fyn
Jylland
Rügen
Mälaren
Vänern
Vättern
Saimaa
Zatoka Gdańska
Kurshskiy Zaliv
Daugava
Projection: Conical with two standard parallels
East from Greenwich
COPYRIGHT GEORGE PHILIP LTD.

DENMARK AND SOUTHERN SWEDEN 1:2 000 000

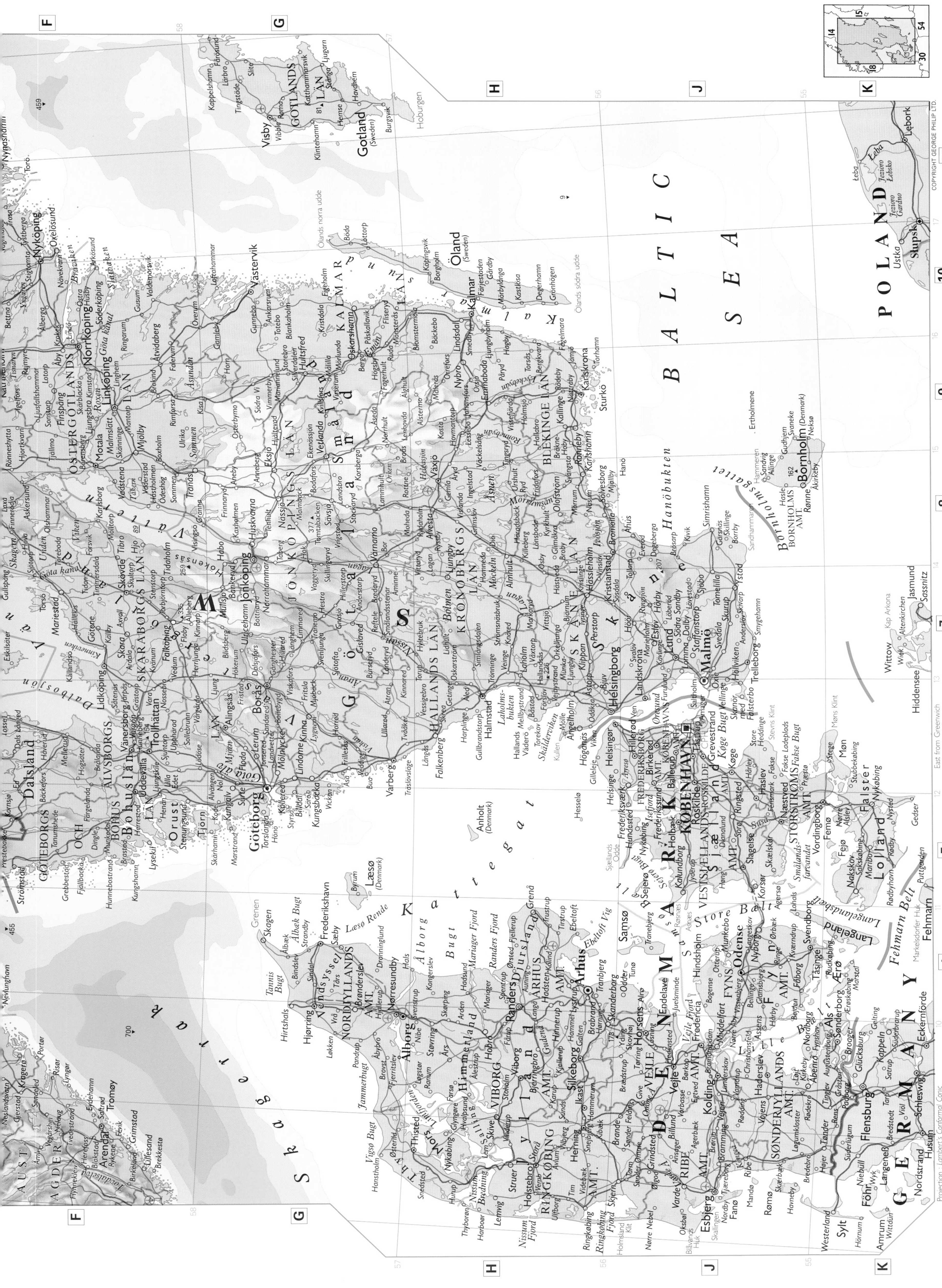
BALTIC SEA
POLAND
GERMANY
DENMARK
Skagerrak
Kattegat
Kalmarsund
Hanöbukten
Bornholmsgattet
Store Bælt
Lille Bælt
Fehmarn Belt
Øresund
Jylland
Sjælland
Fyn
Lolland
Falster
Møn
Bornholm (Denmark)
Gotland (Sweden)
Öland (Sweden)
Anholt (Denmark)
Læsø (Denmark)
Samsø
Langeland
Ærø
Fehmarn
Sylt
Föhr
Amrum
Rømø
Fanø
Rügen
Hiddensee
Vänern
Vättern
Göteborg
Malmö
Helsingborg
Kalmar
Karlskrona
Jönköping
Norrköping
Linköping
Nyköping
Visby
København
Odense
Århus
Ålborg
Esbjerg
Flensburg
Kiel
Słupsk
Lębork
Łeba
Projection : Lambert's Conformal Conic
East from Greenwich
COPYRIGHT GEORGE PHILIP LTD.

SOUTHERN NORWAY 1:2 000 000

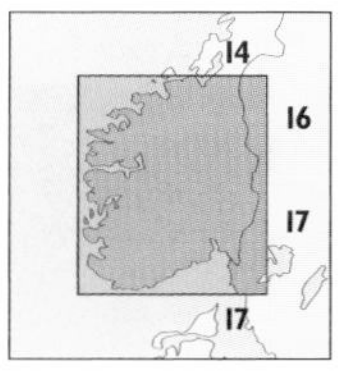

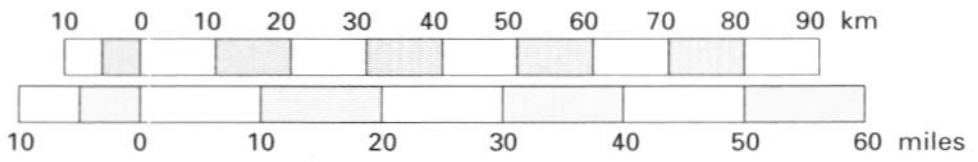

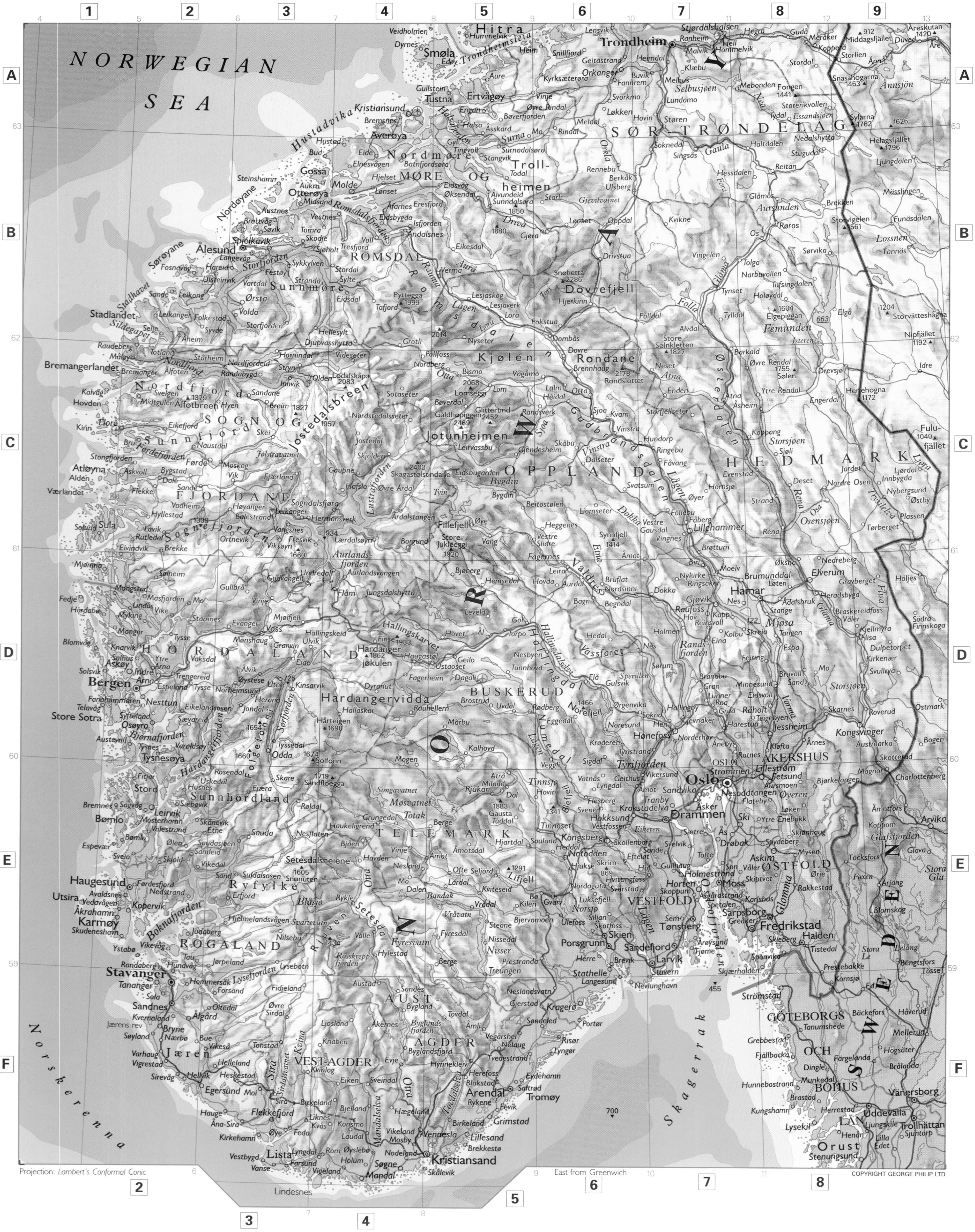

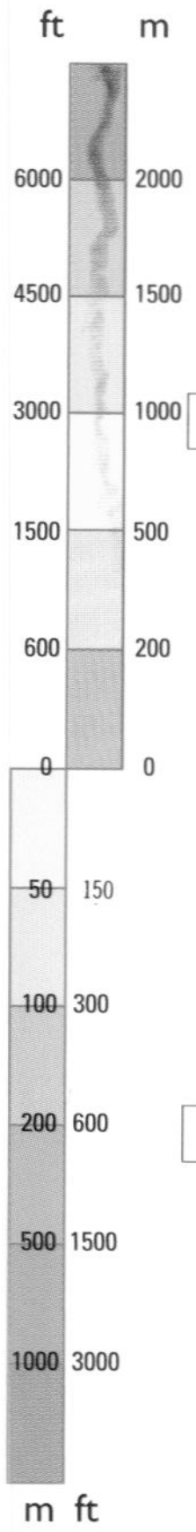

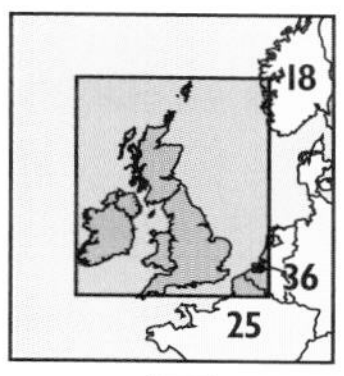
18
36
25

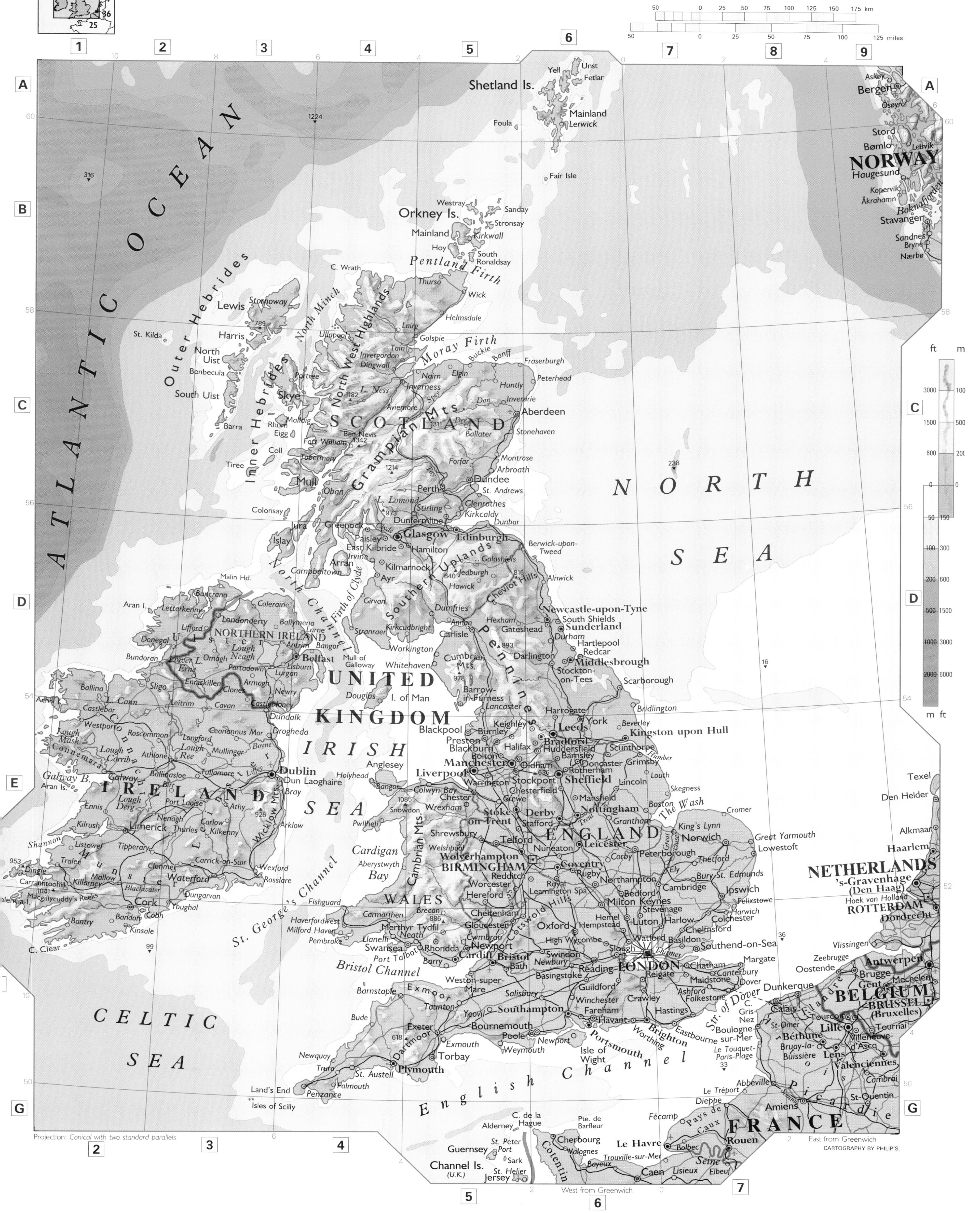
50 0 25 50 75 100 125 150 175 km
50 0 25 50 75 100 125 miles
ATLANTIC OCEAN
NORTH SEA
IRISH SEA
CELTIC SEA
English Channel
Shetland Is.
Yell
Unst
Fetlar
Mainland
Lerwick
Foula
Fair Isle
Orkney Is.
Westray
Sanday
Stronsay
Mainland
Kirkwall
Hoy
South Ronaldsay
Pentland Firth
C. Wrath
Thurso
Wick
Helmsdale
Outer Hebrides
Lewis
Stornoway
Harris
St. Kilda
North Uist
Benbecula
South Uist
Barra
North Minch
Ullapool
North West Highlands
Lairg
Golspie
Tain
Invergordon
Dingwall
Moray Firth
Buckie
Banff
Fraserburgh
Peterhead
Nairn
Elgin
Huntly
Inverurie
Aberdeen
Stonehaven
Inverness
Spey
Don
Dee
L. Ness
Aviemore
Portree
Skye
Inner Hebrides
Rhum
Eigg
Mallaig
Coll
Tiree
Mull
Tobermory
Oban
Fort William
Ben Nevis 1342
SCOTLAND
Grampian Mts.
Ballater
Forfar
Montrose
Arbroath
Dundee
Perth
Tay
St. Andrews
Glenrothes
Kirkcaldy
Dunbar
Stirling
Dunfermline
L. Lomond
Colonsay
Jura
Islay
Greenock
Paisley
Glasgow
Edinburgh
East Kilbride
Hamilton
Irvine
Arran
Kilmarnock
Ayr
Campbeltown
Firth of Clyde
Southern Uplands
Galashiels
Jedburgh
Hawick
Berwick-upon-Tweed
Alnwick
Cheviot Hills
Girvan
Dumfries
Stranraer
Kirkcudbright
Annan
Carlisle
Hexham
Newcastle-upon-Tyne
South Shields
Sunderland
Gateshead
Durham
Hartlepool
Redcar
Middlesbrough
Stockton-on-Tees
Darlington
Scarborough
Pennines
Bridlington
Malin Hd.
Buncrana
Aran I.
Letterkenny
Coleraine
Londonderry
Ballymena
Larne
Lifford
NORTHERN IRELAND
Ulster
Donegal
Antrim
Bangor
Belfast
Lough Neagh
Omagh
Lisburn
Lower L. Erne
Portadown
Lurgan
Bundoran
Enniskillen
Armagh
Newry
Sligo
Clones
Ballina
Leitrim
Cavan
Castleblaney
Achill I.
L. Conn
Castlebar
Westport
Roscommon
Dundalk
Drogheda
Lough Mask
Connemara
Connacht
Lough Corrib
Longford
Lough Ree
Ceanannus Mor
Boyne
Mullingar
Athlone
Leinster
Galway
Galway B.
Aran Is.
Ballinasloe
Tullamore
Liffey
Birr
Dublin
Dun Laoghaire
Bray
IRELAND
Lough Derg
Port Laoise
Wicklow Mts.
Athy
Ennis
Shannon
Kilrush
Limerick
Nenagh
Carlow
Kilkenny
Thurles
Arklow
Munster
Listowel
Tipperary
Tralee
Dingle
Clonmel
Carrick-on-Suir
Wexford
Rosslare
Carrauntoohill
Killarney
Mallow
Waterford
Blackwater
Valencia I.
Macgillycuddy's Reeks
Cork
Cobh
Dungarvan
Youghal
Bantry
Bandon
Kinsale
C. Clear
Mull of Galloway
Workington
Whitehaven
Cumbrian Mts.
Douglas
I. of Man
UNITED KINGDOM
Barrow-in-Furness
Lancaster
Harrogate
York
Leeds
Bradford
Keighley
Burnley
Blackpool
Preston
Blackburn
Bolton
Halifax
Huddersfield
Barnsley
Scunthorpe
Humber
Beverley
Kingston upon Hull
Grimsby
Manchester
Oldham
Doncaster
Rotherham
Sheffield
Liverpool
Warrington
Stockport
Chesterfield
Crewe
Lincoln
Louth
Skegness
Anglesey
Holyhead
Bangor
Colwyn Bay
Chester
Mansfield
Nottingham
Boston
The Wash
Snowdon
Wrexham
Stoke on Trent
Derby
Trent
Grantham
Cromer
King's Lynn
Norwich
Great Yarmouth
Lowestoft
Pwllheli
Cambrian Mts.
Shrewsbury
Stafford
Telford
ENGLAND
Leicester
Peterborough
Cardigan Bay
Aberystwyth
Welshpool
Wolverhampton
BIRMINGHAM
Nuneaton
Coventry
Rugby
Corby
Thetford
Ely
Bury St. Edmunds
Redditch
Worcester
Royal Leamington Spa
Northampton
Bedford
Cambridge
Ipswich
Felixstowe
Harwich
Hereford
Severn
Cotswold Hills
Milton Keynes
Stevenage
Colchester
WALES
Fishguard
Carmarthen
Brecon
Cheltenham
Hemel Hempstead
Luton
Harlow
Chelmsford
Haverfordwest
Milford Haven
Pembroke
Merthyr Tydfil
Neath
Gloucester
Oxford
Watford
Basildon
Southend-on-Sea
Llanelli
Swansea
Port Talbot
Rhondda
Cwmbran
Newport
High Wycombe
Slough
Thames
Barry
Cardiff
Bristol
Bath
Swindon
Newbury
Reading
LONDON
Chatham
Margate
Canterbury
St. George's Channel
Bristol Channel
Weston-super-Mare
Basingstoke
Reigate
Maidstone
Dover
Exmoor
Guildford
Ashford
Folkestone
Barnstaple
Taunton
Salisbury
Winchester
Crawley
Yeovil
Southampton
Fareham
Havant
Hastings
Bude
Exeter
Bournemouth
Poole
Weymouth
Newport
Isle of Wight
Portsmouth
Worthing
Brighton
Eastbourne
Dartmoor
Exmouth
Torbay
Plymouth
Newquay
Truro
St. Austell
Falmouth
Penzance
Land's End
Isles of Scilly
Str. of Dover
C. Gris Nez
Dunkerque
Calais
Boulogne-sur-Mer
Le Touquet-Paris-Plage
St-Omer
Flandre
Béthune
Bruay-la-Buissière
Lille
Lens
Villeneuve-d'Ascq
Tournai
Valenciennes
Cambrai
St-Quentin
Artois
Picardie
Abbeville
Somme
Amiens
Le Tréport
Dieppe
Fécamp
Pays de Caux
FRANCE
Rouen
Bolbec
Seine
Elbeuf
Le Havre
Trouville-sur-Mer
Lisieux
Caen
Bayeux
Cherbourg
Valognes
Cotentin
Pte. de Barfleur
C. de la Hague
Alderney
Guernsey
St. Peter Port
Sark
Channel Is.
(U.K.)
Jersey
St. Helier
NETHERLANDS
Texel
Den Helder
Alkmaar
Haarlem
's-Gravenhage (Den Haag)
Hoek van Holland
ROTTERDAM
Dordrecht
Vlissingen
Zeebrugge
Oostende
Brugge
Gent
Antwerpen
Mechelen
BELGIUM
BRUSSEL (Bruxelles)
NORWAY
Askøy
Bergen
Os
Stord
Bømlo
Leirvik
Haugesund
Kopervik
Åkrahamn
Boknafjorden
Stavanger
Sandnes
Bryne
Nærbø
1224
316
789
1182
1311
1214
973
840
816
893
978
636
1085
926
886
953
1041
618
99
238
16
36
33
ft m
3000 1000
1500 500
600 200
0 0
50 150
100 300
200 600
500 1500
1000 3000
2000 6000
m ft
Projection: Conical with two standard parallels
West from Greenwich
East from Greenwich
CARTOGRAPHY BY PHILIP'S.

ENGLAND AND WALES 1:1 600 000

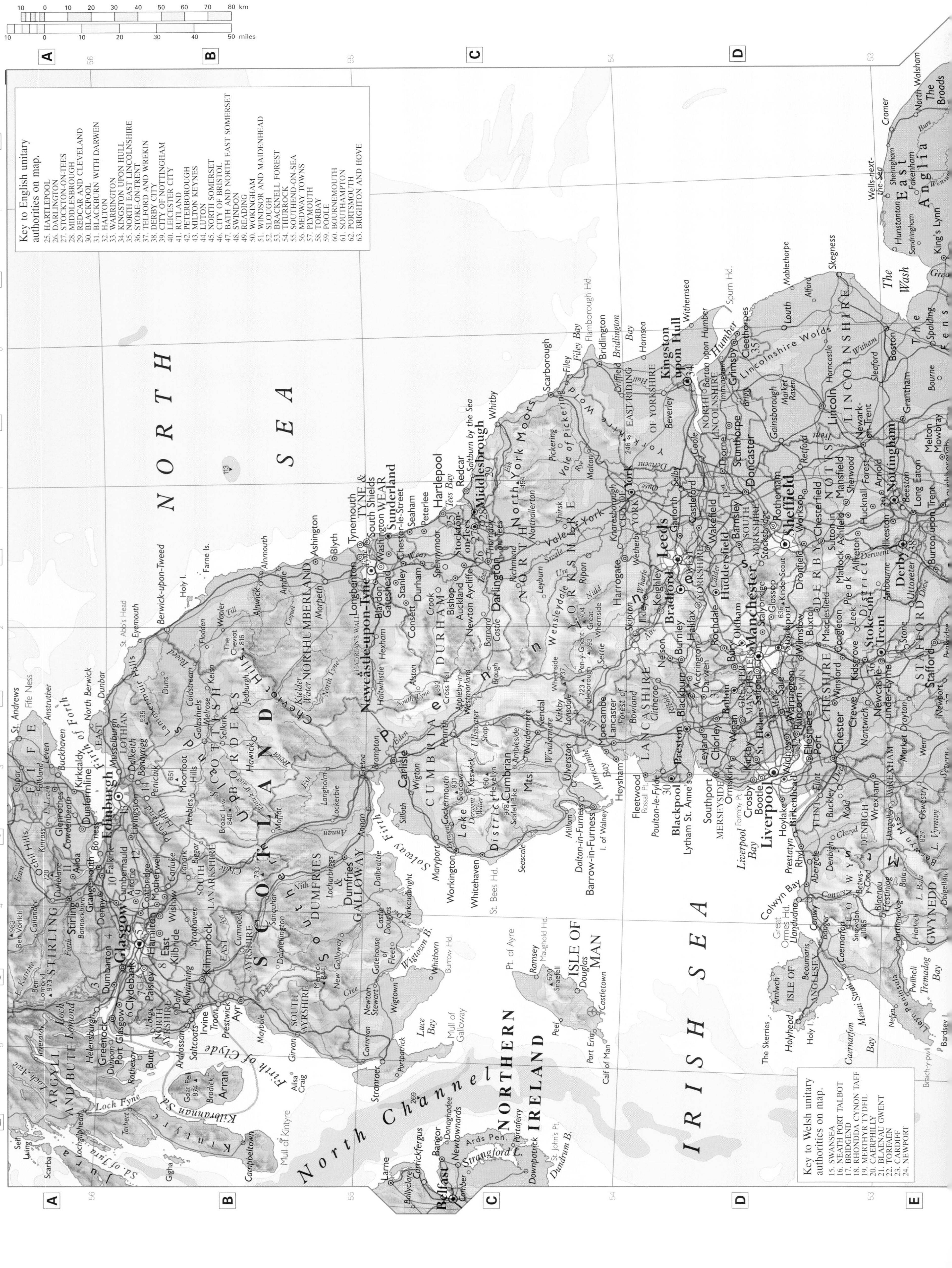
Key to English unitary authorities on map.
25. HARTLEPOOL
26. DARLINGTON
27. STOCKTON-ON-TEES
28. MIDDLESBROUGH
29. REDCAR AND CLEVELAND
30. BLACKPOOL
31. BLACKBURN WITH DARWEN
32. HALTON
33. WARRINGTON
34. KINGSTON UPON HULL
35. NORTH EAST LINCOLNSHIRE
36. STOKE-ON-TRENT
37. TELFORD AND WREKIN
38. DERBY CITY
39. CITY OF NOTTINGHAM
40. LEICESTER CITY
41. RUTLAND
42. PETERBOROUGH
43. MILTON KEYNES
44. LUTON
45. NORTH SOMERSET
46. CITY OF BRISTOL
47. BATH AND NORTH EAST SOMERSET
48. SWINDON
49. READING
50. WOKINGHAM
51. WINDSOR AND MAIDENHEAD
52. SLOUGH
53. BRACKNELL FOREST
54. THURROCK
55. SOUTHEND-ON-SEA
56. MEDWAY TOWNS
57. PLYMOUTH
58. TORBAY
59. POOLE
60. BOURNEMOUTH
61. SOUTHAMPTON
62. PORTSMOUTH
63. BRIGHTON AND HOVE
Key to Welsh unitary authorities on map.
15. SWANSEA
16. NEATH PORT TALBOT
17. BRIDGEND
18. RHONDDA CYNON TAFF
19. MERTHYR TYDFIL
20. CAERPHILLY
21. BLAENAU GWENT
22. TORFAEN
23. CARDIFF
24. NEWPORT

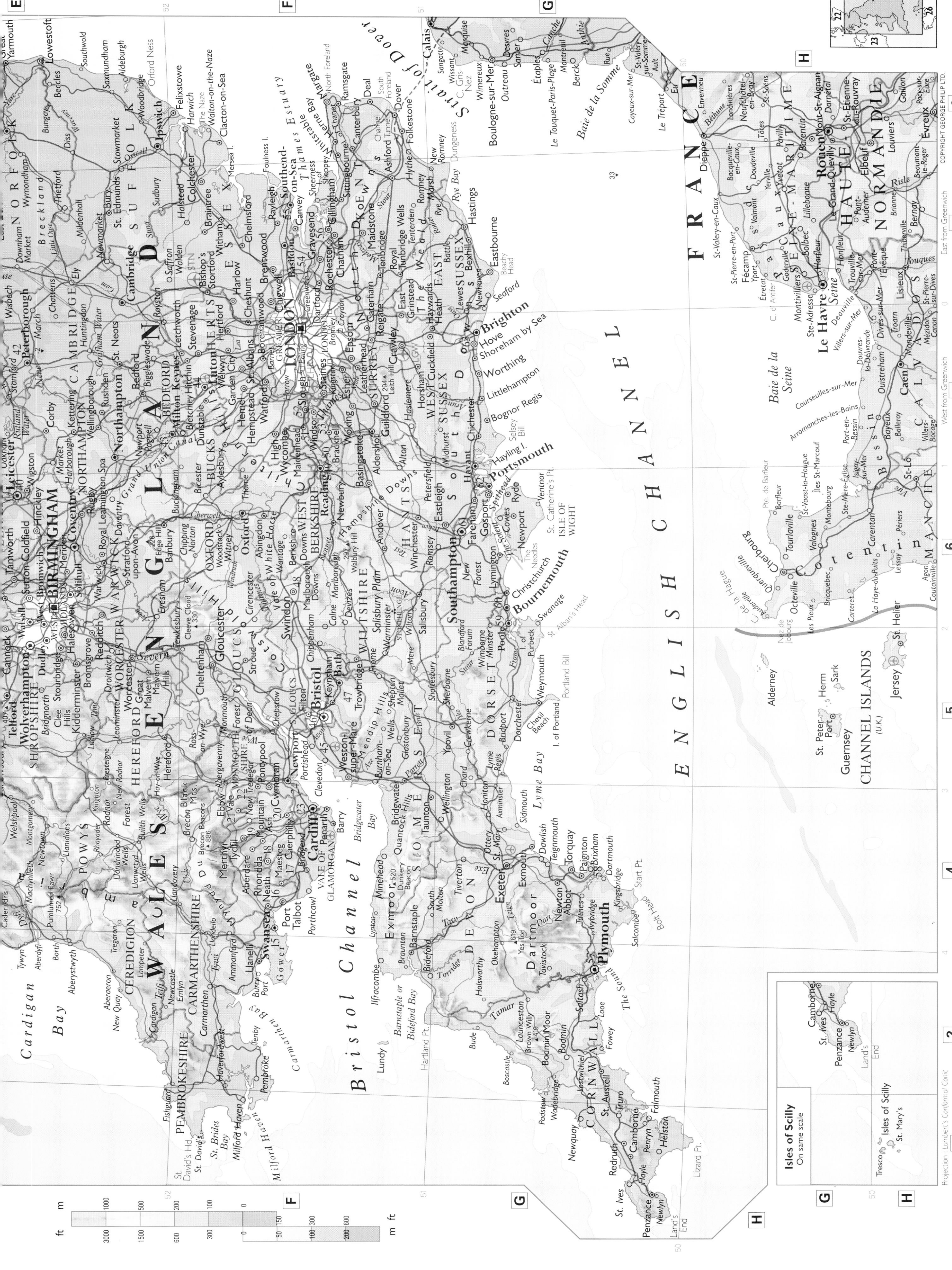
ENGLISH CHANNEL
FRANCE
WALES
ENGLAND
Bristol Channel
Cardigan Bay
Strait of Dover
Thames Estuary
CHANNEL ISLANDS (U.K.)
Guernsey
Jersey
Alderney
Sark
Herm
St. Peter Port
St. Helier
LONDON
BIRMINGHAM
Cardiff
Bristol
Plymouth
Southampton
Portsmouth
Bournemouth
Brighton
Exeter
Swansea
Oxford
Cambridge
Reading
Leicester
Coventry
Wolverhampton
Gloucester
Bath
Ipswich
Norwich
Calais
Boulogne-sur-Mer
Dieppe
Le Havre
Rouen
Caen
Cherbourg
Baie de Seine
Baie de la Somme
Lyme Bay
ISLE OF WIGHT
Isles of Scilly
On same scale
St. Mary's
Tresco
Land's End
Lizard Pt.
Projection: Lambert's Conformal Conic
COPYRIGHT GEORGE PHILIP LTD.
West from Greenwich
East from Greenwich

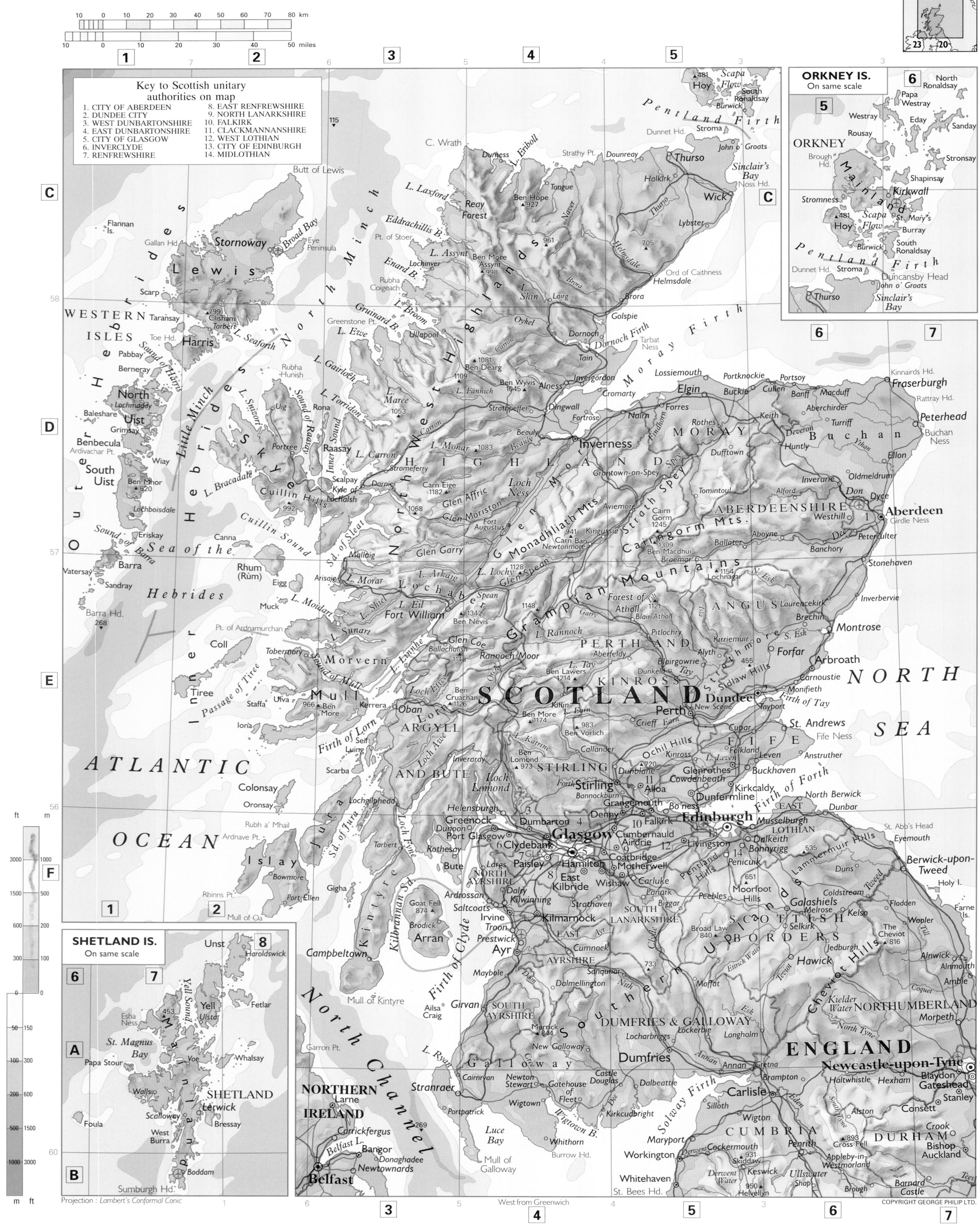

10 0 10 20 30 40 50 60 70 80 km
10 0 10 20 30 40 50 miles
Key to Scottish unitary authorities on map
1. CITY OF ABERDEEN
2. DUNDEE CITY
3. WEST DUNBARTONSHIRE
4. EAST DUNBARTONSHIRE
5. CITY OF GLASGOW
6. INVERCLYDE
7. RENFREWSHIRE
8. EAST RENFREWSHIRE
9. NORTH LANARKSHIRE
10. FALKIRK
11. CLACKMANNANSHIRE
12. WEST LOTHIAN
13. CITY OF EDINBURGH
14. MIDLOTHIAN
ORKNEY IS.
On same scale
SHETLAND IS.
On same scale
SCOTLAND
NORTH SEA
ATLANTIC OCEAN
North Channel
ENGLAND
NORTHERN IRELAND
WESTERN ISLES
Outer Hebrides
Inner Hebrides
Sea of the Hebrides
Little Minch
North Minch
North West Highlands
HIGHLAND
Grampian Mountains
Cairngorm Mts.
Monadhliath Mts.
Southern Uplands
Cheviot Hills
Lammermuir Hills
Pentland Firth
Moray Firth
Firth of Forth
Firth of Tay
Firth of Clyde
Firth of Lorn
Solway Firth
Lewis
Harris
North Uist
South Uist
Benbecula
Barra
Skye
Mull
Islay
Jura
Arran
Kintyre
Stornoway
Inverness
Aberdeen
Dundee
Perth
Stirling
Edinburgh
Glasgow
Fort William
Oban
Thurso
Wick
Kirkwall
Lerwick
Dumfries
Carlisle
Newcastle-upon-Tyne
Belfast
Ben Nevis
1342
Loch Ness
Loch Lomond
MORAY
ABERDEENSHIRE
ANGUS
PERTH AND KINROSS
FIFE
ARGYLL AND BUTE
STIRLING
EAST LOTHIAN
SCOTTISH BORDERS
SOUTH LANARKSHIRE
DUMFRIES & GALLOWAY
SOUTH AYRSHIRE
EAST AYRSHIRE
NORTH AYRSHIRE
NORTHUMBERLAND
CUMBRIA
DURHAM
SHETLAND
ORKNEY
Projection : Lambert's Conformal Conic
West from Greenwich
COPYRIGHT GEORGE PHILIP LTD.

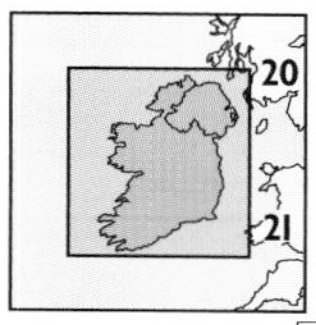

10 0 10 20 30 40 50 60 70 80 km
10 0 10 20 30 40 50 miles

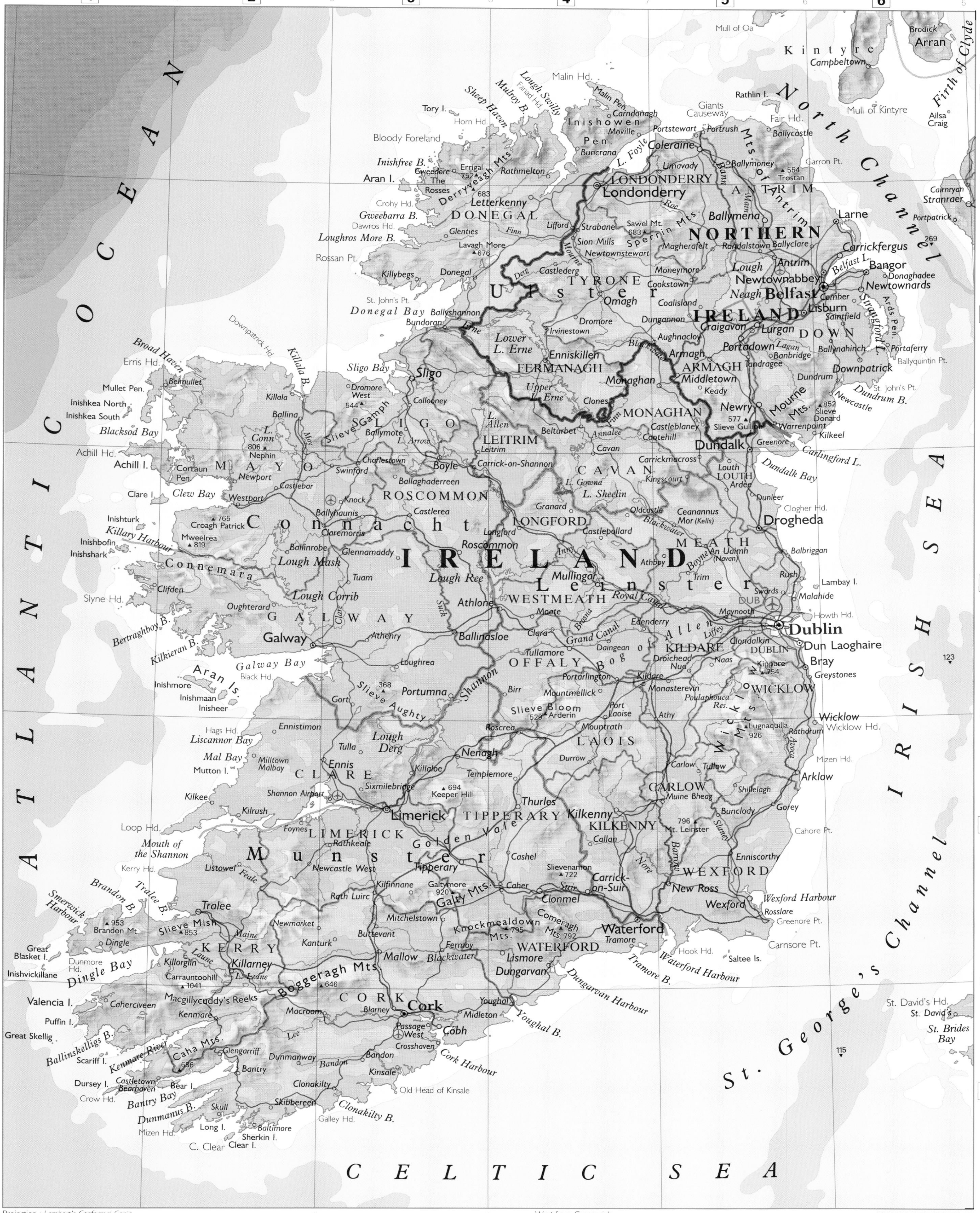

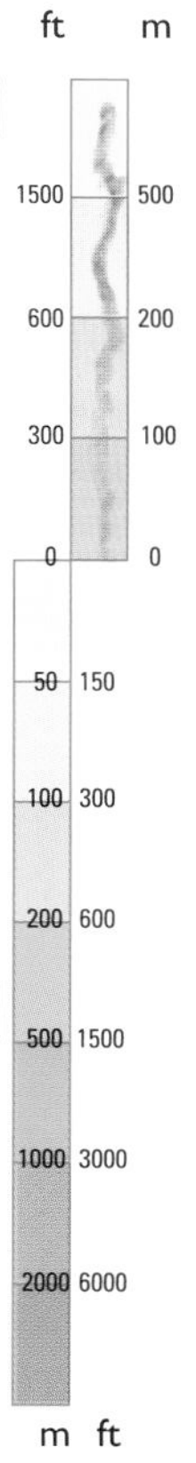

NETHERLANDS, BELGIUM AND LUXEMBOURG 1:2 000 000

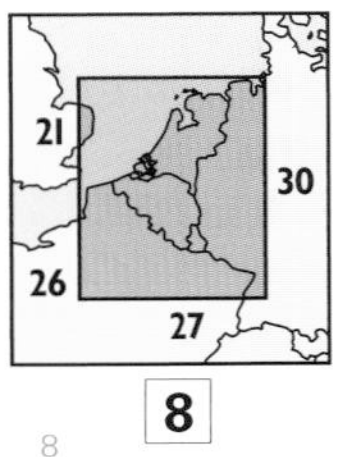

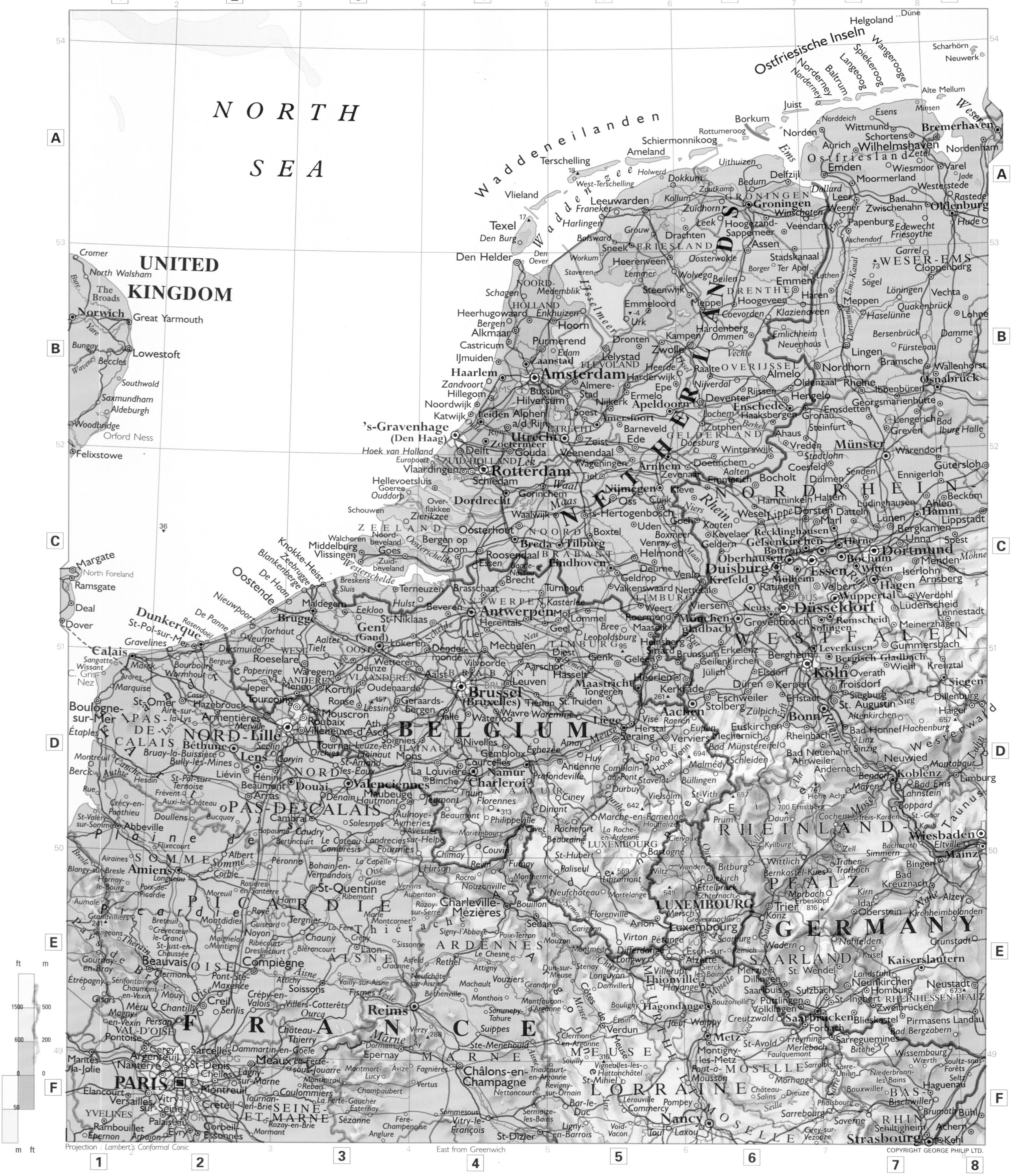

Underlined towns give their name to the administrative area in which they stand.

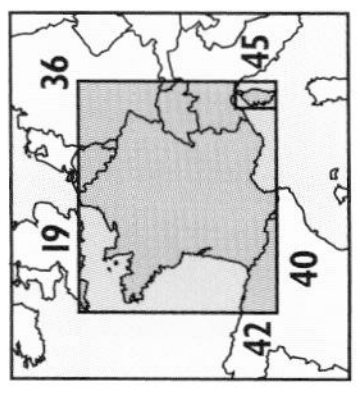
36
45
19
40
42

50 0 25 50 75 100 125 150 175 km
50 0 25 50 75 100 125 miles

UNITED KINGDOM
English Channel
FRANCE
BELGIUM
LUXEMBOURG
GERMANY
SWITZERLAND
ITALY
MONACO
ANDORRA
SPAIN
Bay of Biscay
Golfe de Gascogne
Golfe du Lion
MEDITERRANEAN SEA
Corse (Corsica)
PARIS
LYON
MARSEILLE
Bordeaux
Toulouse
Nantes
Lille
Strasbourg
Massif Central
Pyrénées
Bretagne
Normandie
Channel Is. (U.K.)
Projection: Conical with two standard parallels
West from Greenwich
East from Greenwich
COPYRIGHT GEORGE PHILIP LTD

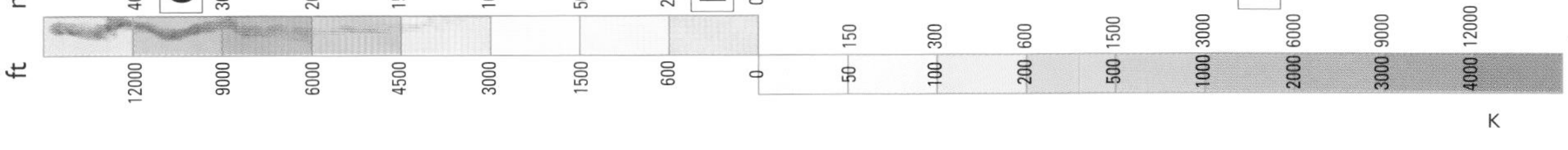
m ft
4000 12000
3000 9000
2000 6000
1500 4500
1000 3000
500 1500
200 600
0 0
50 150
100 300
200 600
500 1500
1000 3000
2000 6000
3000 9000
4000 12000
m ft

DÉPARTEMENTS IN THE PARIS AREA
1. Ville de Paris 3. Val-de-Marne
2. Seine-St-Denis 4. Hauts-de-Seine

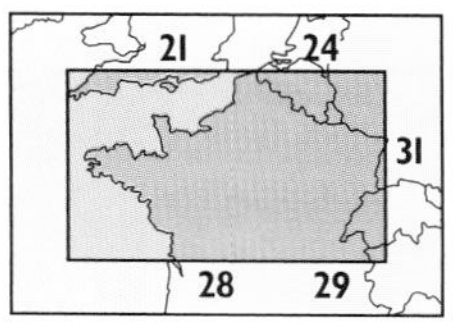

Underlined towns give their name to the administrative area in which they stand.

COPYRIGHT GEORGE PHILIP LTD.

SOUTHERN FRANCE 1:2 000 000

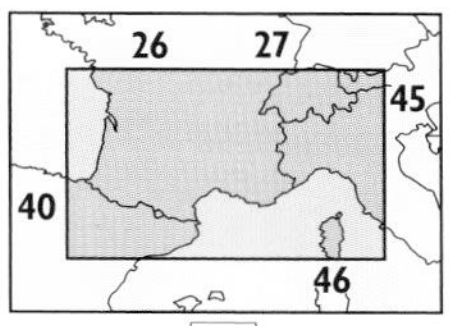
26
27
45
40
46

8
9
10
11
12
13
14
B
C
D
E
F
G
SWITZERLAND
Bern
Luzern
Neuchâtel
Fribourg
Lausanne
Genève
L. Léman
Montreux
Thonon-les-Bains
Sion
Chur
Davos
St. Moritz
GRAUBÜNDEN
VALAIS
TICINO
Alpi Lepontine
Berner Alpen
Alpes Pennine
Locarno
Bellinzona
Lugano
L. Maggiore
Como
Bergamo
Brescia
LOMBARDIA
MILANO
Monza
Novara
Vercelli
Pavia
Piacenza
Cremona
Parma
Torino
PIEMONTE
Asti
Alessandria
Cuneo
Génova
LIGURIA
La Spezia
Savona
Imperia
Sanremo
Golfo di Génova
Riviera di Ponente
Riviera di Levante
Massa
Carrara
Lucca
Pisa
Livorno
Viareggio
Elba
Piombino
Arcipelago Toscano
Capraia
Gorgona
Pianosa
Montecristo
ITALY
FRANCE
RHÔNE-ALPES
SAVOIE
HAUTE-SAVOIE
AIN
ISÈRE
DRÔME
ARDÈCHE
JURA
SAÔNE-ET-LOIRE
Lyon
Villeurbanne
Vénissieux
St-Étienne
Grenoble
Chambéry
Annecy
Valence
Chalon-sur-Saône
Mâcon
Bourg-en-Bresse
Roanne
Montélimar
Orange
Avignon
VAUCLUSE
Nîmes
Arles
Aix-en-Provence
BOUCHES-DU-RHÔNE
Marseille
Toulon
Hyères
Îs. d'Hyères
Camargue
PROVENCE
ALPES-DE-HAUTE-PROVENCE
HAUTES-ALPES
ALPES-MARITIMES
CÔTE D'AZUR
Côte d'Azur
Nice
Cannes
Antibes
Grasse
Fréjus
St-Raphaël
St-Tropez
MONACO
Monte-Carlo
Menton
Ventimiglia
Gap
Briançon
Digne-les-Bains
Massif du Pelvoux
Mont Blanc
Matterhorn
Monte Rosa
VALLE D'AOSTA
Aosta
Mts. du Jura
LIGURIAN SEA
MEDITERRANEAN SEA
CORSE
HAUTE-CORSE
CORSE-DU-SUD
Bastia
Ajaccio
Corte
Calvi
Porto-Vecchio
Bonifacio
Sartène
Bouches de Bonifacio
La Maddalena
Caprera
C. Corse
2940
2650

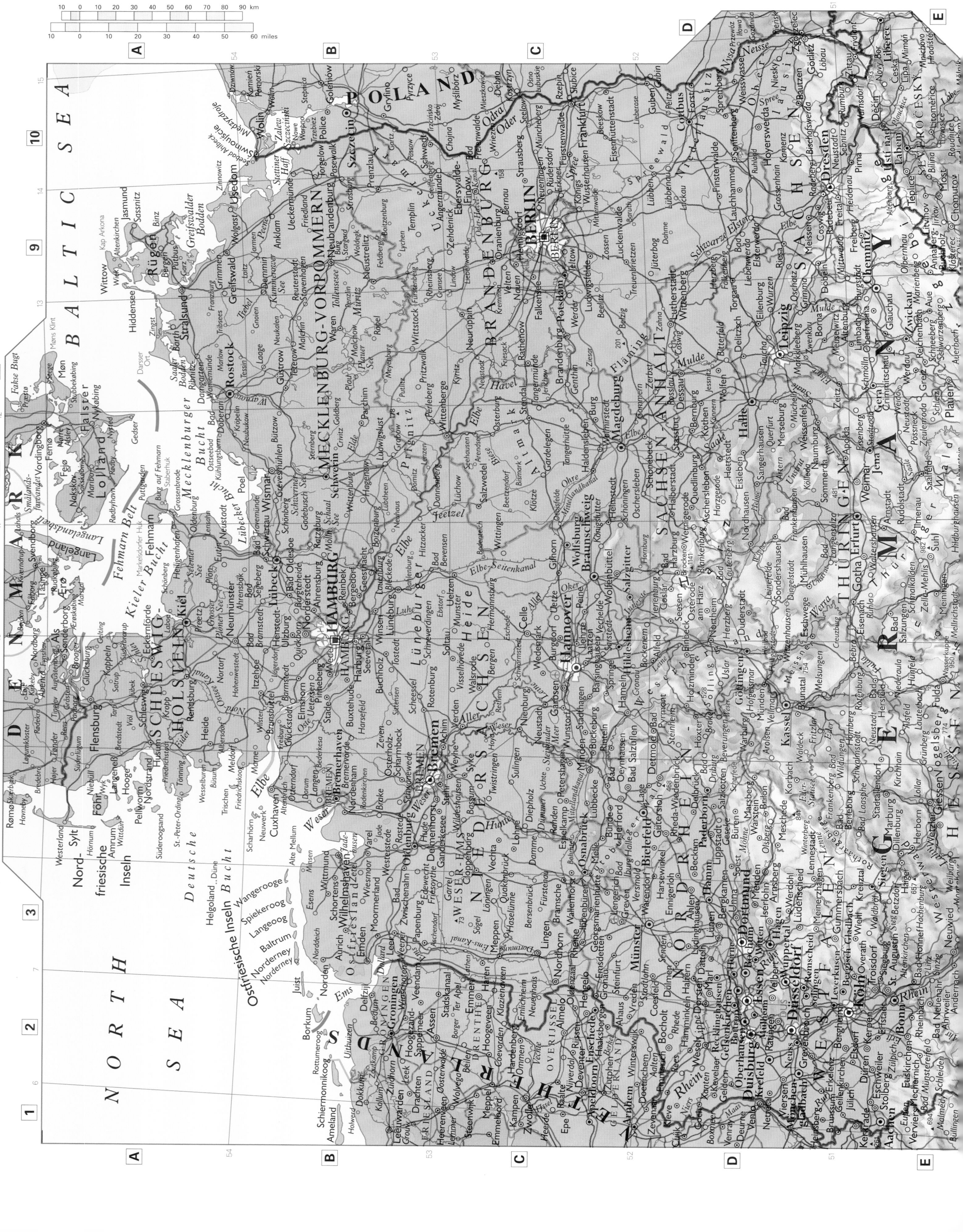
10 0 10 20 30 40 50 60 70 80 90 km
10 0 10 20 30 40 50 60 miles
A B C D E
1 2 3 4 5 6 7 8 9 10
NORTH SEA
BALTIC SEA
DENMARK
POLAND
NEDERLAND
GERMANY
SCHLESWIG-HOLSTEIN
MECKLENBURG-VORPOMMERN
NIEDERSACHSEN
BRANDENBURG
SACHSEN-ANHALT
SACHSEN
THÜRINGEN
NORDRHEIN-WESTFALEN
HESSEN
HAMBURG
BREMEN
BERLIN
Deutsche Bucht
Mecklenburger Bucht
Kieler Bucht
Lübecker Bucht
Fehmarn Belt
Nordfriesische Inseln
Ostfriesische Inseln
Rügen
Fehmarn
Lolland
Falster
Møn
Langeland
Helgoland
Kiel
Lübeck
Rostock
Stralsund
Greifswald
Schwerin
Wismar
Szczecin
Hannover
Braunschweig
Magdeburg
Halle
Leipzig
Dresden
Chemnitz
Erfurt
Kassel
Bielefeld
Münster
Osnabrück
Oldenburg
Bremerhaven
Dortmund
Essen
Duisburg
Düsseldorf
Wuppertal
Köln
Bonn
Aachen
Groningen
Enschede
Cottbus
Frankfurt
Potsdam
Göttingen
Elbe
Weser
Ems
Rhein
Oder
Spree
Havel
Lüneburger Heide
Harz
Altmark
Fläming
Lausitz
Erzgebirge
Thüringer Wald
Vogelsberg
Westerwald

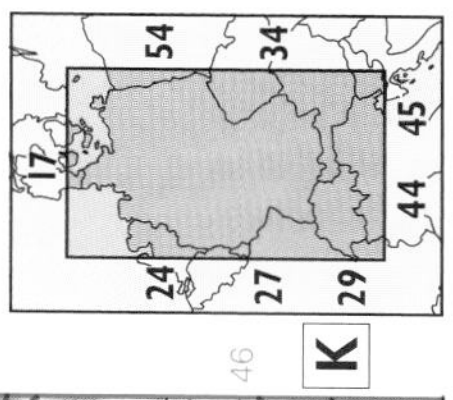
54
34
45
44
29
27
24
17

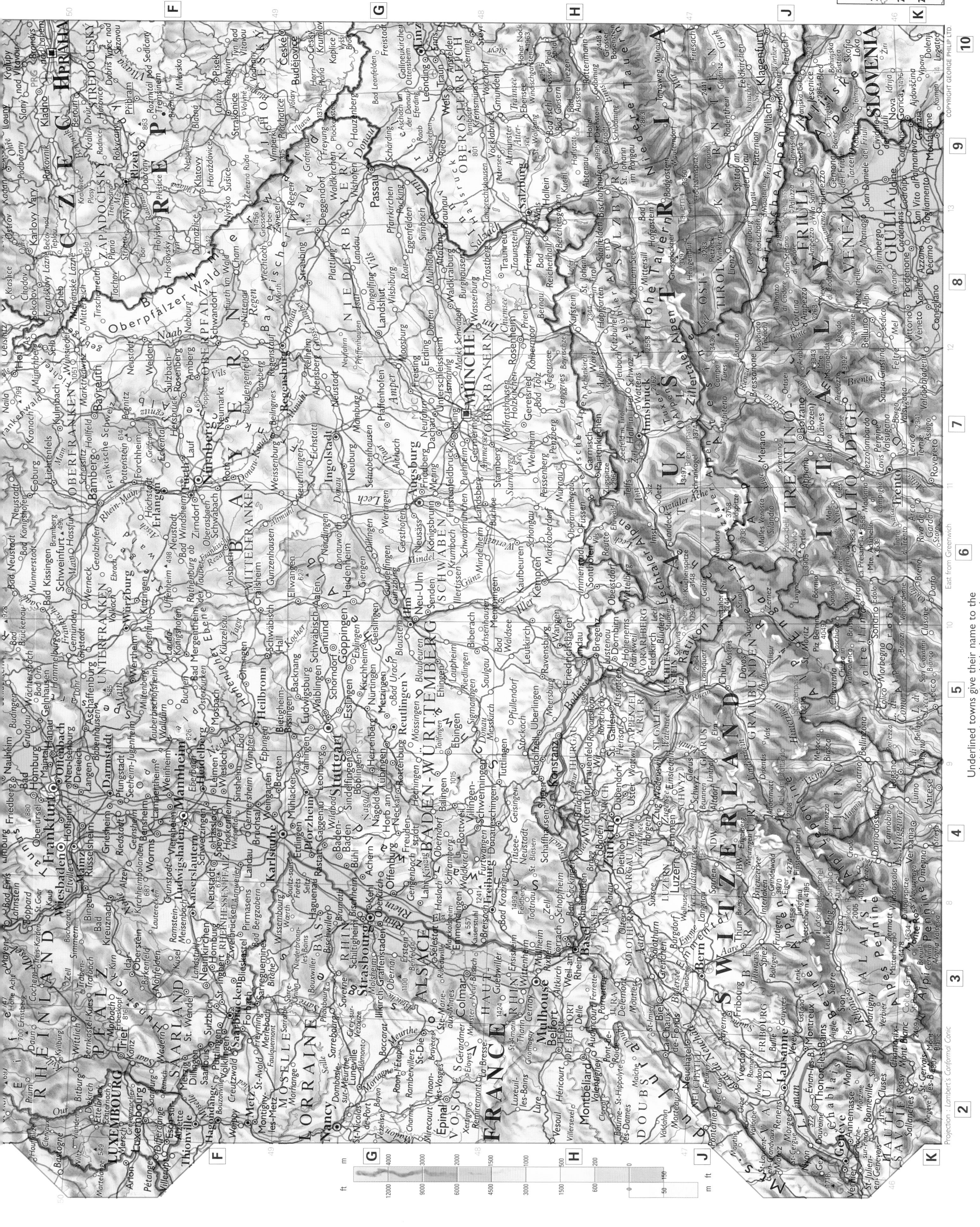
FRANCE
SWITZERLAND
ITALY
AUSTRIA
BAYERN
LUXEMBOURG
SLOVENIA
CZECH REP.
PRAHA
MÜNCHEN
Stuttgart
Frankfurt
Strasbourg
Zürich
Bern
Genève
Lausanne
Luzern
Basel
Innsbruck
Salzburg
Nürnberg
Regensburg
Augsburg
Karlsruhe
Mannheim
Wiesbaden
Mainz
Saarbrücken
Metz
Nancy
Mulhouse
Freiburg
Konstanz
Bolzano
Trento
Udine
Linz
Passau
Plzeň
Klagenfurt
Underlined towns give their name to the administrative area in which they stand.
Projection: Lambert's Conformal Conic
COPYRIGHT GEORGE PHILIP LTD.
East from Greenwich
m
ft
4000
3000
2000
1500
1000
500
200
0
12000
9000
6000
4500
3000
1500
600
0

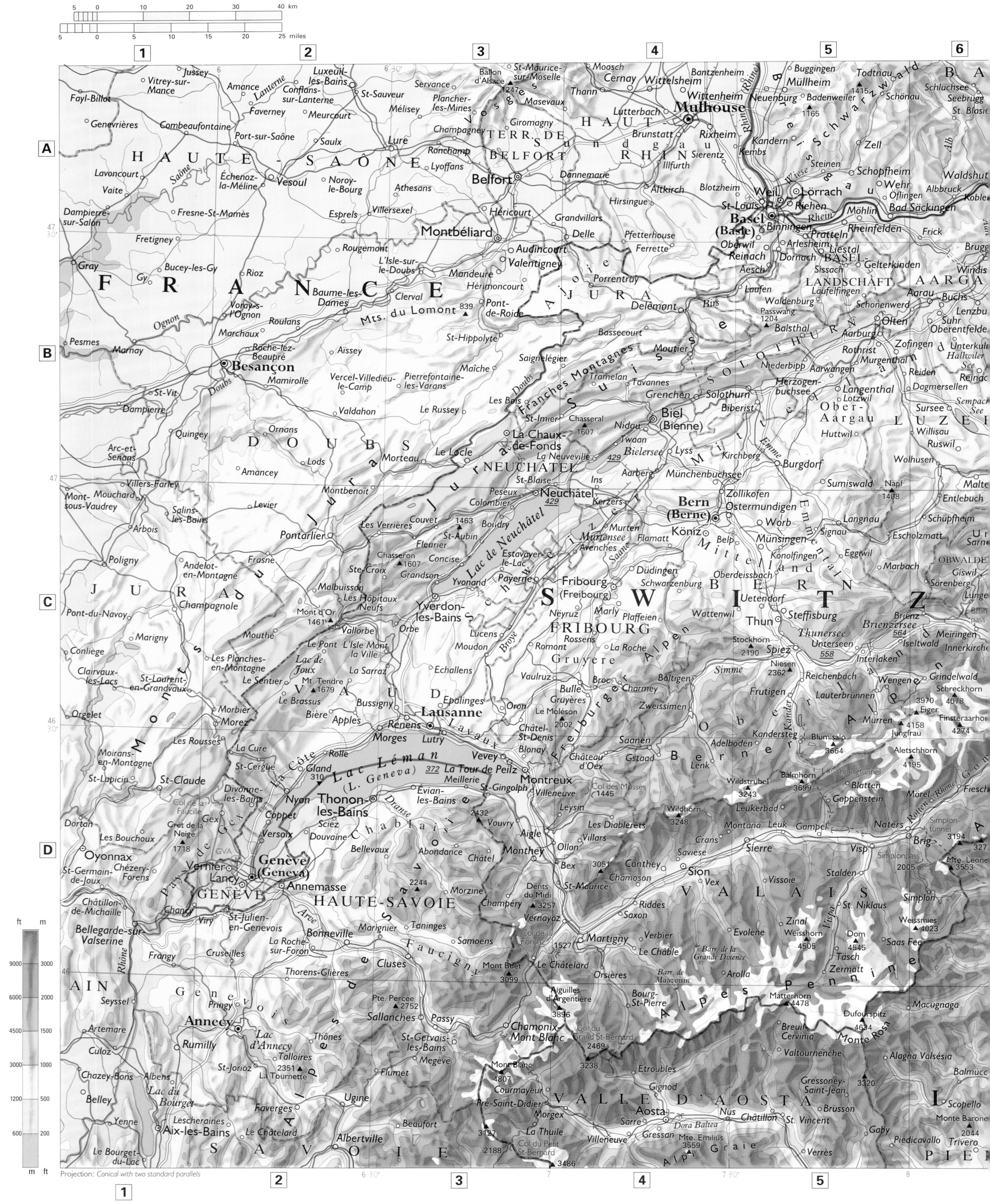

Projection: *Conical with two standard parallels*

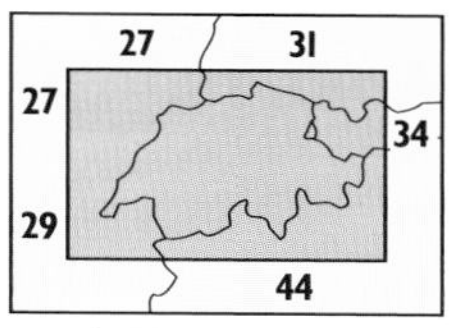
27
31
27
34
29
44

7
8
9
10
11
A
B
C
D
E
6
East from Greenwich
8°30'
9°
9°30'
10°
10°30'
47°30'
47°
46°30'
46°
BADEN WÜRTTEMBERG
GERMANY
BAYERN
AUSTRIA
TIROL
VORARLBERG
LIECHTENSTEIN
SCHAFFHAUSEN
THURGAU
ZÜRICH
ZUG
SCHWYZ
SANKT GALLEN
A.R. APPENZELL I.R.
GLARUS
OBWALDEN
NIDWALDEN
URI
GRAUBÜNDEN
TICINO
TRENTINO-ALTO ÁDIGE
LOMBÁRDIA
ITALY
SWITZERLAND
Blumberg
Engen
Stockach
Bonndorf
Hilzingen
Singen
Radolfzell
Sipplingen
Überlingen
Heiligenberg
Stühlingen
Thayngen
Schaffhausen
Allensbach
Konstanz
Meersburg
Markdorf
Baienfurt
Weingarten
Ravensburg
Wolfegg
Kisslegg
Leutkirch
Altusried
Iller
Obergünzburg
Wildpoldsried
Unterthingau
Wertach
Schongau
Marktoberdorf
Lech
Steingaden
Isny
Kempten
Durach
Buchenberg
Sulzberg
Mittelberg
Nesselwang
Rosshaupten
Forggensee
Meckenbeuren
Tettnang
Argen
Wangen
Friedrichshafen
Langenargen
Kressbronn
Lindenberg
Weiler-Simmerberg
Weitnau
1243
1125
Rettenberg
Wertach
Pfronten
Schwangau
Füssen
Vils
1738
Blaichach
Immenstadt
Oberstaufen
Scheidegg
Lindau
Bodensee (L. Constance)
Neunkirch
Diessenhofen
Stein am Rhein
Steckborn
Neuhausen
Feuerthalen
Tiengen
Kreuzlingen
252
396
Andelfingen
Zurzach
Rhein
Eglisau
Glattfelden
Neftenbach
Thur
Weinfelden
Romanshorn
Döttingen
Würenlingen
Bülach
Seuzach
Frauenfeld
Sulgen
Amriswil
Arbon
Winterthur
Embrach
Kloten
Wängi
Aadorf
Bischofszell
Rorschach
Hard
Bregenz
Wolfurt
Hittisau
Fischen
Sonthofen
Hindelang
Reutte
Weissenbach
Baden
Wettingen
Wallisellen
Effretikon
Elgg
Sirnach
Wil
Uzwil
Sankt Gallen
Gossau
Sankt Margrethen
Rheineck
Widnau
Lustenau
Dornbirn
Egg
Bezau
Oberstdorf
Allgäuer Alpen
2594
Ehrwald
Regensdorf
Limmat
Dübendorf
Turbenthal
Kirchberg
Flawil
Trogen
Teufen
Diepoldsau
Bregenzer Wald
Neuenhof
Dietikon
Schlieren
Zürich
Pfäffikon
Bauma
Degersheim
Herisau
Gais
Altstätten
Hohenems
2282
Mittelberg
Mädelegabel
2645
Häselgehr
Nassereith
Bremgarten
Fällanden
Uster
Bütschwil
Appenzell
Oberriet
Götzis
Hoher Freschen 2004
Au
Schröcken
Bach
2777
Silz
Wohlen
Reuss
Zollikon
Kilchberg
Küsnacht
Wetzikon
Hinwil
Wattwil
Umäsch
Wasserauen
Rankweil
Damüls
Muri
Adliswil
Thalwil
Meilen
Wald
Ebnat-Kappel
Säntis 2501
Feldkirch
Warth
Imst
Affoltern
Horgen
Männedorf
Rüti
Nesslau
Unterwasser
Gams
Lechtaler Alpen
Zürichsee
Stäfa
Wädenswil
Rapperswil
Sins
Baar
Richterswil
Pfäffikon
Kaltbrunn
Speer 1950
Grabs
Buchs
Schaan
Vaduz
Nenzing
Rote Wand 2704
Bludenz
Lech
Parseier-Sp. 3036
Oetz
Cham
Zug
Lachen
Schänis
Walensee
Churfirsten
Sevelen
Langen
Stuben
St. Anton
Zams
Flirsch
Landeck
2974
Hochdorf
Egg
Sihlsee
Walenstadt
Arlbergpass 1793
Dalaas
Rätikon
Montafon
Schruns
Root
Unterägeri
Einsiedeln
Näfels
Trisanna
Prutz
St. Leonhard
Ebikon
Zugersee
Küssnacht
Murg
Kuchenspitze 3148
Emmenbrücke
Arth
Linth
Netstal
Glarus
Mels
Sargans
Schesaplana 2964
Ischgl
Feuchten
Luzern
Kriens
Horw
Rigi
Goldau
Mythen 1899
Schwyz
Weggis
Vitznau
Bad Ragaz
2817
St-Gallenkirch
Gaschurn
Vesul-Sp. 3089
3533
Vierwaldstättersee
434
Brunnen
Muotathal
Glärnisch 2914
Schwanden
Pizol 2844
Schiers
Galtür
Mittelberg
Alpnach
Dorf
Stans
Linthal
Vättis
Landquart
Küblis
Prättigau
2853
Samnaun 3294
Martina
Nauders
Kerns
Bauen
Elm
2794
3247
Klosters
Silvretta Gruppe
3399
Altdorf
Bürglen
Unrotstock 2928
Hausstock 3158
Glarner Alpen
Chur
Flims
Langwies
3312
Piz Buin
Resia
Weisskugel 3736
Erstfeld
Tödi 3614
Domat Ems
Bonaduz
Davos
Arosa
Unter-engadin
Ötztaler Alpen
Engelberg
Titlis 3239
Ilanz
Churwalden
2383
3085
Ardez
Scuol (Schuls)
3602
Oberalpstock 3328
Vorderrhein
Lenzerheide
Flüelapass
Susch
San Valentino alla Muta
Gadmen
Wassen
Disentis (Muster)
Oberland
Thusis
Wiesen
3063
Piz Vadret 3229
Zernez
Málles Venosta
Sluderno
Silandro (Schlanders)
Guttannen
Göschenen
Oberalppass 2044
Sedrun
Filisur
Piz Sesvenna 3205
Val Venosta
Dammastock 3630
Hospental
Andermatt
Vrin
Thalkirch
Tiefencastel
Albula
Piz Kesch 3418
3165
Santa Maria
Adige
Láces
3283
Furkapass
Realp
2431
2108
Pic Medel 3210
3149
Vals
3000
Andeer
Hinterrhein
Savognin
3339
La Punt
Prato allo Stelvio
Grimselpass
2165
P. del San Gottardo
Gletsch
Airolo
3199
Olivone
Adula-Gruppe
Splügen
Splügenpass 2113
Mulegns
Piz d'Err 3378
Samedan
Livigno
Passo dello Stelvio 2757
Ortles 3905
Martello
Ulrichen
Bedretto
Rheinwaldhorn 3402
2065
Sankt Moritz
Julierpass 2284
Pontresina
Münster
Faido
Paso del San Bernardino
San Bernardino
3209
Piz Platta 3392
Silvaplana
Pso. del Bernina 2323
Bórmio
Campo Tencia 3072
Fusio
Malvaglia
3063
Campodolcino 3163
Maloja
Maloja pass 1815
Piz Bernina 4049
3302
Adda
Basodino 3273
Sonogno
Lepontine Alpen
Bodio
Biasca
Mesocco
3025
Pizzo Stella
3131
Vicosoprano
Sóndalo
Formazza
Bignasco
Rossa
Chiavenna
Castasegna
Poschiavo
Grósio
3006
Vermíglio
Dimaro
Cevio
Mera
Monte Disgrazia 3678
Chiesa in Valmalenco
Grosotto
Ponte di Legno
Passo del Tonale
Prémia
2792
Maggia
Mésa
Novate Mezzola
Brusio
Vezza di Oglio
La Presanella 3558
2322
Maggia
Vogorno
Arbedo
Tirano
Edolo
Madonna di Campíglio
Crodo 2237
Varzo
Locarno
Minusio
Bellinzona
Verceia
Sóndrio
Chiuro
Téglio
Mte. Adamello 3554
Crevoladóssola
Intragna
Losone
Ascona
Giubiasco
Gravedona
Morbegno
Talamona
Albosaggia
Aprica
Pinzolo
Masera
Brissago
Vira
Cadenazzo
Pzo. di Gino 2245
Dongo
Cólico
Delébio
Valtellina
Malonno
Domodóssola
Santa Maria Maggiore
Lago di Como
Monte Legnone 2609
Pizzo di Coca 3052
Cedégolo
Villadóssola
Cannóbio
Cànnero Riviera
Maccagno
Porlezza
Gerola Alta
Valbondione
Capo di Ponte
Tione di Trento
Vogogna
Lago Maggiore
193
Agno
Lugano
Menággio
Bellano
Varenna
Alpi Orobie
Schilpário
Ornavasso
Luino
Lago di Lugano
Tremezzo
199
Intróbio
Branzi
Val Camónica
Valli Giudicárie
Pieve di Bono
Gravellona Toce
Pallanza
Ghiffa
Ponte Tresa
Melide
Mte. Generoso 1701
Bellágio
Monte San Primo 1685
Mandello del Lário
Piazza Brembano
Borno
Breno
Riva del Garda
Verbánia
Argegno
Omegna
Laveno
Mendrisio
Nesso
Bienno
Condino
Stresa
Balerna
Chiasso
Gavirate
Moltrásio
Canzo
Lecco
San Giovanni Bianco
Brembo
Valle Seriana
Clusone
Gandino
Monte Colombine 2215
Bagolino
Storo
Limone sul Garda
L. d'Orta
Varallo
Varese
Malnate
Como
Erba
Lóvere
Pisogne
Cóllio
Malcésine
Méina
Arona
Lago di Varese
Olgiate Comasco
Oggiono
Calolziocorte
Zogno
Gazzaniga
Darfo
L. d'Idro
Idro
Borgomanero
Sesto Calende
Brianza
Albino
Casazza
L. d'Iseo
Marone
Gardone Val Trómpia
Vestone
Borgosésia
Tradate
Cantù
Ponte San Pietro
Bérgamo
Gargnano
Serravalle Sésia
Somma Lombardo
Cassano Magnago
Carate Brianza
Merate
Trescore Balneário
Chiese
Vobarno
L. di Garda
Gallarate
Saronno
Meda
Séveso
Seregno
Dálmine
Seriate
Sárnico
Stezzano
Iseo
Sarezzo
Sabbio Chiese
Gardone Riviera
PIEMONTE

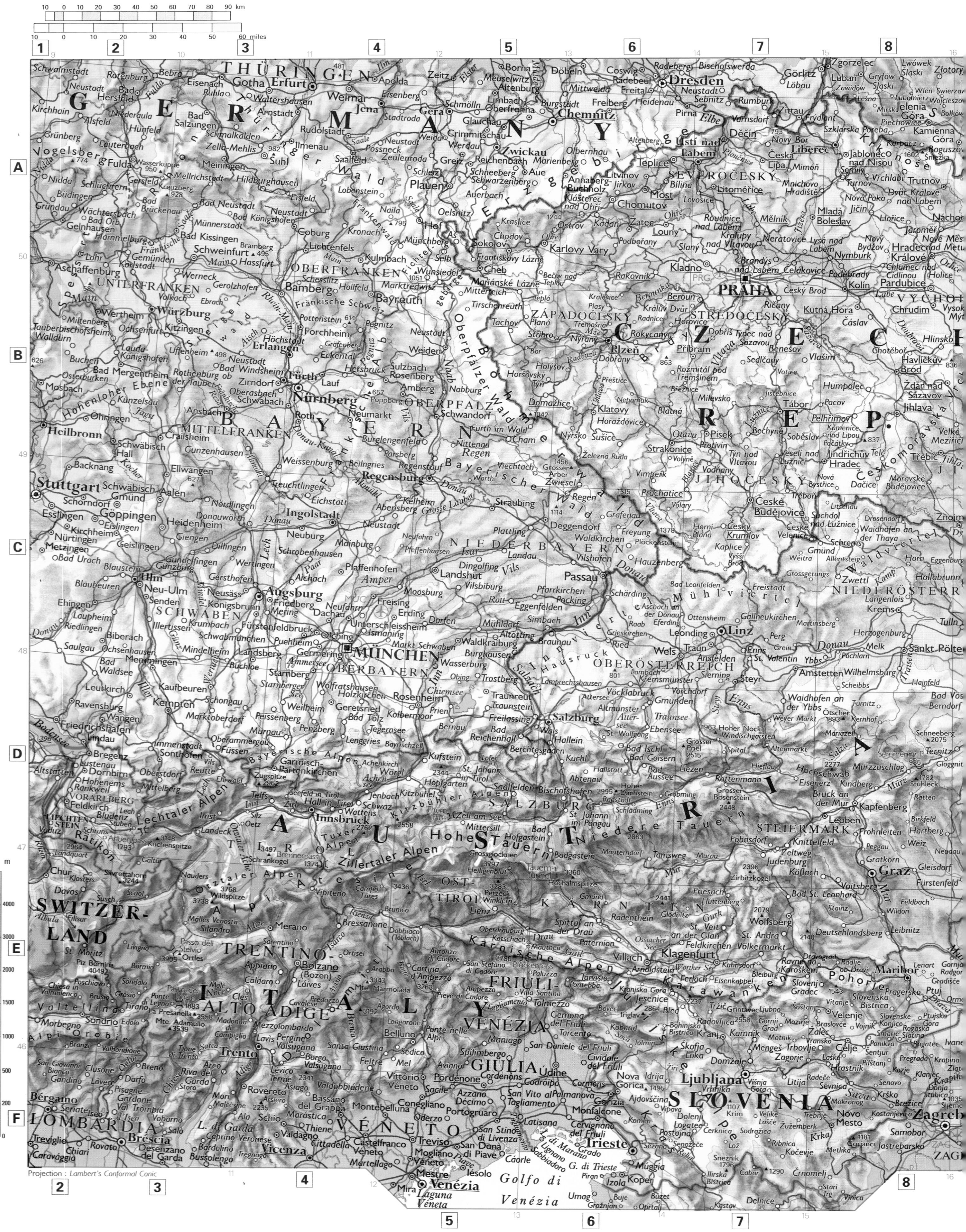

Projection : Lambert's Conformal Conic

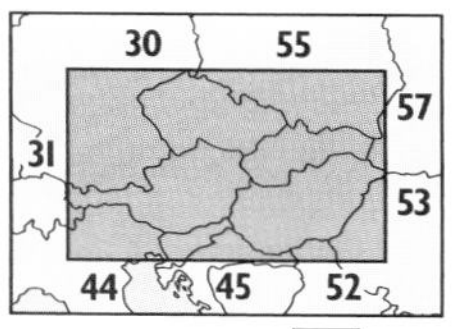

Underlined towns give their name to the administrative area in which they stand.

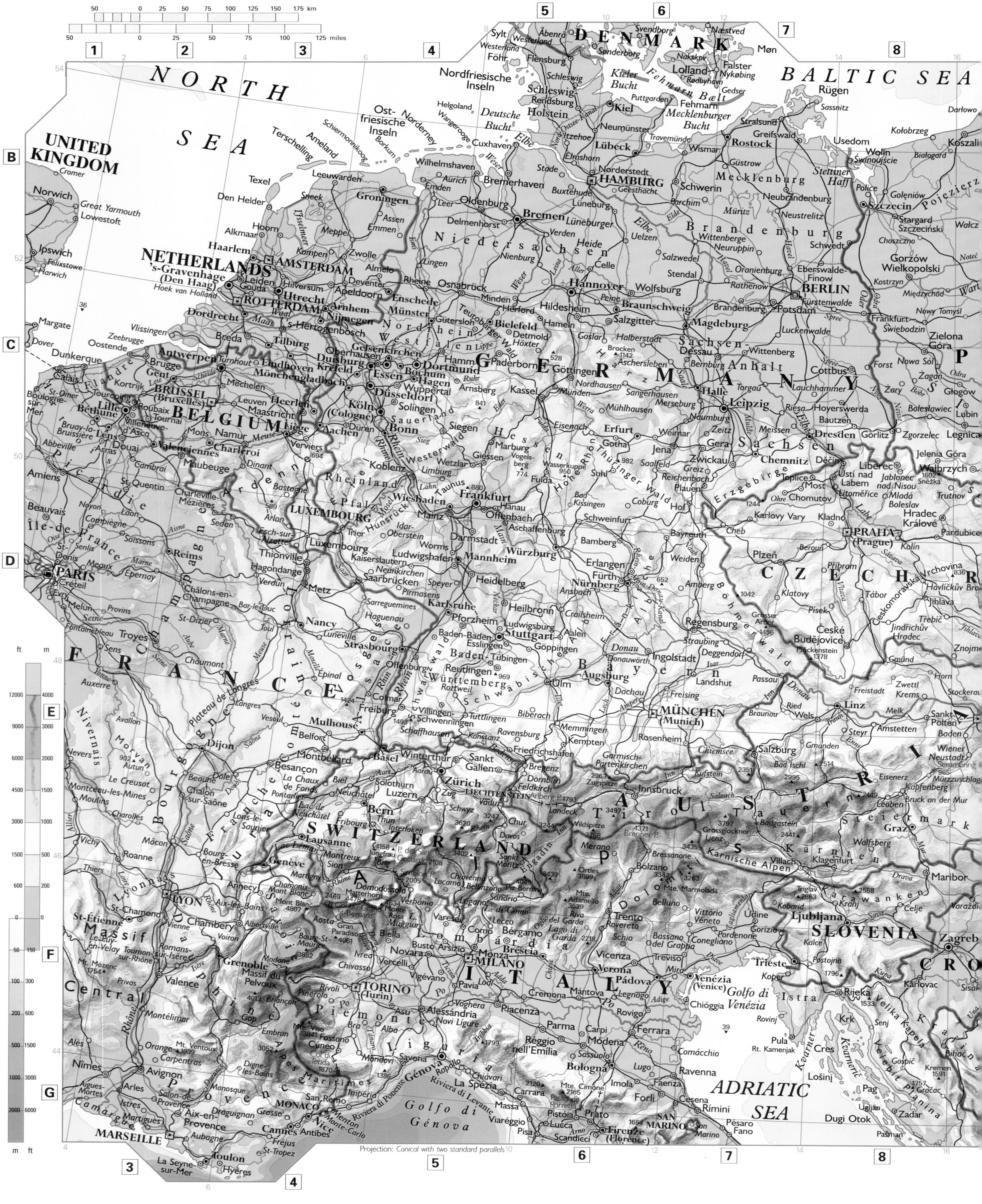

50 0 25 50 75 100 125 150 175 km
50 0 25 50 75 100 125 miles
NORTH SEA
BALTIC SEA
UNITED KINGDOM
NETHERLANDS
BELGIUM
LUXEMBOURG
DENMARK
GERMANY
CZECH R.
AUSTRIA
SWITZERLAND
LIECHTENSTEIN
FRANCE
ITALY
SLOVENIA
MONACO
SAN MARINO
ADRIATIC SEA
Golfo di Génova
Golfo di Venézia
Nordfriesische Inseln
Ostfriesische Inseln
Deutsche Bucht
Kieler Bucht
Mecklenburger Bucht
Fehmarn Bælt
Stettiner Haff
AMSTERDAM
's-Gravenhage (Den Haag)
ROTTERDAM
BRUSSEL (BRUXELLES)
BERLIN
HAMBURG
PRAHA (Prague)
MÜNCHEN (Munich)
PARIS
MILANO
TORINO (Turin)
LYON
MARSEILLE
Ljubljana
Zagreb
Frankfurt
Köln (Cologne)
Düsseldorf
Stuttgart
Nürnberg
Leipzig
Dresden
Hannover
Bremen
Zürich
Bern
Genève
Lausanne
Basel
Innsbruck
Salzburg
Linz
Graz
Venézia (Venice)
Génova
Bologna
Firenze (Florence)
Verona
Trieste
Strasbourg
Nancy
Metz
Reims
Dijon
Grenoble
Avignon
Nice
Niedersachsen
Nordrhein-Westfalen
Hessen
Rheinland-Pfalz
Bayern
Baden-Württemberg
Thüringer Wald
Schwarzwald
Schwäbische Alb
Erzgebirge
Böhmerwald
Harz
Sauerland
Westerwald
Taunus
Hunsrück
Eifel
Ardennes
Mecklenburg
Brandenburg
Sachsen
Sachsen-Anhalt
Tirol
Hohe Tauern
Karnische Alpen
Dolomiti
Steiermark
Kärnten
Karawanken
Lombárdia
Piemonte
Liguria
Provence
Alpes Maritimes
Massif Central
Dauphiné
Jura
Champagne
Lorraine
Bourgogne
Picardie
Île-de-France
Flandre
Istra
Velebit
Projection: Conical with two standard parallels

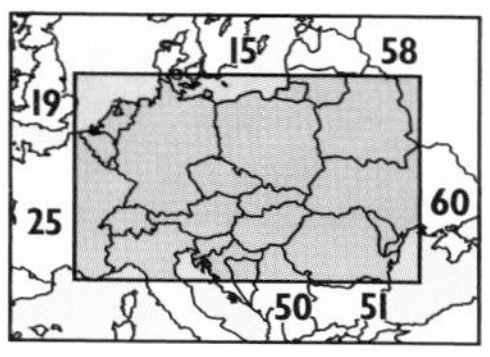
15
58
19
25
60
50
51

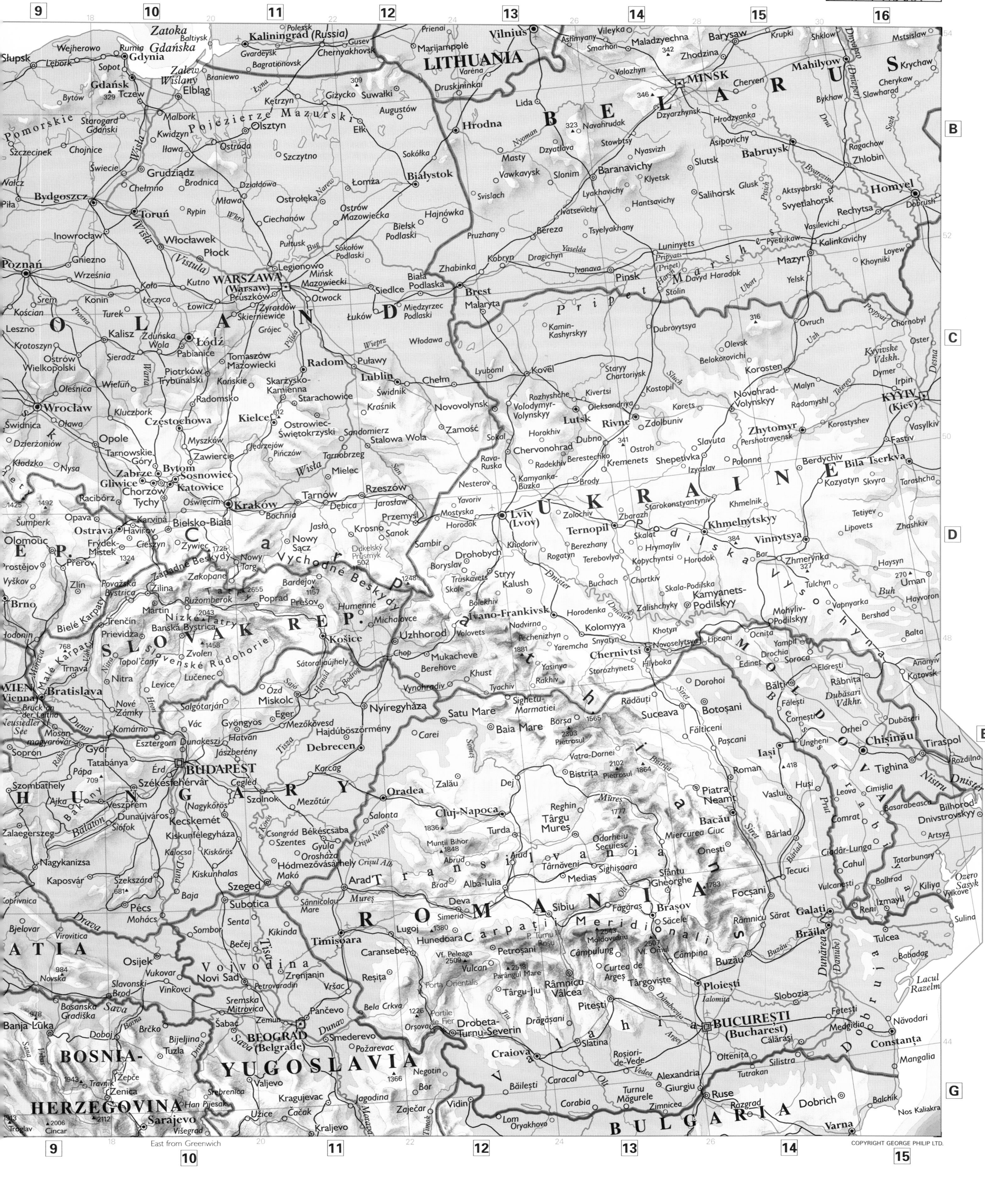
POLAND
LITHUANIA
BELARUS
UKRAINE
SLOVAK REP.
HUNGARY
ROMANIA
MOLDOVA
YUGOSLAVIA
BOSNIA-HERZEGOVINA
BULGARIA
Zatoka Gdańska
Kaliningrad (Russia)
Vilnius
MINSK
WARSZAWA (Warsaw)
Gdańsk
Gdynia
Poznań
Łódź
Wrocław
Kraków
Katowice
Lublin
Białystok
Brest
Hrodna
Homyel
Babruysk
Mahilyow
Pinsk
Pripet Marshes
Lviv (Lvov)
Rivne
Lutsk
Zhytomyr
KYYIV (Kiev)
Vinnytsya
Khmelnytskyy
Ternopil
Chernivtsi
Ivano-Frankivsk
Uzhhorod
Košice
Bratislava
WIEN Vienna
BUDAPEST
Debrecen
Miskolc
Szeged
Chişinău
Iaşi
Cluj-Napoca
Timişoara
Braşov
Ploieşti
BUCUREŞTI (Bucharest)
Constanţa
Craiova
Galaţi
Brăila
BEOGRAD (Belgrade)
Novi Sad
Sarajevo
Ruse
Varna
Carpathians
Transylvania
Carpaţii Meridionali
Vojvodina
Dunărea (Danube)
Dnister
Vistula
East from Greenwich

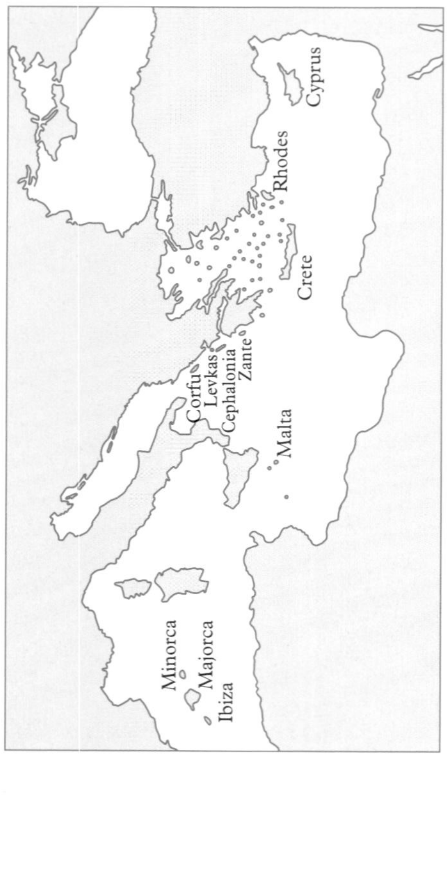
Minorca
Majorca
Ibiza
Corfu
Levkas
Cephalonia
Zante
Malta
Crete
Rhodes
Cyprus

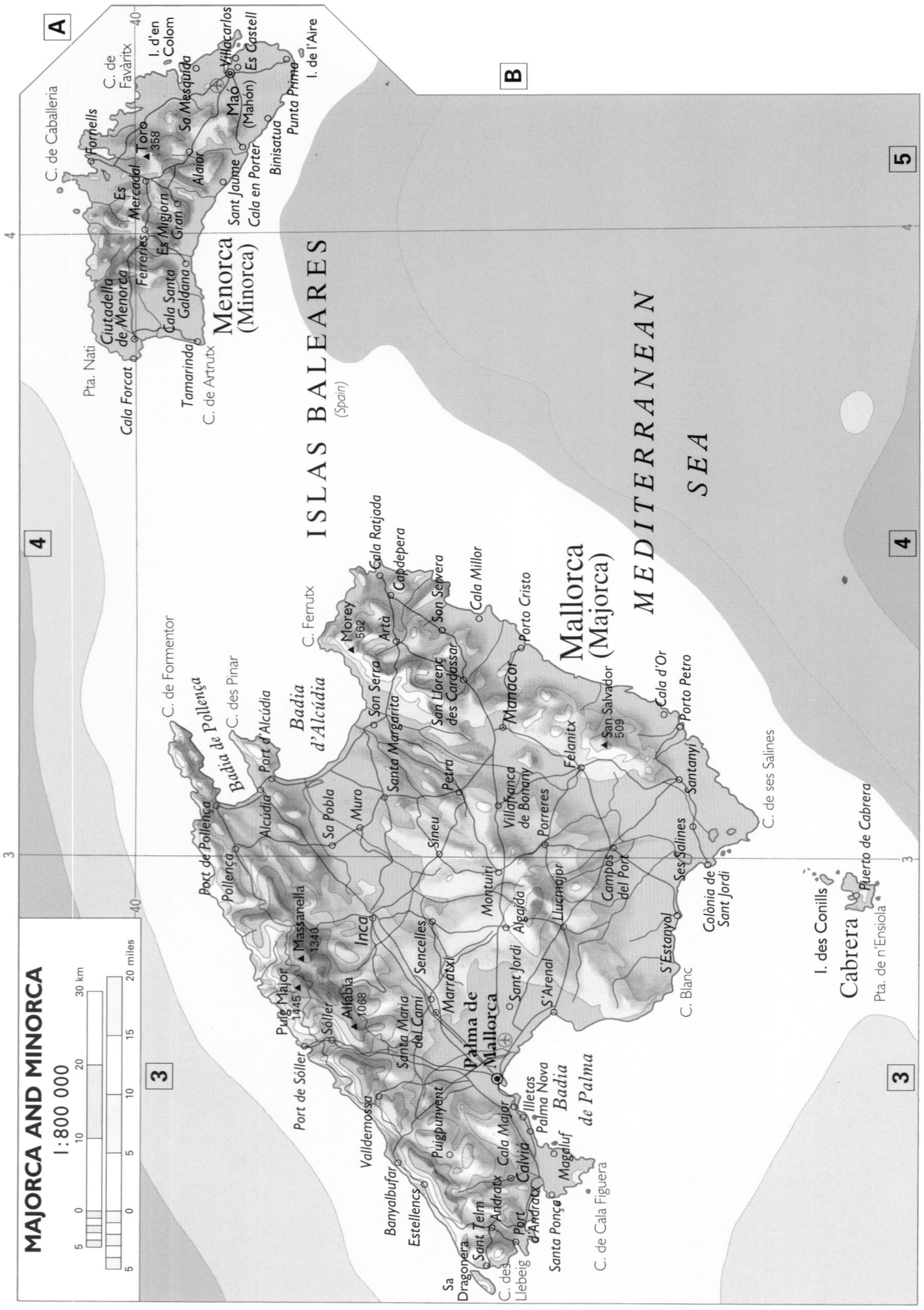
MAJORCA AND MINORCA
1:800 000
ISLAS BALEARES
(Spain)
Mallorca
(Majorca)
Menorca
(Minorca)
MEDITERRANEAN
SEA
Palma de Mallorca
Badia de Palma
Badia d'Alcúdia
Cabrera

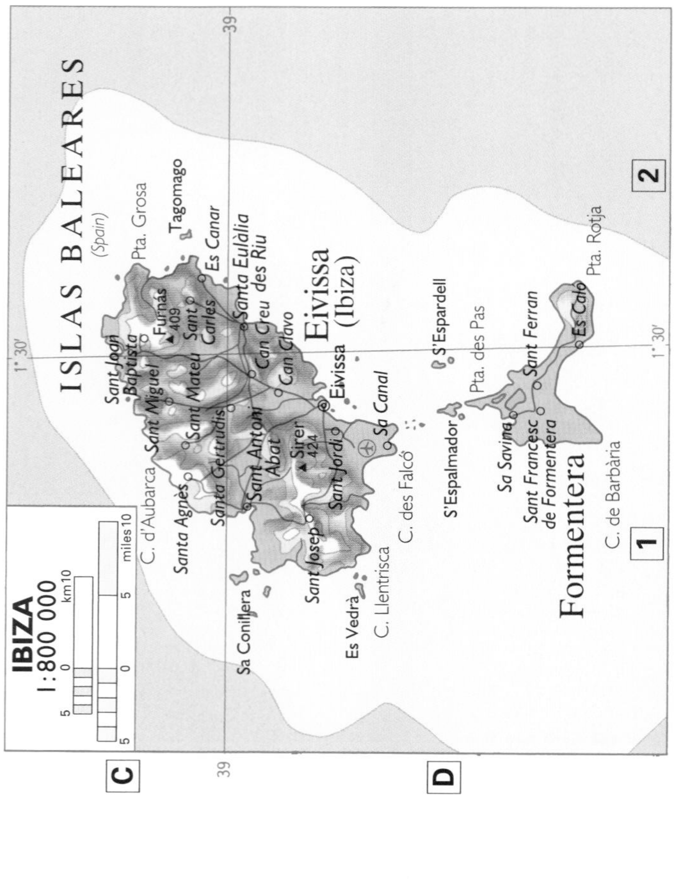
IBIZA
1:800 000
ISLAS BALEARES
(Spain)
Eivissa
(Ibiza)
Formentera

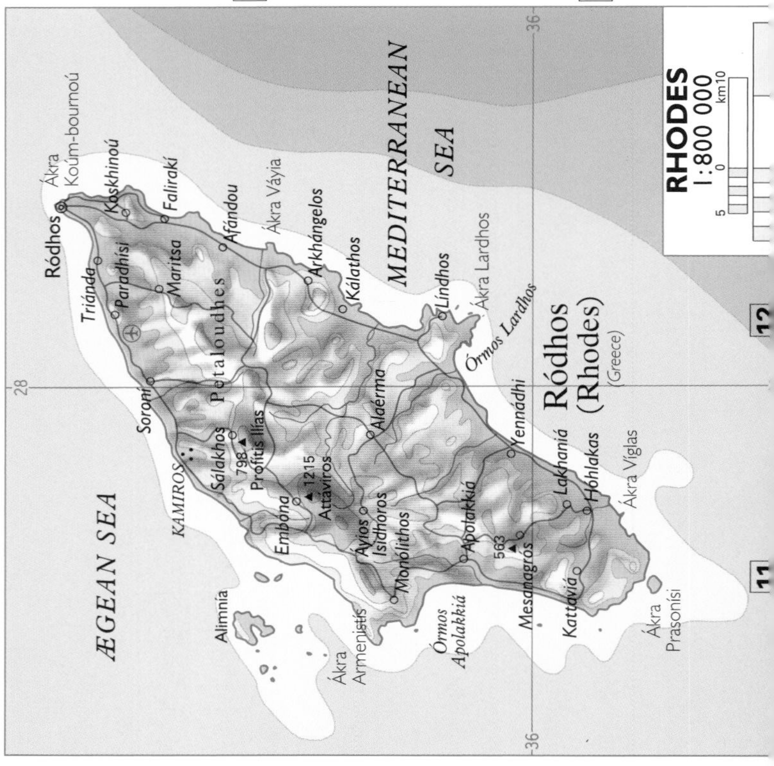
RHODES
1:800 000
Ródhos
(Rhodes)
(Greece)
ÆGEAN SEA
MEDITERRANEAN
SEA

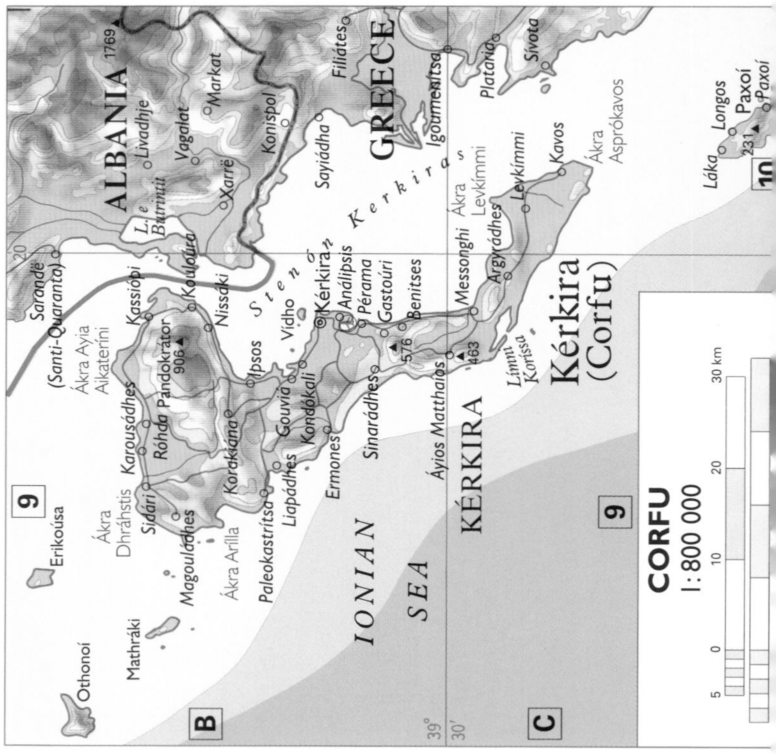
CORFU
1:800 000
Kérkira
(Corfu)
KÉRKIRA
ALBANIA
GREECE
IONIAN
SEA

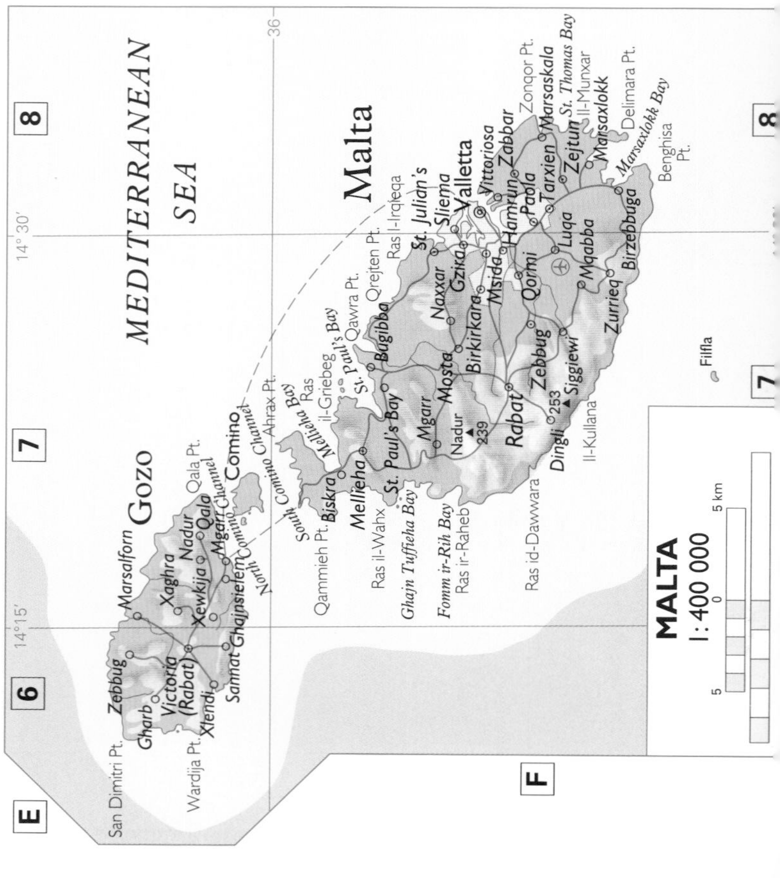
MALTA
1:400 000
Malta
Gozo
Comino
Valletta
MEDITERRANEAN
SEA

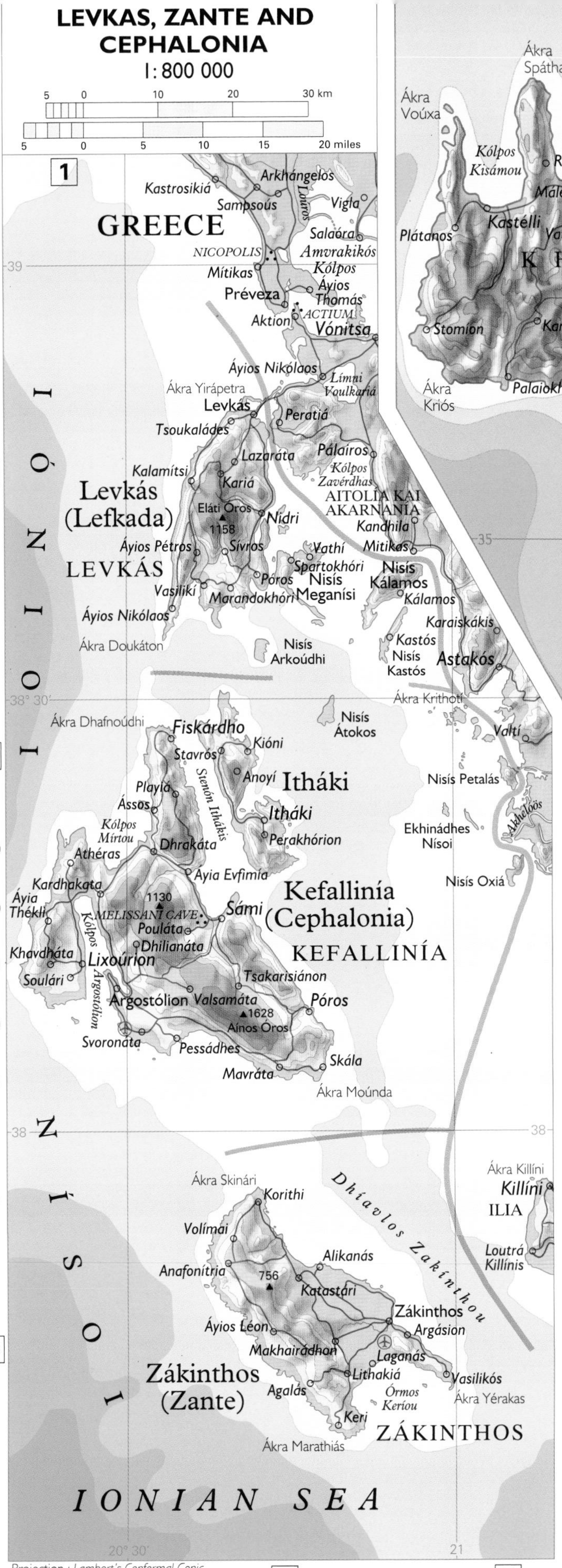

LEVKAS, ZANTE AND CEPHALONIA
1:800 000
GREECE
Levkás (Lefkada)
LEVKÁS
Kefallinía (Cephalonia)
KEFALLINÍA
Itháki
Zákinthos (Zante)
ZÁKINTHOS
AITOLÍA KAI AKARNANÍA
ILIA
IÓNIOI NÍSOI
IONIAN SEA
Préveza
Vónitsa
Argostólion
Lixoúrion
Sámi
Fiskárdho
Projection : Lambert's Conformal Conic

CRETE
1:1 000 000
SEA OF CRETE
MEDITERRANEAN SEA
Kríti (Crete)
(Greece)
KHANIÁ
RÉTHÍMNON
IRÁKLION
LASÍTHI
Khaniá
Réthímnon
Iráklion
Áyios Nikólaos
Ierápetra
Sitía
Gávdhos
Dhíkti Óros
Ídhi Óros
Lévka Óros

CYPRUS
1:1 000 000
CYPRUS
MEDITERRANEAN SEA
Nicosia (Levkôsia)
Limassol
Larnaca
Paphos
Famagusta (Ammochostos)
Kyrenia
Morphou
(Under Turkish Administration)
Troodos
Olympus 1951
Famagusta Bay
Morphou Bay
Larnaca Bay
Akrotiri Bay
AKROTIRI SOVEREIGN BASE AREA
DHEKELIA SOVEREIGN BASE AREA
Mesaoria
Karpasia
East from Greenwich
COPYRIGHT GEORGE PHILIP LTD.

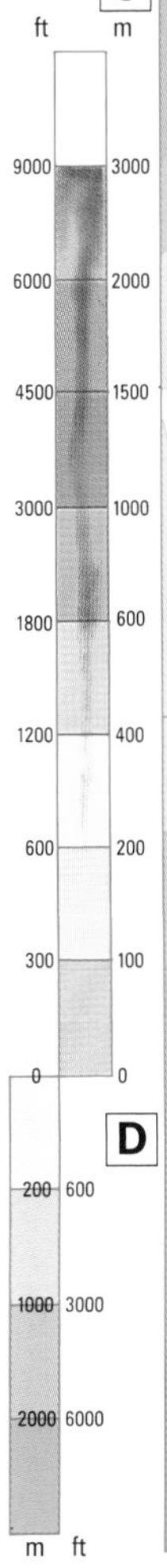

ft
m
9000
3000
6000
2000
4500
1500
3000
1000
1800
600
1200
400
600
200
300
100
0
0
200
600
1000
3000
2000
6000
m
ft

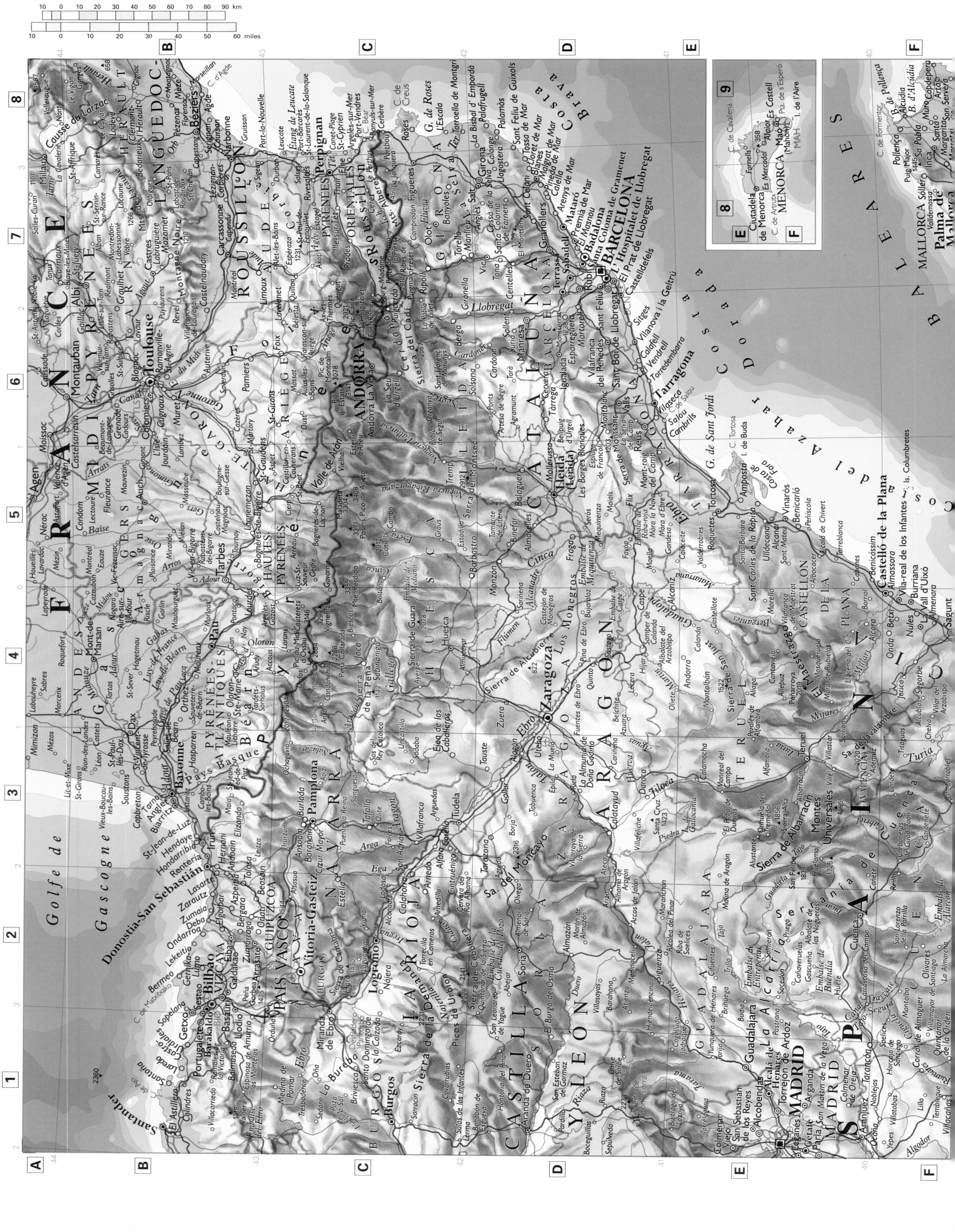
10 0 10 20 30 40 50 60 70 80 90 km
10 0 10 20 30 40 50 60 miles
FRANCE
ESPAÑA
ANDORRA
Golfe de Gascogne
Toulouse
Perpignan
Donostia-San Sebastián
Bilbao
Santander
Vitoria-Gasteiz
Pamplona
Logroño
Burgos
Soria
Zaragoza
Huesca
Lleida
Girona
BARCELONA
Tarragona
Teruel
Castelló de la Plana
Guadalajara
MADRID
Cuenca
PAÍS VASCO
NAVARRA
LA RIOJA
ARAGÓN
CATALUÑA
CASTILLA Y LEÓN
ROUSSILLON
LANGUEDOC
MENORCA
MALLORCA
Palma de Mallorca
BALEARES

M E D I T E R R A N E A N   S E A
A L G E R I A
Golfo de Valencia
Costa Blanca
Costa del Sol
Valencia
Alicante
Murcia
Cartagena
Almería
Granada
Albacete
Oran (Ouahran)
ALGER (Algiers)
Blida
Médéa
Mostaganem
Relizane
Sidi-bel-Abbès
Tiaret
EIVISSA (IBIZA)
Formentera
Cabrera
Melilla (Sp.)
Nador
Alborán (Sp.)
Projection : Lambert's Conformal Conic
West from Greenwich
East from Greenwich

COPYRIGHT GEORGE PHILIP LTD.

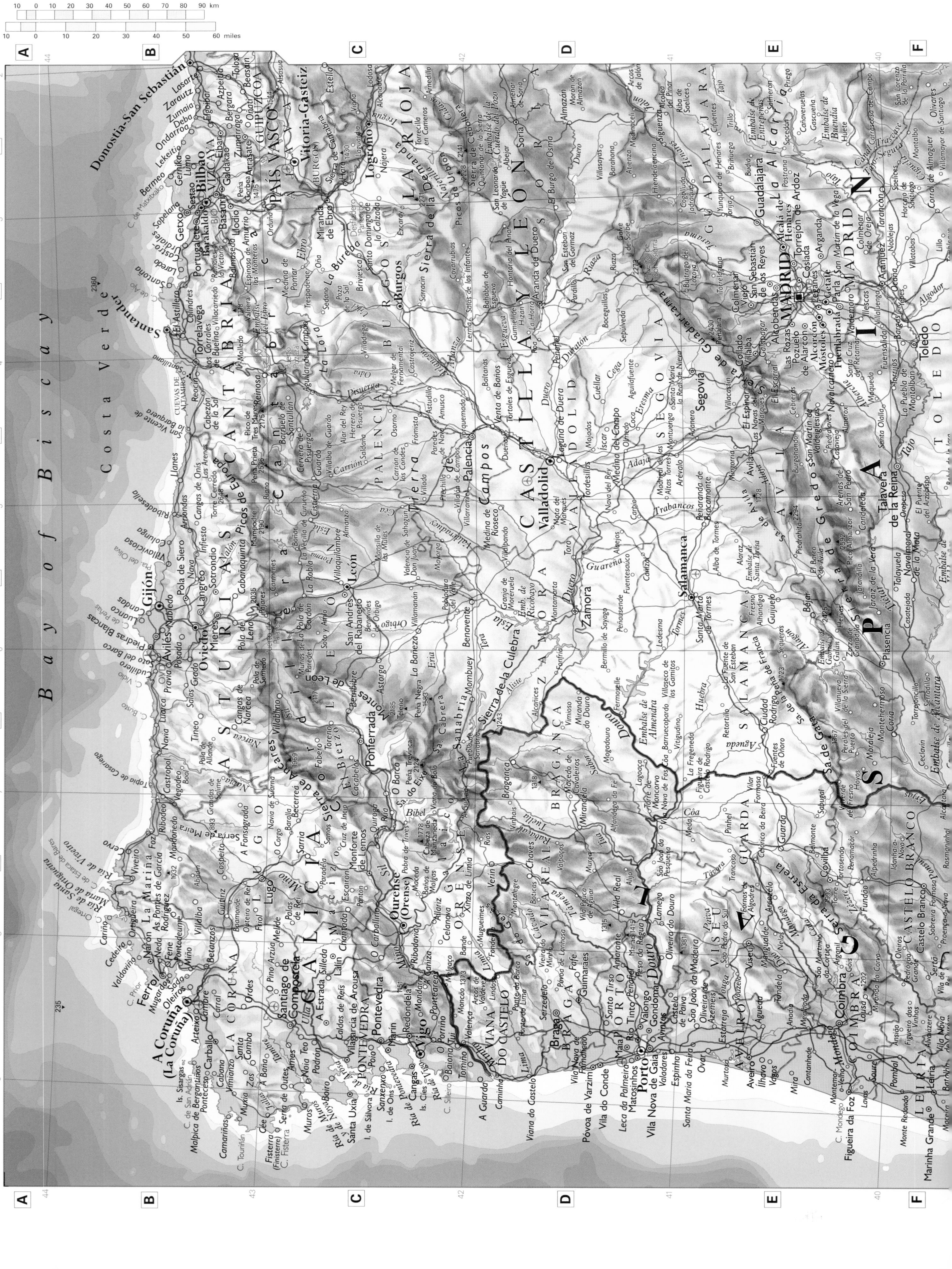
Bay of Biscay
Costa Verde
Donostia-San Sebastián
Bilbao
Santander
Gijón
Oviedo
A Coruña (La Coruña)
Santiago de Compostela
Vigo
Porto
Lugo
Ourense (Orense)
León
Burgos
Valladolid
Salamanca
Zamora
Segovia
Madrid
Toledo
Coimbra
Vitoria-Gasteiz
Logroño
Palencia
Guadalajara
Ávila
CASTILLA Y LEÓN
GALICIA
ASTURIAS
CANTABRIA
PAÍS VASCO
LA RIOJA
MADRID
PORTUGAL
SPAIN

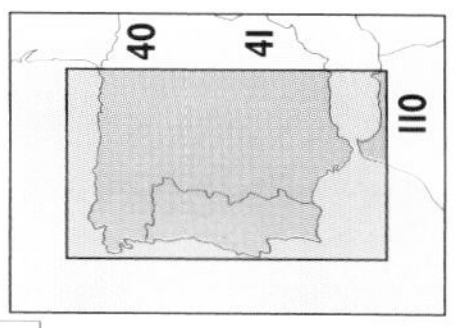
40
41
110

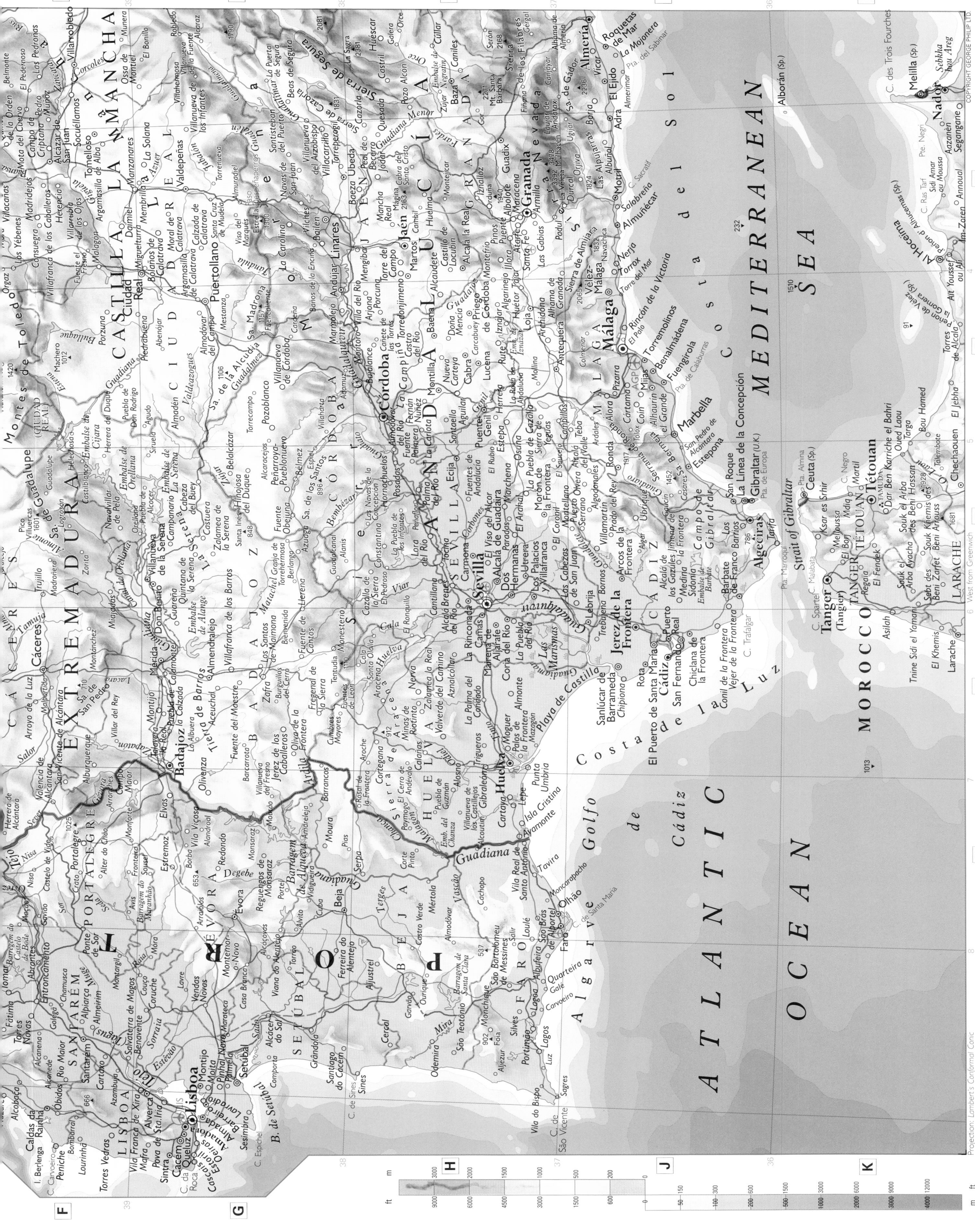
ATLANTIC OCEAN
MEDITERRANEAN SEA
Golfo de Cádiz
Costa de la Luz
Costa del Sol
Strait of Gibraltar
MOROCCO
PORTUGAL
EXTREMADURA
CASTILLA-LA MANCHA
ANDALUCÍA
Sierra Nevada
Sierra de Segura
Montes de Toledo
Sierra Morena
Algarve
LISBOA
SANTARÉM
PORTALEGRE
ÉVORA
SETÚBAL
BEJA
FARO
BADAJOZ
CÁCERES
CIUDAD REAL
CÓRDOBA
JAÉN
GRANADA
MÁLAGA
SEVILLA
HUELVA
CÁDIZ
Lisboa
Setúbal
Évora
Beja
Faro
Badajoz
Mérida
Cáceres
Puertollano
Ciudad Real
Córdoba
Jaén
Linares
Úbeda
Granada
Almería
Málaga
Marbella
Sevilla
Huelva
Jerez de la Frontera
Cádiz
Algeciras
Gibraltar (U.K.)
Tarifa
Ceuta (Sp.)
Tanger
Tétouan
Larache
Melilla (Sp.)
Nador
Guadiana
Guadalquivir
Tejo
Alborán (Sp.)
Projection: Lambert's Conformal Conic
West from Greenwich
COPYRIGHT GEORGE PHILIP LTD.
m
ft

NORTHERN ITALY, SLOVENIA AND CROATIA 1:2 000 000

Projection : Lambert's Conformal Conic

East from Greenwich

Underlined towns give their name to the administrative area in which they stand.

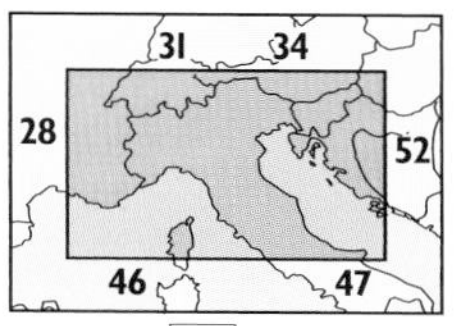

Administrative divisions in Croatia:

1. Brodsko-Posavska	4. Medimurska	8. Virovitičko-Podravska
2. Koprivničko-Križevačka	6. Požeško-Slavonska	10. Zagrebačka
3. Krapinsko-Zagorska	7. Varaždinska	

Inter-entity boundaries as agreed at the 1995 Dayton Peace Agreement.

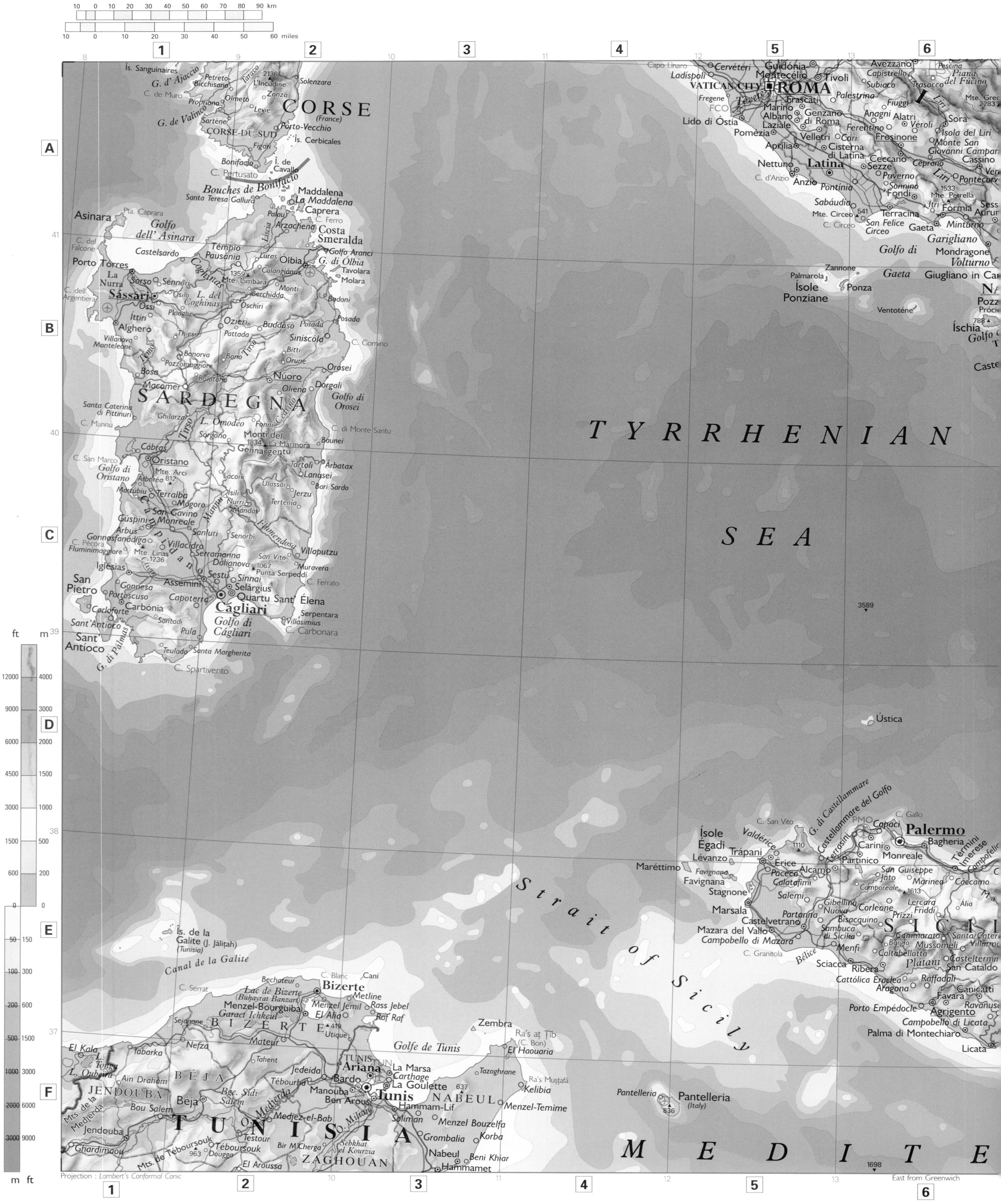

10 0 10 20 30 40 50 60 70 80 90 km
10 0 10 20 30 40 50 60 miles
CORSE
(France)
CORSE-DU-SUD
G. d' Ajaccio
G. de Valinco
Ìs. Sanguinaires
Petreto-Bicchisano
Propriano
Olmeto
Sartène
Levie
Zonza
L'Incudine
2136
Solenzara
Porto-Vecchio
Ìs. Cerbicales
Figari
Bonifacio
Ì. de Cavallo
C. Pertusato
Bouches de Bonifacio
Santa Teresa Gallura
Maddalena
La Maddalena
Caprera
Palau
Arzachena
Costa Smeralda
Asinara
Golfo dell' Asinara
Castelsardo
Tempio Pausania
Olbia
G. di Olbia
Golfo Aranci
Tavolara
Molara
Porto Torres
La Nurra
Sorso
Sennori
Sássari
Ossi
Ittiri
Alghero
Villanova Monteleone
Thiesi
Ozieri
Pattada
Buddusò
Posada
Siniscola
Bitti
Orune
Budoni
C. Comino
Bonorva
Pozzomaggiore
Bosa
Macomer
Bolotana
Nùoro
Oliena
Orosei
Dorgali
Golfo di Orosei
SARDEGNA
Santa Caterina di Pittinuri
C. Mannu
Ghilarza
L. Omodeo
Fonni
Sorgono
Monti del Gennargentu
1834
La Marmora
Baunei
C. di Monte Santu
C. San Marco
Cabras
Oristano
Golfo di Oristano
Mte. Arci
812
Arborea
Terralba
Mogoro
Láconi
Tortolì
Arbatax
Lanusei
Ulassai
Jerzu
Bari Sardo
Tertenia
San Gavino Monreale
Gúspini
Arbus
Gonnosfanádiga
Sanluri
Villacidro
Senorbì
Flumendosa
Villaputzu
Muravera
C. Pécora
Fluminimaggiore
Mte. Linas
1236
Serramanna
Dolianova
San Vito
1067
Punta Serpeddi
Iglesias
Sestu
Sinnai
Selargius
Quartu Sant' Élena
C. Ferrato
San Pietro
Carloforte
Portoscuso
Gonnesa
Carbónia
Assemini
Capoterra
Cágliari
Golfo di Cágliari
Serpentara
Villasimius
C. Carbonara
Sant'Antioco
Santadi
Pula
Teulada
Santa Margherita
C. Spartivento
G. di Palmas
Campidano
Cervéteri
Capo Linaro
Ladispoli
Guidonia Montecélio
Tívoli
VATICAN CITY
ROMA
Fregene
FCO
Frascati
Palestrina
Marino
Albano Laziale
Genzano di Roma
Lido di Óstia
Pomezia
Velletri
Aprilia
Cori
Cisterna di Latina
Anagni
Fiuggi
Alatri
Vèroli
Ferentino
Frosinone
Avezzano
Capistrello
Subiaco
Trasacco
Piana del Fùcino
Sora
Ìsola del Liri
Monte San Giovanni Campano
Cassino
Nettuno
Anzio
C. d'Anzio
Latina
Ceccano
Sezze
Ceprano
Pontecorvo
Priverno
Sonnino
Fondi
Pontinia
Sabáudia
Mte. Circeo
541
C. Circeo
San Felice Circeo
Terracina
Formia
Minturno
Gaeta
Garigliano
Golfo di Gaeta
Mondragone
Volturno
Giugliano in Campania
Palmarola
Zannone
Ìsole Ponziane
Ponza
Ventoténe
Ìschia
788
TYRRHENIAN SEA
3589
Ústica
C. San Vito
G. di Castellammare
Castellammare del Golfo
C. Gallo
PMO
Capaci
Palermo
Bagheria
Carini
Monreale
Termini Imerese
Ìsole Égadi
Lévanzo
Maréttimo
Favignana
Trápani
Érice
Valderice
Alcamo
Partinico
Paceco
Calatafimi
Salemi
Stagnone
Marsala
San Guiseppe Jato
Marineo
Caccamo
Camporeale
1613
Gibellina Nuova
Corleone
Lercara Friddi
Prizzi
Partanna
Castelvetrano
Mazara del Vallo
Campobello di Mazara
Sambuca di Sicilia
Bisacquino
Menfi
C. Granitola
Bélice
Sciacca
Ribera
Cattólica Eraclea
Aragona
Raffadali
Favara
Agrigento
Porto Empédocle
Canicattì
Campobello di Licata
Palma di Montechiaro
Licata
Cammarata
Mussomeli
Villarosa
Caltabellotta
Plátani
San Cataldo
Castelterm
Bíccari
Strait of Sicily
Ìs. de la Galite
(J. Jālitah)
(Tunisia)
Canal de la Galite
C. Serrat
C. Blanc
Cani
Bizerte
Bechateur
Lac de Bizerte
(Buhayrat Banzart)
Menzel-Bourguiba
Garaet Ichkeul
Metline
Menzel Jemil
El Alia
Rass Jebel
Raf Raf
Sejnane
BIZERTE
419
Utique
Zembra
Ra's at Tib
(C. Bon)
El Haouaria
El Kala
Tabarka
Nefza
Mateur
Golfe de Tunis
Tahent
Jedeida
Tébourba
Ariana
La Marsa
Carthage
La Goulette
Bardo
Tunis
TUNIS
Tazoghrane
Ra's Muştafá
Kélibia
Aïn Draham
BÉJA
Béja
JENDOUBA
Bge. Sidi Salem
Medjerda
Manouba
Ben Arous
Hammam-Lif
637
NABEUL
Menzel-Temime
Bou Salem
Mts. de la Medjerda
Jendouba
TUNISIA
Medjez-el-Bab
Soliman
Menzel Bouzelfa
Korba
Grombalia
Beni Khiar
Nabeul
Hammamet
Ghardimaou
Mts. de Téboursouk
963
Téboursouk
Testour
Dougga
Bir M'Cherga
Sebkhat el Kourzia
ZAGHOUAN
El Aroussa
Pantelleria
836
(Italy)
MEDITE
1698
ft m
12000 4000
9000 3000
6000 2000
4500 1500
3000 1000
1500 500
600 200
0 0
50 150
100 300
200 600
500 1500
1000 3000
2000 6000
3000 9000
m ft
Projection : Lambert's Conformal Conic
East from Greenwich

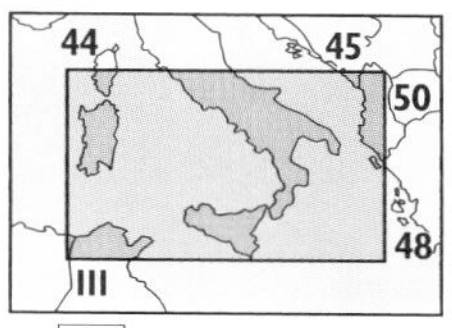
44
45
50
48
III

ADRIATIC SEA
Strait of Otranto
IONIAN SEA
RRANEAN SEA
Golfo di Táranto
Golfo di Manfredónia
Golfo di Salerno
Golfo di Policastro
Golfo di Sant' Eufémia
Golfo di Squillace
Golfo di Gióia
Golfo di Catánia
Golfo di Noto
Golfo di Gela
Str. di Messina
MOLISE
CAMPANIA
PUGLIA
BASILICATA
CALÁBRIA
ALBANIA
GREECE
Tirranë
Durrës
Vlorë
Kérkira (Corfu)
Bari
Fóggia
Barletta
Andria
Trani
Molfetta
Bisceglie
Brindisi
Táranto
Lecce
Otranto
Gallipoli
Matera
Potenza
Salerno
Campobasso
Benevento
Avellino
Caserta
Cosenza
Crotone
Catanzaro
Reggio di Calábria
Messina
Catánia
Siracusa
Ragusa
Enna
Caltanissetta
Gela
Etna
Ísole Eólie
Strómboli
Lípari
Vulcano
Salina
Panarea
Filicudi
Alicudi
Capri
C. Santa Maria di Léuca
C. Passero
C. Spartivento
C. Colonna
C. Rizzuto
Testa del Gargano
Vieste
Manfredónia
Términoli
Lucera
San Severo
Cerignola
Monópoli
Ostuni
Castellaneta
Gióia del Colle
Altamura
Gravina in Púglia
Policoro
Castrovillari
Rossano
Corigliano Cálabro
Paola
Amantea
Vibo Valéntia
Tropea
Palmi
Locri
Siderno
Taormina
Acireale
Augusta
Noto
Módica
Vittória
Comiso
Scicli
Pozzallo
Pachino
Mte. Pollino
Mte. Cervati
Appennino
Monti Nébrodi
Aspromonte
Sila
2248
3323
1956
1928
2005
1898
1055
3065
924
505
15
16
17
18
19
20
41
40
39
38
37
COPYRIGHT GEORGE PHILIP LTD.

Underlined towns give their name to the administrative area in which they stand.

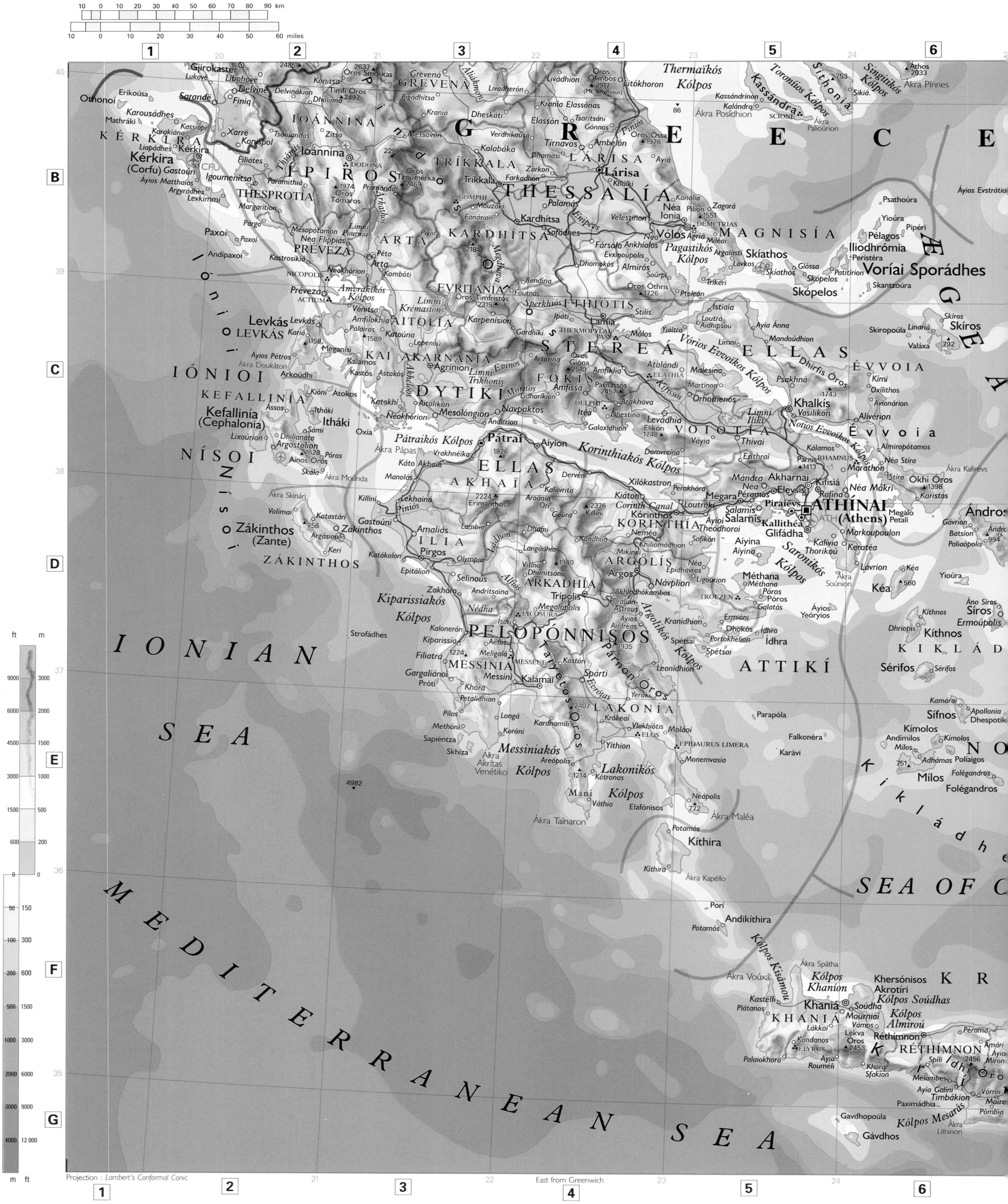

10 0 10 20 30 40 50 60 70 80 90 km
10 0 10 20 30 40 50 60 miles
GREECE
IÓNIOI NÍSOI
IONIAN SEA
MEDITERRANEAN SEA
SEA OF
Thermaïkós Kólpos
Kérkira (Corfu)
Ioánnina
ÍPIROS
THESSALÍA
Lárisa
Vólos
MAGNISÍA
Voríai Sporádhes
Skíathos
Skópelos
Skíros
Levkás
Kefallinía (Cephalonia)
Itháki
Zákinthos (Zante)
STEREÁ ELLAS
Lamía
Pátrai
Pátraikós Kólpos
Korinthiakós Kólpos
Khalkís
Évvoia
ATHÍNAI (Athens)
Piraiévs
Elevsís
Kallithéa
Glifádha
Salamís
Aíyina
Saronikós Kólpos
Argolikós Kólpos
Árgos
Návplion
Trípolis
ARKADHÍA
PELOPÓNNISOS
Kiparissiakós Kólpos
Kalámai
Spárti
LAKONÍA
Messiniakós Kólpos
Lakonikós Kólpos
Kíthira
Andikíthira
ATTIKÍ
Kéa
Kíthnos
Sérifos
Síros
Sífnos
Mílos
Folégandros
Ándros
Khaniá
Réthimnon
Kólpos Khaníon
Kólpos Soúdhas
Gávdhos
Projection : Lambert's Conformal Conic
East from Greenwich

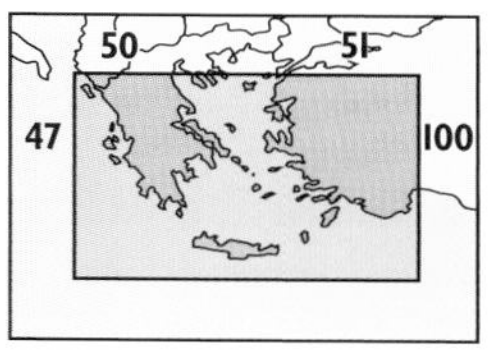
50
51
47
100

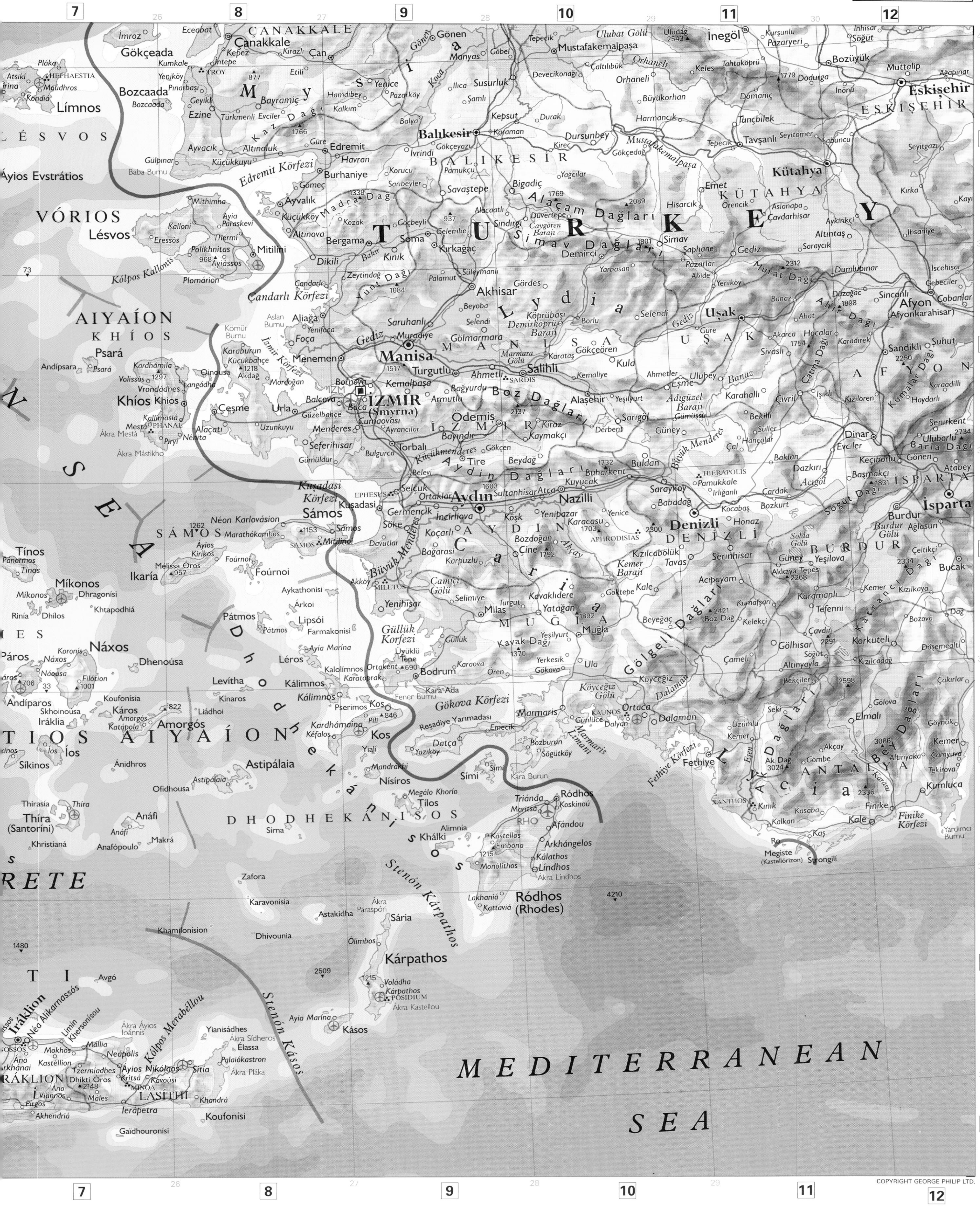
7
8
9
10
11
12
B
C
D
E
F
G
TURKEY
AEGEAN SEA
MEDITERRANEAN SEA
ÇANAKKALE
Çanakkale
Gökçeada
İmroz
Bozcaada
Límnos
LÉSVOS
Áyios Evstrátios
VÓRIOS AIYAÍON
Lésvos
Mitilíni
Kólpos Kallonis
KHÍOS
Khíos
Psará
SÁMOS
Sámos
Ikaría
Foúrnoi
Mikonos
Tínos
Náxos
Páros
Andiparos
Amorgós
Íos
Síkinos
Thíra (Santoríni)
Anáfi
Astipálaia
Kálimnos
Léros
Pátmos
Lipsói
Kos
Nísiros
Tílos
Sími
Khálki
Ródhos (Rhodes)
Lindhos
Kárpathos
Kásos
Sária
DHODHEKÁNISOS
Dhodhekánisos
Stenón Kárpathos
Stenón Kásos
CRETE
Iráklion
Áyios Nikólaos
Sitía
Ierápetra
LASÍTHI
Kólpos Merabéllou
Koufonísi
Gaïdhourونísi
Balıkesir
BALIKESİR
Edremit
Edremit Körfezi
Ayvalık
Bergama
Dikili
Çandarlı Körfezi
Aliağa
Foça
Menemen
Manisa
MANİSA
İZMİR (Smyrna)
İzmir Körfezi
Çeşme
Urla
Torbalı
Ödemiş
Tire
Selçuk
Kuşadası
Kuşadası Körfezi
Söke
Aydın
AYDIN
Aydın Dağları
Nazilli
Denizli
DENİZLİ
Pamukkale
HIERAPOLIS
APHRODISIAS
EPHESUS
MILETUS
Milas
Muğla
MUĞLA
Bodrum
Güllük Körfezi
Gökova Körfezi
Marmaris
Datça
Dalaman
Köyceğiz
Fethiye
Fethiye Körfezi
Kaş
Kalkan
Finike
Megiste (Kastellórizon)
ANTALYA
Ak Dağları
Bey Dağları
Elmalı
Kumluca
Burdur
BURDUR
Isparta
ISPARTA
Eğirdir
Afyon (Afyonkarahisar)
AFYON
Uşak
UŞAK
Kütahya
KÜTAHYA
Eskişehir
ESKİŞEHİR
İnegöl
Mustafakemalpaşa
Susurluk
Gönen
Bandırma
Simav
Simav Dağları
Gediz
Akhisar
Salihli
Alaşehir
Boz Dağları
Büyük Menderes
Küçükmenderes
Lydia
Caria
Mysia
Lycia
Kaz Dağı
Madra Dağı
Yunt Dağı
Alaçam Dağları
Murat Dağı
Uluborlu
Dinar
Acıgöl
Burdur Gölü
Çivril
Kale
Ula
Yatağan
Tavas
Acıpayam
Gölhisar
Tefenni
Kemer
Ortaca
Dalyan
KAUNOS
XANTHOS
Kos
Rodhos
Kárpathos

COPYRIGHT GEORGE PHILIP LTD.

NORTHERN GREECE, BULGARIA AND YUGOSLAVIA 1:2 000 000

Inter-entity boundaries as agreed at the 1995 Dayton Peace Agreement.

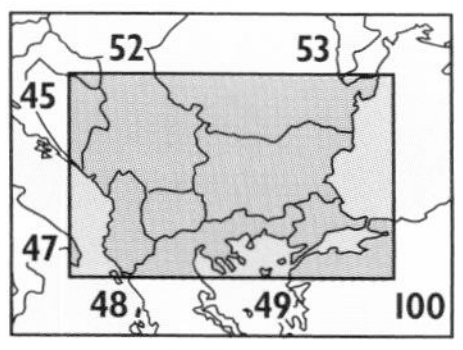

Underlined towns give their name to the administrative area in which they stand.

Administrative divisions in Croatia:
1. Brodsko-Posavska
2. Koprivničko-Križevačka
4. Medimurska
5. Osječko-Baranjska
6. Požeško-Slavonska
8. Virovitičko-Podravska
9. Vukovarsko-Srijemska

Inter-entity boundaries as agreed at the 1995 Dayton Peace Agreement.

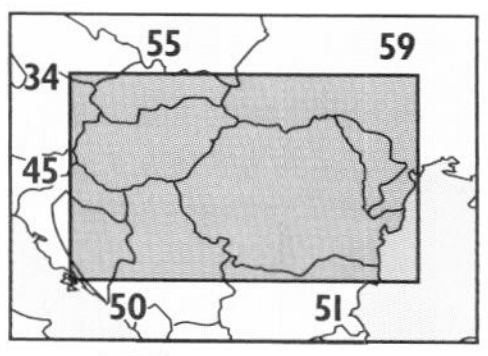

ROMANIA
MOLDOVA
UKRAINE
BULGARIA
BLACK SEA
BUCUREŞTI
Chişinău (Kishinev)
Ivano-Frankivsk
Chernivtsi
Kamyanets-Podilskyy
Mohyliv-Podilskyy
Cluj-Napoca
Baia Mare
Satu Mare
Sighetu Marmaţiei
Suceava
Botoşani
Iaşi
Bălţi
Tiraspol
Tighina
Piatra Neamţ
Bacău
Vaslui
Târgu Mureş
Sibiu
Braşov
Focşani
Galaţi
Brăila
Tulcea
Constanţa
Mangalia
Buzău
Ploieşti
Târgovişte
Piteşti
Râmnicu Vâlcea
Craiova
Slatina
Alexandria
Giurgiu
Ruse
Pleven
Dobrich
Călăraşi
Slobozia
Izmayil
Cahul
Comrat
Carpaţii Meridionali
Transilvania
Valahia
Dunărea
Prut
Siret
Nistru
Dnister
Lacul Razim
ODESKA
Underlined towns give their name to the administrative area in which they stand.
COPYRIGHT GEORGE PHILIP LTD.

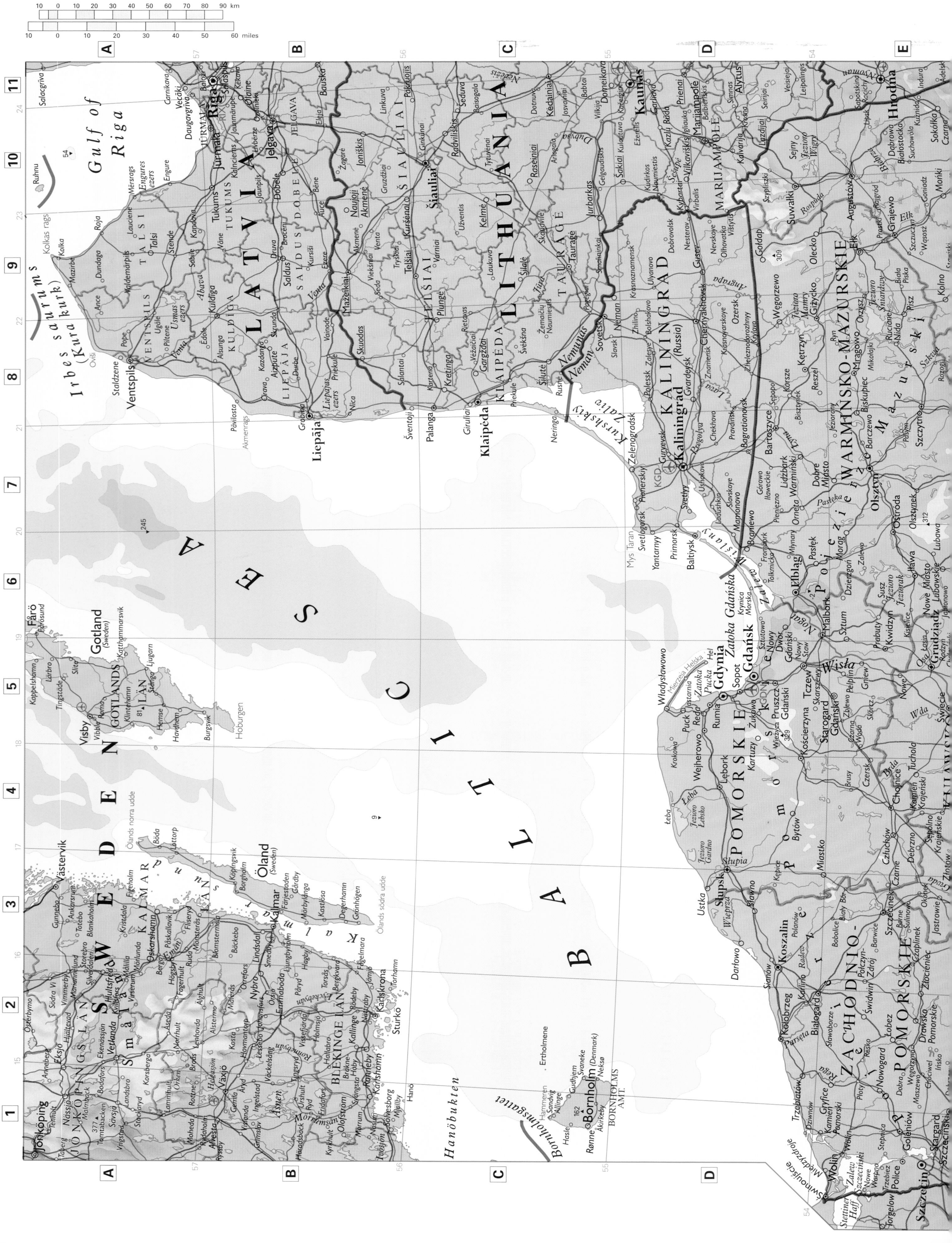

10 0 10 20 30 40 50 60 70 80 90 km
10 0 10 20 30 40 50 60 miles
BALTIC SEA
SWEDEN
Gotland (Sweden)
GOTLANDS LÄN
Visby
Öland (Sweden)
Kalmar
KALMAR LÄN
JÖNKÖPINGS LÄN
BLEKINGE LÄN
Karlskrona
Jönköping
Växjö
Bornholm (Denmark)
BORNHOLMS AMT.
Rønne
Hanöbukten
Gulf of Riga
Irbes šaurums (Kura kurk)
LATVIA
Rīga
Jūrmala
Jelgava
Liepāja
Ventspils
LITHUANIA
Klaipėda
Šiauliai
Kaunas
KALININGRAD (Russia)
Kaliningrad
Sovetsk
POMORSKIE
Gdańsk
Gdynia
Zatoka Gdańska
Elbląg
Olsztyn
WARMIŃSKO-MAZURSKIE
Mazury
Pojezierze Pomorskie
ZACHODNIO-POMORSKIE
Szczecin
Koszalin
Słupsk
Wisła
Hrodna

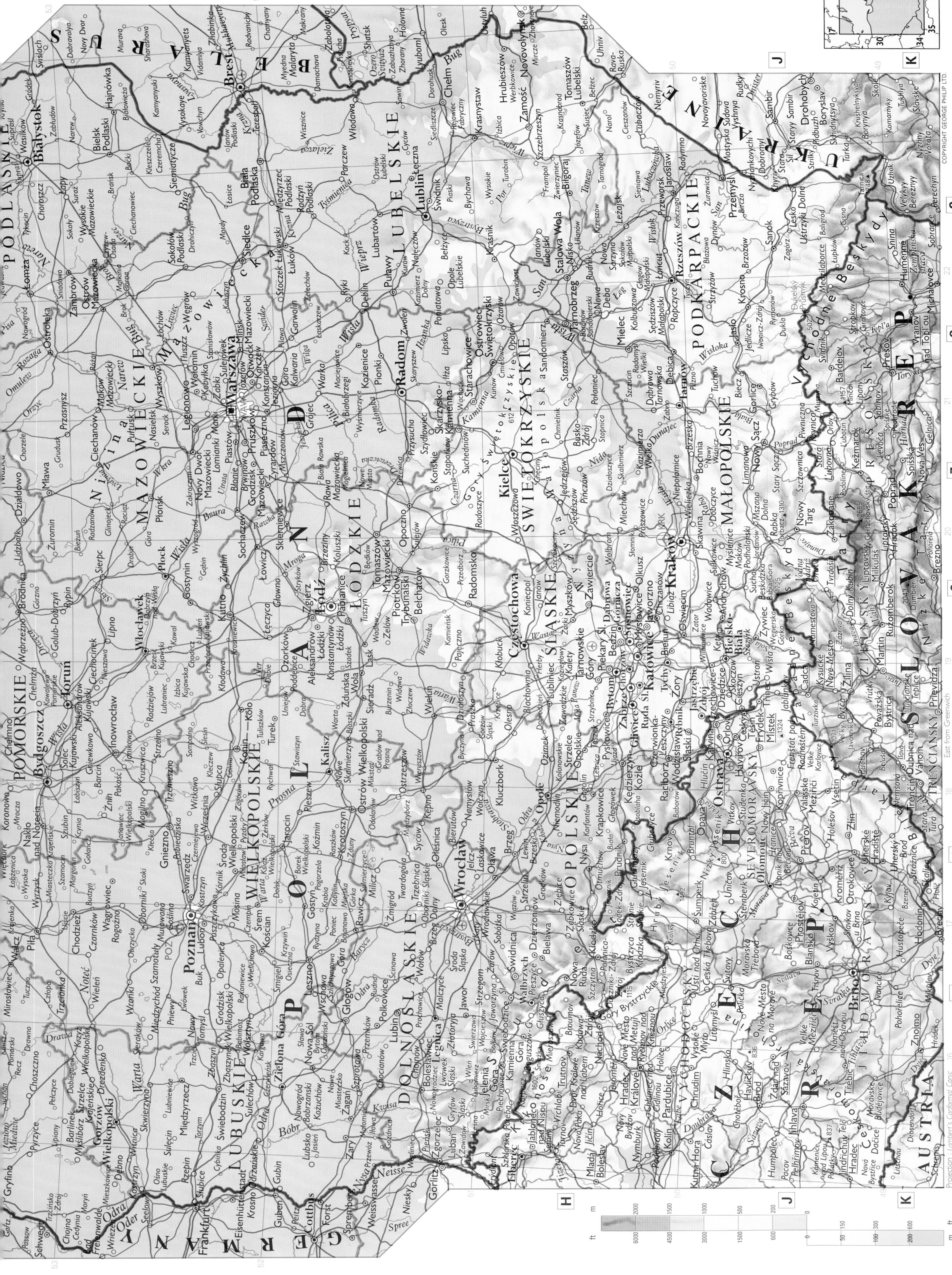

Underlined towns give their name to the administrative area in which they stand.

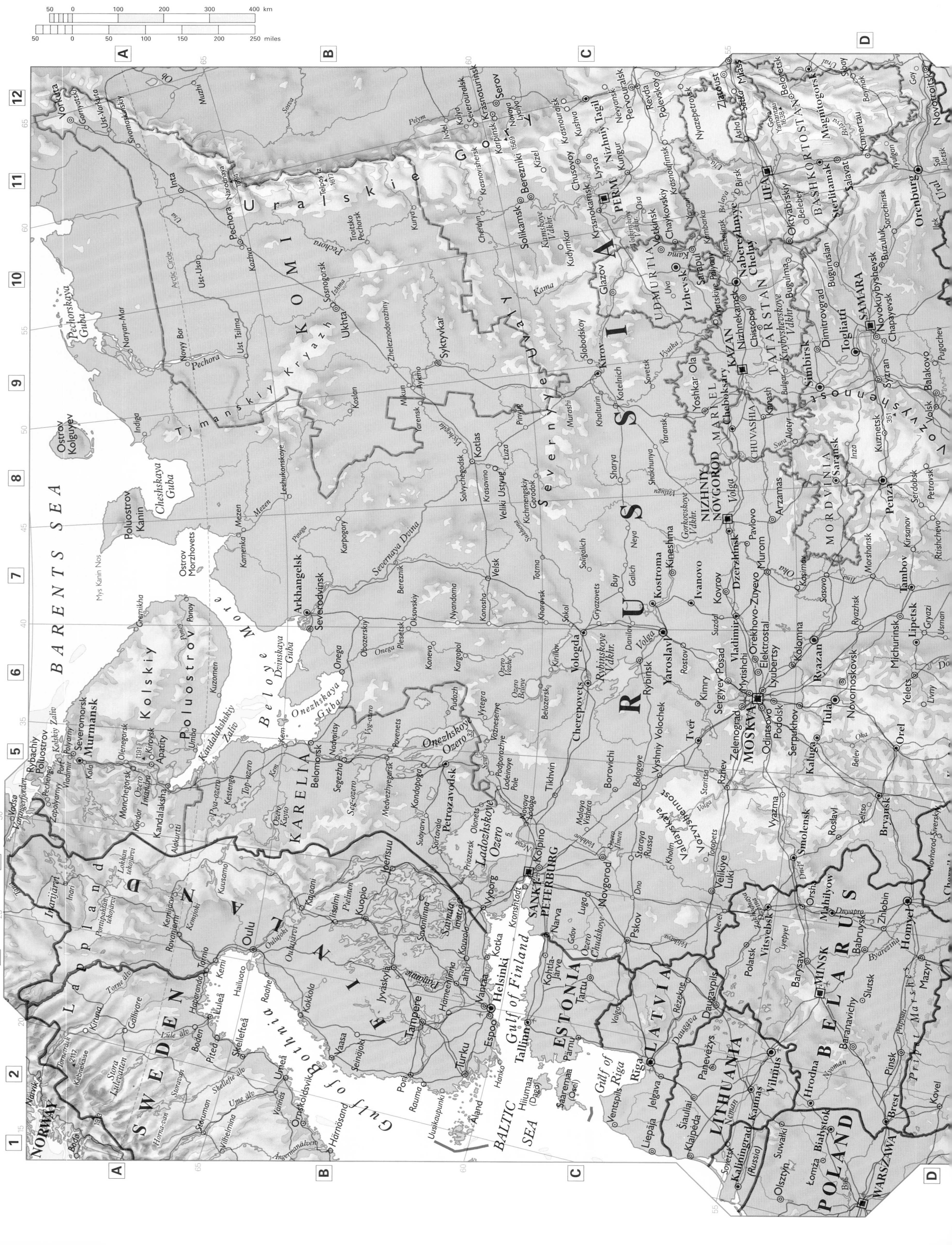
0 100 200 300 400 km
0 50 100 150 200 250 miles
A
B
C
D
1
2
3
4
5
6
7
8
9
10
11
12
BARENTS SEA
BALTIC SEA
Gulf of Bothnia
Gulf of Finland
Gulf of Riga
Beloye More
NORWAY
SWEDEN
FINLAND
ESTONIA
LATVIA
LITHUANIA
BELARUS
POLAND
RUSSIA
KARELIA
KOMI
UDMURTIA
TATARSTAN
CHUVASHIA
MARI EL
MORDVINIA
BASHKORTOSTAN
Lappland
Kolskiy Poluostrov
Timanskiy Kryazh
Ural'skie Gory
Severnye Uvaly
Ostrov Kolguyev
Poluostrov Kanin
Pechorskaya Guba
Cheshskaya Guba
Onezhskoye Ozero
Ladozhskoye Ozero
Rybinskoye Vdkhr.
MOSKVA
SANKT-PETERBURG
NIZHNIY NOVGOROD
KAZAN
PERM
UFA
SAMARA
MINSK
WARSZAWA
Helsinki
Tallinn
Riga
Vilnius
Murmansk
Arkhangelsk
Syktyvkar
Kirov
Vologda
Yaroslavl
Kostroma
Ivanovo
Tula
Ryazan
Smolensk
Bryansk
Orel
Lipetsk
Tambov
Penza
Saransk
Ulyanovsk
Simbirsk
Tolyatti
Orenburg
Izhevsk
Oulu
Tampere
Turku
Kaliningrad (Russia)

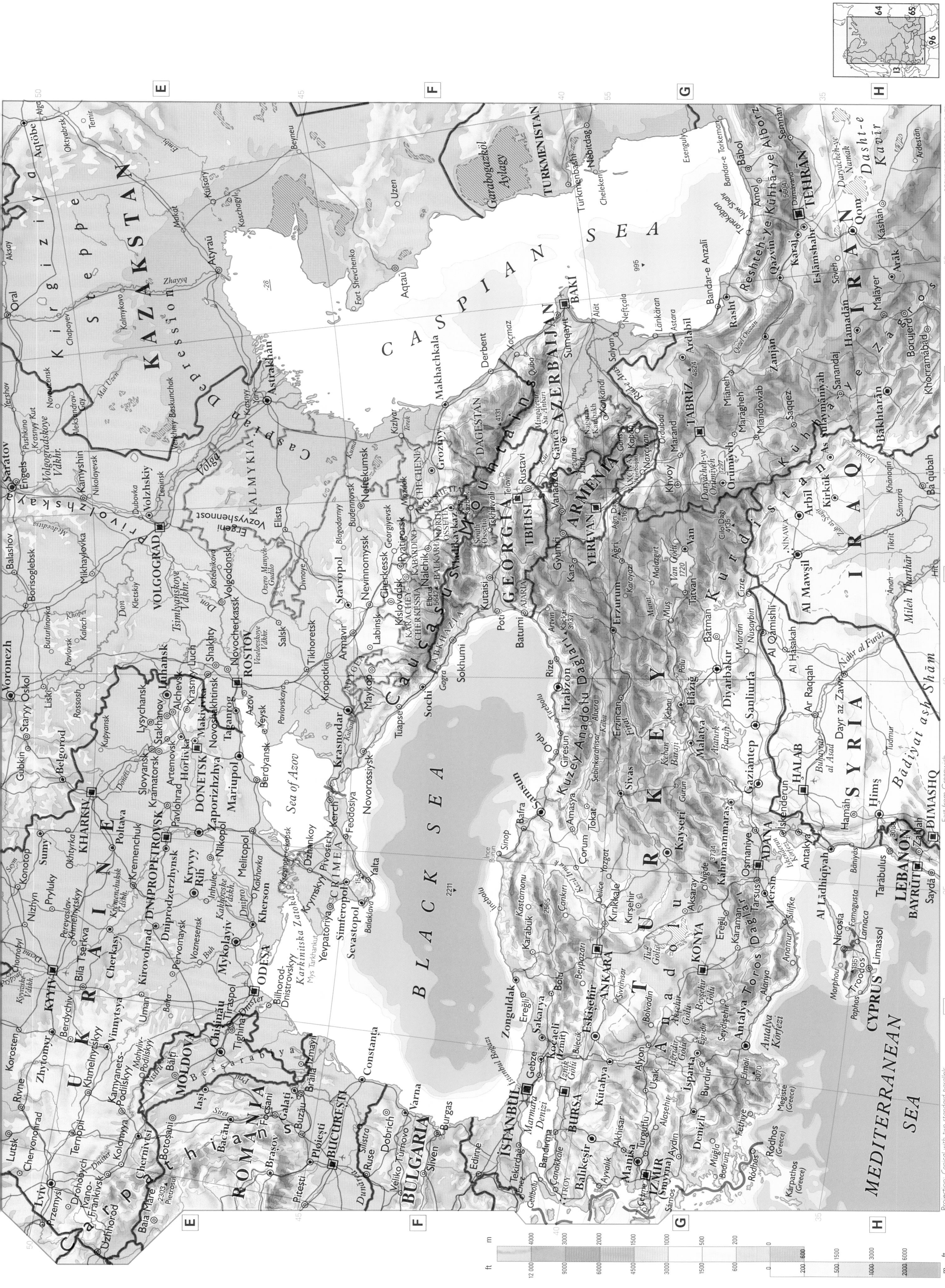
CASPIAN SEA
BLACK SEA
Sea of Azov
MEDITERRANEAN SEA
KAZAKSTAN
UKRAINE
ROMANIA
MOLDOVA
BULGARIA
TURKEY
GEORGIA
ARMENIA
AZERBAIJAN
IRAN
IRAQ
SYRIA
LEBANON
CYPRUS
TURKMENISTAN
KALMYKIA
DAGESTAN
CHECHENIA
CRIMEA
Caucasus Mountains
Caspian Depression
Kirgiz Steppe
Anadolu
Kuzey Anadolu Dağları
Toros Dağları
Kurdistan
Reshteh-ye Kūhhā-ye Alborz
Dasht-e Kavīr
Bādiyat ash Shām
Zāgros
KYYIV
KHARKIV
DNIPROPETROVSK
DONETSK
ODESA
ROSTOV
VOLGOGRAD
Saratov
Astrakhan
BUCUREŞTI
İSTANBUL
ANKARA
İZMIR
BURSA
KONYA
ADANA
TBILISI
YEREVAN
BAKI
TABRĪZ
TEHRĀN
HALAB
DIMASHQ
BAYRŪT
Chişinău
Sevastopol
Krasnodar
Stavropol
Makhachkala
Oral
Aqtöbe
Aqtau
Sochi
Trabzon
Samsun
Erzurum
Kayseri
Sivas
Konstanța
Varna
E
F
G
H
4
5
6
7
8
9
COPYRIGHT GEORGE PHILIP LTD.
Projection: Conical with two standard parallels
East from Greenwich

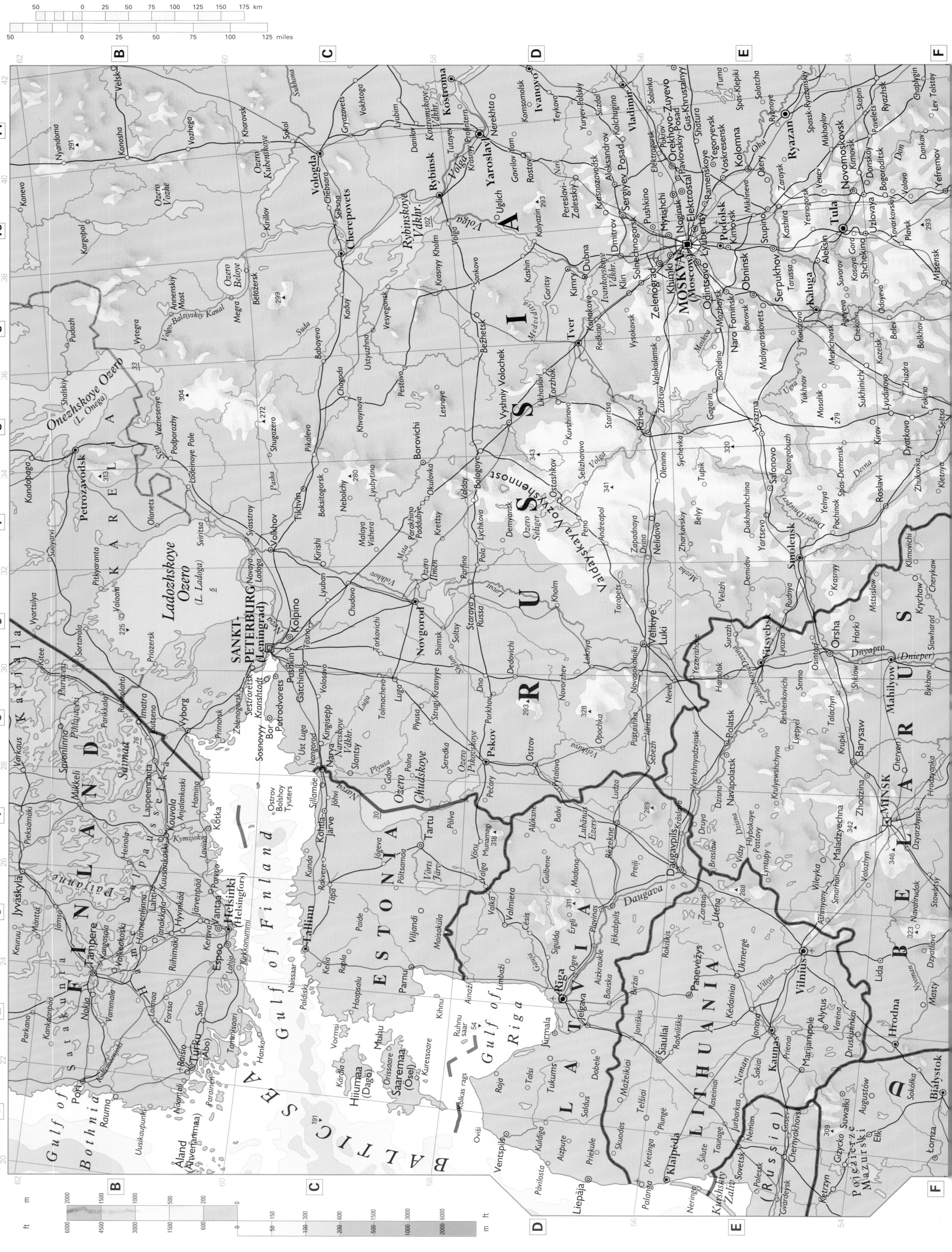
50 0 25 50 75 100 125 150 175 km
50 0 25 50 75 100 125 miles
FINLAND
ESTONIA
LATVIA
LITHUANIA
BELARUS
RUSSIA
KARELIA
BALTIC SEA
Gulf of Finland
Gulf of Riga
Gulf of Bothnia
Ladozhskoye Ozero (L. Ladoga)
Onezhskoye Ozero (L. Onega)
Ozero Chudskoye
Ozero Il'men
Rybinskoye Vdkhr.
Valdayskaya Vozvyshennost
Saaremaa (Ösel)
Hiiumaa (Dagö)
Åland (Ahvenanmaa)
Helsinki (Helsingfors)
Tallinn
Riga
Vilnius
Minsk
Kaunas
Sankt-Peterburg (Leningrad)
Moskva (Moscow)
Novgorod
Pskov
Tver
Smolensk
Vitsyebsk
Mahilyow
Hrodna
Petrozavodsk
Vologda
Cherepovets
Yaroslavl
Kostroma
Ivanovo
Vladimir
Ryazan
Tula
Kaluga
Orsha
Daugavpils
Tartu
Pärnu
Turku (Åbo)
Tampere
Vyborg
Narva
Klaipėda
Šiauliai
Liepāja
Ventspils
Białystok
Volga
Daugava
Dnyapro (Dnieper)
m ft
2000 6000
1500 4500
1000 3000
500 1500
200 600
0

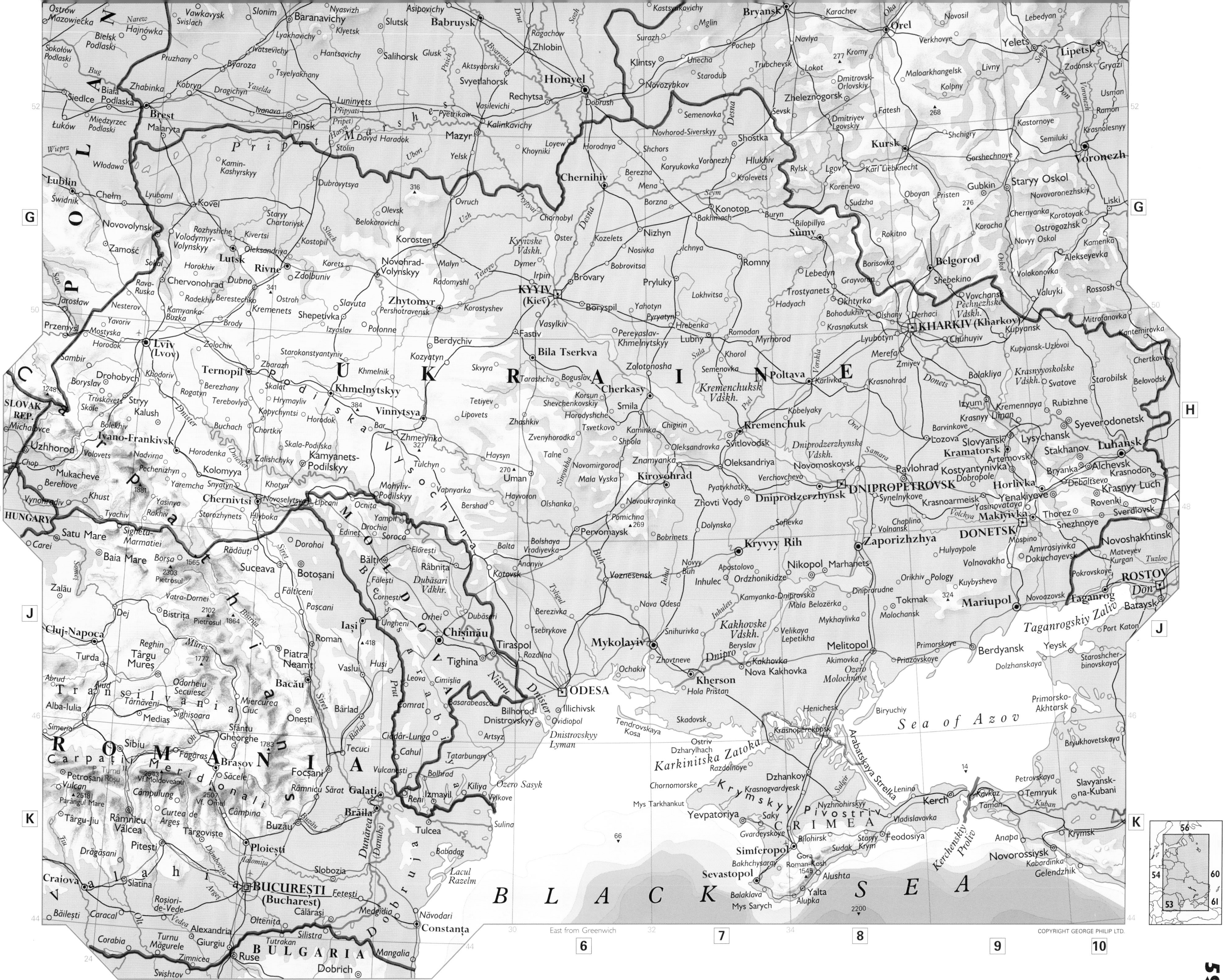

Projection: *Conical with two standard parallels*

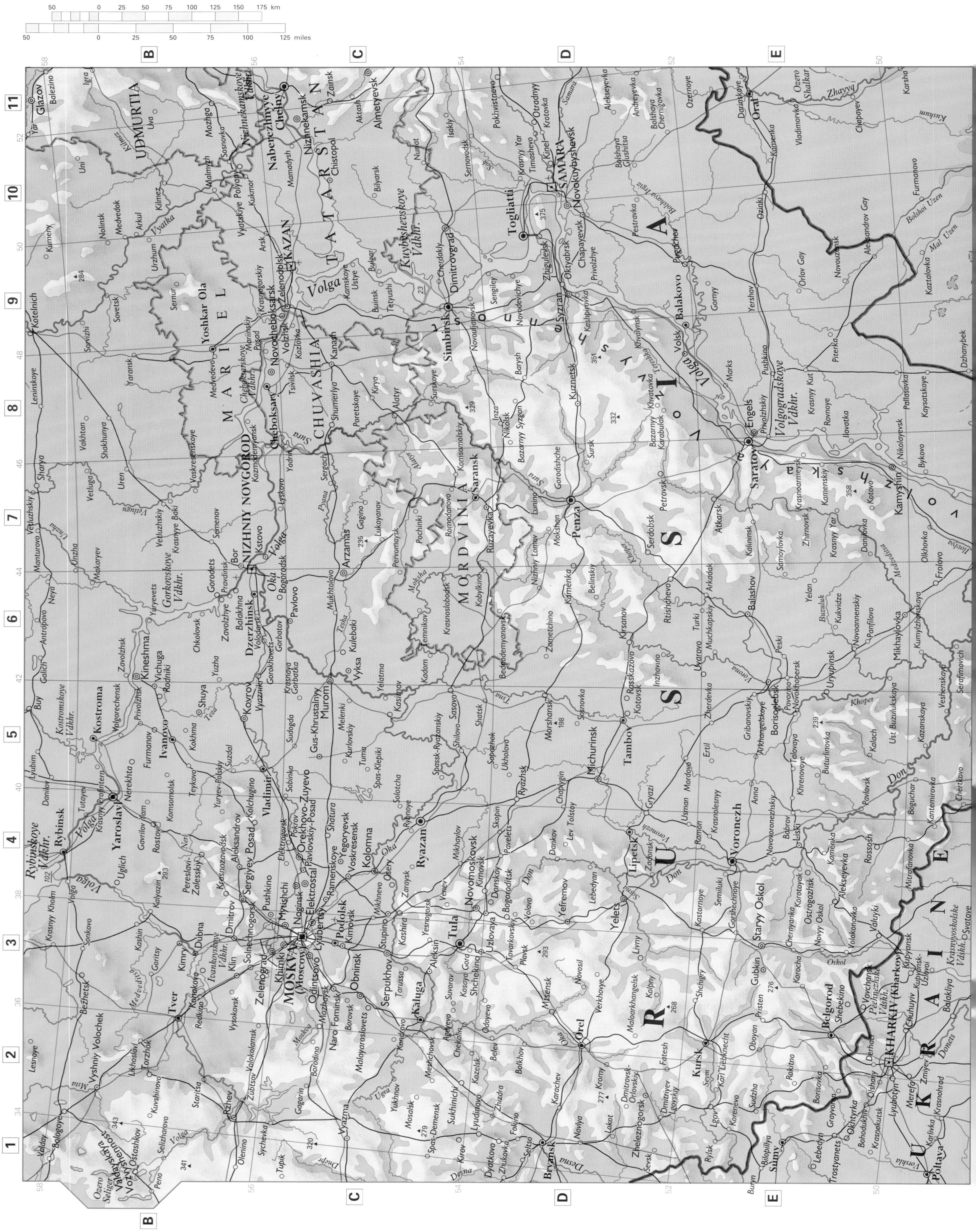
50 0 25 50 75 100 125 150 175 km
50 0 25 50 75 100 125 miles
UDMURTIA
TATARSTAN
MARI EL
CHUVASHIA
MORDVINIA
RUSSIA
UKRAINE
MOSKVA (Moscow)
NIZHNIY NOVGOROD
KAZAN
SAMARA
Naberezhnyye Chelny
Cheboksary
Yoshkar Ola
Simbirsk
Dimitrovgrad
Togliatti
Syzran
Saratov
Engels
Penza
Saransk
Tambov
Voronezh
Lipetsk
Ryazan
Tula
Kaluga
Orel
Kursk
Belgorod
KHARKIV (Kharkov)
Bryansk
Tver
Yaroslavl
Kostroma
Ivanovo
Vladimir
Rybinsk
Kamyshin
Balakovo
Oral
Poltava
Sumy
Volgogradskoye Vdkhr.
Kuybyshevskoye Vdkhr.
Gorkovskoye Vdkhr.
Rybinskoye Vdkhr.
Volga
Oka
Don
Sura
Moksha
Khoper

KAZAKSTAN
KALMYKIA
CASPIAN SEA
BLACK SEA
Sea of Azov
Caucasus Mountains
GEORGIA
ARMENIA
AZERBAIJAN
DAGESTAN
CHECHENIA
INGUSHETIA
NORTH OSSETIA
KABARDINO-BALKARIA
KARACHEY-CHERKESSIA
ADYGEA
ABKHAZIA
AJARIA
CRIMEA
TURKEY
Kuzey Anadolu Dağları
Prikubanskaya Nizmennost
Chernyye Zemli
Ryn Peski
Caspian Depression
Tsimlyanskoye Vdkhr.
VOLGOGRAD
ROSTOV
DONETSK
DNIPROPETROVSK
Zaporizhzhya
Mariupol
Luhansk
Krasnodar
Stavropol
Astrakhan
Elista
Makhachkala
Groznyy
Vladikavkaz
Nalchik
TBILISI
YEREVAN
BAKI
Kutaisi
Batumi
Sochi
Novorossiysk
Trabzon
Samsun
Kerch
Kerchenskiy Proliv
Taganrogskiy Zaliv
Volga
Kuban
Manych
Kuma
Terek
Kür
Projection: Conical with two standard parallels
East from Greenwich
COPYRIGHT GEORGE PHILIP LTD.

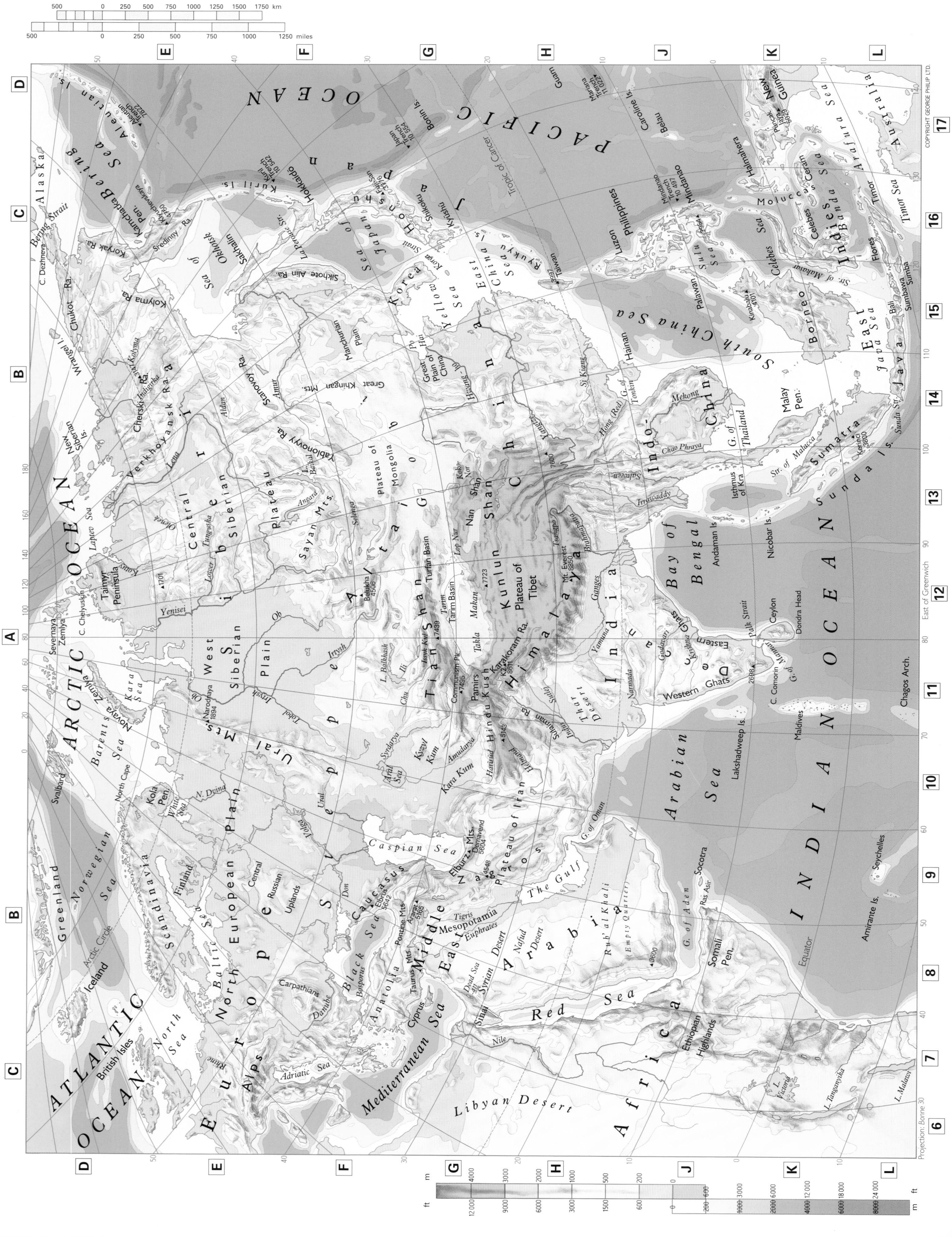

500 0 250 500 750 1000 1250 1500 1750 km
500 0 250 500 750 1000 1250 miles
ARCTIC OCEAN
PACIFIC OCEAN
INDIAN OCEAN
ATLANTIC OCEAN
Bering Sea
Sea of Okhotsk
Sea of Japan
East China Sea
Yellow Sea
South China Sea
Philippines
Bay of Bengal
Arabian Sea
Caspian Sea
Black Sea
Mediterranean Sea
Red Sea
Himalaya
Plateau of Tibet
Kunlun Shan
Tian Shan
Altai
Gobi
Plateau of Mongolia
Central Siberian Plateau
West Siberian Plain
Ural Mts.
North European Plain
Steppe
Plateau of Iran
Arabia
Africa
Europe
India
Indo-China
Borneo
Sumatra
Java
Sri Lanka
Ceylon
Mt. Everest 8850
Tropic of Cancer
Arctic Circle
Equator
Projection: Bonne
East of Greenwich
COPYRIGHT GEORGE PHILIP LTD.
m 4000 3000 2000 1000 500 200 0
ft 12 000 9000 6000 3000 1500 600 0
m 200 1000 2000 4000 6000 8000
ft 600 3000 6000 12 000 18 000 24 000

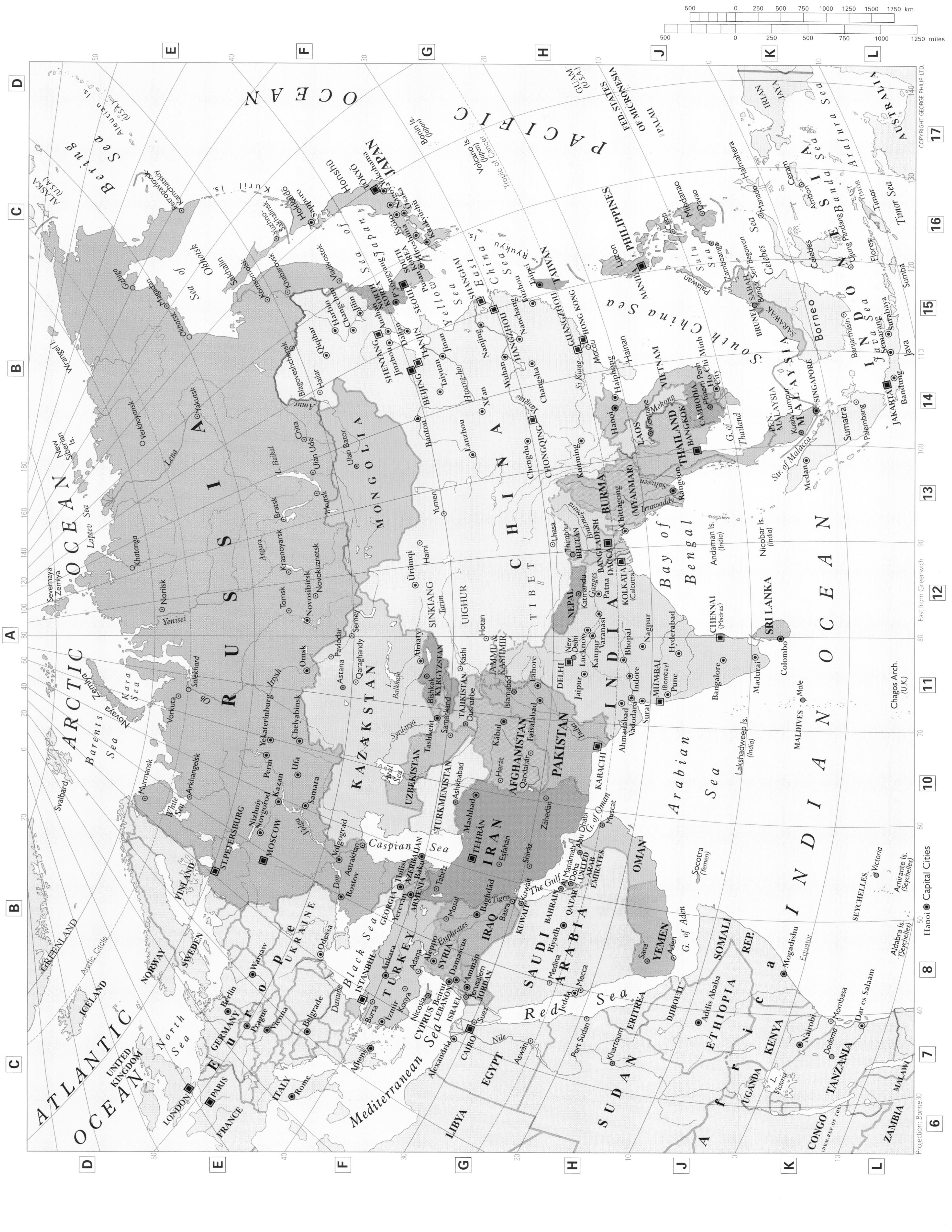

0 250 500 750 1000 1250 1500 1750 km
0 250 500 750 1000 1250 miles
ARCTIC OCEAN
PACIFIC OCEAN
INDIAN OCEAN
ATLANTIC OCEAN
RUSSIA
CHINA
MONGOLIA
KAZAKSTAN
INDIA
PAKISTAN
AFGHANISTAN
IRAN
IRAQ
SAUDI ARABIA
TURKEY
JAPAN
PHILIPPINES
INDONESIA
MALAYSIA
THAILAND
VIETNAM
LAOS
CAMBODIA
BURMA (MYANMAR)
BANGLADESH
NEPAL
BHUTAN
SRI LANKA
UZBEKISTAN
TURKMENISTAN
TAJIKISTAN
KYRGYZSTAN
OMAN
YEMEN
SYRIA
JORDAN
ISRAEL
LEBANON
KUWAIT
QATAR
BAHRAIN
UNITED ARAB EMIRATES
GEORGIA
ARMENIA
AZERBAIJAN
CYPRUS
Caspian Sea
Black Sea
Red Sea
Arabian Sea
Bay of Bengal
South China Sea
East China Sea
Yellow Sea
Sea of Japan
Sea of Okhotsk
Bering Sea
Laptev Sea
Kara Sea
Barents Sea
Mediterranean Sea
BEIJING
TOKYO
MOSCOW
DELHI
TEHRĀN
KARACHI
MUMBAI (Bombay)
KOLKATA (Calcutta)
CHENNAI (Madras)
BANGKOK
JAKARTA
MANILA
SEOUL
SHANGHAI
HONG KONG
SINGAPORE
Hanoi ◙ Capital Cities
East from Greenwich
Projection: Bonne
COPYRIGHT GEORGE PHILIP LTD.

SOUTHERN URALS 1:4 000 000

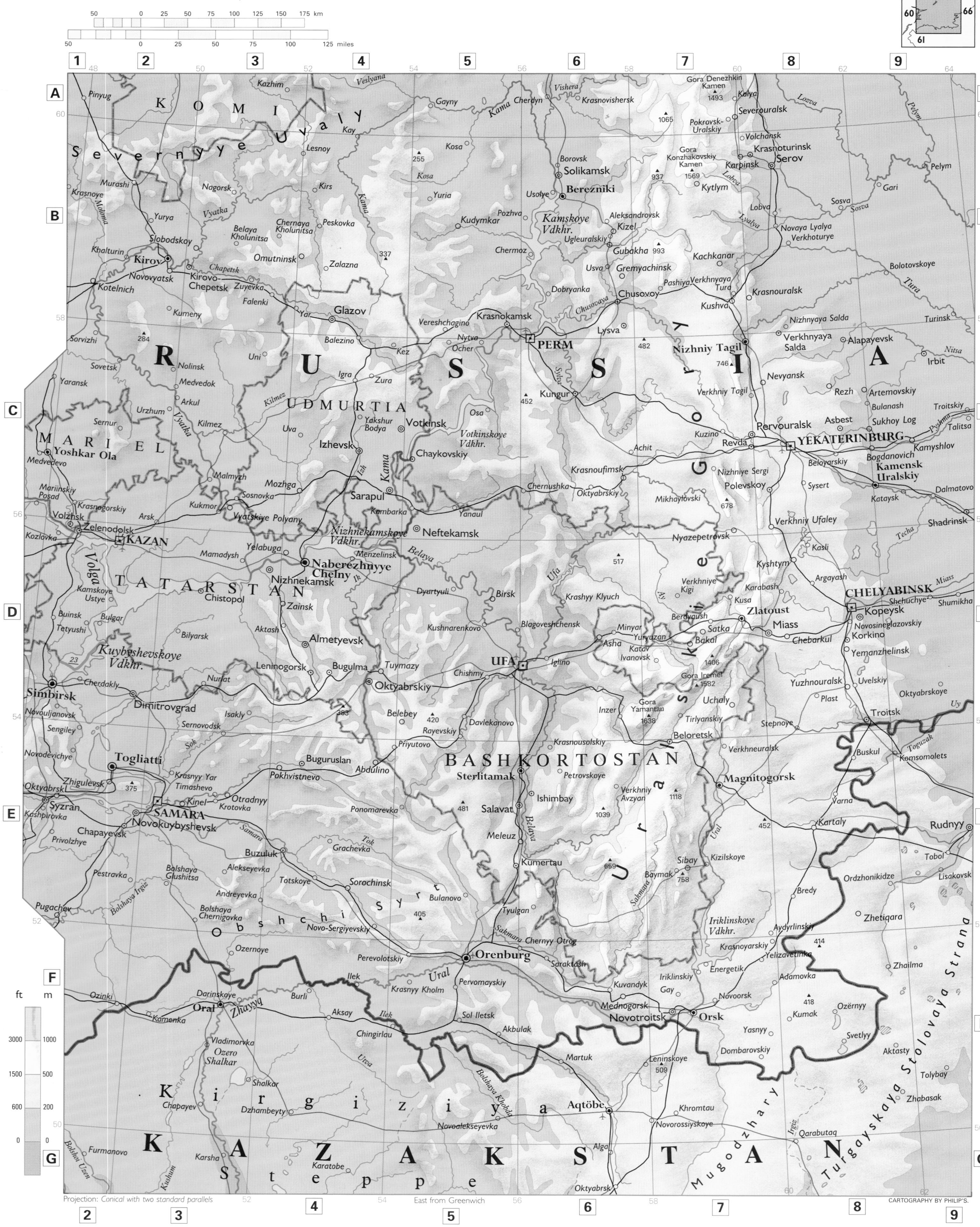

50 0 25 50 75 100 125 150 175 km
50 0 25 50 75 100 125 miles
56
60
66
61
KOMI
Severnyye Uvaly
RUSSIA
UDMURTIA
MARI EL
TATARSTAN
BASHKORTOSTAN
Ural'skiye Gory
Obshchi Syrt
Kirgiziya Steppe
KAZAKSTAN
Mugodzhary
Turgayskaya Stolovaya Strana
Pinyug
Kazhim
Veslyana
Gayny
Kama
Cherdyn
Vishera
Krasnovishersk
Gora Denezhkin Kamen
1493
Kalya
Lozva
Pelym
Kay
1065
Severouralsk
Pokrovsk-Uralskiy
Volchansk
Krasnoturinsk
Serov
Lesnoy
Kosa
255
Borovsk
Solikamsk
Gora Konzhakovskiy Kamen
1569
937
Karpinsk
Lobva
Pelym
Murashi
Nagorsk
Kirs
Yuria
Usolye
Berezniki
Kytlym
Gari
Krasnoye
Moloma
Sosva
Yurya
Vyatka
Pozhva
Kudymkar
Kamskoye Vdkhr.
Aleksandrovsk
Kizel
Lobva
Lyalya
Belaya Kholunitsa
Chernaya Kholunitsa
Peskovka
Ugleuralskiy
Novaya Lyalya
Verkhoturye
Slobodskoy
Gubakha
993
Khalturin
Kirov
Omutninsk
337
Chermoz
Kachkanar
Bolotovskoye
Novovyatsk
Kirovo-Chepetsk
Chapetsk
Zalazna
Usva
Gremyachinsk
Tura
Kotelnich
Zuyevka
Dobryanka
Pashiya
Verkhnyaya Tura
Falenki
Chusovaya
Chusovoy
Krasnouralsk
Kumeny
Yar
Glazov
Krasnokamsk
Kushva
Nizhnyaya Salda
Vereshchagino
Lysva
Turinsk
Sorvizhi
284
Balezino
Nytva
Ocher
PERM
482
Nizhniy Tagil
Verkhnyaya Salda
Alapayevsk
Nitsa
Sovetsk
Nolinsk
Uni
Kez
746
Irbit
Yaransk
Medvedok
Igra
Zura
Sylva
Nevyansk
Kilmez
Kungur
452
Verkhniy Tagil
Rezh
Artemovskiy
Arkul
Urzhum
Bulanash
Troitskiy
Sernur
Yakshur Bodya
Votkinsk
Osa
Asbest
Sukhoy Log
Pyshma
Talitsa
Kilmez
Uva
Votkinskoye Vdkhr.
Pervouralsk
Yoshkar Ola
Izhevsk
Kuzino
Revda
YEKATERINBURG
Kamyshlov
Medvedevo
Chaykovskiy
Achit
Bogdanovich
Malmyzh
Krasnoufimsk
Nizhniye Sergi
Beloyarskiy
Kamensk Uralskiy
Mariinskiy Posad
Mozhga
Izh
Kama
Chernushka
Polevskoy
Sysert
Dalmatovo
Krasnogorskiy
Sosnovka
Sarapul
Oktyabrskiy
Mikhaylovski
678
Kataysk
Kukmor
Kambarka
Yanaul
Volzhsk
Arsk
Vyatskiye Polyany
Verkhniy Ufaley
Shadrinsk
Zelenodolsk
Nizhnekamskoye Vdkhr.
Neftekamsk
Kozlovka
KAZAN
Nyazepetrovsk
Techa
Kasli
Mamadysh
Yelabuga
Menzelinsk
Belaya
517
Kyshtym
Naberezhnyye Chelny
Argayash
Nizhnekamsk
Ik
Ufa
Verkhniye Kigi
Volga
Karabash
CHELYABINSK
Miass
Kamskoye Ustye
Chistopol
Zainsk
Dyurtyuli
Birsk
Krashyy Klyuch
Ay
Kusa
Shchuchye
Shumikha
Buinsk
Bulgar
Zlatoust
Kopeysk
Tetyushi
Aktash
Kushnarenkovo
Blagoveshchensk
Minyar
Berdyaush
Satka
Miass
Novosineglazovskiy
Bilyarsk
Almetyevsk
Asha
Yuryuzan
Bakal
Chebarkul
Korkino
Kuybyshevskoye Vdkhr.
Katav Ivanovsk
Yemanzhelinsk
23
Leninogorsk
Bugulma
Tuymazy
UFA
Iglino
1406
Simbirsk
Cherdakly
Nurlat
Oktyabrskiy
Chishmy
Gora Iremel
1582
Yuzhnouralsk
Uvelskiy
Dimitrovgrad
Uchaly
Plast
Oktyabrskoye
Novoulyanovsk
Isakly
383
Belebey
420
Davlekanovo
Gora Yamantau
1638
Inzer
Tirlyanskiy
Troitsk
Uy
Sengiley
Sernovodsk
Rayevskiy
Stepnoye
Sok
Priyutovo
Krasnousolskiy
Beloretsk
Novodevichye
Bugurulsan
Verkhneuralsk
Buskul
Toguzak
Togliatti
Abdulino
Komsomolets
Krasnyy Yar
Pokhvistnevo
Sterlitamak
Petrovskoye
Zhigulevsk
Timashevo
Magnitogorsk
Oktyabrsk
375
Otradnyy
Verkhniy Avzyan
1118
Syzran
Kinel
Ishimbay
Varna
Kashpirovka
SAMARA
Krotovka
Ponomarevka
481
Salavat
1039
Novokuybyshevsk
Belaya
Ural
Kartaly
Rudnyy
Chapayevsk
Samara
452
Privolzhye
Tok
Meleuz
Grachevka
Buzuluk
Kumertau
Sibay
Kizilskoye
Tobol
659
Pestravka
Bolshaya Glushitsa
Alekseyevka
Baymak
758
Ordzhonikidze
Lisakovsk
Totskoye
Sorochinsk
Sakmara
Bredy
Andreyevka
Bolshaya Irgiz
Bulanovo
Bolshaya Chernigovka
405
Iriklinskoye Vdkhr.
Pugachev
Tyulgan
Zhetiqara
Novo-Sergiyevskiy
Aydyrlinskiy
414
Sakmara
Chernyy Otrog
Ozernoye
Krasnoyarskiy
Yelizavetinka
Perevolotskiy
Orenburg
Saraktash
Zhailma
Ilek
Energetik
Ural
Pervomayskiy
Iriklinskiy
Adamovka
Ozinki
Darinskoye
Burli
Krasnyy Kholm
Kuvandyk
Gay
Novoorsk
Oral
Zhayyq
418
Kamenka
Aksay
Ilek
Sol Iletsk
Mednogorsk
Novotroitsk
Orsk
Kumak
Ozërnyy
Vladimirovka
Chingirlau
Akbulak
Yasnyy
Svetlyy
Ozero Shalkar
Martuk
Dombarovskiy
Aktasty
Utva
Leninskoye
509
Shalkar
Bolshaya Khobda
Tolybay
Chapayev
Dzhambeyty
Aqtöbe
Khromtau
Zhabasak
Novoalekseyevka
Novorossiyskoye
Irgiz
Qarabutaq
Bolshoi Uzen
Furmanovo
Kazhim
Karsha
Karatobe
Alga
Oktyabrsk
ft m
3000 1000
1500 500
600 200
0 0

Projection: *Conical with two standard parallels*

East from Greenwich

CARTOGRAPHY BY PHILIP'S.

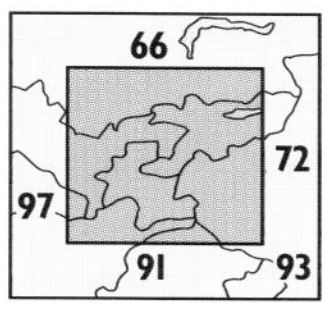

50 0 25 50 75 100 125 150 175 km

50 0 25 50 75 100 125 miles

100 0 100 200 300 400 500 600 700 800 km
100 0 100 200 300 400 500 miles
RUSSIA
1 Adygea
2 Karachey-Cherkessia
3 Kabardino-Balkaria
4 North Ossetia
5 Ingushetia
6 Chechenia
7 Dagestan
8 Mordvinia
9 Chuvashia
10 Mari El
11 Tatarstan
12 Udmurtia
13 Khakassia
AZERBAIJAN
14 Naxçıvan
GEORGIA
15 Ajaria
16 Abkhazia
UKRAINE
17 Crimea
ft m
12 000 4000
9000 3000
6000 2000
3000 1000
1200 400
600 200
0 0
200 600
2000 6000
4000 12 000
m ft
D C B E F G
1 2 3 4 5 6 7 8 9
NORWAY
SWEDEN
FINLAND
ESTONIA
LATVIA
LITHUANIA
POLAND
BELARUS
UKRAINE
MOLDOVA
ROMANIA
GERMANY
DENMARK
RUSSIA
KAZAKSTAN
UZBEKISTAN
TURKMENISTAN
KYRGYZSTAN
TAJIKISTAN
AFGHANISTAN
IRAN
IRAQ
TURKEY
GEORGIA
ARMENIA
AZERBAIJAN
North Sea
Baltic Sea
Gulf of Bothnia
Barents Sea
Kara Sea
ARCTIC
Beloye More
Black Sea
Sea of Azov
Caspian Sea
Aral Sea
Novaya Zemlya
Zemlya Frantsa Iosifa
Poluostrov Yamal
Gydanskiy Poluostrov
Obskaya Guba
Ural
Kyzyl Kum
Kara Kum
Ustyurt Plateau
Pamir
Tarim He
Junggar Pendi
Arctic Circle
MOSKVA
SANKT-PETERBURG
NIZHNIY NOVGOROD
KAZAN
SAMARA
VOLGOGRAD
ROSTOV
KYIV
KHARKIV
DNIPROPETROVSK
DONETSK
ODESA
MINSK
WARSZAWA
STOCKHOLM
Helsinki
Tallinn
Riga
Vilnius
Oslo
KØBENHAVN
BERLIN
HAMBURG
PERM
UFA
YEKATERINBURG
CHELYABINSK
OMSK
NOVOSIBIRSK
Astana
Qaraghandy
ALMATY
Bishkek
TOSHKENT
Dushanbe
Ashgabat
BAKI (Baku)
TBILISI
YEREVAN
TEHRAN
MASHHAD
ESFAHAN
TABRIZ
BAGHDAD
ÜRÜMQI
Arkhangelsk
Murmansk
Vorkuta
Salekhard
Surgut
Nizhnevartovsk
Tomsk
Barnaul
Orenburg
Astrakhan
Saratov
Voronezh
Krasnodar
Makhachkala
Projection: Conical Orthomorphic with two standard parallels
East from Greenwich

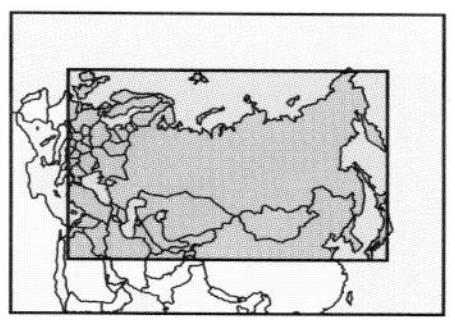

A
B
C
D
E
F
8
9
10
11
12
13
14
15
16
17
18
19
O C E A N
Laptev Sea
East Siberian Sea
Chukchi Sea
Bering Sea
Sea of Okhotsk
Sea of Japan
R U S S I A
Y A K H A
M O N G O L I A
C H I N A
G o b i
D o n g b e i
B U R Y A T I A
TUVA
NORTH KOREA
SOUTH KOREA
JAPAN
Severnaya Zemlya
Ostrov Komsomolets
Ostrov Oktyabrskoy Revolyutsii
Ostrov Bolshevik
Ostrov Shmidta
Ostrov Pioner
Mys Arkticheskiy
Proliv Vilkitskogo
Mys Chelyuskin
Poluostrov Taymyr
Gory Byrranga
Oz. Taymyr
Ostrov Bolshoy Begichev
Nordvik
Novosibirskiye Ostrova
Ostrov Kotelnyy
Ostrov Belkovskiy
Ostrov Stolbovoy
Ostrov Faddeyevskiy
Ostrov Novaya Sibir
Lyakhovskiye Ostrova
Proliv Dmitriya Lapteva
Ostrova Delonga
Ostrov Zhokhova
Ostrov Bennetta
Ostrov Vrangelya
Ostrova Medvezhi
Mys Dezhneva (East C.)
St. Lawrence I. (U.S.A.)
Anadyrskiy Zaliv
Provideniya
Beringovskiy
Chukotskoye Nagorye
Koryakskoye Nagorye
Kolymskoye Nagorye
Verkhoyanskiy Khrebet
Khrebet Cherskogo
Khrebet Dzhugdzur
Stanovoy Khrebet
Yablonovyy Khrebet
Khrebet Sikhote Alin
Da Hinggan Ling
Vostochnyy Sayan
Zapadnyy Sayan
Tannu Ola
Hangayn Nuruu
Hentiyn Nuruu
Gory Putorana
Sredinnyy Khrebet
Poluostrov Kamchatka
Komandorskiye Ostrova
Kurilskiye Ostrova
Sakhalin
Hokkaido
Honshū
Norilsk
Dudinka
Khatanga
Tiksi
Verkhoyansk
Yakutsk
Magadan
Petropavlovsk-Kamchatskiy
Okhotsk
Ayan
Nikolayevsk-na-Amur
Komsomolsk
Khabarovsk
Vladivostok
Nakhodka
Yuzhno-Sakhalinsk
Blagoveshchensk
Chita
Ulan Ude
Irkutsk
Angarsk
Bratsk
Krasnoyarsk
Achinsk
Kansk
Abakan
Kyzyl
Ulaanbaatar
Darhan
Choybalsan
Hailar
Manzhouli
QIQIHAR
HARBIN
Jiamusi
Mudanjiang
JILIN
CHANGCHUN
SHENYANG
FUSHUN
ANSHAN
Dandong
P'YŎNGYANG
Nampo
Chŏngjin
Wŏnsan
SEOUL
INCH'ŎN
TAEJŎN
TAEGU
PUSAN
DALIAN
BEIJING
Zhangjiakou
Baotou
Hohhot
Chengde
Chifeng
Xilinhot
Erenhot
Dalandzadgad
Hami
SAPPORO
Hakodate
Aomori
Hachinohe
Akita
Niigata
Kanazawa
ŌSAKA
Fuji-San 3776
Lena
Olenek
Vilyuy
Aldan
Amur
Kolyma
Indigirka
Yana
Angara
Yenisey
Nizhnyaya Tunguska
Podkamennaya Tunguska
Ozero Baykal
Hövsgöl Nuur
Hulun Nur
Arctic Circle
COPYRIGHT GEORGE PHILIP LTD.

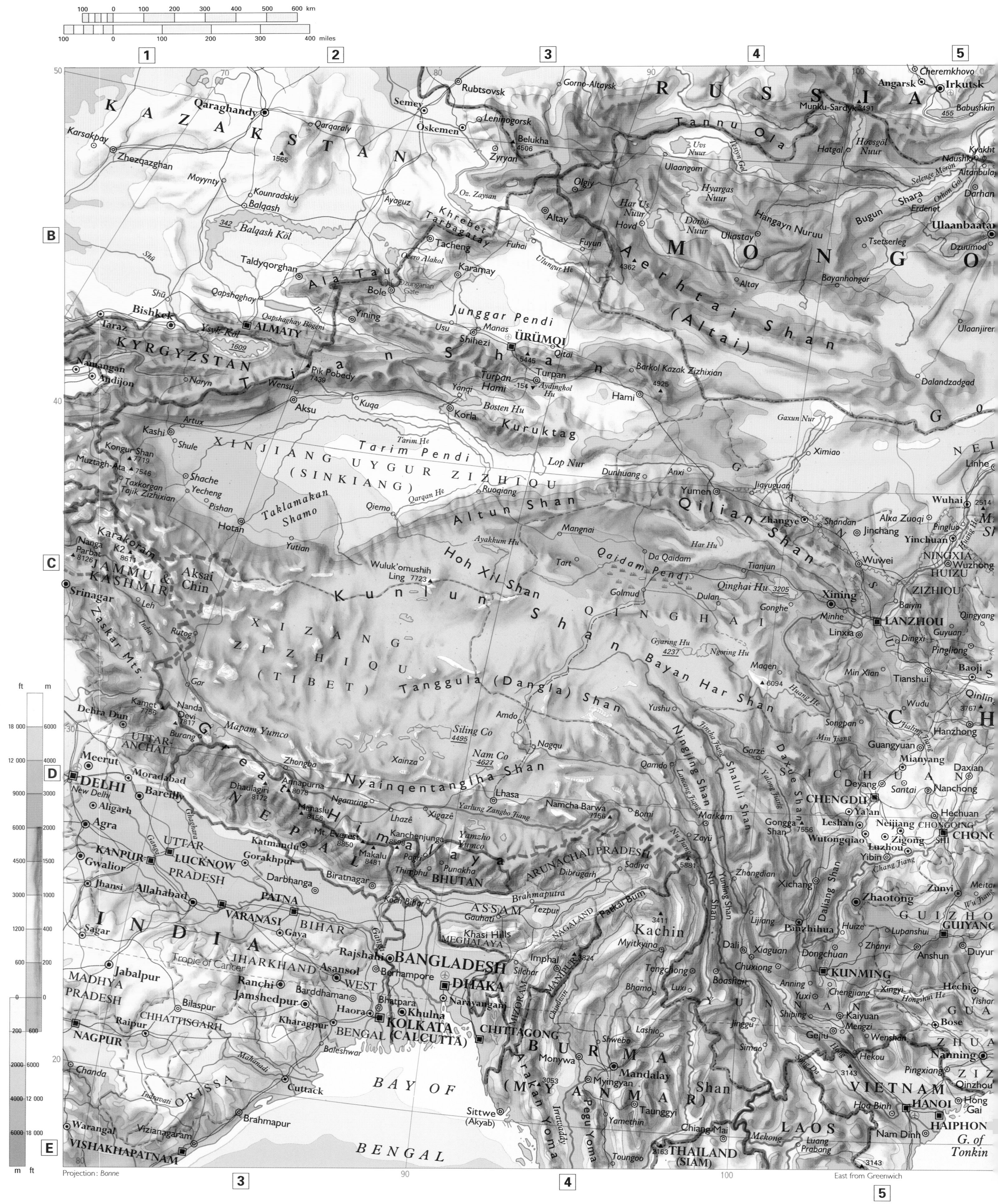
100 0 100 200 300 400 500 600 km
100 0 100 200 300 400 miles
1
2
3
4
5
B
C
D
E
ft m
18 000 6000
12 000 4000
9000 3000
6000 2000
4500 1500
3000 1000
1200 400
600 200
0
200 600
2000 6000
4000 12 000
6000 18 000
m ft
RUSSIA
KAZAKSTAN
KYRGYZSTAN
MONGOLIA
XINJIANG UYGUR ZIZHIQU (SINKIANG)
XIZANG ZIZHIQU (TIBET)
QINGHAI
JAMMU & KASHMIR
Aksai Chin
NEPAL
BHUTAN
BANGLADESH
INDIA
BURMA (MYANMAR)
THAILAND (SIAM)
LAOS
VIETNAM
SICHUAN
YUNNAN
NINGXIA HUIZU ZIZHIQU
Qaraghandy
Karsakpay
Zhezqazghan
Moyynty
Kounradskiy
Balqash
Balqash Köl
Qarqaraly
Semey
Öskemen
Rubtsovsk
Gorno-Altaysk
Leninogorsk
Belukha 4506
Zyryan
Oz. Zaysan
Ayaguz
Khrebet Tarbagatay
Tacheng
Ozero Alakol
Taldyqorghan
Ala Tau
Dzungarian Gate
Bole
Karamay
Fuhai
Ulungur He
Junggar Pendi
Yining
Ili
Qapshaghay
Qapshaghay Bögeni
Bishkek
ALMATY
Ysyk-Köl 1609
Taraz
Namangan
Andijon
Naryn
Pik Pobedy 7439
Wensu
Aksu
Usu
Manas
Shihezi
ÜRÜMQI
5445
Qitai
Turpan
Turpan Hami -154
Aydingkol Hu
Yanqi
Bosten Hu
Korla
Kuqa
Kuruktag
Barkol Kazak Zizhixian
4925
Hami
Tian Shan
Artux
Kashi
Shule
Kongur Shan 7719
Muztagh-Ata 7546
Taxkorgan Tajik Zizhixian
Shache
Yecheng
Pishan
Hotan
Taklamakan Shamo
Tarim He
Tarim Pendi
Qarqan He
Qiemo
Ruoqiang
Lop Nur
Yutian
Karakoram
K2 8611
Nanga Parbat 8126
Srinagar
Leh
Indus
Zaskar Mts.
Rutog
Gar
Kamet 7756
Nanda Devi 7817
Burang
Mapam Yumco
Dehra Dun
UTTAR-ANCHAL
Meerut
Moradabad
DELHI
New Delhi
Bareilly
Aligarh
Agra
Ghaghara
Ganga
UTTAR PRADESH
KANPUR
LUCKNOW
Gwalior
Jhansi
Allahabad
VARANASI
PATNA
BIHAR
Gaya
Sagar
Jabalpur
MADHYA PRADESH
Tropic of Cancer
JHARKHAND
Ranchi
Jamshedpur
Bilaspur
CHHATTISGARH
Raipur
NAGPUR
Mahanadi
Chanda
Indravati
ORISSA
Cuttack
Baleshwar
Brahmapur
Warangal
Vizianagaram
VISHAKHAPATNAM
BAY OF BENGAL
Dhaulagiri 8172
Annapurna 8078
Manaslu 8156
Katmandu
Mt. Everest 8850
Makalu 8481
Kanchenjunga 8598
Great Himalaya
Gorakhpur
Darbhanga
Biratnagar
Thimphu
Punakha
Paro
Yamzho Yumco
Koch Bihar
ASSAM
Gauhati
Khasi Hills
MEGHALAYA
Tezpur
Brahmaputra
Dibrugarh
Sadiya
ARUNACHAL PRADESH
NAGALAND
Patkai Bum
Imphal
MANIPUR
Silchar
MIZORAM
Rajshahi
Asansol
Berhampore
Barddhaman
WEST BENGAL
Haora
Bhatpara
Khulna
KOLKATA (CALCUTTA)
Kharagpur
DHAKA
Narayanganj
CHITTAGONG
Sittwe (Akyab)
Arakan Yoma
Chindwin
Irrawaddy
Pegu Yoma
Monywa
Shwebo
Mandalay
Myingyan
Yamethin
Taunggyi
Toungoo
Shan
3053
3824
3411
Kachin
Myitkyina
Bhamo
Lashio
Chiang Mai
2163
Mekong
Luang Prabang
Altun Shan
Ayakkum Hu
Mangnai
Hoh Xil Shan
Wuluk'omushih Ling 7723
Kunlun Shan
Tanggula (Dangla) Shan
Siling Co 4495
Nam Co 4627
Nagqu
Amdo
Xainza
Zhongba
Nyainqentanglha Shan
Lhasa
Ngamring
Lhazê
Xigazê
Yarlung Zangbo Jiang
Namcha Barwa 7756
Bomi
Qamdo
Markam
Zayü
Nu Jiang
5881
Tart
Qaidam Pendi
Da Qaidam
Har Hu
Tianjun
Golmud
Dulan
Qinghai Hu 3205
Gonghe
Gyaring Hu 4237
Ngoring Hu
Maqen
6094
Bayan Har Shan
Yushu
Huang He
Dunhuang
Anxi
Yumen
Jiayuguan
Qilian Shan
Zhangye
Shandan
Jinchang
Wuwei
Xining
Minhe
LANZHOU
Linxia
Min Xian
Tianshui
Baoji
Qinling
Dingxi
Guyuan
Pingliang
Qingyang
Baiyin
Wuzhong
Yinchuan
Alxa Zuoqi
Wuhai
2514
Pingluo
Linhe
Ximiao
Gaxun Nur
Dalandzadgad
Ulaanjirem
Uvs Nuur
Tannu Ola
Ulaangom
Ölgiy
Har Us Nuur
Hovd
Hyargas Nuur
Döröö Nuur
Uliastay
Hangayn Nuruu
Altay
Fuyun
4362
Aerhtai Shan (Altai)
Bayanhongor
Tsetserleg
Bugun
Shara
Erdenet
Selenge Mörön
Orhon Gol
Darhan
Ulaanbaatar
Dzuumod
Altanbulag
Kyakht
Naushki
Hatgal
Hövsgöl Nuur
Munku-Sardyk 3491
Angarsk
Irkutsk
Cheremkhovo
Babushkin
455
Wudu
3767
Songpan
Hanzhong
Jialing Jiang
Min Jiang
Guangyuan
Mianyang
Daxian
Deyang
Santai
Nanchong
CHENGDU
Ya'an
Leshan
Neijiang
Hechuan
CHONGQING SHI
Gongga Shan 7556
Wutongqiao
Zigong
Luzhou
Yibin
Chang Jiang
Zunyi
Garzê
Daxue Shan
Yalong Jiang
Ningjing Shan
Jinsha Jiang
Shaluli Shan
Lancang Jiang
Nu Shan
Yunling Shan
Zhongdian
Xichang
Daliang Shan
Lijiang
Panzhihua
Zhaotong
Huize
Lupanshui
Zhanyi
GUIZHOU
GUIYANG
Anshun
Duyun
Dali
Xiaguan
Dongchuan
Chuxiong
KUNMING
Tengchong
Luxi
Baoshan
Anning
Yuxi
Chengjiang
Xingyi
Hechi
Hongshui He
Shiping
Kaiyuan
Mengzi
Wenshan
Bose
Jinggu
Simao
Gejiu
Hekou
3143
Song Da
Nanning
Pingxiang
Qinzhou
HANOI
Hoa Binh
Hong Gai
HAIPHONG
Nam Dinh
G. of Tonkin
Projection: Bonne
East from Greenwich
50
40
30
20
70
80
90
100

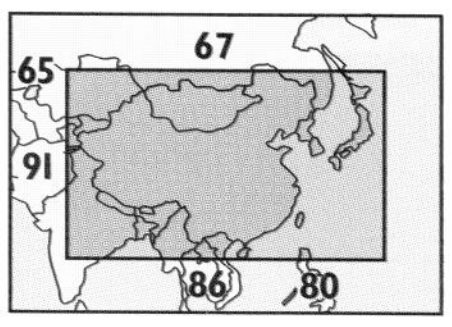
67
65
91
86
80

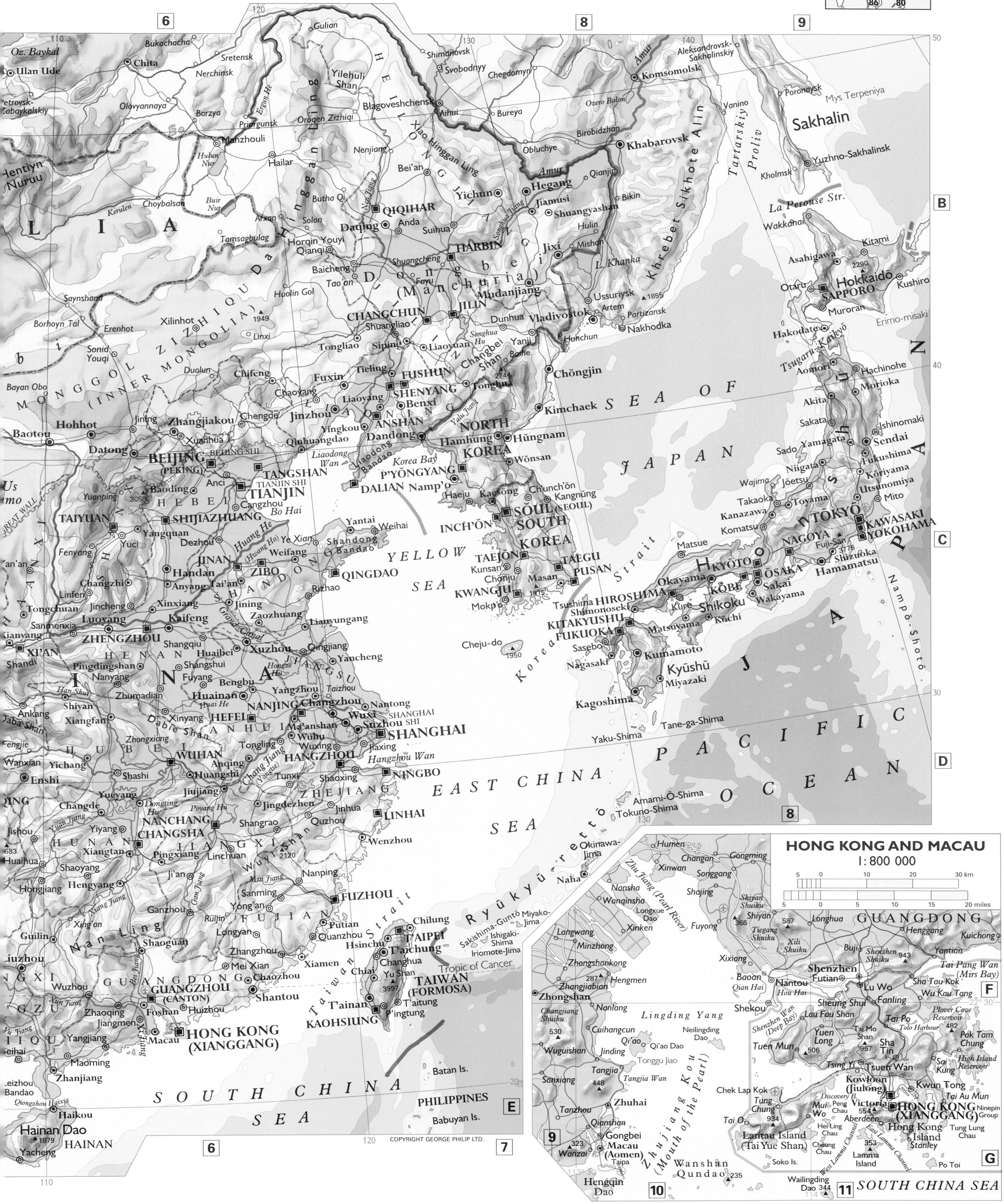
6
7
8
9
B
C
D
E
F
G
10
11
Oz. Baykal
Ulan Ude
Chita
Bukachacha
Sretensk
Nerchinsk
Olovyannaya
Borzya
Priargunsk
Manzhouli
Hailar
Gulian
Yilehuli Shan
Shimanovsk
Svobodnyy
Chegdomyn
Blagoveshchensk
Aihui
Bureya
Amur
Komsomolsk
Aleksandrovsk-Sakhalinskiy
Poronaysk
Mys Terpeniya
Sakhalin
Vanino
Tartarskiy Proliv
Ozero Bolon
Birobidzhan
Obluchye
Khabarovsk
Khrebet Sikhote Alin
Yuzhno-Sakhalinsk
Kholmsk
La Perouse Str.
Wakkanai
Kitami
Asahigawa
2290
Hokkaido
SAPPORO
Otaru
Kushiro
Muroran
Erimo-misaki
Hakodate
Tsugaru-Kaikyō
Aomori
Hachinohe
Morioka
Akita
Ishinomaki
Sakata
Sendai
Yamagata
Sado
Niigata
Fukushima
Kōriyama
Utsunomiya
Mito
Jōetsu
Wajima
Toyama
Takaoka
Kanazawa
Komatsu
TŌKYŌ
KAWASAKI
YOKOHAMA
NAGOYA
Fuji-San
3776
Shizuoka
Hamamatsu
KYŌTO
ŌSAKA
KŌBE
Sakai
Wakayama
Okayama
HIROSHIMA
Matsue
Shikoku
Kōchi
Matsuyama
Kure
Shimonoseki
KITAKYUSHU
FUKUOKA
Sasebo
Nagasaki
Kumamoto
Kyūshū
Miyazaki
Kagoshima
Tane-ga-Shima
Yaku-Shima
Nampō-Shotō
Amami-Ō-Shima
Tokuno-Shima
Okinawa-Jima
Naha
Ryūkyū-rettō
Miyako-Jima
Sakishima-Guntō
Ishigaki-Shima
Iriomote-Jima
Tropic of Cancer
SEA OF JAPAN
PACIFIC OCEAN
EAST CHINA SEA
YELLOW SEA
SOUTH CHINA SEA
Korea Strait
Tsushima
Cheju-do
1950
Hentiyn Nuruu
Hulun Nur
Buir Nur
Kerulen
Choybalsan
Tamsagbulag
Saynshand
Borhoyn Tal
Erenhot
Sonid Youqi
Bayan Obo
Xilinhot
Linxi
1949
Duolun
MONGGOL ZIZHIQU (INNER MONGOLIA)
Da Hinggan Ling
Ergun He
Oroqen Zizhiqi
Xiao Hinggan Ling
HEILONGJIANG
Nenjiang
Bei'an
Yichun
Hegang
Jiamusi
Shuangyashan
Qianjin
Bikin
Hulin
Mishan
Jixi
L. Khanka
Songhua Jiang
Butha Qi
Nen Jiang
QIQIHAR
Anda
Daqing
Suihua
Arxan
Solon
Horqin Youyi Qianqi
HARBIN
Shuangcheng
Baicheng
Tao'an
Fuyu
Huolin Gol
Mudanjiang
Ussuriysk
Artem
Vladivostok
Partizansk
Nakhodka
1855
Dongbei (Manchuria)
JILIN
CHANGCHUN
Shuangliao
Dunhua
Hunchun
Songhua Hu
Siping
Liaoyuan
Changbai Shan
Yanji
2744
Tongliao
Chifeng
Fuxin
Tieling
FUSHUN
SHENYANG
Benxi
Liaoyang
Chaoyang
Tonghua
LIAONING
Jinzhou
Chengde
ANSHAN
Yingkou
Dandong
Yalu Jiang
Qinhuangdao
Liaodong Wan
Liaodong Bandao
Korea Bay
DALIAN
Chŏngjin
Kimchaek
NORTH KOREA
Hamhung
Hŭngnam
Wŏnsan
P'YŎNGYANG
Namp'o
Haeju
Kaesŏng
Ch'unch'ŏn
Kangnŭng
SŎUL (SEOUL)
INCH'ŎN
SOUTH KOREA
TAEJŎN
TAEGU
PUSAN
Kunsan
Chŏnju
KWANGJU
Masan
1915
Mokp'o
Baotou
Hohhot
Jining
Zhangjiakou
Xuanhua
Datong
BEIJING (PEKING)
BEIJING SHI
TANGSHAN
TIANJIN SHI
TIANJIN
Anci
Baoding
HEBEI
3058
Yuanping
TAIYUAN
SHIJIAZHUANG
Cangzhou
Bo Hai
Yangquan
Yuci
Dezhou
Fenyang
JINAN
Huang He (Hwang Ho)
ZIBO
Weifang
Ye Xian
Yantai
Weihai
Shandong Bandao
QINGDAO
SHANDONG
Tai'an
Handan
Anyang
Changzhi
Linfen
Rizhao
Xinxiang
Jining
Tongchuan
Jincheng
Luoyang
Kaifeng
Zaozhuang
Sanmenxia
ZHENGZHOU
Grand Canal
Lianyungang
XI'AN
Shangqiu
Huaibei
Xuzhou
Qingjiang
Yancheng
Shandi
Pingdingshan
HENAN
Shangshui
Hongze Hu
JIANGSU
Nanyang
Fuyang
Bengbu
Huainan
Yangzhou
Taizhou
Nantong
Han Shui
Zhumadian
Huai He
HEFEI
NANJING
Changzhou
Wuxi
Suzhou
SHANGHAI SHI
SHANGHAI
Shiyan
Ankang
Xiangfan
Xinyang
Dabie Shan
ANHUI
Ma'anshan
Wuhu
Wuxing
Jiaxing
HANGZHOU
Hangzhou Wan
Zhongxiang
HUBEI
Tongling
Yichang
WUHAN
Anqing
Huangshi
Chang Jiang (Yangtze)
Tunxi
Shaoxing
NINGBO
Enshi
Shashi
ZHEJIANG
Yueyang
Changde
Dongting Hu
Poyang Hu
Jiujiang
Jingdezhen
Jinhua
LINHAI
NANCHANG
CHANGSHA
Yiyang
Yuan Jiang
Shangrao
Quzhou
HUNAN
Xiangtan
JIANGXI
Wenzhou
Pingxiang
Linchuan
Wuyi Shan
2120
Huaihua
Shaoyang
Hengyang
Ji'an
Gan Jiang
Min Jiang
Nanping
Hongjiang
Sanming
FUZHOU
Ganzhou
Yong'an
FUJIAN
Putian
Xing'an
Guilin
Nan Ling
Ruijin
Longyan
Quanzhou
Chilung
Shaoguan
Zhangzhou
Taiwan Strait
Hsinchu
T'AIPEI
T'aichung
Changhua
Chiai
Yu Shan
3997
Xiamen
Mei Xian
TAIWAN (FORMOSA)
Liuzhou
GUANGDONG
Chaozhou
Shantou
T'aitung
T'ainan
P'ingtung
KAOHSIUNG
Wuzhou
Bei Jiang
GUANGZHOU (CANTON)
Xun Jiang
Zhaoqing
Foshan
Huizhou
Jiangmen
Xi Jiang
Macau
HONG KONG (XIANGGANG)
Yangjiang
Maoming
Zhanjiang
Leizhou Bandao
Qiongzhou Haixia
Haikou
Hainan Dao
1879
HAINAN
Yacheng
Batan Is.
PHILIPPINES
Babuyan Is.
COPYRIGHT GEORGE PHILIP LTD.
110
120
130
140
50
40
30
20
HONG KONG AND MACAU
1: 800 000
5
0
10
20
30 km
5
0
5
10
15
20 miles
Humen
Changan
Gongming
Xinwan
Songgang
Zhu Jiang (Pearl River)
Nansha
Wanqingsha
Longxue Dao
Xinken
Shajing
Fuyong
Shiyan Shuiku
Shiyan
366
587
Longhua
GUANGDONG
Henggang
Kuichong
Tiegang Shuiku
Xili Shuiku
Buji
Shenzhen Shuiku
943
Yantian
Langwang
Minzhong
Zhongshankong
Xixiang
Shenzhen
Futian
Tai Pang Wan (Mirs Bay)
Baoan
Qian Hai
Nantou
Hou Hai
Lu Wo
Sha Tau Kok
Wu Kau Tang
287
Zhangjiabian
Hengmen
Zhongshan
Fanling
Sheung Shui
22° 30'
Lau Fau Shan
Tai Po
Plover Cove Reservoir
Tolo Harbour
482
Changjiang Shuiku
Nanlang
Lingding Yang
Shekou
Shenzhen Wan (Deep Bay)
530
Cuihangcun
Neilingding Dao
Yuen Long
Tai Mo Shan
957
Pak Tam Chung
Wuguishan
Qi'ao
Qi'ao Dao
Tuen Mun
506
Sha Tin
High Island Reservoir
Jinding
Tonggu Jiao
Tsing Yi
Tsuen Wan
Sai Kung
Tangjia
448
Tangjia Wan
Zhujiang Kou (Mouth of the Pearl)
Chek Lap Kok
Kowloon (Jiulong)
Kwun Tong
Sanxiang
Tung Chung
Discovery B.
Peng Chau
Mui Wo
Victoria
HONG KONG (XIANGGANG)
Tai Au Mun
Ninepin Group
Zhuhai
934
554
Tanzhou
Qianshan
Tai O
Aberdeen
Hei Ling Chau
Hong Kong Island
Tung Lung Chau
Gongbei
Lantau Island (Tai Yue Shan)
Cheung Chau
353
Lamma Island
Stanley
323
Wanzai
Macau (Aomen)
Taipa
West Lamma Channel
East Lamma Channel
Wanshan Qundao
235
Soko Is.
Po Toi
113° 30'
Hengqin Dao
Wailingding Dao
344
114
SOUTH CHINA SEA

JAPAN 1:4 000 000

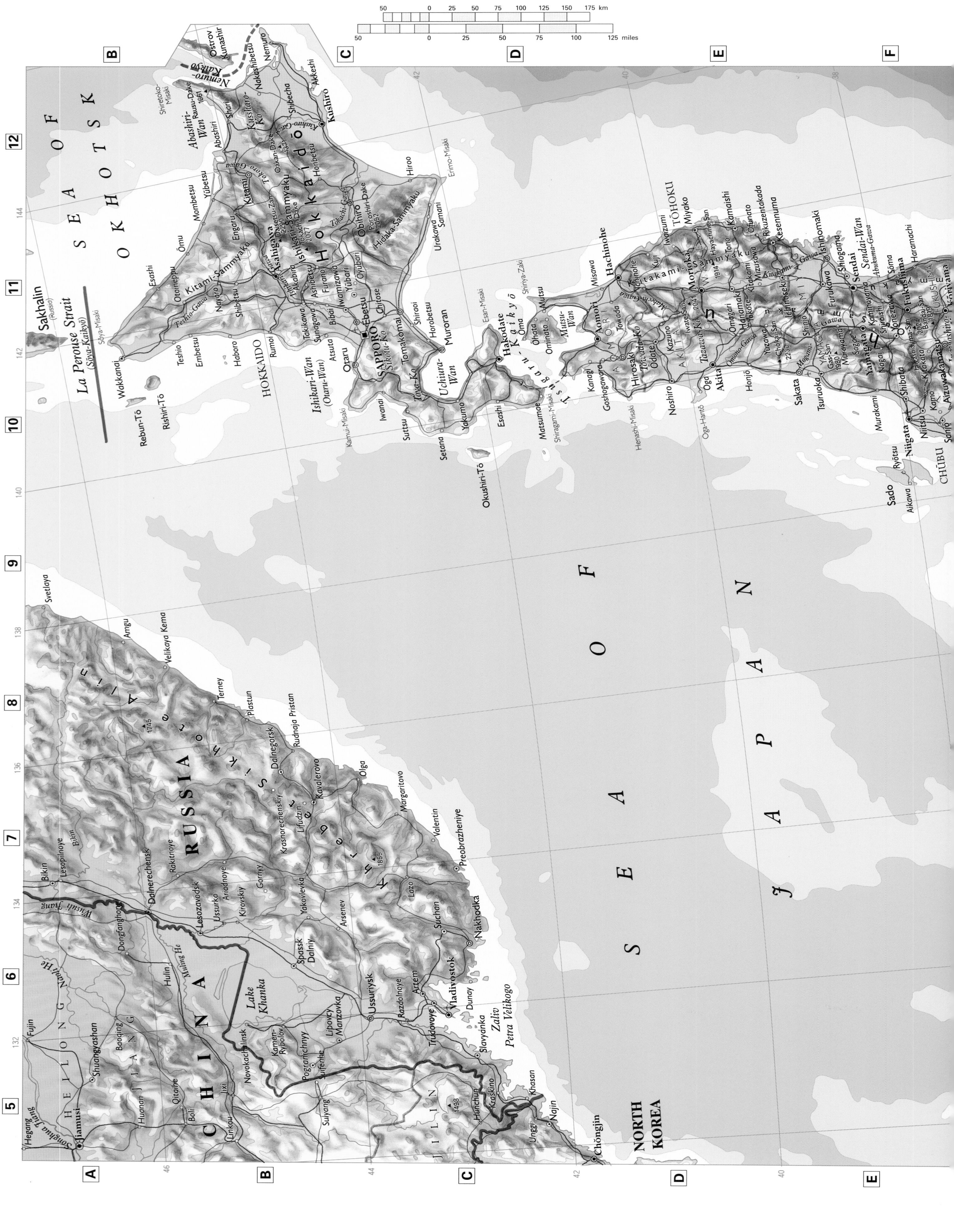
50 0 25 50 75 100 125 150 175 km
50 0 25 50 75 100 125 miles
SEA OF OKHOTSK
SEA OF JAPAN
Sakhalin (Russia)
La Perouse Strait (Sōya-Kaikyō)
Hokkaidō
HOKKAIDO
SAPPORO
Hakodate
Tsugaru-Kaikyō
Aomori
Hachinohe
Morioka
Akita
Sendai
Niigata
Sado
TŌHOKU
CHŪBU
RUSSIA
CHINA
NORTH KOREA
Lake Khanka
Zaliv Petra Velikogo
Vladivostok
Nakhodka
Ussuriysk
Chŏngjin
Jiamusi
Kushiro
Asahikawa
Muroran
Otaru
Wakkanai
Rebun-Tō
Rishiri-Tō
Okushiri-Tō

Projection: *Conical with two standard parallels*

km
miles
SEA OF JAPAN
(EAST SEA)
Yŏngdŏk
Chŏngha
Changgi-Ap
P'ohang
SOUTH KOREA
Oki-Shotō
Dōgo
Daimanji-San 608
Saigō
Honshu
Korea Strait
CHŪGOKU-DISTRICT
Shimane-Hantō
Jizō-Zaki
Matsue
Sakaiminato
Hi-no-Misaki
Hirata
Taisha
Shinji-Ko
Izumo
Yasugi
Yonago
Daito
Kisuki
Dai-Sen 1729
Kurayoshi
TOTTORI
Tottori
Iwami
Kasumi
Toyooka
Hidaka
Suga-no-Sen 1510
Wakasa
Chizu
Wadayama
Ōda
Sanbe-San 1126
Yunotsu
Gōtsu
Hamada
SHIMANE
Chūgoku-Sanchi
Dōgo-San 1269
Bingo-Ochiai
Tōjō
Katsuyama
Niimi
Tsuyama
Ochiai
OKAYAMA
HYOGO
Nishiwaki
Ikuno
Yamasaki
Yanahara
Sayō
Tatsuno
Aioi
Kasai
Himeji
Takasago
Kakogawa
Akashi
Akō
Bizen
Saidaiji
Wake
Takahashi
Shōbara
Miyoshi
HIROSHIMA
Masuda
Kake
Yoshida
Ōta-Gawa
Gō-Gawa
Asahi-Gawa
Takahashi-Gawa
Kanmuri-Yama 1339
Aono-Yama 908
Atō
Hagi
Ōmi-Shima
Mi-Shima
Tsuno-Shima
Nagato
YAMAGUCHI
Yamaguchi
Ōgōri
Mine
San'yō
Hōfu
Tokuji
Shin-Nan'yō
Tokuyama
Kudamatsu
Hikari
Iwakuni
Ōtake
Yanai
HIROSHIMA
Hatsukaichi
Kaita
Higashi-Hiroshima
Kure
Takehara
Mihara
Fukuyama
Onomichi
Fuchū
Ibara
Yakage
Sōja
Okayama
Kurashiki
Kannabe
Konkō
Kasaoka
Tamano
Shōdo-Shima
Tonoshō
Ieshima-Shotō
Harima-Nada
Awaji-Shima
Tsuna
Sumoto
Nandan
Naruto-Kaikyō
Kitano
Hikeru
Naruto
Tokushima
Takamatsu
Shido
Sakaide
Marugame
Tadotsu
Miki
KAGAWA
Zentsūji
Kotohira
Itano
Sanyuki-Sammyaku
Kan'onji
Onohara
Kawanoe
In'noshima
Ōmi-Shima
Ondo
Kurahashi-Jima
Hiroshima-Wan
Aki-Nada
Hiuchi-Nada
Imabari
Niihama
SETO NAIKAI
Hōjō
Tōyō
Saijō
Iyo-Mishima
Ishizuchi-Yama 1981
Shikoku-Sanchi
TOKUSHIMA
Tsurugi-San 1955
Anan
Kii-Suidō
Gamoda-Saki
Ikeda
Waki
Kamojima
Komatsushima
Matsuyama
Iyo
Ōtoya
KŌCHI
EHIME
Yashiro-Jima
Heigun-Tō
Nagahama
Iyo-Nada
Sada-Misaki-Hantō
Ōzu
Uchiko
Yawatahama
Uwa
Kuma
Nankoku
Ino
Kōchi
Tosa-Yamada
Noichi
Sakawa
Tosa
Susaki
Aki
Mugi
Tōyō
Tosa-Wan
Muroto
Muroto-Misaki
Uwajima
Hiromi
Kubokawa
Tsushima
Nishi-Tosa
Mishō
Sukumo
Nakamura
Saga
Tosa-Shimizu
Ashizuri-Zaki
Oki-no-Shima
Shikoku
SHIKOKU-DISTRICT
Hōgo-Kaikyō
Bungo-Suidō
Tsurumi-Saki
Hibiki-Nada
Toyoura
Genkai-Nada
Shimonoseki
Onoda
Ube
KITAKYŪSHŪ
Suō-Nada
Naga-Shima
Iwai-Jima
Hime-Jima
Ō-Shima
Nakama
Munakata
Fukuma
Nōgata
Yukuhashi
Miyata
Iizuka
Tagawa
Nakatsu
Futago-Yama 721
Kunisaki
Buzen
Usa
Bungotakada
Kitsuki
Hiji
Beppu-Wan
Beppu
Tsurusaki
Ōita
Saganoseki
Usuki
Yufu-Dake 1584
ŌITA
Kusu
Oguni
Kujū-San 1787
Tsukumi
Mie
Saiki
Kamae
Taketa
Ichinomiya
Aso
Aso-Zan 1592
Sobo-Yama 1758
Takachiho
Nobeoka
Hinokage
FUKUOKA
Fukuoka
Maebaru
Dazaifu
Kasuga
Yamada
Chikushino
Amagi
Tsukushi-Sanchi
Sefuri-San 1055
Tosu
Kurume
Hita
Chikugo
Kurogi
Ōkawa
Yanagawa
Setaka
Yamaga
Ōmuta
Arao
Kikuchi
Ōzu
Tamana
Kumamoto
KUMAMOTO
Mashiki
Uto
Shimabara
Unzen-Dake 1360
Obama
Katsumoto
Iki
Gō-no-ura
Iki-Kaikyō
Higasi-Suidō
Tsushima
Kara-Saki
Kamiagata
Kamitsushima
Mitsushima
Izuhara
Kō-Saki
Ō-Shima
Yobuko
Karatsu
Ikitsuki-Shima
Hirado
Hirado-Shima
Matsuura
Imari
SAGA
Saga
Taku
Takeo
Arita
Saza
Sasebo
Kashima
Ureshino
Tara
Tara-Dake 1076
Omura-Wan
Ōmura
Isahaya
NAGASAKI
Nishi-Sonogi-Hantō
Nagasaki
Tachibana-Wan
Nomo-Zaki
Kuchinotsu
Misumi
Amakusa-Nada
Amakusa-Shotō
Hondo
Matsushima
Kami-Jima
Shimo-Jima
Yatsushiro-Kai
Yatsushiro
Kunimi-Dake 1739
Itsuki
Shiiba
Hyūga
Taragi
Kyūshū-Sanchi
MIYAZAKI
Hitoyoshi
Ushibuka
Naga-Shima
Minamata
Izumi
Akune
Ōkuchi
Ebino
Saito
Takanabe
Kyūshū
KYŪSHŪ-DISTRICT
Kami-Koshiki-Jima
Miyanojō
Yoshimatsu
Kurino
Kirishima-Yama 1700
Kobayashi
Sadowara
Miyazaki
Koshiki-Rettō
Kushikino
Sendai
Aira
Kokubu
Hayato
Ijūin
Miyakonojō
Shimo-Koshiki-Jima
Kagoshima
KAGOSHIMA
On-Take 1118
Nichinan
Aburatsu
Fukiage
Tarumizu
Shibushi
Noma-Saki
Kaseda
Kanoya
Kushima
Kawanabe
Satsuma-Hantō
Kagoshima-Wan
Kiire
Osaki
Shibushi-Wan
Makurazaki
Bō-no-Misaki
Ibusuki
Kōyama
Kaimon-Dake 924
Yamagawa
Ōsumi-Hantō
Sata-Misaki
Projection: Lambert's Conformal Conic

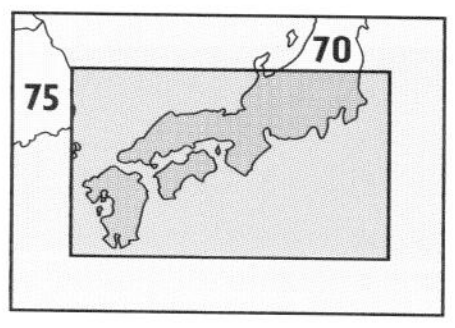
75
70

CHŪBU-DISTRICT
KINKI-DISTRICT
KANTŌ-DISTRICT
P A C I F I C   O C E A N
Enshū-Nada
Kumano-Nada
Sagami-Nada
Kashima-Nada
Wakasa-Wan
Ise-Wan
Suruga-Wan
Sagami-Wan
Tōkyō-Wan
TŌKYŌ
YOKOHAMA
KAWASAKI
NAGOYA
ŌSAKA
KYŌTO
KOBE
Kanazawa
Toyama
Nagano
Fukui
Gifu
Tsu
Nara
Wakayama
Shizuoka
Hamamatsu
Kōfu
Maebashi
Utsunomiya
Mito
Chiba
Urawa
Matsumoto
Takayama
Tsuruga
Maizuru
Ōtsu
Toyohashi
Okazaki
Numazu
Fuji
Odawara
Hiratsuka
Yokosuka
Hachiōji
Kawagoe
Hitachi
Nikkō
Ashikaga
Takasaki
Ueda
Suwa
Iida
Matsusaka
Ise
Toba
Kumano
Tanabe
Shingū
Kushimoto
Shio-no-Misaki
Shimoda
Atami
Itō
Izu-Hantō
Kii-Hantō
Izu-Shotō
Nampō-Shotō
Ō-Shima
To-Shima
Nii-Jima
Shikine-Jima
Kōzu-Shima
Miyake-Jima
Mikura-Jima
Hachijō-Jima
Aoga-Shima
Sumisu-Jima
Omae-Zaki
Irō-Zaki
Nojima-Zaki
Inubō-Zaki
Daiō-Misaki
Echizen-Misaki
Kyō-ga-Saki
Hida-Sammyaku
Kiso-Sammyaku
Akaishi-Sammyaku
Kantō-Sanchi
Ryōhaku-Sanchi
Kii-Sanchi
Fuji-San 3776
Ontake-San 3063
Asama-Yama 2542
Hakken-Zan 1915
ISHIKAWA
TOYAMA
FUKUI
GIFU
NAGANO
GUMMA
TOCHIGI
IBARAKI
SAITAMA
TŌKYŌ
CHIBA
KANAGAWA
YAMANASHI
SHIZUOKA
AICHI
MIE
SHIGA
KYŌTO
ŌSAKA
NARA
WAKAYAMA
East from Greenwich
136
137
138
139
140
35
34
33
32
A
B
C
D
E
F
7
8
9
10
11
12

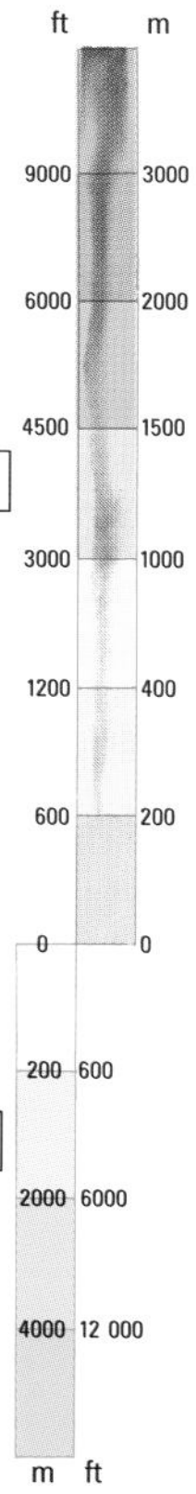
ft
m
9000
3000
6000
2000
4500
1500
3000
1000
1200
400
600
200
0
0
200
600
2000
6000
4000
12 000
m
ft

COPYRIGHT GEORGE PHILIP LTD.

NORTHERN CHINA AND KOREA 1:4 800 000

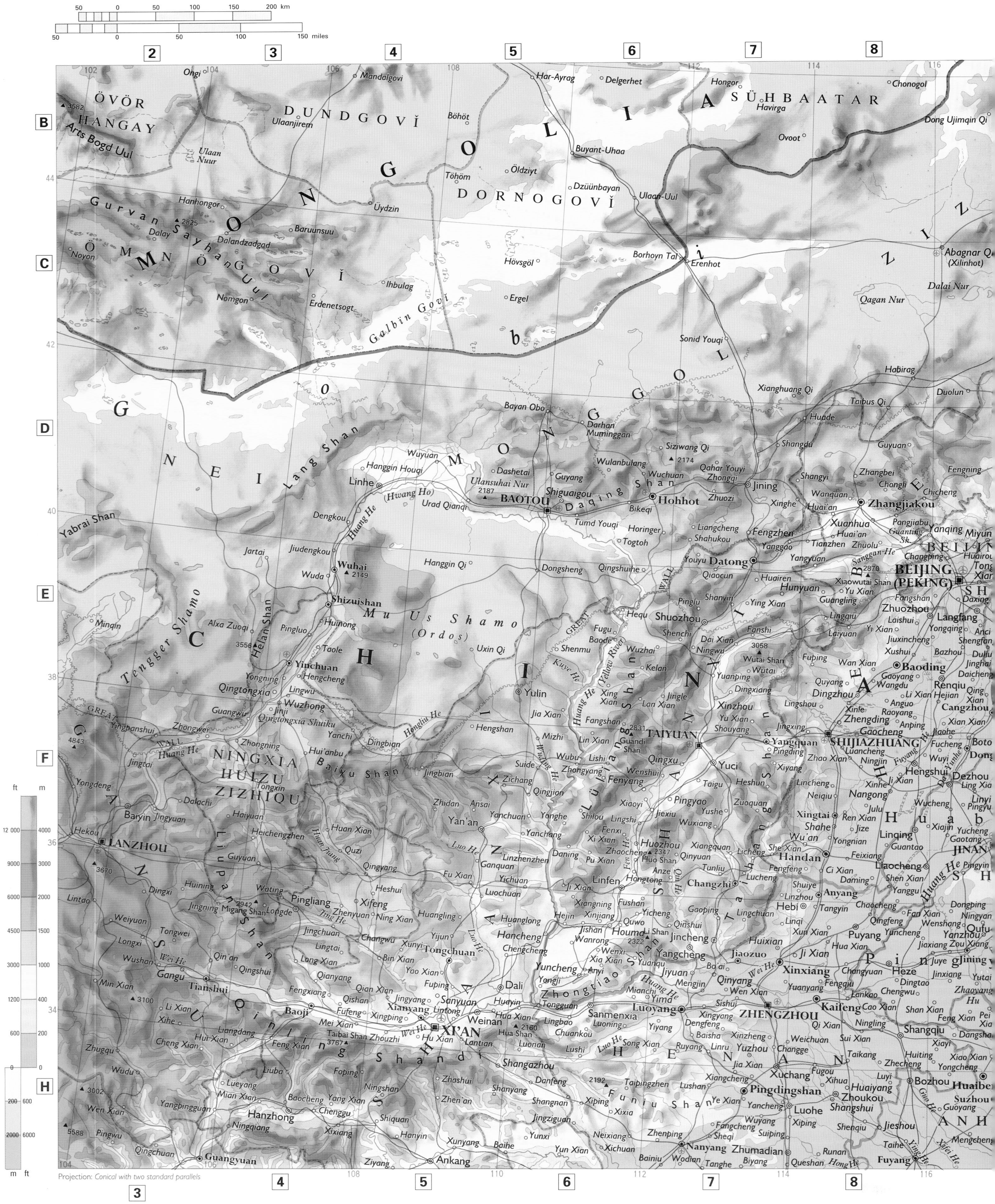

67
68
70
76
77
9
10
11
12
13
14
15
16
B
C
D
E
F
G
H
HARBIN
Bin Xian
Acheng
Shuangcheng
Zhaoyuan
Maoxing
Da'an
Zhenlai
Baicheng
Taonan
Tuquan
Horqin Youyi Qianqi
(Ulanhot)
Hulingol
Hulin He
Anguang
Tao'er He
Nen Jiang
Qagan Nur
Qian Gorlos
Fuyu
Changchunling
Beitaolaizhao
Sanchahe
Yushu
Lalin
Lalin He
Shangzhi
Yanshou
Yimianpo
Wuchang
Shanhetun
Shulan
Zhangguangcai Ling
Hengdaohezi
Mudanjiang
Hailin
Ning'an
Linkou
Jixi
Muling
Turiy Rog
Ozero Khanka
Maqiaohe
Xiachengzi
Pogranichnyy
Suiyang
Suifenhe
Golenki
Dongning
Ussuriysk
Razdolnoye
Artem
Tavrichanka
Vladivostok
Slavyanka
Hunchun
Kraskino
Posyet
RUSSIA
HEILONGJIANG
Qian'an
Shenjingzi
Kaoshan
Nong'an
Dehui
Tongyu
Zhanyu
Beizhengzhen
Changling
Fulongquan
Jiutai
Gangyao
Wulajie
Jarud Qi
1949
Xinkai He
Horqin Zuoyi Zhongqi
Maolin
CHANGCHUN
Huaidezhen
JILIN
Jiaohe
Xinzhan
Emu
Huangsongdian
Jingpo Hu
Dongjingcheng
Luozigou
Chunyang
Dunhua
Daxinggou
Wangqing
Shixian
Tumen
Tumen Jiang
Yanji
Mingyuegue
Longjing
Helong
Namyang
Antu
Bairin Zuoqi
Linxi
2029
Bairin Youqi
Kailu
Tongliao
Xiliao He
Shuangliao
Dongliao He
Fanjiatun
Gongzhuling
Shuangyang
Yitong
Songhua Hu
Manchuria
Xar Moron He
Ongniud Qi
Jargalang
Bamiancheng
Lishu
Siping
Liaoyuan
Panshi
Huadian
Erdao Jiang
Huifa He
Laoha He
Wutonghaolai
Kangping
Zhangwu
Xifeng
Dongfeng
Huinan
Baishan
2020
Xiawa
Hure Qi
Liu He
WALL
Faku
Tiefa
Kaiyuan
Meihekou
Jingyu
Fusong
Baihe
1677
Changbai Shan
Hoeamdong
Unggi
Sŏsura
Najin
Hoeryong
Musan
Puryong
Pugŏdong
Chifeng
Fuxin
Zhangwu
Liao He
Tieling
Shanchengzhen
Qingyuan
Liuhe
Xinlitun
Xinmin
Hunjiang
Linjiang
Chunggang-ŭp
2744
Paektu-san
Lupyongdong
Nanam
2541
Hachon
Chŏngjin
Kyŏngsŏng
Chuuronjang
Ondaejin
Heishui
Beipiao
Qinghemen
Heishan
SHENYANG
FUSHUN
Xinbin
Tonghua
Changbai
Hyesan
Irhyangdong
Weichang
1885
Ningcheng
Chaoyang
Liaozhong
Benxi
Qinghecheng
Dongbei
Inpundong
Huch'ang
Kasan-dong
Hapsu
Simpungdong
Kilchu
Musudan
Daling He
Yi Xian
Beizhen
Goubangzi
Liaoyang
Huanren
1845
Manp'o
Kapsan
Longhua
LIAONING
Anping
Tianshifu
Hun Jiang
Ji'an
Kanggye
Pujon-chŏsuji
Pungsan
Kosŏngni
Kimch'aek
(Songjin)
Chengde
Lingyuan
Jinzhou
Panjin
ANSHAN
Lianshanguan
Yalu Jiang
Kŭup-tong
2522
Ch'ail-bong
Pujon-chŏsuji
Tanch'ŏn
Luanne
Luanping
Pingquan
Liugou
Jianchang
Jinxi
Niuzhuang
Haicheng
Supung Shuiku
Ch'osan
Pyŏktong
Changjin-chŏsuji
Kwangdaeri
Changhŭngni
Pukch'ŏng
Sinch'ang
Shangbancheng
Kuancheng
Tianzhuangtai
Huludao
Yingkou
Dashiqiao
Kuandian
Koin-dong
Changjin
Sinhung
Sinp'o
Sŏhori
Miyun Shuiku
Xinglong
Shuangshanzi
Xingcheng
Liaodong
Gaizhou
Fengcheng
Cao He
Sakchu
NORTH
Oro
Hongwon
Jianchangying
Suizhong
Xiongyuecheng
Wanfu
1131
Xiuyan
Dandong
Sinŭiju
Uiju
Taegwan
Pukchin
Hamhŭng
Hŭngnam
SEA OF
Zunhua
Qinhuangdao
Wan
Buyun Shan
Gushan
Donggou
Yongamp'o
Kusŏng
Kujang
Tŏkch'ŏn
Tongch'ŏn-ni
Tongjosŏn Man
Fengrun
Lulong
Luan Xian
Funing
Chŏngju
Pakch'ŏn
Anju
KOREA
Yutian
Baodi
Changli
Wafangdian
Zhuanghe
Yalu Jiang
Sŏnch'ŏn
Sunch'ŏn
Yŏnghŭng
Kowŏn
Munch'ŏn
TANGSHAN
Luan He
Leting
Sukch'ŏn
Sinchang-ni
Wŏnsan
TIANJIN SHI
Wuqing
Hangu
Pulandian
Pikou
Sunan
Songch'ŏn
Kangdong
Tongyang
Anbyŏn
Kojŏ
JAPAN
TIANJIN
Tanggu
Dagu
Jin Xian
Lüshun
DALIAN
Korea Bay
P'YŎNGYANG
Chunghwa
Koksan
Singosan
Hoeyang
Kosŏng
Namp'o
Songnim
Sepo-ri
1638
Changdo-ri
Kansŏng
Suan
Chiha-ri
Pyŏnggang
Sariwŏn
Kŭmhwa
Sokch'o
Yangyang
Oikou
Bo Hai
Cho-do
Chaeryŏng
Sinmak
Nam-ch'on
Ch'ŏrwŏn
Hwach'ŏn-chŏsuji
1578
Chumunjin
Kangnŭng
Huanghua
Miaodao Qundao
Changyŏn
Sinch'ŏn
Kŭmch'ŏn
Haeju
Kaesŏng
Panmunjŏm
Ch'unch'ŏn
Hongch'ŏn
Yanshan
Paengnyŏng-do
Ongjin
Yŏnan
Munsan
Uijŏngbu
Samch'ŏk
Ullŭng-do
Qingyun
Kanghwa
SOUL
Wudi
Zhanhua
Huang He
Longkou
Penglai
Puch'on
Songnam
Hoengsŏng
Chŏngsŏn
Huimin
Daxindian
Yantai
INCH'ŎN
Anyang
Wŏnju
Yŏngwŏl
Kenli
Laizhou Wan
Huang Xian
Muping
Weihai
Ansan
Suwŏn
Ich'ŏn
Yŏju
Chech'ŏn
Ulchin
Binzhou
Dongying
Fushan
Chengshan Jiao
Osan
Ch'ungju
Yŏngju
Shanghe
Zhaoyuan
Qixia
923
Wendeng
P'yŏngt'aek
SOUTH
Gaoyuan
Guangrao
Laizhou
Rongcheng
Sŏsan
Ch'ŏnan
Chŏngju
Yech'ŏn
Andong
Yŏngdŏk
Huantai
Shouguang
Shandong Bandao
Hongsŏng
Yesan
Uisŏng
Linzi
Changyi
Laiyang
Rushan
Nanhuang
Shidao
Kongju
KOREA
Sangju
Chŏngha
Zhoucun
ZIBO
Yidu
Weifang
Pingdu
Laixi
Haiyang
Anmyŏn-do
Nonsan
TAEJŎN
Sŏnsan
P'ohang
Tai Shan
Boshan
Fangzi
Anqiu
Gaomi
Lancun
Taechŏn-ni
Kanggyŏng
Yŏngdong
Kimch'ŏn
Kumi
Yŏngch'ŏn
Changgi-Ap
Linqu
Jimo
Kyŏngju
1108
SHANDONG
Chengyang
Kunsan
Iri
Chŏnju
Waegwan
TAEGU
Laiwu
Jiaozhou
QINGDAO
Kimje
Chŏngdo
Tai'an
Zhucheng
Jiaozhou Wan
Kochang
Koryŏng
Miryang
Ulsan
Puan
Hamyang
Xintai
Chŏngŭp
Chii-san
Kimhae
Mengyin
Yishui
Wulian
HUANG HAI
Namwŏn
Masan
Tongnae
Sishui
Sagŏ-ri
Tamyang
1915
Chinju
PUSAN
Ju Xian
Liangcheng
(Yellow Sea)
Songjŏng-ni
KWANGJU
Ch'angwon
Pingyi
Yi He
Rizhao
Hadong
Samch'ŏnp'o
Tangtou
Shijiusuo
Naju
Sunch'ŏn
Ch'ungmu
Fei Xian
Andongwei
Korea Strait
Tengzhou
Linyi
Mokp'o
Posong
Polgyo-ri
Yŏsu
Haizhou Wan
Tsushima
Teng Xian
Ganyu
Changhŭng
Izuhara
Lianyungang
Hŭksan-chedo
Haenam
Zaozhuang
Chindo
Weishan
Tancheng
Lianyungang
Hanzhuang
Haizhou
Chenjiagang
Jiawang
Pizhou
Iki
Weishan Hu
Xinyi
Guanyun
Xiangshui
Karatsu
Xuzhou
Yaowan
JIANGSU
Guannan
Imari
Binhai
Cheju-do
JAPAN
Shuanggou
Suqian
Shuyang
Cheju
Sasebo
Onpyŏng-ni
Kashima
Suining
Lianshui
Funing
Hallim
Halla-san
Omura
Da Yunhe
Sheyang
Taejŏng
1950
Isahaya
Nakadōri-Shima
Lingbi
Hongze Hu
Huaiyin
Huai'an
Mosŭlpo
Sŏgwipo
Nagasaki
Yancheng
Kuchinotsu
Guzhen
Suzhou
Grand Canal
Baoying
Liuzhuang
Fukue-Shima
Wuhe
Huaiyuan
Xinghua
Bengbu
Gaoyou Hu
Dongtai
Fengyang
118
120
122
124
126
128
130
132
44
42
40
38
36
34
East from Greenwich
COPYRIGHT GEORGE PHILIP LTD.

50 0 50 100 150 200 km
50 0 50 100 150 miles
ft m
12 000 4000
9000 3000
6000 2000
4500 1500
3000 1000
1200 400
600 200
200 600
2000 6000
m ft
1 2 3 4 5 6 7
A B C D E F G H
GANSU
SHAANXI
SICHUAN
CHONGQING SHI
GUIZHOU
YUNNAN
GUANGXI
KACHIN
SHAN
BURMA (MYANMAR)
LAOS
VIETNAM
THAILAND
Sichuan Pendi
Ningjing Shan
Shaluli Shan
Daxue Shan
Qionglai Shan
Daliang Shan
Dalou Shan
Daba Shan
Wuling Shan
Yun Ling
Nu Shan
Gaoligong Shan
Ailao Shan
Wuliang Shan
Wumeng Shan
Yunnan Gaoyuan
Hoang Lien Son
Gulf of Tonkin
CHENGDU
CHONGQING
GUIYANG
KUNMING
NANNING
HANOI
LIUZHOU
Zigong
Leshan
Yibin
Luzhou
Nanchong
Mianyang
Deyang
Dazhou
Suining
Neijiang
Guangyuan
Hanzhong
Ankang
Zunyi
Anshun
Duyun
Kaili
Tongren
Liupanshui
Qujing
Zhaotong
Panzhihua
Xichang
Dali
Baoshan
Lijiang
Tengchong
Yuxi
Gejiu
Mengzi
Wenshan
Jinghong
Kangding
Ya'an
Baise
Hechi
Qinzhou
Beihai
Fangchenggang
Haiphong
Nam Dinh
Lang Son
Lao Cai
Ha Giang
Cao Bang
Dien Bien
Luang Prabang
Chiang Rai
Keng Tung
Gongga Shan 7556
Hkakabo Razi 5881
Mekong
Salween
Chang Jiang (Yangtse)
Jinsha Jiang (Yangtse)
Lancang Jiang (Mekong)
Nu Jiang
Yalong Jiang
Min Jiang
Dadu He
Jialing Jiang
Wu Jiang
Hongshui He
You Jiang
Zuo Jiang
Yuan Jiang
Song Da
Song Ma
Dao Cai Bau
Fai Tsi Long Archipelago
Weizhou Dao
Leizhou Bandao
Projection: Conical with two standard parallels

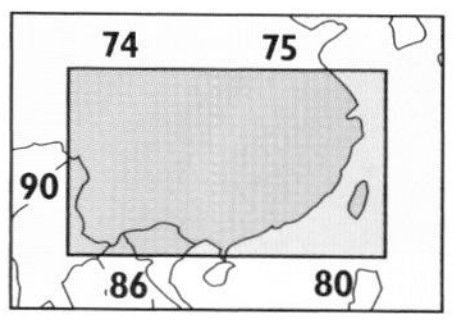
74
75
90
86
80

8
9
10
11
12
13
14
A
B
C
D
E
F
G
H
HENAN
ANHUI
JIANGSU
HUBEI
HUNAN
JIANGXI
ZHEJIANG
FUJIAN
GUANGDONG
TAIWAN
NANJING
WUHAN
SHANGHAI
SHANGHAI SHI
HANGZHOU
NANCHANG
CHANGSHA
GUANGZHOU
HONG KONG (XIANGGANG)
T'AIPEI
KAOHSIUNG
Hefei
Fuzhou
Xiamen
Shantou
Shenzhen
Kowloon
Macau
Zhuhai
Ningbo
Wenzhou
Suzhou
Wuxi
Changzhou
Zhenjiang
Yangzhou
Huainan
Bengbu
Anqing
Jiujiang
Ganzhou
Hengyang
Zhuzhou
Xiangtan
Yueyang
Changde
Yichang
Shashi
Xiangfan
Zhanjiang
Maoming
Wuzhou
Guilin
Chang Jiang (Yangtse)
Poyang Hu
Dongting Hu
Tai Hu
Hongze Hu
Dabie Shan
Wuyi Shan
Nan Ling
Jiuling Shan
Chungyang Shanmo
Taiwan Strait
Luzon Strait
SOUTH CHINA SEA
Dongsha Dao (Pratas I.)
Tropic of Cancer
Matsu Tao (Taiwan)
Chinmen (Quemoy) Tao (Taiwan)
P'enghu Ch'üntou (Pescadores)
Zhoushan Dao
Hainan
Leizhou Wan
East from Greenwich
112
114
116
118
120
122
32
30
28
26
24
22
20
COPYRIGHT GEORGE PHILIP LTD.

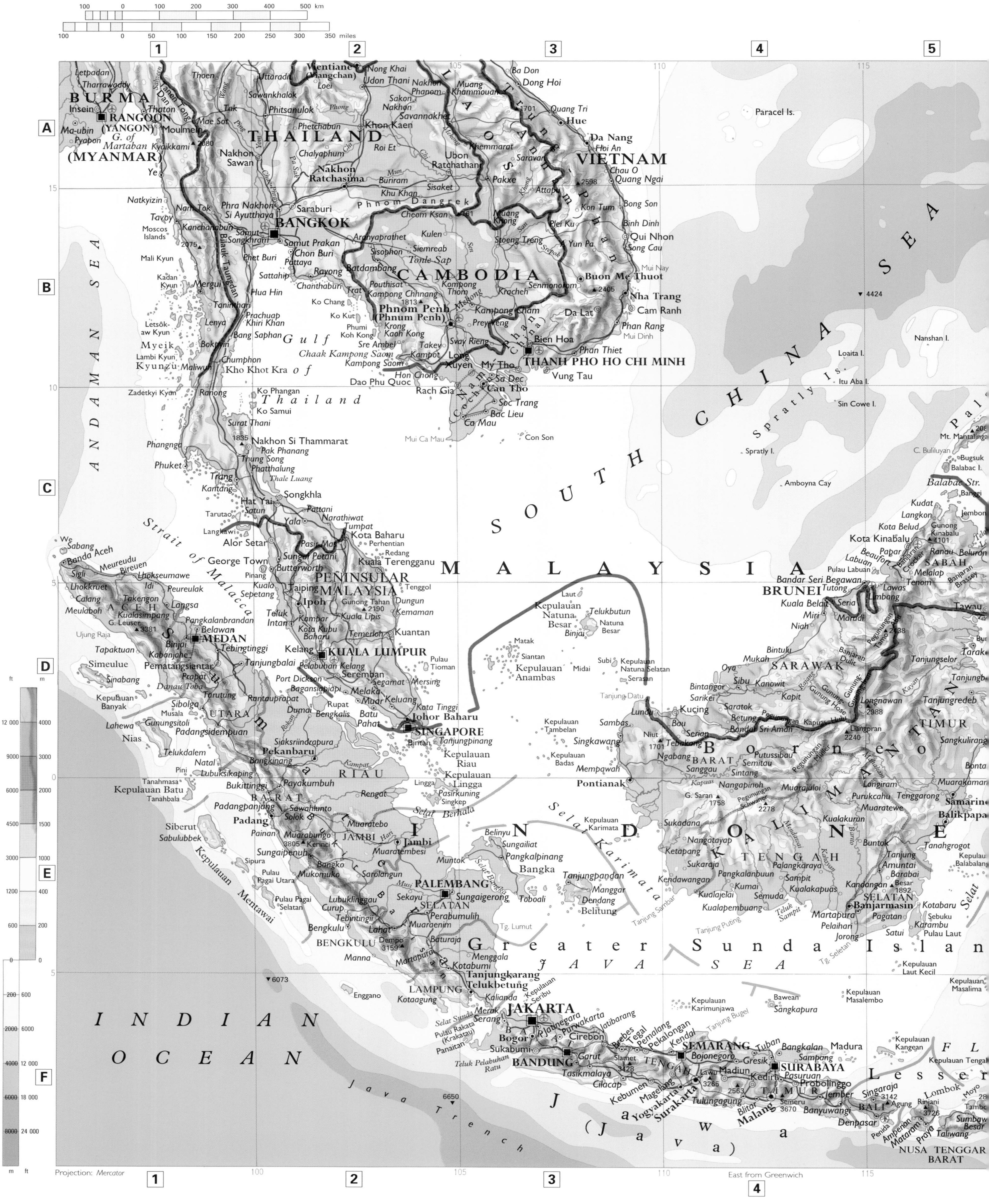
100 0 100 200 300 400 500 km
100 0 50 100 150 200 250 300 350 miles
1 2 3 4 5
A B C D E F
BURMA
RANGOON (YANGON)
(MYANMAR)
G. of Martaban
Moulmein
Letpadan
Tharrawaddy
Insein
Ma-ubin
Pyapon
Kyaikkami
Ye
Thaton
Mae Sot
Tak
Thoen
Uttaradit
Sawankhalok
Phitsanulok
Phetchabun
Loei
Vientiane (Viangchan)
Nong Khai
Udon Thani
Nakhon Phanom
Sakon Nakhon
Savannakhet
Khon Kaen
Muang Khammouan
THAILAND
Nakhon Sawan
Chalyaphum
Nakhon Ratchasima
Roi Et
Ubon Ratchathani
Khemmarat
Buriram
Sisaket
Khu Khan
Phnom Dangrek
Natkyizin
Tavoy
Moscos Islands
Nam Tok
Kanchanaburi
Phra Nakhon Si Ayutthaya
Saraburi
BANGKOK
Samut Songkhram
Samut Prakan
Chon Buri
Pattaya
Phet Buri
Sattahip
Rayong
Chanthaburi
Trat
Aranyaprathet
Sisophon
Siemreab
Tonle Sap
Batdambang
Cheom Ksan
Kulen
CAMBODIA
Pouthisat
Kampong Chhnang
Kampong Thom
Kracheh
Senmonorom
Kampong Cham
Phnom Penh (Phnum Penh)
Prey Veng
Svay Rieng
Takev
Kampot
Kampong Saom
Chaak Kampong Saom
Sre Ambel
Koh Kong
Kaoh Kong
Krong
Phumi
Ko Chang
Ko Kut
Mali Kyun
Kadan Kyun
Mergui
Tanintharyi
Hua Hin
Prachuap Khiri Khan
Bang Saphan
Letsôk-aw Kyun
Lenya
Bokpyin
Myeik
Lambi Kyun
Kyunzu
Maliwun
Chumphon
Kho Khot Kra
Gulf of Thailand
Zadetkyi Kyun
Ranong
Ko Phangan
Ko Samui
Surat Thani
Nakhon Si Thammarat
Pak Phanang
Thung Song
Phatthalung
Thale Luang
Phangnga
Phuket
Trang
Kantang
Hat Yai
Satun
Songkhla
Pattani
Narathiwat
Yala
Tarutao
Langkawi
Alor Setar
Tumpat
Kota Baharu
Perhentian
Redang
Kuala Terengganu
George Town
Pinang
Butterworth
Sungei Petani
Pasir Mas
PENINSULAR MALAYSIA
Tenggol
Kuala Sepetang
Taiping
Ipoh
Gunong Tahan 2190
Kuala Lipis
Dungun
Kemaman
Teluk Intan
Kampar
Kota Kubu Baharu
Temerloh
Kuantan
Kelang
KUALA LUMPUR
Pelabuhan Kelang
Pulau Tioman
Seremban
Port Dickson
Segamat
Mersing
Melaka
Muar
Keluang
Kota Tinggi
Johor Baharu
SINGAPORE
Bintan
Tanjungpinang
Rupat
Bengkalis
Batu Pahat
Dumai
LAOS
Trung Phan
Annam
Ba Don
Dong Hoi
Quang Tri
Hue
Da Nang
Hoi An
VIETNAM
Chau O
Quang Ngai
Saravan
Pakxe
Attapu
Kon Tum
Bong Son
Binh Dinh
Qui Nhon
Song Cau
Pleiku
Muang Khong
Stoeng Treng
A Yun Pa
Buon Me Thuot
Mui Nay
Nha Trang
Cam Ranh
Da Lat
Phan Rang
Mui Dinh
Phan Thiet
Bien Hoa
THANH PHO HO CHI MINH
Vung Tau
Long Xuyen
My Tho
Sa Dec
Can Tho
Soc Trang
Bac Lieu
Ca Mau
Rach Gia
Hon Chong
Dao Phu Quoc
Mui Ca Mau
Con Son
Nam Phan
Cochin China
Paracel Is.
SOUTH CHINA SEA
4424
Nanshan I.
Loaita I.
Itu Aba I.
Spratly Is.
Sin Cowe I.
Spratly I.
Amboyna Cay
Mt. Mantalingan
C. Buliluyan
Bugsuk
Balabac I.
Balabac Str.
Banggi
Kudat
Langkon
Jambongan
Kota Belud
Gunong Kinabalu 4101
Kota Kinabalu
Papar
Ranau
Beaufort
Labuan
SABAH
Pulau Labuan
Melalap
Tenom
Bandar Seri Begawan
BRUNEI
Tutong
Lawas
Limbang
Kuala Belait
Seria
Miri
Marudi
Niah
Tawau
Bintulu
Mukah
SARAWAK
Oya
Sibu
Kanowit
Kapit
Tanjungselor
Bintangor
Sarikei
Saratok
Betong
Kuching
Bandar Sri Aman
Lundu
Bau
Serian
Tebakang
Longnawan
2988
Tanjungredeb
Liangpran 2240
TIMUR
Sangkulirang
Niut 1701
Ngabang
BARAT
Putussibau
Semitau
Sanggau
Sintang
Nangapinoh
Muarajuloi
Longiram
Pontianak
Mempawah
Singkawang
Sambas
Tanjung Datu
MALAYSIA
Laut
Kepulauan Natuna
Natuna Besar
Bunguran
Telukbutun
Matak
Siantan
Kepulauan Anambas
Subi
Midai
Kepulauan Natuna Selatan
Serasan
Kepulauan Tambelan
Kepulauan Badas
Kepulauan Riau
Lingga
Kepulauan Lingga
Pasirkuning
Singkep
Selat Berhala
Selat Karimata
Kepulauan Karimata
G. Saran 1758
Pegunungan Schwaner
2278
Purukcahu
Tenggarong
Samarinda
Muaratewe
Balikpapan
Kualakurun
KALIMANTAN
INDONESIA
Sukadana
Ketapang
Nangatayap
Sukaraja
TENGAH
Palangkaraya
Kendawangan
Pangkalanbuun
Sampit
Kumai
Kualajelai
Kualakapuas
Semuda
Kualapembuang
Teluk Sampit
Tanjung Puting
Buntok
Tanjung
Amuntai
Barabai
Kandangan
Besar 1892
SELATAN
Banjarmasin
Martapura
Pelaihari
Jorong
Pagatan
Kotabaru
Satui
Sebuku
Karambu
Pulau Laut
Tg. Selatan
Kepulauan Laut Kecil
Kepulauan Masalima
We
Sabang
Banda Aceh
Meureudu
Bireuen
Sigli
Lhokseumawe
Lhokkruet
Idi
Calang
Peureulak
Takengon
Langsa
Meulaboh
ACEH
Kualasimpang
G. Leuser 3381
Ujung Raja
Pangkalanbrandan
Belawan
MEDAN
Binjai
Tapaktuan
Kabanjahe
Tebingtinggi
Simeulue
Pematangsiantar
Tanjungbalai
Sinabang
Prapat
Danau Toba
Tarutung
Rantauprapat
Kepulauan Banyak
Sibolga
Musala
UTARA
Gunungsitoli
Padangsidempuan
Lahewa
Nias
Telukdalem
Natal
Pini
Lubuksikaping
Tanahmasa
Kepulauan Batu
Tanahbala
Pekanbaru
Bangkinang
Siaksriindrapura
Kampar
RIAU
Bukittinggi
Payakumbuh
Rengat
BARAT
Padangpanjang
Sawahlunto
Padang
Solok
Siberut
Sabulubbek
Painan
Muaratebo
JAMBI
Muarabungo
Kerinci 3805
Jambi
Muaratembesi
Sungaipenuh
Sipura
Pulau Pagai Utara
Pulau Pagai Selatan
Kepulauan Mentawai
Bangko
Mukomuko
Sarolangun
Muntok
Musi
PALEMBANG
Sungaigerong
Sekayu
Lubuklinggau
SELATAN
Curup
Perabumulih
Tebingtinggi
Muaraenim
Lahat
Bengkulu
BENGKULU
Dempo 3159
Baturaja
Martapura
Manna
Kotabumi
Menggala
Tanjungkarang
Telukbetung
LAMPUNG
Kotaagung
Kalianda
Enggano
Strait of Malacca
Sumatera
Belinyu
Sungailiat
Pangkalpinang
Bangka
Selat Bangka
Toboali
Tg. Lumut
Tanjungpandan
Manggar
Dendang
Belitung
Tanjung Sambar
ANDAMAN SEA
INDIAN OCEAN
6073
Java Trench
6650
Greater Sunda Islands
JAVA SEA
Kepulauan Seribu
Selat Sunda
Merak
Serang
Pulau Rakata (Krakatau)
Panaitan
JAKARTA
Pulau Jawa / Jatinegara
Purwakarta
Jatibarang
Bogor
Cirebon
Sukabumi
BANDUNG
Garut
Tasikmalaya
Cilacap
Teluk Pelabuhan Ratu
Brebes
Tegal
Pemalang
Pekalongan
Kendal
Slamet 3428
Kebumen
Magelang
Yogyakarta
Surakarta
SEMARANG
TENGAH
Bojonegoro
Tuban
Lawu 3265
2563
Madiun
Kediri
Blitar
Tulungagung
Malang
Gresik
SURABAYA
Pasuruan
Probolinggo
Jember
Semeru 3670
Banyuwangi
TIMUR
Bangkalan
Madura
Sampang
Kepulauan Karimunjawa
Tanjung Bugel
Bawean
Sangkapura
Kepulauan Masalembo
Kepulauan Kangean
Kepulauan Tengah
BALI
Singaraja
Agung 3142
Denpasar
Rinjani 3726
Lombok
Mataram
Ampenan
Praya
Penida
Taliwang
Sumbawa Besar
Moyo
NUSA TENGGARA BARAT
Lesser
Jawa (Java)
ft m
12 000 4000
9000 3000
6000 2000
4500 1500
3000 1000
1200 400
600 200
0 0
200 600
2000 6000
4000 12 000
6000 18 000
8000 24 000
m ft
Projection: Mercator
100 105 110 115
15 10 5 0 5
East from Greenwich

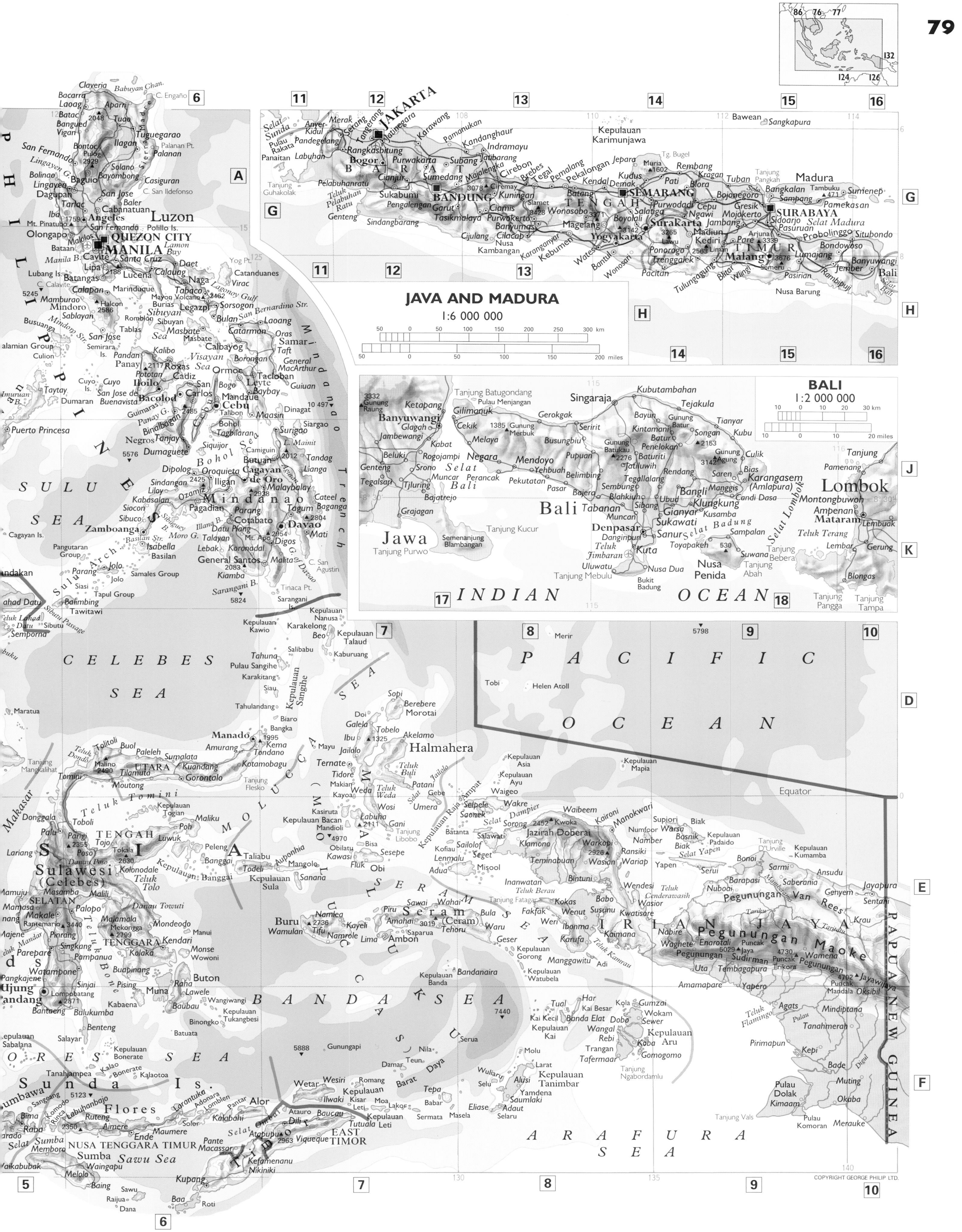
JAVA AND MADURA
1:6 000 000
BALI
1:2 000 000
JAKARTA
BANDUNG
SEMARANG
SURABAYA
Surakarta
Yogyakarta
Malang
BARAT
TENGAH
TIMUR
Madura
Kepulauan Karimunjawa
Bawean
Sangkapura
Selat Sunda
Selat Madura
Nusa Barung
Nusa Kambangan
Singaraja
Denpasar
Kuta
Bali
Jawa
Lombok
Mataram
Nusa Penida
Selat Bali
Selat Badung
Selat Lombok
INDIAN OCEAN
PHILIPPINES
Luzon
QUEZON CITY
MANILA
Mindoro
Samar
Leyte
Cebu
Bohol
Negros
Panay
Mindanao
Zamboanga
Davao
Cagayan de Oro
Iloilo
Bacolod
Tacloban
Visayan Sea
Sibuyan Sea
Bohol Sea
Catanduanes
Masbate
Mindanao Trench
SULU SEA
Sulu Arch.
CELEBES SEA
PACIFIC OCEAN
MOLUCCA SEA
Halmahera
Ternate
Morotai
Manado
Sulawesi (Celebes)
UTARA
TENGAH
SELATAN
TENGGARA
Ujung Pandang
Kendari
Teluk Tomini
Teluk Bone
Buton
Muna
Kepulauan Banggai
Kepulauan Sula
Buru
Seram (Ceram)
Ambon
BANDA SEA
SERAM SEA
Kepulauan Aru
Kepulauan Tanimbar
Kepulauan Kai
IRIAN JAYA
Jayapura
Pegunungan Maoke
Puncak Jaya 5029
Biak
Yapen
Manokwari
Jazirah Doberai
Sorong
Merauke
PAPUA NEW GUINEA
Equator
ARAFURA SEA
FLORES SEA
Flores
Sumbawa
Sumba
Sawu Sea
Timor
Kupang
Dili
EAST TIMOR
NUSA TENGGARA TIMUR
Wetar
Alor
Sunda Is.

COPYRIGHT GEORGE PHILIP LTD.

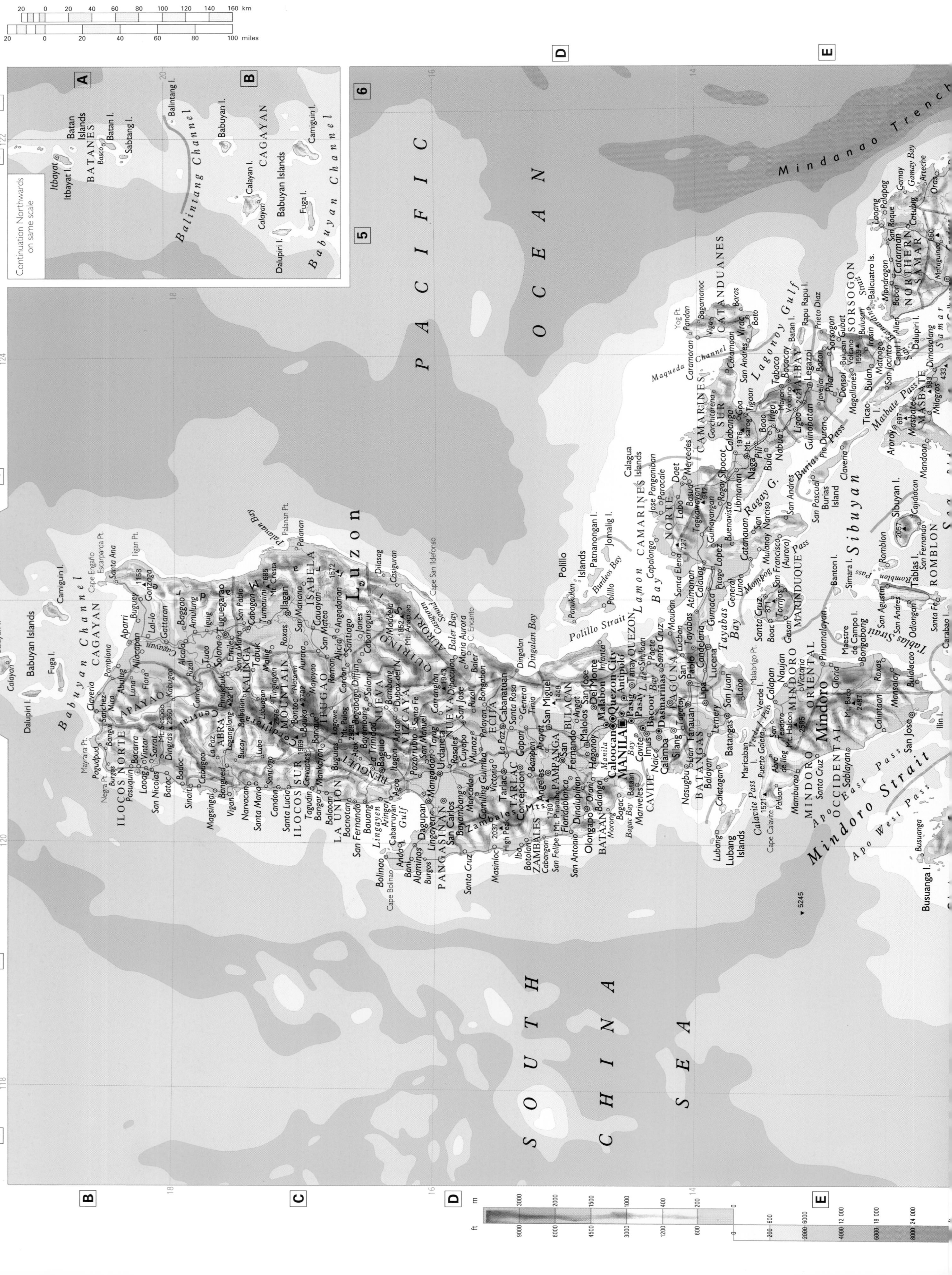

PACIFIC OCEAN
SOUTH CHINA SEA
Luzon
MANILA
Quezon City
Mindoro
Mindoro Strait
Sibuyan Sea
Babuyan Channel
Balintang Channel
Babuyan Islands
Batan Islands
Mindanao Trench
Lamon Bay
Polillo Islands
Tayabas Bay
Lagonoy Gulf
Ragay G.
Lingayen Gulf
Manila Bay
Dingalan Bay
Baler Bay
Burias Pass
San Bernardino Strait
Verde I. Passage
Tablas Strait
ILOCOS NORTE
ILOCOS SUR
LA UNION
PANGASINAN
ZAMBALES
BATAAN
TARLAC
PAMPANGA
BULACAN
NUEVA ECIJA
NUEVA VIZCAYA
IFUGAO
MOUNTAIN
KALINGA-APAYAO
ABRA
CAGAYAN
ISABELA
QUIRINO
AURORA
QUEZON
LAGUNA
CAVITE
BATANGAS
CAMARINES NORTE
CAMARINES SUR
CATANDUANES
ALBAY
SORSOGON
MASBATE
MARINDUQUE
ROMBLON
MINDORO ORIENTAL
MINDORO OCCIDENTAL
NORTHERN SAMAR
Continuation Northwards on same scale
km
miles
m
ft

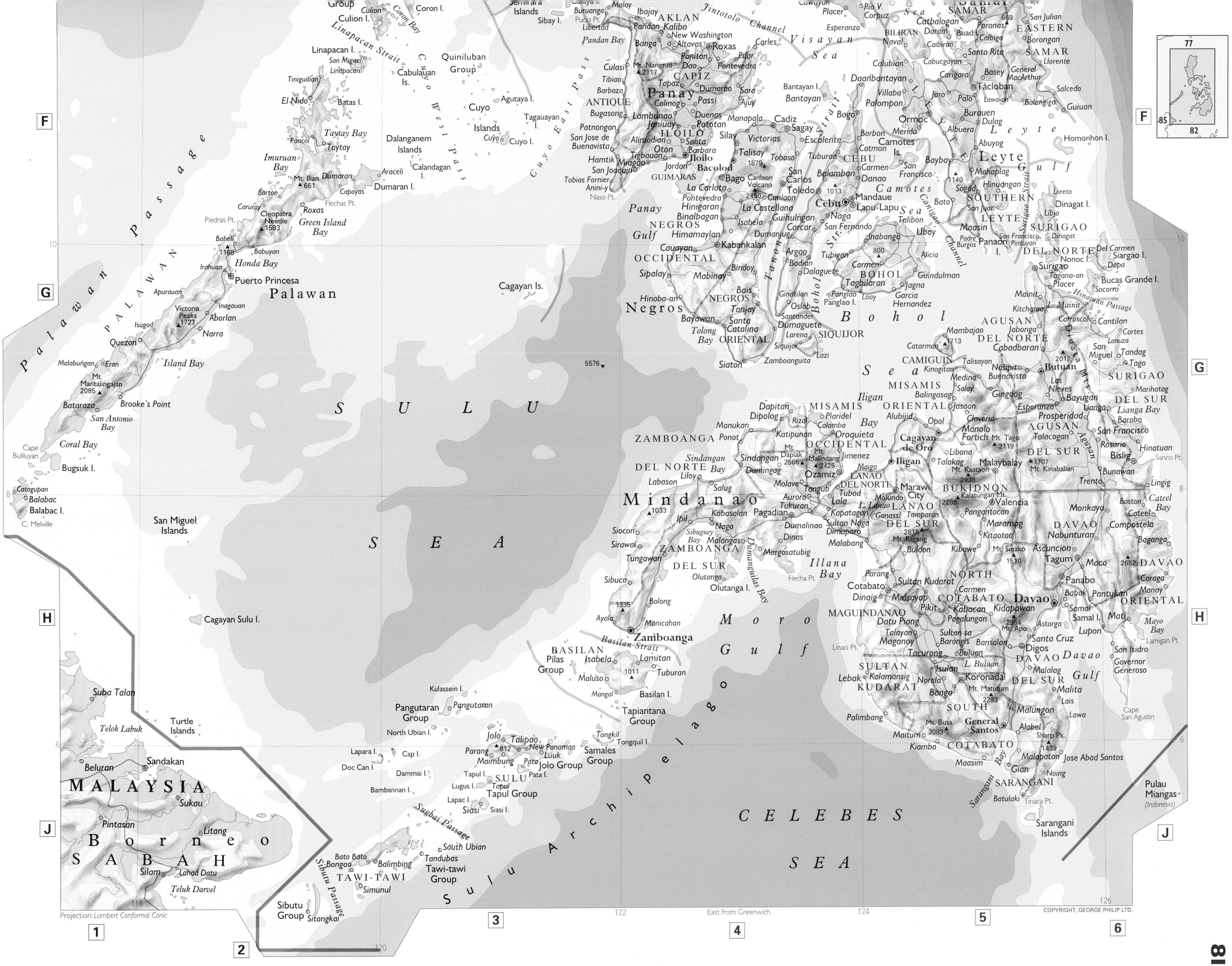
SULU SEA
CELEBES SEA
Mindanao
Palawan
Negros
Panay
Bohol
Leyte
Sea
Visayan Sea
Camotes Sea
Bohol Sea
Moro Gulf
Davao Gulf
Leyte Gulf
Panay Gulf
Illana Bay
Sulu Archipelago
Palawan Passage
Cuyo East Pass
Cuyo West Pass
Linapacan Strait
Jintotolo Channel
Basilan Strait
Sibutu Passage
Sugbai Passage
MALAYSIA
SABAH
Borneo
Puerto Princesa
Zamboanga
Cebu
Davao
Iloilo
Bacolod
Butuan
Cagayan de Oro
Iligan
Tacloban
General Santos
Cotabato
Sandakan
Jolo
Cagayan Is.
Cagayan Sulu I.
San Miguel Islands
Turtle Islands
Cuyo Islands
Quiniluban Group
Tawi-tawi Group
Pangutaran Group
Samales Group
Tapul Group
Jolo Group
Sarangani Islands
Pulau Miangas (Indonesia)
ZAMBOANGA DEL NORTE
ZAMBOANGA DEL SUR
MISAMIS OCCIDENTAL
MISAMIS ORIENTAL
LANAO DEL NORTE
LANAO DEL SUR
BUKIDNON
AGUSAN DEL NORTE
AGUSAN DEL SUR
SURIGAO DEL NORTE
SURIGAO DEL SUR
DAVAO
DAVAO DEL SUR
DAVAO ORIENTAL
NORTH COTABATO
SOUTH COTABATO
SULTAN KUDARAT
MAGUINDANAO
SARANGANI
BASILAN
SULU
TAWI-TAWI
NEGROS OCCIDENTAL
NEGROS ORIENTAL
SIQUIJOR
CAMIGUIN
BOHOL
CEBU
SOUTHERN LEYTE
LEYTE
EASTERN SAMAR
SAMAR
BILIRAN
AKLAN
CAPIZ
ILOILO
ANTIQUE
GUIMARAS
East from Greenwich
Projection: Lambert Conformal Conic
COPYRIGHT, GEORGE PHILIP LTD.

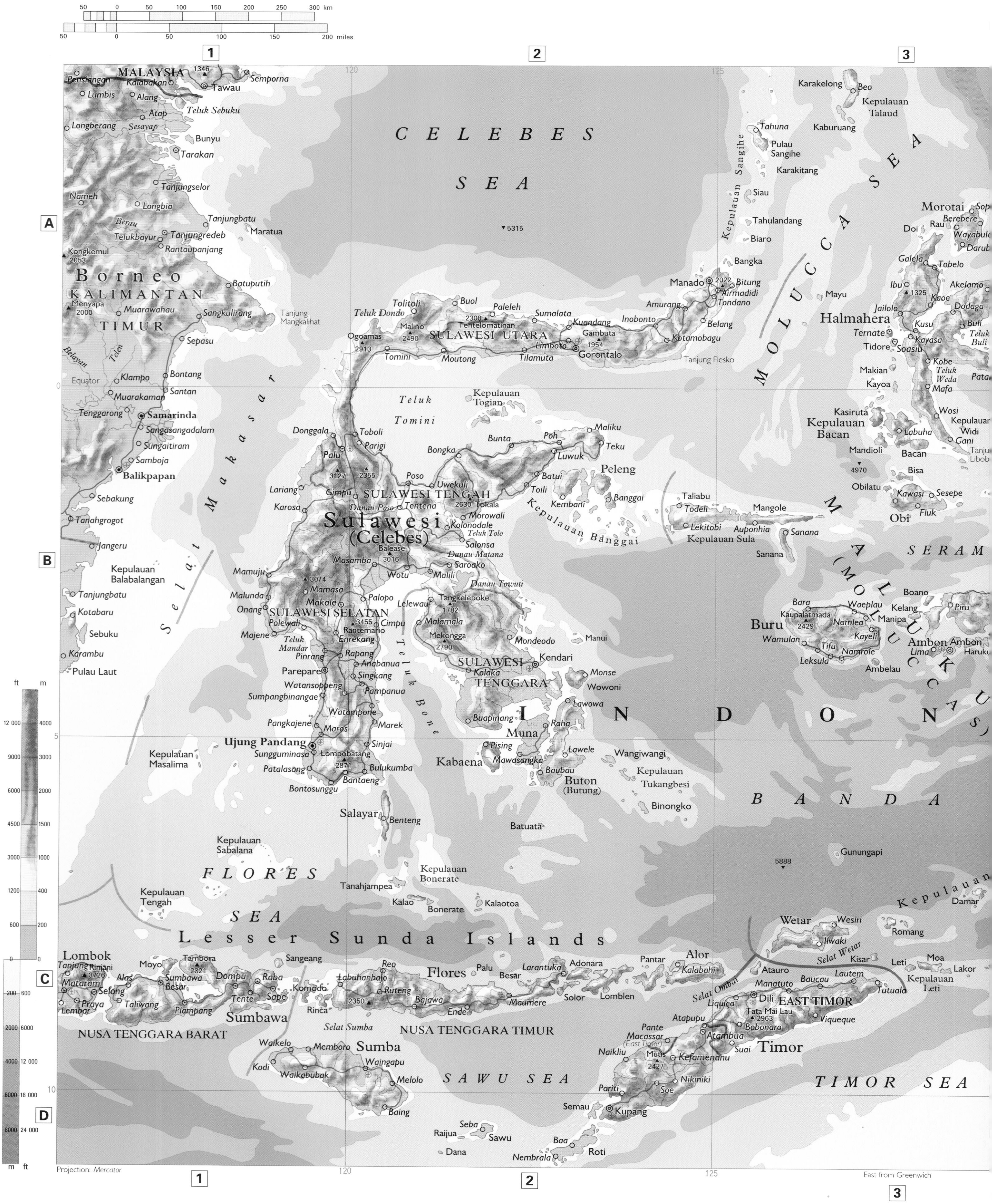
CELEBES SEA
MOLUCCA SEA
BANDA SEA
FLORES SEA
SAWU SEA
TIMOR SEA
SERAM
MALUKU (MOLUCCAS)
INDONESIA
MALAYSIA
Borneo
KALIMANTAN TIMUR
Sulawesi (Celebes)
SULAWESI UTARA
SULAWESI TENGAH
SULAWESI SELATAN
SULAWESI TENGGARA
Lesser Sunda Islands
NUSA TENGGARA BARAT
NUSA TENGGARA TIMUR
EAST TIMOR
Halmahera
Morotai
Obi
Buru
Peleng
Muna
Buton (Butung)
Kabaena
Salayar
Lombok
Sumbawa
Flores
Sumba
Timor
Alor
Wetar
Sawu
Roti
Selat Makasar
Teluk Tomini
Teluk Bone
Teluk Tolo
Teluk Sebuku
Kepulauan Talaud
Kepulauan Sangihe
Kepulauan Togian
Kepulauan Banggai
Kepulauan Sula
Kepulauan Bacan
Kepulauan Balabalangan
Kepulauan Masalima
Kepulauan Sabalana
Kepulauan Tengah
Kepulauan Bonerate
Kepulauan Tukangbesi
Kepulauan Leti
Tarakan
Tawau
Samarinda
Balikpapan
Manado
Gorontalo
Palu
Poso
Kendari
Ujung Pandang
Parepare
Ternate
Ambon
Kupang
Dili
Equator
Projection: Mercator
East from Greenwich

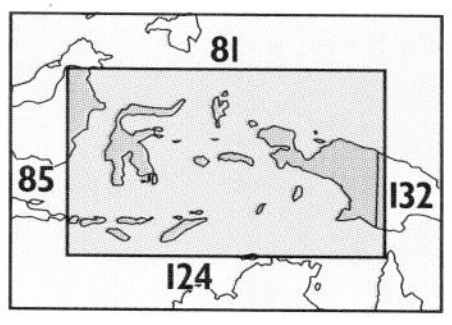
81
85
132
124

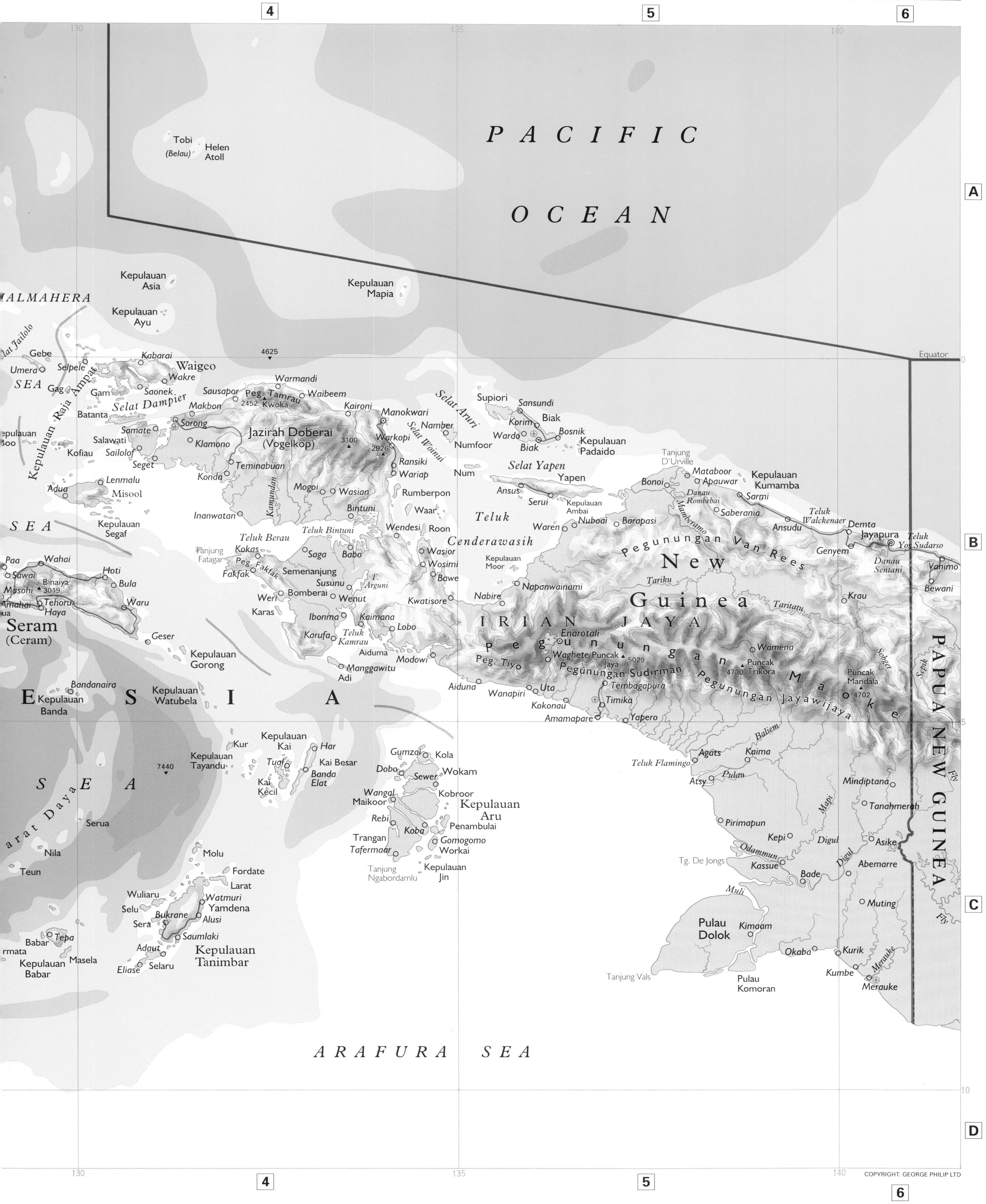
4
5
6
A
B
C
D
130
135
140
10
Equator
PACIFIC
OCEAN
Tobi
(Belau)
Helen Atoll
Kepulauan Asia
Kepulauan Mapia
HALMAHERA
Kepulauan Ayu
4625
Gebe
Umera
Selpele
Kabarai
Waigeo
Wakre
SEA
Gag
Gam
Saonek
Raja Ampat
Selat Dampier
Sausapor
Peg. Tamrau
2452 Kwoka
Warmandi
Waibeem
Makbon
Batanta
Sorong
Samate
Salawati
Kofiau
Sailolof
Seget
Klamono
Kepulauan Raja Ampat
Jazirah Doberai
(Vogelkop)
3100
2926
Kaironi
Manokwari
Warkopi
Ransiki
Wariap
Teminabuan
Konda
Lenmalu
Adua
Misool
Kepulauan Segaf
Inanwatan
Kamundan
Mogoi
Wasian
Bintuni
Rumberpon
Waar
Selat Aruri
Selat Wondama
Namber
Numfoor
Num
Supiori
Sansundi
Korim
Biak
Warda
Bosnik
Kepulauan Padaido
Selat Yapen
Yapen
Ansus
Serui
Kepulauan Ambai
Teluk
Cenderawasih
Waren
Nuboai
Barapasi
Bonoi
Tanjung D'Urville
Mataboor
Apauwar
Kepulauan Kumamba
Danau Rombebai
Sarmi
Mamberamo
Saberania
Teluk Walckenaer
Ansudu
Demta
Jayapura
Teluk Yos Sudarso
Genyem
Danau Sentani
Vanimo
Bewani
Pegunungan Van Rees
New
Guinea
Tariku
Taritatu
Krau
SEA
Paa
Wahai
Sawai
Masohi
Binaiya
3019
Amahai
Tehoru
Haya
Hoti
Bula
Waru
Seram
(Ceram)
Teluk Berau
Teluk Bintuni
Wendesi
Roon
Tanjung Fatagar
Kokas
Peg. Fakfak
Fakfak
Saga
Babo
Semenanjung
Susunu
Bomberai
T. Arguni
Wasior
Wosimi
Bawe
Kepulauan Moor
Napanwainami
Nabire
Weri
Wenut
Kwatisore
Karas
Ibonma
Kaimana
Lobo
Karufa
Teluk Kamrau
Aiduma
Modowi
Manggawitu
Adi
Geser
Kepulauan Gorong
IRIAN
JAYA
Enarotali
Peg. Tiyo
Waghete
Puncak Jaya
5029
Pegunungan Sudirman
Wamena
Puncak Trikora
4730
Pegunungan Jayawijaya
Maoke
Puncak Mandala
4702
Tembagapura
Timika
Aiduna
Wanapiri
Uta
Kokonau
Amamapare
Yapero
Bandanaira
Kepulauan Banda
Kepulauan Watubela
E
S
I
A
Sobger
Sepik
PAPUA NEW GUINEA
Kur
Kepulauan Kai
Har
Kai Besar
Tual
Kai Kecil
Banda Elat
Kepulauan Tayandu
7440
SEA
Gumzai
Kola
Dobo
Sewer
Wokam
Wangal
Maikoor
Kobroor
Kepulauan Aru
Rebi
Koba
Penambulai
Trangan
Tafermaar
Gomogomo
Workai
Tanjung Ngabordamlu
Kepulauan Jin
Baliem
Teluk Flamingo
Agats
Kaima
Atsy
Pulau
Mindiptana
Tanahmerah
Mapi
Pirimapun
Kepi
Digul
Asike
Fly
Tg. De Jongs
Odammun
Kassue
Bade
Abemarre
Muting
Muli
Pulau Dolok
Kimaam
Okaba
Kurik
Kumbe
Maro
Merauke
Tanjung Vals
Pulau Komoran
Serua
Nila
Teun
Damar
Barat Daya
Molu
Fordate
Larat
Wuliaru
Watmuri
Yamdena
Selu
Bukrane
Alusi
Sera
Saumlaki
Babar
Tepa
Adaut
Kepulauan Tanimbar
Marmata
Kepulauan Babar
Masela
Eliase
Selaru
ARAFURA SEA
COPYRIGHT. GEORGE PHILIP LTD

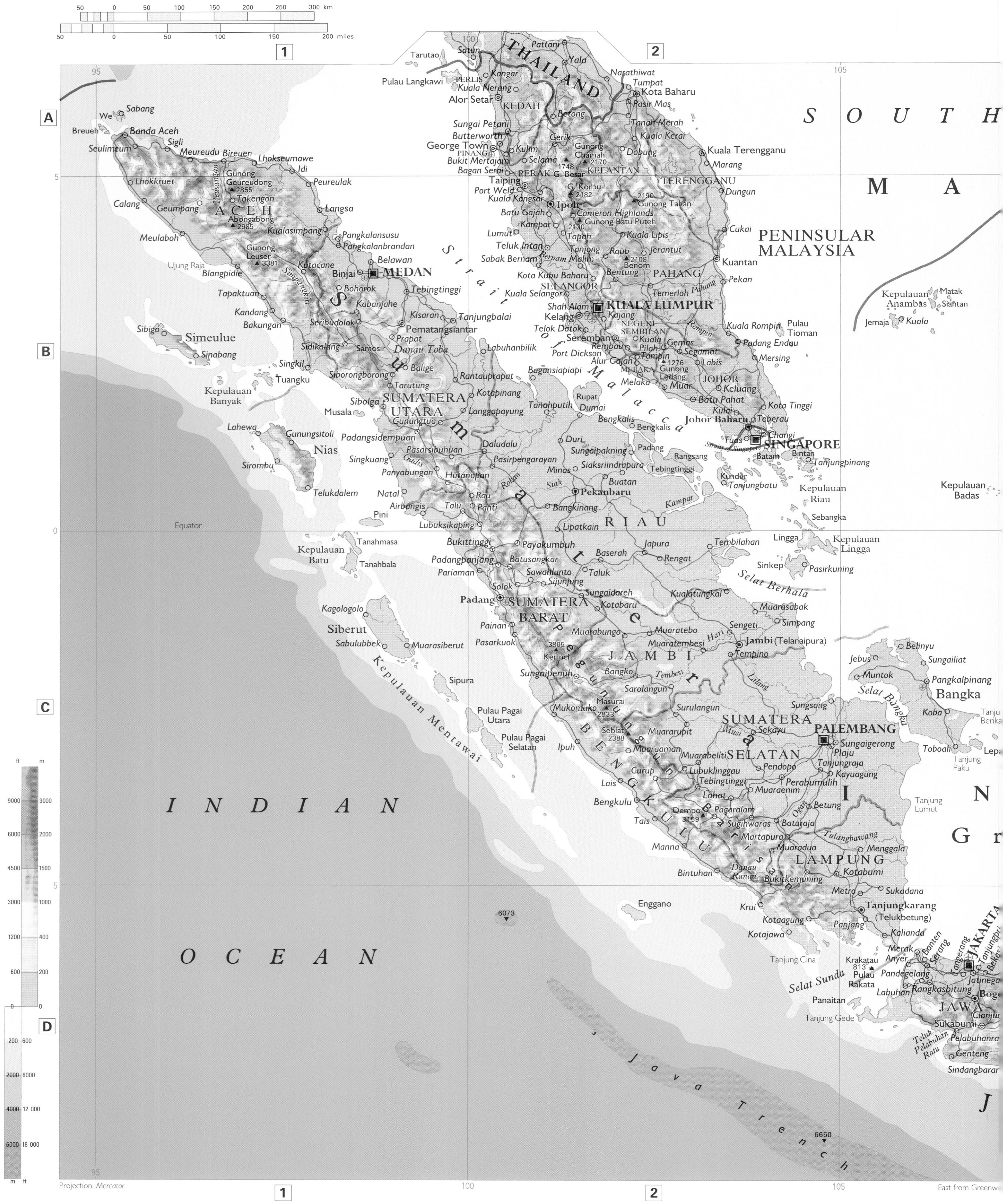

SOUTH
MA
PENINSULAR MALAYSIA
THAILAND
INDIAN OCEAN
Strait of Malacca
Sumatera
Pegunungan Barisan
Kepulauan Mentawai
Java Trench
Selat Berhala
Selat Bangka
Selat Sunda
Equator
ACEH
SUMATERA UTARA
SUMATERA BARAT
RIAU
JAMBI
BENGKULU
SUMATERA SELATAN
LAMPUNG
JAWA
PAHANG
JOHOR
SELANGOR
KELANTAN
TERENGGANU
PERAK
KEDAH
PERLIS
PINANG
MELAKA
NEGERI SEMBILAN
MEDAN
KUALA LUMPUR
SINGAPORE
PALEMBANG
JAKARTA
Banda Aceh
Sabang
Lhokseumawe
Langsa
Meulaboh
Takengon
Binjai
Belawan
Tebingtinggi
Pematangsiantar
Tanjungbalai
Sibolga
Padangsidempuan
Nias
Simeulue
Kepulauan Banyak
Kepulauan Batu
Siberut
Sipura
Pulau Pagai Utara
Pulau Pagai Selatan
Enggano
Pekanbaru
Dumai
Bengkalis
Bukittinggi
Padang
Padangpanjang
Pariaman
Solok
Sawahlunto
Payakumbuh
Jambi (Telanaipura)
Muarabungo
Sungaipenuh
Kerinci
Bengkulu
Curup
Lubuklinggau
Lahat
Muaraenim
Prabumulih
Baturaja
Kotabumi
Metro
Tanjungkarang (Telukbetung)
Kalianda
Krui
Kotaagung
Bangka
Pangkalpinang
Muntok
Koba
Toboali
Kepulauan Riau
Kepulauan Lingga
Lingga
Sinkep
Batam
Bintan
Tanjungpinang
Kepulauan Anambas
Kepulauan Badas
Pulau Tioman
Johor Baharu
Kuantan
Kuala Terengganu
Kota Baharu
Ipoh
Taiping
George Town
Butterworth
Alor Setar
Pulau Langkawi
Tarutao
Satun
Pattani
Yala
Narathiwat
Seremban
Melaka
Kelang
Port Dickson
Kluang
Batu Pahat
Merak
Serang
Anyer
Labuhan
Pandeglang
Rangkasbitung
Sukabumi
Pelabuhanratu
Krakatau
Pulau Rakata
Tanjung Cina
Tanjung Gede
Panaitan
Gunong Leuser 3381
Gunong Tahan
Masurai 2833
Dempo 3159
Kerinci 3805
6073
6650
Projection: Mercator
East from Greenwich

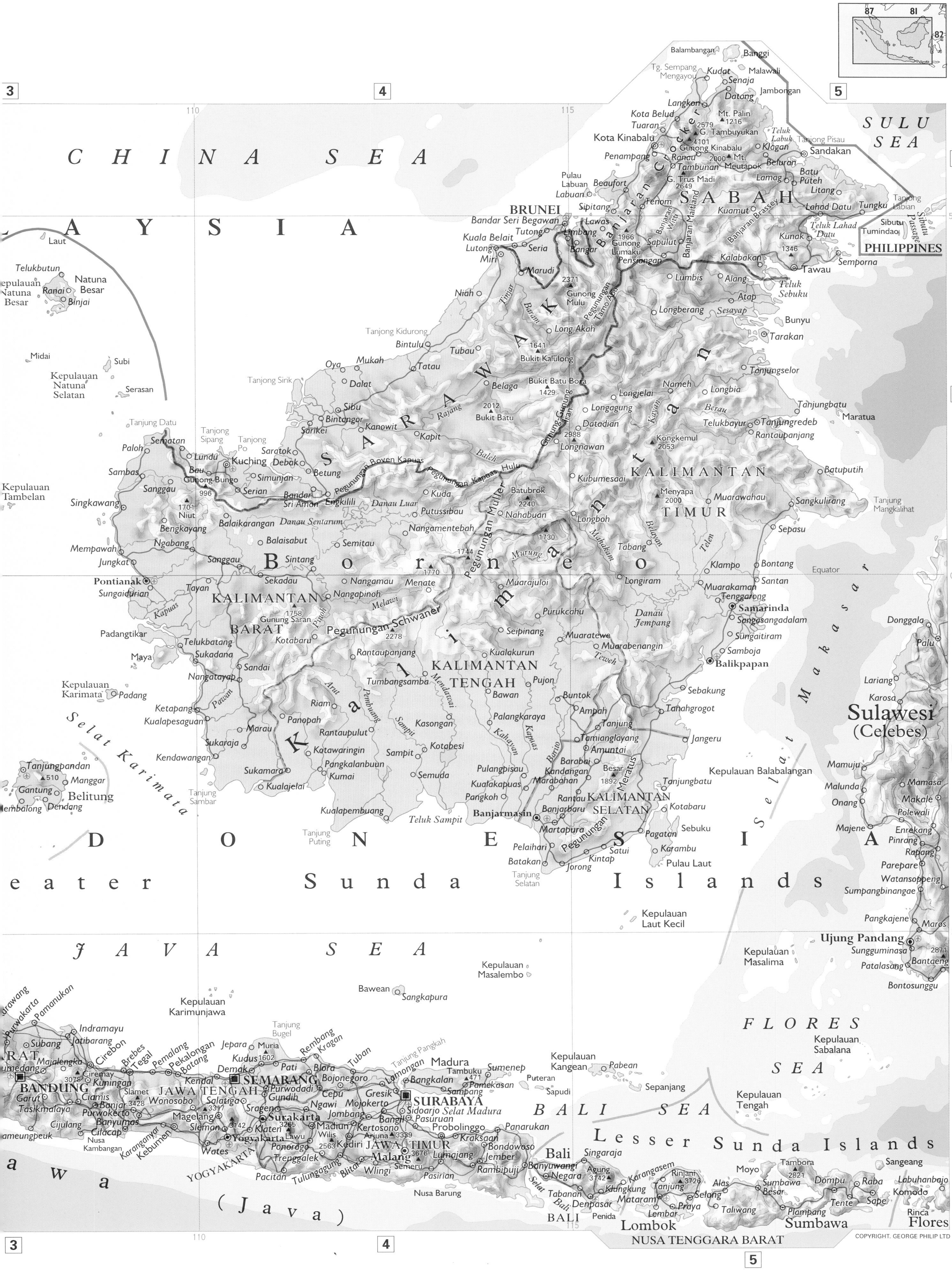
87
81
82
3
4
5
A
B
C
D
110
115
CHINA SEA
SULU SEA
MALAYSIA
BRUNEI
Bandar Seri Begawan
SABAH
SARAWAK
Kota Kinabalu
Sandakan
Tawau
Kudat
Gunong Kinabalu
4101
PHILIPPINES
Kuching
Sibu
Bintulu
Miri
Kuala Belait
Seria
Labuan
Natuna Besar
Kepulauan Natuna Selatan
Kepulauan Tambelan
Borneo
Kalimantan
KALIMANTAN BARAT
KALIMANTAN TENGAH
KALIMANTAN TIMUR
KALIMANTAN SELATAN
Pontianak
Samarinda
Balikpapan
Banjarmasin
Tarakan
Pegunungan Schwaner
Pegunungan Muller
Equator
Selat Karimata
Selat Makasar
Belitung
Sulawesi (Celebes)
Ujung Pandang
INDONESIA
Greater Sunda Islands
JAVA SEA
FLORES SEA
BALI SEA
Lesser Sunda Islands
Jawa (Java)
JAWA TENGAH
JAWA TIMUR
YOGYAKARTA
NUSA TENGGARA BARAT
BANDUNG
SEMARANG
SURABAYA
Yogyakarta
Surakarta
Malang
Madura
Bali
BALI
Denpasar
Lombok
Mataram
Sumbawa
Flores
Kepulauan Karimunjawa
Bawean
Kepulauan Masalembo
Kepulauan Masalima
Kepulauan Laut Kecil
Kepulauan Kangean
Kepulauan Sabalana
Kepulauan Tengah
Pulau Laut
Kepulauan Karimata
Kepulauan Balabalangan
COPYRIGHT. GEORGE PHILIP LTD

50 0 50 100 150 200 km
50 0 50 100 150 miles
A
B
C
D
E
F
1
2
3
4
5
6
7
8
YUNNAN
GUANGXI ZHUANGZU ZIZHIQU
GUANGDONG
HAINAN
VIETNAM
LAOS
THAILAND
CAMBODIA
BURMA (MYANMAR)
SHAN
KAYAH
KAREN
MON
TENASSERIM
PEGU
G. of Tonkin
G. of Martaban
HANOI
Haiphong
Nam Dinh
Thanh Hoa
Vinh
Hue
Da Nang
Qui Nhon
Vientiane (Viangchan)
Luang Prabang
Savannakhet
Pakxe
Ubon Ratchathani
Khon Kaen
Udon Thani
Nakhon Ratchasima
Phitsanulok
Nakhon Sawan
Chiang Mai
Lampang
Chiang Rai
BANGKOK
Thon Buri
Chon Buri
Moulmein
RANGOON (YANGON)
Pegu
Mandalay
Tavoy
Nanning
Zhanjiang
Haikou
Beihai
Maoming
Mekong
Salween
Chao Phraya
Phnom Dangrek
Khorat
Cao Nguyen
Dawna Range
Bilauktaung
Three Pagodas Pass
Tonle Sap
ANGKOR
Siemreab
Battambang
Plaine des Jarres
Tran Ninh
Hong Gai
Dien Bien
Son La
Lao Cai
Kon Tum
Pleiku
Buon Me Thuot

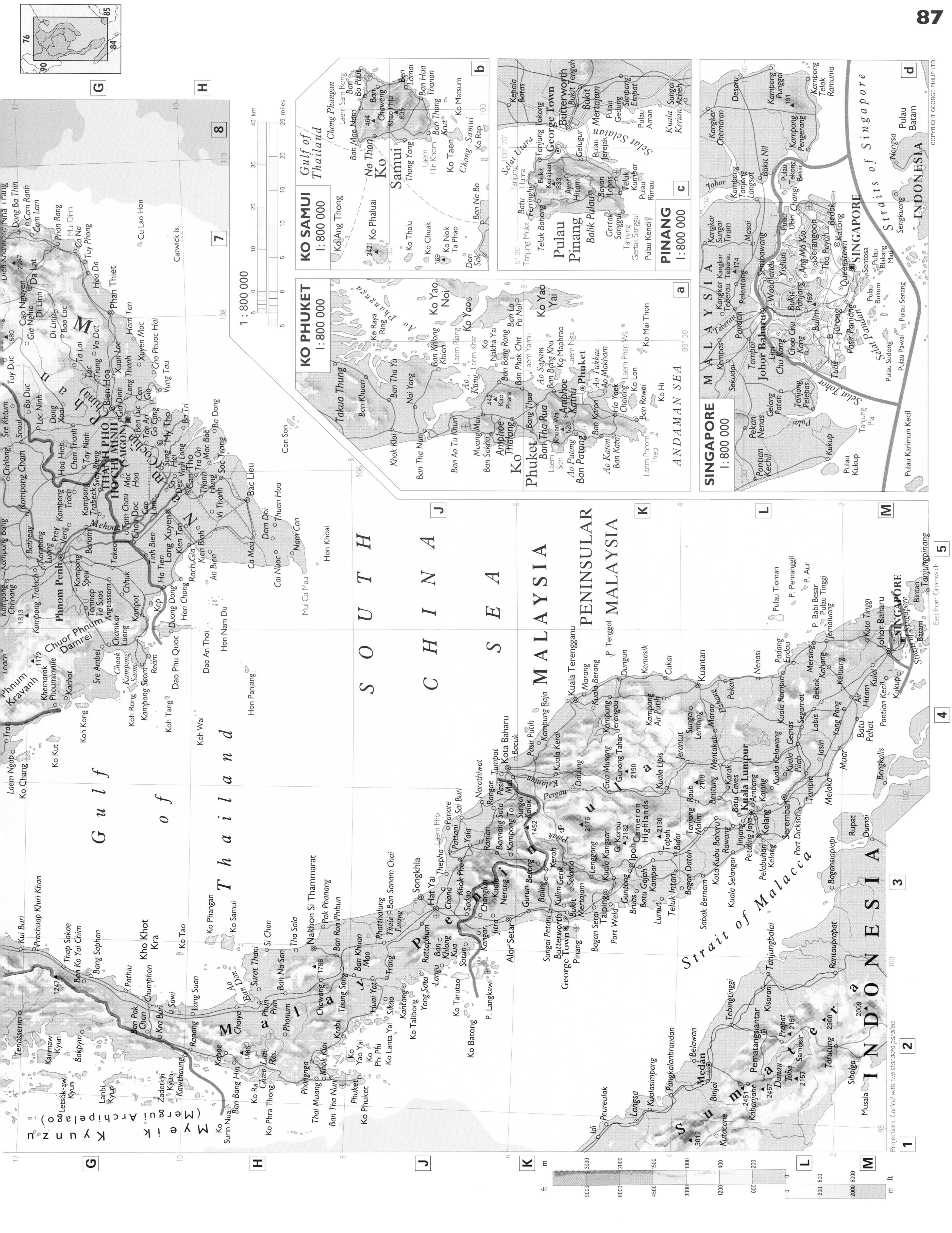

Gulf of Thailand
SOUTH CHINA SEA
MALAYSIA
PENINSULAR MALAYSIA
INDONESIA
Strait of Malacca
Sumatera
Kyunzu (Mergui Archipelago)
Phnom Penh
Thanh Pho Ho Chi Minh (Saigon)
Kuala Lumpur
Singapore
Medan
Mekong
1 : 800 000
KO PHUKET 1: 800 000
KO SAMUI 1: 800 000
PINANG 1: 800 000
SINGAPORE 1: 800 000
ANDAMAN SEA
Projection: Conical with two standard parallels
East from Greenwich
COPYRIGHT GEORGE PHILIP LTD.

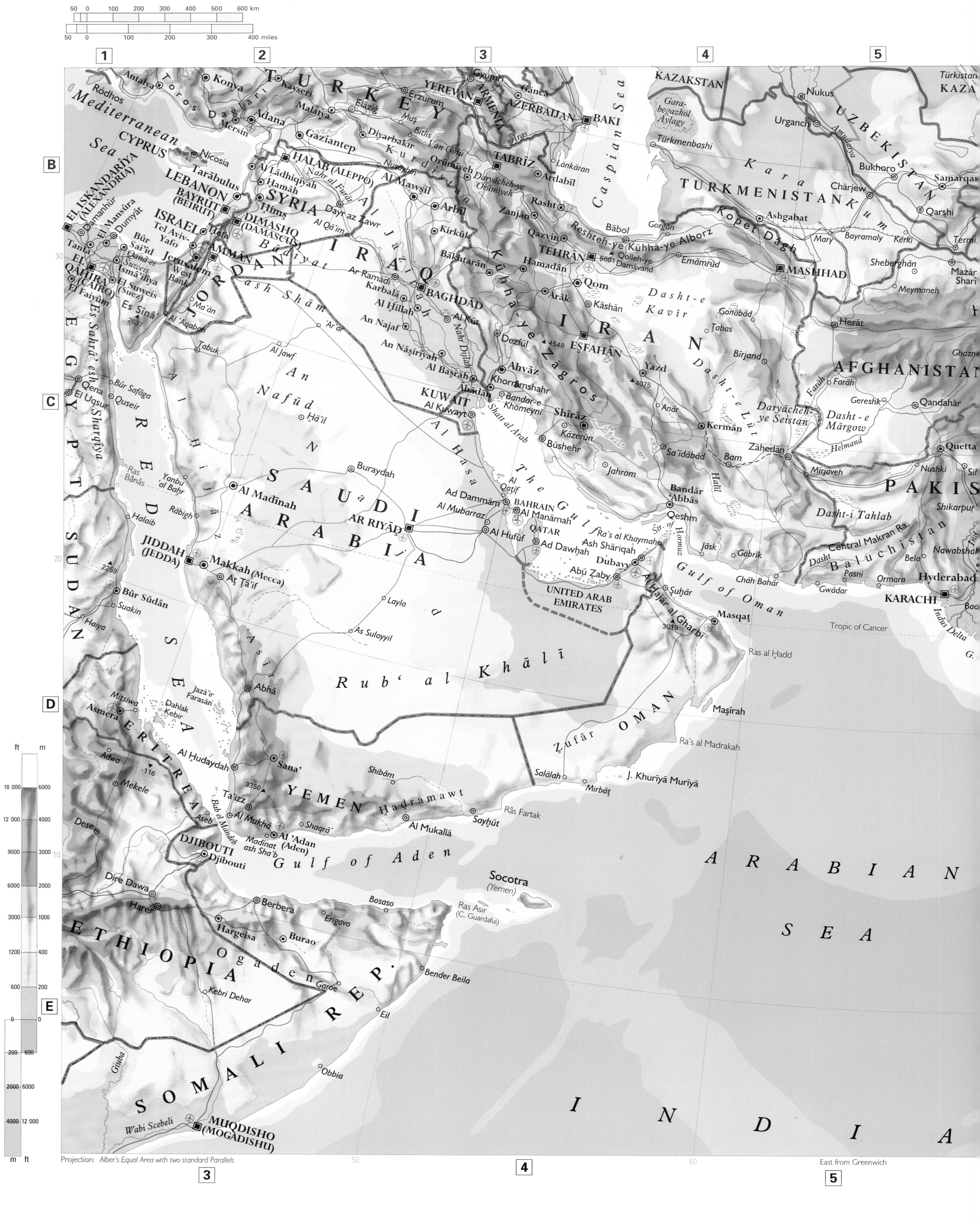
50 0 100 200 300 400 500 600 km
50 0 100 200 300 400 miles
1
2
3
4
5
B
C
D
E
TURKEY
Antalya
Toros Dağları
Konya
Kayseri
Malatya
Elâzığ
Erzurum
Muş
Bitlis
Van Gölü
Adana
Mersin
Gaziantep
Diyarbakır
Kurdistan
Rodhos
Mediterranean Sea
CYPRUS
Nicosia
Tarābulus
LEBANON
BAYRUT (BEIRUT)
SYRIA
ḤALAB (ALEPPO)
Al Lādhiqīyah
Ḥamāh
Ḥimṣ
DIMASHQ (DAMASCUS)
Nahr al Furāt
Dayr az Zawr
Al Qā'im
ISRAEL
Ḥefa
Tel Aviv-Yafo
Jerusalem
West Bank
'AMMĀN
JORDAN
Ma'ān
Al 'Aqabah
EL ISKANDARÎYA (ALEXANDRIA)
Damanhûr
El Mansûra
Dumyât
Bûr Sa'îd
Tanta
Qanâ es Suweis
Ismâ'ilîya
EL QÂHIRA (CAIRO)
El Suweis (Suez)
El Faiyûm
Es Sînâ'
2637
EGYPT
Es Sahrâ' esh Sharqîya
Qena
El Uqsur
Bûr Safâga
Quseir
Ras Bânâs
Halaib
SUDAN
2259
Bûr Sûdân
Suakin
Haiya
YEREVAN
ARMENIA
Gyumri
Gäncä
AZERBAIJAN
BAKI
Aras
Caspian Sea
Lankäran
TABRĪZ
Ardabīl
Orūmīyeh
Daryācheh-ye Orūmīyeh
Al Mawṣil
Arbīl
Kirkūk
Rasht
Zanjān
Qazvīn
TEHRĀN
Bābol
Gorgān
Reshteh-ye Kūhhā-ye Alborz
Qolleh-ye Damāvand
5601
Emāmrūd
Bākhtarān
Hamadān
Qom
Kāshān
Arāk
Dezfūl
4548
IRAN
EṢFAHĀN
Ahvāz
Khorramshahr
Ābādān
Bandar-e Khomeynī
Shatt al Arab
Shīrāz
Kāzerūn
Būshehr
Jahrom
Yazd
4075
Anār
Kermān
Bam
Dasht-e Kavīr
Dasht-e Lūt
Gonābād
Ṭabas
Bīrjand
Kūhhā-ye Zāgros
IRAQ
Bādiyat ash Shām
Ar Ramādī
Karbalā'
BAGHDĀD
Al Ḥillah
Al Kūt
An Najaf
Nahr Dijlah
An Nāṣirīyah
Al Baṣrah
KUWAIT
Al Kuwayt
'Ar'ar
Al Jawf
Tabuk
An Nafūd
Ḥā'il
Nejd
Al Ḥijāz
SAUDI ARABIA
Buraydah
Al Madīnah
Yanbu 'al Baḥr
Rābigh
JIDDAH (JEDDA)
Makkah (Mecca)
Aṭ Ṭā'if
AR RIYĀḌ
Ad Dammām
Al Qaṭīf
Al Mubarraz
Al Hufūf
Al Ḥasā
BAHRAIN
Al Manāmah
QATAR
Ad Dawḥah
The Gulf
Ra's al Khaymah
Ash Shāriqah
Dubayy
Abū Zaby
UNITED ARAB EMIRATES
Layla
As Sulayyil
'Asīr
Abhā
Rub' al Khālī
Bandar 'Abbās
Qeshm
Str. of Hormuz
Jāsk
Gābrīk
Sa'īdābād
Halil
Ṣuḥār
Al Ḥajar al Gharbī
3019
Masqaṭ
Gulf of Oman
Ras al Ḥadd
OMAN
Maṣīrah
Ẓufār
Ra's al Madrakah
Ṣalālah
Mirbāṭ
J. Khurīyā Murīyā
RED SEA
Jazā'ir Farasān
Mitsiwa
Dahlak Kebir
Asmera
ERITREA
Adwa
-116
Mekele
Al Ḥudaydah
Sana'
3350
YEMEN
Shibām
Ḥaḍramawt
Ta'izz
Al Mukhā
Assab
Bab el Mandeb
Shaqrā'
Al Mukallā
Sayḥūt
Râs Fartak
Madīnat ash Sha'b
Al 'Adan (Aden)
Dese
DJIBOUTI
Djibouti
Gulf of Aden
Socotra (Yemen)
Dire Dawa
Harer
ETHIOPIA
Berbera
Bosaso
Erigavo
Ras Asir (C. Guardafui)
Hargeisa
Burao
Ogaden
Garoe
Bender Beila
Kebri Dehar
Eil
SOMALI REP.
Obbia
Giuba
Wabi Scebeli
MUQDISHO (MOGADISHU)
KAZAKSTAN
Garabogazköl Aylagy
Türkmenbashi
Nukus
Urganch
UZBEKISTAN
Amudarya
Bukhoro
Samarqand
Türkistan
KAZA
Qarshi
Kara Kum
TURKMENISTAN
Chärjew
Ashgabat
Kopet Dāgh
Mary
Bayramaly
Kerki
Termiz
MASHHAD
Sheberghān
Mazār-e Sharīf
Meymaneh
Herāt
Ghazni
AFGHANISTAN
Farāh
Gereshk
Qandahār
Daryācheh-ye Seistan
Dasht-e Mārgow
Helmand
Zāhedān
Mīrjāveh
Quetta
Nushki
PAKISTAN
Dasht-i Tahlab
Shikarpur
Central Makran Ra.
Baluchistan
Nawabshah
Dasht
Bela
Hyderabad
Pasni
Ormara
Chāh Bahār
Gwādar
KARACHI
Indus Delta
Tropic of Cancer
ARABIAN SEA
INDIAN
30
20
10
40
50
60
ft m
18 000 6000
12 000 4000
9000 3000
6000 2000
3000 1000
1200 400
600 200
0 0
200 600
2000 6000
4000 12 000
m ft
Projection: Alber's Equal Area with two standard Parallels
East from Greenwich

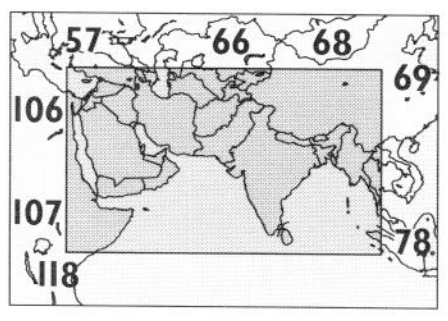
57
66
68
69
106
107
118
78

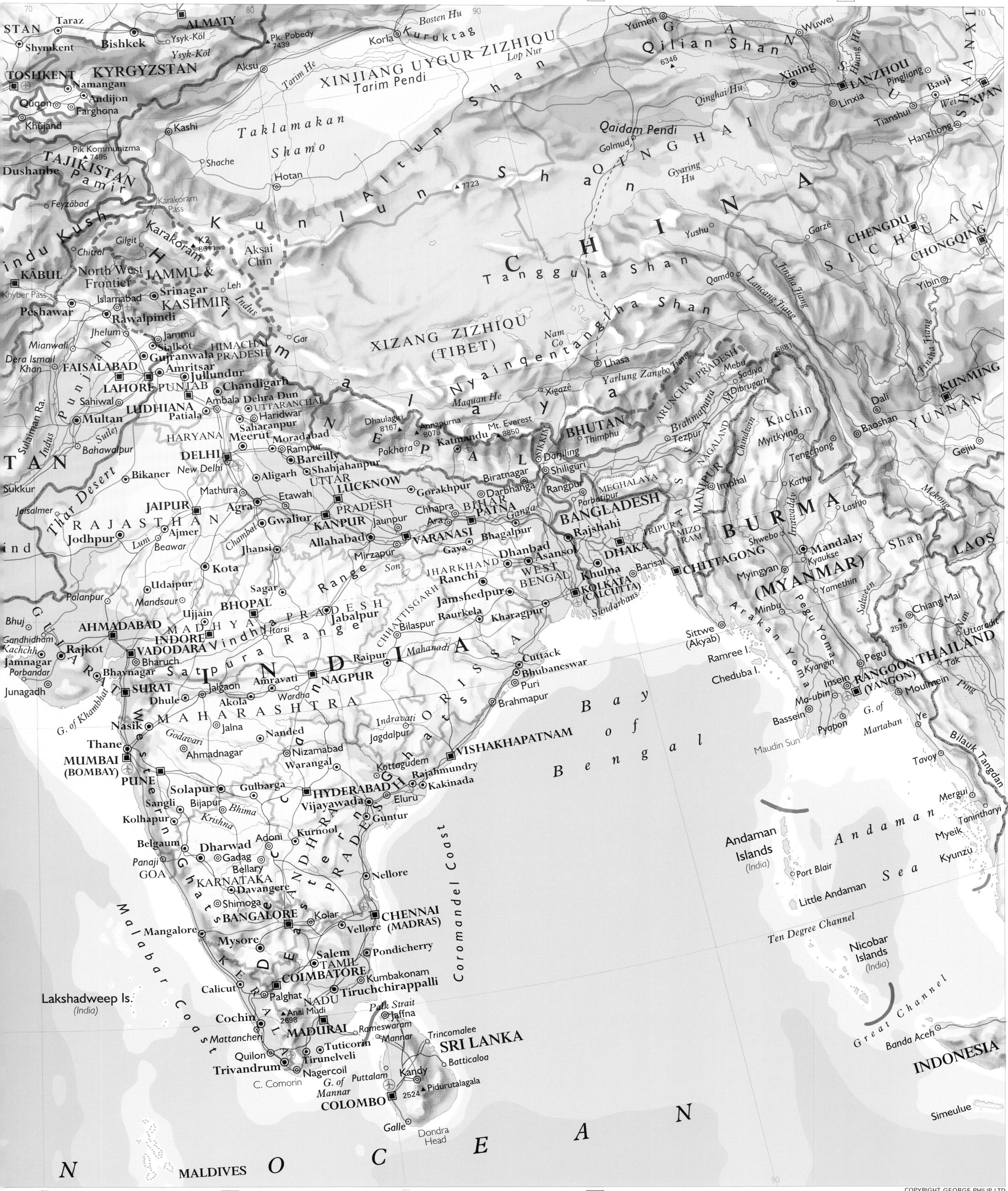
6
7
8
9
B
C
D
E
KYRGYZSTAN
TAJIKISTAN
TOSHKENT
ALMATY
Bishkek
Taraz
Shymkent
Namangan
Andijon
Farghona
Quqon
Khujand
Dushanbe
Pik Kommunizma 7495
Pk. Pobedy 7439
Ysyk-Köl
Aksu
Kashi
Shache
Hotan
Korla
Kuruktag
Bosten Hu
Lop Nur
Tarim He
XINJIANG UYGUR ZIZHIQU
Tarim Pendi
Taklamakan Shamo
Kunlun Shan
Altun Shan
Qilian Shan
Yumen
Wuwei
Xining
LANZHOU
Linxia
Pingliang
Baoji
XI'AN
SHAANXI
Tianshui
Hanzhong
Qinghai Hu
Qaidam Pendi
Golmud
QINGHAI
Gyaring Hu
6346
7723
CHINA
Yushu
Garzê
CHENGDU
SICHUAN
CHONGQING
Yibin
Qamdo
Tanggula Shan
Lancang Jiang
Jinsha Jiang
Nyainqentanglha Shan
XIZANG ZIZHIQU (TIBET)
Nam Co
Lhasa
Yarlung Zangbo Jiang
Xigazê
Maquan He
HIMALAYA
Gar
Pamir
Feyzabad
Hindu Kush
Karakoram Pass
Karakoram
K2 8611
Gilgit
Chitral
Aksai Chin
KABUL
Khyber Pass
North West Frontier
JAMMU & KASHMIR
Srinagar
Leh
Islamabad
Rawalpindi
Peshawar
Indus
Jhelum
Jammu
Mianwali
Dera Ismail Khan
Sialkot
Gujranwala
HIMACHAL PRADESH
FAISALABAD
LAHORE
Amritsar
Jullundur
PUNJAB
Chandigarh
Sahiwal
LUDHIANA
Ambala
Dehra Dun
UTTARANCHAL
Haridwar
Patiala
Saharanpur
Multan
Sulaiman Ra.
Sutlej
Bahawalpur
HARYANA
Meerut
Moradabad
Rampur
Bareilly
Shahjahanpur
DELHI
New Delhi
Aligarh
Bikaner
Sukkur
Thar Desert
Jaisalmer
Mathura
Agra
Etawah
UTTAR PRADESH
LUCKNOW
Gorakhpur
JAIPUR
RAJASTHAN
Ajmer
Jodhpur
Luni
Beawar
Gwalior
Chambal
KANPUR
Jaunpur
Allahabad
VARANASI
Mirzapur
Jhansi
Kota
Udaipur
Mandsaur
Sagar
Palanpur
Ujjain
BHOPAL
MADHYA PRADESH
Jabalpur
AHMADABAD
INDORE
Itarsi
Vindhya Range
Bhuj
Gandhidham
Kachchh
Rajkot
Jamnagar
Porbandar
Junagadh
GUJARAT
VADODARA
Bharuch
Bhavnagar
SURAT
G. of Khambhat
Satpura Range
Dhule
Jalgaon
Amravati
Akola
NAGPUR
Wardha
MAHARASHTRA
Nasik
Jalna
Nanded
Thane
MUMBAI (BOMBAY)
Godavari
Ahmadnagar
Nizamabad
PUNE
Warangal
Solapur
Gulbarga
HYDERABAD
Sangli
Bijapur
Bhima
Kolhapur
Krishna
Vijayawada
Belgaum
Dharwad
Gadag
Adoni
Kurnool
ANDHRA PRADESH
Panaji
GOA
Bellary
KARNATAKA
Davangere
Shimoga
BANGALORE
Kolar
Mangalore
Mysore
Malabar Coast
Western Ghats
Eastern Ghats
Deccan
Lakshadweep Is. (India)
Calicut
COIMBATORE
Salem
TAMIL NADU
Palghat
Cochin
Anai Mudi 2698
KERALA
MADURAI
Mattancheri
Quilon
Trivandrum
Tirunelveli
Nagercoil
C. Comorin
MALDIVES
Tuticorin
Rameswaram
Mannar
G. of Mannar
Palk Strait
Jaffna
Trincomalee
SRI LANKA
Batticaloa
Puttalam
Kandy
2524 Pidurutalagala
COLOMBO
Galle
Dondra Head
CHENNAI (MADRAS)
Vellore
Pondicherry
Kumbakonam
Tiruchchirappalli
Coromandel Coast
Nellore
Guntur
Eluru
Kakinada
Rajahmundry
Kottagudem
VISHAKHAPATNAM
Jagdalpur
Indravati
Raipur
Mahanadi
CHHATTISGARH
Bilaspur
Raurkela
ORISSA
Cuttack
Bhubaneswar
Puri
Brahmapur
INDIA
Son
Range
JHARKHAND
Ranchi
Jamshedpur
Kharagpur
Dhanbad
Asansol
WEST BENGAL
KOLKATA (CALCUTTA)
Sundarbans
Gaya
Bhagalpur
BIHAR
PATNA
Ganga
Chhapra
Ara
Darbhanga
Biratnagar
Pokhara
Katmandu
Dhaulagiri 8167
Annapurna 8078
Mt. Everest 8850
NEPAL
SIKKIM
Darjiling
Shiliguri
BHUTAN
Thimphu
ARUNACHAL PRADESH
Brahmaputra
Tezpur
Dibrugarh
Sadiya
Mebu
ASSAM
NAGALAND
MEGHALAYA
Rangpur
Parbatipur
BANGLADESH
Rajshahi
DHAKA
Khulna
Barisal
TRIPURA
MIZO-RAM
MANIPUR
Imphal
CHITTAGONG
Chindwin
Kachin
Myitkyina
Tengchong
Katha
Irrawaddy
Lashio
Shwebo
Mandalay
Kyaukse
BURMA (MYANMAR)
Myingyan
Minbu
Yamethin
Pegu Yoma
Arakan Yoma
Sittwe (Akyab)
Ramree I.
Cheduba I.
Kyangin
Pegu
Insein
RANGOON (YANGON)
Ma-ubin
Bassein
Pyapon
Moulmein
G. of Martaban
Maudin Sun
Ye
Tavoy
Bilauk Taungdan
Mergui
Myeik
Tanintharyi
Kyunzu
Salween
Shan
THAILAND
Chiang Mai
2576
Uttaradit
Tak
Ping
Nan
LAOS
Mekong
YUNNAN
KUNMING
Dali
Baoshan
Gejiu
5881
Bay of Bengal
Andaman Islands (India)
Port Blair
Little Andaman
Andaman Sea
Ten Degree Channel
Nicobar Islands (India)
Great Channel
Banda Aceh
INDONESIA
Simeulue
INDIAN OCEAN
70
80
90
100
110
10
20
30

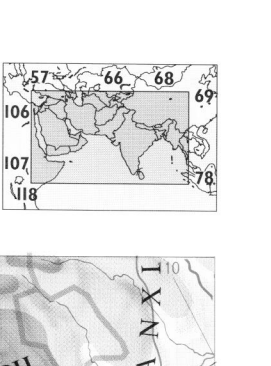

BANGLADESH, NORTH-EASTERN INDIA AND BURMA

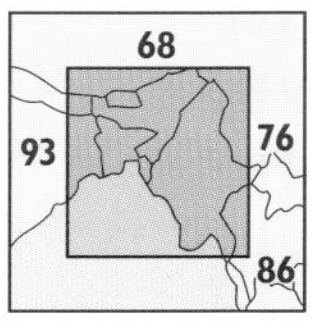

50 0 50 100 150 200 km

50 0 50 100 150 miles

1:4 800 000

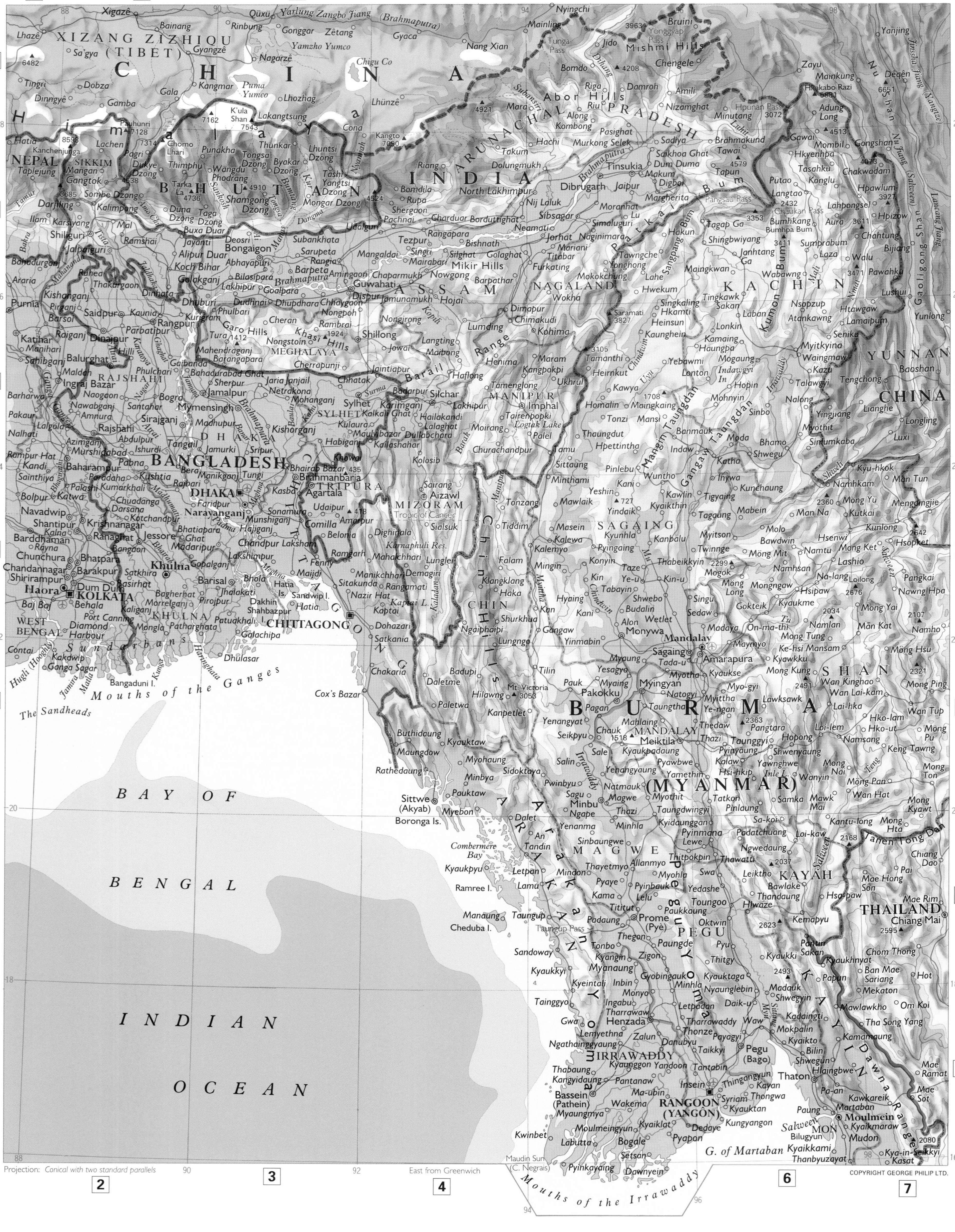

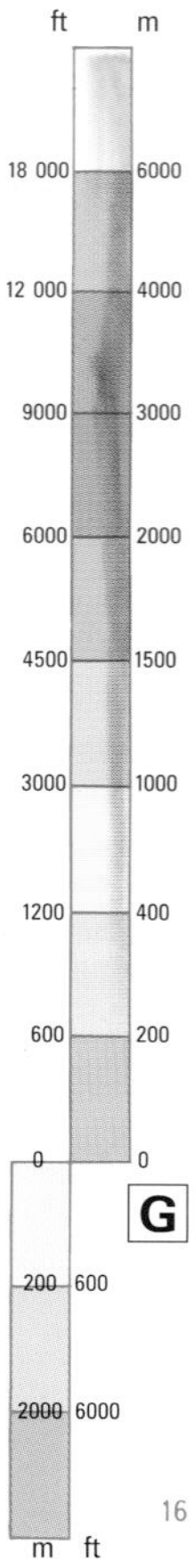

Projection: *Conical with two standard parallels*

East from Greenwich

COPYRIGHT GEORGE PHILIP LTD.

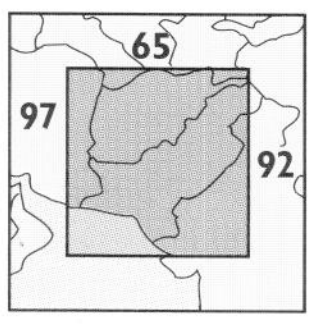

50 0 50 100 150 200 250 300 km
50 0 50 100 150 200 miles

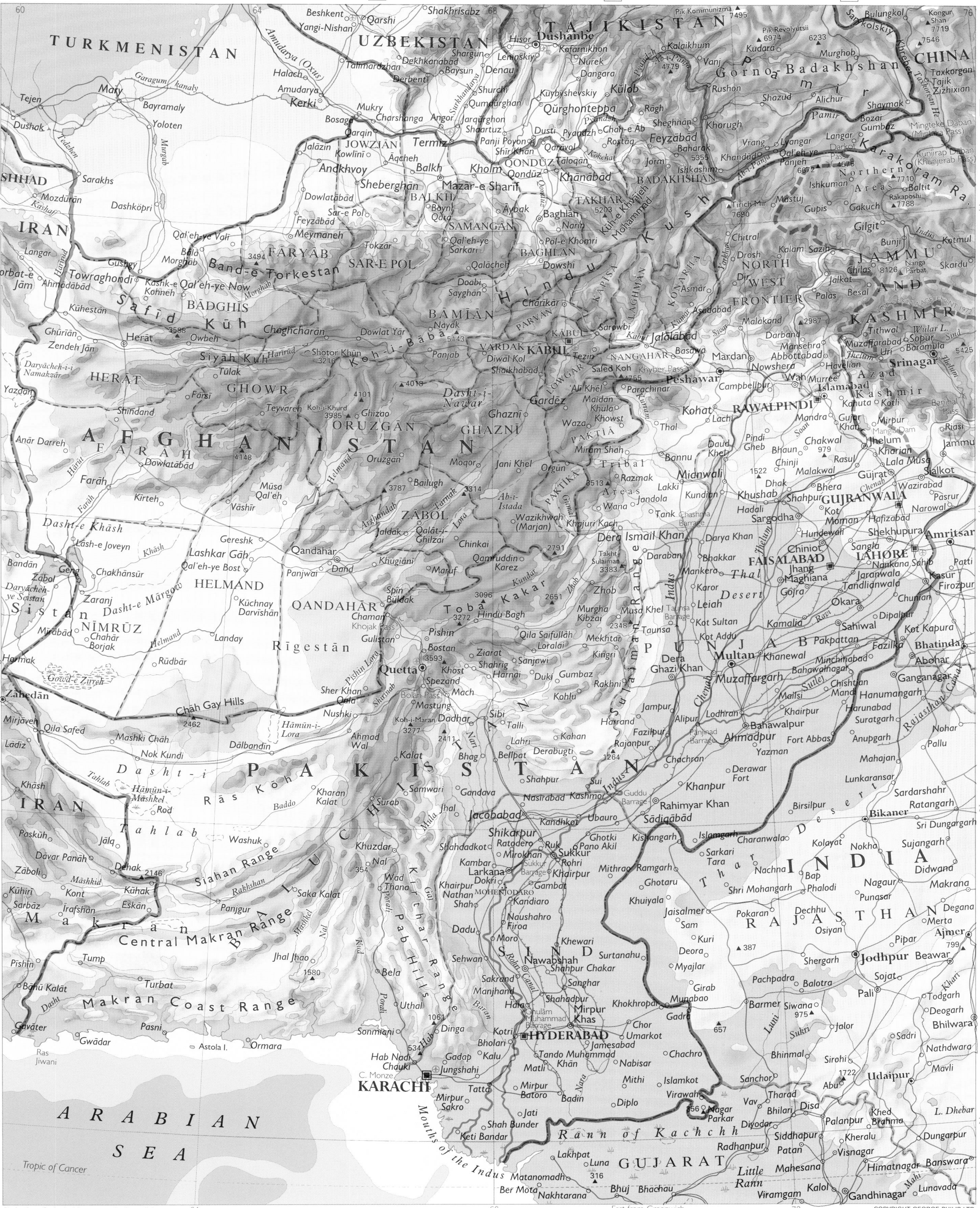

THE INDO-GANGETIC PLAIN 1:4 800 000

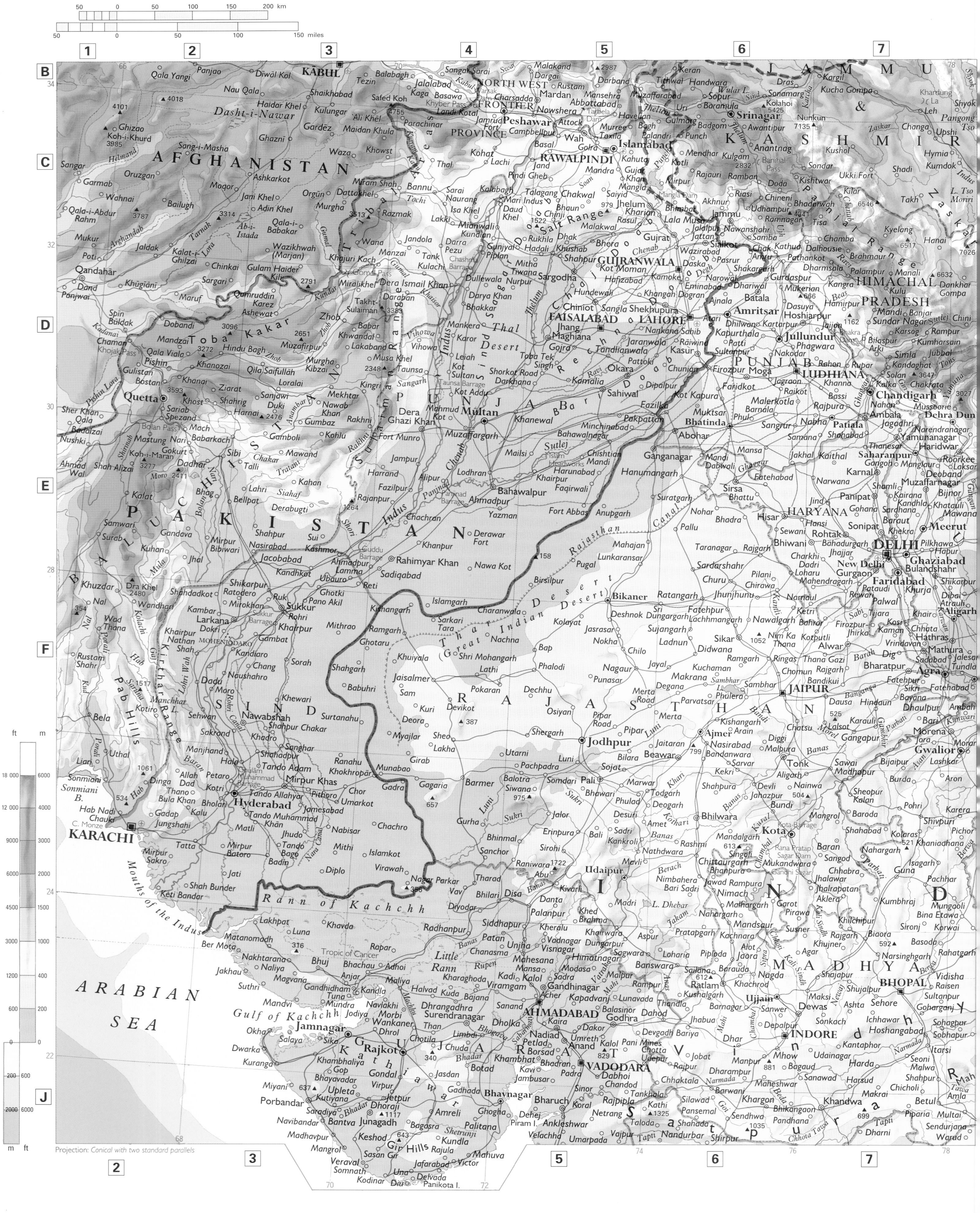

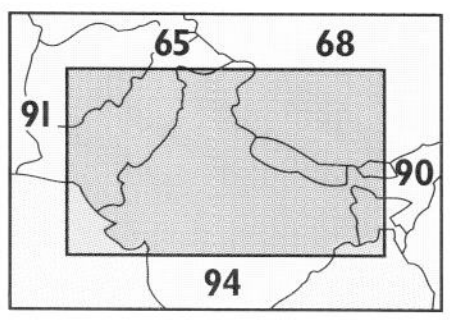
65
68
91
90
94

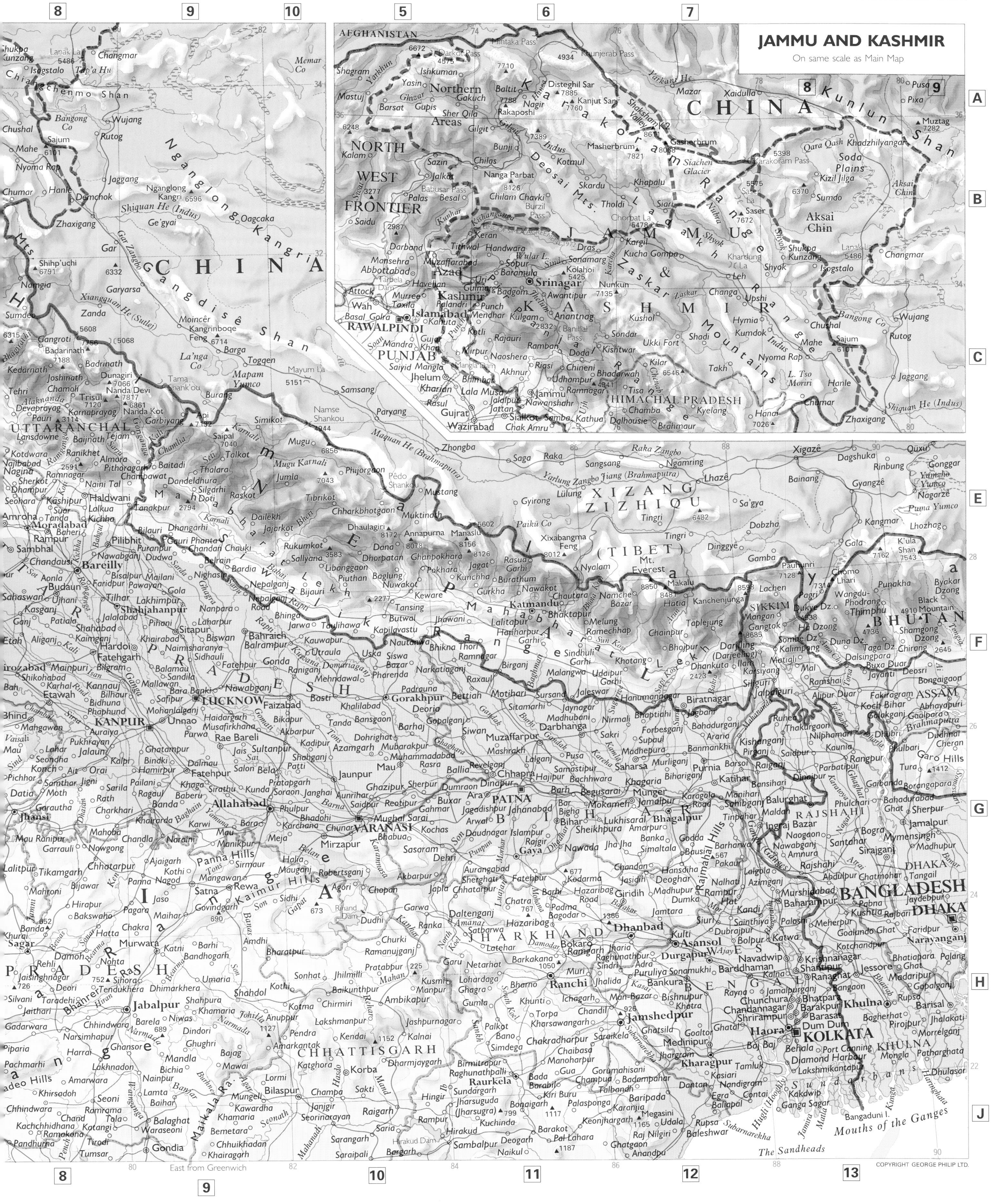
JAMMU AND KASHMIR
On same scale as Main Map
CHINA
Northern Areas
NORTH WEST FRONTIER
AZAD KASHMIR
PUNJAB
JAMMU & KASHMIR
HIMACHAL PRADESH
Karakoram Ra.
Kunlun Shan
Aksai Chin
Srinagar
Islamabad
RAWALPINDI
Jammu
Leh
Kargil
AFGHANISTAN
CHINA
XIZANG ZIZHIQU
(TIBET)
Gangdisê Shan
Nganglong Kangri
UTTARANCHAL
NEPAL
Katmandu
Mt. Everest
SIKKIM
BHUTAN
ASSAM
BANGLADESH
DHAKA
RAJSHAHI
KHULNA
KOLKATA
WEST BENGAL
JHARKHAND
BIHAR
PATNA
UTTAR PRADESH
LUCKNOW
KANPUR
Allahabad
VARANASI
MADHYA PRADESH
Jabalpur
CHHATTISGARH
Ranchi
Jamshedpur
Mouths of the Ganges
The Sandheads
East from Greenwich
COPYRIGHT GEORGE PHILIP LTD.

SOUTHERN INDIA AND SRI LANKA 1:4 800 000

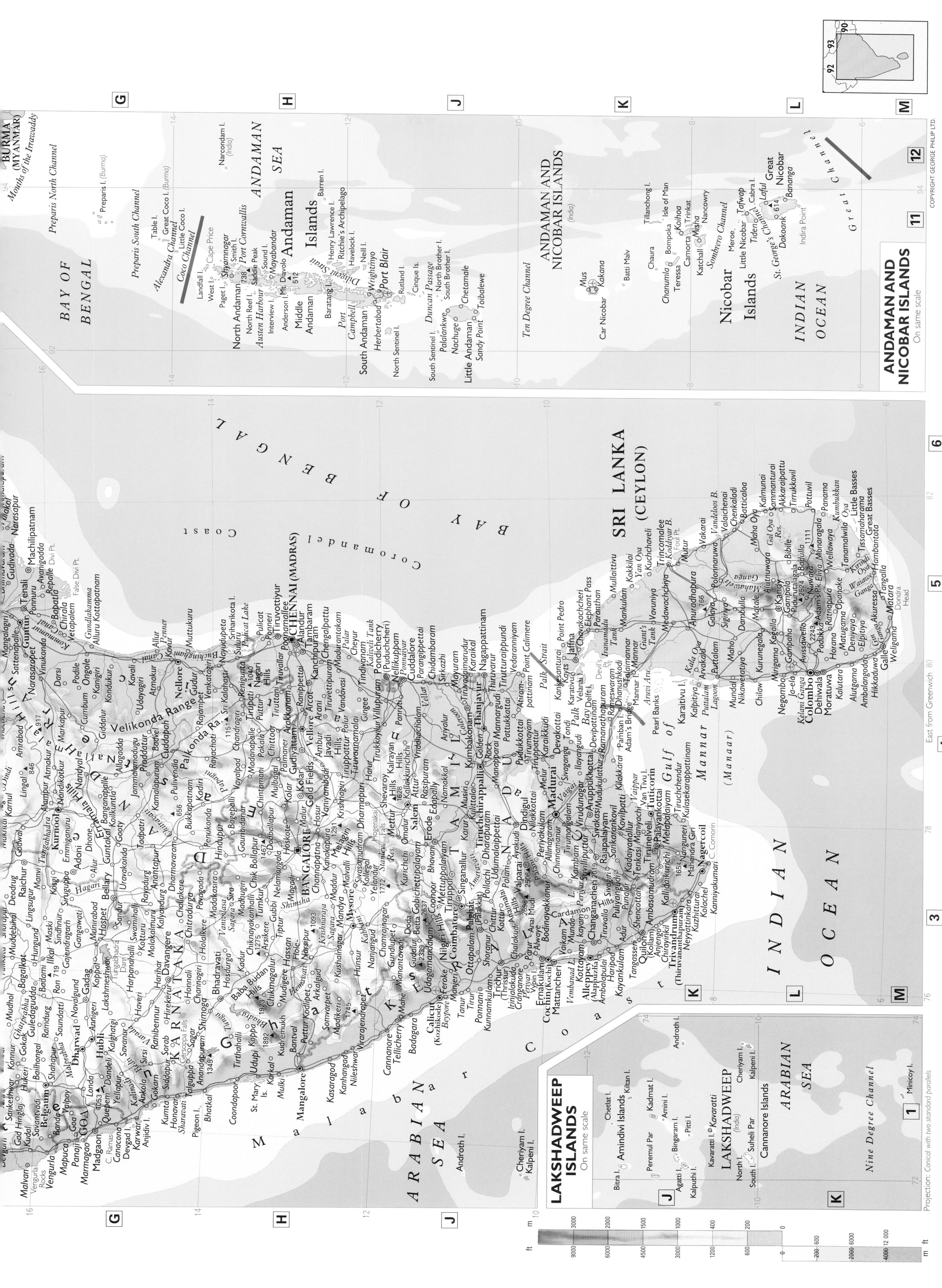

ANDAMAN AND NICOBAR ISLANDS
On same scale
LAKSHADWEEP ISLANDS
On same scale
SRI LANKA (CEYLON)
BAY OF BENGAL
ANDAMAN SEA
INDIAN OCEAN
ARABIAN SEA
Coromandel Coast
Malabar Coast
Gulf of Mannar
Andaman Islands
Nicobar Islands
CHENNAI (MADRAS)
BANGALORE
Colombo
East from Greenwich
Projection: Conical with two standard parallels
COPYRIGHT GEORGE PHILIP LTD.

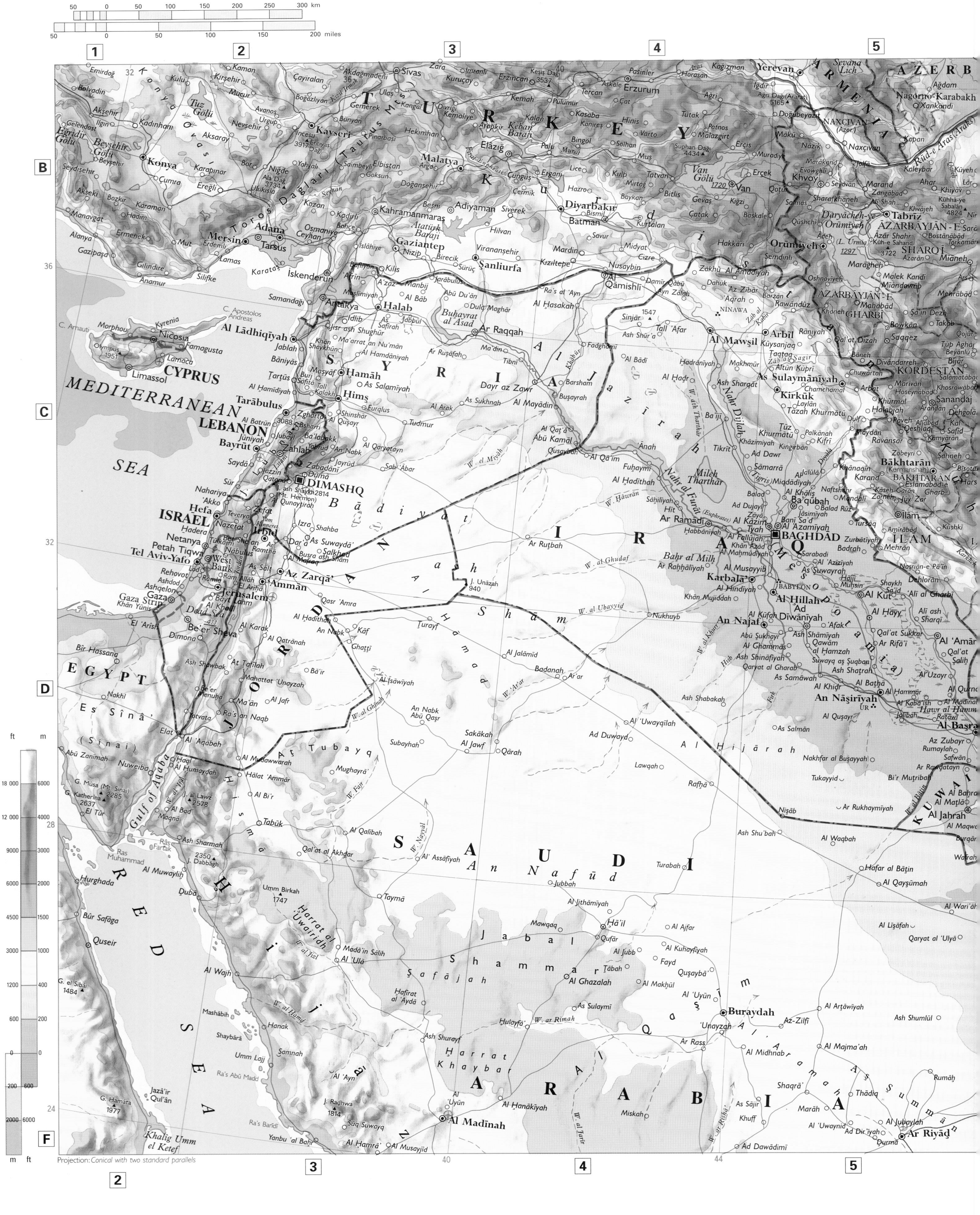

Projection: Conical with two standard parallels

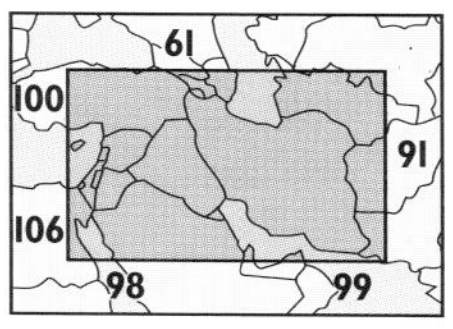
61
100
91
106
98
99

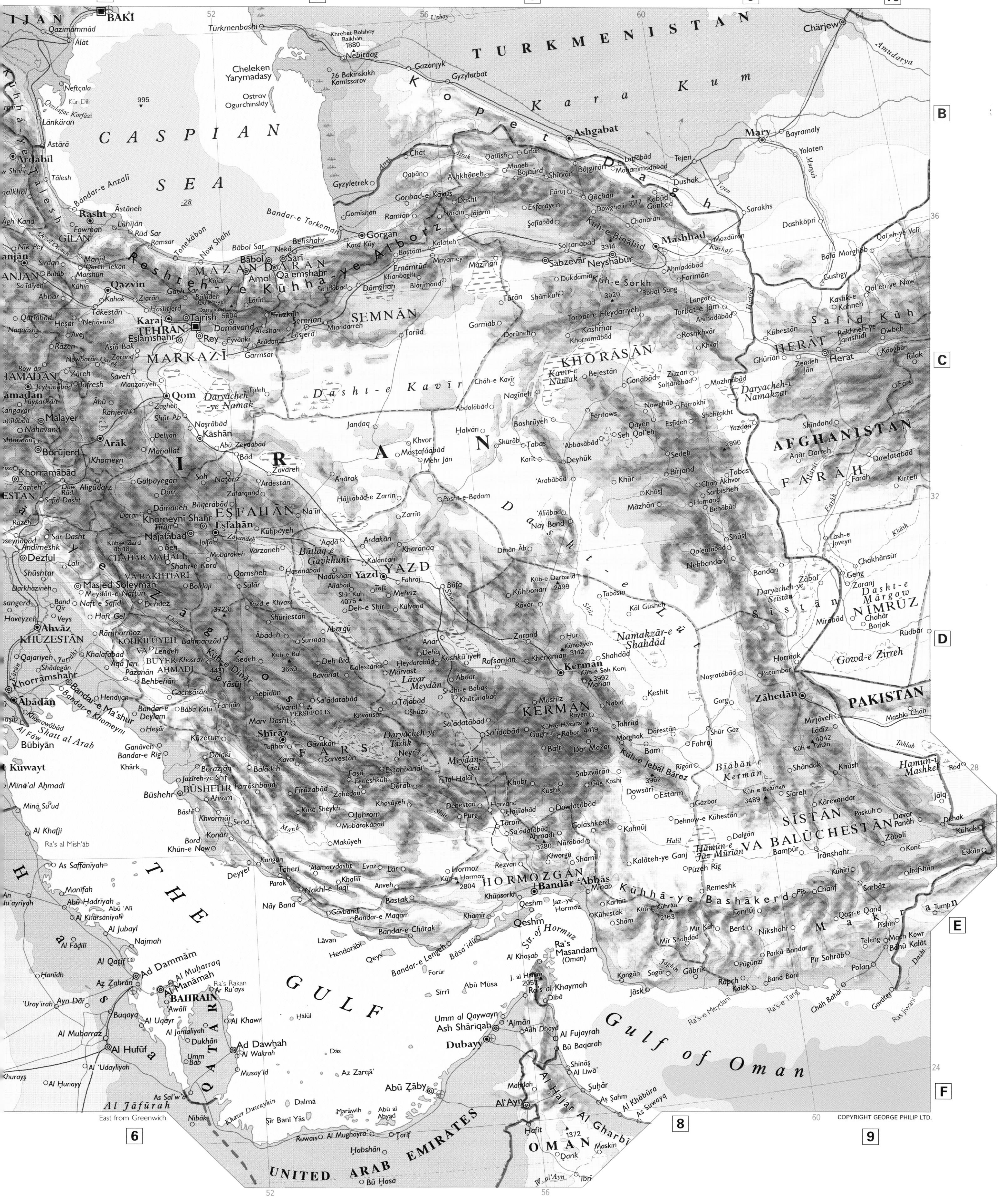
6
7
8
9
10
B
C
D
E
F
TURKMENISTAN
Kara Kum
Kopet Dagh
CASPIAN SEA
Türkmenbashi
Cheleken Yarymadasy
Ostrov Ogurchinskiy
Khrebet Bolshoy Balkhan 1880
Nebitdag
Gazanjyk
Gyzylarbat
26 Bakinskikh Komissarov
Ashgabat
Chärjew
Amudarya
Mary
Bayramaly
Yoloten
Tejen
Dushak
Sarakhs
Gyzyletrek
BAKI
Qazimämmäd
Älät
Neftçala
Länkäran
Ästärä
995
-28
Ardabil
Talesh
Bandar-e Anzalī
Rasht
Āstāneh
Lāhījān
Rūd Sar
Fowman
GĪLĀN
Rāmsar
Tonekābon
Now Shahr
Bābol Sar
Bābol
Behshahr
Bandar-e Torkeman
Gorgān
Sārī
Amol
Qā'emshahr
MĀZANDARĀN
Reshteh-ye Kūhhā-ye Alborz
Gonbad-e Kāvūs
Dasht
Bojnūrd
Shīrvān
Qūchān
Bājgīrān
Mashhad
Kūh-e Binālūd 3314
Neyshābūr
Sabzevār
Kūh-e Sorkh 3020
Torbat-e Heydarīyeh
Torbat-e Jām
Qazvin
Zanjān
Karaj
TEHRĀN
Tajrīsh
Rey
Eslāmshahr
Damāvand 5604
Fīrūzkūh
Semnān
SEMNĀN
Dāmghān
Shāhrūd
Torūd
Garmsār
MARKAZĪ
Qom
Daryācheh-ye Namak
Dasht-e Kavīr
Kāshān
Arāk
Hamadān
Malāyer
Borūjerd
Khorramābād
KHORĀSĀN
Kavīr-e Namak
Gonābād
Ferdows
Tabas
Bīrjand
IRAN
ESFAHĀN
Esfahān
Najafābād
Khomeynī Shahr
Nā'īn
Ardakān
YAZD
Yazd
Bāfq
Mehrīz
Kūh-e Darband 2499
Dasht-e Lūt
Namakzār-e Shahdād
Kermān
KERMĀN
Rafsanjān
Sīrjān
Bam
Kūh-e Hazārān 4419
Kūh-e Jebāl Bārez 3962
Dezfūl
Ahvāz
KHŪZESTĀN
Ābādān
Khorramshahr
Shatt al Arab
Bandar-e Khomeynī
Bandar-e Ma'shur
CHAHĀR MAHALL VA BAKHTIĀRĪ
KOHKĪLŪYEH VA BŪYER AHMADĪ
Yāsūj
Kūh-e Dīnār 4431
Zāgros
Shīrāz
Persepolis
FĀRS
Daryācheh-ye Tashk
Neyrīz
Fasā
Jahrom
Lār
Būshehr
BŪSHEHR
Kāzerūn
Kharg
HORMOZGĀN
Bandar-e 'Abbās
Hormoz
Qeshm
Str. of Hormuz
Bandar-e Lengeh
Kīsh
Kūhhā-ye Bashākerd
SĪSTĀN VA BALŪCHESTĀN
Zāhedān
Zābol
Dasht-e Mārgow
Daryācheh-ye Sīstān
Hāmūn-e Jaz Mūrīān
Īrānshahr
Khāsh
Kūh-e Taftān 4042
Kūh-e Bazman 3489
Chāh Bahār
Jāsk
Makran
Gwadar
Rās Jiwani
PAKISTAN
AFGHANISTAN
HERĀT
Herāt
Safīd Kūh
FARĀH
Farāh
NIMRŪZ
Gowd-e Zirreh
Hamun-i Mashkel
Kuwayt
Būbiyān
Mīnā' al Ahmadī
Al Khafjī
Ra's al Mish'āb
As Saffānīyah
Al Jubayl
Al Qatīf
Ad Dammām
Az Zahrān
Al Manāmah
BAHRAIN
Al Hufūf
Al Mubarraz
QATAR
Ad Dawhah
Dukhān
THE GULF
Abū Mūsá
Dubayy
Ash Shāriqah
Ras al Khaymah
Al Fujayrah
Abū Zaby
Al 'Ayn
UNITED ARAB EMIRATES
OMAN
Ra's Masandam (Oman)
Gulf of Oman
Al Hajar Al Gharbī
Şuhār
Al Jāfūrah
East from Greenwich
52
56
60
64
24
28
32
36
COPYRIGHT GEORGE PHILIP LTD.

SOUTHERN ARABIAN PENINSULA 1:5 600 000

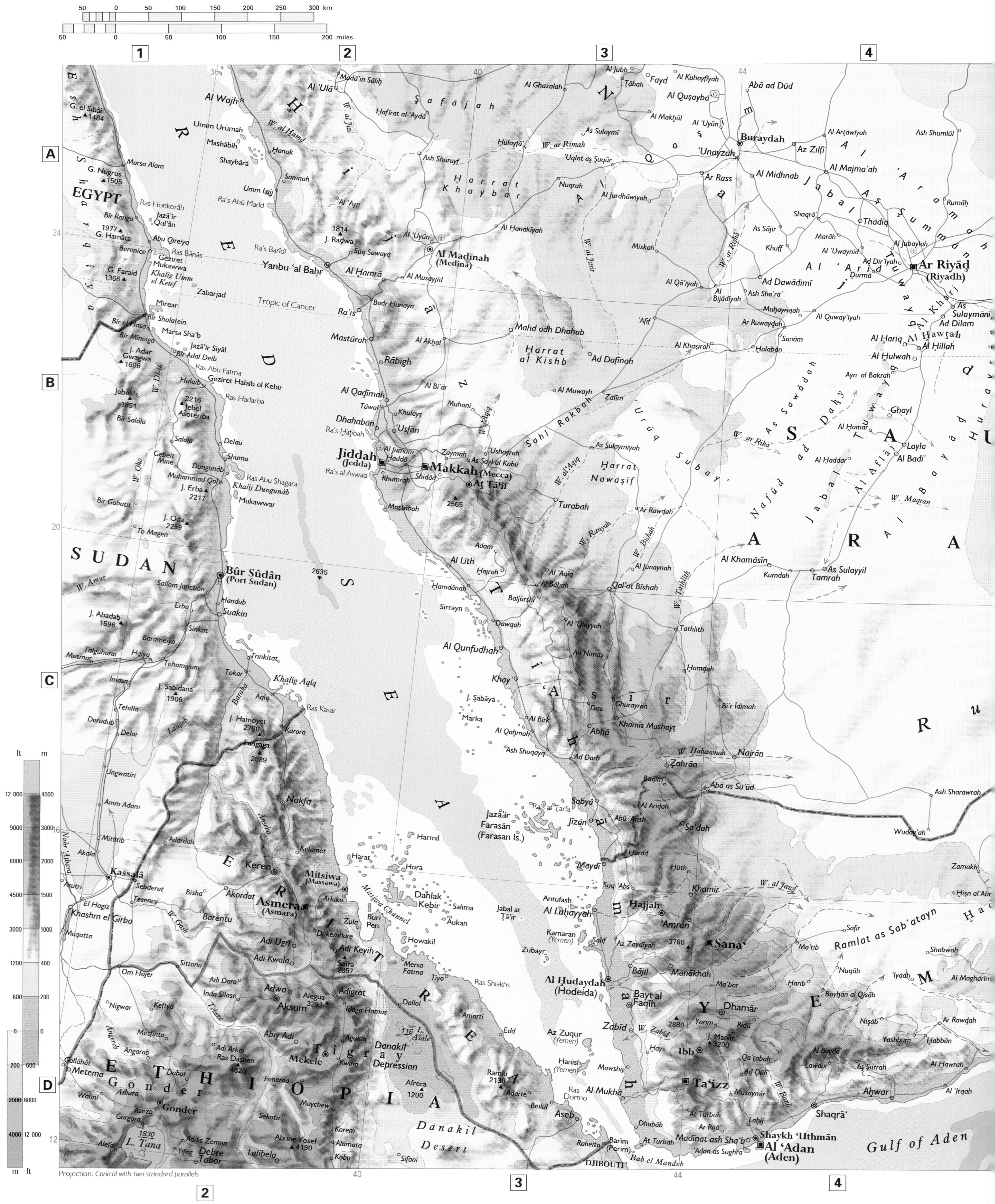

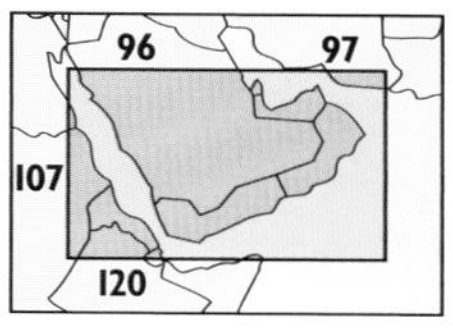
96
97
107
120
8

5
6
7
8
A
B
C
D
THE GULF
Gulf of Oman
IRAN
QATAR
BAHRAIN
UNITED ARAB EMIRATES
OMAN
YEMEN
ARABIAN SEA
Rub' al Khali (Empty Quarter)
Tropic of Cancer
Str. of Hormuz
Abū Ḩadrīyah
Al Jubayl
Al Qaţīf
Ad Dammām
Az Zahrān (Dhahran)
Al Manāmah
Al Muḩarraq
Al Hufūf
Al Mubarraz
Ad Dawḩah
Dukhān
Al Wakrah
Musay'īd
Umm Bāb
Al 'Uḑaylīyah
As Sal'wa
Al Jāfūrah
Ḩaraḑ
Abū Ẓaby (Abu Dhabi)
Dubayy (Dubai)
Ash Shāriqah (Sharjah)
'Ajmān
Umm al Qaywayn
Ra's al Khaymah
Al Fujayrah
Al 'Ayn
Ruwais
Ḩabshān
Bū Ḩasā'
Arādah
Jiwa
Aḑ Ḑafrah
Ra's Musandam (Oman)
Dibā
Khawr Duwayhin
Dalmā
Şīr Banī Yās
Das (U.A.E.)
Ḩālūl (Qatar)
Sirri (Iran)
Abū Mūsa (Iran)
Qeshm
Bandar-e Lengeh
Bastak
Bandar-e Chārak
Kangān
Jāsk
Gavāter
Chāh Bahār
Suḩār
Al Khābūra
Masqaţ (Muscat)
Maţraḩ
Al Qurayyāt
Nazwā
Bahlah
'Ibrī
Izkī
J. ash Shām 3019
Şūr
Ra's al Ḩadd
Al Ḩadd
Ibra
Al Kāmil
Adam
Al Ashkharah
Al Hajar al Gharbī
Jiddat al Ḩarāsīs
Maşīrah
Dawwah
Ḩaymā'
Duqm
Khalīj Maşīrah
Ra's al Madrakah
Ghubbat Şawqirah
Şawqirah
Shuwamiyah
Ghubbat Kuriyā Muriyā
Jazā'ir Khurīyā Murīyā (Kuria Muria Is.)
Ẓufār
Thamarit
Shisur
Fasad
Ma'mūl
Şalālah
Mirbāţ
Ḩāsik
J. al Qamar
J. al Qarā'
Rakhyūt
Ḩabarūt
Damqawt
Al Fayḑamī
Al Ghayḑah
Ghubbat al Qamar
Khalfūt
Ra's Fartak
Qishn
Sayḩūt
Al Ghayl
Tarīm
Shibām
Saywūn
Thamūd
Sanāw
Al Mukallā
Ash Shiḩr
Shuḩayr
Al Ḩasy
Balhaf
W. Ḩaḑramawt
Socotra (Yemen)
Ḩadiboh
Qalansīyah
Ra's Shu'ab
'Abd al Kūri (Yemen)
The Brothers (Yemen)
East from Greenwich
52
56
24
20
16
12
COPYRIGHT, GEORGE PHILIP LTD.

TURKEY AND TRANSCAUCASIA 1:4 000 000

Projection: *Conical with two standard parallels*

Division between Greeks and Turks in Cyprus; Turks to the North.

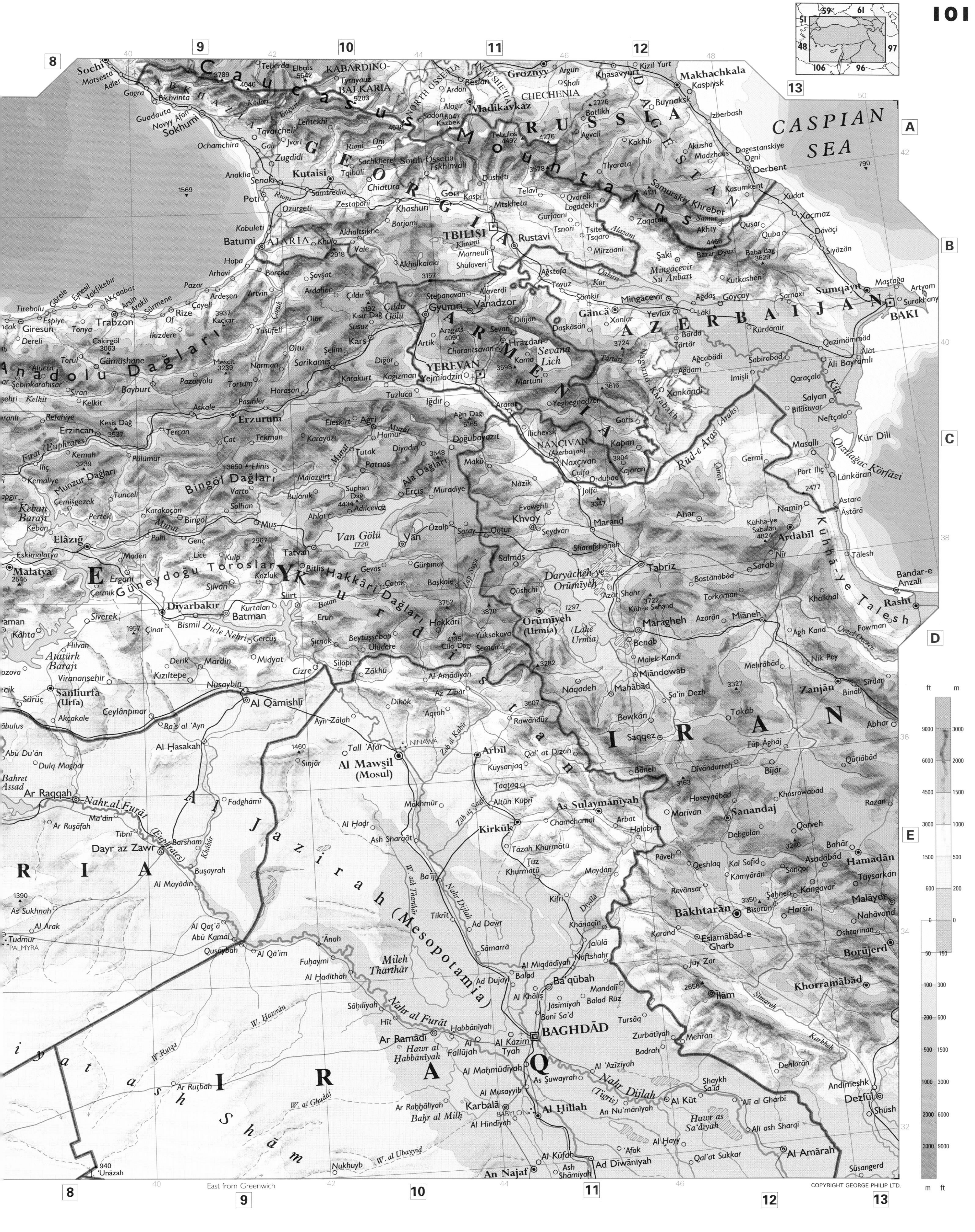
CASPIAN SEA
Caucasus Mountains
RUSSIA
GEORGIA
ARMENIA
AZERBAIJAN
IRAN
IRAQ
TURKEY
SYRIA
Kurdistan
Al Jazirah (Mesopotamia)
Bādiyat ash Shām
Anadolu Dağları
Güneydoğu Toroslar
Hakkâri Dağları
Bingöl Dağları
Munzur Dağları
Ala Dağları
Kūhhā-ye Ţālesh
Samurskiy Khrebet
DAGESTAN
CHECHENIA
INGUSHETIA
NORTH OSSETIA
KABARDINO-BALKARIA
ABKHAZIA
AJARIA
South Ossetia
NAXÇIVAN (Azerbaijan)
Nagorno Karabakh
Sochi
Matsesta
Adler
Gagra
Bichvinta
Gudauta
Novyy Afon
Sokhumi
Ochamchira
Anaklia
Senaki
Poti
Zugdidi
Kutaisi
Tqibuli
Chiatura
Zestaponi
Samtredia
Ozurgeti
Kobuleti
Batumi
Khulo
Akhaltsikhe
Borjomi
Khashuri
Gori
Tskhinvali
Mtskheta
TBILISI
Rustavi
Marneuli
Shulaveri
Akhalkalaki
Telavi
Gurjaani
Lagodekhi
Tsnori
Tsiteli Tsqaro
Mirzaani
Grozny
Argun
Shali
Beslan
Ardon
Alagir
Vladikavkaz
Kazbek
Sadon
Tebulos
Elbrus 5642
Teberda
Tyrnyauz
Khasavyurt
Kizil Yurt
Makhachkala
Kaspiysk
Buynaksk
Izberbash
Botlikh
Agvali
Kakhib
Akusha
Madzhalis
Dagestanskiye Ogni
Derbent
Tlyarata
Kasumkent
Xudat
Xaçmaz
Däväçi
Siyäzän
Quba
Qusar
Akhty
Zaqatala
Şaki
Mingäçevir Su Anbarı
Kutkashen
Baba dag 3629
Bazar Dyuzi
Sumqayıt
Maştağa
Artyom
Surakhany
BAKI
Ağdaş
Göyçay
Şamaxi
Mingäçevir
Yevlax
Läki
Kürdämir
Gäncä
Xanlar
Daşkäsän
Bärdä
Tärtär
Ağcabädi
Ağdam
Xankändi
Qazimämmäd
Älät
Äli Bayramlı
Sabirabad
Imişli
Qaraçala
Salyan
Biläsuvar
Neftçala
Kür Dili
Masallı
Qızılağac Körfäzi
Germi
Port Ilic
Länkäran
Astara
Ästärä
Ağstafa
Tovuz
Şämkir
Alaverdi
Stepanavan
Vanadzor
Gyumri
Dilijan
Sevan
Hrazdan
Aragats 4090
Artik
Charentsavan
YEREVAN
Yejmiadzin
Kamo
Sevana Lich
Martuni
Ararat
Yeghegnadzor
Goris
Kapan
Kajaran
Ilichevsk
Naxçıvan
Culfa
Ordubad
Rūd-e Aras (Araks)
Pazar
Ardeşen
Rize
Çayeli
Of
Sürmene
Araklı
Arsin
Trabzon
Akçaabat
Vakfıkebir
Eynesil
Görele
Tirebolu
Giresun
Espiye
Tonya
Dereli
Çakirgöl 3063
Gümüşhane
Torul
Alucra
Şebinkarahisar
Şiran
Kelkit
Bayburt
Pazaryolu
Mescit 3239
Tortum
İkizdere
Kaçkar 3937
Hopa
Arhavi
Borçka
Artvin
Şavşat
Ardahan
Çıldır
Çıldır Gölü
Kısır Dağ 3192
Susuz
Kars
Yusufeli
Olur
Oltu
Şelim
Sarıkamış
Narman
Horasan
Karakurt
Kağızman
Digor
Tuzluca
Iğdır
Ağrı Dağı 5165
Doğubayazıt
Ağrı
Eleşkirt
Hamur
Tutak
Diyadin
Patnos
Karayazı
Erzurum
Aşkale
Pasinler
Tercan
Tekman
Çat
Hinis 3650
Erzincan
Refahiye
Keşiş Dağ 3537
Kemah 3239
İliç
Kemaliye
Pülümür
Malazgirt
Bulanık
Varto
Solhan
Tunceli
Pertek
Çemişgezek
Keban Barajı
Keban
Elazığ
Palu
Karakoçan
Bingöl
Muş
Genç
Kulp
Lice
Maden
Malatya 2545
Eskimalatya
Ergani
Çermik
Silvan
Kozluk
Diyarbakır
Batman
Kurtalan
Siirt
Bitlis
Tatvan
Ahlat
Adilcevaz
Suphan Dağı 4434
Erciş
Muradiye
Van Gölü 1720
Van
Özalp
Saray
Gevaş
Gürpınar
Çatak
Başkale
Hakkâri
Yüksekova
Şemdinli
Cilo Dağı 4135
Beytüşşebap
Uludere
Şırnak
Eruh
Siverek
Kâhta
Çınar
Bismil
Dicle Nehri
Gercüş
Hilvan
Atatürk Barajı
Viranşehir
Derik
Mardin
Midyat
Kızıltepe
Nusaybin
Cizre
Silopi
Şanlıurfa (Urfa)
Suruç
Akçakale
Ceylânpınar
Fırat (Euphrates)
Murat
Mākū
Khvoy
Evowghlī
Qoţūr
Seydvān
Marand
Jolfa
Ahar
Tabrīz
Salmās
Sharafkhāneh
Daryācheh-ye Orūmīyeh
Qūshchī
Orūmīyeh (Urmia)
Lake Urmia
Āzar Shahr
Kūh-e Sahand 3722
Marāgheh
Bostānābād
Torkamān
Mīāneh
Azarān
Sarāb
Ardabīl
Kūhhā-ye Sabalān 4824
Namīn
Nīr
Tālesh
Bandar-e Anzalī
Rasht
Khalkhāl
Āgh Kand
Qezel Owzan
Fowman
Benāb
Malek Kandī
Mīāndowāb
Mahābād
Naqadeh
Sa'in Dezh
Mehrābād
Nīk Pey
Zanjān
Sīrdān
Bīnāb
Abhar
Bowkān
Takāb
Saqqez
Tūp Āghāj
Qīdār
Qūţībād
Bāneh
Dīvāndarreh
Bījār
Sanandaj
Marīvān
Hoseynābād
Khosrowābād
Razan
Qorveh
Dehgolān
Bahār
Hamadān
Asadābād
Sonqor
Tūysarkān
Pāveh
Qeshlāq
Kal Safīd
Kāmyārān
Ravānsar
Kangāvar
Şahneh
Bīsotūn
Harsīn
Malāyer
Nahāvand
Bākhtarān
Karand
Eslāmābād-e Gharb
Oshtorīnān
Borūjerd
Jūy Zar
Īlām
Khorramābād
Mehrān
Dehlorān
Andīmeshk
Dezfūl
Shūsh
Sūsangerd
Zākhū
Al 'Amādīyah
Dihōk
'Aqrah
Rawāndūz
Arbīl
Qal'at Dīzah
Kūysanjaq
Ţaqţaq
Altūn Kūpri
As Sulaymānīyah
Chamchamal
Arbat
Halabjah
Kirkūk
Ţāzah Khurmātū
Ţūz Khurmātū
Maydān
Kifrī
Khānaqīn
Jalūlā
Naftshahr
Al Miqdādīyah
Ba'qūbah
Balad
Mandalī
Balad Rūz
Jāsimīyah
Banī Sa'd
Al Khāliş
BAGHDĀD
Al Kāzimīyah
Tursāq
Zurbāţīyah
Badrah
Al 'Azīzīyah
Al Kūt
Shaykh Sa'd
'Alī al Gharbī
'Alī ash Sharqī
Hawr as Sa'dīyah
Al 'Amārah
Qal'at Sukkar
Al Hayy
'Afak
Ad Dīwānīyah
Ash Shāmīyah
Al Kūfah
An Najaf
Al Hillah
BABYLON
Al Hindīyah
Karbalā
Bahr al Milh
Ar Rahhālīyah
Al Musayyib
Al Mahmūdīyah
As Şuwayrah
An Nu'mānīyah
Nahr Dijlah (Tigris)
Fallūjah
Ar Ramādī
Hawr al Habbānīyah
Habbānīyah
Hīt
Sāhilīyah
Nahr al Furāt
Al Hadīthah
Fuhaymī
'Ānah
Mileh Tharthār
Ad Dujayl
Sāmarrā
Tikrīt
Ad Dawr
Bayjī
Ash Sharqāţ
Al Hadr
Makhmūr
Al Mawşil (Mosul)
NINAWĀ
Tall 'Afar
Sinjār
Ayn Zālah
Zāb al Kabīr
Zāb aş Şaghīr
W. ath Tharthār
Al Qāmishlī
Ra's al 'Ayn
Al Hasakah
Fadghāmī
Khābūr
Ar Raqqah
Ar Ruşāfah
Ma'din
Tibnī
Barsham
Dayr az Zawr
Buşayrah
Al Mayādīn
Al Qaţ'a
Abū Kamāl
Al Qā'im
Qusaybah
As Sukhnah
Al Arak
Tudmur
PALMYRA
Ar Rutbah
W. Hawrān
W. Rutga
W. al Ghudaf
W. al Ubayyid
Nukhayb
'Unāzah
East from Greenwich
COPYRIGHT GEORGE PHILIP LTD.

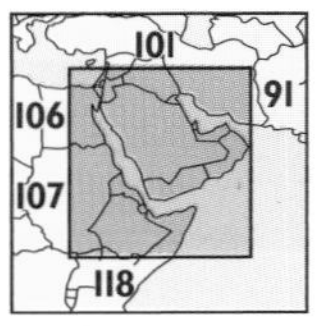
101
91
106
107
118

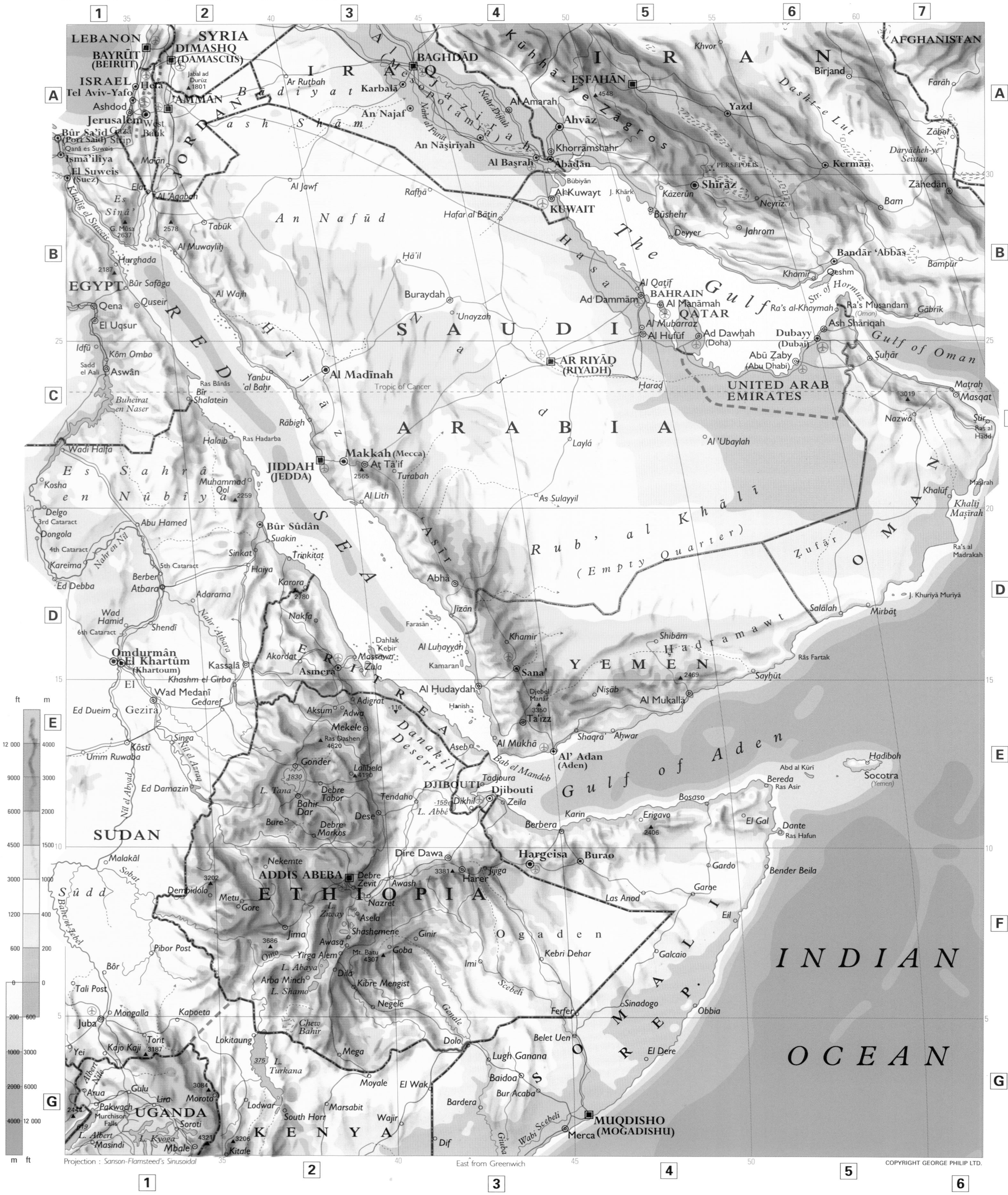
100 0 100 200 300 400 500 600 km
100 0 100 200 300 400 miles
LEBANON
BAYRŪT (BEIRUT)
SYRIA
DIMASHQ (DAMASCUS)
ISRAEL
Tel Aviv-Yafo
Haifa
Ashdod
Jerusalem
West Bank
Gaza Strip
Bûr Sa'îd (Port Said)
Qanâ es Suweis
Ismâ'ilîya
El Suweis (Suez)
'AMMĀN
JORDAN
Jabal ad Durūz 1801
Ma'ān
Elat
Al 'Aqabah
Es Sînâ'
G. Mûsa 2637
2578
Tabūk
Khalîg el Suweis
Al Muwaylih
Hurghada
2187
EGYPT
Bûr Safâga
Quseir
Qena
El Uqsur
Idfū
Kôm Ombo
Sadd el Aali
Aswân
Ras Bânâs
Bîr Shalatein
Buheirat en Naser
Halaib
Ras Hadarba
Wadi Halfa
Es Sahrâ en Nûbîya
Kosha
Delgo
3rd Cataract
Dongola
4th Cataract
Kareima
Nahr en Nil
Ed Debba
Muhammad Qol
2259
Abu Hamed
5th Cataract
Berber
Atbara
Adarama
Nahr 'Atbara
Wad Hamid
6th Cataract
Shendî
Omdurmân
El Khartûm (Khartoum)
Kassalâ
Khashm el Girba
Wad Medanî
Gedaref
Ed Dueim
Gezira
El
Singa
Kôstî
Nil el Azraq
Umm Ruwaba
Ed Damazin
Nil el Abyad
SUDAN
Malakâl
Sobat
Sûdd
Bahr el Jebel
Pibor Post
Bôr
Tali Post
Mongalla
Kapoeta
Juba
Torit
Kajo Kaji
3187
Yei
Albert Nile
Arua
Gulu
Lira
Moroto
3084
Pakwach
Murchison Falls
UGANDA
Soroti
2444
619
L. Albert
Masindi
L. Kyoga
Mbale
4321
3206
Kitale
Lokitaung
L. Turkana
375
Lodwar
South Horr
Marsabit
KENYA
Moyale
El Wak
Wajir
Dif
Bardera
Baidoa
Bur Acaba
Lugh Ganana
Belet Uen
Giuba
Wabi Scebeli
Merca
MUQDISHO (MOGADISHU)
Dolo
Mega
Chew Bahir
Negele
Ganale
Ferfer
Obbia
Sinadogo
El Dere
SOMALI REP.
Imi
Scebeli
Kebri Dehar
Galcaio
Ogaden
Eil
Garoe
Las Anod
Gardo
Bender Beila
Dante
Ras Hafun
El Gal
Bosaso
Bereda
Ras Asir
Erigavo
2406
Karin
Berbera
Burao
Hargeisa
Jijiga
Harer
3381
Dire Dawa
Debre Zevit
ADDIS ABEBA
Nekemte
ETHIOPIA
Awash
Nazret
Asela
L. Ziway
Shashemene
Ginir
Goba
Mt. Batu 4307
Awasa
Yirga Alem
L. Abaya
Arba Minch
L. Shamo
Dila
Kibre Mengist
Jima
3686
Omo
Gore
Metu
Dembidolo
3202
Bure
Debre Markos
Bahir Dar
L. Tana
1830
Debre Tabor
Gonder
Ras Dashen 4620
Lalibela
4190
Dese
Tendaho
L. Abbe
-155
Dikhil
DJIBOUTI
Djibouti
Tadjoura
Zeila
Bab el Mandeb
Aseb
Danakil Desert
-116
Mekele
Adwa
Aksum
Adigrat
Asmera
ERITREA
Akordat
Nakfa
Karora
2780
Massawa
Zula
Dahlak Kebir
Trinkitat
Suakin
Bûr Sûdân
Sinkat
Haiya
RED SEA
Farasan
Jīzān
Abha
'Asir
Al Luhayyah
Kamaran
Al Hudaydah
Hanish
Al Mukhā
Ta'izz
3350
Djebel Manār
Sana'
Khamir
Al' Adan (Aden)
Shaqra'
Ahwar
Nişab
Al Mukallā
2469
Sayhūt
Shibām
Hadramawt
YEMEN
Ras Fartak
Gulf of Aden
Abd al Kūrī
Socotra (Yemen)
Hadiboh
Salālah
Mirbāţ
J. Khuriyā Muriyā
Ra's al Madrakah
Zufār
OMAN
Khalīj Maşīrah
Maşīrah
Khalūf
Nazwá
3019
Maţraḩ
Masqat
Şūr
Ras al Hadd
Gulf of Oman
Şuḩār
UNITED ARAB EMIRATES
Dubayy (Dubai)
Abū Zaby (Abu Dhabi)
Ash Shāriqah
Ra's al-Khaymah
Ra's Musandam (Oman)
Str. of Hormuz
Qeshm
Khamir
Bandar 'Abbās
Gābrik
Bampūr
Ad Dawḩah (Doha)
QATAR
Al Manāmah
BAHRAIN
Al Qaţīf
Ad Dammām
Al Mubarraz
Al Hufūf
Harad
Al 'Ubaylah
Laylá
As Sulayyil
Rub' al Khālī (Empty Quarter)
AR RIYĀD (RIYADH)
SAUDI ARABIA
Najd
Tropic of Cancer
Al Madīnah
Yanbu 'al Bahr
Rābigh
Makkah (Mecca)
JIDDAH (JEDDA)
Aţ Ţā'if
2565
Turabah
Al Līth
Hijāz
'Unayzah
Buraydah
Hā'il
An Nafūd
Al Jawf
Al Wajh
Rafḩā
Hafar al Bāţin
Al Kuwayt
KUWAIT
Al Hasa
The Gulf
Būbiyān
Ar Rutbah
Bādiyat ash Shām
IRAQ
BAGHDĀD
Karbalā'
An Najaf
Al Jazīrah
Mesopotamia
Nahr al Furāt
Nahr Dijlah
An Nāşirīyah
Al Amarah
Al Başrah
Ābādān
Khorrāmshahr
Ahvāz
Kühhā-ye Zāgros
IRAN
EŞFAHĀN
4548
Khvor
Bīrjand
Yazd
Dasht-e Lut
PERSEPOLIS
Shīrāz
Kāzerūn
J. Khārk
Būshehr
Deyyer
Jahrom
Neyrīz
Kermān
Bam
Zābol
Daryācheh-ye Seistan
Zāhedān
Farāh
AFGHANISTAN
INDIAN OCEAN
ft m
12 000 4000
9000 3000
6000 2000
4500 1500
3000 1000
1200 400
600 200
0 0
200 600
1000 3000
2000 6000
4000 12 000
m ft
Projection : Sanson-Flamsteed's Sinusoidal
East from Greenwich

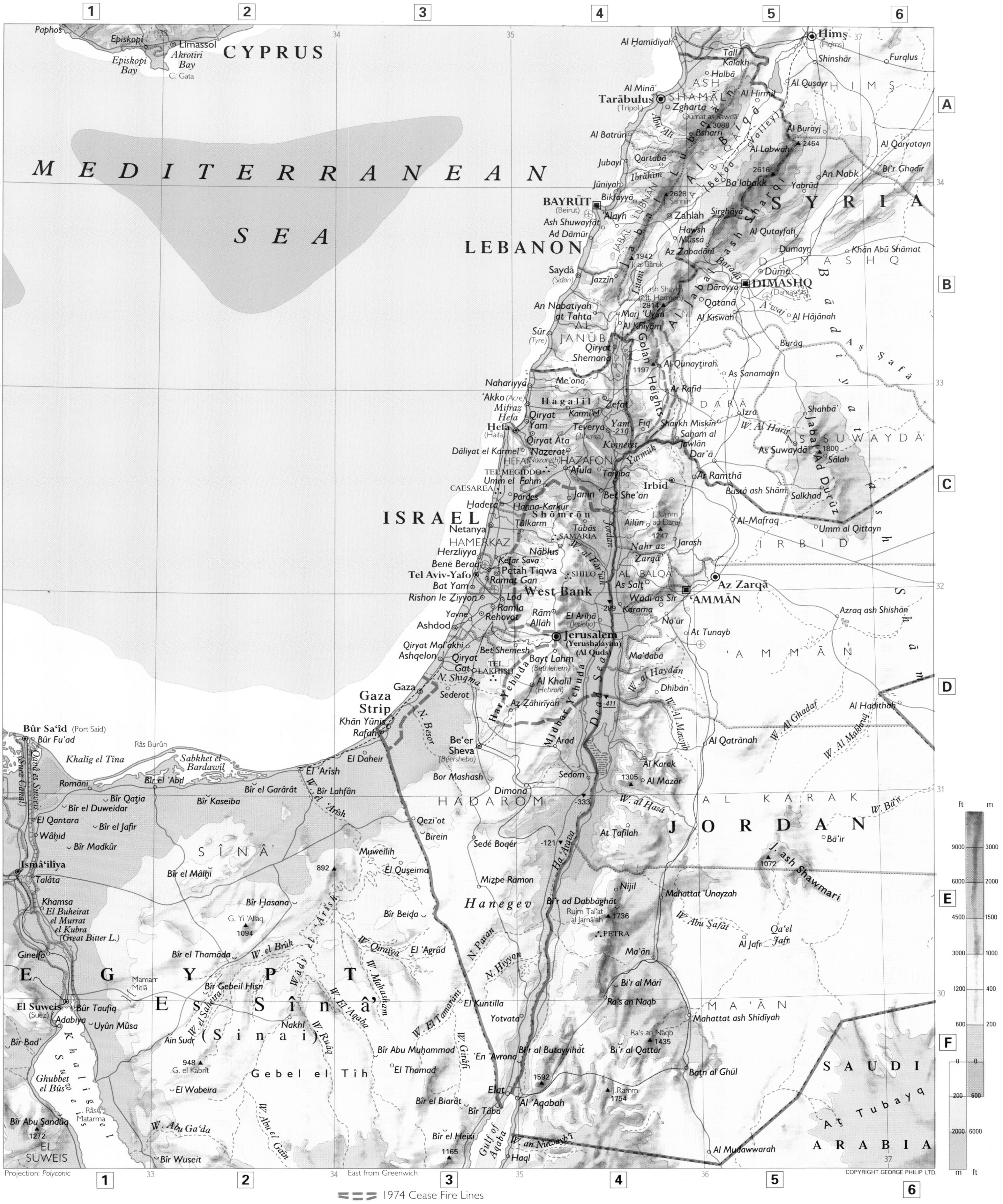
CYPRUS
Paphos
Episkopi
Limassol
Episkopi Bay
Akrotiri Bay
C. Gata
MEDITERRANEAN SEA
LEBANON
SYRIA
ISRAEL
JORDAN
EGYPT
SAUDI ARABIA
West Bank
Gaza Strip
Golan Heights
Dead Sea
Hims
Tarābulus (Tripoli)
BAYRŪT (Beirut)
DIMASHQ (Damascus)
Ṣaydā (Sidon)
Ṣūr (Tyre)
Ḥefa (Haifa)
Tel Aviv-Yafo
Jerusalem (Yerushalayim) (Al Quds)
'AMMĀN
Az Zarqā'
Irbid
Be'er Sheva (Beersheba)
Elat
Al 'Aqabah
Gulf of Aqaba
Gaza
Bûr Sa'îd (Port Said)
Ismâ'ilîya
El Suweis (Suez)
Khalîg el Suweis
Great Bitter L.
Qanâ es Suweis (Suez Canal)
Sînâ' (Sinai)
Gebel el Tîh
Hanegev
HADAROM
AL KARAK
MA'ĀN
Petra
Jabal ad Durūz
1974 Cease Fire Lines
Projection: Polyconic
East from Greenwich
COPYRIGHT GEORGE PHILIP LTD.

See page VIII World: Regions in the News
for a map showing the areas under Palestinian control.

AFRICA : Physical 1:33 600 000

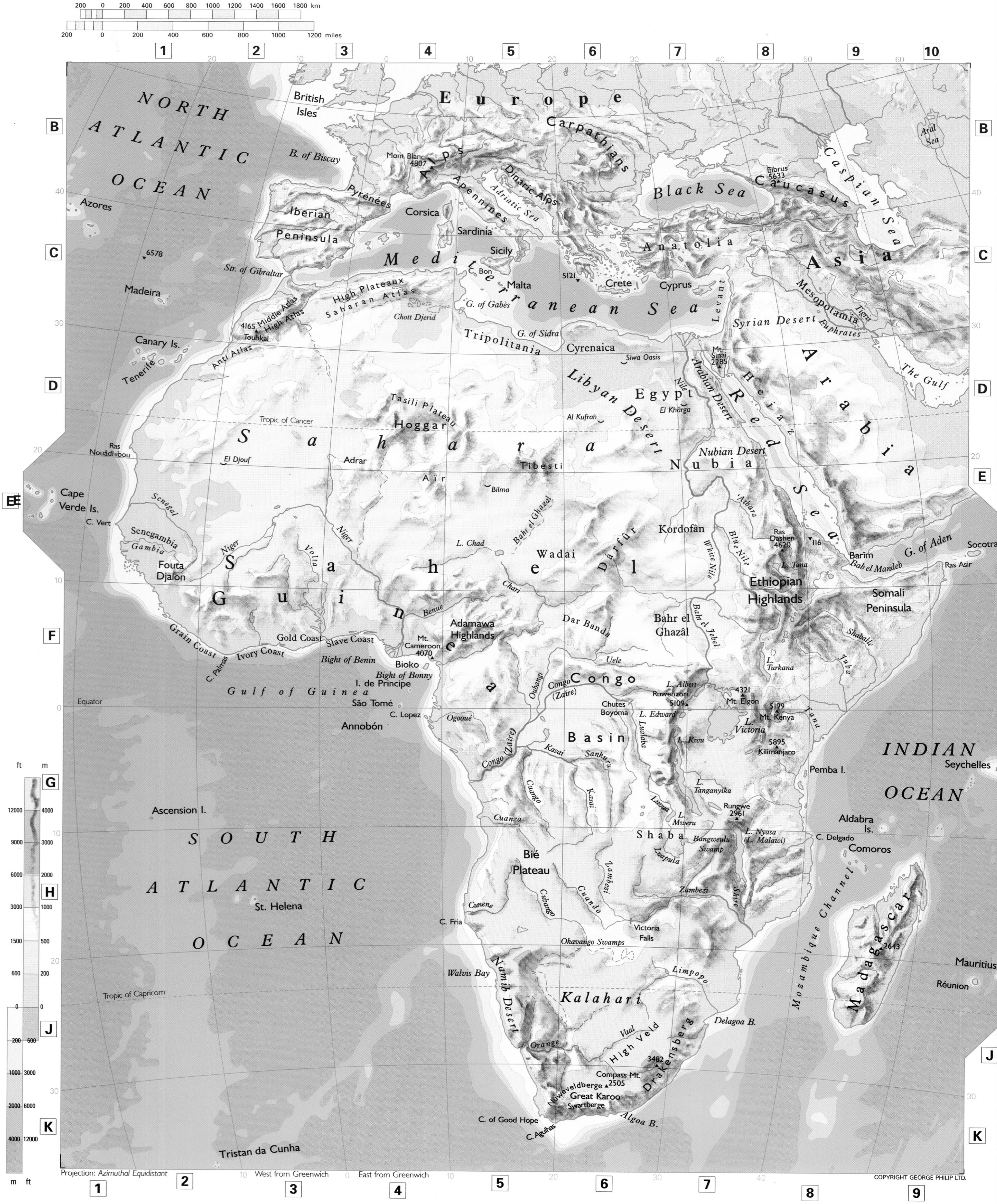
200 0 200 400 600 800 1000 1200 1400 1600 1800 km
200 0 200 400 600 800 1000 1200 miles
NORTH ATLANTIC OCEAN
Azores
6578
Madeira
Canary Is.
Tenerife
Ras Nouâdhibou
Cape Verde Is.
C. Vert
British Isles
B. of Biscay
Europe
Carpathians
Mont Blanc 4807
Alps
Pyrénées
Iberian Peninsula
Corsica
Sardinia
Apennines
Adriatic Sea
Dinaric Alps
Sicily
C. Bon
Malta
5121
Crete
Cyprus
Black Sea
Elbrus 5633
Caucasus
Caspian Sea
Aral Sea
Anatolia
Asia
Mesopotamia
Tigris
Euphrates
Syrian Desert
Levant
Mt. Sinai 2285
Arabia
The Gulf
Hejaz
Str. of Gibraltar
Mediterranean Sea
High Plateaux
Saharan Atlas
Middle Atlas
High Atlas
4165 Toubkal
Anti Atlas
Chott Djerid
G. of Gabès
G. of Sidra
Tripolitania
Cyrenaica
Siwa Oasis
Libyan Desert
Egypt
Nile
El Khârga
Arabian Desert
Red Sea
Al Kufrah
Tasili Plateau
Hoggar
Tropic of Cancer
Sahara
El Djouf
Adrar
Aïr
Bilma
Tibesti
Nubian Desert
Nubia
Atbara
Senegal
Senegambia
Gambia
Fouta Djalon
Niger
Volta
Sahel
L. Chad
Bahr el Ghazal
Wadai
Dârfûr
Kordofân
White Nile
Blue Nile
Ras Dashen 4620
116
L. Tana
Barīm
Bab el Mandeb
G. of Aden
Socotra
Ras Asir
Ethiopian Highlands
Somali Peninsula
Shaballe
Juba
Guinea
Chari
Benue
Adamawa Highlands
Dar Banda
Bahr el Ghazâl
Bahr el Jebel
Grain Coast
Ivory Coast
Gold Coast
Slave Coast
C. Palmas
Bight of Benin
Bight of Bonny
Mt. Cameroon 4070
Bioko
I. de Principe
São Tomé
Gulf of Guinea
Equator
C. Lopez
Annobón
Ogooué
Oubangi
Uele
Congo (Zaïre)
Congo Basin
L. Albert
Ruwenzori 5109
4321 Mt. Elgon
5199 Mt. Kenya
Tana
L. Turkana
Chutes Boyoma
L. Edward
Lualaba
L. Kivu
L. Victoria
5895 Kilimanjaro
Kasai
Sankuru
Cuango
Kasai
L. Tanganyika
Luvua
L. Mweru
Rungwe 2961
Pemba I.
INDIAN OCEAN
Seychelles
Aldabra Is.
C. Delgado
Comoros
Cuanza
Shaba
Bangweulu Swamp
L. Nyasa (L. Malawi)
Luapula
Bié Plateau
Zambezi
Shire
Mozambique Channel
Madagascar
2643
Mauritius
Réunion
Ascension I.
SOUTH ATLANTIC OCEAN
St. Helena
Cunene
Cubango
Cuando
C. Fria
Victoria Falls
Okavango Swamps
Walvis Bay
Namib Desert
Limpopo
Kalahari
Tropic of Capricorn
Delagoa B.
Orange
Vaal
High Veld
Drakensberg
3482
Compass Mt. 2505
Nuweveldberge
Great Karoo
Swartberge
Algoa B.
C. of Good Hope
C. Agulhas
Tristan da Cunha
ft m
12000 4000
9000 3000
6000 2000
3000 1000
1500 500
600 200
0 0
200 600
1000 3000
2000 6000
4000 12000
m ft
Projection: Azimuthal Equidistant
West from Greenwich
East from Greenwich

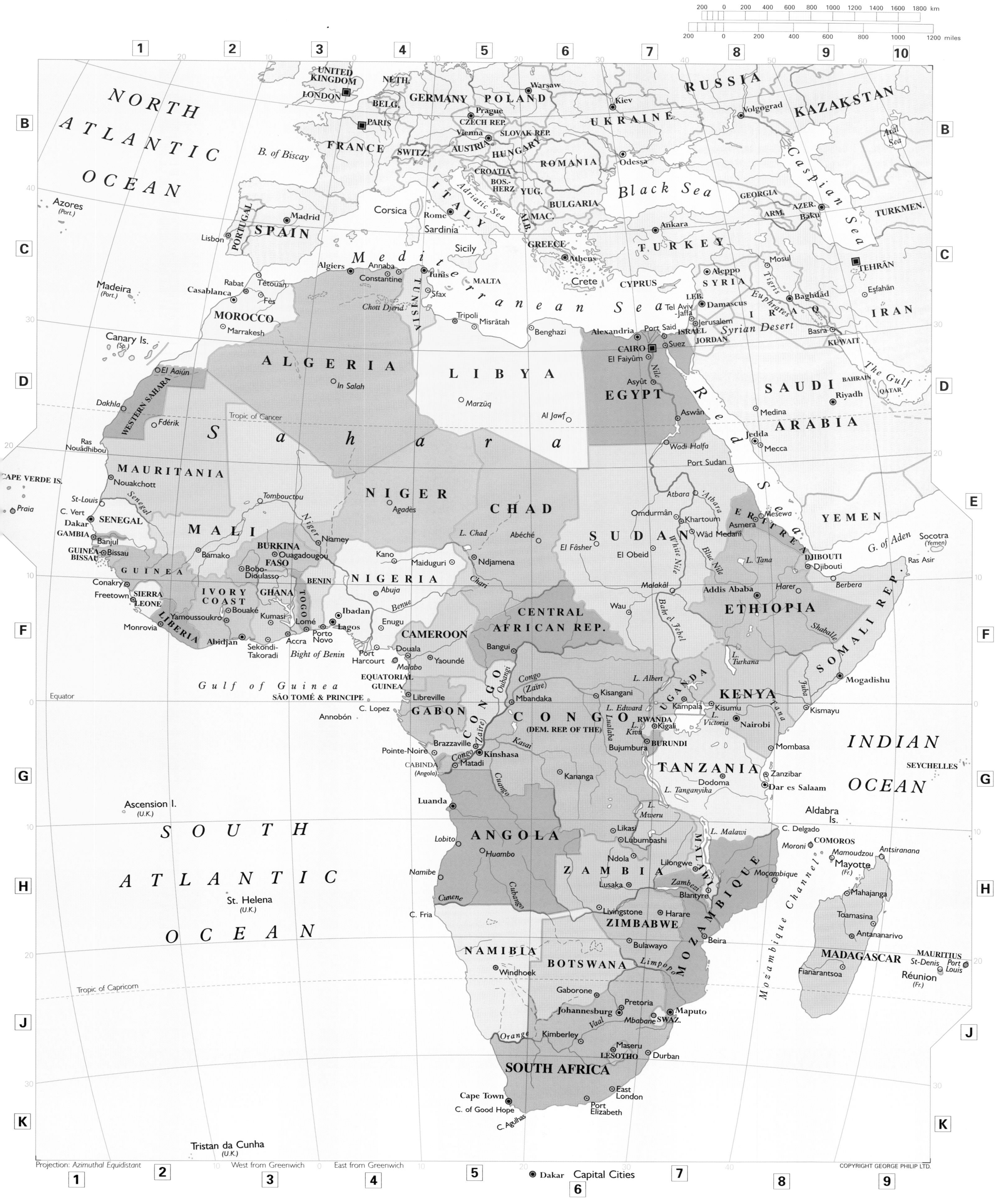

200 0 200 400 600 800 1000 1200 1400 1600 1800 km
200 0 200 400 600 800 1000 1200 miles
NORTH ATLANTIC OCEAN
Azores (Port.)
Madeira (Port.)
Canary Is. (Sp.)
CAPE VERDE IS.
Praia
B. of Biscay
UNITED KINGDOM
LONDON
NETH.
BELG.
PARIS
FRANCE
SWITZ.
GERMANY
POLAND
Warsaw
Prague
CZECH REP.
Vienna
SLOVAK REP.
AUSTRIA
HUNGARY
CROATIA
BOS.-HERZ.
YUG.
ROMANIA
BULGARIA
MAC.
ALB.
GREECE
Athens
Crete
ITALY
Rome
Corsica
Sardinia
Sicily
MALTA
Adriatic Sea
PORTUGAL
Lisbon
SPAIN
Madrid
RUSSIA
Kiev
UKRAINE
Odessa
Volgograd
KAZAKSTAN
Aral Sea
Caspian Sea
Black Sea
GEORGIA
ARM.
AZER.
Baku
TURKMEN.
TURKEY
Ankara
CYPRUS
SYRIA
Aleppo
Mosul
Tigris
Euphrates
Baghdād
TEHRĀN
Esfahān
IRAN
IRAQ
LEB.
Damascus
Tel Aviv-Jaffa
Jerusalem
ISRAEL
JORDAN
Syrian Desert
Basra
KUWAIT
The Gulf
BAHRAIN
QATAR
Riyadh
SAUDI ARABIA
Medina
Jedda
Mecca
YEMEN
Socotra (Yemen)
G. of Aden
Mediterranean Sea
Algiers
Annaba
Tunis
Constantine
Sfax
TUNISIA
Chott Djerid
Tripoli
Misrātah
Benghazi
Rabat
Tétouan
Casablanca
Fès
MOROCCO
Marrakesh
ALGERIA
In Salah
LIBYA
Marzūq
Al Jawf
Alexandria
Port Said
CAIRO
Suez
El Faiyûm
Asyût
Nile
EGYPT
Aswân
Red Sea
El Aaiún
WESTERN SAHARA
Dakhla
Fdérik
Tropic of Cancer
Sahara
Ras Nouâdhibou
MAURITANIA
Nouakchott
Senegal
St-Louis
C. Vert
Dakar
SENEGAL
GAMBIA
Banjul
GUINEA-BISSAU
Bissau
GUINEA
Conakry
Freetown
SIERRA LEONE
Monrovia
LIBERIA
Tombouctou
MALI
Bamako
Niger
BURKINA FASO
Ouagadougou
Bobo-Dioulasso
Niamey
NIGER
Agadès
IVORY COAST
Yamoussoukro
Bouaké
Abidjan
GHANA
Kumasi
Sekondi-Takoradi
Accra
TOGO
Lomé
BENIN
Porto Novo
NIGERIA
Kano
Maiduguri
Abuja
Benue
Ibadan
Lagos
Enugu
Port Harcourt
Bight of Benin
Gulf of Guinea
CHAD
L. Chad
Abéché
Ndjamena
Chari
SUDAN
Wadi Halfa
Port Sudan
Atbara
Omdurmân
Khartoum
Wâd Medanî
El Fâsher
El Obeid
White Nile
Blue Nile
Malakâl
Wau
Bahr el Jebel
ERITREA
Asmera
Mesewa
DJIBOUTI
Djibouti
Ras Asir
Berbera
L. Tana
ETHIOPIA
Addis Ababa
Harer
Shaballe
SOMALI REP.
Mogadishu
Juba
Kismayu
CAMEROON
Douala
Yaoundé
Malabo
EQUATORIAL GUINEA
SÃO TOMÉ & PRINCIPE
Annobón
C. Lopez
Libreville
GABON
CENTRAL AFRICAN REP.
Bangui
Oubangi
Congo (Zaïre)
Mbandaka
CONGO
Brazzaville
Pointe-Noire
CABINDA (Angola)
Kinshasa
Matadi
CONGO (DEM. REP. OF THE)
Kisangani
Kasai
Lualaba
Kananga
Cuango
L. Albert
L. Edward
L. Kivu
UGANDA
Kampala
Kisumu
L. Victoria
KENYA
Nairobi
Tana
Mombasa
RWANDA
Kigali
BURUNDI
Bujumbura
TANZANIA
Dodoma
Zanzibar
Dar es Salaam
L. Tanganyika
L. Mweru
Equator
INDIAN OCEAN
SEYCHELLES
Aldabra Is.
C. Delgado
COMOROS
Moroni
Mamoudzou
Mayotte (Fr.)
Antsiranana
Mahajanga
Toamasina
Antananarivo
MADAGASCAR
Fianarantsoa
MAURITIUS
St-Denis
Port Louis
Réunion (Fr.)
Mozambique Channel
Ascension I. (U.K.)
SOUTH ATLANTIC OCEAN
St. Helena (U.K.)
Tristan da Cunha (U.K.)
Luanda
ANGOLA
Lobito
Huambo
Namibe
Cunene
Cubango
C. Fria
Likasi
Lubumbashi
L. Malawi
MALAWI
Lilongwe
Blantyre
Ndola
ZAMBIA
Lusaka
Zambezi
MOZAMBIQUE
Moçambique
Livingstone
Harare
ZIMBABWE
Bulawayo
Beira
Limpopo
NAMIBIA
Windhoek
BOTSWANA
Gaborone
Tropic of Capricorn
Pretoria
Johannesburg
Maputo
Mbabane
SWAZ.
Vaal
Orange
Kimberley
Maseru
LESOTHO
Durban
SOUTH AFRICA
Cape Town
C. of Good Hope
C. Agulhas
East London
Port Elizabeth
Projection: Azimuthal Equidistant
West from Greenwich
East from Greenwich
Dakar Capital Cities
COPYRIGHT GEORGE PHILIP LTD.

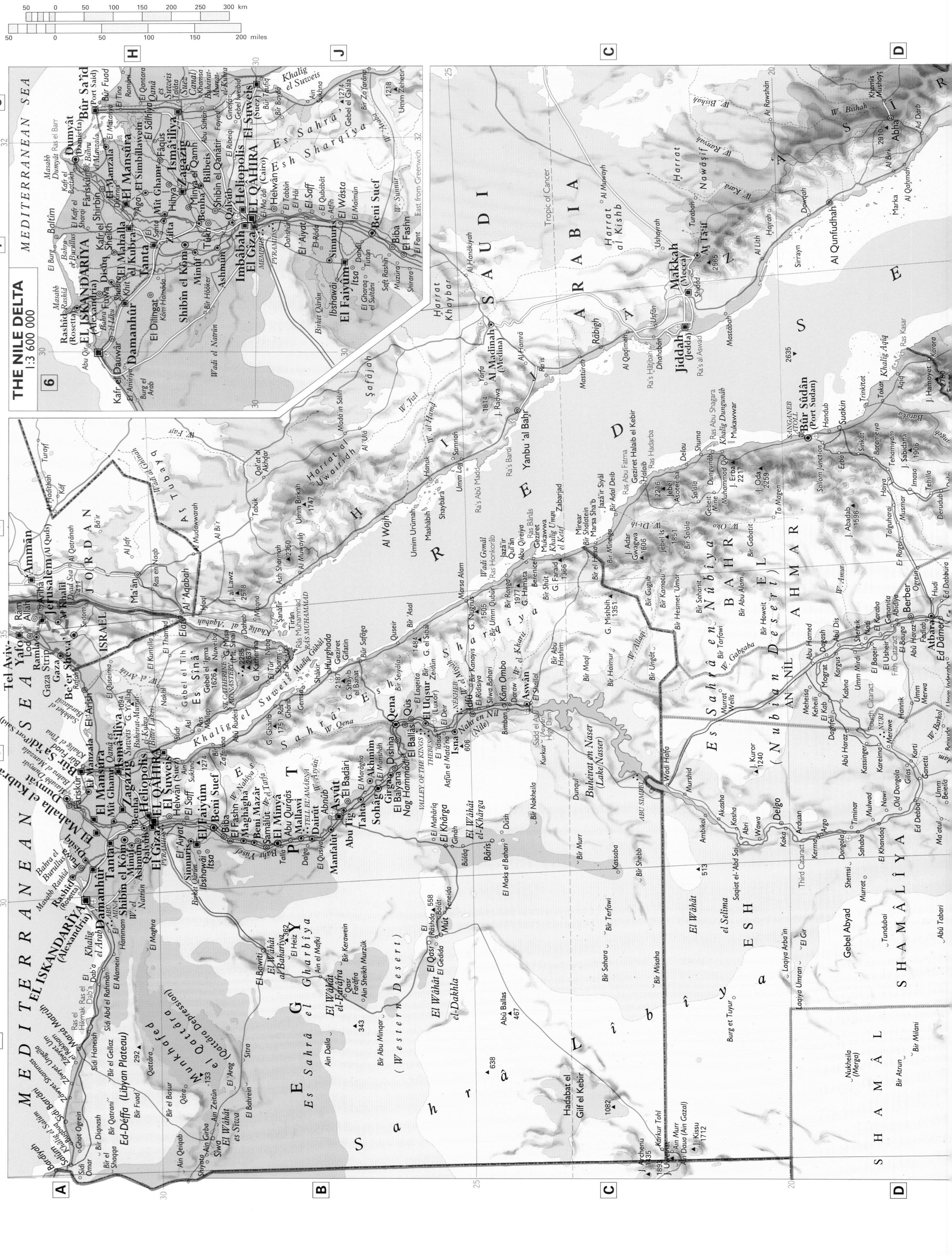
km
miles
THE NILE DELTA
1:3 600 000
MEDITERRANEAN SEA
East from Greenwich
EL ISKANDARÎYA
(Alexandria)
Rashîd
(Rosetta)
Damanhûr
Tanta
El Mansûra
Dumyât
Bûr Sa'îd
(Port Said)
Zagazig
Ismâ'ilîya
Banha
Heliopolis
EL QÂHIRA
(Cairo)
El Gîza
Helwân
El Suweis
(Suez)
El Faiyûm
Beni Suef
MEDITERRANEAN SEA
JORDAN
ISRAEL
Jerusalem
Amman
Tel Aviv-Yafo
Gaza
Be'er Sheva'
Ma'ân
El 'Arîsh
Es Sînâ
Khalîg el Suweis
El Minya
Asyût
Sohâg
Qena
El Uqsur
(Luxor)
Aswân
Buheirat en Naser
(Lake Nasser)
Wadi Halfa
El Wâhât el Khârga
El Wâhât el-Dakhla
El Wâhât el Farâfra
El Wâhât el Bahariya
Siwa
Es Sahrâ el Gharbîya
(Western Desert)
Es Sahrâ esh Sharqîya
Munkhafad el Qattâra
(Qattara Depression)
Ed-Déffa (Libyan Plateau)
Sahrâ' Lîbîya
Hadabat el Gilf el Kebir
Es Sahrâ en Nûbîya
(Nubian Desert)
Bahr el Ahmar
Red Sea
SAUDI ARABIA
Al Madinah
(Medina)
Yanbu 'al Bahr
Makkah
(Mecca)
Jiddah
(Jedda)
At Ta'if
Al Qunfudhah
Abha
Al Wajh
Tabûk
Tropic of Cancer
Bûr Sûdân
(Port Sudan)
Suakin
Atbara
Ed Dâmer
Berber
Dongola
Karima
Merowe
Delgo
Third Cataract
Fourth Cataract
Fifth Cataract
ESH SHAMÂLÎYA
Gebel Abyad
El Wâhât el Selîma

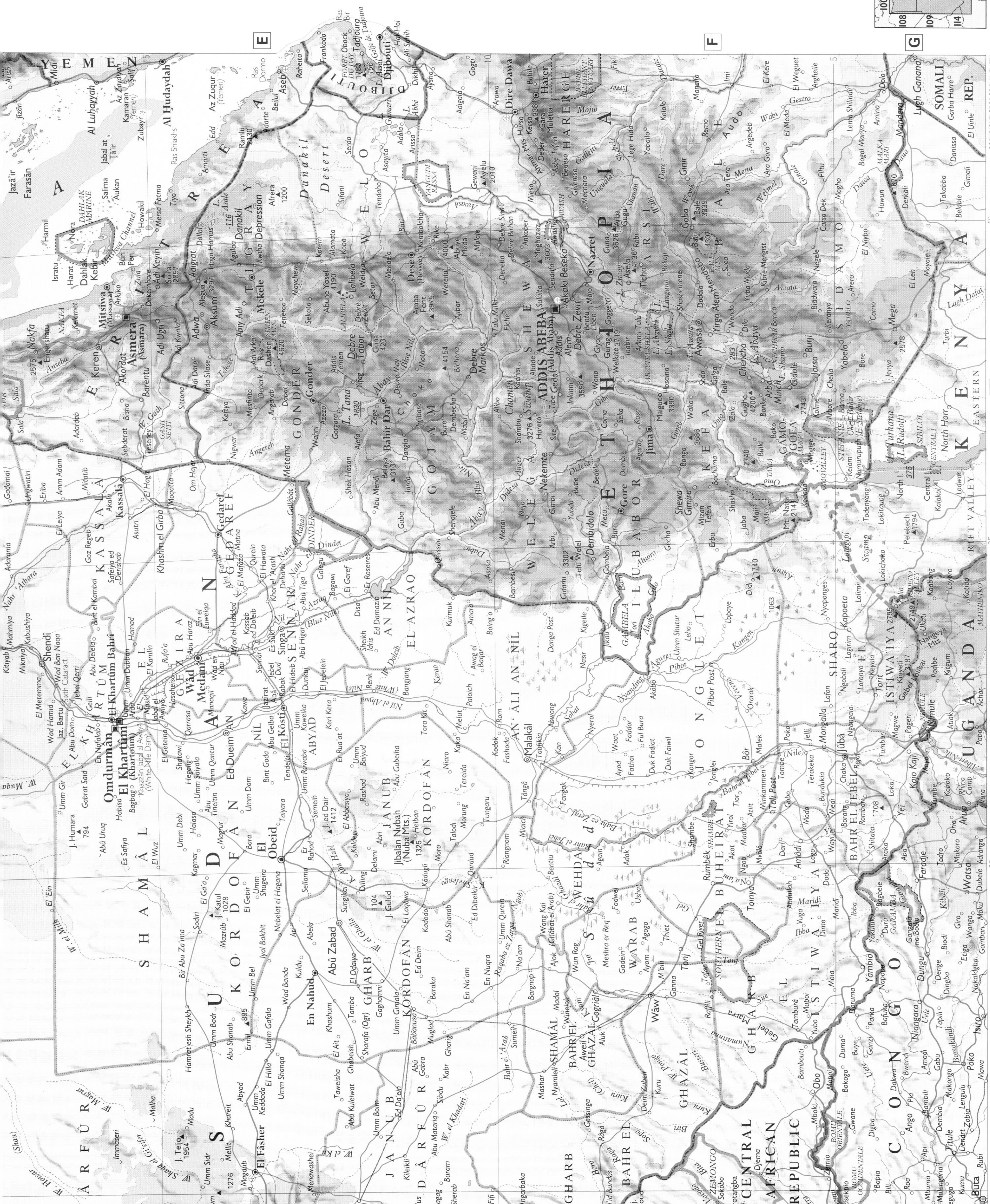

YEMEN
ERITREA
DJIBOUTI
ETHIOPIA
SUDAN
KENYA
UGANDA
CONGO
CENTRAL AFRICAN REPUBLIC
SOMALI REP.
El Khartûm (Khartoum)
Omdurmân
Asmera (Asmara)
Djibouti
ADDIS ABEBA (Addis Ababa)
Dire Dawa
Harer
Gonder
Bahir Dar
Dese
Nazret
Jima
Kassala
Gedaref
Wad Medanî
El Obeid
En Nahud
El Fâsher
Malakâl
Wâw
Juba
L. Tana
L. Turkana (L. Rudolf)
Danakil Depression
Danakil Desert
Mitsiwa (Massawa)
Aseb
Berbera
Dahlak Kebir
Jibalan Nubah (Nuba Mts.)
Sudd
Bahr el Ghazal
Bahr el Jebel
East from Greenwich
Projection: Lambert's Equivalent Azimuthal
COPYRIGHT GEORGE PHILIP LTD.

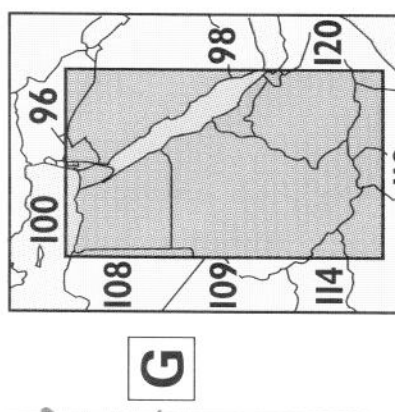

100
96
98
120
108
109
114
118

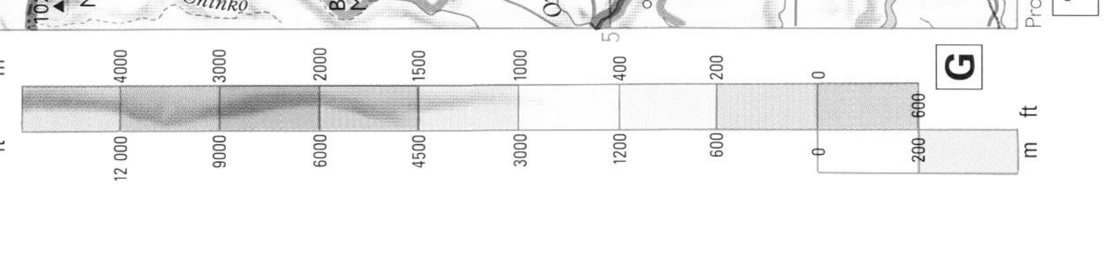

m
4000
3000
2000
1500
1000
400
200
0
200
600
ft
12 000
9000
6000
4500
3000
1200
600
0

National Parks

Nature Reserves and Game Reserves

∴ UNESCO World Heritage Sites

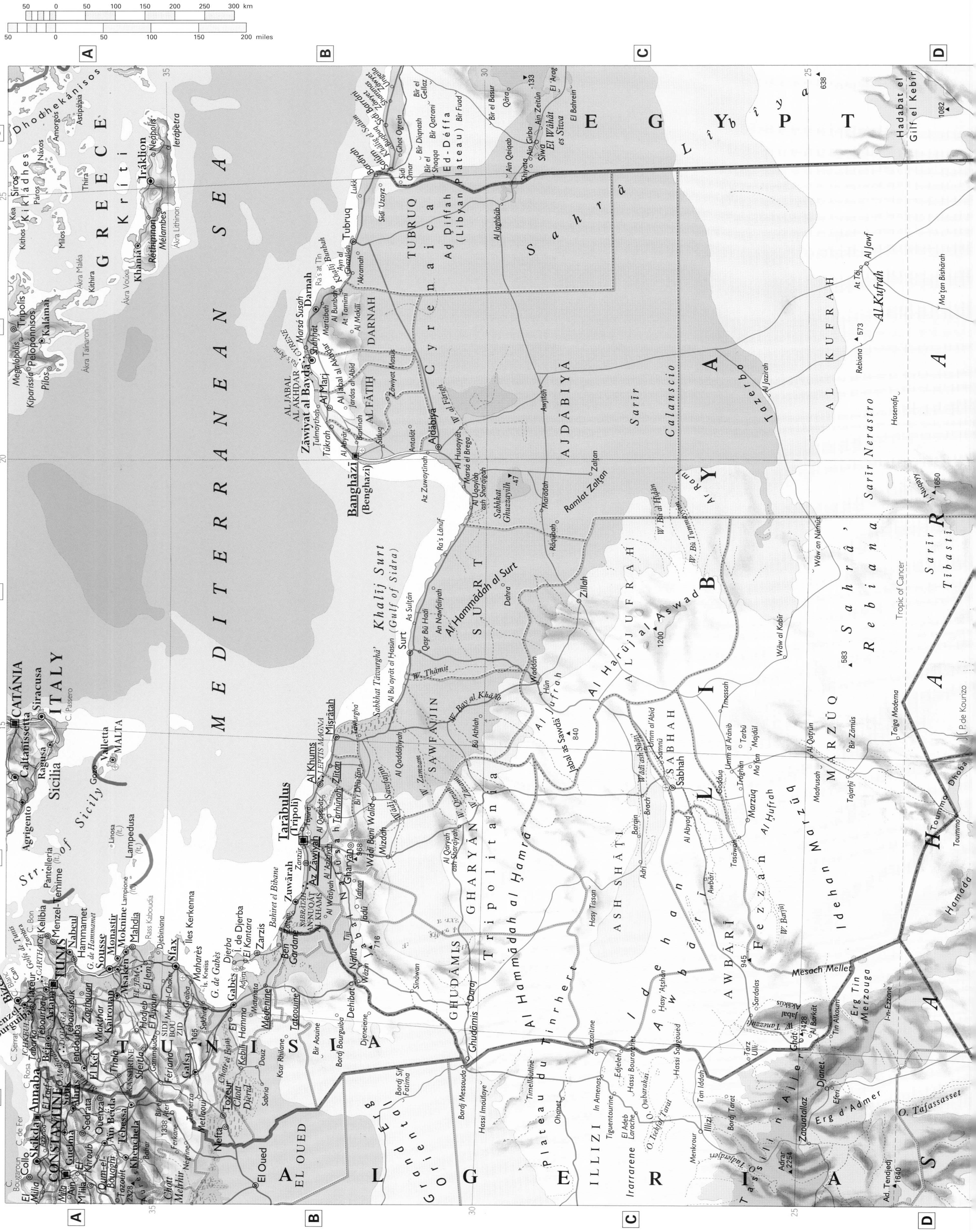
50 0 50 100 150 200 250 300 km
50 0 50 100 150 200 miles
MEDITERRANEAN SEA
GREECE
Kríti
Iráklion
ITALY
CATÁNIA
Sicilia
MALTA
Valletta
Str. of Sicily
TUNIS
Sfax
Sousse
Gabès
Tarābulus (Tripoli)
Banghāzī (Benghazi)
Khalij Surt (Gulf of Sidra)
Tripolitania
Cyrenaica
Fezzan
LIBYA
EGYPT
ALGERIA
Al Kufrah
Sabhah
Tobruq
Darnah
Tropic of Cancer

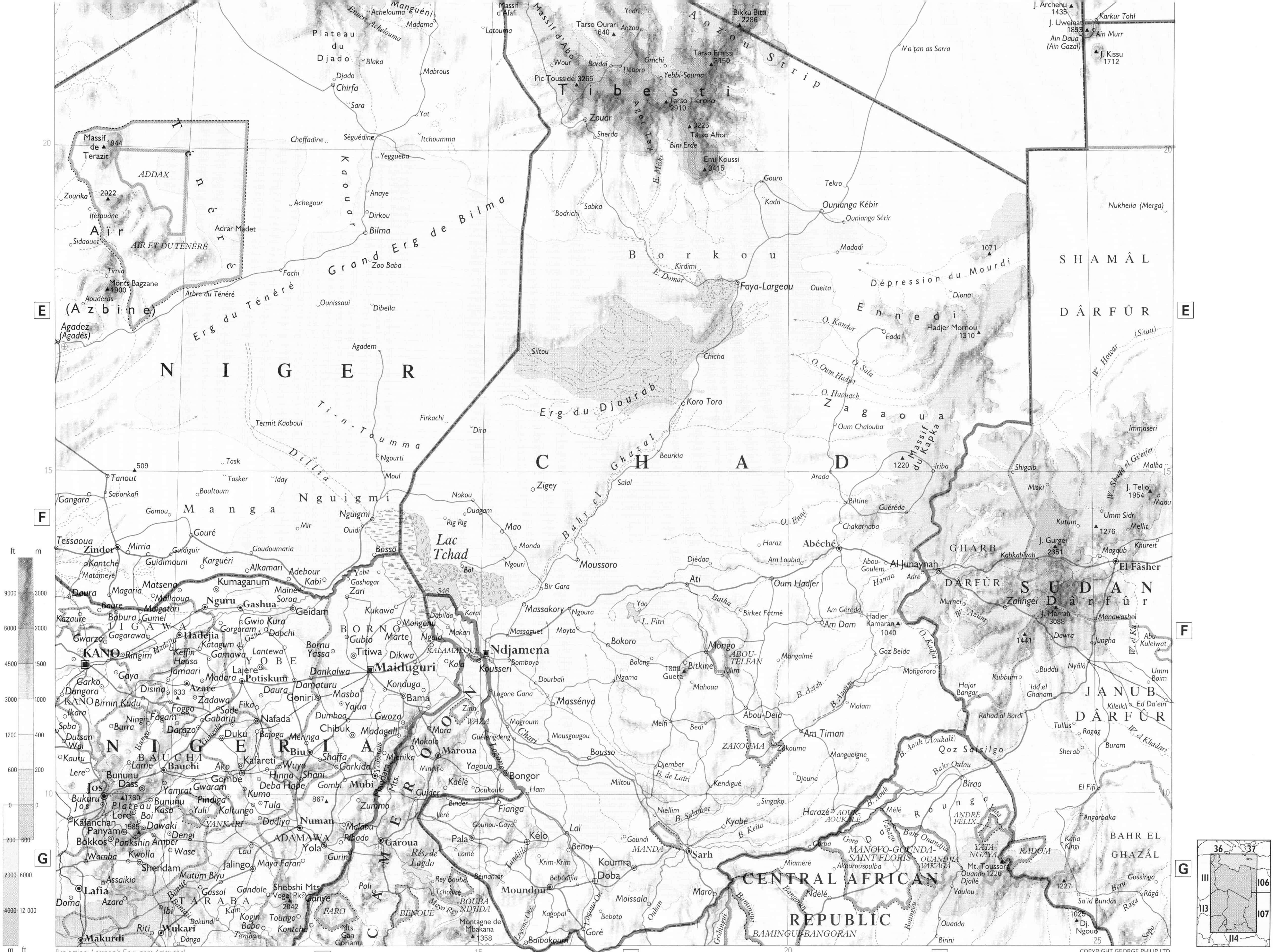
NIGER
CHAD
NIGERIA
CAMEROON
CENTRAL AFRICAN REPUBLIC
SUDAN
SHAMÂL DÂRFÛR
GHARB DÂRFÛR
JANUB DÂRFÛR
BAHR EL GHAZÂL
Tibesti
Aozou Strip
Borkou
Ennedi
Dépression du Mourdi
Zagaoua
Erg du Djourab
Erg du Ténéré
Grand Erg de Bilma
Ténéré
Aïr (Azbine)
Plateau du Djado
Kaouar
Manga
Nguigmi
Ti-n-Toumma
Dillia
Lac Tchad
Bahr el Ghazal
Massif du Kapka
Tarso Emissi 3150
Emi Koussi 3415
Bikku Bitti 2286
Pic Toussidé 3265
Tarso Tieroko 2910
Tarso Ahon 3225
J. Marrah 3088
Agadez (Agadès)
Bilma
Zinder
Faya-Largeau
Abéché
Ndjamena
Maiduguri
KANO
Sarh
Moundou
Bongor
Am Timan
Mongo
Al Junaynah
El Fâsher
Garoua
Maroua
Yola
Jos
Bauchi
Makurdi
Projection: Lambert's Equivalent Azimuthal
COPYRIGHT GEORGE PHILIP LTD.

National Parks

Nature Reserves and Game Reserves

∴ UNESCO World Heritage Sites

Underlined towns give their name to the administrative area in which they stand.

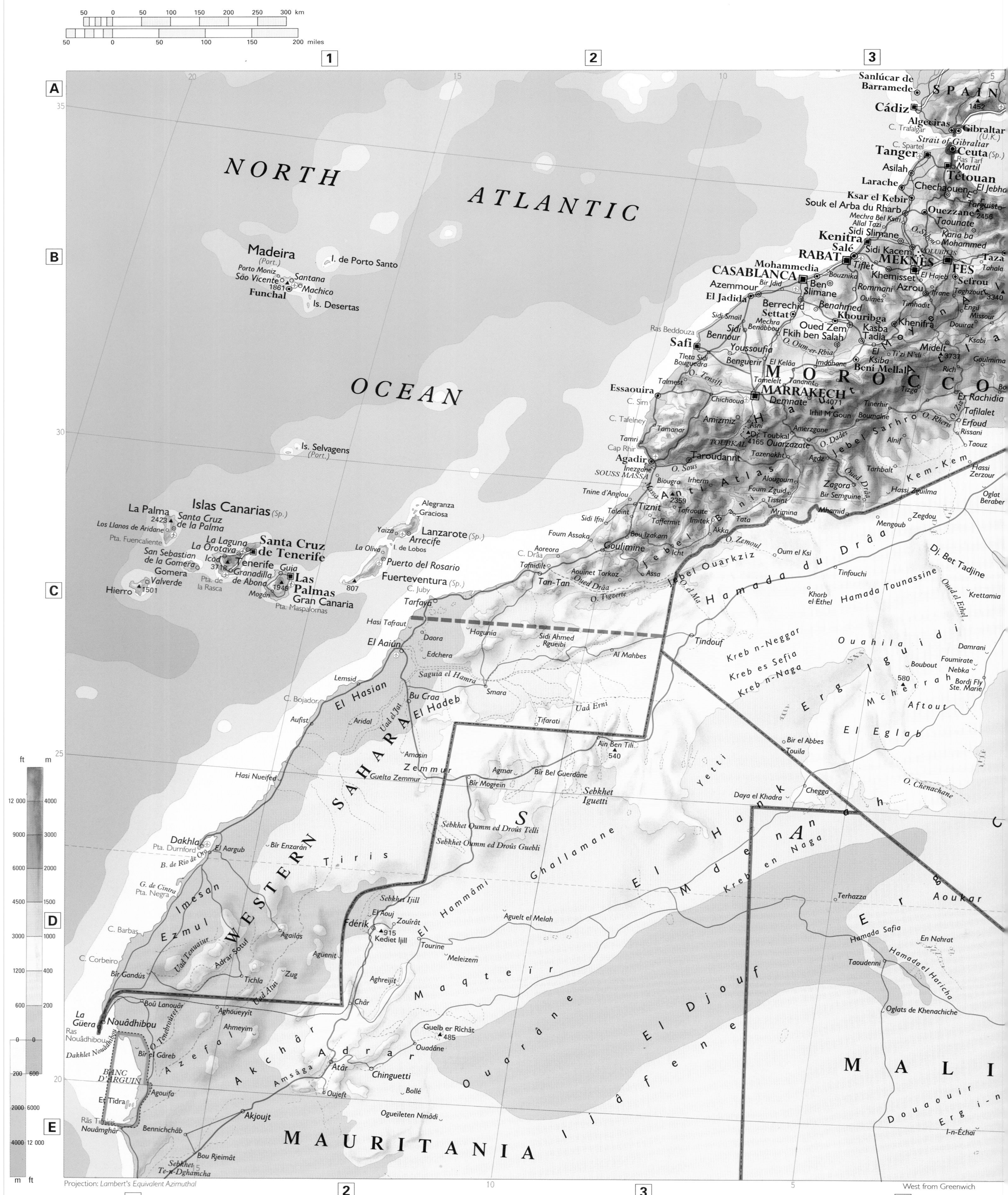
NORTH ATLANTIC OCEAN
Madeira (Port.)
I. de Porto Santo
Funchal
Is. Desertas
Is. Selvagens (Port.)
Islas Canarias (Sp.)
La Palma
Santa Cruz de Tenerife
Las Palmas
Gran Canaria
Tenerife
Gomera
Hierro
Lanzarote (Sp.)
Fuerteventura (Sp.)
Arrecife
Puerto del Rosario
SPAIN
Cádiz
Gibraltar (U.K.)
Strait of Gibraltar
Ceuta (Sp.)
Tanger
Tétouan
Kenitra
RABAT
Salé
MEKNÈS
FES
CASABLANCA
El Jadida
Safi
Essaouira
MARRAKECH
Agadir
MOROCCO
Jebel Toubkal 4165
Ouarzazate
Tiznit
Goulimine
Tan-Tan
Tarfaya
El Aaiún
Smara
Tindouf
WESTERN SAHARA
Dakhla
Zemmur
MAURITANIA
Nouâdhibou
Akjoujt
Atâr
Chinguetti
MALI
Taoudenni
El Djouf
Hamada du Drâa
Erg Iguidi
Projection: Lambert's Equivalent Azimuthal
West from Greenwich

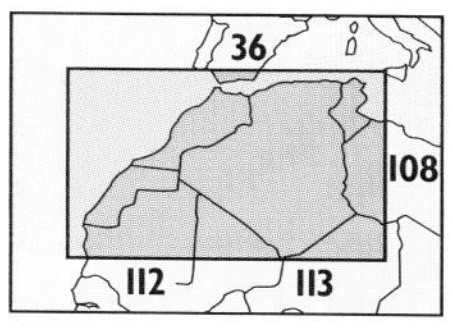
36
108
112
113

4
5
6
7
A
B
C
D
E
MEDITERRANEAN SEA
Granada
Almería
Antequera
MÁLAGA
Motril
Huércal-Overa
C. de Gata
I. de Alborán (Sp.)
ALGER (Algiers)
Blida
Médéa
Tizi-Ouzou
Bejaïa
Jijel
Skikda
Annaba
CONSTANTINE
Sétif
Batna
Biskra
Tébessa
ORAN (Ouahran)
Mostaganem
Arzew (Arseu)
Mascara
Relizane
Tiaret
Sidi-bel-Abbès
Tlemcen
Saïda
Melilla
Nador
Oujda
Al Hoceïma
Taourirt
Guercif
Figuig
Béchar
Beni Ounif
Kenadsa
Abadla
El Bayadh
Mecheria
Naama
Aïn Sefra
Laghouat
Djelfa
Bou Saâda
M'sila
Messaad
Aflou
Ghardaïa
Berriane
Guerara
Ouargla
Hassi Messaoud
Touggourt
El Oued
Guemar
Djamâa
El Meghaier
Tolga
Ouled Djellal
El Goléa
Timimoun
Adrar
In Salah
Zaouiet Reggâne
Beni Abbès
Kerzaz
Tamanrasset
Djanet
Illizi
In Amenas
Bordj Omar Driss
Hassi Tartrat
Bordj Messouda
Tin Alkoum
Abalessa
Silet
Tit
Tahat 2918
Assekrem
Bordj-in-Eker
Idelès
Ifetesene 1680
Garet el Djenoun 2327
Adrar 2254
Adrar Edekel 2306
Adrar Tendjedi 1640
Timeïaouine 598
Tessalit
Aguelhok
Poste Maurice Cortier
Tin Atanai
Aoulef el Arab
Akabli
Taoudrart
A L G E R I A
Grand Erg Occidental
Grand Erg Oriental
Plateau du Tademaït
Plateau du Tinrhert
Erg Iguidi
Erg er Raoui
Tidikelt
Tanezrouft
Ahaggar
Tassili n'Ajjer
Tassili-Oua-n-Ahaggar
Adrar des Iforas
Erg Chech
Hamada Manguéni
Plateau du Djado
Atlas Saharien
Hauts Plateaux
Chott Melrhir
Chott ech Chergui
Chott el Hodna
Tropic of Cancer
TUNIS
Bizerte (Binzert)
Sousse
Sfax
Kairouan
Gabès
Gafsa
Tozeur
Nefta
Kebili
Médenine
Tataouine
Zarzis
Djerba
Monastir
Mahdia
Nabeul
Hammamet
Kelibia
Menzel-Temime
Îles Kerkenna
Chott Djerid
Chott el Fejaj
TUNISIA
Sicilia
Marsala
Pantelleria (It.)
Linosa (It.)
Lampione (It.)
Lampedusa (It.)
TARĀBULUS (Tripoli)
Zuwārah
Az Zāwiyah
Gharyān
Yafran
Nālūt
Ghudāmis
GHUDĀMIS
GHARYĀN
Al Hammādah al Ḥamrā
Idehan Awbārī
AWBĀRĪ
Ghāt
Sardalas
MARZŪQ
Idehān Marzūq
ASH SHAṬI
Adri
LIBYA
NIGER
AÏR ET DU TÉNÉRÉ
ADDAX
Massif de Terazit 1944
Djado
Chirfa
Séguédine
Yat
Bilma
Mabrous
East from Greenwich

COPYRIGHT, GEORGE PHILIP LTD.

National Parks

Nature Reserves and Game Reserves

∴ UNESCO World Heritage Sites

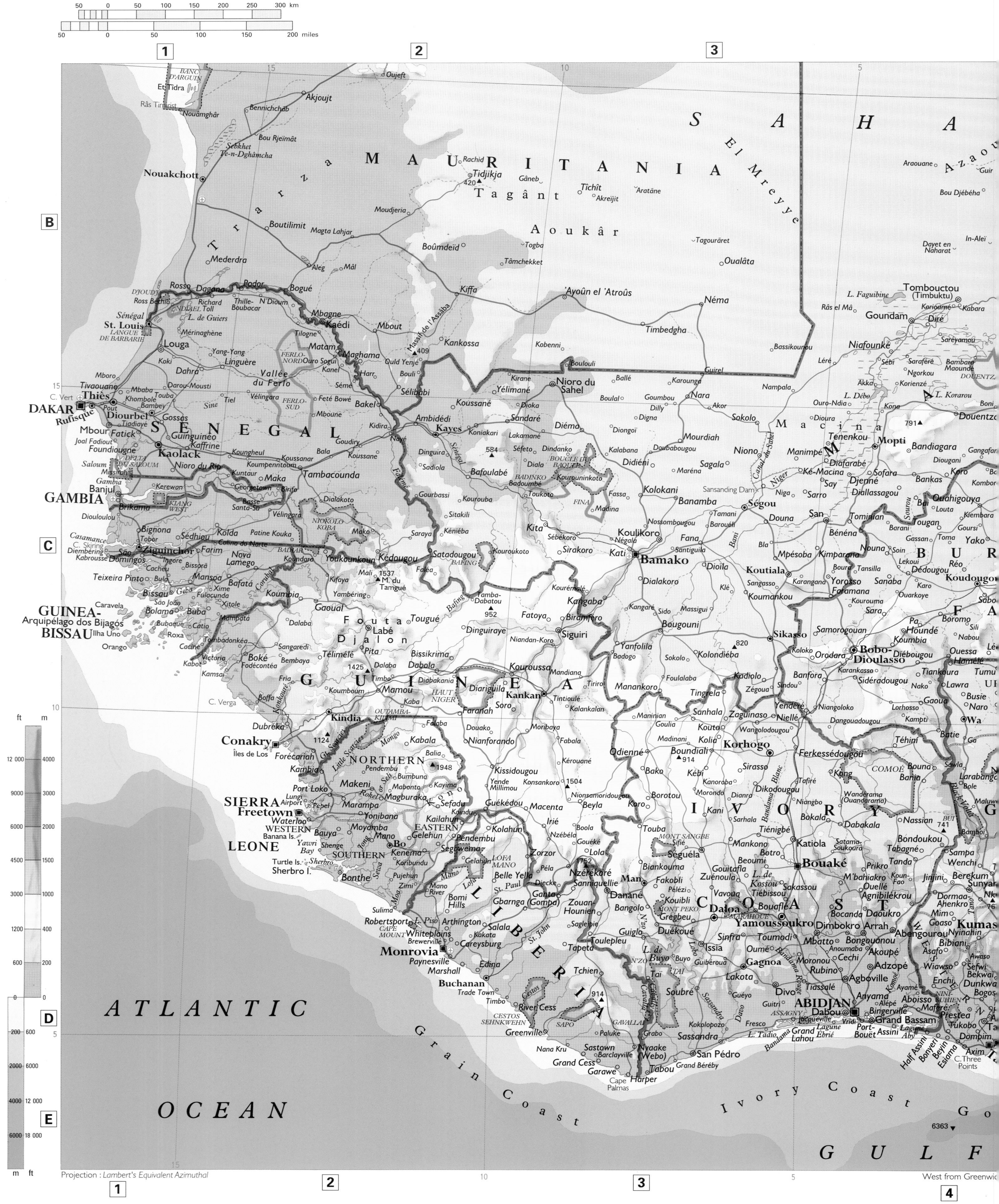

50 0 50 100 150 200 250 300 km
50 0 50 100 150 200 miles
SAHARA
MAURITANIA
Trarza
Tagânt
Aoukâr
El Mreyye
Nouakchott
Akjoujt
Nouâmghâr
Bennichchab
Bou Rjeïmât
Sebkhet Te-n-Dghâmcha
Rachid
Tidjikja
Gâneb
Tîchît
Akreïjit
Aratâne
Moudjeria
Boutilimit
Magta Lahjar
Boûmdeïd
Tâmchekket
Tagouràret
Oualâta
Aleg
Mâl
Mederdra
Rosso
Dagana
Podor
Bogué
Kiffa
'Ayoûn el 'Atroûs
Néma
Timbedgha
Mbagne
Kaédi
Mbout
Kankossa
Kobenni
Boulouli
Sélibabi
Nioro du Sahel
Yélimané
Tombouctou (Timbuktu)
L. Faguibine
Goundam
Diré
Kabara
Niafounké
Araouane
Azaouad
Bou Djébéha
In-Aleï
Dayet en Naharat
SENEGAL
St. Louis
Louga
Linguère
Vallée du Ferlo
Ferlo-Nord
Ferlo-Sud
Matam
Thiès
DAKAR
Rufisque
Diourbel
Fatick
Kaolack
Kaffrine
Tambacounda
Kédougou
GAMBIA
Banjul
Kiang West
Georgetown
Casamance
Ziguinchor
Kolda
Sédhiou
Bignona
GUINEA-BISSAU
Bissau
Bafatá
Gabú
Bolama
Arquipélago dos Bijagós
Catió
GUINEA
Fouta Djalon
Labé
Mamou
Kindia
Conakry
Îles de Los
Boké
Kankan
Siguiri
Faranah
Kissidougou
Guékédou
Macenta
Nzérékoré
Beyla
SIERRA LEONE
Freetown
Bo
Kenema
Makeni
Port Loko
Sherbro I.
Turtle Is.
Banana Is.
NORTHERN
EASTERN
SOUTHERN
WESTERN
LIBERIA
Monrovia
Buchanan
Greenville
Harper
Robertsport
Gbarnga (Gompa)
Zwedru
Tapeta
Cape Palmas
MALI
Kayes
Bamako
Kati
Koulikoro
Ségou
Mopti
Djenné
San
Sikasso
Koutiala
Bougouni
Kita
Nioro du Sahel
Macina
Niono
Douentza
BURKINA FASO
Bobo-Dioulasso
Ouahigouya
Koudougou
Banfora
IVORY COAST
Odienné
Korhogo
Ferkessédougou
Man
Séguéla
Bouaké
Daloa
Yamoussoukro
Gagnoa
Divo
ABIDJAN
Grand Bassam
San Pédro
Sassandra
Tabou
L. de Buyo
L. de Kossou
WESTERN
Kumasi
GHANA
ATLANTIC OCEAN
Grain Coast
Ivory Coast
GULF
6363
Projection: Lambert's Equivalent Azimuthal
West from Greenwich
ft m
12 000 4000
9000 3000
6000 2000
4500 1500
3000 1000
1200 400
600 200
0 0
200 600
2000 6000
4000 12 000
6000 18 000
m ft

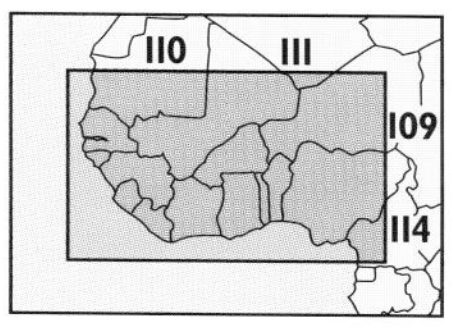

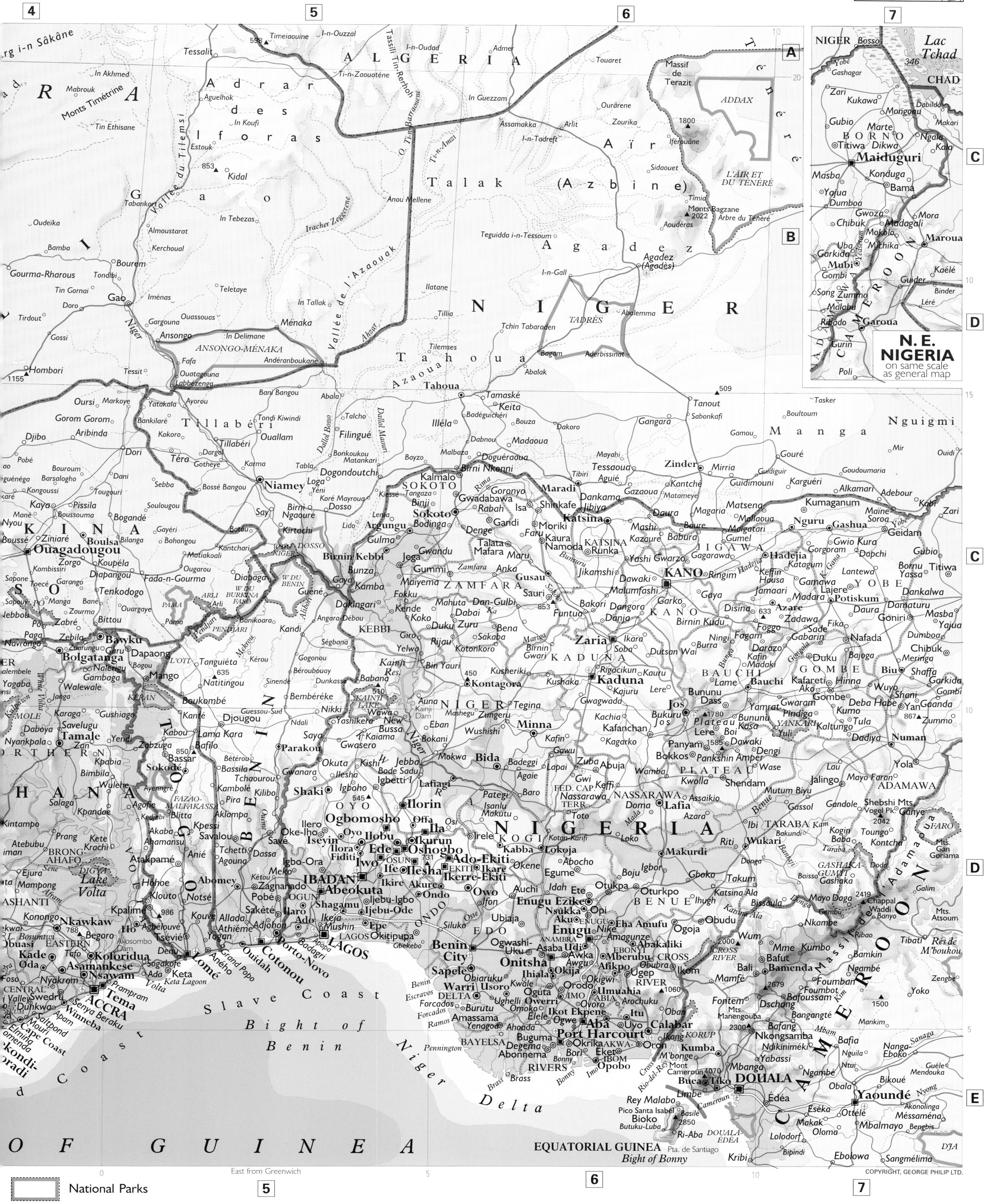

National Parks

Nature Reserves and Game Reserves

∴ UNESCO World Heritage Sites

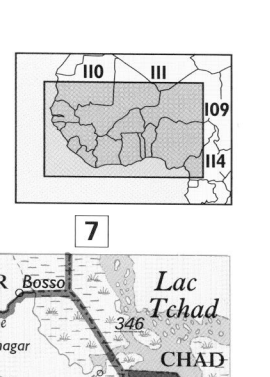

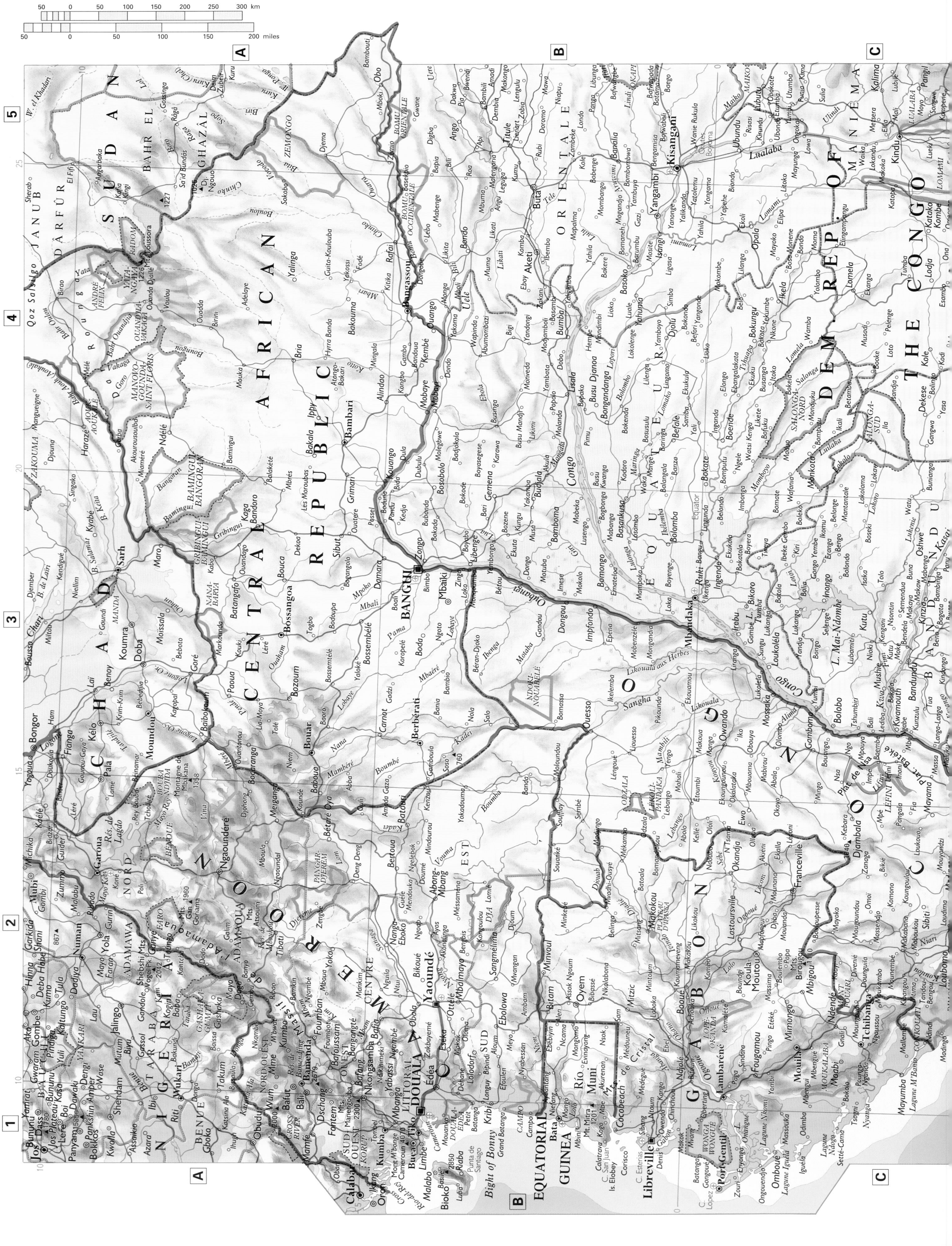

50 0 50 100 150 200 250 300 km
50 0 50 100 150 200 miles
CENTRAL AFRICAN REPUBLIC
CHAD
SUDAN
CAMEROON
NIGERIA
EQUATORIAL GUINEA
GABON
CONGO
DEM. REP. OF THE CONGO
Bangui
Yaoundé
Douala
Libreville
Malabo
Kisangani
Mbandaka
Port-Gentil
Equator
Bight of Bonny

SÃO TOMÉ AND PRÍNCIPE
At the same scale as main map
Príncipe
Santo António
Caroço
948
I. Pedras Tinhosas
Pico de São Tomé 2024
São Tomé
Porto Alegre
Gago Coutinho
ATLANTIC
OCEAN
ANGOLA
ZAMBIA
NAMIBIA
BOTSWANA
CABINDA (Angola)
KINSHASA
Luanda
Lobito
Benguela
Huambo
Lubango
Namibe
Malanje
Kuito
Menongue
Saurimo
Lubumbashi
Kolwezi
Likasi
Kananga
Mbuji-Mayi
Matadi
Boma
Pointe-Noire
Livingstone
Victoria Falls
Hwange
Mongu
Kasempa
Ondjiva
Caprivi Strip
SKELETON COAST
KATANGA
KASAI OCCIDENTAL
KASAI ORIENTAL
LUNDA NORTE
LUNDA SUL
MOXICO
CUANDO CUBANGO
CUNENE
HUÍLA
NORTH WESTERN
WESTERN
SOUTHERN
CENTRAL
COPPERBELT
Projection: Lambert's Equivalent Azimuthal
COPYRIGHT, GEORGE PHILIP LTD.
ft
m
9000
3000
6000
2000
4500
1500
3000
1000
1200
400
600
200
0
0
200
600
2000
6000
4000
12 000
m
ft
109
107
113
118
119
116

National Parks

Nature Reserves and Game Reserves

∴ UNESCO World Heritage Sites

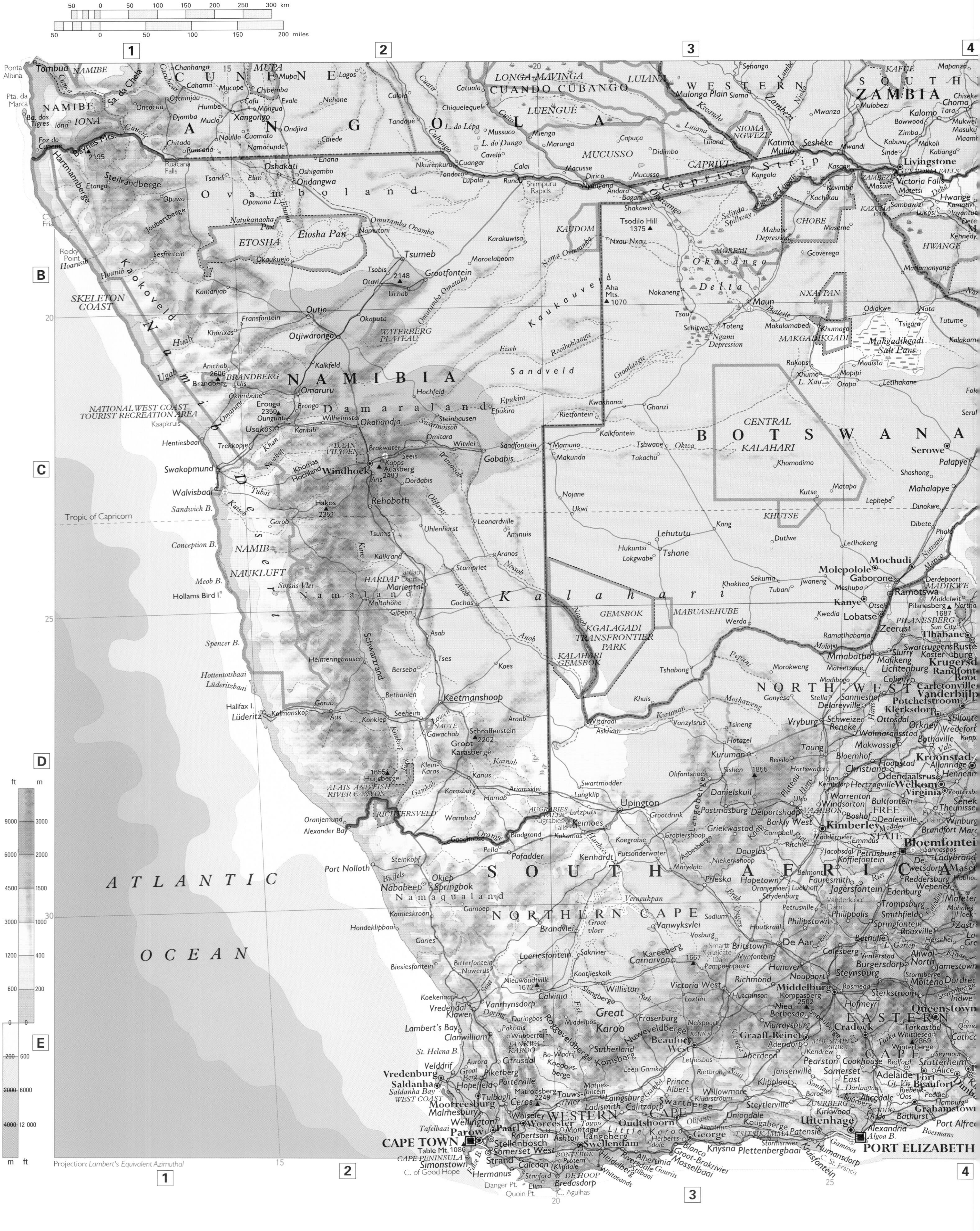

50 0 50 100 150 200 250 300 km
50 0 50 100 150 200 miles
ANGOLA
NAMIBIA
BOTSWANA
ZAMBIA
SOUTH AFRICA
NORTHERN CAPE
NORTH-WEST
WESTERN CAPE
EASTERN CAPE
FREE STATE
ATLANTIC OCEAN
Tropic of Capricorn
SKELETON COAST
Namib Desert
Kalahari
Kaokoveld
Damaraland
Namaqualand
Ovamboland
Okavango Delta
Makgadikgadi Salt Pans
Etosha Pan
Caprivi Strip
Windhoek
Walvisbaai
Swakopmund
Lüderitz
Keetmanshoop
Rehoboth
Gobabis
Tsumeb
Grootfontein
Otjiwarongo
Outjo
Mariental
Maun
Ghanzi
Gaborone
Molepolole
Kanye
Lobatse
Serowe
Palapye
Mahalapye
Francistown
Livingstone
Victoria Falls
Kimberley
Bloemfontein
Upington
Springbok
Port Nolloth
Vredenburg
Saldanha
CAPE TOWN
Stellenbosch
Paarl
Worcester
Swellendam
Oudtshoorn
George
Knysna
Plettenbergbaai
Mosselbaai
Uitenhage
PORT ELIZABETH
Beaufort West
Graaff-Reinet
Middelburg
Colesberg
De Aar
Cradock
Queenstown
Welkom
Klerksdorp
Potchefstroom
Vryburg
Mafikeng
Zeerust
Rustenburg
Orange
Great Karoo
Little Karoo
C. of Good Hope
C. Agulhas
Projection: Lambert's Equivalent Azimuthal
ft m
9000 3000
6000 2000
4500 1500
3000 1000
1200 400
600 200
200 600
2000 6000
4000 12 000

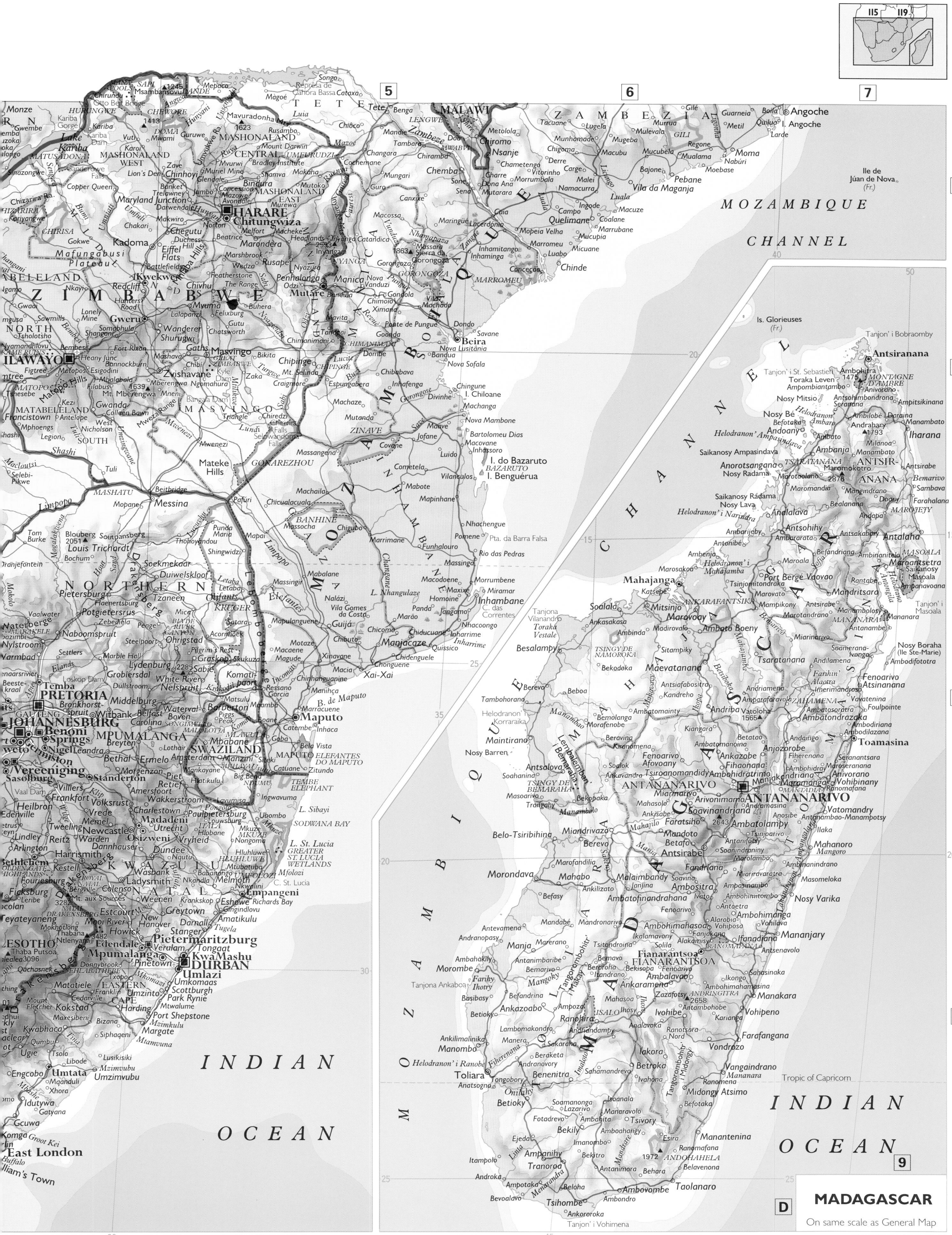

ZIMBABWE
HARARE
Chitungwiza
Bulawayo
Gweru
Masvingo
Mutare
Kadoma
Kwekwe
Messina
MOZAMBIQUE
Beira
Maputo
Tete
Quelimane
Chinde
Inhambane
Xai-Xai
Chimoio
Angoche
MOZAMBIQUE CHANNEL
PRETORIA
JOHANNESBURG
Soweto
Benoni
Springs
Germiston
Vereeniging
Pietersburg
Nelspruit
MPUMALANGA
NORTHERN
KWAZULU NATAL
SWAZILAND
Mbabane
Manzini
LESOTHO
Pietermaritzburg
DURBAN
Umlazi
East London
Port Shepstone
Richards Bay
INDIAN OCEAN
MADAGASCAR
ANTANANARIVO
Antsiranana
Mahajanga
Toamasina
Fianarantsoa
Toliara
Antsirabe
Morondava
Taolanaro
Antalaha
Nosy Boraha (Ile Ste-Marie)
Is. Glorieuses (Fr.)
Ile de Júan de Nova (Fr.)
Tropic of Capricorn
MADAGASCAR
On same scale as General Map
East from Greenwich

National Parks

Nature Reserves and Game Reserves

∴ UNESCO World Heritage Sites

COPYRIGHT GEORGE PHILIP LTD.

EAST AFRICA 1:6 400 000

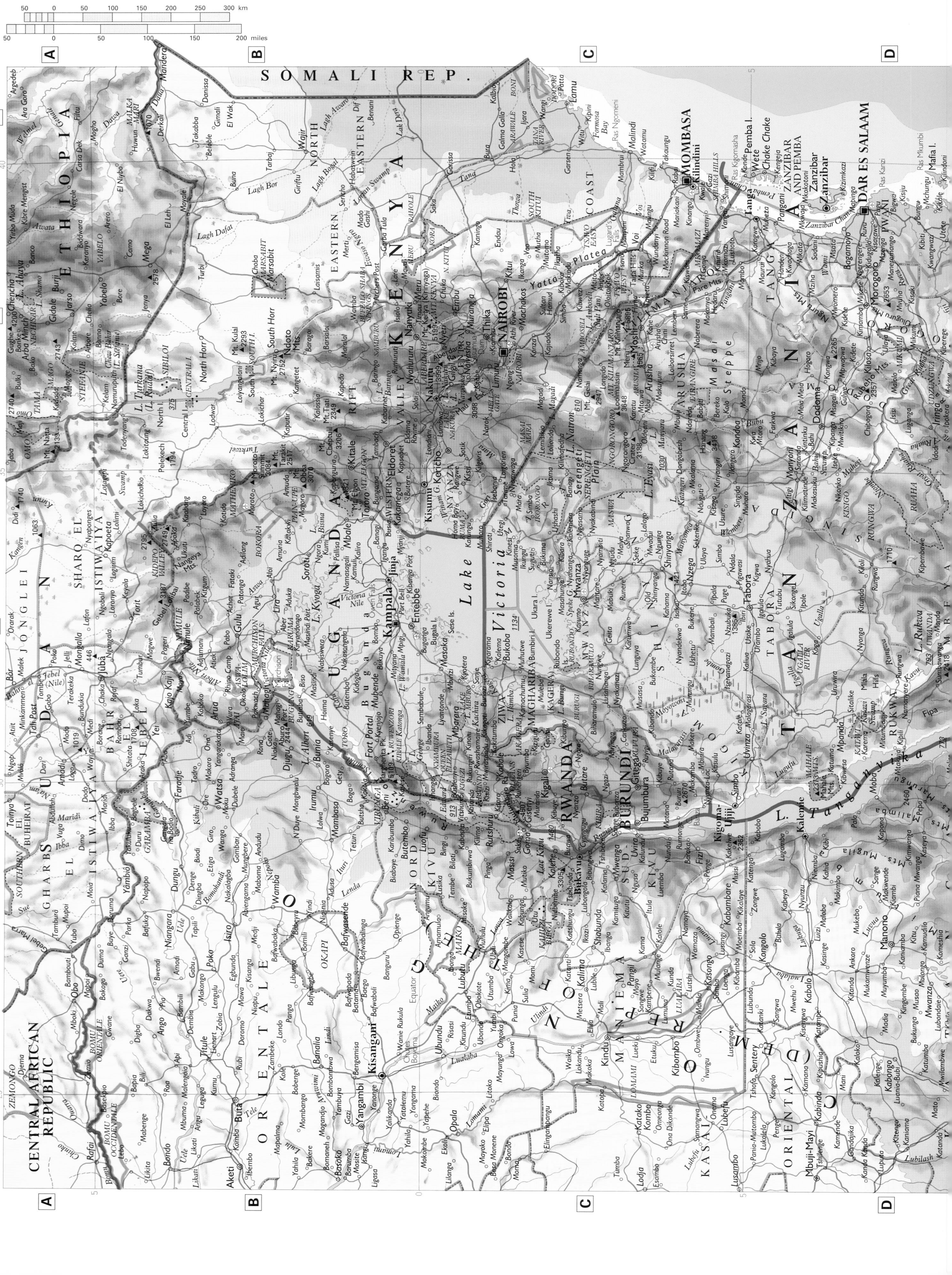

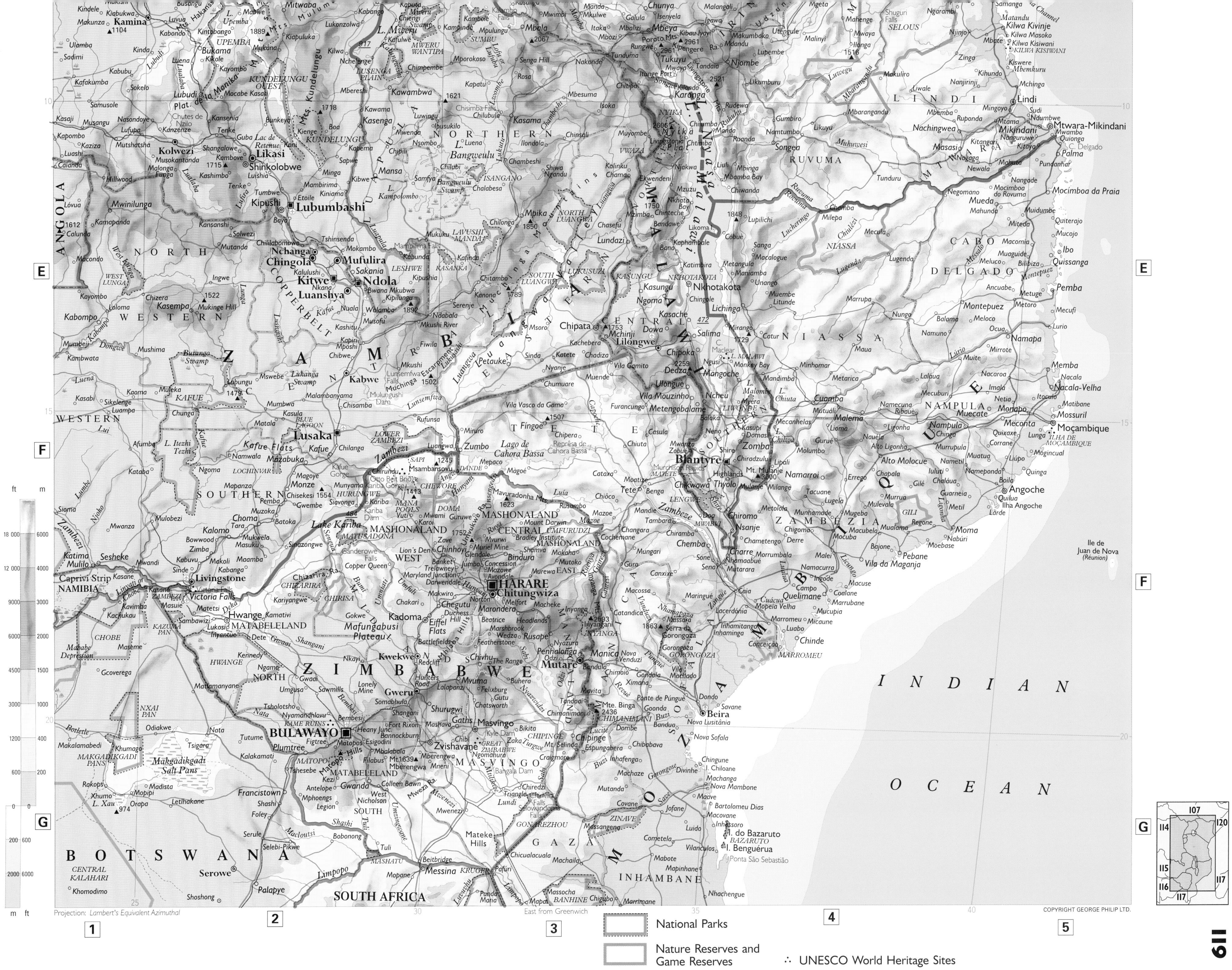
ZAMBIA
MALAWI
MOZAMBIQUE
ZIMBABWE
BOTSWANA
SOUTH AFRICA
NAMIBIA
ANGOLA
INDIAN OCEAN
L. Nyasa / Malawi
Lake Kariba
Lago de Cahora Bassa
Lusaka
Harare
Chitungwiza
Bulawayo
Lubumbashi
Likasi
Kolwezi
Ndola
Kitwe
Mufulira
Chingola
Luanshya
Kabwe
Livingstone
Victoria Falls
Hwange
Gweru
Kwekwe
Kadoma
Masvingo
Mutare
Beira
Quelimane
Nampula
Blantyre
Zomba
Lilongwe
Mzuzu
Chipata
Tete
Lindi
Mtwara-Mikindani
Mbeya
Pemba
Moçambique
Angoche
Francistown
Serowe
Messina
Zambezi
Limpopo
Luangwa
Kafue
Copperbelt
Projection: Lambert's Equivalent Azimuthal
East from Greenwich
COPYRIGHT GEORGE PHILIP LTD.
National Parks
Nature Reserves and Game Reserves
UNESCO World Heritage Sites

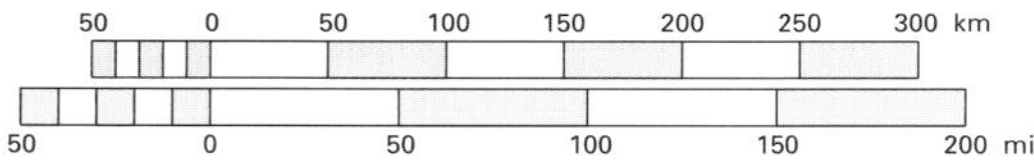

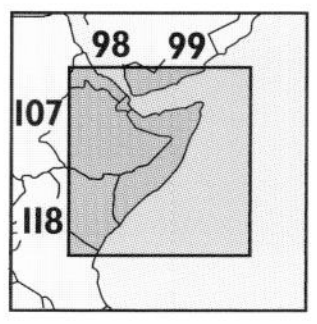

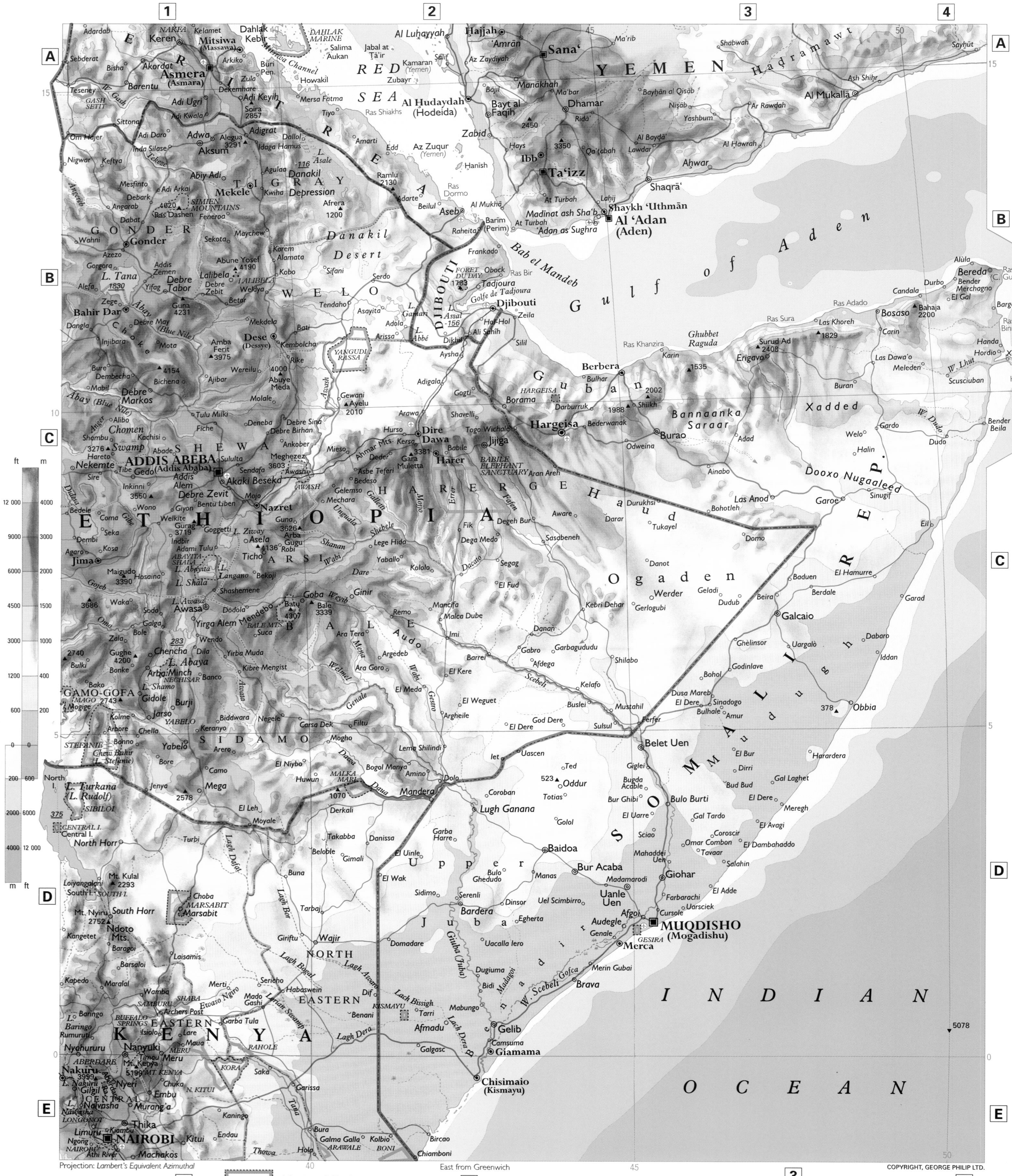

National Parks

Nature Reserves and Game Reserves

∴ UNESCO World Heritage Sites

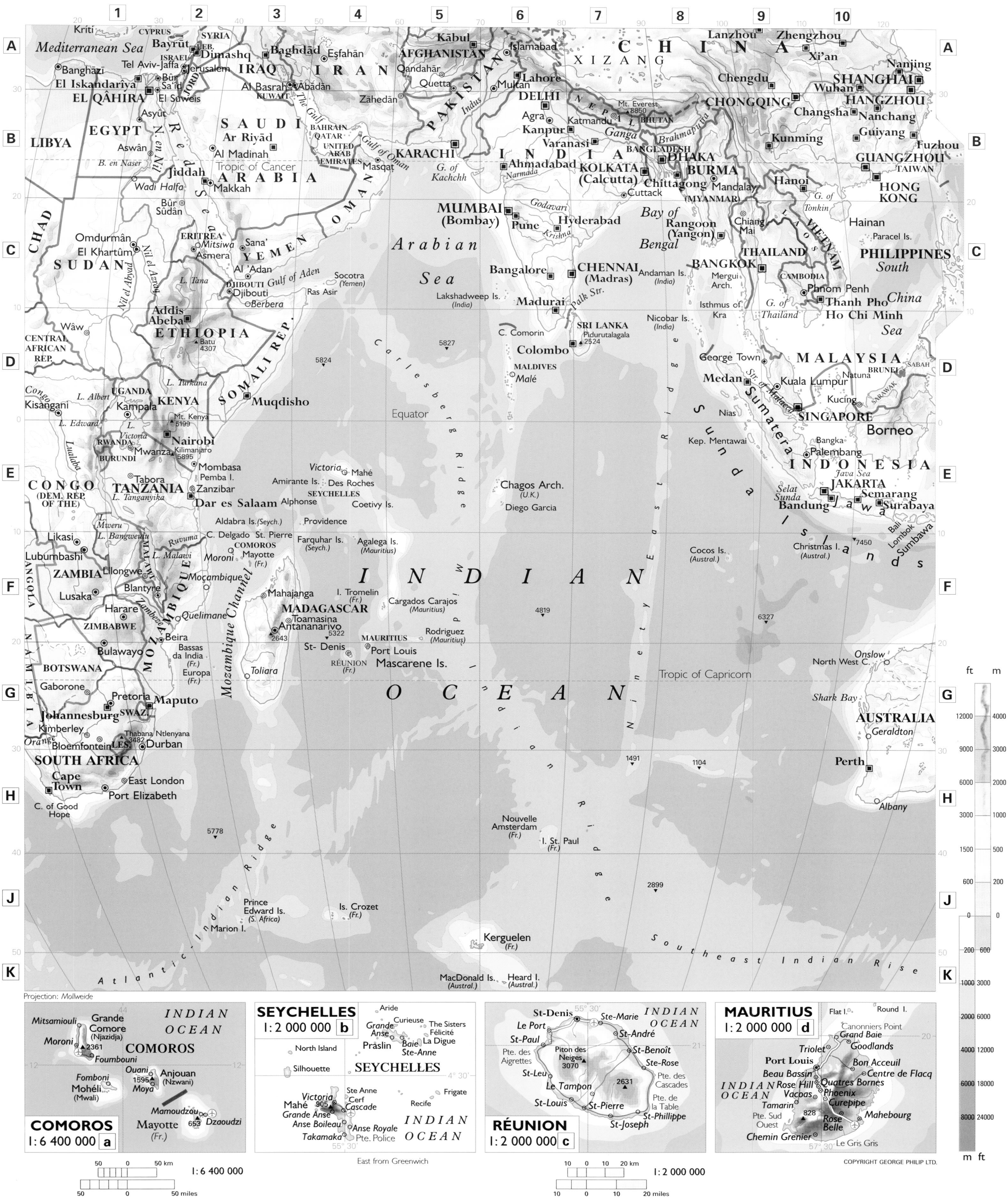
Mediterranean Sea
Kríti
CYPRUS
SYRIA
Bayrūt
LEB.
Dimashq
ISRAEL
Tel Aviv-Jaffa
Jerusalem
Banghāzī
El Iskandarîya
EL QÂHIRA
El Suweis
IRAQ
Baghdād
Al Basrah
KUWAIT
Abādān
Esfahān
I R A N
AFGHANISTAN
Kābul
Qandahār
Quetta
Zāhedān
PAKISTAN
Islamabad
Lahore
Multan
Indus
DELHI
Agra
Kanpur
Varanasi
Katmandu
NEPAL
Mt. Everest 8850
BHUTAN
Ganga
Brahmaputra
BANGLADESH
DHAKA
KOLKATA (Calcutta)
Chittagong
Cuttack
X I Z A N G
C H I N A
Lanzhou
Zhengzhou
Xi'an
Chengdu
CHONGQING
Changsha
Nanjing
SHANGHAI
Wuhan
HANGZHOU
Nanchang
Guiyang
Kunming
Fuzhou
GUANGZHOU
TAIWAN
HONG KONG
Hanoi
G. of Tonkin
Hainan
Paracel Is.
LIBYA
EGYPT
Asyût
Aswân
Nen Nil
Red Sea
B. en Naser
Wadi Halfa
SAUDI ARABIA
Ar Riyād
Al Madinah
Jiddah
Makkah
Tropic of Cancer
The Gulf
BAHRAIN
QATAR
UNITED ARAB EMIRATES
Gulf of Oman
Masqat
OMAN
KARACHI
G. of Kachchh
INDIA
Ahmadabad
Narmada
Godavari
MUMBAI (Bombay)
Pune
Hyderabad
Krishna
Bay of Bengal
BURMA (MYANMAR)
Mandalay
Rangoon (Yangon)
Chiang Mai
LAOS
VIETNAM
THAILAND
BANGKOK
CAMBODIA
Phnom Penh
Thanh Pho Ho Chi Minh
G. of Thailand
PHILIPPINES
South China Sea
CHAD
SUDAN
Omdurmân
El Khartûm
Bûr Sûdân
ERITREA
Mitsiwa
Asmera
Sana'
YEMEN
Al 'Adan
DJIBOUTI
Djibouti
Gulf of Aden
Berbera
Socotra (Yemen)
Ras Asir
Arabian Sea
Nil el Abyad
Nil el Azraq
L. Tana
Addis Abeba
ETHIOPIA
Batu 4307
Wâw
CENTRAL AFRICAN REP.
SOMALI REP.
Muqdisho
Bangalore
CHENNAI (Madras)
Madurai
Palk Str.
Lakshadweep Is. (India)
Andaman Is. (India)
Mergui Arch.
Isthmus of Kra
Nicobar Is. (India)
SRI LANKA
Pidurutalagala 2524
C. Comorin
Colombo
MALDIVES
Malé
5827
5824
Carlesberg Ridge
Congo
Kisangani
UGANDA
L. Albert
Kampala
L. Turkana
KENYA
Mt. Kenya 5199
L. Edward
L. Victoria
RWANDA
BURUNDI
Mwanza
Nairobi
Kilimanjaro 5895
Mombasa
Pemba I.
Zanzibar
Tabora
TANZANIA
L. Tanganyika
Dar es Salaam
CONGO (DEM. REP. OF THE)
Lualaba
Equator
Victoria
Mahé
Amirante Is.
Des Roches
SEYCHELLES
Alphonse
Coetivy Is.
Chagos Arch. (U.K.)
Diego Garcia
George Town
Medan
Str. of Malacca
Kuala Lumpur
MALAYSIA
BRUNEI
SABAH
Natuna
SARAWAK
Kucing
Nias
SINGAPORE
Borneo
Sumatera
Kep. Mentawai
Bangka
Palembang
INDONESIA
Java Sea
JAKARTA
Selat Sunda
Bandung
Semarang
Surabaya
Jawa
Bali
Lombok
Sumbawa
Sunda Islands
Christmas I. (Austral.)
7450
Cocos Is. (Austral.)
L. Mweru
L. Bangweulu
Likasi
Lubumbashi
Ruvuma
L. Malawi
MALAWI
ZAMBIA
Lilongwe
Lusaka
Blantyre
ANGOLA
Harare
ZIMBABWE
Zambezi
MOZAMBIQUE
Moçambique
Quelimane
Beira
Bulawayo
BOTSWANA
NAMIBIA
Gaborone
Pretoria
SWAZ.
Maputo
Johannesburg
Kimberley
Orange
Bloemfontein
LES.
Thabana Ntlenyana 3482
Durban
SOUTH AFRICA
Cape Town
East London
Port Elizabeth
C. of Good Hope
Aldabra Is. (Seych.)
Providence
C. Delgado
St. Pierre
COMOROS
Moroni
Mayotte (Fr.)
Farquhar Is. (Seych.)
Agalega Is. (Mauritius)
Mozambique Channel
Mahajanga
MADAGASCAR
Toamasina
Antananarivo
2643
Toliara
I. Tromelin (Fr.)
Cargados Carajos (Mauritius)
Rodriguez (Mauritius)
MAURITIUS
Port Louis
St- Denis
RÉUNION (Fr.)
Mascarene Is.
Bassas da India (Fr.)
Europa (Fr.)
INDIAN OCEAN
Mid-Indian Ridge
4819
Ninety East Ridge
6327
Tropic of Capricorn
Onslow
North West C.
Shark Bay
AUSTRALIA
Geraldton
Perth
Albany
1491
1104
5778
Nouvelle Amsterdam (Fr.)
I. St. Paul (Fr.)
Southwest Indian Ridge
2899
Prince Edward Is. (S. Africa)
Marion I.
Is. Crozet (Fr.)
Kerguelen (Fr.)
Southeast Indian Rise
Atlantic-Indian Ridge
MacDonald Is. (Austral.)
Heard I. (Austral.)
Projection: Mollweide
ft m
12000 4000
9000 3000
6000 2000
3000 1000
1500 500
600 200
0 0
200 600
1000 3000
2000 6000
4000 12000
6000 18000
8000 24000
m ft
INDIAN OCEAN
Mitsamiouli
Grande Comore (Njazidja)
Moroni
2361
Foumbouni
COMOROS
Fomboni
Mohéli (Mwali)
Ouani
1595
Moya
Anjouan (Nzwani)
Mamoudzou
Dzaoudzi
Mayotte (Fr.)
653
COMOROS
1:6 400 000 a
SEYCHELLES
1:2 000 000 b
Aride
Curieuse
Grande Anse
The Sisters
Félicité
Praslin
Baie Ste-Anne
La Digue
North Island
Silhouette
SEYCHELLES
4° 30'
Ste Anne
Cerf
Victoria
905
Mahé
Cascade
Frigate
Grande Anse
Anse Boileau
Recife
Anse Royale
Pte. Police
Takamaka
INDIAN OCEAN
55° 30'
East from Greenwich
St-Denis
55° 30'
Ste-Marie
INDIAN OCEAN
Le Port
St-André
St-Paul
21
Pte. des Aigrettes
Piton des Neiges 3070
St-Benoît
Ste-Rose
St-Leu
2631
Pte. des Cascades
Le Tampon
Pte. de la Table
St-Louis
St-Pierre
St-Philippe
St-Joseph
RÉUNION
1:2 000 000 c
MAURITIUS
1:2 000 000 d
Flat I.
Round I.
Canonniers Point
Grand Baie
20
Triolet
Goodlands
Port Louis
Bon Acceuil
Beau Bassin
Centre de Flacq
Rose Hill
Quatres Bornes
INDIAN OCEAN
Vacoas
Phoenix
Curepipe
Tamarin
828
Pte. Sud Ouest
Rose Belle
Mahebourg
Chemin Grenier
Le Gris Gris
57° 30'
50 0 50 km
1:6 400 000
50 0 50 miles
10 0 10 20 km
1:2 000 000
10 0 10 20 miles

COPYRIGHT GEORGE PHILIP LTD.

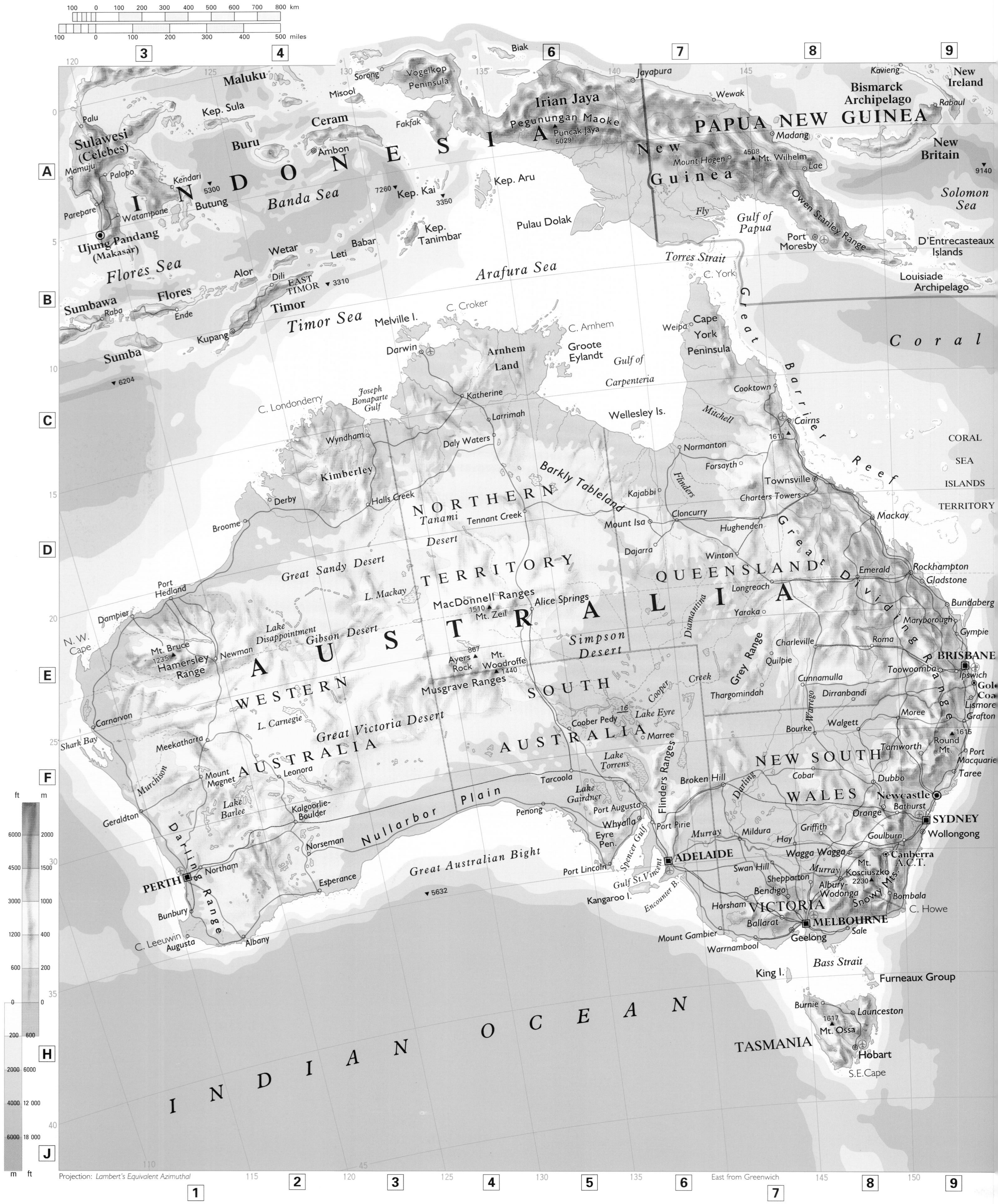
100 0 100 200 300 400 500 600 700 800 km
100 0 100 200 300 400 500 miles
INDONESIA
PAPUA NEW GUINEA
AUSTRALIA
NORTHERN TERRITORY
WESTERN AUSTRALIA
SOUTH AUSTRALIA
QUEENSLAND
NEW SOUTH WALES
VICTORIA
TASMANIA
A.C.T.
CORAL SEA ISLANDS TERRITORY
INDIAN OCEAN
Coral
Maluku
Sulawesi (Celebes)
Kep. Sula
Ceram
Buru
Ambon
Misool
Sorong
Vogelkop Peninsula
Biak
Fakfak
Irian Jaya
Pegunungan Maoke
Puncak Jaya 5029
Jayapura
Wewak
Kavieng
New Ireland
Bismarck Archipelago
Rabaul
New Britain
9140
Solomon Sea
Madang
Mount Hagen
4508 Mt. Wilhelm
Lae
New Guinea
Fly
Gulf of Papua
Owen Stanley Range
Port Moresby
D'Entrecasteaux Islands
Louisiade Archipelago
Palu
Mamuju
Palopo
Kendari
5300
Butung
Parepare
Watampone
Ujung Pandang (Makasar)
Banda Sea
7260 Kep. Kai
3350
Kep. Aru
Kep. Tanimbar
Pulau Dolak
Flores Sea
Wetar
Babar
Leti
Alor
Dili
EAST TIMOR 3310
Timor
Sumbawa
Raba
Flores
Ende
Kupang
Sumba
6204
Timor Sea
Arafura Sea
Torres Strait
C. York
Melville I.
C. Croker
C. Arnhem
Darwin
Arnhem Land
Groote Eylandt
Gulf of Carpenteria
Weipa
Cape York Peninsula
Great Barrier Reef
Cooktown
Mitchell
Cairns
1611
Katherine
Joseph Bonaparte Gulf
C. Londonderry
Larrimah
Wellesley Is.
Normanton
Forsayth
Wyndham
Daly Waters
Kimberley
Barkly Tableland
Flinders
Townsville
Charters Towers
Kajabbi
Derby
Halls Creek
Tanami
Tennant Creek
Cloncurry
Mount Isa
Hughenden
Mackay
Broome
Desert
Dajarra
Winton
Great Dividing Range
Great Sandy Desert
Emerald
Rockhampton
Gladstone
Port Hedland
L. Mackay
MacDonnell Ranges
Alice Springs
1510 Mt. Zeil
Longreach
Diamantina
Bundaberg
Dampier
Yaraka
Maryborough
Gympie
N. W. Cape
Lake Disappointment
Gibson Desert
Simpson Desert
Charleville
Roma
Mt. Bruce 1235
Hamersley Range
Newman
867 Ayers Rock
Mt. Woodroffe 1440
Grey Range
Quilpie
BRISBANE
Toowoomba
Ipswich
Musgrave Ranges
Creek
Cooper
Cunnamulla
Thargomindah
Dirranbandi
Warrego
Lismore
Grafton
Carnarvon
L. Carnegie
Great Victoria Desert
Coober Pedy
-16 Lake Eyre
Moree
Shark Bay
Meekatharra
Marree
Bourke
Walgett
1615 Round Mt.
Port Macquarie
Tamworth
Lake Torrens
Flinders Ranges
Murchison
Mount Magnet
Leonora
Tarcoola
Broken Hill
Darling
Cobar
Dubbo
Taree
Nullarbor Plain
Lake Gairdner
Newcastle
Lake Barlee
Kalgoorlie-Boulder
Penong
Port Augusta
Whyalla
Port Pirie
Bathurst
Orange
SYDNEY
Wollongong
Geraldton
Eyre Pen.
Murray
Mildura
Hay
Griffith
Goulburn
Norseman
Spencer Gulf
ADELAIDE
Wagga Wagga
Canberra
Darling Range
Northam
Great Australian Bight
Port Lincoln
Swan Hill
Mt. Kosciuszko 2230
PERTH
Esperance
Gulf St. Vincent
Shepparton
Albury-Wodonga
Snowy Mts.
5632
Kangaroo I.
Encounter B.
Bendigo
Bombala
Bunbury
Horsham
C. Howe
Ballarat
MELBOURNE
C. Leeuwin
Augusta
Albany
Mount Gambier
Geelong
Sale
Warrnambool
Bass Strait
King I.
Furneaux Group
Burnie
Launceston
1617 Mt. Ossa
Hobart
S.E. Cape
ft m
6000 2000
4500 1500
3000 1000
1200 400
600 200
0 0
200 600
2000 6000
4000 12 000
6000 18 000
m ft
Projection: Lambert's Equivalent Azimuthal
East from Greenwich

KIRIBATI
Tamana
Baker
(U.S.A.)
Equator
6195
Abariringa
Phoenix Is.
Namumea
Carondelet
Melanesia
2743
Mt. Balbi
Bougainville
Choiseul
SOLOMON ISLANDS
Santa Isabel
New Georgia
Malaita
Honiara
2439
Guadalcanal
San Cristóbal
7223
Rennell
Santa Cruz Is.
TUVALU
(Ellice Is.)
Funafuti
Fongafale
Nukulaelae
Fataka
Tokelau Is.
(N.Z.)
Sea
Rotuma
Banks Is.
Espíritu Santo
1879
VANUATU
(New Hebrides)
Malakula
Mata-Utu
Uvea
Wallis & Futuna
(Fr.)
Horn
SAMOA
Savai'i
Apia
'Upolu
American Samoa
Tutuila
Îles D'Entrecasteaux
Port-Vila
Efate
Vanua Levu
Niuafo'ou
Îles Chesterfield
Erromango
Viti Levu
1323
Suva
FIJI
Îles Bélep
Tanna
Kandavu
Lau Group
New Caledonia
(Fr.)
1628
Îles Loyauté
7569
Aneityum
Vava'u Group
TONGA
Ha'apai Group
Noumea
Niue
(N.Z.)
Ceve-i-Ra
Matthew I.
Nuku'alofa
Tongatapu Group
PACIFIC OCEAN
5303
Tonga Trench
10 882
Tropic of Capricorn
Norfolk I.
(Austral.)
Lord Howe I.
(Austral.)
734
Lord Howe Ridge
Raoul
Kermadec Is.
(N.Z.)
Kermadec Trench
10 047
Tasman Sea
North C.
Kaitaia
Whangarei
Auckland
North Island
Bay of Plenty
Hamilton
Tauranga
New Plymouth
Rotorua
Gisborne
NEW ZEALAND
Raupehu
2797
5267
Wanganui
Napier
Palmerston North
Nelson
Cook Strait
Masterton
Wellington
Blenheim
Greymouth
International Date Line
South Island
Aoraki Mt. Cook
3753
Southern Alps
Christchurch
Timaru
Queenstown
Dunedin
Chatham Is.
(N.Z.)
Invercargill
Stewart I.
West from Greenwich
A B C D E F G H J
10 11 12 13 14 15 16 17 18

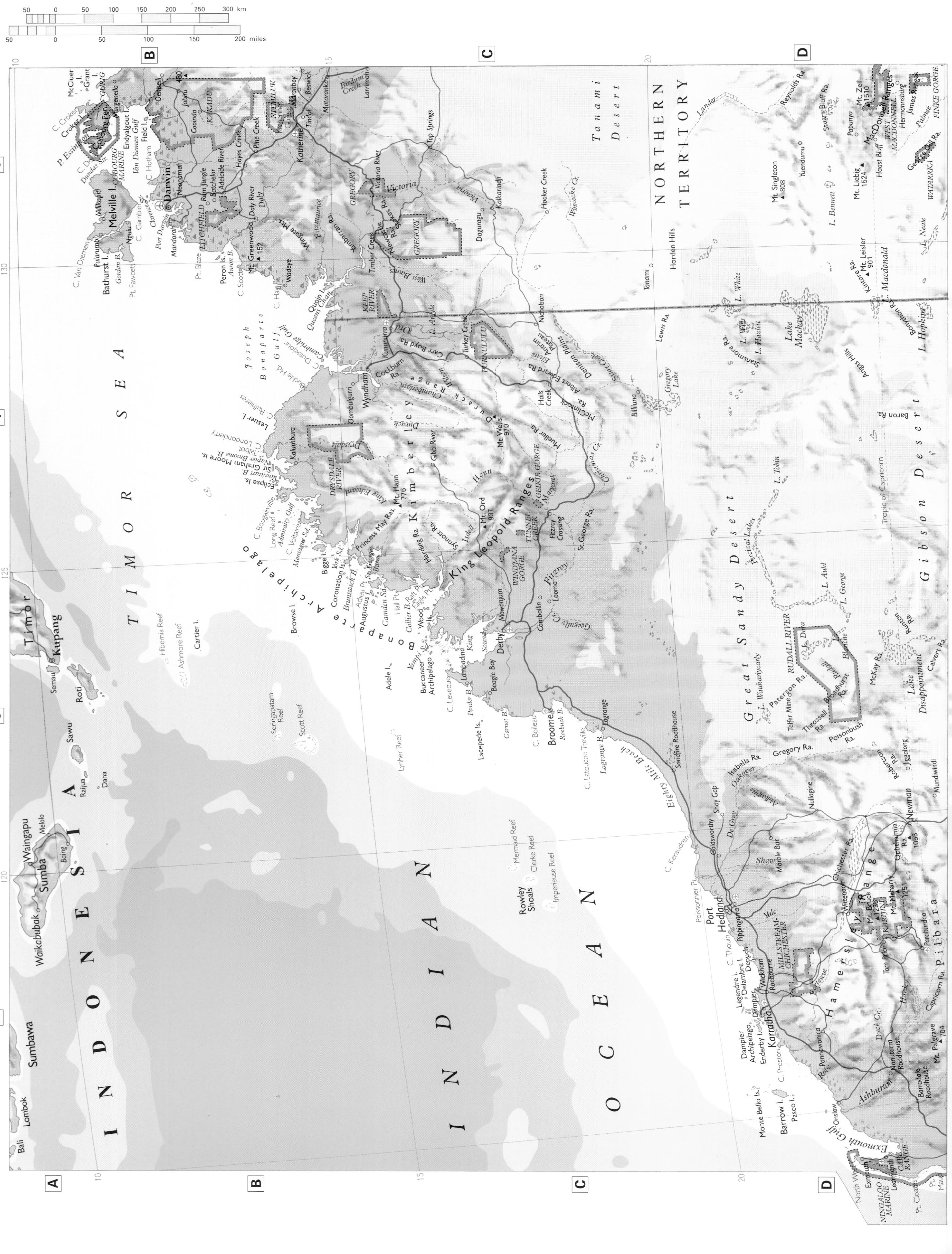

50 0 50 100 150 200 250 300 km
50 0 50 100 150 200 miles
INDONESIA
TIMOR SEA
INDIAN OCEAN
NORTHERN TERRITORY
Tanami Desert
Great Sandy Desert
Gibson Desert
Kimberley
King Leopold Ranges
Bonaparte Archipelago
Joseph Bonaparte Gulf
Hamersley Range
Pilbara
Eighty Mile Beach
Tropic of Capricorn
Darwin
Katherine
Wyndham
Kununurra
Derby
Broome
Port Hedland
Karratha
Newman
Halls Creek
Fitzroy Crossing
Kupang
Timor
Sumba
Sumbawa
Lombok
Bali
Sawu
Roti
Melville I.
Bathurst I.
Exmouth Gulf

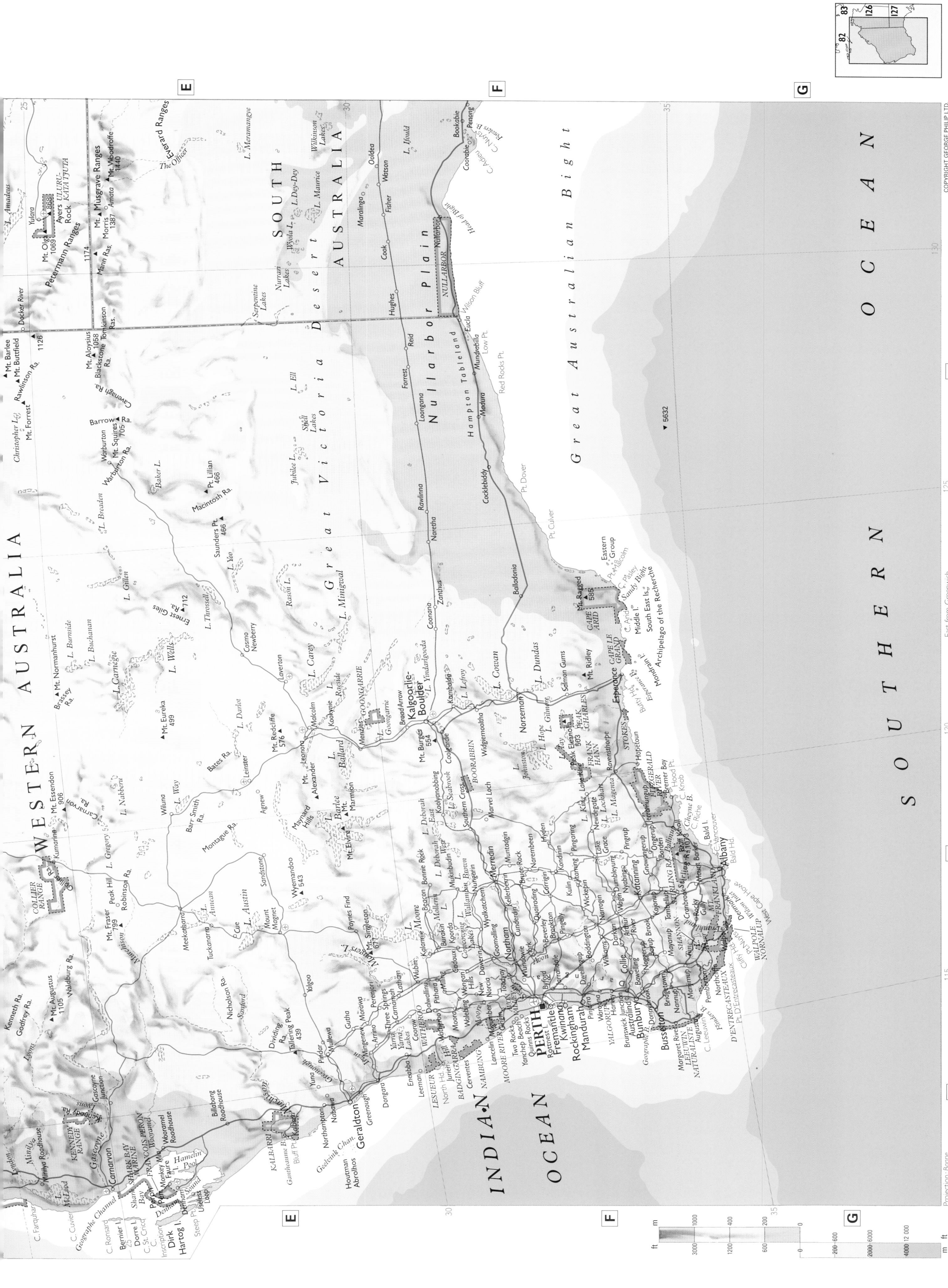
WESTERN AUSTRALIA
SOUTH AUSTRALIA
INDIAN OCEAN
SOUTHERN OCEAN
Great Australian Bight
Great Victoria Desert
Nullarbor Plain
Hampton Tableland
NULLARBOR
PERTH
Fremantle
Rottnest I.
Kwinana
Rockingham
Mandurah
Bunbury
Busselton
Albany
Geraldton
Carnarvon
Kalgoorlie-Boulder
Esperance
Norseman
Merredin
Northam
Collie
Katanning
Narrogin
Moora
Southern Cross
Coolgardie
Menzies
Leonora
Laverton
Meekatharra
Cue
Mount Magnet
Wiluna
Kalbarri
Northampton
Dongara
Jurien
Lancelin
Augusta
Margaret River
Manjimup
Denmark
Walpole
Hopetoun
Ravensthorpe
Eucla
Madura
Mundrabilla
Cocklebiddy
Balladonia
Rawlinna
Naretha
Zanthus
Coonana
Loongana
Forrest
Reid
Hughes
Cook
Fisher
Watson
Ooldea
Maralinga
Nullarbor
Coorabie
Bookabie
Penong
Yulara
Ayers Rock
Mt. Olga 1069
Petermann Ranges
Musgrave Ranges
Mt. Woodroffe 1440
Everard Ranges
Mann Ras.
Tomkinson Ras.
Warburton
Kennedy Ra.
Shark Bay
Dirk Hartog I.
Houtman Abrolhos
Cape Leeuwin
D'Entrecasteaux
Stirling Ra. Bluff Knoll 1073
Archipelago of the Recherche
Cape Arid
Mt. Ragged 585
Head of Bight
Wilson Bluff
L. Barlee
L. Moore
L. Carey
L. Cowan
L. Lefroy
L. Dundas
L. Carnegie
L. Wells
L. Minigwal
L. Austin
Collier Range
Mt. Augustus 1105
Mt. Essendon 906
Robinson Ra.
Carnarvon Ra.
Mt. Eureka 499
Mt. Redcliffe 576
Bates Ra.
Ernest Giles Ra.
Saunders Pt. 466
Pt. Lillian 466
Macintosh Ra.
Mt. Squires 705
Barrow Ra.
Mt. Aloysius 1058
Blackstone Ra.
Mt. Buttfield 1126
Mt. Forrest
Christopher L.
L. Amadeus
L. Meramangye
Wilkinson Lakes
L. Ifould
Serpentine Lakes
Pt. Culver
Pt. Dover
Red Rocks Pt.
Low Pt.
Eastern Group
Sandy Bight
5632
National Parks
East from Greenwich
Projection: Bonne
COPYRIGHT GEORGE PHILIP LTD.
E
F
G
1
2
3
4
5
82
83
126
127
m
ft
3000
1000
1200
400
600
200
0
200
600
2000
6000
4000
12 000

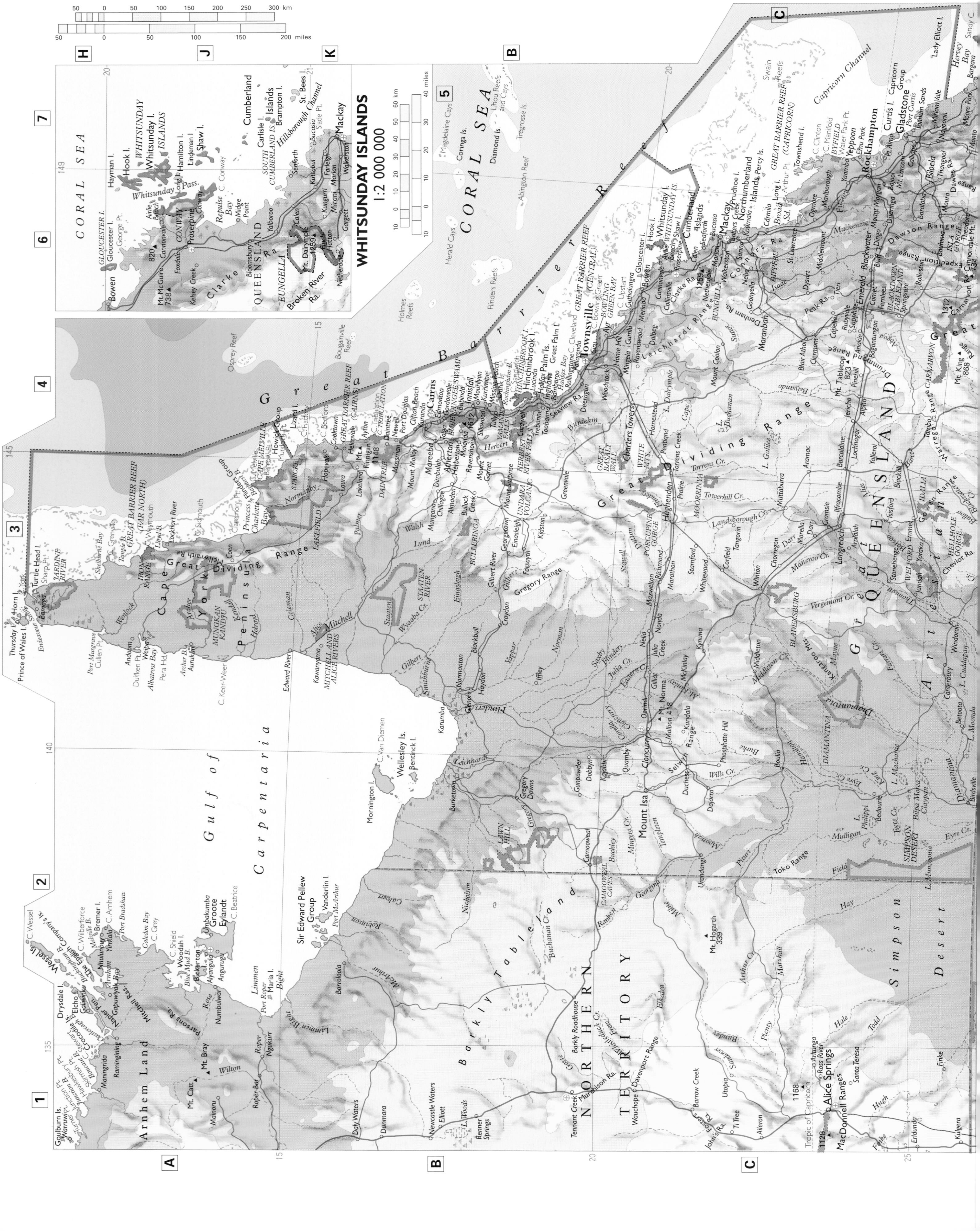
WHITSUNDAY ISLANDS
1:2 000 000
CORAL SEA
Gulf of Carpentaria
Great Barrier Reef
Cape York Peninsula
Arnhem Land
NORTHERN TERRITORY
QUEENSLAND
Barkly Tableland
Simpson Desert
Great Dividing Range
Great Artesian Basin
Townsville
Cairns
Mackay
Rockhampton
Mount Isa
Alice Springs
Tennant Creek
Tropic of Capricorn

SOUTH AUSTRALIA
NEW SOUTH WALES
TASMANIA
TASMAN SEA
Bass Strait
BRISBANE
SYDNEY
CANBERRA
MELBOURNE
ADELAIDE
Newcastle
Wollongong
Gold Coast
Tweed Heads
Toowoomba
Tamworth
Armidale
Dubbo
Orange
Bathurst
Wagga Wagga
Albury
Bendigo
Ballarat
Geelong
Shepparton
Mildura
Broken Hill
Port Augusta
Whyalla
Port Pirie
Port Lincoln
Mount Gambier
Warrnambool
Launceston
Hobart
Devonport
Burnie
Lake Eyre
Lake Torrens
Lake Gairdner
Lake Frome
Kangaroo I.
King Island
Flinders Island
Great Dividing Range
Grey Range
National Parks
On same scale
East from Greenwich
Projection: Bonne
COPYRIGHT, GEORGE PHILIP LTD.
m 1500 1000 400 200 0 200 2000 4000
ft 4500 3000 1200 600 0 600 6000 12 000

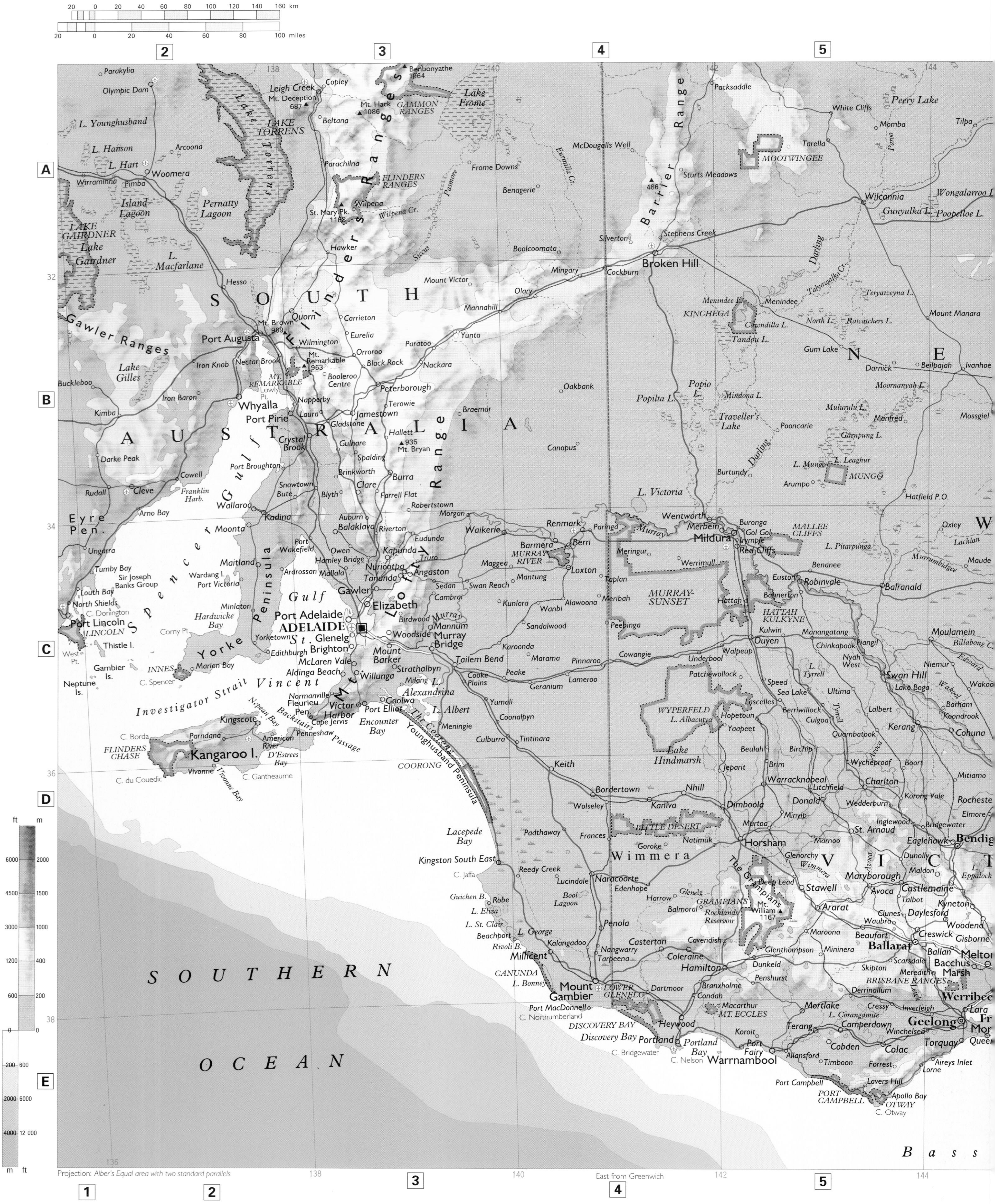

20 0 20 40 60 80 100 120 140 160 km
20 0 20 40 60 80 100 miles
A
B
C
D
E
1
2
3
4
5
136
138
140
142
144
32
34
36
38
S O U T H
A U S T R A L I A
N E W
V I C T
Parakylia
Olympic Dam
L. Younghusband
L. Hanson
L. Hart
Woomera
Arcoona
Wirraminna
Pimba
Island Lagoon
Pernatty Lagoon
LAKE GAIRDNER
Lake Gairdner
L. Macfarlane
Lake Torrens
LAKE TORRENS
Leigh Creek
Copley
Mt. Deception 687
Beltana
Mt. Hack 1086
Benbonyathe 1064
GAMMON RANGES
Lake Frome
Parachilna
FLINDERS RANGES
Wilpena
St. Mary Pk. 1168
Wilpena Cr.
Hawker
Flinders Ranges
Hesso
Gawler Ranges
Port Augusta
Mt. Brown 989
Quorn
Carrieton
Eurelia
Wilmington
Orroroo
Iron Knob
Nectar Brook
Lake Gilles
Mt. Remarkable 963
MT. REMARKABLE
Black Rock
Booleroo Centre
Buckleboo
Iron Baron
Whyalla
Lowly Pt.
Peterborough
Napperby
Terowie
Kimba
Port Pirie
Laura
Jamestown
Gladstone
Crystal Brook
Gulnare
Hallett
935 Mt. Bryan
Spalding
Darke Peak
Port Broughton
Brinkworth
Burra
Clare
Cowell
Franklin Harb.
Rudall
Cleve
Snowtown
Bute
Blyth
Farrell Flat
Spencer Gulf
Wallaroo
Arno Bay
Robertstown
Morgan
Kadina
Eyre Pen.
Moonta
Auburn
Balaklava
Riverton
Port Wakefield
Eudunda
Ungarra
Owen
Kapunda
Tumby Bay
Sir Joseph Banks Group
Wardang I.
Port Victoria
Maitland
Hamley Bridge
Nuriootpa
Truro
Tanunda
Angaston
Ardrossan
Mallala
Yorke Peninsula
Gulf St. Vincent
Louth Bay
North Shields
C. Donington
Port Lincoln
LINCOLN
Gawler
Elizabeth
Port Adelaide
ADELAIDE
Glenelg
Brighton
Minlaton
Hardwicke Bay
Corny Pt.
Yorketown
Edithburgh
Thistle I.
West Pt.
Birdwood
Mannum
Murray
Woodside
Murray Bridge
Mount Barker
McLaren Vale
Aldinga Beach
Willunga
Strathalbyn
Mt. Lofty Ranges
Gambier Is.
INNES
Marion Bay
C. Spencer
Neptune Is.
Investigator Strait
Normanville
Fleurieu Pen.
Victor Harbor
Goolwa
Port Elliot
Cape Jervis
Milang
L. Alexandrina
L. Albert
Meningie
Encounter Bay
Backstairs Passage
Penneshaw
Nepean Bay
Kingscote
American River
D'Estrees Bay
C. Borda
Parndana
FLINDERS CHASE
Kangaroo I.
Vivonne
Vivonne Bay
C. Gantheaume
C. du Couedic
The Coorong
Younghusband Peninsula
COORONG
Mount Victor
Mannahill
Olary
Mingary
Cockburn
Boolcoomata
Yunta
Paratoo
Nackara
Oakbank
Braemar
Canopus
Frome Downs
Benagerie
Pasmore
Siccus
Eurinilla Cr.
McDougalls Well
Barrier Range
486
Sturts Meadows
Silverton
Stephens Creek
Broken Hill
Packsaddle
White Cliffs
Peery Lake
Momba
Paroo
Tilpa
Tarella
MOOTWINGEE
Wilcannia
Wongalarroo L.
Gunyulka L.
Poopelloe L.
Darling
Talyawalka Cr.
Teryaweyna L.
Menindee L.
Menindee
KINCHEGA
Cawndilla L.
Tandou L.
North L.
Ratcatchers L.
Mount Manara
Gum Lake
Darnick
Beilpajah
Ivanhoe
Moornanyah L.
Popio L.
Popilta L.
Mindona L.
Mulurulu L.
Manfred
Mossgiel
Traveller's Lake
Pooncarie
Garnpung L.
L. Mungo
L. Leaghur
MUNGO
Burtundy
Arumpo
Hatfield P.O.
L. Victoria
Wentworth
Merbein
Buronga
Gol Gol
Trymple
Mildura
Red Cliffs
MALLEE CLIFFS
L. Pitarpunga
Oxley
Lachlan
Murrumbidgee
Maude
Renmark
Paringa
Berri
Barmera
MURRAY RIVER
Waikerie
Loxton
Maggea
Mantung
Sedan
Swan Reach
Cambrai
Kunlara
Wanbi
Alawoona
Taplan
Meribah
Meringur
Werrimull
MURRAY-SUNSET
Sandalwood
Peebinga
Hattah
HATTAH KULKYNE
Euston
Robinvale
Benanee
Bannerton
Balranald
Kulwin
Manangatang
Ouyen
Chinkapook
Piangil
Moulamein
Billabong Cr.
Karoonda
Marama
Pinnaroo
Lameroo
Cowangie
Underbool
Walpeup
Nyah West
L. Tyrrell
Niemur
Edward
Tailem Bend
Cooke Plains
Peake
Geranium
Yumali
Coonalpyn
Culburra
Tintinara
Patchewollock
Speed
Sea Lake
Ultima
Swan Hill
Lake Boga
Wakool
Barham
Koondrook
WYPERFELD
L. Albacutya
Lascelles
Hopetoun
Yaapeet
Berriwillock
Culgoa
Tyrrell
Lalbert
Kerang
Quambatook
Cohuna
Lake Hindmarsh
Beulah
Birchip
Avoca
Keith
Jeparit
Brim
Wycheproof
Boort
Warracknabeal
Charlton
Mitiamo
Litchfield
Kingston South East
Lacepede Bay
Bordertown
Nhill
Wolseley
Kaniva
Dimboola
Donald
Korong Vale
Rochester
Minyip
Wedderburn
Elmore
LITTLE DESERT
Padthaway
Frances
Murtoa
St. Arnaud
Inglewood
Bridgewater
Natimuk
Goroke
Wimmera
Horsham
Marnoo
Eaglehawk
Bendigo
Glenorchy
Dunolly
Maldon
Elphinstone
Reedy Creek
C. Jaffa
Lucindale
Naracoorte
Edenhope
The Grampians
Deep Lead
Stawell
Maryborough
Castlemaine
Avoca
Guichen B.
Robe
L. Eliza
L. St. Clair
Bool Lagoon
Harrow
Glenelg
GRAMPIANS
Balmoral
Rocklands Reservoir
Mt. William 1167
Ararat
Talbot
Kyneton
Clunes
Daylesford
Waubra
Woodend
Maroona
Beaufort
Creswick
Gisborne
Ballarat
Ballan
Melton
Bacchus Marsh
Scarsdale
Skipton
Meredith
BRISBANE RANGES
Derrinallum
Werribee
Penola
Beachport
L. George
Rivoli B.
Kalangadoo
Casterton
Cavendish
Glenthompson
Mininera
Nangwarry
Tarpeena
Coleraine
Dunkeld
Millicent
CANUNDA
L. Bonney
Hamilton
Penshurst
Mount Gambier
LOWER GLENELG
Dartmoor
Branxholme
Condah
Macarthur
MT. ECCLES
Mortlake
Cressy
Inverleigh
L. Corangamite
Lara
Port MacDonnell
C. Northumberland
DISCOVERY BAY
Discovery Bay
Heywood
Portland
Portland Bay
Koroit
Port Fairy
Warrnambool
Terang
Camperdown
Geelong
Winchelsea
Torquay
Queenscliff
Cobden
Colac
C. Bridgewater
C. Nelson
Allansford
Timboon
Forrest
Aireys Inlet
Lorne
Port Campbell
PORT CAMPBELL
Lavers Hill
Apollo Bay
OTWAY
C. Otway
SOUTHERN OCEAN
Bass
ft m
6000 2000
4500 1500
3000 1000
1200 400
600 200
0 0
200 600
2000 6000
4000 12 000
m ft
Projection: Alber's Equal area with two standard parallels
East from Greenwich

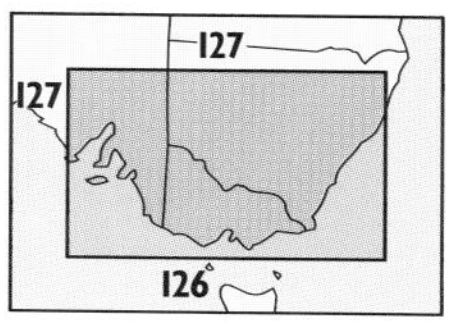

National Parks

COPYRIGHT GEORGE PHILIP LTD.

NEW ZEALAND – NORTH ISLAND 1:2 800 000

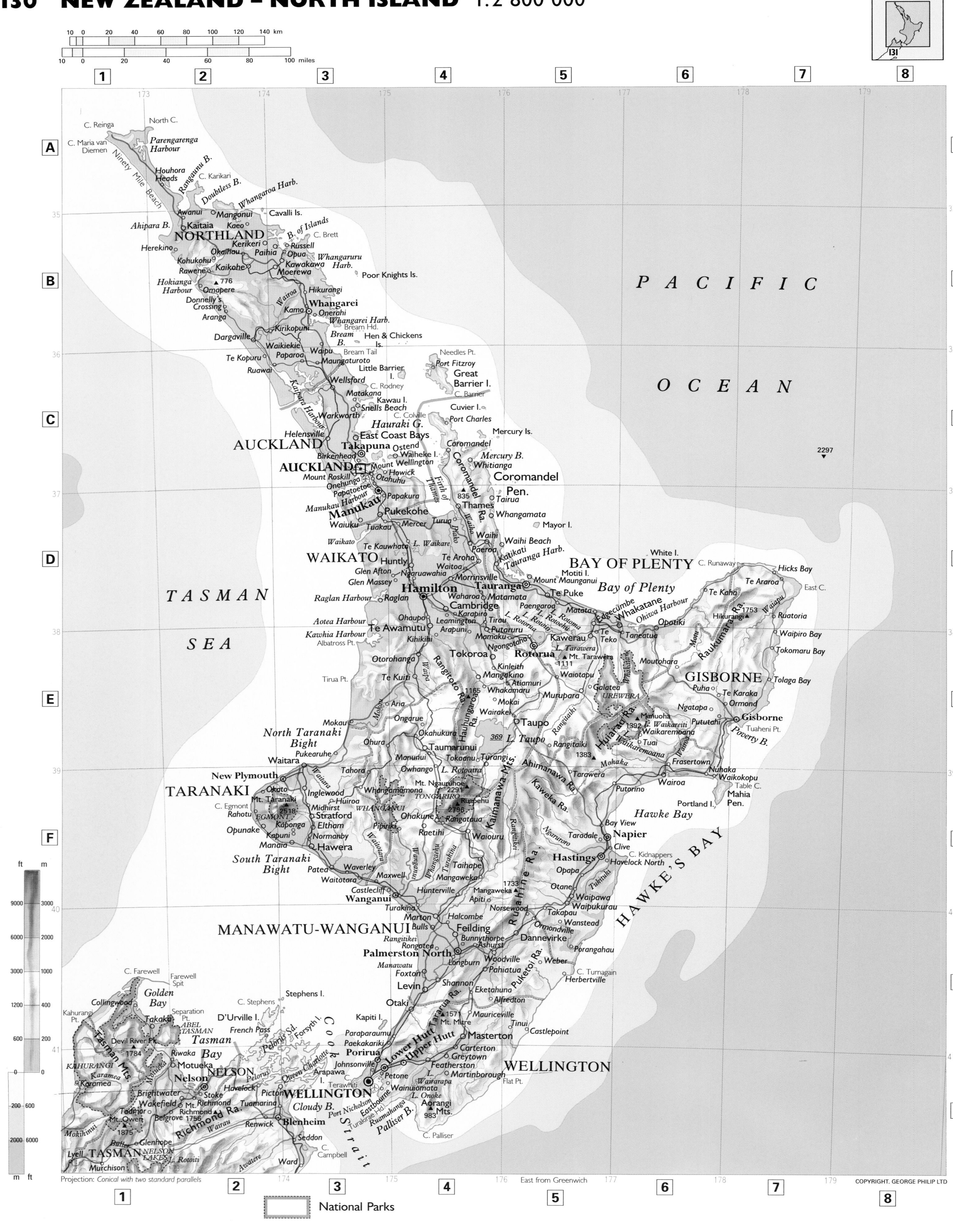
10 0 20 40 60 80 100 120 140 km
10 0 20 40 60 80 100 miles
1 2 3 4 5 6 7 8
A B C D E F G H
131
PACIFIC OCEAN
TASMAN SEA
C. Reinga
North C.
C. Maria van Diemen
Parengarenga Harbour
Rangaunu B.
Ninety Mile Beach
Houhora Heads
C. Karikari
Doubtless B.
Whangaroa Harb.
Awanui
Mangonui
Cavalli Is.
Ahipara B.
Kaitaia
Kaeo
B. of Islands
C. Brett
NORTHLAND
Kerikeri
Russell
Herekino
Okaihau
Paihia
Opua
Whangaruru Harb.
Kohukohu
Kawakawa
Rawene
Kaikohe
Moerewa
Poor Knights Is.
Hokianga Harbour
776
Omapere
Hikurangi
Donnelly's Crossing
Wairoa
Whangarei
Kamo
Onerahi
Aranga
Whangarei Harb.
Bream Hd.
Kirikopuni
Bream B.
Hen & Chickens Is.
Dargaville
Waikiekie
Paparoa
Waipu
Bream Tail
Te Kopuru
Maungaturoto
Needles Pt.
Ruawai
Port Fitzroy
Little Barrier I.
Great Barrier I.
Wellsford
C. Rodney
C. Barrier
Matakana
Kawau I.
Snells Beach
Cuvier I.
Kaipara Harbour
Warkworth
C. Colville
Port Charles
Hauraki G.
Helensville
East Coast Bays
Mercury Is.
AUCKLAND
Takapuna
Ostend
Coromandel
Birkenhead
Waiheke I.
Mercury B.
AUCKLAND
Mount Wellington
Whitianga
Mount Roskill
Howick
Onehunga
Otahuhu
Coromandel Pen.
Papatoetoe
Firth of Thames
835
Manukau Harbour
Manukau
Papakura
Tairua
Thames
Pukekohe
Whangamata
Waiuku
Tuakau
Mercer
Mayor I.
Waikato
Te Kauwhata
L. Waikare
Waihi
Waihi Beach
Paeroa
Katikati
White I.
WAIKATO
Huntly
Te Aroha
Tauranga Harb.
BAY OF PLENTY
C. Runaway
Hicks Bay
Glen Afton
Ngaruawahia
Waitoa
Motiti I.
Glen Massey
Morrinsville
Mount Maunganui
Te Araroa
TASMAN
Hamilton
Tauranga
Bay of Plenty
East C.
Raglan Harbour
Raglan
Waharoa
Matamata
Te Puke
Te Kaha
Cambridge
Paengaroa
Edgecumbe
Whakatane
Ohiwa Harbour
Waiapu
Karapiro
Matata
1753
Aotea Harbour
Ohaupo
Leamington
Tirau
L. Rotoma
Hikurangi
Ruatoria
Te Awamutu
Arapuni
L. Rotoiti
Putaruru
Te Teko
Taneatua
Opotiki
Raukumara Ra.
Waipiro Bay
Kawhia Harbour
Mamaku
Kawerau
Albatross Pt.
Kihikihi
Ngongotaha
L. Tarawera
SEA
Rotorua
Tokomaru Bay
Tokoroa
Mt. Tarawera
1111
Otorohanga
Kinleith
Moutohora
Mangakino
Waiotapu
Tirua Pt.
Te Kuiti
Atiamuri
GISBORNE
Tolaga Bay
Whakamaru
Galatea
Puha
1165
UREWERA
Te Karaka
Murupara
Ormond
Mokai
Aria
Wairakei
Ngatapa
Mokau
Ongarue
Taupo
Manuoha
Gisborne
1392
L. Waikareiti
Waikaremoana
Tuaheni Pt.
North Taranaki Bight
Okahukura
369
L. Taupo
Rangitaiki
Tuai
Poverty B.
Pukearuhe
Ohura
Taumarunui
Huiarau Ra.
L. Waikaremoana
Waitara
Manunui
Tokaanu
Turangi
1383
Mohaka
Frasertown
Nuhaka
New Plymouth
Tahora
Owhango
L. Rotoaira
Ahimanawa Ra.
Tarawera
Wairoa
Waikokopu
Mt. Ngauruhoe
Table C.
TARANAKI
Okato
Inglewood
Whangamomona
2291
Putorino
Mahia Pen.
Mt. Taranaki
Huiroa
TONGARIRO
Ruapehu
Kaweka Ra.
C. Egmont
2518
Midhirst
WHANGANUI
2796
Portland I.
Rahotu
EGMONT
Stratford
Ohakune
Rangataua
Hawke Bay
Kaponga
Eltham
Pipiriki
Kaimanawa Mts.
Bay View
Opunake
Kapuni
Normanby
Raetihi
Waiouru
Taradale
Napier
Manaia
Hawera
Clive
C. Kidnappers
South Taranaki Bight
Patea
Waverley
Taihape
Hastings
Havelock North
HAWKE'S BAY
Waitotara
Maxwell
Mangaweka
Opapa
Castlecliff
1733
Otane
Wanganui
Hunterville
Mangaweka
Apiti
Waipawa
Turakina
Norsewood
Waipukurau
Marton
Halcombe
Takapau
MANAWATU-WANGANUI
Bulls
Feilding
Ruahine Ra.
Ormondville
Wanstead
Rangitikei
Bunnythorpe
Dannevirke
Rongotea
Ashhurst
Porangahau
Palmerston North
Woodville
Weber
Manawatu
Longburn
Pahiatua
C. Turnagain
Foxton
Puketoi Ra.
Herbertville
Levin
Shannon
Eketahuna
C. Farewell
Farewell Spit
Stephens I.
Otaki
Alfredton
Golden Bay
C. Stephens
Collingwood
Tararua Ra.
1571
Mauriceville
Kahurangi Pt.
Separation Pt.
D'Urville I.
Kapiti I.
Mt. Mitre
Tinui
Takaka
ABEL TASMAN
French Pass
Paraparaumu
Masterton
Castlepoint
Tasman Bay
Pelorus Sd.
Cook Strait
Forsyth I.
Paekakariki
Lower Hutt
Upper Hutt
Carterton
Devil River Pk.
1784
Riwaka
Porirua
Greytown
KAHURANGI
Motueka
Queen Charlotte Sd.
Johnsonville
Featherston
WELLINGTON
Karamea
NELSON
Pelorus
Arapawa I.
Martinborough
Nelson
Tasman Mts.
Havelock
Terawhiti
Petone
Flat Pt.
Brightwater
Stoke
Picton
WELLINGTON
Wainuiomata
Wairarapa
Wakefield
Mt. Richmond
Tuamarina
Cloudy B.
Port Nicholson
L. Onoke
Tadmor
Richmond
Eastbourne
Aorangi Mts.
Mt. Owen
Belgrove
1756
Richmond Ra.
Wairau
Turakirae Hd.
Ruamahanga
Palliser B.
983
Mokihinui
1875
Renwick
Blenheim
C. Palliser
Buller
Glenhope
Seddon
Lyell
TASMAN
NELSON LAKES
C. Campbell
L. Rotoiti
Awatere
Ward
Murchison
2297
173 174 175 176 177 178 179
35 36 37 38 39 40 41
ft m
9000 3000
6000 2000
3000 1000
1200 400
600 200
0 0
200 600
2000 6000
m ft
Projection: Conical with two standard parallels
East from Greenwich
COPYRIGHT. GEORGE PHILIP LTD
National Parks

10 0 20 40 60 80 100 120 140 km
10 0 20 40 60 80 100 miles

1 2 3 4 5 6 7 8 9

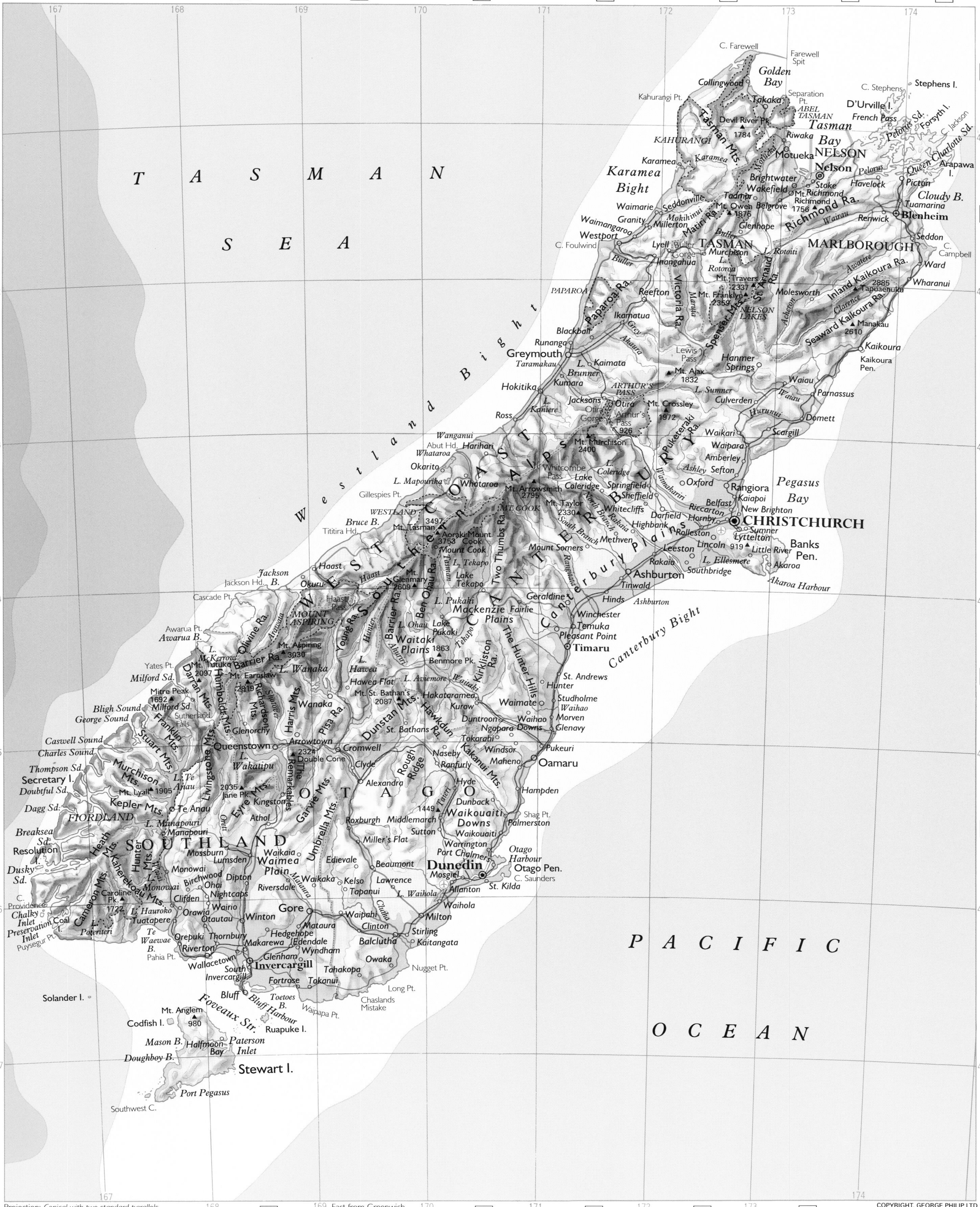
TASMAN SEA
Westland Bight
PACIFIC OCEAN
Canterbury Bight
C. Farewell
Farewell Spit
Golden Bay
Collingwood
Kahurangi Pt.
Takaka
Separation Pt.
ABEL TASMAN
Devil River Pk.
1784
Tasman Mts.
KAHURANGI
Tasman Bay
Riwaka
Motueka
NELSON
Nelson
Karamea
Karamea Bight
Brightwater
Wakefield
Stoke
Mt. Richmond
Richmond 1756
Richmond Ra.
Tadmor
Mt. Owen 1876
Belgrove
Glenhope
Seddonville
Waimarie
Granity
Millerton
Waimangaroa
Westport
C. Foulwind
Matiri Ra.
Mokihinui
Lyell
Buller Gorge
Inangahua
TASMAN
Murchison
Rotoroa
Rotoiti
Mt. Travers 2337
Mt. Franklyn 2359
NELSON LAKES
Spenser Mts.
St. Arnaud Ra.
Victoria Ra.
Maruia
Reefton
PAPAROA
Paparoa Ra.
Ikamatua
Blackball
Runanga
Greymouth
Taramakau
L. Brunner
Kaimata
Kumara
Hokitika
L. Kaniere
Ross
Lewis Pass
Mt. Ajax 1832
Hanmer Springs
L. Sumner
Culverden
ARTHUR'S PASS
Otira
Jacksons
Otira Gorge
Arthur's Pass 926
Mt. Crossley 1972
Stephens I.
C. Stephens
D'Urville I.
French Pass
Pelorus Sd.
Forsyth I.
C. Jackson
Queen Charlotte Sd.
Arapawa I.
Havelock
Picton
Tuamarina
Cloudy B.
Renwick
Blenheim
Wairau
MARLBOROUGH
Seddon
C. Campbell
Ward
Awatere
Inland Kaikoura Ra.
2885 Tapuaenuku
Wharanui
Molesworth
Clarence
Seaward Kaikoura Ra.
Manakau 2610
Kaikoura
Kaikoura Pen.
Waiau
Parnassus
Hurunui
Domett
Waikari
Scargill
Waipara
Amberley
Ashley
Sefton
Oxford
Rangiora
Pegasus Bay
Kaiapoi
Belfast
New Brighton
CHRISTCHURCH
Sumner
Lyttelton
Hornby
Riccarton
Rolleston
Darfield
Lincoln
Leeston
L. Ellesmere
Little River
Banks Pen.
Akaroa
Akaroa Harbour
Southbridge
Rakaia
Ashburton
Tinwald
Wanganui
Abut Hd.
Harihari
Whataroa
Okarito
L. Mapourika
Whataroa
Gillespies Pt.
WESTLAND
Bruce B.
Titritira Hd.
WEST COAST
SOUTHERN ALPS
CANTERBURY
Mt. Murchison 2400
Whitcombe Pass
Lake Coleridge
L. Coleridge
Springfield
Sheffield
Whitecliffs
Mt. Arrowsmith 2795
MT. COOK
Mt. Taylor 2330
Highbank
Methven
Mt. Tasman 3497
Aoraki Mount Cook 3753
Mount Cook
L. Tekapo
Lake Tekapo
Mount Somers
Canterbury Plains
Two Thumbs Ra.
Haast
Jackson B.
Jackson Hd.
Okuru
Mt. Glenmary 2609
Ben Ohau Ra.
Cascade Pt.
Haast Pass
MOUNT ASPIRING
Geraldine
Fairlie
Hinds
L. Pukaki
Mackenzie Plains
Winchester
Temuka
Pleasant Point
Timaru
The Hunter Hills
Awarua Pt.
Awarua B.
Olivine Ra.
Barrier Ra.
Mt. Aspiring 3030
L. Wanaka
Young Ra.
L. Hawea
L. Ohau
Lake Pukaki
Waitaki Plains
1863
Benmore Pk.
Kirkliston Ra.
Yates Pt.
Milford Sd.
L. McKerrow
Mt. Tutuko 2097
Mt. Earnslaw 2819
Darran Mts.
Humboldt Mts.
Richardson Mts.
Mitre Peak 1692
Hawea Flat
L. Aviemore
Waitaki
St. Andrews
Hunter
Studholme
Waimate
Waihao
Morven
Glenavy
Mt. St. Bathan's 2087
Hakataramea
Kurow
Duntroon
Ngapara
Bligh Sound
George Sound
Sutherland Falls
Franklin Mts.
Glenorchy
Harris Mts.
Wanaka
Pisa Ra.
Dunstan Mts.
St. Bathans Ra.
Hawkdun Ra.
Kakanui Mts.
Caswell Sound
Charles Sound
Stuart Mts.
Queenstown
Arrowtown
2324
Double Cone
Cromwell
Naseby
Ranfurly
Pukeuri
Oamaru
Maheno
Thompson Sd.
Secretary I.
Doubtful Sd.
Murchison Mts.
L. Te Anau
Livingstone Mts.
L. Wakatipu
The Remarkables
Clyde
Rough Ridge
Hyde
Mt. Lyall 1905
2035 Jane Pk.
Eyre Mts.
Kingston
Alexandra
OTAGO
Dunback
Hampden
Dagg Sd.
FIORDLAND
Kepler Mts.
Te Anau
Athol
Garvie Mts.
Umbrella Mts.
1449
Waikouaiti Downs
Shag Pt.
Palmerston
L. Manapouri
Manapouri
SOUTHLAND
Roxburgh
Middlemarch
Sutton
Waikouaiti
Breaksea Sd.
Resolution I.
Mossburn
Lumsden
Waikaia
Waimea Plain
Miller's Flat
Warrington
Port Chalmers
Otago Harbour
Otago Pen.
Dusky Sd.
Heath Mts.
Kaherekoau Mts.
Hunter Mts.
Monowai
L. Monowai
Birchwood
Ohai
Dipton
Riversdale
Edievale
Beaumont
Dunedin
Mosgiel
C. Saunders
St. Kilda
Allanton
Lawrence
Kelso
Tapanui
L. Waihola
Waihola
C. Providence
Chalky Inlet
Preservation Inlet
Coal I.
Cameron Mts.
Caroline Pk. 1722
L. Poteriteri
L. Hauroko
Tuatapere
Clifden
Orawia
Nightcaps
Wairio
Otautau
Winton
Gore
Mataura
Waipahi
Clinton
Clutha
Milton
Puysegur Pt.
Te Waewae B.
Pahia Pt.
Orepuki
Thornbury
Riverton
Makarewa
Hedgehope
Edendale
Wyndham
Balclutha
Stirling
Kaitangata
Wallacetown
South Invercargill
Glenham
Invercargill
Owaka
Tahakopa
Fortrose
Tokanui
Nugget Pt.
Long Pt.
Chaslands Mistake
Waipapa Pt.
Toetoes B.
Bluff
Bluff Harbour
Foveaux Str.
Ruapuke I.
Solander I.
Mt. Anglem 980
Codfish I.
Mason B.
Halfmoon Bay
Paterson Inlet
Doughboy B.
Stewart I.
Port Pegasus
Southwest C.
167
168
169
170
171
172
173
174
41
42
43
44
45
46
47
A
B
C
D
E
F
G
H

ft	m
9000	3000
6000	2000
3000	1000
1200	400
600	200
0	0
200	600
2000	6000
4000	12 000
m	ft

Projection: *Conical with two standard parallels*

East from Greenwich

COPYRIGHT. GEORGE PHILIP LTD

1 2 3 4 5 6 7 8 9

National Parks

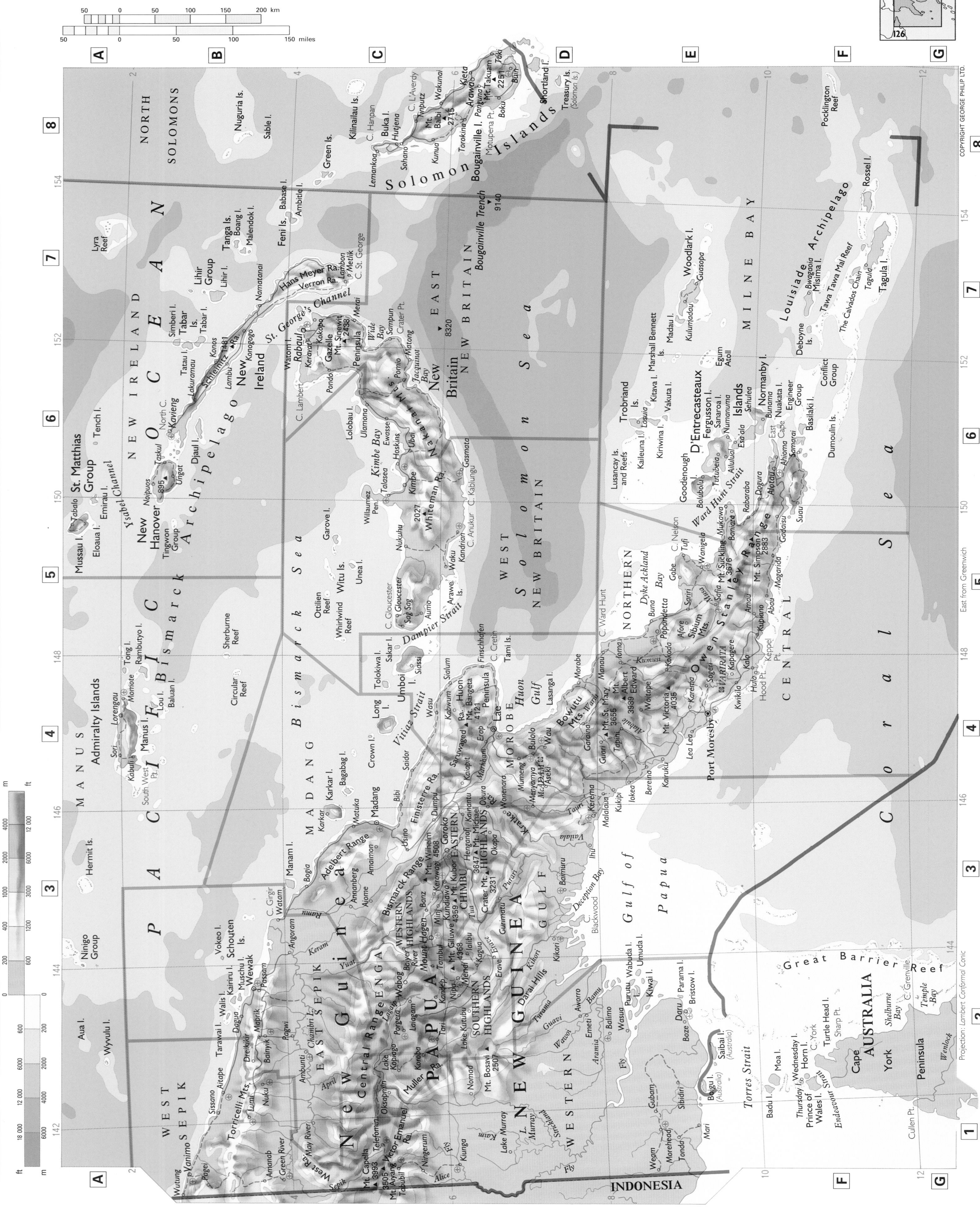
50
0
50
100
150
200 km
50
0
50
100
150 miles
A
B
C
D
E
F
G
1
2
3
4
5
6
7
8
NORTH SOLOMONS
Solomon Islands
Bougainville I.
Bougainville Trench
Buka I.
Arawa
Kieta
Buin
Shortland I.
Treasury Is. (Solomon Is.)
Nuguria Is.
Feni Is.
Tanga Is.
Lihir Group
NEW IRELAND
New Ireland
Kavieng
Namatanai
St. George's Channel
Rabaul
Kokopo
Gazelle Peninsula
EAST NEW BRITAIN
New Britain
WEST NEW BRITAIN
Kimbe Bay
Kimbe
Whiteman Ra.
Nakanai Mts.
Bismarck Archipelago
Bismarck Sea
St. Matthias Group
New Hanover
MANUS
Admiralty Islands
Manus I.
Lorengau
Hermit Is.
Ninigo Group
Wuvulu I.
Aua I.
PACIFIC OCEAN
Solomon Sea
Dampier Strait
Vitiaz Strait
Umboi I.
Long I.
Karkar I.
Madang
MADANG
Adelbert Range
Finisterre Ra.
Huon Peninsula
Huon Gulf
Lae
MOROBE
Wau
Bulolo
Bismarck Range
Mt. Wilhelm 4508
Goroka
EASTERN HIGHLANDS
CHIMBU
WESTERN HIGHLANDS
Mount Hagen
ENGA
Wabag
SOUTHERN HIGHLANDS
Mendi
Central Range
EAST SEPIK
Wewak
WEST SEPIK
Vanimo
Sepik
Fly
Lake Murray
WESTERN
Daru
Torres Strait
PAPUA
Gulf of Papua
GULF
Kerema
CENTRAL
Port Moresby
Owen Stanley Range
Mt. Victoria 4035
Mt. Albert Edward 3990
NORTHERN
Popondetta
Dyke Ackland Bay
MILNE BAY
Alotau
Trobriand Is.
Kiriwina I.
Woodlark I.
D'Entrecasteaux Islands
Goodenough I.
Fergusson I.
Normanby I.
Louisiade Archipelago
Misima I.
Tagula I.
Rossel I.
Coral Sea
Great Barrier Reef
AUSTRALIA
Cape York Peninsula
INDONESIA
Projection: Lambert Conformal Conic
East from Greenwich
Tracks
COPYRIGHT GEORGE PHILIP LTD.
m
ft
83
126

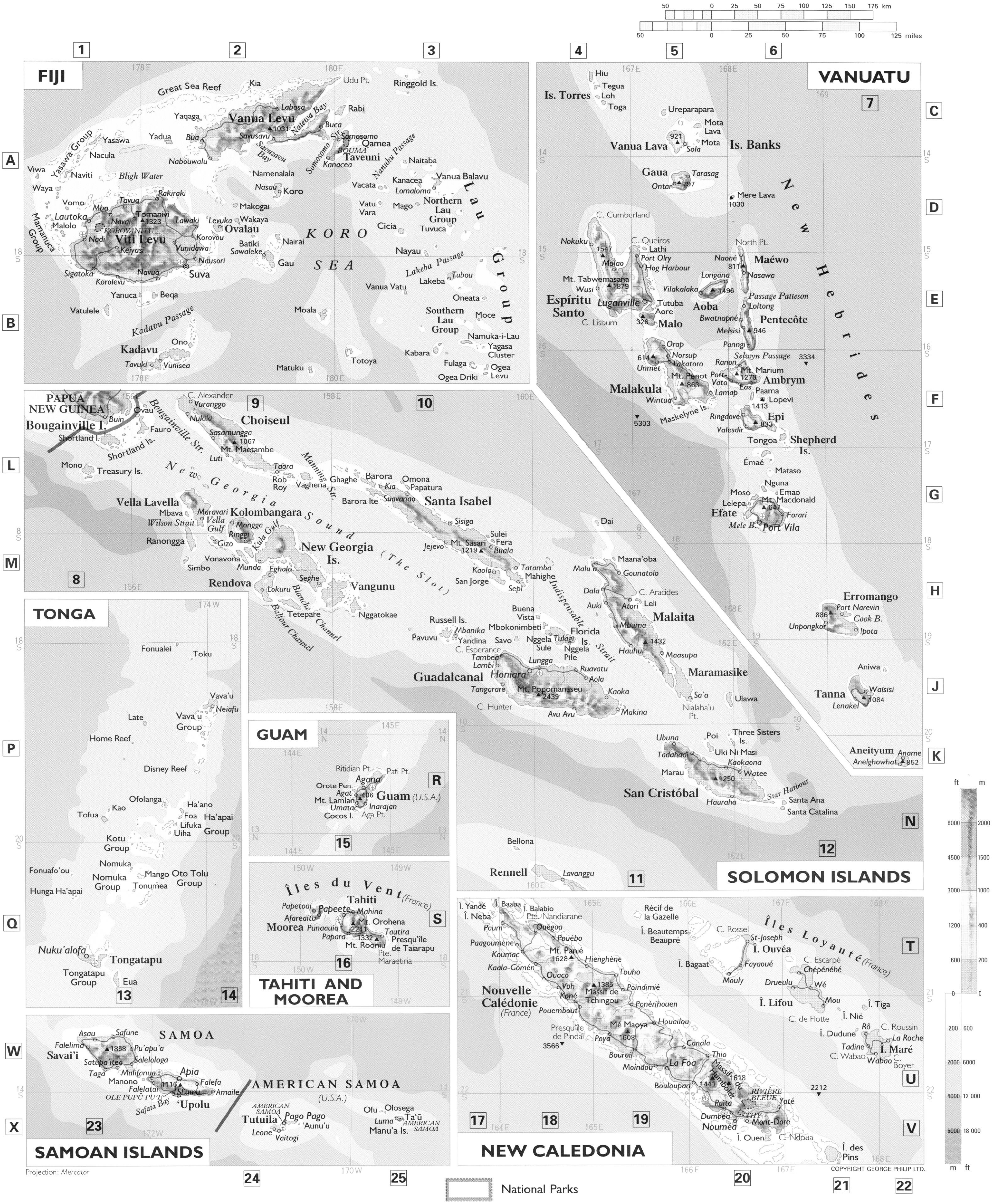
FIJI
Great Sea Reef
Kia
Udu Pt.
Ringgold Is.
Labasa
Yaqaga
Vanua Levu
1031
Natewa Bay
Rabi
Buca
Yadua
Savusavu
Bua
Samosomo
Qamea
Yasawa Group
Yasawa
Savusavu Bay
BOUMA
Taveuni
Somosomo Str.
Nanuku Passage
Nacula
Nabouwalu
Kanacea
Naitaba
Viwa
Naviti
Bligh Water
Namenalala
Vanua Balavu
Kanacea
Vacata
Waya
Nasau
Koro
Lomaloma
Rakiraki
Vatu Vara
Northern Lau Group
Vomo
Tavua
Makogai
Mago
Lau
Mamanuca Group
Lautoka
Mba
Tomanivi 1323
Lawaki
Levuka
Wakaya
Malolo
Navai
Ovalau
Cicia
Tuvuca
KOROYANITU
Korovou
KORO
Nadi
Viti Levu
Batiki
Nairai
Keiyasi
Vunidawa
Sawaleke
Nayau
SEA
Nausori
Gau
Lakeba Passage
Tubou
Group
Sigatoka
Navua
Suva
Lakeba
Korolevu
Vanua Vatu
Oneata
Yanuca
Beqa
Southern Lau Group
Moce
Vatulele
Moala
Kadavu Passage
Namuka-i-Lau
Ono
Yagasa Cluster
Kadavu
Kabara
Totoya
Fulaga
Tavuki
Vunisea
Matuku
Ogea Levu
Ogea Driki
178 E
180 E
18 S
VANUATU
Hiu
Tegua
Is. Torres
Loh
Toga
Ureparapara
Mota
Lava
Vanua Lava
921
Mota
Is. Banks
Sola
Gaua
Tarasag
Ontar
797
Mere Lava
1030
C. Cumberland
New Hebrides
North Pt.
Nokuku
C. Queiros
Lathi
1547
Port Olry
Naoné
Maéwo
Hog Harbour
811
Molao
Longana
Nasawa
Mt. Tabwemasana
1879
Vilakalaka
1496
Wusi
Passage Patteson
Espíritu Santo
Luganville
Tutuba
Aoba
Loltong
Aore
Bwatnapné
Pentecôte
C. Lisburn
326
Malo
Melsisi
946
Orap
Pangi
Norsup
Selwyn Passage
3334
614
Lakatoro
Ranon
Unmet
Mt. Penot
Mt. Marium
Port Vato
1270
Ambrym
863
Malakula
Eas
Lamap
Paama
Wintua
Lopevi
Maskelyne Is.
1413
5303
Ringdove
Epi
Valesdir
833
Tongoa
Shepherd Is.
Émaé
Mataso
Nguna
Moso
Emao
Lelepa
Mt. Macdonald
Efate
647
Forari
Mele B.
Port Vila
Erromango
Port Narevin
886
Cook B.
Unpongkor
Ipota
Aniwa
Tanna
Waïsisi
1084
Lenakel
Aneityum
Aname
Anelghowhat
852
167 E
168 E
169
14 S
15 S
16 S
17 S
18 S
19 S
20 S
SOLOMON ISLANDS
PAPUA NEW GUINEA
C. Alexander
Yuranggo
Buin
Ovau
Bougainville I.
Nukiki
Choiseul
Bougainville Str.
Fauro
Shortland I.
Sasamungga
1067
Shortland Is.
Mt. Maetambe
Luti
Mono
Treasury Is.
New Georgia Sound
Manning Str.
Taora
Barora
Omona
Rob Roy
Kia
Papatura
Vaghena
Ghaghe
Barora Ite
Suavanao
Santa Isabel
Vella Lavella
Mbava
Maravari
Kolombangara
Vella Gulf
Sisiga
Wilson Strait
Mongga
Ringgi
Sulei
Fera
Ranongga
Gizo
Kula Gulf
New Georgia Is.
Jejevo
Mt. Sasari
1219
Buala
(The Slot)
Dai
Vonavona
Munda
Tatamba
Maana'oba
Simbo
Eghol
Kaolo
Mahighe
Malu
Gounatolo
Rendova
Seghe
San Jorge
Sepi
Lokuru
Vangunu
Dala
C. Aracides
Blanche Channel
Auki
Leli
Tetepare
Atori
Malaita
Ngatokae
Buena Vista
Indispensable Strait
Russell Is.
Mbokonimbeti
Florida Is.
Mbanika
Mbuma
Pavuvu
Yandina
Savo
Nggela Sule
Tulagi
1432
C. Esperance
Nggela Pile
Hauhui
Maasupa
Tambea
Lungga
Lambi
Ruavatu
Maramasike
Guadalcanal
Honiara
Aola
Tangarare
Mt. Popomanaseu
2439
Kaoka
Sa'a
C. Hunter
Ulawa
Nialaha'u Pt.
Avu Avu
Makina
Ubuna
Poi
Three Sisters Is.
Tadahadi
Uki Ni Masi
Kaokaona
Marau
Waite
1250
San Cristóbal
Star Harbour
Hauraha
Santa Ana
Santa Catalina
Bellona
Rennell
Lavanggu
156 E
158 E
160 E
162 E
8 S
10 S
TONGA
Fonualei
Toku
Vava'u
Neiafu
Late
Vava'u Group
Home Reef
Disney Reef
Ofolanga
Ha'ano
Kao
Foa
Ha'apai
Tofua
Lifuka
Group
Uiha
Kotu Group
Nomuka
Fonuafo'ou
Mango
Oto Tolu
Nomuka Group
Group
Tonumea
Hunga Ha'apai
Nuku'alofa
Tongatapu
Tongatapu Group
Eua
174 W
18 S
20 S
GUAM
Ritidian Pt.
Pati Pt.
Agana
Orote Pen.
Agat
Guam (U.S.A.)
Mt. Lamlam
406
Umatac
Inarajan
Cocos I.
Aga Pt.
144 E
145 E
13 N
14 N
TAHITI AND MOOREA
Îles du Vent (France)
Tahiti
Papetoai
Papeete
Mahina
Afareaitu
Mt. Orohena
Moorea
Punaauia
2241
Papara
1332
Taiarapu
Mt. Roonui
Presqu'île de Taiarapu
Pte. Maraetiria
150 W
149 W
18 S
SAMOAN ISLANDS
Asau
Safune
SAMOA
Falelima
Savai'i
1858
Pu'apu'a
Salelologa
Satupa'itea
Taga
Mulifanua
Apia
Manono
1116
Falefa
Falelatai
Si'umu
Amaile
OLE PUPŪ PU'E
Safata Bay
'Upolu
AMERICAN SAMOA (U.S.A.)
AMERICAN SAMOA
Ofu
Olosega
Tutuila
Pago Pago
Ta'ū
'Aunu'u
Luma
AMERICAN SAMOA
Leone
Vaitogi
Manu'a Is.
172 W
170 W
14 S
NEW CALEDONIA
Î. Yandé
Î. Baaba
Î. Balabio
Î. Neba
Pte. Nandiarane
Récif de la Gazelle
Poum
Ouégoa
Î. Beautemps-Beaupré
C. Rossel
Îles Loyauté (France)
Pouébo
St-Joseph
Paagoumène
Mt. Panié
Î. Ouvéa
Koumac
1628
Hienghène
C. Escarpé
Fayaoué
Kaala-Gomén
Î. Bagaat
Chépénéhé
Ouaco
Touho
Mouly
1385
Drueulu
Wé
Nouvelle Calédonie (France)
Voh
Massif de Tchingou
Poindimié
Koné
Î. Lifou
Mou
Î. Tiga
Ponérihouen
Pouembout
C. de Flotte
Î. Niè
Houailou
Presqu'île de Pindaï
Mé Maoya
Rô
C. Roussin
Poya
1608
Î. Dudune
La Roche
3566
Canala
Î. Maré
Bourail
Tadine
Thio
C. Wabao
Wabao
C. Boyer
Moindou
La Foa
Massif du Humboldt
1618
Boulouparí
1441
2212
RIVIÈRE BLEUE
Yaté
Païta
Dumbéa
THY
Mont-Dore
Nouméa
Î. Ouen
C. Ndoua
Î. des Pins
164 E
165 E
166 E
167 E
168 E
21 S
22 S
Projection: Mercator
COPYRIGHT GEORGE PHILIP LTD.
National Parks
km
miles
ft
m

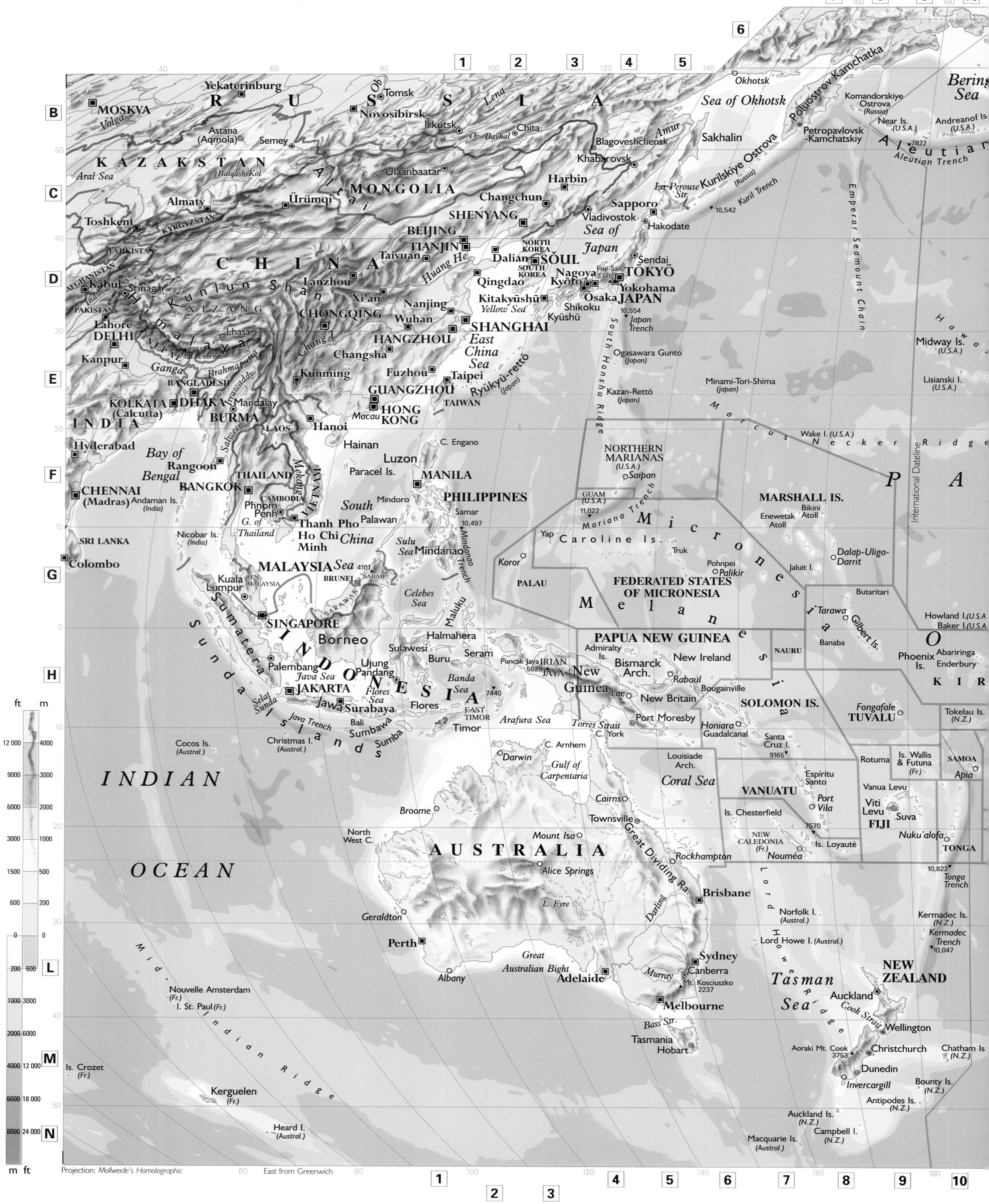
Okhotsk
Sea of Okhotsk
Poluostrov Kamchatka
Bering Sea
Komandorskiye Ostrova (Russia)
Near Is. (U.S.A.)
Andreanof Is. (U.S.A.)
Petropavlovsk -Kamchatskiy
Aleutian
Aleutian Trench
7822
Yekaterinburg
MOSKVA
Volga
RUSSIA
Ob
Tomsk
Novosibirsk
Lena
Irkutsk
Oz. Baykal
Chita
Amur
Blagoveshchensk
Sakhalin
Astana (Aqmola)
Semey
KAZAKSTAN
Aral Sea
Balqash Köl
Ulaanbaatar
Khabarovsk
Kurilskiye Ostrova (Russia)
Kuril Trench
10,542
La Perouse Str.
Harbin
Altai
MONGOLIA
Ürümqi
Almaty
Changchun
Sapporo
Vladivostok
Hakodate
Toshkent
KYRGYZSTAN
SHENYANG
BEIJING
TIANJIN
Taiyuan
Sea of Japan
TAJIKISTAN
CHINA
NORTH KOREA
Dalian
SŎUL
SOUTH KOREA
Sendai
AFGHANISTAN
Kabul
Srinagar
Lanzhou
Huang He
Qingdao
Nagoya
Fuji-San 3776
TŌKYŌ
Yokohama
Indus
Kunlun Shan
Xi'an
Kyōto
Ōsaka
JAPAN
PAKISTAN
XIZANG
Nanjing
Kitakyūshū
Yellow Sea
Shikoku
Kyūshū
10,554
Japan Trench
Lahore
DELHI
Himalaya
Lhasa
CHONGQING
Wuhan
SHANGHAI
NEPAL
8850 Mt. Everest
Chang Jiang
HANGZHOU
East China Sea
South Honshu Ridge
Kanpur
Brahmaputra
Changsha
Ryūkyū-rettō (Japan)
Ogasawara Gunto (Japan)
Ganga
Irrawaddy
Kunming
Fuzhou
Taipei
Minami-Tori-Shima (Japan)
BANGLADESH
GUANGZHOU
Kazan-Rettō (Japan)
KOLKATA (Calcutta)
DHAKA
Mandalay
HONG KONG
Macau
TAIWAN
Marcus Necker Ridge
INDIA
BURMA
Hanoi
LAOS
Wake I. (U.S.A.)
Hyderabad
Salween
Hainan
C. Engano
NORTHERN MARIANAS (U.S.A.)
Bay of Bengal
Rangoon
Mekong
Luzon
Saipan
THAILAND
Paracel Is.
MANILA
VIETNAM
CHENNAI (Madras)
Andaman Is. (India)
BANGKOK
CAMBODIA
Phnom Penh
South China Sea
Mindoro
PHILIPPINES
GUAM (U.S.A.)
11,022
Mariana Trench
MARSHALL IS.
Bikini Atoll
Enewetak Atoll
Samar
10,497
G. of Thailand
Thanh Pho Ho Chi Minh
Palawan
Micronesia
SRI LANKA
Nicobar Is. (India)
Sulu Sea
Mindanao
Mindanao Trench
Yap
Caroline Is.
Truk
Dalap-Uliga-Darrit
Colombo
MALAYSIA
4101
BRUNEI
SABAH
Koror
Pohnpei
Palikir
Jaluit I.
Kuala Lumpur
PEN. MALAYSIA
SARAWAK
Celebes Sea
PALAU
FEDERATED STATES OF MICRONESIA
Butaritari
Sumatera
SINGAPORE
Maluku
Melanesia
Tarawa
Gilbert Is.
Howland I. (U.S.A.)
Baker I. (U.S.A.)
Borneo
INDONESIA
Halmahera
PAPUA NEW GUINEA
Admiralty Is.
Sulawesi
Seram
Banaba
NAURU
Phoenix Is.
Abariringa
Enderbury
KIRIBATI
Sunda Islands
Palembang
Ujung Pandang
Buru
Puncak Jaya 5029
IRIAN JAYA
New Guinea
Bismarck Arch.
New Ireland
Rabaul
Java Sea
Banda Sea
7440
Lae
Bougainville
JAKARTA
Flores Sea
New Britain
SOLOMON IS.
Fongafale
TUVALU
Tokelau Is. (N.Z.)
Selat Sunda
Jawa
Surabaya
Flores
EAST TIMOR
Arafura Sea
Torres Strait
Port Moresby
Java Trench
Bali
Sumbawa
Sumba
Timor
C. York
Honiara
Guadalcanal
Santa Cruz I.
9165
Rotuma
Is. Wallis & Futuna (Fr.)
SAMOA
Apia
Cocos Is. (Austral.)
Christmas I. (Austral.)
C. Arnhem
Darwin
Gulf of Carpentaria
Louisiade Arch.
Coral Sea
Espíritu Santo
Port Vila
VANUATU
Vanua Levu
Viti Levu
Suva
FIJI
INDIAN OCEAN
Broome
Cairns
Is. Chesterfield
Townsville
7570
Nuku'alofa
North West C.
Mount Isa
NEW CALEDONIA (Fr.)
Is. Loyauté
Nouméa
AUSTRALIA
Great Dividing Ra.
Rockhampton
TONGA
Alice Springs
10,822
Tonga Trench
Brisbane
Lord Howe Ridge
L. Eyre
Darling
Norfolk I. (Austral.)
Geraldton
Kermadec Is. (N.Z.)
Kermadec Trench
10,047
Lord Howe I. (Austral.)
Perth
Great Australian Bight
Sydney
Canberra
NEW ZEALAND
Albany
Adelaide
Murray
Mt. Kosciuszko 2237
Tasman Sea
Auckland
Nouvelle Amsterdam (Fr.)
I. St. Paul (Fr.)
Melbourne
Cook Strait
Bass Str.
Wellington
Mid-Indian Ridge
Tasmania
Hobart
Aoraki Mt. Cook 3753
Christchurch
Chatham Is. (N.Z.)
Is. Crozet (Fr.)
Dunedin
Invercargill
Bounty Is. (N.Z.)
Kerguelen (Fr.)
Antipodes Is. (N.Z.)
Auckland Is. (N.Z.)
Campbell I. (N.Z.)
Heard I. (Austral.)
Macquarie Is. (Austral.)
Emperor Seamount Chain
Hawaiian
Midway Is. (U.S.A.)
Lisianski I. (U.S.A.)
International Dateline
PACIFIC OCEAN
ft m
12 000 4000
9000 3000
6000 2000
3000 1000
1500 500
600 200
0 0
200 600
1000 3000
2000 6000
4000 12 000
6000 18 000
8000 24 000
m ft
Projection: Mollweide's Homolographic
East from Greenwich

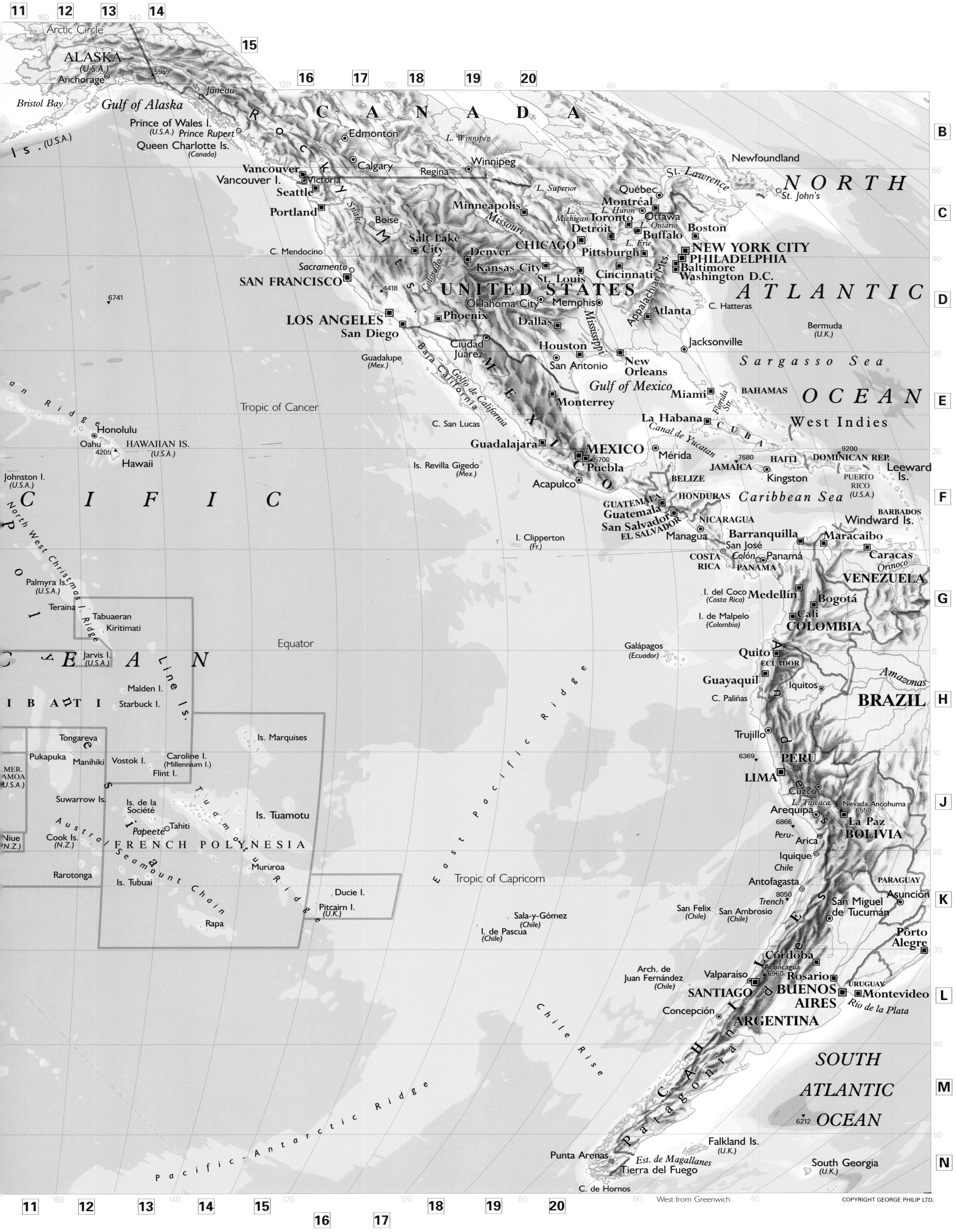

ALASKA
(U.S.A.)
Anchorage
Arctic Circle
Bristol Bay
Gulf of Alaska
Juneau
Prince of Wales I.
(U.S.A.)
Prince Rupert
Queen Charlotte Is.
(Canada)
C A N A D A
Rocky Mts
Edmonton
Calgary
Regina
Winnipeg
L. Winnipeg
Vancouver
Vancouver I.
Victoria
Seattle
Portland
Boise
Snake
Salt Lake City
Denver
Colorado
Minneapolis
Missouri
L. Superior
L. Michigan
L. Huron
L. Ontario
L. Erie
Québec
Montréal
Ottawa
Toronto
Detroit
Buffalo
Boston
CHICAGO
Pittsburgh
NEW YORK CITY
PHILADELPHIA
Baltimore
Washington D.C.
Cincinnati
Appalachian Mts.
St. Lawrence
Newfoundland
St. John's
NORTH
ATLANTIC
OCEAN
C. Mendocino
Sacramento
SAN FRANCISCO
Kansas City
St. Louis
UNITED STATES
Oklahoma City
Memphis
Mississippi
Atlanta
C. Hatteras
Bermuda
(U.K.)
LOS ANGELES
San Diego
Phoenix
Dallas
Ciudad Juárez
Houston
San Antonio
New Orleans
Jacksonville
Sargasso Sea
Gulf of Mexico
Miami
Florida Str.
BAHAMAS
Guadalupe
(Mex.)
Baja California
Golfo de California
MEXICO
Monterrey
Tropic of Cancer
C. San Lucas
Guadalajara
Puebla
5700
Acapulco
Is. Revilla Gigedo
(Mex.)
La Habana
Canal de Yucatan
Mérida
CUBA
West Indies
7680
JAMAICA
Kingston
HAITI
DOMINICAN REP.
9200
PUERTO RICO
(U.S.A.)
Leeward Is.
BELIZE
HONDURAS
GUATEMALA
Guatemala
San Salvador
EL SALVADOR
Caribbean Sea
NICARAGUA
Managua
BARBADOS
Windward Is.
Barranquilla
Maracaibo
Caracas
Orinoco
San José
COSTA RICA
Colón
Panamá
PANAMA
VENEZUELA
I. Clipperton
(Fr.)
I. del Coco
(Costa Rica)
Medellín
Bogotá
Cali
I. de Malpelo
(Colombia)
COLOMBIA
Galápagos
(Ecuador)
Quito
ECUADOR
Equator
Guayaquil
Iquitos
Amazonas
C. Paliñas
BRAZIL
Trujillo
6369
PERU
LIMA
Andes
Cuzco
L. Titicaca
Nevada Ancohuma
6550
La Paz
BOLIVIA
Arequipa
6866
Peru-Chile Trench
Arica
Iquique
Antofagasta
8050
PARAGUAY
Asunción
San Miguel de Tucumán
San Felix
(Chile)
San Ambrosio
(Chile)
Pôrto Alegre
Córdoba
Aconcagua
6960
Rosario
Arch. de Juan Fernández
(Chile)
Valparaíso
SANTIAGO
BUENOS AIRES
URUGUAY
Montevideo
Río de la Plata
Concepción
ARGENTINA
PATAGONIA
SOUTH ATLANTIC OCEAN
6212
Falkland Is.
(U.K.)
Punta Arenas
Est. de Magallanes
Tierra del Fuego
C. de Hornos
South Georgia
(U.K.)
Chile Rise
East Pacific Ridge
Pacific-Antarctic Ridge
Sala-y-Gómez
(Chile)
I. de Pascua
(Chile)
Tropic of Capricorn
Ducie I.
Pitcairn I.
(U.K.)
Is. Marquises
Is. Tuamotu
Tuamotu Ridge
Mururoa
Rapa
FRENCH POLYNESIA
Austral Seamount Chain
Is. Tubuai
Is. de la Société
Tahiti
Papeete
Caroline I.
(Millennium I.)
Flint I.
Vostok I.
Tongareva
Pukapuka
Manihiki
Suwarrow Is.
Cook Is.
(N.Z.)
Rarotonga
Niue
(N.Z.)
AMER. SAMOA
(U.S.A.)
KIRIBATI
Line Is.
Malden I.
Starbuck I.
Jarvis I.
(U.S.A.)
Tabuaeran
Kiritimati
Teraina
Palmyra Is.
(U.S.A.)
North West Christmas I. Ridge
PACIFIC OCEAN
Johnston I.
(U.S.A.)
Hawaiian Ridge
Honolulu
Oahu
HAWAIIAN IS.
(U.S.A.)
4205
Hawaii
6741
4418
5959
West from Greenwich

COPYRIGHT GEORGE PHILIP LTD.

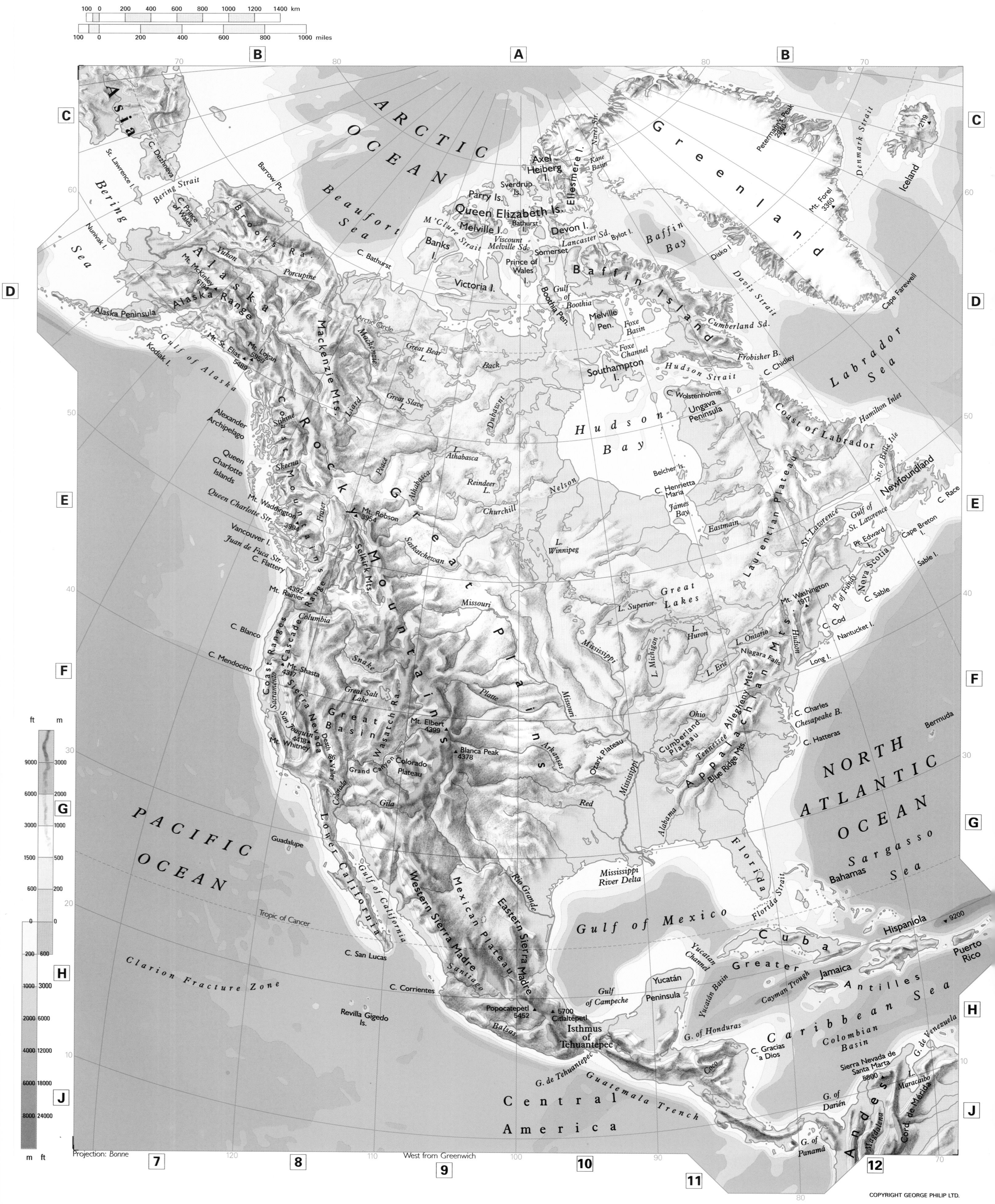

100 0 200 400 600 800 1000 1200 1400 km
100 0 200 400 600 800 1000 miles
A
B
C
D
E
F
G
H
J
7
8
9
10
11
12
ARCTIC OCEAN
Asia
C. Dezhneva
St. Lawrence I.
Bering Strait
Bering Sea
Nunivak I.
C. Prince of Wales
Barrow Pt.
Beaufort Sea
Brooks Ra.
Yukon
Porcupine
Alaska
Mt. McKinley 6194
Alaska Range
Alaska Peninsula
Kodiak I.
Gulf of Alaska
Mt. St. Elias 5489
Mt. Logan 5959
Mackenzie Mts.
Mackenzie
Arctic Circle
Great Bear L.
Great Slave L.
Liard
Stikine
Alexander Archipelago
Queen Charlotte Islands
Skeena
Coast Mountains
Rocky
Mt. Waddington 3994
Queen Charlotte Str.
Vancouver I.
Juan de Fuca Str.
C. Flattery
Fraser
Mt. Robson 3954
Selkirk Mts.
Mountains
Great Plains
Peace
Athabasca
L. Athabasca
Reindeer L.
Churchill
Saskatchewan
Nelson
L. Winnipeg
Missouri
4392 Mt. Rainier
Cascade Range
Columbia
C. Blanco
C. Mendocino
Coast Ranges
Mt. Shasta 4317
Sacramento
San Joaquin
Sierra Nevada
Mt. Whitney 4418
Death Valley -86
Snake
Great Salt Lake
Great Basin
Wasatch Ra.
Mt. Elbert 4399
Blanca Peak 4378
Platte
Colorado Plateau
Grand Canyon
Colorado
Gila
Arkansas
Ozark Plateau
Red
Mississippi
Banks I.
Victoria I.
C. Bathurst
M'Clure Strait
Viscount Melville Sd.
Melville I.
Queen Elizabeth Is.
Parry Is.
Sverdrup Is.
Axel Heiberg I.
Ellesmere I.
Nares Str.
Kane Basin
Bathurst I.
Devon I.
Lancaster Sd.
Bylot I.
Somerset I.
Prince of Wales I.
Gulf of Boothia
Boothia Pen.
Back
Dubawnt
Melville Pen.
Foxe Basin
Foxe Channel
Southampton I.
Baffin Island
Baffin Bay
Cumberland Sd.
Frobisher B.
Hudson Strait
C. Chidley
C. Wolstenholme
Ungava Peninsula
Hudson Bay
Belcher Is.
C. Henrietta Maria
James Bay
Eastmain
Laurentian Plateau
Greenland
Petermann's Peak 2940
Mt. Forel 3360
Disko I.
Davis Strait
Cape Farewell
Denmark Strait
Iceland
2119
Labrador Sea
Coast of Labrador
Hamilton Inlet
Str. of Belle Isle
Newfoundland
C. Race
Gulf of St. Lawrence
St. Lawrence
Pt. Edward I.
Cape Breton I.
Nova Scotia
Sable I.
B. of Fundy
C. Sable
Mt. Washington 1917
C. Cod
Nantucket I.
Long I.
Hudson
Great Lakes
L. Superior
L. Michigan
L. Huron
L. Ontario
L. Erie
Niagara Falls
Allegheny Mts.
Appalachian Mts.
Ohio
Cumberland Plateau
Tennessee
Blue Ridge Mts.
Alabama
C. Charles
Chesapeake B.
C. Hatteras
Bermuda
NORTH ATLANTIC OCEAN
Sargasso Sea
Bahamas
Florida
Florida Strait
Mississippi River Delta
Gulf of Mexico
Cuba
Yucatan Channel
Greater Antilles
Hispaniola
9200
Puerto Rico
Jamaica
Cayman Trough
Yucatán Basin
Yucatán Peninsula
Gulf of Campeche
G. of Honduras
C. Gracias a Dios
Caribbean Sea
Colombian Basin
Coco
G. de Venezuela
L. Maracaibo
Sierra Nevada de Santa Marta 5800
Cord. de Mérida
Magdalena
Andes
G. of Darién
G. of Panamá
Central America
Guatemala Trench
G. de Tehuantepec
Isthmus of Tehuantepec
Popocatepetl 5452
5700 Citlaltépetl
Balsas
Santiago
Western Sierra Madre
Mexican Plateau
Eastern Sierra Madre
Rio Grande
Gulf of California
Lower California
Guadalupe
C. San Lucas
C. Corrientes
Revilla Gigedo Is.
Clarion Fracture Zone
Tropic of Cancer
PACIFIC OCEAN
Projection: Bonne
West from Greenwich
ft m
9000 3000
6000 2000
3000 1000
1500 500
600 200
0 0
200 600
1000 3000
2000 6000
4000 12000
6000 18000
8000 24000
m ft

100 0 200 400 600 800 1000 1200 1400 km
100 0 200 400 600 800 1000 miles
A
B
C
D
E
F
G
H
J
7
8
9
10
11
12
International Date Line
RUSSIA
Asia
St. Lawrence I.
Bering Strait
Bering Sea
ARCTIC OCEAN
Beaufort Sea
Queen Elizabeth Is.
Ellesmere I.
GREENLAND (Denmark)
Denmark Strait
ICELAND
Reykjavík
Baffin Bay
Baffin Island
Davis Strait
Nuuk
Cape Farewell
Victoria I.
NUNAVUT
Yukon
ALASKA (USA)
Porcupine
Fairbanks
Anchorage
Kodiak I.
Gulf of Alaska
NORTHWEST
Arctic Circle
YUKON TERRITORY
Mackenzie
Great Bear L.
Back
TERRITORIES
Whitehorse
Yellowknife
Juneau
Liard
Great Slave L.
Dubawnt
Hudson Strait
Hudson Bay
CANADA
BRITISH COLUMBIA
Skeena
Peace
Athabasca
L. Athabasca
Churchill
Nelson
NEWFOUNDLAND
Labrador
St. John's
Eastmain
QUÉBEC
St. Lawrence
PRINCE EDWARD I.
Charlottetown
St-Pierre Et Miquelon (Fr.)
NEW BRUNSWICK
NOVA SCOTIA
Halifax
Fredericton
C. Sable
Fraser
ALBERTA
Edmonton
MANITOBA
SASKATCHEWAN
Saskatchewan
Calgary
L. Winnipeg
ONTARIO
Québec
Victoria
Vancouver
Regina
Winnipeg
WASHINGTON
Olympia
Seattle
Portland
Salem
Columbia
OREGON
MONTANA
Missouri
Helena
NORTH DAKOTA
Bismarck
MINNESOTA
L. Superior
Montréal
Ottawa
MAINE
Augusta
VER.
N.H.
Concord
Boston
Providence
MASS.
CONN.
R.I.
NEW YORK CITY
Hartford
PHILADELPHIA
IDAHO
Boise
Snake
SOUTH DAKOTA
Minneapolis
WISCONSIN
Madison
L. Michigan
MICHIGAN
Lansing
L. Huron
Toronto
L. Ontario
Buffalo
NEW YORK
Detroit
L. Erie
Cleveland
PA.
Pittsburgh
N.J.
WYOMING
Milwaukee
Toledo
Cheyenne
Salt Lake City
Sacramento
SAN FRANCISCO
San Jose
Carson City
NEVADA
UTAH
UNITED STATES
NEBRASKA
Lincoln
IOWA
CHICAGO
OHIO
Columbus
Baltimore
DE.
MD.
Washington D.C.
W.V.
Richmond
ILLINOIS
INDIANA
Indianapolis
Cincinnati
Springfield
CALIFORNIA
Denver
Kansas City
Topeka
St. Louis
VIRGINIA
COLORADO
KANSAS
MISSOURI
KENTUCKY
Nashville
TENNESSEE
Raleigh
NORTH CAROLINA
Charlotte
Bermuda (U.K.)
Las Vegas
LOS ANGELES
San Diego
Colorado
Santa Fe
Albuquerque
NEW MEXICO
ARIZONA
Phoenix
Tucson
OKLAHOMA
Oklahoma City
ARKANSAS
Little Rock
Memphis
Birmingham
Columbia
Atlanta
SOUTH CAROLINA
GEORGIA
Charleston
Mississippi
MISSISSIPPI
Jackson
Montgomery
ALABAMA
Jacksonville
Tallahassee
NORTH ATLANTIC OCEAN
Dallas
El Paso
TEXAS
Austin
Houston
Baton Rouge
LOUISIANA
New Orleans
FLORIDA
Tampa
Miami
PACIFIC OCEAN
Guadalupe (Mex.)
Hermosillo
Rio Grande
Nassau
BAHAMAS
Turks & Caicos Is. (U.K.)
Florida Str.
Gulf of Mexico
Tropic of Cancer
Culiacan
MEXICO
Monterrey
Havana
CUBA
DOMINICAN REP.
San Juan
PUERTO RICO (U.S.A.)
HAITI
Port-au-Prince
Santo Domingo
Cayman Is. (U.K.)
JAMAICA
Kingston
Mérida
Guadalajara
MÉXICO
Puebla
Revilla Gigedo Is. (Mex.)
Acapulco
Belmopan
BELIZE
Caribbean Sea
GUATEMALA
Guatemala
HONDURAS
Tegucigalpa
San Salvador
EL SALVADOR
NICARAGUA
L. Nicaragua
Managua
Maracaibo
Barranquilla
VENEZUELA
COSTA RICA
San José
Panamá
PANAMA
COLOMBIA
Medellín
South America
Projection: Bonne
West from Greenwich
MÉXICO Capital Cities

COPYRIGHT GEORGE PHILIP LTD.

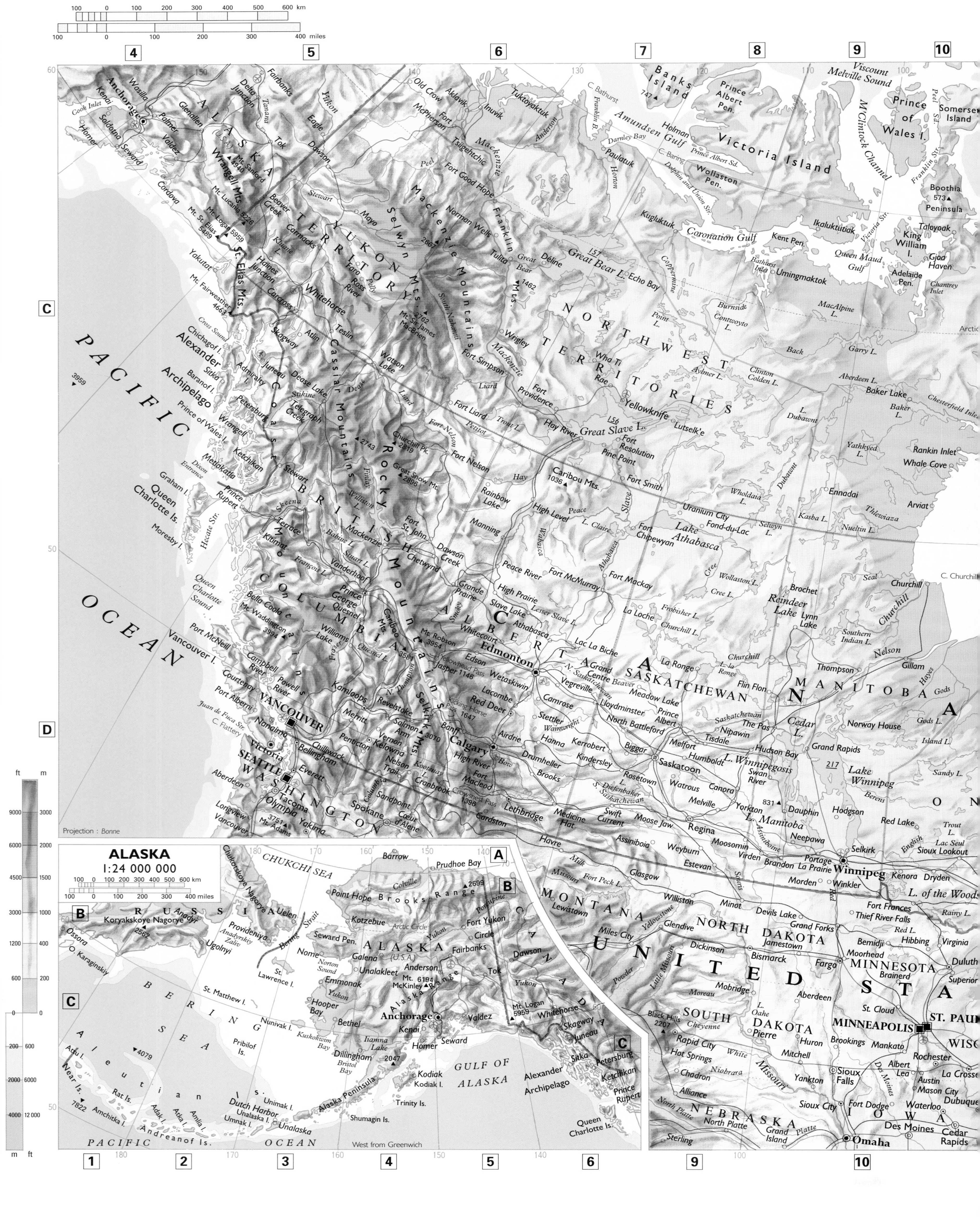
100 0 100 200 300 400 500 600 km
100 0 100 200 300 400 miles
Projection: Bonne
PACIFIC OCEAN
ALASKA
YUKON TERRITORY
NORTHWEST TERRITORIES
BRITISH COLUMBIA
ALBERTA
SASKATCHEWAN
MANITOBA
WASHINGTON
MONTANA
NORTH DAKOTA
SOUTH DAKOTA
MINNESOTA
NEBRASKA
IOWA
UNITED STATES
Banks Island
Victoria Island
Prince of Wales I.
Somerset Island
Viscount Melville Sound
M'Clintock Channel
Amundsen Gulf
Coronation Gulf
Queen Maud Gulf
Great Bear L.
Great Slave L.
Lake Athabasca
Reindeer Lake
Lake Winnipeg
L. Winnipegosis
L. Manitoba
L. of the Woods
Mackenzie Mountains
Selwyn Mts.
Rocky Mountains
Cassiar Mountains
Coast Mountains
Columbia Mountains
Selkirk Mts.
Wrangell Mts.
St. Elias Mts.
Caribou Mts.
Alexander Archipelago
Queen Charlotte Is.
Vancouver I.
Anchorage
Fairbanks
Whitehorse
Dawson
Inuvik
Tuktoyaktuk
Yellowknife
Hay River
Fort Smith
Fort Nelson
Prince Rupert
Prince George
Kamloops
VANCOUVER
Victoria
SEATTLE
Spokane
Edmonton
Calgary
Red Deer
Lethbridge
Medicine Hat
Saskatoon
Regina
Brandon
Winnipeg
Churchill
Thompson
Flin Flon
The Pas
Baker Lake
Rankin Inlet
Arviat
Fort McMurray
Grande Prairie
Dawson Creek
Fort St. John
Mt. Logan 5959
Mt. Robson 3954
Bismarck
Fargo
Grand Forks
MINNEAPOLIS
ST. PAUL
Duluth
Omaha
Des Moines
Pierre
Rapid City
ALASKA
1:24 000 000
100 0 100 200 300 400 500 600 km
100 0 100 200 300 400 miles
CHUKCHI SEA
BERING SEA
GULF OF ALASKA
PACIFIC OCEAN
RUSSIA
CANADA
Brooks Range
Alaska Range
Aleutian Is.
Kodiak I.
Alaska Peninsula
Mt. McKinley 6194
Barrow
Prudhoe Bay
Nome
Kotzebue
Juneau
West from Greenwich
ft m
9000 3000
6000 2000
4500 1500
3000 1000
1200 400
600 200
0 0
200 600
2000 6000
4000 12000

146
147
11
12
13
14
15
16
B
C
D
E
Devon I.
Lancaster Sound
Baffin Bay
Nunavik
Uummannaq
Ilulissat
Qasigiannguit
Tasiilaq
GREENLAND
(KALAALLIT NUNAAT)
(Denmark)
Arctic Bay
Nanisivik
Bylot I.
Pond Inlet
Brodeur Peninsula
Borden Pen.
Eclipse Sd.
C. Adair
Clyde River
Qeqertarsuaq
Kangerlussuaq
Kong Frederik VI's Kyst
Gulf of Boothia
Baffin Island
C. Raper
Home B.
Davis Strait
Sisimiut
Maniitsoq
Fury and Hecla Str.
Igloolik
Qikiqtarjuaq
C. Dyer
Simpson Pen.
Pelly Bay
Committee B.
Melville Peninsula
Sanirajak
Air Force I.
Prince Charles I.
Foxe Basin
Cumberland Peninsula
Pangnirtung
Hoare B.
Nuuk
Qeqertarsuatsiaat
Paamiut
Arsuk
Qaqortoq
Nanortalik
Alluitsup Paa
Uummannarsuaq
Rae Isthmus
Repulse Bay
Nettilling L.
Mercy C.
Cumberland Sd.
NUNAVUT
Circle
C. Dorchester
Amadjuak L.
Wager B.
Roes Welcome Sd.
Foxe Channel
Foxe Pen.
Iqaluit
Hall Peninsula
Meta Incognita Peninsula
Kimmirut
Frobisher Bay
Resolution I.
Southampton I.
Salliq
Bell Pen.
Cape Dorset
Salisbury I.
Nottingham I.
Hudson Strait
Labrador Sea
ATLANTIC OCEAN
Igluligaarjuk
Coats I.
Mansel I.
Ivujivik
Salluit
Kangiqsujuaq
Quaqtaq
Akpatok I.
C. Chidley
Péninsule d'Ungava
Kangirsuk
Ungava Bay
Kangiqsualujjuaq
Hebron
Puvirnituq
Arnaud
L. Payne
Hudson Bay
Ottawa Is.
Feuilles
Koksoak
Kuujjuaq
George
Baleine
Nain
C. Harrison
Hopedale
NEWFOUNDLAND
Inukjuak
Mélèzes
Caniapiscau
L. Minto
Rigolet
Cartwright
Sleeper Is.
King George Is.
Baker's Dozen Is.
Sanikiluaq
Belcher Is.
Smallwood Res.
Labrador
North West River
Happy Valley-Goose Bay
Port Hope Simpson
Belle Isle
C. Bauld
St. Anthony
C. Tatnam
Schefferville
L. Petitsikapau
Esker
Churchill Falls
Churchill
L. à l'Eau Claire
L. Bienville
Kuujjuarapik
Grande Baleine
C. Henrietta Maria
Rés. de Caniapiscau
Labrador City
Fermont
L. Ashuanipi
Natashquan
Romaine
St-Augustin
Str. of Belle Isle
Notre Dame B.
Lewisporte
Gander
Bonavista
Trinity B.
Carbonear
St. John's
Peawanuck
Severn
Winisk
Kanaaupscow
La Grande
Pte. Louis XIV
Chisasibi
James Bay
Gagnon
Moisie
Havre-St-Pierre
Baie Verte
Deer Lake
Grand Falls
Corner Brook
Newfoundland
Stephenville
Placentia B.
Placentia
C. Race
Marystown
Big Trout L.
Akimiski I.
Wemindji
Rés. Manicouagan
Î. d'Anticosti
Attawapiskat
Eastmain
Sept-Îles
Port-Cartier
Fort Albany
Charlton I.
Waskaganish
Rupert
L. Mistassini
L. Albanel
Manicouagan
Gulf of St. Lawrence
Channel-Port aux Basques
C. Ray
Cabot Str.
ST.-PIERRE et MIQUELON (Fr.)
ONTARIO
QUEBEC
Albany
L. St. Joseph
Moosonee
Nottaway
Harricana
Péribonca
Baie Comeau
Matane
Gaspé
Pén. de Gaspé
Îs. de la Madeleine
North C.
Cape Breton I.
Glace Bay
Chibougamau
Rimouski
Campbellton
Bathurst
PR. EDWARD I.
Missinaibi
Nakina
Kenogami
L. Matagami
Matagami
Dolbeau
L. St-Jean
Chicoutimi
Rivière-du-Loup
Edmundston
Miramichi
Summerside
Charlottetown
Sydney
Port Hawkesbury
L. Nipigon
Nipigon
Geraldton
Hearst
Mattagami
Cochrane
Abitibi L.
Amos
Rés. Gouin
Roberval
Jonquière
NEW BRUNSWICK
Northumberland Str.
Antigonish
Marathon
Kapuskasing
Oba
Timmins
Kirkland Lake
Rouyn-Noranda
Val-d'Or
La Tuque
Québec
Grand Falls
Moncton
New Glasgow
Truro
NOVA SCOTIA
Thunder Bay
Chapleau
New Liskeard
Lévis
Thetford Mines
Woodstock
Fredericton
Amherst
Kentville
Dartmouth
Halifax
Sable I. (Nova Scotia)
Lake Superior
Wawa
Rés. Cabonga
Mont-Laurier
Shawinigan
Trois-Rivières
Joliette
Saint John
B. of Fundy
Digby
Bridgewater
Liverpool
Houghton
Sault Ste. Marie
Elliot Lake
Sudbury
Ottawa
MONTRÉAL
St-Hyacinthe
Sherbrooke
MAINE
Bangor
Yarmouth
C. Sable
Ironwood
Marquette
L. Nipissing
North Bay
Parry Sound
Pembroke
Hull
Granby
L. Champlain
Augusta
Lewiston
Portland
Manistique
Manitoulin I.
Georgian Bay
Huntsville
Cornwall
Montpelier
Burlington
VERMONT
NEW HAMPSHIRE
Concord
Manchester
Rhinelander
Escanaba
Menominee
Petoskey
Lake Huron
Barrie
Peterborough
Kingston
WISCONSIN
Wausau
Green Bay
Traverse City
Cadillac
Owen Sound
Oshawa
Belleville
Appleton
Sheboygan
MICHIGAN
L. Michigan
Saginaw
Grand Rapids
Flint
TORONTO
Kitchener
London
Hamilton
L. Ontario
Syracuse
Albany
MASS.
BOSTON
C. Cod
Providence
MILWAUKEE
Madison
Racine
Kenosha
Rockford
Lansing
Sarnia
Niagara Falls
BUFFALO
Rochester
NEW YORK
Springfield
HARTFORD
CONN.
R.I.
New Haven
Elmira
Binghamton
Bridgeport
Windsor
DETROIT
L. Erie
Erie
Jamestown
Scranton
NEW YORK
CHICAGO
Gary
South Bend
Toledo
CLEVELAND
Newark
N.J.
Allentown
Trenton
PENNSYLVANIA
ILLINOIS
INDIANA
OHIO
2136
1890
2850
2591
3809
1652
257
1135
814
1190
6309
183
177
174
75
90
80
70
60
50
40
30
West from Greenwich
COPYRIGHT GEORGE PHILIP LTD.

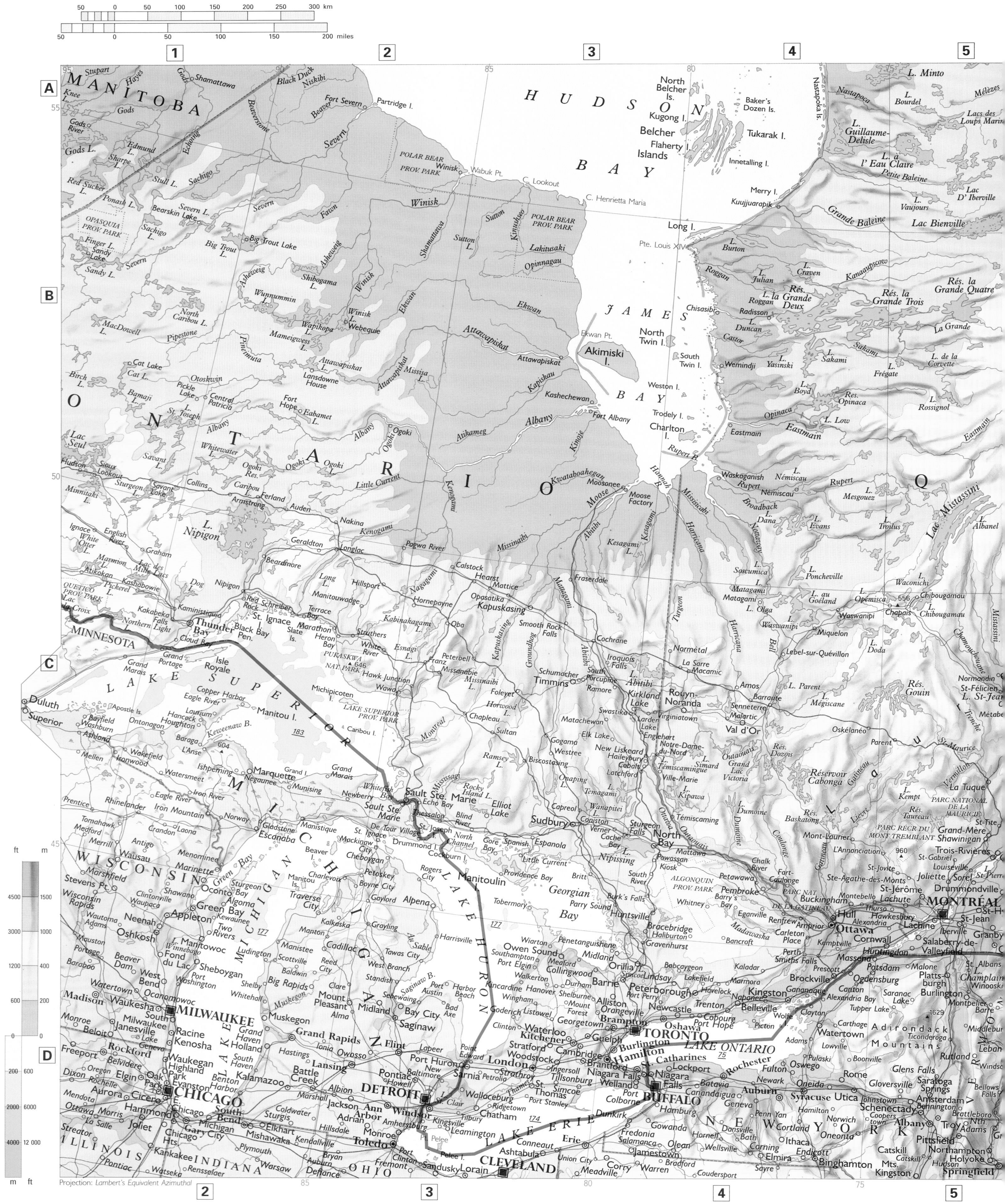
50 0 50 100 150 200 250 300 km
50 0 50 100 150 200 miles
1 2 3 4 5
A B C D
HUDSON BAY
JAMES BAY
MANITOBA
ONTARIO
MINNESOTA
WISCONSIN
MICHIGAN
ILLINOIS
INDIANA
OHIO
NEW YORK
LAKE SUPERIOR
LAKE MICHIGAN
LAKE HURON
LAKE ONTARIO
LAKE ERIE
Georgian Bay
Belcher Islands
Akimiski I.
North Twin I.
South Twin I.
Manitoulin
Isle Royale
L. Nipigon
Lac Seul
L. Mistassini
Réservoir Cabonga
POLAR BEAR PROV. PARK
OPASQUIA PROV. PARK
QUETICO PROV. PARK
PUKASKWA NAT. PARK
LAKE SUPERIOR PROV. PARK
ALGONQUIN PROV. PARK
PARC NATIONAL DE LA MAURICIE
PARC RECR DU MONT TREMBLANT
PARC NAT DE LA GATINEAU
Adirondack Mountains
Winisk
Fort Severn
Attawapiskat
Kashechewan
Fort Albany
Moosonee
Moose Factory
Chisasibi
Radisson
Wemindji
Eastmain
Waskaganish
Kuujjuarapik
Chibougamau
Chapais
Thunder Bay
Nipigon
Geraldton
Longlac
Hearst
Kapuskasing
Cochrane
Timmins
Kirkland Lake
Rouyn-Noranda
Val d'Or
Amos
Wawa
Sault Ste. Marie
Sudbury
North Bay
Duluth
Superior
Marquette
Escanaba
Green Bay
Appleton
Oshkosh
MILWAUKEE
Madison
Racine
Kenosha
CHICAGO
Gary
Grand Rapids
Lansing
Flint
Saginaw
DETROIT
Windsor
Toledo
CLEVELAND
London
Kitchener
Hamilton
TORONTO
Oshawa
Peterborough
Barrie
Kingston
Ottawa
Hull
MONTRÉAL
Trois-Rivières
Cornwall
St. Catharines
Niagara Falls
BUFFALO
Rochester
Syracuse
Utica
Schenectady
Albany
Binghamton
Erie
Watertown
Springfield
ft m
4500 1500
3000 1000
1200 400
600 200
0 0
200 600
2000 6000
4000 12 000
m ft
Projection: Lambert's Equivalent Azimuthal

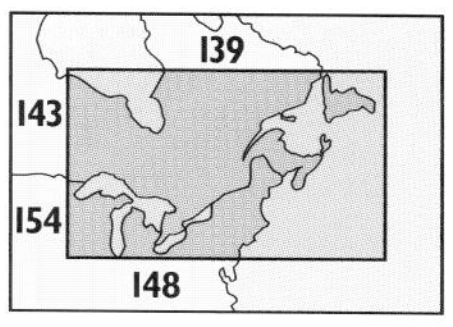
139
143
154
148

6
7
8
9
A
B
C
D
LABRADOR
SEA
NEWFOUNDLAND
Labrador
Newfoundland
QUÉBEC
GULF OF
ST. LAWRENCE
ATLANTIC
OCEAN
UNITED
STATES
MAINE
NEW
BRUNSWICK
NOVA
SCOTIA
PRINCE EDWARD
ISLAND
Cape Breton
Island
Î. d'Anticosti
Pén. de Gaspé
Mts. Chic-Chocs
Smallwood Reservoir
Rés. de
Caniapiscau
Rés.
Manicouagan
Rés.
Pipmuacan
Mealy Mts.
Long Range Mts.
Str. of Belle Isle
Cabot Strait
Bay of Fundy
Northumberland Str.
St. Lawrence
Nain
Davis Inlet
Hopedale
Makkovik
Postville
Rigolet
Cartwright
North West River
Happy Valley-
Goose Bay
Churchill Falls
Twin Falls
Schefferville
Labrador City
Wabush
Fermont
Gagnon
Sept-Îles
Port-Cartier
Baie Comeau
Havre-St-Pierre
Natashquan
Kegaska
Romaine
Harrington Harbour
St-Augustin
Blanc-Sablon
L'Anse au Loup
Red Bay
Mary's Harbour
St. Anthony
Corner Brook
Stephenville
Deer Lake
Gander
Grand Falls
Windsor
Lewisporte
Clarenville
Carbonear
St. John's
Mt. Pearl
Marystown
Burin
Argentia
Placentia
Channel-Port
aux Basques
ST.-PIERRE
ET MIQUELON
(France)
Îs. de la
Madeleine
(Québec)
Gaspé
Matane
Rimouski
Rivière-du-Loup
Chicoutimi
Jonquière
La Baie
Alma
Tadoussac
Québec
Lévis
Montmagny
Thetford
Mines
Sherbrooke
Magog
Edmundston
Campbellton
Bathurst
Miramichi
Moncton
Fredericton
Saint John
Sussex
Charlottetown
Summerside
Souris
Sydney
Glace Bay
Louisbourg
Amherst
Truro
New Glasgow
Antigonish
Halifax
Dartmouth
Kentville
Windsor
Digby
Annapolis
Royal
Yarmouth
Shelburne
Lunenburg
Bridgewater
Liverpool
Sable I.
(Nova Scotia)
C. Sable
Bangor
Augusta
Waterville
Lewiston
Auburn
Brunswick
Portland
Bath
Biddeford
Saco
Sanford
Dover
Rochester
Portsmouth
Concord
Manchester
Nashua
Keene
Haverhill
Lawrence
Lowell
Lynn
Newton
BOSTON
Gloucester
Quincy
Brockton
Worcester
Woonsocket
Presque Isle
Caribou
Houlton
Millinocket
Calais
Eastport
Ellsworth
Bar Harbor
Mount
Desert I.
West from Greenwich
70
65
60
55
50
45

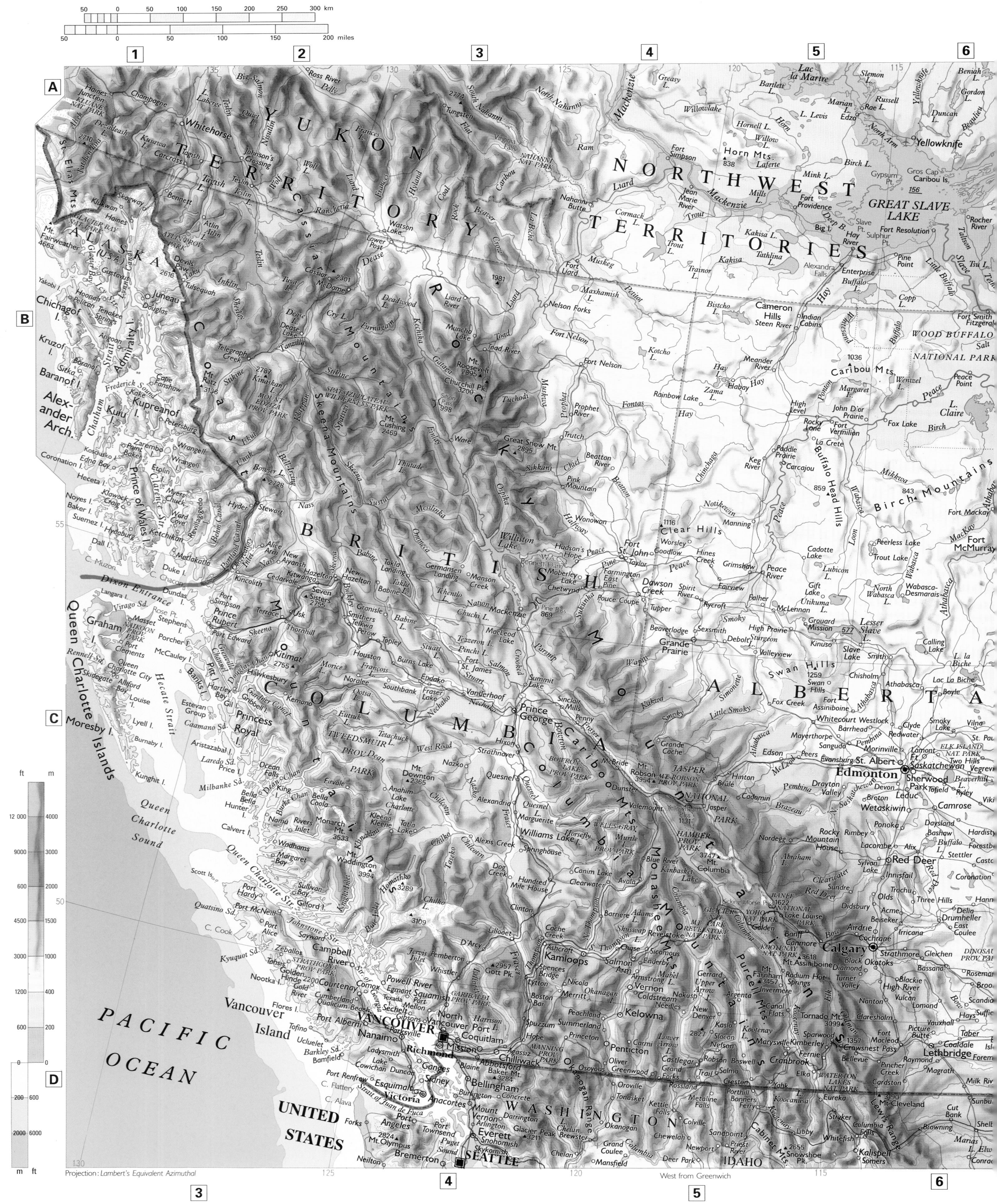
50 0 50 100 150 200 250 300 km
50 0 50 100 150 200 miles
1
2
3
4
5
6
A
B
C
D
YUKON TERRITORY
NORTHWEST TERRITORIES
BRITISH COLUMBIA
ALBERTA
ALASKA (U.S.A.)
WASHINGTON
IDAHO
UNITED STATES
PACIFIC OCEAN
GREAT SLAVE LAKE
WOOD BUFFALO NATIONAL PARK
Whitehorse
Yellowknife
Fort Simpson
Fort Providence
Hay River
Fort Resolution
Fort Smith
Fort Liard
Fort Nelson
Watson Lake
Juneau
Skagway
Haines
Sitka
Petersburg
Wrangell
Ketchikan
Prince Rupert
Kitimat
Terrace
Stewart
Dease Lake
Fort St. John
Dawson Creek
Grande Prairie
Peace River
High Level
Fort McMurray
Prince George
Quesnel
Williams Lake
Kamloops
Kelowna
Penticton
Vernon
Revelstoke
Cranbrook
Jasper
Banff
Calgary
Edmonton
St. Albert
Red Deer
Lethbridge
Medicine Hat
VANCOUVER
Victoria
Nanaimo
Richmond
Bellingham
SEATTLE
Vancouver Island
Queen Charlotte Islands
Queen Charlotte Sound
Hecate Strait
Dixon Entrance
Graham I.
Moresby I.
Chichagof I.
Baranof I.
Admiralty I.
Prince of Wales I.
Alexander Arch.
Coast Mountains
Skeena Mountains
Rocky Mountains
Cassiar Mountains
Omineca Mountains
Columbia Mts.
Cariboo Mts.
Monashee Mts.
Purcell Mts.
Selkirk Mts.
Mackenzie Mountains
Birch Mountains
Caribou Mts.
Clear Hills
Swan Hills
Buffalo Head Hills
Horn Mts.
Cameron Hills
St. Elias Mts.
Mt. Fairweather 4663
Mt. Robson 3954
Mt. Waddington 3994
Mt. Columbia 3747
Mt. Assiniboine 3618
Mt. Olympus 2824
Baker Mt. 3284
Glacier Peak 3211
Mt. Ratz 3136
Mt. Cushing 2469
Great Snow Mt. 2895
Mt. Roosevelt 2895
Churchill Pk. 3200
Yukon
Mackenzie
Liard
Peace
Athabasca
Fraser
Columbia
Skeena
Stikine
Nass
Thompson
Kootenay
Williston Lake
Lesser Slave L.
Kootenay L.
Okanagan L.
Tweedsmuir Prov. Park
Jasper National Park
Banff National Park
Glacier Nat. Park
Yoho Nat. Park
Kootenay Nat. Park
Waterton Lakes Nat. Park
Nahanni Nat. Park
Kluane Nat. Park
Glacier Bay Nat. Park
Projection: Lambert's Equivalent Azimuthal
West from Greenwich
ft m
12 000 4000
9000 3000
6000 2000
4500 1500
3000 1000
1200 400
600 200
0 0
200 600
2000 6000
m ft

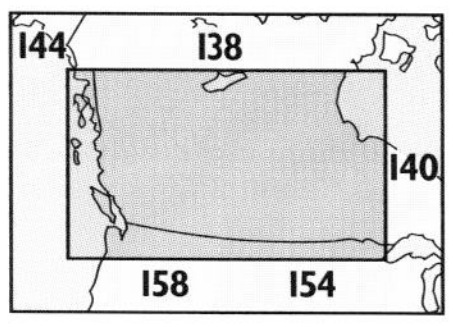

7 8 9 10 11

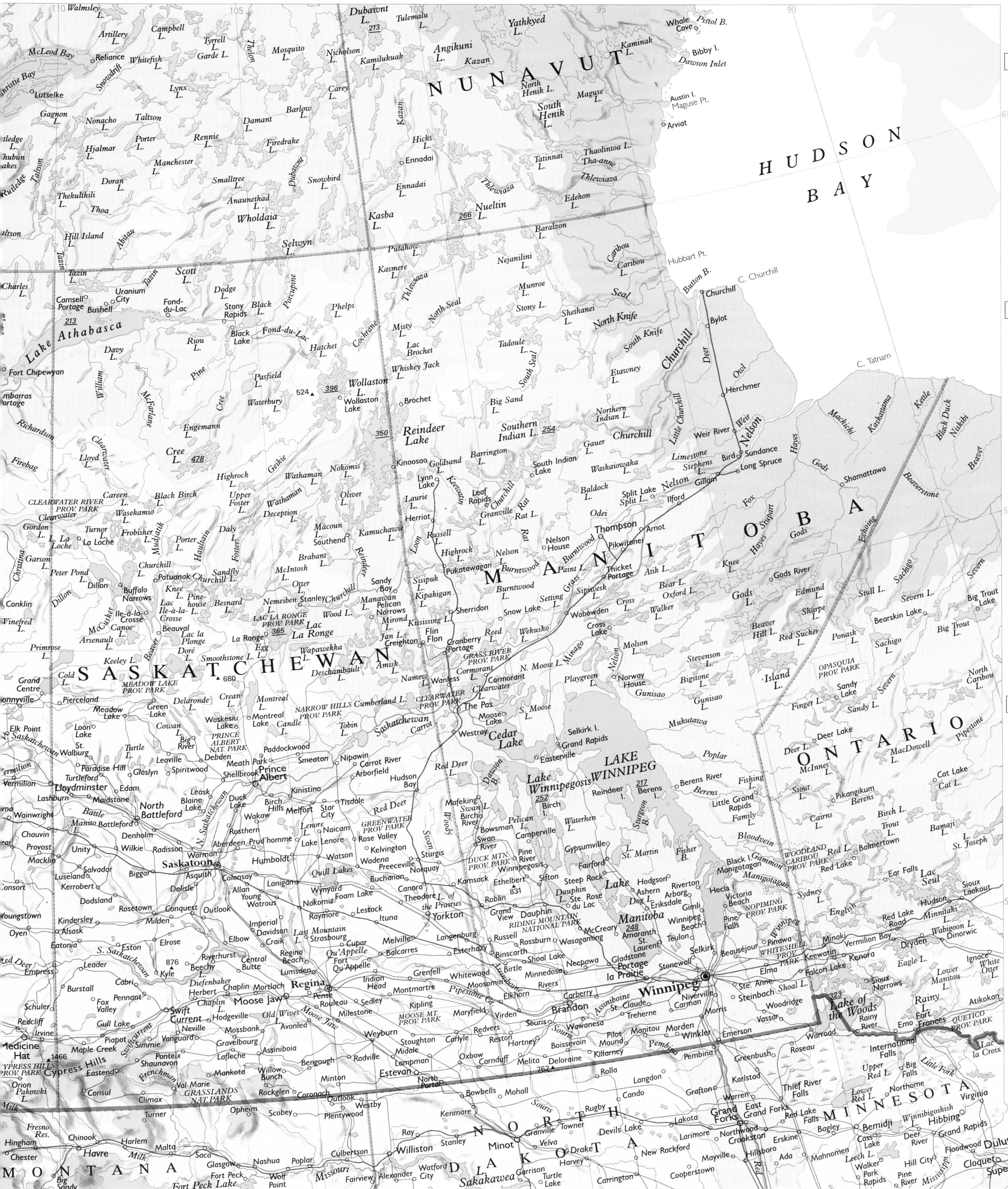

7 8 9 10

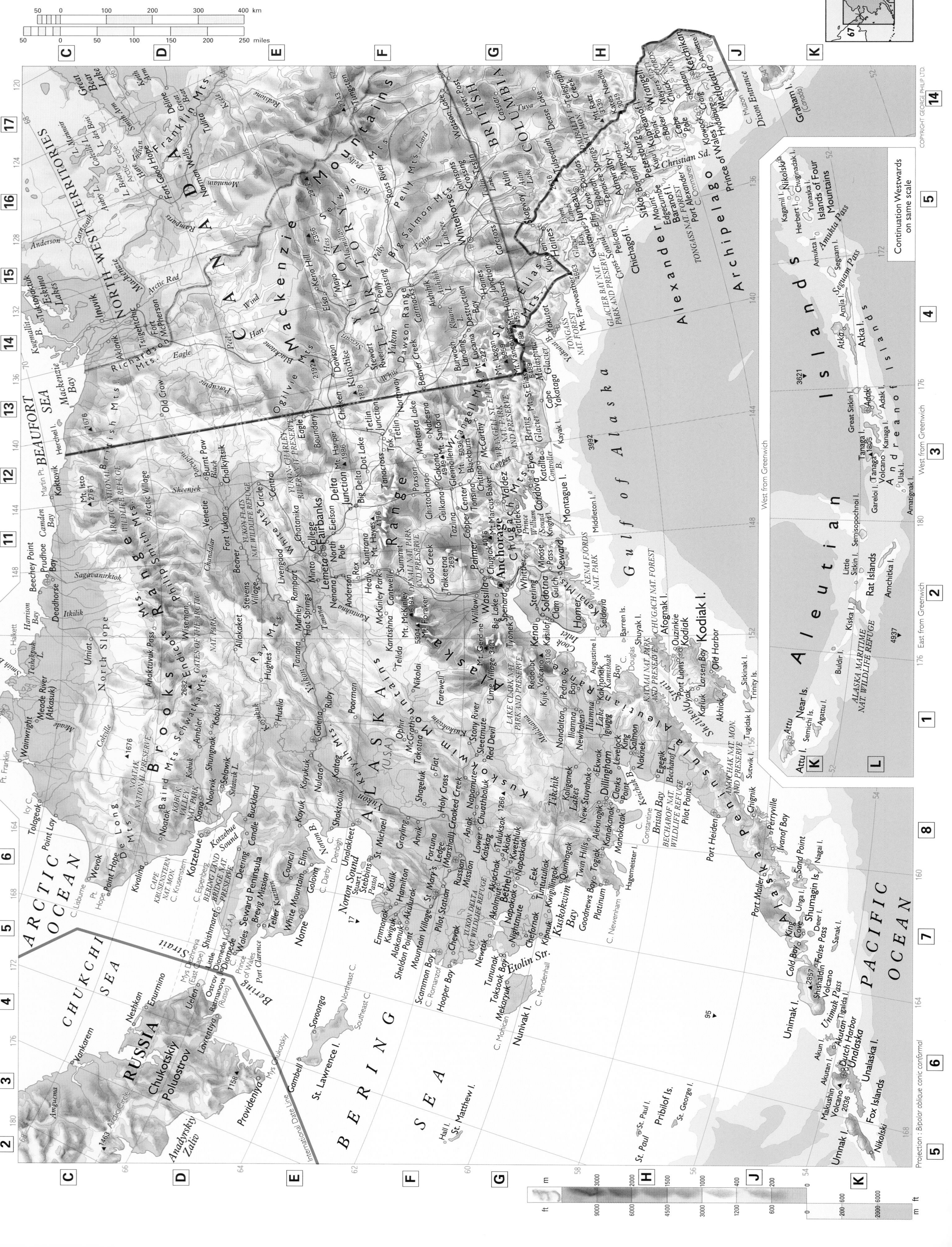
ARCTIC OCEAN
BEAUFORT SEA
CHUKCHI SEA
BERING SEA
PACIFIC OCEAN
Gulf of Alaska
CANADA
RUSSIA
NORTH WEST TERRITORIES
YUKON TERRITORY
BRITISH COLUMBIA
Brooks Range
Alaska Range
Mackenzie Mountains
Alexander Archipelago
Aleutian Islands
Alaska Peninsula
Anchorage
Fairbanks
Juneau
Nome
Kodiak I.
Bering Strait
Continuation Westwards on same scale
Projection : Bipolar oblique conic conformal
COPYRIGHT GEORGE PHILIP LTD.

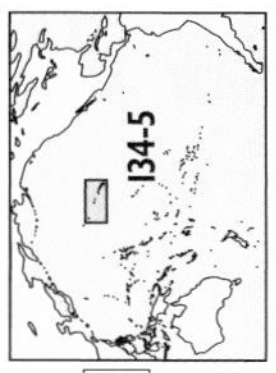
134-5

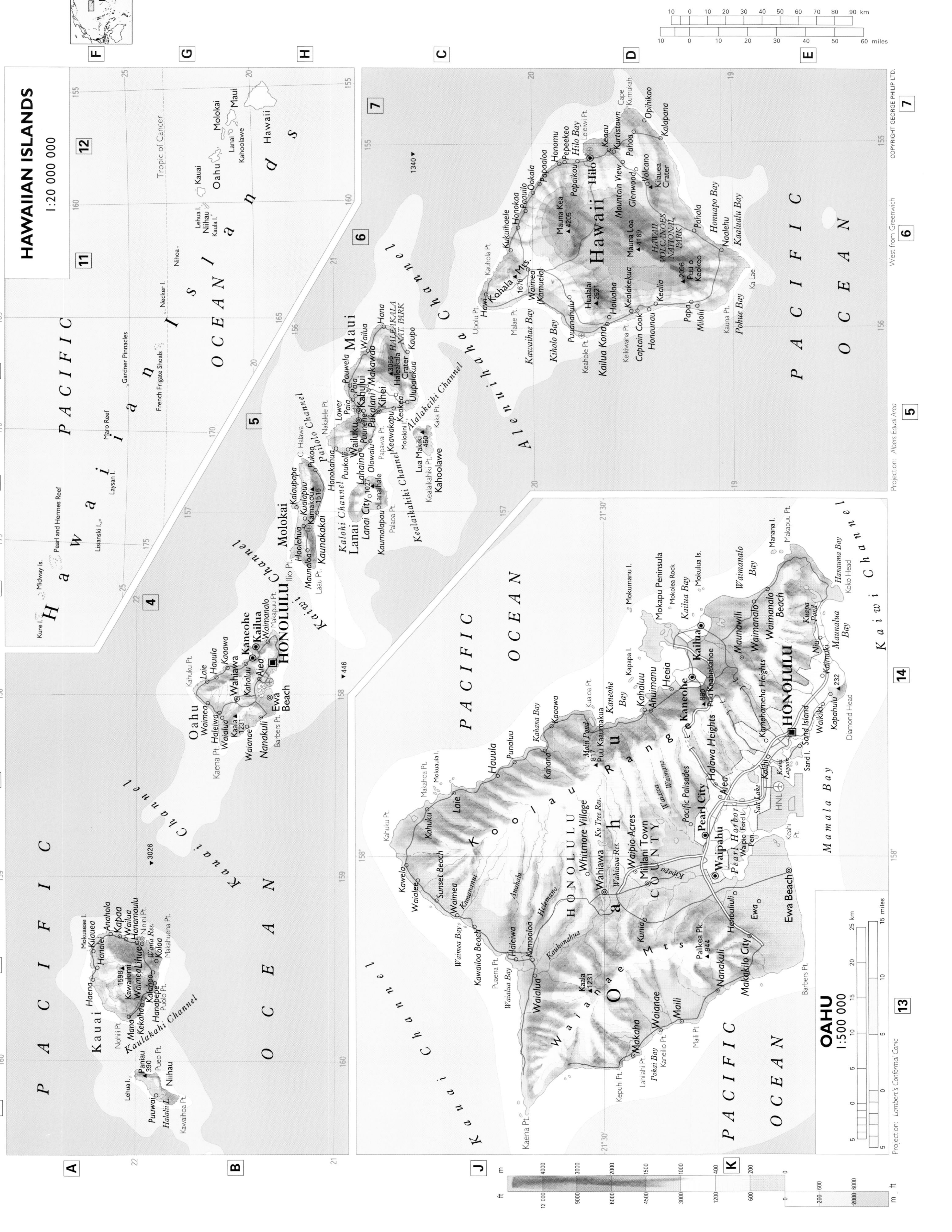
10 0 10 20 30 40 50 60 70 80 90 km
10 0 10 20 30 40 50 60 miles
HAWAIIAN ISLANDS
1:20 000 000
PACIFIC OCEAN
Hawaiian Islands
Tropic of Cancer
Kure I.
Midway Is.
Pearl and Hermes Reef
Lisianski I.
Laysan I.
Maro Reef
Gardner Pinnacles
French Frigate Shoals
Necker I.
Nihoa
Lehua I.
Niihau
Kaula I.
Kauai
Oahu
Molokai
Lanai
Maui
Kahoolawe
Hawaii
Kauai Channel
Kaulakahi Channel
Kaiwi Channel
Kalohi Channel
Pailolo Channel
Auau Channel
Kealaikahiki Channel
Alalakeiki Channel
Alenuihaha Channel
HONOLULU
Hilo
Mauna Kea 4205
Mauna Loa 4169
Kilauea Crater
HAWAII VOLCANOES NATIONAL PARK
HALEAKALA NAT. PARK
Haleakala 3055
OAHU
1:500 000
Projection: Lambert's Conformal Conic
Projection: Albers Equal Area
West from Greenwich
COPYRIGHT GEORGE PHILIP LTD.
Koolau Range
Waianae Mts
HONOLULU COUNTY
Pearl Harbor
Pearl City
Kaneohe Bay
Mamala Bay
Kaiwi Channel
Kauai Channel
m ft
4000 12 000
3000 9000
2000 6000
1500 4500
1000 3000
400 1200
200 600
0 0
200 600
2000 6000

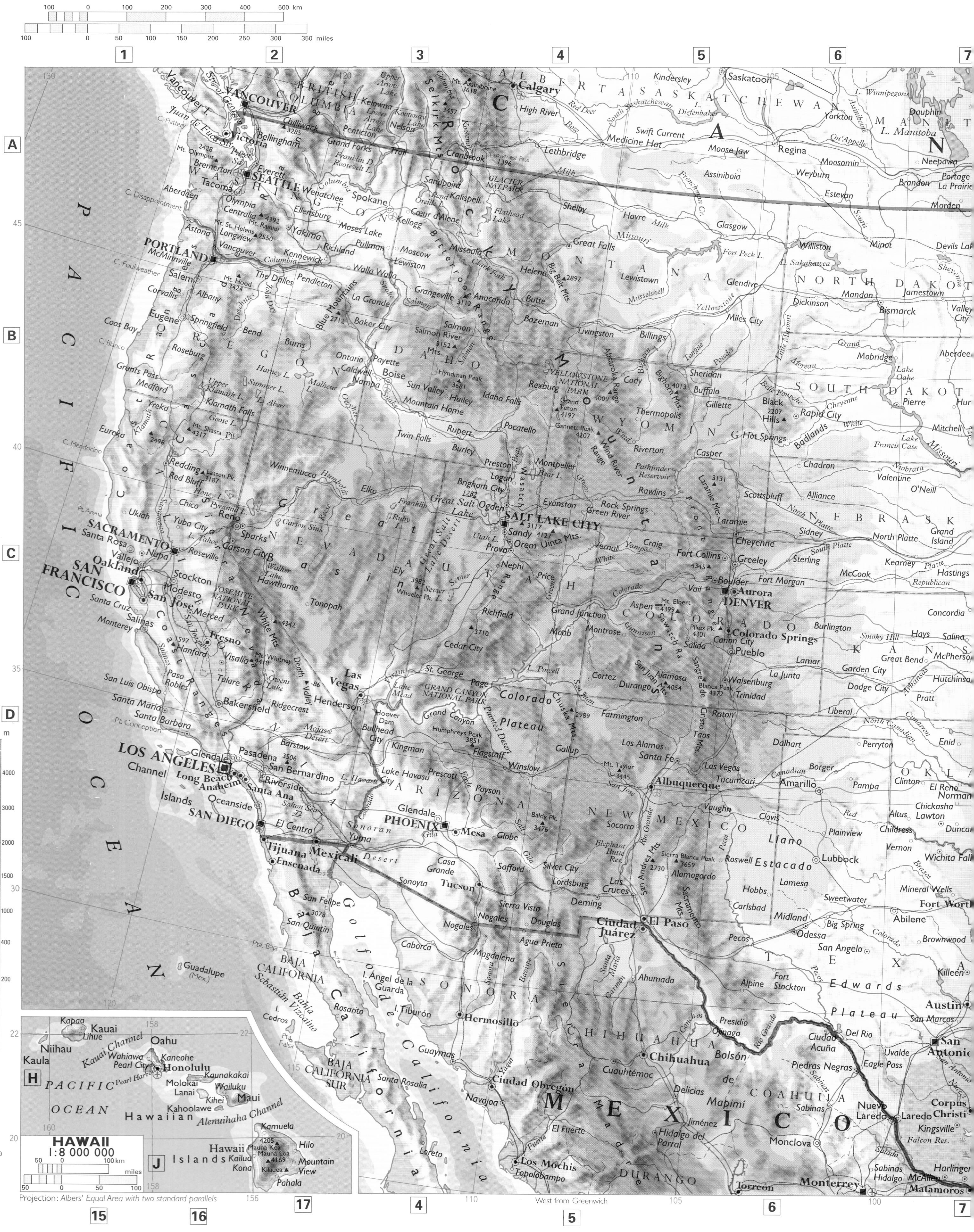

100 0 100 200 300 400 500 km
100 0 50 100 150 200 250 300 350 miles
1 2 3 4 5 6 7
A B C D
PACIFIC OCEAN
CANADA
ALBERTA
SASKATCHEWAN
MANITOBA
BRITISH COLUMBIA
WASHINGTON
OREGON
IDAHO
MONTANA
WYOMING
NEVADA
UTAH
COLORADO
ARIZONA
NEW MEXICO
CALIFORNIA
NORTH DAKOTA
SOUTH DAKOTA
NEBRASKA
KANSAS
TEXAS
MEXICO
SONORA
CHIHUAHUA
COAHUILA
DURANGO
BAJA CALIFORNIA
BAJA CALIFORNIA SUR
Golfo de California
Rocky Mts.
Great Basin
Colorado Plateau
Llano Estacado
Edwards Plateau
Bolsón de Mapimí
Sierra Madre
Sierra Nevada
Coast Ranges
Cascade Ra.
Calgary
Vancouver
Victoria
Seattle
Spokane
Portland
Salem
Eugene
Boise
Helena
Great Falls
Billings
Butte
Bozeman
Regina
Saskatoon
Medicine Hat
Lethbridge
Sacramento
San Francisco
Oakland
San Jose
Fresno
Los Angeles
San Diego
Las Vegas
Reno
Carson City
Salt Lake City
Phoenix
Tucson
Albuquerque
Santa Fe
El Paso
Ciudad Juárez
Denver
Aurora
Colorado Springs
Pueblo
Cheyenne
Casper
Rapid City
Pierre
Bismarck
Amarillo
Lubbock
San Antonio
Austin
Monterrey
Chihuahua
Hermosillo
Tijuana
Mexicali
Ensenada
Torreón
Yellowstone National Park
Grand Canyon National Park
Yosemite National Park
Glacier Nat. Park
Mt. Whitney 4418
Mt. Elbert 4399
Mt. Rainier 4392
Pikes Pk. 4301
Mt. Shasta 4317
Death Valley -86
Salton Sea -72
Great Salt Lake
L. Tahoe
Lake Mead
Missouri
Colorado
Rio Grande
Snake
Columbia
HAWAII
1:8 000 000
50 0 100 km
50 0 50 100 miles
H J
Niihau
Kauai
Oahu
Honolulu
Molokai
Lanai
Maui
Kahoolawe
Hawaii
Mauna Kea 4205
Mauna Loa 4169
Hilo
PACIFIC OCEAN
Hawaiian Islands
Projection: Albers' Equal Area with two standard parallels
West from Greenwich
15 16 17 4 5 6 7

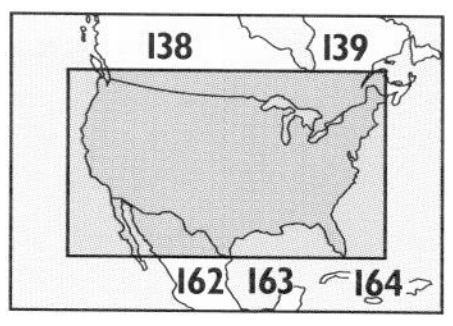
138
139
162
163
164

8
9
10
11
12
13
A
B
C
D
E
F
C A N A D A
O N T A R I O
Q U É B E C
Lake Winnipeg
Winnipeg
Lake of the Woods
Kenora
Dryden
Sioux Lookout
Lake Nipigon
Nipigon
Thunder Bay
Lake Superior
Marathon
Wawa
Hearst
Moosonee
Kapuskasing
Cochrane
Timmins
Kirkland Lake
Rouyn-Noranda
Amos
Chibougamau
L. Chibougamau
L. Matagami
L. Abitibi
Roberval
Jonquière
Chicoutimi
Alma
Baie-Comeau
Matane
Rimouski
Rivière-du-Loup
Edmundston
NEW BRUNSWICK
Québec
La Tuque
Shawinigan
Trois-Rivières
Drummondville
Sherbrooke
MONTRÉAL
Ottawa
Hull
Sudbury
North Bay
Sault Ste. Marie
Manitoulin I.
Georgian Bay
Parry Sound
Huntsville
Orillia
Peterborough
Kingston
Barrie
Oshawa
TORONTO
Kitchener
Hamilton
London
Lake Huron
Lake Michigan
Lake Ontario
Lake Erie
Windsor
DETROIT
Fort Frances
International Falls
Thief River Falls
Grand Forks
Bemidji
Hibbing
Virginia
Duluth
Superior
Two Harbors
Houghton
Marquette
Ishpeming
Iron Mountain
Escanaba
Manistique
Petoskey
Alpena
Traverse City
Saginaw
Bay City
Flint
Lansing
Grand Rapids
Kalamazoo
Battle Creek
Ann Arbor
Toledo
Sandusky
CLEVELAND
Akron
Youngstown
Erie
Buffalo
Niagara Falls
Rochester
Syracuse
Utica
Schenectady
Albany
Troy
Watertown
Oswego
Ithaca
Binghamton
Elmira
Jamestown
Bradford
Scranton
Wilkes-Barre
Williamsport
Altoona
Harrisburg
Allentown
Reading
Lancaster
PHILADELPHIA
NEW YORK
Newark
Paterson
Jersey City
Trenton
Yonkers
Bridgeport
New Haven
HARTFORD
Springfield
Worcester
Providence
Fall River
New Bedford
BOSTON
Lowell
Lawrence
Manchester
Nashua
Concord
Portland
Lewiston
Augusta
Waterville
Bangor
Belfast
Penobscot Bay
Millinocket
Houlton
Presque Isle
Caribou
Saint John
Calais
MAINE
VERMONT
NEW HAMPSHIRE
MASS.
CONN.
R.I.
NEW YORK
PENNSYLVANIA
NEW JERSEY
DEL.
MARYLAND
Burlington
Montpelier
Plattsburgh
Lake Champlain
Adirondack Mts.
White Mts.
Catskill Mts.
Glens Falls
Rutland
Moorhead
Fargo
MINNESOTA
Brainerd
St. Cloud
Fergus Falls
Coon Rapids
MINNEAPOLIS
ST. PAUL
Red Wing
Winona
Rochester
Austin
Mankato
Owatonna
Albert Lea
Willmar
Watertown
Brookings
Madison
Mason City
Charles City
Waterloo
Cedar Rapids
Iowa City
Dubuque
Davenport
Des Moines
Ames
Fort Dodge
Cherokee
Spencer
Sioux City
Norfolk
Columbus
Omaha
Lincoln
Council Bluffs
Ottumwa
Burlington
Galesburg
Rock Island
I O W A
WISCONSIN
Eau Claire
Wausau
Stevens Point
Green Bay
Appleton
Oshkosh
Sheboygan
Manitowoc
La Crosse
Portage
Madison
MILWAUKEE
Janesville
Racine
Kenosha
Rockford
Elgin
Clinton
Aurora
Joliet
CHICAGO
Gary
Kankakee
South Bend
Elkhart
Fort Wayne
Findlay
Lima
Mansfield
Canton
Marion
COLUMBUS
Zanesville
Wheeling
PITTSBURGH
Johnstown
Dayton
Springfield
CINCINNATI
Richmond
Muncie
Kokomo
Lafayette
INDIANAPOLIS
Bloomington
Terre Haute
Columbus
Danville
Champaign
Decatur
Springfield
Peoria
Quincy
Hannibal
Mattoon
Effingham
Midwest
ILLINOIS
INDIANA
OHIO
Beatrice
Maryville
Creston
Red Oak
Kirksville
Chillicothe
St. Joseph
Leavenworth
KANSAS CITY
Topeka
Lawrence
Manhattan
Columbia
Jefferson City
Sedalia
MISSOURI
ST. LOUIS
Alton
East St. Louis
Carbondale
Cape Girardeau
Rolla
Lake of the Ozarks
Lebanon
Springfield
Joplin
Ozark Plateau
Emporia
Newton
Wichita
Fort Scott
Pittsburg
Parsons
Arkansas City
Bartlesville
Ponca City
Tulsa
Muskogee
Oklahoma City
Shawnee
Fort Smith
McAlester
Ardmore
Durant
Sherman
Denton
DALLAS
Arlington
Paris
Texarkana
Hope
Camden
El Dorado
Pine Bluff
Little Rock
Hot Springs
Ouachita Mts.
Stuttgart
Russellville
Conway
Fayetteville
Boston Mts.
West Plains
Poplar Bluff
Paragould
Jonesboro
Blytheville
Newport
ARKANSAS
Memphis
Dyersburg
Jackson
Corinth
Tupelo
Oxford
Clarksdale
Cleveland
Greenwood
Greenville
Yazoo City
Columbus
MISSISSIPPI
Vicksburg
Jackson
Meridian
Natchez
Hattiesburg
Laurel
McComb
Bogalusa
Gulfport
Biloxi
Mobile
Pensacola
Shreveport
Monroe
Alexandria
Natchitoches
Marshall
Longview
Tyler
Corsicana
Waco
Palestine
Nacogdoches
Lufkin
Temple
Bryan
Huntsville
De Ridder
Lake Charles
Beaumont
Port Arthur
HOUSTON
Pasadena
Galveston
Freeport
Victoria
Port Lavaca
Matagorda I.
Aransas Pass
Padre I.
Laguna Madre
Brownsville
Rio Grande
LOUISIANA
Baton Rouge
Lafayette
New Iberia
Morgan City
Houma
NEW ORLEANS
L. Pontchartrain
Breton Sd.
Mississippi River Delta
Atchafalaya B.
Marsh I.
G U L F   O F   M E X I C O
Evansville
Owensboro
Henderson
Paducah
Hopkinsville
Bowling Green
Louisville
Frankfort
Lexington
Richmond
Danville
Somerset
Middlesboro
Hazard
KENTUCKY
Vincennes
Mount Vernon
Clarksville
Nashville
Murfreesboro
Columbia
Oak Ridge
Knoxville
Johnson City
Kingsport
Chattanooga
Huntsville
Florence
Decatur
Athens
TENNESSEE
Cumberland Plateau
Birmingham
Tuscaloosa
Gadsden
Anniston
Demopolis
Selma
Montgomery
Troy
Greenville
Andalusia
Dothan
Auburn
ALABAMA
ATLANTA
Rome
Roswell
Gainesville
Athens
Augusta
Macon
La Grange
Columbus
Dublin
Statesboro
Savannah
Cordele
Albany
Douglas
Waycross
Brunswick
Tifton
Valdosta
Thomasville
GEORGIA
Tallahassee
Panama City
Apalachicola
C. San Blas
Apalachee B.
Lake City
Jacksonville
St. Augustine
Gainesville
Ocala
Daytona Beach
Deltona
Orlando
C. Canaveral
Melbourne
Palm Bay
Fort Pierce
Lakeland
TAMPA
Clearwater
St. Petersburg
Tampa B.
Sarasota
L. Okeechobee
West Palm Beach
Fort Lauderdale
MIAMI
Fort Myers
Cape Coral
Charlotte Harbor
Naples
C. Sable
Florida Bay
Florida Keys
Key West
Straits of Florida
FLORIDA
Grand Bahama I.
Freeport
Little Abaco I.
Great Abaco I.
N.E. Providence Channel
N.W. Providence Channel
BAHAMAS
Nassau
New Providence I.
Eleuthera I.
Cat I.
Exuma Sound
Great Exuma I.
Andros I.
Long I.
A T L A N T I C   O C E A N
Mount Vernon
Marion
Cumberland
Morgantown
Clarksburg
Elkins
Parkersburg
Portsmouth
Huntington
Charleston
Maysville
Beckley
Bluefield
Radford
Pulaski
WEST VIRGINIA
WASHINGTON D.C.
BALTIMORE
Annapolis
Frederick
Wilmington
Dover
Atlantic City
Delaware B.
Salisbury
Harrisonburg
Charlottesville
Richmond
Lynchburg
Roanoke
Petersburg
Danville
Norfolk
Newport News
Virginia Beach
C. Charles
Chesapeake Bay
Elizabeth City
Albemarle Sd.
Pamlico Sd.
C. Hatteras
Rocky Mount
Greenville
Goldsboro
New Bern
Jacksonville
Onslow Bay
Wilmington
C. Fear
Greensboro
Winston-Salem
Durham
Raleigh
Fayetteville
Hickory
CHARLOTTE
Asheville
NORTH CAROLINA
Spartanburg
Greenville
Rock Hill
Anderson
Columbia
Sumter
Florence
Myrtle Beach
Long Bay
Georgetown
C. Romain
Orangeburg
Charleston
SOUTH CAROLINA
Appalachian Mountains
Allegheny Mountains
Blue Ridge
Martha's Vineyard
Nantucket I.
C. Cod
Long I.
C. May
C. Charles
2037
1629
1917
1281
1482
781
811
510
183
177
174
75
95
90
85
80
75
65
45
40
35
30
25

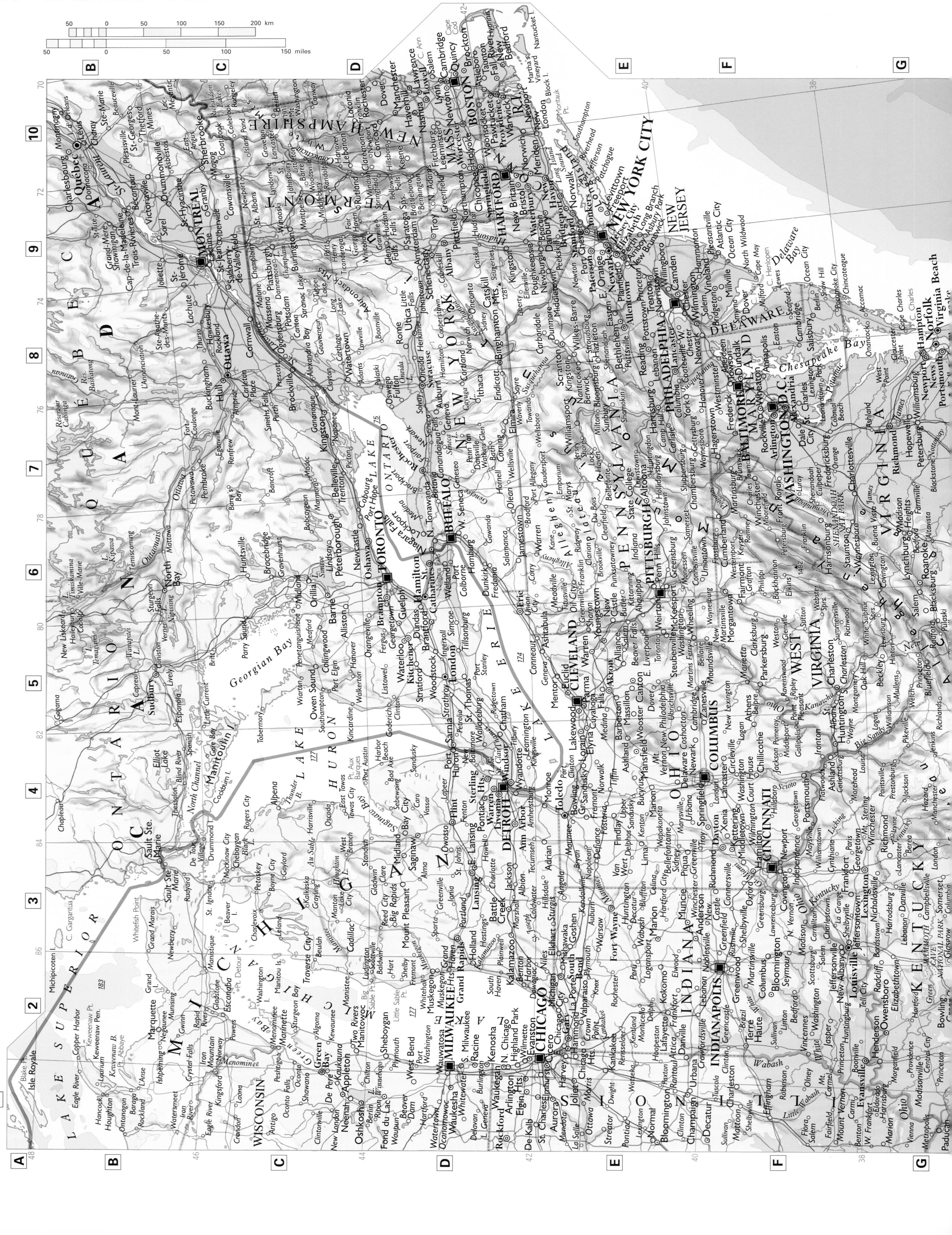

50 0 50 100 150 200 km
50 0 50 100 150 miles
LAKE SUPERIOR
LAKE HURON
LAKE ERIE
LAKE ONTARIO
LAKE MICHIGAN
ONTARIO
QUEBEC
MICHIGAN
WISCONSIN
ILLINOIS
INDIANA
OHIO
KENTUCKY
WEST VIRGINIA
VIRGINIA
PENNSYLVANIA
NEW YORK
NEW JERSEY
DELAWARE
MARYLAND
VERMONT
NEW HAMPSHIRE
MASS.
CONN.
R.I.
Georgian Bay
Chesapeake Bay
Delaware Bay
NEW YORK CITY
CHICAGO
DETROIT
TORONTO
MONTREAL
OTTAWA
CLEVELAND
PITTSBURGH
PHILADELPHIA
BALTIMORE
WASHINGTON D.C.
BOSTON
BUFFALO
COLUMBUS
CINCINNATI
INDIANAPOLIS
MILWAUKEE
HARTFORD

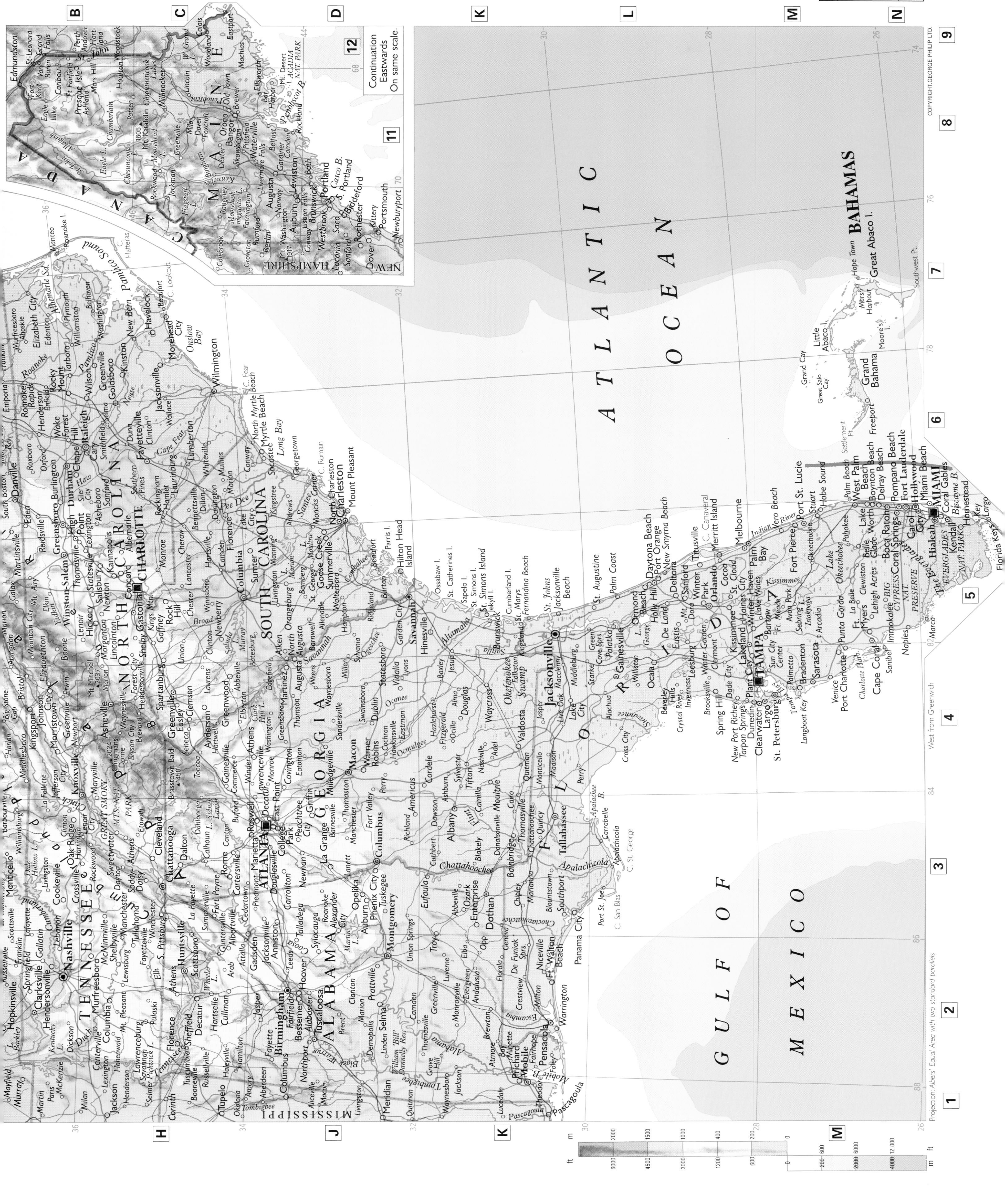
ATLANTIC OCEAN
GULF OF MEXICO
BAHAMAS
TENNESSEE
NORTH CAROLINA
SOUTH CAROLINA
GEORGIA
ALABAMA
MISSISSIPPI
FLORIDA
MAINE
NEW HAMPSHIRE
CANADA
ATLANTA
CHARLOTTE
TAMPA
MIAMI
Nashville
Birmingham
Montgomery
Jacksonville
Columbia
Raleigh
Tallahassee
Savannah
Charleston
Orlando
Chattanooga
Knoxville
Wilmington
Portland
Augusta
Bangor
Grand Bahama
Great Abaco I.
Continuation Eastwards On same scale.
West from Greenwich
Projection: Albers' Equal Area with two standard parallels
COPYRIGHT GEORGE PHILIP LTD.

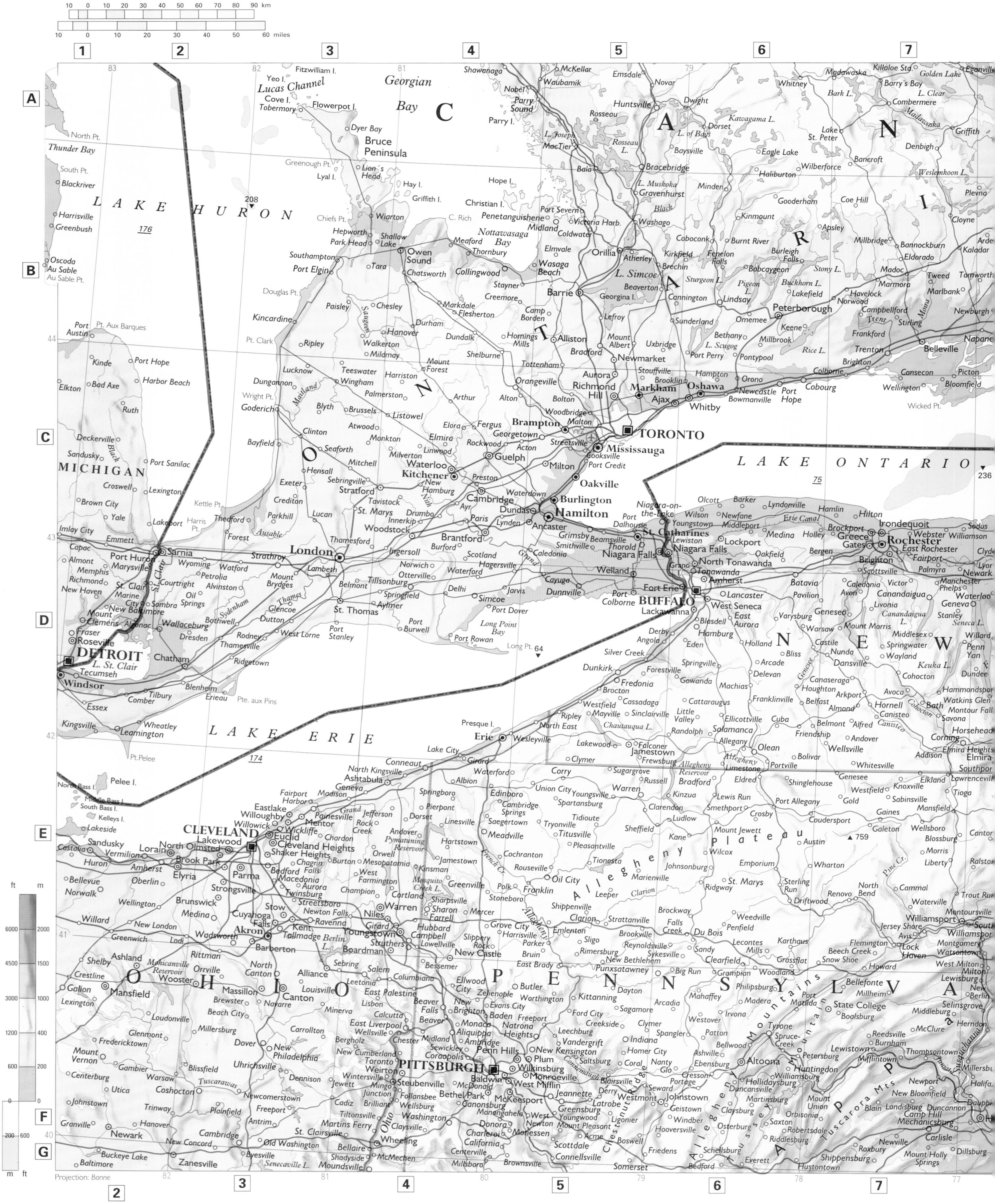
10 0 10 20 30 40 50 60 70 80 90 km
10 0 10 20 30 40 50 60 miles
1 2 3 4 5 6 7
A B C D E F G
LAKE HURON
Georgian Bay
LAKE ONTARIO
LAKE ERIE
CANADA
ONTARIO
MICHIGAN
OHIO
PENNSYLVANIA
NEW YORK
Bruce Peninsula
Allegheny Plateau
Allegheny Mountains
Tussey Mountains
Tuscarora Mts.
TORONTO
Mississauga
Hamilton
Brampton
Oakville
Burlington
St. Catharines
Niagara Falls
BUFFALO
Rochester
DETROIT
Windsor
London
Kitchener
Waterloo
Guelph
Cambridge
Brantford
Sarnia
Port Huron
Oshawa
Peterborough
Barrie
Orillia
Owen Sound
Belleville
CLEVELAND
Akron
Canton
Youngstown
Erie
PITTSBURGH
Altoona
State College
Williamsport
Wheeling
Zanesville
Mansfield
Newark
Projection: Bonne
ft m
6000 2000
4500 1500
3000 1000
1200 400
600 200
0 0
200 600
m ft

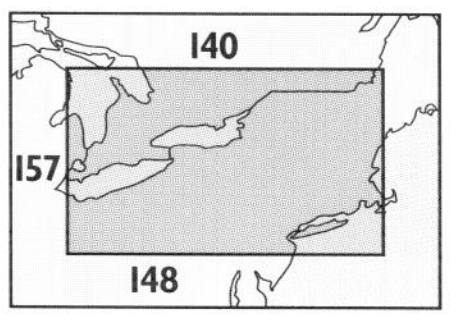
140
157
148

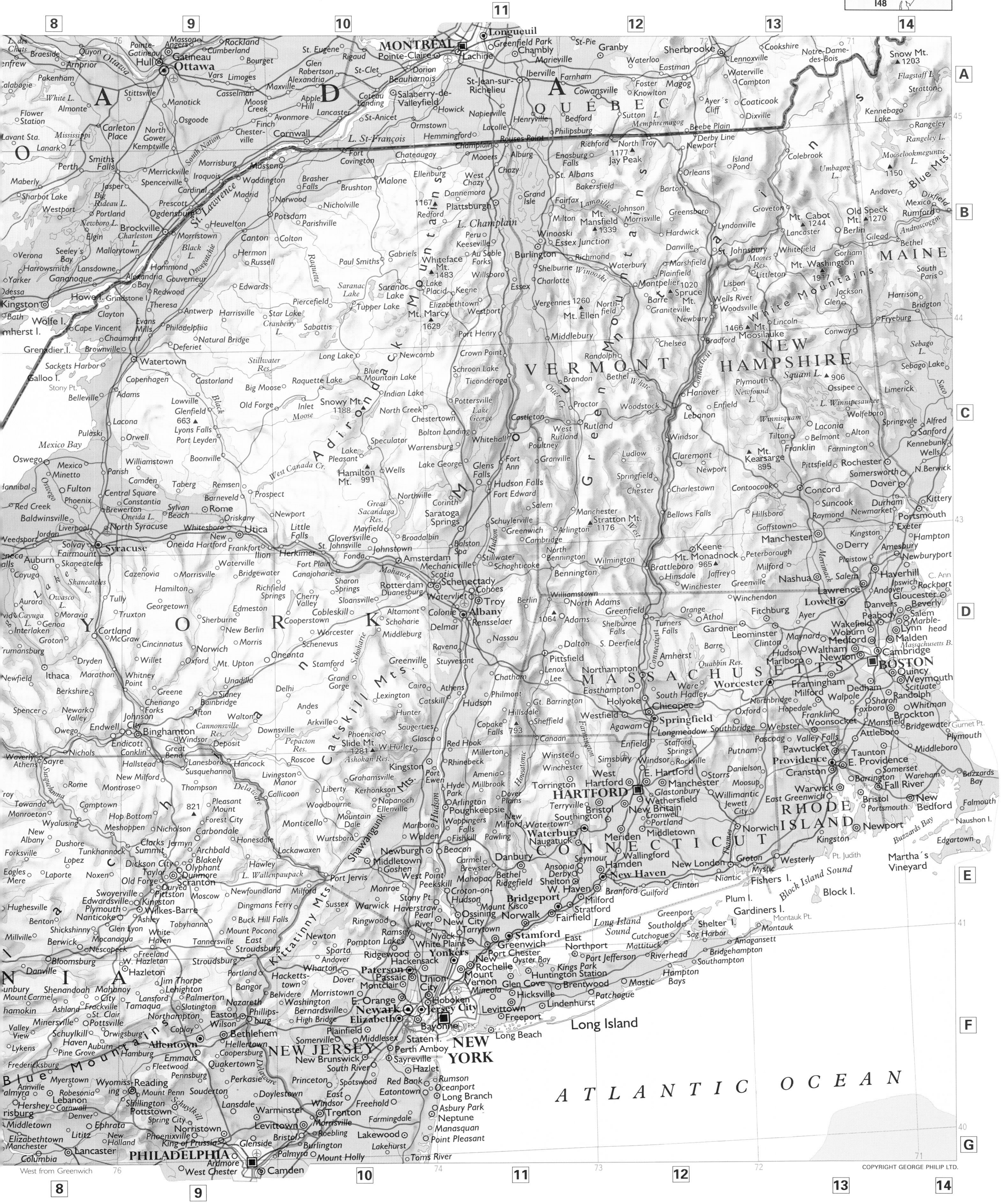
8
9
10
11
12
13
14
A
B
C
D
E
F
G
MONTREAL
Longueuil
Lachine
Pointe-Claire
Ottawa
Hull
Gatineau
QUÉBEC
Sherbrooke
Granby
Magog
St-Jean-sur-Richelieu
Salaberry-de-Valleyfield
Cornwall
L. St-François
Massena
Ogdensburg
Brockville
Kingston
Wolfe I.
St. Lawrence
Plattsburgh
L. Champlain
Burlington
Montpelier
Barre
St. Johnsbury
Mt. Mansfield
1339
Jay Peak
1177
Mt. Marcy
1629
Whiteface Mt.
1483
Saranac Lake
Tupper Lake
Lake Placid
Adirondack Mountains
VERMONT
NEW HAMPSHIRE
MAINE
White Mountains
Mt. Washington
1917
Green Mountains
Rutland
Middlebury
Bennington
Brattleboro
Keene
Concord
Manchester
Nashua
Portsmouth
Dover
Lebanon
Hanover
Mt. Monadnock
965
Watertown
Oswego
Syracuse
Utica
Rome
Oneida L.
Auburn
Cortland
Ithaca
Binghamton
Elmira
Oneonta
Albany
Schenectady
Troy
Saratoga Springs
Glens Falls
Amsterdam
Catskill Mts.
Slide Mt.
1281
Kingston
Poughkeepsie
Newburgh
Hudson
MASSACHUSETTS
BOSTON
Cambridge
Quincy
Lowell
Lawrence
Worcester
Springfield
Pittsfield
North Adams
Fitchburg
Framingham
Brockton
Fall River
New Bedford
Plymouth
Martha's Vineyard
Nantucket
RHODE ISLAND
Providence
Pawtucket
Newport
Block I.
Block Island Sound
CONNECTICUT
HARTFORD
New Haven
Bridgeport
Waterbury
Stamford
Norwalk
Danbury
New London
Long Island Sound
Long Island
Montauk Pt.
Gardiners I.
Fishers I.
NEW YORK
Yonkers
Newark
Jersey City
Elizabeth
Paterson
Bayonne
NEW JERSEY
Trenton
Princeton
New Brunswick
Asbury Park
Long Branch
Toms River
Camden
PHILADELPHIA
Allentown
Bethlehem
Reading
Lancaster
Scranton
Wilkes-Barre
Hazleton
Blue Mountains
Kittatinny Mts.
Delaware
ATLANTIC OCEAN
West from Greenwich
76
74
73
72
71
45
44
43
41
40

COPYRIGHT GEORGE PHILIP LTD.

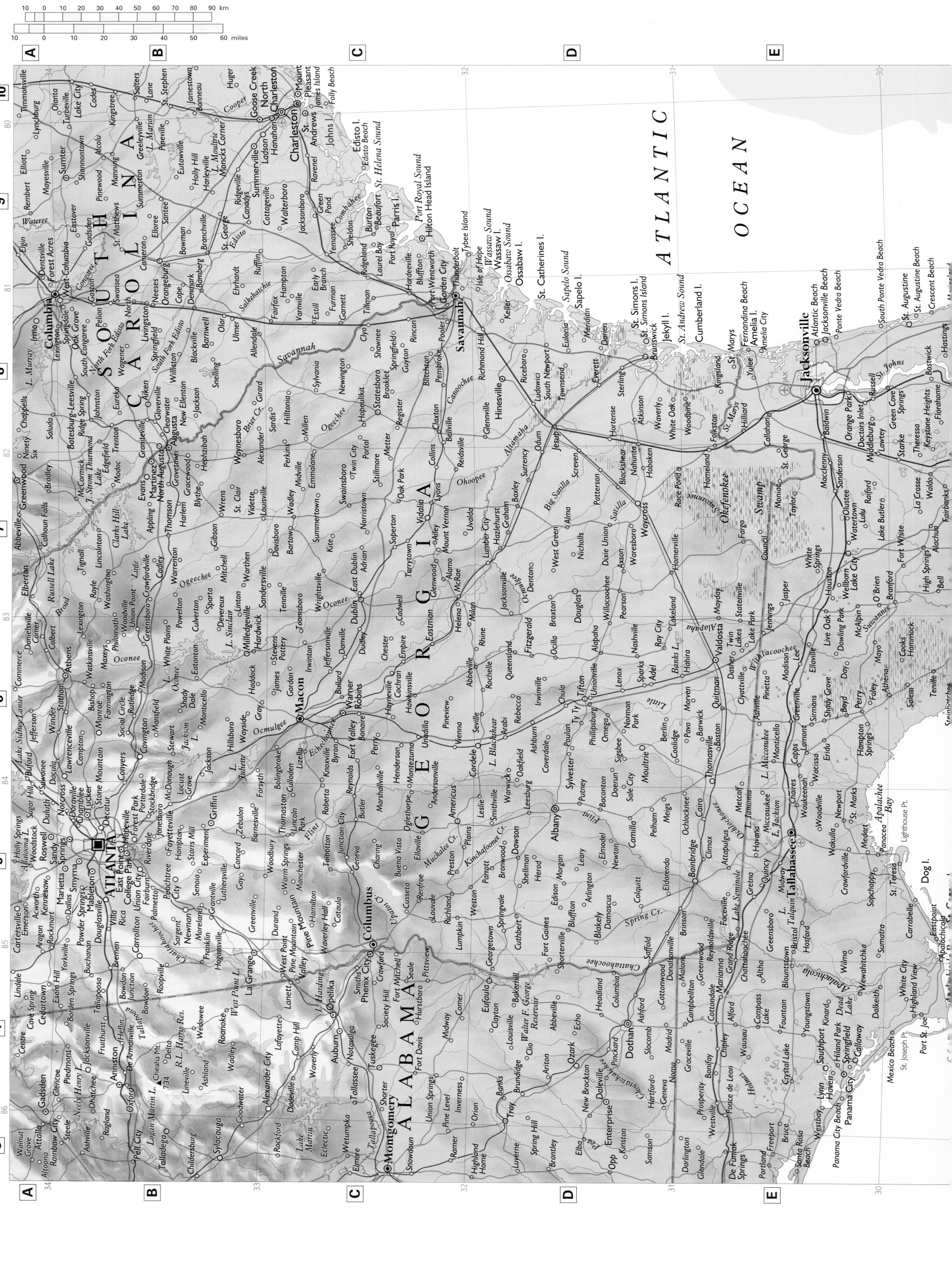
km
miles
SOUTH CAROLINA
GEORGIA
ALABAMA
ATLANTIC
OCEAN
ATLANTA
Columbia
Charleston
Savannah
Augusta
Macon
Columbus
Montgomery
Albany
Tallahassee
Jacksonville
Valdosta
Dothan
Waycross
Brunswick
Athens
Okefenokee Swamp
Apalachee Bay
Hilton Head Island
St. Catherines I.
Cumberland I.
Dog I.

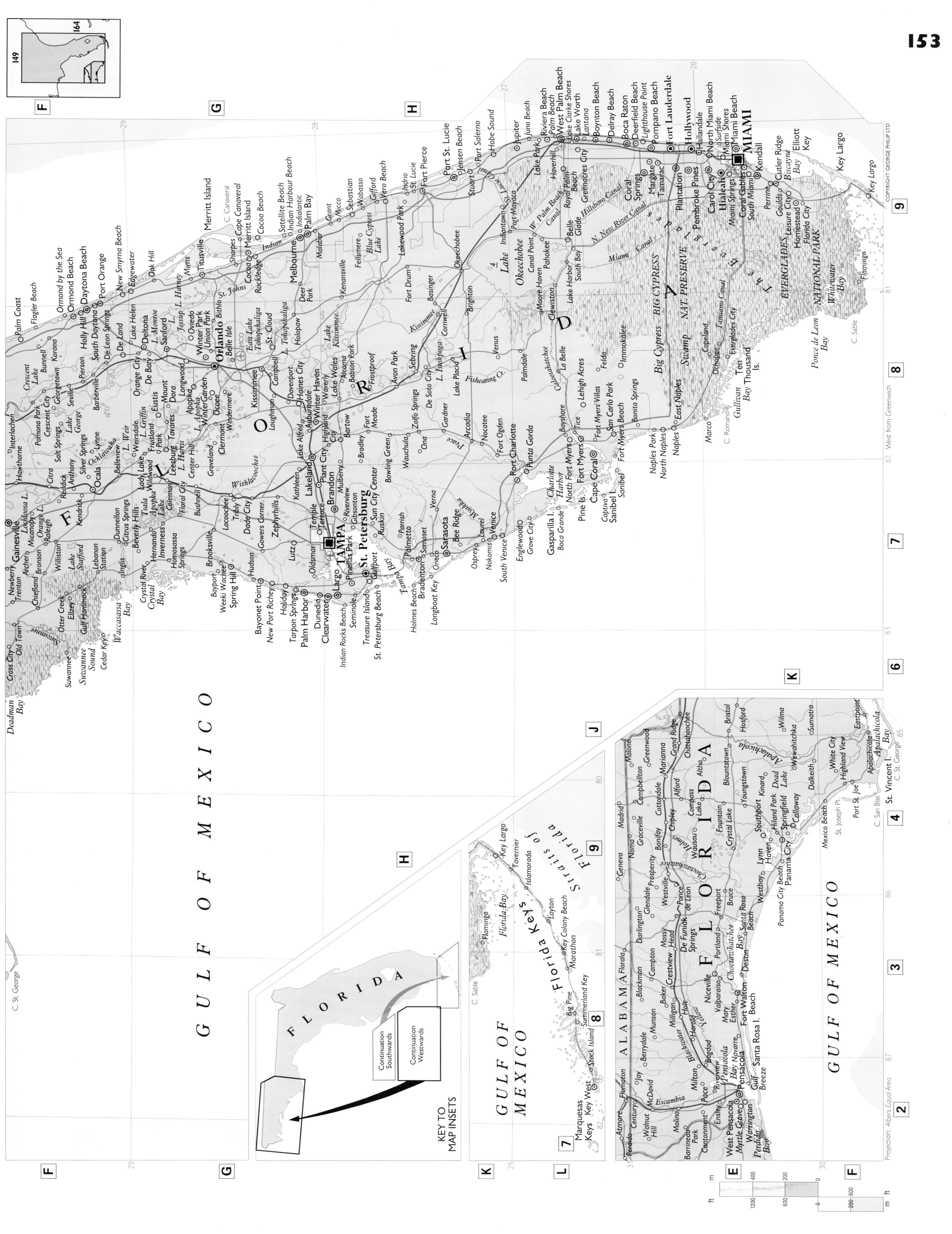
GULF OF MEXICO
F L O R I D A
TAMPA
St. Petersburg
Orlando
MIAMI
Fort Lauderdale
West Palm Beach
Hollywood
Gainesville
Daytona Beach
Melbourne
Lakeland
Sarasota
Fort Myers
Cape Coral
Lake Okeechobee
BIG CYPRESS NAT. PRESERVE
EVERGLADES NATIONAL PARK
Florida Keys
Straits of Florida
Key West
Key Largo
KEY TO MAP INSETS
FLORIDA
Continuation Southwards
Continuation Westwards
ALABAMA
Pensacola
Panama City
Apalachicola
Projection: Albers Equal Area
COPYRIGHT GEORGE PHILIP LTD

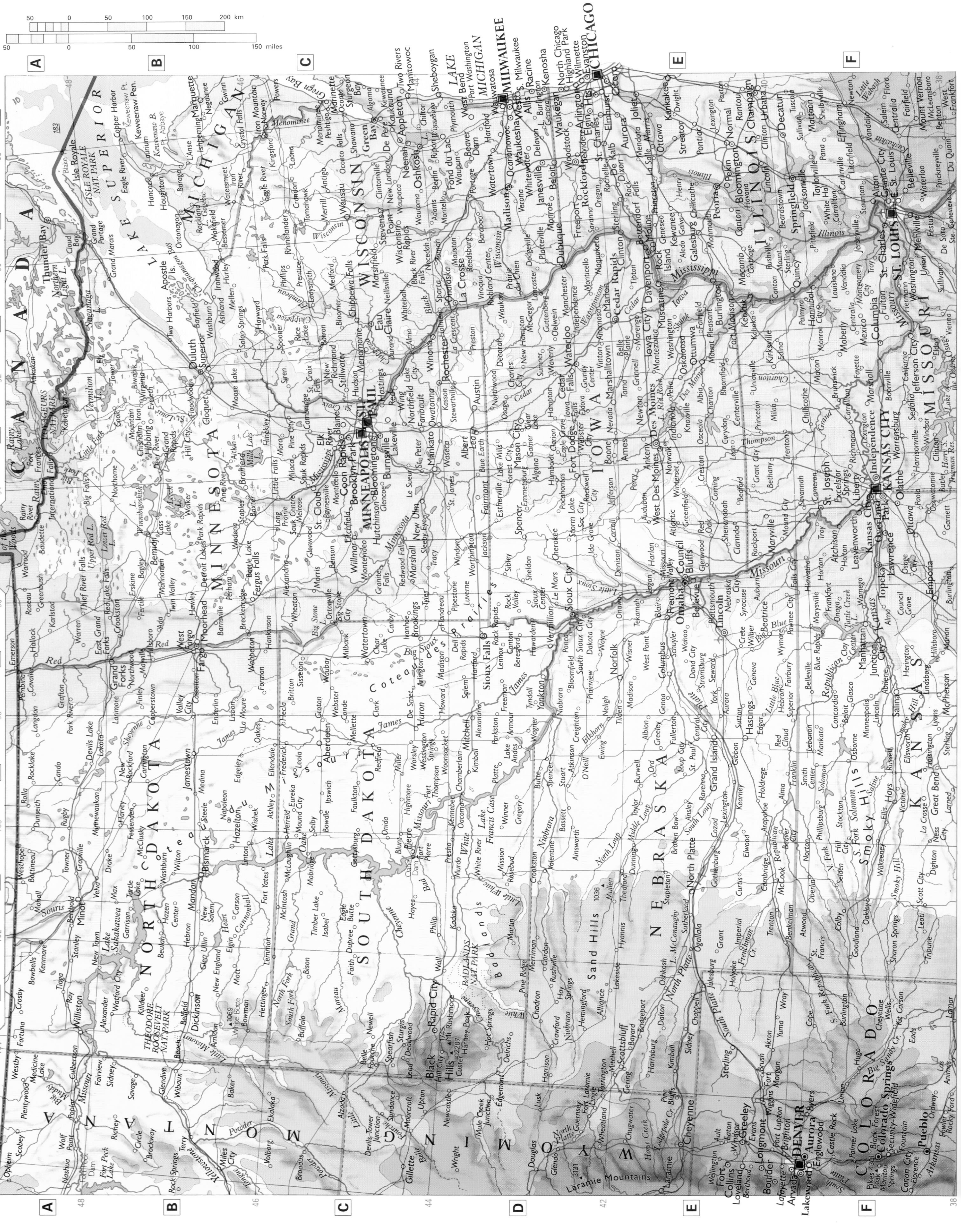
50 0 50 100 150 200 km
50 0 50 100 150 miles
A B C D E F
1 2 3 4 5 6 7 8 9 10 11
CANADA
LAKE SUPERIOR
LAKE MICHIGAN
NORTH DAKOTA
SOUTH DAKOTA
NEBRASKA
KANSAS
MINNESOTA
IOWA
MISSOURI
WISCONSIN
ILLINOIS
MICHIGAN
MONTANA
WYOMING
COLORADO
MILWAUKEE
CHICAGO
MINNEAPOLIS
ST. PAUL
KANSAS CITY
ST. LOUIS
DENVER
Omaha
Des Moines
Lincoln
Topeka
Bismarck
Pierre
Cheyenne
Sioux Falls
Fargo
Duluth
Madison
Springfield
Jefferson City
Colorado Springs
Pueblo
Rapid City
Black Hills
Sand Hills
Smoky Hills
Laramie Mountains
Coteau des Prairies
Badlands
ISLE ROYALE NAT. PARK
VOYAGEURS NAT. PARK
THEODORE ROOSEVELT NAT. PARK
BADLANDS NAT. PARK
Mississippi
Missouri
Lake of the Woods
Lake Sakakawea
Red
Platte
Arkansas

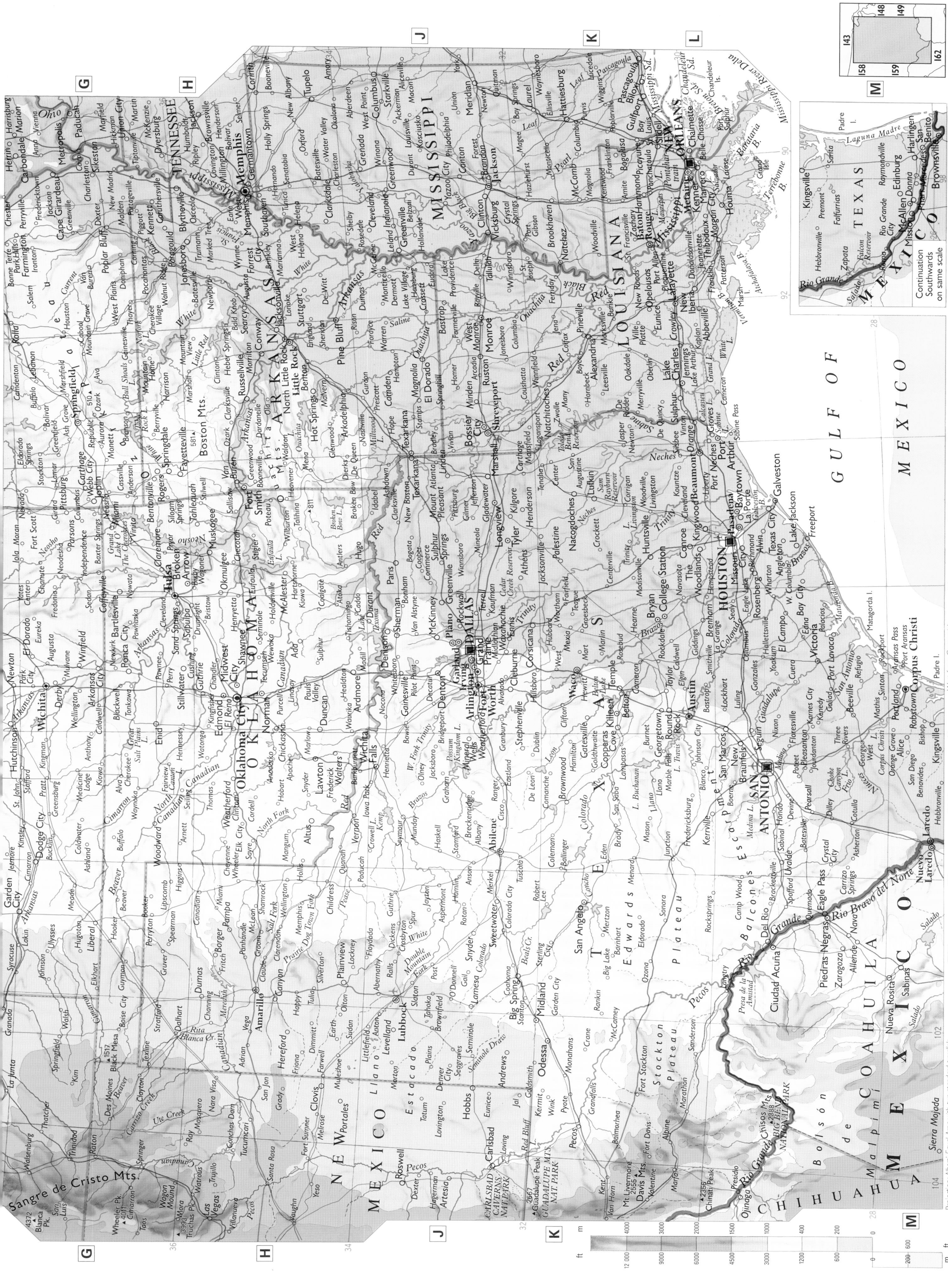
G
H
J
K
L
M
2
3
4
5
6
7
8
OKLAHOMA
ARKANSAS
MISSISSIPPI
TENNESSEE
LOUISIANA
TEXAS
NEW MEXICO
MEXICO
COAHUILA
CHIHUAHUA
GULF OF MEXICO
Sangre de Cristo Mts.
Boston Mts.
Llano Estacado
Edwards Plateau
Stockton Plateau
Balcones Escarpment
Bolsón de Mapimí
CARLSBAD CAVERNS NAT. PARK
GUADALUPE MTS. NAT. PARK
BIG BEND NAT. PARK
Rio Grande
Rio Bravo del Norte
Red
Arkansas
Mississippi
Pecos
Colorado
Brazos
HOUSTON
DALLAS
SAN ANTONIO
NEW ORLEANS
Memphis
Oklahoma City
Tulsa
Wichita
Little Rock
Fort Worth
Austin
Continuation Southwards on same scale
Projection: Albers' Equal Area with two standard parallels
West from Greenwich
COPYRIGHT GEORGE PHILIP LTD.

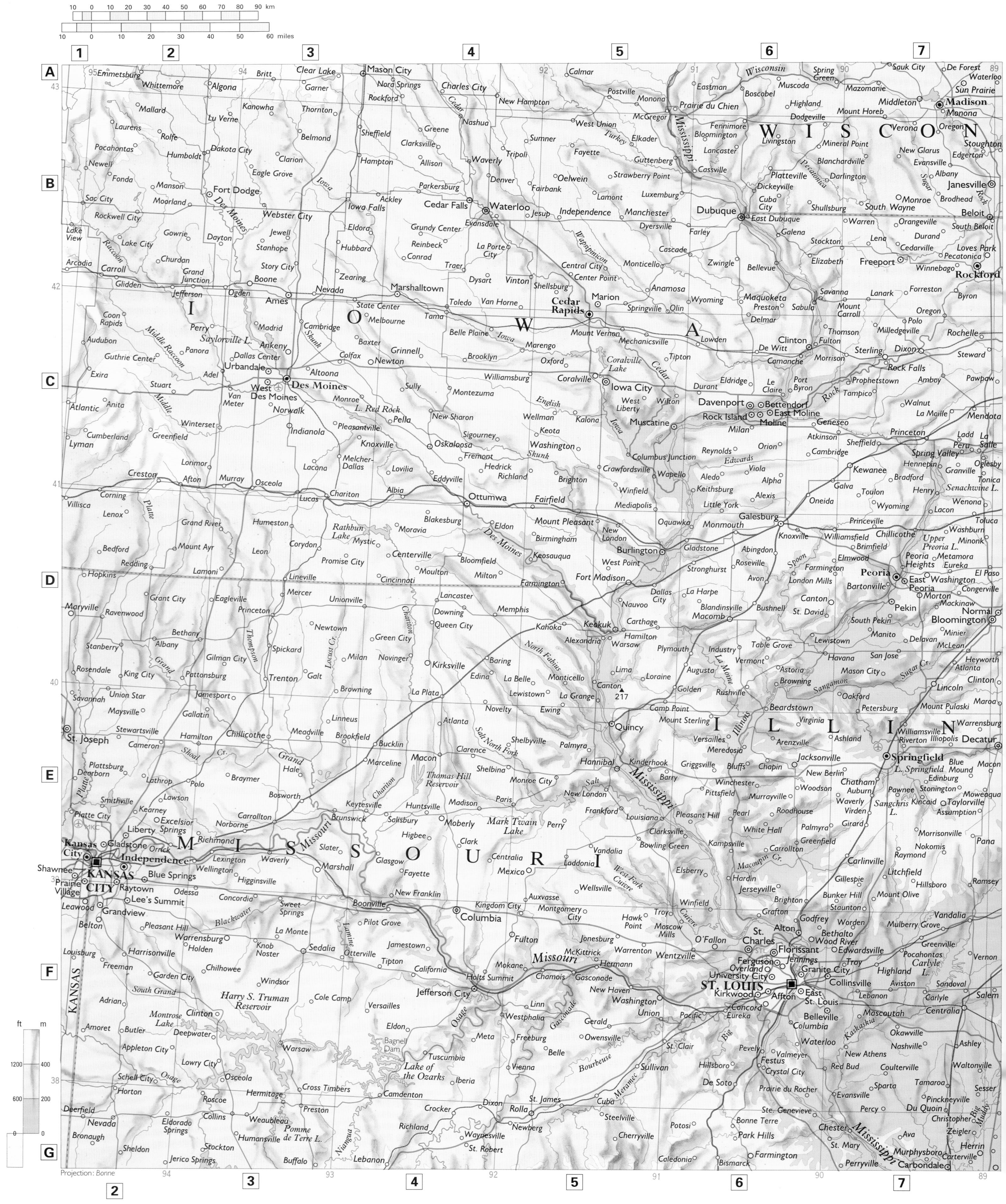

10 0 10 20 30 40 50 60 70 80 90 km
10 0 10 20 30 40 50 60 miles
1 2 3 4 5 6 7
A B C D E F G
IOWA
WISCONSIN
ILLINOIS
MISSOURI
KANSAS
Emmetsburg
Whittemore
Algona
Britt
Clear Lake
Mason City
Nora Springs
Charles City
Calmar
Postville
Eastman
Spring Green
Mazomanie
Sauk City
De Forest
Waterloo
Sun Prairie
Madison
Monona
Middleton
Garner
Rockford
New Hampton
Monona
Prairie du Chien
Muscoda
Boscobel
Highland
Dodgeville
Mount Horeb
Verona
Oregon
Stoughton
Edgerton
Mallard
Kanowha
Thornton
Lu Verne
Laurens
Rolfe
Belmond
Sheffield
Greene
Nashua
McGregor
West Union
Fennimore
Livingston
Mineral Point
New Glarus
Evansville
Albany
Pocahontas
Humboldt
Dakota City
Clarion
Hampton
Clarksville
Allison
Sumner
Fayette
Elkader
Guttenberg
Bloomington
Lancaster
Blanchardville
Darlington
Janesville
Newell
Fonda
Manson
Eagle Grove
Waverly
Tripoli
Denver
Oelwein
Strawberry Point
Platteville
Dickeyville
Cassville
Cuba City
Monroe
Brodhead
Beloit
South Beloit
Sac City
Moorland
Fort Dodge
Des Moines
Webster City
Iowa Falls
Ackley
Parkersburg
Cedar Falls
Waterloo
Fairbank
Lamont
Luxemburg
Dubuque
East Dubuque
Shullsburg
South Wayne
Rockwell City
Lake View
Gowrie
Dayton
Jewell
Eldora
Grundy Center
Evansdale
Jesup
Independence
Manchester
Dyersville
Farley
Galena
Warren
Orangeville
Lena
Durand
Cedarville
Loves Park
Pecatonica
Stanhope
Lake City
Hubbard
Reinbeck
Conrad
La Porte City
Cascade
Zwingle
Bellevue
Stockton
Elizabeth
Freeport
Winnebago
Rockford
Arcadia
Carroll
Churdan
Grand Junction
Story City
Zearing
Traer
Dysart
Vinton
Central City
Center Point
Monticello
Glidden
Jefferson
Boone
Nevada
Marshalltown
Shellsburg
Anamosa
Savanna
Lanark
Forreston
Byron
Ogden
Ames
State Center
Toledo
Van Horne
Cedar Rapids
Marion
Wyoming
Maquoketa
Preston
Sabula
Mount Carroll
Oregon
Coon Rapids
Melbourne
Tama
Springville
Olin
Delmar
Polo
Perry
Saylorville L.
Madrid
Cambridge
Belle Plaine
Mount Vernon
Mechanicsville
Lowden
Clinton
Thomson
Fulton
Milledgeville
Rochelle
Audubon
Panora
Ankeny
Baxter
Iowa
Marengo
De Witt
Sterling
Dixon
Guthrie Center
Dallas Center
Urbandale
Colfax
Grinnell
Newton
Brooklyn
Oxford
Coralville Lake
Tipton
Camanche
Morrison
Steward
Exira
Adel
Altoona
Des Moines
West Des Moines
Williamsburg
Coralville
Iowa City
Eldridge
Durant
Le Claire
Port Byron
Prophetstown
Rock Falls
Amboy
Pawpaw
Stuart
Atlantic
Anita
Van Meter
Norwalk
Monroe
Sully
Montezuma
English
West Liberty
Wilton
Davenport
Bettendorf
East Moline
Rock Island
Moline
Tampico
Walnut
La Moille
Mendota
L. Red Rock
Pella
New Sharon
Winterset
Wellman
Kalona
Muscatine
Milan
Geneseo
Cumberland
Greenfield
Indianola
Pleasantville
Sigourney
Keota
Atkinson
Princeton
Ladd
La Salle
Lyman
Knoxville
Oskaloosa
Washington
Reynolds
Orion
Cambridge
Sheffield
Peru
Spring Valley
Lorimor
Melcher-Dallas
Fremont
Columbus Junction
Edwards
Hennepin
Oglesby
Lacona
Lovilia
Hedrick
Richland
Crawfordsville
Aledo
Viola
Kewanee
Granville
Creston
Afton
Murray
Osceola
Eddyville
Brighton
Wapello
Keithsburg
Alpha
Bradford
Tonica
Corning
Lucas
Chariton
Albia
Ottumwa
Fairfield
Winfield
Galva
Toulon
Henry
Senachwine L.
Villisca
Lenox
Platte
Mediapolis
Alexis
Oneida
Wyoming
Wenona
Grand River
Humeston
Rathbun Lake
Blakesburg
Eldon
Mount Pleasant
Little York
Galesburg
Lacon
Toluca
Moravia
Birmingham
New London
Oquawka
Monmouth
Princeville
Washburn
Bedford
Mount Ayr
Leon
Corydon
Mystic
Centerville
Keosauqua
Burlington
Knoxville
Williamsfield
Chillicothe
Upper Peoria L.
Minonk
Redding
Lamoni
Promise City
Moulton
Bloomfield
West Point
Gladstone
Abingdon
Brimfield
Metamora
Hopkins
Lineville
Cincinnati
Milton
Farmington
Fort Madison
Stronghurst
Roseville
Elmwood
Peoria
Peoria Heights
Eureka
El Paso
Maryville
Grant City
Eagleville
Mercer
Unionville
Lancaster
Memphis
Dallas City
La Harpe
Avon
Farmington
London Mills
East Peoria
Washington
Congerville
Ravenwood
Princeton
Downing
Queen City
Nauvoo
Blandinsville
Bushnell
Canton
Bartonville
Pekin
Morton
Mackinaw
Normal
Bethany
Newtown
Kahoka
Keokuk
Carthage
Macomb
St. David
South Pekin
Bloomington
Stanberry
Albany
Green City
Hamilton
Warsaw
Alexandria
Plymouth
Industry
Table Grove
Lewistown
Manito
Minier
Delavan
McLean
Gilman City
Spickard
Milan
Novinger
Baring
Lima
La Moine
Vermont
Havana
San Jose
Heyworth
Rosendale
King City
Pattonsburg
Trenton
Galt
Kirksville
Edina
La Belle
Monticello
Canton
Loraine
Augusta
Astoria
Mason City
Atlanta
Savannah
Union Star
Jamesport
Browning
La Plata
Lewistown
La Grange
217
Golden
Rushville
Browning
Sangamon
Oakford
Clinton
Lincoln
Maysville
Gallatin
Linneus
Novelty
Ewing
Camp Point
Beardstown
Petersburg
Mount Pulaski
Maroa
Stewartsville
Hamilton
Chillicothe
Meadville
Brookfield
Atlanta
Shelbyville
Quincy
Mount Sterling
Virginia
Williamsville
Riverton
Warrensburg
Illiopolis
Decatur
St. Joseph
Cameron
Bucklin
Clarence
Palmyra
Versailles
Meredosia
Arenzville
Ashland
Springfield
Plattsburg
Dearborn
Macon
Marceline
Shelbina
Hannibal
Kinderhook
Barry
Griggsville
Bluffs
Chapin
Jacksonville
New Berlin
L. Springfield
Blue Mound
Macon
Edinburg
Lathrop
Polo
Braymer
Hale
Thomas Hill Reservoir
Monroe City
New London
Pittsfield
Winchester
Murrayville
Woodson
Chatham
Auburn
Pawnee
Stonington
Moweaqua
Taylorville
Smithville
Lawson
Bosworth
Keytesville
Huntsville
Madison
Paris
Salt
Frankford
Louisiana
Pleasant Hill
Roodhouse
Waverly
Virden
Kincaid
Sangchris L.
Assumption
Platte City
Kearney
Excelsior Springs
Carrollton
Brunswick
Salisbury
Moberly
Mark Twain Lake
Perry
Pearl
White Hall
Palmyra
Girard
Liberty
Norborne
Richmond
Higbee
Clark
Clarksville
Kampsville
Greenfield
Morrisonville
Pana
Kansas City
Gladstone
Orrick
Independence
Lexington
Waverly
Slater
Glasgow
Centralia
Vandalia
Laddonia
Bowling Green
Carrollton
Carlinville
Nokomis
Raymond
Shawnee
Kansas City
Wellington
Marshall
Fayette
Mexico
West Fork Cuivre
Elsberry
Macoupin Cr.
Litchfield
Prairie Village
Blue Springs
Raytown
Odessa
Higginsville
New Franklin
Wellsville
Hardin
Jerseyville
Gillespie
Hillsboro
Ramsey
Leawood
Lee's Summit
Concordia
Sweet Springs
Boonville
Auxvasse
Montgomery City
Winfield
Brighton
Bunker Hill
Mount Olive
Grandview
Blackwater
Kingdom City
Columbia
Troy
Cuivre
Grafton
Staunton
Vandalia
Belton
Pleasant Hill
Pilot Grove
Hawk Point
Moscow Mills
Alton
Godfrey
Worden
Mulberry Grove
Warrensburg
La Monte
Lamine
Jamestown
Fulton
Jonesburg
O'Fallon
St. Charles
Bethalto
Wood River
Greenville
Louisburg
Harrisonville
Holden
Knob Noster
Sedalia
Otterville
Tipton
Mokane
McKittrick
Warrenton
Wentzville
Florissant
Ferguson
Edwardsville
Pocahontas
Vernon
Freeman
Chilhowee
California
Holts Summit
Missouri
Hermann
Jennings
Overland
University City
Granite City
Troy
Carlyle L.
Highland
Garden City
Windsor
Chamois
Gasconade
St. Louis
Collinsville
Aviston
Sandoval
South Grand
Jefferson City
New Haven
Kirkwood
Affton
East St. Louis
Lebanon
Carlyle
Salem
Adrian
Harry S. Truman Reservoir
Cole Camp
Versailles
Linn
Washington
Union
Concord
Belleville
Mascoutah
Centralia
Montrose Lake
Clinton
Eldon
Westphalia
Gerald
Pacific
Eureka
Columbia
Kaskaskia
Amoret
Butler
Deepwater
Osage
Meta
Freeburg
Gasconade
Owensville
Big
Waterloo
Okawville
Ashley
Appleton City
Warsaw
Bagnell Dam
Tuscumbia
Belle
St. Clair
Pevely
Valmeyer
Nashville
New Athens
Lowry City
Bourbeuse
Festus
Crystal City
Waltonville
Schell City
Osceola
Lake of the Ozarks
Iberia
Vienna
Sullivan
Hillsboro
Red Bud
Coulterville
Horton
Hermitage
Cross Timbers
Camdenton
Meramec
De Soto
Tamaroa
Sparta
Sesser
Deerfield
Roscoe
Preston
Crocker
Dixon
Rolla
St. James
Cuba
Prairie du Rocher
Evansville
Pinckneyville
Nevada
Collins
Weaubleau
Pomme de Terre L.
Richland
Newburg
Steelville
Ste. Genevieve
Percy
Du Quoin
Big Muddy
Eldorado Springs
Humansville
Potosi
Bonne Terre
Christopher
Bronaugh
Sheldon
Stockton
Niangua
Waynesville
Cherryville
Park Hills
Chester
Zeigler
Ava
St. Mary
Herrin
Murphysboro
Carterville
Jerico Springs
Buffalo
Lebanon
St. Robert
Caledonia
Bismarck
Farmington
Perryville
Carbondale
Mississippi
Missouri
Illinois
Rock
Pecatonica
Sugar
Cedar
Turkey
Wapsipinicon
Iowa
Skunk
Raccoon
Middle Raccoon
Middle
Grand
Thompson
Locust Cr.
Chariton
North Fabius
Salt North Fork
Spoon
Sugar Cr.
Shoal Cr.
Osage
Lake of the Ozarks
95
94
93
92
91
90
89
43
42
41
40
39
38
ft
m
1200
600
400
200
0
Projection: Bonne

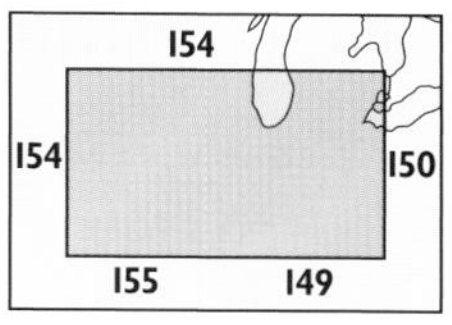

8 9 10 11 12 13 14

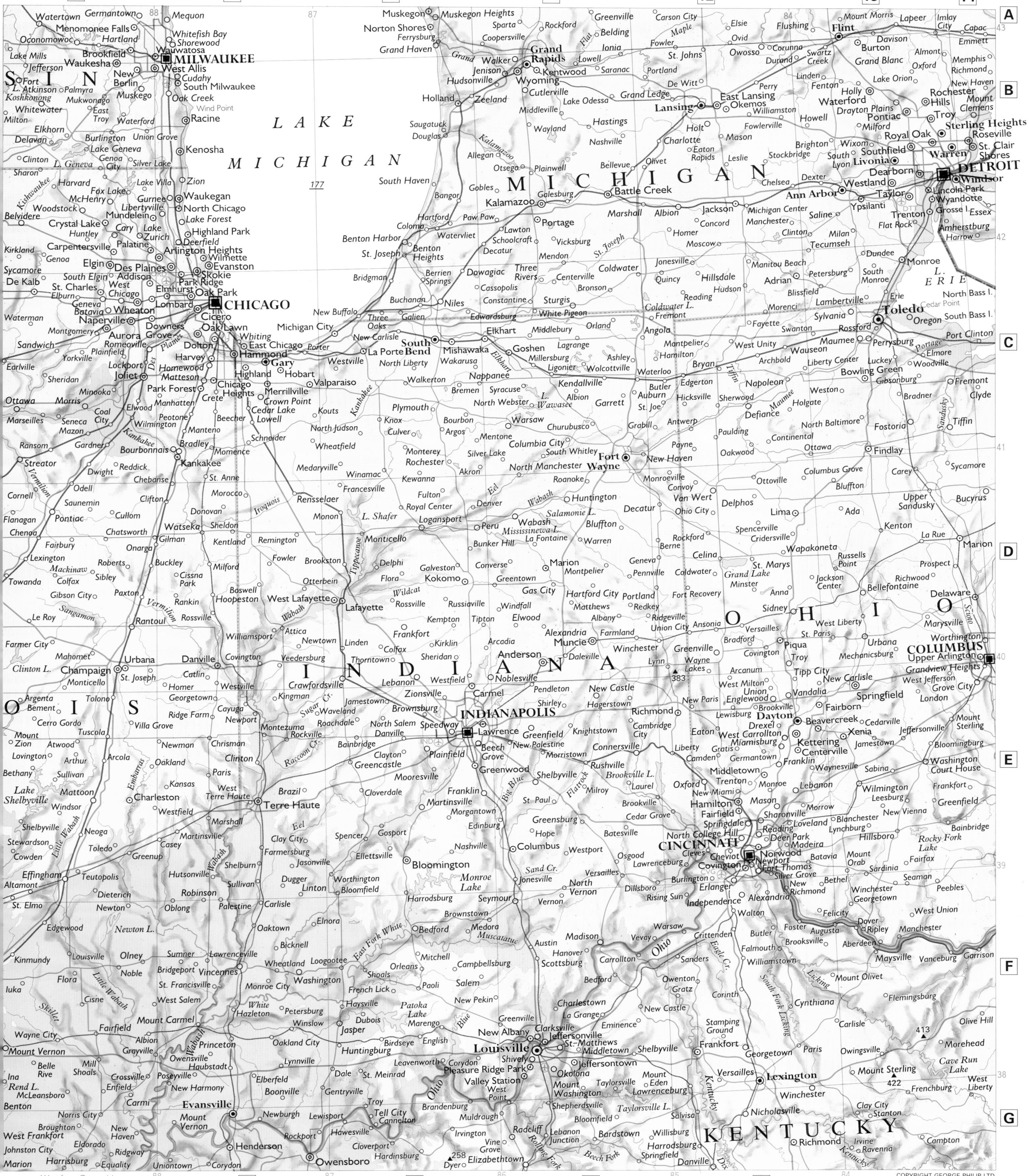

8 9 10 11 12 13

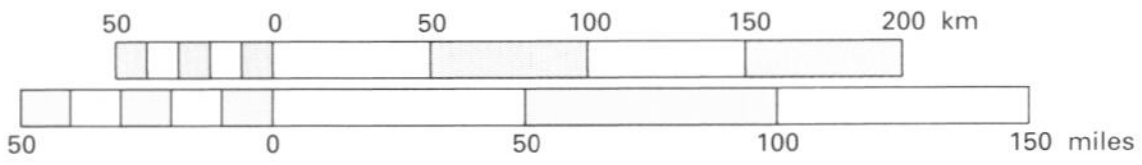
50
0
50
100
150
200 km
50
0
50
100
150 miles

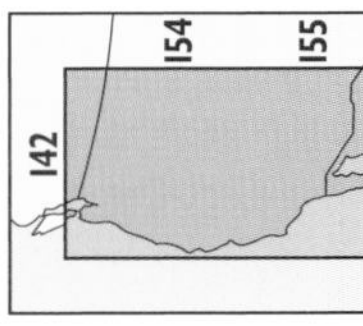
154
155
162
142

A
B
C
D
E
F
1
2
3
4
5
6
7
8
9
10
SASKATCHEWAN
ALBERTA
BRITISH COLUMBIA
WASHINGTON
OREGON
IDAHO
MONTANA
WYOMING
NEVADA
UTAH
SEATTLE
PORTLAND
SACRAMENTO
SALT LAKE CITY
VANCOUVER
Bighorn Mountains
Salmon River Mountains
Sawtooth Range
Blue Mountains
Wallowa Mts.
Cabinet Mountains
Clearwater Mountains
Little Belt Mts.
Big Belt Mts.
Medicine Bow Mts.
Uinta Mountains
Great Salt Lake
Great Salt Lake Desert
Harney Basin
Steens Mountain
Shoshone Mountains
Olympic Mts.
Spokane
Boise
Helena
Billings
Great Falls
Missoula
Butte
Bozeman
Pocatello
Idaho Falls
Ogden
Provo
Reno
Carson City
Salem
Eugene
Medford
Redding
Yakima
Walla Walla
Casper
Laramie
Rock Springs
Elko
Winnemucca

COLORADO
NEW MEXICO
ARIZONA
TEXAS
CHIHUAHUA
SONORA
BAJA CALIFORNIA
MEXICO
PACIFIC OCEAN
Golfo de California
Colorado Plateau
Grand Canyon
Painted Desert
Mohave Desert
Sonoran Desert
Desierto de Altar
Death Valley
Sangre de Cristo Mts.
Sawatch Range
San Juan Mts.
Sacramento Mts.
Mogollon Rim
Chuska Mts.
Rio Grande
Colorado
LOS ANGELES
SAN DIEGO
PHOENIX
Tucson
Albuquerque
Santa Fe
El Paso
Ciudad Juárez
Chihuahua
Hermosillo
Tijuana
Mexicali
Ensenada
Las Vegas
Flagstaff
Yuma
Nogales
Fresno
Bakersfield
San Jose
Oakland
San Francisco
Channel Is.
Isla Guadalupe (Mexico)
Projection: Albers' Equal Area with two standard parallels
COPYRIGHT GEORGE PHILIP LTD.
West from Greenwich
m
ft
4000
3000
2000
1500
1000
400
200
0
12 000
9000
6000
4500
3000
1200
600
2000
6000
12 000

WESTERN WASHINGTON REGION
On same scale
PACIFIC OCEAN
BRITISH COLUMBIA
CANADA
WASHINGTON
OREGON
Vancouver Island
Strait of Juan de Fuca
Olympic Mountains
Cascade Range
SEATTLE
Tacoma
PORTLAND
VANCOUVER
Sierra Nevada
Sacramento Valley
San Joaquin Valley
SACRAMENTO
SAN FRANCISCO
Oakland
San Jose
Fresno
Stockton
Reno
Lake Tahoe
Santa Lucia Range
Diablo Range
Coast Ranges
Inyo Mts.
White Mts.
Pahute Mesa

NEVADA
ARIZONA
CALIFORNIA
MEXICO
BAJA CALIFORNIA
PACIFIC OCEAN
Mojave Desert
Sonoran Desert
Death Valley
Amargosa Range
Panamint Ra.
Temblor Range
San Rafael Mts.
San Gabriel Mts.
San Bernardino Mts.
Chocolate Mts.
Tehachapi Mts.
Providence Mts.
Avawatz Mts.
Imperial Valley
Salton Sea
Lake Mead
Lake Mohave
Lake Havasu
Colorado
Channel Islands
Santa Barbara Channel
San Pedro Channel
Gulf of Santa Catalina
Santa Catalina I.
San Clemente I.
San Nicolas I.
Santa Cruz I.
Santa Rosa I.
San Miguel I.
Santa Barbara I.
Las Vegas
Henderson
North Las Vegas
Boulder City
Kingman
Bullhead City
Needles
Lake Havasu City
Parker
Blythe
Yuma
Barstow
Victorville
Hesperia
Apple Valley
Lancaster
Palmdale
Bakersfield
Santa Clarita
LOS ANGELES
Long Beach
Santa Ana
Anaheim
Riverside
San Bernardino
Palm Springs
Indio
El Centro
Mexicali
Calexico
Oceanside
Escondido
SAN DIEGO
Chula Vista
Tijuana
Tecate
Ensenada
Santa Barbara
Ventura
Oxnard
Santa Maria
San Luis Obispo
Lompoc
Pt. Conception
Pt. Arguello
Ridgecrest
Twentynine Palms
10 0 10 20 30 40 50 60 70 80 90 km
10 0 10 20 30 40 50 60 miles
H
J
K
L
M
N
8
9
10
11
12
13
158
159
162
West from Greenwich
Projection: Bonne
COPYRIGHT GEORGE PHILIP LTD.
m
ft
4000
3000
2000
1500
1000
400
200
0
12 000
9000
6000
4500
3000
1200
600
0
200
2000
6000

REFERENCE TO NUMBERS

1 Distrito Federal
2 Aguascalientes
3 Guanajuato
4 Hidalgo
5 México
6 Morelos
7 Querétaro
8 Tlaxcala

Projection: *Bi-polar oblique Conical Orthomorphic*

West from Greenwich

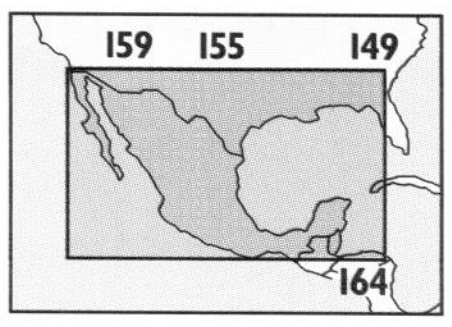
159
155
149
164

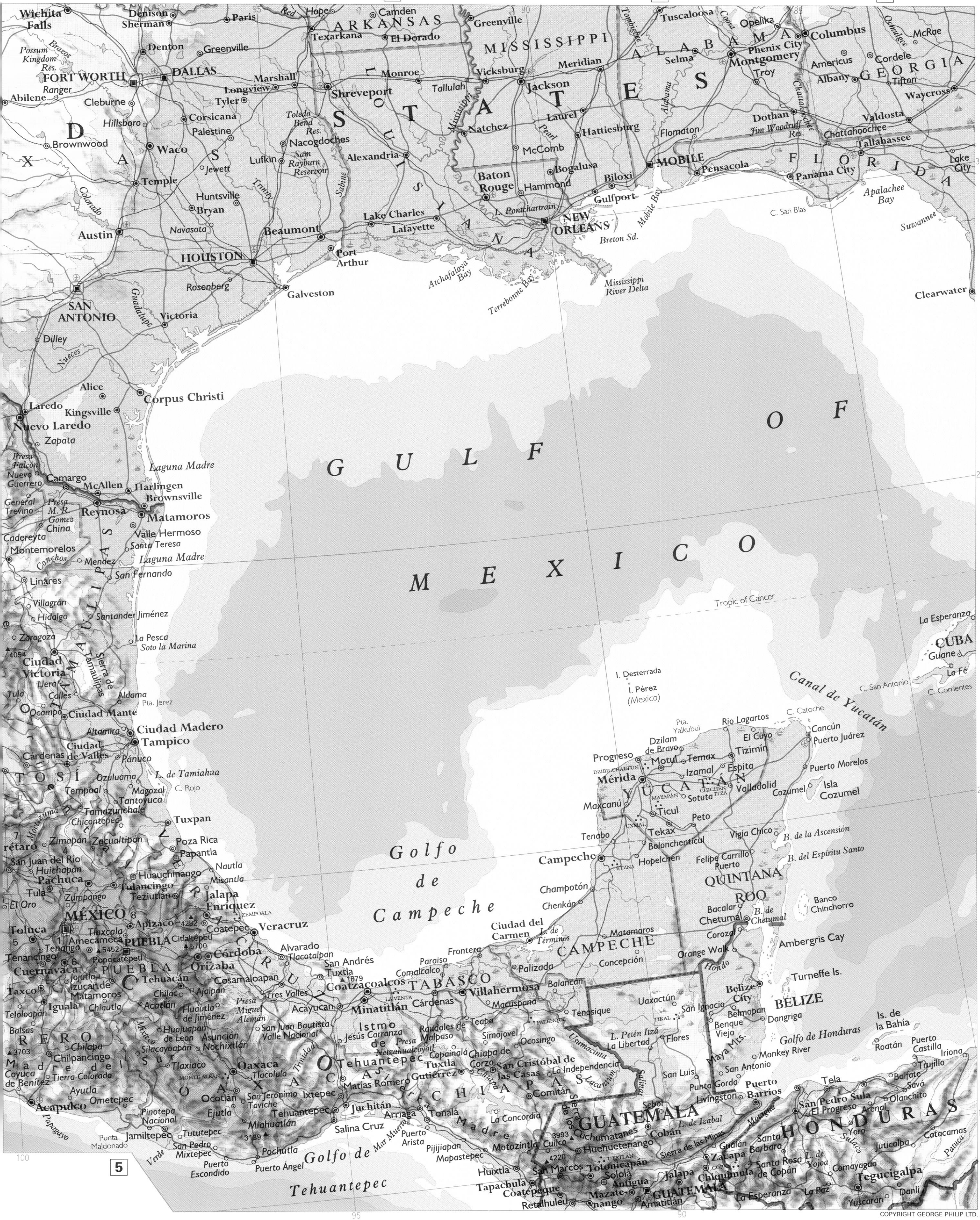
5
6
7
8
A
B
C
D
E
GULF OF MEXICO
Golfo de Campeche
Golfo de Tehuantepec
Golfo de Honduras
Canal de Yucatán
Tropic of Cancer
UNITED STATES
TEXAS
ARKANSAS
LOUISIANA
MISSISSIPPI
ALABAMA
GEORGIA
FLORIDA
MEXICO
TAMAULIPAS
SAN LUIS POTOSÍ
VERACRUZ
PUEBLA
GUERRERO
OAXACA
TABASCO
CHIAPAS
CAMPECHE
YUCATÁN
QUINTANA ROO
BELIZE
GUATEMALA
HONDURAS
CUBA
Wichita Falls
Denison
Sherman
Paris
Hope
Camden
Texarkana
El Dorado
Greenville
Tuscaloosa
Opelika
Columbus
McRae
Denton
Greenville
Possum Kingdom Res.
Brazos
FORT WORTH
DALLAS
Marshall
Monroe
Vicksburg
Jackson
Meridian
Selma
Phenix City
Montgomery
Americus
Cordele
Abilene
Ranger
Cleburne
Longview
Tyler
Shreveport
Tallulah
Troy
Albany
Tifton
Waycross
Corsicana
Hillsboro
Palestine
Toledo Bend Res.
Natchez
Laurel
Hattiesburg
Dothan
Jim Woodruff Res.
Valdosta
Brownwood
Waco
Nacogdoches
Jewett
Lufkin
Sam Rayburn Reservoir
Alexandria
McComb
Flomaton
Chattahoochee
Tallahassee
Temple
Bogalusa
MOBILE
Pensacola
Panama City
Lake City
Baton Rouge
Hammond
Biloxi
Gulfport
Apalachee Bay
Huntsville
Bryan
Colorado
Trinity
Sabine
Mississippi
Pearl
Alabama
Tombigbee
Coosa
Ocmulgee
L. Pontchartrain
NEW ORLEANS
Mobile Bay
C. San Blas
Austin
Navasota
Beaumont
Lake Charles
Lafayette
Breton Sd.
Suwannee
HOUSTON
Port Arthur
Atchafalaya Bay
Terrebonne Bay
Mississippi River Delta
SAN ANTONIO
Rosenberg
Galveston
Clearwater
Victoria
Guadalupe
Dilley
Nueces
Alice
Corpus Christi
Laredo
Kingsville
Nuevo Laredo
Zapata
Presa Falcón
Nuevo Guerrero
Camargo
McAllen
Harlingen
Brownsville
Laguna Madre
General Treviño
Presa M. R. Gómez
Reynosa
Matamoros
China
Cadereyta
Valle Hermoso
Montemorelos
Santa Teresa
Conchos
Mendez
Laguna Madre
Linares
San Fernando
Villagrán
Hidalgo
Santander Jiménez
Zaragoza
La Pesca
Soto la Marina
4054
Ciudad Victoria
Sierra de Tamaulipas
Llera
Tula
Aldama
Pta. Jerez
Ciudad Mante
Ocampo
Altamira
Ciudad Madero
Tampico
Ciudad de Valles
Cárdenas
Pánuco
Ozuluama
L. de Tamiahua
Tempoal
Tantoyuca
C. Rojo
Tamazunchale
Chicontepec
Tuxpan
Zimapán
Zacualtipán
Poza Rica
Papantla
San Juan del Río
Huichapan
Nautla
Pachuca
Huauchinango
Misantla
Tulancingo
Tula
Zumpango
Teziutlán
Jalapa Enríquez
El Oro
MÉXICO
Apizaco
4282
ZEMPOALA
Veracruz
Toluca
Tlaxcala
Amecameca
PUEBLA
Citlaltépetl
5700
Coatepec
Tenancingo
5452
Popocatépetl
Córdoba
Alvarado
Tlacotalpan
San Andrés Tuxtla
Cuernavaca
Orizaba
Jojutla
Izúcar de Matamoros
Tehuacán
Cosamaloapan
Taxco
Chilac
Ajalpan
Tres Valles
Coatzacoalcos
Iguala
Chiautla
Acatlán
Huautla de Jiménez
Presa Miguel Alemán
Acayucan
Minatitlán
Teloloapan
Balsas
Mixteco
Huajuapan de León
San Juan Bautista Valle Nacional
Istmo de Tehuantepec
Chilapa
3703
Chilpancingo
Asunción Nochixtlán
Silacayoapan
Tlaxiaco
Oaxaca
Tlacolula
Coyuca de Benítez
Tierra Colorada
MONTE ALBÁN
Tehuantepec
Ayutla
Ocotlán
San Jerónimo Taviche
Matías Romero
Ixtepec
Acapulco
Ometepec
Ejutla
Tehuantepec
Juchitán
Pinotepa Nacional
Miahuatlán
Salina Cruz
Papagayo
Punta Maldonado
Jamiltepec
Tututepec
3139
Pochutla
San Pedro Mixtepec
Puerto Escondido
Puerto Ángel
Verde
Mar Muerto
Puerto Arista
Pijijiapan
Mapastepec
Huixtla
Tapachula
Coatepeque
Retalhuleu
1879
LA VENTA
Paraíso
Comalcalco
Frontera
Cárdenas
Villahermosa
Macuspana
Palizada
Ciudad del Carmen
L. de Términos
Balancán
Tenosique
PALENQUE
Raudales de Malpaso
Presa Netzahualcóyotl
Jesús Carranza
Teapa
Simojovel
Ocosingo
Tuxtla Gutiérrez
Copainalá
Chiapa de Corzo
San Cristóbal de las Casas
La Independencia
Comitán
Sierra Madre
Tonalá
Arriaga
La Concordia
Motozintla
Cuilco
3993
4220
San Marcos
Huehuetenango
Cuchumatanes
Sierra de los
Totonicapán
Sololá
Antigua
Mazatenango
Amatitlán
GUATEMALA
Jalapa
Chiquimula
Cobán
L. de Izabal
Sierra de las Minas
Gualán
Zacapa
COPÁN
Santa Rosa de Copán
Santa Bárbara
La Esperanza
La Paz
Tegucigalpa
Yuscarán
Danlí
Comayagua
L. de Yojoa
Juticalpa
Catacamas
Patuca
Sulaco
Yoro
Olanchito
Arenal
El Progreso
San Pedro Sula
Tela
Savá
Balfate
Trujillo
Iriona
Puerto Castilla
Roatán
Is. de la Bahía
Motagua
Livingston
Puerto Barrios
Sebol
Punta Gorda
San Luis
San Antonio
Monkey River
Maya Mts.
Dangriga
Belmopan
Benque Viejo
San Ignacio
Belize City
Flores
TIKAL
UAXACTÚN
Uaxactún
L. Petén Itzá
La Libertad
Usumacinta
Lacantún
Salinas
Hondo
Orange Walk
Corozal
Concepción
Matamoros
Chetumal
B. de Chetumal
Bacalar
Banco Chinchorro
Ambergris Cay
Turneffe Is.
Champotón
Chenkán
Campeche
EDZNÁ
Hopelchén
Felipe Carrillo Puerto
B. del Espíritu Santo
Vigía Chico
B. de la Ascensión
Tenabo
Tekax
Bolonchenticul
Peto
UXMAL
Ticul
Maxcanú
MAYAPÁN
Sotuta
CHICHÉN ITZÁ
Valladolid
Cozumel
Isla Cozumel
Mérida
DZIBILCHALTÚN
Progreso
Motul
Temax
Izamal
Espita
Tizimín
Dzilam de Bravo
Pta. Yalkubul
Río Lagartos
El Cuyo
C. Catoche
Cancún
Puerto Juárez
Puerto Morelos
I. Desterrada
I. Pérez
(Mexico)
C. San Antonio
C. Corrientes
La Fe
Guane
La Esperanza
100
95
90
85
30
25
20
15
COPYRIGHT GEORGE PHILIP LTD.

1:6 400 000

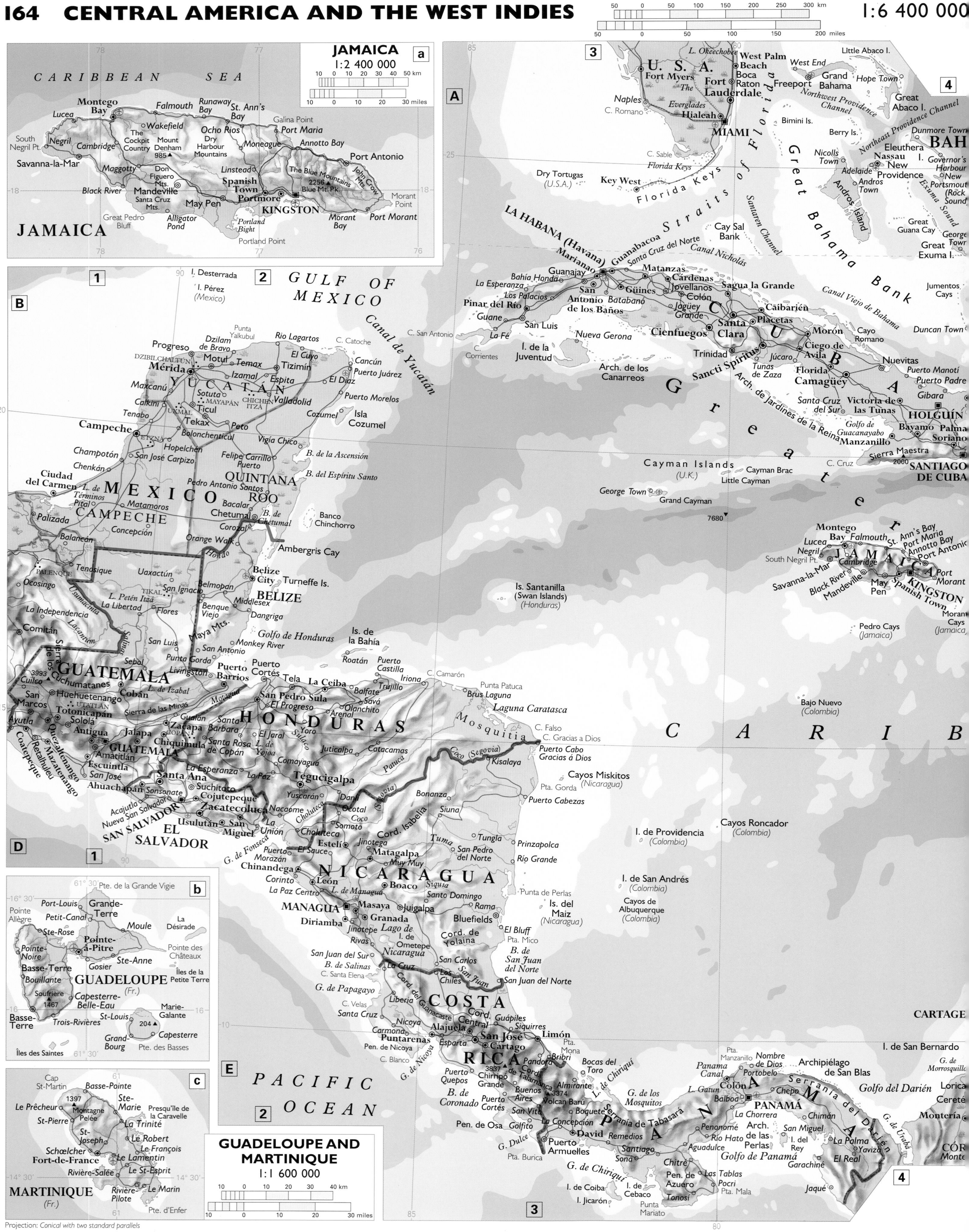
50 0 50 100 150 200 250 300 km
50 0 50 100 150 200 miles
JAMAICA
1:2 400 000
10 0 10 20 30 40 50 km
10 0 10 20 30 miles
a
CARIBBEAN SEA
Montego Bay
Lucea
Falmouth
Runaway Bay
St. Ann's Bay
Galina Point
Port Maria
South Negril Pt.
Negril
Cambridge
The Cockpit Country
Wakefield
Mount Denham 985
Ocho Rios
Dry Harbour Mountains
Moneague
Annotto Bay
Port Antonio
Savanna-la-Mar
Maggotty
Don Figuero Mts.
Linstead
Spanish Town
The Blue Mountains
2256 Blue Mt. Pk.
John Crow Mts.
Black River
Mandeville
Santa Cruz Mts.
Portmore
KINGSTON
Morant Point
May Pen
Great Pedro Bluff
Alligator Pond
Portland Bight
Portland Point
Morant Bay
Port Morant
JAMAICA
3
A
4
L. Okeechobee
U.S.A.
West Palm Beach
Boca Raton
Fort Myers
Fort Lauderdale
The Everglades
Naples
C. Romano
Hialeah
MIAMI
Florida
Freeport
West End
Grand Bahama
Hope Town
Little Abaco I.
Great Abaco I.
Northwest Providence Channel
Northeast Providence Channel
Bimini Is.
Berry Is.
C. Sable
Florida Keys
Dry Tortugas (U.S.A.)
Key West
Florida Keys
Straits of Florida
Santaren Channel
Great Bahama Bank
Nicolls Town
Adelaide
Andros Town
Andros Island
Nassau
New Providence
Eleuthera
Dunmore Town
BAH
Governor's Harbour
New Portsmouth
Exuma Sound
Rock Sound
Great Guana Cay
Great Exuma I.
George Town
Cay Sal Bank
Canal Nicholás
LA HABANA (Havana)
Marianao
Guanabacoa
Santa Cruz del Norte
Matanzas
Cárdenas
Jovellanos
Colón
Jagüey Grande
Sagua la Grande
Caibarién
Bahía Honda
Guanajay
San Antonio de los Baños
Batabanó
Güines
La Esperanza
Los Palacios
Pinar del Río
Guane
San Luis
La Fé
C. Corrientes
C. San Antonio
I. de la Juventud
Nueva Gerona
Arch. de los Canarreos
Cienfuegos
Santa Clara
Placetas
CUBA
Trinidad
Sancti Spíritus
Júcaro
Tunas de Zaza
Arch. de Jardines de la Reina
Florida
Camagüey
Morón
Ciego de Avila
Cayo Romano
Canal Viejo de Bahama
Jumentos Cays
Duncan Town
Nuevitas
Puerto Manatí
Puerto Padre
Gibara
Santa Cruz del Sur
Victoria de las Tunas
HOLGUÍN
Golfo de Guacanayabo
Manzanillo
Bayamo
Palma Soriano
Sierra Maestra
2000
C. Cruz
SANTIAGO DE CUBA
Greater
Cayman Islands (U.K.)
Cayman Brac
Little Cayman
George Town
Grand Cayman
7680
Montego Bay
Falmouth
St. Ann's Bay
Port Maria
Annotto Bay
Port Antonio
Lucea
Negril
South Negril Pt.
Cambridge
JAMAICA
Savanna-la-Mar
Black River
Mandeville
May Pen
Spanish Town
KINGSTON
Port Morant
Morant Cays (Jamaica)
Pedro Cays (Jamaica)
B
1
2
90
I. Desterrada
I. Pérez (Mexico)
GULF OF MEXICO
Canal de Yucatán
Punta Yalkubul
Rio Lagartos
C. Catoche
Progreso
Dzilam de Bravo
DZIBILCHALTÚN
Motul
Temax
El Cuyo
Tizimín
Cancún
Puerto Juárez
Mérida
Izamal
Espita
El Díaz
YUCATÁN
Maxcanú
Sotuta
MAYAPÁN
CHICHÉN ITZÁ
Valladolid
Puerto Morelos
Calkini
UXMAL
Ticul
Tenabo
Tekax
Cozumel
Isla Cozumel
Campeche
Peto
Bolonchenticul
Champotón
Hopelchén
Vigía Chico
San José Carpizo
Felipe Carrillo Puerto
B. de la Ascensión
Chenkán
B. del Espíritu Santo
Ciudad del Carmen
L. de Términos
MEXICO
QUINTANA ROO
Pedro Antonio Santos
Pital
Matamoros
Bacalar
Palizada
CAMPECHE
Chetumal
B. de Chetumal
Banco Chinchorro
Concepción
Corozal
Balancán
Orange Walk
Hondo
Ambergris Cay
PALENQUE
Tenosique
Uaxactún
Belize City
Turneffe Is.
Ocosingo
TIKAL
San Ignacio
Belmopan
Usumacinta
L. Petén Itzá
La Libertad
Benque Viejo
Middlesex
BELIZE
La Independencia
Flores
Dangriga
Lacantún
Maya Mts.
Comitán
Golfo de Honduras
I. de la Bahía
San Luis
Monkey River
San Antonio
Sierra de los Cuchumatanes
Punta Gorda
Roatán
Puerto Castilla
Sebol
Livingston
Puerto Barrios
Puerto Cortés
Tela
La Ceiba
Trujillo
Iriona
C. Camarón
3993
Cuilco
GUATEMALA
UTATLÁN
Cobán
L. de Izabal
San Marcos
Huehuetenango
Sierra de las Minas
Motagua
San Pedro Sula
El Progreso
Balfate
Savá
Olanchito
Arenal
Punta Patuca
Brus Laguna
Laguna Caratasca
Totonicapán
Sololá
Quetzaltenango
Ayutla
Antigua
Guatemala
Guastatoya
Zacapa
Santa Bárbara
HONDURAS
Yoro
Mosquitia
C. Falso
C. Gracias a Dios
Puerto Cabo Gracias á Dios
Coatepeque
Retalhuleu
Mazatenango
Amatitlán
Escuintla
Jalapa
COPÁN
Chiquimula
Santa Rosa de Copán
El Jaral
L. de Yojoa
Sulaco
Juticalpa
Catacamas
Coco (Segovia)
Kisalaya
San José
Ahuachapán
Santa Ana
La Esperanza
Comayagua
La Paz
Tegucigalpa
Patuca
Pta. Gorda
Cayos Miskitos (Nicaragua)
Acajutla
Sonsonate
Suchitoto
Cojutepeque
Yuscarán
Danlí
Bonanza
Puerto Cabezas
Nueva San Salvador
SAN SALVADOR
Zacatecoluca
Nacaome
Choluteca
Ocotal
Coco
Siuna
EL SALVADOR
Usulután
San Miguel
La Unión
Somoto
Cord. Isabelia
Tuma
Tungla
Prinzapolca
G. de Fonseca
Puerto Morazán
El Sauce
Estelí
Jinotega
Matagalpa
Muy Muy
San Pedro del Norte
Río Grande
Chinandega
NICARAGUA
Corinto
León
L. de Managua
Boaco
Siquia
Santo Domingo
La Paz Centro
MANAGUA
Masaya
Juigalpa
Rama
Diriamba
Granada
Bluefields
Jinotepe
Lago de Nicaragua
I. de Ometepe
Cord. de Yolaina
El Bluff
Pta. Mico
Rivas
San Juan del Sur
B. de Salinas
C. Santa Elena
G. de Papagayo
La Cruz
Los Chiles
San Carlos
San Juan
B. de San Juan del Norte
San Juan del Norte
C. Velas
Santa Cruz
Liberia
Cord. del Guanacaste
COSTA RICA
Cord. Central
Guápiles
Siquirres
Limón
Nicoya
Alajuela
Carmona
Puntarenas
San José
Cartago
Pen. de Nicoya
Esparta
C. Blanco
G. de Nicoya
Puerto Quepos
B. de Coronado
Chirripó Grande
3837
Cord. de Talamanca
Pandora
Bribri
Pta. Mona
Bocas del Toro
Almirante
3374
L. de Chiriquí
Buenos Aires
Volcan Barú
San Vito
Puerto Cortés
Golfito
Pen. de Osa
G. Dulce
Pta. Burica
La Concepción
David
Boquete
Puerto Armuelles
G. de Chiriquí
Serranía de Tabasará
Remedios
Santiago
Soná
I. de Coiba
I. de Cebaco
I. Jicarón
Punta Mariato
Chitré
Pen. de Azuero
Las Tablas
Pocrí
Tonosí
Pta. Mala
G. de los Mosquitos
Pta. Manzanillo
Panama Canal
Nombre de Dios
Portobelo
Colón
L. Gatun
Balboa
Chepo
PANAMÁ
PANAMA
La Chorrera
Penonomé
Río Hato
Aguadulce
Arch. de las Perlas
San Miguel
I. del Rey
Golfo de Panamá
Garachiné
Chimán
Serranía del Darién
La Palma
Yaviza
El Real
Jaqué
Archipiélago de San Blas
Golfo del Darién
G. de Urabá
G. de Morrosquillo
I. de San Bernardo
CARTAGE
Lorica
Cereté
Montería
CÓR
Monte
Is. Santanilla (Swan Islands) (Honduras)
Bajo Nuevo (Colombia)
CARIB
Cayos Roncador (Colombia)
I. de Providencia (Colombia)
I. de San Andrés (Colombia)
Cayos de Albuquerque (Colombia)
Punta de Perlas
Is. del Maíz (Nicaragua)
D
E
PACIFIC OCEAN
b
Pte. de la Grande Vigie
Port-Louis
Petit-Canal
Grande-Terre
Pointe Allègre
Ste-Rose
La Désirade
Moule
Pointe-Noire
Pointe-à-Pitre
Pointe des Châteaux
Ste-Anne
Basse-Terre
Gosier
Bouillante
GUADELOUPE (Fr.)
Îles de la Petite Terre
Soufrière 1467
Capesterre-Belle-Eau
Marie-Galante
Basse-Terre
Trois-Rivières
St-Louis
204
Capesterre
Grand-Bourg
Pte. des Basses
Îles des Saintes
c
Cap St-Martin
Basse-Pointe
Le Prêcheur
1397
Montagne Pelée
Ste-Marie
Presqu'île de la Caravelle
St-Pierre
La Trinité
St-Joseph
Le Robert
Schœlcher
Le François
Fort-de-France
Le Lamentin
Rivière-Salée
Le St-Esprit
MARTINIQUE (Fr.)
Rivière-Pilote
Le Marin
Pte. d'Enfer
GUADELOUPE AND MARTINIQUE
1:1 600 000
10 0 10 20 30 40 km
10 0 10 20 30 miles

Projection: *Conical with two standard parallels*

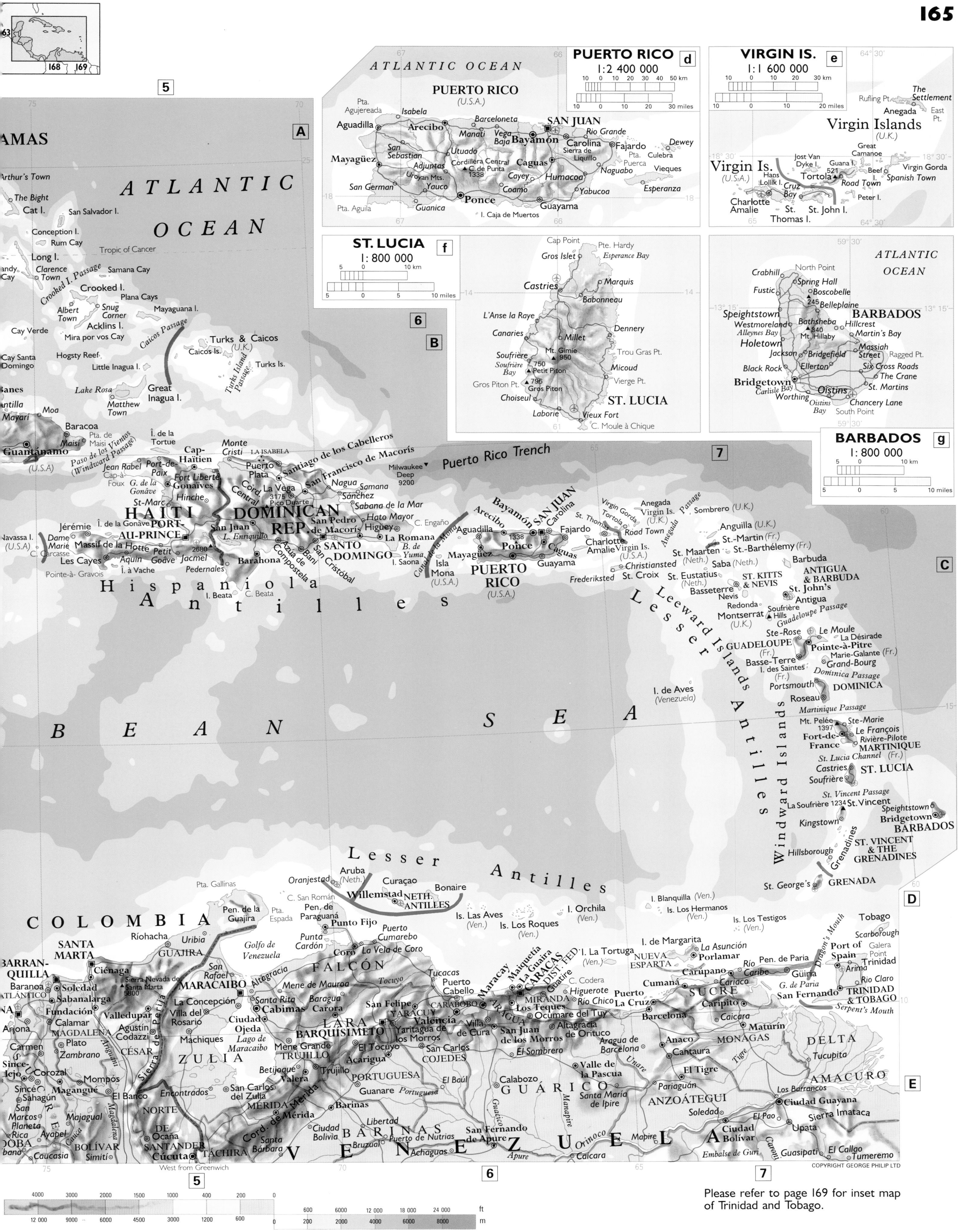

Please refer to page 169 for inset map of Trinidad and Tobago.

100 0 200 400 600 800 1000 1200 1400 km
100 0 200 400 600 800 1000 miles
Tropic of Cancer
Gulf of Campeche
Yucatán Peninsula
Yucatan Channel
Cuba
Greater Antilles
Turks & Caicos Is.
Hispaniola
9200
Puerto Rico
NORTH ATLANTIC OCEAN
Isthmus of Tehuantepec
G. de Honduras
Jamaica
Lesser Antilles
Guadeloupe
Dominica
Martinique
St. Lucia
Barbados
St. Vincent
Caribbean Sea
Guatemala Trench
C. Gracias a Dios
Coco
L. Nicaragua
C. de la Aguja
5800
Sierra Nevada de Santa Marta
L. Maracaibo
I. Margarita
Grenada
Tobago
Trinidad
Panama Canal
G. of Darién
Magdalena
Cord. de Mérida
Llanos
Orinoco
Meta
Gulf of Panama
Cordillera Occidental
Cordillera Central
Cordillera Oriental
Guiana Highlands
2810
Mt. Roraima
Sierra Pacaraima
Essequibo
Courantyne
Serra Tumucumaque
C. Orange
Guaviare
C. de San Francisco
Branco
Negro
Caquetá
Cotopaxi 5897
Chimborazo 6267
Japurá
Putumayo
Amazon
Marajó I.
Equator
Galapagos Is.
Napo
G. of Guayaquil
Marañón
Pta. Pariñas
Pta. Negra
Juruá
Ucayali
Purus
Madeira
Selvas
Aripuanã
Roosevelt
Tapajós
Xingu
Tocantins
Parnaíba
C. de São Roque
Teles Pires
Araguaia
Plat. of Borborema
São Francisco
Huascarán 6768
Chile Peru Trench
Madre de Dios
Arinos
Brazilian Highlands
Guaporé
Mamoré
Plateau of Mato Grosso
Chincha Alta
L. Titicaca
Nevada Ancohuma 6550
Bolivian Plateau
L. de Poopó
PACIFIC OCEAN
Abrolhos Bank
Gran Chaco
Paraguay
Paraná
2890
Serra da Mantiqueira
Pico da Bandeira
C. Frio
8050
Tropic of Capricorn
Atacama Desert
Pilcomayo
Iguaçu Falls
San Félix
San Ambrosio
Cerro Ojos del Salado 6863
Uruguay
Serra do Mar
Salado
Entre Ríos
Salinas Grandes
Sierra de Córdoba
L. Mar Chiquita
L. dos Patos
Mt. Aconcagua 6960
Pampas
Arch. de Juan Fernández
Río de la Plata
Andes
SOUTH ATLANTIC OCEAN
Colorado
Bahía Blanca
Negro
G. San Matías
Chile Rise
Chiloé I.
40
Valdés Peninsula
Chubut
Patagonia
Argentine Basin
Chonos Archipelago
Mte. San Valentín 4058
Taitao Peninsula
Gulf of San Jorge
Gulf of Penas
6212
Wellington I.
Madre de Dios I.
West Falkland
Falkland Is.
East Falkland
Magellan's Str.
Santa Inés I.
Tierra del Fuego
Staten I.
Canal Cockburn
Canal Beagle
C. Horn
South Georgia
ft m
12000 4000
9000 3000
6000 2000
3000 1000
1500 500
600 200
0 0
200 600
1000 3000
2000 6000
4000 12000
6000 18000
8000 24000
m ft
Projection: Lambert's Azimuthal Equal Area
West from Greenwich
CARTOGRAPHY BY PHILIP'S.

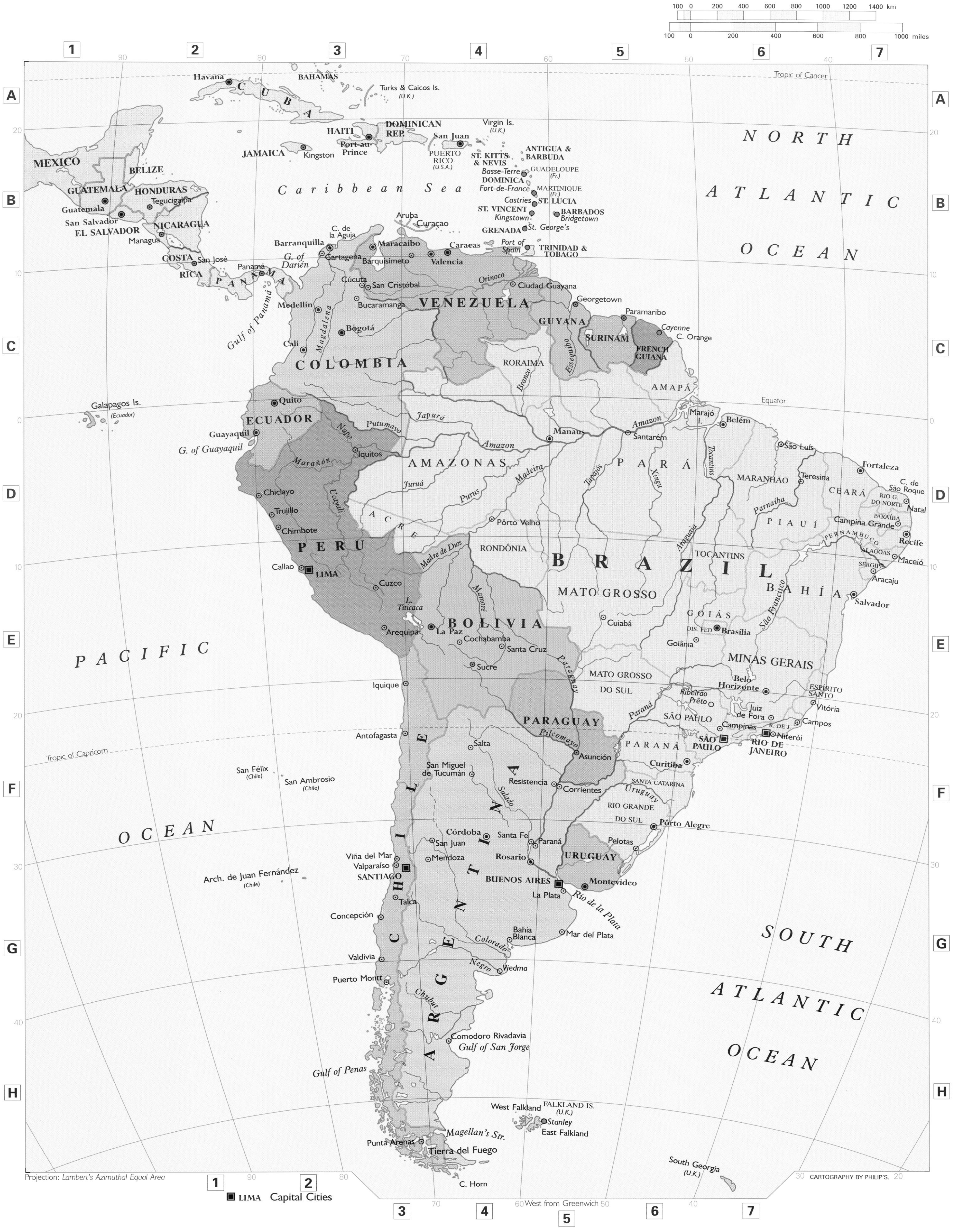

100 0 200 400 600 800 1000 1200 1400 km
100 0 200 400 600 800 1000 miles
Tropic of Cancer
Havana
CUBA
BAHAMAS
Turks & Caicos Is. (U.K.)
MEXICO
BELIZE
GUATEMALA
Guatemala
HONDURAS
Tegucigalpa
San Salvador
EL SALVADOR
NICARAGUA
Managua
COSTA RICA
San José
Panamá
PANAMA
JAMAICA
Kingston
HAITI
Port-au-Prince
DOMINICAN REP.
San Juan
PUERTO RICO (U.S.A.)
Virgin Is. (U.K.)
ST. KITTS & NEVIS
Basse-Terre
ANTIGUA & BARBUDA
GUADELOUPE (Fr.)
DOMINICA
Fort-de-France
MARTINIQUE (Fr.)
Castries
ST. LUCIA
ST. VINCENT
Kingstown
BARBADOS
Bridgetown
GRENADA
St. George's
Port of Spain
TRINIDAD & TOBAGO
Caribbean Sea
NORTH ATLANTIC OCEAN
Aruba
Curaçao
C. de la Aguja
Barranquilla
Cartagena
G. of Darién
Maracaibo
Barquisimeto
Valencia
Caracas
Cúcuta
San Cristóbal
Orinoco
Ciudad Guayana
Medellín
Bucaramanga
VENEZUELA
Georgetown
GUYANA
Paramaribo
SURINAM
Cayenne
C. Orange
FRENCH GUIANA
Gulf of Panamá
Magdalena
Bogotá
Cali
COLOMBIA
RORAIMA
Essequibo
Branco
AMAPÁ
Galapagos Is. (Ecuador)
Quito
ECUADOR
Equator
Guayaquil
G. of Guayaquil
Napo
Putumayo
Japurá
Amazon
Manaus
Marajó I.
Belém
Santarém
Iquitos
Marañón
AMAZONAS
Tapajós
PARÁ
Xingu
Tocantins
São Luís
Fortaleza
Juruá
Purus
Madeira
MARANHÃO
Teresina
CEARÁ
C. de São Roque
RIO G. DO NORTE
Natal
Chiclayo
Trujillo
Chimbote
Ucayali
ACRE
Pôrto Velho
Parnaíba
PIAUÍ
PARAÍBA
Campina Grande
Recife
PERNAMBUCO
ALAGOAS
Maceió
SERGIPE
Aracaju
PERU
Madre de Dios
RONDÔNIA
TOCANTINS
BRAZIL
Araguaia
Callao
LIMA
Cuzco
Mamoré
MATO GROSSO
BAHÍA
São Francisco
Salvador
L. Titicaca
Arequipa
La Paz
BOLIVIA
Cochabamba
Santa Cruz
Sucre
Cuiabá
GOIÁS
DIS. FED.
Brasília
Goiânia
MINAS GERAIS
PACIFIC OCEAN
Iquique
Paraguay
MATO GROSSO DO SUL
Belo Horizonte
ESPÍRITO SANTO
Vitória
Ribeirão Prêto
Juiz de Fora
Paraná
SÃO PAULO
Campinas
R. DE J.
Campos
PARAGUAY
Antofagasta
Salta
Pilcomayo
Asunción
SÃO PAULO
Niterói
RIO DE JANEIRO
PARANÁ
Tropic of Capricorn
San Félix (Chile)
San Ambrosio (Chile)
San Miguel de Tucumán
Curitiba
Resistencia
Corrientes
SANTA CATARINA
Uruguay
Salado
RIO GRANDE DO SUL
Pôrto Alegre
Córdoba
Santa Fe
Paraná
Pelotas
San Juan
Viña del Mar
Valparaíso
Mendoza
Rosario
URUGUAY
SANTIAGO
Arch. de Juan Fernández (Chile)
BUENOS AIRES
Montevideo
La Plata
Rio de la Plata
Talca
Concepción
CHILE
ARGENTINA
Bahía Blanca
Mar del Plata
SOUTH ATLANTIC OCEAN
Colorado
Valdivia
Negro
Viedma
Puerto Montt
Chubut
Comodoro Rivadavia
Gulf of San Jorge
Gulf of Penas
West Falkland
FALKLAND IS. (U.K.)
Stanley
East Falkland
Magellan's Str.
Punta Arenas
Tierra del Fuego
C. Horn
South Georgia (U.K.)
Projection: Lambert's Azimuthal Equal Area
LIMA Capital Cities
West from Greenwich
CARTOGRAPHY BY PHILIP'S.

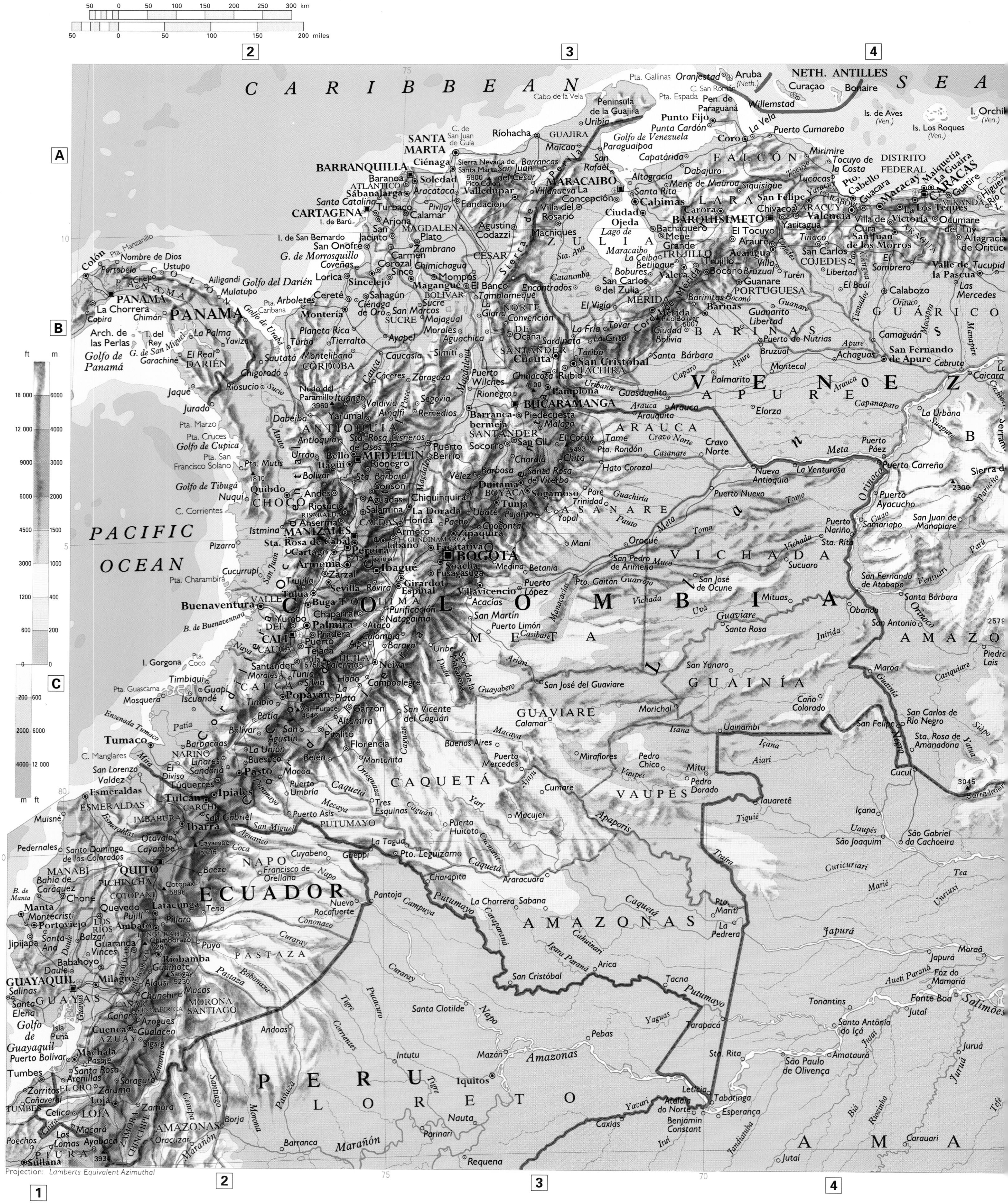

CARIBBEAN SEA
PACIFIC OCEAN
NETH. ANTILLES
Aruba (Neth.)
Curaçao
Bonaire
Willemstad
Oranjestad
VENEZUELA
COLOMBIA
ECUADOR
PERU
PANAMA
CARACAS
BOGOTÁ
QUITO
PANAMÁ
MARACAIBO
BARRANQUILLA
CARTAGENA
SANTA MARTA
MEDELLÍN
CALI
BUCARAMANGA
BARQUISIMETO
GUAYAQUIL
Valencia
Maracay
Cúcuta
Manizales
Pereira
Ibagué
Pasto
Popayán
Ipiales
Tulcán
Ibarra
Ambato
Riobamba
Cuenca
Loja
Machala
Iquitos
Leticia
Tabatinga
Buenaventura
Tumaco
Esmeraldas
San Cristóbal
Mérida
Barinas
Puerto Carreño
Puerto Ayacucho
San Fernando de Apure
Villavicencio
Florencia
Mitú
Pto. Leguízamo
Golfo de Venezuela
Lago de Maracaibo
Golfo del Darién
Golfo de Panamá
Golfo de Guayaquil
Península de la Guajira
Cabo de la Vela
Sierra Nevada de Santa Marta
ANTIOQUIA
CHOCÓ
CAUCA
HUILA
TOLIMA
NARIÑO
PUTUMAYO
CAQUETÁ
META
VICHADA
GUAINÍA
GUAVIARE
VAUPÉS
AMAZONAS
CASANARE
ARAUCA
BOYACÁ
SANTANDER
NORTE DE SANTANDER
CÓRDOBA
SUCRE
BOLÍVAR
MAGDALENA
CESAR
GUAJIRA
ZULIA
FALCÓN
LARA
TRUJILLO
BARINAS
APURE
GUÁRICO
PORTUGUESA
COJEDES
LORETO
PASTAZA
NAPO
AZUAY
LOJA
GUAYAS
MANABÍ
PICHINCHA
Orinoco
Meta
Guaviare
Caquetá
Putumayo
Napo
Amazonas
Marañón
Magdalena
Cauca
Apaporis
Japurá
Solimões
Llanos
Cordillera Oriental
Cordillera Central
Cordillera Occidental
Cordillera de Mérida
Projection: Lamberts Equivalent Azimuthal

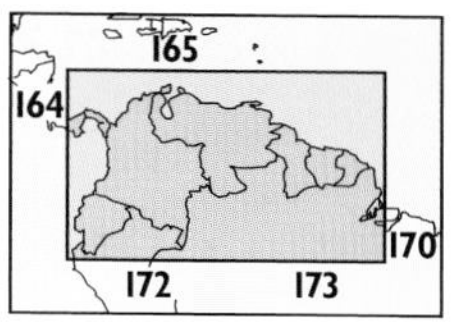

165
164
170
172
173

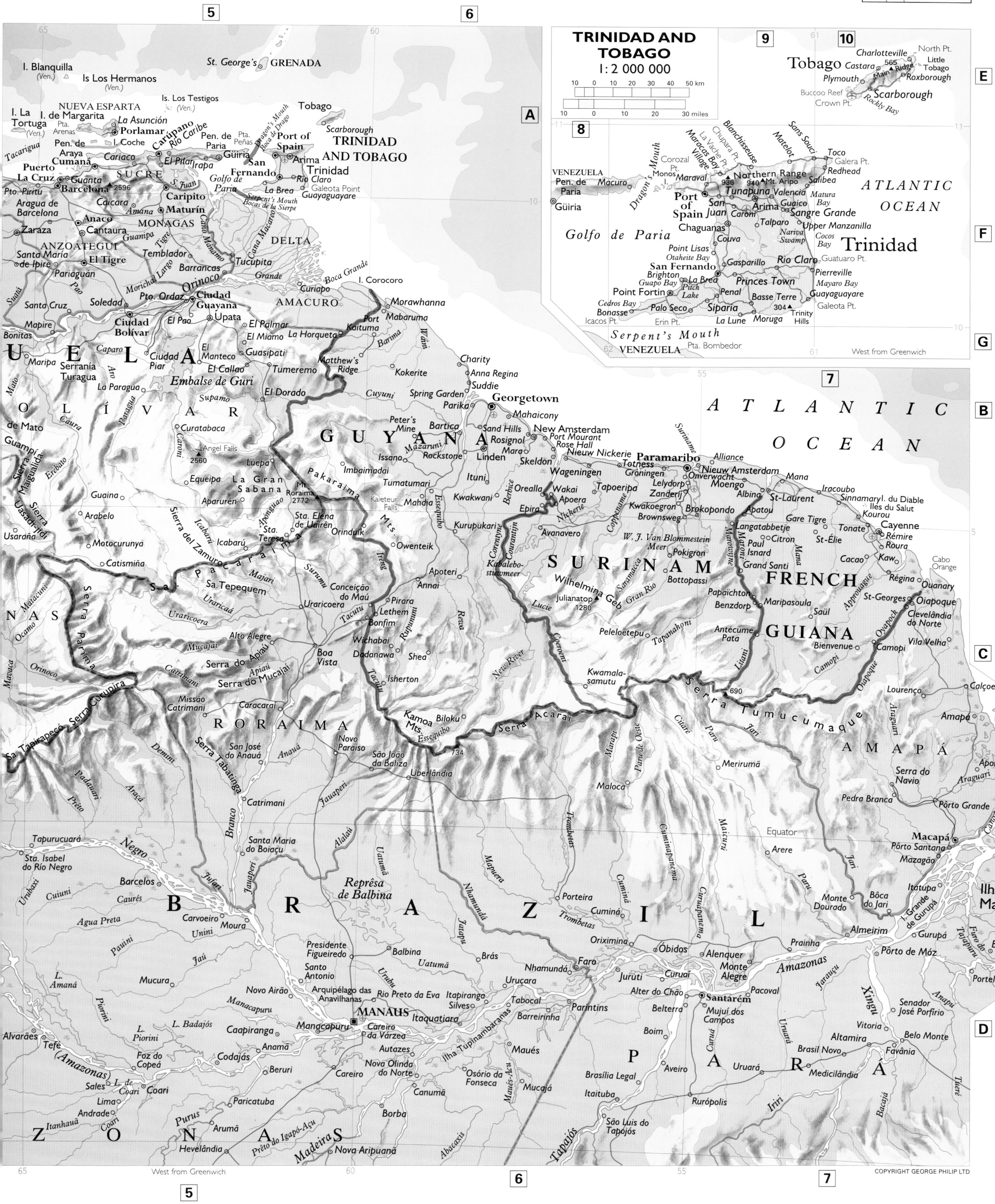

TRINIDAD AND TOBAGO
1 : 2 000 000
10 0 10 20 30 40 50 km
10 0 10 20 30 miles
Tobago
Charlotteville
North Pt.
Little Tobago
Castara
Main Ridge
565
Roxborough
Plymouth
Buccoo Reef
Crown Pt.
Scarborough
Rockly Bay
VENEZUELA
Pen. de Paria
Macuro
Güiria
Dragon's Mouth
Corozal Pt.
Monos I.
Chupara Pt.
La Vache Pt.
Maracas Bay Village
Blanchisseuse
Matelot
Sans Souci
Toco
Galera Pt.
Redhead
Maraval
Northern Range
Mt. Aripo
940
936
Salibea
Port of Spain
San Juan
Tunapuna
Valencia
Matura Bay
ATLANTIC OCEAN
Arima
Guaico
Caroni
Sangre Grande
Golfo de Paria
Chaguanas
Talparo
Upper Manzanilla
Nariva Swamp
Cocos Bay
Couva
Trinidad
Point Lisas
Otaheite Bay
San Fernando
Gasparillo
Rio Claro
Guatuaro Pt.
Brighton
Guapo Bay
La Brea
Pitch Lake
Princes Town
Pierreville
Mayaro Bay
Point Fortin
Cedros Bay
Penal
Basse Terre
Guayaguayare
Bonasse
Palo Seco
Siparia
304
Trinity Hills
Galeota Pt.
Icacos Pt.
Erin Pt.
La Lune
Moruga
Serpent's Mouth
Pta. Bombedor
VENEZUELA
West from Greenwich
I. Blanquilla (Ven.)
Is Los Hermanos (Ven.)
St. George's
GRENADA
Is. Los Testigos (Ven.)
Tobago
Scarborough
TRINIDAD AND TOBAGO
NUEVA ESPARTA
I. La Tortuga (Ven.)
I. de Margarita
La Asunción
Porlamar
Pta. Arenas
Carúpano
Rio Caribe
Pen. de Paria
Pta. Peñas
Dragon's Mouth
Boca de Drago
Port of Spain
Arima
Trinidad
Tacarigua
Pen. de Araya
I. Coche
Cariaco
Cumaná
El Pilar
Irapa
Güiria
San Fernando
Rio Claro
Galeota Point
Guayaguayare
Puerto La Cruz
Guanta
Barcelona
SUCRE
2596
S. Juan
Golfo de Paria
La Brea
Serpent's Mouth
Bocas de la Sierpe
Pto. Píritu
Aragua de Barcelona
Caicara
Caripito
Amana
Maturín
Anaco
Zaraza
Cantaura
MONAGAS
Guanipa
Caño Macareo
Caño Manamo
DELTA
ANZOATEGUI
Tigre
Temblador
Santa María de Ipire
El Tigre
Barrancas
Tucupita
Pariaguán
Morichal Largo
Orinoco
Grande
Curiapo
Boca Grande
I. Corocoro
AMACURO
Pao
Suata
Santa Cruz
Soledad
Pto. Ordaz
Ciudad Guayana
Upata
Morawhanna
Port Kaituma
Mabaruma
Mapire
Ciudad Bolívar
El Pao
El Palmar
Bonitas
Barima
Waini
El Miamo
La Horqueta
Guasipati
Charity
Caparo
Ciudad Piar
El Manteco
El Callao
Tumeremo
Matthew's Ridge
Anna Regina
Maripa
Serranía Turagua
Kokerite
Suddie
Aro
La Paragua
Embalse de Guri
Mato
El Dorado
Cuyuni
Spring Garden
Parika
Georgetown
Supamo
Mahaicony
BOLÍVAR
Caura
Paragua
Peter's Mine
Bartica
New Amsterdam
Port Mourant
Rose Hall
Sand Hills
Rosignol
Curatabaca
GUYANA
Caroni
Mazaruni
Rockstone
Linden
Mara
Skeldon
Angel Falls
2560
Issano
Nieuw Nickerie
Paramaribo
Alliance
Luepa
Imbaimadai
Totness
Groningen
Wageningen
Nieuw Amsterdam
Onverwacht
Mana
Guaipi
Sierra Maigualida
Erebato
Equeipa
La Gran Sabana
Pakaraima
Tumatumari
Ituni
Lelydorp
Zanderij
Moengo
Iracoubo
Sinnamary
I. du Diable
Iles du Salut
Kourou
Mt. Roraima
2772
Aparurén
Kaieteur Falls
Mahdia
Kwakwani
Berbice
Orealla
Wakai
Apoera
Tapoeripa
Albina
St-Laurent
Guaina
Sierra Uasadi-Jidi
Arabelo
Aponguao
Sta. Elena de Uairén
Epira
Kwakoegron
Brokopondo
Apatou
Brownsweg
Gare Tigre
Tonate
Cayenne
Icabaru
Icabarú
Sta. Teresa
Orinduik
Kurupukari
Coppename
Nickerie
Langatabbetje
Rémire
Roura
Usaraña
Motocurunya
Sierra del Zamuro
Owenteik
Avanavero
W. J. Van Blommestein Meer
Pokigron
Paul Isnard
Citron
St-Élie
Mana
Catismiña
Pacaraima
Ireng
Kabalebo-stuwmeer
Corentyne
Courantijn
SURINAM
Marowijne
Maroni
Grand Santi
Cacao
Kaw
Cabo Orange
Majari
Surumu
Apoteri
Annai
Bottopassi
FRENCH
Régina
Ouanary
Sa. Tepequem
Conceição do Maú
Wilhelmina Geb.
Saramacca
Gran Rio
Papaichton
Oiapoque
Uraricaá
Pirara
Julianatop
1280
Lucie
Maripasoula
St-Georges
Matacuni
NAS
Uraricoera
Lethem
Rupununi
Benzdorp
Saül
Approuague
Clevelândia do Norte
Bonfim
Tacutu
Rewa
Peleloetepu
Tapanahoni
Antécume Pata
GUIANA
Ocamo
Serra Parima
Alto Alegre
Mucajaí
Boa Vista
Wichabai
Dadanawa
Shea
Bienvenue
Camopi
Vila Velha
Oyapock
Serra do Apiaú
Apiaú
Coeroeni
Litani
Orinoco
Catrimani
Serra do Mucajaí
New River
Kwamala-samutu
Camopi
Isherton
Marauiá
Sa. Tapirapecó
Serra Curupira
Missão Catrimani
Caracaraí
Serra Tumucumaque
690
Lourenço
Calçoene
Kamoa Mts.
Biloku
Essequibo
Serra Acaraí
RORAIMA
Novo Paraíso
734
Citaré
Paru
Jari
Araguari
Amapá
I. de Maracá
Sucuriju
AMAPÁ
São José do Anauá
Anauá
Serra Tabatinga
Demini
São João da Baliza
Uberlândia
Mapuera
Paru de Oeste
Meriruma
Padauari
Araçá
Preto
Catrimani
Jauaperi
Maloca
Serra do Navio
Aporema
Araguari
Trombetas
Cuminapanema
Maicuru
Pedra Branca
Pôrto Grande
Canal do Norte
I. Janaucu
Tapurucuará
Negro
Branco
Alalaú
Santa Maria do Boiaçu
Equator
Macapá
Pôrto Santana
Mazagão
Caviana
Chaves
Afuá
Sta. Isabel do Rio Negro
Uatumã
Arere
Represa de Balbina
Nhamundá
Jufari
Jauaperi
Barcelos
Urubaxi
Cuiuni
Caurés
Porteira
Cuminá
Curuapanema
Paru
Jari
Monte Dourado
Bôca do Jari
Itatupa
I. Grande de Gurupá
Ilha de Marajo
Anajás
BRAZIL
Agua Preta
Carvoeiro
Moura
Unini
Cuminá
Trombetas
Almeirim
Gurupá
Presidente Figueiredo
Balbina
Pauini
Jatapu
Oriximiná
Prainha
Faro de Tajapuru
Breves
Jaú
Uatumã
Brás
Faro
Óbidos
Alenquer
Pôrto de Móz
Oeiras do Para
L. Amaná
Santo Antonio
Urubu
Nhamundá
Monte Alegre
Amazonas
Mucura
Novo Airão
Arquipélago das Anavilhanas
Rio Preto da Eva
Itapiranga
Silves
Urucara
Juruti
Curuai
Portel
Alter do Chão
Pacoval
Anapu
Manacapuru
Tabocal
Parintins
Santarém
Jarauçu
Xingu
Senador José Porfírio
Piorini
MANAUS
Itaquatiara
Barreirinha
Belterra
Mujuí dos Campos
L. Piorini
L. Badajós
Mangcapuru
Careiro da Várzea
Caapiranga
Vitoria
Alvarães
Tefé
Anamã
Autazes
Ilha Tupinambaranas
Maués
Boim
Uruará
Altamira
Belo Monte
Brasil Novo
Favânia
Foz do Copeá
Codajás
Beruri
(Amazonas)
Nova Olinda do Norte
Osório da Fonseca
Maués-Açu
Mucajá
P
Aveiro
Uruará
Medicilândia
PARÁ
Sales
L. de Coari
Coari
Careiro
Canumã
Brasília Legal
Curuá
Tucuruí
Lima
Paricatuba
Itaituba
Rurópolis
Iriri
Bacajá
Andrade
Itanhauã
Coari
Purus
Borba
São Luis do Tapajós
AMAZONAS
Arumã
Preto do Igapó-Açu
Madeira
Abacaxis
Hevelândia
Nova Aripuanã
Tapajós
West from Greenwich
5
6
7
8
9
10
A
B
C
D
E
F
G

COPYRIGHT GEORGE PHILIP LTD

km
miles
ATLANTIC OCEAN
MARANHÃO
CEARÁ
PIAUÍ
PARÁ
AMAPÁ
TOCANTINS
RIO GRANDE DO NORTE
PARAÍBA
PERNAMBUCO
ALAGOAS
SERGIPE
BRAZIL
Ilha de Marajó
BELÉM
SÃO LUÍS
FORTALEZA
TERESINA
NATAL
João Pessoa
RECIFE
MACEIÓ
Aracaju
Macapá
Chapada das Mangabeiras
Serra do Gurupi
Sa. do Tiracambu
Serra dos Carajás
Tocantins
Xingu
Represa de Sobradinho
Represa de Tucuruí

ATLANTIC OCEAN
BAHIA
GOIÁS
MINAS GERAIS
SÃO PAULO
PARANÁ
ESPÍRITO SANTO
RIO DE JANEIRO
DISTRITO FEDERAL
BRASÍLIA
SALVADOR (Bahia)
BELO HORIZONTE
RIO DE JANEIRO
SÃO PAULO
CURITIBA
GOIÂNIA
VITÓRIA
CAMPINAS
SANTOS
NITERÓI
Tropic of Capricorn
West from Greenwich
Projection : Lambert's Equivalent Azimuthal
COPYRIGHT GEORGE PHILIP LTD

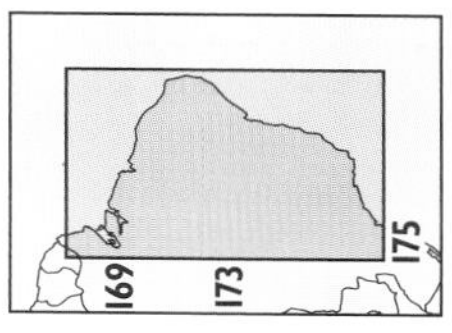

169
173
175

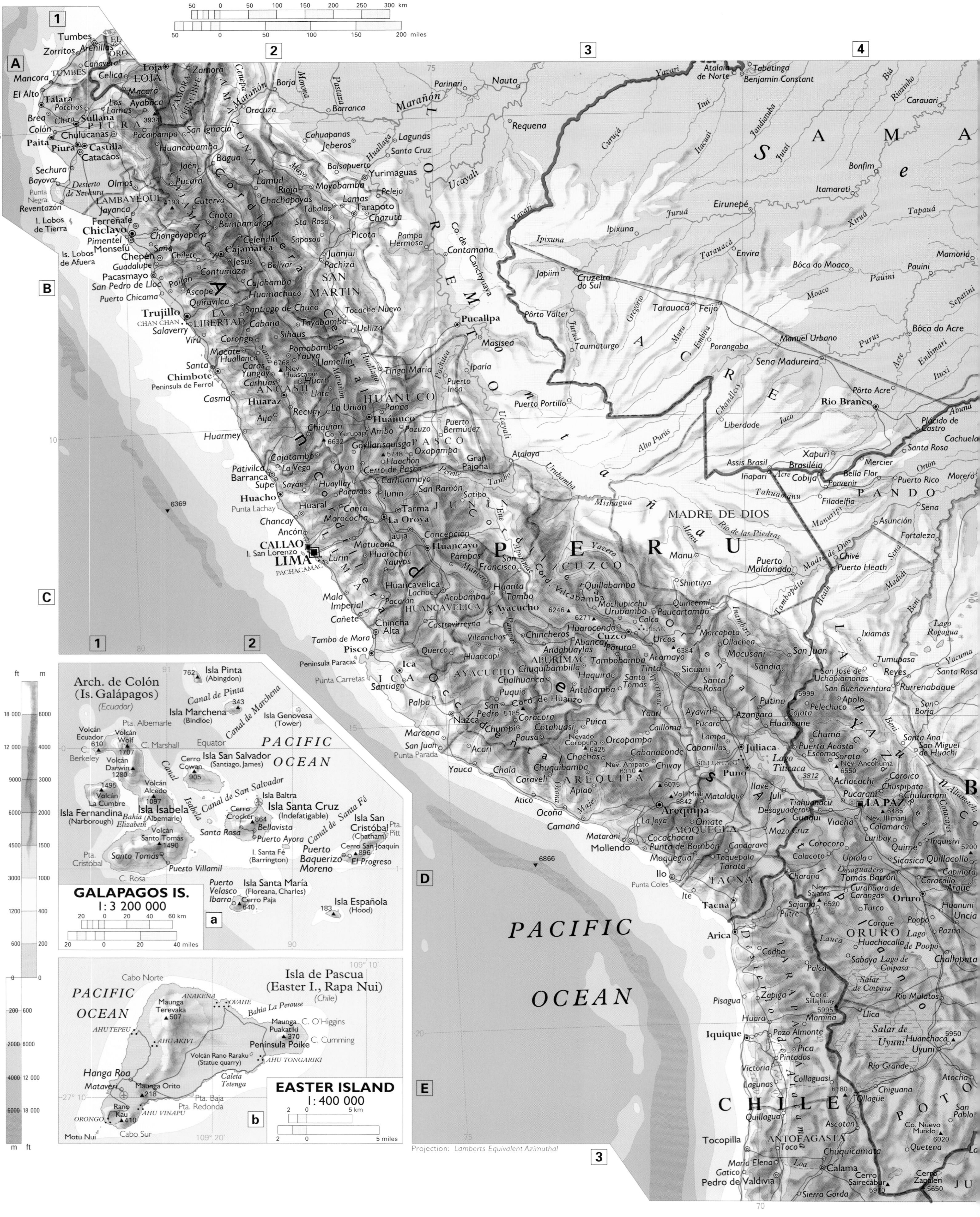
PACIFIC OCEAN
PERU
CHILE
ACRE
PANDO
Lima
Callao
Trujillo
Chiclayo
Piura
Arequipa
Cuzco
Tacna
Arica
Iquique
Tocopilla
Antofagasta
La Paz
Oruro
Rio Branco
Pucallpa
Huancayo
Ayacucho
Lago Titicaca
Salar de Uyuni
Arch. de Colón (Is. Galápagos) (Ecuador)
PACIFIC OCEAN
Isla Isabela (Albemarle)
Isla Santa Cruz (Indefatigable)
Isla Fernandina (Narborough)
Isla San Cristóbal (Chatham)
GALAPAGOS IS.
1: 3 200 000
Isla de Pascua (Easter I., Rapa Nui) (Chile)
Hanga Roa
EASTER ISLAND
1: 400 000
Projection: Lamberts Equivalent Azimuthal

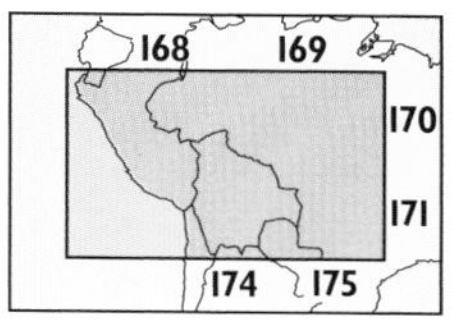
168
169
170
171
174
175

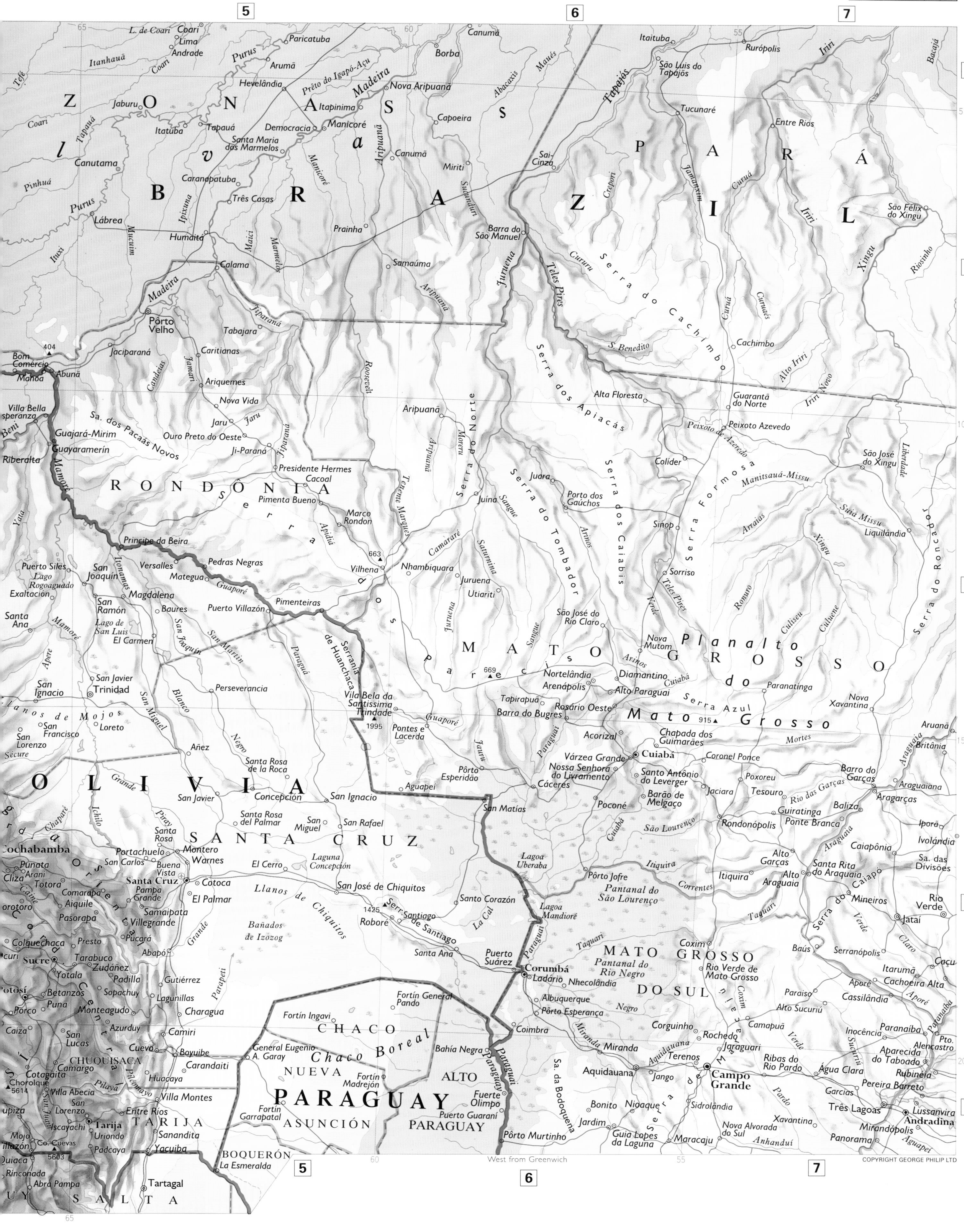
5
6
7
A
B
C
D
E
AMAZONAS
BRAZIL
PARÁ
RONDÔNIA
MATO GROSSO
MATO GROSSO DO SUL
BOLIVIA
SANTA CRUZ
CHUQUISACA
TARIJA
CHACO
Chaco Boreal
NUEVA ASUNCIÓN
PARAGUAY
ALTO PARAGUAY
BOQUERÓN
SALTA
Planalto do Mato Grosso
L. de Coari
Coari
Lima
Andrade
Paricatuba
Canumã
Itaituba
Rurópolis
Iriri
Bacajá
Itanhauã
Arumã
Borba
São Luís do Tapajós
Tapajós
Tefé
Purus
Hevelândia
Prêto do Igapó-Açu
Madeira
Nova Aripuanã
Maués
Abacaxis
Jaburu
Itapinima
Tucunaré
Coari
Tapauá
Itatuba
Democracia
Manicoré
Capoeira
Entre Rios
Santa Maria dos Marmelos
Canumã
Canutama
Aripuanã
Sai-Cinza
Pinhuá
Carana-patuba
Miriti
Crepori
Jamanxim
Curuá
Três Casas
Sucunduri
São Félix do Xingu
Lábrea
Ipixuna
Prainha
Barra do São Manuel
Humaitá
Mucuim
Maici
Marmelos
Iuxi
Calama
Samaúma
Juruena
Teles Pires
Cururu
Serra do Cachimbo
Xingu
Riosinho
Madeira
Jiparaná
Pôrto Velho
Tabajara
Cachimbo
S. Benedito
404
Bom Comércio
Jaciparaná
Caritianas
Alto Iriri
Manoa
Abunã
Candeias
Jamari
Ariquemes
Roosevelt
Serra dos Apiacás
Alta Floresta
Guarantã do Norte
Iriri Novo
Villa Bella
Esperanza
Nova Vida
Aripuanã
Serra do Norte
Jaru
Peixoto de Azevedo
Peixoto Azevedo
Beni
Guajará-Mirim
Sa. dos Pacaás Novos
Ouro Preto do Oeste
Guayaramerín
Ji-Paraná
Colíder
São José do Xingu
Riberalta
Mamoré
Presidente Hermes
Cacoal
Serra dos Caiabis
Serra Formosa
Manitsauá-Missu
Liberdade
Juara
Pimenta Bueno
Serra do Tombador
Porto dos Gaúchos
Marco Rondon
Juína
Sinop
Suiá Missu
Yata
Liquilândia
Apiacás
Serra do Roncador
Príncipe da Beira
Camararé
Saturnina
Arinos
Arraias
663
Puerto Siles
San Joaquín
Pedras Negras
Vilhena
Nhambiquara
Sorriso
Lago Rogoaguado
Itonamas
Versalles
Mategua
Juruena
Exaltación
Magdalena
Guaporé
Utiariti
Teles Pires
Ronuro
Santa Ana
San Ramón
Baures
Puerto Villazón
Pimenteiras
São José do Rio Claro
Culiseu
Culuene
Lago de San Luis
El Carmen
San Joaquín
San Martín
Serranía de Huanchaca
Nova Mutum
Serra dos Parecis
Apere
669
Nortelândia
Diamantino
Cuiabá
Arenápolis
Alto Paraguai
Paranatinga
San Javier
Trinidad
Perseverancia
Vila Bela da Santíssima Trindade
Tapirapuã
Serra Azul
San Ignacio
Llanos de Mojos
Barra do Bugres
Rosário Oeste
Xavantina
1995
Pontes e Lacerda
915
San Francisco
Loreto
Acorizal
Chapada dos Guimarães
Aruanã
San Lorenzo
Mortes
Britânia
Sécure
Añez
Várzea Grande
Cuiabá
Coronel Ponce
Santa Rosa de la Roca
Pôrto Esperidião
Nossa Senhora do Livramento
Santo Antônio do Leverger
Barro do Garças
Araguaia
Aguapeí
Cáceres
Poxoreu
Araguaiana
San Javier
Concepción
San Ignacio
Jaciara
Tesouro
Rio das Garças
Aragarças
Barão de Melgaço
San Matías
Poconé
Santa Rosa del Palmar
San Miguel
San Rafael
Guiratinga
Baliza
Ponte Branca
Iporá
Chaparé
Ichilo
Piray
Santa Rosa
São Lourenço
Rondonópolis
Ivolândia
Cochabamba
Portachuelo
Montero
Warnes
Laguna Concepción
Lagoa Uberaba
Alto Garças
Caiapônia
Sa. das Divisões
Punata
Arani
San Carlos
Buena Vista
El Cerro
Itiquira
Santa Rita do Araguaia
Cliza
Totora
Santa Cruz
Cotoca
Pôrto Jofre
Itiquira
Alto Araguaia
Comarapa
Pampa Grande
San José de Chiquitos
Pantanal do São Lourenço
Correntes
Aiquile
El Palmar
Llanos de Chiquitos
Santo Corazón
Mineiros
Rio Verde
Samaipata
Vallegrande
1425
Serr. Santiago
Roboré
Lagoa Mandioré
Taquari
Serra do Caiapó
Jataí
Pasorapa
Pucará
Bañados de Izozog
Sa. de Santiago
La Cal
Colquechaca
Presto
Abapó
Santa Ana
Coxim
Baús
Serranópolis
Sucre
Tarabuco
Puerto Suárez
Corumbá
Ladário
Rio Verde de Mato Grosso
Caçu
Yotala
Zudañez
Padilla
Parapeti
Pantanal do Rio Negro
Nhecolândia
Itarumã
Potosí
Betanzos
Sopachuy
Gutiérrez
Fortín General Pando
Albuquerque
Aporé
Cachoeira Alta
Puna
Lagunillas
Pôrto Esperança
Paraíso
Cassilândia
Porco
Monteagudo
Charagua
Fortín Ingavi
Negro
Alto Sucuriú
Caiza
Azurduy
Coimbra
Corguinho
Camapuã
San Lucas
Camiri
Bahía Negra
Rochedo
Verde
Paranaíba
Inocência
Pto. Alencastro
Cuevo
General Eugenio A. Garay
Miranda
Jaraguari
Aparecida do Taboado
Boyuibe
Paraguay
Sa. da Bodoquena
Terenos
Ribas do Rio Pardo
Camargo
Carandaiti
Aquidauana
Cotagaita
Pilaya
Pilcomayo
Huacaya
Fortín Madrejón
Aquidauana
Jango
Campo Grande
Água Clara
Rubinéia
Chorolque
5614
Villa Abecia
Villa Montes
Fuerte Olimpo
Sucuriú
Pereira Barreto
Tupiza
San Lorenzo
Entre Ríos
Fortín Garrapatal
Puerto Guaraní
Pardo
Garcias
Três Lagoas
Lussanvira
Iscayachi
Tarija
Sanandita
Bonito
Nioaque
Sidrolândia
Xavantina
Andradina
Mojo
Villazón
Co. Cuevas
Uriondo
Padcaya
Yacuiba
Pôrto Murtinho
Jardim
Guia Lopes da Laguna
Nova Alvorada do Sul
Mirandópolis
Panorama
Aguapeí
Quiaca
5603
La Esmeralda
Maracaju
Anhanduí
Rinconada
Abra Pampa
Tartagal
Serra de Maracaju
65
60
55
West from Greenwich
COPYRIGHT GEORGE PHILIP LTD

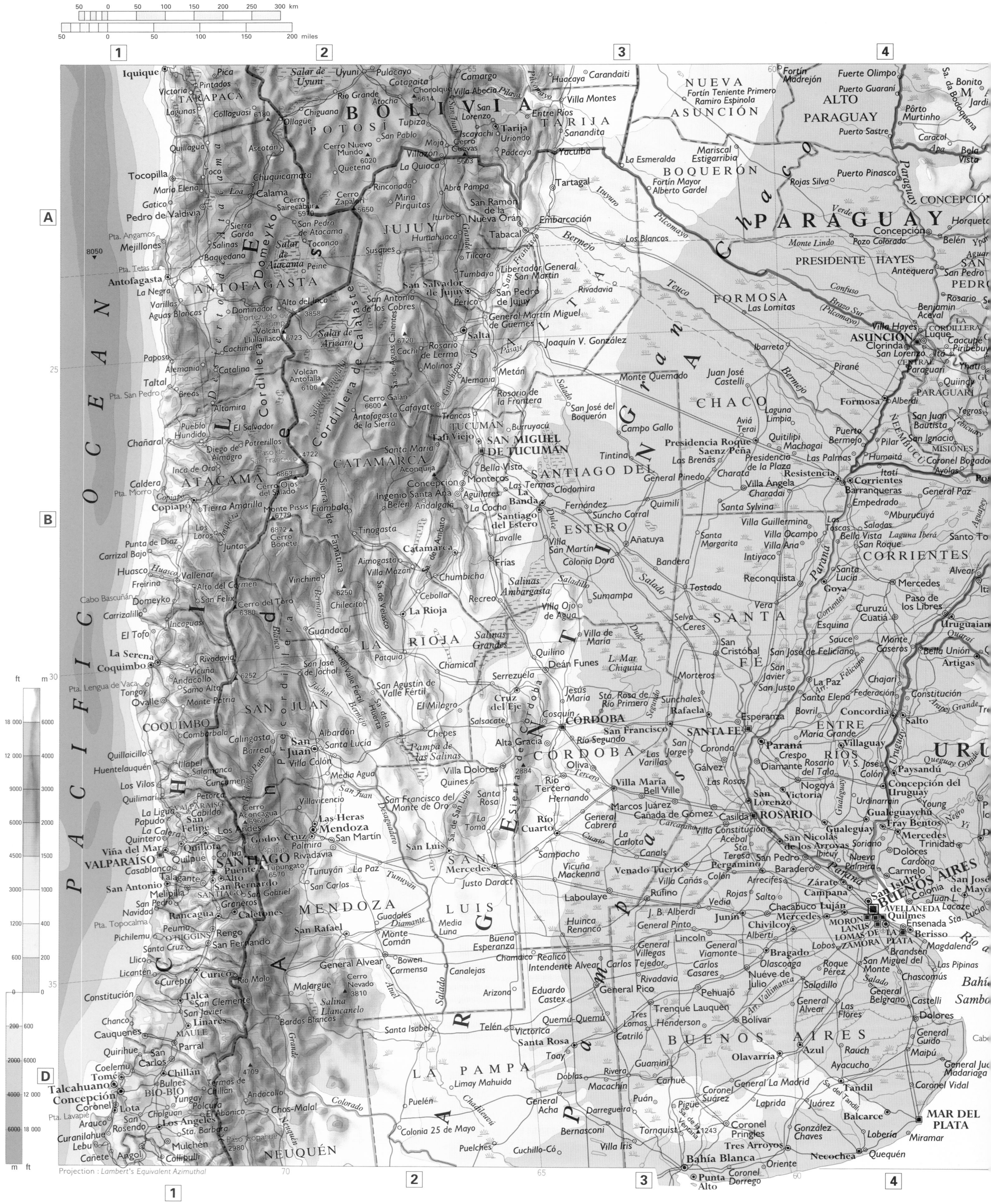

50 0 50 100 150 200 250 300 km
50 0 50 100 150 200 miles
PACIFIC OCEAN
BOLIVIA
PARAGUAY
ARGENTINA
CHILE
URU
POTOSÍ
TARIJA
NUEVA ASUNCIÓN
ALTO PARAGUAY
BOQUERÓN
PRESIDENTE HAYES
TARAPACÁ
ANTOFAGASTA
ATACAMA
COQUIMBO
JUJUY
SALTA
CATAMARCA
TUCUMÁN
FORMOSA
CHACO
SANTIAGO DEL ESTERO
CORRIENTES
LA RIOJA
SAN JUAN
CÓRDOBA
SANTA FÉ
ENTRE RÍOS
MENDOZA
SAN LUIS
LA PAMPA
BUENOS AIRES
NEUQUÉN
Gran Chaco
Pampas
Desierto de Atacama
Cordillera Domeyko
Salar de Uyuni
Salar de Atacama
Iquique
Tocopilla
Antofagasta
Calama
Copiapó
La Serena
Coquimbo
VALPARAÍSO
SANTIAGO
Talca
Chillán
Concepción
Talcahuano
Tarija
Salta
SAN MIGUEL DE TUCUMÁN
Santiago del Estero
Catamarca
La Rioja
San Juan
Mendoza
San Luis
CÓRDOBA
SANTA FE
ROSARIO
Paraná
Resistencia
Corrientes
Formosa
ASUNCIÓN
Concepción
BUENOS AIRES
La Plata
MAR DEL PLATA
Bahía Blanca
Santa Rosa
Cerro Aconcagua 6960
Projection : Lambert's Equivalent Azimuthal

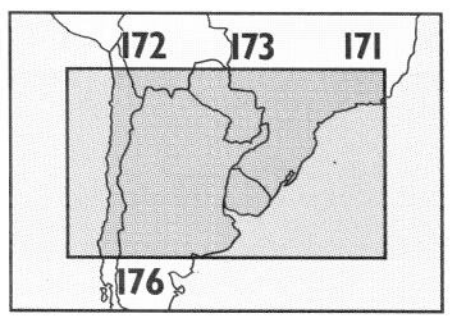
172
173
171
176

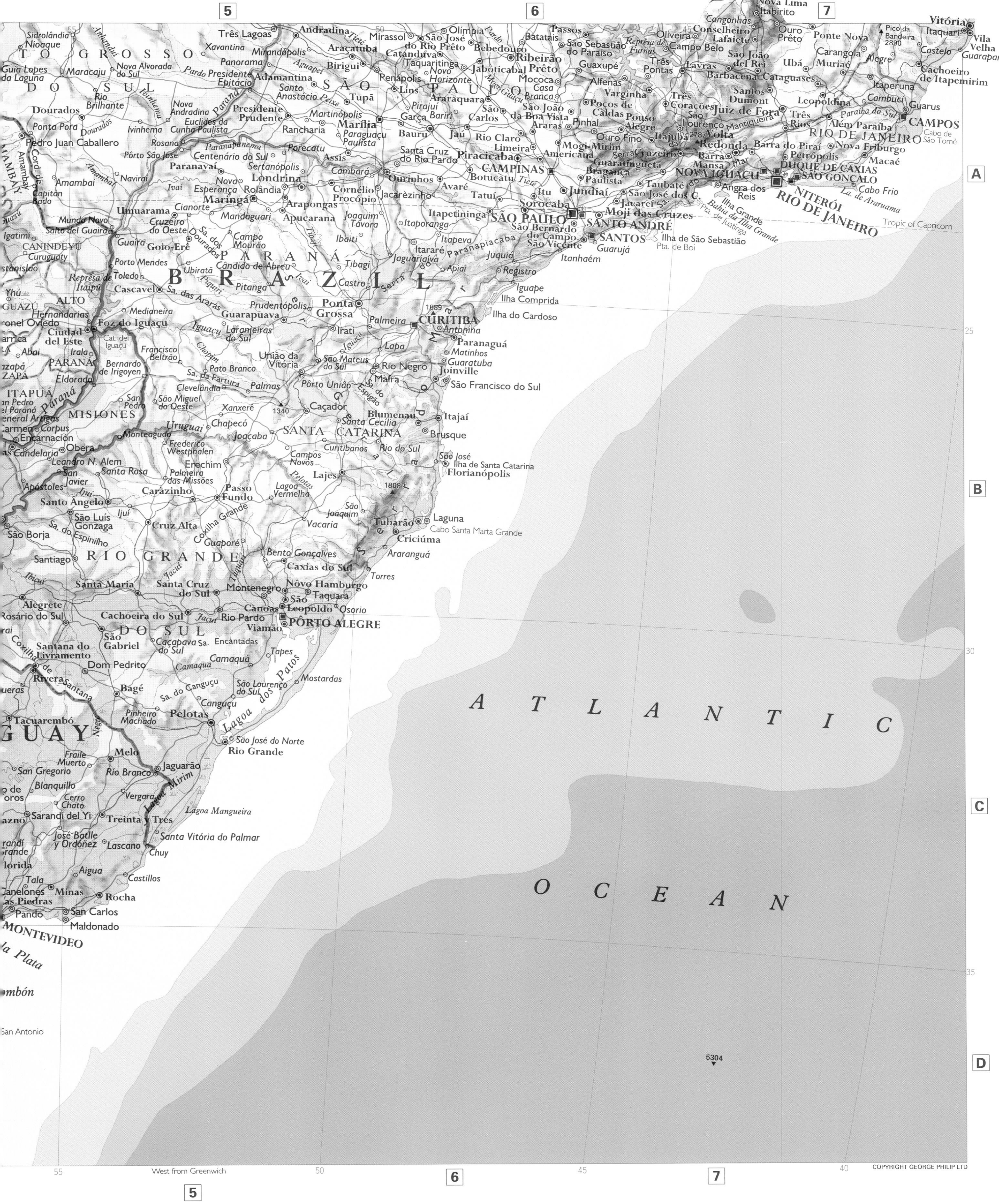
5
6
7
A
B
C
D
BELO HORIZONTE
Nova Lima
Itabirito
Vitória
Vila Velha
Guarapari
Cachoeiro de Itapemirim
Itaperuna
CAMPOS
Cabo de São Tomé
RIO DE JANEIRO
Nova Friburgo
Macaé
Cabo Frio
Petrópolis
DUQUE DE CAXIAS
SÃO GONÇALO
NITERÓI
RIO DE JANEIRO
NOVA IGUAÇU
Juiz de Fora
Barbacena
Volta Redonda
Barra Mansa
Angra dos Reis
Taubaté
Guaratinguetá
Lorena
São José dos C.
Jacareí
Moji das Cruzes
SÃO PAULO
SANTO ANDRÉ
SANTOS
Guarujá
São Bernardo do Campo
São Vicente
Itanhaém
Ilha de São Sebastião
Pta. de Boi
Tropic of Capricorn
Jundiaí
CAMPINAS
Piracicaba
Limeira
Americana
Sorocaba
Itu
Tatuí
Botucatu
Itapetininga
Ribeirão Prêto
Franca
São Carlos
Araraquara
Bauru
Jaú
Rio Claro
Marília
Presidente Prudente
Araçatuba
São José do Rio Prêto
Andradina
Três Lagoas
S Ã O P A U L O
M A T O G R O S S O D O S U L
Dourados
Ponta Porã
Pedro Juan Caballero
Maringá
Londrina
Apucarana
Arapongas
Umuarama
Cascavel
Foz do Iguaçu
Ciudad del Este
Guarapuava
Ponta Grossa
CURITIBA
Paranaguá
Joinville
São Francisco do Sul
P A R A N Á
B R A Z I L
Iguape
Ilha Comprida
Ilha do Cardoso
Registro
Blumenau
Itajaí
Brusque
Florianópolis
Ilha de Santa Catarina
São José
S A N T A C A T A R I N A
Lajes
Chapecó
Joaçaba
Caçador
Tubarão
Laguna
Cabo Santa Marta Grande
Criciúma
Araranguá
Torres
Caxias do Sul
Bento Gonçalves
Passo Fundo
Erechim
Santo Ângelo
Cruz Alta
Santa Maria
Santa Cruz do Sul
Nôvo Hamburgo
São Leopoldo
Canoas
PÔRTO ALEGRE
Viamão
R I O G R A N D E D O S U L
Uruguaiana
Alegrete
Santana do Livramento
Rivera
Bagé
Pelotas
Rio Grande
São José do Norte
Lagoa dos Patos
Lagoa Mirim
Lagoa Mangueira
Jaguarão
Melo
Treinta y Tres
Chuy
Santa Vitória do Palmar
Rocha
Maldonado
San Carlos
MONTEVIDEO
Posadas
Encarnación
MISIONES
A T L A N T I C
O C E A N
5304
West from Greenwich
55
50
45
40
25
30
35
COPYRIGHT GEORGE PHILIP LTD

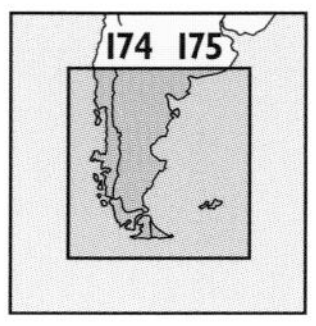
174
175

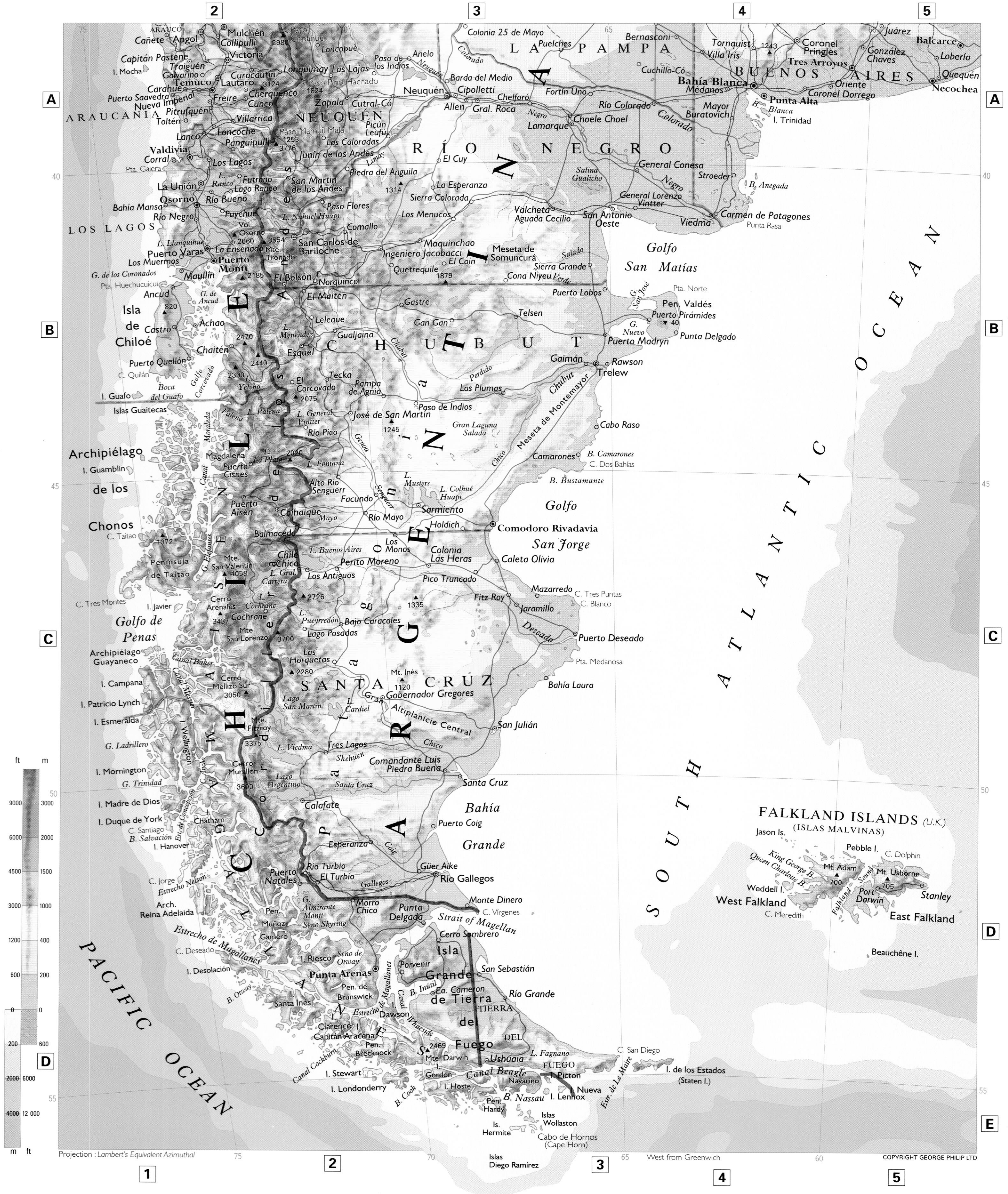
50 0 50 100 150 200 250 300 km
50 0 50 100 150 200 miles
1
2
3
4
5
A
B
C
D
E
LA PAMPA
BUENOS AIRES
NEUQUÉN
RÍO NEGRO
CHUBUT
SANTA CRUZ
TIERRA DEL FUEGO
ARAUCANÍA
LOS LAGOS
AISÉN
MAGALLANES
ARGENTINA
CHILE
Patagonia
Cordillera de los Andes
Golfo San Matías
Golfo San Jorge
Bahía Grande
SOUTH ATLANTIC OCEAN
PACIFIC OCEAN
FALKLAND ISLANDS (U.K.)
(ISLAS MALVINAS)
West Falkland
East Falkland
Stanley
Jason Is.
Pebble I.
C. Dolphin
Mt. Adam 700
Mt. Usborne 705
King George B.
Queen Charlotte B.
Weddell I.
Port Darwin
Falkland Sound
C. Meredith
Beauchêne I.
Colonia 25 de Mayo
Puelches
Bernasconi
Tornquist
Villa Iris
Coronel Pringles
Tres Arroyos
González Chaves
Juárez
Balcarce
Lobería
Quequén
Necochea
Cuchillo-Có
Bahía Blanca
Médanos
Punta Alta
Oriente
Coronel Dorrego
Mayor Buratovich
B. Blanca
I. Trinidad
Río Colorado
Fortín Uno
Choele Choel
Lamarque
Chelforó
Neuquén
Cipolletti
Allen
Gral. Roca
Barda del Medio
Añelo
Paso de los Indios
Cutral-Có
Zapala
Picún Leufú
Las Coloradas
Junín de los Andes
San Martín de los Andes
Piedra del Anguila
El Cuy
La Esperanza
Sierra Colorada
Los Menucos
Valcheta
Aguada Cecilio
San Antonio Oeste
General Conesa
General Lorenzo Vintter
Stroeder
Viedma
Carmen de Patagones
Punta Rasa
B. Anegada
Salina Gualicho
Maquinchao
Ingeniero Jacobacci
El Caín
Meseta de Somuncurá
Sierra Grande
Cona Niyeu
Quetrequile
Comallo
Paso Flores
San Carlos de Bariloche
El Bolsón
Norquinco
El Maitén
Gastre
Gan Gan
Telsen
Puerto Lobos
Pta. Norte
Pen. Valdés
Puerto Pirámides
Punta Delgado
G. San José
G. Nuevo
Puerto Madryn
Rawson
Trelew
Gaimán
Leleque
Gualjaina
Esquel
Tecka
Pampa de Agnía
Las Plumas
Paso de Indios
José de San Martín
Gran Laguna Salada
Meseta de Montemayor
Cabo Raso
Camarones
B. Camarones
C. Dos Bahías
B. Bustamante
Río Pico
Alto Río Senguerr
Facundo
L. Musters
L. Colhué Huapi
Sarmiento
Río Mayo
Holdich
Comodoro Rivadavia
Caleta Olivia
Colonia Las Heras
Los Monos
Perito Moreno
Pico Truncado
Fitz Roy
Jaramillo
Mazarredo
C. Tres Puntas
C. Blanco
Puerto Deseado
Pta. Medanosa
Bahía Laura
Bajo Caracoles
Lago Posadas
Las Horquetas
Mt. Inés 1120
Gobernador Gregores
Gran Altiplanicie Central
San Julián
Tres Lagos
Comandante Luis Piedra Buena
Santa Cruz
Calafate
Puerto Coig
Esperanza
Güer Aike
Río Gallegos
Monte Dinero
C. Vírgenes
Punta Delgada
Strait of Magellan
Cerro Sombrero
Isla Grande de Tierra del Fuego
San Sebastián
Río Grande
Porvenir
Ushuaia
L. Fagnano
C. San Diego
Estr. de Le Maire
I. de los Estados
(Staten I.)
Canal Beagle
I. Navarino
I. Picton
I. Nueva
I. Lennox
B. Nassau
I. Hoste
Pen. Hardy
Is. Hermite
Is. Wollaston
Cabo de Hornos
(Cape Horn)
Islas Diego Ramírez
Mte. Darwin 2469
Gordon
I. Londonderry
I. Stewart
B. Cook
Canal Cockburn
Clarence I.
Capitán Aracena I.
Pen. Brecknock
Dawson I.
Santa Inés I.
Pen. de Brunswick
Punta Arenas
I. Riesco
Seno de Otway
Morro Chico
Puerto Natales
Río Turbio
El Turbio
Estrecho de Magallanes
C. Deseado
I. Desolación
Arch. Reina Adelaida
Estrecho Nelson
C. Jorge
I. Hanover
Chatham
I. Duque de York
I. Madre de Dios
G. Trinidad
I. Mornington
G. Ladrillero
I. Wellington
I. Esmeralda
I. Patricio Lynch
I. Campana
Archipiélago Guayaneco
Golfo de Penas
C. Tres Montes
I. Javier
Península de Taitao
Chonos
C. Taitao
Archipiélago de los Chonos
I. Guamblin
Islas Guaitecas
I. Guafo
Boca del Guafo
Golfo Corcovado
C. Quilán
Puerto Quellón
Chaitén
Isla de Chiloé
Castro
Achao
Ancud
Maullín
Puerto Montt
Puerto Varas
Los Muermos
Osorno
Río Negro
Bahía Mansa
La Unión
Valdivia
Corral
Pta. Galera
Lanco
Panguipulli
Loncoche
Villarrica
Pitrufquén
Toltén
Temuco
Lautaro
Nueva Imperial
Carahue
Puerto Saavedra
I. Mocha
Capitán Pastene
Traiguén
Galvarino
Victoria
Collipulli
Mulchén
Angol
Cañete
Curacautín
Lonquimay
Las Lajas
Loncopué
Puyehue
Vol. Osorno 2660
Mte. Tronador 3554
Puerto Aisén
Coihaique
Balmaceda
Chile Chico
L. Buenos Aires
L. Gral. Carrera
Los Antiguos
Mte. San Valentín 4058
Cochrane
Cerro Arenales 3437
Mte. San Lorenzo 3700
Cerro Mellizo Sur 3050
Mte. Fitzroy 3375
Cerro Murallón 3600
Lago Argentino
L. Viedma
Lago San Martín
L. Cardiel
Puerto Cisnes
Magdalena
L. Palena
Yelcho
L. General Vintter
El Corcovado
2075
Projection : Lambert's Equivalent Azimuthal
West from Greenwich
COPYRIGHT GEORGE PHILIP LTD
ft m
9000 3000
6000 2000
4500 1500
3000 1000
1200 400
600 200
0 0
200 600
2000 6000
4000 12 000
m ft

INDEX TO
WORLD MAPS

How to use the index

The index contains the names of all the principal places and features shown on the World Maps. Each name is followed by an additional entry in italics giving the country or region within which it is located. The alphabetical order of names composed of two or more words is governed primarily by the first word and then by the second. This is an example of the rule:

Mīr Kūh, *Iran*	....	**97 E8**	26 22N 58 55 E
Mīr Shahdād, *Iran*	....	**97 E8**	26 15N 58 29 E
Mira, *Italy*	....	**45 C9**	45 26N 12 8 E
Mira por vos Cay, *Bahamas*	..	**165 B5**	22 9N 74 30W
Miraj, *India*	....	**94 F2**	16 50N 74 45 E

Physical features composed of a proper name (Erie) and a description (Lake) are positioned alphabetically by the proper name. The description is positioned after the proper name and is usually abbreviated:

Erie, L., *N. Amer.*	....	**150 D4**	42 15N 81 0W

Where a description forms part of a settlement or administrative name however, it is always written in full and put in its true alphabetic position:

Mount Olive, *U.S.A.*	....	**156 E7**	39 4N 89 44W

Names beginning with M' and Mc are indexed as if they were spelled Mac. Names beginning St. are alphabetised under Saint, but Sankt, Sint, Sant', Santa and San are all spelt in full and are alphabetised accordingly. If the same place name occurs two or more times in the index and all are in the same country, each is followed by the name of the administrative subdivision in which it is located.

The number in bold type which follows each name in the index refers to the number of the map page where that feature or place will be found. This is usually the largest scale at which the place or feature appears.

The letter and figure which are in bold type immediately after the page number give the grid square on the map page, within which the feature is situated. The letter represents the latitude and the figure the longitude. A lower case letter immediately after the page number refers to an inset map on that page.

In some cases the feature itself may fall within the specified square, while the name is outside. This is usually the case only with features which are larger than a grid square.

The geographical co-ordinates which follow the letter-figure references give the latitude and longitude of each place. The first co-ordinate indicates latitude – the distance north of the Equator. The second co-ordinate indicates longitude – the distance east or west of the Greenwich Meridian. Both latitude and longitude are measured in degrees and minutes (there are 60 minutes in a degree).

The latitude is followed by N(orth) or S(outh) and the longitude by E(ast) or W(est).

Rivers are indexed to their mouths or confluences, and carry the symbol → after their names. A solid square ■ follows the name of a country, while an open square □ refers to a first order administrative area.

How to pronounce place names

English-speaking people usually have no difficulty in reading and pronouncing correctly English place names. However, foreign place name pronunciations may present many problems. Such problems can be minimised by following some simple rules. However, these rules cannot be applied to all situations, and there will be many exceptions.

1. In general, stress each syllable equally, unless your experience suggests otherwise.
2. Pronounce the letter 'a' as a broad 'a' as in 'arm'.
3. Pronounce the letter 'e' as a short 'e' as in 'elm'.
4. Pronounce the letter 'i' as a cross between a short 'i' and long 'e', as the two 'i's in 'California'.
5. Pronounce the letter 'o' as an intermediate 'o' as in 'soft'.
6. Pronounce the letter 'u' as an intermediate 'u' as in 'sure'.
7. Pronounce consonants hard, except in the Romance-language areas where 'g's are likely to be pronounced softly like 'j' in 'jam'; 'j' itself may be pronounced as 'y'; and 'x's may be pronounced as 'h'.
8. For names in mainland China, pronounce 'q' like the 'ch' in 'chin', 'x' like the 'sh' in 'she', 'zh' like the 'j' in 'jam', and 'z' as if it were spelled 'dz'. In general pronounce 'a' as in 'father', 'e' as in 'but', 'i' as in 'keep', 'o' as in 'or', and 'u' as in 'rule'.

Moreover, English has no diacritical marks (accent and pronunciation signs), although some languages do. The following is a brief and general guide to the pronunciation of those most frequently used in the principal Western European languages.

		Pronunciation as in
French	é	day and shows that the e is to be pronounced; e.g. Orléans.
	è	mare
	î	used over any vowel and does not affect pronunciation; shows contraction of the name, usually omission of 's' following a vowel.
	ç	's' before 'a', 'o' and 'u'.
	ë, ï, ü	over 'e', 'i' and 'u' when they are used with another vowel and shows that each is to be pronounced.
German	ä	fate
	ö	fur
	ü	no English equivalent; like French 'tu'
Italian	à, é	over vowels and indicates stress.
Portuguese	ã, õ	vowels pronounced nasally.
	ç	boss
	á	shows stress
	ô	shows that a vowel has an 'i' or 'u' sound combined with it.
Spanish	ñ	canyon
	ü	pronounced as w and separately from adjoining vowels.
	á	usually indicates that this is a stressed vowel.

Abbreviations

A.C.T. – Australian Capital Territory
A.R. – Autonomous Region
Afghan. – Afghanistan
Afr. – Africa
Ala. – Alabama
Alta. – Alberta
Amer. – America(n)
Arch. – Archipelago
Ariz. – Arizona
Ark. – Arkansas
Atl. Oc. – Atlantic Ocean
B. – Baie, Bahía, Bay, Bucht, Bugt
B.C. – British Columbia
Bangla. – Bangladesh
Barr. – Barrage
Bos.-H. – Bosnia-Herzegovina
C. – Cabo, Cap, Cape, Coast
C.A.R. – Central African Republic
C. Prov. – Cape Province
Calif. – California
Cat. – Catarata
Cent. – Central
Chan. – Channel
Colo. – Colorado
Conn. – Connecticut
Cord. – Cordillera
Cr. – Creek
Czech. – Czech Republic
D.C. – District of Columbia
Del. – Delaware
Dem. – Democratic
Dep. – Dependency
Des. – Desert
Dét. – Détroit
Dist. – District
Dj. – Djebel
Domin. – Dominica
Dom. Rep. – Dominican Republic
E. – East
E. Salv. – El Salvador
Eq. Guin. – Equatorial Guinea
Est. – Estrecho
Falk. Is. – Falkland Is.
Fd. – Fjord
Fla. – Florida
Fr. – French
G. – Golfe, Golfo, Gulf, Guba, Gebel
Ga. – Georgia
Gt. – Great, Greater
Guinea-Biss. – Guinea-Bissau
H.K. – Hong Kong
H.P. – Himachal Pradesh
Hants. – Hampshire
Harb. – Harbor, Harbour
Hd. – Head
Hts. – Heights
I.(s). – Île, Ilha, Insel, Isla, Island, Isle
Ill. – Illinois
Ind. – Indiana
Ind. Oc. – Indian Ocean
Ivory C. – Ivory Coast
J. – Jabal, Jebel
Jaz. – Jazīrah
Junc. – Junction
K. – Kap, Kapp
Kans. – Kansas
Kep. – Kepulauan
Ky. – Kentucky
L. – Lac, Lacul, Lago, Lagoa, Lake, Limni, Loch, Lough
La. – Louisiana
Ld. – Land
Liech. – Liechtenstein
Lux. – Luxembourg
Mad. P. – Madhya Pradesh
Madag. – Madagascar
Man. – Manitoba
Mass. – Massachusetts
Md. – Maryland
Me. – Maine
Medit. S. – Mediterranean Sea
Mich. – Michigan
Minn. – Minnesota
Miss. – Mississippi
Mo. – Missouri
Mont. – Montana
Mozam. – Mozambique
Mt.(s) – Mont, Montaña, Mountain
Mte. – Monte
Mti. – Monti
N. – Nord, Norte, North, Northern, Nouveau
N.B. – New Brunswick
N.C. – North Carolina
N. Cal. – New Caledonia
N. Dak. – North Dakota
N.H. – New Hampshire
N.I. – North Island
N.J. – New Jersey
N. Mex. – New Mexico
N.S. – Nova Scotia
N.S.W. – New South Wales
N.W.T. – North West Territory
N.Y. – New York
N.Z. – New Zealand
Nat. – National
Nebr. – Nebraska
Neths. – Netherlands
Nev. – Nevada
Nfld. – Newfoundland
Nic. – Nicaragua
O. – Oued, Ouadi
Occ. – Occidentale
Okla. – Oklahoma
Ont. – Ontario
Or. – Orientale
Oreg. – Oregon
Os. – Ostrov
Oz. – Ozero
P. – Pass, Passo, Pasul, Pulau
P.E.I. – Prince Edward Island
Pa. – Pennsylvania
Pac. Oc. – Pacific Ocean
Papua N.G. – Papua New Guinea
Pass. – Passage
Peg. – Pegunungan
Pen. – Peninsula, Péninsule
Phil. – Philippines
Pk. – Peak
Plat. – Plateau
Prov. – Province, Provincial
Pt. – Point
Pta. – Ponta, Punta
Pte. – Pointe
Qué. – Québec
Queens. – Queensland
R. – Rio, River
R.I. – Rhode Island
Ra. – Range
Raj. – Rajasthan
Recr. – Recreational, Récréatif
Reg. – Region
Rep. – Republic
Res. – Reserve, Reservoir
Rhld-Pfz. – Rheinland-Pfalz
S. – South, Southern, Sur
Si. Arabia – Saudi Arabia
S.C. – South Carolina
S. Dak. – South Dakota
S.I. – South Island
S. Leone – Sierra Leone
Sa. – Serra, Sierra
Sask. – Saskatchewan
Scot. – Scotland
Sd. – Sound
Sev. – Severnaya
Sib. – Siberia
Sprs. – Springs
St. – Saint
Sta. – Santa
Ste. – Sainte
Sto. – Santo
Str. – Strait, Stretto
Switz. – Switzerland
Tas. – Tasmania
Tenn. – Tennessee
Terr. – Territory, Territoire
Tex. – Texas
Tg. – Tanjung
Trin. & Tob. – Trinidad & Tobago
U.A.E. – United Arab Emirates
U.K. – United Kingdom
U.S.A. – United States of America
Ut. P. – Uttar Pradesh
Va. – Virginia
Vdkhr. – Vodokhranilishche
Vdskh. – Vodoskhovyshche
Vf. – Vîrful
Vic. – Victoria
Vol. – Volcano
Vt. – Vermont
W. – Wadi, West
W. Va. – West Virginia
Wall. & F. Is. – Wallis and Futuna Is.
Wash. – Washington
Wis. – Wisconsin
Wlkp. – Wielkopolski
Wyo. – Wyoming
Yorks. – Yorkshire
Yug. – Yugoslavia

A

A Baña, *Spain* **42 C2** 42 58N 8 46W
A Cañiza, *Spain* **42 C2** 42 13N 8 16W
A Coruña, *Spain* **42 B2** 43 20N 8 25W
A Estrada, *Spain* **42 C2** 42 43N 8 27W
A Fonsagrada, *Spain* **42 B3** 43 8N 7 4W
A Guarda, *Spain* **42 D2** 41 56N 8 52W
A Gudiña, *Spain* **42 C3** 42 4N 7 8W
A Rúa, *Spain* **42 C3** 42 24N 7 6W
Aachen, *Germany* **30 E2** 50 45N 6 6 E
Aadorf, *Switz.* **33 B7** 47 30N 8 55 E
Aalborg = Ålborg, *Denmark* **17 G3** 57 2N 9 54 E
Aalen, *Germany* **31 G6** 48 51N 10 6 E
A'Āli an Nīl □, *Sudan* **107 F3** 9 30N 33 0 E
Aalst, *Belgium* **24 D4** 50 56N 4 2 E
Aalten, *Neths.* **24 C6** 51 56N 6 35 E
Aalter, *Belgium* **24 C3** 51 5N 3 28 E
Äänekoski, *Finland* **15 E21** 62 36N 25 44 E
Aarau, *Switz.* **32 B6** 47 23N 8 4 E
Aarberg, *Switz.* **32 B4** 47 2N 7 16 E
Aarburg, *Switz.* **32 B5** 47 19N 7 54 E
Aare →, *Switz.* **32 A6** 47 33N 8 14 E
Aargau □, *Switz.* **32 B6** 47 26N 8 10 E
Aarhus = Århus, *Denmark* **17 H4** 56 8N 10 11 E
Aarschot, *Belgium* **24 D4** 50 59N 4 49 E
Aarwangen, *Switz.* **32 B5** 47 15N 7 46 E
Aasiaat, *Greenland* **10 D5** 68 43N 52 56W
Ab-i-Istada, *Afghan.* **91 B2** 32 29N 67 55 E
Ab-i-Panja = Pyandzh →, *Asia* **65 E4** 37 6N 68 20 E
Aba, *China* **76 A3** 32 59N 101 42 E
Aba, *Dem. Rep. of the Congo* **118 B3** 3 58N 30 17 E
Aba, *Nigeria* **113 D6** 5 10N 7 19 E
Âbâ, Jazîrat, *Sudan* **107 E3** 13 30N 32 31 E
Abacaxis →, *Brazil* **169 D6** 3 54 S 58 47W
Abadab, J., *Sudan* **106 D4** 18 54N 35 56 E
Ābādān, *Iran* **97 D6** 30 22N 48 20 E
Abade, *Ethiopia* **107 F4** 9 22N 38 3 E
Ābādeh, *Iran* **97 D7** 31 8N 52 40 E
Abadin, *Spain* **42 B3** 43 21N 7 29W
Abadla, *Algeria* **111 B4** 31 2N 2 45W
Abaeté, *Brazil* **171 E2** 19 9 S 45 27W
Abaeté →, *Brazil* **171 E2** 18 2 S 45 12W
Abaetetuba, *Brazil* **170 B2** 1 40 S 48 50W
Abagnar Qi, *China* **74 C9** 43 52N 116 2 E
Abah, Tanjung, *Indonesia* **79 K18** 8 46 S 115 38 E
Abai, *Paraguay* **175 B4** 25 58 S 55 54W
Abak, *Nigeria* **113 E6** 4 58N 7 50 E
Abakaliki, *Nigeria* **113 D6** 6 22N 8 2 E
Abakan, *Russia* **67 D10** 53 40N 91 10 E
Abala, *Congo* **114 C3** 1 17 S 15 35 E
Abala, *Niger* **113 C5** 14 56N 3 22 E
Abalak, *Niger* **113 B6** 15 22N 6 21 E
Abalemma, *Algeria* **111 D6** 20 51N 5 59 E
Abalemma, *Niger* **113 B6** 16 12N 7 50 E
Abalessa, *Algeria* **111 D5** 22 58N 4 47 E
Abana, *Turkey* **100 B6** 41 59N 34 1 E
Abancay, *Peru* **172 C3** 13 35 S 72 55W
Abanga →, *Gabon* **114 C2** 0 20 S 10 30 E
Abano Terme, *Italy* **45 C8** 45 22N 11 46 E
Abapó, *Bolivia* **173 D5** 18 48 S 63 25W
Abarán, *Spain* **41 G3** 38 12N 1 23W
Abariringa, *Kiribati* **134 H10** 2 50 S 171 40W
Abarqū, *Iran* **97 D7** 31 10N 53 20 E
Abashiri, *Japan* **70 B12** 44 0N 144 15 E
Abashiri-Wan, *Japan* **70 C12** 44 0N 144 30 E
Abau, *Papua N. G.* **132 F5** 10 11 S 148 46 E
Abaújszántó, *Hungary* **52 B6** 48 16N 21 12 E
Abava →, *Latvia* **54 A8** 57 6N 21 54 E
Ābay = Nîl el Azraq →, *Sudan* **107 D3** 15 38N 32 31 E
Abay, *Kazakstan* **66 E8** 49 38N 72 53 E
Abaya, L., *Ethiopia* **107 F4** 6 30N 37 50 E
Abayita-Shala Lakes Nat. Park, *Ethiopia* **107 F4** 7 40N 38 37 E
Abaza, *Russia* **66 D9** 52 39N 90 6 E
Abba, *C.A.R.* **114 A3** 5 20N 15 11 E
Abbadia San Salvatore, *Italy* **45 F8** 42 53N 11 41 E
'Abbāsābād, *Iran* **97 C8** 33 34N 58 23 E
Abbay = Nîl el Azraq →, *Sudan* **107 D3** 15 38N 32 31 E
Abbaye, Pt., *U.S.A.* **148 B1** 46 58N 88 8W
Abbé, L., *Ethiopia* **107 E5** 11 8N 41 47 E
Abbeville, *France* **27 B8** 50 6N 1 49 E
Abbeville, *Ala., U.S.A.* **152 D4** 31 34N 85 15W
Abbeville, *Ga., U.S.A.* **152 D6** 31 59N 83 18W
Abbeville, *La., U.S.A.* **155 L8** 29 58N 92 8W
Abbeville, *S.C., U.S.A.* **152 A7** 34 11N 82 23W
Abbiategrasso, *Italy* **44 C5** 45 24N 8 54 E
Abbot Ice Shelf, *Antarctica* **7 D16** 73 0 S 92 0W
Abbottabad, *Pakistan* **92 B5** 34 10N 73 15 E
Abbou, O. ben →, *Algeria* **111 C5** 28 32N 5 14 E
Abd al Kūrī, *Yemen* **99 D6** 12 5N 52 20 E
Ābdar, *Iran* **97 D7** 30 16N 55 19 E
'Abdolābād, *Iran* **97 C8** 34 12N 56 30 E
Abdulino, *Russia* **64 E4** 53 42N 53 40 E
Abdulpur, *Bangla.* **90 C2** 24 15N 88 59 E
Abéché, *Chad* **109 F4** 13 50N 20 35 E
Abejar, *Spain* **40 D2** 41 48N 2 47W
Abekr, *Sudan* **107 E2** 12 45N 28 50 E
Abel Tasman Nat. Park, *N.Z.* **131 A8** 40 59 S 173 3 E
Abemarre, *Indonesia* **83 C6** 7 1 S 140 9 E
Abengourou, *Ivory C.* **112 D4** 6 42N 3 27W
Abenójar, *Spain* **43 G6** 38 53N 4 21W
Åbenrå, *Denmark* **17 J3** 55 3N 9 25 E
Abensberg, *Germany* **31 G7** 48 48N 11 51 E
Abeokuta, *Nigeria* **113 D5** 7 3N 3 19 E
Aber, *Uganda* **118 B3** 2 12N 32 25 E
Aberaeron, *U.K.* **21 E3** 52 15N 4 15W
Aberayron = Aberaeron, *U.K.* **21 E3** 52 15N 4 15W
Aberchirder, *U.K.* **22 D6** 57 34N 2 37W
Abercorn = Mbala, *Zambia* **119 D3** 8 46 S 31 24 E
Abercorn, *Australia* **127 D5** 25 12 S 151 5 E
Aberdare, *U.K.* **21 F4** 51 43N 3 27W
Aberdare Nat. Park, *Kenya* **118 C4** 0 22 S 36 44 E
Aberdare Ra., *Kenya* **118 C4** 0 15 S 36 50 E
Aberdeen, *Australia* **129 B9** 32 9 S 150 56 E
Aberdeen, *Canada* **143 C7** 52 20N 106 8W
Aberdeen, *China* **69 G11** 22 15N 114 9 E
Aberdeen, *S. Africa* **116 E3** 32 28 S 24 2 E
Aberdeen, *U.K.* **22 D6** 57 9N 2 5W
Aberdeen, *Ala., U.S.A.* **149 J1** 33 49N 88 33W
Aberdeen, *Idaho, U.S.A.* **158 E7** 42 57N 112 50W
Aberdeen, *Md., U.S.A.* **148 F7** 39 31N 76 10W
Aberdeen, *Ohio, U.S.A.* **157 F13** 38 39N 83 46W
Aberdeen, *S. Dak., U.S.A.* **154 C5** 45 28N 98 29W
Aberdeen, *Wash., U.S.A.* **160 D3** 46 59N 123 50W
Aberdeen, City of □, *U.K.* **22 D6** 57 10N 2 10W
Aberdeenshire □, *U.K.* **22 D6** 57 17N 2 36W
Aberdovey = Aberdyfi, *U.K.* **21 E3** 52 33N 4 3W
Aberdyfi, *U.K.* **21 E3** 52 33N 4 3W
Aberfeldy, *U.K.* **22 E5** 56 37N 3 51W
Abergavenny, *U.K.* **21 F4** 51 49N 3 1W
Abergele, *U.K.* **20 D4** 53 17N 3 35W
Abernathy, *U.S.A.* **155 J4** 33 50N 101 51W
Abert, L., *U.S.A.* **158 E3** 42 38N 120 14W
Aberystwyth, *U.K.* **21 E3** 52 25N 4 5W
Abhā, *Si. Arabia* **98 C3** 18 0N 42 34 E
Abhar, *Iran* **97 B6** 36 9N 49 13 E
Abhayapuri, *India* **90 B3** 26 24N 90 38 E
Abia □, *Nigeria* **113 D6** 5 30N 7 35 E
Abide, *Turkey* **49 C11** 38 55N 29 20 E
Abidiya, *Sudan* **106 D3** 18 18N 34 3 E
Abidjan, *Ivory C.* **112 D4** 5 26N 3 58W
Abilene, *Kans., U.S.A.* **154 F6** 38 55N 97 13W
Abilene, *Tex., U.S.A.* **155 J5** 32 28N 99 43W
Abingdon, *U.K.* **21 F6** 51 40N 1 17W
Abingdon, *Ill., U.S.A.* **156 D6** 40 48N 90 24W
Abingdon, *Va., U.S.A.* **149 G5** 36 43N 81 59W
Abington Reef, *Australia* **126 B4** 18 0 S 149 35 E
Abitau →, *Canada* **143 B7** 59 53N 109 3W
Abitibi →, *Canada* **140 B3** 51 3N 80 55W
Abitibi, L., *Canada* **140 C4** 48 40N 79 40W
Abiy Adi, *Ethiopia* **107 E4** 13 39N 39 3 E
Abkhaz Republic = Abkhazia □, *Georgia* **61 J5** 43 12N 41 5 E
Abkhazia □, *Georgia* **61 J5** 43 12N 41 5 E
Abminga, *Australia* **127 D1** 26 8 S 134 51 E
Abnûb, *Egypt* **106 B3** 27 18N 31 4 E
Åbo = Turku, *Finland* **15 F20** 60 30N 22 19 E
Abo, Massif d', *Chad* **109 D3** 21 41N 16 8 E
Abocho, *Nigeria* **113 D6** 7 35N 6 56 E
Abohar, *India* **92 D6** 30 10N 74 10 E
Aboisso, *Ivory C.* **112 D4** 5 30N 3 5W
Abolo, *Congo* **114 B2** 0 8N 14 16 E
Abomey, *Benin* **113 D5** 7 10N 2 5 E
Abong-Mbang, *Cameroon* **114 B2** 4 0N 13 8 E
Abongabong, *Indonesia* **84 B1** 4 15N 96 48 E
Abonnema, *Nigeria* **113 E6** 4 41N 6 49 E
Abony, *Hungary* **52 C5** 47 12N 20 3 E
Abor Hills, *India* **90 A5** 28 25N 94 46 E
Aborlan, *Phil.* **81 G2** 9 26N 118 33 E
Aboso, *Ghana* **112 D4** 5 23N 1 57W
Abou-Deïa, *Chad* **109 F3** 11 20N 19 20 E
Abou-Goulem, *Chad* **109 F4** 13 37N 21 38 E
Abou-Telfan, Réserve de Faune de l', *Chad* **109 F3** 12 2N 18 58 E
Aboyne, *U.K.* **22 D6** 57 4N 2 47W
Abra □, *Phil.* **80 C3** 17 35N 120 45 E
Abra de Ilog, *Phil.* **80 E3** 13 27N 120 44 E
Abra Pampa, *Argentina* **174 A2** 22 43 S 65 42W
Abraham L., *Canada* **142 C5** 52 15N 116 35W
Abrantes, *Portugal* **43 F2** 39 24N 8 7W
Abreojos, Pta., *Mexico* **162 B2** 26 50N 113 40W
Abri, *Esh Shamâliya, Sudan* **106 C3** 20 50N 30 27 E
Abri, *Janub Kordofân, Sudan* **107 E3** 11 40N 30 21 E
Abrolhos, Banka, *Brazil* **171 E4** 18 0 S [illegible] 0W
Abrud, *Romania* **52 D8** 46 19N 23 5 E
Abruzzo □, *Italy* **45 F10** 42 15N 14 0 E
Absaroka Range, *U.S.A.* **158 D9** 44 45N 109 50W
Abtenau, *Austria* **34 D6** 47 33N 13 21 E
Abu, *India* **92 G5** 24 41N 72 50 E
Abū al Abyad, *U.A.E.* **97 E7** 24 11N 53 50 E
Abū al Khaşīb, *Iraq* **97 D6** 30 25N 48 0 E
Abū 'Alī, *Si. Arabia* **97 E6** 27 20N 49 27 E
Abū 'Alī →, *Lebanon* **103 A4** 34 25N 35 50 E
Abu 'Arīsh, *Si. Arabia* **98 C3** 16 53N 42 48 E
Abu Ballas, *Egypt* **106 C2** 24 26N 27 36 E
Abu Deleiq, *Sudan* **107 D3** 15 57N 33 48 E
Abu Dhabi = Abū Z̧āby, *U.A.E.* **97 E7** 24 28N 54 22 E
Abu Dis, *Sudan* **106 D3** 19 12N 33 38 E
Abu Dom, *Sudan* **107 D3** 16 18N 32 25 E
Abū Du'ān, *Syria* **101 D8** 36 25N 38 15 E
Abu el Gairi, W. →, *Egypt* **103 F2** 29 35N 33 30 E
Abu Fatma, Ras, *Sudan* **106 C4** 22 25N 36 25 E
Abu Gabra, *Sudan* **107 E2** 11 2N 26 50 E
Abu Ga'da, W. →, *Egypt* **103 F1** 29 15N 32 53 E
Abu Gelba, *Sudan* **107 E3** 13 11N 31 52 E
Abu Gubeiha, *Sudan* **107 E3** 11 30N 31 15 E
Abu Habl, Khawr →, *Sudan* **107 E3** 12 37N 31 0 E
Abū Ḩadrīyah, *Si. Arabia* **97 E6** 27 20N 48 58 E
Abu Hamed, *Sudan* **106 D3** 19 32N 33 13 E
Abu Haraz, *An Nîl el Azraq, Sudan* **106 D3** 18 1N 33 58 E
Abu Haraz, *El Gezira, Sudan* **107 E3** 14 35N 33 30 E
Abu Haraz, *Esh Shamâliya, Sudan* **106 D3** 19 8N 32 18 E
Abu Higar, *Sudan* **107 E3** 12 50N 33 59 E
Abū Kamāl, *Syria* **101 E9** 34 30N 41 0 E
Abu Kuleiwat, *Sudan* **107 E2** 12 20N 26 0 E
Abū Madd, Ra's, *Si. Arabia* **96 E3** 24 50N 37 7 E
Abu Matariq, *Sudan* **107 E2** 10 59N 26 9 E
Abu Mendi, *Ethiopia* **107 E4** 11 48N 35 42 E
Abū Mūsā, *U.A.E.* **97 E7** 25 52N 55 3 E
Abū Qaşr, *Si. Arabia* **96 D3** 30 21N 38 34 E
Abu Qir, *Egypt* **106 H7** 31 18N 30 0 E
Abu Qireiya, *Egypt* **106 C4** 24 5N 35 28 E
Abu Qurqâs, *Egypt* **106 B3** 28 1N 30 44 E
Abū Raşāş, Ra's, *Oman* **99 B7** 20 10N 58 38 E
Abu Şafāt, W. →, *Jordan* **103 E5** 30 24N 36 7 E
Abu Shagara, Ras, *Sudan* **106 C4** 21 4N 37 19 E
Abu Shanab, *Sudan* **107 E2** 13 58N 27 49 E
Abu Simbel, *Egypt* **106 C3** 22 18N 31 40 E
Abū Şukhayr, *Iraq* **101 G11** 31 54N 44 30 E
Abu Sultân, *Egypt* **106 H8** 30 24N 32 21 E
Abu Tabari, *Sudan* **106 D2** 17 32N 28 32 E
Abu Tig, *Egypt* **106 B3** 27 4N 31 15 E
Abu Tiga, *Sudan* **107 E3** 12 47N 34 12 E
Abu Tineitin, *Sudan* **107 E3** 14 24N 31 1 E
Abu Uruq, *Sudan* **107 D3** 15 52N 30 25 E
Abu Zabad, *Sudan* **107 E2** 12 25N 29 10 E
Abū Z̧āby, *U.A.E.* **97 E7** 24 28N 54 22 E
Abū Zeydābād, *Iran* **97 C6** 33 54N 51 45 E
Abufari, *Brazil* **173 B5** 5 25 S 62 59W
Abuja, *Nigeria* **113 D6** 9 5N 7 32 E
Abukuma-Gawa →, *Japan* **70 E10** 38 6N 140 52 E
Abukuma-Sammyaku, *Japan* **70 F10** 37 30N 140 45 E
Abulug, *Phil.* **80 B3** 18 27N 121 27 E
Abumombazi, *Dem. Rep. of the Congo* **114 B4** 3 42N 22 10 E
Abunã, *Brazil* **173 B4** 9 40 S 65 20W
Abunã →, *Brazil* **173 B4** 9 41 S 65 20W
Abune Yosef, *Ethiopia* **107 E4** 12 5N 39 12 E
Aburatsu, *Japan* **72 F3** 31 34N 131 24 E
Aburo, *Dem. Rep. of the Congo* **118 B3** 2 4N 30 53 E
Abut Hd., *N.Z.* **131 D5** 43 7 S 170 15 E
Abuye Meda, *Ethiopia* **107 E4** 10 30N 39 49 E
Abuyog, *Phil.* **81 F5** 10 45N 125 0 E
Abwong, *Sudan* **107 F3** 9 2N 32 14 E
Åby, *Sweden* **17 F10** 58 40N 16 10 E
Aby, Lagune, *Ivory C.* **112 D4** 5 15N 3 14W
Abyad, *Sudan* **107 E2** 13 47N 26 24 E
Åbybro, *Denmark* **17 G3** 57 10N 9 44 E
Acacías, *Colombia* **168 C3** 3 59N 73 46W
Acadia Nat. Park, *U.S.A.* **149 C11** 44 20N 68 13W
Acajutla, *El Salv.* **164 D2** 13 36N 89 50W
Açallândia, *Brazil* **170 C2** 5 0 S 47 30W
Acámbaro, *Mexico* **162 D4** 20 0N 100 40W
Acanthus, *Greece* **50 F7** 40 27N 23 47 E
Acaponeta, *Mexico* **162 C3** 22 30N 105 20W
Acapulco, *Mexico* **163 D5** 16 51N 99 56W
Acará, *Brazil* **170 B2** 1 57 S 48 11W
Acarai, Serra, *Brazil* **169 C6** 1 50N 57 50W
Acaraú, *Brazil* **170 B3** 2 53 S 40 7W
Acari, *Brazil* **170 C4** 6 31 S 36 38W
Acarí, *Peru* **172 D3** 15 25 S 74 36W
Acarigua, *Venezuela* **168 B4** 9 33N 69 12W
Acatlán, *Mexico* **163 D5** 18 10N 98 3W
Acayucan, *Mexico* **163 D6** 17 59N 94 58W
Accéglio, *Italy* **44 D4** 44 28N 7 0 E
Accomac, *U.S.A.* **148 G8** 37 43N 75 40W
Accous, *France* **28 E3** 43 0N 0 36W
Accra, *Ghana* **113 D4** 5 35N 0 6W
Accrington, *U.K.* **20 D5** 53 45N 2 22W
Acebal, *Argentina* **174 C3** 33 20 S 60 50W
Aceh □, *Indonesia* **84 B1** 4 15N 97 30 E
Acerra, *Italy* **47 B7** 40 57N 14 22 E
Aceuchal, *Spain* **43 G4** 38 39N 6 30W
Achacachi, *Bolivia* **172 D4** 16 3 S 68 43W
Achaguas, *Venezuela* **168 B4** 7 46N 68 14W
Achalpur, *India* **94 D3** 21 22N 77 32 E
Achao, *Chile* **176 B2** 42 28 S 73 30W
Achegour, *Niger* **109 E2** 19 10N 11 54 E
Achelouma, *Niger* **109 D2** 22 12N 12 50 E
Achelouma, E. →, *Niger* **109 D2** 21 55N 13 35 E
Acheng, *China* **75 B14** 45 30N 126 58 E
Achenkirch, *Austria* **34 D4** 47 32N 11 45 E
Achensee, *Austria* **34 D4** 47 26N 11 45 E
Acher, *India* **92 H5** 23 10N 72 32 E
Achern, *Germany* **31 G4** 48 37N 8 4 E
Acheron →, *N.Z.* **131 C8** 42 16 S 173 4 E
Achill Hd., *Ireland* **23 C1** 53 58N 10 15W
Achill I., *Ireland* **23 C1** 53 58N 10 1W
Achim, *Germany* **30 B5** 53 1N 9 3 E
Achinsk, *Russia* **67 D10** 56 20N 90 20 E
Achisay = Ashchysay, *Kazakstan* **65 B4** 43 35N 68 53 E
Achit, *Russia* **64 C6** 56 48N 57 54 E
Achouka, *Gabon* **114 C2** 0 52 S 9 45 E
Acıgöl, *Turkey* **49 D11** 37 50N 29 50 E
Acıpayam, *Turkey* **49 D11** 37 26N 29 22 E
Acireale, *Italy* **47 E8** 37 37N 15 10 E
Ackerman, *U.S.A.* **155 J10** 33 19N 89 11W
Ackley, *U.S.A.* **156 B3** 42 33N 93 3W
Acklins I., *Bahamas* **165 B5** 22 30N 74 0W
Acme, *Canada* **142 C6** 51 33N 113 30W
Acme, *U.S.A.* **150 F5** 40 8N 79 26W
Acobamba, *Peru* **172 C3** 12 52 S 74 35W
Acomayo, *Peru* **172 C3** 13 55 S 71 38W
Aconcagua, Cerro, *Argentina* **174 C2** 32 39 S 70 0W
Aconquija, Mt., *Argentina* **174 B2** 27 0 S 66 0W
Acopiara, *Brazil* **170 C4** 6 6 S 39 27W
Açores, Is. dos, *Atl. Oc.* **8 C9** 38 0N 27 0W
Acorizal, *Brazil* **173 D6** 15 12 S 56 22W
Acornhoek, *S. Africa* **117 C5** 24 37 S 31 2 E
Acquapendente, *Italy* **45 F8** 42 44N 11 52 E
Acquasanta Terme, *Italy* **45 F10** 42 46N 13 24 E
Acquasparta, *Italy* **45 F9** 42 41N 12 33 E
Acquaviva delle Fonti, *Italy* **47 B9** 40 54N 16 50 E
Ácqui Terme, *Italy* **44 D5** 44 41N 8 28 E
Acraman, L., *Australia* **127 E2** 32 2 S 135 23 E
Acre = 'Akko, *Israel* **103 C4** 32 55N 35 4 E
Acre □, *Brazil* **172 B3** 9 1 S 71 0W
Acre →, *Brazil* **172 B4** 8 45 S 67 22W
Acri, *Italy* **47 C9** 39 29N 16 23 E
Acs, *Hungary* **52 C3** 47 42N 18 2 E
Actæon Mt., *St. Helena* **9 h** 15 58 S 5 42W
Actium, *Greece* **39 B2** 38 57N 20 45 E
Acton, *Canada* **150 C4** 43 38N 80 3W
Açu, *Brazil* **170 C4** 5 34 S 36 54W
Acuña, *Mexico* **162 B4** 29 18N 100 55W
Acworth, *U.S.A.* **152 A5** 34 4N 84 41W
Ad Dafinah, *Si. Arabia* **98 B3** 23 18N 41 58 E
Aḑ Ḑafrah, *U.A.E.* **99 B6** 23 30N 54 30 E
Ad Dahnā, *Si. Arabia* **99 A5** 24 30N 48 10 E
Aḑ Ḑālī', *Yemen* **98 D4** 13 42N 44 44 E
Ad Dammām, *Si. Arabia* **97 E6** 26 20N 50 5 E
Ad Dāmūr, *Lebanon* **103 B4** 33 44N 35 27 E
Ad Darb, *Si. Arabia* **98 C3** 18 2N 43 7 E
Ad Dawādimī, *Si. Arabia* **96 E5** 24 35N 44 15 E
Ad Dawḩah, *Qatar* **97 E6** 25 15N 51 35 E
Ad Dawr, *Iraq* **101 E10** 34 27N 43 47 E
Aḑ Ḑiffah, *Libya* **108 B4** 30 30N 24 30 E
Ad Dilam, *Si. Arabia* **98 B4** 23 55N 47 10 E
Ad Dir'īyah, *Si. Arabia* **96 E5** 24 44N 46 35 E
Ad Dīwānīyah, *Iraq* **101 F11** 32 0N 45 0 E
Ad Dujayl, *Iraq* **101 F11** 33 51N 44 14 E
Ad Duwayd, *Si. Arabia* **96 D4** 30 15N 42 17 E
Ada, *Ghana* **113 D5** 5 44N 0 40 E
Ada, *Serbia, Yug.* **52 E5** 45 49N 20 9 E
Ada, *Minn., U.S.A.* **154 B6** 47 18N 96 31W
Ada, *Ohio, U.S.A.* **157 D13** 40 46N 83 49W
Ada, *Okla., U.S.A.* **155 H6** 34 46N 96 41W
Adabiya, *Egypt* **103 F1** 29 53N 32 28 E
Adad, *Somali Rep.* **120 C3** 9 27N 46 49 E
Adair, C., *Canada* **139 A12** 71 31N 71 24W
Adaja →, *Spain* **42 D6** 41 32N 4 52W
Adak, *U.S.A.* **144 L3** 51 45N 176 45W
Adak I., *U.S.A.* **144 L3** 51 45N 176 45W
Ådalsbruk, *Norway* **18 D8** 60 43N 11 19 E
Adam, *Oman* **99 B7** 22 15N 57 28 E
Adam, Mt., *Falk. Is.* **9 f** 51 34 S 60 4W
Adamantina, *Brazil* **171 F1** 21 42 S 51 4W
Adamaoua, Massif de l', *Cameroon* **113 D7** 7 20N 12 20 E
Adamawa □, *Nigeria* **113 D7** 9 20N 12 30 E
Adamawa Highlands = Adamaoua, Massif de l', *Cameroon* **113 D7** 7 20N 12 20 E
Adamello, Mte., *Italy* **44 B7** 46 9N 10 30 E
Adami Tulu, *Ethiopia* **107 F4** 7 53N 38 41 E
Adaminaby, *Australia* **129 D8** 36 0 S 148 45 E
Adamovka, *Russia* **64 F7** 51 32N 59 56 E
Adams, *Mass., U.S.A.* **151 D11** 42 38N 73 7W
Adams, *N.Y., U.S.A.* **151 C8** 43 49N 76 1W
Adams, *Wis., U.S.A.* **154 D10** 43 57N 89 49W
Adam's Bridge, *Sri Lanka* **95 K4** 9 15N 79 40 E
Adams L., *Canada* **142 C5** 51 10N 119 40W
Adams Mt., *U.S.A.* **160 D5** 46 12N 121 30W
Adam's Peak, *Sri Lanka* **95 L5** 6 48N 80 30 E
Adamuz, *Spain* **43 G6** 38 2N 4 32W
Adana, *Turkey* **100 D6** 37 0N 35 16 E
Adanero, *Spain* **42 E6** 40 56N 4 36W
Adapazarı = Sakarya, *Turkey* **100 B4** 40 48N 30 25 E
Adar Gwagwa, J., *Sudan* **106 C4** 22 15N 35 20 E
Adarama, *Sudan* **107 D3** 17 10N 34 52 E
Adare, C., *Antarctica* **7 D11** 71 0 S 171 0 E
Adarte, *Eritrea* **107 E5** 13 18N 42 8 E
Adaut, *Indonesia* **83 C4** 8 8 S 131 7 E
Adavale, *Australia* **127 D3** 25 52 S 144 32 E
Adda →, *Italy* **44 C6** 45 8N 9 53 E
Addatigala, *India* **94 F6** 17 31N 82 3 E
Addax, Réserve Naturelle, *Niger* **109 E1** 19 17N 9 22 E
Addis Ababa = Addis Abeba, *Ethiopia* **107 F4** 9 2N 38 42 E
Addis Abeba, *Ethiopia* **107 F4** 9 2N 38 42 E
Addis Alem, *Ethiopia* **107 F4** 9 0N 38 17 E
Addis Zemen, *Ethiopia* **107 E4** 12 7N 37 47 E
Addison, *Ill., U.S.A.* **157 C8** 41 55N 88 0W
Addison, *N.Y., U.S.A.* **150 D7** 42 1N 77 14W
Addo, *S. Africa* **116 E4** 33 32 S 25 45 E
Addo Elephant Nat. Park, *S. Africa* **116 E4** 33 30 S 25 50 E
Adebour, *Niger* **113 C7** 13 17N 11 50 E
Ādeh, *Iran* **96 B5** 37 42N 45 11 E
Adel, *Ga., U.S.A.* **152 D6** 31 8N 83 25W
Adel, *Iowa, U.S.A.* **156 C2** 41 37N 94 1W
Adelaide, *Australia* **128 C3** 34 52 S 138 30 E
Adelaide, *Bahamas* **9 b** 25 4N 77 31W
Adelaide, *S. Africa* **116 E4** 32 42 S 26 20 E
Adelaide I., *Antarctica* **7 C17** 67 15 S 68 30W
Adelaide Pen., *Canada* **138 B10** 68 15N 97 30W
Adelaide River, *Australia* **124 B5** 13 15 S 131 7 E
Adelanto, *U.S.A.* **161 L9** 34 35N 117 22W
Adelaye, *C.A.R.* **114 A4** 7 7N 22 49 E
Adelboden, *Switz.* **32 D5** 46 29N 7 33 E
Adele I., *Australia* **124 C3** 15 32 S 123 9 E
Adélie, Terre, *Antarctica* **7 C10** 68 0 S 140 0 E
Adélie Land = Adélie, Terre, *Antarctica* **7 C10** 68 0 S 140 0 E
Adelong, *Australia* **129 C8** 35 16 S 148 4 E
Ademuz, *Spain* **40 E3** 40 5N 1 13W
Aden = Al 'Adan, *Yemen* **98 D4** 12 45N 45 0 E
Aden, G. of, *Asia* **102 E4** 12 30N 47 30 E
Adendorp, *S. Africa* **116 E3** 32 15 S 24 30 E
Aderbissinat, *Niger* **113 B6** 15 34N 7 54 E
Adh Dhayd, *U.A.E.* **97 E7** 25 17N 55 53 E
Adhoi, *India* **92 H4** 23 26N 70 32 E
Adi, *Indonesia* **83 B4** 4 15 S 133 30 E
Adi Arkai, *Ethiopia* **107 E4** 13 35N 37 57 E
Adi Daro, *Ethiopia* **107 E4** 14 20N 38 14 E
Adi Keyih, *Eritrea* **107 E4** 14 51N 39 22 E
Adi Kwala, *Eritrea* **107 E4** 14 38N 38 48 E
Adi Ugri, *Eritrea* **107 E4** 14 58N 38 48 E
Adieu, C., *Australia* **125 F5** 32 0 S 132 10 E
Adieu Pt., *Australia* **124 C3** 15 14 S 124 35 E
Adigala, *Ethiopia* **107 E5** 10 24N 42 15 E
Adige →, *Italy* **45 C9** 45 9N 12 20 E
Adigrat, *Ethiopia* **107 E4** 14 20N 39 26 E
Adıgüzel Barajı, *Turkey* **49 C11** 38 13N 29 14 E
Adilabad, *India* **94 E4** 19 33N 78 20 E
Adilcevaz, *Turkey* **101 C10** 38 47N 42 43 E
Adirondack Mts., *U.S.A.* **151 C10** 44 0N 74 0W
Adıyaman, *Turkey* **101 D8** 37 45N 38 16 E
Adjim, *Tunisia* **108 B2** 33 47N 10 50 E
Adjohon, *Benin* **113 D5** 6 41N 2 32 E
Adjud, *Romania* **53 D12** 46 7N 27 10 E
Adjumani, *Uganda* **118 B3** 3 20N 31 50 E
Adjuntas, *Puerto Rico* **165 d** 18 10N 66 43W
Adlavik Is., *Canada* **141 B8** 55 0N 58 40W
Adler, *Russia* **61 J4** 43 28N 39 52 E
Adliswil, *Switz.* **33 B7** 47 19N 8 32 E
Admer, *Algeria* **111 D6** 20 21N 5 27 E
Admer, Erg d', *Algeria* **111 D6** 24 0N 9 5 E
Admiralty G., *Australia* **124 B4** 14 20 S 125 55 E
Admiralty I., *U.S.A.* **142 B2** 57 30N 134 30W
Admiralty Is., *Papua N. G.* **132 B4** 2 0 S 147 0 E
Ado, *Nigeria* **113 D5** 6 36N 2 56 E
Ado-Ekiti, *Nigeria* **113 D6** 7 38N 5 12 E
Adok, *Sudan* **107 F3** 8 10N 30 20 E
Adola, *Ethiopia* **107 E5** 11 14N 41 44 E
Adonara, *Indonesia* **82 C2** 8 15 S 123 5 E
Adoni, *India* **95 G3** 15 33N 77 18 E
Adony, *Hungary* **52 C3** 47 6N 18 52 E
Adour →, *France* **28 E2** 43 32N 1 32W
Adra, *India* **93 H12** 23 30N 86 42 E
Adra, *Spain* **43 J7** 36 43N 3 3W
Adrano, *Italy* **47 E7** 37 40N 14 50 E
Adrar des Iforas, *Algeria* **111 C4** 27 51N 0 11 E
Adrar Madet, *Niger* **109 E2** 18 54N 10 35 E
Adrasman, *Tajikistan* **65 C4** 40 38N 69 58 E
Adré, *Chad* **109 F4** 13 40N 22 20 E
Adrī, *Libya* **108 C2** 27 32N 13 2 E
Ádria, *Italy* **45 C9** 45 3N 12 3 E
Adrian, *Ga., U.S.A.* **152 C7** 32 33N 82 35W
Adrian, *Mich., U.S.A.* **157 C12** 41 54N 84 2W
Adrian, *Mo., U.S.A.* **156 F2** 38 24N 94 21W
Adrian, *Tex., U.S.A.* **155 H3** 35 16N 102 40W
Adriatic Sea, *Medit. S.* **12 G9** 43 0N 16 0 E
Adua, *Indonesia* **83 B3** 1 45 S 129 50 E
Adula-Gruppe, *Switz.* **33 D8** 46 30N 9 3 E
Adung Long, *Burma* **90 A6** 28 7N 97 42 E
Adur, *India* **95 K3** 9 8N 76 40 E
Adwa, *Ethiopia* **107 E4** 14 15N 38 52 E
Adygea □, *Russia* **61 H5** 45 0N 40 0 E
Adzhar Republic = Ajaria □, *Georgia* **61 K6** 41 30N 42 0 E
Adzopé, *Ivory C.* **112 D4** 6 7N 3 49W
Ægean Sea, *Medit. S.* **49 C7** 38 30N 25 0 E
Aerhtai Shan, *Mongolia* **68 B4** 46 40N 92 45 E
Ærø, *Denmark* **17 K4** 54 52N 10 25 E
Ærøskøbing, *Denmark* **17 K4** 54 53N 10 24 E
Aesch, *Switz.* **32 B5** 47 28N 7 36 E
Aëtós, *Greece* **48 D3** 37 15N 21 50 E
Afafi, Massif d', *Niger* **109 D3** 22 11N 15 10 E
'Afak, *Iraq* **101 F11** 32 4N 45 15 E
Afándou, *Greece* **38 E12** 36 18N 28 12 E
Afarag, Erg, *Algeria* **111 D5** 23 50N 2 47 E
Afareaitu, *Tahiti* **133 S16** 17 33 S 149 47W
Åfarnes, *Norway* **18 B4** 62 40N 7 32 E
Afdega, *Ethiopia* **120 C2** 6 4N 43 30 E
Affoltern, *Switz.* **33 B6** 47 17N 8 27 E
Affreville = Khemis Miliana, *Algeria* **111 A5** 36 11N 2 14 E
Affton, *U.S.A.* **156 F6** 38 33N 90 20W
Afghanistan ■, *Asia* **91 B2** 33 0N 65 0 E
Afgoi, *Somali Rep.* **120 D2** 2 7N 44 59 E
'Afīf, *Si. Arabia* **98 B3** 23 53N 42 56 E
Afikpo, *Nigeria* **113 D6** 5 53N 7 54 E
Aflisses, O. →, *Algeria* **111 C5** 28 40N 0 50 E
Aflou, *Algeria* **111 B5** 34 7N 2 3 E
Afmadu, *Somali Rep.* **120 D2** 0 31N 42 4 E
Afogados da Ingàzeira, *Brazil* **170 C4** 7 45 S 37 39W
Afognak I., *U.S.A.* **144 G9** 58 15N 152 30W
Afore, *Papua N. G.* **132 E5** 9 9 S 148 23 E
Afragóla, *Italy* **47 B7** 40 55N 14 18 E
Afram →, *Ghana* **113 D4** 7 0N 0 52W
Afrera, *Ethiopia* **107 E5** 13 16N 41 5 E
Africa **104 E6** 10 0N 20 0 E
'Afrīn, *Syria* **100 D7** 36 32N 36 50 E
Afşin, *Turkey* **100 C7** 38 14N 36 55 E
Afton, *Iowa, U.S.A.* **156 C2** 41 2N 94 12W
Afton, *N.Y., U.S.A.* **151 D9** 42 14N 75 32W
Afton, *Wyo., U.S.A.* **158 E8** 42 44N 110 56W
Aftout, *Algeria* **110 C4** 26 50N 3 45W
Afuá, *Brazil* **169 D7** 0 15 S 50 20W
'Afula, *Israel* **103 C4** 32 37N 35 17 E
Afumba, *Zambia* **115 F4** 15 38 S 24 56 E
Afyon, *Turkey* **49 C12** 38 45N 30 33 E
Afyon □, *Turkey* **49 C12** 38 25N 30 30 E
Afyonkarahisar = Afyon, *Turkey* **49 C12** 38 45N 30 33 E
Aga, *Egypt* **106 H7** 30 55N 31 10 E
Aga Pt., *Guam* **133 R15** 13 15N 144 43 E
Agadem, *Niger* **109 E2** 16 50N 13 11 E
Agadès = Agadez, *Niger* **113 B6** 16 58N 7 59 E
Agadez, *Niger* **113 B6** 16 58N 7 59 E
Agadir, *Morocco* **110 B3** 30 28N 9 55W
Agaete, *Canary Is.* **9 e1** 28 6N 15 43W
Agaie, *Nigeria* **113 D6** 9 1N 6 18 E
Agailás, *Mauritania* **110 D2** 22 37N 14 22W
Again, *Sudan* **107 F2** 8 28N 29 55 E
Agalás, *Greece* **39 D2** 37 43N 20 47 E
Agalega Is., *Mauritius* **121 F4** 11 0 S 57 0 E
Agana, *Guam* **133 R15** 13 28N 144 45 E
Ağapınar, *Turkey* **49 B12** 39 48N 30 47 E
Agar, *India* **92 H7** 23 40N 76 2 E
Agar →, *India* **94 D6** 21 0N 82 57 E
Agaro, *Ethiopia* **107 F4** 7 50N 36 38 E
Agartala, *India* **90 D3** 23 50N 91 23 E
Agăş, *Romania* **53 D11** 46 28N 26 15 E
Agassiz, *Canada* **142 D4** 49 14N 121 46W
Agat, *Guam* **133 R15** 13 25N 144 40 E
Agats, *Indonesia* **83 C5** 5 33 S 138 0 E
Agatti I., *India* **95 J1** 10 50N 72 12 E
Agattu I., *U.S.A.* **144 K4** 52 25N 173 35 E
Agawam, *U.S.A.* **151 D12** 42 5N 72 37W
Agbélouvé, *Togo* **113 D5** 6 35N 1 14 E
Agboville, *Ivory C.* **112 D4** 5 55N 4 15W
Ağcabädi, *Azerbaijan* **61 K8** 40 5N 47 27 E

Ağdam, *Azerbaijan* **61 L8** 40 0N 46 58 E
Ağdaş, *Azerbaijan* **61 K8** 40 44N 47 22 E
Agde, *France* **28 E7** 43 19N 3 28 E
Agde, C. d', *France* **28 E7** 43 16N 3 28 E
Agdz, *Morocco* **110 B3** 30 47N 6 30W
Agdzhabedi = Ağcabädi, *Azerbaijan* **61 K8** 40 5N 47 27 E
Agen, *France* **28 D4** 44 12N 0 38 E
Ageo, *Japan* **73 B11** 35 58N 139 36 E
Ager Tay, *Chad* **109 E3** 20 0N 17 41 E
Agerbæk, *Denmark* **17 J2** 55 36N 8 48 E
Agersø, *Denmark* **17 J5** 55 13N 11 12 E
Ageyevo, *Russia* **58 E9** 54 10N 36 27 E
Āgh Kand, *Iran* **97 B6** 37 15N 48 4 E
Aghireşu, *Romania* **53 D8** 46 53N 23 15 E
Aghoueyyît, *Mauritania* **110 D1** 21 10N 15 6W
Aghreïjît, *Mauritania* **110 D2** 21 58N 12 11W
Aginskoye, *Russia* **67 D12** 51 6N 114 32 E
Ağlasun, *Turkey* **49 D12** 37 39N 30 31 E
Agly →, *France* **28 F7** 42 46N 3 3 E
Agmar, *Mauritania* **110 C2** 25 18N 10 50W
Agnew, *Australia* **125 E3** 28 1 S 120 31 E
Agnibilékrou, *Ivory C.* **112 D4** 7 10N 3 11W
Agnita, *Romania* **53 E9** 45 59N 24 40 E
Agno, *Switz.* **33 E7** 45 59N 8 53 E
Agnone, *Italy* **45 G11** 41 48N 14 22 E
Ago, *Japan* **73 C8** 34 20N 136 51 E
Agofie, *Ghana* **113 D5** 8 27N 0 15 E
Agogna →, *Italy* **44 C5** 45 4N 8 54 E
Agogo, *Sudan* **107 F2** 7 50N 28 45 E
Agön, *Sweden* **16 C11** 61 34N 17 23 E
Agon Coutainville, *France* **26 C5** 49 2N 1 34W
Agoo, *Phil.* **80 C3** 16 20N 120 22 E
Ágordo, *Italy* **45 B9** 46 18N 12 2 E
Agori, *India* **93 G10** 24 33N 82 57 E
Agouna, *Benin* **113 D5** 7 39N 1 47 E
Agout →, *France* **28 E5** 43 47N 1 41 E
Agra, *India* **92 F7** 27 17N 77 58 E
Agrakhanskiuy Poluostrov, *Russia* **61 J8** 43 42N 47 36 E
Agramunt, *Spain* **40 D6** 41 48N 1 6 E
Agreda, *Spain* **40 D3** 41 51N 1 55W
Ağri, *Turkey* **101 C10** 39 44N 43 3 E
Agri →, *Italy* **47 B9** 40 13N 16 44 E
Ağrı Dağı, *Turkey* **101 C11** 39 50N 44 15 E
Ağri Karakose = Ağri, *Turkey* **101 C10** 39 44N 43 3 E
Agriá, *Greece* **48 B5** 39 20N 23 1 E
Agrigento, *Italy* **46 E6** 37 19N 13 34 E
Agrínion, *Greece* **48 C3** 38 37N 21 27 E
Agrópoli, *Italy* **47 B7** 40 21N 14 59 E
Ağstafa, *Azerbaijan* **61 K7** 41 7N 45 27 E
Água Branca, *Brazil* **170 C3** 5 50 S 42 40W
Agua Caliente, *Baja Calif., Mexico* **161 N10** 32 29N 116 59W
Agua Caliente, *Sinaloa, Mexico* **162 B3** 26 30N 108 20W
Agua Caliente Springs, *U.S.A.* **161 N10** 32 56N 116 19W
Água Clara, *Brazil* **173 E7** 20 25 S 52 45W
Agua Hechicero, *Mexico* **161 N10** 32 26N 116 14W
Agua Preta →, *Brazil* **169 D5** 1 41 S 63 48W
Agua Prieta, *Mexico* **162 A3** 31 20N 109 32W
Aguachica, *Colombia* **168 B3** 8 19N 73 38W
Aguada Cecilio, *Argentina* **176 B3** 40 51 S 65 51W
Aguadas, *Colombia* **168 B2** 5 40N 75 38W
Aguadilla, *Puerto Rico* **165 d** 18 26N 67 10W
Aguadulce, *Panama* **164 E3** 8 15N 80 32W
Aguanga, *U.S.A.* **161 M10** 33 27N 116 51W
Aguanish, *Canada* **141 B7** 50 14N 62 2W
Aguanus →, *Canada* **141 B7** 50 13N 62 5W
Aguapeí, *Brazil* **173 D6** 16 12 S 59 43W
Aguapeí →, *Brazil* **171 F1** 21 0 S 51 0W
Aguapey →, *Argentina* **174 B4** 29 7 S 56 36W
Aguaray Guazú →, *Paraguay* **174 A4** 24 47 S 57 19W
Aguarico →, *Ecuador* **168 D2** 0 59 S 75 11W
Aguas →, *Spain* **40 D4** 41 20N 0 30W
Aguas Blancas, *Chile* **174 A2** 24 15 S 69 55W
Aguas Calientes, Sierra de, *Argentina* **174 B2** 25 26 S 66 40W
Águas Formosas, *Brazil* **171 E3** 17 5 S 40 57W
Aguascalientes, *Mexico* **162 C4** 21 53N 102 12W
Aguascalientes □, *Mexico* **162 C4** 22 0N 102 20W
Agudo, *Spain* **43 G6** 38 59N 4 52W
Águeda, *Portugal* **42 E2** 40 34N 8 27W
Agueda →, *Spain* **42 D4** 41 2N 6 56W
Aguelhok, *Mali* **113 B5** 19 29N 0 52 E
Aguelt el Melah, *Mauritania* **110 D2** 23 3N 8 28W
Agüenit, *W. Sahara* **110 D2** 22 11N 13 8W
Aguié, *Niger* **113 C6** 13 31N 7 46 E
Aguila, Punta, *Puerto Rico* **165 d** 17 57N 67 13W
Aguilafuente, *Spain* **42 D6** 41 13N 4 7W
Aguilar, *Spain* **43 H6** 37 31N 4 40W
Aguilar de Campóo, *Spain* **42 C6** 42 47N 4 15W
Aguilares, *Argentina* **174 B2** 27 26 S 65 35W
Aguilas, *Spain* **41 H3** 37 23N 1 35W
Agüimes, *Canary Is.* **9 e1** 27 58N 15 27W
Aguja, C. de la, *Colombia* **168 A3** 11 18N 74 12W
Agujereada, Pta., *Puerto Rico* **165 d** 18 30N 67 8W
Agulaa, *Ethiopia* **107 E4** 13 40N 39 40 E
Agulhas, C., *S. Africa* **116 E3** 34 52 S 20 0 E
Agulo, *Canary Is.* **9 e1** 28 11N 17 12W
Agung, Gunung, *Indonesia* **85 D5** 8 20 S 115 28 E
Agur, *Uganda* **118 B3** 2 28N 32 55 E
Agusan →, *Phil.* **81 G5** 9 0N 125 30 E
Agusan del Norte □, *Phil.* **81 G5** 9 20N 125 10 E
Agusan del Sur □, *Phil.* **81 G5** 8 30N 125 30 E
Agustín Codazzi, *Colombia* **168 A3** 10 2N 73 14W
Agutaya I., *Phil.* **81 F3** 11 9N 120 58 E
Ağva, *Turkey* **51 E13** 41 8N 29 51 E
Agvali, *Russia* **61 J8** 42 36N 46 8 E
Aha Mts., *Botswana* **116 B3** 19 45 S 21 0 E
Ahaggar, *Algeria* **111 D6** 23 0N 6 30 E
Ahamansu, *Ghana* **113 D5** 7 38N 0 35 E
Ahar, *Iran* **101 C12** 38 35N 47 0 E
Ahat, *Turkey* **49 C11** 38 39N 29 47 E
Ahaura →, *N.Z.* **131 C6** 42 21 S 171 34 E
Ahaus, *Germany* **30 C2** 52 4N 7 0 E
Åheim, *Norway* **18 B2** 62 2N 5 13 E
Ahelledjem, *Algeria* **111 C6** 26 37N 6 58 E
Ahimanawa Ra., *N.Z.* **130 F5** 39 3 S 176 30 E
Ahioma, *Papua N. G.* **132 F6** 10 20 S 150 33 E
Ahipara B., *N.Z.* **130 B2** 35 5 S 173 5 E
Ahir Dağı, *Turkey* **49 C12** 38 45N 30 10 E
Ahiri, *India* **94 E5** 19 30N 80 0 E
Ahlat, *Turkey* **101 C10** 38 45N 42 29 E
Ahlen, *Germany* **30 D3** 51 45N 7 53 E
Ahmad Wal, *Pakistan* **92 E1** 29 18N 65 58 E
Ahmadabad, *India* **92 H5** 23 0N 72 40 E
Aḩmadābād, *Khorāsān, Iran* **97 C9** 35 3N 60 50 E
Aḩmadābād, *Khorāsān, Iran* **97 C8** 35 49N 59 42 E
Aḩmadī, *Iran* **97 E8** 27 56N 56 42 E
Ahmadnagar, *India* **94 E2** 19 7N 74 46 E
Ahmadpur, *India* **94 E3** 18 40N 76 57 E
Ahmadpur, *Pakistan* **92 E4** 29 12N 71 10 E
Ahmadpur Lamma, *Pakistan* **92 E4** 28 19N 70 3 E
Ahmar, *Ethiopia* **107 F5** 9 20N 41 15 E
Ahmedabad = Ahmadabad, *India* **92 H5** 23 0N 72 40 E
Ahmednagar = Ahmadnagar, *India* **94 E2** 19 7N 74 46 E
Ahmetbey, *Turkey* **51 E11** 41 26N 27 34 E
Ahmetler, *Turkey* **49 C11** 38 28N 29 5 E
Ahmetli, *Turkey* **49 C9** 38 32N 27 57 E
Ahmeyim, *Mauritania* **110 D2** 20 51N 14 25W
Ahoada, *Nigeria* **113 D6** 5 8N 6 36 E
Ahome, *Mexico* **162 B3** 25 55N 109 11W
Ahon, Tarso, *Chad* **109 D3** 20 23N 18 18 E
Ahoskie, *U.S.A.* **149 G7** 36 17N 76 59W
Ahr →, *Germany* **30 E3** 50 32N 7 16 E
Ahram, *Iran* **97 D6** 28 52N 51 16 E
Ahrax Pt., *Malta* **38 F7** 36 0N 14 22 E
Ahrensbök, *Germany* **30 A6** 54 2N 10 35 E
Ahrensburg, *Germany* **30 B6** 53 40N 10 13 E
Āhū, *Iran* **97 C6** 34 33N 50 2 E
Ahu Akivi, *Chile* **172 b** 27 7 S 109 24W
Ahu Tepeu, *Chile* **172 b** 27 6 S 109 25W
Ahu Tongariki, *Chile* **172 b** 27 8 S 109 17W
Ahu Vinapu, *Chile* **172 b** 27 10 S 109 25W
Ahuachapán, *El Salv.* **164 D2** 13 54N 89 52W
Ahun, *France* **27 F9** 46 4N 2 5 E
Ahuriri →, *N.Z.* **131 E5** 44 31 S 170 12 E
Åhus, *Sweden* **17 J8** 55 56N 14 18 E
Ahvāz, *Iran* **97 D6** 31 20N 48 40 E
Ahvenanmaa = Åland, *Finland* **15 F19** 60 15N 20 0 E
Aḩwar, *Yemen* **98 D4** 13 30N 46 40 E
Ahzar →, *Mali* **113 B5** 15 30N 3 20 E
Ai →, *India* **90 B3** 26 26N 90 44 E
Ai-Ais, *Namibia* **116 D2** 27 54 S 17 59 E
Ai-Ais and Fish River Canyon Nat. Park, *Namibia* **116 C2** 24 45 S 17 15 E
Aiari →, *Brazil* **168 C4** 1 22N 68 36W
Aichach, *Germany* **31 G7** 48 27N 11 8 E
Aichi □, *Japan* **73 C9** 35 0N 137 15 E
Aiduma, *Indonesia* **83 B4** 4 0 S 134 6 E
Aiduna, *Indonesia* **83 B5** 4 27 S 135 15 E
Aiea, *U.S.A.* **145 K14** 21 23N 157 56W
Aigle, *Switz.* **32 D3** 46 18N 6 58 E
Aignay-le-Duc, *France* **27 E11** 47 40N 4 43 E
Aigoual, Mt., *France* **28 D7** 44 8N 3 35 E
Aigre, *France* **28 C4** 45 54N 0 1 E
Aigrettes, Pte. des, *Réunion* **121 c** 21 3 S 55 13 E
Aigua, *Uruguay* **175 C5** 34 13 S 54 46W
Aigueperse, *France* **27 F10** 46 3N 3 13 E
Aigues →, *France* **29 D8** 44 7N 4 43 E
Aigues-Mortes, *France* **29 E8** 43 35N 4 12 E
Aigues-Mortes, G. d', *France* **29 E8** 43 31N 4 3 E
Aiguilles, *France* **29 D10** 44 47N 6 51 E
Aiguillon, *France* **28 D4** 44 18N 0 21 E
Aigurande, *France* **27 F8** 46 27N 1 49 E
Aihui, *China* **69 A7** 50 10N 127 30 E
Aija, *Peru* **172 B2** 9 50 S 77 45W
Aikawa, *Japan* **70 E9** 38 2N 138 15 E
Aiken, *U.S.A.* **152 B8** 33 34N 81 43W
Ailao Shan, *China* **76 F3** 24 0N 101 20 E
Aileron, *Australia* **126 C1** 22 39 S 133 20 E
Ailey, *U.S.A.* **152 C7** 32 11N 82 34W
Ailigandi, *Panama* **168 B2** 9 14N 78 1W
Aillant-sur-Tholon, *France* **27 E10** 47 52N 3 20 E
Aillik, *Canada* **141 A8** 55 11N 59 18W
Ailsa Craig, *U.K.* **22 F3** 55 15N 5 6W
Ailulual, *Papua N. G.* **132 E6** 9 38 S 150 35 E
'Ailūn, *Jordan* **103 C4** 32 18N 35 47 E
Aim, *Russia* **67 D14** 59 0N 133 55 E
Aimere, *Indonesia* **79 F6** 8 45 S 121 3 E
Aimogasta, *Argentina* **174 B2** 28 33 S 66 50W
Aimorés, *Brazil* **171 E3** 19 30 S 41 4W
Ain □, *France* **27 F12** 46 5N 5 20 E
Ain →, *France* **29 C9** 45 45N 5 11 E
Aïn Beïda, *Algeria* **111 A6** 35 50N 7 29 E
Aïn Ben Khellil, *Algeria* **111 B4** 33 15N 0 49W
Aïn Ben Tili, *Mauritania* **110 C3** 25 59N 9 27W
Aïn Beni Mathar, *Morocco* **111 B4** 34 1N 2 0W
Aïn Benian, *Algeria* **111 A5** 36 48N 2 55 E
Ain Dalla, *Egypt* **106 B2** 27 20N 27 23 E
Ain el Mafki, *Egypt* **106 B2** 27 30N 28 15 E
Ain Girba, *Egypt* **106 B2** 29 20N 25 14 E
Aïn M'lila, *Algeria* **111 A6** 36 2N 6 35 E
Ain Murr, *Sudan* **106 C2** 21 50N 25 9 E
Ain Qeiqab, *Egypt* **106 B1** 29 42N 24 55 E
Aïn Sefra, *Algeria* **111 B4** 32 47N 0 37W
Ain Sheikh Murzûk, *Egypt* **106 B2** 26 47N 27 45 E
Ain Sudr, *Egypt* **103 F2** 29 50N 33 6 E
Ain Sukhna, *Egypt* **106 J8** 29 32N 32 20 E
Aïn Tédelès, *Algeria* **111 A5** 36 0N 0 21 E
Aïn Témouchent, *Algeria* **111 A4** 35 16N 1 8W
Aïn Tikkidine, *Algeria* **111 C5** 25 33N 1 24 E
Aïn Touta, *Algeria* **111 A6** 35 26N 5 54 E
Ain Zeitûn, *Egypt* **106 B2** 29 10N 25 48 E
Aïn Zorah, *Morocco* **111 B4** 34 37N 3 32W
Ainabo, *Somali Rep.* **120 C3** 9 0N 46 25 E
Ainaži, *Latvia* **15 H21** 57 50N 24 24 E
Aínos Óros, *Greece* **39 C2** 38 9N 20 40 E
Ainsworth, *U.S.A.* **154 D5** 42 33N 99 52W
Aioi, *Japan* **72 C6** 34 48N 134 28 E
Aiome, *Papua N. G.* **132 C3** 5 8 S 144 44 E
Aipe, *Colombia* **168 C2** 3 13N 75 15W
Aiquile, *Bolivia* **173 D4** 18 10 S 65 10W
Aïr, *Niger* **113 B6** 18 30N 8 0 E
Aïr et du Ténéré, Réserve Naturelle de L', *Niger* **109 E1** 18 12N 9 56 E
Air Force I., *Canada* **139 B12** 67 58N 74 5W
Air Hitam, *Malaysia* **87 M4** 1 55N 103 11 E
Aira, *Japan* **72 F2** 31 43N 130 43 E
Airaines, *France* **27 C8** 49 58N 1 55 E
Airão, *Brazil* **169 D5** 1 56 S 61 22W
Airdrie, *Canada* **142 C6** 51 18N 114 2W
Airdrie, *U.K.* **22 F5** 55 52N 3 57W
Aire →, *France* **27 C11** 49 18N 4 49 E
Aire →, *U.K.* **20 D7** 53 43N 0 55W
Aire, I. de l', *Spain* **38 B5** 39 48N 4 16 E
Aire-sur-la-Lys, *France* **27 B9** 50 37N 2 22 E
Aire-sur-l'Adour, *France* **28 E3** 43 42N 0 15W
Aireys Inlet, *Australia* **128 E6** 38 29 S 144 5 E
Airlie Beach, *Australia* **126 J6** 20 16 S 148 43 E
Airmadidi, *Indonesia* **82 A3** 1 25N 125 0 E
Airolo, *Switz.* **33 C7** 46 32N 8 37 E
Airvault, *France* **26 F6** 46 50N 0 8W
Aisch →, *Germany* **31 F6** 49 49N 10 58 E
Aisen □, *Chile* **176 C2** 46 30 S 73 0W
Aisne □, *France* **27 C10** 49 42N 3 40 E
Aisne →, *France* **27 C9** 49 26N 2 50 E
Ait, *India* **93 G8** 25 54N 79 14 E
Aitana, Sierra de, *Spain* **41 G4** 38 35N 0 24W
Aitape, *Papua N. G.* **132 B2** 3 11 S 142 22 E
Aitkin, *U.S.A.* **154 B8** 46 32N 93 42W
Aitolía Kai Akarnanía □, *Greece* **48 C3** 38 45N 21 18 E
Aitolikón, *Greece* **48 C3** 38 26N 21 21 E
Aiuaba, *Brazil* **170 C3** 6 38 S 40 7W
Aiud, *Romania* **53 D8** 46 19N 23 44 E
Aix-en-Provence, *France* **29 E9** 43 32N 5 27 E
Aix-la-Chapelle = Aachen, *Germany* **30 E2** 50 45N 6 6 E
Aix-les-Bains, *France* **29 C9** 45 41N 5 53 E
Aixe-sur-Vienne, *France* **28 C5** 45 47N 1 9 E
Aiyang, Mt., *Papua N. G.* **132 C1** 5 10 S 141 20 E
Áíyina, *Greece* **48 D5** 37 45N 23 26 E
Aiyínion, *Greece* **50 F6** 40 28N 22 28 E
Aíyion, *Greece* **48 C4** 38 15N 22 5 E
Aizawl, *India* **90 D4** 23 40N 92 44 E
Aizenay, *France* **26 F5** 46 44N 1 38W
Aizkraukle, *Latvia* **15 H21** 56 36N 25 11 E
Aizpute, *Latvia* **15 H19** 56 43N 21 40 E
Aizuwakamatsu, *Japan* **70 F9** 37 30N 139 56 E
Ajaccio, *France* **29 G12** 41 55N 8 40 E
Ajaccio, G. d', *France* **29 G12** 41 52N 8 40 E
Ajai Game Reserve, *Uganda* **118 B3** 2 52N 31 16 E
Ajaigarh, *India* **93 G9** 24 52N 80 16 E
Ajaju →, *Colombia* **168 C3** 0 59N 72 20W
Ajalpan, *Mexico* **163 D5** 18 22N 97 15W
Ajanta, *India* **94 D2** 20 30N 75 48 E
Ajanta Ra., *India* **94 D2** 20 28N 75 50 E
Ajari Rep. = Ajaria □, *Georgia* **61 K6** 41 30N 42 0 E
Ajaria □, *Georgia* **61 K6** 41 30N 42 0 E
Ajax, *Canada* **150 C5** 43 50N 79 1W
Ajax, Mt., *N.Z.* **131 C7** 42 35 S 172 5 E
Ajdābiyā, *Libya* **108 B4** 30 54N 20 4 E
Ajdovščina, *Slovenia* **45 C10** 45 54N 13 54 E
Ajibar, *Ethiopia* **107 E4** 10 35N 38 36 E
Ajka, *Hungary* **52 C2** 47 4N 17 31 E
'Ajmān, *U.A.E.* **97 E7** 25 25N 55 30 E
Ajmer, *India* **92 F6** 26 28N 74 37 E
Ajnala, *India* **92 D6** 31 50N 74 48 E
Ajo, *U.S.A.* **159 K7** 32 22N 112 52W
Ajo, C. de, *Spain* **42 B7** 43 31N 3 35W
Ajoie, *Switz.* **32 B4** 47 22N 7 0 E
Ajok, *Sudan* **107 F2** 9 15N 28 28 E
Ajuda, Pta. da, *Azores* **9 d3** 37 52N 25 19W
Ajuy, *Phil.* **81 F4** 11 10N 123 1 E
Ak Dağ, *Turkey* **49 E11** 36 30N 29 32 E
Ak Dağları, *Muğla, Turkey* **49 E11** 36 30N 29 30 E
Ak Dağları, *Sivas, Turkey* **100 C7** 39 32N 36 12 E
Ak-Muz, *Kyrgyzstan* **65 C8** 41 15N 76 10 E
Ak-Tüz, *Kyrgyzstan* **65 B8** 42 54N 76 7 E
Akaba, *Togo* **113 D5** 8 10N 1 2 E
Akabira, *Japan* **70 C11** 43 33N 142 5 E
Akabli, *Algeria* **111 C5** 26 49N 1 31 E
Akagera, Parc Nat. d', *Rwanda* **118 C3** 1 31 S 30 33 E
Akaishi-Dake, *Japan* **73 B10** 35 27N 138 9 E
Akaishi-Sammyaku, *Japan* **73 B10** 35 25N 138 10 E
Akaki Beseka, *Ethiopia* **107 F4** 8 55N 38 45 E
Akākūs, Jabal, *Libya* **111 C7** 25 20N 10 30 E
Akala, *Sudan* **107 D4** 15 39N 36 13 E
Akalkot, *India* **94 F3** 17 32N 76 13 E
Akamas, *Cyprus* **39 E8** 35 3N 32 18 E
Akanthou, *Cyprus* **39 E9** 35 22N 33 45 E
Akarca, *Turkey* **49 C11** 38 35N 29 35 E
Akaroa, *N.Z.* **131 D7** 43 49 S 172 59 E
Akaroa Harbour, *N.Z.* **131 D7** 43 50 S 172 55 E
Akasha, *Sudan* **106 C3** 21 10N 30 32 E
Akashi, *Japan* **72 C6** 34 45N 134 58 E
Akbarpur, *Bihar, India* **93 G10** 24 39N 83 58 E
Akbarpur, *Ut. P., India* **93 F10** 26 25N 82 32 E
Akbou, *Algeria* **111 A5** 36 31N 4 31 E
Akbulak, *Russia* **64 F5** 51 1N 55 37 E
Akçaabat, *Turkey* **101 B8** 41 1N 39 34 E
Akçadağ, *Turkey* **100 C7** 38 27N 37 43 E
Akçakale, *Turkey* **101 D8** 36 41N 38 56 E
Akçakoca, *Turkey* **100 B4** 41 5N 31 8 E
Akçaova, *Turkey* **51 E13** 41 3N 29 57 E
Akçay, *Turkey* **49 E11** 36 36N 29 45 E
Akçay →, *Turkey* **49 D10** 37 50N 28 15 E
Akchâr, *Mauritania* **110 D2** 20 20N 14 28W
Akdağ, *Turkey* **49 C8** 38 33N 26 30 E
Akdağmadeni, *Turkey* **100 C6** 39 39N 35 53 E
Akechi, *Japan* **73 B9** 35 18N 137 23 E
Akelamo, *Indonesia* **82 A3** 1 35N 129 40 E
Åkernes, *Norway* **18 F4** 58 45N 7 30 E
Åkers styckebruk, *Sweden* **16 E11** 59 15N 17 5 E
Åkersberga, *Sweden* **16 E12** 59 29N 18 18 E
Akershus □, *Norway* **18 D8** 60 0N 11 10 E
Akeru →, *India* **94 F5** 17 25N 80 5 E
Aketi, *Dem. Rep. of the Congo* **114 B4** 2 38N 23 47 E
Akhaïa □, *Greece* **48 C3** 38 5N 21 45 E
Akhalkalaki, *Georgia* **61 K6** 41 27N 43 25 E
Akhaltsikhe, *Georgia* **61 K6** 41 40N 43 0 E
Akharnaí, *Greece* **48 C5** 38 5N 23 44 E
Akhelóös →, *Greece* **48 C3** 38 19N 21 7 E
Akhendriá, *Greece* **49 G7** 34 59N 25 13 E
Akhiok, *U.S.A.* **144 H9** 56 57N 154 10W
Akhisar, *Turkey* **49 C9** 38 56N 27 48 E
Akhladhókambos, *Greece* **48 D4** 37 31N 22 35 E
Akhmîm, *Egypt* **106 B3** 26 31N 31 47 E
Akhnur, *India* **93 C6** 32 52N 74 45 E
Akhtopol, *Bulgaria* **51 D11** 42 6N 27 56 E
Akhtuba →, *Russia* **61 G8** 47 41N 46 55 E
Akhtubinsk, *Russia* **61 F8** 48 13N 46 7 E
Akhty, *Russia* **61 K8** 41 30N 47 45 E
Akhtyrka = Okhtyrka, *Ukraine* **59 G8** 50 25N 35 0 E
Aki, *Japan* **72 D5** 33 30N 133 54 E
Aki-Nada, *Japan* **72 C4** 34 5N 132 40 E
Akiachak, *U.S.A.* **144 F7** 60 55N 161 26W
Akiak, *U.S.A.* **144 F7** 60 55N 161 13W
Akiéni, *Gabon* **114 C2** 1 11 S 13 53 E
Akimiski I., *Canada* **140 B3** 52 50N 81 30W
Akimovka, *Ukraine* **59 J8** 46 44N 35 0 E
Åkirkeby, *Denmark* **17 J8** 55 4N 14 55 E
Akita, *Japan* **70 E10** 39 45N 140 7 E
Akita □, *Japan* **70 E10** 39 40N 140 30 E
Akjoujt, *Mauritania* **112 B2** 19 45N 14 15W
Akka, *Mali* **112 B4** 15 24N 4 11W
Akka, *Morocco* **110 C3** 29 22N 8 9W
Akkaraipattu, *Sri Lanka* **95 L5** 7 13N 81 51 E
Akkaya Tepesi, *Turkey* **49 D11** 37 25N 29 38 E
Akkeshi, *Japan* **70 C12** 43 2N 144 51 E
'Akko, *Israel* **103 C4** 32 55N 35 4 E
Akkol = Aqköl, *Kazakstan* **65 A7** 45 0N 75 39 E
Akkol = Aqköl, *Kazakstan* **65 B5** 43 36N 70 45 E
Akköy, *Turkey* **49 D9** 37 29N 27 15 E
Aklampa, *Benin* **113 D5** 8 15N 2 10 E
Aklan □, *Phil.* **81 F4** 11 50N 122 30 E
Aklavik, *Canada* **138 B6** 68 12N 135 0W
Aklera, *India* **92 G7** 24 26N 76 32 E
Akmenė, *Lithuania* **54 B9** 56 15N 22 45 E
Akmenrags, *Latvia* **54 B8** 56 50N 21 4 E
Akmeqit, *China* **65 E8** 37 5N 76 55 E
Akmolinsk = Astana, *Kazakstan* **66 D8** 51 10N 71 30 E
Akmonte = Almonte, *Spain* **43 H4** 37 13N 6 38W
Aknoul, *Morocco* **111 B4** 34 40N 3 55W
Akō, *Japan* **72 C6** 34 45N 134 24 E
Ako, *Nigeria* **113 C7** 10 19N 10 48 E
Akôbô, *Sudan* **107 F3** 7 47N 33 1 E
Akobo →, *Ethiopia* **107 F3** 7 48N 33 3 E
Akola, *Maharashtra, India* **94 D3** 20 42N 77 2 E
Akola, *Maharashtra, India* **94 E2** 19 32N 74 3 E
Akolmiut, *U.S.A.* **144 F7** 60 55N 162 20W
Akonolinga, *Cameroon* **113 E7** 3 50N 12 18 E
Akor, *Mali* **112 C3** 14 59N 6 58W
Akordat, *Eritrea* **107 D4** 15 30N 37 40 E
Akosombo Dam, *Ghana* **113 D5** 6 20N 0 5 E
Akot, *India* **94 D3** 21 10N 77 10 E
Akot, *Sudan* **107 F3** 6 31N 30 9 E
Akoupé, *Ivory C.* **112 D4** 6 23N 3 54W
Akourousoulba, *C.A.R.* **114 A4** 8 58N 20 46 E
Akpatok I., *Canada* **139 B13** 60 25N 68 8W
Åkrahamn, *Norway* **15 G11** 59 15N 5 10 E
'Akramah, *Libya* **108 B4** 32 2N 23 41 E
Akranes, *Iceland* **11 C4** 64 19N 22 5W
Akreïjit, *Mauritania* **112 B3** 18 19N 9 11W
Akrítas Venétiko, Ákra, *Greece* **48 E3** 36 43N 21 54 E
Akron, *Colo., U.S.A.* **154 E3** 40 10N 103 13W
Akron, *Ind., U.S.A.* **157 C10** 41 2N 86 1W
Akron, *Ohio, U.S.A.* **150 E3** 41 5N 81 31W
Akrotiri, *Cyprus* **39 F8** 34 36N 32 57 E
Akrotíri, Ákra, *Greece* **51 F9** 40 26N 25 27 E
Akrotiri Bay, *Cyprus* **39 F9** 34 35N 33 10 E
Aksai Chin, *China* **93 B8** 35 15N 79 55 E
Aksaray, *Turkey* **100 C6** 38 25N 34 2 E
Aksay, *Kazakstan* **57 D9** 51 11N 53 0 E
Akşehir, *Turkey* **100 C4** 38 18N 31 30 E
Akşehir Gölü, *Turkey* **100 C4** 38 30N 31 25 E
Akstafa = Ağstafa, *Azerbaijan* **61 K7** 41 7N 45 27 E
Aksu, *China* **68 B3** 41 5N 80 10 E
Aksu →, *Turkey* **100 D4** 36 52N 30 57 E
Aksum, *Ethiopia* **107 E4** 14 5N 38 40 E
Aktash, *Russia* **60 C11** 55 2N 52 0 E
Aktash, *Uzbekistan* **65 D2** 39 55N 65 55 E
Aktasty, *Kazakstan* **64 F8** 50 42N 61 42 E
Aktion, *Greece* **39 B2** 38 57N 20 46 E
Akto, *China* **65 D7** 39 5N 75 59 E
Aktogay, *Kazakstan* **66 E8** 46 57N 79 40 E
Aktsyabrski, *Belarus* **59 F5** 52 38N 28 53 E
Aktyubinsk = Aqtöbe, *Kazakstan* **57 D10** 50 17N 57 10 E
Aktyuz = Ak-Tüz, *Kyrgyzstan* **65 B8** 42 54N 76 7 E
Aku, *Nigeria* **113 D6** 6 40N 7 18 E
Akula, *Dem. Rep. of the Congo* **114 B4** 2 22N 20 12 E
Akun I., *U.S.A.* **144 J6** 54 11N 165 32W
Akune, *Japan* **72 E2** 32 1N 130 12 E
Akure, *Nigeria* **113 D6** 7 15N 5 5 E
Akurenan, *Eq. Guin.* **114 B2** 1 2N 10 40 E
Akuressa, *Sri Lanka* **95 L5** 6 5N 80 29 E
Akureyri, *Iceland* **11 B8** 65 40N 18 6W
Akuseki-Shima, *Japan* **71 K4** 29 27N 129 37 E
Akusha, *Russia* **61 J8** 42 18N 47 30 E
Akutan, *U.S.A.* **144 J6** 54 8N 165 46W
Akutan I., *U.S.A.* **144 J6** 54 7N 165 55W
Akwa-Ibom □, *Nigeria* **113 E6** 4 30N 7 30 E
Akyab = Sittwe, *Burma* **90 E4** 20 18N 92 45 E
Akyazı, *Turkey* **100 B4** 40 40N 30 38 E
Ål, *Norway* **18 D5** 60 38N 8 33 E
Al Abyaḑ, *Libya* **108 C2** 26 49N 14 1 E
Al Abyār, *Libya* **108 B4** 32 9N 20 29 E
Al 'Adan, *Yemen* **98 D4** 12 45N 45 0 E
Al Aḩsā = Hasa □, *Si. Arabia* **97 E6** 25 50N 49 0 E
Al Ajfar, *Si. Arabia* **96 E4** 27 26N 43 0 E
Al Amādīyah, *Iraq* **101 D10** 37 5N 43 30 E
Al 'Amārah, *Iraq* **101 G12** 31 55N 47 15 E
Al 'Aqabah, *Jordan* **103 F4** 29 31N 35 0 E
Al 'Aqīq, *Si. Arabia* **98 B3** 20 39N 41 25 E
Al Arak, *Syria* **101 E8** 34 38N 38 35 E
Al 'Aramah, *Si. Arabia* **96 E5** 25 30N 46 0 E
Al 'Ariḑah, *Si. Arabia* **98 C3** 17 3N 43 5 E
Al Arţāwīyah, *Si. Arabia* **96 E5** 26 31N 45 20 E
Al Ashkhara, *Oman* **99 B7** 21 50N 59 30 E
Al 'Āşimah = 'Ammān □, *Jordan* **103 D5** 31 40N 36 30 E
Al 'Assāfīyah, *Si. Arabia* **96 D3** 28 17N 38 59 E
Al 'Ayn, *Oman* **97 E7** 24 15N 55 45 E
Al 'Ayn, *Si. Arabia* **96 E3** 25 4N 38 6 E
Al 'Aẓamīyah, *Iraq* **96 C5** 33 22N 44 22 E
Al 'Azīzīyah, *Iraq* **101 F11** 32 54N 45 4 E
Al 'Azīzīyah, *Libya* **108 B2** 32 30N 13 1 E
Al Bāb, *Syria* **100 D7** 36 23N 37 29 E
Al Bad', *Si. Arabia* **96 D2** 28 28N 35 1 E
Al Bādī, *Iraq* **96 C4** 35 56N 41 32 E
Al Badī', *Si. Arabia* **98 B4** 22 0N 46 35 E
Al Baḩrah, *Kuwait* **96 D5** 29 40N 47 52 E
Al Baḩral Mayyit = Dead Sea, *Asia* **103 D4** 31 30N 35 30 E
Al Balqā' □, *Jordan* **103 C4** 32 5N 35 45 E
Al Barkāt, *Libya* **108 D2** 24 56N 10 14 E
Al Bārūk, J., *Lebanon* **103 B4** 33 39N 35 40 E
Al Başrah, *Iraq* **96 D5** 30 30N 47 50 E
Al Baţḩā, *Iraq* **96 D5** 31 6N 45 53 E
Al Batinah, *Oman* **99 A7** 24 10N 56 50 E
Al Batrūn, *Lebanon* **103 A4** 34 15N 35 40 E
Al Bayāḑ, *Si. Arabia* **98 B4** 22 0N 47 0 E
Al Bayḑā, *Libya* **108 B4** 32 50N 21 44 E
Al Bayḑā', *Yemen* **98 D4** 14 5N 45 42 E
Al Bi'ār, *Si. Arabia* **98 B2** 22 39N 39 40 E
Al Biqā, *Lebanon* **103 A5** 34 10N 36 10 E
Al Bi'r, *Si. Arabia* **96 D3** 28 51N 36 16 E
Al Birk, *Si. Arabia* **98 C3** 18 13N 41 33 E
Al Bu'ayrāt al Ḩasūn, *Libya* **108 B3** 31 24N 15 44 E
Al Bunbah, *Libya* **108 B4** 32 24N 23 8 E
Al Burayj, *Syria* **103 A5** 34 15N 36 46 E
Al Faḑilī, *Si. Arabia* **97 E6** 26 58N 49 10 E
Al Fallūjah, *Iraq* **101 F10** 33 20N 43 55 E
Al Fātiḩ □, *Libya* **108 B4** 32 0N 21 0 E
Al Fāw, *Iraq* **97 D6** 30 0N 48 30 E
Al Faydamī, *Yemen* **99 C6** 16 25N 52 26 E
Al Fujayrah, *U.A.E.* **97 E8** 25 7N 56 18 E
Al Ghadaf, W. →, *Jordan* **103 D5** 31 26N 36 43 E
Al Ghammās, *Iraq* **96 D5** 31 45N 44 37 E
Al Gharīb, *Libya* **108 B4** 32 35N 21 11 E
Al Ghayḑah, *Yemen* **99 C6** 16 13N 52 11 E
Al Ghayḑah, *Yemen* **99 D5** 14 55N 50 0 E
Al Ghayl, *Yemen* **99 D5** 15 30N 50 54 E
Al Ghazālah, *Si. Arabia* **96 E4** 26 48N 41 19 E
Al Ḩadd, *Oman* **99 B7** 22 32N 59 48 E
Al Ḩaddār, *Si. Arabia* **98 B4** 21 58N 45 57 E
Al Ḩadīthah, *Iraq* **101 E10** 34 0N 41 13 E
Al Ḩadīthah, *Si. Arabia* **103 D6** 31 28N 37 8 E
Al Ḩaḑr, *Iraq* **101 E10** 35 35N 42 44 E
Al Hājānah, *Syria* **103 B5** 33 20N 36 33 E
Al Ḩajar al Gharbī, *Oman* **97 E8** 24 10N 56 15 E
Al Hallānīyah, *Oman* **99 C7** 17 30N 56 1 E
Al Hāmad, *Si. Arabia* **96 D3** 31 30N 39 30 E
Al Ḩamar, *Si. Arabia* **98 B4** 22 26N 46 12 E
Al Hamdāniyah, *Syria* **96 C3** 35 25N 36 50 E
Al Ḩamīdīyah, *Syria* **103 A4** 34 42N 35 57 E
Al Hammādah al Ḩamrā', *Libya* **108 C2** 29 30N 12 0 E
Al Ḩammār, *Iraq* **96 D5** 30 57N 46 51 E
Al Ḩamrā', *Si. Arabia* **96 E3** 24 2N 38 55 E
Al Ḩanākīyah, *Si. Arabia* **96 E4** 24 51N 40 31 E
Al Ḩarīq, *Si. Arabia* **98 B4** 23 29N 46 27 E
Al Harīr, W. →, *Syria* **103 C4** 32 44N 35 59 E
Al Harūj al Aswad, *Libya* **108 C3** 27 0N 17 10 E
Al Ḩasā, W. →, *Jordan* **103 D4** 31 4N 35 29 E
Al Ḩasakah, *Syria* **101 D9** 36 35N 40 45 E
Al Hāsikīyah, *Oman* **99 C6** 17 28N 55 36 E
Al Ḩasy, *Yemen* **99 D5** 14 3N 48 40 E
Al Ḩawrah, *Yemen* **98 D4** 13 50N 47 35 E
Al Ḩawţah, *Si. Arabia* **98 B4** 23 30N 47 0 E
Al Haydān, W. →, *Jordan* **103 D4** 31 29N 35 34 E
Al Ḩayy, *Iraq* **101 F12** 32 5N 46 5 E
Al Ḩijarah, *Asia* **96 D4** 30 0N 44 0 E
Al Ḩillah, *Iraq* **101 F11** 32 30N 44 25 E
Al Ḩillah, *Si. Arabia* **98 B4** 23 35N 46 50 E
Al Hindīyah, *Iraq* **101 F11** 32 30N 44 10 E
Al Hirmil, *Lebanon* **103 A5** 34 26N 36 24 E
Al Hoceïma, *Morocco* **110 A4** 35 8N 3 58W
Al Ḩudaydah, *Yemen* **98 D3** 14 50N 43 0 E
Al Ḩufrah, *Libya* **108 C2** 25 32N 14 1 E
Al Hufūf, *Si. Arabia* **97 E6** 25 25N 49 45 E
Al Ḩulwah, *Si. Arabia* **98 B4** 23 24N 46 48 E
Al Ḩumayḑah, *Si. Arabia* **96 D2** 29 14N 34 56 E
Al Ḩunayy, *Si. Arabia* **97 E6** 25 58N 48 45 E
Al Husayyāt, *Libya* **108 B4** 30 24N 20 37 E
Al 'Irqah, *Yemen* **98 D4** 13 39N 47 22 E
Al Īsāwīyah, *Si. Arabia* **96 D3** 30 43N 37 59 E
Al Ittihad = Madīnat ash Sha'b, *Yemen* **98 D4** 12 50N 45 0 E
Al Jabal al Akhḑar, *Libya* **108 B4** 32 30N 21 30 E
Al Jabal al Akhḑar □, *Libya* **108 B4** 32 30N 21 41 E
Al Jafr, *Jordan* **103 E5** 30 18N 36 14 E
Al Jāfūrah, *Si. Arabia* **97 E7** 25 0N 50 15 E
Al Jaghbūb, *Libya* **108 C4** 29 42N 24 38 E
Al Jahrah, *Kuwait* **96 D5** 29 25N 47 40 E
Al Jalāmīd, *Si. Arabia* **96 D3** 31 20N 40 6 E
Al Jamalīyah, *Qatar* **97 E6** 25 37N 51 5 E
Al Janūb □, *Lebanon* **103 B4** 33 20N 35 20 E
Al Jawf, *Libya* **108 D4** 24 10N 23 24 E

Al Jawf, *Si. Arabia* 96 D3 29 55N 39 40 E
Al Jazirah, *Iraq* 101 E10 33 30N 44 0 E
Al Jazirah, *Libya* 108 C4 26 10N 21 20 E
Al Jithāmīyah, *Si. Arabia* 96 E4 27 41N 41 43 E
Al Jubayl, *Si. Arabia* 97 E6 27 0N 49 50 E
Al Jubaylah, *Si. Arabia* 96 E5 24 55N 46 25 E
Al Jubb, *Si. Arabia* 96 E4 27 11N 42 17 E
Al Jufrah, *Libya* 108 C3 29 10N 16 0 E
Al Jufrah □, *Libya* 108 C3 27 30N 17 30 E
Al Jumūm, *Si. Arabia* 98 B2 21 37N 39 42 E
Al Junaynah, *Sudan* 109 F4 13 27N 22 45 E
Al Kabā'ish, *Iraq* 96 D5 30 58N 47 0 E
Al Kāmil, *Oman* 99 B7 22 13N 59 12 E
Al Karak, *Jordan* 103 D4 31 11N 35 42 E
Al Karak □, *Jordan* 103 E5 31 0N 36 0 E
Al Kāzim Tyah, *Iraq* 101 F11 33 22N 44 12 E
Al Khābūra, *Oman* 97 F8 23 57N 57 5 E
Al Khafji, *Si. Arabia* 97 E6 28 24N 48 29 E
Al Khalīl, *West Bank* 103 D4 31 32N 35 6 E
Al Khāliş, *Iraq* 101 F11 33 49N 44 32 E
Al Khamāsīn, *Si. Arabia* 98 B4 20 29N 44 46 E
Al Kharj, *Si. Arabia* 98 B4 24 0N 47 0 E
Al Kharsānīyah, *Si. Arabia* 97 E6 27 13N 49 18 E
Al Khaşab, *Oman* 97 E8 26 14N 56 15 E
Al Khāşirah, *Si. Arabia* 98 B3 23 30N 43 47 E
Al Khawr, *Qatar* 97 E6 25 41N 51 30 E
Al Khiḑr, *Iraq* 96 D5 31 12N 45 33 E
Al Khiyām, *Lebanon* 103 B4 33 20N 35 36 E
Al Khums, *Libya* 108 B2 32 40N 14 17 E
Al Khums □, *Libya* 108 B2 31 20N 14 10 E
Al Kiswah, *Syria* 103 B5 33 23N 36 14 E
Al Kūfah, *Iraq* 101 F11 32 2N 44 24 E
Al Kufrah, *Libya* 108 D4 24 17N 23 15 E
Al Kuhayfīyah, *Si. Arabia* 96 E4 27 12N 43 3 E
Al Kūt, *Iraq* 101 F11 32 30N 46 0 E
Al Kuwayt, *Kuwait* 96 D5 29 30N 48 0 E
Al Labwah, *Lebanon* 103 A5 34 11N 36 20 E
Al Lādhiqīyah, *Syria* 100 E6 35 30N 35 45 E
Al Līth, *Si. Arabia* 98 B3 20 9N 40 15 E
Al Liwā', *Oman* 97 E8 24 31N 56 36 E
Al Luḩayyah, *Yemen* 98 D3 15 45N 42 40 E
Al Madīnah, *Iraq* 96 D5 30 57N 47 16 E
Al Madīnah, *Si. Arabia* 96 E3 24 35N 39 52 E
Al Mafraq, *Jordan* 103 C5 32 17N 36 14 E
Al Maghārīm, *Yemen* 98 D4 15 1N 47 49 E
Al Mahbes, *W. Sahara* 110 C3 27 10N 9 50W
Al Maḩmūdīyah, *Iraq* 101 F11 33 3N 44 21 E
Al Majma'ah, *Si. Arabia* 96 E5 25 57N 45 22 E
Al Makhruq, W. →, *Jordan* 103 D6 31 28N 37 0 E
Al Makḩūl, *Si. Arabia* 96 E4 26 37N 42 39 E
Al Makīlī, *Libya* 108 B4 32 10N 22 17 E
Al Manāmah, *Bahrain* 97 E6 26 10N 50 30 E
Al Maqwa', *Kuwait* 96 D5 29 10N 47 59 E
Al Marj, *Libya* 108 B4 32 25N 20 30 E
Al Maţlā, *Kuwait* 96 D5 29 24N 47 40 E
Al Mawjib, W. →, *Jordan* 103 D4 31 28N 35 36 E
Al Mawşil, *Iraq* 101 D10 36 15N 43 5 E
Al Mayādin, *Syria* 101 E9 35 1N 40 27 E
Al Mazār, *Jordan* 103 D4 31 4N 35 41 E
Al Midhnab, *Si. Arabia* 96 E5 25 50N 44 18 E
Al Minā', *Lebanon* 103 A4 34 24N 35 49 E
Al Miqdādīyah, *Iraq* 101 E11 34 0N 45 0 E
Al Mubarraz, *Si. Arabia* 97 E6 25 30N 49 40 E
Al Mudawwarah, *Jordan* 103 F5 29 19N 36 0 E
Al Muḑaybī, *Oman* 99 B7 22 34N 58 7 E
Al Mughayrā', *U.A.E.* 97 E7 24 5N 53 32 E
Al Muḩarraq, *Bahrain* 97 E6 26 15N 50 40 E
Al Mukallā, *Yemen* 99 D5 14 33N 49 2 E
Al Mukhā, *Yemen* 98 D3 13 18N 43 15 E
Al Musayjīd, *Si. Arabia* 96 E3 24 5N 39 5 E
Al Musayyib, *Iraq* 101 F11 32 49N 44 20 E
Al Muwayh, *Si. Arabia* 106 C5 22 41N 41 37 E
Al Muwayliḩ, *Si. Arabia* 96 E2 27 40N 35 30 E
Al Owuho = Otukpa, *Nigeria* 113 D6 7 9N 7 41 E
Al Qaddāḩīyah, *Libya* 108 B3 31 15N 15 9 E
Al Qaḑīmah, *Si. Arabia* 98 B2 22 20N 39 13 E
Al Qaḩmah, *Si. Arabia* 98 C3 18 0N 41 41 E
Al Qā'im, *Iraq* 101 E9 34 21N 41 7 E
Al Qalībah, *Si. Arabia* 96 D3 28 24N 37 42 E
Al Qāmishlī, *Syria* 101 D9 37 2N 41 14 E
Al Qaryah ash Sharqīyah, *Libya* 108 B2 30 28N 13 40 E
Al Qaryatayn, *Syria* 103 A6 34 12N 37 13 E
Al Qaşabát, *Libya* 108 B2 32 39N 14 1 E
Al Qaşīm, *Si. Arabia* 96 E4 26 0N 43 0 E
Al Qaţ'ā, *Syria* 101 E9 34 40N 40 48 E
Al Qaţīf, *Si. Arabia* 97 E6 26 35N 50 0 E
Al Qaţn, *Yemen* 99 D5 15 51N 48 26 E
Al Qatrānah, *Jordan* 103 D5 31 12N 36 6 E
Al Qaţrūn, *Libya* 108 D3 24 56N 15 3 E
Al Qayşūmah, *Si. Arabia* 96 D5 28 20N 46 7 E
Al Qiblīyah, *Oman* 99 C7 17 30N 56 20 E
Al Quds = Jerusalem, *Israel* 103 D4 31 47N 35 10 E
Al Qunayţirah, *Syria* 103 C4 32 55N 35 45 E
Al Qunfudhah, *Si. Arabia* 98 C3 19 3N 41 4 E
Al Qurḩ, *Yemen* 99 C5 16 44N 51 29 E
Al Qurnah, *Iraq* 96 D5 31 1N 47 25 E
Al Quşayr, *Iraq* 96 D5 30 39N 45 50 E
Al Quşayr, *Syria* 103 A5 34 31N 36 34 E
Al Quţayfah, *Syria* 103 B5 33 44N 36 36 E
Al Quway'īyah, *Si. Arabia* 98 A4 24 3N 45 15 E
Al 'Ubaylah, *Si. Arabia* 99 B5 21 59N 50 57 E
Al 'Uḑaylīyah, *Si. Arabia* 97 E6 25 8N 49 18 E
Al 'Ulā, *Si. Arabia* 96 E3 26 35N 38 0 E
Al 'Ulayyah, *Si. Arabia* 98 C3 19 39N 41 54 E
Al Uqaylah ash Sharqīgah, *Libya* 108 B3 30 12N 19 10 E
Al 'Uqayr, *Si. Arabia* 97 E6 25 40N 50 15 E
Al 'Uwaynid, *Si. Arabia* 96 E5 24 50N 46 0 E
Al 'Uwayqīlah, *Si. Arabia* 96 D4 30 30N 42 10 E
Al 'Uyūn, *Ḩijāz, Si. Arabia* 96 E3 24 33N 39 35 E
Al 'Uyūn, *Najd, Si. Arabia* 96 E4 26 30N 43 50 E
Al 'Uzayr, *Iraq* 96 D5 31 19N 47 25 E
Al Wajh, *Si. Arabia* 96 E3 26 10N 36 30 E
Al Wakrah, *Qatar* 97 E6 25 10N 51 40 E
Al Waqbah, *Si. Arabia* 96 D5 28 48N 45 33 E
Al Wari'āh, *Si. Arabia* 96 E5 27 51N 47 25 E
Al Wāţīyah, *Libya* 108 B2 32 28N 11 57 E
Ala, *Italy* 44 C8 45 45N 11 0 E
Ala-Buka, *Kyrgyzstan* 65 C5 41 23N 71 30 E
Ala Dağ, *Turkey* 96 B2 37 44N 35 9 E
Ala Dağları, *Turkey* 101 C10 39 15N 43 33 E
Ala Tau Shankou = Dzungarian Gates, *Asia* 68 B3 45 0N 82 0 E
Alabama □, *U.S.A.* 149 J2 33 0N 87 0W
Alabama →, *U.S.A.* 149 K2 31 8N 87 57W
Alabaster, *U.S.A.* 149 J2 33 15N 86 49W
Alabat I., *Phil.* 80 D4 14 7N 122 3 E
Alabel, *Phil.* 81 H5 6 4N 125 16 E
Alabule →, *Papua N. G.* 132 E4 8 31 S 146 56 E
Alaca, *Turkey* 100 B6 40 10N 34 51 E
Alacaatlı, *Turkey* 49 B10 39 15N 28 3 E
Alaçam, *Turkey* 100 B6 41 36N 35 36 E
Alaçam Dağları, *Turkey* 49 B10 39 18N 28 49 E
Alaçatı, *Turkey* 49 C8 38 15N 26 22 E
Alachua, *U.S.A.* 152 F7 29 47N 82 30W
Alaejos, *Spain* 42 D5 41 18N 5 13W
Alaérma, *Greece* 38 E11 36 9N 27 57 E
Alagir, *Russia* 61 J7 43 3N 44 14 E
Alagna Valsésia, *Italy* 44 C4 45 51N 7 56 E
Alagoa Grande, *Brazil* 170 C4 7 3 S 35 35W
Alagoas □, *Brazil* 170 C4 9 0 S 36 0W
Alagoinhas, *Brazil* 171 D4 12 7 S 38 20W
Alagón, *Spain* 40 D3 41 46N 1 12W
Alagón →, *Spain* 42 F4 39 44N 6 53W
Alai Range, *Asia* 65 D5 39 45N 72 0 E
Alaior, *Spain* 38 B5 39 57N 4 8 E
Alajero, *Canary Is.* 9 e1 28 3N 17 13W
Alajuela, *Costa Rica* 164 D3 10 2N 84 8W
Alakamisy, *Madag.* 117 C8 21 19 S 47 14 E
Alakanuk, *U.S.A.* 144 E6 62 41N 164 37W
Alaknanda →, *India* 93 D8 30 8N 78 36 E
Alakurtti, *Russia* 56 A5 67 0N 30 30 E
Alalakeiki Channel, *U.S.A.* 145 C5 20 30N 156 30W
Alalapura, *Surinam* 169 C6 2 20N 56 25W
Alalaú →, *Brazil* 169 D5 0 30 S 61 9W
Alamarvdasht, *Iran* 97 E7 27 37N 52 59 E
Alamata, *Ethiopia* 107 E4 12 25N 39 33 E
Alameda, *Calif., U.S.A.* 160 H4 37 46N 122 15W
Alameda, *N. Mex., U.S.A.* 159 J10 35 11N 106 37W
Alaminos, *Phil.* 80 C2 16 10N 119 59 E
Alamo, *Ga., U.S.A.* 152 C7 32 9N 82 47W
Alamo, *Nev., U.S.A.* 161 J11 37 22N 115 10W
Alamo Crossing, *U.S.A.* 161 L13 34 16N 113 33W
Alamogordo, *U.S.A.* 159 K11 32 54N 105 57W
Alamos, *Mexico* 162 B3 27 0N 109 0W
Alamosa, *U.S.A.* 159 H11 37 28N 105 52W
Alampur, *India* 95 G4 15 55N 78 6 E
Åland, *Finland* 15 F19 60 15N 20 0 E
Aland, *India* 94 F3 17 36N 76 35 E
Alandroal, *Portugal* 43 G3 38 41N 7 24W
Ålands hav, *Sweden* 15 F18 60 0N 19 30 E
Alandur, *India* 95 H5 13 0N 80 15 E
Alange, Presa de, *Spain* 43 G4 38 45N 6 18W
Alania = North Ossetia □, *Russia* 61 J7 43 30N 44 30 E
Alanís, *Spain* 43 G5 38 3N 5 43W
Alanya, *Turkey* 100 D5 36 38N 32 0 E
Alaotra, Farihin', *Madag.* 117 B8 17 30 S 48 30 E
Alapaha, *U.S.A.* 152 D6 31 23N 83 13W
Alapayevsk, *Russia* 64 C8 57 52N 61 42 E
Alappuzha = Alleppey, *India* 95 K3 9 30N 76 28 E
Alar del Rey, *Spain* 42 C6 42 38N 4 20W
Alaraz, *Spain* 42 E5 40 45N 5 17W
Alarcón, Embalse de, *Spain* 40 F2 39 36N 2 10W
Alarobia-Vohiposa, *Madag.* 117 C8 20 59 S 47 9 E
Alaşehir, *Turkey* 49 C10 38 23N 28 30 E
Alaska □, *U.S.A.* 144 E9 64 0N 154 0W
Alaska, G. of, *Pac. Oc.* 144 G11 58 0N 145 0W
Alaska Peninsula, *U.S.A.* 144 J8 56 0N 159 0W
Alaska Range, *U.S.A.* 144 F10 62 50N 151 0W
Alássio, *Italy* 44 E5 44 0N 8 10 E
Älät, *Azerbaijan* 61 L9 39 58N 49 25 E
Alat, *Uzbekistan* 65 D1 39 24N 63 47 E
Alatri, *Italy* 45 G10 41 43N 13 21 E
Alatyr, *Russia* 60 C8 54 55N 46 35 E
Alatyr →, *Russia* 60 C8 54 52N 46 36 E
Alausi, *Ecuador* 168 D2 2 0 S 78 50W
Álava □, *Spain* 40 C2 42 48N 2 28W
Alava, C., *U.S.A.* 158 B1 48 10N 124 44W
Alaverdi, *Armenia* 61 K7 41 15N 44 37 E
Alavus, *Finland* 15 E20 62 35N 23 36 E
Alawoona, *Australia* 128 C4 34 45 S 140 30 E
'Alayh, *Lebanon* 103 B4 33 46N 35 33 E
Alaykuu = Kögart, *Kyrgyzstan* 65 C7 40 15N 74 25 E
Alazani →, *Azerbaijan* 61 K8 41 5N 46 40 E
Alba, *Italy* 44 D5 44 42N 8 2 E
Alba □, *Romania* 53 D8 46 10N 23 30 E
Alba Adriática, *Italy* 45 F10 42 50N 13 56 E
Alba de Tormes, *Spain* 42 E5 40 50N 5 30W
Alba-Iulia, *Romania* 53 D8 46 8N 23 39 E
Albac, *Romania* 52 D7 46 28N 22 58 E
Albacete, *Spain* 41 F3 39 0N 1 50W
Albacete □, *Spain* 41 G3 38 50N 2 0W
Albacutya, L., *Australia* 128 C4 35 45 S 141 58 E
Ålbæk, *Denmark* 17 G4 57 36N 10 25 E
Ålbæk Bugt, *Denmark* 17 G4 57 35N 10 40 E
Albaida, *Spain* 41 G4 38 51N 0 31W
Albalate de las Nogueras, *Spain* 40 E2 40 22N 2 18W
Albalate del Arzobispo, *Spain* 40 D4 41 6N 0 31W
Alban, *France* 28 E6 43 53N 2 28 E
Albanel, L., *Canada* 140 B5 50 55N 73 12W
Albania ■, *Europe* 50 E4 41 0N 20 0 E
Albano Laziale, *Italy* 45 G9 41 44N 12 39 E
Albany, *Australia* 125 G2 35 1 S 117 58 E
Albany, *Ga., U.S.A.* 152 D5 31 35N 84 10W
Albany, *Ind., U.S.A.* 157 D11 40 18N 85 14W
Albany, *Mo., U.S.A.* 156 D2 40 15N 94 20W
Albany, *N.Y., U.S.A.* 151 D11 42 39N 73 45W
Albany, *Oreg., U.S.A.* 158 D2 44 38N 123 6W
Albany, *Tex., U.S.A.* 155 J5 32 44N 99 18W
Albany, *Wis., U.S.A.* 156 B7 42 43N 89 26W
Albany →, *Canada* 140 B3 52 17N 81 31W
Albardón, *Argentina* 174 C2 31 20 S 68 30W
Albarracín, *Spain* 40 E3 40 25N 1 26W
Albarracín, Sierra de, *Spain* 40 E3 40 30N 1 30W
Albatera, *Spain* 41 G4 38 11N 0 52W
Albatross B., *Australia* 126 A3 12 45 S 141 30 E
Albatross Pt., *N.Z.* 130 E3 38 7 S 174 44 E
Albay □, *Phil.* 80 E4 13 13N 123 33 E
Albegna →, *Italy* 45 F8 42 30N 11 11 E
Albemarle, *U.S.A.* 149 H5 35 21N 80 11W
Albemarle, Pta., *Ecuador* 172 a 0 11N 91 21W
Albemarle Sd., *U.S.A.* 149 H7 36 5N 76 0W
Albenga, *Italy* 44 D5 44 3N 8 13 E
Alberche →, *Spain* 42 F6 39 58N 4 46W
Alberdi, *Paraguay* 174 B4 26 14 S 58 20W
Albères, Mts., *France* 28 F6 42 28N 2 56 E
Ålberga, *Sweden* 17 F10 58 44N 16 35 E
Albersdorf, *Germany* 30 A5 54 8N 9 17 E
Albert, *France* 27 C9 50 0N 2 38 E
Albert, L., *Africa* 118 B3 1 30N 31 0 E
Albert, L., *Australia* 128 C3 35 30 S 139 10 E
Albert Edward, Mt., *Papua N. G.* 132 E4 8 20 S 147 24 E
Albert Edward Ra., *Australia* 124 C4 18 17 S 127 57 E
Albert Lea, *U.S.A.* 154 D8 43 39N 93 22W
Albert Nile →, *Uganda* 118 B3 3 36N 32 2 E
Albert Town, *Bahamas* 165 B5 22 37N 74 33W
Alberta □, *Canada* 142 C6 54 40N 115 0W
Alberti, *Argentina* 174 D3 35 1 S 60 16W
Albertinia, *S. Africa* 116 E3 34 11 S 21 34 E
Albertirsa, *Hungary* 52 C4 47 14N 19 37 E
Alberton, *Canada* 141 C7 46 50N 64 0W
Albertville = Kalemie, *Dem. Rep. of the Congo* 118 D2 5 55 S 29 9 E
Albertville, *France* 29 C10 45 40N 6 22 E
Albertville, *U.S.A.* 149 H2 34 16N 86 13W
Albi, *France* 28 E6 43 56N 2 9 E
Albia, *U.S.A.* 156 C4 41 2N 92 48W
Albina, *Surinam* 169 B7 5 37N 54 15W
Albina, Ponta, *Angola* 116 B1 15 52 S 11 44 E
Albino, *Italy* 44 C6 45 46N 9 47 E
Albion, *Ill., U.S.A.* 157 F8 38 23N 88 4W
Albion, *Ind., U.S.A.* 157 C11 41 24N 85 25W
Albion, *Mich., U.S.A.* 157 B12 42 15N 84 45W
Albion, *Nebr., U.S.A.* 154 E6 41 42N 98 0W
Albion, *Pa., U.S.A.* 150 E4 41 53N 80 22W
Albocácer, *Spain* 40 E5 40 21N 0 1 E
Albolote, *Spain* 43 H7 37 14N 3 39W
Alborán, *Medit. S.* 43 K7 35 57N 3 0W
Alborea, *Spain* 41 F3 39 17N 1 24W
Ålborg, *Denmark* 17 G3 57 2N 9 54 E
Ålborg Bugt, *Denmark* 17 H4 56 50N 10 35 E
Alborz, Reshteh-ye Kūhhā-ye, *Iran* 97 C7 36 0N 52 0 E
Albosaggia, *Italy* 33 D9 46 8N 9 51 E
Albox, *Spain* 41 H2 37 23N 2 8W
Albuera, *Phil.* 81 F5 10 55N 124 42 E
Albufeira, *Portugal* 43 H2 37 5N 8 15W
Albula →, *Switz.* 33 C8 46 38N 9 28 E
Albuñol, *Spain* 43 J7 36 48N 3 11W
Albuquerque, *Brazil* 173 D6 19 23 S 57 26W
Albuquerque, *U.S.A.* 159 J10 35 5N 106 39W
Albuquerque, Cayos de, *Caribbean* 164 D3 12 10N 81 50W
Alburg, *U.S.A.* 151 B11 44 59N 73 18W
Alburno, Mte., *Italy* 47 B8 40 33N 15 17 E
Alburquerque, *Spain* 43 F4 39 15N 6 59W
Albury = Albury-Wodonga, *Australia* 129 D7 36 3 S 146 56 E
Albury-Wodonga, *Australia* 129 D7 36 3 S 146 56 E
Alcácer do Sal, *Portugal* 43 G2 38 22N 8 33W
Alcáçovas, *Portugal* 43 G2 38 23N 8 9W
Alcala, *Phil.* 80 C3 17 54N 121 39 E
Alcalá de Chivert, *Spain* 40 E5 40 19N 0 13 E
Alcalá de Guadaira, *Spain* 43 H5 37 20N 5 50W
Alcalá de Henares, *Spain* 42 E7 40 28N 3 22W
Alcalá de los Gazules, *Spain* 43 J5 36 29N 5 43W
Alcalá del Júcar, *Spain* 41 F3 39 12N 1 26W
Alcalá del Río, *Spain* 43 H5 37 31N 5 59W
Alcalá del Valle, *Spain* 43 J5 36 54N 5 10W
Alcalá la Real, *Spain* 43 H7 37 27N 3 57W
Álcamo, *Italy* 46 E5 37 59N 12 55 E
Alcanadre, *Spain* 40 C2 42 24N 2 7W
Alcanadre →, *Spain* 40 D4 41 43N 0 12W
Alcanar, *Spain* 40 E5 40 33N 0 28 E
Alcanede, *Portugal* 43 F2 39 25N 8 49W
Alcanena, *Portugal* 43 F2 39 27N 8 40W
Alcañices, *Spain* 42 D4 41 41N 6 21W
Alcañiz, *Spain* 40 D4 41 2N 0 8W
Alcântara, *Brazil* 170 B3 2 20 S 44 30W
Alcántara, *Spain* 42 F4 39 41N 6 57W
Alcántara, Embalse de, *Spain* 42 F4 39 44N 6 50W
Alcantarilla, *Spain* 41 H3 37 59N 1 12W
Alcaracejos, *Spain* 43 G6 38 24N 4 58W
Alcaraz, *Spain* 41 G2 38 40N 2 29W
Alcaraz, Sierra de, *Spain* 41 G2 38 40N 2 20W
Alcaudete, *Spain* 43 H6 37 35N 4 5W
Alcázar de San Juan, *Spain* 41 F1 39 24N 3 12W
Alcedo, Volcán, *Ecuador* 172 a 0 24 S 91 6W
Alchevsk, *Ukraine* 59 H10 48 30N 38 45 E
Alcira = Alzira, *Spain* 41 F4 39 9N 0 30W
Alcobaça, *Portugal* 43 F2 39 32N 8 58W
Alcobendas, *Spain* 42 E7 40 32N 3 38W
Alcolea del Pinar, *Spain* 40 D2 41 2N 2 28W
Alcoma, *U.S.A.* 153 H8 27 54N 81 29W
Alcora, *Spain* 40 E4 40 5N 0 14W
Alcorcón, *Spain* 42 E7 40 20N 3 50W
Alcoutim, *Portugal* 43 H3 37 25N 7 28W
Alcova, *U.S.A.* 158 E10 42 34N 106 43W
Alcoy, *Spain* 41 G4 38 43N 0 30W
Alcubierre, Sierra de, *Spain* 40 D4 41 45N 0 22W
Alcublas, *Spain* 40 F4 39 48N 0 43W
Alcúdia, *Spain* 38 B4 39 51N 3 7 E
Alcúdia, B. d', *Spain* 38 B4 39 47N 3 15 E
Alcudia, Sierra de la, *Spain* 43 G6 38 34N 4 30W
Aldabra Is., *Seychelles* 105 G8 9 22 S 46 28 E
Aldama, *Mexico* 163 C5 23 0N 98 4W
Aldan, *Russia* 67 D13 58 40N 125 30 E
Aldan →, *Russia* 67 C13 63 28N 129 35 E
Aldea, Pta. de la, *Canary Is.* 9 e1 28 0N 15 50W
Aldeburgh, *U.K.* 21 E9 52 10N 1 37 E
Alden, *Norway* 18 C1 61 19N 4 45 E
Alder Pk., *U.S.A.* 160 K5 35 53N 121 22W
Alderney, *U.K.* 21 H5 49 42N 2 11W
Aldershot, *U.K.* 21 F7 51 15N 0 44W
Aldinga Beach, *Australia* 128 C3 35 17 S 138 27 E
Åled, *Sweden* 17 H6 56 44N 12 57 E
Aledo, *U.S.A.* 156 C6 41 12N 90 45W
Alefa, *Ethiopia* 107 E4 11 55N 36 55 E
Aleg, *Mauritania* 112 B2 17 3N 13 55W
Alegranza, *Canary Is.* 110 C2 29 23N 13 32W
Alegranza, I., *Canary Is.* 9 e2 29 23N 13 32W
Alegre, *Brazil* 171 F3 20 50 S 41 30W
Alegrete, *Brazil* 175 B4 29 40 S 56 0W
Aleisk, *Russia* 66 D9 52 40N 83 0 E
Aleknagik, *U.S.A.* 144 G8 59 17N 158 36W
Aleksandriya = Oleksandriya, *Kirovohrad, Ukraine* 59 H7 48 42N 33 3 E
Aleksandriya = Oleksandriya, *Rivne, Ukraine* 59 G4 50 37N 26 19 E
Aleksandriyskaya, *Russia* 61 J8 43 58N 47 14 E
Aleksandrov, *Russia* 58 D10 56 23N 38 44 E
Aleksandrov Gay, *Russia* 60 E9 50 9N 48 34 E
Aleksandrovac, *Serbia, Yug.* 50 C5 43 28N 21 3 E
Aleksandrovac, *Serbia, Yug.* 50 B5 44 28N 21 13 E
Aleksandrovka = Oleksandrovka, *Ukraine* 59 H7 48 55N 32 20 E
Aleksandrovo, *Bulgaria* 51 C8 43 14N 24 51 E
Aleksandrovsk, *Russia* 64 B6 59 9N 57 33 E
Aleksandrovsk-Sakhalinskiy, *Russia* 67 D15 50 50N 142 20 E
Aleksandrów Kujawski, *Poland* 55 F5 52 53N 18 43 E
Aleksandrów Łódźki, *Poland* 55 G6 51 49N 19 17 E
Alekseyevka, *Samara, Russia* 60 D10 52 35N 51 17 E
Alekseyevka, *Voronezh, Russia* 59 G10 50 43N 38 40 E
Aleksin, *Russia* 58 E9 54 31N 37 9 E
Aleksinac, *Serbia, Yug.* 50 C5 43 31N 21 42 E
Além Paraíba, *Brazil* 171 F3 21 52 S 42 41W
Alemania, *Argentina* 174 B2 25 40 S 65 30W
Alemania, *Chile* 174 B2 25 10 S 69 55W
Alen, *Eq. Guin.* 114 B2 1 58N 11 19 E
Alençon, *France* 26 D7 48 27N 0 4 E
Alenuihaha Channel, *U.S.A.* 145 C6 20 30N 156 0W
Alépé, *Ivory C.* 112 D4 5 29N 3 40W
Aleppo = Ḩalab, *Syria* 100 D7 36 10N 37 15 E
Aléria, *France* 29 F13 42 5N 9 26 E
Aleru, *India* 94 F4 17 39N 79 3 E
Alès, *France* 29 D8 44 9N 4 5 E
Aleşd, *Romania* 52 C7 47 3N 22 22 E
Alessándria, *Italy* 44 D5 44 54N 8 37 E
Ålestrup, *Denmark* 17 H3 56 42N 9 29 E
Ålesund, *Norway* 15 E12 62 28N 6 12 E
Alet-les-Bains, *France* 28 F6 42 59N 2 14 E
Aletschhorn, *Switz.* 32 D6 46 28N 8 0 E
Aleutian Is., *Pac. Oc.* 138 C2 52 0N 175 0W
Aleutian Range, *U.S.A.* 144 G9 60 0N 154 0W
Aleutian Trench, *Pac. Oc.* 134 C10 48 0N 180 0 E
Alexander, *Ga., U.S.A.* 152 B8 33 1N 81 53W
Alexander, *N. Dak., U.S.A.* 154 B3 47 51N 103 39W
Alexander, C., *Solomon Is.* 133 L9 6 34 S 156 32 E
Alexander, Mt., *Australia* 125 E3 28 58 S 120 16 E
Alexander Arch., *U.S.A.* 144 J14 56 0N 136 0W
Alexander Bay, *S. Africa* 116 D2 28 40 S 16 30 E
Alexander City, *U.S.A.* 152 C4 32 56N 85 58W
Alexander I., *Antarctica* 7 C17 69 0 S 70 0W
Alexandra, *Australia* 129 D6 37 8 S 145 40 E
Alexandra, *N.Z.* 131 F4 45 14 S 169 25 E
Alexandra Channel, *Burma* 95 G11 14 7N 93 13 E
Alexandra Falls, *Canada* 142 A5 60 29N 116 18W
Alexandria = El Iskandarîya, *Egypt* 106 H7 31 13N 29 58 E
Alexandria, *B.C., Canada* 142 C4 52 35N 122 27W
Alexandria, *Ont., Canada* 140 C5 45 19N 74 38W
Alexandria, *Romania* 53 G10 43 57N 25 24 E
Alexandria, *S. Africa* 116 E4 33 38 S 26 28 E
Alexandria, *U.K.* 22 F4 55 59N 4 35W
Alexandria, *Ind., U.S.A.* 157 D11 40 16N 85 41W
Alexandria, *Ky., U.S.A.* 157 F12 38 58N 84 23W
Alexandria, *La., U.S.A.* 155 K8 31 18N 92 27W
Alexandria, *Minn., U.S.A.* 154 C7 45 53N 95 22W
Alexandria, *Mo., U.S.A.* 156 D5 40 27N 91 28W
Alexandria, *S. Dak., U.S.A.* 154 D6 43 39N 97 47W
Alexandria, *Va., U.S.A.* 148 F7 38 48N 77 3W
Alexandria Bay, *U.S.A.* 151 B9 44 20N 75 55W
Alexandrina, L., *Australia* 128 C3 35 25 S 139 10 E
Alexandroúpolis, *Greece* 51 F9 40 50N 25 54 E
Alexis, *U.S.A.* 156 C6 41 4N 90 33W
Alexis →, *Canada* 141 B8 52 33N 56 8W
Alexis Creek, *Canada* 142 C4 52 10N 123 20W
Alfabia, *Spain* 38 B3 39 44N 2 44 E
Alfambra, *Spain* 40 E3 40 33N 1 5W
Alfândega da Fé, *Portugal* 42 D4 41 20N 6 59W
Alfaro, *Spain* 40 C3 42 10N 1 50W
Alfatar, *Bulgaria* 51 C11 43 59N 27 13 E
Alfaz del Pi, *Spain* 41 G4 38 35N 0 5W
Alfeld, *Germany* 30 D5 51 59N 9 50 E
Alfenas, *Brazil* 175 A6 21 20 S 46 10W
Alfiós →, *Greece* 48 D3 37 40N 21 33 E
Alföld, *Hungary* 52 D5 46 30N 20 0 E
Alfonsine, *Italy* 45 D9 44 30N 12 3 E
Alfonso XIII = Quezon, *Phil.* 81 G1 9 15N 117 59 E
Alford, *Aberds., U.K.* 22 D6 57 14N 2 41W
Alford, *Lincs., U.K.* 20 D8 53 15N 0 10 E
Alford, *U.S.A.* 152 E4 30 42N 85 24W
Ålfotbreen, *Norway* 18 C2 61 45N 5 39 E
Ålfoten, *Norway* 18 C2 61 51N 5 41 E
Alfred, *Maine, U.S.A.* 151 C14 43 29N 70 43W
Alfred, *N.Y., U.S.A.* 150 D7 42 16N 77 48W
Alfredton, *N.Z.* 130 G4 40 41 S 175 54 E
Alfreton, *U.K.* 20 D6 53 6N 1 24W
Alfta, *Sweden* 16 C10 61 21N 16 4 E
Alga, *Kazakstan* 57 E10 49 53N 57 20 E
Algaida, *Spain* 38 B3 39 33N 2 53 E
Algar, *Spain* 43 J5 36 40N 5 39W
Ålgård, *Norway* 15 G11 58 46N 5 53 E
Algarinejo, *Spain* 43 H6 37 19N 4 9W
Algarve, *Portugal* 43 J2 36 58N 8 20W
Algeciras, *Spain* 43 J5 36 9N 5 28W
Algemesí, *Spain* 41 F4 39 11N 0 27W
Alger, *Algeria* 111 A5 36 42N 3 8 E
Algeria ■, *Africa* 111 C5 28 30N 2 0 E
Alghero, *Italy* 46 B1 40 33N 8 19 E
Älghult, *Sweden* 17 G9 57 0N 15 35 E
Algiers = Alger, *Algeria* 111 A5 36 42N 3 8 E
Algoa B., *S. Africa* 116 E4 33 50 S 25 45 E
Algodonales, *Spain* 43 J5 36 54N 5 24W
Algodor →, *Spain* 42 F7 39 55N 3 53W
Algoma, *U.S.A.* 148 C2 44 36N 87 26W
Algona, *U.S.A.* 156 A2 43 4N 94 14W
Algonac, *U.S.A.* 150 D2 42 37N 82 32W
Algonquin Prov. Park, *Canada* 140 C4 45 50N 78 30W
Alhama de Almería, *Spain* 43 J8 36 57N 2 34W
Alhama de Aragón, *Spain* 40 D3 41 18N 1 54W
Alhama de Granada, *Spain* 43 H7 37 0N 3 59W
Alhama de Murcia, *Spain* 41 H3 37 51N 1 25W
Alhambra, *U.S.A.* 161 L8 34 8N 118 6W
Alhaurín el Grande, *Spain* 43 J6 36 39N 4 41W
Alhucemas = Al Hoceïma, *Morocco* 110 A4 35 8N 3 58W
'Alī al Gharbī, *Iraq* 101 F12 32 30N 46 45 E
'Alī ash Sharqī, *Iraq* 101 F12 32 7N 46 44 E
Äli Bayramlı, *Azerbaijan* 61 L9 39 59N 48 52 E
'Alī Khēl, *Afghan.* 91 B3 33 57N 69 43 E
Ali Sahîh, *Djibouti* 107 E5 11 10N 42 44 E
Alī Shāh, *Iran* 96 B5 38 9N 45 50 E
Ália, *Italy* 46 E6 37 47N 13 43 E
'Alīābād, *Khorāsān, Iran* 97 C8 32 30N 57 30 E
'Alīābād, *Kordestān, Iran* 96 C5 35 4N 46 58 E
'Alīābād, *Yazd, Iran* 97 D7 31 41N 53 49 E
Aliaga, *Spain* 40 E4 40 40N 0 42W
Aliağa, *Turkey* 49 C8 38 47N 26 59 E
Aliákmon →, *Greece* 50 F6 40 30N 22 36 E
Alibag, *India* 94 E1 18 38N 72 56 E
Alibo, *Ethiopia* 107 F4 9 52N 37 5 E
Alibori →, *Benin* 113 C5 11 56N 3 17 E
Alibunar, *Serbia, Yug.* 52 E5 45 5N 20 57 E
Alicante, *Spain* 41 G4 38 23N 0 30W
Alicante □, *Spain* 41 G4 38 30N 0 37W
Alice, *S. Africa* 116 E4 32 48 S 26 55 E
Alice, *U.S.A.* 155 M5 27 45N 98 5W
Alice →, *Queens., Australia* 126 C3 24 2 S 144 50 E
Alice →, *Queens., Australia* 126 B3 15 35 S 142 20 E
Alice →, *Papua N. G.* 132 D1 6 10 S 141 8 E
Alice, Punta, *Italy* 47 C10 39 24N 17 9 E
Alice Arm, *Canada* 142 B3 55 29N 129 31W
Alice Springs, *Australia* 126 C1 23 40 S 133 50 E
Alicedale, *S. Africa* 116 E4 33 15 S 26 4 E
Aliceville, *U.S.A.* 149 J1 33 8N 88 9W
Alichur, *Tajikistan* 65 E6 37 45N 73 33 E
Alicia, *Bohol, Phil.* 81 G5 9 54N 124 26 E
Alicia, *Isabela, Phil.* 80 C3 16 46N 121 42 E
Alicudi, *Italy* 47 D7 38 33N 14 20 E
Aliganj, *India* 93 F8 27 30N 79 10 E
Aligarh, *Raj., India* 92 G7 25 55N 76 15 E
Aligarh, *Ut. P., India* 92 F8 27 55N 78 10 E
Alīgūdarz, *Iran* 97 C6 33 25N 49 45 E
Alijó, *Portugal* 42 D3 41 16N 7 27W
Alikanás, *Greece* 39 D2 37 51N 20 47 E
Alima →, *Congo* 114 C3 1 35 S 16 37 E
Alimnía, *Greece* 38 E11 36 16N 27 43 E
Alimodian, *Phil.* 81 F4 10 49N 122 26 E
Alindao, *C.A.R.* 114 A4 5 2N 21 13 E
Alingsås, *Sweden* 17 G6 57 56N 12 31 E
Alipur, *Pakistan* 92 E4 29 25N 70 55 E
Alipur Duar, *India* 90 B2 26 30N 89 35 E
Aliquippa, *U.S.A.* 150 F4 40 37N 80 15W
Alishan, *Taiwan* 77 F13 23 31N 120 48 E
Aliste →, *Spain* 42 D5 41 34N 5 58W
Alitus = Alytus, *Lithuania* 15 J21 54 24N 24 3 E
Alivérion, *Greece* 48 C6 38 24N 24 2 E
Aliwal North, *S. Africa* 116 E4 30 45 S 26 45 E
Alix, *Canada* 142 C6 52 24N 113 11W
Aljezur, *Portugal* 43 H2 37 18N 8 49W
Aljustrel, *Portugal* 43 H2 37 55N 8 10W
Alkamari, *Niger* 113 C7 13 27N 11 10 E
Alkmaar, *Neths.* 24 B4 52 37N 4 45 E
All American Canal, *U.S.A.* 159 K6 32 45N 115 15W
Allacapan, *Phil.* 80 B3 18 15N 121 35 E
Allada, *Benin* 113 D5 6 41N 2 9 E
Allagadda, *India* 95 G4 15 8N 78 30 E
Allagash →, *U.S.A.* 149 B11 47 5N 69 3W
Allah Dad, *Pakistan* 92 G2 25 38N 67 34 E
Allahabad, *India* 93 G9 25 25N 81 58 E
Allakaket, *U.S.A.* 144 C9 66 34N 152 39W
Allal Tazi, *Morocco* 110 B3 34 30N 6 20W
Allan, *Canada* 143 C7 51 53N 106 4W
Allanche, *France* 28 C6 45 14N 2 57 E
Allanmyo, *Burma* 90 F5 19 30N 95 17 E
Allanridge, *S. Africa* 116 D4 27 45 S 26 40 E
Allansford, *Australia* 128 E5 38 26 S 142 39 E
Allanton, *N.Z.* 131 F5 45 55 S 170 15 E
Allaqi, Wadi →, *Egypt* 106 C3 23 7N 32 47 E
Allariz, *Spain* 42 C3 42 11N 7 50W
Allassac, *France* 28 C5 45 15N 1 29 E
Allatoona L., *U.S.A.* 152 A5 34 10N 84 44W
Ålleberg, *Sweden* 17 F7 58 8N 13 36 E
Allegan, *U.S.A.* 157 B11 42 32N 85 51W

Allegany, U.S.A. 150 D6 42 6N 78 30W
Allegheny →, U.S.A. 150 F5 40 27N 80 1W
Allegheny Mts., U.S.A. 148 G6 38 15N 80 10W
Allegheny Reservoir, U.S.A. 150 E6 41 50N 79 0W
Allègre, France 28 C7 45 12N 3 41 E
Allègre, P., Guadeloupe 164 b 16 22N 61 46W
Allen, Argentina 176 A3 38 58 S 67 50W
Allen, Phil. 80 E5 12 30N 124 17 E
Allen, Bog of, Ireland 23 C5 53 15N 7 0W
Allen, L., Ireland 23 B3 54 8N 8 4W
Allendale, U.S.A. 152 B8 33 1N 81 18W
Allende, Mexico 162 B4 28 20N 100 50W
Allensbach, Germany 33 A8 47 43N 9 4 E
Allentown, U.S.A. 151 F9 40 37N 75 29W
Allentsteig, Austria 34 C8 48 41N 15 20 E
Alleppey, India 95 K3 9 30N 76 28 E
Allepuz, Spain 40 E4 40 29N 0 44W
Aller →, Germany 30 C5 52 56N 9 12 E
Alleynes B., Barbados 165 g 13 13N 59 39W
Alliance, Surinam 169 B7 5 50N 54 50W
Alliance, Nebr., U.S.A. 154 D3 42 6N 102 52W
Alliance, Ohio, U.S.A. 150 F3 40 55N 81 6W
Allier □, France 27 F9 46 25N 2 40 E
Allier →, France 27 F10 46 57N 3 4 E
Alliford Bay, Canada 142 C2 53 12N 131 58W
Alligator Pond, Jamaica 164 a 17 52N 77 34W
Allinagaram, India 95 J3 10 2N 77 30 E
Allinge, Denmark 17 J8 55 17N 14 50 E
Allison, U.S.A. 156 B4 42 45N 92 48W
Alliston, Canada 140 D4 44 9N 79 52W
Alloa, U.K. 22 E5 56 7N 3 47W
Allones, France 26 D8 48 20N 1 40 E
Allora, Australia 127 D5 28 2 S 152 0 E
Allos, France 29 D10 44 15N 6 38 E
Alluitsup Paa, Greenland 10 E6 60 30N 45 35W
Allur, India 95 G5 14 40N 80 4 E
Alluru Kottapatnam, India 95 G5 15 24N 80 7 E
Alma, Canada 141 C5 48 35N 71 40W
Alma, Ga., U.S.A. 152 D7 31 33N 82 28W
Alma, Kans., U.S.A. 154 F6 39 1N 96 17W
Alma, Mich., U.S.A. 148 D3 43 23N 84 39W
Alma, Nebr., U.S.A. 154 E5 40 6N 99 22W
Alma Ata = Almaty, Kazakstan 66 E8 43 15N 76 57 E
Almacelles, Spain 40 D5 41 43N 0 27 E
Almada, Portugal 43 G1 38 40N 9 9W
Almaden, Australia 126 B3 17 22 S 144 40 E
Almadén, Spain 43 G6 38 49N 4 52W
Almalyk = Olmaliq, Uzbekistan 65 C4 40 50N 69 35 E
Almanor, L., U.S.A. 158 F3 40 14N 121 9W
Almansa, Spain 41 G3 38 51N 1 5W
Almanza, Spain 42 C5 42 39N 5 3W
Almanzor, Pico, Spain 42 E5 40 15N 5 18W
Almanzora →, Spain 41 H3 37 14N 1 46W
Almas, Brazil 171 D2 11 33 S 47 9W
Almaş, Munţii, Romania 52 F7 44 49N 22 12 E
Almassora, Spain 40 F4 39 57N 0 3W
Almaty, Kazakstan 66 E8 43 15N 76 57 E
Almazán, Spain 40 D2 41 30N 2 30W
Almeirim, Brazil 169 D7 1 30 S 52 34W
Almeirim, Portugal 43 F2 39 12N 8 37W
Almelo, Neths. 24 B6 52 22N 6 42 E
Almenar de Soria, Spain 40 D2 41 43N 2 12W
Almenara, Brazil 171 E3 16 11 S 40 42W
Almenara, Spain 40 F4 39 46N 0 14W
Almenara, Sierra de la, Spain 41 H3 37 34N 1 32W
Almendra, Embalse de, Spain 42 D4 41 10N 6 5W
Almendralejo, Spain 43 G4 38 41N 6 26W
Almere-Stad, Neths. 24 B5 52 20N 5 15 E
Almería, Spain 43 J8 36 52N 2 27W
Almería □, Spain 41 H2 37 20N 2 20W
Almería, G. de, Spain 41 J2 36 41N 2 28W
Almetyevsk, Russia 60 C11 54 53N 52 20 E
Älmhult, Sweden 17 H8 56 33N 14 8 E
Almirante, Panama 164 E3 9 10N 82 30W
Almirante Montt, G., Chile 176 D2 51 52 S 72 50W
Almirópotamos, Greece 48 C6 38 16N 24 11 E
Almirós, Greece 48 B4 39 11N 22 45 E
Almiroú, Kólpos, Greece 39 E5 35 23N 24 20 E
Almodôvar, Portugal 43 H2 37 31N 8 2W
Almodóvar del Campo, Spain 43 G6 38 43N 4 10W
Almodóvar del Río, Spain 43 H5 37 48N 5 1W
Almond, U.S.A. 150 D7 42 19N 77 44W
Almont, U.S.A. 150 D1 42 55N 83 3W
Almonte, Canada 151 A8 45 14N 76 12W
Almonte, Spain 43 H4 37 13N 6 38W
Almora, India 93 E8 29 38N 79 40 E
Almoradí, Spain 41 G4 38 7N 0 46W
Almorox, Spain 42 E6 40 14N 4 24W
Almoustarat, Mali 113 B5 17 35N 0 8 E
Älmsta, Sweden 16 E12 59 58N 18 50 E
Almudévar, Spain 40 C4 42 3N 0 35W
Almuñécar, Spain 43 J7 36 43N 3 41W
Almunge, Sweden 16 E12 59 53N 18 3 E
Almuradiel, Spain 43 G7 38 32N 3 28W
Alness, U.K. 22 D4 57 41N 4 16W
Alnif, Morocco 110 B3 31 10N 5 8W
Alnmouth, U.K. 20 B6 55 24N 1 37W
Alnwick, U.K. 20 B6 55 24N 1 42W
Aloi, Uganda 118 B3 2 16N 33 10 E
Alon, Burma 90 D5 22 12N 95 5 E
Along, India 90 A5 28 10N 94 46 E
Alor, Indonesia 82 C2 8 15 S 124 30 E
Alor Setar, Malaysia 87 J3 6 7N 100 22 E
Álora, Spain 43 J6 36 49N 4 46W
Alosno, Spain 43 H3 37 33N 7 7W
Alot, India 92 H6 23 56N 75 40 E
Alotau, Papua N. G. 132 F6 10 16 S 150 30 E
Alougoum, Morocco 110 B3 30 17N 6 56W
Aloum, Cameroon 114 B2 2 16N 10 34 E
Aloysius, Mt., Australia 125 E4 26 0 S 128 38 E
Alpaugh, U.S.A. 160 K7 35 53N 119 29W
Alpedrinha, Portugal 42 E3 40 6N 7 27W
Alpena, U.S.A. 148 C4 45 4N 83 27W
Alpercatas →, Brazil 170 C3 6 2 S 44 19W
Alpes-de-Haute-Provence □, France 29 D10 44 8N 6 10 E
Alpes-Maritimes □, France 29 E11 43 55N 7 10 E
Alpha, Australia 126 C4 23 39 S 146 37 E
Alpha, U.S.A. 156 C6 41 12N 90 23W
Alphen aan den Rijn, Neths. 24 B4 52 7N 4 40 E
Alphonse, Seychelles 121 E4 7 0 S 52 45 E
Alpiarça, Portugal 43 F2 39 15N 8 35W
Alpine, Ariz., U.S.A. 159 K9 33 51N 109 9W
Alpine, Calif., U.S.A. 161 N10 32 50N 116 46W
Alpine, Tex., U.S.A. 155 K3 30 22N 103 40W
Alpine Nat. Park, Australia 129 D7 37 15 S 146 45 E
Alpnach Dorf, Switz. 33 C6 46 57N 8 17 E
Alps, Europe 25 C8 46 30N 9 30 E
Alpu, Turkey 100 C4 39 46N 30 58 E
Alqueta, Barragem do, Portugal 43 G3 38 20N 7 25W
Alrø, Denmark 17 J4 55 52N 10 5 E
Als, Denmark 17 K3 54 59N 9 55 E
Alsace, France 27 D14 48 15N 7 25 E
Alsask, Canada 143 C7 51 21N 109 59W
Alsasua, Spain 40 C2 42 54N 2 10W
Alsek →, U.S.A. 142 B1 59 10N 138 12W
Alsfeld, Germany 30 E5 50 44N 9 16 E
Alsten, Norway 14 D15 65 58N 12 40 E
Alstermo, Sweden 17 H9 56 58N 15 38 E
Alston, U.K. 20 C5 54 49N 2 25W
Alta, Norway 14 B20 69 57N 23 10 E
Alta, Sierra, Spain 40 E3 40 31N 1 30W
Alta Floresta, Brazil 173 B6 9 57 S 55 58W
Alta Gracia, Argentina 174 C3 31 40 S 64 30W
Alta Sierra, U.S.A. 161 K8 35 42N 118 33W
Altaelva →, Norway 14 B20 69 54N 23 17 E
Altafjorden, Norway 14 A20 70 5N 23 5 E
Altagracia, Venezuela 168 A3 10 45N 71 30W
Altagracia de Orituco, Venezuela 168 B4 9 52N 66 23W
Altai = Aerhtai Shan, Mongolia 76 B4 46 40N 92 45 E
Altamachi →, Bolivia 172 D4 16 8 S 66 50W
Altamaha →, U.S.A. 152 D8 31 20N 81 20W
Altamira, Brazil 169 D7 3 12 S 52 10W
Altamira, Chile 174 B2 25 47 S 69 51W
Altamira, Colombia 168 C2 2 3N 75 47W
Altamira, Mexico 163 C5 22 24N 97 55W
Altamira, Cuevas de, Spain 42 B6 43 20N 4 5W
Altamont, Ill., U.S.A. 157 E8 39 4N 88 45W
Altamont, N.Y., U.S.A. 151 D10 42 43N 74 3W
Altamura, Italy 45 B9 40 49N 16 33 E
Altanbulag, Mongolia 68 A5 50 16N 106 30 E
Altar, Mexico 162 A2 30 40N 111 50W
Altar, Desierto de, Mexico 162 B2 30 10N 112 0W
Altata, Mexico 162 C3 24 30N 108 0W
Altavas, Phil. 81 F4 11 32N 122 29 E
Altavista, U.S.A. 148 G6 37 6N 79 17W
Altay, China 68 B3 47 48N 88 10 E
Altdorf, Switz. 33 C7 46 52N 8 36 E
Alte Mellum, Germany 30 B4 53 43N 8 10 E
Altea, Spain 41 G4 38 38N 0 2W
Altenberg, Germany 30 E9 50 45N 13 45 E
Altenbruch, Germany 30 B4 53 49N 8 46 E
Altenburg, Germany 30 E8 50 59N 12 25 E
Altenkirchen, Mecklenburg-Vorpommern, Germany 30 A9 54 38N 13 22 E
Altenkirchen, Rhld-Pfz., Germany 30 E3 50 41N 7 39 E
Altenmarkt, Austria 34 D7 47 43N 14 39 E
Alter do Châo, Brazil 169 D6 2 31 S 54 57W
Alter do Châo, Portugal 43 F3 39 12N 7 40W
Altha, U.S.A. 152 E4 30 34N 85 8W
Altınoluk, Turkey 49 B8 39 34N 26 45 E
Altınova, Turkey 49 B8 39 12N 26 47 E
Altıntaş, Turkey 49 B12 39 4N 30 7 E
Altınyaka, Turkey 49 E12 36 33N 30 20 E
Altınyayla, Turkey 49 D11 37 0N 29 33 E
Altiplano = Bolivian Plateau, S. Amer. 166 E4 20 0 S 67 30W
Altiplano, Bolivia 172 D4 17 0 S 68 0W
Altkirch, France 27 E14 47 37N 7 15 E
Altmark, Germany 30 C7 52 45N 11 30 E
Altmühl →, Germany 31 G7 48 54N 11 52 E
Altmunster, Austria 34 D6 47 54N 13 45 E
Alto Adige = Trentino-Alto Adige □, Italy 45 B8 46 30N 11 20 E
Alto Alegre, Brazil 169 C5 2 50N 61 20W
Alto Araguaia, Brazil 173 D7 17 15 S 53 20W
Alto Chicapa, Angola 115 E3 10 52 S 19 17 E
Alto Cuchumatanes = Cuchumatanes, Sierra de los, Guatemala 164 C1 15 35N 91 25W
Alto Cuito = Tempué, Angola 115 E3 13 27 S 18 49 E
Alto del Carmen, Chile 174 B1 28 46 S 70 30W
Alto del Inca, Chile 174 A2 24 10 S 68 10W
Alto Garças, Brazil 173 D7 16 56 S 53 32W
Alto Iriri →, Brazil 173 B7 8 50 S 53 25W
Alto Ligonha, Mozam. 119 F4 15 30 S 38 11 E
Alto Molocue, Mozam. 119 F4 15 50 S 37 35 E
Alto Paraguai, Brazil 173 C6 14 30 S 56 31W
Alto Paraguay □, Paraguay 174 A4 21 0 S 58 30W
Alto Paraiso de Goiás, Brazil 171 D2 14 7 S 47 31W
Alto Paraná □, Paraguay 175 B5 25 30 S 54 50W
Alto Parnaíba, Brazil 170 C2 9 6 S 45 57W
Alto Purús →, Peru 172 B3 9 12 S 70 28W
Alto Río Senguerr, Argentina 176 C2 45 2 S 70 50W
Alto Santo, Brazil 170 C4 5 31 S 38 15W
Alto Sucuriú, Brazil 173 D7 19 19 S 52 47W
Alto Turi, Brazil 170 B2 2 54 S 45 38W
Alton, Canada 150 C4 43 54N 80 5W
Alton, U.K. 21 F7 51 9N 0 59W
Alton, Ill., U.S.A. 156 F6 38 53N 90 11W
Alton, N.H., U.S.A. 151 C13 43 27N 71 13W
Altoona, Ala., U.S.A. 152 A3 34 2N 86 20W
Altoona, Iowa, U.S.A. 156 C3 41 39N 93 28W
Altoona, Pa., U.S.A. 150 F6 40 31N 78 24W
Altos, Brazil 170 C3 5 3 S 42 28W
Altötting, Germany 31 G8 48 12N 12 39 E
Altstätten, Switz. 33 B9 47 22N 9 33 E
Altün Küprī, Iraq 101 E11 35 45N 44 9 E
Altun Shan, China 68 C3 38 30N 88 0 E
Alturas, U.S.A. 158 F3 41 29N 120 32W
Altus, U.S.A. 155 H5 34 38N 99 20W
Alubijid, Phil. 81 G5 8 35N 124 29 E
Alucra, Turkey 101 B8 40 22N 38 47 E
Aluk, Sudan 107 F2 8 25N 27 30 E
Alūksne, Latvia 15 H22 57 24N 27 3 E
Alūla, Somali Rep. 120 B4 11 50N 50 45 E
Alunda, Sweden 16 D12 60 4N 18 5 E
Alunite, U.S.A. 161 K12 35 59N 114 55W
Aluoro →, Ethiopia 107 F3 8 26N 33 24 E
Alupka, Ukraine 59 K8 44 23N 34 2 E
Alur, India 95 E3 15 24N 77 15 E
Alur Gajah, Malaysia 84 B2 2 23N 102 13 E
Alushta, Ukraine 59 K8 44 40N 34 25 E
Alusi, Indonesia 83 C4 7 35 S 131 40 E
Alustante, Spain 40 E3 40 36N 1 40W
Alutgama, Sri Lanka 95 L4 6 26N 79 59 E
Alutnuwara, Sri Lanka 95 L5 7 19N 80 59 E
Alva, U.S.A. 155 G5 36 48N 98 40W
Alvaiázere, Portugal 42 F2 39 49N 8 23W
Älvängen, Sweden 17 G6 57 58N 12 8 E
Alvarado, Mexico 163 D5 18 40N 95 50W
Alvarado, U.S.A. 155 J6 32 24N 97 13W
Alvarães, Brazil 169 D5 3 12 S 64 50W
Alvaro Obregón, Presa, Mexico 162 B3 27 55N 109 52W
Alvdal, Norway 18 B7 62 6N 10 37 E
Älvdalen, Sweden 16 C8 61 13N 14 4 E
Alvear, Argentina 174 B4 29 5 S 56 30W
Alverca, Portugal 43 G1 38 56N 9 1W
Alvesta, Sweden 17 H8 56 54N 14 35 E
Ålvik, Norway 18 D3 60 26N 6 26 E
Alvin, U.S.A. 155 L7 29 26N 95 15W
Alvinston, Canada 150 D3 42 49N 81 52W
Alvito, Portugal 43 G3 38 15N 7 58W
Älvkarleby, Sweden 16 D11 60 34N 17 26 E
Alvorado, Brazil 171 D2 12 28 S 49 6W
Alvord Desert, U.S.A. 158 E4 42 30N 118 25W
Älvros, Sweden 16 B8 62 3N 14 38 E
Älvsbyn, Sweden 14 D19 65 40N 21 0 E
Älvundeid, Norway 18 B5 62 45N 8 33 E
Alwar, India 92 F7 27 38N 76 34 E
Alwaye, India 95 J3 10 8N 76 24 E
Alxa Zuoqi, China 74 E3 38 50N 105 40 E
Alyangula, Australia 126 A2 13 55 S 136 30 E
Alyata = Älät, Azerbaijan 61 L9 39 58N 49 25 E
Alyth, U.K. 22 E5 56 38N 3 13W
Alytus, Lithuania 15 J21 54 24N 24 3 E
Alzada, U.S.A. 154 C2 45 2N 104 25W
Alzey, Germany 31 F4 49 45N 8 7 E
Alzira, Spain 41 F4 39 9N 0 30W
Am Dam, Chad 109 F4 12 40N 20 35 E
Am Géréda, Chad 109 F4 12 53N 21 14 E
Am Loubia, Chad 109 F4 13 39N 20 8 E
Am Timan, Chad 109 F4 11 0N 20 10 E
Amada Gaza, C.A.R. 114 B3 4 46N 15 9 E
Amadeus, L., Australia 125 D5 24 54 S 131 0 E
Amadi, Dem. Rep. of the Congo 118 B2 3 40N 26 40 E
Amâdi, Sudan 107 F3 5 29N 30 25 E
Amadjuak L., Canada 139 B12 65 0N 71 8W
Amadora, Portugal 43 G1 38 45N 9 13W
Amagansett, U.S.A. 151 F12 40 59N 72 9W
Amagasaki, Japan 73 C7 34 42N 135 20 E
Amager, Denmark 17 J6 55 37N 12 35 E
Amagi, Japan 72 D2 33 25N 130 39 E
Amagunze, Nigeria 113 D6 6 20N 7 40 E
Amahai, Indonesia 83 C3 3 20 S 128 55 E
Amaile, Samoa 133 W24 13 59 S 171 22W
Amaimon, Papua N. G. 132 C3 5 12 S 145 30 E
Amakusa-Nada, Japan 72 E2 32 35N 130 5 E
Amakusa-Shotō, Japan 72 E2 32 15N 130 10 E
Åmål, Sweden 16 E6 59 3N 12 42 E
Amalapuram, India 95 F5 16 35N 81 55 E
Amalfi, Colombia 168 B2 6 55N 75 4W
Amalfi, Italy 47 B7 40 38N 14 36 E
Amaliás, Greece 48 D3 37 47N 21 22 E
Amalner, India 94 D2 21 5N 75 5 E
Amamapare, Indonesia 83 B5 4 53 S 136 38 E
Amambaí, Brazil 175 A4 23 5 S 55 13W
Amambaí →, Brazil 175 A5 23 22 S 53 56W
Amambay □, Paraguay 175 A4 23 0 S 56 0W
Amambay, Cordillera de, S. Amer. 175 A4 23 0 S 55 45W
Amami-Guntō, Japan 71 L4 27 16N 129 21 E
Amami-Ō-Shima, Japan 71 L4 28 0N 129 0 E
Aman, Pulau, Malaysia 87 c 5 16N 100 24 E
Amana →, Venezuela 169 B5 9 45N 62 39W
Amaná, L., Brazil 169 D5 2 35 S 64 40W
Amanab, Papua N. G. 132 B1 3 40 S 141 14 E
Amanat →, India 93 G11 24 7N 84 4 E
Amanda Park, U.S.A. 160 C3 47 28N 123 55W
Amangeldy, Kazakstan 66 D7 50 10N 65 10 E
Amantea, Italy 47 C9 39 8N 16 4 E
Amapá, Brazil 169 C7 2 5N 50 50W
Amapá □, Brazil 169 C7 1 40N 52 0W
Amapari, Brazil 169 C7 0 37N 51 39W
Amara, Sudan 107 E3 10 25N 34 10 E
Amarante, Brazil 170 C3 6 14 S 42 50W
Amarante, Portugal 42 D2 41 16N 8 5W
Amarante do Maranhão, Brazil 170 C2 5 36 S 46 45W
Amaranth, Canada 143 C9 50 36N 98 43W
Amarapura, Burma 90 E6 21 54N 96 3 E
Amaravati →, India 95 J4 11 0N 78 15 E
Amareleja, Portugal 43 G3 38 12N 7 13W
Amargosa, Brazil 171 D4 13 2 S 39 36W
Amargosa →, U.S.A. 161 J10 36 14N 116 51W
Amargosa Range, U.S.A. 161 J10 36 20N 116 45W
Amári, Greece 39 E5 35 13N 24 40 E
Amarillo, U.S.A. 155 H4 35 13N 101 50W
Amarkantak, India 93 H9 22 40N 81 45 E
Amârna, Tell el', Sudan 106 B3 27 38N 30 52 E
Amarnath, India 94 E1 19 12N 73 22 E
Amaro, Mte., Italy 45 F11 42 5N 14 5 E
Amaro Leite, Brazil 171 D2 13 58 S 49 9W
Amarpur, Bihar, India 93 G12 25 5N 87 0 E
Amarpur, Tripura, India 90 D3 23 31N 91 39 E
Amarti, Eritrea 107 E5 14 17N 41 6 E
Amarwara, India 93 H8 22 18N 79 10 E
Amasin, W. Sahara 110 C2 25 45N 13 20W
Amasra, Turkey 100 B5 41 45N 32 23 E
Amassama, Nigeria 113 D6 5 1N 6 2 E
Amasya, Turkey 100 B6 40 40N 35 50 E
Amasya □, Turkey 57 F6 40 40N 35 50 E
Amata, Australia 125 E5 26 9 S 131 9 E
Amataurá, Brazil 168 D4 3 29 S 68 6W
Amatignak I., U.S.A. 144 L3 51 16N 179 6W
Amatikulu, S. Africa 117 D5 29 3 S 31 33 E
Amatitlán, Guatemala 164 D1 14 29N 90 38W
Amatrice, Italy 45 F10 42 38N 13 17 E
Amau, Papua N. G. 132 F5 10 2 S 148 34 E
Amay, Belgium 24 D5 50 33N 5 19 E
Amazon = Amazonas →, S. Amer. 169 D7 0 5 S 50 0W
Amazonas □, Brazil 173 B5 5 0 S 65 0W
Amazonas □, Peru 172 B2 5 0 S 78 0W
Amazonas □, Venezuela 168 C4 3 30N 66 0W
Amazonas →, S. Amer. 169 D7 0 5 S 50 0W
Amba Ferit, Ethiopia 107 E4 10 55N 38 50 E
Ambad, India 94 E2 19 38N 75 50 E
Ambagarh Chowki, India 94 D5 20 47N 80 43 E
Ambah, India 92 F8 26 43N 78 13 E
Ambahakily, Madag. 117 C7 21 36 S 43 41 E
Ambahita, Madag. 117 C8 24 1 S 45 16 E
Ambajogal, India 94 E3 18 44N 76 23 E
Ambala, India 92 D7 30 23N 76 56 E
Ambalangoda, Sri Lanka 95 L5 6 15N 80 5 E
Ambalapulai, India 95 K3 9 25N 76 25 E
Ambalavao, Madag. 117 C8 21 50 S 46 56 E
Ambam, Cameroon 114 B2 2 20N 11 15 E
Ambanja, Madag. 117 A8 13 40 S 48 27 E
Ambararata, Madag. 117 B8 15 3 S 48 33 E
Ambarchik, Russia 67 C17 69 40N 162 20 E
Ambarijeby, Madag. 117 A8 14 56 S 47 41 E
Ambaro, Helodranon', Madag. 117 A8 13 23 S 48 38 E
Ambasamudram, India 95 K3 8 43N 77 25 E
Ambato, Ecuador 168 D2 1 5 S 78 42W
Ambato, Madag. 117 A8 13 24 S 48 29 E
Ambato, Sierra de, Argentina 174 B2 28 25 S 66 10W
Ambato Boeny, Madag. 117 B8 16 28 S 46 43 E
Ambatofinandrahana, Madag. 117 C8 20 33 S 46 48 E
Ambatolampy, Madag. 117 B8 19 20 S 47 35 E
Ambatomainty, Madag. 117 B8 17 41 S 45 40 E
Ambatomanoina, Madag. 117 B8 18 18 S 47 37 E
Ambatondrazaka, Madag. 117 B8 17 55 S 48 28 E
Ambatosoratra, Madag. 117 B8 17 37 S 48 31 E
Ambelau, Indonesia 82 B3 3 51 S 127 12 E
Ambelón, Greece 48 B4 39 45N 22 22 E
Ambenja, Madag. 117 B8 15 17 S 46 58 E
Amberg, Germany 31 F7 49 26N 11 52 E
Ambergris Cay, Belize 163 D7 18 0N 88 0W
Ambérieu-en-Bugey, France 29 C9 45 57N 5 20 E
Amberley, N.Z. 131 D7 43 9 S 172 44 E
Ambert, France 28 C7 45 33N 3 44 E
Ambidédi, Mali 112 C2 14 35N 11 47W
Ambikapur, India 93 H10 23 15N 83 15 E
Ambikol, Sudan 106 C3 21 20N 30 50 E
Ambilobé, Madag. 117 A8 13 10 S 49 3 E
Ambinanindrano, Madag. 117 C8 20 5 S 48 23 E
Ambinanitelo, Madag. 117 B8 15 21 S 49 35 E
Ambinda, Madag. 117 B8 16 25 S 45 52 E
Ambitle I., Papua N. G. 132 C7 4 5 S 153 37 E
Amble, U.K. 20 B6 55 20N 1 36W
Ambler, U.S.A. 144 C8 67 5N 157 52W
Ambleside, U.K. 20 C5 54 26N 2 58W
Ambo, Peru 172 C2 10 5 S 76 10W
Amboahangy, Madag. 117 C8 24 15 S 46 22 E
Ambodifototra, Madag. 117 B8 16 59 S 49 52 E
Ambodilazana, Madag. 117 B8 18 6 S 49 10 E
Ambodiriana, Madag. 117 B8 17 55 S 49 18 E
Ambodiriatrimo, Madag. 117 B8 18 50 S 47 26 E
Ambohidray, Madag. 117 B8 18 36 S 48 18 E
Ambohimahamasina, Madag. 117 C8 21 56 S 47 11 E
Ambohimahasoa, Madag. 117 C8 21 7 S 47 13 E
Ambohimanga, Madag. 117 C8 20 52 S 47 36 E
Ambohimitombo, Madag. 117 C8 20 43 S 47 26 E
Ambohitra, Madag. 117 A8 12 30 S 49 10 E
Amboise, France 26 E8 47 24N 1 2 E
Amboiva, Angola 115 E2 11 33 S 14 43 E
Ambon, Indonesia 82 B3 3 43 S 128 12 E
Ambondro, Madag. 117 D8 25 13 S 45 44 E
Amboseli, L., Kenya 118 C4 2 40 S 37 10 E
Amboseli Nat. Park, Kenya 118 C4 2 37 S 37 13 E
Ambositra, Madag. 117 C8 20 31 S 47 25 E
Ambovombe, Madag. 117 D8 25 11 S 46 5 E
Amboy, Calif., U.S.A. 161 L11 34 33N 115 45W
Amboy, Ill., U.S.A. 156 C7 41 44N 89 20W
Amboyna Cay, S. China Sea 78 C4 7 50N 112 50 E
Ambridge, U.S.A. 150 F4 40 36N 80 14W
Ambriz, Angola 115 D2 7 48 S 13 8 E
Ambriz, Reserva de, Angola 115 D2 7 56 S 10 27 E
Ambrym, Vanuatu 133 F6 16 15 S 168 10 E
Ambunti, Papua N. G. 132 C2 4 13 S 142 52 E
Ambur, India 95 H4 12 48N 78 43 E
Amchitka I., U.S.A. 144 L2 51 32N 179 0 E
Amderma, Russia 66 C7 69 45N 61 30 E
Amdhi, India 93 H9 23 51N 81 27 E
Ameca, Mexico 162 C4 20 30N 104 0W
Ameca →, Mexico 162 C3 20 40N 105 15W
Amecameca, Mexico 163 D5 19 7N 98 46W
Ameland, Neths. 24 A5 53 27N 5 45 E
Amélia, Italy 45 F9 42 33N 12 25 E
Amelia City, U.S.A. 152 E8 30 35N 81 28W
Amelia I., U.S.A. 152 E8 30 40N 81 25W
Amendolara, Italy 47 C9 39 57N 16 35 E
Amenia, U.S.A. 151 E11 41 51N 73 33W
American Falls, U.S.A. 158 E7 42 47N 112 51W
American Falls Reservoir, U.S.A. 158 E7 42 47N 112 52W
American Fork, U.S.A. 158 F8 40 23N 111 48W
American Highland, Antarctica 7 D6 73 0 S 75 0 E
American River, Australia 128 C2 35 47 S 137 46 E
American Samoa ■, Pac. Oc. 133 X24 14 20 S 170 40W
American Samoa, Nat. Park of, Amer. Samoa 133 X24 14 15 S 170 28W
Americana, Brazil 175 A6 22 45 S 47 20W
Americus, U.S.A. 152 C5 32 4N 84 14W
Amersfoort, Neths. 24 B5 52 9N 5 23 E
Amersfoort, S. Africa 117 D4 26 59 S 29 53 E
Amery Ice Shelf, Antarctica 7 C6 69 30 S 72 0 E
Amerzgane, Morocco 110 B3 31 4N 7 14W
Ames, Spain 42 C2 42 54N 8 38W
Ames, U.S.A. 156 C3 42 2N 93 37W
Amesbury, U.S.A. 151 D14 42 51N 70 56W
Amet, India 92 G5 25 18N 73 56 E
Amfíklia, Greece 48 C4 38 38N 22 35 E
Amfilokhía, Greece 48 C3 38 52N 21 9 E
Amfípolis, Greece 50 F7 40 48N 23 52 E
Ámfissa, Greece 48 C4 38 32N 22 22 E
Amga, Russia 67 C14 60 50N 132 0 E
Amga →, Russia 67 C14 62 38N 134 32 E
Amgaon, India 94 D5 21 22N 80 22 E
Amgu, Russia 67 E14 45 45N 137 15 E
Amgun →, Russia 67 D14 52 56N 139 38 E
Amherst, Canada 141 C7 45 48N 64 8W
Amherst, Mass., U.S.A. 151 D12 42 23N 72 31W
Amherst, N.Y., U.S.A. 150 D6 42 59N 78 48W
Amherst, Ohio, U.S.A. 150 E2 41 24N 82 14W
Amherst I., Canada 151 B8 44 8N 76 43W
Amherstburg, Canada 140 D3 42 6N 83 6W
Amiata, Mte., Italy 45 F8 42 53N 11 37 E
Amidon, U.S.A. 154 B3 46 29N 103 19W
Amiens, France 27 C9 49 54N 2 16 E
Amili, India 90 A5 28 25N 95 52 E
Amindaion, Greece 50 F5 40 42N 21 42 E
Amindivi Is., India 95 J1 11 23N 72 23 E
Amingaon, India 90 B3 26 11N 91 40 E
Amini I., India 95 J1 11 6N 72 45 E
Åminne, Sweden 17 G7 57 7N 14 0 E
Amino, Ethiopia 107 G5 4 25N 41 52 E
Aminuis, Namibia 116 C2 23 43 S 19 21 E
Āmir, Ra's, Libya 108 B4 32 57N 21 43 E
Amīrābād, Iran 96 C5 33 20N 46 16 E
Amirante Is., Seychelles 62 K9 6 0 S 53 0 E
Amisk L., Canada 143 C8 54 35N 102 15W
Amistad, Presa de la, Mexico 162 B4 29 24N 101 0W
Amite, U.S.A. 155 K9 30 44N 90 30W
Amizmiz, Morocco 110 B3 31 12N 8 15W
Amla, India 92 J8 21 56N 78 7 E
Åmli, Norway 18 F5 58 45N 8 32 E
Amlia I., U.S.A. 144 K4 52 4N 173 30W
Amlwch, U.K. 20 D3 53 24N 4 20W
Amm Adam, Sudan 107 D4 16 20N 36 1 E
'Ammān, Jordan 103 D4 31 57N 35 52 E
'Ammān □, Jordan 103 D5 31 40N 36 30 E
Ammanford, U.K. 21 F4 51 48N 3 59W
Ammassalik = Tasiilaq, Greenland 10 D7 65 40N 37 20W
Ammerån →, Sweden 16 A10 63 9N 16 13 E
Ammersee, Germany 31 G7 48 0N 11 7 E
Ammochostos = Famagusta, Cyprus 39 E9 35 8N 33 55 E
Ammon, U.S.A. 158 E8 43 28N 111 58W
Amnat Charoen, Thailand 86 E5 15 51N 104 38 E
Amnura, Bangla. 93 G13 24 37N 88 25 E
Amo Jiang →, China 76 F3 23 0N 101 50 E
Āmol, Iran 97 B7 36 23N 52 20 E
Amoret, U.S.A. 156 F2 38 15N 94 35W
Amorgós, Greece 49 E7 36 50N 25 57 E
Amory, U.S.A. 149 J1 33 59N 88 29W
Amos, Canada 140 C4 48 35N 78 5W
Åmot, Buskerud, Norway 15 G13 59 57N 9 54 E
Åmot, Oppland, Norway 18 D7 61 0N 10 2 E
Åmot, Telemark, Norway 18 E5 59 34N 8 0 E
Åmotfors, Sweden 16 E6 59 47N 12 22 E
Åmotsdal, Norway 18 E5 59 37N 8 26 E
Amour, Djebel, Algeria 111 B5 33 42N 1 37 E
Amoy = Xiamen, China 77 E12 24 25N 118 4 E
Ampanavoana, Madag. 117 B9 15 41 S 50 22 E
Ampang, Malaysia 87 L3 3 8N 101 45 E
Ampangalana, Lakandranon', Madag. 117 C8 22 48 S 47 50 E
Ampani, India 94 E6 19 35N 82 38 E
Ampanihy, Madag. 117 C7 24 40 S 44 45 E
Amparafaravola, Madag. 117 B8 17 35 S 48 13 E
Ampasinambo, Madag. 117 C8 20 31 S 48 0 E
Ampasindava, Helodranon', Madag. 117 A8 13 40 S 48 15 E
Ampasindava, Saikanosy, Madag. 117 A8 13 42 S 47 55 E
Ampato, Nevado, Peru 172 D3 15 40 S 71 56W
Ampenan, Indonesia 85 D5 8 34 S 116 4 E
Amper, Nigeria 113 D6 9 25N 9 40 E
Amper →, Germany 31 G7 48 29N 11 55 E
Ampezzo, Italy 45 B9 46 25N 12 48 E
Amphoe Kathu, Thailand 87 a 7 55N 98 21 E
Amphoe Thalang, Thailand 87 a 8 1N 98 20 E
Ampitsikinana, Réunion 117 A8 12 57 S 49 49 E
Ampombiantambo, Madag. 117 A8 12 42 S 48 57 E
Amposta, Spain 40 E5 40 43N 0 34 E
Ampotaka, Madag. 117 D7 25 3 S 44 41 E
Ampoza, Madag. 117 C7 22 20 S 44 44 E
Amqui, Canada 141 C6 48 28N 67 27W
Amrabad, India 95 F4 16 23N 78 50 E
'Amrān, Yemen 98 D3 15 41N 43 55 E
Amravati, India 94 D3 20 55N 77 45 E
Amreli, India 92 J4 21 35N 71 17 E
Amrenene el Kasba, Algeria 111 D5 22 10N 0 30 E
Amriswil, Switz. 33 A8 47 33N 9 18 E
Amritsar, India 92 D6 31 35N 74 57 E
Amroha, India 93 E8 28 53N 78 30 E

Amrum, Germany 30 A4 54 38N 8 22 E
Amsâga, Mauritania 110 D2 20 7N 14 10W
Amsel, Algeria 111 D6 22 47N 5 29 E
Amsterdam, Neths. 24 B4 52 23N 4 54 E
Amsterdam, U.S.A. 151 D10 42 56N 74 11W
Amsterdam, I. = Nouvelle-Amsterdam, I., Ind. Oc. 121 H6 38 30 S 77 30 E
Amstetten, Austria 34 C7 48 7N 14 51 E
Amudarya, Turkmenistan 65 E2 37 53N 65 15 E
Amudarya →, Uzbekistan 66 E6 43 58N 59 34 E
Amukta I., U.S.A. 144 K5 52 30N 171 16W
Amukta Pass, U.S.A. 144 L5 52 0N 171 0W
Amulung, Phil. 80 C3 17 50N 121 43 E
Amundsen Gulf, Canada 138 A7 71 0N 124 0W
Amundsen Sea, Antarctica 7 D15 72 0 S 115 0W
Amungen, Sweden 16 C9 61 10N 15 40 E
Amuntai, Indonesia 85 C5 2 28 S 115 25 E
Amur, Somali Rep. 120 C3 5 16N 46 30 E
Amur →, Russia 67 D15 52 56N 141 10 E
Amur, W. →, Sudan 106 D3 18 56N 33 34 E
Amurang, Indonesia 82 A2 1 5N 124 40 E
Amurrio, Spain 40 B1 43 3N 3 0W
Amursk, Russia 67 D14 50 14N 136 54 E
Amusco, Spain 42 C6 42 10N 4 28W
Amvrakikós Kólpos, Greece 48 C2 39 0N 20 55 E
Amvrosiyivka, Ukraine 59 J10 47 43N 38 30 E
Amyderya = Amudarya →, Uzbekistan 66 E6 43 58N 59 34 E
Amzeglouf, Algeria 111 C5 26 50N 0 1 E
An, Burma 90 F5 19 48N 94 0 E
An Bien, Vietnam 87 H5 9 45N 105 0 E
An Hoa, Vietnam 86 E7 15 40N 108 5 E
An Nabatīyah at Tahta, Lebanon 103 B4 33 23N 35 27 E
An Nabk, Si. Arabia 96 D3 31 20N 37 20 E
An Nabk, Syria 103 A5 34 2N 36 44 E
An Nafūd, Si. Arabia 96 D4 28 15N 41 0 E
An Najaf, Iraq 101 G11 32 3N 44 15 E
An Nāşirīyah, Iraq 96 D5 31 0N 46 15 E
An Nawfaliyah, Libya 108 B3 30 54N 17 58 E
An Nhon, Vietnam 86 F7 13 55N 109 7 E
An Nîl □, Sudan 106 D3 19 30N 33 0 E
An Nîl el Abyad □, Sudan 107 E3 14 0N 32 15 E
An Nîl el Azraq □, Sudan 107 E3 11 30N 34 30 E
An Nimāş, Si. Arabia 98 C3 19 7N 42 8 E
An Nu'ayrīyah, Si. Arabia 97 E6 27 30N 48 30 E
An Nu'mānīyah, Iraq 101 F11 32 32N 45 25 E
An Nuwayb'ī, W. →, Si. Arabia 103 F3 29 18N 34 57 E
An Thoi, Dao, Vietnam 87 H4 9 58N 104 0 E
An Uaimh, Ireland 23 C5 53 39N 6 41W
Åna-Sira, Norway 18 F3 58 17N 6 25 E
Anabanua, Indonesia 82 B2 3 57 S 120 4 E
Anabar →, Russia 67 B12 73 8N 113 36 E
'Anabtā, West Bank 103 C4 32 19N 35 7 E
Anaco, Venezuela 169 B5 9 27N 64 28W
Anaconda, U.S.A. 158 C7 46 8N 112 57W
Anacortes, U.S.A. 160 B4 48 30N 122 37W
Anacuao, Mt., Phil. 80 C3 16 16N 121 53 E
Anadarko, U.S.A. 155 H5 35 4N 98 15W
Anadia, Brazil 170 C4 9 42 S 36 18W
Anadia, Portugal 42 E2 40 26N 8 27W
Anadolu, Turkey 100 C5 39 0N 30 0 E
Anadyr, Russia 67 C18 64 35N 177 20 E
Anadyr →, Russia 67 C18 64 55N 176 5 E
Anadyrskiy Zaliv, Russia 67 C19 64 0N 180 0 E
Anáfi, Greece 49 E7 36 22N 25 48 E
Anafonítria, Greece 39 D2 37 51N 20 39 E
Anafópoulo, Greece 49 E7 36 17N 25 50 E
Anaga, Pta. de, Canary Is. 9 e1 28 34N 16 9W
Anagni, Italy 45 G10 41 44N 13 9 E
'Ānah, Iraq 101 E10 34 25N 42 0 E
Anahalu →, U.S.A. 145 J13 21 37N 158 6W
Anaheim, U.S.A. 161 M9 33 50N 117 55W
Anahim Lake, Canada 142 C3 52 28N 125 18W
Anahola, U.S.A. 145 A2 22 9N 159 19W
Anáhuac, Mexico 162 B4 27 14N 100 9W
Anai Mudi, India 95 J3 10 12N 77 4 E
Anaimalai Hills, India 95 J3 10 20N 76 40 E
Anajás, Brazil 170 B2 0 59 S 49 57W
Anajatuba, Brazil 170 B3 3 16 S 44 37W
Anakapalle, India 94 F6 17 42N 83 6 E
Anakena, Chile 172 b 27 5 S 109 20W
Anakie, Australia 126 C4 23 32 S 147 45 E
Anaklia, Georgia 61 J5 42 22N 41 35 E
Anaktuvuk Pass, U.S.A. 144 B10 68 8N 151 45W
Analalava, Madag. 117 A8 14 35 S 48 0 E
Analavoka, Madag. 117 C8 22 23 S 46 30 E
Análipsis, Greece 38 B9 39 36N 19 55 E
Anamã, Brazil 169 D5 3 35 S 61 22W
Anambar →, Pakistan 92 D3 30 15N 68 50 E
Anambas, Kepulauan, Indonesia 84 B3 3 20N 106 30 E
Anambas Is. = Anambas, Kepulauan, Indonesia 84 B3 3 20N 106 30 E
Anambra □, Nigeria 113 D6 6 20N 7 0 E
Aname, Vanuatu 133 K7 20 8 S 169 47 E
Anamosa, U.S.A. 156 B5 42 7N 91 17W
Anamur, Turkey 100 D5 36 8N 32 58 E
Anamur Burnu, Turkey 100 D5 36 2N 32 47 E
Anan, Japan 72 D6 33 54N 134 40 E
Anand, India 92 H5 22 32N 72 59 E
Anandapuram, India 95 G2 14 5N 75 12 E
Anandpur, India 94 D8 21 16N 86 13 E
Anánes, Greece 48 E6 36 33N 24 9 E
Anantapur, India 95 G3 14 39N 77 42 E
Anantnag, India 93 C6 33 45N 75 10 E
Ananyevo, Kyrgyzstan 65 B8 42 45N 77 40 E
Ananyiv, Ukraine 59 J5 47 44N 29 58 E
Anapa, Russia 59 K9 44 55N 37 25 E
Anapodháris →, Greece 39 F6 34 59N 25 20 E
Anápolis, Brazil 171 E2 16 15 S 48 50W
Anapu →, Brazil 169 D7 1 53 S 50 53W
Anār, Iran 97 D7 30 55N 55 13 E
Anār Darreh, Afghan. 91 B1 32 46N 61 39 E
Anārak, Iran 97 C7 33 25N 53 40 E
Anarisfjällen, Sweden 16 A7 63 6N 13 10 E
Anas →, India 92 H5 23 26N 74 0 E
Anatolia = Anadolu, Turkey 100 C5 39 0N 30 0 E
Anatsogno, Madag. 117 C7 23 33 S 43 46 E
Añatuya, Argentina 174 B3 28 20 S 62 50W
Anauá →, Brazil 169 C5 0 58N 61 21W
Anaunethad L., Canada 143 A8 60 55N 104 25W
Anavilhanas, Arquipélago das, Brazil 169 D5 2 42 S 60 45W
Anaye, Niger 109 E2 19 15N 12 50 E
Anbyŏn, N. Korea 75 E14 39 1N 127 35 E
Ancares, Sierra de, Spain 42 C4 42 51N 6 52W
Ancash □, Peru 172 B2 9 30 S 77 45W
Ancaster, Canada 150 C5 43 13N 79 59W
Ancenis, France 26 E5 47 21N 1 10W
Ancho, Canal, Chile 176 D2 50 0 S 74 20W
Anchor Bay, U.S.A. 160 G3 38 48N 123 34W
Anchorage, U.S.A. 144 F10 61 13N 149 54W
Anci, China 74 E9 39 20N 116 40 E
Ancohuma, Nevada, Bolivia 172 D4 16 0 S 68 50W
Ancón, Peru 172 C2 11 50 S 77 10W
Ancona, Italy 45 E10 43 38N 13 30 E
Ancud, Chile 176 B2 42 0 S 73 50W
Ancud, G. de, Chile 176 B2 42 0 S 73 0W
Ancy-le-Franc, France 27 E11 47 46N 4 10 E
Anda, China 69 B7 46 24N 125 19 E
Anda, Phil. 80 C2 16 17N 119 57 E
Andacollo, Argentina 174 D1 37 10 S 70 42W
Andacollo, Chile 174 C1 30 14 S 71 6W
Andahuaylas, Peru 172 C3 13 40 S 73 25W
Andaingo, Madag. 117 B8 18 12 S 48 17 E
Andalgalá, Argentina 174 B2 27 40 S 66 30W
Åndalsnes, Norway 15 E12 62 35N 7 43 E
Andalucía □, Spain 43 H6 37 35N 5 0W
Andalusia = Andalucía □, Spain 43 H6 37 35N 5 0W
Andalusia, U.S.A. 149 K2 31 18N 86 29W
Andaman & Nicobar Is. □, India 95 K11 10 0N 93 0 E
Andaman Is., Ind. Oc. 95 H11 12 30N 92 45 E
Andaman Sea, Ind. Oc. 78 B1 13 0N 96 0 E
Andamooka Opal Fields, Australia 127 E2 30 27 S 137 9 E
Andapa, Madag. 117 A8 14 39 S 49 39 E
Andara, Namibia 116 B3 18 2 S 21 9 E
Andaraí, Brazil 171 D3 12 48 S 41 20W
Andeer, Switz. 33 C8 46 36N 9 26 E
Andelfingen, Switz. 33 A7 47 36N 8 41 E
Andelot-Blancheville, France 27 D12 48 15N 5 18 E
Andenes, Norway 14 B17 69 19N 16 18 E
Andenne, Belgium 24 D5 50 28N 5 5 E
Andéranboukane, Mali 113 B5 15 26N 3 2 E
Andermatt, Switz. 33 C7 46 38N 8 35 E
Andernach, Germany 30 E3 50 26N 7 24 E
Andernos-les-Bains, France 28 D2 44 44N 1 6W
Anderslöv, Sweden 17 J7 55 26N 13 19 E
Anderson, Alaska, U.S.A. 144 D10 64 25N 149 15W
Anderson, Calif., U.S.A. 158 F2 40 27N 122 18W
Anderson, Ind., U.S.A. 157 D11 40 10N 85 41W
Anderson, Mo., U.S.A. 155 G7 36 39N 94 27W
Anderson, S.C., U.S.A. 149 H4 34 31N 82 39W
Anderson →, Canada 138 B7 69 42N 129 0W
Anderson I., India 95 H11 12 46N 92 43 E
Andersonville, U.S.A. 152 C5 32 12N 84 9W
Anderstorp, Sweden 17 G7 57 19N 13 39 E
Andes, Colombia 168 B2 5 39N 75 54W
Andes, U.S.A. 151 D10 42 12N 74 47W
Andes, Cord. de los, S. Amer. 172 C3 20 0 S 68 0W
Andfjorden, Norway 14 B17 69 10N 16 20 E
Andhra, L., India 94 E1 18 54N 73 32 E
Andhra Pradesh □, India 95 F4 18 0N 79 0 E
Andijon, Uzbekistan 66 E8 41 10N 72 15 E
Andikíthira, Greece 48 F5 35 52N 23 15 E
Andilamena, Madag. 117 B8 17 1 S 48 35 E
Andīmeshk, Iran 97 C6 32 27N 48 21 E
Andímilos, Greece 48 E6 36 47N 24 12 E
Andíparos, Greece 49 D7 37 0N 25 3 E
Andípaxoi, Greece 48 B2 39 9N 20 13 E
Andípsara, Greece 49 C7 38 30N 25 29 E
Andírrion, Greece 48 C3 38 20N 21 46 E
Andizhan = Andijon, Uzbekistan 66 E8 41 10N 72 15 E
Andkhvoy, Afghan. 65 E2 36 52N 65 8 E
Andoain, Spain 40 B2 43 13N 2 1W
Andoany, Madag. 117 A8 13 25 S 48 16 E
Andoas, Peru 168 D2 2 55 S 76 25W
Andohahela, Réserve Naturelle Intégrale d', Madag. 117 C8 24 4 S 46 44 E
Andol, India 94 F4 17 51N 78 4 E
Andola, India 94 F3 16 57N 76 50 E
Andong, S. Korea 75 F15 36 40N 128 43 E
Andongwei, China 75 G10 35 6N 119 20 E
Andoom, Australia 126 A3 12 25 S 141 53 E
Andorra, Spain 40 E4 40 59N 0 28W
Andorra ■, Europe 28 F5 42 30N 1 30 E
Andorra La Vella, Andorra 28 F5 42 31N 1 32 E
Andover, U.K. 21 F6 51 12N 1 29W
Andover, Maine, U.S.A. 151 B14 44 38N 70 45W
Andover, Mass., U.S.A. 151 D13 42 40N 71 8W
Andover, N.J., U.S.A. 151 F10 40 59N 74 45W
Andover, N.Y., U.S.A. 150 D7 42 10N 77 48W
Andover, Ohio, U.S.A. 150 E4 41 36N 80 34W
Andøya, Norway 14 B16 69 10N 15 50 E
Andrade, Brazil 169 D5 4 40 S 63 45W
Andradina, Brazil 171 F1 20 54 S 51 23W
Andrahary, Mt., Madag. 117 A8 13 37 S 49 17 E
Andramasina, Madag. 117 B8 19 11 S 47 35 E
Andranopasy, Madag. 117 C7 21 17 S 43 44 E
Andranovory, Madag. 117 C7 23 8 S 44 10 E
Andratx, Spain 38 B3 39 39N 2 25 E
André Félix, Parc Nat. d', C.A.R. 114 A4 9 29N 23 18 E
Andreanof Is., U.S.A. 144 L4 51 30N 176 0W
Andreapol, Russia 58 D7 56 40N 32 17 E
Andrée Land, Greenland 10 C8 73 40N 26 0W
Andrews, S.C., U.S.A. 149 J6 33 27N 79 34W
Andrews, Tex., U.S.A. 155 J3 32 19N 102 33W
Andreyevka, Russia 60 D10 52 19N 51 55 E
Ándria, Italy 47 A9 41 13N 16 17 E
Andriamena, Madag. 117 B8 17 26 S 47 30 E
Andriandampy, Madag. 117 C8 22 45 S 45 41 E
Andriba, Madag. 117 B8 17 30 S 46 58 E
Andrijevica, Montenegro, Yug. 50 D3 42 45N 19 48 E
Andringitra, Réserve Naturelle Intégrale d', Madag. 117 C8 22 13 S 46 5 E
Andrítsaina, Greece 48 D3 37 29N 21 52 E
Androka, Madag. 117 C7 24 58 S 44 2 E
Andropov = Rybinsk, Russia 58 C10 58 5N 38 50 E
Ándros, Greece 48 D6 37 50N 24 57 E
Andros I., Bahamas 164 B4 24 30N 78 0W
Andros Town, Bahamas 164 B4 24 43N 77 47W
Androscoggin →, U.S.A. 151 C14 43 58N 70 0W
Androth I., India 95 J1 10 50N 73 41 E
Andrychów, Poland 55 J6 49 51N 19 18 E
Andselv, Norway 14 B18 69 4N 18 34 E
Andújar, Spain 43 G6 38 3N 4 5W
Andulo, Angola 115 E3 11 25 S 16 45 E
Åneby, Norway 18 D7 60 5N 10 51 E
Aneby, Sweden 17 G8 57 48N 14 49 E
Anegada, B., Argentina 176 B4 40 20 S 62 20W
Anegada I., Br. Virgin Is. 165 e 18 45N 64 20W
Anegada Passage, W. Indies 165 C7 18 15N 63 45W
Aného, Togo 113 D5 6 12N 1 34 E
Aneityum, Vanuatu 133 K7 20 12 S 169 45 E
Anelghowhat, Vanuatu 133 K7 20 19 S 169 43 E
Añelo, Argentina 176 A3 38 20 S 68 45W
Anenni-Noi, Moldova 53 D14 46 53N 29 15 E
Aneto, Pico de, Spain 40 C5 42 37N 0 40 E
Añez, Bolivia 173 D5 15 40 S 63 10W
Anfu, China 77 D10 27 21N 114 40 E
Ang Mo Kio, Singapore 87 d 1 23N 103 50 E
Ang Thong, Thailand 86 E3 14 35N 100 31 E
Ang Thong, Ko, Thailand 87 b 9 37N 99 41 E
Angadanan, Phil. 80 C3 16 45N 121 45 E
Angamos, Punta, Chile 174 A1 23 1 S 70 32W
Angara →, Russia 67 D10 58 5N 94 20 E
Angara-Débou, Benin 113 C5 11 19N 3 3 E
Angarab, Ethiopia 107 E4 13 11N 37 7 E
Angarbaka, Sudan 107 F1 9 44N 24 44 E
Angarsk, Russia 67 D11 52 30N 104 0 E
Angas Hills, Australia 124 D4 23 0 S 127 50 E
Angaston, Australia 128 C3 34 30 S 139 8 E
Angat, Phil. 80 D3 14 56N 121 2 E
Ånge, Sweden 16 B9 62 31N 15 35 E
Ángel, Salto = Angel Falls, Venezuela 169 B5 5 57N 62 30W
Ángel de la Guarda, I., Mexico 162 B2 29 30N 113 30W
Angel Falls, Venezuela 169 B5 5 57N 62 30W
Angeles, Phil. 80 D3 15 9N 120 33 E
Ängelholm, Sweden 17 H6 56 15N 12 58 E
Angels Camp, U.S.A. 160 G6 38 4N 120 32W
Ängelsberg, Sweden 16 E10 59 58N 16 0 E
Anger →, Ethiopia 107 F4 9 37N 36 6 E
Angereb →, Ethiopia 107 E4 13 45N 36 40 E
Ångermanälven →, Sweden 16 B11 62 40N 18 0 E
Ångermanland, Sweden 14 E18 63 36N 17 45 E
Angermünde, Germany 30 B9 53 0N 14 0 E
Angers, Canada 151 A9 45 31N 75 29W
Angers, France 26 E6 47 30N 0 35W
Angerville, France 27 D9 48 19N 2 0 E
Ängesån →, Sweden 14 C20 66 16N 22 47 E
Angical, Brazil 171 D3 12 0 S 44 42W
Angikuni L., Canada 143 A9 62 0N 100 0W
Angkor, Cambodia 86 F4 13 22N 103 50 E
Anglem, Mt., N.Z. 131 G2 46 45 S 167 53 E
Anglès, Spain 40 D7 41 57N 2 38 E
Anglesey, Isle of □, U.K. 20 D3 53 16N 4 18W
Anglet, France 28 E2 43 29N 1 31W
Angleton, U.S.A. 155 L7 29 10N 95 26W
Anglin →, France 28 B4 46 42N 0 52 E
Anglisidhes, Cyprus 39 F9 34 51N 33 27 E
Anglure, France 27 D10 48 35N 3 50 E
Angmagssalik = Tasiilaq, Greenland 10 D7 65 40N 37 20W
Ango, Dem. Rep. of the Congo 118 B2 4 10N 26 5 E
Angoche, Mozam. 119 F4 16 8 S 39 55 E
Angoche, I., Mozam. 119 F4 16 20 S 39 50 E
Angol, Chile 174 D1 37 56 S 72 45W
Angola, Ind., U.S.A. 157 C12 41 38N 85 0W
Angola, N.Y., U.S.A. 150 D5 42 38N 79 2W
Angola ■, Africa 115 E3 12 0 S 18 0 E
Angoon, U.S.A. 144 H14 57 30N 134 35W
Angor, Uzbekistan 65 E3 37 27N 67 9 E
Angoram, Papua N. G. 132 C3 4 4 S 144 4 E
Angoulême, France 28 C4 45 39N 0 10 E
Angoumois, France 28 C4 45 50N 0 25 E
Angra do Heroismo, Azores 9 d1 38 39N 27 13W
Angra dos Reis, Brazil 175 A7 23 0 S 44 10W
Angren, Uzbekistan 66 E8 41 1N 70 12 E
Angtassom, Cambodia 87 G5 11 1N 104 41 E
Angu, Dem. Rep. of the Congo 118 B1 3 23N 24 30 E
Anguang, China 75 B12 45 15N 123 45 E
Anguilla ■, W. Indies 165 C7 18 14N 63 5W
Angul, India 94 D7 20 51N 85 6 E
Anguo, China 74 E8 38 28N 115 15 E
Angurugu, Australia 126 A2 14 0 S 136 25 E
Angus □, U.K. 22 E6 56 46N 2 56W
Angwa →, Zimbabwe 117 B5 16 0 S 30 23 E
Anhanduí →, Brazil 175 A5 21 46 S 52 9W
Anholt, Denmark 17 H5 56 42N 11 33 E
Anhua, China 77 C8 28 23N 111 12 E
Anhui □, China 77 B11 32 0N 117 0 E
Anhwei = Anhui □, China 77 B11 32 0N 117 0 E
Aniak, U.S.A. 144 F8 61 35N 159 32W
Anichab, Namibia 116 C1 21 0 S 14 46 E
Anicuns, Brazil 171 E2 16 28 S 49 58W
Ánidhros, Greece 49 E7 36 38N 25 43 E
Anié, Togo 113 D5 7 42N 1 8 E
Anil, Brazil 170 B3 2 32 S 44 14W
Animas →, U.S.A. 159 H9 36 43N 108 13W
Anina, Romania 52 E6 45 6N 21 51 E
Anini-y, Phil. 81 F3 10 25N 121 55 E
Aninoasa, Romania 53 F9 44 47N 24 10 E
Anita, U.S.A. 156 C2 41 27N 94 46W
Anivorano, Madag. 117 B8 18 44 S 48 58 E
Aniwa, Vanuatu 133 J7 19 17 S 169 35 E
Anjalankoski, Finland 15 F22 60 45N 26 51 E
Anjangaon, India 94 D3 21 10N 77 20 E
Anjar, India 92 H4 23 6N 70 10 E
Anjengo, India 95 K3 8 40N 76 46 E
Anji, China 77 B12 30 46N 119 40 E
Anjidiv I., India 95 G2 14 40N 74 10 E
Anjō, Japan 73 C9 34 57N 137 5 E
Anjou, France 26 E6 47 20N 0 15W
Anjouan, Comoros Is. 121 a 12 15 S 44 20 E
Anjozorobe, Madag. 117 B8 18 22 S 47 52 E
Anju, N. Korea 75 E13 39 36N 125 40 E
Anka, Nigeria 113 C6 12 13N 5 58 E
Ankaboa, Tanjona, Madag. 117 C7 21 58 S 43 20 E
Ankang, China 74 H5 32 40N 109 1 E
Ankara, Turkey 100 C5 39 57N 32 54 E
Ankarafantsika, Réserve Naturelle Intégrale d', Madag. 117 B8 16 8 S 47 5 E
Ankaramena, Madag. 117 C8 21 57 S 46 39 E
Ankarsrum, Sweden 17 G10 57 41N 16 20 E
Ankasakasa, Madag. 117 B7 16 21 S 44 52 E
Ankavandra, Madag. 117 B8 18 46 S 45 18 E
Ankazoabo, Madag. 117 C7 22 18 S 44 31 E
Ankazobe, Madag. 117 B8 18 20 S 47 10 E
Ankeny, U.S.A. 156 C3 41 44N 93 36W
Ankilimalinika, Madag. 117 C7 22 58 S 43 45 E
Ankilizato, Madag. 117 C8 20 25 S 45 1 E
Ankisabe, Madag. 117 B8 19 17 S 46 29 E
Anklam, Germany 30 B9 53 51N 13 41 E
Ankleshwar, India 94 D1 21 38N 73 3 E
Ankober, Ethiopia 107 F4 9 35N 39 40 E
Ankola, India 95 G2 14 40N 74 18 E
Ankoro, Dem. Rep. of the Congo 118 D2 6 45 S 26 55 E
Ankororoka, Madag. 117 D8 25 30 S 45 11 E
Anlong, China 76 E5 25 2N 105 27 E
Anlu, China 77 B9 31 15N 113 45 E
Anmyŏn-do, S. Korea 75 F14 36 25N 126 25 E
Ånn, Sweden 16 A6 63 16N 12 34 E
Ann, C., U.S.A. 151 D14 42 38N 70 35W
Ann Arbor, U.S.A. 157 B13 42 17N 83 45W
Anna, Russia 60 E5 51 28N 40 23 E
Anna, Ill., U.S.A. 155 G10 37 28N 89 15W
Anna, Ohio, U.S.A. 157 D12 40 24N 84 11W
Anna Regina, Guyana 169 B6 7 10N 58 30W
Annaba, Algeria 111 A6 36 50N 7 46 E
Annaberg-Buchholz, Germany 30 E9 50 34N 13 0 E
Annai, Guyana 169 C6 3 57N 59 8W
Annaka, Japan 73 A10 36 19N 138 54 E
Annalee →, Ireland 23 B4 54 2N 7 24W
Annam, Vietnam 86 E7 16 0N 108 0 E
Annamitique, Chaîne, Asia 86 D6 17 0N 106 0 E
Annan, U.K. 22 G5 54 59N 3 16W
Annan →, U.K. 22 G5 54 58N 3 16W
Annanberg, Papua N. G. 132 C3 4 52 S 144 42 E
Annapolis, U.S.A. 148 F7 38 59N 76 30W
Annapolis Royal, Canada 141 D6 44 44N 65 32W
Annapurna, Nepal 93 E10 28 34N 83 50 E
Annean, L., Australia 125 E2 26 54 S 118 14 E
Anneberg, Sweden 17 G8 57 44N 14 49 E
Annecy, France 29 C10 45 55N 6 8 E
Annecy, Lac d', France 29 C10 45 52N 6 10 E
Annemasse, France 27 F13 46 12N 6 16 E
Annenskiy Most, Russia 58 B9 60 45N 37 10 E
Annette I., U.S.A. 144 J15 55 9N 131 28W
Annigeri, India 95 G2 15 26N 75 26 E
Anning, China 76 E4 24 55N 102 26 E
Anniston, U.S.A. 152 B4 33 39N 85 50W
Annobón, Atl. Oc. 105 G4 1 25 S 5 36 E
Annonay, France 29 C8 45 15N 4 40 E
Annot, France 29 E10 43 58N 6 38 E
Annotto Bay, Jamaica 164 a 18 17N 76 45W
Ånnsjön, Sweden 16 A6 63 19N 12 34 E
Annville, U.S.A. 151 F8 40 20N 76 31W
Annweiler, Germany 31 F3 49 12N 7 57 E
Áno Arkhánai, Greece 49 F7 35 16N 25 11 E
Áno Porróia, Greece 50 E7 41 17N 23 2 E
Áno Síros, Greece 48 D6 37 29N 24 56 E
Áno Viánnos, Greece 39 E6 35 2N 25 21 E
Anorotsangana, Madag. 117 A8 13 56 S 47 55 E
Anosibe, Madag. 117 B8 19 26 S 48 13 E
Anou Mellene, Mali 113 B5 17 29N 0 33 E
Anoumaba, Ivory C. 112 D4 6 23N 4 38W
Anoyí, Greece 39 C2 38 25N 20 40 E
Anóyia, Greece 39 E5 35 16N 24 52 E
Anping, Hebei, China 74 E8 38 15N 115 30 E
Anping, Liaoning, China 75 D12 41 5N 123 30 E
Anpu Gang, China 76 G7 21 25N 109 50 E
Anqing, China 77 B11 30 30N 117 3 E
Anqiu, China 75 F10 36 25N 119 10 E
Anren, China 77 D9 26 43N 113 18 E
Ansager, Denmark 17 J2 55 43N 8 45 E
Ansai, China 74 F5 36 50N 109 20 E
Ansbach, Germany 31 F6 49 28N 10 34 E
Anse Boileau, Seychelles 121 b 4 43 S 55 29 E
Anse Royale, Seychelles 121 b 4 44 S 55 31 E
Anseba →, Eritrea 107 D4 16 0N 38 30 E
Anserma, Colombia 168 B2 5 13N 75 48W
Ansfelden, Austria 34 C7 48 12N 14 17 E
Anshan, China 75 D12 41 5N 122 58 E
Anshun, China 76 D5 26 18N 105 57 E
Ansião, Portugal 42 F2 39 56N 8 27W
Ansley, U.S.A. 154 E5 41 18N 99 23W
Ansó, Spain 40 C4 42 51N 0 48W
Ansoain, Spain 40 C3 42 50N 1 38W
Anson, U.S.A. 155 J5 32 45N 99 54W
Anson B., Australia 124 B5 13 20 S 130 6 E
Ansongo, Mali 113 B5 15 25N 0 35 E
Ansongo-Ménaka, Réserve d', Mali 113 B5 15 3N 1 37 E
Ansonia, Conn., U.S.A. 151 E11 41 21N 73 5W
Ansonia, Ohio, U.S.A. 157 D12 40 13N 84 38W
Anstruther, U.K. 22 E6 56 14N 2 41W
Ansudu, Indonesia 83 B5 2 11 S 139 22 E
Ansus, Indonesia 83 B5 1 44 S 135 49 E
Antabamba, Peru 172 C3 14 40 S 73 0W
Antagarh, India 94 D5 20 6N 81 9 E
Antakya, Turkey 100 D7 36 14N 36 10 E
Antalaha, Madag. 117 A9 14 57 S 50 20 E
Antalāt, Libya 108 B4 31 8N 20 42 E
Antalya, Turkey 100 D4 36 52N 30 45 E
Antalya □, Turkey 49 E12 36 30N 30 0 E
Antalya Körfezi, Turkey 100 D4 36 15N 31 30 E
Antambohobe, Madag. 117 C8 22 20 S 46 47 E
Antanambao-Manampotsy, Madag. 117 B8 19 29 S 48 34 E
Antanambe, Madag. 117 B8 16 26 S 49 52 E
Antananarivo, Madag. 117 B8 18 55 S 47 31 E
Antananarivo □, Madag. 117 B8 19 0 S 47 0 E
Antanifotsy, Madag. 117 B8 19 39 S 47 19 E
Antanimbaribe, Madag. 117 C7 21 30 S 44 48 E
Antanimora, Madag. 117 C8 24 49 S 45 40 E
Antarctic Pen., Antarctica 7 C18 67 0 S 60 0W
Antarctica 7 E3 90 0 S 0 0W
Antécume Pata, Fr. Guiana 169 C7 3 17N 54 4W
Antelope, Zimbabwe 119 G2 21 2 S 28 31 E
Antenor Navarro, Brazil 170 C4 6 44 S 38 27W
Antequera, Paraguay 174 A4 24 8 S 57 7W
Antequera, Spain 43 H6 37 5N 4 33W
Antero, Mt., U.S.A. 159 G10 38 41N 106 15W
Antevamena, Madag. 117 C7 21 2 S 44 8 E
Anthemoús, Greece 50 F7 40 31N 23 15 E
Anthony, Fla., U.S.A. 153 F7 29 18N 82 7W
Anthony, Kans., U.S.A. 155 G5 37 9N 98 2W
Anthony, N. Mex., U.S.A. 159 K10 32 0N 106 36W
Anti Atlas, Morocco 110 C3 30 0N 8 30W
Anti-Lebanon = Ash Sharqi, Al Jabal, Lebanon 103 B5 33 40N 36 10 E
Antibes, France 29 E11 43 34N 7 6 E
Antibes, C. d', France 29 E11 43 31N 7 7 E
Anticosti, Î. d', Canada 141 C7 49 30N 63 0W
Antifer, C. d', France 26 C7 49 41N 0 10 E
Antigo, U.S.A. 154 C10 45 9N 89 9W
Antigonish, Canada 141 C7 45 38N 61 58W
Antigua, Canary Is. 9 e2 28 24N 14 1W
Antigua, Guatemala 164 D1 14 34N 90 41W
Antigua, W. Indies 165 C7 17 0N 61 50W
Antigua & Barbuda ■, W. Indies 165 C7 17 20N 61 48W
Antilla, Cuba 164 B4 20 40N 75 50W
Antilles = West Indies, Cent. Amer. 165 D7 15 0N 65 0W
Antioch, U.S.A. 160 G5 38 1N 121 48W
Antioche, Pertuis d', France 28 B2 46 6N 1 20W
Antioquia, Colombia 168 B2 6 40N 75 55W
Antioquia □, Colombia 168 B2 7 0N 75 30W
Antipodes Is., Pac. Oc. 134 M9 49 45 S 178 40 E
Antipolo, Phil. 80 D3 14 35N 121 10 E
Antique □, Phil. 81 F4 11 10N 122 5 E
Antlers, U.S.A. 155 H7 34 14N 95 37W
Antoetra, Madag. 117 C8 20 46 S 47 20 E
Antofagasta, Chile 174 A1 23 50 S 70 30W
Antofagasta □, Chile 174 A2 24 0 S 69 0W
Antofagasta de la Sierra, Argentina 174 B2 26 5 S 67 20W
Antofalla, Argentina 174 B2 25 30 S 68 5W
Antofalla, Salar de, Argentina 174 B2 25 40 S 67 45W
Anton, U.S.A. 155 J3 33 49N 102 10W
Antongila, Helodrano, Madag. 117 B8 15 30 S 49 50 E
Antonibé, Madag. 117 B8 15 7 S 47 24 E
Antonibé, Presqu'île d', Madag. 117 A8 14 55 S 47 20 E
Antonina, Brazil 175 B6 25 26 S 48 42W
Antrain, France 26 D5 48 28N 1 30W
Antrim, U.K. 23 B5 54 43N 6 14W
Antrim, U.S.A. 150 F3 40 7N 81 21W
Antrim □, U.K. 23 B5 54 56N 6 25W
Antrim, Mts. of, U.K. 23 A5 55 3N 6 14W
Antrim Plateau, Australia 124 C4 18 8 S 128 20 E
Antrodoco, Italy 45 F10 42 25N 13 5 E
Antropovo, Russia 60 A6 58 24N 43 6 E
Antsakabary, Madag. 117 B8 15 3 S 48 56 E
Antsalova, Madag. 117 B7 18 40 S 44 37 E
Antsenavolo, Madag. 117 C8 21 24 S 48 3 E
Antsiafabositra, Madag. 117 B8 17 18 S 46 57 E
Antsirabe, Antananarivo, Madag. 117 B8 19 55 S 47 2 E
Antsirabe, Antsiranana, Madag. 117 A8 14 0 S 49 59 E
Antsirabe, Mahajanga, Madag. 117 B8 15 57 S 48 58 E
Antsiranana, Madag. 117 A8 12 25 S 49 20 E
Antsiranana □, Madag. 117 A8 12 16 S 49 17 E
Antsohihy, Madag. 117 A8 14 50 S 47 59 E
Antsohimbondrona Seranana, Madag. 117 A8 13 7 S 48 48 E
Antu, China 75 C15 42 30N 128 20 E
Antufash, Yemen 98 D3 15 42N 42 25 E
Antwerp = Antwerpen, Belgium 24 C4 51 13N 4 25 E
Antwerp, N.Y., U.S.A. 151 B9 44 12N 75 37W
Antwerp, Ohio, U.S.A. 157 C12 41 11N 84 45W
Antwerpen, Belgium 24 C4 51 13N 4 25 E
Antwerpen □, Belgium 24 C4 51 15N 4 40 E
Anukur, C., Papua N. G. 132 D5 6 18 S 149 37 E
Anupgarh, India 92 E5 29 10N 73 10 E
Anuppur, India 93 H9 23 6N 81 41 E
Anuradhapura, Sri Lanka 95 K5 8 22N 80 28 E
Anveh, Iran 97 E7 27 23N 54 11 E
Anvers = Antwerpen, Belgium 24 C4 51 13N 4 25 E
Anvers I., Antarctica 7 C17 64 30 S 63 40W
Anvik, U.S.A. 144 E7 62 39N 160 13W
Anwen, China 77 C13 29 4N 120 26 E
Anxi, Fujian, China 77 E12 25 2N 118 12 E
Anxi, Gansu, China 68 B4 40 30N 95 43 E
Anxian, China 76 B5 31 40N 104 25 E
Anxiang, China 77 C9 29 27N 112 11 E
Anxious B., Australia 127 E1 33 24 S 134 45 E
Anyama, Ivory C. 112 D4 5 30N 4 3W

Anyang, *China* **74 F8** 36 5N 114 21 E
Anyer, *Indonesia* **84 D3** 6 4 S 105 53 E
Anyer-Kidul, *Indonesia* **79 G11** 6 4 S 105 53 E
Anyi, *Jiangxi, China* **77 C10** 28 49N 115 25 E
Anyi, *Shanxi, China* **74 G6** 35 2N 111 2 E
Anyuan, *China* **77 E10** 25 9N 115 21 E
Anyue, *China* **76 B5** 30 9N 105 50 E
Anza, *U.S.A.* **161 M10** 33 35N 116 39W
Anze, *China* **74 F7** 36 10N 112 12 E
Anzhero-Sudzhensk, *Russia* **66 D9** 56 10N 86 0 E
Ánzio, *Italy* **46 A5** 41 27N 12 37 E
Anzoátegui □, *Venezuela* **169 B5** 9 0N 64 30W
Ao Makham, *Thailand* **87 a** 7 50N 98 24 E
Aoba, *Vanuatu* **133 E5** 15 25 S 167 50 E
Aoga-Shima, *Japan* **73 E11** 32 28N 139 46 E
Aoiz, *Spain* **40 C3** 42 46N 1 22W
Aola, *Solomon Is.* **133 M11** 9 30 S 160 30 E
Aomen = Macau, *China* **77 F9** 22 12N 113 33 E
Aomori, *Japan* **70 D10** 40 45N 140 45 E
Aomori □, *Japan* **70 D10** 40 45N 140 40 E
Aonla, *India* **93 E8** 28 16N 79 11 E
Aono-Yama, *Japan* **72 C3** 34 28N 131 48 E
Aoraki Mount Cook, *N.Z.* **131 D5** 43 36 S 170 9 E
Aorangi Mts., *N.Z.* **130 H4** 41 28 S 175 22 E
Aore, *Vanuatu* **133 E5** 15 35 S 167 10 E
Aoreora, *Morocco* **110 C2** 28 51N 10 53W
Aosta, *Italy* **44 C4** 45 45N 7 20 E
Aotea Harbour, *N.Z.* **130 D3** 38 0 S 174 50 E
Aoudéras, *Niger* **113 B6** 17 45N 8 20 E
Aouinet Torkoz, *Morocco* **110 C3** 28 31N 9 46W
Aouk, Bahr ➛, *Africa* **109 G3** 8 51N 18 53 E
Aouk-Aoukalé, Réserve de Faune de l', *C.A.R.* **114 A4** 9 52N 21 25 E
Aoukar, *Mali* **110 D4** 23 50N 2 45W
Aoukâr, *Mauritania* **112 B3** 17 40N 10 0W
Aoulef el Arab, *Algeria* **111 C5** 26 55N 1 2 E
Aozou, *Chad* **109 D3** 21 45N 17 28 E
Aozou Strip, *Chad* **109 D3** 22 0N 19 0 E
Apa ➛, *S. Amer.* **174 A4** 22 6 S 58 2W
Apache, *U.S.A.* **155 H5** 34 54N 98 22W
Apache Junction, *U.S.A.* **159 K8** 33 25N 111 33W
Apalachee B., *U.S.A.* **152 E5** 30 0N 84 0W
Apalachicola, *U.S.A.* **152 F5** 29 43N 84 59W
Apalachicola ➛, *U.S.A.* **152 F5** 29 43N 84 58W
Apalachicola B., *U.S.A.* **152 F3** 29 40N 85 0W
Apam, *Ghana* **113 D4** 5 19N 0 42W
Apapa, *Nigeria* **113 D5** 6 25N 3 25 E
Apaporis ➛, *Colombia* **168 D4** 1 23 S 69 25W
Aparecida do Taboado, *Brazil* **171 F1** 20 5 S 51 5W
Aparri, *Phil.* **80 B3** 18 22N 121 38 E
Aparurén, *Venezuela* **169 B5** 5 6N 62 8W
Apateu, *Romania* **52 D6** 46 36N 21 47 E
Apatin, *Serbia, Yug.* **52 E4** 45 40N 19 0 E
Apatity, *Russia* **56 A5** 67 34N 33 22 E
Apatou, *Fr. Guiana* **169 B7** 5 9N 54 20W
Apatzingán, *Mexico* **162 D4** 19 0N 102 20W
Apauwar, *Indonesia* **83 B5** 1 39 S 138 11 E
Apayao □, *Phil.* **80 B3** 18 10N 121 10 E
Apeldoorn, *Neths.* **24 B5** 52 13N 5 57 E
Apen, *Germany* **30 B3** 53 13N 7 48 E
Apennines = Appennini, *Italy* **44 E7** 44 0N 10 0 E
Apere ➛, *Bolivia* **173 C4** 13 44 S 65 18W
Aphrodisias, *Turkey* **49 D10** 37 42N 28 46 E
Apia, *Samoa* **133 W24** 13 50 S 171 50W
Apiacás, Serra dos, *Brazil* **173 B6** 9 50 S 57 0W
Apiaí, *Brazil* **171 F2** 24 31 S 48 50W
Apiaú ➛, *Brazil* **169 C5** 2 39N 61 12W
Apiaú, Serra do, *Brazil* **169 C5** 2 30N 62 0W
Apidiá ➛, *Brazil* **173 C5** 11 39 S 61 11W
Apies ➛, *S. Africa* **117 D4** 25 15 S 28 8 E
Apinajé, *Brazil* **171 D2** 11 31 S 48 18W
Apiti, *N.Z.* **130 F4** 39 58 S 175 54 E
Apizaco, *Mexico* **163 D5** 19 26N 98 9W
Aplao, *Peru* **172 D3** 16 0 S 72 40W
Apo, Mt., *Phil.* **81 H5** 6 53N 125 14 E
Apo East Pass, *Phil.* **80 E3** 12 40N 120 40 E
Apo West Pass, *Phil.* **80 E3** 12 31N 120 22 E
Apodi, *Brazil* **170 C4** 5 39 S 37 48W
Apoera, *Surinam* **169 B6** 5 12N 57 10W
Apolakkiá, *Greece* **38 E11** 36 5N 27 48 E
Apolakkiá, Órmos, *Greece* **38 E11** 36 5N 27 45 E
Apolda, *Germany* **30 D7** 51 2N 11 32 E
Apollo Bay, *Australia* **128 E5** 38 45 S 143 40 E
Apollonia = Marsá Susah, *Libya* **108 B4** 32 52N 21 59 E
Apollonia, *Greece* **48 E6** 36 58N 24 43 E
Apolo, *Bolivia* **172 C4** 14 30 S 68 30W
Apónguao ➛, *Venezuela* **169 C5** 4 48N 61 36W
Apopka, *U.S.A.* **153 G8** 28 40N 81 31W
Apopka L., *U.S.A.* **153 G8** 28 38N 81 38W
Aporé, *Brazil* **173 D7** 18 58 S 52 1W
Aporé ➛, *Brazil* **171 E1** 19 27 S 50 57W
Aporema, *Brazil* **170 A1** 1 14N 50 49W
Apostle Is., *U.S.A.* **154 B9** 47 0N 90 40W
Apóstoles, *Argentina* **175 B4** 28 0 S 56 0W
Apostolos Andreas, C., *Cyprus* **39 E10** 35 42N 34 35 E
Apostolovo, *Ukraine* **59 J7** 47 39N 33 39 E
Apoteri, *Guyana* **169 C6** 4 2N 58 32W
Appalachian Mts., *U.S.A.* **148 G6** 38 0N 80 0W
Äppelbo, *Sweden* **16 D8** 60 29N 14 1 E
Appennini, *Italy* **44 E7** 44 0N 10 0 E
Appennino Ligure, *Italy* **44 D6** 44 30N 9 0 E
Appenzell, *Switz.* **33 B8** 47 20N 9 25 E
Appenzell-Ausser Rhoden □, *Switz.* **33 B8** 47 23N 9 23 E
Appenzell-Inner Rhoden □, *Switz.* **33 B8** 47 20N 9 25 E
Appiano, *Italy* **45 B8** 46 28N 11 15 E
Apple Hill, *Canada* **151 A10** 45 13N 74 46W
Apple Valley, *U.S.A.* **161 L9** 34 32N 117 14W
Appleby-in-Westmorland, *U.K.* **20 C5** 54 35N 2 29W
Apples, *Switz.* **32 C2** 46 33N 6 26 E
Appleton, *U.S.A.* **148 C1** 44 16N 88 25W
Appleton City, *U.S.A.* **156 F2** 38 11N 94 2W
Appling, *U.S.A.* **152 B7** 33 33N 82 19W
Approuague, *Fr. Guiana* **169 C7** 4 20N 52 0W
Apricena, *Italy* **33 D10** 46 9N 10 6 E
Apricena, *Italy* **45 G12** 41 47N 15 27 E
April ➛, *Papua N. G.* **132 C2** 4 18 S 142 26 E
Aprília, *Italy* **46 A5** 41 36N 12 39 E
Apsheronsk, *Russia* **61 H4** 44 28N 39 42 E
Apsley, *Canada* **150 B6** 44 45N 78 6W
Apt, *France* **29 E9** 43 53N 5 24 E
Apuane, Alpi, *Italy* **44 D7** 44 7N 10 14 E
Apuaú, *Brazil* **169 D5** 2 25 S 60 53W
Apucarana, *Brazil* **175 A5** 23 55 S 51 33W
Apulia = Púglia □, *Italy* **47 A9** 41 15N 16 15 E
Apurauan, *Phil.* **81 G2** 9 35N 118 20 E
Apure □, *Venezuela* **168 B4** 7 10N 68 50W
Apure ➛, *Venezuela* **168 B4** 7 37N 66 25W
Apurímac □, *Peru* **172 C3** 14 0 S 73 0W
Apurimac ➛, *Peru* **172 C3** 12 17 S 73 56W
Apuseni, Munţii, *Romania* **52 D7** 46 30N 22 45 E
Āqā Jarī, *Iran* **97 D6** 30 42N 49 50 E
Aqaba = Al 'Aqabah, *Jordan* **103 F4** 29 31N 35 0 E
Aqaba, G. of, *Red Sea* **96 D2** 28 15N 33 20 E
'Aqabah, Khalīj al = Aqaba, G. of, *Red Sea* **96 D2** 28 15N 33 20 E
Aqbaqay, *Kazakstan* **65 A6** 45 0N 72 47 E
Āqcheh, *Afghan.* **65 E3** 36 56N 66 11 E
'Aqdā, *Iran* **97 C7** 32 26N 53 37 E
Aqīq, *Sudan* **106 D4** 18 14N 38 12 E
Aqīq, Khalīg, *Sudan* **106 D4** 18 20N 38 10 E
'Aqīq, W. al ➛, *Si. Arabia* **98 B3** 20 16N 41 40 E
Aqköl, *Kazakstan* **65 A7** 45 0N 75 39 E
Aqköl, *Kazakstan* **65 B5** 43 36N 70 45 E
Aqmola = Astana, *Kazakstan* **66 D8** 51 10N 71 30 E
Aqqum, *Kazakstan* **65 A2** 44 50N 65 8 E
'Aqrah, *Iraq* **101 D10** 36 46N 43 45 E
Aqshī, *Kazakstan* **65 B8** 43 59N 76 19 E
Aqsū, *Kazakstan* **65 B4** 42 25N 69 50 E
Aqsügek, *Kazakstan* **65 A7** 44 37N 74 30 E
Aqsūmbe, *Kazakstan* **65 A3** 44 26N 67 33 E
Aqtaū, *Kazakstan* **66 E6** 43 39N 51 12 E
Aqtöbe, *Kazakstan* **57 D10** 50 17N 57 10 E
Aquidauana, *Brazil* **173 E6** 20 30 S 55 50W
Aquidauana ➛, *Brazil* **173 D6** 19 44 S 56 50W
Aquiles Serdán, *Mexico* **162 B3** 28 37N 105 54W
Aquin, *Haiti* **165 C5** 18 16N 73 24W
Aquitain, Bassin, *France* **25 D3** 44 0N 0 30W
Aquitaine □, *France* **28 D3** 44 25N 0 30W
Aqviligjuaq = Pelly Bay, *Canada* **139 B11** 68 38N 89 50W
Aqyrtöbe, *Kazakstan* **65 B6** 42 59N 72 7 E
Aqzhar, *Kazakstan* **65 B5** 43 8N 71 37 E
Ar Rachidiya = Er Rachidia, *Morocco* **110 B4** 31 58N 4 20W
Ar Rafid, *Syria* **103 C4** 32 57N 35 52 E
Ar Raḥḥālīyah, *Iraq* **101 F10** 32 44N 43 23 E
Ar Ramādī, *Iraq* **101 F10** 33 25N 43 20 E
Ar Raml, *Libya* **108 C3** 26 45N 19 40 E
Ar Ramthā, *Jordan* **103 C5** 32 34N 36 0 E
Ar Raqqah, *Syria* **101 E8** 35 59N 39 8 E
Ar Rass, *Si. Arabia* **96 E4** 25 50N 43 40 E
Ar Rawḑah, *Si. Arabia* **98 B3** 21 16N 42 50 E
Ar Rawḑah, *Yemen* **98 D4** 14 28N 47 17 E
Ar Rawshān, *Si. Arabia* **106 C5** 20 2N 42 36 E
Ar Rifā'ī, *Iraq* **96 D5** 31 50N 46 10 E
Ar Rijā', *Yemen* **98 D4** 13 1N 44 35 E
Ar Riyāḑ, *Si. Arabia* **96 E5** 24 41N 46 42 E
Ar Ru'ays, *Qatar* **97 E6** 26 8N 51 12 E
Ar Rukhaymīyah, *Iraq* **96 D5** 29 22N 45 38 E
Ar Ruşāfah, *Syria* **101 E8** 35 45N 38 49 E
Ar Ruţbah, *Iraq* **101 F9** 33 0N 40 15 E
Ar Ruwayḑah, *Si. Arabia* **98 B4** 23 40N 44 40 E
Ara, *India* **93 G11** 25 35N 84 32 E
Ara Goro, *Ethiopia* **107 F5** 5 48N 41 18 E
Ara Tera, *Ethiopia* **107 F5** 6 38N 40 57 E
Arab, *U.S.A.* **149 H2** 34 19N 86 30W
'Arab, Bahr el ➛, *Sudan* **107 F2** 9 0N 29 30 E
Arab, Khalîg el, *Egypt* **106 A2** 30 55N 29 0 E
Arab, Shatt al ➛, *Asia* **97 D6** 30 0N 48 31 E
'Araba, W. ➛, *Egypt* **106 J8** 28 19N 33 31 E
'Arabābād, *Iran* **97 C8** 33 2N 57 41 E
'Arabah, W. ➛, *Yemen* **99 C5** 18 5N 51 26 E
Araban, *Turkey* **100 D7** 37 28N 37 44 E
Arabatskaya Strelka, *Ukraine* **59 K8** 45 40N 35 0 E
Arabba, *Italy* **45 B8** 46 30N 11 52 E
Arabelo, *Venezuela* **169 C5** 4 55N 64 13W
Arabi, *U.S.A.* **152 D6** 31 50N 83 44W
Arabia, *Asia* **62 G8** 25 0N 45 0 E
Arabian Desert = Es Sahrâ' Esh Sharqîya, *Egypt* **106 B3** 27 30N 32 30 E
Arabian Gulf = Gulf, The, *Asia* **97 E6** 27 0N 50 0 E
Arabian Sea, *Ind. Oc.* **62 H10** 16 0N 65 0 E
Araç, *Turkey* **100 B5** 41 15N 33 21 E
Aracaju, *Brazil* **170 D4** 10 55 S 37 4W
Aracataca, *Colombia* **168 A3** 10 38N 74 9W
Aracati, *Brazil* **170 B4** 4 30 S 37 44W
Araçatuba, *Brazil* **175 A5** 21 10 S 50 30W
Araceli, *Phil.* **81 F2** 10 33N 119 59 E
Aracena, *Spain* **43 H4** 37 53N 6 38W
Aracena, Sierra de, *Spain* **43 H4** 37 50N 6 50W
Aracides, C., *Solomon Is.* **133 M11** 8 21 S 161 0 E
Aračinovo, *Macedonia* **50 D5** 42 1N 21 34 E
Araçuaí, *Brazil* **171 E3** 16 52 S 42 4W
Araçuaí ➛, *Brazil* **171 E3** 16 46 S 42 2W
'Arad, *Israel* **103 D4** 31 15N 35 12 E
Arad, *Romania* **52 D6** 46 10N 21 20 E
Arad □, *Romania* **52 D6** 46 20N 22 0 E
Arada, *Chad* **109 F4** 15 0N 20 20 E
Arādān, *Iran* **97 C7** 35 21N 52 30 E
Aradhippou, *Cyprus* **39 F9** 34 57N 33 36 E
Arafura Sea, *E. Indies* **83 C5** 9 0 S 135 0 E
Aragarças, *Brazil* **173 D7** 15 55 S 52 15W
Aragats, *Armenia* **61 K7** 40 30N 44 15 E
Aragon, *U.S.A.* **152 A4** 34 2N 85 3W
Aragón □, *Spain* **40 D4** 41 25N 0 40W
Aragón ➛, *Spain* **40 C3** 42 13N 1 44W
Aragona, *Italy* **46 E6** 37 24N 13 27 E
Aragua □, *Venezuela* **168 B4** 10 0N 67 10W
Aragua de Barcelona, *Venezuela* **169 B5** 9 28N 64 49W
Araguacema, *Brazil* **170 C2** 8 50 S 49 20W
Araguaçu, *Brazil* **171 D2** 12 49 S 49 51W
Araguaia ➛, *Brazil* **170 C2** 5 21 S 48 41W
Araguaiana, *Brazil* **173 D7** 15 43 S 51 51W
Araguaína, *Brazil* **170 C2** 7 12 S 48 12W
Araguari, *Brazil* **171 E2** 18 38 S 48 11W
Araguari ➛, *Brazil* **169 C8** 1 15N 49 55W
Araguatins, *Brazil* **170 C2** 5 38 S 48 7W
Arain, *India* **92 F6** 26 27N 75 2 E
Araioses, *Brazil* **170 B3** 2 53 S 41 55W
Arak, *Algeria* **111 C5** 25 20N 3 45 E
Arāk, *Iran* **97 C6** 34 0N 49 40 E
Araka, *Sudan* **107 G3** 4 20N 30 23 E
Arakan □, *Burma* **90 F5** 19 0N 94 15 E
Arakan Yoma, *Burma* **90 F5** 20 0N 94 40 E
Arákhova, *Greece* **48 C4** 38 28N 22 35 E
Arakkonam, *India* **95 H4** 13 7N 79 43 E
Arakli, *Turkey* **101 B8** 41 6N 40 2 E
Araks = Aras, Rūd-e ➛, *Asia* **61 K9** 40 5N 48 29 E
Aral, *Kazakstan* **66 E7** 46 41N 61 45 E
Aral Sea, *Asia* **66 E7** 44 30N 60 0 E
Aral Tengizi = Aral Sea, *Asia* **66 E7** 44 30N 60 0 E
Aralsk = Aral, *Kazakstan* **66 E7** 46 41N 61 45 E
Aralskoye More = Aral Sea, *Asia* **66 E7** 44 30N 60 0 E
Aralsor, Ozero, *Kazakstan* **61 F9** 49 5N 48 12 E
Aramac, *Australia* **126 C4** 22 58 S 145 14 E
Aramia ➛, *Papua N. G.* **132 D2** 7 55 S 143 22 E
Aran ➛, *India* **94 E4** 19 55N 78 12 E
Aran Areh, *Ethiopia* **120 C2** 9 2N 43 54 E
Aran I., *Ireland* **23 A3** 55 0N 8 30W
Aran Is., *Ireland* **23 C2** 53 6N 9 38W
Aranda de Duero, *Spain* **42 D7** 41 39N 3 42W
Arandān, *Iran* **96 C5** 35 23N 46 55 E
Arandelovac, *Serbia, Yug.* **50 B4** 44 18N 20 27 E
Aranga, *N.Z.* **130 B2** 35 44 S 173 40 E
Arani, *Bolivia* **173 D4** 17 34 S 65 46W
Arani, *India* **95 H4** 12 43N 79 19 E
Aranjuez, *Spain* **42 E7** 40 1N 3 40W
Aranos, *Namibia* **116 C2** 24 9 S 19 7 E
Aransas Pass, *U.S.A.* **155 M6** 27 55N 97 9W
Aranyaprathet, *Thailand* **86 F4** 13 41N 102 30 E
Arao, *Japan* **72 E2** 32 59N 130 25 E
Araouane, *Mali* **112 B4** 18 55N 3 30W
Arapahoe, *U.S.A.* **154 E5** 40 18N 99 54W
Arapari, *Brazil* **170 C2** 5 34 S 49 15W
Arapawa I., *N.Z.* **131 B9** 41 11 S 174 17 E
Arapey Grande ➛, *Uruguay* **174 C4** 30 55 S 57 49W
Arapgir, *Turkey* **101 C8** 39 5N 38 30 E
Arapiraca, *Brazil* **170 C4** 9 45 S 36 39W
Arapongas, *Brazil* **175 A5** 23 29 S 51 28W
Arapuni, *N.Z.* **130 E4** 38 4 S 175 39 E
Ar'ar, *Si. Arabia* **96 D4** 30 59N 41 2 E
Araracuara, *Colombia* **168 D3** 0 24 S 72 17W
Araranguá, *Brazil* **175 B6** 29 0 S 49 30W
Araraquara, *Brazil* **171 F2** 21 50 S 48 0W
Araras, *Brazil* **171 F2** 22 22 S 47 23W
Ararás, Serra das, *Brazil* **175 B5** 25 0 S 53 10W
Ararat, *Armenia* **101 C11** 39 48N 44 50 E
Ararat, *Australia* **128 D5** 37 16 S 143 0 E
Ararat, Mt. = Ağrı Dağı, *Turkey* **101 C11** 39 50N 44 15 E
Arari, *Brazil* **170 B3** 3 28 S 44 47W
Araria, *India* **93 F12** 26 9N 87 33 E
Araripe, Chapada do, *Brazil* **170 C3** 7 20 S 40 0W
Araripina, *Brazil* **170 C3** 7 33 S 40 34W
Araruama, L. de, *Brazil* **171 F3** 22 53 S 42 12W
Araruna, *Brazil* **170 C4** 6 52 S 35 44W
Aras, Rūd-e ➛, *Asia* **61 K9** 40 5N 48 29 E
Aratâne, *Mauritania* **112 B3** 18 24N 8 32W
Araticu, *Brazil* **170 B2** 1 58 S 49 51W
Arauca, *Colombia* **168 B3** 7 0N 70 40W
Arauca □, *Colombia* **168 B3** 6 40N 71 0W
Arauca ➛, *Venezuela* **168 B4** 7 24N 66 35W
Arauco, *Chile* **174 D1** 37 16 S 73 25W
Araújos, *Brazil* **171 E2** 19 56 S 45 14W
Arauquita, *Colombia* **168 B3** 7 2N 71 25W
Araure, *Venezuela* **168 B4** 9 34N 69 13W
Arawa, *Ethiopia* **107 F5** 9 57N 41 58 E
Arawale Nat. Reserve, *Kenya* **118 C5** 1 24 S 40 9 E
Arawata ➛, *N.Z.* **131 E3** 44 0 S 168 40 E
Arawe Is., *Papua N. G.* **132 D5** 6 6 S 149 0 E
Araxá, *Brazil* **171 E2** 19 35 S 46 55W
Araya, Pen. de, *Venezuela* **169 A5** 10 40N 64 0W
Arayat, *Phil.* **80 D3** 15 10N 120 46 E
Arba Gugu, *Ethiopia* **107 F5** 8 40N 40 15 E
Arba Minch, *Ethiopia* **107 F4** 6 0N 37 30 E
Arbat, *Iraq* **101 E11** 35 25N 45 35 E
Àrbatax, *Italy* **46 C2** 39 56N 9 42 E
Arbedo, *Switz.* **33 D8** 46 12N 9 3 E
Arbi, *Ethiopia* **107 F4** 9 4N 35 7 E
Arbīl, *Iraq* **101 D11** 36 15N 44 5 E
Arboga, *Sweden* **16 E9** 59 24N 15 52 E
Arbois, *France* **27 F12** 46 55N 5 46 E
Arboletes, *Colombia* **168 B2** 8 51N 76 26W
Arbon, *Switz.* **33 A8** 47 31N 9 26 E
Arbore, *Ethiopia* **107 F4** 5 3N 36 50 E
Arboréa, *Italy* **46 C1** 39 46N 8 35 E
Arborfield, *Canada* **143 C8** 53 6N 103 39W
Arborg, *Canada* **143 C9** 50 54N 97 13W
Arbre du Ténéré, *Niger* **113 B7** 17 50N 10 4 E
Arbroath, *U.K.* **22 E6** 56 34N 2 35W
Arbuckle, *U.S.A.* **160 F4** 39 1N 122 3W
Arbus, *Italy* **46 C1** 39 30N 8 33 E
Arc ➛, *France* **29 C10** 45 34N 6 12 E
Arc-lès-Gray, *France* **27 E12** 47 28N 5 34 E
Arcachon, *France* **28 D2** 44 40N 1 10W
Arcachon, Bassin d', *France* **28 D2** 44 42N 1 10W
Arcade, *Calif., U.S.A.* **161 L8** 34 2N 118 15W
Arcade, *N.Y., U.S.A.* **150 D6** 42 32N 78 25W
Arcadia, *Fla., U.S.A.* **149 M5** 27 13N 81 52W
Arcadia, *Ind., U.S.A.* **157 D10** 40 11N 86 1W
Arcadia, *Iowa, U.S.A.* **156 B1** 42 5N 95 3W
Arcadia, *La., U.S.A.* **155 J8** 32 33N 92 55W
Arcadia, *Pa., U.S.A.* **150 F6** 40 47N 78 51W
Arcanum, *U.S.A.* **157 E12** 39 59N 84 33W
Arcata, *U.S.A.* **158 F1** 40 52N 124 5W
Arcévia, *Italy* **45 E9** 43 30N 12 56 E
Archangel = Arkhangelsk, *Russia* **56 B7** 64 38N 40 36 E
Archar, *Bulgaria* **50 C6** 43 50N 22 54 E
Archbald, *U.S.A.* **151 E9** 41 30N 75 32W
Archbold, *U.S.A.* **157 C12** 41 31N 84 18W
Archena, *Spain* **41 G3** 38 9N 1 16W
Archenu, J., *Chad* **109 D4** 22 15N 24 45 E
Archer, *U.S.A.* **153 F7** 29 32N 82 32W
Archer ➛, *Australia* **126 A3** 13 28 S 141 41 E
Archer B., *Australia* **126 A3** 13 20 S 141 30 E
Archers Post, *Kenya* **118 B4** 0 35N 37 35 E
Arches Nat. Park, *U.S.A.* **159 G9** 38 45N 109 25W
Archidona, *Spain* **43 H6** 37 6N 4 22W
Arci, Mte., *Italy* **46 C1** 39 47N 8 45 E
Arcidosso, *Italy* **45 F8** 42 52N 11 33 E
Arcila = Asilah, *Morocco* **110 A3** 35 29N 6 0W
Arcis-sur-Aube, *France* **27 D11** 48 32N 4 10 E
Arckaringa Cr. ➛, *Australia* **127 D2** 28 10 S 135 22 E
Arco, *Italy* **44 C7** 45 55N 10 53 E
Arco, *U.S.A.* **158 E7** 43 38N 113 18W
Arcola, *U.S.A.* **157 E8** 39 41N 88 19W
Arcoona, *Australia* **128 A2** 31 2 S 137 1 E
Arcos = Arcos de Jalón, *Spain* **40 D2** 41 12N 2 16W
Arcos de Jalón, *Spain* **40 D2** 41 12N 2 16W
Arcos de la Frontera, *Spain* **43 J5** 36 45N 5 49W
Arcos de Valdevez, *Portugal* **42 D2** 41 55N 8 22W
Arcot, *India* **95 H4** 12 53N 79 20 E
Arcoverde, *Brazil* **170 C4** 8 25 S 37 4W
Arcozelo, *Portugal* **42 E3** 40 32N 7 47W
Arctic Bay, *Canada* **139 A11** 73 1N 85 7W
Arctic Ocean, *Arctic* **6 B18** 78 0N 160 0W
Arctic Red River = Tsiigehtchic, *Canada* **138 B6** 67 15N 134 0W
Arctic Village, *U.S.A.* **144 B11** 68 8N 145 32W
Arda ➛, *Bulgaria* **51 E10** 41 40N 26 30 E
Arda ➛, *Italy* **44 C7** 45 2N 10 2 E
Ardabīl, *Iran* **97 B6** 38 15N 48 18 E
Ardahan, *Turkey* **101 B10** 41 7N 42 41 E
Ardakān = Sepīdān, *Iran* **97 D7** 30 20N 52 5 E
Ardakān, *Iran* **97 C7** 32 19N 53 59 E
Ardala, *Sweden* **17 F7** 58 22N 13 19 E
Ardales, *Spain* **43 J6** 36 53N 4 51W
Årdalstangen, *Norway* **18 C4** 61 14N 7 43 E
Ardèche □, *France* **29 D8** 44 42N 4 16 E
Ardèche ➛, *France* **29 D8** 44 16N 4 39 E
Ardee, *Ireland* **23 C5** 53 52N 6 33W
Arden, *Canada* **150 B8** 44 43N 76 56W
Arden, *Denmark* **17 H3** 56 46N 9 52 E
Arden, *Calif., U.S.A.* **160 G5** 38 36N 121 33W
Arden, *Nev., U.S.A.* **161 J11** 36 1N 115 14W
Ardenne, *Belgium* **36 D3** 49 50N 5 5 E
Ardennes = Ardenne, *Belgium* **36 D3** 49 50N 5 5 E
Ardennes □, *France* **27 C11** 49 35N 4 40 E
Ardentes, *France* **27 F8** 46 45N 1 50 E
Arderin, *Ireland* **23 C4** 53 2N 7 39W
Ardeşen, *Turkey* **101 B9** 41 12N 41 2 E
Ardestān, *Iran* **97 C7** 33 20N 52 25 E
Ardez, *Switz.* **33 C10** 46 47N 10 12 E
Árdhas ➛, *Greece* **51 E10** 41 40N 26 30 E
Ardhéa, *Greece* **50 F6** 40 58N 22 3 E
Ardila ➛, *Portugal* **43 G3** 38 12N 7 28W
Ardino, *Bulgaria* **51 E9** 41 34N 25 9 E
Ardivachar Pt., *U.K.* **22 D1** 57 23N 7 26W
Ardlethan, *Australia* **129 C7** 34 22 S 146 53 E
Ardmore, *Okla., U.S.A.* **155 H6** 34 10N 97 8W
Ardmore, *Pa., U.S.A.* **151 G9** 39 58N 75 18W
Ardnamurchan, Pt. of, *U.K.* **22 E2** 56 43N 6 14W
Ardnave Pt., *U.K.* **22 F2** 55 53N 6 20W
Ardon, *Russia* **61 J7** 43 10N 44 18 E
Ardore, *Italy* **47 D9** 38 11N 16 10 E
Ardres, *France* **27 B8** 50 50N 1 59 E
Ardrossan, *Australia* **128 C2** 34 26 S 137 53 E
Ardrossan, *U.K.* **22 F4** 55 39N 4 49W
Ards Pen., *U.K.* **23 B6** 54 33N 5 34W
Arduan, *Sudan* **106 D3** 19 54N 30 20 E
Ardud, *Romania* **52 C7** 47 37N 22 52 E
Åre, *Sweden* **16 A7** 63 22N 13 15 E
Arecibo, *Puerto Rico* **165 d** 18 29N 66 43W
Areia Branca, *Brazil* **170 B4** 5 0 S 37 0W
Arena, Pt., *U.S.A.* **160 G3** 38 57N 123 44W
Arenal, *Honduras* **164 C2** 15 21N 86 50W
Arenales, Cerro, *Chile* **176 C2** 47 5 S 73 40W
Arenápolis, *Brazil* **173 C6** 14 26 S 56 49W
Arenas = Las Arenas, *Spain* **42 B6** 43 17N 4 50W
Arenas, Pta., *Venezuela* **169 A5** 10 31N 64 14W
Arenas de San Pedro, *Spain* **42 E5** 40 12N 5 5W
Arendal, *Norway* **15 G13** 58 28N 8 46 E
Arendsee, *Germany* **30 C7** 52 52N 11 27 E
Arenillas, *Ecuador* **168 D1** 3 33 S 80 10W
Arenys de Mar, *Spain* **40 D7** 41 35N 2 33 E
Arenzano, *Italy* **44 D5** 44 24N 8 41 E
Arenzville, *U.S.A.* **156 E6** 39 53N 90 22W
Areópolis, *Greece* **48 E4** 36 40N 22 22 E
Arequipa, *Peru* **172 D3** 16 20 S 71 30W
Arequipa □, *Peru* **172 D3** 16 0 S 72 50W
Arere, *Brazil* **169 D7** 0 16 S 53 52W
Arero, *Ethiopia* **107 G4** 4 41N 38 50 E
Arès, *France* **28 D2** 44 47N 1 8W
Arévalo, *Spain* **42 D6** 41 3N 4 43W
Arezzo, *Italy* **45 E8** 43 25N 11 53 E
Arga, *Turkey* **96 B3** 38 21N 37 59 E
Arga ➛, *Spain* **40 C3** 42 18N 1 47W
Argalastí, *Greece* **48 B5** 39 13N 23 13 E
Argamakmur, *Indonesia* **84 C2** 3 35 S 102 0 E
Argamasilla de Alba, *Spain* **43 F7** 39 8N 3 5W
Argamasilla de Calatrava, *Spain* **43 G6** 38 44N 4 4W
Arganda, *Spain* **42 E7** 40 19N 3 26W
Arganil, *Portugal* **42 E2** 40 13N 8 3W
Argao, *Phil.* **81 G4** 9 52N 123 36 E
Argásion **39 D2** 37 45N 20 56 E
Argayash, *Russia* **64 D8** 55 29N 60 52 E
Argedeb, *Ethiopia* **107 F5** 6 11N 41 13 E
Argelès-Gazost, *France* **28 E3** 43 0N 0 6W
Argelès-sur-Mer, *France* **28 F7** 42 34N 3 1 E
Argens ➛, *France* **29 E10** 43 24N 6 44 E
Argent-sur-Sauldre, *France* **27 E9** 47 33N 2 25 E
Argenta, *Canada* **142 C5** 50 11N 116 56W
Argenta, *Italy* **45 D8** 44 37N 11 50 E
Argenta, *U.S.A.* **157 E8** 39 59N 88 49W
Argentan, *France* **26 D6** 48 45N 0 1W
Argentário, Mte., *Italy* **45 F8** 42 24N 11 9 E
Argentat, *France* **28 C5** 45 6N 1 56 E
Argentera, *Italy* **44 D4** 44 12N 7 5 E
Argenteuil, *France* **27 D9** 48 57N 2 14 E
Argentia, *Canada* **141 C9** 47 18N 53 58W
Argentiera, C. dell', *Italy* **46 B1** 40 44N 8 8 E
Argentière, Aiguilles d', *Switz.* **32 E4** 45 58N 7 2 E
Argentina ■, *S. Amer.* **176 B3** 35 0 S 66 0W
Argentina Is., *Antarctica* **7 C17** 66 0 S 64 0W
Argentino, L., *Argentina* **176 D2** 50 10 S 73 0W
Argenton-Château, *France* **26 F6** 46 59N 0 27W
Argenton-sur-Creuse, *France* **27 F8** 46 36N 1 30 E
Argeş □, *Romania* **53 F9** 45 0N 24 45 E
Argeş ➛, *Romania* **53 F11** 44 5N 26 38 E
Arghandab ➛, *Afghan.* **91 C2** 31 30N 64 15 E
Argheile, *Ethiopia* **107 F5** 5 19N 42 4 E
Argo, *Sudan* **106 D3** 19 28N 30 30 E
Argolikós Kólpos, *Greece* **48 D4** 37 20N 22 52 E
Argolís □, *Greece* **48 D4** 37 38N 22 50 E
Argonne, *France* **27 C12** 49 10N 5 0 E
Árgos, *Greece* **48 D4** 37 40N 22 43 E
Argos, *U.S.A.* **157 C10** 41 14N 86 15W
Árgos Orestikón, *Greece* **50 F5** 40 27N 21 18 E
Argostólion, *Greece* **39 C2** 38 11N 20 29 E
Argostólion, Kólpos, *Greece* **39 C1** 38 10N 20 27 E
Arguedas, *Spain* **40 C3** 42 11N 1 36W
Arguello, Pt., *U.S.A.* **161 L6** 34 35N 120 39W
Arguineguín, *Canary Is.* **9 e1** 27 46N 15 41W
Argun, *Russia* **61 J7** 43 18N 45 52 E
Argun ➛, *Russia* **67 D13** 53 20N 121 28 E
Argungu, *Nigeria* **113 C5** 12 40N 4 31 E
Arguni, T., *Indonesia* **83 B4** 3 6 S 133 42 E
Argus Pk., *U.S.A.* **161 K9** 35 52N 117 26W
Argyle, L., *Australia* **124 C4** 16 20 S 128 40 E
Argyll & Bute □, *U.K.* **22 E3** 56 13N 5 28W
Arhavi, *Turkey* **101 B9** 41 21N 41 18 E
Århus, *Denmark* **17 H4** 56 8N 10 11 E
Århus Amtskommune □, *Denmark* **17 H4** 56 15N 10 15 E
Aria, *N.Z.* **130 E4** 38 33 S 175 0 E
Ariadnoye, *Russia* **70 B7** 45 8N 134 25 E
Ariamsvlei, *Namibia* **116 D2** 28 9 S 19 51 E
Ariana, *Tunisia* **108 A2** 36 52N 10 12 E
Ariano Irpino, *Italy* **47 A8** 41 9N 15 5 E
Ariari ➛, *Colombia* **168 C3** 2 35N 72 47W
Aribinda, *Burkina Faso* **113 C4** 14 17N 0 52W
Arica, *Chile* **172 D3** 18 32 S 70 20W
Arica, *Colombia* **168 D3** 2 0 S 71 50W
Arico, *Canary Is.* **9 e1** 28 9N 16 29W
Arid, C., *Australia* **125 F3** 34 1 S 123 10 E
Arida, *Japan* **73 C7** 34 5N 135 8 E
Aridal, *W. Sahara* **110 C2** 25 59N 13 54W
Aride, *Seychelles* **121 b** 4 13 S 55 40 E
Ariège □, *France* **28 F5** 42 56N 1 30 E
Ariège ➛, *France* **28 E5** 43 30N 1 25 E
Arieş ➛, *Romania* **53 D8** 46 24N 23 20 E
Arigat el Fersig, *Algeria* **111 C4** 27 35N 2 7W
Arihā, *Israel* **106 A4** 31 51N 35 27 E
Arilje, *Serbia, Yug.* **50 C4** 43 44N 20 7 E
Arílla, Ákra, *Greece* **38 B9** 39 43N 19 39 E
Arima, *Trin. & Tob.* **165 D7** 10 38N 61 17W
Aringay, *Phil.* **80 C3** 16 26N 120 21 E
Arinos ➛, *Brazil* **173 C6** 10 25 S 58 20W
Ario de Rosales, *Mexico* **162 D4** 19 12N 102 0W
Ariogala, *Lithuania* **54 C10** 55 16N 23 28 E
Aripo, Mt., *Trin. & Tob.* **169 F9** 10 45N 61 15W
Aripuanã, *Brazil* **173 B5** 9 25 S 60 30W
Aripuanã ➛, *Brazil* **173 B5** 5 7 S 60 25W
Ariquemes, *Brazil* **173 B5** 9 55 S 63 6W
Arisaig, *U.K.* **22 E3** 56 55N 5 51W
Arîsh, W. el ➛, *Egypt* **106 A3** 31 9N 33 49 E
Arissa, *Ethiopia* **107 E5** 11 10N 41 35 E
Aristazabal I., *Canada* **142 C3** 52 40N 129 10W
Arita, *Japan* **72 D1** 33 11N 129 54 E
Aritao, *Phil.* **80 C3** 16 18N 121 2 E
Ariton, *U.S.A.* **152 D4** 31 36N 85 43W
Arivonimamo, *Madag.* **117 B8** 19 1 S 47 11 E
Ariyalur, *India* **95 J4** 11 8N 79 8 E
Ariza, *Spain* **40 D2** 41 19N 2 3W
Arizaro, Salar de, *Argentina* **174 A2** 24 40 S 67 50W
Arizona, *Argentina* **174 D2** 35 45 S 65 25W
Arizona □, *U.S.A.* **159 J8** 34 0N 112 0W
Arizpe, *Mexico* **162 A2** 30 20N 110 11W
Årjäng, *Sweden* **16 E6** 59 24N 12 8 E
Arjeplog, *Sweden* **14 D18** 66 3N 18 2 E
Arjona, *Colombia* **168 A2** 10 14N 75 22W
Arjona, *Spain* **43 H6** 37 56N 4 4W
Arjuna, *Indonesia* **85 D4** 7 49 S 112 34 E
Arka, *Russia* **67 C15** 60 15N 142 0 E
Arkadak, *Russia* **60 E6** 51 58N 43 30 E
Arkadelphia, *U.S.A.* **155 H8** 34 7N 93 4W
Arkadhía □, *Greece* **48 D4** 37 30N 22 20 E
Arkaig, L., *U.K.* **22 E3** 56 59N 5 10W
Arkalgud, *India* **95 H3** 12 46N 76 3 E
Arkalyk = Arqalyk, *Kazakstan* **66 D7** 50 13N 66 50 E
Arkansas □, *U.S.A.* **155 H8** 35 0N 92 30W
Arkansas ➛, *U.S.A.* **155 J9** 33 47N 91 4W
Arkansas City, *U.S.A.* **155 G6** 37 4N 97 2W
Arkaroola, *Australia* **127 E2** 30 20 S 139 22 E
Árkathos ➛, *Greece* **48 B3** 39 20N 21 4 E

Arkhángelos, *Préveza, Greece* **39 A2** 39 6N 20 42 E
Arkhángelos, *Ródhos, Greece* **38 E12** 36 13N 28 7 E
Arkhangelsk, *Russia* **56 B7** 64 38N 40 36 E
Arkhangelskoye, *Russia* **60 E5** 51 32N 40 58 E
Arki, *India* **92 D7** 31 9N 76 58 E
Arkiko, *Eritrea* **107 D4** 15 33N 39 30 E
Arklow, *Ireland* **23 D5** 52 48N 6 10W
Árkoi, *Greece* **49 D8** 37 24N 26 44 E
Arkona, Kap, *Germany* **30 A9** 54 42N 13 26 E
Arkösund, *Sweden* **17 F10** 58 29N 16 56 E
Arkoúdhi Nisís, *Greece* **39 B2** 38 33N 20 43 E
Arkport, *U.S.A.* **150 D7** 42 24N 77 42W
Arkticheskiy, Mys, *Russia* **67 A10** 81 10N 95 0 E
Arkul, *Russia* **60 B10** 57 17N 50 3 E
Arkville, *U.S.A.* **151 D10** 42 9N 74 37W
Årla, *Sweden* **16 E10** 59 17N 16 40 E
Arlanza →, *Spain* **42 C6** 42 6N 4 9W
Arlanzón →, *Spain* **42 C6** 42 3N 4 17W
Arlbergpass, *Austria* **34 D3** 47 9N 10 12 E
Arles, *France* **29 E8** 43 41N 4 40 E
Arlesheim, *Switz.* **32 B5** 47 30N 7 37 E
Arli, *Burkina Faso* **113 C5** 11 35N 1 28 E
Arli, Parc Nat. de l', *Burkina Faso* **113 C5** 11 35N 1 28 E
Arlington, *S. Africa* **117 D4** 28 1 S 27 53 E
Arlington, *Ga., U.S.A.* **152 D5** 31 26N 84 44W
Arlington, *N.Y., U.S.A.* **151 E11** 41 42N 73 54W
Arlington, *Oreg., U.S.A.* **158 D3** 45 43N 120 12W
Arlington, *S. Dak., U.S.A.* **154 C6** 44 22N 97 8W
Arlington, *Tex., U.S.A.* **155 J6** 32 44N 97 7W
Arlington, *Va., U.S.A.* **148 F7** 38 53N 77 7W
Arlington, *Vt., U.S.A.* **151 C11** 43 5N 73 9W
Arlington, *Wash., U.S.A.* **160 B4** 48 12N 122 8W
Arlington Heights, *U.S.A.* **157 B9** 42 5N 87 59W
Arlon, *Belgium* **24 E5** 49 42N 5 49 E
Arltunga, *Australia* **126 C1** 23 26 S 134 41 E
Armagh, *U.K.* **23 B5** 54 21N 6 39W
Armagh □, *U.K.* **23 B5** 54 18N 6 37W
Armagnac, *France* **28 E4** 43 50N 0 10 E
Armançon →, *France* **27 E10** 47 59N 3 30 E
Armatree, *Australia* **129 A8** 31 26 S 148 28 E
Armavir, *Russia* **61 H5** 45 2N 41 7 E
Armenia, *Colombia* **168 C2** 4 35N 75 45W
Armenia ■, *Asia* **61 K7** 40 20N 45 0 E
Armeniş, *Romania* **52 E7** 45 13N 22 17 E
Armenistís, Ákra, *Greece* **38 E11** 36 8N 27 42 E
Armentières, *France* **27 B9** 50 40N 2 50 E
Armero, *Colombia* **168 C3** 4 58N 74 54W
Armidale, *Australia* **129 A9** 30 30 S 151 40 E
Armilla, *Spain* **43 H7** 37 9N 3 37W
Armori, *India* **94 D4** 20 28N 79 59 E
Armour, *U.S.A.* **154 D5** 43 19N 98 21W
Armstrong, *B.C., Canada* **142 C5** 50 25N 119 10W
Armstrong, *Ont., Canada* **140 B2** 50 18N 89 4W
Armur, *India* **94 E4** 18 48N 78 16 E
Armutlu, *Bursa, Turkey* **51 F12** 40 31N 28 50 E
Armutlu, *İzmir, Turkey* **49 C9** 38 24N 27 34 E
Arnaía, *Greece* **50 F7** 40 30N 23 38 E
Arnarfjörður, *Iceland* **11 B3** 65 48N 23 40W
Arnaud →, *Canada* **139 B12** 60 0N 70 0W
Arnauti, C., *Cyprus* **39 E8** 35 6N 32 17 E
Arnay-le-Duc, *France* **27 E11** 47 10N 4 27 E
Arnedillo, *Spain* **40 C2** 42 13N 2 14W
Arnedo, *Spain* **40 C2** 42 12N 2 5W
Árnes, *Iceland* **11 A5** 66 1N 21 31W
Årnes, *Norway* **18 D8** 60 7N 11 28 E
Árnessýsla □, *Iceland* **11 C6** 64 15N 20 30W
Arnett, *U.S.A.* **155 G5** 36 8N 99 46W
Arnhem, *Neths.* **24 C5** 51 58N 5 55 E
Arnhem, C., *Australia* **126 A2** 12 20 S 137 30 E
Arnhem B., *Australia* **126 A2** 12 20 S 136 10 E
Arnhem Land, *Australia* **126 A1** 13 10 S 134 30 E
Árnissa, *Greece* **50 F5** 40 47N 21 49 E
Arno →, *Italy* **44 E7** 43 41N 10 17 E
Arno Bay, *Australia* **128 B2** 33 54 S 136 34 E
Arnold, *U.K.* **20 D6** 53 1N 1 7W
Arnold, *U.S.A.* **160 G6** 38 15N 120 20W
Arnoldstein, *Austria* **34 E6** 46 33N 13 43 E
Arnon →, *France* **27 E9** 47 13N 2 1 E
Arnot, *Canada* **143 B9** 55 56N 96 41W
Arnøy, *Norway* **14 A19** 70 9N 20 40 E
Arnprior, *Canada* **140 C4** 45 26N 76 21W
Arnsberg, *Germany* **30 D4** 51 24N 8 5 E
Arnstadt, *Germany* **30 E6** 50 50N 10 56 E
Aro →, *Venezuela* **169 B5** 8 1N 64 11W
Aroab, *Namibia* **116 D2** 26 41 S 19 39 E
Aroánia Óri, *Greece* **48 D4** 37 56N 22 12 E
Aroche, *Spain* **43 H4** 37 56N 6 57W
Arochuku, *Nigeria* **113 D6** 5 21N 7 54 E
Aroeiras, *Brazil* **170 C4** 7 31 S 35 41W
Arolla, *Switz.* **32 D4** 46 2N 7 29 E
Arolsen, *Germany* **30 D5** 51 23N 9 2 E
Aron, *India* **92 G6** 25 57N 77 56 E
Aron →, *France* **27 F10** 46 50N 3 28 E
Arona, *Italy* **44 C5** 45 46N 8 34 E
Aroroy, *Phil.* **80 E4** 12 31N 123 24 E
Arosa, *Switz.* **33 C9** 46 47N 9 41 E
Arosa, Ría de, *Spain* **42 C2** 42 28N 8 57W
Årøysund, *Norway* **18 E7** 59 10N 10 27 E
Arpajon, *France* **27 D9** 48 36N 2 15 E
Arpajon-sur-Cère, *France* **28 D6** 44 53N 2 28 E
Arpaşu de Jos, *Romania* **53 E9** 45 47N 24 37 E
Arqalyk, *Kazakstan* **66 D7** 50 13N 66 50 E
Arque, *Bolivia* **172 D4** 17 48 S 66 23W
Arrah = Ara, *India* **93 G11** 25 35N 84 32 E
Arrah, *Ivory C.* **112 D4** 6 40N 3 58W
Arraias, *Brazil* **171 D2** 12 56 S 46 57W
Arraias →, *Mato Grosso, Brazil* **173 C7** 11 10 S 53 35W
Arraias →, *Pará, Brazil* **170 C2** 7 30 S 49 20W
Arraiolos, *Portugal* **43 G3** 38 44N 7 59W
Arran, *U.K.* **22 F3** 55 34N 5 12W
Arras, *France* **27 B9** 50 17N 2 46 E
Arrasate, *Spain* **40 B2** 43 4N 2 30W
Arrats →, *France* **28 D4** 44 6N 0 52 E
Arreau, *France* **28 F4** 42 54N 0 22 E
Arrecife, *Canary Is.* **9 e2** 28 57N 13 37W
Arrecifes, *Argentina* **174 C3** 34 6 S 60 9W
Arrée, Mts. d', *France* **26 D3** 48 26N 3 55W
Arresø, *Denmark* **17 J6** 55 58N 12 6 E
Arriaga, *Chiapas, Mexico* **163 D6** 16 15N 93 52W
Arriaga, *San Luis Potosí, Mexico* **162 C4** 21 55N 101 23W
Arrilalah, *Australia* **126 C3** 23 43 S 143 54 E
Arrino, *Australia* **125 E2** 29 30 S 115 40 E
Arriondas, *Spain* **42 B5** 43 23N 5 11W
Arrojado →, *Brazil* **171 D3** 13 24 S 44 20W
Arromanches-les-Bains, *France* **26 C6** 49 20N 0 38W
Arronches, *Portugal* **43 F3** 39 8N 7 16W
Arros →, *France* **28 E3** 43 40N 0 2W
Arrow, L., *Ireland* **23 B3** 54 3N 8 19W
Arrowhead, L., *U.S.A.* **161 L9** 34 16N 117 10W
Arrowsmith, Mt., *N.Z.* **131 D5** 43 20 S 170 55 E
Arrowtown, *N.Z.* **131 E3** 44 57 S 168 50 E
Arroyo de la Luz, *Spain* **43 F4** 39 30N 6 38W
Arroyo Grande, *U.S.A.* **161 K6** 35 7N 120 35W
Års, *Denmark* **17 H3** 56 48N 9 30 E
Ars, *Iran* **96 B5** 37 9N 47 46 E
Ars-sur-Moselle, *France* **27 C13** 49 5N 6 4 E
Arsenault L., *Canada* **143 B7** 55 6N 108 32W
Arsenev, *Russia* **70 B6** 44 10N 133 15 E
Arsi □, *Ethiopia* **107 F4** 7 45N 39 0 E
Arsiero, *Italy* **45 C8** 45 48N 11 21 E
Arsikere, *India* **95 H3** 13 15N 76 15 E
Arsin, *Turkey* **101 B8** 41 8N 39 55 E
Arsk, *Russia* **60 B9** 56 10N 49 50 E
Árskógssandur, *Iceland* **11 B8** 65 56N 18 27W
Årsunda, *Sweden* **16 D10** 60 31N 16 45 E
Árta, *Greece* **48 B3** 39 8N 21 2 E
Artà, *Spain* **38 B4** 39 41N 3 21 E
Árta □, *Greece* **48 B3** 39 15N 21 5 E
Arteaga, *Mexico* **162 D4** 18 50N 102 20W
Arteche, *Phil.* **80 E5** 12 17N 125 22 E
Arteijo = Arteixo, *Spain* **42 B2** 43 19N 8 29W
Arteixo, *Spain* **42 B2** 43 19N 8 29W
Artem = Artyom, *Azerbaijan* **61 K10** 40 28N 50 20 E
Artem, *Russia* **70 C6** 43 22N 132 13 E
Artemovsk, *Russia* **67 D10** 54 45N 93 35 E
Artemovsk, *Ukraine* **59 H9** 48 35N 38 0 E
Artemovskiy, *Rostov, Russia* **61 G5** 47 45N 40 16 E
Artemovskiy, *Yekaterinburg, Russia* **64 C8** 57 21N 61 54 E
Artenay, *France* **27 D8** 48 5N 1 50 E
Artern, *Germany* **30 D7** 51 22N 11 18 E
Artesa de Segre, *Spain* **40 D6** 41 54N 1 3 E
Artesia = Mosomane, *Botswana* **116 C4** 24 2 S 26 19 E
Artesia, *U.S.A.* **155 J2** 32 51N 104 24W
Arth, *Switz.* **33 B7** 47 4N 8 31 E
Arthington, *Liberia* **112 D2** 6 35N 10 45W
Arthur, *Canada* **150 C4** 43 50N 80 32W
Arthur, *U.S.A.* **157 E8** 39 43N 88 28W
Arthur →, *Australia* **127 G3** 41 2 S 144 40 E
Arthur Cr. →, *Australia* **126 C2** 22 30 S 136 25 E
Arthur Pt., *Australia* **126 C5** 22 7 S 150 3 E
Arthur River, *Australia* **125 F2** 33 20 S 117 2 E
Arthur's Pass, *N.Z.* **131 C6** 42 54 S 171 35 E
Arthur's Pass Nat. Park, *N.Z.* **131 C6** 42 53 S 171 42 E
Arthur's Town, *Bahamas* **165 B4** 24 38N 75 42W
Artigas, *Uruguay* **174 C4** 30 20 S 56 30W
Artik, *Armenia* **61 K6** 40 38N 43 58 E
Artillery L., *Canada* **143 A7** 63 9N 107 52W
Artois, *France* **27 B9** 50 20N 2 30 E
Artotína, *Greece* **48 C4** 38 42N 22 2 E
Artrutx, C. de, *Spain* **38 B4** 39 55N 3 49 E
Artsyz, *Ukraine* **59 J5** 46 4N 29 26 E
Artux, *China* **65 D8** 39 40N 76 10 E
Artvin, *Turkey* **101 B9** 41 14N 41 44 E
Artyom, *Azerbaijan* **61 K10** 40 28N 50 20 E
Aru, Kepulauan, *Indonesia* **83 C4** 6 0 S 134 30 E
Aru Is. = Aru, Kepulauan, *Indonesia* **83 C4** 6 0 S 134 30 E
Arua, *Uganda* **118 B3** 3 1N 30 58 E
Aruanã, *Brazil* **171 D1** 14 54 S 51 10W
Aruba ■, *W. Indies* **165 D6** 12 30N 70 0W
Arudy, *France* **28 E3** 43 7N 0 28W
Arumã, *Brazil* **169 D5** 4 44 S 62 8W
Arumpo, *Australia* **128 B5** 33 48 S 142 55 E
Arun →, *Nepal* **93 F12** 26 55N 87 10 E
Arun →, *U.K.* **21 G7** 50 49N 0 33W
Arunachal Pradesh □, *India* **90 A5** 28 0N 95 0 E
Aruppukkottai, *India* **95 K4** 9 31N 78 8 E
Aruri, Selat, *Indonesia* **83 B5** 0 50 S 135 15 E
Arusha, *Tanzania* **118 C4** 3 20 S 36 40 E
Arusha □, *Tanzania* **118 C4** 4 0 S 36 30 E
Arusha Chini, *Tanzania* **118 C4** 3 32 S 37 20 E
Arusha Nat. Park, *Tanzania* **118 C4** 3 16 S 36 47 E
Arut →, *Indonesia* **85 C4** 2 42 S 111 34 E
Aruvi →, *Sri Lanka* **95 K4** 8 48N 79 53 E
Aruwimi →, *Dem. Rep. of the Congo* **118 B1** 1 13N 23 36 E
Arvada, *Colo., U.S.A.* **154 F2** 39 48N 105 5W
Arvada, *Wyo., U.S.A.* **158 D10** 44 39N 106 8W
Arvakalu, *Sri Lanka* **95 K4** 8 20N 79 58 E
Arve →, *France* **27 F13** 46 11N 6 8 E
Árvi, *Greece* **39 F6** 34 59N 25 28 E
Arvi, *India* **94 D4** 20 59N 78 16 E
Arviat, *Canada* **143 A10** 61 6N 93 59W
Arvidsjaur, *Sweden* **14 D18** 65 35N 19 10 E
Arvika, *Sweden* **16 E6** 59 40N 12 36 E
Arvin, *U.S.A.* **161 K8** 35 12N 118 50W
Arwal, *India* **93 G11** 25 15N 84 41 E
Arxan, *China* **69 B6** 47 11N 119 57 E
Åryd, *Sweden* **17 H8** 56 49N 14 59 E
Aryirádhes, *Greece* **38 C9** 39 27N 19 58 E
Aryiroúpolis, *Greece* **39 E5** 35 17N 24 20 E
Arys, *Kazakstan* **66 E7** 42 26N 68 48 E
Arys →, *Kazakstan* **65 B4** 42 45N 68 15 E
Arzachena, *Italy* **46 A2** 41 5N 9 23 E
Arzamas, *Russia* **60 C6** 55 27N 43 55 E
Arzew, *Algeria* **111 A4** 35 50N 0 23W
Arzgir, *Russia* **61 H7** 45 18N 44 23 E
Arzignano, *Italy* **45 C8** 45 31N 11 20 E
Arzúa, *Spain* **42 C2** 42 56N 8 9W
Aš, *Czech Rep.* **34 A5** 50 13N 12 12 E
Ås, *Norway* **18 E7** 59 40N 10 48 E
Ås, *Sweden* **16 A8** 63 15N 14 34 E
As Pontes de García Rodríguez, *Spain* **42 B3** 43 27N 7 50W
Aş Şafā, *Syria* **103 B6** 33 10N 37 0 E
As Saffānīyah, *Si. Arabia* **97 E6** 27 55N 48 50 E
As Safīrah, *Syria* **100 D7** 36 5N 37 21 E
Aş Şahm, *Oman* **97 E8** 24 10N 56 53 E
As Sājir, *Si. Arabia* **96 E5** 25 11N 44 36 E
As Salamīyah, *Syria* **100 E7** 35 1N 37 2 E
As Salmān, *Iraq* **96 D5** 30 30N 44 32 E
As Salţ, *Jordan* **103 C4** 32 2N 35 43 E
As Sal'w'a, *Qatar* **97 E6** 24 23N 50 50 E
As Samāwah, *Iraq* **96 D5** 31 15N 45 15 E
As Sanamayn, *Syria* **103 B5** 33 3N 36 10 E
As Sawāḑah, *Si. Arabia* **98 B4** 22 24N 44 28 E
As Sayl al Kabīr, *Si. Arabia* **98 B3** 21 38N 40 25 E
As Sohar = Şuḩār, *Oman* **97 E8** 24 20N 56 40 E
As Sukhnah, *Syria* **101 E8** 34 52N 38 52 E
As Sulaymānīyah, *Iraq* **101 E11** 35 35N 45 29 E
As Sulaymānīyah, *Si. Arabia* **98 A4** 24 9N 47 18 E
As Sulaymī, *Si. Arabia* **96 E4** 26 17N 41 21 E
As Sulayyil, *Si. Arabia* **98 B4** 20 27N 45 34 E
As Sulţān, *Libya* **108 B3** 31 4N 17 8 E
As Summān, *Si. Arabia* **96 E5** 25 0N 47 0 E
Aş Şurrah, *Yemen* **98 D4** 13 57N 46 14 E
As Suwaydā', *Syria* **103 C5** 32 40N 36 30 E
As Suwaydā' □, *Syria* **103 C5** 32 45N 36 45 E
As Suwayq, *Oman* **97 F8** 23 51N 57 26 E
As Şuwayrah, *Iraq* **101 F11** 32 55N 45 0 E
Asa, *Kazakstan* **65 B5** 43 2N 71 10 E
Åsa, *Sweden* **17 G6** 57 21N 12 8 E
Asab, *Namibia* **116 D2** 25 30 S 18 0 E
Asaba, *Nigeria* **113 D6** 6 12N 6 38 E
Asad, Buḩayrat al, *Syria* **101 D8** 36 0N 38 15 E
Asadābād, *Iran* **101 E13** 34 47N 48 7 E
Asafo, *Ghana* **112 D4** 6 20N 2 40W
Asahi, *Japan* **73 B12** 35 43N 140 39 E
Asahi-Gawa →, *Japan* **72 C5** 34 36N 133 58 E
Asahigawa, *Japan* **70 C11** 43 46N 142 22 E
Asaka, *Uzbekistan* **65 C6** 40 38N 72 15 E
Asale, L., *Ethiopia* **107 E5** 14 0N 40 20 E
Asama-Yama, *Japan* **73 A10** 36 24N 138 31 E
Asamankese, *Ghana* **113 D4** 5 50N 0 40W
Asan →, *India* **93 F8** 26 37N 78 24 E
Asansol, *India* **93 H12** 23 40N 87 1 E
Åsarna, *Sweden* **16 B8** 62 39N 14 22 E
Asau, *Samoa* **133 W23** 13 27 S 172 33W
Asayita, *Ethiopia* **107 E5** 11 35N 41 23 E
Asbe Teferi, *Ethiopia* **107 F5** 9 4N 40 49 E
Asbesberge, *S. Africa* **116 D3** 29 0 S 23 0 E
Asbest, *Russia* **64 C8** 57 0N 61 30 E
Asbestos, *Canada* **141 C5** 45 47N 71 58W
Asbury Park, *U.S.A.* **151 F10** 40 13N 74 1W
Ascea, *Italy* **47 B8** 40 8N 15 11 E
Ascensión, *Mexico* **162 A3** 31 6N 107 59W
Ascensión, B. de la, *Mexico* **163 D7** 19 50N 87 20W
Ascension I., *Atl. Oc.* **9 g** 7 57 S 14 23W
Aschach an der Donau, *Austria* **34 C7** 48 22N 14 2 E
Aschaffenburg, *Germany* **31 F5** 49 58N 9 6 E
Aschendorf, *Germany* **30 B3** 53 3N 7 19 E
Aschersleben, *Germany* **30 D7** 51 45N 11 29 E
Asciano, *Italy* **45 E8** 43 14N 11 33 E
Áscoli Piceno, *Italy* **45 F10** 42 51N 13 34 E
Áscoli Satriano, *Italy* **47 A8** 41 11N 15 32 E
Ascona, *Switz.* **33 D7** 46 9N 8 46 E
Ascope, *Peru* **172 B2** 7 46 S 79 8W
Ascotán, *Chile* **174 A2** 21 45 S 68 17W
Ascuncion, *Phil.* **81 H5** 7 35N 125 45 E
Aseb, *Eritrea* **107 E5** 13 0N 42 40 E
Åseda, *Sweden* **17 G9** 57 10N 15 20 E
Asedjrad, *Algeria* **111 D5** 24 51N 1 29 E
Aseki, *Papua N. G.* **132 D4** 7 21 S 146 12 E
Asela, *Ethiopia* **107 F4** 8 0N 39 0 E
Åsen, *Sweden* **16 C7** 61 17N 13 50 E
Asenovgrad, *Bulgaria* **51 D8** 42 1N 24 51 E
Aserradero, *Mexico* **162 C3** 23 40N 105 43W
Asfeld, *France* **27 C11** 49 27N 4 5 E
Asfûn el Matâ'na, *Egypt* **106 B3** 25 26N 32 30 E
Åsgårdstrand, *Norway* **18 E7** 59 22N 10 27 E
Asgata, *Cyprus* **39 F9** 34 46N 33 15 E
Ash Fork, *U.S.A.* **159 J7** 35 13N 112 29W
Ash Grove, *U.S.A.* **155 G8** 37 19N 93 35W
Ash Shabakah, *Iraq* **96 D4** 30 49N 43 39 E
Ash Shamāl □, *Lebanon* **103 A5** 34 25N 36 0 E
Ash Shāmīyah, *Iraq* **101 G11** 31 55N 44 35 E
Ash Sha'rā', *Si. Arabia* **98 A4** 24 16N 44 11 E
Ash Shāriqah, *U.A.E.* **97 E7** 25 23N 55 26 E
Ash Sharmah, *Si. Arabia* **96 D2** 28 1N 35 16 E
Ash Sharqāt, *Iraq* **101 E10** 35 27N 43 16 E
Ash Sharqi, Al Jabal, *Lebanon* **103 B5** 33 40N 36 10 E
Ash Shāţi, *Libya* **108 C2** 27 30N 12 30 E
Ash Shaţi □, *Libya* **111 C7** 27 27N 13 37 E
Ash Shaţrah, *Iraq* **96 D5** 31 30N 46 10 E
Ash Shawbak, *Jordan* **96 D2** 30 32N 35 34 E
Ash Shawmari, J., *Jordan* **103 E5** 30 35N 36 35 E
Ash Shiḩr, *Yemen* **99 D5** 14 45N 49 36 E
Ash Shināfīyah, *Iraq* **96 D5** 31 35N 44 39 E
Ash Shu'bah, *Si. Arabia* **96 D5** 28 54N 44 44 E
Ash Shumlūl, *Si. Arabia* **96 E5** 26 31N 47 20 E
Ash Shuqayq, *Si. Arabia* **98 C3** 17 44N 42 1 E
Ash Shūr'a, *Iraq* **96 C4** 35 58N 43 13 E
Ash Shurayf, *Si. Arabia* **96 E3** 25 43N 39 14 E
Ash Shuwayfāt, *Lebanon* **103 B4** 33 45N 35 30 E
Asha, *Russia* **64 D6** 55 0N 57 16 E
Ashanti □, *Ghana* **113 D4** 7 30N 1 30W
Ashau, *Vietnam* **86 D6** 16 6N 107 22 E
Ashbourne, *U.K.* **20 D6** 53 2N 1 43W
Ashburn, *U.S.A.* **152 D6** 31 43N 83 39W
Ashburton, *N.Z.* **131 D6** 43 53 S 171 48 E
Ashburton →, *Australia* **124 D1** 21 40 S 114 56 E
Ashburton, North Branch →, *N.Z.* **131 D6** 43 54 S 171 44 E
Ashburton, South Branch →, *N.Z.* **131 D6** 43 54 S 171 44 E
Ashchysay, *Kazakstan* **65 B4** 43 35N 68 53 E
Ashcroft, *Canada* **142 C4** 50 40N 121 20W
Ashdod, *Israel* **103 D3** 31 49N 34 35 E
Ashdown, *U.S.A.* **155 J7** 33 40N 94 8W
Asheboro, *U.S.A.* **149 H6** 35 43N 79 49W
Åsheim, *Norway* **18 C8** 61 42N 11 11 E
Ashern, *Canada* **143 C9** 51 11N 98 21W
Asherton, *U.S.A.* **155 L5** 28 27N 99 46W
Asheville, *U.S.A.* **149 H4** 35 36N 82 33W
Ashewat, *Pakistan* **92 D3** 31 22N 68 32 E
Asheweig →, *Canada* **140 B2** 54 17N 87 12W
Ashford, *Australia* **127 D5** 29 15 S 151 3 E
Ashford, *U.K.* **21 F8** 51 8N 0 53 E
Ashford, *U.S.A.* **152 D4** 31 11N 85 14W
Ashgabat, *Turkmenistan* **66 F6** 38 0N 57 50 E
Ashibetsu, *Japan* **70 C11** 43 31N 142 11 E
Ashikaga, *Japan* **73 A11** 36 28N 139 29 E
Ashington, *U.K.* **20 B6** 55 11N 1 33W
Ashio, *Japan* **73 A11** 36 38N 139 27 E
Ashizuri-Zaki, *Japan* **72 E5** 32 44N 133 0 E
Ashkarkot, *Afghan.* **92 C2** 33 3N 67 58 E
Ashkhabad = Ashgabat, *Turkmenistan* **66 F6** 38 0N 57 50 E
Āshkhāneh, *Iran* **97 B8** 37 26N 56 55 E
Ashland, *Ala., U.S.A.* **152 B4** 33 16N 85 50W
Ashland, *Ill., U.S.A.* **156 E7** 39 53N 90 1W
Ashland, *Kans., U.S.A.* **155 G5** 37 11N 99 46W
Ashland, *Ky., U.S.A.* **148 F4** 38 28N 82 38W
Ashland, *Mont., U.S.A.* **158 D10** 45 36N 106 16W
Ashland, *Ohio, U.S.A.* **150 F2** 40 52N 82 19W
Ashland, *Oreg., U.S.A.* **158 E2** 42 12N 122 43W
Ashland, *Pa., U.S.A.* **151 F8** 40 45N 76 22W
Ashland, *Va., U.S.A.* **148 G7** 37 46N 77 29W
Ashland, *Wis., U.S.A.* **154 B9** 46 35N 90 53W
Ashley, *Ill., U.S.A.* **156 F7** 38 20N 89 11W
Ashley, *Ind., U.S.A.* **157 C11** 41 32N 85 4W
Ashley, *N. Dak., U.S.A.* **154 B5** 46 2N 99 22W
Ashley, *Pa., U.S.A.* **151 E9** 41 12N 75 55W
Ashley →, *N.Z.* **131 D7** 43 17 S 172 44 E
Ashmore Reef, *Australia* **124 B3** 12 14 S 123 5 E
Ashmûn, *Egypt* **106 H7** 30 18N 30 55 E
Ashmyany, *Belarus* **15 J21** 54 26N 25 52 E
Ashokan Reservoir, *U.S.A.* **151 E10** 41 56N 74 13W
Ashqelon, *Israel* **103 D3** 31 42N 34 35 E
Ashta, *India* **92 H7** 23 1N 76 43 E
Ashtabula, *U.S.A.* **150 E4** 41 52N 80 47W
Ashti, *Maharashtra, India* **94 D4** 21 12N 78 11 E
Ashti, *Maharashtra, India* **94 E2** 18 50N 75 15 E
Ashton, *S. Africa* **116 E3** 33 50 S 20 5 E
Ashton, *U.S.A.* **158 D8** 44 4N 111 27W
Ashuanipi, L., *Canada* **141 B6** 52 45N 66 15W
Ashurst, *N.Z.* **130 G4** 40 16 S 175 45 E
Ashville, *Ala., U.S.A.* **152 B3** 33 50N 86 15W
Ashville, *Fla., U.S.A.* **152 E6** 30 37N 83 39W
Ashville, *Pa., U.S.A.* **150 F6** 40 34N 78 33W
'Āşī →, *Asia* **100 D6** 36 1N 35 59 E
Asia **62 E11** 45 0N 75 0 E
Asia, Kepulauan, *Indonesia* **83 A4** 1 0N 131 13 E
Āsīā Bak, *Iran* **97 C6** 35 19N 50 30 E
Asiago, *Italy* **45 C8** 45 52N 11 30 E
Asidonhoppo, *Surinam* **169 C6** 3 50N 55 30W
Asifabad, *India* **94 E4** 19 20N 79 24 E
Asike, *Indonesia* **83 C6** 6 39 S 140 24 E
Asilah, *Morocco* **110 A3** 35 29N 6 0W
Asinara, *Italy* **46 A1** 41 4N 8 16 E
Asinara, G. dell', *Italy* **46 A1** 41 0N 8 30 E
Asino, *Russia* **66 D9** 57 0N 86 0 E
Asipovichy, *Belarus* **58 F5** 53 19N 28 33 E
'Asīr □, *Si. Arabia* **98 C3** 18 40N 42 30 E
Asir, Ras, *Somali Rep.* **120 B4** 11 55N 51 10 E
Aska, *India* **94 E7** 19 2N 84 42 E
Aşkale, *Turkey* **101 C9** 39 55N 40 41 E
Asker, *Norway* **18 E7** 59 50N 10 29 E
Askersund, *Sweden* **17 F8** 58 53N 14 55 E
Askham, *S. Africa* **116 D3** 26 59 S 20 47 E
Askim, *Norway* **15 G14** 59 35N 11 10 E
Askja, *Iceland* **11 B10** 65 3N 16 48W
Askøy, *Norway* **15 F11** 60 29N 5 10 E
Askvoll, *Norway* **18 C2** 61 21N 5 4 E
Asl, *Egypt* **106 B3** 29 33N 32 44 E
Aslan Burnu, *Turkey* **49 C8** 38 44N 26 45 E
Aslanapa, *Turkey* **49 B11** 39 13N 29 52 E
Āsmār, *Afghan.* **91 B3** 35 10N 71 27 E
Asmara = Asmera, *Eritrea* **107 D4** 15 19N 38 55 E
Asmera, *Eritrea* **107 D4** 15 19N 38 55 E
Asnæs, *Denmark* **17 J4** 55 40N 11 0 E
Åsnen, *Sweden* **17 H8** 56 37N 14 45 E
Asni, *Morocco* **110 B3** 31 17N 7 58W
Aso, *Japan* **72 E3** 32 55N 131 5 E
Aso-Zan, *Japan* **72 E3** 32 53N 131 6 E
Ásola, *Italy* **44 C7** 45 13N 10 24 E
Asosa, *Ethiopia* **107 E3** 10 3N 34 32 E
Asoteriba, Jebel, *Sudan* **106 C4** 21 51N 36 30 E
Aspe, *Spain* **41 G4** 38 20N 0 40W
Aspen, *U.S.A.* **159 G10** 39 11N 106 49W
Aspendos, *Turkey* **100 D4** 36 54N 31 7 E
Aspermont, *U.S.A.* **155 J4** 33 8N 100 14W
Aspet, *France* **28 E4** 43 1N 0 48 E
Aspiring, Mt., *N.Z.* **131 E3** 44 23 S 168 46 E
Aspres-sur-Buëch, *France* **29 D9** 44 32N 5 44 E
Asprókavos, Ákra, *Greece* **38 C10** 39 21N 20 6 E
Aspromonte, *Italy* **47 D9** 38 10N 16 0 E
Aspur, *India* **92 H6** 23 58N 74 7 E
Asquith, *Canada* **143 C7** 52 8N 107 13W
Assa, *Morocco* **110 C3** 28 35N 9 6W
Assab = Aseb, *Eritrea* **107 E5** 13 0N 42 40 E
Assâba, Massif de l', *Mauritania* **112 B2** 16 10N 11 45W
Assagny, Parc Nat. d', *Ivory C.* **112 D4** 5 10N 4 48W
Assaikio, *Nigeria* **113 D6** 8 34N 8 55 E
Assal, L., *Djibouti* **107 E5** 11 40N 42 26 E
Assam □, *India* **90 B4** 26 0N 93 0 E
Assamakka, *Niger* **113 B6** 19 21N 5 38 E
Assaye, *India* **94 D2** 20 15N 75 53 E
Asse, *Belgium* **24 D4** 50 24N 4 10 E
Assekrem, *Algeria* **111 D6** 23 16N 5 49 E
Assémini, *Italy* **46 C1** 39 17N 9 0 E
Assen, *Neths.* **24 A6** 53 0N 6 35 E
Assens, *Denmark* **17 J3** 55 16N 9 55 E
Assini, *Ivory C.* **112 D4** 5 9N 3 17W
Assiniboia, *Canada* **143 D7** 49 40N 105 59W
Assiniboine →, *Canada* **143 D9** 49 53N 97 8W
Assiniboine, Mt., *Canada* **142 C5** 50 52N 115 39W
Assiou, *Algeria* **111 D6** 21 7N 7 36 E
Assis, *Brazil* **175 A5** 22 40 S 50 20W
Assis Brasil, *Brazil* **172 C4** 10 55 S 69 32W
Assisi, *Italy* **45 E9** 43 4N 12 37 E
Åsskard, *Norway* **18 A5** 63 1N 8 30 E
Assok Ngoum, *Gabon* **114 B2** 1 45N 11 39 E
Ássos, *Greece* **39 C2** 38 22N 20 33 E
Assumption, *U.S.A.* **156 E7** 39 31N 89 3W
Assynt, L., *U.K.* **22 C3** 58 10N 5 3W
Astaffort, *France* **28 D4** 44 4N 0 40 E
Astakidha, *Greece* **49 F8** 35 53N 26 50 E
Astakós, *Greece* **39 B3** 38 32N 21 5 E
Astana, *Kazakstan* **66 D8** 51 10N 71 30 E
Āstāneh, *Iran* **97 B6** 37 17N 49 59 E
Astara, *Azerbaijan* **97 B6** 38 30N 48 50 E
Āstārā, *Iran* **101 C13** 38 20N 48 52 E
Asteroúsia, *Greece* **39 F6** 34 59N 25 3 E
Asti, *Italy* **44 D5** 44 54N 8 12 E
Astipálaia, *Greece* **49 E8** 36 32N 26 22 E
Astola I., *Pakistan* **91 D1** 25 7N 63 51 E
Astorga, *Phil.* **81 H5** 6 54N 125 27 E
Astorga, *Spain* **42 C4** 42 29N 6 8W
Astoria, *Ill., U.S.A.* **156 D6** 40 14N 90 21W
Astoria, *Oreg., U.S.A.* **160 D3** 46 11N 123 50W
Åstorp, *Sweden* **17 H6** 56 6N 12 55 E
Astrakhan, *Russia* **61 G9** 46 25N 48 5 E
Astudillo, *Spain* **42 C6** 42 12N 4 22W
Asturias □, *Spain* **42 B5** 43 15N 6 0W
Asunción, *Bolivia* **172 C4** 11 46 S 67 50W
Asunción, *Paraguay* **174 B4** 25 10 S 57 30W
Asunción Nochixtlán, *Mexico* **163 D5** 17 28N 97 14W
Åsunden, *Sweden* **17 F9** 58 0N 15 51 E
Asutri, *Sudan* **107 D4** 15 25N 35 45 E
Aswa →, *Uganda* **118 B3** 3 43N 31 55 E
Aswa-Lolim Game Reserve, *Uganda* **118 B3** 2 43N 31 35 E
Aswad, Ra's al, *Si. Arabia* **98 B2** 21 20N 39 0 E
Aswân, *Egypt* **106 C3** 24 4N 32 57 E
Aswân High Dam = Sadd el Aali, *Egypt* **106 C3** 23 54N 32 54 E
Asyût, *Egypt* **106 B3** 27 11N 31 4 E
Asyûti, Wadi →, *Egypt* **106 B3** 27 11N 31 16 E
Aszód, *Hungary* **52 C4** 47 39N 19 28 E
At-Bashy, *Kyrgyzstan* **65 C7** 41 10N 75 48 E
At-Bashy Kyrka Tooloru, *Kyrgyzstan* **65 C7** 40 50N 75 30 E
At Ţafīlah, *Jordan* **103 E4** 30 45N 35 30 E
Aţ Tā'if, *Si. Arabia* **98 B3** 21 5N 40 27 E
At Tāj, *Libya* **108 D4** 24 13N 23 18 E
At Tamīmī, *Libya* **108 B4** 32 20N 23 4 E
Aţ Ţirāq, *Si. Arabia* **96 E5** 27 19N 44 33 E
Aţ Tubayq, *Si. Arabia* **96 D3** 29 30N 37 0 E
At Turbah, *Yemen* **98 D4** 13 13N 44 7 E
At Turbah, *Yemen* **98 D3** 12 40N 43 30 E
Atabey, *Turkey* **49 D12** 37 57N 30 39 E
Atacama □, *Chile* **174 B2** 27 30 S 70 0W
Atacama, Desierto de, *Chile* **174 A2** 24 0 S 69 20W
Atacama, Salar de, *Chile* **174 A2** 23 30 S 68 20W
Ataco, *Colombia* **168 C2** 3 35N 75 23W
Atakor, *Algeria* **111 D6** 23 27N 5 31 E
Atakpamé, *Togo* **113 D5** 7 31N 1 13 E
Atalaia do Norte, *Brazil* **168 D3** 4 20 S 70 12W
Atalándi, *Greece* **48 C4** 38 39N 22 58 E
Atalaya, *Peru* **172 C3** 10 45 S 73 50W
Atalaya de Femes, *Canary Is.* **9 e2** 28 56N 13 47W
Ataléia, *Brazil* **171 E3** 18 3 S 41 6W
Atambua, *Indonesia* **82 C2** 9 7 S 124 54 E
Atami, *Japan* **73 B11** 35 5N 139 4 E
Atankawng, *Burma* **90 C6** 25 50N 97 47 E
Atapupu, *E. Timor* **82 C2** 9 0 S 124 51 E
Atâr, *Mauritania* **110 D2** 20 30N 13 5W
Ataram, Erg n-, *Algeria* **111 D5** 23 57N 2 0 E
Atarfe, *Spain* **43 H7** 37 13N 3 40W
Atari, *Pakistan* **92 D6** 30 56N 74 2 E
Atascadero, *U.S.A.* **160 K6** 35 29N 120 40W
Atasu, *Kazakstan* **66 E8** 48 30N 71 0 E
Atatürk Barajı, *Turkey* **101 D8** 37 28N 38 30 E
Atauro, *E. Timor* **82 C3** 8 10 S 125 30 E
'Atbara, *Sudan* **106 D3** 17 42N 33 59 E
'Atbara, Nahr →, *Sudan* **106 D3** 17 40N 33 56 E
Atbasar, *Kazakstan* **66 D7** 51 48N 68 20 E
Atbashi = At-Bashy, *Kyrgyzstan* **65 C7** 41 10N 75 48 E
Atça, *Turkey* **49 D10** 37 53N 28 13 E
Atchafalaya B., *U.S.A.* **155 L9** 29 25N 91 25W
Atchison, *U.S.A.* **154 F7** 39 34N 95 7W
Atebubu, *Ghana* **113 D4** 7 47N 1 0W
Ateca, *Spain* **40 D3** 41 20N 1 49W
Aterno →, *Italy* **45 F10** 42 11N 13 51 E
Āteshān, *Iran* **97 C7** 35 35N 52 37 E
Atesine, Alpi, *Italy* **45 B8** 46 55N 11 30 E
Atessa, *Italy* **45 F11** 42 4N 14 27 E
Atfîh, *Egypt* **106 J7** 29 25N 31 15 E
Ath, *Belgium* **24 D3** 50 38N 3 47 E
Athabasca, *Canada* **142 C6** 54 45N 113 20W
Athabasca →, *Canada* **143 B6** 58 40N 110 50W
Athabasca, L., *Canada* **143 B7** 59 15N 109 15W
Athagarh, *India* **94 D7** 20 32N 85 37 E
Athboy, *Ireland* **23 C5** 53 37N 6 56W

Athena, *U.S.A.* **152 F6** 29 59N 83 30W
Athenry, *Ireland* **23 C3** 53 18N 8 44W
Athens = Athínai, *Greece* **48 D5** 37 58N 23 46 E
Athens, *Ala., U.S.A.* **149 H2** 34 48N 86 58W
Athens, *Ga., U.S.A.* **152 B6** 33 57N 83 23W
Athens, *N.Y., U.S.A.* **151 D11** 42 16N 73 49W
Athens, *Ohio, U.S.A.* **148 F4** 39 20N 82 6W
Athens, *Pa., U.S.A.* **151 E8** 41 57N 76 31W
Athens, *Tenn., U.S.A.* **149 H3** 35 27N 84 36W
Athens, *Tex., U.S.A.* **155 J7** 32 12N 95 51W
Athéras, *Greece* **39 C1** 38 19N 20 25 E
Atherley, *Canada* **150 B5** 44 37N 79 20W
Atherton, *Australia* **126 B4** 17 17 S 145 30 E
Athiéme, *Benin* **113 D5** 6 37N 1 40 E
Athienou, *Cyprus* **39 E9** 35 3N 33 32 E
Athínai, *Greece* **48 D5** 37 58N 23 46 E
Athlone, *Ireland* **23 C4** 53 25N 7 56W
Athmalik, *India* **94 D7** 20 43N 84 32 E
Athna, *Cyprus* **39 E9** 35 3N 33 47 E
Athni, *India* **94 F2** 16 44N 75 6 E
Athol, *N.Z.* **131 F3** 45 30 S 168 35 E
Athol, *U.S.A.* **151 D12** 42 36N 72 14W
Athol Is., *Bahamas* **9 b** 25 5N 77 16W
Atholl, Forest of, *U.K.* **22 E5** 56 51N 3 50W
Atholl, Kap, *Greenland* **10 B4** 76 25N 69 30W
Atholville, *Canada* **141 C6** 47 59N 66 43W
Áthos, *Greece* **51 F8** 40 9N 24 22 E
Athy, *Ireland* **23 C5** 53 0N 7 0W
Ati, *Chad* **109 F3** 13 13N 18 20 E
Ati, *Sudan* **107 E2** 13 5N 29 2 E
Atiak, *Uganda* **118 B3** 3 12N 32 2 E
Atiamuri, *N.Z.* **130 E5** 38 24 S 176 5 E
Atico, *Peru* **172 D3** 16 14 S 73 40W
Atienza, *Spain* **40 D2** 41 12N 2 52W
Atiit, *Sudan* **107 F3** 6 10N 30 35 E
Atik L., *Canada* **143 B9** 55 15N 96 0W
Atikameg →, *Canada* **140 B3** 52 30N 82 46W
Atikokan, *Canada* **140 C1** 48 45N 91 37W
Atikonak L., *Canada* **141 B7** 52 40N 64 32W
Atimonan, *Phil.* **80 D3** 14 0N 121 55 E
'Ātinah, W. →, *Oman* **99 C6** 18 23N 53 28 E
Atirampattinam, *India* **95 J4** 10 28N 79 20 E
Atka, *Russia* **67 C16** 60 50N 151 48 E
Atka, *U.S.A.* **144 K4** 52 12N 174 12W
Atka I., *U.S.A.* **144 K4** 52 7N 174 30W
Atkarsk, *Russia* **60 E7** 51 55N 45 2 E
Atkasuk = Meade River, *U.S.A.* **144 A8** 70 28N 157 24W
Atkinson, *Ga., U.S.A.* **152 D8** 31 13N 81 47W
Atkinson, *Ill., U.S.A.* **156 C6** 41 25N 90 1W
Atkinson, *Nebr., U.S.A.* **154 D5** 42 32N 98 59W
Atlanta, *Ga., U.S.A.* **152 B5** 33 45N 84 23W
Atlanta, *Ill., U.S.A.* **156 D7** 40 16N 89 14W
Atlanta, *Mo., U.S.A.* **156 E4** 39 54N 92 29W
Atlanta, *Tex., U.S.A.* **155 J7** 33 7N 94 10W
Atlantic, *U.S.A.* **156 C2** 41 24N 95 1W
Atlantic Beach, *U.S.A.* **152 E8** 30 20N 81 24W
Atlantic City, *U.S.A.* **148 F8** 39 21N 74 27W
Atlantic-Indian Ridge, *Atl. Oc.* **8 M11** 53 0 S 10 0 E
Atlantic Ocean **8 F8** 0 0 20 0W
Atlántico □, *Colombia* **168 A2** 10 45N 75 0W
Atlas Mts. = Haut Atlas, *Morocco* **110 B4** 32 30N 5 0W
Atlin, *Canada* **142 B2** 59 31N 133 41W
Atlin, L., *Canada* **142 B2** 59 26N 133 45W
Atlin Prov. Park, *Canada* **142 B2** 59 10N 134 30W
Atløyna, *Norway* **18 C1** 61 21N 4 58 E
Atmakur, *Andhra Pradesh, India* **94 E4** 18 45N 78 39 E
Atmakur, *Andhra Pradesh, India* **95 G4** 14 37N 79 40 E
Atmakur, *Andhra Pradesh, India* **95 G4** 15 53N 78 35 E
Atmore, *U.S.A.* **149 K2** 31 2N 87 29W
Atna, *Norway* **18 C7** 61 44N 10 49 E
Atna →, *Norway* **18 C7** 61 44N 10 49 E
Atō, *Japan* **72 C3** 34 25N 131 40 E
Atocha, *Bolivia* **172 E4** 20 56 S 66 14W
Atok, *Phil.* **80 C3** 16 35N 120 41 E
Atoka, *U.S.A.* **155 H6** 34 23N 96 8W
Átokos Nisís, *Greece* **39 C2** 38 28N 20 49 E
Atolia, *U.S.A.* **161 K9** 35 19N 117 37W
Atongo-Bakari, *C.A.R.* **114 A4** 5 49N 21 35 E
Atori, *Solomon Is.* **133 M11** 8 42 S 160 59 E
Atrå, *Norway* **18 E5** 59 59N 8 45 E
Atrai →, *Bangla.* **90 C2** 24 7N 89 22 E
Atrak = Atrek →, *Turkmenistan* **97 B8** 37 35N 53 58 E
Ätran, *Sweden* **17 G6** 57 7N 12 57 E
Ätran →, *Sweden* **17 H6** 56 53N 12 30 E
Atrato →, *Colombia* **168 B2** 8 17N 76 58W
Atrauli, *India* **92 E8** 28 2N 78 20 E
Atrek →, *Turkmenistan* **97 B8** 37 35N 53 58 E
Atri, *Italy* **45 F10** 42 35N 13 58 E
Atsikí, *Greece* **49 B7** 39 56N 25 13 E
Atsoum, Mts., *Cameroon* **113 D7** 6 41N 12 57 E
Atsugi, *Japan* **73 B11** 35 25N 139 21 E
Atsumi, *Japan* **73 C9** 34 35N 137 4 E
Atsumi-Wan, *Japan* **73 C9** 34 44N 137 13 E
Atsuta, *Japan* **70 C10** 43 24N 141 26 E
Atsy, *Indonesia* **83 C5** 5 48 S 138 20 E
Attalla, *U.S.A.* **152 A3** 34 1N 86 6W
Attapu, *Laos* **86 E6** 14 48N 106 50 E
Attapulgus, *U.S.A.* **152 E5** 30 45N 84 29W
Attáviros, *Greece* **38 E11** 36 12N 27 50 E
Attawapiskat, *Canada* **140 B3** 52 56N 82 24W
Attawapiskat →, *Canada* **140 B3** 52 57N 82 18W
Attawapiskat L., *Canada* **140 B2** 52 18N 87 54W
Attersee, *Austria* **34 D6** 47 55N 13 32 E
Attica, *Ind., U.S.A.* **157 D9** 40 18N 87 15W
Attica, *Ohio, U.S.A.* **150 E2** 41 4N 82 53W
Attichy, *France* **27 C10** 49 25N 3 3 E
Attigny, *France* **27 C11** 49 28N 4 35 E
Attika = Attikí □, *Greece* **48 D5** 37 10N 23 40 E
Attikamagen L., *Canada* **141 B6** 55 0N 66 30W
Attikí □, *Greece* **48 D5** 37 10N 23 40 E
Attleboro, *U.S.A.* **151 E13** 41 57N 71 17W
Attock, *Pakistan* **92 C5** 33 52N 72 20 E
Attopeu = Attapu, *Laos* **86 E6** 14 48N 106 50 E
Attu, *U.S.A.* **144 K1** 52 56N 173 15 E
Attu I., *U.S.A.* **144 K1** 52 55N 172 55 E
Attunga, *Australia* **129 A9** 30 55 S 150 50 E
Attur, *India* **95 J4** 11 35N 78 30 E
'Atūd, *Yemen* **99 D5** 14 53N 48 10 E
Atuel →, *Argentina* **174 D2** 36 17 S 66 50W
Åtvidaberg, *Sweden* **17 F10** 58 12N 16 0 E
Atwater, *U.S.A.* **160 H6** 37 21N 120 37W
Atwood, *Canada* **150 C3** 43 40N 81 1W
Atwood, *Ill., U.S.A.* **157 E8** 39 48N 88 28W
Atwood, *Kans., U.S.A.* **154 F4** 39 48N 101 3W
Atyraū, *Kazakstan* **57 E9** 47 5N 52 0 E
Au, *Austria* **33 B9** 47 19N 9 59 E
Au Sable, *U.S.A.* **150 B1** 44 25N 83 20W
Au Sable →, *U.S.A.* **148 C4** 44 25N 83 20W
Au Sable Forks, *U.S.A.* **151 B11** 44 27N 73 41W
Au Sable Pt., *U.S.A.* **150 B1** 44 20N 83 20W
Aubagne, *France* **29 E9** 43 17N 5 37 E
Aubarca, C. d', *Spain* **38 C1** 39 4N 1 22 E
Aube □, *France* **27 D11** 48 15N 4 10 E
Aube →, *France* **27 D10** 48 34N 3 43 E
Aubenas, *France* **29 D8** 44 37N 4 24 E
Aubenton, *France* **27 C11** 49 50N 4 12 E
Auberry, *U.S.A.* **160 H7** 37 7N 119 29W
Aubigny-sur-Nère, *France* **27 E9** 47 30N 2 24 E
Aubin, *France* **28 D6** 44 33N 2 15 E
Aubrac, Mts. d', *France* **28 D7** 44 40N 3 2 E
Auburn, *Australia* **128 C3** 34 1 S 138 42 E
Auburn, *Ala., U.S.A.* **152 C4** 32 36N 85 29W
Auburn, *Calif., U.S.A.* **160 G5** 38 54N 121 4W
Auburn, *Ill., U.S.A.* **156 E7** 39 36N 89 45W
Auburn, *Ind., U.S.A.* **157 C11** 41 22N 85 4W
Auburn, *Maine, U.S.A.* **149 C10** 44 6N 70 14W
Auburn, *N.Y., U.S.A.* **151 D8** 42 56N 76 34W
Auburn, *Nebr., U.S.A.* **154 E7** 40 23N 95 51W
Auburn, *Pa., U.S.A.* **151 F8** 40 36N 76 6W
Auburn, *Wash., U.S.A.* **160 C4** 47 18N 122 14W
Auburn Ra., *Australia* **127 D5** 25 15 S 150 30 E
Auburndale, *U.S.A.* **149 L5** 28 4N 81 48W
Aubusson, *France* **28 C6** 45 57N 2 11 E
Auce, *Latvia* **54 B9** 56 28N 22 53 E
Auch, *France* **28 E4** 43 39N 0 36 E
Auchi, *Nigeria* **113 D6** 7 6N 6 13 E
Auckland, *N.Z.* **130 C3** 36 52 S 174 46 E
Auckland □, *N.Z.* **130 E6** 36 50 S 175 0 E
Auckland Is., *Pac. Oc.* **134 N8** 50 40 S 166 5 E
Aude □, *France* **28 E6** 43 8N 2 28 E
Aude →, *France* **28 E7** 43 13N 3 14 E
Audegle, *Somali Rep.* **120 D2** 1 59N 44 50 E
Auden, *Canada* **140 B2** 50 14N 87 53W
Auderville, *France* **26 C5** 49 43N 1 57W
Audierne, *France* **26 D2** 48 1N 4 34W
Audincourt, *France* **27 E13** 47 30N 6 50 E
Audo, *Ethiopia* **107 F5** 6 20N 41 50 E
Audubon, *U.S.A.* **156 C2** 41 43N 94 56W
Aue, *Germany* **30 E8** 50 35N 12 41 E
Auerbach, *Germany* **30 E8** 50 30N 12 24 E
Aueti Paraná →, *Brazil* **168 D4** 1 51 S 65 37W
Aufist, *W. Sahara* **110 C2** 25 44N 14 39W
Augathella, *Australia* **127 D4** 25 48 S 146 35 E
Aughnacloy, *U.K.* **23 B5** 54 25N 6 59W
Augrabies Falls, *S. Africa* **116 D3** 28 35 S 20 20 E
Augrabies Falls Nat. Park, *S. Africa* **116 D3** 28 40 S 20 22 E
Augsburg, *Germany* **31 G6** 48 25N 10 52 E
Augusta, *Australia* **125 F2** 34 19 S 115 9 E
Augusta, *Italy* **47 E8** 37 13N 15 13 E
Augusta, *Ark., U.S.A.* **155 H9** 35 17N 91 22W
Augusta, *Ga., U.S.A.* **152 B8** 33 28N 81 58W
Augusta, *Ill., U.S.A.* **156 D6** 40 14N 90 57W
Augusta, *Kans., U.S.A.* **155 G6** 37 41N 96 59W
Augusta, *Ky., U.S.A.* **157 F12** 38 47N 84 0W
Augusta, *Maine, U.S.A.* **139 D13** 44 19N 69 47W
Augusta, *Mont., U.S.A.* **158 C7** 47 30N 112 24W
Augustenborg, *Denmark* **17 K3** 54 57N 9 53 E
Augustine I., *U.S.A.* **144 G9** 59 22N 153 26W
Augustów, *Poland* **54 E9** 53 51N 23 0 E
Augustus, Mt., *Australia* **125 D2** 24 20 S 116 50 E
Augustus I., *Australia* **124 C3** 15 20 S 124 30 E
Aukan, *Eritrea* **107 D5** 15 29N 40 50 E
Auki, *Solomon Is.* **133 M11** 8 45 S 160 42 E
Aukra, *Norway* **18 B3** 62 47N 6 55 E
Aukum, *U.S.A.* **160 G6** 38 34N 120 43W
Aul, *India* **94 D8** 20 41N 86 39 E
Auld, L., *Australia* **124 D3** 22 25 S 123 50 E
Aulla, *Italy* **44 D6** 44 12N 9 58 E
Aulnay, *France* **28 B3** 46 2N 0 22W
Aulne →, *France* **26 D2** 48 17N 4 16W
Aulnoye-Aymeries, *France* **27 B10** 50 12N 3 50 E
Ault, *France* **26 B8** 50 8N 1 26 E
Ault, *U.S.A.* **154 E2** 40 35N 104 44W
Aulus-les-Bains, *France* **28 F5** 42 49N 1 19 E
Aumale, *France* **27 C8** 49 46N 1 46 E
Aumo, *Papua N. G.* **132 C5** 5 44 S 148 30 E
Aumont-Aubrac, *France* **28 D7** 44 43N 3 17 E
Auna, *Nigeria* **113 C5** 10 9N 4 42 E
Aundah, *India* **94 E3** 19 32N 77 3 E
Aundh, *India* **94 F2** 17 33N 74 23 E
Auning, *Denmark* **17 H4** 56 26N 10 22 E
Aunis, *France* **28 B3** 46 5N 0 50W
'Aunu'u, *Amer. Samoa* **133 X24** 14 20 S 170 31W
Auponhia, *Indonesia* **82 B3** 1 58 S 125 27 E
Aups, *France* **29 E10** 43 37N 6 15 E
Aur, Pulau, *Malaysia* **87 L5** 2 35N 104 10 E
Aura, *Burma* **90 B6** 26 59N 97 57 E
Auraiya, *India* **93 F8** 26 28N 79 33 E
Aurangabad, *Bihar, India* **93 G11** 24 45N 84 18 E
Aurangabad, *Maharashtra, India* **94 E2** 19 50N 75 23 E
Auray, *France* **26 E4** 47 40N 2 59W
Aurdal, *Norway* **18 D6** 60 55N 9 26 E
Aure, *Norway* **18 A5** 63 16N 8 33 E
Aurès, *Algeria* **111 A6** 35 8N 6 30 E
Aurich, *Germany* **30 B3** 53 28N 7 28 E
Aurilândia, *Brazil* **171 E1** 16 44 S 50 28W
Aurillac, *France* **28 D6** 44 55N 2 26 E
Aurlandsfjorden, *Norway* **18 C4** 61 3N 7 1 E
Aurlandsvangen, *Norway* **18 D4** 60 55N 7 12 E
Auronzo di Cadore, *Italy* **45 B9** 46 33N 12 26 E
Aurora = Maéwo, *Vanuatu* **133 E6** 15 10 S 168 10 E
Aurora = San Francisco, *Phil.* **80 E4** 13 21N 122 31 E
Aurora, *Canada* **150 C5** 44 0N 79 28W
Aurora, *Isabela, Phil.* **80 C3** 16 59N 121 38 E
Aurora, *Zamboanga del S., Phil.* **81 H4** 7 57N 123 36 E
Aurora, *S. Africa* **116 E2** 32 40 S 18 29 E
Aurora, *Colo., U.S.A.* **154 F2** 39 44N 104 52W
Aurora, *Ill., U.S.A.* **157 C8** 41 45N 88 19W
Aurora, *Mo., U.S.A.* **155 G8** 36 58N 93 43W
Aurora, *N.Y., U.S.A.* **151 D8** 42 45N 76 42W
Aurora, *Nebr., U.S.A.* **154 E6** 40 52N 98 0W
Aurora, *Ohio, U.S.A.* **150 E3** 41 21N 81 20W
Aurora □, *Phil.* **80 D3** 15 30N 121 30 E
Aursmoen, *Norway* **18 E8** 59 55N 11 26 E
Aursunden, *Norway* **18 B8** 62 40N 11 40 E
Aurukun, *Australia* **126 A3** 13 20 S 141 45 E
Aus, *Namibia* **116 D2** 26 35 S 16 12 E
Ausa, *India* **94 E3** 18 15N 76 30 E
Ausable →, *Canada* **150 C3** 43 19N 81 46W
Auschwitz = Oświęcim, *Poland* **55 H6** 50 2N 19 11 E
Aust-Agder □, *Norway* **18 F4** 58 45N 8 0 E
Austad, *Norway* **18 F4** 58 58N 7 37 E
Austen Harbour, *India* **95 H11** 12 55N 92 45 E
Austerlitz = Slavkov u Brna, *Czech Rep.* **35 B9** 49 10N 16 52 E
Austevoll, *Norway* **18 D2** 60 5N 5 13 E
Austin, *Ind., U.S.A.* **157 F11** 38 45N 85 49W
Austin, *Minn., U.S.A.* **154 D8** 43 40N 92 58W
Austin, *Nev., U.S.A.* **158 G5** 39 30N 117 4W
Austin, *Pa., U.S.A.* **150 E6** 41 38N 78 6W
Austin, *Tex., U.S.A.* **155 K6** 30 17N 97 45W
Austin, L., *Australia* **125 E2** 27 40 S 118 0 E
Austin I., *Canada* **143 A10** 61 10N 94 0W
Austmarka, *Norway* **18 D9** 60 6N 12 21 E
Austnes, *Norway* **18 B3** 62 38N 6 16 E
Austra, *Norway* **14 D14** 65 8N 11 55 E
Austral Is. = Tubuai Is., *Pac. Oc.* **135 K13** 25 0 S 150 0W
Austral Seamount Chain, *Pac. Oc.* **135 K13** 24 0 S 150 0W
Australia ■, *Oceania* **134 K5** 23 0 S 135 0 E
Australian Capital Territory □, *Australia* **129 C8** 35 30 S 149 0 E
Australind, *Australia* **125 F2** 33 17 S 115 42 E
Austria ■, *Europe* **34 E7** 47 0N 14 0 E
Austur-Skaftafellssýsla □, *Iceland* **11 C10** 64 15N 16 0W
Austvågøy, *Norway* **14 B16** 68 20N 14 40 E
Autazes, *Brazil* **169 D6** 3 35 S 59 8W
Auterive, *France* **28 E5** 43 21N 1 29 E
Authie →, *France* **27 B8** 50 22N 1 38 E
Authon-du-Perche, *France* **26 D7** 48 12N 0 54 E
Autlán, *Mexico* **162 D4** 19 40N 104 30W
Autun, *France* **27 F11** 46 58N 4 17 E
Auvergne, *France* **28 C7** 45 20N 3 15 E
Auvergne, Mts. d', *France* **28 C6** 45 20N 2 55 E
Auvézère →, *France* **28 C4** 45 12N 0 50 E
Auxerre, *France* **27 E10** 47 48N 3 32 E
Auxi-le-Château, *France* **27 B9** 50 15N 2 8 E
Auxonne, *France* **27 E12** 47 10N 5 20 E
Auxvasse, *U.S.A.* **156 E5** 39 1N 91 54W
Auzances, *France* **27 F9** 46 2N 2 30 E
Ava, *Ill., U.S.A.* **156 G7** 37 53N 89 30W
Ava, *Mo., U.S.A.* **155 G8** 36 57N 92 40W
Avaldsnes, *Norway* **18 E2** 59 21N 5 20 E
Avallon, *France* **27 E10** 47 30N 3 53 E
Avalon, *U.S.A.* **161 M8** 33 21N 118 20W
Avalon Pen., *Canada* **141 C9** 47 30N 53 20W
Avanavero, *Surinam* **169 C6** 4 51N 57 22W
Avanigadda, *India* **95 G5** 16 0N 80 56 E
Avannaarsua □, *Greenland* **10 B5** 80 0N 55 0W
Avanos, *Turkey* **96 B2** 38 43N 34 51 E
Avaré, *Brazil* **175 A6** 23 4 S 48 58W
Ávas, *Greece* **51 F9** 40 57N 25 56 E
Avawatz Mts., *U.S.A.* **161 K10** 35 40N 116 30W
Avdan Dağı, *Turkey* **51 F13** 40 23N 29 46 E
Aveiro, *Brazil* **169 D6** 3 10 S 55 5W
Aveiro, *Portugal* **42 E2** 40 37N 8 38W
Aveiro □, *Portugal* **42 E2** 40 40N 8 35W
Āvej, *Iran* **97 C6** 35 40N 49 15 E
Avellaneda, *Argentina* **174 C4** 34 50 S 58 10W
Avellino, *Italy* **47 B7** 40 54N 14 47 E
Avenal, *U.S.A.* **160 K6** 36 0N 120 8W
Avenches, *Switz.* **32 C4** 46 53N 7 2 E
Averøya, *Norway* **18 A4** 63 0N 7 35 E
Aversa, *Italy* **47 B7** 40 58N 14 12 E
Avery, *U.S.A.* **158 C6** 47 15N 115 49W
Aves, Is. las, *Venezuela* **165 D6** 12 0N 67 30W
Avesnes-sur-Helpe, *France* **27 B10** 50 8N 3 55 E
Avesta, *Sweden* **16 D10** 60 9N 16 10 E
Aveyron □, *France* **28 D6** 44 22N 2 45 E
Aveyron →, *France* **28 D5** 44 5N 1 16 E
Avezzano, *Italy* **45 F10** 42 2N 13 25 E
Avgó, *Greece* **49 F7** 35 33N 25 37 E
Aviá Terai, *Argentina* **174 B3** 26 45 S 60 50W
Aviano, *Italy* **45 B9** 46 4N 12 36 E
Aviemore, *U.K.* **22 D5** 57 12N 3 50W
Aviemore, L., *N.Z.* **131 E5** 44 37 S 170 18 E
Avigliana, *Italy* **44 C4** 45 5N 7 23 E
Avigliano, *Italy* **47 B8** 40 44N 15 43 E
Avignon, *France* **29 E8** 43 57N 4 50 E
Ávila, *Spain* **42 E6** 40 39N 4 43W
Ávila □, *Spain* **42 E6** 40 30N 5 0W
Ávila, Sierra de, *Spain* **42 E5** 40 40N 5 15W
Avila Beach, *U.S.A.* **161 K6** 35 11N 120 44W
Avilés, *Spain* **42 B5** 43 35N 5 57W
Avintes, *Portugal* **42 D2** 41 7N 8 33W
Avionárion, *Greece* **48 C6** 38 31N 24 8 E
Avis, *Portugal* **43 F3** 39 4N 7 53W
Avis, *U.S.A.* **150 E7** 41 11N 77 19W
Avísio →, *Italy* **44 B8** 46 7N 11 5 E
Avissawella, *Sri Lanka* **95 L5** 6 56N 80 11 E
Aviston, *U.S.A.* **156 F7** 38 36N 89 36W
Aviz = Avis, *Portugal* **43 F3** 39 4N 7 53W
Avize, *France* **27 D11** 48 59N 4 1 E
Avlum, *Denmark* **17 H2** 56 16N 8 47 E
Avoca, *Australia* **128 D5** 37 5 S 143 26 E
Avoca, *U.S.A.* **150 D7** 42 25N 77 25W
Avoca →, *Australia* **128 C5** 35 40 S 143 43 E
Avoca →, *Ireland* **23 D5** 52 48N 6 10W
Avola, *Canada* **142 C5** 51 45N 119 19W
Avola, *Italy* **47 F8** 36 56N 15 7 E
Avon, *Ill., U.S.A.* **156 D6** 40 40N 90 26W
Avon, *N.Y., U.S.A.* **150 D7** 42 55N 77 45W
Avon →, *Australia* **125 F2** 31 40 S 116 7 E
Avon →, *Bristol, U.K.* **21 F5** 51 29N 2 41W
Avon →, *Dorset, U.K.* **21 G6** 50 44N 1 46W
Avon →, *Warks., U.K.* **21 E5** 52 0N 2 8W
Avon Park, *U.S.A.* **153 H8** 27 36N 81 31W
Avondale, *Zimbabwe* **119 F3** 17 43 S 30 58 E
Avonlea, *Canada* **143 D8** 50 0N 105 0W
Avonmore, *Canada* **151 A10** 45 10N 74 58W
Avramov, *Bulgaria* **51 D10** 42 45N 26 38 E
Avranches, *France* **26 D5** 48 40N 1 20W
Avre →, *France* **26 D8** 48 47N 1 22 E
Avrig, *Romania* **53 E9** 45 43N 24 21 E
Avrillé, *France* **26 E6** 47 30N 0 35W
Avtovac, *Bos.-H.* **50 C2** 43 9N 18 35 E
Avu Avu, *Solomon Is.* **133 M11** 9 50 S 160 22 E
Awag el Baqar, *Sudan* **107 E3** 10 10N 33 10 E
A'waj →, *Syria* **103 B5** 33 23N 36 20 E
Awaji, *Japan* **73 C7** 34 32N 135 1 E
Awaji-Shima, *Japan* **72 C6** 34 30N 134 50 E
'Awālī, *Bahrain* **97 E6** 26 0N 50 30 E
Awantipur, *India* **93 C6** 33 55N 75 3 E
Awanui, *N.Z.* **130 B2** 35 4 S 173 17 E
Awarja →, *India* **94 F3** 17 5N 76 15 E
Awarua B., *N.Z.* **131 E3** 44 28 S 168 4 E
Awarua Pt., *N.Z.* **131 E3** 44 15 S 168 5 E
Awasa, *Ethiopia* **107 F4** 7 2N 38 28 E
Awasa, L., *Ethiopia* **107 F4** 7 0N 38 30 E
Awash, *Ethiopia* **107 F5** 9 1N 40 10 E
Awash →, *Ethiopia* **107 E5** 11 45N 41 5 E
Awash Nat. Park and Reserve, *Ethiopia* **107 F5** 9 8N 40 0 E
Awaso, *Ghana* **112 D4** 6 15N 2 22W
Awatere →, *N.Z.* **131 B9** 41 37 S 174 10 E
Awbārī, *Libya* **108 C2** 26 46N 12 57 E
Awbārī □, *Libya* **108 C2** 26 35N 12 46 E
Awbārī, Idehan, *Libya* **108 C2** 27 10N 11 30 E
Awe, L., *U.K.* **22 E3** 56 17N 5 16W
Aweil, *Sudan* **107 F2** 8 42N 27 20 E
Awgu, *Nigeria* **113 D6** 6 4N 7 24 E
Awjilah, *Libya* **108 C4** 29 8N 21 7 E
Awka, *Nigeria* **113 D6** 6 12N 7 5 E
Aworro, *Papua N. G.* **132 D2** 7 43 S 143 11 E
Ax-les-Thermes, *France* **28 F5** 42 44N 1 50 E
Axat, *France* **28 F6** 42 48N 2 13 E
Axe →, *U.K.* **21 F5** 50 42N 3 4W
Axel Heiberg I., *Canada* **6 B3** 80 0N 90 0W
Axim, *Ghana* **112 E4** 4 51N 2 15W
Axinim, *Brazil* **169 D6** 4 2 S 59 22W
Axintele, *Romania* **53 F11** 44 37N 26 47 E
Axioma, *Brazil* **173 B5** 6 45 S 64 31W
Axiós →, *Greece* **50 F6** 40 57N 22 35 E
Axminster, *U.K.* **21 G4** 50 46N 3 0W
Axson, *U.S.A.* **152 D7** 31 17N 82 44W
Axvall, *Sweden* **17 F7** 58 23N 13 34 E
Ay, *France* **27 C11** 49 3N 4 1 E
Ay →, *Russia* **64 C6** 56 8N 57 40 E
Ayaantang, *Eq. Guin.* **114 B2** 1 58N 10 24 E
Ayabaca, *Peru* **172 A2** 4 40 S 79 53W
Ayabe, *Japan* **73 B7** 35 20N 135 20 E
Ayacucho, *Argentina* **174 D4** 37 5 S 58 20W
Ayacucho, *Peru* **172 C3** 13 0 S 74 0W
Ayacucho □, *Peru* **172 C3** 14 0 S 74 0W
Ayaguz, *Kazakstan* **66 E9** 48 10N 80 10 E
Ayakkuduk, *Uzbekistan* **65 C2** 41 12N 65 12 E
Ayakudi, *India* **95 J3** 10 28N 77 56 E
Ayala, *Phil.* **81 H3** 6 57N 121 57 E
Ayamé, *Ivory C.* **112 D4** 5 35N 3 9W
Ayamonte, *Spain* **43 H3** 37 12N 7 24W
Ayan, *Russia* **67 D14** 56 30N 138 16 E
Ayancık, *Turkey* **100 B6** 41 57N 34 35 E
Ayapel, *Colombia* **168 B2** 8 19N 75 9W
Ayas, *Turkey* **100 B5** 40 2N 32 21 E
Ayaviri, *Peru* **172 C3** 14 50 S 70 35W
Āybak, *Afghan.* **91 A3** 36 15N 68 5 E
Aybastı, *Turkey* **100 B7** 40 41N 37 23 E
Aydarkul Ozero, *Uzbekistan* **65 C3** 40 50N 67 10 E
Aydın, *Turkey* **100 D2** 37 51N 27 51 E
Aydin □, *Turkey* **49 D9** 37 50N 28 0 E
Aydin Dağları, *Turkey* **49 D10** 38 0N 28 0 E
Aydyrlinskiy, *Russia* **64 E7** 52 3N 59 50 E
Ayelu, *Ethiopia* **107 E5** 10 5N 40 42 E
Ayenngré, *Togo* **113 D5** 8 40N 1 1 E
Ayer, *U.S.A.* **151 D13** 42 34N 71 35W
Ayer Hitam, *Malaysia* **87 c** 5 24N 100 16 E
Ayerbe, *Spain* **40 C4** 42 17N 0 41W
Ayer's Cliff, *Canada* **151 A12** 45 10N 72 3W
Ayers Rock, *Australia* **125 E5** 25 23 S 131 5 E
Ayiá, *Greece* **48 B4** 39 43N 22 45 E
Ayia Aikateríni, Ákra, *Greece* **38 B9** 39 50N 19 50 E
Ayía Ánna, *Greece* **48 C5** 38 52N 23 24 E
Ayia Dhéka, *Greece* **39 E5** 35 3N 24 58 E
Ayia Gálini, *Greece* **39 E5** 35 6N 24 41 E
Ayía Marína, *Kásos, Greece* **49 F8** 35 27N 26 53 E
Ayía Marína, *Léros, Greece* **49 D8** 37 11N 26 48 E
Áyia Napa, *Cyprus* **39 F10** 34 59N 34 0 E
Ayía Paraskeví, *Greece* **49 B8** 39 14N 26 21 E
Áyia Phyla, *Cyprus* **39 F9** 34 43N 33 1 E
Ayía Rouméli, *Greece* **39 E4** 35 14N 23 58 E
Ayia Varvára, *Greece* **39 E6** 35 8N 25 1 E
Ayiássos, *Greece* **49 B8** 39 5N 26 23 E
Áyioi Theódhoroi, *Greece* **48 D5** 37 55N 23 9 E
Áyion Óros □, *Greece* **51 F8** 40 25N 24 6 E
Áyios Amvrósios, *Cyprus* **39 E9** 35 20N 33 35 E
Áyios Andréas, *Greece* **48 D4** 37 21N 22 45 E
Áyios Evstrátios, *Greece* **48 B6** 39 34N 24 58 E
Áyios Ioánnis, Ákra, *Greece* **39 E6** 35 20N 25 40 E
Áyios Isidhoros, *Greece* **38 E11** 36 9N 27 51 E
Áyios Kiríkos, *Greece* **49 D8** 37 34N 26 17 E
Áyios Léon, *Greece* **39 D2** 37 47N 20 43 E
Áyios Matthaíos, *Greece* **38 C9** 39 30N 19 47 E
Áyios Mírono, *Greece* **39 E6** 35 15N 25 1 E
Áyios Nikólaos, *Aitolía kai Akarnanía, Greece* **39 B2** 38 52N 20 48 E
Áyios Nikólaos, *Kríti, Greece* **39 E6** 35 11N 25 41 E
Áyios Nikólaos, *Levkás, Greece* **39 B2** 38 36N 20 34 E
Áyios Pétros, *Greece* **39 B2** 38 40N 20 36 E
Áyios Seryios, *Cyprus* **39 E9** 35 12N 33 53 E
Áyios Theodhoros, *Cyprus* **39 E10** 35 22N 34 1 E
Áyios Thomás, *Greece* **39 B2** 38 58N 20 47 E
Áyios Yeóryios, *Greece* **48 D5** 37 28N 23 57 E
Aykathonisi, *Greece* **49 D8** 37 28N 27 0 E
Aykino, *Russia* **56 B8** 62 15N 49 56 E
Aykirikçi, *Turkey* **49 B12** 39 8N 30 9 E
Aylesbury, *U.K.* **21 F7** 51 49N 0 49W
Aylmer, *Canada* **150 D4** 42 46N 80 59W
Aylmer, L., *Canada* **138 B8** 64 0N 110 8W
'Ayn, Wādī al, *Oman* **97 F7** 22 15N 55 28 E
'Ayn al Ghazālah, *Libya* **108 B4** 32 10N 23 20 E
Ayn Dār, *Si. Arabia* **97 E7** 25 55N 49 10 E
Ayn Zālah, *Iraq* **101 D10** 36 45N 42 35 E
Ayna, *Spain* **41 G2** 38 34N 2 3W
Aynabulaq, *Kazakstan* **65 A8** 44 36N 77 56 E
Aynāt, *Yemen* **99 C5** 16 4N 49 9 E
Ayni, *Tajikistan* **65 D4** 39 23N 68 32 E
Ayod, *Sudan* **107 F3** 8 7N 31 26 E
Ayolas, *Paraguay* **174 B4** 27 10 S 56 59W
Ayom, *Sudan* **107 F2** 7 49N 28 23 E
Ayon, Ostrov, *Russia* **67 C17** 69 50N 169 0 E
Ayora, *Spain* **41 F3** 39 3N 1 3W
Ayorou, *Niger* **113 C5** 14 53N 1 0 E
Ayos, *Cameroon* **114 B2** 3 53N 12 31 E
'Ayoûn el 'Atroûs, *Mauritania* **112 B3** 16 38N 9 37W
Ayr, *Australia* **126 B4** 19 35 S 147 25 E
Ayr, *Canada* **150 C4** 43 17N 80 27W
Ayr, *U.K.* **22 F4** 55 28N 4 38W
Ayr →, *U.K.* **22 F4** 55 28N 4 38W
Ayrancı, *Turkey* **100 D5** 37 21N 33 41 E
Ayrancılar, *Turkey* **49 C9** 38 15N 27 18 E
Ayre, Pt. of, *U.K.* **20 C3** 54 25N 4 21W
Aysha, *Ethiopia* **107 E5** 10 50N 42 23 E
Ayton, *Australia* **126 B4** 15 56 S 145 22 E
Aytos, *Bulgaria* **51 D11** 42 42N 27 16 E
Aytoska Planina, *Bulgaria* **51 D11** 42 45N 27 30 E
Ayu, Kepulauan, *Indonesia* **83 A4** 0 35N 131 5 E
Ayutla, *Guatemala* **164 D1** 14 40N 92 10W
Ayutla, *Mexico* **163 D5** 16 58N 99 17W
Ayvacık, *Turkey* **100 C2** 39 36N 26 24 E
Ayvalık, *Turkey* **49 B8** 39 20N 26 46 E
Az Zabadānī, *Syria* **103 B5** 33 43N 36 5 E
Aẓ Ẓahirāh, *Asia* **99 B7** 23 40N 56 10 E
Aẓ Ẓāhirīyah, *West Bank* **103 D3** 31 25N 34 58 E
Aẓ Ẓahrān, *Si. Arabia* **97 E6** 26 10N 50 7 E
Az Zarqā, *Jordan* **103 C5** 32 5N 36 4 E
Az Zarqā', *U.A.E.* **97 E7** 24 53N 53 4 E
Az Zāwiyah, *Libya* **108 B2** 32 52N 12 56 E
Az Zaydīyah, *Yemen* **98 D3** 15 20N 43 1 E
Az Zībār, *Iraq* **101 D11** 36 52N 44 4 E
Az Zilfī, *Si. Arabia* **96 E5** 26 12N 44 52 E
Az Zubayr, *Iraq* **96 D5** 30 26N 47 40 E
Az Zuqur, *Yemen* **98 D3** 14 0N 42 45 E
Az Zuwaytīnah, *Libya* **108 B4** 30 58N 20 7 E
Azad Kashmir □, *Pakistan* **93 C5** 33 50N 73 50 E
Azambuja, *Portugal* **43 F2** 39 4N 8 51W
Azamgarh, *India* **93 F10** 26 5N 83 13 E
Azangaro, *Peru* **172 C3** 14 55 S 70 13W
Azaoua, *Niger* **113 B5** 15 50N 4 0 E
Azaouad, *Mali* **112 B4** 19 0N 3 0W
Azaouak, Vallée de l', *Mali* **113 B5** 15 50N 3 20 E
Āzār Shahr, *Iran* **101 D11** 37 45N 45 59 E
Azara, *Nigeria* **113 D6** 8 22N 9 12 E
Azarān, *Iran* **101 D12** 37 25N 47 16 E
Azärbayjan = Azerbaijan ■, *Asia* **61 K9** 40 20N 48 0 E
Āzarbāyjān-e Gharbī □, *Iran* **96 B5** 37 0N 44 30 E
Āzarbāyjān-e Sharqī □, *Iran* **96 B5** 37 20N 47 0 E
Azare, *Nigeria* **113 C7** 11 55N 10 10 E
Azay-le-Rideau, *France* **26 E7** 47 16N 0 30 E
A'zāz, *Syria* **100 D7** 36 36N 37 4 E
Azazga, *Algeria* **111 A5** 36 48N 4 22 E
Azbine = Aïr, *Niger* **113 B6** 18 30N 8 0 E
Azefal, *Mauritania* **110 D2** 21 0N 14 45W
Azeffoun, *Algeria* **111 A5** 36 51N 4 26 E
Azemmour, *Morocco* **110 B3** 33 20N 9 20W
Azennezal, *Algeria* **111 D5** 22 58N 0 43 E
Azerbaijan ■, *Asia* **61 K9** 40 20N 48 0 E
Azerbaijchan = Azerbaijan ■, *Asia* **61 K9** 40 20N 48 0 E
Azezo, *Ethiopia* **107 E4** 12 28N 37 15 E
Azimganj, *India* **93 G13** 24 14N 88 16 E
Aznalcóllar, *Spain* **43 H4** 37 32N 6 17W
Azogues, *Ecuador* **168 D2** 2 35 S 78 0W
Azores = Açores, Is. dos, *Atl. Oc.* **8 C9** 38 0N 27 0W
Azoum, B. →, *Chad* **109 F4** 10 53N 20 15 E
Azov, *Russia* **61 G4** 47 3N 39 25 E
Azov, Sea of, *Europe* **59 J9** 46 0N 36 30 E
Azovskoye More = Azov, Sea of, *Europe* **59 J9** 46 0N 36 30 E
Azpeitia, *Spain* **40 B2** 43 12N 2 19W
Azrak, B. →, *Chad* **109 F4** 10 52N 20 35 E
Azraq ash Shīshān, *Jordan* **103 D5** 31 50N 36 49 E
Azrou, *Morocco* **110 B3** 33 28N 5 19W
Aztec, *U.S.A.* **159 H10** 36 49N 107 59W
Azúa de Compostela, *Dom. Rep.* **165 C5** 18 25N 70 44W
Azuaga, *Spain* **43 G5** 38 16N 5 39W

Azuara, Spain 40 D4 41 15N 0 53W
Azuay □, Ecuador 168 D2 2 55 S 79 0W
Azuer →, Spain 43 F7 39 8N 3 36W
Azuero, Pen. de, Panama 164 E3 7 30N 80 30W
Azuga, Romania 53 E10 45 27N 25 33 E
Azul, Argentina 174 D4 36 42 S 59 43W
Azul, Lagoa, Azores 9 d3 37 52N 25 47W
Azul, Serra, Brazil 173 C7 14 50 S 54 50W
Azurduy, Bolivia 173 D5 19 59 S 64 29W
Azusa, U.S.A. 161 L9 34 8N 117 52W
Azzaba, Algeria 111 A6 36 48N 7 6 E
Azzano Décimo, Italy 45 C9 45 52N 12 56 E
Azzel Mati, Sebkra, Algeria 111 C5 26 10N 0 43 E

B

Ba Don, Vietnam 86 D6 17 45N 106 26 E
Ba Dong, Vietnam 87 H6 9 40N 106 33 E
Ba Ngoi = Cam Lam, Vietnam 87 G7 11 54N 109 10 E
Ba Tri, Vietnam 87 G6 10 2N 106 36 E
Ba Xian = Bazhou, China 74 E9 39 8N 116 22 E
Baa, Indonesia 82 D2 10 50 S 123 0 E
Baaba, Î., N. Cal. 133 T18 20 3 S 163 59 E
Baamonde, Spain 42 B3 43 7N 7 44W
Baao, Phil. 80 E4 13 27N 123 22 E
Baar, Switz. 33 B7 47 12N 8 32 E
Baardeere = Bardera, Somali Rep. 120 D2 2 20N 42 27 E
Baarle-Nassau, Belgium 24 C4 51 27N 4 56 E
Bab el Mandeb, Red Sea 98 D3 12 35N 43 25 E
Baba, Bulgaria 50 D7 42 44N 23 59 E
Baba, B. do, Angola 115 E2 14 50 S 12 14 E
Bābā, Koh-i-, Afghan. 91 B2 34 30N 67 0 E
Baba Budan Hills, India 95 H2 13 30N 75 44 E
Baba Burnu, Turkey 49 B8 39 29N 26 2 E
Baba dag, Azerbaijan 61 K9 41 0N 48 19 E
Bābā Kalū, Iran 97 D6 30 7N 50 49 E
Babaçulândia, Brazil 170 C2 7 13 S 47 46W
Babadag, Romania 53 F13 44 53N 28 44 E
Babadağ, Turkey 49 D10 37 49N 28 52 E
Babadayhan, Turkmenistan 66 F7 37 42N 60 23 E
Babaeski, Turkey 51 E11 41 26N 27 6 E
Babahoyo, Ecuador 168 D2 1 40 S 79 30W
Babai = Sarju →, India 93 F9 27 21N 81 23 E
Babak, Phil. 81 H5 7 8N 125 41 E
Babana, Nigeria 113 C5 10 31N 3 46 E
Babanusa, Sudan 107 E2 11 20N 27 48 E
Babar, Algeria 111 A6 35 10N 7 6 E
Babar, Indonesia 83 C3 8 0 S 129 30 E
Babar, Pakistan 92 D3 31 7N 69 32 E
Babar, Kepulauan, Indonesia 83 C4 8 0 S 131 30 E
Babarkach, Pakistan 92 E3 29 45N 68 0 E
Babase I., Papua N. G. 132 B7 4 0 S 153 42 E
Babayevo, Russia 58 C8 59 24N 35 55 E
Babb, U.S.A. 158 B7 48 51N 113 27W
Babenhausen, Germany 31 F4 49 57N 8 57 E
Băbeni, Romania 53 F9 44 59N 24 11 E
Baberu, India 93 G9 25 33N 80 43 E
Babi Besar, Pulau, Malaysia 87 L4 2 25N 103 59 E
Babia Gora, Europe 55 J6 49 38N 19 38 E
Babian Jiang →, China 76 F3 22 55N 101 47 E
Babile, Ethiopia 107 F5 9 16N 42 11 E
Babile Elephant Sanctuary, Ethiopia 120 C2 8 45N 42 20 E
Babimost, Poland 55 F2 52 10N 15 49 E
Babinda, Australia 126 B4 17 20 S 145 56 E
Babine, Canada 142 B3 55 22N 126 37W
Babine →, Canada 142 B3 55 45N 127 44W
Babine L., Canada 142 C3 54 48N 126 0W
Babo, Indonesia 83 B4 2 30 S 133 30 E
Babócsa, Hungary 52 D2 46 2N 17 21 E
Bābol, Iran 97 B7 36 40N 52 50 E
Bābol Sar, Iran 97 B7 36 45N 52 45 E
Babor, Dj., Algeria 111 A6 36 31N 5 25 E
Baborów, Poland 55 H5 50 7N 18 1 E
Baboua, C.A.R. 114 A2 5 49N 14 58 E
Babruysk, Belarus 59 F5 53 10N 29 15 E
Babson Park, U.S.A. 153 H8 27 49N 81 32W
Babuhri, India 92 F3 26 49N 69 43 E
Babuna, Macedonia 50 E5 41 30N 21 40 E
Babura, Nigeria 113 C6 12 51N 8 59 E
Babusar Pass, Pakistan 93 B5 35 12N 73 59 E
Babušnica, Serbia, Yug. 50 C6 43 7N 22 27 E
Babuyan, Phil. 81 F2 10 0N 118 54 E
Babuyan Chan., Phil. 80 B3 18 40N 121 30 E
Babuyan I., Phil. 80 B3 19 32N 121 57 E
Babuyan Is., Phil. 80 B3 19 10N 121 40 E
Babylon, Iraq 101 F11 32 34N 44 22 E
Bač, Serbia, Yug. 52 E4 45 29N 19 17 E
Bâc →, Moldova 53 D14 46 55N 29 26 E
Bac Can, Vietnam 76 F5 22 8N 105 49 E
Bac Giang, Vietnam 76 G6 21 16N 106 11 E
Bac Lieu, Vietnam 87 H5 9 17N 105 43 E
Bac Ninh, Vietnam 76 G6 21 13N 106 4 E
Bac Phan, Vietnam 86 B5 22 0N 105 0 E
Bac Quang, Vietnam 76 F5 22 30N 104 48 E
Bacabal, Brazil 170 B3 4 15 S 44 45W
Bacacay, Phil. 80 E4 13 18N 123 47 E
Bacajá →, Brazil 169 D7 3 25 S 51 50W
Bacalar, Mexico 163 D7 18 50N 87 27W
Bacan, Indonesia 82 B3 0 50 S 127 30 E
Bacan, Kepulauan, Indonesia 82 B3 0 35 S 127 30 E
Bacarra, Phil. 80 B3 18 15N 120 37 E
Bacău, Romania 53 D11 46 35N 26 55 E
Bacău □, Romania 53 D11 46 30N 26 45 E
Baccarat, France 27 D13 48 28N 6 42 E
Bacchus Marsh, Australia 128 D6 37 43 S 144 27 E
Bacerac, Mexico 162 A3 30 18N 108 50W
Băcești, Romania 53 D12 46 50N 27 11 E
Bach, Austria 33 B10 47 16N 10 25 E
Bach Long Vi, Dao, Vietnam 86 B6 20 10N 107 40 E
Bachaquero, Venezuela 168 B3 9 56N 71 8W
Bacharach, Germany 31 E3 50 3N 7 44 E
Bachelina, Russia 66 D7 57 45N 67 20 E
Bachhwara, India 93 G11 25 35N 85 54 E
Bachuma, Ethiopia 107 F4 6 48N 35 53 E
Bačina, Serbia, Yug. 50 C5 43 42N 21 23 E
Back →, Canada 138 B9 65 10N 104 0W
Bačka Palanka, Serbia, Yug. 52 E4 45 17N 19 27 E
Bačka Topola, Serbia, Yug. 52 E4 45 49N 19 39 E
Bäckebo, Sweden 17 H10 56 53N 16 4 E
Bäckefors, Sweden 17 F6 58 48N 12 9 E
Bäckhammar, Sweden 17 F8 59 10N 14 11 E
Bački Petrovac, Serbia, Yug. 52 E4 45 29N 19 32 E
Backnang, Germany 31 G5 48 56N 9 26 E
Backstairs Passage, Australia 128 C3 35 40 S 138 5 E
Baco, Mt., Phil. 80 E3 12 49N 121 10 E
Bacolod, Phil. 81 F4 10 40N 122 57 E
Bacon, Phil. 80 E5 13 3N 124 3 E
Baconton, U.S.A. 152 D5 31 23N 84 10W
Bacoor, Phil. 80 D3 14 28N 120 56 E
Bacqueville-en-Caux, France 26 C8 49 47N 1 0 E
Bács-Kiskun □, Hungary 52 D4 46 43N 19 30 E
Bácsalmás, Hungary 52 D4 46 8N 19 17 E
Bacuag = Placer, Phil. 81 G5 9 36N 125 38 E
Bacuk, Malaysia 87 J4 6 4N 102 25 E
Bād, Iran 97 C7 33 41N 52 1 E
Bad →, U.S.A. 154 C4 44 21N 100 22W
Bad Aussee, Austria 34 D6 47 43N 13 45 E
Bad Axe, U.S.A. 150 C2 43 48N 83 0W
Bad Bergzabern, Germany 31 F3 49 6N 7 59 E
Bad Berleburg, Germany 30 D4 51 2N 8 26 E
Bad Bevensen, Germany 30 B6 53 5N 10 35 E
Bad Bramstedt, Germany 30 B5 53 55N 9 53 E
Bad Brückenau, Germany 31 E5 50 18N 9 47 E
Bad Doberan, Germany 30 A7 54 6N 11 53 E
Bad Driburg, Germany 30 D5 51 43N 9 1 E
Bad Ems, Germany 31 E3 50 20N 7 43 E
Bad Frankenhausen, Germany 30 D7 51 21N 11 5 E
Bad Freienwalde, Germany 30 C10 52 46N 14 1 E
Bad Goisern, Austria 34 D6 47 38N 13 38 E
Bad Harzburg, Germany 30 D6 51 52N 10 34 E
Bad Hersfeld, Germany 30 E5 50 52N 9 42 E
Bad Hofgastein, Austria 34 D6 47 17N 13 6 E
Bad Homburg, Germany 31 E4 50 13N 8 38 E
Bad Honnef, Germany 30 E3 50 38N 7 13 E
Bad Iburg, Germany 30 C4 52 10N 8 3 E
Bad Ischl, Austria 34 D6 47 44N 13 38 E
Bad Kissingen, Germany 31 E6 50 11N 10 4 E
Bad Königshofen, Germany 31 E6 50 17N 10 28 E
Bad Kreuznach, Germany 31 F3 49 50N 7 51 E
Bad Krozingen, Germany 31 H3 47 54N 7 42 E
Bad Laasphe, Germany 30 E4 50 56N 8 25 E
Bad Lands, U.S.A. 154 D3 43 40N 102 10W
Bad Langensalza, Germany 30 D6 51 5N 10 38 E
Bad Lauterberg, Germany 30 D6 51 38N 10 28 E
Bad Leonfelden, Austria 34 C7 48 31N 14 18 E
Bad Liebenwerda, Germany 30 D9 51 31N 13 24 E
Bad Mergentheim, Germany 31 F5 49 28N 9 42 E
Bad Münstereifel, Germany 30 E2 50 33N 6 46 E
Bad Nauheim, Germany 31 E4 50 21N 8 43 E
Bad Neuenahr-Ahrweiler, Germany 30 E3 50 32N 7 5 E
Bad Neustadt, Germany 31 E6 50 18N 10 13 E
Bad Oeynhausen, Germany 30 C4 52 12N 8 46 E
Bad Oldesloe, Germany 30 B6 53 48N 10 22 E
Bad Orb, Germany 31 E5 50 12N 9 22 E
Bad Pyrmont, Germany 30 D5 51 59N 9 16 E
Bad Ragaz, Switz. 33 C9 47 0N 9 30 E
Bad Reichenhall, Germany 31 H8 47 43N 12 54 E
Bad Säckingen, Germany 31 H3 47 33N 7 56 E
Bad Salzuflen, Germany 30 C4 52 5N 8 45 E
Bad Salzungen, Germany 30 E6 50 48N 10 14 E
Bad Schwartau, Germany 30 B6 53 55N 10 41 E
Bad Segeberg, Germany 30 B6 53 56N 10 17 E
Bad St. Leonhard, Austria 34 E7 46 58N 14 47 E
Bad Tölz, Germany 31 H7 47 45N 11 34 E
Bad Urach, Germany 31 G5 48 29N 9 23 E
Bad Vöslau, Austria 35 D9 47 58N 16 12 E
Bad Waldsee, Germany 31 H5 47 55N 9 45 E
Bad Wildungen, Germany 30 D5 51 6N 9 7 E
Bad Wimpfen, Germany 31 F5 49 13N 9 11 E
Bad Windsheim, Germany 31 F6 49 36N 10 25 E
Bad Zwischenahn, Germany 30 B4 53 12N 8 1 E
Bada Barabil, India 93 H11 22 7N 85 24 E
Badagara, India 95 J2 11 35N 75 40 E
Badagri, Nigeria 113 D5 6 25N 2 55 E
Badajós, L., Brazil 169 D5 3 15 S 62 50W
Badajoz, Spain 43 G4 38 50N 6 59W
Badajoz □, Spain 43 G4 38 40N 6 30W
Badakhshān □, Afghan. 65 E5 36 30N 71 0 E
Badalona, Spain 40 D7 41 26N 2 15 E
Badalzai, Afghan. 92 E1 29 50N 65 35 E
Badami, India 95 G2 15 55N 75 41 E
Badampahar, India 94 C8 22 10N 86 10 E
Badanah, Si. Arabia 96 D4 30 58N 41 30 E
Badarinath, India 93 D8 30 45N 79 30 E
Badarpur, India 90 C4 24 54N 92 36 E
Badas, Kepulauan, Indonesia 84 B3 0 45N 107 5 E
Baddo →, Pakistan 91 D2 28 0N 64 20 E
Bade, Indonesia 83 C5 7 10 S 139 35 E
Badeggi, Nigeria 113 D6 9 1N 6 8 E
Badéguichéri, Niger 113 C6 14 30N 5 22 E
Baden, Austria 35 C9 48 1N 16 13 E
Baden, Switz. 33 B6 47 28N 8 18 E
Baden, U.S.A. 150 F4 40 38N 80 14W
Baden-Baden, Germany 31 G4 48 44N 8 13 E
Baden-Württemberg □, Germany 31 G4 48 20N 8 40 E
Badgastein, Austria 34 D6 47 7N 13 9 E
Badger, Canada 141 C8 49 0N 56 4W
Badger, U.S.A. 160 J7 36 38N 119 1W
Bādghīs □, Afghan. 91 B1 35 0N 63 0 E
Badgingarra Nat. Park, Australia 125 F2 30 23 S 115 22 E
Badgom, India 93 B6 34 1N 74 45 E
Badia Polésine, Italy 45 C8 45 5N 11 29 E
Badian, Phil. 81 G4 9 55N 123 24 E
Badiar, Parc Nat. du, Guinea 112 C2 13 37N 13 11W
Badin, Pakistan 91 D3 24 38N 68 54 E
Badinka, Réserve du, Mali 112 C3 13 31N 9 28W
Badjokola, Dem. Rep. of the Congo 114 B4 3 54N 20 17 E
Badlands Nat. Park, U.S.A. 154 D3 43 38N 102 56W
Badnera, India 94 D3 20 48N 77 44 E
Badoc, Phil. 80 C3 17 56N 120 28 E
Badogo, Mali 112 C3 11 2N 8 13W
Badoumbé, Mali 112 C2 13 42N 10 15W
Badr Ḥunayn, Si. Arabia 98 B2 23 44N 38 46 E
Badrah, Iraq 101 F11 33 6N 45 58 E
Badrinath, India 93 D8 30 44N 79 29 E
Badu I., Papua N. G. 132 F2 10 5 S 142 10 E
Baduen, Somali Rep. 120 C3 7 15N 47 40 E
Badulla, Sri Lanka 95 L5 7 1N 81 7 E
Badung, Selat, Indonesia 79 K18 8 40 S 115 22 E
Badupi, Burma 90 E4 21 36N 93 27 E
Badvel, India 95 G4 14 45N 79 3 E
Baena, Spain 43 H6 37 37N 4 20W
Baerami, N.S.W., Australia 129 B9 32 24 S 150 29 E
Baerami, N.S.W., Australia 129 B9 32 27 S 150 27 E
Baetov, Kyrgyzstan 65 C7 41 13N 74 54 E
Baeza, Ecuador 168 D2 0 25 S 77 53W
Baeza, Spain 43 H7 37 57N 3 25W
Bafang, Cameroon 113 D7 5 9N 10 11 E
Bafatá, Guinea-Biss. 112 C2 12 8N 14 40W
Baffin B., Canada 139 A13 72 0N 64 0W
Baffin I., Canada 139 B12 68 0N 75 0W
Bafia, Cameroon 113 E7 4 40N 11 10 E
Bafilo, Togo 113 D5 9 22N 1 22 E
Bafing →, Mali 112 C2 13 49N 10 50W
Bafing, Parc Nat. du, Mali 112 C2 12 38N 10 28W
Bafliyūn, Syria 96 B3 36 37N 36 59 E
Bafoulabé, Mali 112 C2 13 50N 10 55W
Bafoussam, Cameroon 113 D7 5 28N 10 25 E
Bāfq, Iran 97 D7 31 40N 55 25 E
Bafra, Turkey 100 B6 41 34N 35 54 E
Bafra Burnu, Turkey 100 B7 41 45N 36 2 E
Bāft, Iran 97 D8 29 15N 56 38 E
Bafut, Cameroon 113 D7 6 6N 10 2 E
Bafwasende, Dem. Rep. of the Congo 118 B2 1 3N 27 5 E
Bagaat, Î., N. Cal. 133 K4 20 40 S 166 15 E
Bagabag, Phil. 80 C3 16 30N 121 15 E
Bagabag I., Papua N. G. 132 C4 4 48 S 146 14 E
Bagac, Phil. 80 D3 14 36N 120 23 E
Bagac Bay, Phil. 80 D3 14 36N 120 20 E
Bagalkot, India 95 F2 16 10N 75 40 E
Bagam, Niger 113 B6 15 43N 6 35 E
Bagamanoc, Phil. 80 E5 13 57N 124 17 E
Bagamoyo, Tanzania 118 D4 6 28 S 38 55 E
Bagan Datoh, Malaysia 87 L3 3 59N 100 47 E
Bagan Serai, Malaysia 87 K3 5 1N 100 32 E
Baganga, Phil. 81 H6 7 34N 126 33 E
Bagani, Namibia 116 B3 18 7 S 21 41 E
Bagansiapiapi, Indonesia 84 B2 2 12N 100 50 E
Bagasra, India 92 J4 21 30N 71 0 E
Bagata, Dem. Rep. of the Congo 114 C3 3 44 S 17 57 E
Bagaud, India 92 H6 22 19N 75 53 E
Bagawi, Sudan 107 E3 12 20N 34 18 E
Bagbag, Sudan 107 D3 15 23N 31 30 E
Bagdad, Calif., U.S.A. 161 L11 34 35N 115 53W
Bagdad, Fla., U.S.A. 153 E2 30 36N 87 2W
Bagdarin, Russia 67 D12 54 26N 113 36 E
Bagé, Brazil 175 C5 31 20 S 54 15W
Bagenalstown = Muine Bheag, Ireland 23 D5 52 42N 6 58W
Bagepalli, India 95 H3 13 47N 77 47 E
Bagevadi, India 94 F2 16 35N 75 58 E
Baggao, Phil. 80 B3 17 56N 121 46 E
Baggs, U.S.A. 158 F10 41 2N 107 39W
Bagh, Pakistan 93 C5 33 59N 73 45 E
Baghain →, India 93 G9 25 32N 81 1 E
Baghdād, Iraq 101 F11 33 20N 44 30 E
Bagherhat, Bangla. 90 D2 22 40N 89 47 E
Bagheria, Italy 46 D6 38 5N 13 30 E
Baghlān, Afghan. 91 A3 32 12N 68 46 E
Baghlān □, Afghan. 91 B3 36 0N 68 30 E
Bagley, U.S.A. 154 B7 47 32N 95 24W
Bagn, Norway 18 D6 60 49N 9 34 E
Bagnara Cálabra, Italy 47 D8 38 17N 15 48 E
Bagnasco, Italy 44 D5 44 18N 8 2 E
Bagnell Dam, U.S.A. 156 F4 38 14N 92 36W
Bagnères-de-Bigorre, France 28 E4 43 5N 0 9 E
Bagnères-de-Luchon, France 28 F4 42 47N 0 38 E
Bagni di Lucca, Italy 44 D7 44 1N 10 35 E
Bagno di Romagna, Italy 45 E8 43 50N 11 57 E
Bagnoles-de-l'Orne, France 26 D6 48 32N 0 25W
Bagnols-sur-Cèze, France 29 D8 44 10N 4 36 E
Bagnorégio, Italy 45 F9 42 37N 12 5 E
Bago = Pegu, Burma 90 G6 17 20N 96 29 E
Bago, Phil. 81 F4 10 32N 122 50 E
Bagodar, India 93 G11 24 5N 85 52 E
Bagrationovsk, Russia 15 J19 54 23N 20 39 E
Bagrdan, Serbia, Yug. 50 B5 44 5N 21 11 E
Bagua, Peru 172 B2 5 35 S 78 22W
Baguio, Phil. 80 C3 16 26N 120 34 E
Bağyurdu, Turkey 49 C9 38 25N 27 41 E
Bagzane, Monts, Niger 113 B6 17 43N 8 45 E
Bah, India 93 F8 26 53N 78 36 E
Bahabón de Esgueva, Spain 42 D7 41 52N 3 43W
Bahadurabad Ghat, Bangla. 90 C2 25 11N 89 44 E
Bahadurganj, India 93 F12 26 16N 87 49 E
Bahadurgarh, India 92 E7 28 40N 76 57 E
Bahama, Canal Viejo de, W. Indies 164 B4 22 10N 77 30W
Bahamas ■, N. Amer. 165 B5 24 0N 75 0W
Bahār, Iran 101 E13 34 54N 48 26 E
Bahārak, Afghan. 65 E5 37 0N 70 53 E
Baharampur, India 93 G13 24 2N 88 27 E
Baharîya, El Wâhât al, Egypt 106 B2 28 0N 28 50 E
Bahawalnagar, Pakistan 91 C4 30 0N 73 15 E
Bahawalpur, Pakistan 91 C3 29 24N 71 40 E
Bahçe, Turkey 100 D7 37 13N 36 34 E
Bahçecik, Turkey 51 F13 40 41N 29 44 E
Baheli, Phil. 81 F2 10 0N 118 47 E
Baheri, India 93 E8 28 45N 79 34 E
Bahgul →, India 93 F8 27 45N 79 36 E
Bahi, Tanzania 118 D4 5 58 S 35 21 E
Bahi Swamp, Tanzania 118 D4 6 10 S 35 0 E
Bahia = Salvador, Brazil 171 D4 13 0 S 38 30W
Bahia □, Brazil 171 D3 12 0 S 42 0W
Bahía, Is. de la, Honduras 164 C2 16 45N 86 15W
Bahía Blanca, Argentina 174 D3 38 35 S 62 13W
Bahía de Caráquez, Ecuador 168 D1 0 40 S 80 27W
Bahía Honda, Cuba 164 B3 22 54N 83 10W
Bahía Laura, Argentina 176 C3 48 10 S 66 30W
Bahía Mansa, Chile 176 B2 40 33 S 73 46W
Bahía Negra, Paraguay 173 E6 20 5 S 58 5W
Bahir Dar, Ethiopia 107 E4 11 37N 37 10 E
Bahlah, Oman 99 B7 22 58N 57 18 E
Bahmanzād, Iran 97 D6 31 15N 51 47 E
Bahmer, Algeria 111 C4 27 32N 0 10W
Bahr el Ahmar □, Sudan 106 D4 20 0N 35 0 E
Bahr el Ghazâl □, Sudan 107 F2 7 0N 28 0 E
Bahr el Jabal □, Sudan 107 G3 4 0N 31 0 E
Bahraich, India 93 F9 27 38N 81 37 E
Bahrain ■, Asia 97 E6 26 0N 50 35 E
Bahror, India 92 F7 27 51N 76 20 E
Bāhū Kalāt, Iran 97 E9 25 43N 61 25 E
Bai, Mali 112 C4 13 35N 3 28W
Bai Bung, Mui = Ca Mau, Mui, Vietnam 87 H5 8 38N 104 44 E
Bai Duc, Vietnam 86 C5 18 3N 105 49 E
Bai Thuong, Vietnam 86 C5 19 54N 105 23 E
Baia de Aramă, Romania 52 E7 45 0N 22 50 E
Baía dos Tigres, Angola 115 F2 16 40 S 11 47 E
Baia Farta, Angola 115 E2 12 40 S 13 11 E
Baia Mare, Romania 53 C8 47 40N 23 35 E
Baia-Sprie, Romania 53 C8 47 41N 23 43 E
Baião, Brazil 170 B2 2 40 S 49 40W
Baïbokoum, Chad 109 G3 7 46N 15 43 E
Baicheng, China 75 B12 45 38N 122 42 E
Băicoi, Romania 53 E10 45 3N 25 52 E
Baidoa, Somali Rep. 120 D2 3 8N 43 30 E
Baie Comeau, Canada 141 C6 49 12N 68 10W
Baie-St-Paul, Canada 141 C5 47 28N 70 32W
Baie Ste-Anne, Seychelles 121 b 4 18 S 55 45 E
Baie Trinité, Canada 141 C6 49 25N 67 20W
Baie Verte, Canada 141 C8 49 55N 56 12W
Baignes-Ste-Radegonde, France 28 C3 45 23N 0 25W
Baigneux-les-Juifs, France 27 E11 47 31N 4 39 E
Baihar, India 93 H9 22 6N 80 33 E
Baihe, China 74 H6 32 50N 110 5 E
Ba'ījī, Iraq 101 E10 35 0N 43 30 E
Baijnath, India 93 E8 29 55N 79 37 E
Baikal, L. = Baykal, Oz., Russia 67 D11 53 0N 108 0 E
Baikunthpur, India 93 H10 23 15N 82 33 E
Bailadila, Mt., India 94 E5 18 43N 81 15 E
Baile Atha Cliath = Dublin, Ireland 23 C5 53 21N 6 15W
Băile Govora, Romania 53 E9 45 5N 24 11 E
Băile Herculane, Romania 52 F7 44 53N 22 26 E
Băile Olănești, Romania 53 E9 45 12N 24 14 E
Băile Tușnad, Romania 53 D10 46 9N 25 51 E
Bailén, Spain 43 G7 38 8N 3 48W
Băilești, Romania 53 F8 44 1N 23 20 E
Bailhongal, India 95 G2 15 55N 74 53 E
Bailique, Ilha, Brazil 170 A2 1 2N 49 58W
Bailugh, Afghan. 91 B2 32 40N 66 47 E
Bailundo, Angola 115 E3 12 10 S 15 50 E
Baima, China 76 A3 33 0N 100 26 E
Baimuru, Papua N. G. 132 D3 7 35 S 144 51 E
Bain-de-Bretagne, France 26 E5 47 50N 1 40W
Bainbridge, Ga., U.S.A. 152 E5 30 55N 84 35W
Bainbridge, Ind., U.S.A. 157 E10 39 46N 86 49W
Bainbridge, N.Y., U.S.A. 151 D9 42 18N 75 29W
Bainbridge, Ohio, U.S.A. 157 E13 39 14N 83 16W
Baing, Indonesia 82 D2 10 14 S 120 34 E
Bainiu, China 74 H7 32 50N 112 15 E
Bainyik, Papua N. G. 132 B2 3 40 S 143 4 E
Baiona, Spain 42 C2 42 6N 8 52W
Bā'ir, Jordan 103 E5 30 45N 36 55 E
Baird Mts., U.S.A. 144 C8 67 0N 160 0W
Bairin Youqi, China 75 C10 43 30N 118 35 E
Bairin Zuoqi, China 75 C10 43 58N 119 15 E
Bairnsdale, Australia 129 D7 37 48 S 147 36 E
Bais, Phil. 81 G4 9 35N 123 7 E
Baisha, China 74 G7 34 20N 112 32 E
Baissa, Nigeria 113 D7 7 14N 10 38 E
Baitadi, Nepal 93 E9 29 35N 80 25 E
Baitarani →, India 94 D8 20 45N 86 48 E
Baixa Grande, Brazil 171 D3 11 57 S 40 11W
Baixo-Longa, Angola 115 F3 15 41 S 18 45 E
Baiyer River, Papua N. G. 132 C3 5 32 S 144 9 E
Baiyin, China 74 F3 36 45N 104 14 E
Baiyü, China 76 B2 31 16N 98 50 E
Baiyu Shan, China 74 F4 37 15N 107 30 E
Baiyuda, Sudan 106 D3 17 35N 32 7 E
Baj Baj, India 93 H13 22 30N 88 5 E
Baja, Hungary 52 D3 46 12N 18 59 E
Baja, Pta., Chile 172 b 27 10 S 109 22W
Baja, Pta., Mexico 162 B1 29 50N 116 0W
Baja California, Mexico 162 A1 31 10N 115 12W
Baja California □, Mexico 162 B2 30 0N 115 0W
Baja California Sur □, Mexico 162 B2 25 50N 111 50W
Bajag, India 93 H9 22 40N 81 21 E
Bajamar, Canary Is. 9 e1 28 33N 16 20W
Bajana, India 92 H4 23 7N 71 49 E
Bajatrejo, Indonesia 79 J17 8 29 S 114 19 E
Bajawa, Indonesia 82 C2 8 47 S 120 59 E
Bajera, Indonesia 79 J18 8 31 S 115 2 E
Bājgīrān, Iran 97 B8 37 36N 58 24 E
Bājil, Yemen 98 D3 15 4N 43 17 E
Bajimba, Mt., Australia 127 D5 29 17 S 152 6 E
Bajina Bašta, Serbia, Yug. 50 C3 43 58N 19 35 E
Bajmok, Serbia, Yug. 52 E4 45 57N 19 24 E
Bajo Caracoles, Argentina 176 C2 47 27 S 70 56W
Bajo Nuevo, Caribbean 164 C4 15 40N 78 50W
Bajoga, Nigeria 113 C7 10 57N 11 20 E
Bajool, Australia 126 C5 23 40 S 150 35 E
Bak, Hungary 52 D1 46 43N 16 51 E
Bakal, Russia 64 D7 54 56N 58 48 E
Bakala, C.A.R. 114 A4 6 15N 20 20 E
Bakanas = Baqanas, Kazakstan 65 A8 44 50N 76 15 E
Bakar, Croatia 45 C11 45 18N 14 32 E
Bakel, Senegal 112 C2 14 56N 12 20W
Baker, Calif., U.S.A. 161 K10 35 16N 116 4W
Baker, Fla., U.S.A. 153 E3 30 48N 86 41W
Baker, Mont., U.S.A. 154 B2 46 22N 104 17W
Baker, L., Canada 138 B10 64 0N 96 0W
Baker, Canal, Chile 176 C2 47 45 S 74 45W
Baker City, U.S.A. 158 D5 44 47N 117 50W
Baker I., Pac. Oc. 134 G10 0 10N 176 35W
Baker I., U.S.A. 142 B2 55 20N 133 40W
Baker L., Australia 125 E4 26 54 S 126 5 E
Baker Lake, Canada 138 B10 64 20N 96 3W
Baker Mt., U.S.A. 158 B3 48 50N 121 49W
Bakere, Dem. Rep. of the Congo 114 B4 1 36N 23 50 E
Bakerhill, U.S.A. 152 D4 31 47N 85 18W
Bakers Creek, Australia 126 C4 21 13 S 149 7 E
Baker's Dozen Is., Canada 140 A4 56 45N 78 45W
Bakersfield, Calif., U.S.A. 161 K8 35 23N 119 1W
Bakersfield, Vt., U.S.A. 151 B12 44 45N 72 48W
Bakhchysaray, Ukraine 59 K7 44 40N 33 45 E
Bakhmach, Ukraine 59 G7 51 10N 32 45 E
Bakht, Uzbekistan 65 C4 40 43N 68 42 E
Bākhtarān, Iran 101 E12 34 23N 47 0 E
Bākhtarān □, Iran 96 C5 34 0N 46 30 E
Bakı, Azerbaijan 61 K9 40 29N 49 56 E
Bakır →, Turkey 49 C9 38 55N 27 0 E
Bakırdaği, Turkey 100 C6 38 13N 35 46 E
Bakkafjörður, Iceland 11 A12 66 2N 14 48W
Bakkaflói, Iceland 11 A12 66 10N 14 45W
Baklan, Turkey 49 C11 38 0N 29 36 E
Bako, Ethiopia 107 F4 5 51N 36 23 E
Bako, Ivory C. 112 D3 9 8N 7 40W
Bakony, Hungary 52 C2 47 10N 17 30 E
Bakony Forest = Bakony, Hungary 52 C2 47 10N 17 30 E
Bakori, Nigeria 113 C6 11 34N 7 25 E
Bakouma, C.A.R. 114 A4 5 40N 22 56 E
Bakpakty = Baqbaqty, Kazakstan 65 A8 44 35N 76 40 E
Baksan, Russia 61 J6 43 42N 43 32 E
Bakswaho, India 93 G8 24 15N 79 18 E
Baku = Bakı, Azerbaijan 61 K9 40 29N 49 56 E
Bakundi, Nigeria 113 D7 8 2N 10 45 E
Bakutis Coast, Antarctica 7 D15 74 0 S 120 0W
Bakwa-Kenge, Dem. Rep. of the Congo 115 C4 4 51 S 22 4 E
Baky = Bakı, Azerbaijan 61 K9 40 29N 49 56 E
Bala, Canada 150 A5 45 1N 79 37W
Bala, Senegal 112 C2 14 1N 13 8W
Bâlâ, Turkey 100 C5 39 32N 33 6 E
Bala, U.K. 20 E4 52 54N 3 36W
Bala, L., U.K. 20 E4 52 53N 3 37W
Bālā Morghāb, Afghan. 91 B1 35 35N 63 20 E
Balabac, Phil. 81 H1 7 59N 117 4 E
Balabac I., Phil. 81 G1 8 0N 117 0 E
Balabac Str., E. Indies 78 C5 7 53N 117 5 E
Balabagh, Afghan. 92 B4 34 25N 70 12 E
Ba'labakk, Lebanon 103 B5 34 0N 36 10 E
Balabalangan, Kepulauan, Indonesia 85 C5 2 20 S 117 30 E
Balabio, Î., N. Cal. 133 T18 20 7 S 164 11 E
Bălăcița, Romania 53 F8 44 23N 23 8 E
Balad, Iraq 101 F11 34 1N 44 9 E
Balad Rūz, Iraq 101 F11 33 42N 45 5 E
Bālādeh, Fārs, Iran 97 D6 29 17N 51 56 E
Bālādeh, Māzandaran, Iran 97 B6 36 12N 51 48 E
Balaghat, India 94 D5 21 49N 80 12 E
Balaghat Ra., India 94 E3 18 50N 76 30 E
Balaguer, Spain 40 D5 41 50N 0 50 E
Balaka, Dem. Rep. of the Congo 115 C3 4 52 S 19 57 E
Balakété, C.A.R. 114 A3 6 56N 19 54 E
Balakhna, Russia 60 B6 56 25N 43 32 E
Balaklava, Australia 128 C3 34 7 S 138 22 E
Balaklava, Ukraine 59 K7 44 30N 33 30 E
Balakliya, Ukraine 59 H9 49 28N 36 55 E
Balakovo, Russia 60 D8 52 4N 47 55 E
Balamau, India 93 F9 27 10N 80 21 E
Balamban, Phil. 81 F4 10 30N 123 43 E
Balambangan, Malaysia 85 A5 7 17N 116 55 E
Bălan, Romania 53 D10 46 39N 25 49 E
Balancán, Mexico 163 D6 17 48N 91 32W
Balanga, Phil. 80 D3 14 41N 120 32 E
Balangala, Dem. Rep. of the Congo 114 B3 0 30N 19 56 E
Balangiga, Phil. 81 F5 11 7N 125 23 E
Balangir, India 94 D6 20 43N 83 35 E
Balaoan, Phil. 80 C3 16 49N 120 24 E
Balapur, India 94 D3 20 40N 76 45 E
Balashov, Russia 60 E6 51 30N 43 10 E
Balasinor, India 92 H5 22 57N 73 23 E
Balasore = Baleshwar, India 94 D8 21 35N 87 3 E
Balassagyarmat, Hungary 52 B4 48 4N 19 15 E
Balât, Egypt 106 B2 25 36N 29 19 E
Balaton, Hungary 52 D2 46 50N 17 40 E
Balatonboglár, Hungary 52 D2 46 46N 17 40 E
Balatonfüred, Hungary 52 D2 46 58N 17 54 E
Balatonszentgyörgy, Hungary 52 D2 46 41N 17 19 E
Balayan, Phil. 80 E3 13 57N 120 44 E
Balazote, Spain 41 G2 38 54N 2 9W
Balbalan, Phil. 80 C3 17 27N 121 12 E
Balbi, Mt., Papua N. G. 132 C8 5 55 S 154 58 E
Balbieriškis, Lithuania 54 D10 54 32N 23 53 E
Balbigny, France 29 C8 45 49N 4 11 E
Balbina, Brazil 169 D6 1 58 S 59 29W
Balbina, Represa de, Brazil 169 D6 2 0 S 59 30W

Balboa, *Panama* **164 E4** 8 57N 79 34W
Balbriggan, *Ireland* **23 C5** 53 37N 6 11W
Balcarce, *Argentina* **174 D4** 38 0 S 58 10W
Balcarres, *Canada* **143 C8** 50 50N 103 35W
Bălceşti, *Romania* **53 F8** 44 37N 23 57 E
Balchik, *Bulgaria* **51 C12** 43 28N 28 11 E
Balclutha, *N.Z.* **131 G4** 46 15 S 169 45 E
Balcones Escarpment, *U.S.A.* **155 L5** 29 30N 99 15W
Balçova, *Turkey* **49 C9** 38 22N 27 4 E
Bald Hd., *Australia* **125 G2** 35 6 S 118 1 E
Bald I., *Australia* **125 F2** 34 57 S 118 27 E
Bald Knob, *U.S.A.* **155 H9** 35 19N 91 34W
Baldock L., *Canada* **143 B9** 56 33N 97 57W
Baldwin, *Fla., U.S.A.* **152 E8** 30 18N 81 59W
Baldwin, *Mich., U.S.A.* **148 D3** 43 54N 85 51W
Baldwin, *Pa., U.S.A.* **150 F5** 40 23N 79 59W
Baldwinsville, *U.S.A.* **151 C8** 43 10N 76 20W
Baldy Mt., *U.S.A.* **158 B9** 48 9N 109 39W
Baldy Peak, *U.S.A.* **159 K9** 33 54N 109 34W
Bale, *Croatia* **45 C10** 45 4N 13 46 E
Bale, *Ethiopia* **107 F5** 6 57N 40 8 E
Bale □, *Ethiopia* **107 F5** 6 20N 41 30 E
Bale Mountains Nat. Park,
Ethiopia **107 F4** 6 59N 39 52 E
Baleares, Is., *Spain* **38 B4** 39 30N 3 0 E
Balearic Is. = Baleares, Is., *Spain* **38 B4** 39 30N 3 0 E
Balease, *Indonesia* **82 B2** 2 24 S 120 33 E
Baleia, Pta. da, *Brazil* **171 E4** 17 40 S 39 7W
Baleine = Whale →, *Canada* **141 A6** 58 15N 67 40W
Băleni, *Romania* **53 E12** 45 48N 27 51 E
Baler, *Phil.* **80 D3** 15 46N 121 34 E
Baler Bay, *Phil.* **80 D3** 15 50N 121 35 E
Balerna, *Switz.* **33 E8** 45 52N 9 0 E
Baleshare, *U.K.* **22 D1** 57 31N 7 22W
Baleshwar, *India* **94 D8** 21 35N 87 3 E
Balestrand, *Norway* **18 C3** 61 11N 6 31 E
Balezino, *Russia* **60 B11** 58 2N 53 6 E
Balfate, *Honduras* **164 C2** 15 48N 86 25W
Balfour Channel, *Solomon Is.* **133 M9** 8 43 S 157 27 E
Balharshah, *India* **94 E4** 19 50N 79 23 E
Bali, *Cameroon* **113 D7** 5 54N 10 0 E
Bali, *Dem. Rep. of the Congo* **114 C3** 2 50 S 16 12 E
Balí, *Greece* **39 E5** 35 25N 24 47 E
Bali, *India* **92 G5** 25 11N 73 17 E
Bali, *Indonesia* **85 D4** 8 20 S 115 0 E
Bali □, *Indonesia* **85 D4** 8 20 S 115 0 E
Bali, Selat, *Indonesia* **85 D4** 8 18 S 114 25 E
Bali Sea, *Indonesia* **85 D5** 8 0 S 115 0 E
Balia, *S. Leone* **112 D2** 9 22N 11 1W
Baliapal, *India* **93 J12** 21 40N 87 17 E
Balicuatro Is., *Phil.* **80 E5** 12 39N 124 24 E
Baliem →, *Indonesia* **83 C5** 5 44 S 138 8 E
Baligród, *Poland* **55 J9** 49 20N 22 17 E
Baliguda, *India* **94 D6** 20 12N 83 55 E
Balik Pulau, *Malaysia* **87 c** 5 21N 100 14 E
Balikeşir, *Turkey* **49 B9** 39 39N 27 53 E
Balikeşir □, *Turkey* **49 B9** 39 45N 28 0 E
Balıklıçeşme, *Turkey* **51 F11** 40 18N 27 5 E
Balikpapan, *Indonesia* **85 C5** 1 10 S 116 55 E
Balimbing, *Phil.* **81 J2** 5 5N 119 58 E
Balimo, *Papua N. G.* **132 E2** 8 6 S 142 57 E
Baling, *Malaysia* **87 K3** 5 41N 100 55 E
Balingasag, *Phil.* **81 G5** 8 45N 124 47 E
Balingen, *Germany* **31 G4** 48 16N 8 51 E
Balinţ, *Romania* **52 E6** 45 48N 21 54 E
Balintang Channel, *Phil.* **80 B3** 19 49N 121 40 E
Balintang I., *Phil.* **80 B4** 19 58N 122 9 E
Baliza, *Brazil* **173 D7** 16 0 S 52 20W
Baljurshī, *Si. Arabia* **98 C3** 19 51N 41 33 E
Balkan Mts. = Stara Planina,
Bulgaria **50 C7** 43 15N 23 0 E
Balkh, *Afghan.* **65 E3** 36 44N 66 47 E
Balkh □, *Afghan.* **65 E3** 36 50N 67 0 E
Balkhash = Balqash, *Kazakstan* **66 E8** 46 50N 74 50 E
Balkhash, Ozero = Balqash Köl,
Kazakstan **66 E8** 46 0N 74 50 E
Balkonda, *India* **94 E4** 18 52N 78 21 E
Ballachulish, *U.K.* **22 E3** 56 41N 5 8W
Balladonia, *Australia* **125 F3** 32 27 S 123 51 E
Ballaghaderreen, *Ireland* **23 C3** 53 55N 8 34W
Ballan, *Australia* **128 D6** 37 35 S 144 13 E
Ballarat, *Australia* **128 D5** 37 33 S 143 50 E
Ballard, L., *Australia* **125 E3** 29 20 S 120 40 E
Ballater, *U.K.* **22 D5** 57 3N 3 3W
Ballé, *Mali* **112 B3** 15 18N 8 33W
Ballenas, Canal de, *Mexico* **162 B2** 29 10N 113 45W
Balleny Is., *Antarctica* **7 C11** 66 30 S 163 0 E
Balleroy, *France* **26 C6** 49 11N 0 50W
Ballerup, *Denmark* **17 J6** 55 44N 12 21 E
Ballı, *Turkey* **51 F11** 40 50N 27 3 E
Ballia, *India* **93 G11** 25 46N 84 12 E
Ballina, *Australia* **127 D5** 28 50 S 153 31 E
Ballina, *Ireland* **23 B2** 54 7N 9 9W
Ballinasloe, *Ireland* **23 C3** 53 20N 8 13W
Ballinger, *U.S.A.* **155 K5** 31 45N 99 57W
Ballinrobe, *Ireland* **23 C2** 53 38N 9 13W
Ballinskelligs B., *Ireland* **23 E1** 51 48N 10 13W
Ballon, *France* **26 D7** 48 10N 0 14 E
Ballsh, *Albania* **50 F3** 40 36N 19 44 E
Ballston Spa, *U.S.A.* **151 D11** 43 0N 73 51W
Ballycastle, *U.K.* **23 A5** 55 12N 6 15W
Ballyclare, *U.K.* **23 B5** 54 46N 6 0W
Ballyhaunis, *Ireland* **23 C3** 53 46N 8 46W
Ballymena, *U.K.* **23 B5** 54 52N 6 17W
Ballymoney, *U.K.* **23 A5** 55 5N 6 31W
Ballymote, *Ireland* **23 B3** 54 5N 8 31W
Ballynahinch, *U.K.* **23 B6** 54 24N 5 54W
Ballyquintin Pt., *U.K.* **23 B6** 54 20N 5 30W
Ballyshannon, *Ireland* **23 B3** 54 30N 8 11W
Balmaceda, *Chile* **176 C2** 46 0 S 71 50W
Balmaseda, *Spain* **40 B1** 43 11N 3 12W
Balmazújváros, *Hungary* **52 C6** 47 37N 21 21 E
Balmertown, *Canada* **143 C10** 51 4N 93 41W
Balmhorn, *Switz.* **32 D5** 46 26N 7 42 E
Balmoral, *Australia* **128 D4** 37 15 S 141 48 E
Balmorhea, *U.S.A.* **155 K3** 30 59N 103 45W
Balochistan = Baluchistan □,
Pakistan **91 D2** 27 30N 65 0 E
Balod, *India* **94 D5** 20 44N 81 13 E
Balombo, *Angola* **115 E2** 12 21 S 14 46 E
Balombo →, *Angola* **115 E2** 11 57 S 13 46 E
Balonne →, *Australia* **127 D4** 28 47 S 147 56 E
Balotra, *India* **92 G5** 25 50N 72 14 E
Balpyq Bī, *Kazakstan* **65 A9** 44 52N 78 12 E
Balqash, *Kazakstan* **66 E8** 46 50N 74 50 E
Balqash Köl, *Kazakstan* **66 E8** 46 0N 74 50 E
Balrampur, *India* **93 F10** 27 30N 82 20 E
Balranald, *Australia* **128 C5** 34 38 S 143 33 E
Balş, *Romania* **53 F9** 44 22N 24 5 E
Balsapuerto, *Peru* **172 B2** 5 48 S 76 33W
Balsas, *Mexico* **163 D5** 18 0N 99 40W
Balsas →, *Maranhão, Brazil* **170 C3** 7 15 S 44 35W
Balsas →, *Tocantins, Brazil* **170 C2** 9 58 S 47 52W
Balsas →, *Mexico* **162 D4** 17 55N 102 10W
Bålsta, *Sweden* **16 E11** 59 35N 17 30 E
Balsthal, *Switz.* **32 B5** 47 19N 7 41 E
Balston Spa, *U.S.A.* **151 D11** 43 0N 73 52W
Balta, *Romania* **52 F7** 44 54N 22 38 E
Balta, *Ukraine* **59 J5** 48 2N 29 45 E
Baltanás, *Spain* **42 D6** 41 56N 4 15W
Bălţi, *Moldova* **53 C12** 47 48N 27 58 E
Baltic Sea, *Europe* **15 H18** 57 0N 19 0 E
Baltîm, *Egypt* **106 H7** 31 35N 31 10 E
Baltimore, *Ireland* **23 E2** 51 29N 9 22W
Baltimore, *Md., U.S.A.* **148 F7** 39 17N 76 37W
Baltimore, *Ohio, U.S.A.* **150 G2** 39 51N 82 36W
Baltit, *Pakistan* **93 A6** 36 15N 74 40 E
Baltiysk, *Russia* **15 J18** 54 41N 19 58 E
Baltra, I., *Ecuador* **172 a** 0 26 S 90 16W
Baltrum, *Germany* **30 B3** 53 43N 7 24 E
Baluan I., *Papua N. G.* **132 B4** 2 33 S 147 17 E
Baluchistan □, *Pakistan* **91 D2** 27 30N 65 0 E
Balud, *Phil.* **80 E4** 12 2N 123 12 E
Balurghat, *India* **90 C2** 25 15N 88 44 E
Balvi, *Latvia* **15 H22** 57 8N 27 15 E
Balya, *Turkey* **49 B9** 39 44N 27 35 E
Balykchy, *Kyrgyzstan* **65 B8** 42 26N 76 12 E
Balzar, *Ecuador* **168 D2** 2 2 S 79 54W
Bam, *Iran* **97 D8** 29 7N 58 14 E
Bama, *China* **76 E6** 24 8N 107 12 E
Bama, *Nigeria* **113 C7** 11 33N 13 41 E
Bamaga, *Australia* **126 A3** 10 50 S 142 25 E
Bamaji L., *Canada* **140 B1** 51 9N 91 25W
Bamako, *Mali* **112 C3** 12 34N 7 55W
Bamba, *Dem. Rep. of the Congo* **115 D3** 5 45 S 18 23 E
Bamba, *Mali* **113 B4** 17 5N 1 24W
Bambamarca, *Peru* **172 B2** 6 36 S 78 32W
Bambang, *Phil.* **80 C3** 16 23N 121 6 E
Bambannan I., *Phil.* **81 J3** 5 37N 120 17 E
Bambara Maoundé, *Mali* **112 B4** 13 26N 4 3W
Bambari, *C.A.R.* **114 A4** 5 40N 20 35 E
Bambaroo, *Australia* **126 B4** 18 50 S 146 10 E
Bambaya, *Guinea* **112 D2** 10 55N 13 38W
Bamberg, *Germany* **31 F6** 49 54N 10 54 E
Bamberg, *U.S.A.* **152 B8** 33 18N 81 2W
Bambesi, *Ethiopia* **107 F3** 9 45N 34 40 E
Bambey, *Senegal* **112 C1** 14 42N 16 28W
Bambili, *Dem. Rep. of the Congo* **118 B2** 3 40N 26 0 E
Bambinga, *Dem. Rep. of the Congo* **114 C3** 3 43 S 18 53 E
Bambio, *C.A.R.* **114 B3** 3 55N 16 57 E
Bamboi, *Ghana* **112 D4** 8 13N 2 1W
Bambouti, *C.A.R.* **114 A5** 5 24N 27 12 E
Bambuí, *Brazil* **171 F2** 20 1 S 45 58W
Bamenda, *Cameroon* **113 D7** 5 57N 10 11 E
Bamfield, *Canada* **142 D3** 48 45N 125 10W
Bāmīān □, *Afghan.* **91 B2** 35 0N 67 0 E
Bamiancheng, *China* **75 C13** 43 15N 124 2 E
Bamingui, *C.A.R.* **114 A4** 7 34N 20 11 E
Bamingui →, *C.A.R.* **114 A3** 8 33N 19 5 E
Bamingui-Bangoran, Parc Nat. du,
C.A.R. **114 A3** 8 30N 19 46 E
Bamkin, *Cameroon* **113 D7** 6 3N 11 27 E
Bampan, *Phil.* **80 D3** 15 40N 120 20 E
Bampūr, *Iran* **97 E9** 27 15N 60 21 E
Bamu →, *Papua N. G.* **132 E2** 8 1 S 143 33 E
Ban, *Burkina Faso* **112 C4** 14 5N 2 27W
Ban Ao Tu Khun, *Thailand* **87 a** 8 9N 98 20 E
Ban Ban, *Laos* **86 C4** 19 31N 103 30 E
Ban Bang Hin, *Thailand* **87 H2** 9 32N 98 35 E
Ban Bang Khu, *Thailand* **87 a** 7 57N 98 23 E
Ban Bang Rong, *Thailand* **87 a** 8 3N 98 25 E
Ban Bo Phut, *Thailand* **87 b** 9 33N 100 2 E
Ban Chaweng, *Thailand* **87 b** 9 32N 100 3 E
Ban Chiang Klang, *Thailand* **86 C3** 19 25N 100 55 E
Ban Chik, *Laos* **86 D4** 17 15N 102 22 E
Ban Choho, *Thailand* **86 E4** 15 2N 102 9 E
Ban Dan Lan Hoi, *Thailand* **86 D2** 17 0N 99 35 E
Ban Don = Surat Thani, *Thailand* **87 H2** 9 6N 99 20 E
Ban Don, *Vietnam* **86 F6** 12 53N 107 48 E
Ban Don, Ao →, *Thailand* **87 H2** 9 20N 99 25 E
Ban Dong, *Thailand* **86 C3** 19 30N 100 59 E
Ban Hong, *Thailand* **86 C2** 18 18N 98 50 E
Ban Hua Thanon, *Thailand* **87 b** 9 26N 100 1 E
Ban Kaeng, *Thailand* **86 D3** 17 29N 100 7 E
Ban Kantang, *Thailand* **87 J2** 7 25N 99 31 E
Ban Karon, *Thailand* **87 a** 7 51N 98 18 E
Ban Kata, *Thailand* **87 a** 7 50N 98 18 E
Ban Keun, *Laos* **86 C4** 18 22N 102 35 E
Ban Khai, *Thailand* **86 F3** 12 46N 101 18 E
Ban Kheun, *Laos* **86 B3** 20 13N 101 7 E
Ban Khlong Khian, *Thailand* **87 a** 8 10N 98 26 E
Ban Khlong Kua, *Thailand* **87 J3** 6 57N 100 8 E
Ban Khuan, *Thailand* **87 a** 8 20N 98 25 E
Ban Khuan Mao, *Thailand* **87 J2** 7 50N 99 37 E
Ban Ko Yai Chim, *Thailand* **87 G2** 11 17N 99 26 E
Ban Kok, *Thailand* **86 D4** 16 40N 103 40 E
Ban Laem, *Thailand* **86 F2** 13 13N 99 59 E
Ban Lamai, *Thailand* **87 b** 9 28N 100 3 E
Ban Lao Ngam, *Laos* **86 E6** 15 28N 106 10 E
Ban Le Kathe, *Thailand* **86 E2** 15 49N 98 53 E
Ban Lo Po Noi, *Thailand* **87 a** 8 1N 98 34 E
Ban Mae Chedi, *Thailand* **86 C2** 19 11N 99 31 E
Ban Mae Laeng, *Thailand* **86 B2** 20 1N 99 17 E
Ban Mae Nam, *Thailand* **87 b** 9 34N 100 0 E
Ban Mae Sariang, *Thailand* **86 C1** 18 10N 97 56 E
Ban Mê Thuôt = Buon Ma Thuot,
Vietnam **86 F7** 12 40N 108 3 E
Ban Mi, *Thailand* **86 E3** 15 3N 100 32 E
Ban Muong Mo, *Laos* **86 C4** 19 4N 103 58 E
Ban Na Bo, *Thailand* **87 b** 9 19N 99 41 E
Ban Na Mo, *Laos* **86 D5** 17 7N 105 40 E
Ban Na San, *Thailand* **87 H2** 8 53N 99 52 E
Ban Na Tong, *Laos* **86 B3** 20 56N 101 47 E
Ban Nam Bac, *Laos* **86 B4** 20 38N 102 20 E
Ban Nam Ma, *Laos* **86 A3** 22 2N 101 37 E
Ban Ngang, *Laos* **86 E6** 15 59N 106 11 E
Ban Nong Bok, *Laos* **86 D5** 17 5N 104 48 E
Ban Nong Boua, *Laos* **86 E6** 15 40N 106 33 E
Ban Nong Pling, *Thailand* **86 E3** 15 40N 100 10 E
Ban Pak Chan, *Thailand* **87 G2** 10 32N 98 51 E
Ban Patong, *Thailand* **87 a** 7 54N 98 18 E
Ban Phai, *Thailand* **86 D4** 16 4N 102 44 E
Ban Phak Chit, *Thailand* **87 a** 8 0N 98 24 E
Ban Pong, *Thailand* **86 F2** 13 50N 99 55 E
Ban Rawai, *Thailand* **87 a** 7 47N 98 20 E
Ban Ron Phibun, *Thailand* **87 H2** 8 9N 99 51 E
Ban Sakhu, *Thailand* **87 a** 8 4N 98 18 E
Ban Sanam Chai, *Thailand* **87 J3** 7 33N 100 25 E
Ban Sangkha, *Thailand* **86 E4** 14 37N 103 52 E
Ban Tak, *Thailand* **86 D2** 17 2N 99 4 E
Ban Tako, *Thailand* **86 E4** 14 5N 102 40 E
Ban Tha Dua, *Thailand* **86 D2** 17 59N 98 39 E
Ban Tha Li, *Thailand* **86 D3** 17 37N 101 25 E
Ban Tha Nun, *Thailand* **87 a** 8 12N 98 18 E
Ban Tha Rua, *Thailand* **87 a** 7 59N 98 22 E
Ban Tha Yu, *Thailand* **87 a** 8 17N 98 22 E
Ban Thahine, *Laos* **86 E5** 14 12N 105 33 E
Ban Thong Krut, *Thailand* **87 b** 9 25N 99 57 E
Ban Xien Kok, *Laos* **86 B3** 20 54N 100 39 E
Ban Yen Nhan, *Vietnam* **86 B6** 20 57N 106 2 E
Banā, W. →, *Yemen* **98 D4** 13 3N 45 24 E
Banaba, *Kiribati* **134 H8** 0 45 S 169 50 E
Banalia, *Dem. Rep. of the Congo* **118 B2** 1 32N 25 5 E
Banam, *Cambodia* **87 G5** 11 20N 105 17 E
Banamba, *Mali* **112 C3** 13 29N 7 22W
Banana Is., *S. Leone* **112 D2** 8 7N 13 15W
Bananal, I. do, *Brazil* **171 D1** 11 30 S 50 30W
Bananga, *India* **95 L11** 6 57N 93 54 E
Banaras = Varanasi, *India* **93 G10** 25 22N 83 0 E
Banas →, *Gujarat, India* **92 H4** 23 45N 71 25 E
Banas →, *Mad. P., India* **93 G9** 24 15N 81 30 E
Bânâs, Ras, *Egypt* **106 C4** 23 57N 35 59 E
Banaue, *Phil.* **80 C3** 16 55N 121 4 E
Banaz, *Turkey* **49 C11** 38 46N 29 46 E
Banaz →, *Turkey* **49 C11** 38 12N 29 14 E
Banbridge, *U.K.* **23 B5** 54 22N 6 16W
Banbury, *U.K.* **21 E6** 52 4N 1 20W
Banc d'Arguin, Parc Nat. du,
Mauritania **110 D1** 20 10N 16 20W
Banchory, *U.K.* **22 D6** 57 3N 2 29W
Banco, *Ethiopia* **107 F4** 6 12N 38 13 E
Bancroft, *Canada* **140 C4** 45 3N 77 51W
Band, *Romania* **53 D9** 46 30N 24 25 E
Band Bonī, *Iran* **97 E8** 25 30N 59 33 E
Band-e Torkestan, *Afghan.* **91 B2** 35 30N 64 0 E
Band Qīr, *Iran* **97 D6** 31 39N 48 53 E
Banda, *Cameroon* **114 B2** 3 58N 14 32 E
Banda, *Mad. P., India* **93 G8** 24 3N 78 57 E
Banda, *Maharashtra, India* **95 G1** 15 49N 73 52 E
Banda, *Ut. P., India* **93 G9** 25 30N 80 26 E
Banda, Kepulauan, *Indonesia* **83 B3** 4 37 S 129 50 E
Banda Aceh, *Indonesia* **84 A1** 5 35N 95 20 E
Banda Banda, Mt., *Australia* **129 A10** 31 10 S 152 28 E
Banda Elat, *Indonesia* **83 C4** 5 40 S 133 5 E
Banda Is. = Banda, Kepulauan,
Indonesia **83 B3** 4 37 S 129 50 E
Banda Kani, *Dem. Rep. of*
the Congo **115 C2** 4 48 S 13 52 E
Banda Sea, *Indonesia* **82 C3** 6 0 S 130 0 E
Bandai-San, *Japan* **70 F10** 37 36N 140 4 E
Bandak, *Norway* **18 E5** 59 23N 8 29 E
Bandama →, *Ivory C.* **112 D3** 6 32N 4 30W
Bandama Blanc →, *Ivory C.* **112 D3** 6 55N 5 30W
Bandama Rouge →, *Ivory C.* **112 D4** 6 55N 5 30W
Bandān, *Iran* **97 D9** 31 23N 60 44 E
Bandanaira, *Indonesia* **83 B3** 4 32 S 129 54 E
Bandanwara, *India* **92 F6** 26 9N 74 38 E
Bandar = Machilipatnam, *India* **95 F5** 16 12N 81 8 E
Bandār 'Abbās, *Iran* **97 E8** 27 15N 56 15 E
Bandar-e Anzalī, *Iran* **97 B6** 37 30N 49 30 E
Bandar-e Bushehr = Būshehr, *Iran* **97 D6** 28 55N 50 55 E
Bandar-e Chārak, *Iran* **97 E7** 26 45N 54 20 E
Bandar-e Deylam, *Iran* **97 D6** 30 5N 50 10 E
Bandar-e Khomeynı, *Iran* **97 D6** 30 30N 49 5 E
Bandar-e Lengeh, *Iran* **97 E7** 26 35N 54 58 E
Bandar-e Maqām, *Iran* **97 E7** 26 56N 53 29 E
Bandar-e Ma'shur, *Iran* **97 D6** 30 35N 49 10 E
Bandar-e Rīg, *Iran* **97 D6** 29 29N 50 38 E
Bandar-e Torkeman, *Iran* **97 B7** 37 0N 54 10 E
Bandar Maharani = Muar,
Malaysia **87 L4** 2 3N 102 34 E
Bandar Penggaram = Batu Pahat,
Malaysia **87 M4** 1 50N 102 56 E
Bandar Seri Begawan, *Brunei* **85 B4** 4 52N 115 0 E
Bandar Sri Aman, *Malaysia* **85 B4** 1 15N 111 32 E
Bandawe, *Malawi* **119 E3** 11 58 S 34 5 E
Bande, *Spain* **42 C3** 42 3N 7 58W
Bandeira, Pico da, *Brazil* **171 F3** 20 26 S 41 47W
Bandeirante, *Brazil* **171 D1** 13 41 S 50 48W
Bandera, *Argentina* **174 B3** 28 55 S 62 20W
Banderas, B. de, *Mexico* **162 C3** 20 40N 105 30W
Bandhogarh, *India* **93 H9** 23 40N 81 2 E
Bandi →, *India* **92 F6** 26 12N 75 47 E
Bandia →, *India* **94 E5** 19 2N 80 28 E
Bandiagara, *Mali* **112 C4** 14 12N 3 29W
Bandikui, *India* **92 F7** 27 3N 76 34 E
Bandırma, *Turkey* **51 F11** 40 20N 28 0 E
Bandol, *France* **29 E9** 43 8N 5 46 E
Bandon, *Ireland* **23 E3** 51 44N 8 44W
Bandon →, *Ireland* **23 E3** 51 43N 8 37W
Bandoua, *C.A.R.* **114 B4** 4 39N 21 42 E
Bandula, *Mozam.* **119 F3** 19 0 S 33 7 E
Bandundu, *Dem. Rep. of*
the Congo **114 C3** 3 15 S 17 22 E
Bandundu □, *Dem. Rep. of*
the Congo **114 C3** 3 30 S 17 30 E
Bandung, *Indonesia* **85 D3** 6 54 S 107 36 E
Bané, *Burkina Faso* **113 C4** 11 42N 0 15W
Băneasa, *Romania* **53 E12** 45 56N 27 55 E
Bāneh, *Iran* **101 E11** 35 59N 45 53 E
Bañeres, *Spain* **41 G4** 38 44N 0 38W
Banes, *Cuba* **165 B4** 21 0N 75 42W
Banff, *Canada* **142 C5** 51 10N 115 34W
Banff, *U.K.* **22 D6** 57 40N 2 33W
Banff Nat. Park, *Canada* **142 C5** 51 30N 116 15W
Banfora, *Burkina Faso* **112 C4** 10 40N 4 40W
Bang Fai →, *Laos* **86 D5** 16 57N 104 45 E
Bang Hieng →, *Laos* **86 D5** 16 10N 105 10 E
Bang Krathum, *Thailand* **86 D3** 16 34N 100 18 E
Bang Lamung, *Thailand* **86 F3** 13 3N 100 56 E
Bang Mun Nak, *Thailand* **86 D3** 16 2N 100 23 E
Bang Pa In, *Thailand* **86 E3** 14 14N 100 35 E
Bang Rakam, *Thailand* **86 D3** 16 45N 100 7 E
Bang Saphan, *Thailand* **87 G2** 11 14N 99 28 E
Bang Thao, *Thailand* **87 a** 7 59N 98 18 E
Banga, *Angola* **115 D3** 8 43 S 15 13 E
Banga, *Dem. Rep. of the Congo* **115 D4** 5 25 S 20 28 E
Banga, *Aklan, Phil.* **81 F4** 11 38N 122 20 E
Banga, *S. Cotabato, Phil.* **81 H5** 6 21N 124 47 E
Bangaduni I., *India* **90 E2** 21 34N 88 52 E
Bangala Dam, *Zimbabwe* **119 G3** 21 7 S 31 25 E
Bangalore, *India* **95 H3** 12 59N 77 40 E
Banganapalle, *India* **95 G4** 15 19N 78 14 E
Banganga →, *India* **92 F6** 27 6N 77 25 E
Bangangté, *Cameroon* **113 D7** 5 8N 10 32 E
Bangaon, *India* **93 H13** 23 0N 88 47 E
Bangar, *Phil.* **80 C3** 16 54N 120 25 E
Bangassou, *C.A.R.* **114 B4** 4 55N 23 7 E
Bangeta, Mt., *Papua N. G.* **132 D4** 6 21 S 147 3 E
Banggai, *Indonesia* **82 B2** 1 34 S 123 30 E
Banggai, Kepulauan, *Indonesia* **82 B2** 1 40 S 123 30 E
Banggai Arch. = Banggai,
Kepulauan, *Indonesia* **82 B2** 1 40 S 123 30 E
Banggi, *Malaysia* **85 A5** 7 17N 117 12 E
Banghāzī, *Libya* **108 B4** 32 11N 20 3 E
Banghāzī □, *Libya* **108 B4** 32 7N 20 4 E
Bangil, *Indonesia* **85 D4** 7 36 S 112 50 E
Bangjang, *Sudan* **107 E3** 11 23N 32 41 E
Bangka, *Sulawesi, Indonesia* **82 A3** 1 50N 125 5 E
Bangka, *Sumatera, Indonesia* **84 C3** 2 0 S 105 50 E
Bangka, Selat, *Indonesia* **84 C3** 2 30 S 105 30 E
Bangkalan, *Indonesia* **85 D4** 7 2 S 112 46 E
Bangkinang, *Indonesia* **84 B2** 0 18N 101 5 E
Bangko, *Indonesia* **84 C2** 2 5 S 102 9 E
Bangkok, *Thailand* **86 F3** 13 45N 100 35 E
Bangladesh ■, *Asia* **90 C3** 24 0N 90 0 E
Bangli, *Indonesia* **79 J18** 8 27 S 115 21 E
Bangolo, *Ivory C.* **112 D3** 7 1N 7 29W
Bangong Co, *India* **93 B8** 35 50N 79 20 E
Bangor, *Down, U.K.* **23 B6** 54 40N 5 40W
Bangor, *Gwynedd, U.K.* **20 D3** 53 14N 4 8W
Bangor, *Maine, U.S.A.* **139 D13** 44 48N 68 46W
Bangor, *Mich., U.S.A.* **157 B10** 42 18N 86 7W
Bangor, *Pa., U.S.A.* **151 F9** 40 52N 75 13W
Bangoran →, *C.A.R.* **114 A3** 8 42N 19 6 E
Bangu, *Dem. Rep. of the Congo* **114 C3** 0 3 S 19 12 E
Bangued, *Phil.* **80 C3** 17 40N 120 37 E
Bangui, *C.A.R.* **114 B3** 4 23N 18 35 E
Bangui, *Phil.* **80 B3** 18 32N 120 46 E
Banguru, *Dem. Rep. of the Congo* **118 B2** 0 30N 27 10 E
Bangweulu, L., *Zambia* **119 E3** 11 0 S 30 0 E
Bangweulu Swamp, *Zambia* **119 E3** 11 20 S 30 15 E
Banhine, Parque Nacional de,
Mozam. **117 C5** 22 49 S 32 55 E
Bani, *Dom. Rep.* **165 C5** 18 16N 70 22W
Bani, *Phil.* **80 C2** 16 11N 119 52 E
Bani →, *Mali* **112 C4** 14 30N 4 12W
Bani, Jebel, *Morocco* **110 C3** 29 16N 8 0W
Bani Bangou, *Niger* **113 B5** 15 3N 2 42 E
Banī Sa'd, *Iraq* **101 F11** 33 34N 44 32 E
Bania, *C.A.R.* **114 B3** 4 1N 16 7 E
Bania, *Ivory C.* **112 D4** 9 4N 3 6W
Baniara, *Papua N. G.* **132 E5** 9 44 S 149 54 E
Banihal Pass, *India* **93 C6** 33 30N 75 12 E
Banikoara, *Benin* **113 C5** 11 18N 2 26 E
Banīnah, *Libya* **108 B4** 32 0N 20 12 E
Bāniyās, *Syria* **100 E6** 35 10N 36 0 E
Banja Luka, *Bos.-H.* **52 F2** 44 49N 17 11 E
Banjar, *India* **92 D7** 31 38N 77 21 E
Banjar, *Indonesia* **85 D3** 7 24 S 108 30 E
Banjar →, *India* **93 H9** 22 36N 80 22 E
Banjarmasin, *Indonesia* **85 C4** 3 20 S 114 35 E
Banjarnegara, *Indonesia* **85 D3** 7 24 S 109 42 E
Banjul, *Gambia* **112 C1** 13 28N 16 40W
Banka, *India* **93 G12** 24 53N 86 55 E
Bankas, *Mali* **112 C4** 14 4N 3 31W
Bankeryd, *Sweden* **17 G8** 57 53N 14 6 E
Banket, *Zimbabwe* **119 F3** 17 27 S 30 19 E
Bankilaré, *Niger* **113 C5** 14 35N 0 44 E
Bankot, *India* **94 F1** 17 58N 73 2 E
Banks, *U.S.A.* **152 D4** 31 49N 85 51W
Banks I. = Moa, I., *Papua N. G.* **132 F2** 10 10 S 142 15 E
Banks I., *B.C., Canada* **142 C3** 53 20N 130 0W
Banks I., *N.W.T., Canada* **138 A7** 73 15N 121 30W
Banks Is., *Vanuatu* **133 C5** 13 50 S 167 30 E
Banks L., *U.S.A.* **152 D6** 31 2N 83 6W
Banks Pen., *N.Z.* **131 D8** 43 45 S 173 15 E
Banks Str., *Australia* **127 G4** 40 40 S 148 10 E
Bankumuna, *Dem. Rep. of*
the Congo **115 C3** 4 28 S 19 57 E
Bankura, *India* **93 H12** 23 11N 87 18 E
Bankya, *Bulgaria* **50 D7** 42 43N 23 8 E
Banmankhi, *India* **93 G12** 25 53N 87 11 E
Banmauk, *Burma* **90 C5** 24 24N 95 51 E
Bann →, *Arm., U.K.* **23 B5** 54 30N 6 31W
Bann →, *L'derry., U.K.* **23 A5** 55 8N 6 41W
Bannaanka Saraar, *Somali Rep.* **120 C3** 9 25N 46 17 E
Bannalec, *France* **26 E3** 47 57N 3 42W
Bannang Sata, *Thailand* **87 J3** 6 16N 101 16 E
Bannerton, *Australia* **128 C5** 34 42 S 142 47 E
Banning, *U.S.A.* **161 M10** 33 56N 116 53W
Banningville = Bandundu,
Dem. Rep. of the Congo **114 C3** 3 15 S 17 22 E
Banno, *Ethiopia* **107 G4** 4 51N 37 24 E
Bannockburn, *Canada* **150 B7** 44 39N 77 33W
Bannockburn, *U.K.* **22 E5** 56 5N 3 55W
Bannockburn, *Zimbabwe* **119 G2** 20 17 S 29 48 E
Bannu, *Pakistan* **91 B3** 33 0N 70 18 E
Bano, *India* **93 H11** 22 40N 84 55 E
Bañolas = Banyoles, *Spain* **40 C7** 42 16N 2 44 E
Banon, *France* **29 D9** 44 2N 5 38 E
Baños de la Encina, *Spain* **43 G7** 38 10N 3 46W
Baños de Molgas, *Spain* **42 C3** 42 15N 7 40W
Bánovce nad Bebravou,
Slovak Rep. **35 C11** 48 44N 18 16 E
Banovići, *Bos.-H.* **52 F3** 44 25N 18 32 E
Bansalan, *Phil.* **81 H5** 6 55N 125 13 E
Bansgaon, *India* **93 F10** 26 33N 83 21 E
Banská Bystrica, *Slovak Rep.* **35 C12** 48 46N 19 14 E
Banská Štiavnica, *Slovak Rep.* **35 C11** 48 25N 18 55 E
Bansko, *Bulgaria* **50 E7** 41 52N 23 28 E
Banskobystrický □, *Slovak Rep.* **35 C12** 48 20N 19 0 E
Banswara, *India* **92 H6** 23 32N 74 24 E
Bantaeng, *Indonesia* **82 C1** 5 32 S 119 56 E
Bantaji, *Nigeria* **113 D7** 8 6N 10 5 E
Bantayan, *Phil.* **81 F4** 11 10N 123 43 E
Bantayan I., *Phil.* **81 F4** 11 13N 123 44 E
Banten, *Indonesia* **84 D3** 6 5 S 106 8 E
Banton I., *Phil.* **80 E4** 12 56N 122 4 E
Bantry, *Ireland* **23 E2** 51 41N 9 27W
Bantry B., *Ireland* **23 E2** 51 37N 9 44W
Bantul, *Indonesia* **85 D4** 7 55 S 110 19 E
Bantva, *India* **92 J4** 21 29N 70 12 E
Bantval, *India* **95 H2** 12 55N 75 0 E
Banya, *Bulgaria* **51 D8** 42 33N 24 50 E
Banyak, Kepulauan, *Indonesia* **84 B1** 2 10N 97 10 E
Banyalbufar, *Spain* **38 B3** 39 42N 2 31 E
Banyo, *Cameroon* **113 D7** 6 52N 11 45 E
Banyoles, *Spain* **40 C7** 42 16N 2 44 E
Banyuls-sur-Mer, *France* **28 F7** 42 28N 3 8 E
Banyumas, *Indonesia* **85 D3** 7 32 S 109 18 E
Banyuwangi, *Indonesia* **85 D4** 8 13 S 114 21 E
Banz, *Papua N. G.* **132 C3** 5 47 S 144 37 E
Banza, *Dem. Rep. of the Congo* **114 B4** 0 28N 20 10 E
Banzare Coast, *Antarctica* **7 C9** 68 0 S 125 0 E
Bao Ha, *Vietnam* **76 F5** 22 11N 104 21 E
Bao Lac, *Vietnam* **86 A5** 22 57N 105 40 E
Bao Loc, *Vietnam* **87 G6** 11 32N 107 48 E
Bao'an = Shenzhen, *China* **77 F10** 22 32N 114 5 E
Baocheng, *China* **74 H4** 33 12N 106 56 E
Baode, *China* **74 E6** 39 1N 111 5 E
Baodi, *China* **75 E9** 39 38N 117 20 E
Baoding, *China* **74 E8** 38 50N 115 28 E
Baoji, *China* **74 G4** 34 20N 107 5 E
Baojing, *China* **76 C7** 28 45N 109 41 E
Baokang, *China* **77 B8** 31 54N 111 12 E
Baoro, *C.A.R.* **114 A3** 5 40N 15 58 E
Baoshan, *Shanghai, China* **77 B13** 31 27N 121 26 E
Baoshan, *Yunnan, China* **76 E2** 25 10N 99 5 E
Baotou, *China* **74 D6** 40 32N 110 2 E
Baoxing, *China* **76 B4** 30 24N 102 50 E
Baoying, *China* **75 H10** 33 17N 119 20 E
Bap, *India* **92 F5** 27 23N 72 18 E
Bapatla, *India* **95 G5** 15 55N 80 30 E
Bapaume, *France* **27 B9** 50 7N 2 50 E
Baqanas, *Kazakstan* **65 A8** 44 50N 76 15 E
Baqbaqty, *Kazakstan* **65 A8** 44 35N 76 40 E
Bāqerābād, *Iran* **97 C6** 33 2N 51 58 E
Ba'qūbah, *Iraq* **101 F11** 33 45N 44 50 E
Baquedano, *Chile* **174 A2** 23 20 S 69 52W
Bar, *Montenegro, Yug.* **50 D3** 42 8N 19 6 E
Bar, *Ukraine* **59 H4** 49 4N 27 40 E
Bar Bigha, *India* **93 G11** 25 21N 85 47 E
Bar Harbor, *U.S.A.* **149 C11** 44 23N 68 13W
Bar-le-Duc, *France* **27 D12** 48 47N 5 10 E
Bar-sur-Aube, *France* **27 D11** 48 14N 4 40 E
Bar-sur-Seine, *France* **27 D11** 48 7N 4 20 E
Bara, *India* **93 G9** 25 16N 81 43 E
Bara, *Indonesia* **82 B3** 3 8 S 126 11 E
Bâra, *Romania* **53 C12** 47 2N 27 3 E
Bara Banki, *India* **93 F9** 26 55N 81 12 E
Barabai, *Indonesia* **85 C5** 2 32 S 115 34 E
Baraboo, *U.S.A.* **154 D10** 43 28N 89 45W
Baracoa, *Cuba* **165 B5** 20 20N 74 30W
Baradā →, *Syria* **103 B5** 33 33N 36 34 E
Baradero, *Argentina* **174 C4** 33 52 S 59 29W
Baradine, *Australia* **129 A8** 30 56 S 149 4 E
Baraga, *U.S.A.* **154 B10** 46 47N 88 30W
Bărăganul, *Romania* **53 F12** 44 49N 27 31 E
Barah →, *India* **92 F6** 27 42N 77 5 E
Barahona, *Dom. Rep.* **165 C5** 18 13N 71 7W
Barahona, *Spain* **40 D2** 41 17N 2 39W
Barail Range, *India* **90 C4** 25 15N 93 20 E

Baures, *Bolivia* **173 C5** 13 35 S 63 35W
Bauru, *Brazil* **175 A6** 22 10 S 49 0W
Baús, *Brazil* **173 D7** 18 22 S 52 47W
Bausi, *India* **93 G12** 24 48N 87 1 E
Bauska, *Latvia* **15 H21** 56 24N 24 15 E
Bautino, *Kazakstan* **61 H10** 44 35N 50 14 E
Bautzen, *Germany* **30 D10** 51 10N 14 26 E
Bauya, *S. Leone* **112 D2** 8 12N 12 38W
Baūyrzhan Momyshuly, *Kazakstan* **65 B5** 42 36N 70 47 E
Bavānāt, *Iran* **97 D7** 30 28N 53 27 E
Bavanište, *Serbia, Yug.* **52 F5** 44 49N 20 55 E
Bavaria = Bayern □, *Germany* **31 G7** 48 50N 12 0 E
Båven, *Sweden* **16 E10** 59 0N 16 56 E
Bavispe →, *Mexico* **162 B3** 29 30N 109 11W
Baw Baw Nat. Park, *Australia* **129 D7** 37 50 S 146 17 E
Bawdwin, *Burma* **90 D6** 23 5N 97 20 E
Bawe, *Indonesia* **83 B4** 2 59 S 134 43 E
Bawean, *Indonesia* **85 D4** 5 46 S 112 35 E
Bawku, *Ghana* **113 C4** 11 3N 0 19W
Bawlake, *Burma* **90 F6** 19 11N 97 21 E
Bawolung, *China* **76 C3** 28 50N 101 16 E
Baxley, *U.S.A.* **152 D7** 31 47N 82 21W
Baxoi, *China* **76 B1** 30 1N 96 50 E
Baxter, *Iowa, U.S.A.* **156 C3** 41 49N 93 9W
Baxter, *Minn., U.S.A.* **154 B7** 46 21N 94 17W
Baxter Springs, *U.S.A.* **155 G7** 37 2N 94 44W
Bay, L. de, *Phil.* **80 D3** 14 20N 121 11 E
Bay al Khā'ib, Wādī →, *Libya* **108 B3** 30 55N 15 29 E
Bay City, *Mich., U.S.A.* **148 D4** 43 36N 83 54W
Bay City, *Tex., U.S.A.* **155 L7** 28 59N 95 58W
Bay Minette, *U.S.A.* **149 K2** 30 53N 87 46W
Bay of Plenty □, *N.Z.* **130 D5** 38 0 S 177 0 E
Bay Roberts, *Canada* **141 C9** 47 36N 53 16W
Bay St. Louis, *U.S.A.* **155 K10** 30 19N 89 20W
Bay Springs, *U.S.A.* **155 K10** 31 59N 89 17W
Bay View, *N.Z.* **130 F5** 39 25 S 176 50 E
Baya, *Dem. Rep. of the Congo* **119 E2** 11 53 S 27 25 E
Bayambang, *Phil.* **80 D3** 15 49N 120 27 E
Bayamo, *Cuba* **164 B4** 20 20N 76 40W
Bayamón, *Puerto Rico* **165 d** 18 24N 66 10W
Bayan Har Shan, *China* **68 C4** 34 0N 98 0 E
Bayan Hot = Alxa Zuoqi, *China* **74 E3** 38 50N 105 40 E
Bayan Lepas, *Malaysia* **87 c** 5 17N 100 16 E
Bayan Obo, *China* **74 D5** 41 52N 109 59 E
Bayan-Ovoo = Erdenetsogt, *Mongolia* **74 C4** 42 55N 106 5 E
Bayana, *India* **92 F7** 26 55N 77 18 E
Bayanaūyl, *Kazakstan* **66 D8** 50 45N 75 45 E
Bayandalay, *Mongolia* **74 C2** 43 30N 103 29 E
Bayanhongor, *Mongolia* **68 B5** 46 8N 102 43 E
Bayard, *N. Mex., U.S.A.* **159 K9** 32 46N 108 8W
Bayard, *Nebr., U.S.A.* **154 E3** 41 45N 103 20W
Bayawan, *Phil.* **81 G4** 9 46N 122 45 E
Baybay, *Phil.* **81 F5** 10 40N 124 55 E
Bayburt, *Turkey* **101 B9** 40 15N 40 20 E
Baydhabo = Baidoa, *Somali Rep.* **120 D2** 3 8N 43 30 E
Bayelsa □, *Nigeria* **113 E6** 4 30N 6 0 E
Bayerische Alpen, *Germany* **31 H7** 47 35N 11 30 E
Bayerischer Wald, *Germany* **31 G8** 48 56N 12 50 E
Bayern □, *Germany* **31 G7** 48 50N 12 0 E
Bayeux, *France* **26 C6** 49 17N 0 42W
Bayfield, *Canada* **150 C3** 43 34N 81 42W
Bayfield, *U.S.A.* **154 B9** 46 49N 90 49W
Bäygequm, *Kazakstan* **65 A3** 44 19N 66 27 E
Bayḩān al Qisāb, *Yemen* **98 D4** 15 48N 45 44 E
Bayındır, *Turkey* **49 C9** 38 13N 27 39 E
Baykal, Oz., *Russia* **67 D11** 53 0N 108 0 E
Baykan, *Turkey* **96 B4** 38 7N 41 44 E
Baykonur = Bayqongyr, *Kazakstan* **66 E7** 47 48N 65 50 E
Baykurt, *China* **65 D7** 39 56N 75 33 E
Baymak, *Russia* **64 E7** 52 36N 58 19 E
Baymurat, *Uzbekistan* **65 C3** 41 8N 66 25 E
Baynes Mts., *Namibia* **116 B1** 17 15 S 13 0 E
Bayombong, *Phil.* **80 C3** 16 30N 121 10 E
Bayon, *France* **27 D13** 48 30N 6 20 E
Bayona = Baiona, *Spain* **42 C2** 42 6N 8 52W
Bayonne, *France* **28 E2** 43 30N 1 28W
Bayonne, *U.S.A.* **151 F10** 40 40N 74 7W
Bayovar, *Peru* **172 B1** 5 50 S 81 0W
Bayport, *U.S.A.* **153 G7** 28 32N 82 39W
Bayqongyr, *Kazakstan* **66 E7** 47 48N 65 50 E
Bayram-Ali = Bayramaly, *Turkmenistan* **66 F7** 37 37N 62 10 E
Bayramaly, *Turkmenistan* **66 F7** 37 37N 62 10 E
Bayramiç, *Turkey* **49 B8** 39 48N 26 36 E
Bayreuth, *Germany* **31 F7** 49 56N 11 35 E
Bayrischzell, *Germany* **31 H8** 47 41N 12 0 E
Bayrūt, *Lebanon* **103 B4** 33 53N 35 31 E
Bays, L. of, *Canada* **150 A5** 45 15N 79 4W
Bayshore, *U.S.A.* **153 J8** 26 43N 81 50W
Baysun, *Uzbekistan* **65 D3** 38 12N 67 12 E
Baysville, *Canada* **150 A5** 45 9N 79 7W
Bayt al Faqīh, *Yemen* **98 D3** 14 31N 43 19 E
Bayt Lahm, *West Bank* **103 D4** 31 43N 35 12 E
Baytown, *U.S.A.* **155 L7** 29 43N 94 59W
Bayugan, *Phil.* **81 G5** 8 43N 125 42 E
Bayun, *Indonesia* **79 J18** 8 11 S 115 16 E
Bayyrqum, *Kazakstan* **65 B4** 42 7N 68 3 E
Bayzhansay, *Kazakstan* **65 B4** 43 14N 69 54 E
Bayzo, *Niger* **113 C5** 13 52N 4 35 E
Baza, *Spain* **43 H8** 37 30N 2 47W
Bazar Dyuzi, *Russia* **61 K8** 41 12N 47 50 E
Bazar-Korgon, *Kyrgyzstan* **65 C6** 41 0N 72 43 E
Bazardüzü = Bazar Dyuzi, *Russia* **61 K8** 41 12N 47 50 E
Bazarny Karabulak, *Russia* **60 D8** 52 20N 46 29 E
Bazarnyy Syzgan, *Russia* **60 D8** 53 45N 46 40 E
Bazaruto, I. do, *Mozam.* **117 C6** 21 40 S 35 28 E
Bazaruto, Parque Nacional de, *Mozam.* **117 C6** 21 42 S 35 26 E
Bazas, *France* **28 D3** 44 27N 0 13W
Bazhong, *China* **76 B6** 31 52N 106 46 E
Bazhou, *China* **74 E9** 39 8N 116 22 E
Bazmān, Kūh-e, *Iran* **97 D9** 28 4N 60 1 E
Beach, *U.S.A.* **154 B3** 46 58N 104 0W
Beach City, *U.S.A.* **150 F3** 40 39N 81 35W
Beachport, *Australia* **128 D4** 37 29 S 140 0 E
Beachy Hd., *U.K.* **21 G8** 50 44N 0 15 E
Beacon, *Australia* **125 F2** 30 26 S 117 52 E
Beacon, *U.S.A.* **151 E11** 41 30N 73 58W
Beaconsfield, *Australia* **127 G4** 41 11 S 146 48 E
Beagle, Canal, *S. Amer.* **176 E3** 55 0 S 68 30W
Beagle Bay, *Australia* **124 C3** 16 58 S 122 40 E
Bealanana, *Madag.* **117 A8** 14 33 S 48 44 E
Beals Cr. →, *U.S.A.* **155 J4** 32 10N 100 51W
Beamsville, *Canada* **150 C5** 43 12N 79 28W
Bear →, *Calif., U.S.A.* **160 G5** 38 56N 121 36W
Bear →, *Utah, U.S.A.* **146 B4** 41 30N 112 8W
Béar, C., *France* **28 F7** 42 31N 3 8 E
Bear I., *Ireland* **23 E2** 51 38N 9 50W
Bear L., *Canada* **143 B9** 55 8N 96 0W
Bear L., *U.S.A.* **158 F8** 41 59N 111 21W
Beardmore, *Canada* **140 C2** 49 36N 87 57W
Beardmore Glacier, *Antarctica* **7 E11** 84 30 S 170 0 E
Beardstown, *U.S.A.* **156 E6** 40 1N 90 26W
Bearma →, *India* **93 G8** 24 20N 79 51 E
Béarn, *France* **28 E3** 43 20N 0 30W
Bearpaw Mts., *U.S.A.* **158 B9** 48 12N 109 30W
Bearskin Lake, *Canada* **140 B1** 53 58N 91 2W
Beas →, *India* **92 D6** 31 10N 74 59 E
Beas de Segura, *Spain* **43 G8** 38 15N 2 53W
Beasain, *Spain* **40 B2** 43 3N 2 11W
Beata, C., *Dom. Rep.* **165 C5** 17 40N 71 30W
Beata, I., *Dom. Rep.* **165 C5** 17 34N 71 31W
Beatrice, *U.S.A.* **154 E6** 40 16N 96 45W
Beatrice, *Zimbabwe* **119 F3** 18 15 S 30 55 E
Beatrice, C., *Australia* **126 A2** 14 20 S 136 55 E
Beatton →, *Canada* **142 B4** 56 15N 120 45W
Beatton River, *Canada* **142 B4** 57 26N 121 20W
Beatty, *U.S.A.* **160 J10** 36 54N 116 46W
Beau Bassin, *Mauritius* **121 d** 20 13 S 57 27 E
Beaucaire, *France* **29 E8** 43 48N 4 39 E
Beauce, Plaine de la, *France* **27 D8** 48 10N 1 45 E
Beauceville, *Canada* **141 C5** 46 13N 70 46W
Beauchêne, I., *Falk. Is.* **9 f** 52 55 S 59 15W
Beaudesert, *Australia* **127 D5** 27 59 S 153 0 E
Beaufort, *Australia* **128 D5** 37 25 S 143 25 E
Beaufort, *France* **29 C10** 45 44N 6 34 E
Beaufort, *Malaysia* **85 A5** 5 30N 115 40 E
Beaufort, *N.C., U.S.A.* **149 H7** 34 43N 76 40W
Beaufort, *S.C., U.S.A.* **152 C9** 32 26N 80 40W
Beaufort Sea, *Arctic* **6 B1** 72 0N 140 0W
Beaufort West, *S. Africa* **116 E3** 32 18 S 22 36 E
Beaugency, *France* **27 E8** 47 47N 1 38 E
Beauharnois, *Canada* **151 A11** 45 20N 73 52W
Beaujeu, *France* **27 F11** 46 10N 4 35 E
Beaujolais, *France* **27 F11** 46 0N 4 22 E
Beaulieu →, *Canada* **142 A6** 62 3N 113 11W
Beaulieu-sur-Dordogne, *France* **28 D5** 44 58N 1 50 E
Beaulieu-sur-Mer, *France* **29 E11** 43 42N 7 20 E
Beauly, *U.K.* **22 D4** 57 30N 4 28W
Beauly →, *U.K.* **22 D4** 57 29N 4 27W
Beaumaris, *U.K.* **20 D3** 53 16N 4 6W
Beaumont, *Belgium* **24 D4** 50 15N 4 14 E
Beaumont, *France* **28 D4** 44 45N 0 46 E
Beaumont, *N.Z.* **131 F4** 45 50 S 169 33 E
Beaumont, *U.S.A.* **155 K7** 30 5N 94 6W
Beaumont-de-Lomagne, *France* **28 E5** 43 53N 1 0 E
Beaumont-le-Roger, *France* **26 C7** 49 4N 0 47 E
Beaumont-sur-Sarthe, *France* **26 D7** 48 13N 0 8 E
Beaune, *France* **27 E11** 47 2N 4 50 E
Beaune-la-Rolande, *France* **27 D9** 48 4N 2 25 E
Beaupré, *Canada* **141 C5** 47 3N 70 54W
Beaupréau, *France* **26 E6** 47 12N 1 0W
Beauraing, *Belgium* **24 D4** 50 7N 4 57 E
Beaurepaire, *France* **29 C9** 45 22N 5 1 E
Beauséjour, *Canada* **143 C9** 50 5N 96 35W
Beautemps-Beaupré, Î., *N. Cal.* **133 K4** 20 24 S 166 9 E
Beauvais, *France* **27 C9** 49 25N 2 8 E
Beauval, *Canada* **143 B7** 55 9N 107 37W
Beauvoir-sur-Mer, *France* **26 F4** 46 55N 2 2W
Beauvoir-sur-Niort, *France* **28 B3** 46 12N 0 30W
Beaver, *Alaska, U.S.A.* **144 C11** 66 22N 147 24W
Beaver, *Okla., U.S.A.* **155 G4** 36 49N 100 31W
Beaver, *Pa., U.S.A.* **150 F4** 40 42N 80 19W
Beaver, *Utah, U.S.A.* **159 G7** 38 17N 112 38W
Beaver →, *B.C., Canada* **142 B4** 59 52N 124 20W
Beaver →, *Ont., Canada* **140 A2** 55 55N 87 48W
Beaver →, *Sask., Canada* **143 B7** 55 26N 107 45W
Beaver →, *U.S.A.* **155 G5** 36 35N 99 30W
Beaver City, *U.S.A.* **154 E5** 40 8N 99 50W
Beaver Creek, *Canada* **138 B5** 63 0N 141 0W
Beaver Dam, *U.S.A.* **154 D10** 43 28N 88 50W
Beaver Falls, *U.S.A.* **150 F4** 40 46N 80 20W
Beaver Hill L., *Canada* **143 C10** 54 5N 94 50W
Beaver I., *U.S.A.* **148 C3** 45 40N 85 33W
Beavercreek, *U.S.A.* **157 E12** 39 43N 84 11W
Beaverhill L., *Canada* **142 C6** 53 27N 112 32W
Beaverlodge, *Canada* **142 B5** 55 11N 119 29W
Beaverstone →, *Canada* **140 B2** 54 59N 89 25W
Beaverton, *Canada* **150 B5** 44 26N 79 9W
Beaverton, *U.S.A.* **160 E4** 45 29N 122 48W
Beawar, *India* **92 F6** 26 3N 74 18 E
Bebedouro, *Brazil* **175 A6** 21 0 S 48 25W
Bebera, Tanjung, *Indonesia* **79 K18** 8 44 S 115 51 E
Beboa, *Madag.* **117 B7** 17 22 S 44 33 E
Beboto, *Chad* **109 G3** 8 16N 16 56 E
Bebra, *Germany* **30 E5** 50 58N 9 48 E
Beccles, *U.K.* **21 E9** 52 27N 1 35 E
Bečej, *Serbia, Yug.* **52 E5** 45 36N 20 3 E
Beceni, *Romania* **53 E11** 45 23N 26 48 E
Becerreá, *Spain* **42 C3** 42 51N 7 10W
Béchar, *Algeria* **111 B4** 31 38N 2 18W
Becharof L., *U.S.A.* **144 H8** 57 56N 156 23W
Bechyně, *Czech Rep.* **34 B7** 49 17N 14 29 E
Beckley, *U.S.A.* **148 G5** 37 47N 81 11W
Beckum, *Germany* **30 D4** 51 45N 8 3 E
Beclean, *Romania* **53 C9** 47 11N 24 11 E
Bečov nad Teplou, *Czech Rep.* **34 A5** 50 5N 12 49 E
Bečva →, *Czech Rep.* **35 B10** 49 31N 17 20 E
Bédar, *Spain* **41 H3** 37 11N 1 59W
Bédarieux, *France* **28 E7** 43 37N 3 10 E
Beddouza, Ras, *Morocco* **110 B3** 32 33N 9 9W
Bedele, *Ethiopia* **107 F4** 8 31N 36 23 E
Bederkesa, *Germany* **30 B4** 53 37N 8 50 E
Bederwanak, *Somali Rep.* **120 C2** 9 34N 44 23 E
Bedeso, *Ethiopia* **107 F5** 9 58N 40 52 E
Bedford, *Canada* **151 A12** 45 7N 72 59W
Bedford, *S. Africa* **116 E4** 32 40 S 26 10 E
Bedford, *U.K.* **21 E7** 52 8N 0 28W
Bedford, *Ind., U.S.A.* **157 F10** 38 52N 86 29W
Bedford, *Iowa, U.S.A.* **156 D2** 40 40N 94 44W
Bedford, *Ky., U.S.A.* **157 F11** 38 36N 85 19W
Bedford, *Ohio, U.S.A.* **150 E3** 41 23N 81 32W
Bedford, *Pa., U.S.A.* **150 F6** 40 1N 78 30W
Bedford, *Va., U.S.A.* **148 G6** 37 20N 79 31W
Bedford, C., *Australia* **126 B4** 15 14 S 145 21 E
Bedfordshire □, *U.K.* **21 E7** 52 4N 0 28W
Bedi, *Chad* **109 F3** 11 6N 18 33 E
Będków, *Poland* **55 G6** 51 36N 19 44 E
Bednja →, *Croatia* **45 B13** 46 20N 16 52 E
Bednodemyanovsk, *Russia* **60 D6** 53 55N 43 15 E
Bedok, *Singapore* **87 d** 1 19N 103 56 E
Bedónia, *Italy* **44 D6** 44 30N 9 38 E
Bedourie, *Australia* **126 C2** 24 30 S 139 30 E
Bedretto, *Switz.* **33 C7** 46 31N 8 31 E
Bedti →, *India* **95 G2** 14 50N 74 44 E
Bedum, *Neths.* **24 A6** 53 18N 6 36 E
Będzin, *Poland* **55 H6** 50 19N 19 7 E
Bee Ridge, *U.S.A.* **153 H7** 27 17N 82 29W
Beebe Plain, *Canada* **151 A12** 45 1N 72 9W
Beech Creek, *U.S.A.* **150 E7** 41 5N 77 36W
Beech Fork →, *U.S.A.* **157 G11** 37 46N 85 41W
Beech Grove, *U.S.A.* **157 E10** 39 44N 86 3W
Beecher, *U.S.A.* **157 C9** 41 21N 87 38W
Beechworth, *Australia* **129 D7** 36 22 S 146 43 E
Beef I., *Br. Virgin Is.* **165 e** 18 26N 64 30W
Beelitz, *Germany* **30 C8** 52 14N 12 58 E
Beenleigh, *Australia* **127 D5** 27 43 S 153 10 E
Be'er Menuḩa, *Israel* **96 D2** 30 19N 35 8 E
Be'er Sheva, *Israel* **103 D3** 31 15N 34 48 E
Beersheba = Be'er Sheva, *Israel* **103 D3** 31 15N 34 48 E
Beeskow, *Germany* **30 C10** 52 10N 14 15 E
Beestekraal, *S. Africa* **117 D4** 25 23 S 27 38 E
Beeston, *U.K.* **20 E6** 52 56N 1 14W
Beetzendorf, *Germany* **30 C7** 52 42N 11 6 E
Beeville, *U.S.A.* **155 L6** 28 24N 97 45W
Befale, *Dem. Rep. of the Congo* **114 B4** 0 25N 20 45 E
Befandriana, *Mahajanga, Madag.* **117 B8** 15 16 S 48 32 E
Befandriana, *Toliara, Madag.* **117 C7** 21 55 S 44 0 E
Befasy, *Madag.* **117 C7** 20 33 S 44 23 E
Befori, *Dem. Rep. of the Congo* **114 B4** 0 8N 22 22 E
Befotaka, *Antsiranana, Madag.* **117 A8** 13 15 S 48 16 E
Befotaka, *Fianarantsoa, Madag.* **117 C8** 23 49 S 47 0 E
Bega, *Australia* **129 D8** 36 41 S 149 51 E
Bega, Canalul, *Romania* **52 E5** 45 37N 20 46 E
Bégard, *France* **26 D3** 48 38N 3 18W
Beğendik, *Turkey* **51 F10** 40 55N 26 34 E
Begndal, *Norway* **18 D6** 60 49N 9 46 E
Begoro, *Ghana* **113 D4** 6 23N 0 23W
Begusarai, *India* **93 G12** 25 24N 86 9 E
Behābād, *Iran* **97 C8** 32 24N 59 47 E
Behala, *India* **93 H13** 22 30N 88 20 E
Behara, *Madag.* **117 C8** 24 55 S 46 20 E
Behbehān, *Iran* **97 D6** 30 30N 50 15 E
Behm Canal, *U.S.A.* **142 B2** 55 10N 131 0W
Behshahr, *Iran* **97 B7** 36 45N 53 35 E
Bei Jiang →, *China* **77 F9** 23 2N 112 58 E
Bei'an, *China* **69 B7** 48 10N 126 20 E
Beibei, *China* **76 C6** 29 47N 106 22 E
Beichuan, *China* **76 B5** 31 55N 104 39 E
Beihai, *China* **76 G7** 21 28N 109 6 E
Beijing, *China* **74 E9** 39 55N 116 20 E
Beijing □, *China* **74 E9** 39 55N 116 20 E
Beilen, *Neths.* **24 B6** 52 52N 6 27 E
Beiliu, *China* **77 F8** 22 41N 110 21 E
Beilngries, *Germany* **31 F7** 49 2N 11 28 E
Beilpajah, *Australia* **128 B5** 32 54 S 143 52 E
Beilul, *Eritrea* **107 E5** 13 2N 42 20 E
Béinamar, *Chad* **109 G3** 8 40N 15 23 E
Beinn na Faoghla = Benbecula, *U.K.* **22 D1** 57 26N 7 21W
Beipan Jiang, *China* **76 E5** 25 7N 106 1 E
Beipiao, *China* **75 D11** 41 52N 120 32 E
Beira, *Mozam.* **119 F3** 19 50 S 34 52 E
Beira, *Somali Rep.* **120 C3** 6 57N 47 19 E
Beirut = Bayrūt, *Lebanon* **103 B4** 33 53N 35 31 E
Beiseker, *Canada* **142 C6** 51 23N 113 32W
Beitaolaizhao, *China* **75 B13** 44 58N 125 58 E
Beitbridge, *Zimbabwe* **119 G3** 22 12 S 30 0 E
Beiuş, *Romania* **52 D7** 46 40N 22 21 E
Beizhen = Binzhou, *China* **75 F10** 37 20N 118 2 E
Beizhen, *China* **75 D11** 41 38N 121 54 E
Beizhengzhen, *China* **75 B12** 44 31N 123 30 E
Beja, *Portugal* **43 G3** 38 2N 7 53W
Béja, *Tunisia* **108 A1** 36 43N 9 12 E
Beja □, *Portugal* **43 H3** 37 55N 7 55W
Bejaïa, *Algeria* **111 A6** 36 42N 5 2 E
Béjar, *Spain* **42 E5** 40 23N 5 46W
Bejestān, *Iran* **97 C8** 34 30N 58 5 E
Bekabad, *Uzbekistan* **65 C4** 40 13N 69 14 E
Bekasi, *Indonesia* **84 D3** 6 14 S 106 59 E
Bekçiler, *Turkey* **49 E11** 36 56N 29 44 E
Békés, *Hungary* **52 D6** 46 47N 21 9 E
Békés □, *Hungary* **52 D6** 46 45N 21 0 E
Békéscsaba, *Hungary* **52 D6** 46 40N 21 5 E
Bekilli, *Turkey* **49 C11** 38 17N 29 27 E
Bekily, *Madag.* **117 C8** 24 13 S 45 19 E
Bekisopa, *Madag.* **117 C8** 21 40 S 45 54 E
Bekitro, *Madag.* **117 C8** 24 33 S 45 18 E
Bekodoka, *Madag.* **117 B8** 16 58 S 45 7 E
Bekoji, *Ethiopia* **107 F4** 7 40N 39 17 E
Bekok, *Malaysia* **87 L4** 2 20N 103 7 E
Bekopaka, *Madag.* **117 B7** 19 9 S 44 48 E
Bekuli, *Indonesia* **79 J17** 8 22 S 114 13 E
Bekwai, *Ghana* **113 D4** 6 30N 1 34W
Bela, *India* **93 G10** 25 50N 82 0 E
Bela, *Pakistan* **91 D2** 26 12N 66 20 E
Bela Crkva, *Serbia, Yug.* **52 F6** 44 55N 21 27 E
Bela Palanka, *Serbia, Yug.* **50 C6** 43 13N 22 17 E
Bela Vista, *Brazil* **174 A4** 22 12 S 56 20W
Bela Vista, *Mozam.* **117 D5** 26 10 S 32 44 E
Bélâbre, *France* **28 B5** 46 34N 1 8 E
Belaga, *Malaysia* **85 B4** 2 42N 113 47 E
Belalcázar, *Spain* **43 G5** 38 35N 5 10W
Belan →, *India* **93 G9** 24 2N 81 45 E
Belang, *Indonesia* **82 A2** 0 57N 124 47 E
Belanovica, *Serbia, Yug.* **50 B4** 44 15N 20 23 E
Belarus ■, *Europe* **58 F4** 53 30N 27 0 E
Belas, *Angola* **115 D2** 8 55 S 13 9 E
Belau = Palau ■, *Pac. Oc.* **62 J17** 7 30N 134 30 E
Belavenona, *Madag.* **117 C8** 24 50 S 47 4 E
Belawan, *Indonesia* **84 B1** 3 33N 98 32 E
Belaya, *Ethiopia* **107 E4** 11 25N 36 8 E
Belaya →, *Russia* **64 D6** 54 40N 56 0 E
Belaya Glina, *Russia* **61 G5** 46 5N 40 48 E
Belaya Kalitva, *Russia* **61 F5** 48 13N 40 50 E
Belaya Kholunitsa, *Russia* **64 B3** 58 51N 50 53 E
Belaya Tserkov = Bila Tserkva, *Ukraine* **59 H6** 49 45N 30 10 E
Belayan →, *Indonesia* **85 C5** 0 14 S 116 36 E
Belceşti, *Romania* **53 C12** 47 19N 27 7 E
Bełchatów, *Poland* **55 G6** 51 21N 19 22 E
Belcher Is., *Canada* **140 A3** 56 15N 78 45W
Belchite, *Spain* **40 D4** 41 18N 0 43W
Belden, *U.S.A.* **160 E5** 40 2N 121 17W
Belding, *U.S.A.* **157 A11** 43 6N 85 14W
Belebey, *Russia* **64 D5** 54 7N 54 7 E
Beled Weyne = Belet Uen, *Somali Rep.* **120 D3** 4 30N 45 5 E
Belém, *Brazil* **170 B2** 1 20 S 48 30W
Belém de São Francisco, *Brazil* **170 C4** 8 46 S 38 58W
Belén, *Argentina* **174 B2** 27 40 S 67 5W
Belén, *Colombia* **168 C2** 1 26N 75 56W
Belén, *Paraguay* **174 A4** 23 30 S 57 6W
Belen, *U.S.A.* **159 J10** 34 40N 106 46W
Belene, *Bulgaria* **51 C9** 43 39N 25 10 E
Beleni, *Turkey* **100 D7** 36 31N 36 10 E
Bélep, Is., *N. Cal.* **123 D11** 19 45 S 163 40 E
Bélesta, *France* **28 F5** 42 55N 1 56 E
Belet Uen, *Somali Rep.* **120 D3** 4 30N 45 5 E
Belev, *Russia* **58 F9** 53 50N 36 5 E
Belevi, *Turkey* **49 C9** 38 0N 27 28 E
Belfair, *U.S.A.* **160 C4** 47 27N 122 50W
Belfast, *N.Z.* **131 D7** 43 27 S 172 39 E
Belfast, *S. Africa* **117 D5** 25 42 S 30 2 E
Belfast, *U.K.* **23 B6** 54 37N 5 56W
Belfast, *Maine, U.S.A.* **149 C11** 44 26N 69 1W
Belfast, *N.Y., U.S.A.* **150 D6** 42 21N 78 7W
Belfast L., *U.K.* **23 B6** 54 40N 5 50W
Belfield, *U.S.A.* **154 B3** 46 53N 103 12W
Belfort, *France* **27 E13** 47 38N 6 50 E
Belfort, Territoire de □, *France* **27 E13** 47 40N 6 55 E
Belfry, *U.S.A.* **158 D9** 45 9N 109 1W
Belgaum, *India* **95 G2** 15 55N 74 35 E
Belgioioso, *Italy* **44 C6** 45 10N 9 19 E
Belgium ■, *Europe* **24 D4** 50 30N 5 0 E
Belgodère, *France* **29 F13** 42 35N 9 1 E
Belgorod, *Russia* **59 G9** 50 35N 36 35 E
Belgorod-Dnestrovskiy = Bilhorod-Dnistrovskyy, *Ukraine* **59 J6** 46 11N 30 23 E
Belgrade = Beograd, *Serbia, Yug.* **50 B4** 44 50N 20 37 E
Belgrade, *U.S.A.* **158 D8** 45 47N 111 11W
Belgrove, *N.Z.* **131 B7** 41 27 S 172 59 E
Belhaven, *U.S.A.* **149 H7** 35 33N 76 37W
Beli Drim →, *Europe* **50 D4** 42 6N 20 25 E
Beli Manastir, *Croatia* **52 E3** 45 45N 18 36 E
Beli Timok →, *Serbia, Yug.* **50 C6** 43 53N 22 14 E
Bélice →, *Italy* **46 E5** 37 35N 12 55 E
Belimbing, *Indonesia* **79 J18** 8 24 S 115 2 E
Belinga, *Gabon* **114 B2** 1 10N 13 2 E
Belinskiy, *Russia* **60 D6** 53 0N 43 25 E
Belinyu, *Indonesia* **84 C3** 1 35 S 105 50 E
Beliton Is. = Belitung, *Indonesia* **85 C3** 3 10 S 107 50 E
Belitung, *Indonesia* **85 C3** 3 10 S 107 50 E
Beliu, *Romania* **52 D6** 46 30N 22 0 E
Belize, *Angola* **115 C2** 4 39 S 12 46 E
Belize ■, *Cent. Amer.* **163 D7** 17 0N 88 30W
Belize City, *Belize* **163 D7** 17 25N 88 0W
Beljakovci, *Macedonia* **50 D5** 42 6N 21 59 E
Beljanica, *Serbia, Yug.* **50 B5** 44 8N 21 43 E
Belkovskiy, Ostrov, *Russia* **67 B14** 75 32N 135 44 E
Bell, *U.S.A.* **152 F7** 29 45N 82 52W
Bell →, *Canada* **140 C4** 49 48N 77 38W
Bell I., *Canada* **141 B8** 50 46N 55 35W
Bell-Irving →, *Canada* **142 B3** 56 12N 129 5W
Bell Peninsula, *Canada* **139 B11** 63 50N 82 0W
Bell Ville, *Argentina* **174 C3** 32 40 S 62 40W
Bella, *Italy* **47 B8** 40 45N 15 32 E
Bella Bella, *Canada* **142 C3** 52 10N 128 10W
Bella Coola, *Canada* **142 C3** 52 25N 126 40W
Bella Flor, *Bolivia* **172 C4** 11 9 S 67 49W
Bella Unión, *Uruguay* **174 C4** 30 15 S 57 40W
Bella Vista, *Corrientes, Argentina* **174 B4** 28 33 S 59 0W
Bella Vista, *Tucuman, Argentina* **174 B2** 27 10 S 65 25W
Bellac, *France* **28 B5** 46 7N 1 3 E
Bellágio, *Italy* **44 C6** 45 59N 9 15 E
Bellaire, *U.S.A.* **150 F4** 40 1N 80 45W
Bellária, *Italy* **45 D9** 44 9N 12 28 E
Bellary, *India* **95 G3** 15 10N 76 56 E
Bellata, *Australia* **127 D4** 29 53 S 149 46 E
Bellavista, *Ecuador* **172 a** 0 41 S 90 18W
Belle, *U.S.A.* **156 F5** 38 17N 91 43W
Belle-Chasse, *U.S.A.* **155 L10** 29 51N 89 59W
Belle Fourche, *U.S.A.* **154 C3** 44 40N 103 51W
Belle Fourche →, *U.S.A.* **154 C3** 44 26N 102 18W
Belle Glade, *U.S.A.* **149 M5** 26 41N 80 40W
Belle-Île, *France* **26 E3** 47 20N 3 10W
Belle Isle, *Canada* **141 B8** 51 57N 55 25W
Belle Isle, *U.S.A.* **153 G8** 28 27N 81 21W
Belle Isle, Str. of, *Canada* **141 B8** 51 30N 56 30W
Belle Plaine, *U.S.A.* **156 C4** 41 54N 92 17W
Belle Rive, *U.S.A.* **157 F8** 38 14N 88 45W
Belle Yella, *Liberia* **112 D3** 7 24N 10 0W
Belledonne, *France* **29 C10** 45 20N 6 10 E
Bellefontaine, *U.S.A.* **157 D13** 40 22N 83 46W
Bellefonte, *U.S.A.* **150 F7** 40 55N 77 47W
Bellegarde, *France* **27 E9** 47 59N 2 26 E
Bellegarde-en-Marche, *France* **28 C6** 45 59N 2 18 E
Bellegarde-sur-Valserine, *France* **27 F12** 46 4N 5 50 E
Bellême, *France* **26 D7** 48 22N 0 34 E
Belleoram, *Canada* **141 C8** 47 31N 55 25W
Belleplaine, *Barbados* **165 g** 13 15N 59 34W
Belleview, *U.S.A.* **153 F7** 29 4N 82 3W
Belleville, *Canada* **140 D4** 44 10N 77 23W
Belleville, *France* **27 F11** 46 7N 4 45 E
Belleville, *Ill., U.S.A.* **156 F7** 38 31N 89 59W
Belleville, *Kans., U.S.A.* **154 F6** 39 50N 97 38W
Belleville, *N.Y., U.S.A.* **151 C8** 43 46N 76 10W
Belleville-sur-Vie, *France* **26 F5** 46 46N 1 25W
Bellevue, *Canada* **142 D6** 49 35N 114 22W
Bellevue, *Idaho, U.S.A.* **158 E6** 43 28N 114 16W
Bellevue, *Iowa, U.S.A.* **156 B6** 42 16N 90 26W
Bellevue, *Mich., U.S.A.* **157 B11** 42 27N 85 1W
Bellevue, *Nebr., U.S.A.* **154 E7** 41 8N 95 53W
Bellevue, *Ohio, U.S.A.* **150 E2** 41 17N 82 51W
Bellevue, *Wash., U.S.A.* **160 C4** 47 37N 122 12W
Belley, *France* **29 C9** 45 46N 5 41 E
Bellin = Kangirsuk, *Canada* **139 B13** 60 0N 70 0W
Bellinge, *Denmark* **17 J4** 55 20N 10 20 E
Bellingen, *Australia* **129 A10** 30 25 S 152 50 E
Bellingham, *U.S.A.* **138 D7** 48 46N 122 29W
Bellingshausen Sea, *Antarctica* **7 C17** 66 0 S 80 0W
Bellinzona, *Switz.* **33 D8** 46 11N 9 1 E
Bello, *Colombia* **168 B2** 6 20N 75 33W
Bellona, *Solomon Is.* **133 N10** 11 17 S 159 47 E
Bellows Falls, *U.S.A.* **151 C12** 43 8N 72 27W
Bellpat, *Pakistan* **92 E3** 29 0N 68 5 E
Bellpuig d'Urgell, *Spain* **40 D6** 41 37N 1 1 E
Belluno, *Italy* **45 B9** 46 9N 12 13 E
Bellville, *U.S.A.* **152 C8** 32 9N 81 59W
Bellwood, *U.S.A.* **150 F6** 40 36N 78 20W
Bélmez, *Spain* **43 G5** 38 17N 5 17W
Belmond, *U.S.A.* **156 B3** 42 51N 93 37W
Belmont, *Australia* **129 B9** 33 4 S 151 42 E
Belmont, *Canada* **150 D3** 42 53N 81 5W
Belmont, *S. Africa* **116 D3** 29 28 S 24 22 E
Belmont, *U.S.A.* **150 D6** 42 14N 78 2W
Belmonte, *Brazil* **171 E4** 16 0 S 39 0W
Belmonte, *Portugal* **42 E3** 40 21N 7 20W
Belmonte, *Spain* **41 F2** 39 34N 2 43W
Belmopan, *Belize* **163 D7** 17 18N 88 30W
Belmullet, *Ireland* **23 B2** 54 14N 9 58W
Belo, *Dem. Rep. of the Congo* **114 C4** 0 32 S 23 13 E
Belo Horizonte, *Brazil* **171 E3** 19 55 S 43 56W
Belo Jardim, *Brazil* **170 C4** 8 20 S 36 26W
Belo Monte, *Brazil* **169 D7** 3 5 S 51 46W
Belo-sur-Mer, *Madag.* **117 C7** 20 42 S 44 0 E
Belo-Tsiribihina, *Madag.* **117 B7** 19 40 S 44 30 E
Belogorsk = Bilohirsk, *Ukraine* **59 K8** 45 3N 34 35 E
Belogorsk, *Russia* **67 D13** 51 0N 128 20 E
Belogradchik, *Bulgaria* **50 C6** 43 53N 22 42 E
Belogradets, *Bulgaria* **51 C11** 43 22N 27 18 E
Beloha, *Madag.* **117 D8** 25 10 S 45 3 E
Beloit, *Kans., U.S.A.* **154 F5** 39 28N 98 6W
Beloit, *Wis., U.S.A.* **156 B7** 42 31N 89 2W
Belokorovichi, *Ukraine* **59 G5** 51 7N 28 2 E
Belomorsk, *Russia* **56 B5** 64 35N 34 54 E
Belondo, *Dem. Rep. of the Congo* **114 C3** 0 19 S 19 31 E
Belonge, *Dem. Rep. of the Congo* **114 C3** 2 7 S 19 33 E
Belonia, *India* **90 D3** 23 15N 91 30 E
Belopolye = Bilopillya, *Ukraine* **59 G8** 51 14N 34 20 E
Belorechensk, *Russia* **61 H4** 44 46N 39 52 E
Beloretsk, *Russia* **64 E7** 53 58N 58 24 E
Belorussia = Belarus ■, *Europe* **58 F4** 53 30N 27 0 E
Beloslav, *Bulgaria* **51 C11** 43 11N 27 42 E
Belovo, *Bulgaria* **51 D8** 42 13N 24 1 E
Belovo, *Russia* **66 D9** 54 30N 86 0 E
Belovodsk, *Ukraine* **59 H10** 49 13N 39 36 E
Beloyarskiy, *Russia* **64 C8** 56 45N 61 24 E
Beloye, Ozero, *Russia* **58 B9** 60 10N 37 35 E
Beloye More, *Russia* **56 A6** 66 30N 38 0 E
Belozem, *Bulgaria* **51 D9** 42 12N 25 2 E
Belozersk, *Russia* **58 B9** 60 1N 37 45 E
Belp, *Switz.* **32 C5** 46 53N 7 30 E
Belpasso, *Italy* **47 E7** 37 35N 14 58 E
Belpre, *U.S.A.* **148 F5** 39 17N 81 34W
Belrain, *India* **93 E9** 28 23N 80 55 E
Belt, *U.S.A.* **158 C8** 47 23N 110 55W
Beltana, *Australia* **128 A3** 30 48 S 138 25 E
Belterra, *Brazil* **169 D7** 2 45 S 55 0W
Beltinci, *Slovenia* **45 B13** 46 37N 16 20 E
Belton, *Mo., U.S.A.* **156 F2** 38 49N 94 32W
Belton, *Tex., U.S.A.* **155 K6** 31 3N 97 28W
Belton L., *U.S.A.* **155 K6** 31 8N 97 32W
Beltsy = Bălţi, *Moldova* **53 C12** 47 48N 27 58 E
Belturbet, *Ireland* **23 B4** 54 6N 7 26W
Belukha, *Russia* **66 E9** 49 50N 86 50 E
Beluran, *Malaysia* **78 C5** 5 48N 117 35 E
Beluša, *Slovak Rep.* **35 B11** 49 5N 18 17 E
Belušić, *Serbia, Yug.* **50 C5** 43 50N 21 10 E
Belvedere Maríttimo, *Italy* **47 C8** 39 37N 15 52 E
Belvès, *France* **28 D5** 44 46N 1 0 E
Belvidere, *Ill., U.S.A.* **154 D10** 42 15N 88 50W
Belvidere, *N.J., U.S.A.* **151 F9** 40 50N 75 5W

Belvis de la Jara, *Spain* **42 F6** 39 45N 4 57W
Belyando →, *Australia* **126 C4** 21 38 S 146 50 E
Belyy, *Russia* **58 E7** 55 49N 33 3 E
Belyy, Ostrov, *Russia* **66 B8** 73 30N 71 0 E
Belyy Yar, *Russia* **66 D9** 58 26N 84 39 E
Belyye Vody = Aqsū, *Kazakstan* **65 B4** 42 25N 69 50 E
Bełżec, *Poland* **55 H10** 50 23N 23 26 E
Belzig, *Germany* **30 C8** 52 8N 12 35 E
Belzoni, *U.S.A.* **155 J9** 33 11N 90 29W
Bełżyce, *Poland* **55 G9** 51 11N 22 17 E
Bemaraha, Lembalemban' i, *Madag.* **117 B7** 18 40 S 44 45 E
Bemarivo, *Madag.* **117 C7** 21 45 S 44 45 E
Bemarivo →, *Antsiranana, Madag.* **117 A9** 14 9 S 50 9 E
Bemarivo →, *Mahajanga, Madag.* **117 B8** 15 27 S 47 40 E
Bemavo, *Madag.* **117 C8** 21 33 S 45 25 E
Bembe, *Angola* **115 D2** 7 3 S 14 25 E
Bembéréke, *Benin* **113 C5** 10 11N 2 43 E
Bembesi, *Zimbabwe* **119 G2** 20 0 S 28 58 E
Bembesi →, *Zimbabwe* **119 F2** 18 57 S 27 47 E
Bembézar →, *Spain* **43 H5** 37 45N 5 13W
Bembibre, *Spain* **42 C4** 42 37N 6 25W
Bemboka Nat. Park, *Australia* **129 D8** 36 35 S 149 41 E
Bement, *U.S.A.* **157 E8** 39 55N 88 34W
Bemetara, *India* **93 J9** 21 42N 81 32 E
Bemidji, *U.S.A.* **154 B7** 47 28N 94 53W
Bemolanga, *Madag.* **117 B8** 17 44 S 45 6 E
Ben, *Iran* **97 C6** 32 32N 50 45 E
Ben Boyd Nat. Park, *Australia* **129 D8** 37 0 S 149 55 E
Ben Cruachan, *U.K.* **22 E3** 56 26N 5 8W
Ben Dearg, *U.K.* **22 D4** 57 47N 4 56W
Ben Gardane, *Tunisia* **108 B2** 33 11N 11 11 E
Ben Hope, *U.K.* **22 C4** 58 25N 4 36W
Ben Lawers, *U.K.* **22 E4** 56 32N 4 14W
Ben Lomond, *N.S.W., Australia* **127 E5** 30 1 S 151 43 E
Ben Lomond, *Tas., Australia* **127 G4** 41 38 S 147 42 E
Ben Lomond, *U.K.* **22 E4** 56 11N 4 38W
Ben Lomond Nat. Park, *Australia* **127 G4** 41 33 S 147 39 E
Ben Luc, *Vietnam* **87 G6** 10 39N 106 29 E
Ben Macdhui, *U.K.* **22 D5** 57 4N 3 40W
Ben Mhor, *U.K.* **22 D1** 57 15N 7 18W
Ben More, *Arg. & Bute, U.K.* **22 E2** 56 26N 6 1W
Ben More, *Stirl., U.K.* **22 E4** 56 23N 4 32W
Ben More Assynt, *U.K.* **22 C4** 58 8N 4 52W
Ben Nevis, *U.K.* **22 E3** 56 48N 5 1W
Ben Ohau Ra., *N.Z.* **131 E5** 44 1 S 170 4 E
Ben Quang, *Vietnam* **86 D6** 17 3N 106 55 E
Ben Slimane, *Morocco* **110 B3** 33 38N 7 7W
Ben Vorlich, *U.K.* **22 E4** 56 21N 4 14W
Ben Wyvis, *U.K.* **22 D4** 57 40N 4 35W
Bena, *Nigeria* **113 C6** 11 20N 5 50 E
Bena-Dibele, *Dem. Rep. of the Congo* **115 C4** 4 4 S 22 50 E
Bena-Leka, *Dem. Rep. of the Congo* **115 D4** 5 8 S 22 10 E
Bena-Tshadi, *Dem. Rep. of the Congo* **115 C4** 4 40 S 22 49 E
Benāb, *Iran* **101 D12** 37 20N 46 4 E
Benadir, *Somali Rep.* **120 D2** 1 30N 44 30 E
Benagerie, *Australia* **128 A4** 31 25 S 140 22 E
Benahmed, *Morocco* **110 B3** 33 4N 7 9W
Benalla, *Australia* **129 D7** 36 30 S 146 0 E
Benalmádena, *Spain* **43 J6** 36 36N 4 34W
Benambra, Mt., *Australia* **129 D7** 36 31 S 147 34 E
Benanee, *Australia* **128 C5** 34 31 S 142 52 E
Benares = Varanasi, *India* **93 G10** 25 22N 83 0 E
Bénat, C., *France* **29 E10** 43 5N 6 22 E
Benavente, *Portugal* **43 G2** 38 59N 8 49W
Benavente, *Spain* **42 C5** 42 2N 5 43W
Benavides, *U.S.A.* **155 M5** 27 36N 98 25W
Benavides de Órbigo, *Spain* **42 C5** 42 30N 5 54W
Benbecula, *U.K.* **22 D1** 57 26N 7 21W
Benbonyathe, *Australia* **128 A3** 30 25 S 139 11 E
Bend, *U.S.A.* **158 D3** 44 4N 121 19W
Bendela, *Dem. Rep. of the Congo* **114 C3** 3 18 S 17 36 E
Bendemeer, *Australia* **129 A9** 30 53 S 151 8 E
Bender Beila, *Somali Rep.* **120 C4** 9 30N 50 48 E
Bender Merchagno, *Somali Rep.* **120 B4** 11 41N 50 34 E
Bendery = Tighina, *Moldova* **53 D14** 46 50N 29 30 E
Bendigo, *Australia* **128 D6** 36 40 S 144 15 E
Bendorf, *Germany* **30 E3** 50 25N 7 35 E
Benē Beraq, *Israel* **103 C3** 32 6N 34 51 E
Beneditinos, *Brazil* **170 C3** 5 27 S 42 22W
Benedito Leite, *Brazil* **170 C3** 7 13 S 44 34W
Bénéna, *Mali* **112 C4** 13 9N 4 17W
Benenitra, *Madag.* **117 C8** 23 27 S 45 5 E
Benešov, *Czech Rep.* **34 B7** 49 46N 14 41 E
Benevento, *Italy* **47 A7** 41 8N 14 45 E
Benfeld, *France* **27 D14** 48 22N 7 34 E
Benga, *Mozam.* **119 F3** 16 11 S 33 40 E
Bengal, Bay of, *Ind. Oc.* **62 H12** 15 0N 90 0 E
Bengbis, *Cameroon* **113 E7** 3 27N 12 36 E
Bengbu, *China* **75 H9** 32 58N 117 20 E
Benghazi = Banghāzī, *Libya* **108 B4** 32 11N 20 3 E
Benghisa Point, *Malta* **38 F8** 35 49N 14 33 E
Bengkalis, *Indonesia* **84 B2** 1 30N 102 10 E
Bengkulu, *Indonesia* **84 C2** 3 50 S 102 12 E
Bengkulu □, *Indonesia* **84 C2** 3 48 S 102 16 E
Bengo, *Dem. Rep. of the Congo* **114 C3** 2 11 S 19 5 E
Bengo □, *Angola* **115 D2** 9 0 S 13 10 E
Bengough, *Canada* **143 D7** 49 25N 105 10W
Bengtsfors, *Sweden* **16 E6** 59 2N 12 14 E
Benguela, *Angola* **115 E2** 12 37 S 13 25 E
Benguela □, *Angola* **115 E2** 13 0 S 13 30 E
Benguerir, *Morocco* **110 B3** 32 16N 7 56W
Benguérua, I., *Mozam.* **117 C6** 21 58 S 35 28 E
Benguet □, *Phil.* **80 C3** 16 30N 120 40 E
Benha, *Egypt* **106 H7** 30 26N 31 8 E
Beni, *Dem. Rep. of the Congo* **118 B2** 0 30N 29 27 E
Beni □, *Bolivia* **173 C4** 14 0 S 65 0W
Beni →, *Bolivia* **173 C4** 10 23 S 65 24W
Beni Abbès, *Algeria* **111 B4** 30 5N 2 5W
Beni Haoua, *Algeria* **111 A5** 36 30N 1 30 E
Beni Mazâr, *Egypt* **106 B3** 28 32N 30 44 E
Beni Mellal, *Morocco* **110 B3** 32 21N 6 21W
Beni Ounif, *Algeria* **111 B4** 32 0N 1 10W
Beni Saf, *Algeria* **111 A4** 35 17N 1 15W
Beni Suef, *Egypt* **106 J7** 29 5N 31 6 E
Beniah L., *Canada* **142 A6** 63 23N 112 17W
Benicarló, *Spain* **40 E5** 40 23N 0 23 E
Benicássim, *Spain* **40 E5** 40 3N 0 4 E
Benicia, *U.S.A.* **160 G4** 38 3N 122 9W
Benidorm, *Spain* **41 G4** 38 33N 0 9W
Benin ■, *Africa* **113 D5** 10 0N 2 0 E
Benin →, *Nigeria* **113 D6** 5 45N 5 4 E
Benin, Bight of, *W. Afr.* **113 E5** 5 0N 3 0 E
Benin City, *Nigeria* **113 D6** 6 20N 5 31 E
Benisa, *Spain* **41 G5** 38 43N 0 3 E
Benitses, *Greece* **38 B9** 39 32N 19 55 E
Benjamin Aceval, *Paraguay* **174 A4** 24 58 S 57 34W
Benjamin Constant, *Brazil* **168 D3** 4 40 S 70 15W
Benjamin Hill, *Mexico* **162 A2** 30 10N 111 10W
Benkelman, *U.S.A.* **154 E4** 40 3N 101 32W
Benkovac, *Croatia* **45 D12** 44 2N 15 37 E
Benmore Pk., *N.Z.* **131 E5** 44 25 S 170 8 E
Bennett, *Canada* **142 B2** 59 56N 134 53W
Bennett, L., *Australia* **124 D5** 22 50 S 131 2 E
Bennetta, Ostrov, *Russia* **67 B15** 76 21N 148 56 E
Bennettsville, *U.S.A.* **149 H6** 34 37N 79 41W
Bennichchāb, *Mauritania* **112 B1** 19 32N 15 12W
Bennington, *N.H., U.S.A.* **151 D11** 43 0N 71 55W
Bennington, *Vt., U.S.A.* **151 D11** 42 53N 73 12W
Beno, *Dem. Rep. of the Congo* **114 C3** 3 41 S 17 49 E
Bénodet, *France* **26 E2** 47 53N 4 7W
Benoni, *S. Africa* **117 D4** 26 11 S 28 18 E
Benoud, *Algeria* **111 B5** 32 20N 0 16 E
Benoué, Parc Nat. de la, *Cameroon* **114 A2** 8 30N 13 55 E
Benoy, *Chad* **109 G3** 8 59N 16 19 E
Benque Viejo, *Belize* **163 D7** 17 5N 89 8W
Bensheim, *Germany* **31 F4** 49 40N 8 38 E
Benson, *Ariz., U.S.A.* **159 L8** 31 58N 110 18W
Benson, *Minn., U.S.A.* **154 C7** 45 19N 95 36W
Bent, *Iran* **97 E8** 26 20N 59 31 E
Benteng, *Indonesia* **82 C2** 6 10 S 120 30 E
Bentiaba, *Angola* **115 E2** 14 15 S 12 21 E
Bentinck I., *Australia* **126 B2** 17 3 S 139 35 E
Bentiu, *Sudan* **107 F2** 9 10N 29 55 E
Bento Gonçalves, *Brazil* **175 B5** 29 10 S 51 31W
Benton, *Ark., U.S.A.* **155 H8** 34 34N 92 35W
Benton, *Calif., U.S.A.* **160 H8** 37 48N 118 32W
Benton, *Ill., U.S.A.* **156 G8** 38 0N 88 55W
Benton, *Pa., U.S.A.* **151 E8** 41 12N 76 23W
Benton Harbor, *U.S.A.* **157 B10** 42 6N 86 27W
Benton Heights, *U.S.A.* **157 B10** 42 7N 86 24W
Bentonville, *U.S.A.* **155 G7** 36 22N 94 13W
Bentu Liben, *Ethiopia* **107 F4** 8 32N 38 21 E
Bentung, *Malaysia* **87 L3** 3 31N 101 55 E
Benue □, *Nigeria* **113 D6** 7 20N 8 45 E
Benue →, *Nigeria* **113 D6** 7 48N 6 46 E
Benxi, *China* **75 D12** 41 20N 123 48 E
Benza, *Dem. Rep. of the Congo* **115 D2** 4 49 S 13 17 E
Benzdorp, *Surinam* **169 C7** 3 44N 54 5W
Beo, *Indonesia* **82 A3** 4 25N 126 50 E
Beograd, *Serbia, Yug.* **50 B4** 44 50N 20 37 E
Beoumi, *Ivory C.* **112 D3** 7 45N 5 23W
Bepan Jiang →, *China* **76 E6** 24 55N 106 5 E
Beppu, *Japan* **72 D3** 33 15N 131 30 E
Beppu-Wan, *Japan* **72 D3** 33 18N 131 34 E
Beqa, *Fiji* **133 B2** 18 23 S 178 8 E
Beqaa Valley = Al Biqā, *Lebanon* **103 A5** 34 10N 36 10 E
Ber Mota, *India* **92 H3** 23 27N 68 34 E
Bera, *Bangla.* **90 C2** 24 5N 89 37 E
Berach →, *India* **92 G6** 25 15N 75 2 E
Beraketa, *Madag.* **117 C7** 23 7 S 44 25 E
Béran-Djoko, *Congo* **114 B3** 3 15N 17 0 E
Berane, *Montenegro, Yug.* **50 D3** 42 51N 19 52 E
Berat, *Albania* **50 F3** 40 43N 19 59 E
Berau →, *Indonesia* **85 B5** 2 10N 117 42 E
Berau, Teluk, *Indonesia* **83 B4** 2 30 S 132 30 E
Beravina, *Madag.* **117 B8** 18 10 S 45 14 E
Berber, *Sudan* **106 D3** 18 0N 34 0 E
Berbera, *Somali Rep.* **120 B3** 10 30N 45 2 E
Berbérati, *C.A.R.* **114 B3** 4 15N 15 40 E
Berbice →, *Guyana* **169 B6** 6 20N 57 32W
Berceto, *Italy* **44 D6** 44 31N 9 51 E
Berchidda, *Italy* **46 B2** 40 47N 9 10 E
Berchtesgaden, *Germany* **31 H8** 47 38N 13 0 E
Berck, *France* **27 B8** 50 25N 1 36 E
Berdale, *Somali Rep.* **120 C3** 7 4N 47 51 E
Berdichev = Berdychiv, *Ukraine* **59 H5** 49 57N 28 30 E
Berdsk, *Russia* **66 D9** 54 47N 83 2 E
Berdyansk, *Ukraine* **59 J9** 46 45N 36 50 E
Berdyaush, *Russia* **64 D7** 55 9N 59 9 E
Berdychiv, *Ukraine* **59 H5** 49 57N 28 30 E
Berea, *U.S.A.* **148 G3** 37 34N 84 17W
Berebere, *Indonesia* **82 A3** 2 25N 128 45 E
Bereda, *Somali Rep.* **120 B4** 11 45N 51 0 E
Berehove, *Ukraine* **59 H2** 48 15N 22 35 E
Bereina, *Papua N. G.* **132 E4** 8 39 S 146 30 E
Berekum, *Ghana* **112 D4** 7 29N 2 34W
Berenice, *Egypt* **106 C4** 24 2N 35 25 E
Berens →, *Canada* **143 C9** 52 25N 97 2W
Berens I., *Canada* **143 C9** 52 18N 97 18W
Berens River, *Canada* **143 C9** 52 25N 97 0W
Beresford, *U.S.A.* **154 D6** 43 5N 96 47W
Berestechko, *Ukraine* **59 G3** 50 22N 25 5 E
Bereşti, *Romania* **53 D12** 46 6N 27 50 E
Beretău →, *Romania* **52 C6** 47 10N 21 50 E
Berettyó →, *Hungary* **52 D6** 46 59N 21 7 E
Berettyóújfalu, *Hungary* **52 C6** 47 13N 21 33 E
Berevo, *Mahajanga, Madag.* **117 B7** 17 14 S 44 17 E
Berevo, *Toliara, Madag.* **117 B7** 19 44 S 44 58 E
Bereza = Byaroza, *Belarus* **59 F3** 52 31N 24 51 E
Berezhany, *Ukraine* **59 H3** 49 26N 24 58 E
Berezina = Byarezina →, *Belarus* **59 F6** 52 33N 30 14 E
Berezivka, *Ukraine* **59 J6** 47 14N 30 55 E
Berezna, *Ukraine* **59 G6** 51 35N 31 46 E
Bereznik, *Russia* **56 B7** 62 51N 42 40 E
Berezniki, *Russia* **64 B6** 59 24N 56 46 E
Berezovo, *Russia* **66 C7** 64 0N 65 0 E
Berga, *Spain* **40 C6** 42 6N 1 48 E
Berga, *Sweden* **17 G10** 57 14N 16 3 E
Bergama, *Turkey* **49 B9** 39 8N 27 11 E
Bérgamo, *Italy* **44 C6** 45 41N 9 43 E
Bergaon, *India* **94 D5** 20 41N 80 27 E
Bergara, *Spain* **40 B2** 43 9N 2 28W
Bergby, *Sweden* **16 D11** 60 57N 17 2 E
Bergedorf, *Germany* **30 B6** 53 28N 10 6 E
Bergeforsen, *Sweden* **16 B11** 62 32N 17 23 E
Bergen, *Mecklenburg-Vorpommern, Germany* **30 A9** 54 25N 13 25 E
Bergen, *Niedersachsen, Germany* **30 C5** 52 49N 9 57 E
Bergen, *Neths.* **24 B4** 52 40N 4 43 E
Bergen, *Norway* **15 F11** 60 20N 5 20 E
Bergen, *U.S.A.* **150 C7** 43 5N 77 57W
Bergen op Zoom, *Neths.* **24 C4** 51 28N 4 18 E
Bergerac, *France* **28 D4** 44 51N 0 30 E
Bergheim, *Germany* **30 E2** 50 57N 6 38 E
Bergholz, *U.S.A.* **150 F4** 40 31N 80 53W
Bergisch Gladbach, *Germany* **24 D7** 50 59N 7 8 E
Bergkamen, *Germany* **30 D3** 51 37N 7 38 E
Bergkvara, *Sweden* **17 H10** 56 23N 16 5 E
Bergshamra, *Sweden* **16 E12** 59 38N 18 37 E
Bergsjö, *Sweden* **16 C11** 61 59N 17 3 E
Bergues, *France* **27 B9** 50 58N 2 24 E
Bergviken, *Sweden* **16 C10** 61 15N 16 40 E
Bergville, *S. Africa* **117 D4** 28 52 S 29 18 E
Berhala, Selat, *Indonesia* **84 C2** 1 0 S 104 15 E
Berhampore = Baharampur, *India* **93 G13** 24 2N 88 27 E
Berhampur = Brahmapur, *India* **94 E7** 19 15N 84 54 E
Berheci →, *Romania* **53 E12** 45 58N 27 28 E
Bering Glacier, *U.S.A.* **144 F12** 60 20N 143 30W
Bering Sea, *Pac. Oc.* **138 C1** 58 0N 171 0 E
Bering Strait, *Pac. Oc.* **144 D5** 65 30N 169 0W
Beringen, *Switz.* **33 A7** 47 38N 8 34 E
Beringovskiy, *Russia* **67 C18** 63 3N 179 19 E
Berisso, *Argentina* **174 C4** 34 56 S 57 50W
Berja, *Spain* **43 J8** 36 50N 2 56W
Berkåk, *Norway* **18 B6** 62 50N 10 0 E
Berkane, *Morocco* **111 B4** 34 52N 2 20W
Berkeley, *U.S.A.* **160 H4** 37 52N 122 16W
Berkeley, C., *Ecuador* **172 a** 0 1N 91 35W
Berkner I., *Antarctica* **7 D18** 79 30 S 50 0W
Berkovitsa, *Bulgaria* **50 C7** 43 16N 23 8 E
Berkshire, *U.S.A.* **151 D8** 42 19N 76 11W
Berkshire Downs, *U.K.* **21 F6** 51 33N 1 29W
Berlanga, *Spain* **43 G5** 38 17N 5 50W
Berlenga, I., *Portugal* **43 F1** 39 25N 9 30W
Berlin, *Germany* **30 C9** 52 30N 13 25 E
Berlin, *Ga., U.S.A.* **152 D6** 31 4N 83 37W
Berlin, *Md., U.S.A.* **148 F8** 38 20N 75 13W
Berlin, *N.H., U.S.A.* **151 B13** 44 28N 71 11W
Berlin, *N.Y., U.S.A.* **151 D11** 42 42N 73 23W
Berlin, *Wis., U.S.A.* **148 D1** 43 58N 88 57W
Berlin □, *Germany* **30 C9** 52 30N 13 20 E
Berlin L., *U.S.A.* **150 E4** 41 3N 81 0W
Bermagui, *Australia* **129 D9** 36 25 S 150 4 E
Bermeja, Sierra, *Spain* **43 J5** 36 30N 5 11W
Bermejo →, *Formosa, Argentina* **174 B4** 26 51 S 58 23W
Bermejo →, *San Juan, Argentina* **174 C2** 32 30 S 67 30W
Bermen, L., *Canada* **141 B6** 53 35N 68 55W
Bermeo, *Spain* **40 B2** 43 25N 2 47W
Bermillo de Sayago, *Spain* **42 D4** 41 22N 6 8W
Bermuda ■, *Atl. Oc.* **9 a** 32 45N 65 0W
Bern, *Switz.* **32 C4** 46 57N 7 28 E
Bern □, *Switz.* **32 C5** 46 45N 7 40 E
Bernalda, *Italy* **47 B9** 40 24N 16 41 E
Bernalillo, *U.S.A.* **159 J10** 35 18N 106 33W
Bernam →, *Malaysia* **84 B2** 3 45N 101 5 E
Bernardo de Irigoyen, *Argentina* **175 B5** 26 15 S 53 40W
Bernardo O'Higgins □, *Chile* **174 C1** 34 15 S 70 45W
Bernardsville, *U.S.A.* **151 F10** 40 43N 74 34W
Bernasconi, *Argentina* **174 D3** 37 55 S 63 44W
Bernau, *Bayern, Germany* **31 H8** 47 47N 12 22 E
Bernau, *Brandenburg, Germany* **30 C9** 52 40N 13 35 E
Bernay, *France* **26 C7** 49 5N 0 35 E
Bernburg, *Germany* **30 D7** 51 47N 11 44 E
Berndorf, *Austria* **34 D9** 47 59N 16 1 E
Berne = Bern, *Switz.* **32 C4** 46 57N 7 28 E
Berne = Bern □, *Switz.* **32 C5** 46 45N 7 40 E
Berne, *U.S.A.* **157 D12** 40 39N 84 57W
Berner Alpen, *Switz.* **32 D5** 46 27N 7 35 E
Berneray, *U.K.* **22 D1** 57 43N 7 11W
Bernese Oberland = Oberland, *Switz.* **32 C5** 46 35N 7 38 E
Bernier I., *Australia* **125 D1** 24 50 S 113 12 E
Bernina, Passo del, *Switz.* **33 D10** 46 25N 10 2 E
Bernina, Piz, *Switz.* **33 D9** 46 20N 9 54 E
Bernkastel-Kues, *Germany* **31 F3** 49 55N 7 3 E
Bero →, *Angola* **115 F2** 15 10 S 12 9 E
Beroroha, *Madag.* **117 C8** 21 40 S 45 10 E
Béroubouay, *Benin* **113 C5** 10 34N 2 46 E
Beroun, *Czech Rep.* **34 B7** 49 57N 14 5 E
Berounka →, *Czech Rep.* **34 B7** 50 0N 14 22 E
Berovo, *Macedonia* **50 E6** 41 38N 22 51 E
Berrahal, *Algeria* **111 A6** 36 54N 7 33 E
Berre, Étang de, *France* **29 E9** 43 27N 5 5 E
Berre-l'Étang, *France* **29 E9** 43 27N 5 10 E
Berrechid, *Morocco* **110 B3** 33 18N 7 36W
Berri, *Australia* **128 C4** 34 14 S 140 35 E
Berriane, *Algeria* **111 B5** 32 50N 3 46 E
Berridale, *Australia* **129 D8** 36 22 S 148 48 E
Berrien Springs, *U.S.A.* **157 C10** 41 57N 86 20W
Berrigan, *Australia* **129 C6** 35 38 S 145 49 E
Berriwillock, *Australia* **128 C5** 35 36 S 142 59 E
Berrouaghia, *Algeria* **111 A5** 36 10N 2 53 E
Berry, *Australia* **129 C9** 34 46 S 150 43 E
Berry, *France* **27 F8** 46 50N 2 0 E
Berry Is., *Bahamas* **164 A4** 25 40N 77 50W
Berrydale, *U.S.A.* **153 E2** 30 53N 87 3W
Berryessa L., *U.S.A.* **160 G4** 38 31N 122 6W
Berryville, *U.S.A.* **155 G8** 36 22N 93 34W
Berseba, *Namibia* **116 D2** 26 0 S 17 46 E
Bersenbrück, *Germany* **30 C3** 52 34N 7 56 E
Bershad, *Ukraine* **59 H5** 48 22N 29 31 E
Berthold, *U.S.A.* **154 A4** 48 19N 101 44W
Berthoud, *U.S.A.* **154 E2** 40 19N 105 5W
Bertincourt, *France* **27 B9** 50 5N 2 58 E
Bertolínia, *Brazil* **170 C3** 7 38 S 43 57W
Bertoua, *Cameroon* **114 B2** 4 30N 13 45 E
Bertraghboy B., *Ireland* **23 C2** 53 22N 9 54W
Berufjörður, *Iceland* **11 C12** 64 48N 14 29W
Berunes, *Iceland* **11 C12** 64 42N 14 16W
Beruri, *Brazil* **169 D5** 3 54 S 61 22W
Berwick, *U.S.A.* **151 E8** 41 3N 76 14W
Berwick-upon-Tweed, *U.K.* **20 B6** 55 46N 2 0W
Berwyn Mts., *U.K.* **20 E4** 52 54N 3 26W
Beryslav, *Ukraine* **59 J7** 46 50N 33 30 E
Berzasca, *Romania* **52 F6** 44 39N 21 58 E
Berzence, *Hungary* **52 D2** 46 12N 17 11 E
Besal, *Pakistan* **93 B5** 35 4N 73 56 E
Besalampy, *Madag.* **117 B7** 16 43 S 44 29 E
Besançon, *France* **27 E13** 47 15N 6 2 E
Besar, *Indonesia* **85 C5** 2 40 S 116 0 E
Besar, Gunong, *Malaysia* **84 A2** 5 10N 101 18 E
Besharyk, *Uzbekistan* **65 C5** 40 26N 70 36 E
Beshenkovichi, *Belarus* **58 E5** 55 2N 29 29 E
Beshkent, *Uzbekistan* **65 D2** 38 49N 65 39 E
Beška, *Serbia, Yug.* **52 E5** 45 8N 20 6 E
Beslan, *Russia* **61 J7** 43 15N 44 28 E
Besna Kobila, *Serbia, Yug.* **50 D6** 42 31N 22 10 E
Besnard L., *Canada* **143 B7** 55 25N 106 0W
Besni, *Turkey* **100 D7** 37 41N 37 52 E
Besor, N. →, *Egypt* **103 D3** 31 28N 34 22 E
Bessa Monteiro, *Angola* **115 D2** 7 7 S 13 44 E
Bessarabiya, *Moldova* **59 J5** 47 0N 28 10 E
Bessarabka = Basarabeasca, *Moldova* **53 D13** 46 21N 28 58 E
Bessèges, *France* **29 D8** 44 18N 4 8 E
Bessemer, *Ala., U.S.A.* **149 J2** 33 24N 86 58W
Bessemer, *Mich., U.S.A.* **154 B9** 46 29N 90 3W
Bessemer, *Pa., U.S.A.* **150 F4** 40 59N 80 30W
Bessin, *France* **26 C6** 49 18N 1 0W
Bessines-sur-Gartempe, *France* **28 B5** 46 6N 1 22 E
Beswick, *Australia* **124 B5** 14 34 S 132 53 E
Bet She'an, *Israel* **103 C4** 32 30N 35 30 E
Bet Shemesh, *Israel* **103 D4** 31 44N 35 0 E
Bet Tadjine, Djebel, *Algeria* **110 C4** 29 0N 3 30W
Betafo, *Madag.* **117 B8** 19 50 S 46 51 E
Betamba, *Dem. Rep. of the Congo* **114 C4** 2 17 S 21 24 E
Betancuria, *Canary Is.* **9 e2** 28 25N 14 3W
Betancuria, Mt., *Canary Is.* **9 e2** 28 25N 14 6W
Betania, *Colombia* **168 C3** 4 22N 72 54W
Betanzos, *Bolivia* **173 D4** 19 34 S 65 27W
Betanzos, *Spain* **42 B2** 43 15N 8 12W
Bétaré Oya, *Cameroon* **114 A2** 5 40N 14 5 E
Betatao, *Madag.* **117 B8** 18 11 S 47 52 E
Bétera, *Spain* **41 F4** 39 35N 0 28W
Bétérou, *Benin* **113 D5** 9 12N 2 16 E
Bethal, *S. Africa* **117 D4** 26 27 S 29 28 E
Bethalto, *U.S.A.* **156 F6** 38 55N 90 2W
Bethanien, *Namibia* **116 D2** 26 31 S 17 8 E
Bethany, *Canada* **150 B6** 44 11N 78 34W
Bethany, *Ill., U.S.A.* **157 E8** 39 39N 88 45W
Bethany, *Mo., U.S.A.* **156 D2** 40 16N 94 2W
Bethel, *Alaska, U.S.A.* **144 F7** 60 48N 161 45W
Bethel, *Conn., U.S.A.* **151 E11** 41 22N 73 25W
Bethel, *Maine, U.S.A.* **151 B14** 44 25N 70 47W
Bethel, *Ohio, U.S.A.* **157 F12** 38 58N 84 5W
Bethel, *Vt., U.S.A.* **151 C12** 43 50N 72 38W
Bethel Park, *U.S.A.* **150 F4** 40 20N 80 1W
Béthenville, *France* **27 C11** 49 18N 4 23 E
Bethlehem = Bayt Lahm, *West Bank* **103 D4** 31 43N 35 12 E
Bethlehem, *S. Africa* **117 D4** 28 14 S 28 18 E
Bethlehem, *U.S.A.* **151 F9** 40 37N 75 23W
Bethulie, *S. Africa* **116 E4** 30 30 S 25 59 E
Béthune, *France* **27 B9** 50 30N 2 38 E
Béthune →, *France* **26 C8** 49 53N 1 4 E
Bethungra, *Australia* **129 C7** 34 45 S 147 51 E
Betijoque, *Venezuela* **168 B3** 9 23N 70 44W
Betioky, *Madag.* **117 C7** 23 48 S 44 20 E
Betong, *Thailand* **87 K3** 5 45N 101 5 E
Betoota, *Australia* **126 D3** 25 45 S 140 42 E
Betor, *Ethiopia* **107 E4** 11 37N 39 2 E
Bétou, *Congo* **114 B3** 3 2N 18 32 E
Betroka, *Madag.* **117 C8** 23 16 S 46 0 E
Betsiamites, *Canada* **141 C6** 48 56N 68 40W
Betsiamites →, *Canada* **141 C6** 48 56N 68 38W
Betsiboka →, *Madag.* **117 B8** 16 3 S 46 36 E
Bettendorf, *U.S.A.* **156 C6** 41 32N 90 30W
Bettiah, *India* **93 F11** 26 48N 84 33 E
Bettna, *Sweden* **17 F10** 58 55N 16 38 E
Béttola, *Italy* **44 D6** 44 47N 9 36 E
Betul, *India* **94 D3** 21 58N 77 59 E
Betung, *Malaysia* **85 B4** 1 24N 111 31 E
Betws-y-Coed, *U.K.* **20 D4** 53 5N 3 48W
Betxi, *Spain* **40 F4** 39 56N 0 12W
Betzdorf, *Germany* **30 E3** 50 46N 7 52 E
Béu, *Angola* **115 D3** 6 15 S 15 32 E
Beuil, *France* **29 D10** 44 6N 6 59 E
Beulah, *Australia* **128 C5** 35 58 S 142 29 E
Beulah, *Mich., U.S.A.* **148 C2** 44 38N 86 6W
Beulah, *N. Dak., U.S.A.* **154 B4** 47 16N 101 47W
Beurkia, *Chad* **109 E3** 15 20N 17 56 E
Beuvron →, *France* **26 E8** 47 29N 1 15 E
Beveren, *Belgium* **24 C4** 51 12N 4 16 E
Beverley, *Australia* **125 F2** 32 9 S 116 56 E
Beverley, *U.K.* **20 D7** 53 51N 0 26W
Beverley Hills, *U.S.A.* **149 L4** 28 56N 82 28W
Beverly, *U.S.A.* **151 D14** 42 33N 70 53W
Beverly Hills, *U.S.A.* **161 L8** 34 4N 118 25W
Beverungen, *Germany* **30 D5** 51 39N 9 22 E
Bevoalavo, *Madag.* **117 D7** 25 13 S 45 26 E
Bewani, *Papua N. G.* **83 B6** 3 2 S 141 10 E
Bewas →, *India* **93 H8** 23 59N 79 21 E
Bex, *Switz.* **32 D4** 46 15N 7 1 E
Bexhill, *U.K.* **21 G8** 50 51N 0 29 E
Bey Dağları, *Turkey* **49 E12** 36 38N 30 29 E
Beyānlū, *Iran* **96 C5** 36 0N 47 51 E
Beyazköy, *Turkey* **51 E11** 41 21N 27 42 E
Beyçayırı, *Turkey* **51 F10** 40 15N 26 55 E
Beydağ, *Turkey* **49 C10** 38 5N 28 13 E
Beyeğaç, *Turkey* **49 D10** 37 14N 28 53 E
Beyin, *Ghana* **112 D4** 5 1N 2 41W
Beykoz, *Turkey* **51 E13** 41 8N 29 7 E
Beyla, *Guinea* **112 D3** 8 30N 8 38W
Beynat, *France* **28 C5** 45 8N 1 44 E
Beyneu, *Kazakstan* **57 E10** 45 18N 55 9 E
Beyoba, *Turkey* **49 C9** 38 48N 27 47 E
Beyoğlu, *Turkey* **51 E12** 41 2N 29 0 E
Beypazarı, *Turkey* **100 B4** 40 10N 31 56 E
Beypore →, *India* **95 J2** 11 10N 75 47 E
Beyşehir, *Turkey* **100 D4** 37 41N 31 43 E
Beyşehir Gölü, *Turkey* **100 D4** 37 41N 31 33 E
Beytüşşebap, *Turkey* **101 D10** 37 35N 43 10 E
Bezau, *Austria* **33 B9** 47 23N 9 54 E
Bezdan, *Serbia, Yug.* **52 E3** 45 50N 18 57 E
Bezhetsk, *Russia* **58 D9** 57 47N 36 39 E
Béziers, *France* **28 E7** 43 20N 3 12 E
Bezwada = Vijayawada, *India* **94 F5** 16 31N 80 39 E
Bhabua, *India* **93 G10** 25 3N 83 37 E
Bhadar →, *Gujarat, India* **92 H5** 22 17N 72 20 E
Bhadar →, *Gujarat, India* **92 J3** 21 27N 69 47 E
Bhadarwah, *India* **93 C6** 32 58N 75 46 E
Bhadohi, *India* **93 G10** 25 25N 82 34 E
Bhadra, *India* **92 E6** 29 8N 75 14 E
Bhadra →, *India* **95 H2** 14 0N 75 20 E
Bhadrachalam, *India* **94 F5** 17 40N 80 53 E
Bhadrakh, *India* **94 D8** 21 10N 86 30 E
Bhadran, *India* **92 H5** 22 19N 72 6 E
Bhadravati, *India* **95 H2** 13 49N 75 40 E
Bhag, *Pakistan* **92 E2** 29 2N 67 49 E
Bhagalpur, *India* **93 G12** 25 10N 87 0 E
Bhagirathi →, *Uttaranchal, India* **93 D8** 30 8N 78 35 E
Bhagirathi →, *W. Bengal, India* **93 H13** 23 25N 88 23 E
Bhainsa, *India* **94 E3** 19 10N 77 58 E
Bhairab →, *Bangla.* **90 D2** 22 51N 89 34 E
Bhairab Bazar, *Bangla.* **90 C3** 24 4N 90 58 E
Bhakkar, *Pakistan* **91 C3** 31 40N 71 5 E
Bhakra Dam, *India* **92 D7** 31 30N 76 45 E
Bhaktapur, *Nepal* **93 F11** 27 38N 85 24 E
Bhalki, *India* **94 E3** 18 2N 77 13 E
Bhamo, *Burma* **90 C6** 24 15N 97 15 E
Bhamragarh, *India* **94 E5** 19 30N 80 40 E
Bhandara, *India* **94 D4** 21 5N 79 42 E
Bhanpura, *India* **92 G6** 24 31N 75 44 E
Bhanrer Ra., *India* **93 H8** 23 40N 79 45 E
Bhaptiahi, *India* **93 F12** 26 19N 86 44 E
Bharat = India ■, *Asia* **89 C6** 20 0N 78 0 E
Bharatpur, *Chhattisgarh, India* **93 H9** 23 44N 81 46 E
Bharatpur, *Raj., India* **92 F7** 27 15N 77 30 E
Bharno, *India* **93 H11** 23 14N 84 53 E
Bharuch, *India* **94 D1** 21 47N 73 0 E
Bhatghar L., *India* **94 E1** 18 10N 73 48 E
Bhatiapara Ghat, *Bangla.* **90 D2** 23 13N 89 42 E
Bhatinda, *India* **92 D6** 30 15N 74 57 E
Bhatkal, *India* **95 H2** 13 58N 74 35 E
Bhatpara, *India* **93 H13** 22 50N 88 25 E
Bhattu, *India* **92 E6** 29 36N 75 19 E
Bhaun, *Pakistan* **92 C5** 32 55N 72 40 E
Bhaunagar = Bhavnagar, *India* **94 D1** 21 45N 72 10 E
Bhavani, *India* **95 J3** 11 27N 77 43 E
Bhavnagar, *India* **94 D1** 21 45N 72 10 E
Bhawanipatna, *India* **94 E5** 19 55N 80 10 E
Bhawari, *India* **92 G5** 25 42N 73 4 E
Bhayavadar, *India* **92 J4** 21 51N 70 15 E
Bhera, *Pakistan* **92 C5** 32 29N 72 57 E
Bhikangaon, *India* **92 J6** 21 52N 75 57 E
Bhilai, *India* **94 D5** 21 13N 81 26 E
Bhilsa = Vidisha, *India* **92 H7** 23 28N 77 53 E
Bhilwara, *India* **92 G6** 25 25N 74 38 E
Bhima →, *India* **94 F3** 16 25N 77 17 E
Bhimavaram, *India* **95 F5** 16 30N 81 30 E
Bhimbar, *Pakistan* **93 C6** 32 59N 74 3 E
Bhind, *India* **93 F8** 26 30N 78 46 E
Bhinga, *India* **93 F9** 27 43N 81 56 E
Bhinmal, *India* **92 G5** 25 0N 72 15 E
Bhiwandi, *India* **94 E1** 19 20N 73 0 E
Bhiwani, *India* **92 E7** 28 50N 76 9 E
Bhogava →, *India* **92 H5** 22 26N 72 20 E
Bhokardan, *India* **94 D3** 20 16N 75 46 E
Bhola, *Bangla.* **90 D3** 22 45N 90 35 E
Bholari, *Pakistan* **92 G3** 25 19N 68 13 E
Bhongir, *India* **94 F4** 17 30N 78 56 E
Bhopal, *India* **92 H7** 23 20N 77 30 E
Bhopalpatnam, *India* **94 E5** 18 52N 80 23 E
Bhor, *India* **94 E1** 18 12N 73 53 E
Bhubaneshwar, *India* **94 D7** 20 15N 85 50 E
Bhuj, *India* **92 H3** 23 15N 69 49 E
Bhusaval, *India* **94 D2** 21 3N 75 46 E
Bhutan ■, *Asia* **90 B3** 27 25N 90 30 E
Biá →, *Brazil* **168 D4** 3 28 S 67 23W
Biafra, B. of = Bonny, Bight of, *Africa* **113 E6** 3 30N 9 20 E
Biak, *Indonesia* **83 B5** 1 10 S 136 6 E
Biała, *Poland* **55 H4** 50 24N 17 40 E
Biała →, *Poland* **55 H7** 50 3N 20 55 E
Biała Piska, *Poland* **54 E9** 53 37N 22 5 E
Biała Podlaska, *Poland* **55 F10** 52 4N 23 6 E
Biała Rawska, *Poland* **55 G7** 51 48N 20 29 E
Białobrzegi, *Poland* **55 G7** 51 39N 20 57 E
Białogard, *Poland* **54 D2** 54 2N 15 58 E

Białowieża, *Poland* **55 F10** 52 41N 23 49 E
Biały Bór, *Poland* **54 E3** 53 53N 16 51 E
Białystok, *Poland* **55 E10** 53 10N 23 10 E
Bian →, *Indonesia* **83 C5** 8 6 S 139 58 E
Biancavilla, *Italy* **47 E7** 37 38N 14 52 E
Bianco, *Italy* **47 D9** 38 5N 16 9 E
Biankouma, *Ivory C.* **112 D3** 7 50N 7 40W
Biaora, *India* **92 H7** 23 56N 76 56 E
Bīārjmand, *Iran* **97 B7** 36 6N 55 53 E
Biaro, *Indonesia* **82 A3** 2 5N 125 26 E
Biarritz, *France* **28 E2** 43 29N 1 33W
Bias, *Indonesia* **79 J18** 8 24 S 115 36 E
Biasca, *Switz.* **33 D7** 46 22N 8 58 E
Biavela, *Angola* **115 E3** 14 43 S 19 47 E
Biba, *Egypt* **106 J7** 28 55N 31 0 E
Bibai, *Japan* **70 C10** 43 19N 141 52 E
Bibala, *Angola* **115 E2** 14 44 S 13 24 E
Bibane, Bahiret el, *Tunisia* **108 B2** 33 16N 11 13 E
Bibassé, *Gabon* **114 B2** 1 27N 11 37 E
Bibbiena, *Italy* **45 E8** 43 42N 11 49 E
Bibby I., *Canada* **143 A10** 61 55N 93 0W
Bibel →, *Spain* **42 C3** 42 24N 7 13W
Biberach, *Germany* **31 G5** 48 5N 9 47 E
Biberist, *Switz.* **32 B5** 47 11N 7 34 E
Bibi, *Papua N. G.* **132 C4** 5 30 S 146 2 E
Bibiani, *Ghana* **112 D4** 6 30N 2 8W
Bibile, *Sri Lanka* **95 L5** 7 10N 81 25 E
Bibungwa, *Dem. Rep. of the Congo* **118 C2** 2 40 S 28 15 E
Bic, *Canada* **141 C6** 48 20N 68 41W
Bicaj, *Albania* **50 E4** 41 58N 20 25 E
Bicaz, *Romania* **53 D11** 46 53N 26 5 E
Bicazu Ardelean, *Romania* **53 D10** 46 51N 25 56 E
Bíccari, *Italy* **47 A8** 41 23N 15 12 E
Bicester, *U.K.* **21 F6** 51 54N 1 9W
Bichena, *Ethiopia* **107 E4** 10 28N 38 10 E
Bicheno, *Australia* **127 G4** 41 52 S 148 18 E
Bichia, *India* **93 H9** 22 27N 80 42 E
Bichvinta, *Georgia* **61 J5** 43 9N 40 21 E
Bickerton I., *Australia* **126 A2** 13 45 S 136 10 E
Bicknell, *U.S.A.* **157 F9** 38 47N 87 19W
Bicske, *Hungary* **52 C3** 47 29N 18 38 E
Bicuar, Parque Nacional do, *Angola* **115 F2** 15 14 S 14 45 E
Bida, *Dem. Rep. of the Congo* **114 B3** 4 55N 19 56 E
Bida, *Nigeria* **113 D6** 9 3N 5 58 E
Bidar, *India* **94 F3** 17 55N 77 35 E
Biddeford, *U.S.A.* **149 D10** 43 30N 70 28W
Biddwara, *Ethiopia* **107 F4** 5 11N 38 34 E
Bideford, *U.K.* **21 F3** 51 1N 4 13W
Bideford Bay, *U.K.* **21 F3** 51 5N 4 20W
Bidhuna, *India* **93 F8** 26 49N 79 31 E
Bidon 5 = Poste Maurice Cortier, *Algeria* **111 D5** 22 14N 1 2 E
Bidor, *Malaysia* **87 K3** 4 6N 101 15 E
Bidzar, *Cameroon* **114 A2** 9 54N 14 7 E
Bie, *Sweden* **16 E10** 59 5N 16 12 E
Bié □, *Angola* **115 E3** 12 30 S 17 0 E
Bié, Planalto de, *Angola* **115 E3** 12 0 S 16 0 E
Bieber, *U.S.A.* **158 F3** 41 7N 121 8W
Biebrza →, *Poland* **55 E9** 53 13N 22 25 E
Biecz, *Poland* **55 J8** 49 44N 21 15 E
Biel, *Switz.* **32 B4** 47 8N 7 14 E
Bielawa, *Poland* **55 H3** 50 43N 16 37 E
Bielefeld, *Germany* **30 C4** 52 1N 8 33 E
Bielersee, *Switz.* **32 B4** 47 6N 7 5 E
Biella, *Italy* **44 C5** 45 34N 8 3 E
Bielsk Podlaski, *Poland* **55 F10** 52 47N 23 12 E
Bielsko-Biała, *Poland* **55 J6** 49 50N 19 2 E
Bien Hoa, *Vietnam* **87 G6** 10 57N 106 49 E
Bienne = Biel, *Switz.* **32 B4** 47 8N 7 14 E
Bienno, *Italy* **33 E10** 45 56N 10 18 E
Bienvenida, *Spain* **43 G4** 38 18N 6 12W
Bienvenue, *Fr. Guiana* **169 C7** 3 0N 52 30W
Bienville, L., *Canada* **140 A5** 55 5N 72 40W
Bière, *Switz.* **32 C2** 46 33N 6 20 E
Bierné, *France* **26 E6** 47 48N 0 33W
Bierun, *Poland* **55 H6** 50 6N 19 6 E
Bierutów, *Poland* **55 G4** 51 7N 17 32 E
Biescas, *Spain* **40 C4** 42 37N 0 20W
Biese →, *Germany* **30 C7** 52 53N 11 46 E
Biesiesfontein, *S. Africa* **116 E2** 30 57 S 17 58 E
Bietigheim-Bissingen, *Germany* **31 G5** 48 58N 9 8 E
Bieżuń, *Poland* **55 F6** 52 58N 19 55 E
Biferno →, *Italy* **45 G12** 41 59N 15 2 E
Bifoum, *Gabon* **114 C2** 0 20 S 10 23 E
Big →, *Canada* **141 B8** 54 50N 58 55W
Big →, *U.S.A.* **156 F6** 38 28N 90 37W
Big B., *Canada* **141 A7** 55 43N 60 35W
Big Bear City, *U.S.A.* **161 L10** 34 16N 116 51W
Big Bear Lake, *U.S.A.* **161 L10** 34 15N 116 56W
Big Belt Mts., *U.S.A.* **158 C8** 46 30N 111 25W
Big Bend, *Swaziland* **117 D5** 26 50 S 31 58 E
Big Bend Nat. Park, *U.S.A.* **155 L3** 29 20N 103 5W
Big Black →, *U.S.A.* **155 K9** 32 3N 91 4W
Big Blue →, *Ind., U.S.A.* **157 E11** 39 12N 85 56W
Big Blue →, *Kans., U.S.A.* **154 F6** 39 35N 96 34W
Big Creek, *U.S.A.* **160 H7** 37 11N 119 14W
Big Cypress Nat. Preserve, *U.S.A.* **149 M5** 26 0N 81 10W
Big Cypress Swamp, *U.S.A.* **153 J8** 26 15N 81 30W
Big Delta, *U.S.A.* **144 D11** 64 10N 145 51W
Big Falls, *U.S.A.* **154 A8** 48 12N 93 48W
Big Fork →, *U.S.A.* **154 A8** 48 31N 93 43W
Big Horn Mts. = Bighorn Mts., *U.S.A.* **158 D10** 44 30N 107 30W
Big I., *Canada* **142 A5** 61 7N 116 45W
Big Lake, *U.S.A.* **155 K4** 31 12N 101 28W
Big Moose, *U.S.A.* **151 C10** 43 49N 74 58W
Big Muddy →, *U.S.A.* **156 G8** 38 0N 89 0W
Big Muddy Cr. →, *U.S.A.* **154 A2** 48 8N 104 36W
Big Pine, *Calif., U.S.A.* **160 H8** 37 10N 118 17W
Big Pine, *Fla., U.S.A.* **153 L8** 24 40N 81 21W
Big Piney, *U.S.A.* **158 E8** 42 32N 110 7W
Big Rapids, *U.S.A.* **148 D3** 43 42N 85 29W
Big Rideau L., *Canada* **151 B8** 44 40N 76 15W
Big River, *Canada* **143 C7** 53 50N 107 0W
Big Run, *U.S.A.* **150 F6** 40 57N 78 55W
Big Sable Pt., *U.S.A.* **148 C2** 44 3N 86 1W
Big Salmon →, *Canada* **142 A2** 61 52N 134 55W
Big Sand L., *Canada* **143 B9** 57 45N 99 45W
Big Sandy, *U.S.A.* **158 B8** 48 11N 110 7W
Big Sandy →, *U.S.A.* **148 F4** 38 25N 82 36W
Big Sandy Cr. →, *U.S.A.* **154 F3** 38 7N 102 29W
Big Satilla →, *U.S.A.* **152 D7** 31 27N 82 3W
Big Sioux →, *U.S.A.* **154 D6** 42 29N 96 27W
Big Spring, *U.S.A.* **155 J4** 32 15N 101 28W
Big Stone City, *U.S.A.* **154 C6** 45 18N 96 28W
Big Stone Gap, *U.S.A.* **149 G4** 36 52N 82 47W
Big Stone L., *U.S.A.* **154 C6** 45 30N 96 35W
Big Sur, *U.S.A.* **160 J5** 36 15N 121 48W
Big Timber, *U.S.A.* **158 D9** 45 50N 109 57W
Big Trout L., *Canada* **140 B2** 53 40N 90 0W
Big Trout Lake, *Canada* **140 B2** 53 45N 90 0W
Biğa, *Turkey* **51 F11** 40 13N 27 14 E
Biga →, *Turkey* **51 F11** 40 20N 27 14 E
Bigadiç, *Turkey* **49 B10** 39 22N 28 7 E
Biganos, *France* **28 D3** 44 39N 0 59W
Biggar, *Canada* **143 C7** 52 4N 108 0W
Biggar, *U.K.* **22 F5** 55 38N 3 32W
Bigge I., *Australia* **124 B4** 14 35 S 125 10 E
Biggenden, *Australia* **127 D5** 25 31 S 152 4 E
Biggleswade, *U.K.* **21 E7** 52 5N 0 14W
Biggs, *U.S.A.* **160 F5** 39 25N 121 43W
Bighorn, *U.S.A.* **158 C10** 46 10N 107 27W
Bighorn →, *U.S.A.* **158 C10** 46 10N 107 28W
Bighorn L., *U.S.A.* **158 D9** 44 55N 108 15W
Bighorn Mts., *U.S.A.* **158 D10** 44 30N 107 30W
Bigi, *Dem. Rep. of the Congo* **114 B4** 3 2N 22 25 E
Bignasco, *Switz.* **33 D7** 46 21N 8 37 E
Bignona, *Senegal* **112 C1** 12 52N 16 14W
Bigorre, *France* **28 E4** 43 10N 0 5 E
Bigstone L., *Canada* **143 C9** 53 42N 95 44W
Biguglia, Étang de, *France* **29 F13** 42 36N 9 29 E
Bigwa, *Tanzania* **118 D4** 7 10 S 39 10 E
Bihać, *Bos.-H.* **45 D12** 44 49N 15 57 E
Bihar, *India* **93 G11** 25 5N 85 40 E
Bihar □, *India* **93 G12** 25 0N 86 0 E
Biharamulo, *Tanzania* **118 C3** 2 25 S 31 25 E
Biharamulo Game Reserve, *Tanzania* **118 C3** 2 24 S 31 26 E
Bihariganj, *India* **93 G12** 25 44N 86 59 E
Biharkeresztes, *Hungary* **52 C6** 47 8N 21 44 E
Bihor □, *Romania* **52 D7** 47 0N 22 10 E
Bihor, Munţii, *Romania* **52 D7** 46 29N 22 47 E
Bijagós, Arquipélago dos, *Guinea-Biss.* **112 C1** 11 15N 16 10W
Bijaipur, *India* **92 F7** 26 2N 77 20 E
Bijapur, *Chhattisgarh, India* **94 E5** 18 50N 80 50 E
Bijapur, *Karnataka, India* **94 F2** 16 50N 75 55 E
Bījār, *Iran* **101 E12** 35 52N 47 35 E
Bijawar, *India* **93 G8** 24 38N 79 30 E
Bijeljina, *Bos.-H.* **52 F4** 44 46N 19 14 E
Bijelo Polje, *Montenegro, Yug.* **50 C3** 43 1N 19 45 E
Bijie, *China* **76 D5** 27 20N 105 16 E
Bijnor, *India* **92 E8** 29 27N 78 11 E
Bikaner, *India* **92 E5** 28 2N 73 18 E
Bikapur, *India* **93 F10** 26 30N 82 7 E
Bikeqi, *China* **74 D6** 40 43N 111 20 E
Bikfayyā, *Lebanon* **103 B4** 33 55N 35 41 E
Bikié, *Congo* **114 C2** 3 7 S 13 52 E
Bikin, *Russia* **67 E14** 46 50N 134 20 E
Bikin →, *Russia* **70 A7** 46 51N 134 2 E
Bikini Atoll, *Marshall Is.* **134 F8** 12 0N 167 30 E
Bikita, *Zimbabwe* **117 C5** 20 6 S 31 41 E
Bīkkū Bīttī, *Libya* **109 D3** 22 0N 19 12 E
Bikoro, *Dem. Rep. of the Congo* **114 C3** 0 48 S 18 15 E
Bikoué, *Cameroon* **113 E7** 3 55N 11 50 E
Bila Tserkva, *Ukraine* **59 H6** 49 45N 30 10 E
Bilanga, *Burkina Faso* **113 C4** 12 40N 0 1W
Bilara, *India* **92 F5** 26 14N 73 53 E
Bilasipara, *India* **90 B3** 26 13N 90 14 E
Bilaspur, *Chhattisgarh, India* **93 H10** 22 2N 82 15 E
Bilaspur, *Punjab, India* **92 D7** 31 19N 76 50 E
Biläsuvar, *Azerbaijan* **101 C13** 39 27N 48 32 E
Bilauk Taungdan, *Thailand* **86 F2** 13 0N 99 0 E
Bilbao, *Spain* **40 B2** 43 16N 2 56W
Bilbeis, *Egypt* **106 H7** 30 25N 31 34 E
Bilbo = Bilbao, *Spain* **40 B2** 43 16N 2 56W
Bilbor, *Romania* **53 C10** 47 6N 25 30 E
Bilciureşti, *Romania* **53 F10** 44 44N 25 48 E
Bíldudalur, *Iceland* **11 B3** 65 41N 23 36W
Bílé Karpaty, *Europe* **35 B11** 49 5N 18 0 E
Bileća, *Bos.-H.* **50 D2** 42 53N 18 27 E
Bilecik, *Turkey* **100 B4** 40 5N 30 5 E
Biłgoraj, *Poland* **55 H9** 50 33N 22 42 E
Bilgram, *India* **93 F9** 27 11N 80 2 E
Bilhaur, *India* **93 F9** 26 51N 80 5 E
Bilhorod-Dnistrovskyy, *Ukraine* **59 J6** 46 11N 30 23 E
Bili →, *Dem. Rep. of the Congo* **114 B4** 4 9N 22 29 E
Bilibino, *Russia* **67 C17** 68 3N 166 20 E
Bilibiza, *Mozam.* **119 E5** 12 30 S 40 20 E
Bīliköl, *Kazakstan* **65 B5** 43 5N 70 45 E
Bilimora, *India* **94 D1** 20 45N 72 57 E
Bilin, *Burma* **90 G6** 17 14N 97 15 E
Biliran □, *Phil.* **81 F5** 11 35N 124 28 E
Bilisht, *Albania* **50 F5** 40 37N 21 2 E
Billabalong Roadhouse, *Australia* **125 E2** 27 25 S 115 49 E
Billabong Cr. →, *Australia* **128 C6** 35 5 S 144 2 E
Billdal, *Sweden* **17 G5** 57 35N 11 57 E
Billiluna, *Australia* **124 C4** 19 37 S 127 41 E
Billings, *U.S.A.* **158 D9** 45 47N 108 30W
Billiton Is. = Belitung, *Indonesia* **85 C3** 3 10 S 107 50 E
Billsta, *Sweden* **16 A12** 63 20N 18 28 E
Billund, *Denmark* **17 J3** 55 44N 9 6 E
Bilma, *Niger* **109 E2** 18 50N 13 30 E
Bilo Gora, *Croatia* **52 E2** 45 53N 17 15 E
Biloela, *Australia* **126 C5** 24 24 S 150 31 E
Bilohirsk, *Ukraine* **59 K8** 45 3N 34 35 E
Biloku, *Guyana* **169 C6** 1 50N 58 25W
Biloli, *India* **94 E3** 18 46N 77 44 E
Bilopillya, *Ukraine* **59 G8** 51 14N 34 20 E
Biloxi, *U.S.A.* **155 K10** 30 24N 88 53W
Bilpa Morea Claypan, *Australia* **126 D3** 25 0 S 140 0 E
Biltine, *Chad* **109 F4** 14 40N 20 50 E
Bilugyun, *Burma* **90 G6** 16 24N 97 32 E
Bilyarsk, *Russia* **60 C10** 54 58N 50 22 E
Bima, *Indonesia* **85 D5** 8 22 S 118 49 E
Bimban, *Egypt* **106 C3** 24 24N 32 54 E
Bimbe, *Angola* **115 E3** 11 50 S 15 50 E
Bimberi Pk., *Australia* **129 C8** 35 44 S 148 51 E
Bimbila, *Ghana* **113 D5** 8 54N 0 5 E
Bimbo, *C.A.R.* **114 B3** 4 15N 18 33 E
Bimini Is., *Bahamas* **164 A4** 25 42N 79 25W
Bin Xian, *Heilongjiang, China* **75 B14** 45 42N 127 32 E
Bin Xian, *Shaanxi, China* **74 G5** 35 2N 108 4 E
Bin Yauri, *Nigeria* **113 C5** 10 46N 4 45 E
Bina-Etawah, *India* **92 G8** 24 13N 78 14 E
Bināb, *Iran* **97 B6** 36 35N 48 41 E
Binaiya, *Indonesia* **83 B3** 3 11 S 129 26 E
Binalbagan, *Phil.* **81 F4** 10 12N 122 50 E
Binalong, *Australia* **129 C8** 34 40 S 148 39 E
Bīnālūd, Kūh-e, *Iran* **97 B8** 36 30N 58 30 E
Binatang = Bintangor, *Malaysia* **85 B4** 2 10N 111 40 E
Binche, *Belgium* **24 D4** 50 26N 4 10 E
Binchuan, *China* **76 E3** 25 42N 100 38 E
Binda, *Dem. Rep. of the Congo* **115 D2** 5 52 S 13 14 E
Binder, *Chad* **113 D7** 9 56N 14 27 E
Bindki, *India* **93 F9** 26 2N 80 36 E
Bindoy, *Phil.* **81 G4** 9 48N 123 5 E
Bindslev, *Denmark* **17 G4** 57 33N 10 11 E
Bindura, *Zimbabwe* **119 F3** 17 18 S 31 18 E
Binefar, *Spain* **40 D5** 41 51N 0 18 E
Bingara, *Australia* **127 D5** 29 52 S 150 36 E
Bingaram I., *India* **95 J1** 10 56N 72 17 E
Bingen, *Germany* **31 F3** 49 57N 7 55 E
Bingerville, *Ivory C.* **112 D4** 5 18N 3 49W
Bingham, *U.S.A.* **149 C11** 45 3N 69 53W
Binghamton, *U.S.A.* **151 D9** 42 6N 75 55W
Bingo-Ochiai, *Japan* **72 C4** 34 59N 133 8 E
Bingöl, *Turkey* **101 C9** 38 53N 40 29 E
Bingöl Dağları, *Turkey* **101 C9** 39 16N 41 9 E
Bingsjö, *Sweden* **16 C9** 61 1N 15 39 E
Binh Dinh = An Nhon, *Vietnam* **86 F7** 13 55N 109 7 E
Binh Khe, *Vietnam* **86 F7** 13 57N 108 51 E
Binh Son, *Vietnam* **86 E7** 15 20N 108 40 E
Binhai, *China* **75 G10** 34 2N 119 49 E
Bini Erde, *Chad* **109 D3** 20 6N 18 1 E
Binic, *France* **26 D4** 48 46N 2 50W
Binisatua, *Spain* **38 B5** 39 50N 4 11 E
Binjai, *Indonesia* **84 B1** 3 20N 98 30 E
Binji, *Nigeria* **113 C5** 13 10N 4 55 E
Binka, *India* **94 D6** 21 2N 83 48 E
Binnaway, *Australia* **129 A8** 31 28 S 149 24 E
Binningen, *Switz.* **32 A5** 47 32N 7 34 E
Binongko, *Indonesia* **82 C2** 5 57 S 124 2 E
Binscarth, *Canada* **143 C8** 50 37N 101 17W
Bint Goda, *Sudan* **107 E3** 13 17N 31 33 E
Bintan, *Indonesia* **84 B2** 1 0N 104 0 E
Bintangor, *Malaysia* **85 B4** 2 10N 111 40 E
Bintulu, *Malaysia* **78 D4** 3 10N 113 0 E
Bintuni, *Indonesia* **83 B4** 2 7 S 133 32 E
Bintuni, Teluk, *Indonesia* **83 B4** 2 20 S 133 30 E
Binyang, *China* **76 F7** 23 12N 108 47 E
Binz, *Germany* **30 A9** 54 24N 13 35 E
Binza, *Dem. Rep. of the Congo* **115 C3** 4 21 S 15 14 E
Binzert = Bizerte, *Tunisia* **108 A1** 37 15N 9 50 E
Binzhou, *China* **75 F10** 37 20N 118 2 E
Bío Bío □, *Chile* **174 D1** 37 35 S 72 0W
Biograd na Moru, *Croatia* **45 E12** 43 56N 15 29 E
Bioko, *Eq. Guin.* **113 E6** 3 30N 8 40 E
Biokovo, *Croatia* **45 E14** 43 23N 17 0 E
Biougra, *Morocco* **110 B3** 30 15N 9 14W
Bipindi, *Cameroon* **113 E7** 3 6N 10 30 E
Bir, *India* **94 E2** 19 4N 75 46 E
Bir, Ras, *Djibouti* **107 E5** 12 0N 43 20 E
Bîr Abu Hashim, *Egypt* **106 C3** 23 42N 34 6 E
Bîr Abu Minqar, *Egypt* **106 B2** 26 33N 27 33 E
Bîr Abu Muḩammad, *Egypt* **103 F3** 29 44N 34 14 E
Bi'r ad Dabbāghāt, *Jordan* **103 E4** 30 26N 35 32 E
Bîr Adal Deib, *Sudan* **106 C4** 22 35N 36 10 E
Bi'r al Butayyihāt, *Jordan* **103 F4** 29 47N 35 20 E
Bi'r al Mārī, *Jordan* **103 E4** 30 4N 35 33 E
Bi'r al Qattār, *Jordan* **103 F4** 29 47N 35 32 E
Bir 'Ali, *Yemen* **99 D5** 14 1N 48 20 E
Bir Aouine, *Tunisia* **108 B1** 32 25N 9 18 E
Bîr 'Asal, *Egypt* **106 B3** 25 55N 34 20 E
Bir Atrun, *Sudan* **106 D2** 18 15N 26 40 E
Bîr Beiḍa, *Egypt* **103 E3** 30 25N 34 29 E
Bîr Bel Guerdâne, *Mauritania* **110 C2** 25 24N 10 31W
Bi'r Dhu'fān, *Libya* **108 B2** 31 59N 14 32 E
Bîr Diqnash, *Egypt* **106 A2** 31 3N 25 23 E
Bir el Abbes, *Algeria* **110 C3** 26 7N 6 9W
Bîr el 'Abd, *Egypt* **103 D2** 31 2N 33 0 E
Bir el Ater, *Algeria* **111 B6** 34 46N 8 3 E
Bîr el Basur, *Egypt* **106 B2** 29 51N 25 49 E
Bîr el Biarât, *Egypt* **103 F3** 29 30N 34 43 E
Bîr el Duweidar, *Egypt* **103 E1** 30 56N 32 32 E
Bîr el Garârât, *Egypt* **103 D2** 31 3N 33 34 E
Bîr el Gâreb, *Mauritania* **110 D1** 20 33N 16 12W
Bîr el Gellaz, *Egypt* **106 A2** 30 50N 26 40 E
Bîr el Heisi, *Egypt* **103 F3** 29 22N 34 36 E
Bîr el Jafir, *Egypt* **103 E1** 30 50N 32 41 E
Bîr el Mâlḩi, *Egypt* **103 E2** 30 38N 33 19 E
Bîr el Shaqqa, *Egypt* **106 A2** 30 54N 25 1 E
Bîr el Thamâda, *Egypt* **103 E2** 30 12N 33 27 E
Bîr Enzarán, *W. Sahara* **110 D2** 23 53N 14 32W
Bîr Fuad, *Egypt* **106 A2** 30 35N 26 28 E
Bîr Gandús, *W. Sahara* **110 D1** 21 36N 16 30W
Bir Gara, *Chad* **109 F3** 13 11N 15 58 E
Bîr Gebeil Ḩişn, *Egypt* **103 E2** 30 2N 33 18 E
Bi'r Ghadīr, *Syria* **103 A6** 34 6N 37 3 E
Bîr Haimur, *Egypt* **106 C3** 22 45N 33 40 E
Bîr Ḩasana, *Egypt* **103 E2** 30 29N 33 46 E
Bîr Hōōker, *Egypt* **106 H7** 30 22N 30 21 E
Bi'r Īdimah, *Si. Arabia* **98 C4** 18 31N 44 12 E
Bir Jdid, *Morocco* **110 B3** 33 26N 8 0W
Bîr Kanayis, *Egypt* **106 C3** 24 59N 33 15 E
Bîr Kaseiba, *Egypt* **103 E2** 31 0N 33 17 E
Bîr Kerawein, *Egypt* **106 B2** 27 10N 28 25 E
Bîr Lahfân, *Egypt* **103 E2** 31 0N 33 51 E
Bir Lahrache, *Algeria* **111 B6** 32 1N 8 12 E
Bîr Madkûr, *Egypt* **103 E1** 30 44N 32 33 E
Bîr Maql, *Egypt* **106 C3** 23 7N 33 40 E
Bir Mîneiga, *Sudan* **106 C4** 22 47N 35 12 E
Bîr Misaha, *Egypt* **106 C2** 22 13N 27 59 E
Bîr Mogreïn, *Mauritania* **110 C2** 25 10N 11 25W
Bîr Murr, *Egypt* **106 C3** 23 28N 30 10 E
Bi'r Muţribah, *Kuwait* **96 D5** 29 54N 47 17 E
Bîr Nakheila, *Egypt* **106 C3** 24 1N 30 50 E
Bîr Qaţia, *Egypt* **103 E1** 30 58N 32 45 E
Bîr Qatrani, *Egypt* **106 A2** 30 55N 26 10 E
Bîr Ranga, *Egypt* **106 C4** 24 25N 35 15 E
Bîr Sahara, *Egypt* **106 C2** 22 54N 28 40 E
Bîr Seiyâla, *Egypt* **106 B3** 26 10N 33 50 E
Bir Semguine, *Morocco* **110 B3** 30 1N 5 39W
Bîr Shalatein, *Egypt* **106 C4** 23 5N 35 25 E
Bîr Shebb, *Egypt* **106 C2** 22 25N 29 40 E
Bîr Shût, *Egypt* **106 C4** 23 50N 35 15 E
Bîr Terfawi, *Egypt* **106 C2** 22 57N 28 55 E
Bi'r Tin Abunda, *Libya* **111 C7** 26 28N 12 27 E
Bîr Umm Qubûr, *Egypt* **106 C3** 24 35N 34 2 E
Bîr Ungât, *Egypt* **106 C3** 22 8N 33 48 E
Bîr Za'farâna, *Egypt* **106 J8** 29 10N 32 40 E
Bîr Zāmūs, *Libya* **108 D3** 24 16N 15 6 E
Bîr Zeidûn, *Egypt* **106 B3** 25 45N 33 40 E
Bira, *Indonesia* **83 B4** 2 3 S 132 2 E
Biramféro, *Guinea* **112 C3** 11 40N 9 10W
Birao, *C.A.R.* **114 A4** 10 20N 22 47 E
Biratnagar, *Nepal* **93 F12** 26 27N 87 17 E
Birawa, *Dem. Rep. of the Congo* **118 C2** 2 20 S 28 48 E
Birch →, *Canada* **142 B6** 58 28N 112 17W
Birch Hills, *Canada* **143 C7** 52 59N 105 25W
Birch I., *Canada* **143 C9** 52 26N 99 54W
Birch L., *N.W.T., Canada* **142 A5** 62 4N 116 33W
Birch L., *Ont., Canada* **140 B1** 51 23N 92 18W
Birch Mts., *Canada* **142 B6** 57 30N 113 10W
Birch River, *Canada* **143 C8** 52 24N 101 6W
Birchip, *Australia* **128 C5** 35 56 S 142 55 E
Birchiş, *Romania* **52 E7** 45 58N 22 9 E
Birchwood, *N.Z.* **131 F2** 45 55 S 167 53 E
Bird, *Canada* **143 B10** 56 30N 94 13W
Bird I. = Las Aves, Is., *W. Indies* **165 C7** 15 45N 63 55W
Birdseye, *U.S.A.* **157 F10** 38 19N 86 42W
Birdsville, *Australia* **126 D2** 25 51 S 139 20 E
Birdum Cr. →, *Australia* **124 C5** 15 14 S 133 0 E
Birdwood, *Australia* **128 C3** 34 51 S 138 58 E
Birecik, *Turkey* **101 D8** 37 2N 38 0 E
Birein, *Israel* **103 E3** 30 50N 34 28 E
Bireuen, *Indonesia* **84 A1** 5 14N 96 39 E
Biri, *Norway* **18 D7** 60 58N 10 35 E
Biri →, *Sudan* **107 F2** 7 56N 26 33 E
Birifo, *Gambia* **112 C2** 13 30N 14 0W
Birigui, *Brazil* **175 A5** 21 18 S 50 16W
Birini, *C.A.R.* **114 A4** 7 51N 22 24 E
Birjand, *Iran* **97 C8** 32 53N 59 13 E
Birkeland, *Norway* **18 F4** 58 24N 7 12 E
Birkenfeld, *Germany* **31 F3** 49 38N 7 9 E
Birkenhead, *N.Z.* **130 C3** 36 49 S 174 46 E
Birkenhead, *U.K.* **20 D4** 53 23N 3 2W
Birkerød, *Denmark* **17 J6** 55 50N 12 25 E
Birket Fatmé, *Chad* **109 F3** 12 55N 19 7 E
Birket Qârûn, *Egypt* **106 J7** 29 30N 30 40 E
Birkfeld, *Austria* **34 D8** 47 21N 15 45 E
Birkhadem, *Algeria* **111 A5** 36 43N 3 3 E
Birkirkara, *Malta* **38 F7** 35 54N 14 28 E
Bîrlad = Bârlad, *Romania* **53 D12** 46 15N 27 38 E
Birlik, *Kazakstan* **65 B6** 43 40N 73 49 E
Birlik, *Kazakstan* **65 A6** 44 5N 73 31 E
Birmingham, *U.K.* **21 E6** 52 29N 1 52W
Birmingham, *Ala., U.S.A.* **149 J2** 33 31N 86 48W
Birmingham, *Iowa, U.S.A.* **156 D5** 40 53N 91 57W
Birmitrapur, *India* **94 C7** 22 24N 84 46 E
Birni Ngaouré, *Niger* **113 C5** 13 5N 2 51 E
Birni Nkonni, *Niger* **113 C6** 13 55N 5 15 E
Birnin Gwari, *Nigeria* **113 C6** 11 0N 6 45 E
Birnin Kebbi, *Nigeria* **113 C5** 12 32N 4 12 E
Birnin Kudu, *Nigeria* **113 C6** 11 30N 9 29 E
Birobidzhan, *Russia* **67 E14** 48 50N 132 50 E
Birougou, Mts., *Gabon* **114 C2** 1 51 S 12 20 E
Birr, *Ireland* **23 C4** 53 6N 7 54W
Birrie →, *Australia* **127 D4** 29 43 S 146 37 E
Birs →, *Switz.* **32 B5** 47 24N 7 32 E
Birsilpur, *India* **92 E5** 28 11N 72 15 E
Birsk, *Russia* **64 D5** 55 25N 55 30 E
Birštonas, *Lithuania* **54 D11** 54 37N 24 2 E
Birtle, *Canada* **143 C8** 50 30N 101 5W
Biryuchiy, *Ukraine* **59 J8** 46 10N 35 0 E
Biržai, *Lithuania* **15 H21** 56 11N 24 45 E
Birzebbugga, *Malta* **38 F8** 35 50N 14 32 E
Bisa, *Indonesia* **82 B3** 1 15 S 127 28 E
Bisáccia, *Italy* **47 A8** 41 1N 15 22 E
Bisacquino, *Italy* **46 E6** 37 42N 13 15 E
Bisai, *Japan* **73 B8** 35 16N 136 44 E
Bisalpur, *India* **93 E8** 28 14N 79 48 E
Bisbee, *U.S.A.* **159 L9** 31 27N 109 55W
Biscarrosse, *France* **28 D2** 44 22N 1 20W
Biscarrosse et de Parentis, Étang de, *France* **28 D2** 44 21N 1 10W
Biscay, B. of, *Atl. Oc.* **8 B11** 45 0N 2 0W
Biscayne B., *U.S.A.* **149 N5** 25 40N 80 12W
Biscéglie, *Italy* **47 A9** 41 14N 16 30 E
Bischheim, *France* **27 D14** 48 37N 7 46 E
Bischofshofen, *Austria* **34 D6** 47 26N 13 14 E
Bischofswerda, *Germany* **30 D10** 51 7N 14 10 E
Bischofszell, *Switz.* **33 B8** 47 29N 9 15 E
Bischwiller, *France* **27 D14** 48 46N 7 50 E
Biscoe Bay, *Antarctica* **7 D13** 77 0 S 152 0W
Biscoe Is., *Antarctica* **7 C17** 66 0 S 67 0W
Biscoitos, *Azores* **9 d1** 38 47N 27 15W
Biscostasing, *Canada* **140 C3** 47 18N 82 9W
Biševo, *Croatia* **45 F13** 42 57N 16 3 E
Bisha, *Eritrea* **107 D4** 15 30N 37 31 E
Bishah, W. →, *Si. Arabia* **98 B3** 21 24N 43 26 E
Bishan, *China* **76 C6** 29 33N 106 12 E
Bishanga, *Dem. Rep. of the Congo* **115 C4** 4 31 S 21 2 E
Bishkek, *Kyrgyzstan* **66 E8** 42 54N 74 46 E
Bishnath, *India* **90 B4** 26 40N 93 10 E
Bishnupur, *India* **93 H12** 23 8N 87 20 E
Bisho, *S. Africa* **117 E4** 32 50 S 27 23 E
Bishop, *Calif., U.S.A.* **160 H8** 37 22N 118 24W
Bishop, *Ga., U.S.A.* **152 B6** 33 49N 83 26W
Bishop, *Tex., U.S.A.* **155 M6** 27 35N 97 48W
Bishop Auckland, *U.K.* **20 C6** 54 39N 1 40W
Bishop's Falls, *Canada* **141 C8** 49 2N 55 30W
Bishop's Stortford, *U.K.* **21 F8** 51 52N 0 10 E
Bisignano, *Italy* **47 C9** 39 31N 16 17 E
Bisina, L., *Uganda* **118 B3** 1 38N 33 56 E
Biskra, *Algeria* **111 B6** 34 50N 5 44 E
Biskra, *Malta* **38 F7** 35 58N 14 21 E
Biskupiec, *Poland* **54 E7** 53 53N 20 58 E
Bismarck, *Mo., U.S.A.* **156 G6** 37 46N 90 38W
Bismarck, *N. Dak., U.S.A.* **154 B4** 46 48N 100 47W
Bismarck Arch., *Papua N. G.* **132 B5** 2 30 S 150 0 E
Bismarck Ra., *Papua N. G.* **132 C3** 5 35 S 145 0 E
Bismarck Sea, *Papua N. G.* **132 C4** 4 10 S 146 50 E
Bismark, *Germany* **30 C7** 52 40N 11 33 E
Bismil, *Turkey* **101 D9** 37 51N 40 40 E
Bismo, *Norway* **18 C5** 61 54N 8 15 E
Biso, *Uganda* **118 B3** 1 44N 31 26 E
Bison, *U.S.A.* **154 C3** 45 31N 102 28W
Bīsotūn, *Iran* **101 E12** 34 23N 47 26 E
Bispgården, *Sweden* **16 A10** 63 2N 16 40 E
Bissagos = Bijagós, Arquipélago dos, *Guinea-Biss.* **112 C1** 11 15N 16 10W
Bissam Cuttack, *India* **94 E6** 19 31N 83 31 E
Bissau, *Guinea-Biss.* **112 C1** 11 45N 15 45W
Bissaula, *Nigeria* **113 D7** 7 0N 10 27 E
Bissikrima, *Guinea* **112 C2** 10 50N 10 58W
Bissorã, *Guinea-Biss.* **112 C1** 12 16N 15 35W
Bistcho L., *Canada* **142 B5** 59 45N 118 50W
Bistreţ, *Romania* **53 G8** 43 54N 23 23 E
Bistrica = Ilirska-Bistrica, *Slovenia* **45 C11** 45 34N 14 14 E
Bistriţa, *Romania* **53 C9** 47 9N 24 35 E
Bistriţa →, *Romania* **53 D11** 46 30N 26 57 E
Bistriţa Năsăud □, *Romania* **53 C9** 47 15N 24 30 E
Bistriţei, Munţii, *Romania* **53 C10** 47 15N 25 40 E
Biswan, *India* **93 F9** 27 29N 81 2 E
Bisztynek, *Poland* **54 D7** 54 8N 20 53 E
Bita →, *C.A.R.* **114 A4** 6 26N 24 43 E
Bitam, *Gabon* **114 B2** 2 5N 11 25 E
Bitburg, *Germany* **31 F2** 49 58N 6 31 E
Bitche, *France* **27 C14** 49 2N 7 25 E
Bithlo, *U.S.A.* **153 G8** 28 33N 81 6W
Bithynia, *Turkey* **100 B4** 40 40N 31 0 E
Bitkine, *Chad* **109 F3** 11 59N 18 13 E
Bitlis, *Turkey* **101 C10** 38 20N 42 3 E
Bitola, *Macedonia* **50 E5** 41 1N 21 20 E
Bitolj = Bitola, *Macedonia* **50 E5** 41 1N 21 20 E
Bitonto, *Italy* **47 A9** 41 6N 16 41 E
Bitra I., *India* **95 J1** 11 33N 72 9 E
Bitter Creek, *U.S.A.* **158 F9** 41 33N 108 33W
Bitter L. = Buheirat-Murrat-el-Kubra, *Egypt* **106 H8** 30 18N 32 26 E
Bitterfeld, *Germany* **30 D8** 51 37N 12 20 E
Bitterfontein, *S. Africa* **116 E2** 31 1 S 18 32 E
Bitterroot →, *U.S.A.* **158 C6** 46 52N 114 7W
Bitterroot Range, *U.S.A.* **158 D6** 46 0N 114 20W
Bitterwater, *U.S.A.* **160 J6** 36 23N 121 0W
Bitti, *Italy* **46 B2** 40 29N 9 23 E
Bittou, *Burkina Faso* **113 C4** 11 17N 0 18W
Bitung, *Indonesia* **82 A3** 1 27N 125 11 E
Biu, *Nigeria* **113 C7** 10 40N 12 3 E
Bivolari, *Romania* **53 C12** 47 31N 27 27 E
Bivolu, Vf., *Romania* **53 C10** 47 16N 25 58 E
Biwa-Ko, *Japan* **73 B8** 35 15N 136 10 E
Biwabik, *U.S.A.* **154 B8** 47 32N 92 21W
Bixad, *Romania* **53 C8** 47 56N 23 28 E
Bixby, *U.S.A.* **155 H7** 35 57N 95 53W
Biyang, *China* **74 H7** 32 38N 113 21 E
Biysk, *Russia* **66 D9** 52 40N 85 0 E
Bizana, *S. Africa* **117 E4** 30 50 S 29 52 E
Bizen, *Japan* **72 C6** 34 43N 134 8 E
Bizerte, *Tunisia* **108 A1** 37 15N 9 50 E
Bjåen, *Norway* **18 E4** 59 37N 7 26 E
Bjargtangar, *Iceland* **11 B2** 65 30N 24 30W
Bjarkalundur, *Iceland* **11 B4** 65 33N 22 9W
Bjärnum, *Sweden* **17 H7** 56 17N 13 43 E
Bjästa, *Sweden* **16 A12** 63 12N 18 29 E
Bjelasica, *Montenegro, Yug.* **50 D3** 42 50N 19 40 E
Bjelašnica, *Bos.-H.* **52 G3** 43 43N 18 9 E
Bjelland, *Norway* **18 F4** 58 23N 7 32 E
Bjelovar, *Croatia* **45 C13** 45 56N 16 49 E
Bjerringbro, *Denmark* **17 H3** 56 23N 9 39 E
Bjervamoen, *Norway* **18 E6** 59 17N 9 5 E
Bjøberg, *Norway* **18 D5** 60 56N 8 13 E
Björbo, *Sweden* **16 D8** 60 27N 14 44 E
Bjørkelangen, *Norway* **18 E8** 59 53N 11 34 E
Björklinge, *Sweden* **16 D11** 60 2N 17 33 E
Bjørnafjorden, *Norway* **18 D2** 60 7N 5 28 E
Björneborg, *Sweden* **16 E8** 59 14N 14 16 E
Bjørnevatn, *Norway* **14 B23** 69 40N 30 0 E
Bjørnøya, *Arctic* **6 B8** 74 30N 19 0 E
Bjursås, *Sweden* **16 D9** 60 44N 15 25 E
Bjuv, *Sweden* **17 H6** 56 5N 12 55 E
Bla, *Mali* **112 C3** 12 56N 5 47W

Blace, *Serbia, Yug.* 50 C5 43 18N 21 17 E
Blachownia, *Poland* 55 H5 50 49N 18 56 E
Black = Da →, *Vietnam* 76 G5 21 15N 105 20 E
Black →, *Canada* 150 B5 44 42N 79 19W
Black →, *Alaska, U.S.A.* 144 C11 66 42N 144 42W
Black →, *Ariz., U.S.A.* 159 K8 33 44N 110 13W
Black →, *Ark., U.S.A.* 155 H9 35 38N 91 20W
Black →, *Mich., U.S.A.* 150 D2 42 59N 82 27W
Black →, *N.Y., U.S.A.* 151 C8 43 59N 76 4W
Black →, *Wis., U.S.A.* 154 D9 43 57N 91 22W
Black Bay Pen., *Canada* 140 C2 48 38N 88 21W
Black Birch L., *Canada* 143 B7 56 53N 107 45W
Black Diamond, *Canada* 142 C6 50 45N 114 14W
Black Duck →, *Canada* 140 A2 56 51N 89 2W
Black Forest = Schwarzwald, *Germany* 31 G4 48 30N 8 20 E
Black Forest, *U.S.A.* 154 F2 39 0N 104 43W
Black Hd., *Ireland* 23 C2 53 9N 9 16W
Black Hills, *U.S.A.* 154 D3 44 0N 103 45W
Black I., *Canada* 143 C9 51 12N 96 30W
Black L., *Canada* 143 B7 59 12N 105 15W
Black L., *Mich., U.S.A.* 148 C3 45 28N 84 16W
Black L., *N.Y., U.S.A.* 151 B9 44 31N 75 36W
Black Lake, *Canada* 143 B7 59 11N 105 20W
Black Mesa, *U.S.A.* 155 G3 36 58N 102 58W
Black Mountain, *Australia* 129 A9 30 18 S 151 39 E
Black Mt. = Mynydd Du, *U.K.* 21 F4 51 52N 3 50W
Black Mts., *U.K.* 21 F4 51 55N 3 7W
Black Range, *U.S.A.* 159 K10 33 15N 107 50W
Black River, *Jamaica* 164 a 18 0N 77 50W
Black River Falls, *U.S.A.* 154 C9 44 18N 90 51W
Black Rock, *Australia* 128 B3 32 50 S 138 44 E
Black Rock, *Barbados* 165 g 13 7N 59 37W
Black Sea, *Eurasia* 57 F6 43 30N 35 0 E
Black Tickle, *Canada* 141 B8 53 28N 55 45W
Black Volta →, *Africa* 112 D4 8 41N 1 33W
Black Warrior →, *U.S.A.* 149 J2 32 32N 87 51W
Blackall, *Australia* 126 C4 24 25 S 145 45 E
Blackball, *N.Z.* 131 C6 42 22 S 171 26 E
Blackbull, *Australia* 126 B3 17 55 S 141 45 E
Blackburn, *U.K.* 20 D5 53 45N 2 29W
Blackburn, Mt., *U.S.A.* 144 F12 61 44N 143 26W
Blackburn with Darwen □, *U.K.* 20 D5 53 45N 2 29W
Blackdown Tableland Nat. Park, *Australia* 126 C4 23 52 S 149 8 E
Blackfoot, *U.S.A.* 158 E7 43 11N 112 21W
Blackfoot →, *U.S.A.* 158 C7 46 52N 113 53W
Blackfoot River Reservoir, *U.S.A.* 158 E8 43 0N 111 43W
Blackman, *U.S.A.* 153 E3 30 56N 86 38W
Blackpool, *U.K.* 20 D4 53 49N 3 3W
Blackpool □, *U.K.* 20 D4 53 49N 3 3W
Blackriver, *U.S.A.* 150 B1 44 46N 83 17W
Blacks Harbour, *Canada* 141 C6 45 3N 66 49W
Blacksburg, *U.S.A.* 148 G5 37 14N 80 25W
Blackshear, *U.S.A.* 152 D7 31 18N 82 14W
Blackshear, L., *U.S.A.* 152 D6 31 51N 83 56W
Blacksod B., *Ireland* 23 B1 54 6N 10 0W
Blackstone, *U.S.A.* 148 G7 37 4N 78 0W
Blackstone Ra., *Australia* 125 E4 26 0 S 128 30 E
Blackville, *U.S.A.* 152 B8 33 22N 81 16W
Blackwater, *Australia* 126 C4 23 35 S 148 53 E
Blackwater →, *Cork, Ireland* 19 E3 52 5N 9 3W
Blackwater →, *Meath, Ireland* 23 C4 53 39N 6 41W
Blackwater →, *Waterford, Ireland* 23 D4 52 4N 7 52W
Blackwater →, *U.K.* 23 B5 54 31N 6 35W
Blackwater →, *Fla., U.S.A.* 153 E2 30 36N 87 2W
Blackwater →, *Mo., U.S.A.* 156 F4 38 59N 92 59W
Blackwell, *U.S.A.* 155 G6 36 48N 97 17W
Blackwells Corner, *U.S.A.* 161 K7 35 37N 119 47W
Blackwood, C., *Papua N. G.* 132 D3 7 49 S 144 31 E
Bladensburg Nat. Park, *Australia* 126 C3 22 30 S 142 59 E
Blaenau Ffestiniog, *U.K.* 20 E4 53 0N 3 56W
Blaenau Gwent □, *U.K.* 21 F4 51 48N 3 12W
Bláfell, *Iceland* 11 C7 64 30N 19 51W
Bláfjall, *Iceland* 11 B10 65 26N 16 50W
Blagaj, *Bos.-H.* 50 C1 43 16N 17 55 E
Blagnac, *France* 28 E5 43 37N 1 23 E
Blagodarnoye = Blagodarnyy, *Russia* 61 H6 45 7N 43 37 E
Blagodarnyy, *Russia* 61 H6 45 7N 43 37 E
Blagoevgrad, *Bulgaria* 50 D7 42 2N 23 5 E
Blagoveshchenka, *Kazakstan* 65 B7 43 18N 74 12 E
Blagoveshchensk, *Amur, Russia* 67 D13 50 20N 127 30 E
Blagoveshchensk, *Bashkortostan, Russia* 64 D5 55 1N 55 59 E
Blahkiuh, *Indonesia* 79 J18 8 31 S 115 12 E
Blain, *France* 26 E5 47 29N 1 45W
Blain, *U.S.A.* 150 F7 40 20N 77 31W
Blaine, *Minn., U.S.A.* 154 C8 45 10N 93 13W
Blaine, *Wash., U.S.A.* 160 B4 48 59N 122 45W
Blaine Lake, *Canada* 143 C7 52 51N 106 52W
Blair, *U.S.A.* 154 E6 41 33N 96 8W
Blair Athol, *Australia* 126 C4 22 42 S 147 31 E
Blair Atholl, *U.K.* 22 E5 56 46N 3 50W
Blairgowrie, *U.K.* 22 E5 56 35N 3 21W
Blairsden, *U.S.A.* 160 F6 39 47N 120 37W
Blairsville, *U.S.A.* 150 F5 40 26N 79 16W
Blaj, *Romania* 53 D8 46 10N 23 57 E
Blaka, *Niger* 109 D2 21 21N 12 47 E
Blakang Mati, Pulau, *Singapore* 87 d 1 15N 103 50 E
Blake Pt., *U.S.A.* 154 A10 48 11N 88 25W
Blakely, *Ga., U.S.A.* 152 D5 31 23N 84 56W
Blakely, *Pa., U.S.A.* 151 E9 41 28N 75 37W
Blakesburg, *U.S.A.* 156 D4 40 58N 92 38W
Blakstad, *Norway* 18 F5 58 30N 8 39 E
Blâmont, *France* 27 D13 48 35N 6 50 E
Blanc, C., *Spain* 38 B3 39 21N 2 51 E
Blanc, C., *Tunisia* 108 A1 37 15N 9 56 E
Blanc, Mont, *Alps* 29 C10 45 48N 6 50 E
Blanc-Sablon, *Canada* 141 B8 51 24N 57 12W
Blanca, B., *Argentina* 176 A4 39 10 S 61 30W
Blanca Peak, *U.S.A.* 159 H11 37 35N 105 29W
Blanchardville, *U.S.A.* 156 B7 42 49N 89 52W
Blanche, C., *Australia* 127 E1 33 1 S 134 9 E
Blanche, L., *S. Austral., Australia* 127 D2 29 15 S 139 40 E
Blanche, L., *W. Austral., Australia* 124 D3 22 25 S 123 17 E
Blanche Channel, *Solomon Is.* 133 M9 8 30 S 157 30 E
Blanchester, *U.S.A.* 157 E13 39 17N 83 59W
Blanchisseuse, *Trin. & Tob.* 169 F9 10 48N 61 18W
Blanco, *S. Africa* 116 E3 33 55 S 22 23 E
Blanco, *U.S.A.* 155 K5 30 6N 98 25W
Blanco →, *Argentina* 174 C2 30 20 S 68 42W
Blanco →, *Bolivia* 173 C5 12 30 S 64 18W
Blanco, C., *Costa Rica* 164 E2 9 34N 85 8W
Blanco, C., *U.S.A.* 158 E1 42 51N 124 34W
Blanda →, *Iceland* 11 B6 65 37N 20 9W
Blandford Forum, *U.K.* 21 G5 50 51N 2 9W
Blanding, *U.S.A.* 159 H9 37 37N 109 29W
Blandinsville, *U.S.A.* 156 D6 40 33N 90 52W
Blanes, *Spain* 40 D7 41 40N 2 48 E
Blangy-sur-Bresle, *France* 27 C8 49 55N 1 37 E
Blanice →, *Czech Rep.* 34 B7 49 10N 14 5 E
Blankaholm, *Sweden* 17 G10 57 36N 16 31 E
Blankenberge, *Belgium* 24 C3 51 20N 3 9 E
Blankenburg, *Germany* 30 D6 51 47N 10 57 E
Blanquefort, *France* 28 D3 44 55N 0 38W
Blanquilla, I., *Venezuela* 165 D7 11 51N 64 37W
Blanquillo, *Uruguay* 175 C4 32 53 S 55 37W
Blansko, *Czech Rep.* 35 B9 49 22N 16 40 E
Blantyre, *Malawi* 119 F4 15 45 S 35 0 E
Blarney, *Ireland* 23 E3 51 56N 8 33W
Blasdell, *U.S.A.* 150 D6 42 48N 78 50W
Blåsjø, *Norway* 18 E3 59 20N 6 50 E
Błaszki, *Poland* 55 G5 51 38N 18 30 E
Blatná, *Czech Rep.* 34 B6 49 25N 13 52 E
Blato, *Croatia* 45 F13 42 56N 16 48 E
Blatten, *Switz.* 32 D5 46 20N 7 50 E
Blaubeuren, *Germany* 31 G5 48 24N 9 46 E
Blaustein, *Germany* 31 G5 48 25N 9 53 E
Blåvands Huk, *Denmark* 17 J2 55 33N 8 4 E
Blaydon, *U.K.* 20 C6 54 58N 1 42W
Blaye, *France* 28 C3 45 8N 0 40W
Blaye-les-Mines, *France* 28 D6 44 1N 2 8 E
Blayney, *Australia* 129 B8 33 32 S 149 14 E
Blaze, Pt., *Australia* 124 B5 12 56 S 130 11 E
Błażowa, *Poland* 55 J9 49 53N 22 7 E
Bleckede, *Germany* 30 B6 53 17N 10 43 E
Bled, *Slovenia* 45 B11 46 27N 14 7 E
Blefjell, *Norway* 18 E6 59 48N 9 10 E
Bleiburg, *Austria* 34 E7 46 35N 14 49 E
Blejeşti, *Romania* 53 F10 44 19N 25 27 E
Blekinge, *Sweden* 15 H16 56 25N 15 20 E
Blekinge län □, *Sweden* 17 H9 56 20N 15 20 E
Blenheim, *Canada* 150 D3 42 20N 82 0W
Blenheim, *N.Z.* 131 B8 41 38 S 173 57 E
Bléone →, *France* 29 D10 44 5N 6 0 E
Bléranccourt, *France* 27 C10 49 31N 3 9 E
Bletchley, *U.K.* 21 F7 51 59N 0 44W
Blida, *Algeria* 111 A5 36 30N 2 49 E
Blidet Amor, *Algeria* 111 B6 32 59N 5 58 E
Blidö, *Sweden* 16 E12 59 37N 18 53 E
Blidsberg, *Sweden* 17 G7 57 56N 13 30 E
Blieskastel, *Germany* 31 F3 49 14N 7 12 E
Bligh Sound, *N.Z.* 131 E2 44 47 S 167 32 E
Bligh Water, *Fiji* 133 A2 17 0 S 178 0 E
Blind River, *Canada* 140 C3 46 10N 82 58W
Blinisht, *Albania* 50 E3 41 52N 19 59 E
Blinnenhorn, *Switz.* 33 D6 46 26N 8 19 E
Bliss, *Idaho, U.S.A.* 158 E6 42 56N 114 57W
Bliss, *N.Y., U.S.A.* 150 D6 42 34N 78 15W
Blissfield, *Mich., U.S.A.* 157 C13 41 50N 83 52W
Blissfield, *Ohio, U.S.A.* 150 F3 40 24N 81 58W
Blitar, *Indonesia* 85 D4 8 5 S 112 11 E
Blitchton, *U.S.A.* 152 C8 32 12N 81 26W
Blitta, *Togo* 113 D5 8 23N 1 6 E
Block I., *U.S.A.* 151 E13 41 11N 71 35W
Block Island Sd., *U.S.A.* 151 E13 41 15N 71 40W
Bloemfontein, *S. Africa* 116 D4 29 6 S 26 7 E
Bloemhof, *S. Africa* 116 D4 27 38 S 25 32 E
Blois, *France* 26 E8 47 35N 1 20 E
Blomskog, *Sweden* 16 E6 59 16N 12 2 E
Blomstermåla, *Sweden* 17 H10 56 59N 16 21 E
Blomvåg, *Norway* 18 D1 60 32N 4 50 E
Blonay, *Switz.* 32 D3 46 28N 6 54 E
Blönduós, *Iceland* 11 B6 65 40N 20 12W
Blongas, *Indonesia* 79 K19 8 53 S 116 2 E
Błonie, *Poland* 55 F7 52 12N 20 37 E
Bloodvein →, *Canada* 143 C9 51 47N 96 43W
Bloody Foreland, *Ireland* 23 A3 55 10N 8 17W
Bloomer, *U.S.A.* 154 C9 45 6N 91 29W
Bloomfield, *Canada* 150 C7 43 59N 77 14W
Bloomfield, *Ind., U.S.A.* 157 E10 39 1N 86 57W
Bloomfield, *Iowa, U.S.A.* 156 D4 40 45N 92 25W
Bloomfield, *Ky., U.S.A.* 157 G11 37 55N 85 19W
Bloomfield, *N. Mex., U.S.A.* 159 H10 36 43N 107 59W
Bloomfield, *Nebr., U.S.A.* 154 D6 42 36N 97 39W
Bloomingburg, *U.S.A.* 157 E13 39 36N 83 24W
Bloomington, *Ill., U.S.A.* 156 D8 40 28N 89 0W
Bloomington, *Ind., U.S.A.* 157 E10 39 10N 86 32W
Bloomington, *Minn., U.S.A.* 154 C8 44 50N 93 17W
Bloomington, *Wis., U.S.A.* 156 B6 42 53N 90 55W
Bloomsburg, *U.S.A.* 151 F8 41 0N 76 27W
Bloomsbury, *Australia* 126 J6 20 48 S 148 38 E
Blora, *Indonesia* 85 D4 6 57 S 111 25 E
Blossburg, *U.S.A.* 150 E7 41 41N 77 4W
Blosseville Kyst, *Greenland* 10 D8 68 50N 26 30W
Blotzheim, *France* 32 A4 47 36N 7 29 E
Blouberg, *S. Africa* 117 C4 23 8 S 28 59 E
Blountstown, *U.S.A.* 152 E4 30 27N 85 3W
Bludenz, *Austria* 34 D2 47 10N 9 50 E
Blue →, *U.S.A.* 157 F10 38 11N 86 19W
Blue Cypress L., *U.S.A.* 153 H9 27 44N 80 45W
Blue Earth, *U.S.A.* 154 D8 43 38N 94 6W
Blue Lagoon Nat. Park, *Zambia* 119 F2 15 28 S 27 26 E
Blue Mesa Reservoir, *U.S.A.* 159 G10 38 28N 107 20W
Blue Mound, *U.S.A.* 156 E7 39 42N 89 7W
Blue Mountain Lake, *U.S.A.* 151 C10 43 52N 74 30W
Blue Mountain Pk., *Jamaica* 164 a 18 3N 76 36W
Blue Mountains, The, *Jamaica* 164 a 18 3N 76 36W
Blue Mountains Nat. Park, *Australia* 129 C9 34 2 S 150 15 E
Blue Mts., *Australia* 129 B9 33 40 S 150 15 E
Blue Mts., *Maine, U.S.A.* 151 B14 44 50N 70 35W
Blue Mts., *Oreg., U.S.A.* 158 D4 45 15N 119 0W
Blue Mts., *Pa., U.S.A.* 151 F8 40 30N 76 30W
Blue Mud B., *Australia* 126 A2 13 30 S 136 0 E
Blue Nile = Nîl el Azraq →, *Sudan* 107 D3 15 38N 32 31 E
Blue Rapids, *U.S.A.* 154 F6 39 41N 96 39W
Blue Ridge Mts., *U.S.A.* 149 G5 36 30N 80 15W
Blue River, *Canada* 142 C5 52 6N 119 18W
Blue Springs, *U.S.A.* 156 E2 39 1N 94 17W
Bluefield, *U.S.A.* 148 G5 37 15N 81 17W
Bluefields, *Nic.* 164 D3 12 20N 83 50W
Bluff, *Australia* 126 C4 23 35 S 149 4 E
Bluff, *N.Z.* 131 G3 46 37 S 168 20 E
Bluff, *U.S.A.* 159 H9 37 17N 109 33W
Bluff Harbour, *N.Z.* 131 G3 46 36 S 168 21 E
Bluff Knoll, *Australia* 125 F2 34 24 S 118 15 E
Bluff Pt., *Australia* 125 E1 27 50 S 114 5 E
Bluffs, *U.S.A.* 156 E6 39 45N 90 32W
Bluffton, *Ga., U.S.A.* 152 D5 31 31N 84 52W
Bluffton, *Ind., U.S.A.* 157 D11 40 44N 85 11W
Bluffton, *Ohio, U.S.A.* 157 D13 40 54N 83 54W
Bluffton, *S.C., U.S.A.* 152 C9 32 14N 80 52W
Blumenau, *Brazil* 175 B6 27 0 S 49 0W
Blümisalphorn, *Switz.* 32 D5 46 28N 7 47 E
Blunt, *U.S.A.* 154 C5 44 31N 99 59W
Bly, *U.S.A.* 158 E3 42 24N 121 3W
Blyde River Canyon Nature Reserve, *S. Africa* 117 C5 24 37 S 31 2 E
Blyth, *Australia* 128 B3 33 49 S 138 28 E
Blyth, *Canada* 150 C3 43 44N 81 26W
Blyth, *U.K.* 20 B6 55 8N 1 31W
Blythe, *Calif., U.S.A.* 161 M12 33 37N 114 36W
Blythe, *Ga., U.S.A.* 152 B7 33 17N 82 12W
Blytheville, *U.S.A.* 155 H10 35 56N 89 55W
Bø, *Norway* 18 E6 59 25N 9 3 E
Bo, *S. Leone* 112 D2 7 55N 11 50W
Bo Duc, *Vietnam* 87 G6 11 58N 106 50 E
Bo Hai, *China* 75 E10 39 0N 119 0 E
Bō-no-Misaki, *Japan* 72 F2 31 15N 130 13 E
Bo Xian = Bozhou, *China* 74 H8 33 55N 115 41 E
Boa Esperança, *Brazil* 169 C5 3 21N 61 23W
Boa Esperança, Reprêsa, *Brazil* 170 C3 6 50 S 43 50W
Boa Nova, *Brazil* 171 D3 14 22 S 40 10W
Boa Viagem, *Brazil* 170 C4 5 7 S 39 44W
Boa Vista, *Brazil* 169 C5 2 48N 60 30W
Boa Vista, *C. Verde Is.* 9 j 16 0N 22 49W
Boac, *Phil.* 80 E3 13 27N 121 50 E
Boaco, *Nic.* 164 D2 12 29N 85 35W
Bo'ai, *China* 74 G7 35 10N 113 3 E
Boal, *Spain* 42 B4 43 25N 6 49W
Boali, *C.A.R.* 114 B3 4 48N 18 7 E
Boalsburg, *U.S.A.* 150 F7 40 46N 77 47W
Boane, *Mozam.* 117 D5 26 6 S 32 19 E
Boang I., *Papua N. G.* 132 B7 3 23 S 153 18 E
Boano, *Indonesia* 82 B3 3 0 S 127 56 E
Boardman, *U.S.A.* 150 E4 41 2N 80 40W
Boath, *India* 94 E4 19 20N 78 20 E
Boatswain Bird I., *Ascension I.* 9 g 7 56 S 14 18W
Bobadah, *Australia* 129 B7 32 19 S 146 41 E
Bobai, *China* 76 F7 22 17N 109 59 E
Bobbili, *India* 94 E6 18 35N 83 30 E
Bóbbio, *Italy* 44 D6 44 46N 9 23 E
Bobcaygeon, *Canada* 140 D4 44 33N 78 33W
Boblad, *India* 94 F2 17 13N 75 26 E
Böblingen, *Germany* 31 G5 48 40N 9 1 E
Bobo-Dioulasso, *Burkina Faso* 112 C4 11 8N 4 13W
Bobolice, *Poland* 54 E3 53 58N 16 37 E
Bobon, *Phil.* 80 E5 12 32N 124 34 E
Bobonaro, *E. Timor* 82 C3 9 2 S 125 22 E
Bobonaza →, *Ecuador* 168 D2 2 36 S 76 38W
Boboshevo, *Bulgaria* 50 D7 42 9N 23 0 E
Bobov Dol, *Bulgaria* 50 D6 42 20N 23 0 E
Bóbr →, *Poland* 55 F2 52 4N 15 4 E
Bobraomby, Tanjon' i, *Madag.* 117 A8 12 40 S 49 10 E
Bobrinets, *Ukraine* 59 H7 48 4N 32 5 E
Bobrov, *Russia* 60 E5 51 5N 40 2 E
Bobrovitsa, *Ukraine* 59 G6 50 45N 31 23 E
Bobruysk = Babruysk, *Belarus* 59 F5 53 10N 29 15 E
Bobures, *Venezuela* 168 B3 9 15N 71 11W
Boca de Drago, *Venezuela* 169 F9 11 0N 61 50W
Bôca do Acre, *Brazil* 172 B4 8 50 S 67 27W
Bôca do Jari, *Brazil* 169 D7 1 7 S 51 58W
Bôca do Moaco, *Brazil* 172 B4 7 41 S 68 17W
Boca Grande, *U.S.A.* 153 J7 26 45N 82 16W
Boca Grande, *Venezuela* 169 B5 8 40N 60 40W
Boca Raton, *U.S.A.* 149 M5 26 21N 80 5W
Bocaiúva, *Brazil* 171 E3 17 7 S 43 49W
Bocanda, *Ivory C.* 112 D4 7 5N 4 31W
Bocaranga, *C.A.R.* 114 A3 7 0N 15 35 E
Bocas del Toro, *Panama* 164 E3 9 15N 82 20W
Boceguillas, *Spain* 42 D7 41 20N 3 39W
Bochnia, *Poland* 55 J7 49 58N 20 27 E
Bocholt, *Germany* 30 D2 51 50N 6 36 E
Bochum, *Germany* 30 D3 51 28N 7 13 E
Bockenem, *Germany* 30 C6 52 1N 10 8 E
Boćki, *Poland* 55 F10 52 39N 23 3 E
Bocognano, *France* 29 F13 42 5N 9 4 E
Bocoio, *Angola* 115 E2 12 28 S 14 10 E
Boconó, *Venezuela* 168 B3 9 15N 70 16W
Boconó →, *Venezuela* 168 B4 8 43N 69 34W
Bocoyna, *Mexico* 162 B3 27 52N 107 35W
Bocşa, *Romania* 52 E6 45 21N 21 47 E
Boda, *C.A.R.* 114 B3 4 19N 17 26 E
Boda, *Dalarnas, Sweden* 16 C9 61 1N 15 13 E
Böda, *Kalmar, Sweden* 17 G11 57 15N 17 3 E
Boda, *Västernorrland, Sweden* 16 B10 62 52N 16 39 E
Bodafors, *Sweden* 17 G8 57 48N 14 23 E
Bodaybo, *Russia* 67 D12 57 50N 114 0 E
Boddam, *U.K.* 22 B7 59 56N 1 17W
Boddington, *Australia* 125 F2 32 50 S 116 30 E
Bode Sadu, *Nigeria* 113 D5 9 0N 4 47 E
Bodega Bay, *U.S.A.* 160 G3 38 20N 123 3W
Boden, *Sweden* 14 D19 65 50N 21 42 E
Bodensee, *Europe* 33 A8 47 35N 9 25 E
Bodenteich, *Germany* 30 C6 52 50N 10 42 E
Bodhan, *India* 94 E3 18 40N 77 44 E
Bodinayakkanur, *India* 95 J3 10 2N 77 10 E
Bodinga, *Nigeria* 113 C6 12 58N 5 10 E
Bodio, *Switz.* 33 D7 46 23N 8 55 E
Bodmin, *U.K.* 21 G3 50 28N 4 43W
Bodmin Moor, *U.K.* 21 G3 50 33N 4 36W
Bodø, *Norway* 14 C16 67 17N 14 24 E
Bodoquena, Serra da, *Brazil* 173 E6 21 0 S 56 50W
Bodoupa, *C.A.R.* 114 A3 5 43N 17 36 E
Bodrichi, *Chad* 109 E3 19 11N 15 54 E
Bodrog →, *Hungary* 52 B6 48 11N 21 22 E
Bodrum, *Turkey* 49 D9 37 3N 27 30 E
Boduna, *Dem. Rep. of the Congo* 114 A3 5 5N 19 44 E
Bódva →, *Hungary* 52 B5 48 19N 20 45 E
Boembé, *Congo* 114 C3 2 54 S 15 39 E
Boën, *France* 29 C8 45 44N 4 1 E
Boende, *Dem. Rep. of the Congo* 114 C4 0 24 S 21 12 E
Boerne, *U.S.A.* 155 L5 29 47N 98 44W
Boesmans →, *S. Africa* 116 E4 33 42 S 26 39 E
Boffa, *Guinea* 112 C2 10 16N 14 3W
Bofuku, *Dem. Rep. of the Congo* 114 C4 0 57 S 20 53 E
Bogale, *Burma* 90 E5 16 17N 95 24 E
Bogalusa, *U.S.A.* 155 K10 30 47N 89 52W
Bogan →, *N.S.W., Australia* 127 D4 29 59 S 146 17 E
Bogan →, *N.S.W., Australia* 129 A7 30 20 S 146 55 E
Bogan Gate, *Australia* 129 B7 33 7 S 147 49 E
Bogandé, *Burkina Faso* 113 C4 13 2N 0 8W
Bogangolo, *C.A.R.* 114 A3 5 34N 18 15 E
Bogantungan, *Australia* 126 C4 23 41 S 147 17 E
Bogata, *U.S.A.* 155 J7 33 28N 95 13W
Bogatić, *Serbia, Yug.* 50 B3 44 51N 19 30 E
Boğazkale, *Turkey* 100 B6 40 2N 34 37 E
Boğazlıyan, *Turkey* 100 C6 39 11N 35 14 E
Bogbonga, *Dem. Rep. of the Congo* 114 B3 1 36N 19 24 E
Bogdanovich, *Russia* 64 C9 56 47N 62 1 E
Bogen, *Sweden* 16 D6 60 4N 12 33 E
Bogense, *Denmark* 17 J4 55 34N 10 5 E
Bogetići, *Montenegro, Yug.* 50 D2 42 41N 18 58 E
Boggabilla, *Australia* 127 D5 28 36 S 150 24 E
Boggabri, *Australia* 129 A9 30 45 S 150 5 E
Boggeragh Mts., *Ireland* 23 D3 52 2N 8 55W
Bogia, *Papua N. G.* 132 C3 4 9 S 145 0 E
Boglan = Solhan, *Turkey* 101 C9 38 57N 41 3 E
Bognor Regis, *U.K.* 21 G7 50 47N 0 40W
Bogo, *Phil.* 81 F4 11 3N 124 0 E
Bogodukhov = Bohodukhiv, *Ukraine* 59 G8 50 9N 35 33 E
Bogol Manya, *Ethiopia* 107 G5 4 34N 41 29 E
Bogong, Mt., *Australia* 129 D7 36 47 S 147 17 E
Bogor, *Indonesia* 84 D3 6 36 S 106 48 E
Bogoroditsk, *Russia* 58 F10 53 47N 38 8 E
Bogorodsk, *Russia* 60 B6 56 4N 43 30 E
Bogoso, *Ghana* 112 D4 5 38N 2 3W
Bogotá, *Colombia* 168 C3 4 34N 74 0W
Bogotol, *Russia* 66 D9 56 15N 89 50 E
Bogou, *Togo* 113 C5 10 40N 0 12 E
Bogra, *Bangla.* 90 C2 24 51N 89 22 E
Boguchany, *Russia* 67 D10 58 40N 97 30 E
Boguchar, *Russia* 60 F5 49 55N 40 32 E
Bogué, *Mauritania* 112 B2 16 45N 14 10W
Boguslav, *Ukraine* 59 H6 49 33N 30 56 E
Boguszów-Gorce, *Poland* 55 H3 50 45N 16 12 E
Bohain-en-Vermandois, *France* 27 C10 49 59N 3 28 E
Bohemian Forest = Böhmerwald, *Germany* 31 F9 49 8N 13 14 E
Bohena Cr. →, *Australia* 129 A8 30 17 S 149 42 E
Bohinjska Bistrica, *Slovenia* 45 B11 46 17N 14 1 E
Böhmerwald, *Germany* 31 F9 49 8N 13 14 E
Bohmte, *Germany* 30 C4 52 22N 8 19 E
Bohodukhiv, *Ukraine* 59 G8 50 9N 35 33 E
Bohol, *Somali Rep.* 120 C3 5 45N 46 9 E
Bohol □, *Phil.* 81 G5 9 50N 124 10 E
Bohol Sea, *Phil.* 81 G5 9 0N 124 0 E
Bohol Str., *Phil.* 81 G4 9 45N 123 40 E
Bohongou, *Burkina Faso* 113 C5 13 4N 0 10 E
Böhönye, *Hungary* 52 D2 46 25N 17 28 E
Bohotleh, *Somali Rep.* 120 C3 8 20N 46 25 E
Bohuslän, *Sweden* 17 F5 58 25N 12 0 E
Boi, *Nigeria* 113 D6 9 35N 9 27 E
Boi, Pta. de, *Brazil* 175 A6 23 55 S 45 15W
Boiaçu, *Brazil* 169 D5 0 27 S 61 46W
Boigu I., *Australia* 132 E2 9 15 S 142 14 E
Boileau, C., *Australia* 124 C3 17 40 S 122 7 E
Boim, *Brazil* 169 D6 2 49 S 55 10W
Boing'o, *Sudan* 107 F3 9 58N 33 44 E
Boipariguda, *India* 94 E6 18 46N 82 26 E
Boipeba, I. de, *Brazil* 171 D4 13 39 S 38 55W
Boiro, *Spain* 42 C2 42 39N 8 54W
Bois →, *Brazil* 171 E1 18 35 S 50 2W
Boise, *U.S.A.* 158 E5 43 37N 116 13W
Boise City, *U.S.A.* 155 G3 36 44N 102 31W
Boissevain, *Canada* 143 D8 49 15N 100 5W
Bòite →, *Italy* 45 B9 46 5N 12 5 E
Boitzenburg, *Germany* 30 B9 53 16N 13 35 E
Boizenburg, *Germany* 30 B6 53 23N 10 43 E
Bojador C., *W. Sahara* 110 C2 26 0N 14 30W
Bojana →, *Albania* 50 E3 41 52N 19 22 E
Bojano, *Italy* 47 A7 41 29N 14 29 E
Bojanowo, *Poland* 55 G3 51 43N 16 42 E
Bøjden, *Denmark* 17 J4 55 6N 10 7 E
Bojnūrd, *Iran* 97 B8 37 30N 57 20 E
Bojonegoro, *Indonesia* 85 D4 7 11 S 111 54 E
Boju, *Nigeria* 113 D6 7 22N 7 55 E
Boka, *Serbia, Yug.* 50 B4 45 22N 20 52 E
Boka Kotorska, *Montenegro, Yug.* 50 D2 42 23N 18 32 E
Bokada, *Dem. Rep. of the Congo* 114 B3 4 8N 19 23 E
Bokala, *Dem. Rep. of the Congo* 114 C3 3 8 S 17 4 E
Bokala, *Ivory C.* 112 D4 8 31N 4 33W
Bokani, *Nigeria* 113 D6 9 28N 5 10 E
Bokaro, *India* 93 H11 23 46N 85 55 E
Bokatola, *Dem. Rep. of the Congo* 114 C3 0 38 S 18 46 E
Boké, *Guinea* 112 C2 10 56N 14 17W
Bokela, *Dem. Rep. of the Congo* 114 C4 1 10 S 21 59 E
Bokenda, *Dem. Rep. of the Congo* 114 B4 1 16N 21 22 E
Bokhara →, *Australia* 127 D4 29 55 S 146 42 E
Bokkos, *Nigeria* 113 D6 9 17N 9 1 E
Boknafjorden, *Norway* 15 G11 59 14N 5 40 E
Bokode, *Dem. Rep. of the Congo* 114 B3 3 55N 19 30 E
Bokolo, *Gabon* 114 C2 2 40 S 10 10 E
Bökönbaev, *Kyrgyzstan* 65 B8 42 10N 76 55 E
Bokondo, *Dem. Rep. of the Congo* 114 B4 0 15N 22 32 E
Bokora Game Reserve, *Uganda* 118 B3 2 12N 31 32 E
Bokoro, *Chad* 109 F3 12 25N 17 14 E
Bokota, *Dem. Rep. of the Congo* 114 C4 0 56 S 22 24 E
Bokote, *Dem. Rep. of the Congo* 114 C4 0 12 S 21 8 E
Bokpyin, *Burma* 87 G2 11 18N 98 42 E
Boksitogorsk, *Russia* 58 C7 59 22N 33 50 E
Boku, *Papua N. G.* 132 D8 6 34 S 155 21 E
Bokungu, *Dem. Rep. of the Congo* 114 C4 0 35 S 22 50 E
Bol, *Chad* 109 F2 13 30N 14 40 E
Bol, *Croatia* 45 E13 43 18N 16 38 E
Bolama, *Guinea-Biss.* 112 C1 11 30N 15 30W
Bolan →, *Pakistan* 92 E2 28 38N 67 42 E
Bolan Pass, *Pakistan* 91 C2 29 50N 67 20 E
Bolaños →, *Mexico* 162 C4 21 14N 104 8W
Bolaños de Calatrava, *Spain* 43 G7 38 54N 3 40W
Bolayır, *Turkey* 51 F10 40 31N 26 45 E
Bolbec, *France* 26 C7 49 30N 0 30 E
Boldājī, *Iran* 97 D6 31 56N 51 3 E
Boldeşti-Scăeni, *Romania* 53 E11 45 3N 26 2 E
Bole, *China* 68 B3 45 11N 81 37 E
Bole, *Ethiopia* 107 F4 6 36N 37 20 E
Bole, *Ghana* 112 D4 9 3N 2 23W
Bolekhiv, *Ukraine* 59 H2 49 0N 23 57 E
Boleko, *Dem. Rep. of the Congo* 114 C3 1 35 S 19 50 E
Bolesławiec, *Poland* 55 G2 51 17N 15 37 E
Bolgatanga, *Ghana* 113 C4 10 44N 0 53W
Bolgrad = Bolhrad, *Ukraine* 59 K5 45 40N 28 32 E
Bolhrad, *Ukraine* 59 K5 45 40N 28 32 E
Bolia, *Dem. Rep. of the Congo* 114 C3 1 36 S 18 22 E
Bolinao, *Phil.* 80 C2 16 23N 119 54 E
Bolinao, C., *Phil.* 80 C2 16 23N 119 55 E
Bolingbroke, *U.S.A.* 152 C6 32 57N 83 48W
Bolingo, *Dem. Rep. of the Congo* 114 C4 3 31 S 21 43 E
Bolintin-Vale, *Romania* 53 F10 44 27N 25 46 E
Bolívar, *Argentina* 174 D3 36 15 S 60 53W
Bolívar, *Antioquia, Colombia* 168 B2 5 50N 76 1W
Bolívar, *Cauca, Colombia* 168 C2 2 0N 77 0W
Bolívar, *Peru* 172 B2 7 18 S 77 48W
Bolivar, *Mo., U.S.A.* 155 G8 37 37N 93 25W
Bolivar, *N.Y., U.S.A.* 150 D6 42 4N 78 10W
Bolivar, *Tenn., U.S.A.* 155 H10 35 12N 89 0W
Bolívar □, *Colombia* 168 B3 9 0N 74 40W
Bolívar □, *Ecuador* 168 D2 1 15 S 79 5W
Bolívar □, *Venezuela* 169 B5 6 20N 63 30W
Bolivia ■, *S. Amer.* 173 D5 17 6 S 64 0W
Bolivian Plateau, *S. Amer.* 166 E4 20 0 S 67 30W
Boljevac, *Serbia, Yug.* 50 C5 43 51N 21 58 E
Bolkhov, *Russia* 58 F9 53 25N 36 0 E
Bolków, *Poland* 55 H3 50 55N 16 6 E
Bollé, *Mauritania* 110 D2 20 8N 11 40W
Bollebygd, *Sweden* 17 G6 57 40N 12 35 E
Bollène, *France* 29 D8 44 18N 4 45 E
Bollnäs, *Sweden* 16 C10 61 21N 16 24 E
Bollon, *Australia* 127 D4 28 2 S 147 29 E
Bollstabruk, *Sweden* 16 B11 62 59N 17 40 E
Bolmen, *Sweden* 17 H7 56 55N 13 40 E
Bolobo, *Dem. Rep. of the Congo* 114 C3 2 6 S 16 20 E
Bologna, *Italy* 45 D8 44 29N 11 20 E
Bologoye, *Russia* 58 D8 57 55N 34 5 E
Bolomba, *Dem. Rep. of the Congo* 114 B3 0 35N 19 0 E
Bolombo →, *Dem. Rep. of the Congo* 114 B4 1 32N 21 14 E
Bolonchenticul, *Mexico* 163 D7 20 0N 89 49W
Bolondo, *Dem. Rep. of the Congo* 114 C3 2 12 S 18 42 E
Bolong, *Chad* 109 F3 12 3N 17 45 E
Bolong, *Phil.* 81 H4 7 6N 122 14 E
Bolongongo, *Angola* 115 D3 8 28 S 15 16 E
Bolótana, *Italy* 46 B1 40 20N 8 52 E
Bolotovskoye, *Russia* 64 B9 58 31N 62 28 E
Boloven, Cao Nguyen, *Laos* 86 E6 15 10N 106 30 E
Bolpur, *India* 93 H12 23 40N 87 45 E
Bolsena, *Italy* 45 F8 42 39N 11 59 E
Bolsena, L. di, *Italy* 45 F8 42 36N 11 56 E
Bolshaya Chernigovka, *Russia* 60 D10 52 6N 50 52 E
Bolshaya Glushitsa, *Russia* 60 D10 52 28N 50 30 E
Bolshaya Khobda →, *Kazakstan* 64 F5 50 56N 54 34 E
Bolshaya Martynovka, *Russia* 61 G5 47 19N 41 37 E
Bolshaya Vradiyevka, *Ukraine* 59 J6 47 50N 30 40 E
Bolshevik, Ostrov, *Russia* 67 B11 78 30N 102 0 E
Bolshoi Kavkas = Caucasus Mountains, *Eurasia* 61 J7 42 50N 44 0 E
Bolshoy Anyuy →, *Russia* 67 C17 68 30N 160 49 E
Bolshoy Begichev, Ostrov, *Russia* 67 B12 74 20N 112 30 E
Bolshoy Lyakhovskiy, Ostrov, *Russia* 67 B15 73 35N 142 0 E
Bolshoy Tokmak = Tokmak, *Ukraine* 59 J8 47 16N 35 42 E
Bolshoy Tyuters, Ostrov, *Russia* 15 G22 59 51N 27 13 E
Bólstaðarhlíð, *Iceland* 11 B7 65 31N 19 49W
Bolsward, *Neths.* 24 A5 53 3N 5 32 E
Bolt Head, *U.K.* 21 G4 50 12N 3 48W
Boltaña, *Spain* 40 C5 42 28N 0 4 E
Boltigen, *Switz.* 32 C4 46 38N 7 24 E
Bolton, *Canada* 150 C5 43 54N 79 45W
Bolton, *U.K.* 20 D5 53 35N 2 26W
Bolton Landing, *U.S.A.* 151 C11 43 32N 73 35W

Bolu, *Turkey* 100 B4 40 45N 31 35 E
Bolubolu, *Papua N. G.* 132 E6 9 21 S 150 20 E
Bolungavík, *Iceland* 11 A3 66 9N 23 15W
Boluo, *China* 77 F10 23 3N 114 21 E
Bolvadin, *Turkey* 100 C4 38 45N 31 4 E
Bolzano, *Italy* 45 B8 46 31N 11 22 E
Bom Comércio, *Brazil* 173 B4 9 45 S 65 54W
Bom Conselho, *Brazil* 170 C4 9 10 S 36 41W
Bom Despacho, *Brazil* 171 E2 19 43 S 45 15W
Bom Jesus, *Angola* 115 D2 9 11 S 13 34 E
Bom Jesus, *Brazil* 170 C3 9 4 S 44 22W
Bom Jesus da Gurguéia, Serra, *Brazil* 170 C3 9 0 S 43 0W
Bom Jesus da Lapa, *Brazil* 171 D3 13 15 S 43 25W
Boma, *Dem. Rep. of the Congo* 115 D2 5 50 S 13 4 E
Bomaderry, *Australia* 129 C9 34 52 S 150 37 E
Bomandjokou, *Congo* 114 B2 0 34N 14 23 E
Bomaneh, *Dem. Rep. of the Congo* 114 B4 1 18N 23 47 E
Bomassa, *Congo* 114 B3 2 12N 16 12 E
Bomate, *Dem. Rep. of the Congo* 114 C3 2 14N 25 15 E
Bombala, *Australia* 129 D8 36 56 S 149 15 E
Bombarral, *Portugal* 43 F1 39 15N 9 9W
Bombay = Mumbai, *India* 94 E1 18 55N 72 50 E
Bombedor, Pta., *Venezuela* 169 G9 9 53N 61 37W
Bomberai, Semenanjung, *Indonesia* 83 B4 3 0 S 133 0 E
Bombo Kasani, *Dem. Rep. of the Congo* 115 D4 5 51 S 21 54 E
Bomboma, *Dem. Rep. of the Congo* 114 B3 2 25N 18 55 E
Bombombwa, *Dem. Rep. of the Congo* 118 B2 1 40N 25 40 E
Bomboyo, *Chad* 109 F3 12 1N 15 28 E
Bomdila, *India* 90 B4 27 18N 92 22 E
Bomdo, *India* 90 A5 28 44N 94 54 E
Bomi Hills, *Liberia* 112 D2 7 1N 10 38W
Bomili, *Dem. Rep. of the Congo* 118 B2 1 45N 27 5 E
Bømlo, *Norway* 15 G11 59 37N 5 13 E
Bomokandi →, *Dem. Rep. of the Congo* 118 B2 3 39N 26 8 E
Bomongo, *Dem. Rep. of the Congo* 114 B3 1 27N 18 21 E
Bompoka, *India* 95 K11 8 15N 93 13 E
Bomputu, *Dem. Rep. of the Congo* 114 C4 0 23 S 20 6 E
Bomu →, *C.A.R.* 114 B4 4 40N 22 30 E
Bomu Occidentale, Réserve de Faune de la, *Dem. Rep. of the Congo* 114 B4 4 48N 24 17 E
Bomu Orientale, Réserve de Faune de la, *Dem. Rep. of the Congo* 114 B2 5 0N 25 50 E
Bon, C., *Tunisia* 108 A2 37 1N 11 2 E
Bon Acceuil, *Mauritius* 121 d 20 10 S 57 39 E
Bon Sar Pa, *Vietnam* 86 F6 12 24N 107 35 E
Bonaduz, *Switz.* 33 C8 46 49N 9 25 E
Bonaigarh, *India* 93 J11 21 50N 84 57 E
Bonaire, *Neth. Ant.* 165 D6 12 10N 68 15W
Bonaire, *U.S.A.* 152 C6 32 33N 83 36W
Bonang, *Australia* 129 D8 37 11 S 148 41 E
Bonanza, *Nic.* 164 D3 13 54N 84 35W
Bonaparte Arch., *Australia* 124 B3 14 0 S 124 30 E
Boñar, *Spain* 42 C5 42 52N 5 19W
Bonasse, *Trin. & Tob.* 169 F9 10 5N 61 54W
Bonaventure, *Canada* 141 C6 48 5N 65 32W
Bonavista, *Canada* 141 C9 48 40N 53 5W
Bonavista, C., *Canada* 141 C9 48 42N 53 5W
Bonavista B., *Canada* 141 C9 48 45N 53 25W
Bondeno, *Italy* 45 D8 44 53N 11 25 E
Bondo, *Équateur, Dem. Rep. of the Congo* 114 C4 1 22 S 23 54 E
Bondo, *Orientale, Dem. Rep. of the Congo* 118 B1 3 55N 23 53 E
Bondoukou, *Ivory C.* 112 D4 8 2N 2 47W
Bondowoso, *Indonesia* 85 D4 7 55 S 113 49 E
Bone, Teluk, *Indonesia* 82 B2 4 10 S 120 50 E
Bonefish Pond, *Bahamas* 9 b 25 59N 77 23W
Bonerate, *Indonesia* 82 C2 7 25 S 121 5 E
Bonerate, Kepulauan, *Indonesia* 82 C2 6 30 S 121 10 E
Bo'ness, *U.K.* 22 E5 56 1N 3 37W
Bonete, Cerro, *Argentina* 174 B2 27 55 S 68 40W
Bonfim, *Brazil* 169 C6 3 33N 59 25W
Bong Son = Hoai Nhon, *Vietnam* 86 E7 14 28N 109 1 E
Bonga, *Ethiopia* 107 F4 7 15N 36 14 E
Bongabon, *Phil.* 80 D3 15 38N 121 8 E
Bongabong, *Phil.* 80 E3 12 45N 121 29 E
Bongaigaon, *India* 90 B3 26 28N 90 34 E
Bongandanga, *Dem. Rep. of the Congo* 114 B4 1 24N 21 3 E
Bongao, *Phil.* 81 J2 5 2N 119 46 E
Bongka, *Indonesia* 82 B2 0 58 S 121 27 E
Bongo, *Dem. Rep. of the Congo* 114 C3 1 47 S 17 41 E
Bongo, Sa. de, *Angola* 115 E3 10 3 S 15 15 E
Bongor, *Chad* 109 F3 10 35N 15 20 E
Bongouanou, *Ivory C.* 112 D4 6 42N 4 15W
Bonham, *U.S.A.* 155 J6 33 35N 96 11W
Boni, *Mali* 112 B4 15 3N 2 10W
Boni Nat. Reserve, *Kenya* 118 C5 1 35 S 41 18 E
Bonifacio, *France* 29 G13 41 24N 9 10 E
Bonifacio, Bouches de, *Medit. S.* 46 A2 41 12N 9 15 E
Bonifay, *U.S.A.* 152 E4 30 47N 85 41W
Bonin Is. = Ogasawara Gunto, *Pac. Oc.* 62 G18 27 0N 142 0 E
Bonita Springs, *U.S.A.* 153 J8 26 21N 81 47W
Bonito, *Brazil* 173 21 8 S 56 28W
Bonke, *Ethiopia* 107 F4 6 5N 37 16 E
Bonkoukou, *Niger* 113 C5 14 0N 3 15 E
Bonn, *Germany* 30 E3 50 46N 7 6 E
Bonnat, *France* 27 F8 46 20N 1 54 E
Bonne Terre, *U.S.A.* 155 G9 37 55N 90 33W
Bonneau, *U.S.A.* 152 B10 33 16N 79 58W
Bonners Ferry, *U.S.A.* 158 B5 48 42N 116 19W
Bonnétable, *France* 26 D7 48 11N 0 25 E
Bonneval, *Eure-et-Loir, France* 26 D8 48 11N 1 24 E
Bonneval, *Savoie, France* 29 C11 45 22N 7 3 E
Bonneville, *France* 27 F13 46 4N 6 24 E
Bonney, L., *Australia* 128 D4 37 50 S 140 20 E
Bonnie Doon, *Australia* 129 D6 37 2 S 145 53 E
Bonnie Rock, *Australia* 125 F2 30 29 S 118 22 E
Bonny, *Nigeria* 113 E6 4 25N 7 13 E
Bonny →, *Nigeria* 113 E6 4 20N 7 10 E
Bonny, Bight of, *Africa* 113 E6 3 30N 9 20 E
Bonny Hills, *Australia* 129 A10 31 36 S 152 51 E
Bonny-sur-Loire, *France* 27 E9 47 33N 2 50 E
Bonnyrigg, *U.K.* 22 F5 55 53N 3 6W
Bonnyville, *Canada* 143 C6 54 20N 110 45W
Bono, *Italy* 46 B2 40 25N 9 2 E
Bonoi, *Indonesia* 83 B5 1 45 S 137 41 E
Bonorva, *Italy* 46 B1 40 25N 8 46 E
Bonsall, *U.S.A.* 161 M9 33 16N 117 14W
Bontang, *Indonesia* 85 B5 0 10N 117 30 E
Bontebok Nat. Park, *S. Africa* 116 E3 34 5 S 20 28 E
Bonthe, *S. Leone* 112 D2 7 30N 12 33W
Bontoc, *Phil.* 80 C3 17 7N 120 58 E
Bontosunggu, *Indonesia* 82 C1 5 41 S 119 42 E
Bonyeri, *Ghana* 112 D4 5 1N 2 46W
Bonyhád, *Hungary* 52 D3 46 18N 18 32 E
Bonython Ra., *Australia* 124 D4 23 40 S 128 45 E
Boo, Kepulauan, *Indonesia* 83 B3 1 12 S 129 24 E
Bookabie, *Australia* 125 F5 31 50 S 132 41 E
Booke, *Dem. Rep. of the Congo* 114 C4 2 34 S 22 3 E
Booker, *U.S.A.* 155 G4 36 27N 100 32W
Bool Lagoon, *Australia* 128 D4 37 7 S 140 40 E
Boola, *Guinea* 112 D3 8 22N 8 41 E
Boolcoomata, *Australia* 128 A4 31 57 S 140 33 E
Booleroo Centre, *Australia* 128 B3 32 53 S 138 21 E
Booligal, *Australia* 129 B6 33 58 S 144 53 E
Boonah, *Australia* 127 D5 27 58 S 152 41 E
Boone, *Iowa, U.S.A.* 156 B3 42 4N 93 53W
Boone, *N.C., U.S.A.* 149 G5 36 13N 81 41W
Booneville, *Ark., U.S.A.* 155 H8 35 8N 93 55W
Booneville, *Miss., U.S.A.* 149 H1 34 39N 88 34W
Boonville, *Calif., U.S.A.* 160 F3 39 1N 123 22W
Boonville, *Ind., U.S.A.* 157 F9 38 3N 87 16W
Boonville, *Mo., U.S.A.* 156 F4 38 58N 92 44W
Boonville, *N.Y., U.S.A.* 151 C9 43 29N 75 20W
Boorabbin Nat. Park, *Australia* 125 F4 31 30 S 129 57 E
Boorindal, *Australia* 127 E4 30 22 S 146 11 E
Boorowa, *Australia* 129 C8 34 28 S 148 44 E
Boort, *Australia* 128 D5 36 7 S 143 46 E
Boosaaso = Bosaso, *Somali Rep.* 120 B3 11 12N 49 18 E
Boothia, Gulf of, *Canada* 139 A11 71 0N 90 0W
Boothia Pen., *Canada* 138 A10 71 0N 94 0W
Bootle, *U.K.* 20 D4 53 28N 3 1W
Booué, *Gabon* 114 C2 0 5 S 11 55 E
Bopako, *Dem. Rep. of the Congo* 114 B4 1 53N 21 13 E
Boppard, *Germany* 31 E3 50 13N 7 35 E
Boquerón □, *Paraguay* 173 E5 23 0 S 60 0W
Boquete, *Panama* 164 E3 8 46N 82 27W
Boquilla, Presa de la, *Mexico* 162 B3 27 40N 105 30W
Boquillas del Carmen, *Mexico* 162 B4 29 17N 102 53W
Bor, *Czech Rep.* 34 B5 49 41N 12 45 E
Bor, *Russia* 60 B7 56 28N 43 59 E
Bor, *Serbia, Yug.* 50 B6 44 5N 22 7 E
Bôr, *Sudan* 107 F3 6 10N 31 40 E
Bor, *Sweden* 17 G8 57 9N 14 10 E
Bor, *Turkey* 100 D6 37 54N 34 32 E
Bor Döbö, *Kyrgyzstan* 65 D6 39 31N 73 16 E
Bor Mashash, *Israel* 103 D3 31 7N 34 50 E
Borah Peak, *U.S.A.* 158 D7 44 8N 113 47W
Boralday, *Kazakstan* 65 B8 43 20N 76 51 E
Borama, *Somali Rep.* 120 C2 9 55N 43 7 E
Borang, *Sudan* 107 G3 4 50N 30 59 E
Borangapara, *India* 90 C3 25 14N 90 14 E
Borås, *Sweden* 17 G6 57 43N 12 56 E
Borāzjān, *Iran* 97 D6 29 22N 51 10 E
Borba, *Brazil* 169 D6 4 12 S 59 34W
Borba, *Portugal* 43 G3 38 50N 7 26W
Borbon, *Phil.* 81 F5 10 50N 124 2 E
Borborema, Planalto da, *Brazil* 170 C4 7 0 S 37 0W
Borcea, *Romania* 53 F12 44 20N 27 45 E
Borçka, *Turkey* 101 B9 41 25N 41 41 E
Bord Khūn-e Now, *Iran* 97 D6 28 3N 51 28 E
Borda, C., *Australia* 128 C2 35 45 S 136 34 E
Bordeaux, *France* 28 D3 44 50N 0 36W
Borden, *Australia* 125 F2 34 3 S 118 12 E
Borden, *Canada* 141 C7 46 18N 63 47W
Borden I., *Canada* 6 B2 78 30N 111 30W
Borden Pen., *Canada* 139 A11 73 0N 83 0W
Borden Springs, *U.S.A.* 152 B4 33 56N 85 28W
Border Ranges Nat. Park, *Australia* 127 D5 28 24 S 152 56 E
Borders = Scottish Borders □, *U.K.* 22 F6 55 35N 2 50W
Bordertown, *Australia* 128 D4 36 19 S 140 45 E
Borðeyri, *Iceland* 11 B5 65 12N 21 6W
Bordighera, *Italy* 44 E4 43 46N 7 39 E
Bordj bou Arreridj, *Algeria* 111 A5 36 4N 4 45 E
Bordj Bourguiba, *Tunisia* 108 B2 32 12N 10 2 E
Bordj Fly Ste. Marie, *Algeria* 110 C4 27 19N 2 32W
Bordj-in-Eker, *Algeria* 111 D6 24 9N 5 3 E
Bordj Menaïel, *Algeria* 111 A5 36 46N 3 43 E
Bordj Messouda, *Algeria* 111 B6 30 12N 9 25 E
Bordj Nili, *Algeria* 111 B5 33 28N 3 2 E
Bordj Omar Driss, *Algeria* 111 C6 28 10N 6 40 E
Bordj Sif Fatima, *Algeria* 111 B6 31 6N 8 41 E
Bordj Tarat, *Algeria* 111 C6 25 55N 9 3 E
Bordutttighat, *India* 90 B4 26 57N 93 58 E
Bore, *Ethiopia* 107 G4 4 39N 37 39 E
Borehamwood, *U.K.* 21 F7 51 40N 0 15W
Borek Wielkopolski, *Poland* 55 G4 51 54N 17 11 E
Borensberg, *Sweden* 17 F9 58 34N 15 17 E
Borgå = Porvoo, *Finland* 15 F21 60 24N 25 40 E
Borgampad, *India* 94 F5 17 39N 80 52 E
Borgarfjarðarsýsla □, *Iceland* 11 C5 64 30N 21 30W
Borgarfjörður, *Borgarfjarðarsýsla, Iceland* 11 C4 64 30N 22 0W
Borgarfjörður, *Norður-Múlasýsla, Iceland* 14 D7 65 31N 13 49W
Borgarnes, *Iceland* 11 C5 64 32N 21 55W
Børgefjellet, *Norway* 14 D15 65 20N 13 45 E
Borger, *Neths.* 24 B6 52 54N 6 44 E
Borger, *U.S.A.* 155 H4 35 39N 101 24W
Borgholm, *Sweden* 17 H10 56 52N 16 39 E
Bórgia, *Italy* 47 D9 38 49N 16 30 E
Borgo San Dalmazzo, *Italy* 44 D4 44 20N 7 30 E
Borgo San Lorenzo, *Italy* 45 E8 43 57N 11 23 E
Borgo Val di Taro, *Italy* 44 D6 44 29N 9 46 E
Borgo Valsugana, *Italy* 45 B8 46 3N 11 27 E
Borgomanero, *Italy* 44 C5 45 42N 8 28 E
Borgorose, *Italy* 45 F10 42 11N 13 13 E
Borgosésia, *Italy* 44 C5 45 43N 8 16 E
Borgund, *Norway* 18 C4 61 3N 7 48 E
Borhoyn Tal, *Mongolia* 74 C6 43 50N 111 58 E
Bori, *Nigeria* 113 E6 4 42N 7 21 E
Borigumma, *India* 94 E6 19 3N 82 33 E
Borikhane, *Laos* 86 C4 18 33N 103 43 E
Borisoglebsk, *Russia* 60 E6 51 27N 42 5 E
Borisov = Barysaw, *Belarus* 58 E5 54 17N 28 28 E
Borisovka, *Russia* 59 G9 50 36N 36 1 E
Borja, *Peru* 168 D2 4 20 S 77 40W
Borja, *Spain* 40 D3 41 48N 1 34W
Borjas Blancas = Les Borges Blanques, *Spain* 40 D5 41 31N 0 52 E
Borjomi, *Georgia* 61 K6 41 48N 43 28 E
Børkop, *Denmark* 17 J3 55 39N 9 39 E
Borkou, *Chad* 109 E3 18 15N 18 50 E
Borkum, *Germany* 30 B2 53 34N 6 40 E
Borlänge, *Sweden* 16 D9 60 29N 15 26 E
Borley, C., *Antarctica* 7 C5 66 15 S 52 30 E
Borlu, *Turkey* 49 C10 38 44N 28 27 E
Bormida →, *Italy* 44 D5 44 23N 8 13 E
Bórmio, *Italy* 44 B7 46 28N 10 22 E
Borna, *Germany* 30 D8 51 7N 12 29 E
Borne Sulinowo, *Poland* 54 E3 53 32N 16 36 E
Borneo, *E. Indies* 85 B4 1 0N 115 0 E
Bornholm, *Denmark* 17 J8 55 10N 15 0 E
Bornholms Amtskommune □, *Denmark* 17 J8 55 5N 15 0 E
Bornholmsgattet, *Europe* 17 J8 55 15N 14 20 E
Borno, *Italy* 33 E10 45 56N 10 12 E
Borno □, *Nigeria* 113 C7 11 30N 13 0 E
Bornos, *Spain* 43 J5 36 48N 5 42W
Bornova, *Turkey* 49 C9 38 27N 27 14 E
Bornu Yassa, *Nigeria* 113 C7 12 14N 12 25 E
Boro →, *Sudan* 107 F2 8 52N 26 11 E
Borobudur, *Indonesia* 85 D4 7 36 S 110 13 E
Borodino, *Russia* 58 E8 55 31N 35 40 E
Borogontsy, *Russia* 67 C14 62 42N 131 8 E
Boromo, *Burkina Faso* 112 C4 11 45N 2 58W
Boron, *U.S.A.* 161 L9 35 0N 117 39W
Borong Is., *Burma* 90 F4 19 58N 93 6 E
Borongan, *Phil.* 81 F5 11 37N 125 26 E
Borotangba Mts., *C.A.R.* 107 F2 6 30N 25 0 E
Borotou, *Ivory C.* 112 D3 8 46N 7 30W
Borovan, *Bulgaria* 50 C7 43 27N 23 45 E
Borovichi, *Russia* 58 C7 58 25N 33 55 E
Borovsk, *Berezniki, Russia* 64 B6 59 43N 56 40 E
Borovsk, *Moskva, Russia* 58 E9 55 12N 36 24 E
Borrby, *Sweden* 17 J8 55 27N 14 10 E
Borrego Springs, *U.S.A.* 161 M10 33 15N 116 23W
Borriol, *Spain* 40 E4 40 4N 0 4W
Borroloola, *Australia* 126 B2 16 4 S 136 17 E
Borşa, *Cluj, Romania* 53 D8 46 56N 23 40 E
Borşa, *Maramureş, Romania* 53 C9 47 41N 24 50 E
Borsad, *India* 92 H5 22 25N 72 54 E
Borsec, *Romania* 53 D10 46 57N 25 34 E
Borsod-Abaúj-Zemplén □, *Hungary* 52 B6 48 20N 21 0 E
Bort-les-Orgues, *France* 28 C6 45 24N 2 29 E
Borth, *U.K.* 21 E3 52 29N 4 2W
Börtnan, *Sweden* 16 B7 62 45N 13 50 E
Borūjerd, *Iran* 97 C6 33 55N 48 50 E
Boryslav, *Ukraine* 59 H2 49 18N 23 28 E
Boryspil, *Ukraine* 59 G6 50 21N 30 59 E
Borzhomi = Borjomi, *Georgia* 61 K6 41 48N 43 28 E
Borzna, *Ukraine* 59 G7 51 18N 32 26 E
Borzya, *Russia* 67 D12 50 24N 116 31 E
Bosa, *Italy* 46 B1 40 18N 8 30 E
Bosa Monene, *Dem. Rep. of the Congo* 114 C4 1 16 S 23 40 E
Bosaga, *Turkmenistan* 65 E2 37 33N 65 41 E
Bosambi, *Dem. Rep. of the Congo* 114 B4 2 24N 22 39 E
Bosanska Dubica, *Bos.-H.* 45 C13 45 10N 16 50 E
Bosanska Gradiška, *Bos.-H.* 52 E2 45 10N 17 15 E
Bosanska Kostajnica, *Bos.-H.* 45 C13 45 11N 16 33 E
Bosanska Krupa, *Bos.-H.* 45 D13 44 53N 16 10 E
Bosanski Brod, *Bos.-H.* 52 E2 45 10N 18 0 E
Bosanski Novi, *Bos.-H.* 45 C13 45 2N 16 22 E
Bosanski Petrovac, *Bos.-H.* 45 D13 44 35N 16 21 E
Bosanski Šamac, *Bos.-H.* 52 E3 45 3N 18 29 E
Bosansko Grahovo, *Bos.-H.* 45 D13 44 12N 16 26 E
Bosaso, *Somali Rep.* 120 B3 11 12N 49 18 E
Bosavi, Mt., *Papua N. G.* 132 D2 6 30 S 142 49 E
Boscastle, *U.K.* 21 G3 50 41N 4 42W
Boscobel, *U.S.A.* 156 A6 43 8N 90 42W
Boscobelle, *Barbados* 165 g 13 16N 59 34W
Bose, *China* 76 F6 23 53N 106 35 E
Boseki, *Dem. Rep. of the Congo* 114 C3 2 34 S 19 38 E
Boshan, *China* 75 F9 36 28N 117 49 E
Boshof, *S. Africa* 116 D4 28 31 S 25 13 E
Boshrūyeh, *Iran* 97 C8 33 50N 57 30 E
Bosilegrad, *Serbia, Yug.* 50 D6 42 30N 22 27 E
Boskovice, *Czech Rep.* 35 B9 49 29N 16 40 E
Bosna →, *Bos.-H.* 52 E3 45 4N 18 29 E
Bosna i Hercegovina = Bosnia-Herzegovina ■, *Europe* 52 G2 44 0N 18 0 E
Bosnia-Herzegovina ■, *Europe* 52 G2 44 0N 18 0 E
Bosnik, *Indonesia* 83 B5 1 5 S 136 10 E
Bōsō-Hantō, *Japan* 73 B12 35 20N 140 20 E
Bosobolo, *Dem. Rep. of the Congo* 114 B3 4 15N 19 50 E
Bosporus = İstanbul Boğazı, *Turkey* 51 E13 41 10N 29 10 E
Bosque Farms, *U.S.A.* 159 J10 34 53N 106 40W
Bossangoa, *C.A.R.* 114 A3 6 35N 17 30 E
Bossé Bangou, *Niger* 113 C5 13 20N 1 18 E
Bossembélé, *C.A.R.* 114 A3 5 25N 17 40 E
Bossemtélé, *C.A.R.* 114 A3 5 41N 16 38 E
Bossier City, *U.S.A.* 155 J8 32 31N 93 44W
Bosso, *Niger* 113 C7 13 43N 13 19 E
Bosso, Dallol →, *Niger* 113 C5 12 25N 2 50 E
Bostan, *Pakistan* 92 D2 30 26N 67 2 E
Bostānābād, *Iran* 101 D12 37 50N 46 50 E
Bosten Hu, *China* 68 B3 41 55N 87 40 E
Boston, *Phil.* 81 H6 7 52N 126 22 E
Boston, *U.K.* 20 E7 52 59N 0 2W
Boston, *Ga., U.S.A.* 152 E6 30 47N 83 47W
Boston, *Mass., U.S.A.* 151 D13 42 22N 71 4W
Boston Bar, *Canada* 142 D4 49 52N 121 30W
Boston Mts., *U.S.A.* 155 H8 35 42N 93 15W
Bostwick, *U.S.A.* 152 F8 29 46N 81 38W
Bosumtwi, L., *Ghana* 113 D4 6 30N 1 25W
Bosusulu, *Dem. Rep. of the Congo* 114 B4 0 50N 20 45 E
Bosut →, *Croatia* 52 E3 45 20N 18 45 E
Boswell, *Canada* 142 D5 49 28N 116 45W
Boswell, *Ind., U.S.A.* 157 D9 40 31N 87 23W
Boswell, *Pa., U.S.A.* 150 F5 40 10N 79 2W
Bosworth, *U.S.A.* 156 E3 39 28N 93 20W
Botad, *India* 92 H4 22 15N 71 40 E
Botan →, *Turkey* 101 D10 37 57N 42 2 E
Botene, *Laos* 86 D3 17 35N 101 12 E
Botera, *Angola* 115 E2 11 37 S 14 16 E
Botev, *Bulgaria* 51 D8 42 44N 24 52 E
Botevgrad, *Bulgaria* 50 D7 42 55N 23 47 E
Bothaville, *S. Africa* 116 D4 27 23 S 26 34 E
Bothnia, G. of, *Europe* 14 E19 63 0N 20 15 E
Bothwell, *Australia* 127 G4 42 20 S 147 1 E
Bothwell, *Canada* 150 D3 42 38N 81 52W
Boticas, *Portugal* 42 D3 41 41N 7 40W
Botletle →, *Botswana* 116 C3 20 10 S 23 15 E
Botlikh, *Russia* 61 J8 42 39N 46 11 E
Botna →, *Moldova* 53 D14 46 45N 29 34 E
Botola, *Dem. Rep. of the Congo* 114 C3 1 17 S 18 13 E
Botolan, *Phil.* 80 D3 15 17N 120 1 E
Botoroaga, *Romania* 53 F10 44 8N 25 32 E
Botoşani, *Romania* 53 C11 47 42N 26 41 E
Botoşani □, *Romania* 53 C11 47 50N 26 50 E
Botou, *Burkina Faso* 113 C5 12 42N 1 59 E
Botricello, *Italy* 47 D9 38 56N 16 51 E
Botro, *Ivory C.* 112 D3 7 51N 5 19W
Botswana ■, *Africa* 116 C3 22 0 S 24 0 E
Bottineau, *U.S.A.* 154 A4 48 50N 100 27W
Bottnaryd, *Sweden* 17 G7 57 47N 13 50 E
Bottopassi, *Surinam* 169 C6 4 14N 55 27W
Bottrop, *Germany* 24 C6 51 31N 6 58 E
Botucatu, *Brazil* 175 A6 22 55 S 48 30W
Botwood, *Canada* 141 C8 49 6N 55 23W
Bou Alam, *Algeria* 111 B5 33 50N 1 26 E
Bou Ali, *Algeria* 111 C4 27 11N 0 4W
Bou Djébéha, *Mali* 112 B4 18 25N 2 45W
Bou Guema, *Algeria* 111 C5 28 49N 0 19 E
Bou Ismaïl, *Algeria* 111 A5 36 38N 2 42 E
Bou Izakarn, *Morocco* 110 C3 29 12N 9 46W
Boû Lanouâr, *Mauritania* 110 D1 21 12N 16 34W
Boû Rjeïmât, *Mauritania* 112 B1 19 4N 15 3W
Bou Saâda, *Algeria* 111 A5 35 11N 4 9 E
Bou Salem, *Tunisia* 108 A1 36 45N 9 2 E
Bouaflé, *Ivory C.* 112 D3 7 1N 5 47W
Bouaké, *Ivory C.* 112 D3 7 40N 5 2W
Bouanga, *Congo* 114 C3 2 7 S 16 8 E
Bouar, *C.A.R.* 114 A3 6 0N 15 40 E
Bouârfa, *Morocco* 111 B4 32 32N 1 58W
Bouba Ndjida, Parc Nat. de, *Cameroon* 114 A2 8 50N 14 45 E
Bouboout, *Algeria* 110 C4 27 26N 4 30W
Bouca, *C.A.R.* 114 A3 6 45N 18 25 E
Boucaut B., *Australia* 126 A1 12 0 S 134 25 E
Bouches-du-Rhône □, *France* 29 E9 43 37N 5 2 E
Boucle de Baoule, Parc Nat. de la, *Mali* 112 C3 13 53N 9 0W
Bouda, *Algeria* 111 C4 27 50N 0 27W
Boudenib, *Morocco* 110 B4 31 59N 3 31W
Boudry, *Switz.* 32 C3 46 57N 6 50 E
Boufarik, *Algeria* 111 A5 36 34N 2 58 E
Bougainville, C., *Australia* 124 B4 13 57 S 126 4 E
Bougainville I., *Papua N. G.* 133 L8 6 0 S 155 0 E
Bougainville Reef, *Australia* 126 B4 15 30 S 147 5 E
Bougainville Str., *Solomon Is.* 133 L9 6 40 S 156 10 E
Bougaroun, C., *Algeria* 111 A6 37 6N 6 30 E
Bougie = Bejaïa, *Algeria* 111 A6 36 42N 5 2 E
Bougouni, *Mali* 112 C3 11 30N 7 20W
Bouillon, *Belgium* 24 E5 49 44N 5 3 E
Bouira, *Algeria* 111 A5 36 20N 3 59 E
Boukombé, *Benin* 113 C5 10 13N 1 9 E
Boulal, *Mali* 112 B3 15 8N 8 21W
Boulazac, *France* 28 C4 45 10N 0 47 E
Boulder, *Colo., U.S.A.* 154 E2 40 1N 105 17W
Boulder, *Mont., U.S.A.* 158 C7 46 14N 112 7W
Boulder City, *U.S.A.* 161 K12 35 59N 114 50W
Boulder Creek, *U.S.A.* 160 H4 37 7N 122 7W
Boulder Dam = Hoover Dam, *U.S.A.* 161 K12 36 1N 114 44W
Boulembo, *Gabon* 114 C2 1 26 S 12 0 E
Bouli, *Mauritania* 112 B2 15 17N 12 18W
Boulia, *Australia* 126 C2 22 52 S 139 51 E
Bouligny, *France* 27 C12 49 17N 5 45 E
Boulogne →, *France* 26 E5 47 12N 1 47W
Boulogne-sur-Gesse, *France* 28 E4 43 18N 0 38 E
Boulogne-sur-Mer, *France* 27 B8 50 42N 1 36 E
Bouloire, *France* 26 E7 47 59N 0 45 E
Boulou →, *C.A.R.* 114 A4 6 45N 24 16 E
Boulouli, *Mali* 112 B3 15 30N 9 25W
Bouloupari, *N. Cal.* 133 U20 21 52 S 166 4 E
Bouloupesse, *Congo* 114 C2 1 58 S 12 40 E
Boulsa, *Burkina Faso* 113 C4 12 39N 0 34W
Boultoum, *Niger* 113 C7 14 45N 10 25 E
Bouma Nat. Heritage Park, *Fiji* 133 A2 16 50 S 179 52 E
Boumalne, *Morocco* 110 B3 31 25N 6 0W
Boumba →, *Cameroon* 114 B2 2 2N 15 12 E
Boumbé →, *C.A.R.* 114 B3 4 4N 15 23 E
Boûmdeïd, *Mauritania* 112 B2 17 25N 9 50W
Boun Neua, *Laos* 86 B3 21 38N 101 54 E
Boun Tai, *Laos* 86 B3 21 23N 101 58 E
Bouna, *Ivory C.* 112 D4 9 10N 3 0W
Boundary, *U.S.A.* 144 D12 64 4N 141 6W
Boundary Peak, *U.S.A.* 160 H8 37 51N 118 21W
Boundgi, *Gabon* 114 C2 1 0 S 11 51 E
Boundiali, *Ivory C.* 112 D3 9 30N 6 20W
Boungou →, *C.A.R.* 114 A4 8 21N 23 48 E
Bountiful, *U.S.A.* 158 F8 40 53N 111 53W
Bounty Is., *Pac. Oc.* 134 M9 48 0 S 178 30 E
Boura, *Mali* 112 C4 12 25N 4 33W
Bourail, *N. Cal.* 133 U19 21 34 S 165 30 E
Bourbeuse →, *U.S.A.* 156 F6 38 24N 90 53W
Bourbon, *U.S.A.* 157 C10 41 18N 86 7W
Bourbon-Lancy, *France* 27 F10 46 37N 3 45 E
Bourbon-l'Archambault, *France* 27 F10 46 36N 3 4 E
Bourbonnais, *France* 27 F10 46 28N 3 0 E
Bourbonnais, *U.S.A.* 157 C9 41 9N 87 52W
Bourbonne-les-Bains, *France* 27 E12 47 54N 5 45 E
Bourbourg, *France* 27 B9 50 56N 2 12 E
Bourdel L., *Canada* 140 A5 56 43N 74 10W
Bourem, *Mali* 113 B4 17 0N 0 24W
Bourg, *France* 28 C3 45 3N 0 34W
Bourg-Argental, *France* 29 C8 45 18N 4 32 E
Bourg-de-Péage, *France* 29 C9 45 2N 5 3 E
Bourg-en-Bresse, *France* 27 F12 46 13N 5 12 E
Bourg-Lastic, *France* 28 C6 45 39N 2 35 E
Bourg-Madame, *France* 28 F5 42 26N 1 55 E
Bourg-St-Andéol, *France* 29 D8 44 23N 4 39 E
Bourg-St-Maurice, *France* 29 C10 45 35N 6 46 E
Bourg-St. Pierre, *Switz.* 32 E4 45 57N 7 12 E
Bourganeuf, *France* 28 C5 45 57N 1 45 E
Bourges, *France* 27 E9 47 9N 2 25 E
Bourget, *Canada* 151 A9 45 26N 75 9W
Bourget, Lac du, *France* 29 C9 45 44N 5 52 E
Bourgneuf, B. de, *France* 26 E4 47 3N 2 10W
Bourgneuf-en-Retz, *France* 26 E5 47 2N 1 58W
Bourgogne, *France* 27 F11 47 0N 4 50 E
Bourgoin-Jallieu, *France* 29 C9 45 36N 5 17 E
Bourgueil, *France* 26 E7 47 17N 0 10 E
Bourke, *Australia* 127 E4 30 8 S 145 55 E
Bourne, *U.K.* 20 E7 52 47N 0 22W
Bournemouth, *U.K.* 21 G6 50 43N 1 52W
Bournemouth □, *U.K.* 21 G6 50 43N 1 52W
Bouroum, *Burkina Faso* 113 C4 13 37N 0 39W
Bouse, *U.S.A.* 161 M13 33 56N 114 0W
Boussac, *France* 27 F9 46 22N 2 13 E
Boussé, *Burkina Faso* 113 C4 12 39N 1 53W
Bousso, *Chad* 109 F3 10 34N 16 52 E
Boussouma, *Burkina Faso* 113 C4 12 52N 1 13W
Boutilimit, *Mauritania* 112 B2 17 45N 14 40W
Boutonne →, *France* 28 C3 45 55N 0 50W
Bouvet I. = Bouvetøya, *Antarctica* 8 M12 54 26 S 3 24 E
Bouvetøya, *Antarctica* 8 M12 54 26 S 3 24 E
Bouxwiller, *France* 27 D14 48 49N 7 27 E
Bouza, *Niger* 113 C6 14 29N 6 2 E
Bouznika, *Morocco* 110 B3 33 46N 7 6W
Bouzonville, *France* 27 C13 49 17N 6 32 E
Bova Marina, *Italy* 47 E8 37 56N 15 55 E
Bovalino Marina, *Italy* 47 D9 38 10N 16 10 E
Bovec, *Slovenia* 45 B10 46 20N 13 33 E
Boven Kapuas, Pegunungan, *Malaysia* 85 B4 1 25N 113 15 E
Bøverdal, *Norway* 18 C5 61 44N 8 20 E
Bøverfjorden, *Norway* 18 A5 63 1N 8 32 E
Bovill, *U.S.A.* 158 C5 46 51N 116 24W
Bovino, *Italy* 47 A8 41 15N 15 20 E
Bovril, *Argentina* 174 C4 31 21 S 59 26W
Bow →, *Canada* 142 C6 49 57N 111 41W
Bow Island, *Canada* 142 D6 49 50N 111 23W
Bowbells, *U.S.A.* 154 A3 48 48N 102 15W
Bowdle, *U.S.A.* 154 C5 45 27N 99 39W
Bowdon, *U.S.A.* 152 B4 33 32N 85 15W
Bowdon Junction, *U.S.A.* 152 B4 33 40N 85 9W
Bowelling, *Australia* 125 F2 33 25 S 116 30 E
Bowen, *Argentina* 174 D2 35 0 S 67 31W
Bowen, *Australia* 126 J6 20 0 S 148 16 E
Bowen Mts., *Australia* 129 D7 37 0 S 147 50 E
Bowie, *Ariz., U.S.A.* 159 K9 32 19N 109 29W
Bowie, *Tex., U.S.A.* 155 J6 33 34N 97 51W
Bowkān, *Iran* 101 D12 36 31N 46 12 E
Bowland, Forest of, *U.K.* 20 D5 54 0N 2 30W
Bowling Green, *Fla., U.S.A.* 153 H8 27 38N 81 50W
Bowling Green, *Ky., U.S.A.* 148 G2 36 59N 86 27W
Bowling Green, *Mo., U.S.A.* 156 E5 39 21N 91 12W
Bowling Green, *Ohio, U.S.A.* 157 C13 41 23N 83 39W
Bowling Green, C., *Australia* 126 B4 19 19 S 147 25 E
Bowling Green Bay Nat. Park, *Australia* 126 B4 19 26 S 146 57 E
Bowman, *N. Dak., U.S.A.* 154 B3 46 11N 103 24W
Bowman, *S.C., U.S.A.* 152 B9 33 21N 80 41W
Bowman I., *Antarctica* 7 C8 65 0 S 104 0 E
Bowmanville, *Canada* 150 C6 43 55N 78 41W
Bowmore, *U.K.* 22 F2 55 45N 6 17W
Bowral, *Australia* 129 C9 34 26 S 150 27 E
Bowraville, *Australia* 127 E5 30 37 S 152 52 E
Bowron →, *Canada* 142 C4 54 3N 121 50W
Bowron Lake Prov. Park, *Canada* 142 C4 53 10N 121 5W
Bowser L., *Canada* 142 B3 56 30N 129 30W
Bowsman, *Canada* 143 C8 52 14N 101 12W
Bowutu Mts., *Papua N. G.* 132 D4 7 45 S 147 10 E
Bowwood, *Zambia* 119 F2 17 5 S 26 20 E
Box Cr. →, *Australia* 127 E3 34 10 S 143 50 E
Boxholm, *Sweden* 17 F9 58 12N 15 3 E
Boxmeer, *Neths.* 24 C5 51 38N 5 56 E

Boxtel, Neths. 24 C5 51 36N 5 20 E
Boyabat, Turkey 100 B6 41 28N 34 47 E
Boyabo, Dem. Rep. of the Congo 114 B3 3 43N 18 46 E
Boyaca □, Colombia 168 B3 5 30N 73 20W
Boyalıca, Turkey 51 F13 40 29N 29 33 E
Boyang, China 77 C11 29 0N 116 38 E
Boyasegese, Dem. Rep. of the Congo 114 B4 3 29N 20 33 E
Boyce, U.S.A. 155 K8 31 23N 92 40W
Boyd, U.S.A. 152 E6 30 11N 83 37W
Boyd L., Canada 140 B4 52 46N 76 42W
Boyenge, Dem. Rep. of the Congo 114 B3 0 14N 18 55 E
Boyer, C., N. Cal. 133 U22 21 37 S 168 6 E
Boyera, Dem. Rep. of the Congo 114 C3 0 40 S 19 23 E
Boyle, Canada 142 C6 54 35N 112 49W
Boyle, Ireland 23 C3 53 59N 8 18W
Boyne →, Ireland 23 C5 53 43N 6 15W
Boyne City, U.S.A. 148 C3 45 13N 85 1W
Boyni Qara, Afghan. 91 A2 36 20N 67 0 E
Boynitsa, Bulgaria 50 C6 43 58N 22 32 E
Boynton Beach, U.S.A. 149 M5 26 32N 80 4W
Boyolali, Indonesia 85 D4 7 32 S 110 35 E
Boyoma, Chutes, Dem. Rep. of the Congo 118 B2 0 35N 25 23 E
Boysen Reservoir, U.S.A. 158 E9 43 25N 108 11W
Boyup Brook, Australia 125 F2 33 50 S 116 23 E
Boz Burun, Turkey 51 F12 40 32N 28 46 E
Boz Dağ, Turkey 49 D11 37 18N 29 11 E
Boz Dağları, Turkey 49 C10 38 20N 28 0 E
Bozai Gumbaz, Afghan. 65 E7 37 8N 74 0 E
Bozburun, Turkey 49 E10 36 43N 28 4 E
Bozcaada, Turkey 100 C2 39 49N 26 3 E
Bozdoğan, Turkey 49 D10 37 40N 28 17 E
Boze, Papua N. G. 132 E2 9 3 S 143 3 E
Bozeman, U.S.A. 158 D8 45 41N 111 2W
Bozen = Bolzano, Italy 45 B8 46 31N 11 22 E
Bozene, Dem. Rep. of the Congo 114 B3 2 56N 19 12 E
Boževac, Serbia, Yug. 50 B5 44 32N 21 24 E
Bozhou, China 74 H8 33 55N 115 41 E
Bozkır, Turkey 100 D5 37 11N 32 14 E
Bozkurt, Turkey 49 D11 37 50N 29 37 E
Bozouls, France 28 D6 44 28N 2 43 E
Bozoum, C.A.R. 114 A3 6 25N 16 35 E
Bozova, Antalya, Turkey 49 D12 37 13N 30 18 E
Bozova, Sanliurfa, Turkey 101 D8 37 21N 38 32 E
Bozovici, Romania 52 F7 44 56N 22 0 E
Bozüyük, Turkey 49 B12 39 54N 30 3 E
Bra, Italy 44 D4 44 42N 7 51 E
Braås, Sweden 17 G9 57 4N 15 3 E
Brabant □, Belgium 24 D4 50 46N 4 30 E
Brabant L., Canada 143 B8 55 58N 103 43W
Brabrand, Denmark 17 H4 56 9N 10 7 E
Brač, Croatia 45 E13 43 20N 16 40 E
Bracadale, L., U.K. 22 D2 57 20N 6 30W
Bracciano, Italy 45 F9 42 6N 12 10 E
Bracciano, L. di, Italy 45 F9 42 7N 12 14 E
Bracebridge, Canada 140 C4 45 2N 79 19W
Brach, Libya 108 C2 27 31N 14 20 E
Bracieux, France 26 E8 47 30N 1 30 E
Bräcke, Sweden 16 B9 62 45N 15 26 E
Brackettville, U.S.A. 155 L4 29 19N 100 25W
Bracki Kanal, Croatia 45 E13 43 24N 16 40 E
Bracknell, U.K. 21 F7 51 25N 0 43W
Bracknell Forest □, U.K. 21 F7 51 25N 0 44W
Brad, Romania 52 D7 46 10N 22 50 E
Brádano →, Italy 47 B9 40 23N 16 51 E
Bradenton, U.S.A. 149 M4 27 30N 82 34W
Bradford, Canada 150 B5 44 7N 79 34W
Bradford, U.K. 20 D6 53 47N 1 45W
Bradford, Ill., U.S.A. 156 C7 41 11N 89 39W
Bradford, Ohio, U.S.A. 157 D12 40 8N 84 27W
Bradford, Pa., U.S.A. 150 E6 41 58N 78 38W
Bradford, Vt., U.S.A. 151 C12 43 59N 72 9W
Bradley, Ark., U.S.A. 155 J8 33 6N 93 39W
Bradley, Calif., U.S.A. 160 K6 35 52N 120 48W
Bradley, Fla., U.S.A. 153 H8 27 48N 81 59W
Bradley, Ill., U.S.A. 157 C9 41 9N 87 52W
Bradley Institute, Zimbabwe 119 F3 17 7 S 31 25 E
Bradner, U.S.A. 157 C13 41 20N 83 26W
Brady, U.S.A. 155 K5 31 9N 99 20W
Brædstrup, Denmark 17 J3 55 58N 9 37 E
Braemar, Australia 128 B3 33 12 S 139 35 E
Braeside, Canada 151 A8 45 28N 76 24W
Braga, Portugal 42 D2 41 35N 8 25W
Braga □, Portugal 42 D2 41 30N 8 30W
Bragadiru, Romania 53 G10 43 46N 25 31 E
Bragado, Argentina 174 D3 35 2 S 60 27W
Bragança, Brazil 170 B2 1 0 S 47 2W
Bragança, Portugal 42 D4 41 48N 6 50W
Bragança □, Portugal 42 D4 41 30N 6 45W
Bragança Paulista, Brazil 175 A6 22 55 S 46 32W
Brahmakund, India 90 B6 27 52N 96 22 E
Brahmanbaria, Bangla. 90 D3 23 58N 91 15 E
Brahmani →, India 94 D8 20 39N 86 46 E
Brahmapur, India 94 E7 19 15N 84 54 E
Brahmaputra →, Asia 90 D2 23 58N 89 50 E
Brahmaputra →, India 90 B5 27 48N 95 30 E
Braich-y-pwll, U.K. 20 E3 52 47N 4 46W
Braidwood, Australia 129 C8 35 27 S 149 49 E
Brăila, Romania 53 E12 45 19N 27 59 E
Brăila □, Romania 53 E12 45 5N 27 30 E
Brainerd, U.S.A. 154 B7 46 22N 94 12W
Braintree, U.K. 21 F8 51 53N 0 34 E
Braintree, U.S.A. 151 D14 42 13N 71 0W
Brak →, S. Africa 116 D3 29 35 S 22 55 E
Brake, Germany 30 B4 53 20N 8 28 E
Brakel, Germany 30 D5 51 42N 9 11 E
Bräkne-Hoby, Sweden 17 H9 56 14N 15 6 E
Brakwater, Namibia 116 C2 22 28 S 17 3 E
Brålanda, Sweden 17 F6 58 34N 12 21 E
Bramberg, Germany 31 E6 50 6N 10 40 E
Bramdrupdam, Denmark 17 J3 55 31N 9 28 E
Bramhapuri, India 94 D4 20 36N 79 52 E
Bramming, Denmark 17 J2 55 28N 8 42 E
Brämön, Sweden 16 B11 62 14N 17 40 E
Brampton, Canada 140 D4 43 45N 79 45W
Brampton, U.K. 20 C5 54 57N 2 44W
Bramsche, Germany 30 C3 52 24N 7 59 E
Bramton I., Australia 126 J7 20 50 S 149 17 E
Branchville, U.S.A. 152 B9 33 15N 80 49W
Branco →, Brazil 169 D5 1 20 S 61 50W
Branco, C., Brazil 170 C5 7 9 S 34 47W
Brandberg, Namibia 116 B2 21 10 S 14 33 E
Brandberg Nature Reserve, Namibia 116 C1 21 10 S 14 30 E
Brandbu, Norway 18 D7 60 26N 10 28 E
Brande, Denmark 17 J3 55 57N 9 8 E
Brandenburg = Neubrandenburg, Germany 30 B9 53 33N 13 15 E
Brandenburg, Germany 30 C8 52 25N 12 33 E
Brandenburg, U.S.A. 157 G10 38 0N 86 10W
Brandenburg □, Germany 30 C9 52 50N 13 0 E
Brandfort, S. Africa 116 D4 28 40 S 26 30 E
Brando, France 29 F13 42 47N 9 27 E
Brandon, Canada 143 D9 49 50N 99 57W
Brandon, Fla., U.S.A. 153 H7 27 56N 82 17W
Brandon, Vt., U.S.A. 151 C11 43 48N 73 4W
Brandon B., Ireland 23 D1 52 17N 10 8W
Brandon Mt., Ireland 23 D1 52 15N 10 15W
Brandsen, Argentina 174 D4 35 10 S 58 15W
Brandvlei, S. Africa 116 E3 30 25 S 20 30 E
Brandýs nad Labem, Czech Rep. 34 A7 50 10N 14 40 E
Brănești, Romania 53 F11 44 27N 26 20 E
Branford, Conn., U.S.A. 151 E12 41 17N 72 49W
Branford, Fla., U.S.A. 152 F7 29 58N 82 56W
Braniewo, Poland 54 D6 54 25N 19 50 E
Bransfield Str., Antarctica 7 C18 63 0 S 59 0W
Brańsk, Poland 55 F9 52 45N 22 50 E
Branson, U.S.A. 155 G8 36 39N 93 13W
Brantford, Canada 140 D3 43 10N 80 15W
Brantley, U.S.A. 152 D3 31 35N 86 16W
Brantôme, France 28 C4 45 22N 0 39 E
Branxholme, Australia 128 D4 37 52 S 141 49 E
Branxton, Australia 129 B9 32 38 S 151 21 E
Branzi, Italy 44 B6 46 1N 9 46 E
Brás, Brazil 169 D6 2 5 S 58 10W
Bras d'Or L., Canada 141 C7 45 50N 60 50W
Brasher Falls, U.S.A. 151 B10 44 49N 74 47W
Brasil, Planalto, Brazil 166 E6 18 0 S 46 30W
Brasil Novo, Brazil 169 D7 3 19 S 52 38W
Brasiléia, Brazil 172 C4 11 0 S 68 45W
Brasília, Distrito Federal, Brazil 171 E2 15 47 S 47 55W
Brasília, Minas Gerais, Brazil 171 E3 16 12 S 44 26W
Brasília Legal, Brazil 169 D6 3 49 S 55 36W
Braskereidfoss, Norway 18 D8 60 44N 11 46 E
Braslaw, Belarus 15 J22 55 38N 27 0 E
Braslovče, Slovenia 45 B12 46 21N 15 3 E
Brașov, Romania 53 E10 45 38N 25 35 E
Brașov □, Romania 53 E10 45 45N 25 15 E
Brass, Nigeria 113 E6 4 35N 6 14 E
Brass →, Nigeria 113 E6 4 15N 6 13 E
Brassac-les-Mines, France 28 C7 45 24N 3 20 E
Brasschaat, Belgium 24 C4 51 19N 4 27 E
Brassey, Banjaran, Malaysia 85 B5 5 0N 117 15 E
Brassey Ra., Australia 125 E3 25 8 S 122 15 E
Brasstown Bald, U.S.A. 149 H4 34 53N 83 49W
Brastad, Sweden 17 F5 58 23N 11 30 E
Brastavățu, Romania 53 G9 43 55N 24 24 E
Bratan = Morozov, Bulgaria 51 D9 42 30N 25 10 E
Brateș, Romania 53 E11 45 50N 26 4 E
Bratislava, Slovak Rep. 35 C10 48 10N 17 7 E
Bratislavský □, Slovak Rep. 35 C10 48 15N 17 20 E
Bratsigovo, Bulgaria 51 D8 42 1N 24 22 E
Bratsk, Russia 67 D11 56 10N 101 30 E
Brattleboro, U.S.A. 151 D12 42 51N 72 34W
Brattvåg, Norway 18 B3 62 37N 6 25 E
Bratunac, Bos.-H. 52 F4 44 13N 19 21 E
Braunau, Austria 34 C6 48 15N 13 3 E
Braunschweig, Germany 30 C6 52 15N 10 31 E
Braunton, U.K. 21 F3 51 7N 4 10W
Brava, C. Verde Is. 9 j 15 0N 24 40W
Brava, Somali Rep. 120 D2 1 20N 44 8 E
Bravicea, Moldova 53 C13 47 22N 28 27 E
Bråviken, Sweden 17 F10 58 38N 16 32 E
Bravo del Norte, Rio = Grande, Rio →, U.S.A. 155 N6 25 58N 97 9W
Brawley, U.S.A. 161 N11 32 59N 115 31W
Bray, Ireland 23 C5 53 13N 6 7W
Bray, Mt., Australia 126 A1 14 0 S 134 30 E
Bray, Pays de, France 25 B4 49 46N 1 26 E
Bray-sur-Seine, France 27 D10 48 25N 3 14 E
Braymer, U.S.A. 156 E3 39 35N 93 48W
Brazeau →, Canada 142 C5 52 55N 115 14W
Brazil, U.S.A. 157 E9 39 32N 87 8W
Brazil ■, S. Amer. 171 D2 12 0 S 50 0W
Brazilian Highlands = Brasil, Planalto, Brazil 166 E6 18 0 S 46 30W
Brazo Sur →, S. Amer. 174 B4 25 21 S 57 42W
Brazos →, U.S.A. 155 L7 28 53N 95 23W
Brazzaville, Congo 115 C3 4 9 S 15 12 E
Brčko, Bos.-H. 52 F3 44 54N 18 46 E
Brda →, Poland 55 E5 53 8N 18 8 E
Brdy, Czech Rep. 34 B6 49 43N 13 55 E
Brea, Peru 172 A1 4 40 S 81 7W
Breaden, L., Australia 125 E4 25 51 S 125 28 E
Breaksea Sd., N.Z. 131 F1 45 35 S 166 35 E
Bream B., N.Z. 130 B3 35 56 S 174 28 E
Bream Hd., N.Z. 130 B3 35 51 S 174 36 E
Bream Tail, N.Z. 130 C3 36 3 S 174 36 E
Breas, Chile 174 B1 25 29 S 70 24W
Breaza, Romania 53 E10 45 11N 25 40 E
Brebes, Indonesia 85 D3 6 52 S 109 3 E
Brechin, Canada 150 B5 44 32N 79 10W
Brechin, U.K. 22 E6 56 44N 2 39W
Brecht, Belgium 24 C4 51 21N 4 38 E
Breckenridge, Colo., U.S.A. 158 G10 39 29N 106 3W
Breckenridge, Minn., U.S.A. 154 B6 46 16N 96 35W
Breckenridge, Tex., U.S.A. 155 J5 32 45N 98 54W
Breckland, U.K. 21 E8 52 30N 0 40 E
Brecknock, Pen., Chile 176 D2 54 35 S 71 30W
Břeclav, Czech Rep. 35 C9 48 46N 16 53 E
Brecon, U.K. 21 F4 51 57N 3 23W
Brecon Beacons, U.K. 21 F4 51 53N 3 26W
Breda, Neths. 24 C4 51 35N 4 45 E
Bredaryd, Sweden 17 G7 57 10N 13 45 E
Bredasdorp, S. Africa 116 E3 34 33 S 20 2 E
Bredbo, Australia 129 C8 35 58 S 149 10 E
Bredebro, Denmark 17 J2 55 4N 8 50 E
Bredstedt, Germany 30 A4 54 37N 8 55 E
Bredy, Russia 64 E8 52 26N 60 21 E
Bree, Belgium 24 C5 51 8N 5 35 E
Bregalnica →, Macedonia 50 E6 41 43N 22 9 E
Bregenz, Austria 34 D2 47 30N 9 45 E
Bregenzer Wald, Austria 33 B9 47 20N 10 0 E
Bregovo, Bulgaria 50 B6 44 9N 22 39 E
Bréhal, France 26 D5 48 53N 1 30W
Bréhat, Î. de, France 26 D4 48 51N 3 0W
Breiðafjörður, Iceland 11 B3 65 15N 23 15W
Breiðdalsvík, Iceland 11 C13 64 44N 14 0W
Breil-sur-Roya, France 29 E11 43 56N 7 31 E
Breim, Norway 18 C3 61 44N 6 25 E
Breisach, Germany 31 G3 48 1N 7 36 E
Brejinho de Nazaré, Brazil 170 D2 11 1 S 48 34W
Brejo, Brazil 170 B3 3 41 S 42 47W
Brekke, Norway 18 C2 61 1N 5 26 E
Brekken, Norway 18 B8 62 40N 11 51 E
Brekkestø, Norway 18 F5 58 11N 8 22 E
Bremanger, Norway 18 C1 61 51N 4 58 E
Bremangerlandet, Norway 18 C1 61 51N 5 0 E
Bremen, Germany 30 B4 53 4N 8 47 E
Bremen, Ga., U.S.A. 152 B4 33 43N 85 9W
Bremen, Ind., U.S.A. 157 C10 41 27N 86 9W
Bremen □, Germany 30 B4 53 4N 8 50 E
Bremer Bay, Australia 125 F2 34 21 S 119 20 E
Bremer I., Australia 126 A2 12 5 S 136 45 E
Bremerhaven, Germany 30 B4 53 33N 8 36 E
Bremerton, U.S.A. 160 C4 47 34N 122 38W
Bremervörde, Germany 30 B5 53 29N 9 8 E
Bremgarten, Switz. 33 B6 47 22N 8 20 E
Bremnes, Norway 18 E2 59 47N 5 8 E
Bremsnes, Norway 18 A4 63 6N 7 40 E
Brenes, Spain 43 H5 37 32N 5 54W
Brenham, U.S.A. 155 K6 30 10N 96 24W
Brenne, France 28 B5 46 44N 1 14 E
Brennerpass, Austria 34 D4 47 2N 11 30 E
Brennhaug, Norway 18 C6 61 54N 9 21 E
Breno, Italy 44 C7 45 57N 10 18 E
Brent, U.S.A. 149 J2 32 56N 87 10W
Brenta →, Italy 45 C9 45 11N 12 18 E
Brentwood, U.K. 21 F8 51 37N 0 19 E
Brentwood, Calif., U.S.A. 160 H5 37 56N 121 42W
Brentwood, N.Y., U.S.A. 151 F11 40 47N 73 15W
Bréscia, Italy 44 C7 45 33N 10 15 E
Breskens, Neths. 24 C3 51 23N 3 33 E
Breslau = Wrocław, Poland 55 G4 51 5N 17 5 E
Bresle →, France 26 B8 50 4N 1 22 E
Bressanone, Italy 45 B8 46 43N 11 39 E
Bressay, U.K. 22 A7 60 9N 1 6W
Bresse, France 27 F12 46 50N 5 10 E
Bressuire, France 26 F6 46 51N 0 30W
Brest, Belarus 59 F2 52 10N 23 40 E
Brest, France 26 D2 48 24N 4 31W
Brest-Litovsk = Brest, Belarus 59 F2 52 10N 23 40 E
Bretagne, France 26 D3 48 10N 3 0W
Bretanha, Pta. da, Azores 9 d3 37 54N 25 47W
Breţcu, Romania 53 D11 46 7N 26 18 E
Bretenoux, France 28 D5 44 54N 1 51 E
Breteuil, Eure, France 26 D7 48 50N 0 57 E
Breteuil, Oise, France 27 C9 49 38N 2 18 E
Breton, Canada 142 C6 53 7N 114 28W
Breton, Pertuis, France 28 B2 46 17N 1 25W
Breton Sd., U.S.A. 155 L10 29 35N 89 15W
Brett, C., N.Z. 130 B3 35 10 S 174 20 E
Bretten, Germany 31 F4 49 2N 8 42 E
Breuil-Cervínia, Italy 44 C4 45 56N 7 38 E
Brevard, U.S.A. 149 H4 35 14N 82 44W
Breves, Brazil 170 B1 1 40 S 50 29W
Brevig Mission, U.S.A. 144 D6 65 20N 166 29W
Brevik, Norway 18 E6 59 4N 9 42 E
Brewarrina, Australia 127 E4 30 0 S 146 51 E
Brewer, U.S.A. 149 C11 44 48N 68 46W
Brewer, Mt., U.S.A. 160 J8 36 44N 118 28W
Brewerville, Liberia 112 D2 6 26N 10 47W
Brewster, N.Y., U.S.A. 151 E11 41 23N 73 37W
Brewster, Ohio, U.S.A. 150 F3 40 43N 81 36W
Brewster, Wash., U.S.A. 158 B4 48 6N 119 47W
Brewster, Kap = Kangikajik, Greenland 10 C8 70 7N 22 0W
Brewton, U.S.A. 149 K2 31 7N 87 4W
Breyten, S. Africa 117 D5 26 16 S 30 0 E
Breza, Bos.-H. 52 F3 44 2N 18 16 E
Brezhnev = Naberezhnyye Chelny, Russia 60 C11 55 42N 52 19 E
Brežice, Slovenia 45 C12 45 54N 15 35 E
Brézina, Algeria 111 B5 33 4N 1 14 E
Březnice, Czech Rep. 34 B6 49 32N 13 57 E
Breznik, Bulgaria 50 D6 42 44N 22 55 E
Brezno, Slovak Rep. 35 C12 48 50N 19 40 E
Brezoi, Romania 53 E9 45 21N 24 15 E
Brezovica, Kosovo, Yug. 50 D5 42 15N 21 3 E
Brezovo, Bulgaria 51 D9 42 21N 25 5 E
Bria, C.A.R. 114 A4 6 30N 21 58 E
Briançon, France 29 D10 44 54N 6 39 E
Briare, France 27 E9 47 38N 2 45 E
Briático, Italy 47 D9 38 43N 16 2 E
Bribie I., Australia 127 D5 27 0 S 153 10 E
Bribri, Costa Rica 164 E3 9 38N 82 50W
Briceni, Moldova 53 B12 48 22N 27 6 E
Bricquebec, France 26 C5 49 28N 1 38W
Bridgefield, Barbados 165 g 13 9N 59 36W
Bridgehampton, U.S.A. 151 F12 40 56N 72 19W
Bridgend, U.K. 21 F4 51 30N 3 34W
Bridgend □, U.K. 21 F4 51 36N 3 36W
Bridgeport, Calif., U.S.A. 160 G7 38 15N 119 14W
Bridgeport, Conn., U.S.A. 151 E11 41 11N 73 12W
Bridgeport, Ill., U.S.A. 157 F9 38 43N 87 46W
Bridgeport, Nebr., U.S.A. 154 E3 41 40N 103 6W
Bridgeport, Tex., U.S.A. 155 J6 33 13N 97 45W
Bridger, U.S.A. 158 D9 45 18N 108 55W
Bridgeton, U.S.A. 148 F8 39 26N 75 14W
Bridgetown, Australia 125 F2 33 58 S 116 7 E
Bridgetown, Barbados 165 g 13 5N 59 30W
Bridgetown, Canada 141 D6 44 55N 65 18W
Bridgewater, Australia 128 D5 36 36 S 143 59 E
Bridgewater, Canada 141 D7 44 25N 64 31W
Bridgewater, Mass., U.S.A. 151 E14 41 59N 70 58W
Bridgewater, N.Y., U.S.A. 151 D9 42 53N 75 15W
Bridgewater, C., Australia 128 E4 38 23 S 141 23 E
Bridgewater-Gagebrook, Australia 127 G4 42 44 S 147 14 E
Bridgman, U.S.A. 157 C10 41 57N 86 33W
Bridgnorth, U.K. 21 E5 52 32N 2 25W
Bridgton, U.S.A. 151 B14 44 3N 70 42W
Bridgwater, U.K. 21 F5 51 8N 2 59W
Bridgwater B., U.K. 21 F4 51 15N 3 15W
Bridlington, U.K. 20 C7 54 5N 0 12W
Bridlington B., U.K. 20 C7 54 4N 0 10W
Bridport, Australia 127 G4 40 59 S 147 23 E
Bridport, U.K. 21 G5 50 44N 2 45W
Briec, France 26 D2 48 6N 4 0W
Brienne-le-Château, France 27 D11 48 24N 4 30 E
Brienon-sur-Armançon, France 27 E10 47 59N 3 38 E
Brienz, Switz. 32 C6 46 46N 8 2 E
Brienzersee, Switz. 32 C5 46 44N 7 53 E
Brier Cr. →, U.S.A. 152 C8 32 44N 81 26W
Brig, Switz. 32 D5 46 18N 7 59 E
Brigg, U.K. 20 D7 53 34N 0 28W
Brigham City, U.S.A. 158 F7 41 31N 112 1W
Bright, Australia 129 D7 36 42 S 146 56 E
Brighton, Australia 128 C3 35 5 S 138 30 E
Brighton, Canada 150 B7 44 2N 77 44W
Brighton, Trin. & Tob. 169 F9 10 13N 61 39W
Brighton, U.K. 21 G7 50 49N 0 7W
Brighton, Colo., U.S.A. 154 F2 39 59N 104 49W
Brighton, Fla., U.S.A. 153 H8 27 14N 81 6W
Brighton, Ill., U.S.A. 156 E6 39 2N 90 8W
Brighton, Iowa, U.S.A. 156 C5 41 10N 91 49W
Brighton, Mich., U.S.A. 157 B13 42 32N 83 47W
Brighton, N.Y., U.S.A. 150 C7 43 8N 77 34W
Brightwater, N.Z. 131 B8 41 22 S 173 9 E
Brignogan-Plage, France 26 D2 48 40N 4 20W
Brignoles, France 29 E10 43 25N 6 5 E
Brihuega, Spain 40 E2 40 45N 2 52W
Brikama, Gambia 112 C1 13 15N 16 45W
Brilliant, U.S.A. 150 F4 40 15N 80 39W
Brilon, Germany 30 D4 51 23N 8 35 E
Brim, Australia 128 D5 36 3 S 142 27 E
Brimfield, U.S.A. 156 D7 40 50N 89 53W
Bríndisi, Italy 47 B10 40 39N 17 55 E
Brinje, Croatia 45 D12 44 59N 15 9 E
Brinkley, U.S.A. 155 H9 34 53N 91 12W
Brinkworth, Australia 128 B3 33 42 S 138 26 E
Brinnon, U.S.A. 160 C4 47 41N 122 54W
Brinson, U.S.A. 152 E5 30 59N 84 44W
Brion, I., Canada 141 C7 47 46N 61 26W
Brionne, France 26 C7 49 11N 0 43 E
Brionski, Croatia 45 D10 44 55N 13 45 E
Brioude, France 28 C7 45 18N 3 24 E
Briouze, France 26 D6 48 42N 0 23W
Brisbane, Australia 127 D5 27 25 S 153 2 E
Brisbane →, Australia 127 D5 27 24 S 153 9 E
Brisbane Ranges Nat. Park, Australia 128 D6 37 47 S 144 16 E
Brisighella, Italy 45 D8 44 13N 11 46 E
Brissago, Switz. 33 D7 46 7N 8 43 E
Bristol, U.K. 21 F5 51 26N 2 35W
Bristol, Conn., U.S.A. 151 E12 41 40N 72 57W
Bristol, Fla., U.S.A. 152 E5 30 26N 84 59W
Bristol, Pa., U.S.A. 151 F10 40 6N 74 51W
Bristol, R.I., U.S.A. 151 E13 41 40N 71 16W
Bristol, Tenn., U.S.A. 149 G4 36 36N 82 11W
Bristol, City of □, U.K. 21 F5 51 27N 2 36W
Bristol B., U.S.A. 144 H8 58 0N 160 0W
Bristol Channel, U.K. 21 F3 51 18N 4 30W
Bristol I., Antarctica 7 B1 58 45 S 28 0W
Bristol L., U.S.A. 159 J5 34 23N 116 50W
Bristow, U.S.A. 155 H6 35 50N 96 23W
Bristow I., Papua N. G. 132 E2 9 8 S 143 14 E
Britain = Great Britain, Europe 19 D5 54 0N 2 15W
Britânia, Brazil 173 D7 15 14 S 51 9W
British Columbia □, Canada 142 C3 55 0N 125 15W
British Indian Ocean Terr. = Chagos Arch., Ind. Oc. 62 K11 6 0 S 72 0 E
British Isles, Europe 19 D5 54 0N 4 0W
Brits, S. Africa 117 D4 25 37 S 27 48 E
Britstown, S. Africa 116 E3 30 37 S 23 30 E
Britt, Canada 140 C3 45 46N 80 34W
Britt, U.S.A. 156 A3 43 6N 93 48W
Brittany = Bretagne, France 26 D3 48 10N 3 0W
Britton, U.S.A. 154 C6 45 48N 97 45W
Brive-la-Gaillarde, France 28 C5 45 10N 1 32 E
Briviesca, Spain 42 C7 42 32N 3 19W
Brixen = Bressanone, Italy 45 B8 46 43N 11 39 E
Brixham, U.K. 21 G4 50 23N 3 31W
Brlik = Birlik, Kazakstan 65 B6 43 40N 73 49 E
Brlik = Birlik, Kazakstan 65 A6 44 5N 73 31 E
Brnaze, Croatia 45 E13 43 41N 16 40 E
Brno, Czech Rep. 35 B9 49 10N 16 35 E
Broach = Bharuch, India 94 D1 21 47N 73 0 E
Broad →, Ga., U.S.A. 152 B7 33 59N 82 39W
Broad →, S.C., U.S.A. 149 J5 34 1N 81 4W
Broad Arrow, Australia 125 F3 30 23 S 121 15 E
Broad B., U.K. 22 C2 58 14N 6 18W
Broad Haven, Ireland 23 B2 54 20N 9 55W
Broad Law, U.K. 22 F5 55 30N 3 21W
Broad Sd., Australia 126 C4 22 0 S 149 45 E
Broadalbin, U.S.A. 151 C10 43 4N 74 12W
Broadback →, Canada 140 B4 51 21N 78 52W
Broadford, Australia 129 D6 37 14 S 145 4 E
Broadhurst Ra., Australia 124 D3 22 30 S 122 30 E
Broads, The, U.K. 20 E9 52 45N 1 30 E
Broadus, U.S.A. 154 C2 45 27N 105 25W
Broager, Denmark 17 K3 54 53N 9 40 E
Broby, Sweden 17 H8 56 15N 14 4 E
Broc, Switz. 32 C4 46 37N 7 6 E
Brocēni, Latvia 54 B9 56 42N 22 32 E
Brochet, Canada 143 B8 57 53N 101 40W
Brochet, L., Canada 143 B8 58 36N 101 35W
Brocken, Germany 30 D6 51 47N 10 37 E
Brocklehurst, Australia 129 B8 32 9 S 148 38 E
Brockport, U.S.A. 150 C7 43 13N 77 56W
Brockton, U.S.A. 151 D13 42 5N 71 1W
Brockville, Canada 140 D4 44 35N 75 41W
Brockway, Mont., U.S.A. 154 B2 47 18N 105 45W
Brockway, Pa., U.S.A. 150 E6 41 15N 78 47W
Brocton, U.S.A. 150 D5 42 23N 79 26W
Brod, Macedonia 50 E5 41 32N 21 17 E
Brodarevo, Serbia, Yug. 50 C3 43 14N 19 44 E
Brodeur Pen., Canada 139 A11 72 30N 88 10W
Brodhead, U.S.A. 156 B7 42 37N 89 22W
Brodhead, Mt., U.S.A. 150 E7 41 39N 77 47W
Brodick, U.K. 22 F3 55 35N 5 9W
Brodnica, Poland 55 E6 53 15N 19 25 E
Brody, Ukraine 59 G3 50 5N 25 10 E
Brogan, U.S.A. 158 D5 44 15N 117 31W
Broglie, France 26 C7 49 2N 0 30 E
Brok, Poland 55 F8 52 43N 21 52 E
Broken Arrow, U.S.A. 155 G7 36 3N 95 48W
Broken Bow, Nebr., U.S.A. 154 E5 41 24N 99 38W
Broken Bow, Okla., U.S.A. 155 H7 34 2N 94 44W
Broken Bow Lake, U.S.A. 155 H7 34 9N 94 40W
Broken Hill = Kabwe, Zambia 119 E2 14 30 S 28 29 E
Broken Hill, Australia 128 A4 31 58 S 141 29 E
Broken River Ra., Australia 126 K6 21 0 S 148 22 E
Brokind, Sweden 17 F9 58 13N 15 42 E
Brokopondo, Surinam 169 B7 5 3N 54 59W
Bromley □, U.K. 21 F8 51 24N 0 2 E
Bromölla, Sweden 17 H8 56 5N 14 28 E
Bromsgrove, U.K. 21 E5 52 21N 2 2W
Bronaugh, U.S.A. 156 G2 37 41N 94 28W
Brønderslev, Denmark 17 G3 57 16N 9 57 E
Brong-Ahafo □, Ghana 112 D4 7 50N 2 0W
Broni, Italy 44 C6 45 4N 9 16 E
Bronkhorstspruit, S. Africa 117 D4 25 46 S 28 45 E
Brønnøysund, Norway 14 D15 65 28N 12 14 E
Bronson, Fla., U.S.A. 153 F7 29 27N 82 39W
Bronson, Mich., U.S.A. 157 C11 41 52N 85 12W
Bronte, Italy 47 E7 37 47N 14 50 E
Bronwood, U.S.A. 152 D5 31 50N 84 22W
Brook Park, U.S.A. 150 E4 41 24N 81 51W
Brooke's Point, Phil. 81 G1 8 47N 117 50 E
Brookfield, Mo., U.S.A. 156 E3 39 47N 93 4W
Brookfield, Wis., U.S.A. 157 A8 43 4N 88 9W
Brookhaven, U.S.A. 155 K9 31 35N 90 26W
Brookings, Oreg., U.S.A. 158 E1 42 3N 124 17W
Brookings, S. Dak., U.S.A. 154 C6 44 19N 96 48W
Brooklet, U.S.A. 152 C8 32 23N 81 40W
Brooklin, Canada 150 C6 43 55N 78 55W
Brooklyn, U.S.A. 156 C4 41 44N 92 27W
Brooklyn Park, U.S.A. 154 C8 45 6N 93 23W
Brooks, Canada 142 C6 50 35N 111 55W
Brooks Range, U.S.A. 144 C10 68 0N 152 0W
Brookston, U.S.A. 157 D10 40 36N 86 52W
Brooksville, Fla., U.S.A. 149 L4 28 33N 82 23W
Brooksville, Ky., U.S.A. 157 F12 38 41N 84 4W
Brookton, Australia 125 F2 32 22 S 117 0 E
Brookville, Ind., U.S.A. 157 E12 39 25N 85 1W
Brookville, Ohio, U.S.A. 157 E12 39 50N 84 27W
Brookville, Pa., U.S.A. 150 E5 41 10N 79 5W
Brookville L., U.S.A. 157 E11 39 28N 85 0W
Broom, L., U.K. 22 D3 57 55N 5 15W
Broome, Australia 124 C3 18 0 S 122 15 E
Broons, France 26 D4 48 20N 2 16W
Brora, U.K. 22 C5 58 0N 3 52W
Brora →, U.K. 22 C5 58 0N 3 51W
Brørup, Denmark 17 J2 55 29N 9 1 E
Brösarp, Sweden 17 J8 55 43N 14 6 E
Brosna →, Ireland 23 C4 53 14N 7 58W
Broșteni, Mehedinți, Romania 52 F7 44 45N 22 59 E
Broșteni, Suceava, Romania 53 C10 47 14N 25 43 E
Brostrud, Norway 18 D5 60 18N 8 34 E
Brotas de Macaúbas, Brazil 171 D3 12 0 S 42 38W
Brothers, U.S.A. 158 E3 43 49N 120 36W
Brøttum, Norway 18 C7 61 2N 10 34 E
Brou, France 26 D8 48 13N 1 11 E
Brouage, France 28 C2 45 52N 1 4W
Brough, U.K. 20 C5 54 32N 2 18W
Brough Hd., U.K. 22 B5 59 8N 3 20W
Broughton, U.S.A. 157 G8 37 56N 88 27W
Broughton Island = Qikiqtarjuaq, Canada 139 B13 67 33N 63 0W
Broumov, Czech Rep. 35 A9 50 35N 16 20 E
Brovary, Ukraine 59 G6 50 34N 30 48 E
Brovst, Denmark 17 G3 57 6N 9 31 E
Brown, L., Australia 125 F2 31 5 S 118 15 E
Brown, Mt., Australia 128 B3 32 30 S 138 0 E
Brown, Pt., Australia 127 E1 32 32 S 133 50 E
Brown City, U.S.A. 150 C2 43 13N 82 59W
Brown Willy, U.K. 21 G3 50 35N 4 37W
Brownfield, U.S.A. 155 J3 33 11N 102 17W
Browning, Ill., U.S.A. 156 D6 40 8N 90 22W
Browning, Mo., U.S.A. 156 D3 40 3N 93 12W
Browning, Mont., U.S.A. 158 B7 48 34N 113 1W
Brownsburg, U.S.A. 157 E10 39 51N 86 24W
Brownstown, U.S.A. 157 F10 38 53N 86 3W

Burnt River, Canada 150 B6 44 41N 78 42W
Burntwood →, Canada 143 B9 56 8N 96 34W
Burntwood L., Canada 143 B8 55 22N 100 26W
Buronga, Australia 128 C5 34 18 S 142 20 E
Burqān, Kuwait 96 D5 29 0N 47 57 E
Burra, Australia 128 B3 33 40 S 138 55 E
Burra, Nigeria 113 C6 11 0N 8 56 E
Burragorang, L., Australia 129 B9 33 52 S 150 37 E
Burray, U.K. 22 C6 58 51N 2 54W
Burrel, Albania 50 E4 41 36N 20 1 E
Burren Junction, Australia 127 E4 30 7 S 148 59 E
Burrendong, L., Australia 129 B8 32 45 S 149 10 E
Burriana, Spain 40 F4 39 50N 0 4W
Burrinjuck Res., Australia 129 C8 35 0 S 148 36 E
Burro, Serranías del, Mexico 162 B4 29 0N 102 0W
Burrow Hd., U.K. 22 G4 54 41N 4 24W
Burrowa Pine Mountain Nat. Park, Australia 129 D7 36 6 S 147 45 E
Burrum Coast Nat. Park, Australia 127 D5 25 13 S 152 36 E
Burruyacú, Argentina 174 B3 26 30 S 64 40W
Burry Port, U.K. 21 F3 51 41N 4 15W
Bursa, Turkey 51 F13 40 15N 29 5 E
Burseryd, Sweden 17 G7 57 12N 13 17 E
Burstall, Canada 143 C7 50 39N 109 54W
Burton, Mich., U.S.A. 157 B13 43 0N 83 40W
Burton, Ohio, U.S.A. 150 E3 41 28N 81 8W
Burton, S.C., U.S.A. 149 J5 32 25N 80 45W
Burton, L., Canada 140 B4 54 45N 78 20W
Burton upon Trent, U.K. 20 E6 52 48N 1 38W
Burtundy, Australia 128 B5 33 45 S 142 15 E
Buru, Indonesia 82 B3 3 30 S 126 30 E
Buruanga, Phil. 81 F3 11 51N 121 53 E
Burugi Game Reserve, Tanzania 118 C3 2 20 S 31 6 E
Burullus, Bahra el, Egypt 106 H7 31 25N 31 0 E
Burūm, Yemen 99 D5 14 22N 48 59 E
Burûn, Râs, Egypt 103 D2 31 14N 33 7 E
Burunday = Boralday, Kazakstan 65 B8 43 20N 76 51 E
Burundi ■, Africa 118 C3 3 15 S 30 0 E
Bururi, Burundi 118 C2 3 57 S 29 37 E
Burutu, Nigeria 113 D6 5 20N 5 29 E
Burwell, U.S.A. 154 E5 41 47N 99 8W
Burwick, U.K. 22 C5 58 45N 2 58W
Bury, U.K. 20 D5 53 35N 2 17W
Bury St. Edmunds, U.K. 21 E8 52 15N 0 43 E
Buryatia □, Russia 67 D11 53 0N 110 0 E
Bürylbaytal, Kazakstan 65 A7 45 5N 74 1 E
Buryn, Ukraine 59 G7 51 13N 33 50 E
Burzenin, Poland 55 G5 51 28N 18 47 E
Busa, Mt., Phil. 81 H5 6 8N 124 39 E
Busalla, Italy 44 D5 44 34N 8 57 E
Busan = Pusan, S. Korea 75 G15 35 5N 129 0 E
Busanga, Dem. Rep. of the Congo 114 C4 0 53 S 22 7 E
Busango Swamp, Zambia 119 E2 14 15 S 25 45 E
Buşayrah, Syria 101 E9 35 9N 40 26 E
Busca, Italy 44 D4 44 31N 7 29 E
Bushat, Albania 50 E3 41 58N 19 34 E
Būshehr, Iran 97 D6 28 55N 50 55 E
Būshehr □, Iran 97 D6 28 20N 51 45 E
Bushell, Canada 143 B7 59 31N 108 45W
Bushenyi, Uganda 118 C3 0 35 S 30 10 E
Bushimaie →, Dem. Rep. of the Congo 115 D4 6 2 S 23 45 E
Bushire = Būshehr, Iran 97 D6 28 55N 50 55 E
Bushnell, Fla., U.S.A. 153 G7 28 40N 82 7W
Bushnell, Ill., U.S.A. 156 D6 40 33N 90 31W
Busie, Ghana 112 C4 10 29N 2 22W
Businga, Dem. Rep. of the Congo 114 B4 3 16N 20 59 E
Buskerud □, Norway 18 D5 60 20N 9 0 E
Busko-Zdrój, Poland 55 H7 50 28N 20 42 E
Buskul, Kazakstan 64 E8 53 45N 61 12 E
Buslei, Ethiopia 120 C2 5 28N 44 25 E
Busovača, Bos.-H. 52 F2 44 6N 17 53 E
Buşra ash Shām, Syria 103 C5 32 30N 36 25 E
Busselton, Australia 125 F2 33 42 S 115 15 E
Busseri →, Sudan 107 F2 7 41N 28 3 E
Busseto, Italy 44 D7 44 59N 10 2 E
Bussière-Badil, France 28 C4 45 39N 0 36 E
Bussigny, Switz. 32 C3 46 33N 6 33 E
Bussolengo, Italy 44 C7 45 28N 10 51 E
Bussum, Neths. 24 B5 52 16N 5 10 E
Bustamante, B., Argentina 176 C3 45 5 S 66 18W
Buşteni, Romania 53 E10 45 24N 25 32 E
Busto, C., Spain 42 B4 43 34N 6 28W
Busto Arsízio, Italy 44 C5 45 37N 8 51 E
Busu Djanoa, Dem. Rep. of the Congo 114 B4 1 43N 21 23 E
Busu Kwanga, Dem. Rep. of the Congo 114 B4 1 48N 20 21 E
Busu Mandji, Dem. Rep. of the Congo 114 B4 2 52N 21 14 E
Busuanga, Phil. 80 E2 12 14N 119 52 E
Busuanga I., Phil. 80 E2 12 10N 120 0 E
Büsum, Germany 30 A4 54 7N 8 51 E
Busungbiu, Indonesia 79 J17 8 16 S 114 58 E
Buta, Dem. Rep. of the Congo 118 B1 2 50N 24 53 E
Butare, Rwanda 118 C2 2 31 S 29 52 E
Butaritari, Kiribati 134 G9 3 30N 174 0 E
Bute, Australia 128 B3 33 51 S 138 2 E
Bute, U.K. 22 F3 55 48N 5 2W
Bute Inlet, Canada 142 C4 50 40N 124 53W
Butemba, Uganda 118 B3 1 9N 31 37 E
Butembo, Dem. Rep. of the Congo 118 B2 0 9N 29 18 E
Buteni, Romania 52 D7 46 19N 22 7 E
Butera, Italy 47 E7 37 11N 14 11 E
Butha Qi, China 69 B7 48 0N 122 32 E
Buthidaung, Burma 90 E4 20 52N 92 32 E
Butiaba, Uganda 118 B3 1 50N 31 20 E
Butler, Ga., U.S.A. 152 C5 32 33N 84 14W
Butler, Ind., U.S.A. 157 C12 41 26N 84 52W
Butler, Ky., U.S.A. 157 F12 38 47N 84 22W
Butler, Mo., U.S.A. 156 F2 38 16N 94 20W
Butler, Pa., U.S.A. 150 F5 40 52N 79 54W
Buton, Indonesia 82 C2 5 0 S 122 45 E
Butrintit, L. e, Albania 38 B10 39 43N 20 5 E
Bütschwil, Switz. 33 B8 47 23N 9 5 E
Butte, Mont., U.S.A. 158 C7 46 0N 112 32W
Butte, Nebr., U.S.A. 154 D5 42 58N 98 51W
Butte Creek →, U.S.A. 160 F5 39 12N 121 56W
Butterworth = Gcuwa, S. Africa 117 E4 32 20 S 28 11 E
Butterworth, Malaysia 87 c 5 24N 100 23 E
Buttevant, Ireland 23 D3 52 14N 8 40W
Buttfield, Mt., Australia 125 D4 24 45 S 128 9 E
Button B., Canada 143 B10 58 45N 94 23W
Buttonwillow, U.S.A. 161 K7 35 24N 119 28W
Butty Hd., Australia 125 F3 33 54 S 121 39 E
Butuan, Phil. 81 G5 8 57N 125 33 E
Butuku-Luba, Eq. Guin. 113 E6 3 29N 8 33 E
Butung = Buton, Indonesia 82 C2 5 0 S 122 45 E
Buturlinovka, Russia 60 E5 50 50N 40 35 E
Butzbach, Germany 31 E4 50 25N 8 40 E
Bützow, Germany 30 B7 53 50N 11 58 E
Buulobarde = Bulo Burti, Somali Rep. 120 D3 3 50N 45 33 E
Buur Hakaba = Bur Acaba, Somali Rep. 120 D2 3 12N 44 20 E
Buvik, Norway 18 A7 63 18N 10 11 E
Buxa Duar, India 93 F13 27 45N 89 35 E
Buxar, India 93 G10 25 34N 83 58 E
Buxtehude, Germany 30 B5 53 28N 9 39 E
Buxton, Guyana 169 B6 6 48N 58 2W
Buxton, U.K. 20 D6 53 16N 1 54W
Buxy, France 27 F11 46 44N 4 40 E
Buy, Russia 60 A5 58 28N 41 28 E
Buynaksk, Russia 61 J8 42 48N 47 7 E
Buyo, Ivory C. 112 D3 6 21N 7 5W
Buyo, L. de, Ivory C. 112 D3 6 16N 7 10W
Büyük Menderes →, Turkey 49 D9 37 28N 27 11 E
Büyükçekmece, Turkey 51 E12 41 2N 28 35 E
Büyükkariştiran, Turkey 51 E11 41 18N 27 33 E
Büyükkemikli Burnu, Turkey 51 F10 40 18N 26 14 E
Büyükorhan, Turkey 49 B10 39 46N 28 56 E
Büyükyoncalı, Turkey 51 E11 41 20N 27 55 E
Buzançais, France 26 F8 46 54N 1 25 E
Buzău, Romania 53 E11 45 10N 26 50 E
Buzău □, Romania 53 E11 45 20N 26 30 E
Buzău →, Romania 53 E12 45 26N 27 44 E
Buzău, Pasul, Romania 53 E11 45 35N 26 12 E
Buzen, Japan 72 D3 33 35N 131 5 E
Buzet, Croatia 45 C10 45 24N 13 58 E
Buzi →, Mozam. 119 F3 19 50 S 34 43 E
Buziaş, Romania 52 E6 45 38N 21 36 E
Buzuluk, Russia 64 E4 52 48N 52 12 E
Buzuluk →, Russia 60 E6 50 15N 42 7 E
Buzzards B., U.S.A. 151 E14 41 45N 70 37W
Buzzards Bay, U.S.A. 151 E14 41 44N 70 37W
Bwagaoia, Papua N. G. 132 F7 10 40 S 152 52 E
Bwana Mkubwe, Dem. Rep. of the Congo 119 E2 13 8 S 28 38 E
Bwasa, Dem. Rep. of the Congo 114 C3 3 55 S 18 24 E
Bwatnapné, Vanuatu 133 E6 15 41 S 168 9 E
Bwindi Impenetrable Forest Nat. Park, Uganda 118 C2 1 2 S 29 42 E
Byala, Ruse, Bulgaria 51 C9 43 28N 25 44 E
Byala, Varna, Bulgaria 51 D11 42 53N 27 55 E
Byala Slatina, Bulgaria 50 C7 43 26N 23 58 E
Byarezina →, Belarus 59 F6 52 33N 30 14 E
Byaroza, Belarus 59 F3 52 31N 24 51 E
Bychawa, Poland 55 G9 51 1N 22 36 E
Byczyna, Poland 55 G5 51 7N 18 12 E
Bydgoszcz, Poland 55 E5 53 10N 18 0 E
Byelarus = Belarus ■, Europe 58 F4 53 30N 27 0 E
Byelorussia = Belarus ■, Europe 58 F4 53 30N 27 0 E
Byers, U.S.A. 154 F2 39 43N 104 14W
Byesville, U.S.A. 150 G3 39 58N 81 32W
Byfield Nat. Park, Australia 126 C5 22 52 S 150 45 E
Byford, Australia 125 F2 32 15 S 116 0 E
Bygdin, Norway 18 C5 61 21N 8 32 E
Bygland, Norway 18 F4 58 50N 7 48 E
Byglandsfjorden, Norway 18 F4 58 44N 7 50 E
Bygstad, Norway 18 C2 61 23N 5 40 E
Bykhaw, Belarus 58 F6 53 31N 30 14 E
Bykhov = Bykhaw, Belarus 58 F6 53 31N 30 14 E
Bykle, Norway 18 E4 59 20N 7 22 E
Bykovo, Russia 60 F7 49 50N 45 25 E
Bylas, U.S.A. 159 K8 33 8N 110 7W
Bylot, Canada 143 B10 58 25N 94 8W
Bylot I., Canada 139 A12 73 13N 78 34W
Byrd, C., Antarctica 7 C17 69 38 S 76 7W
Byrock, Australia 129 A7 30 40 S 146 27 E
Byron, Ga., U.S.A. 152 C6 32 39N 83 46W
Byron, Ill., U.S.A. 156 B7 42 8N 89 15W
Byron Bay, Australia 127 D5 28 43 S 153 37 E
Byrranga, Gory, Russia 67 B11 75 0N 100 0 E
Byrranga Mts. = Byrranga, Gory, Russia 67 B11 75 0N 100 0 E
Byrum, Denmark 17 G5 57 16N 11 0 E
Byske, Sweden 14 D19 64 57N 21 11 E
Byske älv →, Sweden 14 D19 64 57N 21 13 E
Bystrovka = Kemin, Kyrgyzstan 65 B7 42 47N 75 42 E
Bystrzyca →, Dolnośląskie, Poland 55 G3 51 12N 16 55 E
Bystrzyca →, Lubelskie, Poland 55 G9 51 21N 22 46 E
Bystrzyca Kłodzka, Poland 55 H3 50 19N 16 39 E
Bytča, Slovak Rep. 35 B11 49 13N 18 34 E
Bytom, Poland 55 H5 50 25N 18 54 E
Bytom Odrzański, Poland 55 G2 51 44N 15 48 E
Bytów, Poland 54 D4 54 10N 17 30 E
Byumba, Rwanda 118 C3 1 35 S 30 4 E
Bzenec, Czech Rep. 35 C10 48 58N 17 18 E
Bzura →, Poland 55 F7 52 25N 20 15 E

C

Ca →, Vietnam 86 C5 18 45N 105 45 E
Ca Mau, Vietnam 87 H5 9 7N 105 8 E
Ca Mau, Mui, Vietnam 87 H5 8 38N 104 44 E
Ca Na, Vietnam 87 G7 11 20N 108 54 E
Caacupé, Paraguay 174 B4 25 23 S 57 5W
Caála, Angola 115 E3 12 46 S 15 30 E
Caamano Sd., Canada 142 C3 52 55N 129 25W
Caapiranga, Brazil 169 D5 3 18 S 61 13W
Caazapá, Paraguay 174 B4 26 8 S 56 19W
Caazapá □, Paraguay 175 B4 26 10 S 56 0W
Cabadbaran, Phil. 81 G5 9 10N 125 38 E
Cabagan, Phil. 80 C3 17 26N 121 46 E
Cabalian = San Juan, Phil. 81 F5 10 16N 125 10 E
Caballeria, C. de, Spain 38 A5 40 5N 4 5 E
Cabana, Peru 172 B2 8 25 S 78 5W
Cabana, Spain 42 B2 43 13N 8 54W
Cabanaconde, Peru 172 D3 15 38 S 71 58W
Cabañaquinta, Spain 42 B5 43 10N 5 38W
Cabanatuan, Phil. 80 D3 15 30N 120 58 E
Cabanes, Spain 40 E5 40 9N 0 2 E
Cabangon, Phil. 80 D3 15 10N 120 3 E
Cabanillas, Peru 172 D3 15 36 S 70 28W
Cabano, Canada 141 C6 47 40N 68 56W
Čabar, Croatia 45 C11 45 36N 14 39 E
Cabarroguis, Phil. 80 C3 16 50N 121 30 E
Cabarruyan I., Phil. 80 C2 16 18N 119 59 E
Cabazon, U.S.A. 161 M10 33 55N 116 47W
Cabedelo, Brazil 170 C5 7 0 S 34 50W
Cabeza del Buey, Spain 43 G5 38 44N 5 13W
Cabezón de la Sal, Spain 42 B6 43 18N 4 14W
Cabildo, Chile 174 C1 32 30 S 71 5W
Cabimas, Venezuela 168 A3 10 23N 71 25W
Cabinda, Angola 115 D2 5 33 S 12 11 E
Cabinda □, Angola 115 D2 5 0 S 12 30 E
Cabinet Mts., U.S.A. 158 C6 48 0N 115 30W
Cabiri, Angola 115 D2 8 52 S 13 39 E
Cable Beach, Bahamas 9 b 25 4N 77 24W
Cabo Blanco, Argentina 176 C3 47 15 S 65 47W
Cabo Frio, Brazil 171 F3 22 51 S 42 3W
Cabo Pantoja, Peru 168 D2 1 0 S 75 10W
Cabo Raso, Argentina 176 B3 44 20 S 65 15W
Cabonga, Réservoir, Canada 140 C4 47 20N 76 40W
Cabool, U.S.A. 155 G8 37 7N 92 6W
Caboolture, Australia 127 D5 27 5 S 152 58 E
Cabora Bassa Dam = Cahora Bassa, Représa de, Mozam. 119 F3 15 20 S 32 50 E
Caborca, Mexico 162 A2 30 40N 112 10W
Cabot, Mt., U.S.A. 151 B13 44 30N 71 25W
Cabot Hd., Canada 150 A3 45 14N 81 17W
Cabot Str., Canada 141 C8 47 15N 59 40W
Cabra, Spain 43 H6 37 30N 4 28W
Cabra del Santo Cristo, Spain 43 H7 37 42N 3 16W
Cabra I., India 95 L11 7 18N 93 50 E
Cábras, Italy 46 C1 39 56N 8 32 E
Cabrera, Spain 38 B3 39 8N 2 57 E
Cabrera, Sierra, Spain 42 C4 42 12N 6 40W
Cabri, Canada 143 C7 50 35N 108 25W
Cabriel →, Spain 41 F3 39 14N 1 3W
Cabruta, Venezuela 168 B4 7 50N 66 10W
Cabucgayan, Phil. 81 F5 11 29N 124 34 E
Cabugao, Phil. 80 C3 17 48N 120 27 E
Cabulauan Is., Phil. 81 F3 11 25N 120 8 E
Cabulo, Angola 115 E3 10 18 S 16 22 E
Caburan = Jose Abad Santos, Phil. 81 J5 5 55N 125 39 E
Cabuta, Angola 115 D2 9 48 S 14 58 E
Cabuyaro, Colombia 168 C3 4 18N 72 49W
Cacabelos, Spain 42 C4 42 36N 6 44W
Caçador, Brazil 175 B5 26 47 S 51 0W
Čačak, Serbia, Yug. 50 C4 43 54N 20 20 E
Cacao, Fr. Guiana 169 C7 4 33N 52 26W
Caçapava do Sul, Brazil 175 C5 30 30 S 53 30W
Cáccamo, Italy 46 E6 37 56N 13 40 E
Cacém, Portugal 43 G1 38 46N 9 18W
Cáceres, Brazil 173 D6 16 5 S 57 40W
Cáceres, Colombia 168 B2 7 35N 75 20W
Cáceres, Spain 43 F4 39 26N 6 23W
Cáceres □, Spain 42 F5 39 45N 6 0W
Cache Bay, Canada 140 C4 46 22N 80 0W
Cache Cr. →, U.S.A. 160 G5 38 42N 121 42W
Cache Creek, Canada 142 C4 50 48N 121 19W
Cacheu, Guinea-Biss. 112 C1 12 14N 16 8W
Cachi, Argentina 174 B2 25 5 S 66 10W
Cachimbo, Brazil 173 B7 8 57 S 54 54W
Cachimbo, Serra do, Brazil 173 B6 9 30 S 55 30W
Cachimo, Angola 115 D4 8 21 S 21 24 E
Cachinal de la Sierra, Chile 174 A2 24 58 S 69 32W
Cachingues, Angola 115 E3 13 5 S 16 43 E
Cachoeira, Brazil 171 D4 12 30 S 39 0W
Cachoeira Alta, Brazil 171 E1 18 48 S 50 58W
Cachoeira do Sul, Brazil 175 C5 30 3 S 52 53W
Cachoeiro de Itapemirim, Brazil 171 F3 20 51 S 41 7W
Cachoeiro do Arari, Brazil 170 B2 1 1 S 48 58W
Cachopo, Portugal 43 H3 37 20N 7 49W
Cachuela Esperanza, Bolivia 173 C4 10 32 S 65 38W
Cacine, Guinea-Biss. 112 C1 11 8N 14 57W
Cacoal, Brazil 173 C5 11 30 S 61 25W
Cacólo, Angola 115 E3 10 9 S 19 21 E
Caconda, Angola 115 E3 13 48 S 15 8 E
Cacongo, Angola 115 D2 5 11 S 12 5 E
Caçu, Brazil 171 E1 18 37 S 51 4W
Cacuaco, Angola 115 D2 8 47 S 13 21 E
Cacuchi →, Angola 115 E3 14 26 S 16 46 E
Cacula, Angola 115 E2 14 29 S 14 10 E
Caculé, Brazil 171 D3 14 30 S 42 13W
Caculuvar →, Angola 115 F2 16 47 S 14 56 E
Cacuso, Angola 115 D3 9 25 S 15 45 E
Čadca, Slovak Rep. 35 B11 49 26N 18 45 E
Caddo, U.S.A. 155 H6 34 7N 96 16W
Cadenazzo, Switz. 33 D7 46 9N 8 57 E
Cader Idris, U.K. 21 E4 52 42N 3 53W
Cadereyta, Mexico 162 B5 25 36N 100 0W
Cades, U.S.A. 152 B10 33 47N 79 47W
Cadí, Sierra del, Spain 40 C6 42 17N 1 42 E
Cadibarrawirracanna, L., Australia 127 D2 28 52 S 135 27 E
Cadillac, France 28 D3 44 38N 0 20W
Cadillac, U.S.A. 148 C3 44 15N 85 24W
Cadiz, Phil. 81 F4 10 57N 123 15 E
Cádiz, Spain 43 J4 36 30N 6 20W
Cadiz, Calif., U.S.A. 161 L11 34 30N 115 28W
Cadiz, Ohio, U.S.A. 150 F4 40 22N 81 0W
Cádiz □, Spain 43 J5 36 36N 5 45W
Cádiz, G. de, Spain 43 J3 36 40N 7 0W
Cadiz L., U.S.A. 159 J6 34 18N 115 24W
Cadley, U.S.A. 152 B7 33 32N 82 40W
Cadney Park, Australia 127 D1 27 55 S 134 3 E
Cadomin, Canada 142 C5 53 2N 117 20W
Cadotte Lake, Canada 142 B5 56 26N 116 23W
Cadours, France 28 E5 43 44N 1 2 E
Cadoux, Australia 125 F2 30 46 S 117 7 E
Cadwell, U.S.A. 152 C6 32 20N 83 3W
Caen, France 26 C6 49 10N 0 22W
Caernarfon, U.K. 20 D3 53 8N 4 16W
Caernarfon, B., U.K. 20 D3 53 4N 4 40W
Caernarvon = Caernarfon, U.K. 20 D3 53 8N 4 16W
Caerphilly, U.K. 21 F4 51 35N 3 13W
Caerphilly □, U.K. 21 F4 51 37N 3 12W
Caesarea, Israel 103 C3 32 30N 34 53 E
Caeté, Brazil 171 E3 19 55 S 43 40W
Caetité, Brazil 171 D3 13 50 S 42 32W
Cafayate, Argentina 174 B2 26 2 S 66 0W
Cafu, Angola 116 B2 16 30 S 15 8 E
Cagayan □, Phil. 80 C3 18 0N 121 50 E
Cagayan →, Phil. 80 B3 18 25N 121 42 E
Cagayan de Oro, Phil. 81 G5 8 30N 124 40 E
Cagayan Is., Phil. 81 G3 9 40N 121 16 E
Cagayan Sulu I., Phil. 81 H2 7 1N 118 30 E
Cagli, Italy 45 E9 43 33N 12 39 E
Cágliari, Italy 46 C2 39 13N 9 7 E
Cágliari, G. di, Italy 46 C2 39 8N 9 11 E
Cagnano Varano, Italy 45 G12 41 49N 15 47 E
Cagnes-sur-Mer, France 29 E11 43 40N 7 9 E
Caguán →, Colombia 168 D3 0 8 S 74 18W
Caguas, Puerto Rico 165 d 18 14N 66 2W
Caha Mts., Ireland 23 E2 51 45N 9 40W
Cahama, Angola 116 B1 16 17 S 14 19 E
Caher, Ireland 23 D4 52 22N 7 56W
Caherciveen, Ireland 23 E1 51 56N 10 14W
Cahora Bassa, L. de, Mozam. 119 F3 15 35 S 32 0 E
Cahora Bassa, Représa de, Mozam. 119 F3 15 20 S 32 50 E
Cahore Pt., Ireland 23 D5 52 33N 6 12W
Cahors, France 28 D5 44 27N 1 27 E
Cahuapanas, Peru 172 B2 5 15 S 77 0W
Cahuinari →, Colombia 168 D3 1 21 S 70 44W
Cahul, Moldova 53 E13 45 50N 28 15 E
Cai Bau, Dao, Vietnam 76 G6 21 10N 107 27 E
Cai Nuoc, Vietnam 87 H5 8 56N 105 1 E
Caia, Mozam. 119 F4 17 51 S 35 24 E
Caiabis, Serra dos, Brazil 173 C6 11 30 S 56 30W
Caianda, Angola 119 E1 11 2 S 23 31 E
Caiapó, Serra do, Brazil 173 D7 17 0 S 52 0W
Caiapônia, Brazil 173 D7 16 57 S 51 49W
Caibarién, Cuba 164 B4 22 30N 79 30W
Caibiran, Phil. 81 F5 11 34N 124 35 E
Caicara, Bolívar, Venezuela 168 B4 7 38N 66 10W
Caicara, Monagas, Venezuela 169 B5 9 52N 63 38W
Caicó, Brazil 170 C4 6 20 S 37 0W
Caicos Is., Turks & Caicos 165 B5 21 40N 71 40W
Caicos Passage, W. Indies 165 B5 22 45N 72 45W
Caidian, China 77 B10 30 35N 114 2 E
Cailloma, Peru 172 D3 15 9 S 71 45W
Căinari, Moldova 53 D14 46 41N 29 3 E
Cainde, Angola 115 F2 15 29 S 13 24 E
Caine →, Bolivia 173 D4 18 23 S 65 21W
Caird Coast, Antarctica 7 D1 75 0 S 25 0W
Cairn Gorm, U.K. 22 D5 57 7N 3 39W
Cairngorm Mts., U.K. 22 D5 57 6N 3 42W
Cairnryan, U.K. 22 G3 54 59N 5 1W
Cairns, Australia 126 B4 16 57 S 145 45 E
Cairns L., Canada 143 C10 51 42N 94 30W
Cairo = El Qâhira, Egypt 106 H7 30 1N 31 14 E
Cairo, Ga., U.S.A. 152 E5 30 52N 84 13W
Cairo, Ill., U.S.A. 155 G10 37 0N 89 11W
Cairo, N.Y., U.S.A. 151 D11 42 18N 74 0W
Cairo Montenotte, Italy 44 D5 44 23N 8 16 E
Cairofa, Angola 115 E2 14 3 S 12 54 E
Caithness, Ord of, U.K. 22 C5 58 8N 3 36W
Caitou, Angola 115 E2 14 28 S 13 7 E
Caiundo, Angola 115 F3 15 50 S 17 28 E
Caiza, Bolivia 173 E4 20 2 S 65 40W
Caja de Muertos, I., Puerto Rico 165 d 17 54N 66 32W
Cajabamba, Peru 172 B2 7 38 S 78 4W
Cajamarca, Peru 172 B2 7 5 S 78 28W
Cajamarca □, Peru 172 B2 6 15 S 78 50W
Cajapió, Brazil 170 B3 2 58 S 44 48W
Cajarc, France 28 D5 44 29N 1 50 E
Cajatambo, Peru 172 C2 10 30 S 77 2W
Cajàzeiras, Brazil 170 C4 6 52 S 38 30W
Čajetina, Serbia, Yug. 50 C3 43 47N 19 42 E
Cajidiocan, Phil. 80 E4 12 22N 122 41 E
Çakirgol, Turkey 101 B8 40 33N 39 40 E
Çakırlar, Turkey 49 E12 36 52N 30 33 E
Čakovec, Croatia 45 B13 46 23N 16 26 E
Çal, Turkey 49 C11 38 4N 29 23 E
Cala, Spain 43 H4 37 59N 6 21W
Cala →, Spain 43 H4 37 38N 6 5W
Cala Cadolar, Punta de = Rotja, Pta., Spain 38 D2 38 38N 1 35 E
Cala d'Or, Spain 38 B4 39 23N 3 14 E
Cala en Porter, Spain 38 B5 39 52N 4 8 E
Cala Figuera, C. de, Spain 38 B3 39 27N 2 31 E
Cala Forcat, Spain 38 B4 40 0N 3 47 E
Cala Major, Spain 38 B3 39 33N 2 37 E
Cala Mezquida = Sa Mesquida, Spain 38 B5 39 55N 4 16 E
Cala Millor, Spain 38 B4 39 35N 3 22 E
Cala Ratjada, Spain 38 B4 39 43N 3 27 E
Cala Santa Galdana, Spain 38 B4 39 56N 3 58 E
Calabanga, Phil. 80 E4 13 42N 123 17 E
Calabar, Nigeria 113 E6 4 57N 8 20 E
Calabogie, Canada 151 A8 45 18N 76 43W
Calabozo, Venezuela 168 B4 9 0N 67 28W
Calábria □, Italy 47 C9 39 0N 16 30 E
Calaburras, Pta. de, Spain 43 J6 36 30N 4 38W
Calaceite, Spain 40 D5 41 1N 0 11 E
Calacoto, Bolivia 172 D4 17 16 S 68 38W
Calacuccia, France 29 F13 42 21N 9 1 E
Calafat, Romania 52 G7 43 58N 22 59 E
Calafate, Argentina 176 D2 50 19 S 72 15W
Calafell, Spain 40 D6 41 11N 1 34 E
Calagua Is., Phil. 80 D4 14 30N 122 55 E
Calahorra, Spain 40 C3 42 18N 1 59W
Calai, Angola 115 F3 17 47 S 19 41 E
Calais, France 27 B8 50 57N 1 56 E
Calais, U.S.A. 149 C12 45 11N 67 17W
Calalaste, Cord. de, Argentina 174 B2 25 0 S 67 0W
Calama, Brazil 173 B5 8 0 S 62 50W
Calama, Chile 174 A2 22 30 S 68 55W
Calamar, Bolívar, Colombia 168 A3 10 15N 74 55W
Calamar, Vaupés, Colombia 168 C3 1 58N 72 32W
Calamarca, Bolivia 172 D4 16 55 S 68 9W
Calamba, Cavite, Phil. 80 D3 14 13N 121 10 E
Calamba, Mis. Occ., Phil. 81 G4 8 35N 123 39 E
Calamian Group, Phil. 81 F2 11 50N 119 55 E
Calamocha, Spain 40 E3 40 50N 1 17W
Calamonte, Spain 43 G4 38 53N 6 23W
Călan, Romania 52 E7 45 44N 22 59 E
Calañas, Spain 43 H4 37 40N 6 53W
Calanda, Spain 40 E4 40 56N 0 15W
Calandagan I., Phil. 81 F3 10 39N 120 15 E
Calandula, Angola 115 D3 9 6 S 15 57 E
Calang, Indonesia 84 B1 4 37N 95 37 E
Calangiánus, Italy 46 B2 40 56N 9 11 E
Calanscio, Sarîr, Libya 108 C4 27 0N 21 30 E
Calapan, Phil. 80 E3 13 25N 121 7 E
Călărasi, Moldova 53 C13 47 16N 28 19 E
Călăraşi, Romania 53 F12 44 12N 27 20 E
Călăraşi □, Romania 53 F12 44 10N 27 0 E
Calasparra, Spain 41 G3 38 14N 1 41W
Calatafimi, Italy 46 E5 37 55N 12 52 E
Calatagan, Phil. 80 E3 13 50N 120 38 E
Calatayud, Spain 40 D3 41 20N 1 40W
Călăţele, Romania 52 D8 46 46N 23 1 E
Calato = Kálathos, Greece 38 E12 36 9N 28 8 E
Calatrava, Eq. Guin. 114 B1 1 6N 9 25 E
Calauag, Phil. 80 E4 13 55N 122 15 E
Calavà, C., Italy 47 D7 38 11N 14 55 E
Calavite, C., Phil. 80 E3 13 26N 120 20 E
Calavite Pass, Phil. 80 E3 13 36N 120 25 E
Calayan, Phil. 80 B3 19 16N 121 28 E
Calayan I., Phil. 80 B3 19 20N 121 27 E
Calbayog, Phil. 80 E5 12 4N 124 38 E
Calbiga, Phil. 81 F5 11 38N 125 0 E
Calca, Peru 172 C3 13 22 S 72 0W
Calcasieu L., U.S.A. 155 L8 29 55N 93 18W
Calcutta = Kolkata, India 93 H13 22 36N 88 24 E
Calcutta, U.S.A. 150 F4 40 40N 80 34W
Caldaro, Italy 45 B8 46 25N 11 14 E
Caldas □, Colombia 168 B2 5 15N 75 30W
Caldas da Rainha, Portugal 43 F1 39 24N 9 8W
Caldas de Reis, Spain 42 C2 42 36N 8 39W
Caldas Novas, Brazil 171 E2 17 45 S 48 38W
Calder →, U.K. 20 D6 53 44N 1 22W
Caldera, Chile 174 B1 27 5 S 70 55W
Caldwell, Idaho, U.S.A. 158 E5 43 40N 116 41W
Caldwell, Kans., U.S.A. 155 G6 37 2N 97 37W
Caldwell, Tex., U.S.A. 155 K6 30 32N 96 42W
Caledon, S. Africa 116 E2 34 14 S 19 26 E
Caledon →, S. Africa 116 E4 30 31 S 26 5 E
Caledon B., Australia 126 A2 12 45 S 137 0 E
Caledonia, Canada 150 C5 43 7N 79 58W
Caledonia, Mo., U.S.A. 156 G6 37 45N 90 46W
Caledonia, N.Y., U.S.A. 150 D7 42 58N 77 51W
Calella, Spain 40 D7 41 37N 2 40 E
Calemba, Angola 116 B2 16 0 S 15 44 E
Calen, Australia 126 J6 20 56 S 148 48 E
Calenzana, France 29 F12 42 31N 8 51 E
Caleta Olivia, Argentina 176 C3 46 25 S 67 25W
Caletones, Chile 174 C1 34 6 S 70 27W
Calexico, U.S.A. 161 N11 32 40N 115 30W
Calf of Man, U.K. 20 C3 54 3N 4 48W
Calgary, Canada 142 C6 51 0N 114 10W
Calheta, Azores 9 d1 38 36N 28 1W
Calheta, Madeira 9 c 32 44N 17 11W
Calheta de Nesquim, Azores 9 d1 38 24N 28 5W
Calhoun, U.S.A. 149 H3 34 30N 84 57W
Calhoun Falls, U.S.A. 152 A7 34 6N 82 36W
Cali, Colombia 168 C2 3 25N 76 35W
Calicut, India 95 J2 11 15N 75 43 E
Caliente, U.S.A. 159 H6 37 37N 114 31W
California, Mo., U.S.A. 156 F4 38 38N 92 34W
California, Pa., U.S.A. 150 F5 40 4N 79 54W
California □, U.S.A. 160 H7 37 30N 119 30W
California, Baja, Mexico 162 A1 32 10N 115 12W
California, Baja, T.N. = Baja California □, Mexico 162 B2 30 0N 115 0W
California, Baja, T.S. = Baja California Sur □, Mexico 162 B2 25 50N 111 50W
California, G. de, Mexico 162 B2 27 0N 111 0W
California City, U.S.A. 161 K9 35 10N 117 55W
California Hot Springs, U.S.A. 161 K8 35 51N 118 41W
Călimăneşti, Romania 53 E9 45 14N 24 20 E
Călimani, Munţii, Romania 53 C10 47 12N 25 0 E
Calingasta, Argentina 174 C2 31 15 S 69 30W
Calinog, Phil. 81 F4 11 7N 122 32 E
Calintaan, Phil. 80 E3 12 35N 120 57 E
Calipatria, U.S.A. 161 M11 33 8N 115 31W
Calistoga, U.S.A. 160 G4 38 35N 122 35W
Calitri, Italy 47 B8 40 54N 15 26 E

Catánia, *Italy* **47 E8** 37 30N 15 6 E
Catánia, G. di, *Italy* **47 E8** 37 24N 15 9 E
Catanzaro, *Italy* **47 D9** 38 54N 16 35 E
Catarman, *Camiguin, Phil.* **81 G5** 9 8N 124 40 E
Catarman, *N. Samar, Phil.* **80 E5** 12 28N 124 35 E
Catatumba →, *Venezuela* **168 B3** 9 21N 71 45W
Cataula, *U.S.A.* **152 C5** 32 39N 84 52W
Catbalogan, *Phil.* **81 F5** 11 46N 124 53 E
Cateco Cangola, *Angola* **115 D3** 8 28 S 15 51 E
Cateel, *Phil.* **81 H6** 7 47N 126 24 E
Cateel Bay, *Phil.* **81 H6** 7 54N 126 25 E
Catembe, *Mozam.* **117 D5** 26 0 S 32 33 E
Catende, *Angola* **115 E4** 11 14 S 21 30 E
Catende, *Brazil* **170 C4** 8 40 S 35 43W
Caterham, *U.K.* **21 F7** 51 15N 0 4W
Catete, *Angola* **115 D2** 9 6 S 13 43 E
Cathcart, *Australia* **129 D8** 36 52 S 149 24 E
Cathcart, *S. Africa* **116 E4** 32 18 S 27 10 E
Cathlamet, *U.S.A.* **160 D3** 46 12N 123 23W
Catio, *Guinea-Biss.* **112 C1** 11 17N 15 15W
Catismiña, *Venezuela* **169 C5** 4 5N 63 40W
Catita, *Brazil* **170 C3** 9 31 S 43 1W
Catlettsburg, *U.S.A.* **148 F4** 38 25N 82 36W
Catlin, *U.S.A.* **157 D9** 40 4N 87 42W
Çatma Dağı, *Turkey* **49 C11** 38 25N 29 50 E
Catmon, *Phil.* **81 F5** 10 43N 124 1 E
Catoche, C., *Mexico* **163 C7** 21 40N 87 8W
Catolé do Rocha, *Brazil* **170 C4** 6 21 S 37 45W
Catota, *Angola* **115 E3** 13 57 S 17 30 E
Cátria, Mte., *Italy* **45 E9** 43 28N 12 42 E
Catriló, *Argentina* **174 D3** 36 26 S 63 24W
Catrimani, *Brazil* **169 C5** 0 27N 61 41W
Catrimani →, *Brazil* **169 C5** 0 28N 61 44W
Catskill, *U.S.A.* **151 D11** 42 14N 73 52W
Catskill Mts., *U.S.A.* **151 D10** 42 10N 74 25W
Catt, Mt., *Australia* **126 A1** 13 49 S 134 23 E
Cattaraugus, *U.S.A.* **150 D6** 42 22N 78 52W
Cattólica, *Italy* **45 E9** 43 58N 12 44 E
Cattólica Eraclea, *Italy* **46 E6** 37 26N 13 24 E
Catu, *Brazil* **171 D4** 12 21 S 38 23W
Catuala, *Angola* **116 B2** 16 25 S 19 2 E
Catuane, *Mozam.* **117 D5** 26 48 S 32 18 E
Catubig, *Phil.* **80 E5** 12 24N 125 3 E
Catumbela, *Angola* **115 E2** 12 25 S 13 34 E
Catumbela →, *Angola* **115 E2** 12 29 S 13 28 E
Catur, *Mozam.* **119 E4** 13 45 S 35 30 E
Catwick Is., *Vietnam* **87 G7** 10 0N 109 0 E
Cauayan, *Isabela, Phil.* **80 C3** 16 56N 121 46 E
Cauayan, *Neg. Occ., Phil.* **81 G4** 9 58N 122 37 E
Cauca ☐, *Colombia* **168 C2** 2 30N 76 50W
Cauca →, *Colombia* **168 B3** 8 54N 74 28W
Caucaia, *Brazil* **170 B4** 3 40 S 38 35W
Caucasia, *Colombia* **168 B2** 8 0N 75 12W
Caucasus Mountains, *Eurasia* **61 J7** 42 50N 44 0 E
Caudete, *Spain* **41 G3** 38 42N 1 2W
Caudry, *France* **27 B10** 50 7N 3 22 E
Caulnes, *France* **26 D4** 48 18N 2 10W
Caulónia, *Italy* **47 D9** 38 23N 16 24 E
Caungula, *Angola* **115 D3** 8 26 S 18 38 E
Cauquenes, *Chile* **174 D1** 36 0 S 72 22W
Caura →, *Venezuela* **169 B5** 7 38N 64 53W
Caurés →, *Brazil* **169 D5** 1 21 S 62 20W
Cauresi →, *Mozam.* **119 F3** 17 8 S 33 0 E
Căuşani, *Moldova* **53 D14** 46 38N 29 25 E
Causapscal, *Canada* **141 C6** 48 19N 67 12W
Caussade, *France* **28 D5** 44 10N 1 33 E
Causse-Méjean, *France* **28 D7** 44 18N 3 42 E
Cauterets, *France* **28 F3** 42 52N 0 8W
Caux, Pays de, *France* **26 C7** 49 38N 0 35 E
Cava de' Tirreni, *Italy* **47 B7** 40 42N 14 42 E
Cávado →, *Portugal* **42 D2** 41 32N 8 48W
Cavaillon, *France* **29 E9** 43 50N 5 2 E
Cavalaire-sur-Mer, *France* **29 E10** 43 10N 6 33 E
Cavalcante, *Brazil* **171 D2** 13 48 S 47 30W
Cavalese, *Italy* **45 B8** 46 17N 11 27 E
Cavalier, *U.S.A.* **154 A6** 48 48N 97 37W
Cavalla = Cavally →, *Africa* **112 E3** 4 22N 7 32W
Cavalli Is., *N.Z.* **130 B2** 35 0 S 173 58 E
Cavallo, I. de, *France* **29 G13** 41 22N 9 16 E
Cavally →, *Africa* **112 E3** 4 22N 7 32W
Cavan, *Ireland* **23 B4** 54 0N 7 22W
Cavan ☐, *Ireland* **23 C4** 54 1N 7 16W
Cavárzere, *Italy* **45 C9** 45 8N 12 5 E
Çavdarhisar, *Turkey* **49 B11** 39 12N 29 37 E
Çavdır, *Turkey* **49 D11** 37 10N 29 42 E
Cave Creek, *U.S.A.* **159 K7** 33 50N 111 57W
Cave Run L., *U.S.A.* **157 F13** 38 5N 83 25W
Cave Spring, *U.S.A.* **152 A4** 34 6N 85 20W
Cavenagh Ra., *Australia* **125 E4** 26 12 S 127 55 E
Cavendish, *Australia* **128 D5** 37 31 S 142 2 E
Caviana, I., *Brazil* **169 C7** 0 10N 50 10W
Cavite, *Phil.* **80 D3** 14 29N 120 55 E
Cavite ☐, *Phil.* **80 D3** 14 15N 120 50 E
Cavnic, *Romania* **53 C8** 47 40N 23 52 E
Cavour, *Italy* **44 D4** 44 47N 7 22 E
Cavtat, *Croatia* **50 D2** 42 35N 18 13 E
Cawayan, *Phil.* **81 F4** 11 56N 123 46 E
Cawndilla L., *Australia* **128 B5** 32 30 S 142 15 E
Cawnpore = Kanpur, *India* **93 F9** 26 28N 80 20 E
Caxias, *Brazil* **170 B3** 4 55 S 43 20W
Caxias do Sul, *Brazil* **175 B5** 29 10 S 51 10W
Caxito, *Angola* **115 D2** 8 30 S 13 30 E
Caxopa, *Angola* **115 E4** 11 52 S 20 52 E
Çay, *Turkey* **100 C4** 38 35N 31 1 E
Cay Pt., *Bahamas* **9 b** 25 59N 77 25W
Cay Sal Bank, *Bahamas* **164 B4** 23 45N 80 0W
Cayambe, *Napo, Ecuador* **168 C2** 0 2N 77 59W
Cayambe, *Quito, Ecuador* **168 C2** 0 3N 78 8W
Çaycuma, *Turkey* **100 B5** 41 25N 32 4 E
Çayeli, *Turkey* **101 B9** 41 5N 40 45 E
Cayenne, *Fr. Guiana* **169 B7** 5 5N 52 18W
Cayenne ☐, *Fr. Guiana* **169 C7** 5 0N 53 0W
Cayey, *Puerto Rico* **165 d** 18 7N 66 10W
Caygören Barajı, *Turkey* **49 B10** 39 15N 28 12 E
Cayiralan, *Turkey* **100 C6** 39 17N 35 38 E
Caylus, *France* **28 D5** 44 15N 1 47 E
Cayman Brac, *Cayman Is.* **164 C4** 19 43N 79 49W
Cayman Is. ■, *W. Indies* **164 C3** 19 40N 80 30W
Cayo Romano, *Cuba* **164 B4** 22 0N 78 0W
Cayres, *France* **28 D7** 44 55N 3 48 E
Cayuga, *Canada* **150 D5** 42 59N 79 50W
Cayuga, *Ind., U.S.A.* **157 E9** 39 57N 87 28W
Cayuga, *N.Y., U.S.A.* **151 D8** 42 54N 76 44W
Cayuga L., *U.S.A.* **151 D8** 42 41N 76 41W
Cazage, *Angola* **115 E4** 11 2 S 20 45 E
Cazalla de la Sierra, *Spain* **43 H5** 37 56N 5 45W
Căzăneşti, *Romania* **53 F12** 44 36N 27 3 E
Cazaubon, *France* **28 E3** 43 56N 0 4W
Cazaux et de Sanguinet, Étang de, *France* **28 D2** 44 29N 1 10W
Cazenovia, *U.S.A.* **151 D9** 42 56N 75 51W
Cazères, *France* **28 E5** 43 13N 1 5 E
Cazin, *Bos.-H.* **45 D12** 44 57N 15 57 E
Čazma, *Croatia* **45 C13** 45 45N 16 39 E
Cazombo, *Angola* **115 E4** 11 54 S 22 56 E
Cazorla, *Spain* **43 H7** 37 55N 3 2W
Cazorla, Sierra de, *Spain* **43 G8** 38 5N 2 55W
Cea →, *Spain* **42 C5** 42 0N 5 36W
Ceamurlia de Jos, *Romania* **53 F13** 44 43N 28 47 E
Ceananus Mor, *Ireland* **23 C5** 53 44N 6 53W
Ceará = Fortaleza, *Brazil* **170 B4** 3 45 S 38 35W
Ceará ☐, *Brazil* **170 C4** 5 0 S 40 0W
Ceará Mirim, *Brazil* **170 C4** 5 38 S 35 25W
Ceauru, L., *Romania* **53 F8** 44 58N 23 11 E
Cebaco, I. de, *Panama* **164 E3** 7 33N 81 9W
Cebollar, *Argentina* **174 B2** 29 10 S 66 35W
Cebollera, Sierra de, *Spain* **40 D2** 42 0N 2 30W
Cebreros, *Spain* **42 E6** 40 27N 4 28W
Cebu, *Phil.* **81 F4** 10 18N 123 54 E
Cebu ☐, *Phil.* **81 F4** 10 20N 123 40 E
Čečava, *Bos.-H.* **52 F2** 44 42N 17 44 E
Ceccano, *Italy* **46 A6** 41 34N 13 20 E
Cece, *Hungary* **52 D3** 46 46N 18 39 E
Cechi, *Ivory C.* **112 D4** 6 15N 4 25W
Cecil Plains, *Australia* **127 D5** 27 30 S 151 11 E
Cécina, *Italy* **44 E7** 43 19N 10 31 E
Cécina →, *Italy* **44 E7** 43 18N 10 29 E
Ceclavín, *Spain* **42 F4** 39 50N 6 45W
Cedar →, *U.S.A.* **156 C5** 41 17N 91 21W
Cedar City, *U.S.A.* **159 H7** 37 41N 113 4W
Cedar Creek Reservoir, *U.S.A.* **155 J6** 32 11N 96 4W
Cedar Falls, *Iowa, U.S.A.* **156 B4** 42 32N 92 27W
Cedar Falls, *Wash., U.S.A.* **160 C5** 47 25N 121 45W
Cedar Grove, *U.S.A.* **157 E12** 39 22N 84 56W
Cedar Key, *U.S.A.* **149 L4** 29 8N 83 2W
Cedar L., *Canada* **143 C9** 53 10N 100 0W
Cedar Lake, *U.S.A.* **157 C9** 41 22N 87 26W
Cedar Point, *U.S.A.* **157 C13** 41 44N 83 21W
Cedar Rapids, *U.S.A.* **156 C5** 41 59N 91 40W
Cedartown, *U.S.A.* **152 A4** 34 1N 85 15W
Cedarvale, *Canada* **142 B3** 55 1N 128 22W
Cedarville, *S. Africa* **117 E4** 30 23 S 29 3 E
Cedarville, *Ill., U.S.A.* **156 B7** 42 23N 89 38W
Cedarville, *Ohio, U.S.A.* **157 E13** 39 44N 83 49W
Cedeira, *Spain* **42 B2** 43 39N 8 2W
Cedral, *Mexico* **162 C4** 23 50N 100 42W
Cedrino →, *Italy* **46 B2** 40 11N 9 24 E
Cedro, *Brazil* **170 C4** 6 34 S 39 3W
Cedros, *Azores* **9 d1** 38 38N 28 42W
Cedros, I. de, *Mexico* **162 B1** 28 10N 115 20W
Cedros B., *Trin. & Tob.* **169 F9** 10 16N 61 54W
Ceduna, *Australia* **127 E1** 32 7 S 133 46 E
Cedynia, *Poland* **55 F1** 52 53N 14 12 E
Cée, *Spain* **42 C1** 42 57N 9 10W
Ceel Dheere = El Dere, *Somali Rep.* **120 C3** 5 22N 46 11 E
Ceerigaabo = Erigavo, *Somali Rep.* **120 B3** 10 35N 47 20 E
Cefalù, *Italy* **47 D7** 38 2N 14 1 E
Cega →, *Spain* **42 D6** 41 33N 4 46W
Cegléd, *Hungary* **52 C4** 47 11N 19 47 E
Céglie Messápico, *Italy* **47 B10** 40 39N 17 31 E
Cehegín, *Spain* **41 G3** 38 6N 1 48W
Ceheng, *China* **76 E5** 24 58N 105 48 E
Cehu-Silvaniei, *Romania* **53 C8** 47 24N 23 9 E
Ceica, *Romania* **52 D7** 46 53N 22 10 E
Ceira →, *Portugal* **42 E2** 40 13N 8 16W
Cekik, *Indonesia* **79 J17** 8 12 S 114 27 E
Cela, *Angola* **115 E3** 11 25 S 15 7 E
Čelákovice, *Czech Rep.* **34 A7** 50 10N 14 46 E
Celano, *Italy* **45 F10** 42 5N 13 33 E
Celanova, *Spain* **42 C3** 42 9N 7 58W
Celaya, *Mexico* **162 C4** 20 31N 100 37W
Celebes = Sulawesi ☐, *Indonesia* **82 B2** 2 0 S 120 0 E
Celebes Sea, *Indonesia* **82 A2** 3 0N 123 0 E
Celendín, *Peru* **172 B2** 6 52 S 78 10W
Čelić, *Bos.-H.* **52 F3** 44 43N 18 49 E
Celica, *Ecuador* **168 D2** 4 7 S 79 59W
Celina, *U.S.A.* **157 D12** 40 33N 84 35W
Celinac, *Bos.-H.* **52 F2** 44 44N 17 22 E
Celje, *Slovenia* **45 B12** 46 16N 15 18 E
Celldömölk, *Hungary* **52 C2** 47 16N 17 10 E
Celle, *Germany* **30 C6** 52 37N 10 4 E
Celorico da Beira, *Portugal* **42 E3** 40 38N 7 24W
Celtic Sea, *Atl. Oc.* **8 A11** 50 9N 9 34W
Çeltikçi, *Turkey* **49 D12** 37 32N 30 29 E
Çemişgezek, *Turkey* **101 C8** 39 3N 38 56 E
Cenderwasih, Teluk, *Indonesia* **79 E9** 3 0 S 135 20 E
Cenepa →, *Peru* **168 D2** 4 40 S 78 10W
Cengong, *China* **76 D7** 27 13N 108 44 E
Ceno →, *Italy* **44 D7** 44 43N 10 5 E
Centallo, *Italy* **44 D4** 44 30N 7 35 E
Centelles, *Spain* **40 D7** 41 50N 2 14 E
Centenário do Sul, *Brazil* **171 F1** 22 48 S 51 36W
Center, *N. Dak., U.S.A.* **154 B4** 47 7N 101 18W
Center, *Tex., U.S.A.* **155 K7** 31 48N 94 11W
Center Hill, *U.S.A.* **153 G7** 28 38N 82 3W
Center Point, *U.S.A.* **156 B5** 42 12N 91 46W
Centerburg, *U.S.A.* **150 F2** 40 18N 82 42W
Centerville, *Calif., U.S.A.* **160 J7** 36 44N 119 30W
Centerville, *Iowa, U.S.A.* **156 D4** 40 44N 92 52W
Centerville, *Mich., U.S.A.* **157 C11** 41 55N 85 32W
Centerville, *Ohio, U.S.A.* **157 E12** 39 38N 84 8W
Centerville, *Pa., U.S.A.* **150 F5** 40 3N 79 59W
Centerville, *Tenn., U.S.A.* **149 H2** 35 47N 87 28W
Centerville, *Tex., U.S.A.* **155 K7** 31 16N 95 59W
Cento, *Italy* **45 D8** 44 43N 11 17 E
Central, *Brazil* **170 D3** 11 8 S 42 8W
Central, *U.S.A.* **144 D11** 65 35N 144 48W
Central ☐, *Ghana* **113 D4** 5 30N 1 0W
Central ☐, *Kenya* **118 C4** 0 30 S 37 30 E
Central ☐, *Malawi* **119 E3** 13 30 S 33 30 E
Central ☐, *Papua N. G.* **132 F5** 10 0 S 148 0 E
Central ☐, *Zambia* **119 E2** 14 25 S 28 50 E
Central, Cordillera, *Bolivia* **173 D5** 18 30 S 64 55W
Central, Cordillera, *Colombia* **168 C2** 5 0N 75 0W
Central, Cordillera, *Costa Rica* **164 D3** 10 10N 84 5W
Central, Cordillera, *Dom. Rep.* **165 C5** 19 15N 71 0W
Central, Cordillera, *Peru* **172 B2** 7 0 S 77 30W
Central, Cordillera, *Phil.* **80 C3** 17 20N 120 57 E
Central, Cordillera, *Puerto Rico* **165 d** 18 8N 66 35W
Central African Rep. ■, *Africa* **114 A4** 7 0N 20 0 E
Central America, *America* **136 H11** 12 0N 85 0W
Central Butte, *Canada* **143 C7** 50 48N 106 31W
Central City, *Colo., U.S.A.* **158 G11** 39 48N 105 31W
Central City, *Iowa, U.S.A.* **156 B5** 42 12N 91 32W
Central City, *Ky., U.S.A.* **148 G2** 37 18N 87 7W
Central City, *Nebr., U.S.A.* **154 E6** 41 7N 98 0W
Central I., *Kenya* **118 B4** 3 30N 36 0 E
Central Island Nat. Park, *Kenya* **118 B4** 2 33N 36 1 E
Central Kalahari Game Reserve, *Botswana* **116 C3** 22 36 S 23 58 E
Central Makran Range, *Pakistan* **91 D2** 26 30N 64 15 E
Central Patricia, *Canada* **140 B1** 51 30N 90 9W
Central Point, *U.S.A.* **158 E2** 42 23N 122 55W
Central Ra., *Papua N. G.* **132 C2** 5 0 S 143 0 E
Central Russian Uplands, *Europe* **12 E13** 54 0N 36 0 E
Central Siberian Plateau, *Russia* **62 C14** 65 0N 105 0 E
Central Square, *U.S.A.* **151 C8** 43 17N 76 9W
Centralia, *Ill., U.S.A.* **156 F7** 38 32N 89 8W
Centralia, *Mo., U.S.A.* **156 E4** 39 13N 92 8W
Centralia, *Wash., U.S.A.* **160 D4** 46 43N 122 58W
Centre, *U.S.A.* **152 A4** 34 9N 85 41W
Centre de Flacq, *Mauritius* **121 d** 20 12 S 57 43 E
Century, *U.S.A.* **153 E2** 30 58N 87 16W
Cenxi, *China* **77 F8** 22 57N 110 57 E
Čeotina →, *Bos.-H.* **50 C2** 43 36N 18 50 E
Cephalonia = Kefallinía, *Greece* **39 C2** 38 15N 20 30 E
Čepin, *Croatia* **52 E3** 45 32N 18 34 E
Ceprano, *Italy* **46 A6** 41 33N 13 31 E
Ceptia, *Angola* **115 E3** 12 56 S 17 35 E
Ceptura, *Romania* **53 E11** 45 1N 26 21 E
Cepu, *Indonesia* **85 D4** 7 9 S 111 35 E
Ceram = Seram, *Indonesia* **83 B3** 3 10 S 129 0 E
Ceram Sea = Seram Sea, *Indonesia* **82 B3** 2 30 S 128 30 E
Cerbère, *France* **28 F7** 42 26N 3 10 E
Cerbicales, Is., *France* **29 G13** 41 33N 9 22 E
Cercal, *Portugal* **43 H2** 37 48N 8 40W
Cerdaña, *Spain* **40 C6** 42 22N 1 35 E
Cère →, *France* **28 D5** 44 55N 1 49 E
Cerea, *Italy* **45 C8** 45 12N 11 13 E
Ceredigion ☐, *U.K.* **21 E3** 52 16N 4 15W
Ceres, *Argentina* **174 B3** 29 55 S 61 55W
Ceres, *Brazil* **171 E2** 15 17 S 49 35W
Ceres, *S. Africa* **116 E2** 33 21 S 19 18 E
Ceres, *U.S.A.* **160 H6** 37 35N 120 57W
Céret, *France* **28 F6** 42 30N 2 42 E
Cereté, *Colombia* **168 B2** 8 53N 75 48W
Cerf, *Seychelles* **121 b** 4 38 S 55 40 E
Cergy, *France* **27 C9** 49 2N 2 4 E
Cerignola, *Italy* **47 A8** 41 17N 15 53 E
Cerigo = Kíthira, *Greece* **48 E5** 36 8N 23 0 E
Cérilly, *France* **27 F9** 46 37N 2 50 E
Cerisiers, *France* **27 D10** 48 8N 3 30 E
Cerizay, *France* **26 F6** 46 50N 0 40W
Çerkeş, *Turkey* **100 B5** 40 49N 32 52 E
Çerkezköy, *Turkey* **51 E12** 41 17N 28 0 E
Cerknica, *Slovenia* **45 C11** 45 48N 14 21 E
Cerkovica, *Bulgaria* **51 C8** 43 41N 24 50 E
Cermerno, *Serbia, Yug.* **50 C4** 43 35N 20 25 E
Çermik, *Turkey* **101 C8** 38 8N 39 26 E
Cerna, *Romania* **53 E13** 45 4N 28 17 E
Cerna →, *Romania* **53 F8** 44 38N 23 58 E
Cernavodă, *Romania* **53 F13** 44 22N 28 3 E
Cernay, *France* **27 E14** 47 44N 7 10 E
Cernik, *Croatia* **52 E2** 45 17N 17 22 E
Cerralvo, I., *Mexico* **162 C3** 24 20N 109 45W
Cërrik, *Albania* **50 E3** 41 2N 19 58 E
Cerritos, *Mexico* **162 C4** 22 27N 100 20W
Cerro Chato, *Uruguay* **175 C4** 33 6 S 55 8W
Cerro Gordo, *U.S.A.* **157 E8** 39 53N 88 44W
Cerro Sombrero, *Chile* **176 D3** 52 45 S 69 15W
Certaldo, *Italy* **44 E8** 43 33N 11 2 E
Cervantes, *Phil.* **80 C3** 17 0N 120 44 E
Cervaro →, *Italy* **47 A8** 41 30N 15 52 E
Cervati, Monte, *Italy* **47 B8** 40 17N 15 29 E
Cerventes, *Australia* **125 F2** 30 31 S 115 3 E
Cervera, *Spain* **40 D6** 41 40N 1 16 E
Cervera de Pisuerga, *Spain* **42 C6** 42 51N 4 30W
Cervera del Río Alhama, *Spain* **40 C3** 42 2N 1 58W
Cervéteri, *Italy* **45 F9** 42 0N 12 6 E
Cérvia, *Italy* **45 D9** 44 15N 12 22 E
Cervignano del Friuli, *Italy* **45 C10** 45 49N 13 20 E
Cervinara, *Italy* **47 A7** 41 1N 14 37 E
Cervione, *France* **29 F13** 42 20N 9 29 E
Cervo, *Spain* **42 B3** 43 40N 7 24W
César ☐, *Colombia* **168 B3** 9 0N 73 30W
Cesarò, *Italy* **47 E7** 37 50N 14 38 E
Cesena, *Italy* **45 D9** 44 8N 12 15 E
Cesenático, *Italy* **45 D9** 44 12N 12 24 E
Cēsis, *Latvia* **15 H21** 57 18N 25 15 E
Česká Lípa, *Czech Rep.* **34 A7** 50 45N 14 30 E
Česká Třebová, *Czech Rep.* **35 B9** 49 54N 16 27 E
České Budějovice, *Czech Rep.* **34 C7** 48 55N 14 25 E
České Velenice, *Czech Rep.* **34 C7** 48 45N 14 57 E
Českomoravská Vrchovina, *Czech Rep.* **34 B8** 49 30N 15 40 E
Český Brod, *Czech Rep.* **34 A7** 50 4N 14 52 E
Český Krumlov, *Czech Rep.* **34 C7** 48 43N 14 21 E
Český Těšín, *Czech Rep.* **35 B11** 49 45N 18 39 E
Česma →, *Croatia* **45 C13** 45 35N 16 29 E
Çeşme, *Turkey* **49 C8** 38 20N 26 23 E
Cessnock, *Australia* **129 B9** 32 50 S 151 21 E
Cesson-Sévigné, *France* **26 D5** 48 7N 1 36W
Cestas, *France* **28 D3** 44 44N 0 41W
Cestos →, *Liberia* **112 D3** 5 40N 9 10W
Cestos Sehnkwehn Nat. Park, *Liberia* **112 D3** 5 40N 9 10W
Cetate, *Romania* **52 F8** 44 7N 23 2 E
Cetin Grad, *Croatia* **45 C12** 45 9N 15 45 E
Cetina →, *Croatia* **45 E13** 43 26N 16 42 E
Cetinje, *Montenegro, Yug.* **50 D2** 42 23N 18 59 E
Cetraro, *Italy* **47 C8** 39 31N 15 55 E
Ceuta, *N. Afr.* **110 A3** 35 52N 5 18W
Ceva, *Italy* **44 D5** 44 23N 8 2 E
Ceve-i-Ra, *Fiji* **123 E13** 21 46 S 174 31 E
Cévennes, *France* **28 D7** 44 10N 3 50 E
Cevio, *Switz.* **33 D7** 46 19N 8 36 E
Ceyhan, *Turkey* **100 D6** 37 4N 35 47 E
Ceyhan →, *Turkey* **100 D6** 36 38N 35 40 E
Ceylânpınar, *Turkey* **101 D9** 36 50N 40 2 E
Ceylon = Sri Lanka ■, *Asia* **95 L5** 7 30N 80 50 E
Cèze →, *France* **29 D8** 44 6N 4 43 E
Cha-am, *Thailand* **86 F2** 12 48N 99 58 E
Cha Pa, *Vietnam* **86 A4** 22 20N 103 47 E
Chá Pungana, *Angola* **115 E3** 13 44 S 18 39 E
Chabanais, *France* **28 C4** 45 52N 0 48 E
Chabeuil, *France* **29 D9** 44 54N 5 3 E
Chablais, *France* **27 F13** 46 20N 6 36 E
Chablis, *France* **27 E10** 47 47N 3 48 E
Chabounia, *Algeria* **111 A5** 35 30N 2 38 E
Chacabuco, *Argentina* **174 C3** 34 40 S 60 27W
Chachapoyas, *Peru* **172 B2** 6 15 S 77 50W
Chachasp, *Peru* **172 D3** 15 30 S 72 15W
Chachoengsao, *Thailand* **86 F3** 13 42N 101 5 E
Chachro, *Pakistan* **92 G4** 25 5N 70 15 E
Chaco ☐, *Argentina* **174 B3** 26 30 S 61 0W
Chaco ☐, *Paraguay* **174 B4** 26 0 S 60 0W
Chaco →, *U.S.A.* **159 H9** 36 46N 108 39W
Chacon, C., *U.S.A.* **142 C2** 54 42N 132 0W
Chad ■, *Africa* **109 F3** 15 0N 17 15 E
Chad, L. = Tchad, L., *Chad* **109 F3** 13 30N 14 30 E
Chadan, *Russia* **67 D10** 51 17N 91 35 E
Chadileuvú →, *Argentina* **174 D2** 37 46 S 66 0W
Chadiza, *Zambia* **119 E3** 14 45 S 32 27 E
Chadron, *U.S.A.* **154 D3** 42 50N 103 0W
Chadyr-Lunga = Ciadâr-Lunga, *Moldova* **53 D13** 46 3N 28 51 E
Chae Hom, *Thailand* **86 C2** 18 43N 99 35 E
Chaek, *Kyrgyzstan* **65 C7** 41 55N 74 30 E
Chaem →, *Thailand* **86 C2** 18 11N 98 38 E
Chaeryŏng, *N. Korea* **75 E13** 38 24N 125 36 E
Chagai Hills = Chāh Gay Hills, *Afghan.* **91 C1** 29 30N 64 0 E
Chagda, *Russia* **67 D14** 58 45N 130 38 E
Chaghcharān, *Afghan.* **91 B2** 34 31N 65 15 E
Chagny, *France* **27 F11** 46 57N 4 45 E
Chagoda, *Russia* **58 C8** 59 10N 35 15 E
Chagos Arch., *Ind. Oc.* **62 K11** 6 0 S 72 0 E
Chagrin Falls, *U.S.A.* **150 E3** 41 26N 81 24W
Chaguanas, *Trin. & Tob.* **169 F9** 10 30N 61 26W
Chāh Ākhvor, *Iran* **97 C8** 32 41N 59 40 E
Chāh Bahar, *Iran* **97 E9** 25 20N 60 40 E
Chāh-e Āb, *Afghan.* **97 C8** 37 23N 69 48 E
Chāh-e Kavīr, *Iran* **97 C8** 34 29N 56 52 E
Chāh Gay Hills, *Afghan.* **91 C1** 29 30N 64 0 E
Chahār Borjak, *Afghan.* **91 C1** 30 17N 62 3 E
Chahār Mahāll va Bakhtīarī ☐, *Iran* **97 C6** 32 0N 49 0 E
Chahtung, *Burma* **90 B7** 26 41N 98 10 E
Chai Wan, *China* **69 G11** 22 16N 114 14 E
Chaillé-les-Marais, *France* **28 B2** 46 25N 1 2W
Chainat, *Thailand* **86 E3** 15 11N 100 8 E
Chaires, *U.S.A.* **152 E5** 30 26N 84 7W
Chaitén, *Chile* **176 B2** 42 55 S 72 43W
Chaiya, *Thailand* **87 H2** 9 23N 99 14 E
Chaj Doab, *Pakistan* **92 C5** 32 15N 73 0 E
Chajari, *Argentina* **174 C4** 30 42 S 58 0W
Chak Amru, *Pakistan* **92 C6** 32 22N 75 11 E
Chaka, *Sudan* **107 G3** 4 49N 31 14 E
Chakar →, *Pakistan* **92 E3** 29 29N 68 2 E
Chakari, *Zimbabwe* **117 B4** 18 5 S 29 51 E
Chakaria, *Bangla.* **90 E4** 21 45N 92 5 E
Chakarnaba, *Chad* **109 F4** 14 13N 20 51 E
Chake Chake, *Tanzania* **118 D4** 5 15 S 39 45 E
Chakhānsūr, *Afghan.* **91 C1** 31 10N 62 0 E
Chakonipau, L., *Canada* **141 A6** 56 18N 68 30W
Chakradharpur, *India* **93 H11** 22 45N 85 40 E
Chakrata, *India* **92 D7** 30 42N 77 51 E
Chakwadam, *Burma* **90 B7** 27 29N 98 31 E
Chakwal, *Pakistan* **91 B4** 32 56N 72 53 E
Chala, *Peru* **172 D3** 15 48 S 74 20W
Chalais, *France* **28 C4** 45 16N 0 3 E
Chalakudi, *India* **95 J3** 10 18N 76 20 E
Chalchihuites, *Mexico* **162 C4** 23 29N 103 53W
Chalcis = Khalkís, *Greece* **48 C5** 38 27N 23 42 E
Châlette-sur-Loing, *France* **27 D9** 48 1N 2 44 E
Chaleur B., *Canada* **141 C6** 47 55N 65 30W
Chalfant, *U.S.A.* **160 H8** 37 32N 118 21W
Chalhuanca, *Peru* **172 C3** 14 15 S 73 15W
Chalindrey, *France* **27 E12** 47 43N 5 26 E
Chaling, *China* **77 D9** 26 58N 113 30 E
Chalisgaon, *India* **94 D2** 20 30N 75 10 E
Chalk River, *Canada* **140 C4** 46 1N 77 27W
Chalkar = Shalkar, *Kazakstan* **64 F3** 50 40N 51 53 E
Chalkar, Ozero = Shalkar, Ozero, *Kazakstan* **64 F3** 50 35N 51 47 E
Chalky Inlet, *N.Z.* **131 G1** 46 3 S 166 31 E
Chalkyitsik, *U.S.A.* **144 C12** 66 39N 143 43W
Challakere, *India* **95 G3** 14 19N 76 39 E
Challans, *France* **26 F5** 46 50N 1 52W
Challapata, *Bolivia* **172 D4** 18 53 S 66 50W
Challis, *U.S.A.* **158 D6** 44 30N 114 14W
Chalmette, *U.S.A.* **155 L10** 29 56N 89 58W
Chalon-sur-Saône, *France* **27 F11** 46 48N 4 50 E
Chalonnes-sur-Loire, *France* **26 E6** 47 20N 0 45W
Châlons-en-Champagne, *France* **27 D11** 48 58N 4 20 E
Châlus, *France* **28 C4** 45 39N 0 58 E
Chalyaphum, *Thailand* **86 E4** 15 48N 102 2 E
Cham, *Germany* **31 F8** 49 13N 12 39 E
Cham, *Switz.* **33 B6** 47 11N 8 28 E
Cham, Cu Lao, *Vietnam* **86 E7** 15 57N 108 30 E
Chama, *U.S.A.* **159 H10** 36 54N 106 35W
Chamah, Gunong, *Malaysia* **84 A2** 5 13N 101 35 E
Chamaicó, *Argentina* **174 D3** 35 3 S 64 58W
Chaman, *Pakistan* **91 C2** 30 58N 66 25 E
Chamba, *India* **92 C7** 32 35N 76 10 E
Chamba, *Tanzania* **119 E4** 11 37 S 37 0 E
Chambal →, *India* **93 F8** 26 29N 79 15 E
Chamberlain, *U.S.A.* **154 D5** 43 49N 99 20W
Chamberlain →, *Australia* **124 C4** 15 30 S 127 54 E
Chamberlain L., *U.S.A.* **149 B11** 46 14N 69 19W
Chambers, *U.S.A.* **159 J9** 35 11N 109 26W
Chambersburg, *U.S.A.* **148 F7** 39 56N 77 40W
Chambéry, *France* **29 C9** 45 34N 5 55 E
Chamblee, *U.S.A.* **152 B5** 33 53N 84 18W
Chambly, *Canada* **151 A11** 45 27N 73 17W
Chambord, *Canada* **141 C5** 48 25N 72 6W
Chamboulive, *France* **28 C5** 45 26N 1 42 E
Chambri L., *Papua N. G.* **132 C2** 4 15 S 143 10 E
Chamchamal, *Iraq* **101 E11** 35 32N 44 50 E
Chamela, *Mexico* **162 D3** 19 32N 105 5W
Chamical, *Argentina* **174 C2** 30 22 S 66 27W
Chamkar Luong, *Cambodia* **87 G4** 11 0N 103 45 E
Chamois, *U.S.A.* **156 F5** 38 41N 91 46W
Chamoli, *India* **93 D8** 30 24N 79 21 E
Chamonix-Mont Blanc, *France* **29 C10** 45 55N 6 51 E
Chamoson, *Switz.* **32 D4** 46 12N 7 13 E
Chamouchouane →, *Canada* **140 C5** 48 37N 72 20W
Champa, *India* **93 H10** 22 2N 82 43 E
Champagne, *Canada* **142 A1** 60 49N 136 30W
Champagne, *France* **27 D11** 48 40N 4 20 E
Champagnole, *France* **27 F12** 46 45N 5 55 E
Champaign, *U.S.A.* **157 D8** 40 7N 88 15W
Champassak, *Laos* **86 E5** 14 53N 105 52 E
Champaubert, *France* **27 D10** 48 50N 3 45 E
Champawat, *India* **93 E9** 29 20N 80 6 E
Champdeniers-St-Denis, *France* **28 B3** 46 29N 0 25W
Champdoré, L., *Canada* **141 A6** 55 55N 65 49W
Champeix, *France* **28 C7** 45 37N 3 8 E
Champéry, *Switz.* **32 D3** 46 11N 6 52 E
Champion, *U.S.A.* **150 E4** 41 19N 80 51W
Champlain, *U.S.A.* **151 B11** 44 59N 73 27W
Champlain, L., *U.S.A.* **151 B11** 44 40N 73 20W
Champlitte, *France* **27 E12** 47 32N 5 31 E
Champotón, *Mexico* **163 D6** 19 20N 90 50W
Champua, *India* **93 H11** 22 5N 85 40 E
Chamrajnagar, *India* **95 J3** 11 52N 76 52 E
Chamusca, *Portugal* **43 F2** 39 21N 8 29W
Chan Chan, *Peru* **172 B2** 8 7 S 79 0W
Chana, *Thailand* **87 J3** 6 55N 100 44 E
Chañaral, *Chile* **174 B1** 26 23 S 70 40W
Chanārān, *Iran* **97 B8** 36 39N 59 6 E
Chanasma, *India* **92 H5** 23 44N 72 5 E
Chancay, *Peru* **172 C2** 11 32 S 77 25W
Chancery Lane, *Barbados* **165 g** 13 4N 59 30W
Chanco, *Chile* **174 D1** 35 44 S 72 32W
Chancy, *Switz.* **32 D1** 46 8N 5 58 E
Chand, *India* **93 J8** 21 57N 79 7 E
Chandalar →, *U.S.A.* **144 C11** 66 37N 146 0W
Chandan, *India* **93 G12** 24 38N 86 40 E
Chandan Chauki, *India* **93 E9** 28 33N 80 47 E
Chandannagar, *India* **93 H13** 22 52N 88 24 E
Chandausi, *India* **93 E8** 28 27N 78 49 E
Chandeleur Is., *U.S.A.* **155 L10** 29 55N 88 57W
Chandeleur Sd., *U.S.A.* **155 L10** 29 55N 89 0W
Chandigarh, *India* **92 D7** 30 43N 76 47 E
Chandil, *India* **93 H12** 22 58N 86 3 E
Chandler, *Australia* **127 D1** 27 0 S 133 19 E
Chandler, *Canada* **141 C7** 48 18N 64 46W
Chandler, *Ariz., U.S.A.* **159 K8** 33 18N 111 50W
Chandler, *Okla., U.S.A.* **155 H6** 35 42N 96 53W
Chandless →, *Brazil* **172 B4** 9 8 S 69 51W
Chandod, *India* **92 J5** 21 59N 73 28 E
Chandpur, *Bangla.* **90 D3** 23 8N 90 45 E
Chandragiri, *India* **95 H4** 13 35N 79 19 E
Chandrapur, *India* **94 E4** 19 57N 79 25 E
Chandrupatla, *India* **94 E5** 18 33N 80 24 E
Chānf, *Iran* **97 E9** 26 38N 60 29 E
Chang, *Pakistan* **92 F3** 26 59N 68 30 E
Chang, Ko, *Thailand* **87 F4** 12 0N 102 23 E
Ch'ang Chiang = Chang Jiang →, *China* **77 B13** 31 48N 121 10 E
Chang Jiang →, *China* **77 B13** 31 48N 121 10 E
Changa, *India* **93 C7** 33 53N 77 35 E
Changan, *China* **69 F10** 22 48N 113 48 E
Changanacheri, *India* **95 K3** 9 25N 76 31 E
Changane →, *Mozam.* **117 C5** 24 30 S 33 30 E
Changbai, *China* **75 D15** 41 25N 128 5 E
Changbai Shan, *China* **75 C15** 42 20N 129 0 E
Changchiak'ou = Zhangjiakou, *China* **74 D8** 40 48N 114 55 E
Ch'angchou = Changzhou, *China* **77 B12** 31 47N 119 58 E
Changchun, *China* **75 C13** 43 57N 125 17 E
Changchunling, *China* **75 B13** 45 18N 125 27 E

Changde, China 77 C8 29 4N 111 35 E
Changdo-ri, N. Korea 75 E14 38 30N 127 40 E
Changfeng, China 77 A11 32 28N 117 10 E
Changhai = Shanghai, China 77 B13 31 15N 121 26 E
Changhua, China 77 B12 30 12N 119 12 E
Changhua, Taiwan 77 E13 24 2N 120 30 E
Changhŭng, S. Korea 75 G14 34 41N 126 52 E
Changhŭngni, N. Korea 75 D15 40 24N 128 19 E
Changi, Malaysia 84 B2 1 23N 103 59 E
Changi, Singapore 87 d 1 23N 103 59 E
Changjiang, China 86 C7 19 20N 108 55 E
Changjiang Shuiku, China 69 G10 22 29N 113 27 E
Changjin, N. Korea 75 D14 40 23N 127 15 E
Changjin-chŏsuji, N. Korea 75 D14 40 30N 127 15 E
Changle, China 77 E12 25 59N 119 27 E
Changli, China 75 E10 39 40N 119 13 E
Changling, China 75 B12 44 20N 123 58 E
Changlun, Malaysia 87 J3 6 25N 100 26 E
Changning, Hunan, China 77 D9 26 28N 112 22 E
Changning, Sichuan, China 76 C5 28 40N 104 56 E
Changning, Yunnan, China 76 E2 24 45N 99 30 E
Changping, China 74 D9 40 14N 116 12 E
Changsha, China 77 C9 28 12N 113 0 E
Changshan, China 77 C12 28 55N 118 27 E
Changshu, China 77 B13 31 38N 120 43 E
Changshun, China 76 D6 26 3N 106 25 E
Changtai, China 77 E11 24 35N 117 42 E
Changting, China 77 E11 25 50N 116 22 E
Changwu, China 74 G4 35 10N 107 45 E
Changxing, China 77 B12 31 0N 119 55 E
Changyang, China 77 B8 30 30N 111 10 E
Changyi, China 75 F10 36 40N 119 30 E
Changyŏn, N. Korea 75 E13 38 15N 125 6 E
Changyuan, China 74 G8 35 15N 114 42 E
Changzhi, China 74 F7 36 10N 113 6 E
Changzhou, China 77 B12 31 47N 119 58 E
Chanhanga, Angola 116 B1 16 0 S 14 8 E
Chanlar = Xanlar, Azerbaijan 61 K8 40 37N 46 12 E
Channagiri, India 95 G2 14 2N 75 56 E
Channapatna, India 95 H3 12 40N 77 15 E
Channel Is., U.K. 21 H5 49 19N 2 24W
Channel Is., U.S.A. 161 M7 33 40N 119 15W
Channel Islands Nat. Park, U.S.A. 161 M8 33 30N 119 0W
Channel-Port aux Basques, Canada 141 C8 47 30N 59 9W
Channel Tunnel, Europe 21 F9 51 0N 1 30 E
Channing, U.S.A. 155 H3 35 41N 102 20W
Chantada, Spain 42 C3 42 36N 7 46W
Chanthaburi, Thailand 86 F4 12 38N 102 12 E
Chantilly, France 27 C9 49 12N 2 29 E
Chantonnay, France 26 F5 46 40N 1 3W
Chantrey Inlet, Canada 138 B10 67 48N 96 20W
Chanumla, India 95 K11 8 19N 93 5 E
Chanute, U.S.A. 155 G7 37 41N 95 27W
Chanza →, Spain 43 H3 37 32N 7 30W
Chao Hu, China 77 B11 31 30N 117 30 E
Chao Phraya →, Thailand 86 F3 13 32N 100 36 E
Chao Phraya Lowlands, Thailand 86 E3 15 30N 100 0 E
Chaocheng, China 74 F8 36 4N 115 37 E
Chaohu, China 77 B11 31 38N 117 50 E
Chaoyang, Guangdong, China 77 F11 23 17N 116 30 E
Chaoyang, Liaoning, China 75 D11 41 35N 120 22 E
Chaozhou, China 77 F11 23 42N 116 32 E
Chapada dos Guimarães, Brazil 173 D6 15 26 S 55 45W
Chapais, Canada 140 C5 49 47N 74 51W
Chapala, Mozam. 119 F4 15 50 S 37 35 E
Chapala, L. de, Mexico 162 C4 20 10N 103 20W
Chaparé →, Bolivia 173 D5 15 58 S 64 42W
Chaparmukh, India 90 B4 26 12N 92 31 E
Chaparral, Colombia 168 C2 3 43N 75 28W
Chapayev, Kazakstan 60 E10 50 25N 51 10 E
Chapayevsk, Russia 60 D9 53 0N 49 40 E
Chapecó, Brazil 175 B5 27 14 S 52 41W
Chapel Hill, U.S.A. 149 H6 35 55N 79 4W
Chapetsk →, Russia 64 B3 58 36N 50 4 E
Chapin, U.S.A. 156 E6 39 46N 90 24W
Chapleau, Canada 140 C3 47 50N 83 24W
Chaplin, Canada 143 C7 50 28N 106 40W
Chaplin L., Canada 143 C7 50 22N 106 36W
Chaplino, Ukraine 59 H9 48 8N 36 15 E
Chaplygin, Russia 58 F11 53 15N 40 0 E
Chappell, U.S.A. 154 E3 41 6N 102 28W
Chappells, U.S.A. 152 A8 34 11N 81 52W
Chapra = Chhapra, India 93 G11 25 48N 84 44 E
Châr, Mauritania 110 D2 21 32N 12 45W
Chara, Russia 67 D12 56 54N 118 20 E
Charadai, Argentina 174 B4 27 35 S 59 55W
Charagua, Bolivia 173 D5 19 45 S 63 10W
Charalá, Colombia 168 B3 6 17N 73 10W
Charambirá, Punta, Colombia 168 C2 4 16N 77 32W
Charaña, Bolivia 172 D4 17 30 S 69 25W
Charantsavan, Armenia 61 K7 40 35N 44 41 E
Charanwala, India 92 F5 27 51N 72 10 E
Charapita, Colombia 168 D3 0 37 S 74 21W
Charata, Argentina 174 B3 27 13 S 61 14W
Charcas, Mexico 162 C4 23 10N 101 20W
Chard, U.K. 21 G5 50 52N 2 58W
Chardon, U.S.A. 150 E3 41 35N 81 12W
Charduar, India 90 B4 26 51N 92 46 E
Chardzhou = Chärjew, Turkmenistan 66 F7 39 6N 63 34 E
Charente □, France 28 C4 45 50N 0 16 E
Charente →, France 28 C2 45 57N 1 5W
Charente-Maritime □, France 28 C3 45 45N 0 45W
Charenton-du-Cher, France 27 F9 46 44N 2 39 E
Chari →, Chad 109 F2 12 58N 14 31 E
Chārīkār, Afghan. 91 B3 35 0N 69 10 E
Charing, U.S.A. 152 C5 32 28N 84 22W
Chariton, U.S.A. 156 C3 41 1N 93 19W
Chariton →, U.S.A. 156 E4 39 19N 92 58W
Charity, Guyana 169 B6 7 24N 58 36W
Chärjew, Turkmenistan 66 F7 39 6N 63 34 E
Charkhari, India 93 G8 25 24N 79 45 E
Charkhi Dadri, India 92 E7 28 37N 76 17 E
Charleroi, Belgium 24 D4 50 24N 4 27 E
Charleroi, U.S.A. 150 F5 40 9N 79 57W
Charles, C., U.S.A. 148 G8 37 7N 75 58W
Charles City, U.S.A. 156 A4 43 4N 92 41W
Charles L., Canada 143 B6 59 50N 110 33W
Charles Sound, N.Z. 131 F2 45 2 S 167 4 E
Charles Town, U.S.A. 148 F7 39 17N 77 52W
Charleston, Ill., U.S.A. 157 E8 39 30N 88 10W
Charleston, Miss., U.S.A. 155 H9 34 1N 90 4W
Charleston, Mo., U.S.A. 155 G10 36 55N 89 21W
Charleston, S.C., U.S.A. 152 C10 32 46N 79 56W
Charleston, W. Va., U.S.A. 148 F5 38 21N 81 38W
Charleston L., Canada 151 B9 44 32N 76 0W
Charleston Peak, U.S.A. 161 J11 36 16N 115 42W
Charlestown, Ireland 23 C3 53 58N 8 48W
Charlestown, S. Africa 117 D4 27 26 S 29 53 E
Charlestown, Ind., U.S.A. 157 F11 38 27N 85 40W
Charlestown, N.H., U.S.A. 151 C12 43 14N 72 25W
Charleville = Rath Luirc, Ireland 23 D3 52 21N 8 40W
Charleville, Australia 127 D4 26 24 S 146 15 E
Charleville-Mézières, France 27 C11 49 44N 4 40 E
Charlevoix, U.S.A. 148 C3 45 19N 85 16W
Charlieu, France 27 F11 46 10N 4 10 E
Charlotte, Mich., U.S.A. 157 B12 42 34N 84 50W
Charlotte, N.C., U.S.A. 149 H5 35 13N 80 51W
Charlotte, Vt., U.S.A. 151 B11 44 19N 73 14W
Charlotte Amalie, U.S. Virgin Is. 165 e 18 21N 64 56W
Charlotte Harbor, U.S.A. 149 M4 26 50N 82 10W
Charlotte L., Canada 142 C3 52 12N 125 19W
Charlottenberg, Sweden 16 E6 59 54N 12 17 E
Charlottesville, U.S.A. 148 F6 38 2N 78 30W
Charlottetown, Nfld., Canada 141 B8 52 46N 56 7W
Charlottetown, P.E.I., Canada 141 C7 46 14N 63 8W
Charlotteville, Trin. & Tob. 169 E10 11 20N 60 33W
Charlton, Australia 128 D5 36 16 S 143 24 E
Charlton, U.S.A. 154 E8 40 59N 93 20W
Charlton I., Canada 140 B4 52 0N 79 20W
Charmes, France 27 D13 48 22N 6 17 E
Charmey, Switz. 32 C4 46 37N 7 10 E
Charny, Canada 141 C5 46 43N 71 15W
Charolles, France 27 F11 46 27N 4 16 E
Chârost, France 27 F9 47 0N 2 7 E
Charouine, Algeria 111 C4 29 0N 0 15W
Charre, Mozam. 119 F4 17 13 S 35 10 E
Charroux, France 28 B4 46 9N 0 25 E
Charsadda, Pakistan 92 B4 34 7N 71 45 E
Charshanga, Turkmenistan 65 E3 37 30N 66 1 E
Charters Towers, Australia 126 C4 20 5 S 146 13 E
Chartres, France 26 D8 48 29N 1 30 E
Charvakskoye Vdkhr., Uzbekistan 65 C5 41 35N 70 0 E
Chascomús, Argentina 174 D4 35 30 S 58 0W
Chasefu, Zambia 119 E3 11 55 S 33 8 E
Chashma Barrage, Pakistan 91 B3 32 27N 71 20 E
Chaslands Mistake, N.Z. 131 G4 46 38 S 169 22 E
Chasseneuil-sur-Bonnieure, France 28 C4 45 52N 0 29 E
Chasseron, Switz. 32 C3 46 52N 6 32 E
Chât, Iran 97 B7 37 59N 55 16 E
Chatal Balkan = Udvoy Balkan, Bulgaria 51 D10 42 50N 26 50 E
Chatanika, U.S.A. 144 D11 65 7N 147 28W
Château-Arnoux, France 29 D10 44 6N 6 0 E
Château-Chinon, France 27 E10 47 4N 3 56 E
Château d'Oex, Switz. 32 D4 46 28N 7 8 E
Château-d'Olonne, France 28 B2 46 30N 1 44W
Château-du-Loir, France 26 E7 47 40N 0 25 E
Château-Gontier, France 26 E6 47 50N 0 48W
Château-la-Vallière, France 26 E7 47 30N 0 20 E
Château-Landon, France 27 D9 48 8N 2 40 E
Château-Renault, France 26 E7 47 36N 0 56 E
Château-Salins, France 27 D13 48 50N 6 30 E
Château-Thierry, France 27 C10 49 3N 3 20 E
Châteaubourg, France 26 D5 48 7N 1 25W
Châteaubriant, France 26 E5 47 43N 1 23W
Châteaudun, France 26 D8 48 3N 1 20 E
Chateaugay, U.S.A. 151 B10 44 56N 74 5W
Châteaugiron, France 26 D5 48 3N 1 30W
Châteauguay, L., Canada 141 A5 56 26N 70 3W
Châteaulin, France 26 D2 48 11N 4 8W
Châteaumeillant, France 27 F9 46 35N 2 12 E
Châteauneuf-du-Faou, France 26 D3 48 11N 3 50W
Châteauneuf-en-Thymerais, France 26 D8 48 35N 1 13 E
Châteauneuf-sur-Charente, France 28 C3 45 36N 0 3W
Châteauneuf-sur-Cher, France 27 F9 46 52N 2 18 E
Châteauneuf-sur-Loire, France 27 E9 47 52N 2 13 E
Châteaurenard, Bouches-du-Rhône, France 29 E8 43 53N 4 51 E
Châteaurenard, Loiret, France 27 E9 47 56N 2 55 E
Châteauroux, France 27 F8 46 50N 1 40 E
Châteauvillain, France 27 D11 48 2N 4 55 E
Châteaux, Pte. des, Guadeloupe 164 b 16 15N 61 10W
Châtel-St-Denis, Switz. 32 C3 46 32N 6 54 E
Châtelaillon-Plage, France 28 B2 46 5N 1 5W
Châtelguyon, France 28 C7 45 55N 3 4 E
Châtellerault, France 26 F7 46 50N 0 30 E
Châtelus-Malvaleix, France 27 F9 46 18N 2 1 E
Chatham = Miramichi, Canada 141 C6 47 2N 65 28W
Chatham, Canada 140 D3 42 24N 82 11W
Chatham, U.K. 21 F8 51 22N 0 32 E
Chatham, Ill., U.S.A. 156 E7 39 40N 89 42W
Chatham, N.Y., U.S.A. 151 D11 42 21N 73 36W
Chatham, I., Chile 176 D2 50 40 S 74 25W
Chatham Is., Pac. Oc. 134 M10 44 0 S 176 40W
Châtillon, Italy 44 C4 45 45N 7 37 E
Châtillon-Coligny, France 27 E9 47 50N 2 51 E
Châtillon-en-Diois, France 29 D9 44 41N 5 29 E
Châtillon-sur-Indre, France 26 F8 46 59N 1 10 E
Châtillon-sur-Loire, France 27 E9 47 35N 2 44 E
Châtillon-sur-Seine, France 27 E11 47 50N 4 33 E
Chatkal →, Uzbekistan 65 C5 41 38N 70 1 E
Chatkal Kyrka Tooloru, Kyrgyzstan 65 C5 41 30N 70 45 E
Chatmohar, Bangla. 93 G13 24 15N 89 15 E
Chatra, India 93 G11 24 12N 84 56 E
Chatrapur, India 94 E7 19 22N 85 2 E
Chats, L. des, Canada 151 A8 45 30N 76 20W
Chatsu, India 92 F6 26 36N 75 57 E
Chatsworth, Canada 150 B4 44 27N 80 54W
Chatsworth, U.S.A. 157 D8 40 45N 88 18W
Chatsworth, Zimbabwe 119 F3 19 38 S 31 13 E
Chatta-Hantō, Japan 73 C8 34 45N 136 55 E
Chattahoochee, U.S.A. 152 E5 30 42N 84 51W
Chattahoochee →, U.S.A. 152 E5 30 54N 84 57W
Chattanooga, U.S.A. 149 H3 35 3N 85 19W
Chatteris, U.K. 21 E8 52 28N 0 2 E
Chaturat, Thailand 86 E3 15 40N 101 51 E
Chatyr-Köl, Kyrgyzstan 65 C7 40 40N 75 18 E
Chatyr-Tash, Kyrgyzstan 65 C8 40 55N 76 25 E
Chau Doc, Vietnam 87 G5 10 42N 105 7 E
Chaudes-Aigues, France 28 D7 44 51N 3 1 E
Chauffailles, France 27 F11 46 13N 4 20 E
Chauk, Burma 90 E5 20 53N 94 49 E
Chaukan Pass, Burma 90 B6 27 8N 97 10 E
Chaumont, France 27 D12 48 7N 5 8 E
Chaumont, U.S.A. 151 B8 44 4N 76 8W
Chaumont-en-Vexin, France 27 C8 49 16N 1 53 E
Chaumont-sur-Loire, France 26 E8 47 29N 1 11 E
Chaunay, France 28 B4 46 13N 0 9 E
Chauny, France 27 C10 49 37N 3 12 E
Chaura, India 95 K11 8 27N 93 2 E
Chausey, Îs., France 26 D5 48 52N 1 49W
Chaussin, France 27 F12 46 59N 5 22 E
Chautauqua L., U.S.A. 150 D5 42 10N 79 24W
Chauvay, Kyrgyzstan 65 C6 40 8N 72 8 E
Chauvigny, France 26 F7 46 34N 0 39 E
Chauvin, Canada 143 C6 52 45N 110 10W
Chavakachcheri, Sri Lanka 95 K5 9 39N 80 9 E
Chavanges, France 27 D11 48 30N 4 35 E
Chavantina, Brazil 173 C7 14 40 S 52 21W
Chaves, Brazil 170 B2 0 15 S 49 55W
Chaves, Portugal 42 D3 41 45N 7 32W
Chavuma, Zambia 115 E4 13 4 S 22 40 E
Chawang, Thailand 87 H2 8 25N 99 30 E
Chayan = Shayan, Kazakstan 65 B4 43 5N 69 25 E
Chaykovskiy, Russia 64 C5 56 47N 54 9 E
Chazelles-sur-Lyon, France 29 C8 45 39N 4 22 E
Chazuta, Peru 172 B2 6 30 S 76 0W
Chazy, U.S.A. 151 B11 44 53N 73 26W
Cheaha Mt., U.S.A. 152 B4 33 29N 85 49W
Cheb, Czech Rep. 34 A5 50 9N 12 28 E
Chebanse, U.S.A. 157 D9 41 0N 87 54W
Chebarkul, Russia 64 D8 55 0N 60 25 E
Cheboksarskoye Vdkhr., Russia 60 B8 56 13N 46 58 E
Cheboksary, Russia 60 B8 56 8N 47 12 E
Cheboygan, U.S.A. 148 C3 45 39N 84 29W
Chebsara, Russia 58 C10 59 10N 38 59 E
Chech, Erg, Africa 110 D4 25 0N 2 15W
Chechaouen, Morocco 110 A3 35 9N 5 15W
Chechen, Ostrov, Russia 61 H8 43 59N 47 40 E
Chechenia □, Russia 61 J7 43 30N 45 29 E
Checheno-Ingush Republic = Chechenia □, Russia 61 J7 43 30N 45 29 E
Chechnya = Chechenia □, Russia 61 J7 43 30N 45 29 E
Chech'ŏn, S. Korea 75 F15 37 8N 128 12 E
Chęciny, Poland 55 H7 50 46N 20 28 E
Checotah, U.S.A. 155 H7 35 28N 95 31W
Chedabucto B., Canada 141 C7 45 25N 61 8W
Cheduba I., Burma 90 F4 18 45N 93 40 E
Cheepie, Australia 127 D4 26 33 S 145 1 E
Chef-Boutonne, France 28 B3 46 7N 0 4W
Cheffadine, Niger 109 D2 19 57N 12 11 E
Chefornak, U.S.A. 144 F6 60 13N 164 12W
Chegdomyn, Russia 67 D14 51 7N 133 1 E
Chegga, Mauritania 110 C3 25 27N 5 40W
Chegutu, Zimbabwe 119 F3 18 10 S 30 14 E
Chehalis, U.S.A. 160 D4 46 40N 122 58W
Chehalis →, U.S.A. 160 D3 46 57N 123 50W
Cheiron, Mt., France 29 E10 43 49N 6 58 E
Cheju do, S. Korea 75 H14 33 29N 126 34 E
Chekalin, Russia 58 E9 54 10N 36 10 E
Chekiang = Zhejiang □, China 77 C13 29 0N 120 0 E
Chel = Kuru, Bahr el →, Sudan 107 F2 8 10N 26 50 E
Chela, Sa. da, Angola 116 B1 16 20 S 13 20 E
Chelan, U.S.A. 158 C3 47 51N 120 1W
Chelan, L., U.S.A. 158 B3 48 11N 120 30W
Chelek, Uzbekistan 65 D3 39 55N 66 51 E
Cheleken, Turkmenistan 57 G9 39 34N 53 16 E
Cheleken Yarymadasy, Turkmenistan 97 B7 39 30N 53 15 E
Chelforó, Argentina 176 A3 39 0 S 66 33W
Chéliff, O. →, Algeria 111 A5 36 0N 0 8 E
Chelkar = Shalqar, Kazakstan 66 E6 47 48N 59 39 E
Chelkar Tengiz, Solonchak, Kazakstan 66 E7 48 5N 63 7 E
Chella, Ethiopia 107 F4 5 0N 37 26 E
Chellala Dahrania, Algeria 111 B5 33 2N 0 1 E
Chelles, France 27 D9 48 52N 2 33 E
Chełm, Poland 55 G10 51 8N 23 30 E
Chełmno, Poland 55 E5 53 20N 18 30 E
Chelmsford, U.K. 21 F8 51 44N 0 29 E
Chełmża, Poland 55 E5 53 10N 18 39 E
Chelsea, Australia 129 E6 38 5 S 145 8 E
Chelsea, Mich., U.S.A. 157 B12 42 19N 84 1W
Chelsea, Vt., U.S.A. 151 C12 43 59N 72 27W
Cheltenham, U.K. 21 F5 51 54N 2 4W
Chelva, Spain 43 F4 39 45N 1 0W
Chelyabinsk, Russia 64 D8 55 10N 61 24 E
Chelyuskin, C., Russia 62 B14 77 30N 103 0 E
Chemainus, Canada 160 B3 48 55N 123 42W
Chembar = Belinskiy, Russia 60 D6 53 0N 43 25 E
Chemillé, France 26 E6 47 14N 0 45W
Chemin Grenier, Mauritius 121 d 20 29 S 57 28 E
Chemnitz, Germany 30 E8 50 51N 12 54 E
Chemult, U.S.A. 158 E3 43 14N 121 47W
Chen, Gora, Russia 67 C15 65 16N 141 50 E
Chenab →, Pakistan 91 C3 30 23N 71 2 E
Chenachane, O. →, Algeria 110 C4 25 20N 3 20W
Chenango Forks, U.S.A. 151 D9 42 15N 75 51W
Chencha, Ethiopia 107 F4 6 15N 37 32 E
Chenchiang = Zhenjiang, China 77 A12 32 11N 119 26 E
Cheney, U.S.A. 158 C5 47 30N 117 35W
Cheng Xian, China 74 H3 33 43N 105 42 E
Chengalpattu, India 95 H4 12 42N 79 58 E
Chengbu, China 77 D8 26 18N 110 16 E
Chengcheng, China 74 G5 35 8N 109 56 E
Chengchou = Zhengzhou, China 74 G7 34 45N 113 34 E
Chengde, China 75 D9 40 59N 117 58 E
Chengdong Hu, China 77 A11 32 15N 116 20 E
Chengdu, China 76 B5 30 38N 104 2 E
Chengele, India 90 A6 28 47N 96 16 E
Chenggong, China 76 E4 24 52N 102 56 E
Chenggu, China 74 H4 33 10N 107 21 E
Chenghai, China 77 F11 23 30N 116 42 E
Chengjiang, China 76 E4 24 39N 103 0 E
Chengkou, China 76 B7 31 54N 108 31 E
Ch'engmai, China 86 C7 19 50N 109 58 E
Ch'engtu = Chengdu, China 76 B5 30 38N 104 2 E
Chengwu, China 74 G8 34 58N 115 50 E
Chengxi Hu, China 77 A11 32 15N 116 10 E
Chengyang, China 75 F11 36 18N 120 21 E
Chenjiagang, China 75 G10 34 23N 119 47 E
Chenkaladi, Sri Lanka 95 L5 7 47N 81 35 E
Chenkán, Mexico 163 D6 19 8N 90 58W
Chennai, India 95 H5 13 8N 80 19 E
Chenoa, U.S.A. 157 D8 40 45N 88 43W
Chenôve, France 27 E12 47 16N 5 1 E
Chenxi, China 77 C8 28 2N 110 12 E
Chenzhou, China 77 D9 25 47N 113 1 E
Cheo Reo, Vietnam 78 B3 13 25N 108 28 E
Cheom Ksan, Cambodia 86 E5 14 13N 104 56 E
Chepelare, Bulgaria 51 E8 41 44N 24 40 E
Chepén, Peru 172 B2 7 15 S 79 23W
Chépénéhé, Vanuatu 133 K5 20 47 S 167 9 E
Chepes, Argentina 174 C2 31 20 S 66 35W
Chepo, Panama 164 E4 9 10N 79 6W
Chepstow, U.K. 21 F5 51 38N 2 41W
Cheptsa → = Chapetsk →, Russia 64 B3 58 36N 50 4 E
Cheptulil, Mt., Kenya 118 B4 1 25N 35 35 E
Chequamegon B., U.S.A. 154 B9 46 40N 90 30W
Cher □, France 27 E9 47 10N 2 30 E
Cher →, France 26 E7 47 21N 0 29 E
Chéradi, Italy 47 B10 40 27N 17 10 E
Cheran, India 90 C3 25 45N 90 44 E
Cherasco, Italy 44 D4 44 39N 7 51 E
Cheraw, U.S.A. 149 H6 34 42N 79 53W
Cherbourg, France 26 C5 49 39N 1 40W
Cherchell, Algeria 111 A5 36 35N 2 12 E
Cherdakly, Russia 60 C9 54 25N 48 50 E
Cherdyn, Russia 64 A6 60 24N 56 29 E
Cheremkhovo, Russia 67 D11 53 8N 103 1 E
Cherepanovo, Russia 66 D9 54 15N 83 30 E
Cherepovets, Russia 58 C9 59 5N 37 55 E
Chergui, Chott ech, Algeria 111 B5 34 21N 0 25 E
Chergui, Zahrez, Algeria 111 B5 35 11N 3 31 E
Cherial, India 94 F4 17 55N 78 59 E
Cherikov = Cherykaw, Belarus 58 F6 53 32N 31 20 E
Cheriyam I., India 95 J1 10 9N 73 40 E
Cherkasy, Ukraine 59 H7 49 27N 32 4 E
Cherkessk, Russia 61 H6 44 15N 42 5 E
Cherla, India 94 E5 18 5N 80 49 E
Cherlak, Russia 66 D8 54 15N 74 55 E
Chermoz, Russia 64 B6 58 46N 56 10 E
Chernak = Shornak, Kazakstan 65 B4 43 24N 68 2 E
Chernaya, Russia 67 B9 70 30N 89 10 E
Chernaya Kholunitsa, Russia 64 B3 58 57N 51 39 E
Cherni, Bulgaria 50 D7 42 35N 23 18 E
Chernigov = Chernihiv, Ukraine 59 G6 51 28N 31 20 E
Chernihiv, Ukraine 59 G6 51 28N 31 20 E
Chernivtsi, Ukraine 59 H3 48 15N 25 52 E
Chernobyl = Chornobyl, Ukraine 59 G6 51 20N 30 15 E
Chernogorsk, Russia 67 D10 53 49N 91 18 E
Chernomorskoye = Chornomorske, Ukraine 59 K7 45 31N 32 40 E
Chernovtsy = Chernivtsi, Ukraine 59 H3 48 15N 25 52 E
Chernushka, Russia 64 C6 56 29N 56 3 E
Chernyakhovsk, Russia 15 J19 54 36N 21 48 E
Chernyanka, Russia 59 G9 50 56N 37 49 E
Chernysheyskiy, Russia 67 C12 63 0N 112 30 E
Chernyy Otrog, Russia 64 F6 51 53N 56 0 E
Chernyye Zemli, Russia 61 H8 46 10N 46 0 E
Cherokee, Iowa, U.S.A. 154 D7 42 45N 95 33W
Cherokee, Okla., U.S.A. 155 G5 36 45N 98 21W
Cherokee Village, U.S.A. 155 G9 36 17N 91 30W
Cherokees, Grand Lake O' The, U.S.A. 155 G7 36 28N 95 2W
Cherquenco, Chile 176 A2 38 35 S 72 0W
Cherrapunji, India 90 C3 25 17N 91 47 E
Cherry Valley, Calif., U.S.A. 161 M10 33 59N 116 57W
Cherry Valley, N.Y., U.S.A. 151 D10 42 48N 74 45W
Cherryville, U.S.A. 156 G5 37 51N 91 16W
Cherskiy, Russia 67 C17 68 45N 161 18 E
Cherskogo Khrebet, Russia 67 C15 65 0N 143 0 E
Chertkovo, Russia 59 H11 49 25N 40 19 E
Cherven, Belarus 58 F5 53 45N 28 28 E
Cherven-Bryag, Bulgaria 51 C8 43 17N 24 7 E
Chervonohrad, Ukraine 59 G3 50 25N 24 10 E
Cherwell →, U.K. 21 F6 51 44N 1 14W
Cherykaw, Belarus 58 F6 53 32N 31 20 E
Chesapeake, U.S.A. 148 G7 36 50N 76 17W
Chesapeake B., U.S.A. 148 G7 38 0N 76 10W
Cheshire □, U.K. 20 D5 53 14N 2 30W
Cheshskaya Guba, Russia 56 A8 67 20N 47 0 E
Cheshunt, U.K. 21 F7 51 43N 0 1W
Chesil Beach, U.K. 21 G5 50 37N 2 33W
Chesley, Canada 150 B3 44 17N 81 5W
Cheste, Spain 41 F4 39 30N 0 41W
Chester, U.K. 20 D5 53 12N 2 53W
Chester, Calif., U.S.A. 158 F3 40 19N 121 14W
Chester, Ga., U.S.A. 152 C6 32 24N 83 9W
Chester, Ill., U.S.A. 155 G10 37 55N 89 49W
Chester, Mont., U.S.A. 158 B8 48 31N 110 58W
Chester, Pa., U.S.A. 148 F8 39 51N 75 22W
Chester, S.C., U.S.A. 149 H5 34 43N 81 12W
Chester, Vt., U.S.A. 151 C12 43 16N 72 36W
Chester, W. Va., U.S.A. 150 F4 40 37N 80 34W
Chester-le-Street, U.K. 20 C6 54 51N 1 34W
Chesterfield, U.K. 20 D6 53 15N 1 25W
Chesterfield, Is., N. Cal. 134 J7 19 52 S 158 15 E
Chesterfield Inlet, Canada 138 B10 63 30N 90 45W
Chesterton Ra., Australia 127 D4 25 30 S 147 27 E
Chesterton Range Nat. Park, Australia 127 D4 26 16 S 147 22 E
Chestertown, U.S.A. 151 C11 43 40N 73 48W
Chesterville, Canada 151 A9 45 6N 75 14W
Chestnut Ridge, U.S.A. 150 F5 40 20N 79 10W
Chesuncook L., U.S.A. 149 C11 46 0N 69 21W
Chetamale, India 95 J11 10 43N 92 33 E
Chéticamp, Canada 141 C7 46 37N 60 59W
Chetlat I., India 95 J1 11 42N 72 42 E
Chetrosu, Moldova 53 B12 48 5N 27 54 E
Chetumal, Mexico 163 D7 18 30N 88 20W
Chetumal, B. de, Mexico 163 D7 18 40N 88 10W
Chetwynd, Canada 142 B4 55 45N 121 36W
Chevak, U.S.A. 144 F6 61 32N 165 35W
Chevanceaux, France 28 C3 45 18N 0 14W
Cheviot, U.S.A. 157 E12 39 10N 84 37W
Cheviot, The, U.K. 20 B5 55 29N 2 9W
Cheviot Hills, U.K. 20 B5 55 20N 2 30W
Cheviot Ra., Australia 126 D3 25 20 S 143 45 E
Chew Bahir, Ethiopia 107 G4 4 40N 36 50 E
Chewelah, U.S.A. 158 B5 48 17N 117 43W
Chewore Safari Area, Zimbabwe 119 F2 16 0 S 29 52 E
Cheyenne, Okla., U.S.A. 155 H5 35 37N 99 40W
Cheyenne, Wyo., U.S.A. 154 E2 41 8N 104 49W
Cheyenne →, U.S.A. 154 C4 44 41N 101 18W
Cheyenne Wells, U.S.A. 154 F3 38 49N 102 21W
Cheyne B., Australia 125 F2 34 35 S 118 50 E
Cheyur, India 95 H5 12 21N 80 0 E
Chhabra, India 92 G7 24 40N 76 54 E
Chhaktala, India 92 H6 22 6N 74 11 E
Chhapra, India 93 G11 25 48N 84 44 E
Chhata, India 92 F7 27 42N 77 30 E
Chhatak, Bangla. 90 C3 25 5N 91 37 E
Chhatarpur, Jharkhand, India 93 G11 24 23N 84 11 E
Chhatarpur, Mad. P., India 93 G8 24 55N 79 35 E
Chhati, India 94 D5 20 47N 81 40 E
Chhattisgarh □, India 93 J10 22 0N 82 0 E
Chhaygaon, India 90 B3 26 3N 91 24 E
Chheg, Cambodia 86 F5 13 45N 105 24 E
Chhindwara, Mad. P., India 93 H8 23 3N 79 29 E
Chhindwara, Mad. P., India 93 H8 22 2N 78 59 E
Chhinhdipada, India 94 D7 21 6N 84 52 E
Chhlong, Cambodia 87 F5 12 15N 105 58 E
Chhota Tawa →, India 92 H7 22 14N 76 36 E
Chhoti Kali Sindh →, India 92 G6 24 2N 75 31 E
Chhuikhadan, India 93 J9 21 32N 80 59 E
Chhuk, Cambodia 87 G5 10 46N 104 28 E
Chi →, Thailand 86 E5 15 11N 104 43 E
Chiai, Taiwan 77 F13 23 29N 120 25 E
Chiali, Taiwan 77 F13 23 10N 120 11 E
Chiamussu = Jiamusi, China 69 B8 46 40N 130 26 E
Chianciano Terme, Italy 45 E8 43 2N 11 49 E
Chiang Dao, Thailand 86 C2 19 22N 98 58 E
Chiang Kham, Thailand 86 C3 19 32N 100 18 E
Chiang Khan, Thailand 86 D3 17 52N 101 36 E
Chiang Khong, Thailand 76 G3 20 17N 100 24 E
Chiang Mai, Thailand 86 C2 18 47N 98 59 E
Chiang Rai, Thailand 76 H2 19 52N 99 50 E
Chiang Saen, Thailand 76 G3 20 16N 100 5 E
Chiange, Angola 115 F2 15 35 S 13 40 E
Chiapa →, Mexico 163 D6 16 42N 93 0W
Chiapa de Corzo, Mexico 163 D6 16 42N 93 0W
Chiapas □, Mexico 163 D6 17 0N 92 45W
Chiaramonte Gulfi, Italy 47 E7 37 2N 14 42 E
Chiaravalle, Italy 45 E10 43 36N 13 19 E
Chiaravalle Centrale, Italy 47 D9 38 41N 16 25 E
Chiari, Italy 44 C6 45 32N 9 56 E
Chiasso, Switz. 33 E8 45 50N 9 2 E
Chiatura, Georgia 61 J6 42 15N 43 17 E
Chiautla, Mexico 163 D5 18 18N 98 34W
Chiávari, Italy 44 D6 44 19N 9 19 E
Chiavenna, Italy 44 B6 46 19N 9 24 E
Chiba, Japan 73 B12 35 30N 140 7 E
Chiba □, Japan 73 B12 35 30N 140 20 E
Chibabava, Mozam. 117 C5 20 17 S 33 35 E
Chibango, Angola 115 E4 13 38 S 21 56 E
Chibemba, Cunene, Angola 115 F2 15 48 S 14 8 E
Chibemba, Huila, Angola 116 B2 16 20 S 15 20 E
Chibi, Zimbabwe 117 C5 20 18 S 30 25 E
Chibia, Angola 115 F2 15 10 S 13 42 E
Chibougamau, Canada 140 C5 49 56N 74 24W
Chibougamau, L., Canada 140 C5 49 50N 74 20W
Chibuk, Nigeria 113 C7 10 52N 12 50 E
Chibuto, Mozam. 117 C5 24 40 S 33 33 E
Chic-Chocs, Mts., Canada 141 C6 48 55N 66 0W
Chicacole = Srikakulam, India 94 E6 18 14N 83 58 E
Chicago, U.S.A. 157 C9 41 53N 87 38W
Chicago Heights, U.S.A. 157 C9 41 30N 87 38W
Chicapa →, Dem. Rep. of the Congo 115 D4 6 25 S 20 48 E
Chicha, Chad 109 E3 16 57N 18 34 E
Chichagof I., U.S.A. 144 H14 57 30N 135 30W
Chichaoua, Morocco 110 B3 31 32N 8 44W
Chichén-Itzá, Mexico 163 C7 20 40N 88 36W
Chicheng, China 74 D8 40 55N 115 55 E
Chichester, U.K. 21 G7 50 50N 0 47W
Chichester Ra., Australia 124 D2 22 12 S 119 15 E
Chichibu, Japan 73 A11 35 59N 139 10 E
Ch'ich'ihaerh = Qiqihar, China 67 E13 47 26N 124 0 E
Chicholi, India 92 H8 22 1N 77 40 E
Chickasha, U.S.A. 155 H6 35 3N 97 58W
Chicken, U.S.A. 144 D12 64 5N 141 56W

Chiclana de la Frontera, *Spain* **43 J4** 36 26N 6 9W
Chiclayo, *Peru* **172 B2** 6 42 S 79 50W
Chico, *U.S.A.* **160 F5** 39 44N 121 50W
Chico →, *Chubut, Argentina* **176 E3** 44 0 S 67 0W
Chico →, *Santa Cruz, Argentina* **176 C3** 50 0 S 68 30W
Chicomba, *Angola* **115 E2** 14 10 S 14 52 E
Chicomo, *Mozam.* **117 C5** 24 31 S 34 6 E
Chicontepec, *Mexico* **163 C5** 20 58N 98 10W
Chicopee, *U.S.A.* **151 D12** 42 9N 72 37W
Chicoutimi, *Canada* **141 C5** 48 28N 71 5W
Chicualacuala, *Mozam.* **117 C5** 22 6 S 31 42 E
Chicuma, *Angola* **115 E2** 13 26 S 14 50 E
Chidambaram, *India* **95 J4** 11 20N 79 45 E
Chidenguele, *Mozam.* **117 C5** 24 55 S 34 11 E
Chidley, C., *Canada* **139 B13** 60 23N 64 26W
Chiducuane, *Mozam.* **117 C5** 24 35 S 34 25 E
Chiede, *Angola* **116 B2** 17 15 S 16 22 E
Chiefland, *U.S.A.* **153 F7** 29 29N 82 52W
Chiefs Pt., *Canada* **150 B3** 44 41N 81 18W
Chiem Hoa, *Vietnam* **86 A5** 22 12N 105 17 E
Chiemsee, *Germany* **31 H8** 47 53N 12 28 E
Chiengi, *Zambia* **119 D2** 8 45 S 29 10 E
Chiengmai = Chiang Mai, *Thailand* **86 C2** 18 47N 98 59 E
Chiengo, *Angola* **115 E4** 13 20 S 21 55 E
Chienti →, *Italy* **45 E10** 43 18N 13 45 E
Chieri, *Italy* **44 C4** 45 1N 7 49 E
Chiers →, *France* **27 C11** 49 39N 4 59 E
Chiesa in Valmalenco, *Italy* **44 B6** 46 16N 9 51 E
Chiese →, *Italy* **44 C7** 45 8N 10 25 E
Chieti, *Italy* **45 F11** 42 21N 14 10 E
Chifeng, *China* **75 C10** 42 18N 118 58 E
Chigasaki, *Japan* **73 B11** 35 19N 139 24 E
Chigirin, *Ukraine* **59 H7** 49 4N 32 38 E
Chignecto B., *Canada* **141 C7** 45 30N 64 40W
Chignik, *U.S.A.* **144 H8** 56 18N 158 24W
Chigorodó, *Colombia* **168 B2** 7 41N 76 42W
Chiguana, *Bolivia* **174 A2** 21 0 S 67 58W
Chigwell, *U.K.* **21 F8** 51 37N 0 5 E
Chiha-ri, *N. Korea* **75 E14** 38 40N 126 30 E
Chihli, G. of = Bo Hai, *China* **75 E10** 39 0N 119 0 E
Chihuahua, *Mexico* **162 B3** 28 40N 106 3W
Chihuahua □, *Mexico* **162 B3** 28 40N 106 3W
Chiili = Shīeli, *Kazakstan* **66 E7** 44 20N 66 15 E
Chik Bollapur, *India* **95 H3** 13 25N 77 45 E
Chikalda, *India* **94 D3** 21 24N 77 19 E
Chikhli, *Ahmadabad, India* **94 D1** 20 45N 73 4 E
Chikhli, *Maharashtra, India* **94 D3** 20 20N 76 18 E
Chikmagalur, *India* **95 H2** 13 15N 75 45 E
Chiknayakanhalli, *India* **95 H3** 13 26N 76 37 E
Chikodi, *India* **95 F2** 16 26N 74 38 E
Chikugo, *Japan* **72 D2** 33 14N 130 28 E
Chikuma-Gawa →, *Japan* **73 A10** 36 59N 138 35 E
Chikushino, *Japan* **72 D2** 33 30N 130 30 E
Chikwawa, *Malawi* **119 F3** 16 2 S 34 50 E
Chila, *Angola* **115 E2** 12 3 S 14 29 E
Chilac, *Mexico* **163 D5** 18 20N 97 24W
Chilam Chavki, *Pakistan* **93 B6** 35 5N 75 5 E
Chilanga, *Zambia* **119 F2** 15 33 S 28 16 E
Chilapa, *Mexico* **163 D5** 17 40N 99 11W
Chilas, *Pakistan* **93 B6** 35 25N 74 5 E
Chilaw, *Sri Lanka* **95 L4** 7 30N 79 50 E
Chilcotin →, *Canada* **142 C4** 51 44N 122 23W
Childers, *Australia* **127 D5** 25 15 S 152 17 E
Childersburg, *U.S.A.* **152 B3** 33 16N 86 21W
Childress, *U.S.A.* **155 H4** 34 25N 100 13W
Chile ■, *S. Amer.* **176 B2** 35 0 S 72 0W
Chile Chico, *Chile* **176 C2** 46 33 S 71 44W
Chile Rise, *Pac. Oc.* **135 L18** 38 0 S 92 0W
Chilecito, *Argentina* **174 B2** 29 10 S 67 30W
Chilesso, *Angola* **115 E3** 11 35 S 16 34 E
Chilete, *Peru* **172 B2** 7 10 S 78 50W
Chilhowee, *U.S.A.* **156 F3** 38 36N 93 51W
Chilia, Braţul →, *Romania* **53 E14** 45 14N 29 42 E
Chilik = Shelek, *Kazakstan* **65 B9** 43 33N 78 17 E
Chililabombwe, *Zambia* **119 E2** 12 18 S 27 43 E
Chilin = Jilin, *China* **75 C14** 43 44N 126 30 E
Chilka L., *India* **94 E7** 19 40N 85 25 E
Chilko →, *Canada* **142 C4** 52 0N 123 40W
Chilko L., *Canada* **142 C4** 51 20N 124 10W
Chillagoe, *Australia* **126 B3** 17 7 S 144 33 E
Chillán, *Chile* **174 D1** 36 40 S 72 10W
Chillicothe, *Ill., U.S.A.* **156 D7** 40 55N 89 29W
Chillicothe, *Mo., U.S.A.* **156 E3** 39 48N 93 33W
Chillicothe, *Ohio, U.S.A.* **148 F4** 39 20N 82 59W
Chilliwack, *Canada* **142 D4** 49 10N 121 54W
Chilo, *India* **92 F5** 27 25N 73 32 E
Chiloane, I., *Mozam.* **117 C5** 20 40 S 34 55 E
Chiloé, I. de, *Chile* **176 B2** 42 30 S 73 50W
Chilonda, *Angola* **115 E3** 11 19 S 16 12 E
Chilongo, *Angola* **115 E3** 13 55 S 16 35 E
Chilpancingo, *Mexico* **163 D5** 17 30N 99 30W
Chiltern, *Australia* **129 D7** 36 10 S 146 36 E
Chiltern Hills, *U.K.* **21 F7** 51 40N 0 53W
Chilton, *U.S.A.* **148 C1** 44 2N 88 10W
Chiluage, *Angola* **115 D4** 9 30 S 21 50 E
Chilubi, *Zambia* **119 E2** 11 5 S 29 58 E
Chilubula, *Zambia* **119 E3** 10 14 S 30 51 E
Chilumba, *Malawi* **119 E3** 10 28 S 34 12 E
Chilung, *Taiwan* **77 E13** 25 3N 121 45 E
Chilwa, L., *Malawi* **119 F4** 15 15 S 35 40 E
Chimakela, *Angola* **115 F3** 15 24 S 16 58 E
Chimakudi, *India* **90 C4** 25 47N 93 48 E
Chimaltitán, *Mexico* **162 C4** 21 46N 103 50W
Chimán, *Panama* **164 E4** 8 45N 78 40W
Chimanimani, *Zimbabwe* **117 B5** 19 48 S 32 52 E
Chimanimani Nat. Park, *Zimbabwe* **119 F3** 19 48 S 33 0 E
Chimay, *Belgium* **24 D4** 50 3N 4 20 E
Chimayo, *U.S.A.* **159 H11** 36 0N 105 56W
Chimbay, *Uzbekistan* **66 E6** 42 57N 59 47 E
Chimborazo, *Ecuador* **168 D2** 1 29 S 78 55W
Chimborazo □, *Ecuador* **168 D2** 1 0 S 78 40W
Chimbote, *Peru* **172 B2** 9 0 S 78 35W
Chimbu □, *Papua N. G.* **132 D3** 6 15 S 144 50 E
Chimichagua, *Colombia* **168 B3** 9 15N 73 49W
Chimion, *Uzbekistan* **65 C5** 40 15N 71 32 E
Chimkent = Shymkent, *Kazakstan* **66 E7** 42 18N 69 36 E
Chimoio, *Mozam.* **119 F3** 19 4 S 33 30 E
Chimpembe, *Zambia* **119 D2** 9 31 S 29 33 E
Chimur, *India* **94 D4** 20 30N 79 23 E
Chin □, *Burma* **90 D4** 22 0N 93 0 E
Chin Hills, *Burma* **90 D4** 22 30N 93 30 E
Chin Ling Shan = Qinling Shandi, *China* **74 H5** 33 50N 108 10 E
China, *Mexico* **163 B5** 25 40N 99 20W
China ■, *Asia* **69 C6** 30 0N 110 0 E
China Lake, *U.S.A.* **161 K9** 35 44N 117 37W
Chinacota, *Colombia* **168 B3** 7 37N 72 36W
Chinan = Jinan, *China* **74 F9** 36 38N 117 1 E
Chinandega, *Nic.* **164 D2** 12 35N 87 12W
Chinati Peak, *U.S.A.* **155 L2** 29 57N 104 29W
Chinaz, *Uzbekistan* **65 C4** 40 56N 68 46 E
Chincha Alta, *Peru* **172 C2** 13 25 S 76 7W
Chinchaga →, *Canada* **142 B5** 58 53N 118 20W
Chincheros, *Peru* **172 C3** 13 30 S 73 44W
Chinchilla, *Australia* **127 D5** 26 45 S 150 38 E
Chinchilla de Monte Aragón, *Spain* **41 G3** 38 53N 1 40W
Chincholi, *India* **94 E3** 17 28N 77 26 E
Chinchorro, Banco, *Mexico* **163 D7** 18 35N 87 20W
Chinchou = Jinzhou, *China* **75 D11** 41 5N 121 3 E
Chinchoua, *Gabon* **114 B1** 0 1N 9 48 E
Chincoteague, *U.S.A.* **148 G8** 37 56N 75 23W
Chinde, *Mozam.* **119 F4** 18 35 S 36 30 E
Chindo, *S. Korea* **75 G14** 34 28N 126 15 E
Chindwin →, *Burma* **90 E5** 21 26N 95 15 E
Chineni, *India* **93 C6** 33 2N 75 15 E
Chinga, *Mozam.* **119 F4** 15 13 S 38 35 E
Chingirlau, *Kazakstan* **64 F5** 51 7N 54 7 E
Chingola, *Zambia* **119 E2** 12 31 S 27 53 E
Chingole, *Malawi* **119 E3** 13 4 S 34 17 E
Chingoroi, *Angola* **115 E2** 13 37 S 14 1 E
Ch'ingtao = Qingdao, *China* **75 F11** 36 5N 120 20 E
Chinguar, *Angola* **115 E3** 12 25 S 16 45 E
Chinguetti, *Mauritania* **110 D2** 20 25N 12 24W
Chingune, *Mozam.* **117 C5** 20 33 S 34 58 E
Chinhae, *S. Korea* **75 G15** 35 9N 128 47 E
Chinhanguanine, *Mozam.* **117 D5** 25 21 S 32 30 E
Chinhoyi, *Zimbabwe* **119 F3** 17 20 S 30 8 E
Chini, *India* **92 D8** 31 32N 78 15 E
Chiniot, *Pakistan* **91 C4** 31 45N 73 0 E
Chínipas, *Mexico* **162 B3** 27 22N 108 32W
Chinji, *Pakistan* **92 C5** 32 42N 72 22 E
Chinju, *S. Korea* **75 G15** 35 12N 128 2 E
Chinkai, *Afghan.* **91 C2** 31 57N 67 26 E
Chinkapook, *Australia* **128 C5** 35 11 S 142 57 E
Chinko →, *C.A.R.* **114 B4** 4 50N 23 53 E
Chinle, *U.S.A.* **159 H9** 36 9N 109 33W
Chinmen, *Taiwan* **77 E13** 24 26N 118 19 E
Chinmen Tao, *Taiwan* **77 E12** 24 27N 118 23 E
Chinnamanur, *India* **95 K3** 9 50N 77 24 E
Chinnampo = Namp'o, *N. Korea* **75 E13** 38 52N 125 10 E
Chinnur, *India* **94 E4** 18 57N 79 49 E
Chino, *Japan* **73 B10** 35 59N 138 9 E
Chino, *U.S.A.* **161 L9** 34 1N 117 41W
Chino Valley, *U.S.A.* **159 J7** 34 45N 112 27W
Chinon, *France* **26 E7** 47 10N 0 15 E
Chinook, *U.S.A.* **158 B9** 48 35N 109 14W
Chinoya, *Zambia* **115 E4** 13 55 S 23 16 E
Chinsali, *Zambia* **119 E3** 10 30 S 32 2 E
Chintalapudi, *India* **94 F5** 17 4N 80 59 E
Chintamani, *India* **95 H4** 13 26N 78 3 E
Chióggia, *Italy* **45 C9** 45 13N 12 17 E
Chíos = Khíos, *Greece* **49 C8** 38 27N 26 9 E
Chipata, *Zambia* **119 E3** 13 38 S 32 28 E
Chiperceni, *Moldova* **53 C13** 47 31N 28 50 E
Chipindo, *Angola* **115 E3** 13 49 S 15 48 E
Chipinge, *Zimbabwe* **119 G3** 20 13 S 32 28 E
Chipinge Safari Area, *Zimbabwe* **119 G3** 20 14 S 33 0 E
Chipiona, *Spain* **43 J4** 36 44N 6 26W
Chipley, *U.S.A.* **152 E4** 30 47N 85 32W
Chiplun, *India* **94 F1** 17 31N 73 34 E
Chipman, *Canada* **141 C6** 46 6N 65 53W
Chipoka, *Malawi* **119 E3** 13 57 S 34 28 E
Chippenham, *U.K.* **21 F5** 51 27N 2 6W
Chippewa →, *U.S.A.* **154 C8** 44 25N 92 5W
Chippewa Falls, *U.S.A.* **154 C9** 44 56N 91 24W
Chipping Norton, *U.K.* **21 F6** 51 56N 1 32W
Chiprovtsi, *Bulgaria* **50 C6** 43 24N 22 52 E
Chiputneticook Lakes, *U.S.A.* **149 C11** 45 35N 67 35W
Chiquelequele, *Angola* **115 F3** 16 44 S 19 5 E
Chiquián, *Peru* **172 C2** 10 10 S 77 0W
Chiquimula, *Guatemala* **164 D2** 14 51N 89 37W
Chiquinquira, *Colombia* **168 B3** 5 37N 73 50W
Chiquitos, Llanos de, *Bolivia* **173 D5** 18 0 S 61 30W
Chir →, *Russia* **61 F6** 48 30N 43 0 E
Chira →, *Peru* **168 D1** 4 54 S 81 8W
Chirala, *India* **95 G5** 15 50N 80 26 E
Chiramba, *Mozam.* **119 F3** 16 55 S 34 39 E
Chirawa, *India* **92 E6** 28 14N 75 42 E
Chirayinkil, *India* **95 K3** 8 41N 76 49 E
Chirchiq, *Uzbekistan* **66 E7** 41 29N 69 35 E
Chiredzi, *Zimbabwe* **117 C5** 21 0 S 31 38 E
Chirfa, *Niger* **109 D2** 20 55N 12 22 E
Chirgua →, *Venezuela* **168 B4** 8 54N 67 58W
Chiricahua Peak, *U.S.A.* **159 L9** 31 51N 109 18W
Chiriquí, G. de, *Panama* **164 E3** 8 0N 82 10W
Chiriquí, L. de, *Panama* **164 E3** 9 10N 82 0W
Chirisa Safari Area, *Zimbabwe* **119 F2** 17 53 S 28 15 E
Chirivira Falls, *Zimbabwe* **119 G3** 21 10 S 32 12 E
Chirnogi, *Romania* **53 F11** 44 7N 26 32 E
Chirpan, *Bulgaria* **51 D9** 42 10N 25 19 E
Chirripó Grande, Cerro, *Costa Rica* **164 E3** 9 29N 83 29W
Chirundu, *Zimbabwe* **117 B4** 16 3 S 28 50 E
Chisamba, *Zambia* **119 E2** 14 55 S 28 20 E
Chisasibi, *Canada* **140 B4** 53 50N 79 0W
Ch'ishan, *Taiwan* **77 F13** 22 44N 120 31 E
Chishmy, *Russia* **64 D5** 54 35N 55 23 E
Chisholm, *Canada* **142 C6** 54 55N 114 10W
Chisholm, *U.S.A.* **154 B8** 47 29N 92 53W
Chishtian Mandi, *Pakistan* **92 E5** 29 50N 72 55 E
Chishui, *China* **76 C5** 28 30N 105 42 E
Chishui He →, *China* **76 C5** 28 49N 105 50 E
Chisimaio, *Somali Rep.* **120 E2** 0 22 S 42 32 E
Chisimba Falls, *Zambia* **119 E3** 10 12 S 30 56 E
Chişinău, *Moldova* **53 C13** 47 2N 28 50 E
Chişineu Criş, *Romania* **52 D6** 46 32N 21 37 E
Chisone →, *Italy* **44 D4** 44 49N 7 25 E
Chisos Mts., *U.S.A.* **155 L3** 29 5N 103 15W
Chissengue, *Angola* **115 D4** 9 13 S 20 34 E
Chissilo, *Angola* **115 E3** 13 48 S 16 31 E
Chistochina, *U.S.A.* **144 E11** 62 34N 144 40W
Chistopol, *Russia* **60 C10** 55 25N 50 38 E
Chita, *Colombia* **168 B3** 6 11N 72 28W
Chita, *Russia* **67 D12** 52 0N 113 35 E
Chitado, *Angola* **115 F2** 17 10 S 14 8 E
Chitanda →, *Angola* **115 F3** 16 1 S 15 12 E
Chitapur, *India* **94 F3** 17 10N 77 5 E
Chitembo, *Angola* **115 E3** 13 30 S 16 50 E
Chitina, *U.S.A.* **144 F11** 61 31N 144 26W
Chitipa, *Malawi* **119 D3** 9 41 S 33 19 E
Chitose, *Japan* **70 C10** 42 49N 141 39 E
Chitradurga, *India* **95 G3** 14 14N 76 24 E
Chitrakot, *India* **94 E5** 19 10N 81 40 E
Chitral, *Pakistan* **91 B3** 35 50N 71 56 E
Chitravati →, *India* **95 G4** 14 45N 78 15 E
Chitré, *Panama* **164 E3** 7 59N 80 27W
Chittagong, *Bangla.* **90 D3** 22 19N 91 48 E
Chittagong □, *Bangla.* **90 C3** 24 5N 91 0 E
Chittaurgarh, *India* **92 G6** 24 52N 74 38 E
Chittoor, *India* **95 H4** 13 15N 79 5 E
Chittur, *India* **95 J3** 10 40N 76 45 E
Chitungwiza, *Zimbabwe* **119 F3** 18 0 S 31 6 E
Chiumbe →, *Dem. Rep. of the Congo* **115 D4** 6 59 S 21 12 E
Chiumbo, *Angola* **115 E3** 12 29 S 16 8 E
Chiume, *Angola* **115 F4** 15 3 S 21 14 E
Chiuro, *Italy* **33 D9** 46 10N 9 59 E
Chiusi, *Italy* **45 E8** 43 1N 11 57 E
Chiva, *Spain* **41 F4** 39 27N 0 41W
Chivacoa, *Venezuela* **168 A4** 10 10N 68 54W
Chivasso, *Italy* **44 C4** 45 11N 7 53 E
Chivay, *Peru* **172 D3** 15 40 S 71 35W
Chivé, *Bolivia* **172 C4** 12 23 S 68 35W
Chivhu, *Zimbabwe* **119 F3** 19 2 S 30 52 E
Chivilcoy, *Argentina* **174 C4** 34 55 S 60 0W
Chiwanda, *Tanzania* **119 E3** 11 23 S 34 55 E
Chixi, *China* **77 G9** 22 0N 112 58 E
Chizarira, *Zimbabwe* **119 F2** 17 36 S 27 45 E
Chizarira Nat. Park, *Zimbabwe* **119 F2** 17 44 S 27 52 E
Chizela, *Zambia* **115 E4** 13 8 S 25 0 E
Chizera, *Zambia* **119 E2** 13 10 S 25 0 E
Chizu, *Japan* **72 B6** 35 16N 134 14 E
Chkalov = Orenburg, *Russia* **64 F5** 51 45N 55 6 E
Chkolovsk, *Russia* **60 B6** 56 50N 43 10 E
Chloride, *U.S.A.* **161 K12** 35 25N 114 12W
Chlumec nad Cidlinou, *Czech Rep.* **34 A8** 50 9N 15 29 E
Chmielnik, *Poland* **55 H7** 50 37N 20 43 E
Cho Bo, *Vietnam* **76 G5** 20 46N 105 10 E
Cho-do, *N. Korea* **75 E13** 38 30N 124 40 E
Cho Phuoc Hai, *Vietnam* **87 G6** 10 26N 107 18 E
Choa Chu Kang, *Singapore* **87 d** 1 22N 103 41 E
Choba, *Kenya* **118 B4** 2 30N 38 5 E
Chobe Nat. Park, *Botswana* **116 B4** 18 37 S 24 23 E
Choch'iwŏn, *S. Korea* **75 F14** 36 37N 127 18 E
Chocianów, *Poland* **55 G2** 51 27N 15 55 E
Chociwel, *Poland* **54 E2** 53 29N 15 21 E
Chocó □, *Colombia* **168 B2** 6 0N 77 0W
Chocolate Mts., *U.S.A.* **161 M11** 33 15N 115 15W
Chocontá, *Colombia* **168 B3** 5 9N 73 41W
Choctawhatchee →, *U.S.A.* **152 E3** 30 25N 86 8W
Chodavaram, *Andhra Pradesh, India* **94 F6** 17 50N 82 57 E
Chodavaram, *Andhra Pradesh, India* **94 F5** 17 27N 81 46 E
Chodecz, *Poland* **55 F6** 52 24N 19 2 E
Chodov, *Czech Rep.* **34 A5** 50 15N 12 45 E
Chodziez, *Poland* **55 F3** 52 58N 16 58 E
Choele Choel, *Argentina* **176 A3** 39 11 S 65 40W
Chōfu, *Japan* **73 B11** 35 39N 139 33 E
Choiseul, *St. Lucia* **165 f** 13 47N 61 3W
Choiseul, *Solomon Is.* **133 L9** 7 0 S 156 40 E
Choix, *Mexico* **162 B3** 26 40N 108 23W
Chojna, *Poland* **55 F1** 52 58N 14 25 E
Chojnice, *Poland* **54 E4** 53 42N 17 32 E
Chojnów, *Poland* **55 G2** 51 18N 15 58 E
Chok-Tal, *Kyrgyzstan* **65 B8** 42 35N 76 45 E
Chōkai-San, *Japan* **70 E10** 39 6N 140 3 E
Choke, *Ethiopia* **107 E4** 11 18N 37 15 E
Choke Canyon L., *U.S.A.* **155 L5** 28 30N 98 20W
Chokurdakh, *Russia* **67 B15** 70 38N 147 55 E
Cholame, *U.S.A.* **160 K6** 35 44N 120 18W
Cholet, *France* **26 E6** 47 4N 0 52W
Cholguan, *Chile* **174 D1** 37 10 S 72 3W
Cholpon-Ata, *Kyrgyzstan* **65 B8** 42 40N 77 6 E
Choluteca, *Honduras* **164 D2** 13 20N 87 14W
Choluteca →, *Honduras* **164 D2** 13 0N 87 20W
Chom Bung, *Thailand* **86 F2** 13 37N 99 36 E
Chom Thong, *Thailand* **86 C2** 18 25N 98 41 E
Choma, *Zambia* **119 F2** 16 48 S 26 59 E
Chomen Swamp, *Ethiopia* **107 F4** 9 20N 37 10 E
Chomun, *India* **92 F6** 27 15N 75 40 E
Chomutov, *Czech Rep.* **34 A6** 50 28N 13 23 E
Chon Buri, *Thailand* **86 F3** 13 21N 101 1 E
Chon Thanh, *Vietnam* **87 G6** 11 24N 106 36 E
Ch'onan, *S. Korea* **75 F14** 36 48N 127 9 E
Chone, *Ecuador* **168 D2** 0 40 S 80 0W
Chong Kai, *Cambodia* **86 F4** 13 57N 103 35 E
Chong Mek, *Thailand* **86 E5** 15 10N 105 27 E
Chong Phangan, *Thailand* **87 b** 9 39N 100 0 E
Chong Samui, *Thailand* **87 b** 9 21N 99 50 E
Chongde, *China* **77 B13** 30 32N 120 26 E
Chŏngdo, *S. Korea* **75 G15** 35 38N 128 42 E
Chŏngha, *S. Korea* **75 F15** 36 12N 129 21 E
Chŏngjin, *N. Korea* **75 D15** 41 47N 129 50 E
Chŏngju, *S. Korea* **75 F14** 36 39N 127 27 E
Chŏngju, *N. Korea* **75 E13** 39 40N 125 5 E
Chongli, *China* **74 D8** 40 58N 115 15 E
Chongming, *China* **77 B13** 31 38N 121 23 E
Chongming Dao, *China* **77 B13** 31 40N 121 30 E
Chongoyape, *Peru* **172 B2** 6 35 S 79 25W
Chongqing, *Chongqing, China* **76 C6** 29 35N 106 25 E
Chongqing, *Sichuan, China* **76 B4** 30 38N 103 40 E
Chongqing Shi □, *China* **76 C6** 30 0N 108 0 E
Chongren, *China* **77 D11** 27 46N 116 3 E
Chonguene, *Mozam.* **117 C5** 25 3 S 33 49 E
Chŏngŭp, *S. Korea* **75 G14** 35 35N 126 50 E
Chongyi, *China* **77 E10** 25 45N 114 29 E
Chongzuo, *China* **76 F6** 22 23N 107 20 E
Chŏnju, *S. Korea* **75 G14** 35 50N 127 4 E
Chonos, Arch. de los, *Chile* **176 C2** 45 0 S 75 0W
Chop, *Ukraine* **59 H2** 48 26N 22 12 E
Chopda, *India* **94 D2** 21 20N 75 15 E
Chopim →, *Brazil* **175 B5** 25 35 S 53 5W
Chor, *Pakistan* **92 G3** 25 31N 69 46 E
Chorbat La, *India* **93 B7** 34 42N 76 37 E
Chorley, *U.K.* **20 D5** 53 39N 2 38W
Chornobyl, *Ukraine* **59 G6** 51 20N 30 15 E
Chornomorske, *Ukraine* **59 K7** 45 31N 32 40 E
Chorolque, Cerro, *Bolivia* **174 A2** 20 59 S 66 5W
Choroszcz, *Poland* **55 E9** 53 10N 22 59 E
Chorregon, *Australia* **126 C3** 22 40 S 143 32 E
Chortkiv, *Ukraine* **59 H3** 49 2N 25 46 E
Ch'ŏrwon, *S. Korea* **75 E14** 38 15N 127 10 E
Chorzele, *Poland* **55 E7** 53 15N 20 55 E
Chorzów, *Poland* **55 H5** 50 18N 18 57 E
Chos-Malal, *Argentina* **174 D1** 37 20 S 70 15W
Ch'osan, *N. Korea* **75 D13** 40 50N 125 47 E
Chōshi, *Japan* **73 B12** 35 45N 140 51 E
Choszczno, *Poland* **55 E2** 53 7N 15 25 E
Chota, *Peru* **172 B2** 6 33 S 78 39W
Choteau, *U.S.A.* **158 C7** 47 49N 112 11W
Chotěboř, *Czech Rep.* **34 B8** 49 43N 15 40 E
Chotila, *India* **92 H4** 22 23N 71 15 E
Chotta Udepur, *India* **92 H6** 22 19N 74 1 E
Chowchilla, *U.S.A.* **160 H6** 37 7N 120 16W
Choybalsan, *Mongolia* **69 B6** 48 4N 114 30 E
Chrisman, *U.S.A.* **157 E9** 39 48N 87 41W
Christchurch, *N.Z.* **131 D7** 43 33 S 172 47 E
Christchurch, *U.K.* **21 G6** 50 44N 1 47W
Christian I., *Canada* **150 B4** 44 50N 80 12W
Christian Sd., *U.S.A.* **144 J14** 55 56N 134 40W
Christiana, *S. Africa* **116 D4** 27 52 S 25 8 E
Christiansfeld, *Denmark* **17 J3** 55 21N 9 29 E
Christianshåb = Qasigiannguit, *Greenland* **10 D5** 68 50N 51 18W
Christiansted, *U.S. Virgin Is.* **165 C7** 17 45N 64 42W
Christie B., *Canada* **143 A6** 62 32N 111 10W
Christina →, *Canada* **143 B6** 56 40N 111 3W
Christmas Cr. →, *Australia* **124 C4** 18 29 S 125 23 E
Christmas I. = Kiritimati, *Kiribati* **135 G12** 1 58N 157 27W
Christmas I., *Ind. Oc.* **121 F9** 10 30 S 105 40 E
Christopher, *U.S.A.* **156 G7** 37 59N 89 3W
Christopher L., *Australia* **125 D4** 24 49 S 127 42 E
Chrudim, *Czech Rep.* **34 B8** 49 58N 15 43 E
Chrzanów, *Poland* **55 H6** 50 10N 19 21 E
Chtimba, *Malawi* **119 E3** 10 35 S 34 13 E
Chu = Shū, *Kazakstan* **66 E8** 43 36N 73 42 E
Chu →, *Vietnam* **86 C5** 19 53N 105 45 E
Chu Lai, *Vietnam* **86 E7** 15 28N 108 45 E
Chuadanga, *Bangla.* **90 D2** 23 38N 88 51 E
Chuak, Ko, *Thailand* **87 b** 9 28N 99 41 E
Ch'uanchou = Quanzhou, *China* **77 E12** 24 55N 118 34 E
Chuankou, *China* **74 G6** 34 20N 110 59 E
Chuathbaluk, *U.S.A.* **144 F8** 61 40N 159 15W
Chubbuck, *U.S.A.* **158 E7** 42 55N 112 28W
Chūbu □, *Japan* **73 A9** 36 45N 137 30 E
Chubut □, *Argentina* **176 B3** 43 30 S 69 0W
Chubut →, *Argentina* **176 B3** 43 20 S 65 5W
Chuchi L., *Canada* **142 B4** 55 12N 124 30W
Chuda, *India* **92 H4** 22 29N 71 41 E
Chudovo, *Russia* **58 C6** 59 10N 31 41 E
Chudskoye, Ozero, *Russia* **15 G22** 58 13N 27 30 E
Chugach Mts., *U.S.A.* **144 F11** 60 45N 147 0W
Chugach Nat. Forest, *U.S.A.* **144 G9** 58 15N 152 45W
Chugiak, *U.S.A.* **144 F10** 61 24N 149 29W
Chuginadak I., *U.S.A.* **144 K5** 52 50N 169 45W
Chūgoku □, *Japan* **72 C5** 35 0N 133 0 E
Chūgoku-Sanchi, *Japan* **72 C5** 35 0N 133 0 E
Chuguyev = Chuhuyiv, *Ukraine* **59 H9** 49 55N 36 45 E
Chugwater, *U.S.A.* **154 E2** 41 46N 104 50W
Chuhuyiv, *Ukraine* **59 H9** 49 55N 36 45 E
Chukchi Sea, *Russia* **67 C19** 68 0N 175 0W
Chukotskoye Nagorye, *Russia* **67 C18** 68 0N 175 0 E
Chula, *U.S.A.* **152 D6** 31 33N 83 32W
Chula Vista, *U.S.A.* **161 N9** 32 39N 117 5W
Chulakkurgan = Sholaqqūrghan, *Kazakstan* **65 B4** 43 46N 69 9 E
Chulband →, *India* **94 D4** 20 40N 79 54 E
Chulucanas, *Peru* **172 B1** 5 8 S 80 10W
Chulumani, *Bolivia* **172 D4** 16 24 S 67 31W
Chulym →, *Russia* **66 D9** 57 43N 83 51 E
Chum Phae, *Thailand* **86 D4** 16 40N 102 6 E
Chum Saeng, *Thailand* **86 E3** 15 55N 100 15 E
Chuma, *Bolivia* **172 D4** 15 24 S 68 56W
Chumar, *India* **93 C8** 32 40N 78 35 E
Chumbicha, *Argentina* **174 B2** 29 0 S 66 10W
Chumerna, *Bulgaria* **51 D9** 42 45N 25 55 E
Chumikan, *Russia* **67 D14** 54 40N 135 10 E
Chumphon, *Thailand* **87 G2** 10 35N 99 14 E
Chumpi, *Peru* **172 D3** 15 4 S 73 46W
Chumuare, *Mozam.* **119 E3** 14 31 S 31 50 E
Chumunjin, *S. Korea* **75 F15** 37 55N 128 54 E
Chuna →, *Russia* **67 D10** 57 47N 94 37 E
Chun'an, *China* **77 C12** 29 35N 119 3 E
Ch'unch'ŏn, *S. Korea* **75 F14** 37 58N 127 44 E
Chunchura, *India* **93 H13** 22 53N 88 27 E
Chunga, *Zambia* **119 F2** 15 0 S 26 2 E
Chunggang-ŭp, *N. Korea* **75 D14** 41 48N 126 48 E
Chunghwa, *N. Korea* **75 E13** 38 52N 125 47 E
Ch'ungju, *S. Korea* **75 F14** 36 58N 127 58 E
Chungking = Chongqing, *China* **76 C6** 29 35N 106 25 E
Chungli, *Taiwan* **77 E13** 24 57N 121 13 E
Ch'ungmu, *S. Korea* **75 G15** 34 50N 128 20 E
Chungt'iaoshan = Zhongtiao Shan, *China* **74 G6** 35 0N 111 10 E
Chungyang Shanmo, *Taiwan* **77 F13** 23 10N 121 0 E
Chunian, *Pakistan* **92 D6** 30 57N 74 0 E
Chunya, *Tanzania* **119 D3** 8 30 S 33 27 E
Chunyang, *China* **75 C15** 43 38N 129 23 E
Chupara Pt., *Trin. & Tob.* **169 F9** 10 49N 61 22W
Chuquibamba, *Peru* **172 D3** 15 47 S 72 44W
Chuquibambilla, *Peru* **172 C3** 14 7 S 72 41W
Chuquicamata, *Chile* **174 A2** 22 15 S 69 0W
Chuquisaca □, *Bolivia* **173 E5** 20 30 S 63 30W
Chur, *Switz.* **33 C9** 46 52N 9 32 E
Churachandpur, *India* **90 C4** 24 20N 93 40 E
Churchill, *Australia* **129 E7** 38 19 S 146 25 E
Churchill, *Canada* **143 B10** 58 47N 94 11W
Churchill →, *Man., Canada* **143 B10** 58 47N 94 12W
Churchill →, *Nfld., Canada* **141 B7** 53 19N 60 10W
Churchill, C., *Canada* **143 B10** 58 46N 93 12W
Churchill Falls, *Canada* **141 B7** 53 36N 64 19W
Churchill L., *Canada* **143 B7** 55 55N 108 20W
Churchill Pk., *Canada* **142 B3** 58 10N 125 10W
Churdan, *U.S.A.* **156 B2** 42 9N 94 29W
Churfisten, *Switz.* **33 B8** 47 8N 9 17 E
Churki, *India* **93 H10** 23 50N 83 12 E
Churu, *India* **92 E6** 28 20N 74 50 E
Churubusco, *U.S.A.* **157 C11** 41 14N 85 19W
Churún Merú = Angel Falls, *Venezuela* **169 B5** 5 57N 62 30W
Churwalden, *Switz.* **33 C9** 46 47N 9 33 E
Chushal, *India* **93 C8** 33 40N 78 40 E
Chuska Mts., *U.S.A.* **159 H9** 36 15N 108 50W
Chusovaya →, *Russia* **64 B6** 58 12N 56 54 E
Chusovoy, *Russia* **64 B6** 58 22N 57 50 E
Chuspipata, *Bolivia* **172 D4** 16 18 S 67 48W
Chust, *Uzbekistan* **65 C5** 41 0N 71 13 E
Chute-aux-Outardes, *Canada* **141 C6** 49 7N 68 24W
Chuuronjang, *N. Korea* **75 D15** 41 35N 129 40 E
Chuvash Republic = Chuvashia □, *Russia* **60 C8** 55 30N 47 0 E
Chuvashia □, *Russia* **60 C8** 55 30N 47 0 E
Chuwārtah, *Iraq* **96 C5** 35 43N 45 34 E
Chuxiong, *China* **76 E3** 25 2N 101 28 E
Chŭy = Shū →, *Kazakstan* **65 A3** 45 0N 67 44 E
Chüy, *Kyrgyzstan* **65 B7** 42 55N 75 15 E
Chuy, *Uruguay* **175 C5** 33 41 S 53 27W
Chuzenji-Ko, *Japan* **73 A11** 36 44N 139 27 E
Chuzhou, *China* **77 A12** 32 19N 118 20 E
Ci Xian, *China* **74 F8** 36 20N 114 25 E
Ciacova, *Romania* **52 E6** 45 35N 21 10 E
Ciadâr-Lunga, *Moldova* **53 D13** 46 3N 28 51 E
Ciamis, *Indonesia* **85 D3** 7 20 S 108 21 E
Cianjur, *Indonesia* **84 D3** 6 49 S 107 8 E
Cianorte, *Brazil* **175 A5** 23 37 S 52 37W
Cibola, *U.S.A.* **161 M12** 33 17N 114 42W
Cicero, *U.S.A.* **157 C9** 41 51N 87 45W
Cícero Dantas, *Brazil* **170 D4** 10 36 S 38 23W
Cicia, *Fiji* **133 A3** 17 45 S 179 18W
Cidacos →, *Spain* **40 C3** 42 21N 1 38W
Cide, *Turkey* **100 B5** 41 53N 33 1 E
Ciechanów, *Poland* **55 F7** 52 52N 20 38 E
Ciechanowiec, *Poland* **55 F9** 52 40N 22 31 E
Ciechocinek, *Poland* **55 F5** 52 53N 18 45 E
Ciego de Avila, *Cuba* **164 B4** 21 50N 78 50W
Ciénaga, *Colombia* **168 A3** 11 1N 74 15W
Ciénaga de Oro, *Colombia* **168 B2** 8 53N 75 37W
Cienfuegos, *Cuba* **164 B3** 22 10N 80 30W
Cierp, *France* **28 F4** 42 55N 0 40 E
Cíes, Is., *Spain* **42 C2** 42 12N 8 55W
Cieszanów, *Poland* **55 H10** 50 14N 23 8 E
Cieszyn, *Poland* **55 J5** 49 45N 18 35 E
Cieza, *Spain* **41 G3** 38 17N 1 23W
Çifteler, *Turkey* **100 C4** 39 22N 31 2 E
Cifuentes, *Spain* **40 E2** 40 47N 2 37W
Cihanbeyli, *Turkey* **100 C5** 38 40N 32 55 E
Cihuatlán, *Mexico* **162 D4** 19 14N 104 35W
Cijara, Embalse de, *Spain* **43 F6** 39 18N 4 52W
Cijulang, *Indonesia* **79 G13** 7 42 S 108 27 E
Cilacap, *Indonesia* **85 D3** 7 43 S 109 0 E
Çıldır, *Turkey* **101 B10** 41 7N 43 8 E
Çıldır Gölü, *Turkey* **101 B10** 41 5N 43 15 E
Cili, *China* **77 C8** 29 30N 111 8 E
Cilibia, *Romania* **53 E12** 45 4N 27 4 E
Cilicia, *Turkey* **100 D5** 36 30N 33 40 E
Cill Chainnigh = Kilkenny, *Ireland* **23 D4** 52 39N 7 15W
Cilo Dağı, *Turkey* **101 D10** 37 28N 43 55 E
Cima, *U.S.A.* **161 K11** 35 14N 115 30W
Cimarron, *Kans., U.S.A.* **155 G4** 37 48N 100 21W
Cimarron, *N. Mex., U.S.A.* **155 G2** 36 31N 104 55W
Cimarron →, *U.S.A.* **155 G6** 36 10N 96 17W
Cimişlia, *Moldova* **53 D13** 46 34N 28 44 E
Cimone, Mte., *Italy* **44 D7** 44 12N 10 42 E
Cimpu, *Indonesia* **82 B2** 3 25 S 120 22 E
Çinar, *Turkey* **101 D9** 37 46N 40 19 E
Çınarcık, *Turkey* **51 F13** 40 38N 29 5 E
Cinca →, *Spain* **40 D5** 41 26N 0 21 E
Cincar, *Bos.-H.* **53 E3** 43 55N 17 5 E
Cincinnati, *Iowa, U.S.A.* **156 D4** 40 38N 92 56W
Cincinnati, *Ohio, U.S.A.* **157 E12** 39 6N 84 31W
Cincinnatus, *U.S.A.* **151 D9** 42 33N 75 54W

Çine, *Turkey* **49 D10** 37 37N 28 2 E
Ciney, *Belgium* **24 D5** 50 18N 5 5 E
Cíngoli, *Italy* **45 E10** 43 23N 13 10 E
Cinigiano, *Italy* **45 F8** 42 53N 11 24 E
Cinque I., *India* **95 J11** 11 16N 92 42 E
Cinto, Mte., *France* **29 F12** 42 24N 8 54 E
Cintra, G. de, *W. Sahara* **110 D1** 23 0N 16 15W
Cintruénigo, *Spain* **40 C3** 42 5N 1 49W
Ciocile, *Romania* **53 F12** 44 49N 27 14 E
Ciolăneşti din Deal, *Romania* **53 F10** 44 19N 25 5 E
Ciorani, *Romania* **53 F11** 44 45N 26 25 E
Čiovo, *Croatia* **45 E13** 43 30N 16 17 E
Cipó, *Brazil* **170 D4** 11 6 S 38 31W
Cipolletti, *Argentina* **176 A3** 38 56 S 67 59W
Circeo, Mte., *Italy* **46 A6** 41 14N 13 3 E
Çirçir, *Turkey* **100 C7** 40 5N 36 47 E
Circle, *Alaska, U.S.A.* **144 D11** 65 50N 144 4W
Circle, *Mont., U.S.A.* **154 B2** 47 25N 105 35W
Circleville, *U.S.A.* **148 F4** 39 36N 82 57W
Circular Reef, *Papua N. G.* **132 B4** 3 25 S 147 47 E
Cirebon, *Indonesia* **85 D3** 6 45 S 108 32 E
Ciremay, *Indonesia* **85 D3** 6 55 S 108 27 E
Cirencester, *U.K.* **21 F6** 51 43N 1 57W
Cireşu, *Romania* **52 F7** 44 47N 22 31 E
Cirey-sur-Vezouze, *France* **27 D13** 48 35N 6 57 E
Ciriè, *Italy* **44 C4** 45 14N 7 36 E
Cirium, *Cyprus* **39 F8** 34 40N 32 53 E
Cirò, *Italy* **47 C10** 39 23N 17 4 E
Cirò Marina, *Italy* **47 C10** 39 22N 17 8 E
Ciron →, *France* **28 D3** 44 36N 0 18W
Cisco, *U.S.A.* **155 J5** 32 23N 98 59W
Cislău, *Romania* **53 E11** 45 14N 26 20 E
Cisna, *Poland* **55 J9** 49 12N 22 20 E
Cisnădie, *Romania* **53 E9** 45 42N 24 9 E
Cisne, *U.S.A.* **157 F8** 38 31N 88 26W
Cisneros, *Colombia* **168 B2** 6 33N 75 4W
Cissna Park, *U.S.A.* **157 D9** 40 34N 87 54W
Cisterna di Latina, *Italy* **46 A5** 41 35N 12 49 E
Cisternino, *Italy* **47 B10** 40 44N 17 25 E
Cistierna, *Spain* **42 C5** 42 48N 5 7W
Citaré →, *Brazil* **169 C7** 1 11N 54 41W
Citeli-Ckaro = Tsiteli-Tsqaro, *Georgia* **61 K8** 41 33N 46 0 E
Citlaltépetl, *Mexico* **163 D5** 19 0N 97 20W
Citra, *U.S.A.* **153 F7** 29 25N 82 7W
Citron, *Fr. Guiana* **169 C7** 4 44N 53 57W
Citrus Heights, *U.S.A.* **160 G5** 38 42N 121 17W
Citrus Springs, *U.S.A.* **153 F7** 29 2N 82 27W
Citrusdal, *S. Africa* **116 E2** 32 35 S 19 0 E
Città della Pieve, *Italy* **45 F9** 42 57N 12 1 E
Città di Castello, *Italy* **45 E9** 43 27N 12 14 E
Città Sant' Angelo, *Italy* **45 F11** 42 32N 14 5 E
Cittadella, *Italy* **45 C8** 45 39N 11 47 E
Cittaducale, *Italy* **45 F9** 42 23N 12 57 E
Cittanova, *Italy* **47 D9** 38 21N 16 5 E
Ciuc, Munţii, *Romania* **53 D11** 46 25N 26 5 E
Ciucaş, Vf., *Romania* **53 E10** 45 31N 25 56 E
Ciucea, *Romania* **52 D7** 46 57N 22 49 E
Ciuciulea, *Moldova* **53 C12** 47 40N 27 29 E
Ciuciuleni, *Moldova* **53 C13** 47 2N 28 25 E
Ciudad Altamirano, *Mexico* **162 D4** 18 20N 100 40W
Ciudad Bolívar, *Venezuela* **169 B5** 8 5N 63 36W
Ciudad Camargo, *Mexico* **162 B3** 27 41N 105 10W
Ciudad de Valles, *Mexico* **163 C5** 22 0N 99 0W
Ciudad del Carmen, *Mexico* **163 D6** 18 38N 91 50W
Ciudad del Este, *Paraguay* **175 B5** 25 30 S 54 50W
Ciudad Delicias = Delicias, *Mexico* **162 B3** 28 10N 105 30W
Ciudad Guayana, *Venezuela* **169 B5** 8 0N 62 30W
Ciudad Guerrero, *Mexico* **162 B3** 28 33N 107 28W
Ciudad Guzmán, *Mexico* **162 D4** 19 40N 103 30W
Ciudad Juárez, *Mexico* **162 A3** 31 40N 106 28W
Ciudad Madero, *Mexico* **163 C5** 22 19N 97 50W
Ciudad Mante, *Mexico* **163 C5** 22 50N 99 0W
Ciudad Obregón, *Mexico* **162 B3** 27 28N 109 59W
Ciudad Ojeda, *Venezuela* **168 A3** 10 12N 71 19W
Ciudad Piar, *Venezuela* **169 B5** 7 27N 63 19W
Ciudad Real, *Spain* **43 G7** 38 59N 3 55W
Ciudad Real □, *Spain* **43 G7** 38 50N 4 0W
Ciudad Rodrigo, *Spain* **42 E4** 40 35N 6 32W
Ciudad Trujillo = Santo Domingo, *Dom. Rep.* **165 C6** 18 30N 69 59W
Ciudad Victoria, *Mexico* **163 C5** 23 41N 99 9W
Ciudadela, *Spain* **38 B4** 40 0N 3 50 E
Ciulniţa, *Romania* **53 F12** 44 26N 27 22 E
Ciumeghiu, *Romania* **52 D6** 46 44N 21 35 E
Ciuperceni, *Romania* **52 F8** 44 54N 23 4 E
Civa Burnu, *Turkey* **100 B7** 41 21N 36 38 E
Cividale del Friuli, *Italy* **45 B10** 46 6N 13 25 E
Civita Castellana, *Italy* **45 F9** 42 18N 12 24 E
Civitanova Marche, *Italy* **45 E10** 43 18N 13 44 E
Civitavécchia, *Italy* **45 F8** 42 6N 11 48 E
Civray, *France* **28 B4** 46 10N 0 17 E
Çivril, *Turkey* **49 C11** 38 20N 29 43 E
Cixerri →, *Italy* **46 C1** 39 17N 8 59 E
Cixi, *China* **77 B13** 30 17N 121 9 E
Cizre, *Turkey* **101 D10** 37 19N 42 10 E
Cizur Mayor, *Spain* **40 C3** 42 47N 1 41W
Clackmannanshire □, *U.K.* **22 E5** 56 10N 3 43W
Clacton-on-Sea, *U.K.* **21 F9** 51 47N 1 11 E
Clain →, *France* **26 F7** 46 47N 0 33 E
Claire, L., *Canada* **142 B6** 58 35N 112 5W
Clairton, *U.S.A.* **150 F5** 40 18N 79 53W
Clairvaux-les-Lacs, *France* **27 F12** 46 35N 5 45 E
Claise →, *France* **28 B5** 46 56N 0 42 E
Clallam Bay, *U.S.A.* **160 B2** 48 15N 124 16W
Clam Gulch, *U.S.A.* **144 F10** 60 15N 151 23W
Clamecy, *France* **27 E10** 47 28N 3 30 E
Clanton, *U.S.A.* **149 J2** 32 51N 86 38W
Clanwilliam, *S. Africa* **116 E2** 32 11 S 18 52 E
Clara, *Ireland* **23 C4** 53 21N 7 37W
Claraville, *U.S.A.* **161 K8** 35 24N 118 20W
Clare, *Australia* **128 B3** 33 50 S 138 37 E
Clare, *U.S.A.* **148 D3** 43 49N 84 46W
Clare □, *Ireland* **23 D3** 52 45N 9 0W
Clare →, *Ireland* **23 C2** 53 20N 9 2W
Clare I., *Ireland* **23 C1** 53 49N 10 0W
Claremont, *Calif., U.S.A.* **161 L9** 34 6N 117 43W
Claremont, *N.H., U.S.A.* **151 C12** 43 23N 72 20W
Claremont Pt., *Australia* **126 A3** 14 1 S 143 41 E
Claremore, *U.S.A.* **155 G7** 36 19N 95 36W
Claremorris, *Ireland* **23 C3** 53 45N 9 0W
Clarence, *U.S.A.* **156 E4** 39 45N 92 16W
Clarence →, *Australia* **127 D5** 29 25 S 153 22 E
Clarence →, *N.Z.* **131 C8** 42 10 S 173 56 E
Clarence, I., *Chile* **176 D2** 54 0 S 72 0W
Clarence, Port, *U.S.A.* **144 D6** 65 15N 166 40W
Clarence B., *Ascension I.* **9 g** 7 55 S 14 25W
Clarence I., *Antarctica* **7 C18** 61 10 S 54 0W
Clarence Str., *Australia* **124 B5** 12 0 S 131 0 E
Clarence Town, *Bahamas* **165 B5** 23 6N 74 59W
Clarendon, *Pa., U.S.A.* **150 E5** 41 47N 79 6W
Clarendon, *Tex., U.S.A.* **155 H4** 34 56N 100 53W
Clarenville, *Canada* **141 C9** 48 10N 54 1W
Claresholm, *Canada* **142 D6** 50 0N 113 33W
Clarie Coast, *Antarctica* **7 C9** 68 0 S 135 0 E
Clarinda, *U.S.A.* **154 E7** 40 44N 95 2W
Clarion, *Iowa, U.S.A.* **156 B3** 42 44N 93 44W
Clarion, *Pa., U.S.A.* **150 E5** 41 13N 79 23W
Clarion →, *U.S.A.* **150 E5** 41 7N 79 41W
Clark, *Mo., U.S.A.* **156 E4** 39 17N 92 21W
Clark, *S. Dak., U.S.A.* **154 C6** 44 53N 97 44W
Clark, Pt., *Canada* **150 B3** 44 4N 81 45W
Clark Fork, *U.S.A.* **158 B5** 48 9N 116 11W
Clark Fork →, *U.S.A.* **158 B5** 48 9N 116 15W
Clarkdale, *U.S.A.* **159 J7** 34 46N 112 3W
Clarke City, *Canada* **141 B6** 50 12N 66 38W
Clarke I., *Australia* **127 G4** 40 32 S 148 10 E
Clarke Ra., *Australia* **126 J6** 20 40 S 148 30 E
Clark's Fork →, *U.S.A.* **158 D9** 45 39N 108 43W
Clark's Harbour, *Canada* **141 D6** 43 25N 65 38W
Clarks Hill L., *U.S.A.* **152 B7** 33 40N 82 12W
Clarks Point, *U.S.A.* **144 G8** 58 51N 158 33W
Clarks Summit, *U.S.A.* **151 E9** 41 30N 75 42W
Clarksburg, *U.S.A.* **148 F5** 39 17N 80 30W
Clarksdale, *U.S.A.* **155 H9** 34 12N 90 35W
Clarksville, *Ark., U.S.A.* **155 H8** 35 28N 93 28W
Clarksville, *Ind., U.S.A.* **157 F11** 38 17N 85 45W
Clarksville, *Iowa, U.S.A.* **156 B4** 42 47N 92 40W
Clarksville, *Mo., U.S.A.* **156 E6** 39 22N 90 54W
Clarksville, *Tenn., U.S.A.* **149 G2** 36 32N 87 21W
Clarksville, *Tex., U.S.A.* **155 J7** 33 37N 95 3W
Claro →, *Brazil* **171 E1** 19 8 S 50 40W
Clatskanie, *U.S.A.* **160 D3** 46 6N 123 12W
Claude, *U.S.A.* **155 H4** 35 7N 101 22W
Claveria, *Cagayan, Phil.* **80 B3** 18 37N 121 4 E
Claveria, *Masbate, Phil.* **80 E4** 12 54N 123 15 E
Claveria, *Mis. Or., Phil.* **81 G5** 8 38N 124 55 E
Clavering Ø, *Greenland* **10 C8** 74 15N 21 0W
Claxton, *U.S.A.* **152 C8** 32 10N 81 55W
Clay, *U.S.A.* **160 G5** 38 17N 121 10W
Clay Center, *U.S.A.* **154 F6** 39 23N 97 8W
Clay City, *Ind., U.S.A.* **157 E9** 39 17N 87 7W
Clay City, *Ky., U.S.A.* **157 G13** 37 52N 83 55W
Claypool, *U.S.A.* **159 K8** 33 25N 110 51W
Claysburg, *U.S.A.* **150 F6** 40 17N 78 27W
Claysville, *U.S.A.* **150 F4** 40 7N 80 25W
Clayton, *Ala., U.S.A.* **152 D4** 31 53N 85 27W
Clayton, *Ind., U.S.A.* **157 E10** 39 41N 86 31W
Clayton, *N. Mex., U.S.A.* **155 G3** 36 27N 103 11W
Clayton, *N.Y., U.S.A.* **151 B8** 44 14N 76 5W
Clear, C., *Ireland* **23 E2** 51 25N 9 32W
Clear, L., *Canada* **150 A7** 45 26N 77 12W
Clear Hills, *Canada* **142 B5** 56 40N 119 30W
Clear I., *Ireland* **23 E2** 51 26N 9 30W
Clear L., *U.S.A.* **160 F4** 39 2N 122 47W
Clear Lake, *Iowa, U.S.A.* **156 A3** 43 8N 93 23W
Clear Lake, *S. Dak., U.S.A.* **154 C6** 44 45N 96 41W
Clear Lake Reservoir, *U.S.A.* **158 F3** 41 56N 121 5W
Clearfield, *Pa., U.S.A.* **150 E6** 41 2N 78 27W
Clearfield, *Utah, U.S.A.* **158 F8** 41 7N 112 2W
Clearlake, *U.S.A.* **158 G2** 38 57N 122 38W
Clearlake Highlands, *U.S.A.* **160 G4** 38 57N 122 38W
Clearwater, *Canada* **142 C4** 51 38N 120 2W
Clearwater, *U.S.A.* **149 M4** 27 58N 82 48W
Clearwater →, *Alta., Canada* **142 C6** 52 22N 114 57W
Clearwater →, *Alta., Canada* **143 B6** 56 44N 111 23W
Clearwater L., *Canada* **143 C9** 53 34N 99 49W
Clearwater Mts., *U.S.A.* **158 C6** 46 5N 115 20W
Clearwater Prov. Park, *Canada* **143 C8** 54 0N 101 0W
Clearwater River Prov. Park, *Canada* **143 B7** 56 55N 109 10W
Cleburne, *U.S.A.* **155 J6** 32 21N 97 23W
Clee Hills, *U.K.* **21 E5** 52 26N 2 35W
Cleethorpes, *U.K.* **20 D7** 53 33N 0 3W
Cleeve Cloud, *U.K.* **21 F6** 51 56N 2 0W
Clelles, *France* **29 D9** 44 50N 5 38 E
Clemson, *U.S.A.* **149 H4** 34 41N 82 50W
Cleopatra Needle, *Phil.* **81 F2** 10 7N 118 58 E
Clerke Reef, *Australia* **124 C2** 17 22 S 119 20 E
Clermont, *Australia* **126 C4** 22 49 S 147 39 E
Clermont, *France* **27 C9** 49 23N 2 24 E
Clermont, *U.S.A.* **153 G8** 28 33N 81 46W
Clermont-en-Argonne, *France* **27 C12** 49 5N 5 4 E
Clermont-Ferrand, *France* **28 C7** 45 46N 3 4 E
Clermont-l'Hérault, *France* **28 E7** 43 38N 3 26 E
Clerval, *France* **27 E13** 47 25N 6 30 E
Clervaux, *Lux.* **24 D6** 50 4N 6 2 E
Cles, *Italy* **44 B8** 46 22N 11 2 E
Cleve, *Australia* **128 B2** 33 43 S 136 30 E
Clevedon, *U.K.* **21 F5** 51 26N 2 52W
Cleveland, *Miss., U.S.A.* **155 J9** 33 45N 90 43W
Cleveland, *Ohio, U.S.A.* **150 E3** 41 30N 81 42W
Cleveland, *Okla., U.S.A.* **155 G6** 36 19N 96 28W
Cleveland, *Tenn., U.S.A.* **149 H3** 35 10N 84 53W
Cleveland, *Tex., U.S.A.* **155 K7** 30 21N 95 5W
Cleveland, C., *Australia* **126 B4** 19 11 S 147 1 E
Cleveland, Mt., *U.S.A.* **158 B7** 48 56N 113 51W
Cleveland Heights, *U.S.A.* **150 E3** 41 30N 81 34W
Clevelândia, *Brazil* **175 B5** 26 24 S 52 23W
Clevelândia do Norte, *Brazil* **169 C7** 3 49N 51 52W
Cleves, *U.S.A.* **157 E12** 39 10N 84 45W
Clew B., *Ireland* **23 C2** 53 50N 9 49W
Clewiston, *U.S.A.* **149 M5** 26 45N 80 56W
Clifden, *Ireland* **23 C1** 53 29N 10 1W
Clifden, *N.Z.* **131 G2** 46 1 S 167 42 E
Cliffdell, *U.S.A.* **160 D5** 46 56N 121 5W
Cliffy Hd., *Australia* **125 G2** 35 1 S 116 29 E
Clifton, *Australia* **127 D5** 27 59 S 151 53 E
Clifton, *Ariz., U.S.A.* **159 K9** 33 3N 109 18W
Clifton, *Colo., U.S.A.* **159 G9** 39 7N 108 25W
Clifton, *Ill., U.S.A.* **157 D9** 40 56N 87 56W
Clifton, *Tex., U.S.A.* **155 K6** 31 47N 97 35W
Clifton Beach, *Australia* **126 B4** 16 46 S 145 39 E
Clifton Pt., *Bahamas* **9 b** 25 1N 77 34W
Climax, *Canada* **143 D7** 49 10N 108 20W
Climax, *U.S.A.* **152 E5** 30 53N 84 26W
Clinch →, *U.S.A.* **149 H3** 35 53N 84 29W
Clingmans Dome, *U.S.A.* **149 H4** 35 34N 83 30W
Clint, *U.S.A.* **159 L10** 31 35N 106 14W
Clinton, *B.C., Canada* **142 C4** 51 6N 121 35W
Clinton, *Ont., Canada* **140 D3** 43 37N 81 32W
Clinton, *N.Z.* **131 G4** 46 12 S 169 23 E
Clinton, *Ark., U.S.A.* **155 H8** 35 36N 92 28W
Clinton, *Conn., U.S.A.* **151 E12** 41 17N 72 32W
Clinton, *Ill., U.S.A.* **156 D8** 40 9N 88 57W
Clinton, *Ind., U.S.A.* **157 E9** 39 40N 87 24W
Clinton, *Iowa, U.S.A.* **156 C6** 41 51N 90 12W
Clinton, *Mass., U.S.A.* **151 D13** 42 25N 71 41W
Clinton, *Mich., U.S.A.* **157 B13** 42 4N 83 58W
Clinton, *Miss., U.S.A.* **155 J9** 32 20N 90 20W
Clinton, *Mo., U.S.A.* **156 F3** 38 22N 93 46W
Clinton, *N.C., U.S.A.* **149 H6** 35 0N 78 22W
Clinton, *Okla., U.S.A.* **155 H5** 35 31N 98 58W
Clinton, *S.C., U.S.A.* **149 H5** 34 29N 81 53W
Clinton, *Tenn., U.S.A.* **149 G3** 36 6N 84 8W
Clinton, *Wash., U.S.A.* **160 C4** 47 59N 122 21W
Clinton, *Wis., U.S.A.* **157 B8** 42 34N 88 52W
Clinton C., *Australia* **126 C5** 22 30 S 150 45 E
Clinton Colden L., *Canada* **138 B9** 63 58N 107 27W
Clinton L., *U.S.A.* **157 D8** 40 15N 88 45W
Clintonville, *U.S.A.* **154 C10** 44 37N 88 46W
Clio, *U.S.A.* **152 D4** 31 43N 85 37W
Clipperton, I., *Pac. Oc.* **135 F17** 10 18N 109 13W
Clisham, *U.K.* **22 D2** 57 57N 6 49W
Clisson, *France* **26 E5** 47 5N 1 16W
Clitheroe, *U.K.* **20 D5** 53 53N 2 22W
Clive, *N.Z.* **130 F5** 39 36 S 176 58 E
Cliza, *Bolivia* **173 D4** 17 36 S 65 56W
Clo-oose, *Canada* **160 B2** 48 39N 124 49W
Cloates, Pt., *Australia* **124 D1** 22 43 S 113 40 E
Clocolan, *S. Africa* **117 D4** 28 55 S 27 34 E
Clodomira, *Argentina* **174 B3** 27 35 S 64 14W
Clogher Hd., *Ireland* **23 C5** 53 48N 6 14W
Clonakilty, *Ireland* **23 E3** 51 37N 8 53W
Clonakilty B., *Ireland* **23 E3** 51 35N 8 51W
Cloncurry, *Australia* **126 C3** 20 40 S 140 28 E
Cloncurry →, *Australia* **126 B3** 18 37 S 140 40 E
Clondalkin, *Ireland* **23 C5** 53 19N 6 25W
Clones, *Ireland* **23 B4** 54 11N 7 15W
Clonmel, *Ireland* **23 D4** 52 21N 7 42W
Cloppenburg, *Germany* **30 C4** 52 51N 8 1 E
Cloquet, *U.S.A.* **154 B8** 46 43N 92 28W
Clorinda, *Argentina* **174 B4** 25 16 S 57 45W
Cloud Bay, *Canada* **140 C2** 48 5N 89 26W
Cloud Peak, *U.S.A.* **158 D10** 44 23N 107 11W
Cloudcroft, *U.S.A.* **159 K11** 32 58N 105 45W
Cloudy B., *N.Z.* **131 B9** 41 25 S 174 10 E
Cloverdale, *Calif., U.S.A.* **160 G4** 38 48N 123 1W
Cloverdale, *Ind., U.S.A.* **157 E10** 39 31N 86 48W
Cloverport, *U.S.A.* **157 G10** 37 50N 86 38W
Clovis, *Calif., U.S.A.* **160 J7** 36 49N 119 42W
Clovis, *N. Mex., U.S.A.* **155 H3** 34 24N 103 12W
Cloyes-sur-le-Loir, *France* **26 E8** 48 0N 1 14 E
Cloyne, *Canada* **150 B7** 44 49N 77 11W
Club Terrace, *Australia* **129 D8** 37 35 S 148 58 E
Cluj □, *Romania* **53 D8** 46 45N 23 30 E
Cluj-Napoca, *Romania* **53 D8** 46 47N 23 38 E
Clunes, *Australia* **128 D5** 37 20 S 143 45 E
Cluny, *France* **27 F11** 46 26N 4 38 E
Cluses, *France* **27 F13** 46 5N 6 35 E
Clusone, *Italy* **44 C6** 45 53N 9 57 E
Clutha →, *N.Z.* **131 G4** 46 20 S 169 49 E
Clwyd →, *U.K.* **20 D4** 53 19N 3 31W
Clyattville, *U.S.A.* **152 E6** 30 42N 83 19W
Clyde, *Canada* **142 C6** 54 9N 113 39W
Clyde, *N.Z.* **131 F4** 45 12 S 169 20 E
Clyde, *N.Y., U.S.A.* **150 C8** 43 5N 76 52W
Clyde, *Ohio, U.S.A.* **157 C14** 41 18N 82 59W
Clyde →, *U.K.* **22 F4** 55 55N 4 30W
Clyde, Firth of, *U.K.* **22 F3** 55 22N 5 1W
Clyde River, *Canada* **139 A13** 70 30N 68 30W
Clydebank, *U.K.* **22 F4** 55 54N 4 23W
Clymer, *N.Y., U.S.A.* **150 D5** 42 1N 79 37W
Clymer, *Pa., U.S.A.* **150 D5** 40 40N 79 1W
Clyo, *U.S.A.* **152 C8** 32 29N 81 16W
Ćmielów, *Poland* **55 H8** 50 53N 21 31 E
Côa →, *Portugal* **42 D3** 41 5N 7 6W
Coachella, *U.S.A.* **161 M10** 33 41N 116 10W
Coachella Canal, *U.S.A.* **161 N12** 32 43N 114 57W
Coahoma, *U.S.A.* **155 J4** 32 18N 101 18W
Coahuayana →, *Mexico* **162 D4** 18 41N 103 45W
Coahuila □, *Mexico* **162 B4** 27 0N 103 0W
Coal →, *Canada* **142 B3** 59 39N 126 57W
Coal City, *U.S.A.* **157 C8** 41 17N 88 17W
Coal I., *N.Z.* **131 G1** 46 8 S 166 40 E
Coalane, *Mozam.* **119 F4** 17 48 S 37 2 E
Coalcomán, *Mexico* **162 D4** 18 40N 103 10W
Coaldale, *Canada* **142 D6** 49 45N 112 35W
Coalgate, *U.S.A.* **155 H6** 34 32N 96 13W
Coalinga, *U.S.A.* **160 J6** 36 9N 120 21W
Coalisland, *U.K.* **23 B5** 54 33N 6 42W
Coalville, *U.K.* **20 E6** 52 44N 1 23W
Coalville, *U.S.A.* **158 F8** 40 55N 111 24W
Coamo, *Puerto Rico* **165 d** 18 5N 66 22W
Coaraci, *Brazil* **171 D4** 14 38 S 39 32W
Coari, *Brazil* **169 D5** 4 8 S 63 7W
Coari →, *Brazil* **169 D5** 4 30 S 63 33W
Coari, L. de, *Brazil* **169 D5** 4 15 S 63 22W
Coast □, *Kenya* **118 C4** 2 40 S 39 45 E
Coast Mts., *Canada* **142 C3** 55 0N 129 20W
Coast Ranges, *U.S.A.* **160 G4** 39 0N 123 0W
Coatbridge, *U.K.* **22 F4** 55 52N 4 6W
Coatepec, *Mexico* **163 D5** 19 27N 96 58W
Coatepeque, *Guatemala* **164 D1** 14 46N 91 55W
Coatesville, *U.S.A.* **148 F8** 39 59N 75 50W
Coaticook, *Canada* **141 C5** 45 10N 71 46W
Coats I., *Canada* **139 B11** 62 30N 83 0W
Coats Land, *Antarctica* **7 D1** 77 0 S 25 0W
Coatzacoalcos, *Mexico* **163 D6** 18 7N 94 25W
Cobadin, *Romania* **53 F13** 44 5N 28 13 E
Cobalt, *Canada* **140 C4** 47 25N 79 42W
Cobán, *Guatemala* **164 C1** 15 30N 90 21W
Çobanlar, *Turkey* **49 C12** 38 41N 30 47 E
Cobar, *Australia* **129 A6** 31 27 S 145 48 E
Cobargo, *Australia* **129 D8** 36 20 S 149 55 E
Cobbannah, *Australia* **129 D7** 37 37 S 147 13 E
Cobberas, Mt., *Australia* **129 D8** 36 53 S 148 12 E
Cobden, *Australia* **128 E5** 38 20 S 143 3 E
Cóbh, *Ireland* **23 E3** 51 51N 8 17W
Cobija, *Bolivia* **172 C4** 11 0 S 68 50W
Cobleskill, *U.S.A.* **151 D10** 42 41N 74 29W
Coboconk, *Canada* **150 B6** 44 39N 78 48W
Cobourg, *Canada* **140 D4** 43 58N 78 10W
Cobourg Marine Park, *Australia* **124 B5** 11 26 S 131 58 E
Cobourg Pen., *Australia* **124 B5** 11 20 S 132 15 E
Cobram, *Australia* **129 C6** 35 54 S 145 40 E
Cóbué, *Mozam.* **119 E3** 12 0 S 34 58 E
Coburg, *Germany* **31 E6** 50 15N 10 58 E
Coca, *Spain* **42 D6** 41 13N 4 32W
Coca →, *Ecuador* **168 D2** 0 29 S 76 58W
Cocachacra, *Peru* **172 D3** 17 5 S 71 45W
Cocal, *Brazil* **170 B3** 3 28 S 41 34W
Cocanada = Kakinada, *India* **94 F6** 16 57N 82 11 E
Cocentaina, *Spain* **41 G4** 38 45N 0 27W
Cochabamba, *Bolivia* **173 D4** 17 26 S 66 10W
Coche, I., *Venezuela* **169 A5** 10 47N 63 56W
Cochem, *Germany* **31 E3** 50 9N 7 9 E
Cochemane, *Mozam.* **119 F3** 17 0 S 32 54 E
Cochin, *India* **95 K3** 9 58N 76 20 E
Cochin China = Nam-Phan, *Vietnam* **87 G6** 10 30N 106 0 E
Cochran, *U.S.A.* **152 C6** 32 23N 83 21W
Cochrane, *Alta., Canada* **142 C6** 51 11N 114 30W
Cochrane, *Ont., Canada* **140 C3** 49 0N 81 0W
Cochrane, *Chile* **176 C2** 47 15 S 72 33W
Cochrane →, *Canada* **143 B8** 59 0N 103 40W
Cochrane, L., *Chile* **176 C2** 47 10 S 72 0W
Cochranton, *U.S.A.* **150 E4** 41 31N 80 3W
Cockburn, *Australia* **128 B4** 32 5 S 141 0 E
Cockburn, Canal, *Chile* **176 D2** 54 30 S 72 0W
Cockburn I., *Canada* **140 C3** 45 55N 83 22W
Cockburn Ra., *Australia* **124 C4** 15 46 S 128 0 E
Cockermouth, *U.K.* **20 C4** 54 40N 3 22W
Cocklebiddy, *Australia* **125 F4** 32 0 S 126 3 E
Cockpit Country, The, *Jamaica* **164 a** 18 15N 77 45W
Côco →, *Brazil* **170 C2** 9 27 S 50 2W
Coco →, *Cent. Amer.* **164 D3** 15 0N 83 8W
Coco, I. del, *Pac. Oc.* **135 G19** 5 25N 87 55W
Coco, Pta., *Colombia* **168 C2** 2 58N 77 43W
Coco Channel, *Asia* **95 H11** 13 45N 93 10 E
Cocoa, *U.S.A.* **149 L5** 28 21N 80 44W
Cocoa Beach, *U.S.A.* **153 G9** 28 19N 80 37W
Cocobeach, *Gabon* **114 B1** 0 59N 9 34 E
Cocoparra Nat. Park, *Australia* **129 C7** 34 10 S 146 12 E
Cocora, *Romania* **53 F12** 44 45N 27 3 E
Côcos, *Brazil* **171 D3** 14 10 S 44 33W
Côcos →, *Brazil* **171 D3** 12 44 S 44 48W
Cocos B., *Trin. & Tob.* **169 F10** 10 25N 61 2W
Cocos I., *Guam* **133 R15** 13 14N 144 39 E
Cocos Is., *Ind. Oc.* **121 F8** 12 10 S 96 55 E
Cod, C., *U.S.A.* **148 D10** 42 5N 70 10W
Codajás, *Brazil* **169 D5** 3 55 S 62 0W
Codera, C., *Venezuela* **168 A4** 10 35N 66 4W
Codfish I., *N.Z.* **131 G2** 46 47 S 167 38 E
Codigoro, *Italy* **45 D9** 44 49N 12 8 E
Codlea, *Romania* **53 E10** 45 42N 25 27 E
Codó, *Brazil* **170 B3** 4 30 S 43 55W
Codogno, *Italy* **44 C6** 45 9N 9 42 E
Codpa, *Chile* **172 D4** 18 50 S 69 44W
Codróipo, *Italy* **45 C10** 45 58N 13 0 E
Codru, Munţii, *Romania* **52 D7** 46 30N 22 15 E
Cody, *U.S.A.* **158 D9** 44 32N 109 3W
Coe Hill, *Canada* **150 B7** 44 52N 77 50W
Coelemu, *Chile* **174 D1** 36 30 S 72 48W
Coelho Neto, *Brazil* **170 B3** 4 15 S 43 0W
Coen, *Australia* **126 A3** 13 52 S 143 12 E
Coeroeni →, *Surinam* **169 C6** 3 21N 57 31W
Coesfeld, *Germany* **30 D3** 51 56N 7 10 E
Coetivy Is., *Seychelles* **121 E4** 7 8 S 56 16 E
Cœur d'Alene, *U.S.A.* **158 C5** 47 45N 116 51W
Cœur d'Alene L., *U.S.A.* **158 C5** 47 32N 116 48W
Coevorden, *Neths.* **24 B6** 52 40N 6 44 E
Cofete, *Canary Is.* **9 e2** 28 6N 14 23W
Coffeyville, *U.S.A.* **155 G7** 37 2N 95 37W
Coffin B., *Australia* **127 E2** 34 38 S 135 28 E
Coffin Bay, *Australia* **127 E2** 34 37 S 135 29 E
Coffin Bay Nat. Park, *Australia* **127 E2** 34 34 S 135 19 E
Coffin Bay Peninsula, *Australia* **127 E2** 34 32 S 135 15 E
Coffs Harbour, *Australia* **129 A10** 30 16 S 153 5 E
Cofrentes, *Spain* **41 F3** 39 13N 1 5W
Cogalnic →, *Moldova* **53 E14** 45 49N 29 40 E
Cogealac, *Romania* **53 F13** 44 36N 28 36 E
Coghinas →, *Italy* **46 B1** 40 55N 8 48 E
Coghinas, L. del, *Italy* **46 B2** 40 46N 9 3 E
Cognac, *France* **28 C3** 45 41N 0 20W
Cogne, *Italy* **44 C4** 45 37N 7 21 E
Cogolin, *France* **29 E10** 43 15N 6 32 E
Cogolludo, *Spain* **40 E1** 40 59N 3 10W
Cohocton, *U.S.A.* **150 D7** 42 30N 77 30W
Cohocton →, *U.S.A.* **150 D7** 42 9N 77 6W
Cohoes, *U.S.A.* **151 D11** 42 46N 73 42W
Cohuna, *Australia* **128 C6** 35 45 S 144 15 E
Coiba, I., *Panama* **164 E3** 7 30N 81 40W
Coig →, *Argentina* **176 D3** 51 0 S 69 10W
Coigeach, Rubha, *U.K.* **22 C3** 58 6N 5 26W
Coihaique, *Chile* **176 C2** 45 30 S 71 45W
Coimbatore, *India* **95 J3** 11 2N 76 59 E
Coimbra, *Brazil* **173 D6** 19 55 S 57 48W
Coimbra, *Portugal* **42 E2** 40 15N 8 27W
Coimbra □, *Portugal* **42 E2** 40 12N 8 25W
Coín, *Spain* **43 J6** 36 40N 4 48W
Coipasa, L. de, *Bolivia* **172 D4** 19 12 S 68 7W
Coipasa, Salar de, *Bolivia* **172 D4** 19 26 S 68 9W
Cojata, *Peru* **172 D4** 15 2 S 69 25W
Cojedes □, *Venezuela* **168 B4** 9 20N 68 20W
Cojedes →, *Venezuela* **168 B4** 8 34N 68 5W
Cojimies, *Ecuador* **168 C1** 0 20N 80 0W
Cojocna, *Romania* **53 D8** 46 45N 23 50 E
Cojutepequé, *El Salv.* **164 D2** 13 41N 88 54W
Čoka, *Serbia, Yug.* **52 E5** 45 57N 20 12 E
Cokeville, *U.S.A.* **158 E8** 42 5N 110 57W
Colaba Pt., *India* **94 E1** 18 54N 72 47 E
Colac, *Australia* **128 E5** 38 21 S 143 35 E
Colachel = Kolachel, *India* **95 K3** 8 10N 77 15 E
Colatina, *Brazil* **171 E3** 19 32 S 40 37W
Colbeck, C., *Antarctica* **7 D13** 77 6 S 157 48W
Colbert, *U.S.A.* **152 A6** 34 2N 83 13W
Colborne, *Canada* **150 C7** 44 0N 77 53W
Colby, *U.S.A.* **154 F4** 39 24N 101 3W
Colchester, *U.K.* **21 F8** 51 54N 0 55 E
Cold Bay, *U.S.A.* **144 J7** 55 12N 162 42W
Cold L., *Canada* **143 C7** 54 33N 110 5W
Coldstream, *Canada* **142 C5** 50 13N 119 11W
Coldstream, *U.K.* **22 F6** 55 39N 2 15W
Coldwater, *Canada* **150 B5** 44 42N 79 40W
Coldwater, *Kans., U.S.A.* **155 G5** 37 16N 99 20W
Coldwater, *Mich., U.S.A.* **157 C11** 41 57N 85 0W
Coldwater, *Ohio, U.S.A.* **157 D12** 40 29N 84 38W
Coldwater, L., *U.S.A.* **157 C12** 41 48N 84 59W
Cole Camp, *U.S.A.* **156 F3** 38 28N 93 12W
Coleambally, *Australia* **129 C6** 34 49 S 145 52 E
Colebrook, *U.S.A.* **151 B13** 44 54N 71 30W
Coleman, *Fla., U.S.A.* **153 G7** 28 48N 82 4W
Coleman, *Tex., U.S.A.* **155 K5** 31 50N 99 26W
Coleman →, *Australia* **126 B3** 15 6 S 141 38 E
Colenso, *S. Africa* **117 D4** 28 44 S 29 50 E
Coleraine, *Australia* **128 D4** 37 36 S 141 40 E
Coleraine, *U.K.* **23 A5** 55 8N 6 41W
Coleridge, L., *N.Z.* **131 D6** 43 17 S 171 30 E
Coleroon →, *India* **95 J4** 11 25N 79 50 E
Colesberg, *S. Africa* **116 E4** 30 45 S 25 5 E
Coleville, *U.S.A.* **160 G7** 38 34N 119 30W
Colfax, *Calif., U.S.A.* **160 F6** 39 6N 120 57W
Colfax, *Ill., U.S.A.* **157 D8** 40 34N 88 37W
Colfax, *Ind., U.S.A.* **157 D10** 40 12N 86 40W
Colfax, *Iowa, U.S.A.* **156 C3** 41 41N 93 14W
Colfax, *La., U.S.A.* **155 K8** 31 31N 92 42W
Colfax, *Wash., U.S.A.* **158 C5** 46 53N 117 22W
Colhué Huapi, L., *Argentina* **176 C3** 45 30 S 69 0W
Colibaşi, *Moldova* **53 E13** 45 43N 28 11 E
Colibaşi, *Romania* **53 F9** 44 56N 24 54 E
Cólico, *Italy* **44 B6** 46 8N 9 22 E
Colíder, *Brazil* **173 C6** 10 45 S 55 25W
Coligny, *France* **27 F12** 46 23N 5 21 E
Coligny, *S. Africa* **117 D4** 26 17 S 26 15 E
Colima, *Mexico* **162 D4** 19 14N 103 43W
Colima □, *Mexico* **162 D4** 19 10N 103 40W
Colima, Nevado de, *Mexico* **162 D4** 19 35N 103 45W
Colina, *Chile* **174 C1** 33 13 S 70 45W
Colina do Norte, *Guinea-Biss.* **112 C2** 12 28N 15 0W
Colinas, *Goiás, Brazil* **171 D2** 14 15 S 48 2W
Colinas, *Maranhão, Brazil* **170 C3** 6 0 S 44 10W
Colindres, *Spain* **42 B7** 43 24N 3 27W
Coll, *U.K.* **22 E2** 56 39N 6 34W
Collaguasi, *Chile* **174 A2** 21 5 S 68 45W
Collarada, Peña, *Spain* **40 C4** 42 43N 0 29W
Collarenebri, *Australia* **127 D4** 29 33 S 148 34 E
Colle di Val d'Elsa, *Italy* **44 E8** 43 25N 11 7 E
Collécchio, *Italy* **44 D7** 44 45N 10 13 E
Colleen Bawn, *Zimbabwe* **119 G2** 21 0 S 29 12 E
College, *U.S.A.* **144 D11** 64 52N 147 49W
College Park, *U.S.A.* **152 B5** 33 40N 84 27W
College Station, *U.S.A.* **155 K6** 30 37N 96 21W
Collesalvetti, *Italy* **44 E7** 43 34N 10 27 E
Collie, *N.S.W., Australia* **129 A8** 31 41 S 148 18 E
Collie, *W. Austral., Australia* **125 F2** 33 22 S 116 8 E
Collier B., *Australia* **124 C3** 16 10 S 124 15 E
Collier Ra., *Australia* **125 D2** 24 45 S 119 10 E
Collier Range Nat. Park, *Australia* **125 D2** 24 39 S 119 7 E
Collina, Passo di, *Italy* **44 D7** 44 2N 10 56 E
Collingwood, *Canada* **140 D3** 44 29N 80 13W
Collingwood, *N.Z.* **131 A7** 40 41 S 172 40 E
Collins, *Canada* **140 B2** 50 17N 89 27W
Collins, *Ga., U.S.A.* **152 C7** 32 11N 82 7W
Collins, *Mo., U.S.A.* **156 G3** 37 54N 93 37W
Collinsville, *Australia* **126 C4** 20 30 S 147 56 E
Collinsville, *U.S.A.* **156 F7** 38 40N 89 59W
Collipulli, *Chile* **174 D1** 37 55 S 72 30W
Collo, *Algeria* **111 A6** 36 58N 6 37 E
Collooney, *Ireland* **23 B3** 54 11N 8 29W
Colmar, *France* **27 D14** 48 5N 7 20 E
Colmars, *France* **29 D10** 44 11N 6 39 E
Colmenar, *Spain* **43 J6** 36 54N 4 20W
Colmenar de Oreja, *Spain* **42 E7** 40 6N 3 25W

Corrèze □, *France* **28 C5** 45 20N 1 45 E
Corrèze →, *France* **28 C5** 45 10N 1 28 E
Corrib, L., *Ireland* **23 C2** 53 27N 9 16W
Corridónia, *Italy* **45 E10** 43 15N 13 30 E
Corrientes, *Argentina* **174 B4** 27 30 S 58 45W
Corrientes □, *Argentina* **174 B4** 28 0 S 57 0W
Corrientes →, *Argentina* **174 C4** 30 42 S 59 38W
Corrientes →, *Peru* **168 D3** 3 43 S 74 35W
Corrientes, C., *Colombia* **168 B2** 5 30N 77 34W
Corrientes, C., *Cuba* **164 B3** 21 43N 84 30W
Corrientes, C., *Mexico* **162 C3** 20 25N 105 42W
Corrigan, *U.S.A.* **155 K7** 31 0N 94 52W
Corrigin, *Australia* **125 F2** 32 20 S 117 53 E
Corry, *U.S.A.* **150 E5** 41 55N 79 39W
Corryong, *Australia* **129 D7** 36 12 S 147 53 E
Corse, *France* **29 G13** 42 0N 9 0 E
Corse, C., *France* **29 E13** 43 1N 9 25 E
Corse-du-Sud □, *France* **29 G13** 41 45N 9 0 E
Corsica = Corse, *France* **29 G13** 42 0N 9 0 E
Corsicana, *U.S.A.* **155 J6** 32 6N 96 28W
Corte, *France* **29 F13** 42 19N 9 11 E
Corte Pinto, *Portugal* **43 H3** 37 42N 7 29W
Cortegana, *Spain* **43 H4** 37 52N 6 49W
Cortes, *Phil.* **81 G6** 9 17N 126 11 E
Cortez, *U.S.A.* **159 H9** 37 21N 108 35W
Cortina d'Ampezzo, *Italy* **45 B9** 46 32N 12 8 E
Cortland, *N.Y., U.S.A.* **151 D8** 42 36N 76 11W
Cortland, *Ohio, U.S.A.* **150 E4** 41 20N 80 44W
Cortona, *Italy* **45 E8** 43 16N 11 59 E
Corubal →, *Guinea-Biss.* **112 C2** 11 57N 15 5W
Coruche, *Portugal* **43 G2** 38 57N 8 30W
Çoruh →, *Turkey* **61 K5** 41 38N 41 38 E
Çorum, *Turkey* **100 B6** 40 30N 34 57 E
Corumbá, *Brazil* **173 D6** 19 0 S 57 30W
Corumbá →, *Brazil* **171 E2** 18 19 S 48 55W
Corumbá de Goiás, *Brazil* **171 E2** 16 0 S 48 50W
Corumbaíba, *Brazil* **171 E2** 18 9 S 48 34W
Corund, *Romania* **53 D10** 46 30N 25 13 E
Corunna = A Coruña, *Spain* **42 B2** 43 20N 8 25W
Corunna, *U.S.A.* **157 B12** 42 59N 84 7W
Corvallis, *U.S.A.* **158 D2** 44 34N 123 16W
Corvette, L. de la, *Canada* **140 B5** 53 25N 74 3W
Corvo, *Azores* **9 d2** 39 42N 31 6W
Corydon, *Ind., U.S.A.* **157 F10** 38 13N 86 7W
Corydon, *Iowa, U.S.A.* **156 D3** 40 46N 93 19W
Corydon, *Ky., U.S.A.* **157 G9** 37 44N 87 43W
Cosalá, *Mexico* **162 C3** 24 28N 106 40W
Cosamaloapan, *Mexico* **163 D5** 18 23N 95 50W
Cosenza, *Italy* **47 C9** 39 18N 16 15 E
Coşereni, *Romania* **53 F11** 44 38N 26 35 E
Coshocton, *U.S.A.* **150 F3** 40 16N 81 51W
Cosmo Newberry, *Australia* **125 E3** 28 0 S 122 54 E
Cosne-Cours-sur-Loire, *France* **27 E9** 47 24N 2 54 E
Coso Junction, *U.S.A.* **161 J9** 36 3N 117 57W
Coso Pk., *U.S.A.* **161 J9** 36 13N 117 44W
Cospeito, *Spain* **42 B3** 43 12N 7 34W
Cosquín, *Argentina* **174 C3** 31 15 S 64 30W
Cossato, *Italy* **44 C5** 45 34N 8 10 E
Cossé-le-Vivien, *France* **26 E6** 47 57N 0 54W
Cosson →, *France* **26 E8** 47 30N 1 15 E
Costa Blanca, *Spain* **41 G4** 38 25N 0 10W
Costa Brava, *Spain* **40 D8** 41 30N 3 0 E
Costa del Sol, *Spain* **43 J6** 36 30N 4 30W
Costa Dorada, *Spain* **40 D6** 41 12N 1 15 E
Costa Mesa, *U.S.A.* **161 M9** 33 38N 117 55W
Costa Rica ■, *Cent. Amer.* **164 E3** 10 0N 84 0W
Costa Smeralda, *Italy* **46 A2** 41 5N 9 35 E
Costeşti, *Romania* **53 F9** 44 40N 24 53 E
Costigliole d'Asti, *Italy* **44 D5** 44 47N 8 11 E
Cosumnes →, *U.S.A.* **160 G5** 38 16N 121 26W
Coswig, *Sachsen, Germany* **30 D9** 51 7N 13 34 E
Coswig, *Sachsen-Anhalt, Germany* **30 D8** 51 53N 12 27 E
Cotabato, *Phil.* **81 H5** 7 14N 124 15 E
Cotabato □, *Phil.* **81 H5** 7 10N 125 0 E
Cotacajes →, *Bolivia* **172 D4** 16 0 S 67 1W
Cotagaita, *Bolivia* **174 A2** 20 45 S 65 40W
Cotahuasi, *Peru* **172 D3** 15 12 S 72 50W
Côte d'Azur, *France* **29 E11** 43 25N 7 10 E
Côte-d'Ivoire = Ivory Coast ■, *Africa* **112 D4** 7 30N 5 0W
Côte d'Or, *France* **27 E11** 47 10N 4 50 E
Côte-d'Or □, *France* **27 E11** 47 30N 4 50 E
Coteau des Prairies, *U.S.A.* **154 C6** 45 20N 97 50W
Coteau du Missouri, *U.S.A.* **154 B4** 47 0N 100 0W
Coteau Landing, *Canada* **151 A10** 45 15N 74 13W
Cotegipe, *Brazil* **171 D3** 12 2 S 44 15W
Cotentin, *France* **26 C5** 49 15N 1 30W
Côtes-d'Armor □, *France* **26 D4** 48 25N 2 40W
Côtes de Meuse, *France* **27 C12** 49 15N 5 22 E
Côtes-du-Nord = Côtes-d'Armor □, *France* **26 D4** 48 25N 2 40W
Cotiella, *Spain* **40 C5** 42 31N 0 19 E
Cotillo, *Canary Is.* **9 e2** 28 41N 14 1W
Cotiujeni, *Moldova* **53 C13** 47 51N 28 33 E
Cotoca, *Bolivia* **173 D5** 17 49 S 63 3W
Cotonou, *Benin* **113 D5** 6 20N 2 25 E
Cotopaxi, *Ecuador* **168 D2** 0 40 S 78 30W
Cotopaxi □, *Ecuador* **168 D2** 0 5 S 78 55W
Cotronei, *Italy* **47 C9** 39 9N 16 47 E
Cotswold Hills, *U.K.* **21 F5** 51 42N 2 10W
Cottage Grove, *U.S.A.* **158 E2** 43 48N 123 3W
Cottageville, *U.S.A.* **152 C9** 32 56N 80 29W
Cottbus, *Germany* **30 D10** 51 45N 14 20 E
Cottondale, *U.S.A.* **152 E4** 30 48N 85 23W
Cottonwood, *Ala., U.S.A.* **152 D4** 31 3N 85 18W
Cottonwood, *Ariz., U.S.A.* **159 J7** 34 45N 112 1W
Cotulla, *U.S.A.* **155 L5** 28 26N 99 14W
Coubre, Pte. de la, *France* **28 C2** 45 42N 1 15W
Couches, *France* **27 F11** 46 53N 4 30 E
Couço, *Portugal* **43 G2** 38 59N 8 17W
Coudersport, *U.S.A.* **150 E6** 41 46N 78 1W
Couedic, C. du, *Australia* **128 D2** 36 5 S 136 40 E
Couëron, *France* **26 E5** 47 13N 1 44W
Couesnon →, *France* **26 D5** 48 38N 1 32W
Couhé, *France* **28 B4** 46 17N 0 11 E
Coulanges-sur-Yonne, *France* **27 E10** 47 31N 3 33 E
Coulee City, *U.S.A.* **158 C4** 47 37N 119 17W
Coulman I., *Antarctica* **7 D11** 73 35 S 170 0 E
Coulommiers, *France* **27 D10** 48 50N 3 3 E
Coulon →, *France* **29 E9** 43 51N 5 0 E
Coulonge →, *Canada* **140 C4** 45 52N 76 46W
Coulonges-sur-l'Autize, *France* **28 B3** 46 29N 0 36W
Coulounieix-Chamiers, *France* **28 C4** 45 11N 0 42 E
Coulterville, *Calif., U.S.A.* **160 H6** 37 43N 120 12W
Coulterville, *Ill., U.S.A.* **156 F7** 38 11N 89 36W
Council, *Ga., U.S.A.* **152 E7** 30 37N 82 31W
Council, *Idaho, U.S.A.* **158 D5** 44 44N 116 26W
Council Bluffs, *U.S.A.* **154 E7** 41 16N 95 52W
Council Grove, *U.S.A.* **154 F6** 38 40N 96 29W
Coupeville, *U.S.A.* **160 B4** 48 13N 122 41W
Courantyne →, *S. Amer.* **169 B6** 5 55N 57 5W
Courcelles, *Belgium* **24 D4** 50 28N 4 22 E
Courçon, *France* **28 B3** 46 15N 0 50W
Courmayeur, *Italy* **44 C3** 45 47N 6 58 E
Couronne, C., *France* **29 E9** 43 19N 5 3 E
Cours-la-Ville, *France* **27 F11** 46 7N 4 19 E
Coursan, *France* **28 E7** 43 14N 3 4 E
Courseulles-sur-Mer, *France* **26 C6** 49 20N 0 29W
Courtenay, *Canada* **142 D4** 49 45N 125 0W
Courtenay, *France* **27 D10** 48 2N 3 3 E
Courtland, *U.S.A.* **160 G5** 38 20N 121 34W
Courtrai = Kortrijk, *Belgium* **24 D3** 50 50N 3 17 E
Courtright, *Canada* **150 D2** 42 49N 82 28W
Coushatta, *U.S.A.* **155 J8** 32 1N 93 21W
Coutances, *France* **26 C5** 49 3N 1 28W
Coutras, *France* **28 C3** 45 3N 0 8W
Coutts Crossing, *Australia* **127 D5** 29 49 S 152 55 E
Couva, *Trin. & Tob.* **169 F9** 10 24N 61 30W
Couvet, *Switz.* **32 C3** 46 57N 6 38 E
Couvin, *Belgium* **24 D4** 50 3N 4 29 E
Covarrubias, *Spain* **42 C7** 42 4N 3 31W
Covasna, *Romania* **53 E11** 45 50N 26 10 E
Covasna □, *Romania* **53 E10** 45 50N 26 0 E
Cove I., *Canada* **150 A3** 45 17N 81 44W
Coveñas, *Colombia* **168 B2** 9 24N 75 44W
Coventry, *U.K.* **21 E6** 52 25N 1 28W
Coverdale, *U.S.A.* **152 D6** 31 38N 83 58W
Covilhã, *Portugal* **42 E3** 40 17N 7 31W
Covington, *Ga., U.S.A.* **152 B6** 33 36N 83 51W
Covington, *Ind., U.S.A.* **157 D9** 40 9N 87 24W
Covington, *Ky., U.S.A.* **157 E12** 39 5N 84 31W
Covington, *Ohio, U.S.A.* **157 D12** 40 7N 84 21W
Covington, *Okla., U.S.A.* **155 G6** 36 18N 97 35W
Covington, *Tenn., U.S.A.* **155 H10** 35 34N 89 39W
Covington, *Va., U.S.A.* **148 G5** 37 47N 79 59W
Cowal, L., *Australia* **129 B7** 33 40 S 147 25 E
Cowan, Cerro, *Ecuador* **172 a** 0 12 S 90 48W
Cowan, L., *Australia* **125 F3** 31 45 S 121 45 E
Cowan L., *Canada* **143 C7** 54 0N 107 15W
Cowangie, *Australia* **128 C4** 35 12 S 141 26 E
Cowansville, *Canada* **140 C5** 45 14N 72 46W
Coward Springs, *Australia* **127 D2** 29 24 S 136 49 E
Cowcowing Lakes, *Australia* **125 F2** 30 55 S 117 20 E
Cowden, *U.S.A.* **157 E8** 39 15N 88 52W
Cowdenbeath, *U.K.* **22 E5** 56 7N 3 21W
Cowell, *Australia* **128 B2** 33 39 S 136 56 E
Cowes, *Australia* **129 E6** 38 28 S 145 14 E
Cowes, *U.K.* **21 G6** 50 45N 1 18W
Cowichan L., *Canada* **160 B2** 48 53N 124 17W
Cowlitz →, *U.S.A.* **160 D4** 46 6N 122 55W
Cowra, *Australia* **129 B8** 33 49 S 148 42 E
Cox, *Spain* **41 G4** 38 8N 0 53W
Coxilha Grande, *Brazil* **175 B5** 28 18 S 51 30W
Coxim, *Brazil* **173 D7** 18 30 S 54 55W
Coxim →, *Brazil* **173 D7** 18 34 S 54 46W
Cox's Bazar, *Bangla.* **90 F3** 21 26N 91 59 E
Coyote Wells, *U.S.A.* **161 N11** 32 44N 115 58W
Coyuca de Benítez, *Mexico* **163 D4** 17 1N 100 8W
Coyuca de Catalan, *Mexico* **162 D4** 18 18N 100 41W
Cozad, *U.S.A.* **154 E5** 40 52N 99 59W
Cozes, *France* **28 C3** 45 34N 0 49W
Cozumel, *Mexico* **163 C7** 20 31N 86 55W
Cozumel, Isla, *Mexico* **163 C7** 20 30N 86 40W
Crabhill, *Barbados* **165 g** 13 19N 59 38W
Cracow = Kraków, *Poland* **55 H6** 50 4N 19 57 E
Cracow, *Australia* **127 D5** 25 17 S 150 17 E
Cradle Mt.-Lake St. Clair Nat. Park, *Australia* **127 G4** 41 49 S 147 56 E
Cradock, *Australia* **127 E2** 32 6 S 138 31 E
Cradock, *S. Africa* **116 E4** 32 8 S 25 36 E
Craig, *Alaska, U.S.A.* **144 J14** 55 29N 133 9W
Craig, *Colo., U.S.A.* **158 F10** 40 31N 107 33W
Craigavon, *U.K.* **23 B5** 54 27N 6 23W
Craigieburn, *Australia* **129 D6** 37 36 S 144 56 E
Craigmore, *Zimbabwe* **119 G3** 20 28 S 32 50 E
Craik, *Canada* **143 C7** 51 3N 105 49W
Crailsheim, *Germany* **31 F6** 49 8N 10 5 E
Craiova, *Romania* **53 F8** 44 21N 23 48 E
Cramsie, *Australia* **126 C3** 23 20 S 144 15 E
Cranberry L., *U.S.A.* **151 B10** 44 11N 74 50W
Cranberry Portage, *Canada* **143 C8** 54 35N 101 23W
Cranbrook, *Australia* **125 F2** 34 18 S 117 33 E
Cranbrook, *Canada* **142 D5** 49 30N 115 46W
Crandon, *U.S.A.* **154 C10** 45 34N 88 54W
Crane, *Oreg., U.S.A.* **158 E4** 43 25N 118 35W
Crane, *Tex., U.S.A.* **155 K3** 31 24N 102 21W
Cranganore, *India* **95 J3** 10 13N 76 13 E
Cranston, *U.S.A.* **151 E13** 41 47N 71 26W
Craon, *France* **26 E6** 47 50N 0 58W
Craonne, *France* **27 C10** 49 27N 3 46 E
Craponne-sur-Arzon, *France* **28 C7** 45 19N 3 51 E
Crasna, *Romania* **53 D12** 46 32N 27 51 E
Crasna →, *Romania* **52 C7** 47 44N 22 35 E
Crasnei, Munţii, *Romania* **53 C8** 47 0N 23 20 E
Crater L., *U.S.A.* **158 E2** 42 56N 122 6W
Crater Lake Nat. Park, *U.S.A.* **158 E2** 42 55N 122 10W
Crater Mt., *Papua N. G.* **132 D3** 6 37 S 145 7 E
Crater Pt., *Papua N. G.* **132 C7** 5 25 S 152 9 E
Crateús, *Brazil* **170 C3** 5 10 S 40 39W
Crati →, *Italy* **47 C9** 39 43N 16 31 E
Crato, *Brazil* **170 C4** 7 10 S 39 25W
Crato, *Portugal* **43 F3** 39 16N 7 39W
Craven, L., *Canada* **140 B4** 54 20N 76 56W
Cravo Norte, *Colombia* **168 B3** 6 18N 70 12W
Cravo Norte →, *Colombia* **168 B3** 6 18N 70 12W
Crawford, *Ala., U.S.A.* **152 C4** 32 27N 85 11W
Crawford, *Nebr., U.S.A.* **154 D3** 42 41N 103 25W
Crawfordsville, *Ind., U.S.A.* **157 D10** 40 2N 86 54W
Crawfordsville, *Iowa, U.S.A.* **156 C5** 41 12N 91 32W
Crawfordville, *Fla., U.S.A.* **152 E5** 30 11N 84 23W
Crawfordville, *Ga., U.S.A.* **152 B7** 33 33N 82 54W
Crawley, *U.K.* **21 F7** 51 7N 0 11W
Crazy Mts., *U.S.A.* **158 C8** 46 12N 110 20W
Crean L., *Canada* **143 C7** 54 5N 106 9W
Crécy-en-Ponthieu, *France* **27 B8** 50 15N 1 53 E
Crediton, *Canada* **150 C3** 43 17N 81 33W
Cree →, *Canada* **143 B7** 58 57N 105 47W
Cree →, *U.K.* **22 G4** 54 55N 4 25W
Cree L., *Canada* **143 B7** 57 30N 106 30W
Creede, *U.S.A.* **159 H10** 37 51N 106 56W
Creekside, *U.S.A.* **150 F5** 40 40N 79 11W
Creel, *Mexico* **162 B3** 27 45N 107 38W
Creemore, *Canada* **150 B4** 44 19N 80 6W
Creighton, *Canada* **143 C8** 54 45N 101 54W
Creighton, *U.S.A.* **154 D6** 42 28N 97 54W
Creil, *France* **27 C9** 49 15N 2 29 E
Crema, *Italy* **44 C6** 45 22N 9 41 E
Cremona, *Italy* **44 C7** 45 7N 10 2 E
Crepaja, *Serbia, Yug.* **52 E5** 45 1N 20 38 E
Crepori →, *Brazil* **173 B6** 5 42 S 57 8W
Crépy, *France* **27 C10** 49 37N 3 32 E
Crépy-en-Valois, *France* **27 C9** 49 14N 2 54 E
Cres, *Croatia* **45 D11** 44 58N 14 25 E
Crescent Beach, *U.S.A.* **152 F8** 29 46N 81 15W
Crescent City, *Calif., U.S.A.* **158 F1** 41 45N 124 12W
Crescent City, *Fla., U.S.A.* **153 F8** 29 26N 81 31W
Crescent Hd., *Australia* **129 A10** 31 11 S 152 59 E
Crescent L., *U.S.A.* **153 F8** 29 28N 81 30W
Crescentino, *Italy* **44 C5** 45 11N 8 6 E
Crespo, *Argentina* **174 C3** 32 2 S 60 19W
Cresson, *U.S.A.* **150 F6** 40 28N 78 36W
Cressy, *Australia* **128 E5** 38 2 S 143 40 E
Crest, *France* **29 D9** 44 44N 5 2 E
Cresta, Mt., *Phil.* **80 C4** 17 17N 122 6 E
Crestline, *Calif., U.S.A.* **161 L9** 34 14N 117 18W
Crestline, *Ohio, U.S.A.* **150 F2** 40 47N 82 44W
Creston, *Canada* **142 D5** 49 10N 116 31W
Creston, *Calif., U.S.A.* **160 K6** 35 32N 120 33W
Creston, *Iowa, U.S.A.* **156 C2** 41 4N 94 22W
Crestview, *Calif., U.S.A.* **160 H8** 37 46N 118 58W
Crestview, *Fla., U.S.A.* **149 K2** 30 46N 86 34W
Creswick, *Australia* **128 D5** 37 25 S 143 58 E
Crêt de la Neige, *France* **27 F12** 46 16N 5 58 E
Crete = Kríti, *Greece* **39 E6** 35 15N 25 0 E
Crete, *Ill., U.S.A.* **157 C9** 41 27N 87 38W
Crete, *Nebr., U.S.A.* **154 E6** 40 38N 96 58W
Crete, Sea of, *Greece* **49 E7** 36 0N 25 0 E
Créteil, *France* **27 D9** 48 47N 2 28 E
Cretin, C., *Papua N. G.* **132 D4** 6 40 S 147 53 E
Creus, C. de, *Spain* **40 C8** 42 20N 3 19 E
Creuse □, *France* **27 F9** 46 10N 2 0 E
Creuse →, *France* **28 B4** 47 0N 0 34 E
Creutzwald, *France* **27 C13** 49 12N 6 42 E
Creuzburg, *Germany* **30 D6** 51 3N 10 14 E
Crèvecœur-le-Grand, *France* **27 C9** 49 37N 2 5 E
Crevillente, *Spain* **41 G4** 38 12N 0 48W
Crewe, *U.K.* **20 D5** 53 6N 2 26W
Crewkerne, *U.K.* **21 G5** 50 53N 2 48W
Criciúma, *Brazil* **175 B6** 28 40 S 49 23W
Cricova, *Moldova* **53 C13** 47 8N 28 52 E
Cridersville, *U.S.A.* **157 D12** 40 39N 84 9W
Crieff, *U.K.* **22 E5** 56 22N 3 50W
Crikvenica, *Croatia* **45 C11** 45 11N 14 40 E
Crimea □, *Ukraine* **59 K8** 45 30N 33 10 E
Crimean Pen. = Krymskyy Pivostriv, *Ukraine* **59 K8** 45 0N 34 0 E
Crimmitschau, *Germany* **30 E8** 50 48N 12 24 E
Cristal, Mts. de, *Gabon* **114 B2** 0 30N 10 30 E
Cristalândia, *Brazil* **170 D2** 10 36 S 49 11W
Cristino Castro, *Brazil* **170 C3** 8 49 S 44 13W
Cristóbal, Pta., *Ecuador* **172 a** 0 54 S 91 30W
Cristuru Secuiesc, *Romania* **53 D10** 46 17N 25 2 E
Crişul Alb →, *Romania* **52 D6** 46 42N 21 17 E
Crişul Negru →, *Romania* **52 D6** 46 42N 21 16 E
Crişul Repede →, *Romania* **52 D5** 46 55N 20 59 E
Crittenden, *U.S.A.* **157 F12** 38 47N 84 36W
Criuleni, *Moldova* **53 C14** 47 13N 29 10 E
Crivitz, *Germany* **30 B7** 53 34N 11 39 E
Crixás, *Brazil* **171 D2** 14 27 S 49 58W
Crna →, *Macedonia* **50 E5** 41 33N 21 59 E
Crna Gora = Montenegro □, *Yugoslavia* **50 D3** 42 40N 19 20 E
Crna Gora, *Macedonia* **50 D5** 42 10N 21 30 E
Crna Reka = Crna →, *Macedonia* **50 E5** 41 33N 21 59 E
Crna Trava, *Serbia, Yug.* **50 D6** 42 49N 22 19 E
Crni Drim →, *Macedonia* **50 E4** 41 17N 20 40 E
Crni Timok →, *Serbia, Yug.* **50 C6** 43 53N 22 15 E
Crnoljeva Planina, *Kosovo, Yug.* **50 D5** 42 20N 21 0 E
Črnomelj, *Slovenia* **45 C12** 45 33N 15 10 E
Croagh Patrick, *Ireland* **23 C2** 53 46N 9 40W
Croajingolong Nat. Park, *Australia* **129 D8** 37 45 S 149 26 E
Croatia ■, *Europe* **45 C13** 45 20N 16 0 E
Crocker, *U.S.A.* **156 G4** 37 57N 92 16W
Crocker, Banjaran, *Malaysia* **85 A5** 5 40N 116 30 E
Crocker, Cerro, *Ecuador* **172 a** 0 36 S 90 21W
Crockett, *U.S.A.* **155 K7** 31 19N 95 27W
Crocodile = Krokodil →, *Mozam.* **117 D5** 25 14 S 32 18 E
Crocodile Is., *Australia* **126 A1** 12 3 S 134 58 E
Crocq, *France* **28 C6** 45 52N 2 21 E
Crodo, *Italy* **44 B5** 46 13N 8 19 E
Crohy Hd., *Ireland* **23 B3** 54 55N 8 26W
Croisette, C., *France* **29 E9** 43 14N 5 22 E
Croisic, Pte. du, *France* **26 E4** 47 19N 2 31W
Croix, L. La, *Canada* **140 C1** 48 20N 92 15W
Croker, C., *Australia* **124 B5** 10 58 S 132 35 E
Croker, C., *Canada* **150 B4** 44 58N 80 59W
Croker I., *Australia* **124 B5** 11 12 S 132 32 E
Cromarty, *U.K.* **22 D4** 57 40N 4 2W
Cromer, *U.K.* **20 E9** 52 56N 1 17 E
Cromwell, *N.Z.* **131 F4** 45 3 S 169 14 E
Cromwell, *U.S.A.* **151 E12** 41 36N 72 39W
Cronat, *France* **27 F10** 46 43N 3 40 E
Crook, *U.K.* **20 C6** 54 43N 1 45W
Crooked →, *Canada* **142 C4** 54 50N 122 54W
Crooked →, *U.S.A.* **158 D3** 44 32N 121 16W
Crooked Creek, *U.S.A.* **144 F8** 61 52N 158 7W
Crooked I., *Bahamas* **165 B5** 22 50N 74 10W
Crooked Island Passage, *Bahamas* **165 B5** 23 0N 74 30W
Crookston, *Minn., U.S.A.* **154 B6** 47 47N 96 37W
Crookston, *Nebr., U.S.A.* **154 D4** 42 56N 100 45W
Crookwell, *Australia* **129 C8** 34 28 S 149 24 E
Crosby, *U.K.* **20 D4** 53 30N 3 3W
Crosby, *N. Dak., U.S.A.* **154 A3** 48 55N 103 18W
Crosby, *Pa., U.S.A.* **150 E6** 41 45N 78 23W
Crosbyton, *U.S.A.* **155 J4** 33 40N 101 14W
Crosía, *Italy* **47 C9** 39 35N 16 45 E
Cross →, *Nigeria* **113 E6** 4 42N 8 21 E
Cross City, *U.S.A.* **153 F6** 29 38N 83 7W
Cross Fell, *U.K.* **20 C5** 54 43N 2 28W
Cross L., *Canada* **143 C9** 54 45N 97 30W
Cross Lake, *Canada* **143 C9** 54 37N 97 47W
Cross River □, *Nigeria* **113 D6** 6 0N 8 0 E
Cross River Nat. Park, *Nigeria* **113 D6** 5 50N 9 0 E
Cross Sound, *U.S.A.* **144 H14** 58 0N 135 0W
Cross Timbers, *U.S.A.* **156 F3** 38 1N 93 14W
Crossett, *U.S.A.* **155 J9** 33 8N 91 58W
Crosshaven, *Ireland* **23 E3** 51 47N 8 17W
Crossley, Mt., *N.Z.* **131 C7** 42 50 S 172 5 E
Crossville, *Ill., U.S.A.* **157 F8** 38 10N 88 4W
Crossville, *Tenn., U.S.A.* **149 G3** 35 57N 85 2W
Croswell, *U.S.A.* **150 C2** 43 16N 82 37W
Croton-on-Hudson, *U.S.A.* **151 E11** 41 12N 73 55W
Crotone, *Italy* **47 C10** 39 5N 17 8 E
Crow →, *Canada* **142 B4** 59 41N 124 20W
Crow Agency, *U.S.A.* **158 D10** 45 36N 107 28W
Crow Hd., *Ireland* **23 E1** 51 35N 10 9W
Crowdy Bay Nat. Park, *Australia* **129 A10** 31 45 S 152 45 E
Crowell, *U.S.A.* **155 J5** 33 59N 99 43W
Crowl Cr. →, *Australia* **129 B6** 32 0 S 145 30 E
Crowley, *U.S.A.* **155 K8** 30 13N 92 22W
Crowley, L., *U.S.A.* **160 H8** 37 35N 118 42W
Crown I., *Papua N. G.* **132 C4** 5 7 S 146 58 E
Crown Point, *Ind., U.S.A.* **157 C9** 41 25N 87 22W
Crown Point, *N.Y., U.S.A.* **151 C11** 43 57N 73 26W
Crown Pt., *Trin. & Tob.* **169 E10** 11 18N 60 51W
Crownpoint, *U.S.A.* **159 J9** 35 41N 108 9W
Crows Landing, *U.S.A.* **160 H5** 37 23N 121 6W
Crows Nest, *Australia* **127 D5** 27 16 S 152 4 E
Crowsnest Pass, *Canada* **142 D6** 49 40N 114 40W
Croydon, *Australia* **126 B3** 18 13 S 142 14 E
Croydon □, *U.K.* **21 F7** 51 22N 0 5W
Crozet, Is., *Ind. Oc.* **121 J4** 46 27 S 52 0 E
Crozon, *France* **26 D2** 48 15N 4 30W
Cruces, Punta, *Colombia* **168 B2** 6 39N 77 32W
Cruz, C., *Cuba* **164 C4** 19 50N 77 50W
Cruz Alta, *Brazil* **175 B5** 28 45 S 53 40W
Cruz Bay, *U.S. Virgin Is.* **165 e** 18 20N 64 48W
Cruz das Almas, *Brazil* **171 D4** 12 0 S 39 6W
Cruz de Incio, *Spain* **42 C3** 42 39N 7 21W
Cruz de Malta, *Brazil* **170 C3** 8 15 S 40 20W
Cruz del Eje, *Argentina* **174 C3** 30 45 S 64 50W
Cruzeiro, *Brazil* **171 F2** 22 33 S 45 0W
Cruzeiro do Oeste, *Brazil* **175 A5** 23 46 S 53 4W
Cruzeiro do Sul, *Brazil* **172 B3** 7 35 S 72 35W
Cry L., *Canada* **142 B3** 58 45N 129 0W
Crystal B., *U.S.A.* **153 G7** 28 50N 82 45W
Crystal Bay, *U.S.A.* **160 F7** 39 15N 120 0W
Crystal Brook, *Australia* **128 B3** 33 21 S 138 12 E
Crystal City, *Mo., U.S.A.* **156 F6** 38 13N 90 23W
Crystal City, *Tex., U.S.A.* **155 L5** 28 41N 99 50W
Crystal Falls, *U.S.A.* **148 B1** 46 5N 88 20W
Crystal Lake, *Fla., U.S.A.* **152 E4** 30 26N 85 42W
Crystal Lake, *Ill., U.S.A.* **157 B8** 42 14N 88 19W
Crystal River, *U.S.A.* **149 L4** 28 54N 82 35W
Crystal Springs, *U.S.A.* **155 K9** 31 59N 90 21W
Csenger, *Hungary* **52 C7** 47 50N 22 41 E
Csongrád, *Hungary* **52 D5** 46 43N 20 12 E
Csongrád □, *Hungary* **52 D5** 46 32N 20 15 E
Csorna, *Hungary* **52 C2** 47 38N 17 18 E
Csurgo, *Hungary* **52 D2** 46 16N 17 9 E
Cu Lao Hon, *Vietnam* **87 G7** 10 54N 108 18 E
Cua Rao, *Vietnam* **86 C5** 19 16N 104 27 E
Cuácua →, *Mozam.* **119 F4** 17 54 S 37 0 E
Cuále, *Angola* **115 D3** 8 22 S 16 10 E
Cuále →, *Angola* **115 D3** 8 29 S 15 1 E
Cuamato, *Angola* **116 B2** 17 2 S 15 7 E
Cuamba, *Mozam.* **119 E4** 14 45 S 36 22 E
Cuando, *Angola* **115 E3** 14 34 S 19 1 E
Cuando →, *Angola* **115 F4** 17 30 S 23 15 E
Cuando Cubango □, *Angola* **116 B3** 16 25 S 20 0 E
Cuangar, *Angola* **116 B2** 17 36 S 18 39 E
Cuango = Kwango →, *Dem. Rep. of the Congo* **114 C3** 3 14 S 17 22 E
Cuango, *Lunda Norte, Angola* **115 D3** 9 8 S 18 3 E
Cuango, *Moxico, Angola* **115 E3** 6 20 S 16 42 E
Cuango, *Uíge, Angola* **115 D3** 6 15 S 16 42 E
Cuanza →, *Angola* **115 D2** 9 21 S 13 9 E
Cuanza Norte □, *Angola* **115 D2** 8 50 S 14 30 E
Cuanza Sul □, *Angola* **115 E2** 10 50 S 14 50 E
Cuao →, *Venezuela* **168 C4** 4 55N 67 40W
Cuarto →, *Argentina* **174 C3** 33 25 S 63 2W
Cuatir →, *Angola* **115 F3** 17 1 S 18 9 E
Cuatrociénegas, *Mexico* **162 B4** 26 59N 102 5W
Cuauhtémoc, *Mexico* **162 B3** 28 25N 106 52W
Cuba, *Portugal* **43 G3** 38 10N 7 54W
Cuba, *Mo., U.S.A.* **156 F5** 38 4N 91 24W
Cuba, *N. Mex., U.S.A.* **159 J10** 36 1N 107 4W
Cuba, *N.Y., U.S.A.* **150 D6** 42 13N 78 17W
Cuba ■, *W. Indies* **164 B4** 22 0N 79 0W
Cuba City, *U.S.A.* **156 B6** 42 36N 90 26W
Cubal, *Angola* **115 E2** 12 26 S 14 3 E
Cubal →, *Angola* **115 E2** 12 13 S 13 39 E
Cubango →, *Africa* **116 B3** 18 50 S 22 25 E
Cubanja, *Angola* **115 E4** 14 49 S 21 20 E
Cubia, *Angola* **115 F4** 15 58 S 21 42 E
Çubuk, *Turkey* **100 B5** 40 14N 33 3 E
Cuchi, *Angola* **115 E3** 14 37 S 16 58 E
Cuchi →, *Angola* **115 F3** 15 13 S 17 20 E
Cuchillo-Có, *Argentina* **176 A4** 38 20 S 64 37W
Cuchivero →, *Venezuela* **168 B4** 7 40N 65 57W
Cuchumatanes, Sierra de los, *Guatemala* **164 C1** 15 35N 91 25W
Cuckfield, *U.K.* **21 F7** 51 1N 0 8W
Cucuí, *Brazil* **168 C4** 1 12N 66 50W
Cucumbi, *Angola* **115 E3** 10 17 S 19 5 E
Cucurpe, *Mexico* **162 A2** 30 20N 110 43W
Cucurrupí, *Colombia* **168 C2** 4 23N 76 56W
Cúcuta, *Colombia* **168 B3** 7 54N 72 31W
Cudahy, *U.S.A.* **157 B9** 42 58N 87 52W
Cudalbi, *Romania* **53 E12** 45 46N 27 41 E
Cuddalore, *India* **95 J4** 11 46N 79 45 E
Cuddapah, *India* **95 G4** 14 30N 78 47 E
Cuddapan, L., *Australia* **126 D3** 25 45 S 141 26 E
Cudgewa, *Australia* **129 D7** 36 10 S 147 42 E
Cudillero, *Spain* **42 B4** 43 33N 6 9W
Cue, *Australia* **125 E2** 27 25 S 117 54 E
Cuebe →, *Angola* **115 F3** 15 46 S 17 32 E
Cuéllar, *Spain* **42 D6** 41 23N 4 21W
Cuemba, *Angola* **115 E3** 11 50 S 17 42 E
Cuenca, *Ecuador* **168 D2** 2 50 S 79 9W
Cuenca, *Spain* **40 E2** 40 5N 2 10W
Cuenca □, *Spain* **40 F3** 40 0N 2 0W
Cuenca, Serranía de, *Spain* **40 F3** 39 55N 1 50W
Cuerdo del Pozo, Embalse de la, *Spain* **40 D2** 41 51N 2 44W
Cuernavaca, *Mexico* **163 D5** 18 55N 99 15W
Cuero, *U.S.A.* **155 L6** 29 6N 97 17W
Cuers, *France* **29 E10** 43 14N 6 5 E
Cuevas, Cerro, *Bolivia* **173 E4** 22 0 S 65 12W
Cuevas del Almanzora, *Spain* **41 H3** 37 18N 1 58W
Cuevo, *Bolivia* **173 E5** 20 15 S 63 30W
Cugir, *Romania* **53 E8** 45 48N 23 25 E
Cugnaux, *France* **28 E5** 43 32N 1 20 E
Cuhai-Bakony →, *Hungary* **52 C2** 47 35N 17 54 E
Cuiabá, *Brazil* **173 D6** 15 30 S 56 0W
Cuiabá →, *Brazil* **173 D6** 17 5 S 56 36W
Cuihangcun, *China* **69 G10** 22 27N 113 32 E
Cuijk, *Neths.* **24 C5** 51 44N 5 50 E
Cuilco, *Guatemala* **164 C1** 15 24N 91 58W
Cuillin Hills, *U.K.* **22 D2** 57 13N 6 15W
Cuillin Sd., *U.K.* **22 D2** 57 4N 6 20W
Cuilo, *Angola* **115 D3** 8 12 S 19 28 E
Cuilo-Futa, *Angola* **115 D3** 6 28 S 15 51 E
Cuima, *Angola* **115 E3** 13 25 S 15 45 E
Cuimba, *Angola* **115 D2** 6 10 S 14 41 E
Cuiseaux, *France* **27 F12** 46 30N 5 22 E
Cuité, *Brazil* **170 C4** 6 29 S 36 9W
Cuito →, *Angola* **115 F4** 18 1 S 20 48 E
Cuito Cuanavale, *Angola* **115 F3** 15 10 S 19 10 E
Cuitzeo, L. de, *Mexico* **162 D4** 19 55N 101 5W
Cuiuni →, *Brazil* **169 D5** 0 45 S 63 7W
Cuivre →, *U.S.A.* **156 F6** 38 55N 90 44W
Cuivre, West Fork →, *U.S.A.* **156 E6** 39 2N 90 58W
Cujmir, *Romania* **52 F7** 44 13N 22 57 E
Cukai, *Malaysia* **87 K4** 4 13N 103 25 E
Culasi, *Phil.* **81 F4** 11 26N 122 3 E
Culbertson, *U.S.A.* **154 A2** 48 9N 104 31W
Culburra, *N.S.W., Australia* **129 C9** 34 56 S 150 46 E
Culburra, *S. Austral., Australia* **128 C3** 35 50 S 139 58 E
Culcairn, *Australia* **129 C7** 35 41 S 147 3 E
Culebra, Isla de, *Puerto Rico* **165 d** 18 19N 65 18W
Culebra, Sierra de la, *Spain* **42 D4** 41 55N 6 20W
Culfa, *Azerbaijan* **101 C11** 38 57N 45 38 E
Culgoa, *Australia* **128 C5** 35 44 S 143 6 E
Culgoa →, *Australia* **127 D4** 29 56 S 146 20 E
Culgoa Flood Plain Nat. Park, *Australia* **127 D4** 28 58 S 147 5 E
Culiacán, *Mexico* **162 C3** 24 50N 107 23W
Culiacán →, *Mexico* **162 C3** 24 30N 107 42W
Culik, *Indonesia* **79 J18** 8 21 S 115 37 E
Culion, *Phil.* **81 F3** 11 54N 119 58 E
Culion I., *Phil.* **81 F2** 11 50N 120 0 E
Culiseu →, *Brazil* **173 C7** 12 14 S 53 17W
Cúllar, *Spain* **43 H8** 37 35N 2 34W
Cullarin Ra., *Australia* **129 C8** 34 30 S 149 30 E
Cullen, *U.K.* **22 D6** 57 42N 2 49W
Cullen Bullen, *Australia* **129 B9** 33 18 S 150 2 E
Cullen Pt., *Australia* **126 A3** 11 57 S 141 54 E
Cullera, *Spain* **41 F4** 39 9N 0 17W
Cullman, *U.S.A.* **149 H2** 34 11N 86 51W
Culloden, *U.S.A.* **152 C5** 32 52N 84 6W
Cullom, *U.S.A.* **157 D8** 40 53N 88 16W
Culo →, *Angola* **115 D3** 6 13 S 15 34 E
Culoz, *France* **29 C9** 45 47N 5 46 E
Culpeper, *U.S.A.* **148 F7** 38 30N 78 0W
Culuene →, *Brazil* **173 C7** 12 56 S 52 51W
Culver, *U.S.A.* **157 C10** 41 13N 86 25W
Culver, Pt., *Australia* **125 F3** 32 54 S 124 43 E
Culverden, *N.Z.* **131 C7** 42 47 S 172 49 E
Culverton, *U.S.A.* **152 B7** 33 19N 82 54W
Cuma, *Angola* **115 E3** 12 52 S 15 5 E
Cumaná, *Venezuela* **169 A5** 10 30N 64 5W
Cumaovası, *Turkey* **49 C9** 38 15N 27 9 E
Cumare, *Colombia* **168 C3** 0 49N 72 32W

D

Daram, *Phil.* **81 F5** 11 38N 124 48 E
Dārān, *Iran* **97 C6** 32 59N 50 24 E
Daraut Kurgan = Daroot-Korgan, *Kyrgyzstan* **65 D6** 39 33N 72 11 E
Daravica, *Kosovo, Yug.* **50 D4** 42 32N 20 8 E
Daraw, *Egypt* **106 C3** 24 22N 32 51 E
Dārayyā, *Syria* **103 B5** 33 28N 36 15 E
Darazo, *Nigeria* **113 C7** 11 1N 10 24 E
Darband, *Pakistan* **92 B5** 34 20N 72 50 E
Darband, Kūh-e, *Iran* **97 D8** 31 34N 57 8 E
Darbhanga, *India* **93 F11** 26 15N 85 55 E
Darburruk, *Somali Rep.* **120 C2** 9 44N 44 31 E
Darby, C., *U.S.A.* **144 D7** 64 19N 162 47W
D'Arcy, *Canada* **142 C4** 50 27N 122 35W
Darda, *Croatia* **52 E3** 45 40N 18 41 E
Dardanelle, *Ark., U.S.A.* **155 H8** 35 13N 93 9W
Dardanelle, *Calif., U.S.A.* **160 G7** 38 20N 119 50W
Dardanelles = Çanakkale Boğazı, *Turkey* **51 F10** 40 17N 26 32 E
Dare →, *Ethiopia* **107 F5** 7 20N 42 11 E
Darende, *Turkey* **100 C7** 38 31N 37 30 E
Dārestān, *Iran* **97 D8** 29 9N 58 42 E
Darfield, *N.Z.* **131 D7** 43 29 S 172 7 E
Darfo, *Italy* **44 C7** 45 53N 10 11 E
Dârfûr, *Sudan* **104 E6** 13 40N 24 0 E
Dargai, *Pakistan* **92 B4** 34 25N 71 55 E
Dargan Ata, *Turkmenistan* **66 E7** 40 29N 62 10 E
Dargaville, *N.Z.* **130 B2** 35 57 S 173 52 E
Dargol, *Niger* **113 C5** 13 54N 1 22 E
Darhan, *Mongolia* **68 B5** 49 37N 106 21 E
Darhan Muminggan Lianheqi, *China* **74 D6** 41 40N 110 28 E
Dari, *Sudan* **107 F3** 5 48N 30 26 E
Darıca, *Turkey* **100 B3** 40 45N 29 23 E
Darien, *U.S.A.* **152 D8** 31 23N 81 26W
Darién, G. del, *Colombia* **168 B2** 9 0N 77 0W
Dariganga = Ovoot, *Mongolia* **74 B7** 45 21N 113 45 E
Daringbadi, *India* **94 E7** 19 54N 84 8 E
Darinskoye, *Kazakstan* **60 E10** 51 20N 51 44 E
Darjeeling = Darjiling, *India* **90 B2** 27 3N 88 18 E
Darjiling, *India* **90 B2** 27 3N 88 18 E
Darkan, *Australia* **125 F2** 33 20 S 116 43 E
Darke Peak, *Australia* **128 B2** 33 27 S 136 12 E
Darkhana, *Pakistan* **92 D5** 30 39N 72 11 E
Darkhazīneh, *Iran* **97 D6** 31 54N 48 39 E
Darkot Pass, *Pakistan* **65 E6** 36 45N 73 26 E
Darling →, *Australia* **128 C4** 34 4 S 141 54 E
Darling Downs, *Australia* **127 D5** 27 30 S 150 30 E
Darling Ra., *Australia* **125 F2** 32 30 S 116 0 E
Darlington, *U.K.* **20 C6** 54 32N 1 33W
Darlington, *Fla., U.S.A.* **152 E3** 30 57N 86 3W
Darlington, *S.C., U.S.A.* **149 H6** 34 18N 79 52W
Darlington, *Wis., U.S.A.* **156 B6** 42 41N 90 7W
Darlington □, *U.K.* **20 C6** 54 32N 1 33W
Darlington, L., *S. Africa* **116 E4** 33 10 S 25 9 E
Darlington Point, *Australia* **129 C7** 34 37 S 146 1 E
Darlot, L., *Australia* **125 E3** 27 48 S 121 35 E
Darłowo, *Poland* **54 D3** 54 25N 16 25 E
Dărmăneşti, *Bacău, Romania* **53 D11** 46 21N 26 33 E
Dărmăneşti, *Suceava, Romania* **53 C11** 47 44N 26 9 E
Darmstadt, *Germany* **31 F4** 49 51N 8 39 E
Darnah, *Libya* **108 B4** 32 45N 22 45 E
Darnah □, *Libya* **108 B4** 31 0N 23 40 E
Darnall, *S. Africa* **117 D5** 29 23 S 31 18 E
Darney, *France* **27 D13** 48 5N 6 2 E
Darnick, *Australia* **128 B5** 32 48 S 143 38 E
Darnley, C., *Antarctica* **7 C6** 68 0 S 69 0 E
Darnley B., *Canada* **138 B7** 69 30N 123 30W
Daroca, *Spain* **40 D3** 41 9N 1 25W
Daroot-Korgan, *Kyrgyzstan* **65 D6** 39 33N 72 11 E
Darou-Mousti, *Senegal* **112 B1** 15 3N 16 3W
Darr →, *Australia* **126 C3** 23 39 S 143 50 E
Darra Pezu, *Pakistan* **92 C4** 32 19N 70 44 E
Darran Mts., *N.Z.* **131 E2** 44 37 S 167 59 E
Darrequeira, *Argentina* **174 D3** 37 42 S 63 10W
Darrington, *U.S.A.* **158 B3** 48 15N 121 36W
Darsana, *Bangla.* **90 D2** 23 35N 88 48 E
Darsi, *India* **95 G4** 15 46N 79 44 E
Darsser Ort, *Germany* **30 A8** 54 28N 12 32 E
Dart →, *U.K.* **21 G4** 50 24N 3 39W
Dart, C., *Antarctica* **7 D14** 73 6 S 126 20W
Dartford, *U.K.* **21 F8** 51 26N 0 13 E
Dartmoor, *Australia* **128 D4** 37 56 S 141 19 E
Dartmoor, *U.K.* **21 G4** 50 38N 3 57W
Dartmouth, *Canada* **141 D7** 44 40N 63 30W
Dartmouth, *U.K.* **21 G4** 50 21N 3 36W
Dartmouth, L., *Australia* **129 D7** 26 4 S 147 22 E
Dartmouth Res., *Australia* **127 D4** 36 34 S 145 18 E
Dartuch, C. = Artrutx, C. de, *Spain* **38 B4** 39 55N 3 49 E
Daru, *Papua N. G.* **132 E2** 9 3 S 143 13 E
Daruba, *Indonesia* **82 A3** 2 5N 128 14 E
Daruvar, *Croatia* **52 E2** 45 35N 17 14 E
Darvaza, *Turkmenistan* **66 E6** 40 11N 58 24 E
Darvel, Teluk = Lahad Datu, Teluk, *Malaysia* **85 B5** 4 50N 118 20 E
Darwen, *U.K.* **20 D5** 53 42N 2 29W
Darwendale, *Zimbabwe* **117 B5** 17 41 S 30 33 E
Darwha, *India* **94 D3** 20 15N 77 45 E
Darwin, *Australia* **124 B5** 12 25 S 130 51 E
Darwin, *U.S.A.* **161 J9** 36 15N 117 35W
Darwin, Mt., *Chile* **176 D3** 54 47 S 69 55W
Darwin, Volcán, *Ecuador* **172 a** 0 10 S 91 18W
Darya Khan, *Pakistan* **92 D4** 31 48N 71 6 E
Daryapur, *India* **94 D3** 20 55N 77 20 E
Daryoi Amu = Amudarya →, *Uzbekistan* **66 E6** 43 58N 59 34 E
Dās, *U.A.E.* **97 E7** 25 20N 53 30 E
Dashen, Ras, *Ethiopia* **107 E4** 13 8N 38 26 E
Dasher, *U.S.A.* **152 E6** 30 45N 83 13W
Dashetai, *China* **74 D5** 41 0N 109 5 E
Dashhowuz, *Turkmenistan* **66 E6** 41 49N 59 58 E
Dashkesan = Daşkäsän, *Azerbaijan* **61 K7** 40 25N 46 0 E
Dashköpri, *Turkmenistan* **97 B9** 36 16N 62 8 E
Dasht, *Iran* **97 B8** 37 17N 56 7 E
Dasht →, *Pakistan* **91 D1** 25 10N 61 40 E
Dasht-i-Tahlab, *Pakistan* **91 C1** 28 40N 62 25 E
Daska, *Pakistan* **92 C6** 32 20N 74 20 E
Daşkäsän, *Azerbaijan* **61 K7** 40 25N 46 0 E
Dasmariñas, *Phil.* **80 D3** 14 20N 120 56 E
Dassa, *Benin* **113 D5** 7 46N 2 14 E
Dasuya, *India* **92 D6** 31 49N 75 38 E
Datça, *Turkey* **49 E9** 36 46N 27 40 E
Datia, *India* **93 G8** 25 39N 78 27 E
Datian, *China* **77 E11** 25 40N 117 50 E
Datong, *Anhui, China* **77 B11** 30 48N 117 44 E
Datong, *Shanxi, China* **74 D7** 40 6N 113 18 E
Dattakhel, *Pakistan* **92 C3** 32 54N 69 46 E
Dattapur = Dhamangaon, *India* **94 D4** 20 48N 78 9 E
Datteln, *Germany* **30 D3** 51 39N 7 21 E
Datu, Tanjung, *Indonesia* **85 B3** 2 5N 109 39 E
Datu Piang, *Phil.* **81 H5** 7 2N 124 30 E
Datuk, Tanjong = Datu, Tanjung, *Indonesia* **85 B3** 2 5N 109 39 E
Daua = Dawa →, *Africa* **107 G5** 4 11N 42 6 E
Daud Khel, *Pakistan* **92 C4** 32 53N 71 34 E
Daudnagar, *India* **93 G11** 25 2N 84 24 E
Daugava →, *Latvia* **15 H21** 57 4N 24 3 E
Daugavpils, *Latvia* **15 J22** 55 53N 26 32 E
Daulatabad, *India* **94 E2** 19 57N 75 15 E
Daule, *Ecuador* **168 D2** 1 56 S 79 56W
Daule →, *Ecuador* **168 D2** 2 10 S 79 52W
Daulpur, *India* **92 F7** 26 45N 77 59 E
Daun, *Germany* **31 E2** 50 11N 6 49 E
Daund, *India* **94 E2** 18 26N 74 40 E
Dauphin, *Canada* **143 C8** 51 9N 100 5W
Dauphin, *U.S.A.* **150 F8** 40 22N 76 56W
Dauphin L., *Canada* **143 C9** 51 20N 99 45W
Dauphiné, *France* **29 C9** 45 15N 5 25 E
Daura, *Borno, Nigeria* **113 C7** 11 31N 11 24 E
Daura, *Katsina, Nigeria* **113 C6** 13 2N 8 21 E
Dausa, *India* **92 F7** 26 52N 76 20 E
Däväçi, *Azerbaijan* **61 K9** 41 15N 48 57 E
Davangere, *India* **95 G2** 14 25N 75 55 E
Davao, *Phil.* **81 H5** 7 0N 125 40 E
Davao □, *Phil.* **81 H5** 7 0N 125 55 E
Davao del Sur □, *Phil.* **81 H5** 6 30N 125 25 E
Davao G., *Phil.* **81 H5** 6 30N 125 48 E
Davao Oriental □, *Phil.* **81 H6** 7 10N 126 30 E
Dāvar Panāh, *Iran* **97 E9** 27 25N 62 15 E
Davenport, *Calif., U.S.A.* **160 H4** 37 1N 122 12W
Davenport, *Fla., U.S.A.* **153 G8** 28 10N 81 36W
Davenport, *Iowa, U.S.A.* **156 C6** 41 32N 90 35W
Davenport, *Wash., U.S.A.* **158 C4** 47 39N 118 9W
Davenport Ra., *Australia* **126 C1** 20 28 S 134 0 E
Daventry, *U.K.* **21 E6** 52 16N 1 10W
David, *Panama* **164 E3** 8 30N 82 30W
David City, *U.S.A.* **154 E6** 41 15N 97 8W
David Gorodok = Davyd Haradok, *Belarus* **59 F4** 52 4N 27 8 E
Davidson, *Canada* **143 C7** 51 16N 105 59W
Davis, *U.S.A.* **160 G5** 38 33N 121 44W
Davis Dam, *U.S.A.* **161 K12** 35 11N 114 34W
Davis Inlet, *Canada* **141 A7** 55 50N 60 59W
Davis Mts., *U.S.A.* **155 K2** 30 50N 103 55W
Davis Sea, *Antarctica* **7 C7** 66 0 S 92 0 E
Davis Str., *N. Amer.* **139 B14** 65 0N 58 0W
Davisboro, *U.S.A.* **152 C7** 32 59N 82 36W
Davison, *U.S.A.* **157 A13** 43 2N 83 31W
Davlekanovo, *Russia* **64 D5** 54 13N 55 3 E
Davo →, *Ivory C.* **112 D3** 5 0N 6 10W
Davos, *Switz.* **33 C9** 46 48N 9 49 E
Davutlar, *Turkey* **49 D9** 37 43N 27 17 E
Davy L., *Canada* **143 B7** 58 53N 108 18W
Davyd Haradok, *Belarus* **59 F4** 52 4N 27 8 E
Dawa →, *Africa* **107 G5** 4 11N 42 6 E
Dawaki, *Bauchi, Nigeria* **113 D6** 9 25N 9 33 E
Dawaki, *Kano, Nigeria* **113 C6** 12 5N 8 23 E
Dawei, *Burma* **86 E2** 14 2N 98 12 E
Dawes Ra., *Australia* **126 C5** 24 40 S 150 40 E
Dawlish, *U.K.* **21 G4** 50 35N 3 28W
Dawna Ra., *Burma* **86 D2** 16 30N 98 30 E
Dawnyein, *Burma* **90 G5** 15 54N 95 36 E
Dawqah, *Si. Arabia* **98 C3** 19 36N 40 54 E
Dawros Hd., *Ireland* **23 B3** 54 50N 8 33W
Dawson, *Canada* **138 B6** 64 10N 139 30W
Dawson, *U.S.A.* **152 D5** 31 46N 84 27W
Dawson, I., *Chile* **176 D2** 53 50 S 70 50W
Dawson B., *Canada* **143 C8** 52 53N 100 49W
Dawson Creek, *Canada* **142 B4** 55 45N 120 15W
Dawson Inlet, *Canada* **143 A10** 61 50N 93 25W
Dawson Ra., *Australia* **126 C4** 24 30 S 149 48 E
Dawu, *Hubei, China* **77 B9** 31 34N 114 7 E
Dawu, *Sichuan, China* **76 B3** 30 55N 101 10 E
Dawwah, *Oman* **99 B7** 20 33N 58 48 E
Dawwara, Ras id-, *Malta* **38 F7** 35 52N 14 21 E
Dax, *France* **28 E2** 43 44N 1 3W
Daxian, *China* **76 B6** 31 15N 107 23 E
Daxin, *China* **76 F6** 22 50N 107 11 E
Daxindian, *China* **75 F11** 37 30N 120 50 E
Daxinggou, *China* **75 C15** 43 25N 129 40 E
Daxue Shan, *Sichuan, China* **76 B3** 30 30N 101 30 E
Daxue Shan, *Yunnan, China* **76 F2** 23 42N 99 48 E
Day, *U.S.A.* **152 E6** 30 12N 83 17W
Daya el Khadra, *Mauritania* **110 C3** 25 14N 6 2W
Dayao, *China* **76 E3** 25 43N 101 20 E
Daye, *China* **77 B10** 30 6N 114 58 E
Dayet en Naharat, *Mali* **112 B4** 17 39N 3 10W
Dayi, *China* **76 B4** 30 41N 103 29 E
Daylesford, *Australia* **128 D6** 37 21 S 144 9 E
Dayong, *China* **77 C8** 29 11N 110 30 E
Dayr az Zawr, *Syria* **101 E9** 35 20N 40 5 E
Daysland, *Canada* **142 C6** 52 50N 112 20W
Dayton, *Iowa, U.S.A.* **156 B2** 42 14N 94 4W
Dayton, *Ky., U.S.A.* **157 E12** 39 47N 84 28W
Dayton, *Nev., U.S.A.* **160 F7** 39 14N 119 36W
Dayton, *Ohio, U.S.A.* **158 F3** 39 45N 84 12W
Dayton, *Pa., U.S.A.* **150 F5** 40 53N 79 15W
Dayton, *Tenn., U.S.A.* **149 H3** 35 30N 85 1W
Dayton, *Wash., U.S.A.* **158 C4** 46 19N 117 59W
Dayton, *Wyo., U.S.A.* **158 D10** 44 53N 107 16W
Daytona Beach, *U.S.A.* **149 L5** 29 13N 81 1W
Dayu, *China* **77 E10** 25 24N 114 22 E
Dayville, *U.S.A.* **158 D4** 44 28N 119 32W
Dazaifu, *Japan* **72 D2** 33 32N 130 32 E
Dazhu, *China* **76 B6** 30 41N 107 15 E
Dazkırı, *Turkey* **49 D11** 37 57N 29 52 E
Dazu, *China* **76 C5** 29 40N 105 42 E
De Aar, *S. Africa* **116 E3** 30 39 S 24 0 E
De Armanville, *U.S.A.* **152 B4** 33 38N 85 45W
De Bary, *U.S.A.* **153 G8** 28 54N 81 18W
De Forest, *U.S.A.* **156 A7** 43 15N 89 20W
De Funiak Springs, *U.S.A.* **152 E3** 30 43N 86 7W
De Grey →, *Australia* **124 D2** 20 12 S 119 13 E
De Haan, *Belgium* **24 C3** 51 16N 3 2 E
De Hoop Nature Reserve, *S. Africa* **116 E3** 34 30 S 20 28 E
De Jongs, Tg., *Indonesia* **83 C5** 6 55 S 138 30 E
De Kalb, *U.S.A.* **154 E10** 41 56N 88 46W
De Land, *U.S.A.* **149 L5** 29 2N 81 18W
De Leon, *U.S.A.* **155 J5** 32 7N 98 32W
De Leon Springs, *U.S.A.* **153 F8** 29 7N 81 21W
De Long Mts., *U.S.A.* **144 B7** 68 30N 163 0W
De Panne, *Belgium* **24 C2** 51 6N 2 34 E
De Pere, *U.S.A.* **148 C1** 44 27N 88 4W
De Queen, *U.S.A.* **155 H7** 34 2N 94 21W
De Quincy, *U.S.A.* **155 K8** 30 27N 93 26W
De Ridder, *U.S.A.* **155 K8** 30 51N 93 17W
De Smet, *U.S.A.* **154 C6** 44 23N 97 33W
De Soto, *U.S.A.* **156 F6** 38 8N 90 34W
De Soto City, *U.S.A.* **153 H8** 27 27N 81 24W
De Tour Village, *U.S.A.* **148 C4** 46 0N 83 56W
De Witt, *Ark., U.S.A.* **155 H9** 34 18N 91 20W
De Witt, *Iowa, U.S.A.* **156 C6** 41 49N 90 33W
De Witt, *Mich., U.S.A.* **157 B12** 42 51N 84 34W
Dead L., *U.S.A.* **152 E4** 30 10N 85 10W
Dead Sea, *Asia* **103 D4** 31 30N 35 30 E
Deadhorse, *U.S.A.* **144 A10** 70 11N 148 27W
Deadman B., *U.S.A.* **153 F6** 29 30N 83 30W
Deadwood, *U.S.A.* **154 C3** 44 23N 103 44W
Deadwood L., *Canada* **142 B3** 59 10N 128 30W
Deal, *U.K.* **21 F9** 51 13N 1 25 E
Deal I., *Australia* **127 F4** 39 30 S 147 20 E
Dealesville, *S. Africa* **116 D4** 28 41 S 25 44 E
De'an, *China* **77 C10** 29 21N 115 46 E
Dean →, *Canada* **142 C3** 52 49N 126 58W
Dean, Forest of, *U.K.* **21 F5** 51 45N 2 33W
Dean Chan., *Canada* **142 C3** 52 30N 127 15W
Deán Funes, *Argentina* **174 C3** 30 20 S 64 20W
Dearborn, *Mich., U.S.A.* **157 B13** 42 19N 83 11W
Dearborn, *Mo., U.S.A.* **156 E2** 39 32N 94 46W
Dease →, *Canada* **142 B3** 59 56N 128 32W
Dease L., *Canada* **142 B2** 58 40N 130 5W
Dease Lake, *Canada* **142 B2** 58 25N 130 6W
Death Valley, *U.S.A.* **161 J10** 36 15N 116 50W
Death Valley Junction, *U.S.A.* **161 J10** 36 20N 116 25W
Death Valley Nat. Park, *U.S.A.* **161 J10** 36 45N 117 15W
Deauville, *France* **26 C7** 49 23N 0 2 E
Deba, *Spain* **40 B2** 43 18N 2 21W
Deba Habe, *Nigeria* **113 C7** 10 14N 11 20 E
Debak, *Malaysia* **85 B4** 1 34N 111 25 E
Debaltsevo, *Ukraine* **59 H10** 48 22N 38 26 E
Debao, *China* **76 F6** 23 21N 106 46 E
Debar, *Macedonia* **50 E4** 41 31N 20 30 E
Debark, *Ethiopia* **107 E4** 13 1N 37 48 E
Debden, *Canada* **143 C7** 53 30N 106 50W
Debdou, *Morocco* **111 B4** 33 59N 3 0W
Dębica, *Poland* **55 H8** 50 2N 21 25 E
Dęblin, *Poland* **55 G8** 51 34N 21 50 E
Dębno, *Poland* **55 F1** 52 44N 14 41 E
Débo, L., *Mali* **112 B4** 15 14N 4 15W
Debolt, *Canada* **142 B5** 55 12N 118 1W
Deborah East, L., *Australia* **125 F2** 30 45 S 119 0 E
Deborah West, L., *Australia* **125 F2** 30 45 S 118 50 E
Deboyne Is., *Papua N. G.* **132 F7** 10 43 S 152 22 E
Debrc, *Serbia, Yug.* **50 B3** 44 38N 19 53 E
Debre Birhan, *Ethiopia* **107 F4** 9 41N 39 31 E
Debre Markos, *Ethiopia* **107 E4** 10 20N 37 40 E
Debre May, *Ethiopia* **107 E4** 11 20N 37 25 E
Debre Sina, *Ethiopia* **107 F4** 9 51N 39 50 E
Debre Tabor, *Ethiopia* **107 E4** 11 50N 38 26 E
Debre Zevit, *Ethiopia* **107 F4** 8 50N 39 0 E
Debre Zeyit, *Ethiopia* **107 E4** 11 48N 38 30 E
Debrecen, *Hungary* **52 C6** 47 33N 21 42 E
Debrzno, *Poland* **54 E4** 53 31N 17 14 E
Dečani, *Kosovo, Yug.* **50 D4** 42 30N 20 18 E
Decatur, *Ala., U.S.A.* **149 H2** 34 36N 86 59W
Decatur, *Ga., U.S.A.* **152 B5** 33 47N 84 18W
Decatur, *Ill., U.S.A.* **156 E8** 39 51N 88 57W
Decatur, *Ind., U.S.A.* **157 D12** 40 50N 84 56W
Decatur, *Mich., U.S.A.* **157 B11** 42 7N 85 58W
Decatur, *Tex., U.S.A.* **155 J6** 33 14N 97 35W
Decazeville, *France* **28 D6** 44 34N 2 15 E
Deccan, *India* **94 F4** 18 0N 79 0 E
Deception, Mt., *Australia* **128 A3** 30 42 S 138 16 E
Deception B., *Papua N. G.* **132 D3** 7 45 S 144 40 E
Deception Bay, *Australia* **127 D5** 27 10 S 153 5 E
Deception L., *Canada* **143 B8** 56 33N 104 13W
Dechang, *China* **76 D4** 27 25N 102 11 E
Dechhu, *India* **92 F5** 26 46N 72 20 E
Děčín, *Czech Rep.* **34 A7** 50 47N 14 12 E
Decize, *France* **27 F10** 46 50N 3 28 E
Deckerville, *U.S.A.* **150 C2** 43 32N 82 44W
Decollatura, *Italy* **47 C9** 39 3N 16 21 E
Decorah, *U.S.A.* **154 D9** 43 18N 91 48W
Deda, *Romania* **53 D9** 46 56N 24 50 E
Dedaye, *Burma* **90 G5** 16 24N 95 53 E
Dedéagach = Alexandroúpolis, *Greece* **51 F9** 40 50N 25 54 E
Deder, *Ethiopia* **107 F5** 9 19N 41 27 E
Dedham, *U.S.A.* **151 D13** 42 15N 71 10W
Dédougou, *Burkina Faso* **112 C4** 12 30N 3 25W
Dedovichi, *Russia* **58 D5** 57 32N 29 56 E
Dedza, *Malawi* **119 E3** 14 20 S 34 20 E
Dee →, *Aberds., U.K.* **22 D6** 57 9N 2 5W
Dee →, *Dumf. & Gall., U.K.* **22 G4** 54 51N 4 3W
Dee →, *Wales, U.K.* **20 D4** 53 22N 3 17W
Deep B., *Canada* **142 A5** 61 15N 116 35W
Deep Lead, *Australia* **128 D5** 37 0 S 142 43 E
Deepwater, *Australia* **127 D5** 29 25 S 151 51 E
Deepwater, *U.S.A.* **156 F3** 38 16N 93 47W
Deer →, *Canada* **143 B10** 58 23N 94 13W
Deer I., *U.S.A.* **144 J7** 54 55N 162 18W
Deer L., *Canada* **143 C10** 52 40N 94 20W
Deer Lake, *Nfld., Canada* **141 C8** 49 11N 57 27W
Deer Lake, *Ont., Canada* **143 C10** 52 36N 94 20W
Deer Lodge, *U.S.A.* **158 C7** 46 24N 112 44W
Deer Park, *Fla., U.S.A.* **153 G9** 28 6N 80 54W
Deer Park, *Ohio, U.S.A.* **157 E12** 39 13N 84 23W
Deer Park, *Wash., U.S.A.* **158 C5** 47 57N 117 28W
Deer River, *U.S.A.* **154 B8** 47 20N 93 48W
Deeragun, *Australia* **126 B4** 19 16 S 146 33 E
Deerdepoort, *S. Africa* **116 C4** 24 37 S 26 27 E
Deerfield, *Ill., U.S.A.* **157 B9** 42 10N 87 51W
Deerfield, *Mo., U.S.A.* **156 G2** 37 50N 94 30W
Deerfield Beach, *U.S.A.* **153 J9** 26 19N 80 6W
Deering, *U.S.A.* **144 C7** 66 4N 162 42W
Deferiet, *U.S.A.* **151 B9** 44 2N 75 41W
Defiance, *U.S.A.* **157 C12** 41 17N 84 22W
Degana, *India* **92 F6** 26 50N 74 20 E
Dêgê, *China* **76 B2** 31 44N 98 39 E
Degebe →, *Portugal* **43 G3** 38 13N 7 29W
Degeberga, *Sweden* **17 J8** 55 51N 14 5 E
Degeh Bur, *Ethiopia* **120 C2** 8 11N 43 31 E
Dégelis, *Canada* **141 C6** 47 30N 68 35W
Degema, *Nigeria* **113 E6** 4 50N 6 48 E
Degerfors, *Sweden* **16 E8** 59 15N 14 27 E
Degerhamn, *Sweden* **17 H10** 56 20N 16 24 E
Degersheim, *Switz.* **33 B8** 47 23N 9 12 E
Deggendorf, *Germany* **31 G8** 48 50N 12 57 E
Degh →, *Pakistan* **92 D5** 31 3N 73 21 E
Değirmendere, *Turkey* **51 F13** 40 42N 29 47 E
Deh Bīd, *Iran* **97 D7** 30 39N 53 11 E
Deh-e Shīr, *Iran* **97 D7** 31 29N 53 45 E
Deh Nugaled = Nugaaleed, Dooxo, *Somali Rep.* **120 C3** 8 35N 48 35 E
Dehaj, *Iran* **97 D7** 30 42N 54 53 E
Dehak, *Iran* **91 D1** 27 11N 62 37 E
Dehane, *Cameroon* **114 B2** 3 30N 10 5 E
Dehdez, *Iran* **97 D6** 31 43N 50 17 E
Dehej, *India* **92 J5** 21 44N 72 40 E
Dehestān, *Iran* **97 D7** 28 30N 55 35 E
Dehgolān, *Iran* **101 E12** 35 17N 47 25 E
Dehibat, *Tunisia* **108 B2** 32 0N 10 47 E
Dehiwala, *Sri Lanka* **95 L4** 6 50N 79 51 E
Dehlorān, *Iran* **101 F12** 32 41N 47 16 E
Dehnow-e Kühestān, *Iran* **97 E8** 27 58N 58 32 E
Dehra Dun, *India* **92 D8** 30 20N 78 4 E
Dehri, *India* **93 G11** 24 50N 84 15 E
Dehua, *China* **77 E12** 25 26N 118 14 E
Dehui, *China* **75 B13** 44 30N 125 40 E
Deim Zubeir, *Sudan* **107 F2** 7 49N 26 16 E
Deinze, *Belgium* **24 D3** 50 59N 3 32 E
Dej, *Romania* **53 C8** 47 10N 23 52 E
Deje, *Sweden* **16 E7** 59 35N 13 29 E
Dejiang, *China* **76 C7** 28 18N 108 7 E
Deka →, *Zimbabwe* **116 B4** 18 4 S 26 42 E
Dekemhare, *Eritrea* **107 D4** 15 6N 39 0 E
Dekese, *Dem. Rep. of the Congo* **114 C4** 3 24 S 21 24 E
Dekhkanabad, *Uzbekistan* **65 D3** 38 21N 66 30 E
Dekoa, *C.A.R.* **114 A3** 6 19N 19 4 E
Del Carmen, *Phil.* **81 G6** 9 50N 126 0 E
Del Mar, *U.S.A.* **161 N9** 32 58N 117 16W
Del Norte, *U.S.A.* **159 H10** 37 41N 106 21W
Del Rio, *U.S.A.* **155 L4** 29 22N 100 54W
Delai, *Sudan* **106 D4** 17 21N 36 6 E
Delambre I., *Australia* **124 D2** 20 26 S 117 5 E
Delami, *Sudan* **107 E3** 11 38N 30 23 E
Delano, *U.S.A.* **161 K7** 35 46N 119 15W
Delano Peak, *U.S.A.* **159 G7** 38 22N 112 22W
Delareyville, *S. Africa* **116 D4** 26 41 S 25 26 E
Delaronde L., *Canada* **143 C7** 54 3N 107 3W
Delavan, *Ill., U.S.A.* **156 D7** 40 22N 89 33W
Delavan, *Wis., U.S.A.* **154 D10** 42 38N 88 39W
Delaware, *U.S.A.* **157 D13** 40 18N 83 4W
Delaware □, *U.S.A.* **148 F8** 39 0N 75 20W
Delaware →, *U.S.A.* **151 G9** 39 15N 75 20W
Delaware B., *U.S.A.* **148 F8** 39 0N 75 10W
Delay →, *Canada* **141 A5** 56 56N 71 28W
Delbrück, *Germany* **30 D4** 51 46N 8 34 E
Delčevo, *Macedonia* **50 E6** 41 58N 22 46 E
Delébio, *Italy* **44 B6** 46 8N 9 27 E
Delegate, *Australia* **129 D8** 37 4 S 148 56 E
Delémont, *Switz.* **32 B4** 47 22N 7 20 E
Delevan, *U.S.A.* **150 D6** 42 29N 78 29W
Delft, *Neths.* **24 B4** 52 1N 4 22 E
Delft I., *Sri Lanka* **95 K4** 9 30N 79 40 E
Delfzijl, *Neths.* **24 A6** 53 20N 6 55 E
Delgada, Punta, *Chile* **176 D3** 52 28 S 69 32W
Delgado, C., *Mozam.* **119 E5** 10 45 S 40 40 E
Delgerhet, *Mongolia* **74 B6** 45 50N 110 30 E
Delgo, *Sudan* **106 C3** 20 6N 30 40 E
Delhi, *Canada* **150 D4** 42 51N 80 30W
Delhi, *India* **92 E7** 28 38N 77 17 E
Delhi, *La., U.S.A.* **155 J9** 32 28N 91 30W
Delhi, *N.Y., U.S.A.* **151 D10** 42 17N 74 55W
Deli Jovan, *Serbia, Yug.* **50 B6** 44 13N 22 9 E
Delia, *Canada* **142 C6** 51 38N 112 23W
Delice, *Turkey* **100 C6** 39 54N 34 2 E
Delicias, *Mexico* **162 B3** 28 10N 105 30W
Delījān, *Iran* **97 C6** 33 59N 50 40 E
Delimara Point, *Malta* **38 F8** 35 49N 14 34 E
Déline, *Canada* **138 B7** 65 10N 123 30W
Delisle, *Canada* **143 C7** 51 55N 107 8W
Delitzsch, *Germany* **30 D8** 51 31N 12 20 E
Dell City, *U.S.A.* **159 L11** 31 56N 105 12W
Dell Rapids, *U.S.A.* **154 D6** 43 50N 96 43W
Delle, *France* **27 E14** 47 30N 7 2 E
Dellys, *Algeria* **111 A5** 36 57N 3 57 E
Delmar, *Iowa, U.S.A.* **156 C6** 42 0N 90 37W
Delmar, *N.Y., U.S.A.* **151 D11** 42 37N 73 47W
Delmenhorst, *Germany* **30 B4** 53 3N 8 37 E
Delmiro Gouveia, *Brazil* **170 C4** 9 24 S 38 6W
Delnice, *Croatia* **45 C11** 45 23N 14 50 E
Delonga, Ostrova, *Russia* **67 B15** 76 40N 149 20 E
Deloraine, *Australia* **127 G4** 41 30 S 146 40 E
Deloraine, *Canada* **143 D8** 49 15N 100 29W
Delphi, *Greece* **48 C4** 38 28N 22 30 E
Delphi, *U.S.A.* **157 D10** 40 36N 86 41W
Delphos, *U.S.A.* **157 D12** 40 51N 84 21W
Delportshoop, *S. Africa* **116 D3** 28 22 S 24 20 E
Delray Beach, *U.S.A.* **149 M5** 26 28N 80 4W
Delsbo, *Sweden* **16 C10** 61 48N 16 32 E
Delta, *Ala., U.S.A.* **152 B4** 33 26N 85 42W
Delta, *Colo., U.S.A.* **159 G9** 38 44N 108 4W
Delta, *Utah, U.S.A.* **158 G7** 39 21N 112 35W
Delta □, *Nigeria* **113 D6** 5 30N 6 0 E
Delta Amacuro □, *Venezuela* **169 B5** 8 30N 61 30W
Delta du Saloum, Parc Nat. du, *Senegal* **112 C1** 13 42N 16 43W
Delta Junction, *U.S.A.* **144 D11** 64 2N 145 44W
Deltona, *U.S.A.* **153 G8** 28 54N 81 16W
Delungra, *Australia* **127 D5** 29 39 S 150 51 E
Delvada, *India* **92 J4** 20 46N 71 2 E
Delvinákion, *Greece* **48 B2** 39 57N 20 32 E
Delvinë, *Albania* **50 G4** 39 59N 20 6 E
Demagiri, *India* **90 D4** 22 55N 92 28 E
Demak, *Indonesia* **85 D4** 6 53 S 110 38 E
Demanda, Sierra de la, *Spain* **40 C2** 42 15N 3 0W
Demavand = Damāvand, *Iran* **97 C7** 35 47N 52 0 E
Demba, *Dem. Rep. of the Congo* **115 D4** 5 28 S 22 15 E
Demba Chio, *Angola* **115 D2** 9 41 S 13 41 E
Dembecha, *Ethiopia* **107 E4** 10 32N 37 30 E
Dembi, *Ethiopia* **107 F4** 8 5N 36 25 E
Dembia, *Dem. Rep. of the Congo* **118 B2** 3 33N 25 48 E
Dembidolo, *Ethiopia* **107 F3** 8 34N 34 50 E
Demchok, *India* **93 C8** 32 42N 79 29 E
Demer →, *Belgium* **24 D4** 50 57N 4 42 E
Demetrias, *Greece* **48 B5** 39 22N 23 1 E
Demidov, *Russia* **58 E6** 55 16N 31 30 E
Deming, *N. Mex., U.S.A.* **159 K10** 32 16N 107 46W
Deming, *Wash., U.S.A.* **160 B4** 48 50N 122 13W
Demini →, *Brazil* **169 D5** 0 46 S 62 56W
Demirci, *Turkey* **49 B10** 39 2N 28 38 E
Demirköprü Barajı, *Turkey* **49 C10** 38 42N 28 25 E
Demirköy, *Turkey* **51 E11** 41 49N 27 45 E
Demmin, *Germany* **30 B9** 53 54N 13 2 E
Demnate, *Morocco* **110 B3** 31 44N 6 59W
Democracia, *Brazil* **173 B5** 5 48 S 61 26W
Demonte, *Italy* **44 D4** 44 19N 7 17 E
Demopolis, *U.S.A.* **149 J2** 32 31N 87 50W
Dempo, *Indonesia* **84 C2** 4 2 S 103 15 E
Demta, *Indonesia* **83 B6** 2 20 S 140 8 E
Demyansk, *Russia* **58 D7** 57 40N 32 27 E
Den Burg, *Neths.* **24 A4** 53 3N 4 47 E
Den Chai, *Thailand* **86 D3** 17 59N 100 4 E
Den Haag = 's-Gravenhage, *Neths.* **24 B4** 52 7N 4 17 E
Den Helder, *Neths.* **24 B4** 52 57N 4 45 E
Den Oever, *Neths.* **24 B5** 52 56N 5 2 E
Denain, *France* **27 B10** 50 20N 3 22 E
Denair, *U.S.A.* **160 H6** 37 32N 120 48W
Denali Nat. Park and Preserve, *U.S.A.* **144 E10** 63 30N 150 0W
Denau, *Uzbekistan* **66 F7** 38 16N 67 54 E
Denbigh, *Canada* **150 A7** 45 8N 77 15W
Denbigh, *U.K.* **20 D4** 53 12N 3 25W
Denbigh, C., *U.S.A.* **144 D7** 64 23N 161 32W
Denbighshire □, *U.K.* **20 D4** 53 8N 3 22W
Dendang, *Indonesia* **85 C3** 3 7 S 107 56 E
Dendé = Ndindi, *Gabon* **114 C2** 3 46 S 11 9 E
Dendermonde, *Belgium* **24 C4** 51 2N 4 5 E
Deneba, *Ethiopia* **107 F4** 9 47N 39 10 E
Denezhkin Kamen, Gora, *Russia* **64 A7** 60 25N 59 32 E
Deng Deng, *Cameroon* **114 A2** 5 12N 13 31 E
Dengchuan, *China* **76 E3** 25 59N 100 3 E
Denge, *Nigeria* **113 C6** 12 52N 5 21 E
Dengfeng, *China* **74 G7** 34 25N 113 2 E
Dengi, *Nigeria* **113 D6** 9 25N 9 55 E
Dengkou, *China* **74 D4** 40 18N 106 55 E
Dengzhou, *China* **77 A9** 32 34N 112 4 E
Denham, *Australia* **125 E1** 25 56 S 113 31 E
Denham, Mt., *Jamaica* **164 a** 18 13N 77 32W
Denham Ra., *Australia* **126 C4** 21 55 S 147 46 E
Denham Sd., *Australia* **125 E1** 25 45 S 113 15 E
Denholm, *Canada* **143 C7** 52 39N 108 1W
Denia, *Spain* **41 G5** 38 49N 0 8 E
Denial B., *Australia* **127 E1** 32 14 S 133 32 E
Deniliquin, *Australia* **129 C6** 35 30 S 144 58 E
Denis, *Gabon* **114 B1** 0 19N 9 22 E
Denison, *Iowa, U.S.A.* **154 E7** 42 1N 95 21W
Denison, *Tex., U.S.A.* **155 J6** 33 45N 96 33W
Denison Plains, *Australia* **124 C4** 18 35 S 128 0 E
Deniyaya, *Sri Lanka* **95 L5** 6 21N 80 33 E
Denizli, *Turkey* **49 D11** 37 42N 29 2 E
Denizli □, *Turkey* **49 D11** 37 45N 29 5 E
Denman, *Australia* **129 B9** 32 24 S 150 42 E
Denman Glacier, *Antarctica* **7 C7** 66 45 S 99 25 E
Denmark, *Australia* **125 F2** 34 59 S 117 25 E
Denmark, *U.S.A.* **152 B8** 33 19N 81 9W
Denmark ■, *Europe* **17 J3** 55 45N 10 0 E
Denmark Str., *Atl. Oc.* **6 C6** 66 0N 30 0W
Dennery, *St. Lucia* **165 f** 13 55N 60 54W
Dennison, *U.S.A.* **150 F3** 40 24N 81 19W
Denny, *U.K.* **22 E5** 56 1N 3 55W

East Riding of Yorkshire □, *U.K.* **20 D7** 53 55N 0 30W
East Rochester, *U.S.A.* **150 C7** 43 7N 77 29W
East St. Louis, *U.S.A.* **156 F6** 38 37N 90 9W
East Schelde = Oosterschelde →, *Neths.* **24 C4** 51 33N 4 0 E
East Sea = Japan, Sea of, *Asia* **70 E7** 40 0N 135 0 E
East Sepik □, *Papua N. G.* **132 C2** 4 0 S 143 45 E
East Siberian Sea, *Russia* **67 B17** 73 0N 160 0 E
East Stroudsburg, *U.S.A.* **151 E9** 41 1N 75 11W
East Sussex □, *U.K.* **21 G8** 50 56N 0 19 E
East Tawas, *U.S.A.* **148 C4** 44 17N 83 29W
East Timor ■, *Asia* **82 C3** 8 50 S 126 0 E
East Tohopekaliga, Lake, *U.S.A.* **153 G8** 28 18N 81 15W
East Toorale, *Australia* **127 E4** 30 27 S 145 28 E
East Troy, *U.S.A.* **157 B8** 42 47N 88 24W
East Walker →, *U.S.A.* **160 G7** 38 52N 119 10W
East Windsor, *U.S.A.* **151 F10** 40 17N 74 34W
Eastbourne, *N.Z.* **130 H3** 41 19 S 174 55 E
Eastbourne, *U.K.* **21 G8** 50 46N 0 18 E
Eastend, *Canada* **143 D7** 49 32N 108 50W
Easter I. = Pascua, I. de, *Chile* **172 b** 27 7 S 109 23W
Eastern □, *Ghana* **113 D4** 6 30N 0 30W
Eastern □, *Kenya* **118 C4** 0 0 38 30 E
Eastern Cape □, *S. Africa* **116 E4** 32 0 S 26 0 E
Eastern Cr. →, *Australia* **126 C3** 20 40 S 141 35 E
Eastern Ghats, *India* **95 H4** 14 0N 78 50 E
Eastern Group = Lau Group, *Fiji* **133 A3** 17 0 S 178 30W
Eastern Group, *Australia* **125 F3** 33 30 S 124 30 E
Eastern Highlands □, *Papua N. G.* **132 D3** 6 30 S 145 35 E
Eastern Province □, *S. Leone* **112 D2** 8 15N 11 0W
Eastern Samar □, *Phil.* **81 F5** 11 40N 125 40 E
Eastern Transvaal = Mpumalanga □, *S. Africa* **117 B5** 26 0 S 30 0 E
Easterville, *Canada* **143 C9** 53 8N 99 49W
Easthampton, *U.S.A.* **151 D12** 42 16N 72 40W
Eastlake, *U.S.A.* **150 E3** 41 40N 81 26W
Eastland, *U.S.A.* **155 J5** 32 24N 98 49W
Eastleigh, *U.K.* **21 G6** 50 58N 1 21W
Eastmain, *Canada* **140 B4** 52 10N 78 30W
Eastmain →, *Canada* **140 B4** 52 27N 78 26W
Eastman, *Canada* **151 A12** 45 18N 72 19W
Eastman, *Ga., U.S.A.* **152 C6** 32 12N 83 11W
Eastman, *Wis., U.S.A.* **156 A5** 43 10N 91 1W
Easton, *Md., U.S.A.* **148 F7** 38 47N 76 5W
Easton, *Pa., U.S.A.* **151 F9** 40 41N 75 13W
Easton, *Wash., U.S.A.* **160 C5** 47 14N 121 11W
Eastover, *U.S.A.* **152 B9** 33 52N 80 41W
Eastpoint, *U.S.A.* **152 F5** 29 44N 84 53W
Eastpointe, *U.S.A.* **150 D2** 42 27N 82 56W
Eastport, *U.S.A.* **149 C12** 44 56N 67 0W
Eastsound, *U.S.A.* **160 B4** 48 42N 122 55W
Eaton, *Colo., U.S.A.* **154 E2** 40 32N 104 42W
Eaton, *Ohio, U.S.A.* **157 E12** 39 45N 84 38W
Eaton Rapids, *U.S.A.* **157 B12** 42 31N 84 39W
Eatonia, *Canada* **143 C7** 51 13N 109 25W
Eatonton, *U.S.A.* **152 B6** 33 20N 83 23W
Eatontown, *U.S.A.* **151 F10** 40 19N 74 4W
Eatonville, *U.S.A.* **160 D4** 46 52N 122 16W
Eau Claire, *Fr. Guiana* **169 C7** 3 30N 53 40W
Eau Claire, *U.S.A.* **154 C9** 44 49N 91 30W
Eau Claire, L. à l', *Canada* **140 A5** 56 10N 74 25W
Eauze, *France* **28 E4** 43 53N 0 7 E
Eban, *Nigeria* **113 D5** 9 40N 4 50 E
Ebanga, *Angola* **115 E2** 12 45 S 14 45 E
Ebangalakata, *Dem. Rep. of the Congo* **114 C4** 0 29 S 21 29 E
Ebbw Vale, *U.K.* **21 F4** 51 46N 3 12W
Ebebiyín, *Eq. Guin.* **114 B2** 2 9N 11 20 E
Ebeggui, *Algeria* **111 C6** 26 2N 6 0 E
Ebel, *Gabon* **114 B2** 0 7N 11 5 E
Ebeltoft, *Denmark* **17 H4** 56 12N 10 41 E
Ebeltoft Vig, *Denmark* **17 H4** 56 10N 10 35 E
Ebensburg, *U.S.A.* **150 F6** 40 29N 78 44W
Ebensee, *Austria* **34 D6** 47 48N 13 46 E
Eber Gölü, *Turkey* **100 C4** 38 38N 31 11 E
Eberbach, *Germany* **31 F4** 49 28N 8 59 E
Eberswalde-Finow, *Germany* **30 C9** 52 50N 13 49 E
Ebetsu, *Japan* **70 C10** 43 7N 141 34 E
Ebian, *China* **76 C4** 29 11N 103 13 E
Ebikon, *Switz.* **33 B6** 47 5N 8 21 E
Ebingen, *Germany* **31 G5** 48 13N 9 1 E
Ebino, *Japan* **72 E2** 32 2N 130 48 E
Ebnat-Kappel, *Switz.* **33 B8** 47 16N 9 7 E
Ebo, *Angola* **115 E2** 11 40 S 14 40 E
Ebola →, *Dem. Rep. of the Congo* **114 B4** 3 20N 20 57 E
Éboli, *Italy* **47 B8** 40 39N 15 2 E
Ebolowa, *Cameroon* **113 E7** 2 55N 11 10 E
Ebonyi □, *Nigeria* **113 D6** 6 20N 8 0 E
Eboy, *Dem. Rep. of the Congo* **114 B4** 2 50N 23 11 E
Ebrach, *Germany* **31 F6** 49 51N 10 29 E
Ébrié, Lagune, *Ivory C.* **112 D4** 5 12N 4 26W
Ebro →, *Spain* **40 E5** 40 43N 0 54 E
Ebro, Embalse del, *Spain* **42 C7** 43 0N 3 58W
Ebstorf, *Germany* **30 B6** 53 2N 10 24 E
Eceabat, *Turkey* **51 F10** 40 11N 26 21 E
Ech Chéliff, *Algeria* **111 A5** 36 10N 1 20 E
Echallens, *Switz.* **32 C3** 46 38N 6 38 E
Echechonnee →, *U.S.A.* **152 C6** 32 39N 83 36W
Echigo-Sammyaku, *Japan* **71 F9** 36 50N 139 50 E
Échirolles, *France* **29 C9** 45 8N 5 44 E
Echizen-Misaki, *Japan* **73 B7** 35 59N 135 57 E
Echmiadzin = Yejmiadzin, *Armenia* **61 K7** 40 12N 44 19 E
Echo, *U.S.A.* **152 D4** 31 29N 85 28W
Echo Bay, *N.W.T., Canada* **138 B8** 66 5N 117 55W
Echo Bay, *Ont., Canada* **140 C3** 46 29N 84 4W
Echoing →, *Canada* **140 B1** 55 51N 92 5W
Echternach, *Lux.* **24 E6** 49 49N 6 25 E
Echuca, *Australia* **129 D6** 36 10 S 144 45 E
Ecija, *Spain* **43 H5** 37 30N 5 10W
Eckental, *Germany* **31 F7** 49 35N 11 12 E
Eckernförde, *Germany* **30 A5** 54 28N 9 50 E
Eclectic, *U.S.A.* **152 C3** 32 38N 86 2W
Eclipse Is., *Australia* **124 B4** 13 54 S 126 19 E
Eclipse Sd., *Canada* **139 A11** 72 38N 79 0W
Écommoy, *France* **26 E7** 47 50N 0 17 E
Ecoporanga, *Brazil* **171 E3** 18 23 S 40 50W
Écouché, *France* **26 D6** 48 42N 0 10W
Ecuador ■, *S. Amer.* **168 D2** 2 0 S 78 0W
Ecuador, Volcán, *Ecuador* **172 a** 1 1 S 91 32W
Écueillé, *France* **26 E8** 47 5N 1 21 E
Ed, *Sweden* **17 F5** 58 55N 11 55 E
Ed Dabbura, *Sudan* **106 D3** 17 40N 34 15 E
Ed Da'ein, *Sudan* **107 E2** 11 26N 26 9 E
Ed Dâmer, *Sudan* **106 D3** 17 27N 34 0 E
Ed Debba, *Sudan* **106 D3** 18 0N 30 51 E
Ed-Déffa, *Egypt* **106 A2** 30 40N 26 30 E
Ed Deim, *Sudan* **107 E2** 10 10N 28 20 E
Ed Dueim, *Sudan* **107 E3** 14 0N 32 10 E
Edam, *Canada* **143 C7** 53 11N 108 46W
Edam, *Neths.* **24 B5** 52 31N 5 3 E
Edane, *Sweden* **16 E6** 59 38N 12 49 E
Edapally, *India* **95 J4** 11 19N 78 3 E
Eday, *U.K.* **22 B6** 59 11N 2 47W
Edchera, *W. Sahara* **110 C2** 27 2N 13 4W
Edd, *Eritrea* **107 E5** 14 0N 41 38 E
Eddrachillis B., *U.K.* **22 C3** 58 17N 5 14W
Eddystone Pt., *Australia* **127 G4** 40 59 S 148 20 E
Eddyville, *U.S.A.* **156 C4** 41 9N 92 38W
Ede, *Neths.* **24 B5** 52 4N 5 40 E
Ede, *Nigeria* **113 D5** 7 45N 4 29 E
Édéa, *Cameroon* **113 E7** 3 51N 10 9 E
Edebäck, *Sweden* **16 D7** 60 4N 13 32 E
Edehon L., *Canada* **143 A9** 60 25N 97 15W
Edekel, Adrar, *Algeria* **111 D6** 23 56N 6 47 E
Edelény, *Hungary* **52 B5** 48 18N 20 44 E
Eden, *Australia* **129 D8** 37 3 S 149 55 E
Eden, *N.C., U.S.A.* **149 G6** 36 29N 79 53W
Eden, *N.Y., U.S.A.* **150 D6** 42 39N 78 55W
Eden, *Tex., U.S.A.* **155 K5** 31 13N 99 51W
Eden →, *U.K.* **20 C4** 54 57N 3 1W
Edenburg, *S. Africa* **116 D4** 29 43 S 25 58 E
Edendale, *N.Z.* **131 G3** 46 19 S 168 48 E
Edendale, *S. Africa* **117 D5** 29 39 S 30 18 E
Edenderry, *Ireland* **23 C4** 53 21N 7 4W
Edenhope, *Australia* **128 D4** 37 4 S 141 19 E
Edenton, *U.S.A.* **149 G7** 36 4N 76 39W
Edenville, *S. Africa* **117 D4** 27 37 S 27 34 E
Eder →, *Germany* **30 D5** 51 12N 9 28 E
Eder-Stausee, *Germany* **30 D4** 51 10N 8 57 E
Edewecht, *Germany* **30 B3** 53 8N 7 58 E
Edgar, *U.S.A.* **154 E6** 40 22N 97 58W
Edgartown, *U.S.A.* **151 E14** 41 23N 70 31W
Edge Hill, *U.K.* **21 E6** 52 8N 1 26W
Edgecumbe, *N.Z.* **130 D5** 37 59 S 176 47 E
Edgefield, *U.S.A.* **152 B8** 33 47N 81 56W
Edgeley, *U.S.A.* **154 B5** 46 22N 98 43W
Edgemont, *U.S.A.* **154 D3** 43 18N 103 50W
Edgeøya, *Svalbard* **6 B9** 77 45N 22 30 E
Edgerton, *Ohio, U.S.A.* **157 C12** 41 27N 84 45W
Edgerton, *Wis., U.S.A.* **156 B7** 42 50N 89 4W
Edgewater, *U.S.A.* **153 G9** 28 59N 80 54W
Edgewood, *U.S.A.* **157 F8** 38 55N 88 40W
Édhessa, *Greece* **50 F6** 40 48N 22 5 E
Edievale, *N.Z.* **131 F4** 45 49 S 169 22 E
Edina, *Liberia* **112 D2** 6 0N 10 10W
Edina, *U.S.A.* **156 D4** 40 10N 92 11W
Edinboro, *U.S.A.* **150 E4** 41 52N 80 8W
Edinburg, *Ill., U.S.A.* **156 E7** 39 39N 89 23W
Edinburg, *Ind., U.S.A.* **157 E11** 39 21N 85 58W
Edinburg, *Tex., U.S.A.* **155 M5** 26 18N 98 10W
Edinburgh, *U.K.* **22 F5** 55 57N 3 13W
Edinburgh, City of □, *U.K.* **22 F5** 55 57N 3 17W
Edineţ, *Moldova* **53 B12** 48 9N 27 18 E
Edirne, *Turkey* **51 E10** 41 40N 26 34 E
Edirne □, *Turkey* **51 E10** 41 12N 26 30 E
Edison, *Ga., U.S.A.* **152 D5** 31 34N 84 44W
Edison, *Wash., U.S.A.* **160 B4** 48 33N 122 27W
Edisto →, *U.S.A.* **152 C9** 32 29N 80 21W
Edisto Beach, *U.S.A.* **152 C9** 32 29N 80 20W
Edisto I., *U.S.A.* **152 C9** 32 35N 80 20W
Edithburgh, *Australia* **128 C2** 35 5 S 137 43 E
Edjeleh, *Algeria* **111 C6** 28 38N 9 50 E
Edmeston, *U.S.A.* **151 D9** 42 42N 75 15W
Edmond, *U.S.A.* **155 H6** 35 39N 97 29W
Edmonds, *U.S.A.* **160 C4** 47 49N 122 23W
Edmonton, *Australia* **126 B4** 17 2 S 145 46 E
Edmonton, *Canada* **142 C6** 53 30N 113 30W
Edmund L., *Canada* **140 B1** 54 45N 93 17W
Edmundston, *Canada* **141 C6** 47 23N 68 20W
Edna, *U.S.A.* **155 L6** 28 59N 96 39W
Edo □, *Nigeria* **113 D6** 6 30N 6 0 E
Edolo, *Italy* **44 B7** 46 10N 10 21 E
Edøy, *Norway* **18 A5** 63 18N 8 10 E
Edremit, *Turkey* **49 B9** 39 34N 27 0 E
Edremit Körfezi, *Turkey* **49 B8** 39 30N 26 45 E
Edsbro, *Sweden* **16 E12** 59 54N 18 29 E
Edsbyn, *Sweden* **16 C9** 61 23N 15 49 E
Edson, *Canada* **142 C5** 53 35N 116 28W
Eduardo Castex, *Argentina* **174 D3** 35 50 S 64 18W
Edward →, *Australia* **128 C5** 35 5 S 143 30 E
Edward, L., *Africa* **118 C2** 0 25 S 29 40 E
Edward River, *Australia* **126 A3** 14 59 S 141 26 E
Edward VII Land, *Antarctica* **7 E13** 80 0 S 150 0W
Edwards, *Calif., U.S.A.* **161 L9** 34 55N 117 51W
Edwards, *N.Y., U.S.A.* **151 B9** 44 20N 75 15W
Edwards →, *U.S.A.* **156 C6** 41 9N 90 59W
Edwards Air Force Base, *U.S.A.* **161 L9** 34 50N 117 40W
Edwards Plateau, *U.S.A.* **155 K4** 30 45N 101 20W
Edwardsburg, *U.S.A.* **157 C10** 41 48N 86 6W
Edwardsville, *Ill., U.S.A.* **156 F7** 38 49N 89 58W
Edwardsville, *Pa., U.S.A.* **151 E9** 41 15N 75 56W
Edzo, *Canada* **142 A5** 62 49N 116 4W
Eek, *U.S.A.* **144 F7** 60 14N 162 2W
Eeklo, *Belgium* **24 C3** 51 11N 3 33 E
Eel →, *Ind., U.S.A.* **157 E10** 39 7N 86 57W
Eel →, *Ind., U.S.A.* **157 D10** 40 45N 86 22W
Efate, *Vanuatu* **133 G6** 17 40 S 168 25 E
Efate, I., *Vanuatu* **133 G6** 17 40 S 168 25 E
Eferding, *Austria* **34 C7** 48 18N 14 1 E
Eferi, *Algeria* **111 D6** 24 30N 9 28 E
Effingham, *U.S.A.* **157 E8** 39 7N 88 33W
Effretikon, *Switz.* **33 B7** 47 25N 8 42 E
Eforie, *Romania* **53 F13** 44 1N 28 37 E
Efoulen, *Cameroon* **114 B2** 2 46N 10 43 E
Efteløt, *Norway* **18 E6** 59 33N 9 49 E
Ega →, *Spain* **40 C3** 42 19N 1 55W
Égadi, Ísole, *Italy* **46 E5** 37 55N 12 16 E
Egan Range, *U.S.A.* **158 G6** 39 35N 114 55W
Eganville, *Canada* **140 C4** 45 32N 77 5W
Egedesminde = Aasiaat, *Greenland* **10 D5** 68 43N 52 56W
Egegik, *U.S.A.* **144 G8** 58 13N 157 22W
Eger = Cheb, *Czech Rep.* **34 A5** 50 9N 12 28 E
Eger, *Hungary* **52 C5** 47 53N 20 27 E
Eger →, *Hungary* **52 C5** 47 38N 20 50 E
Egersund, *Norway* **15 G12** 58 26N 6 1 E
Egg, *Austria* **33 B9** 47 26N 9 54 E
Egg, *Switz.* **33 B7** 47 18N 8 41 E
Egg I., *St. Helena* **9 h** 15 58 S 5 47W
Egg L., *Canada* **143 B7** 55 5N 105 30W
Eggedal, *Norway* **18 D6** 60 14N 9 22 E
Eggenburg, *Austria* **34 C8** 48 38N 15 50 E
Eggenfelden, *Germany* **31 G8** 48 23N 12 46 E
Eggiwil, *Switz.* **32 C5** 46 52N 7 47 E
Egherta, *Somali Rep.* **120 D2** 2 4N 43 11 E
Éghezée, *Belgium* **24 D4** 50 35N 4 55 E
Egholo, *Solomon Is.* **133 M9** 8 25 S 157 25 E
Egilsstaðir, *Iceland* **11 B12** 65 16N 14 25W
Egito, *Angola* **115 E2** 12 4 S 13 58 E
Égletons, *France* **28 C6** 45 24N 2 3 E
Eglisau, *Switz.* **33 A7** 47 35N 8 31 E
Egmont, *Canada* **142 D4** 49 45N 123 56W
Egmont, C., *N.Z.* **130 F2** 39 16 S 173 45 E
Egmont, Mt. = Taranaki, Mt., *N.Z.* **130 F3** 39 17 S 174 5 E
Egmont Nat. Park, *N.Z.* **130 F3** 39 17 S 174 4 E
Egra, *India* **93 J12** 21 54N 87 32 E
Eğridir, *Turkey* **100 D4** 37 52N 30 51 E
Eğridir Gölü, *Turkey* **100 D4** 37 53N 30 50 E
Egtved, *Denmark* **17 J3** 55 38N 9 18 E
Éguas →, *Brazil* **171 D3** 13 26 S 44 14W
Egum Atoll, *Papua N. G.* **132 E7** 9 25 S 152 0 E
Egume, *Nigeria* **113 D6** 7 30N 7 14 E
Éguzon-Chantôme, *France* **27 F8** 46 27N 1 33 E
Egvekinot, *Russia* **67 C19** 66 19N 179 50W
Egyek, *Hungary* **52 C5** 47 39N 20 52 E
Egypt ■, *Africa* **106 B3** 28 0N 31 0 E
Eha Amufu, *Nigeria* **113 D6** 6 30N 7 46 E
Eheli, *Algeria* **111 D5** 22 26N 4 40 E
Ehime □, *Japan* **72 D4** 33 30N 132 40 E
Ehingen, *Germany* **31 G5** 48 16N 9 43 E
Ehrenberg, *U.S.A.* **161 M12** 33 36N 114 31W
Ehrhardt, *U.S.A.* **152 B8** 33 6N 81 1W
Ehrwald, *Austria* **34 D3** 47 24N 10 56 E
Eibar, *Spain* **40 B2** 43 11N 2 28W
Eichstätt, *Germany* **31 G7** 48 54N 11 11 E
Eide, *Hordaland, Norway* **18 D3** 60 31N 6 44 E
Eide, *Møre og Romsdal, Norway* **18 B4** 62 55N 7 27 E
Eider →, *Germany* **30 A4** 54 19N 8 57 E
Eidsbugarden, *Norway* **18 C5** 61 23N 8 16 E
Eidsbygda, *Norway* **18 B4** 62 36N 7 30 E
Eidsdal, *Norway* **18 B4** 62 16N 7 10 E
Eidsvåg, *Norway* **18 B5** 62 46N 8 2 E
Eidsvold, *Australia* **127 D5** 25 25 S 151 12 E
Eidsvoll, *Norway* **15 F14** 60 19N 11 14 E
Eifel, *Germany* **31 E2** 50 15N 6 50 E
Eiffel Flats, *Zimbabwe* **119 F3** 18 20 S 30 0 E
Eiger, *Switz.* **32 C6** 46 34N 8 1 E
Eigg, *U.K.* **22 E2** 56 54N 6 10W
Eighty Mile Beach, *Australia* **124 C3** 19 30 S 120 40 E
Eikefjord, *Norway* **18 C2** 61 35N 5 27 E
Eikelandsosen, *Norway* **18 D2** 60 15N 5 43 E
Eiken, *Norway* **18 F4** 58 29N 7 14 E
Eikeren, *Norway* **18 E6** 59 38N 9 58 E
Eikesdal, *Norway* **18 B5** 62 28N 8 12 E
Eil, *Somali Rep.* **120 C3** 8 0N 49 50 E
Eil, L., *U.K.* **22 E3** 56 51N 5 16W
Eildon, *Australia* **129 D6** 37 14 S 145 55 E
Eildon, L., *Australia* **129 D7** 37 10 S 146 0 E
Eilenburg, *Germany* **30 D8** 51 27N 12 36 E
Ein el Luweiqa, *Sudan* **107 E3** 14 5N 33 50 E
Eina, *Norway* **18 D7** 60 38N 10 35 E
Einarsstaðir, *Iceland* **11 B9** 65 44N 17 24W
Einasleigh, *Australia* **126 B3** 18 32 S 144 5 E
Einasleigh →, *Australia* **126 B3** 17 30 S 142 17 E
Einbeck, *Germany* **30 D5** 51 49N 9 53 E
Eindhoven, *Neths.* **24 C5** 51 26N 5 28 E
Einsiedeln, *Switz.* **33 B7** 47 7N 8 46 E
Eire = Ireland ■, *Europe* **23 C4** 53 50N 7 52W
Eiríksjökull, *Iceland* **11 C6** 64 46N 20 24W
Eiríksstaðir, *Iceland* **11 B11** 65 7N 15 25W
Eirunepé, *Brazil* **172 B4** 6 35 S 69 53W
Eiseb →, *Namibia* **116 C2** 20 33 S 20 59 E
Eisenach, *Germany* **30 E6** 50 58N 10 19 E
Eisenberg, *Germany* **30 E7** 50 58N 11 54 E
Eisenerz, *Austria* **34 D7** 47 32N 14 54 E
Eisenhüttenstadt, *Germany* **30 C10** 52 9N 14 38 E
Eisenkappel, *Austria* **34 E7** 46 29N 14 36 E
Eisenstadt, *Austria* **35 D9** 47 51N 16 31 E
Eisfeld, *Germany* **31 E6** 50 25N 10 54 E
Eisleben, *Germany* **30 D7** 51 32N 11 32 E
Eislingen, *Germany* **31 G5** 48 41N 9 42 E
Eivindvik, *Norway* **18 D2** 60 59N 5 5 E
Eivissa, *Spain* **38 D1** 38 54N 1 26 E
Eixe, Serra do, *Spain* **42 C4** 42 24N 6 54W
Ejea de los Caballeros, *Spain* **40 C3** 42 7N 1 9W
Ejeda, *Madag.* **117 C7** 24 20 S 44 31 E
Ejura, *Ghana* **113 D4** 7 23N 1 15W
Ejutla, *Mexico* **163 D5** 16 34N 96 44W
Ekalaka, *U.S.A.* **154 C2** 45 53N 104 33W
Ekalla, *Gabon* **114 C2** 1 27 S 14 0 E
Ekanga, *Dem. Rep. of the Congo* **114 C4** 2 23 S 23 14 E
Ekenässjön, *Sweden* **17 G9** 57 28N 15 1 E
Ekerö, *Sweden* **16 E11** 59 16N 17 45 E
Eket, *Nigeria* **113 E6** 4 38N 7 56 E
Eketahuna, *N.Z.* **130 G4** 40 38 S 175 43 E
Ekhinádhes Nísoi, *Greece* **39 C3** 38 25N 21 2 E
Ekhínos, *Greece* **51 E9** 41 16N 25 1 E
Ekibastuz, *Kazakstan* **66 D8** 51 50N 75 10 E
Ekiti □, *Nigeria* **113 D6** 7 25N 5 20 E
Ekoli, *Dem. Rep. of the Congo* **118 C1** 0 23 S 24 13 E
Ekoln, *Sweden* **16 E11** 59 45N 17 37 E
Ekouamou, *Congo* **114 B3** 0 8N 16 31 E
Ekoungounou, *Congo* **114 C3** 1 10 S 15 52 E
Ekshärad, *Sweden* **16 D7** 60 10N 13 30 E
Eksjö, *Sweden* **17 G8** 57 40N 14 58 E
Ekukola, *Dem. Rep. of the Congo* **114 C3** 0 31 S 18 56 E
Ekuku, *Dem. Rep. of the Congo* **114 C4** 0 41 S 21 42 E
Ekukula, *Dem. Rep. of the Congo* **114 B4** 0 15N 21 30 E
Ekuma →, *Namibia* **116 B2** 18 40 S 16 2 E
Ekuta, *Dem. Rep. of the Congo* **114 B3** 3 0N 18 50 E
Ekwan →, *Canada* **140 B3** 53 12N 82 15W
Ekwan Pt., *Canada* **140 B3** 53 16N 82 7W
Ekwok, *U.S.A.* **144 G8** 59 22N 157 30W
El Aaiún, *W. Sahara* **110 C2** 27 9N 13 12W
El Aargub, *Mauritania* **110 D1** 23 37N 15 52W
El Abanico, *Chile* **174 D1** 37 20 S 71 31W
El Abbasiya, *Sudan* **107 E3** 12 10N 31 18 E
El Abiodh-Sidi-Cheikh, *Algeria* **111 B5** 32 53N 0 31 E
El Adde, *Somali Rep.* **120 D3** 2 35N 46 9 E
El 'Agrûd, *Egypt* **103 E3** 30 14N 34 24 E
El Aïoun, *Morocco* **111 B4** 34 33N 2 30W
El Ait, *Sudan* **107 E2** 12 22N 27 27 E
El 'Aiyat, *Egypt* **106 J7** 29 36N 31 15 E
El Alamein, *Egypt* **106 A2** 30 48N 28 58 E
El Alto, *Peru* **172 A1** 4 15 S 81 14W
El Aouj, *Mauritania* **110 D2** 22 53N 12 49W
El 'Aqaba, W. →, *Egypt* **103 E2** 30 7N 33 54 E
El 'Arag, *Egypt* **106 B2** 28 40N 26 20 E
El Arahal, *Spain* **43 H5** 37 15N 5 33W
El Aricha, *Algeria* **111 B4** 34 13N 1 10W
El Arīḩā, *West Bank* **103 D4** 31 52N 35 27 E
El 'Arîsh, *Egypt* **103 D2** 31 8N 33 50 E
El 'Arîsh, W. →, *Egypt* **103 D2** 31 8N 33 47 E
El Arrouch, *Algeria* **111 A6** 36 37N 6 53 E
El Asnam = Ech Chéliff, *Algeria* **111 A5** 36 10N 1 20 E
El Astillero, *Spain* **42 B7** 43 24N 3 49W
El Badâri, *Egypt* **106 B3** 27 4N 31 25 E
El Bahrein, *Egypt* **106 B2** 28 30N 26 25 E
El Ballâs, *Egypt* **106 B3** 26 2N 32 43 E
El Balyana, *Egypt* **106 B3** 26 10N 32 3 E
El Banco, *Colombia* **168 B3** 9 0N 73 58W
El Baqeir, *Sudan* **106 D3** 18 40N 33 40 E
El Barco de Ávila, *Spain* **42 E5** 40 21N 5 31W
El Barco de Valdeorras = O Barco, *Spain* **42 C4** 42 23N 6 58W
El Bauga, *Sudan* **106 D3** 18 18N 33 52 E
El Baúl, *Venezuela* **168 B4** 8 57N 68 17W
El Bawiti, *Egypt* **106 B2** 28 25N 28 45 E
El Bayadh, *Algeria* **111 B5** 33 40N 1 1 E
El Bierzo, *Spain* **42 C4** 42 45N 6 30W
El Bluff, *Nic.* **164 D3** 11 59N 83 40W
El Bolsón, *Argentina* **176 B2** 41 55 S 71 30W
El Bonillo, *Spain* **41 G2** 38 57N 2 35W
El Brûk, W. →, *Egypt* **103 E2** 30 15N 33 50 E
El Buheirat □, *Sudan* **107 F3** 7 0N 30 0 E
El Bur, *Somali Rep.* **120 D3** 4 40N 46 37 E
El Burgo de Osma, *Spain* **40 D1** 41 35N 3 4W
El Caín, *Argentina* **176 B3** 41 38 S 68 19W
El Cajon, *U.S.A.* **161 N10** 32 48N 116 58W
El Callao, *Venezuela* **169 B5** 7 18N 61 50W
El Campo, *U.S.A.* **155 L6** 29 12N 96 16W
El Carmen, *Bolivia* **173 C5** 13 40 S 63 55W
El Centro, *U.S.A.* **161 N11** 32 48N 115 34W
El Cerro, *Bolivia* **173 D5** 17 30 S 61 40W
El Cerro de Andévalo, *Spain* **43 H4** 37 45N 6 57W
El Cocuy, *Colombia* **168 B3** 6 25N 72 27W
El Compadre, *Mexico* **161 N10** 32 20N 116 14W
El Corcovado, *Argentina* **176 B2** 43 25 S 71 35W
El Coronil, *Spain* **43 H5** 37 5N 5 38W
El Cuy, *Argentina* **176 A3** 39 55 S 68 25W
El Cuyo, *Mexico* **163 C7** 21 30N 87 40W
El Dab'a, *Egypt* **106 H6** 31 0N 28 27 E
El Daheir, *Egypt* **103 D3** 31 13N 34 10 E
El Dambahaddo, *Somali Rep.* **120 D3** 3 17N 46 40 E
El Dátil, *Mexico* **162 B2** 30 7N 112 15W
El Deir, *Egypt* **106 B3** 25 25N 32 20 E
El Dere, *Ethiopia* **120 C2** 5 6N 43 5 E
El Dere, *Somali Rep.* **120 D3** 3 50N 47 8 E
El Dere, *Somali Rep.* **120 C3** 5 22N 46 11 E
El Descanso, *Mexico* **161 N10** 32 12N 116 58W
El Desemboque, *Mexico* **162 A2** 30 30N 112 57W
El Dilingat, *Egypt* **106 H7** 30 50N 30 31 E
El Diviso, *Colombia* **168 C2** 1 22N 78 14W
El Djouf, *Mauritania* **104 D3** 20 0N 9 0W
El Dorado, *Ark., U.S.A.* **155 J8** 33 12N 92 40W
El Dorado, *Kans., U.S.A.* **155 G6** 37 49N 96 52W
El Dorado, *Venezuela* **169 B5** 6 55N 61 37W
El Eglab, *Algeria* **110 C4** 26 20N 4 30W
El 'Ein, *Sudan* **107 D2** 16 35N 29 22 E
El Ejido, *Spain* **43 J8** 36 47N 2 49W
El Escorial, *Spain* **42 E6** 40 35N 4 7W
El Espinar, *Spain* **42 D6** 41 43N 4 15W
El Eulma, *Algeria* **111 A6** 36 9N 5 42 E
El Faiyûm, *Egypt* **106 J7** 29 19N 30 50 E
El Fâsher, *Sudan* **107 E2** 13 33N 25 26 E
El Fashn, *Egypt* **106 J7** 28 50N 30 54 E
El Ferrol = Ferrol, *Spain* **42 B2** 43 29N 8 15W
El Fifi, *Sudan* **107 E2** 10 4N 25 0 E
El Fud, *Ethiopia* **120 C2** 7 15N 42 52 E
El Fuerte, *Mexico* **162 B3** 26 30N 108 40W
El Ga'a, *Sudan* **107 E2** 14 16N 29 59 E
El Gal, *Somali Rep.* **120 B4** 10 58N 50 20 E
El Garef, *Sudan* **107 E3** 12 3N 34 19 E
El Gebir, *Sudan* **107 E2** 13 40N 29 40 E
El Gedida, *Egypt* **106 B2** 25 40N 28 30 E
El Geneina = Al Junaynah, *Sudan* **109 F4** 13 27N 22 45 E
El Geteina, *Sudan* **107 E3** 14 50N 32 27 E
El Gezira □, *Sudan* **107 E3** 15 0N 33 0 E
El Gir, *Sudan* **106 D2** 19 50N 28 18 E
El Gîza, *Egypt* **106 J7** 30 0N 31 10 E
El Goléa, *Algeria* **111 B5** 30 30N 2 50 E
El Grau, *Spain* **41 G4** 39 0N 0 7W
El Hadeb, *W. Sahara* **110 C2** 25 51N 13 0W
El Hadjira, *Algeria* **111 B6** 32 36N 5 30 E
El Hagiz, *Sudan* **107 D4** 15 15N 35 50 E
El Hâi, *Egypt* **106 J7** 29 39N 31 18 E
El Hajeb, *Morocco* **110 B3** 33 43N 5 13W
El Hamma, *Tunisia* **108 B1** 33 54N 9 48 E
El Hammam, *Egypt* **106 A2** 30 52N 29 25 E
El Hammâmi, *Mauritania* **110 D2** 23 3N 11 30W
El Hamurre, *Somali Rep.* **120 C3** 7 13N 48 54 E
El Hank, *Mauritania* **110 D3** 24 30N 7 0W
El Hasian, *W. Sahara* **110 C2** 26 20N 14 0W
El Hawata, *Sudan* **107 E3** 13 25N 34 42 E
El Heiz, *Egypt* **106 B2** 27 50N 28 40 E
El Hideib, *Sudan* **107 E3** 13 0N 32 50 E
El Hilla, *Sudan* **107 E2** 13 24N 27 2 E
El Homeur, *Algeria* **111 C5** 29 43N 1 45 E
El 'Idisât, *Egypt* **106 B3** 25 30N 32 35 E
El Iskandarîya, *Egypt* **106 H7** 31 13N 29 58 E
El Jadida, *Morocco* **110 B3** 33 11N 8 17W
El Jardal, *Honduras* **164 D2** 14 54N 88 50W
El Jebelein, *Sudan* **107 E3** 12 40N 32 55 E
El Jebha, *Morocco* **110 A4** 35 11N 4 43W
El Jem, *Tunisia* **108 A2** 35 18N 10 42 E
El Kab, *Sudan* **106 D3** 19 27N 32 46 E
El Kabrît, G., *Egypt* **103 F2** 29 42N 33 16 E
El Kafr el Sharqi, *Egypt* **106 H7** 31 16N 31 10 E
El Kala, *Algeria* **111 A6** 36 50N 8 30 E
El Kamlin, *Sudan* **107 D3** 15 3N 33 11 E
El Kantara, *Algeria* **111 A6** 35 14N 5 45 E
El Kantara, *Tunisia* **108 B2** 33 45N 10 58 E
El Karaba, *Sudan* **106 D3** 18 32N 33 41 E
El Kef, *Tunisia* **108 A1** 36 12N 8 47 E
El Kelâa, *Morocco* **110 B3** 32 4N 7 27W
El Kere, *Ethiopia* **107 F5** 5 50N 42 5 E
El Khandaq, *Sudan* **106 D3** 18 30N 30 30 E
El Khârga, *Egypt* **106 B3** 25 30N 30 33 E
El Khartûm, *Sudan* **107 D3** 15 31N 32 35 E
El Khartûm □, *Sudan* **107 D3** 16 0N 33 0 E
El Khartûm Bahrî, *Sudan* **107 D3** 15 40N 32 31 E
El Khroub, *Algeria* **111 A6** 36 10N 6 55 E
El Kseur, *Algeria* **111 A5** 36 46N 4 49 E
El Ksiba, *Morocco* **110 B3** 32 45N 6 1W
El Kuntilla, *Egypt* **103 E3** 30 1N 34 45 E
El Laqâwa, *Sudan* **107 E2** 11 25N 29 1 E
El Laqeita, *Egypt* **106 B3** 25 50N 33 15 E
El Leh, *Ethiopia* **107 G4** 3 46N 39 13 E
El Leiya, *Sudan* **107 D4** 16 15N 35 28 E
El Maestrazgo, *Spain* **40 E4** 40 30N 0 25W
El Mafâza, *Sudan* **107 E3** 13 38N 34 30 E
El Maghra, *Egypt* **106 A2** 30 15N 28 55 E
El Mahalla el Kubra, *Egypt* **106 H7** 31 0N 31 0 E
El Mahârîq, *Egypt* **106 B3** 25 35N 30 35 E
El Maîmûn, *Egypt* **106 J7** 29 14N 31 12 E
El Maitén, *Argentina* **176 B2** 42 3 S 71 10W
El Maiz, *Algeria* **111 C4** 28 19N 0 9W
El Maks el Bahari, *Egypt* **106 C3** 24 30N 30 40 E
El Manshâh, *Egypt* **106 B3** 26 26N 31 50 E
El Mansour, *Algeria* **111 C4** 27 47N 0 14W
El Mansûra, *Egypt* **106 H7** 31 0N 31 19 E
El Manteco, *Venezuela* **169 B5** 7 38N 62 45W
El Manzala, *Egypt* **106 H7** 31 10N 31 50 E
El Marâgha, *Egypt* **106 B3** 26 35N 31 10 E
El Masid, *Sudan* **107 D3** 15 15N 33 0 E
El Masnou, *Spain* **40 D7** 41 28N 2 20 E
El Matariya, *Egypt* **106 H8** 31 15N 32 0 E
El Meda, *Ethiopia* **107 F5** 5 39N 41 47 E
El Medano, *Canary Is.* **9 e1** 28 3N 16 32W
El Meghaier, *Algeria* **111 B6** 33 55N 5 58 E
El Meraguen, *Algeria* **111 C4** 28 0N 0 7W
El Metemma, *Sudan* **107 D3** 16 50N 33 10 E
El Miamo, *Venezuela* **169 B5** 7 39N 61 46W
El Milagro, *Argentina* **174 C2** 30 59 S 65 59W
El Milia, *Algeria* **111 A6** 36 51N 6 13 E
El Minyâ, *Egypt* **106 B3** 28 7N 30 33 E
El Monte, *U.S.A.* **161 L8** 34 4N 118 1W
El Montseny, *Spain* **40 D7** 41 55N 2 25 E
El Mreyye, *Mauritania* **112 B3** 18 0N 6 0W
El Nido, *Phil.* **81 F2** 11 10N 119 25 E
El Niybo, *Ethiopia* **107 G4** 4 40N 39 55 E
El Obeid, *Sudan* **107 E3** 13 8N 30 10 E
El Odaiya, *Sudan* **107 E2** 12 8N 28 12 E
El Oro, *Mexico* **163 D4** 19 48N 100 8W
El Oro □, *Ecuador* **168 D2** 3 30 S 79 50W
El Oued, *Algeria* **111 B6** 33 20N 6 58 E
El Oumi, *Niger* **111 D7** 20 11N 0 15 E
El Palmar, *Bolivia* **173 D5** 17 50 S 63 9W
El Palmar, *Venezuela* **169 B5** 7 58N 61 53W
El Palmito, Presa, *Mexico* **162 B3** 25 40N 105 30W
El Paso, *Ill., U.S.A.* **156 D7** 40 44N 89 1W
El Paso, *Tex., U.S.A.* **159 L10** 31 45N 106 29W
El Paso Robles, *U.S.A.* **160 K6** 35 38N 120 41W
El Pedernoso, *Spain* **41 F2** 39 29N 2 45W
El Pedroso, *Spain* **43 H5** 37 51N 5 45W
El Pilar, *Venezuela* **169 A5** 10 32N 63 9W
El Pobo de Dueñas, *Spain* **40 E3** 40 46N 1 39W
El Portal, *U.S.A.* **160 H7** 37 41N 119 47W
El Porvenir, *Mexico* **162 A3** 31 15N 105 51W
El Prat de Llobregat, *Spain* **40 D7** 41 18N 2 3 E
El Progreso, *Ecuador* **172 a** 0 54 S 89 33W
El Progreso, *Honduras* **164 C2** 15 26N 87 51W
El Pueblito, *Mexico* **162 B3** 29 3N 105 4W

El Pueblo, *Canary Is.* **9 e1** 28 36N 17 47W
El Puente del Arzobispo, *Spain* **42 F5** 39 48N 5 10W
El Puerto de Santa María, *Spain* **43 J4** 36 36N 6 13W
El Qâhira, *Egypt* **106 H7** 30 1N 31 14 E
El Qantara, *Egypt* **103 E1** 30 51N 32 20 E
El Qasr, *Egypt* **106 B2** 25 44N 28 42 E
El Qubâbât, *Egypt* **106 J7** 29 28N 31 16 E
El Quseima, *Egypt* **103 E3** 30 40N 34 15 E
El Qusîya, *Egypt* **106 B3** 27 29N 30 44 E
El Râshda, *Egypt* **106 B2** 25 36N 28 57 E
El Reno, *U.S.A.* **155 H6** 35 32N 97 57W
El Rîdisiya, *Egypt* **106 C3** 24 56N 32 51 E
El Rio, *U.S.A.* **161 L7** 34 14N 119 10W
El Ronquillo, *Spain* **43 H4** 37 44N 6 10W
El Roque, Pta., *Canary Is.* **9 e1** 28 10N 15 25W
El Rosarito, *Mexico* **162 B2** 28 38N 114 4W
El Rubio, *Spain* **43 H5** 37 22N 5 0W
El Saff, *Egypt* **106 J7** 29 34N 31 16 E
El Saheira, W. →, *Egypt* **103 E2** 30 5N 33 25 E
El Salto, *Mexico* **162 C3** 23 47N 105 22W
El Salvador ■, *Cent. Amer.* **164 D2** 13 50N 89 0W
El Sauce, *Nic.* **164 D2** 13 0N 86 40W
El Saucejo, *Spain* **43 H5** 37 4N 5 6W
El Shallal, *Egypt* **106 C3** 24 0N 32 53 E
El Simbillawein, *Egypt* **106 H7** 30 48N 31 13 E
El Sombrero, *Venezuela* **168 B4** 9 23N 67 3W
El Sueco, *Mexico* **162 B3** 29 54N 106 24W
El Suweis, *Egypt* **106 J8** 29 58N 32 31 E
El Tabbin, *Egypt* **106 J7** 29 47N 31 18 E
El Tamarâni, W. →, *Egypt* **103 E3** 30 7N 34 43 E
El Thamad, *Egypt* **103 F3** 29 40N 34 28 E
El Tigre, *Venezuela* **169 B5** 8 44N 64 15W
El Tîh, Gebal, *Egypt* **103 F2** 29 40N 33 50 E
El Tîna, *Egypt* **106 H8** 31 3N 32 22 E
El Tîna, Khalîg, *Egypt* **103 D1** 31 10N 32 40 E
El Tocuyo, *Venezuela* **168 B4** 9 47N 69 48W
El Tofo, *Chile* **174 B1** 29 22 S 71 18W
El Tránsito, *Chile* **174 B1** 28 52 S 70 17W
El Tûr, *Egypt* **96 D2** 28 14N 33 36 E
El Turbio, *Argentina* **176 D2** 51 45 S 72 5W
El Uinle, *Somali Rep.* **120 D2** 3 4N 41 42 E
El Uqsur, *Egypt* **106 B3** 25 41N 32 38 E
El Venado, *Mexico* **162 C4** 22 56N 101 10W
El Vendrell, *Spain* **40 D6** 41 10N 1 30 E
El Vergel, *Mexico* **162 B3** 26 28N 106 22W
El Vigía, *Venezuela* **168 B3** 8 38N 71 39W
El Viso del Alcor, *Spain* **43 H5** 37 23N 5 43W
El Wabeira, *Egypt* **103 F2** 29 34N 33 6 E
El Wak, *Kenya* **118 B5** 2 49N 40 56 E
El Wak, *Somali Rep.* **120 D2** 2 44N 41 1 E
El Waqf, *Egypt* **106 B3** 25 45N 32 15 E
El Weguet, *Ethiopia* **107 F5** 5 28N 42 17 E
El Wuz, *Sudan* **107 D3** 15 5N 30 7 E
Elafónisos, *Greece* **48 E4** 36 29N 22 56 E
Elamanchili, *India* **94 F6** 17 33N 82 50 E
Élancourt, *France* **27 D8** 48 47N 1 58 E
Elands, *Australia* **129 A10** 31 37 S 152 20 E
Élassa, *Greece* **49 F8** 35 18N 26 21 E
Elassón, *Greece* **48 B4** 39 53N 22 12 E
Elat, *Israel* **103 F3** 29 30N 34 56 E
Eláthia, *Greece* **48 C4** 38 37N 22 46 E
Eláti Óros, *Greece* **39 B2** 38 43N 20 39 E
Elâzığ, *Turkey* **101 C8** 38 37N 39 14 E
Elba, *Italy* **44 F7** 42 46N 10 17 E
Elba, *U.S.A.* **152 D3** 31 25N 86 4W
Elbasan, *Albania* **50 E4** 41 9N 20 9 E
Elbe, *U.S.A.* **160 D4** 46 45N 122 10W
Elbe →, *Europe* **30 B4** 53 50N 9 0 E
Elbe-Seitenkanal, *Germany* **30 C6** 52 45N 10 32 E
Elberfeld, *U.S.A.* **157 F9** 38 10N 87 27W
Elbert, Mt., *U.S.A.* **159 G10** 39 7N 106 27W
Elberton, *U.S.A.* **152 A7** 34 7N 82 52W
Elbeuf, *France* **26 C8** 49 17N 1 2 E
Elbidtan, *Turkey* **96 B3** 38 13N 37 12 E
Elbing = Elbląg, *Poland* **54 D6** 54 10N 19 25 E
Elbistan, *Turkey* **100 C7** 38 13N 37 15 E
Elbląg, *Poland* **54 D6** 54 10N 19 25 E
Elbow, *Canada* **143 C7** 51 7N 106 35W
Elbow, Pta., *W. Sahara* **110 D1** 24 5N 15 35W
Elbrus, *Asia* **61 J6** 43 21N 42 30 E
Elburn, *U.S.A.* **157 C8** 41 54N 88 28W
Elburz Mts. = Alborz, Reshteh-ye Kūhhā-ye, *Iran* **97 C7** 36 0N 52 0 E
Elche, *Spain* **41 G4** 38 15N 0 42W
Elche de la Sierra, *Spain* **41 G2** 38 27N 2 3W
Elcho I., *Australia* **126 A2** 11 55 S 135 45 E
Elda, *Spain* **41 G4** 38 29N 0 47W
Elde →, *Germany* **30 B7** 53 7N 11 15 E
Eldon, *Iowa, U.S.A.* **156 D4** 40 55N 92 13W
Eldon, *Mo., U.S.A.* **156 F4** 38 21N 92 35W
Eldon, *Wash., U.S.A.* **160 C3** 47 33N 123 3W
Eldora, *U.S.A.* **156 B3** 42 22N 93 5W
Eldorado, *Argentina* **175 B5** 26 28 S 54 43W
Eldorado, *Canada* **150 B7** 44 35N 77 31W
Eldorado, *Mexico* **162 C3** 24 20N 107 22W
Eldorado, *Ill., U.S.A.* **157 G8** 37 49N 88 26W
Eldorado, *Tex., U.S.A.* **155 K4** 30 52N 100 36W
Eldorado Springs, *U.S.A.* **155 G8** 37 52N 94 1W
Eldorendo, *U.S.A.* **152 D5** 31 3N 84 39W
Eldoret, *Kenya* **118 B4** 0 30N 35 17 E
Eldred, *U.S.A.* **150 E6** 41 58N 78 23W
Eldridge, *U.S.A.* **156 C6** 41 39N 90 35W
Elea, C., *Cyprus* **39 E10** 35 19N 34 4 E
Eleanora, Pk., *Australia* **125 F3** 32 57 S 121 9 E
Elefantes →, *Mozam.* **117 C5** 24 10 S 32 40 E
Elefantes, B. das, *Angola* **115 E2** 13 13 S 12 44 E
Elefantes, G., *Chile* **176 C2** 46 28 S 73 49W
Elefantes do Maputo, Reserva de, *Mozam.* **117 D5** 26 23 S 32 48 E
Elektrogorsk, *Russia* **58 E10** 55 56N 38 50 E
Elektrostal, *Russia* **58 E10** 55 41N 38 32 E
Elele, *Nigeria* **113 D6** 5 5N 6 50 E
Elena, *Bulgaria* **51 D9** 42 55N 25 53 E
Elephant Butte Reservoir, *U.S.A.* **159 K10** 33 9N 107 11W
Elephant I., *Antarctica* **7 C18** 61 0 S 55 0W
Elephant Pass, *Sri Lanka* **95 K5** 9 35N 80 25 E
Elesbão Veloso, *Brazil* **170 C3** 6 13 S 42 8W
Eleshnitsa, *Bulgaria* **50 E7** 41 52N 23 36 E
Eleşkirt, *Turkey* **101 C10** 39 50N 42 50 E
Eleuthera, *Bahamas* **164 B4** 25 0N 76 20W
Elevsís, *Greece* **48 C5** 38 4N 23 26 E
Elevtheroúpolis, *Greece* **51 F8** 40 52N 24 20 E
Elfin Cove, *U.S.A.* **144 G13** 58 12N 136 22W
Elgå, *Norway* **18 B8** 62 10N 11 56 E
Elgepiggen, *Norway* **18 B8** 62 10N 11 21 E
Elgg, *Switz.* **33 B7** 47 29N 8 52 E
Elgin, *Canada* **151 B8** 44 36N 76 13W
Elgin, *U.K.* **22 D5** 57 39N 3 19W
Elgin, *Ill., U.S.A.* **157 B8** 42 2N 88 17W
Elgin, *N. Dak., U.S.A.* **154 B4** 46 24N 101 51W
Elgin, *Oreg., U.S.A.* **158 D5** 45 34N 117 55W
Elgin, *S.C., U.S.A.* **152 A9** 34 10N 80 48W
Elgin, *Tex., U.S.A.* **155 K6** 30 21N 97 22W
Elgoibar, *Spain* **40 B2** 43 13N 2 24W
Elgon, Mt., *Africa* **118 B3** 1 10N 34 30 E
Eliase, *Indonesia* **83 C4** 8 21 S 130 48 E
Elikón, *Greece* **48 C4** 38 18N 22 45 E
Elim, *Namibia* **116 B2** 17 48 S 15 31 E
Elim, *S. Africa* **116 E2** 34 35 S 19 45 E
Elim, *U.S.A.* **144 D7** 64 37N 162 15W
Elin Pelin, *Bulgaria* **50 D7** 42 40N 23 36 E
Elingampangu, *Dem. Rep. of the Congo* **114 C4** 2 0 S 24 4 E
Elipa, *Dem. Rep. of the Congo* **114 C4** 1 3 S 24 20 E
Eliseu Martins, *Brazil* **170 C3** 8 13 S 43 42W
Elista, *Russia* **61 G7** 46 16N 44 14 E
Eliza, L., *Australia* **128 D3** 37 15 S 139 50 E
Elizabeth, *Australia* **128 C3** 34 42 S 138 41 E
Elizabeth, *Ill., U.S.A.* **156 B6** 42 19N 90 13W
Elizabeth, *N.J., U.S.A.* **151 F10** 40 39N 74 13W
Elizabeth, *N.J., U.S.A.* **151 F10** 40 40N 74 13W
Elizabeth, B., *Ecuador* **172 a** 0 36 S 91 12W
Elizabeth City, *U.S.A.* **149 G7** 36 18N 76 14W
Elizabethton, *U.S.A.* **149 G4** 36 21N 82 13W
Elizabethtown, *Ky., U.S.A.* **157 G11** 37 42N 85 52W
Elizabethtown, *N.Y., U.S.A.* **151 B11** 44 13N 73 36W
Elizabethtown, *Pa., U.S.A.* **151 F8** 40 9N 76 36W
Elizondo, *Spain* **40 B3** 43 12N 1 30W
Ełk, *Poland* **54 E9** 53 50N 22 21 E
Elk →, *Canada* **142 C5** 49 11N 115 14W
Ełk →, *Poland* **54 E9** 53 41N 22 28 E
Elk →, *U.S.A.* **149 H2** 34 46N 87 16W
Elk City, *U.S.A.* **155 H5** 35 25N 99 25W
Elk Creek, *U.S.A.* **160 F4** 39 36N 122 32W
Elk Grove, *U.S.A.* **160 G5** 38 25N 121 22W
Elk Island Nat. Park, *Canada* **142 C6** 53 35N 112 59W
Elk Lake, *Canada* **140 C3** 47 40N 80 25W
Elk Point, *Canada* **143 C6** 53 54N 110 55W
Elk River, *Idaho, U.S.A.* **158 C5** 46 47N 116 11W
Elk River, *Minn., U.S.A.* **154 C8** 45 18N 93 35W
Elkader, *U.S.A.* **156 B5** 42 51N 91 24W
Elkedra →, *Australia* **126 C2** 21 8 S 136 22 E
Elkhart, *Ind., U.S.A.* **157 C11** 41 41N 85 58W
Elkhart, *Kans., U.S.A.* **155 G4** 37 0N 101 54W
Elkhart →, *U.S.A.* **157 C11** 41 41N 85 58W
Elkhorn, *Canada* **143 D8** 49 59N 101 14W
Elkhorn, *U.S.A.* **157 B8** 42 40N 88 33W
Elkhorn →, *U.S.A.* **154 E6** 41 8N 96 19W
Elkhovo, *Bulgaria* **51 D10** 42 10N 26 35 E
Elkin, *U.S.A.* **149 G5** 36 15N 80 51W
Elkins, *U.S.A.* **148 F6** 38 55N 79 51W
Elkland, *U.S.A.* **150 E7** 41 59N 77 19W
Elko, *Canada* **142 D5** 49 20N 115 10W
Elko, *U.S.A.* **158 F6** 40 50N 115 46W
Elkton, *U.S.A.* **150 C1** 43 49N 83 11W
Ell, L., *Australia* **125 E4** 29 13 S 127 46 E
Ellaville, *U.S.A.* **152 C5** 32 14N 84 19W
Ellef Ringnes I., *Canada* **6 B2** 78 30N 102 2W
Ellen, Mt., *U.S.A.* **151 B12** 44 9N 72 56W
Ellenburg, *U.S.A.* **151 B11** 44 54N 73 48W
Ellendale, *U.S.A.* **154 B5** 46 0N 98 32W
Ellensburg, *U.S.A.* **158 C3** 46 59N 120 34W
Ellenville, *U.S.A.* **151 E10** 41 43N 74 24W
Ellerton, *Barbados* **165 g** 13 7N 59 33W
Ellery, Mt., *Australia* **129 D8** 37 28 S 148 47 E
Ellesmere, L., *N.Z.* **131 H7** 43 47 S 172 28 E
Ellesmere I., *Canada* **6 B4** 79 30N 80 0W
Ellesmere Port, *U.K.* **20 D5** 53 17N 2 54W
Ellettsville, *U.S.A.* **157 E10** 39 14N 86 38W
Ellice Is. = Tuvalu ■, *Pac. Oc.* **134 H9** 8 0 S 178 0 E
Ellicottville, *U.S.A.* **150 D6** 42 17N 78 40W
Elliot, *Australia* **126 B1** 17 33 S 133 32 E
Elliot, *S. Africa* **117 E4** 31 22 S 27 48 E
Elliot Lake, *Canada* **140 C3** 46 25N 82 35W
Elliotdale = Xhora, *S. Africa* **117 E4** 31 55 S 28 38 E
Elliott, *U.S.A.* **152 A9** 34 6N 80 10W
Elliott Key, *U.S.A.* **153 K9** 25 27N 80 12W
Ellis, *U.S.A.* **154 F5** 38 56N 99 34W
Elliston, *Australia* **127 E1** 33 39 S 134 53 E
Ellisville, *U.S.A.* **155 K10** 31 36N 89 12W
Ellon, *U.K.* **22 D6** 57 22N 2 4W
Ellora, *India* **94 D2** 20 1N 75 10 E
Ellore = Eluru, *India* **94 F5** 16 48N 81 8 E
Elloree, *U.S.A.* **152 B9** 33 32N 80 34W
Ellsworth, *Kans., U.S.A.* **154 F5** 38 44N 98 14W
Ellsworth, *Maine, U.S.A.* **149 C11** 44 33N 68 25W
Ellsworth Land, *Antarctica* **7 D16** 76 0 S 89 0W
Ellsworth Mts., *Antarctica* **7 D16** 78 30 S 85 0W
Ellwangen, *Germany* **31 G6** 48 57N 10 8 E
Ellwood City, *U.S.A.* **150 F4** 40 52N 80 17W
Ellzey, *U.S.A.* **153 F7** 29 19N 82 48W
Elm, *Switz.* **33 C8** 46 54N 9 10 E
Elma, *Canada* **143 D9** 49 52N 95 55W
Elma, *U.S.A.* **160 D3** 47 0N 123 25W
Elmadağ, *Turkey* **100 C5** 39 55N 33 14 E
Elmalı, *Turkey* **49 E11** 36 44N 29 56 E
Elmhurst, *U.S.A.* **157 C9** 41 53N 87 56W
Elmina, *Ghana* **113 D4** 5 5N 1 21W
Elmira, *Canada* **150 C4** 43 36N 80 33W
Elmira, *U.S.A.* **150 D8** 42 6N 76 48W
Elmira Heights, *U.S.A.* **150 D8** 42 8N 76 50W
Elmodel, *U.S.A.* **152 D5** 31 21N 84 29W
Elmore, *Australia* **128 D6** 36 30 S 144 37 E
Elmore, *Ala., U.S.A.* **152 C3** 32 32N 86 19W
Elmore, *Calif., U.S.A.* **161 M11** 33 7N 115 49W
Elmore, *Minn., U.S.A.* **157 C13** 41 29N 83 18W
Elmshorn, *Germany* **30 B5** 53 43N 9 40 E
Elmvale, *Canada* **150 B5** 44 35N 79 52W
Elmwood, *U.S.A.* **156 D7** 40 47N 89 58W
Elne, *France* **28 F6** 42 36N 2 58 E
Elnesvågen, *Norway* **18 B4** 62 52N 7 10 E
Elnora, *U.S.A.* **157 F9** 38 53N 87 5W
Eloaua I., *Papua N. G.* **132 A5** 1 38 S 149 40 E
Elobey, Is., *Eq. Guin.* **114 B1** 1 1N 9 29 E
Elongo, *Dem. Rep. of the Congo* **114 C4** 0 19 S 21 39 E
Elora, *Canada* **150 C4** 43 41N 80 26W
Elorza, *Venezuela* **168 B4** 7 3N 69 31W
Elos, *Greece* **48 E4** 36 46N 22 43 E
Eloúnda, *Greece* **39 E6** 35 16N 25 42 E
Eloy, *U.S.A.* **159 K8** 32 45N 111 33W
Éloyes, *France* **27 D13** 48 6N 6 36 E
Elpitiya, *Sri Lanka* **95 L5** 6 17N 80 10 E
Elrose, *Canada* **143 C7** 51 12N 108 0W
Elsberry, *U.S.A.* **156 E6** 39 10N 90 47W
Elsdorf, *Germany* **30 E2** 50 55N 6 34 E
Elsie, *Mich., U.S.A.* **157 A12** 43 5N 84 23W
Elsie, *Oreg., U.S.A.* **160 E3** 45 52N 123 36W
Elsinore = Helsingør, *Denmark* **17 H6** 56 2N 12 35 E
Elster →, *Germany* **30 D7** 51 25N 11 57 E
Elsterwerda, *Germany* **30 D9** 51 27N 13 31 E
Eltham, *N.Z.* **130 F3** 39 26 S 174 19 E
Elton, *Russia* **61 F8** 49 5N 46 52 E
Elton, Ozero, *Russia* **61 F8** 49 5N 46 42 E
Eltville, *Germany* **31 E4** 50 2N 8 7 E
Eluru, *India* **94 F5** 16 48N 81 8 E
Elvas, *Portugal* **43 G3** 38 50N 7 10W
Elven, *France* **26 E4** 47 44N 2 36W
Elverum, *Norway* **15 F14** 60 53N 11 34 E
Elvire →, *Australia* **124 C4** 17 51 S 128 11 E
Elvire, Mt., *Australia* **125 E2** 29 22 S 119 36 E
Elvo →, *Italy* **44 C5** 45 23N 8 21 E
Elwell, L., *U.S.A.* **158 B8** 48 22N 111 17W
Elwood, *Ill., U.S.A.* **157 C8** 41 24N 88 7W
Elwood, *Ind., U.S.A.* **157 D11** 40 17N 85 50W
Elwood, *Nebr., U.S.A.* **154 E5** 40 36N 99 52W
Elx = Elche, *Spain* **41 G4** 38 15N 0 42W
Ely, *U.K.* **21 E8** 52 24N 0 16 E
Ely, *Minn., U.S.A.* **154 B9** 47 55N 91 51W
Ely, *Nev., U.S.A.* **158 G6** 39 15N 114 54W
Elyria, *U.S.A.* **150 E2** 41 22N 82 7W
Elyrus, *Greece* **48 F5** 35 15N 23 45 E
Elz →, *Germany* **31 G3** 48 18N 7 44 E
Emådalen, *Sweden* **16 C8** 61 20N 14 44 E
Émaé, *Vanuatu* **133 G6** 17 4 S 168 24 E
Emāmrūd, *Iran* **97 B7** 36 30N 55 0 E
Emån →, *Sweden* **17 G10** 57 8N 16 30 E
Emao, *Vanuatu* **133 G6** 17 29 S 168 30 E
Emateloa, *Dem. Rep. of the Congo* **114 B3** 1 16N 18 42 E
Emba, *Kazakstan* **66 E6** 48 50N 58 8 E
Emba →, *Kazakstan* **57 E9** 46 55N 53 28 E
Embarcación, *Argentina* **174 A3** 23 10 S 64 0W
Embarras →, *U.S.A.* **157 F9** 38 39N 87 37W
Embarras Portage, *Canada* **143 B6** 58 27N 111 28W
Embetsu, *Japan* **70 B10** 44 44N 141 47 E
Embi = Emba, *Kazakstan* **66 E6** 48 50N 58 8 E
Embi = Emba →, *Kazakstan* **57 E9** 46 55N 53 28 E
Embira →, *Brazil* **172 B3** 7 19 S 70 15W
Embóna, *Greece* **38 E11** 36 13N 27 51 E
Embrach, *Switz.* **33 B7** 47 30N 8 36 E
Embrun, *France* **29 D10** 44 34N 6 30 E
Embu, *Kenya* **118 C4** 0 32 S 37 38 E
Emden, *Germany* **30 B3** 53 21N 7 12 E
Emecik, *Turkey* **49 E9** 36 46N 27 49 E
Emerald, *Queens., Australia* **126 C4** 23 32 S 148 10 E
Emerald, *Vic., Australia* **122 E8** 37 56 S 145 29 E
Emerson, *Canada* **143 D9** 49 0N 97 10W
Emerson, *U.S.A.* **152 A5** 34 8N 84 45W
Emet, *Turkey* **49 B11** 39 20N 29 15 E
Emeti, *Papua N. G.* **132 D2** 7 53 S 143 15 E
Emi Koussi, *Chad* **109 E3** 19 45N 18 55 E
Emília-Romagna □, *Italy* **44 D8** 44 45N 11 0 E
Emilius, Mte., *Italy* **44 C4** 45 45N 7 20 E
Eminabad, *Pakistan* **92 C6** 32 2N 74 8 E
Emine, Nos, *Bulgaria* **51 D11** 42 40N 27 56 E
Eminence, *U.S.A.* **157 F11** 38 22N 85 11W
Emirau I., *Papua N. G.* **132 A6** 1 40 S 150 0 E
Emirdağ, *Turkey* **100 C4** 39 2N 31 8 E
Emissi, Tarso, *Chad* **109 D3** 21 27N 18 36 E
Emlenton, *U.S.A.* **150 E5** 41 11N 79 43W
Emlichheim, *Germany* **30 C2** 52 37N 6 51 E
Emmaboda, *Sweden* **17 H9** 56 37N 15 32 E
Emmalane, *U.S.A.* **152 C7** 32 46N 82 0W
Emmaus, *S. Africa* **116 D4** 29 2 S 25 15 E
Emmaus, *U.S.A.* **151 F9** 40 32N 75 30W
Emme →, *Switz.* **32 B5** 47 14N 7 32 E
Emmeloord, *Neths.* **24 B5** 52 44N 5 46 E
Emmen, *Neths.* **24 B6** 52 48N 6 57 E
Emmen, *Switz.* **31 H4** 47 5N 8 18 E
Emmenbrücke, *Switz.* **33 B6** 47 4N 8 16 E
Emmendingen, *Germany* **31 G3** 48 6N 7 51 E
Emmental, *Switz.* **32 C4** 46 55N 7 40 E
Emmerich, *Germany* **30 D2** 51 50N 6 14 E
Emmet, *Australia* **126 C3** 24 45 S 144 30 E
Emmetsburg, *U.S.A.* **156 A2** 43 7N 94 41W
Emmett, *Idaho, U.S.A.* **158 E5** 43 52N 116 30W
Emmett, *Mich., U.S.A.* **150 D2** 42 59N 82 46W
Emmiganuru, *India* **95 E3** 15 44N 77 29 E
Emmonak, *U.S.A.* **144 E6** 62 46N 164 30W
Emo, *Canada* **143 D10** 48 38N 93 50W
Emőd, *Hungary* **52 C5** 47 57N 20 47 E
Emona, *Bulgaria* **51 D11** 42 43N 27 53 E
Empalme, *Mexico* **162 B2** 28 1N 110 49W
Empangeni, *S. Africa* **117 D5** 28 50 S 31 52 E
Empedrado, *Argentina* **174 B4** 28 0 S 58 46W
Emperor Seamount Chain, *Pac. Oc.* **134 D9** 40 0N 170 0 E
Empire, *U.S.A.* **152 C6** 32 21N 83 18W
Empoli, *Italy* **44 E7** 43 43N 10 57 E
Emporia, *Kans., U.S.A.* **154 F6** 38 25N 96 11W
Emporia, *Va., U.S.A.* **149 G7** 36 42N 77 32W
Emporium, *U.S.A.* **150 E6** 41 31N 78 14W
Empress, *Canada* **143 C7** 50 57N 110 0W
Empty Quarter = Rub' al Khālī, *Si. Arabia* **99 C5** 19 0N 48 0 E
Ems →, *Germany* **30 B3** 53 20N 7 12 E
Emsdale, *Canada* **150 A5** 45 32N 79 19W
Emsdetten, *Germany* **30 C3** 52 10N 7 32 E
Emu, *China* **75 C15** 43 40N 128 6 E
Emu Park, *Australia* **126 C5** 23 13 S 150 50 E
'En 'Avrona, *Israel* **103 F4** 29 43N 35 0 E
En Nahrat, *Mali* **110 D4** 22 55N 3 36W
En Nahud, *Sudan* **107 E2** 12 45N 28 25 E
En Nofalab, *Sudan* **107 D3** 15 52N 32 32 E
Ena, *Japan* **73 B9** 35 25N 137 25 E
Ena-San, *Japan* **73 B9** 35 26N 137 36 E
Enambú, *Colombia* **168 C3** 1 1N 70 17W
Enana, *Namibia* **116 B2** 17 30 S 16 23 E
Enånger, *Sweden* **16 C11** 61 30N 17 9 E
Enard B., *U.K.* **22 C3** 58 5N 5 20W
Enare = Inarijärvi, *Finland* **14 B22** 69 0N 28 0 E
Enarotali, *Indonesia* **83 B5** 3 55 S 136 21 E
Enbekshi, *Kazakstan* **65 C4** 41 22N 68 3 E
Encampment, *U.S.A.* **158 F10** 41 12N 106 47W
Encantadas, Serra, *Brazil* **175 C5** 30 40 S 53 0W
Encarnación, *Paraguay* **175 B4** 27 15 S 55 50W
Encarnación de Diaz, *Mexico* **162 C4** 21 30N 102 13W
Enchi, *Ghana* **112 D4** 5 53N 2 48W
Encinitas, *U.S.A.* **161 M9** 33 3N 117 17W
Encino, *U.S.A.* **159 J11** 34 39N 105 28W
Encontrados, *Venezuela* **168 B3** 9 3N 72 14W
Encounter B., *Australia* **128 C3** 35 45 S 138 45 E
Encruzilhada, *Brazil* **171 E3** 15 31 S 40 54W
Encs, *Hungary* **52 B6** 48 20N 21 8 E
Endako, *Canada* **142 C3** 54 6N 125 2W
Ende, *Indonesia* **82 C2** 8 45 S 121 40 E
Endeavour Str., *Australia* **126 A3** 10 45 S 142 0 E
Endelave, *Denmark* **17 J4** 55 46N 10 18 E
Enden, *Norway* **17 C4** 61 47N 10 15 E
Enderbury I., *Kiribati* **134 H10** 3 8 S 171 5W
Enderby, *Canada* **142 C5** 50 35N 119 10W
Enderby I., *Australia* **124 D2** 20 35 S 116 30 E
Enderby Land, *Antarctica* **7 C5** 66 0 S 53 0 E
Enderlin, *U.S.A.* **154 B6** 46 38N 97 36W
Endicott, *U.S.A.* **151 D8** 42 6N 76 4W
Endicott Mts., *U.S.A.* **144 C10** 68 0N 152 0W
Endimari →, *Brazil* **172 B4** 8 46 S 66 7W
Endwell, *U.S.A.* **151 D8** 42 6N 76 2W
Endyalgout I., *Australia* **124 B5** 11 40 S 132 35 E
Ene →, *Peru* **172 C3** 11 10 S 74 18W
Eneabba, *Australia* **125 E2** 29 49 S 115 16 E
Energetīcheskīy, *Kazakstan* **65 B8** 43 25N 77 1 E
Energetik, *Russia* **64 F7** 51 45N 58 45 E
Enewetak Atoll, *Marshall Is.* **134 F8** 11 30N 162 15 E
Enez, *Turkey* **51 F10** 40 45N 26 5 E
Enfer, Pte. d', *Martinique* **164 c** 14 22N 60 54W
Enfield, *Canada* **141 D7** 44 56N 63 32W
Enfield, *Conn., U.S.A.* **151 E12** 41 58N 72 36W
Enfield, *Ill., U.S.A.* **157 F8** 38 6N 88 20W
Enfield, *N.H., U.S.A.* **151 C12** 43 39N 72 9W
Enga □, *Papua N. G.* **132 C2** 5 30 S 143 30 E
Engadin, *Switz.* **31 J6** 46 45N 10 10 E
Engan, *Norway* **18 A5** 63 8N 8 31 E
Engaño, C., *Dom. Rep.* **165 C6** 18 30N 68 20W
Engaño, C., *Phil.* **80 B4** 18 35N 122 23 E
Engaru, *Japan* **70 B11** 44 3N 143 31 E
Engcobo, *S. Africa* **117 E4** 31 37 S 28 0 E
Engelberg, *Switz.* **33 C6** 46 48N 8 26 E
Engels, *Russia* **60 E8** 51 28N 46 6 E
Engemann L., *Canada* **143 B7** 58 0N 106 55W
Engerdal, *Norway* **18 C8** 61 45N 11 58 E
Engershatu, *Eritrea* **107 D4** 16 7N 38 34 E
Enggano, *Indonesia* **84 D2** 5 20 S 102 40 E
Engil, *Morocco* **110 B4** 33 12N 4 32W
Engineer Group, *Papua N. G.* **132 F6** 10 35 S 151 20 E
Engkilili, *Malaysia* **85 B4** 1 3N 111 42 E
England, *U.S.A.* **155 H9** 34 33N 91 58W
England □, *U.K.* **20 D7** 53 0N 2 0W
Englee, *Canada* **141 B8** 50 45N 56 5W
Englehart, *Canada* **140 C4** 47 49N 79 52W
Englewood, *Colo., U.S.A.* **154 F2** 39 39N 104 59W
Englewood, *Fla., U.S.A.* **153 J7** 26 58N 82 21W
Englewood, *Ohio, U.S.A.* **157 E12** 39 53N 84 18W
English, *U.S.A.* **157 F10** 38 20N 86 28W
English →, *Canada* **143 C10** 50 35N 93 30W
English →, *U.S.A.* **156 C5** 41 29N 91 32W
English B., *Ascension I.* **9 g** 7 54 S 14 23W
English Bazar = Ingraj Bazar, *India* **93 G13** 24 58N 88 10 E
English Channel, *Europe* **21 G6** 50 0N 2 0W
English River, *Canada* **140 C1** 49 14N 91 0W
Engures ezers, *Latvia* **54 A10** 57 16N 23 6 E
Enguri →, *Georgia* **61 J5** 42 27N 41 38 E
Enid, *U.S.A.* **155 G6** 36 24N 97 53W
Enipévs →, *Greece* **48 B4** 39 22N 22 17 E
Enkhuizen, *Neths.* **24 B5** 52 42N 5 17 E
Enköping, *Sweden* **16 E11** 59 37N 17 4 E
Enle, *China* **76 F3** 24 0N 101 9 E
Enna, *Italy* **47 E7** 37 34N 14 16 E
Ennadai, *Canada* **143 A8** 61 8N 100 53W
Ennadai L., *Canada* **143 A8** 61 0N 101 0W
Enné, O. →, *Chad* **109 F4** 14 24N 18 45 E
Ennedi, *Chad* **109 E4** 17 15N 22 0 E
Enneri Achelouma →, *Niger* **111 D7** 21 55N 13 35 E
Enngonia, *Australia* **127 D4** 29 21 S 145 50 E
Ennigerloh, *Germany* **30 D4** 51 50N 8 2 E
Ennis, *Ireland* **23 D3** 52 51N 8 59W
Ennis, *Mont., U.S.A.* **158 D8** 45 21N 111 44W
Ennis, *Tex., U.S.A.* **155 J6** 32 20N 96 38W
Enniscorthy, *Ireland* **23 D5** 52 30N 6 34W
Enniskillen, *U.K.* **23 B4** 54 21N 7 39W
Ennistimon, *Ireland* **23 D2** 52 57N 9 17W
Enns, *Austria* **34 C7** 48 12N 14 28 E
Enns →, *Austria* **34 C7** 48 14N 14 32 E
Enontekiö, *Finland* **14 B20** 68 23N 23 37 E
Enosburg Falls, *U.S.A.* **151 B12** 44 55N 72 48W
Enping, *China* **77 F9** 22 16N 112 21 E
Enrekang, *Indonesia* **82 B1** 3 34 S 119 47 E
Enrile, *Phil.* **80 C3** 17 34N 121 42 E
Enriquillo, L., *Dom. Rep.* **165 C5** 18 20N 72 5W
Enschede, *Neths.* **24 B6** 52 13N 6 53 E
Ensenada, *Argentina* **174 C4** 34 55 S 57 55W
Ensenada, *Mexico* **162 A1** 31 50N 116 50W
Ensenada de los Muertos, *Mexico* **162 C2** 23 59N 109 50W
Enshi, *China* **76 B7** 30 18N 109 29 E
Enshū-Nada, *Japan* **73 C9** 34 27N 137 38 E
Ensiola, Pta. de n', *Spain* **38 B3** 39 7N 2 55 E
Ensisheim, *France* **27 E14** 47 50N 7 20 E
Ensley, *U.S.A.* **153 E2** 30 31N 87 16W
Entebbe, *Uganda* **118 B3** 0 4N 32 28 E
Enterprise, *Canada* **142 A5** 60 47N 115 45W
Enterprise, *Ala., U.S.A.* **152 D4** 31 19N 85 51W
Enterprise, *Oreg., U.S.A.* **158 D5** 45 25N 117 17W
Entlebuch, *Switz.* **32 C6** 46 59N 8 4 E
Entraygues-sur-Truyère, *France* **28 D6** 44 38N 2 35 E
Entre Ríos, *Bolivia* **174 A3** 21 30 S 64 25W
Entre Rios, *Bahia, Brazil* **171 D4** 11 56 S 38 5W
Entre Rios, *Pará, Brazil* **173 B7** 5 24 S 54 21W
Entre Ríos □, *Argentina* **174 C4** 30 30 S 58 30W
Entrepeñas, Embalse de, *Spain* **40 E2** 40 34N 2 42W
Entroncamento, *Portugal* **43 F2** 39 28N 8 28W
Enugu, *Nigeria* **113 D6** 6 30N 7 30 E
Enugu □, *Nigeria* **113 D6** 6 30N 7 45 E
Enugu Ezike, *Nigeria* **113 D6** 7 0N 7 29 E
Enumclaw, *U.S.A.* **160 C5** 47 12N 121 59W
Envermeu, *France* **26 C8** 49 53N 1 15 E
Envigado, *Colombia* **168 B2** 6 10N 75 35W
Enviken, *Sweden* **16 D9** 60 49N 15 46 E
Envira, *Brazil* **172 B3** 7 18 S 70 13W
Enying, *Hungary* **52 D3** 46 56N 18 15 E
Enyonga, *Gabon* **114 C1** 0 59 S 9 22 E
Enza →, *Italy* **44 D7** 44 54N 10 31 E
Enzan, *Japan* **73 B10** 35 42N 138 44 E
Éolie, Ís., *Italy* **47 D7** 38 30N 14 57 E
Epalinges, *Switz.* **32 C3** 46 33N 6 40 E
Epanomí, *Greece* **50 F6** 40 25N 22 59 E
Epe, *Neths.* **24 B5** 52 21N 5 59 E
Epe, *Nigeria* **113 D5** 6 36N 3 59 E
Epéna, *Congo* **114 B3** 1 22N 17 29 E
Épernay, *France* **27 C10** 49 3N 3 56 E
Épernon, *France* **27 D8** 48 35N 1 40 E
Ephesus, *Turkey* **49 D9** 37 55N 27 22 E
Ephraim, *U.S.A.* **158 G8** 39 22N 111 35W
Ephrata, *Pa., U.S.A.* **151 F8** 40 11N 76 11W
Ephrata, *Wash., U.S.A.* **158 C4** 47 19N 119 33W
Epi, *Vanuatu* **133 F6** 16 43 S 168 15 E
Epidaurus Limera, *Greece* **48 E5** 36 46N 23 0 E
Épila, *Spain* **40 D3** 41 36N 1 17W
Épinac, *France* **27 F11** 46 59N 4 31 E
Épinal, *France* **27 D13** 48 10N 6 27 E
Epira, *Guyana* **169 B6** 5 5N 57 20W
Episkopi, *Cyprus* **39 F8** 34 40N 32 54 E
Episkopí, *Greece* **39 E5** 35 20N 24 20 E
Episkopi Bay, *Cyprus* **39 F8** 34 35N 32 50 E
Epitálion, *Greece* **48 D3** 37 37N 21 30 E
Eppalock, L., *Australia* **128 D6** 36 52 S 144 34 E
Eppan = Appiano, *Italy* **45 B8** 46 28N 11 15 E
Eppingen, *Germany* **31 F4** 49 8N 8 53 E
Epsom, *U.K.* **21 F7** 51 19N 0 16W
Epukiro, *Namibia* **116 C2** 21 40 S 19 9 E
Equality, *U.S.A.* **157 G8** 37 44N 88 20W
Équateur □, *Dem. Rep. of the Congo* **114 B4** 2 0N 21 0 E
Equatorial Guinea ■, *Africa* **114 B1** 2 0N 8 0 E
Equeipa, *Venezuela* **169 B5** 5 22N 62 43W
Er Hai, *China* **76 E3** 25 48N 100 11 E
Er Rachidia, *Morocco* **110 B4** 31 58N 4 20W
Er Rahad, *Sudan* **107 E3** 12 45N 30 32 E
Er Rif, *Morocco* **111 A4** 35 1N 4 1W
Er Rogel, *Sudan* **106 D4** 18 10N 35 25 E
Er Roseires, *Sudan* **107 E3** 11 55N 34 30 E
Er Rua'at, *Sudan* **107 E3** 12 21N 32 17 E
Eraclea, *Italy* **45 C9** 45 35N 12 40 E
Eran, *Phil.* **81 G1** 9 4N 117 42 E
Erandol, *India* **94 D2** 20 56N 75 20 E
Eranga, *Dem. Rep. of the Congo* **114 C3** 1 52 S 18 56 E
Erap, *Papua N. G.* **132 D4** 6 37 S 146 51 E
Erave, *Papua N. G.* **132 D2** 6 39 S 144 0 E
Erave →, *Papua N. G.* **132 D3** 6 54 S 144 47 E
Erāwadī Myit = Irrawaddy →, *Burma* **90 G5** 15 50N 95 6 E
Erāwadī Myitwanya = Irrawaddy, Mouths of the, *Burma* **90 H5** 15 30N 95 0 E
Erba, *Italy* **44 C6** 45 48N 9 15 E
Erba, *Sudan* **106 D4** 19 5N 36 51 E
Erba, J., *Sudan* **106 C4** 20 48N 36 47 E
Erbaa, *Turkey* **100 B7** 40 42N 36 36 E
Erbeskopf, *Germany* **31 F3** 49 44N 7 2 E
Erbil = Arbīl, *Iraq* **101 D11** 36 15N 44 5 E
Erbu, *Ethiopia* **107 E3** 6 44N 34 53 E
Erçek, *Turkey* **96 B4** 38 39N 43 36 E
Erçiş, *Turkey* **101 C10** 39 2N 43 21 E
Erciyaş Dağı, *Turkey* **57 G6** 38 30N 35 30 E
Érd, *Hungary* **52 C3** 47 22N 18 56 E
Erdao Jiang →, *China* **75 C14** 43 0N 127 0 E

Fairplay, *U.S.A.* **159 G11** 39 15N 106 2W
Fairport, *U.S.A.* **150 C7** 43 6N 77 27W
Fairport Harbor, *U.S.A.* **150 E3** 41 45N 81 17W
Fairview, *Canada* **142 B5** 56 5N 118 25W
Fairview, *Mont., U.S.A.* **154 B2** 47 51N 104 3W
Fairview, *Okla., U.S.A.* **155 G5** 36 16N 98 29W
Fairweather, Mt., *U.S.A.* **142 B1** 58 55N 137 32W
Faisalabad, *Pakistan* **91 C4** 31 30N 73 5 E
Faith, *U.S.A.* **154 C3** 45 2N 102 2W
Faizabad, *India* **93 F10** 26 45N 82 10 E
Faizpur, *India* **94 D2** 21 14N 75 49 E
Fajã Grande, *Azores* **9 d2** 39 27N 31 16W
Fajardo, *Puerto Rico* **165 d** 18 20N 65 39W
Fajr, W. →, *Si. Arabia* **96 D3** 29 10N 38 10 E
Fakenham, *U.K.* **20 E8** 52 51N 0 51 E
Fåker, *Sweden* **16 A8** 63 0N 14 34 E
Fakfak, *Indonesia* **83 B4** 2 55 S 132 18 E
Fakfak, Peg., *Indonesia* **83 B4** 2 50 S 132 20 E
Fakiya, *Bulgaria* **51 D11** 42 10N 27 6 E
Fakobli, *Ivory C.* **112 D3** 7 23N 7 23W
Fakse, *Denmark* **17 J6** 55 15N 12 8 E
Fakse Bugt, *Denmark* **17 J6** 55 11N 12 15 E
Fakse Ladeplads, *Denmark* **17 J6** 55 11N 12 9 E
Faku, *China* **75 C12** 42 32N 123 21 E
Falaba, *S. Leone* **112 D2** 9 54N 11 22W
Falaise, *France* **26 D6** 48 54N 0 12W
Falaise, Mui, *Vietnam* **86 C5** 19 6N 105 45 E
Falakrón Óros, *Greece* **50 E7** 41 15N 23 58 E
Falam, *Burma* **90 D4** 23 0N 93 45 E
Falces, *Spain* **40 C3** 42 24N 1 48W
Fălciu, *Romania* **53 D13** 46 17N 28 7 E
Falcó, C. des, *Spain* **38 D1** 38 50N 1 23 E
Falcón □, *Venezuela* **168 A4** 11 0N 69 50W
Falcon, C., *Algeria* **111 A4** 35 50N 0 50W
Falcón, Presa, *Mexico* **163 B5** 26 35N 99 10W
Falcon Lake, *Canada* **143 D9** 49 42N 95 15W
Falcon Reservoir, *U.S.A.* **155 M5** 26 34N 99 10W
Falconara Marittima, *Italy* **45 E10** 43 37N 13 24 E
Falcone, C. del, *Italy* **46 B1** 40 58N 8 12 E
Falconer, *U.S.A.* **150 D5** 42 7N 79 13W
Faléa, *Mali* **112 C2** 12 16N 11 17W
Falefa, *Samoa* **133 W24** 13 54 S 171 31W
Falelatai, *Samoa* **133 W24** 13 55 S 171 59W
Falelima, *Samoa* **133 W23** 13 32 S 172 41W
Falémé →, *Senegal* **112 C2** 14 46N 12 14W
Falenki, *Russia* **64 B3** 58 22N 51 35 E
Falerum, *Sweden* **17 F10** 58 8N 16 13 E
Faleshty = Făleşti, *Moldova* **53 C12** 47 32N 27 44 E
Făleşti, *Moldova* **53 C12** 47 32N 27 44 E
Falfurrias, *U.S.A.* **155 M5** 27 14N 98 9W
Falher, *Canada* **142 B5** 55 44N 117 15W
Falirakí, *Greece* **38 E12** 36 22N 28 12 E
Falkenberg, *Germany* **30 D9** 51 35N 13 14 E
Falkenberg, *Sweden* **17 H6** 56 54N 12 30 E
Falkensee, *Germany* **30 C9** 52 34N 13 4 E
Falkirk, *U.K.* **22 F5** 56 0N 3 47W
Falkirk □, *U.K.* **22 F5** 55 58N 3 49W
Falkland, *U.K.* **22 E5** 56 16N 3 12W
Falkland, East, I., *Falk. Is.* **176 D5** 51 40 S 58 30W
Falkland, West, I., *Falk. Is.* **176 D4** 51 40 S 60 0W
Falkland Is. □, *Atl. Oc.* **9 f** 51 30 S 59 0W
Falkland Sd., *Falk. Is.* **9 f** 52 0 S 60 0W
Falkonéra, *Greece* **48 E5** 36 50N 23 52 E
Falköping, *Sweden* **17 F7** 58 12N 13 33 E
Fall River, *U.S.A.* **151 E13** 41 43N 71 10W
Fällanden, *Switz.* **33 B7** 47 22N 8 38 E
Fallbrook, *U.S.A.* **161 M9** 33 23N 117 15W
Fallon, *U.S.A.* **158 G4** 39 28N 118 47W
Falls City, *U.S.A.* **154 E7** 40 3N 95 36W
Falls Creek, *U.S.A.* **150 E6** 41 9N 78 48W
Falmouth, *Jamaica* **164 a** 18 30N 77 40W
Falmouth, *U.K.* **21 G2** 50 9N 5 5W
Falmouth, *Ky., U.S.A.* **157 F12** 38 41N 84 20W
Falmouth, *Mass., U.S.A.* **151 E14** 41 33N 70 37W
Falsa, Pta., *Mexico* **162 B1** 27 51N 115 3W
False B., *S. Africa* **116 E2** 34 15 S 18 40 E
False Divi Pt., *India* **95 G5** 15 43N 80 50 E
False Pass, *U.S.A.* **144 J7** 54 51N 163 25W
False Pt., *India* **94 D8** 20 18N 86 48 E
Falso, C., *Honduras* **164 C3** 15 12N 83 21W
Falster, *Denmark* **17 K5** 54 45N 11 55 E
Falsterbo, *Sweden* **15 J15** 55 23N 12 50 E
Fălticeni, *Romania* **53 C11** 47 21N 26 20 E
Falun, *Sweden* **16 D9** 60 37N 15 37 E
Famagusta, *Cyprus* **39 E9** 35 8N 33 55 E
Famagusta Bay, *Cyprus* **39 E10** 35 15N 34 0 E
Famatina, Sierra de, *Argentina* **174 B2** 27 30 S 68 0W
Family L., *Canada* **143 C9** 51 54N 95 27W
Famoso, *U.S.A.* **161 K7** 35 37N 119 12W
Fan Xian, *China* **74 G8** 35 55N 115 38 E
Fana, *Mali* **112 C3** 13 0N 6 56W
Fanad Hd., *Ireland* **23 A4** 55 17N 7 38W
Fanahammaren, *Norway* **18 D2** 60 16N 5 20 E
Fanárion, *Greece* **48 B3** 39 24N 21 47 E
Fandriana, *Madag.* **117 C8** 20 14 S 47 21 E
Fang, *Thailand* **76 H2** 19 55N 99 13 E
Fang Xian, *China* **77 A8** 32 3N 110 40 E
Fangaga, *Sudan* **106 D4** 17 40N 37 50 E
Fangak, *Sudan* **107 F3** 9 4N 30 53 E
Fangchang, *China* **77 B12** 31 5N 118 4 E
Fangcheng, *China* **74 H7** 33 18N 112 59 E
Fangchenggang, *China* **76 G7** 21 42N 108 21 E
Fangliao, *Taiwan* **77 F13** 22 22N 120 38 E
Fangshan, *China* **74 E6** 38 3N 111 25 E
Fangzi, *China* **75 F10** 36 33N 119 10 E
Fani i Madh →, *Albania* **50 E4** 41 56N 20 16 E
Fanjakana, *Madag.* **117 C8** 21 10 S 46 53 E
Fanjiatun, *China* **75 C13** 43 40N 125 15 E
Fanling, *China* **69 F11** 22 30N 114 8 E
Fannich, L., *U.K.* **22 D4** 57 38N 4 59W
Fannrem, *Norway* **18 A6** 63 16N 9 50 E
Fannūj, *Iran* **97 E8** 26 35N 59 38 E
Fanø, *Denmark* **17 J2** 55 25N 8 25 E
Fano, *Italy* **45 E10** 43 50N 13 1 E
Fanshi, *China* **74 E7** 39 12N 113 20 E
Fao = Al Fāw, *Iraq* **97 D6** 30 0N 48 30 E
Faqirwali, *Pakistan* **92 E5** 29 27N 73 0 E
Fâqûs, *Egypt* **106 H7** 30 44N 31 47 E
Fara in Sabina, *Italy* **45 F9** 42 12N 12 43 E
Faradje, *Dem. Rep. of the Congo* **118 B2** 3 50N 29 45 E
Farafangana, *Madag.* **117 C8** 22 49 S 47 50 E
Farâfra, El Wâhât el-, *Egypt* **106 B2** 27 15N 28 20 E
Farāh, *Afghan.* **91 B1** 32 20N 62 7 E
Farāh □, *Afghan.* **91 B1** 32 25N 62 10 E
Farahalana, *Madag.* **117 A9** 14 26 S 50 10 E
Faraid, Gebel, *Egypt* **106 C4** 23 33N 35 19 E
Farako, *Ivory C.* **112 D4** 10 45N 6 50W
Faramana, *Burkina Faso* **112 C4** 11 56N 4 45W
Faranah, *Guinea* **112 C2** 10 3N 10 45W
Farap, *Turkmenistan* **65 D1** 39 9N 63 36 E
Farasān, Jazā'ir, *Si. Arabia* **98 C3** 16 45N 41 55 E
Farasan Is. = Farasān, Jazā'ir,
Si. Arabia **98 C3** 16 45N 41 55 E
Faratsiho, *Madag.* **117 B8** 19 24 S 46 57 E
Farbarachi, *Somali Rep.* **120 D3** 2 30N 45 30 E
Fardes →, *Spain* **43 H7** 37 35N 3 0W
Fareham, *U.K.* **21 G6** 50 51N 1 11W
Farewell, *U.S.A.* **144 E9** 62 31N 153 54W
Farewell, C., *N.Z.* **131 A7** 40 29 S 172 43 E
Farewell C. = Nunap Isua,
Greenland **10 F6** 59 48N 43 55W
Farewell Spit, *N.Z.* **131 A8** 40 35 S 173 0 E
Färgelanda, *Sweden* **17 F5** 58 34N 12 0 E
Farghona, *Uzbekistan* **66 E8** 40 23N 71 19 E
Farghonskaya Dolina, *Uzbekistan* **65 C5** 40 50N 71 30 E
Fargo, *Ga., U.S.A.* **152 E7** 30 41N 82 34W
Fargo, *N. Dak., U.S.A.* **154 B6** 46 53N 96 48W
Fār'iah, W. al →, *West Bank* **103 C4** 32 12N 35 27 E
Faribault, *U.S.A.* **154 C8** 44 18N 93 16W
Faridabad, *India* **92 E6** 28 26N 77 19 E
Faridkot, *India* **92 D6** 30 44N 74 45 E
Faridpur, *Bangla.* **90 D2** 23 15N 89 55 E
Faridpur, *India* **93 E8** 28 13N 79 33 E
Fārigh, W. al →, *Libya* **108 B3** 30 28N 20 44 E
Färila, *Sweden* **16 C9** 61 48N 15 50 E
Farim, *Guinea-Biss.* **112 C1** 12 27N 15 9W
Farīmān, *Iran* **97 C8** 35 40N 59 49 E
Farina, *Australia* **127 E2** 30 3 S 138 15 E
Farinha →, *Brazil* **170 C2** 6 51 S 47 30W
Fariones, Pta., *Canary Is.* **9 e2** 29 13N 13 28W
Fâriskûr, *Egypt* **106 H7** 31 20N 31 43 E
Färjestaden, *Sweden* **17 H10** 56 39N 16 27 E
Farkadhón, *Greece* **48 B4** 39 36N 22 4 E
Farkhor = Parkhar, *Tajikistan* **65 E4** 37 30N 69 34 E
Farleigh, *Australia* **126 K7** 21 4 S 149 8 E
Farley, *U.S.A.* **156 B6** 42 27N 91 0W
Farmakonisi, *Greece* **49 D9** 37 17N 27 5 E
Farmer City, *U.S.A.* **157 D8** 40 15N 88 39W
Farmersburg, *U.S.A.* **157 E9** 39 15N 87 23W
Farmerville, *U.S.A.* **155 J8** 32 47N 92 24W
Farmingdale, *U.S.A.* **151 F10** 40 12N 74 10W
Farmington, *Canada* **142 B4** 55 54N 120 30W
Farmington, *Calif., U.S.A.* **160 H6** 37 55N 120 59W
Farmington, *Ga., U.S.A.* **152 B6** 33 47N 83 26W
Farmington, *Ill., U.S.A.* **156 D7** 40 42N 90 0W
Farmington, *Iowa, U.S.A.* **156 D5** 40 38N 91 44W
Farmington, *Maine, U.S.A.* **149 C10** 44 40N 70 9W
Farmington, *Mo., U.S.A.* **155 G9** 37 47N 90 25W
Farmington, *N.H., U.S.A.* **151 C13** 43 24N 71 4W
Farmington, *N. Mex., U.S.A.* **159 H9** 36 44N 108 12W
Farmington, *Utah, U.S.A.* **158 F8** 41 0N 111 12W
Farmington →, *U.S.A.* **151 E12** 41 51N 72 38W
Farmland, *U.S.A.* **157 D11** 40 15N 85 5W
Farmville, *U.S.A.* **148 G6** 37 18N 78 24W
Färnäs, *Sweden* **16 D8** 61 0N 14 39 E
Farne Is., *U.K.* **20 B6** 55 38N 1 37W
Farnham, *Canada* **151 A12** 45 17N 72 59W
Farnham, Mt., *Canada* **142 C5** 50 29N 116 30W
Faro, *Brazil* **169 D6** 2 10 S 56 39W
Faro, *Canada* **138 B6** 62 11N 133 22W
Faro, *Portugal* **43 H3** 37 2N 7 55W
Fårö, *Sweden* **15 H18** 57 55N 19 5 E
Faro □, *Portugal* **43 H2** 37 12N 8 10W
Faro, Réserve de, *Cameroon* **114 A2** 8 15N 12 37 E
Fårösund, *Sweden* **17 G13** 57 52N 19 2 E
Farquhar, C., *Australia* **125 D1** 23 50 S 113 36 E
Farquhar Is., *Seychelles* **121 F4** 11 0 S 52 0 E
Farrars Cr. →, *Australia* **126 D3** 25 35 S 140 43 E
Farrāshband, *Iran* **97 D7** 28 57N 52 5 E
Farrell, *U.S.A.* **150 E4** 41 13N 80 30W
Farrell Flat, *Australia* **128 B3** 33 48 S 138 48 E
Farrokhī, *Iran* **97 C8** 33 50N 59 31 E
Farruch, C. = Ferrutx, C., *Spain* **38 B4** 39 47N 3 21 E
Fārs □, *Iran* **97 D7** 29 30N 55 0 E
Fársala, *Greece* **48 B4** 39 17N 22 23 E
Fārsī, *Afghan.* **91 B1** 33 47N 63 15 E
Farsø, *Denmark* **17 H3** 56 46N 9 19 E
Farson, *U.S.A.* **158 E9** 42 6N 109 27W
Farsund, *Norway* **15 G12** 58 5N 6 55 E
Fartak, Râs, *Si. Arabia* **96 D2** 28 5N 34 34 E
Fartak, Ra's, *Yemen* **99 D6** 15 38N 52 15 E
Fărtăneşti, *Romania* **53 E12** 45 49N 27 59 E
Fartura, Serra da, *Brazil* **175 B5** 26 21 S 52 52W
Faru, *Nigeria* **113 C6** 12 48N 6 12 E
Fārūj, *Iran* **97 B8** 37 14N 58 14 E
Fårup, *Denmark* **17 H3** 56 33N 9 51 E
Farvel, Kap = Nunap Isua,
Greenland **10 F6** 59 48N 43 55W
Farwell, *U.S.A.* **155 H3** 34 23N 103 2W
Fāryāb □, *Afghan.* **65 E2** 36 30N 65 0 E
Fasā, *Iran* **97 D7** 29 0N 53 39 E
Fasano, *Italy* **47 B10** 40 50N 17 22 E
Fashoda, *Sudan* **107 F3** 9 50N 32 2 E
Fassa, *Mali* **112 C3** 13 26N 8 15 E
Fastiv, *Ukraine* **59 G5** 50 7N 29 57 E
Fastov = Fastiv, *Ukraine* **59 G5** 50 7N 29 57 E
Fatagar, Tanjung, *Indonesia* **83 B4** 2 46 S 131 57 E
Fataka, *Solomon Is.* **123 C12** 11 55 S 170 12 E
Fatehabad, *Haryana, India* **92 E6** 29 31N 75 27 E
Fatehabad, *Ut. P., India* **92 F8** 27 1N 78 19 E
Fatehgarh, *India* **93 F8** 27 25N 79 35 E
Fatehpur, *Bihar, India* **93 G11** 24 38N 85 14 E
Fatehpur, *Raj., India* **92 F6** 28 0N 74 40 E
Fatehpur, *Ut. P., India* **93 G9** 25 56N 81 13 E
Fatehpur, *Ut. P., India* **93 F9** 27 10N 81 13 E
Fatehpur Sikri, *India* **92 F6** 27 6N 77 40 E
Fatesh, *Russia* **59 F8** 52 8N 35 57 E
Fathai, *Sudan* **107 F3** 8 5N 31 48 E
Fatick, *Senegal* **112 C1** 14 19N 16 27W
Fatima, *Canada* **141 C7** 47 24N 61 53W
Fátima, *Portugal* **43 F2** 39 37N 8 39W
Fatoya, *Guinea* **112 C3** 11 37N 9 10W
Fatsa, *Turkey* **100 B7** 41 2N 37 31 E
Faucille, Col de la, *France* **27 F13** 46 22N 6 2 E
Faulkton, *U.S.A.* **154 C5** 45 2N 99 8W
Faulquemont, *France* **27 C13** 49 3N 6 36 E
Faure I., *Australia* **125 E1** 25 52 S 113 50 E
Făurei, *Romania* **53 E12** 45 6N 27 19 E
Fauresmith, *S. Africa* **116 D4** 29 44 S 25 17 E
Fauro, *Solomon Is.* **133 L9** 6 55 S 156 7 E
Fauske, *Norway* **14 C16** 67 17N 15 25 E
Fåvang, *Norway* **18 C7** 61 27N 10 11 E
Favânia, *Brazil* **169 D7** 3 7 S 51 48W
Favara, *Italy* **46 E6** 37 19N 13 39 E
Faváritx, C. de, *Spain* **38 B5** 40 0N 4 15 E
Faverges, *France* **29 C10** 45 45N 6 17 E
Favignana, *Italy* **46 E5** 37 56N 12 20 E
Favignana, I., *Italy* **46 E5** 37 56N 12 19 E
Fawcett, Pt., *Australia* **124 B5** 11 46 S 130 2 E
Fawn →, *Canada* **140 A2** 55 20N 87 35W
Fawnskin, *U.S.A.* **161 L10** 34 16N 116 56W
Faxaflói, *Iceland* **11 C3** 64 29N 23 0W
Faxälven →, *Sweden* **16 A10** 63 13N 17 13 E
Faya-Largeau, *Chad* **109 E3** 17 58N 19 6 E
Fayaoué, *Vanuatu* **133 K4** 20 38 S 166 33 E
Fayd, *Si. Arabia* **96 E4** 27 1N 42 52 E
Fayence, *France* **29 E10** 43 38N 6 42 E
Fayette, *Ala., U.S.A.* **149 J2** 33 41N 87 50W
Fayette, *Iowa, U.S.A.* **156 B5** 42 51N 91 48W
Fayette, *La., U.S.A.* **156 E4** 39 9N 92 41W
Fayette, *Mo., U.S.A.* **155 J9** 31 43N 91 4W
Fayette, *Ohio, U.S.A.* **157 C12** 41 40N 84 20W
Fayetteville, *Ark., U.S.A.* **155 G7** 36 4N 94 10W
Fayetteville, *Ga., U.S.A.* **152 B5** 33 27N 84 27W
Fayetteville, *N.C., U.S.A.* **149 H6** 35 3N 78 53W
Fayetteville, *Tenn., U.S.A.* **149 H2** 35 9N 86 34W
Fayied, *Egypt* **106 H8** 30 18N 32 16 E
Fayón, *Spain* **40 D5** 41 15N 0 20 E
Fazao-Malfakassa, Parc Nat. de,
Togo **113 D5** 8 45N 0 50 E
Fazenda Libongo, *Angola* **115 D2** 8 24 S 13 24 E
Fazenda Nova, *Brazil* **171 E1** 16 11 S 50 48W
Fazilka, *India* **92 D6** 30 27N 74 2 E
Fazilpur, *Pakistan* **92 E4** 29 18N 70 29 E
Fdérik, *Mauritania* **110 D2** 22 40N 12 45W
Feale →, *Ireland* **23 D2** 52 27N 9 37W
Fear, C., *U.S.A.* **149 J7** 33 50N 77 58W
Feather →, *U.S.A.* **158 G3** 38 47N 121 36W
Feather Falls, *U.S.A.* **160 F5** 39 36N 121 16W
Featherston, *N.Z.* **130 H4** 41 6 S 175 20 E
Featherstone, *Zimbabwe* **119 F3** 18 42 S 30 55 E
Fécamp, *France* **26 C7** 49 45N 0 22 E
Feda, *Norway* **18 F3** 58 17N 6 50 E
Fedala = Mohammedia, *Morocco* **110 B3** 33 44N 7 21W
Federación, *Argentina* **174 C4** 31 0 S 57 55W
Federal Capital Terr. □, *Nigeria* **113 D6** 9 0N 7 10 E
Federal Way, *U.S.A.* **160 C4** 47 18N 122 19W
Fedeshkūh, *Iran* **97 D7** 28 49N 53 50 E
Fedje, *Norway* **18 D1** 60 47N 4 43 E
Fehérgyarmat, *Hungary* **52 C7** 47 58N 22 30 E
Fehmarn, *Germany* **30 A7** 54 27N 11 7 E
Fehmarn Bælt, *Europe* **17 K5** 54 35N 11 20 E
Fehmarn Belt = Fehmarn Bælt,
Europe **17 K5** 54 35N 11 20 E
Fei Xian, *China* **75 G9** 35 18N 117 59 E
Feijó, *Brazil* **172 B3** 8 9 S 70 21W
Feilding, *N.Z.* **130 G4** 40 13 S 175 35 E
Feira de Santana, *Brazil* **171 D4** 12 15 S 38 57W
Feiring, *Norway* **18 D8** 60 30N 11 10 E
Feixi, *China* **77 B11** 31 43N 117 59 E
Feixiang, *China* **74 F8** 36 30N 114 45 E
Fejaj, Chott el, *Tunisia* **108 B1** 33 52N 9 14 E
Fejér □, *Hungary* **52 C3** 47 9N 18 30 E
Fejø, *Denmark* **17 K5** 54 55N 11 30 E
Feke, *Turkey* **100 D6** 37 48N 35 56 E
Fekete →, *Hungary* **52 E3** 45 47N 18 15 E
Felanitx, *Spain* **38 B4** 39 28N 3 9 E
Felda, *U.S.A.* **153 J8** 26 34N 81 26W
Feldbach, *Austria* **34 E8** 46 57N 15 52 E
Feldberg, *Baden-W., Germany* **31 H3** 47 52N 8 0 E
Feldberg,
Mecklenburg-Vorpommern,
Germany **30 B9** 53 20N 13 25 E
Feldkirch, *Austria* **34 D2** 47 15N 9 37 E
Feldkirchen, *Austria* **34 E7** 46 44N 14 6 E
Felicité, *Seychelles* **121 b** 4 19 S 55 52 E
Felicity, *U.S.A.* **157 F12** 38 51N 84 6W
Felipe Carrillo Puerto, *Mexico* **163 D7** 19 38N 88 3W
Felixburg, *Zimbabwe* **117 B5** 19 29 S 30 51 E
Felixlândia, *Brazil* **171 E3** 18 47 S 44 55W
Felixstowe, *U.K.* **21 F9** 51 58N 1 23 E
Felletin, *France* **28 C6** 45 53N 2 11 E
Fellingsbro, *Sweden* **16 E9** 59 26N 15 37 E
Fellsmere, *U.S.A.* **153 H9** 27 46N 80 36W
Felton, *U.S.A.* **160 H4** 37 3N 122 4W
Feltre, *Italy* **45 B8** 46 1N 11 54 E
Femer Bælt = Fehmarn Bælt,
Europe **17 K5** 54 35N 11 20 E
Femø, *Denmark* **17 K5** 54 58N 11 35 E
Femunden, *Norway* **15 E14** 62 10N 11 53 E
Fen He →, *China* **74 G6** 35 36N 110 42 E
Fene, *Spain* **42 B2** 43 27N 8 9W
Fenelon Falls, *Canada* **150 B6** 44 32N 78 45W
Fener Burnu, *Turkey* **49 E9** 36 58N 27 18 E
Feneroa, *Ethiopia* **107 E4** 13 5N 39 3 E
Feng Xian, *Jiangsu, China* **74 G9** 34 43N 116 35 E
Feng Xian, *Shaanxi, China* **74 H4** 33 54N 106 40 E
Fengári, *Greece* **51 F9** 40 25N 25 32 E
Fengcheng, *Jiangxi, China* **77 C10** 28 12N 115 48 E
Fengcheng, *Liaoning, China* **75 D13** 40 28N 124 5 E
Fengfeng, *China* **74 F8** 36 28N 114 8 E
Fenggang, *China* **76 D6** 27 57N 107 47 E
Fenghua, *China* **77 C13** 29 40N 121 25 E
Fenghuang, *China* **76 D7** 27 57N 109 29 E
Fengkai, *China* **77 F8** 23 24N 111 30 E
Fengkang, *Taiwan* **77 F13** 22 12N 120 41 E
Fengle, *China* **77 B9** 31 29N 112 29 E
Fenglin, *Taiwan* **77 F13** 23 45N 121 26 E
Fengning, *China* **74 D9** 41 10N 116 33 E
Fengqing, *China* **76 E2** 24 38N 99 55 E
Fengqiu, *China* **74 G8** 35 2N 114 25 E
Fengrun, *China* **75 E10** 39 48N 118 8 E
Fengshan, *Guangxi Zhuangzu,*
China **76 E7** 24 39N 109 15 E
Fengshan, *Guangxi Zhuangzu,*
China **76 E6** 24 31N 107 3 E
Fengshan, *Taiwan* **77 F13** 22 38N 120 21 E
Fengshun, *China* **77 F11** 23 46N 116 10 E
Fengtai, *Anhui, China* **77 A11** 32 50N 116 40 E
Fengtai, *Beijing, China* **74 E9** 39 50N 116 18 E
Fengxian, *China* **77 B13** 30 55N 121 26 E
Fengxiang, *China* **74 G4** 34 29N 107 25 E
Fengxin, *China* **77 C10** 28 41N 115 18 E
Fengyang, *China* **75 H9** 32 51N 117 29 E
Fengyi, *China* **76 E3** 25 37N 100 20 E
Fengyüan, *Taiwan* **77 E13** 24 15N 120 35 E
Fengzhen, *China* **74 D7** 40 25N 113 2 E
Feni Is., *Papua N. G.* **132 C7** 4 0 S 153 40 E
Fennimore, *U.S.A.* **156 B6** 42 59N 90 39W
Fenny, *Bangla.* **90 D3** 22 55N 91 32 E
Feno, C. de, *France* **29 G12** 41 58N 8 33 E
Fenoarivo, *Fianarantsoa, Madag.* **117 C8** 21 43 S 46 24 E
Fenoarivo, *Fianarantsoa, Madag.* **117 C8** 20 52 S 46 53 E
Fenoarivo Afovoany, *Madag.* **117 B8** 18 26 S 46 34 E
Fenoarivo Atsinanana, *Madag.* **117 B8** 17 22 S 49 25 E
Fens, The, *U.K.* **20 E7** 52 38N 0 2W
Fensmark, *Denmark* **17 J5** 55 17N 11 48 E
Fenton, *U.S.A.* **157 B13** 42 48N 83 42W
Fenxi, *China* **74 F6** 36 40N 111 31 E
Fenyang, *China* **74 F6** 37 18N 111 48 E
Fenyi, *China* **77 D10** 27 45N 114 47 E
Feodosiya, *Ukraine* **59 K8** 45 2N 35 16 E
Fer, C. de, *Algeria* **111 A6** 37 3N 7 10 E
Fera, *Solomon Is.* **133 M10** 8 6 S 159 37 E
Ferdows, *Iran* **97 C8** 33 58N 58 2 E
Fère-Champenoise, *France* **27 D10** 48 45N 3 59 E
Fère-en-Tardenois, *France* **27 C10** 49 10N 3 30 E
Ferentino, *Italy* **45 G10** 41 42N 13 15 E
Ferfer, *Somali Rep.* **120 C3** 5 4N 45 9 E
Fergana = Farghona, *Uzbekistan* **66 E8** 40 23N 71 19 E
Fergana Range, *Asia* **65 C6** 41 0N 73 50 E
Ferganskaya Dolina =
Farghonskaya Dolina,
Uzbekistan **65 C5** 40 50N 71 30 E
Fergus, *Canada* **150 C4** 43 43N 80 24W
Fergus Falls, *U.S.A.* **154 B6** 46 17N 96 4W
Ferguson, *U.S.A.* **156 F6** 38 45N 90 18W
Fergusson I., *Papua N. G.* **132 E6** 9 30 S 150 45 E
Fériana, *Tunisia* **108 B1** 34 59N 8 33 E
Feričanci, *Croatia* **52 E2** 45 32N 18 0 E
Ferkane, *Algeria* **111 B6** 34 37N 7 26 E
Ferkéssédougou, *Ivory C.* **112 D3** 9 35N 5 6W
Ferlach, *Austria* **34 E7** 46 32N 14 18 E
Ferland, *Canada* **140 B2** 50 19N 88 27W
Ferlo, Vallée du, *Senegal* **112 B2** 15 15N 14 15W
Ferlo-Nord, Réserve de Faune du,
Senegal **112 B2** 15 43N 14 0W
Ferlo-Sud, Réserve de Faune du,
Senegal **112 B2** 15 23N 14 30W
Fermanagh □, *U.K.* **23 B4** 54 21N 7 40W
Fermo, *Italy* **45 E10** 43 9N 13 43 E
Fermont, *Canada* **141 B6** 52 47N 67 5W
Fermoselle, *Spain* **42 D4** 41 19N 6 27W
Fermoy, *Ireland* **23 D3** 52 9N 8 16W
Fernán Nuñéz, *Spain* **43 H6** 37 40N 4 44W
Fernández, *Argentina* **174 B3** 27 55 S 63 50W
Fernandina, I., *Ecuador* **172 a** 0 25 S 91 30W
Fernandina Beach, *U.S.A.* **152 F8** 30 40N 81 27W
Fernando de Noronha, *Brazil* **170 B5** 4 0 S 33 10W
Fernando Póo = Bioko, *Eq. Guin.* **113 E6** 3 30N 8 40 E
Fernandópolis, *Brazil* **171 F1** 20 16 S 50 14W
Ferndale, *U.S.A.* **160 B4** 48 51N 122 36W
Fernie, *Canada* **142 D5** 49 30N 115 5W
Fernlees, *Australia* **126 C4** 23 51 S 148 7 E
Fernley, *U.S.A.* **158 G4** 39 36N 119 15W
Feroke, *India* **95 J2** 11 9N 75 46 E
Ferozepore = Firozpur, *India* **92 D6** 30 55N 74 40 E
Férrai, *Greece* **51 F10** 40 53N 26 10 E
Ferrandina, *Italy* **47 B9** 40 29N 16 27 E
Ferrara, *Italy* **45 D8** 44 50N 11 35 E
Ferrato, C., *Italy* **46 C2** 39 18N 9 38 E
Ferreira do Alentejo, *Portugal* **43 G2** 38 4N 8 6W
Ferreira Gomes, *Brazil* **170 A1** 0 48N 51 8W
Ferreñafe, *Peru* **172 B2** 6 42 S 79 50W
Ferrerías, *Spain* **38 B5** 39 59N 4 1 E
Ferret, C., *France* **28 D2** 44 38N 1 15W
Ferrette, *France* **27 E14** 47 30N 7 20 E
Ferriday, *U.S.A.* **155 K9** 31 38N 91 33W
Ferriere, *Italy* **44 D6** 44 40N 9 30 E
Ferrières, *France* **27 D9** 48 5N 2 48 E
Ferro, Capo, *Italy* **46 A2** 41 9N 9 31 E
Ferrol, *Spain* **42 B2** 43 29N 8 15W
Ferrol, Pen. de, *Peru* **172 B2** 9 10 S 78 35W
Ferron, *U.S.A.* **159 G8** 39 5N 111 8W
Ferros, *Brazil* **171 E3** 19 14 S 43 2W
Ferrutx, C., *Spain* **38 B4** 39 47N 3 21 E
Ferryland, *Canada* **141 C9** 47 2N 52 53W
Ferrysburg, *U.S.A.* **157 A10** 43 5N 86 13W
Fertile, *U.S.A.* **154 B6** 47 32N 96 17W
Fertőszentmiklós, *Hungary* **52 C1** 47 35N 16 53 E
Fès, *Morocco* **110 B4** 34 0N 5 0W
Feshi, *Dem. Rep. of the Congo* **115 D3** 6 8 S 18 10 E
Fessenden, *U.S.A.* **154 B5** 47 39N 99 38W
Festøy, *Norway* **18 B3** 62 22N 6 19 E
Festus, *U.S.A.* **156 F6** 38 13N 90 24W
Feté Bowé, *Senegal* **112 C2** 14 56N 13 30W
Feteşti, *Romania* **53 F12** 44 22N 27 51 E
Fethiye, *Turkey* **49 E11** 36 36N 29 6 E
Fethiye Körfezi, *Turkey* **49 E10** 36 40N 28 50 E
Fetlar, *U.K.* **22 A8** 60 36N 0 52W
Fetsund, *Norway* **18 E8** 59 56N 11 10 E
Feuchten, *Austria* **33 B11** 47 2N 10 44 E
Feuerthalen, *Switz.* **33 A7** 47 37N 8 38 E
Feuilles →, *Canada* **139 C12** 58 47N 70 4W
Feurs, *France* **29 C8** 45 45N 4 13 E
Fevik, *Norway* **18 F5** 58 22N 8 39 E
Feyzābād, *Badākhshān, Afghan.* **65 E5** 37 7N 70 33 E
Feyzābād, *Fāryāb, Afghan.* **91 A2** 36 17N 64 52 E
Fez = Fès, *Morocco* **110 B4** 34 0N 5 0W
Fezzan, *Libya* **108 C2** 27 0N 13 0 E
Fia, *Congo* **114 C2** 3 25 S 14 49 E
Fiambalá, *Argentina* **174 B2** 27 45 S 67 37W
Fianarantsoa, *Madag.* **117 C8** 21 26 S 47 5 E
Fianarantsoa □, *Madag.* **117 B8** 19 30 S 47 0 E
Fianga, *Cameroon* **109 G3** 9 55N 15 9 E
Fiche, *Ethiopia* **107 F4** 9 50N 38 46 E
Fichtelgebirge, *Germany* **31 E7** 50 2N 11 55 E
Ficksburg, *S. Africa* **117 D4** 28 51 S 27 53 E
Fidenza, *Italy* **44 D7** 44 52N 10 3 E
Fiditi, *Nigeria* **113 D5** 7 45N 3 53 E
Fidjeland, *Norway* **18 F3** 58 57N 6 56 E
Field →, *Australia* **126 C2** 23 48 S 138 0 E
Field I., *Australia* **124 B5** 12 5 S 132 23 E
Fieni, *Romania* **53 E10** 45 8N 25 25 E
Fier, *Albania* **50 F3** 40 43N 19 33 E
Fierzë, *Albania* **50 D4** 42 15N 20 1 E
Fiesch, *Switz.* **32 D6** 46 25N 8 12 E
Fife □, *U.K.* **22 E5** 56 16N 3 1W
Fife Ness, *U.K.* **22 E6** 56 17N 2 35W
Fifth Cataract, *Sudan* **106 D3** 18 22N 33 50 E
Figari, *France* **29 G13** 41 29N 9 7 E
Figeac, *France* **28 D6** 44 37N 2 2 E
Figeholm, *Sweden* **17 G10** 57 22N 16 33 E
Figline Valdarno, *Italy* **45 E8** 43 37N 11 28 E
Figtree, *Zimbabwe* **119 G2** 20 22 S 28 20 E
Figueira Castelo Rodrigo, *Portugal* **42 E4** 40 57N 6 58W
Figueira da Foz, *Portugal* **42 E2** 40 7N 8 54W
Figueiró dos Vinhos, *Portugal* **42 F2** 39 55N 8 16W
Figueres, *Spain* **40 C7** 42 18N 2 58 E
Figuig, *Morocco* **111 B4** 32 5N 1 11W
Fihaonana, *Madag.* **117 B8** 18 36 S 47 12 E
Fiherenana, *Madag.* **117 B8** 18 29 S 48 24 E
Fiherenana →, *Madag.* **117 C7** 23 19 S 43 37 E
Fiji ■, *Pac. Oc.* **133 A2** 17 20 S 179 0 E
Fik, *Ethiopia* **107 F5** 8 10N 42 19 E
Fika, *Nigeria* **113 C7** 11 15N 11 13 E
Filabres, Sierra de los, *Spain* **43 H8** 37 13N 2 20W
Filabusi, *Zimbabwe* **117 C4** 20 34 S 29 20 E
Filadelfia, *Bolivia* **172 C4** 11 20 S 68 46W
Filadélfia, *Brazil* **170 C2** 7 21 S 47 30W
Filadélfia, *Italy* **47 D9** 38 47N 16 17 E
Fil'akovo, *Slovak Rep.* **35 C12** 48 17N 19 50 E
Filey, *U.K.* **20 C7** 54 12N 0 18W
Filey B., *U.K.* **20 C7** 54 12N 0 15W
Filfla, *Malta* **38 F7** 35 47N 14 24 E
Filiaşi, *Romania* **53 F8** 44 32N 23 31 E
Filiátes, *Greece* **38 B10** 39 38N 20 16 E
Filiatrá, *Greece* **48 D3** 37 9N 21 35 E
Filicudi, *Italy* **47 D7** 38 35N 14 33 E
Filim, *Oman* **99 B7** 20 37N 58 12 E
Filingué, *Niger* **113 C5** 14 21N 3 22 E
Filiourí →, *Greece* **51 E9** 41 15N 25 40 E
Filipstad, *Sweden* **16 E8** 59 43N 14 9 E
Filisur, *Switz.* **33 C9** 46 41N 9 40 E
Fillefjell, *Norway* **18 C5** 61 8N 8 10 E
Fillmore, *Calif., U.S.A.* **161 L8** 34 24N 118 55W
Fillmore, *Utah, U.S.A.* **159 G7** 38 58N 112 20W
Filótion, *Greece* **49 D7** 37 3N 25 30 E
Filottrano, *Italy* **45 E10** 43 26N 13 21 E
Filtu, *Ethiopia* **107 F5** 5 8N 40 35 E
Fimi →, *Dem. Rep. of the Congo* **114 C3** 3 1 S 16 58 E
Fina, Réserve de, *Mali* **112 C3** 13 15N 8 46W
Finale Emília, *Italy* **45 D8** 44 50N 11 18 E
Finale Lígure, *Italy* **44 D5** 44 10N 8 20 E
Fiñana, *Spain* **43 H8** 37 10N 2 50W
Finch, *Canada* **151 A9** 45 11N 75 7W
Finch Hatton, *Australia* **126 K6** 20 25 S 148 39 E
Findhorn →, *U.K.* **22 D5** 57 38N 3 38W
Findlay, *U.S.A.* **157 C13** 41 2N 83 39W
Finger L., *Canada* **140 B1** 53 33N 93 30W
Finger Lakes, *U.S.A.* **151 D8** 42 40N 76 30W
Fingoè, *Mozam.* **119 E3** 14 55 S 31 50 E
Finike, *Turkey* **49 E12** 36 21N 30 10 E
Finike Körfezi, *Turkey* **49 E12** 36 17N 30 16 E
Finiq, *Albania* **50 G4** 39 54N 20 3 E
Finistère □, *France* **26 D3** 48 20N 4 0W
Finisterre = Fisterra, *Spain* **42 C1** 42 54N 9 16W
Finisterre, C. = Fisterra, C., *Spain* **42 C1** 42 50N 9 19W
Finisterre Ra., *Papua N. G.* **132 D4** 6 0 S 146 30 E
Finke, *Australia* **126 D1** 25 34 S 134 35 E
Finke Gorge Nat. Park, *Australia* **124 D5** 24 8 S 132 49 E
Finland ■, *Europe* **14 E22** 63 0N 27 0 E
Finland, G. of, *Europe* **15 G21** 60 0N 26 0 E
Finlay →, *Canada* **142 B3** 57 0N 125 10W
Finley, *Australia* **129 C6** 35 38 S 145 35 E

Finley, *U.S.A.* **154 B6** 47 31N 97 50W
Finn →, *Ireland* **23 B4** 54 51N 7 28W
Finnerödja, *Sweden* **17 F8** 58 57N 14 24 E
Finnigan, Mt., *Australia* **126 B4** 15 49 S 145 17 E
Finniss, C., *Australia* **127 E1** 33 8 S 134 51 E
Finnmark, *Norway* **14 B20** 69 37N 23 57 E
Finnsnes, *Norway* **14 B18** 69 14N 18 0 E
Finschhafen, *Papua N. G.* **132 D4** 6 33 S 147 50 E
Finse, *Norway* **18 D4** 60 36N 7 30 E
Finspång, *Sweden* **17 F9** 58 43N 15 47 E
Finsteraarhorn, *Switz.* **32 C6** 46 31N 8 10 E
Finsterwalde, *Germany* **30 D9** 51 37N 13 42 E
Fiora →, *Italy* **45 F8** 42 20N 11 34 E
Fiordland Nat. Park, *N.Z.* **131 F2** 45 46 S 167 0 E
Fiorenzuola d'Arda, *Italy* **44 D6** 44 56N 9 55 E
Fîq, *Syria* **103 C4** 32 46N 35 41 E
Firat = Furāt, Nahr al →, *Asia* **96 D5** 31 0N 47 25 E
Firebag →, *Canada* **143 B6** 57 45N 111 21W
Firebaugh, *U.S.A.* **160 J6** 36 52N 120 27W
Firedrake L., *Canada* **143 A8** 61 25N 104 30W
Firenze, *Italy* **45 E8** 43 46N 11 15 E
Firenzuola, *Italy* **45 D8** 44 7N 11 23 E
Firk →, *Iraq* **96 D5** 30 59N 44 34 E
Firkachi, *Niger* **109 E2** 15 40N 14 20 E
Firmi, *France* **28 D6** 44 33N 2 19 E
Firminy, *France* **29 C8** 45 23N 4 18 E
Firozabad, *India* **93 F8** 27 10N 78 25 E
Firozpur, *India* **92 D6** 30 55N 74 40 E
Firozpur-Jhirka, *India* **92 F7** 27 48N 76 57 E
Fīrūzābād, *Iran* **97 D7** 28 52N 52 35 E
Fīrūzkūh, *Iran* **97 C7** 35 50N 52 50 E
Firvale, *Canada* **142 C3** 52 27N 126 13W
Fish →, *Namibia* **116 D2** 28 7 S 17 10 E
Fish →, *S. Africa* **116 E3** 31 30 S 20 16 E
Fish River Canyon, *Namibia* **116 D2** 27 40 S 17 35 E
Fisheating Cr. →, *U.S.A.* **153 J8** 26 57N 81 7W
Fisher, *Australia* **125 F5** 30 30 S 131 0 E
Fisher B., *Canada* **143 C9** 51 35N 97 13W
Fishers I., *U.S.A.* **151 E13** 41 15N 72 0W
Fishguard, *U.K.* **21 E3** 52 0N 4 58W
Fishing L., *Canada* **143 C9** 52 10N 95 24W
Fishkill, *U.S.A.* **151 E11** 41 32N 73 53W
Fiskárdho, *Greece* **39 C2** 38 28N 20 35 E
Fiskenæsset = Qeqertarsuatsiaat, *Greenland* **10 E5** 63 5N 50 45W
Fismes, *France* **27 C10** 49 20N 3 40 E
Fisterra, *Spain* **42 C1** 42 54N 9 16W
Fisterra, C., *Spain* **42 C1** 42 50N 9 19W
Fitchburg, *U.S.A.* **151 D13** 42 35N 71 48W
Fitjar, *Iceland* **11 C5** 64 28N 21 18W
Fitjar, *Norway* **18 E2** 59 55N 5 17 E
Fitri, L., *Chad* **109 F3** 12 50N 17 28 E
Fitz Roy, *Argentina* **176 C3** 47 0 S 67 0W
Fitzgerald, *Canada* **142 B6** 59 51N 111 36W
Fitzgerald, *U.S.A.* **152 D6** 31 43N 83 15W
Fitzgerald River Nat. Park, *Australia* **125 F3** 33 53 S 120 3 E
Fitzmaurice →, *Australia* **124 B5** 14 45 S 130 5 E
Fitzroy →, *Queens., Australia* **126 C5** 23 32 S 150 52 E
Fitzroy →, *W. Austral., Australia* **124 C3** 17 31 S 123 35 E
Fitzroy Crossing, *Australia* **124 C4** 18 9 S 125 38 E
Fitzwilliam I., *Canada* **150 A3** 45 30N 81 45W
Fiuggi, *Italy* **45 G10** 41 48N 13 13 E
Fiume = Rijeka, *Croatia* **45 C11** 45 20N 14 21 E
Five Points, *U.S.A.* **160 J6** 36 26N 120 6W
Fivizzano, *Italy* **44 D7** 44 14N 10 8 E
Fizi, *Dem. Rep. of the Congo* **118 C2** 4 17 S 28 55 E
Fjæra, *Norway* **18 E3** 59 52N 6 22 E
Fjærland, *Norway* **18 C3** 61 24N 6 43 E
Fjällbacka, *Sweden* **17 F5** 58 36N 11 17 E
Fjärdhundra, *Sweden* **16 E10** 59 47N 16 56 E
Fjellerup, *Denmark* **17 H4** 56 29N 10 34 E
Fjerritslev, *Denmark* **17 G3** 57 5N 9 15 E
Fjugesta, *Sweden* **16 E8** 59 11N 14 52 E
Fkih ben Salah, *Morocco* **110 B3** 32 32N 6 45W
Flå, *Norway* **18 D6** 60 25N 9 28 E
Flagler Beach, *U.S.A.* **153 F8** 29 29N 81 8W
Flagstaff, *U.S.A.* **159 J8** 35 12N 111 39W
Flagstaff B., *St. Helena* **9 h** 15 54 S 5 41W
Flagstaff L., *U.S.A.* **149 C10** 45 12N 70 18W
Flaherty I., *Canada* **140 A4** 56 15N 79 15W
Flåm, *Norway* **15 F12** 60 50N 7 7 E
Flamatt, *Switz.* **32 C4** 46 53N 7 19 E
Flambeau →, *U.S.A.* **154 C9** 45 18N 91 14W
Flamborough Hd., *U.K.* **20 C7** 54 7N 0 5W
Flamengos, *Azores* **9 d1** 38 33N 28 39W
Fläming, *Germany* **30 C8** 52 6N 12 23 E
Flaming Gorge Reservoir, *U.S.A.* **158 F9** 41 10N 109 25W
Flamingo, *U.S.A.* **153 K9** 25 8N 80 57W
Flamingo, Teluk, *Indonesia* **83 C5** 5 30 S 138 0 E
Flanagan, *U.S.A.* **157 D8** 40 53N 88 52W
Flanders = Flandre, *Europe* **27 B9** 50 50N 2 30 E
Flandre, *Europe* **27 B9** 50 50N 2 30 E
Flandre Occidentale = West-Vlaanderen □, *Belgium* **24 D2** 51 0N 3 0 E
Flandre Orientale = Oost-Vlaanderen □, *Belgium* **24 C3** 51 5N 3 50 E
Flandreau, *U.S.A.* **154 C6** 44 3N 96 36W
Flanigan, *U.S.A.* **160 E7** 40 10N 119 53W
Flannan Is., *U.K.* **22 C1** 58 9N 7 52W
Flåsjön, *Sweden* **14 D16** 64 5N 15 40 E
Flat, *U.S.A.* **144 E8** 62 28N 158 1W
Flat →, *Canada* **142 A3** 61 33N 125 18W
Flat →, *U.S.A.* **157 B11** 42 56N 85 20W
Flat I., *Mauritius* **121 d** 19 53 S 57 35 E
Flat Pt., *N.Z.* **130 H4** 41 14 S 175 57 E
Flat Rock, *U.S.A.* **157 B13** 42 6N 83 17W
Flateby, *Norway* **18 E6** 59 50N 11 10 E
Flateyri, *Iceland* **11 A3** 66 3N 23 31W
Flathead L., *U.S.A.* **158 C7** 47 51N 114 8W
Flatrock →, *U.S.A.* **157 F10** 39 12N 85 56W
Flattery, C., *Australia* **126 A4** 14 58 S 145 21 E
Flattery, C., *U.S.A.* **160 B2** 48 23N 124 29W
Flatts Village, *Bermuda* **9 a** 32 18N 64 43W
Flatwoods, *U.S.A.* **148 F4** 38 31N 82 43W
Flawil, *Switz.* **33 B8** 47 26N 9 11 E
Flecha Pt., *Phil.* **81 H4** 7 22N 123 24 E
Flechas Pt., *Phil.* **81 F2** 10 22N 119 34 E
Fleetwood, *U.K.* **20 D4** 53 55N 3 1W
Fleetwood, *U.S.A.* **151 F9** 40 27N 75 49W
Flekke, *Norway* **18 C2** 61 19N 5 20 E
Flekkefjord, *Norway* **15 G12** 58 18N 6 39 E
Flemingsburg, *U.S.A.* **157 F13** 38 25N 83 45W
Flemington, *U.S.A.* **150 E7** 41 7N 77 28W
Flemish Cap, *Atl. Oc.* **8 B7** 47 0N 45 0W
Flen, *Sweden* **16 E10** 59 4N 16 35 E
Flensburg, *Germany* **30 A5** 54 47N 9 27 E
Flers, *France* **26 D6** 48 47N 0 33W
Flesberg, *Norway* **18 E6** 59 51N 9 27 E
Flesherton, *Canada* **150 B4** 44 16N 80 33W
Flesko, Tanjung, *Indonesia* **82 A2** 0 29N 124 30 E
Fleurance, *France* **28 E4** 43 52N 0 40 E
Fleurier, *Switz.* **32 C3** 46 54N 6 35 E
Fleurieu Pen., *Australia* **128 C3** 35 40 S 138 5 E
Flevoland □, *Neths.* **24 B5** 52 30N 5 30 E
Flims, *Switz.* **33 C8** 46 50N 9 17 E
Flin Flon, *Canada* **143 C8** 54 46N 101 53W
Flinders →, *Australia* **126 B3** 17 36 S 140 36 E
Flinders B., *Australia* **125 F2** 34 19 S 115 19 E
Flinders Chase Nat. Park, *Australia* **128 C2** 35 50 S 136 42 E
Flinders Group, *Australia* **126 A3** 14 11 S 144 15 E
Flinders I., *S. Austral., Australia* **127 E1** 33 44 S 134 41 E
Flinders I., *Tas., Australia* **127 G4** 40 0 S 148 0 E
Flinders Ranges, *Australia* **128 A3** 31 30 S 138 30 E
Flinders Ranges Nat. Park, *Australia* **128 A3** 31 30 S 138 40 E
Flinders Reefs, *Australia* **126 B4** 17 37 S 148 31 E
Flint, *U.K.* **20 D4** 53 15N 3 8W
Flint, *U.S.A.* **157 A13** 43 1N 83 41W
Flint →, *U.S.A.* **152 E5** 30 57N 84 34W
Flint I., *Kiribati* **135 J12** 11 26 S 151 48W
Flintshire □, *U.K.* **20 D4** 53 17N 3 17W
Flirsch, *Austria* **33 B10** 47 9N 10 24 E
Flisa, *Norway* **18 D9** 60 37N 12 0 E
Flisa →, *Norway* **18 D9** 60 37N 12 0 E
Fliseryd, *Sweden* **17 G10** 57 6N 16 15 E
Flix, *Spain* **40 D5** 41 14N 0 32 E
Flixecourt, *France* **27 B9** 50 1N 2 5 E
Floby, *Sweden* **17 F7** 58 8N 13 20 E
Floda, *Sweden* **17 G6** 57 49N 12 22 E
Flodden, *U.K.* **20 B5** 55 37N 2 8W
Flogny-la-Chapelle, *France* **27 E10** 47 57N 3 57 E
Floodwood, *U.S.A.* **154 B8** 46 55N 92 55W
Flora, *Phil.* **80 B3** 18 14N 121 5 E
Flora, *Ill., U.S.A.* **156 F8** 38 40N 88 29W
Flora, *Ind., U.S.A.* **157 D10** 40 33N 86 31W
Florac, *France* **28 D7** 44 20N 3 37 E
Florahome, *U.S.A.* **152 F8** 29 44N 81 54W
Floral City, *U.S.A.* **153 G7** 28 45N 82 17W
Florala, *U.S.A.* **149 K2** 31 0N 86 20W
Florânia, *Brazil* **170 C4** 6 8 S 36 49W
Florence = Firenze, *Italy* **45 E8** 43 46N 11 15 E
Florence, *Ala., U.S.A.* **149 H2** 34 48N 87 41W
Florence, *Ariz., U.S.A.* **159 K8** 33 2N 111 23W
Florence, *Colo., U.S.A.* **154 F2** 38 23N 105 8W
Florence, *Oreg., U.S.A.* **158 E1** 43 58N 124 7W
Florence, *S.C., U.S.A.* **149 H6** 34 12N 79 46W
Florence, L., *Australia* **127 D2** 28 53 S 138 9 E
Florencia, *Colombia* **168 C2** 1 36N 75 36W
Florennes, *Belgium* **24 D4** 50 15N 4 35 E
Florensac, *France* **28 E7** 43 23N 3 28 E
Florenville, *Belgium* **24 E5** 49 40N 5 19 E
Flores, *Azores* **9 d2** 39 26N 31 13W
Flores, *Brazil* **170 C4** 7 51 S 37 59W
Flores, *Guatemala* **164 C2** 16 59N 89 50W
Flores, *Indonesia* **82 C2** 8 35 S 121 0 E
Flores I., *Canada* **142 D3** 49 20N 126 10W
Flores Sea, *Indonesia* **82 C2** 6 30 S 120 0 E
Floresta, *Brazil* **170 C4** 8 40 S 37 26W
Floreşti, *Moldova* **53 C13** 47 53N 28 17 E
Floresville, *U.S.A.* **155 L5** 29 8N 98 10W
Floriano, *Brazil* **170 C3** 6 50 S 43 0W
Florianópolis, *Brazil* **175 B6** 27 30 S 48 30W
Florida, *Cuba* **164 B4** 21 32N 78 14W
Florida, *Uruguay* **175 C4** 34 7 S 56 10W
Florida □, *U.S.A.* **149 L5** 28 0N 82 0W
Florida, Straits of, *U.S.A.* **164 B4** 25 0N 80 0W
Florida B., *U.S.A.* **164 B3** 25 0N 80 45W
Florida City, *U.S.A.* **153 K9** 25 27N 80 29W
Florida Is., *Solomon Is.* **133 M11** 9 55 S 160 15 E
Florida Keys, *U.S.A.* **153 L8** 24 40N 81 0W
Floridablanca, *Phil.* **80 D3** 14 59N 120 31 E
Florídia, *Italy* **47 E8** 37 5N 15 9 E
Flórina, *Greece* **50 F5** 40 48N 21 26 E
Flórina □, *Greece* **50 F5** 40 45N 21 20 E
Florissant, *U.S.A.* **156 F6** 38 48N 90 20W
Florø, *Norway* **15 F11** 61 35N 5 1 E
Flotte, C. de, *N. Cal.* **133 U21** 21 10 S 167 25 E
Flower Station, *Canada* **151 A8** 45 10N 76 41W
Flowerpot I., *Canada* **150 A3** 45 18N 81 38W
Floydada, *U.S.A.* **155 J4** 33 59N 101 20W
Fludir, *Iceland* **11 C6** 64 7N 20 6W
Flüelapass, *Switz.* **33 C9** 46 46N 9 56 E
Flugumyri, *Iceland* **11 B7** 65 34N 19 19W
Fluk, *Indonesia* **82 B3** 1 42 S 127 44 E
Flúmen →, *Spain* **40 D4** 41 43N 0 9W
Flumendosa →, *Italy* **46 C2** 39 26N 9 37 E
Fluminimaggiore, *Italy* **46 C1** 39 26N 8 30 E
Flushing = Vlissingen, *Neths.* **24 C3** 51 26N 3 34 E
Flushing, *U.S.A.* **157 A13** 43 4N 83 51W
Fluvià →, *Spain* **40 C8** 42 12N 3 7 E
Fly →, *Papua N. G.* **83 C6** 8 25 S 143 0 E
Flying Fish, C., *Antarctica* **7 D15** 72 6 S 102 29W
Foa, *Tonga* **133 P13** 19 45 S 174 18W
Foam Lake, *Canada* **143 C8** 51 40N 103 32W
Foča, *Bos.-H.* **50 C2** 43 31N 18 47 E
Foça, *Turkey* **49 C8** 38 39N 26 46 E
Focşani, *Romania* **53 E12** 45 41N 27 15 E
Fodé, *C.A.R.* **114 A4** 5 29N 23 18 E
Fodécontéa, *Guinea* **112 C2** 10 50N 14 22W
Fogang, *China* **77 F9** 23 52N 113 30 E
Foggaret el Arab, *Algeria* **111 C5** 27 13N 2 49 E
Foggaret ez Zoua, *Algeria* **111 C5** 27 20N 2 53 E
Fóggia, *Italy* **47 A8** 41 27N 15 34 E
Foggo, *Nigeria* **113 C6** 11 21N 9 57 E
Foglia →, *Italy* **45 E9** 43 55N 12 54 E
Fogo, *Canada* **141 C9** 49 43N 54 17W
Fogo, *C. Verde Is.* **9 j** 15 5N 24 20W
Fogo I., *Canada* **141 C9** 49 40N 54 5W
Fohnsdorf, *Austria* **34 D7** 47 12N 14 40 E
Föhr, *Germany* **30 A4** 54 43N 8 30 E
Foia, *Portugal* **43 H2** 37 19N 8 37W
Foix, *France* **28 E5** 42 58N 1 38 E
Fojnica, *Bos.-H.* **52 G2** 43 59N 17 51 E
Fokino, *Russia* **58 F8** 53 30N 34 22 E
Fokís □, *Greece* **48 C4** 38 30N 22 15 E
Fokku, *Nigeria* **113 C5** 11 36N 4 32 E
Fokstua, *Norway* **18 B6** 62 7N 9 17 E
Folda, *Nord-Trøndelag, Norway* **14 D14** 64 32N 10 30 E
Folda, *Nordland, Norway* **14 C16** 67 38N 14 50 E
Földeák, *Hungary* **52 D5** 46 19N 20 30 E
Folégandros, *Greece* **48 E6** 36 40N 24 55 E
Foley, *Botswana* **116 C4** 21 34 S 27 21 E
Foley, *Ala., U.S.A.* **149 K2** 30 24N 87 41W
Foley, *Fla., U.S.A.* **152 E6** 30 4N 83 32W
Foleyet, *Canada* **140 C3** 48 15N 82 25W
Folgefonni, *Norway* **15 F12** 60 3N 6 23 E
Foligno, *Italy* **45 F9** 42 57N 12 42 E
Folkestad, *Norway* **18 B3** 62 7N 6 1 E
Folkestone, *U.K.* **21 F9** 51 5N 1 12 E
Folkston, *U.S.A.* **152 E7** 30 50N 82 0W
Folla →, *Norway* **18 B7** 62 7N 10 37 E
Follansbee, *U.S.A.* **150 F4** 40 19N 80 35W
Folldal, *Norway* **18 B6** 62 8N 10 0 E
Follebu, *Norway* **18 C7** 61 13N 10 16 E
Follónica, *Italy* **44 F7** 42 55N 10 45 E
Follónica, G. di, *Italy* **44 F7** 42 54N 10 43 E
Folsom L., *U.S.A.* **160 G5** 38 42N 121 9W
Folteşti, *Romania* **53 E13** 45 45N 28 3 E
Fomboni, *Comoros Is.* **121 a** 12 18 S 43 46 E
Fomm ir-Rih Bay, *Malta* **38 F7** 35 54N 14 20 E
Fond-du-Lac, *Canada* **143 B7** 59 19N 107 12W
Fond du Lac, *U.S.A.* **154 D10** 43 47N 88 27W
Fond-du-Lac →, *Canada* **143 B7** 59 17N 106 0W
Fonda, *Iowa, U.S.A.* **156 B2** 42 35N 94 51W
Fonda, *N.Y., U.S.A.* **151 D10** 42 57N 74 22W
Fondi, *Italy* **46 A6** 41 21N 13 25 E
Fonfría, *Spain* **42 D4** 41 37N 6 9W
Fongafale, *Tuvalu* **134 H9** 8 31 S 179 13 E
Fongen, *Norway* **18 A8** 63 11N 11 38 E
Fonni, *Italy* **46 B2** 40 7N 9 15 E
Fonsagrada = A Fonsagrada, *Spain* **42 B3** 43 8N 7 4W
Fonseca, G. de, *Cent. Amer.* **164 D2** 13 10N 87 40W
Font-Romeu, *France* **28 F5** 42 31N 2 3 E
Fontaine-Française, *France* **27 E12** 47 32N 5 21 E
Fontainebleau, *France* **27 D9** 48 24N 2 40 E
Fontana, *U.S.A.* **161 L9** 34 6N 117 26W
Fontana, L., *Argentina* **176 B2** 44 55 S 71 30W
Fontas →, *Canada* **142 B4** 58 14N 121 48W
Fonte Boa, *Brazil* **168 D4** 2 33 S 66 0W
Fontem, *Cameroon* **113 D6** 5 32N 9 52 E
Fontenay-le-Comte, *France* **28 B3** 46 28N 0 48W
Fontenelle Reservoir, *U.S.A.* **158 E8** 42 1N 110 3W
Fontur, *Iceland* **14 C6** 66 23N 14 32W
Fonuafo'ou, *Tonga* **133 Q13** 20 19 S 175 25W
Fonualei, *Tonga* **133 P13** 18 1 S 174 19W
Fonyód, *Hungary* **52 D2** 46 44N 17 33 E
Foochow = Fuzhou, *China* **77 D12** 26 5N 119 16 E
Foping, *China* **74 H5** 33 41N 108 0 E
Fora →, *Norway* **18 B7** 62 57N 10 40 E
Foraker, Mt., *U.S.A.* **144 E10** 62 58N 151 24W
Forari, *Vanuatu* **133 G6** 17 40 S 168 31 E
Forbach, *France* **27 C13** 49 10N 6 52 E
Forbes, *Australia* **129 B8** 33 22 S 148 5 E
Forbesganj, *India* **93 F12** 26 17N 87 18 E
Forcados, *Nigeria* **113 D6** 5 26N 5 26 E
Forcados →, *Nigeria* **113 D6** 5 25N 5 19 E
Forcalquier, *France* **29 E9** 43 58N 5 47 E
Forchheim, *Germany* **31 F7** 49 43N 11 2 E
Forclaz, Col de la, *Switz.* **32 D4** 46 3N 7 1 E
Ford City, *Calif., U.S.A.* **161 K7** 35 9N 119 27W
Ford City, *Pa., U.S.A.* **150 F5** 40 46N 79 32W
Ford I., *U.S.A.* **145 K14** 21 22N 157 58W
Fordate, *Indonesia* **83 C4** 7 0 S 131 58 E
Førde, *Hordaland, Norway* **18 E2** 59 36N 5 27 E
Førde, *Sogn og Fjordane, Norway* **15 F11** 61 27N 5 53 E
Førdefjorden, *Norway* **18 C2** 61 29N 5 18 E
Førdesfjord, *Norway* **18 E2** 59 25N 5 20 E
Ford's Bridge, *Australia* **127 D4** 29 41 S 145 29 E
Fordyce, *U.S.A.* **155 J8** 33 49N 92 25W
Forécariah, *Guinea* **112 D2** 9 28N 13 10W
Forel, Mt., *Greenland* **10 D7** 66 52N 36 55W
Foremost, *Canada* **142 D6** 49 26N 111 34W
Forest, *Canada* **150 C3** 43 6N 82 0W
Forest, *U.S.A.* **155 J10** 32 22N 89 29W
Forest Acres, *U.S.A.* **152 A9** 34 1N 80 58W
Forest City, *Iowa, U.S.A.* **154 D8** 43 16N 93 39W
Forest City, *N.C., U.S.A.* **149 H5** 35 20N 81 52W
Forest City, *Pa., U.S.A.* **151 E9** 41 39N 75 28W
Forest Grove, *U.S.A.* **160 E3** 45 31N 123 7W
Forest Park, *U.S.A.* **152 B5** 33 37N 84 22W
Forestburg, *Canada* **142 C6** 52 35N 112 1W
Foresthill, *U.S.A.* **160 F6** 39 1N 120 49W
Forestier Pen., *Australia* **127 G4** 43 0 S 148 0 E
Forestville, *Canada* **141 C6** 48 48N 69 2W
Forestville, *Calif., U.S.A.* **160 G4** 38 28N 122 54W
Forestville, *N.Y., U.S.A.* **150 D5** 42 28N 79 10W
Forêt du Day, Parc Nat. du, *Djibouti* **120 B2** 11 56N 42 40 E
Forez, Mts. du, *France* **28 C7** 45 40N 3 50 E
Forfar, *U.K.* **22 E6** 56 39N 2 53W
Forggensee, *Germany* **33 A11** 47 35N 10 44 E
Forks, *U.S.A.* **160 C2** 47 57N 124 23W
Forksville, *U.S.A.* **151 E8** 41 29N 76 35W
Forlì, *Italy* **45 D9** 44 13N 12 3 E
Forman, *U.S.A.* **154 B6** 46 7N 97 38W
Formazza, *Italy* **44 B5** 46 22N 8 26 E
Formby Pt., *U.K.* **20 D4** 53 33N 3 6W
Formentera, *Spain* **38 D1** 38 43N 1 27 E
Formentor, C. de, *Spain* **38 B4** 39 58N 3 13 E
Former Yugoslav Republic of Macedonia = Macedonia ■, *Europe* **50 E5** 41 53N 21 40 E
Fórmia, *Italy* **46 A6** 41 15N 13 37 E
Formiga, *Brazil* **171 F2** 20 27 S 45 25W
Formígine, *Italy* **44 D7** 44 37N 10 51 E
Formosa = Taiwan ■, *Asia* **77 F13** 23 30N 121 0 E
Formosa, *Argentina* **174 B4** 26 15 S 58 10W
Formosa, *Brazil* **171 E2** 15 32 S 47 20W
Formosa □, *Argentina* **174 B4** 25 0 S 60 0W
Formosa, Serra, *Brazil* **173 C6** 12 0 S 55 0W
Formosa Bay, *Kenya* **118 C5** 2 40 S 40 20 E
Formosa Strait = Taiwan Strait, *Asia* **77 E12** 24 40N 120 0 E
Formoso →, *Brazil* **171 D2** 10 34 S 49 56W
Fornells, *Spain* **38 A5** 40 3N 4 7 E
Fornos de Algodres, *Portugal* **42 E3** 40 38N 7 32W
Fornovo di Taro, *Italy* **44 D7** 44 42N 10 6 E
Føroyar, *Atl. Oc.* **14 F9** 62 0N 7 0W
Forres, *U.K.* **22 D5** 57 37N 3 37W
Forrest, *Vic., Australia* **128 E5** 38 33 S 143 47 E
Forrest, *W. Austral., Australia* **125 F4** 30 51 S 128 6 E
Forrest, Mt., *Australia* **125 D4** 24 48 S 127 45 E
Forrest City, *U.S.A.* **155 H9** 35 1N 90 47W
Forreston, *U.S.A.* **156 B7** 42 8N 89 35W
Fors, *Sweden* **16 D10** 60 14N 16 20 E
Forsand, *Norway* **18 F3** 58 54N 6 5 E
Forsayth, *Australia* **126 B3** 18 33 S 143 34 E
Forshaga, *Sweden* **16 E7** 59 33N 13 29 E
Förslöv, *Sweden* **17 H6** 56 21N 12 48 E
Forsmo, *Sweden* **16 A11** 63 16N 17 11 E
Forssa, *Finland* **15 F20** 60 49N 23 38 E
Forst, *Germany* **30 D10** 51 45N 14 37 E
Forster, *Australia* **129 B10** 32 12 S 152 31 E
Forsvik, *Sweden* **17 F8** 58 35N 14 26 E
Forsyth, *Ga., U.S.A.* **152 B6** 33 2N 83 56W
Forsyth, *Mont., U.S.A.* **158 C10** 46 16N 106 41W
Forsyth I., *N.Z.* **131 A9** 40 58 S 174 5 E
Fort Abbas, *Pakistan* **92 E5** 29 12N 72 52 E
Fort Albany, *Canada* **140 B3** 52 15N 81 35W
Fort Ann, *U.S.A.* **151 C11** 43 25N 73 30W
Fort Assiniboine, *Canada* **142 C6** 54 20N 114 45W
Fort Atkinson, *U.S.A.* **157 B8** 42 56N 88 50W
Fort Augustus, *U.K.* **22 D4** 57 9N 4 42W
Fort Beaufort, *S. Africa* **116 E4** 32 46 S 26 40 E
Fort Benton, *U.S.A.* **158 C8** 47 49N 110 40W
Fort Bragg, *U.S.A.* **158 G2** 39 26N 123 48W
Fort Bridger, *U.S.A.* **158 F8** 41 19N 110 23W
Fort Chipewyan, *Canada* **143 B6** 58 42N 111 8W
Fort Collins, *U.S.A.* **154 E2** 40 35N 105 5W
Fort-Coulonge, *Canada* **140 C4** 45 50N 76 45W
Fort Covington, *U.S.A.* **151 B10** 44 59N 74 29W
Fort Davis, *Ala., U.S.A.* **152 C4** 32 15N 85 43W
Fort Davis, *Tex., U.S.A.* **155 K3** 30 35N 103 54W
Fort-de-France, *Martinique* **164 c** 14 36N 61 2W
Fort Defiance, *U.S.A.* **159 J9** 35 45N 109 5W
Fort Dodge, *U.S.A.* **156 B2** 42 30N 94 11W
Fort Drum, *U.S.A.* **153 H9** 27 32N 80 48W
Fort Edward, *U.S.A.* **151 C11** 43 16N 73 35W
Fort Erie, *Canada* **150 D6** 42 54N 78 56W
Fort Fairfield, *U.S.A.* **149 B12** 46 46N 67 50W
Fort Frances, *Canada* **143 D10** 48 36N 93 24W
Fort Gaines, *U.S.A.* **152 D4** 31 36N 85 3W
Fort Garland, *U.S.A.* **159 H11** 37 26N 105 26W
Fort George = Chisasibi, *Canada* **140 B4** 53 50N 79 0W
Fort Good-Hope, *Canada* **138 B7** 66 14N 128 40W
Fort Hancock, *U.S.A.* **159 L11** 31 18N 105 51W
Fort Hertz = Putao, *Burma* **90 B6** 27 28N 97 30 E
Fort Hope, *Canada* **140 B2** 51 30N 88 0W
Fort Irwin, *U.S.A.* **161 K10** 35 16N 116 34W
Fort Kent, *U.S.A.* **149 B11** 47 15N 68 36W
Fort Klamath, *U.S.A.* **158 E3** 42 42N 122 0W
Fort Laramie, *U.S.A.* **154 D2** 42 13N 104 31W
Fort Lauderdale, *U.S.A.* **149 M5** 26 7N 80 8W
Fort Liard, *Canada* **142 A4** 60 14N 123 30W
Fort Liberté, *Haiti* **165 C5** 19 42N 71 51W
Fort Lupton, *U.S.A.* **154 E2** 40 5N 104 49W
Fort Mackay, *Canada* **142 B6** 57 12N 111 41W
Fort Macleod, *Canada* **142 D6** 49 45N 113 30W
Fort McMurray, *Canada* **142 B6** 56 44N 111 7W
Fort McPherson, *Canada* **138 B6** 67 30N 134 55W
Fort Madison, *U.S.A.* **156 D5** 40 38N 91 27W
Fort Meade, *U.S.A.* **149 M5** 27 45N 81 48W
Fort Mitchell, *U.S.A.* **152 C4** 32 20N 85 1W
Fort Morgan, *U.S.A.* **154 E3** 40 15N 103 48W
Fort Myers, *U.S.A.* **149 M5** 26 39N 81 52W
Fort Myers Beach, *U.S.A.* **153 J8** 26 26N 81 52W
Fort Myers Villas, *U.S.A.* **153 J8** 26 34N 81 52W
Fort Nelson, *Canada* **142 B4** 58 50N 122 44W
Fort Nelson →, *Canada* **142 B4** 59 32N 124 0W
Fort Norman = Tulita, *Canada* **138 B7** 64 57N 125 30W
Fort Payne, *U.S.A.* **149 H3** 34 26N 85 43W
Fort Peck, *U.S.A.* **158 B10** 48 1N 106 27W
Fort Peck Dam, *U.S.A.* **158 C10** 48 0N 106 26W
Fort Peck L., *U.S.A.* **158 C10** 48 0N 106 26W
Fort Pierce, *U.S.A.* **149 M5** 27 27N 80 20W
Fort Pierre, *U.S.A.* **154 C4** 44 21N 100 22W
Fort Pierre Bordes = Ti-n-Zaouatene, *Algeria* **111 E5** 19 55N 2 55 E
Fort Plain, *U.S.A.* **151 D10** 42 56N 74 37W
Fort Portal, *Uganda* **118 B3** 0 40N 30 20 E
Fort Providence, *Canada* **142 A5** 61 3N 117 40W
Fort Qu'Appelle, *Canada* **143 C8** 50 45N 103 50W
Fort Recovery, *U.S.A.* **157 D12** 40 25N 84 47W
Fort Resolution, *Canada* **142 A6** 61 10N 113 40W
Fort Rixon, *Zimbabwe* **119 G2** 20 2 S 29 17 E
Fort Ross, *U.S.A.* **160 G3** 38 32N 123 13W
Fort Rupert = Waskaganish, *Canada* **140 B4** 51 30N 78 40W
Fort St. James, *Canada* **142 C4** 54 30N 124 10W
Fort St. John, *Canada* **142 B4** 56 15N 120 50W
Fort Saskatchewan, *Canada* **142 C6** 53 40N 113 15W
Fort Scott, *U.S.A.* **155 G7** 37 50N 94 42W
Fort Severn, *Canada* **140 A2** 56 0N 87 40W
Fort Shevchenko, *Kazakstan* **61 H10** 44 35N 50 23 E
Fort Simpson, *Canada* **142 A4** 61 45N 121 15W
Fort Smith, *Canada* **142 B6** 60 0N 111 51W
Fort Smith, *U.S.A.* **155 H7** 35 23N 94 25W
Fort Stockton, *U.S.A.* **155 K3** 30 53N 102 53W
Fort Sumner, *U.S.A.* **155 H2** 34 28N 104 15W
Fort Thomas, *U.S.A.* **157 E12** 39 5N 84 27W
Fort Thompson, *U.S.A.* **154 C5** 44 3N 99 26W
Fort Valley, *U.S.A.* **152 C6** 32 33N 83 53W
Fort Vermilion, *Canada* **142 B5** 58 24N 116 0W
Fort Walton Beach, *U.S.A.* **149 K2** 30 25N 86 36W
Fort Wayne, *U.S.A.* **157 C11** 41 4N 85 9W
Fort White, *U.S.A.* **152 F7** 29 55N 82 43W
Fort William, *U.K.* **22 E3** 56 49N 5 7W
Fort Worth, *U.S.A.* **155 J6** 32 45N 97 18W
Fort Yates, *U.S.A.* **154 B4** 46 5N 100 38W
Fort Yukon, *U.S.A.* **144 C11** 66 34N 145 16W
Fortaleza, *Bolivia* **172 C4** 12 6 S 66 49W
Fortaleza, *Brazil* **170 B4** 3 45 S 38 35W
Forteau, *Canada* **141 B8** 51 28N 56 58W
Fortescue →, *Australia* **124 D2** 21 0 S 116 4 E
Forth →, *U.K.* **22 E5** 56 9N 3 50W
Forth, Firth of, *U.K.* **22 E6** 56 5N 2 55W
Forthassa Rharbia, *Algeria* **111 B4** 32 52N 1 18W
Fortín Garrapatal, *Paraguay* **173 E5** 21 27 S 61 30W
Fortín General Pando, *Paraguay* **173 D6** 19 45 S 59 47W
Fortín Ingavi, *Paraguay* **173 D5** 19 55 S 60 47W
Fortín Madrejón, *Paraguay* **173 E6** 20 45 S 59 52W
Fortín Uno, *Argentina* **176 A3** 38 50 S 65 18W
Fortore →, *Italy* **45 G12** 41 55N 15 17 E
Fortrose, *N.Z.* **131 G3** 46 38 S 168 45 E
Fortrose, *U.K.* **22 D4** 57 35N 4 9W
Fortuna, *Spain* **41 G3** 38 11N 1 7W
Fortuna, *Calif., U.S.A.* **158 F1** 40 36N 124 9W
Fortuna, *N. Dak., U.S.A.* **154 A3** 48 55N 103 47W
Fortuna Ledge, *U.S.A.* **144 F7** 61 53N 162 5W
Fortune, *Canada* **141 C8** 47 4N 55 50W
Fortune B., *Canada* **141 C8** 47 30N 55 22W
Forūr, *Iran* **97 E7** 26 17N 54 32 E
Fos-sur-Mer, *France* **29 E8** 43 26N 4 56 E
Foshan, *China* **77 F9** 23 4N 113 5 E
Fosna, *Norway* **14 E14** 63 50N 10 20 E
Fosnavåg, *Norway* **15 E11** 62 22N 5 38 E
Foso, *Ghana* **113 D4** 5 43N 1 15W
Foss, *Iceland* **11 D9** 63 51N 17 52W
Fossano, *Italy* **44 D4** 44 33N 7 43 E
Fossil, *U.S.A.* **158 D3** 45 0N 120 9W
Fossombrone, *Italy* **45 E9** 43 41N 12 48 E
Fossvellir, *Iceland* **11 B12** 65 27N 14 37W
Foster, *Australia* **129 E7** 38 40 S 146 15 E
Foster, *Canada* **151 A12** 45 17N 72 30W
Foster, *U.S.A.* **157 F12** 38 48N 84 13W
Foster →, *Canada* **143 B7** 55 47N 105 49W
Fosters Ra., *Australia* **126 C1** 21 35 S 133 48 E
Fostoria, *U.S.A.* **157 C13** 41 10N 83 25W
Fotadrevo, *Madag.* **117 C8** 24 3 S 45 1 E
Fouesnant, *France* **26 E2** 47 53N 4 1W
Fougamou, *Gabon* **114 C2** 1 16 S 10 30 E
Fougères, *France* **26 D5** 48 21N 1 14W
Foul Pt., *Sri Lanka* **95 K5** 8 35N 81 18 E
Foula, *U.K.* **22 A6** 60 10N 2 5W
Foulalaba, *Mali* **112 C3** 10 40N 7 20W
Foulness I., *U.K.* **21 F8** 51 36N 0 55 E
Foulpointe, *Madag.* **117 B8** 17 41 S 49 31 E
Foulweather, C., *U.S.A.* **146 B2** 44 50N 124 5W
Foulwind, C., *N.Z.* **131 B6** 41 45 S 171 28 E
Foum Assaka, *Morocco* **110 C2** 29 8N 10 24W
Foum Zguid, *Morocco* **110 B3** 30 2N 6 59W
Foumban, *Cameroon* **113 D7** 5 45N 10 50 E
Foumbot, *Cameroon* **113 D7** 5 31N 10 28 E
Foumbouni, *Comoros Is.* **121 a** 11 52 S 43 32 E
Foumirate, *Algeria* **110 C4** 27 30N 3 12W
Foundiougne, *Senegal* **112 C1** 14 5N 16 32W
Fountain, *Colo., U.S.A.* **154 F2** 38 41N 104 42W
Fountain, *Fla., U.S.A.* **152 E4** 30 29N 85 25W
Fountain Springs, *U.S.A.* **161 K8** 35 54N 118 51W
Four Mountains, Is. of, *U.S.A.* **144 K5** 53 0N 170 0W
Fourchambault, *France* **27 E10** 47 2N 3 3 E
Fouriesburg, *S. Africa* **116 D4** 28 38 S 28 14 E
Fourmies, *France* **27 B11** 50 1N 4 2 E
Fournás, *Greece* **48 B3** 39 3N 21 52 E
Foúrnoi, *Greece* **49 D8** 37 36N 26 32 E
Fours, *France* **27 F10** 46 50N 3 42 E
Fourth Cataract, *Sudan* **106 D3** 18 47N 32 3 E
Fouta Djalon, *Guinea* **112 C2** 11 20N 12 10W
Foux, Cap-à-, *Haiti* **165 C5** 19 43N 73 27W
Foveaux Str., *N.Z.* **131 G3** 46 42 S 168 10 E
Fowey, *U.K.* **21 G3** 50 20N 4 39W
Fowler, *Calif., U.S.A.* **160 J7** 36 38N 119 41W
Fowler, *Colo., U.S.A.* **154 F3** 38 8N 104 2W
Fowler, *Ind., U.S.A.* **157 D9** 40 37N 87 19W
Fowler, *Mich., U.S.A.* **157 B12** 43 0N 84 45W
Fowlers B., *Australia* **125 F5** 31 59 S 132 34 E
Fowlerville, *U.S.A.* **157 B12** 42 40N 84 4W
Fowman, *Iran* **97 B6** 37 13N 49 19 E
Fox →, *Canada* **143 B10** 56 3N 93 18W
Fox Creek, *Canada* **142 C5** 54 24N 116 48W
Fox Is., *U.S.A.* **144 K6** 53 0N 168 0W
Fox Lake, *Canada* **142 B6** 58 28N 114 31W
Fox Lake, *U.S.A.* **157 B8** 42 24N 88 11W

G

Galaasiya, *Uzbekistan* **65 D2** 39 51N 64 26 E
Galachipa, *Bangla.* **90 D3** 22 8N 90 26 E
Galala, Gebel el, *Egypt* **106 J8** 29 21N 32 22 E
Galán, Cerro, *Argentina* **174 B2** 25 55 S 66 52W
Galana →, *Kenya* **118 C5** 3 9 S 40 8 E
Galangue, *Angola* **115 E3** 13 42 S 16 9 E
Galangue, Serra, *Angola* **115 E3** 14 18 S 15 52 E
Galanta, *Slovak Rep.* **35 C10** 48 11N 17 45 E
Galapagar, *Spain* **42 E7** 40 36N 3 58W
Galápagos = Colón, Arch. de, *Ecuador* **172 a** 0 0 91 0W
Galashiels, *U.K.* **22 F6** 55 37N 2 49W
Galatás, *Greece* **48 D5** 37 30N 23 26 E
Galatea, *N.Z.* **130 E5** 38 24 S 176 45 E
Galaţi, *Romania* **53 E13** 45 27N 28 2 E
Galaţi □, *Romania* **53 E12** 45 45N 27 30 E
Galatia, *Turkey* **100 C5** 39 30N 33 0 E
Galatina, *Italy* **47 B11** 40 10N 18 10 E
Galátone, *Italy* **47 B11** 40 9N 18 4 E
Galax, *U.S.A.* **149 G5** 36 40N 80 56W
Galaxídhion, *Greece* **48 C4** 38 22N 22 23 E
Galcaio, *Somali Rep.* **120 C3** 6 30N 47 30 E
Galdhøpiggen, *Norway* **15 F12** 61 38N 8 18 E
Galeana, *Chihuahua, Mexico* **162 A3** 30 7N 107 38W
Galeana, *Nuevo León, Mexico* **162 A3** 24 50N 100 4W
Galegu, *Sudan* **107 E4** 12 36N 35 2 E
Galela, *Indonesia* **82 A3** 1 50N 127 49 E
Galena, *Alaska, U.S.A.* **144 D8** 64 44N 156 56W
Galena, *Ill., U.S.A.* **156 B6** 42 25N 90 26W
Galeota Pt., *Trin. & Tob.* **169 F10** 10 8N 60 59W
Galera, *Spain* **41 H2** 37 45N 2 33W
Galera, Pta., *Chile* **176 A2** 39 59 S 73 43W
Galera, Pta. da, *Azores* **9 d3** 37 42N 25 30W
Galera Pt., *Trin. & Tob.* **165 D7** 10 49N 60 54W
Galesburg, *Ill., U.S.A.* **156 D6** 40 57N 90 22W
Galesburg, *Mich., U.S.A.* **157 B11** 42 17N 85 26W
Galeton, *U.S.A.* **150 E7** 41 44N 77 39W
Galga, *Ethiopia* **107 F4** 6 39N 37 47 E
Galgasc, *Somali Rep.* **120 D2** 0 11N 41 38 E
Galheirão →, *Brazil* **171 D2** 12 23 S 45 5W
Galheiros, *Brazil* **171 D2** 13 18 S 46 25W
Gali, *Georgia* **61 J5** 42 37N 41 46 E
Galicea Mare, *Romania* **53 F8** 44 4N 23 19 E
Galich, *Russia* **58 A6** 58 22N 42 24 E
Galiche, *Bulgaria* **50 C7** 43 34N 23 53 E
Galicia □, *Spain* **42 C3** 42 43N 7 45W
Galien, *U.S.A.* **157 C10** 41 48N 86 30W
Galilee = Hagalil, *Israel* **103 C4** 32 53N 35 18 E
Galilee, L., *Australia* **126 C4** 22 20 S 145 50 E
Galilee, Sea of = Yam Kinneret, *Israel* **103 C4** 32 45N 35 35 E
Galim, *Cameroon* **113 D7** 7 6N 12 25 E
Galina Pt., *Jamaica* **164 a** 18 24N 76 58W
Galinoporni, *Cyprus* **39 E10** 35 31N 34 18 E
Galion, *U.S.A.* **150 F2** 40 44N 82 47W
Galite, Îs. de la, *Tunisia* **111 A6** 37 30N 8 59 E
Galiuro Mts., *U.S.A.* **159 K8** 32 30N 110 20W
Galiwinku, *Australia* **126 A2** 12 2 S 135 34 E
Gallabat, *Sudan* **107 E4** 12 58N 36 11 E
Gallan Hd., *U.K.* **22 C1** 58 15N 7 2W
Gallarate, *Italy* **44 C5** 45 40N 8 48 E
Gallatin, *Mo., U.S.A.* **156 E3** 39 55N 93 58W
Gallatin, *Tenn., U.S.A.* **149 G2** 36 24N 86 27W
Galle, *Sri Lanka* **95 L5** 6 5N 80 10 E
Gállego →, *Spain* **40 D4** 41 39N 0 51W
Gallegos →, *Argentina* **176 D3** 51 35 S 69 0W
Galletti →, *Ethiopia* **107 F5** 8 46N 41 10 E
Galley Hd., *Ireland* **23 E3** 51 32N 8 55W
Galliate, *Italy* **44 C5** 45 29N 8 42 E
Gallinas, Pta., *Colombia* **168 A3** 12 28N 71 40W
Gallipoli = Gelibolu, *Turkey* **51 F10** 40 28N 26 43 E
Gallípoli, *Italy* **47 B10** 40 3N 17 58 E
Gallipolis, *U.S.A.* **148 F4** 38 49N 82 12W
Gällivare, *Sweden* **14 C19** 67 9N 20 40 E
Gallneukirchen, *Austria* **34 C7** 48 21N 14 25 E
Gällö, *Sweden* **16 B9** 62 55N 15 13 E
Gallo, C., *Italy* **46 D6** 38 13N 13 19 E
Gallocanta, L. de, *Spain* **40 E3** 40 58N 1 30W
Galloo I., *U.S.A.* **151 C8** 43 55N 76 25W
Galloway, *U.K.* **22 F4** 55 1N 4 29W
Galloway, Mull of, *U.K.* **22 G4** 54 39N 4 52W
Gallup, *U.S.A.* **159 J9** 35 32N 108 45W
Gallur, *Spain* **40 D3** 41 52N 1 19W
Gallyaaral, *Uzbekistan* **65 C3** 40 2N 67 35 E
Galong, *Australia* **129 C8** 34 37 S 148 34 E
Galoya, *Sri Lanka* **95 K5** 8 10N 80 55 E
Galt, *Calif., U.S.A.* **160 G5** 38 15N 121 18W
Galt, *Mo., U.S.A.* **156 D3** 40 8N 93 23W
Galten, *Denmark* **17 H3** 56 9N 9 54 E
Galtür, *Austria* **34 E3** 46 58N 10 11 E
Galty Mts., *Ireland* **23 D3** 52 22N 8 10W
Galtymore, *Ireland* **23 D3** 52 21N 8 11W
Galva, *U.S.A.* **156 C6** 41 10N 90 3W
Galvarino, *Chile* **176 A2** 38 24 S 72 47W
Galve de Sorbe, *Spain* **40 D1** 41 13N 3 10W
Galveston, *Ind., U.S.A.* **157 D10** 40 35N 86 11W
Galveston, *Tex., U.S.A.* **155 L7** 29 18N 94 48W
Galveston B., *U.S.A.* **155 L7** 29 36N 94 50W
Gálvez, *Argentina* **174 C3** 32 0 S 61 14W
Galway, *Ireland* **23 C2** 53 17N 9 3W
Galway □, *Ireland* **23 C2** 53 22N 9 1W
Galway B., *Ireland* **23 C2** 53 13N 9 10W
Gam, *Indonesia* **83 B4** 0 27 S 130 36 E
Gam →, *Vietnam* **86 B5** 21 55N 105 12 E
Gamagōri, *Japan* **73 C9** 34 50N 137 14 E
Gamari, L., *Ethiopia* **107 E5** 11 32N 41 40 E
Gamawa, *Nigeria* **113 C7** 12 10N 10 31 E
Gamay, *Phil.* **80 E5** 12 23N 125 18 E
Gamay Bay, *Phil.* **80 E5** 12 21N 125 21 E
Gamba, *Angola* **115 E3** 11 42 S 17 14 E
Gambaga, *Ghana* **113 C4** 10 30N 0 28W
Gambat, *Pakistan* **92 F3** 27 17N 68 26 E
Gambela, *Ethiopia* **107 F3** 8 14N 34 38 E
Gambela Nat. Park, *Ethiopia* **107 F3** 8 0N 34 0 E
Gambell, *U.S.A.* **144 E5** 63 47N 171 45W
Gambhir →, *India* **92 F6** 26 58N 77 27 E
Gambia ■, *W. Afr.* **112 C1** 13 25N 16 0W
Gambia →, *W. Afr.* **112 C1** 13 28N 16 34W
Gambier, *U.S.A.* **150 F2** 40 22N 82 23W
Gambier, C., *Australia* **124 B5** 11 56 S 130 57 E
Gambier Is., *Australia* **128 C2** 35 3 S 136 30 E
Gambier Village, *Bahamas* **9 b** 25 4N 77 30W
Gambo, *C.A.R.* **114 B4** 4 39N 22 16 E
Gambo, *Canada* **141 C9** 48 47N 54 13W
Gamboli, *Pakistan* **92 E3** 29 53N 68 24 E
Gamboma, *Congo* **114 C3** 1 55 S 15 52 E
Gamboula, *C.A.R.* **114 B3** 4 8N 15 9 E
Gambuta, *Indonesia* **82 A2** 0 30N 123 20 E
Gamka →, *S. Africa* **116 E3** 33 18 S 21 39 E
Gamkab →, *Namibia* **116 D2** 28 4 S 17 54 E
Gamla Uppsala, *Sweden* **16 E11** 59 54N 17 40 E
Gamlakarleby = Kokkola, *Finland* **14 E20** 63 50N 23 8 E
Gamleby, *Sweden* **17 G10** 57 54N 16 24 E
Gammon →, *Canada* **143 C9** 51 24N 95 44W
Gammouda, *Tunisia* **108 A1** 35 3N 9 39 E
Gamo-Gofa □, *Ethiopia* **107 F4** 5 40N 36 40 E
Gamoda-Saki, *Japan* **72 D6** 33 50N 134 45 E
Gamou, *Niger* **113 C6** 14 20N 9 55 E
Gampaha, *Sri Lanka* **95 L4** 7 5N 79 59 E
Gampel, *Switz.* **32 D5** 46 19N 7 44 E
Gampola, *Sri Lanka* **95 L5** 7 10N 80 34 E
Gams, *Switz.* **33 B8** 47 12N 9 26 E
Gamtoos →, *S. Africa* **116 E4** 33 58 S 25 1 E
Gan, *France* **28 E3** 43 12N 0 27W
Gan Gan, *Argentina* **176 B3** 42 30 S 68 10W
Gan Goriama, Mts., *Cameroon* **113 D7** 7 44N 12 45 E
Gan Jiang →, *China* **77 C11** 29 15N 116 0 E
Ganado, *U.S.A.* **159 J9** 35 43N 109 33W
Gananita, *Sudan* **106 D3** 18 22N 33 50 E
Gananoque, *Canada* **140 D4** 44 20N 76 10W
Ganassi, *Phil.* **81 H5** 7 49N 124 6 E
Ganāveh, *Iran* **97 D6** 29 35N 50 35 E
Gäncä, *Azerbaijan* **61 K8** 40 45N 46 20 E
Gancheng, *China* **86 C7** 18 51N 108 37 E
Gand = Gent, *Belgium* **24 C3** 51 2N 3 42 E
Ganda, *Angola* **115 E2** 13 3 S 14 35 E
Gandajika, *Dem. Rep. of the Congo* **115 D4** 6 46 S 23 58 E
Gandak →, *India* **93 G11** 25 39N 85 13 E
Gandara, *Phil.* **80 E5** 12 1N 124 49 E
Gandava, *Pakistan* **91 C2** 28 32N 67 32 E
Gander, *Canada* **141 C9** 48 58N 54 35W
Gander L., *Canada* **141 C9** 48 58N 54 35W
Ganderkesee, *Germany* **30 B4** 53 2N 8 32 E
Ganderowe Falls, *Zimbabwe* **119 F2** 17 20 S 29 10 E
Gandesa, *Spain* **40 D5** 41 3N 0 26 E
Gandhi Sagar, *India* **92 G6** 24 40N 75 40 E
Gandhinagar, *India* **92 H5** 23 15N 72 45 E
Gandi, *Nigeria* **113 C6** 12 55N 5 49 E
Gandía, *Spain* **41 G4** 38 58N 0 9W
Gandino, *Italy* **44 C6** 45 49N 9 54 E
Gando, Pta., *Canary Is.* **9 e1** 27 55N 15 22W
Gandole, *Nigeria* **113 D7** 8 28N 11 35 E
Gandou, *Congo* **114 B3** 2 25N 17 25 E
Gandu, *Brazil* **171 D4** 13 45 S 39 30W
Gâneb, *Mauritania* **112 B2** 18 29N 10 8W
Ganedidalem = Gani, *Indonesia* **82 B3** 0 48 S 128 14 E
Ganetti, *Sudan* **106 D3** 18 0N 31 10 E
Ganga →, *India* **93 H14** 23 20N 90 30 E
Ganga Sagar, *India* **93 J13** 21 38N 88 5 E
Gangafani, *Mali* **112 C4** 14 20N 2 20W
Gangakher, *India* **94 E3** 18 57N 76 45 E
Gangan →, *India* **93 E8** 28 38N 78 58 E
Ganganagar, *India* **92 E5** 29 56N 73 56 E
Gangapur, *Maharashtra, India* **94 E2** 19 41N 75 1 E
Gangapur, *Raj., India* **92 F7** 26 32N 76 49 E
Gangara, *Niger* **113 C6** 14 35N 8 29 E
Gangaw, *Burma* **90 D5** 22 5N 94 5 E
Gangaw Taungdan, *Burma* **90 C6** 24 55N 96 35 E
Gangawati, *India* **95 G3** 15 30N 76 36 E
Ganges = Ganga →, *India* **93 H14** 23 20N 90 30 E
Ganges, *Canada* **142 D4** 48 51N 123 31W
Ganges, *France* **28 E7** 43 56N 3 42 E
Ganges, Mouths of the, *India* **90 E3** 21 30N 90 0 E
Gånghester, *Sweden* **17 G7** 57 42N 13 1 E
Gangi, *Italy* **47 E7** 37 48N 14 12 E
Gângiova, *Romania* **53 G8** 43 54N 23 50 E
Gangoh, *India* **92 E7** 29 46N 77 18 E
Gangroti, *India* **93 D8** 30 50N 79 10 E
Gangtok, *India* **90 B2** 27 20N 88 37 E
Gangu, *China* **74 G3** 34 40N 105 15 E
Gangwa, *Dem. Rep. of the Congo* **114 C4** 3 30 S 20 54 E
Gangyao, *China* **75 B14** 44 12N 126 37 E
Gani, *Indonesia* **82 B3** 0 48 S 128 14 E
Ganj, *India* **93 F8** 27 45N 78 57 E
Ganjam, *India* **94 E7** 19 23N 85 4 E
Ganluc, *China* **76 C4** 28 58N 102 59 E
Ganmain, *Australia* **129 C7** 34 47 S 147 1 E
Gannat, *France* **27 F10** 46 7N 3 11 E
Gannett Peak, *U.S.A.* **158 E9** 43 11N 109 39W
Ganquan, *China* **74 F5** 36 20N 109 20 E
Gänserdorf, *Austria* **35 C9** 48 20N 16 43 E
Ganshui, *China* **76 C6** 28 40N 106 40 E
Gansu □, *China* **74 G3** 36 0N 104 0 E
Ganta, *Liberia* **112 D3** 7 15N 8 59W
Gantheaume, C., *Australia* **128 D2** 36 4 S 137 32 E
Gantheaume B., *Australia* **125 E1** 27 40 S 114 10 E
Gantsevichi = Hantsavichy, *Belarus* **59 F4** 52 49N 26 30 E
Ganye, *Nigeria* **113 D7** 8 25N 12 4 E
Ganyem = Genyem, *Indonesia* **83 B6** 2 46 S 140 12 E
Ganyu, *China* **75 G10** 34 50N 119 8 E
Ganyushkino, *Kazakstan* **61 G9** 46 35N 49 20 E
Ganzhou, *China* **77 E10** 25 51N 114 56 E
Gao, *Mali* **113 B4** 16 15N 0 5W
Gao Xian, *China* **76 C5** 28 21N 104 32 E
Gao'an, *China* **77 C10** 28 26N 115 17 E
Gaochun, *China* **77 B12** 31 20N 118 49 E
Gaohe, *China* **77 F9** 22 46N 112 57 E
Gaohebu, *China* **77 B11** 30 43N 116 49 E
Gaokeng, *China* **77 D9** 27 40N 113 58 E
Gaolan Dao, *China* **77 G9** 21 55N 113 10 E
Gaoligong Shan, *China* **76 E2** 24 45N 98 45 E
Gaomi, *China* **75 F10** 36 20N 119 42 E
Gaoming, *China* **77 F9** 22 50N 112 35 E
Gaoping, *China* **74 G7** 35 45N 112 55 E
Gaotang, *China* **74 F9** 36 50N 116 15 E
Gaoua, *Burkina Faso* **112 C4** 10 20N 3 8W
Gaoual, *Guinea* **112 C2** 11 45N 13 25W
Gaoxiong = Kaohsiung, *Taiwan* **77 F13** 22 35N 120 16 E
Gaoyang, *China* **74 E8** 38 40N 115 45 E
Gaoyao, *China* **77 F9** 23 3N 112 27 E
Gaoyou, *China* **77 A12** 32 47N 119 26 E
Gaoyou Hu, *China* **75 H10** 32 45N 119 20 E
Gaoyuan, *China* **75 F9** 37 8N 117 58 E
Gaozhou, *China* **77 G8** 21 58N 110 50 E
Gap, *France* **29 D10** 44 33N 6 5 E
Gapan, *Phil.* **80 D3** 15 19N 120 57 E
Gapat →, *India* **93 G10** 24 30N 82 28 E
Gapuwiyak, *Australia* **126 A2** 12 25 S 135 43 E
Gar, *China* **68 C2** 32 10N 79 58 E
Garabekewül, *Turkmenistan* **65 D2** 38 30N 64 8 E
Garabogazköl Aylagy, *Turkmenistan* **57 F9** 41 0N 53 30 E
Garachico, *Canary Is.* **9 e1** 28 22N 16 46W
Garachiné, *Panama* **164 E4** 8 0N 78 12W
Garad, *Somali Rep.* **120 C3** 6 57N 49 24 E
Garafia, *Canary Is.* **9 e1** 28 48N 17 57W
Garah, *Australia* **127 D4** 29 5 S 149 38 E
Garaina, *Papua N. G.* **132 D4** 7 53 S 147 8 E
Garajonay, *Canary Is.* **9 e1** 28 7N 17 14W
Garamätnyyaz, *Turkmenistan* **65 E2** 37 45N 64 34 E
Garamba, Parc Nat. de la, *Dem. Rep. of the Congo* **118 B2** 4 10N 29 40 E
Garango, *Burkina Faso* **113 C4** 11 48N 0 34W
Garanhuns, *Brazil* **170 C4** 8 50 S 36 30W
Garautha, *India* **93 G8** 25 34N 79 18 E
Garavuti, *Tajikistan* **65 E4** 37 34N 68 26 E
Garawe, *Liberia* **112 E3** 4 35N 8 0W
Garba Harre, *Somali Rep.* **120 D2** 3 19N 42 13 E
Garba Tula, *Kenya* **118 B4** 0 30N 38 32 E
Garbagududu, *Ethiopia* **120 C2** 6 12N 43 50 E
Garbahaarrey = Garba Harre, *Somali Rep.* **120 D2** 3 19N 42 13 E
Garberville, *U.S.A.* **158 F2** 40 6N 123 48W
Garbiyang, *India* **93 D9** 30 8N 80 54 E
Garbsen, *Germany* **30 C5** 52 26N 9 31 E
Garça, *Brazil* **171 F2** 22 14 S 49 37W
Garças →, *Mato Grosso, Brazil* **173 D7** 15 54 S 52 16W
Garças →, *Pernambuco, Brazil* **170 C4** 8 43 S 39 41W
Garchitorena, *Phil.* **80 E4** 13 52N 123 40 E
Garcia Hernandez, *Phil.* **81 G5** 9 37N 124 18 E
Garcias, *Brazil* **173 E7** 20 34 S 52 13W
Gard □, *France* **29 D8** 44 2N 4 10 E
Gard →, *France* **29 E8** 43 51N 4 37 E
Garda, L. di, *Italy* **44 C7** 45 40N 10 41 E
Gardanne, *France* **29 E9** 43 27N 5 27 E
Gårdby, *Sweden* **17 H10** 56 36N 16 38 E
Garde L., *Canada* **143 A7** 62 50N 106 13W
Gardelegen, *Germany* **30 C7** 52 32N 11 24 E
Garden City, *Ga., U.S.A.* **152 C8** 32 6N 81 9W
Garden City, *Kans., U.S.A.* **155 G4** 37 58N 100 53W
Garden City, *Mo., U.S.A.* **156 F2** 38 34N 94 12W
Garden City, *Tex., U.S.A.* **155 K4** 31 52N 101 29W
Garden Grove, *U.S.A.* **161 M9** 33 47N 117 55W
Gardēz, *Afghan.* **91 B3** 33 37N 69 9 E
Gardhíki, *Greece* **48 C3** 38 50N 21 55 E
Garðhur, *Iceland* **11 A10** 66 4N 16 46W
Gardiner, *Maine, U.S.A.* **149 C11** 44 14N 69 47W
Gardiner, *Mont., U.S.A.* **158 D8** 45 2N 110 22W
Gardiners I., *U.S.A.* **151 E12** 41 6N 72 6W
Gardner, *Fla., U.S.A.* **153 H8** 27 21N 81 48W
Gardner, *Ill., U.S.A.* **157 C8** 41 12N 88 17W
Gardner, *Mass., U.S.A.* **151 D13** 42 34N 71 59W
Gardner Canal, *Canada* **142 C3** 53 27N 128 8W
Gardner Pinnacles, *U.S.A.* **145 G10** 25 0N 167 55W
Gardnerville, *U.S.A.* **160 G7** 38 56N 119 45W
Gardno, Jezioro, *Poland* **54 D4** 54 40N 17 7 E
Gardo, *Somali Rep.* **120 C3** 9 30N 49 6 E
Gardone Val Trómpia, *Italy* **44 C7** 45 41N 10 11 E
Gárdony, *Hungary* **52 C3** 47 12N 18 39 E
Gare Tigre, *Fr. Guiana* **169 C7** 4 58N 53 9W
Gareloi I., *U.S.A.* **144 L3** 51 48N 178 48W
Garešnica, *Croatia* **45 C13** 45 36N 16 56 E
Garéssio, *Italy* **44 D5** 44 12N 8 2 E
Garey, *U.S.A.* **161 L6** 34 53N 120 19W
Garfield, *U.S.A.* **158 C5** 47 1N 117 9W
Garforth, *U.K.* **20 D6** 53 47N 1 24W
Gargaliánoi, *Greece* **48 D3** 37 4N 21 38 E
Gargan, Mt., *France* **28 C5** 45 37N 1 39 E
Gargett, *Australia* **126 K6** 21 9 S 148 46 E
Gargouna, *Mali* **113 B5** 15 56N 0 13 E
Gargždai, *Lithuania* **54 C8** 55 43N 21 24 E
Garhchiroli, *India* **94 D5** 20 10N 80 0 E
Gari, *Russia* **64 B9** 59 26N 62 21 E
Garibaldi Prov. Park, *Canada* **142 D4** 49 50N 122 40W
Gariep, L., *S. Africa* **116 E4** 30 40 S 25 40 E
Garies, *S. Africa* **116 E2** 30 32 S 17 59 E
Garigliano →, *Italy* **46 A6** 41 13N 13 45 E
Garissa, *Kenya* **118 C4** 0 25 S 39 40 E
Garkida, *Nigeria* **113 C7** 10 27N 12 36 E
Garko, *Nigeria* **113 C6** 11 45N 8 35 E
Garland, *Tex., U.S.A.* **155 J6** 32 55N 96 38W
Garland, *Utah, U.S.A.* **158 F7** 41 47N 112 10W
Garlasco, *Italy* **44 C5** 45 12N 8 55 E
Garliava, *Lithuania* **54 D10** 54 49N 23 52 E
Garlin, *France* **28 E3** 43 33N 0 16W
Garm, *Tajikistan* **66 F8** 39 0N 70 20 E
Garmāb, *Iran* **97 C8** 35 25N 56 45 E
Garmisch-Partenkirchen, *Germany* **31 H7** 47 30N 11 6 E
Garmo, Qullai = Kommunizma, Pik, *Tajikistan* **66 F8** 39 0N 72 2 E
Garmsār, *Iran* **97 C7** 35 20N 52 25 E
Garner, *U.S.A.* **156 A3** 43 6N 93 36W
Garnett, *U.S.A.* **154 F7** 38 17N 95 14W
Garnpung L., *Australia* **128 B5** 33 25 S 143 10 E
Garo Hills, *India* **90 C3** 25 30N 90 30 E
Garoe, *Somali Rep.* **120 C3** 8 25N 48 33 E
Garonne →, *France* **28 C3** 45 2N 0 36W
Garonne, Canal Latéral à la, *France* **28 D4** 44 15N 0 18 E
Garoowe = Garoe, *Somali Rep.* **120 C3** 8 25N 48 33 E
Garot, *India* **92 G6** 24 19N 75 41 E
Garoua, *Cameroon* **113 D7** 9 19N 13 21 E
Garove I., *Papua N. G.* **132 C5** 4 42 S 149 30 E
Garpenberg, *Sweden* **16 D10** 60 19N 16 12 E
Garphyttan, *Sweden* **16 E8** 59 18N 14 56 E
Garrauli, *India* **93 G8** 25 5N 79 22 E
Garrel, *Germany* **30 C4** 52 57N 8 1 E
Garrett, *U.S.A.* **157 C11** 41 21N 85 8W
Garrigue = Garrigues, *France* **28 E7** 43 40N 3 55 E
Garrigues, *France* **28 E7** 43 40N 3 55 E
Garrison, *Ky., U.S.A.* **157 F13** 38 36N 83 10W
Garrison, *Mont., U.S.A.* **158 C7** 46 31N 112 49W
Garrison, *N. Dak., U.S.A.* **154 B4** 47 40N 101 25W
Garrison Res. = Sakakawea, L., *U.S.A.* **154 B4** 47 30N 101 25W
Garron Pt., *U.K.* **23 A6** 55 3N 5 59W
Garrovillas, *Spain* **43 F4** 39 40N 6 33W
Garrucha, *Spain* **41 H3** 37 11N 1 49W
Garry →, *U.K.* **22 E5** 56 44N 3 47W
Garry, L., *Canada* **138 B9** 65 58N 100 18W
Garsen, *Kenya* **118 C5** 2 20 S 40 5 E
Gärsnäs, *Sweden* **17 J8** 55 32N 14 10 E
Garson L., *Canada* **143 B6** 56 19N 110 2W
Gartempe →, *France* **28 B4** 46 47N 0 49 E
Gartz, *Germany* **30 B10** 53 13N 14 23 E
Garu, *Ghana* **113 C4** 10 55N 0 11W
Garu, *India* **93 H11** 23 40N 84 14 E
Garub, *Namibia* **116 D2** 26 37 S 16 0 E
Garut, *Indonesia* **85 D3** 7 14 S 107 53 E
Garvão, *Portugal* **43 H2** 37 42N 8 21W
Garvie Mts., *N.Z.* **131 F3** 45 30 S 168 50 E
Garwa = Garoua, *Cameroon* **113 D7** 9 19N 13 21 E
Garwa, *India* **93 G10** 24 11N 83 47 E
Garwolin, *Poland* **55 G8** 51 55N 21 38 E
Gary, *U.S.A.* **157 C9** 41 36N 87 20W
Garz, *Germany* **30 A9** 54 19N 13 20 E
Garzê, *China* **76 B3** 31 38N 100 1 E
Garzón, *Colombia* **168 C2** 2 10N 75 40W
Gas City, *U.S.A.* **157 D11** 40 29N 85 37W
Gas-San, *Japan* **70 E10** 38 32N 140 1 E
Gasan, *Phil.* **80 E3** 13 19N 121 51 E
Gasan Kuli = Esenguly, *Turkmenistan* **66 F6** 37 37N 53 59 E
Gaschurn, *Austria* **33 C10** 46 59N 10 2 E
Gascogne, *France* **28 E4** 43 45N 0 20 E
Gascogne, G. de, *Europe* **28 E2** 44 0N 2 0W
Gasconade, *U.S.A.* **156 F5** 38 40N 91 34W
Gasconade →, *U.S.A.* **156 F5** 38 41N 91 33W
Gascony = Gascogne, *France* **28 E4** 43 45N 0 20 E
Gascoyne →, *Australia* **125 D1** 24 52 S 113 37 E
Gascoyne Junction, *Australia* **125 E2** 25 2 S 115 17 E
Gascueña, *Spain* **40 E2** 40 18N 2 31W
Gash, Wadi →, *Ethiopia* **107 D4** 16 48N 35 51 E
Gash-Setit Wildlife Reserve, *Eritrea* **107 D4** 15 12N 36 58 E
Gashagar, *Nigeria* **113 C7** 13 22N 12 47 E
Gashaka, *Nigeria* **113 D7** 7 20N 11 29 E
Gashaka-Gumti Nat. Park, *Nigeria* **113 D7** 7 23N 11 34 E
Gasherbrum, *Pakistan* **93 B7** 35 40N 76 40 E
Gashua, *Nigeria* **113 C7** 12 54N 11 0 E
Gasmata, *Papua N. G.* **132 D6** 6 17 S 150 20 E
Gasparilla I., *U.S.A.* **153 J7** 26 46N 82 16W
Gasparillo, *Trin. & Tob.* **169 F9** 10 18N 61 26W
Gaspé, *Canada* **141 C7** 48 52N 64 30W
Gaspé, C. de, *Canada* **141 C7** 48 48N 64 7W
Gaspé, Pén. de, *Canada* **141 C6** 48 45N 65 40W
Gaspésie, Parc de Conservation de la, *Canada* **141 C6** 48 55N 65 50W
Gassan, *Burkina Faso* **112 C4** 12 49N 3 12W
Gassol, *Nigeria* **113 D7** 8 34N 10 25 E
Gasteiz = Vitoria-Gasteiz, *Spain* **40 C2** 42 50N 2 41W
Gaston, *U.S.A.* **152 B8** 33 49N 81 5W
Gastonia, *U.S.A.* **149 H5** 35 16N 81 11W
Gastoúni, *Greece* **48 D3** 37 51N 21 15 E
Gastoúri, *Greece* **38 B9** 39 34N 19 54 E
Gastre, *Argentina* **176 B3** 42 20 S 69 15W
Gästrikland, *Sweden* **16 D10** 60 45N 16 40 E
Gata, C., *Cyprus* **39 F9** 34 34N 33 2 E
Gata, C. de, *Spain* **41 J2** 36 41N 2 13W
Gata, Sierra de, *Spain* **42 E4** 40 20N 6 45W
Gataga →, *Canada* **142 B3** 58 35N 126 59W
Gătaia, *Romania* **52 E6** 45 26N 21 30 E
Gatchina, *Russia* **58 C6** 59 35N 30 9 E
Gatehouse of Fleet, *U.K.* **22 G4** 54 53N 4 12W
Gates, *U.S.A.* **150 C7** 43 9N 77 42W
Gateshead, *U.K.* **20 C6** 54 57N 1 35W
Gatesville, *U.S.A.* **155 K6** 31 26N 97 45W
Gaths, *Zimbabwe* **119 G3** 20 2 S 30 32 E
Gatico, *Chile* **174 A1** 22 29 S 70 20W
Gâtinais, *France* **27 D9** 48 5N 2 40 E
Gâtine, Hauteurs de, *France* **28 B3** 46 35N 0 45W
Gatineau, *Canada* **151 A9** 45 29N 75 38W
Gatineau →, *Canada* **140 C4** 45 27N 75 42W
Gatineau, Parc Nat. de la, *Canada* **140 C4** 45 40N 76 0W
Gattaran, *Phil.* **80 B3** 18 4N 121 38 E
Gattinara, *Italy* **44 C5** 45 37N 8 22 E
Gatton, *Australia* **127 D5** 27 32 S 152 17 E
Gatun, L., *Panama* **164 E4** 9 7N 79 56W
Gatyana, *S. Africa* **117 E4** 32 16 S 28 31 E
Gau, *Fiji* **133 B2** 18 2 S 179 18 E
Gaua, *Vanuatu* **133 D5** 14 15 S 167 30 E
Gaucín, *Spain* **43 J5** 36 31N 5 19W
Gauer L., *Canada* **143 B9** 57 0N 97 50W
Gauhati = Guwahati, *India* **90 B3** 26 10N 91 45 E
Gauja →, *Latvia* **15 H21** 57 10N 24 16 E
Gaula →, *Norway* **14 E14** 63 21N 10 14 E
Gaupne, *Norway* **18 C4** 61 25N 7 18 E
Gaurdak = Gowurdak, *Turkmenistan* **65 E3** 37 50N 66 4 E
Gauri Phanta, *India* **93 E9** 28 41N 80 36 E
Gauribidanur, *India* **95 H3** 13 37N 77 32 E
Gausta, *Norway* **15 G13** 59 48N 8 40 E
Gauteng □, *S. Africa* **117 D4** 26 0 S 28 0 E
Gāv Koshī, *Iran* **97 D8** 28 38N 57 12 E
Gāvakān, *Iran* **97 D7** 29 37N 53 10 E
Gavallai Nat. Park, *Liberia* **112 D3** 5 8N 7 20W
Gavarnie, *France* **28 F3** 42 44N 0 1W
Gavāter, *Iran* **97 E9** 25 10N 61 31 E
Gāvbandī, *Iran* **97 E7** 27 12N 53 4 E
Gavdhopoúla, *Greece* **39 F5** 34 56N 24 0 E
Gávdhos, *Greece* **39 F5** 34 50N 24 5 E
Gavi, *Italy* **44 D5** 44 41N 8 49 E
Gavião, *Portugal* **43 F3** 39 28N 7 56W
Gaviota, *U.S.A.* **161 L6** 34 29N 120 13W
Gāvkhūnī, Bāţlāq-e, *Iran* **97 C7** 32 6N 52 52 E
Gävle, *Sweden* **16 D11** 60 40N 17 9 E
Gävleborgs län □, *Sweden* **16 C10** 61 30N 16 15 E
Gävlebukten, *Sweden* **16 D11** 60 40N 17 20 E
Gavorrano, *Italy* **44 F7** 42 55N 10 54 E
Gavray, *France* **26 D5** 48 55N 1 20W
Gavrilov Yam, *Russia* **58 D10** 57 18N 39 49 E
Gávrion, *Greece* **48 D6** 37 54N 24 44 E
Gawachab, *Namibia* **116 D2** 27 4 S 17 55 E
Gawai, *Burma* **90 B6** 27 56N 97 30 E
Gawilgarh Hills, *India* **94 D3** 21 15N 76 45 E
Gawler, *Australia* **128 C3** 34 30 S 138 42 E
Gawler Ranges, *Australia* **128 B2** 32 30 S 136 0 E
Gawu, *Nigeria* **113 D6** 9 14N 6 52 E
Gaxun Nur, *China* **68 B5** 42 22N 100 30 E
Gay, *Russia* **64 F7** 51 27N 58 27 E
Gay, *U.S.A.* **152 B5** 33 6N 84 35W
Gaya, *India* **93 G11** 24 47N 85 4 E
Gaya, *Niger* **113 C5** 11 52N 3 28 E
Gaya, *Nigeria* **113 C6** 11 57N 9 0 E
Gayéri, *Burkina Faso* **113 C5** 12 39N 0 29 E
Gaylord, *U.S.A.* **148 C3** 45 2N 84 41W
Gayndah, *Australia* **127 D5** 25 35 S 151 32 E
Gayny, *Russia* **64 A5** 60 18N 54 19 E
Gaysin = Haysyn, *Ukraine* **59 H5** 48 57N 29 25 E
Gayvoron = Hayvoron, *Ukraine* **59 H5** 48 22N 29 52 E
Gaza, *Gaza Strip* **103 D3** 31 30N 34 28 E
Gaza □, *Mozam.* **117 C5** 23 10 S 32 45 E
Gaza Strip □, *Asia* **103 D3** 31 29N 34 25 E
Gazalkent, *Uzbekistan* **65 C4** 41 33N 69 46 E
Gazanjyk, *Turkmenistan* **97 B7** 39 16N 55 32 E
Gazaoua, *Niger* **113 C6** 13 32N 7 55 E
Gāzbor, *Iran* **97 D8** 28 5N 58 51 E
Gazelle, Récif de la, *N. Cal.* **133 T19** 20 10 S 165 30 E
Gazelle Pen., *Papua N. G.* **132 C6** 4 40 S 152 0 E
Gazi, *Dem. Rep. of the Congo* **118 B1** 1 3N 24 30 E
Gaziantep, *Turkey* **100 D7** 37 6N 37 23 E
Gazipaşa, *Turkey* **100 D5** 36 16N 32 18 E
Gbarnga, *Liberia* **112 D3** 7 19N 9 13W
Gbekebo, *Nigeria* **113 D5** 6 20N 4 56 E
Gboko, *Nigeria* **113 D6** 7 17N 9 4 E
Gbongan, *Nigeria* **113 D5** 7 28N 4 20 E
Gcoverega, *Botswana* **116 B3** 19 8 S 24 18 E
Gcuwa, *S. Africa* **117 E4** 32 20 S 28 11 E
Gdańsk, *Poland* **54 D5** 54 22N 18 40 E
Gdańska, Zatoka, *Poland* **54 D6** 54 30N 19 20 E
Gdov, *Russia* **15 G22** 58 48N 27 55 E
Gdynia, *Poland* **54 D5** 54 35N 18 33 E
Geba →, *Guinea-Biss.* **112 C1** 11 46N 15 36W
Gebe, *Indonesia* **83 A3** 0 5N 129 25 E
Gebeciler, *Turkey* **49 C12** 38 46N 30 46 E
Gebeit Mine, *Sudan* **106 C4** 21 3N 36 29 E
Gebel Abyad, *Sudan* **106 D2** 19 0N 28 0 E
Gebel Iweibid, *Egypt* **106 H8** 30 8N 32 13 E
Gebze, *Turkey* **51 F13** 40 47N 29 25 E
Gecha, *Ethiopia* **107 F4** 7 30N 35 18 E
Gedaref, *Sudan* **107 E4** 14 2N 35 28 E
Gedaref □, *Sudan* **107 E4** 14 0N 35 0 E
Gede, Tanjung, *Indonesia* **84 D3** 6 46 S 105 12 E
Gediz, *Turkey* **49 B11** 39 1N 29 24 E
Gediz →, *Turkey* **49 C8** 38 35N 26 48 E
Gedo, *Ethiopia* **107 F4** 9 2N 37 25 E
Gèdre, *France* **28 F4** 42 47N 0 2 E
Gedser, *Denmark* **17 K5** 54 35N 11 55 E
Gedung, Pulau, *Malaysia* **87 c** 5 17N 100 23 E
Geegully Cr. →, *Australia* **124 C3** 18 32 S 123 41 E
Geel, *Belgium* **24 C4** 51 10N 4 59 E
Geelong, *Australia* **128 E6** 38 10 S 144 22 E
Geelvink B. = Cenderwasih, Teluk, *Indonesia* **79 E9** 3 0 S 135 20 E
Geelvink Chan., *Australia* **125 E1** 28 30 S 114 0 E
Geesthacht, *Germany* **30 B6** 53 26N 10 22 E
Geidam, *Nigeria* **113 C7** 12 57N 11 57 E
Geikie →, *Canada* **143 B8** 57 45N 103 52W
Geikie Gorge Nat. Park, *Australia* **124 C4** 18 3 S 125 41 E
Geilenkirchen, *Germany* **30 E2** 50 57N 6 8 E
Geili, *Sudan* **107 D3** 16 1N 32 37 E
Geilo, *Norway* **18 D5** 60 32N 8 14 E
Geisingen, *Germany* **31 H4** 47 54N 8 38 E
Geislingen, *Germany* **31 G5** 48 37N 9 50 E
Geistown, *U.S.A.* **150 F6** 40 18N 78 52W
Geita, *Tanzania* **118 C3** 2 48 S 32 12 E
Geitastrand, *Norway* **18 A6** 63 22N 9 56 E
Geithus, *Norway* **18 E6** 59 57N 9 59 E
Gejiu, *China* **76 F4** 23 20N 103 10 E
Gel →, *Sudan* **107 F2** 7 5N 29 10 E
Gel, Meydān-e, *Iran* **97 D7** 29 4N 54 50 E
Gel River, *Sudan* **107 F2** 7 5N 29 10 E

Glasgow, *Ky., U.S.A.* **148 G3** 37 0N 85 55W
Glasgow, *Mo., U.S.A.* **156 E4** 39 14N 92 51W
Glasgow, *Mont., U.S.A.* **158 B10** 48 12N 106 38W
Glasgow, City of □, *U.K.* **22 F4** 55 51N 4 12W
Glaslyn, *Canada* **143 C7** 53 22N 108 21W
Glastonbury, *U.K.* **21 F5** 51 9N 2 43W
Glastonbury, *U.S.A.* **151 E12** 41 43N 72 37W
Glatt →, *Switz.* **33 B7** 47 28N 8 32 E
Glattfelden, *Switz.* **33 A7** 47 33N 8 30 E
Glauchau, *Germany* **30 E8** 50 49N 12 31 E
Glava, *Sweden* **16 E6** 59 33N 12 35 E
Glavice, *Croatia* **45 E13** 43 43N 16 41 E
Glazov, *Russia* **60 A11** 58 9N 52 40 E
Gleichen, *Canada* **142 C6** 50 52N 113 3W
Gleisdorf, *Austria* **34 D8** 47 6N 15 44 E
Gleiwitz = Gliwice, *Poland* **55 H5** 50 22N 18 41 E
Glen, *U.S.A.* **151 B13** 44 7N 71 11W
Glen Affric, *U.K.* **22 D3** 57 17N 5 1W
Glen Afton, *N.Z.* **130 D4** 37 37 S 175 4 E
Glen Canyon, *U.S.A.* **159 H8** 37 30N 110 40W
Glen Canyon Dam, *U.S.A.* **159 H8** 36 57N 111 29W
Glen Canyon Nat. Recr. Area, *U.S.A.* **159 H8** 37 15N 111 0W
Glen Coe, *U.K.* **22 E3** 56 40N 5 0W
Glen Cove, *U.S.A.* **151 F11** 40 52N 73 38W
Glen Garry, *U.K.* **22 D3** 57 3N 5 7W
Glen Innes, *Australia* **127 D5** 29 44 S 151 44 E
Glen Lyon, *U.S.A.* **151 E8** 41 10N 76 5W
Glen Massey, *N.Z.* **130 D4** 37 38 S 175 2 E
Glen Mor, *U.K.* **22 D4** 57 9N 4 37W
Glen Moriston, *U.K.* **22 D4** 57 11N 4 52W
Glen Robertson, *Canada* **151 A10** 45 22N 74 30W
Glen Spean, *U.K.* **22 E4** 56 53N 4 40W
Glen Ullin, *U.S.A.* **154 B4** 46 49N 101 50W
Glénan, Îs. de, *France* **26 E3** 47 42N 4 0W
Glenavy, *N.Z.* **131 E6** 44 54 S 171 7 E
Glenburn, *Australia* **129 D6** 37 27 S 145 26 E
Glencoe, *Canada* **150 D3** 42 45N 81 43W
Glencoe, *S. Africa* **117 D5** 28 11 S 30 11 E
Glencoe, *Ala., U.S.A.* **152 B4** 33 57N 85 56W
Glencoe, *Minn., U.S.A.* **154 C7** 44 46N 94 9W
Glendale, *Ariz., U.S.A.* **159 K7** 33 32N 112 11W
Glendale, *Calif., U.S.A.* **161 L8** 34 9N 118 15W
Glendale, *Fla., U.S.A.* **152 E3** 30 52N 86 7W
Glendale, *Zimbabwe* **119 F3** 17 22 S 31 5 E
Glendive, *U.S.A.* **154 B2** 47 7N 104 43W
Glendo, *U.S.A.* **154 D2** 42 30N 105 2W
Glenelg, *Australia* **128 C3** 34 58 S 138 31 E
Glenelg →, *Australia* **128 E4** 38 4 S 140 59 E
Glenfield, *U.S.A.* **151 C9** 43 43N 75 24W
Glengarriff, *Ireland* **23 E2** 51 45N 9 34W
Glenham, *N.Z.* **131 G3** 46 26 S 168 52 E
Glenhope, *N.Z.* **131 B7** 41 40 S 172 39 E
Glenmary, Mt., *N.Z.* **131 D4** 43 55 S 169 55 E
Glenmont, *U.S.A.* **150 F2** 40 31N 82 6W
Glenmorgan, *Australia* **127 D4** 27 14 S 149 42 E
Glenn, *U.S.A.* **160 F4** 39 31N 122 1W
Glennallen, *U.S.A.* **144 E11** 62 7N 145 33W
Glennamaddy, *Ireland* **23 C3** 53 37N 8 33W
Glenns Ferry, *U.S.A.* **158 E6** 42 57N 115 18W
Glennville, *U.S.A.* **152 D8** 31 56N 81 56W
Glenorchy, *Australia* **128 D5** 36 55 S 142 41 E
Glenorchy, *N.Z.* **131 E3** 44 51 S 168 24 E
Glenore, *Australia* **126 B3** 17 50 S 141 12 E
Glenreagh, *Australia* **127 E5** 30 2 S 153 1 E
Glenrock, *U.S.A.* **158 E11** 42 52N 105 52W
Glenrothes, *U.K.* **22 E5** 56 12N 3 10W
Glenrowan, *Australia* **129 D7** 36 29 S 146 13 E
Glens Falls, *U.S.A.* **151 C11** 43 19N 73 39W
Glenside, *U.S.A.* **151 F9** 40 6N 75 9W
Glenthompson, *Australia* **128 D5** 37 38 S 142 38 E
Glenties, *Ireland* **23 B3** 54 49N 8 16W
Glenville, *U.S.A.* **148 F5** 38 56N 80 50W
Glenwood, *Canada* **141 C9** 49 0N 54 58W
Glenwood, *Ark., U.S.A.* **155 H8** 34 20N 93 33W
Glenwood, *Ga., U.S.A.* **152 C7** 32 11N 82 40W
Glenwood, *Hawaii, U.S.A.* **145 D6** 19 29N 155 9W
Glenwood, *Iowa, U.S.A.* **154 E7** 41 3N 95 45W
Glenwood, *Minn., U.S.A.* **154 C7** 45 39N 95 23W
Glenwood, *Wash., U.S.A.* **160 D5** 46 1N 121 17W
Glenwood Springs, *U.S.A.* **158 G10** 39 33N 107 19W
Gletsch, *Switz.* **33 C6** 46 34N 8 22 E
Glettinganes, *Iceland* **11 B13** 65 30N 13 37W
Glidden, *U.S.A.* **156 B2** 42 4N 94 44W
Glifádha, *Greece* **48 D5** 37 52N 23 45 E
Glimåkra, *Sweden* **17 H8** 56 19N 14 7 E
Glina, *Croatia* **45 C13** 45 20N 16 6 E
Glinojeck, *Poland* **55 F7** 52 49N 20 21 E
Glittertind, *Norway* **18 C5** 61 40N 8 32 E
Gliwice, *Poland* **55 H5** 50 22N 18 41 E
Globe, *U.S.A.* **159 K8** 33 24N 110 47W
Glodeanu Siliştea, *Romania* **53 F11** 44 50N 26 48 E
Glodeni, *Moldova* **53 C12** 47 45N 27 31 E
Glödnitz, *Austria* **34 E7** 46 53N 14 7 E
Gloggnitz, *Austria* **34 D8** 47 41N 15 56 E
Głogów, *Poland* **55 G3** 51 37N 16 5 E
Głogówek, *Poland* **55 H4** 50 21N 17 53 E
Glomma →, *Norway* **15 G14** 59 12N 10 57 E
Gloria, *Phil.* **80 E3** 12 59N 121 30 E
Glorieuses, Is., *Ind. Oc.* **117 A8** 11 30 S 47 20 E
Glóssa, *Greece* **48 B5** 39 10N 23 45 E
Glossop, *U.K.* **20 D6** 53 27N 1 56W
Gloucester, *Australia* **129 B9** 32 0 S 151 59 E
Gloucester, *Papua N. G.* **132 C5** 5 31 S 148 31 E
Gloucester, *U.K.* **21 F5** 51 53N 2 15W
Gloucester, *U.S.A.* **151 D14** 42 37N 70 40W
Gloucester, C., *Papua N. G.* **132 C5** 5 26 S 148 21 E
Gloucester I., *Australia* **126 J6** 20 0 S 148 30 E
Gloucester Island Nat. Park, *Australia* **126 J6** 20 2 S 148 30 E
Gloucester Point, *U.S.A.* **148 G7** 37 15N 76 29W
Gloucestershire □, *U.K.* **21 F5** 51 46N 2 15W
Gloversville, *U.S.A.* **151 C10** 43 3N 74 21W
Glovertown, *Canada* **141 C9** 48 40N 54 3W
Gloverville, *U.S.A.* **152 B8** 33 32N 81 48W
Głowno, *Poland* **55 G6** 51 59N 19 42 E
Głubczyce, *Poland* **55 H4** 50 13N 17 52 E
Glubokiy, *Russia* **61 F5** 48 35N 40 25 E
Glubokoye = Hlybokaye, *Belarus* **58 E4** 55 10N 27 45 E
Głuchołazy, *Poland* **55 H4** 50 19N 17 24 E
Glücksburg, *Germany* **30 A5** 54 50N 9 33 E
Glückstadt, *Germany* **30 B5** 53 45N 9 25 E
Glukhov = Hlukhiv, *Ukraine* **59 G7** 51 40N 33 58 E
Glusk, *Belarus* **59 F5** 52 53N 28 41 E
Głuszyca, *Poland* **55 H3** 50 41N 16 23 E
Glyngøre, *Denmark* **17 H2** 56 46N 8 52 E
Gmünd, *Kärnten, Austria* **34 E6** 46 54N 13 31 E
Gmünd, *Niederösterreich, Austria* **34 C8** 48 45N 15 0 E
Gmunden, *Austria* **34 D6** 47 55N 13 48 E
Gnali, *Gabon* **114 C2** 2 34 S 11 18 E
Gnarp, *Sweden* **16 B11** 62 3N 17 16 E
Gnesta, *Sweden* **16 E11** 59 3N 17 17 E
Gniew, *Poland* **54 E5** 53 50N 18 50 E
Gniewkowo, *Poland* **55 F5** 52 54N 18 25 E
Gniezno, *Poland* **55 F4** 52 30N 17 35 E
Gnjilane, *Kosovo, Yug.* **50 D5** 42 28N 21 29 E
Gnoien, *Germany* **30 B8** 53 58N 12 41 E
Gnosjö, *Sweden* **17 G7** 57 22N 13 43 E
Gnowangerup, *Australia* **125 F2** 33 58 S 117 59 E
Go Cong, *Vietnam* **87 G6** 10 22N 106 40 E
Gō-Gawa →, *Japan* **72 B4** 35 2N 132 13 E
Gō-no-ura, *Japan* **72 D1** 33 44N 129 40 E
Goa, *India* **95 G1** 15 33N 73 59 E
Goa, *Phil.* **80 E4** 13 42N 123 29 E
Goa □, *India* **95 G1** 15 33N 73 59 E
Goalen Hd., *Australia* **129 D9** 36 33 S 150 4 E
Goalpara, *India* **90 B3** 26 10N 90 40 E
Goaltor, *India* **93 H12** 22 43N 87 10 E
Goalundo Ghat, *Bangla.* **93 H13** 23 50N 89 47 E
Goaso, *Ghana* **112 D4** 6 48N 2 30W
Goat Fell, *U.K.* **22 F3** 55 38N 5 11W
Goba, *Ethiopia* **107 F4** 7 1N 39 59 E
Goba, *Mozam.* **117 D5** 26 15 S 32 13 E
Gobabis, *Namibia* **116 C2** 22 30 S 19 0 E
Gobe, *Papua N. G.* **132 E5** 9 4 S 149 0 E
Göbel, *Turkey* **51 F12** 40 0N 28 9 E
Gobernador Gregores, *Argentina* **176 C2** 48 46 S 70 15W
Gobi, *Asia* **74 C6** 44 0N 110 0 E
Gobichettipalayam, *India* **95 J3** 11 31N 77 21 E
Gobles, *U.S.A.* **157 B11** 42 22N 85 53W
Gobō, *Japan* **73 D7** 33 53N 135 10 E
Gobo, *Sudan* **107 F3** 5 40N 31 10 E
Göçbeyli, *Turkey* **49 B9** 39 13N 27 25 E
Goch, *Germany* **30 D2** 51 41N 6 9 E
Gochas, *Namibia* **116 C2** 24 59 S 18 55 E
Godavari →, *India* **94 F6** 16 25N 82 18 E
Godavari Pt., *India* **94 F6** 17 0N 82 20 E
Godbout, *Canada* **141 C6** 49 20N 67 38W
Godda, *India* **93 G12** 24 50N 87 13 E
Goddua, *Libya* **108 C2** 26 26N 14 19 E
Godech, *Bulgaria* **50 C7** 43 1N 23 4 E
Goderich, *Canada* **140 D3** 43 45N 81 41W
Goderville, *France* **26 C7** 49 38N 0 22 E
Godfrey, *U.S.A.* **156 F6** 38 58N 90 11W
Godfrey Ra., *Australia* **125 D2** 24 0 S 117 0 E
Goðafoss, *Iceland* **11 B9** 65 41N 17 33W
Godhavn = Qeqertarsuaq, *Greenland* **10 D5** 69 15N 53 38W
Goðdalir, *Iceland* **11 B7** 65 20N 19 6W
Godhra, *India* **92 H5** 22 49N 73 40 E
Godinlave, *Somali Rep.* **120 C3** 5 54N 46 38 E
Gödöllő, *Hungary* **52 C4** 47 38N 19 25 E
Godoy Cruz, *Argentina* **174 C2** 32 56 S 68 52W
Gods →, *Canada* **140 A1** 56 22N 92 51W
Gods L., *Canada* **140 B1** 54 40N 94 15W
Gods River, *Canada* **143 C10** 54 50N 94 5W
Godthåb = Nuuk, *Greenland* **10 E5** 64 10N 51 35W
Godwin Austen = K2, *Pakistan* **93 B7** 35 58N 76 32 E
Goeie Hoop, Kaap die = Good Hope, C. of, *S. Africa* **116 E2** 34 24 S 18 30 E
Goéland, L. au, *Canada* **140 C4** 49 50N 76 48W
Goeree, *Neths.* **24 C3** 51 50N 4 0 E
Goes, *Neths.* **24 C3** 51 30N 3 55 E
Goffstown, *U.S.A.* **151 C13** 43 1N 71 36W
Gogama, *Canada* **140 C3** 47 35N 81 43W
Gogebic, L., *U.S.A.* **154 B10** 46 30N 89 35W
Goggetti, *Ethiopia* **107 F4** 8 11N 38 35 E
Gogolin, *Poland* **55 H5** 50 30N 18 0 E
Gogonou, *Benin* **113 C5** 10 50N 2 50 E
Gogra = Ghaghara →, *India* **93 G11** 25 45N 84 40 E
Gogriâl, *Sudan* **107 F2** 8 30N 28 8 E
Gogti, *Ethiopia* **107 E5** 10 7N 42 51 E
Gohana, *India* **92 E7** 29 8N 76 42 E
Goharganj, *India* **92 H7** 23 1N 77 41 E
Goi →, *India* **92 H6** 22 4N 74 46 E
Goiana, *Brazil* **170 C5** 7 33 S 34 59W
Goianésia, *Brazil* **171 E2** 15 18 S 49 7W
Goiânia, *Brazil* **171 E2** 16 43 S 49 20W
Goiás, *Brazil* **171 E1** 15 55 S 50 10W
Goiás □, *Brazil* **170 D2** 12 10 S 48 0W
Goiatuba, *Brazil* **171 E2** 18 1 S 49 23W
Goio-Erê, *Brazil* **175 A5** 24 12 S 53 1W
Góis, *Portugal* **42 E2** 40 10N 8 6W
Gojam □, *Ethiopia* **107 E4** 10 55N 36 30 E
Gojeb, Wabi →, *Ethiopia* **107 F4** 7 12N 36 40 E
Gojō, *Japan* **73 C7** 34 21N 135 42 E
Gojra, *Pakistan* **92 D5** 31 10N 72 40 E
Gokak, *India* **95 F2** 16 11N 74 52 E
Gokarn, *India* **95 G2** 14 33N 74 17 E
Gökçeada, *Turkey* **51 F9** 40 10N 25 50 E
Gökçedağ, *Turkey* **49 B10** 39 33N 28 56 E
Gökçen, *Turkey* **49 C9** 38 7N 27 53 E
Gökçeören, *Turkey* **49 C10** 38 37N 28 35 E
Gökçeyazı, *Turkey* **49 B9** 39 40N 27 40 E
Gökırmak →, *Turkey* **100 B6** 41 25N 35 8 E
Gökova, *Turkey* **49 D10** 37 1N 28 17 E
Gökova Körfezi, *Turkey* **49 E9** 36 55N 27 50 E
Göksu →, *Turkey* **100 D6** 36 19N 34 5 E
Göksun, *Turkey* **100 C7** 38 2N 36 30 E
Gokteik, *Burma* **90 D6** 22 26N 97 0 E
Göktepe, *Turkey* **49 D10** 37 25N 28 34 E
Gokurt, *Pakistan* **92 E2** 29 40N 67 26 E
Gokwe, *Zimbabwe* **117 B4** 18 7 S 28 58 E
Gol, *Norway* **18 D5** 60 42N 8 55 E
Gol Gol, *Australia* **128 C5** 34 12 S 142 14 E
Gola, *India* **93 E9** 28 3N 80 32 E
Golaghat, *India* **90 B5** 26 30N 94 0 E
Golakganj, *India* **90 B2** 26 8N 89 52 E
Golan Heights = Hagolan, *Syria* **103 C4** 33 0N 35 45 E
Gołańcz, *Poland* **55 F4** 52 57N 17 18 E
Golāshkerd, *Iran* **97 E8** 27 59N 57 16 E
Golaya Pristen = Hola Pristan, *Ukraine* **59 J7** 46 29N 32 32 E
Gölbaşı, *Adiyaman, Turkey* **100 D7** 37 43N 37 25 E
Gölbaşı, *Ankara, Turkey* **100 C5** 39 47N 32 49 E
Golchikha, *Russia* **6 B12** 71 45N 83 30 E
Golconda, *U.S.A.* **158 F5** 40 58N 117 30W
Gölcük, *Kocaeli, Turkey* **51 F13** 40 42N 29 48 E
Gölcük, *Niğde, Turkey* **100 C6** 38 14N 34 47 E
Gold, *U.S.A.* **150 E7** 41 52N 77 50W
Gold Beach, *U.S.A.* **158 E1** 42 25N 124 25W
Gold Coast, *Australia* **122 F9** 28 0 S 153 25 E
Gold Coast, *W. Afr.* **113 E4** 4 0N 1 40W
Gold Creek, *U.S.A.* **144 E10** 62 46N 149 41W
Gold Hill, *U.S.A.* **158 E2** 42 26N 123 3W
Gold River, *Canada* **142 D3** 49 46N 126 3W
Goldach, *Switz.* **33 B8** 47 28N 9 28 E
Gołdap, *Poland* **54 D9** 54 19N 22 18 E
Goldau, *Switz.* **33 B7** 47 3N 8 33 E
Goldberg, *Germany* **30 B8** 53 35N 12 4 E
Golden, *Canada* **142 C5** 51 20N 116 59W
Golden, *U.S.A.* **156 D5** 40 7N 91 1W
Golden B., *N.Z.* **131 A7** 40 40 S 172 50 E
Golden Gate, *U.S.A.* **158 H2** 37 54N 122 30W
Golden Gate Highlands Nat. Park, *S. Africa* **117 D4** 28 40 S 28 40 E
Golden Hinde, *Canada* **142 D3** 49 40N 125 44W
Golden Lake, *Canada* **150 A7** 45 34N 77 21W
Golden Rock, *India* **95 J4** 10 45N 78 48 E
Golden Vale, *Ireland* **23 D3** 52 33N 8 17W
Goldendale, *U.S.A.* **158 D3** 45 49N 120 50W
Goldfield, *U.S.A.* **159 H5** 37 42N 117 14W
Goldsand L., *Canada* **143 B8** 57 2N 101 8W
Goldsboro, *U.S.A.* **149 H7** 35 23N 77 59W
Goldsmith, *U.S.A.* **155 K3** 31 59N 102 37W
Goldsworthy, *Australia* **124 D2** 20 21 S 119 30 E
Goldthwaite, *U.S.A.* **155 K5** 31 27N 98 34W
Golegã, *Portugal* **43 F2** 39 24N 8 29W
Goleniów, *Poland* **54 E1** 53 35N 14 50 E
Golestānak, *Iran* **97 D7** 30 36N 54 14 E
Goleta, *U.S.A.* **161 L7** 34 27N 119 50W
Golfito, *Costa Rica* **164 E3** 8 41N 83 5W
Golfo Aranci, *Italy* **46 B2** 40 59N 9 38 E
Gölgeli Dağları, *Turkey* **49 D10** 37 10N 28 55 E
Gölhisar, *Turkey* **49 D11** 37 8N 29 31 E
Goliad, *U.S.A.* **155 L6** 28 40N 97 23W
Golija, *Montenegro, Yug.* **50 C2** 43 5N 18 45 E
Golija, *Serbia, Yug.* **50 C4** 43 22N 20 15 E
Golina, *Poland* **55 F5** 52 15N 18 4 E
Gölköy, *Turkey* **100 B7** 40 41N 37 37 E
Göllersdorf, *Austria* **34 C9** 48 29N 16 7 E
Gölmarmara, *Turkey* **49 C9** 38 42N 27 55 E
Golo →, *France* **29 F13** 42 31N 9 32 E
Golol, *Somali Rep.* **120 D2** 3 38N 43 49 E
Gölova, *Turkey* **49 E12** 36 48N 30 5 E
Golovin, *U.S.A.* **144 D7** 64 33N 163 2W
Golpāyegān, *Iran* **97 C6** 33 27N 50 18 E
Gölpazarı, *Turkey* **100 B4** 40 16N 30 18 E
Golra, *Pakistan* **92 C5** 33 37N 72 56 E
Golspie, *U.K.* **22 D5** 57 58N 3 59W
Golub-Dobrzyń, *Poland* **55 E6** 53 7N 19 2 E
Golubac, *Serbia, Yug.* **50 B5** 44 38N 21 38 E
Golungo Alto, *Angola* **115 D2** 9 8 S 14 46 E
Golyam Perelik, *Bulgaria* **51 E8** 41 36N 24 33 E
Golyama Kamchiya →, *Bulgaria* **51 C11** 43 10N 27 55 E
Goma, *Dem. Rep. of the Congo* **118 C2** 1 37 S 29 10 E
Gomal Pass, *Pakistan* **92 D3** 31 56N 69 20 E
Gomati →, *India* **93 G10** 25 32N 83 11 E
Gombari, *Dem. Rep. of the Congo* **118 B2** 2 45N 29 3 E
Gombe, *Dem. Rep. of the Congo* **114 C3** 0 45 S 17 36 E
Gombe, *Nigeria* **113 C7** 10 19N 11 2 E
Gömbe, *Turkey* **49 E11** 36 33N 29 38 E
Gombe □, *Nigeria* **113 C7** 10 0N 11 10 E
Gombe →, *Tanzania* **118 C3** 4 38 S 31 40 E
Gombi, *Nigeria* **113 C7** 10 12N 12 30 E
Gomel = Homyel, *Belarus* **59 F6** 52 28N 31 0 E
Gomera, *Canary Is.* **9 e1** 28 7N 17 14W
Gómez Palacio, *Mexico* **162 B4** 25 40N 104 0W
Gomīshān, *Iran* **97 B7** 37 4N 54 6 E
Gommern, *Germany* **30 C7** 52 4N 11 50 E
Gomogomo, *Indonesia* **83 C4** 6 39 S 134 43 E
Gomotartsi, *Bulgaria* **50 B6** 44 6N 22 57 E
Gompa = Ganta, *Liberia* **112 D3** 7 15N 8 59W
Gomphi, *Greece* **48 B3** 39 26N 21 36 E
Goms, *Switz.* **32 D6** 46 27N 8 15 E
Gonābād, *Iran* **97 C8** 34 15N 58 45 E
Gonaïves, *Haiti* **165 C5** 19 20N 72 42W
Gonarezhou Nat. Park, *Zimbabwe* **119 G3** 21 32 S 31 55 E
Gonâve, G. de la, *Haiti* **165 C5** 19 29N 72 42W
Gonâve, I. de la, *Haiti* **165 C5** 18 45N 73 0W
Gonbad-e Kāvūs, *Iran* **97 B7** 37 20N 55 25 E
Gönc, *Hungary* **52 B6** 48 28N 21 14 E
Gonda, *India* **93 F9** 27 9N 81 58 E
Gondal, *India* **92 J4** 21 58N 70 52 E
Gonder, *Ethiopia* **107 E4** 12 39N 37 30 E
Gonder □, *Ethiopia* **107 E4** 12 55N 37 30 E
Gondia, *India* **94 D5** 21 23N 80 10 E
Gondola, *Mozam.* **119 F3** 19 10 S 33 37 E
Gondomar, *Portugal* **42 D2** 41 10N 8 35W
Gondrecourt-le-Château, *France* **27 D12** 48 31N 5 30 E
Gönen, *Balıkesir, Turkey* **51 F11** 40 6N 27 39 E
Gönen, *Isparta, Turkey* **49 D12** 37 57N 30 31 E
Gönen →, *Turkey* **51 F11** 40 6N 27 39 E
Gong Xian, *China* **76 C5** 28 23N 104 47 E
Gong'an, *China* **77 B9** 30 7N 112 12 E
Gongbei, *China* **69 G10** 22 12N 113 32 E
Gongcheng, *China* **77 E8** 24 50N 110 49 E
Gongga Shan, *China* **76 C3** 29 40N 101 55 E
Gongguan, *China* **76 G7** 21 48N 109 36 E
Gonghe, *China* **68 C5** 36 18N 100 32 E
Gongming, *China* **69 F10** 22 47N 113 53 E
Gongo Yembe, *Dem. Rep. of the Congo* **114 C3** 1 58 S 18 40 E
Gongola →, *Nigeria* **113 D7** 9 30N 12 4 E
Gongolgon, *Australia* **127 E4** 30 21 S 146 54 E
Gongoué, *Gabon* **114 C1** 0 31 S 9 13 E
Gongshan, *China* **76 D2** 27 43N 98 29 E
Gongtan, *China* **76 C7** 28 55N 108 20 E
Gongzhuling, *China* **75 C13** 43 30N 124 40 E
Goniadz, *Poland* **54 E9** 53 30N 22 44 E
Goniri, *Nigeria* **113 C7** 11 30N 12 15 E
Gonjo, *China* **76 B2** 30 52N 98 17 E
Gonnesa, *Italy* **46 C1** 39 16N 8 28 E
Gónnos, *Greece* **48 B4** 39 52N 22 29 E
Gonnosfanádiga, *Italy* **46 C1** 39 29N 8 39 E
Gonzaga, *Phil.* **80 B4** 18 16N 122 0 E
Gonzales, *Calif., U.S.A.* **160 J5** 36 30N 121 26W
Gonzales, *Tex., U.S.A.* **155 L6** 29 30N 97 27W
González Chaves, *Argentina* **174 D3** 38 2 S 60 5W
Goobang Nat. Park, *Australia* **129 B8** 33 0 S 148 32 E
Good Hope, C. of, *S. Africa* **116 E2** 34 24 S 18 30 E
Goodenough I., *Papua N. G.* **132 E6** 9 20 S 150 15 E
Gooderham, *Canada* **150 B6** 44 54N 78 21W
Goodhouse, *S. Africa* **116 D2** 28 57 S 18 13 E
Gooding, *U.S.A.* **158 E6** 42 56N 114 43W
Goodland, *U.S.A.* **154 F4** 39 21N 101 43W
Goodlands, *Mauritius* **121 d** 20 2 S 57 39 E
Goodlow, *Canada* **142 B4** 56 20N 120 8W
Goodnews Bay, *U.S.A.* **144 G7** 59 7N 161 35W
Goodooga, *Australia* **127 D4** 29 3 S 147 28 E
Goodsprings, *U.S.A.* **161 K11** 35 49N 115 27W
Goodwater, *U.S.A.* **152 B3** 33 4N 86 3W
Goole, *U.K.* **20 D7** 53 42N 0 53W
Goolgowi, *Australia* **129 B6** 33 58 S 145 41 E
Goolwa, *Australia* **128 C3** 35 30 S 138 47 E
Goomalling, *Australia* **125 F2** 31 15 S 116 49 E
Goomeri, *Australia* **127 D5** 26 12 S 152 6 E
Goonda, *Mozam.* **119 F3** 19 48 S 33 57 E
Goondiwindi, *Australia* **127 D5** 28 30 S 150 21 E
Goongarrie, L., *Australia* **125 F3** 30 3 S 121 9 E
Goongarrie Nat. Park, *Australia* **125 F3** 30 7 S 121 30 E
Goonyella, *Australia* **126 C4** 21 47 S 147 58 E
Goose →, *Canada* **141 B7** 53 20N 60 35W
Goose Creek, *U.S.A.* **152 C9** 32 59N 80 2W
Goose L., *U.S.A.* **158 F3** 41 56N 120 26W
Gooty, *India* **95 G3** 15 7N 77 41 E
Gopalganj, *Bangla.* **90 D2** 23 1N 89 50 E
Gopalganj, *India* **93 F11** 26 28N 84 30 E
Goppenstein, *Switz.* **32 D5** 46 23N 7 46 E
Göppingen, *Germany* **31 G5** 48 42N 9 39 E
Gor, *Spain* **43 H8** 37 23N 2 58W
Góra, *Dolnośląskie, Poland* **55 G3** 51 40N 16 31 E
Góra, *Mazowieckie, Poland* **55 F7** 52 39N 20 6 E
Góra Kalwaria, *Poland* **55 G8** 51 59N 21 14 E
Gorakhpur, *India* **93 F10** 26 47N 83 23 E
Goražde, *Bos.-H.* **52 G3** 43 38N 18 58 E
Gorbatov, *Russia* **60 B6** 56 12N 43 2 E
Gorbea, Peña, *Spain* **40 B2** 43 1N 2 50W
Gorda, *U.S.A.* **160 K5** 35 53N 121 26W
Gorda, Pta., *Canary Is.* **9 e1** 28 45N 18 0W
Gorda, Pta., *Nic.* **164 D3** 14 20N 83 10W
Gordan B., *Australia* **124 B5** 11 35 S 130 10 E
Gördes, *Turkey* **49 C10** 38 54N 28 17 E
Gordon, *Ga., U.S.A.* **152 C6** 32 52N 83 20W
Gordon, *Nebr., U.S.A.* **154 D3** 42 48N 102 12W
Gordon →, *Australia* **127 G4** 42 27 S 145 30 E
Gordon, I., *Chile* **176 D3** 54 55 S 69 30W
Gordon L., *Alta., Canada* **143 B6** 56 30N 110 25W
Gordon L., *N.W.T., Canada* **142 A6** 63 5N 113 11W
Gordonvale, *Australia* **126 B4** 17 5 S 145 50 E
Goré, *Chad* **109 G3** 7 59N 16 31 E
Gore, *Ethiopia* **107 F4** 8 12N 35 32 E
Gore, *N.Z.* **131 G3** 46 5 S 168 58 E
Gore Bay, *Canada* **140 C3** 45 57N 82 28W
Görele, *Turkey* **101 B8** 41 2N 39 0 E
Goreme, *Turkey* **100 C6** 38 35N 34 52 E
Gorey, *Ireland* **23 D5** 52 41N 6 18W
Gorg, *Iran* **97 D8** 29 29N 59 43 E
Gorgān, *Iran* **97 B7** 36 50N 54 29 E
Gorgona, *Italy* **44 E6** 43 26N 9 54 E
Gorgora, *Ethiopia* **107 E4** 12 15N 37 17 E
Gorgoram, *Nigeria* **113 C7** 12 40N 10 45 E
Gorham, *U.S.A.* **151 B13** 44 23N 71 10W
Gori, *Georgia* **61 J7** 42 0N 44 7 E
Goriganga →, *India* **93 E9** 29 45N 80 23 E
Gorinchem, *Neths.* **24 C4** 51 50N 4 59 E
Gorinhatã, *Brazil* **171 E2** 19 15 S 49 45W
Goris, *Armenia* **101 C12** 39 31N 46 22 E
Goritsy, *Russia* **58 D9** 57 4N 36 43 E
Gorízia, *Italy* **45 C10** 45 56N 13 37 E
Gorj □, *Romania* **53 E8** 45 5N 23 25 E
Gorki = Horki, *Belarus* **58 E6** 54 17N 30 59 E
Gorki = Nizhniy Novgorod, *Russia* **60 B7** 56 20N 44 0 E
Gorkiy = Nizhniy Novgorod, *Russia* **60 B7** 56 20N 44 0 E
Gorkovskoye Vdkhr., *Russia* **60 B6** 57 2N 43 4 E
Gorlice, *Poland* **55 J8** 49 35N 21 11 E
Görlitz, *Germany* **30 D10** 51 9N 14 58 E
Gorlovka = Horlivka, *Ukraine* **59 H10** 48 19N 38 5 E
Gorman, *U.S.A.* **161 L8** 34 47N 118 51W
Gorna Dzhumayo = Blagoevgrad, *Bulgaria* **50 D7** 42 2N 23 5 E
Gorna Oryakhovitsa, *Bulgaria* **51 C9** 43 7N 25 40 E
Gornja Radgona, *Slovenia* **45 B13** 46 40N 16 2 E
Gornja Tuzla, *Bos.-H.* **52 F3** 44 35N 18 46 E
Gornji Grad, *Slovenia* **45 B11** 46 20N 14 52 E
Gornji Milanovac, *Serbia, Yug.* **50 B4** 44 3N 20 29 E
Gornji Vakuf, *Bos.-H.* **52 G2** 43 57N 17 34 E
Gorno Ablanovo, *Bulgaria* **51 C9** 43 37N 25 43 E
Gorno-Altay □, *Russia* **66 D9** 51 0N 86 0 E
Gorno-Altaysk, *Russia* **66 D9** 51 50N 86 5 E
Gorno-Badakhshan □, *Tajikistan* **65 D6** 38 30N 73 0 E
Gornyatski, *Russia* **56 A11** 67 32N 64 3 E
Gornyatskiy, *Russia* **61 F5** 48 18N 40 56 E
Gornyy, *Saratov, Russia* **60 E9** 51 50N 48 30 E
Gornyy, *Sib., Russia* **70 B6** 44 57N 133 59 E
Goro →, *C.A.R.* **114 A4** 9 14N 21 16 E
Gorodenka = Horodenka, *Ukraine* **59 H3** 48 41N 25 29 E
Gorodets, *Russia* **60 B6** 56 38N 43 28 E
Gorodishche = Horodyshche, *Ukraine* **59 H6** 49 17N 31 27 E
Gorodishche, *Russia* **60 D7** 53 13N 45 40 E
Gorodnya = Horodnya, *Ukraine* **59 G6** 51 55N 31 33 E
Gorodok = Haradok, *Belarus* **58 E6** 55 30N 30 3 E
Gorodok = Horodok, *Ukraine* **59 H2** 49 46N 23 32 E
Gorodovikovsk, *Russia* **61 G5** 46 8N 41 58 E
Goroka, *Papua N. G.* **132 D3** 6 7 S 145 25 E
Goroke, *Australia* **128 D4** 36 43 S 141 29 E
Gorokhov = Horokhiv, *Ukraine* **59 G3** 50 30N 24 45 E
Gorokhovets, *Russia* **60 B6** 56 13N 42 39 E
Gorom Gorom, *Burkina Faso* **113 C4** 14 26N 0 14W
Goromonzi, *Zimbabwe* **119 F3** 17 52 S 31 22 E
Gorong, Kepulauan, *Indonesia* **83 B4** 3 59 S 131 25 E
Gorongosa, Parque Nacional de, *Mozam.* **117 B5** 18 50 S 34 29 E
Gorongose →, *Mozam.* **117 C5** 20 30 S 34 40 E
Gorongoza, *Mozam.* **119 F3** 18 44 S 34 2 E
Gorongoza, Sa. da, *Mozam.* **119 F3** 18 27 S 34 2 E
Gorontalo, *Indonesia* **82 A2** 0 35N 123 5 E
Goronyo, *Nigeria* **113 C6** 13 29N 5 39 E
Górowo Iławeckie, *Poland* **54 D7** 54 17N 20 30 E
Gorron, *France* **26 D6** 48 25N 0 50W
Gorshechnoye, *Russia* **59 G10** 51 31N 38 2 E
Gort, *Ireland* **23 C3** 53 3N 8 49W
Gortis, *Greece* **39 E5** 35 4N 24 58 E
Gorumahisani, *India* **94 C8** 22 20N 86 24 E
Góry Bystrzyckie, *Poland* **55 H3** 50 16N 16 33 E
Goryachiy Klyuch, *Russia* **61 H4** 44 38N 39 8 E
Gorzkowice, *Poland* **55 G6** 51 13N 19 36 E
Górzno, *Poland* **55 E6** 53 12N 19 38 E
Gorzów Śląski, *Poland* **55 G5** 51 3N 18 22 E
Gorzów Wielkopolski, *Poland* **55 F2** 52 43N 15 15 E
Göschenen, *Switz.* **33 C7** 46 40N 8 36 E
Gose, *Japan* **73 C7** 34 27N 135 44 E
Gosford, *Australia* **129 B9** 33 23 S 151 18 E
Goshen, *Calif., U.S.A.* **160 J7** 36 21N 119 25W
Goshen, *Ind., U.S.A.* **157 C11** 41 35N 85 50W
Goshen, *N.Y., U.S.A.* **151 E10** 41 24N 74 20W
Goshogawara, *Japan* **70 D10** 40 48N 140 27 E
Gosier, *Guadeloupe* **164 b** 16 12N 61 30W
Goslar, *Germany* **30 D6** 51 54N 10 25 E
Gospič, *Croatia* **45 D12** 44 35N 15 23 E
Gosport, *U.K.* **21 G6** 50 48N 1 9W
Gosport, *U.S.A.* **157 E10** 39 21N 86 40W
Gossa, *Norway* **18 B3** 62 52N 6 50 E
Gossas, *Senegal* **112 C1** 14 28N 16 0W
Gossau, *Switz.* **33 B8** 47 25N 9 15 E
Gosse →, *Australia* **126 B1** 19 32 S 134 37 E
Gossi, *Mali* **113 B4** 15 48N 1 20W
Gossinga, *Sudan* **107 F2** 8 36N 25 59 E
Gostivar, *Macedonia* **50 E4** 41 48N 20 57 E
Gostyń, *Poland* **55 G4** 51 50N 17 3 E
Gostynin, *Poland* **55 F6** 52 26N 19 29 E
Göta älv →, *Sweden* **17 G5** 57 42N 11 54 E
Göta kanal, *Sweden* **17 F9** 58 30N 15 58 E
Götaland, *Sweden* **17 G8** 57 30N 14 30 E
Göteborg, *Sweden* **17 G5** 57 43N 11 59 E
Gotemba, *Japan* **73 B10** 35 18N 138 56 E
Götene, *Sweden* **17 F7** 58 32N 13 30 E
Goteşti, *Moldova* **53 D13** 46 9N 28 10 E
Gotha, *Germany* **30 E6** 50 56N 10 42 E
Gothenburg = Göteborg, *Sweden* **17 G5** 57 43N 11 59 E
Gothenburg, *U.S.A.* **154 E4** 40 56N 100 10W
Gothèye, *Niger* **113 C5** 13 52N 1 34 E
Gotland, *Sweden* **17 G12** 57 30N 18 33 E
Gotlands län □, *Sweden* **17 G12** 57 15N 18 30 E
Gotō-Rettō, *Japan* **71 H4** 32 55N 129 5 E
Gotse Delchev, *Bulgaria* **50 E7** 41 36N 23 46 E
Gotska Sandön, *Sweden* **15 G18** 58 24N 19 15 E
Gōtsu, *Japan* **72 C4** 35 0N 132 14 E
Gott Pk., *Canada* **142 C4** 50 18N 122 16W
Gòttero, Monte, *Italy* **44 D6** 44 22N 9 42 E
Göttingen, *Germany* **30 D5** 51 31N 9 55 E
Gottwald = Zmiyev, *Ukraine* **59 H9** 49 39N 36 27 E
Gottwaldov = Zlín, *Czech Rep.* **35 B10** 49 14N 17 40 E
Götzis, *Austria* **33 B9** 47 20N 9 38 E
Goubangzi, *China* **75 D11** 41 20N 121 52 E
Gouda, *Neths.* **24 B4** 52 1N 4 42 E
Goúdhoura, Ákra, *Greece* **39 F7** 34 59N 26 6 E
Goudiry, *Senegal* **112 C2** 14 15N 12 45W
Goudoumaria, *Niger* **113 C7** 13 40N 11 10 E
Gouéké, *Guinea* **112 D3** 8 2N 8 43W
Gough I., *Atl. Oc.* **8 L11** 40 10 S 9 45W
Gouin, Rés., *Canada* **140 C5** 48 35N 74 40W
Gouitafla, *Ivory C.* **112 D3** 7 30N 5 53W
Goulburn, *Australia* **129 C8** 34 44 S 149 44 E
Goulburn Is., *Australia* **126 A1** 11 40 S 133 20 E
Goulburn River Nat. Park, *Australia* **129 B9** 32 19 S 150 10 E
Goulds, *U.S.A.* **153 K9** 25 33N 80 23W
Goulia, *Ivory C.* **112 C3** 10 1N 7 11W
Goulimine, *Morocco* **110 C3** 28 56N 10 0W
Goulmima, *Morocco* **110 B4** 31 41N 4 57W
Goumbou, *Mali* **112 B3** 15 2N 7 25W

Grimmen, *Germany* **30 A9** 54 7N 13 3 E
Grimsay, *U.K.* **22 D1** 57 29N 7 14W
Grimsby, *Canada* **150 C5** 43 12N 79 34W
Grimsby, *U.K.* **20 D7** 53 34N 0 5W
Grimselpass, *Switz.* **33 C6** 46 34N 8 23 E
Grímsey, *Iceland* **11 A9** 66 33N 17 58W
Grimshaw, *Canada* **142 B5** 56 10N 117 40W
Grimslöv, *Sweden* **17 H8** 56 44N 14 34 E
Grímsstaðir, *Iceland* **11 B10** 65 39N 16 7W
Grimstad, *Norway* **15 G13** 58 20N 8 35 E
Grímsvötn, *Iceland* **11 C9** 64 26N 17 22W
Grindavík, *Iceland* **11 D4** 63 50N 22 26W
Grindelwald, *Switz.* **32 C6** 46 38N 8 2 E
Grindsted, *Denmark* **17 J2** 55 46N 8 55 E
Grindstone I., *Canada* **151 B8** 44 43N 76 14W
Grindu, *Romania* **53 F11** 44 44N 26 50 E
Grinnell, *U.S.A.* **156 C4** 41 45N 92 43W
Grintavec, *Slovenia* **45 B11** 46 22N 14 32 E
Gris-Nez, C., *France* **27 B8** 50 52N 1 35 E
Grisolles, *France* **28 E5** 43 49N 1 19 E
Grisons = Graubünden □, *Switz.* **33 C9** 46 45N 9 30 E
Grisslehamn, *Sweden* **16 D12** 60 5N 18 49 E
Grmeč Planina, *Bos.-H.* **45 D13** 44 43N 16 16 E
Groais I., *Canada* **141 B8** 50 55N 55 35W
Grobiņa, *Latvia* **54 B8** 56 33N 21 10 E
Groblersdal, *S. Africa* **117 D4** 25 15 S 29 25 E
Grobming, *Austria* **34 D6** 47 27N 13 54 E
Grocka, *Serbia, Yug.* **50 B4** 44 40N 20 42 E
Gródek, *Poland* **55 E10** 53 6N 23 40 E
Grodków, *Poland* **55 H4** 50 43N 17 21 E
Grodno = Hrodna, *Belarus* **58 F2** 53 42N 23 52 E
Grodzisk Mazowiecki, *Poland* **55 F7** 52 7N 20 37 E
Grodzisk Wielkopolski, *Poland* **55 F3** 52 15N 16 22 E
Grodzyanka = Hrodzyanka, *Belarus* **58 F5** 53 31N 28 42 E
Groesbeck, *U.S.A.* **155 K6** 30 48N 96 31W
Groix, *France* **26 E3** 47 38N 3 29W
Groix, Î. de, *France* **26 E3** 47 38N 3 28W
Grójec, *Poland* **55 G7** 51 50N 20 58 E
Gronau, *Niedersachsen, Germany* **30 C5** 52 5N 9 47 E
Gronau, *Nordrhein-Westfalen, Germany* **30 C3** 52 12N 7 2 E
Grong, *Norway* **14 D15** 64 25N 12 8 E
Grönhögen, *Sweden* **17 H10** 56 16N 16 24 E
Groningen, *Neths.* **24 A6** 53 15N 6 35 E
Groningen, *Surinam* **169 B6** 5 48N 55 28W
Groningen □, *Neths.* **24 A6** 53 16N 6 40 E
Grønnedal = Kangilinnguit, *Greenland* **10 E6** 61 20N 47 57W
Groom, *U.S.A.* **155 H4** 35 12N 101 6W
Groot →, *S. Africa* **116 E3** 33 45 S 24 36 E
Groot Berg →, *S. Africa* **116 E2** 32 47 S 18 8 E
Groot-Brakrivier, *S. Africa* **116 E3** 34 2 S 22 18 E
Groot Karasberge, *Namibia* **116 D2** 27 20 S 18 40 E
Groot-Kei →, *S. Africa* **117 E4** 32 41 S 28 22 E
Groot Vis →, *S. Africa* **116 E4** 33 28 S 27 5 E
Grootdrink, *S. Africa* **116 D3** 28 33 S 21 42 E
Groote Eylandt, *Australia* **126 A2** 14 0 S 136 40 E
Grootfontein, *Namibia* **116 B2** 19 31 S 18 6 E
Grootlaagte →, *Africa* **116 C3** 20 55 S 21 27 E
Grootvloer →, *S. Africa* **116 E3** 30 0 S 20 40 E
Gros C., *Canada* **142 A6** 61 59N 113 32W
Gros Islet, *St. Lucia* **165 f** 14 5N 60 58W
Gros Morne Nat. Park, *Canada* **141 C8** 49 40N 57 50W
Gros Piton, *St. Lucia* **165 f** 13 49N 61 5W
Gros Piton Pt., *St. Lucia* **165 f** 13 49N 61 5W
Grósio, *Italy* **44 B7** 46 18N 10 16 E
Grosne →, *France* **27 F11** 46 42N 4 56 E
Grosotto, *Italy* **33 D10** 46 17N 10 15 E
Grossa, Pta., *Spain* **38 C2** 39 6N 1 36 E
Grosse I., *U.S.A.* **157 B13** 42 8N 83 9W
Grossenbrode, *Germany* **30 A7** 54 21N 11 4 E
Grossenhain, *Germany* **30 D9** 51 17N 13 32 E
Grosser Arber, *Germany* **31 F9** 49 6N 13 8 E
Grosser Plöner See, *Germany* **30 A6** 54 10N 10 22 E
Grosseto, *Italy* **45 F8** 42 46N 11 8 E
Grossgerungs, *Austria* **34 C7** 48 34N 14 57 E
Grossglockner, *Austria* **34 D5** 47 5N 12 40 E
Groswater B., *Canada* **141 B8** 54 20N 57 40W
Grotli, *Norway* **18 B4** 62 2N 7 42 E
Groton, *Conn., U.S.A.* **151 E12** 41 21N 72 5W
Groton, *N.Y., U.S.A.* **151 D8** 42 36N 76 22W
Groton, *S. Dak., U.S.A.* **154 C5** 45 27N 98 6W
Grottáglie, *Italy* **47 B10** 40 32N 17 26 E
Grottaminarda, *Italy* **47 A8** 41 4N 15 2 E
Grottammare, *Italy* **45 F10** 42 59N 13 52 E
Grouard Mission, *Canada* **142 B5** 55 33N 116 9W
Grouin, Pte. du, *France* **26 D5** 48 43N 1 51W
Groundhog →, *Canada* **140 C3** 48 45N 82 58W
Grouw, *Neths.* **24 A5** 53 5N 5 51 E
Grove City, *Ohio, U.S.A.* **157 E13** 39 53N 83 6W
Grove City, *Pa., U.S.A.* **150 E4** 41 10N 80 5W
Grove Hill, *U.S.A.* **149 K2** 31 42N 87 47W
Groveland, *Calif., U.S.A.* **160 H6** 37 50N 120 14W
Groveland, *Fla., U.S.A.* **153 G8** 28 34N 81 51W
Grover City, *U.S.A.* **161 K6** 35 7N 120 37W
Groves, *U.S.A.* **155 L8** 29 57N 93 54W
Groveton, *U.S.A.* **151 B13** 44 36N 71 31W
Grovetown, *U.S.A.* **152 B7** 33 27N 82 12W
Grožnjan, *Croatia* **45 C10** 45 22N 13 43 E
Groznyy, *Russia* **61 J7** 43 20N 45 45 E
Grua, *Norway* **18 D7** 60 16N 10 40 E
Grubišno Polje, *Croatia* **52 E2** 45 44N 17 12 E
Grudovo, *Bulgaria* **51 D11** 42 21N 27 10 E
Grudusk, *Poland* **55 E7** 53 3N 20 38 E
Grudziądz, *Poland* **54 E5** 53 30N 18 47 E
Gruinard B., *U.K.* **22 D3** 57 56N 5 35W
Gruissan, *France* **28 E7** 43 8N 3 7 E
Grumo Áppula, *Italy* **47 A9** 41 1N 16 42 E
Grums, *Sweden* **16 E7** 59 22N 13 5 E
Grünberg, *Germany* **30 E4** 50 35N 8 58 E
Grund, *Iceland* **11 B8** 65 31N 18 9W
Gründau, *Germany* **31 E5** 50 10N 9 9 E
Grundy Center, *U.S.A.* **156 B4** 42 22N 92 47W
Grungedal, *Norway* **18 E4** 59 44N 7 43 E
Grünstadt, *Germany* **31 F4** 49 34N 8 9 E
Gruvberget, *Sweden* **16 C10** 61 6N 16 10 E
Gruver, *U.S.A.* **155 G4** 36 16N 101 24W
Gruyères, *Switz.* **32 C4** 46 35N 7 4 E
Gruža, *Serbia, Yug.* **50 C4** 43 54N 20 46 E
Gryazi, *Russia* **59 F10** 52 30N 39 58 E
Gryazovets, *Russia* **58 C11** 58 50N 40 10 E
Grybów, *Poland* **55 J7** 49 36N 20 55 E
Grycksbo, *Sweden* **16 D9** 60 40N 15 29 E
Gryfice, *Poland* **54 E2** 53 55N 15 13 E
Gryfino, *Poland* **55 E1** 53 16N 14 29 E
Gryfów Śląski, *Poland* **55 G2** 51 2N 15 24 E
Grythyttan, *Sweden* **16 E8** 59 41N 14 32 E
Gstaad, *Switz.* **32 D4** 46 28N 7 18 E
Gua Musang, *Malaysia* **87 K3** 4 53N 101 58 E
Guacanayabo, G. de, *Cuba* **164 B4** 20 40N 77 20W
Guacara, *Venezuela* **168 A4** 10 14N 67 53W
Guachípas →, *Argentina* **174 B2** 25 40 S 65 30W
Guachiría →, *Colombia* **168 B3** 5 27N 70 36W
Guadajoz →, *Spain* **43 H6** 37 50N 4 51W
Guadalajara, *Mexico* **162 C4** 20 40N 103 20W
Guadalajara, *Spain* **40 E1** 40 37N 3 12W
Guadalajara □, *Spain* **40 E2** 40 47N 2 30W
Guadalcanal, *Solomon Is.* **133 M11** 9 32 S 160 12 E
Guadalcanal, *Spain* **43 G5** 38 5N 5 52W
Guadalén →, *Spain* **43 G7** 38 5N 3 32W
Guadales, *Argentina* **174 C2** 34 30 S 67 55W
Guadalete →, *Spain* **43 J4** 36 35N 6 13W
Guadalimar →, *Spain* **43 G7** 38 5N 3 28W
Guadalmena →, *Spain* **43 G8** 38 19N 2 56W
Guadalmez →, *Spain* **43 G5** 38 46N 5 4W
Guadalope →, *Spain* **40 D4** 41 15N 0 3W
Guadalquivir →, *Spain* **43 J4** 36 47N 6 22W
Guadalupe = Guadeloupe ■, *W. Indies* **164 b** 16 20N 61 40W
Guadalupe, *Brazil* **170 C3** 6 44 S 43 47W
Guadalupe, *Mexico* **161 N10** 32 4N 116 32W
Guadalupe, *Spain* **43 F5** 39 27N 5 17W
Guadalupe, *U.S.A.* **161 L6** 34 59N 120 33W
Guadalupe →, *Mexico* **161 N10** 32 6N 116 51W
Guadalupe →, *U.S.A.* **155 L6** 28 27N 96 47W
Guadalupe, Sierra de, *Spain* **43 F5** 39 28N 5 30W
Guadalupe Bravos, *Mexico* **162 A3** 31 20N 106 10W
Guadalupe I., *Pac. Oc.* **136 G8** 29 0N 118 50W
Guadalupe Mts. Nat. Park, *U.S.A.* **155 K2** 32 0N 104 30W
Guadalupe Peak, *U.S.A.* **155 K2** 31 50N 104 52W
Guadalupe y Calvo, *Mexico* **162 B3** 26 6N 106 58W
Guadarrama, Sierra de, *Spain* **42 E7** 41 0N 4 0W
Guadauta, *Georgia* **61 J5** 43 7N 40 32 E
Guadeloupe ■, *W. Indies* **164 b** 16 20N 61 40W
Guadeloupe Passage, *W. Indies* **165 C7** 16 50N 62 15W
Guadelupe, *Peru* **172 B2** 7 15 S 79 29W
Guadiamar →, *Spain* **43 J4** 36 55N 6 24W
Guadiana →, *Portugal* **43 H3** 37 14N 7 22W
Guadiana Menor →, *Spain* **43 H7** 37 56N 3 15W
Guadiaro →, *Spain* **43 J5** 36 17N 5 17W
Guadiato →, *Spain* **43 H5** 37 48N 5 5W
Guadiela →, *Spain* **40 E2** 40 22N 2 49W
Guadix, *Spain* **43 H7** 37 18N 3 11W
Guafo, Boca del, *Chile* **176 B2** 43 35 S 74 0W
Guafo, I., *Chile* **176 B2** 43 35 S 74 50W
Guaico, *Trin. & Tob.* **169 F9** 10 35N 61 9W
Guainía □, *Colombia* **168 C4** 2 30N 69 0W
Guainía →, *Colombia* **168 C4** 2 1N 67 7W
Guaíra, *Brazil* **175 A5** 24 5 S 54 10W
Guaíra □, *Paraguay* **174 B4** 25 45 S 56 30W
Guaitecas, Is., *Chile* **176 B2** 44 0 S 74 30W
Guajará-Mirim, *Brazil* **173 C4** 10 50 S 65 20W
Guajira □, *Colombia* **168 A3** 11 30N 72 30W
Guajira, Pen. de la, *Colombia* **168 A3** 12 0N 72 0W
Gualaceo, *Ecuador* **168 D2** 2 54 S 78 47W
Gualán, *Guatemala* **164 C2** 15 8N 89 22W
Gualdo Tadino, *Italy* **45 E9** 43 14N 12 47 E
Gualeguay, *Argentina* **174 C4** 33 10 S 59 14W
Gualeguaychú, *Argentina* **174 C4** 33 3 S 59 31W
Gualequay →, *Argentina* **174 C4** 33 19 S 59 39W
Gualicho, Salina, *Argentina* **176 B3** 40 25 S 65 20W
Gualjaina, *Argentina* **176 B2** 42 45 S 70 30W
Guam ■, *Pac. Oc.* **133 R15** 13 27N 144 45 E
Guamá, *Brazil* **170 B2** 1 37 S 47 29W
Guamá →, *Brazil* **170 B2** 1 29 S 48 30W
Guamblin, I., *Chile* **176 B1** 44 50 S 75 0W
Guaminí, *Argentina* **174 D3** 37 1 S 62 28W
Guamote, *Ecuador* **168 D2** 1 56 S 78 43W
Guampí, Sierra de, *Venezuela* **169 B4** 6 0N 65 35W
Guamúchil, *Mexico* **162 B3** 25 25N 108 3W
Guana I., *Br. Virgin Is.* **165 e** 18 30N 64 30W
Guanabacoa, *Cuba* **164 B3** 23 8N 82 18W
Guanacaste, Cordillera del, *Costa Rica* **164 D2** 10 40N 85 4W
Guanaceví, *Mexico* **162 B3** 25 40N 106 0W
Guanahani = San Salvador I., *Bahamas* **165 B5** 24 0N 74 40W
Guanajay, *Cuba* **164 B3** 22 56N 82 42W
Guanajuato, *Mexico* **162 C4** 21 0N 101 20W
Guanajuato □, *Mexico* **162 C4** 20 40N 101 20W
Guanambi, *Brazil* **171 D3** 14 13 S 42 47W
Guanare, *Venezuela* **168 B4** 8 42N 69 12W
Guanare →, *Venezuela* **168 B4** 8 13N 67 46W
Guandacol, *Argentina* **174 B2** 29 30 S 68 40W
Guane, *Cuba* **164 B3** 22 10N 84 7W
Guang'an, *China* **76 B6** 30 28N 106 35 E
Guangchang, *China* **77 D11** 26 50N 116 21 E
Guangde, *China* **77 B12** 30 54N 119 25 E
Guangdong □, *China* **77 F9** 23 0N 113 0 E
Guangfeng, *China* **77 C12** 28 20N 118 15 E
Guanghan, *China* **76 B5** 30 58N 104 17 E
Guangling, *China* **74 E8** 39 47N 114 22 E
Guangnan, *China* **76 E5** 24 5N 105 4 E
Guangning, *China* **77 F9** 23 40N 112 22 E
Guangrao, *China* **75 F10** 37 5N 118 25 E
Guangshui, *China* **77 B9** 31 37N 114 0 E
Guangshun, *China* **76 D6** 26 8N 106 21 E
Guangwu, *China* **74 F3** 37 48N 105 57 E
Guangxi Zhuangzu Zizhiqu □, *China* **76 F7** 24 0N 109 0 E
Guangyuan, *China* **76 A5** 32 26N 105 51 E
Guangze, *China* **77 D11** 27 30N 117 12 E
Guangzhou, *China* **77 F9** 23 5N 113 10 E
Guanhães, *Brazil* **171 E3** 18 47 S 42 57W
Guanica, *Puerto Rico* **165 d** 17 59N 66 55W
Guanipa →, *Venezuela* **169 B5** 9 56N 62 26W
Guanling, *China* **76 E5** 25 56N 105 35 E
Guannan, *China* **75 G10** 34 8N 119 21 E
Guanta, *Venezuela* **169 A5** 10 14N 64 36W
Guantánamo, *Cuba* **165 B4** 20 10N 75 14W
Guantao, *China* **74 F8** 36 42N 115 25 E
Guanyang, *China* **77 E8** 25 30N 111 8 E
Guanyun, *China* **75 G10** 34 20N 119 18 E
Guapí, *Colombia* **168 C2** 2 36N 77 54W
Guápiles, *Costa Rica* **164 D3** 10 10N 83 46W
Guapo B., *Trin. & Tob.* **169 F9** 10 12N 61 41W
Guaporé, *Brazil* **175 B5** 28 51 S 51 54W
Guaporé →, *Brazil* **173 C4** 11 55 S 65 4W
Guaqui, *Bolivia* **172 D4** 16 41 S 68 54W
Guara, Sierra de, *Spain* **40 C4** 42 19N 0 15W
Guarabira, *Brazil* **170 C4** 6 51 S 35 29W
Guaranda, *Ecuador* **168 D2** 1 36 S 79 0W
Guarapari, *Brazil* **171 F3** 20 40 S 40 30W
Guarapuava, *Brazil* **171 G1** 25 20 S 51 30W
Guaratinguetá, *Brazil* **175 A6** 22 49 S 45 9W
Guaratuba, *Brazil* **175 B6** 25 53 S 48 38W
Guarda, *Portugal* **42 E3** 40 32N 7 20W
Guarda □, *Portugal* **42 E3** 40 40N 7 20W
Guardafui, C. = Asir, Ras, *Somali Rep.* **120 B4** 11 55N 51 10 E
Guardamar del Segura, *Spain* **41 G4** 38 5N 0 39W
Guardavalle, *Italy* **47 D9** 38 30N 16 30 E
Guárdia Sanframondi, *Italy* **47 A7** 41 15N 14 36 E
Guardiagrele, *Italy* **45 F11** 42 11N 14 13 E
Guardo, *Spain* **42 C6** 42 47N 4 50W
Guareña, *Spain* **43 G4** 38 51N 6 6W
Guareña →, *Spain* **42 D5** 41 29N 5 23W
Guari, *Papua N. G.* **132 E4** 8 3 S 146 52 E
Guárico □, *Venezuela* **168 B4** 8 40N 66 35W
Guarrojo →, *Colombia* **168 C3** 4 6N 70 42W
Guarujá, *Brazil* **175 A6** 24 2 S 46 25W
Guarus, *Brazil* **171 F3** 21 44 S 41 20W
Guasave, *Mexico* **162 B3** 25 34N 108 27W
Guascama, Pta., *Colombia* **168 C2** 2 32N 78 24W
Guasdualito, *Venezuela* **168 B3** 7 15N 70 44W
Guasipati, *Venezuela* **169 B5** 7 28N 61 54W
Guasopa, *Papua N. G.* **132 E7** 9 12 S 152 56 E
Guastalla, *Italy* **44 D7** 44 55N 10 39 E
Guatemala, *Guatemala* **164 D1** 14 40N 90 22W
Guatemala ■, *Cent. Amer.* **164 C1** 15 40N 90 30W
Guatire, *Venezuela* **168 A4** 10 28N 66 32W
Guatuaro Pt., *Trin. & Tob.* **169 F10** 10 19N 60 59W
Guavi →, *Papua N. G.* **132 D2** 7 48 S 143 16 E
Guaviare □, *Colombia* **168 C3** 2 0N 72 30W
Guaviare →, *Colombia* **168 C4** 4 3N 67 44W
Guaxupé, *Brazil* **175 A6** 21 10 S 47 5W
Guayabero →, *Colombia* **168 C3** 2 36N 72 47W
Guayaguayare, *Trin. & Tob.* **169 F9** 10 12N 61 3W
Guayama, *Puerto Rico* **165 d** 17 59N 66 7W
Guayaneco, Arch., *Chile* **176 C1** 47 45 S 75 10W
Guayaquil, *Ecuador* **168 D2** 2 15 S 79 52W
Guayaquil, G. de, *Ecuador* **168 D1** 3 10 S 81 0W
Guayaramerín, *Bolivia* **173 C4** 10 48 S 65 23W
Guayas →, *Ecuador* **168 D2** 2 36 S 79 52W
Guaymas, *Mexico* **162 B2** 27 59N 110 54W
Guba, *Dem. Rep. of the Congo* **119 E2** 10 38 S 26 27 E
Guba, *Ethiopia* **107 E4** 11 17N 35 20 E
Gubakha, *Russia* **64 B6** 58 52N 57 36 E
Gûbâl, Madîq, *Egypt* **106 B3** 27 30N 34 0 E
Gubam, *Papua N. G.* **132 E1** 8 39 S 141 53 E
Guban, *Somali Rep.* **120 B1** 10 30N 44 0 E
Gubat, *Phil.* **80 E5** 12 55N 124 7 E
Gubbi, *India* **95 H3** 13 19N 76 56 E
Gúbbio, *Italy* **45 E9** 43 21N 12 35 E
Guben, *Germany* **30 D10** 51 57N 14 42 E
Gubin, *Poland* **55 G1** 51 57N 14 43 E
Gubio, *Nigeria* **113 C7** 12 30N 12 42 E
Gubkin, *Russia* **59 G9** 51 17N 37 32 E
Guča, *Serbia, Yug.* **50 C4** 43 46N 20 15 E
Gucheng, *China* **77 A8** 32 20N 111 30 E
Gudå, *Norway* **18 A8** 63 27N 11 36 E
Gudalur, *India* **95 J3** 11 30N 76 29 E
Gudata = Guadauta, *Georgia* **61 J5** 43 7N 40 32 E
Gudbrandsdalen, *Norway* **15 F14** 61 33N 10 10 E
Gudenå →, *Denmark* **17 H4** 56 29N 10 13 E
Gudermes, *Russia* **61 J8** 43 24N 46 5 E
Gudhjem, *Denmark* **17 J8** 55 12N 14 58 E
Gudivada, *India* **95 F5** 16 30N 81 3 E
Gudiyattam, *India* **95 H4** 12 57N 78 55 E
Gudur, *India* **95 G4** 14 12N 79 55 E
Gudvangen, *Norway* **18 D3** 60 52N 6 49 E
Guebwiller, *France* **27 E14** 47 55N 7 12 E
Guecho = Getxo, *Spain* **40 B2** 43 21N 2 59W
Guékédou, *Guinea* **112 D2** 8 40N 10 5W
Guelb er Rîchât, *Mauritania* **110 D2** 21 7N 11 24W
Guéle Mendouka, *Cameroon* **113 E7** 4 23N 12 55 E
Guélengdeng, *Chad* **109 F3** 10 55N 15 31 E
Guelma, *Algeria* **111 A6** 36 25N 7 29 E
Guelmine = Goulimine, *Morocco* **110 C3** 28 56N 10 0W
Guelph, *Canada* **140 D3** 43 35N 80 20W
Guelta Zemmur, *W. Sahara* **110 C2** 25 8N 12 22W
Guemar, *Algeria* **111 B6** 33 30N 6 49 E
Guéméné-Penfao, *France* **26 E5** 47 38N 1 50W
Guéméné-sur-Scorff, *France* **26 D3** 48 4N 3 13W
Guéné, *Benin* **113 C5** 11 44N 3 16 E
Güeppí, *Peru* **168 D2** 0 7 S 75 15W
Guer, *France* **26 E4** 47 54N 2 8W
Güer Aike, *Argentina* **176 D3** 51 39 S 69 35W
Guera, *Chad* **109 F3** 11 55N 18 12 E
Guérande, *France* **26 E4** 47 20N 2 26W
Guerara, *Algeria* **111 B5** 32 51N 4 22 E
Guercif, *Morocco* **111 B4** 34 14N 3 21W
Guéréda, *Chad* **109 F4** 14 31N 22 5 E
Guéret, *France* **27 F8** 46 11N 1 51 E
Guérigny, *France* **27 E10** 47 6N 3 10 E
Guerneville, *U.S.A.* **160 G4** 38 30N 123 0W
Guernica = Gernika-Lumo, *Spain* **40 B2** 43 19N 2 40W
Guernsey, *U.K.* **21 H5** 49 26N 2 35W
Guernsey, *U.S.A.* **154 D2** 42 19N 104 45W
Guerrara, *Algeria* **111 C4** 28 5N 0 8W
Guerrero □, *Mexico* **163 D5** 17 30N 100 0W
Guerzim, *Algeria* **111 C4** 29 39N 1 40W
Guessou-Sud, *Benin* **113 C5** 10 3N 2 38 E
Gueugnon, *France* **27 F11** 46 36N 4 4 E
Guéyo, *Ivory C.* **112 D3** 5 25N 6 5W
Gufuðalur, *Iceland* **11 B4** 65 34N 22 25W
Gughe, *Ethiopia* **107 F4** 6 12N 37 30 E
Gūgher, *Iran* **97 D8** 29 28N 56 27 E
Guglionesi, *Italy* **45 G11** 41 55N 14 55 E
Guhakolak, Tanjung, *Indonesia* **79 G11** 6 50 S 105 14 E
Gui Jiang →, *China* **77 F8** 23 30N 111 15 E
Guia, *Canary Is.* **9 e1** 28 8N 15 38W
Guia de Isora, *Canary Is.* **9 e1** 28 12N 16 46W
Guia Lopes da Laguna, *Brazil* **175 A4** 21 26 S 56 7W
Guiana, *S. Amer.* **166 C4** 5 10N 60 40W
Guiana, *Venezuela* **169 B5** 5 9N 63 36W
Guibéroua, *Ivory C.* **112 D3** 6 14N 6 10W
Guichen B., *Australia* **128 D3** 37 10 S 139 45 E
Guichi, *China* **77 B11** 30 39N 117 27 E
Guider, *Cameroon* **113 D7** 9 56N 13 57 E
Guidiguir, *Niger* **113 C6** 13 40N 9 50 E
Guidimouni, *Niger* **113 C6** 13 42N 9 31 E
Guiding, *China* **76 D6** 26 34N 107 11 E
Guidong, *China* **77 D9** 26 7N 113 57 E
Guidónia-Montecélio, *Italy* **45 F9** 42 1N 12 45 E
Guiers, L. de, *Senegal* **112 B1** 16 10N 15 50W
Guigang, *China* **76 F7** 23 8N 109 35 E
Guiglo, *Ivory C.* **112 D3** 6 45N 7 30W
Guihulñgan, *Phil.* **81 F4** 10 7N 123 16 E
Guijá, *Mozam.* **117 C5** 24 27 S 33 0 E
Guijuelo, *Spain* **42 E5** 40 33N 5 40W
Guildford, *U.K.* **21 F7** 51 14N 0 34W
Guilford, *U.S.A.* **151 E12** 41 17N 72 41W
Guilin, *China* **77 E8** 25 18N 110 15 E
Guillaume-Delisle L., *Canada* **140 A4** 56 15N 76 17W
Guillaumes, *France* **29 D10** 44 5N 6 52 E
Guillestre, *France* **29 D10** 44 39N 6 40 E
Guilvinec, *France* **26 E2** 47 48N 4 17W
Güimar, *Canary Is.* **9 e1** 28 18N 16 24W
Guimarães, *Brazil* **170 B3** 2 9 S 44 42W
Guimarães, *Portugal* **42 D2** 41 28N 8 24W
Guimaras □, *Phil.* **81 F4** 10 35N 122 37 E
Guimba, *Phil.* **80 D3** 15 40N 120 46 E
Guinayangan, *Phil.* **80 E4** 13 54N 122 27 E
Guinda, *U.S.A.* **160 G4** 38 50N 122 12W
Guindulman, *Phil.* **81 G5** 9 46N 124 29 E
Guinea, *Africa* **104 F4** 8 0N 8 0 E
Guinea ■, *W. Afr.* **112 C2** 10 20N 11 30W
Guinea, Gulf of, *Atl. Oc.* **113 E5** 3 0N 2 30 E
Guinea-Bissau ■, *Africa* **112 C2** 12 0N 15 0W
Güines, *Cuba* **164 B3** 22 50N 82 0W
Guingamp, *France* **26 D3** 48 34N 3 10W
Guinguinéo, *Senegal* **112 C1** 14 20N 15 57W
Guinobatan, *Phil.* **80 E4** 13 11N 123 36 E
Guipavas, *France* **26 D2** 48 26N 4 29W
Guiping, *China* **77 F8** 23 21N 110 2 E
Guipúzcoa □, *Spain* **40 B2** 43 12N 2 15W
Guir, *Mali* **112 B4** 18 52N 2 52W
Guir, O. →, *Algeria* **111 B4** 31 29N 2 17W
Guiratinga, *Brazil* **173 D7** 16 21 S 53 45W
Guirel, *Mauritania* **112 B3** 15 30N 7 3W
Güiria, *Venezuela* **169 F8** 10 32N 62 18W
Guiscard, *France* **27 C10** 49 40N 3 1 E
Guise, *France* **27 C10** 49 52N 3 35 E
Guita-Koulouba, *C.A.R.* **114 A4** 5 58N 23 21 E
Guitiriz, *Spain* **42 B3** 43 11N 7 50W
Guitri, *Ivory C.* **112 D3** 5 30N 5 14W
Guiuan, *Phil.* **81 F5** 11 5N 125 55 E
Guixi, *China* **77 C11** 28 16N 117 15 E
Guiyang, *Guizhou, China* **76 D6** 26 32N 106 40 E
Guiyang, *Hunan, China* **77 E9** 25 46N 112 42 E
Guizhou □, *China* **76 D6** 27 0N 107 0 E
Gujan-Mestras, *France* **28 D2** 44 38N 1 4W
Gujar Khan, *Pakistan* **92 C5** 33 16N 73 19 E
Gujarat □, *India* **92 H4** 23 20N 71 0 E
Gujiang, *China* **77 D10** 27 11N 114 47 E
Gujranwala, *Pakistan* **91 B4** 32 10N 74 12 E
Gujrat, *Pakistan* **91 B4** 32 40N 74 2 E
Gukovo, *Russia* **61 F5** 48 1N 39 58 E
Gulargambone, *Australia* **129 A8** 31 20 S 148 30 E
Gulbarga, *India* **94 F3** 17 20N 76 50 E
Gulbene, *Latvia* **15 H22** 57 8N 26 52 E
Gülchö, *Kyrgyzstan* **65 C6** 40 19N 73 26 E
Guledagudda, *India* **95 F2** 16 3N 75 48 E
Gulf □, *Papua N. G.* **132 D3** 8 0 S 145 0 E
Gulf, The, *Asia* **97 E6** 27 0N 50 0 E
Gulf Breeze, *U.S.A.* **153 E2** 30 22N 87 9W
Gulf Hammock, *U.S.A.* **153 F7** 29 15N 82 43W
Gulfport, *Fla., U.S.A.* **153 H7** 27 44N 82 43W
Gulfport, *Miss., U.S.A.* **155 K10** 30 22N 89 6W
Gulgong, *Australia* **129 B8** 32 20 S 149 49 E
Gulin, *China* **76 C5** 28 1N 105 50 E
Gulistan, *Pakistan* **92 D2** 30 30N 66 35 E
Guliston, *Uzbekistan* **65 C4** 40 29N 68 46 E
Gulkana, *U.S.A.* **144 E11** 62 16N 145 23W
Gull Lake, *Canada* **143 C7** 50 10N 108 29W
Gullbrå, *Norway* **18 D3** 60 50N 6 17 E
Gullbrandstorp, *Sweden* **17 H6** 56 42N 12 43 E
Gullbringusýsla □, *Iceland* **11 D4** 64 0N 22 0W
Gullfoss, *Iceland* **11 C6** 64 20N 20 8W
Gullhaug, *Norway* **18 E7** 59 30N 10 15 E
Gullivan B., *U.S.A.* **153 K8** 25 45N 81 40W
Gullspång, *Sweden* **17 F8** 58 59N 14 6 E
Gullstein, *Norway* **18 A5** 63 13N 8 9 E
Güllük, *Turkey* **49 D9** 37 14N 27 35 E
Güllük Korfezi, *Turkey* **49 D9** 37 12N 27 30 E
Gulma, *Nigeria* **113 C5** 12 40N 4 23 E
Gulmarg, *India* **93 B6** 34 3N 74 25 E
Gülnar, *Turkey* **100 D5** 36 19N 33 24 E
Gulnare, *Australia* **128 B3** 33 27 S 138 27 E
Gülpınar, *Turkey* **49 B8** 39 32N 26 7 E
Gülşehir, *Turkey* **100 C6** 38 44N 34 37 E
Gulshad, *Kazakstan* **66 E8** 46 45N 74 25 E
Gulsvik, *Norway* **18 D6** 60 24N 9 38 E
Gulu, *Uganda* **118 B3** 2 48N 32 17 E
Gŭlŭbovo, *Bulgaria* **51 D9** 42 8N 25 55 E
Gulud, J., *Sudan* **107 E2** 11 41N 29 31 E
Gulwe, *Tanzania* **118 D4** 6 30 S 36 25 E
Gulyaypole = Hulyaypole, *Ukraine* **59 J9** 47 45N 36 21 E
Gum Lake, *Australia* **128 B5** 32 42 S 143 9 E
Gumaca, *Phil.* **80 E4** 13 55N 122 6 E
Gumal →, *Pakistan* **92 D4** 31 40N 71 50 E
Gumbaz, *Pakistan* **92 D3** 30 2N 69 0 E
Gumel, *Nigeria* **113 C6** 12 39N 9 22 E
Gumiel de Hizán, *Spain* **42 D7** 41 46N 3 41W
Gumla, *India* **93 H11** 23 3N 84 33 E
Gumlu, *Australia* **126 B4** 19 53 S 147 41 E
Gumma □, *Japan* **73 A10** 36 30N 138 20 E
Gummersbach, *Germany* **30 D3** 51 1N 7 34 E
Gummi, *Nigeria* **113 C6** 12 4N 5 9 E
Gümüldür, *Turkey* **49 C9** 38 6N 27 0 E
Gümüşçay, *Turkey* **51 F11** 40 16N 27 17 E
Gümüşhaciköy, *Turkey* **100 B6** 40 50N 35 18 E
Gümüşhane, *Turkey* **101 B8** 40 30N 39 30 E
Gümüşsu, *Turkey* **49 C11** 38 14N 29 1 E
Gumzai, *Indonesia* **83 C4** 5 28 S 134 42 E
Guna, *Ethiopia* **107 F4** 8 18N 39 52 E
Guna, *India* **92 G7** 24 40N 77 19 E
Gundagai, *Australia* **129 C8** 35 3 S 148 6 E
Gundarehi, *India* **94 D5** 20 57N 81 17 E
Gundelfingen, *Germany* **31 G6** 48 34N 10 22 E
Gundih, *Indonesia* **85 D4** 7 10 S 110 56 E
Gundlakamma →, *India* **95 G5** 15 30N 80 15 E
Gundlupet, *India* **95 J3** 11 48N 76 41 E
Gunebang, *Australia* **129 B7** 33 1 S 146 38 E
Güney, *Burdur, Turkey* **49 D11** 37 29N 29 34 E
Güney, *Denizli, Turkey* **49 C11** 38 10N 29 4 E
Güneydoğu Toroslar, *Turkey* **101 C9** 38 20N 40 30 E
Gungal, *Australia* **129 B9** 32 17 S 150 32 E
Gungo, *Angola* **115 E2** 10 58 S 15 30 E
Gungu, *Dem. Rep. of the Congo* **115 D3** 5 43 S 19 20 E
Gunisao →, *Canada* **143 C9** 53 56N 97 53W
Gunisao L., *Canada* **143 C9** 53 33N 96 15W
Gunjyal, *Pakistan* **92 C4** 32 20N 71 55 E
Günlüce, *Turkey* **49 E10** 36 50N 28 20 E
Gunnarskog, *Sweden* **16 E6** 59 49N 12 34 E
Gunnbjørn Fjeld, *Greenland* **10 D8** 68 55N 29 47W
Gunnebo, *Sweden* **17 G10** 57 44N 16 32 E
Gunnedah, *Australia* **129 A9** 30 59 S 150 15 E
Gunnewin, *Australia* **127 D4** 25 59 S 148 33 E
Gunningbar Cr. →, *Australia* **129 A7** 31 14 S 147 6 E
Gunnison, *Colo., U.S.A.* **159 G10** 38 33N 106 56W
Gunnison, *Utah, U.S.A.* **158 G8** 39 9N 111 49W
Gunnison →, *U.S.A.* **159 G9** 39 4N 108 35W
Gunpowder, *Australia* **126 B2** 19 42 S 139 22 E
Guntakal, *India* **95 G3** 15 11N 77 27 E
Guntersville, *U.S.A.* **149 H2** 34 21N 86 18W
Guntong, *Malaysia* **87 K3** 4 36N 101 3 E
Guntur, *India* **95 F5** 16 23N 80 30 E
Gunungapi, *Indonesia* **82 C3** 6 45 S 126 30 E
Gunungsitoli, *Indonesia* **84 B1** 1 15N 97 30 E
Gunupur, *India* **94 E6** 19 5N 83 50 E
Günz →, *Germany* **31 G6** 48 27N 10 16 E
Gunza, *Angola* **115 E2** 10 50 S 13 50 E
Günzburg, *Germany* **31 G6** 48 26N 10 17 E
Gunzenhausen, *Germany* **31 F6** 49 7N 10 44 E
Guo He →, *China* **75 H9** 32 59N 117 10 E
Guoyang, *China* **74 H9** 33 32N 116 12 E
Gupis, *Pakistan* **93 A5** 36 15N 73 20 E
Gura Humorului, *Romania* **53 C10** 47 35N 25 53 E
Gura-Teghii, *Romania* **53 E11** 45 30N 26 25 E
Gurag, *Ethiopia* **107 F4** 8 20N 38 20 E
Gurahonţ, *Romania* **52 D7** 46 16N 22 21 E
Gurdaspur, *India* **92 C6** 32 5N 75 31 E
Gurdon, *U.S.A.* **155 J8** 33 55N 93 9W
Güre, *Balıkesir, Turkey* **49 B8** 39 36N 26 54 E
Güre, *Uşak, Turkey* **49 C11** 38 39N 29 10 E
Gurgaon, *India* **92 E7** 28 27N 77 1 E
Gürgentepe, *Turkey* **100 B7** 40 51N 37 50 E
Gurghiu, Munţii, *Romania* **53 D10** 46 41N 25 15 E
Gurgueia →, *Brazil* **170 C3** 6 50 S 43 24W
Gurha, *India* **92 G4** 25 12N 71 39 E
Guri, Embalse de, *Venezuela* **169 B5** 7 50N 62 52W
Gurig Nat. Park, *Australia* **124 B5** 11 36 S 132 7 E
Gurimatu, *Papua N. G.* **132 D3** 6 45 S 144 45 E
Gurin, *Nigeria* **113 D7** 9 5N 12 54 E
Gurinhatã, *Brazil* **171 E2** 19 14 S 49 48W
Gurjaani, *Georgia* **61 K7** 41 43N 45 52 E
Gurk →, *Austria* **34 E7** 46 35N 14 31 E
Gurkha, *Nepal* **93 E11** 28 5N 84 40 E
Gurley, *Australia* **127 D4** 29 45 S 149 48 E
Gurnee, *U.S.A.* **157 B9** 42 22N 87 55W
Gurnet Point, *U.S.A.* **151 D14** 42 1N 70 34W
Guro, *Mozam.* **119 F3** 17 26 S 32 30 E
Gürpınar, *İst., Turkey* **51 F12** 40 59N 28 37 E
Gürpınar, *Van, Turkey* **101 C10** 38 18N 43 25 E
Gürsu, *Turkey* **51 F13** 40 13N 29 11 E
Gurué, *Mozam.* **119 F4** 15 25 S 36 58 E
Gurun, *Malaysia* **87 K3** 5 49N 100 27 E
Gürün, *Turkey* **100 C7** 38 43N 37 15 E
Gurupá, *Brazil* **169 D7** 1 25 S 51 35W
Gurupá, I. Grande de, *Brazil* **169 D7** 1 25 S 51 45W
Gurupi, *Brazil* **171 D2** 11 43 S 49 4W

Gurupi →, Brazil 170 B2 1 13 S 46 6W
Gurupi, Serra do, Brazil 170 C2 5 0 S 47 50W
Guruwe, Zimbabwe 117 B5 16 40 S 30 42 E
Guryev = Atyraū, Kazakstan 57 E9 47 5N 52 0 E
Gus-Khrustalnyy, Russia 60 C5 55 42N 40 44 E
Gusau, Nigeria 113 C6 12 12N 6 40 E
Gusev, Russia 15 J20 54 35N 22 10 E
Gushan, China 75 E12 39 50N 123 35 E
Gushgy, Turkmenistan 66 F7 35 20N 62 18 E
Gushi, China 77 A10 32 11N 115 41 E
Gushiago, Ghana 113 D4 9 55N 0 15W
Gusinje, Montenegro, Yug. 50 D3 42 35N 19 50 E
Gusinoozersk, Russia 67 D11 51 16N 106 27 E
Gúspini, Italy 46 C1 39 32N 8 37 E
Güssing, Austria 35 D9 47 3N 16 20 E
Gustav Holm, Kap, Greenland 10 D7 66 36N 34 15W
Gustavsberg, Sweden 16 E12 59 19N 18 23 E
Gustavus, U.S.A. 142 B1 58 25N 135 44W
Gustine, U.S.A. 160 H6 37 16N 121 0W
Güstrow, Germany 30 B8 53 47N 12 10 E
Gusum, Sweden 17 F10 58 16N 16 30 E
Guta = Kolárovo, Slovak Rep. 35 D10 47 54N 18 0 E
Gütersloh, Germany 30 D4 51 54N 8 24 E
Gutha, Australia 125 E2 28 58 S 115 55 E
Guthalungra, Australia 126 B4 19 52 S 147 50 E
Guthrie, Okla., U.S.A. 155 H6 35 53N 97 25W
Guthrie, Tex., U.S.A. 155 J4 33 37N 100 19W
Guthrie Center, U.S.A. 156 C2 41 41N 94 30W
Gutian, China 77 D12 26 32N 118 43 E
Gutiérrez, Bolivia 173 D5 19 25 S 63 34W
Guttannen, Switz. 33 C6 46 38N 8 18 E
Guttenberg, U.S.A. 156 B5 42 47N 91 6W
Gutu, Zimbabwe 117 B5 19 41 S 31 9 E
Guwahati, India 90 B3 26 10N 91 45 E
Guy Fawkes River Nat. Park, Australia 127 D5 30 0 S 152 20 E
Guyana ■, S. Amer. 169 B6 5 0N 59 0W
Guyane française = French Guiana ■, S. Amer. 169 C7 4 0N 53 0W
Guyang, China 74 D6 41 0N 110 5 E
Guyenne, France 28 D4 44 30N 0 40 E
Guymon, U.S.A. 155 G4 36 41N 101 29W
Guyra, Australia 127 E5 30 15 S 151 40 E
Guyton, U.S.A. 152 C8 32 20N 81 24W
Guyuan, Hebei, China 74 D8 41 37N 115 40 E
Guyuan, Ningxia Huizu, China 74 G4 36 0N 106 20 E
Guzar, Uzbekistan 65 D3 38 36N 66 15 E
Güzelbahçe, Turkey 49 C8 38 21N 26 54 E
Guzhang, China 76 C7 28 42N 109 58 E
Guzhen, China 75 H9 33 22N 117 18 E
Guzmán, L. de, Mexico 162 A3 31 25N 107 25W
Gvardeysk, Russia 15 J19 54 39N 21 5 E
Gvardeyskoye, Ukraine 59 K8 45 7N 34 1 E
Gvarv, Norway 18 E6 59 23N 9 9 E
Gwa, Burma 90 G5 17 36N 94 34 E
Gwaai, Zimbabwe 119 F2 19 15 S 27 45 E
Gwaai →, Zimbabwe 119 F2 17 59 S 26 52 E
Gwabegar, Australia 129 A8 30 31 S 149 0 E
Gwadabawa, Nigeria 113 C6 13 28N 5 15 E
Gwādar, Pakistan 91 D1 25 10N 62 18 E
Gwagwada, Nigeria 113 C6 10 15N 7 15 E
Gwalior, India 92 F8 26 12N 78 10 E
Gwanara, Nigeria 113 D5 8 55N 3 9 E
Gwanda, Zimbabwe 119 G2 20 55 S 29 0 E
Gwandu, Nigeria 113 C5 12 30N 4 41 E
Gwane, Dem. Rep. of the Congo 118 B2 4 45N 25 48 E
Gwaram, Nigeria 113 C7 10 15N 10 25 E
Gwarzo, Nigeria 113 C6 12 20N 8 55 E
Gwasero, Nigeria 113 D5 9 29N 3 30 E
Gwda →, Poland 55 E3 53 3N 16 44 E
Gweebarra B., Ireland 23 B3 54 51N 8 23W
Gweedore, Ireland 23 A3 55 3N 8 13W
Gweru, Zimbabwe 119 F2 19 28 S 29 45 E
Gwi, Nigeria 113 D6 9 0N 7 10 E
Gwinn, U.S.A. 148 B2 46 19N 87 27W
Gwio Kura, Nigeria 113 C7 12 40N 11 2 E
Gwoza, Nigeria 113 C7 11 5N 13 40 E
Gwydir →, Australia 127 D4 29 27 S 149 48 E
Gwynedd □, U.K. 20 E3 52 52N 4 10W
Gyandzha = Gäncä, Azerbaijan 61 K8 40 45N 46 20 E
Gyaring Hu, China 68 C4 34 50N 97 40 E
Gydanskiy Poluostrov, Russia 66 C8 70 0N 78 0 E
Gyl, Norway 18 B5 62 57N 8 7 E
Gyldenløve Fjord, Greenland 10 E6 64 15N 40 30W
Gympie, Australia 127 D5 26 11 S 152 38 E
Gyobingauk, Burma 90 F5 18 13N 95 39 E
Gyōda, Japan 73 A11 36 10N 139 30 E
Gyomaendrőd, Hungary 52 D5 46 56N 20 50 E
Gyöngyös, Hungary 52 C4 47 48N 19 56 E
Győr, Hungary 52 C2 47 41N 17 40 E
Győr-Moson-Sopron □, Hungary 52 C2 47 40N 17 20 E
Gypsum Pt., Canada 142 A6 61 53N 114 35W
Gypsumville, Canada 143 C9 51 45N 98 40W
Gyueshevo, Bulgaria 50 D6 42 14N 22 28 E
Gyula, Hungary 52 D6 46 38N 21 17 E
Gyumri, Armenia 61 K6 40 47N 43 50 E
Gyzylarbat, Turkmenistan 66 F6 39 4N 56 23 E
Gyzyletrek, Turkmenistan 97 B7 37 36N 54 46 E
Gzhatsk = Gagarin, Russia 58 E8 55 38N 35 0 E
Gzira, Malta 38 F7 35 54N 14 29 E

H

Ha 'Arava →, Israel 103 E4 30 50N 35 20 E
Ha Coi, Vietnam 76 G6 21 26N 107 46 E
Ha Dong, Vietnam 76 G5 20 58N 105 46 E
Ha Giang, Vietnam 76 F5 22 50N 104 59 E
Ha Tien, Vietnam 87 G5 10 23N 104 29 E
Ha Tinh, Vietnam 86 C5 18 20N 105 54 E
Ha Trung, Vietnam 86 C5 19 58N 105 50 E
Ha Yaek Chalong, Thailand 87 a 7 50N 98 22 E
Haaksbergen, Neths. 24 B6 52 9N 6 45 E
Ha'ano, Tonga 133 P13 19 41 S 174 18W
Ha'apai Group, Tonga 133 P13 19 47 S 174 27W
Haapsalu, Estonia 15 G20 58 56N 23 30 E
Haarlem, Neths. 24 B4 52 23N 4 39 E
Haast, N.Z. 131 D4 43 51 S 169 1 E
Haast →, N.Z. 131 D4 43 50 S 169 2 E
Haast Bluff, Australia 124 D5 23 22 S 132 0 E
Haast Pass, N.Z. 131 E4 44 6 S 169 21 E
Hab →, Pakistan 92 G3 24 53N 66 41 E
Hab Nadi Chauki, Pakistan 92 G2 25 0N 66 50 E
Ḥabarūt, Yemen 99 C6 17 18N 52 44 E
Habaswein, Kenya 118 B4 1 2N 39 30 E
Ḥabawnah, W. →, Si. Arabia 98 C4 17 57N 44 58 E
Habay, Canada 142 B5 58 50N 118 44W
Ḥabbān, Yemen 98 D4 14 21N 47 5 E
Ḥabbānīyah, Iraq 101 F10 33 17N 43 29 E
Ḥabbānīyah, Hawr al, Iraq 101 F10 33 17N 43 29 E
Habiganj, Bangla. 90 C3 24 24N 91 30 E
Habo, Sweden 17 G8 57 55N 14 6 E
Haboro, Japan 70 B10 44 22N 141 42 E
Ḥabshān, U.A.E. 97 F7 23 50N 53 37 E
Hachenburg, Germany 30 E3 50 40N 7 49 E
Hachi, India 90 B5 27 48N 94 2 E
Hachijō-Jima, Japan 73 D11 33 5N 139 45 E
Hachiman, Japan 73 B8 35 45N 136 57 E
Hachinohe, Japan 70 D10 40 30N 141 29 E
Hachiōji, Japan 73 B11 35 40N 139 20 E
Hachŏn, N. Korea 75 D15 41 29N 129 2 E
Hacıbektaş, Turkey 100 C6 38 56N 34 33 E
Hacılar, Turkey 100 C6 38 38N 35 26 E
Hack, Mt., Australia 128 A3 30 45 S 138 55 E
Hackås, Sweden 16 B8 62 56N 14 30 E
Hackensack, U.S.A. 151 F10 40 53N 74 3W
Hackettstown, U.S.A. 151 F10 40 51N 74 50W
Haco, Angola 115 E3 10 15 S 15 44 E
Hadali, Pakistan 92 C5 32 16N 72 11 E
Hadano, Japan 73 B11 35 22N 139 14 E
Hadarba, Ras, Sudan 106 C4 22 4N 36 51 E
Hadarom □, Israel 103 E4 31 0N 35 0 E
Ḥaḍbaram, Oman 99 C6 17 27N 55 15 E
Ḥadd, Ra's al, Oman 99 B7 22 35N 59 50 E
Ḥaddā, Si. Arabia 98 B2 21 27N 39 34 E
Haddock, U.S.A. 152 B6 33 2N 83 26W
Haded Plain = Xadded, Somali Rep. 120 C3 9 46N 48 2 E
Hadejia, Nigeria 113 C7 12 30N 10 5 E
Hadejia →, Nigeria 113 C7 12 50N 10 51 E
Ḥadera, Israel 103 C3 32 27N 34 55 E
Ḥadera, N. →, Israel 103 C3 32 28N 34 52 E
Haderslev, Denmark 17 J3 55 15N 9 30 E
Hadgaon, India 94 E3 19 30N 77 40 E
Hadhramaut = Ḥaḍramawt, Yemen 99 D5 15 30N 49 30 E
Hadiboh, Yemen 99 D6 12 39N 54 2 E
Hadım, Turkey 100 D5 36 58N 32 26 E
Hadjadj, O. el →, Algeria 111 C6 28 18N 5 20 E
Hadjeb El Aïoun, Tunisia 108 A1 35 21N 9 32 E
Hadjer Kamaran, Chad 109 F4 12 41N 21 46 E
Hadjer Mornou, Chad 109 E4 17 12N 23 8 E
Hadong, S. Korea 75 G14 35 5N 127 44 E
Ḥaḍramawt, Yemen 99 D5 15 30N 49 30 E
Ḥaḍramawt, W. →, Yemen 99 D5 15 10N 51 8 E
Ḥadrānīyah, Iraq 96 C4 35 38N 43 14 E
Hadrian's Wall, U.K. 20 B5 55 0N 2 30W
Hadsten, Denmark 17 H4 56 19N 10 3 E
Hadsund, Denmark 17 H4 56 44N 10 8 E
Hadyach, Ukraine 59 G8 50 21N 34 0 E
Hægeland, Norway 18 F4 58 22N 7 45 E
Haeju, N. Korea 75 E13 38 3N 125 45 E
Haena, U.S.A. 145 A2 22 14N 159 34W
Haenam, S. Korea 75 G14 34 34N 126 35 E
Haenertsburg, S. Africa 117 C4 24 0 S 29 50 E
Haerhpin = Harbin, China 75 B14 45 48N 126 40 E
Hafar al Bāṭin, Si. Arabia 96 D5 28 32N 45 52 E
Hafik, Turkey 100 C7 39 51N 37 23 E
Ḥafīrat al 'Aydā, Si. Arabia 96 E3 26 26N 39 12 E
Ḥafit, Oman 97 F7 23 59N 55 49 E
Hafizabad, Pakistan 92 C5 32 5N 73 40 E
Haflong, India 90 C4 25 10N 93 5 E
Hafnarfjörður, Iceland 11 C5 64 4N 21 57W
Hafnir, Iceland 11 D4 63 56N 22 41W
Hafslo, Norway 18 C4 61 19N 7 10 E
Haft Gel, Iran 97 D6 31 30N 49 32 E
Hafun, Ras, Somali Rep. 102 E5 10 29N 51 30 E
Hagalil, Israel 103 C4 32 53N 35 18 E
Hagari →, India 95 G3 15 40N 77 0 E
Hagby, Sweden 17 H10 56 34N 16 11 E
Hagemeister I., U.S.A. 144 G7 58 39N 160 54W
Hagen, Germany 30 D3 51 21N 7 27 E
Hagenow, Germany 30 B7 53 26N 11 12 E
Hagerman, U.S.A. 155 J2 33 7N 104 20W
Hagerstown, Ind., U.S.A. 157 E11 39 55N 85 10W
Hagerstown, Md., U.S.A. 148 F7 39 39N 77 43W
Hagersville, Canada 150 D4 42 58N 80 3W
Hagetmau, France 28 E3 43 39N 0 37W
Hagfors, Sweden 16 D7 60 3N 13 45 E
Hagi, Iceland 11 B3 65 28N 23 25W
Hagi, Japan 72 C3 34 30N 131 22 E
Hagolan, Syria 103 C4 33 0N 35 45 E
Hagondange, France 27 C13 49 16N 6 11 E
Hagonoy, Phil. 80 D3 14 50N 120 44 E
Hags Hd., Ireland 23 D2 52 57N 9 28W
Hague, C. de la, France 26 C5 49 44N 1 56W
Hague, The = 's-Gravenhage, Neths. 24 B4 52 7N 4 17 E
Haguenau, France 27 D14 48 49N 7 47 E
Hagunía, W. Sahara 110 C2 27 26N 12 24W
Hahira, U.S.A. 152 E6 30 59N 83 22W
Hai Duong, Vietnam 76 G6 20 56N 106 19 E
Hai'an, Guangdong, China 77 G8 20 18N 110 11 E
Hai'an, Jiangsu, China 77 A13 32 37N 120 27 E
Haicheng, Fujian, China 77 E11 24 23N 117 48 E
Haicheng, Liaoning, China 75 D12 40 50N 122 45 E
Haidar Khel, Afghan. 92 C3 33 58N 68 38 E
Haidargarh, India 93 F9 26 37N 81 22 E
Haifa = Ḥefa, Israel 103 C4 32 46N 35 0 E
Haifeng, China 77 F10 22 58N 115 10 E
Haiger, Germany 30 E4 50 43N 8 12 E
Haikou, China 69 D6 20 1N 110 16 E
Ḥā'il, Si. Arabia 96 E4 27 28N 41 45 E
Hailakandi, India 90 C4 24 42N 92 34 E
Hailar, China 69 B6 49 10N 119 38 E
Hailey, U.S.A. 158 E6 43 31N 114 19W
Haileybury, Canada 140 C4 47 30N 79 38W
Hailin, China 75 B15 44 37N 129 30 E
Hailing Dao, China 77 G8 21 35N 111 47 E
Hailong, China 75 C13 42 32N 125 40 E
Hailuoto, Finland 14 D21 65 3N 24 45 E
Haimen, Guangdong, China 77 F11 23 15N 116 38 E
Haimen, Jiangsu, China 77 B13 31 52N 121 10 E
Hainan □, China 69 E5 19 0N 109 30 E
Hainaut □, Belgium 24 D4 50 30N 4 0 E
Hainburg, Austria 35 C9 48 9N 16 56 E
Haines, Alaska, U.S.A. 142 B1 59 14N 135 26W
Haines, Oreg., U.S.A. 158 D5 44 55N 117 56W
Haines City, U.S.A. 149 L5 28 7N 81 38W
Haines Junction, Canada 142 A1 60 45N 137 30W
Hainfeld, Austria 34 C8 48 3N 15 48 E
Haining, China 77 B13 30 28N 120 40 E
Haiphong, Vietnam 76 G6 20 47N 106 41 E
Haitan Dao, China 77 E12 25 30N 119 45 E
Haiti ■, W. Indies 165 C5 19 0N 72 30W
Haiya, Sudan 106 D4 18 20N 36 21 E
Haiyan, China 77 B13 30 28N 120 58 E
Haiyang, China 75 F11 36 47N 121 9 E
Haiyuan, Guangxi Zhuangzu, China 76 F6 22 8N 107 35 E
Haiyuan, Ningxia Huizu, China 74 F3 36 35N 105 52 E
Haizhou, China 75 G10 34 37N 119 7 E
Haizhou Wan, China 75 G10 34 50N 119 20 E
Hajar Bangar, Sudan 109 F4 10 40N 22 45 E
Hajdú-Bihar □, Hungary 52 C6 47 30N 21 30 E
Hajdúböszörmény, Hungary 52 C6 47 40N 21 30 E
Hajdúdorog, Hungary 52 C6 47 48N 21 30 E
Hajdúhadház, Hungary 52 C6 47 40N 21 40 E
Hajdúnánás, Hungary 52 C6 47 50N 21 26 E
Hajdúsámson, Hungary 52 C6 47 37N 21 42 E
Hajdúszoboszló, Hungary 52 C6 47 27N 21 22 E
Hajiganj, Bangla. 90 D3 23 15N 90 50 E
Hajipur, India 93 G11 25 45N 85 13 E
Ḥājjah, Yemen 98 D3 15 42N 43 36 E
Ḥājjī Muḥsin, Iraq 96 C5 32 35N 45 29 E
Ḥājjīābād, Iran 97 D7 28 19N 55 55 E
Ḥājjīābād-e Zarrīn, Iran 97 C7 33 9N 54 51 E
Hajnówka, Poland 55 F10 52 47N 23 35 E
Ḥajrah, Si. Arabia 98 B3 20 14N 41 3 E
Haka, Burma 90 D4 22 39N 93 37 E
Hakansson, Mts., Dem. Rep. of the Congo 119 D2 8 40 S 25 45 E
Hakataramea, N.Z. 131 E5 44 43 S 170 30 E
Hakkâri, Turkey 101 D10 37 34N 43 44 E
Hakkâri Dağları, Turkey 101 C10 38 2N 42 58 E
Hakken-Zan, Japan 73 C7 34 10N 135 54 E
Hakodate, Japan 70 D10 41 45N 140 44 E
Hakos, Namibia 116 C2 23 13 S 16 21 E
Hakota, Japan 73 A12 36 5N 140 30 E
Håksberg, Sweden 16 D9 60 11N 15 12 E
Haku-San, Japan 73 A8 36 9N 136 46 E
Hakui, Japan 71 F8 36 53N 136 47 E
Hakun, Burma 90 B5 26 46N 95 42 E
Hala, Pakistan 91 D3 25 43N 68 20 E
Ḥalab, Syria 100 D7 36 10N 37 15 E
Ḥalaban, Si. Arabia 98 B4 23 29N 44 23 E
Ḥalabjah, Iraq 101 E11 35 10N 45 58 E
Halach, Turkmenistan 65 D2 38 4N 64 52 E
Halaib, Sudan 106 C4 22 12N 36 30 E
Halalii L., U.S.A. 145 B1 21 52N 160 11W
Halasa, Sudan 107 E3 14 26N 30 39 E
Hālat 'Ammār, Si. Arabia 96 D3 29 10N 36 4 E
Halawa, C., U.S.A. 145 B5 21 10N 156 43W
Halawa Heights, U.S.A. 145 K14 21 23N 157 55W
Halbā, Lebanon 103 A5 34 34N 36 6 E
Halberstadt, Germany 30 D7 51 54N 11 3 E
Halcombe, N.Z. 130 G4 40 8 S 175 30 E
Halcon, Phil. 79 B6 13 0N 121 30 E
Halcon, Mt., Phil. 80 E3 13 16N 121 0 E
Halden, Norway 15 G14 59 9N 11 23 E
Haldensleben, Germany 30 C7 52 17N 11 24 E
Haldwani, India 93 E8 29 31N 79 30 E
Hale, U.S.A. 156 E3 39 36N 93 20W
Hale →, Australia 126 C2 24 56 S 135 53 E
Haleakala Crater, U.S.A. 145 C5 20 43N 156 16W
Haleakala Nat. Park, U.S.A. 145 C5 20 40N 156 15W
Haleiwa, U.S.A. 145 J13 21 36N 158 6W
Halesowen, U.K. 21 E5 52 27N 2 3W
Haleyville, U.S.A. 149 H2 34 14N 87 37W
Half Assini, Ghana 112 D4 5 1N 2 50W
Halfmoon Bay, N.Z. 131 G3 46 50 S 168 5 E
Halfway →, Canada 142 B4 56 12N 121 32W
Halia, India 93 G10 24 50N 82 19 E
Haliburton, Canada 140 C4 45 3N 78 30W
Halifax, Australia 126 B4 18 32 S 146 22 E
Halifax, Canada 141 D7 44 38N 63 35W
Halifax, U.K. 20 D6 53 43N 1 52W
Halifax, U.S.A. 150 F8 40 25N 76 55W
Halifax B., Australia 126 B4 18 50 S 147 0 E
Halifax I., Namibia 116 D2 26 38 S 15 4 E
Halīl →, Iran 97 E8 27 40N 58 30 E
Halin, Somali Rep. 120 C3 9 6N 48 37 E
Halkett, C., U.S.A. 144 A9 70 48N 152 11W
Halkirk, U.K. 22 C5 58 30N 3 29W
Hall Beach = Sanirajak, Canada 139 B11 68 46N 81 12W
Hall I., U.S.A. 144 F4 60 40N 173 6W
Hall in Tirol, Austria 34 D4 47 17N 11 30 E
Hall Pen., Canada 139 B13 63 30N 66 0W
Hall Pt., Australia 124 C3 15 40 S 124 23 E
Hallabro, Sweden 17 H9 56 22N 15 5 E
Halland, Sweden 15 H15 57 8N 12 47 E
Hallandale, U.S.A. 153 K9 25 59N 80 8W
Hallands län □, Sweden 17 H6 57 0N 12 40 E
Hallands Väderö, Sweden 17 H6 56 27N 12 34 E
Hallandsås, Sweden 17 H7 56 22N 13 0 E
Hallaskar, Norway 18 D4 60 15N 7 9 E
Hällbybrunn, Sweden 16 E10 59 24N 16 25 E
Halle, Belgium 24 D4 50 44N 4 13 E
Halle, Nordrhein-Westfalen, Germany 30 C4 52 3N 8 22 E
Halle, Sachsen-Anhalt, Germany 30 D7 51 30N 11 56 E
Hällefors, Sweden 16 E8 59 47N 14 31 E
Hälleforsnäs, Sweden 16 E10 59 10N 16 30 E
Hallein, Austria 34 D6 47 40N 13 5 E
Hällekis, Sweden 17 F7 58 38N 13 27 E
Hallen, Sweden 16 A8 63 11N 14 4 E
Hallett, Australia 128 B3 33 25 S 138 54 E
Hallettsville, U.S.A. 155 L6 29 27N 96 57W
Hallia →, India 94 F4 16 55N 79 20 E
Hallim, S. Korea 75 H14 33 24N 126 15 E
Hallingby, Norway 18 D7 60 7N 10 10 E
Hallingdal, Norway 18 D6 60 40N 9 8 E
Hallingdalselvi →, Norway 15 F13 60 23N 9 35 E
Hallingskarvet, Norway 18 D4 60 36N 7 47 E
Hallingskeid, Norway 18 D4 60 40N 7 17 E
Hallock, U.S.A. 154 A6 48 47N 96 57W
Hallormsstaður, Iceland 11 B12 65 6N 14 45W
Halls Creek, Australia 124 C4 18 16 S 127 38 E
Hallsberg, Sweden 16 E9 59 5N 15 7 E
Hallstahammar, Sweden 16 E10 59 38N 16 15 E
Hallstatt, Austria 34 D6 47 33N 13 38 E
Hallstavik, Sweden 16 D12 60 5N 18 37 E
Hallstead, U.S.A. 151 E9 41 58N 75 45W
Halmahera, Indonesia 82 A3 0 40N 128 0 E
Halmahera Sea, Indonesia 83 B3 0 0 129 0 E
Halmeu, Romania 52 C8 47 57N 23 2 E
Halmstad, Sweden 17 H6 56 41N 12 52 E
Halq el Oued, Tunisia 108 A2 36 53N 10 18 E
Hals, Denmark 17 H4 57 0N 10 18 E
Halsa, Norway 18 A5 63 3N 8 14 E
Halsafjorden, Norway 18 A5 63 5N 8 10 E
Hälsingborg = Helsingborg, Sweden 17 H6 56 3N 12 42 E
Hälsingland, Sweden 16 C10 61 40N 16 5 E
Halstead, U.K. 21 F8 51 57N 0 40 E
Haltdalen, Norway 18 B8 62 56N 11 8 E
Haltern, Germany 30 D3 51 44N 7 11 E
Halti, Finland 14 B19 69 17N 21 18 E
Halton □, U.K. 20 D5 53 22N 2 45W
Haltwhistle, U.K. 20 C5 54 58N 2 26W
Ḥālūl, Qatar 97 E7 25 40N 52 40 E
Halvad, India 92 H4 23 1N 71 11 E
Ḥalvān, Iran 97 C8 33 57N 56 15 E
Ham, Chad 109 F3 10 1N 15 35 E
Ham, France 27 C10 49 45N 3 4 E
Ham Tan, Vietnam 87 G6 10 40N 107 45 E
Ham Yen, Vietnam 86 A5 22 4N 105 3 E
Hamab, Namibia 116 D2 28 7 S 19 16 E
Hamad, Sudan 107 D3 15 20N 33 32 E
Hamada, Japan 72 C4 34 56N 132 4 E
Hamadān, Iran 97 C6 34 52N 48 32 E
Hamadān □, Iran 97 C6 35 0N 49 0 E
Hamadia, Algeria 111 A5 35 28N 1 57 E
Hamāh, Syria 100 E7 35 5N 36 40 E
Hamakita, Japan 73 C9 34 45N 137 47 E
Hamamatsu, Japan 73 C9 34 45N 137 45 E
Hamar, Norway 15 F14 60 48N 11 7 E
Hamâta, Gebel, Egypt 96 E2 24 17N 35 0 E
Hambantota, Sri Lanka 95 L5 6 10N 81 10 E
Hamber Prov. Park, Canada 142 C5 52 20N 118 0W
Hamburg, Germany 30 B5 53 33N 9 59 E
Hamburg, Ark., U.S.A. 155 J9 33 14N 91 48W
Hamburg, N.Y., U.S.A. 150 D6 42 43N 78 50W
Hamburg, Pa., U.S.A. 151 F9 40 33N 75 59W
Hamburg □, Germany 30 B5 53 30N 10 0 E
Ḥamḍ, W. al →, Si. Arabia 96 E3 24 55N 36 20 E
Ḥamḍah, Si. Arabia 98 C3 19 2N 43 36 E
Ḥamdānah, Si. Arabia 98 C3 19 59N 40 34 E
Hamden, U.S.A. 151 E12 41 23N 72 54W
Hamdibey, Turkey 49 B9 39 50N 27 15 E
Häme, Finland 15 F20 61 38N 25 10 E
Hämeenlinna, Finland 15 F21 61 0N 24 28 E
Hamélé, Ghana 112 C4 10 56N 2 45W
Hamelin Pool, Australia 125 E1 26 22 S 114 20 E
Hameln, Germany 30 C5 52 6N 9 21 E
Hamerkaz □, Israel 103 C3 32 15N 34 55 E
Hamersley Ra., Australia 124 D2 22 0 S 117 45 E
Hamhung, N. Korea 75 E14 39 54N 127 30 E
Hami, China 68 B4 42 55N 93 25 E
Hamilton, Australia 128 D5 37 45 S 142 2 E
Hamilton, Bermuda 9 a 32 17N 64 47W
Hamilton, Canada 140 D4 43 15N 79 50W
Hamilton, N.Z. 130 D4 37 47 S 175 19 E
Hamilton, U.K. 22 F4 55 46N 4 2W
Hamilton, Ala., U.S.A. 149 H1 34 9N 87 59W
Hamilton, Alaska, U.S.A. 144 E7 62 54N 163 53W
Hamilton, Ga., U.S.A. 152 C5 32 45N 84 53W
Hamilton, Ill., U.S.A. 156 D5 40 24N 91 21W
Hamilton, Ind., U.S.A. 157 C12 41 33N 84 56W
Hamilton, Mo., U.S.A. 156 E2 39 45N 94 0W
Hamilton, Mont., U.S.A. 158 C6 46 15N 114 10W
Hamilton, N.Y., U.S.A. 151 D9 42 50N 75 33W
Hamilton, Ohio, U.S.A. 157 E12 39 24N 84 34W
Hamilton, Tex., U.S.A. 155 K5 31 42N 98 7W
Hamilton →, Australia 126 C2 23 30 S 139 47 E
Hamilton City, U.S.A. 160 F4 39 45N 122 1W
Hamilton I., Australia 126 J6 20 21 S 148 56 E
Hamilton Inlet, Canada 141 B8 54 0N 57 30W
Hamilton Mt., U.S.A. 151 C10 43 25N 74 22W
Hamina, Finland 15 F22 60 34N 27 12 E
Hamirpur, H.P., India 92 D7 31 41N 76 31 E
Hamirpur, Ut. P., India 93 G9 25 57N 80 9 E
Hamitabat, Turkey 51 E11 41 30N 27 17 E
Hamlet, U.S.A. 149 H6 34 53N 79 42W
Hamley Bridge, Australia 128 C3 34 17 S 138 35 E
Hamlin = Hameln, Germany 30 C5 52 6N 9 21 E
Hamlin, N.Y., U.S.A. 150 C7 43 17N 77 55W
Hamlin, Tex., U.S.A. 155 J4 32 53N 100 8W
Hamm, Germany 30 D3 51 40N 7 50 E
Hammam Bouhadjar, Algeria 111 A4 35 23N 0 58W
Hammamet, Tunisia 108 A2 36 24N 10 38 E
Hammamet, G. de, Tunisia 108 A2 36 10N 10 48 E
Ḥammār, Hawr al, Iraq 96 D5 30 50N 47 10 E
Hammarstrand, Sweden 16 A10 63 7N 16 20 E
Hammelburg, Germany 31 E5 50 6N 9 53 E
Hammeren, Denmark 17 J8 55 18N 14 47 E
Hammerfest, Norway 14 A20 70 39N 23 41 E
Hammerum, Denmark 17 H3 56 8N 9 3 E
Hamminkeln, Germany 30 D2 51 43N 6 35 E
Hammond, Ind., U.S.A. 157 C9 41 38N 87 30W
Hammond, La., U.S.A. 155 K9 30 30N 90 28W
Hammond, N.Y., U.S.A. 151 B9 44 27N 75 42W
Hammondsport, U.S.A. 150 D7 42 25N 77 13W
Hammonton, U.S.A. 148 F8 39 39N 74 48W
Hammeda, Sweden 17 H7 56 41N 13 51 E
Hamoyet, Jebel, Sudan 106 D4 17 33N 38 2 E
Hampden, N.Z. 131 F5 45 18 S 170 50 E
Hampshire □, U.K. 21 F6 51 7N 1 23W
Hampshire Downs, U.K. 21 F6 51 15N 1 10W
Hampton, N.B., Canada 141 C6 45 32N 65 51W
Hampton, Ont., Canada 150 C6 43 58N 78 45W
Hampton, Ark., U.S.A. 155 J8 33 32N 92 28W
Hampton, Ga., U.S.A. 152 B5 33 23N 84 17W
Hampton, Iowa, U.S.A. 156 B3 42 45N 93 13W
Hampton, N.H., U.S.A. 151 D14 42 57N 70 50W
Hampton, S.C., U.S.A. 152 C8 32 52N 81 7W
Hampton, Va., U.S.A. 148 G7 37 2N 76 21W
Hampton Bays, U.S.A. 151 F12 40 53N 72 30W
Hampton Springs, U.S.A. 152 E6 30 5N 83 40W
Hampton Tableland, Australia 125 F4 32 0 S 127 0 E
Hamra, Sweden 16 C8 61 39N 14 59 E
Hamra →, Chad 109 F4 12 52N 21 15 E
Hamrat esh Sheykh, Sudan 107 E2 14 38N 27 55 E
Hamrun, Malta 38 F8 35 53N 14 29 E
Hamtik, Phil. 81 F3 10 42N 121 59 E
Hamur, Turkey 101 C10 39 37N 43 3 E
Hamyang, S. Korea 75 G14 35 32N 127 42 E
Han Jiang →, China 77 F11 23 25N 116 40 E
Han Shui, China 76 A7 30 34N 114 17 E
Han Shui →, China 77 B10 30 35N 114 18 E
Hana, U.S.A. 145 C6 20 45N 155 59W
Hanahan, U.S.A. 152 C10 32 55N 80 0W
Hanak, Si. Arabia 96 E3 25 32N 37 0 E
Hanalei, U.S.A. 145 A2 22 12N 159 30W
Hanamaki, Japan 70 E10 39 23N 141 7 E
Hanamaulu, U.S.A. 145 B2 21 59N 159 22W
Hanang, Tanzania 118 C4 4 30 S 35 25 E
Hanapepe, U.S.A. 145 B2 21 55N 159 35W
Hanau, Germany 31 E4 50 7N 8 56 E
Hanauma B., U.S.A. 145 K14 21 15N 157 40W
Hanbogd = Ihbulag, Mongolia 74 C4 43 11N 107 10 E
Hançalar, Turkey 49 C11 38 8N 29 24 E
Hâncești, Moldova 53 D13 46 50N 28 36 E
Hancheng, China 74 G6 35 31N 110 25 E
Hanchuan, China 77 B9 30 40N 113 50 E
Hancock, Mich., U.S.A. 154 B10 47 8N 88 35W
Hancock, N.Y., U.S.A. 151 E9 41 57N 75 17W
Handa, Japan 73 C8 34 53N 136 55 E
Handa, Somali Rep. 120 B4 10 37N 51 2 E
Handan, China 74 F8 36 35N 114 28 E
Handeni, Tanzania 118 D4 5 25 S 38 2 E
Handlová, Slovak Rep. 35 C11 48 45N 18 35 E
Handub, Sudan 106 D4 19 15N 37 16 E
Handwara, India 93 B6 34 21N 74 20 E
Hanegev, Israel 103 E4 30 50N 35 0 E
Hanford, U.S.A. 160 J7 36 20N 119 39W
Hang Chat, Thailand 86 C2 18 20N 99 21 E
Hang Dong, Thailand 86 C2 18 41N 98 55 E
Hanga Roa, Chile 172 b 27 8 S 109 26W
Hangang →, S. Korea 75 F14 37 50N 126 30 E
Hangayn Nuruu, Mongolia 68 B4 47 30N 99 0 E
Hangchou = Hangzhou, China 77 B13 30 18N 120 11 E
Hanggin Houqi, China 74 D4 40 58N 107 4 E
Hanggin Qi, China 74 E5 39 52N 108 50 E
Hangu, China 75 E9 39 18N 117 53 E
Hangzhou, China 77 B13 30 18N 120 11 E
Hangzhou Wan, China 77 B13 30 15N 120 45 E
Hanhongor, Mongolia 74 C3 43 55N 104 28 E
Ḥanīdh, Si. Arabia 97 E6 26 35N 48 38 E
Ḥanīsh, Yemen 98 D3 13 45N 42 46 E
Haniska, Slovak Rep. 35 C14 48 37N 21 15 E
Hanjiang, China 77 E12 25 26N 119 6 E
Hankinson, U.S.A. 154 B6 46 4N 96 54W
Hanko, Finland 15 G20 59 50N 22 57 E
Hankou, China 77 B10 30 35N 114 30 E
Hanksville, U.S.A. 159 G8 38 22N 110 43W
Hanle, India 93 C8 32 42N 79 4 E
Hanmer Springs, N.Z. 131 C7 42 32 S 172 50 E
Hann →, Australia 124 C4 17 26 S 126 17 E
Hann, Mt., Australia 124 C4 15 45 S 126 0 E
Hanna, Canada 142 C6 51 40N 111 54W
Hanna, U.S.A. 158 F10 41 52N 106 34W
Hannah B., Canada 140 B4 51 40N 80 0W
Hannibal, Mo., U.S.A. 156 E5 39 42N 91 22W
Hannibal, N.Y., U.S.A. 151 C8 43 19N 76 35W
Hannik, Sudan 106 D3 18 12N 32 20 E
Hannover, Germany 30 C5 52 22N 9 46 E
Hanö, Sweden 17 H8 56 1N 14 50 E
Hanöbukten, Sweden 17 J8 55 35N 14 30 E
Hanoi, Vietnam 76 G5 21 5N 105 55 E
Hanover = Hannover, Germany 30 C5 52 22N 9 46 E
Hanover, Canada 140 D3 44 9N 81 2W
Hanover, S. Africa 116 E3 31 4 S 24 29 E

Hanover, *Ind., U.S.A.* **157 F11** 38 43N 85 28W
Hanover, *N.H., U.S.A.* **151 C12** 43 42N 72 17W
Hanover, *Ohio, U.S.A.* **150 F2** 40 4N 82 16W
Hanover, *Pa., U.S.A.* **148 F7** 39 48N 76 59W
Hanover, I., *Chile* **176 D2** 51 0 S 74 50W
Hanpan, C., *Papua N. G.* **132 C8** 5 0 S 154 35 E
Hans Lollik I., *U.S. Virgin Is.* **165 e** 18 24N 64 53W
Hans Meyer Ra., *Papua N. G.* **132 C7** 4 20 S 152 55 E
Hansdiha, *India* **93 G12** 24 36N 87 5 E
Hanshou, *China* **77 C8** 28 56N 111 50 E
Hansi, *India* **92 E6** 29 10N 75 57 E
Hanson, L., *Australia* **128 A2** 31 0 S 136 15 E
Hanstholm, *Denmark* **17 G2** 57 7N 8 36 E
Hantsavichy, *Belarus* **59 F4** 52 49N 26 30 E
Hanumangarh, *India* **92 E6** 29 35N 74 19 E
Hanyin, *China* **76 A7** 32 54N 108 28 E
Hanyū, *Japan* **73 A11** 36 10N 139 32 E
Hanyuan, *China* **76 C4** 29 21N 102 40 E
Hanzhong, *China* **74 H4** 33 10N 107 1 E
Hanzhuang, *China* **75 G9** 34 33N 117 23 E
Haora, *India* **93 H13** 22 37N 88 20 E
Haouach, O. →, *Chad* **109 E4** 16 45N 19 35 E
Haoxue, *China* **77 B9** 30 3N 112 24 E
Haparanda, *Sweden* **14 D21** 65 52N 24 8 E
Hapeville, *U.S.A.* **152 B5** 33 40N 84 25W
Happy, *U.S.A.* **155 H4** 34 45N 101 52W
Happy Camp, *U.S.A.* **158 F2** 41 48N 123 23W
Happy Valley-Goose Bay, *Canada* **141 B7** 53 15N 60 20W
Hapsu, *N. Korea* **75 D15** 41 13N 128 51 E
Hapur, *India* **92 E7** 28 45N 77 45 E
Ḩaql, *Si. Arabia* **103 F3** 29 10N 34 58 E
Haquira, *Peru* **172 C3** 14 14 S 72 12W
Har, *Indonesia* **83 C4** 5 16 S 133 14 E
Har-Ayrag, *Mongolia* **74 B5** 45 47N 109 16 E
Har Hu, *China* **68 C4** 38 20N 97 38 E
Har Us Nuur, *Mongolia* **68 B4** 48 0N 92 0 E
Har Yehuda, *Israel* **103 D3** 31 35N 34 57 E
Ḩaraḑ, *Si. Arabia* **99 A5** 24 22N 49 0 E
Ḩaraḑ, *Yemen* **98 C3** 16 26N 43 5 E
Haradok, *Belarus* **58 E6** 55 30N 30 3 E
Häradsbäck, *Sweden* **17 H8** 56 32N 14 26 E
Haranomachi, *Japan* **70 F10** 37 38N 140 58 E
Harardera, *Somali Rep.* **120 D3** 4 33N 47 38 E
Harare, *Zimbabwe* **119 F3** 17 43 S 31 2 E
Ḩarāsīs, Jiddat al, *Oman* **99 C7** 19 30N 56 0 E
Harat, *Eritrea* **107 D4** 16 5N 39 26 E
Haraz, *Chad* **109 F3** 14 20N 19 12 E
Harazé, *Chad* **109 G4** 9 57N 20 48 E
Harbhanga, *India* **94 D7** 20 38N 84 36 E
Harbin, *China* **75 B14** 45 48N 126 40 E
Harbiye, *Turkey* **100 D7** 36 10N 36 8 E
Harbo, *Sweden* **16 D11** 60 7N 17 12 E
Harboøer, *Denmark* **17 H2** 56 38N 8 10 E
Harbor Beach, *U.S.A.* **150 C2** 43 51N 82 39W
Harbour Breton, *Canada* **141 C8** 47 29N 55 50W
Harbour Deep, *Canada* **141 B8** 50 25N 56 32W
Harburg, *Germany* **30 B5** 53 27N 9 58 E
Hårby, *Denmark* **17 J4** 55 13N 10 7 E
Harda, *India* **92 H7** 22 27N 77 5 E
Hardangerfjorden, *Norway* **15 F12** 60 5N 6 0 E
Hardangerjøkulen, *Norway* **18 D4** 60 30N 7 27 E
Hardangervidda, *Norway* **15 F12** 60 7N 7 20 E
Hardap Dam, *Namibia* **116 C2** 24 32 S 17 50 E
Hardap Recreational Resort, *Namibia* **116 C2** 24 29 S 17 45 E
Hardeeville, *U.S.A.* **152 C8** 32 17N 81 5W
Harden, *Australia* **129 C8** 34 32 S 148 24 E
Hardenberg, *Neths.* **24 B6** 52 34N 6 37 E
Harderwijk, *Neths.* **24 B5** 52 21N 5 38 E
Hardey →, *Australia* **124 D2** 22 45 S 116 8 E
Hardin, *Ill., U.S.A.* **156 E6** 39 10N 90 37W
Hardin, *Mont., U.S.A.* **158 D10** 45 44N 107 37W
Harding, *S. Africa* **117 E4** 30 35 S 29 55 E
Harding, L., *U.S.A.* **152 C4** 32 40N 85 5W
Harding Ra., *Australia* **124 C3** 16 17 S 124 55 E
Hardinsburg, *U.S.A.* **157 G10** 37 47N 86 28W
Hardisty, *Canada* **142 C6** 52 40N 111 18W
Hardoi, *India* **93 F9** 27 26N 80 6 E
Hardwar = Haridwar, *India* **92 E8** 29 58N 78 9 E
Hardwick, *Ga., U.S.A.* **152 B6** 33 4N 83 14W
Hardwick, *Vt., U.S.A.* **151 B12** 44 30N 72 22W
Hardwicke B., *Australia* **128 C2** 34 55 S 137 20 E
Hardy, Pen., *Chile* **176 E3** 55 30 S 68 20W
Hardy, Pte., *St. Lucia* **165 f** 14 6N 60 56W
Hare B., *Canada* **141 B8** 51 15N 55 45W
Hareid, *Norway* **15 E12** 62 22N 6 1 E
Haren, *Germany* **30 C3** 52 47N 7 13 E
Harer, *Ethiopia* **107 F5** 9 20N 42 8 E
Harerge □, *Ethiopia* **107 F5** 7 12N 42 0 E
Harestua, *Norway* **18 D7** 60 11N 10 44 E
Hareto, *Ethiopia* **107 F4** 9 23N 37 6 E
Harfleur, *France* **26 C7** 49 30N 0 10 E
Hargeisa, *Somali Rep.* **120 C2** 9 30N 44 2 E
Hargeisa Game Park, *Somali Rep.* **120 B2** 10 2N 44 2 E
Harghita □, *Romania* **53 D10** 46 30N 25 30 E
Harghita, Munţii, *Romania* **53 D10** 46 25N 25 35 E
Hargshamn, *Sweden* **16 D12** 60 12N 18 30 E
Hari →, *Indonesia* **84 C2** 1 16 S 104 5 E
Haria, *Canary Is.* **9 e2** 29 8N 13 32W
Ḩarīb, *Yemen* **98 D4** 14 56N 45 30 E
Haricha, Hamada el, *Mali* **110 D4** 22 40N 3 15W
Haridwar, *India* **92 E8** 29 58N 78 9 E
Harihar, *India* **95 G2** 14 32N 75 44 E
Harihari, *N.Z.* **131 D5** 43 9 S 170 33 E
Harim, Jabal al, *Oman* **97 E8** 25 58N 56 14 E
Harima-Nada, *Japan* **72 C6** 34 30N 134 35 E
Haringhata →, *Bangla.* **90 E2** 22 0N 89 58 E
Haripad, *India* **95 K3** 9 14N 76 28 E
Harīrūd →, *Asia* **91 A1** 37 24N 60 38 E
Härjedalen, *Sweden* **16 B7** 62 22N 13 5 E
Harlan, *Iowa, U.S.A.* **154 E7** 41 39N 95 19W
Harlan, *Ky., U.S.A.* **149 G4** 36 51N 83 19W
Hârlău, *Romania* **53 C11** 47 23N 26 55 E
Harlech, *U.K.* **20 E3** 52 52N 4 6W
Harlem, *Ga., U.S.A.* **152 B7** 33 25N 82 19W
Harlem, *Mont., U.S.A.* **158 B9** 48 32N 108 47W
Hårlev, *Denmark* **17 J6** 55 21N 12 14 E
Harleyville, *U.S.A.* **152 B9** 33 13N 80 27W
Harlingen, *Neths.* **24 A5** 53 11N 5 25 E
Harlingen, *U.S.A.* **155 M6** 26 12N 97 42W
Harlow, *U.K.* **21 F8** 51 46N 0 8 E
Harlowton, *U.S.A.* **158 C9** 46 26N 109 50W
Harmancık, *Turkey* **49 B11** 39 41N 29 9 E
Harmånger, *Sweden* **16 C11** 61 55N 17 20 E
Harmil, *Eritrea* **107 D5** 16 30N 40 10 E
Harnai, *India* **94 F1** 17 48N 73 6 E
Harnai, *Pakistan* **92 D2** 30 6N 67 56 E
Harney, L., *U.S.A.* **153 G8** 28 45N 81 3W
Harney Basin, *U.S.A.* **158 E4** 43 30N 119 0W
Harney L., *U.S.A.* **158 E4** 43 14N 119 8W
Harney Peak, *U.S.A.* **154 D3** 43 52N 103 32W
Härnön, *Sweden* **16 B12** 62 36N 18 0 E
Härnösand, *Sweden* **16 B11** 62 38N 17 55 E
Haro, *Spain* **40 C2** 42 35N 2 55W
Harold, *U.S.A.* **153 E3** 30 40N 86 53W
Harold Pond, *Bahamas* **9 b** 25 2N 77 22W
Haroldswick, *U.K.* **22 A8** 60 48N 0 50W
Harp L., *Canada* **141 A7** 55 5N 61 50W
Harpanahalli, *India* **95 G3** 14 47N 76 2 E
Harper, *Liberia* **112 E3** 4 25N 7 43W
Harper, Mt., *U.S.A.* **144 D12** 64 14N 143 51W
Harplinge, *Sweden* **17 H6** 56 45N 12 45 E
Harr, *Mauritania* **112 B2** 15 20N 12 28W
Harrai, *India* **93 H8** 22 37N 79 13 E
Harrand, *Pakistan* **92 E4** 29 28N 70 3 E
Ḩarrat Khaybar, *Si. Arabia* **106 B5** 25 30N 39 45 E
Ḩarrat Nawāşīf, *Si. Arabia* **106 C5** 21 20N 42 10 E
Harricana →, *Canada* **140 B4** 50 56N 79 32W
Harriman, *U.S.A.* **149 H3** 35 56N 84 33W
Harrington, *Australia* **129 A10** 31 52 S 152 42 E
Harrington Harbour, *Canada* **141 B8** 50 31N 59 30W
Harrington Sd., *Bermuda* **9 a** 32 20N 64 44W
Harris, *U.K.* **22 D2** 57 50N 6 55W
Harris, L., *U.S.A.* **153 G8** 28 47N 81 49W
Harris, Sd. of, *U.K.* **22 D1** 57 44N 7 6W
Harris L., *Australia* **127 E2** 31 10 S 135 10 E
Harris Mts., *N.Z.* **131 E3** 44 49 S 168 49 E
Harris Pt., *Canada* **150 C2** 43 6N 82 9W
Harrisburg, *Ill., U.S.A.* **155 G10** 37 44N 88 32W
Harrisburg, *Nebr., U.S.A.* **154 E3** 41 33N 103 44W
Harrisburg, *Pa., U.S.A.* **150 F8** 40 16N 76 53W
Harrismith, *S. Africa* **117 D4** 28 15 S 29 8 E
Harrison, *Ark., U.S.A.* **155 G8** 36 14N 93 7W
Harrison, *Maine, U.S.A.* **151 B14** 44 7N 70 39W
Harrison, *Nebr., U.S.A.* **154 D3** 42 41N 103 53W
Harrison, C., *Canada* **141 B8** 54 55N 57 55W
Harrison Bay, *U.S.A.* **144 A10** 70 40N 151 0W
Harrison L., *Canada* **142 D4** 49 33N 121 50W
Harrisonburg, *U.S.A.* **148 F6** 38 27N 78 52W
Harrisonville, *U.S.A.* **156 F2** 38 39N 94 21W
Harriston, *Canada* **150 C4** 43 57N 80 53W
Harrisville, *Mich., U.S.A.* **150 B1** 44 39N 83 17W
Harrisville, *N.Y., U.S.A.* **151 B9** 44 9N 75 19W
Harrisville, *Pa., U.S.A.* **150 E5** 41 8N 80 0W
Harrodsburg, *Ind., U.S.A.* **157 E10** 39 1N 86 33W
Harrodsburg, *Ky., U.S.A.* **157 G12** 37 46N 84 51W
Harrogate, *U.K.* **20 C6** 54 0N 1 33W
Harrow, *Australia* **128 D4** 37 9 S 141 35 E
Harrow, *Canada* **157 B14** 42 2N 82 55W
Harrow □, *U.K.* **21 F7** 51 35N 0 21W
Harrowsmith, *Canada* **151 B8** 44 24N 76 40W
Harry S. Truman Reservoir, *U.S.A.* **156 F3** 38 16N 93 24W
Harsefeld, *Germany* **30 B5** 53 27N 9 30 E
Harsewinkel, *Germany* **30 D4** 51 56N 8 14 E
Harsīn, *Iran* **101 E12** 34 18N 47 33 E
Hârşova, *Romania* **53 F12** 44 40N 27 59 E
Harstad, *Norway* **14 B17** 68 48N 16 30 E
Harsud, *India* **92 H7** 22 6N 76 44 E
Hart, *U.S.A.* **148 D2** 43 42N 86 22W
Hart, L., *Australia* **128 A2** 31 10 S 136 25 E
Hartbees →, *S. Africa* **116 D3** 28 45 S 20 32 E
Hartberg, *Austria* **34 D8** 47 17N 15 58 E
Hårteigen, *Norway* **18 D4** 60 11N 7 3 E
Hartford, *Ala., U.S.A.* **152 D4** 31 6N 85 42W
Hartford, *Conn., U.S.A.* **151 E12** 41 46N 72 41W
Hartford, *Ky., U.S.A.* **148 G2** 37 27N 86 55W
Hartford, *Mich., U.S.A.* **157 B10** 42 13N 86 10W
Hartford, *S. Dak., U.S.A.* **154 D6** 43 38N 96 57W
Hartford, *Wis., U.S.A.* **154 D10** 43 19N 88 22W
Hartford City, *U.S.A.* **157 D11** 40 27N 85 22W
Hartland, *Canada* **141 C6** 46 20N 67 32W
Hartland, *U.S.A.* **157 A8** 43 6N 88 21W
Hartland Pt., *U.K.* **21 F3** 51 1N 4 32W
Hartlepool, *U.K.* **20 C6** 54 42N 1 13W
Hartlepool □, *U.K.* **20 C6** 54 42N 1 17W
Hartley Bay, *Canada* **142 C3** 53 25N 129 15W
Hartmannberge, *Namibia* **116 B1** 17 0 S 13 0 E
Hartney, *Canada* **143 D8** 49 30N 100 35W
Hârtop, *Moldova* **53 D13** 46 39N 28 40 E
Harts →, *S. Africa* **116 D3** 28 24 S 24 17 E
Hartselle, *U.S.A.* **149 H2** 34 27N 86 56W
Hartshorne, *U.S.A.* **155 H7** 34 51N 95 34W
Hartstown, *U.S.A.* **150 E4** 41 33N 80 23W
Hartsville, *U.S.A.* **149 H5** 34 23N 80 4W
Hartswater, *S. Africa* **116 D3** 27 34 S 24 43 E
Hartwell, *U.S.A.* **149 H4** 34 21N 82 56W
Haruku, *Indonesia* **82 B3** 3 34 S 128 29 E
Harunabad, *Pakistan* **92 E5** 29 35N 73 8 E
Harur, *India* **95 H4** 12 3N 78 29 E
Hārūt →, *Afghan.* **91 C1** 31 29N 61 24 E
Harvand, *Iran* **97 D7** 28 25N 55 43 E
Harvard, *U.S.A.* **157 B8** 42 25N 88 37W
Harvey, *Australia* **125 F2** 33 5 S 115 54 E
Harvey, *Ill., U.S.A.* **157 C9** 41 36N 87 50W
Harvey, *N. Dak., U.S.A.* **154 B5** 47 47N 99 56W
Harwich, *U.K.* **21 F9** 51 56N 1 17 E
Haryana □, *India* **92 E7** 29 0N 76 10 E
Haryn →, *Belarus* **59 F4** 52 7N 27 17 E
Harz, *Germany* **30 D6** 51 38N 10 44 E
Harzgerode, *Germany* **30 D7** 51 38N 11 8 E
Hasa □, *Si. Arabia* **97 E6** 25 50N 49 0 E
Hasaheisa, *Sudan* **107 E3** 14 44N 33 20 E
Hasalbag, *China* **65 E8** 37 52N 76 42 E
Ḩasanābād, *Iran* **97 C7** 32 8N 52 44 E
Hasanparti, *India* **94 E4** 18 4N 79 32 E
Hasdo →, *India* **93 J10** 21 44N 82 44 E
Häselgehr, *Austria* **33 B10** 47 19N 10 30 E
Haselünne, *Germany* **30 C3** 52 40N 7 29 E
Hashima, *Japan* **73 B8** 35 20N 136 40 E
Hashimoto, *Japan* **73 C7** 34 19N 135 37 E
Hashtjerd, *Iran* **97 C6** 35 52N 50 40 E
Hasi Nueifed, *W. Sahara* **110 D2** 24 54N 14 49W
Hasi Tafraut, *W. Sahara* **110 C2** 27 24N 13 15W
Ḩāsik, *Oman* **99 C6** 17 22N 55 17 E
Haskell, *U.S.A.* **155 J5** 33 10N 99 44W
Hasköy, *Turkey* **51 E10** 41 38N 26 52 E
Haslach, *Germany* **31 G4** 48 16N 8 5 E
Hasle, *Denmark* **17 J8** 55 11N 14 44 E
Haslemere, *U.K.* **21 F7** 51 5N 0 43W
Haslev, *Denmark* **17 J5** 55 18N 11 57 E
Hasparren, *France* **28 E2** 43 24N 1 18W
Hassa, *Turkey* **100 D7** 36 48N 36 29 E
Hassan, *India* **95 H3** 13 0N 76 5 E
Hassela, *Sweden* **16 B10** 62 7N 16 42 E
Hasselt, *Belgium* **24 D5** 50 56N 5 21 E
Hassene, Adrar, *Algeria* **111 D5** 21 0N 4 0 E
Hassfurt, *Germany* **31 E6** 50 2N 10 30 E
Hassi bou Khelala, *Algeria* **111 B4** 30 17N 0 18W
Hassi Bourarchet, *Algeria* **111 C6** 27 26N 9 19 E
Hassi Djafou, *Algeria* **111 B5** 30 55N 3 35 E
Hassi el Abiod, *Algeria* **111 B5** 31 47N 3 37 E
Hassi el Biod, *Algeria* **111 C6** 28 30N 6 0 E
Hassi el Hadjar, *Algeria* **111 B5** 31 28N 4 45 E
Hassi Imoulaye, *Algeria* **111 C6** 29 54N 9 10 E
Hassi Inifeg, *Algeria* **111 C4** 28 15N 1 30W
Hassi Inifel, *Algeria* **111 C5** 29 50N 3 41 E
Hassi Mana, *Algeria* **111 C4** 28 48N 2 37W
Hassi Messaoud, *Algeria* **111 B6** 31 51N 6 1 E
Hassi Sougoued, *Algeria* **111 C6** 26 50N 9 28 E
Hassi Tartrat, *Algeria* **111 B6** 30 5N 6 28 E
Hassi Zerzour, *Morocco* **110 B4** 30 51N 3 56W
Hassi Zguilma, *Algeria* **111 B4** 30 12N 2 19W
Hässleholm, *Sweden* **17 H7** 56 10N 13 46 E
Hassloch, *Germany* **31 F4** 49 22N 8 16 E
Hästholmen, *Sweden* **17 F8** 58 17N 14 38 E
Hastings, *Australia* **129 E6** 38 18 S 145 12 E
Hastings, *N.Z.* **130 F5** 39 39 S 176 52 E
Hastings, *U.K.* **21 G8** 50 51N 0 35 E
Hastings, *Fla., U.S.A.* **152 F8** 29 43N 81 31W
Hastings, *Mich., U.S.A.* **157 B11** 42 39N 85 17W
Hastings, *Minn., U.S.A.* **154 C8** 44 44N 92 51W
Hastings, *Nebr., U.S.A.* **154 E5** 40 35N 98 23W
Hastings Ra., *Australia* **129 A10** 31 15 S 152 14 E
Hästveda, *Sweden* **17 H7** 56 17N 13 55 E
Ḩasy 'Aţshān, *Libya* **108 C2** 27 20N 10 25 E
Hasy Tissan, *Libya* **111 C7** 28 14N 12 26 E
Hat Yai, *Thailand* **87 J3** 7 1N 100 27 E
Hatanbulag = Ergel, *Mongolia* **74 C5** 43 8N 109 5 E
Hatay = Antalya, *Turkey* **100 D4** 36 52N 30 45 E
Hatch, *U.S.A.* **159 K10** 32 40N 107 9W
Hatchet L., *Canada* **143 B8** 58 36N 103 40W
Haţeg, *Romania* **52 E7** 45 36N 22 55 E
Hateruma-Shima, *Japan* **71 M1** 24 3N 123 47 E
Hatfield P.O., *Australia* **128 B5** 33 54 S 143 49 E
Hatgal, *Mongolia* **68 A5** 50 26N 100 9 E
Hathras, *India* **92 F8** 27 36N 78 6 E
Hatia, *Bangla.* **90 D3** 22 30N 91 5 E
Hatia Is., *Bangla.* **90 D3** 22 30N 91 0 E
Ḩāţibah, Ra's, *Si. Arabia* **106 C4** 21 55N 38 57 E
Hatid, *India* **94 F2** 17 17N 75 3 E
Hato Corozal, *Colombia* **168 B3** 6 11N 71 45W
Hato Mayor, *Dom. Rep.* **165 C6** 18 46N 69 15W
Hatsukaichi, *Japan* **72 C4** 34 22N 132 22 E
Hatta, *India* **93 G8** 24 7N 79 36 E
Hattah, *Australia* **128 C5** 34 48 S 142 17 E
Hattah Kulkyne Nat. Park, *Australia* **128 C5** 35 40 S 142 22 E
Hatteras, C., *U.S.A.* **149 H8** 35 14N 75 32W
Hattiesburg, *U.S.A.* **155 K10** 31 20N 89 17W
Hatvan, *Hungary* **52 C4** 47 40N 19 45 E
Hau Bon = Cheo Reo, *Vietnam* **78 B3** 13 25N 108 28 E
Hau Duc, *Vietnam* **86 E7** 15 20N 108 13 E
Haubstadt, *U.S.A.* **157 F9** 38 12N 87 34W
Haud, *Ethiopia* **120 C2** 8 0N 45 0 E
Hauganes, *Iceland* **11 B8** 65 55N 18 18W
Haugastøl, *Norway* **18 D4** 60 30N 7 50 E
Hauge, *Norway* **18 F3** 58 20N 6 15 E
Haugesund, *Norway* **15 G11** 59 23N 5 13 E
Hauhui, *Solomon Is.* **133 M11** 9 10 S 160 59 E
Hauhungaroa Ra., *N.Z.* **130 E4** 38 42 S 175 40 E
Haukeligrend, *Norway* **18 E4** 59 44N 7 33 E
Haukipudas, *Finland* **14 D21** 65 12N 25 20 E
Haultain →, *Canada* **143 B7** 55 51N 106 46W
Haungpa, *Burma* **90 C6** 25 29N 96 7 E
Hauraha, *Solomon Is.* **133 N11** 10 46 S 161 59 E
Hauraki G., *N.Z.* **130 C4** 36 35 S 175 5 E
Hauroko L., *N.Z.* **131 F2** 45 59 S 167 21 E
Hausruck, *Austria* **34 C6** 48 6N 13 30 E
Hausstock, *Switz.* **33 C8** 46 53N 9 3 E
Haut Atlas, *Morocco* **110 B4** 32 30N 5 0W
Haut Niger, Parc Nat. du, *Guinea* **112 C2** 10 20N 10 20W
Haut-Rhin □, *France* **27 E14** 48 0N 7 15 E
Haut-Zaïre = Orientale □, *Dem. Rep. of the Congo* **118 B2** 2 20N 26 0 E
Haute-Corse □, *France* **29 F13** 42 30N 9 30 E
Haute-Garonne □, *France* **28 E5** 43 30N 1 30 E
Haute-Loire □, *France* **28 C7** 45 5N 3 50 E
Haute-Marne □, *France* **27 D12** 48 10N 5 20 E
Haute-Normandie □, *France* **26 C7** 49 20N 1 0 E
Haute-Saône □, *France* **27 E13** 47 45N 6 10 E
Haute-Savoie □, *France* **29 C10** 46 0N 6 20 E
Haute-Vienne □, *France* **28 C5** 45 50N 1 10 E
Hautes-Alpes □, *France* **29 D10** 44 42N 6 20 E
Hautes Fagnes = Hohe Venn, *Belgium* **24 D6** 50 30N 6 5 E
Hautes-Pyrénées □, *France* **28 F4** 43 0N 0 10 E
Hauteville-Lompnès, *France* **29 C9** 45 58N 5 36 E
Hautmont, *France* **27 B10** 50 15N 3 55 E
Hauts-de-Seine □, *France* **27 D9** 48 52N 2 15 E
Hauts Plateaux, *Algeria* **111 B5** 35 0N 1 0 E
Hauula, *U.S.A.* **145 J14** 21 37N 157 55W
Hauzenberg, *Germany* **31 G9** 48 40N 13 37 E
Havana = La Habana, *Cuba* **164 B3** 23 8N 82 22W
Havana, *Fla., U.S.A.* **152 E5** 30 37N 84 25W
Havana, *Ill., U.S.A.* **156 D6** 40 18N 90 4W
Havant, *U.K.* **21 G7** 50 51N 0 58W
Havârna, *Romania* **53 B11** 48 4N 26 43 E
Havasu, L., *U.S.A.* **161 L12** 34 18N 114 28W
Havdhem, *Sweden* **17 G12** 57 10N 18 20 E
Havel →, *Germany* **30 C8** 52 50N 12 3 E
Havelian, *Pakistan* **92 B5** 34 2N 73 10 E
Havelock, *Canada* **140 D4** 44 26N 77 53W
Havelock, *N.Z.* **131 B8** 41 17 S 173 48 E
Havelock, *U.S.A.* **149 H7** 34 53N 76 54W
Havelock I., *India* **95 J11** 11 58N 93 0 E
Havelock North, *N.Z.* **130 F5** 39 40 S 176 53 E
Haverfordwest, *U.K.* **21 F3** 51 48N 4 58W
Haverhill, *Fla., U.S.A.* **153 J9** 26 42N 80 7W
Haverhill, *Mass., U.S.A.* **151 D13** 42 47N 71 5W
Haveri, *India* **95 G2** 14 53N 75 24 E
Haverstraw, *U.S.A.* **151 E11** 41 12N 73 58W
Håverud, *Sweden* **17 F6** 58 50N 12 28 E
Havirga, *Mongolia* **74 B7** 45 41N 113 5 E
Havířov, *Czech Rep.* **35 B11** 49 46N 18 20 E
Havlíčkův Brod, *Czech Rep.* **34 B8** 49 36N 15 33 E
Havneby, *Denmark* **17 J2** 55 5N 8 34 E
Havran, *Turkey* **49 B9** 39 33N 27 6 E
Havre, *U.S.A.* **158 B9** 48 33N 109 41W
Havre-Aubert, *Canada* **141 C7** 47 12N 61 56W
Havre-St.-Pierre, *Canada* **141 B7** 50 18N 63 33W
Havsa, *Turkey* **51 E10** 41 31N 26 48 E
Havza, *Turkey* **100 B6** 41 0N 35 35 E
Haw →, *U.S.A.* **149 H6** 35 36N 79 3W
Hawaii, *U.S.A.* **145 D6** 19 30N 155 30W
Hawaii □, *U.S.A.* **145 D5** 19 30N 156 30W
Hawaii I., *Pac. Oc.* **146 J17** 20 0N 155 0W
Hawaii Volcanoes Nat. Park, *U.S.A.* **145 D6** 19 23N 155 17W
Hawaiian Is., *Pac. Oc.* **135 E12** 20 30N 156 0W
Hawaiian Ridge, *Pac. Oc.* **135 E11** 24 0N 165 0W
Hawarden, *U.S.A.* **154 D6** 43 0N 96 29W
Hawea, L., *N.Z.* **131 E4** 44 28 S 169 19 E
Hawea Flat, *N.Z.* **131 E4** 44 40 S 169 19 E
Hawera, *N.Z.* **130 F3** 39 35 S 174 19 E
Hawesville, *U.S.A.* **157 G10** 37 54N 86 45W
Hawi, *U.S.A.* **145 C6** 20 14N 155 50W
Hawick, *U.K.* **22 F6** 55 26N 2 47W
Hawk Junction, *Canada* **140 C3** 48 5N 84 38W
Hawk Point, *U.S.A.* **156 F5** 38 58N 91 8W
Hawkdun Ra., *N.Z.* **131 E5** 44 53 S 170 5 E
Hawke B., *N.Z.* **130 F6** 39 25 S 177 20 E
Hawker, *Australia* **128 A3** 31 59 S 138 22 E
Hawke's Bay □, *N.Z.* **130 F5** 39 45 S 176 35 E
Hawkesbury, *Canada* **140 C5** 45 37N 74 37W
Hawkesbury I., *Canada* **142 C3** 53 37N 129 3W
Hawkesbury Pt., *Australia* **126 A1** 11 55 S 134 5 E
Hawkinsville, *U.S.A.* **152 C6** 32 17N 83 28W
Hawks Nest, *Australia* **129 B10** 32 41 S 152 11 E
Hawley, *Minn., U.S.A.* **154 B6** 46 53N 96 19W
Hawley, *Pa., U.S.A.* **151 E9** 41 28N 75 11W
Ḩawrān, W. →, *Iraq* **101 F10** 33 58N 42 34 E
Hawsh Mūssá, *Lebanon* **103 B4** 33 45N 35 55 E
Hawthorne, *Fla., U.S.A.* **153 F7** 29 36N 82 5W
Hawthorne, *Nev., U.S.A.* **158 G4** 38 32N 118 38W
Hay, *Australia* **129 C6** 34 30 S 144 51 E
Hay →, *Australia* **126 C2** 24 50 S 138 0 E
Hay →, *Canada* **142 A5** 60 50N 116 26W
Hay, C., *Australia* **124 B4** 14 5 S 129 29 E
Hay I., *Canada* **150 B4** 44 53N 80 58W
Hay L., *Canada* **142 B5** 58 50N 118 50W
Hay-on-Wye, *U.K.* **21 E4** 52 5N 3 8W
Hay River, *Canada* **142 A5** 60 51N 115 44W
Hay Springs, *U.S.A.* **154 D3** 42 41N 102 41W
Haya = Tehoru, *Indonesia* **83 B3** 3 23 S 129 30 E
Hayachine-San, *Japan* **70 E10** 39 34N 141 29 E
Hayange, *France* **27 C13** 49 20N 6 2 E
Hayato, *Japan* **72 F2** 31 40N 130 43 E
Haydarlı, *Turkey* **49 C12** 38 16N 30 23 E
Hayden, *U.S.A.* **158 F10** 40 30N 107 16W
Haydon, *Australia* **126 B3** 18 0 S 141 30 E
Hayes, *U.S.A.* **154 C4** 44 23N 101 1W
Hayes →, *Canada* **140 A1** 57 3N 92 12W
Hayes, Mt., *U.S.A.* **144 E11** 63 37N 146 43W
Hayes Creek, *Australia* **124 B5** 13 43 S 131 22 E
Hayle, *U.K.* **21 G2** 50 11N 5 26W
Hayling I., *U.K.* **21 G7** 50 48N 0 59W
Haymana, *Turkey* **100 C5** 39 26N 32 31 E
Haymen I., *Australia* **126 J6** 20 3 S 148 52 E
Haynan, *Yemen* **99 D5** 15 50N 48 18 E
Hayneville, *U.S.A.* **152 C6** 32 23N 83 37W
Hayrabolu, *Turkey* **51 E11** 41 12N 27 5 E
Hays, *Canada* **142 C6** 50 6N 111 48W
Hays, *U.S.A.* **154 F5** 38 53N 99 20W
Ḩays, *Yemen* **98 D3** 13 56N 43 29 E
Haysville, *U.S.A.* **157 F10** 38 28N 86 55W
Haysyn, *Ukraine* **59 H5** 48 57N 29 25 E
Hayvoron, *Ukraine* **59 H5** 48 22N 29 52 E
Hayward, *Calif., U.S.A.* **160 H4** 37 40N 122 5W
Hayward, *Wis., U.S.A.* **154 B9** 46 1N 91 29W
Haywards Heath, *U.K.* **21 G7** 51 0N 0 5W
Hazafon □, *Israel* **103 C4** 32 40N 35 20 E
Hazārān, Kūh-e, *Iran* **97 D8** 29 35N 57 20 E
Hazard, *U.S.A.* **148 G4** 37 15N 83 12W
Hazaribag, *India* **93 H11** 23 58N 85 26 E
Hazaribag Road, *India* **93 G11** 24 12N 85 57 E
Hazebrouck, *France* **27 B9** 50 42N 2 31 E
Hazelton, *Canada* **142 B3** 55 20N 127 42W
Hazelton, *U.S.A.* **154 B4** 46 29N 100 17W
Hazen, *U.S.A.* **154 B4** 47 18N 101 38W
Hazlehurst, *Ga., U.S.A.* **152 D7** 31 52N 82 36W
Hazlehurst, *Miss., U.S.A.* **155 K9** 31 52N 90 24W
Hazlet, *U.S.A.* **151 F10** 40 25N 74 12W
Hazleton, *Ind., U.S.A.* **157 F9** 38 29N 87 33W
Hazleton, *Pa., U.S.A.* **151 F9** 40 57N 75 59W
Hazlett, L., *Australia* **124 D4** 21 30 S 128 48 E
Hazro, *Turkey* **96 B4** 38 15N 40 47 E
He Xian, *Anhui, China* **77 B12** 31 45N 118 20 E
He Xian, *Guangxi Zhuangzu, China* **77 E8** 24 27N 111 30 E
Head of Bight, *Australia* **125 F5** 31 30 S 131 25 E
Headland, *U.S.A.* **152 D4** 31 21N 85 21W
Headlands, *Zimbabwe* **119 F3** 18 15 S 32 2 E
Healdsburg, *U.S.A.* **160 G4** 38 37N 122 52W
Healdton, *U.S.A.* **155 H6** 34 14N 97 29W
Healesville, *Australia* **129 D6** 37 35 S 145 30 E
Healy, *U.S.A.* **144 E10** 63 52N 148 58W
Heany Junction, *Zimbabwe* **117 C4** 20 6 S 28 54 E
Heard I., *Ind. Oc.* **121 K6** 53 0 S 74 0 E
Hearne, *U.S.A.* **155 K6** 30 53N 96 36W
Hearst, *Canada* **140 C3** 49 40N 83 41W
Heart →, *U.S.A.* **154 B4** 46 46N 100 50W
Heart's Content, *Canada* **141 C9** 47 54N 53 27W
Heath →, *Bolivia* **172 C4** 12 31 S 68 38W
Heath Mts., *N.Z.* **131 F2** 45 39 S 167 9 E
Heath Pt., *Canada* **141 C7** 49 8N 61 40W
Heathcote, *Australia* **129 D6** 36 56 S 144 45 E
Heavener, *U.S.A.* **155 H7** 34 53N 94 36W
Hebbronville, *U.S.A.* **155 M5** 27 18N 98 41W
Hebei □, *China* **74 E9** 39 0N 116 0 E
Hebel, *Australia* **127 D4** 28 58 S 147 47 E
Heber, *U.S.A.* **161 N11** 32 44N 115 32W
Heber City, *U.S.A.* **158 F8** 40 31N 111 25W
Heber Springs, *U.S.A.* **155 H9** 35 30N 92 2W
Hebert, *Canada* **143 C7** 50 30N 107 10W
Hebgen L., *U.S.A.* **158 D8** 44 52N 111 20W
Hebi, *China* **74 G8** 35 57N 114 7 E
Hebrides, *U.K.* **12 D4** 57 30N 7 0W
Hebrides, Sea of the, *U.K.* **22 D2** 57 5N 7 0W
Hebron = Al Khalīl, *West Bank* **103 D4** 31 32N 35 6 E
Hebron, *Canada* **139 C13** 58 5N 62 30W
Hebron, *N. Dak., U.S.A.* **154 B3** 46 54N 102 3W
Hebron, *Nebr., U.S.A.* **154 E6** 40 10N 97 35W
Heby, *Sweden* **16 E10** 59 56N 16 53 E
Hecate Str., *Canada* **142 C2** 53 10N 130 30W
Heceta I., *U.S.A.* **142 B2** 55 46N 133 40W
Hechi, *China* **76 E7** 24 40N 108 2 E
Hechingen, *Germany* **31 G4** 48 21N 8 57 E
Hechuan, *China* **76 B6** 30 2N 106 12 E
Hecla, *U.S.A.* **154 C5** 45 53N 98 9W
Hecla I., *Canada* **143 C9** 51 10N 96 43W
Hedal, *Norway* **18 D6** 60 37N 9 41 E
Heddal, *Norway* **18 E6** 59 36N 9 9 E
Hédé, *France* **26 D5** 48 18N 1 49W
Hede, *Sweden* **16 B7** 62 23N 13 30 E
Hedemora, *Sweden* **16 D9** 60 18N 15 58 E
Hedensted, *Denmark* **17 J3** 55 46N 9 42 E
Hedesunda, *Sweden* **16 D10** 60 24N 17 0 E
Hedgehope, *N.Z.* **131 G3** 46 12 S 168 34 E
Hedmark □, *Norway* **18 C8** 61 17N 11 40 E
Hedrick, *U.S.A.* **156 C4** 41 11N 92 19W
Heerde, *Neths.* **24 B6** 52 24N 6 2 E
Heerenveen, *Neths.* **24 B5** 52 57N 5 55 E
Heerhugowaard, *Neths.* **24 B4** 52 40N 4 51 E
Heerlen, *Neths.* **24 D5** 50 55N 5 58 E
Ḥefa, *Israel* **103 C4** 32 46N 35 0 E
Ḥefa □, *Israel* **103 C4** 32 40N 35 0 E
Hefei, *China* **77 B11** 31 52N 117 18 E
Hefeng, *China* **77 C8** 29 55N 109 52 E
Heflin, *U.S.A.* **152 B4** 33 39N 85 35W
Hegalig, *Sudan* **107 E3** 14 36N 31 54 E
Hegang, *China* **69 B8** 47 20N 130 19 E
Heggenes, *Norway* **18 C6** 61 9N 9 4 E
Hegra, *Norway* **18 A8** 63 27N 11 8 E
Hei Ling Chau, *China* **69 G11** 22 15N 114 2 E
Heiban, *Sudan* **107 E3** 11 13N 30 31 E
Heichengzhen, *China* **74 F4** 36 24N 106 3 E
Heidal, *Norway* **18 C6** 61 45N 9 19 E
Heide, *Germany* **30 A5** 54 11N 9 6 E
Heidelberg, *Germany* **31 F4** 49 24N 8 42 E
Heidelberg, *S. Africa* **116 E3** 34 6 S 20 59 E
Heidenau, *Germany* **30 E9** 50 57N 13 52 E
Heidenheim, *Germany* **31 G6** 48 41N 10 9 E
Heigun-Tō, *Japan* **72 D4** 33 47N 132 14 E
Heijing, *China* **76 E3** 25 22N 101 44 E
Heilbad Heiligenstadt, *Germany* **30 D6** 51 22N 10 8 E
Heilbron, *S. Africa* **117 D4** 27 16 S 27 59 E
Heilbronn, *Germany* **31 F5** 49 9N 9 13 E
Heiligenblut, *Austria* **34 D5** 47 2N 12 51 E
Heiligenhafen, *Germany* **30 A6** 54 22N 10 59 E
Heilongjiang □, *China* **69 B7** 48 0N 126 0 E
Heilprin Land, *Greenland* **10 A7** 82 5N 33 0W
Heilunkiang = Heilongjiang □, *China* **69 B7** 48 0N 126 0 E
Heim, *Norway* **18 A6** 63 26N 9 5 E
Heimaey, *Iceland* **11 D6** 63 26N 20 17W
Heimdal, *Norway* **18 A7** 63 21N 10 22 E
Heinola, *Finland* **15 F22** 61 13N 26 2 E
Heinsberg, *Germany* **30 D2** 51 3N 6 5 E
Heinsun, *Burma* **90 C5** 25 52N 95 35 E
Heinze Kyun, *Burma* **86 E1** 14 25N 97 45 E
Heirnkut, *Burma* **90 C5** 25 14N 94 44 E
Heishan, *China* **75 D12** 41 40N 122 5 E
Heishui, *Liaoning, China* **75 C10** 42 8N 119 30 E
Heishui, *Sichuan, China* **76 A4** 32 4N 103 2 E

Hejaz = Ḥijāz □, *Si. Arabia* 96 E3 24 0N 40 0 E
Hejian, *China* 74 E9 38 25N 116 5 E
Hejiang, *China* 76 C5 28 43N 105 46 E
Hejin, *China* 74 G6 35 35N 110 42 E
Hekimhan, *Turkey* 100 C7 38 50N 37 55 E
Hekinan, *Japan* 73 C9 34 52N 137 0 E
Hekla, *Iceland* 11 D7 63 56N 19 35W
Hekou, *Guangdong, China* 77 F9 23 13N 112 45 E
Hekou, *Yunnan, China* 76 F4 22 30N 103 59 E
Hel, *Poland* 54 D5 54 37N 18 47 E
Helagsfjället, *Sweden* 16 B6 62 54N 12 25 E
Helan Shan, *China* 74 E3 38 30N 105 55 E
Helechosa, *Spain* 43 F6 39 22N 4 53W
Helemano →, *U.S.A.* 145 J13 21 35N 158 7W
Helen Atoll, *Pac. Oc.* 83 A4 2 40N 132 0 E
Helena, *Ark., U.S.A.* 155 H9 34 32N 90 36W
Helena, *Ga., U.S.A.* 152 C7 32 5N 82 55W
Helena, *Mont., U.S.A.* 158 C7 46 36N 112 2W
Helendale, *U.S.A.* 161 L9 34 44N 117 19W
Helensburgh, *Australia* 129 C9 34 11 S 151 1 E
Helensburgh, *U.K.* 22 E4 56 1N 4 43W
Helensville, *N.Z.* 130 C3 36 41 S 174 29 E
Helenvale, *Australia* 126 B4 15 43 S 145 14 E
Helgasjön, *Sweden* 17 H8 56 55N 14 50 E
Helgeland, *Norway* 14 C15 66 7N 13 29 E
Helgoland, *Germany* 30 A3 54 10N 7 53 E
Heligoland = Helgoland, *Germany* 30 A3 54 10N 7 53 E
Heligoland B. = Deutsche Bucht, *Germany* 30 A4 54 15N 8 0 E
Heliopolis, *Egypt* 106 H7 30 6N 31 17 E
Hell, *Norway* 18 A7 63 26N 10 54 E
Hella, *Iceland* 11 D6 63 50N 20 24W
Helleland, *Norway* 18 F3 58 33N 6 7 E
Hellertown, *U.S.A.* 151 F9 40 35N 75 21W
Hellespont = Çanakkale Boğazı, *Turkey* 51 F10 40 17N 26 32 E
Hellesylt, *Norway* 18 B3 62 6N 6 51 E
Hellevoetsluis, *Neths.* 24 C4 51 50N 4 8 E
Hellhole Gorge Nat. Park, *Australia* 126 D3 25 31 S 144 12 E
Hellín, *Spain* 41 G3 38 31N 1 40W
Hellissandur, *Iceland* 11 C3 64 55N 23 54W
Hell's Gate Nat. Park, *Kenya* 118 C4 0 54 S 36 19 E
Hellvik, *Norway* 18 F2 58 29N 5 52 E
Helmand □, *Afghan.* 91 C2 31 20N 64 0 E
Helmand →, *Afghan.* 91 C1 31 12N 61 34 E
Helme →, *Germany* 30 D7 51 20N 11 21 E
Helmeringhausen, *Namibia* 116 D2 25 54 S 16 57 E
Helmond, *Neths.* 24 C5 51 29N 5 41 E
Helmsdale, *U.K.* 22 C5 58 7N 3 39W
Helmsdale →, *U.K.* 22 C5 58 7N 3 40W
Helmstedt, *Germany* 30 C7 52 12N 11 0 E
Helong, *China* 75 C15 42 40N 129 0 E
Helper, *U.S.A.* 158 G8 39 41N 110 51W
Helsingborg, *Sweden* 17 H6 56 3N 12 42 E
Helsinge, *Denmark* 17 H6 56 2N 12 12 E
Helsingfors = Helsinki, *Finland* 15 F21 60 15N 25 3 E
Helsingør, *Denmark* 17 H6 56 2N 12 35 E
Helsinki, *Finland* 15 F21 60 15N 25 3 E
Helska, Mierzeja, *Poland* 54 D5 54 45N 18 40 E
Helston, *U.K.* 21 G2 50 6N 5 17W
Helvellyn, *U.K.* 20 C4 54 32N 3 1W
Helwân, *Egypt* 106 J7 29 50N 31 20 E
Hemavati →, *India* 95 H3 12 30N 76 20 E
Hemel Hempstead, *U.K.* 21 F7 51 44N 0 28W
Hemet, *U.S.A.* 161 M10 33 45N 116 58W
Hemingford, *U.S.A.* 154 D3 42 19N 103 4W
Hemmingford, *Canada* 151 A11 45 3N 73 35W
Hempe, *Dem. Rep. of the Congo* 114 B4 1 54N 22 42 E
Hempstead, *U.S.A.* 155 K6 30 6N 96 5W
Hemse, *Sweden* 17 G12 57 15N 18 22 E
Hemsedal, *Norway* 18 D5 60 53N 8 30 E
Hemsön, *Sweden* 16 B12 62 42N 18 5 E
Hen, *Norway* 18 D7 60 13N 10 14 E
Hen and Chickens Is., *N.Z.* 130 B3 35 58 S 174 45 E
Henån, *Sweden* 17 F5 58 14N 11 40 E
Henan □, *China* 74 H8 34 0N 114 0 E
Henares →, *Spain* 42 E7 40 24N 3 30W
Henashi-Misaki, *Japan* 70 D9 40 37N 139 51 E
Hendaye, *France* 28 E2 43 23N 1 47W
Hendek, *Turkey* 100 B4 40 48N 30 44 E
Henderson, *Argentina* 174 D3 36 18 S 61 43W
Henderson, *Ga., U.S.A.* 152 C6 32 21N 83 47W
Henderson, *Ky., U.S.A.* 157 G9 37 50N 87 35W
Henderson, *N.C., U.S.A.* 149 G6 36 20N 78 25W
Henderson, *Nev., U.S.A.* 161 J12 36 2N 114 59W
Henderson, *Tenn., U.S.A.* 149 H1 35 26N 88 38W
Henderson, *Tex., U.S.A.* 155 J7 32 9N 94 48W
Hendersonville, *N.C., U.S.A.* 149 H4 35 19N 82 28W
Hendersonville, *Tenn., U.S.A.* 149 G2 36 18N 86 37W
Hendījān, *Iran* 97 D6 30 14N 49 43 E
Hendorābī, *Iran* 97 E7 26 40N 53 37 E
Heng Jiang, *China* 76 C5 28 40N 104 25 E
Heng Xian, *China* 76 F7 22 40N 109 17 E
Henganofi, *Papua N. G.* 132 D3 6 15 S 145 38 E
Hengcheng, *China* 74 E4 38 18N 106 28 E
Hêngchun, *Taiwan* 77 F13 22 0N 120 44 E
Hengdaohezi, *China* 75 B15 44 52N 129 0 E
Hengelo, *Neths.* 24 B6 52 16N 6 48 E
Hengfeng, *China* 77 C10 28 12N 115 48 E
Henggang, *China* 69 F11 22 39N 114 12 E
Hengmen, *China* 69 F10 22 33N 113 35 E
Hengqin Dao, *China* 69 G10 22 7N 113 34 E
Hengshan, *Hunan, China* 77 D9 27 16N 112 45 E
Hengshan, *Shaanxi, China* 74 F5 37 58N 109 5 E
Hengshui, *China* 74 F8 37 41N 115 40 E
Hengyang, *China* 77 D9 26 59N 112 22 E
Henichesk, *Ukraine* 59 J8 46 12N 34 50 E
Henima, *India* 90 C4 25 22N 93 36 E
Hénin-Beaumont, *France* 27 B9 50 25N 2 58 E
Henlopen, C., *U.S.A.* 148 F8 38 48N 75 6W
Hennan, *Sweden* 16 B9 62 2N 15 54 E
Hennebont, *France* 26 E3 47 49N 3 19W
Hennenman, *S. Africa* 116 D4 27 59 S 27 1 E
Hennepin, *U.S.A.* 156 C7 41 15N 89 21W
Hennessey, *U.S.A.* 155 G6 36 6N 97 54W
Hennigsdorf, *Germany* 30 C9 52 38N 13 12 E
Henrietta, *U.S.A.* 155 J5 33 49N 98 12W
Henrietta, Ostrov = Genriyetty, Ostrov, *Russia* 67 B16 77 6N 156 30 E
Henrietta Maria, C., *Canada* 140 A3 55 9N 82 20W
Henry, *U.S.A.* 156 C7 41 7N 89 22W
Henry Lawrence I., *India* 95 H11 12 9N 93 5 E
Henryetta, *U.S.A.* 155 H7 35 27N 95 59W
Henryville, *Canada* 151 A11 45 8N 73 11W
Hensall, *Canada* 150 C3 43 26N 81 30W
Henstedt-Ulzburg, *Germany* 30 B6 53 47N 10 0 E
Hentiesbaai, *Namibia* 116 C1 22 8 S 14 18 E
Hentiyn Nuruu, *Mongolia* 69 B5 48 30N 108 30 E
Henty, *Australia* 129 C7 35 30 S 147 0 E
Henzada, *Burma* 90 G5 17 38N 95 26 E
Hephaestia, *Greece* 49 B7 39 55N 25 14 E
Hephzibah, *U.S.A.* 152 B7 33 19N 82 6W
Heping, *China* 77 E10 24 29N 115 0 E
Heppner, *U.S.A.* 158 D4 45 21N 119 33W
Hepu, *China* 76 G7 21 40N 109 12 E
Hepworth, *Canada* 150 B3 44 37N 81 9W
Heqing, *China* 76 D3 26 37N 100 11 E
Hequ, *China* 74 E6 39 20N 111 15 E
Héraðsflói, *Iceland* 11 B12 65 42N 14 12W
Héraðsvötn →, *Iceland* 11 B7 65 45N 19 25W
Heradsbygd, *Norway* 18 D8 60 49N 11 39 E
Herald Cays, *Australia* 126 B4 16 58 S 149 9 E
Herand, *Norway* 18 D3 60 20N 6 22 E
Herāt, *Afghan.* 91 B1 34 20N 62 7 E
Herāt □, *Afghan.* 91 B1 35 0N 62 0 E
Hérault □, *France* 28 E7 43 34N 3 15 E
Hérault →, *France* 28 E7 43 17N 3 26 E
Herbault, *France* 26 E8 47 36N 1 8 E
Herbert →, *Australia* 126 B4 18 31 S 146 17 E
Herbert I., *U.S.A.* 144 K5 52 45N 170 7W
Herbert River Falls Nat. Park, *Australia* 126 B4 18 15 S 145 32 E
Herbertabad, *India* 95 J11 11 43N 92 37 E
Herberton, *Australia* 126 B4 17 20 S 145 25 E
Herbertsdale, *S. Africa* 116 E3 34 1 S 21 46 E
Herbertville, *N.Z.* 130 G5 40 30 S 176 33 E
Herbignac, *France* 26 E4 47 27N 2 18W
Herborn, *Germany* 30 E4 50 40N 8 18 E
Herby, *Poland* 55 H5 50 45N 18 50 E
Herceg-Novi, *Montenegro, Yug.* 50 D2 42 30N 18 33 E
Herchmer, *Canada* 143 B10 57 22N 94 10W
Herðubreið, *Iceland* 11 B10 65 11N 16 21W
Hereford, *U.K.* 21 E5 52 4N 2 43W
Hereford, *U.S.A.* 155 H3 34 49N 102 24W
Herefordshire □, *U.K.* 21 E5 52 8N 2 40W
Herefoss, *Norway* 18 F5 58 32N 8 23 E
Herehogna, *Sweden* 18 C9 61 44N 12 8 E
Hereke, *Turkey* 51 F13 40 47N 29 38 E
Herekino, *N.Z.* 130 B2 35 18 S 173 11 E
Herencia, *Spain* 43 F7 39 21N 3 22W
Herentals, *Belgium* 24 C4 51 12N 4 51 E
Herford, *Germany* 30 C4 52 7N 8 39 E
Héricourt, *France* 27 E13 47 32N 6 45 E
Herington, *U.S.A.* 154 F6 38 40N 96 57W
Herisau, *Switz.* 33 B8 47 22N 9 17 E
Hérisson, *France* 27 F9 46 32N 2 42 E
Herkimer, *U.S.A.* 151 D10 43 0N 74 59W
Herlong, *U.S.A.* 160 E6 40 8N 120 8W
Herm, *U.K.* 21 H5 49 30N 2 28W
Hermann, *U.S.A.* 156 F5 38 42N 91 27W
Hermannsburg, *Australia* 124 D5 23 57 S 132 45 E
Hermannsburg, *Germany* 30 C6 52 50N 10 5 E
Hermansverk, *Norway* 18 C3 61 11N 6 52 E
Hermanus, *S. Africa* 116 E2 34 27 S 19 12 E
Herment, *France* 28 C6 45 45N 2 24 E
Hermidale, *Australia* 129 A7 31 30 S 146 42 E
Hermiston, *U.S.A.* 158 D4 45 51N 119 17W
Hermit Is., *Papua N. G.* 132 A3 1 32 S 145 5 E
Hermitage, *U.S.A.* 156 G3 37 56N 93 19W
Hermite, I., *Chile* 176 E3 55 50 S 68 0W
Hermon, *U.S.A.* 151 B9 44 28N 75 14W
Hermon, Mt. = Shaykh, J. ash, *Lebanon* 103 B4 33 25N 35 50 E
Hermosillo, *Baja Calif., Mexico* 137 F8 32 27N 114 56W
Hermosillo, *Sonora, Mexico* 162 B2 29 10N 111 0W
Hernád →, *Hungary* 52 C6 47 56N 21 8 E
Hernandarias, *Paraguay* 175 B5 25 20 S 54 40W
Hernandez, *U.S.A.* 160 J6 36 24N 120 46W
Hernando, *Argentina* 174 C3 32 28 S 63 40W
Hernando, *Fla., U.S.A.* 153 G7 28 54N 82 23W
Hernando, *Miss., U.S.A.* 155 H10 34 50N 90 0W
Hernani, *Spain* 40 B3 43 16N 1 58W
Herndon, *U.S.A.* 150 F8 40 43N 76 51W
Herne, *Germany* 24 C7 51 32N 7 14 E
Herne Bay, *U.K.* 21 F9 51 21N 1 8 E
Herning, *Denmark* 17 H2 56 8N 8 58 E
Herod, *U.S.A.* 152 D5 31 42N 84 26W
Heroica = Caborca, *Mexico* 162 A2 30 40N 112 10W
Heroica Nogales = Nogales, *Mexico* 162 A2 31 20N 110 56W
Heron Bay, *Canada* 140 C2 48 40N 86 25W
Herradura, Pta. de la, *Canary Is.* 9 e2 28 26N 14 8W
Herre, *Norway* 18 E6 59 6N 9 34 E
Herreid, *U.S.A.* 154 C4 45 50N 100 4W
Herrenberg, *Germany* 31 G4 48 35N 8 52 E
Herrera, *Spain* 43 H6 37 26N 4 55W
Herrera de Alcántara, *Spain* 43 F3 39 39N 7 25W
Herrera de Pisuerga, *Spain* 42 C6 42 35N 4 20W
Herrera del Duque, *Spain* 43 F5 39 10N 5 3W
Herrestad, *Sweden* 17 F5 58 21N 11 50 E
Herrin, *U.S.A.* 155 G10 37 48N 89 2W
Herriot, *Canada* 143 B8 56 22N 101 16W
Herrljunga, *Sweden* 17 F7 58 5N 13 1 E
Hersbruck, *Germany* 31 F7 49 30N 11 26 E
Hershey, *U.S.A.* 151 F8 40 17N 76 39W
Herstal, *Belgium* 24 D5 50 40N 5 38 E
Hertford, *U.K.* 21 F7 51 48N 0 4W
Hertfordshire □, *U.K.* 21 F7 51 51N 0 5W
's-Hertogenbosch, *Neths.* 24 C5 51 42N 5 17 E
Hertzogville, *S. Africa* 116 D4 28 9 S 25 30 E
Hervás, *Spain* 42 E5 40 16N 5 52W
Hervey B., *Australia* 126 C5 25 0 S 152 52 E
Herzberg, *Brandenburg, Germany* 30 D9 51 41N 13 14 E
Herzberg, *Niedersachsen, Germany* 30 D6 51 38N 10 20 E
Herzliyya, *Israel* 103 C3 32 10N 34 50 E
Herzogenbuchsee, *Switz.* 32 B5 47 11N 7 42 E
Herzogenburg, *Austria* 34 C8 48 17N 15 41 E
Ḥeşār, *Fārs, Iran* 97 D6 29 52N 50 16 E
Ḥeşār, *Markazī, Iran* 97 C6 35 50N 49 12 E
Hesdin, *France* 27 B9 50 21N 2 2 E
Heshan, *China* 76 F7 23 50N 108 53 E
Heshui, *China* 74 G5 35 48N 108 0 E
Heshun, *China* 74 F7 37 22N 113 32 E
Heskestad, *Norway* 18 F3 58 28N 6 22 E
Hesperia, *U.S.A.* 161 L9 34 25N 117 18W
Hessdalen, *Norway* 18 B8 62 48N 11 10 E
Hesse = Hessen □, *Germany* 30 E4 50 30N 9 0 E
Hessen □, *Germany* 30 E4 50 30N 9 0 E
Hesso, *Australia* 128 B2 32 8 S 137 27 E
Hesteyri, *Iceland* 11 A4 66 20N 22 53W
Hestra, *Sweden* 17 G7 57 26N 13 35 E
Hetch Hetchy Aqueduct, *U.S.A.* 160 H5 37 29N 122 19W
Hettinger, *U.S.A.* 154 C3 46 0N 102 42W
Hettstedt, *Germany* 30 D7 51 39N 11 31 E
Heuvelton, *U.S.A.* 151 B9 44 37N 75 25W
Hevelândia, *Brazil* 169 E5 5 12 S 61 50W
Heves, *Hungary* 52 C5 47 36N 20 17 E
Heves □, *Hungary* 52 C5 47 50N 20 0 E
Hewitt, *U.S.A.* 155 K6 31 27N 97 11W
Hexham, *U.K.* 20 C5 54 58N 2 4W
Hexi, *Yunnan, China* 76 E4 24 9N 102 38 E
Hexi, *Zhejiang, China* 77 D12 27 58N 119 38 E
Hexigten Qi, *China* 75 C9 43 18N 117 30 E
Ḥeydarābād, *Iran* 97 D7 30 33N 55 38 E
Heyfield, *Australia* 129 D7 37 59 S 146 47 E
Heysham, *U.K.* 20 C5 54 3N 2 53W
Heyuan, *China* 77 F10 23 39N 114 40 E
Heywood, *Australia* 128 E4 38 8 S 141 37 E
Heyworth, *U.S.A.* 156 D8 40 19N 88 59W
Heze, *China* 74 G8 35 14N 115 20 E
Hezhang, *China* 76 D5 27 8N 104 41 E
Hi, Ko, *Thailand* 87 a 7 44N 98 22 E
Hi-no-Misaki, *Japan* 72 B4 35 26N 132 38 E
Hi Vista, *U.S.A.* 161 L9 34 45N 117 46W
Hialeah, *U.S.A.* 149 N5 25 50N 80 17W
Hiawatha, *U.S.A.* 154 F7 39 51N 95 32W
Hibbing, *U.S.A.* 154 B8 47 25N 92 56W
Hibbs B., *Australia* 127 G4 42 35 S 145 15 E
Hibernia Reef, *Australia* 124 B3 12 0 S 123 23 E
Hibiki-Nada, *Japan* 72 D2 34 0N 130 0 E
Hickman, *U.S.A.* 155 G10 36 34N 89 11W
Hickory, *U.S.A.* 149 H5 35 44N 81 21W
Hicks, Pt., *Australia* 129 D8 37 49 S 149 17 E
Hicks Bay, *N.Z.* 130 D7 37 34 S 178 21 E
Hicks L., *Canada* 143 A9 61 25N 100 0W
Hicksville, *N.Y., U.S.A.* 151 F11 40 46N 73 32W
Hicksville, *Ohio, U.S.A.* 157 C12 41 18N 84 46W
Hida, *Romania* 53 C8 47 10N 23 19 E
Hida-Gawa →, *Japan* 73 B9 35 26N 137 3 E
Hida-Sammyaku, *Japan* 73 A9 36 30N 137 40 E
Hida-Sanchi, *Japan* 73 A9 36 10N 137 0 E
Hidaka, *Japan* 72 B6 35 30N 134 44 E
Hidaka-Sammyaku, *Japan* 70 C11 42 35N 142 45 E
Hidalgo, *Mexico* 163 C5 24 15N 99 26W
Hidalgo □, *Mexico* 163 C5 20 30N 99 10W
Hidalgo, Presa M., *Mexico* 162 B3 26 30N 108 35W
Hidalgo del Parral, *Mexico* 162 B3 26 58N 105 40W
Hiddensee, *Germany* 30 A9 54 32N 13 6 E
Hidrolândia, *Brazil* 171 E2 17 0 S 49 15W
Hieflau, *Austria* 34 D7 47 36N 14 46 E
Hiendelaencina, *Spain* 40 D2 41 5N 3 0W
Hienghène, *N. Cal.* 133 T18 20 41 S 164 56 E
Hierro, *Canary Is.* 9 e1 27 44N 18 0W
Higashi-Hiroshima, *Japan* 72 C4 34 25N 132 45 E
Higashi-Matsuyama, *Japan* 73 A11 36 2N 139 25 E
Higashiajima-San, *Japan* 70 F10 37 40N 140 10 E
Higashiōsaka, *Japan* 73 C7 34 40N 135 37 E
Higasi-Suidō, *Japan* 72 D1 34 0N 129 30 E
Higbee, *U.S.A.* 156 E4 39 19N 92 31W
Higgins, *U.S.A.* 155 G4 36 7N 100 2W
Higgins Corner, *U.S.A.* 160 F5 39 2N 121 5W
Higginsville, *U.S.A.* 156 E3 39 4N 93 43W
High Atlas = Haut Atlas, *Morocco* 110 B4 32 30N 5 0W
High Bridge, *U.S.A.* 151 F10 40 40N 74 54W
High Island Res., *China* 69 G11 22 22N 114 21 E
High Level, *Canada* 142 B5 58 31N 117 8W
High Peak, *Phil.* 80 D3 15 29N 120 7 E
High Pk., *St. Helena* 9 h 15 58 S 5 44W
High Point, *U.S.A.* 149 H6 35 57N 80 0W
High Prairie, *Canada* 142 B5 55 30N 116 30W
High River, *Canada* 142 C6 50 30N 113 50W
High Springs, *U.S.A.* 152 F7 29 50N 82 36W
High Tatra = Tatry, *Slovak Rep.* 35 B13 49 20N 20 0 E
High Veld, *Africa* 104 J6 27 0 S 27 0 E
High Wycombe, *U.K.* 21 F7 51 37N 0 45W
Highbank, *N.Z.* 131 D6 43 37 S 171 45 E
Highland, *Ill., U.S.A.* 156 F7 38 44N 89 41W
Highland, *Ind., U.S.A.* 157 C9 41 33N 87 28W
Highland, *Wis., U.S.A.* 156 A6 43 5N 90 22W
Highland □, *U.K.* 22 D4 57 17N 4 21W
Highland City, *U.S.A.* 153 H8 27 58N 81 53W
Highland Home, *U.S.A.* 152 D3 31°57N 86 19W
Highland Mills = Experiment, *U.S.A.* 152 B5 33 17N 84 17W
Highland Park, *U.S.A.* 157 B9 42 11N 87 48W
Highland View, *U.S.A.* 152 F4 29 50N 85 19W
Highmore, *U.S.A.* 154 C5 44 31N 99 27W
Highrock L., *Man., Canada* 143 B8 55 45N 100 30W
Highrock L., *Sask., Canada* 143 B7 57 5N 105 32W
Higüey, *Dom. Rep.* 165 C6 18 37N 68 42W
Hihya, *Egypt* 106 H7 30 40N 31 36 E
Hiiumaa, *Estonia* 15 G20 58 50N 22 45 E
Híjar, *Spain* 40 D4 41 10N 0 27W
Ḥijāz □, *Si. Arabia* 96 E3 24 0N 40 0 E
Hiji, *Japan* 72 D3 33 22N 131 32 E
Hijo = Tagum, *Phil.* 81 H5 7 33N 125 53 E
Hikari, *Japan* 72 D3 33 58N 131 58 E
Hiketa, *Japan* 72 C6 34 13N 134 24 E
Hikkaduwa, *Sri Lanka* 95 L5 6 8N 80 6 E
Hikmak, Ras el, *Egypt* 106 A2 31 15N 27 51 E
Hiko, *U.S.A.* 160 H11 37 32N 115 14W
Hikone, *Japan* 73 B8 35 15N 136 10 E
Hikurangi, *Gisborne, N.Z.* 130 E5 37 55 S 178 4 E
Hikurangi, *Northland, N.Z.* 130 B3 35 36 S 174 17 E
Hiland Park, *U.S.A.* 152 E4 30 12N 85 33W
Hilawng, *Burma* 90 E4 21 23N 93 48 E
Hildburghausen, *Germany* 30 E6 50 25N 10 42 E
Hildesheim, *Germany* 30 C5 52 9N 9 56 E
Hilðarendi, *Iceland* 11 D7 63 44N 19 57W
Hill →, *Australia* 125 F2 30 23 S 115 3 E
Hill City, *Idaho, U.S.A.* 158 E6 43 18N 115 3W
Hill City, *Kans., U.S.A.* 154 F5 39 22N 99 51W
Hill City, *S. Dak., U.S.A.* 154 D3 43 56N 103 35W
Hill Island L., *Canada* 143 A7 60 30N 109 50W
Hillaby, Mt., *Barbados* 165 g 13 12N 59 35W
Hillared, *Sweden* 17 G7 57 37N 13 10 E
Hillcrest, *Barbados* 165 g 13 13N 59 31W
Hillcrest Center, *U.S.A.* 161 K8 35 23N 118 57W
Hillegom, *Neths.* 24 B4 52 18N 4 35 E
Hillerød, *Denmark* 17 J6 55 56N 12 19 E
Hillerstorp, *Sweden* 17 G7 57 20N 13 52 E
Hilli, *Bangla.* 90 C2 25 17N 89 1 E
Hilliard, *U.S.A.* 152 E8 30 41N 81 55W
Hillsboro, *Ga., U.S.A.* 152 B6 33 11N 83 38W
Hillsboro, *Ill., U.S.A.* 156 E7 39 9N 89 29W
Hillsboro, *Kans., U.S.A.* 154 F6 38 21N 97 12W
Hillsboro, *Mo., U.S.A.* 156 F6 38 14N 90 34W
Hillsboro, *N. Dak., U.S.A.* 154 B6 47 26N 97 3W
Hillsboro, *N.H., U.S.A.* 151 C13 43 7N 71 54W
Hillsboro, *Ohio, U.S.A.* 157 E13 39 12N 83 37W
Hillsboro, *Oreg., U.S.A.* 160 E4 45 31N 122 59W
Hillsboro, *Tex., U.S.A.* 155 J6 32 1N 97 8W
Hillsboro Canal, *U.S.A.* 153 J9 26 30N 80 15W
Hillsborough, *Grenada* 165 D7 12 28N 61 28W
Hillsborough Channel, *Australia* 126 J7 20 56 S 149 15 E
Hillsdale, *Mich., U.S.A.* 157 C12 41 56N 84 38W
Hillsdale, *N.Y., U.S.A.* 151 D11 42 11N 73 32W
Hillsport, *Canada* 140 C2 49 27N 85 34W
Hillston, *Australia* 129 B6 33 30 S 145 31 E
Hilltonia, *U.S.A.* 152 C8 32 53N 81 40W
Hilo, *U.S.A.* 145 D6 19 44N 155 5W
Hilo B., *U.S.A.* 145 D6 19 45N 155 5W
Hilton, *U.S.A.* 150 C7 43 17N 77 48W
Hilton Head Island, *U.S.A.* 152 C9 32 13N 80 45W
Hilvan, *Turkey* 101 D8 37 34N 38 58 E
Hilversum, *Neths.* 24 B5 52 14N 5 10 E
Hilzingen, *Germany* 33 A7 47 46N 8 47 E
Himachal Pradesh □, *India* 92 D7 31 30N 77 0 E
Himalaya, *Asia* 93 E11 29 0N 84 0 E
Himamaylan, *Phil.* 81 F4 10 6N 122 52 E
Himarë, *Albania* 50 F3 40 8N 19 43 E
Hime-Jima, *Japan* 72 D3 33 43N 131 40 E
Himeji, *Japan* 72 C6 34 50N 134 40 E
Himi, *Japan* 73 A8 36 50N 136 55 E
Himmerland, *Denmark* 17 H3 56 45N 9 30 E
Ḥimş, *Syria* 103 A5 34 40N 36 45 E
Ḥimş □, *Syria* 103 A6 34 30N 37 0 E
Hinatuan, *Phil.* 81 G6 8 23N 126 20 E
Hinatuan Passage, *Phil.* 81 G5 9 45N 125 47 E
Hinche, *Haiti* 165 C5 19 9N 72 1W
Hinchinbrook I., *Australia* 126 B4 18 20 S 146 15 E
Hinchinbrook Island Nat. Park, *Australia* 126 B4 18 14 S 146 6 E
Hinckley, *U.K.* 21 E6 52 33N 1 22W
Hinckley, *U.S.A.* 154 B8 46 1N 92 56W
Hindaun, *India* 92 F7 26 44N 77 5 E
Hindmarsh, L., *Australia* 128 D4 36 5 S 141 55 E
Hindol, *India* 94 D7 20 40N 85 10 E
Hinds, *N.Z.* 131 D6 43 59 S 171 36 E
Hindsholm, *Denmark* 17 J4 55 30N 10 40 E
Hindu Bagh, *Pakistan* 91 C2 30 56N 67 50 E
Hindu Kush, *Asia* 65 E5 36 0N 71 0 E
Hindupur, *India* 95 H3 13 49N 77 32 E
Hines Creek, *Canada* 142 B5 56 20N 118 40W
Hinesville, *U.S.A.* 152 D8 31 51N 81 36W
Hinganghat, *India* 94 D4 20 30N 78 52 E
Hingham, *U.S.A.* 158 B8 48 33N 110 25W
Hingir, *India* 93 J10 21 57N 83 41 E
Hingoli, *India* 94 E3 19 41N 77 15 E
Hinigaran, *Phil.* 81 F4 10 16N 122 50 E
Hinis, *Turkey* 101 C9 39 22N 41 43 E
Hinna = Imi, *Ethiopia* 107 F5 6 28N 42 10 E
Hinna, *Nigeria* 113 C7 10 25N 11 35 E
Hinnerup, *Denmark* 17 H4 56 16N 10 4 E
Hinnøya, *Norway* 14 B16 68 35N 15 50 E
Hino, *Japan* 73 C8 35 0N 136 15 E
Hinoba-an, *Phil.* 81 G4 9 35N 122 28 E
Hinojosa del Duque, *Spain* 43 G5 38 30N 5 9W
Hinokage, *Japan* 72 E3 32 39N 131 24 E
Hinsdale, *U.S.A.* 151 D12 42 47N 72 29W
Hinterrhein →, *Switz.* 33 C8 46 40N 9 25 E
Hinton, *Canada* 142 C5 53 26N 117 34W
Hinton, *U.S.A.* 148 G5 37 40N 80 54W
Hinuangan, *Phil.* 81 F5 10 25N 125 12 E
Hinwil, *Switz.* 33 B7 47 18N 8 51 E
Hınzır Burnu, *Turkey* 100 D6 36 19N 35 46 E
Hirado, *Japan* 72 D1 33 22N 129 33 E
Hirado-Shima, *Japan* 72 D1 33 20N 129 30 E
Hirakata, *Japan* 73 C7 34 48N 135 40 E
Hirakud, *India* 94 D6 21 32N 83 51 E
Hirakud Dam, *India* 94 D6 21 32N 83 45 E
Hiran →, *India* 93 H8 23 6N 79 21 E
Hirapur, *India* 93 G8 24 22N 79 13 E
Hirata, *Japan* 72 B4 35 24N 132 49 E
Hiratsuka, *Japan* 73 B11 35 19N 139 21 E
Hirekerur, *India* 95 G2 14 28N 75 23 E
Hirfanlı Barajı, *Turkey* 100 C5 39 18N 33 31 E
Hirhafok, *Algeria* 111 D6 23 49N 5 45 E
Hiromi, *Japan* 72 D4 33 13N 132 36 E
Hiroo, *Japan* 70 C11 42 17N 143 19 E
Hirosaki, *Japan* 70 D10 40 34N 140 28 E
Hiroshima, *Japan* 72 C4 34 24N 132 30 E
Hiroshima □, *Japan* 72 C5 34 50N 133 0 E
Hiroshima-Wan, *Japan* 72 C4 34 5N 132 20 E
Hirson, *France* 27 C11 49 55N 4 4 E
Hirtshals, *Denmark* 17 G3 57 36N 9 57 E
Hisai, *Japan* 73 C8 34 40N 136 28 E
Hisar, *India* 92 E6 29 12N 75 45 E
Hisarcık, *Turkey* 49 B11 39 15N 29 14 E
Hisaria, *Bulgaria* 51 D8 42 30N 24 44 E
Hisb →, *Iraq* 96 D5 31 45N 44 17 E
Ḥismá, *Si. Arabia* 96 D3 28 30N 36 0 E
Ḥişn al 'Abr, *Yemen* 98 C4 16 8N 47 14 E
Hisor, *Tajikistan* 65 D4 38 31N 68 33 E
Hispaniola, *W. Indies* 165 C5 19 0N 71 0W
Hīt, *Iraq* 101 F10 33 38N 42 49 E
Hita, *Japan* 72 D2 33 20N 130 58 E
Hitachi, *Japan* 73 A12 36 36N 140 39 E
Hitachi-Ōta, *Japan* 73 A12 36 30N 140 30 E
Hitchin, *U.K.* 21 F7 51 58N 0 16W
Hitoyoshi, *Japan* 72 E2 32 13N 130 45 E
Hitra, *Norway* 14 E13 63 30N 8 45 E
Hittisau, *Austria* 33 B9 47 28N 9 58 E
Hitzacker, *Germany* 30 B7 53 9N 11 2 E
Hiu, *Vanuatu* 133 C4 13 10 S 166 35 E
Hiuchi-Nada, *Japan* 72 C5 34 5N 133 20 E
Hixon, *Canada* 142 C4 53 25N 122 35W
Ḥiyyon, N. →, *Israel* 103 E4 30 25N 35 10 E
Hjalmar L., *Canada* 143 A7 61 33N 109 25W
Hjälmaren, *Sweden* 16 E9 59 18N 15 40 E
Hjältevad, *Sweden* 17 G9 57 38N 15 20 E
Hjartdal, *Norway* 18 E5 59 37N 8 41 E
Hjelmelandsvågen, *Norway* 18 E3 59 14N 6 10 E
Hjelset, *Norway* 18 B4 62 48N 7 30 E
Hjerkinn, *Norway* 18 B6 62 13N 9 33 E
Hjo, *Sweden* 17 F8 58 22N 14 17 E
Hjørring, *Denmark* 17 G3 57 29N 9 59 E
Hjortkvarn, *Sweden* 17 F9 58 54N 15 26 E
Hjukse, *Norway* 18 E6 59 31N 9 19 E
Hkakabo Razi, *Burma* 90 B6 28 17N 97 46 E
Hko-lam, *Burma* 90 E7 21 7N 98 5 E
Hko-ut, *Burma* 90 E7 20 58N 98 2 E
Hkyenhpa, *Burma* 90 B6 27 43N 97 25 E
Hlaingbwe, *Burma* 90 G6 17 8N 97 50 E
Hlinsko, *Czech Rep.* 34 B8 49 45N 15 54 E
Hlobane, *S. Africa* 117 D5 27 42 S 31 0 E
Hlohovec, *Slovak Rep.* 35 C10 48 26N 17 49 E
Hlučín, *Czech Rep.* 35 B11 49 54N 18 11 E
Hluhluwe, *S. Africa* 117 D5 28 1 S 32 15 E
Hluhluwe Game Reserve, *S. Africa* 117 C5 22 10 S 32 5 E
Hlukhiv, *Ukraine* 59 G7 51 40N 33 58 E
Hlwaze, *Burma* 90 F6 18 54N 96 37 E
Hlyboka, *Ukraine* 59 H3 48 5N 25 56 E
Hlybokaye, *Belarus* 58 E4 55 10N 27 45 E
Hnappadalssýsla □, *Iceland* 11 C4 64 50N 22 30W
Hnífsdalur, *Iceland* 11 A3 66 7N 23 8W
Hnúšťa, *Slovak Rep.* 35 C12 48 35N 19 58 E
Ho, *Ghana* 113 D5 6 37N 0 27 E
Ho Chi Minh City = Thanh Pho Ho Chi Minh, *Vietnam* 87 G6 10 58N 106 40 E
Ho Thuong, *Vietnam* 86 C5 19 32N 105 48 E
Hoa Binh, *Vietnam* 76 G5 20 50N 105 20 E
Hoa Da, *Vietnam* 87 G7 11 16N 108 40 E
Hoa Hiep, *Vietnam* 87 G5 11 34N 105 51 E
Hoai Nhon, *Vietnam* 86 E7 14 28N 109 1 E
Hoang Lien Son, *Vietnam* 76 F4 22 0N 104 0 E
Hoanib →, *Namibia* 116 B2 19 27 S 12 46 E
Hoare B., *Canada* 139 B13 65 17N 62 30W
Hoarusib →, *Namibia* 116 B2 19 3 S 12 36 E
Hobart, *Australia* 127 G4 42 50 S 147 21 E
Hobart, *Ind., U.S.A.* 157 C9 41 32N 87 15W
Hobart, *Okla., U.S.A.* 155 H5 35 1N 99 6W
Hobbs, *U.S.A.* 155 J3 32 42N 103 8W
Hobbs Coast, *Antarctica* 7 D14 74 50 S 131 0W
Hobe Sound, *U.S.A.* 153 H9 27 4N 80 8W
Hobo, *Colombia* 168 C2 2 35N 75 30W
Hoboken, *Ga., U.S.A.* 152 D7 31 11N 82 8W
Hoboken, *N.J., U.S.A.* 151 F10 40 45N 74 4W
Hobro, *Denmark* 17 H3 56 39N 9 46 E
Hoburgen, *Sweden* 17 H12 56 55N 18 7 E
Hocalar, *Turkey* 49 C11 38 36N 30 0 E
Hochdorf, *Switz.* 33 B6 47 10N 8 17 E
Hochfeld, *Namibia* 116 C2 21 28 S 17 58 E
Hochschwab, *Austria* 34 D8 47 35N 15 0 E
Höchstadt, *Germany* 31 F6 49 42N 10 47 E
Hockenheim, *Germany* 31 F4 49 19N 8 32 E
Hodaka-Dake, *Japan* 73 A9 36 17N 137 39 E
Hodeida = Al Ḥudaydah, *Yemen* 98 D3 14 50N 43 0 E
Hodgeville, *Canada* 143 C7 50 7N 106 58W
Hodgson, *Canada* 143 C9 51 13N 97 36W
Hódmezővásárhely, *Hungary* 52 D5 46 28N 20 22 E
Hodna, Chott el, *Algeria* 111 A6 35 26N 4 43 E
Hodna, Monts du, *Algeria* 111 A5 35 52N 4 42 E
Hodonín, *Czech Rep.* 35 C10 48 50N 17 10 E
Hodzhambas, *Turkmenistan* 65 D2 38 7N 65 0 E
Hoeamdong, *N. Korea* 75 C16 42 30N 130 16 E
Hœdic, Î. de, *France* 26 E4 47 20N 2 53W
Hoek van Holland, *Neths.* 24 C4 52 0N 4 7 E
Hoengsŏng, *S. Korea* 75 F14 37 29N 127 59 E
Hoeryong, *N. Korea* 75 C15 42 30N 129 45 E
Hoeyang, *N. Korea* 75 E14 38 43N 127 36 E
Hof, *Germany* 31 E7 50 19N 11 55 E
Hof, *Norður-Múlasýsla, Iceland* 11 B11 65 39N 15 0W

Hof, *Suður-Múlasýsla, Iceland* 11 C12 64 33N 14 40W
Hof, *Norway* 18 E7 59 32N 10 5 E
Hoffell, *Iceland* 11 C11 64 23N 15 20W
Hofgeismar, *Germany* 30 D5 51 29N 9 23 E
Hofheim, *Germany* 31 E4 50 5N 8 26 E
Hofmeyr, *S. Africa* 116 E4 31 39 S 25 50 E
Höfn, *Iceland* 11 C11 64 15N 15 13W
Hofors, *Sweden* 16 D10 60 31N 16 15 E
Hofsjökull, *Iceland* 11 C8 64 49N 18 48W
Hofsós, *Iceland* 11 B7 65 53N 19 26W
Hōfu, *Japan* 72 C3 34 3N 131 34 E
Hog Harbour, *Vanuatu* 133 E5 15 8 S 167 6 E
Hogan Group, *Australia* 127 F4 39 13 S 147 1 E
Höganäs, *Sweden* 17 H6 56 12N 12 33 E
Hogansville, *U.S.A.* 152 B5 33 10N 84 55W
Hogarth, Mt., *Australia* 126 C2 21 48 S 136 58 E
Hogenakai Falls, *India* 95 H3 12 6N 77 50 E
Hoggar = Ahaggar, *Algeria* 111 D6 23 0N 6 30 E
Högsäter, *Sweden* 17 F6 58 38N 12 5 E
Högsby, *Sweden* 17 G10 57 10N 16 1 E
Högsjö, *Sweden* 16 E9 59 4N 15 44 E
Hogsty Reef, *Bahamas* 165 B5 21 41N 73 48W
Hoh →, *U.S.A.* 160 C2 47 45N 124 29W
Hohe Acht, *Germany* 31 E3 50 22N 7 0 E
Hohe Tauern, *Austria* 34 D5 47 11N 12 40 E
Hohe Venn, *Belgium* 24 D6 50 30N 6 5 E
Hohenau, *Austria* 35 C9 48 36N 16 55 E
Hohenems, *Austria* 34 D2 47 22N 9 42 E
Hohenloher Ebene, *Germany* 31 F5 49 14N 9 36 E
Hohenwald, *U.S.A.* 149 H2 35 33N 87 33W
Hohenwestedt, *Germany* 30 A5 54 5N 9 40 E
Hoher Freschen, *Austria* 33 B9 47 18N 9 46 E
Hoher Rhön = Rhön, *Germany* 30 E5 50 24N 9 58 E
Hohhot, *China* 74 D6 40 52N 111 40 E
Hóhlakas, *Greece* 38 F11 35 57N 27 53 E
Hohoe, *Ghana* 113 D5 7 8N 0 32 E
Hoi An, *Vietnam* 86 E7 15 30N 108 19 E
Hoi Xuan, *Vietnam* 76 G5 20 25N 105 9 E
Hoisington, *U.S.A.* 154 F5 38 31N 98 47W
Hojai, *India* 90 B4 26 2N 92 54 E
Højer, *Denmark* 17 K2 54 58N 8 42 E
Hōjō, *Japan* 72 D4 33 58N 132 46 E
Hok, *Sweden* 17 G8 57 31N 14 16 E
Hökensås, *Sweden* 17 G8 58 0N 14 5 E
Hökerum, *Sweden* 17 G7 57 51N 13 16 E
Hokianga Harbour, *N.Z.* 130 B2 35 31 S 173 22 E
Hokitika, *N.Z.* 131 C5 42 42 S 171 0 E
Hokkaidō □, *Japan* 70 C11 43 30N 143 0 E
Hokksund, *Norway* 18 E6 59 48N 9 54 E
Hokuriko Tunnel, *Japan* 73 B8 35 40N 136 6 E
Hol-Hol, *Djibouti* 107 E5 11 20N 42 50 E
Hola Pristan, *Ukraine* 59 J7 46 29N 32 32 E
Holalkere, *India* 95 G3 14 2N 76 11 E
Hólar, *Iceland* 11 B7 65 44N 19 8W
Holbæk, *Denmark* 17 J5 55 43N 11 43 E
Holbrook, *Australia* 129 C7 35 42 S 147 18 E
Holbrook, *U.S.A.* 159 J8 34 54N 110 10W
Holden, *Mo., U.S.A.* 156 F3 38 43N 94 0W
Holden, *Utah, U.S.A.* 158 G7 39 6N 112 16W
Holdenville, *U.S.A.* 155 H6 35 5N 96 24W
Holdich, *Argentina* 176 C3 45 57 S 68 13W
Holdrege, *U.S.A.* 154 E5 40 26N 99 23W
Hole-Narsipur, *India* 95 H3 12 48N 76 16 E
Holešov, *Czech Rep.* 35 B10 49 20N 17 35 E
Holetown, *Barbados* 165 g 13 11N 59 38W
Holgate, *U.S.A.* 157 C12 41 15N 84 8W
Holguín, *Cuba* 164 B4 20 50N 76 20W
Holíč, *Slovak Rep.* 35 C10 48 49N 17 10 E
Holice, *Czech Rep.* 34 A8 50 5N 16 0 E
Holiday, *U.S.A.* 153 G7 28 13N 82 43W
Höljes, *Sweden* 16 D6 60 50N 12 35 E
Hollabrunn, *Austria* 34 C9 48 34N 16 5 E
Hollams Bird I., *Namibia* 116 C1 24 40 S 14 30 E
Holland, *Mich., U.S.A.* 157 B10 42 47N 86 7W
Holland, *N.Y., U.S.A.* 150 D6 42 38N 78 32W
Hollandale, *U.S.A.* 155 J9 33 10N 90 51W
Hollandia = Jayapura, *Indonesia* 83 B6 2 28 S 140 38 E
Holley, *U.S.A.* 150 C6 43 14N 78 2W
Hollfeld, *Germany* 31 F7 49 56N 11 18 E
Hollidaysburg, *U.S.A.* 150 F6 40 26N 78 24W
Hollis, *U.S.A.* 155 H5 34 41N 99 55W
Hollister, *Calif., U.S.A.* 160 J5 36 51N 121 24W
Hollister, *Idaho, U.S.A.* 158 E6 42 21N 114 35W
Höllviken = Höllviksnäs, *Sweden* 17 J6 55 26N 12 58 E
Höllviksnäs, *Sweden* 17 J6 55 26N 12 58 E
Holly, *U.S.A.* 157 B13 42 48N 83 38W
Holly Hill, *Fla., U.S.A.* 149 L5 29 16N 81 3W
Holly Hill, *S.C., U.S.A.* 152 B9 33 19N 80 25W
Holly Springs, *Ga., U.S.A.* 152 A5 34 10N 84 30W
Holly Springs, *Miss., U.S.A.* 155 H10 34 46N 89 27W
Hollywood, *U.S.A.* 149 N5 26 1N 80 9W
Holman, *Canada* 138 A8 70 44N 117 44W
Hólmavík, *Iceland* 14 D3 65 42N 21 40W
Holmen, *Norway* 18 D7 60 40N 10 22 E
Holmen, *U.S.A.* 154 D9 43 58N 91 15W
Holmes →, *U.S.A.* 152 E4 30 30N 85 50W
Holmes Beach, *U.S.A.* 153 H7 27 31N 82 43W
Holmes Reefs, *Australia* 126 B4 16 27 S 148 0 E
Holmestrand, *Norway* 18 E7 59 31N 10 14 E
Holmsjö, *Sweden* 17 H9 56 25N 15 32 E
Holmsjön, *Västernorrland, Sweden* 16 B10 62 41N 16 33 E
Holmsjön, *Västernorrland, Sweden* 16 B9 62 26N 15 20 E
Holmsland Klit, *Denmark* 17 J2 56 0N 8 5 E
Holmsund, *Sweden* 14 E19 63 41N 20 20 E
Holod, *Romania* 52 D7 46 49N 22 8 E
Holopaw, *U.S.A.* 153 G8 28 8N 81 5W
Holøydal, *Norway* 18 B8 62 12N 11 27 E
Holroyd →, *Australia* 126 A3 14 10 S 141 36 E
Holstebro, *Denmark* 17 H2 56 22N 8 37 E
Holsteinsborg = Sisimiut, *Greenland* 10 D5 66 40N 53 30W
Holsworthy, *U.K.* 21 G3 50 48N 4 22W
Holt, *Iceland* 11 D7 63 33N 19 48W
Holt, *Fla., U.S.A.* 153 E3 30 43N 86 45W
Holt, *Mich., U.S.A.* 157 B12 42 39N 84 31W
Holton, *Canada* 141 B8 54 31N 57 12W
Holton, *U.S.A.* 154 F7 39 28N 95 44W
Holts Summit, *U.S.A.* 156 F4 38 38N 92 7W
Holtville, *U.S.A.* 161 N11 32 49N 115 23W
Holualoa, *U.S.A.* 145 D6 19 37N 155 57W
Holum, *Norway* 18 F4 58 6N 7 32 E
Holwerd, *Neths.* 24 A5 53 22N 5 54 E
Holy Cross, *U.S.A.* 144 E8 62 12N 159 46W
Holy I., *Angl., U.K.* 20 D3 53 17N 4 37W
Holy I., *Northumb., U.K.* 20 B6 55 40N 1 47W
Holyhead, *U.K.* 20 D3 53 18N 4 38W
Holyoke, *Colo., U.S.A.* 154 E3 40 35N 102 18W
Holyoke, *Mass., U.S.A.* 151 D12 42 12N 72 37W
Holyrood, *Canada* 141 C9 47 27N 53 8W
Holzkirchen, *Germany* 31 H7 47 52N 11 42 E
Holzminden, *Germany* 30 D5 51 50N 9 28 E
Homa Bay, *Kenya* 118 C3 0 36 S 34 30 E
Homalin, *Burma* 90 C5 24 55N 95 0 E
Homand, *Iran* 97 C8 32 28N 59 37 E
Homathko →, *Canada* 142 C4 51 0N 124 56W
Homberg, *Germany* 30 D5 51 2N 9 25 E
Hombori, *Mali* 113 B4 15 20N 1 38W
Homburg, *Germany* 31 F3 49 28N 7 18 E
Home B., *Canada* 139 B13 68 40N 67 10W
Home Hill, *Australia* 126 B4 19 43 S 147 25 E
Home Reef, *Tonga* 133 P13 18 59 S 174 47W
Homedale, *U.S.A.* 158 E5 43 37N 116 56W
Homeland, *U.S.A.* 152 E7 30 51N 82 1W
Homer, *Alaska, U.S.A.* 144 G10 59 39N 151 33W
Homer, *Ill., U.S.A.* 157 D9 40 4N 87 57W
Homer, *La., U.S.A.* 155 J8 32 48N 93 4W
Homer, *Mich., U.S.A.* 157 B12 42 9N 84 49W
Homer City, *U.S.A.* 150 F5 40 32N 79 10W
Homerville, *U.S.A.* 152 D7 31 2N 82 45W
Homestead, *Australia* 126 C4 20 20 S 145 40 E
Homestead, *U.S.A.* 149 N5 25 28N 80 29W
Homewood, *Calif., U.S.A.* 160 F6 39 4N 120 8W
Homewood, *Ill., U.S.A.* 157 C9 41 34N 87 40W
Hommelvik, *Norway* 18 A7 63 25N 10 48 E
Hommersåk, *Norway* 18 F2 58 56N 5 50 E
Homnabad, *India* 94 F3 17 45N 77 11 E
Homoine, *Mozam.* 117 C6 23 55 S 35 8 E
Homoljske Planina, *Serbia, Yug.* 50 B5 44 10N 21 45 E
Homonhon I., *Phil.* 81 F5 10 44N 125 43 E
Homorod, *Romania* 53 D10 46 5N 25 15 E
Homosassa Springs, *U.S.A.* 153 G7 28 48N 82 35W
Homs = Ḥimş, *Syria* 103 A5 34 40N 36 45 E
Homyel, *Belarus* 59 F6 52 28N 31 0 E
Hon Chong, *Vietnam* 87 G5 10 25N 104 30 E
Hon Me, *Vietnam* 86 C5 19 23N 105 56 E
Honan = Henan □, *China* 74 H8 34 0N 114 0 E
Honaunau, *U.S.A.* 145 D6 19 26N 155 55W
Honavar, *India* 95 G2 14 17N 74 27 E
Honaz, *Turkey* 49 D11 37 46N 29 18 E
Honbetsu, *Japan* 70 C11 43 7N 143 37 E
Honcut, *U.S.A.* 160 F5 39 20N 121 32W
Honda, *Colombia* 168 B3 5 12N 74 45W
Honda Bay, *Phil.* 81 G2 9 53N 118 49 E
Hondarribia, *Spain* 40 B3 43 22N 1 47W
Hondeklipbaai, *S. Africa* 116 E2 30 19 S 17 17 E
Hondo, *Japan* 72 E2 32 27N 130 12 E
Hondo, *U.S.A.* 155 L5 29 21N 99 9W
Hondo →, *Belize* 163 D7 18 25N 88 21W
Honduras ■, *Cent. Amer.* 164 D2 14 40N 86 30W
Honduras, G. de, *Caribbean* 164 C2 16 50N 87 0W
Hønefoss, *Norway* 15 F14 60 10N 10 18 E
Honesdale, *U.S.A.* 151 E9 41 34N 75 16W
Honey L., *U.S.A.* 160 E6 40 15N 120 19W
Honfleur, *France* 26 C7 49 25N 0 13 E
Høng, *Denmark* 17 J5 55 31N 11 18 E
Hong →, *Vietnam* 76 F5 22 0N 104 0 E
Hong Gai, *Vietnam* 76 G6 20 57N 107 5 E
Hong He →, *China* 74 H8 32 25N 115 35 E
Hong Hu, *China* 77 C9 29 54N 113 24 E
Hong Kong □, *China* 77 F10 22 11N 114 14 E
Hong Kong I., *China* 69 G11 22 16N 114 12 E
Honga, *Angola* 115 F3 15 9 S 15 12 E
Hong'an, *China* 77 B10 31 20N 114 40 E
Hongch'ŏn, *S. Korea* 75 F14 37 44N 127 53 E
Honghai Wan, *China* 77 F10 22 40N 115 0 E
Honghe, *China* 76 F4 23 25N 102 25 E
Honghu, *China* 77 C9 29 50N 113 30 E
Hongjiang, *China* 76 D7 27 7N 109 59 E
Hongliu He →, *China* 74 F5 38 0N 109 50 E
Hongor, *Mongolia* 74 B7 45 45N 112 50 E
Hongsa, *Laos* 86 C3 19 43N 101 20 E
Hongshui He →, *China* 76 F7 23 48N 109 30 E
Hongsŏng, *S. Korea* 75 F14 36 37N 126 38 E
Hongtong, *China* 74 F6 36 16N 111 40 E
Honguedo, Détroit d', *Canada* 141 C7 49 15N 64 0W
Hongwon, *N. Korea* 75 E14 40 0N 127 56 E
Hongya, *China* 76 C4 29 57N 103 22 E
Hongyuan, *China* 76 A4 32 51N 102 40 E
Hongze Hu, *China* 75 H10 33 15N 118 35 E
Honiara, *Solomon Is.* 133 M10 9 27 S 159 57 E
Honiton, *U.K.* 21 G4 50 47N 3 11W
Honjō, *Akita, Japan* 70 E10 39 23N 140 3 E
Honjō, *Gumma, Japan* 73 A11 36 14N 139 11 E
Honkawane, *Japan* 73 B10 35 5N 138 5 E
Honkorâb, Ras, *Egypt* 106 C4 24 35N 35 10 E
Honnali, *India* 95 G2 14 15N 75 40 E
Honningsvåg, *Norway* 14 A21 70 59N 25 59 E
Hönö, *Sweden* 17 G5 57 41N 11 39 E
Honokaa, *U.S.A.* 145 C6 20 5N 155 28W
Honokahua, *U.S.A.* 145 C5 21 0N 156 40W
Honolulu, *U.S.A.* 145 K14 21 19N 157 52W
Honomu, *U.S.A.* 145 D6 19 52N 155 7W
Honouliuli, *U.S.A.* 145 K13 21 22N 158 2W
Honshū, *Japan* 73 A8 36 0N 138 0 E
Hontoria del Pinar, *Spain* 40 D1 41 50N 3 10W
Honuapo B., *U.S.A.* 145 D6 19 5N 155 33W
Hood, Mt., *U.S.A.* 158 D3 45 23N 121 42W
Hood, Pt., *Australia* 125 F2 34 23 S 119 34 E
Hood Pt., *Papua N. G.* 132 F4 10 4 S 147 45 E
Hood River, *U.S.A.* 158 D3 45 43N 121 31W
Hoodsport, *U.S.A.* 160 C3 47 24N 123 9W
Hooge, *Germany* 30 A4 54 34N 8 33 E
Hoogeveen, *Neths.* 24 B6 52 44N 6 28 E
Hoogezand-Sappemeer, *Neths.* 24 A6 53 9N 6 45 E
Hooghly = Hugli →, *India* 93 J13 21 56N 88 4 E
Hooghly-Chinsura = Chunchura, *India* 93 H13 22 53N 88 27 E
Hook Hd., *Ireland* 23 D5 52 7N 6 56W
Hook I., *Australia* 126 J6 20 4 S 149 0 E
Hook of Holland = Hoek van Holland, *Neths.* 24 C4 52 0N 4 7 E
Hooker, *U.S.A.* 155 G4 36 52N 101 13W
Hooker Creek, *Australia* 124 C5 18 23 S 130 38 E
Hoolehua, *U.S.A.* 145 B4 21 10N 157 5W
Hoonah, *U.S.A.* 142 B1 58 7N 135 27W
Hooper Bay, *U.S.A.* 144 F6 61 32N 166 6W
Hoopeston, *U.S.A.* 157 D9 40 28N 87 40W
Hoopstad, *S. Africa* 116 D4 27 50 S 25 55 E
Höör, *Sweden* 17 J7 55 56N 13 33 E
Hoorn, *Neths.* 24 B5 52 38N 5 4 E
Hoover, *U.S.A.* 149 J2 33 20N 86 11W
Hoover Dam, *U.S.A.* 161 K12 36 1N 114 44W
Hooversville, *U.S.A.* 150 F6 40 9N 78 55W
Hop Bottom, *U.S.A.* 151 E9 41 42N 75 46W
Hopa, *Turkey* 101 B9 41 28N 41 30 E
Hope, *Canada* 142 D4 49 25N 121 25W
Hope, *Ariz., U.S.A.* 161 M13 33 43N 113 42W
Hope, *Ark., U.S.A.* 155 J8 33 40N 93 36W
Hope, *Ind., U.S.A.* 157 E11 39 18N 85 46W
Hope, L., *S. Austral., Australia* 127 D2 28 24 S 139 18 E
Hope, L., *W. Austral., Australia* 125 F3 32 35 S 120 15 E
Hope I., *Canada* 150 B4 44 55N 80 11W
Hope Town, *Bahamas* 164 A4 26 35N 76 57W
Hopedale, *Canada* 141 A7 55 28N 60 13W
Hopedale, *U.S.A.* 151 D13 42 8N 71 33W
Hopefield, *S. Africa* 116 E2 33 3 S 18 22 E
Hopei = Hebei □, *China* 74 E9 39 0N 116 0 E
Hopelchén, *Mexico* 163 D7 19 46N 89 50W
Hopetoun, *Vic., Australia* 128 C5 35 42 S 142 22 E
Hopetoun, *W. Austral., Australia* 125 F3 33 57 S 120 7 E
Hopetown, *S. Africa* 116 D3 29 34 S 24 3 E
Hopevale, *Australia* 126 B4 15 16 S 145 20 E
Hopewell, *U.S.A.* 148 G7 37 18N 77 17W
Hopfgarten, *Austria* 34 D5 47 27N 12 10 E
Hopin, *Burma* 90 C6 24 58N 96 30 E
Hopkins, *U.S.A.* 156 D2 40 33N 94 49W
Hopkins, L., *Australia* 124 D4 24 15 S 128 35 E
Hopkinsville, *U.S.A.* 149 G2 36 52N 87 29W
Hopland, *U.S.A.* 160 G3 38 58N 123 7W
Hopong, *Burma* 90 E6 20 47N 97 11 E
Hoque, *Angola* 115 F2 14 25 S 13 50 E
Hoquiam, *U.S.A.* 160 D3 46 59N 123 53W
Hōrai, *Japan* 73 C9 34 58N 137 32 E
Horana, *Sri Lanka* 95 L5 6 43N 80 4 E
Horasan, *Turkey* 101 B10 40 3N 42 11 E
Horažďovice, *Czech Rep.* 34 B6 49 19N 13 42 E
Horb, *Germany* 31 G4 48 26N 8 47 E
Hörby, *Sweden* 17 J7 55 51N 13 40 E
Horcajo de Santiago, *Spain* 40 F1 39 50N 3 1W
Hordabø, *Norway* 18 D1 60 42N 4 54 E
Hordaland □, *Norway* 18 D3 60 25N 6 15 E
Horden Hills, *Australia* 124 D5 20 15 S 130 0 E
Hordio, *Somali Rep.* 120 B4 10 33N 51 6 E
Horezu, *Romania* 53 E8 45 6N 24 0 E
Horgen, *Switz.* 33 B7 47 15N 8 35 E
Horgoš, *Serbia, Yug.* 52 D4 46 10N 20 0 E
Hořice, *Czech Rep.* 34 A8 50 21N 15 39 E
Horinger, *China* 74 D6 40 28N 111 48 E
Horki, *Belarus* 58 E6 54 17N 30 59 E
Horlick Mts., *Antarctica* 7 E15 84 0 S 102 0W
Horlivka, *Ukraine* 59 H10 48 19N 38 5 E
Hormak, *Iran* 97 D9 29 58N 60 51 E
Hormoz, *Iran* 97 E7 27 35N 55 0 E
Hormoz, Jaz.-ye, *Iran* 97 E8 27 8N 56 28 E
Hormozgān □, *Iran* 97 E8 27 30N 56 0 E
Hormuz, Kūh-e, *Iran* 97 E7 27 27N 55 10 E
Hormuz, Str. of, *The Gulf* 97 E8 26 30N 56 30 E
Horn, *Austria* 34 C8 48 39N 15 40 E
Horn, *Iceland* 14 C2 66 28N 22 28W
Horn, *Sweden* 17 G9 57 54N 15 51 E
Horn →, *Canada* 142 A5 61 30N 118 1W
Horn, Cape = Hornos, C. de, *Chile* 176 E3 55 50 S 67 30W
Horn, Is., *Wall. & F. Is.* 123 C15 14 16 S 178 6W
Horn Head, *Ireland* 23 A3 55 14N 8 0W
Horn I., *Australia* 126 A3 10 37 S 142 17 E
Horn Mts., *Canada* 142 A5 62 15N 119 15W
Hornachuelos, *Spain* 43 H5 37 50N 5 14W
Hornavan, *Sweden* 14 C17 66 15N 17 30 E
Hornbeck, *U.S.A.* 155 K8 31 20N 93 24W
Hornbjarg, *Iceland* 11 A4 66 28N 22 25W
Hornbrook, *U.S.A.* 158 F2 41 55N 122 33W
Hornburg, *Germany* 30 C6 52 2N 10 37 E
Hornby, *N.Z.* 131 D7 43 33 S 172 33 E
Horncastle, *U.K.* 20 D7 53 13N 0 7W
Horndal, *Sweden* 16 D10 60 18N 16 23 E
Hornell, *U.S.A.* 150 D7 42 20N 77 40W
Hornell L., *Canada* 142 A5 62 20N 119 25W
Hornepayne, *Canada* 140 C3 49 14N 84 48W
Horní Planá, *Czech Rep.* 34 C7 48 46N 14 2 E
Hornindal, *Norway* 18 C3 61 58N 6 30 E
Hornings Mills, *Canada* 150 B4 44 9N 80 12W
Hornitos, *U.S.A.* 160 H6 37 30N 120 14W
Hornos, C. de, *Chile* 176 E3 55 50 S 67 30W
Hornos Is., *Papua N. G.* 132 B4 2 12 S 147 45 E
Hornoy-le-Bourg, *France* 27 C8 49 50N 1 54 E
Hornsby, *Australia* 129 B9 33 42 S 151 2 E
Hornsea, *U.K.* 20 D7 53 55N 0 11W
Hornsjø, *Norway* 18 C7 61 19N 10 38 E
Hornslandet, *Sweden* 16 C11 61 35N 17 37 E
Hörnum, *Germany* 30 A4 54 45N 8 17 E
Horobetsu, *Japan* 70 C10 42 24N 141 6 E
Horodenka, *Ukraine* 59 H3 48 41N 25 29 E
Horodnya, *Ukraine* 59 G6 51 55N 31 33 E
Horodok, *Khmelnytskyy, Ukraine* 59 H4 49 10N 26 34 E
Horodok, *Lviv, Ukraine* 59 H2 49 46N 23 32 E
Horodyshche, *Ukraine* 59 H6 49 17N 31 27 E
Horokhiv, *Ukraine* 59 G3 50 30N 24 45 E
Horovice, *Czech Rep.* 34 B6 49 48N 13 53 E
Horqin Youyi Qianqi, *China* 75 A12 46 5N 122 3 E
Horqueta, *Paraguay* 174 A4 23 15 S 56 55W
Horred, *Sweden* 17 G6 57 22N 12 28 E
Horse Creek, *U.S.A.* 154 E3 41 57N 105 10W
Horse Is., *Canada* 141 B8 50 15N 55 50W
Horsefly L., *Canada* 142 C4 52 25N 121 0W
Horseheads, *U.S.A.* 150 D8 42 10N 76 49W
Horsens, *Denmark* 17 J3 55 52N 9 51 E
Horsham, *Australia* 128 D5 36 44 S 142 13 E
Horsham, *U.K.* 21 F7 51 4N 0 20W
Horšovský Týn, *Czech Rep.* 34 B5 49 31N 12 58 E
Horta, *Azores* 9 d1 38 32N 28 38W
Horten, *Norway* 15 G14 59 25N 10 32 E
Hortense, *U.S.A.* 152 D8 31 20N 81 57W
Horti, *India* 94 F2 17 7N 75 47 E
Hortobágy →, *Hungary* 52 C6 47 30N 21 6 E
Horton, *Kans., U.S.A.* 154 F7 39 40N 95 32W
Horton, *Mo., U.S.A.* 156 G2 37 58N 94 22W
Horton →, *Canada* 138 B7 69 56N 126 52W
Horw, *Switz.* 33 B6 47 1N 8 19 E
Horwood L., *Canada* 140 C3 48 5N 82 20W
Hosaina, *Ethiopia* 107 F4 7 30N 37 47 E
Hosdurga, *India* 95 H3 13 49N 76 17 E
Hose, Gunung-Gunung, *Malaysia* 78 D4 2 5N 114 6 E
Hosenofu, *Libya* 108 D4 23 41N 21 4 E
Ḥoseynābād, *Khuzestān, Iran* 97 C6 32 45N 48 20 E
Ḥoseynābād, *Kordestān, Iran* 101 E12 35 33N 47 8 E
Hosford, *U.S.A.* 152 E5 30 23N 84 48W
Hoshangabad, *India* 92 H7 22 45N 77 45 E
Hoshiarpur, *India* 92 D6 31 30N 75 58 E
Hoskins, *Papua N. G.* 132 C6 5 29 S 150 27 E
Hoskote, *India* 95 H3 13 4N 77 48 E
Hospental, *Switz.* 33 C7 46 37N 8 34 E
Hospet, *India* 95 G3 15 15N 76 20 E
Hoste, I., *Chile* 176 E3 55 0 S 69 0W
Hostens, *France* 28 D3 44 30N 0 40W
Hosur, *India* 95 H3 12 43N 77 49 E
Hot, *Thailand* 86 C2 18 8N 98 29 E
Hot Creek Range, *U.S.A.* 158 G6 38 40N 116 20W
Hot Springs, *Ark., U.S.A.* 155 H8 34 31N 93 3W
Hot Springs, *S. Dak., U.S.A.* 154 D3 43 26N 103 29W
Hotagen, *Sweden* 14 E16 63 50N 14 30 E
Hotan, *China* 68 C2 37 25N 79 55 E
Hotazel, *S. Africa* 116 D3 27 17 S 22 58 E
Hotchkiss, *U.S.A.* 159 G10 38 48N 107 43W
Hotham, C., *Australia* 124 B5 12 2 S 131 18 E
Hoti, *Indonesia* 83 B4 3 0 S 130 22 E
Hoting, *Sweden* 14 D17 64 8N 16 15 E
Hotolisht, *Albania* 50 E4 41 10N 20 25 E
Hotte, Massif de la, *Haiti* 165 C5 18 30N 73 45W
Hottentotsbaai, *Namibia* 116 D1 26 8 S 14 59 E
Hou Hai, *China* 69 F10 22 32N 113 56 E
Houailou, *N. Cal.* 133 U19 21 17 S 165 38 E
Houat, Î. de, *France* 26 E4 47 24N 2 58W
Houdan, *France* 27 D8 48 48N 1 35 E
Houei Sai, *Laos* 76 G3 20 18N 100 26 E
Houeillès, *France* 28 D4 44 12N 0 2 E
Houffalize, *Belgium* 24 D5 50 8N 5 48 E
Houghton, *Mich., U.S.A.* 154 B10 47 7N 88 34W
Houghton, *N.Y., U.S.A.* 150 D6 42 25N 78 10W
Houghton L., *U.S.A.* 148 C3 44 21N 84 44W
Houhora Heads, *N.Z.* 130 A2 34 49 S 173 9 E
Houlton, *U.S.A.* 149 B12 46 8N 67 51W
Houma, *U.S.A.* 155 L9 29 36N 90 43W
Houndé, *Burkina Faso* 112 C4 11 34N 3 31W
Hourtin, *France* 28 C2 45 11N 1 4W
Hourtin-Carcans, Étang d', *France* 28 C2 45 10N 1 6W
Housatonic →, *U.S.A.* 151 E11 41 10N 73 7W
Houston, *Canada* 142 C3 54 25N 126 39W
Houston, *Fla., U.S.A.* 152 E7 30 15N 82 54W
Houston, *Mo., U.S.A.* 155 G9 37 22N 91 58W
Houston, *Tex., U.S.A.* 155 L7 29 46N 95 22W
Hout →, *S. Africa* 117 C4 23 4 S 29 36 E
Houtkraal, *S. Africa* 116 E3 30 23 S 24 5 E
Houtman Abrolhos, *Australia* 125 E1 28 43 S 113 48 E
Hov, *Norway* 18 D7 60 42N 10 20 E
Hovd, *Mongolia* 68 B4 48 2N 91 37 E
Hovda, *Norway* 18 D6 60 53N 9 11 E
Hovden, *Aust-Agder, Norway* 18 E4 59 33N 7 22 E
Hovden, *Sogn og Fjordane, Norway* 18 C1 61 41N 4 52 E
Hove, *U.K.* 21 G7 50 50N 0 10W
Hovet, *Norway* 18 D5 60 38N 8 8 E
Hoveyzeh, *Iran* 97 D6 31 27N 48 4 E
Hovgaard Ø, *Greenland* 10 B9 79 55N 18 50W
Hovin, *Norway* 18 E6 59 51N 9 0 E
Hovmantorp, *Sweden* 17 H9 56 47N 15 7 E
Hövsgöl, *Mongolia* 74 C5 43 37N 109 39 E
Hövsgöl Nuur, *Mongolia* 68 A5 51 0N 100 30 E
Hovsta, *Sweden* 16 E9 59 22N 15 15 E
Howakil, *Eritrea* 107 D5 15 10N 40 16 E
Howar, Wadi →, *Sudan* 107 D2 17 30N 27 8 E
Howard, *Australia* 127 D5 25 16 S 152 32 E
Howard, *Pa., U.S.A.* 150 F7 41 1N 77 40W
Howard, *S. Dak., U.S.A.* 154 C6 44 1N 97 32W
Howe, *U.S.A.* 158 E7 43 48N 113 0W
Howe, C., *Australia* 129 D9 37 30 S 150 0 E
Howe I., *Canada* 151 B8 44 16N 76 17W
Howell, *U.S.A.* 157 B13 42 36N 83 56W
Howick, *Canada* 151 A11 45 11N 73 51W
Howick, *N.Z.* 130 C3 36 54 S 174 56 E
Howick, *S. Africa* 117 D5 29 28 S 30 14 E
Howick Group, *Australia* 126 A4 14 20 S 145 30 E
Howitt, L., *Australia* 127 D2 27 40 S 138 40 E
Howland I., *Pac. Oc.* 134 G10 0 48N 176 38W
Howlong, *Australia* 129 C7 35 59 S 146 38 E
Howrah = Haora, *India* 93 H13 22 37N 88 20 E
Howth Hd., *Ireland* 23 C5 53 22N 6 3W
Höxter, *Germany* 30 D5 51 46N 9 22 E
Hoy, *U.K.* 22 C5 58 50N 3 15W
Hoya, *Germany* 30 C5 52 49N 9 8 E
Høyanger, *Norway* 15 F12 61 13N 6 4 E
Hoyerswerda, *Germany* 30 D10 51 26N 14 14 E
Hoylake, *U.K.* 20 D4 53 24N 3 10W
Hōyo-Kaikyō, *Japan* 72 D3 33 20N 131 58 E
Hoyos, *Spain* 42 E4 40 9N 6 45W
Hpa-an = Pa-an, *Burma* 90 G6 16 51N 97 40 E
Hpawlum, *Burma* 90 B7 27 12N 98 12 E
Hpettintha, *Burma* 90 C5 24 14N 95 23 E
Hpizow, *Burma* 90 B7 26 57N 98 24 E
Hpunan Pass, *India* 90 A6 28 9N 97 20 E
Hradec Králové, *Czech Rep.* 34 A8 50 15N 15 50 E
Hrádek, *Czech Rep.* 35 C9 48 46N 16 16 E
Hrafnseyri, *Iceland* 11 B3 65 46N 23 28W
Hranice, *Czech Rep.* 35 B10 49 34N 17 45 E
Hrazdan, *Armenia* 61 K7 40 30N 44 46 E
Hrebenka, *Ukraine* 59 G7 50 9N 32 22 E
Hrífunes, *Iceland* 11 D8 63 38N 18 30W
Hrísey, *Iceland* 11 B8 66 0N 18 23W
Hrodna, *Belarus* 58 F2 53 42N 23 52 E
Hrodzyanka, *Belarus* 58 F5 53 31N 28 42 E
Hron →, *Slovak Rep.* 35 D11 47 49N 18 45 E
Hrubieszów, *Poland* 55 H10 50 49N 23 51 E
Hrubý Jeseník, *Czech Rep.* 35 A10 50 5N 17 10 E
Hrvatska = Croatia ■, *Europe* 45 C13 45 20N 16 0 E
Hrymayliv, *Ukraine* 59 H4 49 20N 26 5 E
Hsa-paw, *Burma* 90 F6 19 1N 97 30 E
Hsenwi, *Burma* 90 D6 23 22N 97 55 E
Hsi-hkip, *Burma* 90 E6 20 25N 96 42 E
Hsiamen = Xiamen, *China* 77 E12 24 25N 118 4 E
Hsian = Xi'an, *China* 74 G5 34 15N 109 0 E
Hsinchu, *Taiwan* 77 E13 24 48N 120 58 E
Hsinhailien = Lianyungang, *China* 75 G10 34 40N 119 11 E
Hsinying, *Taiwan* 77 F13 23 18N 120 19 E
Hsipaw, *Burma* 90 D6 22 37N 97 18 E
Hsopket, *Burma* 76 F2 23 11N 98 26 E
Hsüchou = Xuzhou, *China* 75 G9 34 18N 117 10 E
Htawgaw, *Burma* 90 C7 25 57N 98 23 E
Hu Xian, *China* 74 G5 34 8N 108 42 E
Hua Hin, *Thailand* 86 F2 12 34N 99 58 E
Hua Xian, *Henan, China* 74 G8 35 30N 114 30 E
Hua Xian, *Shaanxi, China* 74 G5 34 30N 109 48 E
Hua'an, *China* 77 E11 25 1N 117 32 E
Huab →, *Namibia* 116 B2 20 52 S 13 25 E
Huacaya, *Bolivia* 173 E5 20 45 S 63 43W
Huachacalla, *Bolivia* 172 D4 18 45 S 68 17W
Huacheng, *China* 77 E10 24 4N 115 37 E
Huachinera, *Mexico* 162 A3 30 9N 108 55W
Huacho, *Peru* 172 C2 11 10 S 77 35W
Huachón, *Peru* 172 C2 10 35 S 76 0W
Huade, *China* 74 D7 41 55N 113 59 E
Huadian, *China* 75 C14 43 0N 126 40 E
Huadu, *China* 77 F9 23 22N 113 12 E
Huai He →, *China* 77 A12 33 0N 118 30 E
Huai Yot, *Thailand* 87 J2 7 45N 99 37 E
Huai'an, *Hebei, China* 74 D8 40 30N 114 20 E
Huai'an, *Jiangsu, China* 75 H10 33 30N 119 10 E
Huaibei, *China* 74 G9 34 0N 116 48 E
Huaibin, *China* 77 A10 32 32N 115 27 E
Huaide = Gongzhuling, *China* 75 C13 43 30N 124 40 E
Huaidezhen, *China* 75 C13 43 48N 124 50 E
Huaihua, *China* 76 D7 27 32N 109 57 E
Huaiji, *China* 77 F9 23 55N 112 12 E
Huainan, *China* 77 A11 32 38N 116 58 E
Huaining, *China* 77 B11 30 24N 116 40 E
Huairen, *China* 74 E7 39 48N 113 20 E
Huairou, *China* 74 D9 40 20N 116 35 E
Huaiyang, *China* 74 H8 33 40N 114 52 E
Huaiyin, *China* 75 H10 33 30N 119 2 E
Huaiyuan, *Anhui, China* 75 H9 32 55N 117 10 E
Huaiyuan, *Guangxi Zhuangzu, China* 76 E7 24 31N 108 22 E
Huajianzi, *China* 75 D13 41 23N 125 20 E
Huajuapan de Leon, *Mexico* 163 D5 17 50N 97 48W
Hualalai, *U.S.A.* 145 D6 19 42N 155 52W
Hualapai Peak, *U.S.A.* 159 J7 35 5N 113 54W
Hualien, *Taiwan* 77 E13 24 0N 121 30 E
Huallaga →, *Peru* 172 B2 5 15 S 75 30W
Huallanca, *Peru* 172 B2 8 50 S 77 56W
Huamachuco, *Peru* 172 B2 7 50 S 78 5W
Huambo, *Angola* 115 E3 12 42 S 15 54 E
Huambo □, *Angola* 115 E3 13 0 S 16 0 E
Huan Jiang →, *China* 74 G5 34 28N 109 0 E
Huan Xian, *China* 74 F4 36 33N 107 7 E
Huancabamba, *Peru* 172 B2 5 10 S 79 15W
Huancane, *Peru* 172 D4 15 10 S 69 44W
Huancapi, *Peru* 172 C3 13 40 S 74 0W
Huancavelica, *Peru* 172 C2 12 50 S 75 5W
Huancavelica □, *Peru* 172 C3 13 0 S 75 0W
Huancayo, *Peru* 172 C2 12 5 S 75 12W
Huanchaca, *Bolivia* 172 E4 20 15 S 66 40W
Huanchaca, Serranía de, *Bolivia* 173 C5 14 30 S 60 39W
Huang Hai = Yellow Sea, *China* 75 G12 35 0N 123 0 E
Huang He →, *China* 75 F10 37 55N 118 50 E
Huang Xian, *China* 75 F11 37 38N 120 30 E
Huangchuan, *China* 77 A10 32 15N 115 10 E
Huanggang, *China* 77 B10 30 29N 114 52 E
Huangguoshu, *China* 76 E5 26 0N 105 40 E
Huangling, *China* 74 G5 35 34N 109 15 E
Huanglong, *China* 74 G5 35 30N 109 59 E
Huanglongtan, *China* 77 A8 32 40N 110 33 E
Huangmei, *China* 77 B10 30 5N 115 56 E
Huangpi, *China* 77 B10 30 50N 114 22 E
Huangping, *China* 76 D6 26 52N 107 54 E
Huangshan, *China* 77 C12 29 42N 118 25 E
Huangshi, *China* 77 B10 30 10N 115 3 E

Huangsongdian, *China* **75 C14** 43 45N 127 25 E
Huangyan, *China* **77 C13** 28 38N 121 19 E
Huangyangsi, *China* **77 D8** 26 33N 111 39 E
Huaning, *China* **76 E4** 24 17N 102 56 E
Huanjiang, *China* **76 E7** 24 50N 108 18 E
Huanta, *Peru* **172 C3** 12 55 S 74 20W
Huantai, *China* **75 F9** 36 58N 117 56 E
Huánuco, *Peru* **172 B2** 9 55 S 76 15W
Huánuco □, *Peru* **172 B2** 9 55 S 76 14W
Huanuni, *Bolivia* **172 D4** 18 16 S 66 51W
Huanzo, Cordillera de, *Peru* **172 C3** 14 35 S 73 20W
Huaping, *China* **76 D3** 26 46N 101 25 E
Huara, *Chile* **172 D4** 19 59 S 69 47W
Huaral, *Peru* **172 C2** 11 32 S 77 13W
Huaraz, *Peru* **172 B2** 9 30 S 77 32W
Huari, *Peru* **172 B2** 9 14 S 77 14W
Huarmey, *Peru* **172 C2** 10 5 S 78 5W
Huarochirí, *Peru* **172 C2** 12 9 S 76 15W
Huarocondo, *Peru* **172 C3** 13 26 S 72 14W
Huarong, *China* **77 C9** 29 29N 112 30 E
Huascarán, *Peru* **172 B2** 9 8 S 77 36W
Huascarán, Nevado, *Peru* **172 B2** 9 7 S 77 37W
Huasco, *Chile* **174 B1** 28 30 S 71 15W
Huasco ~, *Chile* **174 B1** 28 27 S 71 13W
Huasna, *U.S.A.* **161 K6** 35 6N 120 24W
Huatabampo, *Mexico* **162 B3** 26 50N 109 50W
Huauchinango, *Mexico* **163 C5** 20 11N 98 3W
Huautla de Jiménez, *Mexico* **163 D5** 18 8N 96 51W
Huaxi, *China* **76 D6** 26 25N 106 40 E
Huay Namota, *Mexico* **162 C4** 21 56N 104 30W
Huayin, *China* **74 G6** 34 35N 110 5 E
Huayllay, *Peru* **172 C2** 11 3 S 76 21W
Huayuan, *China* **76 C7** 28 37N 109 29 E
Huayun, *China* **76 B6** 30 14N 106 40 E
Huazhou, *China* **77 G8** 21 33N 110 33 E
Hubbard, *Iowa, U.S.A.* **156 B3** 42 18N 93 18W
Hubbard, *Ohio, U.S.A.* **150 E4** 41 9N 80 34W
Hubbard, *Tex., U.S.A.* **155 K6** 31 51N 96 48W
Hubbart Pt., *Canada* **143 B10** 59 21N 94 41W
Hubei □, *China* **77 B9** 31 0N 112 0 E
Hubli, *India* **95 G2** 15 22N 75 15 E
Huch'ang, *N. Korea* **75 D14** 41 25N 127 2 E
Hucknall, *U.K.* **20 D6** 53 3N 1 13W
Huddersfield, *U.K.* **20 D6** 53 39N 1 47W
Hude, *Germany* **30 B4** 53 7N 8 26 E
Hudi, *Sudan* **106 D3** 17 43N 34 18 E
Hudiksvall, *Sweden* **16 C11** 61 43N 17 10 E
Hudson, *Canada* **140 B1** 50 6N 92 9W
Hudson, *Fla., U.S.A.* **153 G7** 28 22N 82 42W
Hudson, *Mass., U.S.A.* **151 D13** 42 23N 71 34W
Hudson, *Mich., U.S.A.* **157 C12** 41 51N 84 21W
Hudson, *N.Y., U.S.A.* **151 D11** 42 15N 73 46W
Hudson, *Wis., U.S.A.* **154 C8** 44 58N 92 45W
Hudson, *Wyo., U.S.A.* **158 E9** 42 54N 108 35W
Hudson ~, *U.S.A.* **151 F10** 40 42N 74 2W
Hudson Bay, *Nunavut, Canada* **139 C11** 60 0N 86 0W
Hudson Bay, *Sask., Canada* **143 C8** 52 51N 102 23W
Hudson Falls, *U.S.A.* **151 C11** 43 18N 73 35W
Hudson Mts., *Antarctica* **7 D16** 74 32 S 99 20W
Hudson Str., *Canada* **139 B13** 62 0N 70 0W
Hudson's Hope, *Canada* **142 B4** 56 0N 121 54W
Hudsonville, *U.S.A.* **157 B11** 42 52N 85 52W
Hue, *Vietnam* **86 D6** 16 30N 107 35 E
Huebra ~, *Spain* **42 D4** 41 2N 6 48W
Huechucuicui, Pta., *Chile* **176 B2** 41 48 S 74 2W
Huedin, *Romania* **52 D8** 46 52N 23 2 E
Huehuetenango, *Guatemala* **164 C1** 15 20N 91 28W
Huejúcar, *Mexico* **162 C4** 22 21N 103 13W
Huélamo, *Spain* **40 E3** 40 17N 1 48W
Huelgoat, *France* **26 D3** 48 22N 3 46W
Huelma, *Spain* **43 H7** 37 39N 3 28W
Huelva, *Spain* **43 H4** 37 18N 6 57W
Huelva □, *Spain* **43 H4** 37 40N 7 0W
Huelva ~, *Spain* **43 H5** 37 27N 6 0W
Huentelauquén, *Chile* **174 C1** 31 38 S 71 33W
Huércal-Overa, *Spain* **41 H3** 37 23N 1 57W
Huerta, Sa. de la, *Argentina* **174 C2** 31 10 S 67 30W
Huertas, C. de las, *Spain* **41 G4** 38 21N 0 24W
Huerva ~, *Spain* **40 D4** 41 39N 0 52W
Huesca, *Spain* **40 C4** 42 8N 0 25W
Huesca □, *Spain* **40 C5** 42 20N 0 1 E
Huéscar, *Spain* **41 H2** 37 44N 2 35W
Huetamo, *Mexico* **162 D4** 18 36N 100 54W
Huete, *Spain* **40 E2** 40 10N 2 43W
Huger, *U.S.A.* **152 B10** 33 6N 79 48W
Hugh ~, *Australia* **126 D1** 25 1 S 134 1 E
Hughenden, *Australia* **126 C3** 20 52 S 144 10 E
Hughes, *Australia* **125 F4** 30 42 S 129 31 E
Hughes, *U.S.A.* **144 C9** 66 3N 154 15W
Hughesville, *U.S.A.* **151 E8** 41 14N 76 44W
Hugli ~, *India* **93 J13** 21 56N 88 4 E
Hugo, *Colo., U.S.A.* **154 F3** 39 8N 103 28W
Hugo, *Okla., U.S.A.* **155 H7** 34 1N 95 31W
Hugoton, *U.S.A.* **155 G4** 37 11N 101 21W
Hui Xian = Huixian, *China* **74 G7** 35 27N 113 12 E
Hui Xian, *China* **74 H4** 33 50N 106 4 E
Hui'an, *China* **77 E12** 25 1N 118 43 E
Hui'anbu, *China* **74 F4** 37 28N 106 38 E
Huiarau Ra., *N.Z.* **130 E5** 38 45 S 176 55 E
Huichang, *China* **77 E10** 25 32N 115 45 E
Huichapán, *Mexico* **163 C5** 20 24N 99 40W
Huidong, *Guangdong, China* **77 F10** 22 58N 114 43 E
Huidong, *Sichuan, China* **76 D4** 26 34N 102 35 E
Huifa He ~, *China* **75 C14** 43 0N 127 50 E
Huíla, *Angola* **115 F2** 15 4 S 13 32 E
Huíla □, *Angola* **115 E2** 14 0 S 15 0 E
Huila □, *Colombia* **168 C2** 2 30N 75 45W
Huila, Nevado del, *Colombia* **168 C2** 3 0N 76 0W
Huilai, *China* **77 F11** 23 0N 116 18 E
Huili, *China* **76 D4** 26 35N 102 17 E
Huimin, *China* **75 F9** 37 27N 117 28 E
Huinan, *China* **75 C14** 42 40N 126 2 E
Huinca Renancó, *Argentina* **174 C3** 34 51 S 64 22W
Huining, *China* **74 G3** 35 38N 105 0 E
Huinong, *China* **74 E4** 39 5N 106 35 E
Huiroa, *N.Z.* **130 F3** 39 15 S 174 30 E
Huisache, *Mexico* **162 C4** 22 55N 100 25W
Huishui, *China* **76 D6** 26 7N 106 38 E
Huisne ~, *France* **26 E7** 47 59N 0 11 E
Huiting, *China* **74 G9** 34 5N 116 5 E
Huitong, *China* **76 D7** 26 51N 109 45 E
Huixian, *China* **74 G7** 35 27N 113 12 E
Huixtla, *Mexico* **163 D6** 15 9N 92 28W
Huize, *China* **76 D4** 26 24N 103 15 E
Huizhou, *China* **77 F10** 23 0N 114 23 E
Hukeri, *India* **95 F2** 16 14N 74 36 E
Hukou, *China* **77 C11** 29 45N 116 21 E
Hŭksan-chedo, *S. Korea* **75 G13** 34 40N 125 30 E
Hukuntsi, *Botswana* **116 C3** 23 58 S 21 45 E
Hula, *Papua N. G.* **132 F4** 10 5 S 147 43 E
Ḥulayfā', *Si. Arabia* **96 E4** 25 58N 40 45 E
Huld = Ulaanjirem, *Mongolia* **74 B3** 45 5N 105 30 E
Hulin He ~, *China* **75 B12** 45 0N 122 10 E
Hull = Kingston upon Hull, *U.K.* **20 D7** 53 45N 0 21W
Hull, *Canada* **140 C4** 45 25N 75 44W
Hull ~, *U.K.* **20 D7** 53 44N 0 20W
Hulst, *Neths.* **24 C4** 51 17N 4 2 E
Hultsfred, *Sweden* **17 G9** 57 30N 15 52 E
Hulun Nur, *China* **69 B6** 49 0N 117 30 E
Hulyaypole, *Ukraine* **59 J9** 47 45N 36 21 E
Huma, Tanjung, *Malaysia* **87 c** 5 29N 100 16 E
Humacao, *Puerto Rico* **165 d** 18 9N 65 50W
Humahuaca, *Argentina* **174 A2** 23 10 S 65 25W
Humaitá, *Brazil* **173 B5** 7 35 S 63 1W
Humaitá, *Paraguay* **174 B4** 27 2 S 58 31W
Humansdorp, *S. Africa* **116 E3** 34 2 S 24 46 E
Humansville, *U.S.A.* **156 G3** 37 48N 93 35W
Humara, J., *Sudan* **107 D3** 16 16N 30 59 E
Humbe, *Angola* **116 B1** 16 40 S 14 55 E
Humber ~, *U.K.* **20 D7** 53 42N 0 27W
Humboldt, *Canada* **143 C7** 52 15N 105 9W
Humboldt, *Iowa, U.S.A.* **156 B2** 42 44N 94 13W
Humboldt, *Tenn., U.S.A.* **155 H10** 35 50N 88 55W
Humboldt ~, *U.S.A.* **158 F4** 39 59N 118 36W
Humboldt, Massif du, *N. Cal.* **133 U20** 21 53 S 166 25 E
Humboldt Gletscher, *Greenland* **10 B4** 79 30N 62 0W
Humboldt Mts., *N.Z.* **131 E3** 44 30 S 168 15 E
Hume, *U.S.A.* **160 J8** 36 48N 118 54W
Hume, L., *Australia* **129 D7** 36 0 S 147 5 E
Humen, *China* **69 F10** 22 50N 113 40 E
Humenné, *Slovak Rep.* **35 C14** 48 55N 21 50 E
Humeston, *U.S.A.* **156 D3** 40 52N 93 30W
Hummelsta, *Sweden* **16 E10** 59 34N 16 58 E
Hummelvik, *Norway* **18 A5** 63 29N 8 19 E
Humpata, *Angola* **115 F2** 15 2 S 13 24 E
Humphreys, Mt., *U.S.A.* **160 H8** 37 17N 118 40W
Humphreys Peak, *U.S.A.* **159 J8** 35 21N 111 41W
Humpolec, *Czech Rep.* **34 B8** 49 31N 15 20 E
Humptulips, *U.S.A.* **160 C3** 47 14N 123 57W
Humula, *Australia* **129 C7** 35 30 S 147 46 E
Hūn, *Libya* **108 C3** 29 2N 16 0 E
Hun Jiang ~, *China* **75 D13** 40 50N 125 38 E
Húnaflói, *Iceland* **11 B6** 65 50N 20 50W
Hunan □, *China* **77 D9** 27 30N 112 0 E
Húnavatnssýsla □, *Iceland* **11 B6** 65 30N 20 25W
Hunchun, *China* **75 C16** 42 52N 130 28 E
Hundested, *Denmark* **17 J5** 55 58N 11 52 E
Hundewali, *Pakistan* **92 D5** 31 55N 72 38 E
Hundorp, *Norway* **18 C7** 61 33N 9 59 E
Hundred Mile House, *Canada* **142 C4** 51 38N 121 18W
Hundvåg, *Norway* **18 E2** 59 0N 5 43 E
Hunedoara, *Romania* **52 E7** 45 40N 22 50 E
Hunedoara □, *Romania* **52 E7** 45 50N 22 54 E
Hünfeld, *Germany* **30 E5** 50 39N 9 46 E
Hung Yen, *Vietnam* **76 G6** 20 39N 106 4 E
Hunga Ha'apai, *Tonga* **133 Q13** 20 41 S 175 7W
Hungary ■, *Europe* **35 D12** 47 20N 19 20 E
Hungary, Plain of, *Europe* **12 F10** 47 0N 20 0 E
Hungerford, *Australia* **127 D3** 28 58 S 144 24 E
Hŭngnam, *N. Korea* **75 E14** 39 49N 127 45 E
Hungt'ou Hsü, *Taiwan* **77 G13** 22 0N 121 30 E
Hungund, *India* **95 F3** 16 4N 76 3 E
Huni Valley, *Ghana* **112 D4** 5 33N 1 56W
Hunneberg, *Sweden* **17 F6** 58 18N 12 30 E
Hunnebostrand, *Sweden* **17 F5** 58 27N 11 18 E
Hunsberge, *Namibia* **116 D2** 27 45 S 17 12 E
Hunsrück, *Germany* **31 F3** 49 56N 7 27 E
Hunstanton, *U.K.* **20 E8** 52 56N 0 29 E
Hunsur, *India* **95 H3** 12 16N 76 16 E
Hunte ~, *Germany* **30 B4** 53 14N 8 28 E
Hunter, *N.Z.* **131 E6** 44 36 S 171 2 E
Hunter, *U.S.A.* **151 D10** 42 13N 74 13W
Hunter ~, *Australia* **129 B9** 32 52 S 151 46 E
Hunter ~, *N.Z.* **131 E4** 44 21 S 169 27 E
Hunter, C., *Solomon Is.* **133 M10** 9 48 S 159 50 E
Hunter I., *Australia* **127 G3** 40 30 S 144 45 E
Hunter I., *Canada* **142 C3** 51 55N 128 0W
Hunter Mts., *N.Z.* **131 F2** 45 43 S 167 25 E
Hunter Ra., *Australia* **129 B9** 32 45 S 150 15 E
Hunters Road, *Zimbabwe* **119 F2** 19 9 S 29 49 E
Hunterville, *N.Z.* **130 F4** 39 56 S 175 35 E
Huntingburg, *U.S.A.* **157 F10** 38 18N 86 57W
Huntingdon, *Canada* **140 C5** 45 6N 74 10W
Huntingdon, *U.K.* **21 E7** 52 20N 0 11W
Huntingdon, *U.S.A.* **150 F6** 40 30N 78 1W
Huntington, *Ind., U.S.A.* **157 D11** 40 53N 85 30W
Huntington, *Oreg., U.S.A.* **158 D5** 44 21N 117 16W
Huntington, *Utah, U.S.A.* **158 G8** 39 20N 110 58W
Huntington, *W. Va., U.S.A.* **148 F4** 38 25N 82 27W
Huntington Beach, *U.S.A.* **161 M9** 33 40N 118 5W
Huntington Station, *U.S.A.* **151 F11** 40 52N 73 26W
Huntley, *U.S.A.* **157 B8** 42 10N 88 26W
Huntly, *N.Z.* **130 D4** 37 34 S 175 11 E
Huntly, *U.K.* **22 D6** 57 27N 2 47W
Huntsville, *Canada* **140 C4** 45 20N 79 14W
Huntsville, *Ala., U.S.A.* **149 H2** 34 44N 86 35W
Huntsville, *Mo., U.S.A.* **156 E4** 39 26N 92 33W
Huntsville, *Tex., U.S.A.* **155 K7** 30 43N 95 33W
Hunyani ~, *Zimbabwe* **119 F3** 15 57 S 30 39 E
Hunyuan, *China* **74 E7** 39 42N 113 42 E
Hunza ~, *India* **93 B6** 35 54N 74 20 E
Huo Xian = Huozhou, *China* **74 F6** 36 36N 111 42 E
Huon G., *Papua N. G.* **132 D4** 7 0 S 147 30 E
Huon Pen., *Papua N. G.* **132 D4** 6 20 S 147 30 E
Huong Hoa, *Vietnam* **86 D6** 16 37N 106 45 E
Huong Khe, *Vietnam* **86 C5** 18 13N 105 41 E
Huonville, *Australia* **127 G4** 43 0 S 147 5 E
Huoqiu, *China* **77 A11** 32 20N 116 12 E
Huoshan, *Anhui, China* **77 A12** 32 28N 118 30 E
Huoshan, *Anhui, China* **77 B11** 31 25N 116 20 E
Huoshao Dao = Lü-Tao, *Taiwan* **77 F13** 22 40N 121 30 E
Huozhou, *China* **74 F6** 36 36N 111 42 E
Hupeh = Hubei □, *China* **77 B9** 31 0N 112 0 E
Ḥūr, *Iran* **97 D8** 30 50N 57 7 E
Hurbanovo, *Slovak Rep.* **35 D11** 47 51N 18 11 E
Hurd, C., *Canada* **150 A3** 45 13N 81 44W
Hure Qi, *China* **75 C11** 42 45N 121 45 E
Hurezani, *Romania* **53 F8** 44 49N 23 40 E
Hurghada, *Egypt* **106 B3** 27 15N 33 50 E
Hurley, *N. Mex., U.S.A.* **159 K9** 32 42N 108 8W
Hurley, *Wis., U.S.A.* **154 B9** 46 27N 90 11W
Huron, *Calif., U.S.A.* **160 J6** 36 12N 120 6W
Huron, *Ohio, U.S.A.* **150 E2** 41 24N 82 33W
Huron, *S. Dak., U.S.A.* **154 C5** 44 22N 98 13W
Huron, L., *U.S.A.* **150 B2** 44 30N 82 40W
Hurricane, *U.S.A.* **159 H7** 37 11N 113 17W
Hurso, *Ethiopia* **107 F5** 9 35N 41 33 E
Hurstbridge, *Australia* **129 D6** 37 40 S 145 12 E
Hurunui ~, *N.Z.* **131 C8** 42 54 S 173 18 E
Hurup, *Denmark* **17 H2** 56 46N 8 25 E
Húsafell, *Iceland* **11 C6** 64 42N 20 53W
Húsavík, *Iceland* **11 A9** 66 3N 17 21W
Huşi, *Romania* **53 D13** 46 41N 28 7 E
Huskisson, *Australia* **129 C9** 35 2 S 150 41 E
Huskvarna, *Sweden* **17 G8** 57 47N 14 15 E
Huslia, *U.S.A.* **144 D8** 65 41N 156 24W
Husnes, *Norway* **18 E2** 59 52N 5 46 E
Hustad, *Norway* **18 B4** 62 57N 7 6 E
Hustadvika, *Norway* **14 E12** 63 0N 7 0 E
Hustontown, *U.S.A.* **150 F6** 40 3N 78 2W
Hustopeče, *Czech Rep.* **35 C9** 48 57N 16 43 E
Husum, *Germany* **30 A5** 54 28N 9 4 E
Husum, *Sweden* **16 A13** 63 21N 19 12 E
Hutchinson, *Kans., U.S.A.* **155 F6** 38 5N 97 56W
Hutchinson, *Minn., U.S.A.* **154 C7** 44 54N 94 22W
Ḥūth, *Yemen* **98 C3** 16 14N 43 58 E
Hutjena, *Papua N. G.* **132 C8** 5 23 S 154 42 E
Hutsonville, *U.S.A.* **157 E9** 39 7N 87 40W
Hutte Sauvage, L. de la, *Canada* **141 A7** 56 15N 64 45W
Hüttenberg, *Austria* **34 E7** 46 56N 14 33 E
Hutton, Mt., *Australia* **127 D4** 25 51 S 148 20 E
Huttwil, *Switz.* **32 B5** 47 7N 7 50 E
Huwun, *Ethiopia* **107 G5** 4 23N 40 6 E
Huy, *Belgium* **24 D5** 50 31N 5 15 E
Huzhou, *China* **77 B13** 30 51N 120 8 E
Huzurabad, *India* **94 E4** 18 12N 79 25 E
Huzurnagar, *India* **94 F4** 16 54N 79 53 E
Hvalpsund, *Denmark* **17 H3** 56 42N 9 11 E
Hvammsfjörður, *Iceland* **11 B4** 65 4N 22 5W
Hvammstangi, *Iceland* **11 B6** 65 24N 20 57W
Hvammur, *Mýrasýsla, Iceland* **11 C5** 64 50N 21 21W
Hvammur, *Skagafjarðarsýsla, Iceland* **11 B7** 65 53N 19 51W
Hvannadalshnúkur, *Iceland* **11 C10** 64 1N 16 41W
Hvanneyri, *Iceland* **11 C5** 64 34N 21 36W
Hvar, *Croatia* **45 E13** 43 11N 16 28 E
Hvarski Kanal, *Croatia* **45 E13** 43 15N 16 35 E
Hveragerði, *Iceland* **11 C5** 64 0N 21 12W
Hvítá ~, *Iceland* **11 C5** 64 30N 21 58W
Hvítárvatn, *Iceland* **11 C7** 64 37N 19 50W
Hvittingfoss, *Norway* **18 E7** 59 29N 10 0 E
Hvolsvöllur, *Iceland* **11 D6** 63 45N 20 14W
Hwachŏn-chŏsuji, *S. Korea* **75 E14** 38 5N 127 50 E
Hwang Ho = Huang He ~, *China* **75 F10** 37 55N 118 50 E
Hwange, *Zimbabwe* **119 F2** 18 18 S 26 30 E
Hwange Nat. Park, *Zimbabwe* **116 B4** 19 0 S 26 30 E
Hwekum, *Burma* **90 B5** 26 7N 95 22 E
Hyaing, *Burma* **90 D5** 22 39N 94 44 E
Hyannis, *Mass., U.S.A.* **148 E10** 41 39N 70 17W
Hyannis, *Nebr., U.S.A.* **154 E4** 42 0N 101 46W
Hyargas Nuur, *Mongolia* **68 B4** 49 0N 93 0 E
Hybo, *Sweden* **16 C10** 61 49N 16 15 E
Hydaburg, *U.S.A.* **142 B2** 55 15N 132 50W
Hyde, *N.Z.* **131 F5** 45 18 S 170 16 E
Hyde Park, *Guyana* **169 B6** 6 30N 58 16W
Hyde Park, *U.S.A.* **151 E11** 41 47N 73 56W
Hyden, *Australia* **125 F2** 32 24 S 118 53 E
Hyder, *U.S.A.* **142 B2** 55 55N 130 5W
Hyderabad, *India* **94 F4** 17 22N 78 29 E
Hyderabad, *Pakistan* **91 D3** 25 23N 68 24 E
Hyen, *Norway* **18 C2** 61 44N 5 56 E
Hyères, *France* **29 E10** 43 8N 6 9 E
Hyères, Îs. d', *France* **29 F10** 43 0N 6 20 E
Hyesan, *N. Korea* **75 D15** 41 20N 128 10 E
Hyland ~, *Canada* **142 B3** 59 52N 128 12W
Hyllestad, *Norway* **18 E4** 59 6N 7 29 E
Hyllestad, *Norway* **18 C2** 61 10N 5 17 E
Hyltebruk, *Sweden* **17 H7** 56 59N 13 15 E
Hymia, *India* **93 C8** 33 40N 78 2 E
Hyndman Peak, *U.S.A.* **158 E6** 43 45N 114 8W
Hynnekleiv, *Norway* **18 F5** 58 36N 8 25 E
Hyōgo □, *Japan* **72 B6** 35 15N 134 50 E
Hyrra Banda, *C.A.R.* **114 A4** 5 58N 22 1 E
Hyrum, *U.S.A.* **158 F8** 41 38N 111 51W
Hysham, *U.S.A.* **158 C10** 46 18N 107 14W
Hythe, *U.K.* **21 F9** 51 4N 1 5 E
Hyūga, *Japan* **72 E3** 32 25N 131 35 E
Hyvinge = Hyvinkää, *Finland* **15 F21** 60 38N 24 50 E
Hyvinkää, *Finland* **15 F21** 60 38N 24 50 E

I

I-n-Azaoua, *Illizi, Algeria* **111 C6** 25 42N 6 54 E
I-n-Azaoua, *Tamanrasset, Algeria* **111 D6** 20 46N 7 32 E
I-n-Échaï, *Mali* **110 D4** 20 10N 2 5W
I-n-Gall, *Niger* **113 B6** 16 51N 7 1 E
I-n-Kelemet, *Algeria* **111 C6** 26 57N 5 47 E
I-n-Oudad, *Algeria* **111 D5** 20 17N 4 38 E
I-n-Ouzzal, *Algeria* **113 A5** 20 40N 2 35 E
I-n-Quzzal, *Algeria* **111 D5** 20 41N 2 34 E
I-n-Tadreft, *Niger* **113 B6** 19 5N 6 38 E
Iabès, Erg, *Algeria* **111 C4** 27 30N 2 2W
Iablanița, *Romania* **52 F7** 44 57N 22 19 E
Iaco ~, *Brazil* **172 B4** 9 3 S 68 34W
Iacobeni, *Romania* **53 C10** 47 25N 25 20 E
Iaçu, *Brazil* **171 D3** 12 45 S 40 13W
Iakora, *Madag.* **117 C8** 23 6 S 46 40 E
Ialibu, *Papua N. G.* **132 D2** 6 17 S 143 59 E
Ialomița □, *Romania* **53 F12** 44 30N 27 30 E
Ialomița ~, *Romania* **53 F12** 44 42N 27 51 E
Ialoveni, *Moldova* **53 D13** 46 56N 28 47 E
Ialpug ~, *Moldova* **53 E13** 45 41N 28 35 E
Iamonia L., *U.S.A.* **152 E5** 30 38N 84 14W
Ianca, *Romania* **53 E12** 45 6N 27 29 E
Iara, *Romania* **53 D8** 46 31N 23 35 E
Iarda, *Ethiopia* **107 E4** 11 9N 35 53 E
Iargara, *Moldova* **53 D13** 46 24N 28 23 E
Iași, *Romania* **53 C12** 47 10N 27 40 E
Iași □, *Romania* **53 C12** 47 20N 27 0 E
Íasmos, *Greece* **51 E9** 41 8N 25 11 E
Iauaretê, *Colombia* **168 C4** 0 36N 69 12W
Ib ~, *India* **93 J10** 21 34N 83 48 E
Iba, *Phil.* **80 D2** 15 22N 120 0 E
Ibadan, *Nigeria* **113 D5** 7 22N 3 58 E
Ibagué, *Colombia* **168 C2** 4 20N 75 20W
Ibaiti, *Brazil* **171 F1** 23 50 S 50 10W
Ibajay, *Phil.* **81 F4** 11 49N 122 10 E
Iballë, *Albania* **50 D4** 42 12N 20 2 E
Ibănești, *Botoșani, Romania* **53 B11** 48 4N 26 22 E
Ibănești, *Mureș, Romania* **53 D9** 46 45N 24 57 E
Ibanshe, *Dem. Rep. of the Congo* **115 C4** 4 58 S 21 30 E
Ibar ~, *Serbia, Yug.* **50 C4** 43 43N 20 45 E
Ibara, *Japan* **72 C5** 34 36N 133 28 E
Ibaraki, *Japan* **73 C7** 34 49N 135 34 E
Ibaraki □, *Japan* **73 A12** 36 10N 140 10 E
Ibarra, *Ecuador* **168 C2** 0 21N 78 7W
Ibb, *Yemen* **98 D4** 14 2N 44 10 E
Ibba, *Sudan* **107 G2** 4 49N 29 2 E
Ibba, Bahr el ~, *Sudan* **107 F2** 5 30N 28 55 E
Ibbenbüren, *Germany* **30 C3** 52 16N 7 43 E
Ibeke Gembo, *Dem. Rep. of the Congo* **114 C3** 1 24 S 18 51 E
Ibembo, *Dem. Rep. of the Congo* **118 B1** 2 35N 23 35 E
Ibenga ~, *Congo* **114 B3** 2 19N 18 9 E
Ibera, L., *Argentina* **174 B4** 28 30 S 57 9W
Iberia, *U.S.A.* **156 F4** 38 5N 92 18W
Iberian Peninsula, *Europe* **12 H5** 40 0N 5 0W
Iberville, *Canada* **140 C5** 45 19N 73 17W
Iberville, Lac d', *Canada* **140 A5** 55 55N 73 15W
Ibi, *Nigeria* **113 D6** 8 15N 9 44 E
Ibi, *Spain* **41 G4** 38 38N 0 34W
Ibiá, *Brazil* **171 E2** 19 30 S 46 30W
Ibiapaba, Sa. da, *Brazil* **170 B3** 4 0 S 41 30W
Ibicaraí, *Brazil* **171 D4** 14 51 S 39 36W
Ibicuí, *Brazil* **171 D4** 14 51 S 39 59W
Ibicuí ~, *Brazil* **175 B4** 29 25 S 56 47W
Ibicuy, *Argentina* **174 C4** 33 55 S 59 10W
Ibipetuba, *Brazil* **170 D3** 11 0 S 44 32W
Ibitiara, *Brazil* **171 D3** 12 39 S 42 13W
Ibiza = Eivissa, *Spain* **38 D1** 38 54N 1 26 E
Íblei, Monti, *Italy* **47 E7** 37 15N 14 45 E
Ibo, *Mozam.* **119 E5** 12 22 S 40 40 E
Ibonma, *Indonesia* **83 B4** 3 29 S 133 31 E
Ibotirama, *Brazil* **171 D3** 12 13 S 43 12W
Ibrāhīm ~, *Lebanon* **103 A4** 34 4N 35 38 E
'Ibrī, *Oman* **97 F8** 23 14N 56 30 E
İbriktepe, *Turkey* **51 E10** 41 0N 26 30 E
Ibshawâi, *Egypt* **106 J7** 29 21N 30 40 E
Ibu, *Indonesia* **82 A3** 1 35N 127 33 E
Ibuki-Sanchi, *Japan* **73 B8** 35 25N 136 18 E
Ibusuki, *Japan* **72 F2** 31 12N 130 40 E
Ica, *Peru* **172 C2** 14 0 S 75 48W
Ica □, *Peru* **172 C2** 14 20 S 75 30W
Iça ~, *Brazil* **172 A4** 2 55 S 67 58W
Icabarú, *Venezuela* **169 C5** 4 20N 61 45W
Icabarú ~, *Venezuela* **169 C5** 4 45N 62 15W
Icacos Pt., *Trin. & Tob.* **169 F9** 10 3N 61 57W
Içana, *Brazil* **168 C4** 0 21N 67 19W
Içana ~, *Brazil* **168 C4** 0 26N 67 19W
Icatu, *Brazil* **170 B3** 2 46 S 44 4W
Içel = Mersin, *Turkey* **100 D6** 36 51N 34 36 E
Iceland ■, *Europe* **11 C8** 64 45N 19 0W
Ichalkaranji, *India* **94 F2** 16 40N 74 33 E
Ich'ang = Yichang, *China* **77 B8** 30 40N 111 20 E
Ichchapuram, *India* **94 E7** 19 10N 84 40 E
Ichhawar, *India* **92 H7** 23 1N 77 1 E
Ichihara, *Japan* **73 B12** 35 28N 140 5 E
Ichikawa, *Japan* **73 B11** 35 44N 139 55 E
Ichilo ~, *Bolivia* **173 D5** 15 57 S 64 50W
Ichinohe, *Japan* **70 D10** 40 13N 141 17 E
Ichinomiya, *Gifu, Japan* **73 B8** 35 18N 136 48 E
Ichinomiya, *Kumamoto, Japan* **72 E3** 32 58N 131 5 E
Ichinoseki, *Japan* **70 E10** 38 55N 141 8 E
Ichkeul Nat. Park, *Tunisia* **108 A1** 37 5N 9 37 E
Ichnya, *Ukraine* **59 G7** 50 52N 32 24 E
Icht, *Morocco* **110 C3** 29 6N 8 54W
Icó, *Brazil* **170 C4** 6 24 S 38 51W
Icoca, *Angola* **115 D3** 6 12 S 16 20 E
Icod, *Canary Is.* **9 e1** 28 22N 16 43W
Icoraci, *Brazil* **170 B2** 1 18 S 48 28W
Icy C., *U.S.A.* **144 A7** 70 20N 161 52W
Ida Grove, *U.S.A.* **154 D7** 42 21N 95 28W
Idabel, *U.S.A.* **155 J7** 33 54N 94 50W
Idaga Hamus, *Ethiopia* **107 E4** 14 13N 39 48 E
Idah, *Nigeria* **113 D6** 7 5N 6 40 E
Idaho □, *U.S.A.* **158 D7** 45 0N 115 0W
Idaho City, *U.S.A.* **158 E6** 43 50N 115 50W
Idaho Falls, *U.S.A.* **158 E7** 43 30N 112 2W
Idalia Nat. Park, *Australia* **126 C3** 24 49 S 144 36 E
Idanha-a-Nova, *Portugal* **42 F3** 39 50N 7 15W
Idar-Oberstein, *Germany* **31 F3** 49 43N 7 16 E
Iday, *Niger* **109 F2** 14 54N 11 33 E
'Idd el Ghanam, *Sudan* **109 F4** 11 30N 24 19 E
Iddan, *Somali Rep.* **120 C3** 6 10N 48 55 E
Idelès, *Algeria* **111 D6** 23 50N 5 53 E
Idfû, *Egypt* **106 C3** 24 55N 32 49 E
Ídhi Óros, *Greece* **39 E5** 35 15N 24 45 E
Ídhra, *Greece* **48 D5** 37 20N 23 28 E
Idi, *Indonesia* **84 A1** 5 2N 97 37 E
Idiofa, *Dem. Rep. of the Congo* **115 C3** 4 55 S 19 42 E
Idkerberget, *Sweden* **16 D9** 60 22N 15 15 E
Idku, Bahra el, *Egypt* **106 H7** 31 18N 30 18 E
Idlib, *Syria* **100 E7** 35 55N 36 36 E
Idre, *Sweden* **16 C6** 61 52N 12 42 E
Idria, *U.S.A.* **160 J6** 36 25N 120 41W
Idrija, *Slovenia* **45 C11** 46 0N 14 5 E
Idritsa, *Russia* **58 D5** 56 17N 28 53 E
Idro, *Italy* **33 E10** 45 44N 10 29 E
Idutywa, *S. Africa* **117 E4** 32 8 S 28 18 E
Ieper, *Belgium* **24 D2** 50 51N 2 53 E
Ierápetra, *Greece* **39 F6** 35 1N 25 44 E
Ierissós, *Greece* **50 F7** 40 22N 23 52 E
Ierissóu Kólpos, *Greece* **50 F7** 40 27N 23 57 E
Iernut, *Romania* **53 D9** 46 27N 24 15 E
Ieshima-Shotō, *Japan* **72 C6** 34 40N 134 32 E
Iesi, *Italy* **45 E10** 43 31N 13 14 E
Iésolo, *Italy* **45 C9** 45 32N 12 38 E
Ifach, Peñón de, *Spain* **41 G5** 38 38N 0 5 E
'Ifāl, W. al ~, *Si. Arabia* **96 D2** 28 7N 35 3 E
Ifanadiana, *Madag.* **117 C8** 21 19 S 47 39 E
Ife, *Nigeria* **113 D5** 7 30N 4 31 E
Iférouâne, *Niger* **113 B6** 19 5N 8 24 E
Ifetesene, *Algeria* **111 C5** 25 30N 4 33 E
Iffley, *Australia* **126 B3** 18 53 S 141 12 E
Ifon, *Nigeria* **113 D6** 6 58N 5 40 E
Iforas, Adrar des, *Africa* **111 D5** 19 40N 1 40 E
Ifould, L., *Australia* **125 F5** 30 52 S 132 6 E
Ifrane, *Morocco* **110 B3** 33 33N 5 7W
Ifugao □, *Phil.* **80 C3** 16 40N 121 10 E
Iga, *Japan* **73 C8** 34 45N 136 10 E
Iganga, *Uganda* **118 B3** 0 37N 33 28 E
Igara Paraná ~, *Colombia* **168 D3** 2 9 S 71 47W
Igarapava, *Brazil* **171 F2** 20 3 S 47 47W
Igarapé Açu, *Brazil* **170 B2** 1 4 S 47 33W
Igarapé-Mirim, *Brazil* **170 B2** 1 59 S 48 58W
Igarka, *Russia* **66 C9** 67 30N 86 33 E
Igatimi, *Paraguay* **175 A4** 24 5 S 55 40W
Igatpuri, *India* **94 E1** 19 40N 73 35 E
Igbetti, *Nigeria* **113 D5** 8 44N 4 8 E
Igbo-Ora, *Nigeria* **113 D5** 7 29N 3 15 E
Igboho, *Nigeria* **113 D5** 8 53N 3 50 E
Igbor, *Nigeria* **113 D6** 7 27N 8 34 E
Iğdır, *Turkey* **101 C11** 39 55N 44 2 E
Igelfors, *Sweden* **17 F9** 58 52N 15 41 E
Iggesund, *Sweden* **16 C11** 61 39N 17 10 E
Ighil Izane = Relizane, *Algeria* **111 A5** 35 44N 0 31 E
Igiugig, *U.S.A.* **144 G9** 59 20N 155 55W
Iglésias, *Italy* **46 C1** 39 19N 8 32 E
Igli, *Algeria* **111 B4** 30 25N 2 19W
Iglino, *Russia* **64 D6** 54 50N 56 26 E
Igloolik, *Canada* **139 B11** 69 20N 81 49W
Iglulgaarjuk, *Canada* **139 B10** 63 21N 90 42W
Iglulik = Igloolik, *Canada* **139 B11** 69 20N 81 49W
'Igma, Gebel el, *Egypt* **106 B3** 28 55N 34 0 E
Ignace, *Canada* **140 C1** 49 30N 91 40W
İğneada, *Turkey* **51 E11** 41 52N 27 59 E
İğneada Burnu, *Turkey* **51 E12** 41 53N 28 2 E
Igoumenítsa, *Greece* **38 B10** 39 32N 20 18 E
Igra, *Russia* **60 B11** 57 33N 53 7 E
Iguaçu ~, *Brazil* **175 B5** 25 36 S 54 36W
Iguaçu, Cat. del, *Brazil* **175 B5** 25 41 S 54 26W
Iguaçu Falls = Iguaçu, Cat. del, *Brazil* **175 B5** 25 41 S 54 26W
Iguala, *Mexico* **163 D5** 18 20N 99 40W
Igualada, *Spain* **40 D6** 41 37N 1 37 E
Iguape, *Brazil* **171 F2** 24 43 S 47 33W
Iguassu = Iguaçu ~, *Brazil* **175 B5** 25 36 S 54 36W
Iguatu, *Brazil* **170 C4** 6 20 S 39 18W
Iguéla, *Gabon* **114 C1** 2 0 S 9 16 E
Iguéla, Lagune, *Gabon* **114 C2** 1 48 S 9 16 E
Iguetti, Sebkhet, *Mauritania* **110 C3** 25 5N 9 50W
Iguig, *Phil.* **80 C3** 17 45N 121 44 E
Iharana, *Madag.* **117 A9** 13 25 S 50 0 E
Ihbulag, *Mongolia* **74 C4** 43 11N 107 10 E
Iheya-Shima, *Japan* **71 L3** 27 4N 127 58 E
Ihiala, *Nigeria* **113 D6** 5 51N 6 55 E
Ihirene ~, *Algeria* **111 D5** 20 28N 4 37 E
Ihosy, *Madag.* **117 C8** 22 24 S 46 8 E
Ihotry, Farihy, *Madag.* **117 C7** 21 56 S 43 41 E
Ihu, *Papua N. G.* **132 D3** 7 55 S 145 24 E
Ihugh, *Nigeria* **113 D6** 7 2N 9 0 E
Ii, *Finland* **14 D21** 65 19N 25 22 E
Ii-Shima, *Japan* **71 L3** 26 43N 127 47 E
Iida, *Japan* **73 B9** 35 35N 137 50 E
Iijoki ~, *Finland* **14 D21** 65 20N 25 20 E
Iisalmi, *Finland* **14 E22** 63 32N 27 10 E
Iiyama, *Japan* **71 F9** 36 51N 138 22 E
Iizuka, *Japan* **72 D2** 33 38N 130 42 E
Ijâfene, *Mauritania* **110 D3** 20 40N 8 0W
Ijebu-Igbo, *Nigeria* **113 D5** 6 56N 4 1 E
Ijebu-Ode, *Nigeria* **113 D5** 6 47N 3 58 E

Ijill, Sebkhet, *Mauritania* **110 D2** 22 47N 12 53W
IJmuiden, *Neths.* **24 B4** 52 28N 4 35 E
IJssel →, *Neths.* **24 B5** 52 35N 5 50 E
IJsselmeer, *Neths.* **24 B5** 52 45N 5 20 E
Ijuí, *Brazil* **175 B5** 28 23 S 53 55W
Ijuí →, *Brazil* **175 B4** 27 58 S 55 20W
Ijūin, *Japan* **72 F2** 31 37N 130 24 E
Ik →, *Russia* **64 D4** 55 41N 53 29 E
Ikalamavony, *Madag.* **117 C8** 21 9 S 46 35 E
Ikale, *Nigeria* **113 D6** 7 40N 5 37 E
Ikali, *Dem. Rep. of the Congo* **114 C4** 2 2 S 21 4 E
Ikaluktutiak, *Canada* **138 B9** 69 10N 105 0W
Ikamatua, *N.Z.* **131 C6** 42 16 S 171 41 E
Ikang, *Nigeria* **113 E6** 4 49N 8 30 E
Ikara, *Nigeria* **113 C6** 11 12N 8 15 E
Ikare, *Nigeria* **113 D6** 7 32N 5 40 E
Ikaría, *Greece* **49 D8** 37 35N 26 10 E
Ikast, *Denmark* **17 H3** 56 8N 9 10 E
Ikeda, *Japan* **72 C5** 34 1N 133 48 E
Ikeja, *Nigeria* **113 D5** 6 36N 3 23 E
Ikela, *Dem. Rep. of the Congo* **114 C4** 1 6 S 23 6 E
Ikélemba, *Congo* **114 B3** 1 12N 16 38 E
Ikélemba →, *Dem. Rep. of the Congo* **114 B3** 0 7N 18 17 E
Ikengo, *Dem. Rep. of the Congo* **114 C3** 0 8 S 18 8 E
Ikerre-Ekiti, *Nigeria* **113 D6** 7 25N 5 19 E
Ikhtiman, *Bulgaria* **50 D7** 42 27N 23 48 E
Iki, *Japan* **72 D1** 33 45N 129 42 E
Iki-Kaikyō, *Japan* **72 D1** 33 40N 129 45 E
Ikimba L., *Tanzania* **118 C3** 1 30 S 31 20 E
Ikire, *Nigeria* **113 D5** 7 23N 4 15 E
Ikitsuki-Shima, *Japan* **72 D1** 33 23N 129 26 E
İkizdere, *Turkey* **101 B9** 40 46N 40 32 E
Iko, *Congo* **114 C3** 0 35 S 16 0 E
Ikom, *Nigeria* **113 D6** 6 0N 8 42 E
Ikomu, *Dem. Rep. of the Congo* **114 C3** 1 54 S 19 40 E
Ikongo, *Madag.* **117 C8** 21 52 S 47 27 E
Ikopa →, *Madag.* **117 B8** 16 45 S 46 40 E
Ikorongo Game Reserve, *Tanzania* **118 C3** 1 50 S 34 53 E
Ikot Ekpene, *Nigeria* **113 D6** 5 12N 7 40 E
Ikungu, *Tanzania* **118 C3** 1 33 S 33 42 E
Ikuno, *Japan* **72 B6** 35 10N 134 48 E
Ikurun, *Nigeria* **113 D5** 7 54N 4 40 E
Il-Kullana, *Malta* **38 F7** 35 50N 14 24 E
Il-Munxar, *Malta* **38 F8** 35 51N 14 34 E
Ila, *Dem. Rep. of the Congo* **114 C4** 2 53 S 21 7 E
Ila, *Nigeria* **113 D5** 8 0N 4 39 E
Ilafer, *Algeria* **111 D5** 21 40N 1 58 E
Ilagan, *Phil.* **80 C3** 17 7N 121 53 E
Ilaka, *Madag.* **117 B8** 19 33 S 48 52 E
Īlām, *Iran* **101 F12** 33 36N 46 36 E
Ilam, *Nepal* **93 F12** 26 58N 87 58 E
Ilam □, *Iran* **96 C5** 33 0N 47 0 E
Ilan, *Taiwan* **77 E13** 24 45N 121 44 E
Ilanskiy, *Russia* **67 D10** 56 14N 96 3 E
Ilanz, *Switz.* **33 C8** 46 46N 9 12 E
Ilaro, *Nigeria* **113 D5** 6 53N 3 3 E
Ilatane, *Niger* **113 B5** 16 30N 4 45 E
Ilave, *Peru* **172 D4** 16 5 S 69 40W
Iława, *Poland* **54 E6** 53 36N 19 34 E
Ilayangudi, *India* **95 K4** 9 34N 78 37 E
Ile →, *Kazakstan* **66 E8** 45 53N 77 10 E
Ile-à-la-Crosse, *Canada* **143 B7** 55 27N 107 53W
Ile-à-la-Crosse, Lac, *Canada* **143 B7** 55 40N 107 45W
Île-de-France □, *France* **27 D9** 49 0N 2 20 E
Ileanda, *Romania* **53 C8** 47 20N 23 38 E
Ilebo, *Dem. Rep. of the Congo* **115 C4** 4 17 S 20 55 E
Ilek, *Russia* **64 F4** 51 32N 53 21 E
Ilek →, *Russia* **64 F4** 51 30N 53 22 E
Iler, *Algeria* **111 D5** 20 57N 3 21 E
Iler, O. →, *Algeria* **111 D5** 20 59N 3 14 E
Ilero, *Nigeria* **113 D5** 8 0N 3 20 E
Ilesha, *Kwara, Nigeria* **113 D5** 8 57N 3 28 E
Ilesha, *Oyo, Nigeria* **113 D5** 7 37N 4 40 E
Ilford, *Canada* **143 B9** 56 4N 95 35W
Ilfracombe, *Australia* **126 C3** 23 30 S 144 30 E
Ilfracombe, *U.K.* **21 F3** 51 12N 4 8W
Ilgaz, *Turkey* **100 B5** 40 55N 33 37 E
Ilgaz Dağları, *Turkey* **100 B5** 41 10N 33 50 E
Ilgın, *Turkey* **100 C4** 38 16N 31 55 E
Ilha, Pta. da, *Azores* **9 d1** 38 25N 28 3W
Ilha de Moçambique, *Mozam.* **119 F5** 15 4 S 40 52 E
Ilha Grande, *Brazil* **169 D4** 0 27 S 65 2W
Ilha Grande, B. da, *Brazil* **171 F3** 23 9 S 44 30W
Ílhavo, *Portugal* **42 E2** 40 33N 8 43W
Ilhéus, *Brazil* **171 D4** 14 49 S 39 2W
Ili = Ile →, *Kazakstan* **66 E8** 45 53N 77 10 E
Ilia, *Romania* **52 E7** 45 57N 22 40 E
Ilia □, *Greece* **48 D3** 37 45N 21 35 E
Iliamna, *U.S.A.* **144 G9** 59 45N 154 55W
Iliamna L., *U.S.A.* **144 G9** 59 30N 155 0W
Ilian, Mt., *Phil.* **81 F2** 10 26N 119 33 E
Iliç, *Turkey* **101 C8** 39 27N 38 33 E
Ilıca, *Turkey* **49 B9** 39 52N 27 46 E
Īlīch, *Kazakstan* **65 C4** 40 50N 68 27 E
Ilichevsk, *Azerbaijan* **101 C11** 39 22N 45 5 E
Iligan, *Phil.* **81 G5** 8 12N 124 13 E
Iligan Bay, *Phil.* **81 G5** 8 25N 124 5 E
Iligan Pt., *Phil.* **80 B4** 18 25N 122 25 E
Ilíkí, L., *Greece* **48 C5** 38 24N 23 15 E
Ilin I., *Phil.* **80 E3** 12 14N 121 5 E
Ilio Pt., *U.S.A.* **145 B4** 21 13N 157 16W
Iliodhrómia, *Greece* **48 B5** 39 12N 23 50 E
Ilion, *U.S.A.* **151 D9** 43 1N 75 2W
Ilirska-Bistrica, *Slovenia* **45 C11** 45 34N 14 14 E
Ilkal, *India* **95 G3** 15 57N 76 8 E
Ilkeston, *U.K.* **20 E6** 52 58N 1 19W
Ilkley, *U.K.* **20 D6** 53 56N 1 48W
Illampu = Ancohuma, Nevada, *Bolivia* **172 D4** 16 0 S 68 50W
Illana B., *Phil.* **81 H4** 7 35N 123 45 E
Illapel, *Chile* **174 C1** 32 0 S 71 10W
Ille-et-Vilaine □, *France* **26 D5** 48 10N 1 30W
Ille-sur-Têt, *France* **28 F6** 42 40N 2 38 E
Illéla, *Niger* **113 C6** 14 32N 5 20 E
Iller →, *Germany* **31 G5** 48 23N 9 58 E
Illertissen, *Germany* **31 G6** 48 12N 10 7 E
Illescas, *Spain* **42 E7** 40 8N 3 51W
Illetas, *Spain* **38 B3** 39 32N 2 35 E
Illichivsk, *Ukraine* **59 J6** 46 20N 30 35 E
Illiers-Combray, *France* **26 D8** 48 18N 1 15 E
Illimani, Nevado, *Bolivia* **172 D4** 16 30 S 67 50W
Illinois □, *U.S.A.* **156 D7** 40 15N 89 30W
Illinois →, *U.S.A.* **156 F6** 38 58N 90 28W
Illiopolis, *U.S.A.* **156 E7** 39 51N 89 15W
Illium = Troy, *Turkey* **49 B8** 39 57N 26 12 E
Illizi, *Algeria* **111 C6** 26 31N 8 32 E
Illkirch-Graffenstaden, *France* **27 D14** 48 34N 7 42 E
Íllora, *Spain* **43 H7** 37 17N 3 53W
Illulissat, *Greenland* **10 D5** 69 12N 51 10W
Ilm →, *Germany* **30 D7** 51 6N 11 40 E
Ilmajoki, *Finland* **15 E20** 62 44N 22 34 E
Ilmen, Ozero, *Russia* **58 C6** 58 15N 31 10 E
Ilmenau, *Germany* **30 E6** 50 41N 10 54 E
Ilo, *Peru* **172 D3** 17 40 S 71 20W
Ilobu, *Nigeria* **113 D5** 7 45N 4 25 E
Ilocos Norte □, *Phil.* **80 B3** 18 10N 120 45 E
Ilocos Sur □, *Phil.* **80 C3** 17 20N 120 35 E
Iloilo, *Phil.* **81 F4** 10 45N 122 33 E
Iloilo □, *Phil.* **81 F4** 11 0N 122 40 E
Ilora, *Nigeria* **113 D5** 7 45N 3 50 E
Ilorin, *Nigeria* **113 D5** 8 30N 4 35 E
Ilovatka, *Russia* **60 E7** 50 30N 45 50 E
Ilovlya, *Russia* **61 F7** 49 15N 44 2 E
Ilovlya →, *Russia* **61 F7** 49 14N 44 0 E
Iłowa, *Poland* **55 G2** 51 30N 15 10 E
Ilubabor □, *Ethiopia* **107 F4** 7 25N 35 0 E
Ilva Mică, *Romania* **53 C9** 47 17N 24 40 E
Ilwaco, *U.S.A.* **160 D2** 46 19N 124 3W
Ilwaki, *Indonesia* **82 C3** 7 55 S 126 30 E
Ilyichevsk = Illichivsk, *Ukraine* **59 J6** 46 20N 30 35 E
Iłża, *Poland* **55 G8** 51 10N 21 15 E
Iłzanka →, *Poland* **55 G8** 51 14N 21 48 E
Imabari, *Japan* **72 C5** 34 4N 133 0 E
Imaichi, *Japan* **73 A11** 36 43N 139 46 E
Imaloto →, *Madag.* **117 C8** 23 27 S 45 13 E
İmamoğlu, *Turkey* **100 D6** 37 15N 35 38 E
Imandra, Ozero, *Russia* **56 A5** 67 30N 33 0 E
Imanombo, *Madag.* **117 C8** 24 26 S 45 49 E
Imari, *Japan* **72 D1** 33 15N 129 52 E
Imasa, *Sudan* **106 D4** 18 0N 36 12 E
Imathía □, *Greece* **50 F6** 40 30N 22 15 E
Imatra, *Finland* **58 B5** 61 12N 28 48 E
Imazu, *Japan* **73 B8** 35 24N 136 2 E
Imbabura □, *Ecuador* **168 C2** 0 30N 78 45W
Imbaimadai, *Guyana* **169 B5** 5 44N 60 17W
Imbil, *Australia* **127 D5** 26 22 S 152 32 E
Imbonga, *Dem. Rep. of the Congo* **114 C3** 0 43 S 19 44 E
Imdahane, *Morocco* **110 B3** 32 8N 7 0W
Iménas, *Mali* **113 B5** 16 20N 0 40 E
imeni 26 Bakinskikh Komissarov = Neftçala, *Azerbaijan* **97 B6** 39 19N 49 12 E
imeni 26 Bakinskikh Komissarov, *Turkmenistan* **97 B7** 39 22N 54 10 E
Imeri, Serra, *Brazil* **168 C4** 0 50N 65 25W
Imerimandroso, *Madag.* **117 B8** 17 26 S 48 35 E
Imesan, *Mauritania* **110 D1** 22 54N 15 30W
Imese, *Dem. Rep. of the Congo* **114 B3** 2 6N 18 9 E
Imi, *Ethiopia* **107 F5** 6 28N 42 10 E
Imishly = Imişli, *Azerbaijan* **61 L9** 39 55N 48 4 E
Imişli, *Azerbaijan* **61 L9** 39 55N 48 4 E
Imitek, *Morocco* **110 C3** 29 43N 8 10W
Imlay, *U.S.A.* **158 F4** 40 40N 118 9W
Imlay City, *U.S.A.* **150 D1** 43 2N 83 5W
Immaseri, *Sudan* **107 D2** 15 40N 25 31 E
Immenstadt, *Germany* **31 H6** 47 33N 10 13 E
Immingham, *U.K.* **20 D7** 53 37N 0 13W
Immokalee, *U.S.A.* **149 M5** 26 25N 81 25W
Imo □, *Nigeria* **113 D6** 5 30N 7 10 E
Imo →, *Nigeria* **113 E6** 4 36N 7 35 E
Ímola, *Italy* **45 D8** 44 20N 11 42 E
Imotski, *Croatia* **45 E14** 43 27N 17 12 E
Impé, *Congo* **114 C3** 2 45 S 15 16 E
Imperatriz, *Amazonas, Brazil* **172 B4** 5 18 S 67 11W
Imperatriz, *Maranhão, Brazil* **170 C2** 5 30 S 47 29W
Impéria, *Italy* **44 E5** 43 53N 8 3 E
Imperial, *Canada* **143 C7** 51 21N 105 28W
Imperial, *Peru* **172 C2** 13 4 S 76 21W
Imperial, *Calif., U.S.A.* **161 N11** 32 51N 115 34W
Imperial, *Nebr., U.S.A.* **154 E4** 40 31N 101 39W
Imperial Beach, *U.S.A.* **161 N9** 32 35N 117 8W
Imperial Dam, *U.S.A.* **161 N12** 32 55N 114 25W
Imperial Reservoir, *U.S.A.* **161 N12** 32 53N 114 28W
Imperial Valley, *U.S.A.* **161 N11** 33 0N 115 30W
Imperieuse Reef, *Australia* **124 C2** 17 36 S 118 50 E
Impfondo, *Congo* **114 B3** 1 40N 18 0 E
Imphal, *India* **90 C4** 24 48N 93 56 E
Imphy, *France* **27 F10** 46 55N 3 16 E
Impulo, *Angola* **115 E2** 13 51 S 13 39 E
Imranlı, *Turkey* **101 C8** 39 54N 38 7 E
İmroz = Gökçeada, *Turkey* **51 F9** 40 10N 25 50 E
İmroz, *Turkey* **51 F9** 40 10N 25 55 E
Imst, *Austria* **34 D3** 47 15N 10 44 E
Imuris, *Mexico* **162 A2** 30 47N 110 52W
Imuruan B., *Phil.* **81 F2** 10 40N 119 10 E
Imus, *Phil.* **80 D3** 14 26N 120 56 E
In Akhmed, *Mali* **113 B4** 19 49N 0 56W
In Aleï, *Mali* **112 B4** 17 42N 2 30W
In Amenas, *Algeria* **111 C6** 28 5N 9 33 E
In Atei, *Algeria* **111 D6** 20 33N 6 4 E
In Belbel, *Algeria* **111 C5** 27 55N 1 12 E
In Dekkar, O. →, *Algeria* **111 C6** 27 12N 6 16 E
In Delimane, *Mali* **113 B5** 15 52N 1 31 E
In Guezzam, *Algeria* **111 E6** 19 37N 5 52 E
In Koufi, *Mali* **113 B5** 19 11N 1 25 E
In Rhar, *Algeria* **111 C5** 27 10N 1 59 E
In Salah, *Algeria* **111 C5** 27 10N 2 32 E
In Tallak, *Mali* **113 B5** 16 19N 3 15 E
In Tebezas, *Mali* **113 B5** 17 49N 1 53 E
Ina, *Japan* **73 B9** 35 50N 137 55 E
Ina, *U.S.A.* **157 F8** 38 9N 88 54W
Ina-Bonchi, *Japan* **73 B9** 35 45N 137 58 E
Inabanga, *Phil.* **81 F5** 10 2N 124 4 E
Inagauan, *Phil.* **81 G2** 9 33N 118 39 E
Inajá, *Brazil* **170 C4** 8 54 S 37 49W
Inambari →, *Peru* **172 C4** 12 41 S 69 44W
Inangahua, *N.Z.* **131 B6** 41 52 S 171 59 E
Inanwatan, *Indonesia* **83 B4** 2 8 S 132 10 E
Iñapari, *Peru* **172 C4** 11 0 S 69 40W
Inarajan, *Guam* **133 R15** 13 16N 144 45 E
Inari, *Finland* **14 B22** 68 54N 27 5 E
Inarijärvi, *Finland* **14 B22** 69 0N 28 0 E
Inawashiro-Ko, *Japan* **70 F10** 37 29N 140 6 E
Inazawa, *Japan* **73 B8** 35 15N 136 47 E
Inbin, *Burma* **90 F5** 18 6N 95 16 E
Inca, *Spain* **38 B3** 39 43N 2 54 E
Inca de Oro, *Chile* **174 B2** 26 45 S 69 54W
Incaguasi, *Chile* **174 B1** 29 12 S 71 5W
İnce Burun, *Turkey* **100 A6** 42 7N 34 56 E
İncekum Burnu, *Turkey* **100 D5** 36 13N 33 57 E
İncesu, *Turkey* **96 B2** 38 38N 35 11 E
Inch'ŏn, *S. Korea* **75 F14** 37 27N 126 40 E
Incio = Cruz de Incio, *Spain* **42 C3** 42 39N 7 21W
İncirliova, *Turkey* **49 D9** 37 50N 27 41 E
Incline Village, *U.S.A.* **158 G4** 39 10N 119 58W
Incomáti →, *Mozam.* **117 D5** 25 46 S 32 43 E
Inda Silase, *Ethiopia* **107 E4** 14 10N 38 15 E
Indal, *Sweden* **16 B11** 62 35N 17 5 E
Indalsälven →, *Sweden* **16 B11** 62 36N 17 30 E
Indaw, *Burma* **90 C6** 24 15N 96 5 E
Indawgyi In, *Burma* **90 C6** 25 8N 96 20 E
Indbir, *Ethiopia* **107 F4** 8 7N 37 52 E
Independence, *Calif., U.S.A.* **160 J8** 36 48N 118 12W
Independence, *Iowa, U.S.A.* **156 B5** 42 28N 91 54W
Independence, *Kans., U.S.A.* **155 G7** 37 14N 95 42W
Independence, *Ky., U.S.A.* **157 F12** 38 57N 84 33W
Independence, *Mo., U.S.A.* **156 E2** 39 6N 94 25W
Independence Fjord, *Greenland* **10 A8** 82 10N 29 0W
Independence Mts., *U.S.A.* **158 F5** 41 20N 116 0W
Independência, *Brazil* **170 C3** 5 23 S 40 19W
Independenţa, *Romania* **53 E12** 45 25N 27 42 E
Index, *U.S.A.* **160 C5** 47 50N 121 33W
Indi, *India* **94 F2** 17 10N 75 58 E
India ■, *Asia* **89 C6** 20 0N 78 0 E
Indialantic, *U.S.A.* **153 G9** 28 6N 80 34W
Indian →, *Fla., U.S.A.* **149 M5** 27 59N 80 34W
Indian →, *Fla., U.S.A.* **153 H9** 27 10N 80 10W
Indian Cabins, *Canada* **142 B5** 59 52N 117 40W
Indian Harbour, *Canada* **141 B8** 54 27N 57 13W
Indian Harbour Beach, *U.S.A.* **153 G9** 28 10N 80 35W
Indian Head, *Canada* **143 C8** 50 30N 103 41W
Indian Lake, *U.S.A.* **151 C10** 43 47N 74 16W
Indian Ocean **62 K11** 5 0 S 75 0 E
Indian Rocks Beach, *U.S.A.* **153 H7** 27 53N 82 51W
Indian Springs, *U.S.A.* **161 J11** 36 35N 115 40W
Indiana, *U.S.A.* **150 F5** 40 37N 79 9W
Indiana □, *U.S.A.* **157 E11** 40 0N 86 0W
Indianapolis, *U.S.A.* **157 E10** 39 46N 86 9W
Indianola, *Iowa, U.S.A.* **156 C3** 41 22N 93 34W
Indianola, *Miss., U.S.A.* **155 J9** 33 27N 90 39W
Indiantown, *U.S.A.* **153 H9** 27 1N 80 28W
Indiapora, *Brazil* **171 E1** 19 57 S 50 17W
Indiga, *Russia* **56 A8** 67 38N 49 9 E
Indigirka →, *Russia* **67 B15** 70 48N 148 54 E
Inđija, *Serbia, Yug.* **52 E5** 45 6N 20 7 E
Indio, *U.S.A.* **161 M10** 33 43N 116 13W
Indira Pt., *India* **95 L11** 6 44N 93 49 E
Indispensable Strait, *Solomon Is.* **133 M11** 9 0 S 160 30 E
Indo-China, *Asia* **62 H14** 15 0N 102 0 E
Indonesia ■, *Asia* **85 C4** 5 0 S 115 0 E
Indore, *India* **92 H6** 22 42N 75 53 E
Indramayu, *Indonesia* **85 D3** 6 20 S 108 19 E
Indravati →, *India* **94 E5** 19 20N 80 20 E
Indre □, *France* **27 F8** 46 50N 1 39 E
Indre →, *France* **26 E7** 47 16N 0 11 E
Indre Arna, *Norway* **18 D2** 60 26N 5 30 E
Indre-et-Loire □, *France* **26 E7** 47 20N 0 40 E
Indrio, *U.S.A.* **153 H9** 27 31N 80 21W
Indulkana, *Australia* **127 D1** 26 58 S 133 5 E
Indungo, *Angola* **115 E3** 14 48 S 16 17 E
Indus →, *Pakistan* **91 D2** 24 20N 67 47 E
Indus, Mouths of the, *Pakistan* **91 E3** 24 0N 68 0 E
Industry, *U.S.A.* **156 D6** 40 20N 90 36W
İnebolu, *Turkey* **100 B5** 41 55N 33 40 E
İnecik, *Turkey* **51 F11** 40 56N 27 16 E
İnegöl, *Turkey* **51 F13** 40 5N 29 31 E
Inés, Mt., *Argentina* **176 C3** 48 30 S 69 40W
Ineu, *Romania* **52 D6** 46 26N 21 51 E
Inezgane, *Morocco* **110 B3** 30 25N 9 29W
Infanta, *Phil.* **80 D3** 14 45N 121 39 E
Infantes = Villanueva de los Infantes, *Spain* **43 G7** 38 43N 3 1W
Infiernillo, Presa del, *Mexico* **162 D4** 18 9N 102 0W
Infiesto, *Spain* **42 B5** 43 21N 5 21W
Inga, Barrage d', *Dem. Rep. of the Congo* **115 D2** 5 39 S 13 39 E
Ingabu, *Burma* **90 G5** 17 37N 95 20 E
Inganda, *Dem. Rep. of the Congo* **114 C4** 0 5 S 20 57 E
Ingapirca, *Ecuador* **168 D2** 2 38 S 78 56W
Ingelstad, *Sweden* **17 H8** 56 45N 14 56 E
Ingende, *Dem. Rep. of the Congo* **114 C3** 0 12 S 18 57 E
Ingeniero Jacobacci, *Argentina* **176 B3** 41 20 S 69 36W
Ingenio, *Canary Is.* **9 e1** 27 55N 15 26W
Ingenio Santa Ana, *Argentina* **174 B2** 27 25 S 65 40W
Ingersoll, *Canada* **140 D3** 43 4N 80 55W
Ingham, *Australia* **126 B4** 18 43 S 146 10 E
Ingichka, *Uzbekistan* **65 D2** 39 47N 65 58 E
Ingleborough, *U.K.* **20 C5** 54 10N 2 22W
Inglefield Land, *Greenland* **10 B4** 78 30N 70 0W
Inglewood, *Queens., Australia* **127 D5** 28 25 S 151 2 E
Inglewood, *Vic., Australia* **128 D5** 36 29 S 143 53 E
Inglewood, *N.Z.* **130 F3** 39 9 S 174 14 E
Inglewood, *U.S.A.* **161 M8** 33 58N 118 21W
Inglis, *U.S.A.* **153 F7** 29 2N 82 40W
Ingolf Fjord, *Greenland* **10 A9** 80 35N 17 30W
Ingólfshöfði, *Iceland* **14 E5** 63 48N 16 39W
Ingolstadt, *Germany* **31 G7** 48 46N 11 26 E
Ingomar, *U.S.A.* **158 C10** 46 35N 107 23W
Ingonish, *Canada* **141 C7** 46 42N 60 18W
Ingore, *Guinea-Biss.* **112 C1** 12 24N 15 48W
Ingraj Bazar, *India* **93 G13** 24 58N 88 10 E
Ingrid Christensen Coast, *Antarctica* **7 C6** 69 30 S 76 0 E
Ingul → = Inhul →, *Ukraine* **59 J7** 46 50N 32 0 E
Ingulec = Inhulec, *Ukraine* **59 J7** 47 42N 33 14 E
Ingulets → = Inhulets →, *Ukraine* **59 J7** 46 46N 32 47 E
Inguri → = Enguri →, *Georgia* **61 J5** 42 27N 41 38 E
Ingushetia □, *Russia* **61 J7** 43 20N 44 50 E
Ingwavuma, *S. Africa* **117 D5** 27 9 S 31 59 E
Inhaca, *Mozam.* **117 D5** 26 1 S 32 57 E
Inhafenga, *Mozam.* **117 C5** 20 36 S 33 53 E
Inhambane, *Mozam.* **117 C6** 23 54 S 35 30 E
Inhambane □, *Mozam.* **117 C5** 22 30 S 34 20 E
Inhambupe, *Brazil* **171 D4** 11 47 S 38 21W
Inhaminga, *Mozam.* **119 F4** 18 26 S 35 0 E
Inharrime, *Mozam.* **117 C6** 24 30 S 35 0 E
Inharrime →, *Mozam.* **117 C6** 24 30 S 35 0 E
Inhisar, *Turkey* **49 A12** 40 3N 30 23 E
Inhul →, *Ukraine* **59 J7** 46 50N 32 0 E
Inhulec, *Ukraine* **59 J7** 47 42N 33 14 E
Inhulets →, *Ukraine* **59 J7** 46 46N 32 47 E
Inhuma, *Brazil* **170 C3** 6 40 S 41 42W
Inhumas, *Brazil* **171 E2** 16 22 S 49 30W
Iniesta, *Spain* **41 F3** 39 27N 1 45W
Ining = Yining, *China* **66 E9** 43 58N 81 10 E
Inini □, *Fr. Guiana* **169 C7** 4 0N 53 0W
Inírida →, *Colombia* **168 C4** 3 55N 67 52W
Inishbofin, *Ireland* **23 C1** 53 37N 10 13W
Inisheer, *Ireland* **23 C2** 53 3N 9 32W
Inishfree B., *Ireland* **23 A3** 55 4N 8 23W
Inishkea North, *Ireland* **23 B1** 54 9N 10 11W
Inishkea South, *Ireland* **23 B1** 54 7N 10 12W
Inishmaan, *Ireland* **23 C2** 53 5N 9 35W
Inishmore, *Ireland* **23 C2** 53 8N 9 45W
Inishowen Pen., *Ireland* **23 A4** 55 14N 7 15W
Inishshark, *Ireland* **23 C1** 53 37N 10 16W
Inishturk, *Ireland* **23 C1** 53 42N 10 7W
Inishvickillane, *Ireland* **23 D1** 52 3N 10 37W
Injibara, *Ethiopia* **107 E4** 10 59N 37 0 E
Injune, *Australia* **127 D4** 25 53 S 148 32 E
Inkisi →, *Dem. Rep. of the Congo* **115 D3** 4 46 S 14 52 E
Inklin →, *Canada* **142 B2** 58 50N 133 10W
Inland Kaikoura Ra., *N.Z.* **131 B8** 41 59 S 173 41 E
Inland Sea = Setonaikai, *Japan* **72 C5** 34 20N 133 30 E
Inle L., *Burma* **90 E6** 20 30N 96 58 E
Inlet, *U.S.A.* **151 C10** 43 45N 74 48W
Inn →, *Austria* **34 C6** 48 35N 13 28 E
Innamincka, *Australia* **127 D3** 27 44 S 140 46 E
Innbygda, *Norway* **18 C9** 61 19N 12 17 E
Inner Hebrides, *U.K.* **22 E2** 57 0N 6 30W
Inner Mongolia = Nei Monggol Zizhiqu □, *China* **74 D7** 42 0N 112 0 E
Inner Sound, *U.K.* **22 D3** 57 30N 5 55W
Innerkip, *Canada* **150 C4** 43 13N 80 42W
Innerkirchen, *Switz.* **32 C6** 46 43N 8 14 E
Innes Nat. Park, *Australia* **128 C2** 35 52 S 136 53 E
Innetalling I., *Canada* **140 A4** 56 0N 79 0W
Innisfail, *Australia* **126 B4** 17 33 S 146 5 E
Innisfail, *Canada* **142 C6** 52 0N 113 57W
In'noshima, *Japan* **72 C5** 34 19N 133 10 E
Innsbruck, *Austria* **34 D4** 47 16N 11 23 E
Innviertel, *Austria* **34 C6** 48 15N 13 15 E
Innvik, *Norway* **18 C3** 61 51N 6 37 E
Inny →, *Ireland* **23 C4** 53 30N 7 50W
Ino, *Japan* **72 D5** 33 33N 133 26 E
Inobonto, *Indonesia* **82 A2** 0 52N 123 57 E
Inocência, *Brazil* **171 E1** 19 47 S 51 48W
Inongo, *Dem. Rep. of the Congo* **114 C3** 1 55 S 18 30 E
Inoni, *Congo* **114 C3** 3 4 S 15 39 E
İnönü, *Turkey* **49 B12** 39 48N 30 9 E
Inoucdjouac = Inukjuak, *Canada* **139 C12** 58 25N 78 15W
Inowrocław, *Poland* **55 F5** 52 50N 18 12 E
Inpundong, *N. Korea* **75 D14** 41 25N 126 34 E
Inquisivi, *Bolivia* **172 D4** 16 50 S 67 10W
Ins, *Switz.* **32 B4** 47 1N 7 7 E
Inscription, C., *Australia* **125 E1** 25 29 S 112 59 E
Insein, *Burma* **90 G6** 16 50N 96 5 E
Insjön, *Sweden* **16 D9** 60 41N 15 6 E
Ińsko, *Poland* **54 E2** 53 25N 15 32 E
Însurăţei, *Romania* **53 F12** 44 50N 27 40 E
Inta, *Russia* **56 A11** 66 5N 60 8 E
Intendente Alvear, *Argentina* **174 D3** 35 12 S 63 32W
İntepe, *Turkey* **49 A8** 40 1N 26 20 E
Interlachen, *U.S.A.* **153 F8** 29 37N 81 53W
Interlaken, *Switz.* **32 C5** 46 41N 7 50 E
Interlaken, *U.S.A.* **151 D8** 42 37N 76 44W
International Falls, *U.S.A.* **154 A8** 48 36N 93 25W
Interview I., *India* **95 H11** 12 55N 92 43 E
Intiyaco, *Argentina* **174 B3** 28 43 S 60 5W
Întorsura Buzăului, *Romania* **53 E11** 45 41N 26 2 E
Intragna, *Switz.* **33 D7** 46 11N 8 42 E
Intutu, *Peru* **168 D3** 3 32 S 74 48W
Inubō-Zaki, *Japan* **73 B12** 35 42N 140 52 E
Inukjuak, *Canada* **139 C12** 58 25N 78 15W
Inútil, B., *Chile* **176 D2** 53 30 S 70 15W
Inuvik, *Canada* **138 B6** 68 16N 133 40W
Inuyama, *Japan* **73 B8** 35 23N 136 56 E
Inveraray, *U.K.* **22 E3** 56 14N 5 5W
Inverbervie, *U.K.* **22 E6** 56 51N 2 17W
Invercargill, *N.Z.* **131 G3** 46 24 S 168 24 E
Inverclyde □, *U.K.* **22 F4** 55 55N 4 49W
Inverell, *Australia* **127 D5** 29 45 S 151 8 E
Invergordon, *U.K.* **22 D4** 57 41N 4 10W
Inverleigh, *Australia* **128 E6** 38 6 S 144 3 E
Inverloch, *Australia* **127 F4** 38 38 S 145 45 E
Invermere, *Canada* **142 C5** 50 30N 116 2W
Inverness, *Canada* **141 C7** 46 15N 61 19W
Inverness, *U.K.* **22 D4** 57 29N 4 13W
Inverness, *Ala., U.S.A.* **152 C4** 32 1N 85 45W
Inverness, *Fla., U.S.A.* **149 L4** 28 50N 82 20W
Inverurie, *U.K.* **22 D6** 57 17N 2 23W
Investigator Group, *Australia* **127 E1** 34 45 S 134 20 E
Investigator Str., *Australia* **128 C2** 35 30 S 137 0 E
Inya, *Russia* **66 D9** 50 28N 86 37 E
Inyanga, *Zimbabwe* **119 F3** 18 12 S 32 40 E
Inyangani, *Zimbabwe* **119 F3** 18 5 S 32 50 E
Inyantue, *Zimbabwe* **116 B4** 18 33 S 26 39 E
Inyo Mts., *U.S.A.* **160 J9** 36 40N 118 0W
Inyokern, *U.S.A.* **161 K9** 35 39N 117 49W
Inywa, *Burma* **90 D6** 23 56N 96 17 E
Inza, *Russia* **60 D8** 53 55N 46 25 E
Inzer, *Russia* **64 D6** 54 14N 57 34 E
Inzhavino, *Russia* **60 D6** 52 22N 42 30 E
Inzia →, *Dem. Rep. of the Congo* **115 C3** 3 45 S 17 57 E
Iō-Jima, *Japan* **71 J5** 30 48N 130 18 E
Ioánnina, *Greece* **48 B2** 39 42N 20 47 E
Ioánnina □, *Greece* **48 B2** 39 39N 20 57 E
Iokea, *Papua N. G.* **132 E4** 8 25 S 146 16 E
Iola, *U.S.A.* **155 G7** 37 55N 95 24W
Ioma, *Papua N. G.* **132 E4** 8 19 S 147 52 E
Ion Corvin, *Romania* **53 F12** 44 7N 27 50 E
Iôna, *Angola* **115 F2** 16 54 S 12 34 E
Iona, *U.K.* **22 E2** 56 20N 6 25W
Iona, Parque Nacional do, *Angola* **115 F2** 16 47 S 12 20 E
Ione, *U.S.A.* **160 G6** 38 21N 120 56W
Iongo, *Angola* **115 D3** 9 11 S 17 45 E
Ionia, *U.S.A.* **157 B11** 42 59N 85 4W
Ionian Is. = Iónioi Nísoi, *Greece* **39 B1** 38 40N 20 0 E
Ionian Sea, *Medit. S.* **12 H9** 37 30N 17 30 E
Iónioi Nísoi, *Greece* **39 B1** 38 40N 20 0 E
Iónioi Nísoi □, *Greece* **39 B2** 38 40N 20 0 E
Íos, *Greece* **49 E7** 36 41N 25 20 E
Iowa □, *U.S.A.* **156 C3** 42 18N 93 30W
Iowa →, *U.S.A.* **156 C5** 41 10N 91 1W
Iowa City, *U.S.A.* **156 C5** 41 40N 91 32W
Iowa Falls, *U.S.A.* **156 B3** 42 31N 93 16W
Iowa Park, *U.S.A.* **155 J5** 33 57N 98 40W
Ipala, *Tanzania* **118 C3** 4 30 S 32 52 E
Ipameri, *Brazil* **171 E2** 17 44 S 48 9W
Ipanema, *Brazil* **171 E3** 19 47 S 41 44W
Iparía, *Peru* **172 B3** 9 17 S 74 29W
Ipáti, *Greece* **48 C4** 38 52N 22 14 E
Ipatinga, *Brazil* **171 E3** 19 32 S 42 30W
Ipatovo, *Russia* **61 H6** 45 45N 42 50 E
Ipel' →, *Europe* **35 D11** 47 48N 18 53 E
Ipiales, *Colombia* **168 C2** 0 50N 77 37W
Ipiaú, *Brazil* **171 D4** 14 8 S 39 44W
Ipil, *Phil.* **81 H4** 7 47N 122 35 E
Ipin = Yibin, *China* **76 C5** 28 45N 104 32 E
Ipirá, *Brazil* **171 D4** 12 10 S 39 44W
Ipiranga, *Brazil* **168 D4** 3 13 S 65 57W
Ípiros □, *Greece* **48 B2** 39 30N 20 30 E
Ipixuna, *Brazil* **172 B3** 7 0 S 71 40W
Ipixuna →, *Amazonas, Brazil* **172 B3** 7 11 S 71 51W
Ipixuna →, *Amazonas, Brazil* **173 B5** 5 45 S 63 2W
Ipoh, *Malaysia* **87 K3** 4 35N 101 5 E
Iporá, *Brazil* **173 D7** 16 28 S 51 7W
Ipota, *Vanuatu* **133 H7** 18 52 S 169 20 E
Ippy, *C.A.R.* **114 A4** 6 5N 21 7 E
İpsala, *Turkey* **51 F10** 40 55N 26 23 E
Ipsárion, Óros, *Greece* **51 F8** 40 40N 24 40 E
Ipsos, *Greece* **38 B9** 39 43N 19 48 E
Ipswich, *Australia* **127 D5** 27 35 S 152 40 E
Ipswich, *U.K.* **21 E9** 52 4N 1 10 E
Ipswich, *Mass., U.S.A.* **151 D14** 42 41N 70 50W
Ipswich, *S. Dak., U.S.A.* **154 C5** 45 27N 99 2W
Ipu, *Brazil* **170 B3** 4 23 S 40 44W
Ipueiras, *Brazil* **170 B3** 4 33 S 40 43W
Ipupiara, *Brazil* **171 D3** 11 49 S 42 37W
Iqaluit, *Canada* **139 B13** 63 44N 68 31W
Iquique, *Chile* **172 E3** 20 19 S 70 5W
Iquitos, *Peru* **168 D3** 3 45 S 73 10W
Irabu-Jima, *Japan* **71 M2** 24 50N 125 10 E
Iracoubo, *Fr. Guiana* **169 B7** 5 30N 53 10W
Īrafshān, *Iran* **97 E9** 26 42N 61 56 E
Irahuan, *Phil.* **81 G2** 9 48N 118 41 E
Iráklia, *Kikládhes, Greece* **49 E7** 36 50N 25 28 E
Iráklia, *Sérrai, Greece* **50 E7** 41 10N 23 16 E
Iráklion, *Greece* **39 E6** 35 20N 25 12 E
Iráklion □, *Greece* **39 E6** 35 10N 25 10 E
Irako-Zaki, *Japan* **73 C9** 34 35N 137 1 E
Irala, *Paraguay* **175 B5** 25 55 S 54 35W
Iran ■, *Asia* **97 C7** 33 0N 53 0 E
Iran, Gunung-Gunung, *Malaysia* **85 B4** 2 20N 114 50 E
Iran, Plateau of, *Asia* **62 F9** 32 0N 55 0 E
Iran Ra. = Iran, Gunung-Gunung, *Malaysia* **85 B4** 2 20N 114 50 E
Iranamadu Tank, *Sri Lanka* **95 K5** 9 23N 80 29 E
Īrānshahr, *Iran* **97 E9** 27 15N 60 40 E
Irapa, *Venezuela* **169 A5** 10 34N 62 35W
Irapuato, *Mexico* **162 C4** 20 40N 101 30W
Iraq ■, *Asia* **101 F10** 33 0N 44 0 E
Irarrar, O. →, *Mali* **111 E5** 20 0N 1 30 E
Irarrarene, *Algeria* **111 C6** 27 37N 7 30 E
Irati, *Brazil* **175 B5** 25 25 S 50 38W
Irbes saurums, *Latvia* **54 A9** 57 45N 22 5 E
Irbid, *Jordan* **103 C4** 32 35N 35 48 E
Irbid □, *Jordan* **103 C5** 32 15N 36 35 E
Irbit, *Russia* **64 C9** 57 41N 63 3 E
Irebu, *Dem. Rep. of the Congo* **114 C3** 0 40 S 17 46 E
Irecê, *Brazil* **170 D3** 11 18 S 41 52W
Iregua →, *Spain* **40 C7** 42 27N 2 24 E
Ireland ■, *Europe* **23 C4** 53 50N 7 52W
Ireland I., *Bermuda* **9 a** 32 19N 64 50W

Irele, *Nigeria* **113 D6** 7 40N 5 40 E
Iremel, Gora, *Russia* **64 D7** 54 33N 58 50 E
Ireng →, *Brazil* **169 C6** 3 33N 59 51W
Irerrer, O. →, *Algeria* **111 E6** 19 25N 5 47 E
Irgiz, Bolshaya →, *Russia* **60 D9** 52 10N 49 10 E
Irharrhar, O. →, *Algeria* **111 C6** 28 3N 6 15 E
Irherm, *Morocco* **110 B3** 30 7N 8 18W
Irhil M'Goun, *Morocco* **110 B3** 31 30N 6 28W
Irhyangdong, *N. Korea* **75 D15** 41 15N 129 30 E
Iri, *S. Korea* **75 G14** 35 59N 127 0 E
Irian Jaya □, *Indonesia* **83 B5** 4 0 S 137 0 E
Iriba, *Chad* **109 E4** 15 7N 22 15 E
Irié, *Guinea* **112 D3** 8 15N 9 10W
Iriga, *Phil.* **80 E4** 13 25N 123 25 E
Iriklinskiy, *Russia* **64 F7** 51 39N 58 38 E
Iriklinskoye Vdkhr., *Russia* **64 F7** 52 0N 59 0 E
Iringa, *Tanzania* **118 D4** 7 48 S 35 43 E
Iringa □, *Tanzania* **118 D4** 7 48 S 35 43 E
Irinjalakuda, *India* **95 J3** 10 21N 76 14 E
Iriomote-Jima, *Japan* **71 M1** 24 19N 123 48 E
Iriona, *Honduras* **164 C2** 15 57N 85 11W
Iriri →, *Brazil* **169 D7** 3 52 S 52 37W
Iriri Novo →, *Brazil* **173 B7** 8 46 S 53 22W
Irish Republic ■, *Europe* **23 C3** 53 0N 8 0W
Irish Sea, *U.K.* **20 D3** 53 38N 4 48W
Irkeshtam = Erkech-Tam, *Kyrgyzstan* **65 D6** 39 41N 73 55 E
Irkutsk, *Russia* **67 D11** 52 18N 104 20 E
Irlığanlı, *Turkey* **49 D11** 37 53N 29 12 E
Irma, *Canada* **143 C6** 52 55N 111 14W
Irō-Zaki, *Japan* **73 C10** 34 36N 138 51 E
Iroise, Mer d', *France* **26 D2** 48 15N 4 45W
Iron Baron, *Australia* **128 B2** 32 58 S 137 11 E
Iron Gate = Portile de Fier, *Europe* **52 F7** 44 44N 22 30 E
Iron Knob, *Australia* **128 B2** 32 46 S 137 8 E
Iron Mountain, *U.S.A.* **148 C1** 45 49N 88 4W
Iron Range Nat. Park, *Australia* **126 A3** 12 34 S 143 18 E
Iron River, *U.S.A.* **154 B10** 46 6N 88 39W
Irondequoit, *U.S.A.* **150 C7** 43 13N 77 35W
Ironton, *Mo., U.S.A.* **155 G9** 37 36N 90 38W
Ironton, *Ohio, U.S.A.* **148 F4** 38 32N 82 41W
Ironwood, *U.S.A.* **154 B9** 46 27N 90 9W
Iroquois, *Canada* **151 B9** 44 51N 75 19W
Iroquois →, *U.S.A.* **157 C9** 41 5N 87 49W
Iroquois Falls, *Canada* **140 C3** 48 46N 80 41W
Irosin, *Phil.* **80 E5** 12 42N 124 2 E
Irpin, *Ukraine* **59 G6** 50 30N 30 15 E
Irqieqa, Ras I-, *Malta* **38 F7** 35 56N 14 29 E
Irrara Cr. →, *Australia* **127 D4** 29 35 S 145 31 E
Irrawaddy □, *Burma* **90 G5** 17 0N 95 0 E
Irrawaddy →, *Burma* **90 G5** 15 50N 95 6 E
Irrawaddy, Mouths of the, *Burma* **90 H5** 15 30N 95 0 E
Irricana, *Canada* **142 C6** 51 19N 113 37W
Irsina, *Italy* **47 B9** 40 45N 16 14 E
Irtysh →, *Russia* **66 C7** 61 4N 68 52 E
Irumu, *Dem. Rep. of the Congo* **118 B2** 1 32N 29 53 E
Irún, *Spain* **40 B3** 43 20N 1 52W
Irunea = Pamplona, *Spain* **40 C3** 42 48N 1 38W
Irurzun, *Spain* **40 C3** 42 55N 1 50W
Irvine, *U.K.* **22 F4** 55 37N 4 41W
Irvine, *Calif., U.S.A.* **161 M9** 33 41N 117 46W
Irvine, *Ky., U.S.A.* **157 G13** 37 42N 83 58W
Irvinestown, *U.K.* **23 B4** 54 28N 7 39W
Irving, *U.S.A.* **155 J6** 32 49N 96 56W
Irvington, *U.S.A.* **157 G10** 37 53N 86 17W
Irvona, *U.S.A.* **150 F6** 40 46N 78 33W
Irwin →, *Australia* **125 E1** 29 15 S 114 54 E
Irwinton, *U.S.A.* **152 C6** 32 49N 83 10W
Irwinville, *U.S.A.* **152 D6** 31 39N 83 23W
Irymple, *Australia* **128 C5** 34 14 S 142 8 E
Is, Jebel, *Sudan* **106 C4** 22 3N 35 28 E
Is-sur-Tille, *France* **27 E12** 47 30N 5 8 E
Isa, *Nigeria* **113 C6** 13 14N 6 24 E
Isa Khel, *Pakistan* **92 C4** 32 41N 71 17 E
Isaac →, *Australia* **126 C4** 22 55 S 149 20 E
Isabel, *U.S.A.* **154 C4** 45 24N 101 26W
Isabela, *Basilan, Phil.* **81 H3** 6 40N 121 59 E
Isabela, *Negros, Phil.* **81 F4** 10 12N 122 59 E
Isabela, *Puerto Rico* **165 d** 18 30N 67 2W
Isabela □, *Phil.* **80 C4** 17 0N 122 0 E
Isabela, Canal, *Ecuador* **172 a** 0 20 S 90 55W
Isabela, I., *Ecuador* **172 a** 0 30 S 91 4W
Isabela, I., *Mexico* **162 C3** 21 51N 105 55W
Isabela, Cord., *Nic.* **164 D2** 13 30N 85 25W
Isabella Ra., *Australia* **124 D3** 21 0 S 121 4 E
Isaccea, *Romania* **53 E13** 45 16N 28 28 E
Ísafjarðardjúp, *Iceland* **11 A3** 66 10N 23 0W
Ísafjarðarsýsla □, *Iceland* **11 B3** 66 0N 23 0W
Ísafjörður, *Iceland* **11 A3** 66 5N 23 9W
Isagarh, *India* **92 G7** 24 48N 77 51 E
Isahaya, *Japan* **72 E2** 32 52N 130 2 E
Isaka, *Dem. Rep. of the Congo* **114 C3** 2 33 S 18 54 E
Isaka, *Tanzania* **118 C3** 3 56 S 32 59 E
Isakly, *Russia* **60 C10** 54 8N 51 32 E
Işalniţa, *Romania* **53 F8** 44 24N 23 44 E
Isalo, Parc Nat. de l', *Madag.* **117 C8** 22 23 S 45 16 E
Isan →, *India* **93 F9** 26 51N 80 7 E
Isana = Içana →, *Brazil* **168 C4** 0 26N 67 19W
Isandja, *Dem. Rep. of the Congo* **114 C4** 2 59 S 21 59 E
Isangano Nat. Park, *Zambia* **119 E3** 11 8 S 30 35 E
Isangi, *Dem. Rep. of the Congo* **114 B4** 0 52N 24 10 E
Isanlu Makutu, *Nigeria* **113 D6** 8 20N 5 50 E
Isar →, *Germany* **31 G8** 48 48N 12 57 E
Isarco →, *Italy* **45 B8** 46 27N 11 18 E
Ísari, *Greece* **48 D3** 37 22N 22 0 E
Isarog, Mt., *Phil.* **80 E4** 13 39N 123 23 E
Íscar, *Spain* **42 D6** 41 22N 4 32W
Iscayachi, *Bolivia* **173 E4** 21 31 S 65 3W
Iscehisar, *Turkey* **49 C12** 38 51N 30 45 E
Ischgl, *Austria* **33 B10** 47 1N 10 17 E
Íschia, *Italy* **46 B6** 40 44N 13 57 E
Iscuandé, *Colombia* **168 C2** 2 28N 77 59W
Isdell →, *Australia* **124 C3** 16 27 S 124 51 E
Ise, *Japan* **73 C8** 34 25N 136 45 E
Ise-Wan, *Japan* **73 C8** 34 43N 136 43 E
Isefjord, *Denmark* **17 J5** 55 53N 11 50 E
Isel →, *Austria* **34 E5** 46 50N 12 47 E
Iseltwald, *Switz.* **32 C5** 46 43N 7 58 E
Isenthal, *Switz.* **33 C7** 46 55N 8 34 E
Iseo, *Italy* **44 C7** 45 39N 10 3 E
Iseo, L. d', *Italy* **44 C7** 45 43N 10 4 E
Iseramagazi, *Tanzania* **118 C3** 4 37 S 32 10 E
Isère □, *France* **29 C9** 45 15N 5 40 E
Isère →, *France* **29 D8** 44 59N 4 51 E
Iserlohn, *Germany* **30 D3** 51 22N 7 41 E
Isérnia, *Italy* **47 A7** 41 36N 14 14 E
Isesaki, *Japan* **73 A11** 36 19N 139 12 E
Iseyin, *Nigeria* **113 D5** 8 0N 3 36 E
Isfahan = Eşfahān, *Iran* **97 C6** 32 39N 51 43 E
Isfana, *Kyrgyzstan* **65 D4** 39 50N 69 31 E
Isfara, *Tajikistan* **65 C5** 40 7N 70 38 E
Isfjorden, *Norway* **18 B4** 62 35N 7 49 E
Ishëm, *Albania* **50 E3** 41 33N 19 34 E
Ishenga Oshwe, *Dem. Rep. of the Congo* **114 C4** 3 57 S 22 33 E
Isherton, *Guyana* **169 C6** 2 20N 59 25W
Ishigaki-Shima, *Japan* **71 M2** 24 20N 124 10 E
Ishikari-Gawa →, *Japan* **70 C10** 43 15N 141 23 E
Ishikari-Sammyaku, *Japan* **70 C11** 43 30N 143 0 E
Ishikari-Wan, *Japan* **70 C10** 43 25N 141 1 E
Ishikawa □, *Japan* **73 A8** 36 30N 136 30 E
Ishim, *Russia* **66 D7** 56 10N 69 30 E
Ishim →, *Russia* **66 D8** 57 45N 71 10 E
Ishimbay, *Russia* **64 E6** 53 28N 56 2 E
Ishinomaki, *Japan* **70 E10** 38 32N 141 20 E
Ishioka, *Japan* **73 A12** 36 11N 140 16 E
Ishizuchi-Yama, *Japan* **72 D5** 33 45N 133 6 E
Ishkashim, *Tajikistan* **65 E5** 36 44N 71 37 E
Ishkuman, *Pakistan* **93 A5** 36 30N 73 50 E
Ishpeming, *U.S.A.* **148 B2** 46 29N 87 40W
Ishtykhan, *Uzbekistan* **65 D3** 39 58N 66 29 E
Ishurdi, *Bangla.* **90 C2** 24 9N 89 3 E
Isigny-sur-Mer, *France* **26 C5** 49 19N 1 6W
Isıklar Dağı, *Turkey* **51 F11** 40 45N 27 15 E
Işıklı, *Turkey* **49 C11** 38 19N 29 51 E
Isil Kul, *Russia* **66 D8** 54 55N 71 16 E
Ísili, *Italy* **46 C2** 39 44N 9 6 E
Isiolo, *Kenya* **118 B4** 0 24N 37 33 E
Isiro, *Dem. Rep. of the Congo* **118 B2** 2 53N 27 40 E
Isisford, *Australia* **126 C3** 24 15 S 144 21 E
Iskandar, *Uzbekistan* **65 C4** 41 36N 69 41 E
Iskenderun, *Turkey* **100 D7** 36 32N 36 10 E
Iskenderun Körfezi, *Turkey* **100 D6** 36 40N 35 50 E
Iski-Naukat = Eski-Nookat, *Kyrgyzstan* **65 C6** 40 16N 72 36 E
Iskilip, *Turkey* **100 B6** 40 45N 34 29 E
Iskŭr →, *Bulgaria* **51 C8** 43 45N 24 25 E
Iskŭr, Yazovir, *Bulgaria* **50 D7** 42 23N 23 30 E
Iskut →, *Canada* **142 B2** 56 45N 131 49W
Isla →, *U.K.* **22 E5** 56 32N 3 20W
Isla Cristina, *Spain* **43 H3** 37 13N 7 17W
Isla Gorge Nat. Park, *Australia* **126 D4** 25 10 S 149 57 E
Isla Vista, *U.S.A.* **161 L7** 34 25N 119 53W
Islâhiye, *Turkey* **100 D7** 37 0N 36 35 E
Islam Headworks, *Pakistan* **92 E5** 29 49N 72 33 E
Islamabad, *Pakistan* **91 B4** 33 40N 73 10 E
Islamgarh, *Pakistan* **92 F4** 27 51N 70 48 E
Islamkot, *Pakistan* **92 G4** 24 42N 70 13 E
Islamorada, *U.S.A.* **153 L9** 24 56N 80 37W
Islampur, *Bihar, India* **93 G11** 25 9N 85 12 E
Islampur, *Maharashtra, India* **94 F2** 17 2N 74 20 E
Island Bay, *Phil.* **81 G2** 9 6N 118 10 E
Island L., *Canada* **143 C10** 53 47N 94 25W
Island Lagoon, *Australia* **128 A2** 31 30 S 136 40 E
Island Pond, *U.S.A.* **151 B13** 44 49N 71 53W
Islands, B. of, *Canada* **141 C8** 49 11N 58 15W
Islands, B. of, *N.Z.* **130 B3** 35 15 S 174 6 E
Islay, *U.K.* **22 F2** 55 46N 6 10W
Isle →, *France* **28 D3** 44 55N 0 15W
Isle aux Morts, *Canada* **141 C8** 47 35N 59 0W
Isle of Hope, *U.S.A.* **152 D8** 31 58N 81 5W
Isle of Wight □, *U.K.* **21 G6** 50 41N 1 17W
Isle Royale Nat. Park, *U.S.A.* **154 B10** 48 0N 88 55W
Isleton, *U.S.A.* **160 G5** 38 10N 121 37W
Ismail = Izmayil, *Ukraine* **59 K5** 45 22N 28 46 E
Ismâ'ilîya, *Egypt* **106 H8** 30 37N 32 18 E
Ismaning, *Germany* **31 G7** 48 13N 11 40 E
Isna, *Egypt* **106 B3** 25 17N 32 30 E
Isoanala, *Madag.* **117 C8** 23 50 S 45 44 E
Isogstalo, *India* **93 B8** 34 15N 78 46 E
Ísola del Liri, *Italy* **45 G10** 41 41N 13 34 E
Ísola della Scala, *Italy* **44 C7** 45 16N 11 0 E
Ísola di Capo Rizzuto, *Italy* **47 D10** 38 58N 17 6 E
Isparta, *Turkey* **49 D12** 37 47N 30 30 E
Isperikh, *Bulgaria* **51 C10** 43 43N 26 50 E
Íspica, *Italy* **47 F7** 36 47N 14 55 E
Israel ■, *Asia* **103 D3** 32 0N 34 50 E
Isratu, *Eritrea* **107 D4** 16 20N 39 53 E
Issano, *Guyana* **169 B6** 5 49N 59 26W
Issia, *Ivory C.* **112 D3** 6 33N 6 33W
Issoire, *France* **28 C7** 45 32N 3 15 E
Issoudun, *France* **27 F8** 46 57N 1 59 E
Issyk-Kul = Balykchy, *Kyrgyzstan* **65 B8** 42 26N 76 12 E
Issyk-Kul, Ozero = Ysyk-Köl, *Kyrgyzstan* **66 E8** 42 25N 77 15 E
Ist, *Croatia* **45 D11** 44 17N 14 47 E
Istaihah, *U.A.E.* **99 B6** 23 19N 54 4 E
Istállós-kő, *Hungary* **52 B5** 48 4N 20 26 E
İstanbul, *Turkey* **51 E12** 41 0N 29 0 E
İstanbul □, *Turkey* **51 E12** 41 0N 29 0 E
İstanbul Boğazı, *Turkey* **51 E13** 41 10N 29 10 E
Isteren, *Norway* **18 B8** 61 58N 11 47 E
Istiaía, *Greece* **48 C5** 38 57N 23 9 E
Istmina, *Colombia* **168 B2** 5 10N 76 39W
Isto, Mt., *U.S.A.* **144 B12** 69 12N 143 48W
Istok, *Kosovo, Yug.* **50 D4** 42 45N 20 24 E
Istokpoga, L., *U.S.A.* **149 M5** 27 23N 81 17W
Istra, *Croatia* **45 C10** 45 10N 14 0 E
Istres, *France* **29 E8** 43 31N 4 59 E
Istria = Istra, *Croatia* **45 C10** 45 10N 14 0 E
Isugod, *Phil.* **81 G2** 9 19N 118 5 E
Isulan, *Phil.* **81 H5** 6 30N 124 29 E
Itá, *Paraguay* **174 B4** 25 29 S 57 21W
Itabaiana, *Paraíba, Brazil* **170 C4** 7 18 S 35 19W
Itabaiana, *Sergipe, Brazil* **170 D4** 10 41 S 37 37W
Itabaianinha, *Brazil* **170 D4** 11 16 S 37 47W
Itaberaba, *Brazil* **171 D3** 12 32 S 40 18W
Itaberaí, *Brazil* **171 E2** 16 2 S 49 48W
Itabira, *Brazil* **171 E3** 19 37 S 43 13W
Itabirito, *Brazil* **171 F3** 20 15 S 43 48W
Itaboca, *Brazil* **169 D5** 4 50 S 62 40W
Itabuna, *Brazil* **171 D4** 14 48 S 39 16W
Itacajá, *Brazil* **170 C2** 8 19 S 47 46W
Itacaunas →, *Brazil* **170 C2** 5 21 S 49 8W
Itacuaí →, *Brazil* **172 A3** 4 20 S 70 12W
Itaguaçu, *Brazil* **171 E3** 19 48 S 40 51W
Itaguari →, *Brazil* **171 D3** 14 11 S 44 40W
Itaguatins, *Brazil* **170 C2** 5 47 S 47 29W
Itaim →, *Brazil* **170 C3** 7 2 S 42 2W
Itainópolis, *Brazil* **170 C3** 7 24 S 41 31W
Itaipú, Represa de, *Brazil* **175 B5** 25 30 S 54 30W
Itaituba, *Brazil* **169 D6** 4 10 S 55 50W
Itajaí, *Brazil* **175 B6** 27 50 S 48 39W
Itajubá, *Brazil* **171 F2** 22 24 S 45 30W
Itajuípe, *Brazil* **171 D4** 14 41 S 39 22W
Itaka, *Tanzania* **119 D3** 8 50 S 32 49 E
Itako, *Japan* **73 B12** 35 56N 140 33 E
Itala Nature Reserve, *S. Africa* **117 D5** 27 30 S 31 7 E
Italy ■, *Europe* **13 G8** 42 0N 13 0 E
Itamaraju, *Brazil* **171 E4** 17 4 S 39 32W
Itamarati, *Brazil* **172 B4** 6 24 S 68 15W
Itamataré, *Brazil* **170 B2** 2 16 S 46 24W
Itambacuri, *Brazil* **171 E3** 18 1 S 41 42W
Itambé, *Brazil* **171 E3** 15 15 S 40 37W
Itami, *Japan* **73 C7** 34 46N 135 25 E
Itampolo, *Madag.* **117 C7** 24 41 S 43 57 E
Itandrano, *Madag.* **117 C8** 21 47 S 45 17 E
Itanhaém, *Brazil* **171 F2** 24 11 S 46 47W
Itanhauã →, *Brazil* **169 D5** 4 45 S 63 48W
Itanhém, *Brazil* **171 E3** 17 9 S 40 20W
Itano, *Japan* **72 C6** 34 7N 134 28 E
Itapaci, *Brazil* **171 D2** 14 57 S 49 34W
Itapagé, *Brazil* **170 B4** 3 41 S 39 34W
Itaparica, I. de, *Brazil* **171 D4** 12 54 S 38 42W
Itapebi, *Brazil* **171 E4** 15 56 S 39 32W
Itapecuru-Mirim, *Brazil* **170 B3** 3 24 S 44 20W
Itaperuna, *Brazil* **171 F3** 21 10 S 41 54W
Itapetinga, *Brazil* **171 E3** 15 15 S 40 15W
Itapetininga, *Brazil* **175 A6** 23 36 S 48 7W
Itapeva, *Brazil* **175 A6** 23 59 S 48 59W
Itapicuru →, *Bahia, Brazil* **170 D4** 11 47 S 37 32W
Itapicuru →, *Maranhão, Brazil* **170 B3** 2 52 S 44 12W
Itapinima, *Brazil* **173 B5** 5 25 S 60 44W
Itapipoca, *Brazil* **170 B4** 3 30 S 39 35W
Itapiranga, *Brazil* **169 D6** 2 45 S 58 1W
Itapiúna, *Brazil* **170 B4** 4 33 S 38 57W
Itaporanga, *Paraíba, Brazil* **170 C4** 7 18 S 38 0W
Itaporanga, *São Paulo, Brazil* **171 F2** 23 42 S 49 29W
Itapuá □, *Paraguay* **175 B4** 26 40 S 55 40W
Itapuranga, *Brazil* **171 E2** 15 40 S 49 59W
Itaquari, *Brazil* **171 F3** 20 20 S 40 25W
Itaquatiara, *Brazil* **169 D6** 2 58 S 58 30W
Itaquí, *Brazil* **174 B4** 29 8 S 56 30W
Itararé, *Brazil* **175 A6** 24 6 S 49 23W
Itarsi, *India* **92 H7** 22 36N 77 51 E
Itarumã, *Brazil* **171 E1** 18 42 S 51 25W
Itatí, *Argentina* **174 B4** 27 16 S 58 15W
Itatira, *Brazil* **170 B4** 4 30 S 39 37W
Itatuba, *Brazil* **173 B5** 5 46 S 63 20W
Itatupa, *Brazil* **169 D7** 0 37 S 51 12W
Itaueira, *Brazil* **170 C3** 7 36 S 43 2W
Itaueira →, *Brazil* **170 C3** 6 41 S 42 55W
Itaúna, *Brazil* **171 F3** 20 4 S 44 34W
Itbayat, *Phil.* **80 A3** 20 47N 121 51 E
Itbayat I., *Phil.* **80 A3** 20 45N 121 50 E
Itchen →, *U.K.* **21 G6** 50 55N 1 22W
Itchouma, *Niger* **111 D7** 20 14N 13 32 E
Itchoumma, *Niger* **109 D2** 20 14N 13 32 E
Ite, *Peru* **172 D3** 17 55 S 70 57W
Itéa, *Greece* **48 C4** 38 25N 22 25 E
Itezhi Tezhi, L., *Zambia* **119 F2** 15 30 S 25 30 E
Ithaca = Itháki, *Greece* **48 C2** 38 25N 20 40 E
Ithaca, *U.S.A.* **151 D8** 42 27N 76 30W
Itháki, *Greece* **48 C2** 38 25N 20 40 E
Itinga, *Brazil* **171 E3** 16 36 S 41 47W
Itiquira, *Brazil* **173 D7** 17 12 S 54 7W
Itiquira →, *Brazil* **173 D6** 17 18 S 56 44W
Itiruçu, *Brazil* **171 D3** 13 31 S 40 9W
Itiúba, *Brazil* **170 D4** 10 43 S 39 51W
Itkilik →, *U.S.A.* **144 A10** 70 9N 150 56W
Itō, *Japan* **73 C11** 34 58N 139 5 E
Itogon, *Phil.* **80 C3** 16 22N 120 41 E
Itoigawa, *Japan* **71 F8** 37 2N 137 51 E
Itoko, *Dem. Rep. of the Congo* **114 C4** 1 0 S 21 48 E
Iton →, *France* **26 C8** 49 9N 1 12 E
Itonamas →, *Bolivia* **173 C5** 12 28 S 64 24W
Itri, *Italy* **46 A6** 41 17N 13 32 E
Itsa, *Egypt* **106 J7** 29 15N 30 47 E
Itsuki, *Japan* **72 E2** 32 24N 130 50 E
Íttiri, *Italy* **46 B1** 40 36N 8 34 E
Ittoqqortoormiit, *Greenland* **10 C8** 70 20N 23 0W
Itu, *Brazil* **175 A6** 23 17 S 47 15W
Itu, *Nigeria* **113 D6** 5 10N 7 58 E
Itu Aba I., *S. China Sea* **78 B4** 10 23N 114 21 E
Ituaçu, *Brazil* **171 D3** 13 50 S 41 18W
Ituango, *Colombia* **168 B2** 7 4N 75 45W
Ituí →, *Brazil* **168 D3** 4 38 S 70 19W
Ituiutaba, *Brazil* **171 E2** 19 0 S 49 25W
Itumbiara, *Brazil* **171 E2** 18 20 S 49 10W
Ituna, *Canada* **143 C8** 51 10N 103 24W
Itunge Port, *Tanzania* **119 D3** 9 40 S 33 55 E
Ituni, *Guyana* **169 B6** 5 28N 58 15W
Itupiranga, *Brazil* **170 C2** 5 9 S 49 20W
Iturama, *Brazil* **171 E1** 19 44 S 50 11W
Iturbe, *Argentina* **174 A2** 23 0 S 65 25W
Ituri →, *Dem. Rep. of the Congo* **118 B2** 1 40N 27 1 E
Iturup, Ostrov, *Russia* **67 E15** 45 0N 148 0 E
Ituverava, *Brazil* **171 F2** 20 20 S 47 47W
Ituxi →, *Brazil* **173 B5** 7 18 S 64 51W
Ituyuro →, *Argentina* **174 A3** 22 40 S 63 50W
Itzehoe, *Germany* **30 B5** 53 55N 9 31 E
Iuka, *U.S.A.* **157 F8** 38 37N 88 47W
Ivahona, *Madag.* **117 C8** 23 27 S 46 10 E
Ivaí →, *Brazil* **175 A5** 23 18 S 53 42W
Ivalo, *Finland* **14 B22** 68 38N 27 35 E
Ivalojoki →, *Finland* **14 B22** 68 40N 27 40 E
Ivanava, *Belarus* **59 F3** 52 7N 25 29 E
Ivančice, *Czech Rep.* **35 B9** 49 6N 16 23 E
Ivăneşti, *Romania* **53 D12** 46 39N 27 27 E
Ivangorod, *Russia* **58 C5** 59 27N 28 13 E
Ivanhoe, *N.S.W., Australia* **128 B6** 32 56 S 144 20 E
Ivanhoe, *Vic., Australia* **129 D6** 37 46 S 145 3 E
Ivanhoe, *Calif., U.S.A.* **160 J7** 36 23N 119 13W
Ivanhoe, *Minn., U.S.A.* **154 C6** 44 28N 96 15W
Ivanić Grad, *Croatia* **45 C13** 45 41N 16 25 E
Ivanjica, *Serbia, Yug.* **50 C4** 43 35N 20 12 E
Ivanjska, *Bos.-H.* **52 F2** 44 55N 17 4 E
Ivankoyskoye Vdkhr., *Russia* **58 D9** 56 37N 36 32 E
Ivano-Frankivsk, *Ukraine* **59 H3** 48 40N 24 40 E
Ivano-Frankovsk = Ivano-Frankivsk, *Ukraine* **59 H3** 48 40N 24 40 E
Ivanof Bay, *U.S.A.* **144 J8** 55 54N 159 29W
Ivanovka, *Kyrgyzstan* **65 B7** 42 53N 75 6 E
Ivanovo = Ivanava, *Belarus* **59 F3** 52 7N 25 29 E
Ivanovo, *Russia* **58 D11** 57 5N 41 0 E
Ivanšćica, *Croatia* **45 B13** 46 12N 16 13 E
Ivato, *Madag.* **117 C8** 20 37 S 47 10 E
Ivatsevichy, *Belarus* **59 F3** 52 43N 25 21 E
Ivaylovgrad, *Bulgaria* **51 E10** 41 32N 26 8 E
Ivdel, *Russia* **56 B11** 60 42N 60 24 E
Ivindo →, *Gabon* **114 C2** 0 9 S 12 9 E
Ivinheima →, *Brazil* **175 A5** 23 14 S 53 42W
Ivinhema, *Brazil* **175 A5** 22 10 S 53 37W
Ivittuut, *Greenland* **10 E6** 61 14N 48 12W
Ivohibe, *Madag.* **117 C8** 22 31 S 46 57 E
Ivolândia, *Brazil* **171 E1** 16 34 S 50 51W
Ivory Coast, *W. Afr.* **112 E4** 4 20N 5 0W
Ivory Coast ■, *Africa* **112 D4** 7 30N 5 0W
Ivösjön, *Sweden* **17 H8** 56 8N 14 25 E
Ivrea, *Italy* **44 C4** 45 28N 7 52 E
Ivrindi, *Turkey* **49 B9** 39 34N 27 30 E
Ivujivik, *Canada* **139 B12** 62 24N 77 55W
Ivybridge, *U.K.* **21 G4** 50 23N 3 56W
Iwai-Jima, *Japan* **72 D3** 33 47N 131 58 E
Iwaizumi, *Japan* **70 E10** 39 50N 141 45 E
Iwaki, *Japan* **71 F10** 37 3N 140 55 E
Iwakuni, *Japan* **72 C4** 34 15N 132 8 E
Iwami, *Japan* **72 B6** 35 32N 134 15 E
Iwamizawa, *Japan* **70 C10** 43 12N 141 46 E
Iwanai, *Japan* **70 C10** 42 58N 140 30 E
Iwase, *Japan* **73 A12** 36 21N 140 6 E
Iwata, *Japan* **73 C9** 34 42N 137 51 E
Iwate □, *Japan* **70 E10** 39 30N 141 30 E
Iwate-San, *Japan* **70 E10** 39 51N 141 0 E
Iwo, *Nigeria* **113 D5** 7 39N 4 9 E
Iwonicz-Zdrój, *Poland* **55 J8** 49 37N 21 47 E
Iwungu, *Dem. Rep. of the Congo* **115 D3** 5 16 S 19 17 E
Ixiamas, *Bolivia* **172 C4** 13 50 S 68 5W
Ixopo, *S. Africa* **117 E5** 30 11 S 30 5 E
Ixtepec, *Mexico* **163 D5** 16 32N 95 10W
Ixtlán del Río, *Mexico* **162 C4** 21 5N 104 21W
'Iyādh, *Yemen* **98 D4** 14 59N 46 51 E
Iyal Bakhit, *Sudan* **107 E2** 13 20N 28 39 E
Iyo, *Japan* **72 D4** 33 45N 132 45 E
Iyo-Mishima, *Japan* **72 D5** 33 58N 133 30 E
Iyo-Nada, *Japan* **72 D4** 33 40N 132 20 E
Izabal, L. de, *Guatemala* **164 C2** 15 30N 89 10W
Izamal, *Mexico* **163 C7** 20 56N 89 1W
Izberbash, *Russia* **61 J8** 42 35N 47 52 E
Izbica, *Poland* **55 H10** 50 53N 23 10 E
Izbica Kujawska, *Poland* **55 F5** 52 25N 18 40 E
Izbiceni, *Romania* **53 G9** 43 45N 24 40 E
Izena-Shima, *Japan* **71 L3** 26 56N 127 56 E
Izgrev, *Bulgaria* **51 C10** 43 36N 26 58 E
Izh →, *Russia* **64 C4** 56 9N 53 0 E
Izhevsk, *Russia* **64 C4** 56 51N 53 14 E
Izhma →, *Russia* **56 A9** 65 19N 52 54 E
Izileg, *Algeria* **111 D6** 20 20N 6 4 E
Izkī, *Oman* **99 B7** 22 56N 57 46 E
Izmayil, *Ukraine* **59 K5** 45 22N 28 46 E
Izmir, *Turkey* **49 C9** 38 25N 27 8 E
Izmir □, *Turkey* **49 C9** 38 15N 27 40 E
Izmir Körfezi, *Turkey* **49 C8** 38 30N 26 50 E
Izmit = Kocaeli, *Turkey* **51 F13** 40 45N 29 50 E
Iznájar, *Spain* **43 H6** 37 15N 4 19W
Iznalloz, *Spain* **43 H7** 37 24N 3 30W
Iznik, *Turkey* **100 B3** 40 23N 29 46 E
Iznik Gölü, *Turkey* **51 F13** 40 27N 29 30 E
Izobil'nyy, *Russia* **61 H5** 45 25N 41 44 E
Izola, *Slovenia* **45 C10** 45 32N 13 39 E
Izozog, Bañados de, *Bolivia* **173 D5** 18 48 S 62 10W
Izra, *Syria* **103 C5** 32 51N 36 15 E
Iztochni Rodopi, *Bulgaria* **51 E9** 41 45N 25 30 E
Izu-Hantō, *Japan* **73 C11** 34 45N 139 0 E
Izu-Shotō, *Japan* **71 G10** 34 30N 140 0 E
Izúcar de Matamoros, *Mexico* **163 D5** 18 36N 98 28W
Izuhara, *Japan* **72 C1** 34 12N 129 17 E
Izumi, *Kagoshima, Japan* **72 E2** 32 5N 130 22 E
Izumi, *Ōsaka, Japan* **73 C7** 34 28N 135 24 E
Izumi-Sano, *Japan* **73 C7** 34 23N 135 18 E
Izumo, *Japan* **72 B4** 35 20N 132 46 E
Izyaslav, *Ukraine* **59 G4** 50 5N 26 50 E
Izyum, *Ukraine* **59 H9** 49 12N 37 19 E

J

J.F. Rodrigues, *Brazil* **170 B1** 2 55 S 50 20W
J.P. Koch Fjord, *Greenland* **10 A6** 82 45N 44 0W
Ja-ela, *Sri Lanka* **95 L4** 7 5N 79 53 E
Jaba, *Ethiopia* **107 F4** 6 20N 35 7 E
Jabal at Ta'ir, *Red Sea* **107 D5** 15 35N 41 52 E
Jabalón →, *Spain* **43 G6** 38 53N 4 5W
Jabalpur, *India* **93 H8** 23 9N 79 58 E
Jabbūl, *Syria* **96 B3** 36 4N 37 30 E
Jabiru, *Australia* **124 B5** 12 40 S 132 53 E
Jablah, *Syria* **100 E6** 35 20N 36 0 E
Jablanac, *Croatia* **45 D11** 44 42N 14 56 E
Jablanica, *Bos.-H.* **52 G2** 43 40N 17 45 E
Jablonec nad Nisou, *Czech Rep.* **34 A8** 50 43N 15 10 E
Jablonica, *Slovak Rep.* **35 C10** 48 37N 17 26 E
Jabłonowo Pomorskie, *Poland* **54 E6** 53 23N 19 10 E
Jablunkov, *Czech Rep.* **35 B11** 49 35N 18 46 E
Jaboatão, *Brazil* **170 C4** 8 7 S 35 1W
Jabonga, *Phil.* **81 G5** 9 20N 125 32 E
Jaboticabal, *Brazil* **175 A6** 21 15 S 48 17W
Jabukovac, *Serbia, Yug.* **50 B6** 44 22N 22 21 E
Jaburu, *Brazil* **173 B5** 5 30 S 64 0W
Jaca, *Spain* **40 C4** 42 35N 0 33W
Jacaré →, *Brazil* **170 D3** 10 3 S 42 13W
Jacareí, *Brazil* **175 A6** 23 20 S 46 0W
Jacarèzinho, *Brazil* **175 A6** 23 5 S 49 58W
Jaciara, *Brazil* **173 D7** 15 59 S 54 57W
Jacinto, *Brazil* **171 E3** 16 10 S 40 17W
Jaciparaná, *Brazil* **173 B5** 9 15 S 64 23W
Jackman, *U.S.A.* **149 C10** 45 35N 70 17W
Jacksboro, *U.S.A.* **155 J5** 33 14N 98 15W
Jackson, *Barbados* **165 g** 13 7N 59 36W
Jackson, *Ala., U.S.A.* **149 K2** 31 31N 87 53W
Jackson, *Calif., U.S.A.* **160 G6** 38 21N 120 46W
Jackson, *Ga., U.S.A.* **152 B6** 33 20N 83 57W
Jackson, *Ky., U.S.A.* **148 G4** 37 33N 83 23W
Jackson, *Mich., U.S.A.* **157 B12** 42 15N 84 24W
Jackson, *Minn., U.S.A.* **154 D7** 43 37N 95 1W
Jackson, *Miss., U.S.A.* **155 J9** 32 18N 90 12W
Jackson, *Mo., U.S.A.* **155 G10** 37 23N 89 40W
Jackson, *N.H., U.S.A.* **151 B13** 44 10N 71 11W
Jackson, *Ohio, U.S.A.* **148 F4** 39 3N 82 39W
Jackson, *S.C., U.S.A.* **152 B8** 33 20N 81 47W
Jackson, *Tenn., U.S.A.* **149 H1** 35 37N 88 49W
Jackson, *Wyo., U.S.A.* **158 E8** 43 29N 110 46W
Jackson, C., *N.Z.* **131 A9** 40 59 S 174 20 E
Jackson B., *N.Z.* **131 D3** 43 58 S 168 42 E
Jackson Center, *U.S.A.* **157 D12** 40 27N 84 4W
Jackson Hd., *N.Z.* **131 D3** 43 58 S 168 37 E
Jackson L., *Fla., U.S.A.* **152 E5** 30 30N 84 17W
Jackson L., *Ga., U.S.A.* **152 B6** 33 19N 83 50W
Jackson L., *Wyo., U.S.A.* **158 E8** 43 52N 110 36W
Jacksons, *N.Z.* **131 C6** 42 46 S 171 32 E
Jackson's Arm, *Canada* **141 C8** 49 52N 56 47W
Jacksonville, *Ala., U.S.A.* **152 B4** 33 49N 85 46W
Jacksonville, *Ark., U.S.A.* **155 H8** 34 52N 92 7W
Jacksonville, *Calif., U.S.A.* **160 H6** 37 52N 120 24W
Jacksonville, *Fla., U.S.A.* **152 E8** 30 20N 81 39W
Jacksonville, *Ga., U.S.A.* **152 D7** 31 49N 82 59W
Jacksonville, *Ill., U.S.A.* **156 E6** 39 44N 90 14W
Jacksonville, *N.C., U.S.A.* **149 H7** 34 45N 77 26W
Jacksonville, *Tex., U.S.A.* **155 K7** 31 58N 95 17W
Jacksonville Beach, *U.S.A.* **152 E8** 30 17N 81 24W
Jacmel, *Haiti* **165 C5** 18 14N 72 32W
Jacob Lake, *U.S.A.* **159 H7** 36 43N 112 13W
Jacobabad, *Pakistan* **91 C3** 28 20N 68 29 E
Jacobina, *Brazil* **170 D3** 11 11 S 40 30W
Jacques Cartier, Dét. de, *Canada* **141 C7** 50 0N 63 30W
Jacques Cartier, Mt., *Canada* **141 C6** 48 57N 66 0W
Jacques Cartier, Parc Prov., *Canada* **141 C5** 47 15N 71 33W
Jacqueville, *Ivory C.* **112 D4** 5 12N 4 25W
Jacuí →, *Brazil* **175 C5** 30 2 S 51 15W
Jacumba, *U.S.A.* **161 N10** 32 37N 116 11W
Jacundá →, *Brazil* **170 B1** 1 57 S 50 26W
Jadcherla, *India* **94 F4** 16 46N 78 9 E
Jade, *Germany* **30 B4** 53 20N 8 14 E
Jadebusen, *Germany* **30 B4** 53 29N 8 12 E
Jadotville = Likasi, *Dem. Rep. of the Congo* **119 E2** 10 55 S 26 48 E
Jadovnik, *Serbia, Yug.* **50 C3** 43 20N 19 45 E
Jadraque, *Spain* **40 E2** 40 55N 2 55W
Jādū, *Libya* **108 B2** 32 0N 12 0 E
Jaén, *Peru* **172 B2** 5 25 S 78 40W
Jaén, *Spain* **43 H7** 37 44N 3 43W
Jaén □, *Spain* **43 H7** 37 50N 3 30W
Jæren, *Norway* **18 F2** 58 42N 5 47 E
Jærens rev, *Norway* **18 F2** 58 45N 5 45 E
Jafarabad, *India* **92 J4** 20 52N 71 22 E
Jafène, *Africa* **110 D3** 20 35N 5 30W
Jaffa = Tel Aviv-Yafo, *Israel* **103 C3** 32 4N 34 48 E
Jaffa, C., *Australia* **128 D3** 36 58 S 139 40 E
Jaffna, *Sri Lanka* **95 K5** 9 45N 80 2 E
Jaffrey, *U.S.A.* **151 D12** 42 49N 72 2W
Jagadhri, *India* **92 D7** 30 10N 77 20 E
Jagadishpur, *India* **93 G11** 25 30N 84 21 E
Jagdalpur, *India* **94 E6** 19 3N 82 0 E
Jagersfontein, *S. Africa* **116 D4** 29 44 S 25 27 E
Jaghīn →, *Iran* **97 E8** 27 17N 57 13 E
Jagna, *Phil.* **81 G5** 9 39N 124 22 E
Jagodina, *Serbia, Yug.* **50 B5** 44 5N 21 15 E
Jagst →, *Germany* **31 F5** 49 14N 9 10 E
Jagtial, *India* **94 E4** 18 50N 79 0 E
Jaguaquara, *Brazil* **171 D4** 13 32 S 39 58W
Jaguariaíva, *Brazil* **175 A6** 24 10 S 49 50W
Jaguaribe, *Brazil* **170 C4** 5 53 S 38 37W

Jaguaribe →, Brazil 170 B4 4 25 S 37 45W
Jaguaruana, Brazil 170 B4 4 50 S 37 47W
Jagüey Grande, Cuba 164 B3 22 35N 81 7W
Jagungal, Mt., Australia 129 D8 36 8 S 148 22 E
Jahanabad, India 93 G11 25 13N 84 59 E
Jahazpur, India 92 G6 25 37N 75 17 E
Jahrom, Iran 97 D7 28 30N 53 31 E
Jaicós, Brazil 170 C3 7 21 S 41 8W
Jaigarh, India 94 F1 17 17N 73 13 E
Jaijon, India 92 D7 31 21N 76 9 E
Jailolo, Indonesia 82 A3 1 5N 127 30 E
Jailolo, Selat, Indonesia 83 A3 0 5N 129 5 E
Jaintiapur, Bangla. 90 C4 25 8N 92 7 E
Jaipur, Assam, India 90 B5 27 16N 95 24 E
Jaipur, Raj., India 92 F6 27 0N 75 50 E
Jais, India 93 F9 26 15N 81 32 E
Jaisalmer, India 92 F4 26 55N 70 54 E
Jaisinghnagar, India 93 H8 23 38N 78 34 E
Jaitaran, India 92 F5 26 12N 73 56 E
Jaithari, India 93 H8 23 14N 78 37 E
Jājarm, Iran 97 B8 36 58N 56 27 E
Jajce, Bos.-H. 52 F2 44 19N 17 17 E
Jajpur, India 94 D8 20 53N 86 22 E
Jakam →, India 92 H6 23 54N 74 13 E
Jakarta, Indonesia 84 D3 6 9 S 106 49 E
Jakhal, India 92 E6 29 48N 75 50 E
Jakhau, India 92 H3 23 13N 68 43 E
Jakobshavn = Ilulissat, Greenland 10 D5 69 12N 51 10W
Jakobstad = Pietarsaari, Finland 14 E20 63 40N 22 43 E
Jakupica, Macedonia 50 E5 41 45N 21 22 E
Jal, U.S.A. 155 J3 32 7N 103 12W
Jalal-Abad, Kyrgyzstan 65 C6 40 56N 73 0 E
Jalālābād, Afghan. 91 B3 34 30N 70 29 E
Jalalabad, India 93 F8 27 41N 79 42 E
Jalalpur Jattan, Pakistan 92 C6 32 38N 74 11 E
Jalama, U.S.A. 161 L6 34 29N 120 29W
Jalapa, Guatemala 164 D2 14 39N 89 59W
Jalapa Enríquez, Mexico 163 D5 19 32N 96 55W
Jalasjärvi, Finland 15 E20 62 29N 22 47 E
Jalaun, India 93 F8 26 8N 79 25 E
Jalāzin, Afghan. 65 E2 37 2N 64 49 E
Jaldak, Afghan. 91 C2 31 58N 66 43 E
Jaldhaka →, Bangla. 90 B2 26 16N 89 16 E
Jales, Brazil 171 F1 20 10 S 50 33W
Jalesar, India 92 F8 27 29N 78 19 E
Jaleswar, Nepal 93 F11 26 38N 85 48 E
Jalgaon, India 94 D2 21 0N 75 42 E
Jalībah, Iraq 96 D5 30 35N 46 32 E
Jalingo, Nigeria 113 D7 8 55N 11 25 E
Jalisco □, Mexico 162 D4 20 0N 104 0W
Jalkot, Pakistan 93 B5 35 14N 73 24 E
Jallas →, Spain 42 C1 42 54N 9 8W
Jalna, India 94 E2 19 48N 75 38 E
Jalón →, Spain 40 D3 41 47N 1 4W
Jalor, India 92 G5 25 21N 72 37 E
Jalpa, Mexico 162 C4 21 38N 102 58W
Jalpaiguri, India 90 B2 26 32N 88 46 E
Jālq, Iran 91 D1 27 35N 62 46 E
Jaluit I., Marshall Is. 134 G8 6 0N 169 30 E
Jalūlā, Iraq 101 E11 34 16N 45 10 E
Jamaame = Giamama, Somali Rep. 120 D2 0 4N 42 44 E
Jamaari, Nigeria 113 C6 11 44N 9 53 E
Jamaica ■, W. Indies 164 a 18 10N 77 30W
Jamalpur, Bangla. 90 C2 24 52N 89 56 E
Jamalpur, India 93 G12 25 18N 86 28 E
Jamalpurganj, India 93 H13 23 2N 87 59 E
Jamanxim →, Brazil 173 A6 4 43 S 56 18W
Jamari, Brazil 173 B5 8 45 S 63 27W
Jamari →, Brazil 173 B5 8 27 S 63 30W
Jamba, Angola 115 E3 14 40 S 16 2 E
Jambewangi, Indonesia 79 J17 8 17 S 114 7 E
Jambi, Indonesia 84 C2 1 38 S 103 30 E
Jambi □, Indonesia 84 C2 1 30 S 102 30 E
Jambusar, India 92 H5 22 3N 72 51 E
James, U.S.A. 152 C6 32 58N 83 29W
James →, S. Dak., U.S.A. 154 D6 42 52N 97 18W
James →, Va., U.S.A. 148 G7 36 56N 76 27W
James B., Canada 140 B3 54 0N 80 0W
James Island, U.S.A. 152 C10 32 45N 79 55W
James Ranges, Australia 124 D5 24 10 S 132 30 E
James Ross I., Antarctica 7 C18 63 58 S 57 50W
Jamesabad, Pakistan 92 G3 25 17N 69 15 E
Jameson Land, Greenland 10 C8 71 0N 23 30W
Jamesport, U.S.A. 156 E3 39 58N 93 48W
Jamestown, Australia 128 B3 33 10 S 138 32 E
Jamestown, St. Helena 9 h 15 55 S 5 43W
Jamestown, S. Africa 116 E4 31 6 S 26 45 E
Jamestown, Ind., U.S.A. 157 E10 39 56N 86 38W
Jamestown, Mo., U.S.A. 156 F4 38 48N 92 30W
Jamestown, N. Dak., U.S.A. 154 B5 46 54N 98 42W
Jamestown, N.Y., U.S.A. 150 D5 42 6N 79 14W
Jamestown, Ohio, U.S.A. 157 E13 39 39N 83 33W
Jamestown, Pa., U.S.A. 150 E4 41 29N 80 27W
Jamestown, S.C., U.S.A. 152 B10 33 17N 79 42W
Jamīlābād, Iran 97 C6 34 24N 48 28 E
Jamiltepec, Mexico 163 D5 16 17N 97 49W
Jamira →, India 93 J13 21 35N 88 28 E
Jämjö, Sweden 17 H9 56 12N 15 49 E
Jamkhandi, India 94 F2 16 30N 75 15 E
Jamkhed, India 94 E2 18 43N 75 19 E
Jammalamadugu, India 95 G4 14 51N 78 25 E
Jammerbugt, Denmark 17 G3 57 15N 9 20 E
Jammu, India 92 C6 32 43N 74 54 E
Jammu & Kashmir □, India 93 B7 34 25N 77 0 E
Jamnagar, India 92 H4 22 30N 70 6 E
Jamner, India 94 D2 20 45N 75 52 E
Jamni →, India 93 G8 25 13N 78 35 E
Jampur, Pakistan 91 C3 29 39N 70 40 E
Jamrud, Pakistan 92 C4 33 59N 71 24 E
Jämsä, Finland 15 F21 61 53N 25 10 E
Jamshedpur, India 93 H12 22 44N 86 12 E
Jamtara, India 93 H12 23 59N 86 49 E
Jämtland, Sweden 14 E15 63 31N 14 0 E
Jämtlands län □, Sweden 16 B7 62 40N 13 50 E
Jamuna →, Bangla. 90 D2 23 51N 89 45 E
Jamunamukh, India 90 B4 26 6N 92 44 E
Jamurki, Bangla. 90 C3 24 9N 90 2 E
Jan L., Canada 143 C8 54 56N 102 55W
Jan Mayen, Arctic 6 B7 71 0N 9 0W
Janakkala, Finland 15 F21 60 54N 24 36 E
Janaúba, Brazil 171 E3 15 48 S 43 19W
Janaucu, I., Brazil 170 A1 0 30N 50 10W
Jand, Pakistan 92 C5 33 30N 72 6 E
Jandaia, Brazil 171 E1 17 6 S 50 7W
Jandaq, Iran 97 C7 34 3N 54 22 E
Jandia, Canary Is. 9 e2 28 6N 14 21W
Jandia, Pta. de, Canary Is. 9 e2 28 3N 14 31W
Jandiatuba →, Brazil 168 D4 3 28 S 68 42W
Jandola, Pakistan 92 C4 32 20N 70 9 E
Jandowae, Australia 127 D5 26 45 S 151 7 E
Jándula →, Spain 43 G6 38 3N 4 6W
Jane Pk., N.Z. 131 F3 45 15 S 168 20 E
Janesville, U.S.A. 156 B7 42 41N 89 1W
Janga, Ghana 113 C4 10 5N 1 0W
Jangamo, Mozam. 117 C6 24 6 S 35 21 E
Janghai, India 93 G10 25 33N 82 19 E
Jango, Brazil 173 E6 20 27 S 55 29W
Jangoon, India 94 F4 17 44N 79 5 E
Jangy-Bazar, Kyrgyzstan 65 C5 41 40N 70 53 E
Jangy-Jol, Kyrgyzstan 65 C6 41 36N 72 9 E
Janhtang Ga, Burma 90 B6 26 32N 96 38 E
Jani Khel, Afghan. 91 B3 32 46N 68 24 E
Janikowo, Poland 55 F5 52 45N 18 7 E
Janīn, West Bank 103 C4 32 28N 35 18 E
Janinà = Ioánnina □, Greece 48 B2 39 39N 20 57 E
Janiuay, Phil. 81 F4 10 58N 122 30 E
Janja, Bos.-H. 52 F4 44 40N 19 14 E
Janjevo, Kosovo, Yug. 50 D5 42 35N 21 19 E
Janjgir, India 93 J10 22 1N 82 34 E
Janjina, Croatia 45 F14 42 58N 17 25 E
Janjina, Madag. 117 C8 20 30 S 45 50 E
Janos, Mexico 162 A3 30 45N 108 10W
Jánoshalma, Hungary 52 D4 46 18N 19 21 E
Jánosháza, Hungary 52 C2 47 8N 17 12 E
Jánossomorja, Hungary 52 C2 47 47N 17 11 E
Janów, Poland 55 H6 50 44N 19 27 E
Janów Lubelski, Poland 55 H9 50 48N 22 23 E
Janów Podlaski, Poland 55 F10 52 11N 23 11 E
Janowiec Wielkopolski, Poland 55 F4 52 45N 17 30 E
Januária, Brazil 171 E3 15 25 S 44 25W
Janub Dârfûr □, Sudan 107 E2 11 0N 25 0 E
Janub Kordofân □, Sudan 107 E3 12 0N 30 0 E
Janubio, Canary Is. 9 e2 28 56N 13 50W
Janville, France 27 D8 48 10N 1 50 E
Janwada, India 94 E3 18 0N 77 29 E
Janzé, France 26 E5 47 55N 1 28W
Jaora, India 92 H6 23 40N 75 10 E
Japan ■, Asia 71 G8 36 0N 136 0 E
Japan, Sea of, Asia 70 E7 40 0N 135 0 E
Japan Trench, Pac. Oc. 62 F18 32 0N 142 0 E
Japen = Yapen, Indonesia 83 B5 1 50 S 136 0 E
Japiim, Brazil 172 B3 7 37 S 72 54W
Japla, India 93 G11 24 33N 84 1 E
Japurá, Brazil 168 D4 1 48 S 66 34W
Japurá →, Brazil 168 D4 3 8 S 65 46W
Jaquarão, Brazil 175 C5 32 34 S 53 23W
Jaqué, Panama 164 E4 7 27N 78 8W
Jarābulus, Syria 101 D8 36 49N 38 1 E
Jaraguá, Brazil 171 E2 15 45 S 49 20W
Jaraguari, Brazil 173 E7 20 9 S 54 35W
Jaraicejo, Spain 43 F5 39 40N 5 49W
Jaraíz de la Vera, Spain 42 E5 40 4N 5 45W
Jarama →, Spain 42 E7 40 24N 3 32W
Jaramānah, Syria 100 F7 33 29N 36 21 E
Jaramillo, Argentina 176 C3 47 10 S 67 7W
Jarandilla, Spain 42 E5 40 8N 5 39W
Jaranwala, Pakistan 91 C4 31 15N 73 26 E
Jarash, Jordan 103 C4 32 17N 35 54 E
Jarauçu →, Brazil 169 D7 1 48 S 52 22W
Järbo, Sweden 16 D10 60 43N 16 36 E
Jardas al 'Abīd, Libya 108 B4 32 18N 20 59 E
Jardim, Brazil 174 A4 21 28 S 56 2W
Jardín →, Spain 41 G2 38 50N 2 10W
Jardine River Nat. Park, Australia 126 A3 11 9 S 142 21 E
Jardines de la Reina, Arch. de los, Cuba 164 B4 20 50N 78 50W
Jargalang, China 75 C12 43 5N 122 55 E
Jargalant = Hovd, Mongolia 68 B4 48 2N 91 37 E
Jari →, Brazil 169 D7 1 9 S 51 54W
Jaria Janjail, Bangla. 90 C3 25 0N 90 40 E
Jarīr, W. al →, Si. Arabia 96 E4 25 38N 42 30 E
Järlåsa, Sweden 16 E11 59 53N 17 12 E
Jarmen, Germany 30 B9 53 54N 13 20 E
Järna, Dalarnas, Sweden 16 D8 60 33N 14 26 E
Järna, Stockholm, Sweden 16 E11 59 6N 17 34 E
Jarnac, France 28 C3 45 40N 0 11W
Jarny, France 27 C12 49 9N 5 53 E
Jaro, Phil. 81 F5 11 11N 124 47 E
Jarocin, Poland 55 G4 51 59N 17 29 E
Jaroměř, Czech Rep. 34 A8 50 22N 15 52 E
Jarosław, Poland 55 H9 50 2N 22 42 E
Järpås, Sweden 17 F6 58 23N 12 57 E
Järpen, Sweden 16 A7 63 21N 13 26 E
Jarqūrghon, Uzbekistan 65 E3 37 31N 67 25 E
Jarrahdale, Australia 125 F2 32 24 S 116 5 E
Jarrahi →, Iran 97 D6 30 49N 48 48 E
Jarres, Plaine des, Laos 86 C4 19 27N 103 10 E
Jarso, Ethiopia 107 F4 5 15N 37 30 E
Jartai, China 74 E3 39 45N 105 48 E
Jaru, Brazil 173 C5 10 26 S 62 27W
Jaru →, Brazil 173 C5 10 5 S 61 59W
Jarud Qi, China 75 B11 44 28N 120 50 E
Järvenpää, Finland 15 F21 60 29N 25 5 E
Jarvis, Canada 150 D4 42 53N 80 6W
Jarvis I., Pac. Oc. 135 H12 0 15 S 160 5W
Jarvorník, Czech Rep. 35 A10 50 23N 17 2 E
Järvsö, Sweden 16 C10 61 43N 16 10 E
Jarwa, India 93 F10 27 38N 82 30 E
Jaša Tomić, Serbia, Yug. 52 E5 45 26N 20 50 E
Jasaan, Phil. 81 G5 8 39N 124 45 E
Jasdan, India 92 H4 22 2N 71 12 E
Jashpurnagar, India 93 H11 22 54N 84 9 E
Jasidih, India 93 G12 24 31N 86 39 E
Jasień, Poland 55 G2 51 46N 15 0 E
Jāsimīyah, Iraq 101 F11 33 45N 44 41 E
Jasin, Malaysia 87 L4 2 20N 102 26 E
Jāsk, Iran 97 E8 25 38N 57 45 E
Jasło, Poland 55 J8 49 45N 21 30 E
Jasmund, Germany 30 A9 54 32N 13 35 E
Jaso, India 93 G9 24 30N 80 29 E
Jason Is., Falk. Is. 176 G4 51 0 S 61 0W
Jasonville, U.S.A. 157 E9 39 10N 87 12W
Jasper, Alta., Canada 142 C5 52 55N 118 5W
Jasper, Ont., Canada 151 B9 44 52N 75 57W
Jasper, Ala., U.S.A. 149 J2 33 50N 87 17W
Jasper, Fla., U.S.A. 152 E7 30 31N 82 57W
Jasper, Ind., U.S.A. 157 F10 38 24N 86 56W
Jasper, Tex., U.S.A. 155 K8 30 56N 94 1W
Jasper Nat. Park, Canada 142 C5 52 50N 118 8W
Jasrasar, India 92 F5 27 43N 73 49 E
Jastarnia, Poland 54 D5 54 42N 18 40 E
Jastrebarsko, Croatia 45 C12 45 41N 15 39 E
Jastrowie, Poland 54 E3 53 26N 16 49 E
Jastrzębie Zdrój, Poland 55 J5 49 57N 18 35 E
Jász-Nagykun-Szolnok □, Hungary 52 C5 47 15N 20 30 E
Jászapáti, Hungary 52 C5 47 32N 20 10 E
Jászárokszállás, Hungary 52 C4 47 39N 19 58 E
Jászberény, Hungary 52 C4 47 30N 19 55 E
Jászkisér, Hungary 52 C5 47 27N 20 20 E
Jászladány, Hungary 52 C5 47 23N 20 10 E
Jataí, Brazil 171 E1 17 58 S 51 48W
Jatapu →, Brazil 169 D6 2 13 S 58 17W
Jath, India 94 F2 17 3N 75 13 E
Jati, Pakistan 92 G3 24 20N 68 19 E
Jatibarang, Indonesia 85 D3 6 28 S 108 18 E
Jatiluwih, Indonesia 79 J18 8 23 S 115 8 E
Jatinegara, Indonesia 84 D3 6 13 S 106 52 E
Játiva = Xátiva, Spain 41 G4 38 59N 0 32W
Jättendal, Sweden 16 C11 61 58N 17 15 E
Jaú, Angola 115 F2 15 12 S 13 31 E
Jaú, Brazil 175 A6 22 10 S 48 30W
Jaú →, Brazil 169 D5 1 54 S 61 26W
Jauaperí →, Brazil 169 D5 1 26 S 61 35W
Jauja, Peru 172 C2 11 45 S 75 15W
Jaunpur, India 93 G10 25 46N 82 44 E
Jauru →, Brazil 173 D6 16 22 S 57 46W
Java = Jawa, Indonesia 85 D4 7 0 S 110 0 E
Java Barat □, Indonesia 79 G12 7 0 S 107 0 E
Java Sea, Indonesia 85 C3 4 35 S 107 15 E
Java Tengah □, Indonesia 79 G14 7 0 S 110 0 E
Java Timur □, Indonesia 79 G15 8 0 S 113 0 E
Java Trench, Ind. Oc. 84 D2 9 0 S 105 0 E
Javadi Hills, India 95 H4 12 40N 78 40 E
Javalambre, Sa. de, Spain 40 E4 40 6N 1 0W
Jávea, Spain 41 G5 38 48N 0 10 E
Javhlant = Ulyasutay, Mongolia 68 B4 47 56N 97 28 E
Javier, I., Chile 176 C2 47 5 S 74 25W
Javla, India 94 F2 17 18N 75 9 E
Jawa, Indonesia 85 D4 7 0 S 110 0 E
Jawad, India 92 G6 24 36N 74 51 E
Jawf, W. al →, Yemen 98 D4 15 50N 45 30 E
Jawhar, India 94 E1 19 55N 73 14 E
Jawor, Poland 55 G3 51 4N 16 11 E
Jaworzno, Poland 55 H6 50 13N 19 11 E
Jaworzyna Śląska, Poland 55 H3 50 55N 16 28 E
Jay, U.S.A. 153 E2 30 57N 87 9W
Jay Peak, U.S.A. 151 B12 44 55N 72 32W
Jaya, Puncak, Indonesia 83 B5 3 57 S 137 17 E
Jayanca, Peru 172 B2 6 24 S 79 50W
Jayanti, India 90 B2 26 45N 89 40 E
Jayapura, Indonesia 83 B6 2 28 S 140 38 E
Jayawijaya, Pegunungan, Indonesia 83 B5 5 0 S 139 0 E
Jayrūd, Syria 100 F7 33 49N 36 44 E
Jayton, U.S.A. 155 J4 33 15N 100 34W
Jāz Mūrīān, Hāmūn-e, Iran 97 E8 27 20N 58 55 E
Jazīreh-ye Shīf, Iran 97 D6 29 4N 50 54 E
Jazminal, Mexico 162 C4 24 56N 101 25W
Jazzīn, Lebanon 103 B4 33 31N 35 35 E
Jean, U.S.A. 161 K11 35 47N 115 20W
Jean Marie River, Canada 142 A4 61 32N 120 38W
Jean Rabel, Haiti 165 C5 19 50N 73 5W
Jeanerette, U.S.A. 155 L9 29 55N 91 40W
Jeanette, Ostrov = Zhannetty, Ostrov, Russia 67 B16 76 43N 158 0 E
Jeannette, U.S.A. 150 F5 40 20N 79 36W
Jebāl Bārez, Kūh-e, Iran 97 D8 28 30N 58 20 E
Jebba, Nigeria 113 D5 9 9N 4 48 E
Jebel, Bahr el →, Sudan 107 F3 9 30N 30 25 E
Jebel Dud, Sudan 107 E3 13 25N 33 9 E
Jebel Qerri, Sudan 107 D3 16 16N 32 50 E
Jeberos, Peru 172 B2 5 15 S 76 10W
Jedburgh, U.K. 22 F6 55 29N 2 33W
Jedda = Jiddah, Si. Arabia 98 B2 21 29N 39 10 E
Jeddore L., Canada 141 C8 48 3N 55 55W
Jedlicze, Poland 55 J8 49 43N 21 40 E
Jędrzejów, Poland 55 H7 50 35N 20 15 E
Jedwabne, Poland 55 E9 53 17N 22 18 E
Jeetzel →, Germany 30 B7 53 9N 11 3 E
Jefferson, Ga., U.S.A. 152 A6 34 7N 83 35W
Jefferson, Iowa, U.S.A. 156 B2 42 1N 94 23W
Jefferson, Ohio, U.S.A. 150 E4 41 44N 80 46W
Jefferson, Tex., U.S.A. 155 J7 32 46N 94 21W
Jefferson, Wis., U.S.A. 157 B8 43 0N 88 48W
Jefferson, Mt., Nev., U.S.A. 158 G5 38 51N 117 0W
Jefferson, Mt., Oreg., U.S.A. 158 D3 44 41N 121 48W
Jefferson City, Mo., U.S.A. 156 F4 38 34N 92 10W
Jefferson City, Tenn., U.S.A. 149 G4 36 7N 83 30W
Jeffersontown, U.S.A. 157 F11 38 12N 85 35W
Jeffersonville, Ga., U.S.A. 152 C6 32 41N 83 20W
Jeffersonville, Ind., U.S.A. 157 F11 38 17N 85 44W
Jeffersonville, Ohio, U.S.A. 157 E13 39 39N 83 34W
Jeffrey City, U.S.A. 158 E10 42 30N 107 49W
Jega, Nigeria 113 C5 12 15N 4 23 E
Jejevo, Solomon Is. 133 M10 8 6 S 159 8 E
Jēkabpils, Latvia 15 H21 56 29N 25 57 E
Jekyll I., U.S.A. 152 D8 31 4N 81 25W
Jelcz-Laskowice, Poland 55 G4 51 2N 17 19 E
Jelenia Góra, Poland 55 H2 50 50N 15 45 E
Jelgava, Latvia 15 H20 56 41N 23 49 E
Jelgava □, Latvia 54 B10 56 35N 23 45 E
Jelica, Serbia, Yug. 50 C4 43 50N 20 17 E
Jelli, Sudan 107 F3 5 25N 31 45 E
Jelšava, Slovak Rep. 35 C13 48 37N 20 15 E
Jemaja, Indonesia 87 L5 3 5N 105 45 E
Jemaluang, Malaysia 87 L4 2 16N 103 52 E
Jember, Indonesia 85 D4 8 11 S 113 41 E
Jembongan, Malaysia 78 C5 6 45N 117 20 E
Jena, Germany 30 E7 50 54N 11 35 E
Jena, U.S.A. 155 K8 31 41N 92 8W
Jenbach, Austria 34 D4 47 24N 11 47 E
Jendouba, Tunisia 108 A1 36 29N 8 47 E
Jenison, U.S.A. 157 B11 42 54N 85 47W
Jenkins, U.S.A. 148 G4 37 10N 82 38W
Jenner, U.S.A. 160 G3 38 27N 123 7W
Jennings, Fla., U.S.A. 152 E6 30 36N 83 6W
Jennings, La., U.S.A. 155 K8 30 13N 92 40W
Jennings, Mo., U.S.A. 156 F6 38 43N 90 16W
Jensen Beach, U.S.A. 153 H9 27 15N 80 14W
Jepara, Indonesia 85 D3 7 40 S 109 14 E
Jeparit, Australia 128 D5 36 8 S 142 1 E
Jequié, Brazil 171 D3 13 51 S 40 5W
Jequitaí →, Brazil 171 E3 17 4 S 44 50W
Jequitinhonha, Brazil 171 E3 16 30 S 41 0W
Jequitinhonha →, Brazil 171 E4 15 51 S 38 53W
Jerada, Morocco 111 B4 34 17N 2 10W
Jerantut, Malaysia 87 L4 3 56N 102 22 E
Jerejak, Pulau, Malaysia 87 c 5 19N 100 19 E
Jérémie, Haiti 165 C5 18 40N 74 10W
Jeremoabo, Brazil 170 D4 10 4 S 38 21W
Jerez, Punta, Mexico 163 C5 22 58N 97 40W
Jerez de García Salinas, Mexico 162 C4 22 39N 103 0W
Jerez de la Frontera, Spain 43 J4 36 41N 6 7W
Jerez de los Caballeros, Spain 43 G4 38 20N 6 45W
Jericho = El Arīḩā, West Bank 103 D4 31 52N 35 27 E
Jericho, Australia 126 C4 23 38 S 146 6 E
Jerichow, Germany 30 C8 52 30N 12 2 E
Jerico Springs, U.S.A. 156 G2 37 37N 94 1W
Jerid, Chott el = Djerid, Chott, Tunisia 108 B1 33 42N 8 30 E
Jerilderie, Australia 129 C6 35 20 S 145 41 E
Jermyn, U.S.A. 151 E9 41 31N 75 31W
Jerome, U.S.A. 158 E6 42 44N 114 31W
Jerramungup, Australia 125 F2 33 55 S 118 55 E
Jersey, U.K. 21 H5 49 11N 2 7W
Jersey City, U.S.A. 151 F10 40 44N 74 4W
Jersey Shore, U.S.A. 150 E7 41 12N 77 15W
Jerseyville, U.S.A. 156 E6 39 7N 90 20W
Jerumenha, Brazil 170 C3 7 5 S 43 30W
Jerusalem, Israel 103 D4 31 47N 35 10 E
Jervis B., Australia 129 C9 35 8 S 150 46 E
Jervis Inlet, Canada 142 C4 50 0N 123 57W
Jerzu, Italy 46 C2 39 47N 9 31 E
Jesenice, Slovenia 45 B11 46 28N 14 3 E
Jeseník, Czech Rep. 35 A10 50 14N 17 8 E
Jesenké, Slovak Rep. 35 C13 48 20N 20 10 E
Jesi = Iesi, Italy 45 E10 43 31N 13 14 E
Jesselton = Kota Kinabalu, Malaysia 85 A5 6 0N 116 4 E
Jessheim, Norway 14 F8 60 9N 11 10 E
Jessnitz, Germany 30 D8 51 40N 12 18 E
Jessore, Bangla. 90 D2 23 10N 89 10 E
Jessup L., U.S.A. 153 G8 28 43N 81 14W
Jesup, Ga., U.S.A. 152 D8 31 36N 81 53W
Jesup, Iowa, U.S.A. 156 B4 42 29N 92 4W
Jesús, Peru 172 B2 7 15 S 78 25W
Jesús Carranza, Mexico 163 D5 17 28N 95 1W
Jesús María, Argentina 174 C3 30 59 S 64 5W
Jetmore, U.S.A. 155 F5 38 4N 99 54W
Jetpur, India 92 J4 21 45N 70 10 E
Jeumont, France 27 B11 50 18N 4 6 E
Jevnaker, Norway 15 F14 60 15N 10 26 E
Jewell, U.S.A. 156 B3 42 20N 93 39W
Jewett, U.S.A. 150 F3 40 22N 81 2W
Jewett City, U.S.A. 151 E13 41 36N 72 0W
Jeyḩūnābād, Iran 97 C6 34 58N 48 59 E
Jeypore, India 94 E6 18 50N 82 38 E
Jeziorak, Jezioro, Poland 54 E6 53 40N 19 35 E
Jeziorany, Poland 54 E7 53 58N 20 46 E
Jeziorka →, Poland 55 F8 52 8N 21 9 E
Jha Jha, India 93 G12 24 46N 86 22 E
Jhaarkand = Jharkhand □, India 93 H11 24 0N 85 50 E
Jhabua, India 92 H6 22 46N 74 36 E
Jhajjar, India 92 E7 28 37N 76 42 E
Jhal, Pakistan 92 E2 28 17N 67 27 E
Jhal Jhao, Pakistan 91 D2 26 20N 65 35 E
Jhalakati, Bangla. 90 D3 22 39N 90 12 E
Jhalawar, India 92 G7 24 40N 76 10 E
Jhalida, India 93 H11 23 22N 85 58 E
Jhalrapatan, India 92 G7 24 33N 76 10 E
Jhang Maghiana, Pakistan 91 C4 31 15N 72 22 E
Jhansi, India 93 G8 25 30N 78 36 E
Jhargram, India 93 H12 22 27N 86 59 E
Jharia, India 93 H12 23 45N 86 26 E
Jharkhand □, India 93 H11 24 0N 85 50 E
Jharsuguda, India 94 D7 21 56N 84 5 E
Jhelum, Pakistan 91 B4 33 0N 73 45 E
Jhelum →, Pakistan 92 D5 31 20N 72 10 E
Jhilmilli, India 93 H10 23 24N 82 51 E
Jhudo, Pakistan 92 G3 24 58N 69 18 E
Jhunjhunu, India 92 E6 28 10N 75 30 E
Ji-Paraná, Brazil 173 C5 10 50 S 61 58W
Ji Xian, Hebei, China 74 F8 37 35N 115 30 E
Ji Xian, Henan, China 74 G8 35 22N 114 5 E
Ji Xian, Shanxi, China 74 F6 36 7N 110 40 E
Jia Xian, Henan, China 74 H7 33 59N 113 12 E
Jia Xian, Shaanxi, China 74 E6 38 12N 110 28 E
Jiading, China 77 B13 31 22N 121 15 E
Jiahe, China 77 E9 25 38N 112 19 E
Jialing Jiang →, China 76 C6 29 30N 106 20 E
Jiamusi, China 69 B8 46 40N 130 26 E
Ji'an, Jiangxi, China 77 D10 27 6N 114 59 E
Ji'an, Jilin, China 75 D14 41 5N 126 10 E
Jianchang, China 75 D11 40 55N 120 35 E
Jianchangying, China 75 D10 40 10N 118 50 E
Jianchuan, China 76 D2 26 38N 99 55 E
Jiande, China 77 C12 29 23N 119 15 E
Jiang'an, China 76 C5 28 40N 105 3 E
Jiangbei, China 76 C6 29 40N 106 34 E
Jiangcheng, China 76 F3 22 36N 101 52 E
Jiangchuan, China 76 E4 24 8N 102 39 E
Jiangdi, China 76 D4 26 57N 103 37 E
Jiangdu, China 77 A12 32 27N 119 36 E
Jiange, China 76 A5 32 4N 105 32 E
Jianghua, China 77 E8 25 0N 111 47 E
Jiangjin, China 76 C6 29 14N 106 14 E
Jiangkou, China 76 D7 27 40N 108 49 E
Jiangle, China 77 D11 26 42N 117 23 E
Jiangling, China 77 B9 30 25N 112 12 E
Jiangmen, China 77 F9 22 32N 113 0 E
Jiangning, China 77 B12 31 55N 118 50 E
Jiangshan, China 77 C12 28 40N 118 37 E
Jiangsu □, China 75 H11 33 0N 120 0 E
Jiangxi □, China 77 D11 27 30N 116 0 E
Jiangyan, China 77 A13 32 30N 120 7 E
Jiangyin, China 77 B13 31 54N 120 17 E
Jiangyong, China 77 E8 25 20N 111 22 E
Jiangyou, China 76 B5 31 44N 104 43 E
Jianhe, China 76 D7 26 37N 108 31 E
Jianli, China 77 C9 29 46N 112 56 E
Jianning, China 77 D11 26 50N 116 50 E
Jian'ou, China 77 D12 27 3N 118 17 E
Jianshi, China 76 B7 30 37N 109 38 E
Jianshui, China 76 F4 23 36N 102 43 E
Jianyang, Fujian, China 77 D12 27 20N 118 5 E
Jianyang, Sichuan, China 76 B5 30 24N 104 33 E
Jiao Xian = Jiaozhou, China 75 F11 36 18N 120 1 E
Jiaohe, Hebei, China 74 E9 38 2N 116 20 E
Jiaohe, Jilin, China 75 C14 43 40N 127 22 E
Jiaojiang, China 77 C13 28 40N 121 24 E
Jiaoling, China 77 E11 24 41N 116 12 E
Jiaozhou, China 75 F11 36 18N 120 1 E
Jiaozhou Wan, China 75 F11 36 5N 120 10 E
Jiaozuo, China 74 G7 35 16N 113 12 E
Jiashan, China 77 B13 30 55N 120 55 E
Jiashi, China 65 D8 39 29N 76 39 E
Jiawang, China 75 G9 34 28N 117 26 E
Jiaxiang, China 74 G9 35 25N 116 20 E
Jiaxing, China 77 B13 30 49N 120 45 E
Jiayi = Chiai, Taiwan 77 F13 23 29N 120 25 E
Jiayu, China 77 C9 29 55N 113 55 E
Jibão, Serra do, Brazil 171 D3 14 48 S 45 0W
Jibiya, Nigeria 113 C6 13 5N 7 12 E
Jibou, Romania 53 C8 47 15N 23 17 E
Jibuti = Djibouti ■, Africa 107 E5 12 0N 43 0 E
Jicarón, I., Panama 164 E3 7 10N 81 50W
Jičín, Czech Rep. 34 A8 50 25N 15 28 E
Jiddah, Si. Arabia 98 B2 21 29N 39 10 E
Jido, India 90 A5 29 2N 94 58 E
Jieshou, China 74 H8 33 18N 115 22 E
Jiexiu, China 74 F6 37 2N 111 55 E
Jieyang, China 77 F11 23 35N 116 21 E
Jigawa □, Nigeria 113 C6 12 0N 9 45 E
Jiggalong, Australia 124 D3 23 21 S 120 47 E
Jigni, India 93 G8 25 45N 79 25 E
Jihlava, Czech Rep. 34 B8 49 28N 15 35 E
Jihlava →, Czech Rep. 35 C9 48 55N 16 36 E
Jihočeský □, Czech Rep. 34 B7 49 8N 14 35 E
Jihomoravský □, Czech Rep. 35 B9 49 5N 16 30 E
Jijel, Algeria 111 A6 36 52N 5 50 E
Jijiga, Ethiopia 120 C2 9 20N 42 50 E
Jikamshi, Nigeria 113 C6 12 12N 7 45 E
Jikau, Sudan 107 F3 8 28N 33 47 E
Jilib = Gelib, Somali Rep. 120 D2 0 29N 42 46 E
Jilin, China 75 C14 43 44N 126 30 E
Jilin □, China 75 C14 44 0N 127 0 E
Jiloca →, Spain 40 D3 41 21N 1 39W
Jilong = Chilung, Taiwan 77 E13 25 3N 121 45 E
Jim Thorpe, U.S.A. 151 F9 40 52N 75 44W
Jima, Ethiopia 107 F4 7 40N 36 47 E
Jimbaran, Teluk, Indonesia 79 K18 8 46 S 115 9 E
Jimbolia, Romania 52 E5 45 47N 20 43 E
Jimena de la Frontera, Spain 43 J5 36 27N 5 24W
Jiménez, Mexico 162 B4 27 10N 104 54W
Jimenez, Phil. 81 G4 8 20N 123 50 E
Jimo, China 75 F11 36 23N 120 30 E
Jin, Kepulauan, Indonesia 83 C4 6 20 S 134 40 E
Jin Jiang →, China 77 C10 28 24N 115 48 E
Jin Xian = Jinzhou, China 74 E8 38 2N 115 2 E
Jin Xian, China 75 E11 38 55N 121 42 E
Jinan, China 74 F9 36 38N 117 1 E
Jinchang, China 68 C5 38 30N 102 10 E
Jincheng, China 74 G7 35 29N 112 50 E
Jinchuan, China 76 B4 31 30N 102 3 E
Jind, India 92 E7 29 19N 76 22 E
Jindabyne, Australia 129 D8 36 25 S 148 35 E
Jinding, China 69 G10 22 22N 113 33 E
Jindřichův Hradec, Czech Rep. 34 B8 49 10N 15 2 E
Jing He →, China 74 G5 34 27N 109 4 E
Jing Shan, China 77 B8 31 20N 111 35 E
Jing Xian, China 77 B12 30 38N 118 25 E
Jing'an, China 77 C10 28 50N 115 17 E
Jingbian, China 74 F5 37 20N 108 30 E
Jingchuan, China 74 G4 35 20N 107 20 E
Jingde, China 77 B12 30 15N 118 27 E

Jingdezhen, China 77 C11 29 20N 117 11 E
Jingdong, China 76 E3 24 23N 100 47 E
Jinggangshan, China 77 D10 26 58N 114 15 E
Jinggu, China 76 F3 23 35N 100 41 E
Jinghai, China 74 E9 38 55N 116 55 E
Jinghong, China 76 G3 22 0N 100 45 E
Jingjiang, China 77 A13 32 2N 120 16 E
Jingle, China 74 E6 38 20N 111 55 E
Jingmen, China 77 B9 31 0N 112 10 E
Jingning, China 74 G3 35 30N 105 43 E
Jingpo Hu, China 75 C15 43 55N 128 55 E
Jingshan, China 77 B9 31 1N 113 7 E
Jingtai, China 74 F3 37 10N 104 6 E
Jingxi, China 76 F6 23 8N 106 27 E
Jingxing, China 74 E8 38 2N 114 8 E
Jingyang, China 74 G5 34 30N 108 50 E
Jingyu, China 75 C14 42 25N 126 45 E
Jingyuan, China 74 F3 36 30N 104 40 E
Jingzhou, China 76 D7 26 33N 109 40 E
Jingziguan, China 74 H6 33 15N 111 0 E
Jinhua, China 77 C12 29 8N 119 38 E
Jining, Nei Monggol Zizhiqu, China 74 D7 41 5N 113 0 E
Jining, Shandong, China 74 G9 35 22N 116 34 E
Jinja, Uganda 118 B3 0 25N 33 12 E
Jinjang, Malaysia 87 L3 3 13N 101 39 E
Jinji, China 74 F4 37 58N 106 8 E
Jinjiang, Fujian, China 77 E12 24 43N 118 33 E
Jinjiang, Yunnan, China 76 D3 26 14N 100 34 E
Jinjini, Ghana 112 D4 7 26N 2 42W
Jinkou, China 77 B10 30 20N 114 8 E
Jinkouhe, China 76 C4 29 18N 103 4 E
Jinmen Dao, China 77 E12 24 25N 118 25 E
Jinning, China 76 E4 24 38N 102 38 E
Jinotega, Nic. 164 D2 13 6N 85 59W
Jinotepe, Nic. 164 D2 11 50N 86 10W
Jinping, Guizhou, China 76 D7 26 41N 109 10 E
Jinping, Yunnan, China 76 F4 22 45N 103 18 E
Jinsha, China 76 D6 27 29N 106 12 E
Jinsha Jiang →, China 76 C5 28 50N 104 36 E
Jinshan, China 77 B13 30 54N 121 10 E
Jinshi, China 77 C8 29 40N 111 50 E
Jintan, China 77 B12 31 42N 119 36 E
Jintotolo Channel, Phil. 81 F4 11 48N 123 5 E
Jintur, India 94 E3 19 37N 76 42 E
Jinxi, Jiangxi, China 77 D11 27 56N 116 45 E
Jinxi, Liaoning, China 75 D11 40 52N 120 50 E
Jinxian, China 77 C11 28 26N 116 17 E
Jinxiang, China 74 G9 35 5N 116 22 E
Jinyang, China 76 D4 27 28N 103 5 E
Jinyun, China 77 C13 28 35N 120 5 E
Jinzhai, China 77 B10 31 40N 115 53 E
Jinzhou, Hebei, China 74 E8 38 2N 115 2 E
Jinzhou, Liaoning, China 75 D11 41 5N 121 3 E
Jiparaná →, Brazil 173 B5 8 3 S 62 52W
Jipijapa, Ecuador 168 D1 1 0 S 80 40W
Jiquilpan, Mexico 162 D4 19 57N 102 42W
Jishan, China 74 G6 35 34N 110 58 E
Jishou, China 76 C7 28 21N 109 43 E
Jishui, China 77 D10 27 12N 115 8 E
Jisr ash Shughūr, Syria 100 E7 35 49N 36 18 E
Jitarning, Australia 125 F2 32 48 S 117 57 E
Jitra, Malaysia 87 J3 6 16N 100 25 E
Jiu →, Romania 53 G8 43 47N 23 48 E
Jiudengkou, China 74 E4 39 56N 106 40 E
Jiujiang, Guangdong, China 77 F9 22 50N 113 0 E
Jiujiang, Jiangxi, China 77 C10 29 42N 115 58 E
Jiuling Shan, China 77 C10 28 40N 114 40 E
Jiulong = Kowloon, H.K. 77 F10 22 19N 114 11 E
Jiulong, China 76 C3 28 57N 101 31 E
Jiutai, China 75 B13 44 10N 125 50 E
Jiuxincheng, China 74 E8 39 17N 115 59 E
Jiuyuhang, China 77 B12 30 18N 119 56 E
Jiwa, U.A.E. 99 B6 23 0N 54 10 E
Jiwani, Ras, Pakistan 91 D1 25 1N 61 44 E
Jixi, Anhui, China 77 B12 30 5N 118 34 E
Jixi, Heilongjiang, China 75 B16 45 20N 130 50 E
Jiyang, China 75 F9 37 0N 117 12 E
Jiyuan, China 74 G7 35 7N 112 57 E
Jiz', W. →, Yemen 99 C6 16 12N 52 14 E
Jīzān, Si. Arabia 98 C3 17 0N 42 20 E
Jize, China 74 F8 36 54N 114 56 E
Jizera →, Czech Rep. 34 A7 50 10N 14 43 E
Jizl, W. →, Si. Arabia 106 B4 25 39N 38 25 E
Jizl, Wādī al, Si. Arabia 96 E3 25 39N 38 25 E
Jizō-Zaki, Japan 72 B5 35 34N 133 20 E
Jizzakh, Uzbekistan 66 E7 40 6N 67 50 E
Joaçaba, Brazil 175 B5 27 5 S 51 31W
Joaíma, Brazil 171 E3 16 39 S 41 2W
Joal Fadiout, Senegal 112 C1 14 9N 16 50W
João Amaro, Brazil 171 D3 12 46 S 40 22W
João Câmara, Brazil 170 C4 5 32 S 35 48W
João Pessoa, Brazil 170 C5 7 10 S 34 52W
João Pinheiro, Brazil 171 E2 17 45 S 46 10W
Joaquim Távora, Brazil 171 F2 23 30 S 49 58W
Joaquín V. González, Argentina 174 B3 25 10 S 64 0W
Jobat, India 92 H6 22 25N 74 34 E
Jobourg, Nez de, France 26 C5 49 41N 1 57W
Jódar, Spain 43 H7 37 50N 3 21W
Jodhpur, India 92 F5 26 23N 73 8 E
Jodiya, India 92 H4 22 42N 70 18 E
Joensuu, Finland 56 B4 62 37N 29 49 E
Jōetsu, Japan 73 F9 37 12N 138 10 E
Jœuf, France 27 C12 49 12N 6 0 E
Jofane, Mozam. 117 C5 21 15 S 34 18 E
Jogbani, India 93 F12 26 25N 87 15 E
Jõgeva, Estonia 15 G22 58 45N 26 24 E
Jogjakarta = Yogyakarta, Indonesia 85 D4 7 49 S 110 22 E
Jōhana, Japan 73 A8 36 30N 136 57 E
Johannesburg, S. Africa 117 D4 26 10 S 28 2 E
Johannesburg, U.S.A. 161 K9 35 22N 117 38W
Johansfors, Sweden 17 H9 56 42N 15 32 E
Johilla →, India 93 H9 23 37N 81 14 E
John Crow Mts., Jamaica 164 a 18 5N 76 25W
John Day, U.S.A. 158 D4 44 25N 118 57W
John Day →, U.S.A. 158 D3 45 44N 120 39W
John D'Or Prairie, Canada 142 B5 58 30N 115 8W
John H. Kerr Reservoir, U.S.A. 149 G6 36 36N 78 18W
John o' Groats, U.K. 22 C5 58 38N 3 4W
Johnnie, U.S.A. 161 J10 36 25N 116 5W
Johns I., U.S.A. 152 C9 32 40N 80 10W
John's Ra., Australia 126 C1 21 55 S 133 23 E
Johnson, Kans., U.S.A. 155 G4 37 34N 101 45W
Johnson, Vt., U.S.A. 151 B12 44 38N 72 41W
Johnson City, N.Y., U.S.A. 151 D9 42 7N 75 58W
Johnson City, Tenn., U.S.A. 149 G4 36 19N 82 21W
Johnson City, Tex., U.S.A. 155 K5 30 17N 98 25W
Johnsonburg, U.S.A. 150 E6 41 29N 78 41W
Johnsondale, U.S.A. 161 K8 35 58N 118 32W
Johnson's Crossing, Canada 142 A2 60 29N 133 18W
Johnsonville, N.Z. 130 H3 41 13 S 174 48 E
Johnston, U.S.A. 152 B8 33 50N 81 48W
Johnston, L., Australia 125 F3 32 25 S 120 30 E
Johnston City, U.S.A. 156 G8 37 49N 88 56W
Johnston Falls = Mambilima Falls, Zambia 119 E2 10 31 S 28 45 E
Johnston I., Pac. Oc. 135 F11 17 10N 169 8W
Johnstone Str., Canada 142 C3 50 28N 126 0W
Johnstown, N.Y., U.S.A. 151 C10 43 0N 74 22W
Johnstown, Ohio, U.S.A. 150 F2 40 9N 82 41W
Johnstown, Pa., U.S.A. 150 F6 40 20N 78 55W
Johor □, Malaysia 84 B2 2 5N 103 20 E
Johor, Selat, Asia 87 d 1 28N 103 47 E
Johor Baharu, Malaysia 87 d 1 28N 103 46 E
Jõhvi, Estonia 15 G22 59 22N 27 27 E
Joigny, France 27 E10 47 58N 3 20 E
Joinville, Brazil 175 B6 26 15 S 48 55W
Joinville, France 27 D12 48 27N 5 10 E
Joinville I., Antarctica 7 C18 65 0 S 55 30W
Jojutla, Mexico 163 D5 18 37N 99 11W
Jokkmokk, Sweden 14 C18 66 35N 19 50 E
Jökulsá á Bru →, Iceland 11 B12 65 40N 14 16W
Jökulsá á Fjöllum →, Iceland 11 A10 66 10N 16 30W
Jolfā, Āzarbājān-e Sharqī, Iran 101 C11 38 57N 45 38 E
Jolfā, Eşfahan, Iran 97 C6 32 58N 51 37 E
Joliet, U.S.A. 157 C8 41 32N 88 5W
Joliette, Canada 140 C5 46 3N 73 24W
Jolo, Phil. 81 H3 6 0N 121 0 E
Jolo Group, Phil. 81 J3 6 0N 121 9 E
Jolon, U.S.A. 160 K5 35 58N 121 9W
Jølstravatnet, Norway 18 C3 61 32N 6 23 E
Jomalig I., Phil. 80 D4 14 42N 122 22 E
Jombang, Indonesia 85 D4 7 33 S 112 14 E
Jomda, China 76 B2 31 28N 98 12 E
Jona, Switz. 33 B7 47 14N 8 51 E
Jonava, Lithuania 15 J21 55 8N 24 12 E
Jondal, Norway 18 D3 60 16N 6 15 E
Jones, Phil. 80 C3 16 33N 121 42 E
Jones Sound, Canada 6 B3 76 0N 85 0W
Jonesboro, Ark., U.S.A. 155 H9 35 50N 90 42W
Jonesboro, Ga., U.S.A. 152 B5 33 31N 84 22W
Jonesboro, La., U.S.A. 155 J8 32 15N 92 43W
Jonesburg, U.S.A. 156 F5 38 51N 91 18W
Jonesville, Ind., U.S.A. 157 E11 39 5N 85 54W
Jonesville, Mich., U.S.A. 157 C12 41 59N 84 40W
Jong →, S. Leone 112 D2 7 32N 12 23W
Jonglei, Sudan 107 F3 6 25N 30 50 E
Jonglei □, Sudan 107 F3 7 30N 32 30 E
Joniškis, Lithuania 15 H20 56 13N 23 35 E
Jönköping, Sweden 17 G8 57 45N 14 8 E
Jönköpings län □, Sweden 17 G8 57 30N 14 30 E
Jonquière, Canada 141 C5 48 27N 71 14W
Jonsered, Sweden 17 G6 57 45N 12 10 E
Jonzac, France 28 C3 45 27N 0 28W
Joplin, U.S.A. 155 G7 37 6N 94 31W
Jora, India 92 F6 26 20N 77 49 E
Jordan, Phil. 81 F4 10 40N 122 35 E
Jordan, Mont., U.S.A. 158 C10 47 19N 106 55W
Jordan, N.Y., U.S.A. 151 C8 43 4N 76 29W
Jordan ■, Asia 103 E5 31 0N 36 0 E
Jordan →, Asia 103 D4 31 48N 35 32 E
Jordan Valley, U.S.A. 158 E5 42 59N 117 3W
Jordânia, Brazil 171 E3 15 55 S 40 11W
Jordanów, Poland 55 J6 49 41N 19 49 E
Jordet, Norway 18 C9 61 25N 12 8 E
Jorge, C., Chile 176 D1 51 40 S 75 35W
Jorgen Brønlund Fjord, Greenland 10 A8 82 30N 29 0W
Jorhat, India 90 B5 26 45N 94 12 E
Jorm, Afghan. 65 E5 36 50N 70 52 E
Jörn, Sweden 14 D19 65 4N 20 1 E
Jorong, Indonesia 85 C4 3 58 S 114 56 E
Jørpeland, Norway 15 G11 59 3N 6 1 E
Jorquera →, Chile 174 B2 28 3 S 69 58W
Jos, Nigeria 113 D6 9 53N 8 51 E
Jos Plateau, Nigeria 113 D6 9 55N 9 0 E
Jošanička Banja, Serbia, Yug. 50 C4 43 24N 20 47 E
Jose Abad Santos, Phil. 81 J5 5 55N 125 39 E
José Batlle y Ordóñez, Uruguay 175 C4 33 20 S 55 10W
José de San Martín, Argentina 176 B2 44 4 S 70 26W
Jose Panganiban, Phil. 80 D4 14 17N 122 41 E
Joseni, Romania 53 D10 46 42N 25 29 E
Joseph, L., Nfld., Canada 141 B6 52 45N 65 18W
Joseph, L., Ont., Canada 150 A5 45 10N 79 44W
Joseph Bonaparte G., Australia 124 B4 14 35 S 128 50 E
Joshinath, India 93 D8 30 34N 79 34 E
Joshua Tree, U.S.A. 161 L10 34 8N 116 19W
Joshua Tree Nat. Park, U.S.A. 161 M10 33 55N 116 0W
Josselin, France 26 E4 47 57N 2 33W
Jost Van Dyke, Br. Virgin Is. 165 e 18 29N 64 47W
Jostedal, Norway 18 C4 61 35N 7 15 E
Jostedalsbreen, Norway 15 F12 61 40N 6 59 E
Jotunheimen, Norway 15 F13 61 35N 8 25 E
Joubertberge, Namibia 116 B1 18 30 S 14 0 E
Joué-lès-Tours, France 26 E7 47 21N 0 40 E
Jourdanton, U.S.A. 155 L5 28 55N 98 33W
Joutseno, Finland 58 B5 61 7N 28 31 E
Jovellanos, Cuba 164 B3 22 40N 81 10W
Jovellar, Phil. 80 E4 13 4N 123 36 E
Jowai, India 90 C4 25 26N 92 12 E
Jowhar = Giohar, Somali Rep. 120 D3 2 48N 45 30 E
Jowzjān □, Afghan. 65 E3 36 10N 66 0 E
Joyeuse, France 29 D8 44 29N 4 16 E
Jōyō, Japan 73 C7 34 50N 135 47 E
Józefów, Lubelskie, Poland 55 H10 50 28N 23 2 E
Józefów, Mazowieckie, Poland 55 F8 52 10N 21 11 E
Ju Xian, China 75 F10 36 35N 118 20 E
Juan Aldama, Mexico 162 C4 24 20N 103 23W
Juan Bautista Alberdi, Argentina 174 C3 34 26 S 61 48W
Juan de Fuca Str., Canada 160 B3 48 15N 124 0W
Juan de Nova, Ind. Oc. 117 B7 17 3 S 43 45 E
Juan Fernández, Arch. de, Pac. Oc. 135 L20 33 50 S 80 0W
Juan José Castelli, Argentina 174 B3 25 27 S 60 57W
Juan L. Lacaze, Uruguay 174 C4 34 26 S 57 25W
Juanjuí, Peru 172 B2 7 10 S 76 45W
Juankoski, Finland 14 E23 63 3N 28 19 E
Juara, Brazil 173 C6 11 20 S 57 25W
Juárez, Argentina 174 D4 37 40 S 59 43W
Juárez, Mexico 161 N11 32 20N 115 57W
Juárez, Sierra de, Mexico 162 A1 32 0N 116 0W
Juatinga, Ponta de, Brazil 171 F3 23 17 S 44 30W
Juàzeiro, Brazil 170 C3 9 30 S 40 30W
Juàzeiro do Norte, Brazil 170 C4 7 10 S 39 18W
Juba = Giuba →, Somali Rep. 120 D2 1 30N 42 35 E
Juba, Sudan 107 G3 4 50N 31 35 E
Jubayl, Lebanon 103 A4 34 5N 35 39 E
Jubbah, Si. Arabia 96 D4 28 2N 40 56 E
Jubbal, India 92 D7 31 5N 77 40 E
Jubbulpore = Jabalpur, India 93 H8 23 9N 79 58 E
Jübek, Germany 30 A5 54 33N 9 22 E
Jubga, Russia 61 H4 44 19N 38 48 E
Jubilee L., Australia 125 E4 29 0 S 126 50 E
Juby, C., Morocco 110 C2 28 0N 12 59W
Júcar = Xúquer →, Spain 41 F4 39 5N 0 10W
Júcaro, Cuba 164 B4 21 37N 78 51W
Juchitán, Mexico 163 D5 16 27N 95 5W
Judaberg, Norway 18 E2 59 10N 5 51 E
Judaea = Har Yehuda, Israel 103 D3 31 35N 34 57 E
Judenburg, Austria 34 D7 47 12N 14 38 E
Judith →, U.S.A. 158 C9 47 44N 109 39W
Judith, Pt., U.S.A. 151 E13 41 22N 71 29W
Judith Gap, U.S.A. 158 C9 46 41N 109 45W
Juelsminde, Denmark 17 J4 55 43N 10 1 E
Jufari →, Brazil 169 D5 1 13 S 62 0W
Jugoslavia = Yugoslavia ■, Europe 50 C4 43 20N 20 0 E
Juigalpa, Nic. 164 D2 12 6N 85 26W
Juillac, France 28 C5 45 20N 1 19 E
Juist, Germany 30 B2 53 40N 6 59 E
Juiz de Fora, Brazil 171 F3 21 43 S 43 19W
Jujuy □, Argentina 174 A2 23 20 S 65 40W
Julesburg, U.S.A. 154 E3 40 59N 102 16W
Juli, Peru 172 D4 16 10 S 69 25W
Julia Cr. →, Australia 126 C3 20 0 S 141 11 E
Julia Creek, Australia 126 C3 20 39 S 141 44 E
Juliaca, Peru 172 D3 15 25 S 70 10W
Julian, U.S.A. 161 M10 33 4N 116 38W
Julian Alps = Julijske Alpe, Slovenia 45 B11 46 15N 14 1 E
Julian L., Canada 140 B4 54 25N 77 57W
Julianatop, Surinam 169 C6 3 40N 56 30W
Julianehåb = Qaqortoq, Greenland 10 E6 60 43N 46 0W
Jülich, Germany 30 E2 50 55N 6 22 E
Julierpass, Switz. 33 D9 46 28N 9 32 E
Juliette, L., U.S.A. 152 B6 33 2N 83 50W
Julijske Alpe, Slovenia 45 B11 46 15N 14 1 E
Julimes, Mexico 162 B3 28 25N 105 27W
Jullundur, India 92 D6 31 20N 75 40 E
Julu, China 74 F8 37 15N 115 2 E
Jumbo, Zimbabwe 119 F3 17 30 S 30 58 E
Jumbo Pk., U.S.A. 161 J12 36 12N 114 11W
Jumentos Cays, Bahamas 164 B4 23 0N 75 40W
Jumilla, Spain 41 G3 38 28N 1 19W
Jumla, Nepal 93 E10 29 15N 82 13 E
Jumna = Yamuna →, India 93 G9 25 30N 81 53 E
Junagadh, India 92 J4 21 30N 70 30 E
Junction, Tex., U.S.A. 155 K5 30 29N 99 46W
Junction, Utah, U.S.A. 159 G7 38 14N 112 13W
Junction B., Australia 126 A1 11 52 S 133 55 E
Junction City, Ga., U.S.A. 152 C5 32 36N 84 28W
Junction City, Kans., U.S.A. 154 F6 39 2N 96 50W
Junction City, Oreg., U.S.A. 158 D2 44 13N 123 12W
Junction Pt., Australia 126 A1 11 45 S 133 50 E
Jundah, Australia 126 C3 24 46 S 143 2 E
Jundiaí, Brazil 175 A6 24 30 S 47 0W
Juneau, U.S.A. 142 B2 58 18N 134 25W
Junee, Australia 129 C7 34 53 S 147 35 E
Jungfrau, Switz. 32 C5 46 32N 7 58 E
Junggar Pendi, China 68 B3 44 30N 86 0 E
Jungsdalshytta, Norway 18 D4 60 49N 7 55 E
Jungshahi, Pakistan 92 G2 24 52N 67 44 E
Juniata →, U.S.A. 150 F7 40 30N 77 40W
Junín, Argentina 174 C3 34 33 S 60 57W
Junín, Peru 172 C2 11 12 S 76 0W
Junín □, Peru 172 C3 11 30 S 75 0W
Junín de los Andes, Argentina 176 A2 39 45 S 71 0W
Jūnīyah, Lebanon 103 B4 33 59N 35 38 E
Junlian, China 76 C5 28 8N 104 29 E
Junnar, India 94 E1 19 12N 73 58 E
Juno Beach, U.S.A. 153 J9 26 52N 80 3W
Juntas, Chile 174 B2 28 24 S 69 58W
Juntura, U.S.A. 158 E4 43 45N 118 5W
Juparanã, L., Brazil 171 E3 19 16 S 40 8W
Jupiter, U.S.A. 153 J9 26 57N 80 6W
Juquiá, Brazil 171 F2 24 19 S 47 38W
Jur, Nahr el →, Sudan 107 F2 8 45N 29 15 E
Jura = Jura, Mts. du, Europe 27 F13 46 40N 6 5 E
Jura = Schwäbische Alb, Germany 31 G5 48 20N 9 30 E
Jura, U.K. 22 F3 56 0N 5 50W
Jura □, France 27 F12 46 47N 5 45 E
Jura □, Switz. 31 H3 47 20N 7 20 E
Jūra →, Lithuania 54 C9 55 3N 22 9 E
Jura, Mts. du, Europe 27 F13 46 40N 6 5 E
Jura, Sd. of, U.K. 22 F3 55 57N 5 45W
Jura Suisse, Switz. 32 B4 47 10N 7 0 E
Jurado, Colombia 168 B2 7 7N 77 46W
Jurbarkas, Lithuania 15 J20 55 4N 22 46 E
Jurien, Australia 125 F2 30 18 S 115 2 E
Jurilovca, Romania 53 F13 44 46N 28 52 E
Jūrmala, Latvia 15 H20 56 58N 23 34 E
Jurong, China 77 B12 31 57N 119 9 E
Jurong, Singapore 87 d 1 19N 103 42 E
Juruá, Brazil 168 D4 3 27 S 66 3W
Juruá →, Brazil 168 D4 2 37 S 65 44W
Juruena, Brazil 173 C6 13 0 S 58 10W
Juruena →, Brazil 173 B6 7 20 S 58 3W
Juruti, Brazil 169 D6 2 9 S 56 4W
Jussey, France 27 E12 47 50N 5 55 E
Justo Daract, Argentina 174 C2 33 52 S 65 12W
Jutaí, Amazonas, Brazil 168 D4 2 44 S 66 57W
Jutaí, Amazonas, Brazil 172 B4 5 11 S 68 54W
Jutaí →, Brazil 168 D4 2 43 S 66 57W
Jüterbog, Germany 30 D9 51 59N 13 5 E
Juticalpa, Honduras 164 D2 14 40N 86 12W
Jutland = Jylland, Denmark 17 H3 56 25N 9 30 E
Juventud, I. de la, Cuba 164 B3 21 40N 82 40W
Juvigny-sous-Andaine, France 26 D6 48 32N 0 30W
Jūy Zar, Iran 101 F12 33 50N 46 18 E
Juye, China 74 G9 35 22N 116 5 E
Juzennecourt, France 27 D11 48 10N 4 58 E
Jvari, Georgia 61 J6 42 42N 42 4 E
Jyderup, Denmark 17 J5 55 40N 11 26 E
Jylland, Denmark 17 H3 56 25N 9 30 E
Jyväskylä, Finland 15 E21 62 14N 25 50 E

K

K2, Pakistan 93 B7 35 58N 76 32 E
Ka →, Nigeria 113 C5 11 40N 4 10 E
Ka Lae, U.S.A. 145 E6 18 55N 155 41W
Kaaawa, U.S.A. 145 J14 21 33N 157 51W
Kaala, U.S.A. 145 J13 21 31N 158 9W
Kaala-Gomén, N. Cal. 133 T18 20 40 S 164 25 E
Kaalualu B., U.S.A. 145 E6 18 58N 155 37W
Kaap Plateau, S. Africa 116 D3 28 30 S 24 0 E
Kaapkruis, Namibia 116 C1 21 55 S 13 57 E
Kaapstad = Cape Town, S. Africa 116 E2 33 55 S 18 22 E
Kaataon, Mt., Phil. 81 G5 8 10N 124 52 E
Kaba, Guinea 112 C2 10 9N 11 40W
Kabacan, Phil. 81 H5 7 8N 124 49 E
Kabaena, Indonesia 82 C2 5 15 S 122 0 E
Kabala, S. Leone 112 D2 9 38N 11 37W
Kabale, Uganda 118 C3 1 15 S 30 0 E
Kabalebostuwmeer, Surinam 169 C6 4 45N 57 30W
Kabalo, Dem. Rep. of the Congo 118 D2 6 0 S 27 0 E
Kabambare, Dem. Rep. of the Congo 118 C2 4 41 S 27 39 E
Kabango, Dem. Rep. of the Congo 119 D2 8 35 S 28 30 E
Kabanjahe, Indonesia 84 B1 3 6N 98 30 E
Kabankalan, Phil. 81 G4 9 59N 122 49 E
Kabara, Fiji 133 B3 18 59 S 178 56W
Kabara, Mali 112 B4 16 40N 2 50W
Kabarai, Indonesia 83 B4 0 4 S 130 58 E
Kabardinka, Russia 59 K10 44 40N 37 57 E
Kabardino-Balkar Republic = Kabardino-Balkaria □, Russia 61 J6 43 30N 43 30 E
Kabardino-Balkaria □, Russia 61 J6 43 30N 43 30 E
Kabarega Falls = Murchison Falls, Uganda 118 B3 2 15N 31 30 E
Kabasalan, Phil. 81 H4 7 47N 122 44 E
Kabat, Indonesia 79 J17 8 16 S 114 19 E
Kabba, Nigeria 113 D6 7 50N 6 3 E
Kabbani →, India 95 H3 12 13N 76 54 E
Kabetogama, U.S.A. 154 A8 48 28N 92 59W
Kabi, Niger 113 C7 13 30N 12 35 E
Kabin Buri, Thailand 86 F3 13 57N 101 43 E
Kabinakagami L., Canada 140 C3 48 54N 84 25W
Kabinda, Dem. Rep. of the Congo 115 D4 6 10 S 24 29 E
Kabkabīyah, Sudan 109 F4 13 50N 24 0 E
Kablungu, C., Papua N. G. 132 D6 6 20 S 150 1 E
Kabna, Sudan 106 D3 19 6N 32 40 E
Kabo, C.A.R. 114 A3 7 35N 18 38 E
Kabompo, Zambia 119 E1 13 36 S 24 14 E
Kabompo →, Zambia 115 E4 14 11 S 23 11 E
Kabondo, Dem. Rep. of the Congo 119 D2 8 58 S 25 40 E
Kabongo, Dem. Rep. of the Congo 118 D2 7 22 S 25 33 E
Kabot, Guinea 112 C2 10 48N 14 57W
Kabou, Togo 113 D5 9 28N 0 55 E
Kaboudia, Rass, Tunisia 108 A2 35 13N 11 10 E
Kabr, Sudan 107 E2 10 54N 26 50 E
Kabrousse, Senegal 112 C1 12 25N 16 45W
Kabubu, Dem. Rep. of the Congo 115 D4 9 42 S 24 40 E
Kabūd Gonbad, Iran 97 B8 37 5N 59 45 E
Kabugao, Phil. 80 B3 18 2N 121 11 E
Kābul, Afghan. 91 B3 34 28N 69 11 E
Kābul □, Afghan. 91 B3 34 30N 69 0 E
Kābul →, Pakistan 91 B4 33 55N 72 14 E
Kabuli, Papua N. G. 132 B4 2 7 S 146 40 E
Kabunga, Dem. Rep. of the Congo 118 C2 1 38 S 28 3 E
Kaburuang, Indonesia 82 A3 3 50N 126 30 E
Kabushiya, Sudan 107 D3 16 54N 33 41 E
Kabwanga, Dem. Rep. of the Congo 115 D4 7 2 S 22 36 E
Kabwe, Zambia 119 E2 14 30 S 28 29 E
Kabwum, Papua N. G. 132 D4 6 11 S 147 15 E
Kačanik, Kosovo, Yug. 50 D5 42 13N 21 12 E
Kačerginė, Lithuania 54 D10 54 56N 23 42 E
Kachchh, Gulf of, India 92 H3 22 50N 69 15 E
Kachchh, Rann of, India 92 H4 24 0N 70 0 E
Kachchhidhana, India 93 J8 21 44N 78 46 E
Kachebera, Zambia 119 E3 13 50 S 32 50 E
Kachia, Nigeria 113 D6 9 50N 7 55 E
Kachikau, Botswana 116 B3 18 8 S 24 26 E
Kachin □, Burma 76 D1 26 0N 97 30 E
Kachira, L., Uganda 118 C3 0 40 S 31 7 E
Kachiry, Kazakstan 66 D8 53 10N 75 50 E
Kachisi, Ethiopia 107 F4 9 40N 37 50 E
Kachkanar, Russia 64 B7 58 42N 59 33 E
Kachnara, India 92 H6 23 50N 75 6 E
Kachot, Cambodia 87 G4 11 30N 103 3 E
Kaçkar, Turkey 101 B9 40 45N 41 10 E
Kada, Chad 109 E3 19 20N 19 39 E
Kadaingti, Burma 90 G6 17 37N 97 32 E
Kadaiyanallur, India 95 K3 9 3N 77 22 E
Kadan, Czech Rep. 34 A6 50 23N 13 16 E
Kadan Kyun, Burma 86 F2 12 30N 98 20 E
Kadanai →, Afghan. 92 D1 31 22N 65 45 E
Kadarkút, Hungary 52 D2 46 13N 17 39 E
Kadavu, Fiji 133 B2 19 0 S 178 15 E
Kadavu Passage, Fiji 133 B2 18 45 S 178 0 E
Kade, Ghana 113 D4 6 7N 0 56W
Kadei →, C.A.R. 114 B3 3 31N 16 3 E
Kadi, India 92 H5 23 18N 72 23 E
Kadina, Australia 128 B2 33 55 S 137 43 E
Kadınhanı, Turkey 100 C5 38 14N 32 13 E
Kadiolo, Mali 112 C3 10 35N 7 41W
Kadipur, India 93 F10 26 10N 82 23 E
Kadirabad, India 94 E2 19 51N 75 54 E
Kadiri, India 95 G4 14 12N 78 13 E
Kadirli, Turkey 100 D7 37 23N 36 5 E
Kadiyevka = Stakhanov, Ukraine 59 H10 48 35N 38 40 E
Kadja, O. →, Chad 109 F4 12 2N 22 28 E
Kadmat I., India 95 J1 11 14N 72 47 E
Kadodo, Sudan 107 E2 11 4N 29 31 E
Kadoka, U.S.A. 154 D4 43 50N 101 31W
Kadom, Russia 60 C6 54 37N 42 30 E
Kadoma, Zimbabwe 119 F2 18 20 S 29 52 E
Kâdugli, Sudan 107 E2 11 0N 29 45 E
Kaduna, Nigeria 113 C6 10 30N 7 21 E
Kaduna □, Nigeria 113 C6 11 0N 7 30 E
Kadur, India 95 H3 13 34N 76 1 E
Kaduy, Russia 58 C9 59 12N 37 9 E
Kaédi, Mauritania 112 B2 16 9N 13 28W
Kaélé, Cameroon 113 C7 10 7N 14 27 E
Kaélé, Cent. Amer. 109 F2 10 7N 14 27 E
Kaena Pt., U.S.A. 145 J13 21 35N 158 17W
Kaeng Khoï, Thailand 86 E3 14 35N 101 0 E
Kaeo, N.Z. 130 B2 35 6 S 173 49 E
Kaesŏng, N. Korea 75 F14 37 58N 126 35 E
Kāf, Si. Arabia 96 D3 31 25N 37 29 E
Kafakumba, Dem. Rep. of the Congo 115 D4 9 38 S 23 46 E
Kafan = Kapan, Armenia 101 C12 39 18N 46 27 E
Kafanchan, Nigeria 113 D6 9 40N 8 20 E
Kafareti, Nigeria 113 C7 10 25N 11 12 E
Kaffrine, Senegal 112 C1 14 8N 15 36W
Kafia Kingi, Sudan 114 A4 9 20N 24 25 E
Kafin, Nigeria 113 D6 9 30N 7 4 E
Kafin Madaki, Nigeria 113 C6 10 41N 9 46 E
Kafinda, Zambia 119 E3 12 32 S 30 20 E
Kafirévs, Ákra, Greece 48 C6 38 9N 24 38 E
Kafr el Battikh, Egypt 106 H7 31 25N 31 44 E
Kafr el Dauwâr, Egypt 106 H7 31 8N 30 8 E
Kafr el Sheikh, Egypt 106 H7 31 15N 30 50 E
Kafue, Zambia 119 F2 15 46 S 28 9 E
Kafue Flats, Zambia 119 F2 15 40 S 27 25 E
Kafue Nat. Park, Zambia 119 F2 15 12 S 25 38 E
Kafulwe, Zambia 119 D2 9 0 S 29 1 E
Kafumba, Dem. Rep. of the Congo 115 D3 5 23 S 18 55 E
Kaga, Afghan. 92 B4 34 14N 70 10 E
Kaga, Japan 73 A8 36 16N 136 15 E
Kaga Bandoro, C.A.R. 114 A3 7 0N 19 10 E
Kagamil I., U.S.A. 144 K5 53 0N 169 43W
Kagan, Uzbekistan 66 F7 39 43N 64 33 E
Kagarko, Nigeria 113 D6 9 28N 7 36 E
Kagawa □, Japan 72 C6 34 15N 134 0 E
Kagera = Ziwa Maghariba □, Tanzania 118 C3 2 0 S 31 30 E
Kagera →, Uganda 118 C3 0 57 S 31 47 E
Kağızman, Turkey 101 B10 40 5N 43 10 E
Kagmar, Sudan 107 E3 14 24N 30 25 E
Kagopal, Chad 109 G3 8 16N 16 23 E
Kagoshima, Japan 72 F2 31 35N 130 33 E
Kagoshima □, Japan 72 F2 31 30N 130 30 E
Kagoshima-Wan, Japan 72 F2 31 25N 130 40 E
Kagua, Papua N. G. 132 D2 6 26 S 143 48 E
Kagul = Cahul, Moldova 53 E13 45 50N 28 15 E
Kahak, Iran 97 B6 36 6N 49 46 E
Kahaluu, U.S.A. 145 K14 21 28N 157 50W
Kahama, Tanzania 118 C3 4 8 S 32 30 E
Kahan, Pakistan 92 E3 29 18N 68 54 E
Kahana, U.S.A. 145 J14 21 34N 157 53W
Kahana B., U.S.A. 145 J14 21 35N 157 50W
Kahang, Malaysia 87 L4 2 12N 103 32 E
Kahayan →, Indonesia 85 C4 3 40 S 114 0 E
Kahe, Tanzania 118 C4 3 30 S 37 25 E
Kahemba, Dem. Rep. of the Congo 115 D3 7 18 S 18 55 E
Kaherekoau Mts., N.Z. 131 F2 45 45 S 167 15 E
Kahil, Djebel bou, Algeria 111 B5 34 26N 4 0 E
Kahnūj, Iran 97 E8 27 55N 57 40 E
Kahoka, U.S.A. 156 D5 40 25N 91 44W
Kahoolawe, U.S.A. 145 C5 20 33N 156 37W
Kahramanmaraş, Turkey 100 D7 37 37N 36 53 E
Kâhta, Turkey 101 D8 37 46N 38 36 E
Kahuku, U.S.A. 145 J14 21 41N 157 57W
Kahuku Pt., U.S.A. 145 J14 21 43N 157 59W
Kahului, U.S.A. 145 C5 20 54N 156 28W
Kahurangi Nat. Park, N.Z. 131 B7 41 15 S 172 32 E
Kahurangi Pt., N.Z. 131 A7 40 50 S 172 10 E
Kahuta, Pakistan 92 C5 33 35N 73 24 E
Kahuzi-Biega, Parc Nat. du, Dem. Rep. of the Congo 118 C2 1 50 S 27 55 E
Kai, Kepulauan, Indonesia 83 C4 5 55 S 132 45 E

Kai Besar, *Indonesia* **83 C4** 5 35 S 133 0 E
Kai Is. = Kai, Kepulauan, *Indonesia* **83 C4** 5 55 S 132 45 E
Kai Kecil, *Indonesia* **83 C4** 5 45 S 132 40 E
Kai Xian, *China* **76 B7** 31 11N 108 21 E
Kaiama, *Nigeria* **113 D5** 9 36N 4 1 E
Kaiapit, *Papua N. G.* **132 D4** 6 18 S 146 18 E
Kaiapoi, *N.Z.* **131 D7** 43 24 S 172 40 E
Kaieteur Falls, *Guyana* **169 B6** 5 1N 59 10W
Kaifeng, *China* **74 G8** 34 48N 114 21 E
Kaihua, *China* **77 C12** 29 12N 118 20 E
Kaijiang, *China* **76 B6** 31 7N 107 55 E
Kaikohe, *N.Z.* **130 B2** 35 25 S 173 49 E
Kaikoura, *N.Z.* **131 C8** 42 25 S 173 43 E
Kaikoura Pen., *N.Z.* **131 C8** 42 25 S 173 43 E
Kailahun, *S. Leone* **112 D2** 8 18N 10 39W
Kailashahar, *India* **90 C4** 24 19N 92 0 E
Kaileuna I., *Papua N. G.* **132 E6** 8 32 S 150 57 E
Kaili, *China* **76 D6** 26 33N 107 59 E
Kailu, *China* **75 C11** 43 38N 121 18 E
Kailua, *U.S.A.* **145 K14** 21 24N 157 44W
Kailua B., *U.S.A.* **145 K14** 21 25N 157 40W
Kailua Kona, *U.S.A.* **145 D6** 19 39N 155 59W
Kaim →, *Papua N. G.* **132 D1** 6 55 S 141 33 E
Kaima, *Indonesia* **83 C5** 5 32 S 138 48 E
Kaimana, *Indonesia* **83 B4** 3 39 S 133 45 E
Kaimanawa Mts., *N.Z.* **130 F4** 39 15 S 175 56 E
Kaimata, *N.Z.* **131 C6** 42 34 S 171 28 E
Kaimganj, *India* **93 F8** 27 33N 79 24 E
Kaimon-Dake, *Japan* **72 F2** 31 11N 130 32 E
Kaimuki, *U.S.A.* **145 K14** 21 17N 157 48W
Kaimur Hills, *India* **93 G10** 24 30N 82 0 E
Kainab →, *Namibia* **116 D2** 28 32 S 19 34 E
Kainan, *Japan* **73 C7** 34 9N 135 12 E
Kainantu, *Papua N. G.* **132 D3** 6 18 S 145 52 E
Kainji Dam, *Nigeria* **113 D5** 9 55N 4 35 E
Kainji Lake Nat. Park, *Nigeria* **113 C5** 10 5N 4 6 E
Kainji Res., *Nigeria* **113 C5** 10 1N 4 40 E
Kainuu, *Finland* **14 D23** 64 30N 29 7 E
Kaipara Harbour, *N.Z.* **130 C3** 36 25 S 174 14 E
Kaiping, *China* **77 F9** 22 23N 112 42 E
Kaipokok B., *Canada* **141 B8** 54 54N 59 47W
Kaira, *India* **92 H5** 22 45N 72 50 E
Kairana, *India* **92 E7** 29 24N 77 15 E
Kairiru I., *Papua N. G.* **132 B2** 3 21 S 143 34 E
Kaironi, *Indonesia* **83 B4** 0 47 S 133 40 E
Kairouan, *Tunisia* **108 A2** 35 45N 10 5 E
Kairuku, *Papua N. G.* **132 E4** 8 51 S 146 35 E
Kaiserslautern, *Germany* **31 F3** 49 26N 7 45 E
Kaiserstuhl, *Germany* **31 G3** 48 4N 7 40 E
Kaita, *Japan* **72 C4** 34 22N 132 32 E
Kaitaia, *N.Z.* **130 B2** 35 8 S 173 17 E
Kaitangata, *N.Z.* **131 G4** 46 17 S 169 51 E
Kaithal, *India* **92 E7** 29 48N 76 26 E
Kaitu →, *Pakistan* **92 C4** 33 10N 70 30 E
Kaiwi Channel, *U.S.A.* **145 K14** 21 15N 157 30W
Kaiyang, *China* **76 D6** 27 4N 106 59 E
Kaiyuan, *Liaoning, China* **75 C13** 42 28N 124 1 E
Kaiyuan, *Yunnan, China* **76 F4** 23 40N 103 12 E
Kaiyuh Mts., *U.S.A.* **144 D8** 64 30N 158 0W
Kajaani, *Finland* **14 D22** 64 17N 27 46 E
Kajabbi, *Australia* **126 C3** 20 0 S 140 1 E
Kajana = Kajaani, *Finland* **14 D22** 64 17N 27 46 E
Kajang, *Malaysia* **87 L3** 2 59N 101 48 E
Kajaran, *Armenia* **101 C12** 39 10N 46 7 E
Kajiado, *Kenya* **118 C4** 1 53 S 36 48 E
Kajo Kaji, *Sudan* **107 G3** 3 58N 31 40 E
Kajuru, *Nigeria* **113 C6** 10 15N 7 34 E
Kajy-Say, *Kyrgyzstan* **65 B8** 42 8N 77 10 E
Kaka, *Sudan* **107 E3** 10 38N 32 10 E
Kaka Pt., *U.S.A.* **145 C5** 20 31N 156 33W
Kakabeka Falls, *Canada* **140 C2** 48 24N 89 37W
Kakadu Nat. Park, *Australia* **124 B5** 12 0 S 132 3 E
Kakamas, *S. Africa* **116 D3** 28 45 S 20 33 E
Kakamega, *Kenya* **118 B3** 0 20N 34 46 E
Kakamigahara, *Japan* **73 B8** 35 28N 136 48 E
Kakana, *India* **95 K11** 9 7N 92 48 E
Kakanj, *Bos.-H.* **52 F3** 44 4N 18 4 E
Kakanui Mts., *N.Z.* **131 F5** 45 10 S 170 30 E
Kakata, *Liberia* **112 D2** 6 35N 10 20W
Kakdwip, *India* **93 J13** 21 53N 88 11 E
Kake, *Japan* **72 C4** 34 36N 132 19 E
Kake, *U.S.A.* **142 B2** 56 59N 133 57W
Kakegawa, *Japan* **73 C10** 34 45N 138 1 E
Kakeroma-Jima, *Japan* **71 K4** 28 8N 129 14 E
Kakhib, *Russia* **61 J8** 42 28N 46 34 E
Kakhonak, *U.S.A.* **144 G9** 59 26N 154 51W
Kakhovka, *Ukraine* **59 J7** 46 45N 33 30 E
Kakhovske Vdskh., *Ukraine* **59 J7** 47 5N 34 0 E
Kakinada, *India* **94 F6** 16 57N 82 11 E
Kakisa →, *Canada* **142 A5** 61 3N 118 10W
Kakisa L., *Canada* **142 A5** 60 56N 117 43W
Kakogawa, *Japan* **72 C6** 34 46N 134 51 E
Kaktovik, *U.S.A.* **144 A12** 70 8N 143 38W
Kakum Nat. Park, *Ghana* **113 D4** 5 24N 1 20W
Kakwa →, *Canada* **142 C5** 54 37N 118 28W
Kāl Gūsheh, *Iran* **97 D8** 30 59N 58 12 E
Kal Safīd, *Iran* **101 E12** 34 52N 47 23 E
Kala, *Nigeria* **113 C7** 12 2N 14 40 E
Kala Oya →, *Sri Lanka* **95 K4** 8 20N 79 45 E
Kalaa-Kebira, *Tunisia* **108 A2** 35 59N 10 32 E
Kalaallit Nunaat = Greenland ■, *N. Amer.* **10 D6** 66 0N 45 0W
Kalabagh, *Pakistan* **92 C4** 33 0N 71 28 E
Kalabahi, *Indonesia* **82 C2** 8 13 S 124 31 E
Kalabáka, *Greece* **48 B3** 39 42N 21 39 E
Kalabakan, *Malaysia* **85 B5** 4 25N 117 29 E
Kalabana, *Mali* **112 C3** 14 10N 8 35W
Kalabo, *Zambia* **115 E4** 14 58 S 22 40 E
Kalach, *Russia* **60 E5** 50 22N 41 0 E
Kalach na Donu, *Russia* **61 F6** 48 43N 43 32 E
Kaladan →, *Burma* **90 E4** 20 20N 93 5 E
Kaladar, *Canada* **140 D4** 44 37N 77 5W
Kalahari, *Africa* **116 C3** 24 0 S 21 30 E
Kalahari Gemsbok Nat. Park, *S. Africa* **116 D3** 25 30 S 20 30 E
Kalaheo, *U.S.A.* **145 B2** 21 56N 159 32W
Kalaikhum, *Tajikistan* **65 D5** 38 28N 70 46 E
Kalajoki, *Finland* **14 D20** 64 12N 24 10 E
Kālak, *Iran* **97 E8** 25 29N 59 22 E
Kalakamati, *Botswana* **117 C4** 20 40 S 27 25 E
Kalakan, *Russia* **67 D12** 55 15N 116 45 E
K'alak'unlun Shank'ou = Karakoram Pass, *Asia* **93 B7** 35 33N 77 50 E
Kalam, *Pakistan* **93 B5** 35 34N 72 30 E
Kalama, *Dem. Rep. of the Congo* **118 C2** 2 52 S 28 35 E
Kalama, *U.S.A.* **160 E4** 46 1N 122 51W
Kalámai, *Greece* **48 D4** 37 3N 22 10 E
Kalamaloué, Parc Nat. de, *Cameroon* **109 F2** 12 9N 14 58 E
Kalamansig, *Phil.* **81 H5** 6 33N 124 3 E
Kalamariá, *Greece* **50 F6** 40 33N 22 55 E
Kalamata = Kalámai, *Greece* **48 D4** 37 3N 22 10 E
Kalamazoo, *U.S.A.* **157 B11** 42 17N 85 35W
Kalamazoo →, *U.S.A.* **157 B10** 42 40N 86 10W
Kalamb, *India* **94 E2** 18 3N 74 48 E
Kalambo Falls, *Tanzania* **119 D3** 8 37 S 31 35 E
Kalamítsi, *Greece* **39 B2** 38 45N 20 36 E
Kalamnuri, *India* **94 E3** 19 40N 77 20 E
Kálamos, *Attikí, Greece* **48 C5** 38 17N 23 52 E
Kálamos, *Levkás, Greece* **39 B2** 38 37N 20 56 E
Kálamos Nisís, *Greece* **39 B2** 38 37N 20 55 E
Kalan, *Turkey* **96 B3** 39 7N 39 32 E
Kalangadoo, *Australia* **128 D4** 37 34 S 140 41 E
Kalankalan, *Guinea* **112 C3** 10 7N 8 54W
Kalannie, *Australia* **125 F2** 30 22 S 117 5 E
Kalāntarī, *Iran* **97 C7** 32 10N 54 8 E
Kalao, *Indonesia* **82 C2** 7 21 S 121 0 E
Kalaotoa, *Indonesia* **82 C2** 7 20 S 121 50 E
Kalapana, *U.S.A.* **145 D7** 19 21N 154 59W
Kälarne, *Sweden* **16 B10** 62 59N 16 5 E
Kalasin, *Thailand* **86 D4** 16 26N 103 30 E
Kalat, *Pakistan* **91 C2** 29 8N 66 31 E
Kalāteh, *Iran* **97 B7** 36 33N 55 41 E
Kalāteh-ye Ganj, *Iran* **97 E8** 27 31N 57 55 E
Kálathos, *Greece* **38 E12** 36 9N 28 8 E
Kalatungan Mt., *Phil.* **81 H5** 7 54N 124 50 E
Kalaupapa, *U.S.A.* **145 B5** 21 12N 156 59W
Kalaus →, *Russia* **61 H7** 45 40N 44 7 E
Kalávrita, *Greece* **48 C4** 38 3N 22 8 E
Kalaw, *Burma* **90 E6** 20 38N 96 34 E
Kalbān, *Oman* **99 B7** 20 18N 58 38 E
Kalbarri, *Australia* **125 E1** 27 40 S 114 10 E
Kalbarri Nat. Park, *Australia* **125 E1** 27 51 S 114 30 E
Kalce, *Slovenia* **36 F8** 45 54N 14 13 E
Kaldrananes, *Iceland* **11 B5** 65 45N 21 25W
Kale, *Antalya, Turkey* **49 E12** 36 14N 30 0 E
Kale, *Denizli, Turkey* **49 D10** 37 27N 28 49 E
Kalecik, *Turkey* **100 B5** 40 4N 33 26 E
Kalehe, *Dem. Rep. of the Congo* **118 C2** 2 6 S 28 50 E
Kalema, *Tanzania* **118 C3** 1 12 S 31 55 E
Kalemie, *Dem. Rep. of the Congo* **118 D2** 5 55 S 29 9 E
Kalemyo, *Burma* **90 D5** 23 11N 94 4 E
Kalety, *Poland* **55 H5** 50 35N 18 52 E
Kalewa, *Burma* **90 D5** 23 10N 94 15 E
Kaleybar, *Iran* **96 B5** 38 47N 47 2 E
Kálfafell, *Iceland* **11 D9** 63 57N 17 41W
Kalgan = Zhangjiakou, *China* **74 D8** 40 48N 114 55 E
Kalghatgi, *India* **95 G2** 15 11N 74 58 E
Kalgoorlie-Boulder, *Australia* **125 F3** 30 40 S 121 22 E
Kalhovd, *Norway* **18 D5** 60 4N 8 21 E
Kali →, *India* **93 F8** 27 6N 79 55 E
Kali Sindh →, *India* **92 G6** 25 32N 76 17 E
Kaliakra, Nos, *Bulgaria* **51 C12** 43 21N 28 30 E
Kalianda, *Indonesia* **84 D3** 5 50 S 105 45 E
Kalibo, *Phil.* **81 F4** 11 43N 122 22 E
Kaliganj, *Bangla.* **90 D2** 22 25N 89 8 E
Kalihi, *U.S.A.* **145 K14** 21 20N 157 53W
Kalima, *Dem. Rep. of the Congo* **118 C2** 2 33 S 26 32 E
Kalimantan ☐, *Indonesia* **85 C4** 0 0 114 0 E
Kalimantan Barat ☐, *Indonesia* **85 C4** 0 0 110 30 E
Kalimantan Selatan ☐, *Indonesia* **85 C5** 2 30 S 115 30 E
Kalimantan Tengah ☐, *Indonesia* **85 C4** 2 0 S 113 30 E
Kalimantan Timur ☐, *Indonesia* **85 B5** 1 30N 116 30 E
Kálimnos, *Greece* **49 D8** 37 0N 27 0 E
Kalimpong, *India* **90 B2** 27 4N 88 35 E
Kalinadi →, *India* **95 G2** 14 50N 74 7 E
Kalinga ☐, *Phil.* **80 C3** 17 30N 121 20 E
Kalinin = Tver, *Russia* **58 D8** 56 55N 35 55 E
Kaliningrad, *Russia* **15 J19** 54 42N 20 32 E
Kalininsk, *Russia* **60 E7** 51 30N 44 40 E
Kalininskoye = Kara-Balta, *Kyrgyzstan* **65 B6** 42 50N 73 49 E
Kalinkavichy, *Belarus* **59 F5** 52 12N 29 20 E
Kalinkovichi = Kalinkavichy, *Belarus* **59 F5** 52 12N 29 20 E
Kalinovik, *Bos.-H.* **50 C2** 43 31N 18 25 E
Kalipetrovo, *Bulgaria* **51 B11** 44 5N 27 14 E
Kaliro, *Uganda* **118 B3** 0 56N 33 30 E
Kalirrákhi, *Greece* **51 F8** 40 40N 24 35 E
Kalispell, *U.S.A.* **158 B6** 48 12N 114 19W
Kalisz, *Poland* **55 G5** 51 45N 18 8 E
Kalisz Pomorski, *Poland* **55 E2** 53 17N 15 55 E
Kaliua, *Tanzania* **118 D3** 5 5 S 31 48 E
Kaliveli Tank, *India* **95 H4** 12 5N 79 50 E
Kalívia Thorikoú, *Greece* **48 D5** 37 50N 23 55 E
Kalix, *Sweden* **14 D20** 65 53N 23 12 E
Kalix →, *Sweden* **14 D20** 65 50N 23 11 E
Kalka, *India* **92 D7** 30 46N 76 57 E
Kalkali Ghat, *India* **90 C4** 24 36N 92 20 E
Kalkan, *Turkey* **49 E11** 36 15N 29 23 E
Kalkarindji, *Australia* **124 C5** 17 30 S 130 47 E
Kalkaska, *U.S.A.* **148 C3** 44 44N 85 11W
Kalkfeld, *Namibia* **116 C2** 20 57 S 16 14 E
Kalkfontein, *Botswana* **116 C3** 22 4 S 20 57 E
Kalkım, *Turkey* **49 B9** 39 48N 27 13 E
Kalkrand, *Namibia* **116 C2** 24 1 S 17 35 E
Kallakkurichchi, *India* **95 J4** 11 44N 79 1 E
Kallam, *India* **94 E3** 18 36N 76 2 E
Kållandsö, *Sweden* **17 F7** 58 40N 13 5 E
Kallavesi, *Finland* **14 E22** 62 58N 27 30 E
Källby, *Sweden* **17 F7** 58 30N 13 8 E
Kållered, *Sweden* **17 G6** 57 32N 12 4 E
Kallidaikurichi, *India* **95 K3** 8 38N 77 31 E
Kallimasiá, *Greece* **49 C8** 38 18N 26 6 E
Kallinge, *Sweden* **17 H9** 56 15N 15 18 E
Kallithéa, *Greece* **48 D5** 37 55N 23 41 E
Kallmet, *Albania* **50 E3** 41 51N 19 41 E
Kalloní, *Greece* **49 B8** 39 14N 26 12 E
Kallonís, Kólpos, *Greece* **49 B8** 39 10N 26 10 E
Kallsjön, *Sweden* **14 E15** 63 38N 13 0 E
Kalmalo, *Nigeria* **113 C6** 13 40N 5 20 E
Kalmanstunga, *Iceland* **11 C6** 64 44N 20 48W
Kalmar, *Sweden* **17 H10** 56 40N 16 20 E
Kalmar län ☐, *Sweden* **17 G10** 57 25N 16 0 E
Kalmar sund, *Sweden* **17 H10** 56 40N 16 25 E
Kalmunai, *Sri Lanka* **95 L5** 7 25N 81 49 E
Kalmyk Republic = Kalmykia ☐, *Russia* **61 G8** 46 5N 46 1 E
Kalmykia ☐, *Russia* **61 G8** 46 5N 46 1 E
Kalmykovo, *Kazakstan* **57 E9** 49 0N 51 47 E
Kalna, *India* **93 H13** 23 13N 88 25 E
Kalnai, *India* **93 H10** 22 46N 83 30 E
Kalni →, *Bangla.* **90 C3** 24 21N 91 13 E
Kalo, *Papua N. G.* **132 F4** 10 1 S 147 48 E
Kalocsa, *Hungary* **52 D4** 46 32N 19 0 E
Kalofer, *Bulgaria* **51 D8** 42 37N 24 59 E
Kalohi Channel, *U.S.A.* **145 C5** 21 0N 157 0W
Kalokhorio, *Cyprus* **39 F9** 34 51N 33 2 E
Kaloko, *Dem. Rep. of the Congo* **118 D2** 6 47 S 25 48 E
Kalol, *Gujarat, India* **92 H5** 22 37N 73 31 E
Kalol, *Gujarat, India* **92 H5** 23 15N 72 33 E
Kalolímnos, *Greece* **49 D9** 37 4N 27 5 E
Kalomo, *Zambia* **119 F2** 17 0 S 26 30 E
Kalona, *U.S.A.* **156 C5** 41 29N 91 43W
Kalonerón, *Greece* **48 D3** 37 20N 21 38 E
Kalpeni I., *India* **95 J1** 10 5N 73 38 E
Kalpi, *India* **93 F8** 26 8N 79 47 E
Kalpitiya, *Sri Lanka* **95 K4** 8 14N 79 46 E
Kalputhi I., *India* **95 J1** 10 49N 72 10 E
Kalrayan Hills, *India* **95 J4** 11 45N 78 40 E
Kalsubai, *India* **94 E1** 19 35N 73 45 E
Kaltag, *U.S.A.* **144 D8** 64 20N 158 43W
Kaltbrunn, *Switz.* **33 B8** 47 13N 9 2 E
Kaltern = Caldaro, *Italy* **45 B8** 46 25N 11 14 E
Kaltungo, *Nigeria* **113 D7** 9 48N 11 19 E
Kalu, *Pakistan* **92 G2** 25 5N 67 39 E
Kaluga, *Russia* **58 E9** 54 35N 36 10 E
Kalulong, Bukit, *Malaysia* **85 B4** 3 14N 114 39 E
Kalulushi, *Zambia* **119 E2** 12 50 S 28 3 E
Kalundborg, *Denmark* **17 J5** 55 41N 11 5 E
Kalush, *Ukraine* **59 H3** 49 3N 24 23 E
Kałuszyn, *Poland* **55 F8** 52 13N 21 52 E
Kalutara, *Sri Lanka* **95 L5** 6 35N 80 0 E
Kalvåg, *Norway* **18 C1** 61 46N 4 51 E
Kalvarija, *Lithuania* **54 D10** 54 24N 23 14 E
Kalwakurti, *India* **94 F4** 16 41N 78 30 E
Kalya, *Russia* **64 A7** 60 15N 59 59 E
Kalyan, *Maharashtra, India* **94 D2** 20 30N 74 3 E
Kalyan, *Maharashtra, India* **94 E1** 19 15N 73 9 E
Kalyandurg, *India* **95 G3** 14 33N 77 6 E
Kalyani, *India* **94 F3** 17 52N 76 57 E
Kalyansingapuram, *India* **94 E6** 19 30N 83 19 E
Kalyazin, *Russia* **58 D9** 57 15N 37 55 E
Kam, *Albania* **50 D4** 42 17N 20 18 E
Kam →, *Nigeria* **113 D7** 8 15N 1 10 E
Kama, *Burma* **90 F5** 19 1N 95 4 E
Kama, *Dem. Rep. of the Congo* **118 C2** 3 30 S 27 5 E
Kama →, *Russia* **64 C5** 55 45N 52 0 E
Kamachumu, *Tanzania* **118 C3** 1 37 S 31 37 E
Kamae, *Japan* **72 E3** 32 48N 131 56 E
Kamaing, *Burma* **90 C6** 25 26N 96 35 E
Kamaishi, *Japan* **70 E10** 39 16N 141 53 E
Kamakou, *U.S.A.* **145 B5** 21 7N 156 52W
Kamakura, *Japan* **73 B11** 35 19N 139 33 E
Kamalapurum, *India* **95 G4** 14 35N 78 39 E
Kamalété, *Gabon* **114 C2** 0 43 S 11 49 E
Kamalia, *Pakistan* **92 D5** 30 44N 72 42 E
Kaman, *India* **92 F6** 27 39N 77 16 E
Kaman, *Turkey* **100 C5** 39 22N 33 44 E
Kamana, *Dem. Rep. of the Congo* **115 D4** 5 59 S 24 58 E
Kamananui →, *U.S.A.* **145 J13** 21 38N 158 4W
Kamanjab, *Namibia* **116 B2** 19 35 S 14 51 E
Kamapanda, *Zambia* **119 E1** 12 5 S 24 0 E
Kamarān, *Yemen* **98 D3** 15 21N 42 35 E
Kamareddi, *India* **94 E4** 18 19N 78 21 E
Kamashi, *Uzbekistan* **65 D2** 38 51N 65 23 E
Kamativi, *Zimbabwe* **116 B4** 18 20 S 27 6 E
Kamba, *Dem. Rep. of the Congo* **115 C4** 4 0 S 22 22 E
Kamba, *Nigeria* **113 C5** 11 50N 3 45 E
Kambalda, *Australia* **125 F3** 31 10 S 121 37 E
Kambam, *India* **95 K3** 9 45N 77 16 E
Kambar, *Pakistan* **92 F3** 27 37N 68 1 E
Kambarka, *Russia* **64 C5** 56 15N 54 11 E
Kambia, *S. Leone* **112 D2** 9 3N 12 53W
Kambolé, *Togo* **113 D5** 8 43N 1 39 E
Kambolé, *Zambia* **119 D3** 8 47 S 30 48 E
Kambos, *Cyprus* **39 E8** 35 2N 32 44 E
Kambove, *Dem. Rep. of the Congo* **119 E2** 10 51 S 26 33 E
Kambuie, *Dem. Rep. of the Congo* **115 D4** 6 59 S 22 19 E
Kambwata, *Zambia* **115 E4** 14 3 S 23 43 E
Kamchatka, Poluostrov, *Russia* **67 D16** 57 0N 160 0 E
Kamchatka Pen. = Kamchatka, Poluostrov, *Russia* **67 D16** 57 0N 160 0 E
Kamchiya →, *Bulgaria* **51 C11** 43 4N 27 44 E
Kame Ruins, *Zimbabwe* **119 G2** 20 7 S 28 25 E
Kamehameha Heights, *U.S.A.* **145 K14** 21 21N 157 52W
Kamen, *Russia* **66 D9** 53 50N 81 30 E
Kamen-Rybolov, *Russia* **70 B6** 44 46N 132 2 E
Kamende, *Dem. Rep. of the Congo* **115 D4** 6 26 S 24 35 E
Kamenica, *Serbia, Yug.* **50 C6** 43 27N 22 27 E
Kamenica, *Serbia, Yug.* **50 B3** 44 25N 19 45 E
Kamenice nad Lipou, *Czech Rep.* **34 B8** 49 18N 15 2 E
Kamenjak, Rt, *Croatia* **45 D10** 44 47N 13 55 E
Kamenka = Kaminka, *Ukraine* **59 H7** 49 3N 32 6 E
Kamenka, *Kazakstan* **60 E10** 51 7N 50 19 E
Kamenka, *Arkhangelsk, Russia* **56 A7** 65 58N 44 0 E
Kamenka, *Penza, Russia* **60 D6** 53 10N 44 5 E
Kamenka, *Voronezh, Russia* **59 G10** 50 47N 39 20 E
Kamenka Bugskaya = Kamyanka-Buzka, *Ukraine* **59 G3** 50 8N 24 16 E
Kamenka Dneprovskaya = Kamyanka-Dniprovska, *Ukraine* **59 J8** 47 29N 34 28 E
Kamennomostskiy, *Russia* **61 H5** 44 18N 40 13 E
Kameno, *Bulgaria* **51 D11** 42 34N 27 18 E
Kamenolomini, *Russia* **61 G5** 47 40N 40 14 E
Kamensk-Shakhtinskiy, *Russia* **61 F5** 48 23N 40 20 E
Kamensk Uralskiy, *Russia* **64 C9** 56 25N 62 2 E
Kamenskiy, *Russia* **60 E7** 50 48N 45 25 E
Kamenskoye, *Russia* **67 C17** 62 45N 165 30 E
Kamenyak, *Bulgaria* **51 C10** 43 24N 26 57 E
Kamenz, *Germany* **30 D10** 51 15N 14 5 E
Kameoka, *Japan* **73 C7** 35 0N 135 35 E
Kameyama, *Japan* **73 C8** 34 51N 136 27 E
Kami-Jima, *Japan* **72 E2** 32 27N 130 20 E
Kami-Koshiki-Jima, *Japan* **72 F1** 31 50N 129 52 E
Kamiagata, *Japan* **72 C1** 34 47N 129 24 E
Kamiah, *U.S.A.* **158 C5** 46 14N 116 2W
Kamień Krajeński, *Poland* **54 E4** 53 32N 17 32 E
Kamień Pomorski, *Poland* **54 E1** 53 57N 14 43 E
Kamienna →, *Poland* **55 G8** 51 6N 21 47 E
Kamienna Góra, *Poland* **55 H3** 50 47N 16 2 E
Kamieńsk, *Poland* **55 G6** 51 12N 19 29 E
Kamieskroon, *S. Africa* **116 E2** 30 9 S 17 56 E
Kamilukuak, L., *Canada* **143 A8** 62 22N 101 40W
Kamin-Kashyrskyy, *Ukraine* **59 G3** 51 39N 24 56 E
Kamina, *Dem. Rep. of the Congo* **119 D2** 8 45 S 25 0 E
Kaminak L., *Canada* **143 A10** 62 10N 95 0W
Kaministiquia, *Canada* **140 C1** 48 32N 89 35W
Kaminka, *Ukraine* **59 H7** 49 3N 32 6 E
Kaminoyama, *Japan* **70 E10** 38 9N 140 17 E
Kamioka, *Japan* **73 A9** 36 25N 137 15 E
Kamiros, *Greece* **38 E11** 36 20N 27 56 E
Kamishak Bay, *U.S.A.* **144 G9** 59 15N 153 45W
Kamitsushima, *Japan* **72 C1** 34 50N 129 28 E
Kamituga, *Dem. Rep. of the Congo* **118 C2** 3 2 S 28 10 E
Kamla →, *India* **93 G12** 25 35N 86 36 E
Kamloops, *Canada* **142 C4** 50 40N 120 20W
Kamnik, *Slovenia* **45 B11** 46 14N 14 37 E
Kamo, *Armenia* **61 K7** 40 21N 45 7 E
Kamo, *Japan* **70 F9** 37 39N 139 3 E
Kamo, *N.Z.* **130 B3** 35 42 S 174 20 E
Kamoa Mts., *Guyana* **169 C6** 1 30N 59 0W
Kamogawa, *Japan* **73 B12** 35 5N 140 5 E
Kamojima, *Japan* **72 C6** 34 4N 134 21 E
Kamoke, *Pakistan* **92 C6** 32 4N 74 4 E
Kamooloa, *U.S.A.* **145 J13** 21 34N 158 7W
Kamp →, *Austria* **34 C8** 48 23N 15 42 E
Kampala, *Uganda* **118 B3** 0 20N 32 30 E
Kampang Chhnang, *Cambodia* **87 F5** 12 20N 104 35 E
Kampar, *Malaysia* **87 K3** 4 18N 101 9 E
Kampar →, *Indonesia* **84 B2** 0 30N 103 8 E
Kampen, *Neths.* **24 B5** 52 33N 5 53 E
Kamphaeng Phet, *Thailand* **86 D2** 16 28N 99 30 E
Kampolombo, L., *Zambia* **119 E2** 11 37 S 29 42 E
Kampong Pengerang, *Malaysia* **87 d** 1 22N 104 7 E
Kampong Punggai, *Malaysia* **87 d** 1 27N 104 18 E
Kampong Saom, *Cambodia* **87 G4** 10 38N 103 30 E
Kampong Saom, Chaak, *Cambodia* **87 G4** 10 50N 103 32 E
Kampong Tanjong Langsat, *Malaysia* **87 d** 1 28N 104 1 E
Kampong Telok Ramunia, *Malaysia* **87 d** 1 22N 104 15 E
Kampong To, *Thailand* **87 J3** 6 3N 101 13 E
Kampot, *Cambodia* **87 G5** 10 36N 104 10 E
Kampsville, *U.S.A.* **156 E6** 39 18N 90 37W
Kampti, *Burkina Faso* **112 C4** 10 7N 3 25W
Kampuchea = Cambodia ■, *Asia* **86 F5** 12 15N 105 0 E
Kampung Air Putih, *Malaysia* **87 K4** 4 15N 103 10 E
Kampung Jerangau, *Malaysia* **87 K4** 4 50N 103 10 E
Kampung Raja, *Malaysia* **87 K4** 5 45N 102 35 E
Kampungbaru = Tolitoli, *Indonesia* **82 A2** 1 5N 120 50 E
Kamrau, Teluk, *Indonesia* **83 B4** 3 30 S 133 36 E
Kamsack, *Canada* **143 C8** 51 34N 101 54W
Kamsai, *Guinea* **112 C2** 10 40N 14 36W
Kamskoye Ustye, *Russia* **60 C9** 55 10N 49 20 E
Kamskoye Vdkhr., *Russia* **64 B6** 58 41N 56 7 E
Kamthi, *India* **94 D4** 21 9N 79 19 E
Kamuchawie L., *Canada* **143 B8** 56 18N 101 59W
Kamuela, *U.S.A.* **145 C6** 20 1N 155 41W
Kamui-Misaki, *Japan* **70 C10** 43 20N 140 21 E
Kamundan →, *Indonesia* **83 B4** 2 17 S 132 39 E
Kamyanets-Podilskyy, *Ukraine* **59 H4** 48 45N 26 40 E
Kamyanka-Buzka, *Ukraine* **59 G3** 50 8N 24 16 E
Kamyanka-Dniprovska, *Ukraine* **59 J8** 47 29N 34 28 E
Kāmyārān, *Iran* **101 E12** 34 47N 46 56 E
Kamyshin, *Russia* **60 E7** 50 10N 45 24 E
Kamyshlov, *Russia* **64 C9** 56 50N 62 43 E
Kamyzyak, *Russia* **61 G9** 46 4N 48 10 E
Kan, *Burma* **90 D5** 22 25N 94 5 E
Kan, *Sudan* **107 F3** 9 1N 31 47 E
Kanaaupscow, *Canada* **140 B4** 54 2N 76 30W
Kanaaupscow →, *Canada* **139 C12** 53 39N 77 9W
Kanab, *U.S.A.* **159 H7** 37 3N 112 32W
Kanab →, *U.S.A.* **159 H7** 36 24N 112 38W
Kanacea, *Lau Group, Fiji* **133 A3** 17 15 S 179 6W
Kanacea, *Taveuni, Fiji* **133 A2** 16 59 S 179 56 E
Kanaga I., *U.S.A.* **144 L3** 51 45N 177 22W
Kanagawa ☐, *Japan* **73 B11** 35 20N 139 20 E
Kanagi, *Japan* **70 D10** 40 54N 140 27 E
Kanairiktok →, *Canada* **141 A7** 55 2N 60 18W
Kanakapura, *India* **95 H3** 12 33N 77 28 E
Kanália, *Greece* **48 B4** 39 30N 22 53 E
Kananga, *Dem. Rep. of the Congo* **115 D4** 5 55 S 22 18 E
Kanangra-Boyd Nat. Park, *Australia* **129 B9** 33 57 S 150 15 E
Kanash, *Russia* **60 C8** 55 30N 47 32 E
Kanaskat, *U.S.A.* **160 C5** 47 19N 121 54W
Kanastraíon, Ákra = Palioúrion, Ákra, *Greece* **50 G7** 39 57N 23 45 E
Kanawha →, *U.S.A.* **148 F4** 38 50N 82 9W
Kanazawa, *Japan* **73 A8** 36 30N 136 38 E
Kanbalu, *Burma* **90 D5** 23 12N 95 31 E
Kanchanaburi, *Thailand* **86 E2** 14 2N 99 31 E
Kanchenjunga, *Nepal* **93 F13** 27 50N 88 10 E
Kanchipuram, *India* **95 H4** 12 52N 79 45 E
Kańczuga, *Poland* **55 J9** 49 59N 22 25 E
Kanda Kanda, *Dem. Rep. of the Congo* **115 D4** 6 52 S 23 48 E
Kandaghat, *India* **92 D7** 30 59N 77 7 E
Kandahar = Qandahār, *Afghan.* **91 C2** 31 32N 65 43 E
Kandahar, *India* **94 E3** 18 52N 77 12 E
Kandala, *Dem. Rep. of the Congo* **115 D3** 6 20 S 19 40 E
Kandalaksha, *Russia* **56 A5** 67 9N 32 30 E
Kandalakshskiy Zaliv, *Russia* **56 A6** 66 0N 35 0 E
Kandangan, *Indonesia* **85 C5** 2 50 S 115 20 E
Kandanghaur, *Indonesia* **79 G13** 6 21 S 108 6 E
Kandanos, *Greece* **39 E4** 35 19N 23 44 E
Kandava, *Latvia* **54 A9** 57 2N 22 46 E
Kandavu = Kadavu, *Fiji* **133 B2** 19 0 S 178 15 E
Kandavu Passage = Kadavu Passage, *Fiji* **133 B2** 18 45 S 178 0 E
Kandep, *Papua N. G.* **132 C2** 5 54 S 143 32 E
Kander →, *Switz.* **32 C5** 46 33N 7 38 E
Kandersteg, *Switz.* **32 D5** 46 28N 7 40 E
Kandhíla, *Greece* **39 B2** 38 42N 20 56 E
Kandhíla, *Greece* **48 D4** 37 46N 22 22 E
Kandhkot, *Pakistan* **92 E3** 28 16N 69 8 E
Kandhla, *India* **92 E7** 29 18N 77 19 E
Kandi, *Benin* **113 C5** 11 7N 2 55 E
Kandi, *India* **93 H13** 23 58N 88 5 E
Kandiaro, *Pakistan* **92 F3** 27 4N 68 13 E
Kandıra, *Turkey* **100 B4** 41 4N 30 9 E
Kandla, *India* **92 H4** 23 0N 70 10 E
Kandor, O. →, *Chad* **109 E4** 17 13N 20 52 E
Kandos, *Australia* **129 B8** 32 45 S 149 58 E
Kandreho, *Madag.* **117 B8** 17 29 S 46 6 E
Kandrian, *Papua N. G.* **132 D5** 6 14 S 149 37 E
Kandy, *Sri Lanka* **95 L5** 7 18N 80 43 E
Kane, *U.S.A.* **150 E6** 41 40N 78 49W
Kane Basin, *Greenland* **10 B4** 79 1N 70 0W
Kaneilio Pt., *U.S.A.* **145 K13** 21 27N 158 12W
Kanel, *Senegal* **112 B2** 15 30N 13 18W
Kaneohe, *U.S.A.* **145 K14** 21 25N 157 48W
Kaneohe B., *U.S.A.* **145 K14** 21 30N 157 50W
Kanevskaya, *Russia* **61 G4** 46 3N 38 57 E
Kanfanar, *Croatia* **45 C10** 45 7N 13 50 E
Kang, *Botswana* **116 C3** 23 41 S 22 50 E
Kangaamiut, *Greenland* **10 D5** 65 50N 53 20W
Kangaba, *Mali* **112 C3** 11 56N 8 25W
Kangal, *Turkey* **100 C7** 39 14N 37 23 E
Kangān, *Fārs, Iran* **97 E7** 27 50N 52 3 E
Kangān, *Hormozgān, Iran* **97 E8** 25 48N 57 28 E
Kangar, *Malaysia* **87 J3** 6 27N 100 12 E
Kangaré, *Mali* **112 C3** 11 36N 8 4W
Kangaroo I., *Australia* **128 C2** 35 45 S 137 0 E
Kangaroo Mts., *Australia* **126 C3** 23 29 S 141 51 E
Kangasala, *Finland* **15 F21** 61 28N 24 4 E
Kangāvar, *Iran* **97 C6** 34 40N 48 0 E
Kangding, *China* **76 B3** 30 2N 101 57 E
Kangdong, *N. Korea* **75 E14** 39 9N 126 5 E
Kangean, Kepulauan, *Indonesia* **85 D5** 6 55 S 115 23 E
Kangean Is. = Kangean, Kepulauan, *Indonesia* **85 D5** 6 55 S 115 23 E
Kangen →, *Sudan* **107 F3** 6 47N 33 9 E
Kangerdlugssuak, *Greenland* **10 D7** 68 10N 32 20W
Kangerluarsoruseq, *Greenland* **10 E5** 63 45N 51 27W
Kangerluarsoruset = Kangerluarsoruseq, *Greenland* **10 E5** 63 45N 51 27W
Kangerlussuaq, *Greenland* **10 D5** 66 59N 50 40W
Kanggye, *N. Korea* **75 D14** 41 0N 126 35 E
Kanggyŏng, *S. Korea* **75 F14** 36 10N 127 0 E
Kanghwa, *S. Korea* **75 F14** 37 45N 126 30 E
Kangikajik, *Greenland* **10 C8** 70 7N 22 0W
Kangilinnguit, *Greenland* **10 E6** 61 20N 47 57W
Kangiqsliniq = Rankin Inlet, *Canada* **138 B10** 62 30N 93 0W
Kangiqsualujjuaq, *Canada* **139 C13** 58 30N 65 59W
Kangiqsujuaq, *Canada* **139 B12** 61 30N 72 0W
Kangiqtugaapik = Clyde River, *Canada* **139 A13** 70 30N 68 30W
Kangirsuk, *Canada* **139 B13** 60 0N 70 0W
Kangkar Chemaran, *Malaysia* **87 d** 1 34N 104 12 E
Kangkar Sungai Tiram, *Malaysia* **87 d** 1 35N 103 55 E
Kangkar Teberau, *Malaysia* **87 d** 1 32N 103 51 E
Kangnŭng, *S. Korea* **75 F15** 37 45N 128 54 E
Kango, *Gabon* **114 B2** 0 11N 10 5 E
Kangoya, *Dem. Rep. of the Congo* **115 D4** 9 55 S 22 48 E
Kangping, *China* **75 C12** 42 43N 123 18 E
Kangpokpi, *India* **90 C4** 25 8N 93 58 E
Kangra, *India* **92 C7** 32 6N 76 16 E
Kangyidaung, *Burma* **90 G5** 16 56N 94 54 E
Kanhan →, *India* **94 D4** 21 4N 79 34 E
Kanhangad, *India* **95 H2** 12 21N 74 58 E
Kanhar →, *India* **93 G10** 24 28N 83 8 E
Kanheri, *India* **94 E1** 19 13N 72 50 E
Kani, *Sagaing, Burma* **90 D5** 23 52N 95 22 E
Kani, *Sagaing, Burma* **90 D5** 22 26N 94 51 E
Kani, *Ivory C.* **112 D3** 8 29N 6 36W
Kaniama, *Dem. Rep. of the Congo* **118 D1** 7 30 S 24 12 E
Kaniapiskau = Caniapiscau →, *Canada* **141 A6** 56 40N 69 30W
Kaniapiskau, Res. = Caniapiscau, Rés. de, *Canada* **141 B6** 54 10N 69 55W

Kings Park, *U.S.A.* 151 F11 40 53N 73 16W
King's Peak, *U.S.A.* 158 F8 40 46N 110 27W
Kingsbridge, *U.K.* 21 G4 50 17N 3 47W
Kingsburg, *U.S.A.* 160 J7 36 31N 119 33W
Kingscote, *Australia* 128 C2 35 40 S 137 38 E
Kingscourt, *Ireland* 23 C5 53 55N 6 48W
Kingsford, *U.S.A.* 148 C1 45 48N 88 4W
Kingsland, *U.S.A.* 152 E8 30 48N 81 41W
Kingsley, *U.S.A.* 154 D7 42 35N 95 58W
Kingsport, *U.S.A.* 149 G4 36 33N 82 33W
Kingston, *Canada* 140 D4 44 14N 76 30W
Kingston, *Jamaica* 164 a 18 0N 76 50W
Kingston, *N.Z.* 131 F3 45 20 S 168 43 E
Kingston, *N.H., U.S.A.* 151 D13 42 56N 71 3W
Kingston, *N.Y., U.S.A.* 151 E11 41 56N 73 59W
Kingston, *Pa., U.S.A.* 151 E9 41 16N 75 54W
Kingston, *R.I., U.S.A.* 151 E13 41 29N 71 30W
Kingston Pk., *U.S.A.* 161 K11 35 45N 115 54W
Kingston South East, *Australia* 128 D3 36 51 S 139 55 E
Kingston upon Hull, *U.K.* 20 D7 53 45N 0 21W
Kingston upon Hull □, *U.K.* 20 D7 53 45N 0 21W
Kingston-upon-Thames □, *U.K.* 21 F7 51 24N 0 17W
Kingstown, *Australia* 129 A9 30 29 S 151 6 E
Kingstown, *St. Vincent* 165 D7 13 10N 61 10W
Kingstree, *U.S.A.* 152 B10 33 40N 79 50W
Kingsville, *Canada* 140 D3 42 2N 82 45W
Kingsville, *U.S.A.* 155 M6 27 31N 97 52W
Kingunda, *Dem. Rep. of the Congo* 115 D3 6 36 S 16 58 E
Kingussie, *U.K.* 22 D4 57 6N 4 2W
Kingwood, *U.S.A.* 155 K7 29 54N 95 18W
Kınık, *Antalya, Turkey* 49 E11 36 20N 29 20 E
Kınık, *İzmir, Turkey* 49 B9 39 6N 27 24 E
Kinistino, *Canada* 143 C7 52 57N 105 2W
Kinkala, *Congo* 115 C2 4 18 S 14 49 E
Kinki □, *Japan* 73 D8 33 45N 136 0 E
Kinleith, *N.Z.* 130 E4 38 20 S 175 56 E
Kinmount, *Canada* 150 B6 44 48N 78 45W
Kinmundy, *U.S.A.* 157 F8 38 46N 88 51W
Kinn, *Norway* 18 C1 61 34N 4 45 E
Kinna, *Sweden* 17 G6 57 32N 12 42 E
Kinnairds Hd., *U.K.* 22 D6 57 43N 2 1W
Kinnared, *Sweden* 17 G7 57 2N 13 7 E
Kinnarodden, *Norway* 12 A11 71 8N 27 40 E
Kinnarp, *Sweden* 17 F7 58 5N 13 32 E
Kinneviken, *Sweden* 17 F7 58 35N 13 15 E
Kinngait = Cape Dorset, *Canada* 139 B12 64 14N 76 32W
Kino, *Mexico* 162 B2 28 45N 111 59W
Kinogitan, *Phil.* 81 G5 9 0N 124 48 E
Kinoje →, *Canada* 140 B3 52 8N 81 25W
Kinomoto, *Japan* 73 B8 35 30N 136 13 E
Kinoni, *Uganda* 118 C3 0 41 S 30 28 E
Kinoosao, *Canada* 143 B8 57 5N 102 1W
Kinross, *U.K.* 22 E5 56 13N 3 25W
Kinsale, *Ireland* 23 E3 51 42N 8 31W
Kinsale, Old Hd. of, *Ireland* 23 E3 51 37N 8 33W
Kinsarvik, *Norway* 18 D3 60 22N 6 43 E
Kinsha = Chang Jiang →, *China* 77 B13 31 48N 121 10 E
Kinshasa, *Dem. Rep. of the Congo* 115 C3 4 20 S 15 15 E
Kinsley, *U.S.A.* 155 G5 37 55N 99 25W
Kinsman, *U.S.A.* 150 E4 41 26N 80 35W
Kinston, *Ala., U.S.A.* 152 D3 31 13N 86 10W
Kinston, *N.C., U.S.A.* 149 H7 35 16N 77 35W
Kintamani, *Indonesia* 79 J18 8 14 S 115 19 E
Kintampo, *Ghana* 113 D4 8 5N 1 41W
Kintap, *Indonesia* 85 C5 3 51 S 115 13 E
Kintore Ra., *Australia* 124 D4 23 15 S 128 47 E
Kintshua, *Dem. Rep. of the Congo* 115 C3 4 27 S 19 38 E
Kintyre, *U.K.* 22 F3 55 30N 5 35W
Kintyre, Mull of, *U.K.* 22 F3 55 17N 5 47W
Kinu-Gawa →, *Japan* 73 B11 35 36N 139 57 E
Kinushseo →, *Canada* 140 A3 55 15N 83 45W
Kinuso, *Canada* 142 B5 55 20N 115 25W
Kinwat, *India* 94 E4 19 38N 78 12 E
Kinyangiri, *Tanzania* 118 C3 4 25 S 34 37 E
Kinyeti, *Sudan* 107 G3 3 57N 32 54 E
Kinzia, *Dem. Rep. of the Congo* 114 C3 3 36 S 18 26 E
Kinzig →, *Germany* 31 G3 48 36N 7 49 E
Kinzua, *U.S.A.* 150 E6 41 52N 78 58W
Kinzua Dam, *U.S.A.* 150 E6 41 53N 79 0W
Kióni, *Greece* 39 C2 38 27N 20 41 E
Kiosk, *Canada* 140 C4 46 6N 78 53W
Kiowa, *Kans., U.S.A.* 155 G5 37 1N 98 29W
Kiowa, *Okla., U.S.A.* 155 H7 34 43N 95 54W
Kipahigan L., *Canada* 143 B8 55 20N 101 55W
Kipanga, *Tanzania* 118 D4 6 15 S 35 20 E
Kipapa →, *U.S.A.* 145 K13 21 24N 158 1W
Kiparissía, *Greece* 48 D3 37 15N 21 40 E
Kiparissiakós Kólpos, *Greece* 48 D3 37 25N 21 25 E
Kipawa, L., *Canada* 140 C4 46 50N 79 0W
Kipembawe, *Tanzania* 118 D3 7 38 S 33 27 E
Kipengere Ra., *Tanzania* 119 D3 9 12 S 34 15 E
Kipili, *Tanzania* 118 D3 7 28 S 30 32 E
Kipini, *Kenya* 118 C5 2 30 S 40 32 E
Kipling, *Canada* 143 C8 50 6N 102 38W
Kipnuk, *U.S.A.* 144 G6 59 56N 164 3W
Kippure, *Ireland* 23 C5 53 11N 6 21W
Kipushi, *Dem. Rep. of the Congo* 119 E2 11 48 S 27 12 E
Kiraddul, *India* 94 E5 18 33N 81 10 E
Kirane, *Mali* 112 B2 15 20N 10 20W
Kiranomena, *Madag.* 117 B8 18 17 S 46 2 E
Kiraz, *Turkey* 49 C10 38 14N 28 13 E
Kirazlı, *Turkey* 51 F10 40 2N 26 41 E
Kirchberg, *Bern, Switz.* 32 B5 47 5N 7 35 E
Kirchberg, *St. Gallen, Switz.* 33 B8 47 25N 9 2 E
Kirchhain, *Germany* 30 E4 50 47N 8 56 E
Kirchheim, *Germany* 31 G5 48 39N 9 27 E
Kirchheimbolanden, *Germany* 31 F3 49 40N 8 0 E
Kirchschlag, *Austria* 35 D9 47 30N 16 19 E
Kirdimi, *Chad* 109 E3 18 11N 18 31 E
Kireç, *Turkey* 49 B10 39 33N 28 22 E
Kirensk, *Russia* 67 D11 57 50N 107 55 E
Kirghiz Range, *Asia* 65 B6 42 40N 73 40 E
Kirghizia = Kyrgyzstan ■, *Asia* 66 E8 42 0N 75 0 E
Kirghizstan = Kyrgyzstan ■, *Asia* 66 E8 42 0N 75 0 E
Kirgiziya Steppe, *Eurasia* 57 E10 50 0N 55 0 E
Kiri, *Dem. Rep. of the Congo* 114 C3 1 29 S 19 0 E
Kiri Buru, *India* 94 D7 22 0N 85 0 E
Kiribati ■, *Pac. Oc.* 134 H10 5 0 S 180 0 E
Kırıkhan, *Turkey* 100 D7 36 31N 36 21 E
Kırıkkale, *Turkey* 100 C5 39 51N 33 32 E
Kirikopuni, *N.Z.* 130 B3 35 50 S 174 1 E
Kirillov, *Russia* 58 C10 59 49N 38 24 E
Kirin = Jilin, *China* 75 C14 43 44N 126 30 E
Kirindi Oya →, *Sri Lanka* 95 L5 6 15N 81 20 E
Kirinyaga = Kenya, Mt., *Kenya* 118 C4 0 10 S 37 18 E
Kirishi, *Russia* 58 C7 59 28N 31 59 E
Kirishima-Yama, *Japan* 72 F2 31 58N 130 55 E
Kiritimati, *Kiribati* 135 G12 1 58N 157 27W
Kiriwina I., *Papua N. G.* 132 E6 8 40 S 151 6 E
Kırka, *Turkey* 49 B12 39 17N 30 33 E
Kırkağaç, *Turkey* 49 B9 39 8N 27 40 E
Kirkby, *U.K.* 20 D5 53 30N 2 54W
Kirkby Lonsdale, *U.K.* 20 C5 54 12N 2 36W
Kirkcaldy, *U.K.* 22 E5 56 7N 3 9W
Kirkcudbright, *U.K.* 22 G4 54 50N 4 2W
Kirkee, *India* 94 E1 18 34N 73 56 E
Kirkehamn, *Norway* 18 F3 58 14N 6 31 E
Kirkenær, *Norway* 18 D9 60 27N 12 3 E
Kirkenes, *Norway* 14 B23 69 40N 30 5 E
Kirkfield, *Canada* 150 B6 44 34N 78 59W
Kirkjubæjarklaustur, *Iceland* 11 D8 63 47N 18 4W
Kirkkonummi, *Finland* 15 F21 60 8N 24 26 E
Kirkland, *U.S.A.* 157 B8 42 6N 88 51W
Kirkland Lake, *Canada* 140 C3 48 9N 80 2W
Kırklareli, *Turkey* 51 E11 41 44N 27 15 E
Kırklareli □, *Turkey* 51 E11 41 45N 27 15 E
Kirklin, *U.S.A.* 157 D10 40 12N 86 22W
Kirkliston Ra., *N.Z.* 131 E5 44 25 S 170 34 E
Kirksville, *U.S.A.* 156 D4 40 12N 92 35W
Kirkük, *Iraq* 101 E11 35 30N 44 21 E
Kirkwall, *U.K.* 22 C6 58 59N 2 58W
Kirkwood, *S. Africa* 116 E4 33 22 S 25 15 E
Kirkwood, *U.S.A.* 156 F6 38 35N 90 24W
Kirlampudi, *India* 94 F6 17 12N 82 12 E
Kirn, *Germany* 31 F3 49 47N 7 26 E
Kirov, *Kaluga, Russia* 58 E8 54 3N 34 20 E
Kirov, *Kirov, Russia* 64 B2 58 35N 49 40 E
Kirovabad = Gäncä, *Azerbaijan* 61 K8 40 45N 46 20 E
Kirovakan = Vanadzor, *Armenia* 61 K7 40 48N 44 30 E
Kirovo-Chepetsk, *Russia* 64 B3 58 28N 50 0 E
Kirovograd = Kirovohrad, *Ukraine* 59 H7 48 35N 32 20 E
Kirovohrad, *Ukraine* 59 H7 48 35N 32 20 E
Kirovsk = Babadayhan, *Turkmenistan* 66 F7 37 42N 60 23 E
Kirovsk, *Russia* 56 A5 67 32N 33 41 E
Kirovskiy = Balpyq Bī, *Kazakstan* 65 A9 44 52N 78 12 E
Kirovskiy, *Astrakhan, Russia* 61 H9 45 51N 48 11 E
Kirovskiy, *Kamchatka, Russia* 67 D16 54 27N 155 42 E
Kirovskiy, *Primorsk, Russia* 70 B6 45 7N 133 30 E
Kirriemuir, *U.K.* 22 E5 56 41N 3 1W
Kirs, *Russia* 64 B4 59 21N 52 14 E
Kirsanov, *Russia* 60 D6 52 35N 42 40 E
Kırşehir, *Turkey* 100 C6 39 14N 34 5 E
Kirtachi, *Niger* 113 C5 12 52N 2 30 E
Kīrteh, *Afghan.* 91 B1 32 15N 63 0 E
Kirthar Range, *Pakistan* 91 D2 27 0N 67 0 E
Kirtland, *U.S.A.* 159 H9 36 44N 108 21W
Kiruna, *Sweden* 14 C19 67 52N 20 15 E
Kirundu, *Dem. Rep. of the Congo* 118 C2 0 50 S 25 35 E
Kirya, *Russia* 60 C8 55 8N 46 55 E
Kiryū, *Japan* 73 A11 36 24N 139 20 E
Kisa, *Sweden* 17 G9 58 0N 15 39 E
Kisaga, *Tanzania* 118 C4 4 30 S 34 23 E
Kisalaya, *Nic.* 164 D3 14 40N 84 3W
Kisalföld, *Hungary* 52 C2 47 30N 17 0 E
Kisambo, *Dem. Rep. of the Congo* 115 D3 6 25 S 18 14 E
Kisámou, Kólpos, *Greece* 39 E4 35 30N 23 38 E
Kisandji, *Dem. Rep. of the Congo* 115 D3 6 18 S 19 16 E
Kisanga, *Dem. Rep. of the Congo* 118 B2 2 30N 26 35 E
Kisangani, *Dem. Rep. of the Congo* 118 B2 0 35N 25 15 E
Kisantu, *Dem. Rep. of the Congo* 115 D3 5 7 S 15 5 E
Kisar, *Indonesia* 82 C3 8 5 S 127 10 E
Kisaran, *Indonesia* 84 B1 3 0N 99 37 E
Kisarawe, *Tanzania* 118 D4 6 53 S 39 0 E
Kisarazu, *Japan* 73 B11 35 23N 139 55 E
Kisbér, *Hungary* 52 C3 47 30N 18 2 E
Kishanganga →, *Pakistan* 93 B5 34 18N 73 28 E
Kishanganj, *India* 90 B2 26 3N 88 14 E
Kishangarh, *Raj., India* 92 F6 26 34N 74 52 E
Kishangarh, *Raj., India* 92 F4 27 50N 70 30 E
Kishb, Ḩarrat al, *Si. Arabia* 98 B3 22 30N 40 15 E
Kishi, *Nigeria* 113 D5 9 1N 3 52 E
Kishinev = Chişinău, *Moldova* 53 C13 47 2N 28 50 E
Kishiwada, *Japan* 73 C7 34 28N 135 22 E
Kishorganj, *Bangla.* 90 C3 24 26N 90 40 E
Kishtwar, *India* 93 C6 33 20N 75 48 E
Kishwaukee →, *U.S.A.* 156 B7 42 12N 89 8W
Kisielice, *Poland* 54 E6 53 36N 19 16 E
Kisigo Game Reserve, *Tanzania* 118 D3 6 27 S 34 17 E
Kisii, *Kenya* 118 C3 0 40 S 34 45 E
Kisiju, *Tanzania* 118 D4 7 23 S 39 19 E
Kısır, *Turkey* 101 B10 41 0N 43 5 E
Kisizi, *Uganda* 118 C2 1 0S 29 58 E
Kiska I., *U.S.A.* 144 L2 51 59N 177 30 E
Kiskomárom = Zalakomár, *Hungary* 52 D2 46 33N 17 10 E
Kiskőrei-víztároló, *Hungary* 52 C5 47 31N 20 36 E
Kiskőrös, *Hungary* 52 D4 46 37N 19 20 E
Kiskundorozsma, *Hungary* 52 D5 46 16N 20 5 E
Kiskunfélegyháza, *Hungary* 52 D4 46 42N 19 53 E
Kiskunhalas, *Hungary* 52 D4 46 28N 19 37 E
Kiskunmajsa, *Hungary* 52 D4 46 30N 19 48 E
Kislovodsk, *Russia* 61 J6 43 50N 42 45 E
Kismayu = Chisimaio, *Somali Rep.* 120 E2 0 22 S 42 32 E
Kismayu Nat. Park, *Somali Rep.* 120 D2 1 25N 41 30 E
Kiso-Gawa →, *Japan* 73 B8 35 20N 136 45 E
Kiso-Sammyaku, *Japan* 73 B9 35 45N 137 45 E
Kisofukushima, *Japan* 73 B9 35 52N 137 43 E
Kisoro, *Uganda* 118 C2 1 17 S 29 48 E
Kissidougou, *Guinea* 112 D2 9 5N 10 5W
Kissimmee, *U.S.A.* 149 L5 28 18N 81 24W
Kissimmee →, *U.S.A.* 149 M5 27 9N 80 52W
Kissimmee, L., *U.S.A.* 153 H8 27 55N 81 17W
Kississing L., *Canada* 143 B8 55 10N 101 20W
Kissónerga, *Cyprus* 39 F8 34 49N 32 24 E
Kissu, J., *Sudan* 106 C2 21 37N 25 10 E
Kistanje, *Croatia* 45 E12 43 58N 15 55 E
Kisújszállás, *Hungary* 52 C5 47 12N 20 50 E
Kisuki, *Japan* 72 B4 35 17N 132 54 E
Kisumu, *Kenya* 118 C3 0 3S 34 45 E
Kisvárda, *Hungary* 52 B7 48 14N 22 4 E
Kiswani, *Tanzania* 118 C4 4 5S 37 57 E
Kiswere, *Tanzania* 119 D4 9 27 S 39 30 E
Kit Carson, *U.S.A.* 154 F3 38 46N 102 48W
Kita, *Mali* 112 C3 13 5N 9 25W
Kita-Ura, *Japan* 73 B12 36 0N 140 34 E
Kitaa □, *Greenland* 10 C6 70 0N 47 0W
Kitab, *Uzbekistan* 65 D3 39 7N 66 52 E
Kitaibaraki, *Japan* 71 F10 36 50N 140 45 E
Kitakami, *Japan* 70 E10 39 20N 141 10 E
Kitakami-Gawa →, *Japan* 70 E10 38 25N 141 19 E
Kitakami-Sammyaku, *Japan* 70 E10 39 30N 141 30 E
Kitakata, *Japan* 70 F9 37 39N 139 52 E
Kitakyūshū, *Japan* 72 D2 33 50N 130 50 E
Kitale, *Kenya* 118 B4 1 0N 35 0 E
Kitami, *Japan* 70 C11 43 48N 143 54 E
Kitami-Sammyaku, *Japan* 70 B11 44 22N 142 43 E
Kitangiri, L., *Tanzania* 118 C3 4 5 S 34 20 E
Kitano-Kaikyō, *Japan* 72 C6 34 17N 134 58 E
Kitaotao, *Phil.* 81 H5 7 40N 125 1 E
Kitava I., *Papua N. G.* 132 E6 8 40 S 151 20 E
Kitaya, *Tanzania* 119 E5 10 38 S 40 8 E
Kitcharao, *Phil.* 81 G5 9 27N 125 36 E
Kitchener, *Canada* 140 D3 43 27N 80 29W
Kitee, *Finland* 58 A6 62 5N 30 8 E
Kitega = Gitega, *Burundi* 118 C2 3 26 S 29 56 E
Kitengo, *Dem. Rep. of the Congo* 118 D1 7 26 S 24 8 E
Kitgum, *Uganda* 118 B3 3 17N 32 52 E
Kíthira, *Greece* 48 E5 36 8N 23 0 E
Kíthnos, *Greece* 48 D6 37 26N 24 27 E
Kiti, *Cyprus* 39 F9 34 50N 33 34 E
Kiti, C., *Cyprus* 39 F9 34 48N 33 36 E
Kitimat, *Canada* 142 C3 54 3N 128 38W
Kitinen →, *Finland* 14 C22 67 14N 27 27 E
Kitiyab, *Sudan* 107 D3 17 13N 33 35 E
Kitombe, *Dem. Rep. of the Congo* 115 D3 5 22 S 18 59 E
Kítros, *Greece* 50 F6 40 22N 22 34 E
Kitsuki, *Japan* 72 D3 33 25N 131 37 E
Kittakittaooloo, L., *Australia* 127 D2 28 3 S 138 14 E
Kittanning, *U.S.A.* 150 F5 40 49N 79 31W
Kittatinny Mts., *U.S.A.* 151 F10 41 0N 75 0W
Kittery, *U.S.A.* 149 D10 43 5N 70 45W
Kittilä, *Finland* 14 C21 67 40N 24 51 E
Kitui, *Kenya* 118 C4 1 17 S 38 0 E
Kitwanga, *Canada* 142 B3 55 6N 128 4W
Kitwe, *Zambia* 119 E2 12 54 S 28 13 E
Kitzbühel, *Austria* 34 D5 47 27N 12 24 E
Kitzbühler Alpen, *Austria* 34 D5 47 20N 12 20 E
Kitzingen, *Germany* 31 F6 49 44N 10 9 E
Kiunga, *Papua N. G.* 132 D1 6 7 S 141 18 E
Kivalina, *U.S.A.* 144 C6 67 44N 164 33W
Kivarli, *India* 92 G5 24 33N 72 46 E
Kivertsi, *Ukraine* 59 G3 50 50N 25 28 E
Kividhes, *Cyprus* 39 F8 34 46N 32 51 E
Kivik, *Sweden* 17 J8 55 41N 14 13 E
Kivotós, *Greece* 50 F5 40 13N 21 26 E
Kivu, L., *Dem. Rep. of the Congo* 118 C2 1 48 S 29 0 E
Kiwai I., *Papua N. G.* 132 E2 8 35 S 143 30 E
Kiyev = Kyyiv, *Ukraine* 59 G6 50 30N 30 28 E
Kiyevskoye Vdkhr. = Kyyivske Vdskh., *Ukraine* 59 G6 51 0N 30 25 E
Kıyıköy, *Turkey* 51 E12 41 38N 28 5 E
Kizel, *Russia* 64 B6 59 3N 57 40 E
Kiziguru, *Rwanda* 118 C3 1 46 S 30 23 E
Kızıl Adalar, *Turkey* 51 F13 40 52N 29 5 E
Kızıl Irmak →, *Turkey* 100 B6 41 44N 35 58 E
Kizil Jilga, *China* 93 B8 35 26N 78 50 E
Kizil Yurt, *Russia* 61 J8 43 13N 46 54 E
Kızılcabölük, *Turkey* 49 D11 37 37N 29 1 E
Kızılcadağ, *Turkey* 49 D11 37 1N 29 58 E
Kızılcahamam, *Turkey* 100 B5 40 30N 32 30 E
Kızılhisar, *Turkey* 100 D3 37 32N 29 17 E
Kızılırmak, *Turkey* 100 B5 40 21N 33 59 E
Kızılkaya, *Turkey* 49 D12 37 18N 30 27 E
Kızılören, *Turkey* 49 C12 38 15N 30 10 E
Kizilskoye, *Russia* 64 E7 52 44N 58 54 E
Kızıltepe, *Turkey* 101 D9 37 12N 40 35 E
Kizimkazi, *Tanzania* 118 D4 6 28 S 39 30 E
Kizlyar, *Russia* 61 J8 43 51N 46 40 E
Kizyl-Arvat = Gyzylarbat, *Turkmenistan* 66 F6 39 4N 56 23 E
Kjellerup, *Denmark* 17 H3 56 17N 9 25 E
Kjellmyra, *Norway* 18 D9 60 39N 12 1 E
Kjølen, *Norway* 18 C5 62 3N 8 43 E
Kjölur, *Iceland* 11 C7 64 50N 19 25W
Kjósarsýsla □, *Iceland* 11 C5 64 15N 21 30W
Kladanj, *Bos.-H.* 52 F3 44 14N 18 42 E
Kladnica, *Serbia, Yug.* 50 C4 43 23N 20 2 E
Kladno, *Czech Rep.* 34 A7 50 10N 14 7 E
Kladovo, *Serbia, Yug.* 50 B6 44 36N 22 33 E
Klæbu, *Norway* 18 A7 63 18N 10 29 E
Klaeng, *Thailand* 86 F3 12 47N 101 39 E
Klagan, *Malaysia* 85 A5 5 58N 117 27 E
Klagenfurt, *Austria* 34 E7 46 38N 14 20 E
Klaipėda, *Lithuania* 15 J19 55 43N 21 10 E
Klaipėda □, *Lithuania* 54 C8 55 43N 21 7 E
Klaksvík, *Færoe Is.* 14 E9 62 14N 6 35W
Klamath →, *U.S.A.* 158 F1 41 33N 124 5W
Klamath Falls, *U.S.A.* 158 E3 42 13N 121 46W
Klamath Mts., *U.S.A.* 158 F2 41 20N 123 0W
Klamono, *Indonesia* 83 B4 1 8 S 131 30 E
Klangklang, *Burma* 90 D4 22 41N 93 26 E
Klanjec, *Croatia* 45 B12 46 3N 15 45 E
Klappan →, *Canada* 142 B3 58 0N 129 43W
Klara = Trysilelva →, *Norway* 18 C9 61 2N 12 35 E
Klarälven →, *Sweden* 16 E7 59 23N 13 32 E
Klässbol, *Sweden* 16 E6 59 33N 12 45 E
Klaten, *Indonesia* 85 D4 7 43 S 110 36 E
Klatovy, *Czech Rep.* 34 B6 49 23N 13 18 E
Klawer, *S. Africa* 116 E2 31 44 S 18 36 E
Klawock, *U.S.A.* 144 J14 55 33N 133 6W
Klazienaveen, *Neths.* 24 B6 52 44N 7 0 E
Klé, *Mali* 112 C3 12 10N 6 28W
Klecko, *Poland* 55 F4 52 38N 17 25 E
Kleczew, *Poland* 55 F5 52 22N 18 9 E
Kleena Kleene, *Canada* 142 C4 52 0N 124 59W
Klein-Karas, *Namibia* 116 D2 27 33 S 18 7 E
Klekovača, *Bos.-H.* 45 D13 44 25N 16 32 E
Klenoec, *Macedonia* 50 E4 41 32N 20 49 E
Klenovec, *Slovak Rep.* 35 C12 48 36N 19 54 E
Klerksdorp, *S. Africa* 116 D4 26 53 S 26 38 E
Kleszczele, *Poland* 55 F10 52 35N 23 19 E
Kletnya, *Russia* 58 F7 53 23N 33 12 E
Kletsk = Klyetsk, *Belarus* 59 F4 53 5N 26 45 E
Kletskiy, *Russia* 61 F6 49 16N 43 11 E
Kleve, *Germany* 30 D2 51 47N 6 7 E
Klickitat, *U.S.A.* 158 D3 45 49N 121 9W
Klickitat →, *U.S.A.* 158 E5 45 42N 121 17W
Klidhes, *Cyprus* 39 E10 35 42N 34 36 E
Klimovichi, *Belarus* 58 F6 53 36N 32 0 E
Klin, *Russia* 58 D9 56 20N 36 48 E
Klina, *Kosovo, Yug.* 50 D4 42 37N 20 35 E
Klinaklini →, *Canada* 142 C3 51 21N 125 40W
Klintehamn, *Sweden* 17 G12 57 24N 18 12 E
Klintsy, *Russia* 59 F7 52 50N 32 10 E
Klip →, *S. Africa* 117 D4 27 3 S 29 3 E
Klipdale, *S. Africa* 116 E2 34 19 S 19 57 E
Klippan, *Sweden* 17 H7 56 8N 13 10 E
Klipplaat, *S. Africa* 116 E3 33 1 S 24 22 E
Klisura, *Bulgaria* 51 D8 42 40N 24 28 E
Kljajićevo, *Serbia, Yug.* 52 E4 45 45N 19 17 E
Ključ, *Bos.-H.* 45 D13 44 32N 16 48 E
Kłobuck, *Poland* 55 H5 50 55N 18 55 E
Klockestrand, *Sweden* 16 B11 62 53N 17 55 E
Kłodawa, *Poland* 55 F5 52 15N 18 55 E
Kłodzko, *Poland* 55 H3 50 28N 16 38 E
Kløfta, *Norway* 18 D8 60 4N 11 10 E
Klos, *Albania* 50 E4 41 28N 20 10 E
Klosterneuburg, *Austria* 35 C9 48 18N 16 19 E
Klosters, *Switz.* 33 C9 46 52N 9 52 E
Kloten, *Switz.* 33 B7 47 27N 8 35 E
Klötze, *Germany* 30 C7 52 37N 11 10 E
Klouto, *Togo* 113 D5 6 57N 0 44 E
Kluane L., *Canada* 138 B6 61 15N 138 40W
Kluane Nat. Park, *Canada* 142 A1 60 45N 139 30W
Kluczbork, *Poland* 55 H5 50 58N 18 12 E
Klukwan, *U.S.A.* 142 B1 59 24N 135 54W
Klungkung, *Indonesia* 79 K18 8 32 S 115 24 E
Klyetsk, *Belarus* 59 F4 53 5N 26 45 E
Klyuchevskaya, Gora, *Russia* 67 D17 55 50N 160 30 E
Knaben, *Norway* 18 F4 58 40N 7 4 E
Knappavellir, *Iceland* 11 D10 63 54N 16 36W
Knäred, *Sweden* 17 H7 56 31N 13 19 E
Knaresborough, *U.K.* 20 C6 54 1N 1 28W
Knarvik, *Norway* 18 D2 60 32N 5 19 E
Knee L., *Man., Canada* 140 A1 55 3N 94 45W
Knee L., *Sask., Canada* 143 B7 55 51N 107 0W
Kneïss, Is., *Tunisia* 108 B2 34 22N 10 18 E
Knezha, *Bulgaria* 51 C8 43 30N 24 5 E
Knić, *Serbia, Yug.* 50 C4 43 53N 20 42 E
Knight I., *U.S.A.* 144 F11 60 21N 147 45W
Knight Inlet, *Canada* 142 C3 50 45N 125 40W
Knighton, *U.K.* 21 E4 52 21N 3 3W
Knights Ferry, *U.S.A.* 160 H6 37 50N 120 40W
Knights Landing, *U.S.A.* 160 G5 38 48N 121 43W
Knightstown, *U.S.A.* 157 E11 39 48N 85 32W
Knin, *Croatia* 45 D13 44 3N 16 17 E
Knislinge, *Sweden* 17 H8 56 12N 14 5 E
Knittelfeld, *Austria* 34 D7 47 13N 14 51 E
Knivsta, *Sweden* 16 E11 59 43N 17 48 E
Knjaževac, *Serbia, Yug.* 50 C6 43 35N 22 18 E
Knob, C., *Australia* 125 F2 34 32 S 119 16 E
Knob Noster, *U.S.A.* 156 F3 38 46N 93 33W
Knock, *Ireland* 23 C3 53 48N 8 55W
Knockmealdown Mts., *Ireland* 23 D4 52 14N 7 56W
Knokke-Heist, *Belgium* 24 C3 51 21N 3 17 E
Knossós, *Greece* 39 E6 35 16N 25 10 E
Knowlton, *Canada* 151 A12 45 13N 72 31W
Knox, *U.S.A.* 157 C10 41 18N 86 37W
Knox Coast, *Antarctica* 7 C8 66 30 S 108 0 E
Knoxville, *Ga., U.S.A.* 152 C6 32 47N 83 59W
Knoxville, *Ill., U.S.A.* 156 D6 40 55N 90 17W
Knoxville, *Iowa, U.S.A.* 156 C4 41 19N 93 6W
Knoxville, *Pa., U.S.A.* 150 E7 41 57N 77 27W
Knoxville, *Tenn., U.S.A.* 149 H4 35 58N 83 55W
Knud Rasmussen Land, *Greenland* 10 B4 79 0N 60 0W
Knysna, *S. Africa* 116 E3 34 2 S 23 2 E
Knyszyn, *Poland* 54 E9 53 20N 22 56 E
Ko Kha, *Thailand* 86 C2 18 11N 99 24 E
Kō-Saki, *Japan* 72 C1 34 5N 129 13 E
Ko Yao, *Thailand* 87 a 8 7N 98 35 E
Koartac = Quaqtaq, *Canada* 139 B13 60 55N 69 40W
Koba, *Aru, Indonesia* 83 C4 6 37 S 134 37 E
Koba, *Bangka, Indonesia* 84 C3 2 26 S 106 14 E
Kobarid, *Slovenia* 45 B10 46 15N 13 30 E
Kobayashi, *Japan* 72 F2 31 56N 130 59 E
Kobdo = Hovd, *Mongolia* 68 B4 48 2N 91 37 E
Kobe, *Indonesia* 82 A3 0 26N 127 54 E
Kōbe, *Japan* 73 C7 34 45N 135 10 E
Kobelyaky, *Ukraine* 59 H8 49 11N 34 9 E
København, *Denmark* 17 J6 55 41N 12 34 E
Københavns Amtskommune □, *Denmark* 17 J6 55 42N 12 21 E
Kobenni, *Mauritania* 112 B3 15 58N 9 24W
Kōbi-Sho, *Japan* 71 M1 25 56N 123 41 E
Koblenz, *Germany* 31 E3 50 21N 7 36 E
Koblenz, *Switz.* 32 A6 47 37N 8 14 E
Kobo, *Dem. Rep. of the Congo* 115 C3 4 54 S 17 9 E
Kobo, *Ethiopia* 107 E4 12 2N 39 56 E
Kobroor, *Indonesia* 83 C4 6 10 S 134 30 E
Kobryn, *Belarus* 59 F3 52 15N 24 22 E
Kobuchizawa, *Japan* 73 B10 35 52N 138 19 E
Kobuk, *U.S.A.* 144 C8 66 55N 156 52W
Kobuk →, *U.S.A.* 144 C7 66 54N 160 38W
Kobuleti, *Georgia* 61 K5 41 55N 41 45 E
Kobylin, *Poland* 55 G4 51 43N 17 12 E
Kobyłka, *Poland* 55 F8 52 21N 21 10 E
Kobylkino, *Russia* 60 C6 54 8N 43 56 E
Koca →, *Turkey* 51 F11 40 8N 27 57 E
Kocabaş, *Turkey* 49 D11 37 49N 29 20 E
Kocaeli, *Turkey* 51 F13 40 45N 29 50 E
Kocaeli □, *Turkey* 51 F13 40 45N 29 55 E
Kočane, *Serbia, Yug.* 50 C5 43 12N 21 52 E
Kočani, *Macedonia* 50 E6 41 55N 22 25 E
Koçarlı, *Turkey* 49 D9 37 45N 27 43 E
Koceljevo, *Serbia, Yug.* 50 B3 44 28N 19 50 E
Kočevje, *Slovenia* 45 C11 45 39N 14 50 E
Koch Bihar, *India* 90 B2 26 22N 89 29 E
Kochang, *S. Korea* 75 G14 35 41N 127 55 E
Kochas, *India* 93 G10 25 15N 83 56 E
Kocher →, *Germany* 31 F5 49 13N 9 12 E
Kochi = Cochin, *India* 95 K3 9 58N 76 20 E
Kōchi, *Japan* 72 D5 33 30N 133 35 E
Kōchi □, *Japan* 72 D5 33 40N 133 30 E
Kochiu = Gejiu, *China* 76 F4 23 20N 103 10 E
Kochkor, *Kyrgyzstan* 65 B7 42 13N 75 46 E
Kochkor-Ata, *Kyrgyzstan* 65 C6 41 1N 72 29 E
Kock, *Poland* 55 G9 51 38N 22 27 E
Kodaira, *Japan* 73 B11 35 44N 139 29 E
Kodala, *India* 94 E7 19 38N 84 57 E
Kodarma, *India* 93 G11 24 28N 85 36 E
Koddiyar B., *Sri Lanka* 95 K5 8 33N 81 15 E
Kode, *Sweden* 17 G5 57 57N 11 51 E
Kodi, *Dem. Rep. of the Congo* 114 C4 3 34 S 22 12 E
Kodi, *Indonesia* 82 C1 9 33 S 119 0 E
Kodiak, *U.S.A.* 144 H9 57 47N 152 24W
Kodiak I., *U.S.A.* 144 H9 57 30N 152 45W
Kodinar, *India* 92 J4 20 46N 70 46 E
Kodlipet, *India* 95 H2 12 48N 75 53 E
Kodok, *Sudan* 107 F3 9 53N 32 7 E
Kodori →, *Georgia* 61 J5 42 47N 41 10 E
Kodoro, *Dem. Rep. of the Congo* 114 B4 1 16N 20 6 E
Koedoesberge, *S. Africa* 116 E3 32 40 S 20 11 E
Koes, *Namibia* 116 D2 26 0 S 19 15 E
Kofarnikhon, *Tajikistan* 65 D4 38 34N 69 1 E
Kofçaz, *Turkey* 51 E11 41 58N 27 12 E
Koffiefontein, *S. Africa* 116 D4 29 30 S 25 0 E
Kofiau, *Indonesia* 83 B3 1 11 S 129 50 E
Köflach, *Austria* 34 D8 47 4N 15 5 E
Koforidua, *Ghana* 113 D4 6 3N 0 17W
Kōfu, *Japan* 73 B10 35 40N 138 30 E
Koga, *Japan* 73 A11 36 11N 139 43 E
Kogaluk →, *Canada* 141 A7 56 12N 61 44W
Kögart, *Kyrgyzstan* 65 C7 40 15N 74 25 E
Køge, *Denmark* 17 J6 55 27N 12 11 E
Køge Bugt, *Denmark* 17 J6 55 30N 12 20 E
Kogi □, *Nigeria* 113 D6 7 45N 6 45 E
Kogin Baba, *Nigeria* 113 D7 7 55N 11 35 E
Koh, *Eq. Guin.* 114 B1 1 5N 9 42 E
Koh-i-Khurd, *Afghan.* 91 B2 33 30N 65 59 E
Koh-i-Maran, *Pakistan* 92 E2 29 18N 66 50 E
Kohala Mts., *U.S.A.* 145 C6 20 5N 155 45W
Kohat, *Pakistan* 91 B3 33 40N 71 29 E
Kohima, *India* 90 C5 25 35N 94 10 E
Kohkīlūyeh va Būyer Aḩmadi □, *Iran* 97 D6 31 30N 50 30 E
Kohler Ra., *Antarctica* 7 D15 77 0 S 110 0W
Kohlu, *Pakistan* 92 E3 29 54N 69 15 E
Kohtla-Järve, *Estonia* 15 G22 59 20N 27 20 E
Kohukohu, *N.Z.* 130 B2 35 22 S 173 38 E
Koihoa, *India* 95 K11 8 12N 93 29 E
Koilkuntla, *India* 95 G4 15 14N 78 19 E
Koillismaa, *Finland* 14 D23 65 44N 28 36 E
Koin-dong, *N. Korea* 75 D14 40 28N 126 18 E
Koinare, *Bulgaria* 51 C8 43 21N 24 8 E
Koindu, *S. Leone* 112 D2 8 26N 10 19W
Kojetín, *Czech Rep.* 35 B10 49 21N 17 20 E
Kojŏ, *N. Korea* 75 E14 38 58N 127 58 E
Kojonup, *Australia* 125 F2 33 48 S 117 10 E
Kojūr, *Iran* 97 B6 36 23N 51 43 E
Kök-Aygyr, *Kyrgyzstan* 65 C7 40 42N 75 32 E
Kök-Jangak, *Kyrgyzstan* 65 C6 41 2N 73 12 E
Koka, *Sudan* 106 C3 20 5N 30 35 E
Kokand = Qŭqon, *Uzbekistan* 66 E8 40 30N 70 57 E
Kokas, *Indonesia* 83 B4 2 42 S 132 26 E
Kokava, *Slovak Rep.* 35 C12 48 35N 19 50 E
Kokcha →, *Afghan.* 91 A3 37 9N 69 24 E
Kokchetav = Kökshetaū, *Kazakstan* 66 D7 53 20N 69 25 E
Kokemäenjoki →, *Finland* 15 F19 61 32N 21 44 E
Kokerite, *Guyana* 169 B6 7 12N 59 35W
Kokhma, *Russia* 60 B5 56 57N 41 8 E
Koki, *Senegal* 112 B1 15 30N 15 59W
Kokkilai, *Sri Lanka* 95 K5 9 0N 80 57 E
Kokkola, *Finland* 14 E20 63 50N 23 8 E
Koko, *Nigeria* 113 C5 11 28N 4 29 E
Koko Head, *U.S.A.* 145 K14 21 16N 157 43W
Kokoda, *Papua N. G.* 132 E4 8 54 S 147 47 E
Kokolopozo, *Ivory C.* 112 D3 5 8N 6 5W
Kokomo, *U.S.A.* 157 D10 40 29N 86 8W
Kokonau, *Indonesia* 83 B5 4 43 S 136 26 E
Kokopo, *Papua N. G.* 132 C7 4 22 S 152 19 E
Kokoro, *Niger* 113 C5 14 12N 0 55 E
Koksan, *N. Korea* 75 E14 38 46N 126 40 E

Köksaray, *Kazakstan* **65 B4** 42 38N 68 9 E
Kökshetaū, *Kazakstan* **66 D7** 53 20N 69 25 E
Koksoak →, *Canada* **139 C13** 58 30N 68 10W
Kokstad, *S. Africa* **117 E4** 30 32 S 29 29 E
Köksü, *Kazakstan* **65 C4** 41 28N 68 1 E
Köktal, *Kazakstan* **65 B5** 43 16N 70 18 E
Kokubu, *Japan* **72 F2** 31 44N 130 46 E
Kokyar, *China* **65 E8** 37 23N 77 10 E
Kola, *Indonesia* **83 C4** 5 35 S 134 30 E
Kola, *Russia* **56 A5** 68 45N 33 8 E
Kola Pen. = Kolskiy Poluostrov, *Russia* **56 A6** 67 30N 38 0 E
Kolachel, *India* **95 K3** 8 10N 77 15 E
Kolachi →, *Pakistan* **92 F2** 27 8N 67 2 E
Kolahoi, *India* **93 B6** 34 12N 75 22 E
Kolahun, *Liberia* **112 D2** 8 15N 10 4W
Kolaka, *Indonesia* **82 B2** 4 3 S 121 46 E
Kolar, *India* **95 H4** 13 12N 78 15 E
Kolar Gold Fields, *India* **95 H4** 12 58N 78 16 E
Kolaras, *India* **92 G6** 25 14N 77 36 E
Kolari, *Finland* **14 C20** 67 20N 23 48 E
Kolárovo, *Slovak Rep.* **35 D10** 47 54N 18 0 E
Kolašin, *Montenegro, Yug.* **50 D3** 42 50N 19 31 E
Kolbäck, *Sweden* **16 E10** 59 34N 16 15 E
Kolbäcksån →, *Sweden* **16 E10** 59 36N 16 16 E
Kolbeinsstaðir, *Iceland* **11 C4** 64 59N 22 16W
Kolbermoor, *Germany* **31 H8** 47 51N 12 4 E
Kolbu, *Norway* **18 D7** 60 39N 10 45 E
Kolbuszowa, *Poland* **55 H8** 50 15N 21 46 E
Kolchugino = Leninsk-Kuznetskiy, *Russia* **66 D9** 54 44N 86 10 E
Kolchugino, *Russia* **58 D10** 56 17N 39 22 E
Kolda, *Senegal* **112 C2** 12 55N 14 57W
Koldegi, *Sudan* **107 E3** 12 3N 30 16 E
Kolding, *Denmark* **17 J3** 55 30N 9 29 E
Kole, *Dem. Rep. of the Congo* **114 C4** 3 16 S 22 42 E
Koléa, *Algeria* **111 A5** 36 38N 2 46 E
Kolepom = Dolak, Pulau, *Indonesia* **83 C5** 8 0 S 138 30 E
Kolguyev, Ostrov, *Russia* **56 A8** 69 20N 48 30 E
Kolhapur, *India* **94 F2** 16 43N 74 15 E
Kolia, *Ivory C.* **112 D3** 9 46N 6 28W
Koliganek, *U.S.A.* **144 G8** 59 48N 157 25W
Kolín, *Czech Rep.* **34 A8** 50 2N 15 9 E
Kolind, *Denmark* **17 H4** 56 21N 10 34 E
Kolkas rags, *Latvia* **15 H20** 57 46N 22 37 E
Kolkata, *India* **93 H13** 22 36N 88 24 E
Kolkhozobod, *Tajikistan* **65 E4** 37 35N 68 40 E
Kollam = Quilon, *India* **95 K3** 8 50N 76 38 E
Kölleda, *Germany* **30 D7** 51 11N 11 15 E
Kollegal, *India* **95 H3** 12 9N 77 9 E
Kolleru L., *India* **94 F5** 16 40N 81 10 E
Kollum, *Neths.* **24 A6** 53 17N 6 10 E
Kolmanskop, *Namibia* **116 D2** 26 45 S 15 14 E
Köln, *Germany* **30 E2** 50 56N 6 57 E
Kolno, *Poland* **54 E8** 53 25N 21 56 E
Koło, *Poland* **55 F5** 52 14N 18 40 E
Koloa, *U.S.A.* **145 B2** 21 55N 159 28W
Kołobrzeg, *Poland* **54 D2** 54 10N 15 35 E
Kolokani, *Mali* **112 C3** 13 35N 7 45W
Koloko, *Burkina Faso* **112 C3** 11 5N 5 19W
Kololo, *Ethiopia* **107 F5** 7 29N 41 58 E
Kolombangara, *Solomon Is.* **133 M9** 8 0 S 157 5 E
Kolomna, *Russia* **58 E10** 55 8N 38 45 E
Kolomyya, *Ukraine* **59 H3** 48 31N 25 2 E
Kolondiéba, *Mali* **112 C3** 11 5N 6 54W
Kolonodale, *Indonesia* **82 B2** 2 0 S 121 19 E
Kolonowskie, *Poland* **55 H5** 50 39N 18 22 E
Kolosib, *India* **90 C4** 24 15N 92 45 E
Kolpashevo, *Russia* **66 D9** 58 20N 83 5 E
Kolpino, *Russia* **58 C6** 59 44N 30 39 E
Kolpny, *Russia* **59 F9** 52 17N 37 1 E
Kolskiy Poluostrov, *Russia* **56 A6** 67 30N 38 0 E
Kolskiy Zaliv, *Russia* **56 A5** 69 23N 34 0 E
Kolsva, *Sweden* **16 E9** 59 36N 15 51 E
Kolubara →, *Serbia, Yug.* **50 B4** 44 35N 20 15 E
Koluszki, *Poland* **55 G6** 51 45N 19 46 E
Kolwezi, *Dem. Rep. of the Congo* **119 E2** 10 40 S 25 25 E
Kolyma →, *Russia* **67 C17** 69 30N 161 0 E
Kolymskoye Nagorye, *Russia* **67 C16** 63 0N 157 0 E
Kôm Hamâda, *Egypt* **106 H7** 30 46N 30 41 E
Kôm Ombo, *Egypt* **106 C3** 24 25N 32 52 E
Komadugu Gana →, *Nigeria* **113 C7** 13 5N 12 24 E
Komagane, *Japan* **73 B9** 35 44N 137 58 E
Komaki, *Japan* **73 B8** 35 17N 136 55 E
Komandorskiye Is. = Komandorskiye Ostrova, *Russia* **67 D17** 55 0N 167 0 E
Komandorskiye Ostrova, *Russia* **67 D17** 55 0N 167 0 E
Komárno, *Slovak Rep.* **35 D11** 47 49N 18 5 E
Komárom, *Hungary* **52 C3** 47 43N 18 7 E
Komárom-Esztergom □, *Hungary* **52 C3** 47 35N 18 20 E
Komatipoort, *S. Africa* **117 D5** 25 25 S 31 55 E
Komatou Yialou, *Cyprus* **39 E10** 35 25N 34 8 E
Komatsu, *Japan* **73 A8** 36 25N 136 30 E
Komatsushima, *Japan* **72 D6** 34 0N 134 35 E
Komba, *Dem. Rep. of the Congo* **114 B4** 2 52N 24 3 E
Kombissiri, *Burkina Faso* **113 C4** 12 4N 1 20W
Kombo, *Gabon* **114 C2** 0 20 S 12 22 E
Kombong, *India* **90 A5** 28 7N 94 51 E
Kombori, *Burkina Faso* **112 C4** 13 26N 3 56W
Komboti, *Greece* **48 B3** 39 6N 21 5 E
Komen, *Slovenia* **45 C10** 45 49N 13 45 E
Komenda, *Ghana* **113 D4** 5 4N 1 28W
Komi □, *Russia* **56 B10** 64 0N 55 0 E
Komiža, *Croatia* **45 E13** 43 3N 16 11 E
Komló, *Hungary* **52 D3** 46 15N 18 16 E
Kommamur Canal, *India* **95 G5** 16 0N 80 25 E
Kommunarsk = Alchevsk, *Ukraine* **59 H10** 48 30N 38 45 E
Kommunizma, Pik, *Tajikistan* **66 F8** 39 0N 72 2 E
Komodo, *Indonesia* **82 C1** 8 37 S 119 20 E
Komoé →, *Ivory C.* **112 D4** 5 12N 3 44W
Komono, *Congo* **114 C2** 3 10 S 13 20 E
Komoran, Pulau, *Indonesia* **83 C5** 8 18 S 138 45 E
Komoro, *Japan* **73 A10** 36 19N 138 26 E
Komotini, *Greece* **51 E9** 41 9N 25 26 E
Komovi, *Montenegro, Yug.* **50 D3** 42 41N 19 39 E
Kompasberg, *S. Africa* **116 E3** 31 45 S 24 32 E
Kompong Bang, *Cambodia* **87 F5** 12 24N 104 40 E
Kompong Cham, *Cambodia* **87 F5** 12 0N 105 30 E
Kompong Chhnang = Kampang Chhnang, *Cambodia* **87 F5** 12 20N 104 35 E
Kompong Chikreng, *Cambodia* **86 F5** 13 5N 104 18 E
Kompong Kleang, *Cambodia* **86 F5** 13 6N 104 8 E
Kompong Luong, *Cambodia* **87 G5** 11 49N 104 48 E
Kompong Pranak, *Cambodia* **86 F5** 13 35N 104 55 E
Kompong Som = Kampong Saom, *Cambodia* **87 G4** 10 38N 103 30 E
Kompong Som, Chhung = Kampong Saom, Chaak, *Cambodia* **87 G4** 10 50N 103 32 E
Kompong Speu, *Cambodia* **87 G5** 11 26N 104 32 E
Kompong Sralao, *Cambodia* **86 E5** 14 5N 105 46 E
Kompong Thom, *Cambodia* **86 F5** 12 35N 104 51 E
Kompong Trabeck, *Cambodia* **86 F5** 13 6N 105 14 E
Kompong Trabeck, *Cambodia* **87 G5** 11 9N 105 28 E
Kompong Trach, *Cambodia* **87 G5** 11 25N 105 48 E
Kompong Tralach, *Cambodia* **87 G5** 11 54N 104 47 E
Komrat = Comrat, *Moldova* **53 D13** 46 18N 28 40 E
Komsberg, *S. Africa* **116 E3** 32 40 S 20 45 E
Komsomolabad, *Tajikistan* **65 D4** 38 50N 69 55 E
Komsomolets, *Kazakstan* **64 E9** 53 45N 62 2 E
Komsomolets, Ostrov, *Russia* **67 A10** 80 30N 95 0 E
Komsomolsk, *Amur, Russia* **67 D14** 50 30N 137 0 E
Komsomolsk, *Ivanovo, Russia* **58 D11** 57 2N 40 20 E
Komsomolsk, *Turkmenistan* **65 D1** 39 2N 63 36 E
Komsomolskiy, *Russia* **60 C7** 54 27N 45 33 E
Kömür Burnu, *Turkey* **49 C8** 38 39N 26 12 E
Kon Tum, *Vietnam* **86 E7** 14 24N 108 0 E
Kon Tum, Plateau du, *Vietnam* **86 E7** 14 30N 108 30 E
Kona, *Mali* **112 C4** 14 57N 3 53W
Konakovo, *Russia* **58 D9** 56 40N 36 51 E
Konarak, *India* **94 E8** 19 54N 86 7 E
Konarhā □, *Afghan.* **91 B3** 35 30N 71 3 E
Konārī, *Iran* **97 D6** 28 13N 51 36 E
Konch, *India* **93 G8** 26 0N 79 10 E
Konda, *Indonesia* **83 B4** 1 34 S 131 57 E
Kondagaon, *India* **94 E5** 19 35N 81 35 E
Konde, *Tanzania* **118 C4** 4 57 S 39 45 E
Kondiá, *Greece* **49 B7** 39 49N 25 10 E
Kondinin, *Australia* **125 F2** 32 34 S 118 8 E
Kondo, *Dem. Rep. of the Congo* **115 D2** 5 35 S 13 0 E
Kondoa, *Tanzania* **118 C4** 4 55 S 35 50 E
Kondókali, *Greece* **38 B9** 39 38N 19 51 E
Kondopaga, *Russia* **58 A8** 62 12N 34 17 E
Kondratyevo, *Russia* **67 D10** 57 22N 98 15 E
Kondrovo, *Russia* **58 E8** 54 48N 35 56 E
Konduga, *Nigeria* **113 C7** 11 35N 13 26 E
Kondukur, *India* **95 G4** 15 12N 79 57 E
Koné, *Cameroon* **114 A2** 8 50N 13 17 E
Koné, *N. Cal.* **133 U18** 21 4 S 164 52 E
Köneürgench, *Turkmenistan* **66 E6** 42 19N 59 10 E
Konevo, *Russia* **58 A10** 62 8N 39 20 E
Kong = Khong →, *Cambodia* **86 F5** 13 32N 105 58 E
Kong, *Ivory C.* **112 D4** 8 54N 4 36W
Kong, Koh, *Cambodia* **87 G4** 11 20N 103 0 E
Kong Christian IX Land, *Greenland* **10 D7** 68 0N 36 0W
Kong Christian X Land, *Greenland* **10 C8** 74 0N 29 0W
Kong Frederik IX Land, *Greenland* **10 D5** 67 0N 52 0W
Kong Frederik VI Kyst, *Greenland* **10 E6** 63 0N 43 0W
Kong Frederik VIII Land, *Greenland* **10 B8** 78 30N 26 0W
Kong Oscar Fjord, *Greenland* **10 C8** 72 20N 24 0W
Kongbo, *C.A.R.* **114 B4** 4 44N 21 23 E
Kongeå →, *Denmark* **17 J2** 55 23N 8 39 E
Kongerslev, *Denmark* **17 H4** 56 54N 10 6 E
Kongju, *S. Korea* **75 F14** 36 30N 127 0 E
Kongkemul, *Indonesia* **85 B4** 1 52N 112 11 E
Konglu, *Burma* **90 B6** 27 13N 97 57 E
Kongola, *Namibia* **116 B3** 17 45 S 23 20 E
Kongolo, *Kasai-Or., Dem. Rep. of the Congo* **118 D1** 5 26 S 24 49 E
Kongolo, *Katanga, Dem. Rep. of the Congo* **118 D2** 5 22 S 27 0 E
Kongor, *Sudan* **107 F3** 7 1N 31 27 E
Kongoulou, *Cameroon* **114 B2** 2 59N 11 7 E
Kongoussi, *Burkina Faso* **113 C4** 13 19N 1 32W
Kongsberg, *Norway* **15 G13** 59 39N 9 39 E
Kongsvinger, *Norway* **15 F15** 60 12N 12 2 E
Kongwa, *Tanzania* **118 D4** 6 11 S 36 26 E
Koni, *Dem. Rep. of the Congo* **119 E2** 10 40 S 27 11 E
Koni, Mts., *Dem. Rep. of the Congo* **119 E2** 10 36 S 27 10 E
Koniakari, *Mali* **112 C2** 14 35N 10 50W
Koniecpol, *Poland* **55 H6** 50 46N 19 40 E
Königs Wusterhausen, *Germany* **30 C9** 52 19N 13 38 E
Königsberg = Kaliningrad, *Russia* **15 J19** 54 42N 20 32 E
Königsbrunn, *Germany* **31 G6** 48 16N 10 54 E
Königslutter, *Germany* **30 C6** 52 15N 10 49 E
Konin, *Poland* **55 F5** 52 12N 18 15 E
Konispol, *Albania* **38 B10** 39 42N 20 10 E
Kónitsa, *Greece* **48 A2** 40 5N 20 48 E
Köniz, *Switz.* **32 C4** 46 56N 7 25 E
Konjic, *Bos.-H.* **52 G2** 43 42N 17 58 E
Konkiep, *Namibia* **116 D2** 26 49 S 17 15 E
Konkō, *Japan* **72 C4** 34 33N 133 36 E
Konkouré →, *Guinea* **112 D2** 9 50N 13 42W
Könnern, *Germany* **30 D7** 51 41N 11 47 E
Konnur, *India* **95 F2** 16 14N 74 49 E
Kono, *S. Leone* **112 D2** 8 30N 11 5W
Konogogo, *Papua N. G.* **132 B7** 3 29 S 152 10 E
Konolfingen, *Switz.* **32 C5** 46 54N 7 38 E
Konongo, *Ghana* **113 D4** 6 40N 1 15W
Konos, *Papua N. G.* **132 B6** 3 10 S 151 44 E
Konosha, *Russia* **58 B11** 61 0N 40 5 E
Kōnosu, *Japan* **73 A11** 36 3N 139 31 E
Konotop, *Ukraine* **59 G7** 51 12N 33 7 E
Konsankoro, *Guinea* **112 D3** 9 2N 9 0W
Końskie, *Poland* **55 G7** 51 15N 20 23 E
Konsmo, *Norway* **18 F4** 58 16N 7 23 E
Konstancin-Jeziorna, *Poland* **55 F8** 52 5N 21 7 E
Konstantinovka = Kostyantynivka, *Ukraine* **59 H9** 48 32N 37 39 E
Konstantinovsk, *Russia* **61 G5** 47 33N 41 10 E
Konstantynów Łódźki, *Poland* **55 G6** 51 45N 19 20 E
Konstanz, *Germany* **31 H5** 47 40N 9 10 E
Kont, *Iran* **97 E9** 26 55N 61 50 E
Konta, *India* **94 F5** 17 48N 81 23 E
Kontagora, *Nigeria* **113 C6** 10 23N 5 27 E
Kontcha, *Cameroon* **113 D7** 7 59N 12 15 E
Konya, *Turkey* **100 D5** 37 52N 32 35 E
Konya Ovası, *Turkey* **100 C5** 38 30N 33 5 E
Konyin, *Burma* **90 D5** 22 58N 94 42 E
Konz, *Germany* **31 F2** 49 42N 6 34 E
Konza, *Kenya* **118 C4** 1 45 S 37 7 E
Konzhakovskiy Kamen, Gora, *Russia* **64 B7** 59 38N 59 8 E
Koo-wee-rup, *Australia* **129 E6** 38 13 S 145 28 E
Koocanusa, L., *Canada* **158 B6** 49 20N 115 15W
Kookynie, *Australia* **125 E3** 29 17 S 121 22 E
Koolau Range, *U.S.A.* **145 J14** 21 35N 157 50W
Koolyanobbing, *Australia* **125 F2** 30 48 S 119 36 E
Koondrook, *Australia* **128 C6** 35 33 S 144 8 E
Koonibba, *Australia* **127 E1** 31 54 S 133 25 E
Koorawatha, *Australia* **129 C8** 34 2 S 148 33 E
Koorda, *Australia* **125 F2** 30 48 S 117 35 E
Kooskia, *U.S.A.* **158 C6** 46 9N 115 59W
Kootenay →, *U.S.A.* **142 D5** 49 19N 117 39W
Kootenay L., *Canada* **142 D5** 49 45N 116 50W
Kootenay Nat. Park, *Canada* **142 C5** 51 0N 116 0W
Kootingal, *Australia* **129 A9** 31 3 S 151 4 E
Kootjieskolk, *S. Africa* **116 E3** 31 15 S 20 21 E
Kopa = Qopa, *Kazakstan* **65 B7** 43 31N 75 50 E
Kopanovka, *Russia* **61 G8** 47 28N 46 50 E
Kopaonik, *Yugoslavia* **50 C4** 43 10N 20 50 E
Kopargaon, *India* **94 E2** 19 51N 74 28 E
Kópasker, *Iceland* **11 A10** 66 18N 16 27W
Kópavogur, *Iceland* **11 C5** 64 6N 21 55W
Koper, *Slovenia* **45 C10** 45 31N 13 44 E
Kopervik, *Norway* **15 G11** 59 17N 5 17 E
Kopet Dagh, *Asia* **97 B8** 38 0N 58 0 E
Kopeysk, *Russia* **64 D8** 55 7N 61 37 E
Kopi, *Australia* **127 E2** 33 24 S 135 40 E
Köping, *Sweden* **16 E10** 59 31N 16 3 E
Köpingsvik, *Sweden* **17 H10** 56 53N 16 43 E
Kopište, *Croatia* **45 F13** 42 48N 16 42 E
Koplik, *Albania* **50 D3** 42 15N 19 25 E
Köpmanholmen, *Sweden* **16 A12** 63 10N 18 35 E
Koppa, *India* **95 H2** 13 33N 75 21 E
Koppal, *India* **95 G3** 15 23N 76 5 E
Koppang, *Norway* **18 C8** 61 34N 11 3 E
Kopparberg, *Sweden* **16 E9** 59 52N 15 0 E
Koppeh Dāgh = Kopet Dagh, *Asia* **97 B8** 38 0N 58 0 E
Kopperå, *Norway* **18 A8** 63 24N 11 50 E
Koppies, *S. Africa* **117 D4** 27 20 S 27 30 E
Koppom, *Sweden* **16 E6** 59 43N 12 10 E
Koprivlen, *Bulgaria* **50 E7** 41 31N 23 53 E
Koprivnica, *Croatia* **45 B13** 46 12N 16 45 E
Kopřivnice, *Czech Rep.* **35 B11** 49 36N 18 9 E
Koprivshtitsa, *Bulgaria* **51 D8** 42 40N 24 19 E
Köprübaşı, *Turkey* **49 C10** 38 43N 28 23 E
Kopychyntsi, *Ukraine* **59 H3** 49 7N 25 58 E
Kora Nat. Park, *Kenya* **118 C4** 0 14 S 38 44 E
Korab, *Macedonia* **50 E4** 41 44N 20 40 E
Korakiána, *Greece* **38 B9** 39 42N 19 45 E
Koral, *India* **92 J5** 21 50N 73 12 E
Korangal, *India* **94 E3** 17 6N 77 38 E
Koraput, *India* **94 E6** 18 50N 82 40 E
Korarou, L., *Mali* **112 B4** 15 15N 3 15W
Korba, *India* **93 H10** 22 20N 82 45 E
Korbach, *Germany* **30 D4** 51 16N 8 52 E
Korbu, G., *Malaysia* **87 K3** 4 41N 101 18 E
Korce = Korçë, *Albania* **50 F4** 40 37N 20 50 E
Korçë, *Albania* **50 F4** 40 37N 20 50 E
Korčula, *Croatia* **45 F13** 42 56N 16 57 E
Korčulanski Kanal, *Croatia* **45 E13** 43 3N 16 40 E
Kord Küy, *Iran* **97 B7** 36 48N 54 7 E
Kord Sheykh, *Iran* **97 D7** 28 31N 52 53 E
Korday, *Kazakstan* **65 B7** 43 3N 74 43 E
Kordestān □, *Iran* **96 C5** 36 0N 47 0 E
Koré Mayroua, *Niger* **113 C5** 13 18N 3 55 E
Korea, North ■, *Asia* **75 E14** 40 0N 127 0 E
Korea, South ■, *Asia* **75 G15** 36 0N 128 0 E
Korea Bay, *Korea* **75 E13** 39 0N 124 0 E
Korea Strait, *Asia* **75 H15** 34 0N 129 30 E
Koregaon, *India* **94 F2** 17 40N 74 10 E
Korem, *Ethiopia* **107 E4** 12 30N 39 32 E
Korenevo, *Russia* **59 G8** 51 27N 34 55 E
Korenovsk, *Russia* **61 H4** 45 30N 39 22 E
Korets, *Ukraine* **59 G4** 50 40N 27 5 E
Korfantów, *Poland* **55 H4** 50 29N 17 36 E
Korgan, *Turkey* **100 B7** 40 44N 37 13 E
Korgus, *Sudan* **106 D3** 19 16N 33 29 E
Korhogo, *Ivory C.* **112 D3** 9 29N 5 28W
Koribundu, *S. Leone* **112 D2** 7 41N 11 46W
Korienzé, *Mali* **112 B4** 15 22N 3 50W
Korim, *Indonesia* **83 B5** 0 58 S 136 10 E
Korinthía □, *Greece* **48 D4** 37 50N 22 35 E
Korinthiakós Kólpos, *Greece* **48 C4** 38 16N 22 30 E
Kórinthos, *Greece* **48 D4** 37 56N 22 55 E
Korioumé, *Mali* **112 B4** 16 35N 3 0W
Koríssa, Límni, *Greece* **38 C9** 39 27N 19 53 E
Korithi, *Greece* **39 D2** 37 55N 20 42 E
Kōriyama, *Japan* **70 F10** 37 24N 140 23 E
Korkino, *Russia* **64 D8** 54 54N 61 23 E
Korkuteli, *Turkey* **49 D12** 37 4N 30 13 E
Korla, *China* **68 B3** 41 45N 86 4 E
Kormakiti, C., *Cyprus* **39 E8** 35 23N 32 56 E
Körmend, *Hungary* **52 C1** 47 5N 16 35 E
Kornat, *Croatia* **45 E12** 43 50N 15 20 E
Korneshty = Corneşti, *Moldova* **53 C13** 47 21N 28 1 E
Korneuburg, *Austria* **35 C9** 48 20N 16 20 E
Kórnik, *Poland* **55 F4** 52 15N 17 6 E
Kornsjø, *Norway* **18 F8** 58 57N 11 39 E
Koro, *Fiji* **133 A2** 17 19 S 179 23 E
Koro, *Ivory C.* **112 D3** 8 32N 7 30W
Koro, *Mali* **112 C4** 14 1N 2 58W
Koro Sea, *Fiji* **133 A3** 17 30 S 179 45W
Koro Toro, *Chad* **109 E3** 16 5N 18 30 E
Koroba, *Papua N. G.* **132 C2** 5 44 S 142 47 E
Korocha, *Russia* **59 G9** 50 54N 37 19 E
Köroğlu Dağları, *Turkey* **100 B5** 40 38N 33 0 E
Korogwe, *Tanzania* **118 D4** 5 5 S 38 25 E
Koroit, *Australia* **128 E5** 38 18 S 142 24 E
Korolevu, *Fiji* **133 B1** 18 12 S 177 46 E
Korona, *U.S.A.* **153 F8** 29 25N 81 12W
Koronadal, *Phil.* **81 H5** 6 12N 125 1 E
Korong Vale, *Australia* **128 D5** 36 22 S 143 45 E
Koróni, *Greece* **48 E3** 36 48N 21 57 E
Korónia, Límni, *Greece* **50 F7** 40 47N 23 10 E
Koronís, *Greece* **49 D7** 37 12N 25 35 E
Koronowo, *Poland* **55 E4** 53 19N 17 55 E
Koropelé, *C.A.R.* **114 B4** 4 44N 17 11 E
Koror, *Palau* **134 G5** 7 20N 134 28 E
Körös →, *Hungary* **52 D5** 46 43N 20 12 E
Köröstarcsa, *Hungary* **52 D6** 46 53N 21 3 E
Korosten, *Ukraine* **59 G5** 50 54N 28 36 E
Korostyshev, *Ukraine* **59 G5** 50 19N 29 4 E
Korotoyak, *Russia* **59 G10** 51 1N 39 2 E
Korovou, *Fiji* **133 A2** 17 47 S 178 32 E
Koroyanitu Nat. Heritage Park, *Fiji* **133 A1** 17 40 S 177 35 E
Korraraika, Helodranon' i, *Madag.* **117 B7** 17 45 S 43 57 E
Korsakov, *Russia* **67 E15** 46 36N 142 42 E
Korsberga, *Sweden* **17 G9** 57 19N 15 7 E
Korshunovo, *Russia* **67 D12** 58 37N 110 10 E
Korsør, *Denmark* **17 J5** 55 20N 11 9 E
Korsun Shevchenkovskiy, *Ukraine* **59 H6** 49 26N 31 16 E
Korsze, *Poland* **54 D8** 54 11N 21 9 E
Korti, *Sudan* **106 D3** 18 6N 31 33 E
Kortrijk, *Belgium* **24 D3** 50 50N 3 17 E
Korucu, *Turkey* **49 B9** 39 28N 27 22 E
Korumburra, *Australia* **129 E6** 38 26 S 145 50 E
Korup, Parc Nat. du, *Cameroon* **114 A1** 5 15N 9 2 E
Korwai, *India* **92 G8** 24 7N 78 5 E
Koryakskoye Nagorye, *Russia* **67 C18** 61 0N 171 0 E
Koryŏng, *S. Korea* **75 G15** 35 44N 128 15 E
Koryukovka, *Ukraine* **59 G7** 51 46N 32 16 E
Kos, *Greece* **49 E9** 36 50N 27 15 E
Kosa, *Ethiopia* **107 F4** 7 50N 36 50 E
Kosa, *Russia* **64 B5** 59 56N 55 0 E
Kosa →, *Russia* **64 A5** 60 11N 55 10 E
Kosai, *Japan* **73 C9** 34 42N 137 32 E
Kosaya Gora, *Russia* **58 E9** 54 10N 37 30 E
Koschagyl, *Kazakstan* **57 E9** 46 40N 54 0 E
Kościan, *Poland* **55 F3** 52 5N 16 40 E
Kościerzyna, *Poland* **54 D4** 54 8N 17 59 E
Kosciusko, *U.S.A.* **155 J10** 33 4N 89 35W
Kosciusko Nat. Park, *Australia* **129 D8** 36 30 S 148 20 E
Kosciuszko, Mt., *Australia* **129 D8** 36 27 S 148 16 E
Kosély →, *Hungary* **52 C6** 47 25N 21 5 E
Kosgi, *Andhra Pradesh, India* **94 F3** 16 58N 77 43 E
Kosgi, *Andhra Pradesh, India* **95 G3** 15 51N 77 16 E
Kosh-Döbö, *Kyrgyzstan* **65 C7** 41 5N 74 15 E
Kosha, *Sudan* **106 C3** 20 50N 30 30 E
Koshava, *Bulgaria* **50 B7** 44 4N 23 2 E
Koshigaya, *Japan* **73 B11** 35 54N 139 48 E
K'oshih = Kashi, *China* **65 D8** 39 30N 76 2 E
Koshiki-Rettō, *Japan* **72 F1** 31 45N 129 49 E
Koshkonong L., *U.S.A.* **157 B8** 42 52N 88 58W
Kōshoku, *Japan* **73 A10** 36 38N 138 6 E
Koshrabad, *Uzbekistan* **65 C3** 40 18N 66 32 E
Kosi, *India* **92 F7** 27 48N 77 29 E
Kosi →, *India* **93 E8** 28 41N 78 57 E
Košice, *Slovak Rep.* **35 C14** 48 42N 21 15 E
Košický □, *Slovak Rep.* **35 C14** 48 45N 21 0 E
Kosjerić, *Serbia, Yug.* **50 B3** 44 0N 19 55 E
Köşk, *Turkey* **49 D10** 37 50N 28 3 E
Koskinoú, *Greece* **38 E12** 36 23N 28 13 E
Koslan, *Russia* **56 B8** 63 34N 49 14 E
Kosŏng, *N. Korea* **75 E15** 38 40N 128 22 E
Kosovo □, *Yugoslavia* **50 D4** 42 30N 21 0 E
Kosovo Polje, *Kosovo, Yug.* **50 D5** 42 40N 21 5 E
Kosovska Kamenica, *Kosovo, Yug.* **50 D5** 42 35N 21 35 E
Kosovska Mitrovica, *Kosovo, Yug.* **50 D4** 42 54N 20 52 E
Kosrap, *China* **65 E8** 38 0N 76 12 E
Kossou, L. de, *Ivory C.* **112 D3** 6 59N 5 31W
Kosta, *Sweden* **17 H9** 56 50N 15 24 E
Kostajnica, *Croatia* **45 C13** 45 17N 16 30 E
Kostanjevica, *Slovenia* **45 C12** 45 51N 15 27 E
Kostenets, *Bulgaria* **50 D7** 42 15N 23 52 E
Koster, *S. Africa* **116 D4** 25 52 S 26 54 E
Kôstî, *Sudan* **107 E3** 13 8N 32 43 E
Kostinbrod, *Bulgaria* **50 D7** 42 49N 23 13 E
Kostolac, *Serbia, Yug.* **50 B5** 44 37N 21 15 E
Kostopil, *Ukraine* **59 G4** 50 51N 26 22 E
Kostroma, *Russia* **58 D11** 57 50N 40 58 E
Kostromskoye Vdkhr., *Russia* **58 D11** 57 52N 40 49 E
Kostrzyn, *Lubuskie, Poland* **55 F1** 52 35N 14 39 E
Kostrzyn, *Wielkopolskie, Poland* **55 F4** 52 24N 17 14 E
Kostyantynivka, *Ukraine* **59 H9** 48 32N 37 39 E
Kostyukovichi = Kastsyukovichy, *Belarus* **58 F7** 53 20N 32 4 E
Koszalin, *Poland* **54 D3** 54 11N 16 8 E
Kőszeg, *Hungary* **52 C1** 47 23N 16 33 E
Kot Addu, *Pakistan* **91 C3** 30 30N 71 0 E
Kot Kapura, *India* **92 D6** 30 35N 74 50 E
Kot Moman, *Pakistan* **92 C5** 32 13N 73 0 E
Kot Sultan, *Pakistan* **92 D4** 30 46N 70 56 E
Kota, *India* **92 G6** 25 14N 75 49 E
Kota Baharu, *Malaysia* **87 J4** 6 7N 102 14 E
Kota Barrage, *India* **92 G6** 25 6N 75 51 E
Kota Belud, *Malaysia* **85 A5** 6 21N 116 26 E
Kota Kinabalu, *Malaysia* **85 A5** 6 0N 116 4 E
Kota Kubu Baharu, *Malaysia* **87 L3** 3 34N 101 39 E
Kota Tinggi, *Malaysia* **87 M4** 1 44N 103 53 E
Kotaagung, *Indonesia* **84 D2** 5 38 S 104 29 E
Kotabaru, *Indonesia* **85 C5** 3 20 S 116 20 E
Kotabumi, *Indonesia* **84 C2** 4 49 S 104 54 E
Kotagede, *Indonesia* **85 D4** 7 54 S 110 26 E
Kotamobagu, *Indonesia* **82 A2** 0 57N 124 31 E
Kotapad, *India* **94 E6** 19 9N 82 21 E
Kotawaringin, *Indonesia* **85 C4** 2 28 S 111 27 E
Kotchandpur, *Bangla.* **90 D2** 23 24N 89 1 E
Kotcho L., *Canada* **142 B4** 59 7N 121 12W
Kotdwara, *India* **93 E8** 29 45N 78 32 E
Kotel, *Bulgaria* **51 D10** 42 52N 26 26 E
Kotelnich, *Russia* **60 A9** 58 22N 48 24 E
Kotelnikovo, *Russia* **61 G6** 47 38N 43 8 E
Kotelnyy, Ostrov, *Russia* **67 B14** 75 10N 139 0 E
Kothagudam, *India* **94 F5** 17 30N 80 40 E
Kothapet, *India* **94 E4** 19 21N 79 28 E
Kothari →, *India* **92 G6** 25 20N 75 4 E
Köthen, *Germany* **30 D7** 51 45N 11 59 E
Kothi, *Chhattisgarh, India* **93 H10** 23 21N 82 3 E
Kothi, *Mad. P., India* **93 G9** 24 45N 80 40 E
Kotiro, *Pakistan* **92 F2** 26 17N 67 13 E
Kotka, *Finland* **15 F22** 60 28N 26 58 E
Kotlas, *Russia* **56 B8** 61 17N 46 43 E
Kotlenska Planina, *Bulgaria* **51 D10** 42 56N 26 30 E
Kotli, *Pakistan* **92 C5** 33 30N 73 55 E
Kotlik, *U.S.A.* **144 E7** 63 2N 163 33W
Kotma, *India* **93 H9** 23 12N 81 58 E
Kotmul, *Pakistan* **93 B6** 35 32N 75 10 E
Kotohira, *Japan* **72 C5** 34 11N 133 49 E
Koton-Karifi, *Nigeria* **113 D6** 8 0N 6 48 E
Kotonkoro, *Nigeria* **113 C6** 11 3N 5 58 E
Kotor, *Montenegro, Yug.* **50 D2** 42 25N 18 47 E
Kotor Varoš, *Bos.-H.* **52 F2** 44 38N 17 22 E
Kotoriba, *Croatia* **45 B13** 46 23N 16 48 E
Kotovo, *Russia* **60 E7** 50 22N 44 45 E
Kotovsk, *Russia* **60 D5** 52 36N 41 32 E
Kotovsk, *Ukraine* **59 J5** 47 45N 29 35 E
Kotputli, *India* **92 F7** 27 43N 76 12 E
Kotri, *Pakistan* **91 D3** 25 22N 68 22 E
Kotri →, *India* **94 E5** 19 15N 80 35 E
Kótronas, *Greece* **48 E4** 36 38N 22 29 E
Kötschach-Mauthen, *Austria* **34 E6** 46 41N 13 1 E
Kottayam, *India* **95 K3** 9 35N 76 33 E
Kotto →, *C.A.R.* **114 B4** 4 14N 22 2 E
Kottur, *India* **95 J3** 10 34N 76 56 E
Kotu Group, *Tonga* **133 Q14** 20 0 S 173 25W
Kotuy →, *Russia* **67 B11** 71 54N 102 6 E
Kotzebue, *U.S.A.* **144 C7** 66 53N 162 39W
Kotzebue Sound, *U.S.A.* **144 C7** 66 20N 163 0W
Kouango, *C.A.R.* **114 B4** 5 0N 20 10 E
Koudougou, *Burkina Faso* **112 C4** 12 10N 2 20W
Koufonísi, *Greece* **39 F7** 34 56N 26 8 E
Koufonísia, *Greece* **49 E7** 36 57N 25 35 E
Kougaberge, *S. Africa* **116 E3** 33 48 S 23 50 E
Kouibli, *Ivory C.* **112 D3** 7 15N 7 14W
Kouilou →, *Congo* **115 C2** 4 10 S 12 5 E
Kouki, *C.A.R.* **114 A3** 7 22N 17 3 E
Koula Moutou, *Gabon* **114 C2** 1 15 S 12 25 E
Koulen = Kulen, *Cambodia* **86 F5** 13 50N 104 40 E
Koulikoro, *Mali* **112 C3** 12 40N 7 50W
Kouloúra, *Greece* **38 B9** 39 42N 19 54 E
Koúm-bournoú, Ákra, *Greece* **38 E12** 36 15N 28 11 E
Koumac, *N. Cal.* **133 T18** 20 33 S 164 17 E
Koumala, *Australia* **126 C4** 21 38 S 149 15 E
Koumameyong, *Gabon* **114 B2** 0 11N 11 51 E
Koumankou, *Mali* **112 C3** 11 58N 6 6W
Koumbia, *Burkina Faso* **112 C4** 11 10N 3 50W
Koumbia, *Guinea* **112 C2** 11 48N 13 29W
Koumboum, *Guinea* **112 C2** 10 25N 13 0W
Koumpenntoum, *Senegal* **112 C2** 13 59N 14 34W
Koumra, *Chad* **109 G3** 8 50N 17 35 E
Koun-Fao, *Ivory C.* **112 D4** 7 30N 3 15W
Koundara, *Guinea* **112 C2** 12 29N 13 18W
Koundé, *C.A.R.* **114 A2** 6 7N 14 38 E
Koundian, *Guinea* **112 C3** 13 10N 10 35W
Koungheul, *Senegal* **112 C2** 14 0N 14 50W
Koungoulou, *Congo* **114 C2** 3 31 S 13 20 E
Kounradskiy, *Kazakstan* **66 E8** 46 59N 75 0 E
Kountze, *U.S.A.* **155 K7** 30 22N 94 19W
Koupéla, *Burkina Faso* **113 C4** 12 11N 0 21W
Kourémalé, *Mali* **112 C3** 11 59N 8 42W
Kouris →, *Cyprus* **39 F8** 34 38N 32 54 E
Kourizo, P. de, *Chad* **108 D3** 22 28N 15 27 E
Kourou, *Fr. Guiana* **169 B7** 5 9N 52 39W
Kourouba, *Mali* **112 C2** 13 22N 10 57W
Kouroukoto, *Mali* **112 C2** 13 20N 10 5W
Kouroumа, *Burkina Faso* **112 C4** 11 35N 4 50W
Kourouninkoto, *Mali* **112 C3** 13 52N 9 35W
Kouroussa, *Guinea* **112 C3** 10 45N 9 45W
Koussanar, *Senegal* **112 C2** 13 52N 14 5W
Koussané, *Mali* **112 C2** 14 53N 11 14W
Koussane, *Senegal* **112 C2** 14 10N 12 22W
Kousseri, *Cameroon* **109 F2** 12 0N 14 55 E
Koutiala, *Mali* **112 C3** 12 25N 5 23W
Kouto, *Ivory C.* **112 D3** 9 53N 6 25W
Kouts, *U.S.A.* **157 C9** 41 19N 87 2W
Kouvé, *Togo* **113 D5** 6 25N 1 25 E
Kouvola, *Finland* **15 F22** 60 52N 26 43 E
Kouyi, *Congo* **114 C2** 2 29 S 12 25 E
Kouyou →, *Congo* **114 C3** 0 44 S 16 38 E
Kovačica, *Serbia, Yug.* **52 E5** 45 5N 20 38 E
Kovdor, *Russia* **56 A5** 67 34N 30 24 E
Kovel, *Ukraine* **59 G3** 51 11N 24 38 E
Kovilpatti, *India* **95 K3** 9 10N 77 50 E
Kovin, *Serbia, Yug.* **52 F5** 44 44N 20 59 E
Kovrov, *Russia* **60 B5** 56 25N 41 25 E
Kovur, *Andhra Pradesh, India* **94 F5** 17 3N 81 39 E

Küre, *Turkey* **100 B5** 41 48N 33 43 E
Küre Dağları, *Turkey* **100 B6** 41 50N 34 10 E
Kure I., *U.S.A.* **145 F8** 28 25N 178 25W
Kuressaare, *Estonia* **15 G20** 58 15N 22 30 E
Kurgan, *Russia* **66 D7** 55 26N 65 18 E
Kurgan-Tyube = Qŭrghonteppa, *Tajikistan* **65 E4** 37 50N 68 47 E
Kurganinsk, *Russia* **61 H5** 44 54N 40 34 E
Kurgannaya = Kurganinsk, *Russia* **61 H5** 44 54N 40 34 E
Kuri, *India* **92 F4** 26 37N 70 43 E
Kuria Maria Is. = Khurīyā Murīyā, Jazā'ir, *Oman* **99 C6** 17 30N 55 58 E
Kurichchi, *India* **95 J3** 11 36N 77 35 E
Kuridala, *Australia* **126 C3** 21 16 S 140 29 E
Kurigram, *Bangla.* **90 C2** 25 49N 89 39 E
Kurik, *Indonesia* **83 C5** 8 9 S 139 59 E
Kurikka, *Finland* **15 E20** 62 36N 22 24 E
Kuril Is. = Kurilskiye Ostrova, *Russia* **67 E15** 45 0N 150 0 E
Kuril Trench, *Pac. Oc.* **62 E19** 44 0N 153 0 E
Kurilsk, *Russia* **67 E15** 45 14N 147 53 E
Kurilskiye Ostrova, *Russia* **67 E15** 45 0N 150 0 E
Kurino, *Japan* **72 F2** 31 57N 130 43 E
Kurinskaya Kosa = Kür Dili, *Azerbaijan* **97 B6** 39 3N 49 13 E
Kurkheda, *India* **94 D5** 20 37N 80 12 E
Kurkur, *Egypt* **106 C3** 23 50N 32 0 E
Kurla, *India* **94 E1** 19 5N 72 52 E
Kurlovskiy, *Russia* **60 C5** 55 25N 40 40 E
Kurmuk, *Sudan* **107 E3** 10 33N 34 21 E
Kurnool, *India* **95 G4** 15 45N 78 0 E
Kuro-Shima, *Kagoshima, Japan* **71 J4** 30 50N 129 57 E
Kuro-Shima, *Okinawa, Japan* **71 M2** 24 14N 124 1 E
Kurobe-Gawe →, *Japan* **73 A9** 36 55N 137 25 E
Kurogi, *Japan* **72 D2** 33 12N 130 40 E
Kuror, J., *Sudan* **106 C3** 20 27N 31 30 E
Kurow, *N.Z.* **131 E5** 44 44 S 170 29 E
Kurów, *Poland* **55 G9** 51 23N 22 12 E
Kurrajong, *Australia* **129 B9** 33 33 S 150 42 E
Kurram →, *Pakistan* **91 B3** 32 36N 71 20 E
Kurri Kurri, *Australia* **129 B9** 32 50 S 151 28 E
Kurrimine, *Australia* **126 B4** 17 47 S 146 6 E
Kursavka, *Russia* **61 H6** 44 29N 42 32 E
Kurse Korhi, *India* **94 D5** 20 14N 80 46 E
Kurshskiy Zaliv, *Russia* **15 J19** 55 9N 21 6 E
Kursk, *Russia* **59 G9** 51 42N 36 11 E
Kuršumlija, *Serbia, Yug.* **50 C5** 43 9N 21 19 E
Kuršumlijska Banja, *Serbia, Yug.* **50 C5** 43 3N 21 11 E
Kurşunlu, *Bursa, Turkey* **51 F13** 40 3N 29 40 E
Kurşunlu, *Çankırı, Turkey* **100 B5** 40 51N 33 15 E
Kurtalan, *Turkey* **101 D9** 37 56N 41 44 E
Kurtbey, *Turkey* **51 E10** 41 9N 26 35 E
Kürti →, *Kazakstan* **65 A8** 44 16N 76 42 E
Kurtistown, *U.S.A.* **145 D6** 19 36N 155 4W
Kuru, *Sudan* **107 F2** 7 43N 26 31 E
Kuru, Bahr el →, *Sudan* **107 F2** 8 10N 26 50 E
Kurucaşile, *Turkey* **100 B5** 41 49N 32 42 E
Kuruçay, *Turkey* **96 B3** 39 39N 38 29 E
Kuruktag, *China* **68 B3** 41 0N 89 0 E
Kuruman, *S. Africa* **116 D3** 27 28 S 23 28 E
Kuruman →, *S. Africa* **116 D3** 26 56 S 20 39 E
Kurume, *Japan* **72 D2** 33 15N 130 30 E
Kurun →, *Sudan* **107 F3** 5 30N 34 17 E
Kurunegala, *Sri Lanka* **95 L5** 7 30N 80 23 E
Kurupukari, *Guyana* **169 C6** 4 43N 58 37W
Kurya, *Russia* **56 B10** 61 42N 57 9 E
Kus Gölü, *Turkey* **51 F11** 40 10N 27 55 E
Kusa, *Russia* **64 D7** 55 20N 59 29 E
Kuşadası, *Turkey* **100 D2** 37 52N 27 15 E
Kuşadası Körfezı, *Turkey* **49 D8** 37 56N 27 0 E
Kusamba, *Indonesia* **79 K18** 8 34 S 115 27 E
Kusatsu, *Gumma, Japan* **73 A10** 36 37N 138 36 E
Kusatsu, *Shiga, Japan* **73 C7** 34 58N 135 57 E
Kusawa L., *Canada* **142 A1** 60 20N 136 13W
Kusel, *Germany* **31 F3** 49 32N 7 24 E
Kushạka, *Nigeria* **113 C6** 10 32N 6 48 E
Kushalgarh, *India* **92 H6** 23 10N 74 27 E
Kushalnagar, *India* **95 H2** 12 14N 75 57 E
Kushchevskaya, *Russia* **61 G4** 46 33N 39 35 E
Kusheriki, *Nigeria* **113 C6** 10 33N 6 28 E
Kushikino, *Japan* **72 F2** 31 44N 130 16 E
Kushima, *Japan* **72 F3** 31 29N 131 14 E
Kushimoto, *Japan* **73 D7** 33 28N 135 47 E
Kushiro, *Japan* **70 C12** 43 0N 144 25 E
Kushiro-Gawa →, *Japan* **70 C12** 42 59N 144 23 E
Kūshk, *Iran* **97 D8** 28 46N 56 51 E
Kushka = Gushgy, *Turkmenistan* **66 F7** 35 20N 62 18 E
Kūshkī, *Iran* **96 C5** 33 31N 47 13 E
Kushnarenkovo, *Russia* **64 D5** 55 6N 55 22 E
Kushol, *India* **93 C7** 33 40N 76 36 E
Kushrabat = Koshrabad, *Uzbekistan* **65 C3** 40 18N 66 32 E
Kushtia, *Bangla.* **90 D2** 23 55N 89 5 E
Kushum →, *Kazakstan* **60 F10** 49 20N 50 30 E
Kushva, *Russia* **64 B7** 58 18N 59 45 E
Kuskokwim →, *U.S.A.* **144 F7** 60 5N 162 25W
Kuskokwim B., *U.S.A.* **144 G7** 59 45N 162 25W
Kuskokwim Mts., *U.S.A.* **144 E9** 62 30N 156 0W
Kusmi, *India* **93 H10** 23 17N 83 55 E
Küsnacht, *Switz.* **33 B7** 47 19N 8 35 E
Kussharo-Ko, *Japan* **70 C12** 43 38N 144 21 E
Küssnacht, *Switz.* **33 B6** 47 5N 8 26 E
Kustanay = Qostanay, *Kazakstan* **66 D7** 53 10N 63 35 E
Kusu, *Indonesia* **82 A3** 0 53N 127 43 E
Kusu, *Japan* **72 D3** 33 16N 131 9 E
Kut, Ko, *Thailand* **87 G4** 11 40N 102 35 E
Kuta, *Indonesia* **79 K18** 8 43 S 115 11 E
Kutacane, *Indonesia* **84 B1** 3 50N 97 50 E
Kütahya, *Turkey* **49 B12** 39 30N 30 2 E
Kütahya □, *Turkey* **49 B11** 39 10N 29 30 E
Kutaisi, *Georgia* **61 J6** 42 19N 42 40 E
Kutaraja = Banda Aceh, *Indonesia* **84 A1** 5 35N 95 20 E
Kutch, Gulf of = Kachchh, Gulf of, *India* **92 H3** 22 50N 69 15 E
Kutch, Rann of = Kachchh, Rann of, *India* **92 H4** 24 0N 70 0 E
Kutina, *Croatia* **45 C13** 45 29N 16 48 E
Kutiyana, *India* **92 J4** 21 36N 70 2 E
Kutjevo, *Croatia* **52 E2** 45 23N 17 55 E
Kutkai, *Burma* **90 D6** 23 27N 97 56 E
Kutkashen, *Azerbaijan* **61 K8** 40 58N 47 47 E
Kutná Hora, *Czech Rep.* **34 B8** 49 57N 15 16 E
Kutno, *Poland* **55 F6** 52 15N 19 23 E
Kutru, *India* **94 E5** 19 5N 80 46 E
Kutse, *Botswana* **116 C3** 21 7 S 22 16 E
Kuttabul, *Australia* **126 K6** 21 1 S 148 54 E
Kutu, *Dem. Rep. of the Congo* **114 C3** 2 40 S 18 11 E
Kutu Moke, *Dem. Rep. of the Congo* **114 C3** 3 12 S 17 21 E
Kutum, *Sudan* **107 E1** 14 10N 24 40 E
Kúty, *Slovak Rep.* **35 C10** 48 40N 17 3 E
Kuujjuaq, *Canada* **139 C13** 58 6N 68 15W
Kuujjuarapik, *Canada* **140 A4** 55 20N 77 35W
Kuŭp-tong, *N. Korea* **75 D14** 40 45N 126 1 E
Kuusamo, *Finland* **14 D23** 65 57N 29 8 E
Kuusankoski, *Finland* **15 F22** 60 55N 26 38 E
Kuvandyk, *Russia* **64 F6** 51 28N 57 21 E
Kuvango, *Angola* **115 E3** 14 28 S 16 20 E
Kuvasay, *Uzbekistan* **65 C5** 40 18N 71 59 E
Kuvshinovo, *Russia* **58 D8** 57 2N 34 11 E
Kuwait = Al Kuwayt, *Kuwait* **96 D5** 29 30N 48 0 E
Kuwait ■, *Asia* **96 D5** 29 30N 47 30 E
Kuwana, *Japan* **73 B8** 35 5N 136 43 E
Kuwana →, *India* **93 F10** 26 25N 83 15 E
Kuybyshev = Samara, *Russia* **60 D10** 53 8N 50 6 E
Kuybyshev, *Russia* **66 D8** 55 27N 78 19 E
Kuybyshevo, *Ukraine* **59 J9** 47 25N 36 40 E
Kuybyshevskiy, *Tajikistan* **65 E4** 37 52N 68 44 E
Kuybyshevskoye Vdkhr., *Russia* **60 C9** 55 2N 49 30 E
Kuye He →, *China* **74 E6** 38 23N 110 46 E
Kūyeh, *Iran* **96 B5** 38 45N 47 57 E
Kuylyuk, *Uzbekistan* **65 C4** 41 14N 69 17 E
Kūysanjaq, *Iraq* **101 D11** 36 5N 44 38 E
Kuyto, Ozero, *Russia* **56 B5** 65 6N 31 20 E
Kuyucak, *Turkey* **49 D10** 37 55N 28 28 E
Kuyumba, *Russia* **67 C10** 60 58N 96 59 E
Kuzey Anadolu Dağları, *Turkey* **100 B7** 41 30N 35 0 E
Kuzhitturai, *India* **95 K3** 8 18N 77 11 E
Kuzino, *Russia* **64 C7** 57 1N 59 27 E
Kuzitrin →, *U.S.A.* **144 D6** 65 10N 165 25W
Kuzmin, *Serbia, Yug.* **52 E4** 45 2N 19 25 E
Kuznetsk, *Russia* **60 D8** 53 12N 46 40 E
Kuzomen, *Russia* **56 A6** 66 22N 36 50 E
Kvænangen, *Norway* **14 A19** 70 5N 21 15 E
Kværndrup, *Denmark* **17 J4** 55 10N 10 31 E
Kvaløy, *Norway* **14 B18** 69 40N 18 30 E
Kvam, *Norway* **18 C6** 61 40N 9 42 E
Kvänum, *Sweden* **17 F7** 58 18N 13 11 E
Kvareli = Qvareli, *Georgia* **61 K7** 41 57N 45 47 E
Kvarner, *Croatia* **45 D11** 44 50N 14 10 E
Kvarnerič, *Croatia* **45 D11** 44 43N 14 37 E
Kvås, *Norway* **18 F4** 58 16N 7 14 E
Kvernaland, *Norway* **18 F2** 58 47N 5 45 E
Kvichak B., *U.S.A.* **144 G8** 58 48N 157 30W
Kvicksund, *Sweden* **16 E10** 59 27N 16 19 E
Kvikne, *Norway* **18 B7** 62 35N 10 16 E
Kvillsfors, *Sweden* **17 G9** 57 24N 15 29 E
Kvina →, *Norway* **18 F3** 58 19N 6 55 E
Kvinlog, *Norway* **18 F3** 58 31N 6 55 E
Kvismare kanal, *Sweden* **16 E9** 59 11N 15 35 E
Kvissleby, *Sweden* **16 B11** 62 18N 17 22 E
Kviteseid, *Norway* **18 E5** 59 24N 8 29 E
Kwabhaca, *S. Africa* **117 E4** 30 51 S 29 0 E
Kwakhanai, *Botswana* **116 C3** 21 39 S 21 16 E
Kwakoegron, *Surinam* **169 B6** 5 12N 55 25W
Kwale, *Kenya* **118 C4** 4 15 S 39 31 E
Kwale, *Nigeria* **113 D6** 5 46N 6 26 E
Kwamalasamutu, *Surinam* **169 C6** 2 20N 56 47W
KwaMashu, *S. Africa* **117 D5** 29 45 S 30 58 E
Kwamouth, *Dem. Rep. of the Congo* **114 C3** 3 9 S 16 12 E
Kwando →, *Africa* **116 B3** 18 27 S 23 32 E
Kwangdaeri, *N. Korea* **75 D14** 40 31N 127 32 E
Kwangju, *S. Korea* **75 G14** 35 9N 126 54 E
Kwango →, *Dem. Rep. of the Congo* **114 C3** 3 14 S 17 22 E
Kwangsi-Chuang = Guangxi Zhuangzu Zizhiqu □, *China* **76 F7** 24 0N 109 0 E
Kwangtung = Guangdong □, *China* **77 F9** 23 0N 113 0 E
Kwara □, *Nigeria* **113 D6** 8 45N 4 30 E
Kwataboahegan →, *Canada* **140 B3** 51 9N 80 50W
Kwatisore, *Indonesia* **83 B4** 3 18 S 134 50 E
KwaZulu Natal □, *S. Africa* **117 D5** 29 0 S 30 0 E
Kweichow = Guizhou □, *China* **76 D6** 27 0N 107 0 E
Kwekwe, *Zimbabwe* **119 F2** 18 58 S 29 48 E
Kwenge →, *Dem. Rep. of the Congo* **115 C3** 4 50 S 18 44 E
Kwethluk, *U.S.A.* **144 F7** 60 49N 161 26W
Kwidzyn, *Poland* **54 E5** 53 44N 18 55 E
Kwigillingok, *U.S.A.* **144 G7** 59 51N 163 8W
Kwiguk, *U.S.A.* **144 E6** 62 46N 164 30W
Kwiha, *Ethiopia* **107 E4** 13 29N 39 32 E
Kwikila, *Papua N. G.* **132 E4** 9 49 S 147 38 E
Kwilu →, *Dem. Rep. of the Congo* **115 C3** 3 22 S 17 22 E
Kwinana New Town, *Australia* **125 F2** 32 15 S 115 47 E
Kwinbet, *Burma* **90 G5** 16 20N 94 14 E
Kwisa →, *Poland* **55 G2** 51 34N 15 24 E
Kwoka, *Indonesia* **83 B4** 0 31 S 132 27 E
Kwolla, *Nigeria* **113 D6** 9 0N 9 15 E
Kwun Tong, *China* **69 G11** 22 19N 114 13 E
Kya-in-Seikkyi, *Burma* **90 G7** 16 2N 98 8 E
Kyabé, *Chad* **109 G3** 9 30N 19 0 E
Kyabra Cr. →, *Australia* **127 D3** 25 36 S 142 55 E
Kyabram, *Australia* **129 D6** 36 19 S 145 4 E
Kyaikkami, *Burma* **90 G6** 16 4N 97 34 E
Kyaiklat, *Burma* **90 G5** 16 25N 95 40 E
Kyaikmaraw, *Burma* **90 G6** 16 23N 97 44 E
Kyaikthin, *Burma* **90 D5** 23 32N 95 40 E
Kyaikto, *Burma* **86 D1** 17 20N 97 3 E
Kyakhta, *Russia* **67 D11** 50 30N 106 25 E
Kyambura Game Reserve, *Uganda* **118 C3** 0 7 S 30 9 E
Kyancutta, *Australia* **127 E2** 33 8 S 135 33 E
Kyangin, *Burma* **90 F5** 18 20N 95 20 E
Kyaukhnyat, *Burma* **90 F6** 18 15N 97 31 E
Kyaukki, *Burma* **90 F6** 18 27N 96 56 E
Kyaukkyi, *Burma* **90 F5** 18 15N 94 29 E
Kyaukme, *Burma* **90 D6** 22 32N 97 2 E
Kyaukpadaung, *Burma* **90 E5** 20 52N 95 8 E
Kyaukpyu, *Burma* **90 F4** 19 28N 93 30 E
Kyaukse, *Burma* **90 E6** 21 36N 96 10 E
Kyauktaga, *Burma* **90 F6** 18 10N 96 37 E
Kyauktan, *Burma* **90 G6** 16 38N 96 19 E
Kyauktaw, *Burma* **90 E4** 20 51N 92 59 E
Kyaunggon, *Burma* **90 G5** 17 6N 95 11 E
Kyawkku, *Burma* **90 E6** 21 48N 96 56 E
Kybartai, *Lithuania* **54 D9** 54 39N 22 45 E
Kyburz, *U.S.A.* **160 G6** 38 47N 120 18W
Kyeintali, *Burma* **90 G5** 18 0N 94 29 E
Kyelang, *India* **92 C7** 32 35N 77 2 E
Kyenjojo, *Uganda* **118 B3** 0 40N 30 37 E
Kyidaunggan, *Burma* **90 F6** 19 53N 96 12 E
Kyjov, *Czech Rep.* **35 B10** 49 1N 17 7 E
Kyle, *Canada* **143 C7** 50 50N 108 2W
Kyle Dam, *Zimbabwe* **119 G3** 20 15 S 31 0 E
Kyle of Lochalsh, *U.K.* **22 D3** 57 17N 5 44W
Kyll →, *Germany* **31 F2** 49 48N 6 41 E
Kyllburg, *Germany* **31 E2** 50 2N 6 34 E
Kymijoki →, *Finland* **15 F22** 60 30N 26 55 E
Kyneton, *Australia* **128 D6** 37 10 S 144 29 E
Kynuna, *Australia* **126 C3** 21 37 S 141 55 E
Kyō-ga-Saki, *Japan* **73 B7** 35 45N 135 15 E
Kyoga, L., *Uganda* **118 B3** 1 35N 33 0 E
Kyogle, *Australia* **127 D5** 28 40 S 153 0 E
Kyom →, *Sudan* **107 F2** 8 58N 28 13 E
Kyongju, *S. Korea* **75 G15** 35 51N 129 14 E
Kyŏngsŏng, *N. Korea* **75 D15** 41 35N 129 36 E
Kyōto, *Japan* **73 C7** 35 0N 135 45 E
Kyōto □, *Japan* **73 B7** 35 15N 135 45 E
Kyparissovouno, *Cyprus* **39 E9** 35 19N 33 10 E
Kyperounda, *Cyprus* **39 F8** 34 56N 32 58 E
Kyrenia, *Cyprus* **39 E9** 35 20N 33 20 E
Kyrgyzstan ■, *Asia* **66 E8** 42 0N 75 0 E
Kyritz, *Germany* **30 C8** 52 56N 12 24 E
Kyrkhult, *Sweden* **17 H8** 56 22N 14 34 E
Kyrksæterøra, *Norway* **18 A6** 63 18N 9 5 E
Kyrönjoki →, *Finland* **14 E19** 63 14N 21 45 E
Kyshtym, *Russia* **64 D8** 55 42N 60 34 E
Kystatyam, *Russia* **67 C13** 67 20N 123 10 E
Kysucké Nové Mesto, *Slovak Rep.* **35 B11** 49 18N 18 47 E
Kythréa, *Cyprus* **39 E9** 35 15N 33 29 E
Kytlym, *Russia* **64 B7** 59 30N 59 12 E
Kyu-hkok, *Burma* **90 C7** 24 4N 98 4 E
Kyunhla, *Burma* **90 D5** 23 25N 95 15 E
Kyuquot Sound, *Canada* **142 D3** 50 2N 127 22W
Kyurdamir = Kürdämir, *Azerbaijan* **61 K9** 40 25N 48 3 E
Kyūshū, *Japan* **72 E3** 33 0N 131 0 E
Kyūshū □, *Japan* **72 E3** 33 0N 131 0 E
Kyūshū-Sanchi, *Japan* **72 E3** 32 35N 131 17 E
Kyustendil, *Bulgaria* **50 D6** 42 16N 22 41 E
Kyusyur, *Russia* **67 B13** 70 19N 127 30 E
Kywong, *Australia* **129 C7** 34 58 S 146 44 E
Kyyiv, *Ukraine* **59 G6** 50 30N 30 28 E
Kyyivske Vdskh., *Ukraine* **59 G6** 51 0N 30 25 E
Kyzyl, *Russia* **67 D10** 51 50N 94 30 E
Kyzyl-Adyr, *Kyrgyzstan* **65 B5** 42 39N 71 35 E
Kyzyl Kum, *Uzbekistan* **66 E7** 42 30N 65 0 E
Kyzyl-Kyya, *Kyrgyzstan* **66 E8** 40 16N 72 8 E
Kyzyl-Suu, *Kyrgyzstan* **65 B9** 42 20N 78 0 E
Kyzyl-Suu →, *Kyrgyzstan* **65 D6** 38 50N 70 0 E
Kyzyltepa, *Uzbekistan* **65 C2** 40 1N 64 51 E
Kzyl-Orda = Qyzylorda, *Kazakstan* **66 E7** 44 48N 65 28 E

L

La Albuera, *Spain* **43 G4** 38 45N 6 49W
La Alcarria, *Spain* **40 E2** 40 31N 2 45W
La Almarcha, *Spain* **40 F2** 39 41N 2 24W
La Almunia de Doña Godina, *Spain* **40 D3** 41 29N 1 23W
La Asunción, *Venezuela* **169 A5** 11 2N 63 53W
La Baie, *Canada* **141 C5** 48 19N 70 53W
La Banda, *Argentina* **174 B3** 27 45 S 64 10W
La Bañeza, *Spain* **42 C5** 42 17N 5 54W
La Barca, *Mexico* **162 C4** 20 20N 102 40W
La Barge, *U.S.A.* **158 E8** 42 16N 110 12W
La Bastide-Puylaurent, *France* **28 D7** 44 35N 3 55 E
La Baule-Escoubiac, *France* **26 E4** 47 17N 2 24W
La Belle, *Fla., U.S.A.* **149 M5** 26 46N 81 26W
La Belle, *Mo., U.S.A.* **156 D5** 40 7N 91 55W
La Biche →, *Canada* **142 B4** 59 57N 123 50W
La Biche, L., *Canada* **142 C6** 54 50N 112 5W
La Bisbal d'Empordà, *Spain* **40 D8** 41 58N 3 2 E
La Bomba, *Mexico* **162 A1** 31 53N 115 2W
La Brea, *Trin. & Tob.* **169 F9** 10 15N 61 37W
La Brède, *France* **28 D3** 44 41N 0 32W
La Bresse, *France* **27 D13** 48 2N 6 53 E
La Bureba, *Spain* **42 C7** 42 36N 3 24W
La Cal →, *Bolivia* **173 D6** 17 27 S 58 15W
La Calera, *Chile* **174 C1** 32 50 S 71 10W
La Campiña, *Spain* **43 H6** 37 45N 4 45W
La Canal = Sa Canal, *Spain* **38 D1** 38 51N 1 23 E
La Cañiza = A Cañiza, *Spain* **42 C2** 42 13N 8 16W
La Canourgue, *France* **28 D7** 44 26N 3 13 E
La Capelle, *France* **27 C10** 49 59N 3 50 E
La Carlota, *Argentina* **174 C3** 33 30 S 63 20W
La Carlota, *Phil.* **81 F4** 10 25N 122 55 E
La Carlota, *Spain* **43 H6** 37 40N 4 56W
La Carolina, *Spain* **43 G7** 38 17N 3 38W
La Castellana, *Phil.* **81 F4** 10 20N 123 3 E
La Cavalerie, *France* **28 D7** 44 1N 3 10 E
La Ceiba, *Honduras* **164 C2** 15 40N 86 50W
La Ceiba, *Venezuela* **168 C3** 9 28N 71 4W
La Chaise-Dieu, *France* **28 C7** 45 18N 3 42 E
La Chapelle d'Angillon, *France* **27 E9** 47 21N 2 25 E
La Chapelle-St-Luc, *France* **27 D11** 48 20N 4 3 E
La Chapelle-sur-Erdre, *France* **26 E5** 47 18N 1 34W
La Charité-sur-Loire, *France* **27 E10** 47 10N 3 1 E
La Chartre-sur-le-Loir, *France* **26 E7** 47 44N 0 34 E
La Châtaigneraie, *France* **28 B3** 46 39N 0 44W
La Châtre, *France* **27 F9** 46 35N 2 0 E
La Chaux-de-Fonds, *Switz.* **32 B3** 47 7N 6 50 E
La Chorrera, *Colombia* **168 D3** 0 44 S 73 1W
La Chorrera, *Panama* **164 E4** 8 53N 79 47W
La Ciotat, *France* **29 E9** 43 10N 5 37 E
La Clayette, *France* **27 F11** 46 17N 4 19 E
La Cocha, *Argentina* **174 B2** 27 50 S 65 40W
La Concepción = Ri-Aba, *Eq. Guin.* **113 E6** 3 28N 8 40 E
La Concepción, *Panama* **164 E3** 8 31N 82 37W
La Concepción, *Venezuela* **168 A3** 10 30N 71 50W
La Concordia, *Mexico* **163 D6** 16 8N 92 38W
La Coruña = A Coruña, *Spain* **42 B2** 43 20N 8 25W
La Coruña □, *Spain* **42 B2** 43 10N 8 30W
La Côte, *Switz.* **32 D2** 46 25N 6 15 E
La Côte-St-André, *France* **29 C9** 45 24N 5 15 E
La Courtine-le-Trucq, *France* **28 C6** 45 41N 2 15 E
La Crau, *Bouches-du-Rhône, France* **29 E8** 43 32N 4 40 E
La Crau, *Var, France* **29 E10** 43 9N 6 4 E
La Crescent, *U.S.A.* **154 D9** 43 50N 91 18W
La Crete, *Canada* **142 B5** 58 11N 116 24W
La Crosse, *Fla., U.S.A.* **152 F7** 29 51N 82 24W
La Crosse, *Kans., U.S.A.* **154 F5** 38 32N 99 18W
La Crosse, *Wis., U.S.A.* **154 D9** 43 48N 91 15W
La Cruz, *Costa Rica* **164 D2** 11 4N 85 39W
La Cruz, *Mexico* **162 C3** 23 55N 106 54W
La Cumbre, Volcán, *Ecuador* **172 a** 0 21 S 91 32W
La Désirade, *Guadeloupe* **164 b** 16 18N 61 3W
La Digue, *Seychelles* **121 b** 4 20 S 55 51 E
La Dorada, *Colombia* **168 B3** 5 30N 74 40W
La Ensenada, *Chile* **176 B2** 41 12 S 72 33W
La Escondida, *Mexico* **162 C5** 24 6N 99 55W
La Esmeralda, *Paraguay* **174 A3** 22 16 S 62 33W
La Esperanza, *Argentina* **176 B3** 40 26 S 68 32W
La Esperanza, *Cuba* **164 B3** 22 46N 83 44W
La Esperanza, *Honduras* **164 D2** 14 15N 88 10W
La Estrada = A Estrada, *Spain* **42 C2** 42 43N 8 27W
La Faouët, *France* **26 D3** 48 2N 3 30W
La Fayette, *U.S.A.* **149 H3** 34 42N 85 17W
La Fé, *Cuba* **164 B3** 22 2N 84 15W
La Fère, *France* **27 C10** 49 39N 3 21 E
La Ferté-Bernard, *France* **26 D7** 48 10N 0 40 E
La Ferté-Gaucher, *France* **27 D10** 48 47N 3 19 E
La Ferté-Macé, *France* **26 D6** 48 35N 0 22W
La Ferté-St-Aubin, *France* **27 E8** 47 42N 1 57 E
La Ferté-sous-Jouarre, *France* **27 D10** 48 56N 3 8 E
La Ferté-Vidame, *France* **26 D7** 48 37N 0 53 E
La Flèche, *France* **26 E6** 47 42N 0 4W
La Foa, *N. Cal.* **133 U19** 21 43 S 165 50 E
La Follette, *U.S.A.* **149 G3** 36 23N 84 7W
La Fontaine, *U.S.A.* **157 D11** 40 40N 85 43W
La Fregeneda, *Spain* **42 E4** 40 58N 6 54W
La Fría, *Venezuela* **168 B3** 8 13N 72 15W
La Fuente de San Esteban, *Spain* **42 E4** 40 49N 6 15W
La Gacilly, *France* **26 E4** 47 45N 2 8W
La Gineta, *Spain* **41 F2** 39 8N 2 1W
La Gloria, *Colombia* **168 B3** 8 37N 73 48W
La Gran Sabana, *Venezuela* **169 B5** 5 30N 61 30W
La Grand-Combe, *France* **29 D8** 44 13N 4 2 E
La Grande, *U.S.A.* **158 D4** 45 20N 118 5W
La Grande →, *Canada* **140 B5** 53 50N 79 0W
La Grande Deux, Rés., *Canada* **140 B4** 53 40N 76 55W
La Grande-Motte, *France* **29 E8** 43 23N 4 5 E
La Grande Quatre, Rés., *Canada* **140 B5** 54 0N 73 15W
La Grande Trois, Rés., *Canada* **140 B4** 53 40N 75 10W
La Grange, *Calif., U.S.A.* **160 H6** 37 42N 120 27W
La Grange, *Ga., U.S.A.* **152 B4** 33 2N 85 2W
La Grange, *Ky., U.S.A.* **148 F3** 38 25N 85 23W
La Grange, *Ky., U.S.A.* **157 F11** 38 24N 85 22W
La Grange, *Mo., U.S.A.* **156 D5** 40 3N 91 35W
La Grange, *Tex., U.S.A.* **155 L6** 29 54N 96 52W
La Grave, *France* **29 C10** 45 3N 6 18 E
La Grita, *Venezuela* **168 B3** 8 8N 71 59W
La Guaira, *Venezuela* **168 A4** 10 36N 66 56W
La Guardia = A Guarda, *Spain* **42 D2** 41 56N 8 52W
La Gudiña = A Gudiña, *Spain* **42 C3** 42 4N 7 8W
La Güera, *Mauritania* **110 D1** 20 51N 17 0W
La Guerche-de-Bretagne, *France* **26 E5** 47 57N 1 16W
La Guerche-sur-l'Aubois, *France* **27 F9** 46 58N 2 56 E
La Habana, *Cuba* **164 B3** 23 8N 82 22W
La Harpe, *U.S.A.* **156 D6** 40 35N 90 58W
La Haye-du-Puits, *France* **26 C5** 49 17N 1 33W
La Horqueta, *Venezuela* **169 B5** 7 55N 60 20W
La Horra, *Spain* **42 D7** 41 44N 3 53W
La Independencia, *Mexico* **163 D6** 16 31N 91 47W
La Isabela, *Dom. Rep.* **165 C5** 19 58N 71 2W
La Jonquera, *Spain* **40 C7** 42 25N 2 53 E
La Joya, *Peru* **172 D3** 16 43 S 71 52W
La Junta, *U.S.A.* **155 F3** 37 59N 103 33W
La Laguna, *Canary Is.* **9 e1** 28 28N 16 18W
La Libertad, *Guatemala* **164 C1** 16 47N 90 7W
La Libertad, *Mexico* **162 B2** 29 55N 112 41W
La Libertad □, *Peru* **172 B2** 8 0 S 78 30W
La Ligua, *Chile* **174 C1** 32 30 S 71 16W
La Línea de la Concepción, *Spain* **43 J5** 36 15N 5 23W
La Loche, *Canada* **143 B7** 56 29N 109 26W
La Londe-les-Maures, *France* **29 E10** 43 8N 6 14 E
La Lora, *Spain* **42 C7** 42 45N 4 0W
La Loupe, *France* **26 D8** 48 29N 1 0 E
La Louvière, *Belgium* **24 D4** 50 27N 4 10 E
La Lune, *Trin. & Tob.* **169 F9** 10 3N 61 22W
La Machine, *France* **27 F10** 46 54N 3 27 E
La Maddalena, *Italy* **46 A2** 41 13N 9 24 E
La Malbaie, *Canada* **141 C5** 47 40N 70 10W
La Mancha, *Spain* **41 F2** 39 10N 2 54W
La Mariña, *Spain* **42 B3** 43 30N 7 40W
La Martre, L., *Canada* **142 A5** 63 15N 117 55W
La Mesa, *U.S.A.* **161 N9** 32 46N 117 3W
La Misión, *Mexico* **162 A1** 32 5N 116 50W
La Moille, *U.S.A.* **156 C7** 41 32N 89 17W
La Moine →, *U.S.A.* **156 E6** 39 59N 90 31W
La Monte, *U.S.A.* **156 F3** 38 46N 93 26W
La Mothe-Achard, *France* **26 F5** 46 37N 1 40W
La Motte, *France* **29 D10** 44 20N 6 3 E
La Motte-Chalançon, *France* **29 D9** 44 30N 5 21 E
La Motte-Servolex, *France* **29 C9** 45 35N 5 53 E
La Moure, *U.S.A.* **154 B5** 46 21N 98 18W
La Muela, *Spain* **40 D3** 41 36N 1 7W
La Mure, *France* **29 D9** 44 55N 5 48 E
La Negra, *Chile* **174 A1** 23 46 S 70 18W
La Neuveville, *Switz.* **32 B4** 47 4N 7 6 E
La Oliva, *Canary Is.* **9 e2** 28 36N 13 57W
La Oraya, *Peru* **172 C2** 11 32 S 75 54W
La Orotava, *Canary Is.* **9 e1** 28 22N 16 31W
La Oroya, *Peru* **172 C2** 11 32 S 75 54W
La Pacaudière, *France* **27 F10** 46 11N 3 52 E
La Palma, *Canary Is.* **9 e1** 28 40N 17 50W
La Palma, *Panama* **164 E4** 8 15N 78 0W
La Palma del Condado, *Spain* **43 H4** 37 21N 6 38W
La Paloma, *Chile* **174 C1** 30 35 S 71 0W
La Pampa □, *Argentina* **174 D2** 36 50 S 66 0W
La Paragua, *Venezuela* **169 B5** 6 50N 63 20W
La Paz, *Entre Ríos, Argentina* **174 C4** 30 50 S 59 45W
La Paz, *San Luis, Argentina* **174 C2** 33 30 S 67 20W
La Paz, *Bolivia* **172 D4** 16 20 S 68 10W
La Paz, *Honduras* **164 D2** 14 20N 87 47W
La Paz, *Mexico* **162 C2** 24 10N 110 20W
La Paz, *Abra, Phil.* **80 C3** 17 40N 120 41 E
La Paz, *Tarlac, Phil.* **80 D3** 15 26N 120 45 E
La Paz □, *Bolivia* **172 D4** 15 30 S 68 0W
La Paz Centro, *Nic.* **164 D2** 12 20N 86 41W
La Pedrera, *Colombia* **168 D4** 1 18 S 69 43W
La Pérade, *Canada* **141 C5** 46 35N 72 12W
La Perouse, Bahía, *Chile* **172 b** 27 5 S 109 18W
La Perouse Str., *Asia* **70 B11** 45 40N 142 0 E
La Pesca, *Mexico* **163 C5** 23 46N 97 47W
La Piedad, *Mexico* **162 C4** 20 20N 102 1W
La Pine, *U.S.A.* **158 E3** 43 40N 121 30W
La Plata, *Argentina* **174 D4** 35 0 S 57 55W
La Plata, *Colombia* **168 C2** 2 23N 75 53W
La Plata, *U.S.A.* **156 D4** 40 2N 92 29W
La Plata, L., *Argentina* **176 B2** 44 55 S 71 50W
La Pobla de Lillet, *Spain* **40 C6** 42 16N 1 59 E
La Pocatière, *Canada* **141 C5** 47 22N 70 2W
La Pola de Gordón, *Spain* **42 C5** 42 51N 5 41W
La Porta, *France* **29 F13** 42 25N 9 21 E
La Porte, *Ind., U.S.A.* **157 C10** 41 36N 86 43W
La Porte, *Tex., U.S.A.* **155 L7** 29 39N 95 1W
La Porte City, *U.S.A.* **156 B4** 42 19N 92 12W
La Presanella, *Italy* **44 B7** 46 13N 10 40 E
La Puebla = Sa Pobla, *Spain* **38 B4** 39 46N 3 1 E
La Puebla de Cazalla, *Spain* **43 H5** 37 10N 5 20W
La Puebla de los Infantes, *Spain* **43 H5** 37 47N 5 24W
La Puebla de Montalbán, *Spain* **42 F6** 39 52N 4 22W
La Puebla del Río, *Spain* **43 H4** 37 16N 6 3W
La Puerta de Segura, *Spain* **43 G8** 38 22N 2 45W
La Punt, *Switz.* **33 C9** 46 35N 9 56 E
La Purísima, *Mexico* **162 B2** 26 10N 112 4W
La Push, *U.S.A.* **160 C2** 47 55N 124 38W
La Quiaca, *Argentina* **174 A2** 22 5 S 65 35W
La Réole, *France* **28 D3** 44 35N 0 1W
La Restinga, *Canary Is.* **9 e1** 27 38N 17 59W
La Rioja, *Argentina* **174 B2** 29 20 S 67 0W
La Rioja □, *Argentina* **174 B2** 29 30 S 67 0W
La Rioja □, *Spain* **40 C2** 42 20N 2 20W
La Robla, *Spain* **42 C5** 42 50N 5 41W
La Roche, *N. Cal.* **133 U22** 21 26 S 168 2 E
La Roche, *Switz.* **32 C4** 46 42N 7 7 E
La Roche-Bernard, *France* **26 E4** 47 31N 2 19W
La Roche-Canillac, *France* **28 C5** 45 12N 1 57 E
La Roche-en-Ardenne, *Belgium* **24 D5** 50 11N 5 35 E
La Roche-sur-Foron, *France* **27 F13** 46 4N 6 19 E
La Roche-sur-Yon, *France* **26 F5** 46 40N 1 25W
La Rochefoucauld, *France* **28 C4** 45 44N 0 24 E
La Rochelle, *France* **28 B2** 46 10N 1 9W
La Roda, *Spain* **41 F2** 39 13N 2 15W
La Roda de Andalucía, *Spain* **43 H6** 37 12N 4 46W
La Romana, *Dom. Rep.* **165 C6** 18 27N 68 57W
La Ronge, *Canada* **143 B7** 55 5N 105 20W
La Rue, *U.S.A.* **157 D13** 40 35N 83 23W
La Rumorosa, *Mexico* **161 N10** 32 33N 116 4W
La Sabina = Sa Savina, *Spain* **38 D1** 38 44N 1 25 E
La Sagra, *Spain* **41 H2** 37 57N 2 35W
La Salle, *U.S.A.* **156 C7** 41 20N 89 6W
La Sanabria, *Spain* **42 C4** 42 0N 6 30W
La Santa, *Canary Is.* **9 e2** 29 5N 13 40W
La Sarraz, *Switz.* **32 C3** 46 38N 6 32 E
La Sarre, *Canada* **140 C4** 48 45N 79 15W
La Scie, *Canada* **141 C8** 49 57N 55 36W
La Selva, *Spain* **40 C7** 42 0N 2 45 E
La Selva Beach, *U.S.A.* **160 J5** 36 56N 121 51W
La Selva del Camp, *Spain* **40 D6** 41 13N 1 8 E
La Serena, *Chile* **174 B1** 29 55 S 71 10W
La Serena, *Spain* **43 G5** 38 45N 5 40W
La Seu d'Urgell, *Spain* **40 C6** 42 22N 1 23 E
La Seyne-sur-Mer, *France* **29 E9** 43 7N 5 52 E
La Sila, *Italy* **47 C9** 39 15N 16 35 E
La Solana, *Spain* **43 G7** 38 59N 3 14W
La Soufrière, *St. Vincent* **165 D7** 13 20N 61 11W
La Souterraine, *France* **27 F8** 46 15N 1 30 E

La Spézia, *Italy* **44 D6** 44 7N 9 50 E
La Suze-sur-Sarthe, *France* **26 E7** 47 53N 0 2 E
La Tagua, *Colombia* **168 C3** 0 3N 74 40W
La Teste, *France* **28 D2** 44 37N 1 8W
La Tortuga, *Venezuela* **165 D6** 11 0N 65 22W
La Tour de Peilz, *Switz.* **32 D3** 46 27N 6 52 E
La Tour-du-Pin, *France* **29 C9** 45 33N 5 27 E
La Tournette, *France* **32 E2** 45 36N 6 30 E
La Tranche-sur-Mer, *France* **26 F5** 46 20N 1 27W
La Tremblade, *France* **28 C2** 45 46N 1 8W
La Trinidad, *Phil.* **80 C3** 16 28N 120 35 E
La Trinité, *Martinique* **164 c** 14 43N 60 58W
La Tuque, *Canada* **140 C5** 47 30N 72 50W
La Unión, *Chile* **176 B2** 40 10 S 73 0W
La Unión, *Colombia* **168 C2** 1 35N 77 5W
La Unión, *El Salv.* **164 D2** 13 20N 87 50W
La Unión, *Mexico* **162 D4** 17 58N 101 49W
La Unión, *Peru* **172 B2** 9 43 S 76 45W
La Unión, *Spain* **41 H4** 37 38N 0 53W
La Union □, *Phil.* **80 C3** 16 30N 120 25 E
La Urbana, *Venezuela* **168 B4** 7 8N 66 56W
La Vache Pt., *Trin. & Tob.* **169 F9** 10 47N 61 37W
La Vall d'Uixó, *Spain* **40 F4** 39 49N 0 15W
La Vecilla de Curveño, *Spain* **42 C5** 42 51N 5 27W
La Vega, *Dom. Rep.* **165 C5** 19 20N 70 30W
La Vega, *Peru* **172 C2** 10 41 S 77 44W
La Vela de Coro, *Venezuela* **168 A4** 11 27N 69 34W
La Veleta, *Spain* **43 H7** 37 1N 3 22W
La Venta, *Mexico* **163 D6** 18 8N 94 3W
La Ventura, *Mexico* **162 C4** 24 38N 100 54W
La Venturosa, *Colombia* **168 B4** 6 8N 68 48W
La Victoria, *Venezuela* **168 A4** 10 14N 67 20W
La Voulte-sur-Rhône, *France* **29 D8** 44 48N 4 46 E
Laa an der Thaya, *Austria* **35 C9** 48 43N 16 23 E
Laaber, Grosse →, *Germany* **31 G8** 48 55N 12 30 E
Laage, *Germany* **30 B8** 53 55N 12 21 E
Laas Caanood = Las Anod, *Somali Rep.* **120 C3** 8 26N 47 19 E
Laatzen, *Germany* **30 C5** 52 19N 9 48 E
Laau Pt., *U.S.A.* **145 B4** 21 6N 157 19W
Laba →, *Russia* **61 H4** 45 11N 39 42 E
Laban, *Burma* **90 C6** 25 52N 96 40 E
Labasa, *Fiji* **133 A2** 16 30 S 179 27 E
Labason, *Phil.* **81 G4** 8 4N 122 31 E
Labastide-Murat, *France* **28 D5** 44 39N 1 33 E
Labastide-Rouairoux, *France* **28 E6** 43 28N 2 39 E
Labbézenga, *Mali* **113 B5** 15 2N 0 48 E
Labdah = Leptis Magna, *Libya* **108 B2** 32 40N 14 12 E
Labe = Elbe →, *Europe* **30 B4** 53 50N 9 0 E
Labé, *Guinea* **112 C2** 11 24N 12 16W
Laberge, L., *Canada* **142 A1** 61 11N 135 12W
Labian, Tanjong, *Malaysia* **85 A5** 5 9N 119 13 E
Labig Pt. = Iligan Pt., *Phil.* **80 B4** 18 25N 122 25 E
Labin, *Croatia* **45 C11** 45 5N 14 8 E
Labinsk, *Russia* **61 H5** 44 40N 40 48 E
Labis, *Malaysia* **87 L4** 2 22N 103 2 E
Łabiszyn, *Poland* **55 F4** 52 57N 17 54 E
Labo, *Phil.* **80 D4** 14 9N 122 51 E
Laboe, *Germany* **30 A6** 54 24N 10 13 E
Laboka, *Gabon* **114 B2** 0 19N 11 32 E
Laborec →, *Slovak Rep.* **35 C14** 48 37N 21 58 E
Laborie, *St. Lucia* **165 f** 13 45N 61 2W
Labouheyre, *France* **28 D3** 44 13N 0 55W
Laboulaye, *Argentina* **174 C3** 34 10 S 63 30W
Labrador, *Canada* **141 B7** 53 20N 61 0W
Labrador City, *Canada* **141 B6** 52 57N 66 55W
Labrador Sea, *Atl. Oc.* **139 C14** 57 0N 54 0W
Lábrea, *Brazil* **173 B5** 7 15 S 64 51W
Labruguière, *France* **28 E6** 43 31N 2 16 E
Labuan, *Malaysia* **85 A5** 5 20N 115 14 E
Labuan, Pulau, *Malaysia* **85 A5** 5 21N 115 13 E
Labuha, *Indonesia* **82 B3** 0 30 S 127 30 E
Labuhan, *Indonesia* **84 D3** 6 22 S 105 50 E
Labuhanbajo, *Indonesia* **82 C2** 8 28 S 119 54 E
Labuk, Telok, *Malaysia* **85 A5** 6 10N 117 50 E
Labutta, *Burma* **90 G5** 16 9N 94 46 E
Labyrinth, L., *Australia* **127 E2** 30 40 S 135 11 E
Labytnangi, *Russia* **66 C7** 66 39N 66 21 E
Laç, *Albania* **50 E3** 41 38N 19 43 E
Lac Bouchette, *Canada* **141 C5** 48 16N 72 11W
Lac Édouard, *Canada* **140 C5** 47 40N 72 16W
Lac La Biche, *Canada* **142 C6** 54 45N 111 58W
Lac la Martre = Wha Ti, *Canada* **138 B8** 63 8N 117 16W
Lac La Ronge Prov. Park, *Canada* **143 B7** 55 9N 104 41W
Lac-Mégantic, *Canada* **141 C5** 45 35N 70 53W
Lac Thien, *Vietnam* **86 F7** 12 25N 108 11 E
Lacanau, *France* **28 D2** 44 58N 1 5W
Lacanau, Étang de, *France* **28 D2** 44 58N 1 7W
Lacantúm →, *Mexico* **163 D6** 16 36N 90 40W
Lacara →, *Spain* **43 G4** 38 55N 6 25W
Lacaune, *France* **28 E6** 43 43N 2 40 E
Lacaune, Mts. de, *France* **28 E6** 43 43N 2 50 E
Laccadive Is. = Lakshadweep Is., *India* **95 J1** 10 0N 72 30 E
Lacepede B., *Australia* **128 D3** 36 40 S 139 40 E
Lacepede Is., *Australia* **124 C3** 16 55 S 122 0 E
Lacerdónia, *Mozam.* **119 F4** 18 3 S 35 35 E
Lacey, *U.S.A.* **160 C4** 47 7N 122 49W
Lachay, Pta., *Peru* **172 C2** 11 17 S 77 44W
Lachen, *India* **90 B2** 27 46N 88 36 E
Lachen, *Switz.* **33 B7** 47 12N 8 51 E
Lachhmangarh, *India* **92 F6** 27 50N 75 4 E
Lachi, *Pakistan* **92 C4** 33 25N 71 20 E
Lachine, *Canada* **140 C5** 45 30N 73 40W
Lachlan →, *Australia* **128 C5** 34 22 S 143 55 E
Lachoc, *Peru* **172 C2** 12 50 S 75 6W
Lachute, *Canada* **140 C5** 45 39N 74 21W
Lackawanna, *U.S.A.* **150 D6** 42 50N 78 50W
Lackawaxen, *U.S.A.* **151 E10** 41 29N 74 59W
Lacolle, *Canada* **151 A11** 45 5N 73 22W
Lacombe, *Canada* **142 C6** 52 30N 113 44W
Lacon, *U.S.A.* **156 C7** 41 2N 89 24W
Lacona, *Iowa, U.S.A.* **156 C3** 41 12N 93 23W
Lacona, *N.Y., U.S.A.* **151 C8** 43 39N 76 10W
Láconi, *Italy* **46 C2** 39 54N 9 4 E
Laconia, *U.S.A.* **151 C13** 43 32N 71 28W
Lacoochee, *U.S.A.* **153 G7** 28 28N 82 11W
Lacq, *France* **28 E3** 43 25N 0 35W
Ladakh Ra., *India* **93 C8** 34 0N 78 0 E
Ladário, *Brazil* **173 D6** 19 1 S 57 35W
Ladd, *U.S.A.* **156 C7** 41 23N 89 13W
Laddonia, *U.S.A.* **156 E5** 39 15N 91 39W
Lądek-Zdrój, *Poland* **55 H3** 50 21N 16 53 E
Ládhon →, *Greece* **48 D3** 37 40N 21 50 E
Ladik, *Turkey* **100 B6** 40 57N 35 58 E
Ladismith, *S. Africa* **116 E3** 33 28 S 21 15 E
Ladíspoli, *Italy* **45 G9** 41 56N 12 5 E
Lādīz, *Iran* **97 D9** 28 55N 61 15 E
Ladnun, *India* **92 F6** 27 38N 74 25 E
Ladoga, L. = Ladozhskoye Ozero, *Russia* **58 B6** 61 15N 30 30 E
Ladozhskoye Ozero, *Russia* **58 B6** 61 15N 30 30 E
Ladrillero, G., *Chile* **176 C1** 49 20 S 75 35W
Ladson, *U.S.A.* **152 C9** 32 59N 80 6W
Lady Elliott I., *Australia* **126 C5** 24 7 S 152 42 E
Lady Grey, *S. Africa* **116 E4** 30 43 S 27 13 E
Lady Lake, *U.S.A.* **153 G8** 28 55N 81 55W
Ladybrand, *S. Africa* **116 D4** 29 9 S 27 29 E
Ladysmith, *Canada* **142 D4** 49 0N 123 49W
Ladysmith, *S. Africa* **117 D4** 28 32 S 29 46 E
Ladysmith, *U.S.A.* **154 C9** 45 28N 91 12W
Lae, *Papua N. G.* **132 D4** 6 40 S 147 2 E
Laem Hin Khom, *Thailand* **87 b** 9 25N 99 56 E
Laem Khat, *Thailand* **87 a** 8 6N 98 26 E
Laem Nga, *Thailand* **87 a** 7 55N 98 27 E
Laem Ngop, *Thailand* **87 F4** 12 10N 102 26 E
Laem Phan Wa, *Thailand* **87 a** 7 47N 98 25 E
Laem Pho, *Thailand* **87 J3** 6 55N 101 19 E
Laem Phrom Thep, *Thailand* **87 a** 7 45N 98 19 E
Laem Riang, *Thailand* **87 a** 8 7N 98 27 E
Laem Sam Rong, *Thailand* **87 b** 9 35N 100 4 E
Laem Son, *Thailand* **87 a** 7 59N 98 16 E
Laem Yamu, *Thailand* **87 a** 7 59N 98 26 E
Lærdalsøyri, *Norway* **18 C4** 61 6N 7 28 E
Læsø, *Denmark* **17 G5** 57 15N 11 5 E
Læsø Rende, *Denmark* **17 G4** 57 20N 10 45 E
Lafayette, *Ala., U.S.A.* **152 C4** 32 54N 85 24W
Lafayette, *Colo., U.S.A.* **154 F2** 39 58N 105 12W
Lafayette, *Ind., U.S.A.* **157 D10** 40 25N 86 54W
Lafayette, *La., U.S.A.* **155 K9** 30 14N 92 1W
Lafayette, *Tenn., U.S.A.* **149 G2** 36 31N 86 2W
Laferte →, *Canada* **142 A5** 61 53N 117 44W
Lafia, *Nigeria* **113 D6** 8 30N 8 34 E
Lafiagi, *Nigeria* **113 D6** 8 52N 5 20 E
Lafleche, *Canada* **143 D7** 49 45N 106 40W
Lafon, *Sudan* **107 F3** 5 5N 32 29 E
Laful, *India* **95 L11** 7 10N 93 52 E
Lagaip →, *Papua N. G.* **132 C2** 5 4 S 142 52 E
Lagan, *Sweden* **17 H7** 56 56N 13 58 E
Lagan →, *Sweden* **17 H6** 56 30N 12 58 E
Lagan →, *U.K.* **23 B6** 54 36N 5 55W
Laganás, *Greece* **39 D2** 37 44N 20 53 E
Lagangilang, *Phil.* **80 C3** 17 37N 120 44 E
Lagarfljót →, *Iceland* **11 B12** 65 40N 14 18W
Lagarto, *Brazil* **170 D4** 10 54 S 37 41W
Lagawe, *Phil.* **80 C3** 16 49N 121 6 E
Lagdo, Rés. de, *Cameroon* **114 A2** 8 40N 14 0 E
Lage, *Germany* **30 D4** 51 59N 8 48 E
Lågen →, *Oppland, Norway* **15 F14** 61 8N 10 25 E
Lågen →, *Vestfold, Norway* **15 G14** 59 3N 10 3 E
Lägerdorf, *Germany* **30 B5** 53 53N 9 34 E
Laghmān □, *Afghan.* **91 B3** 34 20N 70 0 E
Laghouat, *Algeria* **111 B5** 33 50N 2 59 E
Lagnieu, *France* **29 C9** 45 55N 5 20 E
Lagny-sur-Marne, *France* **27 D9** 48 52N 2 44 E
Lago, *Italy* **47 C9** 39 10N 16 9 E
Lago Posadas, *Argentina* **176 C2** 47 30 S 71 40W
Lago Ranco, *Chile* **176 B2** 40 19 S 72 30W
Lagoa, *Azores* **9 d3** 37 45N 25 20W
Lagôa, *Portugal* **43 H2** 37 8N 8 27W
Lagoa Vermelha, *Brazil* **175 B5** 28 13 S 51 32W
Lagoaça, *Portugal* **42 D4** 41 11N 6 44W
Lagodekhi, *Georgia* **61 K8** 41 50N 46 22 E
Lagónegro, *Italy* **47 B8** 40 8N 15 45 E
Lagonoy G., *Phil.* **80 E4** 13 35N 123 50 E
Lagos, *Angola* **115 F3** 16 3 S 16 35 E
Lagos, *Nigeria* **113 D5** 6 25N 3 27 E
Lagos, *Portugal* **43 H2** 37 5N 8 41W
Lagos □, *Nigeria* **113 D5** 6 28N 3 25 E
Lagos de Moreno, *Mexico* **162 C4** 21 21N 101 55W
Lagrange, *Australia* **124 C3** 18 45 S 121 43 E
Lagrange, *U.S.A.* **157 C11** 41 39N 85 25W
Lagrange B., *Australia* **124 C3** 18 38 S 121 42 E
Laguardia, *Spain* **40 C2** 42 33N 2 35W
Laguépie, *France* **28 D5** 44 8N 1 57 E
Laguna, *Brazil* **175 B6** 28 30 S 48 50W
Laguna, *U.S.A.* **159 J10** 35 2N 107 25W
Laguna □, *Phil.* **80 D3** 14 10N 121 20 E
Laguna Beach, *U.S.A.* **161 M9** 33 33N 117 47W
Laguna de Duera, *Spain* **42 D6** 41 35N 4 43W
Laguna Limpia, *Argentina* **174 B4** 26 32 S 59 45W
Lagunas, *Chile* **174 A2** 21 0 S 69 45W
Lagunas, *Peru* **172 B2** 5 10 S 75 35W
Lagunillas, *Bolivia* **173 D5** 19 38 S 63 43W
Lahad Datu, *Malaysia* **85 A5** 5 0N 118 20 E
Lahad Datu, Teluk, *Malaysia* **85 B5** 4 50N 118 20 E
Lahaina, *U.S.A.* **145 C5** 20 53N 156 41W
Lahan Sai, *Thailand* **86 E4** 14 25N 102 52 E
Lahanam, *Laos* **86 D5** 16 16N 105 16 E
Lahar, *India* **93 F8** 26 12N 78 57 E
Laharpur, *India* **93 F9** 27 43N 80 56 E
Lahat, *Indonesia* **84 C2** 3 45 S 103 30 E
Lahe, *Burma* **90 B5** 26 20N 95 26 E
Lahewa, *Indonesia* **84 B1** 1 22N 97 12 E
Laḩij, *Yemen* **98 D4** 13 4N 44 53 E
Lāhījān, *Iran* **97 B6** 37 10N 50 6 E
Lahilahi Pt., *U.S.A.* **145 K13** 21 28N 158 13W
Lahn →, *Germany* **31 E3** 50 19N 7 37 E
Lahnstein, *Germany* **31 E3** 50 19N 7 37 E
Laholm, *Sweden* **17 H7** 56 30N 13 2 E
Laholmsbukten, *Sweden* **17 H6** 56 30N 12 45 E
Lahore, *Pakistan* **91 C4** 31 32N 74 22 E
Lahpongsel, *Burma* **90 B7** 27 7N 98 25 E
Lahr, *Germany* **31 G3** 48 20N 7 53 E
Lahri, *Pakistan* **92 E3** 29 11N 68 13 E
Lahti, *Finland* **15 F21** 60 58N 25 40 E
Lahtis = Lahti, *Finland* **15 F21** 60 58N 25 40 E
Laï, *Chad* **109 G3** 9 25N 16 18 E
Lai Chau, *Vietnam* **76 F4** 22 5N 103 3 E
Lai-hka, *Burma* **90 E6** 21 16N 97 40 E
Laiagam, *Papua N. G.* **132 C2** 5 33 S 143 30 E
Lai'an, *China* **77 A12** 32 28N 118 30 E
Laibin, *China* **76 F7** 23 42N 109 14 E
Laie, *U.S.A.* **145 J14** 21 39N 157 56W
Laifeng, *China* **76 C7** 29 27N 109 20 E
L'Aigle, *France* **26 D7** 48 46N 0 38 E
Laignes, *France* **27 E11** 47 50N 4 20 E
L'Aiguillon-sur-Mer, *France* **28 B2** 46 20N 1 18W
Laila = Layla, *Si. Arabia* **98 B4** 22 10N 46 40 E
Laingsburg, *S. Africa* **116 E3** 33 9 S 20 52 E
Lainio älv →, *Sweden* **14 C20** 67 35N 22 40 E
Lairg, *U.K.* **22 C4** 58 2N 4 24W
Laïri, B. de, *Chad* **109 F3** 12 28N 16 45 E
Lais, *Phil.* **81 H5** 6 20N 125 39 E
Laishui, *China* **74 E8** 39 23N 115 45 E
Laissac, *France* **28 D6** 44 23N 2 50 E
Láives, *Italy* **45 B8** 46 26N 11 20 E
Laiwu, *China* **75 F9** 36 15N 117 40 E
Laixi, *China* **75 F11** 36 50N 120 31 E
Laiyang, *China* **75 F11** 36 59N 120 45 E
Laiyuan, *China* **74 E8** 39 20N 114 40 E
Laizhou, *China* **75 F10** 37 8N 119 57 E
Laizhou Wan, *China* **75 F10** 37 30N 119 30 E
Laja →, *Mexico* **162 C4** 20 55N 100 46W
Lajedo, *Azores* **9 d2** 39 23N 31 15W
Lajere, *Nigeria* **113 C7** 12 10N 11 25 E
Lajes, *Azores* **9 d1** 38 46N 27 6W
Lajes, *Rio Grande do N., Brazil* **170 C4** 5 41 S 36 14W
Lajes, *Sta. Catarina, Brazil* **175 B5** 27 48 S 50 20W
Lajes das Flores, *Azores* **9 d2** 39 23N 31 10W
Lajes do Pico, *Azores* **9 d1** 38 23N 28 16W
Lajinha, *Brazil* **171 F3** 20 9 S 41 37W
Lajkovac, *Serbia, Yug.* **50 B4** 44 27N 20 14 E
Lajosmizse, *Hungary* **52 C4** 47 3N 19 32 E
Lak Sao, *Laos* **86 C5** 18 11N 104 59 E
Láka, *Greece* **38 C10** 39 17N 20 9 E
Lakaband, *Pakistan* **92 D3** 31 2N 69 15 E
Lakamané, *Mali* **112 C3** 14 35N 9 44W
Lakatoro, *Vanuatu* **133 F5** 16 6 S 167 25 E
Lake Alfred, *U.S.A.* **153 G8** 28 6N 81 44W
Lake Alpine, *U.S.A.* **160 G7** 38 29N 120 0W
Lake Andes, *U.S.A.* **154 D5** 43 9N 98 32W
Lake Arthur, *U.S.A.* **155 K8** 30 5N 92 41W
Lake Bindegolly Nat. Park, *Australia* **127 D3** 28 0 S 144 12 E
Lake Boga, *Australia* **128 C5** 35 26 S 143 38 E
Lake Butler, *U.S.A.* **152 E7** 30 1N 82 21W
Lake Cargelligo, *Australia* **129 B7** 33 15 S 146 22 E
Lake Charles, *U.S.A.* **155 K8** 30 14N 93 13W
Lake City, *Colo., U.S.A.* **159 G10** 38 2N 107 19W
Lake City, *Fla., U.S.A.* **152 E7** 30 11N 82 38W
Lake City, *Iowa, U.S.A.* **156 B2** 42 16N 94 44W
Lake City, *Mich., U.S.A.* **148 C3** 44 20N 85 13W
Lake City, *Minn., U.S.A.* **154 C8** 44 27N 92 16W
Lake City, *Pa., U.S.A.* **150 D4** 42 1N 80 21W
Lake City, *S.C., U.S.A.* **152 B10** 33 52N 79 45W
Lake Clarke Shores, *U.S.A.* **153 J9** 26 39N 80 5W
Lake Coleridge, *N.Z.* **131 D6** 43 17 S 171 30 E
Lake Cowichan, *Canada* **142 D4** 48 49N 124 3W
Lake District, *U.K.* **20 C4** 54 35N 3 20 E
Lake Elsinore, *U.S.A.* **161 M9** 33 38N 117 20W
Lake Eyre Nat. Park, *Australia* **127 D2** 28 40 S 137 31 E
Lake Forest, *U.S.A.* **157 B9** 42 15N 87 50W
Lake Gairdner Nat. Park, *Australia* **127 E2** 31 41 S 135 51 E
Lake Geneva, *U.S.A.* **157 B8** 42 36N 88 26W
Lake George, *U.S.A.* **151 C11** 43 26N 73 43W
Lake Grace, *Australia* **125 F2** 33 7 S 118 28 E
Lake Harbor, *U.S.A.* **153 J9** 26 42N 80 48W
Lake Harbour = Kimmirut, *Canada* **139 B13** 62 50N 69 50W
Lake Havasu City, *U.S.A.* **161 L12** 34 27N 114 22W
Lake Helen, *U.S.A.* **153 G8** 28 59N 81 14W
Lake Hughes, *U.S.A.* **161 L8** 34 41N 118 26W
Lake Isabella, *U.S.A.* **161 K8** 35 38N 118 28W
Lake Jackson, *U.S.A.* **155 L7** 29 3N 95 27W
Lake Junction, *U.S.A.* **158 D8** 44 35N 110 28W
Lake King, *Australia* **125 F2** 33 5 S 119 45 E
Lake Kopiago, *Papua N. G.* **132 C2** 5 23 S 142 31 E
Lake Kutubu, *Papua N. G.* **132 D2** 6 20 S 143 18 E
Lake Lenore, *Canada* **143 C8** 52 24N 104 59W
Lake Louise, *Canada* **142 C5** 51 30N 116 10W
Lake Malawi Nat. Park, *Malawi* **119 E3** 14 2 S 34 53 E
Lake Mburo Nat. Park, *Uganda* **118 C3** 0 33 S 30 56 E
Lake Mead Nat. Recr. Area, *U.S.A.* **161 K12** 36 15N 114 30W
Lake Mills, *Iowa, U.S.A.* **154 D8** 43 25N 93 32W
Lake Mills, *Wis., U.S.A.* **157 A8** 43 5N 88 55W
Lake Murray, *Papua N. G.* **132 D1** 6 48 S 141 29 E
Lake Nakura Nat. Park, *Kenya* **118 C4** 0 21 S 36 8 E
Lake Odessa, *U.S.A.* **157 B11** 42 47N 85 8W
Lake Orion, *U.S.A.* **157 B13** 42 47N 83 14W
Lake Park, *Fla., U.S.A.* **153 J9** 26 48N 80 3W
Lake Park, *Ga., U.S.A.* **152 E6** 30 41N 83 11W
Lake Placid, *Fla., U.S.A.* **153 H8** 27 18N 81 22W
Lake Placid, *N.Y., U.S.A.* **151 B11** 44 17N 73 59W
Lake Pleasant, *U.S.A.* **151 C10** 43 28N 74 25W
Lake Providence, *U.S.A.* **155 J9** 32 48N 91 10W
Lake Pukaki, *N.Z.* **131 E5** 44 11 S 170 8 E
Lake St. Peter, *Canada* **150 A6** 45 18N 78 2W
Lake Superior Prov. Park, *Canada* **140 C3** 47 45N 84 45W
Lake Tekapo, *N.Z.* **131 D5** 44 0 S 170 30 E
Lake View, *U.S.A.* **156 B1** 42 18N 95 3W
Lake Villa, *U.S.A.* **157 B8** 42 25N 88 5W
Lake Village, *U.S.A.* **155 J9** 33 20N 91 17W
Lake Wales, *U.S.A.* **149 M5** 27 54N 81 35W
Lake Worth, *U.S.A.* **149 M5** 26 37N 80 3W
Lake Zurich, *U.S.A.* **157 B8** 42 12N 88 5W
Lakeba, *Fiji* **133 B3** 18 13 S 178 47W
Lakeba Passage, *Fiji* **133 B3** 18 0 S 178 45W
Lakefield, *Canada* **140 D4** 44 25N 78 16W
Lakefield Nat. Park, *Australia* **126 B3** 15 24 S 144 26 E
Lakehurst, *U.S.A.* **151 F10** 40 1N 74 19W
Lakeland, *Australia* **126 B3** 15 49 S 144 57 E
Lakeland, *Fla., U.S.A.* **149 M5** 28 3N 81 57W
Lakeland, *Ga., U.S.A.* **152 D6** 31 2N 83 4W
Lakemba = Lakeba, *Fiji* **133 B3** 18 13 S 178 47W
Lakeport, *Calif., U.S.A.* **160 F4** 39 3N 122 55W
Lakeport, *Mich., U.S.A.* **150 C2** 43 7N 82 30W
Lakes Entrance, *Australia* **129 D8** 37 50 S 148 0 E
Lakeside, *Ariz., U.S.A.* **159 J9** 34 9N 109 58W
Lakeside, *Calif., U.S.A.* **161 N10** 32 52N 116 55W
Lakeside, *Nebr., U.S.A.* **154 D3** 42 3N 102 26W
Lakeside, *Ohio, U.S.A.* **150 E2** 41 32N 82 46W
Lakeview, *U.S.A.* **158 E3** 42 11N 120 21W
Lakeville, *U.S.A.* **154 C8** 44 39N 93 14W
Lakewood, *Colo., U.S.A.* **154 F2** 39 44N 105 5W
Lakewood, *N.J., U.S.A.* **151 F10** 40 6N 74 13W
Lakewood, *N.Y., U.S.A.* **150 D5** 42 6N 79 19W
Lakewood, *Ohio, U.S.A.* **150 E3** 41 29N 81 48W
Lakewood, *Wash., U.S.A.* **160 C4** 47 11N 122 32W
Lakha, *India* **92 F4** 26 9N 70 54 E
Lakhaniá, *Greece* **38 F11** 35 58N 27 54 E
Lakhimpur, *India* **93 F9** 27 57N 80 46 E
Lakhipur, *Assam, India* **90 C4** 24 48N 93 0 E
Lakhipur, *Assam, India* **90 B3** 26 2N 90 18 E
Lakhnadon, *India* **93 H8** 22 36N 79 36 E
Lakhonpheng, *Laos* **86 E5** 15 54N 105 34 E
Lakhpat, *India* **92 H3** 23 48N 68 47 E
Läki, *Azerbaijan* **61 K8** 40 34N 47 22 E
Laki, *Iceland* **11 C8** 64 4N 18 14W
Lakin, *U.S.A.* **155 G4** 37 57N 101 15W
Lakitusaki →, *Canada* **140 B3** 54 21N 82 25W
Lakki, *Pakistan* **92 C4** 32 36N 70 55 E
Lákkoi, *Greece* **39 E4** 35 24N 23 57 E
Lakonía □, *Greece* **48 E4** 36 55N 22 30 E
Lakonikós Kólpos, *Greece* **48 E4** 36 40N 22 40 E
Lakor, *Indonesia* **82 C3** 8 15 S 128 17 E
Lakota, *Ivory C.* **112 D3** 5 50N 5 30W
Lakota, *U.S.A.* **154 A5** 48 2N 98 21W
Laksar, *India* **92 E8** 29 46N 78 3 E
Laksefjorden, *Norway* **14 A22** 70 45N 26 50 E
Lakselv, *Norway* **14 A21** 70 2N 25 0 E
Laksettipet, *India* **94 E4** 18 52N 79 13 E
Lakshadweep □, *India* **95 J1** 10 0N 72 30 E
Lakshadweep Is., *India* **95 J1** 10 0N 72 30 E
Laksham, *Bangla.* **90 D3** 23 14N 91 8 E
Lakshimpur, *Bangla.* **90 D3** 22 58N 90 50 E
Lakshmanpur, *India* **93 H10** 22 58N 83 3 E
Lakshmeshwar, *India* **95 G2** 15 9N 75 28 E
Lakshmikantapur, *India* **93 H13** 22 5N 88 20 E
Lakuramau, *Papua N. G.* **132 B6** 2 54 S 151 15 E
Lal-lo, *Phil.* **80 B3** 18 12N 121 40 E
Lala, *Dem. Rep. of the Congo* **115 C4** 4 10 S 20 30 E
Lala, *Phil.* **81 H4** 7 59N 123 46 E
Lala Musa, *Pakistan* **92 C5** 32 40N 73 57 E
Lalaghat, *India* **90 C4** 24 30N 92 40 E
Lalago, *Tanzania* **118 C3** 3 28 S 33 58 E
Lalapanzi, *Zimbabwe* **119 F3** 19 20 S 30 15 E
Lalapaşa, *Turkey* **51 E10** 41 49N 26 44 E
Lalbenque, *France* **28 D5** 44 19N 1 34 E
Lalbert, *Australia* **128 C5** 35 38 S 143 20 E
L'Albufera, *Spain* **41 F4** 39 20N 0 27W
Lalganj, *India* **93 G11** 25 52N 85 13 E
Lalgola, *India* **93 G13** 24 25N 88 15 E
Lālī, *Iran* **97 C6** 32 21N 49 6 E
Lalibela, *Ethiopia* **107 E4** 12 3N 39 0 E
Lalin, *China* **75 B14** 45 12N 127 0 E
Lalín, *Spain* **42 C2** 42 40N 8 5W
Lalin He →, *China* **75 B13** 45 32N 125 40 E
Lalinde, *France* **28 D4** 44 50N 0 44 E
Lalitapur, *Nepal* **93 F11** 27 40N 85 20 E
Lalitpur, *India* **93 G8** 24 42N 78 28 E
Lalkua, *India* **93 E8** 29 5N 79 31 E
Lalm, *Norway* **18 C6** 61 50N 9 17 E
Lalsot, *India* **92 F7** 26 34N 76 20 E
Lam, *Vietnam* **86 B6** 21 21N 106 31 E
Lam Pao Res., *Thailand* **86 D4** 16 50N 103 15 E
Lama Kara, *Togo* **113 D5** 9 30N 1 15 E
Lamag, *Malaysia* **85 A5** 5 29N 117 49 E
Lamaipum, *Burma* **90 C6** 25 40N 97 57 E
Lamap, *Vanuatu* **133 F5** 16 26 S 167 43 E
Lamar, *Colo., U.S.A.* **154 F3** 38 5N 102 37W
Lamar, *Mo., U.S.A.* **155 G7** 37 30N 94 16W
Lamarque, *Argentina* **176 A3** 39 24 S 65 40W
Lamas, *Peru* **172 B2** 6 28 S 76 31W
Lamastre, *France* **29 D8** 44 59N 4 35 E
Lambach, *Austria* **34 C6** 48 6N 13 51 E
Lamballe, *France* **26 D4** 48 29N 2 31W
Lambaréné, *Gabon* **114 C2** 0 41 S 10 12 E
Lambasa = Labasa, *Fiji* **133 A2** 16 30 S 179 27 E
Lambay I., *Ireland* **23 C5** 53 29N 6 1W
Lambayeque □, *Peru* **172 B2** 6 45 S 80 0W
Lambert, C., *Papua N. G.* **132 C6** 4 11 S 151 31 E
Lambert Glacier, *Antarctica* **7 D6** 71 0 S 70 0 E
Lambert's Bay, *S. Africa* **116 E2** 32 5 S 18 17 E
Lambertville, *U.S.A.* **157 C13** 41 46N 83 35W
Lambesc, *France* **29 E9** 43 39N 5 16 E
Lambeth, *Canada* **150 D3** 42 54N 81 18W
Lambi, *Solomon Is.* **133 M10** 9 22 S 159 39 E
Lámbia, *Greece* **48 D3** 37 52N 21 53 E
Lambomakondro, *Madag.* **117 C7** 22 41 S 44 44 E
Lambon, *Papua N. G.* **132 C7** 4 45 S 152 48 E
Lambro →, *Italy* **44 C6** 45 8N 9 32 E
Lambu, *Papua N. G.* **132 B6** 3 18 S 151 43 E
Lambunao, *Phil.* **81 F4** 11 3N 122 29 E
Lamé, *Chad* **109 G2** 9 15N 14 32 E
Lame, *Nigeria* **113 C6** 10 30N 9 20 E
Lame Deer, *U.S.A.* **158 D10** 45 37N 106 40W
Lamego, *Portugal* **42 D3** 41 5N 7 52W
Lamèque, *Canada* **141 C7** 47 45N 64 38W
Lameroo, *Australia* **128 C4** 35 19 S 140 33 E
Lamesa, *U.S.A.* **155 J4** 32 44N 101 58W
Lamía, *Greece* **48 C4** 38 55N 22 26 E
Lamigan Pt., *Phil.* **81 H6** 6 48N 126 21 E
Lamine →, *U.S.A.* **156 F4** 38 59N 92 51W
Lamington Nat. Park, *Australia* **127 D5** 28 13 S 153 12 E
Lamitan, *Phil.* **81 H4** 6 39N 122 8 E
Lamlan, Mt., *Guam* **133 R15** 13 22N 144 41 E
Lamma I., *China* **69 G11** 22 12N 114 8 E
Lammermuir Hills, *U.K.* **22 F6** 55 50N 2 40W
Lammhult, *Sweden* **17 G8** 57 10N 14 35 E
Lamoille →, *U.S.A.* **151 B11** 44 38N 73 13W
Lamon B., *Phil.* **80 D4** 14 30N 122 20 E
Lamongan, *Indonesia* **85 D4** 7 7 S 112 25 E
Lamoni, *U.S.A.* **156 D3** 40 37N 93 56W
Lamont, *Canada* **142 C6** 53 46N 112 50W
Lamont, *Calif., U.S.A.* **161 K8** 35 15N 118 55W
Lamont, *Fla., U.S.A.* **152 E6** 30 23N 83 49W
Lamont, *Iowa, U.S.A.* **156 B5** 42 35N 91 40W
Lamont, *Wyo., U.S.A.* **158 E10** 42 13N 107 29W
Lamotte-Beuvron, *France* **27 E9** 47 36N 2 2 E
Lampa, *Peru* **172 D3** 15 22 S 70 22W
Lampang, *Thailand* **86 C2** 18 16N 99 32 E
Lampasas, *U.S.A.* **155 K5** 31 4N 98 11W
Lampazos de Naranjo, *Mexico* **162 B4** 27 2N 100 32W
Lampedusa, *Medit. S.* **111 A7** 35 36N 12 40 E
Lampertheim, *Germany* **31 F4** 49 35N 8 27 E
Lampeter, *U.K.* **21 E3** 52 7N 4 4W
Lampione, *Medit. S.* **108 A2** 35 33N 12 20 E
Lampman, *Canada* **143 D8** 49 25N 102 50W
Lamprechtshausen, *Austria* **34 D5** 48 0N 12 58 E
Lampung □, *Indonesia* **84 D2** 5 30 S 104 30 E
Lamta, *India* **93 H9** 22 8N 80 7 E
Lamu, *Burma* **90 F5** 19 14N 94 10 E
Lamu, *Kenya* **118 C5** 2 16 S 40 55 E
Lamud, *Peru* **172 B2** 6 10 S 77 57W
Lamy, *U.S.A.* **159 J11** 35 29N 105 53W
Lan Xian, *China* **74 E6** 38 15N 111 35 E
Lan Yu = Hungt'ou Hsü, *Taiwan* **77 G13** 22 0N 121 30 E
Lanai, *U.S.A.* **145 C5** 20 50N 156 55W
Lanai City, *U.S.A.* **145 C5** 20 50N 156 55W
Lanaihale, *U.S.A.* **145 C5** 20 49N 156 53W
Lanak La, *China* **93 B8** 34 27N 79 32 E
Lanak'o Shank'ou = Lanak La, *China* **93 B8** 34 27N 79 32 E
Lanao, L., *Phil.* **81 H5** 7 52N 124 15 E
Lanao del Norte □, *Phil.* **81 H5** 8 0N 124 10 E
Lanao del Sur □, *Phil.* **81 H5** 7 40N 124 15 E
Lanark, *Canada* **151 A8** 45 1N 76 22W
Lanark, *U.K.* **22 F5** 55 40N 3 47W
Lanark, *U.S.A.* **156 B7** 42 6N 89 50W
Lanbi Kyun, *Burma* **87 G2** 10 50N 98 20 E
Lancang, *China* **76 F2** 22 36N 99 58 E
Lancang Jiang →, *China* **76 G3** 21 40N 101 10 E
Lancashire □, *U.K.* **20 D5** 53 50N 2 48W
Lancaster, *Canada* **151 A10** 45 10N 74 30W
Lancaster, *U.K.* **20 C5** 54 3N 2 48W
Lancaster, *Calif., U.S.A.* **161 L8** 34 42N 118 8W
Lancaster, *Ky., U.S.A.* **148 G3** 37 37N 84 35W
Lancaster, *Mo., U.S.A.* **156 D4** 40 31N 92 32W
Lancaster, *N.H., U.S.A.* **151 B13** 44 29N 71 34W
Lancaster, *N.Y., U.S.A.* **150 D6** 42 54N 78 40W
Lancaster, *Ohio, U.S.A.* **148 F4** 39 43N 82 36W
Lancaster, *Pa., U.S.A.* **151 F8** 40 2N 76 19W
Lancaster, *S.C., U.S.A.* **149 H5** 34 43N 80 46W
Lancaster, *Wis., U.S.A.* **156 B6** 42 51N 90 43W
Lancaster Sd., *Canada* **139 A11** 74 13N 84 0W
Lancelin, *Australia* **125 F2** 31 0 S 115 18 E
Lanchow = Lanzhou, *China* **74 F2** 36 1N 103 52 E
Lanciano, *Italy* **45 F11** 42 14N 14 23 E
Lanco, *Chile* **176 A2** 39 24 S 72 46W
Lancones, *Peru* **172 A1** 4 30 S 80 30W
Lancun, *China* **75 F11** 36 25N 120 10 E
Łańcut, *Poland* **55 H9** 50 10N 22 13 E
Lancy, *Switz.* **32 D2** 46 12N 6 8 E
Landau, *Bayern, Germany* **31 G8** 48 40N 12 41 E
Landau, *Rhld-Pfz., Germany* **31 F4** 49 12N 8 6 E
Landay, *Afghan.* **91 C1** 30 31N 63 47 E
Landeck, *Austria* **34 D3** 47 9N 10 34 E
Lander, *U.S.A.* **158 E9** 42 50N 108 44W
Lander →, *Australia* **124 D5** 22 0 S 132 0 E
Landerneau, *France* **26 D2** 48 28N 4 17W
Landeryd, *Sweden* **17 G7** 57 7N 13 15 E
Landes, *France* **28 D2** 44 0N 1 0W
Landes □, *France* **28 E3** 43 57N 0 48W
Landete, *Spain* **40 F3** 39 56N 1 25W
Landfall I., *India* **95 H11** 13 40N 93 2 E
Landi Kotal, *Pakistan* **92 B4** 34 7N 71 6 E
Landisburg, *U.S.A.* **150 F7** 40 21N 77 19W
Landivisiau, *France* **26 D2** 48 31N 4 6W
Landquart, *Switz.* **33 C9** 46 58N 9 32 E
Landquart →, *Switz.* **33 C9** 46 50N 9 47 E
Landrecies, *France* **27 B10** 50 7N 3 40 E
Land's End, *U.K.* **21 G2** 50 4N 5 44W
Landsberg, *Germany* **31 G6** 48 2N 10 53 E
Landsborough Cr. →, *Australia* **126 C3** 22 28 S 144 35 E
Landsbro, *Sweden* **17 G8** 57 24N 14 56 E
Landshut, *Germany* **31 G8** 48 34N 12 8 E
Landskrona, *Sweden* **17 J6** 55 53N 12 50 E
Landstuhl, *Germany* **31 F3** 49 24N 7 33 E
Landvetter, *Sweden* **17 G6** 57 41N 12 17 E
Lane, *U.S.A.* **152 B10** 33 32N 79 53W
Lanesboro, *U.S.A.* **151 E9** 41 57N 75 34W
Lanester, *France* **26 E3** 47 46N 3 22W

Lanett, *U.S.A.* **152 C4** 32 52N 85 12W
Lang Qua, *Vietnam* **86 A5** 22 16N 104 27 E
Lang Shan, *China* **74 D4** 41 0N 106 30 E
Lang Son, *Vietnam* **76 G6** 21 52N 106 42 E
Lang Suan, *Thailand* **87 H2** 9 57N 99 4 E
Langå, *Denmark* **17 H3** 56 23N 9 54 E
Langa-Langa, *Dem. Rep. of the Congo* **114 C3** 3 50 S 15 59 E
Lángadhás, *Greece* **50 F7** 40 46N 23 6 E
Langádhia, *Greece* **48 D4** 37 43N 22 1 E
Långan →, *Sweden* **16 A8** 63 19N 14 44 E
Langanes, *Iceland* **11 A12** 66 20N 14 53W
Langano, L., *Ethiopia* **107 F4** 7 36N 38 43 E
Langar, *Afghan.* **65 E6** 37 2N 73 47 E
Langar, *Iran* **97 C9** 35 23N 60 25 E
Langara I., *Canada* **142 C2** 54 14N 133 1W
Långås, *Sweden* **17 H6** 56 58N 12 26 E
Langatabbetje, *Surinam* **169 C7** 4 59N 54 28W
Langdai, *China* **76 D5** 26 6N 105 21 E
Langdon, *U.S.A.* **154 A5** 48 45N 98 22W
Långe Jan = Ölands södra udde, *Sweden* **17 H10** 56 12N 16 23 E
Langeac, *France* **28 C7** 45 7N 3 29 E
Langeais, *France* **26 E7** 47 20N 0 24 E
Langeb Baraka →, *Sudan* **106 D4** 17 28N 36 50 E
Langeberg, *S. Africa* **116 E3** 33 55 S 21 0 E
Langeberge, *S. Africa* **116 D3** 28 15 S 22 33 E
Langeland, *Denmark* **17 K4** 54 56N 10 48 E
Langelands Bælt, *Denmark* **17 K4** 54 50N 10 55 E
Langen, *Austria* **33 B10** 47 8N 10 7 E
Langen, *Hessen, Germany* **31 F4** 49 59N 8 40 E
Langen, *Niedersachsen, Germany* **30 B4** 53 36N 8 36 E
Langenargen, *Germany* **33 A9** 47 36N 9 33 E
Langenburg, *Canada* **143 C8** 50 51N 101 43W
Langeneß, *Germany* **30 A4** 54 38N 8 36 E
Langenlois, *Austria* **34 C8** 48 29N 15 40 E
Langenthal, *Switz.* **32 B5** 47 13N 7 47 E
Langeoog, *Germany* **30 B3** 53 45N 7 32 E
Langeskov, *Denmark* **17 J4** 55 22N 10 35 E
Langesund, *Norway* **18 F6** 59 0N 9 45 E
Langevåg, *Norway* **18 B3** 62 26N 6 13 E
Länghem, *Sweden* **17 G7** 57 36N 13 14 E
Langhirano, *Italy* **44 D7** 44 37N 10 16 E
Langholm, *U.K.* **22 F5** 55 9N 3 0W
Langisjór, *Iceland* **11 C8** 64 11N 18 15W
Langjökull, *Iceland* **11 C6** 64 39N 20 12W
Langkawi, Pulau, *Malaysia* **87 J2** 6 25N 99 45 E
Langklip, *S. Africa* **116 D3** 28 12 S 20 20 E
Langkon, *Malaysia* **85 A5** 6 30N 116 40 E
Langlade, *St- P. & M.* **141 C8** 46 50N 56 20W
Langley, *Canada* **160 A4** 49 7N 122 39W
Langnau, *Switz.* **32 C5** 46 56N 7 47 E
Langogne, *France* **28 D7** 44 43N 3 50 E
Langon, *France* **28 D3** 44 33N 0 16W
Langøya, *Norway* **14 B16** 68 45N 14 50 E
Langreo, *Spain* **42 B5** 43 18N 5 40W
Langres, *France* **27 E12** 47 52N 5 20 E
Langres, Plateau de, *France* **27 E12** 47 45N 5 3 E
Langsa, *Indonesia* **84 B1** 4 30N 97 57 E
Långsele, *Sweden* **16 A11** 63 12N 17 4 E
Långshyttan, *Sweden* **16 D10** 60 27N 16 2 E
Langtao, *Burma* **90 B6** 27 15N 97 34 E
Langting, *India* **90 C4** 25 31N 93 7 E
Langtry, *U.S.A.* **155 L4** 29 49N 101 34W
Langu, *Thailand* **87 J2** 6 53N 99 47 E
Langue de Barbarie, Parc Nat. de la, *Senegal* **112 C1** 14 54N 16 30W
Languedoc, *France* **28 E7** 43 58N 3 55 E
Languedoc-Roussillon □, *France* **28 E6** 43 25N 3 0 E
Langwang, *China* **69 F9** 22 38N 113 27 E
Langwies, *Switz.* **33 C9** 46 50N 9 44 E
Langxi, *China* **77 B12** 31 10N 119 12 E
Langxiangzhen, *China* **74 E9** 39 43N 116 8 E
Langzhong, *China* **76 B5** 31 38N 105 58 E
Lanigan, *Canada* **143 C7** 51 51N 105 2W
Lanjigarh, *India* **94 E6** 19 43N 83 23 E
Lankao, *China* **74 G8** 34 48N 114 50 E
Länkäran, *Azerbaijan* **97 B6** 38 48N 48 52 E
Lanmeur, *France* **26 D3** 48 39N 3 43W
Lannemezan, *France* **28 E4** 43 8N 0 23 E
Lannilis, *France* **26 D2** 48 35N 4 32W
Lannion, *France* **26 D3** 48 46N 3 29W
L'Annonciation, *Canada* **140 C5** 46 25N 74 55W
Lanouaille, *France* **28 C5** 45 24N 1 9 E
Lanping, *China* **76 D2** 26 28N 99 15 E
Lansdale, *U.S.A.* **151 F9** 40 14N 75 17W
Lansdowne, *Australia* **129 A10** 31 48 S 152 30 E
Lansdowne, *Canada* **151 B8** 44 24N 76 1W
Lansdowne, *India* **93 E8** 29 50N 78 41 E
Lansdowne House, *Canada* **140 B2** 52 14N 87 53W
L'Anse, *U.S.A.* **148 B1** 46 45N 88 27W
L'Anse au Loup, *Canada* **141 B8** 51 32N 56 50W
L'Anse aux Meadows, *Canada* **141 B8** 51 36N 55 32W
L'Anse la Raye, *St. Lucia* **165 f** 13 55N 61 19W
Lansford, *U.S.A.* **151 F9** 40 50N 75 53W
Lanshan, *China* **77 E9** 25 24N 112 10 E
Lansing, *U.S.A.* **157 B12** 42 44N 84 33W
Lanslebourg-Mont-Cenis, *France* **29 C10** 45 17N 6 52 E
Lanta Yai, Ko, *Thailand* **87 J2** 7 35N 99 3 E
Lantana, *U.S.A.* **153 J9** 26 35N 80 3W
Lantau I., *China* **69 G10** 22 15N 113 56 E
Lantewa, *Nigeria* **113 C7** 12 16N 11 44 E
Lantian, *China* **74 G5** 34 11N 109 20 E
Lanus, *Argentina* **174 C4** 34 44 S 58 27W
Lanusei, *Italy* **46 C2** 39 52N 9 34 E
Lanuza, *Phil.* **81 G6** 9 14N 126 4 E
Lanxi, *China* **77 C12** 29 13N 119 28 E
Lanzarote, *Canary Is.* **9 e2** 29 0N 13 40W
Lanzhou, *China* **74 F2** 36 1N 103 52 E
Lanzo Torinese, *Italy* **44 C4** 45 16N 7 28 E
Lao →, *Italy* **47 C8** 39 47N 15 48 E
Lao Bao, *Laos* **86 D6** 16 35N 106 30 E
Lao Cai, *Vietnam* **76 F4** 22 30N 103 57 E
Laoag, *Phil.* **80 B3** 18 7N 120 34 E
Laoang, *Phil.* **80 E5** 12 32N 125 8 E
Laoha He →, *China* **75 C11** 43 25N 120 35 E
Laohekou, *China* **77 A8** 32 22N 111 38 E
Laois □, *Ireland* **23 D4** 52 57N 7 36W
Laon, *France* **27 C10** 49 33N 3 35 E
Laona, *U.S.A.* **148 C1** 45 34N 88 40W
Laos ■, *Asia* **86 D5** 17 45N 105 0 E
Lapa, *Brazil* **175 B6** 25 46 S 49 44W
Lapac I., *Phil.* **81 J3** 5 32N 120 47 E
Lapai, *Nigeria* **113 D6** 9 5N 6 32 E
Lapalisse, *France* **27 F10** 46 15N 3 38 E
Lapap I., *Phil.* **81 J2** 5 57N 120 0 E
Lapeer, *U.S.A.* **157 A13** 43 3N 83 19W
Lapeyrade, *France* **28 D3** 44 4N 0 3W
Lapithos, *Cyprus* **39 E9** 35 21N 33 11 E
Lapland = Lappland, *Europe* **14 B21** 68 7N 24 0 E
Laporte, *U.S.A.* **151 E8** 41 25N 76 30W
Lapovo, *Serbia, Yug.* **50 B5** 44 10N 21 7 E
Lappeenranta, *Finland* **15 F23** 61 3N 28 12 E
Lappland, *Europe* **14 B21** 68 7N 24 0 E
Laprida, *Argentina* **174 D3** 37 34 S 60 45W
Lapseki, *Turkey* **51 F10** 40 20N 26 41 E
Laptev Sea, *Russia* **67 B13** 76 0N 125 0 E
Lapu-Lapu, *Phil.* **81 F4** 10 20N 123 55 E
Lapua, *Finland* **14 E20** 62 58N 23 0 E
Lăpuş →, *Romania* **53 C8** 47 25N 23 40 E
Lapuş, Munţii, *Romania* **53 C8** 47 20N 23 50 E
Lăpuşna, *Moldova* **53 D13** 46 53N 28 25 E
Łapy, *Poland* **55 F9** 52 59N 22 52 E
Laqiya Arba'in, *Sudan* **106 C2** 20 1N 28 1 E
Laqiya Umran, *Sudan* **106 D2** 19 55N 28 18 E
L'Áquila, *Italy* **45 F10** 42 22N 13 22 E
Lār, *Āzarbājān-e Sharqī, Iran* **96 B5** 38 30N 47 52 E
Lār, *Fārs, Iran* **97 E7** 27 40N 54 14 E
Lara, *Australia* **128 E6** 38 2 S 144 26 E
Lara □, *Venezuela* **168 A4** 10 10N 69 50W
Larabanga, *Ghana* **112 D4** 9 16N 1 56W
Larache, *Morocco* **110 A3** 35 10N 6 5W
Laragne-Montéglin, *France* **29 D9** 44 18N 5 49 E
Laramie, *U.S.A.* **154 E2** 41 19N 105 35W
Laramie →, *U.S.A.* **158 F11** 42 13N 104 33W
Laramie Mts., *U.S.A.* **154 E2** 42 0N 105 30W
Laranjeiras, *Brazil* **170 D4** 10 48 S 37 10W
Laranjeiras do Sul, *Brazil* **175 B5** 25 23 S 52 23W
Larantuka, *Indonesia* **82 C2** 8 21 S 122 55 E
Larat, *Indonesia* **83 C4** 7 0 S 132 0 E
L'Arbresle, *France* **29 C8** 45 50N 4 36 E
Lärbro, *Sweden* **17 G12** 57 47N 18 50 E
Lårdal, *Norway* **18 E5** 59 25N 8 10 E
Larde, *Mozam.* **119 F4** 16 28 S 39 43 E
Larder Lake, *Canada* **140 C4** 48 5N 79 40W
Lardhos, Ákra = Líndhos, Ákra, *Greece* **38 E12** 36 4N 28 10 E
Lardhos, Órmos, *Greece* **38 E12** 36 4N 28 2 E
Laredo, *Spain* **42 B7** 43 26N 3 28W
Laredo, *U.S.A.* **155 M5** 27 30N 99 30W
Laredo Sd., *Canada* **142 C3** 52 30N 128 53W
Larena, *Phil.* **81 G4** 9 15N 123 35 E
Largentière, *France* **29 D8** 44 34N 4 18 E
L'Argentière-la-Bessée, *France* **29 D10** 44 47N 6 33 E
Largo, *U.S.A.* **149 M4** 27 55N 82 47W
Largo, Key, *U.S.A.* **153 K9** 25 15N 80 15W
Largs, *U.K.* **22 F4** 55 47N 4 52W
Lari, *Italy* **44 E7** 43 34N 10 35 E
Lariang, *Indonesia* **82 B1** 1 26 S 119 17 E
Larimore, *U.S.A.* **154 B6** 47 54N 97 38W
Lārīn, *Iran* **97 C7** 35 55N 52 19 E
Larino, *Italy* **45 G11** 41 48N 14 54 E
Lárisa, *Greece* **48 B4** 39 36N 22 27 E
Lárisa □, *Greece* **48 B4** 39 39N 22 24 E
Larkana, *Pakistan* **91 D3** 27 32N 68 18 E
Larnaca, *Cyprus* **39 F9** 34 55N 33 38 E
Larnaca Bay, *Cyprus* **39 F9** 34 53N 33 45 E
Larne, *U.K.* **23 B6** 54 51N 5 51W
Larned, *U.S.A.* **154 F5** 38 11N 99 6W
Laroquebrou, *France* **28 D6** 44 58N 2 12 E
Larose, *U.S.A.* **155 L9** 29 34N 90 23W
Larrimah, *Australia* **124 C5** 15 35 S 133 12 E
Larsen Bay, *U.S.A.* **144 H9** 57 32N 153 59W
Larsen Ice Shelf, *Antarctica* **7 C17** 67 0 S 62 0W
Laruns, *France* **28 F3** 43 0N 0 26W
Larvik, *Norway* **15 G14** 59 4N 10 2 E
Larzac, Causse du, *France* **28 E7** 43 50N 3 17 E
Las Alpujarras, *Spain* **41 J1** 36 55N 3 20W
Las Animas, *U.S.A.* **154 F3** 38 4N 103 13W
Las Anod, *Somali Rep.* **120 C3** 8 26N 47 19 E
Las Arenas, *Spain* **42 B6** 43 17N 4 50W
Las Aves, Is., *W. Indies* **165 C7** 15 45N 63 55W
Las Bonitas, *Venezuela* **168 B4** 7 52N 65 40W
Las Brenãs, *Argentina* **174 B3** 27 5 S 61 7W
Las Cabezas de San Juan, *Spain* **43 J5** 36 57N 5 58W
Las Chimeneas, *Mexico* **161 N10** 32 8N 116 5W
Las Coloradas, *Argentina* **176 A2** 39 34 S 70 36W
Las Cruces, *U.S.A.* **159 K10** 32 19N 106 47W
Las Flores, *Argentina* **174 D4** 36 10 S 59 7W
Las Heras, *Argentina* **174 C2** 32 51 S 68 49W
Las Horquetas, *Argentina* **176 C2** 48 14 S 71 11W
Las Khoreh, *Somali Rep.* **120 B3** 11 10N 48 20 E
Las Lajas, *Argentina* **176 A2** 38 30 S 70 25W
Las Lomas, *Peru* **172 A1** 4 40 S 80 10W
Las Lomitas, *Argentina* **174 A3** 24 43 S 60 35W
Las Marismas, *Spain* **43 H4** 37 5N 6 20W
Las Mercedes, *Venezuela* **168 B4** 9 7N 66 24W
Las Minas, *Spain* **41 G3** 38 20N 1 41W
Las Navas de la Concepción, *Spain* **43 H5** 37 56N 5 30W
Las Navas del Marqués, *Spain* **42 E6** 40 36N 4 20W
Las Nieves, *Phil.* **81 G5** 8 46N 125 34 E
Las Palmas, *Argentina* **174 B4** 27 8 S 58 45W
Las Palmas, *Canary Is.* **9 e1** 28 7N 15 26W
Las Palmas →, *Mexico* **161 N10** 32 26N 116 54W
Las Pedroñas, *Spain* **41 F2** 39 26N 2 40W
Las Piedras, *Uruguay* **175 C4** 34 44 S 56 14W
Las Pipinas, *Argentina* **174 D4** 35 30 S 57 19W
Las Plumas, *Argentina* **176 B3** 43 40 S 67 15W
Las Rosas, *Argentina* **174 C3** 32 30 S 61 35W
Las Rozas, *Spain* **42 E7** 40 29N 3 52W
Las Tablas, *Panama* **164 E3** 7 49N 80 14W
Las Termas, *Argentina* **174 B3** 27 29 S 64 52W
Las Toscas, *Argentina* **174 B4** 28 21 S 59 18W
Las Truchas, *Mexico* **162 D4** 17 57N 102 13W
Las Varillas, *Argentina* **174 C3** 31 50 S 62 50W
Las Vegas, *N. Mex., U.S.A.* **159 J11** 35 36N 105 13W
Las Vegas, *Nev., U.S.A.* **161 J11** 36 10N 115 9W
Lasanga I., *Papua N. G.* **132 D4** 7 25 S 147 15 E
Lasarte, *Spain* **40 B2** 43 16N 2 1W
Lascano, *Uruguay* **175 C5** 33 35 S 54 12W
Lascelles, *Australia* **128 C5** 35 34 S 142 34 E
Lash-e Joveyn, *Afghan.* **91 C1** 31 45N 61 30 E
Lashburn, *Canada* **143 C7** 53 10N 109 40W
Lashio, *Burma* **90 D6** 22 56N 97 45 E
Lashkar, *India* **92 F8** 26 10N 78 10 E
Lashkar Gāh, *Afghan.* **91 C2** 31 35N 64 21 E
Łasin, *Poland* **54 E6** 53 30N 19 2 E
Lasíthi, *Greece* **39 E6** 35 11N 25 31 E
Lasíthi □, *Greece* **39 E6** 35 5N 25 50 E
Lāsjerd, *Iran* **97 C7** 35 24N 53 4 E
Lask, *Poland* **55 G6** 51 34N 19 8 E
Łaskarzew, *Poland* **55 G8** 51 48N 21 36 E
Laško, *Slovenia* **45 B12** 46 10N 15 16 E
Lassance, *Brazil* **171 E3** 17 54 S 44 34W
Lassay-les-Châteaux, *France* **26 D6** 48 27N 0 30W
Lassen Pk., *U.S.A.* **158 F3** 40 29N 121 31W
Lassen Volcanic Nat. Park, *U.S.A.* **158 F3** 40 30N 121 20W
Lassongo, *Angola* **115 E4** 12 5 S 22 46 E
Last Mountain L., *Canada* **143 C7** 51 5N 105 14W
Lastchance Cr. →, *U.S.A.* **160 E5** 40 2N 121 15W
Lastoursville, *Gabon* **114 C2** 0 55 S 12 38 E
Lastovo, *Croatia* **45 F13** 42 46N 16 55 E
Lastovski Kanal, *Croatia* **45 F14** 42 50N 17 0 E
Lat Yao, *Thailand* **86 E2** 15 45N 99 48 E
Latacunga, *Ecuador* **168 D2** 0 50 S 78 35W
Latakia = Al Lādhiqīyah, *Syria* **100 E6** 35 30N 35 45 E
Latchford, *Canada* **140 C4** 47 20N 79 50W
Late, *Tonga* **133 P13** 18 48 S 174 39W
Latehar, *India* **93 H11** 23 45N 84 30 E
Laterza, *Italy* **47 B9** 40 37N 16 48 E
Latham, *Australia* **125 E2** 29 44 S 116 20 E
Lathen, *Germany* **30 C3** 52 52N 7 19 E
Lathi, *India* **92 F4** 27 43N 71 23 E
Lathi, *Vanuatu* **133 D5** 14 57 S 167 8 E
Lathrop, *U.S.A.* **156 E2** 39 33N 94 20W
Lathrop Wells, *U.S.A.* **161 J10** 36 39N 116 24W
Latiano, *Italy* **47 B10** 40 33N 17 43 E
Latina, *Italy* **46 A5** 41 28N 12 52 E
Latisana, *Italy* **45 C10** 45 47N 13 0 E
Latium = Lazio □, *Italy* **45 F9** 42 10N 12 30 E
Laton, *U.S.A.* **160 J7** 36 26N 119 41W
Latorytsya →, *Slovak Rep.* **35 C14** 48 28N 21 50 E
Latouche Treville, C., *Australia* **124 C3** 18 27 S 121 49 E
Latouma, *Niger* **109 D2** 22 10N 14 50 E
Látrar, *Iceland* **11 A3** 66 24N 23 2W
Latrobe, *Australia* **127 G4** 41 14 S 146 30 E
Latrobe, *U.S.A.* **150 F5** 40 19N 79 23W
Latrónico, *Italy* **47 B9** 40 5N 16 1 E
Latur, *India* **94 E3** 18 25N 76 40 E
Latvia ■, *Europe* **15 H20** 56 50N 24 0 E
Lau, *Nigeria* **113 D7** 9 11N 11 19 E
Lau Fau Shan, *China* **69 G10** 22 28N 113 59 E
Lau Group, *Fiji* **133 A3** 17 0 S 178 30W
Lauca →, *Bolivia* **172 D4** 19 9 S 68 10W
Lauchhammer, *Germany* **30 D9** 51 29N 13 47 E
Lauda-Königshofen, *Germany* **31 F5** 49 33N 9 42 E
Laudal, *Norway* **18 F4** 58 15N 7 30 E
Lauenburg, *Germany* **30 B6** 53 22N 10 32 E
Lauf, *Germany* **31 F7** 49 30N 11 16 E
Laufás, *Iceland* **11 B8** 65 53N 18 4W
Läufelfingen, *Switz.* **32 B5** 47 24N 7 52 E
Laufen, *Switz.* **32 B5** 47 25N 7 30 E
Laugar, *Iceland* **11 B5** 65 15N 21 48W
Laugarás, *Iceland* **11 C6** 64 7N 20 30W
Laugarbakki, *Iceland* **11 B6** 65 20N 20 55W
Laugarvatn, *Iceland* **11 C6** 64 13N 20 44W
Laughlin, *U.S.A.* **159 J6** 35 8N 114 35W
Laujar de Andarax, *Spain* **41 H2** 37 0N 2 54W
Laukaa, *Finland* **15 E21** 62 24N 25 56 E
Launceston, *Australia* **127 G4** 41 24 S 147 8 E
Launceston, *U.K.* **21 G3** 50 38N 4 22W
Laune →, *Ireland* **23 D2** 52 7N 9 47W
Launglon Bok, *Burma* **86 F1** 13 50N 97 54 E
Laupheim, *Germany* **31 G5** 48 14N 9 52 E
Laura, *Queens., Australia* **126 B3** 15 32 S 144 32 E
Laura, *S. Austral., Australia* **128 B3** 33 10 S 138 18 E
Laureana di Borrello, *Italy* **47 D9** 38 30N 16 5 E
Laurel, *Fla., U.S.A.* **153 H7** 27 8N 82 27W
Laurel, *Ind., U.S.A.* **157 E11** 39 31N 85 11W
Laurel, *Miss., U.S.A.* **155 K10** 31 41N 89 8W
Laurel, *Mont., U.S.A.* **158 D9** 45 40N 108 46W
Laurel Bay, *U.S.A.* **152 C9** 32 27N 80 47W
Laurencekirk, *U.K.* **22 E6** 56 50N 2 28W
Laurens, *Iowa, U.S.A.* **156 B2** 42 51N 94 52W
Laurens, *S.C., U.S.A.* **149 H4** 34 30N 82 1W
Laurentian Plateau, *Canada* **141 B6** 52 0N 70 0W
Lauria, *Italy* **47 B8** 40 2N 15 50 E
Laurie L., *Canada* **143 B8** 56 35N 101 57W
Laurinburg, *U.S.A.* **149 H6** 34 47N 79 28W
Laurium, *U.S.A.* **148 B1** 47 14N 88 27W
Lausanne, *Switz.* **32 C3** 46 32N 6 38 E
Laut, *Indonesia* **85 B3** 4 45N 108 0 E
Laut, Pulau, *Indonesia* **85 C5** 3 40 S 116 10 E
Laut Kecil, Kepulauan, *Indonesia* **85 C5** 4 45 S 115 40 E
Lautaro, *Chile* **176 A2** 38 31 S 72 27W
Lautem, *E. Timor* **82 C3** 8 22 S 126 54 E
Lauterbach, *Germany* **30 E5** 50 37N 9 24 E
Lauterbrunnen, *Switz.* **32 C5** 46 36N 7 55 E
Lauterecken, *Germany* **31 F3** 49 38N 7 35 E
Lautoka, *Fiji* **133 A1** 17 37 S 177 27 E
Lauzès, *France* **28 D5** 44 34N 1 35 E
Lavagh More, *Ireland* **23 B3** 54 46N 8 6W
Lavagna, *Italy* **44 D6** 44 18N 9 20 E
Laval, *France* **26 D6** 48 4N 0 48W
Lavalle, *Argentina* **174 B2** 28 15 S 65 15W
Lavanggu, *Solomon Is.* **133 N11** 11 36 S 160 16 E
Lavant Station, *Canada* **151 A8** 45 3N 76 42W
Lāvar Meydān, *Iran* **97 D7** 30 20N 54 30 E
Lávara, *Greece* **51 E10** 41 19N 26 22 E
Lavardac, *France* **28 D4** 44 12N 0 20 E
Lavaur, *France* **28 E5** 43 40N 1 49 E
Lavaux, *Switz.* **32 D3** 46 30N 6 45 E
Lavelanet, *France* **28 F5** 42 57N 1 51 E
Lavello, *Italy* **47 A8** 41 3N 15 48 E
L'Averdy, C., *Papua N. G.* **132 C8** 5 33 S 155 4 E
Lavers Hill, *Australia* **128 E5** 38 40 S 143 25 E
Laverton, *Australia* **125 E3** 28 44 S 122 29 E
Lavik, *Norway* **18 C2** 61 6N 5 25 E
Lavis, *Italy* **44 B8** 46 8N 11 7 E
Lávkos, *Greece* **48 B5** 39 9N 23 14 E
Lavos, *Portugal* **42 E2** 40 6N 8 49W
Lavradio, *Portugal* **43 G1** 38 40N 9 3W
Lavras, *Brazil* **171 F3** 21 20 S 45 0W
Lavre, *Portugal* **43 G2** 38 46N 8 22W
Lávrion, *Greece* **48 D6** 37 40N 24 4 E
Lávris, *Greece* **39 E5** 35 25N 24 40 E
Lavumisa, *Swaziland* **117 D5** 27 20 S 31 55 E
Lavushi Manda Nat. Park, *Zambia* **119 E3** 12 46 S 31 0 E
Lawa, *Phil.* **81 H5** 6 12N 125 41 E
Lawa-an, *Phil.* **81 F5** 11 51N 125 5 E
Lawaki, *Fiji* **133 A2** 17 40 S 178 35 E
Lawas, *Malaysia* **85 B5** 4 55N 115 25 E
Lawdar, *Yemen* **98 D4** 13 53N 45 52 E
Lawele, *Indonesia* **82 C2** 5 13 S 122 57 E
Lawksawk, *Burma* **90 E6** 21 15N 96 52 E
Lawn Hill Nat. Park, *Australia* **126 B2** 18 15 S 138 6 E
Lawowa, *Indonesia* **82 B2** 4 26 S 122 56 E
Lawqah, *Si. Arabia* **96 D4** 29 49N 42 45 E
Lawra, *Ghana* **112 C4** 10 39N 2 51W
Lawrence, *N.Z.* **131 F4** 45 55 S 169 41 E
Lawrence, *Ind., U.S.A.* **157 E10** 39 50N 86 2W
Lawrence, *Kans., U.S.A.* **154 F7** 38 58N 95 14W
Lawrence, *Mass., U.S.A.* **151 D13** 42 43N 71 10W
Lawrenceburg, *Ind., U.S.A.* **157 E12** 39 6N 84 52W
Lawrenceburg, *Ky., U.S.A.* **157 F12** 38 2N 84 54W
Lawrenceburg, *Tenn., U.S.A.* **149 H2** 35 14N 87 20W
Lawrenceville, *Ga., U.S.A.* **152 B6** 33 57N 83 59W
Lawrenceville, *Ill., U.S.A.* **157 F9** 38 44N 87 41W
Lawrenceville, *Pa., U.S.A.* **150 E7** 41 59N 77 8W
Laws, *U.S.A.* **160 H8** 37 24N 118 20W
Lawson, *U.S.A.* **156 E2** 39 26N 94 12W
Lawtey, *U.S.A.* **152 E7** 30 3N 82 5W
Lawton, *Mich., U.S.A.* **157 B11** 42 10N 85 50W
Lawton, *Okla., U.S.A.* **155 H5** 34 37N 98 25W
Lawu, *Indonesia* **85 D4** 7 40 S 111 13 E
Lawz, J. al, *Si. Arabia* **106 B4** 28 39N 35 18 E
Laxå, *Sweden* **17 F8** 58 59N 14 37 E
Laxamýri, *Iceland* **11 B9** 65 58N 17 24W
Laxford, L., *U.K.* **22 C3** 58 24N 5 6W
Laxou, *France* **27 D13** 48 41N 6 8 E
Lay →, *France* **28 B2** 46 18N 1 17W
Layla, *Si. Arabia* **98 B4** 22 10N 46 40 E
Laylān, *Iraq* **96 C5** 35 18N 44 31 E
Layon →, *France* **26 E6** 47 20N 0 45W
Laysan I., *U.S.A.* **145 F9** 25 50N 171 50W
Layton, *Fla., U.S.A.* **153 L9** 24 50N 80 47W
Layton, *Utah, U.S.A.* **158 F7** 41 4N 111 58W
Laytonville, *U.S.A.* **158 G2** 39 41N 123 29W
Laza, *Burma* **90 B6** 26 30N 97 38 E
Lazaráta, *Greece* **39 B2** 38 47N 20 40 E
Lazarevac, *Serbia, Yug.* **50 B4** 44 23N 20 17 E
Lazarevskoye, *Russia* **61 J4** 43 55N 39 21 E
Lazarivo, *Madag.* **117 C8** 23 54 S 44 59 E
Lazdijai, *Lithuania* **54 D10** 54 14N 23 31 E
Lazi, *Phil.* **81 G4** 9 8N 123 38 E
Lazio □, *Italy* **45 F9** 42 10N 12 30 E
Lazo, *Moldova* **53 C13** 47 33N 28 2 E
Lazo, *Russia* **70 C6** 43 25N 133 55 E
Le Beausset, *France* **29 E9** 43 12N 5 48 E
Le Blanc, *France* **28 B5** 46 37N 1 3 E
Le Bleymard, *France* **28 D7** 44 30N 3 42 E
Le Bourgneuf-la-Fôret, *France* **26 D6** 48 10N 0 59W
Le Brassus, *Switz.* **32 C2** 46 35N 6 13 E
Le Bugue, *France* **28 D4** 44 55N 0 56 E
Le Canourgue = La Canourgue, *France* **28 D7** 44 26N 3 13 E
Le Cateau Cambrésis, *France* **27 B10** 50 7N 3 32 E
Le Caylar, *France* **28 E7** 43 51N 3 19 E
Le Châble, *Switz.* **32 D4** 46 5N 7 12 E
Le Chambon-Feugerolles, *France* **29 C8** 45 24N 4 19 E
Le Châtelard, *Switz.* **32 D3** 46 4N 6 57 E
Le Châtelet, *France* **27 F9** 46 38N 2 16 E
Le Chesne, *France* **27 C11** 49 30N 4 45 E
Le Cheylard, *France* **29 D8** 44 55N 4 25 E
Le Claire, *Iowa, U.S.A.* **156 C6** 41 36N 90 21W
Le Claire, *Iowa, U.S.A.* **156 C6** 41 36N 90 20W
Le Conquet, *France* **26 D2** 48 21N 4 46W
Le Creusot, *France* **27 F11** 46 48N 4 24 E
Le Croisic, *France* **26 E4** 47 18N 2 30W
Le Donjon, *France* **27 F10** 46 22N 3 48 E
Le Dorat, *France* **28 B5** 46 14N 1 5 E
Le François, *Martinique* **164 c** 14 38N 60 57W
Le Grand-Lucé, *France* **26 E7** 47 52N 0 28 E
Le Grand-Pressigny, *France* **26 F7** 46 55N 0 48 E
Le Grand-Quevilly, *France* **26 C8** 49 24N 1 3 E
Le Gris Gris, *Mauritius* **121 d** 20 31 S 57 32 E
Le Havre, *France* **26 C7** 49 30N 0 5 E
Le Lamentin, *Martinique* **164 c** 14 35N 61 2W
Le Lavandou, *France* **29 E10** 43 8N 6 22 E
Le Lion-d'Angers, *France* **26 E6** 47 37N 0 43W
Le Locle, *Switz.* **32 B3** 47 3N 6 44 E
Le Louroux-Béconnais, *France* **26 E6** 47 30N 0 55W
Le Luc, *France* **29 E10** 43 23N 6 21 E
Le Lude, *France* **26 E7** 47 39N 0 9 E
Le Maire, Estr. de, *Argentina* **176 D4** 54 50 S 65 0W
Le Mans, *France* **26 E7** 48 0N 0 10 E
Le Marin, *Martinique* **164 c** 14 27N 60 55W
Le Mars, *U.S.A.* **154 D6** 42 47N 96 10W
Le Mayet-de-Montagne, *France* **27 F10** 46 4N 3 40 E
Le Mêle-sur-Sarthe, *France* **26 D7** 48 31N 0 22 E
Le Moléson, *Switz.* **32 C4** 46 33N 7 1 E
Le Monastier-sur-Gazeille, *France* **28 D7** 44 57N 3 59 E
Le Monêtier-les-Bains, *France* **29 D10** 44 58N 6 30 E
Le Mont-Dore, *France* **28 C6** 45 35N 2 49 E
Le Mont-St-Michel, *France* **26 D5** 48 40N 1 30W
Le Muy, *France* **29 E10** 43 28N 6 34 E
Le Palais, *France* **26 E3** 47 20N 3 10W
Le Perthus, *France* **28 F6** 42 30N 2 53 E
Le Pont, *Switz.* **32 C2** 46 41N 6 20 E
Le Port, *Réunion* **121 c** 20 56 S 55 18 E
Le Prêcheur, *Martinique* **164 c** 14 50N 61 12W
Le Puy-en-Velay, *France* **28 C7** 45 3N 3 52 E
Le Robert, *Martinique* **164 c** 14 40N 60 56W
Le Roy, *U.S.A.* **157 D8** 40 21N 88 46W
Le St-Esprit, *Martinique* **164 c** 14 34N 60 56W
Le Sentier, *Switz.* **32 C2** 46 37N 6 15 E
Le Sueur, *U.S.A.* **154 C8** 44 28N 93 55W
Le Tampon, *Réunion* **121 c** 21 16 S 55 32 E
Le Teil, *France* **29 D8** 44 33N 4 40 E
Le Teilleul, *France* **26 D6** 48 32N 0 53W
Le Theil, *France* **26 D7** 48 16N 0 42 E
Le Thillot, *France* **27 E13** 47 52N 6 46 E
Le Thuy, *Vietnam* **86 D6** 17 14N 106 49 E
Le Touquet-Paris-Plage, *France* **27 B8** 50 30N 1 36 E
Le Tréport, *France* **26 B8** 50 3N 1 20 E
Le Val-d'Ajol, *France* **27 E13** 47 55N 6 30 E
Le Verdon-sur-Mer, *France* **28 C2** 45 33N 1 4W
Le Vigan, *France* **28 E7** 43 59N 3 36 E
Lea →, *U.K.* **21 F8** 51 31N 0 1 E
Lea Lea, *Papua N. G.* **132 E4** 9 17 S 146 59 E
Leach, *Cambodia* **87 F4** 12 21N 103 46 E
Lead, *U.S.A.* **154 C3** 44 21N 103 46W
Leader, *Canada* **143 C7** 50 50N 109 30W
Leadville, *U.S.A.* **159 G10** 39 15N 106 18W
Leaf →, *U.S.A.* **155 K10** 30 59N 88 44W
Leaf Rapids, *Canada* **143 B9** 56 30N 99 59W
Leaghur, L., *Australia* **128 B5** 33 35 S 143 3 E
Lealui, *Zambia* **115 F4** 15 10 S 23 2 E
Leamington, *Canada* **140 D3** 42 3N 82 36W
Leamington, *N.Z.* **130 D4** 37 55 S 175 30 E
Leamington, *U.S.A.* **158 G7** 39 32N 112 17W
Leamington Spa = Royal Leamington Spa, *U.K.* **21 E6** 52 18N 1 31W
Le'an, *China* **77 D10** 27 22N 115 48 E
Leandro Norte Alem, *Argentina* **175 B4** 27 34 S 55 15W
Leane, L., *Ireland* **23 D2** 52 2N 9 32W
Learmonth, *Australia* **124 D1** 22 13 S 114 10 E
Leary, *U.S.A.* **152 D5** 31 29N 84 31W
Leask, *Canada* **143 C7** 53 5N 106 45W
Leatherhead, *U.K.* **21 F7** 51 18N 0 20W
Leavenworth, *Ind., U.S.A.* **157 F10** 38 12N 86 21W
Leavenworth, *Kans., U.S.A.* **154 F7** 39 19N 94 55W
Leavenworth, *Wash., U.S.A.* **158 C3** 47 36N 120 40W
Leawood, *U.S.A.* **156 F2** 38 57N 94 37W
Łeba, *Poland* **54 D4** 54 45N 17 32 E
Łeba →, *Poland* **54 D4** 54 46N 17 33 E
Lebach, *Germany* **31 F2** 49 25N 6 54 E
Lebak, *Phil.* **81 H5** 6 32N 124 5 E
Lebam, *U.S.A.* **160 D3** 46 34N 123 33W
Lebane, *Serbia, Yug.* **50 D5** 42 56N 21 44 E
Lebango, *Congo* **114 B2** 0 39N 14 21 E
Lebango →, *Congo* **114 B2** 0 2N 14 52 E
Lebanon, *Ill., U.S.A.* **156 F7** 38 38N 89 49W
Lebanon, *Ind., U.S.A.* **157 D10** 40 3N 86 28W
Lebanon, *Kans., U.S.A.* **154 F5** 39 49N 98 33W
Lebanon, *Ky., U.S.A.* **148 G3** 37 34N 85 15W
Lebanon, *Mo., U.S.A.* **155 G8** 37 41N 92 40W
Lebanon, *N.H., U.S.A.* **151 C12** 43 39N 72 15W
Lebanon, *Ohio, U.S.A.* **157 E12** 39 26N 84 13W
Lebanon, *Oreg., U.S.A.* **158 D2** 44 32N 122 55W
Lebanon, *Pa., U.S.A.* **151 F8** 40 20N 76 26W
Lebanon, *Tenn., U.S.A.* **149 G2** 36 12N 86 18W
Lebanon ■, *Asia* **103 B5** 34 0N 36 0 E
Lebanon Junction, *U.S.A.* **157 G11** 37 50N 85 44W
Lebec, *U.S.A.* **161 L8** 34 50N 118 52W
Lebedyan, *Russia* **59 F10** 53 0N 39 10 E
Lebedyn, *Ukraine* **59 G8** 50 35N 34 30 E
Lebel-sur-Quévillon, *Canada* **140 C4** 49 3N 76 59W
Lebo, *Dem. Rep. of the Congo* **114 B4** 4 30N 23 58 E
Lebomboberge, *S. Africa* **117 C5** 24 30 S 32 0 E
Lębork, *Poland* **54 D4** 54 33N 17 46 E
Lebrija, *Spain* **43 J4** 36 53N 6 5W
Łebsko, Jezioro, *Poland* **54 D4** 54 40N 17 25 E
Lebu, *Chile* **174 D1** 37 40 S 73 47W
Leca da Palmeira, *Portugal* **42 D2** 41 12N 8 42W
Lecce, *Italy* **47 B11** 40 23N 18 11 E
Lecco, *Italy* **44 C6** 45 51N 9 23 E
Lecco, L. di, *Italy* **44 C6** 45 55N 9 19 E
Lécera, *Spain* **40 D4** 41 13N 0 43W
Lech, *Austria* **34 D3** 47 13N 10 9 E
Lech →, *Germany* **31 G6** 48 43N 10 56 E
Lechang, *China* **77 E9** 25 10N 113 20 E
Lechtaler Alpen, *Austria* **34 D3** 47 15N 10 30 E
Léconi, *Gabon* **114 C2** 1 35 S 14 14 E
Léconi →, *Gabon* **114 C2** 1 11 S 13 16 E
Lecontes Mills, *U.S.A.* **150 E6** 41 5N 78 17W
Lectoure, *France* **28 E4** 43 56N 0 38 E
Łęczna, *Poland* **55 G9** 51 18N 22 53 E
Łęczyca, *Poland* **55 F6** 52 5N 19 15 E
Ledang, Gunong, *Malaysia* **84 B2** 2 22N 102 37 E
Ledesma, *Spain* **42 D5** 41 6N 5 59W
Lediba, *Dem. Rep. of the Congo* **114 C3** 3 1 S 16 34 E
Lédo, Cabo, *Angola* **115 D2** 9 43 S 13 12 E
Ledong, *China* **86 C7** 18 41N 109 5 E

Leduc, Canada 142 C6 53 15N 113 30W
Lee, Fla., U.S.A. 152 E6 30 25N 83 18W
Lee, Mass., U.S.A. 151 D11 42 19N 73 15W
Lee →, Ireland 23 E3 51 53N 8 56W
Lee Vining, U.S.A. 160 H7 37 58N 119 7W
Leech L., U.S.A. 154 B7 47 10N 94 24W
Leechburg, U.S.A. 150 F5 40 37N 79 36W
Leeds, U.K. 20 D6 53 48N 1 33W
Leeds, U.S.A. 149 J2 33 33N 86 33W
Leek, Neths. 24 A6 53 10N 6 24 E
Leek, U.K. 20 D5 53 7N 2 1W
Leeman, Australia 125 E1 29 57 S 114 58 E
Leeper, U.S.A. 150 E5 41 22N 79 18W
Leer, Germany 30 B3 53 13N 7 26 E
Lee's Summit, U.S.A. 156 F2 38 55N 94 23W
Leesburg, Fla., U.S.A. 149 L5 28 49N 81 53W
Leesburg, Ga., U.S.A. 152 D5 31 44N 84 10W
Leesburg, Ohio, U.S.A. 157 E13 39 21N 83 33W
Leeston, N.Z. 131 D7 43 45 S 172 19 E
Leesville, U.S.A. 155 K8 31 9N 93 16W
Leeton, Australia 129 C7 34 33 S 146 23 E
Leetonia, U.S.A. 150 F4 40 53N 80 45W
Leeu Gamka, S. Africa 116 E3 32 47 S 21 59 E
Leeuwarden, Neths. 24 A5 53 15N 5 48 E
Leeuwin, C., Australia 125 F2 34 20 S 115 9 E
Leeuwin Naturaliste Nat. Park,
Australia 125 F2 34 6 S 115 3 E
Leeward Is., Atl. Oc. 165 C7 16 30N 63 30W
Léfini, Congo 114 C3 2 55 S 15 39 E
Léfini →, Congo 114 C3 2 56 S 16 9 E
Léfini, Réserve de Chasse de la,
Congo 114 C3 2 55 S 15 20 E
Lefka, Cyprus 39 E8 35 6N 32 51 E
Lefkoniko, Cyprus 39 E9 35 18N 33 44 E
Lefroy, Canada 150 B5 44 16N 79 34W
Lefroy, L., Australia 125 F3 31 21 S 121 40 E
Łeg →, Poland 55 H8 50 42N 21 50 E
Leganés, Spain 42 E7 40 19N 3 45W
Legazpi, Phil. 80 E4 13 10N 123 45 E
Lège-Cap-Ferret, France 28 D2 44 48N 1 9W
Lege Hida, Ethiopia 107 F5 7 56N 41 4 E
Legendre I., Australia 124 D2 20 22 S 116 55 E
Leghorn = Livorno, Italy 44 E7 43 33N 10 19 E
Legionowo, Poland 55 F7 52 25N 20 50 E
Legnago, Italy 45 C8 45 11N 11 18 E
Legnano, Italy 44 C5 45 36N 8 54 E
Legnica, Poland 55 G3 51 12N 16 10 E
Legrad, Croatia 45 B13 46 17N 16 51 E
Leh, India 93 B7 34 9N 77 35 E
Lehigh Acres, U.S.A. 153 J8 26 36N 81 39W
Lehighton, U.S.A. 151 F9 40 50N 75 43W
Lehliu, Romania 53 F11 44 29N 26 50 E
Leho, Sudan 107 F3 7 7N 33 52 E
Lehrte, Germany 30 C5 52 22N 9 58 E
Lehua I., U.S.A. 145 A1 22 1N 160 6W
Lehututu, Botswana 116 C3 23 54 S 21 55 E
Lei Shui →, China 77 D9 26 55N 112 35 E
Leiah, Pakistan 91 C3 30 58N 70 58 E
Leibnitz, Austria 34 E8 46 47N 15 34 E
Leibo, China 76 C4 28 11N 103 34 E
Leicester, U.K. 21 E6 52 38N 1 8W
Leicester City □, U.K. 21 E6 52 38N 1 8W
Leicestershire □, U.K. 21 E6 52 41N 1 17W
Leichhardt →, Australia 126 B2 17 35 S 139 48 E
Leichhardt Ra., Australia 126 C4 20 46 S 147 40 E
Leiden, Neths. 24 B4 52 9N 4 30 E
Leie →, Belgium 24 C3 51 2N 3 45 E
Leifers = Láives, Italy 45 B8 46 26N 11 20 E
Leigh →, Australia 128 E6 38 18 S 144 30 E
Leigh Creek, Australia 128 A3 30 38 S 138 26 E
Leikanger, Sogn og Fjordane,
Norway 18 B2 62 8N 5 18 E
Leikanger, Sogn og Fjordane,
Norway 18 C3 61 10N 6 51 E
Leikong, Norway 18 B2 62 15N 5 47 E
Leiktho, Burma 90 F6 19 13N 96 35 E
Leimen, Germany 31 F4 49 21N 8 41 E
Leine →, Germany 30 C5 52 43N 9 36 E
Leinefelde, Germany 30 D6 51 23N 10 19 E
Leinster, Australia 125 E3 27 51 S 120 36 E
Leinster □, Ireland 23 C4 53 3N 7 8W
Leinster, Mt., Ireland 23 D5 52 37N 6 46W
Leipalingis, Lithuania 54 D10 54 5N 23 51 E
Leipzig, Germany 30 D8 51 18N 12 22 E
Leira, Norway 18 D6 60 58N 9 17 E
Leiria, Portugal 42 F2 39 46N 8 53W
Leiria □, Portugal 42 F2 39 46N 8 53W
Leirvassbu, Norway 18 C5 61 33N 8 13 E
Leirvik, Norway 15 G11 59 47N 5 28 E
Leishan, China 76 D7 26 15N 108 20 E
Leisler, Mt., Australia 124 D4 23 23 S 129 20 E
Leisure City, U.S.A. 153 K9 25 31N 80 26W
Leith, U.K. 22 F5 55 59N 3 11W
Leith Hill, U.K. 21 F7 51 11N 0 22W
Leitha →, Europe 35 D10 47 50N 17 15 E
Leitrim, Ireland 23 B3 54 0N 8 5W
Leitrim □, Ireland 23 B4 54 8N 8 0W
Leitza, Spain 40 B3 43 5N 1 55W
Leiyang, China 77 D9 26 27N 112 45 E
Leizhou, China 77 G8 20 52N 110 8 E
Leizhou Bandao, China 76 G7 21 0N 110 0 E
Leizhou Wan, China 77 G8 20 50N 110 20 E
Lek →, Neths. 24 C4 51 54N 4 35 E
Leka, Norway 14 D14 65 5N 11 35 E
Lekáni, Greece 51 E8 41 10N 24 35 E
Lekbibaj, Albania 50 D3 42 17N 19 56 E
Lekeitio, Spain 40 B2 43 20N 2 32W
Lekhainá, Greece 48 D3 37 57N 21 16 E
Lekitobi, Indonesia 82 B2 1 58 S 124 33 E
Lékoli-Pandaka, Réserve de Faune
de la, Congo 114 B2 0 41N 14 50 E
Lekoui, Burkina Faso 112 C4 12 37N 3 40W
Leksand, Sweden 16 D9 60 44N 15 1 E
Leksula, Indonesia 82 B3 3 46 S 126 31 E
Lékva Óros, Greece 39 E5 35 18N 24 3 E
Leland, Mich., U.S.A. 148 C3 45 1N 85 45W
Leland, Miss., U.S.A. 155 J9 33 24N 90 54W
Lelång, Sweden 16 E6 59 10N 12 5 E
Leleiwi Pt., U.S.A. 145 D7 19 44N 155 0W
Lelepa, Vanuatu 133 G6 17 35 S 168 11 E
Leleque, Argentina 176 B2 42 28 S 71 0W
Lelewau, Indonesia 82 B2 3 2 S 121 5 E
Leli, Solomon Is. 133 M11 8 42 S 161 4 E
Lelu, Burma 90 F5 19 4N 95 30 E
Lelydorp, Surinam 169 B6 5 42N 55 14W
Lelystad, Neths. 24 B5 52 30N 5 25 E
Lem, Denmark 17 H2 56 1N 8 24 E
Lema, Nigeria 113 C5 12 58N 4 13 E
Lema Shilindi, Ethiopia 107 G5 4 50N 42 6 E
Léman, L., Europe 27 F13 46 26N 6 30 E
Lemankoa, Papua N. G. 132 C8 5 3 S 154 34 E
Lembar, Indonesia 79 K19 8 45 S 116 4 E
Lembuak, Indonesia 79 K19 8 36 S 116 11 E
Lemera, Dem. Rep. of the Congo 118 C2 3 0 S 28 55 E
Lemery, Phil. 80 E3 13 51N 120 56 E
Lemeta, U.S.A. 144 D11 64 52N 147 44W
Lemfu, Dem. Rep. of the Congo 115 D3 5 18 S 15 13 E
Lemhi Ra., U.S.A. 158 D7 44 30N 113 30W
Lemmer, Neths. 24 B5 52 51N 5 43 E
Lemmon, U.S.A. 154 C3 45 57N 102 10W
Lemon Grove, U.S.A. 161 N9 32 45N 117 2W
Lemoore, U.S.A. 160 J7 36 18N 119 46W
Lempdes, France 28 C7 45 22N 3 17 E
Lemsid, W. Sahara 110 C2 26 33N 13 51W
Lemvig, Denmark 17 H2 56 33N 8 20 E
Lemyethna, Burma 90 G5 17 36N 95 9 E
Lena, U.S.A. 156 B7 42 23N 89 49W
Lena →, Russia 67 B13 72 52N 126 40 E
Lenakel, Vanuatu 133 J7 19 38 S 169 16 E
Lenart, Slovenia 45 B12 46 36N 15 48 E
Lenartovce, Slovak Rep. 35 C13 48 18N 20 19 E
Lencloître, France 26 F7 46 50N 0 20 E
Lençóis, Brazil 171 D3 12 35 S 41 24W
Léndas, Greece 39 F5 34 56N 24 56 E
Lendava, Slovenia 45 B13 46 35N 16 25 E
Lendeh, Iran 97 D6 30 58N 50 25 E
Lendinara, Italy 45 C8 45 5N 11 36 E
Lenger, Kazakstan 65 B4 42 12N 69 54 E
Lengerich, Germany 30 C3 52 11N 7 52 E
Lenggong, Malaysia 87 K3 5 6N 100 58 E
Lenggries, Germany 31 H7 47 41N 11 35 E
Léngoué, Congo 114 B3 1 15N 15 38 E
Lengshuijiang, China 77 D8 27 40N 111 26 E
Lengshuitan, China 77 D8 26 27N 111 35 E
Lengua de Vaca, Pta., Chile 174 C1 30 14 S 71 38W
Lengwe Nat. Park, Malawi 119 F3 16 14 S 34 45 E
Lengyeltóti, Hungary 52 D2 46 40N 17 40 E
Lenhovda, Sweden 17 G9 57 0N 15 16 E
Lenina, Kanal →, Russia 61 J7 43 44N 45 17 E
Lenina, Pik, Kyrgyzstan 65 D6 39 20N 72 55 E
Leninabad = Khŭjand, Tajikistan 66 E7 40 17N 69 37 E
Leninakan = Gyumri, Armenia 61 K6 40 47N 43 50 E
Leningrad = Sankt-Peterburg,
Russia 58 C6 59 55N 30 20 E
Leningradskiy, Tajikistan 65 D5 38 6N 70 1 E
Lenino, Ukraine 59 K8 45 17N 35 46 E
Leninogorsk, Kazakstan 66 D9 50 20N 83 30 E
Leninogorsk, Russia 64 D4 54 36N 52 30 E
Leninpol, Kyrgyzstan 65 B5 42 29N 71 55 E
Leninsk = Asaka, Uzbekistan 65 C6 40 38N 72 15 E
Leninsk, Russia 61 F7 48 40N 45 15 E
Leninsk-Kuznetskiy, Russia 66 D9 54 44N 86 10 E
Leninskiy, Tajikistan 65 D4 38 26N 68 46 E
Leninskoe, Kyrgyzstan 65 C6 40 40N 73 9 E
Leninskoye = Qazyghurt,
Kazakstan 65 C4 41 45N 69 23 E
Leninskoye, Kazakstan 64 F6 50 44N 57 53 E
Leninskoye, Russia 60 A8 58 23N 47 3 E
Lenk, Switz. 32 D4 46 27N 7 28 E
Lenkoran = Länkäran, Azerbaijan 97 B6 38 48N 48 52 E
Lenmalu, Indonesia 83 B4 1 45 S 130 15 E
Lenne →, Germany 30 D3 51 25N 7 29 E
Lennestadt, Germany 30 D4 51 8N 8 2 E
Lennox, U.S.A. 154 D6 43 21N 96 53W
Lennox, I., Chile 176 E3 55 18 S 66 50W
Lennoxville, Canada 151 A13 45 22N 71 51W
Leno, Italy 44 C7 45 22N 10 13 E
Lenoir, U.S.A. 149 H5 35 55N 81 32W
Lenoir City, U.S.A. 149 H3 35 48N 84 16W
Lenore L., Canada 143 C8 52 30N 104 59W
Lenox, Ga., U.S.A. 152 D6 31 16N 83 28W
Lenox, Iowa, U.S.A. 156 D2 40 53N 94 34W
Lenox, Mass., U.S.A. 151 D11 42 22N 73 17W
Lens, France 27 B9 50 26N 2 50 E
Lensahn, Germany 30 A6 54 13N 10 53 E
Lensk, Russia 67 C12 60 48N 114 55 E
Lensvik, Norway 18 A6 63 31N 9 48 E
Lentekhi, Georgia 61 J6 42 47N 42 45 E
Lenti, Hungary 52 D1 46 37N 16 33 E
Lentini, Italy 47 E8 37 17N 15 0 E
Lenwood, U.S.A. 161 L9 34 53N 117 7W
Lenya, Burma 78 B1 11 33N 98 57 E
Lenzburg, Switz. 32 B6 47 23N 8 11 E
Lenzen, Germany 30 B7 53 5N 11 29 E
Lenzerheide, Switz. 33 C9 46 44N 9 34 E
Léo, Burkina Faso 112 C4 11 3N 2 2W
Leoben, Austria 34 D8 47 22N 15 5 E
Leodhas = Lewis, U.K. 22 C2 58 9N 6 40W
Leola, U.S.A. 154 C5 45 43N 98 56W
Leominster, U.K. 21 E5 52 14N 2 43W
Leominster, U.S.A. 151 D13 42 32N 71 46W
Léon, France 28 E2 43 53N 1 18W
León, Mexico 162 C4 21 7N 101 40W
León, Nic. 164 D2 12 20N 86 51W
León, Spain 42 C5 42 38N 5 34W
Leon, U.S.A. 156 D3 40 44N 93 45W
León □, Spain 42 C5 42 40N 5 55W
Leon →, U.S.A. 155 K6 31 14N 97 28W
León, Montes de, Spain 42 C4 42 30N 6 18W
Leonardtown, U.S.A. 148 F7 38 17N 76 38W
Leonardville, Namibia 116 C2 23 29 S 18 49 E
Leonberg, Germany 31 G5 48 48N 9 1 E
Leonding, Austria 34 C7 48 16N 14 15 E
Leone, Amer. Samoa 133 X24 14 23 S 170 48W
Leone, Mte., Switz. 32 D6 46 15N 8 5 E
Leonessa, Italy 45 F9 42 34N 12 58 E
Leonforte, Italy 47 E7 37 38N 14 23 E
Leongatha, Australia 129 E6 38 30 S 145 58 E
Leonia, U.S.A. 152 E3 30 55N 86 1W
Leonídhion, Greece 48 D4 37 9N 22 52 E
Leonora, Australia 125 E3 28 49 S 121 19 E
Leopoldina, Brazil 171 F3 21 28 S 42 40W
Leopoldo Bulhões, Brazil 171 E2 16 37 S 48 46W
Leopoldsburg, Belgium 24 C5 51 7N 5 13 E
Leoti, U.S.A. 154 F4 38 29N 101 21W
Leova, Moldova 53 D13 46 28N 28 15 E
Leoville, Canada 143 C7 53 39N 107 33W
Lepe, Spain 43 H3 37 15N 7 12W
Lepel = Lyepyel, Belarus 58 E5 54 50N 28 40 E
Lepenoú, Greece 48 C3 38 42N 21 17 E
Leping, China 77 C11 28 47N 117 7 E
Lépo, L. do, Angola 116 B2 17 0 S 19 0 E
Lepontine, Alpi, Italy 33 D6 46 22N 8 27 E
Leppävirta, Finland 15 E22 62 29N 27 46 E
Lepsény, Hungary 52 D3 47 0N 18 15 E
Leptis Magna, Libya 108 B2 32 40N 14 12 E
Lequeitio = Lekeitio, Spain 40 B2 43 20N 2 32W
Lercara Friddi, Italy 46 E6 37 45N 13 36 E
Lerdo, Mexico 162 B4 25 32N 103 32W
Léré, C.A.R. 114 A3 6 46N 17 25 E
Léré, Chad 113 D7 9 39N 14 13 E
Léré, Mali 112 B4 15 45N 4 55W
Lere, Bauchi, Nigeria 113 D6 9 43N 9 18 E
Lere, Kaduna, Nigeria 113 C6 10 23N 8 35 E
Leribe, Lesotho 117 D4 28 51 S 28 3 E
Lérici, Italy 44 D6 44 4N 9 55 E
Lérida = Lleida, Spain 40 D5 41 37N 0 39 E
Lérins, Îs. de, France 29 E11 43 31N 7 3 E
Lerma, Spain 42 C7 42 0N 3 47W
Léros, Greece 49 D8 37 10N 26 50 E
Lérouville, France 27 D12 48 44N 5 30 E
Lerum, Sweden 17 G6 57 46N 12 16 E
Lerwick, U.K. 22 A7 60 9N 1 9W
Leş, Romania 52 D6 46 58N 21 50 E
Les Abrets, France 29 C9 45 32N 5 35 E
Les Andelys, France 26 C8 49 15N 1 25 E
Les Bois, Switz. 32 B3 47 11N 6 50 E
Les Borges Blanques, Spain 40 D5 41 31N 0 52 E
Les Cayes, Haiti 165 C5 18 15N 73 46W
Les Diablerets, Switz. 32 D4 46 22N 7 10 E
Les Essarts, France 26 F5 46 47N 1 12W
Les Herbiers, France 26 F5 46 52N 1 1W
Les Minquiers, Plateau des,
Chan. Is. 26 D4 48 58N 2 8W
Les Moroubas, C.A.R. 114 A4 6 11N 20 13 E
Les Pieux, France 26 C5 49 30N 1 48W
Les Ponts-de-Cé, France 26 E6 47 25N 0 30W
Les Riceys, France 27 E11 47 59N 4 22 E
Les Sables-d'Olonne, France 28 B2 46 30N 1 45W
Les Vans, France 29 D8 44 25N 4 7 E
Les Verrières, Switz. 32 C2 46 55N 6 28 E
Lesbos = Lésvos, Greece 49 B8 39 10N 26 20 E
L'Escala, Spain 40 C8 42 7N 3 8 E
Leshan, China 76 C4 29 33N 103 41 E
Leshukonskoye, Russia 56 B8 64 54N 45 46 E
Leshwe, Demalisques de,
Dem. Rep. of the Congo 119 E2 12 45 S 29 30 E
Lésina, Italy 45 G12 41 52N 15 21 E
Lésina, L. di, Italy 45 G12 41 53N 15 26 E
Lesjaskog, Norway 18 B5 62 14N 8 22 E
Lesjaverk, Norway 18 B5 62 12N 8 34 E
Lesjöfors, Sweden 16 E8 59 58N 14 11 E
Lesko, Poland 55 J9 49 30N 22 23 E
Leskov I., Antarctica 7 B1 56 0 S 28 0W
Leskovac, Serbia, Yug. 50 C5 43 0N 21 58 E
Leskovik, Albania 50 F4 40 10N 20 34 E
Leslie, Ga., U.S.A. 152 D5 31 57N 84 5W
Leslie, Mich., U.S.A. 157 B12 42 27N 84 26W
Leśna, Poland 55 G2 51 1N 15 15 E
Lesneven, France 26 D2 48 35N 4 20W
Leśnica, Poland 55 H5 50 26N 18 11 E
Lešnica, Serbia, Yug. 50 B3 44 39N 19 20 E
Lesnoy, Russia 64 B4 59 47N 52 9 E
Lesnoye, Russia 58 C8 58 15N 35 18 E
Lesopilnoye, Russia 70 A7 46 44N 134 20 E
Lesotho ■, Africa 117 D4 29 40 S 28 0 E
Lesozavodsk, Russia 67 E14 45 30N 133 29 E
Lesparre-Médoc, France 28 C3 45 18N 0 57W
Lessay, France 26 C5 49 14N 1 30W
Lesse →, Belgium 24 D5 50 15N 4 54 E
Lessebo, Sweden 17 H9 56 45N 15 16 E
Lesser Antilles, W. Indies 165 D7 15 0N 61 0W
Lesser Slave L., Canada 142 B5 55 30N 115 25W
Lesser Sunda Is., Indonesia 82 C1 8 0 S 120 0 E
Lessines, Belgium 24 D3 50 42N 3 50 E
Lester, U.S.A. 160 C5 47 12N 121 29W
Lestock, Canada 143 C8 51 19N 103 59W
Lesuer I., Australia 124 B4 13 50 S 127 17 E
Lesueur Nat. Park, Australia 125 F2 30 11 S 115 10 E
Lésvos, Greece 49 B8 39 10N 26 20 E
Leszno, Poland 55 G3 51 50N 16 30 E
Letaba, S. Africa 117 C5 23 59 S 31 50 E
Letälven, Sweden 16 E8 59 5N 14 20 E
Létavértes, Hungary 52 C6 47 23N 21 55 E
Letchworth, U.K. 21 F7 51 59N 0 13W
Letea, Ostrov, Romania 53 E14 45 18N 29 20 E
Lethbridge, Canada 142 D6 49 45N 112 45W
Lethem, Guyana 169 C6 3 20N 59 50W
Leti, Kepulauan, Indonesia 82 C3 8 10 S 128 0 E
Leti Is. = Leti, Kepulauan,
Indonesia 82 C3 8 10 S 128 0 E
Letiahau →, Botswana 116 C3 21 16 S 24 0 E
Leticia, Colombia 168 D4 4 9 S 70 0W
Leting, China 75 E10 39 23N 118 55 E
Letjiesbos, S. Africa 116 E3 32 34 S 22 16 E
Letlhakane, Botswana 116 C4 21 27 S 25 30 E
Letlhakeng, Botswana 116 C3 24 0 S 24 59 E
Letong, Indonesia 78 D3 2 58N 105 42 E
Letpadan, Burma 90 G5 17 45N 95 45 E
Letpan, Burma 90 F5 19 28N 94 10 E
Letsôk-aw Kyun, Burma 87 G2 11 30N 98 25 E
Letterkenny, Ireland 23 B4 54 57N 7 45W
Leu, Romania 53 F9 44 10N 24 0 E
Léua, Angola 115 E4 11 34 S 20 32 E
Leucadia, U.S.A. 161 M9 33 4N 117 18W
Leucate, France 28 F7 42 56N 3 3 E
Leucate, Étang de, France 28 F7 42 50N 3 0 E
Leuk, Switz. 32 D5 46 19N 7 37 E
Leukerbad, Switz. 32 D5 46 24N 7 36 E
Leuşeni, Moldova 53 D13 46 49N 28 12 E
Leuser, G., Indonesia 84 B1 3 46N 97 12 E
Leutkirch, Germany 31 H6 47 49N 10 1 E
Leuven, Belgium 24 D4 50 52N 4 42 E
Leuze-en-Hainaut, Belgium 24 D3 50 36N 3 37 E
Lev Tolstoy, Russia 58 F10 53 13N 39 29 E
Levádhia, Greece 49 C4 38 27N 22 54 E
Levan, Albania 50 F3 40 40N 19 28 E
Levanger, Norway 14 E14 63 45N 11 19 E
Levant, Î. du, France 29 E10 43 3N 6 28 E
Lévanto, Italy 44 D6 44 10N 9 38 E
Lévanzo, Italy 46 D5 38 0N 12 20 E
Leveld, Norway 18 D5 60 44N 8 33 E
Levelland, U.S.A. 155 J3 33 35N 102 23W
Leven, U.K. 22 E6 56 12N 3 0W
Leven, L., U.K. 22 E5 56 12N 3 22W
Leven, Toraka, Madag. 117 A8 12 30 S 47 45 E
Leveque C., Australia 124 C3 16 20 S 123 0 E
Leverano, Italy 47 B10 40 17N 18 0 E
Leverkusen, Germany 30 D3 51 1N 7 1 E
Levice, Slovak Rep. 35 C11 48 13N 18 35 E
Lévico Terme, Italy 45 B8 46 0N 11 18 E
Levie, France 29 G13 41 40N 9 7 E
Levier, France 27 F13 46 58N 6 8 E
Levin, N.Z. 130 G4 40 37 S 175 18 E
Lévis, Canada 141 C5 46 48N 71 9W
Levis, L., Canada 142 A5 62 37N 117 58W
Levítha, Greece 49 D8 37 0N 26 28 E
Levittown, N.Y., U.S.A. 151 F11 40 44N 73 31W
Levittown, Pa., U.S.A. 151 F10 40 9N 74 51W
Levka, Bulgaria 51 E10 41 52N 26 15 E
Levkás, Greece 39 B2 38 40N 20 43 E
Levkás □, Greece 39 B2 38 45N 20 40 E
Levkímmi, Greece 38 C10 39 25N 20 3 E
Levkímmi, Ákra, Greece 38 C10 39 29N 20 4 E
Levkôsia = Nicosia, Cyprus 39 E9 35 10N 33 25 E
Levoča, Slovak Rep. 35 B13 49 2N 20 35 E
Levroux, France 27 F8 46 59N 1 38 E
Levski, Bulgaria 51 C9 43 21N 25 10 E
Levskigrad = Karlovo, Bulgaria 51 D8 42 38N 24 47 E
Levuka, Fiji 133 A2 17 34 S 179 0 E
Lewe, Burma 90 F6 19 38N 96 7 E
Lewes, U.K. 21 G8 50 52N 0 1 E
Lewes, U.S.A. 148 F8 38 46N 75 9W
Lewin Brzeski, Poland 55 H4 50 45N 17 37 E
Lewis, U.K. 22 C2 58 9N 6 40W
Lewis →, U.S.A. 160 E4 45 51N 122 48W
Lewis, Butt of, U.K. 22 C2 58 31N 6 16W
Lewis Pass, N.Z. 131 C7 42 31 S 172 11 E
Lewis Ra., Australia 124 D4 20 3 S 128 50 E
Lewis Range, U.S.A. 158 C7 48 5N 113 5W
Lewis Run, U.S.A. 150 E6 41 52N 78 40W
Lewisburg, Ohio, U.S.A. 157 E12 39 51N 84 33W
Lewisburg, Pa., U.S.A. 150 F8 40 58N 76 54W
Lewisburg, Tenn., U.S.A. 149 H2 35 27N 86 48W
Lewisburg, W. Va., U.S.A. 148 G5 37 48N 80 27W
Lewisport, U.S.A. 157 G10 37 56N 86 54W
Lewisporte, Canada 141 C8 49 15N 55 3W
Lewiston, Idaho, U.S.A. 158 C5 46 25N 117 1W
Lewiston, Maine, U.S.A. 149 C11 44 6N 70 13W
Lewiston, N.Y., U.S.A. 150 C5 43 11N 79 3W
Lewistown, Ill., U.S.A. 156 D6 40 24N 90 9W
Lewistown, Mo., U.S.A. 156 D5 40 5N 91 49W
Lewistown, Mont., U.S.A. 158 C9 47 4N 109 26W
Lewistown, Pa., U.S.A. 150 F7 40 36N 77 34W
Lexington, Ga., U.S.A. 152 B6 33 52N 83 7W
Lexington, Ill., U.S.A. 154 E10 40 39N 88 47W
Lexington, Ky., U.S.A. 157 F12 38 3N 84 30W
Lexington, Mich., U.S.A. 150 C2 43 16N 82 32W
Lexington, Mo., U.S.A. 156 E3 39 11N 93 52W
Lexington, N.C., U.S.A. 149 H5 35 49N 80 15W
Lexington, N.Y., U.S.A. 151 D10 42 15N 74 22W
Lexington, Nebr., U.S.A. 154 E5 40 47N 99 45W
Lexington, Ohio, U.S.A. 150 F2 40 41N 82 35W
Lexington, S.C., U.S.A. 152 B8 33 59N 81 11W
Lexington, Tenn., U.S.A. 149 H1 35 39N 88 24W
Lexington, Va., U.S.A. 148 G6 37 47N 79 27W
Lexington Park, U.S.A. 148 F7 38 16N 76 27W
Leyburn, U.K. 20 C6 54 19N 1 48W
Leye, China 76 E6 24 48N 106 29 E
Leyland, U.K. 20 D5 53 42N 2 43W
Leyre →, France 28 D2 44 39N 1 1W
Leysin, Switz. 32 D4 46 21N 7 1 E
Leyte, Phil. 81 F5 10 30N 125 0 E
Leyte □, Phil. 81 F5 11 0N 125 0 E
Leyte Gulf, Phil. 81 F5 10 50N 125 25 E
Leżajsk, Poland 55 H9 50 16N 22 25 E
Lezay, France 28 B3 46 15N 0 1W
Lezhë, Albania 50 E3 41 47N 19 39 E
Lezhi, China 76 B5 30 19N 104 58 E
Lézignan-Corbières, France 28 E6 43 13N 2 43 E
Lezoux, France 28 C7 45 49N 3 21 E
Lgov, Russia 59 G8 51 42N 35 16 E
Lhasa, China 68 D4 29 25N 90 58 E
Lhazê, China 68 D3 29 5N 87 38 E
Lhokkruet, Indonesia 84 B1 4 55N 95 24 E
Lhokseumawe, Indonesia 84 A1 5 10N 97 10 E
L'Hospitalet de Llobregat, Spain 40 D7 41 21N 2 6 E
Lhuntsi Dzong, Bhutan 90 B3 27 39N 91 10 E
Li, Thailand 86 D2 17 48N 98 57 E
Li Shui →, China 77 C9 29 24N 112 1 E
Li Xian, Gansu, China 74 G3 34 10N 105 5 E
Li Xian, Hebei, China 74 E8 38 30N 115 35 E
Li Xian, Hunan, China 77 C8 29 36N 111 42 E
Lia-Moya, C.A.R. 114 A3 6 54N 16 17 E
Liádhoi, Greece 49 E8 36 50N 26 11 E
Lian, Phil. 80 D3 14 3N 120 39 E
Liancheng, China 77 E11 25 42N 116 40 E
Lianga, Phil. 81 G6 8 38N 126 6 E
Lianga Bay, Phil. 81 G6 8 37N 126 12 E
Liangcheng, Nei Monggol Zizhiqu,
China 74 D7 40 28N 112 25 E
Liangcheng, Shandong, China 75 G10 35 32N 119 37 E
Liangdang, China 74 H4 33 56N 106 18 E
Lianghe, China 76 E2 24 50N 98 20 E
Lianghekou, China 76 C7 29 11N 108 44 E
Liangping, China 76 B6 30 38N 107 47 E
Liangpran, Indonesia 78 D4 1 4N 114 23 E
Lianhua, China 77 D9 27 3N 113 54 E
Lianjiang, Fujian, China 77 D12 26 12N 119 27 E
Lianjiang, Guangdong, China 77 G8 21 40N 110 20 E
Lianping, China 77 E10 24 26N 114 30 E
Lianshan, China 77 E9 24 38N 112 8 E
Lianshanguan, China 75 D12 40 53N 123 43 E
Lianshui, China 75 H10 33 42N 119 20 E
Lianyuan, China 77 D8 27 40N 111 38 E
Lianyungang, China 75 G10 34 40N 119 11 E
Lianzhou, China 77 E9 24 51N 112 22 E
Liao He →, China 75 D11 41 0N 121 50 E
Liaocheng, China 74 F8 36 28N 115 58 E
Liaodong Bandao, China 75 E12 40 0N 122 30 E
Liaodong Wan, China 75 D11 40 20N 121 10 E
Liaoning □, China 75 D12 41 40N 122 30 E
Liaoyang, China 75 D12 41 15N 122 58 E
Liaoyuan, China 75 C13 42 58N 125 2 E
Liaozhong, China 75 D12 41 23N 122 50 E
Liapádhes, Greece 38 B9 39 42N 19 40 E
Liard →, Canada 142 A4 61 51N 121 18W
Liard River, Canada 142 B3 59 25N 126 5W
Liari, Pakistan 92 G2 25 37N 66 30 E
Libano, Colombia 168 C2 4 55N 75 4W
Libau = Liepāja, Latvia 15 H19 56 30N 21 0 E
Libby, U.S.A. 158 B6 48 23N 115 33W
Libenge, Dem. Rep. of the Congo 114 B3 3 40N 18 55 E
Liberal, U.S.A. 155 G4 37 3N 100 55W
Liberdade, Brazil 172 C3 10 5 S 70 20W
Liberdade →, Brazil 173 B7 9 40 S 52 17W
Liberec, Czech Rep. 34 A8 50 47N 15 7 E
Liberia, Costa Rica 164 D2 10 40N 85 30W
Liberia ■, W. Afr. 112 D3 6 30N 9 30W
Libertad, Phil. 81 F3 11 46N 121 55 E
Libertad, Venezuela 168 B4 8 20N 69 37W
Liberty, Ind., U.S.A. 157 E12 39 38N 84 56W
Liberty, Mo., U.S.A. 156 E2 39 15N 94 25W
Liberty, N.Y., U.S.A. 151 E10 41 48N 74 45W
Liberty, Pa., U.S.A. 150 E7 41 34N 77 6W
Liberty, Tex., U.S.A. 155 K7 30 3N 94 48W
Liberty Center, U.S.A. 157 C12 41 27N 84 1W
Libertyville, U.S.A. 157 B9 42 18N 87 57W
Libiąż, Poland 55 H6 50 7N 19 21 E
Libibi, Angola 115 E3 14 42 S 17 44 E
Lîbîya, Sahrâ', Africa 108 C4 25 0N 25 0 E
Libjo, Phil. 81 F5 10 12N 125 32 E
Libmanan, Phil. 80 E4 13 42N 123 4 E
Libo, China 76 E6 25 22N 107 53 E
Libobo, Tanjung, Indonesia 82 B3 0 54 S 128 28 E
Libode, S. Africa 117 E4 31 33 S 29 2 E
Libohovë, Albania 50 F4 40 3N 20 10 E
Libona, Phil. 81 G5 8 20N 124 44 E
Libonda, Zambia 115 E4 14 28 S 23 12 E
Libourne, France 28 D3 44 55N 0 14W
Libramont, Belgium 24 E5 49 55N 5 23 E
Librazhd, Albania 50 E4 41 12N 20 22 E
Libreville, Gabon 114 B1 0 25N 9 26 E
Libya ■, N. Afr. 108 C3 27 0N 17 0 E
Libyan Desert = Lîbîya, Sahrâ',
Africa 108 C4 25 0N 25 0 E
Libyan Plateau = Ed-Déffa, Egypt 106 A2 30 40N 26 30 E
Licantén, Chile 174 D1 35 55 S 72 0W
Licata, Italy 46 E6 37 6N 13 56 E
Lice, Turkey 101 C9 38 27N 40 39 E
Licheng, China 74 F7 36 28N 113 20 E
Lichfield, U.K. 21 E6 52 41N 1 49W
Lichinga, Mozam. 119 E4 13 13 S 35 11 E
Lichtenburg, S. Africa 116 D4 26 8 S 26 8 E
Lichtenfels, Germany 31 E7 50 8N 11 4 E
Lichuan, Hubei, China 76 B7 30 18N 108 57 E
Lichuan, Jiangxi, China 77 D11 27 18N 116 55 E
Licking →, U.S.A. 157 F12 39 6N 84 30W
Licosa, Punta, Italy 47 B7 40 15N 14 54 E
Licungo →, Mozam. 119 F4 17 40 S 37 15 E
Lida, Belarus 15 K21 53 53N 25 15 E
Liden, Sweden 16 B10 62 42N 16 48 E
Lidhorikion, Greece 48 C4 38 32N 22 12 E
Lidhult, Sweden 17 H7 56 50N 13 27 E
Lidköping, Sweden 17 F7 58 31N 13 7 E
Lido, Italy 45 C9 45 25N 12 22 E
Lido, Niger 113 C5 12 54N 3 44 E
Lido di Roma = Óstia, Lido di,
Italy 45 G9 41 43N 12 17 E
Lidzbark, Poland 55 E6 53 15N 19 49 E
Lidzbark Warmiński, Poland 54 D7 54 7N 20 34 E
Liebenwalde, Germany 30 C9 52 52N 13 24 E
Lieberose, Germany 30 D10 51 59N 14 17 E
Liebig, Mt., Australia 124 D5 23 18 S 131 22 E

Liebling, *Romania* **52 E6** 45 36N 21 20 E
Liechtenstein ■, *Europe* **33 B9** 47 8N 9 35 E
Liège, *Belgium* **24 D5** 50 38N 5 35 E
Liège □, *Belgium* **24 D5** 50 32N 5 35 E
Liegnitz = Legnica, *Poland* **55 G3** 51 12N 16 10 E
Lienart, *Dem. Rep. of the Congo* **118 B2** 3 3N 25 31 E
Lienyünchiangshih = Lianyungang, *China* **75 G10** 34 40N 119 11 E
Lienz, *Austria* **34 E5** 46 50N 12 46 E
Liepāja, *Latvia* **15 H19** 56 30N 21 0 E
Liepāja □, *Latvia* **54 B8** 56 30N 21 30 E
Liepājas ezers, *Latvia* **54 B8** 56 27N 21 3 E
Lier, *Belgium* **24 C4** 51 7N 4 34 E
Liernais, *France* **27 E11** 47 13N 4 16 E
Liestal, *Switz.* **32 B5** 47 29N 7 44 E
Lieşti, *Romania* **53 E12** 45 38N 27 34 E
Liévin, *France* **27 B9** 50 24N 2 47 E
Lièvre →, *Canada* **140 C4** 45 31N 75 26W
Liezen, *Austria* **34 D7** 47 34N 14 15 E
Liffey →, *Ireland* **23 C5** 53 21N 6 13W
Lifford, *Ireland* **23 B4** 54 51N 7 29W
Liffré, *France* **26 D5** 48 12N 1 30W
Lifjell, *Norway* **18 E5** 59 27N 8 45 E
Lifou, I., *N. Cal.* **133 K5** 20 53 S 167 13 E
Lifudzin, *Russia* **70 B7** 44 21N 134 58 E
Lifuka, *Tonga* **133 P13** 19 48 S 174 21W
Ligao, *Phil.* **80 E4** 13 14N 123 32 E
Ligasa, *Dem. Rep. of the Congo* **114 B4** 0 44N 23 49 E
Lighthouse Point, *U.S.A.* **153 J9** 26 15N 80 7W
Lighthouse Pt., *U.S.A.* **152 F5** 29 54N 84 21W
Lightning Ridge, *Australia* **127 D4** 29 22 S 148 0 E
Lignano Sabbiadoro, *Italy* **45 C10** 45 42N 13 9 E
Ligny-en-Barrois, *France* **27 D12** 48 36N 5 20 E
Ligonha →, *Mozam.* **119 F4** 16 54 S 39 9 E
Ligonier, *Ind., U.S.A.* **157 C11** 41 28N 85 35W
Ligonier, *Pa., U.S.A.* **150 F5** 40 15N 79 14W
Ligoúrion, *Greece* **48 D5** 37 37N 23 4 E
Ligueil, *France* **26 E7** 47 2N 0 49 E
Liguria □, *Italy* **44 D5** 44 30N 8 50 E
Ligurian Sea, *Medit. S.* **12 G7** 43 20N 9 0 E
Lihir Group, *Papua N. G.* **132 B7** 3 0 S 152 35 E
Lihir I., *Papua N. G.* **132 B7** 3 5 S 152 35 E
Lihou Reefs and Cays, *Australia* **126 B5** 17 25 S 151 40 E
Lihue, *U.S.A.* **145 B2** 21 59N 159 23W
Lijiang, *China* **76 D3** 26 55N 100 20 E
Likasi, *Dem. Rep. of the Congo* **119 E2** 10 55 S 26 48 E
Likati, *Dem. Rep. of the Congo* **114 B4** 3 20N 24 0 E
Likati →, *Dem. Rep. of the Congo* **114 B4** 2 53N 24 3 E
Likenäs, *Sweden* **16 D8** 60 37N 13 3 E
Likete, *Dem. Rep. of the Congo* **114 C4** 0 48 S 21 31 E
Likhoslavl, *Russia* **58 D8** 57 12N 35 30 E
Likhovskoy, *Russia* **59 H11** 48 10N 40 10 E
Likimi, *Dem. Rep. of the Congo* **114 B4** 2 44N 20 47 E
Likisia = Liquica, *E. Timor* **82 C3** 8 36 S 125 19 E
Likita, *Dem. Rep. of the Congo* **114 B4** 4 15N 23 36 E
Liknes, *Norway* **18 F3** 58 19N 6 59 E
Likokou, *Gabon* **114 C2** 0 12 S 12 48 E
Likoma I., *Malawi* **119 E3** 12 3 S 34 45 E
Likouala →, *Congo* **114 C3** 0 2N 14 53 E
Likouala aux Herbes →, *Congo* **114 C3** 0 52 S 17 8 E
Likumburu, *Tanzania* **119 D4** 9 43 S 35 8 E
Lilanga, *Dem. Rep. of the Congo* **114 C4** 0 34 S 23 56 E
L'Île-Bouchard, *France* **26 E7** 47 7N 0 26 E
L'Île-Rousse, *France* **29 F12** 42 38N 8 57 E
Lilenga, *Dem. Rep. of the Congo* **114 B4** 1 4N 22 2 E
Liling, *China* **77 D9** 27 42N 113 29 E
Lilla Edet, *Sweden* **17 F6** 58 9N 12 8 E
Lille, *France* **27 B10** 50 38N 3 3 E
Lille Bælt, *Denmark* **17 J3** 55 20N 9 45 E
Lillebonne, *France* **26 C7** 49 30N 0 32 E
Lillehammer, *Norway* **15 F14** 61 8N 10 30 E
Lillesand, *Norway* **15 G13** 58 15N 8 23 E
Lillestrøm, *Norway* **18 E8** 59 58N 11 5 E
Lillhärdal, *Sweden* **16 C8** 61 51N 14 5 E
Lillian Pt., *Australia* **125 E4** 27 40 S 126 6 E
Lillo, *Spain* **42 F7** 39 45N 3 20W
Lillooet, *Canada* **142 C4** 50 44N 121 57W
Lillooet →, *Canada* **142 D4** 49 15N 121 57W
Lilongwe, *Malawi* **119 E3** 14 0 S 33 48 E
Liloy, *Phil.* **81 G4** 8 4N 122 39 E
Lim →, *Bos.-H.* **50 C3** 43 45N 19 15 E
Lim Chu Kang, *Singapore* **87 d** 1 26N 103 43 E
Lima, *Brazil* **169 D5** 4 36 S 63 40W
Lima, *Indonesia* **82 B3** 3 39 S 127 58 E
Lima, *Peru* **172 C2** 12 0 S 77 0W
Lima, *Ill., U.S.A.* **156 D5** 40 11N 91 23W
Lima, *Mont., U.S.A.* **158 D7** 44 38N 112 36W
Lima, *Ohio, U.S.A.* **157 D12** 40 44N 84 6W
Lima □, *Peru* **172 C2** 12 3 S 77 3W
Lima →, *Portugal* **42 D2** 41 41N 8 50W
Liman, *Indonesia* **79 G14** 7 48 S 111 45 E
Liman, *Russia* **61 H8** 45 45N 47 12 E
Limanowa, *Poland* **55 J7** 49 42N 20 22 E
Limassol, *Cyprus* **39 F9** 34 42N 33 1 E
Limavady, *U.K.* **23 A5** 55 3N 6 56W
Limay →, *Argentina* **176 A3** 39 0 S 68 0W
Limay Mahuida, *Argentina* **174 D2** 37 10 S 66 45W
Limbach-Oberfrohna, *Germany* **30 E8** 50 52N 12 43 E
Limbang, *Brunei* **85 B5** 4 42N 115 6 E
Limbara, Mte., *Italy* **46 B2** 40 51N 9 10 E
Limbaži, *Latvia* **15 H21** 57 31N 24 42 E
Limbdi, *India* **92 H4** 22 34N 71 51 E
Limbe, *Cameroon* **113 E6** 4 1N 9 10 E
Limboto, *Indonesia* **82 A2** 0 37N 122 57 E
Limbueta, *Angola* **115 E3** 12 30 S 18 42 E
Limburg, *Germany* **31 E4** 50 22N 8 4 E
Limburg □, *Belgium* **24 C5** 51 2N 5 25 E
Limburg □, *Neths.* **24 C5** 51 20N 5 55 E
Lime Village, *U.S.A.* **144 F9** 61 21N 155 28W
Limedsforsen, *Sweden* **16 D7** 60 52N 13 25 E
Limeira, *Brazil* **175 A6** 22 35 S 47 28W
Limenária, *Greece* **51 F8** 40 38N 24 32 E
Limerick, *Ireland* **23 D3** 52 40N 8 37W
Limerick, *U.S.A.* **151 C14** 43 41N 70 48W
Limerick □, *Ireland* **23 D3** 52 30N 8 50W
Limestone, *U.S.A.* **150 D6** 42 2N 78 38W
Limestone →, *Canada* **143 B10** 56 31N 94 7W
Limfjorden, *Denmark* **17 H3** 56 55N 9 0 E
Limia = Lima →, *Portugal* **42 D2** 41 41N 8 50W
Limín Khersonísou, *Greece* **39 E6** 35 18N 25 21 E
Limingen, *Norway* **14 D15** 64 48N 13 35 E
Limmared, *Sweden* **17 G7** 57 34N 13 20 E
Limmat →, *Switz.* **33 B6** 47 26N 8 20 E
Limmen Bight, *Australia* **126 A2** 14 40 S 135 35 E
Limmen Bight →, *Australia* **126 B2** 15 7 S 135 44 E
Límni, *Greece* **48 C5** 38 43N 23 18 E
Límni Voulkariá, *Greece* **39 B2** 38 52N 20 50 E
Límnos, *Greece* **49 B7** 39 50N 25 5 E
Limoeiro, *Brazil* **170 C4** 7 52 S 35 27W
Limoeiro do Norte, *Brazil* **170 C4** 5 5 S 38 0W
Limoges, *Canada* **151 A9** 45 20N 75 16W
Limoges, *France* **28 C5** 45 50N 1 15 E
Limón, *Costa Rica* **164 E3** 10 0N 83 2W
Limon, *U.S.A.* **154 F3** 39 16N 103 41W
Limone Piemonte, *Italy* **44 D4** 44 12N 7 34 E
Limousin, *France* **28 C5** 45 30N 1 30 E
Limousin, Plateaux du, *France* **28 C5** 45 45N 1 15 E
Limoux, *France* **28 E6** 43 4N 2 12 E
Limpopo →, *Africa* **117 D5** 25 5 S 33 30 E
Limuru, *Kenya* **118 C4** 1 2 S 36 35 E
Lin Xian, *China* **74 F6** 37 57N 110 58 E
Lin'an, *China* **77 B12** 30 15N 119 42 E
Linao Pt., *Phil.* **81 H4** 6 46N 123 58 E
Linapacan, *Phil.* **81 F2** 11 30N 119 52 E
Linapacan I., *Phil.* **81 F2** 11 27N 119 49 E
Linapacan Str., *Phil.* **81 F2** 11 37N 119 56 E
Linares, *Chile* **174 D1** 35 50 S 71 40W
Linares, *Colombia* **168 C2** 1 23N 77 31W
Linares, *Mexico* **163 C5** 24 50N 99 40W
Linares, *Spain* **43 G7** 38 10N 3 40W
Linaro, Capo, *Italy* **45 F8** 42 2N 11 50 E
Línas Mte., *Italy* **46 C1** 39 25N 8 38 E
Lincang, *China* **76 F3** 23 58N 100 1 E
Lincheng, *China* **74 F8** 37 25N 114 30 E
Linchuan, *China* **77 D11** 27 57N 116 15 E
Lincoln, *Argentina* **174 C3** 34 55 S 61 30W
Lincoln, *N.Z.* **131 D7** 43 38 S 172 30 E
Lincoln, *U.K.* **20 D7** 53 14N 0 32W
Lincoln, *Calif., U.S.A.* **160 G5** 38 54N 121 17W
Lincoln, *Ill., U.S.A.* **156 D7** 40 9N 89 22W
Lincoln, *Kans., U.S.A.* **154 F5** 39 3N 98 9W
Lincoln, *Maine, U.S.A.* **149 C11** 45 22N 68 30W
Lincoln, *N.H., U.S.A.* **151 B13** 44 3N 71 40W
Lincoln, *N. Mex., U.S.A.* **159 K11** 33 30N 105 23W
Lincoln, *Nebr., U.S.A.* **154 E6** 40 49N 96 41W
Lincoln City, *U.S.A.* **158 D1** 44 57N 124 1W
Lincoln Hav = Lincoln Sea, *Arctic* **10 A5** 84 0N 55 0W
Lincoln Park, *Ga., U.S.A.* **152 C5** 32 52N 84 20W
Lincoln Park, *Mich., U.S.A.* **157 B13** 42 15N 83 11W
Lincoln Sea, *Arctic* **10 A5** 84 0N 55 0W
Lincolnshire □, *U.K.* **20 D7** 53 14N 0 32W
Lincolnshire Wolds, *U.K.* **20 D7** 53 26N 0 13W
Lincolnton, *Ga., U.S.A.* **152 B7** 33 48N 82 29W
Lincolnton, *N.C., U.S.A.* **149 H5** 35 29N 81 16W
L'Incudine, *France* **29 G13** 41 50N 9 12 E
Lind, *U.S.A.* **158 C4** 46 58N 118 37W
Linda, *U.S.A.* **160 F5** 39 8N 121 34W
Lindale, *U.S.A.* **152 A4** 34 11N 85 11W
Lindås, *Norway* **18 D2** 60 44N 5 9 E
Lindau, *Germany* **31 H5** 47 33N 9 42 E
Lindeman I., *Australia* **126 J7** 20 27 S 149 3 E
Linden, *Guyana* **169 B6** 6 0N 58 10W
Linden, *Ala., U.S.A.* **149 J2** 32 18N 87 48W
Linden, *Calif., U.S.A.* **160 G5** 38 1N 121 5W
Linden, *Ind., U.S.A.* **157 D10** 40 11N 86 54W
Linden, *Mich., U.S.A.* **157 B13** 42 49N 83 47W
Linden, *Tex., U.S.A.* **155 J7** 33 1N 94 22W
Lindenhurst, *U.S.A.* **151 F11** 40 41N 73 23W
Lindenow Fjord, *Greenland* **10 E6** 60 30N 43 25W
Lindesberg, *Sweden* **16 E9** 59 36N 15 15 E
Lindesnes, *Norway* **15 H12** 57 58N 7 3 E
Líndhos, *Greece* **38 E12** 36 6N 28 4 E
Líndhos, Ákra, *Greece* **38 E12** 36 4N 28 10 E
Lindi, *Tanzania* **119 D4** 9 58 S 39 38 E
Lindi □, *Tanzania* **119 D4** 9 40 S 38 30 E
Lindi →, *Dem. Rep. of the Congo* **118 B2** 0 33N 25 5 E
Lindö, *Sweden* **17 F10** 58 37N 16 15 E
Lindome, *Sweden* **17 G6** 57 35N 12 5 E
Lindoso, *Portugal* **42 D2** 41 52N 8 11W
Lindow, *Germany* **30 C8** 52 58N 12 59 E
Lindsay, *Canada* **140 D4** 44 22N 78 43W
Lindsay, *Calif., U.S.A.* **160 J7** 36 12N 119 5W
Lindsay, *Okla., U.S.A.* **155 H6** 34 50N 97 38W
Lindsborg, *U.S.A.* **154 F6** 38 35N 97 40W
Lindsdal, *Sweden* **17 H10** 56 44N 16 18 E
Linesville, *U.S.A.* **150 E4** 41 39N 80 26W
Lineville, *Ala., U.S.A.* **152 B4** 33 19N 85 45W
Lineville, *Iowa, U.S.A.* **156 D3** 40 35N 93 32W
Linfen, *China* **74 F6** 36 3N 111 30 E
Ling Xian, *Hunan, China* **77 D9** 26 29N 113 48 E
Ling Xian, *Shandong, China* **74 F9** 37 22N 116 30 E
Lingal, *India* **95 F4** 16 17N 78 31 E
Lingao, *China* **86 C7** 19 56N 109 42 E
Lingayen, *Phil.* **80 C3** 16 1N 120 14 E
Lingayen G., *Phil.* **80 C3** 16 10N 120 15 E
Lingbi, *China* **75 H9** 33 33N 117 33 E
Lingbo, *Sweden* **16 C10** 61 3N 16 41 E
Lingchuan, *Guangxi Zhuangzu, China* **77 E8** 25 26N 110 21 E
Lingchuan, *Shanxi, China* **74 G7** 35 45N 113 12 E
Lingding Yang, *China* **69 G10** 22 25N 113 44 E
Lingen, *Germany* **30 C3** 52 31N 7 19 E
Lingga, *Indonesia* **84 C2** 0 12 S 104 37 E
Lingga, Kepulauan, *Indonesia* **84 C2** 0 10 S 104 30 E
Lingga Arch. = Lingga, Kepulauan, *Indonesia* **84 C2** 0 10 S 104 30 E
Linghem, *Sweden* **17 F9** 58 26N 15 47 E
Lingig, *Phil.* **81 G6** 8 2N 126 24 E
Lingle, *U.S.A.* **154 D2** 42 8N 104 21W
Lingomo, *Dem. Rep. of the Congo* **114 B4** 0 38N 22 3 E
Lingqiu, *China* **74 E8** 39 28N 114 22 E
Lingshan, *China* **76 F7** 22 25N 109 18 E
Lingshi, *China* **74 F6** 36 48N 111 48 E
Lingshou, *China* **74 E8** 38 20N 114 20 E
Lingshui, *China* **86 C8** 18 27N 110 0 E
Lingsugur, *India* **95 F3** 16 10N 76 31 E
Lingtai, *China* **74 G4** 35 0N 107 40 E
Linguère, *Senegal* **112 B1** 15 25N 15 5W
Lingui, *China* **77 E8** 25 12N 110 2 E
Lingunda, *Dem. Rep. of the Congo* **114 C3** 0 49N 21 8 E
Lingwu, *China* **74 E4** 38 6N 106 20 E
Lingyuan, *China* **75 D10** 41 10N 119 15 E
Lingyun, *China* **76 E6** 25 2N 106 35 E
Linhai, *China* **77 C13** 28 50N 121 8 E
Linhares, *Brazil* **171 E3** 19 25 S 40 4W
Linhe, *China* **74 D4** 40 48N 107 20 E
Linjiang, *China* **75 D14** 41 50N 127 0 E
Linköping, *Sweden* **17 F9** 58 28N 15 36 E
Linkou, *China* **75 B16** 45 15N 130 18 E
Linli, *China* **77 C8** 29 27N 111 30 E
Linn, *U.S.A.* **156 F5** 38 29N 91 51W
Linneus, *U.S.A.* **156 E3** 39 53N 93 11W
Linnhe, L., *U.K.* **22 E3** 56 36N 5 25W
Linosa, *Medit. S.* **108 A2** 35 51N 12 50 E
Linqi, *China* **74 G7** 35 45N 113 52 E
Linqing, *China* **74 F8** 36 50N 115 42 E
Linqu, *China* **75 F10** 36 25N 118 30 E
Linru, *China* **74 G7** 34 11N 112 52 E
Lins, *Brazil* **175 A6** 21 40 S 49 44W
Linshui, *China* **76 B6** 30 21N 106 57 E
Linstead, *Jamaica* **164 a** 18 8N 77 2W
Linta →, *Madag.* **117 D7** 25 2 S 44 5 E
Linth →, *Switz.* **31 H5** 47 7N 9 7 E
Linthal, *Switz.* **33 C8** 46 54N 9 0 E
Linton, *Ind., U.S.A.* **157 F9** 39 2N 87 10W
Linton, *N. Dak., U.S.A.* **154 B4** 46 16N 100 14W
Lintong, *China* **74 G5** 34 20N 109 10 E
Linwood, *Canada* **150 C4** 43 35N 80 43W
Linwu, *China* **77 E9** 25 19N 112 31 E
Linxi, *China* **75 C10** 43 36N 118 2 E
Linxia, *China* **68 C5** 35 36N 103 10 E
Linxiang, *China* **77 C9** 29 28N 113 23 E
Linyanti →, *Africa* **116 B4** 17 50 S 25 5 E
Linyi, *China* **75 G10** 35 5N 118 21 E
Linz, *Austria* **34 C7** 48 18N 14 18 E
Linz, *Germany* **30 E3** 50 34N 7 17 E
Linzhenzhen, *China* **74 F5** 36 30N 109 59 E
Linzi, *China* **75 F10** 36 50N 118 20 E
Lioko, *Équateur, Dem. Rep. of the Congo* **114 B4** 0 2N 22 4 E
Lioko, *Orientale, Dem. Rep. of the Congo* **114 B4** 1 25N 23 7 E
Liomseter, *Norway* **18 C6** 61 15N 9 35 E
Lion, G. du, *France* **28 E7** 43 10N 4 0 E
Lionárisso, *Cyprus* **39 E10** 35 28N 34 8 E
Lioni, *Italy* **47 B8** 40 52N 15 11 E
Lions, G. of = Lion, G. du, *France* **28 E7** 43 10N 4 0 E
Lion's Den, *Zimbabwe* **119 F3** 17 15 S 30 5 E
Lion's Head, *Canada* **150 B3** 44 58N 81 15W
Liouesso, *Congo* **114 B3** 1 2N 15 43 E
Liozno = Lyozna, *Belarus* **58 E6** 55 0N 30 50 E
Lipa, *Phil.* **80 E3** 13 57N 121 10 E
Lipali, *Mozam.* **119 F4** 15 50 S 35 50 E
Lipany, *Slovak Rep.* **35 B13** 49 9N 20 58 E
Lípari, *Italy* **47 D7** 38 26N 14 58 E
Lípari, I., *Italy* **47 D7** 38 29N 14 56 E
Lípari, Is. = Eólie, Ís., *Italy* **47 D7** 38 30N 14 57 E
Lipcani, *Moldova* **53 B11** 48 14N 26 48 E
Lipetsk, *Russia* **59 F10** 52 37N 39 35 E
Lipiany, *Poland* **55 E1** 53 2N 14 58 E
Liping, *China* **76 D7** 26 15N 109 7 E
Lipkany = Lipcani, *Moldova* **53 B11** 48 14N 26 48 E
Lipljan, *Kosovo, Yug.* **50 D5** 42 31N 21 7 E
Lipník nad Bečvou, *Czech Rep.* **35 B10** 49 32N 17 36 E
Lipno, *Poland* **55 F6** 52 49N 19 15 E
Lipova, *Romania* **52 D6** 46 8N 21 42 E
Lipovcy Manzovka, *Russia* **70 B6** 44 12N 132 26 E
Lipovets, *Ukraine* **59 H5** 49 12N 29 1 E
Lippe →, *Germany* **30 D2** 51 39N 6 36 E
Lippstadt, *Germany* **30 D4** 51 41N 8 22 E
Lipscomb, *U.S.A.* **155 G4** 36 14N 100 16W
Lipsk, *Poland* **54 E10** 53 44N 23 24 E
Lipsko, *Poland* **55 G8** 51 9N 21 40 E
Lipsói, *Greece* **49 D8** 37 19N 26 50 E
Liptovský Hrádok, *Slovak Rep.* **35 B12** 49 2N 19 44 E
Liptovský Milkuláš, *Slovak Rep.* **35 B12** 49 6N 19 35 E
Liptrap C., *Australia* **129 E6** 38 50 S 145 55 E
Lipu, *China* **77 E8** 24 30N 110 22 E
Liquica, *E. Timor* **82 C3** 8 36 S 125 19 E
Liquillo, Sierra de, *Puerto Rico* **165 d** 18 20N 65 47W
Lira, *Uganda* **118 B3** 2 17N 32 57 E
Liranga, *Congo* **114 C3** 0 43 S 17 32 E
Liri →, *Italy* **46 A6** 41 25N 13 52 E
Liria = Llíria, *Spain* **41 F4** 39 37N 0 35W
Lisakovsk, *Kazakstan* **64 E9** 52 33N 62 37 E
Lisala, *Dem. Rep. of the Congo* **114 B4** 2 12N 21 38 E
Lisboa, *Portugal* **43 G1** 38 42N 9 10W
Lisboa □, *Portugal* **43 F1** 39 0N 9 12W
Lisbon = Lisboa, *Portugal* **43 G1** 38 42N 9 10W
Lisbon, *N. Dak., U.S.A.* **154 B6** 46 27N 97 41W
Lisbon, *N.H., U.S.A.* **151 B13** 44 13N 71 55W
Lisbon, *Ohio, U.S.A.* **150 F4** 40 46N 80 46W
Lisbon Falls, *U.S.A.* **149 D10** 44 0N 70 4W
Lisburn, *U.K.* **23 B5** 54 31N 6 3W
Lisburn, C., *Vanuatu* **133 E4** 15 39 S 166 46 E
Liscannor B., *Ireland* **23 D2** 52 55N 9 24W
Liscia →, *Italy* **46 A2** 41 11N 9 9 E
Lishe Jiang →, *China* **76 E3** 24 15N 101 35 E
Lishi, *China* **74 F6** 37 31N 111 8 E
Lishu, *China* **75 C13** 43 20N 124 18 E
Lishui, *Jiangsu, China* **77 B12** 31 38N 119 2 E
Lishui, *Zhejiang, China* **77 C12** 28 28N 119 54 E
Lisianski I., *Pac. Oc.* **134 E10** 26 2N 174 0W
Lisianski I., *U.S.A.* **145 F9** 26 2N 174 0W
Lisichansk = Lysychansk, *Ukraine* **59 H10** 48 55N 38 30 E
Lisieux, *France* **26 C7** 49 10N 0 12 E
Liski, *Russia* **59 G10** 51 3N 39 30 E
L'Isle-Jourdain, *Gers, France* **28 E5** 43 36N 1 5 E
L'Isle-Jourdain, *Vienne, France* **28 B4** 46 13N 0 31 E
L'Isle-Mont-la-Ville, *Switz.* **32 C2** 46 37N 6 25 E
L'Isle-sur-la-Sorgue, *France* **29 E9** 43 54N 5 2 E
Lisle-sur-Tarn, *France* **28 E5** 43 52N 1 49 E
Lismore, *Australia* **127 D5** 28 44 S 153 21 E
Lismore, *Ireland* **23 D4** 52 8N 7 55W
Lista, *Norway* **15 G12** 58 7N 6 39 E
Lister, Mt., *Antarctica* **7 D11** 78 0 S 162 0 E
Liston, *Australia* **127 D5** 28 39 S 152 6 E
Listowel, *Canada* **140 D3** 43 44N 80 58W
Listowel, *Ireland* **23 D2** 52 27N 9 29W
Lit, *Sweden* **16 A8** 63 19N 14 51 E
Lit-et-Mixe, *France* **28 D2** 44 2N 1 15W
Litang, *Guangxi Zhuangzu, China* **76 F7** 23 12N 109 8 E
Litang, *Sichuan, China* **76 B3** 30 1N 100 17 E
Litang, *Malaysia* **85 A5** 5 27N 118 31 E
Litang Qu →, *China* **76 C3** 28 4N 101 32 E
Litani →, *Lebanon* **103 B4** 33 20N 35 15 E
Litchfield, *Australia* **128 D5** 36 18 S 142 52 E
Litchfield, *Calif., U.S.A.* **160 E6** 40 24N 120 23W
Litchfield, *Conn., U.S.A.* **151 E11** 41 45N 73 11W
Litchfield, *Ill., U.S.A.* **156 E7** 39 11N 89 39W
Litchfield, *Minn., U.S.A.* **154 C7** 45 8N 94 32W
Litchfield Nat. Park, *Australia* **124 B5** 13 14 S 131 1 E
Liteni, *Romania* **53 C11** 47 32N 26 32 E
Lithakiá, *Greece* **39 D2** 37 43N 20 50 E
Lithgow, *Australia* **129 B9** 33 25 S 150 8 E
Líthinon, Ákra, *Greece* **39 F5** 34 55N 24 44 E
Lithuania ■, *Europe* **15 J20** 55 30N 24 0 E
Litija, *Slovenia* **45 B11** 46 3N 14 50 E
Lititz, *U.S.A.* **151 F8** 40 9N 76 18W
Litókhoron, *Greece* **50 F6** 40 8N 22 34 E
Litoko, *Dem. Rep. of the Congo* **114 C4** 1 13 S 24 47 E
Litoměřice, *Czech Rep.* **34 A7** 50 33N 14 10 E
Litomyšl, *Czech Rep.* **35 B9** 49 52N 16 20 E
Litschau, *Austria* **34 C8** 48 58N 15 4 E
Little Abaco I., *Bahamas* **164 A4** 26 50N 77 30W
Little Andaman I., *India* **95 J11** 10 45N 92 30 E
Little Barrier I., *N.Z.* **130 C4** 36 12 S 175 8 E
Little Basses, *Sri Lanka* **95 L5** 6 24N 81 43 E
Little Belt Mts., *U.S.A.* **158 C8** 46 40N 110 45W
Little Blue →, *U.S.A.* **154 F6** 39 42N 96 41W
Little Buffalo →, *Canada* **142 A6** 61 0N 113 46W
Little Cayman, *Cayman Is.* **164 C3** 19 41N 80 3W
Little Churchill →, *Canada* **143 B9** 57 30N 95 22W
Little Coco I., *Burma* **95 H11** 14 0N 93 13 E
Little Colorado →, *U.S.A.* **159 H8** 36 12N 111 48W
Little Current, *Canada* **140 C3** 45 55N 82 0W
Little Current →, *Canada* **140 B3** 50 57N 84 36W
Little Desert Nat. Park, *Australia* **128 D4** 37 25 S 141 30 E
Little Diomede I., *U.S.A.* **144 D5** 65 45N 168 56W
Little Falls, *Minn., U.S.A.* **154 C7** 45 59N 94 22W
Little Falls, *N.Y., U.S.A.* **151 C10** 43 3N 74 51W
Little Fork →, *U.S.A.* **154 A8** 48 31N 93 35W
Little Grand Rapids, *Canada* **143 C9** 52 0N 95 29W
Little Humboldt →, *U.S.A.* **158 F5** 41 1N 117 43W
Little Inagua I., *Bahamas* **165 B5** 21 40N 73 50W
Little Karoo, *S. Africa* **116 E3** 33 45 S 21 0 E
Little Lake, *U.S.A.* **161 K9** 35 56N 117 55W
Little Laut Is. = Laut Kecil, Kepulauan, *Indonesia* **85 C5** 4 45 S 115 40 E
Little Mecatina = Petit-Mécatina →, *Canada* **141 B8** 50 40N 59 30W
Little Minch, *U.K.* **22 D2** 57 35N 6 45W
Little Missouri →, *U.S.A.* **154 B3** 47 36N 102 25W
Little Nicobar, *India* **95 L11** 7 20N 93 40 E
Little Ouse →, *U.K.* **21 E9** 52 22N 1 12 E
Little Rann, *India* **92 H4** 23 25N 71 25 E
Little Red →, *U.S.A.* **155 H9** 35 11N 91 27W
Little River, *N.Z.* **131 D7** 43 45 S 172 49 E
Little Rock, *U.S.A.* **155 H8** 34 45N 92 17W
Little Ruaha →, *Tanzania* **118 D4** 7 57 S 37 53 E
Little Sable Pt., *U.S.A.* **148 D2** 43 38N 86 33W
Little Scarcies →, *S. Leone* **112 D2** 8 50N 13 15W
Little Sioux →, *U.S.A.* **154 E6** 41 48N 96 4W
Little Sitkin I., *U.S.A.* **144 L2** 51 57N 178 31 E
Little Smoky →, *Canada* **142 C5** 54 44N 117 11W
Little Snake →, *U.S.A.* **158 F9** 40 27N 108 26W
Little Sound, *Bermuda* **9 a** 32 15N 64 50W
Little Tobago, *Trin. & Tob.* **169 E10** 11 18N 60 30W
Little Valley, *U.S.A.* **150 D6** 42 15N 78 48W
Little Wabash →, *U.S.A.* **157 G8** 37 55N 88 5W
Little White →, *U.S.A.* **154 D4** 43 40N 100 40W
Little York, *U.S.A.* **156 C6** 41 1N 90 45W
Littlefield, *U.S.A.* **155 J3** 33 55N 102 20W
Littlehampton, *U.K.* **21 G7** 50 49N 0 32W
Littleton, *U.S.A.* **151 B13** 44 18N 71 46W
Litunga, *Angola* **115 E3** 13 19 S 16 48 E
Litvinov, *Czech Rep.* **34 A6** 50 36N 13 37 E
Liu He →, *China* **75 D11** 40 55N 121 35 E
Liu Jiang →, *China* **76 F7** 23 55N 109 30 E
Liuba, *China* **74 H4** 33 38N 106 55 E
Liucheng, *China* **76 E7** 24 38N 109 14 E
Liugou, *China* **75 D10** 40 57N 118 15 E
Liuhe, *China* **75 C13** 42 17N 125 43 E
Liuheng Dao, *China* **77 C14** 29 40N 122 5 E
Liujiang, *China* **76 E7** 24 26N 109 11 E
Liukang Tenggaja = Sabalana, Kepulauan, *Indonesia* **82 C1** 6 45 S 118 50 E
Liuli, *Tanzania* **119 E3** 11 3 S 34 38 E
Liuwa Plain, *Zambia* **115 E4** 14 20 S 22 30 E
Liuwa Plain Nat. Park, *Zambia* **115 E4** 14 45 S 22 35 E
Liuyang, *China* **77 C9** 28 10N 113 37 E
Liuzhou, *China* **76 E7** 24 22N 109 22 E
Liuzhuang, *China* **75 H11** 33 12N 120 18 E
Livada, *Romania* **52 C8** 47 52N 23 5 E
Livadherón, *Greece* **50 F5** 40 2N 21 57 E
Livadhia, *Cyprus* **39 F9** 34 57N 33 38 E
Livádhion, *Greece* **48 A4** 40 8N 22 9 E
Livadhje, *Albania* **38 B10** 39 47N 20 7 E
Livarot, *France* **26 D7** 48 58N 0 9 E
Live Oak, *Calif., U.S.A.* **160 F5** 39 17N 121 40W
Live Oak, *Fla., U.S.A.* **152 E7** 30 18N 82 59W
Livengood, *U.S.A.* **144 D10** 65 32N 148 33W
Liveras, *Cyprus* **39 E8** 35 23N 32 57 E
Livermore, *U.S.A.* **160 H5** 37 41N 121 47W
Livermore, Mt., *U.S.A.* **155 K2** 30 38N 104 11W
Livermore Falls, *U.S.A.* **149 C11** 44 29N 70 11W
Liverpool, *Australia* **129 B9** 33 54 S 150 58 E
Liverpool, *Canada* **141 D7** 44 5N 64 41W
Liverpool, *U.K.* **20 D4** 53 25N 3 0W
Liverpool, *U.S.A.* **151 C8** 43 6N 76 13W
Liverpool Bay, *U.K.* **20 D4** 53 30N 3 20W
Liverpool Plains, *Australia* **129 A9** 31 15 S 150 15 E
Liverpool Ra., *Australia* **129 A9** 31 50 S 150 30 E
Livigno, *Italy* **44 B7** 46 35N 10 10 E
Livingston, *Guatemala* **164 C2** 15 50N 88 50W
Livingston, *U.K.* **22 F5** 55 54N 3 30W
Livingston, *Ala., U.S.A.* **149 J1** 32 35N 88 11W
Livingston, *Calif., U.S.A.* **160 H6** 37 23N 120 43W
Livingston, *Mont., U.S.A.* **158 D8** 45 40N 110 34W
Livingston, *S.C., U.S.A.* **149 J5** 33 32N 80 53W
Livingston, *Tenn., U.S.A.* **149 G3** 36 23N 85 19W
Livingston, *Tex., U.S.A.* **155 K7** 30 43N 94 56W
Livingston, *Wis., U.S.A.* **156 B6** 42 54N 90 26W
Livingston, L., *U.S.A.* **155 K7** 30 50N 95 10W
Livingston Manor, *U.S.A.* **151 E10** 41 54N 74 50W
Livingstone, *Zambia* **119 F2** 17 46 S 25 52 E
Livingstone Mts., *N.Z.* **131 F3** 45 15 S 168 9 E
Livingstone Mts., *Tanzania* **119 D3** 9 40 S 34 20 E
Livingstonia, *Malawi* **119 E3** 10 38 S 34 5 E
Livno, *Bos.-H.* **52 G2** 43 50N 17 1 E
Livny, *Russia* **59 F9** 52 30N 37 30 E
Livonia, *Mich., U.S.A.* **157 B13** 42 23N 83 23W
Livonia, *N.Y., U.S.A.* **150 D7** 42 49N 77 40W
Livorno, *Italy* **44 E7** 43 33N 10 19 E
Livramento, *Brazil* **175 C4** 30 55 S 55 30W
Livramento do Brumado, *Brazil* **171 D3** 13 39 S 41 50W
Livron-sur-Drôme, *France* **29 D8** 44 46N 4 51 E
Liwale, *Tanzania* **119 D4** 9 48 S 37 58 E
Liwiec →, *Poland* **55 F8** 52 36N 21 34 E
Liwonde Nat. Park, *Malawi* **119 E4** 14 48 S 35 20 E
Lixi, *China* **76 D3** 26 23N 101 59 E
Lixian, *China* **76 B4** 31 23N 103 13 E
Lixoúrion, *Greece* **39 C2** 38 12N 20 26 E
Liyang, *China* **77 B12** 31 26N 119 28 E
Lizard I., *Australia* **126 A4** 14 42 S 145 30 E
Lizard Pt., *U.K.* **21 H2** 49 57N 5 13W
Lizarda, *Brazil* **170 C2** 9 36 S 46 41W
Lizella, *U.S.A.* **152 C6** 32 48N 83 49W
Lizzano, *Italy* **47 B10** 40 23N 17 27 E
Ljig, *Serbia, Yug.* **50 B4** 44 13N 20 18 E
Ljøra →, *Norway* **18 C9** 61 24N 12 35 E
Ljørdal, *Norway* **18 C9** 61 23N 12 41 E
Ljosland, *Norway* **18 F4** 58 47N 7 22 E
Ljubija, *Bos.-H.* **45 D13** 44 55N 16 35 E
Ljubinje, *Bos.-H.* **50 D2** 42 58N 18 5 E
Ljubljana, *Slovenia* **45 B11** 46 4N 14 33 E
Ljubno, *Slovenia* **45 B11** 46 25N 14 46 E
Ljubovija, *Serbia, Yug.* **50 B3** 44 11N 19 22 E
Ljugarn, *Sweden* **17 G12** 57 20N 18 43 E
Ljung, *Sweden* **17 G7** 57 59N 13 3 E
Ljungan →, *Sweden* **16 B11** 62 18N 17 23 E
Ljungaverk, *Sweden* **16 B10** 62 30N 16 5 E
Ljungby, *Sweden* **15 H15** 56 49N 13 55 E
Ljungbyholm, *Sweden* **17 H10** 56 39N 16 5 E
Ljungdalen, *Sweden* **16 B6** 62 51N 12 47 E
Ljungsbro, *Sweden* **17 F9** 58 31N 15 30 E
Ljungskile, *Sweden* **17 F5** 58 14N 11 55 E
Ljusdal, *Sweden* **16 C10** 61 46N 16 3 E
Ljusfallshammar, *Sweden* **17 F9** 58 48N 15 30 E
Ljusnan →, *Sweden* **16 C11** 61 12N 17 8 E
Ljusne, *Sweden* **16 C11** 61 13N 17 7 E
Ljutomer, *Slovenia* **45 B13** 46 31N 16 11 E
Llagostera, *Spain* **40 D7** 41 50N 2 54 E
Llamellín, *Peru* **172 B2** 9 0 S 76 54W
Llancanelo, Salina, *Argentina* **174 D2** 35 40 S 69 8W
Llandeilo, *U.K.* **21 F4** 51 53N 3 59W
Llandovery, *U.K.* **21 F4** 51 59N 3 48W
Llandrindod Wells, *U.K.* **21 E4** 52 14N 3 22W
Llandudno, *U.K.* **20 D4** 53 19N 3 50W
Llanelli, *U.K.* **21 F3** 51 41N 4 10W
Llanes, *Spain* **42 B6** 43 25N 4 50W
Llangollen, *U.K.* **20 E4** 52 58N 3 11W
Llanidloes, *U.K.* **21 E4** 52 27N 3 31W
Llano, *U.S.A.* **155 K5** 30 45N 98 41W
Llano →, *U.S.A.* **155 K5** 30 39N 98 26W
Llano Estacado, *U.S.A.* **155 J3** 33 30N 103 0W
Llanos, *S. Amer.* **166 C3** 5 0N 71 35W
Llanquihue, L., *Chile* **176 B1** 41 10 S 72 50W
Llanwrtyd Wells, *U.K.* **21 E4** 52 7N 3 38W
Llata, *Peru* **172 B2** 9 25 S 76 47W
Llebeig, C. des, *Spain* **38 B3** 39 33N 2 18 E
Lleida, *Spain* **40 D5** 41 37N 0 39 E
Lleida □, *Spain* **40 C6** 42 6N 1 0 E
Llentrisca, C., *Spain* **38 D1** 38 52N 1 15 E
Llera, *Mexico* **163 C5** 23 19N 99 1W
Llerena, *Spain* **43 G5** 38 17N 6 0W
Lleyn Peninsula, *U.K.* **20 E3** 52 51N 4 36W
Llica, *Bolivia* **172 D4** 19 52 S 68 16W
Llico, *Chile* **174 C1** 34 46 S 72 5W
Llíria, *Spain* **41 F4** 39 37N 0 35W
Llobregat →, *Spain* **40 D7** 41 19N 2 9 E
Llodio, *Spain* **40 B2** 43 9N 2 58W
Llorente, *Phil.* **81 F5** 11 25N 125 33 E
Lloret de Mar, *Spain* **40 D7** 41 41N 2 53 E

Lowa →, Dem. Rep. of the Congo 118 C2 1 24 S 25 51 E
Lowden, U.S.A. 156 C6 41 52N 90 56W
Lowell, Ind., U.S.A. 157 C9 41 18N 87 25W
Lowell, Mass., U.S.A. 151 D13 42 38N 71 19W
Lowell, Mich., U.S.A. 157 B11 42 56N 85 20W
Lowellville, U.S.A. 150 E4 41 2N 80 32W
Löwen →, Namibia 116 D2 26 51 S 18 17 E
Lower Alkali L., U.S.A. 158 F3 41 16N 120 2W
Lower Arrow L., Canada 142 D5 49 40N 118 5W
Lower Austria = Niederösterreich □, Austria 34 C8 48 25N 15 40 E
Lower California = Baja California, Mexico 162 A1 31 10N 115 12W
Lower Glenelg Nat. Park, Australia 128 E4 38 4 S 141 41 E
Lower Hutt, N.Z. 130 H3 41 10 S 174 55 E
Lower Kalskag, U.S.A. 144 F7 61 31N 160 22W
Lower Lake, U.S.A. 160 G4 38 55N 122 37W
Lower Manitou L., Canada 143 D10 49 15N 93 0W
Lower Paia, U.S.A. 145 C5 20 55N 156 23W
Lower Post, Canada 142 B3 59 58N 128 30W
Lower Red L., U.S.A. 154 B7 47 58N 95 0W
Lower Saxony = Niedersachsen □, Germany 30 C4 52 50N 9 0 E
Lower Tunguska = Tunguska, Nizhnyaya →, Russia 67 C9 65 48N 88 4 E
Lower Zambezi Nat. Park, Zambia 119 F2 15 25 S 29 40 E
Lowestoft, U.K. 21 E9 52 29N 1 45 E
Lowgar □, Afghan. 91 B3 34 0N 69 0 E
Łowicz, Poland 55 F6 52 6N 19 55 E
Lowly, Pt., Australia 128 B2 33 0 S 137 46 E
Lowry City, U.S.A. 156 F3 38 8N 93 44W
Lowville, U.S.A. 151 C9 43 47N 75 29W
Loxton, Australia 128 C4 34 28 S 140 31 E
Loxton, S. Africa 116 E3 31 30 S 22 22 E
Loyalton, U.S.A. 160 F6 39 41N 120 14W
Loyalty Is. = Loyauté, Îs., N. Cal. 133 K4 20 50 S 166 30 E
Loyang = Luoyang, China 74 G7 34 40N 112 26 E
Loyauté, Îs., N. Cal. 133 K4 20 50 S 166 30 E
Loyev = Loyew, Belarus 59 G6 51 56N 30 46 E
Loyew, Belarus 59 G6 51 56N 30 46 E
Loyoro, Uganda 118 B3 3 22N 34 14 E
Lož, Slovenia 45 C11 45 43N 14 30 E
Lozère □, France 28 D7 44 35N 3 30 E
Loznica, Serbia, Yug. 50 B3 44 32N 19 12 E
Lozova, Ukraine 59 H9 49 0N 36 20 E
Lozva →, Russia 64 B9 59 36N 62 20 E
Lu, India 90 B5 26 58N 95 14 E
Lü Shan, China 77 C11 29 30N 115 55 E
Lü-Tao, Taiwan 77 F13 22 40N 121 30 E
Lu Verne, U.S.A. 156 B2 42 55N 94 5W
Lu Wo, China 69 F11 22 33N 114 6 E
Lua →, Dem. Rep. of the Congo 114 B3 2 46N 18 26 E
Lua Makika, U.S.A. 145 C5 20 33N 156 37W
Luachimo, Angola 115 D4 7 23 S 20 48 E
Luacono, Angola 115 E4 11 15 S 21 37 E
Luajan →, India 93 G11 24 44N 85 1 E
Lualaba →, Dem. Rep. of the Congo 118 B2 0 26N 25 20 E
Luale, Dem. Rep. of the Congo 114 B4 1 9N 23 5 E
Luampa, Zambia 119 F1 15 4 S 24 20 E
Lu'an, China 77 B11 31 45N 116 29 E
Luan Chau, Vietnam 76 G4 21 38N 103 24 E
Luan He →, China 75 E10 39 20N 119 5 E
Luan Xian, China 75 E10 39 40N 118 40 E
Luancheng, Guangxi Zhuangzu, China 76 F7 22 48N 108 55 E
Luancheng, Hebei, China 74 F8 37 53N 114 40 E
Luanco, Spain 42 B5 43 37N 5 48W
Luanda, Angola 115 D2 8 50 S 13 15 E
Luando, Reserva Natural Integral do, Angola 115 E3 11 0 S 17 32 E
Luang, Thale, Thailand 87 J3 7 30N 100 15 E
Luang Prabang, Laos 76 H4 19 52N 102 10 E
Luanginga →, Zambia 115 F4 15 11 S 22 55 E
Luangwa, Zambia 119 F3 15 35 S 30 16 E
Luangwa →, Zambia 119 E3 14 25 S 30 25 E
Luangwa Valley, Zambia 119 E3 13 30 S 31 30 E
Luania-Bubi, Dem. Rep. of the Congo 115 D4 7 28 S 24 49 E
Luanne, China 75 D9 40 55N 117 40 E
Luanping, China 75 D9 40 53N 117 23 E
Luanshya, Zambia 119 E2 13 3 S 28 28 E
Luapula □, Zambia 119 E2 11 0 S 29 0 E
Luapula →, Africa 119 D2 9 26 S 28 33 E
Luarca, Spain 42 B4 43 32N 6 32W
Luashi, Dem. Rep. of the Congo 119 E1 10 50 S 23 36 E
Luatamba, Angola 115 E4 12 6 S 20 19 E
Luatira, Angola 115 E3 12 52 S 17 14 E
Luau, Angola 115 E4 10 40 S 22 10 E
Luba, Phil. 80 C3 17 19N 120 42 E
Lubaczów, Poland 55 H10 50 10N 23 8 E
Lubalo, Angola 115 D3 9 10 S 19 15 E
Lubamiti, Dem. Rep. of the Congo 114 C3 2 28 S 17 47 E
Lubań, Poland 55 G2 51 5N 15 15 E
Lubana, Ozero = Lubānas Ezers, Latvia 15 H22 56 45N 27 0 E
Lubānas Ezers, Latvia 15 H22 56 45N 27 0 E
Lubang, Phil. 80 E3 13 52N 120 7 E
Lubang Is., Phil. 80 E3 13 50N 120 12 E
Lubango, Angola 115 E2 14 55 S 13 30 E
Lubao, Dem. Rep. of the Congo 118 D2 5 17 S 25 42 E
Lubartów, Poland 55 G9 51 28N 22 42 E
Lubawa, Poland 54 E6 53 30N 19 48 E
Lübbecke, Germany 30 C4 52 18N 8 37 E
Lübben, Germany 30 D9 51 56N 13 54 E
Lübbenau, Germany 30 D9 51 52N 13 57 E
Lubbock, U.S.A. 155 J4 33 35N 101 51W
Lübeck, Germany 30 B6 53 52N 10 40 E
Lübecker Bucht, Germany 30 A6 54 3N 10 54 E
Lubefu, Dem. Rep. of the Congo 118 C1 4 47 S 24 27 E
Lubefu →, Dem. Rep. of the Congo 118 C1 4 10 S 23 0 E
Lubelskie □, Poland 55 G9 51 20N 22 50 E
Lubero = Luofu, Dem. Rep. of the Congo 118 C2 0 10 S 29 15 E
Lubersac, France 28 C5 45 26N 1 23 E
Lubicon L., Canada 142 B5 56 23N 115 56W
Lubień Kujawski, Poland 55 F6 52 23N 19 9 E
Lubilash →, Dem. Rep. of the Congo 115 D4 6 2 S 23 45 E
Lubin, Poland 55 G3 51 24N 16 11 E
Lublin, Poland 55 G9 51 12N 22 38 E
Lubliniec, Poland 55 H5 50 43N 18 45 E
Lubnān, Jabal, Lebanon 103 B4 33 45N 35 40 E
Lubniewice, Poland 55 F2 52 31N 15 15 E
Lubny, Ukraine 59 G7 50 3N 32 58 E
Lubomierz, Poland 55 G2 51 1N 15 31 E
Luboń, Poland 55 F3 52 21N 16 51 E
Lubondaie, Dem. Rep. of the Congo 115 D4 8 1 S 26 32 E
Lubongola, Dem. Rep. of the Congo 118 C2 2 35 S 27 50 E
L'ubotín, Slovak Rep. 35 B13 49 17N 20 53 E
Lubraniec, Poland 55 F5 52 33N 18 50 E
Lubsko, Poland 55 G1 51 45N 14 57 E
Lübtheen, Germany 30 B7 53 18N 11 5 E
Lubuagan, Phil. 80 C3 17 21N 121 10 E
Lubudi, Dem. Rep. of the Congo 115 D4 6 51 S 21 18 E
Lubudi →, Kasai-Occ., Dem. Rep. of the Congo 115 C4 4 19 S 20 23 E
Lubudi →, Katanga, Dem. Rep. of the Congo 119 D2 9 0 S 25 35 E
Lubuklinggau, Indonesia 84 C2 3 15 S 102 55 E
Lubuksikaping, Indonesia 84 B2 0 10N 100 15 E
Lubumbashi, Dem. Rep. of the Congo 119 E2 11 40 S 27 28 E
Lubunda, Dem. Rep. of the Congo 118 D2 5 12 S 26 41 E
Lubungu, Zambia 119 E2 14 35 S 26 24 E
Lubuskie □, Poland 55 F2 52 10N 15 20 E
Lubutu, Dem. Rep. of the Congo 118 C2 0 45 S 26 30 E
Luc An Chau, Vietnam 86 A5 22 6N 104 43 E
Luc-en-Diois, France 29 D9 44 36N 5 28 E
Lucala, Angola 115 D3 9 7 S 15 58 E
Lucala →, Angola 115 D2 9 38 S 14 14 E
Lucan, Canada 150 C3 43 11N 81 24W
Lucania, Mt., Canada 138 B5 61 1N 140 29W
Lucapa, Angola 115 D4 8 25 S 20 45 E
Lucas, U.S.A. 156 C3 41 2N 93 29W
Lucas Channel, Canada 150 A3 45 21N 81 45W
Lucban, Phil. 80 D3 14 6N 121 33 E
Lucca, Italy 44 E7 43 50N 10 29 E
Lucé, France 26 D8 48 26N 1 27 E
Luce Bay, U.K. 22 G4 54 45N 4 48W
Lucea, Jamaica 164 a 18 25N 78 10W
Lucedale, U.S.A. 149 K1 30 56N 88 35W
Lucena, Phil. 80 E3 13 56N 121 37 E
Lucena, Spain 43 H6 37 27N 4 31W
Lučenec, Slovak Rep. 35 C12 48 18N 19 42 E
Lucens, Switz. 32 C3 46 43N 6 51 E
Lucera, Italy 47 A8 41 30N 15 20 E
Lucerne = Luzern, Switz. 33 B6 47 3N 8 18 E
Lucerne, U.S.A. 160 F4 39 6N 122 48W
Lucerne Valley, U.S.A. 161 L10 34 27N 116 57W
Lucero, Mexico 162 A3 30 49N 106 30W
Luchena →, Spain 41 H3 37 44N 1 50W
Lucheng, China 74 F7 36 20N 113 11 E
Lucheringo →, Mozam. 119 E4 11 43 S 36 17 E
Lüchow, Germany 30 C7 52 58N 11 8 E
Luchuan, China 77 F8 22 21N 110 12 E
Lucia, U.S.A. 160 J5 36 2N 121 33W
Lucie →, Surinam 169 C6 3 35N 57 38W
Lucinda, Australia 126 B4 18 32 S 146 20 E
Lucindale, Australia 128 D4 36 58 S 140 26 E
Lucira, Angola 115 E2 14 0 S 12 35 E
Luciras, B. das, Angola 115 E2 13 52 S 12 31 E
Luckau, Germany 30 D9 51 50N 13 42 E
Luckenwalde, Germany 30 C9 52 5N 13 10 E
Luckey, U.S.A. 157 C13 41 27N 83 29W
Luckhoff, S. Africa 116 D3 29 44 S 24 43 E
Lucknow, Canada 150 C3 43 57N 81 31W
Lucknow, India 93 F9 26 50N 81 0 E
Luçon, France 28 B2 46 28N 1 10W
Lucusse, Angola 115 E4 12 32 S 20 48 E
Lüda = Dalian, China 75 E11 38 50N 121 40 E
Luda Kamchiya →, Bulgaria 51 C11 43 3N 27 29 E
Ludbreg, Croatia 45 B13 46 15N 16 38 E
Lüdenscheid, Germany 30 D3 51 13N 7 37 E
Lüderitz, Namibia 116 D2 26 41 S 15 8 E
Lüderitzbaai, Namibia 116 D2 26 36 S 15 8 E
Ludhiana, India 92 D6 30 57N 75 56 E
Ludian, China 76 D4 27 10N 103 33 E
Luding Qiao, China 76 C4 29 53N 102 12 E
Lüdinghausen, Germany 30 D3 51 46N 7 27 E
Ludington, U.S.A. 148 D2 43 57N 86 27W
Ludlow, U.K. 21 E5 52 22N 2 42W
Ludlow, Calif., U.S.A. 161 L10 34 43N 116 10W
Ludlow, Pa., U.S.A. 150 E6 41 43N 78 56W
Ludlow, Vt., U.S.A. 151 C12 43 24N 72 42W
Ludowici, U.S.A. 152 D8 31 43N 81 45W
Ludus, Romania 53 D9 46 29N 24 5 E
Ludvika, Sweden 16 D9 60 8N 15 14 E
Ludwigsburg, Germany 31 G5 48 53N 9 11 E
Ludwigsfelde, Germany 30 C9 52 17N 13 17 E
Ludwigshafen, Germany 31 F4 49 29N 8 26 E
Ludwigslust, Germany 30 B7 53 19N 11 30 E
Ludza, Latvia 58 D4 56 32N 27 43 E
Lue, Australia 129 B8 32 38 S 149 50 E
Luebo, Dem. Rep. of the Congo 115 D4 5 21 S 21 23 E
Lueki, Dem. Rep. of the Congo 118 C2 3 20 S 25 48 E
Luena, Angola 115 E3 12 13 S 19 51 E
Luena, Dem. Rep. of the Congo 119 D2 9 28 S 25 43 E
Luena, Zambia 119 E3 10 40 S 30 25 E
Luena →, Angola 115 E4 12 30 S 22 34 E
Luena →, Zambia 115 E4 14 46 S 23 30 E
Luena Flats, Zambia 115 E4 14 47 S 23 17 E
Luengué, Coutada Pública do, Angola 115 F3 16 55 S 19 55 E
Luepa, Venezuela 169 B5 5 43N 61 31W
Lueta →, Dem. Rep. of the Congo 115 D4 7 4 S 21 40 E
Luete →, Zambia 115 F4 15 46 S 23 10 E
Lüeyang, China 74 H4 33 22N 106 10 E
Lufeng, Guangdong, China 77 F10 22 57N 115 38 E
Lufeng, Yunnan, China 76 E4 25 0N 102 5 E
Lufico, Angola 115 D2 6 24 S 13 23 E
Lufira →, Dem. Rep. of the Congo 119 D2 9 30 S 27 0 E
Lufkin, U.S.A. 155 K7 31 21N 94 44W
Lufupa, Dem. Rep. of the Congo 119 E1 10 37 S 24 56 E
Luga, Russia 58 C5 58 40N 29 55 E
Luga →, Russia 58 C5 59 40N 28 18 E
Lugano, Switz. 33 E7 46 1N 8 57 E
Lugano, L. di, Switz. 33 E8 46 0N 9 0 E
Lugansk = Luhansk, Ukraine 59 H10 48 38N 39 15 E
Luganville, Vanuatu 133 E5 15 27 S 167 10 E
Lugard's Falls, Kenya 118 C4 3 6 S 38 41 E
Lugela, Mozam. 119 F4 16 25 S 36 43 E
Lugenda →, Mozam. 119 E4 11 25 S 38 33 E
Lugh Ganana, Somali Rep. 120 D2 3 48N 42 34 E
Lugnaquilla, Ireland 23 D5 52 58N 6 28W
Lugo, Italy 45 D8 44 25N 11 54 E
Lugo, Spain 42 B3 43 2N 7 35W
Lugo □, Spain 42 C3 43 0N 7 30W
Lugoj, Romania 52 E6 45 42N 21 57 E
Lugovoy = Qulan, Kazakstan 66 E8 42 55N 72 43 E
Lugus I., Phil. 81 J3 5 41N 120 50 E
Luhansk, Ukraine 59 H10 48 38N 39 15 E
Luhe, China 77 A12 32 19N 118 50 E
Luhe →, Germany 30 B6 53 23N 10 13 E
Luhit →, India 90 B5 27 48N 95 28 E
Luhuo, China 76 B3 31 21N 100 48 E
Lui →, Angola 115 D3 8 21 S 17 33 E
Lui →, Zambia 115 F4 16 18 S 23 17 E
Luia, Angola 115 D4 8 10 S 21 32 E
Luia →, Angola 115 D4 8 32 S 21 47 E
Luiana, Angola 116 B3 17 25 S 22 59 E
Luiana →, Angola 115 F4 17 24 S 23 3 E
Luiana, Coutada Pública do, Angola 115 F4 16 55 S 22 20 E
Luilaka →, Dem. Rep. of the Congo 114 C4 0 52 S 20 12 E
Luimneach = Limerick, Ireland 23 D3 52 40N 8 37W
Luing, U.K. 22 E3 56 14N 5 39W
Luino, Italy 44 C5 45 59N 8 44 E
Luio →, Angola 115 E4 13 17 S 21 37 E
Luís Correia, Brazil 170 B3 3 0 S 41 35W
Luís Gonçalves, Brazil 170 C1 5 37 S 50 25W
Luitpold Coast, Antarctica 7 D1 78 30 S 32 0W
Luiza, Dem. Rep. of the Congo 115 D4 7 40 S 22 30 E
Luizi, Dem. Rep. of the Congo 118 D2 6 0 S 27 25 E
Luján, Argentina 174 C4 34 45 S 59 5W
Lujiang, China 77 B11 31 20N 117 15 E
Lukala, Dem. Rep. of the Congo 115 D2 5 31 S 14 32 E
Lukang, Taiwan 77 E13 24 1N 120 22 E
Lukanga, Bandundu, Dem. Rep. of the Congo 114 C3 1 41 S 18 9 E
Lukanga, Équateur, Dem. Rep. of the Congo 114 C3 1 0 S 18 8 E
Lukanga Swamp, Zambia 119 E2 14 30 S 27 40 E
Lukavac, Bos.-H. 52 F3 44 33N 18 32 E
Lukenie →, Dem. Rep. of the Congo 114 C3 3 0 S 18 50 E
Lukhisaral, India 93 G12 25 11N 86 5 E
Lŭki, Bulgaria 51 E8 41 50N 24 43 E
Lukk, Libya 108 B4 32 1N 24 46 E
Lukolela, Équateur, Dem. Rep. of the Congo 114 C3 1 10 S 17 12 E
Lukolela, Kasai-Or., Dem. Rep. of the Congo 118 D1 5 23 S 24 32 E
Lukosi, Zimbabwe 119 F2 18 30 S 26 30 E
Lukovë, Albania 50 G3 39 59N 19 54 E
Lukovit, Bulgaria 51 C8 43 13N 24 11 E
Łuków, Poland 55 G9 51 55N 22 23 E
Lukoyanov, Russia 60 C7 55 2N 44 29 E
Luksefjell, Norway 18 E6 59 23N 9 34 E
Lukuni, Dem. Rep. of the Congo 115 D3 5 50 S 17 16 E
Lukusuzi Nat. Park, Zambia 119 E3 12 43 S 32 36 E
Lula, Dem. Rep. of the Congo 115 D3 5 22 S 16 2 E
Lule älv →, Sweden 14 D19 65 35N 22 10 E
Luleå, Sweden 14 D20 65 35N 22 10 E
Lüleburgaz, Turkey 51 E11 41 23N 27 22 E
Luliang, China 76 E4 25 0N 103 40 E
Luling, U.S.A. 155 L6 29 41N 97 39W
Lulong, China 75 E10 39 53N 118 51 E
Lulonga →, Dem. Rep. of the Congo 114 B3 1 0N 18 10 E
Lulu, U.S.A. 152 E7 30 7N 82 29W
Lulu →, Dem. Rep. of the Congo 114 B4 1 18N 23 42 E
Lulua →, Dem. Rep. of the Congo 115 C4 4 30 S 20 30 E
Luma, Amer. Samoa 133 X25 14 16 S 169 33W
Lumai, Angola 115 E4 13 13 S 21 25 E
Lumajang, Indonesia 85 D4 8 8 S 113 13 E
Lumaku, Gunong, Malaysia 85 B5 4 52N 115 38 E
Lumbala →, Angola 115 E4 12 39 S 22 35 E
Lumbala Kaquengue, Angola 115 E4 12 39 S 22 34 E
Lumbala N'guimbo, Angola 115 E4 14 18 S 21 18 E
Lumbe →, Zambia 115 F4 16 44 S 23 41 E
Lumber City, U.S.A. 152 D7 31 56N 82 41W
Lumberton, U.S.A. 149 H6 34 37N 79 0W
Lumbwa, Kenya 118 C4 0 12 S 35 28 E
Lumding, India 90 C4 25 46N 93 10 E
Lumi, Papua N. G. 132 B2 3 30 S 142 2 E
Lumpkin, U.S.A. 152 C5 32 3N 84 48W
Lumsden, Canada 143 C8 50 39N 104 52W
Lumsden, N.Z. 131 F3 45 44 S 168 27 E
Lumut, Malaysia 87 K3 4 13N 100 37 E
Lumut, Tanjung, Indonesia 84 C3 3 50 S 105 58 E
Luna, India 92 H3 23 43N 69 16 E
Luna, Phil. 80 B3 18 18N 121 21 E
Lunan, China 76 E4 24 40N 103 18 E
Lunavada, India 92 H5 23 8N 73 37 E
Lunca, Romania 53 C10 47 22N 25 1 E
Lunca Corbului, Romania 53 F9 44 42N 24 45 E
Lund, Sweden 17 J7 55 44N 13 12 E
Lunda Norte □, Angola 115 D3 8 0 S 20 0 E
Lunda Sul □, Angola 115 D4 10 0 S 20 0 E
Lundamo, Norway 18 A7 63 9N 10 19 E
Lundazi, Zambia 119 E3 12 20 S 33 7 E
Lunderskov, Denmark 17 J3 55 29N 9 19 E
Lundi →, Zimbabwe 119 G3 21 43 S 32 34 E
Lundu, Malaysia 85 B3 1 40N 109 50 E
Lundy, U.K. 21 F3 51 10N 4 41W
Lune →, U.K. 20 C5 54 0N 2 51W
Lüneburg, Germany 30 B6 53 15N 10 24 E
Lüneburg Heath = Lüneburger Heide, Germany 30 B6 53 10N 10 12 E
Lüneburger Heide, Germany 30 B6 53 10N 10 12 E
Lunel, France 29 E8 43 39N 4 9 E
Lünen, Germany 30 D3 51 37N 7 32 E
Lunenburg, Canada 141 D7 44 22N 64 18W
Lunéville, France 27 D13 48 36N 6 30 E
Lunga, Dem. Rep. of the Congo 115 C4 5 46 S 12 14 E
Lunga →, Zambia 119 E2 14 34 S 26 25 E
Lunge, Angola 115 E3 12 13 S 16 7 E
Lungern, Switz. 32 C6 46 48N 8 10 E
Lungga, Solomon Is. 133 M11 9 25 S 160 3 E
Lungi Airport, S. Leone 112 D2 8 40N 13 17W
Lunglei, India 90 D4 22 55N 92 45 E
Lungngo, Burma 90 E4 21 57N 93 36 E
Lungwebungu →, Zambia 115 E4 14 19 S 23 14 E
Luni, India 92 G5 26 0N 73 6 E
Luni →, India 92 G4 24 41N 71 14 E
Luninets = Luninyets, Belarus 59 F4 52 15N 26 50 E
Luning, U.S.A. 158 G4 38 30N 118 11W
Lunino, Russia 60 D7 53 38N 45 18 E
Luninyets, Belarus 59 F4 52 15N 26 50 E
Lunkaransar, India 92 E5 28 29N 73 44 E
Lunner, Norway 18 D7 60 19N 10 35 E
Lunsemfwa →, Zambia 119 E3 14 54 S 30 12 E
Lunsemfwa Falls, Zambia 119 E2 14 30 S 29 6 E
Luo He →, China 74 G6 34 35N 110 20 E
Luocheng, China 76 E7 24 48N 108 53 E
Luochuan, China 74 G5 35 45N 109 26 E
Luoci, China 76 E4 25 19N 102 18 E
Luodian, China 76 E6 25 24N 106 43 E
Luoding, China 77 F8 22 45N 111 40 E
Luofu, Dem. Rep. of the Congo 118 C2 0 10 S 29 15 E
Luohe, China 74 H8 33 32N 114 2 E
Luojiang, China 76 B5 31 18N 104 33 E
Luonan, China 74 G6 34 5N 110 10 E
Luoning, China 74 G6 34 35N 111 40 E
Luoshan, China 77 A10 32 13N 114 30 E
Luotian, China 77 B10 30 46N 115 22 E
Luoxiao Shan, China 77 D10 26 30N 114 1 E
Luoyang, China 74 G7 34 40N 112 26 E
Luoyuan, China 77 D12 26 28N 119 30 E
Luozi, Dem. Rep. of the Congo 115 C2 4 54 S 14 0 E
Luozigou, China 75 C16 43 42N 130 18 E
Lupanshui, China 76 D5 26 38N 104 48 E
Lupeni, Romania 53 E8 45 21N 23 13 E
Lupilichi, Mozam. 119 E4 11 47 S 35 13 E
Lupire, Angola 115 E3 14 36 S 19 29 E
Łupków, Poland 55 J9 49 15N 22 4 E
Lupoing, China 76 E5 24 53N 104 21 E
Lupon, Phil. 81 H6 6 54N 126 0 E
Luputa, Dem. Rep. of the Congo 115 D4 7 7 S 23 43 E
Luqa, Malta 38 F7 35 52N 14 29 E
Luquan, China 76 E4 25 35N 102 25 E
Luque, Paraguay 174 B4 25 19 S 57 25W
Luquembo, Angola 115 E3 10 44 S 17 43 E
Lūras, Italy 46 B2 40 56N 9 10 E
Luray, U.S.A. 148 F6 38 40N 78 28W
Lure, France 27 E13 47 40N 6 30 E
Luremo, Angola 115 D3 8 30 S 17 50 E
Lurgan, U.K. 23 B5 54 28N 6 19W
Luribay, Bolivia 172 D4 17 6 S 67 39W
Lurin, Peru 172 C2 12 17 S 76 52W
Lusaka, Zambia 119 F2 15 28 S 28 16 E
Lusambo, Dem. Rep. of the Congo 118 C1 4 58 S 23 28 E
Lusancay Is. and Reefs, Papua N. G. 132 E6 8 30 S 150 30 E
Lusangaye, Dem. Rep. of the Congo 118 C2 4 54 S 26 0 E
Luseland, Canada 143 C7 52 5N 109 24W
Lusenga Plain Nat. Park, Zambia 119 D2 9 22 S 29 14 E
Lusengo, Dem. Rep. of the Congo 114 B3 1 47N 19 31 E
Lushan, Henan, China 74 H7 33 45N 112 55 E
Lushan, Sichuan, China 76 B4 30 12N 102 52 E
Lushi, China 74 G6 34 3N 111 3 E
Lushnjë, Albania 50 F3 40 55N 19 41 E
Lushoto, Tanzania 118 C4 4 47 S 38 20 E
Lushui, China 76 E2 25 58N 98 44 E
Lüshun, China 75 E11 38 45N 121 15 E
Lusignan, France 28 B4 46 26N 0 8 E
Lusigny-sur-Barse, France 27 D11 48 16N 4 15 E
Lusiye, Zambia 115 F4 16 30 S 27 57 E
Lusk, U.S.A. 154 D2 42 46N 104 27W
Lussac-les-Châteaux, France 28 B4 46 24N 0 43 E
Lustenau, Austria 34 D2 47 26N 9 39 E
Lustrafjorden, Norway 18 C4 61 23N 7 25 E
Lūt, Dasht-e, Iran 97 D8 31 30N 58 0 E
Luta = Dalian, China 75 E11 38 50N 121 40 E
Lutembo, Angola 115 E4 13 26 S 21 16 E
Lutherstadt Wittenberg, Germany 30 D8 51 53N 12 39 E
Luthersville, U.S.A. 152 B5 33 13N 84 45W
Luti, Solomon Is. 133 L9 7 14 S 157 0 E
Luton, U.K. 21 F7 51 53N 0 24W
Luton □, U.K. 21 F7 51 53N 0 24W
Lutong, Malaysia 85 B4 4 28N 114 0 E
Lutry, Switz. 32 C3 46 31N 6 42 E
Lutselke, Canada 143 A6 62 24N 110 44W
Lutshima →, Dem. Rep. of the Congo 115 D3 5 22 S 18 59 E
Lutsk, Ukraine 59 G3 50 50N 25 15 E
Lutuai, Angola 115 E4 12 41 S 20 7 E
Lutz, U.S.A. 153 G7 28 9N 82 28W
Lützow Holmbukta, Antarctica 7 C4 69 10 S 37 30 E
Lutzputs, S. Africa 116 D3 28 3 S 20 40 E
Luuk, Phil. 81 J3 5 58N 121 18 E
Luuq = Lugh Ganana, Somali Rep. 120 D2 3 48N 42 34 E
Luverne, Ala., U.S.A. 152 D3 31 43N 86 16W
Luverne, Minn., U.S.A. 154 D6 43 39N 96 13W
Luvo, Angola 115 D2 5 51 S 14 5 E
Lúvua, Angola 115 E4 8 49 S 25 19 E
Luvua, Dem. Rep. of the Congo 119 D2 8 48 S 25 17 E
Luvua →, Dem. Rep. of the Congo 118 D2 6 50 S 27 30 E
Luvuvhu →, S. Africa 117 C5 22 25 S 31 18 E
Luwegu →, Tanzania 119 D4 8 31 S 37 23 E
Luwuk, Indonesia 82 B2 0 56 S 122 47 E
Luxembourg, Lux. 24 E6 49 37N 6 9 E
Luxembourg □, Belgium 24 E5 49 58N 5 30 E
Luxembourg ■, Europe 25 B7 49 45N 6 0 E
Luxemburg, U.S.A. 156 B5 44 32N 91 5W
Luxeuil-les-Bains, France 27 E13 47 49N 6 24 E
Luxi, Hunan, China 77 C8 28 20N 110 7 E
Luxi, Yunnan, China 76 E4 24 40N 103 55 E
Luxi, Yunnan, China 76 E2 24 27N 98 36 E
Luxor = El Uqsur, Egypt 106 B3 25 41N 32 38 E
Luy-de-Béarn →, France 28 E3 43 39N 0 48W
Luy-de-France →, France 28 E3 43 39N 0 48W
Luyi, China 74 H8 33 50N 115 35 E
Luz, Azores 9 d1 39 1N 28 0W
Luz-St-Sauveur, France 28 F4 42 53N 0 0W
Luza, Russia 56 B8 60 39N 47 10 E
Luzern, Switz. 33 B6 47 3N 8 18 E
Luzern □, Switz. 32 B5 47 2N 7 55 E
Luzhai, China 76 E7 24 29N 109 42 E
Luzhi, China 76 D5 26 21N 105 16 E
Luzhou, China 76 C5 28 52N 105 20 E
Luziânia, Brazil 171 E2 16 20 S 48 0W
Luzilândia, Brazil 170 B3 3 28 S 42 22W
Lužnice →, Czech Rep. 34 B7 49 14N 14 23 E
Luzon, Phil. 80 C3 16 0N 121 0 E
Luzy, France 27 F10 46 47N 3 58 E
Luzzi, Italy 47 C9 39 27N 16 17 E
Lviv, Ukraine 59 H3 49 50N 24 0 E
Lvov = Lviv, Ukraine 59 H3 49 50N 24 0 E
Lwówek, Poland 55 F3 52 28N 16 10 E
Lwówek Śląski, Poland 55 G2 51 7N 15 38 E
Lyakhavichy, Belarus 59 F4 53 2N 26 32 E
Lyakhovskiye, Ostrova, Russia 67 B15 73 40N 141 0 E
Lyaki = Läki, Azerbaijan 61 K8 40 34N 47 22 E
Lyal I., Canada 150 B3 44 57N 81 24W
Lyall Mt., N.Z. 131 F2 45 16 S 167 32 E
Lyallpur = Faisalabad, Pakistan 91 C4 31 30N 73 5 E
Lyalya →, Russia 64 B8 59 9N 61 29 E
Lyangar, Tajikistan 65 E6 37 3N 72 40 E
Lyaskovets, Bulgaria 51 C9 43 6N 25 44 E
Lybster, U.K. 22 C5 58 18N 3 15W
Lycaonia, Turkey 100 D5 38 0N 33 0 E
Lychen, Germany 30 B9 53 12N 13 18 E
Lychkova, Russia 58 D7 57 55N 32 24 E
Lycia, Turkey 49 E11 36 30N 29 30 E
Lyckebyån →, Sweden 17 H9 56 12N 15 39 E
Lycksele, Sweden 14 D18 64 38N 18 40 E
Lycosura, Greece 48 D4 37 20N 22 3 E
Lydda = Lod, Israel 103 D3 31 57N 34 54 E
Lydenburg, S. Africa 117 D5 25 10 S 30 29 E
Lydia, Turkey 49 C10 38 48N 28 19 E
Łydynia →, Poland 55 F7 52 43N 20 26 E
Lyell, N.Z. 131 B7 41 48 S 172 4 E
Lyell I., Canada 142 C2 52 40N 131 35W
Lyepyel, Belarus 58 E5 54 50N 28 40 E
Lyford Cay, Bahamas 9 b 25 2N 77 33W
Lygnern, Sweden 17 G6 57 30N 12 15 E
Lykens, U.S.A. 151 F8 40 34N 76 42W
Lyman, Iowa, U.S.A. 156 C2 30 29N 94 59W
Lyman, Wyo., U.S.A. 158 F8 41 20N 110 18W
Lyme B., U.K. 21 G4 50 42N 2 53W
Lyme Regis, U.K. 21 G5 50 43N 2 57W
Lymington, U.K. 21 G6 50 45N 1 32W
Łyna →, Poland 15 J19 54 37N 21 14 E
Lynchburg, Ohio, U.S.A. 157 E13 39 15N 83 48W
Lynchburg, S.C., U.S.A. 152 A9 34 3N 80 4W
Lynchburg, Va., U.S.A. 148 G6 37 25N 79 9W
Lynd →, Australia 126 B3 16 28 S 143 18 E
Lynd Ra., Australia 127 D4 25 30 S 149 20 E
Lynden, Canada 150 C4 43 14N 80 9W
Lynden, U.S.A. 160 B4 48 57N 122 27W
Lyndhurst, Australia 127 E2 30 15 S 138 18 E
Lyndon →, Australia 125 D1 23 29 S 114 6 E
Lyndonville, N.Y., U.S.A. 150 C6 43 20N 78 23W
Lyndonville, Vt., U.S.A. 151 B12 44 31N 72 1W
Lyngdal, Buskerud, Norway 18 E6 59 54N 9 32 E
Lyngdal, Vest-Agder, Norway 18 F4 58 8N 7 7 E
Lyngen, Norway 14 B19 69 45N 20 30 E
Lyngør, Norway 18 F6 58 38N 9 8 E
Lynher Reef, Australia 124 C3 15 27 S 121 55 E
Lynn, Ind., U.S.A. 157 D12 40 3N 84 56W
Lynn, Mass., U.S.A. 151 D14 42 28N 70 57W
Lynn Canal, U.S.A. 144 G14 58 50N 135 15W
Lynn Haven, U.S.A. 152 E4 30 15N 85 39W
Lynn Lake, Canada 143 B8 56 51N 101 3W
Lynne, U.S.A. 153 F8 29 12N 81 55W
Lynnville, U.S.A. 157 F9 38 12N 87 19W
Lynnwood, U.S.A. 160 C4 47 49N 122 19W
Lynton, U.K. 21 F4 51 13N 3 50W
Lyntupy, Belarus 15 J22 55 4N 26 23 E
Lynx L., Canada 143 A7 62 25N 106 15W
Lyon, France 29 C8 45 46N 4 50 E
Lyonnais, France 29 C8 45 45N 4 15 E
Lyons = Lyon, France 29 C8 45 46N 4 50 E
Lyons, Ga., U.S.A. 152 C7 32 12N 82 19W
Lyons, Kans., U.S.A. 154 F5 38 21N 98 12W
Lyons, N.Y., U.S.A. 150 C8 43 5N 77 0W

Lyons →, *Australia* **125 E2** 25 2 S 115 9 E
Lyons Falls, *U.S.A.* **151 C9** 43 37N 75 22W
Lyozna, *Belarus* **58 E6** 55 0N 30 50 E
Lyra Reef, *Papua N. G.* **132 A7** 1 50 S 153 35 E
Lys = Leie →, *Belgium* **24 C3** 51 2N 3 45 E
Lysá nad Labem, *Czech Rep.* **34 A7** 50 11N 14 51 E
Lysebotn, *Norway* **18 E3** 59 3N 6 37 E
Lysefjorden, *Norway* **18 E3** 59 0N 6 23 E
Lysekil, *Sweden* **17 F5** 58 17N 11 26 E
Lyskovo, *Russia* **60 B7** 56 0N 45 3 E
Lyss, *Switz.* **32 B4** 47 4N 7 19 E
Lystrup, *Denmark* **17 H4** 56 14N 10 14 E
Lysva, *Russia* **64 B6** 58 7N 57 49 E
Lysvik, *Sweden* **16 D7** 60 1N 13 9 E
Lysychansk, *Ukraine* **59 H10** 48 55N 38 30 E
Lytham St. Anne's, *U.K.* **20 D4** 53 45N 3 0W
Lyttelton, *N.Z.* **131 D7** 43 35 S 172 44 E
Lytton, *Canada* **142 C4** 50 13N 121 31W
Lyuban, *Russia* **58 C6** 59 16N 31 18 E
Lyubertsy, *Russia* **58 E9** 55 39N 37 50 E
Lyubim, *Russia* **58 C11** 58 20N 40 39 E
Lyubimets, *Bulgaria* **51 E10** 41 50N 26 5 E
Lyuboml, *Ukraine* **59 G3** 51 11N 24 4 E
Lyubotyn, *Ukraine* **59 H8** 50 0N 36 0 E
Lyubytino, *Russia* **58 C7** 58 50N 33 16 E
Lyudinovo, *Russia* **58 F8** 53 52N 34 28 E

M

M.R. Gomez, Presa, *Mexico* **163 B5** 26 10N 99 0W
Ma →, *Vietnam* **76 H5** 19 47N 105 56 E
Ma, O. el →, *Algeria* **110 C3** 27 45N 7 52W
Ma-ubin, *Burma* **90 G5** 16 44N 95 39 E
Ma'adaba, *Jordan* **103 E4** 30 43N 35 47 E
Maamba, *Zambia* **116 B4** 17 17 S 26 28 E
Ma'ān, *Jordan* **103 E4** 30 12N 35 44 E
Ma'ān □, *Jordan* **103 F5** 30 0N 36 0 E
Maana'oba, *Solomon Is.* **133 M11** 8 17 S 160 50 E
Maanselkä, *Finland* **14 C23** 63 52N 28 32 E
Ma'anshan, *China* **77 B12** 31 44N 118 29 E
Maarianhamina, *Finland* **15 F18** 60 5N 19 55 E
Maarmorilik, *Greenland* **10 C5** 71 3N 51 0W
Ma'arrat an Nu'mān, *Syria* **100 E7** 35 43N 36 43 E
Maas →, *Neths.* **24 C4** 51 45N 4 32 E
Maaseik, *Belgium* **24 C5** 51 6N 5 45 E
Maasim, *Phil.* **81 J5** 5 52N 125 0 E
Maasin, *Phil.* **79 B6** 10 8N 124 50 E
Maastricht, *Neths.* **24 D5** 50 50N 5 40 E
Maasupa, *Solomon Is.* **133 M11** 9 16 S 161 17 E
Maave, *Mozam.* **117 C5** 21 4 S 34 47 E
Mababe Depression, *Botswana* **116 B3** 18 50 S 24 15 E
Mabaia, *Angola* **115 D2** 7 12 S 14 2 E
Mabalane, *Mozam.* **117 C5** 23 37 S 32 31 E
Mabanga, *Dem. Rep. of the Congo* **114 B3** 1 30N 19 6 E
Ma'bar, *Yemen* **98 D4** 14 48N 44 17 E
Mabaruma, *Guyana* **169 B6** 8 10N 59 50W
Mabein, *Burma* **90 D6** 23 29N 96 37 E
Mabel L., *Canada* **142 C5** 50 35N 118 43W
Mabenga, *Dem. Rep. of the Congo* **114 C3** 3 39 S 18 40 E
Mabenge, *Dem. Rep. of the Congo* **118 B1** 4 15N 24 12 E
Maberly, *Canada* **151 B8** 44 50N 76 32W
Mabian, *China* **76 C4** 28 47N 103 37 E
Mabil, *Ethiopia* **107 E4** 10 26N 36 52 E
Mabinay, *Phil.* **81 G4** 9 48N 122 54 E
Mabirou, *Congo* **114 C3** 1 3S 15 42 E
Mablethorpe, *U.K.* **20 D8** 53 20N 0 15 E
Mableton, *U.S.A.* **152 B5** 33 49N 84 35W
Mably, *France* **27 F11** 46 5N 4 4 E
Maboma, *Dem. Rep. of the Congo* **118 B2** 2 30N 28 10 E
Mabonto, *S. Leone* **112 D2** 8 53N 11 50W
Maboukou, *Congo* **114 C2** 3 39 S 12 31 E
Mabrouk, *Mali* **113 B4** 19 29N 1 15W
Mabrous, *Niger* **109 D2** 21 14N 13 35 E
Mabuasehube Game Reserve, *Botswana* **116 D3** 25 5 S 21 10 E
Mabungo, *Somali Rep.* **120 D2** 0 49N 42 35 E
Mac Bac, *Vietnam* **87 H6** 9 46N 106 7 E
Macachín, *Argentina* **174 D3** 37 10 S 63 43W
Macaé, *Brazil* **171 F3** 22 20 S 41 43W
Macael, *Spain* **41 H2** 37 20N 2 18W
Macaíba, *Brazil* **170 C4** 5 51 S 35 21W
Macajuba, *Brazil* **171 D3** 12 9 S 40 22W
McAlester, *U.S.A.* **155 H7** 34 56N 95 46W
McAllen, *U.S.A.* **155 M5** 26 12N 98 14W
McAlpin, *U.S.A.* **152 E7** 30 8N 82 57W
MacAlpine L., *Canada* **138 B9** 66 40N 102 50W
Macamic, *Canada* **140 C4** 48 45N 79 0W
Macao = Macau, *China* **77 F9** 22 12N 113 33 E
Macão, *Portugal* **43 F3** 39 35N 7 59W
Macapá, *Brazil* **169 C7** 0 5N 51 4W
Macará, *Ecuador* **168 D2** 4 23 S 79 57W
Macarani, *Brazil* **171 E3** 15 33 S 40 24W
Macarena, Serranía de la, *Colombia* **168 C3** 2 45N 73 55W
Macareo, Caño →, *Venezuela* **169 B5** 9 47N 61 36W
Macarthur, *Australia* **128 E5** 38 5 S 142 0 E
McArthur →, *Australia* **126 B2** 15 54 S 136 40 E
McArthur, Port, *Australia* **126 B2** 16 4 S 136 23 E
Macas, *Ecuador* **168 D2** 2 19 S 78 7W
Macate, *Peru* **172 B2** 8 48 S 78 7W
Macau, *Brazil* **170 C4** 5 15 S 36 40W
Macau, *China* **77 F9** 22 12N 113 33 E
Macaúbas, *Brazil* **171 D3** 13 2 S 42 42W
Macaya →, *Colombia* **168 C3** 0 59N 72 20W
McBride, *Canada* **142 C4** 53 20N 120 19W
McCall, *U.S.A.* **158 D5** 44 55N 116 6W
McCamey, *U.S.A.* **155 K3** 31 8N 102 14W
McCammon, *U.S.A.* **158 E7** 42 39N 112 12W
McCarthy, *U.S.A.* **144 F12** 61 26N 142 56W
McCauley I., *Canada* **142 C2** 53 40N 130 15W
McCleary, *U.S.A.* **160 C3** 47 3N 123 16W
Macclenny, *U.S.A.* **152 E7** 30 17N 82 7W
Macclesfield, *U.K.* **20 D5** 53 15N 2 8W
M'Clintock Chan., *Canada* **138 A9** 72 0N 102 0W
McClintock Ra., *Australia* **124 C4** 18 44 S 127 38 E
McCloud, *U.S.A.* **158 F2** 41 15N 122 8W
McCluer I., *Australia* **124 B5** 11 5 S 133 0 E
McClure, *U.S.A.* **150 F7** 40 42N 77 19W
McClure, L., *U.S.A.* **160 H6** 37 35N 120 16W
M'Clure Str., *Canada* **6 B2** 75 0N 119 0W
McClusky, *U.S.A.* **154 B4** 47 29N 100 27W
McComb, *U.S.A.* **155 K9** 31 15N 90 27W
McConaughy, L., *U.S.A.* **154 E4** 41 14N 101 40W
McCook, *U.S.A.* **154 E4** 40 12N 100 38W
McCormick, *U.S.A.* **152 B7** 33 55N 82 17W
McCreary, *Canada* **143 C9** 50 47N 99 29W
McCullough Mt., *U.S.A.* **161 K11** 35 35N 115 13W
McCusker →, *Canada* **143 B7** 55 32N 108 39W
McDame, *Canada* **142 B3** 59 44N 128 59W
McDavid, *U.S.A.* **153 E2** 30 52N 87 19W
McDermitt, *U.S.A.* **158 F5** 41 59N 117 43W
McDonald, *U.S.A.* **150 F4** 40 22N 80 14W
Macdonald, L., *Australia* **124 D4** 23 30 S 129 0 E
Macdonald, Mt., *Vanuatu* **133 G6** 17 36 S 168 23 E
McDonald Is., *Ind. Oc.* **121 K6** 53 0 S 73 0 E
MacDonnell Ranges, *Australia* **124 D5** 23 40 S 133 0 E
McDonough, *U.S.A.* **152 B5** 33 27N 84 9W
McDougalls Well, *Australia* **128 A4** 31 8 S 141 15 E
MacDowell L., *Canada* **140 B1** 52 15N 92 45W
Macduff, *U.K.* **22 D6** 57 40N 2 31W
Maceda, *Spain* **42 C3** 42 16N 7 39W
Macedonia, *U.S.A.* **150 E3** 41 19N 81 31W
Macedonia ■, *Europe* **50 E5** 41 53N 21 40 E
Maceió, *Brazil* **170 C4** 9 40 S 35 41W
Maceira, *Portugal* **42 F2** 39 41N 8 55W
Macenta, *Guinea* **112 D3** 8 35N 9 32W
Macerata, *Italy* **45 E10** 43 18N 13 27 E
McFarland, *U.S.A.* **161 K7** 35 41N 119 14W
McFarlane →, *Canada* **143 B7** 59 12N 107 58W
Macfarlane, L., *Australia* **128 B2** 32 0 S 136 40 E
McGehee, *U.S.A.* **155 J9** 33 38N 91 24W
McGill, *U.S.A.* **158 G6** 39 23N 114 47W
Macgillycuddy's Reeks, *Ireland* **23 E2** 51 58N 9 45W
McGrath, *U.S.A.* **144 E9** 62 58N 155 36W
McGraw, *U.S.A.* **151 D8** 42 36N 76 8W
McGregor, *U.S.A.* **156 A5** 43 1N 91 11W
McGregor Ra., *Australia* **127 D3** 27 0 S 142 45 E
McGuire, Mt, *Australia* **126 J6** 20 18 S 148 23 E
Mach Kowr, *Iran* **97 E9** 25 48N 61 28 E
Machacalis, *Brazil* **171 E3** 17 5 S 40 45W
Machado = Jiparaná →, *Brazil* **173 B5** 8 3 S 62 52W
Machagai, *Argentina* **174 B3** 26 56 S 60 2W
Machakos, *Kenya* **118 C4** 1 30 S 37 15 E
Machala, *Ecuador* **168 D2** 3 20 S 79 57W
Machanga, *Mozam.* **117 C6** 20 59 S 35 0 E
Machattie, L., *Australia* **126 C2** 24 50 S 139 48 E
Machault, *France* **27 C11** 49 21N 4 29 E
Machava, *Mozam.* **117 D5** 25 54 S 32 28 E
Machece, *Mozam.* **119 F4** 19 15 S 35 32 E
Machecoul, *France* **26 F5** 47 0N 1 49W
Macheke, *Zimbabwe* **117 B5** 18 5 S 31 51 E
Macheng, *China* **77 B10** 31 12N 115 2 E
McHenry, *U.S.A.* **157 B8** 42 21N 88 16W
Macherla, *India* **94 F4** 16 29N 79 26 E
Machero, *Spain* **43 F6** 39 21N 4 20W
Machgaon, *India* **94 D8** 20 5N 86 17 E
Machhu →, *India* **92 H4** 23 6N 70 46 E
Machias, *Maine, U.S.A.* **149 C12** 44 43N 67 28W
Machias, *N.Y., U.S.A.* **150 D6** 42 25N 78 30W
Machichi →, *Canada* **143 B10** 57 3N 92 6W
Machico, *Madeira* **9 c** 32 43N 16 44W
Machida, *Japan* **73 B11** 35 28N 139 23 E
Machilipatnam, *India* **95 F5** 16 12N 81 8 E
Machiques, *Venezuela* **168 A3** 10 4N 72 34W
Machupicchu, *Peru* **172 C3** 13 8 S 72 30W
Machynlleth, *U.K.* **21 E4** 52 35N 3 50W
Macia, *Mozam.* **117 D5** 25 2 S 33 8 E
Maciejowice, *Poland* **55 G8** 51 36N 21 26 E
McIlwraith Ra., *Australia* **126 A3** 13 50 S 143 20 E
Măcin, *Romania* **53 E13** 45 16N 28 8 E
Macina, *Mali* **112 C4** 14 50N 5 0W
McInnes L., *Canada* **143 C10** 52 13N 93 45W
McIntosh, *U.S.A.* **154 C4** 45 55N 101 21W
McIntosh L., *Canada* **143 B8** 55 45N 105 0W
Macintosh Ra., *Australia* **125 E4** 27 39 S 125 32 E
Macintyre →, *Australia* **127 D5** 28 37 S 150 47 E
Macizo Galaico, *Spain* **42 C3** 42 30N 7 30W
Mackay, *Australia* **126 K7** 21 8 S 149 11 E
Mackay, *U.S.A.* **158 E7** 43 55N 113 37W
MacKay →, *Canada* **142 B6** 57 10N 111 38W
Mackay, L., *Australia* **124 D4** 22 30 S 129 0 E
McKay Ra., *Australia* **124 D3** 23 0 S 122 30 E
McKeesport, *U.S.A.* **150 F5** 40 21N 79 52W
McKellar, *Canada* **150 A5** 45 30N 79 55W
McKenna, *U.S.A.* **160 D4** 46 56N 122 33W
Mackenzie, *Canada* **142 B4** 55 20N 123 5W
Mackenzie, *Guyana* **169 B6** 6 0N 58 17W
McKenzie, *U.S.A.* **149 G1** 36 8N 88 31W
Mackenzie →, *Australia* **126 C4** 23 38 S 149 46 E
Mackenzie →, *Canada* **138 B6** 69 10N 134 20W
McKenzie →, *U.S.A.* **158 D2** 44 7N 123 6W
Mackenzie Bay, *Canada* **6 B1** 69 0N 137 30W
Mackenzie City = Linden, *Guyana* **169 B6** 6 0N 58 10W
Mackenzie Mts., *Canada* **138 B6** 64 0N 130 0W
Mackenzie Plains, *N.Z.* **131 E5** 44 10 S 170 25 E
McKerrow, L., *N.Z.* **131 E3** 44 25 S 168 5 E
Mackinaw, *U.S.A.* **156 D7** 40 32N 89 21W
Mackinaw →, *U.S.A.* **156 D7** 40 33N 89 44W
Mackinaw City, *U.S.A.* **148 C3** 45 47N 84 44W
McKinlay, *Australia* **126 C3** 21 16 S 141 18 E
McKinlay →, *Australia* **126 C3** 20 50 S 141 28 E
McKinley, Mt., *U.S.A.* **144 E10** 63 4N 151 0W
McKinley Park, *U.S.A.* **144 E10** 63 44N 148 55W
McKinley Sea, *Arctic* **10 A11** 82 0N 0 0W
McKinney, *U.S.A.* **155 J6** 33 12N 96 37W
Mackinnon Road, *Kenya* **118 C4** 3 40 S 39 1 E
McKittrick, *Calif., U.S.A.* **161 K7** 35 18N 119 37W
McKittrick, *Mo., U.S.A.* **156 F5** 38 44N 91 27W
Macklin, *Canada* **143 C7** 52 20N 109 56W
Macksville, *Australia* **129 A10** 30 40 S 152 56 E
McLaren Vale, *Australia* **128 C3** 35 13 S 138 31 E
McLaughlin, *U.S.A.* **154 C4** 45 49N 100 49W
Maclean, *Australia* **127 D5** 29 26 S 153 16 E
McLean, *Ill., U.S.A.* **156 D7** 40 19N 89 10W
McLean, *Tex., U.S.A.* **155 H4** 35 14N 100 36W
McLeansboro, *U.S.A.* **154 F10** 38 6N 88 32W
Maclear, *S. Africa* **117 E4** 31 2 S 28 23 E
Maclear, C., *Malawi* **119 E3** 13 58 S 34 49 E
Macleay →, *Australia* **129 A10** 30 56 S 153 0 E
McLennan, *Canada* **142 B5** 55 42N 116 50W
McLeod →, *Canada* **142 C5** 54 9N 115 44W
MacLeod, B., *Canada* **143 A7** 62 53N 110 0W
McLeod, L., *Australia* **125 D1** 24 9 S 113 47 E
MacLeod Lake, *Canada* **142 C4** 54 58N 123 0W
McLoughlin, Mt., *U.S.A.* **158 E2** 42 27N 122 19W
McMechen, *U.S.A.* **150 G4** 39 57N 80 44W
McMinnville, *Oreg., U.S.A.* **158 D2** 45 13N 123 12W
McMinnville, *Tenn., U.S.A.* **149 H3** 35 41N 85 46W
McMurdo Sd., *Antarctica* **7 D11** 77 0 S 170 0 E
McMurray = Fort McMurray, *Canada* **142 B6** 56 44N 111 7W
McMurray, *U.S.A.* **160 B4** 48 19N 122 14W
Maco, *Phil.* **81 H5** 7 20N 125 50 E
Macocolo, *Angola* **115 D3** 6 47 S 16 8 E
Macodoene, *Mozam.* **117 C6** 23 32 S 35 5 E
Macolo, *Angola* **115 D3** 7 5 S 16 42 E
Macomb, *U.S.A.* **156 D6** 40 27N 90 40W
Macomer, *Italy* **46 B1** 40 16N 8 47 E
Mâcon, *France* **27 F11** 46 19N 4 50 E
Macon, *Ga., U.S.A.* **152 C6** 32 51N 83 38W
Macon, *Ill., U.S.A.* **156 E8** 39 43N 89 0W
Macon, *Miss., U.S.A.* **149 J1** 33 7N 88 34W
Macon, *Mo., U.S.A.* **156 E4** 39 44N 92 28W
Macondo, *Angola* **115 E4** 12 37 S 23 46 E
Macossa, *Mozam.* **119 F3** 17 55 S 33 56 E
Macoun L., *Canada* **143 B8** 56 32N 103 40W
Macoupin Cr. →, *U.S.A.* **156 E6** 39 11N 90 38W
Macovane, *Mozam.* **117 C6** 21 30 S 35 2 E
McPherson, *U.S.A.* **154 F6** 38 22N 97 40W
McPherson Pk., *U.S.A.* **161 L7** 34 53N 119 53W
McPherson Ra., *Australia* **127 D5** 28 15 S 153 15 E
Macquarie →, *N.S.W., Australia* **127 E4** 30 5 S 147 30 E
Macquarie →, *N.S.W., Australia* **129 A7** 30 7 S 147 24 E
Macquarie Harbour, *Australia* **127 G4** 42 15 S 145 23 E
Macquarie Is., *Pac. Oc.* **134 N7** 54 36 S 158 55 E
McRae, *U.S.A.* **152 C7** 32 4N 82 54W
MacRobertson Land, *Antarctica* **7 D6** 71 0 S 64 0 E
Macroom, *Ireland* **23 E3** 51 54N 8 57W
MacTier, *Canada* **150 A5** 45 9N 79 46W
Macubela, *Mozam.* **119 F4** 16 53 S 37 49 E
Macugnaga, *Italy* **44 C4** 45 58N 7 58 E
Macuiza, *Mozam.* **119 F3** 18 7 S 34 29 E
Macujer, *Colombia* **168 C3** 0 24N 73 10W
Macuro, *Venezuela* **169 F9** 10 42N 61 55W
Macusani, *Peru* **172 C3** 14 4 S 70 29W
Macuse, *Mozam.* **119 F4** 17 45 S 37 10 E
Macuspana, *Mexico* **163 D6** 17 46N 92 36W
Macusse, *Angola* **116 B3** 17 48 S 20 23 E
Mada →, *Nigeria* **113 D6** 7 59N 7 55 E
Madadeni, *S. Africa* **117 D5** 27 43 S 30 3 E
Madadi, *Chad* **109 E4** 18 28N 20 45 E
Madagali, *Nigeria* **113 C7** 10 56N 13 33 E
Madagascar ■, *Africa* **117 C8** 20 0 S 47 0 E
Madā'in Sālih, *Si. Arabia* **96 E3** 26 46N 37 57 E
Madakasira, *India* **95 H3** 13 56N 77 16 E
Madalena, *Azores* **9 d1** 38 32N 28 32W
Madama, *Niger* **109 D2** 22 0N 13 40 E
Madame I., *Canada* **141 C7** 45 30N 60 58W
Madan, *Bulgaria* **51 E8** 41 30N 24 57 E
Madanapalle, *India* **95 H4** 13 33N 78 28 E
Madang, *Papua N. G.* **132 C3** 5 12 S 145 49 E
Madang □, *Papua N. G.* **132 C3** 5 0 S 145 30 E
Madaoua, *Niger* **113 C6** 14 5N 6 27 E
Madara, *Nigeria* **113 C7** 11 45N 10 35 E
Madaripur, *Bangla.* **90 D3** 23 19N 90 15 E
Madau I., *Papua N. G.* **132 E7** 8 58 S 152 28 E
Madauk, *Burma* **90 G6** 17 56N 96 52 E
Madawaska, *Canada* **150 A7** 45 30N 78 0W
Madawaska →, *Canada* **140 C4** 45 27N 76 21W
Madaya, *Burma* **90 D6** 22 12N 96 10 E
Madbar, *Sudan* **107 F3** 6 17N 30 45 E
Maddalena, *Italy* **46 A2** 41 16N 9 23 E
Maddaloni, *Italy* **47 A7** 41 2N 14 23 E
Maddela, *Phil.* **80 C3** 16 21N 121 41 E
Maddur, *India* **95 H3** 12 36N 77 4 E
Madeira, *Atl. Oc.* **9 c** 32 50N 17 0W
Madeira, *U.S.A.* **157 E12** 39 11N 84 22W
Madeira →, *Brazil* **169 D6** 3 22 S 58 45W
Mädelegabel, *Germany* **33 B10** 47 18N 10 18 E
Madeleine, Îs. de la, *Canada* **141 C7** 47 30N 61 40W
Maden, *Turkey* **101 C8** 38 23N 39 40 E
Madera, *Mexico* **162 B3** 29 12N 108 7W
Madera, *Calif., U.S.A.* **160 J6** 36 57N 120 3W
Madera, *Pa., U.S.A.* **150 F6** 40 49N 78 26W
Madgaon, *India* **95 G1** 15 12N 73 58 E
Madha, *India* **94 F2** 18 0N 75 30 E
Madhavpur, *India* **92 J3** 21 15N 69 58 E
Madhepura, *India* **93 F12** 26 11N 86 23 E
Madhira, *India* **94 F5** 16 55N 80 22 E
Madhubani, *India* **93 F12** 26 21N 86 7 E
Madhugiri, *India* **95 H3** 13 40N 77 12 E
Madhumati →, *Bangla.* **90 D2** 22 53N 89 52 E
Madhupur, *Bangla.* **90 C3** 24 37N 90 2 E
Madhupur, *India* **93 G12** 24 16N 86 39 E
Madhya Pradesh □, *India* **92 J8** 22 50N 78 0 E
Madidi →, *Bolivia* **172 C4** 12 32 S 66 52W
Madikeri, *India* **95 H2** 12 30N 75 45 E
Madikwe Game Reserve, *S. Africa* **117 D5** 27 38 S 32 15 E
Madill, *U.S.A.* **155 H6** 34 6N 96 46W
Madimba, *Angola* **115 D2** 6 36 S 14 23 E
Madimba, *Dem. Rep. of the Congo* **115 C3** 4 58 S 15 5 E
Ma'din, *Syria* **101 E8** 35 45N 39 36 E
Madina, *Mali* **112 C3** 13 25N 8 50W
Madinani, *Ivory C.* **112 D3** 9 37N 6 57W
Madīnat ash Sha'b, *Yemen* **98 D4** 12 50N 45 0 E
Madingo, *Congo* **114 C2** 4 5 S 11 24 E
Madingou, *Congo* **114 C2** 4 10 S 13 33 E
Madirovalo, *Madag.* **117 B8** 16 26 S 46 32 E
Madison, *Calif., U.S.A.* **160 G5** 38 41N 121 59W
Madison, *Fla., U.S.A.* **152 E6** 30 28N 83 25W
Madison, *Ga., U.S.A.* **152 B6** 33 36N 83 28W
Madison, *Ind., U.S.A.* **157 F11** 38 44N 85 23W
Madison, *Mo., U.S.A.* **156 E4** 39 28N 92 13W
Madison, *Nebr., U.S.A.* **154 E6** 41 50N 97 27W
Madison, *Ohio, U.S.A.* **150 E3** 41 46N 81 3W
Madison, *S. Dak., U.S.A.* **154 D6** 44 0N 97 7W
Madison, *Wis., U.S.A.* **156 A7** 43 4N 89 24W
Madison →, *U.S.A.* **158 D8** 45 56N 111 31W
Madison Heights, *U.S.A.* **148 G6** 37 25N 79 8W
Madisonville, *Ky., U.S.A.* **148 G2** 37 20N 87 30W
Madisonville, *Tex., U.S.A.* **155 K7** 30 57N 95 55W
Madista, *Botswana* **116 C4** 21 15 S 25 6 E
Madiun, *Indonesia* **85 D4** 7 38 S 111 32 E
Madjingo, *Gabon* **114 B2** 1 20N 14 4 E
Madoc, *Canada* **150 B7** 44 30N 77 28W
Madol, *Sudan* **107 F2** 9 3N 27 45 E
Madon →, *France* **27 D13** 48 36N 6 6 E
Madona, *Latvia* **15 H22** 56 53N 26 5 E
Madonie, *Italy* **46 E6** 37 50N 13 50 E
Madonna di Campíglio, *Italy* **33 D11** 46 14N 10 49 E
Madra Dağı, *Turkey* **49 B9** 39 23N 27 12 E
Madrakah, Ra's al, *Oman* **99 C7** 19 0N 57 50 E
Madras = Chennai, *India* **95 H5** 13 8N 80 19 E
Madras = Tamil Nadu □, *India* **95 J3** 11 0N 77 0 E
Madras, *U.S.A.* **158 D3** 44 38N 121 8W
Madre, Laguna, *U.S.A.* **155 M6** 27 0N 97 30W
Madre, Sierra, *Phil.* **80 C4** 17 0N 122 0 E
Madre de Dios □, *Peru* **172 C3** 12 0 S 70 15W
Madre de Dios →, *Bolivia* **172 C4** 10 59 S 66 8W
Madre de Dios, I., *Chile* **176 D1** 50 20 S 75 10W
Madre del Sur, Sierra, *Mexico* **163 D5** 17 30N 100 0W
Madre Occidental, Sierra, *Mexico* **162 B3** 27 0N 107 0W
Madre Oriental, Sierra, *Mexico* **162 C5** 25 0N 100 0W
Madri, *India* **92 G5** 24 16N 73 32 E
Madrid, *Spain* **42 E7** 40 25N 3 45W
Madrid, *Ala., U.S.A.* **152 D4** 31 2N 85 24W
Madrid, *Iowa, U.S.A.* **156 C3** 41 53N 93 49W
Madrid, *N.Y., U.S.A.* **151 B9** 44 45N 75 8W
Madrid □, *Spain* **42 E7** 40 30N 3 45W
Madridejos, *Spain* **43 F7** 39 28N 3 33W
Madrigal de las Altas Torres, *Spain* **42 D6** 41 5N 5 0W
Madrona, Sierra, *Spain* **43 G6** 38 27N 4 16W
Madroñera, *Spain* **43 F5** 39 26N 5 42W
Madrusah, *Libya* **108 D2** 24 48N 14 32 E
Madu, *Sudan* **107 E2** 14 37N 26 4 E
Maduo, *Dem. Rep. of the Congo* **114 C4** 1 24 S 20 44 E
Madura, *Australia* **125 F4** 31 55 S 127 0 E
Madura, *Indonesia* **79 G15** 7 30 S 114 0 E
Madura, Selat, *Indonesia* **85 D4** 7 30 S 113 20 E
Madurai, *India* **95 K4** 9 55N 78 10 E
Madurantakam, *India* **95 H4** 12 30N 79 50 E
Madzhalis, *Russia* **61 J8** 42 9N 47 47 E
Mae Chan, *Thailand* **86 B2** 20 9N 99 52 E
Mae Hong Son, *Thailand* **86 C2** 19 16N 97 56 E
Mae Khlong →, *Thailand* **86 F3** 13 24N 100 0 E
Mae Phrik, *Thailand* **86 D2** 17 27N 99 7 E
Mae Ramat, *Thailand* **86 D2** 16 58N 98 31 E
Mae Rim, *Thailand* **86 C2** 18 54N 98 57 E
Mae Sot, *Thailand* **86 D2** 16 43N 98 34 E
Mae Suai, *Thailand* **76 H2** 19 39N 99 33 E
Mae Tha, *Thailand* **86 C2** 18 28N 99 8 E
Maebaru, *Japan* **72 D2** 33 33N 130 12 E
Maebashi, *Japan* **73 A11** 36 24N 139 4 E
Maella, *Spain* **40 D5** 41 8N 0 7 E
Maesteg, *U.K.* **21 F4** 51 36N 3 40W
Maestra, Sierra, *Cuba* **164 B4** 20 15N 77 0W
Maestre de Campo I., *Phil.* **80 E3** 12 56N 121 42 E
Maetambe, Mt., *Solomon Is.* **133 L9** 7 3 S 157 1 E
Maevatanana, *Madag.* **117 B8** 16 56 S 46 49 E
Maéwo, *Vanuatu* **133 E6** 15 10 S 168 10 E
Mafa, *Indonesia* **82 A3** 0 3N 127 53 E
Ma'fan, *Libya* **108 C2** 25 56N 14 29 E
Mafeking = Mafikeng, *S. Africa* **116 D4** 25 50 S 25 38 E
Mafeking, *Canada* **143 C8** 52 40N 101 10W
Maféré, *Ivory C.* **112 D4** 5 30N 3 2W
Mafeteng, *Lesotho* **116 D4** 29 51 S 27 15 E
Maffra, *Australia* **129 D7** 37 53 S 146 58 E
Mafia I., *Tanzania* **118 D4** 7 45 S 39 50 E
Mafikeng, *S. Africa* **116 D4** 25 50 S 25 38 E
Mafra, *Brazil* **175 B6** 26 10 S 49 55W
Mafra, *Portugal* **43 G1** 38 55N 9 20W
Mafungabusi Plateau, *Zimbabwe* **119 F2** 18 30 S 29 8 E
Magadan, *Russia* **67 D16** 59 38N 150 50 E
Magadi, *India* **95 H3** 12 58N 77 14 E
Magadi, *Kenya* **118 C4** 1 54 S 36 19 E
Magadi, L., *Kenya* **118 C4** 1 54 S 36 19 E
Magaliesburg, *S. Africa* **117 D4** 26 0 S 27 32 E
Magallanes, *Phil.* **80 E4** 12 50N 123 50 E
Magallanes □, *Chile* **176 D2** 52 0 S 72 0W
Magallanes, Estrecho de, *Chile* **176 D2** 52 30 S 75 0W
Magaluf, *Spain* **38 B3** 39 29N 2 32 E
Magangué, *Colombia* **168 B3** 9 14N 74 45W
Maganoy, *Phil.* **81 H5** 6 51N 124 31 E
Magaria, *Niger* **113 C6** 13 4N 9 5 E
Magarida, *Papua N. G.* **132 F5** 10 18 S 149 20 E
Magburaka, *S. Leone* **112 D2** 8 47N 12 0W
Magdalen Is. = Madeleine, Îs. de la, *Canada* **141 C7** 47 30N 61 40W
Magdalena, *Argentina* **174 D4** 35 5 S 57 30W
Magdalena, *Bolivia* **173 C5** 13 13 S 63 57W
Magdalena, *Malaysia* **83 B5** 4 25N 117 55 E
Magdalena, *Mexico* **162 A2** 30 50N 112 0W
Magdalena, *U.S.A.* **159 J10** 34 7N 107 15W
Magdalena □, *Colombia* **168 A3** 10 0N 74 0W
Magdalena →, *Colombia* **168 A3** 11 6N 74 51W
Magdalena →, *Mexico* **162 A2** 30 40N 112 25W
Magdalena, B., *Mexico* **162 C2** 24 30N 112 10W
Magdalena, I., *Chile* **176 B2** 44 40 S 73 0W
Magdalena, Llano de la, *Mexico* **162 C2** 25 0N 111 30W
Magdeburg, *Germany* **30 C7** 52 7N 11 38 E
Magdelaine Cays, *Australia* **126 B5** 16 33 S 150 18 E
Magdub, *Sudan* **107 E2** 13 42N 25 5 E
Magee, *U.S.A.* **155 K10** 31 52N 89 44W
Magelang, *Indonesia* **85 D4** 7 29 S 110 13 E
Magellan's Str. = Magallanes, Estrecho de, *Chile* **176 D2** 52 30 S 75 0W
Magenta, *Italy* **44 C5** 45 28N 8 53 E
Magenta, L., *Australia* **125 F2** 33 30 S 119 2 E
Magerøya, *Norway* **14 A21** 71 3N 25 40 E
Maggea, *Australia* **128 C4** 34 28 S 140 2 E
Maggia, *Switz.* **33 D7** 46 15N 8 42 E
Maggia →, *Switz.* **33 D7** 46 18N 8 36 E
Maggiorasca, Mte., *Italy* **44 D6** 44 33N 9 29 E
Maggiore, Lago, *Italy* **44 C5** 45 57N 8 39 E
Maggotty, *Jamaica* **164 a** 18 9N 77 46W
Maghâgha, *Egypt* **106 B3** 28 38N 30 50 E
Maghama, *Mauritania* **112 B2** 15 32N 12 57W
Magherafelt, *U.K.* **23 B5** 54 45N 6 37W
Maghnia, *Algeria* **111 B4** 34 50N 1 43W
Magione, *Italy* **45 E9** 43 8N 12 12 E
Magistralnyy, *Russia* **67 D11** 56 16N 107 36 E
Maglaj, *Bos.-H.* **52 F3** 44 33N 18 7 E
Magliano in Toscana, *Italy* **45 F8** 42 36N 11 17 E
Máglie, *Italy* **47 B11** 40 7N 18 18 E
Magnac-Laval, *France* **28 B5** 46 13N 1 11 E
Magnetic Pole (North) = North Magnetic Pole, *Canada* **6 B2** 77 58N 102 8W
Magnetic Pole (South) = South Magnetic Pole, *Antarctica* **7 C9** 64 8 S 138 8 E
Magnisía □, *Greece* **48 B5** 39 15N 23 0 E
Magnitogorsk, *Russia* **64 E7** 53 27N 59 4 E
Magnolia, *Ark., U.S.A.* **155 J8** 33 16N 93 14W
Magnolia, *Miss., U.S.A.* **155 K9** 31 9N 90 28W
Magnor, *Norway* **18 E9** 59 56N 12 15 E
Magny-en-Vexin, *France* **27 C8** 49 9N 1 47 E
Mago, *Fiji* **133 A3** 17 26 S 179 8W
Mago Nat. Park, *Ethiopia* **107 F4** 5 40N 36 18 E
Magog, *Canada* **141 C5** 45 18N 72 9W
Magoro, *Uganda* **118 B3** 1 45N 34 12 E
Magosa = Famagusta, *Cyprus* **39 E9** 35 8N 33 55 E
Magouládhes, *Greece* **38 B9** 39 45N 19 42 E
Magoye, *Zambia* **119 F2** 16 1 S 27 30 E
Magozal, *Mexico* **163 C5** 21 34N 97 59W
Magpie, L., *Canada* **141 B7** 51 0N 64 41W
Magrath, *Canada* **142 D6** 49 25N 112 50W
Magre →, *Spain* **41 F4** 39 11N 0 25W
Magrur, *Sudan* **107 E3** 14 1N 30 27 E
Magrur, Wadi →, *Sudan* **107 D2** 16 5N 26 30 E
Magsingal, *Phil.* **80 C3** 17 41N 120 25 E
Magta Lahjar, *Mauritania* **112 B2** 17 28N 13 17W
Maguan, *China* **76 F5** 23 0N 104 21 E
Maguarinho, C., *Brazil* **170 B2** 0 15 S 48 30W
Magude, *Mozam.* **117 D5** 25 2 S 32 40 E
Maguindanao □, *Phil.* **81 H5** 7 5N 124 0 E
Mağusa = Famagusta, *Cyprus* **39 E9** 35 8N 33 55 E
Maguse L., *Canada* **143 A9** 61 40N 95 10W
Maguse Pt., *Canada* **143 A10** 61 20N 93 50W
Magvana, *India* **92 H3** 23 13N 69 22 E
Magwe, *Burma* **90 E5** 20 10N 95 0 E
Magwe, *Sudan* **107 G3** 4 8N 32 17 E
Magwe □, *Burma* **90 F5** 20 0N 95 0 E
Maha Oya, *Sri Lanka* **95 L5** 7 31N 81 22 E
Maha Sarakham, *Thailand* **86 D4** 16 12N 103 16 E
Mahābād, *Iran* **101 D11** 36 50N 45 45 E
Mahabaleshwar, *India* **94 F1** 17 58N 73 43 E
Mahabharat Lekh, *Nepal* **93 E10** 28 30N 82 0 E
Mahabo, *Madag.* **117 C7** 20 23 S 44 40 E
Mahad, *India* **94 E1** 18 6N 73 29 E
Mahaddei Uen, *Somali Rep.* **120 D3** 2 58N 45 32 E
Mahadeo Hills, *India* **93 H8** 22 20N 78 30 E
Mahadeopur, *India* **94 E5** 18 48N 80 0 E
Mahaffey, *U.S.A.* **150 F6** 40 53N 78 44W
Mahagi, *Dem. Rep. of the Congo* **118 B3** 2 20N 31 0 E
Mahaicony, *Guyana* **169 B6** 6 36N 57 48W
Mahajamba →, *Madag.* **117 B8** 15 33 S 47 8 E
Mahajamba, Helodranon' i, *Madag.* **117 B8** 15 24 S 47 5 E
Mahajan, *India* **92 E5** 28 48N 73 56 E
Mahajanga, *Madag.* **117 B8** 15 40 S 46 25 E
Mahajanga □, *Madag.* **117 B8** 17 0 S 47 0 E
Mahajilo →, *Madag.* **117 B8** 19 42 S 45 22 E
Mahakam →, *Indonesia* **85 C5** 0 35 S 117 17 E
Mahalapye, *Botswana* **116 C4** 23 1 S 26 51 E
Mahalchhar, *Bangla.* **90 D4** 22 55N 92 2 E
Mahale Mountains Nat. Park, *Tanzania* **118 D2** 6 10 S 29 50 E
Mahale Mts., *Tanzania* **118 D3** 6 20 S 30 0 E
Mahallāt, *Iran* **97 C6** 33 55N 50 30 E
Māhān, *Iran* **97 D8** 30 5N 57 18 E
Mahan →, *India* **93 H10** 23 30N 82 50 E
Mahanadi →, *India* **94 D8** 20 20N 86 25 E
Mahananda →, *India* **93 G12** 25 12N 87 52 E
Mahanoro, *Madag.* **117 B8** 19 54 S 48 48 E
Mahanoy City, *U.S.A.* **151 F8** 40 49N 76 9W
Mahaplag, *Phil.* **81 F5** 10 35N 124 57 E
Maharashtra □, *India* **94 D2** 20 30N 75 30 E
Maharès, *Tunisia* **108 B2** 34 32N 10 29 E
Mahasamund, *India* **94 D6** 21 6N 82 6 E
Mahasham, W. →, *Egypt* **103 E3** 30 15N 34 10 E
Mahasoa, *Madag.* **117 C8** 22 12 S 46 6 E
Mahasolo, *Madag.* **117 B8** 19 7 S 46 22 E
Mahattat ash Shīdīyah, *Jordan* **103 F4** 29 55N 35 55 E

Mahattat ‘Unayzah, *Jordan* **103 E4** 30 30N 35 47 E
Mahavavy →, *Madag.* **117 B8** 15 57 S 45 54 E
Mahaweli Ganga →, *Sri Lanka* **95 K5** 8 27N 81 13 E
Mahaxay, *Laos* **86 D5** 17 22N 105 12 E
Mahbubabad, *India* **94 F5** 17 42N 80 2 E
Mahbubnagar, *India* **94 F3** 16 45N 77 59 E
Mahd adh Dhahab, *Si. Arabia* **98 B3** 23 30N 40 52 E
Maḩḑah, *Oman* **97 E7** 24 24N 55 59 E
Mahdia, *Guyana* **169 B6** 5 13N 59 8W
Mahdia, *Tunisia* **108 A2** 35 28N 11 0 E
Mahe, *Jammu & Kashmir, India* **93 C8** 33 10N 78 32 E
Mahé, *Pondicherry, India* **95 J2** 11 42N 75 34 E
Mahé, *Seychelles* **121 b** 5 0 S 55 30 E
Mahebourg, *Mauritius* **121 d** 20 24 S 57 42 E
Mahendra Giri, *India* **95 K3** 8 20N 77 30 E
Mahendraganj, *India* **90 C2** 25 20N 89 45 E
Mahendragarh, *India* **92 E7** 28 17N 76 14 E
Mahenge, *Tanzania* **119 D4** 8 45 S 36 41 E
Maheno, *N.Z.* **131 F5** 45 10 S 170 50 E
Mahesana, *India* **92 H5** 23 39N 72 26 E
Maheshwar, *India* **92 H6** 22 11N 75 35 E
Mahgawan, *India* **93 F8** 26 29N 78 37 E
Mahi →, *India* **92 H5** 22 15N 72 55 E
Mahia Pen., *N.Z.* **130 F6** 39 9 S 177 55 E
Mahighe, *Solomon Is.* **133 M10** 8 30 S 159 58 E
Mahilyow, *Belarus* **58 F6** 53 55N 30 18 E
Mahim, *India* **94 E1** 19 39N 72 44 E
Mahina, *Tahiti* **133 S16** 17 30 S 149 27W
Mahirija, *Morocco* **111 B4** 34 0N 3 16W
Mahlaing, *Burma* **90 E5** 21 6N 95 39 E
Mahmiya, *Sudan* **107 D3** 17 12N 33 43 E
Mahmud Kot, *Pakistan* **92 D4** 30 16N 71 0 E
Mahmudia, *Romania* **53 E14** 45 5N 29 5 E
Mahmudiye, *Turkey* **49 B12** 39 48N 30 15 E
Mahmutbey, *Turkey* **51 E12** 41 3N 28 49 E
Mahnomen, *U.S.A.* **154 B7** 47 19N 95 58W
Maho, *Sri Lanka* **95 L5** 7 49N 80 16 E
Mahoba, *India* **93 G8** 25 15N 79 55 E
Mahomet, *U.S.A.* **157 D8** 40 12N 88 24W
Mahón = Maó, *Spain* **38 B5** 39 53N 4 16 E
Mahone Bay, *Canada* **141 D7** 44 30N 64 20W
Mahopac, *U.S.A.* **151 E11** 41 22N 73 45W
Mahoua, *Chad* **109 F3** 11 49N 18 26 E
Mahuta, *Nigeria* **113 C5** 11 32N 4 58 E
Mahuva, *India* **92 J4** 21 5N 71 48 E
Mahya Daği, *Turkey* **51 E11** 41 47N 27 36 E
Mai-Ndombe, L., *Dem. Rep. of the Congo* **114 C3** 2 0 S 18 20 E
Mai-Sai, *Thailand* **76 G2** 20 20N 99 55 E
Mai Thon, Ko, *Thailand* **87 a** 7 40N 98 28 E
Maia, *Azores* **9 d4** 36 56N 25 1W
Maia, *Portugal* **42 D2** 41 14N 8 37W
Maia, *Spain* **40 B3** 43 12N 1 29W
Maials, *Spain* **40 D5** 41 22N 0 30 E
Maibong, *India* **90 C4** 25 18N 93 10 E
Maicao, *Colombia* **168 A3** 11 23N 72 13W
Maîche, *France* **27 E13** 47 16N 6 48 E
Maici →, *Brazil* **173 B5** 6 30 S 61 43W
Maicurú →, *Brazil* **169 D7** 2 14 S 54 17W
Máida, *Italy* **47 D9** 38 51N 16 22 E
Maidan Khula, *Afghan.* **91 B3** 33 36N 69 50 E
Maidenhead, *U.K.* **21 F7** 51 31N 0 42W
Maidstone, *Canada* **143 C7** 53 5N 109 20W
Maidstone, *U.K.* **21 F8** 51 16N 0 32 E
Maiduguri, *Nigeria* **113 C7** 12 0N 13 20 E
Măieruş, *Romania* **53 E10** 45 53N 25 31 E
Maigatari, *Nigeria* **113 C6** 12 46N 9 27 E
Maignelay Montigny, *France* **27 C9** 49 32N 2 30 E
Maigo, *Phil.* **81 G4** 8 10N 123 57 E
Maigualida, Sierra, *Venezuela* **169 B4** 5 30N 65 10W
Maigudo, *Ethiopia* **107 F4** 7 30N 37 8 E
Maihar, *India* **93 G9** 24 16N 80 45 E
Maihara, *Japan* **73 B8** 35 19N 136 17 E
Maijdi, *Bangla.* **90 D3** 22 48N 91 10 E
Maikala Ra., *India* **94 D5** 22 0N 81 0 E
Maiko, Parc Nat. de la, *Dem. Rep. of the Congo* **118 C2** 0 30 S 27 50 E
Maikoor, *Indonesia* **83 C4** 6 8 S 134 6 E
Mailani, *India* **93 E9** 28 17N 80 21 E
Maili, *U.S.A.* **145 K13** 21 25N 158 11W
Maili Pt, *U.S.A.* **145 K13** 21 24N 158 11W
Maillezais, *France* **28 B3** 46 22N 0 45W
Mailsi, *Pakistan* **92 E5** 29 48N 72 15 E
Maimbung, *Phil.* **81 J3** 5 56N 121 2 E
Main →, *Germany* **31 F4** 50 0N 8 18 E
Main →, *U.K.* **23 B5** 54 48N 6 18W
Main Range Nat. Park, *Australia* **127 D5** 28 11 S 152 27 E
Main Ridge, *Trin. & Tob.* **169 E10** 11 16N 60 40W
Mainburg, *Germany* **31 G7** 48 38N 11 47 E
Maindargi, *India* **94 F3** 17 28N 76 18 E
Maine, *France* **26 D6** 48 20N 0 15W
Maine □, *U.S.A.* **149 C11** 45 20N 69 0W
Maine →, *Ireland* **23 D2** 52 9N 9 45W
Maine-et-Loire □, *France* **26 E6** 47 31N 0 30W
Maïne-Soroa, *Niger* **113 C7** 13 13N 12 2 E
Maingkaing, *Burma* **90 C5** 24 48N 95 16 E
Maingkwan, *Burma* **90 B6** 26 15N 96 37 E
Mainit, *Phil.* **81 G5** 9 32N 125 32 E
Mainit, L., *Phil.* **81 G5** 9 31N 125 30 E
Mainland, *Orkney, U.K.* **22 C5** 58 59N 3 8W
Mainland, *Shet., U.K.* **22 A7** 60 15N 1 22W
Mainoru, *Australia* **126 A1** 14 0 S 134 6 E
Mainpuri, *India* **93 F8** 27 18N 79 4 E
Maintal, *Germany* **31 E4** 50 7N 8 52 E
Maintenon, *France* **27 D8** 48 35N 1 35 E
Maintirano, *Madag.* **117 B7** 18 3 S 44 1 E
Mainz, *Germany* **31 E4** 50 1N 8 14 E
Maio, *C. Verde Is.* **9 j** 15 10N 23 10W
Maipú, *Argentina* **174 D4** 36 52 S 57 50W
Maiquetía, *Venezuela* **168 A4** 10 36N 66 57W
Máira →, *Italy* **44 D4** 44 49N 7 38 E
Mairabari, *India* **90 B4** 26 30N 92 22 E
Mairipotaba, *Brazil* **171 E2** 17 18 S 49 28W
Maisí, *Cuba* **165 B5** 20 17N 74 9W
Maisí, Pta. de, *Cuba* **165 B5** 20 10N 74 10W
Maitland, *N.S.W., Australia* **129 B9** 32 33 S 151 36 E
Maitland, *S. Austral., Australia* **128 C2** 34 23 S 137 40 E
Maitland →, *Canada* **150 C3** 43 45N 81 43W
Maitland, Banjaran, *Malaysia* **85 B5** 4 55N 116 37 E
Maitum, *Phil.* **81 H5** 6 2N 124 30 E
Maiyema, *Nigeria* **113 C5** 12 5N 4 25 E
Maiyuan, *China* **77 E11** 25 34N 117 28 E
Maiz, Is. del, *Nic.* **164 D3** 12 15N 83 4W
Maizuru, *Japan* **73 B7** 35 25N 135 22 E
Majagual, *Colombia* **168 B3** 8 33N 74 38W
Majalengka, *Indonesia* **85 D3** 6 50 S 108 13 E
Majari →, *Brazil* **169 C5** 3 29N 60 58W
Majdūl, *Libya* **108 C3** 25 51N 15 7 E
Majene, *Indonesia* **82 B1** 3 38 S 118 57 E
Majes →, *Peru* **172 D3** 16 40 S 72 44W
Majete Game Reserve, *Malawi* **119 F3** 15 54 S 34 34 E
Majevica, *Bos.-H.* **52 F3** 44 45N 18 50 E
Maji, *Ethiopia* **107 F4** 6 12N 35 30 E
Majiang, *China* **76 D6** 26 28N 107 32 E
Majorca = Mallorca, *Spain* **38 B4** 39 30N 3 0 E
Majors Creek, *Australia* **129 C8** 35 33 S 149 45 E
Majuriã, *Brazil* **173 B5** 7 30 S 64 55W
Maka, *Senegal* **112 C2** 13 40N 14 10W
Makaha, *U.S.A.* **145 K13** 21 29N 158 13W
Makaha, *Zimbabwe* **117 B5** 17 20 S 32 39 E
Makahoa Pt., *U.S.A.* **145 J14** 21 41N 157 56W
Makahuena Pt., *U.S.A.* **145 B2** 21 52N 159 27W
Makak, *Cameroon* **113 E7** 3 36N 11 0 E
Makakilo City, *U.S.A.* **145 K13** 21 22N 158 5W
Makakou, *Gabon* **114 C2** 0 11 S 12 12 E
Makalamabedi, *Botswana* **116 C3** 20 19 S 23 51 E
Makale, *Indonesia* **82 B1** 3 6 S 119 51 E
Makamba, *Burundi* **118 C2** 4 8 S 29 49 E
Makapuu Pt., *U.S.A.* **145 K14** 21 19N 157 39W
Makarewa, *N.Z.* **131 G3** 46 20 S 168 21 E
Makari, *Cameroon* **113 C7** 12 35N 10 27 E
Makari, *Cent. Amer.* **109 F2** 12 35N 10 27 E
Makarikari = Makgadikgadi Salt Pans, *Botswana* **116 C4** 20 40 S 25 45 E
Makarovo, *Russia* **67 D11** 57 40N 107 45 E
Makarska, *Croatia* **45 E14** 43 20N 17 2 E
Makaryev, *Russia* **60 B6** 57 52N 43 50 E
Makasar = Ujung Pandang, *Indonesia* **82 C1** 5 10 S 119 20 E
Makasar, Selat, *Indonesia* **85 C5** 1 0 S 118 20 E
Makasar, Str. of = Makasar, Selat, *Indonesia* **85 C5** 1 0 S 118 20 E
Makat, *Kazakstan* **57 E9** 47 39N 53 19 E
Makaw, *Dem. Rep. of the Congo* **114 C3** 3 29 S 18 20 E
Makawao, *U.S.A.* **145 C5** 20 52N 156 17W
Makaya, *Dem. Rep. of the Congo* **114 C3** 3 21 S 18 1 E
Makbon, *Indonesia* **83 B4** 0 45 S 131 32 E
Makedonija = Macedonia ■, *Europe* **50 E5** 41 53N 21 40 E
Makeni, *S. Leone* **112 D2** 8 55N 12 5W
Makeyevka = Makiyivka, *Ukraine* **59 H9** 48 0N 38 0 E
Makgadikgadi Nat. Park, *Botswana* **116 C3** 20 27 S 24 47 E
Makgadikgadi Salt Pans, *Botswana* **116 C4** 20 40 S 25 45 E
Makhachkala, *Russia* **61 J8** 43 0N 47 30 E
Makhairádhon, *Greece* **39 D2** 37 46N 20 49 E
Makharadze = Ozurgeti, *Georgia* **61 K5** 41 55N 42 2 E
Makhmūr, *Iraq* **101 E10** 35 46N 43 35 E
Makhtal, *India* **95 E3** 16 30N 77 31 E
Makhyah, W. →, *Yemen* **99 C5** 17 40N 49 1 E
Makian, *Indonesia* **82 A3** 0 20N 127 20 E
Makina, *Solomon Is.* **133 M11** 9 50 S 160 50 E
Makindu, *Kenya* **118 C4** 2 18 S 37 50 E
Makinsk, *Kazakstan* **66 D8** 52 37N 70 26 E
Makiyivka, *Ukraine* **59 H9** 48 0N 38 0 E
Makkah, *Si. Arabia* **98 B2** 21 30N 39 54 E
Makkovik, *Canada* **141 A8** 55 10N 59 10W
Makó, *Hungary* **52 D5** 46 14N 20 33 E
Mako, *Senegal* **112 C2** 12 52N 12 20W
Makogai, *Fiji* **133 A2** 17 28 S 179 0 E
Makok, *Gabon* **114 C1** 0 1 S 9 35 E
Makokou, *Gabon* **114 B2** 0 40N 12 50 E
Makongo, *Dem. Rep. of the Congo* **118 B2** 3 25N 26 17 E
Makoro, *Dem. Rep. of the Congo* **118 B2** 3 10N 29 59 E
Makoua, *Congo* **114 C3** 0 5 S 15 50 E
Maków Mazowiecki, *Poland* **55 F8** 52 52N 21 6 E
Maków Podhalański, *Poland* **55 J6** 49 43N 19 45 E
Makrá, *Greece* **49 E7** 36 15N 25 54 E
Makran, *Asia* **91 D1** 26 13N 61 30 E
Makran Coast Range, *Pakistan* **91 D2** 25 40N 64 0 E
Makrana, *India* **92 F6** 27 2N 74 46 E
Mákri, *Greece* **51 F9** 40 52N 25 40 E
Makri, *India* **94 E5** 19 46N 81 55 E
Makriyialos, *Greece* **39 E6** 35 2N 25 59 E
Maktar, *Tunisia* **108 A1** 35 48N 9 12 E
Mākū, *Iran* **101 C11** 39 15N 44 31 E
Makum, *India* **90 B5** 27 30N 95 23 E
Makumbi, *Dem. Rep. of the Congo* **115 D4** 5 50 S 20 43 E
Makunda, *Botswana* **116 C3** 22 30 S 20 7 E
Makung, *Taiwan* **77 F12** 23 34N 119 34 E
Makunza, *Dem. Rep. of the Congo* **115 D4** 8 52 S 24 19 E
Makurazaki, *Japan* **72 F2** 31 15N 130 20 E
Makurdi, *Nigeria* **113 D6** 7 43N 8 35 E
Makushin Volcano, *U.S.A.* **144 K6** 53 53N 166 55W
Makūyeh, *Iran* **97 D7** 28 7N 53 9 E
Makwassie, *S. Africa* **116 D4** 27 17 S 26 0 E
Makwiro, *Zimbabwe* **117 B5** 17 58 S 30 25 E
Mal, *India* **90 B2** 26 51N 88 45 E
Mâl, *Mauritania* **112 B2** 16 58N 13 23W
Mal B., *Ireland* **23 D2** 52 50N 9 30W
Mala, *Peru* **172 C2** 12 40 S 76 38W
Mala, Pta., *Panama* **164 E3** 7 28N 80 2W
Mala Belozërka, *Ukraine* **59 J8** 47 12N 34 56 E
Mala Kapela, *Croatia* **45 D12** 44 45N 15 30 E
Mała Panew →, *Poland* **55 H4** 50 43N 17 54 E
Mala Vyska, *Ukraine* **59 H6** 48 39N 31 36 E
Malabang, *Phil.* **81 H5** 7 36N 124 3 E
Malabar, *U.S.A.* **153 H9** 28 0N 80 34W
Malabar Coast, *India* **95 J2** 11 0N 75 0 E
Malabo = Rey Malabo, *Eq. Guin.* **113 E6** 3 45N 8 50 E
Malabon, *Phil.* **80 D3** 14 21N 121 0 E
Malabrigo Pt., *Phil.* **80 E3** 13 36N 121 15 E
Malabu, *Nigeria* **113 D7** 9 32N 12 48 E
Malabuñgan, *Phil.* **81 G1** 9 3N 117 38 E
Malacca, Str. of, *Indonesia* **87 L3** 3 0N 101 0 E
Malacky, *Slovak Rep.* **35 C10** 48 27N 17 0 E
Malad City, *U.S.A.* **158 E7** 42 12N 112 15W
Maladeta, *Spain* **40 C5** 42 39N 0 39 E
Maladzyechna, *Belarus* **58 E4** 54 20N 26 50 E
Malae Pt., *U.S.A.* **145 C6** 20 7N 155 53W
Málaga, *Colombia* **168 B3** 6 42N 72 44W
Málaga, *Spain* **43 J6** 36 43N 4 23W
Málaga □, *Spain* **43 J6** 36 38N 4 58W
Malagarasi, *Tanzania* **118 D3** 5 5 S 30 50 E
Malagarasi →, *Tanzania* **118 D2** 5 12 S 29 47 E
Malagasy Rep. = Madagascar ■, *Africa* **117 C8** 20 0 S 47 0 E
Malagón, *Spain* **43 F7** 39 11N 3 52W
Malagón →, *Spain* **43 H3** 37 35N 7 29W
Malahide, *Ireland* **23 C5** 53 26N 6 9W
Malaimbandy, *Madag.* **117 C8** 20 20 S 45 36 E
Malaita, *Solomon Is.* **133 M11** 9 0 S 161 0 E
Malakâl, *Sudan* **107 F3** 9 33N 31 40 E
Malakanagiri, *India* **94 E5** 18 21N 81 54 E
Malakand, *Pakistan* **91 B3** 34 40N 71 55 E
Malakula, *Vanuatu* **133 F5** 16 15 S 167 30 E
Malakwal, *Pakistan* **92 C5** 32 34N 73 13 E
Malalag, *Phil.* **81 H5** 6 36N 125 24 E
Malalaua, *Papua N. G.* **132 E4** 8 4 S 146 10 E
Malam, *Chad* **109 F4** 11 27N 20 59 E
Malamala, *Indonesia* **82 B2** 3 21 S 120 55 E
Malanda, *Australia* **126 B4** 17 22 S 145 35 E
Malang, *Indonesia* **85 D4** 7 59 S 112 45 E
Malangas, *Phil.* **81 H4** 7 37N 123 1 E
Malange □, *Angola* **115 D3** 9 30 S 16 0 E
Malangen, *Norway* **14 B18** 69 24N 18 37 E
Malanje, *Angola* **115 D3** 9 36 S 16 17 E
Malapatan, *Phil.* **81 J5** 5 59N 125 18 E
Mälaren, *Sweden* **16 E11** 59 30N 17 10 E
Malargüe, *Argentina* **174 D2** 35 32 S 69 30W
Malartic, *Canada* **140 C4** 48 9N 78 9W
Malaryta, *Belarus* **59 G3** 51 50N 24 3 E
Malaspina Glacier, *U.S.A.* **144 G12** 59 50N 140 30W
Malatya, *Turkey* **101 C8** 38 25N 38 20 E
Malawali, *Malaysia* **85 A5** 7 3N 117 18 E
Malawi ■, *Africa* **119 E3** 11 55 S 34 0 E
Malawi, L. = Nyasa, L., *Africa* **119 E3** 12 30 S 34 30 E
Malay, *Phil.* **81 F3** 11 54N 121 55 E
Malay Pen., *Asia* **87 J3** 7 25N 100 0 E
Malaya Belozërka = Mala Belozërka, *Ukraine* **59 J8** 47 12N 34 56 E
Malaya Vishera, *Russia* **58 C7** 58 55N 32 25 E
Malaya Viska = Mala Vyska, *Ukraine* **59 H6** 48 39N 31 36 E
Malaybalay, *Phil.* **81 G5** 8 5N 125 7 E
Malāyer, *Iran* **97 C6** 34 19N 48 51 E
Malaysia ■, *Asia* **81 J1** 5 0N 110 0 E
Malazgirt, *Turkey* **101 C10** 39 10N 42 33 E
Malbaza, *Niger* **113 C6** 13 59N 5 38 E
Malbon, *Australia* **126 C3** 21 5 S 140 17 E
Malbooma, *Australia* **127 E1** 30 41 S 134 11 E
Malbork, *Poland* **54 D6** 54 3N 19 1 E
Malca Dube, *Ethiopia* **120 C2** 6 47N 42 4 E
Malcésine, *Italy* **44 C7** 45 46N 10 48 E
Malchin, *Germany* **30 B8** 53 44N 12 44 E
Malchow, *Germany* **30 B8** 53 28N 12 25 E
Malcolm, *Australia* **125 E3** 28 51 S 121 25 E
Malcolm, Pt., *Australia* **125 F3** 33 48 S 123 45 E
Malczyce, *Poland* **55 G3** 51 14N 16 29 E
Maldah, *India* **93 G13** 25 2N 88 9 E
Maldegem, *Belgium* **24 C3** 51 14N 3 26 E
Malden, *Mass., U.S.A.* **151 D13** 42 26N 71 4W
Malden, *Mo., U.S.A.* **155 G10** 36 34N 89 57W
Malden I., *Kiribati* **135 H12** 4 3 S 155 1W
Maldives ■, *Ind. Oc.* **62 J11** 5 0N 73 0 E
Maldon, *Australia* **128 D6** 37 0 S 144 6 E
Maldonado, *Uruguay* **175 C5** 34 59 S 55 0W
Maldonado, Punta, *Mexico* **163 D5** 16 19N 98 35W
Malè, *Italy* **44 B7** 46 21N 10 55 E
Malé, *Maldives* **63 J11** 4 0N 73 28 E
Malé Karpaty, *Slovak Rep.* **35 C10** 48 30N 17 20 E
Maléa, Ákra, *Greece* **48 E5** 36 28N 23 7 E
Malebo, Pool, *Africa* **115 C3** 4 17 S 15 20 E
Malegaon, *India* **94 D2** 20 30N 74 38 E
Malei, *Mozam.* **119 F4** 17 12 S 36 58 E
Malek, *Sudan* **107 F3** 6 4N 31 36 E
Malek Kandī, *Iran* **101 D12** 37 9N 46 6 E
Malela, *Bas-Congo, Dem. Rep. of the Congo* **115 D2** 5 59 S 12 37 E
Malela, *Maniema, Dem. Rep. of the Congo* **118 C2** 4 22 S 26 8 E
Malema, *Mozam.* **119 E4** 14 57 S 37 20 E
Máleme, *Greece* **39 E4** 35 31N 23 49 E
Malendok I., *Papua N. G.* **132 B7** 3 28 S 153 13 E
Maleny, *Australia* **127 D5** 26 45 S 152 52 E
Målerås, *Sweden* **17 H9** 56 54N 15 34 E
Malerkotla, *India* **92 D6** 30 32N 75 58 E
Máles, *Greece* **39 E6** 35 6N 25 35 E
Malesherbes, *France* **27 D9** 48 15N 2 24 E
Maleshevska Planina, *Europe* **50 E7** 41 38N 23 7 E
Malesína, *Greece* **48 C5** 38 37N 23 14 E
Malestroit, *France* **26 E4** 47 49N 2 25W
Malfa, *Italy* **47 D7** 38 35N 14 50 E
Malgobek, *Russia* **61 J7** 43 30N 44 34 E
Malgomaj, *Sweden* **14 D17** 64 40N 16 30 E
Malgrat = Malgrat de Mar, *Spain* **40 D7** 41 39N 2 46 E
Malgrat de Mar, *Spain* **40 D7** 41 39N 2 46 E
Malha, *Sudan* **107 D2** 15 8N 25 10 E
Malhada, *Brazil* **171 D3** 14 21 S 43 47W
Malhargarh, *India* **92 G6** 24 17N 74 59 E
Malheur →, *U.S.A.* **158 D5** 44 4N 116 59W
Malheur L., *U.S.A.* **158 E4** 43 20N 118 48W
Mali, *Guinea* **112 C2** 12 10N 12 20W
Mali ■, *Africa* **112 B4** 17 0N 3 0W
Mali →, *Burma* **90 C6** 25 42N 97 30 E
Mali Kanal, *Serbia, Yug.* **52 E4** 45 36N 19 24 E
Mali Kyun, *Burma* **86 F2** 13 0N 98 20 E
Malibu, *U.S.A.* **161 L8** 34 2N 118 41W
Maligaya = Gloria, *Phil.* **80 E3** 12 59N 121 30 E
Maliku, *Indonesia* **82 B2** 0 39 S 123 16 E
Malili, *Indonesia* **82 B2** 2 42 S 121 6 E
Målilla, *Sweden* **17 G9** 57 23N 15 48 E
Malimba, Mts., *Dem. Rep. of the Congo* **118 D2** 7 30 S 29 30 E
Malin Hd., *Ireland* **23 A4** 55 23N 7 23W
Malin Pen., *Ireland* **23 A4** 55 20N 7 17W
Malindang, Mt., *Phil.* **81 G4** 8 13N 123 38 E
Malindi, *Kenya* **118 C5** 3 12 S 40 5 E
Malines = Mechelen, *Belgium* **24 C4** 51 2N 4 29 E
Malino, *Indonesia* **82 A2** 1 0N 121 0 E
Malinyi, *Tanzania* **119 D4** 8 56 S 36 0 E
Malipo, *China* **76 F5** 23 7N 104 42 E
Maliq, *Albania* **50 F4** 40 45N 20 48 E
Malita, *Phil.* **81 H5** 6 19N 125 39 E
Maliwun, *Burma* **78 B1** 10 17N 98 40 E
Maliya, *India* **92 H4** 23 5N 70 46 E
Maljenik, *Serbia, Yug.* **50 C5** 43 54N 21 43 E
Malka Mari Nat. Park, *Kenya* **118 B5** 4 11N 40 46 E
Malkapur, *India* **94 D1** 20 53N 73 58 E
Malkara, *Turkey* **51 F10** 40 53N 26 53 E
Małkinia Górna, *Poland* **55 F9** 52 42N 22 5 E
Malko Tŭrnovo, *Bulgaria* **51 E11** 41 59N 27 31 E
Mallacoota, *Australia* **129 D8** 37 40 S 149 40 E
Mallacoota Inlet, *Australia* **129 D8** 37 34 S 149 40 E
Mallaig, *U.K.* **22 D3** 57 0N 5 50W
Mallala, *Australia* **128 C3** 34 26 S 138 30 E
Mallaoua, *Niger* **113 C6** 13 2N 9 36 E
Mallard, *U.S.A.* **156 B2** 42 56N 94 41W
Mallawan, *India* **93 F9** 27 4N 80 12 E
Mallawi, *Egypt* **106 B3** 27 44N 30 44 E
Mallee Cliffs Nat. Park, *Australia* **128 C5** 34 16 S 142 32 E
Mallembe, *Gabon* **114 C2** 3 34 S 10 53 E
Mallemort, *France* **29 E9** 43 43N 5 11 E
Málles Venosta, *Italy* **44 B7** 46 41N 10 32 E
Mállia, *Greece* **39 E6** 35 17N 25 32 E
Mallicolo = Malakula, *Vanuatu* **133 F5** 16 15 S 167 30 E
Mallión, Kólpos, *Greece* **39 E6** 35 19N 25 27 E
Mallorca, *Spain* **38 B4** 39 30N 3 0 E
Mallorytown, *Canada* **151 B9** 44 29N 75 53W
Mallow, *Ireland* **23 D3** 52 8N 8 39W
Malmbäck, *Sweden* **17 G8** 57 34N 14 28 E
Malmberget, *Sweden* **14 C19** 67 11N 20 40 E
Malmédy, *Belgium* **24 D6** 50 25N 6 2 E
Malmesbury, *S. Africa* **116 E2** 33 28 S 18 41 E
Malmköping, *Sweden* **16 E10** 59 8N 16 44 E
Malmö, *Sweden* **17 J6** 55 36N 12 59 E
Malmslätt, *Sweden* **17 F9** 58 27N 15 33 E
Malmyzh, *Russia* **60 B10** 56 31N 50 41 E
Malnaş, *Romania* **53 D10** 46 2N 25 49 E
Malo, *Vanuatu* **133 E5** 15 40 S 167 11 E
Malo Konare, *Bulgaria* **51 D8** 42 12N 24 24 E
Maloarkhangelsk, *Russia* **59 F9** 52 28N 36 30 E
Maloca, *Brazil* **169 C6** 0 43N 55 57W
Maloja, *Switz.* **33 D9** 46 25N 9 35 E
Malojapass, *Switz.* **33 D9** 46 23N 9 42 E
Malolo, *Fiji* **133 A1** 17 45 S 177 11 E
Malolos, *Phil.* **80 D3** 14 50N 120 49 E
Malolotja Nature Reserve, *Swaziland* **117 D5** 26 4 S 31 6 E
Malombe L., *Malawi* **119 E4** 14 40 S 35 15 E
Małomice, *Poland* **55 G2** 51 34N 15 29 E
Malomir, *Bulgaria* **51 D10** 42 16N 26 32 E
Malone, *Fla., U.S.A.* **152 E4** 30 57N 85 10W
Malone, *N.Y., U.S.A.* **151 B10** 44 51N 74 18W
Malong, *China* **76 E4** 25 24N 103 34 E
Malonga, *Dem. Rep. of the Congo* **115 E4** 10 24 S 23 10 E
Malonno, *Italy* **33 D10** 46 7N 10 18 E
Małopolskie □, *Poland* **55 J7** 49 50N 20 20 E
Malorad, *Bulgaria* **50 C7** 43 28N 23 41 E
Måløy, *Norway* **15 F11** 61 57N 5 6 E
Maloyaroslovets, *Russia* **58 E9** 55 2N 36 20 E
Malpartida, *Spain* **43 F4** 39 26N 6 30W
Malpaso, *Canary Is.* **9 e1** 27 43N 18 3W
Malpelo, I. de, *Colombia* **135 G19** 4 3N 81 35W
Malpica de Bergantiños, *Spain* **42 B2** 43 19N 8 50W
Malprabha →, *India* **95 F3** 16 20N 76 5 E
Malpur, *India* **92 H5** 23 21N 73 27 E
Malpura, *India* **92 F6** 26 17N 75 23 E
Mals = Málles Venosta, *Italy* **44 B7** 46 41N 10 32 E
Malsiras, *India* **94 F2** 17 52N 74 55 E
Malta, *Brazil* **170 C4** 6 54 S 37 31W
Malta, *Idaho, U.S.A.* **158 E7** 42 18N 113 22W
Malta, *Mont., U.S.A.* **158 B10** 48 21N 107 52W
Malta ■, *Europe* **38 F7** 35 55N 14 26 E
Maltahöhe, *Namibia* **116 C2** 24 55 S 17 0 E
Maltepe, *Turkey* **51 F13** 40 55N 29 8 E
Malters, *Switz.* **32 B6** 47 3N 8 11 E
Malton, *Canada* **150 C5** 43 42N 79 38W
Malton, *U.K.* **20 C7** 54 8N 0 49W
Malu'a, *Solomon Is.* **133 M11** 8 20 S 160 38 E
Maluku, *Dem. Rep. of the Congo* **114 C3** 4 3 S 15 34 E
Maluku, *Indonesia* **79 E7** 1 0 S 127 0 E
Maluku □, *Indonesia* **82 B3** 3 0 S 128 0 E
Maluku Sea = Molucca Sea, *Indonesia* **82 A3** 0 0 125 0 E
Malumfashi, *Nigeria* **113 C6** 11 48N 7 39 E
Malunda, *Indonesia* **82 B1** 3 0 S 118 50 E
Malundo, *Angola* **115 E4** 14 51 S 22 0 E
Malung, *Sweden* **16 D7** 60 42N 13 44 E
Malungon, *Phil.* **81 H5** 6 16N 125 14 E
Malungsfors, *Sweden* **16 D7** 60 44N 13 33 E
Malur, *India* **95 H3** 13 0N 77 55 E
Maluso, *Phil.* **81 H3** 6 33N 121 53 E
Maluwe, *Ghana* **112 D4** 8 40N 2 17W
Malvaglia, *Switz.* **33 D7** 46 24N 8 59 E
Malvalli, *India* **95 H3** 12 28N 77 8 E
Malvan, *India* **95 F1** 16 2N 73 30 E
Malvern, *U.S.A.* **155 H8** 34 22N 92 49W
Malvern Hills, *U.K.* **21 E5** 52 0N 2 19W
Malvik, *Norway* **18 A7** 63 25N 10 40 E
Malvinas, Is. = Falkland Is. □, *Atl. Oc.* **9 f** 51 30 S 59 0W
Malý Dunaj →, *Slovak Rep.* **35 D11** 47 45N 18 9 E
Malya, *Tanzania* **118 C3** 3 5 S 33 38 E
Malybay, *Kazakstan* **65 B9** 43 30N 78 25 E
Malyn, *Ukraine* **59 G5** 50 46N 29 3 E
Malyy Lyakhovskiy, Ostrov, *Russia* **67 B15** 74 7N 140 36 E
Mama, *Russia* **67 D12** 58 18N 112 54 E
Mamadysh, *Russia* **60 C10** 55 44N 51 23 E
Mamaku, *N.Z.* **130 E5** 38 5 S 176 8 E
Mamala B., *U.S.A.* **145 K14** 21 15N 157 55W
Mamanguape, *Brazil* **170 C4** 6 50 S 35 4W
Mamanuca Group, *Fiji* **133 A1** 17 35 S 177 5 E
Mamanutha Group, *Fiji* **133 A1** 17 34 S 177 4 E
Mamarr Mitlā, *Egypt* **103 E1** 30 2N 32 54 E
Mamasa, *Indonesia* **82 B1** 2 55 S 119 20 E
Mambajao, *Phil.* **81 G5** 9 15N 124 43 E
Mambasa, *Dem. Rep. of the Congo* **118 B2** 1 22N 29 3 E
Mamberamo →, *Indonesia* **83 B5** 2 0 S 137 50 E
Mambéré →, *C.A.R.* **114 B3** 3 31N 16 3 E
Mambili →, *Congo* **114 B3** 0 6N 16 5 E
Mambilima Falls, *Zambia* **119 E2** 10 31 S 28 45 E
Mambirima, *Dem. Rep. of the Congo* **119 E2** 11 25 S 27 33 E
Mambo, *Tanzania* **118 C4** 4 52 S 38 22 E
Mambrui, *Kenya* **118 C5** 3 5 S 40 5 E
Mamburao, *Phil.* **80 E3** 13 13N 120 39 E
Mameigwess L., *Canada* **140 B2** 52 35N 87 50W
Mamers, *France* **26 D7** 48 21N 0 22 E
Mamfé, *Cameroon* **113 D6** 5 50N 9 15 E
Māmī, Ra's, *Yemen* **99 D6** 12 32N 54 30 E
Mamiña, *Chile* **172 E4** 20 5 S 69 14W
Mammoth, *U.S.A.* **159 K8** 32 43N 110 39W
Mammoth Cave Nat. Park, *U.S.A.* **148 G3** 37 8N 86 13W
Mamoré →, *Bolivia* **173 C4** 10 23 S 65 53W
Mamou, *Guinea* **112 C2** 10 15N 12 0W
Mamoudzou, *Mayotte* **105 H8** 12 48 S 45 14 E
Mampatá, *Guinea-Biss.* **112 C2** 11 54N 14 53W
Mampikony, *Madag.* **117 B8** 16 6 S 47 38 E
Mampoko, *Dem. Rep. of the Congo* **114 B3** 0 51N 18 42 E
Mampong, *Ghana* **113 D4** 7 6N 1 26W
Mamry, Jezioro, *Poland* **54 D8** 54 5N 21 50 E
Mamuil Malal, Paso, *S. Amer.* **176 A2** 39 35 S 71 28W
Mamuju, *Indonesia* **82 B1** 2 41 S 118 50 E
Ma'mūl, *Oman* **99 C6** 18 8N 55 16 E
Mamuno, *Botswana* **116 C3** 22 16 S 20 1 E
Mamuras, *Albania* **50 E3** 41 34N 19 41 E
Man, *Ivory C.* **112 D3** 7 30N 7 40W
Man →, *India* **94 F2** 17 31N 75 32 E
Man, I. of, *India* **95 K11** 8 28N 93 36 E
Man, I. of, *U.K.* **20 C3** 54 15N 4 30W
Man-Bazar, *India* **93 H12** 23 4N 86 39 E
Mān Kat, *Burma* **90 D7** 22 5N 98 1 E
Man Na, *Burma* **90 D6** 23 27N 97 19 E
Man Tun, *Burma* **90 D7** 23 52N 98 38 E
Mana, *Fr. Guiana* **169 B7** 5 45N 53 55W
Mana, *U.S.A.* **145 A2** 22 2N 159 47W
Mana →, *Fr. Guiana* **169 B7** 5 45N 53 55W
Mana Pools Nat. Park, *Zimbabwe* **119 F2** 15 56 S 29 25 E
Manaar, G. of = Mannar, G. of, *Asia* **95 K4** 8 30N 79 0 E
Manabí □, *Ecuador* **168 D1** 0 40 S 80 5W
Manacacías →, *Colombia* **168 C3** 4 23N 72 4W
Manacapuru, *Brazil* **169 D5** 3 16 S 60 37W
Manacapuru →, *Brazil* **169 D5** 3 18 S 60 37W
Manacor, *Spain* **38 B4** 39 34N 3 13 E
Manadas, *Azores* **9 d1** 38 38N 28 6W
Manado, *Indonesia* **82 A2** 1 29N 124 51 E
Managua, *Nic.* **164 D2** 12 6N 86 20W
Managua, L. de, *Nic.* **164 D2** 12 20N 86 30W
Manaia, *N.Z.* **130 F3** 39 33 S 174 8 E
Manakara, *Madag.* **117 C8** 22 8 S 48 1 E
Manakau, *N.Z.* **131 C8** 42 15 S 173 42 E
Manākhah, *Yemen* **98 D3** 15 5N 43 44 E
Manali, *India* **92 C7** 32 16N 77 10 E
Manam I., *Papua N. G.* **132 C3** 4 5 S 145 0 E
Manama = Al Manāmah, *Bahrain* **97 E6** 26 10N 50 30 E
Manambao →, *Madag.* **117 B7** 17 35 S 44 0 E
Manambato, *Madag.* **117 A8** 13 43 S 49 7 E
Manambolo →, *Madag.* **117 B7** 19 18 S 44 22 E
Manambolosy, *Madag.* **117 B8** 16 2 S 49 40 E
Mánamo, Caño →, *Venezuela* **169 B5** 9 55N 62 16W
Manana I., *U.S.A.* **145 K14** 21 20N 157 40W
Mananara, *Madag.* **117 B8** 16 10 S 49 46 E
Mananara →, *Madag.* **117 C8** 23 21 S 47 42 E
Mananara, Réserve Naturelle Intégrale de, *Madag.* **117 B8** 16 14 S 49 45 E
Manangatang, *Australia* **128 C5** 35 5 S 142 54 E
Mananjary, *Madag.* **117 C8** 21 13 S 48 20 E
Manankoro, *Mali* **112 C3** 10 28N 7 25W
Manantavadi, *India* **95 J3** 11 49N 76 1 E
Manantenina, *Madag.* **117 C8** 24 17 S 47 19 E
Manaos = Manaus, *Brazil* **169 D6** 3 0 S 60 0W
Manapala, *Phil.* **81 F4** 10 58N 123 5 E
Manapire →, *Venezuela* **168 B4** 7 42N 66 7W
Manapouri, *N.Z.* **131 F2** 45 34 S 167 39 E
Manapouri, L., *N.Z.* **131 F2** 45 32 S 167 32 E
Manapparai, *India* **95 J4** 10 36N 78 25 E
Manaqil, *Sudan* **107 E3** 14 15N 32 59 E
Manar →, *India* **94 E3** 18 50N 77 20 E
Manār, Jabal, *Yemen* **98 D4** 14 2N 44 17 E
Manaravolo, *Madag.* **117 C8** 23 59 S 45 39 E

Manas, *China* 68 B3 44 17N 85 56 E
Manas, *Somali Rep.* 120 D2 2 57N 43 28 E
Manas →, *India* 90 B3 26 12N 90 40 E
Manas, Gora, *Kyrgyzstan* 65 B5 42 22N 71 2 E
Manaslu, *Nepal* 93 E11 28 33N 84 33 E
Manasquan, *U.S.A.* 151 F10 40 8N 74 3W
Manassa, *U.S.A.* 159 H11 37 11N 105 56W
Manatí, *Puerto Rico* 165 d 18 26N 66 29W
Manati B., *St. Helena* 9 h 16 0S 5 46W
Manatuto, *E. Timor* 82 C3 8 30S 126 1 E
Manau, *Papua N. G.* 132 E4 8 4S 148 0 E
Manaung, *Burma* 90 F4 18 45N 93 40 E
Manaus, *Brazil* 169 D6 3 0S 60 0W
Manavgat, *Turkey* 100 D4 36 47N 31 26 E
Manawan L., *Canada* 143 B8 55 24N 103 14W
Manawatu →, *N.Z.* 130 G4 40 28S 175 12 E
Manawatu-Wanganui □, *N.Z.* 130 F4 39 50S 175 30 E
Manay, *Phil.* 81 H6 7 17N 126 33 E
Manbij, *Syria* 100 D7 36 31N 37 57 E
Mancha Real, *Spain* 43 H7 37 48N 3 39W
Manche □, *France* 26 C5 49 10N 1 20W
Manchegorsk, *Russia* 66 C4 67 54N 32 58 E
Manchester, *U.K.* 20 D5 53 29N 2 12W
Manchester, *Calif., U.S.A.* 160 G3 38 58N 123 41W
Manchester, *Conn., U.S.A.* 151 E12 41 47N 72 31W
Manchester, *Ga., U.S.A.* 152 C5 32 51N 84 37W
Manchester, *Iowa, U.S.A.* 156 B5 42 29N 91 27W
Manchester, *Ky., U.S.A.* 148 G4 37 9N 83 46W
Manchester, *Mich., U.S.A.* 157 B12 42 9N 84 2W
Manchester, *N.H., U.S.A.* 151 D13 42 59N 71 28W
Manchester, *N.Y., U.S.A.* 150 D7 42 56N 77 16W
Manchester, *Ohio, U.S.A.* 157 F13 38 41N 83 36W
Manchester, *Pa., U.S.A.* 151 F8 40 4N 76 43W
Manchester, *Tenn., U.S.A.* 149 H2 35 29N 86 5W
Manchester, *Vt., U.S.A.* 151 C11 43 10N 73 5W
Manchester L., *Canada* 143 A7 61 28N 107 29W
Manchhar L., *Pakistan* 92 F2 26 25N 67 39 E
Manchuria = Dongbei, *China* 75 D13 45 0N 125 0 E
Manchurian Plain, *China* 62 E16 47 0N 124 0 E
Manciano, *Italy* 45 F8 42 35N 11 31 E
Mancifa, *Ethiopia* 107 F5 6 53N 41 50 E
Mancora, *Peru* 172 A1 4 9S 81 1W
Mand →, *India* 93 J10 21 42N 83 15 E
Mand →, *Iran* 97 D7 28 20N 52 30 E
Manda, *Ludewe, Tanzania* 119 E3 10 30S 34 40 E
Manda, *Mbeya, Tanzania* 118 D3 7 58S 32 29 E
Manda, *Mbeya, Tanzania* 119 D3 8 30S 32 49 E
Manda, Parc Nat. de, *Chad* 109 G3 9 45N 17 52 E
Mandabé, *Madag.* 117 C7 21 0S 44 55 E
Mandaguari, *Brazil* 175 A5 23 32S 51 42W
Mandah = Töhöm, *Mongolia* 74 B5 44 27N 108 2 E
Mandal, *Norway* 15 G12 58 2N 7 25 E
Mandala, Puncak, *Indonesia* 83 B6 4 44S 140 20 E
Mandalay, *Burma* 90 D6 22 0N 96 4 E
Mandalay □, *Burma* 90 E5 22 0N 96 5 E
Mandale = Mandalay, *Burma* 90 D6 22 0N 96 4 E
Mandalgarh, *India* 92 G6 25 12N 75 6 E
Mandalgovi, *Mongolia* 74 B4 45 45N 106 10 E
Mandalī, *Iraq* 101 F11 33 43N 45 28 E
Mandan, *U.S.A.* 154 B4 46 50N 100 54W
Mandaon, *Phil.* 80 E4 12 13N 123 17 E
Mandar, Teluk, *Indonesia* 82 B1 3 35S 119 15 E
Mandara Mts., *Nigeria* 109 F2 10 40N 13 40 E
Mandas, *Italy* 46 C2 39 40N 9 8 E
Mandaue, *Phil.* 81 F4 10 20N 123 56 E
Mandelieu-la-Napoule, *France* 29 E10 43 34N 6 57 E
Mandera, *Kenya* 118 B5 3 55N 41 53 E
Mandeville, *Jamaica* 164 a 18 2N 77 31W
Mandi, *India* 92 D7 31 39N 76 58 E
Mandi Dabwali, *India* 92 E6 29 58N 74 42 E
Mandiana, *Guinea* 112 C3 10 37N 8 39W
Mandimba, *Mozam.* 119 E4 14 20S 35 40 E
Mandioli, *Indonesia* 82 B3 0 40S 127 20 E
Mandioré, L., *S. Amer.* 173 D6 18 8S 57 33W
Mandla, *India* 93 H9 22 39N 80 30 E
Mandø, *Denmark* 17 J2 55 18N 8 33 E
Mandorah, *Australia* 124 B5 12 32S 130 42 E
Mandoto, *Madag.* 117 B8 19 34S 46 17 E
Mandoúdhion, *Greece* 48 C5 38 48N 23 29 E
Mándra, *Greece* 48 C5 38 4N 23 30 E
Mandra, *Pakistan* 92 C5 33 23N 73 12 E
Mandrákhi, *Greece* 49 E9 36 36N 27 11 E
Mandrare →, *Madag.* 117 D8 25 10S 46 30 E
Mandritsara, *Madag.* 117 B8 15 50S 48 49 E
Mandronarivo, *Madag.* 117 C8 21 7S 45 38 E
Mandsaur, *India* 92 G6 24 3N 75 8 E
Mandurah, *Australia* 125 F2 32 36S 115 48 E
Mandúria, *Italy* 47 B10 40 24N 17 38 E
Mandvi, *India* 92 H3 22 51N 69 22 E
Mandya, *India* 95 H3 12 30N 77 0 E
Mandzai, *Pakistan* 92 D2 30 55N 67 6 E
Mané, *Burkina Faso* 113 C4 12 59N 1 21W
Maneh, *Iran* 97 B8 37 39N 57 7 E
Manengouba, Mts., *Cameroon* 113 E6 5 0N 9 50 E
Maner →, *India* 94 E4 18 30N 79 40 E
Manera, *Madag.* 117 C7 22 55S 44 20 E
Manérbio, *Italy* 44 C7 45 21N 10 8 E
Maneroo Cr. →, *Australia* 126 C3 23 21S 143 53 E
Manfalût, *Egypt* 106 B3 27 20N 30 52 E
Manfred, *Australia* 128 B5 33 19S 143 45 E
Manfredónia, *Italy* 45 G12 41 38N 15 55 E
Manfredónia, G. di, *Italy* 45 G13 41 35N 16 5 E
Manga, *Brazil* 171 D3 14 46S 43 56W
Manga, *Burkina Faso* 113 C4 11 40N 1 4W
Manga, *Congo* 114 C3 0 13S 16 5 E
Manga, *Niger* 113 C7 15 0N 14 0 E
Mangabeiras, Chapada das, *Brazil* 170 D2 10 0S 46 30W
Mangai, *Dem. Rep. of the Congo* 115 C3 4 2S 19 33 E
Mangakino, *N.Z.* 130 E4 38 22S 175 47 E
Mangal, *Phil.* 81 H3 6 25N 121 58 E
Mangalagiri, *India* 95 F5 16 26N 80 36 E
Mangaldai, *India* 90 B4 26 26N 92 2 E
Mangaldan, *Phil.* 80 C3 16 4N 120 24 E
Mangalia, *Romania* 53 G13 43 50N 28 35 E
Mangalmé, *Chad* 109 F3 12 26N 19 37 E
Mangalore, *India* 95 H2 12 55N 74 47 E
Mangalvedha, *India* 94 F2 17 31N 75 28 E
Mangan, *India* 90 B2 27 31N 88 32 E
Mangaon, *India* 94 E1 18 15N 73 20 E
Mangawan, *India* 93 G9 24 41N 81 33 E
Mangaweka, *N.Z.* 130 F4 39 48S 175 47 E
Mangaweka, Mt., *N.Z.* 130 F5 39 49S 176 5 E
Mange, *Dem. Rep. of the Congo* 114 B4 0 54N 20 30 E
Manger, *Norway* 18 D2 60 38N 5 3 E
Manggar, *Indonesia* 85 C3 2 50S 108 10 E
Manggawitu, *Indonesia* 83 B4 4 8S 133 32 E
Manggis, *Indonesia* 79 J18 8 29S 115 31 E
Mangin Taungdan, *Burma* 90 C5 24 15N 95 45 E
Mangindrano, *Madag.* 117 A8 14 17S 48 58 E
Mangkalihat, Tanjung, *Indonesia* 85 B5 1 2N 118 59 E
Mangla, *Pakistan* 92 C5 33 7N 73 39 E
Mangla Dam, *Pakistan* 93 C5 33 9N 73 44 E
Manglares, C., *Colombia* 168 C2 1 36N 79 2W
Manglaur, *India* 92 E7 29 44N 77 49 E
Mangnai, *China* 68 C4 37 52N 91 43 E
Mango, *Togo* 113 C5 10 20N 0 30 E
Mango, *Tonga* 133 Q14 20 17S 173 25W
Mangoche, *Malawi* 119 E4 14 25S 35 16 E
Mangoky →, *Madag.* 117 C7 21 29S 43 41 E
Mangole, *Indonesia* 82 B3 1 50S 125 55 E
Mangombe, *Dem. Rep. of the Congo* 118 C2 1 20S 26 48 E
Mangonui, *N.Z.* 130 B2 35 1S 173 32 E
Mangoro →, *Madag.* 117 B8 20 0S 48 45 E
Mangrol, *Mad. P., India* 92 J4 21 7N 70 7 E
Mangrol, *Raj., India* 92 G6 25 20N 76 31 E
Mangrul Pir, *India* 94 D3 20 19N 77 21 E
Mangualde, *Portugal* 42 E3 40 38N 7 48W
Mangueigne, *Chad* 109 F4 10 30N 21 15 E
Mangueira, L. da, *Brazil* 175 C5 33 0S 52 50W
Manguéni, Hamada, *Niger* 108 D2 22 35N 12 40 E
Mangum, *U.S.A.* 155 H5 34 53N 99 30W
Mangungu, *Dem. Rep. of the Congo* 115 D3 5 16S 19 36 E
Mangyshlak Poluostrov, *Kazakstan* 66 E6 44 30N 52 30 E
Manhattan, *U.S.A.* 154 F6 39 11N 96 35W
Manhatten, *U.S.A.* 157 C9 41 26N 87 59W
Manhiça, *Mozam.* 117 D5 25 23S 32 49 E
Manhuaçu, *Brazil* 171 F3 20 15S 42 2W
Manhumirim, *Brazil* 171 F3 20 22S 41 57W
Maní, *Colombia* 168 C3 4 49N 72 17W
Mania →, *Madag.* 117 B8 19 42S 45 22 E
Maniago, *Italy* 45 B9 46 10N 12 43 E
Manica, *Mozam.* 117 B5 18 58S 32 59 E
Manica □, *Mozam.* 117 B5 19 10S 33 45 E
Manicaland □, *Zimbabwe* 119 F3 19 0S 32 30 E
Manicoré, *Brazil* 173 B5 5 48S 61 16W
Manicoré →, *Brazil* 173 B5 5 51S 61 19W
Manicouagan →, *Canada* 141 C6 49 30N 68 30W
Manicouagan, Rés., *Canada* 141 B6 51 5N 68 40W
Maniema □, *Dem. Rep. of the Congo* 118 C2 3 0S 26 0 E
Manīfah, *Si. Arabia* 97 E6 27 44N 49 0 E
Manifold, C., *Australia* 126 C5 22 41S 150 50 E
Maniganggo, *China* 76 B2 31 56N 99 10 E
Manigotagan, *Canada* 143 C9 51 6N 96 18W
Manigotagan →, *Canada* 143 C9 51 7N 96 20W
Manihari, *India* 93 G12 25 21N 87 38 E
Manihiki, *Cook Is.* 135 J11 10 24S 161 1W
Maniitsoq, *Greenland* 10 D5 65 26N 52 55W
Manika, Plateau de la, *Dem. Rep. of the Congo* 119 E2 10 0S 25 5 E
Manikchhari, *Bangla.* 90 D3 22 51N 91 50 E
Manikganj, *Bangla.* 90 D3 23 52N 90 0 E
Manikpur, *India* 93 G9 25 4N 81 7 E
Manila, *Phil.* 80 D3 14 40N 121 3 E
Manila, *U.S.A.* 158 F9 40 59N 109 43W
Manila B., *Phil.* 80 D3 14 40N 120 35 E
Manildra, *Australia* 129 B8 33 11S 148 41 E
Manilla, *Australia* 129 A9 30 45S 150 43 E
Maninpé, *Mali* 112 C3 14 11N 5 28W
Maningrida, *Australia* 126 A1 12 3S 134 13 E
Maninian, *Ivory C.* 112 C3 10 3N 7 52W
Manipa, *Indonesia* 82 B3 3 17S 127 35 E
Manipur □, *India* 90 C4 25 0N 94 0 E
Manipur →, *Burma* 90 D5 23 45N 94 20 E
Manisa, *Turkey* 49 C9 38 38N 27 30 E
Manisa □, *Turkey* 49 C9 38 40N 28 0 E
Manistee, *U.S.A.* 148 C2 44 15N 86 19W
Manistee →, *U.S.A.* 148 C2 44 15N 86 21W
Manistique, *U.S.A.* 148 C2 45 57N 86 15W
Manito, *U.S.A.* 156 D7 40 26N 89 47W
Manito L., *Canada* 143 C7 52 43N 109 43W
Manitoba □, *Canada* 143 B9 55 30N 97 0W
Manitoba, L., *Canada* 143 C9 51 0N 98 45W
Manitou, *Canada* 143 D9 49 15N 98 32W
Manitou, L., *Canada* 141 B6 50 55N 65 17W
Manitou Beach, *U.S.A.* 157 C12 41 58N 84 19W
Manitou Is., *U.S.A.* 148 C3 45 8N 86 0W
Manitou Springs, *U.S.A.* 154 F2 38 52N 104 55W
Manitoulin I., *Canada* 140 C3 45 40N 82 30W
Manitouwadge, *Canada* 140 C2 49 8N 85 48W
Manitowoc, *U.S.A.* 148 C2 44 5N 87 40W
Manitsauá-Missu →, *Brazil* 173 C7 10 58S 53 20W
Maniyachi, *India* 95 K3 8 51N 77 55 E
Manizales, *Colombia* 168 B2 5 5N 75 32W
Manja, *Madag.* 117 C7 21 26S 44 20 E
Manjacaze, *Mozam.* 117 C5 24 45S 34 0 E
Manjakandriana, *Madag.* 117 B8 18 55S 47 47 E
Manjeri, *India* 95 J3 11 7N 76 11 E
Manjhand, *Pakistan* 91 D3 25 50N 68 10 E
Manjil, *Iran* 97 B6 36 46N 49 30 E
Manjimup, *Australia* 125 F2 34 15S 116 6 E
Manjlegaon, *India* 94 E3 19 9N 76 14 E
Manjra →, *India* 94 E3 18 49N 77 52 E
Mankato, *Kans., U.S.A.* 154 F5 39 47N 98 13W
Mankato, *Minn., U.S.A.* 154 C8 44 10N 94 0W
Mankayan, *Phil.* 80 C3 16 52N 120 47 E
Mankayane, *Swaziland* 117 D5 26 40S 31 4 E
Mankera, *Pakistan* 92 D4 31 23N 71 26 E
Mankim, *Cameroon* 113 D7 5 6N 12 3 E
Mankono, *Ivory C.* 112 D3 8 1N 6 10W
Mankota, *Canada* 143 D7 49 25N 107 5W
Mankulam, *Sri Lanka* 95 K5 9 8N 80 26 E
Manlay = Üydzin, *Mongolia* 74 B4 44 9N 107 0 E
Manley Hot Springs, *U.S.A.* 144 D10 65 0N 150 38W
Manlleu, *Spain* 40 C7 42 2N 2 17 E
Manly, *Australia* 129 B9 33 48S 151 17 E
Manmad, *India* 94 D2 20 18N 74 28 E
Mann Ranges, *Australia* 125 E5 26 6S 130 5 E
Manna, *Indonesia* 84 C2 4 25S 102 55 E
Mannahill, *Australia* 128 B4 32 25S 140 0 E
Mannar, *Sri Lanka* 95 K4 9 1N 79 54 E
Mannar, G. of, *Asia* 95 K4 8 30N 79 0 E
Mannar I., *Sri Lanka* 95 K4 9 5N 79 45 E
Mannargudi, *India* 95 J4 10 45N 79 51 E
Männedorf, *Switz.* 33 B7 47 15N 8 43 E
Mannheim, *Germany* 31 F4 49 29N 8 29 E
Manning, *Canada* 142 B5 56 53N 117 39W
Manning, *Oreg., U.S.A.* 160 E3 45 45N 123 13W
Manning, *S.C., U.S.A.* 152 B9 33 42N 80 13W
Manning →, *Australia* 129 A10 31 52S 152 43 E
Manning Prov. Park, *Canada* 142 D4 49 5N 120 45W
Manning Str., *Solomon Is.* 133 L10 7 30S 158 0 E
Mannu →, *Italy* 46 C2 39 16N 9 0 E
Mannu, C., *Italy* 46 B1 40 3N 8 21 E
Mannum, *Australia* 128 C3 34 50S 139 20 E
Mano, *S. Leone* 112 D2 8 3N 12 2W
Mano →, *Liberia* 112 D2 6 56N 11 30W
Mano River, *Liberia* 112 D2 7 20N 11 6W
Manoa, *Bolivia* 173 B4 9 40S 65 27W
Manoharpur, *India* 93 H11 22 23N 85 12 E
Manokotak, *U.S.A.* 144 G8 58 58N 159 3W
Manokwari, *Indonesia* 83 B4 0 54S 134 0 E
Manolás, *Greece* 48 C3 38 4N 21 21 E
Manolo Fortich, *Phil.* 81 G5 8 28N 124 50 E
Manombo, *Madag.* 117 C7 22 57S 43 28 E
Manono, *Dem. Rep. of the Congo* 118 D2 7 15S 27 25 E
Manono, *Samoa* 133 W23 13 50S 172 5W
Manoppello, *Italy* 45 F11 42 15N 14 3 E
Manosque, *France* 29 E9 43 49N 5 47 E
Manotick, *Canada* 151 A9 45 13N 75 41W
Manouane →, *Canada* 141 C5 49 30N 71 10W
Manouane, L., *Canada* 141 B5 50 45N 70 45W
Manovo-Gounda Saint Floris, Parc Nat. du, *C.A.R.* 114 A4 9 30N 21 25 E
Manp'o, *N. Korea* 75 D14 41 6N 126 24 E
Manpojin = Manp'o, *N. Korea* 75 D14 41 6N 126 24 E
Manpur, *Chhattisgarh, India* 93 H10 23 17N 83 35 E
Manpur, *Chhattisgarh, India* 94 D5 20 22N 80 43 E
Manpur, *Mad. P., India* 92 H6 22 26N 75 37 E
Manresa, *Spain* 40 D6 41 48N 1 50 E
Mansa, *Gujarat, India* 92 H5 23 27N 72 45 E
Mansa, *Punjab, India* 92 E6 30 0N 75 27 E
Mansa, *Zambia* 119 E2 11 13S 28 55 E
Mansalay, *Phil.* 80 E3 12 31N 121 26 E
Månsåsen, *Sweden* 16 A8 63 5N 14 18 E
Mansehra, *Pakistan* 92 B5 34 20N 73 15 E
Mansel I., *Canada* 139 B11 62 0N 80 0W
Mansfield, *Australia* 129 D7 37 4S 146 6 E
Mansfield, *U.K.* 20 D6 53 9N 1 11W
Mansfield, *Ga., U.S.A.* 152 B6 33 31N 83 44W
Mansfield, *La., U.S.A.* 155 J8 32 2N 93 43W
Mansfield, *Mass., U.S.A.* 151 D13 42 2N 71 13W
Mansfield, *Ohio, U.S.A.* 150 F2 40 45N 82 31W
Mansfield, *Pa., U.S.A.* 150 E7 41 48N 77 5W
Mansfield, Mt., *U.S.A.* 151 B12 44 33N 72 49W
Mansi, *Burma* 90 C5 24 48N 95 52 E
Mansidão, *Brazil* 170 D3 10 43S 44 2W
Mansilla de las Mulas, *Spain* 42 C5 42 30N 5 25W
Mansle, *France* 28 C4 45 52N 0 12 E
Manso →, *Brazil* 171 D2 13 50S 47 0W
Mansoa, *Guinea-Biss.* 112 C1 12 0N 15 20W
Manson, *U.S.A.* 156 B2 42 32N 94 32W
Manson Creek, *Canada* 142 B4 55 37N 124 32W
Mansoura, *Algeria* 111 A5 36 1N 4 31 E
Manta, *Ecuador* 168 D1 1 0S 80 40W
Manta, B. de, *Ecuador* 168 D1 0 54S 80 44W
Mantadia, Parc Nat. de, *Madag.* 117 B8 18 54S 48 21 E
Mantalingajan, Mt., *Phil.* 81 G1 8 55N 117 45 E
Mantantale, *Dem. Rep. of the Congo* 114 C4 2 10S 20 11 E
Mantare, *Tanzania* 118 C3 2 42S 33 13 E
Mantaro →, *Peru* 172 C3 12 16S 73 57W
Manteca, *U.S.A.* 160 H5 37 48N 121 13W
Mantecal, *Venezuela* 168 B4 7 34N 69 17W
Mantena, *Brazil* 171 E3 18 47S 40 59W
Manteno, *U.S.A.* 157 C9 41 15N 87 50W
Manteo, *U.S.A.* 149 H8 35 55N 75 40W
Mantes-la-Jolie, *France* 27 D8 48 58N 1 41 E
Mantha, *India* 94 E3 19 40N 76 23 E
Manthani, *India* 94 E4 18 40N 79 35 E
Manti, *U.S.A.* 158 G8 39 16N 111 38W
Mantiqueira, Serra da, *Brazil* 171 F3 22 0S 44 0W
Manton, *U.S.A.* 148 C3 44 25N 85 24W
Mantorp, *Sweden* 17 F9 58 21N 15 20 E
Mántova, *Italy* 44 C7 45 9N 10 48 E
Mänttä, *Finland* 15 E21 62 0N 24 40 E
Mantua = Mántova, *Italy* 44 C7 45 9N 10 48 E
Mantung, *Australia* 128 C4 34 35S 140 3 E
Manturovo, *Russia* 60 A7 58 23N 44 45 E
Manu, *Peru* 172 C3 12 10S 70 51W
Manu →, *Peru* 172 C3 12 16S 70 55W
Manu'a Is., *Amer. Samoa* 133 X25 14 13S 169 35W
Manuel Alves →, *Brazil* 171 D2 11 19S 48 28W
Manuel Alves Grande →, *Brazil* 170 C2 7 27S 47 35W
Manuel Urbano, *Brazil* 172 B4 8 53S 69 18W
Manui, *Indonesia* 82 B2 3 35S 123 5 E
Manukan, *Phil.* 81 G4 8 32N 123 12 E
Manukau, *N.Z.* 130 D3 37 0S 174 52 E
Manukau Harbour, *N.Z.* 130 D3 37 3S 174 45 E
Manunui, *N.Z.* 130 E4 38 54S 175 21 E
Manuoha, *N.Z.* 130 E6 38 39S 177 7 E
Manuripi →, *Bolivia* 172 C4 11 6S 67 36W
Manus □, *Papua N. G.* 132 B4 2 0S 147 0 E
Manus I., *Papua N. G.* 132 B4 2 0S 147 0 E
Manvi, *India* 95 G3 15 57N 76 59 E
Manwath, *India* 94 E3 19 19N 76 32 E
Many, *U.S.A.* 155 K8 31 34N 93 29W
Manyara, L., *Tanzania* 118 C4 3 40S 35 50 E
Manyas, *Turkey* 51 F11 40 2N 27 59 E
Manych →, *Russia* 61 G5 47 13N 40 40 E
Manych-Gudilo, Ozero, *Russia* 61 G6 46 24N 42 38 E
Manyonga →, *Tanzania* 118 C3 4 10S 34 15 E
Manyoni, *Tanzania* 118 D3 5 45S 34 55 E
Manzai, *Pakistan* 92 C4 32 12N 70 15 E
Manzala, Bahra el, *Egypt* 106 H7 31 10N 31 56 E
Manzanares, *Spain* 43 F7 39 2N 3 22W
Manzaneda, *Spain* 42 C3 42 12N 7 15W
Manzanillo, *Cuba* 164 B4 20 20N 77 31W
Manzanillo, *Mexico* 162 D4 19 0N 104 20W
Manzanillo, Pta., *Panama* 164 E4 9 30N 79 40W
Manzano Mts., *U.S.A.* 159 J10 34 40N 106 20W
Manzarīyeh, *Iran* 97 C6 34 53N 50 50 E
Manzhouli, *China* 69 B6 49 35N 117 25 E
Manzini, *Swaziland* 117 D5 26 30S 31 25 E
Mao, *Chad* 109 F3 14 4N 15 19 E
Maó, *Spain* 38 B5 39 53N 4 16 E
Maoke, Pegunungan, *Indonesia* 83 B5 3 40S 137 30 E
Maolin, *China* 75 C12 43 58N 123 30 E
Maoming, *China* 77 G8 21 50N 110 54 E
Maopi T'ou, *China* 77 G13 21 56N 120 43 E
Maouri, Dallol →, *Niger* 113 C5 12 5N 3 30 E
Maoxian, *China* 76 B4 31 41N 103 49 E
Maoxing, *China* 75 B13 45 28N 124 40 E
Mapalma, *Dem. Rep. of the Congo* 114 B4 2 3N 24 30 E
Mapam Yumco, *China* 68 C3 30 45N 81 28 E
Mapastepec, *Mexico* 163 D6 15 26N 92 54W
Mapfongui, *Gabon* 114 C2 1 15S 12 59 E
Maphrao, Ko, *Thailand* 87 a 7 56N 98 26 E
Mapi →, *Indonesia* 83 C5 6 55S 139 14 E
Mapia, Kepulauan, *Indonesia* 83 A4 0 50N 134 20 E
Mapimí, *Mexico* 162 B4 25 50N 103 50W
Mapimí, Bolsón de, *Mexico* 162 B4 27 30N 104 15W
Maping, *China* 77 B9 31 34N 113 32 E
Mapinga, *Tanzania* 118 D4 6 40S 39 12 E
Mapinhane, *Mozam.* 117 C6 22 20S 35 0 E
Mapire, *Venezuela* 169 B5 7 45N 64 42W
Maple →, *U.S.A.* 157 B12 42 59N 84 57W
Maple Creek, *Canada* 143 D7 49 55N 109 29W
Maple Valley, *U.S.A.* 160 C4 47 25N 122 3W
Mapleton, *U.S.A.* 158 D2 44 2N 123 52W
Mapourika, L., *N.Z.* 131 D5 43 16S 170 12 E
Maprik, *Papua N. G.* 132 B2 3 44S 143 3 E
Mapuca, *India* 95 G1 15 36N 73 46 E
Mapuera →, *Brazil* 169 D6 1 5S 57 2W
Mapulanguene, *Mozam.* 117 C5 24 29S 32 6 E
Maputo, *Mozam.* 117 D5 25 58S 32 32 E
Maputo □, *Mozam.* 117 D5 26 0S 32 25 E
Maputo, B. de, *Mozam.* 117 D5 25 50S 32 45 E
Maqiaohe, *China* 75 B16 44 40N 130 30 E
Maqnā, *Si. Arabia* 96 D2 28 25N 34 50 E
Maqran, W. →, *Si. Arabia* 98 B4 20 55N 47 12 E
Maqteïr, *Mauritania* 110 D2 21 50N 11 40W
Maqueda, *Spain* 42 E6 40 4N 4 22W
Maqueda Channel, *Phil.* 80 E5 13 42N 124 1 E
Maquela do Zombo, *Angola* 114 D3 6 0S 15 15 E
Maquinchao, *Argentina* 176 B3 41 15S 68 50W
Maquoketa, *U.S.A.* 156 B6 42 4N 90 40W
Mar, Serra do, *Brazil* 175 B6 25 30S 49 0W
Mar Chiquita, L., *Argentina* 174 C3 30 40S 62 50W
Mar del Plata, *Argentina* 174 D4 38 0S 57 30W
Mar Menor, *Spain* 41 H4 37 40N 0 45W
Mara, *Guyana* 169 B6 6 0N 57 36W
Mara, *India* 90 A5 28 11N 94 14 E
Mara, *Tanzania* 118 C3 1 30S 34 32 E
Mara □, *Tanzania* 118 C3 1 45S 34 20 E
Maraã, *Brazil* 168 D4 1 52S 65 25W
Marabá, *Brazil* 170 C2 5 20S 49 5W
Maracá, I. de, *Brazil* 169 C7 2 10N 50 30W
Maracaibo, *Venezuela* 168 A3 10 40N 71 37W
Maracaibo, L. de, *Venezuela* 168 B3 9 40N 71 30W
Maracaju, *Brazil* 175 A4 21 38S 55 9W
Maracajú, Serra de, *Brazil* 173 E6 23 57S 55 1W
Maracanã, *Brazil* 170 B2 0 46S 47 27W
Maracás, *Brazil* 171 D3 13 26S 40 18W
Maracas Bay Village, *Trin. & Tob.* 169 F9 10 46N 61 28W
Maracay, *Venezuela* 168 A4 10 15N 67 28W
Maracena, *Spain* 43 H7 37 12N 3 38W
Marādah, *Libya* 108 C3 29 15N 19 15 E
Maradi, *Niger* 113 C6 13 29N 7 20 E
Maraetiria, Pte., *Tahiti* 133 S16 17 51S 149 10W
Marāgheh, *Iran* 101 D12 37 30N 46 12 E
Maragogipe, *Brazil* 171 D4 12 46S 38 55W
Marāh, *Si. Arabia* 96 E5 25 0N 45 35 E
Marahoue, Parc Nat. de la, *Ivory C.* 112 D3 8 0N 7 8W
Marajó, B. de, *Brazil* 170 B2 1 0S 48 30W
Marajó, I. de, *Brazil* 170 B2 1 0S 49 30W
Marākand, *Iran* 96 B5 38 51N 45 16 E
Marakele Nat. Park, *S. Africa* 117 E4 32 14S 25 27 E
Maralal, *Kenya* 118 B4 1 0N 36 38 E
Maralinga, *Australia* 125 F5 30 13S 131 32 E
Maram, *India* 90 C5 25 25N 94 6 E
Marama, *Australia* 128 C4 35 10S 140 10 E
Maramag, *Phil.* 81 H5 7 46N 125 0 E
Maramaraereğlisi, *Turkey* 51 F11 40 57N 27 57 E
Maramasike, *Solomon Is.* 133 M11 9 30S 161 25 E
Marampa, *S. Leone* 112 D2 8 45N 12 28W
Maramureș □, *Romania* 53 C9 47 45N 24 0 E
Maran, *Malaysia* 87 L4 3 35N 102 45 E
Marana, *U.S.A.* 159 K8 32 27N 111 13W
Maranboy, *Australia* 124 B5 14 40S 132 39 E
Maranchón, *Spain* 40 D2 41 6N 2 15W
Marand, *Iran* 101 C11 38 30N 45 45 E
Marandokhóri, *Greece* 39 B2 38 38N 20 39 E
Marang, *Malaysia* 87 K4 5 12N 103 13 E
Maranguape, *Brazil* 170 B4 3 55S 38 50W
Maranhão = São Luís, *Brazil* 170 B3 2 39S 44 15W
Maranhão □, *Brazil* 170 B2 5 0S 46 0W
Marano, L. di, *Italy* 45 C10 45 44N 13 10 E
Maranoa →, *Australia* 127 D4 27 50S 148 37 E
Marañón →, *Peru* 172 A3 4 30S 73 35W
Marão, *Mozam.* 117 C5 24 18S 34 2 E
Marapi →, *Brazil* 169 C6 0 37N 55 58W
Marari, *Brazil* 172 B4 5 43S 67 47W
Maraş = Kahramanmaraş, *Turkey* 100 D7 37 37N 36 53 E
Mărășești, *Romania* 53 E12 45 52N 27 14 E
Maratea, *Italy* 47 C8 39 59N 15 43 E
Marateca, *Portugal* 43 G2 38 34N 8 40W
Marathasa, *Cyprus* 39 F8 34 59N 32 51 E
Marathiás, Ákra, *Greece* 39 D2 37 39N 20 50 E
Marathókambos, *Greece* 49 D8 37 43N 26 42 E
Marathon, *Australia* 126 C3 20 51S 143 32 E
Marathon, *Canada* 140 C2 48 44N 86 23W
Marathón, *Greece* 48 C5 38 11N 23 58 E
Marathon, *Fla., U.S.A.* 153 L8 24 43N 81 5W
Marathon, *N.Y., U.S.A.* 151 D8 42 27N 76 2W
Marathon, *Tex., U.S.A.* 155 K3 30 12N 103 15W
Marathóvouno, *Cyprus* 39 E9 35 13N 33 37 E
Maratua, *Indonesia* 85 B5 2 10N 118 35 E
Maraú, *Brazil* 171 D4 14 6S 39 0W
Marau, *Solomon Is.* 133 N11 10 31S 161 31 E
Maraval, *Trin. & Tob.* 169 F9 10 43N 61 32W
Maravari, *Solomon Is.* 133 L9 7 50S 156 42 E
Maravatío, *Mexico* 162 D4 19 51N 100 25W
Marawi City, *Phil.* 81 G5 8 0N 124 21 E
Marāwih, *U.A.E.* 97 E7 24 18N 53 18 E
Marbach, *Switz.* 32 C5 46 51N 7 53 E
Marbella, *Spain* 43 J6 36 30N 4 57W
Marble Bar, *Australia* 124 D2 21 9S 119 44 E
Marble Falls, *U.S.A.* 155 K5 30 35N 98 16W
Marblehead, *U.S.A.* 151 D14 42 30N 70 51W
Mårbu, *Norway* 18 D5 60 11N 8 9 E
Marburg, *Germany* 30 E4 50 47N 8 46 E
Marcal →, *Hungary* 52 C2 47 41N 17 40 E
Marcali, *Hungary* 52 D2 46 35N 17 25 E
Marcapata, *Peru* 172 C3 13 31S 70 52W
Marcaria, *Italy* 44 C7 45 7N 10 32 E
Mărcăuţi, *Moldova* 53 B12 48 20N 27 14 E
Marceline, *U.S.A.* 156 E4 39 43N 92 57W
March, *U.K.* 21 E8 52 33N 0 5 E
Marchal, *Dem. Rep. of the Congo* 115 D2 5 16S 14 58 E
Marchand = Rommani, *Morocco* 110 B3 33 31N 6 40W
Marche, *France* 28 B5 46 5N 1 20 E
Marche □, *Italy* 45 E10 43 30N 13 15 E
Marche-en-Famenne, *Belgium* 24 D5 50 14N 5 19 E
Marchena, *Spain* 43 H5 37 18N 5 23W
Marchena, Canal de, *Ecuador* 172 a 0 19N 90 12W
Marchena, I., *Ecuador* 172 a 0 19N 90 29W
Marches = Marche □, *Italy* 45 E10 43 30N 13 15 E
Marciana Marina, *Italy* 44 F7 42 48N 10 12 E
Marcianise, *Italy* 47 A7 41 2N 14 17 E
Marcigny, *France* 27 F11 46 17N 4 2 E
Marcillat-en-Combraille, *France* 27 F9 46 12N 2 38 E
Marck, *France* 27 B8 50 57N 1 57 E
Marckolsheim, *France* 27 D14 48 10N 7 30 E
Marco, *U.S.A.* 153 K8 25 58N 81 44W
Marco Rondon, *Brazil* 173 C5 12 0S 60 56W
Marcona, *Peru* 172 D2 15 10S 75 0W
Marcos Juárez, *Argentina* 174 C3 32 42S 62 5W
Mărculeşti, *Moldova* 53 C13 47 52N 28 14 E
Marcus Baker, Mt., *U.S.A.* 144 F11 61 26N 147 45W
Marcus I. = Minami-Tori-Shima, *Pac. Oc.* 134 E7 24 20N 153 58 E
Marcus Necker Ridge, *Pac. Oc.* 134 F9 20 0N 175 0 E
Marcy, Mt., *U.S.A.* 151 B11 44 7N 73 56W
Mardan, *Pakistan* 91 B4 34 20N 72 0 E
Mardin, *Turkey* 101 D9 37 20N 40 43 E
Mårdsjön, *Sweden* 16 A9 63 18N 15 35 E
Maré, Î., *N. Cal.* 133 U22 21 30S 168 0 E
Marécchia →, *Italy* 45 D9 44 4N 12 34 E
Marechal Deodoro, *Brazil* 170 C4 9 43S 35 54W
Maree, L., *U.K.* 22 D3 57 40N 5 26W
Mareeba, *Australia* 126 B4 16 59S 145 28 E
Mareetsane, *S. Africa* 116 D4 26 9S 25 25 E
Marek, *Indonesia* 82 B2 4 41S 120 24 E
Maremma, *Italy* 45 F8 42 30N 11 30 E
Maréna, *Kayes, Mali* 112 C2 14 36N 10 45W
Maréna, *Koulikouro, Mali* 112 C3 13 55N 7 20W
Marengo, *Ind., U.S.A.* 157 F10 38 22N 86 21W
Marengo, *Iowa, U.S.A.* 156 C4 41 48N 92 4W
Marennes, *France* 28 C2 45 49N 1 7W
Marenyi, *Kenya* 118 C4 4 22S 39 8 E
Marerano, *Madag.* 117 C7 21 23S 44 52 E
Maréttimo, *Italy* 46 E5 37 58N 12 4 E
Mareuil, *France* 28 C4 45 26N 0 29 E
Marfa, *U.S.A.* 155 K2 30 19N 104 1W
Marganets = Marhanets, *Ukraine* 59 J8 47 40N 34 40 E
Margaret →, *Australia* 124 C4 18 9S 125 41 E
Margaret Bay, *Canada* 142 C3 51 20N 127 35W
Margaret L., *Canada* 142 B5 58 56N 115 25W
Margaret River, *Australia* 125 F2 33 57S 115 4 E
Margarita, I. de, *Venezuela* 169 A5 11 0N 64 0W
Margaritíon, *Greece* 48 B2 39 22N 20 26 E
Margaritovo, *Russia* 70 C7 43 25N 134 45 E
Margate, *S. Africa* 117 E5 30 50S 30 20 E
Margate, *U.K.* 21 F9 51 23N 1 23 E
Margate, *U.S.A.* 153 J9 26 15N 80 12W
Margeride, Mts. de la, *France* 28 D7 44 43N 3 38 E
Margherita, *India* 90 B5 27 16N 95 40 E
Margherita di Savóia, *Italy* 47 A9 41 22N 16 9 E
Margherita Pk., *Uganda* 118 B3 0 22N 29 51 E

Marghilon = Margilan, Uzbekistan 65 C5 40 27N 71 42 E
Marghita, Romania 52 C7 47 22N 22 22 E
Margilan, Uzbekistan 65 C5 40 27N 71 42 E
Margonin, Poland 55 F4 52 58N 17 5 E
Margosatubig, Phil. 81 H4 7 34N 123 10 E
Mārgow, Dasht-e, Afghan. 91 C1 30 40N 62 30 E
Marguerite, Canada 142 C4 52 30N 122 25W
Marhanets, Ukraine 59 J8 47 40N 34 40 E
Marhoum, Algeria 111 B4 34 27N 0 11W
Mari, Papua N. G. 132 E1 9 11 S 141 42 E
Mari El □, Russia 60 B8 56 30N 48 0 E
Mari Indus, Pakistan 92 C4 32 57N 71 34 E
Mari Republic = Mari El □, Russia 60 B8 56 30N 48 0 E
María, Sa. de, Spain 41 H2 37 39N 2 14W
Maria Aurora, Phil. 80 D3 15 48N 121 28 E
María Elena, Chile 174 A2 22 18 S 69 40W
María Grande, Argentina 174 C4 31 45 S 59 55W
Maria I., N. Terr., Australia 126 A2 14 52 S 135 45 E
Maria I., Tas., Australia 127 G4 42 35 S 148 0 E
Maria Island Nat. Park, Australia 127 G4 42 38 S 148 5 E
Maria van Diemen, C., N.Z. 130 A1 34 29 S 172 40 E
Mariager, Denmark 17 H3 56 40N 9 59 E
Mariager Fjord, Denmark 17 H4 56 42N 10 19 E
Mariakani, Kenya 118 C4 3 50 S 39 27 E
Mariala Nat. Park, Australia 127 D4 25 57 S 145 2 E
Marian, Australia 126 K6 21 9 S 148 57 E
Marian L., Canada 142 A5 63 0N 116 15W
Mariana Trench, Pac. Oc. 62 H18 13 0N 145 0 E
Marianao, Cuba 164 B3 23 8N 82 24W
Mariani, India 90 B5 26 39N 94 19 E
Marianna, Ark., U.S.A. 155 H9 34 46N 90 46W
Marianna, Fla., U.S.A. 152 E4 30 46N 85 14W
Mariannelund, Sweden 17 G9 57 37N 15 35 E
Mariánské Lázně, Czech Rep. 34 B5 49 58N 12 41 E
Marias →, U.S.A. 158 C8 47 56N 110 30W
Mariato, Punta, Panama 164 E3 7 12N 80 52W
Mariazell, Austria 34 D8 47 47N 15 19 E
Ma'rib, Yemen 98 D4 15 25N 45 21 E
Maribo, Denmark 17 K5 54 48N 11 30 E
Maribor, Slovenia 45 B12 46 36N 15 40 E
Maricaban I., Phil. 80 E3 13 39N 120 53 E
Marico →, Africa 116 C4 23 35 S 26 57 E
Maricopa, Ariz., U.S.A. 159 K7 33 4N 112 3W
Maricopa, Calif., U.S.A. 161 K7 35 4N 119 24W
Marîdî, Sudan 107 G2 4 55N 29 25 E
Marîdî, Wadi →, Sudan 107 F2 6 15N 29 21 E
Marié →, Brazil 168 D4 0 27 S 66 26W
Marie Byrd Land, Antarctica 7 D14 79 30 S 125 0W
Marie-Galante, Guadeloupe 164 b 15 56N 61 16W
Mariecourt = Kangiqsujuaq, Canada 139 B12 61 30N 72 0W
Mariefred, Sweden 16 E11 59 15N 17 12 E
Marieholm, Sweden 17 J7 55 53N 13 10 E
Mariembourg, Belgium 24 D4 50 6N 4 31 E
Marienbad = Mariánské Lázně, Czech Rep. 34 B5 49 58N 12 41 E
Marienberg, Germany 30 E9 50 39N 13 9 E
Mariental, Namibia 116 C2 24 36 S 18 0 E
Marienville, U.S.A. 150 E5 41 28N 79 8W
Mariestad, Sweden 17 F7 58 43N 13 50 E
Marietta, Ga., U.S.A. 152 B5 33 57N 84 33W
Marietta, Ohio, U.S.A. 148 F5 39 25N 81 27W
Marieville, Canada 151 A11 45 26N 73 10W
Mariga →, Nigeria 113 C6 9 40N 5 55 E
Marignane, France 29 E9 43 25N 5 13 E
Marignier, France 32 D3 46 6N 6 31 E
Marihatag, Phil. 81 G6 8 48N 126 18 E
Mariinsk, Russia 66 D9 56 10N 87 20 E
Mariinskiy Posad, Russia 60 B8 56 10N 47 45 E
Marijampolė, Lithuania 15 J20 54 33N 23 19 E
Marijampolės □, Lithuania 54 D10 54 34N 23 21 E
Marília, Brazil 175 A6 22 13 S 50 0W
Marimba, Angola 115 D3 8 28 S 17 8 E
Marín, Spain 42 C2 42 23N 8 42W
Marina, U.S.A. 160 J5 36 41N 121 48W
Marinduque, Phil. 79 B6 13 25N 122 0 E
Marinduque □, Phil. 80 E4 13 18N 122 0 E
Marine City, U.S.A. 150 D2 42 43N 82 30W
Marineland, U.S.A. 152 F8 29 40N 81 13W
Marineo, Italy 46 E6 37 57N 13 25 E
Marinette, U.S.A. 148 C2 45 6N 87 38W
Maringá, Brazil 175 A5 23 26 S 52 2W
Maringa →, Dem. Rep. of the Congo 114 B3 1 14N 19 48 E
Marinha Grande, Portugal 42 F2 39 45N 8 56W
Marino, Italy 45 G9 41 46N 12 39 E
Marion, Ala., U.S.A. 149 J2 32 38N 87 19W
Marion, Ill., U.S.A. 155 G10 37 44N 88 56W
Marion, Ind., U.S.A. 157 D11 40 32N 85 40W
Marion, Iowa, U.S.A. 156 B5 42 2N 91 36W
Marion, Kans., U.S.A. 154 F6 38 21N 97 1W
Marion, N.C., U.S.A. 149 H5 35 41N 82 1W
Marion, Ohio, U.S.A. 157 D13 40 35N 83 8W
Marion, S.C., U.S.A. 149 H6 34 11N 79 24W
Marion, Va., U.S.A. 149 G5 36 50N 81 31W
Marion, L., U.S.A. 152 B9 33 28N 80 10W
Marion Bay, Australia 128 C2 35 12 S 136 59 E
Marion I., Ind. Oc. 121 J2 47 0 S 38 0 E
Maripa, Venezuela 169 B4 7 26N 65 9W
Maripasoula, Fr. Guiana 169 C7 3 40N 54 4W
Mariposa, U.S.A. 160 H7 37 29N 119 58W
Mariscal Estigarribia, Paraguay 174 A3 22 3 S 60 40W
Maritime Alps = Maritimes, Alpes, Europe 29 D11 44 10N 7 10 E
Maritimes, Alpes, Europe 29 D11 44 10N 7 10 E
Maritsa = Évros →, Greece 100 B2 41 40N 26 34 E
Maritsá, Greece 38 E12 36 22N 28 8 E
Marium, Mt., Vanuatu 133 F6 16 15 S 168 7 E
Mariupol, Ukraine 59 J9 47 5N 37 31 E
Marīvān, Iran 101 E12 35 30N 46 25 E
Mariveles, Phil. 80 D3 14 26N 120 29 E
Marj 'Uyūn, Lebanon 103 B4 33 20N 35 35 E
Mark Twain L., U.S.A. 156 E5 39 28N 91 55W
Marka = Merca, Somali Rep. 120 D2 1 48N 44 50 E
Marka, Si. Arabia 106 D5 18 14N 41 19 E
Markam, China 76 C2 29 42N 98 38 E
Markapur, India 95 G4 15 44N 79 19 E
Markaryd, Sweden 17 H7 56 28N 13 35 E
Markat, Albania 38 B10 39 44N 20 12 E
Markazī □, Iran 97 C6 35 0N 49 30 E
Markdale, Canada 150 B4 44 19N 80 39W
Marked Tree, U.S.A. 155 H9 35 32N 90 25W
Markelsdorfer Huk, Germany 30 A7 54 33N 11 4 E
Market Drayton, U.K. 20 E5 52 54N 2 29W
Market Harborough, U.K. 21 E7 52 29N 0 55W
Market Rasen, U.K. 20 D7 53 24N 0 20W
Markham, Canada 150 C5 43 52N 79 16W
Markham →, Papua N. G. 132 D4 6 41 S 147 2 E
Markham, Mt., Antarctica 7 E11 83 0 S 164 0 E
Marki, Poland 55 F8 52 20N 21 2 E
Markit, China 65 D8 38 53N 77 35 E
Markkleeberg, Germany 30 D8 51 16N 12 23 E
Markleeville, U.S.A. 160 G7 38 42N 119 47W
Markounda, C.A.R. 114 A3 7 39N 16 55 E
Markoupoulon, Greece 48 D5 37 53N 23 57 E
Markovac, Serbia, Yug. 50 B5 44 14N 21 7 E
Markovo, Russia 67 C17 64 40N 170 24 E
Markoye, Burkina Faso 113 C5 14 39N 0 2 E
Marks, Russia 60 E8 51 45N 46 50 E
Marksville, U.S.A. 155 K8 31 8N 92 4W
Markt Schwaben, Germany 31 G7 48 11N 11 52 E
Marktoberdorf, Germany 31 H6 47 45N 10 37 E
Marktredwitz, Germany 31 E8 50 1N 12 6 E
Marl, Germany 30 D3 51 39N 7 4 E
Marla, Australia 127 D1 27 19 S 133 33 E
Marlbank, Canada 150 B7 44 26N 77 6W
Marlboro, Mass., U.S.A. 151 D13 42 19N 71 33W
Marlboro, N.Y., U.S.A. 151 E11 41 36N 73 59W
Marlborough, Australia 126 C4 22 46 S 149 52 E
Marlborough, U.K. 21 F6 51 25N 1 43W
Marlborough □, N.Z. 131 B8 41 40 S 173 50 E
Marlborough Downs, U.K. 21 F6 51 27N 1 53W
Marle, France 27 C10 49 43N 3 47 E
Marlin, U.S.A. 155 K6 31 18N 96 54W
Marlow, Germany 30 A8 54 9N 12 33 E
Marlow, U.S.A. 155 H6 34 39N 97 58W
Marly, Switz. 32 C4 46 47N 7 10 E
Marmagao, India 95 G1 15 25N 73 56 E
Marmande, France 28 D4 44 30N 0 10 E
Marmara, Turkey 51 F11 40 35N 27 34 E
Marmara, Sea of = Marmara Denizi, Turkey 51 F12 40 45N 28 15 E
Marmara Denizi, Turkey 51 F12 40 45N 28 15 E
Marmara Gölü, Turkey 49 C10 38 37N 28 2 E
Marmaris, Turkey 49 E10 36 50N 28 14 E
Marmaris Limanı, Turkey 49 E10 36 50N 28 19 E
Marmelos →, Brazil 173 B5 6 6 S 61 46W
Marmion, Mt., Australia 125 E2 29 16 S 119 50 E
Marmion L., Canada 140 C1 48 55N 91 20W
Marmolada, Mte., Italy 45 B8 46 26N 11 51 E
Marmolejo, Spain 43 G6 38 3N 4 13W
Marmora, Canada 140 D4 44 28N 77 41W
Mármora, La, Italy 46 C2 39 59N 9 20 E
Marnay, France 27 E12 47 16N 5 48 E
Marne, Germany 30 B5 53 56N 9 2 E
Marne □, France 27 D11 48 50N 4 10 E
Marne →, France 27 D9 48 48N 2 24 E
Marneuli, Georgia 61 K7 41 30N 44 48 E
Marnoo, Australia 128 D5 36 40 S 142 52 E
Maro, Chad 109 G3 8 30N 19 0 E
Maro Reef, U.S.A. 145 F9 25 25N 170 35W
Maroa, U.S.A. 156 D8 40 2N 88 57W
Maroa, Venezuela 168 C4 2 43N 67 33W
Maroala, Madag. 117 B8 15 23 S 47 59 E
Maroantsetra, Madag. 117 B8 15 26 S 49 44 E
Maroelaboom, Namibia 116 B2 19 15 S 18 53 E
Marofandilia, Madag. 117 C7 20 7 S 44 34 E
Marojejy, Réserve de, Madag. 117 A8 14 26 S 49 21 E
Marolambo, Madag. 117 C8 20 2 S 48 7 E
Maromandia, Madag. 117 A8 14 13 S 48 5 E
Marondera, Zimbabwe 119 F3 18 5 S 31 42 E
Maroni →, Fr. Guiana 169 B7 5 30N 54 0W
Marónia, Greece 51 F9 40 53N 25 30 E
Maronne →, France 28 C5 45 5N 1 56 E
Maroochydore, Australia 127 D5 26 29 S 153 5 E
Maroona, Australia 128 D5 37 27 S 142 54 E
Maros, Indonesia 82 C1 5 0 S 119 34 E
Maros →, Hungary 52 D5 46 15N 20 13 E
Marosakoa, Madag. 117 B8 15 26 S 46 38 E
Maroseranana, Madag. 117 B8 18 32 S 48 51 E
Maróstica, Italy 45 C8 45 44N 11 40 E
Marotandrano, Madag. 117 B8 16 10 S 48 50 E
Marotaolano, Madag. 117 A8 12 47 S 49 15 E
Maroua, Cameroon 113 C7 10 40N 14 20 E
Marovato, Madag. 117 B8 15 48 S 48 5 E
Marovoay, Madag. 117 B8 16 6 S 46 39 E
Marowijne □, Surinam 169 C7 4 0N 55 0W
Marowijne →, Surinam 169 B7 5 45N 53 58W
Marquard, S. Africa 116 D4 28 40 S 27 28 E
Marquesas Is. = Marquises, Is., Pac. Oc. 135 H14 9 30 S 140 0W
Marquesas Keys, U.S.A. 153 L7 24 35N 82 10W
Marquette, U.S.A. 148 B2 46 33N 87 24W
Marquis, St. Lucia 165 f 14 2N 60 54W
Marquise, France 27 B8 50 50N 1 40 E
Marquises, Is., Pac. Oc. 135 H14 9 30 S 140 0W
Marra, Gebel, Sudan 107 F2 7 20N 27 35 E
Marra, Pta. da, Angola 115 F2 16 31 S 11 43 E
Marra Cr. →, Australia 129 A7 30 8 S 147 15 E
Marra Marra Nat. Park, Australia 129 B9 33 30 S 151 4 E
Marracuene, Mozam. 117 D5 25 45 S 32 35 E
Marradi, Italy 45 D8 44 4N 11 37 E
Marrakech, Morocco 110 B3 31 9N 8 0W
Marratxi, Spain 38 B3 39 39N 2 48 E
Marrawah, Australia 127 G3 40 55 S 144 42 E
Marrecas, Serra das, Brazil 170 C3 9 0 S 41 0W
Marree, Australia 127 D2 29 39 S 138 1 E
Marrero, U.S.A. 155 L9 29 54N 90 6W
Marrimane, Mozam. 117 C5 22 58 S 33 34 E
Marromeu, Mozam. 117 B6 18 15 S 36 25 E
Marroquí, Punta, Spain 43 K5 36 0N 5 37W
Marrowie Cr. →, Australia 129 B6 33 23 S 145 40 E
Marrubane, Mozam. 119 F4 18 0 S 37 0 E
Marrūbiu, Italy 46 C1 39 40N 8 35 E
Marrupa, Mozam. 119 E4 13 8 S 37 30 E
Mars B., Ascension I. 9 g 7 59 S 14 24W
Mars Hill, U.S.A. 149 B12 46 31N 67 52W
Marsá 'Alam, Egypt 106 B3 25 5N 34 54 E
Marsá el Brega, Libya 108 B3 30 24N 19 37 E
Marsá Matrûh, Egypt 106 A2 31 19N 27 9 E
Marsá Sha'b, Sudan 106 C4 22 52N 35 47 E
Marsá Susah, Libya 108 B4 32 52N 21 59 E
Marsabit, Kenya 118 B4 2 18N 38 0 E
Marsabit Nat. Park and Reserve, Kenya 118 B4 2 23N 37 56 E
Marsala, Italy 46 E5 37 48N 12 26 E
Marsalforn, Malta 38 E7 36 4N 14 16 E
Mârşani, Romania 53 F9 44 1N 24 1 E
Marsaskala, Malta 38 F8 35 52N 14 34 E
Marsaxlokk, Malta 38 F8 35 51N 14 33 E
Marsaxlokk Bay, Malta 38 F8 35 49N 14 33 E
Marsberg, Germany 30 D4 51 28N 8 52 E
Marsciano, Italy 45 F9 42 54N 12 20 E
Marsden, Australia 129 B7 33 47 S 147 32 E
Marseillan, France 28 E7 43 23N 3 31 E
Marseille, France 29 E9 43 18N 5 23 E
Marseilles = Marseille, France 29 E9 43 18N 5 23 E
Marseilles, U.S.A. 157 C8 41 20N 88 43W
Marsh I., U.S.A. 155 L9 29 34N 91 53W
Marshall = Fortuna Ledge, U.S.A. 144 F7 61 53N 162 5W
Marshall, Liberia 112 D2 6 8N 10 22W
Marshall, Ark., U.S.A. 155 H8 35 55N 92 38W
Marshall, Ill., U.S.A. 157 E9 39 23N 87 42W
Marshall, Mich., U.S.A. 157 B12 42 16N 84 58W
Marshall, Minn., U.S.A. 154 C7 44 25N 95 45W
Marshall, Mo., U.S.A. 156 E3 39 7N 93 12W
Marshall, Tex., U.S.A. 155 J7 32 33N 94 23W
Marshall →, Australia 126 C2 22 59 S 136 59 E
Marshall, C., Ecuador 172 a 0 1 S 91 12W
Marshall Bennett Is., Papua N. G. 132 E6 8 50 S 151 55 E
Marshall Is. ■, Pac. Oc. 134 G9 9 0N 171 0 E
Marshalltown, U.S.A. 156 B4 42 3N 92 55W
Marshallville, U.S.A. 152 C6 32 27N 83 56W
Marshbrook, Zimbabwe 117 B5 18 33 S 31 9 E
Marshfield, Mo., U.S.A. 155 G8 37 15N 92 54W
Marshfield, Vt., U.S.A. 151 B12 44 20N 72 20W
Marshfield, Wis., U.S.A. 154 C9 44 40N 90 10W
Marshūn, Iran 97 B6 36 19N 49 23 E
Mársico Nuovo, Italy 47 B8 40 25N 15 44 E
Märsta, Sweden 16 E11 59 37N 17 52 E
Marstal, Denmark 17 K4 54 51N 10 30 E
Marstrand, Sweden 17 G5 57 53N 11 35 E
Mart, U.S.A. 155 K6 31 33N 96 50W
Marta →, Italy 45 F8 42 14N 11 42 E
Martaban, Burma 90 G6 16 30N 97 35 E
Martaban, G. of, Burma 90 G6 16 5N 96 30 E
Martano, Italy 47 B11 40 12N 18 18 E
Martapura, Kalimantan, Indonesia 85 C4 3 22 S 114 47 E
Martapura, Sumatera, Indonesia 84 C2 4 19 S 104 22 E
Marte, Nigeria 113 C7 12 23N 13 46 E
Martel, France 28 D5 44 57N 1 37 E
Martelange, Belgium 24 E5 49 49N 5 43 E
Martellago, Italy 45 C9 45 33N 12 9 E
Martés, Sierra, Spain 41 F4 39 20N 1 0W
Martfű, Hungary 52 C5 47 1N 20 17 E
Marthaguy Cr. →, Australia 129 A7 30 16 S 147 35 E
Marthapal, India 94 E5 19 24N 81 37 E
Martha's Vineyard, U.S.A. 151 E14 41 25N 70 38W
Martigné-Ferchaud, France 26 E5 47 50N 1 20W
Martigny, Switz. 32 D4 46 6N 7 3 E
Martigues, France 29 E9 43 24N 5 4 E
Martil, Morocco 110 A3 35 36N 5 15W
Martin, Slovak Rep. 35 B11 49 6N 18 58 E
Martin, S. Dak., U.S.A. 154 D4 43 11N 101 44W
Martin, Tenn., U.S.A. 155 G10 36 21N 88 51W
Martín →, Spain 40 D4 41 18N 0 19W
Martin, L., U.S.A. 152 C4 32 41N 85 55W
Martin Pt., U.S.A. 144 A12 70 8N 143 16W
Martina, Switz. 33 C10 46 53N 10 28 E
Martina Franca, Italy 47 B10 40 42N 17 20 E
Martinborough, N.Z. 130 H4 41 14 S 175 29 E
Martinez, Calif., U.S.A. 160 G4 38 1N 122 8W
Martinez, Ga., U.S.A. 149 J4 33 31N 82 4W
Martinho Campos, Brazil 171 E2 19 20 S 45 13W
Martinique ■, W. Indies 164 c 14 40N 61 0W
Martinique Passage, W. Indies 165 C7 15 15N 61 0W
Martínon, Greece 48 C5 38 35N 23 12 E
Martinópolis, Brazil 175 A5 22 11 S 51 12W
Martin's Bay, Barbados 165 g 13 12N 59 29W
Martins Ferry, U.S.A. 150 F4 40 6N 80 44W
Martinsberg, Austria 34 C8 48 22N 15 9 E
Martinsburg, Pa., U.S.A. 150 F6 40 19N 78 20W
Martinsburg, W. Va., U.S.A. 148 F7 39 27N 77 58W
Martinsicuro, Italy 45 F10 42 54N 13 54 E
Martinsville, Ill., U.S.A. 157 E9 39 20N 87 53W
Martinsville, Ind., U.S.A. 157 E10 39 26N 86 25W
Martinsville, Va., U.S.A. 149 G6 36 41N 79 52W
Marton, N.Z. 130 G4 40 4 S 175 23 E
Martorell, Spain 40 D6 41 28N 1 56 E
Martos, Spain 43 H7 37 44N 3 58W
Martūbah, Libya 108 B4 32 35N 22 46 E
Martuk, Kazakstan 64 F6 50 46N 56 31 E
Martuni, Armenia 61 K7 40 8N 45 20 E
Maru, Nigeria 113 C6 12 22N 6 22 E
Marudi, Malaysia 85 B4 4 11N 114 19 E
Maruf, Afghan. 91 C2 31 30N 67 6 E
Marugame, Japan 72 C5 34 15N 133 40 E
Marui = Pagwi, Papua N. G. 132 C2 4 4 S 143 2 E
Maruia →, N.Z. 131 B7 41 47 S 172 13 E
Maruim, Brazil 170 D4 10 45 S 37 5W
Marulan, Australia 129 C9 34 43 S 150 3 E
Marunga, Angola 116 B3 17 28 S 20 2 E
Marungu, Mts., Dem. Rep. of the Congo 118 D3 7 30 S 30 0 E
Maruoka, Japan 73 A8 36 9N 136 16 E
Marv Dasht, Iran 97 D7 29 50N 52 40 E
Marvast, Iran 97 D7 30 30N 54 15 E
Marvejols, France 28 D7 44 33N 3 19 E
Marvel Loch, Australia 125 F2 31 28 S 119 29 E
Marwar, India 92 G5 25 43N 73 45 E
Mary, Turkmenistan 66 F7 37 40N 61 50 E
Maryborough = Port Laoise, Ireland 23 C4 53 2N 7 18W
Maryborough, Queens., Australia 127 D5 25 31 S 152 37 E
Maryborough, Vic., Australia 128 D5 37 0 S 143 44 E
Maryfield, Canada 143 D8 49 50N 101 35W
Maryland □, U.S.A. 148 F7 39 0N 76 30W
Maryland Junction, Zimbabwe 119 F3 17 45 S 30 31 E
Maryport, U.K. 20 C4 54 44N 3 28W
Mary's Harbour, Canada 141 B8 52 18N 55 51W
Marystown, Canada 141 C8 47 10N 55 10W
Marysvale, Canada 142 D5 49 35N 116 0W
Marysville, Calif., U.S.A. 160 F5 39 9N 121 35W
Marysville, Kans., U.S.A. 154 F6 39 51N 96 39W
Marysville, Mich., U.S.A. 150 D2 42 54N 82 29W
Marysville, Ohio, U.S.A. 157 D13 40 14N 83 22W
Marysville, Wash., U.S.A. 160 B4 48 3N 122 11W
Maryville, Mo., U.S.A. 156 D2 40 21N 94 52W
Maryville, Tenn., U.S.A. 149 H4 35 46N 83 58W
Marzo, Punta, Colombia 168 B2 6 50N 77 42W
Marzūq, Libya 108 C2 25 53N 13 57 E
Marzūq □, Libya 108 D3 25 0N 16 0 E
Marzūq, Idehan, Libya 108 D2 24 50N 13 51 E
Masahunga, Tanzania 118 C3 2 6 S 33 18 E
Masai, Malaysia 87 d 1 29N 103 53 E
Masai Mara Nat. Reserve, Kenya 118 C4 1 25 S 35 5 E
Masai Steppe, Tanzania 118 C4 4 30 S 36 30 E
Masaka, Uganda 118 C3 0 21 S 31 45 E
Masalembo, Kepulauan, Indonesia 85 D4 5 35 S 114 30 E
Masalima, Kepulauan, Indonesia 85 D5 5 4 S 117 5 E
Masallı, Azerbaijan 101 C13 39 3N 48 40 E
Masamba, Indonesia 82 B2 2 30 S 120 15 E
Masan, S. Korea 75 G15 35 11N 128 32 E
Masandam, Ra's, Oman 97 E8 26 30N 56 30 E
Masasi, Tanzania 119 E4 10 45 S 38 52 E
Masaya, Nic. 164 D2 12 0N 86 7W
Masba, Nigeria 113 C7 11 35N 13 1 E
Masbate, Phil. 80 E4 12 21N 123 36 E
Masbate □, Phil. 80 E4 12 20N 123 30 E
Masbate Pass, Phil. 80 E4 12 30N 123 35 E
Máscali, Italy 47 E8 37 45N 15 12 E
Mascara, Algeria 111 A5 35 26N 0 6 E
Mascarene Is., Ind. Oc. 121 G4 22 0 S 55 0 E
Mascota, Mexico 162 C4 20 30N 104 50W
Mascoutah, U.S.A. 156 F7 38 29N 89 48W
Masein, Burma 90 D5 23 22N 94 21 E
Masela, Indonesia 83 C3 8 9 S 129 51 E
Maseru, Lesotho 116 D4 29 18 S 27 30 E
Masfjorden, Norway 18 D2 60 48N 5 18 E
Mashaba, Zimbabwe 119 G3 20 2 S 30 29 E
Mashābih, Si. Arabia 96 E3 25 35N 36 30 E
Mashan, China 76 F7 23 40N 108 11 E
Mashar, Sudan 107 F2 9 16N 26 51 E
Mashatu Game Reserve, Botswana 117 C4 22 5 S 29 5 E
Mashegu, Nigeria 113 D6 10 0N 5 35 E
Masherbrum, Pakistan 93 B7 35 38N 76 18 E
Mashhad, Iran 97 B8 36 20N 59 35 E
Mashi, Nigeria 113 C6 13 0N 7 54 E
Mashiki, Japan 72 E2 32 51N 130 53 E
Mashīz, Iran 97 D8 29 56N 56 37 E
Mashkai →, Pakistan 91 D2 26 2N 65 19 E
Māshkel, Hāmūn-i-, Pakistan 91 C1 28 20N 62 56 E
Mashki Chāh, Pakistan 91 C1 29 5N 62 30 E
Mashonaland Central □, Zimbabwe 117 B5 17 30 S 31 0 E
Mashonaland East □, Zimbabwe 117 B5 18 0 S 32 0 E
Mashonaland West □, Zimbabwe 117 B4 17 30 S 29 30 E
Mashrakh, India 93 F11 26 7N 84 48 E
Mashtaga = Maştağa, Azerbaijan 61 K10 40 35N 49 57 E
Masi Manimba, Dem. Rep. of the Congo 115 C3 4 40 S 17 54 E
Masibi, Angola 115 E4 11 6 S 22 41 E
Masindi, Uganda 118 B3 1 40N 31 43 E
Masindi Port, Uganda 118 B3 1 43N 32 2 E
Masinloc, Phil. 80 D2 15 32N 119 57 E
Maşīrah, Oman 99 B7 21 0N 58 50 E
Maşīrah, Khalīj, Oman 99 B7 20 10N 58 10 E
Maşīrah, Tur'at, Oman 99 B7 20 30N 58 40 E
Masisea, Peru 172 B3 8 35 S 74 22W
Masisi, Dem. Rep. of the Congo 118 C2 1 23 S 28 49 E
Masjed Soleyman, Iran 97 D6 31 55N 49 18 E
Mask, L., Ireland 23 C2 53 36N 9 22W
Maskelyne Is., Vanuatu 133 F5 16 32 S 167 49 E
Maski, India 95 G3 15 56N 76 46 E
Maskin, Oman 97 F8 23 30N 56 50 E
Maslen Nos, Bulgaria 51 D11 42 18N 27 48 E
Maslinica, Croatia 45 E13 43 24N 16 13 E
Maşna'ah, Yemen 99 D5 14 27N 48 17 E
Masnou = El Masnou, Spain 40 D7 41 28N 2 20 E
Masoala, Parc Nat. de, Madag. 117 B9 15 30 S 50 12 E
Masoala, Tanjon' i, Madag. 117 B9 15 59 S 50 13 E
Masoarivo, Madag. 117 B7 19 3 S 44 19 E
Maşohi = Amahai, Indonesia 83 C3 3 20 S 128 55 E
Masomeloka, Madag. 117 C8 20 17 S 48 37 E
Mason, Mich., U.S.A. 157 B12 42 35N 84 27W
Mason, Nev., U.S.A. 160 G7 38 56N 119 8W
Mason, Ohio, U.S.A. 157 E12 39 22N 84 19W
Mason, Tex., U.S.A. 155 K5 30 45N 99 14W
Mason B., N.Z. 131 G2 46 55 S 167 45 E
Mason City, Ill., U.S.A. 156 D7 40 12N 89 42W
Mason City, Iowa, U.S.A. 156 A3 43 9N 93 12W
Maspalomas, Canary Is. 9 e1 27 46N 15 35W
Maspalomas, Pta., Canary Is. 9 e1 27 43N 15 36W
Masqat, Oman 99 B7 23 37N 58 36 E
Massa, Congo 114 C3 3 45 S 15 29 E
Massa, Italy 44 D7 44 1N 10 9 E
Massa, O. →, Morocco 110 B3 30 2N 9 40W
Massa Maríttima, Italy 44 E7 43 3N 10 52 E
Massachusetts □, U.S.A. 151 D13 42 30N 72 0W
Massachusetts B., U.S.A. 151 D14 42 20N 70 50W
Massafra, Italy 47 B10 40 35N 17 7 E
Massaguet, Chad 109 F3 12 28N 15 26 E
Massakory, Chad 109 F3 13 0N 15 49 E
Massanella, Spain 38 B3 39 48N 2 51 E
Massangano, Angola 115 D2 9 40 S 14 13 E
Massangena, Mozam. 117 C5 21 34 S 33 0 E
Massango, Angola 115 D3 8 1 S 16 10 E
Massapê, Brazil 170 B3 3 31 S 40 19W
Massat, France 28 F5 42 53N 1 21 E
Massawa = Mitsiwa, Eritrea 107 D4 15 35N 39 25 E
Massena, U.S.A. 151 B10 44 56N 74 54W
Massénya, Chad 109 F3 11 21N 16 9 E
Masset, Canada 142 C2 54 2N 132 10W
Masseube, France 28 E4 43 25N 0 34 E
Massiac, France 28 C7 45 15N 3 11 E
Massiah Street, Barbados 165 g 13 9N 59 29W
Massif Central, France 28 D7 44 55N 3 0 E
Massigui, Mali 112 C3 11 48N 6 50W
Massillon, U.S.A. 150 F3 40 48N 81 32W
Massima, Gabon 114 C2 1 27 S 11 33 E
Massine, O. →, Algeria 111 C5 36 13N 2 12 E
Massinga, Mozam. 117 C6 23 15 S 35 22 E
Massingir, Mozam. 117 C5 23 51 S 32 4 E
Mässlingen, Sweden 16 B6 62 40N 12 50 E
Masson, Canada 151 A9 45 32N 75 25W
Masson I., Antarctica 7 C7 66 10 S 93 20 E
Massouka, Gabon 114 C1 1 37 S 9 56 E
Mastābah, Si. Arabia 98 B2 20 49N 39 26 E
Maştağa, Azerbaijan 61 K10 40 35N 49 57 E
Mastanli = Momchilgrad, Bulgaria 51 E9 41 33N 25 23 E
Masterton, N.Z. 130 G4 40 56 S 175 39 E
Mastic, U.S.A. 151 F12 40 47N 72 54W
Mástikho, Ákra, Greece 49 C8 38 10N 26 2 E
Mastuj, Pakistan 93 A5 36 20N 72 36 E
Mastung, Pakistan 91 C2 29 50N 66 56 E
Mastūrah, Si. Arabia 98 B2 23 7N 38 52 E
Masty, Belarus 58 F3 53 27N 24 38 E
Masuda, Japan 72 C3 34 40N 131 51 E
Masuika, Dem. Rep. of the Congo 115 D4 7 37 S 22 32 E
Masvingo, Zimbabwe 119 G3 20 8 S 30 49 E
Masvingo □, Zimbabwe 119 G3 21 0 S 31 30 E
Maswa Game Reserve, Tanzania 118 C3 2 58 S 34 19 E
Maşyāf, Syria 100 E7 35 4N 36 20 E
Maszewo, Poland 54 E2 53 29N 15 3 E
Mat →, Albania 50 E3 41 40N 19 35 E
Mata de São João, Brazil 171 D4 12 31 S 38 17W
Mata Utu, Wall. & F. Is. 123 C15 13 17 S 176 8W
Matabele Plain, Zambia 115 F4 16 20 S 23 10 E
Matabeleland North □, Zimbabwe 119 F2 19 0 S 28 0 E
Matabeleland South □, Zimbabwe 119 G2 21 0 S 29 0 E
Mataboor, Indonesia 83 B5 1 41 S 138 3 E
Matachel →, Spain 43 G4 38 50N 6 17W
Matachewan, Canada 140 C3 47 56N 80 39W
Matacuni →, Venezuela 169 C4 3 2N 65 16W
Matadi, Dem. Rep. of the Congo 115 D2 5 52 S 13 31 E
Matagalpa, Nic. 164 D2 13 0N 85 58W
Matagami, Canada 140 C4 49 45N 77 34W
Matagami, L., Canada 140 C4 49 50N 77 40W
Matagorda B., U.S.A. 155 L6 28 40N 96 0W
Matagorda I., U.S.A. 155 L6 28 15N 96 30W
Mataguinao, Phil. 80 E5 12 5N 124 55 E
Matak, Indonesia 84 B3 3 18N 106 16 E
Matakana, Australia 129 B6 32 59 S 145 54 E
Matakana, N.Z. 130 C3 36 21 S 174 43 E
Matala, Angola 115 E3 14 46 S 15 4 E
Mátala, Greece 39 F5 34 59N 24 45 E
Matalaque, Peru 172 D3 16 26 S 70 49W
Matale, Sri Lanka 95 L5 7 30N 80 37 E
Matam, Senegal 112 B2 15 34N 13 17W
Matamata, N.Z. 130 D4 37 48 S 175 47 E
Matameye, Niger 113 C6 13 26N 8 28 E
Matamoros, Campeche, Mexico 163 D6 18 50N 90 50W
Matamoros, Coahuila, Mexico 162 B4 25 33N 103 15W
Matamoros, Tamaulipas, Mexico 163 B5 25 50N 97 30W
Ma'ţan as Sarra, Libya 109 D4 21 45N 22 0 E
Ma'ţan Bishārah, Libya 108 D4 23 0N 22 32 E
Matana, Danau, Indonesia 82 B2 2 28 S 121 20 E
Matandu →, Tanzania 119 D3 8 45 S 34 19 E
Matane, Canada 141 C6 48 50N 67 33W
Matang, China 76 F5 23 30N 104 7 E
Matankari, Niger 113 C5 13 46N 4 1 E
Matanomadh, India 92 H3 23 33N 68 57 E
Matanzas, Cuba 164 B3 23 0N 81 40W
Matapa, Botswana 116 C3 23 11 S 24 39 E
Matapan, C. = Taínaron, Ákra, Greece 48 E4 36 22N 22 27 E
Matapédia, Canada 141 C6 48 0N 66 59W
Matapo Nat. Park, Zimbabwe 119 G2 20 30 S 29 40 E
Matara, Sri Lanka 95 M5 5 58N 80 30 E
Mataram, Indonesia 85 D5 8 35 S 116 7 E
Matarani, Peru 172 D3 17 0 S 72 10W
Mataranka, Australia 124 B5 14 55 S 133 4 E
Matarma, Râs, Egypt 103 E1 30 27N 32 44 E
Mataró, Spain 40 D7 41 32N 2 29 E
Matarraña →, Spain 40 D5 41 14N 0 22 E
Mataruška Banja, Serbia, Yug. 50 C4 43 40N 20 40 E
Mataso, Vanuatu 133 G6 17 14 S 168 26 E
Matata, N.Z. 130 D5 37 54 S 176 48 E
Matatiele, S. Africa 117 E4 30 20 S 28 49 E
Mataura, N.Z. 131 G3 46 11 S 168 51 E
Mataura →, N.Z. 131 G3 46 34 S 168 44 E
Mataveri, Chile 172 b 27 9 S 109 27W
Mategua, Bolivia 173 C5 13 1 S 62 48W
Matehuala, Mexico 162 C4 23 40N 100 40W

Mateira, *Brazil* **171 E1** 18 54 S 50 30W
Mateke, *Dem. Rep. of the Congo* **114 C3** 4 52 S 24 25 E
Mateke Hills, *Zimbabwe* **119 G3** 21 48 S 31 0 E
Matelot, *Trin. & Tob.* **169 F9** 10 50N 61 7W
Matera, *Italy* **47 B9** 40 40N 16 36 E
Matese, Monti del, *Italy* **47 A7** 41 27N 14 22 E
Mátészalka, *Hungary* **52 C7** 47 58N 22 20 E
Matetsi, *Zimbabwe* **119 F2** 18 12 S 26 0 E
Mateur, *Tunisia* **108 A1** 37 0N 9 40 E
Matfors, *Sweden* **16 B11** 62 21N 17 2 E
Matha, *France* **28 C3** 45 52N 0 20W
Matheniko Game Reserve, *Uganda* **118 B3** 2 49N 34 27 E
Mathis, *U.S.A.* **155 L6** 28 6N 97 50W
Mathoura, *Australia* **129 C6** 35 50 S 144 55 E
Mathráki, *Greece* **38 B9** 39 48N 19 31 E
Mathura, *India* **92 F7** 27 30N 77 40 E
Mati, *Phil.* **81 H6** 6 55N 126 15 E
Matiakoali, *Burkina Faso* **113 C5** 12 28N 1 2 E
Matiali, *India* **93 F13** 26 56N 88 49 E
Matías Romero, *Mexico* **163 D5** 16 53N 95 2W
Matibane, *Mozam.* **119 E5** 14 49 S 40 45 E
Matima, *Botswana* **116 C3** 20 15 S 24 26 E
Matinhos, *Brazil* **171 G2** 25 49 S 48 32W
Matiri Ra., *N.Z.* **131 B7** 41 38 S 172 20 E
Matjiesfontein, *S. Africa* **116 E3** 33 14 S 20 35 E
Matla →, *India* **93 J13** 21 40N 88 40 E
Matlamanyane, *Botswana* **116 B4** 19 33 S 25 57 E
Matli, *Pakistan* **92 G3** 25 2N 68 39 E
Matlock, *U.K.* **20 D6** 53 9N 1 33W
Matmata, *Tunisia* **108 B1** 33 37N 9 59 E
Matna, *Sudan* **107 E4** 13 49N 35 10 E
Matnog, *Phil.* **80 E5** 12 35N 124 5 E
Mato, *Dem. Rep. of the Congo* **115 D4** 8 1 S 24 24 E
Mato →, *Venezuela* **169 B4** 7 9N 65 7W
Mato, Serrania de, *Venezuela* **168 B4** 6 25N 65 25W
Mato Grosso □, *Brazil* **173 C6** 14 0 S 55 0W
Mato Grosso, Planalto do, *Brazil* **173 C7** 15 0 S 55 0W
Mato Grosso do Sul □, *Brazil* **173 D7** 18 0 S 55 0W
Mato Verde, *Brazil* **171 D1** 11 13 S 50 40W
Matochkin Shar, *Russia* **66 B6** 73 10N 56 40 E
Matong, *Papua N. G.* **132 C6** 5 36 S 151 50 E
Matopo Hills, *Zimbabwe* **119 G2** 20 36 S 28 20 E
Matopos, *Zimbabwe* **119 G2** 20 20 S 28 29 E
Matosinhos, *Portugal* **42 D2** 41 11N 8 42W
Matour, *France* **27 F11** 46 19N 4 29 E
Matroosberg, *S. Africa* **116 E2** 33 23 S 19 40 E
Maţruḩ, *Oman* **99 B7** 23 37N 58 30 E
Matsena, *Nigeria* **113 C7** 13 5N 10 5 E
Matsesta, *Russia* **61 J4** 43 34N 39 51 E
Matsu Tao, *Taiwan* **77 E13** 26 9N 119 56 E
Matsudo, *Japan* **73 B11** 35 47N 139 54 E
Matsue, *Japan* **72 B5** 35 25N 133 10 E
Matsum, Ko, *Thailand* **87 b** 9 22N 99 59 E
Matsumae, *Japan* **70 D10** 41 26N 140 7 E
Matsumoto, *Japan* **73 A10** 36 15N 138 0 E
Matsusaka, *Japan* **73 C8** 34 34N 136 32 E
Matsushima, *Japan* **72 E2** 32 30N 130 25 E
Matsuura, *Japan* **72 D1** 33 20N 129 49 E
Matsuyama, *Japan* **72 D4** 33 45N 132 45 E
Matsuzaki, *Japan* **73 C10** 34 43N 138 50 E
Mattagami →, *Canada* **140 B3** 50 43N 81 29W
Mattancheri, *India* **95 K3** 9 50N 76 15 E
Mattawa, *Canada* **140 C4** 46 20N 78 45W
Matterhorn, *Switz.* **32 E5** 45 58N 7 39 E
Mattersburg, *Austria* **35 D9** 47 44N 16 24 E
Matteson, *U.S.A.* **157 C9** 41 30N 87 42W
Matthew, I., *N. Cal.* **123 E13** 22 29 S 171 15 E
Matthew Town, *Bahamas* **165 B5** 20 57N 73 40W
Matthews, *U.S.A.* **157 D11** 40 23N 85 30W
Matthew's Ridge, *Guyana* **169 B5** 7 37N 60 10W
Mattice, *Canada* **140 C3** 49 40N 83 20W
Mattili, *India* **94 E6** 18 33N 82 12 E
Mattituck, *U.S.A.* **151 F12** 40 59N 72 32W
Mattō, *Japan* **73 A8** 36 31N 136 34 E
Mattoon, *U.S.A.* **154 F10** 39 29N 88 23W
Matuba, *Mozam.* **117 C5** 24 28 S 32 49 E
Matucana, *Peru* **172 C2** 11 55 S 76 25W
Matugama, *Sri Lanka* **95 L5** 6 31N 80 7 E
Matuka, *Papua N. G.* **132 C3** 4 54 S 145 47 E
Matuku, *Fiji* **133 B2** 19 10 S 179 44 E
Matūn = Khowst, *Afghan.* **91 B3** 33 22N 69 58 E
Matura B., *Trin. & Tob.* **169 F10** 10 39N 61 1W
Maturín, *Venezuela* **169 B5** 9 45N 63 11W
Matusadona Nat. Park, *Zimbabwe* **119 F2** 16 58 S 28 42 E
Matutum, Mt., *Phil.* **81 H5** 6 22N 125 5 E
Matveyev Kurgan, *Russia* **59 J10** 47 35N 38 57 E
Matxitxako, C., *Spain* **40 B2** 43 28N 2 47W
Mau, *Mad. P., India* **93 F8** 26 17N 78 41 E
Mau, *Ut. P., India* **93 G10** 25 56N 83 33 E
Mau, *Ut. P., India* **93 G9** 25 17N 81 23 E
Mau Escarpment, *Kenya* **118 C4** 0 40 S 36 0 E
Mau Ranipur, *India* **93 G8** 25 16N 79 8 E
Mauban, *Phil.* **80 D3** 14 12N 121 44 E
Maubeuge, *France* **27 B10** 50 17N 3 57 E
Maubourguet, *France* **28 E4** 43 29N 0 1 E
Maud, Pt., *Australia* **124 D1** 23 6 S 113 45 E
Maude, *Australia* **128 C6** 34 29 S 144 18 E
Maudin Sun, *Burma* **90 G5** 16 0N 94 12 E
Maués, *Brazil* **169 D6** 3 20 S 57 45W
Maués-Acu →, *Brazil* **169 D6** 3 22 S 57 44W
Maughold Hd., *U.K.* **20 C3** 54 18N 4 18W
Mauguio, *France* **28 E7** 43 37N 4 1 E
Maui, *U.S.A.* **145 C5** 20 48N 156 20W
Maulamyaing = Moulmein, *Burma* **90 G6** 16 30N 97 40 E
Maule □, *Chile* **174 D1** 36 5 S 72 30W
Mauléon-Licharre, *France* **28 E3** 43 14N 0 54W
Maullín, *Chile* **176 B2** 41 38 S 73 37W
Maulvibazar, *Bangla.* **90 C3** 24 29N 91 42 E
Maumee, *U.S.A.* **157 C13** 41 34N 83 39W
Maumee →, *U.S.A.* **157 C13** 41 42N 83 28W
Maumere, *Indonesia* **82 C2** 8 38 S 122 13 E
Maumusson, Pertuis de, *France* **28 C2** 45 48N 1 14W
Maun, *Botswana* **116 C3** 20 0 S 23 26 E
Mauna Kea, *U.S.A.* **145 D6** 19 50N 155 28W
Mauna Loa, *U.S.A.* **145 D6** 19 30N 155 35W
Maunaloa, *U.S.A.* **145 B4** 21 8N 157 13W
Maunalua B., *U.S.A.* **145 K14** 21 15N 157 45W
Maunawili, *U.S.A.* **145 K14** 21 23N 157 46W
Maunga Orito, *Chile* **172 b** 27 10 S 109 25W
Maunga Puakatiki, *Chile* **172 b** 27 6 S 109 15W
Maunga Terevaka, *Chile* **172 b** 27 5 S 109 23W
Maungaturoto, *N.Z.* **130 C3** 36 6 S 174 23 E
Maungdow, *Burma* **90 E4** 20 50N 92 21 E
Maungmagan Kyunzu, *Burma* **86 E1** 14 0N 97 48 E
Maupin, *U.S.A.* **158 D3** 45 11N 121 5W
Maure-de-Bretagne, *France* **26 E5** 47 59N 1 58W
Maurepas, L., *U.S.A.* **155 K9** 30 15N 90 30W
Maures, *France* **29 E10** 43 15N 6 15 E
Mauriac, *France* **28 C6** 45 13N 2 19 E
Maurice, L., *Australia* **125 E5** 29 30 S 131 0 E
Mauriceville, *N.Z.* **130 G4** 40 45 S 175 42 E
Mauricie, Parc Nat. de la, *Canada* **140 C5** 46 45N 73 0W
Maurienne, *France* **29 C10** 45 13N 6 30 E
Mauritania ■, *Africa* **110 D3** 20 50N 10 0W
Mauritius ■, *Ind. Oc.* **105 J9** 20 0 S 57 0 E
Mauron, *France* **26 D4** 48 9N 2 18W
Maurs, *France* **28 D6** 44 43N 2 12 E
Mauston, *U.S.A.* **154 D9** 43 48N 90 5W
Mauterndorf, *Austria* **34 D6** 47 9N 13 40 E
Mauthen, *Austria* **34 E6** 46 40N 13 0 E
Mauvezin, *France* **28 E4** 43 44N 0 53 E
Mauvoisin, Barr. de, *Switz.* **32 E4** 45 58N 7 20 E
Mauzé-sur-le-Mignon, *France* **28 B3** 46 12N 0 41W
Mavaca →, *Venezuela* **169 C4** 2 31N 65 11W
Mavinga, *Angola* **115 F4** 15 50 S 20 21 E
Mavli, *India* **92 G5** 24 45N 73 55 E
Mavráta, *Greece* **39 C2** 38 4N 20 44 E
Mavrovë, *Albania* **50 F3** 40 26N 19 32 E
Mavuradonha Mts., *Zimbabwe* **119 F3** 16 30 S 31 30 E
Mawa, *Dem. Rep. of the Congo* **118 B2** 2 45N 26 40 E
Mawai, *India* **93 H9** 22 30N 81 4 E
Mawana, *India* **92 E7** 29 6N 77 58 E
Mawand, *Pakistan* **92 E3** 29 33N 68 38 E
Mawasangka, *Indonesia* **82 C2** 5 17 S 122 18 E
Mawk Mai, *Burma* **90 E6** 20 14N 97 37 E
Mawlaik, *Burma* **90 D5** 23 40N 94 26 E
Mawlamyine = Moulmein, *Burma* **90 G6** 16 30N 97 40 E
Mawlawkho, *Burma* **90 G6** 17 50N 97 38 E
Mawqaq, *Si. Arabia* **96 E4** 27 25N 41 8 E
Mawshij, *Yemen* **98 D3** 13 43N 43 17 E
Mawson Coast, *Antarctica* **7 C6** 68 30 S 63 0 E
Max, *U.S.A.* **154 B4** 47 49N 101 18W
Maxcanú, *Mexico* **163 C6** 20 40N 92 0W
Maxesibeni, *S. Africa* **117 E4** 30 49 S 29 23 E
Maxeys, *U.S.A.* **152 B6** 33 45N 83 11W
Maxhamish L., *Canada* **142 B4** 59 50N 123 17W
Maxixe, *Mozam.* **117 C6** 23 54 S 35 17 E
Maxville, *Canada* **151 A10** 45 17N 74 51W
Maxwell, *N.Z.* **130 F3** 39 51 S 174 49 E
Maxwell, *U.S.A.* **160 F4** 39 17N 122 11W
Maxwelton, *Australia* **126 C3** 20 43 S 142 41 E
May, C., *U.S.A.* **148 F8** 38 56N 74 58W
May Jirgui, *Niger* **109 F1** 13 44N 8 8 E
May Pen, *Jamaica* **164 a** 17 58N 77 15W
May River, *Papua N. G.* **132 C1** 4 19 S 141 58 E
Maya, *Indonesia* **85 C3** 1 10 S 109 35 E
Maya →, *Russia* **67 D14** 60 28N 134 28 E
Maya Mts., *Belize* **163 D7** 16 30N 89 0W
Mayabandar, *India* **95 H11** 12 56N 92 56 E
Mayaguana, *Bahamas* **165 B5** 22 30N 72 44W
Mayagüez, *Puerto Rico* **165 d** 18 12N 67 9W
Mayahi, *Niger* **113 C6** 13 58N 7 40 E
Mayals = Maials, *Spain* **40 D5** 41 22N 0 30 E
Mayama, *Congo* **114 C2** 3 51 S 14 54 E
Mayāmey, *Iran* **97 B7** 36 24N 55 42 E
Mayang, *China* **76 D7** 27 53N 109 49 E
Mayanup, *Australia* **125 F2** 33 57 S 116 27 E
Mayapan, *Mexico* **163 C7** 20 30N 89 25W
Mayaqum, *Kazakstan* **65 B4** 42 51N 68 3 E
Mayarí, *Cuba* **165 B4** 20 40N 75 41W
Mayaro B., *Trin. & Tob.* **169 F10** 10 14N 61 0W
Mayavaram = Mayuram, *India* **95 J4** 11 3N 79 42 E
Maybell, *U.S.A.* **158 F9** 40 31N 108 5W
Maybole, *U.K.* **22 F4** 55 21N 4 42W
Maychew, *Ethiopia* **107 E4** 12 50N 39 31 E
Maydān, *Iraq* **101 E11** 34 55N 45 37 E
Maydena, *Australia* **127 G4** 42 45 S 146 30 E
Maydī, *Yemen* **98 C3** 16 19N 42 48 E
Mayen, *Germany* **31 E3** 50 19N 7 13 E
Mayenne, *France* **26 D6** 48 20N 0 38W
Mayenne □, *France* **26 D6** 48 10N 0 40W
Mayenne →, *France* **26 E6** 47 30N 0 32W
Mayer, *U.S.A.* **159 J7** 34 24N 112 14W
Mayerthorpe, *Canada* **142 C5** 53 57N 115 8W
Mayesville, *U.S.A.* **152 A9** 34 0N 80 12W
Mayfield, *Ky., U.S.A.* **149 G1** 36 44N 88 38W
Mayfield, *N.Y., U.S.A.* **151 C10** 43 6N 74 16W
Mayhill, *U.S.A.* **159 K11** 32 53N 105 29W
Maykop, *Russia* **61 H5** 44 35N 40 10 E
Mayli-Say = Mayluu-Suu, *Kyrgyzstan* **65 C6** 41 17N 72 24 E
Mayluu-Suu, *Kyrgyzstan* **65 C6** 41 17N 72 24 E
Maymak, *Kyrgyzstan* **65 B5** 42 42N 71 13 E
Maymyo, *Burma* **86 A1** 22 2N 96 28 E
Maynard, *Mass., U.S.A.* **151 D13** 42 26N 71 27W
Maynard, *Wash., U.S.A.* **160 C4** 47 59N 122 55W
Maynard Hills, *Australia* **125 E2** 28 28 S 119 49 E
Mayne →, *Australia* **126 C3** 23 40 S 141 55 E
Maynooth, *Ireland* **23 C5** 53 23N 6 34W
Mayo, *Canada* **138 B6** 63 38N 135 57W
Mayo, *U.S.A.* **152 E6** 30 3N 83 10W
Mayo □, *Ireland* **23 C2** 53 53N 9 3W
Mayo →, *Argentina* **176 C3** 45 45 S 69 45W
Mayo →, *Peru* **172 B2** 6 38 S 76 15W
Mayo Bay, *Phil.* **81 H6** 6 56N 126 22 E
Mayo Daga, *Nigeria* **113 D7** 6 59N 11 25 E
Mayo Faran, *Nigeria* **113 D7** 8 57N 12 4 E
Mayoko, *Congo* **114 C2** 2 18 S 12 49 E
Mayoko, *Dem. Rep. of the Congo* **114 C4** 1 6 S 23 50 E
Mayon Volcano, *Phil.* **80 E4** 13 15N 123 41 E
Mayor Buratovich, *Argentina* **176 A4** 39 15 S 62 37W
Mayor I., *N.Z.* **130 D5** 37 16 S 176 17 E
Mayorga, *Spain* **42 C5** 42 10N 5 16W
Mayotte, *Ind. Oc.* **105 H8** 12 50 S 45 10 E
Mayoyao, *Phil.* **80 C3** 16 59N 121 14 E
Mayraira Pt., *Phil.* **80 B3** 18 39N 120 51 E
Mayskiy, *Russia* **61 J7** 43 47N 44 2 E
Maysville, *Ky., U.S.A.* **157 F13** 38 39N 83 46W
Maysville, *Mo., U.S.A.* **156 E2** 39 53N 94 22W
Mayu, *Indonesia* **82 A3** 1 30N 126 30 E
Mayumba, *Gabon* **114 C2** 3 25 S 10 39 E
Mayuram, *India* **95 J4** 11 3N 79 42 E
Mayville, *N. Dak., U.S.A.* **154 B6** 47 30N 97 20W
Mayville, *N.Y., U.S.A.* **150 D5** 42 15N 79 30W
Mayya, *Russia* **67 C14** 61 44N 130 18 E
Mazabuka, *Zambia* **119 F2** 15 52 S 27 44 E
Mazagán = El Jadida, *Morocco* **110 B3** 33 11N 8 17W
Mazagão, *Brazil* **169 D7** 0 7 S 51 16W
Mazamet, *France* **28 E6** 43 30N 2 20 E
Mazán, *Peru* **168 D3** 3 30 S 73 0W
Māzandarān □, *Iran* **97 B7** 36 30N 52 0 E
Mazapil, *Mexico* **162 C4** 24 38N 101 34W
Mazar, *China* **65 E8** 36 32N 77 1 E
Mazar, O. →, *Algeria* **111 B5** 31 50N 1 36 E
Mazār-e Sharīf, *Afghan.* **65 E3** 36 41N 67 0 E
Mazara del Vallo, *Italy* **46 E5** 37 39N 12 35 E
Mazarredo, *Argentina* **176 C3** 47 10 S 66 50W
Mazarrón, *Spain* **41 H3** 37 38N 1 19W
Mazarrón, G. de, *Spain* **41 H3** 37 27N 1 19W
Mazaruni →, *Guyana* **169 B6** 6 25N 58 35W
Mazatán, *Mexico* **162 B2** 29 0N 110 8W
Mazatenango, *Guatemala* **164 D1** 14 35N 91 30W
Mazatlán, *Mexico* **162 C3** 23 13N 106 25W
Mažeikiai, *Lithuania* **15 H20** 56 20N 22 20 E
Māzhān, *Iran* **97 C8** 32 30N 59 0 E
Mazīnān, *Iran* **97 B8** 36 19N 56 56 E
Mazo Cruz, *Peru* **172 D4** 16 45 S 69 44W
Mazoe, *Mozam.* **119 F3** 16 42 S 33 7 E
Mazoe →, *Mozam.* **119 F3** 16 20 S 33 30 E
Mazomanie, *U.S.A.* **156 A7** 43 11N 89 48W
Mazon, *U.S.A.* **157 C8** 41 14N 88 25W
Mazowe, *Zimbabwe* **119 F3** 17 28 S 30 58 E
Mazowieckie □, *Poland* **55 F8** 52 40N 21 0 E
Mazrûb, *Sudan* **107 E2** 14 0N 29 20 E
Mazu Dao, *China* **77 D12** 26 10N 119 55 E
Mazurian Lakes = Mazurski, Pojezierze, *Poland* **54 E7** 53 50N 21 0 E
Mazurski, Pojezierze, *Poland* **54 E7** 53 50N 21 0 E
Mazyr, *Belarus* **59 F5** 51 59N 29 15 E
Mba, *Fiji* **133 A1** 17 33 S 177 41 E
Mbaba, *Senegal* **112 C1** 14 59N 16 44W
Mbabane, *Swaziland* **117 D5** 26 18 S 31 6 E
Mbaéré →, *C.A.R.* **114 B3** 3 47N 17 31 E
Mbagne, *Mauritania* **112 B2** 16 6N 14 47W
M'bahiakro, *Ivory C.* **112 D4** 7 33N 4 19W
Mbaïki, *C.A.R.* **114 B3** 3 53N 18 1 E
Mbakana, Mt. de, *Cameroon* **114 A3** 7 57N 15 6 E
Mbala, *Zambia* **119 D3** 8 46 S 31 24 E
Mbalabala, *Zimbabwe* **117 C4** 20 27 S 29 3 E
Mbale, *Uganda* **118 B3** 1 8N 34 12 E
Mbali →, *C.A.R.* **114 B3** 4 27N 18 20 E
Mbalmayo, *Cameroon* **113 E7** 3 33N 11 33 E
Mbam →, *Cameroon* **113 E7** 4 24N 11 17 E
Mbamba Bay, *Tanzania* **119 E3** 11 13 S 34 49 E
Mbandaka, *Dem. Rep. of the Congo* **114 B3** 0 1N 18 18 E
Mbanga, *Cameroon* **113 E6** 4 30N 9 33 E
Mbanika, *Solomon Is.* **133 M10** 9 3 S 159 13 E
M'Banio, Lagune, *Gabon* **114 C2** 3 35 S 11 0 E
Mbanza Congo, *Angola* **115 D2** 6 18 S 14 16 E
Mbanza Ngungu, *Dem. Rep. of the Congo* **115 D2** 5 12 S 14 53 E
Mbarangandu, *Tanzania* **119 D4** 10 11 S 36 48 E
Mbarara, *Uganda* **118 C3** 0 35 S 30 40 E
Mbari →, *C.A.R.* **114 B4** 4 34N 22 43 E
Mbashe →, *S. Africa* **117 E4** 32 15 S 28 54 E
Mbatto, *Ivory C.* **112 D4** 6 28N 4 22W
Mbava, *Solomon Is.* **133 L9** 7 47 S 156 33 E
Mbé, *Congo* **114 C3** 3 14 S 15 50 E
Mbe, *Eq. Guin.* **114 B1** 1 47N 9 56 E
Mbengga = Beqa, *Fiji* **133 B2** 18 23 S 178 8 E
Mbengué, *Gabon* **114 C2** 2 2 S 11 7 E
Mbengui, *Gabon* **114 C2** 2 3 S 10 4 E
Mbenkuru →, *Tanzania* **119 D4** 9 25 S 39 50 E
Mbéré →, *Cameroon* **114 A3** 7 45N 15 36 E
Mberengwa, *Zimbabwe* **119 G2** 20 29 S 29 57 E
Mberengwa, Mt., *Zimbabwe* **119 G2** 20 37 S 29 55 E
Mberubu, *Nigeria* **113 D6** 6 10N 7 38 E
Mbesuma, *Zambia* **119 E3** 10 0 S 32 2 E
Mbeya, *Tanzania* **119 D3** 8 54 S 33 29 E
Mbeya □, *Tanzania* **118 D3** 8 15 S 33 30 E
Mbigou, *Gabon* **114 C2** 1 53 S 11 56 E
M'bili, *Sudan* **107 F2** 7 35N 28 15 E
Mbinga, *Tanzania* **119 E4** 10 50 S 35 0 E
Mbini = Río Muni □, *Eq. Guin.* **114 B2** 1 30N 10 0 E
Mbini, *Eq. Guin.* **114 B1** 1 35N 9 37 E
Mboi, *Dem. Rep. of the Congo* **115 D4** 6 57 S 21 54 E
Mboki, *C.A.R.* **107 F2** 5 19N 25 58 E
Mbokonimbeti, *Solomon Is.* **133 M11** 8 57 S 160 7 E
Mboli, *Dem. Rep. of the Congo* **114 B4** 4 8N 23 9 E
M'bonge, *Cameroon* **113 E6** 4 33N 9 5 E
Mboro, *Senegal* **112 B1** 15 9N 16 54W
Mboua, *Cameroon* **114 A2** 4 25N 14 16 E
M'boukou, Rés. de, *Cameroon* **113 D7** 6 23N 12 50 E
Mboune, *Senegal* **112 C2** 14 42N 13 34W
Mbouoma, *Congo* **114 C3** 0 52 S 15 4 E
Mbour, *Senegal* **112 C1** 14 22N 16 54W
Mbout, *Mauritania* **112 B2** 16 1N 12 38W
Mbrés, *C.A.R.* **114 A3** 6 40N 19 48 E
M'Bridge →, *Angola* **115 D2** 7 12 S 12 51 E
Mbuji-Mayi, *Dem. Rep. of the Congo* **118 D1** 6 9 S 23 40 E
Mbulu, *Tanzania* **118 C4** 3 45 S 35 30 E
Mbuma, *Dem. Rep. of the Congo* **114 B4** 3 32N 24 50 E
Mbuma, *Solomon Is.* **133 M11** 8 59 S 160 46 E
Mburucuyá, *Argentina* **174 B4** 28 1 S 58 14W
M'bwat, *Cameroon* **114 A2** 6 29N 10 45 E
Mcherrah, *Algeria* **110 C4** 27 0N 4 30W
Mchinja, *Tanzania* **119 D4** 9 44 S 39 45 E
Mchinji, *Malawi* **119 E3** 13 47 S 32 58 E
Mdennah, *Mauritania* **110 D3** 24 37N 6 0W
Mé Maoya, *N. Cal.* **133 U19** 21 22 S 165 22 E
Mead, L., *U.S.A.* **161 J12** 36 1N 114 44W
Meade, *U.S.A.* **155 G4** 37 17N 100 20W
Meade →, *U.S.A.* **144 A9** 70 52N 155 55W
Meade River, *U.S.A.* **144 A8** 70 28N 157 24W
Meadow Lake, *Canada* **143 C7** 54 10N 108 26W
Meadow Lake Prov. Park, *Canada* **143 C7** 54 27N 109 0W
Meadow Valley Wash →, *U.S.A.* **161 J12** 36 40N 114 34W
Meadville, *Mo., U.S.A.* **156 E3** 39 47N 93 18W
Meadville, *Pa., U.S.A.* **150 E4** 41 39N 80 9W
Meaford, *Canada* **140 D3** 44 36N 80 35W
Mealhada, *Portugal* **42 E2** 40 22N 8 27W
Mealy Mts., *Canada* **141 B8** 53 10N 58 0W
Meander River, *Canada* **142 B5** 59 2N 117 42W
Meares, C., *U.S.A.* **158 D2** 45 37N 124 0W
Mearim →, *Brazil* **170 B3** 3 4 S 44 35W
Meath □, *Ireland* **23 C5** 53 40N 6 57W
Meath Park, *Canada* **143 C7** 53 27N 105 22W
Meaulne, *France* **27 F9** 46 36N 2 36 E
Meaux, *France* **27 D9** 48 58N 2 50 E
Mebechi-Gawa →, *Japan* **70 D10** 40 31N 141 31 E
Mebonden, *Norway* **18 A8** 63 13N 11 2 E
Mebulu, Tanjung, *Indonesia* **79 K18** 8 50 S 115 5 E
Mecanhelas, *Mozam.* **119 F4** 15 12 S 35 54 E
Mecaya →, *Colombia* **168 C2** 0 29N 75 11W
Mecca = Makkah, *Si. Arabia* **98 B2** 21 30N 39 54 E
Mecca, *U.S.A.* **161 M10** 33 34N 116 5W
Mechanicsburg, *Ohio, U.S.A.* **157 D13** 40 4N 83 33W
Mechanicsburg, *Pa., U.S.A.* **150 F8** 40 13N 77 1W
Mechanicsville, *U.S.A.* **156 C5** 41 54N 91 16W
Mechanicville, *U.S.A.* **151 D11** 42 54N 73 41W
Mechara, *Ethiopia* **107 F5** 8 36N 40 20 E
Mechelen, *Belgium* **24 C4** 51 2N 4 29 E
Mecheria, *Algeria* **111 B4** 33 35N 0 18W
Mechernich, *Germany* **30 E2** 50 35N 6 39 E
Mechetinskaya, *Russia* **61 G5** 46 45N 40 32 E
Mechra Bel Ksiri, *Morocco* **110 B3** 34 34N 5 57W
Mechra Benâbbou, *Morocco* **110 B3** 32 39N 7 48W
Mecidiye, *Turkey* **51 F10** 40 38N 26 32 E
Mecitözü, *Turkey* **100 B6** 40 32N 35 17 E
Mecklenburg, *Germany* **36 B6** 53 33N 11 40 E
Mecklenburg-Vorpommern □, *Germany* **30 B8** 53 45N 12 15 E
Mecklenburger Bucht, *Germany* **30 A7** 54 20N 11 40 E
Meconta, *Mozam.* **119 E4** 14 59 S 39 50 E
Mecsek, *Hungary* **52 D3** 46 10N 18 18 E
Meda, *Portugal* **42 E3** 40 57N 7 18W
Medak, *India* **94 E4** 18 1N 78 15 E
Medan, *Indonesia* **84 B1** 3 40N 98 38 E
Médanos, *Argentina* **176 A4** 38 50 S 62 42W
Medanosa, Pta., *Argentina* **176 C3** 48 8 S 66 0W
Medart, *U.S.A.* **152 E5** 30 5N 84 23W
Medaryville, *U.S.A.* **157 C10** 41 5N 86 55W
Medawachchiya, *Sri Lanka* **95 K5** 8 30N 80 30 E
Medchal, *India* **94 F4** 17 37N 78 29 E
Mede, *Italy* **44 C5** 45 6N 8 44 E
Médéa, *Algeria* **111 A5** 36 12N 2 50 E
Mededa, *Bos.-H.* **52 G4** 43 44N 19 10 E
Médégué, *Gabon* **114 B2** 0 37N 10 8 E
Medeiros Neto, *Brazil* **171 E3** 17 20 S 40 14W
Medel, Pic, *Switz.* **33 C7** 46 34N 8 55 E
Medellín, *Colombia* **168 B2** 6 15N 75 35W
Medelpad, *Sweden* **16 B10** 62 33N 16 30 E
Medemblik, *Neths.* **24 B5** 52 46N 5 8 E
Médenine, *Tunisia* **108 B2** 33 21N 10 30 E
Mederdra, *Mauritania* **112 B1** 17 0N 15 38W
Medford, *Mass., U.S.A.* **151 D13** 42 25N 71 7W
Medford, *Oreg., U.S.A.* **158 E2** 42 19N 122 52W
Medford, *Wis., U.S.A.* **154 C9** 45 9N 90 20W
Medgidia, *Romania* **53 F13** 44 15N 28 19 E
Medi, *Sudan* **107 F3** 5 4N 30 42 E
Media Agua, *Argentina* **174 C2** 31 58 S 68 25W
Media Luna, *Argentina* **174 C2** 34 45 S 66 44W
Medianeira, *Brazil* **175 B5** 25 17 S 54 5W
Mediapolis, *U.S.A.* **156 D5** 41 0N 91 10W
Mediaş, *Romania* **53 D9** 46 9N 24 22 E
Medicilândia, *Brazil* **169 D7** 3 33 S 53 8W
Medicina, *Italy* **45 D8** 44 28N 11 38 E
Medicine Bow, *U.S.A.* **158 F10** 41 54N 106 12W
Medicine Bow Pk., *U.S.A.* **158 F10** 41 21N 106 19W
Medicine Bow Ra., *U.S.A.* **158 F10** 41 10N 106 25W
Medicine Hat, *Canada* **143 D6** 50 0N 110 45W
Medicine Lake, *U.S.A.* **154 A2** 48 30N 104 30W
Medicine Lodge, *U.S.A.* **155 G5** 37 17N 98 35W
Medina = Al Madīnah, *Si. Arabia* **96 E3** 24 35N 39 52 E
Medina, *Brazil* **171 E3** 16 15 S 41 29W
Medina, *Colombia* **168 C3** 4 30N 73 21W
Medina, *Phil.* **81 G5** 8 55N 125 0 E
Medina, *N. Dak., U.S.A.* **154 B5** 46 54N 99 18W
Medina, *N.Y., U.S.A.* **150 C6** 43 13N 78 23W
Medina, *Ohio, U.S.A.* **150 E3** 41 8N 81 52W
Medina →, *U.S.A.* **155 L5** 29 16N 98 29W
Medina de Pomar, *Spain* **42 C7** 42 56N 3 29W
Medina de Ríoseco, *Spain* **42 D5** 41 53N 5 3W
Medina del Campo, *Spain* **42 D6** 41 18N 4 55W
Medina L., *U.S.A.* **155 L5** 29 32N 98 56W
Medina Sidonia, *Spain* **43 J5** 36 28N 5 57W
Medinaceli, *Spain* **40 D2** 41 12N 2 30W
Medinipur, *India* **93 H12** 22 25N 87 21 E
Mediterranean Sea, *Europe* **12 H7** 35 0N 15 0 E
Medjerda, O. →, *Tunisia* **108 A2** 37 7N 10 13 E
Mednogorsk, *Russia* **64 F6** 51 24N 57 37 E
Médoc, *France* **28 C3** 45 10N 0 50W
Medora, *U.S.A.* **157 F10** 38 49N 86 10W
Médouneu, *Gabon* **114 B2** 0 57N 10 47 E
Medulin, *Croatia* **45 D10** 44 49N 13 55 E
Medveđa, *Serbia, Yug.* **50 D5** 42 50N 21 32 E
Medvedevo, *Russia* **60 B8** 56 37N 47 47 E
Medveditsa →, *Tver, Russia* **58 D9** 57 5N 37 30 E
Medveditsa →, *Volgograd, Russia* **60 F6** 49 35N 42 41 E
Medvedok, *Russia* **60 B10** 57 20N 50 1 E
Medvezhi, Ostrava, *Russia* **67 B17** 71 0N 161 0 E
Medvezhyegorsk, *Russia* **56 B5** 63 0N 34 25 E
Medway □, *U.K.* **21 F8** 51 25N 0 32 E
Medway →, *U.K.* **21 F8** 51 27N 0 46 E
Medzev, *Slovak Rep.* **35 C13** 48 43N 20 55 E
Medzilaborce, *Slovak Rep.* **35 B14** 49 17N 21 52 E
Medžitlija, *Macedonia* **50 F5** 40 56N 21 26 E
Meekatharra, *Australia* **125 E2** 26 32 S 118 29 E
Meeker, *U.S.A.* **158 F10** 40 2N 107 55W
Meelpaeg Res., *Canada* **141 C8** 48 15N 56 33W
Meeniyan, *Australia* **129 E7** 38 35 S 146 0 E
Meersburg, *Germany* **31 H5** 47 41N 9 16 E
Meerut, *India* **92 E7** 29 1N 77 42 E
Meeteetse, *U.S.A.* **158 D9** 44 9N 108 52W
Mega, *Ethiopia* **107 G4** 3 57N 38 19 E
Megálo Khorío, *Greece* **49 E9** 36 27N 27 24 E
Megálo Petalí, *Greece* **48 D6** 38 0N 24 15 E
Megalópolis, *Greece* **48 D4** 37 25N 22 7 E
Meganísi Nisís, *Greece* **39 B2** 38 38N 20 46 E
Mégara, *Greece* **48 D5** 37 58N 23 22 E
Megasini, *India* **93 J12** 21 38N 86 21 E
Megdhova →, *Greece* **48 B3** 39 10N 21 45 E
Megève, *France* **29 C10** 45 51N 6 37 E
Meghalaya □, *India* **90 C3** 25 50N 91 0 E
Meghezez, *Ethiopia* **107 F4** 9 18N 39 26 E
Meghna →, *Bangla.* **90 D3** 22 50N 90 50 E
Mégiscane, L., *Canada* **140 C4** 48 35N 75 55W
Megiste, *Greece* **49 E11** 36 8N 29 34 E
Megra, *Russia* **58 B9** 60 11N 37 14 E
Mehadia, *Romania* **52 F7** 44 56N 22 23 E
Mehaïguene, O. →, *Algeria* **111 B5** 32 15N 2 59 E
Meharry, Mt., *Australia* **124 D2** 22 59 S 118 35 E
Mehedeby, *Sweden* **16 D11** 60 27N 17 25 E
Mehedinţi □, *Romania* **52 F7** 44 40N 22 45 E
Meheisa, *Sudan* **106 D3** 19 38N 32 57 E
Mehekar, *India* **94 D3** 20 9N 76 34 E
Mehlville, *U.S.A.* **154 F9** 38 30N 90 19W
Mehndawal, *India* **93 F10** 26 58N 83 5 E
Mehr Jān, *Iran* **97 C7** 33 50N 55 6 E
Mehrābād, *Iran* **101 D12** 36 53N 47 55 E
Mehrān, *Iran* **101 F12** 33 7N 46 10 E
Mehrīz, *Iran* **97 D7** 31 35N 54 28 E
Mehun-sur-Yèvre, *France* **27 E9** 47 10N 2 13 E
Mei Jiang →, *China* **77 E11** 24 25N 116 35 E
Mei Xian, *China* **74 G4** 34 18N 107 55 E
Meia Ponte →, *Brazil* **171 E2** 18 32 S 49 36W
Meicheng, *China* **77 C12** 29 29N 119 16 E
Meichengzhen, *China* **77 C8** 28 9N 111 40 E
Meichuan, *China* **77 B10** 30 8N 115 31 E
Meiganga, *Cameroon* **114 A2** 6 30N 14 25 E
Meigs, *U.S.A.* **152 D5** 31 4N 84 6W
Meigu, *China* **76 C4** 28 16N 103 20 E
Meiktila, *Burma* **90 E5** 20 53N 95 54 E
Meilen, *Switz.* **33 B7** 47 16N 8 39 E
Meinerzhagen, *Germany* **30 D3** 51 6N 7 38 E
Meiningen, *Germany* **30 E6** 50 34N 10 25 E
Meio →, *Brazil* **171 D3** 13 36 S 44 7W
Meira, Serra de, *Spain* **42 B3** 43 15N 7 15W
Meiringen, *Switz.* **32 C6** 46 43N 8 12 E
Meishan, *China* **76 B4** 30 3N 103 23 E
Meissen, *Germany* **30 D9** 51 9N 13 29 E
Meissner, *Germany* **30 D5** 51 14N 9 50 E
Meitan, *China* **76 D6** 27 45N 107 29 E
Meizhou, *China* **77 E11** 24 16N 116 6 E
Meja, *India* **93 G10** 25 9N 82 7 E
Mejillones, *Chile* **174 A1** 23 10 S 70 30W
Mékambo, *Gabon* **114 B2** 1 2N 13 50 E
Mekdela, *Ethiopia* **107 E4** 11 24N 39 10 E
Mekele, *Ethiopia* **107 E4** 13 33N 39 30 E
Mekerghene, Sebkra, *Algeria* **111 C5** 26 21N 1 30 E
Mekhtar, *Pakistan* **91 C3** 30 30N 69 15 E
Meknès, *Morocco* **110 B3** 33 57N 5 33W
Meko, *Nigeria* **113 D5** 7 27N 2 52 E
Mekong →, *Asia* **87 H6** 9 30N 106 15 E
Mekongga, *Indonesia* **82 B2** 3 39 S 121 15 E
Mekoryuk, *U.S.A.* **144 F6** 60 23N 166 11W
Mekrou →, *Benin* **113 C5** 12 25N 2 50 E
Mekvari = Kür →, *Azerbaijan* **101 C13** 39 29N 49 15 E
Mel, *Italy* **45 B9** 46 4N 12 5 E
Melagiri Hills, *India* **95 H3** 12 20N 77 30 E
Melah, Oued el →, *Algeria* **111 C6** 32 20N 2 28 E
Melah, Sebkhet el, *Algeria* **111 C4** 29 20N 1 30W
Melaka, *Malaysia* **87 L4** 2 15N 102 15 E
Melaka □, *Malaysia* **84 B2** 2 15N 102 15 E
Melalap, *Malaysia* **78 C5** 5 10N 116 5 E
Mélambes, *Greece* **39 E5** 35 8N 24 40 E
Melanesia, *Pac. Oc.* **134 H7** 4 0 S 155 0 E
Melapalaiyam, *India* **95 K3** 8 39N 77 44 E
Melawi →, *Indonesia* **85 B4** 0 5N 111 29 E
Melaya, *Indonesia* **79 J17** 8 17 S 114 30 E
Melbourne, *Australia* **129 D6** 37 50 S 145 0 E
Melbourne, *Fla., U.S.A.* **149 L5** 28 5N 80 37W
Melbourne, *Iowa, U.S.A.* **156 C3** 41 57N 93 6W
Melcher-Dallas, *U.S.A.* **156 C3** 41 14N 93 15W
Melchor Múzquiz, *Mexico* **162 B4** 27 50N 101 30W
Melchor Ocampo, *Mexico* **162 C4** 24 52N 101 40W
Meldal, *Norway* **18 A6** 63 3N 9 44 E
Méldola, *Italy* **45 D9** 44 7N 12 5 E
Meldorf, *Germany* **30 A5** 54 5N 9 5 E
Mélé, *C.A.R.* **114 A4** 9 46N 21 33 E
Mele B., *Vanuatu* **133 G6** 17 44 S 168 14 E

Meleden, Somali Rep. 120 B3 10 25N 49 51 E
Melegnano, Italy 44 C6 45 21N 9 19 E
Meleizem, Mauritania 110 D2 22 19N 11 24W
Melenci, Serbia, Yug. 52 E5 45 32N 20 20 E
Melenki, Russia 60 C5 55 20N 41 37 E
Meleuz, Russia 64 E6 52 58N 55 55 E
Mélèzes →, Canada 140 A5 57 40N 69 29W
Melfi, Chad 109 F3 11 0N 17 59 E
Melfi, Italy 47 B8 41 0N 15 39 E
Melfort, Canada 143 C8 52 50N 104 37W
Melfort, Zimbabwe 119 F3 18 0S 31 25 E
Melgaço, Portugal 42 C2 42 7N 8 15W
Melgar de Fernamental, Spain 42 C6 42 27N 4 17W
Melgraseyri, Iceland 11 A4 66 1N 22 27W
Melhus, Norway 14 E14 63 17N 10 18 E
Melide, Spain 42 C2 42 55N 8 1W
Melide, Switz. 33 E7 45 57N 8 57 E
Meligalá, Greece 48 D3 37 15N 21 59 E
Melilla, N. Afr. 111 A4 35 21N 2 57W
Melilli, Italy 47 E8 37 11N 15 7 E
Melipilla, Chile 174 C1 33 42S 71 15W
Mélissa, Ákra, Greece 49 E5 35 6N 24 33 E
Mélissa Óros, Greece 49 D8 37 32N 26 4 E
Mélissani Cave, Greece 39 C2 38 15N 20 38 E
Melita, Canada 143 D8 49 15N 101 0W
Mélito di Porto Salvo, Italy 47 E8 37 55N 15 47 E
Melitopol, Ukraine 59 J8 46 50N 35 22 E
Melk, Austria 34 C8 48 13N 15 20 E
Mellan Fryken, Sweden 16 E7 59 45N 13 10 E
Mellansel, Sweden 14 E18 63 25N 18 17 E
Mellbystrand, Sweden 17 H6 56 30N 12 56 E
Melle, France 28 B3 46 14N 0 10W
Melle, Germany 30 C4 52 12N 8 20 E
Mellègue, O. →, Tunisia 108 A1 36 36N 9 14 E
Mellen, U.S.A. 154 B9 46 20N 90 40W
Mellerud, Sweden 17 F6 58 41N 12 28 E
Mellette, U.S.A. 154 C5 45 9N 98 30W
Mellid = Melide, Spain 42 C2 42 55N 8 1W
Mellieha, Malta 38 F7 35 57N 14 22 E
Mellieha Bay, Malta 38 F7 35 59N 14 22 E
Mellit, Sudan 107 E2 14 7N 25 34 E
Mellizo Sur, Cerro, Chile 176 C2 48 33S 73 10W
Mellrichstadt, Germany 30 E6 50 25N 10 17 E
Melnik, Bulgaria 50 E7 41 30N 23 25 E
Mělník, Czech Rep. 34 A7 50 22N 14 23 E
Melo, Uruguay 175 C5 32 20S 54 10W
Melolo, Indonesia 82 C2 9 53S 120 40 E
Melouprey, Cambodia 86 F5 13 48N 105 16 E
Melrhir, Chott, Algeria 111 B6 34 13N 6 30 E
Melrose, Australia 129 B7 32 42S 146 57 E
Melrose, U.K. 22 F6 55 36N 2 43W
Melrose, Minn., U.S.A. 154 C7 45 40N 94 49W
Melrose, N. Mex., U.S.A. 155 H3 34 26N 103 38W
Mels, Switz. 33 B8 47 3N 9 25 E
Melsisi, Vanuatu 133 E6 15 46S 168 10 E
Melstone, U.S.A. 158 C10 46 36N 107 52W
Melsungen, Germany 30 D5 51 7N 9 32 E
Melton, Australia 128 D6 37 41S 144 35 E
Melton Mowbray, U.K. 20 E7 52 47N 0 54W
Melun, France 27 D9 48 32N 2 39 E
Melur, India 95 J4 10 2N 78 23 E
Melut, Sudan 107 E3 10 30N 32 13 E
Melville, Canada 143 C8 50 55N 102 50W
Melville, C., Australia 126 A3 14 11S 144 30 E
Melville, C., Phil. 81 H1 7 49N 117 0 E
Melville, L., Canada 141 B8 53 30N 60 0W
Melville B., Australia 126 A2 12 0S 136 45 E
Melville B., Greenland 10 B4 75 30N 63 0W
Melville I., Australia 124 B5 11 30S 131 0 E
Melville I., Canada 6 B2 75 30N 112 0W
Melville Pen., Canada 139 B11 68 0N 84 0W
Mélykút, Hungary 52 D4 46 11N 19 25 E
Memaliaj, Albania 50 F3 40 25N 19 56 E
Memba, Mozam. 119 E5 14 11S 40 30 E
Memboro, Indonesia 82 C1 9 30S 119 30 E
Membrilla, Spain 43 G7 38 59N 3 21W
Memel = Klaipėda, Lithuania 15 J19 55 43N 21 10 E
Memel, S. Africa 117 D4 27 38S 29 36 E
Memmingen, Germany 31 H6 47 58N 10 10 E
Mempawah, Indonesia 85 B3 0 30N 109 5 E
Memphis, Egypt 106 J7 29 52N 31 12 E
Memphis, Mich., U.S.A. 150 D2 42 54N 82 46W
Memphis, Mo., U.S.A. 156 D4 40 28N 92 10W
Memphis, Tenn., U.S.A. 155 H10 35 8N 90 3W
Memphis, Tex., U.S.A. 155 H4 34 44N 100 33W
Memphremagog, L., U.S.A. 151 B12 45 0N 72 12W
Mena, Ukraine 59 G7 51 31N 32 13 E
Mena, U.S.A. 155 H7 34 35N 94 15W
Mena →, Ethiopia 107 F5 5 40N 40 50 E
Menai Strait, U.K. 20 D3 53 11N 4 13W
Ménaka, Mali 113 B5 15 59N 2 18 E
Menan = Chao Phraya →, Thailand 86 F3 13 32N 100 36 E
Menarandra →, Madag. 117 D7 25 17S 44 30 E
Menard, U.S.A. 155 K5 30 55N 99 47W
Menate, Indonesia 85 C4 0 12S 113 3 E
Menawashei, Sudan 107 E1 12 41N 24 59 E
Mendawai →, Indonesia 85 C4 3 30S 113 0 E
Mende, France 28 D7 44 31N 3 30 E
Mendebo, Ethiopia 107 F4 7 0N 39 22 E
Menden, Germany 30 D3 51 26N 7 47 E
Mendenhall, C., U.S.A. 144 G6 59 45N 166 10W
Menderes, Turkey 49 C9 38 14N 27 8 E
Mendez, Mexico 163 B5 25 7N 98 34W
Mendhar, India 93 C6 33 35N 74 10 E
Mendi, Ethiopia 107 F4 9 47N 35 4 E
Mendi, Papua N. G. 132 D2 6 11S 143 39 E
Mendip Hills, U.K. 21 F5 51 17N 2 40W
Mendocino, U.S.A. 158 G2 39 19N 123 48W
Mendocino, C., U.S.A. 158 F1 40 26N 124 25W
Mendon, U.S.A. 157 B11 42 0N 85 27W
Mendooran, Australia 129 A8 31 50S 149 6 E
Mendota, Calif., U.S.A. 160 J6 36 45N 120 23W
Mendota, Ill., U.S.A. 156 C7 41 33N 89 7W
Mendoyo, Indonesia 79 J17 8 23S 114 42 E
Mendoza, Argentina 174 C2 32 50S 68 52W
Mendoza □, Argentina 174 C2 33 0S 69 0W
Mendrisio, Switz. 33 E7 45 52N 8 59 E
Mene Grande, Venezuela 168 B3 9 49N 70 56W
Menemen, Turkey 49 C9 38 34N 27 3 E
Menen, Belgium 24 D3 50 47N 3 7 E
Menéndez, L., Argentina 176 B2 42 40S 71 51W
Menfi, Italy 46 E5 37 36N 12 58 E
Mengdingjie, China 76 F2 23 31N 98 58 E
Mengeš, Slovenia 45 B11 46 10N 14 35 E
Menggala, Indonesia 84 C3 4 30S 105 15 E
Menghai, China 76 G3 21 49N 100 55 E
Mengíbar, Spain 43 H7 37 58N 3 48W
Mengjin, China 74 G7 34 55N 112 45 E
Mengla, China 76 G3 21 20N 101 25 E
Menglian, China 76 F2 22 21N 99 27 E
Mengoub, Algeria 110 C3 29 49N 5 26W
Mengshan, China 77 E8 24 14N 110 55 E
Mengyin, China 75 G9 35 40N 117 58 E
Mengzhe, China 76 F3 22 2N 100 15 E
Mengzi, China 76 F4 23 20N 103 22 E
Menihek, Canada 141 B6 54 28N 56 36W
Menihek L., Canada 141 B6 54 0N 67 0W
Menin = Menen, Belgium 24 D3 50 47N 3 7 E
Menindee, Australia 128 B5 32 20S 142 25 E
Menindee L., Australia 128 B5 32 20S 142 25 E
Meningie, Australia 128 C3 35 50S 139 18 E
Menjangan, Pulau, Indonesia 79 J17 8 7S 114 31 E
Menkrour, Algeria 111 C6 26 27N 8 9 E
Menlo Park, U.S.A. 160 H4 37 27N 122 12W
Menominee, U.S.A. 148 C2 45 6N 87 37W
Menominee →, U.S.A. 148 C2 45 6N 87 36W
Menomonee Falls, U.S.A. 157 A8 43 11N 88 7W
Menomonie, U.S.A. 154 C9 44 53N 91 55W
Menongue, Angola 115 E3 14 48S 17 52 E
Menorca, Spain 38 B5 40 0N 4 0 E
Mentakab, Malaysia 87 L4 3 29N 102 21 E
Mentasta Lake, U.S.A. 144 E12 62 55N 143 45W
Mentawai, Kepulauan, Indonesia 84 C1 2 0S 99 0 E
Menton, France 29 E11 43 50N 7 29 E
Mentone, U.S.A. 157 C10 41 10N 86 2W
Mentor, U.S.A. 150 E3 41 40N 81 21W
Menyamya, Papua N. G. 132 D3 7 10S 145 59 E
Menzel-Bourguiba, Tunisia 108 A1 37 9N 9 49 E
Menzel-Chaker, Tunisia 108 B2 35 0N 10 26 E
Menzel-Temime, Tunisia 108 A2 36 46N 11 0 E
Menzelinsk, Russia 64 D4 55 47N 53 11 E
Menzies, Australia 125 E3 29 40S 121 2 E
Meob B., Namibia 116 B2 24 25S 14 34 E
Me'ona, Israel 103 B4 33 1N 35 15 E
Meoqui, Mexico 162 B3 28 17N 105 29W
Mepaco, Mozam. 119 F3 15 57S 30 48 E
Meppel, Neths. 24 B6 52 42N 6 12 E
Meppen, Germany 30 C3 52 42N 7 17 E
Mequinenza, Spain 40 D5 41 22N 0 17 E
Mequinenza, Embalse de, Spain 40 D5 41 25N 0 15 E
Mequon, U.S.A. 157 A9 43 14N 87 59W
Mer, France 26 E8 47 42N 1 30 E
Merabéllou, Kólpos, Greece 39 E6 35 10N 25 50 E
Merai, Papua N. G. 132 C7 4 52S 152 19 E
Merak, Indonesia 79 F12 6 10N 106 26 E
Meråker, Norway 18 A8 63 25N 11 46 E
Meramangye, L., Australia 125 E5 28 25S 132 13 E
Meramec →, U.S.A. 156 F6 38 24N 90 21W
Meran = Merano, Italy 45 B8 46 40N 11 9 E
Merano, Italy 45 B8 46 40N 11 9 E
Merate, Italy 44 C6 45 42N 9 25 E
Merauke, Indonesia 83 C6 8 29S 140 24 E
Merauke →, Indonesia 83 C6 8 30S 140 24 E
Merbabu, Indonesia 85 D4 7 30S 110 40 E
Merbein, Australia 128 C5 34 10S 142 2 E
Merbuk, Gunung, Indonesia 79 J17 8 13S 114 39 E
Merca, Somali Rep. 120 D2 1 48N 44 50 E
Mercato Saraceno, Italy 45 E9 43 57N 12 12 E
Merced, U.S.A. 160 H6 37 18N 120 29W
Merced →, U.S.A. 160 H6 37 21N 120 59W
Merced Pk., U.S.A. 160 H7 37 36N 119 24W
Mercedes, Buenos Aires, Argentina 174 C4 34 40S 59 30W
Mercedes, Corrientes, Argentina 174 B4 29 10S 58 5W
Mercedes, San Luis, Argentina 174 C2 33 40S 65 21W
Mercedes, Phil. 80 D4 14 7N 123 1 E
Mercedes, Uruguay 174 C4 33 12S 58 0W
Mercedes, U.S.A. 155 M6 26 9N 97 55W
Merceditas, Chile 174 B1 28 20S 70 35W
Mercer, N.Z. 130 D4 37 16S 175 5 E
Mercer, Mo., U.S.A. 156 D3 40 31N 93 32W
Mercer, Pa., U.S.A. 150 E4 41 14N 80 15W
Mercer Island, U.S.A. 160 C4 47 35N 122 15W
Mercier, Bolivia 172 C4 10 42S 68 5W
Mercury, U.S.A. 161 J11 36 40N 115 58W
Mercury B., N.Z. 130 C4 36 48S 175 45 E
Mercury Is., N.Z. 130 C4 36 37S 175 52 E
Mercy C., Canada 139 B13 65 0N 63 30W
Merdrignac, France 26 D4 48 11N 2 27W
Mere, U.K. 21 F5 51 6N 2 16W
Mere Lava, Vanuatu 133 D6 14 25S 168 3 E
Meredith, Australia 128 D6 37 49S 144 5 E
Meredith, C., Falk. Is. 9 f 52 15S 60 40W
Meredith, L., U.S.A. 155 H4 35 43N 101 33W
Meredosia, U.S.A. 156 E6 39 50N 90 34W
Merefa, Ukraine 59 H9 49 48N 36 3 E
Meregh, Somali Rep. 120 D3 3 46N 47 18 E
Merei, Romania 53 E11 45 7N 26 43 E
Merga = Nukheila, Sudan 106 D2 19 1N 26 21 E
Mergui, Burma 86 F2 12 26N 98 34 E
Mergui Arch. = Myeik Kyunzu, Burma 87 G1 11 30N 97 30 E
Meribah, Australia 128 C4 34 43S 140 51 E
Meriç, Turkey 51 E10 41 11N 26 25 E
Meriç →, Turkey 51 F10 40 52N 26 12 E
Mérida, Mexico 163 C7 20 58N 89 37W
Merida, Phil. 81 F5 10 55N 124 32 E
Mérida, Spain 43 G4 38 55N 6 25W
Mérida, Venezuela 168 B3 8 24N 71 8W
Mérida □, Venezuela 168 B3 8 30N 71 10W
Mérida, Cord. de, Venezuela 168 B3 9 0N 71 0W
Meriden, U.K. 21 E6 52 26N 1 38W
Meriden, U.S.A. 151 E12 41 32N 72 48W
Meridian, Calif., U.S.A. 160 F5 39 9N 121 55W
Meridian, Ga., U.S.A. 152 D8 31 27N 81 23W
Meridian, Idaho, U.S.A. 158 E5 43 37N 116 24W
Meridian, Miss., U.S.A. 153 J1 32 22N 88 42W
Mérignac, France 28 D3 44 51N 0 39W
Merimbula, Australia 129 D8 36 53S 149 54 E
Mérinaghène, Senegal 112 B1 15 57N 15 55W
Merinda, Australia 126 C4 20 2S 148 11 E
Mering, Germany 31 G6 48 16N 10 59 E
Meringa, Nigeria 113 C7 10 44N 12 9 E
Meringur, Australia 128 C4 34 20S 141 19 E
Merir, Pac. Oc. 79 D8 4 10N 132 30 E
Merirumã, Brazil 169 C7 1 15N 54 50W
Merke, Kazakstan 65 B6 42 52N 73 11 E
Merkel, U.S.A. 155 J5 32 28N 100 1W
Mermaid Reef, Australia 124 C2 17 6S 119 36 E
Meroe, India 95 L11 7 33N 93 33 E
Merowe, Sudan 106 D3 18 29N 31 46 E
Merredin, Australia 125 F2 31 28S 118 18 E
Merrick, U.K. 22 F4 55 8N 4 28W
Merrickville, Canada 151 B9 44 55N 75 50W
Merrill, Oreg., U.S.A. 158 E3 42 1N 121 36W
Merrill, Wis., U.S.A. 154 C10 45 11N 89 41W
Merrillville, U.S.A. 157 C9 41 29N 87 20W
Merrimack →, U.S.A. 151 D14 42 49N 70 49W
Merriman, U.S.A. 154 D4 42 55N 101 42W
Merritt, Canada 142 C4 50 10N 120 45W
Merritt Island, U.S.A. 153 G9 28 21N 80 42W
Merriwa, Australia 129 B9 32 6S 150 22 E
Merriwagga, Australia 129 B6 33 47S 145 43 E
Merry I., Canada 140 A4 55 29N 77 31W
Merrygoen, Australia 129 A8 31 51S 149 12 E
Merryville, U.S.A. 155 K8 30 45N 93 33W
Mersa Fatma, Eritrea 107 E5 14 57N 40 17 E
Mersch, Lux. 24 E6 49 44N 6 7 E
Merse →, Italy 45 E8 43 5N 11 22 E
Mersea I., U.K. 21 F8 51 47N 0 58 E
Merseburg, Germany 30 D7 51 22N 11 59 E
Mersey →, U.K. 20 D4 53 25N 3 1W
Merseyside □, U.K. 20 D4 53 31N 3 2W
Mersin, Turkey 100 D6 36 51N 34 36 E
Mersing, Malaysia 87 L4 2 25N 103 50 E
Merta, India 92 F6 26 39N 74 4 E
Merta Road, India 92 F5 26 43N 73 55 E
Merthyr Tydfil, U.K. 21 F4 51 45N 3 22W
Merthyr Tydfil □, U.K. 21 F4 51 46N 3 21W
Mértola, Portugal 43 H3 37 40N 7 40W
Mertzon, U.S.A. 155 K4 31 16N 100 49W
Méru, France 27 C9 49 13N 2 8 E
Meru, Kenya 118 B4 0 3N 37 40 E
Meru, Tanzania 118 C4 3 15S 36 46 E
Meru Nat. Park, Kenya 118 B4 0 5N 38 10 E
Merville, France 27 B9 50 38N 2 38 E
Méry-sur-Seine, France 27 D10 48 31N 3 54 E
Merzifon, Turkey 100 B6 40 53N 35 32 E
Merzig, Germany 31 F2 49 26N 6 38 E
Merzouga, Erg Tin, Algeria 111 D7 24 0N 11 4 E
Mesa, U.S.A. 159 K8 33 25N 111 50W
Mesa Verde Nat. Park, U.S.A. 159 H9 37 11N 108 29W
Mesach Mellet, Libya 108 D2 24 30N 11 30 E
Mesagne, Italy 47 B10 40 34N 17 48 E
Mesanagrós, Greece 38 E11 36 1N 27 49 E
Mesaoría, Cyprus 39 E9 35 12N 33 14 E
Mesarás, Kólpos, Greece 39 E5 35 6N 24 47 E
Meschede, Germany 30 D4 51 20N 8 18 E
Mescit, Turkey 101 B9 40 21N 41 11 E
Mesfinto, Ethiopia 107 E4 13 20N 37 22 E
Mesgouez, L., Canada 140 B5 51 20N 75 0W
Meshchovsk, Russia 58 E8 54 22N 35 17 E
Meshed = Mashhad, Iran 97 B8 36 20N 59 35 E
Meshoppen, U.S.A. 151 E8 41 36N 76 3W
Meshra er Req, Sudan 107 F2 8 25N 29 18 E
Mesilinka →, Canada 142 B4 56 6N 124 30W
Mesilla, U.S.A. 159 K10 32 16N 106 48W
Meslay-du-Maine, France 26 E6 47 58N 0 33W
Mesocco, Switz. 33 D8 46 23N 9 12 E
Mesolóngion, Greece 48 C3 38 21N 21 28 E
Mesopotamia = Al Jazirah, Iraq 101 E10 33 30N 44 0 E
Mesopotamia, U.S.A. 150 E4 41 27N 80 57W
Mesopótamon, Greece 48 B2 39 14N 20 32 E
Mesoraca, Italy 47 C9 39 5N 16 48 E
Mésou Volímais = Volímai, Greece 39 D2 37 52N 20 39 E
Mesquite, U.S.A. 159 H6 36 47N 114 6W
Messaad, Algeria 111 B5 34 8N 3 30 E
Messac, France 26 E5 47 49N 1 50W
Messalo →, Mozam. 119 E4 12 25S 39 15 E
Méssaména, Cameroon 113 E7 3 48N 12 49 E
Messeue, Greece 48 D3 37 12N 21 58 E
Messier, Canal, Chile 176 C2 48 20S 74 33W
Messina, Italy 47 D8 38 11N 15 34 E
Messina, S. Africa 117 C5 22 20S 30 5 E
Messina, Str. di, Italy 47 D8 38 15N 15 35 E
Messíni, Greece 48 D4 37 4N 22 1 E
Messínia □, Greece 48 D3 37 10N 22 0 E
Messiniakós Kólpos, Greece 48 E4 36 45N 22 5 E
Messkirch, Germany 31 H5 47 59N 9 7 E
Messonghi, Greece 38 C9 39 29N 19 56 E
Mesta →, Bulgaria 50 E7 40 54N 24 49 E
Mestá, Ákra, Greece 49 C7 38 16N 25 53 E
Mestanza, Spain 43 G6 38 35N 4 4W
Mestersvig, Greenland 10 C8 72 10N 23 40W
Mestre, Italy 45 C9 45 29N 12 15 E
Mestre, Espigão, Brazil 171 D2 12 30S 46 10W
Mesudiye, Turkey 100 B7 40 28N 37 46 E
Meta, U.S.A. 156 F4 38 19N 92 10W
Meta □, Colombia 168 C3 3 30N 73 0W
Meta →, S. Amer. 168 B4 6 12N 67 28W
Meta Incognita Peninsula, Canada 139 B13 62 40N 68 0W
Metabetchouan, Canada 141 C5 48 26N 71 52W
Metairie, U.S.A. 155 L9 29 58N 90 10W
Metalici, Munţii, Romania 52 D7 46 15N 22 50 E
Metaline Falls, U.S.A. 158 B5 48 52N 117 22W
Metallifere, Colline, Italy 44 E8 43 10N 11 0 E
Metamora, U.S.A. 156 D7 40 47N 89 22W
Metán, Argentina 174 B3 25 30S 65 0W
Metangula, Mozam. 119 E3 12 40S 34 50 E
Metauro →, Italy 45 E10 43 50N 13 3 E
Metcalf, U.S.A. 152 E6 30 43N 83 59W
Metema, Ethiopia 107 E4 12 56N 36 13 E
Metengobalame, Mozam. 119 E3 14 49S 34 30 E
Méthana, Greece 48 D5 37 35N 23 23 E
Methóni, Greece 48 E3 36 49N 21 42 E
Methven, N.Z. 131 D6 43 38S 171 40 E
Metil, Mozam. 119 F4 16 24S 39 0 E
Metkovets, Bulgaria 50 C7 43 37N 23 10 E
Metković, Croatia 45 E14 43 6N 17 39 E
Metlakatla, U.S.A. 144 J15 55 8N 131 35W
Metlaoui, Tunisia 108 B1 34 24N 8 24 E
Metlik, Papua N. G. 132 C7 4 46S 152 55 E
Metlika, Slovenia 45 C12 45 40N 15 20 E
Metro, Indonesia 84 D3 5 5S 105 20 E
Metropolis, U.S.A. 155 G10 37 9N 88 44W
Métsovon, Greece 48 B3 39 48N 21 12 E
Metter, U.S.A. 152 C7 32 24N 82 3W
Mettuppalaiyam, India 95 J3 11 18N 76 59 E
Mettur, India 95 J3 11 48N 77 47 E
Metu, Ethiopia 107 F4 8 18N 35 35 E
Metz, France 27 C13 49 8N 6 10 E
Metzingen, Germany 31 G5 48 31N 9 17 E
Meulaboh, Indonesia 84 B1 4 11N 96 3 E
Meung-sur-Loire, France 27 E8 47 50N 1 40 E
Meurcourt, France 32 A2 47 46N 6 14 E
Meureudu, Indonesia 84 A1 5 19N 96 10 E
Meurthe →, France 27 D13 48 47N 6 9 E
Meurthe-et-Moselle □, France 27 D13 48 52N 6 0 E
Meuse □, France 27 C12 49 8N 5 25 E
Meuse →, Europe 24 D5 50 45N 5 41 E
Meuselwitz, Germany 30 D8 51 2N 12 17 E
Meutapok, Mt., Malaysia 85 A5 5 40N 117 0 E
Mexia, U.S.A. 155 K6 31 41N 96 29W
Mexiana, I., Brazil 170 A2 0 0 49 30W
Mexicali, Mexico 161 N11 32 40N 115 30W
Mexican Plateau, Mexico 136 G9 25 0N 104 0W
Mexican Water, U.S.A. 159 H9 36 57N 109 32W
México, Mexico 163 D5 19 20N 99 10W
Mexico, Maine, U.S.A. 151 B14 44 34N 70 33W
Mexico, Mo., U.S.A. 156 E5 39 10N 91 53W
Mexico, N.Y., U.S.A. 151 C8 43 28N 76 18W
México □, Mexico 163 D5 19 20N 99 10W
Mexico ■, Cent. Amer. 162 C4 25 0N 105 0W
Mexico, G. of, Cent. Amer. 163 C7 25 0N 90 0W
Mexico B., U.S.A. 151 C8 43 35N 76 20W
Mexico Beach, U.S.A. 152 F4 29 57N 85 25W
Meydān-e Naftūn, Iran 97 D6 31 56N 49 18 E
Meydani, Ra's-e, Iran 97 E8 25 24N 59 6 E
Meyenburg, Germany 30 B8 53 18N 12 14 E
Meyers Chuck, U.S.A. 144 J14 55 45N 132 15W
Meymac, France 28 C6 45 32N 2 10 E
Meymaneh, Afghan. 91 B2 35 53N 64 38 E
Meyo, Cameroon 114 B2 2 50N 11 1 E
Meyrueis, France 28 D7 44 12N 3 27 E
Meyssac, France 28 C5 45 3N 1 40 E
Meyzieu, France 29 C8 45 46N 4 59 E
Mezdra, Bulgaria 50 C7 43 12N 23 42 E
Mèze, France 28 E7 43 27N 3 36 E
Mezen, Russia 56 A7 65 50N 44 20 E
Mezen →, Russia 56 A7 65 44N 44 22 E
Mézenc, Mt., France 29 D8 44 54N 4 11 E
Mezeş, Munţii, Romania 52 C8 47 5N 23 5 E
Mezha →, Russia 58 E6 55 44N 31 33 E
Mezhdurechenskiy, Russia 66 D7 59 36N 65 56 E
Mézidon-Canon, France 26 C6 49 5N 0 1W
Mézières-en-Brenne, France 28 B5 46 49N 1 13 E
Mézilhac, France 29 D8 44 49N 4 21 E
Mézin, France 28 D4 44 4N 0 16 E
Mezőberény, Hungary 52 D6 46 49N 21 3 E
Mezőfalva, Hungary 52 D3 46 55N 18 49 E
Mezőhegyes, Hungary 52 D5 46 19N 20 49 E
Mezőkövácsháza, Hungary 52 D5 46 25N 20 57 E
Mezőkövesd, Hungary 52 C5 47 49N 20 35 E
Mézos, France 28 D2 44 5N 1 10W
Mezőtúr, Hungary 52 C5 47 1N 20 41 E
Mezquital, Mexico 162 C4 23 29N 104 23W
Mezzolombardo, Italy 44 B8 46 13N 11 5 E
Mfolozi →, S. Africa 117 D5 28 25S 32 26 E
Mgarr, Malta 38 F7 35 55N 14 22 E
Mgarr, Gozo, Malta 38 E7 36 2N 14 18 E
Mgeta, Tanzania 119 D4 8 22S 36 6 E
Mglin, Russia 59 F7 53 2N 32 50 E
Mhlaba Hills, Zimbabwe 119 F3 18 30S 30 30 E
Mhow, India 92 H6 22 33N 75 50 E
Mi-Shima, Japan 72 C3 34 46N 131 9 E
Miagao, Phil. 81 F4 10 39N 122 14 E
Miahuatlán, Mexico 163 D5 16 21N 96 36W
Miajadas, Spain 43 F5 39 9N 5 54W
Miami, Fla., U.S.A. 149 N5 25 47N 80 11W
Miami, Okla., U.S.A. 155 G7 36 53N 94 53W
Miami, Tex., U.S.A. 155 H4 35 42N 100 38W
Miami Beach, U.S.A. 149 N5 25 47N 80 8W
Miami Canal, U.S.A. 153 J9 26 30N 80 45W
Miami Shores, U.S.A. 153 K9 25 52N 80 12W
Miami Springs, U.S.A. 153 K9 25 49N 80 17W
Miamisburg, U.S.A. 157 E12 39 38N 84 17W
Mian Xian, China 74 H4 33 10N 106 32 E
Mianchi, China 74 G6 34 48N 111 48 E
Mīāndarreh, Iran 97 C7 35 37N 53 39 E
Mīāndowāb, Iran 101 D12 37 0N 46 5 E
Miandrivazo, Madag. 117 B8 19 31S 45 29 E
Mīāneh, Iran 101 D12 37 30N 47 40 E
Mianning, China 76 C4 28 32N 102 9 E
Mianwali, Pakistan 91 B3 32 38N 71 28 E
Mianyang, China 76 B5 31 22N 104 47 E
Mianzhu, China 76 B5 31 22N 104 7 E
Miaoli, Taiwan 77 E13 24 37N 120 49 E
Miarinarivo, Antananarivo, Madag. 117 B8 18 57S 46 55 E
Miarinarivo, Toamasina, Madag. 117 B8 16 38S 48 15 E
Miarivaratra, Madag. 117 C8 20 13S 47 31 E
Miass, Russia 64 D8 54 59N 60 6 E
Miasteczko Krajeńskie, Poland 55 E4 53 7N 17 1 E
Miastko, Poland 54 E3 54 0N 16 58 E
Mica, S. Africa 117 C5 24 10S 30 48 E
Micanopy, U.S.A. 153 F7 29 30N 82 17W
Micăsasa, Romania 53 D9 46 7N 24 7 E
Micco, U.S.A. 153 H9 27 53N 80 30W
Miccosukee, U.S.A. 152 E5 30 36N 84 3W
Miccosukee, L., U.S.A. 152 E6 30 33N 83 53W
Michael, Mt., Papua N. G. 132 D3 6 27S 145 22 E
Michalovce, Slovak Rep. 35 C14 48 47N 21 58 E
Michigan □, U.S.A. 148 C3 44 0N 85 0W
Michigan, L., U.S.A. 157 B9 44 0N 87 0W
Michigan Center, U.S.A. 157 B12 42 14N 84 20W
Michigan City, U.S.A. 157 C10 41 43N 86 54W
Michika, Nigeria 113 C7 10 36N 13 23 E
Michipicoten I., Canada 140 C2 47 40N 85 40W
Michoacan □, Mexico 162 D4 19 0N 102 0W
Michurin, Bulgaria 51 D11 42 9N 27 51 E
Michurinsk, Russia 60 D5 52 58N 40 27 E
Mico, Pta., Nic. 164 D3 12 0N 83 30W
Miconje, Angola 115 C2 4 26S 12 48 E
Micoud, St. Lucia 165 f 13 49N 60 54W
Micronesia, Pac. Oc. 134 G7 11 0N 160 0 E
Micronesia, Federated States of ■, Pac. Oc. 134 G7 9 0N 150 0 E
Mid-Indian Ridge, Ind. Oc. 121 H6 30 0S 75 0 E
Midai, Indonesia 85 B3 3 0N 107 47 E
Midale, Canada 143 D8 49 25N 103 20W
Middelburg, Neths. 24 C3 51 30N 3 36 E
Middelburg, Eastern Cape, S. Africa 116 E4 31 30S 25 0 E
Middelburg, Mpumalanga, S. Africa 117 D4 25 49S 29 28 E
Middelfart, Denmark 17 J3 55 30N 9 43 E
Middelpos, S. Africa 116 E3 31 55S 20 13 E
Middelwit, S. Africa 116 C4 24 51S 27 3 E
Middle →, U.S.A. 156 C3 41 26N 93 30W
Middle Alkali L., U.S.A. 158 F3 41 27N 120 5W
Middle Andaman I., India 95 H11 12 30N 92 50 E
Middle Bass I., U.S.A. 150 E2 41 41N 82 49W
Middle East, Asia 62 F7 38 0N 40 0 E
Middle Fork Feather →, U.S.A. 160 F5 38 33N 121 30W
Middle I., Australia 125 F3 34 6S 123 11 E
Middle Loup →, U.S.A. 154 E5 41 17N 98 24W
Middle Raccoon →, U.S.A. 156 C3 41 35N 93 35W
Middle Sackville, Canada 141 D7 44 47N 63 42W
Middleboro, U.S.A. 151 E14 41 54N 70 55W
Middleburg, Fla., U.S.A. 152 E8 30 4N 81 52W
Middleburg, N.Y., U.S.A. 151 D10 42 36N 74 20W
Middleburg, Pa., U.S.A. 150 F7 40 47N 77 3W
Middlebury, Ind., U.S.A. 157 C11 41 41N 85 42W
Middlebury, Vt., U.S.A. 151 B11 44 1N 73 10W
Middlemarch, N.Z. 131 F5 45 30S 170 9 E
Middlemount, Australia 126 C4 22 50S 148 40 E
Middleport, N.Y., U.S.A. 150 C6 43 13N 78 29W
Middleport, Ohio, U.S.A. 148 F4 39 0N 82 3W
Middlesboro, U.S.A. 149 G4 36 36N 83 43W
Middlesbrough, U.K. 20 C6 54 35N 1 13W
Middlesbrough □, U.K. 20 C6 54 28N 1 13W
Middlesex, Belize 164 C2 17 2N 88 31W
Middlesex, N.J., U.S.A. 151 F10 40 36N 74 30W
Middlesex, N.Y., U.S.A. 150 D7 42 42N 77 16W
Middleton, Australia 126 C3 22 22S 141 32 E
Middleton, Canada 141 D6 44 57N 65 4W
Middleton, U.S.A. 156 A7 43 6N 89 30W
Middleton Cr. →, Australia 126 C3 22 35S 141 51 E
Middleton I., U.S.A. 144 G11 59 26N 146 20W
Middletown, U.K. 23 B5 54 17N 6 51W
Middletown, Calif., U.S.A. 160 G4 38 45N 122 37W
Middletown, Conn., U.S.A. 151 E12 41 34N 72 39W
Middletown, Ky., U.S.A. 157 F11 38 14N 85 32W
Middletown, N.Y., U.S.A. 151 E10 41 27N 74 25W
Middletown, Ohio, U.S.A. 157 E12 39 31N 84 24W
Middletown, Pa., U.S.A. 151 F8 40 12N 76 44W
Middleville, U.S.A. 157 B11 42 43N 85 28W
Midelt, Morocco 110 B4 32 46N 4 44W
Midge Point, Australia 126 J6 20 39S 148 43 E
Midhirst, N.Z. 130 F3 39 17S 174 18 E
Miðsandur, Iceland 11 C5 64 24N 21 28W
Midhurst, U.K. 21 G7 50 59N 0 44W
Midi, Yemen 107 D5 16 20N 42 45 E
Midi, Canal du →, France 28 E5 43 45N 1 21 E
Midi d'Ossau, Pic du, France 28 F3 42 50N 0 26W
Midi-Pyrénées □, France 28 E5 43 55N 1 45 E
Midland, Canada 140 D4 44 45N 79 50W
Midland, Calif., U.S.A. 161 M12 33 52N 114 48W
Midland, Mich., U.S.A. 148 D3 43 37N 84 14W
Midland, Pa., U.S.A. 150 F4 40 39N 80 27W
Midland, Tex., U.S.A. 155 K3 32 0N 102 3W
Midlands □, Zimbabwe 119 F2 19 40S 29 0 E
Midleton, Ireland 23 E3 51 55N 8 10W
Midlothian, U.S.A. 155 J6 32 30N 97 0W
Midlothian □, U.K. 22 F5 55 51N 3 5W
Midongy, Tangorombohitr' i, Madag. 117 C8 23 30S 47 0 E
Midongy Atsimo, Madag. 117 C8 23 35S 47 1 E
Midou →, France 28 E3 43 54N 0 30W
Midouze →, France 28 E3 43 48N 0 51W
Midsayap, Phil. 81 H5 7 12N 124 32 E
Midsund, Norway 18 B3 62 41N 6 40 E
Midtgulen, Norway 18 C2 61 44N 5 11 E
Midu, China 76 E3 25 18N 100 30 E

Midville, U.S.A. 152 C7 32 49N 82 14W
Midway, Ala., U.S.A. 152 C4 32 5N 85 31W
Midway, Fla., U.S.A. 152 E5 30 30N 84 27W
Midway Is., Pac. Oc. 134 E10 28 13N 177 22W
Midway Is., U.S.A. 145 F8 28 13N 177 22W
Midway Wells, U.S.A. 161 N11 32 41N 115 7W
Midwest, U.S.A. 158 E10 43 25N 106 16W
Midwest City, U.S.A. 155 H6 35 27N 97 24W
Midyat, Turkey 101 D9 37 25N 41 23 E
Midžor, Bulgaria 50 C6 43 24N 22 40 E
Mie, Japan 72 E3 32 58N 131 35 E
Mie □, Japan 73 C8 34 30N 136 10 E
Miechów, Poland 55 H7 50 21N 20 5 E
Miedwie, Jezioro, Poland 55 E1 53 17N 14 54 E
Międzybórz, Poland 55 G4 51 25N 17 34 E
Międzychód, Poland 55 F2 52 35N 15 53 E
Międzylesie, Poland 55 H3 50 8N 16 40 E
Międzyrzec Podlaski, Poland 55 G9 51 58N 22 45 E
Międzyrzecz, Poland 55 F2 52 26N 15 35 E
Międzyzdroje, Poland 54 E1 53 56N 14 26 E
Miejska Górka, Poland 55 G3 51 39N 16 58 E
Miélan, France 28 E4 43 27N 0 19 E
Mielec, Poland 55 H8 50 15N 21 25 E
Mienga, Angola 116 B2 17 12 S 19 48 E
Miercurea-Ciuc, Romania 53 D10 46 21N 25 48 E
Miercurea Sibiului, Romania 53 E8 45 53N 23 48 E
Mieres, Spain 42 B5 43 18N 5 48W
Mieroszów, Poland 55 H3 50 40N 16 11 E
Mieso, Ethiopia 107 F5 9 15N 40 43 E
Mieszkowice, Poland 55 F1 52 47N 14 30 E
Mifflintown, U.S.A. 150 F7 40 34N 77 24W
Mifraz Ḥefa, Israel 103 C4 32 52N 35 0 E
Migennes, France 27 E10 47 58N 3 31 E
Migliarino, Italy 45 D8 44 46N 11 56 E
Miguel Alemán, Presa, Mexico 163 D5 18 15N 96 40W
Miguel Alves, Brazil 170 B3 4 11 S 42 55W
Miguel Calmon, Brazil 170 D3 11 26 S 40 36W
Miguelturra, Spain 43 G7 38 58N 3 53W
Mihăileni, Romania 53 C11 47 58N 26 9 E
Mihăileşti, Romania 53 F10 44 20N 25 54 E
Mihailovca, Moldova 53 D13 46 33N 28 56 E
Mihalgazi, Turkey 49 A12 40 2N 30 34 E
Mihaliççık, Turkey 100 C4 39 53N 31 30 E
Mihara, Japan 72 C5 34 24N 133 5 E
Mihara-Yama, Japan 73 C11 34 43N 139 23 E
Miheşu de Cîmpie, Romania 53 D9 46 41N 24 9 E
Mijas, Spain 43 J6 36 36N 4 40W
Mikese, Tanzania 118 D4 6 48 S 37 55 E
Mikha-Tskhakaya = Senaki, Georgia 61 J6 42 15N 42 7 E
Mikhailovka = Mykhaylivka, Ukraine 59 J8 47 12N 35 15 E
Mikhaylov, Russia 58 E10 54 14N 39 0 E
Mikhaylovgrad = Montana, Bulgaria 50 C7 43 27N 23 16 E
Mikhaylovka, Kyrgyzstan 65 B9 42 37N 78 20 E
Mikhaylovka, Russia 60 E6 50 3N 43 5 E
Mikhaylovski, Russia 64 C7 56 27N 59 7 E
Mikhnevo, Russia 58 E9 55 4N 37 59 E
Miki, Hyōgo, Japan 72 C6 34 48N 134 59 E
Miki, Kagawa, Japan 72 C6 34 12N 134 7 E
Mikínai, Greece 48 D4 37 43N 22 46 E
Mikir Hills, India 90 B4 26 10N 93 30 E
Mikkeli, Finland 15 F22 61 43N 27 15 E
Mikkwa →, Canada 142 B6 58 25N 114 46W
Mikniya, Sudan 107 D3 17 0N 33 45 E
Mikołajki, Poland 54 E8 53 49N 21 37 E
Míkonos, Greece 49 D7 37 30N 25 25 E
Mikope, Dem. Rep. of the Congo 115 C4 4 58 S 20 43 E
Mikrí Préspa, Límni, Greece 50 F5 40 47N 21 3 E
Mikrón Dhérion, Greece 51 E10 41 19N 26 6 E
Mikstat, Poland 55 G4 51 32N 17 59 E
Mikulov, Czech Rep. 35 C9 48 48N 16 39 E
Mikumi, Tanzania 118 D4 7 26 S 37 0 E
Mikumi Nat. Park, Tanzania 118 D4 7 35 S 37 15 E
Mikun, Russia 56 B9 62 20N 50 0 E
Mikuni, Japan 73 A8 36 13N 136 9 E
Mikuni-Tōge, Japan 73 A10 36 50N 138 50 E
Mikura-Jima, Japan 73 D11 33 52N 139 36 E
Milaca, U.S.A. 154 C8 45 45N 93 39W
Milagro, Ecuador 168 D2 2 11 S 79 36W
Milagros, Phil. 80 E4 12 13N 123 30 E
Milan = Milano, Italy 44 C6 45 28N 9 12 E
Milan, Ga., U.S.A. 152 C6 32 1N 83 4W
Milan, Ill., U.S.A. 156 C6 41 27N 90 34W
Milan, Mich., U.S.A. 157 B13 42 5N 83 41W
Milan, Mo., U.S.A. 156 D3 40 12N 93 7W
Milan, Tenn., U.S.A. 149 H1 35 55N 88 46W
Miland, Norway 18 E5 59 54N 8 45 E
Milando, Angola 115 D3 8 45 S 17 36 E
Milando, Reserva Parcial de, Angola 115 D3 8 45 S 17 10 E
Milang, Australia 128 C3 35 24 S 138 58 E
Milange, Mozam. 119 F4 16 3 S 35 45 E
Milano, Italy 44 C6 45 28N 9 12 E
Milanoa, Madag. 117 A8 13 35 S 49 47 E
Milâs, Turkey 49 D9 37 20N 27 50 E
Milatos, Greece 39 E6 35 18N 25 34 E
Milazzo, Italy 47 D8 38 13N 15 15 E
Milbank, U.S.A. 154 C6 45 13N 96 38W
Milbanke Sd., Canada 142 C3 52 15N 128 35W
Milden, Canada 143 C7 51 29N 107 32W
Mildenhall, U.K. 21 E8 52 21N 0 32 E
Mildmay, Canada 150 B3 44 3N 81 7W
Mildura, Australia 128 C5 34 13 S 142 9 E
Mile, China 76 E4 24 28N 103 20 E
Miléai, Greece 48 B5 39 20N 23 9 E
Miles, Australia 127 D5 26 40 S 150 9 E
Miles City, U.S.A. 154 B2 46 25N 105 51W
Mileşti, Moldova 53 C13 47 13N 28 3 E
Milestone, Canada 143 D8 49 59N 104 31W
Mileto, Italy 47 D9 38 36N 16 4 E
Miletto, Mte., Italy 47 A7 41 27N 14 22 E
Miletus, Turkey 49 D9 37 30N 27 18 E
Milevsko, Czech Rep. 34 B7 49 27N 14 21 E
Milford, Calif., U.S.A. 160 E6 40 10N 120 22W
Milford, Conn., U.S.A. 151 E11 41 14N 73 3W
Milford, Del., U.S.A. 148 F8 38 55N 75 26W
Milford, Ill., U.S.A. 157 D9 40 38N 87 42W
Milford, Mass., U.S.A. 151 D13 42 8N 71 31W
Milford, Mich., U.S.A. 157 B13 42 35N 83 36W
Milford, N.H., U.S.A. 151 D13 42 50N 71 39W
Milford, Pa., U.S.A. 151 E10 41 19N 74 48W
Milford, Utah, U.S.A. 159 G7 38 24N 113 1W
Milford Haven, U.K. 21 F2 51 42N 5 7W
Milford Sd., N.Z. 131 E2 44 41 S 167 47 E
Milḩ, Baḩr al, Iraq 101 F10 32 40N 43 35 E
Miliana, Aïn Salah, Algeria 111 C5 27 20N 2 32 E
Miliana, Médéa, Algeria 111 A5 36 20N 2 15 E
Milicz, Poland 55 G4 51 31N 17 19 E
Milikapiti, Australia 124 B5 11 26 S 130 40 E
Mililani Town, U.S.A. 145 K13 21 28N 158 1W
Miling, Australia 125 F2 30 30 S 116 17 E
Militello in Val di Catánia, Italy 47 E7 37 16N 14 48 E
Milk →, U.S.A. 158 B10 48 4N 106 19W
Milk, Wadi el →, Sudan 107 D3 17 55N 30 20 E
Milk River, Canada 142 D6 49 10N 112 5W
Mill I., Antarctica 7 C8 66 0 S 101 30 E
Mill Shoals, U.S.A. 157 F8 38 15N 88 21W
Mill Valley, U.S.A. 160 H4 37 54N 122 32W
Millárs →, Spain 40 F4 39 55N 0 1W
Millau, France 28 D7 44 8N 3 4 E
Millbridge, Canada 150 B7 44 41N 77 36W
Millbrook, Canada 150 B6 44 10N 78 29W
Millbrook, U.S.A. 151 E11 41 47N 73 42W
Mille Lacs, L. des, Canada 140 C1 48 45N 90 35W
Mille Lacs L., U.S.A. 154 B8 46 15N 93 39W
Milledgeville, Ga., U.S.A. 152 B6 33 5N 83 14W
Milledgeville, Ill., U.S.A. 156 C7 41 58N 89 46W
Millen, U.S.A. 152 C8 32 48N 81 57W
Millennium I. = Caroline I., Kiribati 135 H12 9 58 S 150 13W
Miller, U.S.A. 154 C5 44 31N 98 59W
Millerovo, Russia 61 F5 48 57N 40 28 E
Miller's Flat, N.Z. 131 F4 45 39 S 169 23 E
Millersburg, Ind., U.S.A. 157 C11 41 32N 85 42W
Millersburg, Ohio, U.S.A. 150 F3 40 33N 81 55W
Millersburg, Pa., U.S.A. 150 F8 40 32N 76 58W
Millerton, N.Z. 131 B6 41 39 S 171 54 E
Millerton, U.S.A. 151 E11 41 57N 73 31W
Millerton L., U.S.A. 160 J7 37 1N 119 41W
Millet, St. Lucia 165 f 13 55N 60 59W
Millevaches, Plateau de, France 28 C6 45 45N 2 0 E
Millheim, U.S.A. 150 F7 40 54N 77 29W
Millicent, Australia 128 D4 37 34 S 140 21 E
Milligan, U.S.A. 153 E3 30 45N 86 38W
Millington, U.S.A. 153 H10 35 20N 89 53W
Millinocket, U.S.A. 149 C11 45 39N 68 43W
Millmerran, Australia 127 D5 27 53 S 151 16 E
Millom, U.K. 20 C4 54 13N 3 16W
Mills L., Canada 142 A5 61 30N 118 20W
Millsboro, U.S.A. 150 G5 40 0N 80 0W
Millstream-Chichester Nat. Park, Australia 124 D2 21 35 S 117 6 E
Millthorpe, Australia 129 B8 33 26 S 149 12 E
Milltown Malbay, Ireland 23 D2 52 52N 9 24W
Millville, N.J., U.S.A. 148 F8 39 24N 75 2W
Millville, Pa., U.S.A. 151 E8 41 7N 76 32W
Millwood L., U.S.A. 155 J8 33 42N 93 58W
Milna, Croatia 45 E13 43 20N 16 28 E
Milne →, Australia 126 C2 21 10 S 137 33 E
Milne Bay □, Papua N. G. 132 E7 10 0 S 152 30 E
Milne Land, Greenland 10 C8 70 40N 26 30W
Milo, U.S.A. 149 C11 45 15N 68 59W
Milolii, U.S.A. 145 D6 19 11N 155 55W
Mílos, Greece 48 E6 36 44N 24 25 E
Miłosław, Poland 55 F4 52 12N 17 32 E
Milot, Albania 50 E3 41 41N 19 43 E
Milparinka, Australia 127 D3 29 46 S 141 57 E
Milroy, U.S.A. 157 E11 39 30N 85 28W
Miltenberg, Germany 31 F5 49 41N 9 16 E
Milton, Australia 129 C9 35 20 S 150 27 E
Milton, N.S., Canada 141 D7 44 4N 64 45W
Milton, Ont., Canada 150 C5 43 31N 79 53W
Milton, N.Z. 131 G4 46 7 S 169 59 E
Milton, Calif., U.S.A. 160 G6 38 3N 120 51W
Milton, Fla., U.S.A. 149 K2 30 38N 87 3W
Milton, Iowa, U.S.A. 156 D4 40 41N 92 10W
Milton, Pa., U.S.A. 150 F8 41 1N 76 51W
Milton, Vt., U.S.A. 151 B11 44 38N 73 7W
Milton, Wis., U.S.A. 157 B8 42 47N 88 56W
Milton-Freewater, U.S.A. 158 D4 45 56N 118 23W
Milton Keynes, U.K. 21 E7 52 1N 0 44W
Milton Keynes □, U.K. 21 E7 52 1N 0 44W
Miltou, Chad 109 F3 10 14N 17 26 E
Miluo, China 77 C9 29 0N 112 59 E
Milverton, Canada 150 C4 43 34N 80 55W
Milwaukee, U.S.A. 157 A9 43 2N 87 55W
Milwaukee Deep, Atl. Oc. 165 C6 19 50N 68 0W
Milwaukie, U.S.A. 160 E4 45 27N 122 38W
Mim, Ghana 112 D4 6 57N 2 33W
Mimizan, France 28 D2 44 12N 1 13W
Mimoň, Czech Rep. 34 A7 50 38N 14 43 E
Mimongo, Gabon 114 C2 1 11 S 11 36 E
Mimoso, Brazil 171 E2 15 10 S 48 5W
Mims, U.S.A. 153 G9 28 40N 80 51W
Min Jiang →, Fujian, China 77 E12 26 0N 119 35 E
Min Jiang →, Sichuan, China 76 C5 28 45N 104 40 E
Min Xian, China 74 G3 34 25N 104 5 E
Mina Pirquitas, Argentina 174 A2 22 40 S 66 30W
Mīnā Su'ud, Si. Arabia 97 D6 28 45N 48 28 E
Mīnā'al Aḩmadī, Kuwait 97 D6 29 5N 48 10 E
Minago →, Canada 143 C9 54 33N 98 59W
Minakami, Japan 73 A10 36 49N 138 59 E
Minaki, Canada 143 D10 49 59N 94 40W
Minakuchi, Japan 73 C8 34 58N 136 10 E
Minamata, Japan 72 E2 32 10N 130 30 E
Minami-Tori-Shima, Pac. Oc. 134 E7 24 20N 153 58 E
Minas, Uruguay 175 C4 34 20 S 55 10W
Minas, Sierra de las, Guatemala 164 C2 15 9N 89 31W
Minas Basin, Canada 141 C7 45 20N 64 12W
Minas de Rio Tinto = Minas de Riotinto, Spain 43 H4 37 42N 6 35W
Minas de Riotinto, Spain 43 H4 37 42N 6 35W
Minas Gerais □, Brazil 171 E2 18 50 S 46 0W
Minas Novas, Brazil 171 E3 17 15 S 42 36W
Minatitlán, Mexico 163 D6 17 59N 94 31W
Minbu, Burma 90 E5 20 10N 94 52 E
Minbya, Burma 90 E4 20 22N 93 16 E
Minchinabad, Pakistan 92 D5 30 10N 73 34 E
Mincio →, Italy 44 C7 45 4N 10 59 E
Minčol, Slovak Rep. 35 B13 49 15N 20 58 E
Mindanao, Phil. 81 H5 8 0N 125 0 E
Mindanao Sea = Bohol Sea, Phil. 81 G5 9 0N 124 0 E
Mindanao Trench, Pac. Oc. 80 E5 12 0N 126 6 E
Mindel →, Germany 31 G6 48 31N 10 23 E
Mindelheim, Germany 31 G6 48 2N 10 29 E
Mindelo, C. Verde Is. 9 j 16 24N 25 0W
Minden, Canada 150 B6 44 55N 78 43W
Minden, Germany 30 C4 52 17N 8 55 E
Minden, La., U.S.A. 155 J8 32 37N 93 17W
Minden, Nev., U.S.A. 160 G7 38 57N 119 46W
Mindiptana, Indonesia 83 C6 5 55 S 140 22 E
Mindon, Burma 90 F5 19 21N 94 44 E
Mindona L., Australia 128 B5 33 6 S 142 6 E
Mindoro, Phil. 80 E3 13 0N 121 0 E
Mindoro Occidental □, Phil. 80 E3 13 0N 120 55 E
Mindoro Oriental □, Phil. 80 E3 13 0N 121 5 E
Mindoro Str., Phil. 80 E3 12 30N 120 30 E
Mindouli, Congo 115 C2 4 12 S 14 28 E
Mindourou, Cameroon 114 B2 3 29N 13 26 E
Mine, Japan 72 C3 34 12N 131 7 E
Minehead, U.K. 21 F4 51 12N 3 29W
Mineiros, Brazil 173 D7 17 34 S 52 34W
Mineola, N.Y., U.S.A. 151 F11 40 45N 73 39W
Mineola, Tex., U.S.A. 155 J7 32 40N 95 29W
Mineral King, U.S.A. 160 J8 36 27N 118 36W
Mineral Point, U.S.A. 156 B6 42 52N 90 11W
Mineral Wells, U.S.A. 155 J5 32 48N 98 7W
Mineralnyye Vody, Russia 61 H6 44 15N 43 8 E
Minersville, U.S.A. 151 F8 40 41N 76 16W
Minerva, U.S.A. 150 F3 40 44N 81 6W
Minervino Murge, Italy 47 A9 41 5N 16 5 E
Minetto, U.S.A. 151 C8 43 24N 76 28W
Ming-Kush, Kyrgyzstan 65 C7 41 40N 74 28 E
Mingäçevir, Azerbaijan 61 K8 40 45N 47 0 E
Mingäçevir Su Anbarı, Azerbaijan 61 K8 40 57N 46 50 E
Mingala, C.A.R. 114 A4 5 6N 21 49 E
Mingan, Canada 141 B7 50 20N 64 0W
Mingary, Australia 128 B4 32 8 S 140 45 E
Mingechaur = Mingäçevir, Azerbaijan 61 K8 40 45N 47 0 E
Mingechaurskoye Vdkhr. = Mingäçevir Su Anbarı, Azerbaijan 61 K8 40 57N 46 50 E
Mingela, Australia 126 B4 19 52 S 146 38 E
Mingenew, Australia 125 E2 29 12 S 115 21 E
Mingera Cr. →, Australia 126 C2 20 38 S 137 45 E
Minggang, China 77 A10 32 24N 114 3 E
Mingguang, China 77 A11 32 46N 117 59 E
Mingin, Burma 90 D5 22 50N 94 30 E
Mingir, Moldova 53 D13 46 40N 28 20 E
Minglanilla, Spain 41 F3 39 34N 1 38W
Minglun, China 76 E7 25 10N 108 21 E
Mingo, Congo 114 C3 1 55 S 15 1 E
Mingo Junction, U.S.A. 150 F4 40 19N 80 37W
Mingorria, Spain 42 E6 40 45N 4 40W
Mingshan, China 76 B4 30 6N 103 10 E
Mingteke, China 65 E7 37 7N 75 4 E
Mingteke Daban = Mintaka Pass, Pakistan 65 E7 37 0N 74 58 E
Mingxi, China 77 D11 26 18N 117 12 E
Mingyuegue, China 75 C15 43 2N 128 50 E
Minhla, Magwe, Burma 90 F5 19 58N 95 3 E
Minhla, Pegu, Burma 90 G5 17 59N 95 43 E
Minho = Miño →, Spain 42 D2 41 52N 8 40W
Minhou, China 77 E12 26 0N 119 15 E
Miničevo, Serbia, Yug. 50 C6 43 42N 22 18 E
Minicoy I., India 95 K1 8 17N 73 2 E
Minidoka, U.S.A. 158 E7 42 45N 113 29W
Minier, U.S.A. 156 D7 40 26N 89 19W
Minigwal, L., Australia 125 E3 29 31 S 123 14 E
Minilya →, Australia 125 D1 23 45 S 114 0 E
Minilya Roadhouse, Australia 125 D1 23 55 S 114 0 E
Mininera, Australia 128 D5 37 37 S 142 58 E
Minipi L., Canada 141 B7 52 25N 60 45W
Minj, Papua N. G. 132 C3 5 54 S 144 37 E
Mink L., Canada 142 A5 61 54N 117 40W
Minkammen, Sudan 107 F3 6 3N 31 32 E
Minkebé, Gabon 114 B2 1 45N 12 45 E
Minlaton, Australia 128 C2 34 45 S 137 35 E
Minna, Nigeria 113 D6 9 37N 6 30 E
Minneapolis, Kans., U.S.A. 154 F6 39 8N 97 42W
Minneapolis, Minn., U.S.A. 154 C8 44 59N 93 16W
Minnedosa, Canada 143 C9 50 14N 99 50W
Minnesota □, U.S.A. 154 B8 46 0N 94 15W
Minnesota →, U.S.A. 154 C8 44 54N 93 9W
Minnesund, Norway 18 D8 60 23N 11 14 E
Minnewaukan, U.S.A. 154 A5 48 4N 99 15W
Minnipa, Australia 127 E2 32 51 S 135 9 E
Minnitaki L., Canada 140 C1 49 57N 92 10W
Mino, Japan 73 B8 35 32N 136 55 E
Miño, Spain 42 B2 43 21N 8 12W
Miño →, Spain 42 D2 41 52N 8 40W
Mino-Kamo, Japan 73 B9 35 23N 137 2 E
Mino-Mikawa-Kōgen, Japan 73 B9 35 10N 137 23 E
Minoa, Greece 49 F7 35 6N 25 45 E
Minobu, Japan 73 B10 35 22N 138 26 E
Minobu-Sanchi, Japan 73 B10 35 14N 138 20 E
Minonk, U.S.A. 156 D7 40 54N 89 2W
Minooka, U.S.A. 157 C8 41 27N 88 16W
Minorca = Menorca, Spain 38 B5 40 0N 4 0 E
Minore, Australia 129 B8 32 14 S 148 27 E
Minot, U.S.A. 154 A4 48 14N 101 18W
Minqin, China 74 E2 38 38N 103 20 E
Minqing, China 77 D12 26 15N 118 50 E
Minsen, Germany 30 B3 53 41N 7 58 E
Minsk, Belarus 58 F4 53 52N 27 30 E
Mińsk Mazowiecki, Poland 55 F8 52 10N 21 33 E
Minster, U.S.A. 157 D12 40 24N 84 23W
Mintabie, Australia 127 D1 27 15 S 133 7 E
Mintaka Pass, Pakistan 65 E7 37 0N 74 58 E
Minthami, Burma 90 D5 23 55N 94 16 E
Minto, Canada 141 C6 46 5N 66 5W
Minto, U.S.A. 144 D10 64 53N 149 11W
Minto, L., Canada 140 A5 57 13N 75 0W
Minton, Canada 143 D8 49 10N 104 35W
Mintoum, Gabon 114 B2 0 27N 12 16 E
Minturn, U.S.A. 158 G10 39 35N 106 26W
Minturno, Italy 46 A6 41 15N 13 45 E
Minûf, Egypt 106 H7 30 26N 30 52 E
Minusinsk, Russia 67 D10 53 43N 91 20 E
Minusio, Switz. 33 D7 46 11N 8 49 E
Minutang, India 90 A6 28 15N 96 30 E
Minvoul, Gabon 114 B2 2 9N 12 8 E
Minwakh, Yemen 99 C5 16 48N 48 6 E
Minya el Qamh, Egypt 106 H7 30 31N 31 21 E
Minyar, Russia 64 D6 55 4N 57 33 E
Minyip, Australia 128 D5 36 29 S 142 36 E
Minzhong, China 69 F10 22 37N 113 30 E
Mionica, Bos.-H. 52 F3 44 51N 18 29 E
Mionica, Serbia, Yug. 50 B4 44 14N 20 6 E
Miquelon, Canada 140 C4 49 25N 76 27W
Miquelon, St- P. & M. 141 C8 47 8N 56 22W
Mir, Niger 113 C7 14 5N 11 59 E
Mīr Kūh, Iran 97 E8 26 22N 58 55 E
Mīr Shahdād, Iran 97 E8 26 15N 58 29 E
Mira, Italy 45 C9 45 26N 12 8 E
Mira, Portugal 42 E2 40 26N 8 44W
Mira →, Colombia 168 C2 1 36N 79 1W
Mira →, Portugal 43 H2 37 43N 8 47W
Mira por vos Cay, Bahamas 165 B5 22 9N 74 30W
Mirābād, Afghan. 91 C1 30 25N 61 50 E
Mirabella Eclano, Italy 47 A7 41 2N 14 59 E
Miracema do Norte, Brazil 170 C2 9 33 S 48 24W
Mirador, Brazil 170 C3 6 22 S 44 22W
Miraflores, Colombia 168 C3 1 25N 72 13W
Miraj, India 94 F2 16 50N 74 45 E
Miram Shah, Pakistan 91 B3 33 0N 70 2 E
Miramar, Argentina 174 D4 38 15 S 57 50W
Miramar, Mozam. 117 C6 23 50 S 35 35 E
Miramas, France 29 E8 43 33N 4 59 E
Mirambeau, France 28 C3 45 23N 0 35W
Miramichi, Canada 141 C6 47 2N 65 28W
Miramichi B., Canada 141 C7 47 15N 65 0W
Miramont-de-Guyenne, France 28 D4 44 37N 0 21 E
Miranda, Brazil 173 E6 20 10 S 56 15W
Miranda □, Venezuela 168 A4 10 15N 66 25W
Miranda →, Brazil 173 D6 19 25 S 57 20W
Miranda de Ebro, Spain 40 C2 42 41N 2 57W
Miranda do Corvo, Portugal 42 E2 40 6N 8 20W
Miranda do Douro, Portugal 42 D4 41 30N 6 16W
Mirande, France 28 E4 43 31N 0 25 E
Mirandela, Portugal 42 D3 41 32N 7 10W
Mirándola, Italy 44 D8 44 53N 11 4 E
Mirandópolis, Brazil 175 A5 21 9 S 51 6W
Mirango, Malawi 119 E3 13 32 S 34 58 E
Mirani, Australia 126 K6 21 8 S 148 53 E
Mirano, Italy 45 C9 45 30N 12 7 E
Miras, Albania 50 F4 40 30N 20 56 E
Mirassol, Brazil 175 A6 20 46 S 49 28W
Mirbāţ, Oman 99 C6 17 0N 54 36 E
Mirbou North, Australia 129 E7 38 24 S 146 10 E
Mirear, Egypt 106 C4 23 15N 35 41 E
Mirebeau, Côte-d'Or, France 27 E12 47 25N 5 20 E
Mirebeau, Vienne, France 26 F7 46 49N 0 10 E
Mirecourt, France 27 D13 48 20N 6 10 E
Mirgorod = Myrhorod, Ukraine 59 H7 49 58N 33 37 E
Miri, Malaysia 85 B4 4 23N 113 59 E
Mirialguda, India 94 F4 16 52N 79 35 E
Miriam Vale, Australia 126 C5 24 20 S 151 33 E
Miribel, France 27 G11 45 50N 4 57 E
Mirigama, Sri Lanka 95 L5 7 15N 80 8 E
Mirim, L., S. Amer. 175 C5 32 45 S 52 50W
Mirimire, Venezuela 168 A4 11 10N 68 43W
Miriti, Brazil 173 B6 6 15 S 59 0W
Mirnyy, Russia 67 C12 62 33N 113 53 E
Miroč, Serbia, Yug. 50 B6 44 32N 22 16 E
Mirokhan, Pakistan 92 F3 27 46N 68 6 E
Mirond L., Canada 143 B8 55 6N 102 47W
Mirosławiec, Poland 54 E3 53 20N 16 5 E
Mirpur, Pakistan 93 C5 33 32N 73 56 E
Mirpur Batoro, Pakistan 92 G3 24 44N 68 16 E
Mirpur Bibiwari, Pakistan 92 E2 28 33N 67 44 E
Mirpur Khas, Pakistan 91 D3 25 30N 69 0 E
Mirpur Sakro, Pakistan 92 G2 24 33N 67 41 E
Mirria, Niger 113 C6 13 43N 9 7 E
Mirrool, Australia 129 C7 34 19 S 147 10 E
Mirs Bay = Tai Pang Wan, H.K. 69 F11 22 33N 114 24 E
Mirsk, Poland 55 H2 50 58N 15 23 E
Mirtağ, Turkey 96 B4 38 23N 41 56 E
Mírtou, Kólpos, Greece 39 C1 38 20N 20 27 E
Miryang, S. Korea 75 G15 35 31N 128 44 E
Mirzaani, Georgia 61 K8 41 24N 46 5 E
Mirzapur, India 93 G10 25 10N 82 34 E
Mirzapur-cum-Vindhyachal = Mirzapur, India 93 G10 25 10N 82 34 E
Misaki, Japan 73 C7 34 18N 135 9 E
Misamis Occidental □, Phil. 81 G4 8 20N 123 42 E
Misamis Oriental □, Phil. 81 G5 8 45N 125 0 E
Misantla, Mexico 163 D5 19 56N 96 50W
Misawa, Japan 70 D10 40 41N 141 24 E
Miscou I., Canada 141 C7 47 57N 64 31W
Misha, India 95 L10 7 59N 93 20 E
Mish'āb, Ra's al, Si. Arabia 97 D6 28 15N 48 43 E
Mishagua →, Peru 172 C3 11 12 S 72 58W
Mishan, China 69 B8 45 37N 131 48 E
Mishawaka, U.S.A. 157 C10 41 40N 86 11W
Mishbih, Gebel, Egypt 106 C3 22 38N 34 44 E
Mishima, Japan 73 B10 35 10N 138 52 E
Mishmi Hills, India 90 A5 29 0N 96 0 E
Mishō, Japan 72 E4 32 57N 132 35 E
Misima I., Papua N. G. 132 F7 10 40 S 152 45 E
Misión, Mexico 161 N10 32 6N 116 53W
Misión Fagnano, Argentina 176 D3 54 32 S 67 17W
Misiones □, Argentina 175 B5 27 0 S 55 0W
Misiones □, Paraguay 174 B4 27 0 S 56 0W
Miskah, Si. Arabia 96 E4 24 49N 42 56 E
Miski, E. →, Chad 109 E3 20 0N 17 55 E
Miskitos, Cayos, Nic. 164 D3 14 26N 82 50W
Miskolc, Hungary 52 B5 48 7N 20 50 E
Misoke, Dem. Rep. of the Congo 118 C2 0 42 S 28 2 E
Misool, Indonesia 83 B4 1 52 S 130 10 E
Mişrātah, Libya 108 B3 32 24N 15 3 E
Mişrātah □, Libya 108 C3 33 30N 15 0 E
Missanabie, Canada 140 C3 48 20N 84 6W
Missão Catrimani, Brazil 169 C5 2 48N 62 18W
Missão Velha, Brazil 170 C4 7 15 S 39 10W
Missinaibi →, Canada 140 B3 50 43N 81 29W
Missinaibi L., Canada 140 C3 48 23N 83 40W
Mission, Canada 142 D4 49 10N 122 15W
Mission, S. Dak., U.S.A. 154 D4 43 18N 100 39W
Mission, Tex., U.S.A. 155 M5 26 13N 98 20W
Mission Beach, Australia 126 B4 17 53 S 146 6 E
Mission Viejo, U.S.A. 161 M9 33 36N 117 40W
Missirah, Senegal 112 C1 13 40N 16 30W
Missisa L., Canada 140 B2 52 20N 85 7W
Missisicabi →, Canada 140 B4 51 14N 79 31W
Mississagi →, Canada 140 C3 46 15N 83 9W
Mississauga, Canada 150 C5 43 32N 79 35W
Mississinewa L., U.S.A. 157 D10 40 46N 86 3W
Mississippi □, U.S.A. 155 J10 33 0N 90 0W
Mississippi →, U.S.A. 155 L10 29 9N 89 15W
Mississippi L., Canada 151 A8 45 5N 76 10W
Mississippi River Delta, U.S.A. 155 L9 29 10N 89 15W
Mississippi Sd., U.S.A. 155 K10 30 20N 89 0W
Missoula, U.S.A. 158 C7 46 52N 114 1W
Missour, Morocco 110 B4 33 3N 4 0W
Missouri □, U.S.A. 156 E3 38 25N 92 30W
Missouri →, U.S.A. 156 F6 38 49N 90 7W
Missouri City, U.S.A. 155 L7 29 37N 95 32W
Missouri Valley, U.S.A. 154 E7 41 34N 95 53W
Mist, U.S.A. 160 E3 45 59N 123 15W
Mistassibi →, Canada 141 B5 48 53N 72 13W
Mistassini, Canada 141 C5 48 53N 72 12W
Mistassini →, Canada 141 C5 48 42N 72 20W
Mistassini, L., Canada 140 B5 51 0N 73 30W
Mistastin L., Canada 141 A7 55 57N 63 20W
Mistelbach, Austria 35 C9 48 34N 16 34 E
Misterbianco, Italy 47 E8 37 31N 15 1 E
Misti, Volcán, Peru 172 D3 16 18 S 71 24W
Mistinibi, L., Canada 141 A7 55 56N 64 17W
Mistretta, Italy 47 E7 37 56N 14 22 E
Misty L., Canada 143 B8 58 53N 101 40W
Misugi, Japan 73 C8 34 31N 136 16 E
Misumi, Japan 72 E2 32 37N 130 27 E
Misurata = Mişrātah, Libya 108 B3 32 24N 15 3 E
Mît Ghamr, Egypt 106 H7 30 42N 31 12 E
Mitaka, Japan 73 B11 35 40N 139 33 E
Mitatib, Sudan 107 D4 15 59N 36 12 E
Mitchell, Australia 127 D4 26 29 S 147 58 E
Mitchell, Canada 150 C3 43 28N 81 12W
Mitchell, Ga., U.S.A. 152 B7 33 13N 82 42W
Mitchell, Ind., U.S.A. 157 F10 38 44N 86 28W
Mitchell, Nebr., U.S.A. 154 E3 41 57N 103 49W
Mitchell, Oreg., U.S.A. 158 D3 44 34N 120 9W
Mitchell, S. Dak., U.S.A. 154 D6 43 43N 98 2W
Mitchell →, Australia 126 B3 15 12 S 141 35 E
Mitchell, Mt., U.S.A. 149 H4 35 46N 82 16W
Mitchell and Alice Rivers Nat. Park, Australia 126 B3 15 28 S 142 5 E
Mitchell Ranges, Australia 126 A2 12 49 S 135 36 E
Mitchell River Nat. Park, Australia 129 D7 37 37 S 147 22 E
Mitchelstown, Ireland 23 D3 52 15N 8 16W
Mitha Tiwana, Pakistan 92 C5 32 13N 72 6 E
Mithi, Pakistan 92 G3 24 44N 69 48 E
Míthimna, Greece 49 B8 39 20N 26 12 E
Mithrao, Pakistan 92 F3 27 28N 69 40 E
Mitiamo, Australia 128 D6 36 12 S 144 15 E
Mítikas, Greece 39 B2 38 40N 20 56 E
Mítikas, Greece 39 B2 39 0N 20 42 E
Mitilíni, Greece 49 B8 39 6N 26 35 E
Mitilinoí, Greece 49 D8 37 42N 26 56 E
Mito, Japan 73 A12 36 20N 140 30 E
Mitra, Mt., Eq. Guin. 114 B1 1 23N 9 19 E
Mitre, Mt., N.Z. 130 G4 40 50 S 175 30 E
Mitrofanovka, Russia 59 H10 49 58N 39 42 E
Mitrovica = Kosovska Mitrovica, Kosovo, Yug. 50 D4 42 54N 20 52 E
Mitsamiouli, Comoros Is. 121 a 11 20 S 43 16 E
Mitsang, Gabon 114 B2 0 42N 12 33 E
Mitsinjo, Madag. 117 B8 16 1 S 45 52 E
Mitsiwa, Eritrea 107 D4 15 35N 39 25 E
Mitsiwa Channel, Eritrea 107 D5 15 30N 40 0 E
Mitsukaidō, Japan 73 A11 36 1N 139 59 E
Mitsushima, Japan 72 C1 34 15N 129 20 E
Mittagong, Australia 129 C9 34 28 S 150 29 E
Mittelberg, Tirol, Austria 33 C11 46 57N 10 53 E
Mittelberg, Vorarlberg, Austria 33 B10 47 20N 10 10 E
Mittelberg, Germany 33 A10 47 38N 10 26 E
Mittelfranken □, Germany 31 F6 49 25N 10 40 E
Mittelland, Switz. 32 C4 46 50N 7 23 E
Mittellandkanal →, Germany 30 C4 52 20N 8 28 E
Mittenwalde, Germany 30 C9 52 15N 13 31 E

Mittersill, Austria 34 D5 47 16N 12 29 E
Mitterteich, Germany 31 F8 49 57N 12 14 E
Mittimatalik = Pond Inlet, Canada 139 A12 72 40N 77 0W
Mittweida, Germany 30 E8 50 59N 12 59 E
Mitú, Colombia 168 C3 1 15N 70 13W
Mituas, Colombia 168 C4 3 52N 68 49W
Mitumba, Tanzania 118 D3 7 8S 31 2 E
Mitumba, Mts., Dem. Rep. of the Congo 118 D2 7 0S 27 30 E
Mitwaba, Dem. Rep. of the Congo 119 D2 8 2S 27 17 E
Mityana, Uganda 118 B3 0 23N 32 2 E
Mitzic, Gabon 114 B2 0 45N 11 40 E
Miura, Japan 73 B11 35 12N 139 40 E
Mixteco →, Mexico 163 D5 18 11N 98 30W
Miyagi □, Japan 70 E10 38 15N 140 45 E
Miyāh, W. el →, Egypt 106 C3 25 0N 33 23 E
Miyāh, W. el →, Syria 96 C3 34 44N 39 57 E
Miyake-Jima, Japan 73 C11 34 5N 139 30 E
Miyako, Japan 70 E10 39 40N 141 59 E
Miyako-Jima, Japan 71 M2 24 45N 125 20 E
Miyako-Rettō, Japan 71 M2 24 24N 125 0 E
Miyakonojō, Japan 72 F3 31 40N 131 5 E
Miyani, India 92 J3 21 50N 69 26 E
Miyanojō, Japan 72 F2 31 54N 130 27 E
Miyanoura-Dake, Japan 71 J5 30 20N 130 31 E
Miyata, Japan 72 D2 33 49N 130 42 E
Miyazaki, Japan 72 F3 31 56N 131 30 E
Miyazaki □, Japan 72 E3 32 30N 131 30 E
Miyazu, Japan 73 B7 35 35N 135 10 E
Miyet, Bahr el = Dead Sea, Asia 103 D4 31 30N 35 30 E
Miyi, China 76 D4 26 47N 102 9 E
Miyoshi, Japan 72 C4 34 48N 132 51 E
Miyun, China 74 D9 40 28N 116 50 E
Miyun Shuiku, China 75 D9 40 30N 117 0 E
Mizan Teferi, Ethiopia 107 F4 6 57N 35 3 E
Mizdah, Libya 108 B2 31 30N 13 0 E
Mizen Hd., Cork, Ireland 23 E2 51 27N 9 50W
Mizen Hd., Wick., Ireland 23 D5 52 51N 6 4W
Mizhi, China 74 F6 37 47N 110 12 E
Mizil, Romania 53 F11 44 59N 26 29 E
Mizoram □, India 90 D4 23 30N 92 40 E
Mizpe Ramon, Israel 103 E3 30 34N 34 49 E
Mizuho, Japan 73 B7 35 6N 135 17 E
Mizunami, Japan 73 B9 35 22N 137 15 E
Mizusawa, Japan 70 E10 39 8N 141 8 E
Mjällby, Sweden 17 H8 56 3N 14 40 E
Mjöbäck, Sweden 17 G6 57 28N 12 53 E
Mjölby, Sweden 17 F9 58 20N 15 10 E
Mjølfjell, Norway 18 D3 60 41N 6 55 E
Mjømna, Norway 18 D1 60 55N 4 55 E
Mjörn, Sweden 17 G6 57 55N 12 25 E
Mjøsa, Norway 15 F14 60 40N 11 0 E
Mkata, Tanzania 118 D4 5 45 S 38 20 E
Mkhaya Nature Reserve, Swaziland 117 D5 26 34 S 34 45 E
Mkokotoni, Tanzania 118 D4 5 55 S 39 15 E
Mkomazi, Tanzania 118 C4 4 40 S 38 7 E
Mkomazi →, S. Africa 117 E5 30 12 S 30 50 E
Mkomazi Game Reserve, Tanzania 118 C3 4 4 S 30 2 E
Mkulwe, Tanzania 119 D3 8 37 S 32 20 E
Mkumbi, Ras, Tanzania 118 D4 7 38 S 39 55 E
Mkushi, Zambia 119 E2 14 25 S 29 15 E
Mkushi River, Zambia 119 E2 13 32 S 29 45 E
Mkuze, S. Africa 117 D5 27 10 S 32 0 E
Mkuze Game Reserve, S. Africa 117 D4 29 27 S 29 30 E
Mladá Boleslav, Czech Rep. 34 A7 50 27N 14 53 E
Mladenovac, Serbia, Yug. 50 B4 44 28N 20 44 E
Mlala Hills, Tanzania 118 D3 6 50 S 31 40 E
Mlange = Mulanje, Malawi 119 F4 16 2 S 35 33 E
Mlava →, Serbia, Yug. 50 B5 44 45N 21 13 E
Mława, Poland 55 E7 53 9N 20 25 E
Mlawula Nature Reserve, Swaziland 117 D5 26 12 S 32 2 E
Mliništa, Bos.-H. 45 D13 44 15N 16 50 E
Mljet, Croatia 45 F14 42 43N 17 30 E
Mljetski Kanal, Croatia 45 F14 42 48N 17 35 E
Mlynary, Poland 54 D6 54 12N 19 46 E
Mmabatho, S. Africa 116 D4 25 49 S 25 30 E
Mme, Cameroon 113 D7 6 18N 10 14 E
Mnichovo Hradiště, Czech Rep. 34 A7 50 32N 14 59 E
Mo, Hordaland, Norway 18 D2 60 49N 5 48 E
Mo, Møre og Romsdal, Norway 18 A5 63 0N 8 59 E
Mo, Telemark, Norway 18 E4 59 28N 7 50 E
Mo i Rana, Norway 14 C16 66 20N 14 7 E
Moa, Cuba 165 B4 20 40N 74 56W
Moa, Indonesia 82 C3 8 0 S 128 0 E
Moa →, S. Leone 112 D2 6 59N 11 36W
Moa, I., Papua N. G. 132 F2 10 10 S 142 15 E
Moab, U.S.A. 159 G9 38 35N 109 33W
Moabi, Gabon 114 C2 2 24 S 10 59 E
Moaco →, Brazil 172 B4 7 41 S 68 18W
Moala, Fiji 133 B2 18 36 S 179 53 E
Moama, Australia 127 F3 36 7 S 144 46 E
Moamba, Mozam. 117 D5 25 36 S 32 15 E
Moapa, U.S.A. 161 J12 36 40N 114 37W
Moate, Ireland 23 C4 53 24N 7 44W
Moba, Dem. Rep. of the Congo 118 D2 7 0 S 29 48 E
Mobara, Japan 73 B12 35 25N 140 18 E
Mobārakābād, Iran 97 D7 28 24N 53 20 E
Mobaye, C.A.R. 114 B4 4 25N 21 5 E
Mobayi, Dem. Rep. of the Congo 114 B4 4 15N 21 8 E
Mobeka, Dem. Rep. of the Congo 114 B3 1 52N 19 49 E
Mobenzélé, Congo 114 B3 0 56N 17 50 E
Moberley Lake, Canada 142 B4 55 50N 121 44W
Moberly, U.S.A. 156 E4 39 25N 92 26W
Mobile, U.S.A. 149 K1 30 41N 88 3W
Mobile B., U.S.A. 149 K2 30 30N 88 0W
Mobridge, U.S.A. 154 C4 45 32N 100 26W
Mobutu Sese Seko, L. = Albert, L., Africa 118 B3 1 30N 31 0 E
Moc Chau, Vietnam 86 B5 20 50N 104 38 E
Moc Hoa, Vietnam 87 G5 10 46N 105 56 E
Mocabe, Sa. de, Angola 115 D3 7 12 S 15 0 E
Mocabe Kasari, Dem. Rep. of the Congo 119 D2 9 58 S 26 12 E
Mocajuba, Brazil 170 B2 2 35 S 49 30W
Moçambique, Mozam. 119 F5 15 3 S 40 42 E
Moçâmedes = Namibe, Angola 115 F2 15 7 S 12 11 E
Mocanaqua, U.S.A. 151 E8 41 9N 76 8W
Mocapra →, Venezuela 168 B4 7 56N 66 46W
Moce, Fiji 133 B3 18 40 S 178 29W
Mocha, I., Chile 176 A2 38 22 S 73 56W
Mochudi, Botswana 116 C4 24 27 S 26 7 E
Mocimboa da Praia, Mozam. 119 E5 11 25 S 40 20 E
Mociu, Romania 53 D9 46 46N 24 3 E
Möckeln, Sweden 17 H8 56 40N 14 15 E
Mockfjärd, Sweden 16 D8 60 30N 14 57 E
Moclips, U.S.A. 160 C2 47 14N 124 13W
Mocoa, Colombia 168 C2 1 7N 76 35W
Mococa, Brazil 175 A6 21 28 S 47 0W
Mocorito, Mexico 162 B3 25 30N 107 53W
Moctezuma, Mexico 162 B3 29 50N 109 0W
Moctezuma →, Mexico 163 C5 21 59N 98 34W
Mocuba, Mozam. 119 F4 16 54 S 36 57 E
Mocúzari, Presa, Mexico 162 B3 27 10N 109 10W
Moda, Burma 90 C6 24 22N 96 29 E
Modane, France 29 C10 45 12N 6 40 E
Modasa, India 92 H5 23 30N 73 21 E
Modder →, S. Africa 116 D3 29 2 S 24 37 E
Modderrivier, S. Africa 116 D3 29 2 S 24 38 E
Módena, Italy 44 D7 44 40N 10 55 E
Modena, U.S.A. 159 H7 37 48N 113 56W
Modesto, U.S.A. 160 H6 37 39N 121 0W
Möðrudalur, Iceland 11 B11 65 22N 15 53W
Möðruvellir, Iceland 11 B8 65 46N 18 15W
Módica, Italy 47 F7 36 52N 14 46 E
Modjamboli, Dem. Rep. of the Congo 114 B4 2 28N 22 6 E
Mödling, Austria 35 C9 48 5N 16 17 E
Modo, Sudan 107 F3 5 31N 30 33 E
Modoc, U.S.A. 152 B7 33 44N 82 13W
Modowi, Indonesia 83 B4 4 5 S 134 39 E
Modra, Slovak Rep. 35 C10 48 19N 17 20 E
Modriča, Bos.-H. 52 F3 44 57N 18 17 E
Moe, Australia 129 E7 38 12 S 146 19 E
Moebase, Mozam. 119 F4 17 3 S 38 41 E
Moëlan-sur-Mer, France 26 E3 47 49N 3 38W
Moelv, Norway 18 D7 60 56N 10 43 E
Moengo, Surinam 169 B7 5 45N 54 20W
Moerewa, N.Z. 130 B3 35 8 S 174 1 E
Moësa →, Switz. 33 D8 46 12N 9 10 E
Moffat, U.K. 22 F5 55 21N 3 27W
Moga, India 92 D6 30 48N 75 8 E
Mogadishu = Muqdisho, Somali Rep. 120 D3 2 2N 45 25 E
Mogador = Essaouira, Morocco 110 B3 31 32N 9 42W
Mogadouro, Portugal 42 D4 41 22N 6 47W
Mogalakwena →, S. Africa 117 C4 22 38 S 28 40 E
Mogami-Gawa →, Japan 70 E10 38 45N 140 0 E
Mogán, Canary Is. 9 e1 27 53N 15 43W
Mogandjo, Dem. Rep. of the Congo 114 B4 1 23N 24 15 E
Mogaung, Burma 90 C6 25 20N 97 0 E
Mogen, Norway 18 D4 60 2N 7 52 E
Mogente = Moixent, Spain 41 G4 38 52N 0 45W
Mogho, Ethiopia 107 G5 4 54N 40 16 E
Mogi das Cruzes, Brazil 175 A6 23 31 S 46 11W
Mogi-Guaçu →, Brazil 175 A6 20 53 S 48 10W
Mogi-Mirim, Brazil 175 A6 22 29 S 47 0W
Mogielnica, Poland 55 G7 51 42N 20 41 E
Mogige, Ethiopia 107 F4 5 24N 36 14 E
Mogilev = Mahilyow, Belarus 58 F6 53 55N 30 18 E
Mogilev-Podolskiy = Mohyliv-Podilskyy, Ukraine 59 H4 48 26N 27 48 E
Mogilno, Poland 55 F4 52 39N 17 55 E
Mogincual, Mozam. 119 F5 15 35 S 40 25 E
Mogliano Véneto, Italy 45 C9 45 33N 12 14 E
Mogocha, Russia 67 D12 53 40N 119 50 E
Mogoi, Indonesia 83 B4 1 55 S 133 10 E
Mogok, Burma 90 D6 23 0N 96 40 E
Mogollon Rim, U.S.A. 159 J8 34 10N 110 50W
Mógoro, Italy 46 C1 39 41N 8 47 E
Mograt, Sudan 106 D3 19 28N 33 16 E
Mogroum, Chad 109 F3 11 6N 15 25 E
Moguer, Spain 43 H4 37 15N 6 52W
Mogumber, Australia 125 F2 31 2 S 116 3 E
Mohács, Hungary 52 E3 45 58N 18 41 E
Mohaka →, N.Z. 130 F6 39 7 S 177 12 E
Mohala, India 94 D5 20 35N 80 44 E
Mohales Hoek, Lesotho 116 E4 30 7 S 27 26 E
Mohali, Congo 114 B3 0 15N 15 29 E
Mohall, U.S.A. 154 A4 48 46N 101 31W
Moḥammadābād, Iran 97 B8 37 52N 59 5 E
Mohammadia, Algeria 111 A5 35 33N 0 3 E
Mohammedia, Morocco 110 B3 33 44N 7 21W
Mohana, India 94 E7 19 27N 84 16 E
Mohana →, India 93 G11 24 43N 85 0 E
Mohanganj, Bangla. 90 C3 24 54N 90 59 E
Mohanlalganj, India 93 F9 26 41N 80 58 E
Mohave, L., U.S.A. 161 K12 35 12N 114 34W
Mohawk →, U.S.A. 151 D11 42 47N 73 41W
Moheda, Sweden 17 G8 57 1N 14 35 E
Mohéli, Comoros Is. 121 a 12 20 S 43 40 E
Mohenjodaro, Pakistan 91 D3 27 19N 68 7 E
Mohican, C., U.S.A. 144 F6 60 12N 167 25W
Mohicanville Reservoir, U.S.A. 150 F3 40 45N 82 0W
Möhlin, Switz. 32 A5 47 33N 7 51 E
Möhne →, Germany 30 D3 51 29N 7 57 E
Mohnyin, Burma 90 C6 24 47N 96 22 E
Mohoro, Tanzania 118 D4 8 6 S 39 8 E
Mohyliv-Podilskyy, Ukraine 59 H4 48 26N 27 48 E
Moi, Norway 18 F3 58 27N 6 32 E
Moia, Sudan 107 F2 5 3N 28 2 E
Moidart, L., U.K. 22 E3 56 47N 5 52W
Moinabad, India 94 F3 17 44N 77 16 E
Moindou, N. Cal. 133 U19 21 42 S 165 41 E
Moineşti, Romania 53 D11 46 28N 26 31 E
Moira →, Canada 150 B7 44 21N 77 24W
Moirang, India 90 C4 24 30N 93 46 E
Moirans, France 29 C9 45 20N 5 33 E
Moirans-en-Montagne, France 27 F12 46 26N 5 43 E
Moíres, Greece 39 E5 35 4N 24 56 E
Moisaküla, Estonia 15 G21 58 3N 25 12 E
Moisie, Canada 141 B6 50 12N 66 1W
Moisie →, Canada 141 B6 50 14N 66 5W
Moissac, France 28 D5 44 7N 1 5 E
Moïssala, Chad 109 G3 8 21N 17 46 E
Moita, Portugal 43 G2 38 38N 8 58W
Moixent, Spain 41 G4 38 52N 0 45W
Möja, Sweden 16 E12 59 26N 18 55 E
Mojácar, Spain 41 H3 37 6N 1 55W
Mojados, Spain 42 D6 41 26N 4 40W
Mojave, U.S.A. 161 K8 35 3N 118 10W
Mojave Desert, U.S.A. 161 L10 35 0N 116 30W
Moji, China 65 D7 39 0N 74 27 E
Mojiang, China 76 F3 23 37N 101 35 E
Mojjo →, Ethiopia 107 F5 7 55N 42 0 E
Mojkovac, Montenegro, Yug. 50 D3 42 58N 19 35 E
Mojo, Bolivia 174 A2 21 48 S 65 33W
Mojo, Ethiopia 107 F4 8 35N 39 5 E
Mojokerto, Indonesia 85 D4 7 28 S 112 26 E
Mojos, Llanos de, Bolivia 173 D5 15 10 S 65 0W
Moju, Brazil 170 B2 1 53 S 48 46W
Moju →, Brazil 170 B2 1 40 S 48 25W
Mokai, N.Z. 130 E4 38 32 S 175 56 E
Mokambo, Dem. Rep. of the Congo 119 E2 12 25 S 28 20 E
Mokameh, India 93 G11 25 24N 85 55 E
Mokane, U.S.A. 156 F5 38 41N 91 53W
Mokapu Peninsula, U.S.A. 145 K14 21 25N 157 45W
Mokau, N.Z. 130 E3 38 42 S 174 39 E
Mokau →, N.Z. 130 E3 38 35 S 174 35 E
Mokelumne →, U.S.A. 160 G5 38 13N 121 28W
Mokelumne Hill, U.S.A. 160 G6 38 18N 120 43W
Mokhós, Greece 39 E6 35 16N 25 27 E
Mokhotlong, Lesotho 117 D4 29 22 S 29 2 E
Mokihinui →, N.Z. 131 B6 41 33 S 171 58 E
Möklinta, Sweden 16 D10 60 4N 16 33 E
Moknine, Tunisia 108 A2 35 35N 10 58 E
Mokoan, L., Australia 129 D7 36 27 S 146 5 E
Mokokchung, India 90 B5 26 15N 94 30 E
Mokolea Rock, U.S.A. 145 K14 21 27N 157 44W
Mokolo, Cameroon 113 C7 10 50N 13 55 E
Mokolo, Cent. Amer. 109 F2 10 49N 13 54 E
Mokolo, Dem. Rep. of the Congo 114 B3 1 55N 18 6 E
Mokolo →, S. Africa 117 C4 23 14 S 27 43 E
Mokombe, Dem. Rep. of the Congo 114 C4 0 14 S 23 48 E
Mokpalin, Burma 90 G6 17 26N 96 53 E
Mokp'o, S. Korea 75 G14 34 50N 126 25 E
Mokra Gora, Yugoslavia 50 D4 42 50N 20 30 E
Mokronog, Slovenia 45 C12 45 57N 15 9 E
Moksha →, Russia 60 C6 54 45N 41 53 E
Mokshan, Russia 60 D7 53 25N 44 35 E
Mokuaeae I., U.S.A. 145 A2 22 14N 159 25W
Mokuauia I., U.S.A. 145 J14 21 40N 157 56W
Mokulua Is., U.S.A. 145 K14 21 24N 157 42W
Mokwa, Nigeria 113 D6 9 19N 5 0 E
Mol, Belgium 24 C5 51 11N 5 5 E
Mola di Bari, Italy 47 A10 41 4N 17 5 E
Molakalmuru, India 95 G3 14 55N 76 50 E
Molale, Ethiopia 107 E4 10 10N 39 41 E
Molanda, Dem. Rep. of the Congo 114 B4 2 28N 20 48 E
Moláoi, Greece 48 E4 36 49N 22 56 E
Molara, Italy 46 B2 40 52N 9 43 E
Molat, Croatia 45 D11 44 15N 14 50 E
Molave, Phil. 81 G4 8 5N 123 30 E
Molchanovo, Russia 66 D9 57 40N 83 50 E
Mold, U.K. 20 D4 53 9N 3 8W
Moldava nad Bodvou, Slovak Rep. 35 C14 48 38N 21 0 E
Moldavia = Moldova ■, Europe 53 C13 47 0N 28 0 E
Moldavia, Romania 53 D12 46 30N 27 0 E
Molde, Norway 14 E12 62 45N 7 9 E
Moldo Too, Kyrgyzstan 65 C7 41 35N 75 0 E
Moldotau = Moldo Too, Kyrgyzstan 65 C7 41 35N 75 0 E
Moldova ■, Europe 53 C13 47 0N 28 0 E
Moldova Nouă, Romania 52 F6 44 45N 21 41 E
Moldoveanu, Vf., Romania 53 E9 45 36N 24 45 E
Moldoviţa, Romania 53 C10 47 41N 25 32 E
Mole →, U.K. 21 F7 51 24N 0 21W
Mole Creek, Australia 127 G4 41 34 S 146 24 E
Mole Nat. Park, Ghana 113 D4 9 43N 1 44W
Molegbwe, Dem. Rep. of the Congo 114 B4 4 12N 20 53 E
Molepolole, Botswana 116 C4 24 28 S 25 28 E
Molesworth, N.Z. 131 C8 42 5 S 173 16 E
Molfetta, Italy 47 A9 41 12N 16 36 E
Molii Pond, U.S.A. 145 J14 21 31N 157 51W
Molina de Aragón, Spain 40 E3 40 46N 1 52W
Molina de Segura, Spain 41 G3 38 3N 1 12W
Moline, U.S.A. 156 C6 41 30N 90 31W
Molinella, Italy 45 D8 44 37N 11 40 E
Molino, U.S.A. 153 E2 30 43N 87 20W
Molinos, Argentina 174 B2 25 28 S 66 15W
Moliro, Dem. Rep. of the Congo 118 D3 8 12 S 30 30 E
Moliterno, Italy 47 B8 40 14N 15 52 E
Molkom, Sweden 16 E7 59 37N 13 44 E
Mölle, Sweden 17 H6 56 17N 12 31 E
Molledo, Spain 42 B6 43 8N 4 6W
Mollendo, Peru 172 D3 17 0 S 72 0W
Mollerin, L., Australia 125 F2 30 30 S 117 35 E
Mollerussa, Spain 40 D5 41 37N 0 54 E
Mollina, Spain 43 H6 37 8N 4 38W
Mölln, Germany 30 B6 53 39N 10 32 E
Mölltorp, Sweden 17 F8 58 30N 14 26 E
Mölnlycke, Sweden 17 G6 57 40N 12 8 E
Molo, Burma 90 D6 23 22N 96 53 E
Molochansk, Ukraine 59 J8 47 15N 35 35 E
Molochnoye, Ozero, Ukraine 59 J8 46 30N 35 20 E
Molodechno = Maladzyechna, Belarus 58 E4 54 20N 26 50 E
Molokai, U.S.A. 145 B5 21 8N 157 0W
Molokini I., U.S.A. 145 C5 20 38N 156 30W
Moloma →, Russia 64 B2 58 29N 48 33 E
Molong, Australia 129 B8 33 5 S 148 54 E
Molopo →, Africa 116 D3 27 30 S 20 13 E
Mólos, Greece 48 C4 38 47N 22 37 E
Molotov = Perm, Russia 64 C6 58 0N 56 10 E
Moloundou, Cameroon 114 B3 2 8N 15 15 E
Molowaie, Dem. Rep. of the Congo 115 D4 5 47 S 23 18 E
Molsheim, France 27 D14 48 33N 7 29 E
Molson L., Canada 143 C9 54 22N 96 40W
Molteno, S. Africa 116 E4 31 22 S 26 22 E
Moltrásio, Italy 33 E8 45 52N 9 6 E
Molu, Indonesia 83 C4 6 45 S 131 40 E
Molucca Sea, Indonesia 82 A3 0 0 125 0 E
Moluccas = Maluku, Indonesia 79 E7 1 0 S 127 0 E
Molundo, Phil. 81 H5 7 57N 124 23 E
Moma, Dem. Rep. of the Congo 118 C1 1 35 S 23 52 E
Moma, Mozam. 119 F4 16 47 S 39 4 E
Momba, Australia 128 A5 30 58 S 143 30 E
Mombaça, Brazil 170 C4 5 43 S 39 45W
Mombango, Dem. Rep. of the Congo 114 B4 1 45N 24 26 E
Mombasa, Kenya 118 C4 4 2 S 39 43 E
Mombetsu, Japan 70 B11 44 21N 143 22 E
Mombil, Burma 90 B7 27 46N 98 6 E
Momboyo →, Dem. Rep. of the Congo 114 C3 0 16 S 19 0 E
Mombuey, Spain 42 C4 42 3N 6 20W
Momchilgrad, Bulgaria 51 E9 41 33N 25 23 E
Momence, U.S.A. 157 C9 41 10N 87 40W
Momi, Dem. Rep. of the Congo 118 C2 1 42 S 27 0 E
Momote, Papua N. G. 132 B4 2 4 S 147 27 E
Mompog Pass, Phil. 80 E4 13 34N 122 13 E
Mompós, Colombia 168 B3 9 14N 74 26W
Møn, Denmark 17 K6 54 57N 12 20 E
Mon □, Burma 90 G6 16 0N 97 30 E
Mona, Canal de la, W. Indies 165 C6 18 30N 67 45W
Mona, Isla, Puerto Rico 165 C6 18 5N 67 54W
Mona, Pta., Costa Rica 164 E3 9 37N 82 36W
Mona Quimbundo, Angola 115 D3 9 55 S 19 58 E
Monaca, U.S.A. 150 F4 40 41N 80 17W
Monaco ■, Europe 29 E11 43 46N 7 23 E
Monadhliath Mts., U.K. 22 D4 57 10N 4 4W
Monadnock, Mt., U.S.A. 151 D12 42 52N 72 7W
Monagas □, Venezuela 169 B5 9 20N 63 0W
Monaghan, Ireland 23 B5 54 15N 6 57W
Monaghan □, Ireland 23 B5 54 11N 6 56W
Monahans, U.S.A. 155 K3 31 36N 102 54W
Monapo, Mozam. 119 E5 14 56 S 40 19 E
Monar, L., U.K. 22 D3 57 26N 5 8W
Monaragala, Sri Lanka 95 L5 6 52N 81 22 E
Monarch Mt., Canada 142 C3 51 55N 125 57W
Monashee Mts., Canada 142 C5 51 0N 118 43W
Monasterevin, Ireland 23 C4 53 8N 7 4W
Monastir = Bitola, Macedonia 50 E5 41 1N 21 20 E
Monastir, Tunisia 108 A2 35 50N 10 49 E
Moncada, Phil. 80 D3 15 44N 120 34 E
Moncalieri, Italy 44 D4 45 0N 7 41 E
Moncalvo, Italy 44 C5 45 3N 8 16 E
Monção, Portugal 42 C2 42 4N 8 27W
Moncarapacho, Portugal 43 H3 37 5N 7 46W
Moncayo, Sierra del, Spain 40 D3 41 48N 1 50W
Monchegorsk, Russia 56 A5 67 54N 32 58 E
Mönchengladbach, Germany 30 D2 51 11N 6 27 E
Monchique, Portugal 43 H2 37 19N 8 38W
Moncks Corner, U.S.A. 152 B9 33 12N 80 1W
Monclova, Mexico 162 B4 26 50N 101 30W
Moncontour, France 26 D4 48 22N 2 38W
Moncton, Canada 141 C7 46 7N 64 51W
Mondariz, Spain 42 C2 42 14N 8 27W
Mondego →, Portugal 42 E2 40 9N 8 52W
Mondego, C., Portugal 42 E2 40 11N 8 54W
Mondeodo, Indonesia 82 B2 3 34 S 122 9 E
Mondeville, France 26 C6 49 10N 0 18W
Mondimbi, Dem. Rep. of the Congo 114 B4 1 48N 22 46 E
Mondjuku, Dem. Rep. of the Congo 114 C4 1 41 S 21 12 E
Mondo, Chad 109 F3 13 47N 15 32 E
Mondolfo, Italy 45 E10 43 45N 13 6 E
Mondoñedo, Spain 42 B3 43 25N 7 23W
Mondovì, Italy 44 D4 44 23N 7 49 E
Mondragon, Phil. 80 E5 12 31N 124 45 E
Mondragone, Italy 46 A6 41 7N 13 53 E
Mondrain I., Australia 125 F3 34 9 S 122 14 E
Moneague, Jamaica 164 a 18 16N 77 7W
Monemvasía, Greece 48 E5 36 41N 23 3 E
Monessen, U.S.A. 150 F5 40 9N 79 54W
Monesterio, Spain 43 G4 38 6N 6 15W
Monestier-de-Clermont, France 29 D9 44 55N 5 38 E
Monett, U.S.A. 155 G8 36 55N 93 55W
Moneymore, U.K. 23 B5 54 41N 6 40W
Monfalcone, Italy 45 C10 45 49N 13 32 E
Monflanquin, France 28 D4 44 32N 0 47 E
Monforte, Portugal 43 F3 39 6N 7 25W
Monforte de Lemos, Spain 42 C3 42 31N 7 33W
Möng Hsu, Burma 76 G2 21 54N 98 30 E
Mong Hta, Burma 90 F7 19 50N 98 35 E
Mong Ket, Burma 90 D7 23 8N 98 22 E
Mong Kung, Burma 90 E6 21 35N 97 35 E
Mong Kyawt, Burma 90 F7 19 56N 98 45 E
Möng long, Burma 90 D6 22 47N 96 37 E
Möng Mit, Burma 90 D6 23 7N 96 41 E
Möng Nai, Burma 90 E6 20 32N 97 46 E
Mong Pan, Burma 90 E7 20 19N 98 22 E
Mong Ping, Burma 76 G2 21 22N 99 2 E
Mong Pu, Burma 90 E7 20 55N 98 44 E
Mong Ton, Burma 90 E7 20 17N 98 45 E
Mong Tung, Burma 90 D6 22 2N 97 41 E
Möng Yai, Burma 90 D7 22 21N 98 3 E
Möng Yu, Burma 90 D6 23 30N 97 47 E
Monga, Dem. Rep. of the Congo 114 B4 4 12N 22 49 E
Mongala →, Dem. Rep. of the Congo 114 B3 1 53N 19 46 E
Mongalla, Sudan 107 F3 5 8N 31 42 E
Mongandia, Congo 114 B3 0 45N 17 11 E
Mongers, L., Australia 125 E2 29 25 S 117 5 E
Mongga, Solomon Is. 133 L9 7 52 S 157 0 E
Monghyr = Munger, India 93 G12 25 23N 86 30 E
Mongibello = Etna, Italy 47 E7 37 50N 14 55 E
Mongla, Bangla. 90 D2 22 8N 89 35 E
Mongngaw, Burma 90 D6 22 47N 96 59 E
Mongo, Chad 109 F3 12 14N 18 43 E
Mongo, Eq. Guin. 114 B2 1 52N 10 10 E
Mongo →, S. Leone 112 D2 9 35N 12 10W
Mongolia ■, Asia 67 E10 47 0N 103 0 E
Mongomo, Eq. Guin. 114 B2 1 38N 11 19 E
Mongonu, Nigeria 113 C7 12 40N 13 32 E
Mongororo, Chad 109 F4 12 3N 22 26 E
Mongstad, Norway 18 D2 60 49N 5 2 E
Mongu, Zambia 115 F4 15 16 S 23 12 E
Mônguà, Angola 116 B2 16 43 S 15 20 E
Moniac, U.S.A. 152 E7 30 31N 82 14W
Monifieth, U.K. 22 E6 56 30N 2 48W
Monistrol-sur-Loire, France 29 C8 45 17N 4 11 E
Monkayo, Phil. 81 H6 7 50N 126 5 E
Monkey Bay, Malawi 119 E4 14 7 S 35 1 E
Monkey Mia, Australia 125 E1 25 48 S 113 43 E
Monkey River, Belize 163 D7 16 22N 88 29W
Mońki, Poland 54 E9 53 23N 22 48 E
Monkoto, Dem. Rep. of the Congo 114 C4 1 38 S 20 35 E
Monkton, Canada 150 C3 43 35N 81 5W
Monmouth, U.K. 21 F5 51 48N 2 42W
Monmouth, Ill., U.S.A. 156 D6 40 55N 90 39W
Monmouth, Oreg., U.S.A. 158 D2 44 51N 123 14W
Monmouthshire □, U.K. 21 F5 51 48N 2 54W
Mono, Solomon Is. 133 L8 7 20 S 155 35 E
Mono L., U.S.A. 160 H7 38 1N 119 1W
Monolith, U.S.A. 161 K8 35 7N 118 22W
Monólithos, Greece 38 E11 36 7N 27 45 E
Monon, U.S.A. 157 D10 40 52N 86 53W
Monona, Iowa, U.S.A. 156 A5 43 3N 91 23W
Monona, Wis., U.S.A. 156 A7 43 4N 89 20W
Monongahela, U.S.A. 150 F5 40 12N 79 56W
Monópoli, Italy 47 B10 40 57N 17 18 E
Monor, Hungary 52 C4 47 21N 19 27 E
Monos I., Trin. & Tob. 169 F9 10 42N 61 44W
Monóvar, Spain 41 G4 38 28N 0 53W
Monowai, N.Z. 131 F2 45 53 S 167 31 E
Monowai, L., N.Z. 131 F2 45 53 S 167 25 E
Monqoumba, C.A.R. 114 B3 3 33N 18 40 E
Monreal del Campo, Spain 40 E3 40 47N 1 20W
Monreale, Italy 46 D6 38 5N 13 17 E
Monroe, Ga., U.S.A. 152 B6 33 47N 83 43W
Monroe, Iowa, U.S.A. 156 C3 41 31N 93 6W
Monroe, La., U.S.A. 155 J8 32 30N 92 7W
Monroe, Mich., U.S.A. 157 C13 41 55N 83 24W
Monroe, N.C., U.S.A. 149 H5 34 59N 80 33W
Monroe, N.Y., U.S.A. 151 E10 41 20N 74 11W
Monroe, Ohio, U.S.A. 157 E12 39 27N 84 22W
Monroe, Utah, U.S.A. 159 G7 38 38N 112 7W
Monroe, Wash., U.S.A. 160 C5 47 51N 121 58W
Monroe, Wis., U.S.A. 156 B7 42 36N 89 38W
Monroe, L., U.S.A. 153 G8 28 50N 81 19W
Monroe City, Ind., U.S.A. 157 F9 38 37N 87 20W
Monroe City, Mo., U.S.A. 156 E5 39 39N 91 44W
Monroe L., U.S.A. 157 E10 39 1N 86 31W
Monroeton, U.S.A. 151 E8 41 43N 76 29W
Monroeville, Ala., U.S.A. 149 K2 31 31N 87 20W
Monroeville, Ind., U.S.A. 157 D12 40 59N 84 52W
Monroeville, Pa., U.S.A. 150 F5 40 26N 79 45W
Monrovia, Liberia 112 D2 6 18N 10 47W
Mons, Belgium 24 D3 50 27N 3 58 E
Møns Klint, Denmark 17 K6 54 57N 12 33 E
Monsaraz, Portugal 43 G3 38 28N 7 22W
Monse, Indonesia 82 B2 4 7 S 123 15 E
Monsefú, Peru 172 B2 6 52 S 79 52W
Monségur, France 28 D4 44 38N 0 4 E
Monsélice, Italy 45 C8 45 14N 11 45 E
Mønshaug, Norway 18 D3 60 37N 6 31 E
Mönsterås, Sweden 17 G10 57 3N 16 26 E
Mont Cenis, Col du, France 29 C10 45 15N 6 55 E
Mont-de-Marsan, France 28 E3 43 54N 0 31W
Mont-Dore, N. Cal. 133 V20 22 16 S 166 34 E
Mont Fouari, Réserve du, Congo 114 C2 2 52 S 11 32 E
Mont-Joli, Canada 141 C6 48 37N 68 10W
Mont-Laurier, Canada 140 C4 46 35N 75 30W
Mont-Louis, Canada 141 C6 49 15N 65 44W
Mont Peko, Parc Nat. du, Ivory C. 112 D3 9 5N 7 15W
Mont-roig del Camp, Spain 40 D5 41 5N 0 58 E
Mont-St-Michel, Le = Le Mont-St-Michel, France 26 D5 48 40N 1 30W
Mont Sangbe, Parc Nat. du, Ivory C. 112 D3 8 0N 7 10W
Mont Tremblant, Parc Recr. du, Canada 140 C5 46 30N 74 30W
Montabaur, Germany 30 E3 50 25N 7 50 E
Montagnac, France 28 E7 43 29N 3 28 E
Montagnana, Italy 45 C8 45 14N 11 28 E
Montagne d'Ambre, Parc Nat. de la, Madag. 117 A8 12 37 S 49 8 E
Montagu, S. Africa 116 E3 33 45 S 20 8 E
Montagu I., Antarctica 7 B1 58 25 S 26 20W
Montague, Canada 141 C7 46 10N 62 39W
Montague, I., Mexico 162 A2 31 40N 114 56W
Montague I., Australia 129 D9 36 16 S 150 13 E
Montague I., U.S.A. 144 G11 60 0N 147 30W
Montague Ra., Australia 125 E2 27 15 S 119 30 E
Montague Sd., Australia 124 B4 14 28 S 125 20 E
Montaigu, France 26 F5 46 59N 1 18W
Montalbán, Spain 40 E4 40 50N 0 45W

Mossbank, *Canada* **143 D7** 49 56N 105 56W
Mossburn, *N.Z.* **131 F3** 45 41 S 168 15 E
Mosselbaai, *S. Africa* **116 E3** 34 11 S 22 8 E
Mossendjo, *Congo* **114 C2** 2 55 S 12 42 E
Mosses, Col des, *Switz.* **32 D4** 46 25N 7 7 E
Mossfellsbær, *Iceland* **11 C5** 64 11N 21 45W
Mossgiel, *Australia* **128 B6** 33 15 S 144 5 E
Mossingen, *Germany* **31 G5** 48 24N 9 4 E
Mossman, *Australia* **126 B4** 16 21 S 145 15 E
Mossoró, *Brazil* **170 C4** 5 10 S 37 15W
Mossuril, *Mozam.* **119 E5** 14 58 S 40 42 E
Mossy Head, *U.S.A.* **153 E3** 30 45N 86 19W
Mossy Point, *Australia* **129 C9** 35 50 S 150 11 E
Most, *Czech Rep.* **34 A6** 50 31N 13 38 E
Mosta, *Malta* **38 F7** 35 55N 14 26 E
Mostaganem, *Algeria* **111 A5** 35 54N 0 5 E
Mostar, *Bos.-H.* **52 G2** 43 22N 17 50 E
Mostardas, *Brazil* **175 C5** 31 2 S 50 51W
Mostefa, Rass, *Tunisia* **108 A2** 36 55N 11 3 E
Mosteiros, *Azores* **9 d3** 37 53N 25 49W
Mosterhamn, *Norway* **18 E2** 59 42N 5 21 E
Mostiska = Mostyska, *Ukraine* **59 H2** 49 48N 23 4 E
Móstoles, *Spain* **42 E7** 40 19N 3 53W
Mosty = Masty, *Belarus* **58 F3** 53 27N 24 38 E
Mostyska, *Ukraine* **59 H2** 49 48N 23 4 E
Mosul = Al Mawşil, *Iraq* **101 D10** 36 15N 43 5 E
Mosŭlpo, *S. Korea* **75 H14** 33 20N 126 17 E
Møsvatnet, *Norway* **18 E5** 59 52N 8 5 E
Mota, *Ethiopia* **107 E4** 11 5N 37 52 E
Mota, *Vanuatu* **133 C5** 13 49 S 167 42 E
Mota del Cuervo, *Spain* **41 F2** 39 30N 2 52W
Mota del Marqués, *Spain* **42 D5** 41 38N 5 11W
Mota Lava, *Vanuatu* **133 C5** 13 40 S 167 40 E
Motaba, *Congo* **114 B3** 2 6N 18 2 E
Motagua →, *Guatemala* **164 C2** 15 44N 88 14W
Motala, *Sweden* **17 F9** 58 32N 15 1 E
Motaze, *Mozam.* **117 C5** 24 48 S 32 52 E
Moţca, *Romania* **53 C11** 47 15N 26 37 E
Motegi, *Japan* **73 A12** 36 32N 140 11 E
Moth, *India* **93 G8** 25 43N 78 57 E
Motherwell, *U.K.* **22 F5** 55 47N 3 58W
Motihari, *India* **93 F11** 26 30N 84 55 E
Motilla del Palancar, *Spain* **41 F3** 39 34N 1 55W
Motiti I., *N.Z.* **130 D5** 37 38 S 176 25 E
Motnik, *Slovenia* **45 B11** 46 14N 14 54 E
Motocurunya, *Venezuela* **169 C5** 4 24N 64 5W
Motovun, *Croatia* **45 C10** 45 20N 13 50 E
Motozintla de Mendoza, *Mexico* **163 D6** 15 21N 92 14W
Motril, *Spain* **43 J7** 36 31N 3 37W
Motru, *Romania* **52 F7** 44 48N 22 59 E
Motru →, *Romania* **53 F8** 44 32N 23 31 E
Mott, *U.S.A.* **154 B3** 46 23N 102 20W
Móttola, *Italy* **47 B10** 40 38N 17 2 E
Motu →, *N.Z.* **130 D6** 37 51 S 177 35 E
Motu Nui, *Chile* **172 b** 27 12 S 109 28W
Motuba, *Dem. Rep. of the Congo* **114 B3** 2 20N 18 34 E
Motueka, *N.Z.* **131 B8** 41 7 S 173 1 E
Motueka →, *N.Z.* **131 B8** 41 5 S 173 1 E
Motul, *Mexico* **163 C7** 21 0N 89 20W
Motupena Pt., *Papua N. G.* **132 D8** 6 30 S 155 10 E
Mou, *N. Cal.* **133 U19** 21 5 S 165 26 E
Mouanda, *Gabon* **114 C2** 1 28 S 13 7 E
Mouchalagane →, *Canada* **141 B6** 50 56N 68 41W
Moúdhros, *Greece* **49 B7** 39 50N 25 18 E
Mouding, *China* **76 E3** 25 20N 101 28 E
Moudjeria, *Mauritania* **112 B2** 17 50N 12 28W
Moudon, *Switz.* **32 C3** 46 40N 6 49 E
Mougoundou, *Congo* **114 C2** 2 40 S 12 41 E
Mouila, *Gabon* **114 C2** 1 50 S 11 0 E
Mouka, *C.A.R.* **114 A4** 7 16N 21 52 E
Moukalaba, Réserve de la, *Gabon* **114 C2** 2 50 S 10 35 E
Moukambo, *Gabon* **114 C2** 3 5 S 11 38 E
Moul, *Niger* **109 F2** 15 5N 13 11 E
Moulamein, *Australia* **128 C6** 35 3 S 144 1 E
Moule, *Guadeloupe* **164 b** 16 20N 61 21W
Moule à Chique, C., *St. Lucia* **165 f** 13 43N 60 57W
Moulianá, *Greece* **39 E6** 35 10N 25 59 E
Moulins, *France* **27 F10** 46 35N 3 19 E
Moulmein, *Burma* **90 G6** 16 30N 97 40 E
Moulmeingyun, *Burma* **90 G5** 16 23N 95 16 E
Moulouya, O. →, *Morocco* **111 A4** 35 5N 2 25W
Moulton, *U.S.A.* **156 D4** 40 41N 92 41W
Moultrie, *U.S.A.* **152 D6** 31 11N 83 47W
Moultrie, L., *U.S.A.* **152 B9** 33 20N 80 5W
Mouly, *N. Cal.* **133 K4** 20 47 S 166 26 E
Mounana, *Gabon* **114 C2** 1 18 S 13 13 E
Mound City, *Mo., U.S.A.* **154 E7** 40 7N 95 14W
Mound City, *S. Dak., U.S.A.* **154 C4** 45 44N 100 4W
Moúnda, Ákra, *Greece* **39 C2** 38 3N 20 47 E
Moundou, *Chad* **109 G3** 8 40N 16 10 E
Moundsville, *U.S.A.* **150 G4** 39 55N 80 44W
Mounembé, *Congo* **114 C2** 3 20 S 12 32 E
Moung, *Cambodia* **86 F4** 12 46N 103 27 E
Moungoudi, *Congo* **114 C2** 2 45 S 11 46 E
Mount Airy, *U.S.A.* **149 G5** 36 31N 80 37W
Mount Albert, *Canada* **150 B5** 44 8N 79 19W
Mount Aspiring Nat. Park, *N.Z.* **131 E3** 44 19 S 168 47 E
Mount Ayr, *U.S.A.* **156 D2** 40 43N 94 14W
Mount Barker, *S. Austral., Australia* **128 C3** 35 5 S 138 52 E
Mount Barker, *W. Austral., Australia* **125 F2** 34 38 S 117 40 E
Mount Beauty, *Australia* **129 D7** 36 47 S 147 10 E
Mount Brydges, *Canada* **150 D3** 42 54N 81 29W
Mount Buffalo Nat. Park, *Australia* **129 D7** 36 43 S 146 46 E
Mount Burr, *Australia* **127 F3** 37 34 S 140 26 E
Mount Carmel, *Ill., U.S.A.* **157 F9** 38 25N 87 46W
Mount Carmel, *Pa., U.S.A.* **151 F8** 40 47N 76 24W
Mount Carroll, *U.S.A.* **156 B7** 42 6N 89 59W
Mount Charleston, *U.S.A.* **161 J11** 36 16N 115 37W
Mount Clemens, *U.S.A.* **150 D2** 42 35N 82 53W
Mount Cook, *N.Z.* **131 D5** 43 44 S 170 5 E
Mount Cook Nat. Park, *N.Z.* **131 D5** 43 35 S 170 15 E
Mount Coolon, *Australia* **126 C4** 21 25 S 147 25 E
Mount Darwin, *Zimbabwe* **119 F3** 16 47 S 31 38 E
Mount Desert I., *U.S.A.* **149 C11** 44 21N 68 20W
Mount Dora, *U.S.A.* **149 L5** 28 48N 81 38W
Mount Eccles Nat. Park, *Australia* **128 E4** 38 5 S 141 54 E
Mount Eden, *U.S.A.* **157 F11** 38 3N 85 9W
Mount Edgecumbe, *U.S.A.* **144 H14** 57 3N 135 21W
Mount Edziza Prov. Park, *Canada* **142 B2** 57 30N 130 45W
Mount Elgon Nat. Park, *Kenya* **118 B3** 1 4N 34 42 E
Mount Elgon Nat. Park, *Uganda* **118 B3** 1 20N 34 30 E
Mount Field Nat. Park, *Australia* **127 G4** 42 39 S 146 35 E
Mount Fletcher, *S. Africa* **117 E4** 30 40 S 28 30 E
Mount Forest, *Canada* **140 D3** 43 59N 80 43W
Mount Gambier, *Australia* **128 D4** 37 50 S 140 46 E
Mount Garnet, *Australia* **126 B4** 17 37 S 145 6 E
Mount Hagen, *Papua N. G.* **132 C3** 5 52 S 144 16 E
Mount Holly, *U.S.A.* **151 G10** 39 59N 74 47W
Mount Holly Springs, *U.S.A.* **150 F7** 40 7N 77 12W
Mount Hope, *N.S.W., Australia* **129 B6** 32 51 S 145 51 E
Mount Hope, *S. Austral., Australia* **127 E2** 34 7 S 135 23 E
Mount Horeb, *U.S.A.* **156 B7** 43 1N 89 44W
Mount Isa, *Australia* **126 C2** 20 42 S 139 26 E
Mount Jewett, *U.S.A.* **150 E6** 41 44N 78 39W
Mount Kaputar Nat. Park, *Australia* **127 E5** 30 16 S 150 10 E
Mount Kenya Nat. Park, *Kenya* **118 C4** 0 7 S 37 21 E
Mount Kilimanjaro Nat. Park, *Tanzania* **118 C4** 3 2 S 37 19 E
Mount Kisco, *U.S.A.* **151 E11** 41 12N 73 44W
Mount Laguna, *U.S.A.* **161 N10** 32 52N 116 25W
Mount Larcom, *Australia* **126 C5** 23 48 S 150 59 E
Mount Lofty Ra., *Australia* **128 C3** 34 35 S 139 5 E
Mount Magnet, *Australia* **125 E2** 28 2 S 117 47 E
Mount Manara, *Australia* **128 B5** 32 29 S 143 58 E
Mount Maunganui, *N.Z.* **130 D5** 37 40 S 176 14 E
Mount Molloy, *Australia* **126 B4** 16 42 S 145 20 E
Mount Morgan, *Australia* **126 C5** 23 40 S 150 25 E
Mount Morris, *Mich., U.S.A.* **157 A13** 43 7N 83 42W
Mount Morris, *N.Y., U.S.A.* **150 D7** 42 44N 77 52W
Mount Olive, *U.S.A.* **156 E7** 39 4N 89 44W
Mount Olivet, *U.S.A.* **157 F12** 38 32N 84 2W
Mount Orab, *U.S.A.* **157 E13** 39 2N 83 55W
Mount Pearl, *Canada* **141 C9** 47 31N 52 47W
Mount Penn, *U.S.A.* **151 F9** 40 20N 75 54W
Mount Perry, *Australia* **127 D5** 25 13 S 151 42 E
Mount Pleasant, *Iowa, U.S.A.* **156 D5** 40 58N 91 33W
Mount Pleasant, *Mich., U.S.A.* **148 D3** 43 36N 84 46W
Mount Pleasant, *Pa., U.S.A.* **150 F5** 40 9N 79 33W
Mount Pleasant, *S.C., U.S.A.* **152 C10** 32 47N 79 52W
Mount Pleasant, *Tenn., U.S.A.* **149 H2** 35 32N 87 12W
Mount Pleasant, *Tex., U.S.A.* **155 J7** 33 9N 94 58W
Mount Pleasant, *Utah, U.S.A.* **158 G8** 39 33N 111 27W
Mount Pocono, *U.S.A.* **151 E9** 41 7N 75 22W
Mount Pulaski, *U.S.A.* **156 D7** 40 1N 89 17W
Mount Rainier Nat. Park, *U.S.A.* **160 D5** 46 55N 121 50W
Mount Remarkable Nat. Park, *Australia* **128 B3** 32 47 S 138 3 E
Mount Revelstoke Nat. Park, *Canada* **142 C5** 51 5N 118 30W
Mount Robson Prov. Park, *Canada* **142 C5** 53 0N 119 0W
Mount Roskill, *N.Z.* **130 C3** 36 55 S 174 45 E
Mount Selinda, *Zimbabwe* **117 C5** 20 24 S 32 43 E
Mount Shasta, *U.S.A.* **158 F2** 41 19N 122 19W
Mount Signal, *U.S.A.* **161 N11** 32 39N 115 37W
Mount Somers, *N.Z.* **131 D6** 43 45 S 171 27 E
Mount Sterling, *Ill., U.S.A.* **156 E6** 39 59N 90 45W
Mount Sterling, *Ky., U.S.A.* **157 F13** 38 4N 83 56W
Mount Sterling, *Ohio, U.S.A.* **157 E13** 39 43N 83 16W
Mount Surprise, *Australia* **126 B3** 18 10 S 144 17 E
Mount Union, *U.S.A.* **150 F7** 40 23N 77 53W
Mount Upton, *U.S.A.* **151 D9** 42 26N 75 23W
Mount Vernon, *Ga., U.S.A.* **152 C7** 32 11N 82 36W
Mount Vernon, *Ill., U.S.A.* **148 F1** 38 19N 88 55W
Mount Vernon, *Ind., U.S.A.* **154 F10** 38 17N 88 57W
Mount Vernon, *Ind., U.S.A.* **157 G9** 37 56N 87 54W
Mount Vernon, *Iowa, U.S.A.* **156 C5** 41 55N 91 23W
Mount Vernon, *N.Y., U.S.A.* **151 F11** 40 55N 73 50W
Mount Vernon, *Ohio, U.S.A.* **150 F2** 40 23N 82 29W
Mount Vernon, *Wash., U.S.A.* **160 B4** 48 25N 122 20W
Mount Victor, *Australia* **128 B3** 32 11 S 139 44 E
Mount Washington, *U.S.A.* **157 F11** 38 3N 85 33W
Mount Wellington, *N.Z.* **130 C3** 36 55 S 174 52 E
Mount William Nat. Park, *Australia* **127 G4** 40 56 S 148 14 E
Mount Zion, *U.S.A.* **157 E8** 39 46N 88 53W
Mountain □, *Phil.* **80 C3** 17 20N 121 10 E
Mountain Ash, *U.K.* **21 F4** 51 40N 3 23W
Mountain Center, *U.S.A.* **161 M10** 33 42N 116 44W
Mountain City, *Nev., U.S.A.* **158 F6** 41 50N 115 58W
Mountain City, *Tenn., U.S.A.* **149 G5** 36 29N 81 48W
Mountain Dale, *U.S.A.* **151 E10** 41 41N 74 32W
Mountain Grove, *U.S.A.* **155 G8** 37 8N 92 16W
Mountain Home, *Ark., U.S.A.* **155 G8** 36 20N 92 23W
Mountain Home, *Idaho, U.S.A.* **158 E6** 43 8N 115 41W
Mountain Iron, *U.S.A.* **154 B8** 47 32N 92 37W
Mountain Pass, *U.S.A.* **161 K11** 35 29N 115 35W
Mountain View, *Ark., U.S.A.* **155 H8** 35 52N 92 7W
Mountain View, *Calif., U.S.A.* **160 H4** 37 23N 122 5W
Mountain View, *Hawaii, U.S.A.* **145 D6** 19 33N 155 7W
Mountain Village, *U.S.A.* **144 E7** 62 5N 163 43W
Mountain Zebra Nat. Park, *S. Africa* **116 E4** 32 14 S 25 27 E
Mountainair, *U.S.A.* **159 J10** 34 31N 106 15W
Mountlake Terrace, *U.S.A.* **160 C4** 47 47N 122 19W
Mountmellick, *Ireland* **23 C4** 53 7N 7 20W
Mountrath, *Ireland* **23 D4** 53 0N 7 28W
Moura, *Australia* **126 C4** 24 35 S 149 58 E
Moura, *Brazil* **169 D5** 1 32 S 61 38W
Moura, *Portugal* **43 G3** 38 7N 7 30W
Mourão, *Portugal* **43 G3** 38 22N 7 22W
Mourdi, Dépression du, *Chad* **109 E4** 18 10N 23 0 E
Mourdiah, *Mali* **112 C3** 14 35N 7 25W
Mourenx, *France* **28 E3** 43 22N 0 38W
Mouri, *Ghana* **113 D4** 5 6N 1 14W
Mourilyan, *Australia* **126 B4** 17 35 S 146 3 E
Mourmelon-le-Grand, *France* **27 C11** 49 8N 4 22 E
Mourne →, *U.K.* **23 B4** 54 52N 7 26W
Mourne Mts., *U.K.* **23 B5** 54 10N 6 0W
Mourniaí, *Greece* **39 E5** 35 29N 24 1 E
Mournies = Mourniaí, *Greece* **39 E5** 35 29N 24 1 E
Mouscron, *Belgium* **24 D3** 50 45N 3 12 E
Mousgougou, *Chad* **109 F3** 10 47N 16 9 E
Moussoro, *Chad* **109 F3** 13 41N 16 35 E
Mouthe, *France* **27 F13** 46 44N 6 12 E
Moutier, *Switz.* **32 B4** 47 16N 7 21 E
Moûtiers, *France* **29 C10** 45 29N 6 32 E
Moutohara, *N.Z.* **130 E6** 38 27 S 177 32 E
Moutong, *Indonesia* **82 A2** 0 28N 121 13 E
Mouy, *France* **27 C9** 49 18N 2 20 E
Mouyondzi, *Congo* **114 C2** 4 1 S 13 59 E
Mouzáki, *Greece* **48 B3** 39 25N 21 37 E
Mouzon, *France* **27 C12** 49 36N 5 3 E
Movas, *Mexico* **162 B3** 28 10N 109 25W
Moville, *Ireland* **23 A4** 55 11N 7 3W
Mowandjum, *Australia* **124 C3** 17 22 S 123 40 E
Moweaqua, *U.S.A.* **156 E7** 39 38N 89 1W
Moxico □, *Angola* **115 E4** 12 0 S 20 30 E
Moxotó →, *Brazil* **170 C4** 9 19 S 38 14W
Moy →, *Ireland* **23 B2** 54 8N 9 8W
Moya, *Comoros Is.* **121 a** 12 18 S 44 18 E
Moyale, *Kenya* **107 G4** 3 30N 39 0 E
Moyamba, *S. Leone* **112 D2** 8 4N 12 30W
Moyen Atlas, *Morocco* **110 B4** 33 0N 5 0W
Moyne, L. le, *Canada* **141 A6** 56 45N 68 47W
Moyo, *Indonesia* **85 D5** 8 10 S 117 40 E
Moyobamba, *Peru* **172 B2** 6 0 S 77 0W
Moyto, *Chad* **109 F3** 12 35N 16 33 E
Moyyero →, *Russia* **67 C11** 68 44N 103 42 E
Moyynqum, *Kazakstan* **65 A6** 44 17N 72 57 E
Moyynty, *Kazakstan* **66 E8** 47 10N 73 18 E
Mozambique = Moçambique, *Mozam.* **119 F5** 15 3 S 40 42 E
Mozambique ■, *Africa* **119 F4** 19 0 S 35 0 E
Mozambique Chan., *Africa* **117 B7** 17 30 S 42 30 E
Mozdok, *Russia* **61 J7** 43 45N 44 48 E
Mozdūrān, *Iran* **97 B9** 36 9N 60 35 E
Mozhaysk, *Russia* **58 E9** 55 30N 36 2 E
Mozhga, *Russia* **60 B11** 56 26N 52 15 E
Mozhnābād, *Iran* **97 C9** 34 7N 60 6 E
Mozirje, *Slovenia* **45 B11** 46 22N 14 58 E
Mozyr = Mazyr, *Belarus* **59 F5** 51 59N 29 15 E
Mpanda, *Tanzania* **118 D3** 6 23 S 31 1 E
Mpé, *Congo* **114 C2** 2 58 S 14 38 E
Mpese, *Dem. Rep. of the Congo* **115 D3** 5 16 S 15 30 E
Mpésoba, *Mali* **112 C3** 12 31N 5 39W
Mphoengs, *Zimbabwe* **117 C4** 21 10 S 27 51 E
Mpika, *Zambia* **119 E3** 11 51 S 31 25 E
Mpoko →, *C.A.R.* **114 B3** 4 19N 18 33 E
Mpouya, *Congo* **114 C3** 2 38 S 16 13 E
Mpulungu, *Zambia* **119 D3** 8 51 S 31 5 E
Mpumalanga, *S. Africa* **117 D5** 29 50 S 30 33 E
Mpumalanga □, *S. Africa* **117 B5** 26 0 S 30 0 E
Mpwapwa, *Tanzania* **118 D4** 6 23 S 36 30 E
Mqabba, *Malta* **38 F7** 35 51N 14 28 E
Mqanduli, *S. Africa* **117 E4** 31 49 S 28 45 E
Mqinvartsveri = Kazbek, *Russia* **61 J7** 42 42N 44 30 E
Mrągowo, *Poland* **54 E8** 53 52N 21 18 E
Mramor, *Serbia, Yug.* **50 C5** 43 20N 21 45 E
Mrimina, *Morocco* **110 C3** 29 50N 7 9W
Mrkonjić Grad, *Bos.-H.* **52 F2** 44 26N 17 4 E
Mrkopalj, *Croatia* **45 C11** 45 21N 14 52 E
Mrocza, *Poland* **55 E4** 53 16N 17 35 E
Msaken, *Tunisia* **108 A2** 35 49N 10 33 E
Msambansovu, *Zimbabwe* **119 F3** 15 50 S 30 3 E
Msida, *Malta* **38 F7** 35 54N 14 29 E
M'sila, *Algeria* **111 A5** 35 46N 4 30 E
Msoro, *Zambia* **119 E3** 13 35 S 31 50 E
Msta →, *Russia* **58 C6** 58 25N 31 20 E
Mstislavl = Mstsislaw, *Belarus* **58 E6** 54 0N 31 50 E
Mstsislaw, *Belarus* **58 E6** 54 0N 31 50 E
Mszana Dolna, *Poland* **55 J7** 49 41N 20 5 E
Mszczonów, *Poland* **55 G7** 51 58N 20 33 E
Mtama, *Tanzania* **119 E4** 10 17 S 39 21 E
Mtamvuna →, *S. Africa* **117 E5** 31 6 S 30 12 E
Mtilikwe →, *Zimbabwe* **119 G3** 21 9 S 31 30 E
Mtima, *Congo* **114 C2** 3 49 S 12 7 E
Mtsensk, *Russia* **58 F9** 53 17N 36 36 E
Mtskheta, *Georgia* **61 K7** 41 52N 44 45 E
Mtubatuba, *S. Africa* **117 D5** 28 30 S 32 8 E
Mtwalume, *S. Africa* **117 E5** 30 30 S 30 38 E
Mtwara-Mikindani, *Tanzania* **119 E5** 10 20 S 40 20 E
Mu →, *Burma* **90 E5** 21 56N 95 38 E
Mu Gia, Deo, *Vietnam* **86 D5** 17 40N 105 47 E
Mu Us Shamo, *China* **74 E5** 39 0N 109 0 E
Muacandala, *Angola* **115 E3** 10 2 S 19 40 E
Muaná, *Brazil* **170 B2** 1 25 S 49 15W
Muanda, *Dem. Rep. of the Congo* **115 D2** 6 0 S 12 20 E
Muang Chiang Rai = Chiang Rai, *Thailand* **76 H2** 19 52N 99 50 E
Muang Khong, *Laos* **86 E5** 14 7N 105 51 E
Muang Lamphun, *Thailand* **86 C2** 18 40N 99 2 E
Muang Mai, *Thailand* **87 a** 8 5N 98 21 E
Muang Pak Beng, *Laos* **76 H3** 19 54N 101 8 E
Muangai, *Angola* **115 E3** 12 32 S 19 55 E
Muar, *Malaysia* **87 L4** 2 3N 102 34 E
Muarabungo, *Indonesia* **84 C2** 1 28 S 102 52 E
Muaraenim, *Indonesia* **84 C2** 3 40 S 103 50 E
Muarajuloi, *Indonesia* **85 C4** 0 12 S 114 3 E
Muarakaman, *Indonesia* **85 C5** 0 2 S 116 45 E
Muaratebo, *Indonesia* **84 C2** 1 30 S 102 26 E
Muaratembesi, *Indonesia* **84 C2** 1 42 S 103 8 E
Muaratewe, *Indonesia* **85 C4** 0 58 S 114 52 E
Mubarakpur, *India* **93 F10** 26 6N 83 18 E
Mubarek, *Uzbekistan* **65 D2** 39 15N 65 9 E
Mubarraz = Al Mubarraz, *Si. Arabia* **97 E6** 25 30N 49 40 E
Mubende, *Uganda* **118 B3** 0 33N 31 22 E
Mubi, *Nigeria* **113 C7** 10 18N 13 16 E
Mucajá, *Brazil* **169 D6** 3 57 S 57 32W
Mucajaí →, *Brazil* **169 C5** 2 25N 60 52W
Mucajaí, Serra do, *Brazil* **169 C5** 2 23N 61 10W
Mucari, *Angola* **115 D3** 9 30 S 16 54 E
Muchachos, Roque de los, *Canary Is.* **9 e1** 28 44N 17 52W
Mücheln, *Germany* **30 D7** 51 17N 11 47 E
Muchinga Mts., *Zambia* **119 E3** 11 30 S 31 30 E
Muchkapskiy, *Russia* **60 E6** 51 52N 42 28 E
Muchuan, *China* **76 C5** 28 57N 103 55 E
Muck, *U.K.* **22 E2** 56 50N 6 15W
Muckadilla, *Australia* **127 D4** 26 35 S 148 23 E
Muckalee Cr. →, *U.S.A.* **152 D5** 31 38N 84 9W
Muco →, *Colombia* **168 C3** 4 15N 70 21W
Mucoma, *Angola* **115 F2** 15 18 S 13 39 E
Muconda, *Angola* **115 E4** 10 31 S 21 15 E
Mucope, *Angola* **115 F2** 16 24 S 14 52 E
Mucugê, *Brazil* **171 D3** 13 0 S 41 23W
Mucuim →, *Brazil* **173 B5** 6 33 S 64 18W
Mucur, *Turkey* **100 C6** 39 3N 34 22 E
Mucura, *Brazil* **169 D5** 2 31 S 62 43W
Mucuri, *Brazil* **171 E4** 18 0 S 39 36W
Mucurici, *Brazil* **171 E3** 18 6 S 40 31W
Mucusso, *Angola* **116 B3** 18 1 S 21 25 E
Mucusso, Coutada Pública do, *Angola* **115 F4** 17 27 S 21 0 E
Muda, *Canary Is.* **9 e2** 28 34N 13 57W
Mudanjiang, *China* **75 B15** 44 38N 129 30 E
Mudanya, *Turkey* **51 F12** 40 25N 28 50 E
Muddebihal, *India* **95 F3** 16 20N 76 8 E
Muddy Cr. →, *U.S.A.* **159 H8** 38 24N 110 42W
Mudgee, *Australia* **129 B8** 32 32 S 149 31 E
Mudhol, *Andhra Pradesh, India* **94 E3** 18 58N 77 55 E
Mudhol, *Karnataka, India* **95 F2** 16 21N 75 17 E
Mudiata, *Dem. Rep. of the Congo* **115 D4** 7 15 S 22 1 E
Mudigere, *India* **95 H2** 13 8N 75 38 E
Mudjatik →, *Canada* **143 B7** 56 1N 107 36W
Mudon, *Burma* **90 G6** 16 15N 97 44 E
Mudugh, *Somali Rep.* **120 C3** 7 0N 47 30 E
Mudukulattur, *India* **95 K4** 9 21N 78 31 E
Mudurnu, *Turkey* **100 B4** 40 27N 31 12 E
Muecate, *Mozam.* **119 E4** 14 55 S 39 40 E
Mueda, *Mozam.* **119 E4** 11 36 S 39 28 E
Mueller Ra., *Australia* **124 C4** 18 18 S 126 46 E
Muende, *Mozam.* **119 E3** 14 28 S 33 0 E
Muerto, Mar, *Mexico* **163 D6** 16 10N 94 10W
Mufu Shan, *China* **77 C10** 29 20N 114 30 E
Mufulira, *Zambia* **119 E2** 12 32 S 28 15 E
Mufuma, *Angola* **115 D3** 9 12 S 16 29 E
Mufumbiro Range, *Africa* **118 C2** 1 25 S 29 30 E
Mugardos, *Spain* **42 B2** 43 27N 8 15W
Muge →, *Portugal* **43 F2** 39 8N 8 44W
Múggia, *Italy* **45 C10** 45 36N 13 46 E
Mughal Sarai, *India* **93 G10** 25 18N 83 7 E
Mughayrā', *Si. Arabia* **96 D3** 29 17N 37 41 E
Mugi, *Japan* **72 D6** 33 40N 134 25 E
Mugia = Muxía, *Spain* **42 B1** 43 3N 9 10W
Mugila, Mts., *Dem. Rep. of the Congo* **118 D2** 7 0 S 28 50 E
Muginga, *Angola* **115 D3** 8 21 S 17 36 E
Muğla, *Turkey* **49 D10** 37 15N 28 22 E
Muğla □, *Turkey* **49 D10** 37 15N 28 0 E
Muglad, *Sudan* **107 E2** 11 1N 27 50 E
Müglizh, *Bulgaria* **51 D9** 42 37N 25 32 E
Mugodzhary, *Kazakstan* **64 G7** 49 0N 58 40 E
Mugu, *Nepal* **93 E10** 29 45N 82 30 E
Muhammad, Râs, *Egypt* **96 E2** 27 44N 34 16 E
Muhammad Qol, *Sudan* **106 C4** 20 53N 37 9 E
Muhammadabad, *India* **93 F10** 26 4N 83 25 E
Muḩayriqah, *Si. Arabia* **98 B4** 23 59N 45 4 E
Muhesi →, *Tanzania* **118 D4** 7 0 S 35 20 E
Mühlacker, *Germany* **31 G4** 48 57N 8 51 E
Mühldorf, *Germany* **31 G8** 48 14N 12 32 E
Mühlhausen, *Germany* **30 D6** 51 12N 10 27 E
Mühlig Hofmann fjell, *Antarctica* **7 D3** 72 30 S 5 0 E
Mühlviertel, *Austria* **34 C7** 48 30N 14 10 E
Muhos, *Finland* **14 D22** 64 47N 25 59 E
Muhu, *Estonia* **15 G20** 58 36N 23 11 E
Muhutwe, *Tanzania* **118 C3** 1 35 S 31 45 E
Mui Wo, *China* **69 G10** 22 16N 113 59 E
Muie, *Angola* **115 E4** 14 23 S 20 25 E
Muine Bheag, *Ireland* **23 D5** 52 42N 6 58W
Muir, L., *Australia* **125 F2** 34 30 S 116 40 E
Muisné, *Ecuador* **168 C1** 0 36N 80 2W
Mujnak = Muynak, *Uzbekistan* **66 E6** 43 44N 59 10 E
Mujuí dos Campos, *Brazil* **169 D7** 2 35 S 54 41W
Muka, Tanjung, *Malaysia* **87 c** 5 28N 100 11 E
Mukacheve, *Ukraine* **59 H2** 48 27N 22 45 E
Mukachevo = Mukacheve, *Ukraine* **59 H2** 48 27N 22 45 E
Mukah, *Malaysia* **85 B4** 2 55N 112 5 E
Mukandwara, *India* **92 G6** 24 49N 75 59 E
Mukawa, *Papua N. G.* **132 E5** 9 38 S 149 59 E
Mukawwa, Geziret, *Egypt* **106 C4** 23 55N 35 53 E
Mukawwar, *Sudan* **106 C4** 20 50N 37 17 E
Mukdahan, *Thailand* **86 D5** 16 32N 104 43 E
Mukden = Shenyang, *China* **75 D12** 41 48N 123 27 E
Mukerian, *India* **92 D6** 31 57N 75 37 E
Mukher, *India* **94 E3** 18 42N 77 22 E
Mukhtolovo, *Russia* **60 C6** 55 29N 43 15 E
Mukhtuya = Lensk, *Russia* **67 C12** 60 48N 114 55 E
Mukinbudin, *Australia* **125 F2** 30 55 S 118 5 E
Mukishi, *Kasai-Occ., Dem. Rep. of the Congo* **115 D4** 5 39 S 21 3 E
Mukishi, *Katanga, Dem. Rep. of the Congo* **119 D1** 8 30 S 24 44 E
Mukomuko, *Indonesia* **84 C2** 2 30 S 101 10 E
Mukomwenze, *Dem. Rep. of the Congo* **118 D2** 6 49 S 27 15 E
Mukry, *Turkmenistan* **65 E2** 37 54N 65 12 E
Muktsar, *India* **92 D6** 30 30N 74 30 E
Mukur = Moqor, *Afghan.* **91 B2** 32 50N 67 42 E
Mukutawa →, *Canada* **143 C9** 53 10N 97 24W
Mukwela, *Zambia* **119 F2** 17 0 S 26 40 E
Mukwonago, *U.S.A.* **157 B8** 42 52N 88 20W
Mul, *India* **94 D4** 20 4N 79 40 E
Mula, *Spain* **41 G3** 38 3N 1 33W
Mula →, *India* **94 E2** 18 34N 74 21 E
Mula →, *Pakistan* **92 F2** 27 57N 67 36 E
Mulamba, *Dem. Rep. of the Congo* **115 D4** 6 21 S 21 13 E
Mulanay, *Phil.* **80 E4** 13 31N 122 24 E
Mulange, *Dem. Rep. of the Congo* **118 C2** 3 40 S 27 10 E
Mulanje, *Malawi* **119 F4** 16 2 S 35 33 E
Mulanje, Mt., *Malawi* **119 F4** 16 0 S 35 30 E
Mulatupo, *Panama* **168 B2** 8 57N 77 45W
Mulbagal, *India* **95 H4** 13 10N 78 24 E
Mulberry, *U.S.A.* **153 H8** 27 54N 81 59W
Mulberry Grove, *U.S.A.* **156 F7** 38 56N 89 16W
Mulchatna →, *U.S.A.* **144 G8** 59 40N 157 7W
Mulchén, *Chile* **174 D1** 37 45 S 72 20W
Mulde →, *Germany* **30 D8** 51 53N 12 15 E
Muldraugh, *U.S.A.* **157 G11** 37 56N 85 59W
Mule Creek Junction, *U.S.A.* **154 D2** 43 19N 104 8W
Muleba, *Tanzania* **118 C3** 1 50 S 31 37 E
Mulegns, *Switz.* **33 C9** 46 32N 9 38 E
Mulejé, *Mexico* **162 B2** 26 53N 112 1W
Muleshoe, *U.S.A.* **155 H3** 34 13N 102 43W
Muletta, Gara, *Ethiopia* **107 F5** 9 15N 41 44 E
Mulgrave, *Canada* **141 C7** 45 38N 61 31W
Mulgrave I. = Badu I., *Papua N. G.* **132 F2** 10 5 S 142 10 E
Mulhacén, *Spain* **43 H7** 37 4N 3 20W
Mülheim, *Germany* **30 D2** 51 25N 6 54 E
Mulhouse, *France* **27 E14** 47 40N 7 20 E
Muli, *China* **76 D3** 27 52N 101 8 E
Muli →, *Indonesia* **83 C5** 7 16 S 138 45 E
Mulifanua, *Samoa* **133 W24** 13 50 S 171 59W
Muling, *China* **75 B16** 44 35N 130 10 E
Mulki, *India* **95 H2** 13 6N 74 48 E
Mull, *U.K.* **22 E3** 56 25N 5 56W
Mull, Sound of, *U.K.* **22 E3** 56 30N 5 50W
Mullaittivu, *Sri Lanka* **95 K5** 9 15N 80 49 E
Mullen, *U.S.A.* **154 D4** 42 3N 101 1W
Mullens, *U.S.A.* **148 G5** 37 35N 81 23W
Muller, Pegunungan, *Indonesia* **85 B4** 0 30N 113 30 E
Muller Ra., *Papua N. G.* **132 C2** 5 35 S 142 20 E
Mullet Pen., *Ireland* **23 B1** 54 13N 10 2W
Mullewa, *Australia* **125 E2** 28 29 S 115 30 E
Müllheim, *Germany* **31 H3** 47 47N 7 36 E
Mulligan →, *Australia* **126 D2** 25 0 S 139 0 E
Mullingar, *Ireland* **23 C4** 53 31N 7 21W
Mullins, *U.S.A.* **149 H6** 34 12N 79 15W
Mullsjö, *Sweden* **17 G7** 57 56N 13 55 E
Mullumbimby, *Australia* **127 D5** 28 30 S 153 30 E
Mulobezi, *Zambia* **119 F2** 16 45 S 25 7 E
Mulondo, *Angola* **115 F3** 15 41 S 15 12 E
Mulonga Plain, *Zambia* **115 F4** 16 20 S 22 40 E
Mulroy B., *Ireland* **23 A4** 55 15N 7 46W
Multai, *India* **94 E1** 18 30N 73 48 E
Multai, *India* **94 D4** 21 50N 78 21 E
Multan, *Pakistan* **91 C3** 30 15N 71 36 E
Mulu, Gunong, *Malaysia* **85 B4** 4 3N 114 56 E
Mulug, *India* **94 E4** 18 11N 79 57 E
Mulumbe, Mts., *Dem. Rep. of the Congo* **119 D2** 8 40 S 27 30 E
Mulundu, *Dem. Rep. of the Congo* **115 D4** 6 40 S 20 33 E
Mulungushi Dam, *Zambia* **119 E2** 14 48 S 28 48 E
Mulurulu L., *Australia* **128 B5** 33 15 S 143 20 E
Mulvane, *U.S.A.* **155 G6** 37 29N 97 15W
Mulwad, *Sudan* **106 D3** 18 45N 30 39 E
Mulwala, *Australia* **129 C7** 35 59 S 146 0 E
Muma, *Dem. Rep. of the Congo* **114 B4** 3 25N 23 21 E
Mumbai, *India* **94 E1** 18 55N 72 50 E
Mumbeji, *Zambia* **115 E4** 13 51 S 23 39 E
Mumbondo, *Angola* **115 E2** 10 9 S 14 15 E
Mumbwa, *Zambia* **119 F2** 15 0 S 27 0 E
Mumeng, *Papua N. G.* **132 D4** 7 1 S 146 37 E
Mumra, *Russia* **61 H8** 45 45N 47 41 E
Mun →, *Thailand* **86 E5** 15 19N 105 30 E
Muna, *Indonesia* **82 B2** 5 0 S 122 30 E
Munabao, *India* **92 G4** 25 45N 70 17 E
Munakata, *Japan* **72 D2** 33 48N 130 38 E
Munamagi, *Estonia* **15 H22** 57 43N 27 4 E
Muncan, *Indonesia* **79 K18** 8 34 S 115 11 E
Muncar, *Indonesia* **79 J17** 8 26 S 114 20 E
Münchberg, *Germany* **31 E7** 50 11N 11 47 E
Müncheberg, *Germany* **30 C10** 52 30N 14 9 E
München, *Germany* **31 G7** 48 8N 11 34 E
Munchen-Gladbach = Mönchengladbach, *Germany* **30 D2** 51 11N 6 27 E
Münchenbuchsee, *Switz.* **32 B4** 47 1N 7 27 E
Muncho Lake, *Canada* **142 B3** 59 0N 125 50W
Munch'ŏn, *N. Korea* **75 E14** 39 14N 127 19 E
Münchwilen, *Switz.* **33 B7** 47 28N 8 59 E
Muncie, *U.S.A.* **157 D11** 40 12N 85 23W
Muncoonie, L., *Australia* **126 D2** 25 12 S 138 40 E
Munda, *Solomon Is.* **133 M9** 8 20 S 157 16 E
Mundabbera, *Australia* **127 D5** 25 36 S 151 18 E
Mundakayam, *India* **95 K3** 9 30N 76 50 E
Mundal, *Sri Lanka* **95 L4** 7 48N 79 48 E
Munday, *U.S.A.* **155 J5** 33 27N 99 38W
Mundelein, *U.S.A.* **157 B8** 42 16N 88 0W
Münden, *Germany* **30 D5** 51 25N 9 38 E
Mundiwindi, *Australia* **124 D3** 23 47 S 120 9 E
Mundo →, *Spain* **41 G2** 38 30N 2 15W
Mundo Novo, *Brazil* **171 D3** 11 50 S 40 29W
Mundra, *India* **92 H3** 22 54N 69 48 E
Mundrabilla, *Australia* **125 F4** 31 52 S 127 51 E
Munducurus, *Brazil* **169 D6** 4 47 S 58 16W
Munenga, *Angola* **115 E2** 10 2 S 14 41 E
Munera, *Spain* **41 F2** 39 2N 2 29W
Muneru →, *India* **94 F5** 16 45N 80 3 E
Mungallala, *Australia* **127 D4** 26 28 S 147 34 E
Mungallala Cr. →, *Australia* **127 D4** 28 53 S 147 5 E
Mungana, *Australia* **126 B3** 17 8 S 144 27 E

Mungaoli, *India* **92 G8** 24 24N 78 7 E
Mungari, *Mozam.* **119 F3** 17 12 S 33 30 E
Mungbere, *Dem. Rep. of the Congo* **118 B2** 2 36N 28 28 E
Mungeli, *India* **93 H9** 22 4N 81 41 E
Munger, *India* **93 G12** 25 23N 86 30 E
Mungkan Kandju Nat. Park, *Australia* **126 A3** 13 35 S 142 52 E
Mungo, *Angola* **115 E3** 11 49 S 16 16 E
Mungo, L., *Australia* **128 B5** 33 45 S 143 0 E
Mungo Nat. Park, *Australia* **128 B5** 33 44 S 143 6 E
Munhango, *Angola* **115 E3** 12 10 S 18 38 E
Munhango →, *Angola* **115 E4** 11 17 S 19 44 E
Munich = München, *Germany* **31 G7** 48 8N 11 34 E
Munirabad, *India* **95 F3** 15 20N 76 20 E
Munising, *U.S.A.* **148 B2** 46 25N 86 40W
Munka-Ljungby, *Sweden* **17 H6** 56 16N 12 58 E
Munkebo, *Denmark* **17 J4** 55 27N 10 34 E
Munkedal, *Sweden* **17 F5** 58 28N 11 40 E
Munkfors, *Sweden* **16 E7** 59 47N 13 30 E
Munku-Sardyk, *Russia* **67 D11** 51 45N 100 20 E
Münnerstadt, *Germany* **31 E6** 50 14N 10 12 E
Munoz, *Phil.* **80 D3** 15 43N 120 54 E
Muñoz Gamero, Pen., *Chile* **176 D2** 52 30 S 73 5W
Munroe L., *Canada* **143 B9** 59 13N 98 35W
Munsan, *S. Korea* **75 F14** 37 51N 126 48 E
Munshiganj, *Bangla.* **90 D3** 23 33N 90 32 E
Münsingen, *Switz.* **32 C5** 46 52N 7 32 E
Munson, *U.S.A.* **153 E3** 30 52N 86 52W
Munster, *France* **27 D14** 48 2N 7 8 E
Munster, *Niedersachsen, Germany* **30 C6** 52 58N 10 5 E
Münster, *Nordrhein-Westfalen, Germany* **30 D3** 51 58N 7 37 E
Münster, *Switz.* **33 D6** 46 29N 8 17 E
Munster □, *Ireland* **23 D3** 52 18N 8 44W
Muntadgin, *Australia* **125 F2** 31 45 S 118 33 E
Muntele Mare, Vf., *Romania* **53 D8** 46 30N 23 12 E
Muntok, *Indonesia* **84 C3** 2 5 S 105 10 E
Munyama, *Zambia* **119 F2** 16 5 S 28 31 E
Munzur Dağları, *Turkey* **101 C8** 39 30N 39 10 E
Muong Beng, *Laos* **76 G3** 20 23N 101 46 E
Muong Boum, *Vietnam* **76 F4** 22 24N 102 49 E
Muong Et, *Laos* **86 B5** 20 49N 104 1 E
Muong Hai, *Laos* **76 G3** 21 3N 101 49 E
Muong Hiem, *Laos* **86 B4** 20 5N 103 22 E
Muong Houn, *Laos* **76 G3** 20 8N 101 23 E
Muong Hung, *Vietnam* **76 G4** 20 56N 103 53 E
Muong Kau, *Laos* **86 E5** 15 6N 105 47 E
Muong Khao, *Laos* **86 C4** 19 38N 103 32 E
Muong Khoua, *Laos* **76 G4** 21 5N 102 31 E
Muong Liep, *Laos* **86 C3** 18 29N 101 40 E
Muong May, *Laos* **86 E6** 14 49N 106 56 E
Muong Ngeun, *Laos* **76 G3** 20 36N 101 3 E
Muong Ngoi, *Laos* **76 G4** 20 43N 102 41 E
Muong Nhie, *Vietnam* **76 F4** 22 12N 102 28 E
Muong Nong, *Laos* **86 D6** 16 22N 106 30 E
Muong Ou Tay, *Laos* **76 F3** 22 7N 101 48 E
Muong Oua, *Laos* **86 C3** 18 18N 101 20 E
Muong Peun, *Laos* **76 G4** 20 13N 103 52 E
Muong Phalane, *Laos* **86 D5** 16 39N 105 34 E
Muong Phieng, *Laos* **86 C3** 19 6N 101 32 E
Muong Phine, *Laos* **86 D6** 16 32N 106 2 E
Muong Sai, *Laos* **76 G3** 20 42N 101 59 E
Muong Saiapoun, *Laos* **86 C3** 18 24N 101 31 E
Muong Sen, *Vietnam* **86 C5** 19 24N 104 8 E
Muong Sing, *Laos* **76 G3** 21 11N 101 9 E
Muong Son, *Laos* **76 G4** 20 27N 103 19 E
Muong Soui, *Laos* **86 C4** 19 33N 102 52 E
Muong Va, *Laos* **76 G4** 21 53N 102 19 E
Muong Xia, *Vietnam* **86 B5** 20 19N 104 50 E
Muonio, *Finland* **14 C20** 67 57N 23 40 E
Muonionjoki →, *Finland* **14 C20** 67 11N 23 34 E
Muotathal, *Switz.* **33 C7** 46 58N 8 46 E
Mupa, *Angola* **115 F3** 16 5 S 15 50 E
Mupa, Parque Nacional da, *Angola* **115 F3** 15 55 S 15 35 E
Muping, *China* **75 F11** 37 22N 121 36 E
Mupoi, *Sudan* **107 F2** 5 28N 27 40 E
Muqaddam, Wadi →, *Sudan* **106 D3** 18 4N 31 30 E
Muqdisho, *Somali Rep.* **120 D3** 2 2N 45 25 E
Muqshin, W. →, *Oman* **99 C6** 19 44N 55 14 E
Muquequete, *Angola* **115 E2** 14 50 S 14 16 E
Mur →, *Austria* **35 E9** 46 18N 16 52 E
Mur-de-Bretagne, *France* **26 D4** 48 12N 3 0W
Muradiye, *Manisa, Turkey* **49 C9** 38 39N 27 21 E
Muradiye, *Van, Turkey* **101 C10** 39 0N 43 44 E
Murakami, *Japan* **70 E9** 38 14N 139 29 E
Murallón, Cerro, *Chile* **176 C2** 49 48 S 73 30W
Muranda, *Rwanda* **118 C2** 1 52 S 29 20 E
Murang'a, *Kenya* **118 C4** 0 45 S 37 9 E
Murashi, *Russia* **64 B2** 59 30N 49 0 E
Murat, *France* **28 C6** 45 7N 2 53 E
Murat →, *Turkey* **101 C9** 38 46N 40 0 E
Murat Dağı, *Turkey* **49 C11** 38 55N 29 43 E
Muratlı, *Turkey* **51 E11** 41 10N 27 29 E
Murato, *France* **29 F13** 42 35N 9 20 E
Murau, *Austria* **34 D7** 47 6N 14 10 E
Muravera, *Italy* **46 C2** 39 25N 9 34 E
Murayama, *Japan* **70 E10** 38 30N 140 25 E
Murça, *Portugal* **42 D3** 41 24N 7 28W
Murchison, *N.Z.* **131 B7** 41 49 S 172 21 E
Murchison →, *Australia* **125 E1** 27 45 S 114 0 E
Murchison, Mt., *Antarctica* **7 D11** 73 0 S 168 0 E
Murchison, Mt., *N.Z.* **131 D6** 43 0 S 171 22 E
Murchison Falls, *Uganda* **118 B3** 2 15N 31 30 E
Murchison Falls Nat. Park, *Uganda* **118 B3** 2 17N 31 48 E
Murchison Mts., *N.Z.* **131 F2** 45 13 S 167 23 E
Murchison Ra., *Australia* **126 C1** 20 0 S 134 10 E
Murchison Rapids, *Malawi* **119 F3** 15 55 S 34 35 E
Murcia, *Spain* **41 G3** 38 5N 1 10W
Murcia □, *Spain* **41 H3** 37 50N 1 30W
Murdo, *U.S.A.* **154 D4** 43 53N 100 43W
Murdoch Pt., *Australia* **126 A3** 14 37 S 144 55 E
Mürefte, *Turkey* **51 F11** 40 40N 27 14 E
Mureş □, *Romania* **53 D9** 46 45N 24 40 E
Mureş →, *Romania* **52 D5** 46 15N 20 13 E
Mureşul = Mureş →, *Romania* **52 D5** 46 15N 20 13 E
Muret, *France* **28 E5** 43 30N 1 20 E
Murewa, *Zimbabwe* **117 B5** 17 39 S 31 47 E
Murfreesboro, *N.C., U.S.A.* **149 G7** 36 27N 77 6W
Murfreesboro, *Tenn., U.S.A.* **149 H2** 35 51N 86 24W
Murg, *Switz.* **33 B8** 47 6N 9 13 E
Murgab = Murghob, *Tajikistan* **66 F8** 38 10N 74 2 E
Murgab →, *Turkmenistan* **97 B9** 38 18N 61 12 E
Murgenella, *Australia* **124 B5** 11 34 S 132 56 E
Murgeni, *Romania* **53 D13** 46 12N 28 1 E
Murgenthal, *Switz.* **32 B5** 47 16N 7 50 E
Murgha Kibzai, *Pakistan* **92 D3** 30 44N 69 25 E
Murghob, *Tajikistan* **66 F8** 38 10N 74 2 E
Murgon, *Australia* **127 D5** 26 15 S 151 54 E
Muri, *India* **93 H11** 23 22N 85 52 E
Muri, *Switz.* **33 B6** 47 17N 8 21 E
Muria, *Indonesia* **85 D4** 6 36 S 110 53 E
Muriaé, *Brazil* **171 F3** 21 8 S 42 23W
Murias de Paredes, *Spain* **42 C4** 42 52N 6 11W
Murici, *Brazil* **170 C4** 9 19 S 35 56W
Muriége, *Angola* **115 D4** 9 58 S 21 11 E
Muriel Mine, *Zimbabwe* **119 F3** 17 14 S 30 40 E
Murila, *Angola* **115 E4** 10 44 S 20 20 E
Müritz, *Germany* **30 B8** 53 25N 12 42 E
Murka, *Kenya* **118 C4** 3 27 S 38 0 E
Murkong Selek, *India* **90 B5** 27 44N 95 18 E
Murliganj, *India* **93 G12** 25 54N 86 59 E
Murmansk, *Russia* **56 A5** 68 57N 33 10 E
Murnau, *Germany* **31 H7** 47 40N 11 12 E
Muro, *France* **29 F12** 42 34N 8 54 E
Muro, *Spain* **38 B4** 39 44N 3 3 E
Muro, C. de, *France* **29 G12** 41 44N 8 37 E
Muro de Alcoy, *Spain* **41 G4** 38 46N 0 26W
Muro Lucano, *Italy* **47 B8** 40 45N 15 29 E
Murom, *Russia* **60 C6** 55 35N 42 3 E
Muroran, *Japan* **70 C10** 42 25N 141 0 E
Muros, *Spain* **42 C1** 42 45N 9 5W
Muros y de Noya, Ría de, *Spain* **42 C1** 42 45N 9 0W
Muroto, *Japan* **72 D6** 33 18N 134 9 E
Muroto-Misaki, *Japan* **72 D6** 33 15N 134 10 E
Murowana Goślina, *Poland* **55 F3** 52 35N 17 0 E
Murphy, *U.S.A.* **158 E5** 43 13N 116 33W
Murphys, *U.S.A.* **160 G6** 38 8N 120 28W
Murphysboro, *U.S.A.* **156 G7** 37 46N 89 20W
Murrat, *Sudan* **106 D2** 18 51N 29 33 E
Murrat Wells, *Sudan* **106 C3** 21 3N 32 55 E
Murray, *Iowa, U.S.A.* **156 C3** 41 3N 93 57W
Murray, *Ky., U.S.A.* **149 G1** 36 37N 88 19W
Murray, *Utah, U.S.A.* **158 F8** 40 40N 111 53W
Murray →, *Australia* **128 C3** 35 20 S 139 22 E
Murray, L., *Papua N. G.* **132 D1** 7 0 S 141 35 E
Murray, L., *U.S.A.* **152 A8** 34 3N 81 13W
Murray Bridge, *Australia* **128 C3** 35 6 S 139 14 E
Murray Harbour, *Canada* **141 C7** 46 0N 62 28W
Murray River Nat. Park, *Australia* **127 E3** 34 23 S 140 32 E
Murray-Sunset Nat. Park, *Australia* **128 C4** 34 45 S 141 30 E
Murraysburg, *S. Africa* **116 E3** 31 58 S 23 47 E
Murrayville, *Ill., U.S.A.* **156 E6** 39 35N 90 15W
Murrayville, *Ill., U.S.A.* **156 E6** 39 35N 90 15W
Murree, *Pakistan* **92 C5** 33 56N 73 28 E
Murren, *Switz.* **32 C5** 46 34N 7 53 E
Murrieta, *U.S.A.* **161 M9** 33 33N 117 13W
Murro di Porco, Capo, *Italy* **47 F8** 37 0N 15 20 E
Murrumbateman, *Australia* **129 C8** 34 58 S 149 0 E
Murrumbidgee →, *Australia* **128 C5** 34 43 S 143 12 E
Murrumburrah, *Australia* **129 C8** 34 32 S 148 22 E
Murrurundi, *Australia* **129 A9** 31 42 S 150 51 E
Murshid, *Sudan* **106 C3** 21 40N 31 10 E
Murshidabad, *India* **93 G13** 24 11N 88 19 E
Murska Sobota, *Slovenia* **45 B13** 46 39N 16 12 E
Murtazapur, *India* **94 D3** 20 40N 77 25 E
Murten, *Switz.* **32 C4** 46 56N 7 4 E
Murtensee, *Switz.* **32 C4** 46 56N 7 7 E
Murtle L., *Canada* **142 C5** 52 8N 119 38W
Murtoa, *Australia* **128 D5** 36 35 S 142 28 E
Murtosa, *Portugal* **42 E2** 40 44N 8 40W
Muru →, *Brazil* **172 B3** 8 9 S 70 45W
Murud, *India* **94 E1** 18 19N 72 58 E
Murungu, *Tanzania* **118 C3** 4 12 S 31 10 E
Muruntau, *Uzbekistan* **65 C2** 41 30N 64 37 E
Murupara, *N.Z.* **130 E5** 38 28 S 176 42 E
Mururoa, *Pac. Oc.* **135 K14** 21 52 S 138 55W
Murwara, *India* **93 H9** 23 46N 80 28 E
Murwillumbah, *Australia* **127 D5** 28 18 S 153 27 E
Mürz →, *Austria* **34 D8** 47 30N 15 25 E
Mürzzuschlag, *Austria* **34 D8** 47 36N 15 41 E
Mus, *India* **95 K11** 9 14N 92 47 E
Muş, *Turkey* **101 C9** 38 45N 41 30 E
Musa, *Dem. Rep. of the Congo* **114 B3** 2 40N 19 18 E
Musa →, *Papua N. G.* **132 E5** 9 3 S 148 55 E
Mûsa, Gebel, *Egypt* **96 D2** 28 33N 33 59 E
Musa Khel, *Pakistan* **92 D3** 30 59N 69 52 E
Mūsa Qal'eh, *Afghan.* **91 B2** 32 20N 64 50 E
Musadi, *Dem. Rep. of the Congo* **114 C4** 2 31 S 22 50 E
Musafirkhana, *India* **93 F9** 26 22N 81 48 E
Musala, *Bulgaria* **50 D7** 42 13N 23 37 E
Musala, *Indonesia* **84 B1** 1 41N 98 28 E
Musan, *N. Korea* **75 C15** 42 12N 129 12 E
Musandam, Ra's, *Oman* **99 A7** 26 20N 56 20 E
Musangu, *Dem. Rep. of the Congo* **119 E1** 10 28 S 23 55 E
Musasa, *Tanzania* **118 C3** 3 25 S 31 30 E
Musashino, *Japan* **73 B11** 35 42N 139 34 E
Musay'īd, *Qatar* **97 E6** 25 0N 51 33 E
Musaymīr, *Yemen* **98 D4** 13 27N 44 37 E
Muscat = Masqat, *Oman* **99 B7** 23 37N 58 36 E
Muscat & Oman = Oman ■, *Asia* **99 B7** 23 0N 58 0 E
Muscatatuc →, *U.S.A.* **157 F10** 38 47N 86 9W
Muscatine, *U.S.A.* **156 C5** 41 25N 91 3W
Muschu I., *Papua N. G.* **132 B2** 3 25 S 143 35 E
Muscoda, *U.S.A.* **156 A6** 43 11N 90 27W
Musgrave Harbour, *Canada* **141 C9** 49 27N 53 58W
Musgrave Ranges, *Australia* **125 E5** 26 0 S 132 0 E
Mushie, *Dem. Rep. of the Congo* **114 C3** 2 56 S 16 55 E
Mushima, *Zambia* **115 E4** 14 10 S 24 56 E
Mushin, *Nigeria* **113 D5** 6 32N 3 21 E
Musi →, *India* **94 F4** 16 41N 79 40 E
Musi →, *Indonesia* **84 C2** 2 20 S 104 56 E
Musiri, *India* **95 J4** 10 56N 78 27 E
Muskeg →, *Canada* **142 A4** 60 20N 123 20W
Muskego, *U.S.A.* **157 B8** 42 55N 88 8W
Muskegon, *U.S.A.* **157 A10** 43 14N 86 16W
Muskegon →, *U.S.A.* **148 D2** 43 14N 86 21W
Muskegon Heights, *U.S.A.* **157 A10** 43 12N 86 16W
Muskogee, *U.S.A.* **155 H7** 35 45N 95 22W
Muskoka, L., *Canada* **150 B5** 45 0N 79 25W
Muskwa →, *Canada* **142 B4** 58 47N 122 48W
Muslīmiyah, *Syria* **96 B3** 36 19N 37 12 E
Musmar, *Sudan* **106 D4** 18 13N 35 40 E
Musofu, *Zambia* **119 E2** 13 30 S 29 0 E
Musoma, *Tanzania* **118 C3** 1 30 S 33 48 E
Musquaro, L., *Canada* **141 B7** 50 38N 61 5W
Musquodoboit Harbour, *Canada* **141 D7** 44 50N 63 9W
Mussau I., *Papua N. G.* **132 A5** 1 30 S 149 40 E
Musselburgh, *U.K.* **22 F5** 55 57N 3 2W
Musselshell →, *U.S.A.* **158 C10** 47 21N 107 57W
Mussende, *Angola* **115 E3** 10 32 S 16 5 E
Mussidan, *France* **28 C4** 45 2N 0 22 E
Mussolo, *Angola* **115 D3** 9 59 S 17 19 E
Mussomeli, *Italy* **46 E6** 37 35N 13 45 E
Mussoorie, *India* **92 D8** 30 27N 78 6 E
Mussuco, *Angola* **116 B2** 17 2 S 19 3 E
Mustafakemalpaşa, *Turkey* **51 F12** 40 2N 28 24 E
Mustahil, *Ethiopia* **120 C2** 5 16N 44 45 E
Mustang, *Nepal* **93 E10** 29 10N 83 55 E
Musters, L., *Argentina* **176 C3** 45 20 S 69 25W
Musudan, *N. Korea* **75 D15** 40 50N 129 43 E
Muswellbrook, *Australia* **129 B9** 32 16 S 150 56 E
Muszyna, *Poland* **55 J7** 49 22N 20 55 E
Mût, *Egypt* **106 B2** 25 28N 28 58 E
Mut, *Turkey* **100 D5** 36 40N 33 28 E
Mutanda, *Dem. Rep. of the Congo* **115 D3** 5 17 S 16 34 E
Mutanda, *Mozam.* **117 C5** 21 0 S 33 34 E
Mutanda, *Zambia* **119 E2** 12 24 S 26 13 E
Mutare, *Zimbabwe* **119 F3** 18 58 S 32 38 E
Muting, *Indonesia* **83 C6** 7 23 S 140 20 E
Mutis, *Indonesia* **82 C2** 9 30 S 124 14 E
Mutoko, *Zimbabwe* **117 B5** 17 24 S 32 13 E
Mutoray, *Russia* **67 C11** 60 56N 101 0 E
Mutoto, *Dem. Rep. of the Congo* **115 D4** 5 42 S 22 42 E
Mutoxo, *Angola* **115 E4** 12 17 S 21 40 E
Mutshatsha, *Dem. Rep. of the Congo* **119 E1** 10 35 S 24 20 E
Mutsu, *Japan* **70 D10** 41 5N 140 55 E
Mutsu-Wan, *Japan* **70 D10** 41 5N 140 55 E
Muttaburra, *Australia* **126 C3** 22 38 S 144 29 E
Muttalip, *Turkey* **49 B12** 39 50N 30 32 E
Mutton I., *Ireland* **23 D2** 52 49N 9 32W
Muttukuru, *India* **95 G5** 14 16N 80 6 E
Mutuáli, *Mozam.* **119 E4** 14 55 S 37 0 E
Mutum Biyu, *Nigeria* **113 D7** 8 40N 10 50 E
Mutunópolis, *Brazil* **171 D2** 13 40 S 49 15W
Mutur, *Sri Lanka* **95 K5** 8 27N 81 16 E
Muweilih, *Egypt* **103 E3** 30 42N 34 19 E
Muxaluando, *Angola* **115 D2** 8 8 S 14 18 E
Muxía, *Spain* **42 B1** 43 3N 9 10W
Muxima, *Angola* **115 D2** 9 33 S 13 58 E
Muy Muy, *Nic.* **164 D2** 12 39N 85 36W
Muyinga, *Burundi* **118 C3** 3 14 S 30 33 E
Muynak, *Uzbekistan* **66 E6** 43 44N 59 10 E
Muyunkum, Peski, *Kazakstan* **65 A4** 44 12N 71 0 E
Muzaffarabad, *Pakistan* **93 B5** 34 25N 73 30 E
Muzaffargarh, *Pakistan* **91 C3** 30 5N 71 14 E
Muzaffarnagar, *India* **92 E7** 29 26N 77 40 E
Muzaffarpur, *India* **93 F11** 26 7N 85 23 E
Muzafirpur, *Pakistan* **92 D3** 30 58N 69 9 E
Muzeze, *Angola* **115 F3** 15 3 S 17 43 E
Muzhi, *Russia* **56 A11** 65 25N 64 40 E
Muzillac, *France* **26 E4** 47 35N 2 30W
Muzon, C., *U.S.A.* **144 J14** 54 40N 132 42W
Muztagh-Ata, *China* **65 D7** 38 17N 75 7 E
Muzūra, *Egypt* **106 J7** 28 53N 30 48 E
Mvadhi-Ousyé, *Gabon* **114 B2** 1 13N 13 12 E
Mvam, *Gabon* **114 C1** 0 13 S 9 39 E
Mvangan, *Cameroon* **114 B2** 2 17N 11 43 E
Mvôlô, *Sudan* **107 F2** 6 2N 29 53 E
Mvuma, *Zimbabwe* **119 F3** 19 16 S 30 30 E
Mvurwi, *Zimbabwe* **119 F3** 17 0 S 30 57 E
Mwabvi Game Reserve, *Malawi* **119 F3** 16 42 S 35 0 E
Mwadi-Kalumbu, *Dem. Rep. of the Congo* **115 D3** 7 53 S 18 43 E
Mwadui, *Tanzania* **118 C3** 3 26 S 33 32 E
Mwali = Mohéli, *Comoros Is.* **121 a** 12 20 S 43 40 E
Mwambo, *Tanzania* **119 E5** 10 30 S 40 22 E
Mwandi, *Zambia* **119 F1** 17 30 S 24 51 E
Mwanza, *Dem. Rep. of the Congo* **118 D2** 7 55 S 26 43 E
Mwanza, *Tanzania* **118 C3** 2 30 S 32 58 E
Mwanza, *Zambia* **119 F1** 16 58 S 24 28 E
Mwanza □, *Tanzania* **118 C3** 2 0 S 33 0 E
Mwaya, *Tanzania* **119 D3** 9 32 S 33 55 E
Mweelrea, *Ireland* **23 C2** 53 39N 9 49W
Mweka, *Dem. Rep. of the Congo* **115 C4** 4 50 S 21 34 E
Mwendjila, *Dem. Rep. of the Congo* **115 D3** 7 12 S 18 51 E
Mwene-Ditu, *Dem. Rep. of the Congo* **115 D4** 6 35 S 22 27 E
Mwenezi, *Zimbabwe* **119 G3** 21 15 S 30 48 E
Mwenezi →, *Mozam.* **119 G3** 22 40 S 31 50 E
Mwenga, *Dem. Rep. of the Congo* **118 C2** 3 1 S 28 28 E
Mweru, L., *Zambia* **119 D2** 9 0 S 28 40 E
Mwetshi, *Dem. Rep. of the Congo* **115 C4** 4 50 S 22 38 E
Mweza Range, *Zimbabwe* **119 G3** 21 0 S 30 0 E
Mwilambwe, *Dem. Rep. of the Congo* **118 D2** 8 7 S 25 5 E
Mwimbi, *Tanzania* **119 D3** 8 38 S 31 39 E
Mwinilunga, *Zambia* **119 E1** 11 43 S 24 25 E
My Tho, *Vietnam* **87 G6** 10 29N 106 23 E
Mya, O. →, *Algeria* **111 B5** 30 46N 4 54 E
Myajlar, *India* **92 F4** 26 15N 70 20 E
Myakka →, *U.S.A.* **153 J7** 26 56N 82 11W
Myall Lakes Nat. Park, *Australia* **129 B10** 32 25 S 152 30 E
Myanaung, *Burma* **90 F5** 18 18N 95 22 E
Myanmar = Burma ■, *Asia* **90 E6** 21 0N 96 30 E
Myaung, *Burma* **90 E5** 21 50N 95 25 E
Myaungmya, *Burma* **90 G5** 16 30N 94 40 E
Myebon, *Burma* **90 E4** 20 3N 93 22 E
Myeik Kyunzu, *Burma* **87 G1** 11 30N 97 30 E
Myers Chuck, *U.S.A.* **142 B2** 55 44N 132 11W
Myerstown, *U.S.A.* **151 F8** 40 22N 76 19W
Myingyan, *Burma* **90 E5** 21 30N 95 20 E
Myitkyina, *Burma* **90 C6** 25 24N 97 26 E
Myitson, *Burma* **90 D6** 23 16N 96 34 E
Myittha, *Burma* **90 E6** 21 25N 96 8 E
Myittha →, *Burma* **90 D5** 23 12N 94 17 E
Myjava, *Slovak Rep.* **35 C10** 48 41N 17 37 E
Mykhaylivka, *Ukraine* **59 J8** 47 12N 35 15 E
Mykines, *Færoe Is.* **14 E9** 62 7N 7 35W
Myking, *Norway* **18 D2** 60 41N 5 19 E
Mykolayiv, *Ukraine* **59 J7** 46 58N 32 0 E
Mylius Erichsen Land, *Greenland* **10 A8** 81 30N 27 0W
Mymensingh, *Bangla.* **90 C3** 24 45N 90 24 E
Mynydd Du, *U.K.* **21 F4** 51 52N 3 50W
Myo-gyi, *Burma* **90 E6** 21 27N 96 22 E
Myohaung, *Burma* **90 E4** 20 35N 93 11 E
Myohla, *Burma* **90 F5** 19 16N 95 25 E
Myotha, *Burma* **90 E5** 21 41N 95 43 E
Myothit, *Kachin, Burma* **90 C6** 24 24N 97 24 E
Myothit, *Magwe, Burma* **90 E5** 20 12N 95 27 E
Myrasýsla □, *Iceland* **11 C5** 64 45N 21 30W
Mýrdalsjökull, *Iceland* **11 D7** 63 40N 19 6W
Myrhorod, *Ukraine* **59 H7** 49 58N 33 37 E
Mýri, *Iceland* **11 B9** 65 23N 17 23W
Myrtle Beach, *U.S.A.* **149 J6** 33 42N 78 53W
Myrtle Creek, *U.S.A.* **158 E2** 43 1N 123 17W
Myrtle Grove, *U.S.A.* **153 E2** 30 23N 87 17W
Myrtle Point, *U.S.A.* **158 E1** 43 4N 124 8W
Myrtleford, *Australia* **129 D7** 36 34 S 146 44 E
Myrtou, *Cyprus* **39 E9** 35 18N 33 4 E
Myrzakent, *Kazakstan* **65 C4** 40 40N 68 32 E
Mysen, *Norway* **18 E8** 59 33N 11 20 E
Mysia, *Turkey* **51 G11** 39 50N 27 0 E
Myślenice, *Poland* **55 J6** 49 51N 19 57 E
Myślibórz, *Poland* **55 F1** 52 55N 14 50 E
Mysłowice, *Poland* **55 H6** 50 15N 19 12 E
Mysore = Karnataka □, *India* **95 H3** 13 15N 77 0 E
Mysore, *India* **95 H3** 12 17N 76 41 E
Mystic, *Conn., U.S.A.* **151 E13** 41 21N 71 58W
Mystic, *Iowa, U.S.A.* **156 D4** 40 47N 92 57W
Myszków, *Poland* **55 H6** 50 45N 19 22 E
Myszyniec, *Poland* **54 E8** 53 23N 21 21 E
Mythen, *Switz.* **33 B7** 47 2N 8 42 E
Mytishchi, *Russia* **58 E9** 55 50N 37 50 E
Mývatn, *Iceland* **11 B10** 65 36N 17 0W
Mzab, Oued en →, *Algeria* **111 B6** 32 15N 5 0 E
Mže →, *Czech Rep.* **34 B6** 49 46N 13 24 E
Mzimba, *Malawi* **119 E3** 11 55 S 33 39 E
Mzimkulu →, *S. Africa* **117 E5** 30 44 S 30 28 E
Mzimvubu →, *S. Africa* **117 E4** 31 38 S 29 33 E
Mzuzu, *Malawi* **119 E3** 11 30 S 33 55 E

N

Na Hearadh = Harris, *U.K.* **22 D2** 57 50N 6 55W
Na-lang, *Burma* **90 D6** 22 42N 97 33 E
Na Noi, *Thailand* **86 C3** 18 19N 100 43 E
Na Phao, *Laos* **86 D5** 17 35N 105 44 E
Na Sam, *Vietnam* **76 F6** 22 3N 106 37 E
Na San, *Vietnam* **86 B5** 21 12N 104 2 E
Na Thon, *Thailand* **87 b** 9 32N 99 56 E
Naab →, *Germany* **31 F8** 49 1N 12 2 E
Naalehu, *U.S.A.* **145 D6** 19 4N 155 35W
Na'am, *Sudan* **107 F2** 9 42N 28 27 E
Na'am →, *Sudan* **107 F2** 6 48N 29 57 E
Naantali, *Finland* **15 F19** 60 29N 22 2 E
Naas, *Ireland* **23 C5** 53 12N 6 40W
Nababeep, *S. Africa* **116 D2** 29 36 S 17 46 E
Nabadwip = Navadwip, *India* **93 H13** 23 34N 88 20 E
Nabari, *Japan* **73 C8** 34 37N 136 5 E
Nabawa, *Australia* **125 E1** 28 30 S 114 48 E
Nabberu, L., *Australia* **125 E3** 25 50 S 120 30 E
Nabburg, *Germany* **31 F8** 49 27N 12 11 E
Naberezhnyye Chelny, *Russia* **60 C11** 55 42N 52 19 E
Nabesna, *U.S.A.* **144 E12** 62 22N 143 0W
Nabeul, *Tunisia* **108 A2** 36 30N 10 44 E
Nabha, *India* **92 D7** 30 26N 76 14 E
Nabīd, *Iran* **97 D8** 29 40N 57 38 E
Nabire, *Indonesia* **83 B5** 3 15 S 135 26 E
Nabisar, *Pakistan* **92 G3** 25 8N 69 40 E
Nabisipi →, *Canada* **141 B7** 50 14N 62 13W
Nabiswera, *Uganda* **118 B3** 1 27N 32 15 E
Nablus = Nābulus, *West Bank* **103 C4** 32 14N 35 15 E
Naboomspruit, *S. Africa* **117 C4** 24 32 S 28 40 E
Nabou, *Burkina Faso* **112 C4** 11 25N 2 50W
Nabouwalu, *Fiji* **133 A2** 17 0 S 178 45 E
Nabua, *Phil.* **80 E4** 13 24N 123 22 E
Nābulus, *West Bank* **103 C4** 32 14N 35 15 E
Nabunturan, *Phil.* **81 H5** 7 35N 125 58 E
Nacala, *Mozam.* **119 E5** 14 31 S 40 34 E
Nacala-Velha, *Mozam.* **119 E5** 14 32 S 40 34 E
Nacaome, *Honduras* **164 D2** 13 31N 87 30W
Nacaroa, *Mozam.* **119 E4** 14 22 S 39 56 E
Naches, *U.S.A.* **158 C3** 46 44N 120 42W
Naches →, *U.S.A.* **160 D6** 46 38N 120 31W
Nachicapau, L., *Canada* **141 A6** 56 40N 68 5W
Nachikatsuura, *Japan* **73 D7** 33 33N 135 58 E
Nachingwea, *Tanzania* **119 E4** 10 23 S 38 49 E
Nachna, *India* **92 F4** 27 34N 71 41 E
Náchod, *Czech Rep.* **34 A9** 50 25N 16 8 E
Nachuge, *India* **95 J11** 10 47N 92 21 E
Nacimiento L., *U.S.A.* **160 K6** 35 46N 120 53W
Nackara, *Australia* **128 B3** 32 48 S 139 12 E
Naco, *Mexico* **162 A3** 31 20N 109 56W
Nacogdoches, *U.S.A.* **155 K7** 31 36N 94 39W
Nácori Chico, *Mexico* **162 B3** 29 39N 109 1W
Nacozari, *Mexico* **162 A3** 30 24N 109 39W
Nacula, *Fiji* **133 A1** 16 54 S 177 27 E
Nadi, *Fiji* **133 A1** 17 42 S 177 20 E
Nadi, *Sudan* **106 D3** 18 40N 33 41 E
Nadiad, *India* **92 H5** 22 41N 72 56 E
Nădlac, *Romania* **52 D5** 46 10N 20 50 E
Nador, *Morocco* **111 A4** 35 14N 2 58W
Nadur, *Malta* **38 F7** 35 54N 14 22 E
Nadur, *Gozo, Malta* **38 E7** 36 2N 14 18 E
Nadūshan, *Iran* **97 C7** 32 2N 53 35 E
Nadvirna, *Ukraine* **59 H3** 48 37N 24 30 E
Nadvoitsy, *Russia* **56 B5** 63 52N 34 14 E
Nadvornaya = Nadvirna, *Ukraine* **59 H3** 48 37N 24 30 E
Nadym, *Russia* **66 C8** 65 35N 72 42 E
Nadym →, *Russia* **66 C8** 66 12N 72 0 E
Nærbø, *Norway* **15 G11** 58 40N 5 39 E
Næstved, *Denmark* **17 J5** 55 13N 11 44 E
Nafada, *Nigeria* **113 C7** 11 8N 11 20 E
Näfels, *Switz.* **33 B8** 47 6N 9 4 E
Naft-e Safīd, *Iran* **97 D6** 31 40N 49 17 E
Naftshahr, *Iran* **101 E11** 34 0N 45 30 E
Nafud Desert = An Nafūd, *Si. Arabia* **96 D4** 28 15N 41 0 E
Nafūsah, Jabal, *Libya* **108 B2** 32 12N 12 30 E
Nag Hammâdi, *Egypt* **106 B3** 26 2N 32 18 E
Naga, *Camarines S., Phil.* **80 E4** 13 38N 123 15 E
Naga, *Cebu, Phil.* **81 F4** 10 13N 123 45 E
Naga, *Zamboanga del S., Phil.* **81 H4** 7 46N 122 45 E
Naga, Kreb en, *Africa* **110 D3** 24 12N 6 0W
Naga-Shima, *Kagoshima, Japan* **72 E2** 32 10N 130 9 E
Naga-Shima, *Yamaguchi, Japan* **72 D4** 33 49N 132 5 E
Nagahama, *Ehime, Japan* **72 D4** 33 36N 132 29 E
Nagahama, *Shiga, Japan* **73 B8** 35 23N 136 16 E
Nagai, *Japan* **70 E10** 38 6N 140 2 E
Nagai I., *U.S.A.* **144 J8** 55 5N 160 0W
Nagaland □, *India* **90 B5** 26 0N 94 30 E
Nagambie, *Australia* **129 D6** 36 47 S 145 10 E
Nagano, *Japan* **73 A10** 36 40N 138 10 E
Nagano □, *Japan* **73 A10** 36 15N 138 0 E
Nagaoka, *Japan* **71 F9** 37 27N 138 51 E
Nagappattinam, *India* **95 J4** 10 46N 79 51 E
Nagar →, *Bangla.* **90 C2** 24 27N 89 12 E
Nagar Karnul, *India* **95 F4** 16 29N 78 20 E
Nagar Parkar, *Pakistan* **92 G4** 24 28N 70 46 E
Nagara-Gawa →, *Japan* **73 B8** 35 40N 136 43 E
Nagaram, *India* **94 E5** 18 21N 80 26 E
Nagari Hills, *India* **95 H4** 13 3N 79 45 E
Nagasaki, *Japan* **72 E1** 32 47N 129 50 E
Nagasaki □, *Japan* **72 E1** 32 50N 129 40 E
Nagato, *Japan* **72 C3** 34 19N 131 5 E
Nagaur, *India* **92 F5** 27 15N 73 45 E
Nagbhir, *India* **94 D4** 20 34N 79 55 E
Nagda, *India* **92 H6** 23 27N 75 25 E
Nagercoil, *India* **95 K3** 8 12N 77 26 E
Nagina, *India* **93 E8** 29 30N 78 30 E
Nagīneh, *Iran* **97 C8** 34 20N 57 15 E
Naginimara, *India* **90 B5** 26 49N 94 50 E
Nagir, *Pakistan* **93 A6** 36 12N 74 42 E
Naglarby, *Sweden* **16 D9** 60 25N 15 34 E
Nagod, *India* **93 G9** 24 34N 80 36 E
Nagold, *Germany* **31 G4** 48 32N 8 43 E
Nagold →, *Germany* **31 G4** 48 52N 8 42 E
Nagoorin, *Australia* **126 C5** 24 17 S 151 15 E
Nagorno-Karabakh, *Azerbaijan* **101 C12** 39 55N 46 45 E
Nagornyy, *Russia* **67 D13** 55 58N 124 57 E
Nagorsk, *Russia* **64 B3** 59 18N 50 48 E
Nagoya, *Japan* **73 B8** 35 10N 136 50 E
Nagpur, *India* **94 D4** 21 8N 79 10 E
Nagua, *Dom. Rep.* **165 C6** 19 23N 69 50W
Naguabo, *Puerto Rico* **165 d** 18 13N 65 44W
Nagyatád, *Hungary* **52 D2** 46 14N 17 22 E
Nagyecsed, *Hungary* **52 C7** 47 53N 22 24 E
Nagykálló, *Hungary* **52 C6** 47 53N 21 51 E
Nagykanizsa, *Hungary* **52 D2** 46 28N 17 0 E
Nagykáta, *Hungary* **52 C4** 47 25N 19 45 E
Nagykőrös, *Hungary* **52 C4** 47 5N 19 48 E
Naha, *Japan* **71 L3** 26 13N 127 42 E
Nahan, *India* **92 D7** 30 33N 77 18 E
Nahanni Butte, *Canada* **142 A4** 61 2N 123 31W
Nahanni Nat. Park, *Canada* **142 A4** 61 15N 125 0W
Nahargarh, *Mad. P., India* **92 G6** 24 10N 75 14 E
Nahargarh, *Raj., India* **92 G7** 24 55N 76 50 E
Nahariyya, *Israel* **100 F6** 33 1N 35 5 E
Nahāvand, *Iran* **97 C6** 34 10N 48 22 E
Nahe →, *Germany* **31 F3** 49 58N 7 54 E
Nahîya, W. →, *Egypt* **106 B3** 28 55N 31 0 E
Nahuel Huapi, L., *Argentina* **176 B2** 41 0 S 71 32W
Nahunta, *U.S.A.* **152 D8** 31 12N 81 59W
Nai Yong, *Thailand* **87 a** 8 14N 98 22 E
Naic, *Phil.* **80 D3** 14 19N 120 46 E
Naicá, *Mexico* **162 B3** 27 53N 105 31W
Naicam, *Canada* **143 C8** 52 30N 104 30W
Naikliu, *Indonesia* **82 C2** 9 30 S 123 50 E
Naikoon Prov. Park, *Canada* **142 C2** 53 55N 131 55W
Naikul, *India* **94 D7** 21 20N 84 58 E
Naila, *Germany* **31 E7** 50 19N 11 42 E
Naimisharanya, *India* **93 F9** 27 21N 80 30 E
Nain, *Canada* **141 A7** 56 34N 61 40W
Nā'īn, *Iran* **97 C7** 32 54N 53 0 E
Naini Tal, *India* **93 E8** 29 30N 79 30 E
Naintré, *France* **26 F7** 46 46N 0 29 E
Nainwa, *India* **92 G6** 25 46N 75 51 E
Naipu, *Romania* **53 F10** 44 12N 25 47 E

Nairai, *Fiji* **133 A2** 17 49 S 179 15 E
Nairn, *U.K.* **22 D5** 57 35N 3 53W
Nairobi, *Kenya* **118 C4** 1 17 S 36 48 E
Nairobi Nat. Park, *Kenya* **118 C4** 1 22 S 36 50 E
Naissaar, *Estonia* **15 G21** 59 34N 24 29 E
Naita, Mt., *Ethiopia* **107 F4** 5 30N 35 18 E
Naitaba, *Fiji* **133 A3** 17 0 S 179 16W
Naivasha, *Kenya* **118 C4** 0 40 S 36 30 E
Naivasha, L., *Kenya* **118 C4** 0 48 S 36 20 E
Najac, *France* **28 D5** 44 14N 1 58 E
Najafābād, *Iran* **97 C6** 32 40N 51 15 E
Najd, *Si. Arabia* **102 B3** 26 30N 42 0 E
Nájera, *Spain* **40 C2** 42 26N 2 48W
Najerilla →, *Spain* **40 C2** 42 32N 2 48W
Najibabad, *India* **92 E8** 29 40N 78 20 E
Najin, *N. Korea* **75 C16** 42 12N 130 15 E
Najmah, *Si. Arabia* **97 E6** 26 42N 50 6 E
Najrān, *Si. Arabia* **98 C4** 17 34N 44 18 E
Naju, *S. Korea* **75 G14** 35 3N 126 43 E
Naka-Gawa →, *Japan* **73 A12** 36 20N 140 36 E
Nakadōri-Shima, *Japan* **71 H4** 32 57N 129 4 E
Nakalagba, *Dem. Rep. of the Congo* **118 B2** 2 50N 27 58 E
Nakalele Pt., *U.S.A.* **145 B5** 21 2N 156 35W
Nakama, *Japan* **72 D2** 33 56N 130 43 E
Nakaminato, *Japan* **73 A12** 36 21N 140 36 E
Nakamura, *Japan* **72 E4** 32 59N 132 56 E
Nakanai Mts., *Papua N. G.* **132 C6** 5 40 S 151 0 E
Nakano, *Japan* **73 A10** 36 45N 138 22 E
Nakano-Shima, *Japan* **71 K4** 29 51N 129 52 E
Nakanojō, *Japan* **73 A10** 36 35N 138 51 E
Nakashibetsu, *Japan* **70 C12** 43 33N 144 59 E
Nakatsu, *Japan* **72 D3** 33 34N 131 15 E
Nakatsugawa, *Japan* **73 B9** 35 29N 137 30 E
Nakfa, *Eritrea* **107 D4** 16 40N 38 32 E
Nakfa Wildlife Reserve, *Eritrea* **107 D4** 17 28N 38 55 E
Nakha Yai, Ko, *Thailand* **87 a** 8 3N 98 28 E
Nakhfar al Buşayyah, *Iraq* **96 D5** 30 0N 46 10 E
Nakhichevan = Naxçıvan, *Azerbaijan* **101 C11** 39 12N 45 15 E
Nakhichevan Republic = Naxçıvan □, *Azerbaijan* **101 C11** 39 25N 45 26 E
Nakhl, *Egypt* **103 F2** 29 55N 33 43 E
Nakhl-e Taqī, *Iran* **97 E7** 27 28N 52 36 E
Nakhodka, *Russia* **67 E14** 42 53N 132 54 E
Nakhon Nayok, *Thailand* **86 E3** 14 12N 101 13 E
Nakhon Pathom, *Thailand* **86 F3** 13 49N 100 3 E
Nakhon Phanom, *Thailand* **86 D5** 17 23N 104 43 E
Nakhon Ratchasima, *Thailand* **86 E4** 14 59N 102 12 E
Nakhon Sawan, *Thailand* **86 E3** 15 35N 100 10 E
Nakhon Si Thammarat, *Thailand* **87 H3** 8 29N 100 0 E
Nakhon Thai, *Thailand* **86 D3** 17 5N 100 44 E
Nakhtarana, *India* **92 H3** 23 20N 69 15 E
Nakina, *Canada* **140 B2** 50 10N 86 40W
Nakło nad Notecią, *Poland* **55 E4** 53 9N 17 38 E
Naknek, *U.S.A.* **144 G8** 58 44N 157 1W
Nako, *Burkina Faso* **112 C4** 10 40N 3 4W
Nakodar, *India* **92 D6** 31 8N 75 31 E
Nakskov, *Denmark* **17 K5** 54 50N 11 8 E
Naktong →, *S. Korea* **75 G15** 35 7N 128 57 E
Nakuru, *Kenya* **118 C4** 0 15 S 36 4 E
Nakuru, L., *Kenya* **118 C4** 0 23 S 36 5 E
Nakusp, *Canada* **142 C5** 50 20N 117 45W
Nal, *Pakistan* **92 F2** 27 40N 66 12 E
Nal →, *Pakistan* **91 D2** 25 20N 65 30 E
Nalázi, *Mozam.* **117 C5** 24 3 S 33 20 E
Nalchik, *Russia* **61 J6** 43 30N 43 33 E
Nałęczów, *Poland* **55 G9** 51 17N 22 9 E
Nalerigu, *Ghana* **113 C4** 10 35N 0 25W
Nalgonda, *India* **94 F4** 17 6N 79 15 E
Nalhati, *India* **93 G12** 24 17N 87 52 E
Naliya, *India* **92 H3** 23 16N 68 50 E
Nallamalai Hills, *India* **95 G4** 15 30N 78 50 E
Nallıhan, *Turkey* **100 B4** 40 11N 31 20 E
Nalolo, *Zambia* **115 F4** 15 33 S 23 7 E
Nalón →, *Spain* **42 B4** 43 32N 6 4W
Nalong, *Burma* **90 C6** 24 44N 97 28 E
Nālūt, *Libya* **108 B2** 31 54N 11 0 E
Nam Can, *Vietnam* **87 H5** 8 46N 104 59 E
Nam-ch'on, *N. Korea* **75 E14** 38 15N 126 26 E
Nam Co, *China* **68 C4** 30 30N 90 45 E
Nam Dinh, *Vietnam* **76 G6** 20 25N 106 5 E
Nam Du, Hon, *Vietnam* **87 H5** 9 41N 104 21 E
Nam Ngum Dam, *Laos* **86 C4** 18 35N 102 34 E
Nam-Phan, *Vietnam* **87 G6** 10 30N 106 0 E
Nam Phong, *Thailand* **86 D4** 16 42N 102 52 E
Nam Tha, *Laos* **76 G3** 20 58N 101 30 E
Nam Tok, *Thailand* **86 E2** 14 21N 99 4 E
Namacunde, *Angola* **115 E4** 11 26 S 22 43 E
Namacunde, *Angola* **116 B2** 17 18 S 15 50 E
Namacurra, *Mozam.* **117 B6** 17 30 S 36 50 E
Namadgi Nat. Park, *Australia* **129 C8** 35 42 S 149 0 E
Namak, Daryācheh-ye, *Iran* **97 C7** 34 30N 52 0 E
Namak, Kavir-e, *Iran* **97 C8** 34 30N 57 30 E
Namakkal, *India* **95 J4** 11 13N 78 13 E
Namakzār, Daryācheh-ye, *Iran* **91 B1** 34 0N 60 30 E
Namaland, *Namibia* **116 C2** 26 0 S 17 0 E
Namangan, *Uzbekistan* **66 E8** 41 0N 71 40 E
Namapa, *Mozam.* **119 E4** 13 43 S 39 50 E
Namaqualand, *S. Africa* **116 E2** 30 0 S 17 25 E
Namasagali, *Uganda* **118 B3** 1 2N 33 0 E
Namatanai, *Papua N. G.* **132 B7** 3 40 S 152 29 E
Namber, *Indonesia* **83 B4** 1 2 S 134 49 E
Nambour, *Australia* **127 D5** 26 32 S 152 58 E
Nambouwalu = Nabouwalu, *Fiji* **133 A2** 17 0 S 178 45 E
Nambuangongo, *Angola* **115 D2** 8 1 S 14 12 E
Nambucca Heads, *Australia* **129 A10** 30 37 S 153 0 E
Nambung Nat. Park, *Australia* **125 F2** 30 30 S 115 5 E
Namcha Barwa, *China* **68 D4** 29 40N 95 10 E
Namche Bazar, *Nepal* **93 F12** 27 51N 86 47 E
Namchonjŏm = Nam-ch'on, *N. Korea* **75 E14** 38 15N 126 26 E
Namecunda, *Mozam.* **119 E4** 14 54 S 37 37 E
Nameh, *Indonesia* **85 B5** 2 34N 116 21 E
Namenalala, *Fiji* **133 A2** 17 8 S 179 9 E
Nameponda, *Mozam.* **119 F4** 15 50 S 39 50 E
Namerikawa, *Japan* **73 A9** 36 46N 137 20 E
Náměšť' nad Oslavou, *Czech Rep.* **35 B9** 49 12N 16 10 E
Námestovo, *Slovak Rep.* **35 B12** 49 24N 19 25 E
Nametil, *Mozam.* **119 F4** 15 40 S 39 21 E
Namew L., *Canada* **143 C8** 54 14N 101 56W
Namgia, *India* **93 D8** 31 48N 78 40 E
Namhkam, *Burma* **76 E1** 23 50N 97 41 E
Namho, *Burma* **90 D7** 22 4N 99 1 E
Namhsan, *Burma* **90 D6** 22 48N 97 2 E
Namib Desert, *Namibia* **116 C2** 22 30 S 15 0 E
Namib-Naukluft Park, *Namibia* **116 C2** 24 40 S 15 16 E
Namibe, *Angola* **115 F2** 15 7 S 12 11 E
Namibe □, *Angola* **116 B1** 16 35 S 12 30 E
Namibe, Reserva Parcial de, *Angola* **115 F2** 16 35 S 12 20 E
Namibia ■, *Africa* **116 C2** 22 0 S 18 9 E
Namibwoestyn = Namib Desert, *Namibia* **116 C2** 22 30 S 15 0 E
Namīn, *Iran* **101 C13** 38 25N 48 30 E
Namlan, *Burma* **90 D6** 22 15N 97 24 E
Namlea, *Indonesia* **82 B3** 3 18 S 127 5 E
Namoi →, *N.S.W., Australia* **129 A8** 30 12 S 149 30 E
Namoi →, *N.S.W., Australia* **129 A9** 30 0 S 148 7 E
Namous, O. en →, *Algeria* **111 B4** 31 0N 0 15W
Nampa, *U.S.A.* **158 E5** 43 34N 116 34W
Nampala, *Mali* **112 B3** 15 20N 5 30W
Namp'o, *N. Korea* **75 E13** 38 52N 125 10 E
Nampō-Shotō, *Japan* **71 J10** 32 0N 140 0 E
Nampula, *Mozam.* **119 F4** 15 6 S 39 15 E
Namrole, *Indonesia* **82 B3** 3 46 S 126 46 E
Namsang, *Burma* **90 E6** 20 53N 97 43 E
Namsen →, *Norway* **14 D14** 64 28N 11 37 E
Namsos, *Norway* **14 D14** 64 29N 11 30 E
Namtsy, *Russia* **67 C13** 62 43N 129 37 E
Namtu, *Burma* **90 D6** 23 5N 97 28 E
Namtumbo, *Tanzania* **119 E4** 10 30 S 36 4 E
Namu, *Canada* **142 C3** 51 52N 127 50W
Namuka-i-Lau, *Fiji* **133 B3** 18 53 S 178 37W
Namumea, *Tuvalu* **123 B14** 5 41 S 176 9 E
Namur, *Belgium* **24 D4** 50 27N 4 52 E
Namur □, *Belgium* **24 D4** 50 17N 5 0 E
Namutoni, *Namibia* **116 B2** 18 49 S 16 55 E
Namwala, *Zambia* **119 F2** 15 44 S 26 30 E
Namwŏn, *S. Korea* **75 G14** 35 23N 127 23 E
Namysłów, *Poland* **55 G4** 51 6N 17 42 E
Nan, *Thailand* **86 C3** 18 48N 100 46 E
Nan →, *Thailand* **86 E3** 15 42N 100 9 E
Nan-ch'ang = Nanchang, *China* **77 C10** 28 42N 115 55 E
Nan Ling, *China* **77 E8** 25 0N 112 30 E
Nan Xian, *China* **77 C9** 29 20N 112 22 E
Nana, *C.A.R.* **114 A3** 5 0N 15 50 E
Nana, *Romania* **53 F11** 44 17N 26 34 E
Nana-Barya, Réserve de Faune de la, *C.A.R.* **114 A3** 7 40N 17 29 E
Nana Kru, *Liberia* **112 E3** 4 55N 8 45W
Nanaimo, *Canada* **142 D4** 49 10N 124 0W
Nanakuli, *U.S.A.* **145 K13** 21 24N 158 9W
Nanam, *N. Korea* **75 D15** 41 44N 129 40 E
Nanan, *China* **77 E12** 24 59N 118 21 E
Nanango, *Australia* **127 D5** 26 40 S 152 0 E
Nan'ao, *China* **77 F11** 23 28N 117 5 E
Nanao, *Japan* **71 F8** 37 0N 137 0 E
Nanbu, *China* **76 B6** 31 18N 106 3 E
Nanchang, *Jiangxi, China* **77 C10** 28 42N 115 55 E
Nanchang, *Kiangsi, China* **77 C10** 28 34N 115 48 E
Nancheng, *China* **77 D11** 27 33N 116 35 E
Nanching = Nanjing, *China* **77 A12** 32 2N 118 47 E
Nanchong, *China* **76 B6** 30 43N 106 2 E
Nanchuan, *China* **76 C6** 29 9N 107 6 E
Nancowry, *India* **95 L11** 7 59N 93 32 E
Nancy, *France* **27 D13** 48 42N 6 12 E
Nanda Devi, *India* **93 D8** 30 23N 79 59 E
Nanda Kot, *India* **93 D9** 30 17N 80 5 E
Nandan, *China* **76 E6** 24 58N 107 29 E
Nandan, *Japan* **72 C6** 34 10N 134 42 E
Nanded, *India* **94 E3** 19 10N 77 20 E
Nandewar Ra., *Australia* **127 E5** 30 15 S 150 35 E
Nandgaon, *India* **94 D2** 20 19N 74 39 E
Nandi = Nadi, *Fiji* **133 A1** 17 42 S 177 20 E
Nandiarane, Pte., *N. Cal.* **133 T18** 20 14 S 164 19 E
Nandigama, *India* **94 F5** 16 47N 80 18 E
Nandigram, *India* **93 H12** 22 1N 87 58 E
Nandikotkur, *India* **95 G4** 15 52N 78 18 E
Nandura, *India* **94 D3** 20 52N 76 25 E
Nandurbar, *India* **94 D2** 21 20N 74 15 E
Nandyal, *India* **95 G4** 15 30N 78 30 E
Nanfeng, *Guangdong, China* **77 F8** 23 45N 111 47 E
Nanfeng, *Jiangxi, China* **77 D11** 27 12N 116 28 E
Nanga-Eboko, *Cameroon* **113 E7** 4 41N 12 22 E
Nanga Parbat, *Pakistan* **93 B6** 35 10N 74 35 E
Nangade, *Mozam.* **119 E4** 11 5 S 39 36 E
Nangapinoh, *Indonesia* **85 C4** 0 20 S 111 44 E
Nangarhār □, *Afghan.* **91 B3** 34 20N 70 0 E
Nangatayap, *Indonesia* **85 C4** 1 32 S 110 34 E
Nangeya Mts., *Uganda* **118 B3** 3 30N 33 30 E
Nangis, *France* **27 D10** 48 33N 3 1 E
Nangong, *China* **74 F8** 37 23N 115 22 E
Nangtud, Mt., *Phil.* **81 F4** 11 17N 122 11 E
Nanguneri, *India* **95 K3** 8 29N 77 40 E
Nangwarry, *Australia* **128 D4** 37 33 S 140 48 E
Nanhua, *China* **76 E3** 25 13N 101 21 E
Nanhuang, *China* **75 F11** 36 58N 121 48 E
Nanhui, *China* **77 B13** 31 5N 121 44 E
Nanjangud, *India* **95 H3** 12 6N 76 43 E
Nanjeko, *Zambia* **119 F1** 15 31 S 23 30 E
Nanji Shan, *China* **77 D13** 27 27N 121 4 E
Nanjian, *China* **76 E3** 25 2N 100 25 E
Nanjiang, *China* **76 A6** 32 28N 106 51 E
Nanjing, *Fujian, China* **77 E11** 24 25N 117 20 E
Nanjing, *Jiangsu, China* **77 A12** 32 2N 118 47 E
Nanjirinji, *Tanzania* **119 D4** 9 41 S 39 5 E
Nankana Sahib, *Pakistan* **92 D5** 31 27N 73 38 E
Nankang, *China* **77 E10** 25 40N 114 45 E
Nanking = Nanjing, *China* **77 A12** 32 2N 118 47 E
Nankoku, *Japan* **72 D5** 33 39N 133 44 E
Nanlang, *China* **69 G10** 22 30N 113 32 E
Nanling, *China* **77 B12** 30 55N 118 20 E
Nannial, *India* **94 E4** 19 4N 79 38 E
Nanning, *China* **76 F7** 22 48N 108 20 E
Nannup, *Australia* **125 F2** 33 59 S 115 48 E
Nanortalik, *Greenland* **10 E6** 60 10N 45 17W
Nanpan Jiang →, *China* **76 E6** 25 10N 106 5 E
Nanpara, *India* **93 F9** 27 52N 81 33 E
Nanpi, *China* **74 E9** 38 2N 116 45 E
Nanping, *Fujian, China* **77 D12** 26 38N 118 10 E
Nanping, *Henan, China* **77 C9** 29 55N 112 3 E
Nanri Dao, *China* **77 E12** 25 15N 119 25 E
Nanripe, *Mozam.* **119 E4** 13 52 S 38 52 E
Nansei-Shotō = Ryūkyū-rettō, *Japan* **71 M3** 26 0N 126 0 E
Nansen Land, *Greenland* **10 A6** 83 0N 43 0W
Nansen Sd., *Canada* **6 A3** 81 0N 91 0W
Nansha, *China* **69 F10** 22 45N 113 34 E
Nanshan I., *S. China Sea* **78 B5** 10 45N 115 49 E
Nansio, *Tanzania* **118 C3** 2 3 S 33 4 E
Nant, *France* **28 D7** 44 1N 3 18 E
Nanterre, *France* **27 D9** 48 53N 2 13 E
Nantes, *France* **26 E5** 47 12N 1 33W
Nantiat, *France* **28 B5** 46 1N 1 11 E
Nanticoke, *U.S.A.* **151 E8** 41 12N 76 0W
Nanton, *Canada* **142 C6** 50 21N 113 46W
Nantong, *China* **77 A13** 32 1N 120 52 E
Nantou, *China* **69 F10** 22 32N 113 55 E
Nantou, *Taiwan* **77 F13** 23 57N 120 35 E
Nantua, *France* **27 F12** 46 10N 5 35 E
Nantucket I., *U.S.A.* **148 E10** 41 16N 70 5W
Nantwich, *U.K.* **20 D5** 53 4N 2 31W
Nanty Glo, *U.S.A.* **150 F6** 40 28N 78 50W
Nanuku Passage, *Fiji* **133 A3** 16 45 S 179 15W
Nanuque, *Brazil* **171 E3** 17 50 S 40 21W
Nanusa, Kepulauan, *Indonesia* **79 D7** 4 45N 127 1 E
Nanutarra Roadhouse, *Australia* **124 D2** 22 32 S 115 30 E
Nanxi, *China* **76 C5** 28 54N 104 59 E
Nanxiong, *China* **77 E10** 25 6N 114 15 E
Nanyang, *China* **74 H7** 33 11N 112 30 E
Nanyi Hu, *China* **77 B12** 31 5N 119 0 E
Nanyuki, *Kenya* **118 B4** 0 2N 37 4 E
Nanzhang, *China* **77 B8** 31 45N 111 50 E
Nao, C. de la, *Spain* **41 G5** 38 44N 0 14 E
Naococane, L., *Canada* **141 B5** 52 50N 70 45W
Naogaon, *Bangla.* **90 C2** 24 52N 88 52 E
Naoné, *Vanuatu* **133 E6** 15 0 S 168 8 E
Náousa, *Imathía, Greece* **50 F6** 40 42N 22 9 E
Náousa, *Kikládhes, Greece* **49 D7** 37 7N 25 14 E
Naozhou Dao, *China* **77 G8** 20 55N 110 20 E
Napa, *U.S.A.* **160 G4** 38 18N 122 17W
Napa →, *U.S.A.* **160 G4** 38 10N 122 19W
Napakiak, *U.S.A.* **144 F7** 60 42N 161 57W
Napamute, *U.S.A.* **144 F8** 61 33N 158 42W
Napanee, *Canada* **140 D4** 44 15N 77 0W
Napanoch, *U.S.A.* **151 E10** 41 44N 74 22W
Napanwainami, *Indonesia* **83 B5** 3 3 S 135 45 E
Napaskiak, *U.S.A.* **144 F7** 60 43N 161 55W
Nape, *Laos* **86 C5** 18 18N 105 6 E
Nape Pass = Keo Neua, Deo, *Vietnam* **86 C5** 18 23N 105 10 E
Naperville, *U.S.A.* **157 C8** 41 46N 88 9W
Napf, *Switz.* **32 B5** 47 1N 7 56 E
Napier, *N.Z.* **130 F5** 39 30 S 176 56 E
Napier Broome B., *Australia* **124 B4** 14 2 S 126 37 E
Napier Pen., *Australia* **126 A2** 12 4 S 135 43 E
Napierville, *Canada* **151 A11** 45 11N 73 25W
Naples = Nápoli, *Italy* **47 B7** 40 50N 14 15 E
Naples, *U.S.A.* **149 M5** 26 8N 81 48W
Naples Park, *U.S.A.* **153 J8** 26 17N 81 46W
Napo, *China* **76 F5** 23 22N 105 50 E
Napo □, *Ecuador* **168 D2** 0 30 S 77 0W
Napo →, *Peru* **168 D3** 3 20 S 72 40W
Napoleon, *N. Dak., U.S.A.* **154 B5** 46 30N 99 46W
Napoleon, *Ohio, U.S.A.* **157 C12** 41 23N 84 8W
Napoleon's Tomb, *St. Helena* **9 h** 15 56 S 5 42W
Nápoli, *Italy* **47 B7** 40 50N 14 15 E
Nápoli, G. di, *Italy* **47 B7** 40 43N 14 10 E
Napopo, *Dem. Rep. of the Congo* **118 B2** 4 15N 28 0 E
Nappanee, *U.S.A.* **157 C11** 41 27N 86 0W
Napperby, *Australia* **128 B3** 33 9 S 138 7 E
Naqāda, *Egypt* **106 B3** 25 53N 32 42 E
Naqadeh, *Iran* **101 D11** 36 57N 45 23 E
Naqb, Ra's an, *Jordan* **103 F4** 30 0N 35 29 E
Naqqāsh, *Iran* **97 C6** 35 40N 49 6 E
Nara, *Japan* **73 C7** 34 40N 135 49 E
Nara, *Mali* **112 B3** 15 10N 7 20W
Nara □, *Japan* **73 C8** 34 30N 136 0 E
Nara Canal, *Pakistan* **92 G3** 24 30N 69 20 E
Nara Visa, *U.S.A.* **155 H3** 35 37N 103 6W
Naracoorte, *Australia* **128 D4** 36 58 S 140 45 E
Naradhan, *Australia* **129 B7** 33 34 S 146 17 E
Naraini, *India* **93 G9** 25 11N 80 29 E
Narasannapeta, *India* **94 E7** 18 25N 84 3 E
Narasapur, *India* **95 F5** 16 26N 81 40 E
Narasaropet, *India* **95 F5** 16 14N 80 4 E
Narathiwat, *Thailand* **87 J3** 6 30N 101 48 E
Narayanapatnam, *India* **94 E6** 18 53N 83 10 E
Narayanganj, *Bangla.* **90 D3** 23 40N 90 33 E
Narayanpet, *India* **94 F3** 16 45N 77 30 E
Narbonne, *France* **28 E7** 43 11N 3 0 E
Narbuvollen, *Norway* **18 B8** 62 21N 11 27 E
Narcea →, *Spain* **42 B4** 43 33N 6 44W
Narcondam I., *India* **95 H12** 13 20N 94 16 E
Nardīn, *Iran* **97 B7** 37 3N 55 59 E
Nardò, *Italy* **47 B11** 40 11N 18 2 E
Narembeen, *Australia* **125 F2** 32 7 S 118 24 E
Narendranagar, *India* **92 D8** 30 10N 78 18 E
Nares Str., *Arctic* **10 B3** 80 0N 70 0W
Naretha, *Australia* **125 F3** 31 0 S 124 45 E
Narew →, *Poland* **55 F7** 52 26N 20 41 E
Nari →, *Pakistan* **92 F2** 28 0N 67 40 E
Narin, *Afghan.* **91 A3** 36 5N 69 0 E
Narindra, Helodranon' i, *Madag.* **117 A8** 14 55 S 47 30 E
Narino □, *Colombia* **168 C2** 1 30N 78 0W
Narita, *Japan* **73 B12** 35 47N 140 19 E
Nariva Swamp, *Trin. & Tob.* **169 F9** 10 26N 61 4W
Närke, *Sweden* **16 E8** 59 10N 15 0 E
Narmada →, *India* **92 J5** 21 38N 72 36 E
Narman, *Turkey* **101 B9** 40 26N 41 57 E
Narmland, *Sweden* **15 F15** 60 0N 13 30 E
Narnaul, *India* **92 E7** 28 5N 76 11 E
Narni, *Italy* **45 F9** 42 30N 12 30 E
Naro, *Ghana* **112 C4** 10 22N 2 27W
Naro Fominsk, *Russia* **58 E9** 55 23N 36 43 E
Narodnaya, *Russia* **56 A10** 65 5N 59 58 E
Narok, *Kenya* **118 C4** 1 55 S 35 52 E
Narón, *Spain* **42 B2** 43 32N 8 9W
Narooma, *Australia* **129 D9** 36 14 S 150 4 E
Narowal, *Pakistan* **91 B4** 32 6N 74 52 E
Narra, *Phil.* **81 G2** 9 18N 118 28 E
Narrabri, *Australia* **127 E4** 30 19 S 149 46 E
Narran →, *Australia* **127 D4** 28 37 S 148 12 E
Narrandera, *Australia* **129 C7** 34 42 S 146 31 E
Narrogin, *Australia* **125 F2** 32 58 S 117 14 E
Narromine, *Australia* **129 B8** 32 12 S 148 12 E
Narrow Hills Prov. Park, *Canada* **143 C8** 54 0N 104 37W
Narsampet, *India* **94 F4** 17 57N 79 58 E
Narsaq, *Greenland* **10 E6** 60 57N 46 4W
Narsimhapur, *India* **93 H8** 22 54N 79 14 E
Narsinghgarh, *India* **92 H7** 23 45N 76 40 E
Narsinghpur, *India* **94 D7** 20 28N 85 5 E
Narsipatnam, *India* **94 F6** 17 40N 82 37 E
Nartes, L. e, *Albania* **50 F3** 40 32N 19 25 E
Nartkala, *Russia* **61 J6** 43 33N 43 51 E
Naruto, *Kantō, Japan* **72 C6** 34 11N 134 37 E
Narutō, *Shikoku, Japan* **73 B12** 35 36N 140 25 E
Naruto-Kaikyō, *Japan* **72 C6** 34 14N 134 39 E
Narva, *Estonia* **58 C5** 59 23N 28 12 E
Narva →, *Russia* **15 G22** 59 27N 28 2 E
Narva Bay, *Estonia* **15 G19** 59 35N 27 35 E
Narvacan, *Phil.* **80 C3** 17 25N 120 28 E
Narvik, *Norway* **14 B17** 68 28N 17 26 E
Narvskoye Vdkhr., *Russia* **58 C5** 59 18N 28 14 E
Narwana, *India* **92 E7** 29 39N 76 6 E
Naryan-Mar, *Russia* **56 A9** 67 42N 53 12 E
Narym, *Russia* **66 D9** 59 0N 81 30 E
Naryn, *Kyrgyzstan* **66 E8** 41 26N 75 58 E
Naryn →, *Uzbekistan* **65 C5** 40 52N 71 36 E
Nasa, *Norway* **14 C16** 66 29N 15 23 E
Nasau, *Fiji* **133 A2** 17 19 S 179 27 E
Năsăud, *Romania* **53 C9** 47 19N 24 29 E
Nasawa, *Vanuatu* **133 E6** 15 12 S 168 9 E
Naseby, *N.Z.* **131 F5** 45 1 S 170 10 E
Naselle, *U.S.A.* **160 D3** 46 22N 123 49W
Naser, Buheirat en, *Egypt* **106 C3** 23 0N 32 30 E
Nashua, *Iowa, U.S.A.* **156 B4** 42 57N 92 32W
Nashua, *Mont., U.S.A.* **158 B10** 48 8N 106 22W
Nashua, *N.H., U.S.A.* **151 D13** 42 45N 71 28W
Nashville, *Ark., U.S.A.* **155 J8** 33 57N 93 51W
Nashville, *Ga., U.S.A.* **152 D6** 31 12N 83 15W
Nashville, *Ill., U.S.A.* **156 F7** 38 21N 89 23W
Nashville, *Ind., U.S.A.* **157 E10** 39 12N 86 15W
Nashville, *Mich., U.S.A.* **157 B11** 42 36N 85 5W
Nashville, *Tenn., U.S.A.* **149 G2** 36 10N 86 47W
Našice, *Croatia* **52 E3** 45 32N 18 4 E
Nasielsk, *Poland* **55 F7** 52 35N 20 50 E
Nasik, *India* **94 E1** 19 58N 73 50 E
Nasipit, *Phil.* **81 G5** 8 57N 125 19 E
Nasir, *Sudan* **107 F3** 8 36N 33 4 E
Nasirabad, *India* **92 F6** 26 15N 74 45 E
Nasirabad, *Pakistan* **92 E3** 28 23N 68 24 E
Naskaupi →, *Canada* **141 B7** 53 47N 60 51W
Naso, *Italy* **47 D7** 38 7N 14 47 E
Naso Pt., *Phil.* **81 F3** 10 25N 121 57 E
Naşrābād, *Iran* **97 C6** 34 8N 51 26 E
Naşrīān-e Pā'īn, *Iran* **96 C5** 32 52N 46 52 E
Nass →, *Canada* **142 C3** 55 0N 129 40W
Nassarawa, *Nigeria* **113 D6** 8 32N 7 41 E
Nassarawa □, *Nigeria* **113 D6** 8 30N 8 20 E
Nassau, *Bahamas* **9 b** 25 5N 77 20W
Nassau, *U.S.A.* **151 D11** 42 31N 73 37W
Nassau, B., *Chile* **176 E3** 55 20 S 68 0W
Nasser, L. = Naser, Buheirat en, *Egypt* **106 C3** 23 0N 32 30 E
Nasser City = Kôm Ombo, *Egypt* **106 C3** 24 25N 32 52 E
Nassereith, *Austria* **33 B11** 47 19N 10 50 E
Nassian, *Ivory C.* **112 D4** 8 28N 3 28W
Nässjö, *Sweden* **17 G8** 57 39N 14 42 E
Nastapoka →, *Canada* **140 A4** 56 55N 76 33W
Nastapoka, Is., *Canada* **140 A4** 56 55N 76 50W
Nasugbu, *Phil.* **80 D3** 14 5N 120 38 E
Näsum, *Sweden* **17 H8** 56 10N 14 29 E
Näsviken, *Sweden* **16 C10** 61 46N 16 52 E
Nata, *Botswana* **116 C4** 20 12 S 26 12 E
Nata →, *Botswana* **116 C4** 20 14 S 26 10 E
Natagaima, *Colombia* **168 C2** 3 37N 75 6W
Natal, *Brazil* **170 C4** 5 47 S 35 13W
Natal, *Indonesia* **84 B1** 0 35N 99 7 E
Natal Drakensberg Park, *S. Africa* **117 D4** 29 27 S 29 30 E
Natalinci, *Serbia, Yug.* **52 F5** 44 15N 20 49 E
Naţanz, *Iran* **97 C6** 33 30N 51 55 E
Natashquan, *Canada* **141 B7** 50 14N 61 46W
Natashquan →, *Canada* **141 B7** 50 7N 61 50W
Natchez, *U.S.A.* **155 K9** 31 34N 91 24W
Natchitoches, *U.S.A.* **155 K8** 31 46N 93 5W
Naters, *Switz.* **32 D5** 46 19N 7 58 E
Natewa B., *Fiji* **133 A2** 16 35 S 179 40 E
Nathalia, *Australia* **129 D6** 36 1 S 145 13 E
Nathdwara, *India* **92 G5** 24 55N 73 50 E
Nati, Pta., *Spain* **38 A4** 40 3N 3 50 E
Natimuk, *Australia* **128 D5** 36 42 S 142 0 E
Nation →, *Canada* **142 B4** 55 30N 123 32W
National Capital District □, *Papua N. G.* **132 E4** 9 25 S 147 10 E
National City, *U.S.A.* **161 N9** 32 41N 117 6W
National West Coast Tourist Recr. Area, *Namibia* **116 C1** 21 53 S 14 14 E
Natitingou, *Benin* **113 C5** 10 20N 1 26 E
Natividad, I., *Mexico* **162 B1** 27 50N 115 10W
Natividade, *Brazil* **171 D2** 11 43 S 47 47W
Natkyizin, *Burma* **86 E1** 14 57N 97 59 E
Natmauk, *Burma* **90 E5** 20 20N 95 24 E
Natogyi, *Burma* **90 E5** 21 25N 95 39 E
Natonin, *Phil.* **80 C3** 17 6N 121 18 E
Natron, L., *Tanzania* **118 C4** 2 20 S 36 0 E
Natrona Heights, *U.S.A.* **150 F5** 40 37N 79 44W
Natrûn, W. el →, *Egypt* **106 H7** 30 25N 30 13 E
Nattai Nat. Park, *Australia* **129 C9** 34 12 S 150 22 E
Nättraby, *Sweden* **17 H9** 56 13N 15 31 E
Natukanaoka Pan, *Namibia* **116 B2** 18 40 S 15 45 E
Natuna Besar, Kepulauan, *Indonesia* **84 B3** 4 0N 108 15 E
Natuna Is. = Natuna Besar, Kepulauan, *Indonesia* **84 B3** 4 0N 108 15 E
Natuna Selatan, Kepulauan, *Indonesia* **85 B3** 2 45N 109 0 E
Natural Bridge, *U.S.A.* **151 B9** 44 5N 75 30W
Naturaliste, C., *Australia* **127 G4** 40 50 S 148 15 E
Nau, *Tajikistan* **65 C4** 40 9N 69 22 E
Nau Qala, *Afghan.* **92 B3** 34 5N 68 5 E
Naucelle, *France* **28 D6** 44 13N 2 20 E
Nauders, *Austria* **34 E3** 46 54N 10 30 E
Nauen, *Germany* **30 C8** 52 36N 12 52 E
Naugatuck, *U.S.A.* **151 E11** 41 30N 73 3W
Naujaat = Repulse Bay, *Canada* **139 B11** 66 30N 86 30W
Naujan, *Phil.* **80 E3** 13 20N 121 18 E
Naujoji Akmenė, *Lithuania* **54 B9** 56 19N 22 54 E
Naulila, *Angola* **115 F2** 17 13 S 14 39 E
Naumburg, *Germany* **30 D7** 51 9N 11 47 E
Naupada, *India* **94 E7** 18 34N 84 18 E
Nā'ūr at Tunayb, *Jordan* **103 D4** 31 48N 35 57 E
Nauru ■, *Pac. Oc.* **134 H8** 1 0 S 166 0 E
Naushahra = Nowshera, *Pakistan* **91 B3** 34 0N 72 0 E
Naushahro, *Pakistan* **92 F3** 26 50N 68 7 E
Naushon I., *U.S.A.* **151 E14** 41 29N 70 45W
Nausori, *Fiji* **133 A2** 18 2 S 178 32 E
Naustdal, *Norway* **18 C2** 61 31N 5 43 E
Nauta, *Peru* **168 D3** 4 31 S 73 35W
Naute Recreational Resort, *Namibia* **116 D2** 26 55 S 17 57 E
Nautla, *Mexico* **163 C5** 20 20N 96 50W
Nauvoo, *U.S.A.* **156 D5** 40 33N 91 23W
Nava, *Mexico* **162 B4** 28 25N 100 46W
Nava, *Spain* **42 B5** 43 21N 5 31W
Nava del Rey, *Spain* **42 D5** 41 22N 5 6W
Navadwip, *India* **93 H13** 23 34N 88 20 E
Navahermosa, *Spain* **43 F6** 39 41N 4 28W
Navahrudak, *Belarus* **58 F3** 53 40N 25 50 E
Navai, *Fiji* **133 A1** 17 36 S 177 57 E
Navajo Reservoir, *U.S.A.* **159 H10** 36 48N 107 36W
Naval, *Phil.* **81 F5** 11 34N 124 23 E
Navalcarnero, *Spain* **42 E6** 40 17N 4 5W
Navalgund, *India* **95 G2** 15 34N 75 22 E
Navalmoral de la Mata, *Spain* **42 F5** 39 52N 5 33W
Navalvillar de Pela, *Spain* **43 F5** 39 9N 5 24W
Navan = An Uaimh, *Ireland* **23 C5** 53 39N 6 41W
Navapolatsk, *Belarus* **58 E5** 55 32N 28 37 E
Navarino, I., *Chile* **176 E3** 55 0 S 67 40W
Navarra □, *Spain* **40 C3** 42 40N 1 40W
Navarre, *Fla., U.S.A.* **153 E3** 30 24N 86 52W
Navarre, *Ohio, U.S.A.* **150 F3** 40 43N 81 31W
Navarro →, *U.S.A.* **160 F3** 39 11N 123 45W
Navas de San Juan, *Spain* **43 G7** 38 30N 3 19W
Navasota, *U.S.A.* **155 K6** 30 23N 96 5W
Navassa I., *W. Indies* **165 C5** 18 30N 75 0W
Nävekvarn, *Sweden* **17 F10** 58 38N 16 49 E
Naver →, *U.K.* **22 C4** 58 32N 4 14W
Navia, *Spain* **42 B4** 43 35N 6 42W
Navia →, *Spain* **42 B4** 43 15N 6 50W
Navia de Suarna, *Spain* **42 C3** 42 58N 7 3W
Navibandar, *India* **92 J3** 21 26N 69 48 E
Navidad, *Chile* **174 C1** 33 57 S 71 50W
Naviraí, *Brazil* **175 A5** 23 8 S 54 13W
Naviti, *Fiji* **133 A1** 17 7 S 177 15 E
Navlakhi, *India* **92 H4** 22 58N 70 28 E
Navlya, *Russia* **59 F8** 52 53N 34 30 E
Năvodari, *Romania* **53 F13** 44 19N 28 36 E
Navoi = Nawoiy, *Uzbekistan* **66 E7** 40 9N 65 22 E
Navojoa, *Mexico* **162 B3** 27 0N 109 30W
Navolato, *Mexico* **162 C3** 24 47N 107 42W
Návpaktos, *Greece* **48 C3** 38 24N 21 50 E
Návplion, *Greece* **48 D4** 37 33N 22 50 E
Navrongo, *Ghana* **113 C4** 10 51N 1 3W
Navsari, *India* **94 D1** 20 57N 72 59 E
Navua, *Fiji* **133 B2** 18 12 S 178 11 E
Nawa Kot, *Pakistan* **92 E4** 28 21N 71 24 E
Nawab Khan, *Pakistan* **92 D3** 30 17N 69 12 E
Nawabganj, *Bangla.* **90 C2** 24 35N 88 14 E
Nawabganj, *Ut. P., India* **93 F9** 26 56N 81 14 E
Nawabganj, *Ut. P., India* **93 E8** 28 32N 79 40 E
Nawabshah, *Pakistan* **91 D3** 26 15N 68 25 E
Nawada, *India* **93 G11** 24 50N 85 33 E
Nāwah, *Afghan.* **92 C3** 32 19N 67 53 E
Nawakot, *Nepal* **93 F11** 27 55N 85 10 E
Nawalgarh, *India* **92 F6** 27 50N 75 15 E
Nawanshahr, *India* **93 C6** 32 33N 74 48 E
Nawapara, *India* **94 D6** 20 46N 82 33 E
Nawar, Dasht-i-, *Afghan.* **91 B2** 33 52N 68 0 E
Nawāsīf, Ḩarrat, *Si. Arabia* **98 B3** 21 20N 42 10 E
Nawi, *Sudan* **106 D3** 18 32N 30 50 E
Nawng Hpa, *Burma* **90 D7** 22 10N 98 57 E
Nawoiy, *Uzbekistan* **66 E7** 40 9N 65 22 E

Nawş, Ra's, *Oman* **99 C6** 17 15N 55 16 E
Naxçıvan, *Azerbaijan* **101 C11** 39 12N 45 15 E
Naxçıvan □, *Azerbaijan* **101 C11** 39 25N 45 26 E
Náxos, *Greece* **49 D7** 37 8N 25 25 E
Naxxar, *Malta* **38 F7** 35 55N 14 27 E
Nay, *France* **28 E3** 43 10N 0 18W
Nay, Mui, *Vietnam* **78 B3** 12 55N 109 23 E
Nāy Band, *Būshehr, Iran* **97 E7** 27 20N 52 40 E
Nāy Band, *Khorāsān, Iran* **97 C8** 32 20N 57 34 E
Naya →, *Colombia* **168 C2** 3 13N 77 22W
Nayagarh, *India* **94 D7** 20 8N 85 6 E
Nayakhan, *Russia* **67 C16** 61 56N 159 0 E
Nayarit □, *Mexico* **162 C4** 22 0N 105 0W
Nayau, *Fiji* **133 B2** 18 6 S 178 10 E
Nayé, *Senegal* **112 C2** 14 28N 12 12W
Nayong, *China* **76 D5** 26 50N 105 20 E
Nayoro, *Japan* **70 B11** 44 21N 142 28 E
Nayudupeta, *India* **95 H4** 13 54N 79 54 E
Nayyāl, W. →, *Si. Arabia* **96 D3** 28 35N 39 4 E
Nazaré, *Bahia, Brazil* **171 D4** 13 2 S 39 0W
Nazaré, *Pará, Brazil* **173 B7** 6 25 S 52 29W
Nazaré, *Tocantins, Brazil* **170 C2** 6 23 S 47 40W
Nazaré, *Portugal* **43 F1** 39 36N 9 4W
Nazareth = Nazerat, *Israel* **103 C4** 32 42N 35 17 E
Nazareth, *U.S.A.* **151 F9** 40 44N 75 19W
Nazas, *Mexico* **162 B4** 25 10N 104 6W
Nazas →, *Mexico* **162 B4** 25 35N 103 25W
Nazca, *Peru* **172 C3** 14 50 S 74 57W
Naze, The, *U.K.* **21 F9** 51 53N 1 18 E
Nazerat, *Israel* **103 C4** 32 42N 35 17 E
Nāzīk, *Iran* **101 C11** 39 1N 45 4 E
Nazilli, *Turkey* **49 D10** 37 55N 28 15 E
Nazir Hat, *Bangla.* **90 D3** 22 35N 91 49 E
Nazko, *Canada* **142 C4** 53 1N 123 37W
Nazko →, *Canada* **142 C4** 53 7N 123 34W
Nazret, *Ethiopia* **107 F4** 8 32N 39 22 E
Nazwa, *Oman* **99 B7** 22 56N 57 32 E
Ncama, *Eq. Guin.* **114 B2** 1 55N 10 56 E
Nchanga, *Zambia* **119 E2** 12 30 S 27 49 E
Ncheu, *Malawi* **119 E3** 14 50 S 34 47 E
Ndala, *Tanzania* **118 C3** 4 45 S 33 15 E
Ndalatando, *Angola* **115 D2** 9 12 S 14 48 E
Ndali, *Benin* **113 D5** 9 50N 2 46 E
Ndareda, *Tanzania* **118 C4** 4 12 S 35 30 E
Ndélé, *C.A.R.* **114 A4** 8 25N 20 36 E
Ndendé, *Gabon* **114 C2** 2 22 S 11 23 E
Ndiael, Réserve de Faune du, *Senegal* **112 B1** 16 15N 16 0W
Ndikinimeki, *Cameroon* **113 E7** 4 46N 10 50 E
Ndindi, *Gabon* **114 C2** 3 46 S 11 9 E
N'Dioum, *Senegal* **112 B2** 16 31N 14 39W
Ndjamena, *Chad* **109 F2** 12 10N 14 59 E
Ndjolé, *Gabon* **114 C2** 0 10 S 10 45 E
Ndogo, Lagune, *Gabon* **114 C2** 2 35 S 10 0 E
Ndoki-Nouabalé, Réserve de Faune de, *Congo* **114 B3** 2 32N 16 32 E
Ndola, *Zambia* **119 E2** 13 0 S 28 34 E
Ndoto Mts., *Kenya* **118 B4** 2 0N 37 0 E
Ndoua, C., *N. Cal.* **133 V20** 22 24 S 166 56 E
Ndouba, *Congo* **114 C2** 0 9 S 14 4 E
Nduguti, *Tanzania* **118 C3** 4 18 S 34 41 E
Ndumu Game Reserve, *S. Africa* **117 D5** 26 52 S 32 15 E
Nea →, *Norway* **18 A8** 63 15N 11 0 E
Néa Alikarnassós, *Greece* **49 F7** 35 18N 25 13 E
Néa Ankhíalos, *Greece* **48 B4** 39 16N 22 49 E
Néa Epídhavros, *Greece* **48 D5** 37 40N 23 7 E
Néa Flippiás, *Greece* **48 B2** 39 12N 20 53 E
Néa Ionia, *Greece* **48 B4** 39 21N 22 56 E
Néa Kallikrátia, *Greece* **50 F7** 40 21N 23 3 E
Néa Mákri, *Greece* **48 C5** 38 5N 23 59 E
Néa Moudhaniá, *Greece* **50 F7** 40 15N 23 17 E
Néa Péramos, *Attikí, Greece* **48 C5** 38 0N 23 26 E
Néa Péramos, *Kavála, Greece* **51 F8** 40 50N 24 18 E
Néa Víssi, *Greece* **51 E10** 41 34N 26 33 E
Néa Zíkhna, *Greece* **50 E7** 41 2N 23 49 E
Neagari, *Japan* **73 A8** 36 26N 136 25 E
Neagh, Lough, *U.K.* **23 B5** 54 37N 6 25W
Neah Bay, *U.S.A.* **160 B2** 48 22N 124 37W
Neale, L., *Australia* **124 D5** 24 15 S 130 0 E
Neamati, *India* **90 B5** 26 50N 94 20 E
Neamţ □, *Romania* **53 C11** 47 0N 26 20 E
Neápolis, *Kozáni, Greece* **50 F5** 40 20N 21 24 E
Neápolis, *Kríti, Greece* **39 E6** 35 15N 25 37 E
Neápolis, *Lakonía, Greece* **48 E5** 36 27N 23 8 E
Near Is., *U.S.A.* **144 K1** 52 30N 174 0 E
Neath, *U.K.* **21 F4** 51 39N 3 48W
Neath Port Talbot □, *U.K.* **21 F4** 51 42N 3 45W
Neba, Î., *N. Cal.* **133 T17** 20 10 S 163 57 E
Nebbou, *Burkina Faso* **113 C4** 11 9N 1 51W
Nebelat el Hagana, *Sudan* **107 E2** 13 13N 29 2 E
Nebine Cr. →, *Australia* **127 D4** 29 27 S 146 56 E
Nebitdag, *Turkmenistan* **57 G9** 39 30N 54 22 E
Nebka, *Algeria* **110 C4** 27 28N 3 12W
Nebo, *Australia* **126 C4** 21 42 S 148 42 E
Nebolchy, *Russia* **58 C7** 59 8N 33 18 E
Nebraska □, *U.S.A.* **154 E5** 41 30N 99 30W
Nebraska City, *U.S.A.* **154 E7** 40 41N 95 52W
Nébrodi, Monti, *Italy* **47 E7** 37 54N 14 35 E
Necedah, *U.S.A.* **154 C9** 44 2N 90 4W
Nechako →, *Canada* **142 C4** 53 30N 122 44W
Neches →, *U.S.A.* **155 L8** 29 58N 93 51W
Nechisar Nat. Park, *Ethiopia* **107 F4** 5 58N 37 55 E
Neckar →, *Germany* **31 F4** 49 27N 8 29 E
Necker I., *U.S.A.* **145 G11** 23 35N 164 42W
Necochea, *Argentina* **174 D4** 38 30 S 58 50W
Nectar Brook, *Australia* **128 B2** 32 43 S 137 57 E
Neda, *Spain* **42 B2** 43 30N 8 9W
Nedalshytta, *Norway* **18 B9** 62 59N 12 3 E
Nedelino, *Bulgaria* **51 E9** 41 27N 25 3 E
Nedelišće, *Croatia* **45 B13** 46 23N 16 22 E
Nédha →, *Greece* **48 D3** 37 25N 21 45 E
Nedreberg, *Norway* **18 D8** 60 59N 11 41 E
Nedroma, *Algeria* **111 A4** 35 1N 1 45W
Nedstrand, *Norway* **18 E2** 59 21N 5 49 E
Needles, *Canada* **142 D5** 49 53N 118 7W
Needles, *U.S.A.* **161 L12** 34 51N 114 37W
Needles, The, *U.K.* **21 G6** 50 39N 1 35W
Needles Pt., *N.Z.* **130 C4** 36 3 S 175 25 E
Neely Henry L., *U.S.A.* **152 B3** 33 55N 86 2W
Ñeembucú □, *Paraguay* **174 B4** 27 0 S 58 0W
Neemuch = Nimach, *India* **92 G6** 24 30N 74 56 E
Neenah, *U.S.A.* **148 C1** 44 11N 88 28W
Neepawa, *Canada* **143 C9** 50 15N 99 30W
Neeses, *U.S.A.* **152 B8** 33 33N 81 7W
Nefta, *Tunisia* **108 B1** 33 53N 7 50 E
Neftah Sidi Boubekeur, *Algeria* **111 A5** 35 1N 0 4 E
Neftçala, *Azerbaijan* **97 B6** 39 19N 49 12 E
Neftegorsk, *Russia* **61 H4** 44 25N 39 45 E
Neftekamsk, *Russia* **64 C5** 56 6N 54 17 E
Neftekumsk, *Russia* **61 H7** 44 46N 44 50 E
Neftenbach, *Switz.* **33 A7** 47 32N 8 41 E
Nefyn, *U.K.* **20 E3** 52 56N 4 31W
Négala, *Mali* **112 C3** 12 52N 8 30W
Negapatam = Nagappattinam, *India* **95 J4** 10 46N 79 51 E
Negara, *Indonesia* **79 J17** 8 22 S 114 37 E
Negaunee, *U.S.A.* **148 B2** 46 30N 87 36W
Negele, *Ethiopia* **107 F4** 5 20N 39 36 E
Negeri Sembilan □, *Malaysia* **84 B2** 2 45N 102 10 E
Negev Desert = Hanegev, *Israel* **103 E4** 30 50N 35 0 E
Negoiul, Vf., *Romania* **53 E9** 45 38N 24 35 E
Negombo, *Sri Lanka* **95 L4** 7 12N 79 50 E
Negotin, *Serbia, Yug.* **50 B6** 44 16N 22 37 E
Negotino, *Macedonia* **50 E6** 41 29N 22 7 E
Negra, Peña, *Spain* **42 C4** 42 11N 6 30W
Negra, Pta., *Mauritania* **110 D1** 22 54N 16 18W
Negra, Pta., *Peru* **172 B1** 6 6 S 81 10W
Negra Pt., *Phil.* **80 B3** 18 40N 120 50 E
Negrais C. = Maudin Sun, *Burma* **90 G5** 16 0N 94 12 E
Negreşti, *Romania* **53 D12** 46 50N 27 30 E
Negreşti-Oaş, *Romania* **53 C8** 47 52N 23 26 E
Negril, *Jamaica* **164 a** 18 22N 78 20W
Négrine, *Algeria* **111 B6** 34 30N 7 30 E
Negro →, *Argentina* **176 B4** 41 2 S 62 47W
Negro →, *Bolivia* **173 C5** 14 11 S 63 7W
Negro →, *Brazil* **169 D6** 3 0 S 60 0W
Negro →, *Uruguay* **175 C4** 33 24 S 58 22W
Negros, *Phil.* **81 G4** 9 30N 122 40 E
Negros Occidental □, *Phil.* **81 F4** 10 0N 122 55 E
Negros Oriental □, *Phil.* **81 G4** 9 45N 123 0 E
Negru Vodă, *Romania* **53 G13** 43 47N 28 21 E
Neguac, *Canada* **141 C6** 47 15N 65 5W
Nehalem →, *U.S.A.* **160 E3** 45 40N 123 56W
Nehāvand, *Iran* **97 C6** 35 56N 49 31 E
Nehbandān, *Iran* **97 D9** 31 35N 60 5 E
Nehoiu, *Romania* **53 E11** 45 24N 26 20 E
Nei Monggol Zizhiqu □, *China* **74 D7** 42 0N 112 0 E
Neiafu, *Tonga* **133 P14** 18 39 S 173 59W
Neiges, Piton des, *Réunion* **121 c** 21 5 S 55 29 E
Neijiang, *China* **76 C5** 29 35N 104 55 E
Neilingding Dao, *China* **69 G10** 22 25N 113 48 E
Neill I., *India* **95 J11** 11 50N 93 3 E
Neillsville, *U.S.A.* **154 C9** 44 34N 90 36W
Neilton, *U.S.A.* **158 C2** 47 25N 123 53W
Neiqiu, *China* **74 F8** 37 15N 114 30 E
Neiva, *Colombia* **168 C2** 2 56N 75 18W
Neixiang, *China* **74 H6** 33 10N 111 52 E
Nejanilini L., *Canada* **143 B9** 59 33N 97 48W
Nejd = Najd, *Si. Arabia* **102 B3** 26 30N 42 0 E
Nejo, *Ethiopia* **107 F4** 9 30N 35 28 E
Nekā, *Iran* **97 B7** 36 39N 53 19 E
Nekemte, *Ethiopia* **107 F4** 9 4N 36 30 E
Nêkheb, *Egypt* **106 B3** 25 10N 32 48 E
Neksø, *Denmark* **17 J9** 55 4N 15 8 E
Nelamangala, *India* **95 H3** 13 6N 77 24 E
Nelas, *Portugal* **42 E3** 40 32N 7 52W
Nelaug, *Norway* **18 F5** 58 39N 8 40 E
Nelia, *Australia* **126 C3** 20 39 S 142 12 E
Nelidovo, *Russia* **58 D7** 56 13N 32 49 E
Neligh, *U.S.A.* **154 D5** 42 8N 98 2W
Nelkan, *Russia* **67 D14** 57 40N 136 4 E
Nellikuppam, *India* **95 J4** 11 46N 79 43 E
Nellore, *India* **95 G4** 14 27N 79 59 E
Nelson, *Canada* **142 D5** 49 30N 117 20W
Nelson, *N.Z.* **131 B8** 41 18 S 173 16 E
Nelson, *U.K.* **20 D5** 53 50N 2 13W
Nelson, *Ariz., U.S.A.* **159 J7** 35 31N 113 19W
Nelson, *Nev., U.S.A.* **161 K12** 35 42N 114 50W
Nelson □, *N.Z.* **131 B8** 41 20 S 173 20 E
Nelson →, *Canada* **143 C9** 54 33N 98 2W
Nelson, C., *Australia* **128 E4** 38 26 S 141 32 E
Nelson, C., *Papua N. G.* **132 E5** 9 0 S 149 20 E
Nelson, Estrecho, *Chile* **176 D2** 51 30 S 75 0W
Nelson Bay, *Australia* **129 B10** 32 43 S 152 9 E
Nelson Forks, *Canada* **142 B4** 59 30N 124 0W
Nelson House, *Canada* **143 B9** 55 47N 98 51W
Nelson L., *Canada* **143 B8** 55 48N 100 7W
Nelson Lakes Nat. Park, *N.Z.* **131 B7** 41 55 S 172 44 E
Nelspoort, *S. Africa* **116 E3** 32 7 S 23 0 E
Nelspruit, *S. Africa* **117 D5** 25 29 S 30 59 E
Néma, *Mauritania* **112 B3** 16 40N 7 15W
Neman, *Russia* **15 J20** 55 2N 22 2 E
Neman →, *Lithuania* **15 J19** 55 25N 21 10 E
Nembrala, *Indonesia* **82 D2** 10 53 S 122 50 E
Neméa, *Greece* **48 D4** 37 49N 22 40 E
Nemeiben L., *Canada* **143 B7** 55 20N 105 20W
Nemërçkë, Mal, *Albania* **50 F4** 40 15N 20 15 E
Nemira, Vf., *Romania* **53 D11** 46 17N 26 19 E
Némiscau, *Canada* **140 B4** 51 18N 76 54W
Némiscau, L., *Canada* **140 B4** 51 25N 76 40W
Nemours, *France* **27 D9** 48 16N 2 40 E
Nemšová, *Slovak Rep.* **35 C11** 48 58N 18 7 E
Nemunas = Neman →, *Lithuania* **15 J19** 55 25N 21 10 E
Nemuro, *Japan* **70 C12** 43 20N 145 35 E
Nemuro-Kaikyō, *Japan* **70 C12** 43 30N 145 30 E
Nen Jiang →, *China* **75 B13** 45 28N 124 30 E
Nenagh, *Ireland* **23 D3** 52 52N 8 11W
Nenana, *U.S.A.* **144 D10** 64 34N 149 5W
Nenasi, *Malaysia* **87 L4** 3 9N 103 23 E
Nene →, *U.K.* **21 E8** 52 49N 0 11 E
Nénita, *Greece* **49 C8** 38 14N 26 6 E
Nenjiang, *China* **69 B7** 49 10N 125 10 E
Neno, *Malawi* **119 F3** 15 25 S 34 40 E
Nenzing, *Austria* **33 B9** 47 11N 9 42 E
Neodesha, *U.S.A.* **155 G7** 37 25N 95 41W
Neoga, *U.S.A.* **157 E8** 39 19N 88 27W
Neokhórion, *Aitolía kai Akarnanía, Greece* **48 C3** 38 25N 21 17 E
Neokhórion, *Árta, Greece* **48 B2** 39 4N 21 0 E
Néon Karlovásion, *Greece* **49 D8** 37 45N 26 42 E
Néon Petrítsi, *Greece* **50 E7** 41 16N 23 15 E
Neópolis, *Brazil* **170 D4** 10 18 S 36 35W
Neosho, *U.S.A.* **155 G7** 36 52N 94 22W
Neosho →, *U.S.A.* **155 H7** 36 48N 95 18W
Nepal ■, *Asia* **93 F11** 28 0N 84 30 E
Nepalganj, *Nepal* **93 E9** 28 5N 81 40 E
Nepalganj Road, *India* **93 E9** 28 1N 81 41 E
Nepean B., *Australia* **128 C2** 35 42 S 137 37 E
Nephi, *U.S.A.* **158 G8** 39 43N 111 50W
Nephin, *Ireland* **23 B2** 54 1N 9 22W
Nepi, *Italy* **45 F9** 42 14N 12 21 E
Nepomuk, *Czech Rep.* **34 B6** 49 29N 13 35 E
Neptune, *U.S.A.* **151 F10** 40 13N 74 2W
Neptune Is., *Australia* **128 C2** 35 17 S 136 10 E
Nera →, *Italy* **45 F9** 42 26N 12 24 E
Nera →, *Romania* **52 F6** 44 48N 21 25 E
Nérac, *France* **28 D4** 44 8N 0 21 E
Nerang, *Australia* **127 D5** 27 58 S 153 20 E
Nerastro, Sarīr, *Libya* **108 D4** 24 20N 20 37 E
Neratovice, *Czech Rep.* **34 A7** 50 16N 14 31 E
Nerchinsk, *Russia* **67 D12** 52 0N 116 39 E
Nereju, *Romania* **53 E11** 45 43N 26 43 E
Nerekhta, *Russia* **58 D11** 57 26N 40 38 E
Néret, L., *Canada* **141 B5** 54 45N 70 44W
Neretvanski Kanal, *Croatia* **45 E14** 43 7N 17 10 E
Neringa, *Lithuania* **15 J19** 55 20N 21 5 E
Nerja, *Spain* **43 J7** 36 43N 3 55W
Nerl →, *Russia* **58 D11** 56 11N 40 34 E
Nerpio, *Spain* **41 G2** 38 11N 2 16W
Nerva, *Spain* **43 H4** 37 42N 6 30W
Nervi, *Italy* **44 D6** 44 23N 9 2 E
Neryungri, *Russia* **67 D13** 57 38N 124 28 E
Nes, *Iceland* **11 B9** 65 53N 17 24W
Nes, *Norway* **18 D6** 60 34N 9 59 E
Nesbyen, *Norway* **18 D6** 60 34N 9 8 E
Nescopeck, *U.S.A.* **151 E8** 41 3N 76 12W
Nesebŭr, *Bulgaria* **51 D11** 42 41N 27 46 E
Neset, *Norway* **18 C7** 61 53N 10 7 E
Nesflaten, *Norway* **18 E3** 59 38N 6 48 E
Neskaupstaður, *Iceland* **11 B13** 65 9N 13 42W
Nesland, *Norway* **18 E4** 59 31N 7 59 E
Neslandsvatn, *Norway* **18 F6** 58 57N 9 10 E
Nesoddtangen, *Norway* **18 E7** 59 48N 10 40 E
Ness, L., *U.K.* **22 D4** 57 15N 4 32W
Ness City, *U.S.A.* **154 F5** 38 27N 99 54W
Nesslau, *Switz.* **33 B8** 47 14N 9 13 E
Nesterov, *Poland* **59 G2** 50 4N 23 58 E
Nestórion, *Greece* **50 F5** 40 24N 21 5 E
Néstos →, *Greece* **51 E8** 41 20N 24 35 E
Nesttun, *Norway* **18 D2** 60 19N 5 20 E
Nesvady, *Slovak Rep.* **35 D11** 47 56N 18 7 E
Nesvizh = Nyasvizh, *Belarus* **59 F4** 53 14N 26 38 E
Netanya, *Israel* **103 C3** 32 20N 34 51 E
Netarhat, *India* **93 H11** 23 29N 84 16 E
Nete →, *Belgium* **24 C4** 51 7N 4 14 E
Netherdale, *Australia* **126 K6** 21 10 S 148 33 E
Netherlands ■, *Europe* **24 C5** 52 0N 5 30 E
Netherlands Antilles ■, *W. Indies* **168 A4** 12 15N 69 0W
Neto →, *Italy* **47 C10** 39 12N 17 9 E
Netrakona, *Bangla.* **90 C3** 24 53N 90 47 E
Netrang, *India* **92 J5** 21 39N 73 21 E
Netstal, *Switz.* **33 B8** 47 3N 9 3 E
Nettancourt, *France* **27 D11** 48 51N 4 57 E
Nettetal, *Germany* **30 D2** 51 19N 6 12 E
Nettilling L., *Canada* **139 B12** 66 30N 71 0W
Nettuno, *Italy* **46 A5** 41 27N 12 39 E
Netzahualcoyotl, Presa, *Mexico* **163 D6** 17 10N 93 30W
Neu-Isenburg, *Germany* **31 E4** 50 3N 8 42 E
Neu-Ulm, *Germany* **31 G6** 48 22N 10 0 E
Neubrandenburg, *Germany* **30 B9** 53 33N 13 15 E
Neubukow, *Germany* **30 A7** 54 2N 11 39 E
Neuburg, *Germany* **31 G7** 48 44N 11 11 E
Neuchâtel, *Switz.* **32 C3** 47 0N 6 55 E
Neuchâtel □, *Switz.* **32 C3** 47 0N 6 55 E
Neuchâtel, Lac de, *Switz.* **32 C3** 46 53N 6 50 E
Neudau, *Austria* **34 D9** 47 11N 16 6 E
Neuenegg, *Switz.* **32 C4** 46 54N 7 18 E
Neuenhagen, *Germany* **30 C9** 52 30N 13 38 E
Neuenhaus, *Germany* **30 C2** 52 30N 6 58 E
Neuenhof, *Switz.* **33 B6** 47 27N 8 19 E
Neuf-Brisach, *France* **27 D14** 48 1N 7 30 E
Neufahrn, *Bayern, Germany* **31 G8** 48 41N 12 11 E
Neufahrn, *Bayern, Germany* **31 G7** 48 18N 11 40 E
Neufchâteau, *Belgium* **24 E5** 49 50N 5 25 E
Neufchâteau, *France* **27 D12** 48 21N 5 40 E
Neufchâtel-en-Bray, *France* **26 C8** 49 44N 1 26 E
Neufchâtel-sur-Aisne, *France* **27 C11** 49 26N 4 1 E
Neuhaus, *Germany* **30 B6** 53 17N 10 56 E
Neuhausen, *Switz.* **33 A7** 47 41N 8 37 E
Neuillé-Pont-Pierre, *France* **26 E7** 47 33N 0 33 E
Neuilly-St-Front, *France* **27 C10** 49 10N 3 15 E
Neukalen, *Germany* **30 B8** 53 49N 12 46 E
Neumarkt, *Germany* **31 F7** 49 26N 11 27 E
Neumünster, *Germany* **30 A5** 54 4N 9 58 E
Neung-sur-Beuvron, *France* **27 E8** 47 30N 1 50 E
Neunkirch, *Switz.* **33 A7** 47 42N 8 30 E
Neunkirchen, *Austria* **34 D9** 47 43N 16 4 E
Neunkirchen, *Germany* **31 F3** 49 20N 7 9 E
Neuquén, *Argentina* **176 A3** 38 55 S 68 0W
Neuquén □, *Argentina* **174 D2** 38 0 S 69 50W
Neuquén →, *Argentina* **176 A3** 38 59 S 68 0W
Neuruppin, *Germany* **30 C8** 52 55N 12 48 E
Neusäss, *Germany* **31 G6** 48 24N 10 50 E
Neuse →, *U.S.A.* **149 H7** 35 6N 76 29W
Neusiedl, *Austria* **35 D9** 47 57N 16 50 E
Neusiedler See, *Austria* **35 D9** 47 50N 16 47 E
Neuss, *Germany* **30 D2** 51 11N 6 42 E
Neussargues-Moissac, *France* **28 C7** 45 9N 3 0 E
Neustadt, *Bayern, Germany* **31 F8** 49 44N 12 10 E
Neustadt, *Bayern, Germany* **31 G7** 48 48N 11 46 E
Neustadt, *Bayern, Germany* **31 F6** 49 34N 10 37 E
Neustadt, *Bayern, Germany* **31 E7** 50 19N 11 7 E
Neustadt, *Brandenburg, Germany* **30 C8** 52 50N 12 27 E
Neustadt, *Hessen, Germany* **30 E5** 50 51N 9 9 E
Neustadt, *Niedersachsen, Germany* **30 C5** 52 30N 9 30 E
Neustadt, *Rhld-Pfz., Germany* **31 F4** 49 21N 8 10 E
Neustadt, *Sachsen, Germany* **30 D10** 51 2N 14 12 E
Neustadt, *Schleswig-Holstein, Germany* **30 A6** 54 6N 10 49 E
Neustadt, *Thüringen, Germany* **30 E7** 50 45N 11 43 E
Neustrelitz, *Germany* **30 B9** 53 21N 13 4 E
Neuvic, *France* **28 C6** 45 23N 2 16 E
Neuville-sur-Saône, *France* **29 C8** 45 52N 4 51 E
Neuvy-le-Roi, *France* **26 E7** 47 36N 0 36 E
Neuvy-St-Sépulchre, *France* **27 F8** 46 35N 1 48 E
Neuvy-sur-Barangeon, *France* **27 E9** 47 20N 2 15 E
Neuwerk, *Germany* **30 B4** 53 55N 8 30 E
Neuwied, *Germany* **30 E3** 50 26N 7 29 E
Neva →, *Russia* **58 C6** 59 50N 30 30 E
Nevada, *Iowa, U.S.A.* **156 B3** 42 1N 93 27W
Nevada, *Mo., U.S.A.* **155 G7** 37 51N 94 22W
Nevada □, *U.S.A.* **158 G5** 39 0N 117 0W
Nevada City, *U.S.A.* **160 F6** 39 16N 121 1W
Nevado, Cerro, *Argentina* **174 D2** 35 30 S 68 32W
Nevasa, *India* **94 E2** 19 34N 75 0 E
Neve, Sa. da, *Angola* **115 E2** 13 43 S 13 10 E
Nevel, *Russia* **58 D5** 56 0N 29 55 E
Nevers, *France* **27 F10** 47 0N 3 9 E
Nevertire, *Australia* **129 A7** 31 50 S 147 44 E
Nevesinje, *Bos.-H.* **50 C2** 43 14N 18 6 E
Neville, *Canada* **143 D7** 49 58N 107 39W
Nevinnomyssk, *Russia* **61 H6** 44 40N 42 0 E
Nevis, *St. Kitts & Nevis* **165 C7** 17 0N 62 30W
Nevlunghavn, *Norway* **18 F6** 58 58N 9 53 E
Nevrokop = Gotse Delchev, *Bulgaria* **50 E7** 41 36N 23 46 E
Nevşehir, *Turkey* **100 C6** 38 33N 34 40 E
Nevyansk, *Russia* **64 C8** 57 30N 60 13 E
New →, *Guyana* **169 C6** 3 20N 57 37W
New →, *U.S.A.* **148 F5** 38 10N 81 12W
New Aiyansh, *Canada* **142 B3** 55 12N 129 4W
New Albany, *Ind., U.S.A.* **157 F11** 38 18N 85 49W
New Albany, *Miss., U.S.A.* **155 H10** 34 29N 89 0W
New Albany, *Pa., U.S.A.* **151 E8** 41 36N 76 27W
New Amsterdam, *Guyana* **169 B6** 6 15N 57 36W
New Angledool, *Australia* **127 D4** 29 5 S 147 55 E
New Athens, *U.S.A.* **156 F7** 38 19N 89 53W
New Baltimore, *U.S.A.* **150 D2** 42 41N 82 44W
New Bedford, *U.S.A.* **151 E14** 41 38N 70 56W
New Berlin, *Ill., U.S.A.* **156 E7** 39 44N 89 55W
New Berlin, *N.Y., U.S.A.* **151 D9** 42 37N 75 20W
New Berlin, *Pa., U.S.A.* **150 F8** 40 50N 76 57W
New Berlin, *Wis., U.S.A.* **157 B8** 42 59N 88 6W
New Bern, *U.S.A.* **149 H7** 35 7N 77 3W
New Bethlehem, *U.S.A.* **150 F5** 41 0N 79 20W
New Bloomfield, *U.S.A.* **150 F7** 40 25N 77 11W
New Boston, *U.S.A.* **155 J7** 33 28N 94 25W
New Braunfels, *U.S.A.* **155 L5** 29 42N 98 8W
New Brighton, *N.Z.* **131 D7** 43 29 S 172 43 E
New Brighton, *U.S.A.* **150 F4** 40 42N 80 19W
New Britain, *Papua N. G.* **132 C6** 5 50 S 150 20 E
New Britain, *U.S.A.* **151 E12** 41 40N 72 47W
New Brockton, *U.S.A.* **152 D4** 31 23N 85 56W
New Brunswick, *U.S.A.* **151 F10** 40 30N 74 27W
New Brunswick □, *Canada* **141 C6** 46 50N 66 30W
New Buffalo, *U.S.A.* **157 C10** 41 47N 86 45W
New Bussa, *Nigeria* **113 D5** 9 53N 4 31 E
New Caledonia ■, *Pac. Oc.* **133 U19** 21 0 S 165 0 E
New Carlisle, *Ind., U.S.A.* **157 C10** 41 45N 86 32W
New Carlisle, *Ohio, U.S.A.* **157 E12** 39 56N 84 2W
New Castile = Castilla-La Mancha □, *Spain* **12 H5** 39 30N 3 30W
New Castle, *Ind., U.S.A.* **157 E11** 39 55N 85 22W
New Castle, *Ky., U.S.A.* **157 F11** 38 26N 85 10W
New Castle, *Pa., U.S.A.* **150 F4** 41 0N 80 21W
New City, *U.S.A.* **151 E11** 41 9N 73 59W
New Concord, *U.S.A.* **150 G3** 39 59N 81 54W
New Cumberland, *U.S.A.* **150 F4** 40 30N 80 36W
New Cuyama, *U.S.A.* **161 L7** 34 57N 119 38W
New Delhi, *India* **92 E7** 28 37N 77 13 E
New Denver, *Canada* **142 D5** 50 0N 117 25W
New Don Pedro Reservoir, *U.S.A.* **160 H6** 37 43N 120 24W
New Ellenton, *U.S.A.* **152 B8** 33 28N 81 41W
New England, *U.S.A.* **154 B3** 46 32N 102 52W
New England Nat. Park, *Australia* **129 A10** 30 25 S 152 30 E
New England Ra., *Australia* **127 E5** 30 20 S 151 45 E
New Forest, *U.K.* **21 G6** 50 53N 1 34W
New Franklin, *U.S.A.* **156 E4** 39 1N 92 44W
New Galloway, *U.K.* **22 F4** 55 5N 4 9W
New Georgia Is., *Solomon Is.* **133 M9** 8 15 S 157 30 E
New Georgia Sound, *Solomon Is.* **133 L9** 8 0 S 158 20 E
New Glarus, *U.S.A.* **156 B7** 42 49N 89 38W
New Glasgow, *Canada* **141 C7** 45 35N 62 36W
New Guinea, *Oceania* **132 C1** 4 0 S 136 0 E
New Hamburg, *Canada* **150 C4** 43 23N 80 42W
New Hampshire □, *U.S.A.* **151 C13** 44 0N 71 30W
New Hampton, *U.S.A.* **156 A4** 43 3N 92 19W
New Hanover, *Papua N. G.* **132 B6** 2 30 S 150 10 E
New Hanover, *S. Africa* **117 D5** 29 22 S 30 31 E
New Harmony, *U.S.A.* **157 F9** 38 8N 87 56W
New Hartford, *U.S.A.* **151 C9** 43 4N 75 18W
New Haven, *Conn., U.S.A.* **151 E12** 41 18N 72 55W
New Haven, *Ill., U.S.A.* **157 G8** 37 55N 88 8W
New Haven, *Ind., U.S.A.* **157 C11** 41 4N 85 1W
New Haven, *Mich., U.S.A.* **150 D2** 42 44N 82 48W
New Haven, *Mo., U.S.A.* **156 F5** 38 37N 91 13W
New Hazelton, *Canada* **142 B3** 55 20N 127 30W
New Hebrides = Vanuatu ■, *Pac. Oc.* **133 E6** 15 0 S 168 0 E
New Hebrides, *Vanuatu* **133 D6** 15 0 S 168 0 E
New Holland, *U.S.A.* **151 F8** 40 6N 76 5W
New Iberia, *U.S.A.* **155 K9** 30 1N 91 49W
New Ireland, *Papua N. G.* **132 B6** 3 20 S 151 50 E
New Ireland □, *Papua N. G.* **132 B6** 3 0 S 151 30 E
New Jersey □, *U.S.A.* **148 E8** 40 0N 74 30W
New Kensington, *U.S.A.* **150 F5** 40 34N 79 46W
New Lexington, *U.S.A.* **148 F4** 39 43N 82 13W
New Liskeard, *Canada* **140 C4** 47 31N 79 41W
New London, *Conn., U.S.A.* **151 E12** 41 22N 72 6W
New London, *Iowa, U.S.A.* **156 D5** 40 55N 91 24W
New London, *Mo., U.S.A.* **156 E5** 39 35N 91 24W
New London, *Ohio, U.S.A.* **150 E2** 41 5N 82 24W
New London, *Wis., U.S.A.* **154 C10** 44 23N 88 45W
New Madrid, *U.S.A.* **155 G10** 36 36N 89 32W
New Martinsville, *U.S.A.* **148 F5** 39 39N 80 52W
New Meadows, *U.S.A.* **158 D5** 44 58N 116 18W
New Melones L., *U.S.A.* **160 H6** 37 57N 120 31W
New Mexico □, *U.S.A.* **159 J10** 34 30N 106 0W
New Miami, *U.S.A.* **157 E12** 39 26N 84 32W
New Milford, *Conn., U.S.A.* **151 E11** 41 35N 73 25W
New Milford, *Pa., U.S.A.* **151 E9** 41 52N 75 44W
New Norcia, *Australia* **125 F2** 30 57 S 116 13 E
New Norfolk, *Australia* **127 G4** 42 46 S 147 2 E
New Orleans, *U.S.A.* **155 L9** 29 58N 90 4W
New Palestine, *U.S.A.* **157 E11** 39 45N 85 52W
New Panamao, *Phil.* **81 J3** 5 59N 121 13 E
New Paris, *U.S.A.* **157 E12** 39 51N 84 48W
New Pekin, *U.S.A.* **157 F10** 38 31N 86 2W
New Philadelphia, *U.S.A.* **150 F3** 40 30N 81 27W
New Plymouth, *N.Z.* **130 F3** 39 4 S 174 5 E
New Plymouth, *U.S.A.* **158 E5** 43 58N 116 49W
New Port Richey, *U.S.A.* **153 G7** 28 16N 82 43W
New Providence, *Bahamas* **164 A4** 25 25N 78 35W
New Providence I., *Bahamas* **9 b** 25 3N 77 25W
New Quay, *U.K.* **21 E3** 52 13N 4 21W
New Radnor, *U.K.* **21 E4** 52 15N 3 9W
New Richmond, *Canada* **141 C6** 48 15N 65 45W
New Richmond, *Ohio, U.S.A.* **157 F12** 38 57N 84 17W
New Richmond, *Wis., U.S.A.* **154 C8** 45 7N 92 32W
New Roads, *U.S.A.* **155 K9** 30 42N 91 26W
New Rochelle, *U.S.A.* **151 F11** 40 55N 73 47W
New Rockford, *U.S.A.* **154 B5** 47 41N 99 8W
New Romney, *U.K.* **21 G8** 50 59N 0 57 E
New Ross, *Ireland* **23 D5** 52 23N 6 57W
New Salem, *U.S.A.* **154 B4** 46 51N 101 25W
New Scone, *U.K.* **22 E5** 56 25N 3 24W
New Sharon, *U.S.A.* **156 C4** 41 28N 92 39W
New Siberian I. = Novaya Sibir, Ostrov, *Russia* **67 B16** 75 10N 150 0 E
New Siberian Is. = Novosibirskiye Ostrova, *Russia* **67 B15** 75 0N 142 0 E
New Smyrna Beach, *U.S.A.* **149 L5** 29 1N 80 56W
New South Wales □, *Australia* **129 B7** 33 0 S 146 0 E
New Stuyahok, *U.S.A.* **144 G8** 59 29N 157 20W
New Town, *U.S.A.* **154 B3** 47 59N 102 30W
New Tredegar, *U.K.* **21 F4** 51 44N 3 16W
New Ulm, *U.S.A.* **154 C7** 44 19N 94 28W
New Vienna, *U.S.A.* **157 E13** 39 19N 83 42W
New Washington, *Phil.* **81 F4** 11 39N 122 26 E
New Waterford, *Canada* **141 C7** 46 13N 60 4W
New Westminster, *Canada* **160 A4** 49 13N 122 55W
New York, *U.S.A.* **151 F11** 40 45N 74 0W
New York □, *U.S.A.* **151 D9** 43 0N 75 0W
New York Mts., *U.S.A.* **159 J6** 35 0N 115 20W
New Zealand ■, *Oceania* **130 G5** 40 0 S 176 0 E
Newaj →, *India* **92 G7** 24 24N 76 49 E
Newala, *Tanzania* **119 E4** 10 58 S 39 18 E
Newark, *Del., U.S.A.* **148 F8** 39 41N 75 46W
Newark, *N.J., U.S.A.* **151 F10** 40 44N 74 10W
Newark, *N.Y., U.S.A.* **150 C7** 43 3N 77 6W
Newark, *Ohio, U.S.A.* **150 F2** 40 3N 82 24W
Newark-on-Trent, *U.K.* **20 D7** 53 5N 0 48W
Newark Valley, *U.S.A.* **151 D8** 42 14N 76 11W
Newberg, *Mo., U.S.A.* **156 G5** 37 55N 91 54W
Newberg, *Oreg., U.S.A.* **158 D2** 45 18N 122 58W
Newberry, *Fla., U.S.A.* **153 F7** 29 39N 82 37W
Newberry, *Mich., U.S.A.* **148 B3** 46 21N 85 30W
Newberry, *S.C., U.S.A.* **149 H5** 34 17N 81 37W
Newberry Springs, *U.S.A.* **161 L10** 34 50N 116 41W
Newboro L., *Canada* **151 B8** 44 38N 76 20W
Newbridge = Droichead Nua, *Ireland* **23 C5** 53 11N 6 48W
Newburgh, *Canada* **150 B8** 44 19N 76 52W
Newburgh, *Ind., U.S.A.* **157 G9** 37 57N 87 24W
Newburgh, *N.Y., U.S.A.* **151 E10** 41 30N 74 1W
Newbury, *U.K.* **21 F6** 51 24N 1 20W
Newbury, *N.H., U.S.A.* **151 B12** 43 19N 72 3W
Newbury, *Vt., U.S.A.* **151 B12** 44 5N 72 4W
Newburyport, *U.S.A.* **149 D10** 42 49N 70 53W
Newcastle, *Australia* **129 B9** 33 0 S 151 46 E
Newcastle, *N.B., Canada* **141 C6** 47 1N 65 38W
Newcastle, *Ont., Canada* **140 D4** 43 55N 78 35W
Newcastle, *S. Africa* **117 D4** 27 45 S 29 58 E
Newcastle, *U.K.* **23 B6** 54 13N 5 54W
Newcastle, *Calif., U.S.A.* **160 G5** 38 53N 121 8W
Newcastle, *Wyo., U.S.A.* **154 D2** 43 50N 104 11W
Newcastle Emlyn, *U.K.* **21 E3** 52 2N 4 28W
Newcastle Ra., *Australia* **124 C5** 15 45 S 130 15 E
Newcastle-under-Lyme, *U.K.* **20 D5** 53 1N 2 14W
Newcastle-upon-Tyne, *U.K.* **20 C6** 54 58N 1 36W
Newcastle Waters, *Australia* **126 B1** 17 30 S 133 28 E
Newcastle West, *Ireland* **23 D2** 52 27N 9 3W
Newcomb, *U.S.A.* **151 C10** 43 58N 74 10W
Newcomerstown, *U.S.A.* **150 F3** 40 16N 81 36W

Newdegate, Australia 125 F2 33 6 S 119 0 E
Newell, Australia 126 B4 16 20 S 145 16 E
Newell, Iowa, U.S.A. 156 B1 42 36N 95 0W
Newell, S. Dak., U.S.A. 154 C3 44 43N 103 25W
Newenham, C., U.S.A. 144 G7 58 39N 162 11W
Newfane, U.S.A. 150 C6 43 17N 78 43W
Newfield, U.S.A. 151 D8 42 18N 76 33W
Newfound L., U.S.A. 151 C13 43 40N 71 47W
Newfoundland, Canada 136 E14 49 0N 55 0W
Newfoundland, U.S.A. 151 E9 41 18N 75 19W
Newfoundland □, Canada 141 B8 53 0N 58 0W
Newhalen, U.S.A. 144 G9 59 43N 154 54W
Newhall, U.S.A. 161 L8 34 23N 118 32W
Newhaven, U.K. 21 G8 50 47N 0 3 E
Newington, U.S.A. 152 C8 32 35N 81 30W
Newkirk, U.S.A. 155 G6 36 53N 97 3W
Newlyn, U.K. 21 G2 50 6N 5 34W
Newman, Australia 124 D2 23 18 S 119 45 E
Newman, Calif., U.S.A. 160 H5 37 19N 121 1W
Newman, Ill., U.S.A. 157 E9 39 48N 87 59W
Newmarket, Canada 150 B5 44 3N 79 28W
Newmarket, Ireland 23 D2 52 13N 9 0W
Newmarket, U.K. 21 E8 52 15N 0 25 E
Newmarket, U.S.A. 151 C14 43 4N 70 56W
Newnan, U.S.A. 152 B5 33 23N 84 48W
Newport, Ireland 23 C2 53 53N 9 33W
Newport, I. of W., U.K. 21 G6 50 42N 1 17W
Newport, Newp., U.K. 21 F5 51 35N 3 0W
Newport, Ark., U.S.A. 155 H9 35 37N 91 16W
Newport, Ind., U.S.A. 157 E9 39 53N 87 25W
Newport, Ky., U.S.A. 157 E12 39 5N 84 30W
Newport, N.H., U.S.A. 151 C12 43 22N 72 10W,
Newport, N.Y., U.S.A. 151 C9 43 11N 75 1W
Newport, Oreg., U.S.A. 158 D1 44 39N 124 3W
Newport, Pa., U.S.A. 150 F7 40 29N 77 8W
Newport, R.I., U.S.A. 151 E13 41 29N 71 19W
Newport, Tenn., U.S.A. 149 H4 35 58N 83 11W
Newport, Vt., U.S.A. 151 B12 44 56N 72 13W
Newport, Wash., U.S.A. 158 B5 48 11N 117 3W
Newport □, U.K. 21 F4 51 33N 3 1W
Newport Beach, U.S.A. 161 M9 33 37N 117 56W
Newport News, U.S.A. 148 G7 36 59N 76 25W
Newport Pagnell, U.K. 21 E7 52 5N 0 43W
Newquay, U.K. 21 G2 50 25N 5 6W
Newry, U.K. 23 B5 54 11N 6 21W
Newtok, U.S.A. 144 F6 60 56N 164 38W
Newton, Ga., U.S.A. 152 D5 31 19N 84 20W
Newton, Ill., U.S.A. 154 F10 38 59N 88 10W
Newton, Iowa, U.S.A. 156 C3 41 42N 93 3W
Newton, Kans., U.S.A. 155 F6 38 3N 97 21W
Newton, Mass., U.S.A. 151 D13 42 21N 71 12W
Newton, Miss., U.S.A. 155 J10 32 19N 89 10W
Newton, N.C., U.S.A. 149 H5 35 40N 81 13W
Newton, N.J., U.S.A. 151 E10 41 3N 74 45W
Newton, Tex., U.S.A. 155 K8 30 51N 93 46W
Newton Abbot, U.K. 21 G4 50 32N 3 37W
Newton Aycliffe, U.K. 20 C6 54 37N 1 34W
Newton Falls, U.S.A. 150 E4 41 11N 80 59W
Newton L., U.S.A. 157 F8 38 55N 88 15W
Newton Stewart, U.K. 22 G4 54 57N 4 30W
Newtonmore, U.K. 22 D4 57 4N 4 8W
Newtown, U.K. 21 E4 52 31N 3 19W
Newtown, Ind., U.S.A. 157 D9 40 13N 87 9W
Newtown, Mo., U.S.A. 156 D3 40 22N 93 20W
Newtownabbey, U.K. 23 B6 54 40N 5 56W
Newtownards, U.K. 23 B6 54 36N 5 42W
Newtownbarry = Bunclody, Ireland 23 D5 52 39N 6 40W
Newtownstewart, U.K. 23 B4 54 43N 7 23W
Newville, U.S.A. 150 F7 40 10N 77 24W
Nexon, France 28 C5 45 41N 1 11 E
Neya, Russia 60 A6 58 21N 43 49 E
Neyrīz, Iran 97 D7 29 15N 54 19 E
Nëyruz, Switz. 32 C4 46 47N 7 4 E
Neyshābūr, Iran 97 B8 36 10N 58 50 E
Neyyattinkara, India 95 K3 8 26N 77 5 E
Nezhin = Nizhyn, Ukraine 59 G6 51 5N 31 55 E
Nezperce, U.S.A. 158 C5 46 14N 116 14W
Ngabang, Indonesia 85 B3 0 23N 109 55 E
Ngabe, Congo 114 C3 3 12 S 16 12 E
Ngabordamlu, Tanjung, Indonesia 83 C4 6 56 S 134 11 E
N'Gage, Angola 115 D3 7 46 S 15 15 E
Ngaiphaipi, Burma 90 D4 22 14N 93 15 E
Ngala, Nigeria 113 C7 12 20N 14 11 E
Ngama, Chad 109 F3 11 45N 17 6 E
Ngambé, Centre, Cameroon 113 D7 5 48N 11 29 E
Ngambé, Littoral, Cameroon 113 E7 4 21N 10 40 E
Ngami Depression, Botswana 116 C3 20 30 S 22 46 E
Ngamo, Zimbabwe 119 F2 19 3 S 27 32 E
Ngangala, Sudan 107 G3 4 42N 31 55 E
Nganjuk, Indonesia 85 D4 7 32 S 111 55 E
Ngao, Thailand 86 C2 18 46N 99 59 E
Ngaoundéré, Cameroon 114 A2 7 15N 13 35 E
Ngapara, N.Z. 131 E5 44 57 S 170 46 E
Ngape, Burma 90 E5 20 2N 94 28 E
Ngara, Tanzania 118 C3 2 29 S 30 40 E
Ngaruawahia, N.Z. 130 D4 37 42 S 175 11 E
Ngaruroro →, N.Z. 130 F5 39 34 S 176 55 E
Ngatapa, N.Z. 130 E6 38 32 S 177 45 E
Ngathainggyaung, Burma 90 G5 17 24N 95 5 E
Ngauruhoe, Mt., N.Z. 130 F4 39 13 S 175 45 E
Ngawi, Indonesia 85 D4 7 24 S 111 26 E
Ngele, Dem. Rep. of the Congo 114 C4 0 30 S 20 22 E
Ngelebok, Cameroon 114 B2 4 16N 14 3 E
Nggatokae, Solomon Is. 133 M10 8 45 S 158 15 E
Nggela, Solomon Is. 133 M11 9 5 S 160 15 E
Nggela Pile, Solomon Is. 133 M11 9 5 S 160 20 E
Nggela Sule, Solomon Is. 133 M11 9 2 S 160 12 E
Nghia Lo, Vietnam 76 G5 21 33N 104 28 E
Ngidinga, Dem. Rep. of the Congo 115 D3 5 37 S 15 17 E
Ngo, Congo 114 C3 2 29 S 15 45 E
Ngoap, Cameroon 114 B2 4 9N 12 51 E
Ngoboli, Sudan 107 G3 4 57N 32 37 E
N'Gola, Angola 115 E2 14 10 S 14 30 E
Ngoma, Malawi 119 E3 13 8 S 33 45 E
Ngomahura, Zimbabwe 119 G3 20 26 S 30 43 E
Ngomba, Tanzania 119 D3 8 20 S 32 53 E
Ngongotaha, N.Z. 130 E5 38 5 S 176 12 E
Ngop, Sudan 107 F3 6 17N 30 9 E
Ngoring Hu, China 68 C4 34 55N 97 5 E
Ngorkou, Mali 112 B4 15 40N 3 41W
Ngorongoro, Tanzania 118 C4 3 11 S 35 32 E
Ngorongoro Conservation Area, Tanzania 118 C4 2 40 S 35 30 E
Ngoto, C.A.R. 114 B3 3 59N 17 19 E
Ngouo, Dj., C.A.R. 114 A4 7 55N 24 38 E
Ngoura, Chad 109 F3 12 44N 16 21 E
Ngouri, Chad 109 F3 13 38N 15 22 E
Ngourti, Niger 109 E2 15 19N 13 12 E
Ngoussou, Gabon 114 C2 3 0 S 11 7 E
Ngozi, Burundi 118 C2 2 54 S 29 50 E
Ngudu, Tanzania 118 C3 2 58 S 33 25 E
Nguigmi, Niger 109 F2 14 20N 13 20 E
Nguila, Cameroon 113 E7 4 41N 11 43 E
Nguiu, Australia 124 B5 11 46 S 130 38 E
Ngukurr, Australia 126 A1 14 44 S 134 44 E
Nguna, Vanuatu 133 G6 17 26 S 168 22 E
Ngunga, Tanzania 118 C3 3 37 S 33 37 E
Nguru, Nigeria 113 C7 12 56N 10 29 E
Nguru Mts., Tanzania 118 D4 6 0 S 37 30 E
Ngusi, Malawi 119 E3 14 0 S 34 50 E
Nguyen Binh, Vietnam 76 F5 22 39N 105 56 E
Ngwedaung, Burma 90 F6 19 31N 97 9 E
Nha Trang, Vietnam 87 F7 12 16N 109 10 E
Nhacoongo, Mozam. 117 C6 24 18 S 35 14 E
Nhamaabué, Mozam. 119 F4 17 25 S 35 5 E
Nhambiquara, Brazil 173 C6 12 50 S 59 49W
Nhamundá, Brazil 169 D6 2 14 S 56 43W
Nhamundá →, Brazil 169 D6 2 12 S 56 41W
Nhangulaze, L., Mozam. 117 C5 24 0 S 34 30 E
Nharêa, Angola 115 E3 11 38 S 16 58 E
Nhecolândia, Brazil 173 D6 19 17 S 56 58W
Nhill, Australia 128 D4 36 18 S 141 40 E
Nho Quan, Vietnam 76 G5 20 18N 105 45 E
Nhulunbuy, Australia 126 A2 12 10 S 137 20 E
Nhundo, Angola 115 E4 14 25 S 21 23 E
Nia-nia, Dem. Rep. of the Congo 118 B2 1 30N 27 40 E
Niafounké, Mali 112 B4 16 0N 4 5W
Niagara Falls, Canada 140 D4 43 7N 79 5W
Niagara Falls, U.S.A. 150 C6 43 5N 79 4W
Niagara-on-the-Lake, Canada 150 C5 43 15N 79 4W
Niah, Malaysia 85 B4 3 58N 113 46 E
Nialaha'u Pt., Solomon Is. 133 M11 9 47 S 161 34 E
Niamey, Niger 113 C5 13 27N 2 6 E
Niandan-Koro, Guinea 112 C3 11 5N 9 15W
Nianforando, Guinea 112 D2 9 37N 10 36W
Niangara, Dem. Rep. of the Congo 118 B2 3 42N 27 50 E
Niangbo, Ivory C. 112 D3 8 49N 5 10W
Niangoloko, Burkina Faso 112 C4 10 15N 4 55W
Niangua →, U.S.A. 156 G4 38 0N 92 48W
Niantic, U.S.A. 151 E12 41 20N 72 11W
Niari, Congo 114 C2 4 9 S 14 9 E
Niaro, Sudan 107 E3 10 38N 31 31 E
Nias, Indonesia 84 B1 1 0N 97 30 E
Niassa □, Mozam. 119 E4 13 30 S 36 0 E
Niassa, Reserva do, Mozam. 119 E4 12 4 S 36 57 E
Nibāk, Si. Arabia 97 E7 24 25N 50 50 E
Nibe, Denmark 17 H3 56 59N 9 38 E
Nicaragua ■, Cent. Amer. 164 D2 11 40N 85 30W
Nicaragua, L. de, Nic. 164 D2 12 0N 85 30W
Nicastro, Italy 47 D9 38 59N 16 19 E
Nice, France 29 E11 43 42N 7 14 E
Niceville, U.S.A. 149 K2 30 31N 86 30W
Nichicun, L., Canada 141 B5 53 5N 71 0W
Nichinan, Japan 72 F3 31 38N 131 23 E
Nicholás, Canal, W. Indies 164 B3 23 30N 80 5W
Nicholasville, U.S.A. 157 G12 37 53N 84 34W
Nicholls, U.S.A. 152 D7 31 31N 82 38W
Nichols, U.S.A. 151 D8 42 1N 76 22W
Nicholson, Australia 124 C4 18 2 S 128 54 E
Nicholson, U.S.A. 151 E9 41 37N 75 47W
Nicholson →, Australia 126 B2 17 31 S 139 36 E
Nicholson L., Canada 143 A8 62 40N 102 40W
Nicholson Ra., Australia 125 E2 27 15 S 116 45 E
Nicholville, U.S.A. 151 B10 44 41N 74 39W
Nickerie →, Surinam 169 B6 5 58N 57 0W
Nicobar Is., Ind. Oc. 95 L11 8 0N 93 30 E
Nicola, Canada 142 C4 50 12N 120 40W
Nicolls Town, Bahamas 164 A4 25 8N 78 0W
Nicopolis, Greece 39 A2 39 5N 20 43 E
Nicosia, Cyprus 39 E9 35 10N 33 25 E
Nicosia, Italy 47 E7 37 45N 14 24 E
Nicótera, Italy 47 D8 38 33N 15 56 E
Nicoya, Costa Rica 164 D2 10 9N 85 27W
Nicoya, G. de, Costa Rica 164 E3 10 0N 85 0W
Nicoya, Pen. de, Costa Rica 164 E2 9 45N 85 40W
Nidau, Switz. 32 B4 47 7N 7 15 E
Nidd →, U.K. 20 D6 53 59N 1 23W
Nidda, Germany 31 E5 50 23N 9 1 E
Nidda →, Germany 31 E4 50 17N 8 48 E
Nidri, Greece 39 B2 38 43N 20 42 E
Nidwalden □, Switz. 33 C6 46 50N 8 25 E
Nidzica, Poland 55 E7 53 25N 20 28 E
Niè, Î., N. Cal. 133 U21 21 8 S 167 35 E
Niebüll, Germany 30 A4 54 46N 8 48 E
Nied →, Germany 27 C13 49 23N 6 40 E
Niederaula, Germany 30 E5 50 47N 9 36 E
Niederbayern □, Germany 31 G8 48 40N 12 50 E
Niederbipp, Switz. 32 B5 47 16N 7 42 E
Niederbronn-les-Bains, France 27 D14 48 57N 7 39 E
Niedere Tauern, Austria 34 D7 47 20N 14 0 E
Niederlausitz, Germany 30 D9 51 42N 13 59 E
Niederösterreich □, Austria 34 C8 48 25N 15 40 E
Niedersachsen □, Germany 30 C4 52 50N 9 0 E
Niefang, Eq. Guin. 114 B2 1 50N 10 14 E
Niekerkshoop, S. Africa 116 D3 29 19 S 22 51 E
Niellé, Ivory C. 112 C3 10 5N 5 38W
Niellim, Chad 109 G3 9 42N 17 49 E
Niem, C.A.R. 114 A3 6 12N 15 14 E
Niemba, Dem. Rep. of the Congo 118 D2 5 58 S 28 24 E
Niemen = Neman →, Lithuania 15 J19 55 25N 21 10 E
Niemodlin, Poland 55 H4 50 38N 17 38 E
Niemur, Australia 128 C6 35 17 S 144 9 E
Nienburg, Germany 30 C5 52 39N 9 13 E
Niepołomice, Poland 55 H7 50 3N 20 13 E
Niers →, Germany 30 D1 51 43N 5 57 E
Niesen, Switz. 32 C5 46 38N 7 39 E
Niesky, Germany 30 D10 51 17N 14 49 E
Nieszawa, Poland 55 F5 52 52N 18 50 E
Nieu Bethesda, S. Africa 116 E3 31 51 S 24 34 E
Nieuw Amsterdam, Surinam 169 B6 5 53N 55 5W
Nieuw Nickerie, Surinam 169 B6 6 0N 56 59W
Nieuwoudtville, S. Africa 116 E2 31 23 S 19 7 E
Nieuwpoort, Belgium 24 C2 51 8N 2 45 E
Nieves, Pico de las, Canary Is. 9 e1 27 57N 15 35W
Nièvre □, France 27 E10 47 10N 3 40 E
Niga, Mali 112 C3 13 36N 5 27W
Niğde, Turkey 100 D6 37 58N 34 40 E
Nigel, S. Africa 117 D4 26 27 S 28 25 E
Niger □, Nigeria 113 D6 10 0N 5 30 E
Niger ■, W. Afr. 113 B7 17 30N 10 0 E
Niger →, W. Afr. 113 D6 5 33N 6 33 E
Niger Delta, Africa 113 E6 5 0N 6 0 E
Nigeria ■, W. Afr. 113 D6 8 30N 8 0 E
Nighasin, India 93 E9 28 14N 80 52 E
Nightcaps, N.Z. 131 F3 45 57 S 168 2 E
Nightmute, U.S.A. 144 F6 60 29N 164 44W
Nigrita, Greece 50 F7 40 56N 23 29 E
Nihoa, U.S.A. 145 G11 23 6N 161 58W
Nii-Jima, Japan 73 C11 34 20N 139 15 E
Niigata, Japan 72 F9 37 58N 139 0 E
Niigata □, Japan 71 F9 37 15N 138 45 E
Niihama, Japan 72 D5 33 55N 133 16 E
Niihau, U.S.A. 145 B1 21 54N 160 9W
Niimi, Japan 72 C5 34 59N 133 28 E
Niitsu, Japan 70 F9 37 48N 139 7 E
Nij Laluk, India 90 B4 27 7N 93 56 E
Níjar, Spain 41 J2 36 53N 2 15W
Nijil, Jordan 103 E4 30 32N 35 33 E
Nijkerk, Neths. 24 B5 52 13N 5 30 E
Nijmegen, Neths. 24 C5 51 50N 5 52 E
Nijverdal, Neths. 24 B6 52 22N 6 28 E
Nīk Pey, Iran 97 B6 36 50N 48 10 E
Nikaweratiya, Sri Lanka 95 L5 7 45N 80 7 E
Nike, Nigeria 113 D6 6 26N 7 29 E
Nikiniki, Indonesia 82 C2 9 49 S 124 30 E
Nikísiani, Greece 51 F8 40 57N 24 29 E
Nikítas, Greece 50 F7 40 13N 23 43 E
Nikki, Benin 113 D5 9 58N 3 12 E
Nikkō, Japan 73 A11 36 45N 139 35 E
Nikolai, U.S.A. 144 E9 62 58N 154 10W
Nikolayev = Mykolayiv, Ukraine 59 J7 46 58N 32 0 E
Nikolayevsk, Russia 60 E7 50 0N 45 35 E
Nikolayevsk-na-Amur, Russia 67 D15 53 8N 140 44 E
Nikolsk, Russia 60 D8 53 49N 46 4 E
Nikolski, U.S.A. 144 K5 52 56N 168 52W
Nikolskoye, Russia 67 D17 55 12N 166 0 E
Nikopol, Bulgaria 51 C8 43 43N 24 54 E
Nikopol, Ukraine 59 J8 47 35N 34 25 E
Niksar, Turkey 100 B7 40 31N 37 2 E
Nīkshahr, Iran 97 E9 26 15N 60 10 E
Nikšić, Montenegro, Yug. 50 D2 42 50N 18 57 E
Nîl, Nahr en →, Africa 106 H7 30 10N 31 6 E
Nîl el Abyad →, Sudan 107 D3 15 38N 32 31 E
Nîl el Azraq →, Sudan 107 D3 15 38N 32 31 E
Nila, Indonesia 83 C3 6 44 S 129 31 E
Nilakkottai, India 95 J3 10 10N 77 52 E
Niland, U.S.A. 161 M11 33 14N 115 31W
Nilanga, India 94 E3 18 6N 76 46 E
Nile = Nîl, Nahr en →, Africa 106 H7 30 10N 31 6 E
Niles, Mich., U.S.A. 157 C10 41 50N 86 15W
Niles, Ohio, U.S.A. 150 E4 41 11N 80 46W
Nileshwar, India 95 H2 12 15N 75 6 E
Nilgiri Hills, India 95 J3 11 30N 76 30 E
Nilo Peçanha, Brazil 171 D4 13 37 S 39 6W
Nilsebu, Norway 18 E3 59 11N 6 39 E
Nilüfer →, Turkey 51 F12 40 18N 28 27 E
Nim Ka Thana, India 92 F6 27 44N 75 48 E
Nimach, India 92 G6 24 30N 74 56 E
Nimbahera, India 92 G6 24 37N 74 45 E
Nîmes, France 29 E8 43 50N 4 23 E
Nimfaíon, Ákra = Pínnes, Ákra, Greece 51 F8 40 5N 24 20 E
Nimmitabel, Australia 129 D8 36 29 S 149 15 E
Nīmrūz □, Afghan. 91 C1 30 0N 62 0 E
Nimule, Sudan 107 G3 3 32N 32 3 E
Nimule Nat. Park, Sudan 107 G3 3 38N 32 2 E
Nin, Croatia 45 D12 44 16N 15 12 E
Nīnawá, Iraq 101 D10 36 25N 43 10 E
Ninda, Angola 115 E4 14 47 S 21 24 E
Nindigully, Australia 127 D4 28 21 S 148 50 E
Nine Degree Channel, India 95 K1 9 0N 73 0 E
Ninepin Group, China 69 G11 22 16N 114 21 E
Ninety East Ridge, Ind. Oc. 121 E7 1 0 S 90 0 E
Ninety Mile Beach, N.Z. 130 A1 34 48 S 173 0 E
Ninety Mile Beach, The, Australia 129 E7 38 15 S 147 24 E
Ninety Six, U.S.A. 152 A7 34 11N 82 1W
Nineveh = Nīnawá, Iraq 101 D10 36 25N 43 10 E
Ning Xian, China 74 G4 35 30N 107 58 E
Ningaloo Marine Park, Australia 124 D1 22 23 S 113 32 E
Ning'an, China 75 B15 44 22N 129 20 E
Ningbo, China 77 C13 29 51N 121 28 E
Ningcheng, China 75 D10 41 32N 119 53 E
Ningde, China 77 D12 26 38N 119 23 E
Ningdu, China 77 D10 26 25N 115 59 E
Ningerum, Papua N. G. 132 C1 5 41 S 141 8 E
Ninggang, China 77 D9 26 42N 113 55 E
Ningguo, China 77 B12 30 35N 119 0 E
Ninghai, China 77 C13 29 15N 121 27 E
Ninghua, China 77 D11 26 14N 116 45 E
Ningi, Nigeria 113 C6 10 55N 9 30 E
Ningjin, China 74 F8 37 35N 114 57 E
Ningjing Shan, China 76 C2 30 0N 98 20 E
Ninglang, China 76 D3 27 20N 100 55 E
Ningling, China 74 G8 34 25N 115 22 E
Ningming, China 76 F6 22 8N 107 4 E
Ningnan, China 76 D4 27 5N 102 36 E
Ningpo = Ningbo, China 77 C13 29 51N 121 28 E
Ningqiang, China 74 H4 32 47N 106 15 E
Ningshan, China 74 H5 33 21N 108 21 E
Ningsia Hui A.R. = Ningxia Huizu Zizhiqu □, China 74 F4 38 0N 106 0 E
Ningwu, China 74 E7 39 0N 112 18 E
Ningxia Huizu Zizhiqu □, China 74 F4 38 0N 106 0 E
Ningxiang, China 77 C9 28 15N 112 30 E
Ningyang, China 74 G9 35 47N 116 45 E
Ningyuan, China 77 E8 25 37N 111 57 E
Ninh Binh, Vietnam 76 G5 20 15N 105 55 E
Ninh Giang, Vietnam 86 B6 20 44N 106 24 E
Ninh Hoa, Vietnam 86 F7 12 30N 109 7 E
Ninh Ma, Vietnam 86 F7 12 48N 109 21 E
Nini-Suhien Nat. Park, Ghana 112 D4 5 20N 2 34W
Ninigo Group, Papua N. G. 132 A3 1 22 S 144 17 E
Ninini Pt., U.S.A. 145 B2 21 58N 159 20W
Ninove, Belgium 24 D4 50 51N 4 2 E
Nioaque, Brazil 175 A4 21 5 S 55 50W
Niobrara, U.S.A. 154 D6 42 45N 98 2W
Niobrara →, U.S.A. 154 D6 42 46N 98 3W
Nioki, Dem. Rep. of the Congo 114 C3 2 47 S 17 40 E
Niokolo-Koba, Parc Nat. du, Senegal 112 C2 13 3N 13 2W
Niono, Mali 112 C3 14 15N 6 0W
Nionsamoridougou, Guinea 112 D3 8 45N 8 50W
Nioro du Rip, Senegal 112 C1 13 40N 15 50W
Nioro du Sahel, Mali 112 B3 15 15N 9 30W
Niort, France 28 B3 46 19N 0 29W
Nipa, Papua N. G. 132 D2 6 9 S 143 29 E
Nipani, India 95 F2 16 20N 74 25 E
Nipawin, Canada 143 C8 53 20N 104 0W
Nipfjället, Sweden 16 C6 61 59N 12 50 E
Nipigon, Canada 140 C2 49 0N 88 17W
Nipigon, L., Canada 140 C2 49 50N 88 30W
Nipishish L., Canada 141 B7 54 12N 60 45W
Nipissing, L., Canada 140 C4 46 20N 80 0W
Nipomo, U.S.A. 161 K6 35 3N 120 29W
Nipton, U.S.A. 161 K11 35 28N 115 16W
Niquelândia, Brazil 171 D2 14 33 S 48 23W
Nīr, Iran 101 C12 38 2N 47 59 E
Nira →, India 94 F2 17 58N 75 8 E
Nirasaki, Japan 73 B10 35 42N 138 27 E
Nirmal, India 94 E4 19 3N 78 20 E
Nirmali, India 93 F12 26 20N 86 35 E
Niš, Serbia, Yug. 50 C5 43 19N 21 58 E
Nisa, Portugal 43 F3 39 30N 7 41W
Nisāb, Si. Arabia 96 D5 29 11N 44 43 E
Nişāb, Yemen 98 D4 14 25N 46 29 E
Nišava →, Serbia, Yug. 50 C5 43 20N 21 46 E
Niscemi, Italy 47 E7 37 9N 14 23 E
Nishi-Sonogi-Hantō, Japan 72 E1 32 55N 129 45 E
Nishi-Tosa, Japan 72 D4 33 13N 132 46 E
Nishinomiya, Japan 73 C7 34 45N 135 20 E
Nishino'omote, Japan 71 J5 30 43N 130 59 E
Nishio, Japan 73 C9 34 52N 137 3 E
Nishiwaki, Japan 72 C6 34 59N 134 58 E
Nísiros, Greece 49 E9 36 35N 27 12 E
Niška Banja, Serbia, Yug. 50 C6 43 18N 22 1 E
Niskibi →, Canada 140 A2 56 29N 88 9W
Nisko, Poland 55 H9 50 35N 22 7 E
Nisporeni, Moldova 53 C13 47 4N 28 10 E
Nisqually →, U.S.A. 160 C4 47 6N 122 42W
Nissáki, Greece 38 B9 39 43N 19 52 E
Nissan →, Sweden 17 H6 56 40N 12 51 E
Nissedal, Norway 18 E5 59 10N 8 30 E
Nisser, Norway 18 E5 59 7N 8 28 E
Nissum Bredning, Denmark 17 H2 56 40N 8 20 E
Nissum Fjord, Denmark 17 H2 56 20N 8 11 E
Nistru = Dnister →, Europe 59 J6 46 18N 30 17 E
Nisutlin →, Canada 142 A2 60 14N 132 34W
Nitchequon, Canada 141 B5 53 10N 70 58W
Niterói, Brazil 171 F3 22 52 S 43 0W
Nith →, Canada 150 C4 43 12N 80 23W
Nith →, U.K. 22 F5 55 14N 3 33W
Nitmiluk Nat. Park, Australia 124 B5 14 6 S 132 15 E
Nitra, Slovak Rep. 35 C11 48 19N 18 4 E
Nitra →, Slovak Rep. 35 D11 47 46N 18 10 E
Nitriansky □, Slovak Rep. 35 C11 48 10N 18 30 E
Nittenau, Germany 31 F8 49 12N 12 16 E
Niu, U.S.A. 145 K14 21 19N 157 44W
Niuafo'ou, Tonga 123 D15 15 30 S 175 58W
Niue, Cook Is. 135 J11 19 2 S 169 54W
Niulan Jiang →, China 76 D4 27 30N 103 5 E
Niut, Indonesia 85 B4 0 55N 110 6 E
Niutou Shan, China 77 C13 29 5N 121 59 E
Niuzhuang, China 75 D12 40 58N 122 28 E
Nivala, Finland 14 E21 63 56N 24 57 E
Nivelles, Belgium 24 D4 50 35N 4 20 E
Nivernais, France 27 E10 47 15N 3 30 E
Niwas, India 93 H9 23 3N 80 26 E
Nixon, U.S.A. 155 L6 29 16N 97 46W
Nizam Sagar, India 94 E3 18 10N 77 58 E
Nizamabad, India 94 E4 18 45N 78 7 E
Nizamghat, India 90 A5 28 20N 95 45 E
Nizhne Kolymsk, Russia 67 C17 68 34N 160 55 E
Nizhnegorskiy = Nyzhnohirskyy, Ukraine 59 K8 45 27N 34 38 E
Nizhnekamsk, Russia 60 C10 55 38N 51 49 E
Nizhnekamskoye Vdkhr., Russia 64 D4 55 56N 52 56 E
Nizhneudinsk, Russia 67 D10 54 54N 99 3 E
Nizhnevartovsk, Russia 66 C8 60 56N 76 38 E
Nizhniy Chir, Russia 61 F6 48 22N 43 5 E
Nizhniy Lomov, Russia 60 D6 53 34N 43 38 E
Nizhniy Novgorod, Russia 60 B7 56 20N 44 0 E
Nizhniy Tagil, Russia 64 C7 57 55N 59 57 E
Nizhniye Sergi, Russia 64 C7 56 40N 59 18 E
Nizhnyaya Salda, Russia 64 B8 58 8N 60 42 E
Nizhyn, Ukraine 59 G6 51 5N 31 55 E
Nizina Mazowiecka, Poland 55 F8 52 30N 21 0 E
Nizip, Turkey 100 D7 37 5N 37 50 E
Nízké Tatry, Slovak Rep. 35 C12 48 55N 19 30 E
Nízký Jeseník, Czech Rep. 35 B10 49 50N 17 30 E
Nizza Monferrato, Italy 44 D5 44 46N 8 21 E
Njakwa, Malawi 119 E3 11 1 S 33 56 E
Njanji, Zambia 119 E3 14 25 S 31 46 E
Njarðvíkur, Iceland 11 D4 63 59N 22 32W
Njazidja = Grande Comore, Comoros Is. 121 a 11 35 S 43 20 E
Njegoš, Montenegro, Yug. 50 D2 42 53N 18 45 E
Njinjo, Tanzania 119 D4 8 48 S 38 54 E
Njoko →, Zambia 115 F4 17 8 S 24 4 E
Njombe, Tanzania 119 D3 9 20 S 34 50 E
Njombe →, Tanzania 118 D4 6 56 S 35 6 E
Njurundabommen, Sweden 16 B11 62 15N 17 25 E
Nkambe, Cameroon 113 D7 6 35N 10 40 E
Nkana, Zambia 119 E2 12 50 S 28 8 E
Nkandla, S. Africa 117 D5 28 37 S 31 5 E
Nkawkaw, Ghana 113 D4 6 36N 0 49W
Nkayi, Zimbabwe 119 F2 19 41 S 29 20 E
Nkhotakota, Malawi 119 E3 12 56 S 34 15 E
Nkhotakota Game Reserve, Malawi 119 E3 12 50 S 34 0 E
Nkolabona, Gabon 114 B2 1 14N 11 43 E
Nkomi, Lagune, Gabon 114 C1 1 35 S 9 17 E
Nkone, Dem. Rep. of the Congo 114 C4 1 2 S 22 20 E
Nkongsamba, Cameroon 113 E6 4 55N 9 55 E
Nkunga, Dem. Rep. of the Congo 115 C3 4 41 S 18 34 E
Nkurenkuru, Namibia 116 B2 17 42 S 18 32 E
Nkwanta, Ghana 112 D4 6 10N 2 10W
Nmai →, Burma 76 F2 25 30N 97 25 E
Noakhali = Maijdi, Bangla. 90 D3 22 48N 91 10 E
Noatak, U.S.A. 144 C7 67 34N 162 58W
Nobel, Canada 150 A4 45 25N 80 6W
Nobeoka, Japan 72 E3 32 36N 131 41 E
Noble, U.S.A. 157 F8 38 42N 88 14W
Noblejas, Spain 42 F7 39 58N 3 26W
Noblesville, U.S.A. 157 D11 40 3N 86 1W
Nocatee, U.S.A. 153 H8 27 10N 81 53W
Noce →, Italy 44 B8 46 9N 11 4 E
Nocera Inferiore, Italy 47 B7 40 44N 14 38 E
Nocera Umbra, Italy 45 E9 43 5N 12 47 E
Noci, Italy 47 B10 40 48N 17 7 E
Nocona, U.S.A. 155 J6 33 47N 97 44W
Nocrich, Romania 53 E9 45 55N 24 26 E
Noda, Japan 73 B11 35 56N 139 52 E
Nodeland, Norway 18 F4 58 8N 7 51 E
Nogal Valley = Nugaaleed, Dooxo, Somali Rep. 120 C3 8 35N 48 35 E
Nogales, Mexico 162 A2 31 20N 110 56W
Nogales, U.S.A. 159 L8 31 20N 110 56W
Nogaro, France 28 E3 43 45N 0 2W
Nogat →, Poland 54 D6 54 17N 19 17 E
Nōgata, Japan 72 D2 33 48N 130 44 E
Nogent, France 27 D12 48 1N 5 20 E
Nogent-le-Rotrou, France 26 D7 48 20N 0 50 E
Nogent-sur-Seine, France 27 D10 48 30N 3 30 E
Noggerup, Australia 125 F2 33 32 S 116 5 E
Noginsk, Moskva, Russia 58 E10 55 50N 38 25 E
Noginsk, Tunguska, Russia 67 C10 64 30N 90 50 E
Nogoa →, Australia 126 C4 23 40 S 147 55 E
Nogoyá, Argentina 174 C4 32 24 S 59 48W
Nógrád □, Hungary 52 C4 48 0N 19 30 E
Noguera Pallaresa →, Spain 40 D5 41 55N 0 55 E
Noguera Ribagorzana →, Spain 40 D5 41 40N 0 43 E
Nohar, India 92 E6 29 11N 74 49 E
Nohfelden, Germany 31 F3 49 35N 7 7 E
Nohili Pt., U.S.A. 145 A2 22 4N 159 47W
Nohta, India 93 H8 23 40N 79 34 E
Noia, Spain 42 C2 42 48N 8 53W
Noichi, Japan 72 D5 33 33N 133 42 E
Noing, Phil. 81 J5 5 40N 125 28 E
Noipuos, Papua N. G. 132 B6 2 25 S 150 7 E
Noire, Montagne, France 28 E6 43 28N 2 18 E
Noires, Mts., France 26 D3 48 11N 3 40W
Noirétable, France 28 C7 45 48N 3 46 E
Noirmoutier, Î. de, France 26 F4 46 58N 2 10W
Noirmoutier-en-l'Île, France 26 F4 47 0N 2 14W
Nojane, Botswana 116 C3 23 15 S 20 14 E
Nojima-Zaki, Japan 73 C11 34 54N 139 53 E
Nok Kundi, Pakistan 91 C1 28 50N 62 45 E
Nok Ta Phao, Ko, Thailand 87 b 9 23N 99 40 E
Nokaneng, Botswana 116 B3 19 40 S 22 17 E
Nokia, Finland 15 F20 61 30N 23 30 E
Nokomis, Canada 143 C8 51 35N 105 0W
Nokomis, Fla., U.S.A. 153 H7 27 7N 82 27W
Nokomis, Ill., U.S.A. 156 E7 39 18N 89 18W
Nokomis L., Canada 143 B8 57 0N 103 0W
Nokou, Chad 109 F2 14 35N 14 47 E
Nokuku, Vanuatu 133 E4 14 54 S 166 35 E
Nol, Sweden 17 G6 57 56N 12 5 E
Nola, C.A.R. 114 B3 3 35N 16 4 E
Nola, Italy 47 B7 40 55N 14 33 E
Nolay, France 27 F11 46 58N 4 35 E
Noli, C. di, Italy 44 D5 44 12N 8 25 E
Nolinsk, Russia 60 B9 57 28N 49 57 E
Noma, U.S.A. 152 E4 30 59N 85 37W
Noma Omuramba →, Namibia 116 B3 18 52 S 20 53 E
Noma-Saki, Japan 72 F2 31 25N 130 7 E
Nomad, Papua N. G. 132 D2 6 19 S 142 13 E
Nombre de Dios, Panama 164 E4 9 34N 79 28W
Nome, U.S.A. 144 D6 64 30N 165 25W
Nomo-Zaki, Japan 72 E1 32 35N 129 44 E
Nomuka, Tonga 133 Q13 20 17 S 174 48W
Nomuka Group, Tonga 133 Q13 20 20 S 174 48W
Nonacho L., Canada 143 A7 61 42N 109 40W
Nonancourt, France 26 D8 48 47N 1 11 E

Novska, *Croatia* **45 C14** 45 19N 17 0 E
Novvy Urengoy, *Russia* **66 C8** 65 48N 76 52 E
Nový Bor, *Czech Rep.* **34 A7** 50 46N 14 35 E
Novy Bug = Novyy Buh, *Ukraine* **59 J7** 47 34N 32 29 E
Nový Bydžov, *Czech Rep.* **34 A8** 50 14N 15 29 E
Novy Dwór Mazowiecki, *Poland* **55 F7** 52 26N 20 44 E
Nový Jičín, *Czech Rep.* **35 B11** 49 30N 18 2 E
Novyy Afon, *Georgia* **61 J5** 43 7N 40 50 E
Novyy Bor, *Russia* **56 A9** 66 43N 52 19 E
Novyy Buh, *Ukraine* **59 J7** 47 34N 32 29 E
Novyy Oskol, *Russia* **59 G9** 50 44N 37 55 E
Novyy Port, *Russia* **66 C8** 67 40N 72 30 E
Now Shahr, *Iran* **97 B6** 36 40N 51 30 E
Nowa Deba, *Poland* **55 H8** 50 26N 21 41 E
Nowa Nowa, *Australia* **129 D8** 37 44 S 148 3 E
Nowa Ruda, *Poland* **55 H3** 50 35N 16 30 E
Nowa Sarzyna, *Poland* **55 H9** 50 21N 22 21 E
Nowa Sól, *Poland* **55 G2** 51 48N 15 44 E
Nowata, *U.S.A.* **155 G7** 36 42N 95 38W
Nowbarān, *Iran* **97 C6** 35 8N 49 42 E
Nowe, *Poland* **54 E5** 53 41N 18 44 E
Nowe Miasteczko, *Poland* **55 G2** 51 42N 15 42 E
Nowe Miasto, *Poland* **55 G7** 51 38N 20 34 E
Nowe Miasto Lubawskie, *Poland* **54 E6** 53 27N 19 33 E
Nowe Skalmierzyce, *Poland* **55 G4** 51 43N 18 0 E
Nowe Warpno, *Poland* **54 E1** 53 42N 14 18 E
Nowendoc, *Australia* **129 A9** 31 32 S 151 44 E
Nowghāb, *Iran* **97 C8** 33 53N 59 4 E
Nowgong, *Assam, India* **90 B4** 26 20N 92 50 E
Nowgong, *Mad. P., India* **93 G8** 25 4N 79 27 E
Nowogard, *Poland* **54 E2** 53 41N 15 10 E
Nowogród, *Poland* **55 E8** 53 14N 21 53 E
Nowogród Bobrzanski, *Poland* **55 G2** 51 48N 15 15 E
Nowogrodziec, *Poland* **55 G2** 51 12N 15 24 E
Nowra, *Australia* **129 C9** 34 53 S 150 35 E
Nowrangapur, *India* **94 E6** 19 14N 82 33 E
Nowshera, *Pakistan* **91 B3** 34 0N 72 0 E
Nowy Dwór Gdański, *Poland* **54 D6** 54 13N 19 7 E
Nowy Sącz, *Poland* **55 J7** 49 40N 20 41 E
Nowy Staw, *Poland* **54 D6** 54 13N 19 2 E
Nowy Targ, *Poland* **55 J7** 49 29N 20 2 E
Nowy Tomyśl, *Poland* **55 F3** 52 19N 16 10 E
Nowy Wiśnicz, *Poland* **55 J7** 49 55N 20 28 E
Noxen, *U.S.A.* **151 E8** 41 25N 76 4W
Noxon, *U.S.A.* **158 C6** 48 0N 115 43W
Noyabr'sk, *Russia* **66 C8** 64 34N 76 21 E
Noyant, *France* **26 E7** 47 30N 0 6 E
Noyers, *France* **27 E10** 47 40N 4 0 E
Noyon, *France* **27 C9** 49 34N 2 59 E
Noyon, *Mongolia* **74 C2** 43 2N 102 4 E
Nozay, *France* **26 E5** 47 34N 1 38W
Nqutu, *S. Africa* **117 D5** 28 13 S 30 32 E
Nsa, *Congo* **114 C3** 2 22 S 15 19 E
Nsa, O. en →, *Algeria* **111 B6** 32 28N 5 24 E
Nsa, Plateau de, *Congo* **114 C3** 2 26 S 15 20 E
Nsanje, *Malawi* **119 F4** 16 55 S 35 12 E
Nsawam, *Ghana* **113 D4** 5 50N 0 24W
Nsok, *Eq. Guin.* **114 B2** 1 10N 11 19 E
Nsomba, *Zambia* **119 E2** 10 45 S 29 51 E
Nsontin, *Dem. Rep. of the Congo* **114 C3** 3 7 S 17 56 E
Nsopzup, *Burma* **90 C6** 25 51N 97 30 E
Nsukka, *Nigeria* **113 D6** 6 51N 7 29 E
Ntem →, *Cameroon* **114 B2** 2 21N 9 49 E
Ntoum, *Gabon* **114 B1** 0 22N 9 47 E
N'Tsama, *Congo* **114 C2** 0 53 S 14 44 E
Ntui, *Cameroon* **113 E7** 4 27N 11 38 E
Nu Jiang →, *China* **76 E2** 29 58N 97 25 E
Nu Shan, *China* **76 E2** 26 0N 99 20 E
Nuakata I., *Papua N. G.* **132 F6** 10 17 S 151 2 E
Nuba Mts. = Nubah, Jibalan, *Sudan* **107 E3** 12 0N 31 0 E
Nubah, Jibalan, *Sudan* **107 E3** 12 0N 31 0 E
Nubia, *Africa* **104 D7** 21 0N 32 0 E
Nubian Desert = Nûbîya, Es Sahrâ en, *Sudan* **106 C3** 21 30N 33 30 E
Nûbîya, Es Sahrâ en, *Sudan* **106 C3** 21 30N 33 30 E
Nubledo, *Spain* **42 B5** 43 31N 5 52W
Nuboai, *Indonesia* **83 B5** 2 10 S 136 30 E
Nubra →, *India* **93 B7** 34 35N 77 35 E
Nucet, *Romania* **52 D7** 46 28N 22 35 E
Nueces →, *U.S.A.* **155 M6** 27 51N 97 30W
Nueltin L., *Canada* **143 A9** 60 30N 99 30W
Nueva, I., *Chile* **176 E3** 55 13 S 66 30W
Nueva Antioquia, *Colombia* **168 B4** 6 5N 69 26W
Nueva Asunción □, *Paraguay* **174 A3** 21 0 S 61 0W
Nueva Carteya, *Spain* **43 H6** 37 35N 4 28W
Nueva Ecija □, *Phil.* **80 D3** 15 35N 121 0 E
Nueva Esparta □, *Venezuela* **169 A5** 11 0N 64 0W
Nueva Gerona, *Cuba* **164 B3** 21 53N 82 49W
Nueva Imperial, *Chile* **176 A2** 38 45 S 72 58W
Nueva Palmira, *Uruguay* **174 C4** 33 52 S 58 20W
Nueva Rosita, *Mexico* **162 B4** 28 0N 101 11W
Nueva San Salvador, *El Salv.* **164 D2** 13 40N 89 18W
Nueva Tabarca, *Spain* **41 G4** 38 17N 0 30W
Nueva Vizcaya □, *Phil.* **80 C3** 16 20N 121 20 E
Nuéve de Julio, *Argentina* **174 D3** 35 30 S 61 0W
Nuevitas, *Cuba* **164 B4** 21 30N 77 20W
Nuevo, G., *Argentina* **176 B4** 43 0 S 64 30W
Nuevo Casas Grandes, *Mexico* **162 A3** 30 22N 108 0W
Nuevo Guerrero, *Mexico* **163 B5** 26 34N 99 15W
Nuevo Laredo, *Mexico* **163 B5** 27 30N 99 30W
Nuevo León □, *Mexico* **162 C5** 25 0N 100 0W
Nuevo Mundo, Cerro, *Bolivia* **172 E4** 21 55 S 66 53W
Nuevo Rocafuerte, *Ecuador* **168 D2** 0 55 S 75 27W
Nugaaleed, Dooxo, *Somali Rep.* **120 C3** 8 35N 48 35 E
Nugget Pt., *N.Z.* **131 G4** 46 27 S 169 50 E
Nugrus, Gebel, *Egypt* **106 C3** 24 47N 34 35 E
Nuguria Is., *Papua N. G.* **132 B8** 3 20 S 154 45 E
Nuhaka, *N.Z.* **130 F6** 39 3 S 177 45 E
Nuits-St-Georges, *France* **27 E11** 47 10N 4 56 E
Nukey Bluff, *Australia* **127 E2** 32 26 S 135 29 E
Nukheila, *Sudan* **106 D2** 19 1N 26 21 E
Nukhuyb, *Iraq* **101 F10** 32 4N 42 3 E
Nukiki, *Solomon Is.* **133 L9** 6 46 S 156 35 E
Nuku, *Papua N. G.* **132 B2** 3 41 S 142 28 E
Nuku'alofa, *Tonga* **133 Q14** 21 10 S 174 0W
Nukuhu, *Papua N. G.* **132 C5** 5 34 S 149 22 E
Nukulaelae, *Tuvalu* **123 B14** 9 23 S 179 52 E
Nukus, *Uzbekistan* **66 E6** 42 27N 59 41 E
Nulato, *U.S.A.* **144 D8** 64 43N 158 6W
Nules, *Spain* **40 F4** 39 51N 0 9W
Nullagine, *Australia* **124 D3** 21 53 S 120 7 E
Nullagine →, *Australia* **124 D3** 21 20 S 120 20 E
Nullarbor, *Australia* **125 F5** 31 28 S 130 55 E
Nullarbor Nat. Park, *Australia* **125 F2** 32 39 S 115 37 E
Nullarbor Plain, *Australia* **125 F4** 31 10 S 129 0 E
Num, *Indonesia* **83 B5** 1 30 S 135 13 E
Numalla, L., *Australia* **127 D3** 28 43 S 144 20 E
Numan, *Nigeria* **113 D7** 9 29N 12 3 E
Numanuma, *Papua N. G.* **132 E6** 9 41 S 150 55 E
Numata, *Japan* **73 A11** 36 45N 139 4 E
Numatinna →, *Sudan* **107 F2** 7 38N 27 20 E
Numazu, *Japan* **73 B10** 35 7N 138 51 E
Numbulwar, *Australia* **126 A2** 14 15 S 135 45 E
Numedal, *Norway* **18 D6** 60 6N 9 6 E
Numfoor, *Indonesia* **83 B4** 1 0 S 134 50 E
Numurkah, *Australia* **129 D6** 36 5 S 145 26 E
Nunaksaluk I., *Canada* **141 A7** 55 49N 60 20W
Nunap Isua, *Greenland* **10 F6** 59 48N 43 55W
Nunavut □, *Canada* **139 B11** 66 0N 85 0W
Nunda, *U.S.A.* **150 D7** 42 35N 77 56W
Nuneaton, *U.K.* **19 E6** 52 32N 1 27W
Nungarin, *Australia* **125 F2** 31 12 S 118 6 E
Nungo, *Mozam.* **119 E4** 13 23 S 37 43 E
Nungwe, *Tanzania* **118 C3** 2 48 S 32 2 E
Nunivak I., *U.S.A.* **144 F6** 60 10N 166 30W
Nunkun, *India* **93 C7** 33 57N 76 2 E
Núoro, *Italy* **46 B2** 40 20N 9 20 E
Núpur, *Iceland* **11 B3** 65 56N 23 36W
Nuqayy, Jabal, *Libya* **108 D3** 23 11N 19 30 E
Nuqūb, *Yemen* **98 D4** 14 59N 45 48 E
Nuquí, *Colombia* **168 B2** 5 42N 77 17W
Nūrābād, *Iran* **97 E8** 27 47N 57 12 E
Nurabad, *Uzbekistan* **65 D3** 39 36N 66 17 E
Nurata, *Uzbekistan* **65 C2** 40 33N 65 41 E
Nurata Tizmasi, *Uzbekistan* **65 C3** 40 40N 66 30 E
Nure →, *Italy* **44 C6** 45 3N 9 49 E
Nurek, *Tajikistan* **65 D4** 38 23N 69 19 E
Nuremberg = Nürnberg, *Germany* **31 F7** 49 27N 11 3 E
Nuri, *Mexico* **162 B3** 28 2N 109 22W
Nuri, *Sudan* **106 D3** 18 29N 31 59 E
Nuriootpa, *Australia* **128 C3** 34 27 S 139 0 E
Nurlat, *Russia* **60 C10** 54 29N 50 45 E
Nurmes, *Finland* **14 E23** 63 33N 29 10 E
Nürnberg, *Germany* **31 F7** 49 27N 11 3 E
Nurpur, *Pakistan* **92 D4** 31 53N 71 54 E
Nurra, La, *Italy* **46 B1** 40 45N 8 15 E
Nurran, L. = Terewah, L., *Australia* **127 D4** 29 52 S 147 35 E
Nurrari Lakes, *Australia* **125 E5** 29 1 S 130 5 E
Nurri, *Italy* **46 C2** 39 43N 9 14 E
Nürtingen, *Germany* **31 G5** 48 37N 9 19 E
Nurzec →, *Poland* **55 F9** 52 37N 22 25 E
Nus, *Italy* **44 C4** 45 45N 7 28 E
Nusa Barung, *Indonesia* **85 D4** 8 30 S 113 30 E
Nusa Dua, *Indonesia* **79 K18** 8 48 S 115 14 E
Nusa Kambangan, *Indonesia* **85 D3** 7 40 S 108 10 E
Nusa Tenggara Barat □, *Indonesia* **85 D5** 8 50 S 117 30 E
Nusa Tenggara Timur □, *Indonesia* **82 C2** 9 30 S 122 0 E
Nusaybin, *Turkey* **101 D9** 37 3N 41 10 E
Nushki, *Pakistan* **91 C2** 29 35N 66 0 E
Nuuk, *Greenland* **10 E5** 64 10N 51 35W
Nuussauq, *Greenland* **10 C5** 74 8N 57 3W
Nuwakot, *Nepal* **93 E10** 28 10N 83 55 E
Nuwara Eliya, *Sri Lanka* **95 L5** 6 58N 80 48 E
Nuweiba', *Egypt* **96 D2** 28 59N 34 39 E
Nuwerus, *S. Africa* **116 E2** 31 8 S 18 24 E
Nuweveldberge, *S. Africa* **116 E3** 32 10 S 21 45 E
Nuyts, C., *Australia* **125 F5** 32 2 S 132 21 E
Nuyts, Pt., *Australia* **125 G2** 35 4 S 116 38 E
Nuyts Arch., *Australia* **127 E1** 32 35 S 133 20 E
Nuzvid, *India* **94 F5** 16 47N 80 53 E
N'Vinda, *Angola* **115 E3** 13 8 S 19 2 E
Nxai Pan Nat. Park, *Botswana* **116 B3** 19 50 S 24 46 E
Nxau-Nxau, *Botswana* **116 B3** 18 57 S 21 4 E
Nyaake, *Liberia* **112 E3** 4 52N 7 37W
Nyabessan, *Cameroon* **114 B2** 2 28N 10 24 E
Nyabing, *Australia* **125 F2** 33 33 S 118 9 E
Nyack, *U.S.A.* **151 E11** 41 5N 73 55W
Nyagan, *Russia* **66 C7** 62 30N 65 38 E
Nyah West, *Australia* **128 C5** 35 16 S 143 21 E
Nyahanga, *Tanzania* **118 C3** 2 20 S 33 37 E
Nyahua, *Tanzania* **118 D3** 5 25 S 33 23 E
Nyahururu, *Kenya* **118 B4** 0 2N 36 27 E
Nyainqentanglha Shan, *China* **68 D4** 30 0N 90 0 E
Nyakanazi, *Tanzania* **118 C3** 3 2 S 31 10 E
Nyakrom, *Ghana* **113 D4** 5 40N 0 50W
Nyâlâ, *Sudan* **107 E1** 12 2N 24 58 E
Nyamandhlovu, *Zimbabwe* **119 F2** 19 55 S 28 16 E
Nyambiti, *Tanzania* **118 C3** 2 48 S 33 27 E
Nyamlell, *Sudan* **107 F2** 9 7N 26 59 E
Nyamwaga, *Tanzania* **118 C3** 1 27 S 34 33 E
Nyandekwa, *Tanzania* **118 C3** 3 57 S 32 32 E
Nyanding →, *Sudan* **107 F3** 8 40N 32 41 E
Nyandoma, *Russia* **58 B11** 61 40N 40 12 E
Nyanga →, *Gabon* **114 C2** 2 58 S 10 15 E
Nyanga Nat. Park, *Zimbabwe* **119 F3** 18 17 S 32 46 E
Nyangana, *Namibia* **116 B3** 18 0 S 20 40 E
Nyanguge, *Tanzania* **118 C3** 2 30 S 33 12 E
Nyankpala, *Ghana* **113 D4** 9 21N 0 58W
Nyanza, *Rwanda* **118 C2** 2 20 S 29 42 E
Nyanza □, *Kenya* **118 C3** 0 10 S 34 15 E
Nyanza-Lac, *Burundi* **118 C2** 4 21 S 29 36 E
Nyaponges, *Sudan* **107 F3** 5 5N 33 45 E
Nyasa, L., *Africa* **119 E3** 12 30 S 34 30 E
Nyasvizh, *Belarus* **59 F4** 53 14N 26 38 E
Nyaunglebin, *Burma* **90 G6** 17 52N 96 42 E
Nyazepetrovsk, *Russia* **64 C7** 56 3N 59 36 E
Nyazura, *Zimbabwe* **119 F3** 18 40 S 32 16 E
Nyazwidzi →, *Zimbabwe* **119 G3** 20 0 S 31 17 E
Nybergsund, *Norway* **18 C9** 61 15N 12 19 E
Nyborg, *Denmark* **17 J4** 55 18N 10 47 E
Nybro, *Sweden* **17 H9** 56 44N 15 55 E
Nyda, *Russia* **66 C8** 66 40N 72 58 E
Nyeboe Land, *Greenland* **10 A5** 82 0N 57 0W
Nyengo Swamp, *Zambia* **115 E4** 14 51 S 22 7 E
Nyeri, *Kenya* **118 C4** 0 23 S 36 56 E
Nyerol, *Sudan* **107 F3** 8 41N 32 1 E
Nyhammar, *Sweden* **16 D8** 60 17N 14 58 E
Nyika Nat. Park, *Malawi* **119 E3** 10 30 S 33 53 E
Nyinahin, *Ghana* **112 D4** 6 43N 2 3W
Nyíradony, *Hungary* **52 C6** 47 41N 21 55 E
Nyírbátor, *Hungary* **52 C7** 47 49N 22 9 E
Nyíregyháza, *Hungary* **52 C6** 47 58N 21 47 E
Nykirke, *Norway* **18 D7** 60 54N 10 19 E
Nykøbing, *Storstrøm, Denmark* **17 K5** 54 56N 11 52 E
Nykøbing, *Vestsjælland, Denmark* **17 J5** 55 55N 11 40 E
Nykøbing, *Viborg, Denmark* **17 H2** 56 48N 8 51 E
Nyköping, *Sweden* **17 F11** 58 45N 17 1 E
Nykroppa, *Sweden* **16 E8** 59 37N 14 18 E
Nykvarn, *Sweden* **16 E11** 59 11N 17 25 E
Nyland, *Sweden* **16 A11** 63 1N 17 45 E
Nylstroom, *S. Africa* **117 C4** 24 42 S 28 22 E
Nymagee, *Australia* **129 B7** 32 7 S 146 20 E
Nymboida Nat. Park, *Australia* **127 D5** 29 38 S 152 26 E
Nymburk, *Czech Rep.* **34 A8** 50 10N 15 1 E
Nynäshamn, *Sweden* **17 F11** 58 54N 17 57 E
Nyngan, *Australia* **129 A7** 31 30 S 147 8 E
Nyoma Rap, *India* **93 C8** 33 10N 78 40 E
Nyoman = Neman →, *Lithuania* **15 J19** 55 25N 21 10 E
Nyon, *Switz.* **32 D2** 46 23N 6 14 E
Nyong →, *Cameroon* **113 E6** 3 17N 9 54 E
Nyons, *France* **29 D9** 44 22N 5 10 E
Nyou, *Burkina Faso* **113 C4** 12 42N 2 1W
Nýrsko, *Czech Rep.* **34 B6** 49 18N 13 9 E
Nysa, *Poland* **55 H4** 50 30N 17 22 E
Nysa →, *Europe* **30 C10** 52 4N 14 46 E
Nysa Kłodzka →, *Poland* **55 H4** 50 49N 17 40 E
Nysäter, *Sweden* **16 E6** 59 17N 12 47 E
Nyseter, *Norway* **18 B5** 62 2N 8 20 E
Nyssa, *U.S.A.* **158 E5** 43 53N 117 0W
Nysted, *Denmark* **17 K5** 54 40N 11 44 E
Nytva, *Russia* **64 C5** 57 56N 55 20 E
Nyunzu, *Dem. Rep. of the Congo* **118 D2** 5 57 S 27 58 E
Nyurba, *Russia* **67 C12** 63 17N 118 28 E
Nyzhnohirskyy, *Ukraine* **59 K8** 45 27N 34 38 E
Nzébéla, *Guinea* **112 D3** 8 9N 9 7W
Nzega, *Tanzania* **118 C3** 4 10 S 33 12 E
N'zérékoré, *Guinea* **112 D3** 7 49N 8 48W
Nzeto, *Angola* **115 D2** 7 10 S 12 52 E
Nzilo, Chutes de, *Dem. Rep. of the Congo* **119 E2** 10 18 S 25 27 E
Nzo →, *Ivory C.* **112 D3** 6 15N 7 3W
N'Zo, Réserve de Faune du, *Ivory C.* **112 D3** 6 15N 7 15W
Nzubuka, *Tanzania* **118 C3** 4 45 S 32 50 E
Nzwani = Anjouan, *Comoros Is.* **121 a** 12 15 S 44 20 E

O

O Barco, *Spain* **42 C4** 42 23N 6 58W
O Carballiño, *Spain* **42 C2** 42 26N 8 5W
O Corgo, *Spain* **42 C3** 42 56N 7 25W
O Le Pupū Pu'e Nat. Park, *Samoa* **133 W24** 13 59 S 171 43W
O Pino, *Spain* **42 C2** 42 56N 8 20W
O Porriño, *Spain* **42 C2** 42 10N 8 37W
Ō-Shima, *Fukuoka, Japan* **72 D2** 30 53N 130 28 E
Ō-Shima, *Nagasaki, Japan* **72 C1** 33 29N 129 33 E
Ō-Shima, *Shizuoka, Japan* **73 C11** 34 44N 139 24 E
Oa, Mull of, *U.K.* **22 F2** 55 35N 6 20W
Oacoma, *U.S.A.* **154 D5** 43 48N 99 24W
Oahe, L., *U.S.A.* **154 C4** 44 27N 100 24W
Oahe Dam, *U.S.A.* **154 C4** 44 27N 100 24W
Oahu, *U.S.A.* **145 K14** 21 28N 157 58W
Oak Creek, *U.S.A.* **157 B9** 42 52N 87 55W
Oak Harbor, *U.S.A.* **160 B4** 48 18N 122 39W
Oak Hill, *Fla., U.S.A.* **153 G9** 28 52N 80 51W
Oak Hill, *W. Va., U.S.A.* **148 G5** 37 59N 81 9W
Oak Lawn, *U.S.A.* **157 C9** 41 43N 87 44W
Oak Park, *Ga., U.S.A.* **152 C7** 32 22N 82 19W
Oak Park, *Ill., U.S.A.* **157 C9** 41 53N 87 47W
Oak Ridge, *U.S.A.* **149 G3** 36 1N 84 16W
Oak View, *U.S.A.* **161 L7** 34 24N 119 18W
Oakan-Dake, *Japan* **70 C12** 43 27N 144 10 E
Oakbank, *Australia* **128 B4** 33 4 S 140 33 E
Oakdale, *Calif., U.S.A.* **160 H6** 37 46N 120 51W
Oakdale, *La., U.S.A.* **155 K8** 30 49N 92 40W
Oakes, *U.S.A.* **154 B5** 46 8N 98 6W
Oakesdale, *U.S.A.* **158 C5** 47 8N 117 15W
Oakey, *Australia* **127 D5** 27 25 S 151 43 E
Oakfield, *Ga., U.S.A.* **152 D6** 31 47N 83 58W
Oakfield, *N.Y., U.S.A.* **150 C6** 43 4N 78 16W
Oakford, *U.S.A.* **156 D7** 40 6N 89 58W
Oakham, *U.K.* **21 E7** 52 40N 0 43W
Oakhurst, *U.S.A.* **160 H7** 37 19N 119 40W
Oakland, *Calif., U.S.A.* **160 H4** 37 49N 122 16W
Oakland, *Ill., U.S.A.* **157 E8** 39 39N 88 2W
Oakland City, *U.S.A.* **157 F9** 38 20N 87 21W
Oaklands, *Australia* **129 C7** 35 34 S 146 10 E
Oakley, *Idaho, U.S.A.* **158 E7** 42 15N 113 53W
Oakley, *Kans., U.S.A.* **154 F4** 39 8N 100 51W
Oakover →, *Australia* **124 D3** 21 0 S 120 40 E
Oakridge, *U.S.A.* **158 E2** 43 45N 122 28W
Oaktown, *U.S.A.* **157 F9** 38 52N 87 27W
Oakville, *Canada* **150 C5** 43 27N 79 41W
Oakville, *U.S.A.* **160 D3** 46 51N 123 14W
Oakwood, *U.S.A.* **157 C12** 41 6N 84 23W
Oamaru, *N.Z.* **131 F5** 45 5 S 170 59 E
Ōamishirasato, *Japan* **73 B12** 35 31N 140 18 E
Oancea, *Romania* **53 E12** 45 21N 27 42 E
Oarai, *Japan* **73 A12** 36 21N 140 34 E
Oasis, *Calif., U.S.A.* **161 M10** 33 28N 116 6W
Oasis, *Nev., U.S.A.* **160 H9** 37 29N 117 55W
Oates Land, *Antarctica* **7 C11** 69 0 S 160 0 E
Oatlands, *Australia* **127 G4** 42 17 S 147 21 E
Oatman, *U.S.A.* **161 K12** 35 1N 114 19W
Oaxaca, *Mexico* **163 D5** 17 2N 96 40W
Oaxaca □, *Mexico* **163 D5** 17 0N 97 0W
Ob →, *Russia* **66 C7** 66 45N 69 30 E
Oba, *Canada* **140 C3** 49 4N 84 7W
Obala, *Cameroon* **113 E7** 4 9N 11 32 E
Obama, *Fukui, Japan* **73 B7** 35 30N 135 45 E
Obama, *Nagasaki, Japan* **72 E2** 32 43N 130 13 E
Oban, *Nigeria* **113 D6** 5 17N 8 33 E
Oban, *U.K.* **22 E3** 56 25N 5 29W
Obbia, *Somali Rep.* **120 C3** 5 25N 48 30 E
Ober-Aargau, *Switz.* **32 B5** 47 10N 7 45 E
Ober-engadin, *Switz.* **33 C9** 46 35N 9 55 E
Obera, *Argentina* **175 B4** 27 21 S 55 2W
Oberalppass, *Switz.* **33 C7** 46 39N 8 35 E
Oberalpstock, *Switz.* **33 C7** 46 45N 8 47 E
Oberammergau, *Germany* **31 H7** 47 36N 11 4 E
Oberasbach, *Germany* **31 F6** 49 25N 10 57 E
Oberbayern □, *Germany* **31 G7** 48 5N 11 50 E
Oberdiessbach, *Switz.* **32 C5** 46 5[illegible]N 7 40 E
Oberdrauburg, *Austria* **34 E5** 46 4[illegible]N 12 58 E
Oberentfelden, *Switz.* **32 B6** 47 [illegible]N 8 2 E
Oberfranken □, *Germany* **31 E7** 50 10N 11 20 E
Oberhausen, *Germany* **30 D2** 51 28N 6 51 E
Oberkirch, *Germany* **31 G4** 48 31N 8 4 E
Oberland, *Switz.* **32 C5** 46 35N 7 38 E
Oberlausitz, *Germany* **30 D10** 51 16N 14 18 E
Oberlin, *Kans., U.S.A.* **154 F4** 39 49N 100 32W
Oberlin, *La., U.S.A.* **155 K8** 30 37N 92 46W
Oberlin, *Ohio, U.S.A.* **150 E2** 41 18N 82 13W
Obernai, *France* **27 D14** 48 28N 7 30 E
Oberndorf, *Germany* **31 G4** 48 17N 8 34 E
Oberon, *Australia* **129 B8** 33 45 S 149 52 E
Oberösterreich □, *Austria* **34 C7** 48 10N 14 0 E
Oberpfalz □, *Germany* **31 F8** 49 20N 12 10 E
Oberpfälzer Wald, *Germany* **31 F8** 49 30N 12 30 E
Oberriet, *Switz.* **33 B9** 47 19N 9 34 E
Obersiggenthal, *Switz.* **33 B6** 47 29N 8 18 E
Oberstdorf, *Germany* **31 H6** 47 24N 10 15 E
Oberting, *Gabon* **114 C1** 0 22 S 9 46 E
Oberursel, *Germany* **31 E4** 50 11N 8 35 E
Oberwart, *Austria* **35 D9** 47 17N 16 12 E
Oberwil, *Switz.* **32 A5** 47 32N 7 33 E
Obi, *Indonesia* **82 B3** 1 23 S 127 45 E
Obiaruku, *Nigeria* **113 D6** 5 51N 6 9 E
Óbidos, *Brazil* **169 D6** 1 50 S 55 30W
Óbidos, *Portugal* **43 F1** 39 19N 9 10W
Obigarm, *Tajikistan* **65 D4** 38 43N 69 42 E
Obihiro, *Japan* **70 C11** 42 56N 143 12 E
Obikiik, *Tajikistan* **65 D4** 38 9N 68 39 E
Obilatu, *Indonesia* **82 B3** 1 25 S 127 20 E
Obilnoye, *Russia* **61 G7** 47 32N 44 30 E
Obing, *Germany* **31 G8** 48 0N 12 24 E
Objat, *France* **28 C5** 45 16N 1 24 E
Oblong, *U.S.A.* **157 F9** 39 0N 87 55W
Obluchye, *Russia* **67 E14** 49 1N 131 4 E
Obninsk, *Russia* **58 E9** 55 8N 36 37 E
Obo, *C.A.R.* **118 A2** 5 20N 26 32 E
Oboa, Mt., *Uganda* **118 B3** 1 45N 34 45 E
Obock, *Djibouti* **107 E5** 12 0N 43 20 E
Oborniki, *Poland* **55 F3** 52 39N 16 50 E
Oborniki Śląskie, *Poland* **55 G3** 51 17N 16 53 E
Obouya, *Congo* **114 C3** 0 56 S 15 43 E
Oboyan, *Russia* **59 G9** 51 15N 36 21 E
Obozerskaya = Obozerskiy, *Russia* **56 B7** 63 34N 40 21 E
Obozerskiy, *Russia* **56 B7** 63 34N 40 21 E
Obrenovac, *Serbia, Yug.* **50 B4** 44 40N 20 11 E
O'Brien, *U.S.A.* **152 E7** 30 2N 82 57W
Obrovac, *Croatia* **45 D12** 44 11N 15 41 E
Obruk, *Turkey* **100 C5** 38 7N 33 12 E
Obrzycko, *Poland* **55 F3** 52 42N 16 32 E
Observatory Inlet, *Canada* **142 B3** 55 10N 129 54W
Obshchi Syrt, *Russia* **64 E4** 52 0N 53 0 E
Obskaya Guba, *Russia* **66 C8** 69 0N 73 0 E
Obuasi, *Ghana* **113 D4** 6 17N 1 40W
Obubra, *Nigeria* **113 D6** 6 8N 8 20 E
Obudu, *Nigeria* **113 D6** 6 38N 9 5 E
Obura, *Papua N. G.* **132 D3** 6 33 S 145 58 E
Obwalden □, *Switz.* **32 C6** 46 55N 8 15 E
Obzor, *Bulgaria* **51 D11** 42 50N 27 52 E
Ocala, *U.S.A.* **149 L4** 29 11N 82 8W
Ocamo →, *Venezuela* **169 C4** 2 48N 65 14W
Ocampo, *Chihuahua, Mexico* **162 B3** 28 9N 108 24W
Ocampo, *Tamaulipas, Mexico* **163 C5** 22 50N 99 20W
Ocaña, *Colombia* **168 B3** 8 15N 73 20W
Ocaña, *Spain* **42 F7** 39 55N 3 30W
Ocanomowoc, *U.S.A.* **154 D10** 43 7N 88 30W
Occidental, Cordillera, *Colombia* **168 C3** 5 0N 76 0W
Occidental, Cordillera, *Peru* **172 C3** 14 0 S 74 0W
Occidental, Grand Erg, *Algeria* **111 B5** 30 20N 1 0 E
Ocean City, *Md., U.S.A.* **148 F8** 38 20N 75 5W
Ocean City, *N.J., U.S.A.* **148 F8** 39 17N 74 35W
Ocean City, *Wash., U.S.A.* **160 C2** 47 4N 124 10W
Ocean Falls, *Canada* **142 C3** 52 18N 127 48W
Ocean I. = Banaba, *Kiribati* **134 H8** 0 45 S 169 50 E
Ocean Park, *U.S.A.* **160 D2** 46 30N 124 3W
Oceano, *U.S.A.* **161 K6** 35 6N 120 37W
Oceanport, *U.S.A.* **151 F10** 40 19N 74 3W
Oceanside, *U.S.A.* **161 M9** 33 12N 117 23W
Ochagavía, *Spain* **40 C3** 42 55N 1 5W
Ochakiv, *Ukraine* **59 J6** 46 37N 31 33 E
Ochamchira, *Georgia* **61 J5** 42 46N 41 32 E
Ocher, *Russia* **64 C5** 57 53N 54 42 E
Ochiai, *Japan* **72 B5** 35 1N 133 45 E
Ochil Hills, *U.K.* **22 E5** 56 14N 3 40W
Ochlocknee, *U.S.A.* **152 E5** 30 58N 84 3W
Ochlockonee →, *U.S.A.* **152 F5** 29 59N 84 26W
Ocho Rios, *Jamaica* **164 a** 18 24N 77 6W
Ochopee, *U.S.A.* **153 K8** 25 54N 81 18W
Ochsenfurt, *Germany* **31 F6** 49 40N 10 4 E
Ochsenhausen, *Germany* **31 G5** 48 4N 9 57 E
Ocilla, *U.S.A.* **152 D6** 31 36N 83 15W
Ockelbo, *Sweden* **16 D10** 60 54N 16 45 E
Ocmulgee →, *U.S.A.* **152 D7** 31 58N 82 33W
Ocna Mureş, *Romania* **53 D8** 46 23N 23 55 E
Ocna Sibiului, *Romania* **53 E9** 45 52N 24 2 E
Ocnele Mari, *Romania* **53 E9** 45 8N 24 18 E
Ocniţa, *Moldova* **53 B12** 48 25N 27 30 E
Ocoee, *U.S.A.* **153 G8** 28 34N 81 33W
Ocoña, *Peru* **172 D3** 16 26 S 73 8W
Ocoña →, *Peru* **172 D3** 16 28 S 73 8W
Oconee →, *U.S.A.* **152 D7** 31 58N 82 33W
Oconee, L., *U.S.A.* **152 B6** 33 28N 83 15W
Oconomowoc, *U.S.A.* **157 A8** 43 7N 88 30W
Oconto, *U.S.A.* **148 C2** 44 53N 87 52W
Oconto Falls, *U.S.A.* **148 C1** 44 52N 88 9W
Ocosingo, *Mexico* **163 D6** 17 10N 92 15W
Ocotal, *Nic.* **164 D2** 13 41N 86 31W
Ocotlán, *Mexico* **162 C4** 20 21N 102 42W
Ocotlán de Morelos, *Mexico* **163 D5** 16 48N 96 40W
Ocreza →, *Portugal* **43 F3** 39 32N 7 50W
Öcsa, *Hungary* **52 C4** 47 17N 19 15 E
Octeville, *France* **26 C5** 49 38N 1 40W
Ocumare del Tuy, *Venezuela* **168 A4** 10 7N 66 46W
Ocuri, *Bolivia* **173 D4** 18 45 S 65 50W
Oda, *Ghana* **113 D4** 5 50N 0 51W
Ōda, *Japan* **72 B4** 35 11N 132 30 E
Oda, J., *Sudan* **106 C4** 20 21N 36 39 E
Ódáðahraun, *Iceland* **11 B9** 65 5N 17 0W
Ödåkra, *Sweden* **17 H6** 56 7N 12 45 E
Odammun →, *Indonesia* **83 C5** 6 50 S 138 45 E
Odate, *Japan* **70 D10** 40 16N 140 34 E
Odawara, *Japan* **73 B11** 35 20N 139 6 E
Odda, *Norway* **15 F12** 60 3N 6 35 E
Odder, *Denmark* **17 J4** 55 58N 10 10 E
Oddur, *Somali Rep.* **120 D2** 4 11N 43 52 E
Odei →, *Canada* **143 B9** 56 6N 96 54W
Odell, *U.S.A.* **157 C8** 41 0N 88 31W
Odemira, *Portugal* **43 H2** 37 35N 8 40W
Ödemiş, *Turkey* **49 C9** 38 15N 28 0 E
Odendaalsrus, *S. Africa* **116 D4** 27 48 S 26 45 E
Odensbacken, *Sweden* **16 E9** 59 10N 15 32 E
Odense, *Denmark* **17 J4** 55 22N 10 23 E
Odenwald, *Germany* **31 F5** 49 35N 9 0 E
Oder →, *Europe* **30 B10** 53 33N 14 38 E
Oder-Havel Kanal, *Germany* **30 C10** 52 52N 14 2 E
Oderzo, *Italy* **45 C9** 45 47N 12 29 E
Odesa, *Ukraine* **59 J6** 46 30N 30 45 E
Ödeshög, *Sweden* **17 F8** 58 14N 14 39 E
Odessa = Odesa, *Ukraine* **59 J6** 46 30N 30 45 E
Odessa, *Canada* **151 B8** 44 17N 76 43W
Odessa, *Mo., U.S.A.* **156 F3** 39 0N 93 57W
Odessa, *Tex., U.S.A.* **155 K3** 31 52N 102 23W
Odessa, *Wash., U.S.A.* **158 C4** 47 20N 118 41W
Odiakwe, *Botswana* **116 C4** 20 12 S 25 17 E
Odiel →, *Spain* **43 H4** 37 10N 6 55W
Odienné, *Ivory C.* **112 D3** 9 30N 7 34W
Odimba, *Gabon* **114 C2** 2 2 S 9 33 E
Odintsovo, *Russia* **58 E9** 55 39N 37 15 E
Odiongan, *Phil.* **80 E3** 12 24N 121 59 E
Odobeşti, *Romania* **53 E12** 45 43N 27 4 E
Odolanów, *Poland* **55 G4** 51 34N 17 40 E
O'Donnell, *U.S.A.* **155 J4** 32 58N 101 50W
Odorheiu Secuiesc, *Romania* **53 D10** 46 21N 25 21 E
Odoyevo, *Russia* **58 F9** 53 56N 36 42 E
Odra = Oder →, *Europe* **30 B10** 53 33N 14 38 E
Odra →, *Spain* **42 C6** 42 14N 4 17W
Odum, *U.S.A.* **152 D7** 31 40N 82 2W
Odweina, *Somali Rep.* **120 C3** 9 25N 45 4 E
Odžaci, *Serbia, Yug.* **52 E4** 45 30N 19 17 E
Odžak, *Bos.-H.* **52 E3** 45 3N 18 18 E
Odzala, *Congo* **114 B2** 0 37N 14 37 E
Odzala, Parc Nat. d', *Congo* **114 B2** 0 55N 14 55 E
Odzi, *Zimbabwe* **117 B5** 19 0 S 32 20 E
Odzi →, *Zimbabwe* **117 B5** 19 45 S 32 23 E
Oebisfelde, *Germany* **30 C6** 52 27N 10 57 E
Oeiras, *Brazil* **170 C3** 7 0 S 42 8W
Oeiras, *Portugal* **43 G1** 38 41N 9 18W
Oeiras do Para, *Brazil* **169 D8** 1 58 S 49 51W
Oelrichs, *U.S.A.* **154 D3** 43 11N 103 14W
Oelsnitz, *Germany* **31 E8** 50 24N 12 10 E
Oelwein, *U.S.A.* **156 B5** 42 41N 91 55W
Oenpelli, *Australia* **124 B5** 12 20 S 133 4 E
Oetz, *Austria* **34 D3** 47 13N 10 53 E
Of, *Turkey* **101 B9** 40 59N 40 23 E
O'Fallon, *U.S.A.* **156 F6** 38 49N 90 42W
Ofanto →, *Italy* **47 A9** 41 22N 16 13 E
Offa, *Nigeria* **113 D5** 8 13N 4 42 E
Offaly □, *Ireland* **23 C4** 53 15N 7 30W
Offenbach, *Germany* **31 E4** 50 6N 8 44 E
Offenburg, *Germany* **31 G3** 48 28N 7 56 E
Offida, *Italy* **45 F10** 42 56N 13 41 E
Offoué →, *Gabon* **114 C2** 0 4 S 11 44 E
Ofidhousa, *Greece* **49 E8** 36 33N 26 8 E
Öflingen, *Germany* **32 A5** 47 36N 7 55 E
Ofolanga, *Tonga* **133 P14** 19 38 S 173 35W
Ofotfjorden, *Norway* **14 B17** 68 27N 17 0 E
Ofte, *Norway* **18 E5** 59 30N 8 13 E
Ofu, *Amer. Samoa* **133 X25** 14 11 S 169 41W
Ōfunato, *Japan* **70 E10** 39 4N 141 43 E
Oga, *Japan* **70 E9** 39 55N 139 50 E
Oga-Hantō, *Japan* **70 E9** 39 58N 139 47 E
Ogaden, *Ethiopia* **120 C3** 7 30N 45 30 E
Ōgaki, *Japan* **73 B8** 35 21N 136 37 E
Ogallala, *U.S.A.* **154 E4** 41 8N 101 43W

Ogan →, *Indonesia* **84 C2** 3 1 S 104 44 E
Ogasawara Gunto, *Pac. Oc.* **62 G18** 27 0N 142 0 E
Ogbomosho, *Nigeria* **113 D5** 8 1N 4 11 E
Ogden, *Iowa, U.S.A.* **156 B2** 42 2N 94 2W
Ogden, *Utah, U.S.A.* **158 F7** 41 13N 111 58W
Ogdensburg, *U.S.A.* **151 B9** 44 42N 75 30W
Ogea Driki, *Fiji* **133 B3** 19 12 S 178 27W
Ogea Levu, *Fiji* **133 B3** 19 8 S 178 24W
Ogeechee →, *U.S.A.* **152 D8** 31 50N 81 3W
Ogilby, *U.S.A.* **161 N12** 32 49N 114 50W
Oglat Beraber, *Algeria* **110 B4** 30 15N 3 34W
Oglats de Khenachiche, *Mali* **110 D4** 21 51N 3 58W
Oglesby, *U.S.A.* **156 C7** 41 18N 89 4W
Oglethorpe, *U.S.A.* **152 C5** 32 18N 84 4W
Oglio →, *Italy* **44 C7** 45 2N 10 39 E
Ogmore, *Australia* **126 C4** 22 37 S 149 35 E
Ognon →, *France* **27 E12** 47 16N 5 28 E
Ogoamas, *Indonesia* **82 A2** 0 50N 120 5 E
Ogoja, *Nigeria* **113 D6** 6 38N 8 39 E
Ogoki, *Canada* **140 B2** 51 38N 85 58W
Ogoki →, *Canada* **140 B2** 51 38N 85 57W
Ogoki L., *Canada* **140 B2** 50 50N 87 10W
Ogoki Res., *Canada* **140 B2** 50 45N 88 15W
Ogooué →, *Gabon* **114 C1** 1 0 S 9 0 E
Ogōri, *Japan* **72 C3** 34 6N 131 24 E
Ogosta →, *Bulgaria* **50 C7** 43 48N 23 55 E
Ogowe = Ogooué →, *Gabon* **114 C1** 1 0 S 9 0 E
Ogr = Sharafa, *Sudan* **107 E2** 11 59N 27 7 E
Ograźden, *Macedonia* **50 E6** 41 30N 22 50 E
Ogre, *Latvia* **15 H21** 56 49N 24 36 E
Ogrein, *Sudan* **106 D3** 17 55N 34 50 E
Ogulin, *Croatia* **45 C12** 45 16N 15 16 E
Ogun □, *Nigeria* **113 D5** 7 0N 3 0 E
Oguni, *Japan* **72 D3** 33 11N 131 8 E
Ogur, *Iceland* **11 A4** 66 2N 22 44W
Ogurchinskiy, Ostrov, *Turkmenistan* **97 B7** 38 55N 53 2 E
Oguta, *Nigeria* **113 D6** 5 44N 6 44 E
Ogwashi-Uku, *Nigeria* **113 D6** 6 15N 6 30 E
Ogwe, *Nigeria* **113 E6** 5 0N 7 14 E
Ohai, *N.Z.* **131 F3** 45 55 S 168 0 E
Ohakune, *N.Z.* **130 F4** 39 24 S 175 24 E
Ohanet, *Algeria* **111 C6** 28 44N 8 46 E
Ōhara, *Japan* **73 B12** 35 15N 140 23 E
Ohata, *Japan* **70 D10** 41 24N 141 10 E
Ohatchee, *U.S.A.* **152 B4** 33 47N 86 0W
Ohau, L., *N.Z.* **131 E4** 44 15 S 169 53 E
Ohaupo, *N.Z.* **130 D4** 37 56 S 175 20 E
O'Higgins, C., *Chile* **172 b** 27 5 S 109 15W
Ohio □, *U.S.A.* **150 F2** 40 15N 82 45W
Ohio →, *U.S.A.* **157 G8** 36 59N 89 8W
Ohio City, *U.S.A.* **157 D12** 40 46N 84 37W
Ohiwa Harbour, *N.Z.* **130 D6** 37 59 S 177 10 E
Ohře →, *Czech Rep.* **34 A7** 50 30N 14 10 E
Ohre →, *Germany* **30 C7** 52 18N 11 46 E
Ohrid, *Macedonia* **50 E4** 41 8N 20 52 E
Ohridsko Jezero, *Macedonia* **50 E4** 41 8N 20 52 E
Ohrigstad, *S. Africa* **117 C5** 24 39 S 30 36 E
Öhringen, *Germany* **31 F5** 49 12N 9 31 E
Ohura, *N.Z.* **130 E3** 38 51 S 174 59 E
Oi Qu, *China* **76 C2** 28 37N 98 16 E
Oiapoque, *Brazil* **169 C7** 3 50N 51 50W
Oiapoque →, *Brazil* **169 C7** 4 8N 51 40W
Oikou, *China* **75 E9** 38 35N 117 42 E
Oil City, *U.S.A.* **150 E5** 41 26N 79 42W
Oil Springs, *Canada* **150 D2** 42 47N 82 7W
Oildale, *U.S.A.* **161 K7** 35 25N 119 1W
Oinousa, *Greece* **49 C8** 38 33N 26 14 E
Oise □, *France* **27 C9** 49 28N 2 30 E
Oise →, *France* **27 C9** 49 0N 2 4 E
Oiseaux du Djoudj, Parc Nat. aux, *Senegal* **112 B1** 16 24N 16 14W
Oistins, *Barbados* **165 g** 13 4N 59 33W
Oistins B., *Barbados* **165 g** 13 4N 59 33W
Ōita, *Japan* **72 D3** 33 14N 131 36 E
Ōita □, *Japan* **72 D3** 33 15N 131 30 E
Oiticica, *Brazil* **170 C3** 5 3 S 41 5W
Ojacaliente, *Mexico* **162 C4** 22 34N 102 15W
Ojai, *U.S.A.* **161 L7** 34 27N 119 15W
Ojhar, *India* **94 D1** 20 6N 73 56 E
Ojinaga, *Mexico* **162 B4** 29 34N 104 25W
Ojiya, *Japan* **71 F9** 37 18N 138 48 E
Ojos del Salado, Cerro, *Argentina* **174 B2** 27 0 S 68 40W
Oka →, *Russia* **60 B7** 56 20N 43 59 E
Okaba, *Indonesia* **83 C5** 8 6 S 139 42 E
Okahandja, *Namibia* **116 C2** 22 0 S 16 59 E
Okahukura, *N.Z.* **130 E4** 38 48 S 175 14 E
Okaihau, *N.Z.* **130 B2** 35 19 S 173 47 E
Okalataka, *Congo* **114 C2** 0 18 S 14 54 E
Okanagan L., *Canada* **142 D5** 50 0N 119 30W
Okandja, *Gabon* **114 C2** 0 35 S 13 45 E
Okano →, *Gabon* **114 C2** 0 5 S 10 57 E
Okanogan, *U.S.A.* **158 B4** 48 22N 119 35W
Okanogan →, *U.S.A.* **158 B4** 48 6N 119 44W
Okány, *Hungary* **52 D6** 46 52N 21 21 E
Okapa, *Papua N. G.* **132 D3** 6 38 S 145 39 E
Okapi, Parc Nat. d', *Dem. Rep. of the Congo* **118 B2** 2 30N 27 20 E
Okaputa, *Namibia* **116 C2** 20 5 S 17 0 E
Okara, *Pakistan* **91 C4** 30 50N 73 31 E
Okarito, *N.Z.* **131 D5** 43 15 S 170 9 E
Okato, *N.Z.* **130 F2** 39 12 S 173 53 E
Okaukuejo, *Namibia* **116 B2** 19 10 S 16 0 E
Okavango Delta, *Botswana* **116 B3** 18 45 S 22 45 E
Okavango Swamp = Okavango Delta, *Botswana* **116 B3** 18 45 S 22 45 E
Ōkawa, *Japan* **72 D2** 33 9N 130 21 E
Okawville, *U.S.A.* **156 F7** 38 26N 89 33W
Okaya, *Japan* **73 A10** 36 5N 138 10 E
Okayama, *Japan* **72 C5** 34 40N 133 54 E
Okayama □, *Japan* **72 C5** 35 0N 133 50 E
Okazaki, *Japan* **73 C9** 34 57N 137 10 E
Oke-Iho, *Nigeria* **113 D5** 8 1N 3 18 E
Okeechobee, *U.S.A.* **149 M5** 27 15N 80 50W
Okeechobee, L., *U.S.A.* **149 M5** 27 0N 80 50W
Okefenokee Swamp, *U.S.A.* **152 E7** 30 40N 82 20W
Okehampton, *U.K.* **21 G4** 50 44N 4 0W
Okemos, *U.S.A.* **157 B12** 42 43N 84 26W
Okene, *Nigeria* **113 D6** 7 32N 6 11 E
Oker →, *Germany* **30 C6** 52 32N 10 22 E
Okha, *India* **92 H3** 22 27N 69 4 E
Okha, *Russia* **67 D15** 53 40N 143 0 E
Ōkhi Óros, *Greece* **48 C6** 38 5N 24 25 E
Okhotsk, *Russia* **67 D15** 59 20N 143 10 E
Okhotsk, Sea of, *Asia* **67 D15** 55 0N 145 0 E
Okhotskiy Perevoz, *Russia* **67 C14** 61 52N 135 35 E
Okhtyrka, *Ukraine* **59 G8** 50 25N 35 0 E
Oki-no-Shima, *Japan* **72 E4** 32 44N 132 33 E
Oki-Shotō, *Japan* **72 A5** 36 5N 133 15 E
Okiep, *S. Africa* **116 D2** 29 39 S 17 53 E
Okigwi, *Nigeria* **113 D6** 5 52N 7 20 E
Okija, *Nigeria* **113 D6** 5 54N 6 55 E
Okinawa □, *Japan* **71 L4** 26 40N 128 0 E
Okinawa-Guntō, *Japan* **71 L4** 26 40N 128 0 E
Okinawa-Jima, *Japan* **71 L4** 26 32N 128 0 E
Okino-erabu-Shima, *Japan* **71 L4** 27 21N 128 33 E
Okitipupa, *Nigeria* **113 D5** 6 31N 4 50 E
Oklahoma □, *U.S.A.* **155 H6** 35 20N 97 30W
Oklahoma City, *U.S.A.* **155 H6** 35 30N 97 30W
Oklawaha →, *U.S.A.* **153 F8** 29 28N 81 41W
Okmulgee, *U.S.A.* **155 H7** 35 37N 95 58W
Oknitsa = Ocniţa, *Moldova* **53 B12** 48 25N 27 30 E
Oko, W. →, *Sudan* **106 C4** 21 15N 35 56 E
Okolo, *Uganda* **118 B3** 2 37N 31 8 E
Okolona, *Ky., U.S.A.* **157 F11** 38 8N 85 41W
Okolona, *Miss., U.S.A.* **155 J10** 34 0N 88 45W
Okombahe, *Namibia* **116 C2** 21 23 S 15 22 E
Okonek, *Poland* **54 E3** 53 32N 16 51 E
Okotoks, *Canada* **142 C6** 50 43N 113 58W
Okoyo, *Congo* **114 C3** 1 28 S 15 0 E
Okrika, *Nigeria* **113 E6** 4 40N 7 10 E
Oksapmin, *Papua N. G.* **132 C2** 5 17 S 142 15 E
Øksendal, *Norway* **18 B5** 62 42N 8 27 E
Oksibil, *Indonesia* **83 B6** 4 59 S 140 35 E
Øksna, *Norway* **18 D8** 60 58N 11 27 E
Oksovskiy, *Russia* **56 B6** 62 33N 39 57 E
Oktabrsk = Oktyabrsk, *Kazakstan* **57 E10** 49 28N 57 25 E
Oktwin, *Burma* **90 F6** 18 49N 96 26 E
Oktyabr, *Kazakstan* **65 B8** 43 41N 77 12 E
Oktyabrsk, *Kazakstan* **57 E10** 49 28N 57 25 E
Oktyabrsk, *Russia* **60 D9** 53 11N 48 40 E
Oktyabrskiy = Aktsyabrski, *Belarus* **59 F5** 52 38N 28 53 E
Oktyabrskiy, *Bashkortostan, Russia* **64 D4** 54 28N 53 28 E
Oktyabrskiy, *Perm, Russia* **64 C6** 56 31N 57 12 E
Oktyabrskiy, *Rostov, Russia* **61 G5** 47 30N 40 4 E
Oktyabrskoy Revolyutsii, Ostrov, *Russia* **67 B10** 79 30N 97 0 E
Oktyabrskoye = Zhovtneve, *Ukraine* **59 J7** 46 54N 32 3 E
Oktyabrskoye, *Russia* **64 D9** 54 26N 62 44 E
Ōkuchi, *Japan* **72 E2** 32 4N 130 37 E
Okulovka, *Russia* **58 C7** 58 25N 33 19 E
Okuru, *N.Z.* **131 D3** 43 55 S 168 55 E
Okushiri-Tō, *Japan* **70 C9** 42 15N 139 30 E
Okuta, *Nigeria* **113 D5** 9 14N 3 12 E
Okwa →, *Botswana* **116 C3** 22 30 S 23 0 E
Ola, *U.S.A.* **155 H8** 35 2N 93 13W
Ólafsfjörður, *Iceland* **11 A8** 66 4N 18 39W
Ólafsvík, *Iceland* **11 C3** 64 53N 23 43W
Olaine, *Latvia* **56 D3** 56 48N 23 59 E
Olancha, *U.S.A.* **161 J8** 36 17N 118 1W
Olancha Pk., *U.S.A.* **161 J8** 36 15N 118 7W
Olanchito, *Honduras* **164 C2** 15 30N 86 30W
Öland, *Sweden* **17 H10** 56 45N 16 38 E
Ölands norra udde, *Sweden* **17 G11** 57 22N 17 5 E
Ölands södra udde, *Sweden* **17 H10** 56 12N 16 23 E
Olanta, *U.S.A.* **152 B10** 33 56N 79 56W
Olar, *U.S.A.* **152 B8** 33 11N 81 11W
Olargues, *France* **28 E6** 43 34N 2 53 E
Olary, *Australia* **128 B4** 32 18 S 140 19 E
Olascoaga, *Argentina* **174 D3** 35 15 S 60 39W
Olathe, *U.S.A.* **154 F7** 38 53N 94 49W
Olavarría, *Argentina* **174 D3** 36 55 S 60 20W
Oława, *Poland* **55 H4** 50 57N 17 20 E
Olbernhau, *Germany* **30 E9** 50 40N 13 19 E
Ólbia, *Italy* **46 B2** 40 55N 9 31 E
Ólbia, G. di, *Italy* **46 B2** 40 55N 9 39 E
Olching, *Germany* **31 G7** 48 12N 11 21 E
Olcott, *U.S.A.* **150 C6** 43 20N 78 42W
Old Bahama Chan. = Bahama, Canal Viejo de, *W. Indies* **164 B4** 22 10N 77 30W
Old Baldy Pk. = San Antonio, Mt., *U.S.A.* **161 L9** 34 17N 117 38W
Old Bar, *Australia* **129 A10** 31 58 S 152 35 E
Old Castile = Castilla y Leon □, *Spain* **42 D6** 42 0N 5 0W
Old Crow, *Canada* **138 B6** 67 30N 139 55W
Old Dale, *U.S.A.* **161 L11** 34 8N 115 47W
Old Dongola, *Sudan* **106 D3** 18 11N 30 44 E
Old Forge, *N.Y., U.S.A.* **151 C10** 43 43N 74 58W
Old Forge, *Pa., U.S.A.* **151 E9** 41 22N 75 45W
Old Fort B., *Bahamas* **9 b** 25 3N 77 32W
Old Harbor, *U.S.A.* **144 H9** 57 12N 153 18W
Old Perlican, *Canada* **141 C9** 48 5N 53 1W
Old Shinyanga, *Tanzania* **118 C3** 3 33 S 33 27 E
Old Speck Mt., *U.S.A.* **151 B14** 44 34N 70 57W
Old Town, *Fla., U.S.A.* **153 F7** 29 36N 82 59W
Old Town, *Maine, U.S.A.* **149 C11** 44 56N 68 39W
Old Washington, *U.S.A.* **150 F3** 40 2N 81 27W
Old Wives L., *Canada* **143 C7** 50 5N 106 0W
Oldbury, *U.K.* **21 F5** 51 38N 2 33W
Oldcastle, *Ireland* **23 C4** 53 46N 7 10W
Oldeani, *Tanzania* **118 C4** 3 22 S 35 35 E
Olden, *Norway* **18 C3** 61 49N 6 49 E
Oldenburg, *Niedersachsen, Germany* **30 B4** 53 9N 8 13 E
Oldenburg, *Schleswig-Holstein, Germany* **30 A6** 54 17N 10 52 E
Oldenzaal, *Neths.* **24 B6** 52 19N 6 53 E
Oldham, *U.K.* **20 D5** 53 33N 2 7W
Oldman →, *Canada* **142 D6** 49 57N 111 42W
Oldmeldrum, *U.K.* **22 D6** 57 20N 2 19W
Olds, *Canada* **142 C6** 51 50N 114 10W
Oldsmar, *U.S.A.* **153 G7** 28 2N 82 40W
Oldziyt, *Mongolia* **74 B5** 44 40N 109 1 E
Ole Rømer Land, *Greenland* **10 C8** 74 10N 24 30W
Olean, *U.S.A.* **150 D6** 42 5N 78 26W
Olecko, *Poland* **54 D9** 54 2N 22 31 E
Oléggio, *Italy* **44 C5** 45 36N 8 38 E
Oleiros, *Portugal* **42 F3** 39 56N 7 56W
Oleiros, *Spain* **42 B2** 43 20N 8 19W
Olekma →, *Russia* **67 C13** 60 22N 120 42 E
Olekminsk, *Russia* **67 C13** 60 25N 120 30 E
Oleksandriya, *Kirovohrad, Ukraine* **59 H7** 48 42N 33 3 E
Oleksandriya, *Rivne, Ukraine* **59 G4** 50 37N 26 19 E
Oleksandrovka, *Ukraine* **59 H7** 48 55N 32 20 E
Olema, *U.S.A.* **160 G4** 38 3N 122 47W
Ølen, *Norway* **18 E2** 59 36N 5 48 E
Olenegorsk, *Russia* **56 A5** 68 9N 33 18 E
Olenek, *Russia* **67 C12** 68 28N 112 18 E
Olenek →, *Russia* **67 B13** 73 0N 120 10 E
Olenino, *Russia* **58 D7** 56 15N 33 30 E
Oléron, Î. d', *France* **28 C2** 45 55N 1 15W
Oleśnica, *Poland* **55 G4** 51 13N 17 22 E
Olesno, *Poland* **55 H5** 50 51N 18 26 E
Olevsk, *Ukraine* **59 G4** 51 12N 27 39 E
Olga, *Russia* **67 E14** 43 50N 135 14 E
Olga, L., *Canada* **140 C4** 49 47N 77 15W
Olga, Mt., *Australia* **125 E5** 25 20 S 130 50 E
Ølgod, *Denmark* **17 J2** 55 49N 8 36 E
Olhão, *Portugal* **43 H3** 37 3N 7 48W
Olib, *Croatia* **45 D11** 44 23N 14 44 E
Oliena, *Italy* **46 B2** 40 16N 9 24 E
Oliete, *Spain* **40 D4** 41 1N 0 41W
Olifants →, *Africa* **117 C5** 23 57 S 31 58 E
Olifants →, *Namibia* **116 C2** 25 30 S 19 30 E
Olifantshoek, *S. Africa* **116 D3** 27 57 S 22 42 E
Ólimbos, *Greece* **49 F9** 35 44N 27 11 E
Ólimbos, Óros, *Greece* **50 F6** 40 6N 22 23 E
Olímpia, *Brazil* **175 A6** 20 44 S 48 54W
Olin, *U.S.A.* **156 C5** 42 0N 91 9W
Olinda, *Brazil* **170 C5** 8 1 S 34 51W
Olindiná, *Brazil* **170 D4** 11 22 S 38 21W
Olite, *Spain* **40 C3** 42 29N 1 40W
Oliva, *Argentina* **174 C3** 32 0 S 63 38W
Oliva, *Spain* **41 G4** 38 58N 0 9W
Oliva, Punta del, *Spain* **42 B5** 43 37N 5 28W
Oliva de la Frontera, *Spain* **43 G4** 38 17N 6 54W
Olivares, *Spain* **40 F2** 39 46N 2 20W
Olive Hill, *U.S.A.* **157 F13** 38 18N 83 13W
Olivehurst, *U.S.A.* **160 F5** 39 6N 121 34W
Oliveira, *Brazil* **171 F3** 20 39 S 44 50W
Oliveira de Azeméis, *Portugal* **42 E2** 40 49N 8 29W
Oliveira do Douro, *Portugal* **42 D2** 41 5N 8 2W
Oliveira dos Brejinhos, *Brazil* **171 D3** 12 19 S 42 54W
Olivenza, *Spain* **43 G3** 38 41N 7 9W
Oliver, *Canada* **142 D5** 49 13N 119 37W
Oliver L., *Canada* **143 B8** 56 56N 103 22W
Olivet, *France* **27 E8** 47 51N 1 55 E
Olivet, *U.S.A.* **157 B12** 42 27N 84 56W
Olivine Ra., *N.Z.* **131 E3** 44 15 S 168 30 E
Olivone, *Switz.* **33 C7** 46 32N 8 57 E
Olkhovka, *Russia* **60 F7** 49 48N 44 32 E
Olkusz, *Poland* **55 H6** 50 18N 19 33 E
Ollachea, *Peru* **172 C3** 13 49 S 70 29W
Ollagüe, *Chile* **174 A2** 21 15 S 68 10W
Ollon, *Switz.* **32 D3** 46 18N 7 0 E
Olloua, *Congo* **114 C2** 0 54 S 14 34 E
Olmaliq, *Uzbekistan* **65 C4** 40 50N 69 35 E
Olmedo, *Spain* **42 D6** 41 20N 4 43W
Olmeto, *France* **29 G12** 41 43N 8 55 E
Olmos, *Peru* **172 B2** 5 59 S 79 46W
Olney, *Ill., U.S.A.* **157 F8** 38 44N 88 5W
Olney, *Tex., U.S.A.* **155 J5** 33 22N 98 45W
Olofström, *Sweden* **17 H8** 56 17N 14 32 E
Ololi, *Congo* **114 C2** 0 15 S 14 36 E
Oloma, *Cameroon* **113 E7** 3 29N 11 19 E
Olomane →, *Canada* **141 B7** 50 14N 60 37W
Olombo, *Congo* **114 C3** 1 18 S 15 53 E
Olomouc, *Czech Rep.* **35 B10** 49 38N 17 12 E
Olonets, *Russia* **58 B7** 61 0N 32 54 E
Olongapo, *Phil.* **80 D3** 14 50N 120 18 E
Olonne-sur-Mer, *France* **28 B2** 46 32N 1 47W
Oloron, Gave d' →, *France* **28 E2** 43 33N 1 5W
Oloron-Ste-Marie, *France* **28 E3** 43 11N 0 38W
Olosega, *Amer. Samoa* **133 X25** 14 12 S 169 40W
Olot, *Spain* **40 C7** 42 11N 2 30 E
Olovo, *Bos.-H.* **52 F3** 44 8N 18 35 E
Olovyannaya, *Russia* **67 D12** 50 58N 115 35 E
Olowalu, *U.S.A.* **145 C5** 20 49N 156 38W
Oloy →, *Russia* **67 C16** 66 29N 159 29 E
Olsberg, *Germany* **30 D4** 51 21N 8 31 E
Olshammar, *Sweden* **17 F8** 58 45N 14 48 E
Olshanka, *Ukraine* **59 H6** 48 16N 30 58 E
Olshany, *Ukraine* **59 G8** 50 3N 35 53 E
Olsztyn, *Poland* **54 E7** 53 48N 20 29 E
Olsztynek, *Poland* **54 E7** 53 34N 20 19 E
Olt □, *Romania* **53 F9** 44 20N 24 30 E
Olt →, *Romania* **53 G9** 43 43N 24 51 E
Oltedal, *Norway* **18 F3** 58 49N 6 2 E
Olten, *Switz.* **32 B5** 47 21N 7 53 E
Olteniţa, *Romania* **53 F11** 44 7N 26 42 E
Olton, *U.S.A.* **155 H3** 34 11N 102 8W
Oltu, *Turkey* **101 B9** 40 35N 41 58 E
Oluanpi, *Taiwan* **77 G13** 21 54N 120 51 E
Olula del Rio, *Spain* **41 H2** 37 21N 2 18W
Olur, *Turkey* **101 B10** 40 49N 42 8 E
Olustee, *U.S.A.* **152 E7** 30 12N 82 26W
Olutanga, *Phil.* **81 H4** 7 26N 122 54 E
Olutanga I., *Phil.* **81 H4** 7 22N 122 52 E
Olvega, *Spain* **40 D2** 41 47N 2 0W
Olvera, *Spain* **43 J5** 36 55N 5 18W
Olymbos, *Cyprus* **39 E9** 35 21N 33 45 E
Olympia, *Greece* **48 D3** 37 39N 21 39 E
Olympia, *U.S.A.* **160 D4** 47 3N 122 53W
Olympic Dam, *S. Austral., Australia* **127 E2** 30 30 S 136 55 E
Olympic Dam, *S. Austral., Australia* **128 A2** 30 29 S 136 52 E
Olympic Mts., *U.S.A.* **160 C3** 47 55N 123 45W
Olympic Nat. Park, *U.S.A.* **160 C3** 47 48N 123 30W
Olympus, *Cyprus* **39 F8** 34 56N 32 52 E
Olympus, Mt. = Ólimbos, Óros, *Greece* **50 F6** 40 6N 22 23 E
Olympus, Mt. = Uludağ, *Turkey* **51 F13** 40 4N 29 13 E
Olympus, Mt., *U.S.A.* **160 C3** 47 48N 123 43W
Olyphant, *U.S.A.* **151 E9** 41 27N 75 36W
Om →, *Russia* **66 D8** 54 59N 73 22 E
Om Hajer, *Eritrea* **107 E4** 14 20N 36 41 E
Om Koi, *Thailand* **86 D2** 17 48N 98 22 E
Ōma, *Japan* **70 D10** 41 45N 141 5 E
Ōmachi, *Japan* **73 A9** 36 30N 137 50 E
Omae-Zaki, *Japan* **73 C10** 34 36N 138 14 E
Ōmagari, *Japan* **70 E10** 39 27N 140 29 E
Omagh, *U.K.* **23 B4** 54 36N 7 19W
Omagh □, *U.K.* **23 B4** 54 35N 7 15W
Omaha, *U.S.A.* **154 E7** 41 17N 95 58W
Omak, *U.S.A.* **158 B4** 48 25N 119 31W
Omalos, *Greece* **39 E4** 35 19N 23 55 E
Omalur, *India* **95 J4** 11 44N 78 4 E
Oman ■, *Asia* **99 B7** 23 0N 58 0 E
Oman, G. of, *Asia* **97 E8** 24 30N 58 30 E
Omapere, *N.Z.* **130 B2** 35 37 S 173 25 E
Omar Combon, *Somali Rep.* **120 D3** 3 10N 45 47 E
Omaruru, *Namibia* **116 C2** 21 26 S 16 0 E
Omaruru →, *Namibia* **116 C1** 22 7 S 14 15 E
Omate, *Peru* **172 D3** 16 45 S 71 0W
Ombai, Selat, *Indonesia* **82 C2** 8 30 S 124 50 E
Omboué, *Gabon* **114 C1** 1 35 S 9 15 E
Ombrone →, *Italy* **44 F8** 42 42N 11 5 E
Omchi, *Chad* **109 D3** 21 22N 17 53 E
Omdurmân, *Sudan* **107 D3** 15 40N 32 28 E
Ōme, *Japan* **73 B11** 35 47N 139 15 E
Omega, *U.S.A.* **152 D6** 31 21N 83 36W
Omegna, *Italy* **44 C5** 45 53N 8 24 E
Omemee, *Canada* **150 B6** 44 18N 78 33W
Omeo, *Australia* **129 D7** 37 6 S 147 36 E
Omeonga, *Dem. Rep. of the Congo* **118 C1** 3 40 S 24 22 E
Ometepe, I. de, *Nic.* **164 D2** 11 32N 85 35W
Ometepec, *Mexico* **163 D5** 16 39N 98 23W
Ōmi-Shima, *Ehime, Japan* **72 C5** 34 15N 133 0 E
Ōmi-Shima, *Yamaguchi, Japan* **72 C3** 34 25N 131 9 E
Omihachiman, *Japan* **73 B8** 35 7N 136 3 E
Ominato, *Japan* **70 D10** 41 17N 141 10 E
Omineca →, *Canada* **142 B4** 56 3N 124 16W
Omiš, *Croatia* **45 E13** 43 28N 16 40 E
Omišalj, *Croatia* **45 C11** 45 13N 14 32 E
Omitara, *Namibia* **116 C2** 22 16 S 18 2 E
Ōmiya, *Japan* **73 B11** 35 54N 139 38 E
Ommaney, C., *U.S.A.* **144 H14** 56 10N 134 40W
Ommen, *Neths.* **24 B6** 52 31N 6 26 E
Ömnögovĭ □, *Mongolia* **74 C3** 43 15N 104 0 E
Omo →, *Ethiopia* **107 F4** 6 25N 36 10 E
Omo Nat. Park, *Ethiopia* **107 F4** 5 54N 35 55 E
Omo Valley, *Ethiopia* **107 F4** 5 7N 36 0 E
Omodeo, L., *Italy* **46 B1** 40 8N 8 56 E
Omodhos, *Cyprus* **39 F8** 34 51N 32 48 E
Omoï, *Congo* **114 C2** 2 56 S 13 13 E
Omoko, *Nigeria* **113 D6** 5 19N 6 40 E
Omolon →, *Russia* **67 C16** 68 42N 158 36 E
Omona, *Solomon Is.* **133 L10** 7 30 S 158 43 E
Omono-Gawa →, *Japan* **70 E10** 39 46N 140 3 E
Omsk, *Russia* **66 D8** 55 0N 73 12 E
Omsukchan, *Russia* **67 C16** 62 32N 155 48 E
Ōmu, *Japan* **70 B11** 44 34N 142 58 E
Omul, Vf., *Romania* **53 E10** 45 27N 25 29 E
Omulew →, *Poland* **55 E8** 53 5N 21 33 E
Ōmura, *Japan* **72 E1** 32 56N 129 57 E
Ōmura-Wan, *Japan* **72 E1** 32 57N 129 52 E
Omuramba Omatako →, *Namibia* **116 B2** 17 45 S 20 25 E
Omuramba Ovambo →, *Namibia* **116 B2** 18 45 S 16 59 E
Omurtag, *Bulgaria* **51 C10** 43 8N 26 26 E
Ōmuta, *Japan* **72 D2** 33 5N 130 26 E
Omutninsk, *Russia* **64 B4** 58 45N 52 4 E
On-ma-thi, *Burma* **90 D6** 22 17N 96 41 E
On-Take, *Japan* **72 F2** 31 35N 130 39 E
Oña, *Spain* **42 C7** 42 43N 3 25W
Ona, *U.S.A.* **153 H8** 27 29N 81 55W
Ona Dikonde, *Dem. Rep. of the Congo* **114 C4** 3 51 S 24 11 E
Onaga, *U.S.A.* **154 F6** 39 29N 96 10W
Onalaska, *U.S.A.* **154 D9** 43 53N 91 14W
Onancock, *U.S.A.* **148 G8** 37 43N 75 45W
Onang, *Indonesia* **82 B1** 3 2 S 118 49 E
Onangue, L., *Gabon* **114 C1** 0 57 S 10 4 E
Onaping L., *Canada* **140 C3** 47 3N 81 30W
Onarga, *U.S.A.* **157 D8** 40 43N 88 1W
Oñati, *Spain* **40 B2** 43 3N 2 25W
Onavas, *Mexico* **162 B3** 28 28N 109 30W
Onawa, *U.S.A.* **154 D6** 42 2N 96 6W
Oncócua, *Angola* **116 B1** 16 30 S 13 25 E
Onda, *Spain* **40 F4** 39 55N 0 17W
Ondaejin, *N. Korea* **75 D15** 41 34N 129 40 E
Ondangwa, *Namibia* **116 B2** 17 57 S 16 4 E
Ondarroa, *Spain* **40 B2** 43 19N 2 25W
Ondas →, *Brazil* **171 D3** 12 8 S 44 55W
Ondava →, *Slovak Rep.* **35 C14** 48 27N 21 48 E
Ondjiva, *Angola* **116 B2** 16 48 S 15 50 E
Ondo, *Japan* **72 C4** 34 11N 132 32 E
Ondo, *Nigeria* **113 D5** 7 4N 4 47 E
Ondo □, *Nigeria* **113 D6** 6 45N 5 0 E
Öndörshil, *Mongolia* **74 B5** 45 13N 108 5 E
Öndverðarnes, *Iceland* **11 C2** 64 52N 24 0W
One Tree, *Australia* **127 E3** 34 11 S 144 43 E
Oneata, *Fiji* **133 B3** 18 26 S 178 25W
Oneco, *U.S.A.* **153 H7** 27 25N 82 31W
Onega, *Russia* **56 B6** 64 0N 38 10 E
Onega →, *Russia* **56 B6** 63 58N 38 2 E
Onega, G. of = Onezhskaya Guba, *Russia* **56 B6** 64 24N 36 38 E
Onega, L. = Onezhskoye Ozero, *Russia* **58 B8** 61 44N 35 22 E
Onehunga, *N.Z.* **130 C3** 36 55 S 174 48 E
Oneida, *Ill., U.S.A.* **156 C6** 41 4N 90 13W
Oneida, *N.Y., U.S.A.* **151 C9** 43 6N 75 39W
Oneida L., *U.S.A.* **151 C9** 43 12N 75 54W
O'Neill, *U.S.A.* **154 D5** 42 27N 98 39W
Onekotan, Ostrov, *Russia* **67 E16** 49 25N 154 45 E
Onema, *Dem. Rep. of the Congo* **118 C1** 4 35 S 24 30 E
Oneonta, *U.S.A.* **151 D9** 42 27N 75 4W
Onerahi, *N.Z.* **130 B3** 35 45 S 174 22 E
Oneşti, *Romania* **53 D11** 46 17N 26 47 E
Onezhskaya Guba, *Russia* **56 B6** 64 24N 36 38 E
Onezhskoye Ozero, *Russia* **58 B8** 61 44N 35 22 E
Ongarue, *N.Z.* **130 E4** 38 42 S 175 19 E
Ongea Levu = Ogea Levu, *Fiji* **133 B3** 19 8 S 178 24W
Ongers →, *S. Africa* **116 E3** 31 4 S 23 13 E
Ongerup, *Australia* **125 F2** 33 58 S 118 28 E
Ongjin, *N. Korea* **75 F13** 37 56N 125 21 E
Ongkharak, *Thailand* **86 E3** 14 8N 101 1 E
Ongniud Qi, *China* **75 C10** 43 0N 118 38 E
Ongoka, *Dem. Rep. of the Congo* **118 C2** 1 20S 26 0 E
Ongole, *India* **95 G5** 15 33N 80 2 E
Ongon = Havirga, *Mongolia* **74 B7** 45 41N 113 5 E
Ongouendjo, *Gabon* **114 C1** 1 23 S 9 5 E
Oni, *Georgia* **61 J6** 42 33N 43 26 E
Onida, *U.S.A.* **154 C4** 44 42N 100 4W
Onilahy →, *Madag.* **117 C7** 23 34 S 43 45 E
Onitsha, *Nigeria* **113 D6** 6 6N 6 42 E
Ono, *Fiji* **133 B2** 18 55 S 178 29 E
Ono, *Fukui, Japan* **73 B8** 35 59N 136 29 E
Ono, *Hyōgo, Japan* **72 C6** 34 51N 134 56 E
Onoda, *Japan* **72 C3** 33 59N 131 11 E
Onohara, *Japan* **72 C5** 34 5N 133 40 E
Onoke, L., *N.Z.* **130 H4** 41 22 S 175 8 E
Onomichi, *Japan* **72 C5** 34 25N 133 12 E
Onpyŏng-ni, *S. Korea* **75 H14** 33 25N 126 55 E
Ons, I. de, *Spain* **42 C2** 42 23N 8 55W
Onslow, *Australia* **124 D2** 21 40 S 115 12 E
Onslow B., *U.S.A.* **149 H7** 34 20N 77 15W
Ontake-San, *Japan* **73 B9** 35 53N 137 29 E
Ontar, *Vanuatu* **133 D5** 14 17 S 167 27 E
Ontario, *Calif., U.S.A.* **161 L9** 34 4N 117 39W
Ontario, *Oreg., U.S.A.* **158 D5** 44 2N 116 58W
Ontario □, *Canada* **140 B2** 48 0N 83 0W
Ontario, L., *N. Amer.* **150 C7** 43 20N 78 0W
Ontinyent, *Spain* **41 G4** 38 50N 0 35W
Ontonagon, *U.S.A.* **154 B10** 46 52N 89 19W
Ontur, *Spain* **41 G3** 38 38N 1 29W
Onverwacht, *Surinam* **169 B6** 5 35N 55 11W
Onyx, *U.S.A.* **161 K8** 35 41N 118 14W
Oodnadatta, *Australia* **127 D2** 27 33 S 135 30 E
Ookala, *U.S.A.* **145 C6** 20 1N 155 17W
Ooldea, *Australia* **125 F5** 30 27 S 131 50 E
Oombulgurri, *Australia* **124 C4** 15 15 S 127 45 E
Oorindi, *Australia* **126 C3** 20 40 S 141 1 E
Oost-Vlaanderen □, *Belgium* **24 C3** 51 5N 3 50 E
Oostende, *Belgium* **24 C2** 51 15N 2 54 E
Oosterhout, *Neths.* **24 C4** 51 39N 4 47 E
Oosterschelde →, *Neths.* **24 C4** 51 33N 4 0 E
Oosterwolde, *Neths.* **24 B6** 53 0N 6 17 E
Ootacamund = Udagamandalam, *India* **95 J3** 11 30N 76 44 E
Ootha, *Australia* **129 B7** 33 6 S 147 29 E
Ootsa L., *Canada* **142 C3** 53 50N 126 2W
Opaka, *Bulgaria* **51 C10** 43 28N 26 10 E
Opala, *Dem. Rep. of the Congo* **118 C1** 0 40 S 24 20 E
Opalenica, *Poland* **55 F3** 52 18N 16 24 E
Opan, *Bulgaria* **51 D9** 42 13N 25 41 E
Opanake, *Sri Lanka* **95 L5** 6 35N 80 40 E
Opapa, *N.Z.* **130 F5** 39 47 S 176 42 E
Opasatika, *Canada* **140 C3** 49 30N 82 50W
Opasquia Prov. Park, *Canada* **140 B1** 53 33N 93 5W
Opatija, *Croatia* **45 C11** 45 21N 14 17 E
Opatów, *Poland* **55 H8** 50 50N 21 27 E
Opava, *Czech Rep.* **35 B10** 49 57N 17 58 E
Opelika, *U.S.A.* **152 C4** 32 39N 85 23W
Opelousas, *U.S.A.* **155 K8** 30 32N 92 5W
Opémisca, L., *Canada* **140 C5** 49 56N 74 52W
Opheim, *U.S.A.* **158 B10** 48 51N 106 24W
Ophir, *U.S.A.* **144 E8** 63 10N 156 31W
Ophthalmia Ra., *Australia* **124 D2** 23 15 S 119 30 E
Opi, *Nigeria* **113 D6** 6 36N 7 28 E
Opihikao, *U.S.A.* **145 D7** 19 26N 154 53W
Opinaca →, *Canada* **140 B4** 52 15N 78 2W
Opinaca, Rés., *Canada* **140 B4** 52 39N 76 20W
Opinnagau →, *Canada* **140 B3** 54 12N 82 25W
Opiscoteo, L., *Canada* **141 B6** 53 10N 68 10W
Opobo, *Nigeria* **113 E6** 4 35N 7 34 E
Opochka, *Russia* **58 D5** 56 42N 28 45 E
Opoczno, *Poland* **55 G7** 51 22N 20 18 E
Opol, *Phil.* **81 G5** 8 31N 124 34 E
Opole, *Poland* **55 H4** 50 42N 17 58 E
Opole Lubelskie, *Poland* **55 G8** 51 9N 21 58 E
Opolskie □, *Poland* **55 H5** 50 30N 18 0 E
Opon = Lapu-Lapu, *Phil.* **81 F4** 10 20N 123 55 E
Opononо L., *Namibia* **116 B2** 18 8 S 15 45 E
Oporto = Porto, *Portugal* **42 D2** 41 8N 8 40W
Opotiki, *N.Z.* **130 E6** 38 1 S 177 19 E
Opp, *U.S.A.* **152 D3** 31 17N 86 16W

Oppdal, *Norway* 15 E13 62 35N 9 41 E
Oppido Mamertina, *Italy* 47 D8 38 16N 15 59 E
Oppland □, *Norway* 18 C6 61 15N 9 40 E
Opportunity, *U.S.A.* 158 C5 47 39N 117 15W
Oprişor, *Romania* 52 F8 44 17N 23 5 E
Oprtalj, *Croatia* 45 C10 45 23N 13 50 E
Opua, *N.Z.* 130 B3 35 19 S 174 9 E
Opunake, *N.Z.* 130 F2 39 26 S 173 52 E
Opuwo, *Namibia* 116 B1 18 3 S 13 45 E
Opuzen, *Croatia* 45 E14 43 1N 17 34 E
Oquawka, *U.S.A.* 156 D6 40 56N 90 57W
Ora, *Cyprus* 39 F9 34 51N 33 12 E
Oracle, *U.S.A.* 159 K8 32 37N 110 46W
Oracuzar, *Peru* 168 D2 4 42 S 78 6W
Oradea, *Romania* 52 C6 47 2N 21 58 E
Öræfajökull, *Iceland* 11 C10 64 2N 16 39W
Orahovac, *Kosovo, Yug.* 50 D4 42 24N 20 40 E
Orahovica, *Croatia* 52 E2 45 35N 17 52 E
Orai, *India* 93 G8 25 58N 79 30 E
Oraison, *France* 29 E9 43 55N 5 55 E
Oral = Zhayyq →, *Kazakstan* 57 E9 47 0N 51 48 E
Oral, *Kazakstan* 60 E10 51 20N 51 20 E
Oran, *Algeria* 111 A4 35 45N 0 39W
Orange, *Australia* 129 B8 33 15 S 149 7 E
Orange, *France* 29 D8 44 8N 4 47 E
Orange, *Calif., U.S.A.* 161 M9 33 47N 117 51W
Orange, *Mass., U.S.A.* 151 D12 42 35N 72 19W
Orange, *Tex., U.S.A.* 155 K8 30 6N 93 44W
Orange, *Va., U.S.A.* 148 F6 38 15N 78 7W
Orange →, *S. Africa* 116 D2 28 41 S 16 28 E
Orange, C., *Brazil* 169 C7 4 20N 51 30W
Orange City, *U.S.A.* 153 G8 28 57N 81 18W
Orange Cove, *U.S.A.* 160 J7 36 38N 119 19W
Orange Free State = Free State □, *S. Africa* 116 D4 28 30 S 27 0 E
Orange Grove, *U.S.A.* 155 M6 27 58N 97 56W
Orange L., *U.S.A.* 153 F7 29 25N 82 13W
Orange Park, *U.S.A.* 152 E8 30 10N 81 42W
Orange Walk, *Belize* 163 D7 18 6N 88 33W
Orangeburg, *U.S.A.* 152 B9 33 30N 80 52W
Orangeville, *Canada* 140 D3 43 55N 80 5W
Orangeville, *U.S.A.* 156 B7 42 28N 89 39W
Orango, *Guinea-Biss.* 112 C1 11 5N 16 0W
Orani, *Phil.* 80 D3 14 49N 120 32 E
Oranienburg, *Germany* 30 C9 52 45N 13 14 E
Oranje = Orange →, *S. Africa* 116 D2 28 41 S 16 28 E
Oranje Vrystaat = Free State □, *S. Africa* 116 D4 28 30 S 27 0 E
Oranjemund, *Namibia* 116 D2 28 38 S 16 29 E
Oranjerivier, *S. Africa* 116 D3 29 40 S 24 12 E
Oranjestad, *Aruba* 165 D5 12 32N 70 2W
Orap, *Vanuatu* 133 E5 15 58 S 167 20 E
Orarak, *Sudan* 107 F3 6 15N 32 23 E
Oras, *Phil.* 80 E5 12 9N 125 28 E
Orašje, *Bos.-H.* 52 E3 45 1N 18 42 E
Orăştie, *Romania* 53 E8 45 50N 23 10 E
Oraşul Stalin = Braşov, *Romania* 53 E10 45 38N 25 35 E
Orava →, *Slovak Rep.* 35 B12 49 9N 19 8 E
Orava, Vodna nádrž, *Slovak Rep.* 35 B12 49 25N 19 35 E
Oraviţa, *Romania* 52 E6 45 2N 21 43 E
Orawia, *N.Z.* 131 G2 46 1 S 167 50 E
Orb →, *France* 28 E7 43 15N 3 18 E
Orba →, *Italy* 44 D5 44 53N 8 37 E
Ørbæk, *Denmark* 17 J4 55 17N 10 39 E
Orbe, *Switz.* 32 C3 46 43N 6 32 E
Orbec, *France* 26 C7 49 1N 0 23 E
Orbetello, *Italy* 45 F8 42 27N 11 13 E
Órbigo →, *Spain* 42 C5 42 5N 5 42W
Orbisonia, *U.S.A.* 150 F7 40 15N 77 54W
Orbost, *Australia* 129 D8 37 40 S 148 29 E
Örbyhus, *Sweden* 16 D11 60 15N 17 43 E
Orcas I., *U.S.A.* 160 B4 48 42N 122 56W
Orce, *Spain* 41 H2 37 44N 2 28W
Orce →, *Spain* 41 H2 37 44N 2 28W
Orchard City, *U.S.A.* 159 G10 38 50N 107 58W
Orchies, *France* 27 B10 50 28N 3 14 E
Orchila, I., *Venezuela* 165 D6 11 48N 66 10W
Órcia →, *Italy* 45 F8 42 58N 11 21 E
Orco →, *Italy* 44 C4 45 10N 7 52 E
Orcopampa, *Peru* 172 D3 15 20 S 72 23W
Orcutt, *U.S.A.* 161 L6 34 52N 120 27W
Ord, *U.S.A.* 154 E5 41 36N 98 56W
Ord →, *Australia* 124 C4 15 33 S 128 15 E
Ord, Mt., *Australia* 124 C4 17 20 S 125 34 E
Ordenes = Ordes, *Spain* 42 B2 43 5N 8 29W
Orderville, *U.S.A.* 159 H7 37 17N 112 38W
Ordes, *Spain* 42 B2 43 5N 8 29W
Ording = St-Peter-Ording, *Germany* 30 A4 54 20N 8 36 E
Ordos = Mu Us Shamo, *China* 74 E5 39 0N 109 0 E
Ordu, *Turkey* 100 B7 40 55N 37 53 E
Ordubad, *Azerbaijan* 101 C12 38 54N 46 1 E
Orduña, *Álava, Spain* 40 C2 42 58N 2 58W
Orduña, *Granada, Spain* 43 H7 37 20N 3 30W
Ordway, *U.S.A.* 154 F3 38 13N 103 46W
Ordzhonikidze = Vladikavkaz, *Russia* 61 J7 43 0N 44 35 E
Ordzhonikidze, *Kazakstan* 64 E8 52 27N 61 39 E
Ordzhonikidze, *Ukraine* 59 J8 47 39N 34 3 E
Ordzhonikidzeabad = Kofarnikhon, *Tajikistan* 65 D4 38 34N 69 1 E
Ore, *Dem. Rep. of the Congo* 118 B2 3 17N 29 30 E
Ore Mts. = Erzgebirge, *Germany* 30 E8 50 27N 12 55 E
Orealla, *Guyana* 169 B6 5 15N 57 23W
Orebić, *Croatia* 45 F14 43 0N 17 11 E
Örebro, *Sweden* 16 E9 59 20N 15 18 E
Örebro län □, *Sweden* 16 E8 59 27N 15 0 E
Oregon, *Ill., U.S.A.* 156 B7 42 1N 89 20W
Oregon, *Ohio, U.S.A.* 157 C13 41 38N 83 25W
Oregon, *Wis., U.S.A.* 156 B7 42 56N 89 23W
Oregon □, *U.S.A.* 158 E3 44 0N 121 0W
Oregon City, *U.S.A.* 160 E4 45 21N 122 36W
Öregrund, *Sweden* 16 D12 60 21N 18 30 E
Öregrundsgrepen, *Sweden* 16 D12 60 25N 18 15 E
Orekhov = Orikhiv, *Ukraine* 59 J8 47 30N 35 48 E
Orekhovo-Zuyevo, *Russia* 58 E10 55 50N 38 55 E
Orel, *Russia* 59 F9 52 57N 36 3 E
Orel →, *Ukraine* 59 H8 48 40N 34 39 E
Orellana, *Spain* 43 F5 39 1N 5 32W
Orellana, Canal de, *Spain* 43 F5 39 2N 6 0W
Orellana, Embalse de, *Spain* 43 F5 39 5N 5 10W
Orem, *U.S.A.* 158 F8 40 19N 111 42W
Ören, *Turkey* 49 D9 37 3N 27 57 E
Orenburg, *Russia* 64 F5 51 45N 55 6 E
Örencik, *Turkey* 49 B11 39 16N 29 33 E
Orense = Ourense, *Spain* 42 C3 42 19N 7 55W
Orense □, *Spain* 42 C3 42 15N 7 51W
Orepuki, *N.Z.* 131 G2 46 19 S 167 46 E
Orestiás, *Greece* 51 E10 41 30N 26 33 E
Orestos Pereyra, *Mexico* 162 B3 26 31N 105 40W
Øresund, *Europe* 17 J6 55 45N 12 45 E
Oreti →, *N.Z.* 131 G3 46 28 S 168 14 E
Orford Ness, *U.K.* 21 E9 52 5N 1 35 E
Organà = Organyà, *Spain* 40 C6 42 13N 1 20 E
Organos, Pta. de los, *Canary Is.* 9 e1 28 12N 17 17W
Organyà, *Spain* 40 C6 42 13N 1 20 E
Orgaz, *Spain* 43 F7 39 39N 3 53W
Ørgenvika, *Norway* 18 D6 60 17N 9 42 E
Orgeyev = Orhei, *Moldova* 53 C13 47 24N 28 50 E
Orgūn, *Afghan.* 91 B3 32 55N 69 12 E
Orhaneli, *Turkey* 51 G12 39 54N 28 59 E
Orhaneli →, *Turkey* 51 G12 39 50N 28 55 E
Orhangazi, *Turkey* 51 F13 40 29N 29 18 E
Orhei, *Moldova* 53 C13 47 24N 28 50 E
Orhon Gol →, *Mongolia* 68 A5 50 21N 106 0 E
Ória, *Italy* 47 B10 40 30N 17 38 E
Orida, *Niger* 111 D7 21 20N 12 15 E
Oriental, Cordillera, *Bolivia* 173 D4 17 0 S 66 0W
Oriental, Cordillera, *Colombia* 168 B3 6 0N 73 0W
Oriental, Grand Erg, *Algeria* 111 C6 30 0N 6 30 E
Orientale □, *Dem. Rep. of the Congo* 118 B2 2 20N 26 0 E
Oriente, *Argentina* 174 D3 38 44 S 60 37W
Orihuela, *Spain* 41 G4 38 7N 0 55W
Orihuela del Tremedal, *Spain* 40 E3 40 33N 1 39W
Orikhiv, *Ukraine* 59 J8 47 30N 35 48 E
Orikum, *Albania* 50 F3 40 20N 19 26 E
Orillia, *Canada* 140 D4 44 40N 79 24W
Orinduik, *Guyana* 169 C5 4 40N 60 3W
Orinoco →, *Venezuela* 169 B5 9 15N 61 30W
Orion, *Canada* 143 D6 49 27N 110 49W
Orion, *Ala., U.S.A.* 152 D4 31 58N 86 0W
Orion, *Ill., U.S.A.* 156 C6 41 21N 90 23W
Oriskany, *U.S.A.* 151 C9 43 10N 75 20W
Orissa □, *India* 94 E7 20 0N 84 0 E
Orissaare, *Estonia* 15 G20 58 34N 23 5 E
Oristano, *Italy* 46 C1 39 54N 8 36 E
Oristano, G. di, *Italy* 46 C1 39 50N 8 29 E
Orituco →, *Venezuela* 168 B4 8 45N 67 27W
Oriximina, *Brazil* 169 D6 1 45 S 55 52W
Orizaba, *Mexico* 163 D5 18 51N 97 6W
Orizare, *Bulgaria* 51 D11 42 44N 27 39 E
Orizona, *Brazil* 171 E2 17 3 S 48 18W
Ørje, *Norway* 18 E8 59 29N 11 39 E
Orjen, *Bos.-H.* 50 D2 42 35N 18 34 E
Orjiva, *Spain* 43 J7 36 53N 3 24W
Orkanger, *Norway* 14 E13 63 18N 9 52 E
Örkelljunga, *Sweden* 17 H7 56 17N 13 17 E
Örken, *Sweden* 17 G9 57 6N 15 1 E
Örkény, *Hungary* 52 C4 47 9N 19 26 E
Orkla →, *Norway* 14 E13 63 18N 9 51 E
Orkney, *S. Africa* 116 D4 26 58 S 26 40 E
Orkney □, *U.K.* 22 B5 59 2N 3 13W
Orkney Is., *U.K.* 22 B6 59 0N 3 0W
Orland, *Calif., U.S.A.* 160 F4 39 45N 122 12W
Orland, *Ind., U.S.A.* 157 C11 41 47N 85 12W
Orlando, *U.S.A.* 149 L5 28 33N 81 23W
Orlando, C. d', *Italy* 47 D7 38 10N 14 43 E
Orléanais, *France* 27 E9 48 0N 2 0 E
Orléans, *France* 27 E8 47 54N 1 52 E
Orleans, *Ind., U.S.A.* 157 F10 38 40N 86 27W
Orleans, *Vt., U.S.A.* 151 B12 44 49N 72 12W
Orléans, I. d', *Canada* 141 C5 46 54N 70 58W
Orlice →, *Czech Rep.* 34 A8 50 13N 15 50 E
Orlov, *Slovak Rep.* 35 B13 49 17N 20 51 E
Orlov Gay, *Russia* 60 E9 50 56N 48 19 E
Orlová, *Czech Rep.* 35 B11 49 51N 18 26 E
Orlovat, *Serbia, Yug.* 52 E5 45 14N 20 33 E
Orlovka, *Kyrgyzstan* 65 B7 42 45N 75 36 E
Ormara, *Pakistan* 91 D2 25 16N 64 33 E
Ormea, *Italy* 44 D4 44 9N 7 54 E
Ormília, *Greece* 50 F7 40 16N 23 39 E
Ormoc, *Phil.* 81 F5 11 0N 124 37 E
Ormond, *N.Z.* 130 E6 38 33 S 177 56 E
Ormond Beach, *U.S.A.* 149 L5 29 17N 81 3W
Ormond by the Sea, *U.S.A.* 153 F8 29 21N 81 4W
Ormondville, *N.Z.* 130 G5 40 5 S 176 19 E
Órmos Keríou, *Greece* 39 D2 37 42N 20 53 E
Ormož, *Slovenia* 45 B13 46 25N 16 10 E
Ormskirk, *U.K.* 20 D5 53 35N 2 54W
Ormstown, *Canada* 151 A11 45 8N 74 0W
Ornans, *France* 27 E13 47 7N 6 10 E
Ornavasso, *Italy* 33 E6 45 58N 8 24 E
Orne □, *France* 26 D7 48 40N 0 5 E
Orne →, *France* 26 C6 49 18N 0 15W
Orneta, *Poland* 54 D7 54 8N 20 9 E
Ornö, *Sweden* 16 E12 59 4N 18 24 E
Örnsköldsvik, *Sweden* 16 A12 63 17N 18 40 E
Oro, *N. Korea* 75 D14 40 1N 127 27 E
Oro →, *Mexico* 162 B3 25 35N 105 2W
Oro Grande, *U.S.A.* 161 L9 34 36N 117 20W
Oro Valley, *U.S.A.* 159 K8 32 26N 110 58W
Orobie, Alpi, *Italy* 44 B6 46 7N 10 0 E
Orocué, *Colombia* 168 C3 4 48N 71 20W
Orodara, *Burkina Faso* 112 C4 11 0N 4 55W
Orodo, *Nigeria* 113 D6 5 34N 7 4 E
Orofino, *U.S.A.* 158 C5 46 29N 116 15W
Orohena, Mt., *Tahiti* 133 S16 17 37 S 149 28W
Orol Dengizi = Aral Sea, *Asia* 66 E7 44 30N 60 0 E
Oromocto, *Canada* 141 C6 45 54N 66 29W
Oron, *Nigeria* 113 E6 4 48N 8 14 E
Oron, *Switz.* 32 C3 46 34N 6 50 E
Orongo, *Chile* 172 b 27 11 S 109 27W
Orono, *Canada* 150 C6 43 59N 78 37W
Orono, *U.S.A.* 149 C11 44 53N 68 40W
Oronsay, *U.K.* 22 E2 56 1N 6 15W
Oropesa, *Spain* 42 F5 39 57N 5 10W
Oroqen Zizhiqi, *China* 69 A7 50 34N 123 43 E
Oroquieta, *Phil.* 81 G4 8 32N 123 44 E
Orós, *Brazil* 170 C4 6 15 S 38 55W
Orosei, *Italy* 46 B2 40 23N 9 42 E
Orosei, G. di, *Italy* 46 B2 40 15N 9 44 E
Orosháza, *Hungary* 52 D5 46 32N 20 42 E
Oroszlány, *Hungary* 52 C3 47 29N 18 19 E
Orote Pen., *Guam* 133 R15 13 26N 144 38 E
Orotukan, *Russia* 67 C16 62 16N 151 42 E
Oroville, *Calif., U.S.A.* 160 F5 39 31N 121 33W
Oroville, *Wash., U.S.A.* 158 B4 48 56N 119 26W
Oroville, L., *U.S.A.* 160 F5 39 33N 121 29W
Orrefors, *Sweden* 17 H9 56 50N 15 45 E
Orrick, *U.S.A.* 156 E2 39 13N 94 7W
Orroroo, *Australia* 128 B3 32 43 S 138 38 E
Orrviken, *Sweden* 16 A8 63 6N 14 26 E
Orrville, *U.S.A.* 150 F3 40 50N 81 46W
Orsa, *Sweden* 16 C8 61 7N 14 37 E
Orsara di Púglia, *Italy* 47 A8 41 17N 15 16 E
Orsasjön, *Sweden* 16 C8 61 7N 14 37 E
Orsha, *Belarus* 58 E6 54 30N 30 25 E
Orsières, *Switz.* 32 D4 46 2N 7 9 E
Örsjö, *Sweden* 17 H9 56 42N 15 45 E
Orsk, *Russia* 64 F7 51 12N 58 34 E
Orşova, *Romania* 52 F7 44 41N 22 25 E
Ørsta, *Norway* 18 B3 62 13N 6 8 E
Ørsted, *Denmark* 17 H4 56 30N 10 20 E
Örsundsbro, *Sweden* 16 E11 59 44N 17 18 E
Orta, L. d', *Italy* 44 C5 45 49N 8 24 E
Orta Nova, *Italy* 47 A8 41 19N 15 42 E
Ortaca, *Turkey* 49 E10 36 49N 28 45 E
Ortakent, *Turkey* 49 D9 37 5N 27 21 E
Ortaklar, *Turkey* 49 D9 37 53N 27 30 E
Ortaköy, *Çorum, Turkey* 100 B6 40 16N 35 15 E
Ortaköy, *Niğde, Turkey* 100 C6 38 44N 34 3 E
Orte, *Italy* 45 F9 42 27N 12 23 E
Ortegal, C., *Spain* 42 B3 43 43N 7 52W
Orteguaza →, *Colombia* 168 C2 0 43N 75 16W
Orthez, *France* 28 E3 43 29N 0 48W
Ortigueira, *Spain* 42 B3 43 40N 7 50W
Orting, *U.S.A.* 160 C4 47 6N 122 12W
Ortisei, *Italy* 45 B8 46 34N 11 40 E
Ortles, *Italy* 44 B7 46 31N 10 33 E
Ortnevik, *Norway* 18 C3 61 8N 6 7 E
Orto-Tokoy, *Kyrgyzstan* 65 B8 42 20N 76 1 E
Ortón →, *Bolivia* 172 C4 10 50 S 67 0W
Ortona, *Italy* 45 F11 42 21N 14 24 E
Ortonville, *U.S.A.* 154 C6 45 19N 96 27W
Orūmīyeh, *Iran* 101 D11 37 40N 45 0 E
Orūmīyeh, Daryācheh-ye, *Iran* 101 D11 37 50N 45 30 E
Orune, *Italy* 46 B2 40 24N 9 22 E
Oruro, *Bolivia* 172 D4 18 0 S 67 9W
Oruro □, *Bolivia* 172 D4 18 40 S 67 30W
Orust, *Sweden* 17 F5 58 10N 11 40 E
Oruzgān □, *Afghan.* 91 B2 33 30N 66 0 E
Orvault, *France* 26 E5 47 17N 1 38W
Orvieto, *Italy* 45 F9 42 43N 12 7 E
Orwell, *N.Y., U.S.A.* 151 C9 43 35N 75 50W
Orwell, *Ohio, U.S.A.* 150 E4 41 32N 80 52W
Orwell →, *U.K.* 21 F9 51 59N 1 18 E
Orwigsburg, *U.S.A.* 151 F8 40 38N 76 6W
Oryakhovo, *Bulgaria* 50 C7 43 40N 23 57 E
Orzinuovi, *Italy* 44 C6 45 24N 9 55 E
Orzyc →, *Poland* 55 F8 52 46N 21 14 E
Orzysz, *Poland* 54 E8 53 50N 21 58 E
Os, *Norway* 18 B8 62 30N 11 14 E
Osa, *Russia* 64 C5 57 17N 55 26 E
Osa →, *Norway* 18 C8 61 18N 11 46 E
Osa →, *Poland* 54 E5 53 33N 18 46 E
Osa, Pen. de, *Costa Rica* 164 E3 8 0N 84 0W
Osage, *U.S.A.* 156 A4 43 17N 92 49W
Osage →, *U.S.A.* 156 F5 38 35N 91 57W
Osage City, *U.S.A.* 154 F7 38 38N 95 50W
Ōsaka, *Japan* 73 C7 34 40N 135 30 E
Ōsaka □, *Japan* 73 C7 34 30N 135 30 E
Ōsaka-Wan, *Japan* 73 C7 34 30N 135 18 E
Osaki, *Japan* 72 F3 31 25N 131 2 E
Osan, *S. Korea* 75 F14 37 11N 127 4 E
Osawatomie, *U.S.A.* 154 F7 38 31N 94 57W
Osborne, *U.S.A.* 154 F5 39 26N 98 42W
Osby, *Sweden* 17 H7 56 23N 13 59 E
Osceola, *Ark., U.S.A.* 155 H10 35 42N 89 58W
Osceola, *Iowa, U.S.A.* 156 C3 41 2N 93 46W
Osceola, *Mo., U.S.A.* 156 F3 38 3N 93 42W
Oschatz, *Germany* 30 D9 51 17N 13 6 E
Oschersleben, *Germany* 30 C7 52 2N 11 14 E
Óschiri, *Italy* 46 B2 40 43N 9 6 E
Oscoda, *U.S.A.* 150 B1 44 26N 83 20W
Osečina, *Serbia, Yug.* 50 B3 44 23N 19 34 E
Ösel = Saaremaa, *Estonia* 15 G20 58 30N 22 30 E
Osensjøen, *Norway* 18 C8 61 13N 11 50 E
Osery, *Russia* 58 E10 54 52N 38 28 E
Osgood, *U.S.A.* 157 E11 39 8N 85 18W
Osgoode, *Canada* 151 A9 45 8N 75 36W
Osh, *Kyrgyzstan* 66 E8 40 37N 72 49 E
Oshawa, *Canada* 140 D4 43 50N 78 50W
Oshigambo, *Namibia* 116 B2 17 45 S 16 5 E
Oshkosh, *Nebr., U.S.A.* 154 E3 41 24N 102 21W
Oshkosh, *Wis., U.S.A.* 154 C10 44 1N 88 33W
Oshmyany = Ashmyany, *Belarus* 15 J21 54 26N 25 52 E
Oshnovīyeh, *Iran* 96 B5 37 2N 45 6 E
Oshogbo, *Nigeria* 113 D5 7 48N 4 37 E
Oshtorīnān, *Iran* 97 C6 34 1N 48 38 E
Oshwe, *Dem. Rep. of the Congo* 114 C3 3 25 S 19 28 E
Osi, *Nigeria* 113 D6 8 8N 5 14 E
Osieczna, *Poland* 55 G3 51 55N 16 40 E
Osijek, *Croatia* 52 E3 45 34N 18 41 E
Ósilo, *Italy* 46 B1 40 45N 8 40 E
Ósimo, *Italy* 45 E10 43 28N 13 30 E
Osintorf, *Belarus* 58 E6 54 40N 30 39 E
Osipenko = Berdyansk, *Ukraine* 59 J9 46 45N 36 50 E
Osipovichi = Asipovichy, *Belarus* 58 F5 53 19N 28 33 E
Osiyan, *India* 92 F5 26 43N 72 55 E
Osizweni, *S. Africa* 117 D5 27 49 S 30 7 E
Oskaloosa, *U.S.A.* 156 C4 41 18N 92 39W
Oskarshamn, *Sweden* 17 G10 57 15N 16 27 E
Oskarström, *Sweden* 17 H6 56 48N 12 58 E
Oskélanéo, *Canada* 140 C4 48 5N 75 15W
Öskemen, *Kazakstan* 66 E9 50 0N 82 36 E
Oskol →, *Ukraine* 59 H9 49 6N 37 25 E
Oslo, *Norway* 15 G14 59 55N 10 45 E
Oslo □, *Norway* 18 D7 59 54N 10 43 E
Oslob, *Phil.* 81 G4 9 31N 123 26 E
Oslofjorden, *Norway* 15 G14 59 20N 10 35 E
Osmanabad, *India* 94 E3 18 5N 76 10 E
Osmancık, *Turkey* 100 B6 40 58N 34 47 E
Osmaniye, *Turkey* 100 D7 37 5N 36 10 E
Osmanlı, *Turkey* 51 E10 41 35N 26 51 E
Osmannagar, *India* 94 E4 18 [illegible] 79 20 E
Ösmo, *Sweden* 16 F11 58 [illegible] 17 55 E
Osnabrück, *Germany* 30 C4 52 [illegible] 8 3 E
Ośno Lubuskie, *Poland* 55 F1 52 28N 14 51 E
Osoblaha, *Czech Rep.* 35 A10 50 17N 17 44 E
Osogovska Planina, *Macedonia* 50 D6 42 10N 22 30 E
Osor, *Italy* 45 D11 44 42N 14 24 E
Osorio, *Brazil* 175 B5 29 53 S 50 17W
Osório da Fonseca, *Brazil* 169 D6 3 52 S 58 14W
Osorno, *Chile* 176 B2 40 25 S 73 0W
Osorno, *Spain* 42 C6 42 24N 4 22W
Osorno □, *Chile* 176 B2 40 34 S 73 9W
Osorno, Vol., *Chile* 176 B2 41 0 S 72 30W
Osoyoos, *Canada* 142 D5 49 0N 119 30W
Osøyro, *Norway* 15 F11 60 9N 5 30 E
Ospakseyri, *Iceland* 11 B5 65 27N 21 26W
Ospika →, *Canada* 142 B4 56 20N 124 0W
Osprey, *U.S.A.* 153 H7 27 12N 82 29W
Osprey Reef, *Australia* 126 A4 13 52 S 146 36 E
Oss, *Neths.* 24 C5 51 46N 5 32 E
Ossa, Mt., *Australia* 127 G4 41 52 S 146 3 E
Óssa, Óros, *Greece* 48 B4 39 47N 22 42 E
Ossa de Montiel, *Spain* 41 G2 38 58N 2 45W
Ossabaw I., *U.S.A.* 152 D8 31 50N 81 5W
Ossabaw Sd., *U.S.A.* 152 D8 31 50N 81 6W
Osse →, *France* 28 D4 44 7N 0 17 E
Osse →, *Nigeria* 113 D6 6 10N 5 20 E
Ossi, *Italy* 46 B1 40 40N 8 35 E
Ossining, *U.S.A.* 151 E11 41 10N 73 55W
Ossipee, *U.S.A.* 151 C13 43 41N 71 7W
Ossokmanuan L., *Canada* 141 B7 53 25N 65 0W
Ossora, *Russia* 67 D17 59 20N 163 13 E
Ostashkov, *Russia* 58 D7 57 4N 33 2 E
Östavall, *Sweden* 16 B9 62 26N 15 29 E
Østby, *Norway* 18 C9 61 15N 12 33 E
Oste →, *Germany* 30 B5 53 49N 9 2 E
Ostend = Oostende, *Belgium* 24 C2 51 15N 2 54 E
Ostend, *N.Z.* 130 C4 36 48 S 175 2 E
Oster, *Ukraine* 59 G6 50 57N 30 53 E
Osterburg, *Germany* 30 C7 52 47N 11 45 E
Osterburg, *U.S.A.* 150 F6 40 16N 78 31W
Osterburken, *Germany* 31 F5 49 25N 9 26 E
Österbybruk, *Sweden* 16 D11 60 13N 17 55 E
Österbymo, *Sweden* 17 G9 57 49N 15 15 E
Österdalälven, *Sweden* 16 C7 61 30N 13 45 E
Østerdalen, *Norway* 15 F14 61 40N 10 50 E
Österfärnebo, *Sweden* 16 D10 60 19N 16 48 E
Österforse, *Sweden* 16 A11 63 9N 17 3 E
Östergötlands län □, *Sweden* 17 F9 58 35N 15 45 E
Osterholz-Scharmbeck, *Germany* 30 B4 53 13N 8 47 E
Østerild, *Denmark* 17 G2 57 2N 8 51 E
Ostermundigen, *Switz.* 32 C4 46 58N 7 27 E
Osterode, *Germany* 30 D6 51 43N 10 15 E
Östersund, *Sweden* 16 A8 63 10N 14 38 E
Östervåla, *Sweden* 16 D11 60 11N 17 11 E
Østfold □, *Norway* 18 E8 59 25N 11 25 E
Ostfriesische Inseln, *Germany* 30 B3 53 42N 7 0 E
Ostfriesland, *Germany* 30 B3 53 20N 7 30 E
Östhammar, *Sweden* 16 D12 60 16N 18 22 E
Óstia, Lido di, *Italy* 45 G9 41 43N 12 17 E
Ostíglia, *Italy* 45 C8 45 4N 11 8 E
Östmark, *Sweden* 16 D6 60 17N 12 45 E
Östra Husby, *Sweden* 17 F10 58 35N 16 33 E
Ostrava, *Czech Rep.* 35 B11 49 51N 18 18 E
Ostróda, *Poland* 54 E6 53 42N 19 58 E
Ostrogozhsk, *Russia* 59 G10 50 55N 39 7 E
Ostroh, *Ukraine* 59 G4 50 20N 26 30 E
Ostrołęka, *Poland* 55 E8 53 4N 21 32 E
Ostrov, *Bulgaria* 51 C8 43 40N 24 9 E
Ostrov, *Czech Rep.* 34 A5 50 18N 12 57 E
Ostrov, *Romania* 53 F12 44 6N 27 24 E
Ostrov, *Russia* 58 D5 57 25N 28 20 E
Ostrów Lubelski, *Poland* 55 G9 51 29N 22 51 E
Ostrów Mazowiecka, *Poland* 55 F8 52 50N 21 51 E
Ostrów Wielkopolski, *Poland* 55 G4 51 36N 17 44 E
Ostrowiec-Świętokrzyski, *Poland* 55 H8 50 55N 21 22 E
Ostrožac, *Bos.-H.* 52 G2 43 43N 17 49 E
Ostrzeszów, *Poland* 55 G4 51 25N 17 52 E
Ostseebad Kühlungsborn, *Germany* 30 A7 54 8N 11 44 E
Osttirol □, *Austria* 34 E5 46 50N 12 30 E
Ostuni, *Italy* 47 B10 40 44N 17 35 E
Osum →, *Albania* 50 F4 40 40N 20 10 E
Osŭm →, *Bulgaria* 51 C8 43 40N 24 50 E
Ōsumi-Hantō, *Japan* 72 F2 31 20N 130 55 E
Ōsumi-Kaikyō, *Japan* 71 J5 30 55N 131 0 E
Ōsumi-Shotō, *Japan* 71 J5 30 30N 130 0 E
Osun □, *Nigeria* 113 D5 7 30N 4 30 E
Osuna, *Spain* 43 H5 37 14N 5 8W
Oswegatchie →, *U.S.A.* 151 B9 44 42N 75 30W
Oswego, *U.S.A.* 151 C8 43 27N 76 31W
Oswego →, *U.S.A.* 151 C8 43 27N 76 30W
Oswestry, *U.K.* 20 E4 52 52N 3 3W
Oświęcim, *Poland* 55 H6 50 2N 19 11 E
Ōta, *Fukui, Japan* 73 B8 35 57N 136 3 E
Ōta, *Gumma, Japan* 73 A11 36 18N 139 22 E
Ōta-Gawa →, *Japan* 72 C4 34 21N 132 18 E
Otaci, *Moldova* 53 B12 48 27N 27 47 E
Otago □, *N.Z.* 131 E4 45 15 S 170 0 E
Otago Harbour, *N.Z.* 131 F5 45 47 S 170 42 E
Otago Pen., *N.Z.* 131 F5 45 48 S 170 39 E
Otaheite B., *Trin. & Tob.* 169 F9 10 20N 61 30W
Otahuhu, *N.Z.* 130 C3 36 56 S 174 51 E
Ōtake, *Japan* 72 C4 34 12N 132 13 E
Ōtaki, *Japan* 73 B12 35 17N 140 15 E
Otaki, *N.Z.* 130 G4 40 45 S 175 10 E
Otane, *N.Z.* 130 F5 39 54 S 176 39 E
Otar, *Kazakstan* 65 B7 43 32N 75 12 E
Otaru, *Japan* 70 C10 43 10N 141 0 E
Otaru-Wan = Ishikari-Wan, *Japan* 70 C10 43 25N 141 1 E
Otautau, *N.Z.* 131 G3 46 9 S 168 1 E
Otava →, *Czech Rep.* 34 B7 49 26N 14 12 E
Otavalo, *Ecuador* 168 C2 0 13N 78 20W
Otavi, *Namibia* 116 B2 19 40 S 17 24 E
Otchinjau, *Angola* 116 B1 16 30 S 13 56 E
Otelec, *Romania* 52 E5 45 36N 20 50 E
Otelnuk L., *Canada* 141 A6 56 9N 68 12W
Oţelu Roşu, *Romania* 52 E7 45 32N 22 22 E
Otero de Rey = Outeiro de Rei, *Spain* 42 B3 43 6N 7 36W
Othello, *U.S.A.* 158 C4 46 50N 119 10W
Othonoí, *Greece* 38 B9 39 52N 19 22 E
Óthris, Óros, *Greece* 48 B4 39 2N 22 37 E
Oti, Réserve de Faune de l', *Togo* 113 C5 10 40N 0 35 E
Otira, *N.Z.* 131 C6 42 49 S 171 35 E
Otira Gorge, *N.Z.* 131 C6 42 53 S 171 33 E
Otjiwarongo, *Namibia* 116 C2 20 30 S 16 33 E
Ötmök, *Kyrgyzstan* 65 B6 42 20N 73 10 E
Otmuchów, *Poland* 55 H4 50 28N 17 10 E
Oto Tolu Group, *Tonga* 133 Q13 20 21 S 174 32W
Otočac, *Croatia* 45 D12 44 53N 15 12 E
Otoineppu, *Japan* 70 B11 44 44N 142 16 E
Otok, *Croatia* 45 E13 43 42N 16 44 E
Oton, *Phil.* 81 F4 10 42N 122 29 E
Otorohanga, *N.Z.* 130 E4 38 12 S 175 14 E
Otoskwin →, *Canada* 140 B2 52 13N 88 6W
Ōtoyo, *Japan* 72 D5 33 43N 133 45 E
Otra →, *Norway* 15 G13 58 9N 8 1 E
Otradnyy, *Russia* 60 D10 53 22N 51 21 E
Otranto, *Italy* 47 B11 40 9N 18 28 E
Otranto, C. d', *Italy* 47 B11 40 7N 18 30 E
Otranto, Str. of, *Italy* 47 B11 40 15N 18 40 E
Otrokovice, *Czech Rep.* 35 B10 49 12N 17 32 E
Otse, *S. Africa* 116 D4 25 2 S 25 45 E
Otsego, *U.S.A.* 157 B11 42 27N 85 42W
Ōtsu, *Japan* 73 C7 35 0N 135 50 E
Ōtsuki, *Japan* 73 B10 35 36N 138 57 E
Otta, *Norway* 18 C6 61 46N 9 32 E
Otta →, *Norway* 18 C6 61 46N 9 31 E
Ottapalam, *India* 95 J3 10 46N 76 23 E
Ottawa = Outaouais →, *Canada* 140 C5 45 27N 74 8W
Ottawa, *Canada* 140 C4 45 27N 75 42W
Ottawa, *Ill., U.S.A.* 154 E10 41 21N 88 51W
Ottawa, *Kans., U.S.A.* 154 F7 38 37N 95 16W
Ottawa, *Ohio, U.S.A.* 157 C12 41 1N 84 3W
Ottawa Is., *Canada* 139 C11 59 35N 80 10W
Ottélé, *Cameroon* 113 E7 3 38N 11 19 E
Ottensheim, *Austria* 34 C7 48 21N 14 12 E
Otter Cr. →, *U.S.A.* 151 B11 44 13N 73 17W
Otter Creek, *U.S.A.* 153 F7 29 19N 82 46W
Otter L., *Canada* 143 B8 55 35N 104 39W
Otterbein, *U.S.A.* 157 D9 40 29N 87 6W
Otterndorf, *Germany* 30 B4 53 48N 8 53 E
Otterøya, *Norway* 18 B3 62 45N 6 50 E
Otterup, *Denmark* 17 J4 55 30N 10 22 E
Otterville, *Canada* 150 D4 42 55N 80 36W
Otterville, *U.S.A.* 156 F4 38 42N 93 0W
Ottery St. Mary, *U.K.* 21 G4 50 44N 3 17W
Ottilien Reef, *Papua N. G.* 132 C5 4 33 S 148 49 E
Otto Beit Bridge, *Zimbabwe* 119 F2 15 59 S 28 56 E
Ottosdal, *S. Africa* 116 D4 26 46 S 25 59 E
Ottoville, *U.S.A.* 157 D12 40 57N 84 22W
Ottumwa, *U.S.A.* 156 D4 41 1N 92 25W
Otu, *Nigeria* 113 D5 8 14N 3 22 E
Otukpa, *Nigeria* 113 D6 7 9N 7 41 E
Oturkpo, *Nigeria* 113 D6 7 16N 8 8 E
Otway, B., *Chile* 176 D2 53 30 S 74 0W
Otway, C., *Australia* 128 E5 38 52 S 143 30 E
Otway, Seno de, *Chile* 176 D2 53 0 S 71 30W
Otway Nat. Park, *Australia* 128 E5 38 47 S 143 34 E
Otwock, *Poland* 55 F8 52 5N 21 20 E
Ötztaler Ache →, *Austria* 34 D3 47 14N 10 50 E
Ötztaler Alpen, *Austria* 34 E3 46 56N 11 0 E
Ou →, *Laos* 86 B4 20 4N 102 13 E
Ou Neua, *Laos* 76 F3 22 18N 101 48 E
Ou-Sammyaku, *Japan* 70 E10 39 20N 140 35 E
Ouachita →, *U.S.A.* 155 K9 31 38N 91 49W
Ouachita, L., *U.S.A.* 155 H8 34 34N 93 12W
Ouachita Mts., *U.S.A.* 155 H7 34 40N 94 25W
Ouaco, *N. Cal.* 133 T18 20 50 S 164 29 E
Ouadâne, *Mauritania* 110 D2 20 50N 11 40W
Ouadda, *C.A.R.* 114 A4 8 15N 22 20 E
Ouagadougou, *Burkina Faso* 113 C4 12 25N 1 30W
Ouagam, *Chad* 109 F2 14 22N 14 42 E
Ouaham →, *C.A.R.* 114 A3 6 35N 15 12 E
Ouahigouya, *Burkina Faso* 112 C4 13 31N 2 25W
Ouahila, *Algeria* 110 C4 27 50N 5 0W
Ouahran = Oran, *Algeria* 111 A4 35 45N 0 39W
Oualâta, *Mauritania* 112 B3 17 20N 6 55W

Ouallam, Niger **113 C5** 14 23N 2 10 E
Ouallene, Algeria **111 D5** 24 41N 1 11 E
Ouanary, Fr. Guiana **169 C7** 4 13N 51 40W
Ouanda Djallé, C.A.R. **114 A4** 8 55N 22 53 E
Ouandago, C.A.R. **114 A3** 7 13N 18 50 E
Ouandjia, Bahr →, C.A.R. **114 A4** 9 35N 21 43 E
Ouandjia-Vakaga, Réserve de Faune de la, C.A.R. **114 A4** 9 2N 22 18 E
Ouango, C.A.R. **114 B4** 4 19N 22 30 E
Ouani, Comoros Is. **121 a** 12 9 S 44 18 E
Ouantonou, C.A.R. **114 A3** 7 19N 15 18 E
Ouarâne, Mauritania **110 D2** 21 0N 10 30W
Ouargaye, Burkina Faso **113 C5** 11 40N 0 5 E
Ouargla, Algeria **111 B6** 31 59N 5 16 E
Ouarkoye, Burkina Faso **112 C4** 12 5N 3 40W
Ouarkziz, Jebel, Algeria **110 C3** 28 50N 8 0W
Ouarra →, C.A.R. **114 A4** 5 5N 24 26 E
Ouarzazate, Morocco **110 B3** 30 55N 6 50W
Ouassouas, Mali **113 B5** 16 10N 1 23 E
Ouatagouna, Mali **113 B5** 15 11N 0 43 E
Ouatere, C.A.R. **114 A3** 5 30N 19 8 E
Oubangi →, Dem. Rep. of the Congo **114 C3** 0 30 S 17 50 E
Oubarakai, O. →, Algeria **111 C6** 27 20N 9 0 E
Ouche →, France **27 E12** 47 6N 5 16 E
Ouddorp, Neths. **24 C3** 51 50N 3 57 E
Oude Rijn →, Neths. **24 B4** 52 12N 4 24 E
Oudeïka, Mali **113 B4** 17 30N 1 40W
Oudenaarde, Belgium **24 D3** 50 50N 3 37 E
Oudon →, France **26 E6** 47 41N 0 53W
Oudtshoorn, S. Africa **116 E3** 33 35 S 22 14 E
Oued Zem, Morocco **110 B3** 32 52N 6 34W
Ouégoa, N. Cal. **133 T18** 20 20 S 164 26 E
Oueita, Chad **109 E4** 17 47N 20 39 E
Ouellé, Ivory C. **112 D4** 7 26N 4 1W
Ouéme →, Benin **113 D5** 6 30N 2 30 E
Ouen, Î., N. Cal. **133 V20** 22 26 S 166 49 E
Ouenza, Algeria **111 A6** 35 57N 8 4 E
Ouessa, Burkina Faso **112 C4** 11 4N 2 47W
Ouessant, Î. d', France **26 D1** 48 28N 5 6W
Ouesso, Congo **114 B3** 1 37N 16 5 E
Ouest, Pte. de l', Canada **141 C7** 49 52N 64 40W
Ouezzane, Morocco **110 B3** 34 51N 5 35W
Ougarou, Burkina Faso **113 C5** 12 10N 0 58 E
Oughterard, Ireland **23 C2** 53 26N 9 18W
Ouhan →, Chad **109 G3** 9 18N 18 14 E
Ouidah, Benin **113 D5** 6 25N 2 0 E
Ouidi, Niger **113 C7** 14 10N 13 0 E
Ouissongo, Angola **115 E3** 7 40 S 15 41 E
Ouistreham, France **26 C6** 49 17N 0 18W
Oujda, Morocco **111 B4** 34 41N 1 55W
Oujeft, Mauritania **112 A2** 20 2N 13 0W
Oulainen, Finland **14 D21** 64 17N 24 47 E
Ould Yenjé, Mauritania **112 B2** 15 38N 12 16W
Ouled Djellal, Algeria **111 B6** 34 28N 5 2 E
Ouled Naïl, Mts. des, Algeria **111 B5** 34 30N 3 30 E
Ouli, Cameroon **114 A2** 5 12N 14 33 E
Oullins, France **29 C8** 45 43N 4 49 E
Oulmès, Morocco **110 B3** 33 17N 6 0W
Oulou, Bahr →, C.A.R. **114 A4** 9 48N 21 32 E
Oulu, Finland **14 D21** 65 1N 25 29 E
Oulujärvi, Finland **14 D22** 64 25N 27 15 E
Oulujoki →, Finland **14 D21** 65 1N 25 30 E
Oulx, Italy **44 C3** 45 2N 6 50 E
Oum Chalouba, Chad **109 E4** 15 48N 20 46 E
Oum-el-Bouaghi, Algeria **111 A6** 35 55N 7 6 E
Oum-el-Ksi, Algeria **110 C3** 29 4N 6 59W
Oum-er-Rbia, O. →, Morocco **110 B3** 33 19N 8 21W
Oum Hadjer, Chad **109 F3** 13 18N 19 41 E
Oum Hadjer, O. →, Chad **109 E4** 16 38N 20 14 E
Oumé, Ivory C. **112 D3** 6 21N 5 27W
Oumm ed Droûs Guebli, Sebkhet, Mauritania **110 D2** 24 3N 11 45W
Oumm ed Droûs Telli, Sebkhet, Mauritania **110 D2** 24 20N 11 30W
Ounane, Dj., Algeria **111 C6** 25 4N 7 19 E
Ounasjoki →, Finland **14 C21** 66 31N 25 40 E
Ounguati, Namibia **116 C2** 22 0 S 15 46 E
Ounianga Kébir, Chad **109 E4** 19 4N 20 29 E
Ounianga Sérir, Chad **109 E4** 18 54N 20 51 E
Ounissoui, Niger **109 E2** 17 34N 12 13 E
Our →, Lux. **24 E6** 49 55N 6 5 E
Ouranópolis, Greece **50 F7** 40 20N 23 59 E
Ourârene, Niger **113 B6** 19 30N 7 10 E
Ourari, Tarso, Chad **109 D3** 21 27N 17 27 E
Ouray, U.S.A. **159 G10** 38 1N 107 40W
Ourcq →, France **27 C10** 49 1N 3 1 E
Ourém, Brazil **170 B2** 1 33 S 47 6W
Ourense, Spain **42 C3** 42 19N 7 55W
Ouricuri, Brazil **170 C3** 7 53 S 40 5W
Ourinhos, Brazil **175 A6** 23 0 S 49 54W
Ourique, Portugal **43 H2** 37 38N 8 16W
Ouro Fino, Brazil **175 A6** 22 16 S 46 25W
Ouro-Ndia, Mali **112 B4** 15 8N 4 35W
Ouro Prêto, Brazil **171 F3** 20 20 S 43 30W
Ouro Prêto do Oeste, Brazil **173 C5** 10 40 S 62 18W
Ouro Sogui, Senegal **112 B2** 15 36N 13 19W
Oursi, Burkina Faso **113 C4** 14 41N 0 27W
Ourthe →, Belgium **24 D5** 50 29N 5 35 E
Ouse →, E. Susx., U.K. **21 G8** 50 47N 0 4 E
Ouse →, N. Yorks., U.K. **20 D7** 53 44N 0 55W
Oust, France **28 F5** 42 52N 1 13 E
Oust →, France **26 E4** 47 35N 2 6W
Outamba-Kilimi Nat. Park, S. Leone **112 D2** 9 50N 12 40W
Outaouais →, Canada **140 C5** 45 27N 74 8W
Outardes →, Canada **141 C6** 49 24N 69 30W
Outat Oulad el Haj, Morocco **111 B4** 33 22N 3 42W
Outeiro de Rei, Spain **42 B3** 43 6N 7 36W
Outer Hebrides, U.K. **22 D1** 57 30N 7 40W
Outes = Serra de Outes, Spain **42 C2** 42 52N 8 55W
Outjo, Namibia **116 C2** 20 5 S 16 7 E
Outlook, Canada **143 C7** 51 30N 107 0W
Outokumpu, Finland **14 E23** 62 43N 29 1 E
Outreau, France **27 B8** 50 40N 1 36 E
Ouvéa, Î., N. Cal. **133 K4** 20 35 S 166 35 E
Ouvèze →, France **29 E8** 43 59N 4 51 E
Ouyen, Australia **128 C5** 35 1 S 142 22 E
Ouzinkie, U.S.A. **144 H9** 57 56N 152 30W
Ouzouer-le-Marché, France **27 E8** 47 54N 1 32 E
Ovada, Italy **44 D5** 44 38N 8 38 E
Ovahe, Chile **172 b** 27 5 S 109 19W
Ovalau, Fiji **133 A2** 17 40 S 178 48 E
Ovalle, Chile **174 C1** 30 33 S 71 18W
Ovamboland, Namibia **116 B2** 18 30 S 16 0 E
Ovar, Portugal **42 E2** 40 51N 8 40W
Ovau, Solomon Is. **133 L9** 6 40 S 156 8 E
Overath, Germany **30 E3** 50 56N 7 17 E
Overflakkee, Neths. **24 C4** 51 44N 4 10 E
Overijssel □, Neths. **24 B6** 52 25N 6 35 E
Overland, U.S.A. **156 F6** 38 41N 90 22W
Overland Park, U.S.A. **154 F7** 38 55N 94 50W
Overton, U.S.A. **161 J12** 36 33N 114 27W
Övertorneå, Sweden **14 C20** 66 23N 23 38 E
Överum, Sweden **17 F10** 58 0N 16 20 E
Ovid, Mich., U.S.A. **157 A12** 43 1N 84 22W
Ovid, N.Y., U.S.A. **151 D8** 42 41N 76 49W
Ovidiopol, Ukraine **59 J6** 46 15N 30 30 E
Ovidiu, Romania **53 F13** 44 16N 28 34 E
Oviedo, Spain **42 B5** 43 25N 5 50W
Oviedo, U.S.A. **153 G8** 28 40N 81 13W
Oviksfjällen, Sweden **16 A7** 63 0N 13 49 E
Oviši, Latvia **15 H19** 57 33N 21 44 E
Ovoot, Mongolia **74 B7** 45 21N 113 45 E
Övör Hangay □, Mongolia **74 B2** 45 0N 102 30 E
Ovoro, Nigeria **113 D6** 5 26N 7 16 E
Øvre Årdal, Norway **15 F12** 61 19N 7 48 E
Övre Fryken, Sweden **16 E7** 60 0N 13 7 E
Øvre Rendal, Norway **18 C8** 61 54N 11 4 E
Øvre Rindal, Norway **18 A6** 63 6N 9 10 E
Øvre Sirdal, Norway **18 F3** 58 48N 6 43 E
Ovruch, Ukraine **59 G5** 51 25N 28 45 E
Owaka, N.Z. **131 G4** 46 27 S 169 40 E
Owambo = Ovamboland, Namibia **116 B2** 18 30 S 16 0 E
Owando, Congo **114 C3** 0 29 S 15 55 E
Owasco L., U.S.A. **151 D8** 42 50N 76 31W
Owase, Japan **73 C8** 34 7N 136 12 E
Owatonna, U.S.A. **154 C8** 44 5N 93 14W
Owbeh, Afghan. **91 B1** 34 28N 63 10 E
Owego, U.S.A. **151 D8** 42 6N 76 16W
Owen, Australia **128 C3** 34 15 S 138 32 E
Owen, Mt., N.Z. **131 B7** 41 35 S 172 33 E
Owen Falls Dam, Uganda **118 B3** 0 30N 33 5 E
Owen Sound, Canada **140 D3** 44 35N 80 55W
Owen Stanley Ra., Papua N. G. **132 E4** 8 30 S 147 0 E
Owendo, Gabon **114 B1** 0 17N 9 30 E
Owens →, U.S.A. **160 J9** 36 32N 117 59W
Owens L., U.S.A. **161 J9** 36 26N 117 57W
Owensboro, U.S.A. **157 G9** 37 46N 87 7W
Owensville, Ind., U.S.A. **157 F9** 38 16N 87 41W
Owensville, Mo., U.S.A. **156 F5** 38 21N 91 30W
Owenteik, Guyana **169 C6** 4 27N 59 35W
Owenton, U.S.A. **157 F12** 38 32N 84 50W
Owerri, Nigeria **113 D6** 5 29N 7 0 E
Owhango, N.Z. **130 F4** 39 0 S 175 23 E
Owingsville, U.S.A. **157 F13** 38 9N 83 46W
Owl →, Canada **143 B10** 57 51N 92 44W
Owo, Nigeria **113 D6** 7 10N 5 39 E
Owosso, U.S.A. **157 B12** 43 0N 84 10W
Owyhee, U.S.A. **158 F5** 41 57N 116 6W
Owyhee →, U.S.A. **158 E5** 43 49N 117 2W
Owyhee, L., U.S.A. **158 E5** 43 38N 117 14W
Ox Mts. = Slieve Gamph, Ireland **23 B3** 54 6N 9 0W
Oxapampa, Peru **172 C2** 10 33 S 75 26W
Öxarfjörður, Iceland **11 A10** 66 15N 16 45W
Oxbow, Canada **143 D8** 49 14N 102 10W
Oxelösund, Sweden **17 F11** 58 43N 17 5 E
Oxford, N.Z. **131 D7** 43 18 S 172 11 E
Oxford, U.K. **21 F6** 51 46N 1 15W
Oxford, Ala., U.S.A. **152 B4** 33 36N 85 51W
Oxford, Iowa, U.S.A. **156 C5** 41 43N 91 47W
Oxford, Mass., U.S.A. **151 D13** 42 7N 71 52W
Oxford, Mich., U.S.A. **157 B13** 42 49N 83 16W
Oxford, Miss., U.S.A. **155 H10** 34 22N 89 31W
Oxford, N.C., U.S.A. **149 G6** 36 19N 78 35W
Oxford, N.Y., U.S.A. **151 D9** 42 27N 75 36W
Oxford, Ohio, U.S.A. **157 E12** 39 31N 84 45W
Oxford L., Canada **143 C9** 54 51N 95 37W
Oxfordshire □, U.K. **21 F6** 51 48N 1 16W
Oxía Nisís, Greece **39 C3** 38 18N 21 6 E
Oxie, Sweden **17 J7** 55 33N 13 6 E
Oxílithos, Greece **48 C6** 38 35N 24 7 E
Oxley, Australia **128 C6** 34 11 S 144 6 E
Oxley Wild Rivers Nat. Park, Australia **129 A10** 30 57 S 152 12 E
Oxnard, U.S.A. **161 L7** 34 12N 119 11W
Oxsjövålen, Sweden **16 B7** 62 34N 13 57 E
Oxus = Amudarya →, Uzbekistan **66 E6** 43 58N 59 34 E
Oy-Tal, Kyrgyzstan **65 C7** 40 24N 74 6 E
Oya, Malaysia **85 B4** 2 55N 111 55 E
Oyabe, Japan **73 A8** 36 47N 136 56 E
Oyama, Japan **73 A11** 36 18N 139 48 E
Oyapock →, Fr. Guiana **169 C7** 4 8N 51 40W
Øye, Norway **18 F3** 58 16N 6 49 E
Oyem, Gabon **114 B2** 1 34N 11 31 E
Oyen, Canada **143 C6** 51 22N 110 28W
Øyer, Norway **18 C7** 61 16N 10 25 E
Øyeren, Norway **18 E8** 59 50N 11 15 E
Oykel →, U.K. **22 D4** 57 56N 4 26W
Oymyakon, Russia **67 C15** 63 25N 142 44 E
Oyo, Nigeria **113 D5** 7 46N 3 56 E
Oyo □, Nigeria **113 D5** 8 15N 3 30 E
Oyón, Peru **172 C2** 10 37 S 76 47W
Oyonnax, France **27 F12** 46 16N 5 40 E
Øyslebø, Norway **18 F4** 58 9N 7 34 E
Oyster Bay, U.S.A. **151 F11** 40 52N 73 32W
Øystese, Norway **18 D3** 60 22N 6 9 E
Oytal, Kazakstan **65 B6** 42 54N 73 17 E
Ōyūbari, Japan **70 C11** 43 1N 142 5 E
Oyyq, Kazakstan **65 B5** 43 36N 71 16 E
Özalp, Turkey **101 C10** 38 39N 43 59 E
Ozamiz, Phil. **81 G4** 8 15N 123 50 E
Ozark, Ala., U.S.A. **152 D4** 31 28N 85 39W
Ozark, Ark., U.S.A. **155 H8** 35 29N 93 50W
Ozark, Mo., U.S.A. **155 G8** 37 1N 93 12W
Ozark Plateau, U.S.A. **155 G9** 37 20N 91 40W
Ozarks, L. of the, U.S.A. **156 F4** 38 12N 92 38W
Ożarów, Poland **55 H8** 50 53N 21 40 E
Ózd, Hungary **52 B5** 48 14N 20 15 E
Ozernoye, Russia **60 E10** 51 46N 51 28 E
Ozërnyy, Russia **64 F8** 51 8N 60 50 E
Ozette L., U.S.A. **160 B2** 48 6N 124 38W
Özgön, Kyrgyzstan **65 C6** 40 46N 73 18 E
Ozieri, Italy **46 B2** 40 35N 9 0 E
Ozimek, Poland **55 H5** 50 41N 18 11 E
Ozinki, Russia **60 E9** 51 12N 49 44 E
Ozona, U.S.A. **155 K4** 30 43N 101 12W
Ozorków, Poland **55 G6** 51 57N 19 16 E
Ozren, Bos.-H. **52 G3** 43 55N 18 29 E
Ōzu, Ehime, Japan **72 D4** 33 30N 132 33 E
Ōzu, Kumamoto, Japan **72 E2** 32 52N 130 52 E
Ozuluama, Mexico **163 C5** 21 40N 97 50W
Ozun, Romania **53 E10** 45 47N 25 50 E
Ozurgeti, Georgia **61 K5** 41 55N 42 2 E

P

Pa, Burkina Faso **112 C4** 11 33N 3 19W
Pa-an, Burma **90 G6** 16 51N 97 40 E
Pa Mong Dam, Thailand **86 D4** 18 0N 102 22 E
Pa Sak →, Thailand **78 B2** 15 30N 101 0 E
Paagoumène, N. Cal. **133 T18** 20 29 S 164 11 E
Paama, Vanuatu **133 F6** 16 28 S 168 14 E
Paamiut, Greenland **10 E6** 62 0N 49 43W
Paar →, Germany **31 G7** 48 46N 11 36 E
Paarl, S. Africa **116 E2** 33 45 S 18 56 E
Paauilo, U.S.A. **145 C6** 20 2N 155 22W
Pab Hills, Pakistan **91 D2** 26 30N 66 45 E
Pabbay, U.K. **22 D1** 57 46N 7 14W
Pabianice, Poland **55 G6** 51 40N 19 20 E
Pabna, Bangla. **90 C2** 24 1N 89 18 E
Pabo, Uganda **118 B3** 3 1N 32 10 E
Pacaás Novos, Serra dos, Brazil **173 C5** 10 45 S 64 15W
Pacaipampa, Peru **172 B2** 5 35 S 79 39W
Pacaja →, Brazil **170 B1** 1 56 S 50 50W
Pacajus, Brazil **170 B4** 4 10 S 38 31W
Pacaraima, Sa., S. Amer. **169 C5** 4 0N 62 30W
Pacarán, Peru **172 C2** 12 50 S 76 3W
Pacaraos, Peru **172 C2** 11 12 S 76 42W
Pacasmayo, Peru **172 B2** 7 20 S 79 35W
Pace, U.S.A. **153 E2** 30 36N 87 10W
Paceco, Italy **46 E5** 37 59N 12 33 E
Pachacamac, Peru **172 C2** 12 14 S 77 53W
Pachhar, India **92 G7** 24 40N 77 42 E
Pachino, Italy **47 F8** 36 43N 15 5 E
Pachitea →, Peru **172 B3** 8 46 S 74 33W
Pachiza, Peru **172 B2** 7 16 S 76 46W
Pachmarhi, India **93 H8** 22 28N 78 26 E
Pachnai, India **90 B4** 26 57N 92 19 E
Pacho, Colombia **168 B3** 5 8N 74 10W
Pachora, India **94 D2** 20 38N 75 29 E
Pachuca, Mexico **163 C5** 20 10N 98 40W
Pacific, Canada **142 C3** 54 48N 128 28W
Pacific, U.S.A. **156 F6** 38 29N 90 45W
Pacific-Antarctic Ridge, Pac. Oc. **135 M16** 43 0 S 115 0W
Pacific Grove, U.S.A. **160 J5** 36 38N 121 56W
Pacific Ocean, Pac. Oc. **80 D5** 10 0N 140 0W
Pacific Palisades, U.S.A. **145 K14** 21 25N 157 58W
Pacific Rim Nat. Park, Canada **160 B2** 48 40N 124 45W
Pacifica, U.S.A. **160 H4** 37 36N 122 30W
Pacitan, Indonesia **85 D4** 8 12 S 111 7 E
Packsaddle, Australia **128 A4** 30 36 S 141 58 E
Packwood, U.S.A. **160 D5** 46 36N 121 40W
Pacov, Czech Rep. **34 B8** 49 27N 15 0 E
Pacoval, Brazil **169 D7** 2 40 S 54 11W
Pacuí →, Brazil **171 E2** 16 46 S 45 1W
Pacy-sur-Eure, France **26 C8** 49 1N 1 23 E
Padaido, Kepulauan, Indonesia **83 B5** 1 15 S 136 30 E
Padampur, India **94 D6** 20 59N 83 4 E
Padang, Indonesia **84 C2** 1 0 S 100 20 E
Padang Endau, Malaysia **87 L4** 2 40N 103 38 E
Padangpanjang, Indonesia **84 C2** 0 40 S 100 20 E
Padangsidempuan, Indonesia **84 B1** 1 30N 99 15 E
Padangtikar, Indonesia **85 C3** 0 44 S 109 15 E
Padatchaung, Burma **90 F5** 19 46N 94 48 E
Padauari →, Brazil **169 D5** 0 15 S 64 5W
Padaung, Burma **90 F5** 18 43N 95 9 E
Padborg, Denmark **17 K3** 54 49N 9 21 E
Padcaya, Bolivia **173 E5** 21 52 S 64 48W
Paddle Prairie, Canada **142 B5** 57 57N 117 29W
Paddockwood, Canada **143 C7** 53 30N 105 30W
Paderborn, Germany **30 D4** 51 42N 8 45 E
Paderoo, India **94 E6** 18 5N 82 40 E
Padeş, Vf., Romania **52 E7** 45 40N 22 22 E
Padilla, Bolivia **173 D5** 19 19 S 64 20W
Padina, Romania **53 F12** 44 50N 27 8 E
Padma, India **93 G11** 24 12N 85 22 E
Padma →, Bangla. **90 D3** 23 22N 90 32 E
Pádova, Italy **45 C8** 45 25N 11 53 E
Padra, India **92 H5** 22 15N 73 7 E
Padrauna, India **93 F10** 26 54N 83 59 E
Padre Burgos, Phil. **81 F5** 10 1N 125 0 E
Padre I., U.S.A. **155 M6** 27 10N 97 25W
Padrón, Spain **42 C2** 42 41N 8 39W
Padstow, U.K. **21 G3** 50 33N 4 58W
Padthaway, Australia **128 D4** 36 36 S 140 31 E
Padua = Pádova, Italy **45 C8** 45 25N 11 53 E
Paducah, Ky., U.S.A. **148 G1** 37 5N 88 37W
Paducah, Tex., U.S.A. **155 H4** 34 1N 100 18W
Padukka, Sri Lanka **95 L5** 6 50N 80 5 E
Padul, Spain **43 H7** 37 1N 3 38W
Padwa, India **94 E6** 18 27N 82 47 E
Paekakariki, N.Z. **130 G3** 40 59 S 174 58 E
Paengaroa, N.Z. **130 D5** 37 49 S 176 29 E
Paengnyŏng-do, S. Korea **75 F13** 37 57N 124 40 E
Paeroa, N.Z. **130 D4** 37 23 S 175 41 E
Paesana, Italy **44 D4** 44 41N 7 16 E
Paete, Phil. **80 D3** 14 23N 121 29 E
Pafúri, Mozam. **117 C5** 22 28 S 31 17 E
Pag, Croatia **45 D12** 44 25N 15 3 E
Paga, Gabon **114 C2** 0 45 S 10 21 E
Paga, Ghana **113 C4** 11 1N 1 8W
Pagadian, Phil. **81 H4** 7 55N 123 30 E
Pagai Selatan, Pulau, Indonesia **84 C2** 3 0 S 100 15 E
Pagai Utara, Pulau, Indonesia **84 C2** 2 35 S 100 0 E
Pagalu = Annobón, Atl. Oc. **105 G4** 1 25 S 5 36 E
Pagalungan, Phil. **81 H5** 7 4N 124 41 E
Pagan, Burma **90 E5** 21 10N 94 52 E
Pagara, India **93 G9** 24 22N 80 1 E
Pagastikós Kólpos, Greece **48 B5** 39 15N 23 0 E
Pagatan, Indonesia **85 C5** 3 33 S 115 59 E
Page, U.S.A. **159 H8** 36 57N 111 27W
Pagėgiai, Lithuania **54 C8** 55 9N 21 54 E
Pagei, Papua N. G. **132 B1** 3 2 S 141 10 E
Paget I., India **95 H11** 13 26N 92 50 E
Pago Pago, Amer. Samoa **133 X24** 14 16 S 170 43W
Pagosa Springs, U.S.A. **159 H10** 37 16N 107 1W
Pagudpud, Phil. **80 B3** 18 34N 120 47 E
Pagwa River, Canada **140 B2** 50 2N 85 14W
Pagwi, Papua N. G. **132 C2** 4 4 S 143 2 E
Pahala, U.S.A. **145 D6** 19 12N 155 29W
Pahang □, Malaysia **84 B2** 3 30N 102 45 E
Pahang →, Malaysia **87 L4** 3 30N 103 9 E
Pahia Pt., N.Z. **131 G2** 46 20 S 167 41 E
Pahiatua, N.Z. **130 G4** 40 27 S 175 50 E
Pahoa, U.S.A. **145 D7** 19 30N 154 57W
Pahokee, U.S.A. **149 M5** 26 50N 80 40W
Pahrump, U.S.A. **161 J11** 36 12N 115 59W
Pahute Mesa, U.S.A. **160 H10** 37 20N 116 45W
Pai, Thailand **86 C2** 19 19N 98 27 E
Paia, U.S.A. **145 C5** 20 54N 156 22W
Paicines, U.S.A. **160 J5** 36 44N 121 17W
Paide, Estonia **15 G21** 58 57N 25 31 E
Paignton, U.K. **21 G4** 50 26N 3 35W
Paihia, N.Z. **130 B3** 35 17 S 174 6 E
Paiho, Taiwan **77 F13** 23 21N 120 25 E
Paiján, Peru **172 B2** 7 42 S 79 20W
Päijänne, Finland **15 F21** 61 30N 25 30 E
Pailani, India **93 G9** 25 45N 80 26 E
Pailin, Cambodia **86 F4** 12 46N 102 36 E
Pailolo Channel, U.S.A. **145 C5** 21 0N 156 40W
Paimpol, France **26 D3** 48 48N 3 4W
Painan, Indonesia **84 C2** 1 21 S 100 34 E
Painesville, U.S.A. **150 E3** 41 43N 81 15W
Paint Hills = Wemindji, Canada **140 B4** 53 0N 78 49W
Paint L., Canada **143 B9** 55 28N 97 57W
Painted Desert, U.S.A. **159 J8** 36 0N 111 0W
Paintsville, U.S.A. **148 G4** 37 49N 82 48W
País Vasco □, Spain **40 C2** 42 50N 2 45W
Paisley, Canada **150 B3** 44 18N 81 16W
Paisley, U.K. **22 F4** 55 50N 4 25W
Paisley, U.S.A. **158 E3** 42 42N 120 32W
Païta, N. Cal. **133 V20** 22 8 S 166 22 E
Paita, Peru **172 B1** 5 11 S 81 9W
Paithan, India **94 E2** 19 29N 75 23 E
Paiva →, Portugal **42 D2** 41 4N 8 16W
Paizhou, China **77 B9** 30 12N 113 55 E
Paja, Cerro, Ecuador **172 a** 1 17 S 90 26W
Pajares, Spain **42 B5** 43 1N 5 46W
Pajares, Puerto de, Spain **42 C5** 42 58N 5 46W
Pajarito, Colombia **168 B3** 5 17N 72 43W
Pajęczno, Poland **55 G5** 51 10N 19 0 E
Pak Lay, Laos **86 C3** 18 15N 101 27 E
Pak Phanang, Thailand **87 H3** 8 21N 100 12 E
Pak Sane, Laos **86 C4** 18 22N 103 39 E
Pak Song, Laos **86 E6** 15 11N 106 14 E
Pak Suong, Laos **76 H4** 19 58N 102 15 E
Pak Tam Chung, China **69 G11** 22 24N 114 19 E
Pakala, India **95 H4** 13 29N 79 8 E
Pakaraima Mts., Guyana **169 B5** 6 0N 60 0W
Pakaur, India **93 G12** 24 38N 87 51 E
Pakenham, Australia **129 E6** 38 6 S 145 30 E
Pakenham, Canada **151 A8** 45 18N 76 18W
Pákhnes, Greece **39 E5** 35 16N 24 4 E
Pakhtaabad, Uzbekistan **65 C6** 40 55N 72 29 E
Pakhuis, S. Africa **116 E2** 32 9 S 19 5 E
Pakistan ■, Asia **91 C3** 30 0N 70 0 E
Pakkading, Laos **86 C4** 18 19N 103 59 E
Pakokku, Burma **90 E5** 21 20N 95 0 E
Pakość, Poland **55 F5** 52 48N 18 6 E
Pakowki L., Canada **143 D6** 49 20N 111 0W
Pakpattan, Pakistan **91 C4** 30 25N 73 27 E
Pakrac, Croatia **52 E2** 45 27N 17 12 E
Pakruojis, Lithuania **54 C10** 55 58N 23 52 E
Paks, Hungary **52 D3** 46 38N 18 55 E
Paktīā □, Afghan. **91 B3** 33 0N 69 15 E
Paktīkā □, Afghan. **91 B3** 32 30N 69 0 E
Pakwach, Uganda **118 B3** 2 28N 31 27 E
Pakxe, Laos **86 E5** 15 5N 105 52 E
Pal Lahara, India **93 J11** 21 27N 85 11 E
Pala, Chad **109 G3** 9 25N 15 5 E
Pala, Dem. Rep. of the Congo **118 D2** 6 45 S 29 30 E
Pala, U.S.A. **161 M9** 33 22N 117 5W
Palabek, Uganda **118 B3** 3 22N 32 33 E
Palacios, U.S.A. **155 L6** 28 42N 96 13W
Palafrugell, Spain **40 D8** 41 55N 3 10 E
Palagiano, Italy **47 B10** 40 35N 17 2 E
Palagonía, Italy **47 E7** 37 19N 14 45 E
Palagruža, Croatia **45 F13** 42 24N 16 15 E
Palaiókastron, Greece **39 E7** 35 12N 26 15 E
Palaiokhóra, Greece **39 E4** 35 16N 23 39 E
Pálairos, Greece **39 B2** 38 47N 20 53 E
Palaiseau, France **27 D9** 48 43N 2 15 E
Palakol, India **95 F5** 16 31N 81 46 E
Palalankwe, India **95 J11** 10 52N 92 29 E
Palam, India **94 E3** 19 0N 77 0 E
Palamás, Greece **48 B4** 39 26N 22 4 E
Palamòs, Spain **40 D8** 41 50N 3 10 E
Palampur, India **92 C7** 32 10N 76 30 E
Palamut, Turkey **49 C9** 38 59N 27 41 E
Palana, Australia **127 F4** 39 45 S 147 55 E
Palana, Russia **67 D16** 59 10N 159 59 E
Palanan, Phil. **80 C4** 17 8N 122 29 E
Palanan Bay, Phil. **80 C4** 17 9N 122 27 E
Palanan Pt., Phil. **80 C4** 17 17N 122 30 E
Palandri, Pakistan **93 C5** 33 42N 73 40 E
Palanga, Lithuania **15 J19** 55 58N 21 3 E
Palanganene, Dem. Rep. of the Congo **115 D3** 6 32 S 18 52 E
Palangkaraya, Indonesia **85 C4** 2 16 S 113 56 E
Palani, India **95 J3** 10 30N 77 30 E
Palani Hills, India **95 J3** 10 14N 77 33 E
Palanpur, India **92 G5** 24 10N 72 25 E
Palanro, Indonesia **82 B1** 3 21 S 119 23 E
Palaoa Pt., U.S.A. **145 C5** 20 44N 156 58W
Palapag, Phil. **80 E5** 12 33N 125 7 E
Palapye, Botswana **116 C4** 22 30 S 27 7 E
Palar →, India **95 H5** 12 27N 80 13 E
Palas, Pakistan **93 B5** 35 4N 73 14 E
Palas de Rei, Spain **42 C3** 42 52N 7 52W
Palashi, India **93 H13** 23 47N 88 15 E
Palasponga, India **93 J11** 21 47N 85 34 E
Palatine, U.S.A. **157 B8** 42 7N 88 3W
Palatka, Russia **67 C16** 60 6N 150 54 E
Palatka, U.S.A. **152 F8** 29 39N 81 38W
Palau, Italy **46 A2** 41 11N 9 23 E
Palau, Mexico **63 J17** 27 53N 101 25W
Palau ■, Pac. Oc. **62 J17** 7 30N 134 30 E
Palauk, Burma **86 F2** 13 10N 98 40 E
Palawan, Phil. **81 G2** 9 30N 118 30 E
Palawan □, Phil. **81 G2** 10 0N 119 0 E
Palawan Passage, Phil. **81 G2** 10 0N 118 0 E
Palayan, Phil. **80 D3** 15 36N 121 8 E
Palayankottai, India **95 K3** 8 45N 77 45 E
Palazzo, Pte., France **29 F12** 42 28N 8 30 E
Palazzo San Gervásio, Italy **47 B8** 40 56N 15 59 E
Palazzolo Acréide, Italy **47 E7** 37 4N 14 54 E
Palca, Chile **172 D4** 19 7 S 69 9W
Paldiski, Estonia **15 G21** 59 23N 24 9 E
Pale, Bos.-H. **52 G3** 43 50N 18 38 E
Palel, India **90 C5** 24 27N 94 2 E
Paleleh, Indonesia **82 A2** 1 10N 121 50 E
Palembang, Indonesia **84 C2** 3 0 S 104 50 E
Palena →, Chile **176 B2** 43 50 S 73 50W
Palena, L., Chile **176 B2** 43 55 S 71 40W
Palencia, Spain **42 C6** 42 1N 4 34W
Palencia □, Spain **42 C6** 42 31N 4 33W
Palenque, Mexico **163 D6** 17 31N 91 58W
Paleokastrítsa, Greece **38 B9** 39 40N 19 41 E
Paleometokho, Cyprus **39 E9** 35 7N 33 11 E
Palermo, Colombia **168 C2** 2 54N 75 26W
Palermo, Italy **46 D6** 38 7N 13 22 E
Palermo, U.S.A. **158 G3** 39 26N 121 33W
Palestine, Asia **103 D4** 32 0N 35 0 E
Palestine, Ill., U.S.A. **157 F9** 39 0N 87 37W
Palestine, Tex., U.S.A. **155 K7** 31 46N 95 38W
Palestrina, Italy **45 G9** 41 50N 12 53 E
Paletwa, Burma **90 E4** 21 10N 92 50 E
Palghat, India **95 J3** 10 46N 76 42 E
Palgrave, Mt., Australia **124 D2** 23 22 S 115 58 E
Pali, India **92 G5** 25 50N 73 20 E
Palikea Pk., U.S.A. **145 K13** 21 26N 158 6W
Palikir, Micronesia **134 G7** 6 55N 158 9 E
Palimbang, Phil. **81 H5** 6 12N 124 12 E
Palin, Mt., Malaysia **85 A5** 6 10N 117 10 E
Palinuro, Italy **47 B8** 40 2N 15 17 E
Palinuro, C., Italy **47 B8** 40 2N 15 16 E
Palioúrion, Ákra, Greece **50 G7** 39 57N 23 45 E
Palisades Reservoir, U.S.A. **158 E8** 43 20N 111 12W
Paliseul, Belgium **24 E5** 49 54N 5 8 E
Palitana, India **92 J4** 21 32N 71 49 E
Palizada, Mexico **163 D6** 18 18N 92 8W
Palk Bay, Asia **95 K4** 9 30N 79 15 E
Palk Strait, Asia **95 K4** 10 0N 79 45 E
Palkānah, Iraq **96 C5** 35 49N 44 26 E
Palkonda, India **94 E6** 18 36N 83 48 E
Palkonda Ra., India **95 H4** 13 50N 79 20 E
Palkot, India **93 H11** 22 53N 84 39 E
Palla Road = Dinokwe, Botswana **116 C4** 23 29 S 26 37 E
Pallanza = Verbánia, Italy **44 C5** 45 56N 8 33 E
Pallarenda, Australia **126 B4** 19 12 S 146 46 E
Pallasovka, Russia **60 E8** 50 4N 47 0 E
Palleru →, India **94 F5** 16 45N 80 2 E
Pallës, Bishti i, Albania **50 E3** 41 24N 19 24 E
Pallinup →, Australia **125 F2** 34 27 S 118 50 E
Pallisa, Uganda **118 B3** 1 12N 33 43 E
Palliser, C., N.Z. **130 H4** 41 37 S 175 14 E
Palliser B., N.Z. **130 H4** 41 26 S 175 5 E
Pallu, India **92 E6** 28 59N 74 14 E
Palm Bay, U.S.A. **149 L5** 28 2N 80 35W
Palm Beach, U.S.A. **149 M6** 26 43N 80 2W
Palm Coast, U.S.A. **149 L5** 29 32N 81 10W
Palm Desert, U.S.A. **161 M10** 33 43N 116 22W
Palm Harbor, U.S.A. **153 G7** 28 5N 82 47W
Palm Is., Australia **126 B4** 18 40 S 146 35 E
Palm Springs, U.S.A. **161 M10** 33 50N 116 33W
Palma, Mozam. **119 E5** 10 46 S 40 29 E
Palma →, Brazil **171 D2** 12 33 S 47 52W
Palma, B. de, Spain **38 B3** 39 30N 2 39 E
Palma de Mallorca, Spain **38 B3** 39 35N 2 39 E
Palma del Río, Spain **43 H5** 37 43N 5 17W
Palma di Montechiaro, Italy **46 E6** 37 11N 13 46 E

Palma Nova, *Spain* **38 B3** 39 32N 2 34 E
Palma Soriano, *Cuba* **164 B4** 20 15N 76 0W
Palmaner, *India* **95 H4** 13 12N 78 45 E
Palmares, *Brazil* **170 C4** 8 41 S 35 28W
Palmarito, *Venezuela* **168 B3** 7 37N 70 10W
Palmarola, *Italy* **46 B5** 40 56N 12 51 E
Palmas, *Brazil* **175 B5** 26 29 S 52 0W
Palmas, C., *Liberia* **112 E3** 4 27N 7 46W
Pálmas, G. di, *Italy* **46 D1** 39 0N 8 30 E
Palmas de Monte Alto, *Brazil* **171 D3** 14 16 S 43 10W
Palmdale, *Calif., U.S.A.* **161 L8** 34 35N 118 7W
Palmdale, *Fla., U.S.A.* **153 J8** 26 57N 81 19W
Palmeira, *Brazil* **171 G2** 25 25 S 50 0W
Palmeira das Missões, *Brazil* **175 B5** 27 55 S 53 17W
Palmeira dos Índios, *Brazil* **170 C4** 9 25 S 36 37W
Palmeirais, *Brazil* **170 C3** 6 0 S 43 0W
Palmeiras, *Brazil* **171 D3** 12 31 S 41 34W
Palmeiras →, *Brazil* **171 D2** 12 22 S 47 8W
Palmeirinhas, Pta. das, *Angola* **115 D2** 9 2 S 12 57 E
Palmela, *Portugal* **43 G2** 38 32N 8 57W
Palmelo, *Brazil* **171 E2** 17 20 S 48 27W
Palmer, *U.S.A.* **144 F10** 61 36N 149 7W
Palmer →, *Australia* **126 B3** 16 0 S 142 26 E
Palmer Arch., *Antarctica* **7 C17** 64 15 S 65 0W
Palmer Lake, *U.S.A.* **154 F2** 39 7N 104 55W
Palmer Land, *Antarctica* **7 D18** 73 0 S 63 0W
Palmerston, *Canada* **150 C4** 43 50N 80 51W
Palmerston, *N.Z.* **131 F5** 45 29 S 170 43 E
Palmerston North, *N.Z.* **130 G4** 40 21 S 175 39 E
Palmerton, *U.S.A.* **151 F9** 40 48N 75 37W
Palmetto, *Fla., U.S.A.* **149 M4** 27 31N 82 34W
Palmetto, *Ga., U.S.A.* **152 B5** 33 31N 84 40W
Palmi, *Italy* **47 D8** 38 21N 15 51 E
Palmira, *Argentina* **174 C2** 32 59 S 68 34W
Palmira, *Colombia* **168 C2** 3 32N 76 16W
Palmyra = Tudmur, *Syria* **101 E8** 34 36N 38 15 E
Palmyra, *Ill., U.S.A.* **156 E7** 39 26N 90 0W
Palmyra, *Mo., U.S.A.* **156 E5** 39 48N 91 32W
Palmyra, *N.J., U.S.A.* **151 F9** 40 1N 75 1W
Palmyra, *N.Y., U.S.A.* **150 C7** 43 5N 77 18W
Palmyra, *Pa., U.S.A.* **151 F8** 40 18N 76 36W
Palmyra, *Wis., U.S.A.* **157 B8** 42 52N 88 36W
Palmyra Is., *Pac. Oc.* **135 G11** 5 52N 162 5W
Palmyras Pt., *India* **94 D8** 20 46N 87 1 E
Palo, *Phil.* **81 F5** 11 10N 124 59 E
Palo Alto, *U.S.A.* **160 H4** 37 27N 122 10W
Palo Seco, *Trin. & Tob.* **169 F9** 10 4N 61 36W
Palo Verde, *U.S.A.* **161 M12** 33 26N 114 44W
Paloich, *Sudan* **107 E3** 10 28N 32 32 E
Palompon, *Phil.* **81 F5** 11 3N 124 23 E
Palopo, *Indonesia* **82 B2** 3 0 S 120 16 E
Palos, C. de, *Spain* **41 H4** 37 38N 0 40W
Palos de la Frontera, *Spain* **43 H4** 37 14N 6 53W
Palos Verdes, *U.S.A.* **161 M8** 33 48N 118 23W
Palos Verdes, Pt., *U.S.A.* **161 M8** 33 43N 118 26W
Palpa, *Peru* **172 C2** 14 30 S 75 15W
Pålsboda, *Sweden* **16 E9** 59 3N 15 22 E
Palu, *Indonesia* **82 B1** 1 0 S 119 52 E
Palu, *Turkey* **101 C9** 38 45N 40 0 E
Paluan, *Phil.* **80 E3** 13 26N 120 29 E
Paluke, *Liberia* **112 D3** 5 2N 8 5W
Paluzza, *Italy* **45 B10** 46 32N 13 1 E
Palwal, *India* **92 E7** 28 8N 77 19 E
Pama, *Burkina Faso* **113 C5** 11 19N 0 44 E
Pama →, *C.A.R.* **114 B3** 4 23N 18 43 E
Pama, Réserve de, *Burkina Faso* **113 C5** 11 27N 0 40 E
Pamanukan, *Indonesia* **85 D3** 6 16 S 107 49 E
Pamban I., *India* **95 K4** 9 15N 79 20 E
Pamekasan, *Indonesia* **85 D4** 7 10 S 113 28 E
Pamenang, *Indonesia* **79 J19** 8 24 S 116 6 E
Pamiers, *France* **28 E5** 43 7N 1 39 E
Pamir, *Tajikistan* **66 F8** 37 40N 73 0 E
Pamir →, *Tajikistan* **65 E6** 37 1N 72 41 E
Pamlico →, *U.S.A.* **149 H7** 35 20N 76 28W
Pamlico Sd., *U.S.A.* **149 H8** 35 20N 76 0W
Pampa, *U.S.A.* **155 H4** 35 32N 100 58W
Pampa de Agma, *Argentina* **176 B3** 43 45 S 69 40W
Pampa de las Salinas, *Argentina* **174 C2** 32 1 S 66 58W
Pampa Grande, *Bolivia* **173 D5** 18 5 S 64 6W
Pampa Hermosa, *Peru* **172 B2** 7 7 S 75 4W
Pampanga □, *Phil.* **80 D3** 15 4N 120 40 E
Pampanua, *Indonesia* **82 B2** 4 16 S 120 8 E
Pampas, *Argentina* **174 D3** 35 0 S 63 0W
Pampas, *Peru* **172 C3** 12 20 S 74 50W
Pampas →, *Peru* **172 C3** 13 24 S 73 12W
Pamphylia, *Turkey* **100 D4** 37 0N 31 20 E
Pamplona, *Colombia* **168 B3** 7 23N 72 39W
Pamplona, *Phil.* **80 B3** 18 31N 121 20 E
Pamplona, *Spain* **40 C3** 42 48N 1 38W
Pampoenpoort, *S. Africa* **116 E3** 31 3 S 22 40 E
Pamukçu, *Turkey* **49 B9** 39 30N 27 54 E
Pamukkale, *Turkey* **49 D11** 37 55N 29 8 E
Pan Xian, *China* **76 E5** 25 46N 104 38 E
Pana, *U.S.A.* **156 E7** 39 23N 89 5W
Panabo, *Phil.* **81 H5** 7 19N 125 42 E
Panaca, *U.S.A.* **159 H6** 37 47N 114 23W
Panacea, *U.S.A.* **152 E5** 30 2N 84 23W
Panagyurishte, *Bulgaria* **51 D8** 42 30N 24 15 E
Panaitan, *Indonesia* **84 D3** 6 36 S 105 12 E
Panaji, *India* **95 G1** 15 25N 73 50 E
Panamá, *Panama* **164 E4** 9 0N 79 25W
Panama, *Sri Lanka* **95 L5** 6 45N 81 48 E
Panama ■, *Cent. Amer.* **164 E4** 8 48N 79 55W
Panamá, G. de, *Panama* **164 E4** 8 4N 79 20W
Panama Canal, *Panama* **164 E4** 9 10N 79 37W
Panama City, *U.S.A.* **152 E4** 30 10N 85 40W
Panama City Beach, *U.S.A.* **152 E4** 30 11N 85 48W
Panamint Range, *U.S.A.* **161 J9** 36 20N 117 20W
Panamint Springs, *U.S.A.* **161 J9** 36 20N 117 28W
Panão, *Peru* **172 B2** 9 55 S 75 55W
Panaon I., *Phil.* **81 F5** 10 3N 125 13 E
Panare, *Thailand* **87 J3** 6 51N 101 30 E
Panarea, *Italy* **47 D8** 38 38N 15 4 E
Panaro →, *Italy* **45 D8** 44 55N 11 25 E
Panarukan, *Indonesia* **85 D4** 7 42 S 113 56 E
Panay, *Phil.* **81 F4** 11 10N 122 30 E
Panay, G., *Phil.* **79 B6** 11 0N 122 30 E
Pančevo, *Serbia, Yug.* **52 F5** 44 52N 20 41 E
Panch'iao, *Taiwan* **77 E13** 25 1N 121 27 E
Panciu, *Romania* **53 E12** 45 54N 27 8 E
Pancol, *Phil.* **81 F2** 10 52N 119 25 E
Pancorbo, Desfiladero, *Spain* **42 C7** 42 32N 3 5W
Pâncota, *Romania* **52 D6** 46 20N 21 45 E
Panda, *Mozam.* **117 C5** 24 2 S 34 45 E
Pandan, *Malaysia* **87 d** 1 32N 103 46 E
Pandan, *Antique, Phil.* **81 F4** 11 45N 122 10 E
Pandan, *Catanduanes, Phil.* **80 D5** 14 3N 124 10 E
Pandan, Selat, *Singapore* **87 d** 1 15N 103 44 E
Pandan Bay, *Phil.* **81 F4** 11 43N 122 0 E
Pandegelang, *Indonesia* **84 D3** 6 25 S 106 5 E
Pandhana, *India* **92 J7** 21 42N 76 13 E
Pandharkawada, *India* **94 D4** 20 1N 78 32 E
Pandharpur, *India* **94 F2** 17 41N 75 20 E
Pandhurna, *India* **94 D4** 21 36N 78 35 E
Pando, *Uruguay* **175 C4** 34 44 S 56 0W
Pando □, *Bolivia* **172 C4** 11 20 S 67 40W
Pando, L. = Hope, L., *Australia* **127 D2** 28 24 S 139 18 E
Pandokrátor, *Greece* **38 B9** 39 45N 19 50 E
Pandora, *Costa Rica* **164 E3** 9 43N 83 3W
Pandrup, *Denmark* **17 G3** 57 14N 9 40 E
Pandu, *Dem. Rep. of the Congo* **114 B3** 4 59N 19 16 E
Panevėžys, *Lithuania* **15 J21** 55 42N 24 25 E
Panfilov, *Kazakstan* **66 E8** 44 10N 80 0 E
Panfilov Atyndaghy, *Kazakstan* **65 B8** 43 23N 77 7 E
Panfilovo, *Russia* **60 E6** 50 25N 42 46 E
Panga, *Dem. Rep. of the Congo* **118 B2** 1 52N 26 18 E
Pangaíon Óros, *Greece* **51 F8** 40 50N 24 0 E
Pangala, *Congo* **114 C2** 3 16 S 14 34 E
Pangalanes, Canal des = Ampangalana, Lakandranon', *Madag.* **117 C8** 22 48 S 47 50 E
Pangani, *Tanzania* **118 D4** 5 25 S 38 58 E
Pangani →, *Tanzania* **118 D4** 5 26 S 38 58 E
Pangantocan, *Phil.* **81 H5** 7 50N 124 49 E
Pangar Djérem, Réserve de, *Cameroon* **114 A2** 5 50N 13 10 E
Pangasinan □, *Phil.* **80 D3** 15 55N 120 20 E
Pangfou = Bengbu, *China* **75 H9** 32 58N 117 20 E
Pangil, *Dem. Rep. of the Congo* **118 C2** 3 10 S 26 35 E
Pangkah, Tanjung, *Indonesia* **85 D4** 6 51 S 112 33 E
Pangkai, *Burma* **90 D7** 22 40N 98 40 E
Pangkajene, *Indonesia* **82 B1** 4 46 S 119 34 E
Pangkalanbrandan, *Indonesia* **84 B1** 4 1N 98 20 E
Pangkalanbuun, *Indonesia* **85 C4** 2 41 S 111 37 E
Pangkalansusu, *Indonesia* **84 B1** 4 2N 98 13 E
Pangkalpinang, *Indonesia* **84 C3** 2 0 S 106 0 E
Pangkoh, *Indonesia* **85 C4** 3 5 S 114 8 E
Panglao, *Phil.* **81 G4** 9 35N 123 45 E
Panglao I., *Phil.* **81 G4** 9 35N 123 48 E
Pangnirtung, *Canada* **139 B13** 66 8N 65 54W
Pango Alucuem, *Angola* **115 D2** 8 43 S 14 33 E
Pangong Tso, *India* **92 B8** 34 40N 78 40 E
Pangrango, *Indonesia* **84 D3** 6 46 S 107 1 E
Pangsau Pass, *Burma* **90 B6** 27 15N 96 10 E
Pangtara, *Burma* **90 E6** 20 57N 96 40 E
Panguipulli, *Chile* **176 A2** 39 38 S 72 20W
Panguitch, *U.S.A.* **159 H7** 37 50N 112 26W
Panguna, *Papua N. G.* **132 D8** 6 21 S 155 25 E
Pangutaran, *Phil.* **81 H3** 6 18N 120 35 E
Pangutaran Group, *Phil.* **81 H3** 6 18N 120 34 E
Panhala, *India* **94 F2** 16 49N 74 7 E
Panhandle, *U.S.A.* **155 H4** 35 21N 101 23W
Pani Mines, *India* **92 H5** 22 29N 73 50 E
Pania-Mutombo, *Dem. Rep. of the Congo* **118 D1** 5 11 S 23 51 E
Paniau, *U.S.A.* **145 B1** 21 56N 160 5W
Panié, Mt., *N. Cal.* **133 T18** 20 36 S 164 46 E
Panikota I., *India* **92 J4** 20 46N 71 21 E
Panipat, *India* **92 E7** 29 25N 77 2 E
Panitan, *Phil.* **81 F4** 11 28N 122 46 E
Panj = Pyandzh, *Tajikistan* **65 E4** 37 14N 69 6 E
Panj = Pyandzh →, *Asia* **65 E4** 37 6N 68 20 E
Panjab, *Afghan.* **91 B2** 34 23N 67 1 E
Panjakent = Pendzhikent, *Tajikistan* **65 D3** 39 29N 67 37 E
Panjal Range = Pir Panjal Range, *India* **92 C7** 32 30N 76 50 E
Panjang, Hon, *Vietnam* **87 H4** 9 20N 103 28 E
Panjgur, *Pakistan* **91 D2** 27 0N 64 5 E
Panjhra →, *India* **94 D2** 21 13N 74 57 E
Panji Poyon, *Tajikistan* **65 E4** 37 12N 68 35 E
Panjim = Panaji, *India* **95 G1** 15 25N 73 50 E
Panjin, *China* **75 D12** 41 3N 122 2 E
Panjnad →, *Pakistan* **92 E4** 28 57N 70 30 E
Panjwai, *Afghan.* **91 C2** 31 26N 65 27 E
Pankshin, *Nigeria* **113 D6** 9 16N 9 25 E
Panmunjŏm, *N. Korea* **75 F14** 37 59N 126 38 E
Panna, *India* **93 G9** 24 40N 80 15 E
Panna Hills, *India* **93 G9** 24 40N 81 15 E
Pannawonica, *Australia* **124 D2** 21 39 S 116 19 E
Pannga, Tanjung, *Indonesia* **79 K19** 8 54 S 116 2 E
Panngi, *Vanuatu* **133 E6** 15 58 S 168 12 E
Pannirtuuq = Pangnirtung, *Canada* **139 B13** 66 8N 65 54W
Pano Akil, *Pakistan* **92 F3** 27 51N 69 7 E
Pano Lefkara, *Cyprus* **39 F9** 34 53N 33 20 E
Pano Panayia, *Cyprus* **39 F8** 34 55N 32 38 E
Panora, *U.S.A.* **156 C2** 41 42N 94 22W
Panorama, *Brazil* **175 A5** 21 21 S 51 51W
Pánormon, *Greece* **39 E5** 35 25N 24 41 E
Panruti, *India* **95 J4** 11 46N 79 35 E
Pansemal, *India* **92 J6** 21 39N 74 42 E
Panshan = Panjin, *China* **75 D12** 41 3N 122 2 E
Panshi, *China* **75 C14** 42 58N 126 5 E
Pantanaw, *Burma* **90 G5** 16 59N 95 28 E
Pantar, *Indonesia* **82 C2** 8 28 S 124 10 E
Pante Macassar, *E. Timor* **82 C2** 9 30 S 123 58 E
Pante Makasar = Pante Macassar, *E. Timor* **82 C2** 9 30 S 123 58 E
Pantelleria, *Italy* **46 F4** 36 50N 11 57 E
Pantin Sakan, *Burma* **90 F6** 18 38N 97 33 E
Pantoja, *Peru* **168 D2** 0 58 S 75 10W
Pantón, *Spain* **42 C3** 42 31N 7 37W
Pantukan, *Phil.* **81 H5** 7 9N 125 54 E
Panu, *Dem. Rep. of the Congo* **114 C3** 3 50 S 19 10 E
Pánuco, *Mexico* **163 C5** 22 0N 98 15W
Panukulan, *Phil.* **80 D3** 14 56N 121 49 E
Panvel, *India* **94 E1** 18 59N 73 4 E
Panyam, *Nigeria* **113 D6** 9 27N 9 8 E
Panyu, *China* **77 F9** 22 51N 113 20 E
Panzhihua, *China* **76 D3** 26 33N 101 44 E
Panzi, *Dem. Rep. of the Congo* **115 D3** 7 17 S 18 1 E
Pao →, *Anzoátegui, Venezuela* **169 B5** 8 6N 64 17W
Pao →, *Apure, Venezuela* **168 B4** 8 33N 68 1W
Páola, *Italy* **47 C9** 39 21N 16 2 E
Paola, *Malta* **38 F8** 35 52N 14 30 E
Paola, *U.S.A.* **154 F7** 38 35N 94 53W
Paoli, *U.S.A.* **157 F10** 38 33N 86 28W
Paonia, *U.S.A.* **159 G10** 38 52N 107 36W
Paoting = Baoding, *China* **74 E8** 38 50N 115 28 E
Paot'ou = Baotou, *China* **74 D6** 40 32N 110 2 E
Paoua, *C.A.R.* **114 A3** 7 9N 16 20 E
Pap, *Uzbekistan* **65 C5** 40 52N 71 6 E
Pápa, *Hungary* **52 C2** 47 22N 17 30 E
Papa, *U.S.A.* **145 D6** 19 13N 155 52W
Papa Stour, *U.K.* **22 A7** 60 20N 1 42W
Papa Westray, *U.K.* **22 B6** 59 20N 2 55W
Papaaloa, *U.S.A.* **145 D6** 19 59N 155 13W
Papagayo →, *Mexico* **163 D5** 16 36N 99 43W
Papagayo, G. de, *Costa Rica* **164 D2** 10 30N 85 50W
Papagni →, *India* **95 G3** 15 35N 77 45 E
Papaïchton, *Fr. Guiana* **169 C7** 3 48N 54 10W
Papaikou, *U.S.A.* **145 D6** 19 47N 155 6W
Papakura, *N.Z.* **130 D3** 37 4 S 174 59 E
Papantla, *Mexico* **163 C5** 20 30N 97 30W
Papar, *Malaysia* **78 C5** 5 45N 116 0 E
Papara, *Tahiti* **133 S16** 17 43 S 149 22W
Paparoa, *N.Z.* **130 C3** 36 6 S 174 16 E
Paparoa Nat. Park, *N.Z.* **131 C6** 42 7 S 171 26 E
Paparoa Ra., *N.Z.* **131 C6** 42 5 S 171 35 E
Pápas, Ákra, *Greece* **48 C3** 38 13N 21 20 E
Papatoetoe, *N.Z.* **130 C3** 36 59 S 174 51 E
Papatura, *Solomon Is.* **133 L10** 7 32 S 158 47 E
Papawai Pt., *U.S.A.* **145 C5** 20 47N 156 32W
Papeete, *Tahiti* **133 S16** 17 32 S 149 34W
Papenburg, *Germany* **30 B3** 53 5N 7 23 E
Papetoai, *Tahiti* **133 S16** 17 29 S 149 52W
Paphlagonia, *Turkey* **100 B5** 41 30N 33 0 E
Paphos, *Cyprus* **39 F8** 34 46N 32 25 E
Papien Chiang = Da →, *Vietnam* **76 G5** 21 15N 105 20 E
Papigochic →, *Mexico* **162 B3** 29 9N 109 40W
Paposo, *Chile* **174 B1** 25 0 S 70 30W
Papoutsa, *Cyprus* **39 F9** 34 54N 33 4 E
Papua, G. of, *Papua N. G.* **132 E3** 9 0 S 144 50 E
Papua New Guinea ■, *Oceania* **132 D3** 8 0 S 145 0 E
Papudo, *Chile* **174 C1** 32 29 S 71 27W
Papuk, *Croatia* **52 E2** 45 30N 17 30 E
Papun, *Burma* **90 F6** 18 2N 97 30 E
Papunya, *Australia* **124 D5** 23 15 S 131 54 E
Pará = Belém, *Brazil* **170 B2** 1 20 S 48 30W
Pará □, *Brazil* **173 A7** 3 20 S 52 0W
Paraburdoo, *Australia* **124 D2** 23 14 S 117 32 E
Paracale, *Phil.* **80 D4** 14 17N 122 48 E
Paracas, Pen., *Peru* **172 C2** 13 53 S 76 20W
Paracatu, *Brazil* **171 E2** 17 10 S 46 50W
Paracatu →, *Brazil* **171 E2** 16 30 S 45 4W
Paracel Is., *S. China Sea* **78 A4** 15 50N 112 0 E
Parachilna, *Australia* **128 A3** 31 10 S 138 21 E
Parachinar, *Pakistan* **91 B3** 33 55N 70 5 E
Paraćin, *Serbia, Yug.* **50 C5** 43 54N 21 27 E
Paracuru, *Brazil* **170 B4** 3 24 S 39 4W
Parada, Punta, *Peru* **172 D2** 15 22 S 75 11W
Paradas, *Spain* **43 H5** 37 18N 5 29W
Paradela, *Spain* **42 C3** 42 44N 7 37W
Paradhísi, *Greece* **38 E12** 36 18N 28 7 E
Paradip, *India* **94 D8** 20 15N 86 35 E
Paradise, *Calif., U.S.A.* **160 F5** 39 46N 121 37W
Paradise, *Nev., U.S.A.* **161 J11** 36 9N 115 10W
Paradise →, *Canada* **141 B8** 53 27N 57 19W
Paradise Hill, *Canada* **143 C7** 53 32N 109 28W
Paradise I., *Bahamas* **9 b** 25 6N 77 19W
Paradise River, *Canada* **141 B8** 53 27N 57 17W
Paradise Valley, *U.S.A.* **158 F5** 41 30N 117 32W
Parado, *Indonesia* **85 D5** 8 42 S 118 30 E
Paragould, *U.S.A.* **155 G9** 36 3N 90 29W
Paraguá →, *Bolivia* **173 C5** 13 34 S 61 53W
Paragua →, *Venezuela* **169 B5** 6 55N 62 55W
Paraguaçu →, *Brazil* **171 D4** 12 45 S 38 54W
Paraguaçu Paulista, *Brazil* **175 A5** 22 22 S 50 35W
Paraguaipoa, *Venezuela* **168 A3** 11 21N 71 57W
Paraguaná, Pen. de, *Venezuela* **168 A3** 12 0N 70 0W
Paraguarí, *Paraguay* **174 B4** 25 36 S 57 0W
Paraguarí □, *Paraguay* **174 B4** 26 0 S 57 10W
Paraguay ■, *S. Amer.* **174 A4** 23 0 S 57 0W
Paraguay →, *Paraguay* **174 B4** 27 18 S 58 38W
Paraíba = João Pessoa, *Brazil* **170 C5** 7 10 S 34 52W
Paraíba □, *Brazil* **170 C4** 7 0 S 36 0W
Paraíba do Sul →, *Brazil* **171 F3** 21 37 S 41 3W
Parainen, *Finland* **15 F20** 60 18N 22 18 E
Paraiso, *Brazil* **173** 19 3 S 52 59W
Paraiso, *Mexico* **163 D6** 18 24N 93 14W
Parak, *Iran* **97 E7** 27 38N 52 25 E
Parakhino Paddubye, *Russia* **58 C7** 58 26N 33 10 E
Parakou, *Benin* **113 D5** 9 25N 2 40 E
Parakylia, *Australia* **128 A2** 30 24 S 136 25 E
Paralimni, *Cyprus* **39 E9** 35 2N 33 58 E
Parálion-Astrous, *Greece* **48 D4** 37 25N 22 45 E
Paralkote, *India* **94 E5** 19 47N 80 41 E
Parama I., *Papua N. G.* **132 E2** 9 0 S 143 25 E
Paramaribo, *Surinam* **169 B6** 5 50N 55 10W
Parambu, *Brazil* **170 C3** 6 13 S 40 43W
Paramillo, Nudo del, *Colombia* **168 B2** 7 4N 75 55W
Paramirim, *Brazil* **171 D3** 13 26 S 42 15W
Paramirim →, *Brazil* **171 D3** 11 34 S 43 18W
Paramithiá, *Greece* **48 B2** 39 30N 20 35 E
Paramushir, Ostrov, *Russia* **67 D16** 50 24N 156 0 E
Paran →, *Israel* **103 E4** 30 20N 35 10 E
Paraná, *Argentina* **174 C3** 31 45 S 60 30W
Paraná, *Brazil* **171 D2** 12 30 S 47 48W
Paraná □, *Brazil* **175 A5** 24 30 S 51 0W
Paraná →, *Argentina* **174 C4** 33 43 S 59 15W
Paranã →, *Brazil* **171 D2** 12 30 S 48 14W
Paranaguá, *Brazil* **175 B6** 25 30 S 48 30W
Paranaíba, *Brazil* **173 D7** 19 40 S 51 11W
Paranaíba →, *Brazil* **171 F1** 20 6 S 51 4W
Paranapanema →, *Brazil* **175 A5** 22 40 S 53 9W
Paranapiacaba, Serra do, *Brazil* **175 A6** 24 31 S 48 35W
Paranas, *Phil.* **81 F5** 11 42N 125 2 E
Paranavaí, *Brazil* **175 A5** 23 4 S 52 56W
Parang, *Maguindanao, Phil.* **81 H5** 7 23N 124 16 E
Parang, *Sulu, Phil.* **81 J3** 5 55N 120 54 E
Parangaba, *Brazil* **170 B4** 3 45 S 38 33W
Parangippettai, *India* **95 J4** 11 30N 79 38 E
Parângul Mare, Vf., *Romania* **53 E8** 45 20N 23 37 E
Paranthan, *Sri Lanka* **95 K5** 9 26N 80 24 E
Paraparaumu, *N.Z.* **130 G4** 40 57 S 175 3 E
Parapetí →, *Bolivia* **173 D5** 18 58 S 62 21W
Parapóla, *Greece* **48 E5** 36 55N 23 27 E
Paraspóri, Ákra, *Greece* **49 F9** 35 55N 27 15 E
Paratinga, *Brazil* **171 D3** 12 40 S 43 10W
Paratoo, *Australia* **128 B3** 32 42 S 139 20 E
Paraúna, *Brazil* **171 E1** 16 55 S 50 26W
Paray-le-Monial, *France* **27 F11** 46 27N 4 7 E
Parbati →, *Mad. P., India* **92 G7** 25 50N 76 30 E
Parbati →, *Raj., India* **92 F7** 26 54N 77 53 E
Parbatipur, *Bangla.* **90 C2** 25 39N 88 55 E
Parbhani, *India* **94 E3** 19 8N 76 52 E
Parchim, *Germany* **30 B7** 53 26N 11 52 E
Parczew, *Poland* **55 G9** 51 40N 22 52 E
Pardes Hanna-Karkur, *Israel* **103 C3** 32 28N 34 57 E
Pardilla, *Spain* **42 D7** 41 33N 3 43W
Pardo →, *Bahia, Brazil* **171 E4** 15 40 S 39 0W
Pardo →, *Mato Grosso, Brazil* **175 A5** 21 46 S 52 9W
Pardo →, *Minas Gerais, Brazil* **171 E3** 15 48 S 44 48W
Pardo →, *São Paulo, Brazil* **171 F2** 20 10 S 48 38W
Pardubice, *Czech Rep.* **34 A8** 50 3N 15 45 E
Pare, *Indonesia* **85 D4** 7 43 S 112 12 E
Pare Mts., *Tanzania* **118 C4** 4 0 S 37 45 E
Parecis, Serra dos, *Brazil* **173 C6** 13 0 S 60 0W
Paredes de Nava, *Spain* **42 C6** 42 9N 4 42W
Parelhas, *Brazil* **170 C4** 6 41 S 36 39W
Paren, *Russia* **67 C17** 62 30N 163 15 E
Parenda, *India* **94 E2** 18 16N 75 28 E
Parengarenga Harbour, *N.Z.* **130 A1** 34 31 S 173 0 E
Parent, *Canada* **140 C5** 47 55N 74 35W
Parent, L., *Canada* **140 C4** 48 31N 77 1W
Parentis-en-Born, *France* **28 D2** 44 21N 1 4W
Parepare, *Indonesia* **82 B1** 4 0 S 119 40 E
Parfino, *Russia* **58 D6** 57 59N 31 34 E
Párga, *Greece* **48 B2** 39 15N 20 29 E
Pargi, *India* **94 E3** 17 11N 77 53 E
Pargo, Pta. do, *Madeira* **9 c** 32 49N 17 17W
Paria, G. de, *Venezuela* **169 A5** 10 20N 62 0W
Paria, Pen. de, *Venezuela* **169 A5** 10 50N 62 30W
Pariaguán, *Venezuela* **169 B5** 8 51N 64 34W
Pariaman, *Indonesia* **84 C2** 0 47 S 100 11 E
Paricatuba, *Brazil* **169 D5** 4 26 S 61 53W
Paricutín, Cerro, *Mexico* **162 D4** 19 28N 102 15W
Parigi, *Java, Indonesia* **85 D3** 7 42 S 108 29 E
Parigi, *Sulawesi, Indonesia* **82 B2** 0 50 S 120 5 E
Parika, *Guyana* **169 B6** 6 50N 58 20W
Parikkala, *Finland* **58 B5** 61 33N 29 31 E
Parima, Serra, *Brazil* **169 C5** 2 30N 64 0W
Parinari, *Peru* **172 A3** 4 35 S 74 25W
Pariñas, Pta., *S. Amer.* **166 D2** 4 30 S 82 0W
Parincea, *Romania* **53 D12** 46 27N 27 9 E
Paringa, *Australia* **128 C4** 34 10 S 140 46 E
Parintins, *Brazil* **169 D6** 2 40 S 56 50W
Paris, *Canada* **150 C4** 43 12N 80 25W
Paris, *France* **27 D9** 48 50N 2 20 E
Paris, *Idaho, U.S.A.* **158 E8** 42 14N 111 24W
Paris, *Ill., U.S.A.* **157 E9** 39 36N 87 42W
Paris, *Ky., U.S.A.* **157 F12** 38 13N 84 15W
Paris, *Mo., U.S.A.* **156 E5** 39 29N 92 0W
Paris, *Tenn., U.S.A.* **149 G1** 36 18N 88 19W
Paris, *Tex., U.S.A.* **155 J7** 33 40N 95 33W
Paris, Ville de □, *France* **27 D9** 48 50N 2 20 E
Parish, *U.S.A.* **151 C8** 43 25N 76 8W
Parishville, *U.S.A.* **151 B10** 44 38N 74 49W
Pariti, *Indonesia* **82 D2** 10 1 S 123 45 E
Park, *U.S.A.* **160 B4** 48 45N 122 18W
Park City, *U.S.A.* **155 G6** 37 48N 97 20W
Park Falls, *U.S.A.* **154 C9** 45 56N 90 27W
Park Forest, *U.S.A.* **157 C9** 41 29N 87 40W
Park Head, *Canada* **150 B3** 44 36N 81 9W
Park Hills, *Mo., U.S.A.* **155 G9** 37 53N 90 28W
Park Hills, *Mo., U.S.A.* **156 G6** 37 51N 90 31W
Park Range, *U.S.A.* **158 G10** 40 0N 106 30W
Park Rapids, *U.S.A.* **154 B7** 46 55N 95 4W
Park Ridge, *U.S.A.* **157 B9** 42 2N 87 51W
Park River, *U.S.A.* **154 A6** 48 24N 97 45W
Park Rynie, *S. Africa* **117 E5** 30 25 S 30 45 E
Parkā Bandar, *Iran* **97 E8** 25 55N 59 35 E
Parkal, *India* **94 E4** 18 12N 79 43 E
Parkano, *Finland* **15 E20** 62 1N 23 0 E
Parkent, *Uzbekistan* **65 C4** 41 18N 69 40 E
Parker, *Ariz., U.S.A.* **161 L12** 34 9N 114 17W
Parker, *Pa., U.S.A.* **150 E5** 41 5N 79 41W
Parker Dam, *U.S.A.* **161 L12** 34 18N 114 8W
Parkersburg, *Iowa, U.S.A.* **156 B4** 42 35N 92 47W
Parkersburg, *W. Va., U.S.A.* **148 F5** 39 16N 81 34W
Parkes, *Australia* **129 B8** 33 9 S 148 11 E
Parkfield, *U.S.A.* **160 K6** 35 54N 120 26W
Parkhar, *Tajikistan* **65 E4** 37 30N 69 34 E
Parkhill, *Canada* **150 C3** 43 15N 81 38W
Parkland, *U.S.A.* **160 C4** 47 9N 122 26W
Parkston, *U.S.A.* **154 D6** 43 24N 97 59W
Parksville, *Canada* **142 D4** 49 20N 124 21W
Parla, *Spain* **42 E7** 40 14N 3 46W
Parlakimidi, *India* **94 E7** 18 45N 84 5 E
Parli, *India* **94 E3** 18 50N 76 35 E
Pârliţa, *Moldova* **53 C12** 47 19N 27 52 E
Parma, *Italy* **44 D7** 44 48N 10 20 E
Parma, *Idaho, U.S.A.* **158 E5** 43 47N 116 57W
Parma, *Ohio, U.S.A.* **150 E3** 41 23N 81 43W
Parma →, *Italy* **44 D7** 44 56N 10 26 E
Parnaguá, *Brazil* **170 D3** 10 10 S 44 38W
Parnaíba, *Piauí, Brazil* **170 B3** 2 54 S 41 47W
Parnaíba, *São Paulo, Brazil* **173 D7** 19 34 S 51 14W
Parnaíba →, *Brazil* **170 B3** 3 0 S 41 50W
Parnamirim, *Brazil* **170 C4** 8 5 S 39 34W
Parnarama, *Brazil* **170 C3** 5 31 S 43 6W
Parnassós, *Greece* **48 C4** 38 35N 22 30 E
Parnassus, *N.Z.* **131 C8** 42 42 S 173 23 E
Parndana, *Australia* **128 C2** 35 48 S 137 12 E
Parner, *India* **94 E2** 19 0N 74 26 E
Párnis, *Greece* **48 C5** 38 14N 23 45 E
Párnon Óros, *Greece* **48 D4** 37 15N 22 45 E
Pärnu, *Estonia* **15 G21** 58 28N 24 33 E
Parola, *India* **94 D2** 20 47N 75 7 E
Paroo →, *Australia* **128 A5** 31 28 S 143 32 E
Páros, *Greece* **49 D7** 37 5N 25 12 E
Parowan, *U.S.A.* **159 H7** 37 51N 112 50W
Parpaillon, *France* **29 D10** 44 30N 6 40 E
Parral, *Chile* **174 D1** 36 10 S 71 52W
Parramatta, *Australia* **129 B9** 33 48 S 151 1 E
Parras, *Mexico* **162 B4** 25 30N 102 20W
Parrett →, *U.K.* **21 F4** 51 12N 3 1W
Parris I., *U.S.A.* **152 C9** 32 20N 80 41W
Parrish, *U.S.A.* **153 H7** 27 35N 82 26W
Parrott, *U.S.A.* **152 D5** 31 54N 84 31W
Parrsboro, *Canada* **141 C7** 45 30N 64 25W
Parry I., *Canada* **150 A4** 45 18N 80 10W
Parry Is., *Canada* **6 B2** 77 0N 110 0W
Parry Sound, *Canada* **140 C4** 45 20N 80 0W
Parsberg, *Germany* **31 F7** 49 10N 11 43 E
Parseier Spitze, *Austria* **33 B10** 47 10N 10 28 E
Parsęta →, *Poland* **54 D2** 54 11N 15 34 E
Parsnip →, *Canada* **142 B4** 55 10N 123 2W
Parsons, *U.S.A.* **155 G7** 37 20N 95 16W
Parsons Ra., *Australia* **126 A2** 13 30 S 135 15 E
Partabpur, *India* **94 E5** 20 0N 80 42 E
Partanna, *Italy* **46 E5** 37 43N 12 53 E
Parthenay, *France* **26 F6** 46 38N 0 16W
Partinico, *Italy* **46 D6** 38 3N 13 7 E
Partizánske, *Slovak Rep.* **35 C11** 48 38N 18 23 E
Partridge I., *Canada* **140 A2** 55 59N 87 37W
Partur, *India* **94 E3** 19 40N 76 14 E
Paru →, *Brazil* **169 D7** 1 33 S 52 38W
Parú →, *Venezuela* **168 C4** 4 20N 66 27W
Paru de Oeste →, *Brazil* **169 C6** 1 30N 56 0W
Parucito →, *Venezuela* **168 B4** 5 18N 65 59W
Parur, *India* **95 J3** 10 13N 76 14 E
Paruro, *Peru* **172 C3** 13 45 S 71 50W
Parvān □, *Afghan.* **91 B3** 35 0N 69 0 E
Parvatipuram, *India* **94 E6** 18 50N 83 25 E
Parvatsar, *India* **92 F6** 26 52N 74 49 E
Påryd, *Sweden* **17 H9** 56 34N 15 55 E
Parys, *S. Africa* **116 D4** 26 52 S 27 29 E
Pas, Pta. des, *Spain* **38 D1** 38 46N 1 26 E
Pas-de-Calais □, *France* **27 B9** 50 30N 2 10 E
Pasada, *Spain* **42 B5** 43 23N 5 40W
Pasadena, *Canada* **141 C8** 49 1N 57 36W
Pasadena, *Calif., U.S.A.* **161 L8** 34 9N 118 9W
Pasadena, *Tex., U.S.A.* **155 L7** 29 43N 95 13W
Pasaje, *Ecuador* **168 D2** 3 23 S 79 50W
Pasaje →, *Argentina* **174 B3** 25 39 S 63 56W
Paşalimanı, *Turkey* **51 F11** 40 29N 27 36 E
Pasar, *Indonesia* **79 J17** 8 27 S 114 54 E
Pasay, *Phil.* **80 D3** 14 33N 121 0 E
Pascagoula, *U.S.A.* **155 K10** 30 21N 88 33W
Pascagoula →, *U.S.A.* **155 K10** 30 23N 88 37W
Paşcani, *Romania* **53 C11** 47 14N 26 45 E
Pasco, *U.S.A.* **158 C4** 46 14N 119 6W
Pasco □, *Peru* **172 C2** 10 40 S 75 0W
Pasco, Cerro de, *Peru* **172 C2** 10 45 S 76 10W
Pasco I., *Australia* **124 D2** 20 57 S 115 20 E
Pascoag, *U.S.A.* **151 E13** 41 57N 71 42W
Pascua, I. de, *Chile* **172 b** 27 7 S 109 23W
Pasewalk, *Germany* **30 B9** 53 30N 13 58 E
Pasfield L., *Canada* **143 B7** 58 24N 105 20W
Pasha →, *Russia* **58 B7** 60 29N 32 55 E
Pashiya, *Russia* **64 B7** 58 33N 58 26 E
Pashmakli = Smolyan, *Bulgaria* **51 E8** 41 36N 24 38 E
Pasig, *Phil.* **80 D3** 14 35N 121 5 E
Pasighat, *India* **90 A5** 28 4N 95 21 E
Pasinler, *Turkey* **101 C9** 39 59N 41 41 E
Pasir Mas, *Malaysia* **87 J4** 6 2N 102 8 E
Pasir Panjang, *Singapore* **87 d** 1 18N 103 46 E
Pasir Putih, *Malaysia* **87 K4** 5 50N 102 24 E
Pasirian, *Indonesia* **85 D4** 8 13 S 113 8 E
Pasirkuning, *Indonesia* **84 C2** 0 30 S 104 33 E
Påskallavik, *Sweden* **17 G10** 57 10N 16 26 E
Paskūh, *Iran* **97 E9** 27 34N 61 39 E
Pasłęk, *Poland* **54 D6** 54 3N 19 41 E
Pasłęka →, *Poland* **54 D6** 54 26N 19 46 E
Pasley, C., *Australia* **125 F3** 33 52 S 123 35 E
Pašman, *Croatia* **45 E12** 43 58N 15 20 E
Pasmore →, *Australia* **128 A3** 31 5 S 139 49 E
Pasni, *Pakistan* **91 D1** 25 15N 63 27 E
Paso Cantinela, *Mexico* **161 N11** 32 33N 115 47W
Paso de Indios, *Argentina* **176 B3** 43 55 S 69 0W
Paso de los Indios, *Argentina* **176 A3** 38 32 S 69 25W
Paso de los Libres, *Argentina* **174 B4** 29 44 S 57 10W
Paso de los Toros, *Uruguay* **174 C4** 32 45 S 56 30W

Paso Flores, *Argentina* **176 B2** 40 35 S 70 38W
Paso Robles, *U.S.A.* **159 J3** 35 38N 120 41W
Pasorapa, *Bolivia* **173 D5** 18 16 S 64 37W
Paspébiac, *Canada* **141 C6** 48 3N 65 17W
Pasrur, *Pakistan* **92 C6** 32 16N 74 43 E
Passage West, *Ireland* **23 E3** 51 52N 8 21W
Passaic, *U.S.A.* **151 F10** 40 51N 74 7W
Passam, *Papua N. G.* **132 B2** 3 41 S 143 38 E
Passau, *Germany* **31 G9** 48 34N 13 28 E
Passero, C., *Italy* **47 F8** 36 41N 15 10 E
Passi, *Phil.* **81 F4** 11 6N 122 38 E
Passo Fundo, *Brazil* **175 B5** 28 10 S 52 20W
Passos, *Brazil* **171 F2** 20 45 S 46 37W
Passow, *Germany* **30 B10** 53 8N 14 6 E
Passwang, *Switz.* **32 B5** 47 22N 7 41 E
Passy, *France* **29 C10** 45 55N 6 41 E
Pastavy, *Belarus* **15 J22** 55 4N 26 50 E
Pastaza □, *Ecuador* **168 D2** 2 0 S 77 0W
Pastaza →, *Peru* **168 D2** 4 50 S 76 52W
Pasto, *Colombia* **168 C2** 1 13N 77 17W
Pastol B., *U.S.A.* **144 E7** 63 7N 163 15W
Pastos Bons, *Brazil* **170 C3** 6 36 S 44 5W
Pastrana, *Spain* **40 E2** 40 27N 2 53W
Pasuquin, *Phil.* **80 B3** 18 20N 120 37 E
Pasuruan, *Indonesia* **85 D4** 7 40 S 112 44 E
Pasym, *Poland* **54 E7** 53 48N 20 49 E
Pásztó, *Hungary* **52 C4** 47 52N 19 43 E
Pata, *Phil.* **81 J3** 5 51N 121 10 E
Pata I., *Phil.* **81 J3** 5 49N 121 10 E
Patagonia, *Argentina* **176 C2** 45 0 S 69 0W
Patagonia, *U.S.A.* **159 L8** 31 33N 110 45W
Patalasang, *Indonesia* **82 C1** 5 26 S 119 26 E
Patambar, *Iran* **97 D9** 29 45N 60 17 E
Patan = Lalitapur, *Nepal* **93 F11** 27 40N 85 20 E
Patan, *Gujarat, India* **94 F1** 17 22N 73 57 E
Patan, *Maharashtra, India* **92 H5** 23 54N 72 14 E
Patani, *Indonesia* **82 A3** 0 20N 128 50 E
Pătârlagele, *Romania* **53 E11** 45 19N 26 21 E
Pataudi, *India* **92 E7** 28 18N 76 48 E
Patchewollock, *Australia* **128 C5** 35 22 S 142 12 E
Patchogue, *U.S.A.* **151 F11** 40 46N 73 1W
Patea, *N.Z.* **130 F3** 39 45 S 174 30 E
Pategi, *Nigeria* **113 D6** 8 50N 5 45 E
Patensie, *S. Africa* **116 E3** 33 46 S 24 49 E
Paterna, *Spain* **41 F4** 39 30N 0 26W
Paternion, *Austria* **34 E6** 46 43N 13 38 E
Paternò, *Italy* **47 E7** 37 34N 14 54 E
Pateros, *U.S.A.* **158 B4** 48 3N 119 54W
Paterson, *Australia* **129 B9** 32 35 S 151 36 E
Paterson, *U.S.A.* **151 F10** 40 55N 74 11W
Paterson Inlet, *N.Z.* **131 G3** 46 56 S 168 12 E
Paterson Ra., *Australia* **124 D3** 21 45 S 122 10 E
Pathankot, *India* **92 C6** 32 18N 75 45 E
Pathardi, *India* **94 E2** 19 10N 75 11 E
Patharghata, *Bangla.* **90 D2** 22 2N 89 58 E
Pathein = Bassein, *Burma* **90 G5** 16 45N 94 30 E
Pathfinder Reservoir, *U.S.A.* **158 E10** 42 28N 106 51W
Pathiu, *Thailand* **87 G2** 10 42N 99 19 E
Pathri, *India* **94 E3** 19 15N 76 27 E
Pathum Thani, *Thailand* **86 E3** 14 1N 100 32 E
Pati, *Indonesia* **85 D4** 6 45 S 111 1 E
Pati Pt., *Guam* **133 R15** 13 40N 144 50 E
Patía, *Colombia* **168 C2** 2 4N 77 4W
Patía →, *Colombia* **168 C2** 2 13N 78 40W
Patiala, *Punjab, India* **92 D7** 30 23N 76 26 E
Patiala, *Ut. P., India* **93 F8** 27 43N 79 1 E
Patine Kouka, *Senegal* **112 C2** 12 45N 13 45W
Patitírion, *Greece* **48 B5** 39 8N 23 50 E
Pativilca, *Peru* **172 C2** 10 42 S 77 48W
Patkai Bum, *India* **90 B5** 27 0N 95 30 E
Pátmos, *Greece* **49 D8** 37 21N 26 36 E
Patna, *India* **93 G11** 25 35N 85 12 E
Patnagarh, *India* **94 D6** 20 43N 83 9 E
Patnanongan I., *Phil.* **80 D4** 14 48N 122 11 E
Patnongon, *Phil.* **81 F4** 10 55N 122 0 E
Patnos, *Turkey* **101 C10** 39 13N 42 51 E
Pato Branco, *Brazil* **175 B5** 26 13 S 52 40W
Patoka L., *U.S.A.* **157 F10** 38 20N 86 40W
Patong, Ao, *Thailand* **87 a** 7 54N 98 17 E
Patonga, *Uganda* **118 B3** 2 45N 33 15 E
Patos, *Albania* **50 F3** 40 42N 19 38 E
Patos, *Brazil* **170 C4** 6 55 S 37 16W
Patos, L. dos, *Brazil* **175 C5** 31 20 S 51 0W
Patos, Río de los →, *Argentina* **174 C2** 31 18 S 69 25W
Patos de Minas, *Brazil* **171 E2** 18 35 S 46 32W
Patquía, *Argentina* **174 C2** 30 2 S 66 55W
Pátrai, *Greece* **48 C3** 38 14N 21 47 E
Pátraikós Kólpos, *Greece* **48 C3** 38 17N 21 30 E
Patras = Pátrai, *Greece* **48 C3** 38 14N 21 47 E
Patreksfjörður, *Iceland* **11 B2** 65 34N 24 0W
Patricio Lynch, I., *Chile* **176 C1** 48 35 S 75 30W
Patrocínio, *Brazil* **171 E2** 18 57 S 47 0W
Patta, *Kenya* **118 C5** 2 10 S 41 0 E
Pattada, *Italy* **46 B2** 40 35N 9 6 E
Pattani, *Thailand* **87 J3** 6 48N 101 15 E
Pattaya, *Thailand* **78 B2** 12 52N 100 55 E
Patten, *U.S.A.* **149 C11** 46 0N 68 38W
Patterson, *Calif., U.S.A.* **160 H5** 37 28N 121 8W
Patterson, *Ga., U.S.A.* **152 D7** 31 23N 82 8W
Patterson, *La., U.S.A.* **155 L9** 29 42N 91 18W
Patterson, Mt., *U.S.A.* **160 G7** 38 29N 119 20W
Patteson, Passage, *Vanuatu* **133 E6** 15 26 S 168 12 E
Patti, *Punjab, India* **92 D6** 31 17N 74 54 E
Patti, *Ut. P., India* **93 G10** 25 55N 82 12 E
Patti, *Italy* **47 D7** 38 8N 14 58 E
Pattoki, *Pakistan* **92 D5** 31 5N 73 52 E
Patton, *U.S.A.* **150 F6** 40 38N 78 39W
Pattonsburg, *U.S.A.* **156 D2** 40 3N 94 8W
Pattukkattai, *India* **95 J4** 10 25N 79 20 E
Patu, *Brazil* **170 C4** 6 6 S 37 38W
Patuakhali, *Bangla.* **90 D3** 22 20N 90 25 E
Patuanak, *Canada* **143 B7** 55 55N 107 43W
Patuca →, *Honduras* **164 C3** 15 50N 84 18W
Patuca, Punta, *Honduras* **164 C3** 15 49N 84 14W
Pătulele, *Romania* **52 F7** 44 21N 22 47 E
Patur, *India* **94 D3** 20 27N 76 56 E
Pátzcuaro, *Mexico* **162 D4** 19 30N 101 40W
Pau, *France* **28 E3** 43 19N 0 25W
Pau, Gave de →, *France* **28 E2** 43 33N 1 12W
Pau d' Arco, *Brazil* **170 C2** 7 30 S 49 22W
Pau dos Ferros, *Brazil* **170 C4** 6 7 S 38 10W
Paucartambo, *Peru* **172 C3** 13 19 S 71 35W
Pauillac, *France* **28 C3** 45 11N 0 46W
Pauini, *Brazil* **172 B4** 7 40 S 66 58W
Pauini →, *Brazil* **169 D5** 1 42 S 62 50W
Pauk, *Burma* **90 E5** 21 27N 94 30 E
Paukkaung, *Burma* **90 F5** 18 54N 95 33 E
Pauktaw, *Burma* **90 E4** 20 11N 93 4 E
Paul I., *Canada* **141 A7** 56 30N 61 20W
Paul Isnard, *Fr. Guiana* **169 C7** 4 47N 54 1W
Paul Smiths, *U.S.A.* **151 B10** 44 26N 74 15W
Paulatuk, *Canada* **138 B7** 69 25N 124 0W
Paulding, *U.S.A.* **157 C12** 41 8N 84 35W
Paulhan, *France* **28 E7** 43 33N 3 28 E
Paulis = Isiro, *Dem. Rep. of the Congo* **118 B2** 2 53N 27 40 E
Paulista, *Brazil* **170 C5** 7 57 S 34 53W
Paulistana, *Brazil* **170 C3** 8 9 S 41 9W
Paulo Afonso, *Brazil* **170 C4** 9 21 S 38 15W
Paulo de Faria, *Brazil* **171 F2** 20 2 S 49 24W
Paulpietersburg, *S. Africa* **117 D5** 27 23 S 30 50 E
Pauls Valley, *U.S.A.* **155 H6** 34 44N 97 13W
Pauma Valley, *U.S.A.* **161 M10** 33 16N 116 58W
Paung, *Burma* **90 G5** 16 37N 94 28 E
Paungde, *Burma* **90 F5** 18 29N 95 30 E
Pauni, *India* **94 D4** 20 48N 79 40 E
Pauri, *India* **93 D8** 30 9N 78 47 E
Pausa, *Peru* **172 D3** 15 16 S 73 22W
Pauto →, *Colombia* **168 B3** 5 9N 70 55W
Pauwela, *U.S.A.* **145 C5** 20 56N 156 19W
Pavagada, *India* **95 G3** 14 6N 77 16 E
Pāveh, *Iran* **101 E12** 35 3N 46 22 E
Pavelets, *Russia* **58 F10** 53 49N 39 14 E
Pavia, *Italy* **44 C6** 45 7N 9 8 E
Pavilion, *U.S.A.* **150 D6** 42 52N 78 1W
Pavilly, *France* **26 C7** 49 34N 0 57 E
Pāvilosta, *Latvia* **15 H19** 56 53N 21 14 E
Pavlikeni, *Bulgaria* **51 C9** 43 14N 25 20 E
Pavlodar, *Kazakstan* **66 D8** 52 33N 77 0 E
Pavlograd = Pavlohrad, *Ukraine* **59 H8** 48 30N 35 52 E
Pavlohrad, *Ukraine* **59 H8** 48 30N 35 52 E
Pavlovo, *Russia* **60 C6** 55 58N 43 5 E
Pavlovsk, *Russia* **60 E5** 50 26N 40 5 E
Pavlovskaya, *Russia* **61 G4** 46 17N 39 47 E
Pavlovskiy-Posad, *Russia* **58 E10** 55 47N 38 42 E
Pavo, *U.S.A.* **152 E6** 30 58N 83 45W
Pavullo nel Frignano, *Italy* **44 D7** 44 20N 10 50 E
Pavuvu, *Solomon Is.* **133 M10** 9 4 S 159 8 E
Paw Paw, *U.S.A.* **157 B11** 42 13N 85 53W
Pawahku, *Burma* **90 B7** 26 11N 98 40 E
Pawai, Pulau, *Singapore* **87 d** 1 11N 103 44 E
Pawan →, *Indonesia* **85 C4** 1 55 S 110 0 E
Pawayan, *India* **93 E9** 28 4N 80 6 E
Pawhuska, *U.S.A.* **155 G6** 36 40N 96 20W
Pawling, *U.S.A.* **151 E11** 41 34N 73 36W
Pawnee, *Ill., U.S.A.* **156 E7** 39 36N 89 35W
Pawnee, *Okla., U.S.A.* **155 G6** 36 20N 96 48W
Pawnee City, *U.S.A.* **154 E6** 40 7N 96 9W
Pawpaw, *U.S.A.* **156 C8** 41 41N 88 59W
Pawtucket, *U.S.A.* **151 E13** 41 53N 71 23W
Paximádhia, *Greece* **39 F5** 35 0N 24 35 E
Paxoí, *Greece* **38 C10** 39 14N 20 12 E
Paxson, *U.S.A.* **144 E11** 63 2N 145 30W
Paxton, *Ill., U.S.A.* **157 D8** 40 27N 88 6W
Paxton, *Nebr., U.S.A.* **154 E4** 41 7N 101 21W
Payagyi, *Burma* **90 G6** 17 29N 96 32 E
Payakumbuh, *Indonesia* **84 C2** 0 20 S 100 35 E
Payerne, *Switz.* **32 C3** 46 49N 6 56 E
Payette, *U.S.A.* **158 D5** 44 5N 116 56W
Paymogo, *Spain* **43 H3** 37 44N 7 21W
Payne, *U.S.A.* **157 C12** 41 5N 84 44W
Payne Bay = Kangirsuk, *Canada* **139 B13** 60 0N 70 0W
Payne L., *Canada* **139 C12** 59 30N 74 30W
Payne Pt., *Ascension I.* **9 g** 7 57 S 14 25W
Paynes Find, *Australia* **125 E2** 29 15 S 117 42 E
Paynesville, *Liberia* **112 D2** 6 20N 10 45W
Paynesville, *U.S.A.* **154 C7** 45 23N 94 43W
Pays de la Loire □, *France* **26 E6** 47 45N 0 25W
Paysandú, *Uruguay* **174 C4** 32 19 S 58 8W
Payshanba, *Uzbekistan* **65 C3** 40 0N 66 14 E
Payson, *U.S.A.* **159 J8** 34 14N 111 20W
Paz →, *Guatemala* **164 D1** 13 44N 90 10W
Paz, B. de la, *Mexico* **162 C2** 24 15N 110 25W
Pāzanān, *Iran* **97 D6** 30 35N 49 59 E
Pazar, *Turkey* **101 B9** 41 10N 40 50 E
Pazarcık, *Turkey* **100 D7** 37 30N 37 17 E
Pazardzhik, *Bulgaria* **51 D8** 42 12N 24 20 E
Pazarköy, *Turkey* **49 B9** 39 51N 27 24 E
Pazarlar, *Turkey* **49 C11** 39 0N 29 7 E
Pazaryeri, *Turkey* **49 B11** 40 0N 29 56 E
Pazaryolu, *Turkey* **101 B9** 40 21N 40 47 E
Pazin, *Croatia* **45 C10** 45 14N 13 56 E
Pazña, *Bolivia* **172 D4** 18 36 S 66 55W
Pčinja →, *Macedonia* **50 E5** 41 50N 21 45 E
Pe Ell, *U.S.A.* **160 D3** 46 34N 123 18W
Pea →, *U.S.A.* **152 D4** 31 1N 85 51W
Peabody, *U.S.A.* **151 D14** 42 31N 70 56W
Peace →, *Canada* **142 B6** 59 0N 111 25W
Peace →, *U.S.A.* **153 J7** 26 56N 82 6W
Peace Point, *Canada* **142 B6** 59 7N 112 27W
Peace River, *Canada* **142 B5** 56 15N 117 18W
Peach Springs, *U.S.A.* **159 J7** 35 32N 113 25W
Peachland, *Canada* **142 D5** 49 47N 119 45W
Peachtree City, *U.S.A.* **152 B5** 33 25N 84 35W
Peak, The = Kinder Scout, *U.K.* **20 D6** 53 24N 1 52W
Peak, The, *Ascension I.* **9 g** 7 57 S 14 20W
Peak Charles Nat. Park, *Australia* **125 F3** 32 42 S 121 10 E
Peak District, *U.K.* **20 D6** 53 10N 1 50W
Peak Hill, *N.S.W., Australia* **129 B8** 32 47 S 148 11 E
Peak Hill, *W. Austral., Australia* **125 E2** 25 35 S 118 43 E
Peak Ra., *Australia* **126 C4** 22 50 S 148 20 E
Peake, *Australia* **128 C3** 35 25 S 139 55 E
Peake Cr. →, *Australia* **127 D2** 28 2 S 136 7 E
Peal de Becerro, *Spain* **43 H7** 37 55N 3 7W
Peale, Mt., *U.S.A.* **159 G9** 38 26N 109 14W
Pearblossom, *U.S.A.* **161 L9** 34 30N 117 55W
Pearl, *U.S.A.* **156 E6** 39 28N 90 38W
Pearl →, *U.S.A.* **155 K10** 30 11N 89 32W
Pearl and Hermes Reef, *U.S.A.* **145 F8** 27 55N 175 45W
Pearl Banks, *Sri Lanka* **95 K4** 8 45N 79 45 E
Pearl City, *U.S.A.* **145 K14** 21 24N 157 59W
Pearl Harbor, *U.S.A.* **145 K14** 21 21N 157 57W
Pearl River = Zhu Jiang →, *China* **77 F9** 22 45N 113 37 E
Pearl River, *U.S.A.* **151 E10** 41 4N 74 2W
Pearsall, *U.S.A.* **155 L5** 28 54N 99 6W
Pearson, *U.S.A.* **152 D7** 31 18N 82 51W
Peary Land, *Greenland* **10 A7** 82 40N 33 0W
Pease →, *U.S.A.* **155 H5** 34 12N 99 2W
Peawanuck, *Canada* **139 C11** 55 15N 85 12W
Pebane, *Mozam.* **119 F4** 17 10 S 38 8 E
Pebas, *Peru* **168 D3** 3 10 S 71 46W
Pebble, I., *Falk. Is.* **9 f** 51 20 S 59 40W
Pebble Beach, *U.S.A.* **160 J5** 36 34N 121 57W
Peć, *Kosovo, Yug.* **50 D4** 42 40N 20 17 E
Peçanha, *Brazil* **171 E3** 18 33 S 42 34W
Pecatonica, *U.S.A.* **156 B7** 42 19N 89 22W
Pecatonica →, *U.S.A.* **156 B7** 42 26N 89 12W
Péccioli, *Italy* **44 E7** 43 33N 10 43 E
Pechea, *Romania* **53 E12** 45 36N 27 49 E
Pechenga, *Russia* **56 A5** 69 29N 31 4 E
Pechenizhyn, *Ukraine* **59 H3** 48 30N 24 48 E
Pechiguera, Pta., *Canary Is.* **9 e2** 28 51N 13 53W
Pechnezhskoye Vdkhr., *Ukraine* **59 G9** 50 5N 36 54 E
Pechora, *Russia* **56 A10** 65 10N 57 11 E
Pechora →, *Russia* **56 A9** 68 13N 54 15 E
Pechorskaya Guba, *Russia* **56 A9** 68 40N 54 0 E
Pecica, *Romania* **52 D6** 46 10N 21 3 E
Pecka, *Serbia, Yug.* **50 B3** 44 18N 19 33 E
Pécora, C., *Italy* **46 C1** 39 27N 8 23 E
Pečory, *Russia* **15 H22** 57 48N 27 40 E
Pecos, *U.S.A.* **155 K3** 31 26N 103 30W
Pecos →, *U.S.A.* **155 L3** 29 42N 101 22W
Pécs, *Hungary* **52 D3** 46 5N 18 15 E
Pedda Bellala, *India* **94 E4** 19 4N 78 49 E
Peddapalli, *India* **94 E4** 18 40N 79 24 E
Peddapuram, *India* **94 F6** 17 6N 82 8 E
Pedder, L., *Australia* **127 G4** 42 55 S 146 10 E
Peddie, *S. Africa* **117 E4** 33 14 S 27 7 E
Pedernales, *Dom. Rep.* **165 C5** 18 2N 71 44W
Pedernales, *Ecuador* **168 C1** 0 5N 80 3W
Pedieos →, *Cyprus* **39 E9** 35 10N 33 54 E
Pedirka, *Australia* **127 D2** 26 40 S 135 14 E
Pedra Azul, *Brazil* **171 E3** 16 2 S 41 17W
Pedra Branca, *Brazil* **169 C7** 0 51N 51 58W
Pedra Grande, Recifes de, *Brazil* **171 E4** 17 45 S 38 58W
Pedra Lume, *C. Verde Is.* **9 j** 16 40N 22 52W
Pedras Negras, *Brazil* **173 C5** 12 51 S 62 54W
Pedras Tinhosas, I., *São Tomé & Principe* **115 G6** 1 22N 7 17 E
Pedreguer, *Spain* **41 G5** 38 48N 0 3 E
Pedreiras, *Brazil* **170 B3** 4 32 S 44 40W
Pedro Afonso, *Brazil* **170 C2** 9 0 S 48 10W
Pedro Bay, *U.S.A.* **144 G9** 59 47N 154 7W
Pedro Cays, *Jamaica* **164 C4** 17 5N 77 48W
Pedro Chico, *Colombia* **168 C3** 1 4N 70 25W
Pedro de Valdivia, *Chile* **174 A2** 22 55 S 69 38W
Pedro Dorado, *Colombia* **168 C3** 1 0N 70 14W
Pedro Juan Caballero, *Paraguay* **175 A4** 22 30 S 55 40W
Pedro Muñoz, *Spain* **43 F8** 39 25N 2 56W
Pedrógão Grande, *Portugal* **42 F2** 39 55N 8 9W
Pee Dee →, *U.S.A.* **149 J6** 33 22N 79 16W
Peebinga, *Australia* **128 C4** 34 52 S 140 57 E
Peebles, *U.K.* **22 F5** 55 40N 3 11W
Peebles, *U.S.A.* **157 F13** 38 57N 83 24W
Peekskill, *U.S.A.* **151 E11** 41 17N 73 55W
Peel, *U.K.* **20 C3** 54 13N 4 40W
Peel →, *Australia* **129 A9** 30 50 S 150 29 E
Peel →, *Canada* **138 B6** 67 0N 135 0W
Peel Sound, *Canada* **138 A10** 73 0N 96 0W
Peene →, *Germany* **30 A9** 54 9N 13 46 E
Peera Peera Poolanna L., *Australia* **127 D2** 26 30 S 138 0 E
Peerless Lake, *Canada* **142 B6** 56 37N 114 40W
Peers, *Canada* **142 C5** 53 40N 116 0W
Peery L., *Australia* **128 A5** 30 45 S 143 35 E
Pegasus Bay, *N.Z.* **131 D8** 43 20 S 173 10 E
Peggau, *Austria* **34 D8** 47 12N 15 21 E
Pegnitz, *Germany* **31 F7** 49 44N 11 31 E
Pegnitz →, *Germany* **31 F6** 49 30N 10 59 E
Pego, *Spain* **41 G4** 38 51N 0 8W
Pegu, *Burma* **90 G6** 17 20N 96 29 E
Pegu □, *Burma* **90 G6** 17 30N 96 30 E
Pegu Yoma, *Burma* **90 F5** 19 0N 96 0 E
Pehčevo, *Macedonia* **50 E6** 41 41N 22 55 E
Pehlıvanköy, *Turkey* **51 E10** 41 20N 26 55 E
Pehuajó, *Argentina* **174 D3** 35 45 S 62 0W
Pei Xian = Pizhou, *China* **74 G9** 34 44N 116 55 E
Peine, *Chile* **174 A2** 23 45 S 68 8W
Peine, *Germany* **30 C6** 52 19N 10 14 E
Peip'ing = Beijing, *China* **74 E9** 39 55N 116 20 E
Peipus, L. = Chudskoye, Ozero, *Russia* **15 G22** 58 13N 27 30 E
Peissenberg, *Germany* **31 H7** 47 48N 11 4 E
Peitz, *Germany* **30 D10** 51 51N 14 24 E
Peixe, *Brazil* **171 D2** 12 0 S 48 40W
Peixe →, *Brazil* **171 F1** 21 31 S 51 58W
Peixoto de Azeredo →, *Brazil* **173 C6** 10 6 S 55 31W
Pek →, *Serbia, Yug.* **50 B5** 44 45N 21 29 E
Pekalongan, *Indonesia* **85 D3** 6 53 S 109 40 E
Pekan, *Malaysia* **87 L4** 3 30N 103 25 E
Pekan Nenas, *Malaysia* **87 d** 1 31N 103 31 E
Pekanbaru, *Indonesia* **84 B2** 0 30N 101 15 E
Pekang, *Taiwan* **77 F13** 23 34N 120 18 E
Pekin, *U.S.A.* **156 D7** 40 35N 89 40W
Peking = Beijing, *China* **74 E9** 39 55N 116 20 E
Pekutatan, *Indonesia* **79 J17** 8 25 S 114 49 E
Péla, *Guinea* **112 D3** 7 37N 9 7W
Pelabuhan Kelang, *Malaysia* **87 L3** 3 0N 101 23 E
Pelabuhan Ratu, Teluk, *Indonesia* **84 D3** 7 5 S 106 30 E
Pelabuhanratu, *Indonesia* **84 D3** 7 0 S 106 32 E
Pélagos, *Greece* **48 B6** 39 17N 24 4 E
Pelaihari, *Indonesia* **85 C4** 3 55 S 114 45 E
Pelat, Mt., *France* **29 D10** 44 16N 6 42 E
Pełczyce, *Poland* **55 E2** 53 3N 15 16 E
Peleaga, Vf., *Romania* **52 E7** 45 22N 22 55 E
Pelechuco, *Bolivia* **172 C4** 14 48 S 69 4W
Pelée, Mt., *Martinique* **164 c** 14 48N 61 10W
Pelee, Pt., *Canada* **140 D3** 41 54N 82 31W
Pelee I., *Canada* **140 D3** 41 47N 82 40W
Pelejo, *Peru* **172 B2** 6 10 S 75 49W
Pelekech, *Kenya* **118 B4** 3 52N 35 8 E
Peleng, *Indonesia* **82 B2** 1 20 S 123 30 E
Pelenge, *Dem. Rep. of the Congo* **114 C4** 2 44 S 22 39 E
Pelentong, *Malaysia* **87 d** 1 32N 103 49 E
Pélézi, *Ivory C.* **112 D3** 7 17N 6 54W
Pelham, *U.S.A.* **152 D5** 31 8N 84 9W
Pelhřimov, *Czech Rep.* **34 B8** 49 24N 15 12 E
Pelican, *U.S.A.* **142 B1** 57 58N 136 14W
Pelican L., *Canada* **143 C8** 52 28N 100 20W
Pelican Narrows, *Canada* **143 B8** 55 10N 102 56W
Pelion, *U.S.A.* **152 B8** 33 46N 81 15W
Pelješac, *Croatia* **45 F14** 42 55N 17 25 E
Pelkosenniemi, *Finland* **14 C22** 67 6N 27 28 E
Pell City, *U.S.A.* **152 B3** 33 35N 86 17W
Pella, *Greece* **50 F6** 40 46N 22 23 E
Pella, *S. Africa* **116 D2** 29 1 S 19 6 E
Pella, *U.S.A.* **156 C4** 41 25N 92 55W
Pélla □, *Greece* **50 F6** 40 52N 22 0 E
Pello, *Finland* **14 C21** 66 47N 23 59 E
Pellworm, *Germany* **30 A4** 54 31N 8 39 E
Pelly →, *Canada* **138 B6** 62 47N 137 19W
Pelly Bay, *Canada* **139 B11** 68 38N 89 50W
Peloponnese = Pelopónnisos □, *Greece* **48 D4** 37 10N 22 0 E
Pelopónnisos □, *Greece* **48 D4** 37 10N 22 0 E
Peloritani, Monti, *Italy* **47 D8** 38 3N 15 20 E
Pelorus →, *N.Z.* **131 B8** 41 16 S 173 45 E
Pelorus Sd., *N.Z.* **131 A8** 40 59 S 173 59 E
Pelotas, *Brazil* **175 C5** 31 42 S 52 23W
Pelotas →, *Brazil* **175 B5** 27 28 S 51 55W
Pelovo, *Bulgaria* **51 C8** 43 26N 24 17 E
Pelplin, *Poland* **54 E5** 53 55N 18 42 E
Pelvoux, Massif du, *France* **29 D10** 44 52N 6 20 E
Pelym, *Russia* **64 B9** 59 34N 63 27 E
Pelym →, *Russia* **64 B9** 59 39N 63 26 E
Pemalang, *Indonesia* **85 D3** 6 53 S 109 23 E
Pemanggil, Pulau, *Malaysia* **87 L5** 2 37N 104 21 E
Pematangsiantar, *Indonesia* **84 B1** 2 57N 99 5 E
Pemba, *Mozam.* **119 E5** 12 58 S 40 30 E
Pemba, *Zambia* **119 F2** 16 30 S 27 28 E
Pemba Channel, *Tanzania* **118 D4** 5 0 S 39 37 E
Pemba I., *Tanzania* **118 D4** 5 0 S 39 45 E
Pemberton, *Australia* **125 F2** 34 30 S 116 0 E
Pemberton, *Canada* **142 C4** 50 25N 122 50W
Pembina, *U.S.A.* **154 A6** 48 58N 97 15W
Pembroke, *Canada* **140 C4** 45 50N 77 7W
Pembroke, *U.K.* **21 F3** 51 41N 4 55W
Pembroke, *U.S.A.* **152 C8** 32 8N 81 37W
Pembroke Pines, *U.S.A.* **153 J9** 26 5N 80 14W
Pembrokeshire □, *U.K.* **21 F3** 51 52N 4 56W
Pembuang →, *Indonesia* **85 C4** 3 24 S 112 33 E
Pen, *India* **94 E1** 18 45N 73 5 E
Pen-y-Ghent, *U.K.* **20 C5** 54 10N 2 14W
Peña, Sierra de la, *Spain* **40 C4** 42 32N 0 45W
Peña de Francia, Sierra de la, *Spain* **42 E4** 40 32N 6 10W
Penafiel, *Portugal* **42 D2** 41 12N 8 17W
Peñafiel, *Spain* **42 D6** 41 35N 4 7W
Peñaflor, *Spain* **43 H5** 37 43N 5 21W
Penal, *Trin. & Tob.* **169 F9** 10 9N 61 29W
Peñalara, *Spain* **42 E7** 40 51N 3 57W
Penalva, *Brazil* **170 B2** 3 18 S 45 10W
Penamacôr, *Portugal* **42 E3** 40 10N 7 10W
Penambulai, *Indonesia* **83 C4** 6 24 S 134 48 E
Penang = Pinang, *Malaysia* **87 c** 5 25N 100 15 E
Penápolis, *Brazil* **175 A6** 21 30 S 50 0W
Peñaranda de Bracamonte, *Spain* **42 E5** 40 53N 5 13W
Peñarroya, *Spain* **40 E4** 40 25N 0 40W
Peñarroya-Pueblonuevo, *Spain* **43 G5** 38 19N 5 16W
Penarth, *U.K.* **21 F4** 51 26N 3 11W
Peñas, C. de, *Spain* **42 B5** 43 42N 5 52W
Penas, G. de, *Chile* **176 C2** 47 0 S 75 0W
Peñas, Pta., *Venezuela* **169 A5** 11 17N 62 0W
Peñas de San Pedro, *Spain* **41 G3** 38 44N 2 0W
Peñas del Chache, *Canary Is.* **9 e2** 29 6N 13 33W
Peñausende, *Spain* **42 D5** 41 17N 5 52W
Pench →, *India* **94 D4** 21 17N 79 10 E
Pench'i = Benxi, *China* **75 D12** 41 20N 123 48 E
Pend Oreille →, *U.S.A.* **158 B5** 49 4N 117 37W
Pend Oreille, L., *U.S.A.* **158 C5** 48 10N 116 21W
Pendálofon, *Greece* **50 F5** 40 14N 21 12 E
Pendé →, *C.A.R.* **114 A3** 7 55N 16 36 E
Pendembu, *Eastern, S. Leone* **112 D2** 8 10N 10 42W
Pendembu, *Northern, S. Leone* **112 D2** 9 7N 11 14W
Pendências, *Brazil* **170 C4** 5 15 S 36 43W
Pender B., *Australia* **124 C3** 16 45 S 122 42 E
Pendik, *Turkey* **51 F13** 40 53N 29 13 E
Pendjari →, *Benin* **113 C5** 10 55N 0 50 E
Pendjari, Parc Nat. de la, *Benin* **113 C5** 11 15N 1 32 E
Pendleton, *Ind., U.S.A.* **157 E11** 40 0N 85 45W
Pendleton, *Oreg., U.S.A.* **158 D4** 45 40N 118 47W
Pendra, *India* **93 H9** 22 46N 81 57 E
Pendzhikent, *Tajikistan* **65 D3** 39 29N 67 37 E
Penedo, *Brazil* **170 D4** 10 15 S 36 36W
Penelokan, *Indonesia* **79 J18** 8 17 S 115 22 E
Penetanguishene, *Canada* **140 D4** 44 50N 79 55W
Penfield, *U.S.A.* **150 E6** 41 13N 78 35W
Peng Chau, *China* **69 G11** 22 17N 114 2 E
Pengalengan, *Indonesia* **85 D3** 7 9 S 107 30 E
Penganga →, *India* **94 E4** 19 53N 79 9 E
Penge, *Kasai-Or., Dem. Rep. of the Congo* **118 D1** 5 30 S 24 33 E
Penge, *Sud-Kivu, Dem. Rep. of the Congo* **118 C2** 4 27 S 28 25 E
P'enghu Ch'üntou, *Taiwan* **77 F12** 23 34N 119 30 E
Penglai, *China* **75 F11** 37 48N 120 42 E
Pengshan, *China* **76 B4** 30 14N 103 58 E
Pengshui, *China* **76 C7** 29 17N 108 12 E
Penguin, *Australia* **127 G4** 41 8 S 146 6 E
Pengxi, *China* **76 B5** 30 44N 105 45 E
Pengze, *China* **77 C11** 29 52N 116 32 E
Penhalonga, *Zimbabwe* **119 F3** 18 52 S 32 40 E
Peniche, *Portugal* **43 F1** 39 19N 9 22W
Penicuik, *U.K.* **22 F5** 55 50N 3 13W
Penida, Nusa, *Indonesia* **85 D5** 8 45 S 115 30 E
Peninnes, Alpes = Pennine, Alpi, *Alps* **31 J3** 46 4N 7 30 E
Peninsular Malaysia □, *Malaysia* **87 L4** 4 0N 102 0 E
Peñíscola, *Spain* **40 E5** 40 22N 0 24 E
Penitente, Serra do, *Brazil* **170 C2** 8 45 S 46 20W
Penkridge, *U.K.* **20 E5** 52 44N 2 6W
Penmarch, *France* **26 E2** 47 49N 4 21W
Penmarch, Pte. de, *France* **26 E2** 47 48N 4 22W
Penn Hills, *U.S.A.* **150 F5** 40 28N 79 52W
Penn Yan, *U.S.A.* **150 D7** 42 40N 77 3W
Penna, Punta della, *Italy* **45 F11** 42 10N 14 43 E
Pennant, *Canada* **143 C7** 50 32N 108 14W
Penne, *Italy* **45 F10** 42 27N 13 55 E
Penner →, *India* **95 G5** 14 35N 80 10 E
Penneshaw, *Australia* **128 C2** 35 44 S 137 56 E
Pennine, Alpi, *Alps* **31 J3** 46 4N 7 30 E
Pennines, *U.K.* **20 C5** 54 45N 2 27W
Pennington, *U.S.A.* **160 F5** 39 15N 121 47W
Pennington →, *Nigeria* **113 E6** 4 45N 5 35 E
Pennino, Mte., *Italy* **45 E9** 43 6N 12 53 E
Pennsburg, *U.S.A.* **151 F9** 40 23N 75 29W
Pennsylvania □, *U.S.A.* **148 E7** 40 45N 77 30W
Pennville, *U.S.A.* **157 D11** 40 30N 85 9W
Penny, *Canada* **142 C4** 53 51N 121 20W
Peno, *Russia* **58 D7** 57 2N 32 49 E
Penobscot →, *U.S.A.* **149 C11** 44 30N 68 48W
Penobscot B., *U.S.A.* **149 C11** 44 35N 68 50W
Penola, *Australia* **128 D4** 37 25 S 140 48 E
Penong, *Australia* **125 F5** 31 56 S 133 1 E
Penonomé, *Panama* **164 E3** 8 31N 80 21W
Penot, Mt., *Vanuatu* **133 F5** 16 20 S 167 31 E
Penrith, *Australia* **129 B9** 33 43 S 150 38 E
Penrith, *U.K.* **20 C5** 54 40N 2 45W
Penryn, *U.K.* **21 G2** 50 9N 5 7W
Pensacola, *U.S.A.* **149 K2** 30 25N 87 13W
Pensacola Mts., *Antarctica* **7 E1** 84 0 S 40 0W
Pense, *Canada* **143 C8** 50 25N 104 59W
Penshurst, *Australia* **128 D5** 37 49 S 142 20 E
Pensiangan, *Malaysia* **85 B5** 4 33N 116 19 E
Pentecost = Pentecôte, *Vanuatu* **133 E6** 15 42 S 168 10 E
Pentecoste, *Brazil* **170 B4** 3 48 S 39 17W
Pentecôte, *Vanuatu* **133 E6** 15 42 S 168 10 E
Penticton, *Canada* **142 D5** 49 30N 119 38W
Pentland, *Australia* **126 C4** 20 32 S 145 25 E
Pentland Firth, *U.K.* **22 C5** 58 43N 3 10W
Pentland Hills, *U.K.* **22 F5** 55 48N 3 25W
Penukonda, *India* **95 G3** 14 5N 77 38 E
Penza, *Russia* **60 D7** 53 15N 45 5 E
Penzance, *U.K.* **21 G2** 50 7N 5 33W
Penzberg, *Germany* **31 H7** 47 45N 11 22 E
Penzhino, *Russia* **67 C17** 63 30N 167 55 E
Penzhinskaya Guba, *Russia* **67 C17** 61 30N 163 0 E
Penzhou, *China* **76 B4** 31 4N 103 32 E
Penzlin, *Germany* **30 B9** 53 30N 13 5 E
Peoria, *Ariz., U.S.A.* **159 K7** 33 35N 112 14W
Peoria, *Ill., U.S.A.* **156 D7** 40 42N 89 36W
Peoria Heights, *U.S.A.* **156 D7** 40 45N 89 35W
Peotone, *U.S.A.* **157 C9** 41 20N 87 48W
Pepacton Reservoir, *U.S.A.* **151 D10** 42 5N 74 58W
Pepani →, *S. Africa* **116 D3** 25 49 S 22 47 E
Pepeekeo, *U.S.A.* **145 D6** 19 51N 155 6W
Pepel, *S. Leone* **112 D2** 8 40N 13 5W
Peqin, *Albania* **50 E3** 41 3N 19 44 E
Pera Hd., *Australia* **126 A3** 12 55 S 141 37 E
Perabumulih, *Indonesia* **84 C2** 3 27 S 104 15 E
Perak □, *Malaysia* **84 A2** 5 0N 101 0 E
Perak →, *Malaysia* **87 K3** 4 0N 100 50 E
Perakhóra, *Greece* **48 C4** 38 2N 22 56 E
Perakhórion, *Greece* **39 C2** 38 21N 20 43 E
Perales de Alfambra, *Spain* **40 E4** 40 38N 1 0W
Perales del Puerto, *Spain* **42 E4** 40 10N 6 40W
Pérama, *Kérkira, Greece* **38 B9** 39 34N 19 54 E
Pérama, *Kríti, Greece* **39 E5** 35 20N 24 40 E
Perancak, *Indonesia* **79 J17** 8 24 S 114 37 E
Peräpohjola, *Finland* **14 C22** 66 16N 26 10 E
Perast, *Montenegro, Yug.* **50 D2** 42 31N 18 47 E
Peratiá, *Greece* **39 B2** 38 49N 20 45 E
Percé, *Canada* **141 C7** 48 31N 64 13W
Perche, *France* **26 D8** 48 31N 1 1 E
Perche, Collines du, *France* **25 B4** 48 30N 0 40 E
Perchtoldsdorf, *Austria* **35 C9** 48 7N 16 16 E
Percival Lakes, *Australia* **124 D4** 21 25 S 125 0 E
Percy, *France* **26 D5** 48 55N 1 11W
Percy, *U.S.A.* **156 F7** 38 5N 89 41W
Percy Is., *Australia* **126 C5** 21 39 S 150 16 E
Perdido →, *Argentina* **176 B3** 42 55 S 67 0W
Perdido, Mte., *Spain* **40 C5** 42 40N 0 5 E
Perdu, Mt. = Perdido, Mte., *Spain* **40 C5** 42 40N 0 5 E
Pereira, *Colombia* **168 C2** 4 49N 75 43W

Perelazovskiy, *Russia* **61 F6** 49 8N 42 35 E
Peremul Par, *India* **95 J1** 11 10N 72 4 E
Perené →, *Peru* **172 C3** 11 9 S 74 14W
Perenjori, *Australia* **125 E2** 29 26 S 116 16 E
Peresecina, *Moldova* **53 C13** 47 16N 28 46 E
Pereslavi-Zalesskiy, *Russia* **58 D10** 56 45N 38 50 E
Peretu, *Romania* **53 F10** 44 3N 25 5 E
Perevolotskiy, *Russia* **64 F5** 51 51N 54 12 E
Pereyaslav-Khmelnytskyy, *Ukraine* **59 G6** 50 3N 31 28 E
Pérez, I., *Mexico* **163 C7** 22 24N 89 42W
Perg, *Austria* **34 C7** 48 15N 14 38 E
Pergamino, *Argentina* **174 C3** 33 52 S 60 30W
Pergau →, *Malaysia* **87 K3** 5 23N 102 2 E
Pérgine Valsugana, *Italy* **45 B8** 46 4N 11 14 E
Pérgola, *Italy* **45 E9** 43 34N 12 50 E
Perham, *U.S.A.* **154 B7** 46 36N 95 34W
Perhentian, Kepulauan, *Malaysia* **78 C2** 5 54N 102 42 E
Periam, *Romania* **52 D5** 46 2N 20 52 E
Péribonca →, *Canada* **141 C5** 48 45N 72 5W
Péribonca, L., *Canada* **141 B5** 50 1N 71 10W
Perico, *Argentina* **174 A2** 24 20 S 65 5W
Pericos, *Mexico* **162 B3** 25 3N 107 42W
Périers, *France* **26 C5** 49 11N 1 25W
Périgord, *France* **28 D4** 45 0N 0 40 E
Périgueux, *France* **28 C4** 45 10N 0 42 E
Perijá, Sierra de, *Colombia* **168 B3** 9 30N 73 3W
Peristéra, *Greece* **48 B5** 39 15N 23 58 E
Peristerona →, *Cyprus* **39 E9** 35 8N 33 5 E
Perito Moreno, *Argentina* **176 C2** 46 36 S 70 56W
Peritoró, *Brazil* **170 B3** 4 20 S 44 18W
Perivol = Dragovishtitsa, *Bulgaria* **50 D6** 42 22N 22 39 E
Periyakulam, *India* **95 J3** 10 5N 77 30 E
Periyar →, *India* **95 J3** 10 15N 76 10 E
Periyar, L., *India* **95 K3** 9 25N 77 10 E
Perkasie, *U.S.A.* **151 F9** 40 22N 75 18W
Perković, *Croatia* **45 E13** 43 41N 16 10 E
Perlas, Arch. de las, *Panama* **164 E4** 8 41N 79 7W
Perlas, Punta de, *Nic.* **164 D3** 12 30N 83 30W
Perleberg, *Germany* **30 B7** 53 5N 11 52 E
Perlez, *Serbia, Yug.* **52 E5** 45 11N 20 22 E
Perlis □, *Malaysia* **84 A2** 6 30N 100 15 E
Perm, *Russia* **64 C6** 58 0N 56 10 E
Përmet, *Albania* **50 F4** 40 15N 20 21 E
Pernambuco = Recife, *Brazil* **170 C5** 8 0 S 35 0W
Pernambuco □, *Brazil* **170 C4** 8 0 S 37 0W
Pernatty Lagoon, *Australia* **128 A2** 31 30 S 137 12 E
Pernik, *Bulgaria* **50 D7** 42 35N 23 2 E
Peron Is., *Australia* **124 B5** 13 9 S 130 4 E
Peron Pen., *Australia* **125 E1** 26 0 S 113 10 E
Péronne, *France* **27 C9** 49 55N 2 57 E
Perosa Argentina, *Italy* **44 D4** 44 58N 7 10 E
Perow, *Canada* **142 C3** 54 35N 126 10W
Perpendicular Pt., *Australia* **127 E5** 31 37 S 152 52 E
Perpignan, *France* **28 F6** 42 42N 2 53 E
Perrine, *U.S.A.* **153 K9** 25 36N 80 21W
Perris, *U.S.A.* **161 M9** 33 47N 117 14W
Perros-Guirec, *France* **26 D3** 48 49N 3 28W
Perry, *Fla., U.S.A.* **152 E6** 30 7N 83 35W
Perry, *Ga., U.S.A.* **152 C6** 32 28N 83 44W
Perry, *Iowa, U.S.A.* **156 C2** 41 51N 94 6W
Perry, *Mich., U.S.A.* **157 B12** 42 50N 84 13W
Perry, *Mo., U.S.A.* **156 E5** 39 26N 91 40W
Perry, *Okla., U.S.A.* **155 G6** 36 17N 97 14W
Perrysburg, *U.S.A.* **157 C13** 41 34N 83 38W
Perryton, *U.S.A.* **155 G4** 36 24N 100 48W
Perryville, *Alaska, U.S.A.* **144 J8** 55 55N 159 9W
Perryville, *Mo., U.S.A.* **155 G10** 37 43N 89 52W
Persan, *France* **27 C9** 49 9N 2 16 E
Persberg, *Sweden* **16 E8** 59 47N 14 15 E
Perşembe, *Turkey* **100 B7** 41 5N 37 46 E
Persepolis, *Iran* **97 D7** 29 55N 52 50 E
Perseverancia, *Bolivia* **173 C5** 14 44 S 62 48W
Pershotravensk, *Ukraine* **59 G4** 50 13N 27 40 E
Persia = Iran ■, *Asia* **97 C7** 33 0N 53 0 E
Persian Gulf = Gulf, The, *Asia* **97 E6** 27 0N 50 0 E
Perstorp, *Sweden* **17 H7** 56 10N 13 25 E
Pertek, *Turkey* **101 C8** 38 51N 39 19 E
Perth, *Australia* **125 F2** 31 57 S 115 52 E
Perth, *Canada* **140 D4** 44 55N 76 15W
Perth, *U.K.* **22 E5** 56 24N 3 26W
Perth & Kinross □, *U.K.* **22 E5** 56 45N 3 55W
Perth Amboy, *U.S.A.* **151 F10** 40 31N 74 16W
Perth-Andover, *Canada* **141 C6** 46 44N 67 42W
Pertuis, *France* **29 E9** 43 42N 5 30 E
Pertusato, C., *France* **29 G13** 41 21N 9 11 E
Peru, *Ill., U.S.A.* **156 C7** 41 20N 89 8W
Peru, *Ind., U.S.A.* **157 D10** 40 45N 86 4W
Peru, *N.Y., U.S.A.* **151 B11** 44 35N 73 32W
Peru ■, *S. Amer.* **168 D2** 4 0 S 75 0W
Peru Basin, *Pac. Oc.* **135 J18** 20 0 S 95 0W
Peru-Chile Trench, *Pac. Oc.* **135 K20** 20 0 S 72 0W
Perúgia, *Italy* **45 E9** 43 7N 12 23 E
Perušić, *Croatia* **45 D12** 44 40N 15 22 E
Pervomaysk, *Russia* **60 C6** 54 56N 43 58 E
Pervomaysk, *Ukraine* **59 H6** 48 10N 30 46 E
Pervomayskiy, *Russia* **64 F5** 51 32N 55 2 E
Pervouralsk, *Russia* **64 C7** 56 59N 59 59 E
Pésaro, *Italy* **45 E9** 43 54N 12 55 E
Pescadores = P'enghu Ch'üntou, *Taiwan* **77 F12** 23 34N 119 30 E
Pescara, *Italy* **45 F11** 42 28N 14 13 E
Pescara →, *Italy* **45 F11** 42 28N 14 13 E
Peschanokopskoye, *Russia* **61 G5** 46 14N 41 4 E
Péscia, *Italy* **44 E7** 43 54N 10 41 E
Pescina, *Italy* **45 F10** 42 2N 13 39 E
Peseux, *Switz.* **32 C3** 46 59N 6 53 E
Peshawar, *Pakistan* **91 B3** 34 2N 71 37 E
Peshkopi, *Albania* **50 E4** 41 41N 20 25 E
Peshtera, *Bulgaria* **51 D8** 42 2N 24 18 E
Peshtigo, *U.S.A.* **148 C2** 45 4N 87 46W
Peski, *Russia* **60 E6** 51 14N 42 29 E
Peskovka, *Russia* **64 B4** 59 4N 52 22 E
Pêso da Régua, *Portugal* **42 D3** 41 10N 7 47W
Pesqueira, *Brazil* **170 C4** 8 20 S 36 42W
Pessac, *France* **28 D3** 44 48N 0 37W
Pessádhes, *Greece* **39 C2** 38 7N 20 35 E
Pest □, *Hungary* **52 C4** 47 29N 19 5 E
Pestovo, *Russia* **58 C8** 58 33N 35 42 E
Pestravka, *Russia* **60 D9** 52 28N 49 57 E
Péta, *Greece* **48 B3** 39 10N 21 2 E
Petah Tiqwa, *Israel* **103 C3** 32 6N 34 53 E
Petalás, Nisís, *Greece* **39 C3** 38 25N 21 5 E
Petalídhion, *Greece* **48 E3** 36 57N 21 55 E
Petaling Jaya, *Malaysia* **87 L3** 3 4N 101 42 E
Petaloudhes, *Greece* **38 E12** 36 18N 28 5 E
Petaluma, *U.S.A.* **160 G4** 38 14N 122 39W
Pétange, *Lux.* **24 E5** 49 33N 5 55 E
Petaro, *Pakistan* **92 G3** 25 31N 68 18 E
Petatlán, *Mexico* **162 D4** 17 31N 101 16W
Petauke, *Zambia* **119 E3** 14 14 S 31 20 E
Petawawa, *Canada* **140 C4** 45 54N 77 17W
Petén Itzá, L., *Guatemala* **164 C2** 16 58N 89 50W
Peter I., *Br. Virgin Is.* **165 e** 18 22N 64 32W
Peter I.s Øy, *Antarctica* **7 C16** 69 0 S 91 0W
Peter Pond L., *Canada* **143 B7** 55 55N 108 44W
Peterbell, *Canada* **140 C3** 48 36N 83 21W
Peterborough, *Australia* **128 B3** 32 58 S 138 51 E
Peterborough, *Canada* **140 D4** 44 20N 78 20W
Peterborough, *U.K.* **21 E7** 52 35N 0 15W
Peterborough, *U.S.A.* **151 D13** 42 53N 71 57W
Peterborough □, *U.K.* **21 E7** 52 35N 0 15W
Peterculter, *U.K.* **22 D6** 57 6N 2 16W
Peterhead, *U.K.* **22 D7** 57 31N 1 48W
Peterlee, *U.K.* **20 C6** 54 47N 1 20W
Petermann Bjerg, *Greenland* **10 C8** 73 7N 28 25W
Petermann Gletscher, *Greenland* **10 A4** 80 30N 60 0W
Petermann Ranges, *Australia* **124 E5** 26 0 S 130 30 E
Peter's Mine, *Guyana* **169 B6** 6 14N 59 20W
Petersburg, *Alaska, U.S.A.* **144 H14** 56 48N 132 58W
Petersburg, *Ill., U.S.A.* **156 D7** 40 1N 89 51W
Petersburg, *Ind., U.S.A.* **157 F9** 38 30N 87 17W
Petersburg, *Mich., U.S.A.* **157 C13** 41 54N 83 43W
Petersburg, *Pa., U.S.A.* **150 F6** 40 34N 78 3W
Petersburg, *Va., U.S.A.* **148 G7** 37 14N 77 24W
Petersburg, *W. Va., U.S.A.* **148 F6** 39 1N 79 5W
Petersfield, *U.K.* **21 F7** 51 1N 0 56W
Petershagen, *Germany* **30 C4** 52 23N 8 58 E
Petília Policastro, *Italy* **47 C9** 39 7N 16 48 E
Petit Batanga, *Cameroon* **114 B1** 3 15N 9 54 E
Petit-Canal, *Guadeloupe* **164 b** 16 25N 61 31W
Petit Goâve, *Haiti* **165 C5** 18 27N 72 51W
Petit Jardin, *Canada* **141 C8** 48 28N 59 14W
Petit Lac Manicouagan, *Canada* **141 B6** 51 25N 67 40W
Petit-Mécatina →, *Canada* **141 B8** 50 40N 59 30W
Petit-Mécatina, I. du, *Canada* **141 B8** 50 30N 59 25W
Petit Piton, *St. Lucia* **165 f** 13 51N 61 5W
Petit Saint Bernard, Col du, *Italy* **29 C10** 45 40N 6 52 E
Petitcodiac, *Canada* **141 C6** 45 57N 65 11W
Petite Baleine →, *Canada* **140 A4** 56 0N 76 45W
Petite Saguenay, *Canada* **141 C5** 48 15N 70 4W
Petite Terre, Iles de la, *Guadeloupe* **164 b** 16 13N 61 9W
Petitot →, *Canada* **142 A4** 60 14N 123 29W
Petitsikapau L., *Canada* **141 B6** 54 37N 66 25W
Petlad, *India* **92 H5** 22 30N 72 45 E
Peto, *Mexico* **163 C7** 20 10N 88 53W
Petone, *N.Z.* **130 H3** 41 13 S 174 53 E
Petorca, *Chile* **174 C1** 32 15 S 70 56W
Petoskey, *U.S.A.* **148 C3** 45 22N 84 57W
Petra, *Jordan* **103 E4** 30 20N 35 22 E
Petra, *Spain* **38 B4** 39 37N 3 6 E
Petra, Ostrova, *Russia* **6 B13** 76 15N 118 30 E
Petra Velikogo, Zaliv, *Russia* **70 C6** 42 40N 132 0 E
Petrel = Petrer, *Spain* **41 G4** 38 30N 0 46W
Petrella, Monte, *Italy* **46 A6** 41 18N 13 40 E
Petrer, *Spain* **41 G4** 38 30N 0 46W
Petreto-Bicchisano, *France* **29 G12** 41 47N 8 58 E
Petrich, *Bulgaria* **50 E7** 41 24N 23 13 E
Petrified Forest Nat. Park, *U.S.A.* **159 J9** 35 0N 109 30W
Petrijanec, *Croatia* **45 B13** 46 23N 16 17 E
Petrikov = Pyetrikaw, *Belarus* **59 F5** 52 11N 28 29 E
Petrila, *Romania* **53 E8** 45 29N 23 29 E
Petrinja, *Croatia* **45 C13** 45 28N 16 18 E
Petrodvorets, *Russia* **58 C5** 59 52N 29 54 E
Petrograd = Sankt-Peterburg, *Russia* **58 C6** 59 55N 30 20 E
Petrolândia, *Brazil* **170 C4** 9 5 S 38 20W
Petrolia, *Canada* **140 D3** 42 54N 82 9W
Petrolina, *Brazil* **170 C3** 9 24 S 40 30W
Petropavl, *Kazakstan* **66 D7** 54 53N 69 13 E
Petropavlovsk = Petropavl, *Kazakstan* **66 D7** 54 53N 69 13 E
Petropavlovsk-Kamchatskiy, *Russia* **67 D16** 53 3N 158 43 E
Petropavlovskiy = Akhtubinsk, *Russia* **61 F8** 48 13N 46 7 E
Petrópolis, *Brazil* **171 F3** 22 33 S 43 9W
Petroşani, *Romania* **53 E8** 45 28N 23 20 E
Petrova Gora, *Croatia* **45 C12** 45 15N 15 45 E
Petrovac, *Montenegro, Yug.* **50 D2** 42 13N 18 57 E
Petrovac, *Serbia, Yug.* **50 B5** 44 22N 21 26 E
Petrovaradin, *Serbia, Yug.* **52 E4** 45 16N 19 55 E
Petrovsk, *Russia* **60 D7** 52 22N 45 19 E
Petrovsk-Zabaykalskiy, *Russia* **67 D11** 51 20N 108 55 E
Petrovskaya, *Russia* **59 K9** 45 25N 37 58 E
Petrovskoye = Svetlograd, *Russia* **61 H6** 45 25N 42 58 E
Petrovskoye, *Russia* **64 E6** 53 37N 56 23 E
Petrozavodsk, *Russia* **58 B8** 61 41N 34 20 E
Petrus Steyn, *S. Africa* **117 D4** 27 38 S 28 8 E
Petrusburg, *S. Africa* **116 D4** 29 4 S 25 26 E
Petzeck, *Austria* **34 E5** 46 57N 12 48 E
Peumo, *Chile* **174 C1** 34 21 S 71 12W
Peureulak, *Indonesia* **84 B1** 4 48N 97 45 E
Peusangan →, *Indonesia* **84 A1** 5 16N 96 51 E
Pevek, *Russia* **67 C18** 69 41N 171 19 E
Pevely, *U.S.A.* **156 F6** 38 17N 90 24W
Peveragno, *Italy* **44 D4** 44 20N 7 37 E
Peyrehorade, *France* **28 E2** 43 34N 1 7W
Peyruis, *France* **29 D9** 44 1N 5 56 E
Pézenas, *France* **28 E7** 43 28N 3 24 E
Pezinok, *Slovak Rep.* **35 C10** 48 17N 17 17 E
Pfaffenhofen, *Germany* **31 G7** 48 31N 11 31 E
Pfäffikon, *Schwyz, Switz.* **33 B7** 47 13N 8 46 E
Pfäffikon, *Zürich, Switz.* **33 B7** 47 22N 8 47 E
Pfarrkirchen, *Germany* **31 G8** 48 25N 12 56 E
Pfeffenhausen, *Germany* **31 G7** 48 39N 11 58 E
Pforzheim, *Germany* **31 G4** 48 52N 8 41 E
Pfullendorf, *Germany* **31 H5** 47 55N 9 15 E
Pfungstadt, *Germany* **31 F4** 49 48N 8 35 E
Phaistós, *Greece* **39 E5** 35 2N 24 50 E
Phala, *Botswana* **116 C4** 23 45 S 26 50 E
Phalera = Phulera, *India* **92 F6** 26 52N 75 16 E
Phalodi, *India* **92 F5** 27 12N 72 24 E
Phalsbourg, *France* **27 D14** 48 46N 7 15 E
Phaltan, *India* **94 F2** 17 59N 74 26 E
Phaluai, Ko, *Thailand* **87 b** 9 32N 99 41 E
Phan, *Thailand* **86 C2** 19 28N 99 43 E
Phan Rang, *Vietnam* **87 G7** 11 34N 109 0 E
Phan Ri = Hoa Da, *Vietnam* **87 G7** 11 16N 108 40 E
Phan Thiet, *Vietnam* **87 G7** 11 1N 108 9 E
Phanae, *Greece* **49 C7** 38 8N 25 57 E
Phanat Nikhom, *Thailand* **86 F3** 13 27N 101 11 E
Phangan, Ko, *Thailand* **87 H3** 9 45N 100 0 E
Phangnga, *Thailand* **87 H2** 8 28N 98 30 E
Phangnga, Ao, *Thailand* **87 a** 8 16N 98 33 E
Phanom Sarakham, *Thailand* **86 F3** 13 45N 101 21 E
Phaphund, *India* **93 F8** 26 36N 79 28 E
Pharenda, *India* **93 F10** 27 5N 83 17 E
Pharr, *U.S.A.* **155 M5** 26 12N 98 11W
Phatthalung, *Thailand* **87 J3** 7 39N 100 6 E
Phayao, *Thailand* **86 C2** 19 11N 99 55 E
Phelps, *U.S.A.* **150 D7** 42 58N 77 3W
Phelps L., *Canada* **143 B8** 59 15N 103 15W
Phenix City, *U.S.A.* **149 J3** 32 28N 85 0W
Phet Buri, *Thailand* **86 F2** 13 1N 99 55 E
Phetchabun, *Thailand* **86 D3** 16 25N 101 8 E
Phetchabun, Thiu Khao, *Thailand* **86 E3** 16 0N 101 20 E
Phetchaburi = Phet Buri, *Thailand* **86 F2** 13 1N 99 55 E
Phi Phi, Ko, *Thailand* **87 J2** 7 45N 98 46 E
Phiafay, *Laos* **86 E6** 14 48N 106 0 E
Phibun Mangsahan, *Thailand* **86 E5** 15 14N 105 14 E
Phichai, *Thailand* **86 D3** 17 22N 100 10 E
Phichit, *Thailand* **86 D3** 16 26N 100 22 E
Philadelphia, *Miss., U.S.A.* **155 J10** 32 46N 89 7W
Philadelphia, *N.Y., U.S.A.* **151 B9** 44 9N 75 43W
Philadelphia, *Pa., U.S.A.* **151 G9** 39 57N 75 10W
Philip, *U.S.A.* **154 C4** 44 2N 101 40W
Philip Smith Mts., *U.S.A.* **144 C11** 68 0N 148 0W
Philippeville, *Belgium* **24 D4** 50 12N 4 33 E
Philippi, *Greece* **51 E8** 41 1N 24 16 E
Philippi, *U.S.A.* **148 F5** 39 9N 80 3W
Philippi L., *Australia* **126 C2** 24 20 S 138 55 E
Philippines ■, *Asia* **80 E4** 12 0N 123 0 E
Philippolis, *S. Africa* **116 E4** 30 15 S 25 16 E
Philippopolis = Plovdiv, *Bulgaria* **51 D8** 42 8N 24 44 E
Philipsburg, *Canada* **151 A11** 45 2N 73 5W
Philipsburg, *Mont., U.S.A.* **158 C7** 46 20N 113 18W
Philipsburg, *Pa., U.S.A.* **150 F6** 40 54N 78 13W
Philipstown = Daingean, *Ireland* **23 C4** 53 18N 7 17W
Philipstown, *S. Africa* **116 E3** 30 28 S 24 30 E
Phillip I., *Australia* **129 E6** 38 30 S 145 12 E
Phillips, *U.S.A.* **154 C9** 45 42N 90 24W
Phillipsburg, *Ga., U.S.A.* **152 D6** 31 25N 83 30W
Phillipsburg, *Kans., U.S.A.* **154 F5** 39 45N 99 19W
Phillipsburg, *N.J., U.S.A.* **151 F9** 40 42N 75 12W
Philmont, *U.S.A.* **151 D11** 42 15N 73 39W
Philomath, *Ga., U.S.A.* **152 B7** 33 44N 82 59W
Philomath, *Oreg., U.S.A.* **158 D2** 44 32N 123 22W
Phimai, *Thailand* **86 E4** 15 13N 102 30 E
Phitsanulok, *Thailand* **86 D3** 16 50N 100 12 E
Phnom Dangrek, *Thailand* **78 B2** 14 20N 104 0 E
Phnom Penh, *Cambodia* **87 G5** 11 33N 104 55 E
Phnum Penh = Phnom Penh, *Cambodia* **87 G5** 11 33N 104 55 E
Phoenicia, *U.S.A.* **151 D10** 42 5N 74 14W
Phoenix, *Mauritius* **121 d** 20 17 S 57 30 E
Phoenix, *Ariz., U.S.A.* **159 K7** 33 27N 112 4W
Phoenix, *N.Y., U.S.A.* **151 C8** 43 14N 76 18W
Phoenix Is., *Kiribati* **134 H10** 3 30 S 172 0W
Phoenixville, *U.S.A.* **151 F9** 40 8N 75 31W
Phon, *Thailand* **86 E4** 15 49N 102 36 E
Phon Tiou, *Laos* **86 D5** 17 53N 104 37 E
Phong →, *Thailand* **86 D4** 16 23N 102 56 E
Phong Saly, *Laos* **76 G4** 21 42N 102 9 E
Phong Tho, *Vietnam* **86 A4** 22 32N 103 21 E
Phonhong, *Laos* **86 C4** 18 30N 102 25 E
Phonum, *Thailand* **87 H2** 8 49N 98 48 E
Phosphate Hill, *Australia* **126 C2** 21 53 S 139 58 E
Photharam, *Thailand* **86 F2** 13 41N 99 51 E
Phra Nakhon Si Ayutthaya, *Thailand* **86 E3** 14 25N 100 30 E
Phra Thong, Ko, *Thailand* **87 H2** 9 5N 98 17 E
Phrae, *Thailand* **86 C3** 18 7N 100 9 E
Phrom Phiram, *Thailand* **86 D3** 17 2N 100 12 E
Phrygia, *Turkey* **100 C4** 38 40N 30 0 E
Phu Dien, *Vietnam* **86 C5** 18 58N 105 31 E
Phu Loi, *Laos* **86 B4** 20 14N 103 14 E
Phu Ly, *Vietnam* **76 G5** 20 35N 105 50 E
Phu Quoc, Dao, *Vietnam* **87 G4** 10 20N 104 0 E
Phu Tho, *Vietnam* **76 G5** 21 24N 105 13 E
Phuc Yen, *Vietnam* **76 G5** 21 16N 105 45 E
Phuket, *Thailand* **87 a** 7 53N 98 24 E
Phuket, Ko, *Thailand* **87 a** 8 0N 98 22 E
Phul, *India* **92 D6** 30 19N 75 14 E
Phulad, *India* **92 G5** 25 38N 73 49 E
Phulbani, *India* **94 D7** 20 28N 84 14 E
Phulbari, *India* **90 C3** 25 55N 90 2 E
Phulchari, *Bangla.* **90 C2** 25 11N 89 37 E
Phulera, *India* **92 F6** 26 52N 75 16 E
Phulpur, *India* **93 G10** 25 31N 82 49 E
Phun Phin, *Thailand* **87 H2** 9 7N 99 12 E
Piacá, *Brazil* **170 C2** 7 42 S 47 18W
Piacenza, *Italy* **44 C6** 45 1N 9 40 E
Piaçubaçu, *Brazil* **170 D4** 10 24 S 36 25W
Piai, Tanjung, *Malaysia* **87 d** 1 17N 103 30 E
Piako →, *N.Z.* **130 D4** 37 12 S 175 30 E
Pian Cr. →, *Australia* **127 E4** 30 2 S 148 12 E
Pian-Upe Game Reserve, *Uganda* **118 B3** 1 44N 34 20 E
Piana, *France* **29 F12** 42 15N 8 34 E
Pianella, *Italy* **45 F11** 42 24N 14 2 E
Piangil, *Australia* **128 C5** 35 5 S 143 20 E
Pianosa, *Puglia, Italy* **45 F12** 42 12N 15 44 E
Pianosa, *Toscana, Italy* **44 F7** 42 35N 10 5 E
Piapot, *Canada* **143 D7** 49 59N 109 8W
Pias, *Portugal* **43 G3** 38 1N 7 29W
Piaseczno, *Poland* **55 F8** 52 5N 21 2 E
Piaski, *Poland* **55 G9** 51 8N 22 52 E
Piastów, *Poland* **55 F7** 52 12N 20 48 E
Piatã, *Brazil* **171 D3** 13 9 S 41 48W
Piatra, *Romania* **53 G10** 43 51N 25 9 E
Piatra Neamţ, *Romania* **53 D11** 46 56N 26 21 E
Piatra Olt, *Romania* **53 F9** 44 22N 24 16 E
Piauí □, *Brazil* **170 C3** 7 0 S 43 0W
Piauí →, *Brazil* **170 C3** 6 38 S 42 42W
Piave →, *Italy* **45 C9** 45 32N 12 44 E
Piazza Ármerina, *Italy* **47 E7** 37 21N 14 20 E
Pibor →, *Sudan* **107 F3** 7 35N 33 0 E
Pibor Post, *Sudan* **107 F3** 6 47N 33 3 E
Pica, *Chile* **172 E4** 20 35 S 69 25W
Picardie, *France* **27 C10** 49 50N 3 0 E
Picardie, Plaine de, *France* **27 C9** 50 0N 2 0 E
Picardy = Picardie, *France* **27 C10** 49 50N 3 0 E
Picayune, *U.S.A.* **155 K10** 30 32N 89 41W
Picerno, *Italy* **47 B8** 40 38N 15 38 E
Pichhor, *India* **93 G8** 25 58N 78 20 E
Pichilemu, *Chile* **174 C1** 34 22 S 72 0W
Pichincha, □, *Ecuador* **168 D2** 0 10 S 78 40W
Pichor, *India* **92 G8** 25 11N 78 11 E
Pickerel L., *Canada* **140 C1** 48 40N 91 25W
Pickering, *U.K.* **20 C7** 54 15N 0 46W
Pickering, Vale of, *U.K.* **20 C7** 54 14N 0 45W
Pickle Lake, *Canada* **140 B1** 51 30N 90 12W
Pickwick L., *U.S.A.* **149 H1** 35 4N 88 15W
Pico, *Azores* **9 d1** 38 28N 28 20W
Pico, Ponta do, *Azores* **9 d1** 38 28N 28 25W
Pico Truncado, *Argentina* **176 C3** 46 40 S 68 0W
Picos, *Brazil* **170 C3** 7 5 S 41 28W
Picota, *Peru* **172 B2** 6 54 S 76 24W
Picton, *Australia* **129 C9** 34 12 S 150 34 E
Picton, *Canada* **140 D4** 44 1N 77 9W
Picton, *N.Z.* **131 B9** 41 18 S 174 3 E
Picton, I., *Chile* **176 E3** 55 2 S 66 57W
Pictou, *Canada* **141 C7** 45 41N 62 42W
Picture Butte, *Canada* **142 D6** 49 55N 112 45W
Picuí, *Brazil* **170 C4** 6 31 S 36 21W
Picún Leufú, *Argentina* **176 A3** 39 30 S 69 5W
Pidurutalagala, *Sri Lanka* **95 L5** 7 10N 80 50 E
Piechowice, *Poland* **55 H2** 50 51N 15 36 E
Piedecuesta, *Colombia* **168 B3** 6 59N 73 3W
Piedmont = Piemonte □, *Italy* **44 D5** 45 0N 8 0 E
Piedmont, *Ala., U.S.A.* **152 B4** 33 55N 85 37W
Piedmont, *S.C., U.S.A.* **147 D10** 34 0N 81 30W
Piedmonte Matese, *Italy* **47 A7** 41 22N 14 22 E
Piedra →, *Spain* **40 D3** 41 18N 1 47W
Piedra del Anguila, *Argentina* **176 B2** 40 2 S 70 4W
Piedra Lais, *Venezuela* **168 C4** 3 10N 65 50W
Piedrabuena, *Spain* **43 G6** 39 0N 4 10W
Piedrahita, *Spain* **42 E5** 40 28N 5 23W
Piedralaves, *Spain* **42 E6** 40 19N 4 42W
Piedras, R. de las →, *Peru* **172 C4** 12 30 S 69 15W
Piedras Blancas, *Spain* **42 B5** 43 33N 5 58W
Piedras Negras, *Mexico* **162 B4** 28 42N 100 31W
Piedras Pt., *Phil.* **81 F2** 10 11N 118 48 E
Piekary Śląskie, *Poland* **55 H5** 50 24N 18 57 E
Pieksämäki, *Finland* **15 E22** 62 18N 27 10 E
Piemonte □, *Italy* **44 D5** 45 0N 8 0 E
Pienaarsrivier, *S. Africa* **117 D4** 25 15 S 28 18 E
Pieniężno, *Poland* **54 D7** 54 14N 20 8 E
Pieńsk, *Poland* **55 G2** 51 16N 15 2 E
Piercefield, *U.S.A.* **151 B10** 44 13N 74 35W
Pierceland, *Canada* **143 C7** 54 20N 109 46W
Piería □, *Greece* **50 F6** 40 13N 22 25 E
Pierpont, *U.S.A.* **150 E4** 41 45N 80 34W
Pierre, *U.S.A.* **154 C4** 44 22N 100 21W
Pierre-Buffière, *France* **28 C5** 45 41N 1 22 E
Pierre-de-Bresse, *France* **27 F12** 46 54N 5 13 E
Pierre E. Trudeau, Mt. = Logan, Mt., *Canada* **138 B5** 60 31N 140 22W
Pierrefontaine-les-Varans, *France* **27 E13** 47 14N 6 32 E
Pierrefort, *France* **28 D6** 44 55N 2 50 E
Pierrelatte, *France* **29 D8** 44 23N 4 43 E
Pierreville, *Trin. & Tob.* **169 F9** 10 16N 61 0W
Pierson, *U.S.A.* **153 F8** 29 14N 81 28W
Pieštany, *Slovak Rep.* **35 C10** 48 38N 17 55 E
Piesting →, *Austria* **35 C9** 48 6N 16 40 E
Pieszyce, *Poland* **55 H3** 50 43N 16 33 E
Piet Retief, *S. Africa* **117 D5** 27 1 S 30 50 E
Pietarsaari, *Finland* **14 E20** 63 40N 22 43 E
Pietermaritzburg, *S. Africa* **117 D5** 29 35 S 30 25 E
Pietersburg, *S. Africa* **117 C4** 23 54 S 29 25 E
Pietragalla, *Italy* **47 B8** 40 45N 15 53 E
Pietrasanta, *Italy* **44 E7** 43 57N 10 14 E
Pietroşiţa, *Romania* **53 E10** 45 11N 25 26 E
Pietrosul, Vf., *Maramureş, Romania* **53 C9** 47 35N 24 43 E
Pietrosul, Vf., *Suceava, Romania* **53 C10** 47 12N 25 18 E
Pieve di Cadore, *Italy* **45 B9** 46 26N 12 22 E
Pieve di Teco, *Italy* **44 D4** 44 3N 7 56 E
Pievepélago, *Italy* **44 D7** 44 12N 10 37 E
Pigadhítsa, *Greece* **50 G5** 39 59N 21 23 E
Pigeon I., *India* **95 G2** 14 2N 74 20 E
Pigeon L., *Canada* **150 B6** 44 27N 78 30W
Piggott, *U.S.A.* **155 G9** 36 23N 90 11W
Pigna, *Italy* **44 E4** 43 56N 7 40 E
Pigüe, *Argentina* **174 D3** 37 36 S 62 25W
Pihani, *India* **93 F9** 27 36N 80 15 E
Pihlajavesi, *Finland* **15 F23** 61 45N 28 45 E
Pijijiapan, *Mexico* **163 D6** 15 42N 93 14W
Pikalevo, *Russia* **58 C8** 59 37N 34 9 E
Pikangikum Berens, *Canada* **143 C10** 51 49N 94 0W
Pikes Peak, *U.S.A.* **154 F2** 38 50N 105 3W
Piketberg, *S. Africa* **116 E2** 32 55 S 18 40 E
Pikeville, *U.S.A.* **148 G4** 37 29N 82 31W
Pikit, *Phil.* **81 H5** 7 4N 124 41 E
Pikou, *China* **75 E12** 39 18N 122 22 E
Pikounda, *Congo* **114 B3** 0 30N 16 44 E
Pikwitonei, *Canada* **143 B9** 55 35N 97 9W
Piła, *Poland* **55 E3** 53 10N 16 48 E
Pila, *Spain* **41 G3** 38 16N 1 11W
Pilaía, *Greece* **50 F6** 40 32N 22 59 E
Pilanesberg Nat. Park, *S. Africa* **116 D4** 25 15 S 27 4 E
Pilani, *India* **92 E6** 28 22N 75 33 E
Pilar, *Brazil* **170 C4** 9 36 S 35 56W
Pilar, *Paraguay* **174 B4** 26 50 S 58 20W
Pilar, *Capiz, Phil.* **81 F4** 11 29N 123 0 E
Pilar, *Sorsogon, Phil.* **80 E4** 12 56N 123 40 E
Pilar de la Horadada, *Spain* **41 H4** 37 52N 0 47W
Pilas Group, *Phil.* **81 H3** 6 45N 121 35 E
Pilawa, *Poland* **55 G8** 51 57N 21 32 E
Pilaya →, *Bolivia* **173 E5** 20 55 S 64 4W
Pilbara, *Australia* **124 D2** 23 35 S 117 25 E
Pilcomayo →, *Paraguay* **174 B4** 25 21 S 57 42W
Pilgrim's Rest, *S. Africa* **117 C5** 24 55 S 30 44 E
Pilgrimstad, *Sweden* **16 B9** 62 57N 15 2 E
Píli, *Greece* **49 E9** 36 50N 27 15 E
Pili, *Phil.* **80 E4** 13 33N 123 19 E
Pilibhit, *India* **93 E8** 28 40N 79 50 E
Pilica →, *Poland* **55 G8** 51 52N 21 17 E
Pilion, *Greece* **48 B5** 39 27N 23 3 E
Pilis, *Hungary* **52 C4** 47 17N 19 35 E
Pilisvörösvár, *Hungary* **52 C3** 47 38N 18 56 E
Pilkhawa, *India* **92 E7** 28 43N 77 42 E
Pillar B., *Ascension I.* **9 g** 7 59 S 14 21W
Pillaro, *Ecuador* **168 D2** 1 10 S 78 32W
Pilliga, *Australia* **127 E4** 30 21 S 148 54 E
Pílos, *Greece* **48 E3** 36 55N 21 42 E
Pilot Grove, *U.S.A.* **156 F4** 38 53N 92 55W
Pilot Mound, *Canada* **143 D9** 49 15N 98 54W
Pilot Point, *Alaska, U.S.A.* **144 H8** 57 34N 157 35W
Pilot Point, *Tex., U.S.A.* **155 J6** 33 24N 96 58W
Pilot Rock, *U.S.A.* **158 D4** 45 29N 118 50W
Pilot Station, *U.S.A.* **144 F7** 61 56N 162 53W
Pilsen = Plzeň, *Czech Rep.* **34 B6** 49 45N 13 22 E
Pilštanj, *Slovenia* **45 B12** 46 8N 15 39 E
Piltene, *Latvia* **54 A8** 57 13N 21 40 E
Pilzno, *Poland* **55 J8** 49 58N 21 16 E
Pima, *U.S.A.* **159 K9** 32 54N 109 50W
Pimba, *Australia* **128 A2** 31 18 S 136 46 E
Pimenta Bueno, *Brazil* **173 C5** 11 35 S 61 10W
Pimenteiras, *Brazil* **173 C5** 13 40 S 60 58W
Pimentel, *Peru* **172 B2** 6 45 S 79 55W
Pimu, *Dem. Rep. of the Congo* **114 B4** 1 42N 20 58 E
Pina de Ebro, *Spain* **40 D4** 41 29N 0 33W
Pinamalayan, *Phil.* **80 E3** 13 2N 121 29 E
Pinang, *Malaysia* **87 c** 5 25N 100 15 E
Pinang □, *Malaysia* **84 A2** 5 20N 100 20 E
Pinar, C. des, *Spain* **38 B4** 39 53N 3 12 E
Pinar del Río, *Cuba* **164 B3** 22 26N 83 40W
Pınarbaşı, *Çanakkale, Turkey* **49 B8** 39 53N 26 15 E
Pınarbaşı, *Kayseri, Turkey* **100 C7** 38 43N 36 23 E
Pınarhisar, *Turkey* **51 E11** 41 37N 27 30 E
Pinatubo, Mt., *Phil.* **80 D3** 15 8N 120 21 E
Pincehely, *Hungary* **52 D3** 46 41N 18 27 E
Pinchang, *China* **76 B6** 31 36N 107 3 E
Pincher Creek, *Canada* **142 D6** 49 30N 113 57W
Pinchi L., *Canada* **142 C4** 54 38N 124 30W
Pinckard, *U.S.A.* **152 D4** 31 19N 85 33W
Pinckneyville, *U.S.A.* **156 F7** 38 5N 89 23W
Pińczów, *Poland* **55 H7** 50 32N 20 32 E
Pindaï, Presqu'île de, *N. Cal.* **133 U18** 21 20 S 164 56 E
Pindar, *Australia* **125 E2** 28 30 S 115 47 E
Pindaré →, *Brazil* **170 B3** 3 17 S 44 47W
Pindaré Mirim, *Brazil* **170 B2** 3 37 S 45 21W
Pindi Gheb, *Pakistan* **92 C5** 33 14N 72 21 E
Pindiga, *Nigeria* **113 D7** 9 58N 10 53 E
Pindobal, *Brazil* **170 B2** 3 16 S 48 25W
Pindos Óros, *Greece* **48 B3** 40 0N 21 0 E
Pindus Mts. = Pindos Óros, *Greece* **48 B3** 40 0N 21 0 E
Pine →, *B.C., Canada* **142 B4** 56 8N 120 43W
Pine →, *Sask., Canada* **143 B7** 58 50N 105 38W
Pine, C., *Canada* **141 C9** 46 37N 53 32W
Pine Bluff, *U.S.A.* **155 H9** 34 13N 92 1W
Pine Bluffs, *U.S.A.* **154 E2** 41 11N 104 4W
Pine City, *U.S.A.* **154 C8** 45 50N 92 59W
Pine Cr. →, *U.S.A.* **150 E7** 41 10N 77 16W
Pine Creek, *Australia* **124 B5** 13 50 S 131 50 E
Pine Falls, *Canada* **143 C9** 50 34N 96 11W
Pine Flat Res., *U.S.A.* **160 J7** 36 50N 119 20W
Pine Grove, *U.S.A.* **151 F8** 40 33N 76 23W
Pine Is., *U.S.A.* **153 J7** 26 36N 82 7W
Pine Level, *U.S.A.* **152 C3** 32 4N 86 4W
Pine Mountain, *U.S.A.* **152 C5** 32 52N 84 51W
Pine Pass, *Canada* **142 B4** 55 25N 122 42W
Pine Point, *Canada* **142 A6** 60 50N 114 28W
Pine Ridge, *Australia* **129 A9** 31 30 S 150 28 E
Pine Ridge, *U.S.A.* **154 D3** 43 2N 102 33W
Pine River, *Canada* **143 C8** 51 45N 100 30W
Pine River, *U.S.A.* **154 B7** 46 43N 94 24W
Pine Valley, *U.S.A.* **161 N10** 32 50N 116 32W
Pinecrest, *U.S.A.* **160 G6** 38 12N 120 1W
Pineda de Mar, *Spain* **40 D7** 41 37N 2 42 E
Pinedale, *Calif., U.S.A.* **160 J7** 36 50N 119 48W
Pinedale, *Wyo., U.S.A.* **158 E9** 42 52N 109 52W
Pinega →, *Russia* **56 B8** 64 30N 44 19 E

Polillo Is., *Phil.* 80 D4 14 56N 122 0 E
Polillo Strait, *Phil.* 80 D4 14 44N 121 51 E
Polis, *Cyprus* 39 E8 35 2N 32 26 E
Polístena, *Italy* 47 D9 38 24N 16 4 E
Políyiros, *Greece* 50 F7 40 23N 23 25 E
Polk, *U.S.A.* 150 E5 41 22N 79 56W
Polkowice, *Poland* 55 G3 51 29N 16 3 E
Polla, *Italy* 47 B8 40 31N 15 29 E
Pollachi, *India* 95 J3 10 35N 77 0 E
Pollença, *Spain* 38 B4 39 54N 3 1 E
Pollença, B. de, *Spain* 38 B4 39 53N 3 8 E
Pollfoss, *Norway* 18 C4 61 58N 7 54 E
Póllica, *Italy* 47 B8 40 11N 15 3 E
Pollino, Mte., *Italy* 47 C9 39 55N 16 11 E
Polna, *Russia* 58 C5 58 31N 28 5 E
Polnovat, *Russia* 66 C7 63 50N 65 54 E
Polo, *Ill., U.S.A.* 156 C7 41 59N 89 35W
Polo, *Mo., U.S.A.* 156 E2 39 33N 94 3W
Pology, *Ukraine* 59 J9 47 29N 36 15 E
Polonnaruwa, *Sri Lanka* 95 L5 7 56N 81 0 E
Polonne, *Ukraine* 59 G4 50 6N 27 30 E
Polonnoye = Polonne, *Ukraine* 59 G4 50 6N 27 30 E
Polski Trŭmbesh, *Bulgaria* 51 C9 43 20N 25 38 E
Polsko Kosovo, *Bulgaria* 51 C9 43 23N 25 38 E
Polson, *U.S.A.* 158 C6 47 41N 114 9W
Poltár, *Slovak Rep.* 35 C12 48 26N 19 48 E
Poltava, *Ukraine* 59 H8 49 35N 34 35 E
Põltsamaa, *Estonia* 15 G21 58 41N 25 58 E
Polunochnoye, *Russia* 66 C7 60 52N 60 25 E
Polur, *India* 95 H4 12 32N 79 11 E
Põlva, *Estonia* 15 G22 58 3N 27 3 E
Polyarny, *Russia* 56 A5 69 8N 33 20 E
Polynesia, *Pac. Oc.* 135 J11 10 0 S 162 0W
Polynésie française = French Polynesia ■, *Pac. Oc.* 135 K13 20 0 S 145 0W
Pomabamba, *Peru* 172 B2 8 50 S 77 28W
Pomarance, *Italy* 44 E7 43 18N 10 52 E
Pomaro, *Mexico* 162 D4 18 20N 103 18W
Pombal, *Brazil* 170 C4 6 45 S 37 50W
Pombal, *Portugal* 42 F2 39 55N 8 40W
Pómbia, *Greece* 39 F5 35 0N 24 51 E
Pombos, B. dos, *Angola* 115 E2 11 40 S 13 47 E
Pomene, *Mozam.* 117 C6 22 53 S 35 33 E
Pomeroy, *Ohio, U.S.A.* 148 F4 39 2N 82 2W
Pomeroy, *Wash., U.S.A.* 158 C5 46 28N 117 36W
Pomézia, *Italy* 46 A5 41 40N 12 30 E
Pomichna, *Ukraine* 59 H6 48 13N 31 36 E
Pomio, *Papua N. G.* 132 C6 5 32 S 151 33 E
Pomme de Terre L., *U.S.A.* 156 G3 37 54N 93 19W
Pomona, *Australia* 127 D5 26 22 S 152 52 E
Pomona, *U.S.A.* 161 L9 34 4N 117 45W
Pomona Park, *U.S.A.* 153 F8 29 30N 81 36W
Pomorie, *Bulgaria* 51 D11 42 32N 27 41 E
Pomorskie □, *Poland* 54 D5 54 30N 18 0 E
Pomorskie, Pojezierze, *Poland* 54 E3 53 40N 16 37 E
Pomos, *Cyprus* 39 E8 35 9N 32 33 E
Pomos, C., *Cyprus* 39 E8 35 10N 32 33 E
Pompano Beach, *U.S.A.* 149 M5 26 14N 80 8W
Pompei, *Italy* 47 B7 40 45N 14 30 E
Pompey, *France* 27 D13 48 46N 6 6 E
Pompeys Pillar, *U.S.A.* 158 D10 45 59N 107 57W
Pompton Lakes, *U.S.A.* 151 F10 41 0N 74 17W
Ponape = Pohnpei, *Micronesia* 134 G7 6 55N 158 10 E
Ponask L., *Canada* 140 B1 54 0N 92 41W
Ponca, *U.S.A.* 154 D6 42 34N 96 43W
Ponca City, *U.S.A.* 155 G6 36 42N 97 5W
Ponce, *Puerto Rico* 165 d 18 1N 66 37W
Ponce de Leon, *U.S.A.* 152 E4 30 44N 85 56W
Ponce de Leon B., *U.S.A.* 153 K8 25 15N 81 10W
Ponchatoula, *U.S.A.* 155 K9 30 26N 90 26W
Poncheville, L., *Canada* 140 B4 50 10N 76 55W
Pond, *U.S.A.* 161 K7 35 43N 119 20W
Pond Inlet, *Canada* 139 A12 72 40N 77 0W
Pondicherry, *India* 95 J4 11 59N 79 50 E
Pondo, *Papua N. G.* 132 C6 4 33 S 151 38 E
Ponds, I. of, *Canada* 141 B8 53 27N 55 52W
Ponérihouen, *N. Cal.* 133 U19 21 5 S 165 24 E
Ponferrada, *Spain* 42 C4 42 32N 6 35W
Pongo, Wadi →, *Sudan* 107 F2 8 42N 27 40 E
Poniatowa, *Poland* 55 G9 51 11N 22 3 E
Poniec, *Poland* 55 G3 51 48N 16 50 E
Ponikva, *Slovenia* 45 B12 46 16N 15 26 E
Ponnaiyar →, *India* 95 J4 11 50N 79 45 E
Ponnani, *India* 95 J2 10 45N 75 59 E
Ponneri, *India* 95 H5 13 20N 80 15 E
Ponnuru, *India* 95 F5 16 5N 80 34 E
Ponoka, *Canada* 142 C6 52 42N 113 40W
Ponomarevka, *Russia* 64 E5 53 19N 54 8 E
Ponorogo, *Indonesia* 85 D4 7 52 S 111 27 E
Ponot, *Phil.* 81 G4 8 25N 123 0 E
Ponoy, *Russia* 56 A7 67 0N 41 13 E
Ponoy →, *Russia* 56 A7 66 59N 41 17 E
Pons = Ponts, *Spain* 40 D6 41 55N 1 12 E
Pons, *France* 28 C3 45 35N 0 34W
Ponsul →, *Portugal* 42 F3 39 40N 7 31W
Pont-à-Mousson, *France* 27 D13 48 54N 6 1 E
Pont-Audemer, *France* 26 C7 49 21N 0 30 E
Pont-Aven, *France* 26 E3 47 51N 3 47W
Pont Canavese, *Italy* 44 C4 45 25N 7 36 E
Pont-d'Ain, *France* 27 F12 46 3N 5 21 E
Pont-de-Roide, *France* 27 E13 47 23N 6 45 E
Pont-de-Salars, *France* 28 D6 44 18N 2 44 E
Pont-de-Vaux, *France* 27 F11 46 26N 4 56 E
Pont-de-Veyle, *France* 27 F11 46 17N 4 53 E
Pont-du-Château, *France* 27 G10 45 47N 3 15 E
Pont-l'Abbé, *France* 26 E2 47 52N 4 15W
Pont-l'Évêque, *France* 26 C7 49 18N 0 11 E
Pont-St-Esprit, *France* 29 D8 44 16N 4 40 E
Pont-St-Martin, *Italy* 44 C4 45 36N 7 48 E
Pont-Ste-Maxence, *France* 27 C9 49 18N 2 35 E
Pont-sur-Yonne, *France* 27 D10 48 18N 3 10 E
Ponta de Pedras, *Brazil* 170 B2 1 23 S 48 52W
Ponta Delgada, *Flores, Azores* 9 d2 39 31N 31 13W
Ponta Delgada, *São Miguel, Azores* 9 d3 37 44N 25 40W
Ponta do Sol, *Madeira* 9 c 32 42N 17 7W
Ponta Grossa, *Brazil* 175 B5 25 7 S 50 10W
Ponta Pora, *Brazil* 175 A4 22 20 S 55 35W
Pontacq, *France* 28 E3 43 11N 0 8W
Pontailler-sur-Saône, *France* 27 E12 47 13N 5 25 E
Pontal →, *Brazil* 170 C3 9 8 S 40 12W
Pontalina, *Brazil* 171 E2 17 31 S 49 27W
Pontarlier, *France* 27 F13 46 54N 6 20 E
Pontassieve, *Italy* 45 E8 43 46N 11 26 E
Pontaumur, *France* 28 C6 45 52N 2 40 E
Pontcharra, *France* 29 C10 45 26N 6 1 E
Pontchartrain L., *U.S.A.* 155 K10 30 5N 90 5W
Pontchâteau, *France* 26 E4 47 25N 2 5W
Ponte Alta, Serra do, *Brazil* 171 E2 19 42 S 47 40W
Ponte Alta do Norte, *Brazil* 170 D2 10 45 S 47 34W
Ponte Branca, *Brazil* 173 D7 16 27 S 52 40W
Ponte da Barca, *Portugal* 42 D2 41 48N 8 25W
Ponte de Sor, *Portugal* 43 F2 39 17N 8 1W
Ponte dell'Ólio, *Italy* 44 D6 44 52N 9 39 E
Ponte di Legno, *Italy* 44 B7 46 16N 10 31 E
Ponte do Lima, *Portugal* 42 D2 41 46N 8 35W
Ponte do Pungué, *Mozam.* 119 F3 19 30 S 34 33 E
Ponte-Leccia, *France* 29 F13 42 28N 9 13 E
Ponte nelle Alpi, *Italy* 45 B9 46 11N 12 16 E
Ponte Nova, *Brazil* 171 F3 20 25 S 42 54W
Ponte Tresa, *Italy* 33 E7 45 58N 8 51 E
Ponte Vedra Beach, *U.S.A.* 152 E8 30 15N 81 23W
Ponteareas, *Spain* 42 C2 42 10N 8 28W
Pontebba, *Italy* 45 B10 46 30N 13 18 E
Ponteceso, *Spain* 42 B2 43 15N 8 54W
Pontecorvo, *Italy* 46 A6 41 27N 13 40 E
Pontedeume, *Spain* 42 B2 43 24N 8 10W
Ponteix, *Canada* 143 D7 49 46N 107 29W
Pontes e Lacerda, *Brazil* 173 D6 15 12 S 59 22W
Pontevedra, *Capiz, Phil.* 81 F4 11 29N 122 50 E
Pontevedra, *Neg. Occ., Phil.* 81 F4 10 22N 122 52 E
Pontevedra, *Spain* 42 C2 42 26N 8 40W
Pontevedra □, *Spain* 42 C2 42 25N 8 39W
Pontevedra, R. de →, *Spain* 42 C2 42 22N 8 45W
Pontevico, *Italy* 44 C7 45 16N 10 5 E
Pontiac, *Ill., U.S.A.* 154 E10 40 53N 88 38W
Pontiac, *Mich., U.S.A.* 157 B13 42 38N 83 18W
Pontian Kecil, *Malaysia* 87 d 1 29N 103 23 E
Pontianak, *Indonesia* 85 C3 0 3 S 109 15 E
Pontine Is. = Ponziane, Ísole, *Italy* 46 B5 40 55N 12 57 E
Pontine Mts. = Kuzey Anadolu Dağları, *Turkey* 100 B7 41 30N 35 0 E
Pontínia, *Italy* 46 A6 41 25N 13 2 E
Pontivy, *France* 26 D4 48 5N 2 58W
Pontoise, *France* 27 C9 49 3N 2 5 E
Ponton →, *Canada* 142 B5 58 27N 116 11W
Pontorson, *France* 26 D5 48 34N 1 30W
Pontrémoli, *Italy* 44 D6 44 22N 9 53 E
Pontresina, *Switz.* 33 D9 46 29N 9 48 E
Pontrieux, *France* 26 D3 48 42N 3 10W
Ponts, *Spain* 40 D6 41 55N 1 12 E
Pontypool, *Canada* 150 B6 44 6N 78 38W
Pontypool, *U.K.* 21 F4 51 42N 3 2W
Ponza, *Italy* 46 B5 40 54N 12 58 E
Ponziane, Ísole, *Italy* 46 B5 40 55N 12 57 E
Poochera, *Australia* 127 E1 32 43 S 134 51 E
Poole, *U.K.* 21 G6 50 43N 1 59W
Poole □, *U.K.* 21 G6 50 43N 1 59W
Pooler, *U.S.A.* 152 C8 32 7N 81 15W
Poona = Pune, *India* 94 E1 18 29N 73 57 E
Poonamallee, *India* 95 H5 13 3N 80 10 E
Pooncarie, *Australia* 128 B5 33 22 S 142 31 E
Poopelloe L., *Australia* 128 A6 31 40 S 144 0 E
Poopó, *Bolivia* 172 D4 18 23 S 66 59W
Poopó, L. de, *Bolivia* 172 D4 18 30 S 67 35W
Poor Knights Is., *N.Z.* 130 B3 35 29 S 174 43 E
Popa, *Gabon* 114 C2 1 35 S 12 32 E
Popayán, *Colombia* 168 C2 2 27N 76 36W
Poperinge, *Belgium* 24 D2 50 51N 2 42 E
Popilta L., *Australia* 128 B4 33 10 S 141 42 E
Popina, *Bulgaria* 51 B10 44 7N 26 57 E
Popio L., *Australia* 128 B4 33 10 S 141 52 E
Poplar, *U.S.A.* 154 A2 48 7N 105 12W
Poplar →, *Canada* 143 C9 53 0N 97 19W
Poplar Bluff, *U.S.A.* 155 G9 36 46N 90 24W
Poplarville, *U.S.A.* 155 K10 30 51N 89 32W
Popocatépetl, Volcán, *Mexico* 163 D5 19 2N 98 38W
Popokabaka, *Dem. Rep. of the Congo* 115 D3 5 41 S 16 40 E
Pópoli, *Italy* 45 F10 42 10N 13 50 E
Popolo, *Dem. Rep. of the Congo* 114 B4 2 22N 21 8 E
Popomanaseu, Mt., *Solomon Is.* 133 M11 9 40 S 160 1 E
Popondetta, *Papua N. G.* 132 E5 8 48 S 148 17 E
Popovača, *Croatia* 45 C13 45 30N 16 41 E
Popovo, *Bulgaria* 51 C10 43 21N 26 18 E
Poppberg, *Germany* 31 F7 49 26N 11 37 E
Poppi, *Italy* 45 E8 43 43N 11 46 E
Poprad, *Slovak Rep.* 35 B13 49 3N 20 18 E
Poprad →, *Slovak Rep.* 35 B13 49 38N 20 42 E
Poradaha, *Bangla.* 90 D2 23 51N 89 1 E
Porali →, *Pakistan* 91 D2 25 58N 66 26 E
Porangaba, *Brazil* 172 B3 8 48 S 70 36W
Porangahau, *N.Z.* 130 G5 40 17 S 176 37 E
Porangatu, *Brazil* 171 D2 13 26 S 49 10W
Porbandar, *India* 92 J3 21 44N 69 43 E
Porce →, *Colombia* 168 B3 7 28N 74 53W
Porcher I., *Canada* 142 C2 53 50N 130 30W
Porco, *Bolivia* 173 D4 19 50 S 65 59W
Porcos →, *Brazil* 171 D2 12 42 S 45 7W
Porcuna, *Spain* 43 H6 37 52N 4 11W
Porcupine →, *Canada* 143 B8 59 11N 104 46W
Porcupine →, *U.S.A.* 144 C11 66 34N 145 19W
Porcupine Gorge Nat. Park, *Australia* 126 C3 20 22 S 144 26 E
Pordenone, *Italy* 45 C9 45 57N 12 39 E
Pordim, *Bulgaria* 51 C8 43 23N 24 51 E
Pore, *Colombia* 168 B3 5 43N 72 0W
Poreč, *Croatia* 45 C10 45 14N 13 36 E
Porecatu, *Brazil* 171 F1 22 43 S 51 24W
Poretskoye, *Russia* 60 C8 55 9N 46 21 E
Porgera, *Papua N. G.* 132 C2 5 28 S 143 12 E
Pori, *Finland* 15 F19 61 29N 21 48 E
Porí, *Greece* 48 F5 35 58N 23 13 E
Porkhov, *Russia* 58 D5 57 45N 29 38 E
Porlamar, *Venezuela* 169 A5 10 57N 63 51W
Porlezza, *Italy* 44 B6 46 2N 9 7 E
Porma →, *Spain* 42 C5 42 49N 5 28W
Pornic, *France* 26 E4 47 7N 2 5W
Poronaysk, *Russia* 67 E15 49 13N 143 0 E
Póros, 39 C2 38 9N 20 47 E
Póros, *Attikí, Greece* 48 D5 37 30N 23 30 E
Póros, *Levkás, Greece* 39 B2 38 38N 20 43 E
Poroshiri-Dake, *Japan* 70 C11 42 41N 142 52 E
Poroszló, *Hungary* 52 C5 47 39N 20 40 E
Poroto Mts., *Tanzania* 119 D3 9 0 S 33 30 E
Porpoise B., *Antarctica* 7 C9 66 0 S 127 0 E
Porpoise Pt., *Ascension I.* 9 g 7 54 S 14 21W
Porquerolles, Î. de, *France* 29 F10 43 0N 6 13 E
Porrentruy, *Switz.* 32 B4 47 25N 7 6 E
Porreres, *Spain* 38 B4 39 31N 3 2 E
Porsangen, *Norway* 14 A21 70 40N 25 40 E
Porsgrunn, *Norway* 15 G13 59 10N 9 40 E
Port Adelaide, *Australia* 128 C3 34 46 S 138 30 E
Port Alberni, *Canada* 142 D4 49 14N 124 50W
Port Albert, *Australia* 129 E7 38 42 S 146 42 E
Port Alexander, *U.S.A.* 144 H14 56 15N 134 38W
Port Alfred, *S. Africa* 116 E4 33 36 S 26 55 E
Port Alice, *Canada* 142 C3 50 20N 127 25W
Port Allegany, *U.S.A.* 150 E6 41 48N 78 17W
Port Allen, *U.S.A.* 155 K9 30 27N 91 12W
Port Alma, *Australia* 126 C5 23 38 S 150 53 E
Port Angeles, *U.S.A.* 160 B3 48 7N 123 27W
Port Antonio, *Jamaica* 164 a 18 10N 76 30W
Port Aransas, *U.S.A.* 155 M6 27 50N 97 4W
Port Arthur = Lüshun, *China* 75 E11 38 45N 121 15 E
Port Arthur, *Australia* 127 G4 43 7 S 147 50 E
Port Arthur, *U.S.A.* 155 L8 29 54N 93 56W
Port au Choix, *Canada* 141 B8 50 43N 57 22W
Port au Port B., *Canada* 141 C8 48 40N 58 50W
Port-au-Prince, *Haiti* 165 C5 18 40N 72 20W
Port Augusta, *Australia* 128 B2 32 30 S 137 50 E
Port Austin, *U.S.A.* 150 B2 44 3N 83 1W
Port Bell, *Uganda* 118 B3 0 18N 32 35 E
Port Bergé Vaovao, *Madag.* 117 B8 15 33 S 47 40 E
Port Blair, *India* 95 J11 11 40N 92 45 E
Port Blandford, *Canada* 141 C9 48 20N 54 10W
Port-Bouët, *Ivory C.* 112 D4 5 16N 3 57W
Port Bradshaw, *Australia* 126 A2 12 30 S 137 20 E
Port Broughton, *Australia* 128 B2 33 37 S 137 56 E
Port Burwell, *Canada* 150 D4 42 40N 80 48W
Port Byron, *U.S.A.* 156 C6 41 37N 90 19W
Port Campbell, *Australia* 128 E5 38 37 S 143 1 E
Port Campbell, *India* 95 J11 11 56N 92 37 E
Port Campbell Nat. Park, *Australia* 128 E5 38 8 S 143 6 E
Port Canning, *India* 93 H13 22 23N 88 40 E
Port-Cartier, *Canada* 141 B6 50 2N 66 50W
Port Chalmers, *N.Z.* 131 F5 45 49 S 170 30 E
Port Charles, *N.Z.* 130 C4 36 33 S 175 30 E
Port Charlotte, *U.S.A.* 153 J7 26 59N 82 6W
Port Chester, *U.S.A.* 151 F11 41 0N 73 40W
Port Clements, *Canada* 142 C2 53 40N 132 10W
Port Clinton, *U.S.A.* 157 C14 41 31N 82 56W
Port Colborne, *Canada* 140 D4 42 50N 79 10W
Port Coquitlam, *Canada* 142 D4 49 15N 122 45W
Port Cornwallis, *India* 95 H11 13 17N 93 5 E
Port Credit, *Canada* 150 C5 43 33N 79 35W
Port Curtis, *Australia* 126 C5 23 57 S 151 20 E
Port d'Alcúdia, *Spain* 38 B4 39 50N 3 7 E
Port Dalhousie, *Canada* 150 C5 43 13N 79 16W
Port d'Andratx, *Spain* 38 B3 39 32N 2 23 E
Port Darwin, *Australia* 124 B5 12 24 S 130 45 E
Port Darwin, *Falk. Is.* 9 f 51 50 S 59 0W
Port Davey, *Australia* 127 G4 43 16 S 145 55 E
Port-de-Bouc, *France* 29 E8 43 24N 4 59 E
Port-de-Paix, *Haiti* 165 C5 19 50N 72 50W
Port de Pollença, *Spain* 38 B4 39 54N 3 4 E
Port de Sóller, *Spain* 38 B3 39 48N 2 42 E
Port Dickson, *Malaysia* 87 L3 2 30N 101 49 E
Port Douglas, *Australia* 126 B4 16 30 S 145 30 E
Port Dover, *Canada* 150 D4 42 47N 80 12W
Port Edward, *Canada* 142 C2 54 12N 130 10W
Port Elgin, *Canada* 140 D3 44 25N 81 25W
Port Elizabeth, *S. Africa* 116 E4 33 58 S 25 40 E
Port Ellen, *U.K.* 22 F2 55 38N 6 11W
Port Elliot, *Australia* 128 C3 35 32 S 138 41 E
Port-en-Bessin, *France* 26 C6 49 21N 0 45W
Port Erin, *U.K.* 20 C3 54 5N 4 45W
Port Essington, *Australia* 124 B5 11 15 S 132 10 E
Port Etienne = Nouâdhibou, *Mauritania* 110 D1 20 54N 17 0W
Port Ewen, *U.S.A.* 151 E11 41 54N 73 59W
Port Fairy, *Australia* 128 E5 38 22 S 142 12 E
Port Fitzroy, *N.Z.* 130 C4 36 8 S 175 20 E
Port Fouâd = Bûr Fuad, *Egypt* 106 H8 31 15N 32 20 E
Port Gamble, *U.S.A.* 160 C4 47 51N 122 35W
Port-Gentil, *Gabon* 114 C1 0 40 S 8 50 E
Port Germein, *Australia* 127 E2 33 1 S 138 1 E
Port Gibson, *U.S.A.* 155 K9 31 58N 90 59W
Port Glasgow, *U.K.* 22 F4 55 56N 4 41W
Port Harcourt, *Nigeria* 113 E6 4 40N 7 10 E
Port Hardy, *Canada* 142 C3 50 41N 127 30W
Port Harrison = Inukjuak, *Canada* 139 C12 58 25N 78 15W
Port Hawkesbury, *Canada* 141 C7 45 36N 61 22W
Port Hedland, *Australia* 124 D2 20 25 S 118 35 E
Port Heiden, *U.S.A.* 144 H8 56 55N 158 41W
Port Henry, *U.S.A.* 151 B11 44 3N 73 28W
Port Hood, *Canada* 141 C7 46 0N 61 32W
Port Hope, *Canada* 140 D4 43 56N 78 20W
Port Hope, *U.S.A.* 150 C2 43 57N 82 43W
Port Hope Simpson, *Canada* 141 B8 52 33N 56 18W
Port Hueneme, *U.S.A.* 161 L7 34 7N 119 12W
Port Huron, *U.S.A.* 150 D2 42 58N 82 26W
Port Ilıç, *Azerbaijan* 101 C13 38 53N 48 47 E
Port Jefferson, *U.S.A.* 151 F11 40 57N 73 3W
Port Jervis, *U.S.A.* 151 E10 41 22N 74 41W
Port-Joinville, *France* 26 F4 46 45N 2 23W
Port Katon, *Russia* 59 J10 46 52N 38 46 E
Port Kelang = Pelabuhan Kelang, *Malaysia* 87 L3 3 0N 101 23 E
Port Kembla, *Australia* 129 C9 34 52 S 150 49 E
Port Kenny, *Australia* 127 E1 33 10 S 134 41 E
Port-la-Nouvelle, *France* 28 E7 43 1N 3 3 E
Port Lairge = Waterford, *Ireland* 23 D4 52 15N 7 8W
Port Laoise, *Ireland* 23 C4 53 2N 7 18W
Port Lavaca, *U.S.A.* 155 L6 28 37N 96 38W
Port Leyden, *U.S.A.* 151 C9 43 35N 75 21W
Port Lincoln, *Australia* 128 C1 34 42 S 135 52 E
Port Lions, *U.S.A.* 144 H9 57 52N 152 53W
Port Loko, *S. Leone* 112 D2 8 48N 12 46W
Port Louis, *France* 26 E3 47 42N 3 22W
Port-Louis, *Guadeloupe* 164 b 16 28N 61 32W
Port Louis, *Mauritius* 105 H9 20 10 S 57 30 E
Port MacDonnell, *Australia* 128 E4 38 5 S 140 48 E
Port McNeill, *Canada* 142 C3 50 35N 127 6W
Port Macquarie, *Australia* 129 A10 31 25 S 152 25 E
Port Maria, *Jamaica* 164 a 18 25N 76 55W
Port Matilda, *U.S.A.* 150 F6 40 48N 78 3W
Port Mayaca, *U.S.A.* 153 J9 26 59N 80 36W
Port Mellon, *Canada* 142 D4 49 32N 123 31W
Port-Menier, *Canada* 141 C7 49 51N 64 15W
Port Moller, *U.S.A.* 144 J7 55 59N 160 34W
Port Moody, *Canada* 160 A4 49 17N 122 51W
Port Morant, *Jamaica* 164 a 17 54N 76 19W
Port Moresby, *Papua N. G.* 132 E4 9 24 S 147 8 E
Port Mourant, *Guyana* 169 B6 6 15N 57 20W
Port Musgrave, *Australia* 126 A3 11 55 S 141 50 E
Port Narevin, *Vanuatu* 133 H7 18 45 S 169 10 E
Port-Navalo, *France* 26 E4 47 34N 2 54W
Port Neches, *U.S.A.* 155 L8 30 0N 93 59W
Port Nicholson, *N.Z.* 130 H3 41 20 S 174 52 E
Port Nolloth, *S. Africa* 116 D2 29 17 S 16 52 E
Port Nouveau-Québec = Kangiqsualujjuaq, *Canada* 139 C13 58 30N 65 59W
Port of Spain, *Trin. & Tob.* 165 D7 10 40N 61 31W
Port Olry, *Vanuatu* 133 E5 15 1 S 167 4 E
Port Orange, *U.S.A.* 153 F9 29 9N 80 59W
Port Orchard, *U.S.A.* 160 C4 47 32N 122 38W
Port Orford, *U.S.A.* 158 E1 42 45N 124 30W
Port Pegasus, *N.Z.* 131 H2 47 12 S 167 41 E
Port Perry, *Canada* 140 D4 44 6N 78 56W
Port Phillip B., *Australia* 129 E6 38 10 S 144 50 E
Port Pirie, *Australia* 128 B3 33 10 S 138 1 E
Port Radium = Echo Bay, *Canada* 138 B8 66 5N 117 55W
Port Renfrew, *Canada* 142 D4 48 30N 124 20W
Port Roper, *Australia* 126 A2 14 45 S 135 25 E
Port Rowan, *Canada* 150 D4 42 40N 80 30W
Port Royal Sd., *U.S.A.* 152 C9 32 15N 80 40W
Port Safaga = Bûr Safâga, *Egypt* 96 E2 26 43N 33 57 E
Port Said = Bûr Sa'îd, *Egypt* 106 H8 31 16N 32 18 E
Port St. Joe, *U.S.A.* 152 F4 29 49N 85 18W
Port St. Johns = Umzimvubu, *S. Africa* 117 E4 31 38 S 29 33 E
Port-St-Louis-du-Rhône, *France* 29 E8 43 23N 4 49 E
Port St. Lucie, *U.S.A.* 149 M5 27 20N 80 20W
Port-Ste-Marie, *France* 28 D4 44 15N 0 25 E
Port Salerno, *U.S.A.* 153 H9 27 9N 80 12W
Port Sanilac, *U.S.A.* 150 C2 43 26N 82 33W
Port Severn, *Canada* 150 B5 44 48N 79 43W
Port Shepstone, *S. Africa* 117 E5 30 44 S 30 28 E
Port Simpson, *Canada* 142 C2 54 30N 130 20W
Port Stanley = Stanley, *Falk. Is.* 9 f 51 40 S 59 51W
Port Stanley, *Canada* 140 D3 42 40N 81 10W
Port Sudan = Bûr Sûdân, *Sudan* 106 D4 19 32N 37 9 E
Port Sulphur, *U.S.A.* 155 L10 29 29N 89 42W
Port-sur-Saône, *France* 27 E13 47 42N 6 2 E
Port Talbot, *U.K.* 21 F4 51 35N 3 47W
Port Taufiq = Bûr Taufiq, *Egypt* 106 J8 29 54N 32 32 E
Port Townsend, *U.S.A.* 160 B4 48 7N 122 45W
Port-Vato, *Vanuatu* 133 F6 16 20 S 168 1 E
Port-Vendres, *France* 28 F7 42 32N 3 8 E
Port Victoria, *Australia* 128 C2 34 30 S 137 29 E
Port Vila, *Vanuatu* 133 G6 17 45 S 168 18 E
Port Vladimir, *Russia* 56 A5 69 25N 33 6 E
Port Wakefield, *Australia* 128 C3 34 12 S 138 10 E
Port Washington, *U.S.A.* 148 D2 43 23N 87 53W
Port Weld = Kuala Sepetang, *Malaysia* 87 K3 4 49N 100 28 E
Port Wentworth, *U.S.A.* 152 C8 32 9N 81 10W
Porta Orientalis, *Romania* 37 F12 45 6N 22 18 E
Portachuelo, *Bolivia* 173 D5 17 10 S 63 20W
Portadown, *U.K.* 23 B5 54 25N 6 27W
Portaferry, *U.K.* 23 B6 54 23N 5 33W
Portage, *Mich., U.S.A.* 157 B11 42 12N 85 35W
Portage, *Pa., U.S.A.* 150 F6 40 23N 78 41W
Portage, *Wis., U.S.A.* 154 D10 43 33N 89 28W
Portage →, *U.S.A.* 157 C14 41 31N 83 5W
Portage La Prairie, *Canada* 143 D9 49 58N 98 18W
Portageville, *U.S.A.* 155 G10 36 26N 89 42W
Portal, *U.S.A.* 152 C8 32 33N 81 56W
Portalegre, *Portugal* 43 F3 39 19N 7 25W
Portalegre □, *Portugal* 43 F3 39 20N 7 40W
Portales, *U.S.A.* 155 H3 34 11N 103 20W
Portarlington, *Ireland* 23 C4 53 9N 7 14W
Portbou, *Spain* 40 C8 42 25N 3 9 E
Porteira, *Brazil* 169 D6 1 5 S 57 4W
Porteirinha, *Brazil* 171 E3 15 44 S 43 2W
Portel, *Brazil* 170 B1 1 57 S 50 49W
Portel, *Portugal* 43 G3 38 19N 7 41W
Porter, *U.S.A.* 157 C9 41 36N 87 4W
Porter L., *N.W.T., Canada* 143 A7 61 41N 108 5W
Porter L., *Sask., Canada* 143 B7 56 20N 107 20W
Porterville, *S. Africa* 116 E2 33 0 S 19 0 E
Porterville, *U.S.A.* 160 J8 36 4N 119 1W
Portes-lès-Valence, *France* 29 D8 44 52N 4 54 E
Porthcawl, *U.K.* 21 F4 51 29N 3 42W
Porthill, *U.S.A.* 158 B5 48 59N 116 30W
Porthmadog, *U.K.* 20 E3 52 55N 4 8W
Portile de Fier, *Europe* 52 F7 44 44N 22 30 E
Portimão, *Portugal* 43 H2 37 8N 8 32W
Portishead, *U.K.* 21 F5 51 29N 2 46W
Portiţei, Gura, *Romania* 53 F14 44 41N 29 0 E
Portknockie, *U.K.* 22 D6 57 42N 2 51W
Portland, *N.S.W., Australia* 129 B9 33 20 S 150 0 E
Portland, *Vic., Australia* 128 E4 38 20 S 141 35 E
Portland, *Canada* 151 B8 44 42N 76 12W
Portland, *Conn., U.S.A.* 151 E12 41 34N 72 38W
Portland, *Fla., U.S.A.* 152 E3 30 31N 86 12W
Portland, *Ind., U.S.A.* 157 D12 40 26N 84 59W
Portland, *Maine, U.S.A.* 139 D12 43 39N 70 16W
Portland, *Mich., U.S.A.* 157 B12 42 52N 84 54W
Portland, *Oreg., U.S.A.* 160 E4 45 32N 122 37W
Portland, *Pa., U.S.A.* 151 F9 40 55N 75 6W
Portland, *Tex., U.S.A.* 155 M6 27 53N 97 20W
Portland, I. of, *U.K.* 21 G5 50 33N 2 26W
Portland B., *Australia* 128 E4 38 15 S 141 45 E
Portland Bight, *Jamaica* 164 a 17 52N 77 5W
Portland Bill, *U.K.* 21 G5 50 31N 2 28W
Portland Canal, *U.S.A.* 142 B2 55 56N 130 0W
Portland I., *N.Z.* 130 F6 39 20 S 177 51 E
Portland Pt., *Ascension I.* 9 g 7 59 S 14 25W
Portland Pt., *Jamaica* 164 a 17 42N 77 11W
Portmadoc = Porthmadog, *U.K.* 20 E3 52 55N 4 8W
Portmore, *Jamaica* 164 a 17 53N 77 53W
Pôrto, *Brazil* 170 B3 3 54 S 42 42W
Porto, *France* 29 F12 42 16N 8 42 E
Porto, *Portugal* 42 D2 41 8N 8 40W
Porto □, *Portugal* 42 D2 41 8N 8 20W
Porto, G. de, *France* 29 F12 42 17N 8 34 E
Pôrto Acre, *Brazil* 172 B4 9 34 S 67 31W
Pôrto Alegre, *Pará, Brazil* 169 D7 4 22 S 52 44W
Pôrto Alegre, *Rio Grande do S., Brazil* 175 C5 30 5 S 51 10W
Porto Alegre, *São Tomé & Principe* 115 G6 0 2N 6 32 E
Porto Amboim = Gunza, *Angola* 115 E2 10 50 S 13 50 E
Porto Azzurro, *Italy* 44 F7 42 46N 10 24 E
Pôrto Cajueiro, *Brazil* 173 C6 11 3 S 55 53W
Porto Cristo, *Spain* 38 B4 39 33N 3 20 E
Pôrto da Fôlha, *Brazil* 170 C4 9 55 S 37 17W
Pôrto de Móz, *Brazil* 169 D7 1 41 S 52 13W
Pôrto de Pedras, *Brazil* 170 C4 9 10 S 35 17W
Pôrto des Meinacos, *Brazil* 173 C7 12 33 S 53 7W
Pôrto dos Gaúchos, *Brazil* 173 C6 11 32 S 57 16W
Porto Empédocle, *Italy* 46 E6 37 17N 13 32 E
Pôrto Esperança, *Brazil* 173 D6 19 37 S 57 29W
Pôrto Esperidão, *Brazil* 173 D6 15 51 S 58 28W
Porto Formoso, *Azores* 9 d3 37 49N 25 25W
Pôrto Franco, *Brazil* 170 C2 6 20 S 47 24W
Pôrto Grande, *Brazil* 169 C7 0 42N 51 24W
Porto Inglês, *C. Verde Is.* 9 j 15 21N 23 10W
Pôrto Jofre, *Brazil* 173 D6 17 20 S 56 48W
Pórto Lágos, *Greece* 51 E9 41 1N 25 6 E
Pôrto Mendes, *Brazil* 175 A5 24 30 S 54 15W
Porto Moniz, *Madeira* 9 c 32 52N 17 11W
Pôrto Murtinho, *Brazil* 173 E6 21 45 S 57 55W
Pôrto Nacional, *Brazil* 170 D2 10 40 S 48 30W
Porto-Novo, *Benin* 113 D5 6 23N 2 42 E
Porto Petro, *Spain* 38 B4 39 22N 3 13 E
Porto San Giórgio, *Italy* 45 E10 43 11N 13 48 E
Porto Sant' Elpídio, *Italy* 45 E10 43 15N 13 43 E
Pôrto Santana, *Brazil* 169 D7 0 3 S 51 11W
Porto Santo, I. de, *Madeira* 110 B1 33 45N 16 25W
Porto Santo Stéfano, *Italy* 44 F8 42 26N 11 7 E
Pôrto São José, *Brazil* 175 A5 22 43 S 53 10W
Pôrto Seguro, *Brazil* 171 E4 16 26 S 39 5W
Porto Tolle, *Italy* 45 D9 44 56N 12 22 E
Porto Tórres, *Italy* 46 B1 40 50N 8 24 E
Pôrto União, *Brazil* 175 B5 26 10 S 51 10W
Pôrto Válter, *Brazil* 172 B3 8 15 S 72 40W
Porto-Vecchio, *France* 29 G13 41 35N 9 16 E
Pôrto Velho, *Brazil* 173 B5 8 46 S 63 54W
Portobelo, *Panama* 164 E4 9 35N 79 42W
Portoferráio, *Italy* 44 F7 42 48N 10 20 E
Portogruaro, *Italy* 45 C9 45 47N 12 50 E
Portola, *U.S.A.* 160 F6 39 49N 120 28W
Portomaggiore, *Italy* 45 D8 44 42N 11 48 E
Portør, *Norway* 18 F6 58 48N 9 28 E
Portoscuso, *Italy* 46 C1 39 12N 8 24 E
Portovénere, *Italy* 44 D6 44 3N 9 51 E
Portoviejo, *Ecuador* 168 D1 1 7 S 80 28W
Portpatrick, *U.K.* 22 G3 54 51N 5 7W
Portree, *U.K.* 22 D2 57 25N 6 12W
Portrush, *U.K.* 23 A5 55 12N 6 40W
Portsmouth, *Domin.* 165 C7 15 34N 61 27W
Portsmouth, *U.K.* 21 G6 50 48N 1 6W
Portsmouth, *N.H., U.S.A.* 149 D10 43 5N 70 45W
Portsmouth, *Ohio, U.S.A.* 148 F4 38 44N 82 57W
Portsmouth, *R.I., U.S.A.* 151 E13 41 36N 71 15W
Portsmouth, *Va., U.S.A.* 148 G7 36 50N 76 18W
Portsmouth □, *U.K.* 21 G6 50 48N 1 6W
Portsoy, *U.K.* 22 D6 57 41N 2 41W
Portstewart, *U.K.* 23 A5 55 11N 6 43W
Porttipahtan tekojärvi, *Finland* 14 B22 68 5N 26 40 E
Portugal ■, *Europe* 42 F3 40 0N 8 0W
Portugalete, *Spain* 40 B1 43 19N 3 4W
Portuguesa □, *Venezuela* 168 B4 9 10N 69 15W
Portumna, *Ireland* 23 C3 53 6N 8 14W
Portville, *U.S.A.* 150 D6 42 3N 78 20W
Porvenir, *Bolivia* 172 C4 11 10 S 68 50W
Porvenir, *Chile* 176 D2 53 10 S 70 16W
Porvoo, *Finland* 15 F21 60 24N 25 40 E
Porzuna, *Spain* 43 F6 39 9N 4 9W
Posada, *Italy* 46 B2 40 38N 9 43 E
Posada →, *Italy* 46 B2 40 39N 9 45 E

Posadas, *Argentina* **175 B4** 27 30 S 55 50W
Posadas, *Spain* **43 H5** 37 47N 5 11W
Poschiavo, *Switz.* **33 D10** 46 19N 10 4 E
Posets, *Spain* **40 C5** 42 39N 0 25 E
Poseyville, *U.S.A.* **157 F9** 38 10N 87 47W
Poshan = Boshan, *China* **75 F9** 36 28N 117 49 E
Posht-e-Badam, *Iran* **97 C7** 33 2N 55 23 E
Posídhion, Ákra, *Greece* **50 G7** 39 57N 23 30 E
Posidium, *Greece* **49 F9** 35 30N 27 10 E
Poso, *Indonesia* **82 B2** 1 20 S 120 55 E
Poso, Danau, *Indonesia* **82 B2** 1 52 S 120 35 E
Posoegroenoe, *Surinam* **169 C6** 4 23N 55 43W
Posong, *S. Korea* **75 G14** 34 46N 127 5 E
Posse, *Brazil* **171 D2** 14 4 S 46 18W
Possel, *C.A.R.* **114 A3** 5 5N 19 10 E
Possession I., *Antarctica* **7 D11** 72 4 S 172 0 E
Pössneck, *Germany* **30 E7** 50 42N 11 35 E
Possum Kingdom L., *U.S.A.* **155 J5** 32 52N 98 26W
Post, *U.S.A.* **155 J4** 33 12N 101 23W
Post Falls, *U.S.A.* **158 C5** 47 43N 116 57W
Postavy = Pastavy, *Belarus* **15 J22** 55 4N 26 50 E
Poste-de-la-Baleine = Kuujjuarapik, *Canada* **140 A4** 55 20N 77 35W
Poste Maurice Cortier, *Algeria* **111 D5** 22 14N 1 2 E
Postmasburg, *S. Africa* **116 D3** 28 18 S 23 5 E
Postojna, *Slovenia* **45 C11** 45 46N 14 12 E
Poston, *U.S.A.* **161 M12** 34 0N 114 24W
Postville, *Canada* **141 B8** 54 54N 59 47W
Postville, *U.S.A.* **156 A5** 43 5N 91 34W
Potamós, *Andikíthira, Greece* **48 F5** 35 52N 23 15 E
Potamós, *Kíthira, Greece* **48 E4** 36 15N 22 58 E
Potchefstroom, *S. Africa* **116 D4** 26 41 S 27 7 E
Potcoava, *Romania* **53 F9** 44 30N 24 39 E
Poté, *Brazil* **171 E3** 17 49 S 41 49W
Poteau, *U.S.A.* **155 H7** 35 3N 94 37W
Poteet, *U.S.A.* **155 L5** 29 2N 98 35W
Potenza, *Italy* **47 B8** 40 38N 15 48 E
Potenza →, *Italy* **45 E10** 43 25N 13 40 E
Potenza Picena, *Italy* **45 E10** 43 22N 13 37 E
Poteriteri, L., *N.Z.* **131 G2** 46 5 S 167 10 E
Potgietersrus, *S. Africa* **117 C4** 24 10 S 28 55 E
Poti, *Georgia* **61 J5** 42 10N 41 38 E
Potiraguá, *Brazil* **171 E4** 15 36 S 39 53W
Potiskum, *Nigeria* **113 C7** 11 39N 11 2 E
Potlogi, *Romania* **53 F10** 44 34N 25 34 E
Potomac →, *U.S.A.* **148 G7** 38 0N 76 23W
Potosí, *Bolivia* **173 D4** 19 38 S 65 50W
Potosi, *U.S.A.* **156 G6** 37 56N 90 47W
Potosí □, *Bolivia* **172 E4** 20 31 S 67 0W
Potosi Mt., *U.S.A.* **161 K11** 35 57N 115 29W
Pototan, *Phil.* **81 F4** 10 54N 122 38 E
Potrerillos, *Chile* **174 B2** 26 30 S 69 30W
Potsdam, *Germany* **30 C9** 52 25N 13 4 E
Potsdam, *U.S.A.* **151 B10** 44 40N 74 59W
Pottangi, *India* **94 E6** 18 34N 82 58 E
Pottenstein, *Germany* **31 F7** 49 46N 11 24 E
Pottersville, *U.S.A.* **151 C11** 43 43N 73 50W
Pottery Hill = Abu Ballas, *Egypt* **106 C2** 24 26N 27 36 E
Pottstown, *U.S.A.* **151 F9** 40 15N 75 39W
Pottsville, *U.S.A.* **151 F8** 40 41N 76 12W
Pottuvil, *Sri Lanka* **95 L5** 6 55N 81 50 E
P'otzu, *Taiwan* **77 F13** 23 30N 120 25 E
Pouancé, *France* **26 E5** 47 44N 1 10W
Pouce Coupé, *Canada* **142 B4** 55 40N 120 10W
Pouébo, *N. Cal.* **133 T18** 20 24 S 164 36 E
Pouembout, *N. Cal.* **133 U18** 21 8 S 164 53 E
Poughkeepsie, *U.S.A.* **151 E11** 41 42N 73 56W
Pouilly-sur-Loire, *France* **27 E9** 47 17N 2 57 E
Poulan, *U.S.A.* **152 D6** 31 31N 83 47W
Poulaphouca Res., *Ireland* **23 C5** 53 8N 6 30W
Pouláta, *Greece* **39 C2** 38 14N 20 36 E
Poulsbo, *U.S.A.* **160 C4** 47 44N 122 39W
Poultney, *U.S.A.* **151 C11** 43 31N 73 14W
Poulton-le-Fylde, *U.K.* **20 D5** 53 51N 2 58W
Poum, *N. Cal.* **133 T18** 20 14 S 164 2 E
Pounga-Nganda, *Gabon* **114 C2** 2 58 S 10 51 E
Pouso Alegre, *Mato Grosso, Brazil* **173 C6** 11 46 S 57 16W
Pouso Alegre, *Minas Gerais, Brazil* **175 A6** 22 14 S 45 57W
Pout, *Senegal* **112 C1** 14 45N 17 0W
Pouthisat, *Cambodia* **86 F4** 12 34N 103 50 E
Pouzauges, *France* **26 F6** 46 47N 0 50W
Pova de Sta. Iria, *Portugal* **43 G1** 38 51N 9 4W
Považská Bystrica, *Slovak Rep.* **35 B11** 49 8N 18 27 E
Povenets, *Russia* **56 B5** 62 50N 34 50 E
Poverty B., *N.Z.* **130 E7** 38 43 S 178 2 E
Povlen, *Serbia, Yug.* **50 B3** 44 9N 19 44 E
Póvoa de Lanhosa, *Portugal* **42 D2** 41 33N 8 15W
Póvoa de Varzim, *Portugal* **42 D2** 41 25N 8 46W
Povoação, *Azores* **9 d3** 37 45N 25 15W
Povorino, *Russia* **60 E6** 51 12N 42 5 E
Povungnituk = Puvirnituq, *Canada* **139 B12** 60 2N 77 10W
Powassan, *Canada* **140 C4** 46 5N 79 25W
Poway, *U.S.A.* **161 N9** 32 58N 117 2W
Powder →, *U.S.A.* **154 B2** 46 45N 105 26W
Powder River, *U.S.A.* **158 E10** 43 2N 106 59W
Powder Springs, *U.S.A.* **152 B5** 33 52N 84 41W
Powell, *U.S.A.* **158 D9** 44 45N 108 46W
Powell, L., *U.S.A.* **159 H8** 36 57N 111 29W
Powell River, *Canada* **142 D4** 49 50N 124 35W
Powelton, *U.S.A.* **152 B7** 33 26N 82 52W
Powers, *U.S.A.* **148 C2** 45 41N 87 32W
Powys □, *U.K.* **21 E4** 52 20N 3 20W
Poxoreu, *Brazil* **173 D7** 15 50 S 54 23W
Poya, *N. Cal.* **133 U19** 21 19 S 165 7 E
Poyang Hu, *China* **77 C11** 29 5N 116 20 E
Poyarkovo, *Russia* **67 E13** 49 36N 128 41 E
Poysdorf, *Austria* **35 C9** 48 40N 16 37 E
Poza de la Sal, *Spain* **42 C7** 42 35N 3 31W
Poza Rica, *Mexico* **163 C5** 20 33N 97 27W
Pozanti, *Turkey* **100 D6** 37 25N 34 50 E
Požarevac, *Serbia, Yug.* **50 B5** 44 35N 21 18 E
Pozazal, Puerto, *Spain* **42 C6** 42 56N 4 10W
Požega, *Croatia* **52 E2** 45 20N 17 40 E
Požega, *Serbia, Yug.* **50 C4** 43 53N 20 2 E
Pozhva, *Russia* **64 B6** 59 5N 56 5 E
Poznań, *Poland* **55 F3** 52 25N 16 55 E
Pozo, *U.S.A.* **161 K6** 35 20N 120 24W
Pozo Alcón, *Spain* **43 H8** 37 42N 2 56W
Pozo Almonte, *Chile* **172 E4** 20 10 S 69 50W
Pozo Colorado, *Paraguay* **174 A4** 23 30 S 58 45W
Pozoblanco, *Spain* **43 G6** 38 23N 4 51W
Pozorrubio, *Phil.* **80 C3** 16 7N 120 33 E
Pozuzo, *Peru* **172 C2** 10 5 S 75 35W
Pozzallo, *Italy* **47 F7** 36 43N 14 51 E
Pozzomaggiore, *Italy* **46 B1** 40 24N 8 39 E
Pozzuoli, *Italy* **47 B7** 40 49N 14 7 E
Pra →, *Ghana* **113 D4** 5 1N 1 37W
Prabuty, *Poland* **54 E6** 53 47N 19 15 E
Prača, *Bos.-H.* **52 G3** 43 47N 18 43 E
Prachatice, *Czech Rep.* **34 B6** 49 1N 14 0 E
Prachin Buri, *Thailand* **86 E3** 14 0N 101 25 E
Prachuap Khiri Khan, *Thailand* **87 G2** 11 49N 99 48 E
Pradelles, *France* **28 D7** 44 46N 3 52 E
Pradera, *Colombia* **168 C2** 3 25N 76 15W
Prades, *France* **28 F6** 42 38N 2 23 E
Prado, *Brazil* **171 E4** 17 20 S 39 13W
Prado del Rey, *Spain* **43 J5** 36 48N 5 33W
Præstø, *Denmark* **17 J6** 55 8N 12 2 E
Pragersko, *Slovenia* **45 B12** 46 27N 15 42 E
Prague = Praha, *Czech Rep.* **34 A7** 50 5N 14 22 E
Praha, *Czech Rep.* **34 A7** 50 5N 14 22 E
Prahecq, *France* **28 B3** 46 19N 0 26W
Prahita →, *India* **94 E4** 19 0N 79 55 E
Prahova □, *Romania* **53 E10** 45 10N 26 0 E
Prahova →, *Romania* **53 F10** 44 50N 25 50 E
Prahovo, *Serbia, Yug.* **50 B6** 44 18N 22 39 E
Praia, *Azores* **9 d1** 39 3N 27 58W
Praia, *C. Verde Is.* **9 j** 15 2N 23 34W
Práia a Mare, *Italy* **47 C8** 39 50N 15 45 E
Praia da Vitória, *Azores* **9 d1** 38 44N 27 4W
Praia do Norte, *Azores* **9 d1** 38 36N 28 46W
Praid, *Romania* **53 D10** 46 32N 25 10 E
Prainha, *Azores* **9 d1** 38 27N 28 12W
Prainha, *Amazonas, Brazil* **173 B5** 7 10 S 60 30W
Prainha, *Pará, Brazil* **169 D7** 1 45 S 53 30W
Prairie, *Australia* **126 C3** 20 50 S 144 35 E
Prairie City, *U.S.A.* **158 D4** 44 28N 118 43W
Prairie Dog Town Fork →, *U.S.A.* **155 H5** 34 30N 99 23W
Prairie du Chien, *U.S.A.* **156 A5** 43 3N 91 9W
Prairie du Rocher, *U.S.A.* **156 F6** 38 5N 90 6W
Prairie Village, *U.S.A.* **156 F2** 38 58N 94 38W
Prairies, L. of the, *Canada* **143 C8** 51 16N 101 32W
Pramánda, *Greece* **48 B3** 39 32N 21 8 E
Prampram, *Ghana* **113 D5** 5 43N 0 8 E
Pran Buri, *Thailand* **86 F2** 12 23N 99 55 E
Prándarjökull, *Iceland* **11 C12** 64 40N 14 55W
Prang, *Ghana* **113 D4** 8 1N 0 56W
Prapat, *Indonesia* **78 D1** 2 41N 98 58 E
Praslin, *Seychelles* **121 b** 4 18 S 55 45 E
Prasonísi, Ákra, *Greece* **38 F11** 35 42N 27 46 E
Prästmon, *Sweden* **16 A11** 63 5N 17 45 E
Praszka, *Poland* **55 G5** 51 5N 18 31 E
Prata, *Brazil* **171 E2** 19 25 S 48 54W
Pratabpur, *India* **93 H10** 23 28N 83 15 E
Pratapgarh, *Raj., India* **92 G6** 24 2N 74 40 E
Pratapgarh, *Ut. P., India* **93 G9** 25 56N 81 59 E
Pratas Is. = Dongsha Dao, *China* **77 G11** 20 45N 116 43 E
Prätigau, *Switz.* **33 C9** 46 56N 9 44 E
Prato, *Italy* **44 E8** 43 53N 11 6 E
Prato allo Stelvio, *Italy* **33 C11** 46 37N 10 35 E
Prátola Peligna, *Italy* **45 F10** 42 6N 13 52 E
Prats-de-Mollo-la-Preste, *France* **28 F6** 42 25N 2 27 E
Pratt, *U.S.A.* **155 G5** 37 39N 98 44W
Pratteln, *Switz.* **32 A5** 47 31N 7 41 E
Prattville, *U.S.A.* **149 J2** 32 28N 86 29W
Pravara →, *India* **94 E2** 19 35N 74 45 E
Pravdinsk, *Russia* **60 B6** 56 29N 43 28 E
Pravets, *Bulgaria* **50 D7** 42 53N 23 55 E
Pravia, *Spain* **42 B4** 43 30N 6 12W
Praya, *Indonesia* **85 D5** 8 39 S 116 17 E
Pré-en-Pail, *France* **26 D6** 48 28N 0 12W
Precipice Nat. Park, *Australia* **127 D5** 25 18 S 150 5 E
Precordillera, *Argentina* **174 C2** 30 0 S 69 1W
Predáppio, *Italy* **45 D8** 44 6N 11 59 E
Predazzo, *Italy* **45 B8** 46 19N 11 36 E
Predeal, *Romania* **53 E10** 45 30N 25 34 E
Predejane, *Serbia, Yug.* **50 D6** 42 51N 22 9 E
Preeceville, *Canada* **143 C8** 51 57N 102 40W
Preetz, *Germany* **30 A6** 54 14N 10 18 E
Pregrada, *Croatia* **45 B12** 46 11N 15 45 E
Preiļi, *Latvia* **15 H22** 56 18N 26 43 E
Preko, *Croatia* **45 D12** 44 7N 15 10 E
Prelog, *Croatia* **45 B13** 46 18N 16 32 E
Premer, *Australia* **129 A8** 31 29 S 149 56 E
Prémery, *France* **27 E10** 47 10N 3 18 E
Prémia, *Italy* **33 D6** 46 17N 8 20 E
Premià de Mar, *Spain* **40 D7** 41 29N 2 22 E
Premont, *U.S.A.* **155 M5** 27 22N 98 7W
Premuda, *Croatia* **45 D11** 44 20N 14 36 E
Prentice, *U.S.A.* **154 C9** 45 33N 90 17W
Prenzlau, *Germany* **30 B9** 53 19N 13 50 E
Preobrazheniye, *Russia* **70 C6** 42 54N 133 54 E
Preparis I., *Burma* **95 G11** 14 52N 93 41 E
Preparis North Channel, *Burma* **95 G11** 15 27N 94 5 E
Preparis South Channel, *Burma* **95 G11** 14 33N 93 30 E
Přerov, *Czech Rep.* **35 B10** 49 28N 17 27 E
Prescott, *Canada* **140 D4** 44 45N 75 30W
Prescott, *Ariz., U.S.A.* **159 J7** 34 33N 112 28W
Prescott, *Ark., U.S.A.* **155 J8** 33 48N 93 23W
Prescott Valley, *U.S.A.* **159 J7** 34 40N 112 18W
Preservation Inlet, *N.Z.* **131 G1** 46 8 S 166 35 E
Preševo, *Serbia, Yug.* **50 D5** 42 19N 21 39 E
Presho, *U.S.A.* **154 D4** 43 54N 100 3W
Presicce, *Italy* **47 C11** 39 54N 18 16 E
Presidencia de la Plaza, *Argentina* **174 B4** 27 0 S 59 50W
Presidencia Roque Saenz Peña, *Argentina* **174 B3** 26 45 S 60 30W
Presidente Dutra, *Brazil* **170 C3** 5 15 S 44 30W
Presidente Epitácio, *Brazil* **171 F1** 21 56 S 52 6W
Presidente Figueiredo, *Brazil* **169 D5** 1 57 S 60 2W
Presidente Hayes □, *Paraguay* **174 A4** 24 0 S 59 0W
Presidente Hermes, *Brazil* **173 C5** 11 17 S 61 55W
Presidente Prudente, *Brazil* **175 A5** 22 5 S 51 25W
Presidio, *Mexico* **162 B4** 29 29N 104 23W
Presidio, *U.S.A.* **155 L2** 29 34N 104 22W
Preslav, *Bulgaria* **51 C10** 43 10N 26 52 E
Preslavska Planina, *Bulgaria* **51 C10** 43 10N 26 45 E
Prešov, *Slovak Rep.* **35 B14** 49 0N 21 15 E
Prešovský □, *Slovak Rep.* **35 B13** 49 10N 21 0 E
Prespa, *Bulgaria* **51 E8** 41 44N 24 55 E
Prespa, L. = Prespansko Jezero, *Macedonia* **50 F5** 40 55N 21 0 E
Prespansko Jezero, *Macedonia* **50 F5** 40 55N 21 0 E
Presque I., *U.S.A.* **150 D4** 42 9N 80 6W
Presque Isle, *U.S.A.* **149 B12** 46 41N 68 1W
Prestatyn, *U.K.* **20 D4** 53 20N 3 24W
Prestea, *Ghana* **112 D4** 5 22N 2 7W
Presteigne, *U.K.* **21 E5** 52 17N 3 0W
Přeštice, *Czech Rep.* **34 B6** 49 34N 13 20 E
Presto, *Bolivia* **173 D5** 18 55 S 64 56W
Preston, *Canada* **150 C4** 43 23N 80 21W
Preston, *U.K.* **20 D5** 53 46N 2 42W
Preston, *Ga., U.S.A.* **152 C5** 32 4N 84 32W
Preston, *Idaho, U.S.A.* **158 E8** 42 6N 111 53W
Preston, *Iowa, U.S.A.* **156 B6** 42 3N 90 24W
Preston, *Minn., U.S.A.* **154 D8** 43 40N 92 5W
Preston, *Mo., U.S.A.* **156 G3** 37 56N 93 13W
Preston, C., *Australia* **124 D2** 20 51 S 116 12 E
Prestonburg, *U.S.A.* **148 G4** 37 39N 82 46W
Prestranda, *Norway* **18 E6** 59 6N 9 4 E
Prestwick, *U.K.* **22 F4** 55 29N 4 37W
Prêto →, *Amazonas, Brazil* **169 D5** 0 8 S 64 6W
Prêto →, *Bahia, Brazil* **170 D3** 11 21 S 43 52W
Prêto do Igapó-Açu →, *Brazil* **169 D6** 4 26 S 59 48W
Pretoria, *S. Africa* **117 D4** 25 44 S 28 12 E
Preuilly-sur-Claise, *France* **26 F7** 46 51N 0 56 E
Préveza, *Greece* **39 B2** 38 57N 20 45 E
Préveza □, *Greece* **48 B2** 39 10N 20 40 E
Prey Veng, *Cambodia* **87 G5** 11 35N 105 29 E
Priazovskoye, *Ukraine* **59 J8** 46 44N 35 40 E
Pribilof Is., *U.S.A.* **144 H5** 57 0N 170 0W
Priboj, *Serbia, Yug.* **50 C3** 43 35N 19 32 E
Příbram, *Czech Rep.* **34 B7** 49 41N 14 2 E
Price, *U.S.A.* **158 G8** 39 36N 110 49W
Price, C., *India* **95 H11** 13 34N 93 3 E
Price I., *Canada* **142 C3** 52 23N 128 41W
Prichard, *U.S.A.* **149 K1** 30 44N 88 5W
Priego, *Spain* **40 E2** 40 26N 2 21W
Priego de Córdoba, *Spain* **43 H6** 37 27N 4 12W
Priekule, *Latvia* **15 H19** 56 26N 21 35 E
Prien, *Germany* **31 H8** 47 51N 12 20 E
Prienai, *Lithuania* **15 J20** 54 38N 23 57 E
Prieska, *S. Africa* **116 D3** 29 40 S 22 42 E
Priest L., *U.S.A.* **158 B5** 48 35N 116 52W
Priest River, *U.S.A.* **158 B5** 48 10N 116 54W
Priest Valley, *U.S.A.* **160 J6** 36 10N 120 39W
Prieto Diaz, *Phil.* **80 E5** 13 2N 124 12 E
Prievidza, *Slovak Rep.* **35 C11** 48 46N 18 36 E
Prignitz, *Germany* **30 B7** 53 6N 11 45 E
Prijedor, *Bos.-H.* **45 D13** 44 58N 16 41 E
Prijepolje, *Serbia, Yug.* **50 C3** 43 27N 19 40 E
Prikaspiyskaya Nizmennost = Caspian Depression, *Eurasia* **61 G9** 47 0N 48 0 E
Prikro, *Ivory C.* **112 D4** 7 40N 3 59W
Prikubanskaya Nizmennost, *Russia* **61 H4** 45 39N 38 33 E
Prilep, *Macedonia* **50 E5** 41 21N 21 32 E
Priluki = Pryluky, *Ukraine* **59 G7** 50 30N 32 24 E
Prime Seal I., *Australia* **127 G4** 40 3 S 147 43 E
Primeira Cruz, *Brazil* **170 B3** 2 30 S 43 26W
Primorsk, *Russia* **58 B5** 60 22N 28 37 E
Primorsko, *Bulgaria* **51 D11** 42 15N 27 44 E
Primorsko-Akhtarsk, *Russia* **59 J10** 46 2N 38 10 E
Primorskoye, *Ukraine* **59 J9** 46 48N 36 20 E
Primrose L., *Canada* **143 C7** 54 55N 109 45W
Prince Albert, *Canada* **143 C7** 53 15N 105 50W
Prince Albert, *S. Africa* **116 E3** 33 12 S 22 2 E
Prince Albert Mts., *Antarctica* **7 D11** 76 0 S 161 30 E
Prince Albert Nat. Park, *Canada* **143 C7** 54 0N 106 25W
Prince Albert Pen., *Canada* **138 A8** 72 30N 116 0W
Prince Albert Sd., *Canada* **138 A8** 70 25N 115 0W
Prince Alfred, C., *Canada* **6 B1** 74 20N 124 40W
Prince Charles I., *Canada* **139 B12** 67 47N 76 12W
Prince Charles Mts., *Antarctica* **7 D6** 72 0 S 67 0 E
Prince Edward I. □, *Canada* **141 C7** 46 20N 63 20W
Prince Edward Is., *Ind. Oc.* **121 J2** 46 35 S 38 0 E
Prince Edward Pt., *Canada* **150 C8** 43 56N 76 52W
Prince George, *Canada* **142 C4** 53 55N 122 50W
Prince of Wales, C., *U.S.A.* **144 D5** 65 36N 168 5W
Prince of Wales I., *Australia* **126 A3** 10 40 S 142 10 E
Prince of Wales I., *Canada* **138 A10** 73 0N 99 0W
Prince of Wales I., *U.S.A.* **144 J14** 55 47N 132 50W
Prince Patrick I., *Canada* **6 B2** 77 0N 120 0W
Prince Regent Inlet, *Canada* **6 B3** 73 0N 90 0W
Prince Rupert, *Canada* **142 C2** 54 20N 130 20W
Prince William Sd., *U.S.A.* **144 F11** 60 40N 147 0W
Princes Town, *Trin. & Tob.* **169 F9** 10 16N 61 23W
Princesa Isabel, *Brazil* **170 C4** 7 44 S 38 0W
Princess Charlotte B., *Australia* **126 A3** 14 25 S 144 0 E
Princess May Ranges, *Australia* **124 C4** 15 30 S 125 30 E
Princess Royal I., *Canada* **142 C3** 53 0N 128 40W
Princeton, *Canada* **142 D4** 49 27N 120 30W
Princeton, *Calif., U.S.A.* **160 F4** 39 24N 122 1W
Princeton, *Ill., U.S.A.* **156 C7** 41 23N 89 28W
Princeton, *Ind., U.S.A.* **157 F9** 38 21N 87 34W
Princeton, *Ky., U.S.A.* **148 G2** 37 7N 87 53W
Princeton, *Mo., U.S.A.* **156 D3** 40 24N 93 35W
Princeton, *N.J., U.S.A.* **151 F10** 40 21N 74 39W
Princeton, *W. Va., U.S.A.* **148 G5** 37 22N 81 6W
Princeville, *U.S.A.* **156 D7** 40 56N 89 46W
Príncipe, *São Tomé & Principe* **115 G6** 1 37N 7 25 E
Principe, I. de, *Atl. Oc.* **104 F4** 1 37N 7 27 E
Principe da Beira, *Brazil* **173 C5** 12 20 S 64 30W
Prineville, *U.S.A.* **158 D3** 44 18N 120 51W
Prins Christian Sund, *Greenland* **10 E6** 60 4N 43 10W
Prins Harald Kyst, *Antarctica* **7 D4** 70 0 S 35 1 E
Prinsesse Astrid Kyst, *Antarctica* **7 D3** 70 45 S 12 30 E
Prinsesse Ragnhild Kyst, *Antarctica* **7 D4** 70 15 S 27 30 E
Prinzapolca, *Nic.* **164 D3** 13 20N 83 35W
Prior, C., *Spain* **42 B2** 43 34N 8 17W
Priozersk, *Russia* **58 B6** 61 2N 30 7 E
Pripet = Prypyat →, *Europe* **59 G6** 51 20N 30 15 E
Pripet Marshes, *Europe* **59 F5** 52 10N 28 10 E
Pripyat Marshes = Pripet Marshes, *Europe* **59 F5** 52 10N 28 10 E
Pripyats = Prypyat →, *Europe* **59 G6** 51 20N 30 15 E
Prislop, Pasul, *Romania* **53 C9** 47 37N 24 48 E
Pristen, *Russia* **59 G9** 51 15N 36 44 E
Priština, *Kosovo, Yug.* **50 D5** 42 40N 21 13 E
Pritzwalk, *Germany* **30 B8** 53 9N 12 10 E
Privas, *France* **29 D8** 44 45N 4 37 E
Priverno, *Italy* **46 A6** 41 28N 13 11 E
Privolzhsk, *Russia* **60 B5** 57 23N 41 16 E
Privolzhskaya Vozvyshennost, *Russia* **60 E7** 51 0N 46 0 E
Privolzhskiy, *Russia* **60 E8** 51 25N 46 3 E
Privolzhye, *Russia* **60 D9** 52 52N 48 33 E
Priyutnoye, *Russia* **61 G6** 46 12N 43 40 E
Priyutovo, *Russia* **64 E4** 53 55N 53 59 E
Prizren, *Kosovo, Yug.* **50 D4** 42 13N 20 45 E
Prizzi, *Italy* **46 E6** 37 43N 13 26 E
Prnjavor, *Bos.-H.* **52 F2** 44 52N 17 43 E
Probolinggo, *Indonesia* **85 D4** 7 46 S 113 13 E
Prochowice, *Poland* **55 G3** 51 17N 16 20 E
Proctor, *U.S.A.* **151 C11** 43 40N 73 2W
Proddatur, *India* **95 G4** 14 45N 78 30 E
Prodhromos, *Cyprus* **39 F8** 34 57N 32 50 E
Proença-a-Nova, *Portugal* **42 F3** 39 45N 7 54W
Profítis Ilías, *Greece* **38 E11** 36 17N 27 56 E
Profondeville, *Belgium* **24 D4** 50 23N 4 52 E
Progreso, *Coahuila, Mexico* **162 B4** 27 28N 101 4W
Progreso, *Yucatán, Mexico* **163 C7** 21 20N 89 40W
Prokhladnyy, *Russia* **61 J7** 43 50N 44 2 E
Prokletije, *Albania* **50 D3** 42 30N 19 45 E
Prokopyevsk, *Russia* **66 D9** 54 0N 86 45 E
Prokuplje, *Serbia, Yug.* **50 C5** 43 16N 21 36 E
Proletarsk, *Russia* **61 G5** 46 42N 41 50 E
Proletarskaya = Proletarsk, *Russia* **61 G5** 46 42N 41 50 E
Prome, *Burma* **90 F5** 18 49N 95 13 E
Promise City, *U.S.A.* **156 D3** 40 45N 93 9W
Prophet →, *Canada* **142 B4** 58 48N 122 40W
Prophet River, *Canada* **142 B4** 58 6N 122 43W
Prophetstown, *U.S.A.* **156 C7** 41 40N 89 56W
Propriá, *Brazil* **170 D4** 10 13 S 36 51W
Propriano, *France* **29 G12** 41 41N 8 52 E
Proserpine, *Australia* **126 J6** 20 21 S 148 36 E
Prosna →, *Poland* **55 F4** 52 6N 17 44 E
Prospect, *N.Y., U.S.A.* **151 C9** 43 18N 75 9W
Prospect, *Ohio, U.S.A.* **157 D13** 40 27N 83 11W
Prosperidad, *Phil.* **81 G5** 8 34N 125 52 E
Prosperous B., *St. Helena* **9 h** 15 56 S 5 39W
Prosser, *U.S.A.* **158 C4** 46 12N 119 46W
Prostějov, *Czech Rep.* **35 B10** 49 30N 17 9 E
Prostki, *Poland* **54 E9** 53 42N 22 25 E
Proston, *Australia* **127 D5** 26 8 S 151 32 E
Proszowice, *Poland* **55 H7** 50 13N 20 16 E
Próti, *Greece* **48 D3** 37 5N 21 32 E
Provadiya, *Bulgaria* **51 C11** 43 12N 27 30 E
Provence, *France* **29 E9** 43 40N 5 46 E
Provence-Alpes-Côte d'Azur □, *France* **29 D10** 44 0N 6 15 E
Providence, *Seychelles* **121 E4** 9 14 S 51 2 E
Providence, *Ky., U.S.A.* **148 G2** 37 24N 87 46W
Providence, *R.I., U.S.A.* **151 E13** 41 49N 71 24W
Providence, C., *N.Z.* **131 F1** 45 59 S 166 29 E
Providence Bay, *Canada* **140 C3** 45 41N 82 15W
Providence Mts., *U.S.A.* **161 K11** 35 10N 115 15W
Providencia, I. de, *Colombia* **164 D3** 13 25N 81 26W
Provideniya, *Russia* **67 C19** 64 23N 173 18W
Provins, *France* **27 D10** 48 33N 3 15 E
Provo, *U.S.A.* **158 F8** 40 14N 111 39W
Provost, *Canada* **143 C6** 52 25N 110 20W
Prozor, *Bos.-H.* **52 G2** 43 50N 17 34 E
Prrenjas, *Albania* **50 E4** 41 4N 20 32 E
Prudentópolis, *Brazil* **171 G1** 25 12 S 50 57W
Prudhoe Bay, *U.S.A.* **144 A10** 70 18N 148 22W
Prudhoe I., *Australia* **126 C4** 21 19 S 149 41 E
Prud'homme, *Canada* **143 C7** 52 20N 105 54W
Prudnik, *Poland* **55 H4** 50 20N 17 38 E
Prüm, *Germany* **31 E2** 50 12N 6 25 E
Prundu, *Romania* **53 F11** 44 6N 26 14 E
Pruszcz Gdański, *Poland* **54 D5** 54 17N 18 40 E
Pruszków, *Poland* **55 F7** 52 9N 20 49 E
Prut →, *Romania* **53 E13** 45 28N 28 10 E
Prutz, *Austria* **33 B11** 47 5N 10 40 E
Pruzhany, *Belarus* **59 F3** 52 33N 24 28 E
Prvič, *Croatia* **45 D11** 44 55N 14 47 E
Prydz B., *Antarctica* **7 C6** 69 0 S 74 0 E
Pryluky, *Ukraine* **59 G7** 50 30N 32 24 E
Pryor, *U.S.A.* **155 G7** 36 19N 95 19W
Prypyat →, *Europe* **59 G6** 51 20N 30 15 E
Przasnysz, *Poland* **55 E7** 53 2N 20 54 E
Przedbórz, *Poland* **55 G6** 51 6N 19 53 E
Przedecz, *Poland* **55 F5** 52 20N 18 53 E
Przemków, *Poland* **55 G2** 51 31N 15 48 E
Przemyśl, *Poland* **55 J9** 49 50N 22 45 E
Przeworsk, *Poland* **55 H9** 50 6N 22 32 E
Przewóz, *Poland* **55 G1** 51 28N 14 57 E
Przhevalsk = Karakol, *Kyrgyzstan* **66 E8** 42 30N 78 20 E
Przysucha, *Poland* **55 G7** 51 22N 20 38 E
Psakhná, *Greece* **48 C5** 38 34N 23 35 E
Psará, *Greece* **49 C7** 38 37N 25 38 E
Psathoúra, *Greece* **48 B6** 39 30N 24 12 E
Psel →, *Ukraine* **59 H7** 49 10N 33 37 E
Pserimos, *Greece* **49 E9** 36 56N 27 8 E
Psíra, *Greece* **39 E6** 35 12N 25 52 E
Pskem →, *Uzbekistan* **65 C5** 41 38N 70 1 E
Pskem Tizmasi, *Uzbekistan* **65 C5** 42 0N 70 45 E
Pskent, *Uzbekistan* **65 C4** 40 54N 69 20 E
Pskov, *Russia* **58 D5** 57 50N 28 25 E
Pskovskoye, Ozero, *Russia* **58 D5** 58 0N 27 58 E
Psunj, *Croatia* **52 E2** 45 25N 17 19 E
Pteleón, *Greece* **48 B4** 39 3N 22 57 E
Ptich = Ptsich →, *Belarus* **59 F5** 52 9N 28 52 E
Ptolemaís, *Greece* **50 F5** 40 30N 21 43 E
Ptsich →, *Belarus* **59 F5** 52 9N 28 52 E
Ptuj, *Slovenia* **45 B12** 46 28N 15 50 E
Ptujska Gora, *Slovenia* **45 B12** 46 23N 15 47 E
Pu Xian, *China* **74 F6** 36 24N 111 6 E
Pua, *Thailand* **86 C3** 19 11N 100 55 E
Puaena Pt., *U.S.A.* **145 J13** 21 36N 158 6W
Puán, *Argentina* **174 D3** 37 30 S 62 45W
Pu'an, *China* **76 E5** 25 46N 104 57 E
Puan, *S. Korea* **75 G14** 35 44N 126 44 E
Pu'apu'a, *Samoa* **133 W23** 13 34 S 172 9W
Pubei, *China* **76 F7** 22 16N 109 31 E
Pucacuro →, *Peru* **168 D3** 3 20 S 74 58W
Pucallpa, *Peru* **172 B3** 8 25 S 74 30W
Pucará, *Bolivia* **173 D5** 18 43 S 64 11W
Pucará, *Cajamarca, Peru* **172 B2** 6 0 S 79 7W
Pucará, *Puno, Peru* **172 D3** 15 5 S 70 24W
Pucarani, *Bolivia* **172 D4** 16 23 S 68 30W
Pucheng, *China* **77 D12** 27 59N 118 31 E
Pucheni, *Romania* **53 E10** 45 12N 25 17 E
Puchheim, *Germany* **31 G7** 48 9N 11 21 E
Púchov, *Slovak Rep.* **35 B11** 49 8N 18 20 E
Pucio Pt., *Phil.* **81 F3** 11 46N 121 51 E
Pucioasa, *Romania* **53 E10** 45 5N 25 25 E
Pučišća, *Croatia* **45 E13** 43 22N 16 43 E
Puck, *Poland* **54 D5** 54 45N 18 23 E
Pucka, Zatoka, *Poland* **54 D5** 54 30N 18 40 E
Puçol, *Spain* **41 F4** 39 37N 0 18W
Pudasjärvi, *Finland* **14 D22** 65 23N 26 53 E
Puding, *China* **76 D5** 26 18N 105 44 E
Pudozh, *Russia* **58 B9** 61 48N 36 32 E
Puduchcheri = Pondicherry, *India* **95 J4** 11 59N 79 50 E
Pudukkottai, *India* **95 J4** 10 28N 78 47 E
Puebla, *Mexico* **163 D5** 19 3N 98 12W
Puebla □, *Mexico* **163 D5** 18 30N 98 0W
Puebla de Alcocer, *Spain* **43 G5** 38 59N 5 14W
Puebla de Don Fadrique, *Spain* **41 H2** 37 58N 2 25W
Puebla de Don Rodrigo, *Spain* **43 F6** 39 5N 4 37W
Puebla de Guzmán, *Spain* **43 H3** 37 37N 7 15W
Puebla de la Calzada, *Spain* **43 G4** 38 54N 6 37W
Puebla de Sanabria, *Spain* **42 C4** 42 4N 6 38W
Puebla de Trives = Pobra de Trives, *Spain* **42 C3** 42 20N 7 10W
Pueblo, *U.S.A.* **154 F2** 38 16N 104 37W
Pueblo Hundido, *Chile* **174 B1** 26 20 S 70 5W
Puelches, *Argentina* **174 D2** 38 5 S 65 51W
Puelén, *Argentina* **174 D2** 37 32 S 67 38W
Puente Alto, *Chile* **174 C1** 33 32 S 70 35W
Puente-Genil, *Spain* **43 H6** 37 22N 4 47W
Puente la Reina, *Spain* **40 C3** 42 40N 1 49W
Puenteareas = Ponteareas, *Spain* **42 C2** 42 10N 8 28W
Puentedeume = Pontedeume, *Spain* **42 B2** 43 24N 8 10W
Puentes de Garcia Rodriguez = As Pontes de García Rodríguez, *Spain* **42 B3** 43 27N 7 50W
Pueo Pt., *U.S.A.* **145 B1** 21 54N 160 4W
Pu'er, *China* **76 F3** 23 0N 101 15 E
Puerca, Pta., *Puerto Rico* **165 d** 18 13N 65 36W
Puerco →, *U.S.A.* **159 J10** 34 22N 107 50W
Puerta Galera, *Phil.* **80 E3** 13 30N 120 57 E
Puerto, *Canary Is.* **9 e1** 28 5N 17 20W
Puerto Acosta, *Bolivia* **172 D4** 15 32 S 69 15W
Puerto Aisén, *Chile* **176 C2** 45 27 S 73 0W
Puerto Ángel, *Mexico* **163 D5** 15 40N 96 29W
Puerto Arista, *Mexico* **163 D6** 15 56N 93 48W
Puerto Armuelles, *Panama* **164 E3** 8 20N 82 51W
Puerto Asis, *Colombia* **168 C2** 0 30N 76 30W
Puerto Ayacucho, *Venezuela* **168 B4** 5 40N 67 35W
Puerto Ayora, *Ecuador* **172 a** 0 45 S 90 19W
Puerto Baquerizo Moreno, *Ecuador* **172 a** 0 54 S 89 36W
Puerto Barrios, *Guatemala* **164 C2** 15 40N 88 32W
Puerto Bermejo, *Argentina* **174 B4** 26 55 S 58 34W
Puerto Bermúdez, *Peru* **172 C3** 10 20 S 74 58W
Puerto Bolívar, *Ecuador* **168 D2** 3 19 S 79 55W
Puerto Cabello, *Venezuela* **168 A4** 10 28N 68 1W
Puerto Cabezas, *Nic.* **164 D3** 14 0N 83 30W
Puerto Cabo Gracias á Dios, *Nic.* **164 D3** 15 0N 83 10W
Puerto Capaz = El Jebha, *Morocco* **110 A4** 35 11N 4 43W
Puerto Carreño, *Colombia* **168 B4** 6 12N 67 22W
Puerto Castilla, *Honduras* **164 C2** 16 0N 86 0W
Puerto Chicama, *Peru* **172 B2** 7 45 S 79 20W
Puerto Cisnes, *Chile* **176 B2** 44 45 S 72 42W
Puerto Coig, *Argentina* **176 D3** 50 54 S 69 15W
Puerto Cortés, *Costa Rica* **164 E3** 8 55N 84 0W
Puerto Cortés, *Honduras* **164 C2** 15 51N 88 0W
Puerto Cumarebo, *Venezuela* **168 A4** 11 29N 69 30W
Puerto de Alcudia = Port d'Alcúdia, *Spain* **38 B4** 39 50N 3 7 E
Puerto de Cabrera, *Spain* **38 B3** 39 8N 2 56 E
Puerto de Gran Tarajal, *Canary Is.* **9 e2** 28 13N 14 1W
Puerto de la Cruz, *Canary Is.* **9 e1** 28 24N 16 32W
Puerto de Mazarrón, *Spain* **41 H3** 37 34N 1 15W
Puerto de Pozo Negro, *Canary Is.* **9 e2** 28 19N 13 55W
Puerto de Sóller = Port de Sóller, *Spain* **38 B3** 39 48N 2 42 E
Puerto de Somosierra, *Spain* **42 D7** 41 9N 3 35W
Puerto del Carmen, *Canary Is.* **9 e2** 28 55N 13 38W
Puerto del Rosario, *Canary Is.* **9 e2** 28 30N 13 52W

Q

Queen Alexandra Ra., *Antarctica* **7 E11** 85 0 S 170 0 E
Queen Charlotte B., *Falk. Is.* **9 f** 51 50 S 60 40W
Queen Charlotte City, *Canada* **142 C2** 53 15N 132 2W
Queen Charlotte Is., *Canada* **142 C2** 53 20N 132 10W
Queen Charlotte Sd., *Canada* **142 C3** 51 0N 128 0W
Queen Charlotte Sd., *N.Z.* **131 B9** 41 10 S 174 15 E
Queen Charlotte Strait, *Canada* **142 C3** 50 45N 127 10W
Queen City, *U.S.A.* **156 D4** 40 25N 92 34W
Queen Elizabeth Is., *Canada* **136 B10** 76 0N 95 0W
Queen Elizabeth Nat. Park, *Uganda* **118 C3** 0 0 30 0 E
Queen Mary Land, *Antarctica* **7 D7** 70 0 S 95 0 E
Queen Maud G., *Canada* **138 B9** 68 15N 102 30W
Queen Maud Land, *Antarctica* **7 D3** 72 30 S 12 0 E
Queen Maud Mts., *Antarctica* **7 E13** 86 0 S 160 0W
Queens Chan., *Australia* **124 C4** 15 0 S 129 30 E
Queenscliff, *Australia* **128 E6** 38 16 S 144 39 E
Queensland, *U.S.A.* **152 D6** 31 46N 83 14W
Queensland □, *Australia* **126 C3** 22 0 S 142 0 E
Queenstown, *Australia* **127 G4** 42 4 S 145 35 E
Queenstown, *N.Z.* **131 F3** 45 1 S 168 40 E
Queenstown, *Singapore* **87 d** 1 18N 103 48 E
Queenstown, *S. Africa* **116 E4** 31 52 S 26 52 E
Queets, *U.S.A.* **160 C2** 47 32N 124 20W
Queguay Grande →, *Uruguay* **174 C4** 32 9 S 58 9W
Queimada, Pta. da, *Azores* **9 d1** 38 23N 28 14W
Queimadas, *Brazil* **170 D4** 11 0 S 39 38W
Queiros, C., *Vanuatu* **133 D5** 14 55 S 167 1 E
Quela, *Angola* **115 D3** 9 10 S 16 56 E
Quelimane, *Mozam.* **119 F4** 17 53 S 36 58 E
Quelo, *Angola* **115 D2** 6 29 S 12 36 E
Quelpart = Cheju do, *S. Korea* **75 H14** 33 29N 126 34 E
Queluz, *Portugal* **43 G1** 38 45N 9 15W
Quemado, *N. Mex., U.S.A.* **159 J9** 34 20N 108 30W
Quemado, *Tex., U.S.A.* **155 L4** 28 58N 100 35W
Quemoy = Chinmen, *Taiwan* **77 E13** 24 26N 118 19 E
Quemú-Quemú, *Argentina* **174 D3** 36 3 S 63 36W
Quepem, *India* **95 G2** 15 13N 74 3 E
Quequén, *Argentina* **174 D4** 38 30 S 58 30W
Querco, *Peru* **172 C3** 13 50 S 74 52W
Querétaro, *Mexico* **162 C4** 20 36N 100 23W
Querétaro □, *Mexico* **162 C5** 20 30N 100 0W
Querfurt, *Germany* **30 D7** 51 23N 11 35 E
Quérigut, *France* **28 F6** 42 42N 2 6 E
Querqueville, *France* **26 C5** 49 40N 1 42W
Quesada, *Spain* **43 H7** 37 51N 3 4W
Queshan, *China* **74 H8** 32 55N 114 2 E
Quesnel, *Canada* **142 C4** 53 0N 122 30W
Quesnel →, *Canada* **142 C4** 52 58N 122 29W
Quesnel L., *Canada* **142 C4** 52 30N 121 20W
Questa, *U.S.A.* **159 H11** 36 42N 105 36W
Questembert, *France* **26 E4** 47 40N 2 28W
Quetena, *Bolivia* **172 E4** 22 10 S 67 25W
Quetico Prov. Park, *Canada* **140 C1** 48 30N 91 45W
Quetrequile, *Argentina* **176 B3** 41 33 S 69 22W
Quetta, *Pakistan* **91 C2** 30 15N 66 55 E
Quevedo, *Ecuador* **168 D2** 1 2 S 79 29W
Quezaltenango, *Guatemala* **164 D1** 14 50N 91 30W
Quezon, *Phil.* **81 G1** 9 15N 117 59 E
Quezon □, *Phil.* **80 D3** 14 40N 121 30 E
Quezon City, *Phil.* **80 D3** 14 38N 121 0 E
Qufār, *Si. Arabia* **96 E4** 27 26N 41 37 E
Qui Nhon, *Vietnam* **86 F7** 13 40N 109 13 E
Quibala, *Angola* **115 E2** 10 46 S 14 59 E
Quibaxe, *Angola* **115 D2** 8 24 S 14 27 E
Quibdo, *Colombia* **168 B2** 5 42N 76 40W
Quiberon, *France* **26 E3** 47 29N 3 9W
Quiberon, Presqu'île de, *France* **26 E3** 47 30N 3 8W
Quiçama, Parque Nacional da, *Angola* **115 D2** 9 41 S 13 35 E
Quickborn, *Germany* **30 B5** 53 42N 9 52 E
Quiet L., *Canada* **142 A2** 61 5N 133 5W
Quiindy, *Paraguay* **174 B4** 25 58 S 57 14W
Quila, *Mexico* **162 C3** 24 23N 107 13W
Quilán, C., *Chile* **176 B2** 43 15 S 74 30W
Quilcene, *U.S.A.* **160 C4** 47 49N 122 53W
Quilenda, *Angola* **115 E2** 10 39 S 14 23 E
Quilengues, *Angola* **115 E2** 14 12 S 14 12 E
Quilimarí, *Chile* **174 C1** 32 5 S 71 30W
Quilino, *Argentina* **174 C3** 30 14 S 64 29W
Quill Lakes, *Canada* **143 C8** 51 55N 104 13W
Quillabamba, *Peru* **172 C3** 12 50 S 72 50W
Quillacollo, *Bolivia* **172 D4** 17 26 S 66 17W
Quillagua, *Chile* **174 A2** 21 40 S 69 40W
Quillaicillo, *Chile* **174 C1** 31 17 S 71 40W
Quillan, *France* **28 F6** 42 53N 2 10 E
Quillota, *Chile* **174 C1** 32 54 S 71 16W
Quilmes, *Argentina* **174 C4** 34 43 S 58 15W
Quilon, *India* **95 K3** 8 50N 76 38 E
Quilpie, *Australia* **127 D3** 26 35 S 144 11 E
Quilpué, *Chile* **174 C1** 33 5 S 71 33W
Quilua, *Mozam.* **119 F4** 16 17 S 39 54 E
Quimbele, *Angola* **115 D3** 6 17 S 16 41 E
Quimbo, *Angola* **115 E3** 14 4 S 16 11 E
Quimbonge, *Angola* **115 D3** 8 36 S 18 30 E
Quime, *Bolivia* **172 D4** 17 2 S 67 15W
Quimilí, *Argentina* **174 B3** 27 40 S 62 30W
Quimper, *France* **26 E2** 48 0N 4 9W
Quimperlé, *France* **26 E3** 47 53N 3 33W
Quinault →, *U.S.A.* **160 C2** 47 21N 124 18W
Quincemil, *Peru* **172 C3** 13 15 S 70 40W
Quincy, *Calif., U.S.A.* **160 F6** 39 56N 120 57W
Quincy, *Fla., U.S.A.* **152 E5** 30 35N 84 34W
Quincy, *Ill., U.S.A.* **156 E5** 39 56N 91 23W
Quincy, *Mass., U.S.A.* **151 D14** 42 15N 71 0W
Quincy, *Mich., U.S.A.* **157 C12** 41 57N 84 53W
Quincy, *Wash., U.S.A.* **158 C4** 47 22N 119 56W
Quines, *Argentina* **174 C2** 32 13 S 65 48W
Quinga, *Mozam.* **119 F5** 15 49 S 40 15 E
Quingey, *France* **27 E12** 47 7N 5 52 E
Quingombe, *Angola* **115 D2** 6 38 S 13 1 E
Quinhagak, *U.S.A.* **144 G7** 59 45N 161 54W
Quiniluban Group, *Phil.* **81 F3** 11 27N 120 48 E
Quinns Rocks, *Australia* **125 F2** 31 40 S 115 42 E
Quintana de la Serena, *Spain* **43 G5** 38 45N 5 40W
Quintana Roo □, *Mexico* **163 D7** 19 0N 88 0W
Quintanar de la Orden, *Spain* **43 F7** 39 36N 3 5W
Quintanar de la Sierra, *Spain* **40 D2** 41 57N 2 55W
Quintanar del Rey, *Spain* **41 F3** 39 21N 1 56W
Quintero, *Chile* **174 C1** 32 45 S 71 30W
Quintin, *France* **26 D4** 48 26N 2 56W
Quinto, *Spain* **40 D4** 41 25N 0 32W
Quinzáu, *Angola* **115 D2** 6 51 S 12 44 E
Quípar →, *Spain* **41 G3** 38 15N 1 40W
Quipeio, *Angola* **115 E3** 12 27 S 15 30 E
Quirihue, *Chile* **174 D1** 36 15 S 72 35W
Quirima, *Angola* **115 E3** 10 47 S 18 6 E
Quirimbo, *Angola* **115 E2** 10 36 S 14 12 E
Quirindi, *Australia* **129 A9** 31 28 S 150 40 E
Quirino □, *Phil.* **80 C3** 16 15N 121 40 E
Quirinopolis, *Brazil* **171 E1** 18 32 S 50 30W
Quiroga, *Spain* **42 C3** 42 28N 7 18W
Quiruvilca, *Peru* **172 B2** 8 1 S 78 19W
Quissac, *France* **29 E8** 43 55N 4 0 E
Quissanga, *Mozam.* **119 E5** 12 24 S 40 28 E
Quissico, *Mozam.* **117 C5** 24 42 S 34 44 E
Quitapa, *Angola* **115 E3** 10 20 S 18 19 E
Quitilipi, *Argentina* **174 B3** 26 50 S 60 13W
Quitman, *U.S.A.* **152 E6** 30 47N 83 34W
Quito, *Ecuador* **168 D2** 0 15 S 78 35W
Quixadá, *Brazil* **170 B4** 4 55 S 39 0W
Quixaxe, *Mozam.* **119 F5** 15 17 S 40 4 E
Quixeramobim, *Brazil* **170 C4** 5 12 S 39 17W
Quixico, *Angola* **115 D2** 7 59 S 14 25 E
Quixinge, *Angola* **115 D2** 9 52 S 14 23 E
Quizenga, *Angola* **115 D3** 9 21 S 15 28 E
Qujing, *China* **76 E4** 25 32N 103 41 E
Qulan, *Kazakstan* **66 E8** 42 55N 72 43 E
Qul'ân, Jazâ'ir, *Egypt* **96 E2** 24 22N 35 31 E
Qumbu, *S. Africa* **117 E4** 31 10 S 28 48 E
Qumqŭrghan, *Uzbekistan* **65 E3** 37 49N 67 35 E
Quneitra, *Syria* **103 B4** 33 7N 35 48 E
Qŭnghirot, *Uzbekistan* **66 E6** 43 6N 58 54 E
Qu'nyido, *China* **76 B2** 31 15N 98 6 E
Quoin I., *Australia* **124 B4** 14 54 S 129 32 E
Quoin Pt., *S. Africa* **116 E2** 34 46 S 19 37 E
Quorn, *Australia* **128 B3** 32 25 S 138 5 E
Qŭqon, *Uzbekistan* **66 E8** 40 30N 70 57 E
Qurein, *Sudan* **107 E3** 13 30N 34 50 E
Qŭrghonteppa, *Tajikistan* **65 E4** 37 50N 68 47 E
Qurnat as Sawdā', *Lebanon* **103 A5** 34 18N 36 6 E
Qûs, *Egypt* **106 B3** 25 55N 32 50 E
Qusar, *Azerbaijan* **61 K9** 41 25N 48 26 E
Quşaybā', *Si. Arabia* **96 E4** 26 53N 43 35 E
Qusaybah, *Iraq* **101 E9** 34 24N 40 59 E
Quşay'ir, *Yemen* **99 D5** 14 55N 50 20 E
Quseir, *Egypt* **96 E2** 26 7N 34 16 E
Qūshchī, *Iran* **101 D11** 37 59N 45 3 E
Quthing, *Lesotho* **117 E4** 30 25 S 27 36 E
Qūţīābād, *Iran* **97 C6** 35 47N 48 30 E
Quwo, *China* **74 G6** 35 38N 111 25 E
Quyang, *China* **74 E8** 38 35N 114 40 E
Quynh Nhai, *Vietnam* **86 B4** 21 49N 103 33 E
Quyon, *Canada* **151 A8** 45 31N 76 14W
Quzhou, *China* **77 C12** 28 57N 118 54 E
Quzi, *China* **74 F4** 36 20N 107 20 E
Qvareli, *Georgia* **61 K7** 41 57N 45 47 E
Qytet Stalin = Kuçovë, *Albania* **50 F3** 40 47N 19 57 E
Qyzylorda, *Kazakstan* **66 E7** 44 48N 65 28 E

R

Ra, Ko, *Thailand* **87 H2** 9 13N 98 16 E
Raab, *Austria* **34 C6** 48 21N 13 39 E
Raahe, *Finland* **14 D21** 64 40N 24 28 E
Raalte, *Neths.* **24 B6** 52 23N 6 16 E
Raasay, *U.K.* **22 D2** 57 25N 6 4W
Raasay, Sd. of, *U.K.* **22 D2** 57 30N 6 8W
Rab, *Croatia* **45 D11** 44 45N 14 45 E
Raba, *Indonesia* **85 D5** 8 36 S 118 55 E
Rába →, *Hungary* **52 C2** 47 38N 17 38 E
Raba →, *Poland* **55 H7** 50 8N 20 30 E
Rabaçal →, *Portugal* **42 D3** 41 30N 7 12W
Rabah, *Nigeria* **113 C6** 13 5N 5 30 E
Rabai, *Kenya* **118 C4** 3 50 S 39 31 E
Rabak, *Sudan* **107 E3** 13 9N 32 44 E
Rabaraba, *Papua N. G.* **132 E5** 9 58 S 149 49 E
Rabastens, *France* **28 E5** 43 50N 1 43 E
Rabastens-de-Bigorre, *France* **28 E4** 43 23N 0 9 E
Rabat = Victoria, *Malta* **38 E6** 36 3N 14 14 E
Rabat, *Kazakstan* **65 B4** 42 2N 69 31 E
Rabat, *Malta* **38 F7** 35 53N 14 24 E
Rabat, *Morocco* **110 B3** 34 2N 6 48W
Rabaul, *Papua N. G.* **132 C7** 4 24 S 152 18 E
Rabi, *Fiji* **133 A3** 16 30 S 179 59W
Rābigh, *Si. Arabia* **98 B2** 22 50N 39 5 E
Rabka, *Poland* **55 J6** 49 37N 19 59 E
Râbniţa, *Moldova* **53 C14** 47 45N 29 0 E
Rābor, *Iran* **97 D8** 29 17N 56 55 E
Rabyānah, *Libya* **108 D4** 24 15N 22 0 E
Rača, *Serbia, Yug.* **50 B4** 44 14N 21 0 E
Răcăciuni, *Romania* **53 D11** 46 20N 26 59 E
Răcăşdia, *Romania* **52 F6** 44 59N 21 36 E
Racconigi, *Italy* **44 D4** 44 46N 7 46 E
Raccoon →, *U.S.A.* **156 C3** 41 35N 93 37W
Raccoon Cr. →, *U.S.A.* **157 E9** 39 47N 87 23W
Race, C., *Canada* **141 C9** 46 40N 53 5W
Rach Gia, *Vietnam* **87 G5** 10 5N 105 5 E
Rachid, *Mauritania* **112 B2** 18 45N 11 35W
Raciąż, *Poland* **55 F7** 52 46N 20 10 E
Racibórz, *Poland* **55 H5** 50 7N 18 18 E
Racine, *U.S.A.* **157 B9** 42 41N 87 51W
Rackerby, *U.S.A.* **160 F5** 39 26N 121 22W
Radama, Nosy, *Madag.* **117 A8** 14 0 S 47 47 E
Radama, Saikanosy, *Madag.* **117 A8** 14 16 S 47 53 E
Radan, *Serbia, Yug.* **50 D5** 42 59N 21 29 E
Rădăuţi, *Romania* **53 C10** 47 50N 25 59 E
Rădăuţi-Prut, *Romania* **53 B11** 48 14N 26 48 E
Radbuza →, *Czech Rep.* **34 B6** 49 45N 13 22 E
Radcliff, *U.S.A.* **157 G11** 37 51N 85 57W
Radeberg, *Germany* **30 D9** 51 7N 13 53 E
Radebeul, *Germany* **30 D9** 51 6N 13 39 E
Radeče, *Slovenia* **45 B12** 46 5N 15 14 E
Radekhiv, *Ukraine* **59 G3** 50 25N 24 32 E
Radekhov = Radekhiv, *Ukraine* **59 G3** 50 25N 24 32 E
Radenthein, *Austria* **34 E6** 46 48N 13 43 E
Radew →, *Poland* **54 D2** 54 2N 15 52 E
Radford, *U.S.A.* **148 G5** 37 8N 80 34W
Radhanpur, *India* **92 H4** 23 50N 71 38 E
Radhwa, Jabal, *Si. Arabia* **96 E3** 24 34N 38 18 E
Radika →, *Macedonia* **50 E4** 41 38N 20 37 E
Radisson, *Qué., Canada* **140 B4** 53 47N 77 37W
Radisson, *Sask., Canada* **143 C7** 52 30N 107 20W
Radium Hot Springs, *Canada* **142 C5** 50 35N 116 2W
Radlje ob Dravi, *Slovenia* **45 B12** 46 38N 15 13 E
Radnevo, *Bulgaria* **51 D9** 42 17N 25 58 E
Radnice, *Czech Rep.* **34 B6** 49 51N 13 35 E
Radnor Forest, *U.K.* **21 E4** 52 17N 3 10W
Radolfzell, *Germany* **31 H4** 47 39N 8 59 E
Radom, *Poland* **55 G8** 51 23N 21 12 E
Radom Nat. Park, *Sudan* **114 A4** 9 20N 23 50 E
Radomir, *Bulgaria* **50 D6** 42 37N 22 59 E
Radomka →, *Poland* **55 G8** 51 43N 21 28 E
Radomsko, *Poland* **55 G6** 51 5N 19 28 E
Radomyshl, *Ukraine* **59 G5** 50 30N 29 12 E
Radomyśl Wielki, *Poland* **55 H8** 50 14N 21 15 E
Radoszyce, *Poland* **55 G7** 51 4N 20 15 E
Radoviš, *Macedonia* **50 E6** 41 38N 22 28 E
Radovljica, *Slovenia* **45 B11** 46 22N 14 12 E
Radstadt, *Austria* **34 D6** 47 24N 13 28 E
Radstock, C., *Australia* **127 E1** 33 12 S 134 20 E
Răducăneni, *Romania* **53 D12** 46 58N 27 54 E
Raduša, *Macedonia* **50 D5** 42 7N 21 15 E
Radviliškis, *Lithuania* **15 J20** 55 49N 23 33 E
Radville, *Canada* **143 D8** 49 30N 104 15W
Raḑwá, J., *Si. Arabia* **106 C4** 24 34N 38 18 E
Radymno, *Poland* **55 J9** 49 59N 22 52 E
Radzanów, *Poland* **55 F7** 52 56N 20 8 E
Radziejów, *Poland* **55 F5** 52 40N 18 30 E
Radzyń Chełmiński, *Poland* **54 E5** 53 23N 18 55 E
Radzyń Podlaski, *Poland* **55 G9** 51 47N 22 37 E
Rae, *Canada* **142 A5** 62 50N 116 3W
Rae Bareli, *India* **93 F9** 26 18N 81 20 E
Rae Isthmus, *Canada* **139 B11** 66 40N 87 30W
Raeren, *Belgium* **24 D6** 50 41N 6 7 E
Raeside, L., *Australia* **125 E3** 29 20 S 122 0 E
Raetihi, *N.Z.* **130 F4** 39 25 S 175 17 E
Rafaela, *Argentina* **174 C3** 31 10 S 61 30W
Rafah, *Gaza Strip* **103 D3** 31 18N 34 14 E
Rafai, *C.A.R.* **118 B1** 4 59N 23 58 E
Raffadali, *Italy* **46 E6** 37 24N 13 32 E
Raffili, *Sudan* **107 F2** 6 50N 28 0 E
Rafḩā, *Si. Arabia* **96 D4** 29 35N 43 35 E
Rafsanjān, *Iran* **97 D8** 30 30N 56 5 E
Raft Pt., *Australia* **124 C3** 16 4 S 124 26 E
Râgâ, *Sudan* **107 F2** 8 28N 25 41 E
Raga →, *Sudan* **107 F2** 8 41N 25 52 E
Ragachow, *Belarus* **59 F6** 53 8N 30 5 E
Ragag, *Sudan* **107 E1** 10 59N 24 40 E
Ragang, Mt., *Phil.* **81 H5** 7 43N 124 32 E
Ragay, *Phil.* **80 E4** 13 49N 122 47 E
Ragay G., *Phil.* **80 E4** 13 30N 122 45 E
Ragged, Mt., *Australia* **125 F3** 33 27 S 123 25 E
Ragged Pt., *Barbados* **165 g** 13 10N 59 10W
Rāgh, *Afghan.* **65 E5** 37 32N 70 27 E
Raghunathpalli, *India* **93 H11** 22 14N 84 48 E
Raghunathpur, *India* **93 H12** 23 33N 86 40 E
Raglan, *N.Z.* **130 D3** 37 55 S 174 55 E
Raglan Harbour, *N.Z.* **130 D3** 37 47 S 174 50 E
Ragland, *U.S.A.* **152 B3** 33 45N 86 9W
Ragusa, *Italy* **47 F7** 36 55N 14 44 E
Raha, *Indonesia* **82 B2** 4 55 S 123 0 E
Rahad, Nahr ed →, *Sudan* **107 E3** 14 28N 33 31 E
Rahad al Bardī, *Sudan* **109 F4** 11 20N 23 40 E
Rahaeng = Tak, *Thailand* **86 D2** 16 52N 99 8 E
Rahatgarh, *India* **93 H8** 23 47N 78 22 E
Rahden, *Germany* **30 C4** 52 26N 8 36 E
Raheb, Ras ir-, *Malta* **38 F7** 35 54N 14 20 E
Raheita, *Eritrea* **107 E5** 12 46N 43 4 E
Rahimyar Khan, *Pakistan* **91 C3** 28 30N 70 25 E
Rāhjerd, *Iran* **97 C6** 34 22N 50 22 E
Rahole Nat. Reserve, *Kenya* **118 B4** 0 5N 38 57 E
Råholt, *Norway* **18 D8** 60 16N 11 11 E
Rahon, *India* **92 D7** 31 3N 76 7 E
Rahotu, *N.Z.* **130 F2** 39 20 S 173 49 E
Rahuri, *India* **94 E2** 19 23N 74 39 E
Raichur, *India* **95 F3** 16 10N 77 20 E
Raiford, *U.S.A.* **152 E7** 30 4N 82 14W
Raiganj, *India* **93 G13** 25 37N 88 10 E
Raigarh, *India* **94 D6** 21 56N 83 25 E
Raighar, *India* **94 E6** 19 51N 82 6 E
Raijua, *Indonesia* **82 D2** 10 37 S 121 36 E
Raikot, *India* **92 D6** 30 41N 75 42 E
Railton, *Australia* **127 G4** 41 25 S 146 28 E
Rainbow City, *U.S.A.* **152 B3** 33 57N 86 5W
Rainbow Lake, *Canada* **142 B5** 58 30N 119 23W
Rainier, *U.S.A.* **160 D4** 46 53N 122 41W
Rainier, Mt., *U.S.A.* **160 D5** 46 52N 121 46W
Rainy L., *Canada* **143 D10** 48 42N 93 10W
Rainy River, *Canada* **143 D10** 48 43N 94 29W
Raippaluoto, *Finland* **14 E19** 63 13N 21 14 E
Raipur, *India* **94 D5** 21 17N 81 45 E
Rairakhol, *India* **94 D7** 21 4N 84 21 E
Ra'is, *Si. Arabia* **106 C4** 23 33N 38 43 E
Raisen, *India* **92 H8** 23 20N 77 48 E
Raisio, *Finland* **15 F20** 60 28N 22 11 E
Raj Nandgaon, *India* **94 D5** 21 5N 81 5 E
Raj Nilgiri, *India* **93 J12** 21 28N 86 46 E
Raja, Ujung, *Indonesia* **84 B1** 3 40N 96 25 E
Raja Ampat, Kepulauan, *Indonesia* **83 B4** 0 30 S 130 0 E
Rajahmundry, *India* **94 F5** 17 1N 81 48 E
Rajampet, *India* **95 G4** 14 11N 79 10 E
Rajang →, *Malaysia* **85 B4** 2 30N 112 0 E
Rajanpur, *Pakistan* **92 E4** 29 6N 70 19 E
Rajapalaiyam, *India* **95 K3** 9 25N 77 35 E
Rajapur, *India* **94 F1** 16 40N 73 31 E
Rajasthan □, *India* **92 F5** 26 45N 73 30 E
Rajasthan Canal, *India* **92 F5** 28 0N 72 0 E
Rajauri, *India* **93 C6** 33 25N 74 21 E
Rajbari, *Bangla.* **90 D2** 23 47N 89 41 E
Rajgarh, *Mad. P., India* **92 G7** 24 2N 76 45 E
Rajgarh, *Raj., India* **92 F7** 27 14N 76 38 E
Rajgarh, *Raj., India* **92 E6** 28 40N 75 25 E
Rajgir, *India* **93 G11** 25 2N 85 25 E
Rajgród, *Poland* **54 E9** 53 42N 22 42 E
Rajim, *India* **94 D5** 20 58N 81 53 E
Rajkot, *India* **92 H4** 22 15N 70 56 E
Rajmahal Hills, *India* **93 G12** 24 30N 87 30 E
Rajpipla, *India* **94 D1** 21 50N 73 30 E
Rajpur, *India* **92 H6** 22 18N 74 21 E
Rajpura, *India* **92 D7** 30 25N 76 32 E
Rajshahi, *Bangla.* **90 C2** 24 22N 88 39 E
Rajshahi □, *Bangla.* **90 C2** 25 0N 89 0 E
Rajula, *India* **92 J4** 21 3N 71 26 E
Rajur, *India* **94 D4** 20 7N 78 55 E
Rajura, *India* **94 E4** 19 47N 79 22 E
Rakaia, *N.Z.* **131 D7** 43 45 S 172 1 E
Rakaia →, *N.Z.* **131 D7** 43 36 S 172 15 E
Rakan, Ra's, *Qatar* **97 E6** 26 10N 51 20 E
Rakaposhi, *Pakistan* **93 A6** 36 10N 74 25 E
Rakata, Pulau, *Indonesia* **84 D3** 6 10 S 105 20 E
Rakhiv, *Ukraine* **59 H3** 48 3N 24 12 E
Rakhni, *Pakistan* **92 D3** 30 4N 69 56 E
Rakhni →, *Pakistan* **92 E3** 29 31N 69 36 E
Rakhyūt, *Oman* **99 C6** 16 44N 53 20 E
Rakiraki, *Fiji* **133 A2** 17 22 S 178 11 E
Rakitnoye, *Russia* **70 B7** 45 36N 134 17 E
Rakitovo, *Bulgaria* **51 E8** 41 59N 24 5 E
Rakkestad, *Norway* **18 E8** 59 25N 11 21 E
Rakoniewice, *Poland* **55 F3** 52 10N 16 16 E
Rakops, *Botswana* **116 C3** 21 1 S 24 28 E
Rakovica, *Croatia* **45 D12** 44 59N 15 38 E
Rakovník, *Czech Rep.* **34 A6** 50 6N 13 42 E
Rakovski, *Bulgaria* **51 D8** 42 21N 24 57 E
Rakshan →, *Pakistan* **91 D1** 27 10N 63 25 E
Rakvere, *Estonia* **15 G22** 59 20N 26 25 E
Raleigh, *Fla., U.S.A.* **153 F7** 29 25N 82 32W
Raleigh, *N.C., U.S.A.* **149 H6** 35 47N 78 39W
Rali Salem, *Algeria* **111 D5** 21 3N 1 9 E
Ralja, *Serbia, Yug.* **50 B4** 44 33N 20 34 E
Ralls, *U.S.A.* **155 J4** 33 41N 101 24W
Ralston, *U.S.A.* **150 E8** 41 30N 76 57W
Ram →, *Canada* **142 A4** 62 1N 123 41W
Rām Allāh, *West Bank* **103 D4** 31 55N 35 10 E
Rama, *Nic.* **164 D3** 12 9N 84 15W
Ramacca, *Italy* **47 E7** 37 23N 14 42 E
Ramachandrapuram, *India* **94 F6** 16 50N 82 4 E
Ramagiri Udayagiri, *India* **94 E7** 19 5N 84 18 E
Ramakona, *India* **93 J8** 21 43N 78 50 E
Ramales de la Victoria, *Spain* **42 B7** 43 15N 3 28W
Ramalho, Serra do, *Brazil* **171 D3** 13 45 S 44 0W
Raman, *Thailand* **87 J3** 6 29N 101 18 E
Ramanathapuram, *India* **95 K4** 9 25N 78 55 E
Ramanetaka, B. de, *Madag.* **117 A8** 14 13 S 47 52 E
Ramanujganj, *India* **93 H10** 23 48N 83 42 E
Ramas C., *India* **95 G1** 15 5N 73 55 E
Ramat Gan, *Israel* **103 C3** 32 4N 34 48 E
Ramatlhabama, *S. Africa* **116 D4** 25 37 S 25 33 E
Ramban, *India* **93 C6** 33 14N 75 12 E
Rambervillers, *France* **27 D13** 48 20N 6 38 E
Rambi = Rabi, *Fiji* **133 A3** 16 30 S 179 59W
Rambipuji, *Indonesia* **85 D4** 8 12 S 113 37 E
Rambouillet, *France* **27 D8** 48 39N 1 50 E
Rambrai, *India* **90 C3** 25 40N 91 19 E
Rambutyo I., *Papua N. G.* **132 B4** 2 18 S 147 49 E
Ramdurg, *India* **95 G2** 15 58N 75 22 E
Rame Hd., *Australia* **129 D8** 37 47 S 149 30 E
Ramechhap, *Nepal* **93 F12** 27 25N 86 10 E
Ramenskoye, *Russia* **58 E10** 55 32N 38 15 E
Ramer, *U.S.A.* **152 C3** 32 3N 86 13W
Rameswaram, *India* **95 K4** 9 17N 79 18 E
Ramganga →, *India* **93 F8** 27 5N 79 58 E
Ramgarh, *Bangla.* **90 D3** 22 59N 91 44 E
Ramgarh, *Jharkhand, India* **93 H11** 23 40N 85 35 E
Ramgarh, *Raj., India* **92 F6** 27 16N 75 14 E
Ramgarh, *Raj., India* **92 F4** 27 30N 70 36 E
Rāmhormoz, *Iran* **97 D6** 31 15N 49 35 E
Ramīān, *Iran* **97 B7** 37 3N 55 16 E
Ramingining, *Australia* **126 A2** 12 19 S 135 3 E
Ramla, *Israel* **103 D3** 31 55N 34 52 E
Ramlat Zalţan, *Libya* **108 C3** 28 30N 19 30 E
Ramlu, *Eritrea* **107 E5** 13 32N 41 40 E
Ramm, Jabal, *Jordan* **103 F4** 29 35N 35 24 E
Râmna →, *Romania* **53 E12** 45 36N 27 3 E
Ramnad = Ramanathapuram, *India* **95 K4** 9 25N 78 55 E
Ramnagar, *Jammu & Kashmir, India* **93 C6** 32 47N 75 18 E
Ramnagar, *Uttaranchal, India* **93 E8** 29 24N 79 7 E
Ramnäs, *Sweden* **16 E10** 59 46N 16 12 E
Râmnicu Sărat, *Romania* **53 E12** 45 26N 27 3 E
Râmnicu Vâlcea, *Romania* **53 E9** 45 9N 24 21 E
Ramon, *Phil.* **80 C3** 16 50N 121 31 E
Ramon, *Russia* **59 G10** 51 55N 39 21 E
Ramona, *U.S.A.* **161 M10** 33 2N 116 52W
Ramonville-St-Agne, *France* **28 E5** 43 33N 1 28 E
Ramore, *Canada* **140 C3** 48 30N 80 25W
Ramos →, *Nigeria* **113 D6** 5 8N 5 22 E
Ramotswa, *Botswana* **116 C4** 24 50 S 25 52 E
Rampart, *U.S.A.* **144 D10** 65 30N 150 10W
Rampur, *H.P., India* **92 D7** 31 26N 77 43 E
Rampur, *Mad. P., India* **92 H5** 23 25N 73 53 E
Rampur, *Orissa, India* **94 D6** 21 48N 83 58 E
Rampur, *Ut. P., India* **93 E8** 28 50N 79 5 E
Rampur Hat, *India* **93 G12** 24 10N 87 50 E
Rampura, *India* **92 G6** 24 30N 75 27 E
Ramrama Tola, *India* **93 J8** 21 52N 79 55 E
Ramree I., *Burma* **90 F5** 19 0N 93 40 E
Rāmsar, *Iran* **97 B6** 36 53N 50 41 E
Ramsey, *U.K.* **20 C3** 54 20N 4 22W
Ramsey, *Ill., U.S.A.* **156 E7** 39 8N 89 7W
Ramsey, *N.J., U.S.A.* **151 E10** 41 4N 74 9W
Ramsey L., *Canada* **140 C3** 47 13N 82 15W
Ramsgate, *U.K.* **21 F9** 51 20N 1 25 E
Ramshai, *India* **90 B2** 26 44N 88 51 E
Ramsjö, *Sweden* **16 B9** 62 11N 15 37 E
Ramstein, *Germany* **31 F3** 49 27N 7 32 E
Ramtek, *India* **94 D4** 21 20N 79 15 E
Ramu →, *Papua N. G.* **132 C3** 4 0 S 144 41 E
Ramvik, *Sweden* **16 B11** 62 49N 17 51 E
Rana Pratap Sagar Dam, *India* **92 G6** 24 58N 75 38 E
Ranaghat, *India* **93 H13** 23 15N 88 35 E
Ranahu, *Pakistan* **92 G3** 25 55N 69 45 E
Ranau, *Malaysia* **78 C5** 6 2N 116 40 E
Rancagua, *Chile* **174 C1** 34 10 S 70 50W
Rance →, *France* **26 D5** 48 34N 1 59W
Rancharia, *Brazil* **171 F1** 22 15 S 50 55W
Rancheria →, *Canada* **142 A3** 60 13N 129 7W
Ranchester, *U.S.A.* **158 D10** 44 54N 107 10W
Ranchi, *India* **93 H11** 23 19N 85 27 E
Rancho Cucamonga, *U.S.A.* **161 L9** 34 10N 117 30W
Ranco, L., *Chile* **176 B2** 40 15 S 72 25W
Rand, *Australia* **129 C7** 35 33 S 146 32 E
Randaberg, *Norway* **18 E2** 59 1N 5 36 E
Randabygd, *Norway* **18 C3** 61 51N 6 20 E
Randalstown, *U.K.* **23 B5** 54 45N 6 19W
Randan, *France* **27 F10** 46 2N 3 21 E
Randazzo, *Italy* **47 E7** 37 53N 14 57 E
Rander, *India* **94 D1** 21 14N 72 47 E
Randers, *Denmark* **17 H4** 56 29N 10 1 E
Randers Fjord, *Denmark* **17 H4** 56 37N 10 20 E
Randfontein, *S. Africa* **117 D4** 26 8 S 27 45 E
Randle, *U.S.A.* **160 D5** 46 32N 121 57W
Randolph, *Mass., U.S.A.* **151 D13** 42 10N 71 2W
Randolph, *N.Y., U.S.A.* **150 D6** 42 10N 78 59W
Randolph, *Utah, U.S.A.* **158 F8** 41 40N 111 11W
Randolph, *Vt., U.S.A.* **151 C12** 43 55N 72 40W
Randsburg, *U.S.A.* **161 K9** 35 22N 117 39W
Randsfjorden, *Norway* **18 D7** 60 25N 10 24 E
Randsverk, *Norway* **18 C6** 61 44N 9 3 E
Råne älv →, *Sweden* **14 D20** 65 50N 22 20 E
Ranfurly, *N.Z.* **131 F5** 45 7 S 170 6 E
Rangae, *Thailand* **87 J3** 6 19N 101 44 E
Rangamati, *Bangla.* **90 D4** 22 38N 92 12 E
Rangapara, *India* **90 B4** 26 49N 92 39 E
Rangárvallasýsla □, *Iceland* **11 D7** 63 55N 20 0W
Rangataua, *N.Z.* **130 F4** 39 26 S 175 28 E
Rangaunu B., *N.Z.* **130 A2** 34 51 S 173 15 E
Rangeley, *U.S.A.* **151 B14** 44 58N 70 39W
Rangeley L., *U.S.A.* **151 B14** 44 55N 70 43W
Rangely, *U.S.A.* **158 F9** 40 5N 108 48W
Ranger, *U.S.A.* **155 J5** 32 28N 98 41W
Rangia, *India* **90 B3** 26 28N 91 38 E
Rangiora, *N.Z.* **131 D7** 43 19 S 172 36 E
Rangitaiki, *N.Z.* **130 E5** 38 52 S 176 24 E
Rangitaiki →, *N.Z.* **130 D5** 37 54 S 176 49 E
Rangitata →, *N.Z.* **131 D6** 43 45 S 171 15 E
Rangitikei →, *N.Z.* **130 G4** 40 17 S 175 15 E
Rangitoto Ra., *N.Z.* **130 E4** 38 25 S 175 35 E
Rangkasbitung, *Indonesia* **84 D3** 6 21 S 106 15 E
Rangoon, *Burma* **90 G6** 16 45N 96 20 E
Rangpur, *Bangla.* **90 C2** 25 42N 89 22 E
Rangsang, *Indonesia* **84 B2** 1 20N 103 30 E
Rangsit, *Thailand* **86 F3** 13 59N 100 37 E
Ranheim, *Norway* **18 A7** 63 26N 10 32 E
Ranibennur, *India* **95 G2** 14 35N 75 30 E
Raniganj, *India* **93 F9** 27 3N 82 13 E
Ranikhet, *India* **93 E8** 29 39N 79 25 E
Ranippettai, *India* **95 H4** 12 56N 79 23 E
Rāniyah, *Iraq* **96 B5** 36 15N 44 53 E
Ranka, *India* **93 H10** 23 59N 83 47 E
Ranken →, *Australia* **126 C2** 20 31 S 137 36 E
Rankin, *Ill., U.S.A.* **157 D9** 40 28N 87 54W
Rankin, *Tex., U.S.A.* **155 K4** 31 13N 101 56W
Rankin Inlet, *Canada* **138 B10** 62 30N 93 0W
Rankins Springs, *Australia* **129 B7** 33 49 S 146 14 E
Rankweil, *Austria* **34 D2** 47 17N 9 39 E
Rannoch, L., *U.K.* **22 E4** 56 41N 4 20W
Rannoch Moor, *U.K.* **22 E4** 56 38N 4 48W
Rano Kau, *Chile* **172 b** 27 11 S 109 26W
Rano Raraku, Volcán, *Chile* **172 b** 27 7 S 109 17W
Ranobe, Helodranon' i, *Madag.* **117 C7** 23 3 S 43 33 E
Ranohira, *Madag.* **117 C8** 22 29 S 45 24 E
Ranomafana, *Toamasina, Madag.* **117 B8** 18 57 S 48 50 E
Ranomafana, *Toliara, Madag.* **117 C8** 24 34 S 47 0 E
Ranomafana, Parc Nat. de, *Madag.* **117 C8** 21 16 S 47 25 E
Ranomena, *Madag.* **117 C8** 23 25 S 47 17 E
Ranon, *Vanuatu* **133 F6** 16 8 S 168 7 E
Ranong, *Thailand* **87 H2** 9 56N 98 40 E
Ranongga, *Solomon Is.* **133 M9** 8 5 S 156 35 E
Ranotsara Nord, *Madag.* **117 C8** 22 48 S 46 36 E
Ranpur, *India* **94 D7** 20 5N 85 20 E
Rānsa, *Iran* **97 C6** 33 39N 48 18 E
Ransiki, *Indonesia* **83 B4** 1 30 S 134 10 E
Ransom, *U.S.A.* **157 C8** 41 9N 88 39W
Rantabe, *Madag.* **117 B8** 15 42 S 49 39 E
Rantau, *Indonesia* **85 C5** 2 56 S 115 9 E
Rantauprapat, *Indonesia* **84 B1** 2 15N 99 50 E
Rantemario, *Indonesia* **82 B1** 3 15 S 119 57 E
Rantoul, *U.S.A.* **157 D8** 40 19N 88 9W
Ranum, *Denmark* **17 H3** 56 54N 9 14 E

Ranyah, W. →, *Si. Arabia* **98 B3** 21 18N 43 20 E
Raon l'Étape, *France* **27 D13** 48 24N 6 50 E
Raoping, *China* **77 F11** 23 42N 117 1 E
Raoui, Erg er, *Algeria* **111 C4** 29 0N 2 0W
Raoyang, *China* **74 E8** 38 15N 115 45 E
Rap, Ko, *Thailand* **87 b** 9 19N 99 58 E
Rapa, *Pac. Oc.* **135 K13** 27 35 S 144 20W
Rapa Nui = Pascua, I. de, *Chile* **172 b** 27 7 S 109 23W
Rapallo, *Italy* **44 D6** 44 21N 9 14 E
Rapang, *Indonesia* **82 B1** 3 50 S 119 48 E
Rapar, *India* **92 H4** 23 34N 70 38 E
Rāpch, *Iran* **97 E8** 25 40N 59 15 E
Raper, C., *Canada* **139 B13** 69 44N 67 6W
Rapid City, *U.S.A.* **154 D3** 44 5N 103 14W
Rapid River, *U.S.A.* **148 C2** 45 55N 86 58W
Rapla, *Estonia* **15 G21** 59 1N 24 52 E
Rapperswil, *Switz.* **33 B7** 47 14N 8 45 E
Rapti →, *India* **93 F10** 26 18N 83 41 E
Rapu Rapu I., *Phil.* **80 E5** 13 12N 124 9 E
Raqaba ez Zarqa →, *Sudan* **107 F2** 9 14N 29 44 E
Râqûbah, *Libya* **108 C3** 28 58N 19 2 E
Raquette →, *U.S.A.* **151 B10** 45 0N 74 42W
Raquette Lake, *U.S.A.* **151 C10** 43 49N 74 40W
Rarotonga, *Cook Is.* **135 K12** 21 30 S 160 0W
Ra's al 'Ayn, *Syria* **101 D9** 36 45N 40 12 E
Ra's al Khaymah, *U.A.E.* **97 E7** 25 50N 55 59 E
Ras el Ma, *Algeria* **111 B4** 34 26N 0 50W
Râs el Mâ, *Mali* **112 B4** 16 35N 4 30W
Râs Ghârib, *Egypt* **108 C3** 28 6N 33 18 E
Râs Kōh, *Pakistan* **91 C2** 28 43N 64 55 E
Ra's Lānūf, *Libya* **108 B3** 30 46N 18 11 E
Râs Mallap, *Egypt* **106 B3** 29 18N 32 50 E
Râs Muhammad Nat. Park, *Egypt* **106 B3** 27 45N 34 16 E
Rasa, Punta, *Argentina* **176 B4** 40 50 S 62 15W
Rasca, Pta. de la, *Canary Is.* **9 e1** 27 59N 16 41W
Râşcani, *Moldova* **53 C12** 47 58N 27 33 E
Raseiniai, *Lithuania* **15 J20** 55 25N 23 5 E
Rashad, *Sudan* **107 E3** 11 55N 31 0 E
Rashîd, *Egypt* **106 H7** 31 21N 30 22 E
Rashîd, Masabb, *Egypt* **106 H7** 31 22N 30 17 E
Rashmi, *India* **92 G6** 25 4N 74 22 E
Rasht, *Iran* **97 B6** 37 20N 49 40 E
Rasi Salai, *Thailand* **86 E5** 15 20N 104 9 E
Rasipuram, *India* **95 J4** 11 30N 78 15 E
Raška, *Serbia, Yug.* **50 C4** 43 19N 20 39 E
Râsnov, *Romania* **53 E10** 45 35N 25 27 E
Rason L., *Australia* **125 E3** 28 45 S 124 25 E
Raşova, *Romania* **53 F12** 44 15N 27 55 E
Rasovo, *Bulgaria* **50 C7** 43 42N 23 17 E
Rasra, *India* **93 G10** 25 50N 83 50 E
Rass el Oued, *Algeria* **111 A6** 35 57N 5 2 E
Rasskazovo, *Russia* **60 D5** 52 35N 41 50 E
Rast, *Romania* **53 G8** 43 53N 23 16 E
Rastatt, *Germany* **31 G4** 48 50N 8 11 E
Rastede, *Germany* **30 B4** 53 15N 8 12 E
Răstolița, *Romania* **53 D9** 46 59N 24 58 E
Rasul, *Pakistan* **92 C5** 32 42N 73 34 E
Raszków, *Poland* **55 G4** 51 43N 17 40 E
Rat Buri, *Thailand* **86 F2** 13 30N 99 54 E
Rat Islands, *U.S.A.* **144 L2** 52 0N 178 0 E
Rat L., *Canada* **143 B9** 56 10N 99 40W
Ratangarh, *India* **92 E6** 28 5N 74 35 E
Rätansbyn, *Sweden* **16 B8** 62 29N 14 33 E
Raţāwī, *Iraq* **96 D5** 30 38N 47 13 E
Ratcatchers L., *Australia* **128 B5** 32 30 S 143 12 E
Rath, *India* **93 G8** 25 36N 79 37 E
Rath Luirc, *Ireland* **23 D3** 52 21N 8 40W
Rathbun L., *U.S.A.* **156 D4** 40 49N 92 53W
Rathdrum, *Ireland* **23 D5** 52 56N 6 14W
Rathedaung, *Burma* **90 G2** 20 29N 92 45 E
Rathenow, *Germany* **30 C8** 52 37N 12 19 E
Rathkeale, *Ireland* **23 D3** 52 32N 8 56W
Rathlin I., *U.K.* **23 A5** 55 18N 6 14W
Rathmelton, *Ireland* **23 A4** 55 2N 7 38W
Ratibor = Racibórz, *Poland* **55 H5** 50 7N 18 18 E
Rätikon, *Austria* **33 B9** 47 0N 9 55 E
Ratingen, *Germany* **30 D2** 51 18N 6 52 E
Ratlam, *India* **92 H6** 23 20N 75 0 E
Ratnagiri, *India* **94 F1** 16 57N 73 18 E
Ratnapura, *Sri Lanka* **95 L5** 6 40N 80 20 E
Ratodero, *Pakistan* **92 F3** 27 48N 68 18 E
Raton, *U.S.A.* **155 G2** 36 54N 104 24W
Rattaphum, *Thailand* **87 J3** 7 8N 100 16 E
Ratten, *Austria* **34 D8** 47 28N 15 44 E
Rattray Hd., *U.K.* **22 D7** 57 38N 1 50W
Rättvik, *Sweden* **16 D9** 60 52N 15 7 E
Ratz, Mt., *Canada* **142 B2** 57 23N 132 12W
Ratzeburg, *Germany* **30 B6** 53 40N 10 46 E
Rau, *Indonesia* **82 A3** 2 20N 128 10 E
Raub, *Malaysia* **87 L3** 3 47N 101 52 E
Rauch, *Argentina* **174 D4** 36 45 S 59 5W
Raudales de Malpaso, *Mexico* **163 D6** 17 30N 23 30W
Raudeberg, *Norway* **18 C2** 61 59N 5 7 E
Raufarhöfn, *Iceland* **11 A11** 66 27N 15 57W
Raufoss, *Norway* **15 F14** 60 44N 10 37 E
Rauhellern, *Norway* **18 D4** 60 15N 7 50 E
Raukumara Ra., *N.Z.* **130 E6** 38 5 S 177 55 E
Raul Soares, *Brazil* **171 F3** 20 5 S 42 22W
Rauma, *Finland* **15 F19** 61 10N 21 30 E
Rauma →, *Norway* **18 B4** 62 34N 7 43 E
Raung, Gunung, *Indonesia* **79 J17** 8 8 S 114 3 E
Raurkela, *India* **93 H11** 22 14N 84 50 E
Rausu-Dake, *Japan* **70 B12** 44 4N 145 7 E
Răut →, *Moldova* **53 C14** 47 15N 29 9 E
Rava-Ruska, *Poland* **59 G2** 50 15N 23 42 E
Rava Russkaya = Rava-Ruska, *Poland* **59 G2** 50 15N 23 42 E
Ravalli, *U.S.A.* **158 C6** 47 17N 114 11W
Ravānsar, *Iran* **101 E12** 34 43N 46 40 E
Ravanusa, *Italy* **46 E6** 37 16N 13 58 E
Rāvar, *Iran* **97 D8** 31 20N 56 51 E
Ravena, *U.S.A.* **151 D11** 42 28N 73 49W
Ravenel, *U.S.A.* **152 C9** 32 46N 80 15W
Ravenna, *Italy* **45 D9** 44 25N 12 12 E
Ravenna, *Ky., U.S.A.* **157 G13** 37 42N 83 55W
Ravenna, *Nebr., U.S.A.* **154 E5** 41 1N 98 55W
Ravenna, *Ohio, U.S.A.* **150 E3** 41 9N 81 15W
Ravensburg, *Germany* **31 H5** 47 46N 9 36 E
Ravenshoe, *Australia* **126 B4** 17 37 S 145 29 E
Ravensthorpe, *Australia* **125 F3** 33 35 S 120 2 E
Ravenswood, *Australia* **126 C4** 20 6 S 146 54 E
Ravenswood, *U.S.A.* **148 F5** 38 57N 81 46W
Ravensworth, *Australia* **129 B9** 32 26 S 151 4 E
Ravenwood, *U.S.A.* **156 D2** 40 22N 94 41W
Raver, *India* **94 D3** 21 15N 76 2 E
Ravi →, *Pakistan* **92 D4** 30 35N 71 49 E
Ravna Gora, *Croatia* **45 C11** 45 24N 14 50 E
Ravna Reka, *Serbia, Yug.* **50 B5** 44 1N 21 35 E
Ravne na Koroškem, *Slovenia* **45 B11** 46 36N 14 59 E
Rawa Mazowiecka, *Poland* **55 G7** 51 46N 20 12 E
Rawalpindi, *Pakistan* **91 B4** 33 38N 73 8 E
Rawāndūz, *Iraq* **101 D11** 36 40N 44 30 E
Rawang, *Malaysia* **87 L3** 3 20N 101 35 E
Rawene, *N.Z.* **130 B2** 35 25 S 173 32 E
Rawicz, *Poland* **55 G3** 51 36N 16 52 E
Rawka →, *Poland* **55 F7** 52 9N 20 8 E
Rawlinna, *Australia* **125 F4** 30 58 S 125 28 E
Rawlins, *U.S.A.* **158 F10** 41 47N 107 14W
Rawlinson Ra., *Australia* **125 D4** 24 40 S 128 30 E
Rawson, *Argentina* **176 B3** 43 15 S 65 5W
Raxaul, *India* **93 F11** 26 59N 84 51 E
Ray, *U.S.A.* **154 A3** 48 21N 103 10W
Ray, C., *Canada* **141 C8** 47 33N 59 15W
Ray City, *U.S.A.* **152 D6** 31 5N 83 11W
Ray Mts., *U.S.A.* **144 D10** 66 0N 152 0W
Raya Ring, Ko, *Thailand* **87 a** 8 18N 98 29 E
Rayachoti, *India* **95 G4** 14 4N 78 50 E
Rayadurg, *India* **95 G3** 14 40N 76 50 E
Rayagada, *India* **94 E6** 19 15N 83 20 E
Raychikhinsk, *Russia* **67 E13** 49 46N 129 25 E
Rāyen, *Iran* **97 D8** 29 34N 57 26 E
Rayevskiy, *Russia* **64 D5** 54 4N 54 56 E
Rayle, *U.S.A.* **152 B7** 33 48N 82 54W
Rayleigh, *U.K.* **21 F8** 51 36N 0 37 E
Raymond, *Canada* **142 D6** 49 30N 112 35W
Raymond, *Calif., U.S.A.* **160 H7** 37 13N 119 54W
Raymond, *Ill., U.S.A.* **156 E7** 39 19N 89 34W
Raymond, *N.H., U.S.A.* **151 C13** 43 2N 71 11W
Raymond, *Wash., U.S.A.* **160 D3** 46 41N 123 44W
Raymond Terrace, *Australia* **129 B9** 32 45 S 151 44 E
Raymondville, *U.S.A.* **155 M6** 26 29N 97 47W
Raymore, *Canada* **143 C8** 51 25N 104 31W
Rayón, *Mexico* **162 B2** 29 43N 110 35W
Rayong, *Thailand* **86 F3** 12 40N 101 20 E
Raytown, *U.S.A.* **156 E2** 39 1N 94 28W
Rayville, *U.S.A.* **155 J9** 32 29N 91 46W
Raz, Pte. du, *France* **26 D2** 48 2N 4 47W
Razan, *Iran* **97 C6** 35 23N 49 2 E
Ražana, *Serbia, Yug.* **50 B3** 44 6N 19 55 E
Ražanj, *Serbia, Yug.* **50 C5** 43 40N 21 31 E
Razdelna, *Bulgaria* **51 C11** 43 13N 27 41 E
Razdel'naya = Rozdilna, *Ukraine* **59 J6** 46 50N 30 2 E
Razdolnoye, *Russia* **70 C5** 43 30N 131 52 E
Razdolnoye, *Ukraine* **59 K7** 45 46N 33 29 E
Razeh, *Iran* **97 C6** 32 47N 48 9 E
Razgrad, *Bulgaria* **51 C10** 43 33N 26 34 E
Razim, Lacul, *Romania* **53 F14** 44 50N 29 0 E
Razlog, *Bulgaria* **50 E7** 41 53N 23 28 E
Razmak, *Pakistan* **91 B3** 32 45N 69 50 E
Ré, Î. de, *France* **28 B2** 46 12N 1 30W
Reading, *U.K.* **21 F7** 51 27N 0 58W
Reading, *Mich., U.S.A.* **157 C12** 41 50N 84 45W
Reading, *Ohio, U.S.A.* **157 E12** 39 13N 84 26W
Reading, *Pa., U.S.A.* **151 F9** 40 20N 75 56W
Reading □, *U.K.* **21 F7** 51 27N 0 58W
Real, Cordillera, *Bolivia* **172 D4** 17 0 S 67 10W
Realicó, *Argentina* **174 D3** 35 0 S 64 15W
Réalmont, *France* **28 E6** 43 48N 2 10 E
Realp, *Switz.* **33 C6** 46 36N 8 30 E
Ream, *Cambodia* **87 G4** 10 34N 103 39 E
Reata, *Mexico* **162 B4** 26 8N 101 5W
Reay Forest, *U.K.* **22 C4** 58 22N 4 55W
Rebais, *France* **27 D10** 48 50N 3 10 E
Rebi, *Indonesia* **83 C4** 6 23 S 134 7 E
Rebiana, *Libya* **108 D4** 24 12N 22 10 E
Rebiana, Sahrâ, *Libya* **108 D3** 24 0N 23 0 E
Rebun-Tō, *Japan* **70 B10** 45 23N 141 2 E
Recanati, *Italy* **45 E10** 43 24N 13 32 E
Recaş, *Romania* **52 E6** 45 46N 21 30 E
Recco, *Italy* **44 D6** 44 22N 9 9 E
Recherche, Arch. of the, *Australia* **125 F3** 34 15 S 122 50 E
Rechna Doab, *Pakistan* **92 D5** 31 35N 73 30 E
Rechytsa, *Belarus* **59 F6** 52 21N 30 24 E
Recife, *Brazil* **170 C5** 8 0 S 35 0W
Recife, *Seychelles* **121 b** 4 36 S 55 42 E
Recklinghausen, *Germany* **24 C7** 51 37N 7 12 E
Reconquista, *Argentina* **174 B4** 29 10 S 59 45W
Recreio, *Brazil* **173 B6** 8 0 S 58 25W
Recreo, *Argentina* **174 B2** 29 25 S 65 10W
Recuay, *Peru* **172 B2** 9 43 S 77 28W
Recz, *Poland* **55 E2** 53 16N 15 31 E
Red →, *La., U.S.A.* **155 K9** 31 1N 91 45W
Red →, *N. Dak., U.S.A.* **138 C10** 49 0N 97 15W
Red Bank, *U.S.A.* **151 F10** 40 21N 74 5W
Red Bay, *Canada* **141 B8** 51 44N 56 25W
Red Bluff, *U.S.A.* **158 F2** 40 11N 122 15W
Red Bluff L., *U.S.A.* **155 K3** 31 54N 103 55W
Red Bud, *U.S.A.* **156 F7** 38 13N 89 59W
Red Cliffs, *Australia* **128 C5** 34 19 S 142 11 E
Red Cloud, *U.S.A.* **154 E5** 40 5N 98 32W
Red Creek, *U.S.A.* **151 C8** 43 14N 76 45W
Red Deer, *Canada* **142 C6** 52 20N 113 50W
Red Deer →, *Alta., Canada* **143 C7** 50 58N 110 0W
Red Deer →, *Man., Canada* **143 C8** 52 53N 101 1W
Red Deer L., *Canada* **143 C8** 52 55N 101 20W
Red Devil, *U.S.A.* **144 F8** 61 46N 157 19W
Red Hook, *U.S.A.* **151 E11** 41 55N 73 53W
Red Indian L., *Canada* **141 C8** 48 35N 57 0W
Red L., *Canada* **143 C10** 51 3N 93 49W
Red Lake, *Canada* **143 C10** 51 3N 93 49W
Red Lake Falls, *U.S.A.* **154 B6** 47 53N 96 16W
Red Lake Road, *Canada* **143 C10** 49 59N 93 25W
Red Lodge, *U.S.A.* **158 D9** 45 11N 109 15W
Red Mountain, *U.S.A.* **161 K9** 35 37N 117 38W
Red Oak, *U.S.A.* **154 E7** 41 1N 95 14W
Red Rock, *Canada* **140 C2** 48 55N 88 15W
Red Rock, L., *U.S.A.* **156 C3** 41 22N 92 59W
Red Rocks Pt., *Australia* **125 F4** 32 13 S 127 32 E
Red Sea, *Asia* **102 C2** 25 0N 36 0 E
Red Slate Mt., *U.S.A.* **160 H8** 37 31N 118 52W
Red Sucker L., *Canada* **140 B1** 54 9N 93 40W
Red Tower Pass = Turnu Roşu, P., *Romania* **53 E9** 45 33N 24 17 E
Red Wing, *U.S.A.* **154 C8** 44 34N 92 31W
Reda, *Poland* **54 D5** 54 40N 18 19 E
Redang, *Malaysia* **78 C2** 5 49N 103 2 E
Redange, *Lux.* **24 E5** 49 46N 5 52 E
Redcar, *U.K.* **20 C6** 54 37N 1 4W
Redcar & Cleveland □, *U.K.* **20 C7** 54 29N 1 0W
Redcliff, *Canada* **143 C6** 50 10N 110 50W
Redcliffe, *Australia* **127 D5** 27 12 S 153 0 E
Redcliffe, Mt., *Australia* **125 E3** 28 30 S 121 30 E
Reddersburg, *S. Africa* **116 D4** 29 41 S 26 10 E
Reddick, *Fla., U.S.A.* **153 F7** 29 22N 82 12W
Reddick, *Ill., U.S.A.* **157 C8** 41 6N 88 15W
Redding, *Calif., U.S.A.* **158 F2** 40 35N 122 24W
Redding, *Iowa, U.S.A.* **156 D2** 40 36N 94 23W
Redditch, *U.K.* **21 E6** 52 18N 1 55W
Redenção, *Brazil* **170 B4** 4 13 S 38 43W
Redfield, *U.S.A.* **154 C5** 44 53N 98 31W
Redford, *U.S.A.* **151 B11** 44 38N 73 48W
Redhead, *Trin. & Tob.* **169 F10** 10 48N 60 3W
Redkey, *U.S.A.* **157 D11** 40 21N 85 9W
Redkino, *Russia* **58 D9** 56 39N 36 16 E
Redlands, *U.S.A.* **161 M9** 34 4N 117 11W
Redmond, *Oreg., U.S.A.* **158 D3** 44 17N 121 11W
Redmond, *Wash., U.S.A.* **160 C4** 47 41N 122 7W
Redon, *France* **26 E4** 47 40N 2 6W
Redonda, *Antigua* **165 C7** 16 58N 62 19W
Redonda, Pta., *Chile* **172 b** 27 10 S 109 22W
Redondela, *Spain* **42 C2** 42 15N 8 38W
Redondo, *Portugal* **43 G3** 38 39N 7 37W
Redondo Beach, *U.S.A.* **161 M8** 33 50N 118 23W
Redoubt Volcano, *U.S.A.* **144 F9** 60 29N 152 45W
Redruth, *U.K.* **21 G2** 50 14N 5 14W
Redvers, *Canada* **143 D8** 49 35N 101 40W
Redwater, *Canada* **142 C6** 53 55N 113 6W
Redwood, *U.S.A.* **151 B9** 44 18N 75 48W
Redwood City, *U.S.A.* **160 H4** 37 30N 122 15W
Redwood Falls, *U.S.A.* **154 C7** 44 32N 95 7W
Redwood Nat. Park, *U.S.A.* **158 F1** 41 40N 124 5W
Ree, L., *Ireland* **23 C3** 53 35N 8 0W
Reed, L., *Canada* **143 C8** 54 38N 100 30W
Reed City, *U.S.A.* **148 D3** 43 53N 85 31W
Reedley, *U.S.A.* **160 J7** 36 36N 119 27W
Reedsburg, *U.S.A.* **154 D9** 43 32N 90 0W
Reedsport, *U.S.A.* **158 E1** 43 42N 124 6W
Reedsville, *U.S.A.* **150 F7** 40 39N 77 35W
Reedy Creek, *Australia* **128 D4** 36 58 S 140 2 E
Reefton, *N.Z.* **131 C6** 42 6 S 171 51 E
Rees, *Germany* **30 D2** 51 46N 6 24 E
Reese →, *U.S.A.* **158 F5** 40 48N 117 4W
Refahiye, *Turkey* **101 C8** 39 54N 38 47 E
Reftele, *Sweden* **17 G7** 57 11N 13 35 E
Refugio, *U.S.A.* **155 L6** 28 18N 97 17W
Rega →, *Poland* **54 D2** 54 10N 15 18 E
Regalbuto, *Italy* **47 E7** 37 39N 14 38 E
Regen, *Germany* **31 G9** 48 58N 13 8 E
Regen →, *Germany* **31 F8** 49 1N 12 6 E
Regeneração, *Brazil* **170 C3** 6 15 S 42 41W
Regensburg, *Germany* **31 F8** 49 1N 12 6 E
Regensdorf, *Switz.* **33 B6** 47 26N 8 28 E
Regenstauf, *Germany* **31 F8** 49 7N 12 8 E
Reggâne = Zaouiet Reggâne, *Algeria* **111 C5** 26 32N 0 3 E
Reggello, *Italy* **45 E8** 43 41N 11 32 E
Réggio di Calábria, *Italy* **47 D8** 38 6N 15 39 E
Réggio nell'Emília, *Italy* **44 D7** 44 43N 10 36 E
Reghin, *Romania* **53 D9** 46 46N 24 42 E
Regina, *Canada* **143 C8** 50 27N 104 35W
Régina, *Fr. Guiana* **169 C7** 4 19N 52 8W
Regina Beach, *Canada* **143 C8** 50 47N 105 0W
Register, *U.S.A.* **152 C8** 32 22N 81 53W
Registro, *Brazil* **175 A6** 24 29 S 47 49W
Reguengos de Monsaraz, *Portugal* **43 G3** 38 25N 7 32W
Reh, Erg er, *Algeria* **111 C5** 27 48N 4 30 E
Rehar →, *India* **93 H10** 23 55N 82 40 E
Rehli, *India* **93 H8** 23 38N 79 5 E
Rehoboth, *Namibia* **116 C2** 23 15 S 17 4 E
Rehovot, *Israel* **103 D3** 31 54N 34 48 E
Reichenbach, *Germany* **30 E8** 50 37N 12 17 E
Reichenbach, *Switz.* **32 C5** 46 38N 7 42 E
Reid, *Australia* **125 F4** 30 49 S 128 26 E
Reiden, *Switz.* **32 B5** 47 14N 7 59 E
Reidsville, *Ga., U.S.A.* **152 C7** 32 6N 82 7W
Reidsville, *N.C., U.S.A.* **149 G6** 36 21N 79 40W
Reigate, *U.K.* **21 F7** 51 14N 0 12W
Reillo, *Spain* **40 F3** 39 54N 1 53W
Reims, *France* **27 C11** 49 15N 4 1 E
Reina Adelaida, Arch., *Chile* **176 D2** 52 20 S 74 0W
Reinach, *Aargau, Switz.* **32 B6** 47 14N 8 11 E
Reinach, *Basel, Switz.* **32 B5** 47 29N 7 35 E
Reinbeck, *U.S.A.* **156 B4** 42 19N 92 36W
Reinbek, *Germany* **30 B6** 53 30N 10 15 E
Reindeer →, *Canada* **143 B8** 55 36N 103 11W
Reindeer I., *Canada* **143 C9** 52 30N 98 0W
Reindeer L., *Canada* **143 B8** 57 15N 102 15W
Reinga, C., *N.Z.* **130 A1** 34 25 S 172 43 E
Reinosa, *Spain* **42 B6** 43 2N 4 15W
Reinsvoll, *Norway* **18 D7** 60 40N 10 38 E
Reitan, *Norway* **18 B8** 62 49N 11 22 E
Reitz, *S. Africa* **117 D4** 27 48 S 28 29 E
Reivilo, *S. Africa* **116 D3** 27 36 S 24 8 E
Rejaf, *Sudan* **107 G3** 4 45N 31 35 E
Rejmyre, *Sweden* **17 F9** 58 50N 15 55 E
Rejowiec Fabryczny, *Poland* **55 G10** 51 5N 23 17 E
Reka →, *Slovenia* **45 C11** 45 40N 14 0 E
Rekovac, *Serbia, Yug.* **50 C5** 43 51N 21 3 E
Reliance, *Canada* **143 A7** 63 0N 109 20W
Relizane, *Algeria* **111 A5** 35 44N 0 31 E
Remad, Oued →, *Algeria* **111 B4** 33 28N 1 20W
Rémalard, *France* **26 D7** 48 26N 0 47 E
Remarkable, Mt., *Australia* **128 B3** 32 48 S 138 10 E
Rembang, *Indonesia* **85 D4** 6 42 S 111 21 E
Rembau, *Malaysia* **84 B2** 2 35N 102 6 E
Rembert, *U.S.A.* **152 A9** 34 6N 80 32W
Remchi, *Algeria* **111 A4** 35 2N 1 26W
Remedios, *Colombia* **168 B3** 7 2N 74 41W
Remedios, *Panama* **164 E3** 8 15N 81 50W
Remeshk, *Iran* **97 E8** 26 55N 58 50 E
Remetea, *Romania* **53 D10** 46 45N 25 29 E
Remich, *Lux.* **24 E6** 49 32N 6 22 E
Remington, *U.S.A.* **157 D9** 40 46N 87 9W
Rémire, *Fr. Guiana* **169 C7** 4 53N 52 17W
Remiremont, *France* **27 D13** 48 2N 6 36 E
Remo, *Ethiopia* **107 F5** 6 48N 41 20 E
Remontnoye, *Russia* **61 G6** 46 34N 43 37 E
Remoulins, *France* **29 E8** 43 55N 4 35 E
Remscheid, *Germany* **24 C7** 51 11N 7 12 E
Ren Xian, *China* **74 F8** 37 8N 114 40 E
Rena, *Norway* **18 C8** 61 8N 11 20 E
Rena →, *Norway* **18 C8** 61 8N 11 23 E
Renascença, *Brazil* **168 D4** 3 50 S 66 21W
Rend Lake, *U.S.A.* **156 F8** 38 2N 88 58W
Rendang, *Indonesia* **79 J18** 8 26 S 115 25 E
Rende, *Italy* **47 C9** 39 20N 16 11 E
Rendína, *Greece* **48 B3** 39 4N 21 58 E
Rendova, *Solomon Is.* **133 M9** 8 33 S 157 17 E
Rendsburg, *Germany* **30 A5** 54 17N 9 39 E
Renens, *Switz.* **32 C3** 46 32N 6 35 E
Renfrew, *Canada* **140 C4** 45 30N 76 40W
Renfrewshire □, *U.K.* **22 F4** 55 49N 4 38W
Renfroe, *U.S.A.* **152 C5** 32 14N 84 43W
Rengat, *Indonesia* **84 C2** 0 30 S 102 45 E
Rengo, *Chile* **174 C1** 34 24 S 70 50W
Renhua, *China* **77 E9** 25 5N 113 40 E
Renhuai, *China* **76 D6** 27 48N 106 24 E
Reni, *Ukraine* **59 K5** 45 28N 28 15 E
Renigunta, *India* **95 H4** 13 38N 79 30 E
Renk, *Sudan* **107 E3** 11 50N 32 50 E
Renland, *Greenland* **10 C8** 71 10N 26 30W
Renmark, *Australia* **128 C4** 34 11 S 140 43 E
Rennebu, *Norway* **18 B6** 62 52N 9 49 E
Rennell, *Solomon Is.* **133 N11** 11 40 S 160 10 E
Rennell Sd., *Canada* **142 C2** 53 23N 132 35W
Renner Springs, *Australia* **126 B1** 18 20 S 133 47 E
Rennes, *France* **26 D5** 48 7N 1 41W
Rennie L., *Canada* **143 A7** 61 32N 105 35W
Reno, *U.S.A.* **160 F7** 39 31N 119 48W
Reno →, *Italy* **45 D9** 44 38N 12 16 E
Renovo, *U.S.A.* **150 E7** 41 20N 77 45W
Renqiu, *China* **74 E9** 38 43N 116 5 E
Rens, *Denmark* **17 K3** 54 54N 9 5 E
Renshou, *China* **76 C5** 30 3N 104 9 E
Rensselaer, *Ind., U.S.A.* **157 D9** 40 57N 87 9W
Rensselaer, *N.Y., U.S.A.* **151 D11** 42 38N 73 45W
Rentería, *Spain* **40 B3** 43 19N 1 54W
Renton, *U.S.A.* **160 C4** 47 29N 122 12W
Renwick, *N.Z.* **131 B8** 41 30 S 173 51 E
Réo, *Burkina Faso* **112 C4** 12 28N 2 35W
Reo, *Indonesia* **82 C2** 8 19 S 120 30 E
Reocín, *Spain* **42 B6** 43 21N 4 5W
Reotipur, *India* **93 G10** 25 33N 83 45 E
Repalle, *India* **95 F5** 16 2N 80 45 E
Répcelak, *Hungary* **52 C2** 47 24N 17 1 E
Republic, *Mo., U.S.A.* **155 G8** 37 7N 93 29W
Republic, *Wash., U.S.A.* **158 B4** 48 39N 118 44W
Republican →, *U.S.A.* **154 F6** 39 4N 96 48W
Republiek, *Surinam* **169 B6** 5 30N 55 13W
Repulse B., *Australia* **126 J6** 20 35 S 148 46 E
Repulse Bay, *Canada* **139 B11** 66 30N 86 30W
Requena, *Peru* **172 B3** 5 5 S 73 52W
Requena, *Spain* **41 F3** 39 30N 1 4W
Réquista, *France* **28 D6** 44 1N 2 32 E
Reşadiye = Datça, *Turkey* **49 E9** 36 46N 27 40 E
Reşadiye, *Turkey* **100 B7** 40 23N 37 20 E
Reşadiye Yarımadası, *Turkey* **49 E9** 36 40N 27 45 E
Resavica, *Serbia, Yug.* **50 B5** 44 4N 21 31 E
Resen, *Macedonia* **50 E5** 41 5N 21 0 E
Reserve, *U.S.A.* **159 K9** 33 43N 108 45W
Resht = Rasht, *Iran* **97 B6** 37 20N 49 40 E
Résia, *Italy* **33 C11** 46 50N 10 31 E
Resistencia, *Argentina* **174 B4** 27 30 S 59 0W
Reşiţa, *Romania* **52 E6** 45 18N 21 53 E
Resko, *Poland* **54 E2** 53 47N 15 25 E
Resolution I., *Canada* **139 B13** 61 30N 65 0W
Resolution I., *N.Z.* **131 F1** 45 40 S 166 40 E
Resplandes, *Brazil* **170 C2** 6 17 S 45 13W
Resplendor, *Brazil* **171 E3** 19 20 S 41 15W
Ressano Garcia, *Mozam.* **117 D5** 25 25 S 32 0 E
Reston, *Canada* **143 D8** 49 33N 101 6W
Reszel, *Poland* **54 D8** 54 4N 21 10 E
Retalhuleu, *Guatemala* **164 D1** 14 33N 91 46W
Retenue, L. de, *Dem. Rep. of the Congo* **119 E2** 11 0 S 27 0 E
Retezat, Munţii, *Romania* **52 E8** 45 25N 23 0 E
Retford, *U.K.* **20 D7** 53 19N 0 56W
Rethel, *France* **27 C11** 49 30N 4 20 E
Rethem, *Germany* **30 C5** 52 47N 9 22 E
Réthímnon, *Greece* **39 E5** 35 18N 24 30 E
Réthímnon □, *Greece* **39 E5** 35 23N 24 28 E
Reti, *Pakistan* **92 E3** 28 5N 69 48 E
Retiche, Alpi, *Switz.* **33 D10** 46 30N 10 0 E
Retiers, *France* **26 E5** 47 55N 1 23W
Retortillo, *Spain* **42 E4** 40 48N 6 21W
Retournac, *France* **29 C8** 45 12N 4 2 E
Rétság, *Hungary* **52 C4** 47 58N 19 10 E
Rettenberg, *Germany* **33 A10** 47 35N 10 18 E
Réunion ■, *Ind. Oc.* **105 J9** 21 0 S 56 0 E
Reus, *Spain* **40 D6** 41 10N 1 5 E
Reuss →, *Switz.* **33 B6** 47 16N 8 24 E
Reuterstadt Stavenhagen, *Germany* **30 B8** 53 42N 12 54 E
Reutlingen, *Germany* **31 G5** 48 29N 9 12 E
Reutte, *Austria* **34 D3** 47 29N 10 42 E
Reval = Tallinn, *Estonia* **15 G21** 59 22N 24 48 E
Revda, *Russia* **64 C7** 56 48N 59 57 E
Revel, *France* **28 E6** 43 28N 2 1 E
Revelganj, *India* **93 G11** 25 50N 84 40 E
Revelstoke, *Canada* **142 C5** 51 0N 118 10W
Reventazón, *Peru* **172 B1** 6 10 S 80 58W
Revigny-sur-Ornain, *France* **27 D11** 48 49N 4 59 E
Revillagigedo, Is. de, *Pac. Oc.* **162 D2** 18 40N 112 0W
Revin, *France* **27 C11** 49 55N 4 39 E
Revolyutsii, Pik, *Tajikistan* **65 D6** 38 31N 72 21 E
Revolyutsiya, Qullai = Revolyutsii, Pik, *Tajikistan* **65 D6** 38 31N 72 21 E
Revúca, *Slovak Rep.* **35 C13** 48 41N 20 7 E
Revuè →, *Mozam.* **119 F3** 19 50 S 34 0 E
Rewa, *India* **93 G9** 24 33N 81 25 E
Rewa →, *Guyana* **169 C6** 3 19N 58 42W
Rewari, *India* **92 E7** 28 15N 76 40 E
Rexburg, *U.S.A.* **158 E8** 43 49N 111 47W
Rey, *Iran* **97 C6** 35 35N 51 25 E
Rey, I. del, *Panama* **164 E4** 8 20N 78 30W
Rey, Mayo →, *Cameroon* **114 A2** 8 47N 14 1 E
Rey, Rio-del-→, *Cameroon* **114 B1** 4 31N 8 45 E
Rey Bouba, *Cameroon* **114 A2** 8 40N 14 15 E
Rey Malabo, *Eq. Guin.* **113 E6** 3 45N 8 50 E
Reyðarfjörður, *Iceland* **11 B12** 65 2N 14 13W
Reyes, *Bolivia* **172 C4** 14 19 S 67 23W
Reyes, Pt., *U.S.A.* **160 H3** 38 0N 123 0W
Reyhanlı, *Turkey* **100 D7** 36 16N 36 35 E
Reykholt, *Árnessýsla, Iceland* **11 C5** 64 40N 21 18W
Reykholt, *Borgarfjarðarsýsla, Iceland* **11 C6** 64 10N 20 25W
Reykjahlið, *Iceland* **11 B10** 65 40N 16 55W
Reykjanes, *Iceland* **11 D4** 63 48N 22 40W
Reykjavík, *Iceland* **11 C5** 64 10N 21 57W
Reynolds, *Ga., U.S.A.* **152 C5** 32 33N 84 6W
Reynolds, *Ill., U.S.A.* **156 C6** 41 20N 90 40W
Reynolds Ra., *Australia* **124 D5** 22 30 S 133 0 E
Reynoldsville, *Ga., U.S.A.* **152 E5** 30 51N 84 47W
Reynoldsville, *Pa., U.S.A.* **150 E6** 41 5N 78 58W
Reynosa, *Mexico* **163 B5** 26 5N 98 18W
Rēzekne, *Latvia* **15 H22** 56 30N 27 17 E
Rezh, *Russia* **64 C8** 57 23N 61 24 E
Rezina, *Moldova* **53 C13** 47 45N 28 58 E
Rezovo, *Bulgaria* **51 D12** 42 0N 28 0 E
Rezvān, *Iran* **97 E8** 27 34N 56 6 E
Rgotina, *Serbia, Yug.* **50 B6** 44 1N 22 17 E
Rhamnus, *Greece* **48 C6** 38 12N 24 3 E
Rharbi, Zahrez, *Algeria* **111 B5** 34 50N 2 55 E
Rharis, O. →, *Algeria* **111 C6** 26 0N 5 4 E
Rhayader, *U.K.* **21 E4** 52 18N 3 29W
Rheda-Wiedenbrück, *Germany* **30 D4** 51 50N 8 20 E
Rhede, *Germany* **30 D2** 51 50N 6 42 E
Rhein →, *Europe* **24 C6** 51 52N 6 2 E
Rhein-Main-Donau-Kanal, *Germany* **31 F7** 49 1N 11 27 E
Rheinbach, *Germany* **30 E2** 50 38N 6 57 E
Rheine, *Germany* **30 C3** 52 17N 7 26 E
Rheineck, *Switz.* **33 B9** 47 28N 9 31 E
Rheinfelden, *Germany* **31 H3** 47 33N 7 47 E
Rheinfelden, *Switz.* **32 A5** 47 32N 7 47 E
Rheinhessen-Pfalz □, *Germany* **31 F3** 49 20N 8 0 E
Rheinland-Pfalz □, *Germany* **31 E2** 50 0N 7 0 E
Rheinsberg, *Germany* **30 B8** 53 6N 12 54 E
Rheinwaldhorn, *Switz.* **33 D8** 46 30N 9 3 E
Rheris, Oued →, *Morocco* **110 B4** 30 50N 4 34W
Rhin = Rhein →, *Europe* **24 C6** 51 52N 6 2 E
Rhine = Rhein →, *Europe* **24 C6** 51 52N 6 2 E
Rhine, *U.S.A.* **152 D6** 31 59N 83 12W
Rhinebeck, *U.S.A.* **151 E11** 41 56N 73 55W
Rhineland-Palatinate = Rheinland-Pfalz □, *Germany* **31 E2** 50 0N 7 0 E
Rhinelander, *U.S.A.* **154 C10** 45 38N 89 25W
Rhinns Pt., *U.K.* **22 F2** 55 40N 6 29W
Rhino Camp, *Uganda* **118 B3** 3 0N 31 22 E
Rhir, Cap, *Morocco* **110 B3** 30 38N 9 54W
Rho, *Italy* **44 C6** 45 32N 9 2 E
Rhode Island □, *U.S.A.* **151 E13** 41 40N 71 30W
Rhodes = Ródhos, *Greece* **38 E12** 36 15N 28 10 E
Rhodesia = Zimbabwe ■, *Africa* **119 F3** 19 0 S 30 0 E
Rhodope Mts. = Rhodopi Planina, *Bulgaria* **51 E8** 41 40N 24 20 E
Rhodopi Planina, *Bulgaria* **51 E8** 41 40N 24 20 E
Rhön, *Germany* **30 E5** 50 24N 9 58 E
Rhondda, *U.K.* **21 F4** 51 39N 3 31W
Rhondda Cynon Taff □, *U.K.* **21 F4** 51 42N 3 27W
Rhône □, *France* **29 C8** 45 54N 4 35 E
Rhône →, *France* **29 E8** 43 28N 4 42 E
Rhône-Alpes □, *France* **29 C9** 45 40N 6 0 E
Rhum, *U.K.* **22 E2** 57 0N 6 20W
Rhyl, *U.K.* **20 D4** 53 20N 3 29W
Ri-Aba, *Eq. Guin.* **113 E6** 3 28N 8 40 E
Riachão, *Brazil* **170 C2** 7 20 S 46 37W
Riacho de Santana, *Brazil* **171 D3** 13 37 S 42 57W
Rialma, *Brazil* **171 E2** 15 18 S 49 34W
Riang, *India* **90 B4** 27 31N 92 56 E
Riangnom, *Sudan* **107 F3** 9 55N 30 1 E
Riaño, *Spain* **42 C6** 42 59N 4 59W
Rians, *France* **29 E9** 43 37N 5 44 E
Riansáres →, *Spain* **43 F7** 39 32N 3 18W

Rokan →, Indonesia 84 B2 2 0N 100 50 E
Rokel →, S. Leone 112 D2 8 30N 12 48W
Rokiškis, Lithuania 15 J21 55 55N 25 35 E
Rokitno, Russia 59 G8 50 57N 35 56 E
Rokycany, Czech Rep. 34 B6 49 43N 13 35 E
Rolândia, Brazil 175 A5 23 18 S 51 23W
Røldal, Norway 18 E3 59 47N 6 50 E
Rolfe, U.S.A. 156 B2 42 49N 94 31W
Rolla, U.S.A. 155 G9 37 57N 91 46W
Rolle, Switz. 32 D2 46 28N 6 20 E
Rolleston, Australia 126 C4 24 28 S 148 35 E
Rolleston, N.Z. 131 D7 43 35 S 172 24 E
Rolling Fork →, U.S.A. 157 G11 37 55N 85 50W
Rollingstone, Australia 126 B4 19 2 S 146 24 E
Rom, Norway 18 F4 58 8N 7 5 E
Rom, Sudan 107 F3 9 54N 32 16 E
Roma, Australia 127 D4 26 32 S 148 49 E
Roma, Italy 45 G9 41 54N 12 29 E
Roma, Sweden 17 G12 57 32N 18 26 E
Roma, U.S.A. 155 M5 26 25N 99 1W
Romain C., U.S.A. 149 J6 33 0N 79 22W
Romaine, Canada 141 B7 50 13N 60 40W
Romaine →, Canada 141 B7 50 18N 63 47W
Roman, Bulgaria 50 C7 43 8N 23 57 E
Roman, Romania 53 D11 46 57N 26 55 E
Roman-Kosh, Gora, Ukraine 59 K8 44 37N 34 15 E
Romanche →, France 29 C9 45 5N 5 43 E
Romang, Indonesia 82 C3 7 30 S 127 20 E
Români, Egypt 103 E1 30 59N 32 38 E
Romania ■, Europe 53 D10 46 0N 25 0 E
Romanija, Bos.-H. 52 G3 43 50N 18 45 E
Romano, C., U.S.A. 153 K8 25 51N 81 41W
Romano, Cayo, Cuba 164 B4 22 0N 77 30W
Romanovka = Basarabeasca, Moldova 53 D13 46 21N 28 58 E
Romans-sur-Isère, France 29 C9 45 3N 5 3 E
Romanshorn, Switz. 33 A8 47 33N 9 22 E
Romanzof C., U.S.A. 144 F6 61 49N 166 6W
Rombari, Sudan 107 G3 4 33N 31 2 E
Rombebai, Danau, Indonesia 83 B5 1 50 S 137 53 E
Romblon, Phil. 80 E4 12 33N 122 17 E
Romblon □, Phil. 80 E4 12 30N 122 15 E
Romblon Pass, Phil. 80 E4 12 27N 122 12 E
Rome = Roma, Italy 45 G9 41 54N 12 29 E
Rome, Ga., U.S.A. 149 H3 34 15N 85 10W
Rome, N.Y., U.S.A. 151 C9 43 13N 75 27W
Rome, Pa., U.S.A. 151 E8 41 51N 76 21W
Romeoville, U.S.A. 157 C8 41 39N 88 3W
Rometta, Italy 47 D8 38 10N 15 25 E
Romilly-sur-Seine, France 27 D10 48 31N 3 44 E
Romitan, Uzbekistan 65 D2 39 56N 64 23 E
Rommani, Morocco 110 B3 33 31N 6 40W
Romney, U.S.A. 148 F6 39 21N 78 45W
Romney Marsh, U.K. 21 F8 51 2N 0 54 E
Romny, Ukraine 59 G7 50 48N 33 28 E
Rømø, Denmark 17 J2 55 10N 8 30 E
Romodan, Ukraine 59 G7 49 55N 33 15 E
Romodanovo, Russia 60 C7 54 26N 45 23 E
Romont, Switz. 32 C3 46 42N 6 54 E
Romorantin-Lanthenay, France 27 E8 47 21N 1 45 E
Rompin →, Malaysia 84 B2 2 49N 103 29 E
Romsdalen, Norway 15 E12 62 25N 7 52 E
Romsdalsfjorden, Norway 18 B4 62 38N 7 20 E
Romsey, U.K. 21 G6 51 0N 1 29W
Ron, India 95 G2 15 40N 75 44 E
Ron, Vietnam 86 D6 17 53N 106 27 E
Rona, U.K. 22 D3 57 34N 5 59W
Ronan, U.S.A. 158 C6 47 32N 114 6W
Roncador, Cayos, Colombia 164 D3 13 32N 80 4W
Roncador, Serra do, Brazil 171 D1 12 30 S 52 30W
Ronciglione, Italy 45 F9 42 17N 12 13 E
Ronco →, Italy 45 D9 44 24N 12 12 E
Ronda, Spain 43 J5 36 46N 5 12W
Ronda, Serranía de, Spain 43 J5 36 44N 5 3W
Rondane, Norway 15 F13 61 57N 9 50 E
Rondón, Colombia 168 B3 6 17N 71 6W
Rondônia, Brazil 173 C5 10 52 S 61 57W
Rondônia □, Brazil 173 C5 11 0 S 63 0W
Rondonópolis, Brazil 173 D7 16 28 S 54 38W
Rondslottet, Norway 18 C6 61 55N 9 45 E
Rong, Koh, Cambodia 87 G4 10 45N 103 15 E
Rong Jiang →, China 76 E7 24 35N 109 20 E
Rong Xian, Guangxi Zhuangzu, China 77 F8 22 50N 110 31 E
Rong Xian, Sichuan, China 76 C5 29 23N 104 22 E
Rong'an, China 76 E7 25 14N 109 22 E
Rongchang, China 76 C5 29 20N 105 32 E
Ronge, L. la, Canada 143 B7 55 6N 105 17W
Rongjiang, China 76 E7 25 57N 108 28 E
Rongotea, N.Z. 130 G4 40 19 S 175 25 E
Rongshui, China 76 E7 25 5N 109 12 E
Rønne, Denmark 17 J8 55 6N 14 43 E
Ronne Ice Shelf, Antarctica 7 D18 78 0 S 60 0W
Ronneby, Sweden 17 H9 56 12N 15 17 E
Ronnebyån →, Sweden 17 H9 56 11N 15 18 E
Rönneshytta, Sweden 17 F9 58 56N 15 2 E
Ronsard, C., Australia 125 D1 24 46 S 113 10 E
Ronse, Belgium 24 D3 50 45N 3 35 E
Ronuro →, Brazil 173 C7 11 56 S 53 33W
Roodepoort, S. Africa 117 D4 26 11 S 27 54 E
Roodhouse, U.S.A. 156 E6 39 29N 90 24W
Roof Butte, U.S.A. 159 H9 36 28N 109 5W
Rooiboklaagte →, Namibia 116 C3 20 50 S 21 0 E
Roon, Indonesia 83 B4 2 23 S 134 33 E
Rooniu, Mt., Tahiti 133 S16 17 49 S 149 12W
Roopville, U.S.A. 152 B4 33 27N 85 8W
Roorkee, India 92 E7 29 52N 77 59 E
Roosendaal, Neths. 24 C4 51 32N 4 29 E
Roosevelt, U.S.A. 158 F8 40 18N 109 59W
Roosevelt →, Brazil 173 B5 7 35 S 60 20W
Roosevelt, Mt., Canada 142 B3 58 26N 125 20W
Roosevelt I., Antarctica 7 D12 79 30 S 162 0W
Root, Switz. 33 B6 47 5N 8 23 E
Ropczyce, Poland 55 H8 50 4N 21 38 E
Roper →, Australia 126 A2 14 43 S 135 27 E
Roper Bar, Australia 126 A1 14 44 S 134 44 E
Roque Pérez, Argentina 174 D4 35 25 S 59 24W
Roquefort, France 28 D3 44 2N 0 20W
Roquemaure, France 29 D8 44 3N 4 48 E
Roquetas de Mar, Spain 41 J2 36 46N 2 36W
Roquetes, Spain 40 E5 40 50N 0 30 E
Roquevaire, France 29 E9 43 20N 5 36 E
Roraima □, Brazil 169 C5 2 0N 61 30W
Roraima, Mt., Venezuela 169 B5 5 10N 60 40W
Røros, Norway 15 E14 62 35N 11 23 E
Rorschach, Switz. 33 B8 47 28N 9 28 E
Rosa, Zambia 119 D3 9 33 S 31 15 E
Rosa, C., Algeria 111 A6 37 0N 8 16 E
Rosa, C., Ecuador 172 a 1 4 S 91 10W
Rosa, L., Bahamas 165 B5 21 0N 73 30W
Rosa, Monte, Europe 32 E5 45 57N 7 53 E
Rosais, Pta. dos, Azores 9 d1 38 45N 28 19W
Rosal de la Frontera, Spain 43 H3 37 59N 7 13W
Rosales, Phil. 80 D3 15 54N 120 38 E
Rosalia, U.S.A. 158 C5 47 14N 117 22W
Rosamond, U.S.A. 161 L8 34 52N 118 10W
Rosans, France 29 D9 44 24N 5 29 E
Rosario, Argentina 174 C3 33 0 S 60 40W
Rosário, Brazil 170 B3 3 0 S 44 15W
Rosario, Baja Calif., Mexico 162 B1 30 0N 115 50W
Rosario, Sinaloa, Mexico 162 C3 23 0N 105 52W
Rosario, Paraguay 174 A4 24 30 S 57 35W
Rosario, Phil. 81 G5 8 24N 125 59 E
Rosario, Villa del, Venezuela 168 A3 10 19N 72 19W
Rosario de la Frontera, Argentina 174 B3 25 50 S 65 0W
Rosario de Lerma, Argentina 174 A2 24 59 S 65 35W
Rosario del Tala, Argentina 174 C4 32 20 S 59 10W
Rosário do Sul, Brazil 175 C5 30 15 S 54 55W
Rosário Oeste, Brazil 173 C6 14 50 S 56 25W
Rosarito, Mexico 161 N9 32 18N 117 4W
Rosarno, Italy 47 D8 38 29N 15 58 E
Rosas = Roses, Spain 40 C8 42 19N 3 10 E
Roscoe, Miss., U.S.A. 156 G3 37 58N 93 48W
Roscoe, N.Y., U.S.A. 151 E10 41 56N 74 55W
Roscoff, France 26 D3 48 44N 3 58W
Roscommon, Ireland 23 C3 53 38N 8 11W
Roscommon □, Ireland 23 C3 53 49N 8 23W
Roscrea, Ireland 23 D4 52 57N 7 49W
Rose →, Australia 126 A2 14 16 S 135 45 E
Rose Belle, Mauritius 121 d 20 24 S 57 36 E
Rose Blanche, Canada 141 C8 47 38N 58 45W
Rose Hill, Mauritius 121 d 20 14 S 57 27 E
Rose Pt., Canada 142 C2 54 11N 131 39W
Rose Valley, Canada 143 C8 52 19N 103 49W
Roseau, Domin. 165 C7 15 20N 61 24W
Roseau, U.S.A. 154 A7 48 51N 95 46W
Rosebery, Australia 127 G4 41 46 S 145 33 E
Rosebud, Australia 128 E6 38 21 S 144 54 E
Rosebud, S. Dak., U.S.A. 154 D4 43 14N 100 51W
Rosebud, Tex., U.S.A. 155 K6 31 4N 96 59W
Roseburg, U.S.A. 158 E2 43 13N 123 20W
Rosedale, U.S.A. 155 J9 33 51N 91 2W
Roseland, U.S.A. 160 G4 38 25N 122 43W
Rosemary, Canada 142 C6 50 46N 112 5W
Rosenberg, U.S.A. 155 L7 29 34N 95 49W
Rosendaël, France 27 A9 51 3N 2 24 E
Rosendal, Norway 18 E3 59 59N 6 0 E
Rosendale, U.S.A. 156 D2 40 4N 94 51W
Rosenheim, Germany 31 H8 47 51N 12 7 E
Roses, Spain 40 C8 42 19N 3 10 E
Roses, G. de, Spain 40 C8 42 10N 3 15 E
Roseto degli Abruzzi, Italy 45 F11 42 41N 14 1 E
Rosetown, Canada 143 C7 51 35N 107 59W
Rosetta = Rashîd, Egypt 106 H7 31 21N 30 22 E
Roseville, Calif., U.S.A. 160 G5 38 45N 121 17W
Roseville, Ill., U.S.A. 156 D6 40 44N 90 40W
Roseville, Mich., U.S.A. 150 D2 42 30N 82 56W
Rosewood, Australia 127 D5 27 38 S 152 36 E
Roshkhvār, Iran 97 C8 34 58N 59 37 E
Roshtqala, Tajikistan 65 E5 37 16N 71 49 E
Rosières-en-Santerre, France 27 C9 49 49N 2 42 E
Rosignano Maríttimo, Italy 44 E7 43 24N 10 28 E
Rosignol, Guyana 169 B6 6 15N 57 30W
Roşiori de Vede, Romania 53 F10 44 9N 25 0 E
Rositsa, Bulgaria 51 C11 43 57N 27 57 E
Rositsa →, Bulgaria 51 C9 43 10N 25 30 E
Roskilde, Denmark 17 J6 55 38N 12 3 E
Roskilde Amtskommune □, Denmark 17 J6 55 35N 12 5 E
Roskovec, Albania 50 F3 40 44N 19 43 E
Roslavl, Russia 58 F7 53 57N 32 55 E
Rosmaninhal, Portugal 42 F3 39 44N 7 5W
Rosmead, S. Africa 116 E4 31 29 S 25 8 E
Røsnæs, Denmark 17 J4 55 44N 10 55 E
Rosolini, Italy 47 F7 36 49N 14 57 E
Rosporden, France 26 E3 47 57N 3 50W
Ross, Australia 127 G4 42 2 S 147 30 E
Ross, N.Z. 131 C5 42 53 S 170 49 E
Ross Béthio, Mauritania 112 B1 16 15N 16 8W
Ross I., Antarctica 7 D11 77 30 S 168 0 E
Ross Ice Shelf, Antarctica 7 E12 80 0 S 180 0 E
Ross L., U.S.A. 158 B3 48 44N 121 4W
Ross-on-Wye, U.K. 21 F5 51 54N 2 34W
Ross River, Australia 126 C1 23 44 S 134 30 E
Ross River, Canada 142 A2 62 30N 131 30W
Ross Sea, Antarctica 7 D11 74 0 S 178 0 E
Rossa, Switz. 33 D8 46 23N 9 8 E
Rossall Pt., U.K. 20 D4 53 55N 3 3W
Rossan Pt., Ireland 23 B3 54 42N 8 47W
Rossano, Italy 47 C9 39 36N 16 39 E
Rossburn, Canada 143 C8 50 40N 100 49W
Rosseau, Canada 150 A5 45 16N 79 39W
Rosseau L., Canada 150 A5 45 10N 79 35W
Rossel, C., Vanuatu 133 K4 20 23 S 166 36 E
Rossel I., Papua N. G. 132 F8 11 21 S 154 9 E
Rossens, Switz. 32 C4 46 43N 7 7 E
Rosses, The, Ireland 23 A3 55 2N 8 20W
Rossford, U.S.A. 157 C13 41 36N 83 34W
Rossignol, L., Canada 140 B5 52 43N 73 40W
Rossignol Res., Canada 141 D6 44 12N 65 10W
Rosskreppfjorden, Norway 18 E4 59 4N 7 10 E
Rossland, Canada 142 D5 49 6N 117 50W
Rosslare, Ireland 23 D5 52 17N 6 24W
Rosslau, Germany 30 D8 51 52N 12 15 E
Rosso, Mauritania 112 B1 16 40N 15 45W
Rosso, C., France 29 F12 42 13N 8 32 E
Rossosh, Russia 59 G10 50 15N 39 28 E
Røssvatnet, Norway 14 D16 65 45N 14 5 E
Rossville, Ill., U.S.A. 157 D9 40 23N 87 40W
Rossville, Ind., U.S.A. 157 D10 40 25N 86 36W
Røst, Norway 14 C15 67 32N 12 0 E
Rostāq, Afghan. 65 E4 37 7N 69 49 E
Rosthern, Canada 143 C7 52 40N 106 20W
Rostock, Germany 30 A8 54 5N 12 8 E
Rostov, Don, Russia 59 J10 47 15N 39 45 E
Rostov, Yaroslavl, Russia 58 D10 57 14N 39 25 E
Rostrenen, France 26 D3 48 14N 3 21W
Roswell, Ga., U.S.A. 152 A5 34 2N 84 22W
Roswell, N. Mex., U.S.A. 155 J2 33 24N 104 32W
Rota, Spain 43 J4 36 37N 6 20W
Rotan, U.S.A. 155 J4 32 51N 100 28W
Rote Wand, Austria 33 B9 47 11N 9 59 E
Rotenburg, Hessen, Germany 30 E5 50 59N 9 44 E
Rotenburg, Niedersachsen, Germany 30 B5 53 6N 9 25 E
Roth, Germany 31 F7 49 15N 11 5 E
Rothaargebirge, Germany 30 D4 51 2N 8 13 E
Rothenburg, Switz. 33 B6 47 6N 8 16 E
Rothenburg ob der Tauber, Germany 31 F6 49 23N 10 11 E
Rother →, U.K. 21 G8 50 59N 0 45 E
Rotherham, U.K. 20 D6 53 26N 1 20W
Rothes, U.K. 22 D5 57 32N 3 13W
Rothesay, Canada 141 C6 45 23N 66 0W
Rothesay, U.K. 22 F3 55 50N 5 3W
Rothrist, Switz. 32 B5 47 18N 7 54 E
Roti, Indonesia 82 D2 10 50 S 123 0 E
Rotja, Pta., Spain 38 D2 38 38N 1 35 E
Rotnes, Norway 18 D7 60 3N 10 51 E
Roto, Australia 129 B6 33 0 S 145 30 E
Rotoaira, L., N.Z. 130 F4 39 3 S 175 45 E
Rotoehu, L., N.Z. 130 E5 38 1 S 176 32 E
Rotoiti, L., Bay of Plenty, N.Z. 130 E5 38 2 S 176 26 E
Rotoiti, L., W. Coast, N.Z. 131 B7 41 51 S 172 49 E
Rotoma, L., N.Z. 130 E5 38 2 S 176 35 E
Rotondo, Mte., France 29 F13 42 14N 9 8 E
Rotoroa, L., N.Z. 131 B7 41 55 S 172 39 E
Rotorua, N.Z. 130 E5 38 9 S 176 16 E
Rotorua, L., N.Z. 130 E5 38 5 S 176 18 E
Rott →, Germany 31 G9 48 27N 13 25 E
Rotten →, Switz. 32 D5 46 18N 7 36 E
Rottenburg, Germany 31 G4 48 28N 8 55 E
Rottenmann, Austria 34 D7 47 31N 14 22 E
Rotterdam, Neths. 24 C4 51 55N 4 30 E
Rotterdam, U.S.A. 151 D10 42 48N 74 1W
Rottne, Sweden 17 G8 57 1N 14 54 E
Rottnest I., Australia 125 F2 32 0 S 115 27 E
Rottumeroog, Neths. 24 A6 53 33N 6 34 E
Rottweil, Germany 31 G4 48 9N 8 37 E
Rotuma, Fiji 134 J9 12 25 S 177 5 E
Roubaix, France 27 B10 50 40N 3 10 E
Roudnice nad Labem, Czech Rep. 34 A7 50 25N 14 15 E
Rouen, France 26 C8 49 27N 1 4 E
Rouergue, France 28 D5 44 15N 2 0 E
Rough Ridge, N.Z. 131 F4 45 10 S 169 55 E
Rouillac, France 28 C3 45 47N 0 4W
Rouleau, Canada 143 C8 50 10N 104 56W
Round I., Mauritius 121 d 19 51 S 57 45 E
Round Mountain, U.S.A. 158 G5 38 43N 117 4W
Round Mt., N.S.W., Australia 127 E5 30 26 S 152 16 E
Round Mt., N.S.W., Australia 129 A9 30 15 S 152 15 E
Round Rock, U.S.A. 155 K6 30 31N 97 41W
Roundup, U.S.A. 158 C9 46 27N 108 33W
Roura, Fr. Guiana 169 C7 4 44N 52 20W
Rousay, U.K. 22 B5 59 10N 3 2W
Rouses Point, U.S.A. 151 B11 44 59N 73 22W
Rouseville, U.S.A. 150 E5 41 28N 79 42W
Roussillon, Isère, France 29 C8 45 24N 4 49 E
Roussillon, Pyrénées-Or., France 28 F6 42 30N 2 35 E
Roussin, C., N. Cal. 133 U21 21 20 S 167 59 E
Rouxville, S. Africa 116 E4 30 25 S 26 50 E
Rouyn-Noranda, Canada 140 C4 48 20N 79 0W
Rovaniemi, Finland 14 C21 66 29N 25 41 E
Rovato, Italy 44 C7 45 34N 10 0 E
Rovenki, Ukraine 59 H10 48 5N 39 21 E
Rovereto, Italy 44 C8 45 53N 11 3 E
Roverud, Norway 18 D9 60 15N 12 3 E
Rovigo, Italy 45 C8 45 4N 11 47 E
Rovinj, Croatia 45 C10 45 5N 13 40 E
Rovìra, Colombia 168 C2 4 15N 75 20W
Rovno = Rivne, Ukraine 59 G4 50 40N 26 10 E
Rovnoye, Russia 60 E8 50 52N 46 3 E
Rovuma = Ruvuma →, Tanzania 119 E5 10 29 S 40 28 E
Row'ān, Iran 97 C6 35 8N 48 51 E
Rowena, Australia 127 D4 29 48 S 148 55 E
Rowley Shoals, Australia 124 C2 17 30 S 119 0 E
Roxa, Guinea-Biss. 112 C1 11 15N 15 45W
Roxas, Capiz, Phil. 81 F4 11 36N 122 49 E
Roxas, Isabela, Phil. 80 C3 17 8N 121 36 E
Roxas, Mind. Or., Phil. 80 E3 12 35N 121 31 E
Roxas, Palawan, Phil. 81 F2 10 20N 119 21 E
Roxboro, U.S.A. 149 G6 36 24N 78 59W
Roxborough, Trin. & Tob. 169 E10 11 15N 60 35W
Roxburgh, N.Z. 131 F4 45 33 S 169 19 E
Roxbury, U.S.A. 150 F7 40 6N 77 39W
Roxen, Sweden 17 F9 58 30N 15 40 E
Roy, Mont., U.S.A. 158 C9 47 20N 108 58W
Roy, N. Mex., U.S.A. 155 H2 35 57N 104 12W
Roy, Utah, U.S.A. 158 F7 41 10N 112 2W
Royal Canal, Ireland 23 C4 53 30N 7 13W
Royal Center, U.S.A. 157 D10 40 52N 86 30W
Royal Leamington Spa, U.K. 21 E6 52 18N 1 31W
Royal Nat. Park, Australia 129 C9 34 5 S 151 5 E
Royal Natal Nat. Park, S. Africa 117 D4 28 43 S 28 51 E
Royal Oak, U.S.A. 157 B13 42 30N 83 9W
Royal Tunbridge Wells, U.K. 21 F8 51 7N 0 16 E
Royale, Isle, U.S.A. 154 B10 48 0N 88 54W
Royalla, Australia 129 C8 35 30 S 149 9 E
Royan, France 28 C2 45 37N 1 2W
Roye, France 27 C9 49 42N 2 48 E
Royston, U.K. 21 E7 52 3N 0 0W
Rožaj, Montenegro, Yug. 50 D4 42 50N 20 11 E
Różan, Poland 55 F8 52 52N 21 25 E
Rozay-en-Brie, France 27 D9 48 41N 2 58 E
Rozdilna, Ukraine 59 J6 46 50N 30 2 E
Rozhyshche, Ukraine 59 G3 50 54N 25 15 E
Rožmitál pod Třemšínem, Czech Rep. 34 B6 49 36N 13 53 E
Rožňava, Slovak Rep. 35 C13 48 37N 20 35 E
Rozogi, Poland 54 E8 53 28N 21 19 E
Rozoy-sur-Serre, France 27 C11 49 40N 4 8 E
Rozzano, Italy 44 C6 45 22N 9 10 E
Rrëshen, Albania 50 E3 41 47N 19 49 E
Rrogozhine, Albania 50 E3 41 4N 19 50 E
Rtanj, Serbia, Yug. 50 C5 43 45N 21 50 E
Rtem, O. el →, Algeria 111 B6 33 29N 5 38 E
Rtishchevo, Russia 60 D6 52 18N 43 46 E
Rúa = A Rúa, Spain 42 C3 42 24N 7 6W
Ruacaná, Namibia 116 B1 17 27 S 14 21 E
Ruaha Nat. Park, Tanzania 118 D3 7 41 S 34 30 E
Ruahine Ra., N.Z. 130 F5 39 55 S 176 2 E
Ruamahanga →, N.Z. 130 H4 41 24 S 175 8 E
Ruapehu, N.Z. 130 F4 39 17 S 175 35 E
Ruapuke I., N.Z. 131 G3 46 46 S 168 31 E
Ruâq, W. →, Egypt 103 F2 30 0N 33 49 E
Ruatoria, N.Z. 130 D7 37 55 S 178 20 E
Ruavatu, Solomon Is. 133 M11 9 26 S 160 26 E
Ruawai, N.Z. 130 C2 36 8 S 173 59 E
Rub' al Khālī, Si. Arabia 99 C5 19 0N 48 0 E
Rubeho Mts., Tanzania 118 D4 6 50 S 36 25 E
Rubezhnoye = Rubizhne, Ukraine 59 H10 49 6N 38 25 E
Rubh a' Mhail, U.K. 22 F2 55 56N 6 8W
Rubha Hunish, U.K. 22 D2 57 42N 6 20W
Rubha Robhanais = Lewis, Butt of, U.K. 22 C2 58 31N 6 16W
Rubi, Spain 40 D7 41 29N 2 2 E
Rubiataba, Brazil 171 E2 15 8 S 49 48W
Rubicon →, U.S.A. 160 G5 38 53N 121 4W
Rubicone →, Italy 45 D9 44 8N 12 28 E
Rubik, Albania 50 E3 41 46N 19 47 E
Rubinéia, Brazil 171 F1 20 13 S 51 2W
Rubino, Ivory C. 112 D4 6 4N 4 18W
Rubio, Venezuela 168 B3 7 43N 72 22W
Rubizhne, Ukraine 59 H10 49 6N 38 25 E
Rubondo Nat. Park, Tanzania 118 C3 2 18 S 31 58 E
Rubtsovsk, Russia 66 D9 51 30N 81 10 E
Ruby, U.S.A. 144 D9 64 45N 155 30W
Ruby L., U.S.A. 158 F6 40 10N 115 28W
Ruby Mts., U.S.A. 158 F6 40 30N 115 20W
Rubyvale, Australia 126 C4 23 25 S 147 42 E
Rucheng, China 77 E9 25 33N 113 38 E
Ruciane-Nida, Poland 54 E8 53 40N 21 32 E
Rūd Sar, Iran 97 B6 37 8N 50 18 E
Ruda, Sweden 17 G10 57 6N 16 7 E
Ruda Śląska, Poland 55 H5 50 16N 18 50 E
Rudall, Australia 128 B2 33 43 S 136 17 E
Rudall →, Australia 124 D3 22 34 S 122 13 E
Rudall River Nat. Park, Australia 124 D3 22 38 S 122 30 E
Rūdbār, Afghan. 91 C1 30 9N 62 36 E
Rüdersdorf, Germany 30 C9 52 27N 13 47 E
Rudewa, Tanzania 119 E3 10 7 S 34 40 E
Rudkøbing, Denmark 17 K4 54 56N 10 41 E
Rudna, Poland 55 G3 51 30N 16 17 E
Rūdnīchnyy, Kazakstan 65 A9 44 40N 78 54 E
Rudnik, Bulgaria 51 D11 42 36N 27 30 E
Rudnik, Poland 55 H9 50 26N 22 15 E
Rudnik, Serbia, Yug. 50 B4 44 7N 20 35 E
Rudnya, Russia 58 E6 54 55N 31 7 E
Rudnyy, Kazakstan 64 E9 52 57N 63 7 E
Rudo, Bos.-H. 52 G4 43 41N 19 23 E
Rudolfa, Ostrov, Russia 66 A6 81 45N 58 30 E
Rudolstadt, Germany 30 E7 50 44N 11 19 E
Rudong, China 77 A13 32 20N 121 12 E
Rudozem, Bulgaria 51 E8 41 29N 24 51 E
Rudyard, U.S.A. 148 B3 46 14N 84 36W
Rue, France 27 B8 50 15N 1 40 E
Ruenya →, Africa 119 F3 16 24 S 33 48 E
Rufa'a, Sudan 107 E3 14 44N 33 22 E
Rufflin, U.S.A. 152 B9 33 0N 80 49W
Rufiji →, Tanzania 118 D4 7 50 S 39 15 E
Rufino, Argentina 174 C3 34 20 S 62 50W
Rufisque, Senegal 112 C1 14 40N 17 15W
Rufling Pt., Br. Virgin Is. 165 e 18 44N 64 27W
Rufunsa, Zambia 119 F2 15 4 S 29 34 E
Rugao, China 77 A13 32 23N 120 31 E
Rugby, U.K. 21 E6 52 23N 1 16W
Rugby, U.S.A. 154 A5 48 22N 100 0W
Rügen, Germany 30 A9 54 22N 13 24 E
Rugles, France 26 D7 48 50N 0 40 E
Ruhea, Bangla. 90 B2 26 10N 88 25 E
Ruhengeri, Rwanda 118 C2 1 30 S 29 36 E
Ruhla, Germany 30 E6 50 54N 10 23 E
Ruhland, Germany 30 D9 51 27N 13 51 E
Ruhnu, Estonia 15 H20 57 48N 23 15 E
Ruhr →, Germany 30 D2 51 27N 6 43 E
Ruhuhu →, Tanzania 119 E3 10 31 S 34 34 E
Rui Barbosa, Brazil 171 D3 12 18 S 40 27W
Rui'an, China 77 D13 27 47N 120 40 E
Ruichang, China 77 C10 29 40N 115 39 E
Ruidoso, U.S.A. 159 K11 33 20N 105 41W
Ruijin, China 77 E10 25 48N 116 0 E
Ruili, China 76 E1 24 1N 97 43 E
Ruivo, Pico, Madeira 9 c 32 45N 16 56W
Ruj, Bulgaria 50 D6 42 52N 22 34 E
Rujen, Macedonia 50 D6 42 9N 22 30 E
Rujm Tal'at al Jamā'ah, Jordan 103 E4 30 24N 35 30 E
Ruk, Pakistan 92 F3 27 50N 68 42 E
Rukhla, Pakistan 92 C4 32 27N 71 57 E
Rukwa □, Tanzania 118 D3 7 0 S 31 30 E
Rukwa, L., Tanzania 118 D3 8 0 S 32 20 E
Rulhieres, C., Australia 124 B4 13 56 S 127 22 E
Rum = Rhum, U.K. 22 E2 57 0N 6 20W
Rum Cay, Bahamas 165 B5 23 40N 74 58W
Rum Jungle, Australia 124 B5 13 0 S 130 59 E
Ruma, Serbia, Yug. 52 E4 45 0N 19 50 E
Ruma Nat. Park, Kenya 118 C3 0 39 S 34 18 E
Rumāḩ, Si. Arabia 96 E5 25 29N 47 10 E
Rumania = Romania ■, Europe 53 D10 46 0N 25 0 E
Rumaylah, Iraq 96 D5 30 47N 47 37 E
Rumbêk, Sudan 107 F2 6 54N 29 37 E
Rumberpon, Indonesia 83 B4 1 50 S 134 15 E
Rumburk, Czech Rep. 34 A7 50 57N 14 32 E
Rumford, U.S.A. 149 C10 44 33N 70 33W
Rumia, Poland 54 D5 54 37N 18 25 E
Rumilly, France 29 C9 45 53N 5 56 E
Rumoi, Japan 70 C10 43 56N 141 39 E
Rumonge, Burundi 118 C2 3 59 S 29 26 E
Rumson, U.S.A. 151 F11 40 23N 74 0W
Rumuruti, Kenya 118 B4 0 17N 36 32 E
Runan, China 74 H8 33 0N 114 30 E
Runanga, N.Z. 131 C6 42 25 S 171 15 E
Runaway, C., N.Z. 130 D6 37 32 S 177 59 E
Runaway Bay, Jamaica 164 a 18 27N 77 20W
Runcorn, U.K. 20 D5 53 21N 2 44W
Rundu, Namibia 116 B2 17 52 S 19 43 E
Rungwa, Tanzania 118 D3 6 55 S 33 32 E
Rungwa →, Tanzania 118 D3 7 36 S 31 50 E
Rungwa Game Reserve, Tanzania 118 D3 6 53 S 34 2 E
Rungwe, Tanzania 119 D3 9 11 S 33 32 E
Runka, Nigeria 113 C6 12 28N 7 20 E
Runn, Sweden 16 D9 60 30N 15 40 E
Runton Ra., Australia 124 D3 23 31 S 123 6 E
Ruokolahti, Finland 58 B5 61 17N 28 50 E
Ruoqiang, China 68 C3 38 55N 88 10 E
Rupa, India 90 B4 27 15N 92 21 E
Rupar, India 92 D7 31 2N 76 38 E
Rupat, Indonesia 84 B2 1 45N 101 40 E
Rupea, Romania 53 D10 46 2N 25 13 E
Rupen →, India 92 H4 23 28N 71 31 E
Rupert, U.S.A. 158 E7 42 37N 113 41W
Rupert →, Canada 140 B4 51 29N 78 45W
Rupert B., Canada 140 B4 51 35N 79 0W
Rupert House = Waskaganish, Canada 140 B4 51 30N 78 40W
Rupsa, India 93 J12 21 37N 87 1 E
Rupununi →, Guyana 169 C6 4 3N 58 35W
Rur →, Germany 30 D1 51 11N 5 59 E
Rurópolis, Brazil 169 D7 4 3 S 54 59W
Rurrenabaque, Bolivia 172 C4 14 30 S 67 32W
Rus →, Spain 41 F2 39 30N 2 30W
Rusambo, Zimbabwe 119 F3 16 30 S 32 4 E
Rusape, Zimbabwe 119 F3 18 35 S 32 8 E
Ruschuk = Ruse, Bulgaria 51 C9 43 48N 25 59 E
Ruse, Bulgaria 51 C9 43 48N 25 59 E
Ruse □, Bulgaria 51 C10 43 35N 26 20 E
Ruşeţu, Romania 53 F12 44 57N 27 14 E
Rush, Ireland 23 C5 53 31N 6 6W
Rushan, China 75 F11 36 56N 121 30 E
Rushden, U.K. 21 E7 52 18N 0 35W
Rushikulya →, India 94 E7 19 23N 85 5 E
Rushmore, Mt., U.S.A. 154 D3 43 53N 103 28W
Rushon, Tajikistan 65 E5 37 57N 71 33 E
Rushville, Ill., U.S.A. 156 D6 40 7N 90 34W
Rushville, Ind., U.S.A. 157 E11 39 37N 85 27W
Rushville, Nebr., U.S.A. 154 D3 42 43N 102 28W
Rushworth, Australia 129 D6 36 32 S 145 1 E
Ruskin, U.S.A. 153 H7 27 43N 82 26W
Russas, Brazil 170 B4 4 55 S 37 50W
Russell, Canada 143 C8 50 50N 101 20W
Russell, N.Z. 130 B3 35 16 S 174 10 E
Russell, Fla., U.S.A. 152 E8 30 3N 81 45W
Russell, Kans., U.S.A. 154 F5 38 54N 98 52W
Russell, N.Y., U.S.A. 151 B9 44 27N 75 9W
Russell, Pa., U.S.A. 150 E5 41 56N 79 8W
Russell Is., Solomon Is. 133 M10 9 4 S 159 12 E
Russell L., Man., Canada 143 B8 56 15N 101 30W
Russell L., N.W.T., Canada 142 A5 63 5N 115 44W
Russellkonda, India 94 E7 19 57N 84 42 E
Russells Point, U.S.A. 157 D13 40 28N 83 54W
Russellville, Ala., U.S.A. 149 H2 34 30N 87 44W
Russellville, Ark., U.S.A. 155 H8 35 17N 93 8W
Russellville, Ky., U.S.A. 149 G2 36 51N 86 53W
Rüsselsheim, Germany 31 F4 49 59N 8 23 E
Russi, Italy 45 D9 44 22N 12 2 E
Russia ■, Eurasia 67 C11 62 0N 105 0 E
Russian →, U.S.A. 160 G3 38 27N 123 8W
Russian Mission, U.S.A. 144 F7 61 47N 161 19W
Russiaville, U.S.A. 157 D10 40 25N 86 16W
Russkoye Ustie, Russia 6 B15 71 0N 149 0 E
Rust, Austria 35 D9 47 49N 16 42 E
Rustam, Pakistan 92 B5 34 25N 72 13 E
Rustam Shahr, Pakistan 92 F2 26 58N 66 6 E
Rustavi, Georgia 61 K7 41 30N 45 0 E
Rustenburg, S. Africa 116 D4 25 41 S 27 14 E
Ruston, U.S.A. 155 J8 32 32N 92 38W
Ruswil, Switz. 32 B6 47 5N 8 8 E
Rutana, Burundi 118 C3 3 55 S 30 0 E
Rute, Spain 43 H6 37 19N 4 23W
Ruteng, Indonesia 82 C2 8 35 S 120 30 E
Ruth, U.S.A. 150 C2 43 42N 82 45W
Rutherford, U.S.A. 160 G4 38 26N 122 24W
Rutherglen, Australia 129 D7 36 5 S 146 29 E
Rüti, Switz. 33 B7 47 16N 8 51 E

S

St-Jean-de-Maurienne, France 29 C10 45 16N 6 21 E
St-Jean-de-Monts, France 26 F4 46 47N 2 4W
St-Jean-du-Gard, France 28 D7 44 7N 3 52 E
St-Jean-en-Royans, France 29 C9 45 1N 5 18 E
St-Jean-Pied-de-Port, France 28 E2 43 10N 1 14W
St-Jean-Port-Joli, Canada 141 C5 47 15N 70 13W
St-Jean-sur-Richelieu, Canada 140 C5 45 20N 73 20W
St-Jérôme, Canada 140 C5 45 47N 74 0W
St. Joe, U.S.A. 157 C12 41 19N 84 54W
St. John, Canada 141 C6 45 20N 66 8W
St. John, U.S.A. 155 G5 38 0N 98 46W
St. John →, Liberia 112 D2 6 40N 9 10W
St. John →, U.S.A. 149 C12 45 12N 66 5W
St. John, C., Canada 141 C8 50 0N 55 32W
St. John I., U.S. Virgin Is. 165 e 18 20N 64 42W
St. John's, Antigua 165 C7 17 6N 61 51W
St. John's, Canada 141 C9 47 35N 52 40W
St. Johns, Ariz., U.S.A. 159 J9 34 30N 109 22W
St. Johns, Mich., U.S.A. 157 B12 43 0N 84 33W
St. Johns →, U.S.A. 152 E8 30 24N 81 24W
St. John's Pt., Ireland 23 B3 54 34N 8 27W
St. Johnsbury, U.S.A. 151 B12 44 25N 72 1W
St. Johnsville, U.S.A. 151 D10 43 0N 74 43W
St-Joseph, Martinique 164 c 14 39N 61 4W
St-Joseph, N. Cal. 133 K4 20 27 S 166 36 E
St-Joseph, Réunion 121 c 21 22 S 55 37 E
St. Joseph, Ill., U.S.A. 157 D8 40 7N 88 2W
St. Joseph, La., U.S.A. 155 K9 31 55N 91 14W
St. Joseph, Mich., U.S.A. 157 B10 42 6N 86 29W
St. Joseph, Mo., U.S.A. 156 E2 39 46N 94 50W
St. Joseph →, U.S.A. 157 B10 42 7N 86 29W
St. Joseph, I., Canada 140 C3 46 12N 83 58W
St. Joseph, L., Canada 140 B1 51 10N 90 35W
St. Joseph Pt., U.S.A. 152 F4 29 52N 85 24W
St-Jovite, Canada 140 C5 46 8N 74 38W
St-Juéry, France 28 E6 43 57N 2 12 E
St. Julian's, Malta 38 F7 35 55N 14 29 E
St-Julien-Chapteuil, France 29 C8 45 2N 4 4 E
St-Julien-de-Vouvantes, France 26 E5 47 38N 1 13W
St-Julien-en-Genevois, France 27 F13 46 9N 6 5 E
St-Junien, France 28 C4 45 53N 0 55 E
St-Just-en-Chaussée, France 27 C9 49 30N 2 25 E
St-Just-en-Chevalet, France 28 C7 45 55N 3 50 E
St. Kilda, N.Z. 131 F5 45 53 S 170 31 E
St. Kilda, U.K. 19 C2 57 49N 8 34W
St. Kitts & Nevis ■, W. Indies 165 C7 17 20N 62 40W
St. Laurent, Canada 143 C9 50 25N 97 58W
St-Laurent, Fr. Guiana 169 B7 5 29N 54 3W
St-Laurent-de-la-Salanque, France 28 F6 42 46N 2 59 E
St-Laurent-du-Pont, France 29 C9 45 23N 5 45 E
St-Laurent-en-Grandvaux, France 27 F12 46 35N 5 58 E
St-Laurent-Médoc, France 28 C3 45 8N 0 49W
St. Lawrence, Australia 126 C4 22 16 S 149 31 E
St. Lawrence, Canada 141 C8 46 54N 55 23W
St. Lawrence →, Canada 141 C6 49 30N 66 0W
St. Lawrence, Gulf of, Canada 141 C7 48 25N 62 0W
St. Lawrence I., U.S.A. 144 E5 63 30N 170 30W
St. Leonard, Canada 141 C6 47 12N 67 58W
St-Léonard-de-Noblat, France 28 C5 45 49N 1 29 E
St. Leonhard im Pitztal, Austria 33 B11 47 4N 10 51 E
St-Leu, Réunion 121 c 21 9 S 55 18 E
St. Lewis →, Canada 141 B8 52 26N 56 11W
St-Lô, France 26 C5 49 7N 1 5W
St-Louis, France 27 E14 47 30N 7 34 E
St-Louis, Guadeloupe 164 b 15 56N 61 19W
St-Louis, Réunion 121 c 21 16 S 55 25 E
St. Louis, Senegal 112 B1 16 8N 16 27W
St. Louis, U.S.A. 156 F6 38 37N 90 12W
St. Louis →, U.S.A. 154 B8 47 15N 92 45W
St-Loup-sur-Semouse, France 27 E13 47 53N 6 16 E
St. Lucia ■, W. Indies 165 f 14 0N 60 50W
St. Lucia, L., S. Africa 117 D5 28 5 S 32 30 E
St. Lucia Channel, W. Indies 165 D7 14 15N 61 0W
St. Lucie, U.S.A. 153 H9 27 29N 80 20W
St. Lucie Canal, U.S.A. 153 H9 27 10N 80 18W
St. Maarten, W. Indies 165 C7 18 0N 63 5W
St. Magnus B., U.K. 22 A7 60 25N 1 35W
St-Maixent-l'École, France 28 B3 46 24N 0 12W
St-Malo, France 26 D4 48 39N 2 1W
St-Malo, G. de, France 26 D4 48 50N 2 30W
St-Mandrier-sur-Mer, France 29 E9 43 4N 5 57 E
St-Marc, Haiti 165 C5 19 10N 72 41W
St-Marcellin, France 29 C9 45 9N 5 20 E
St-Marcouf, Îs., France 26 C5 49 30N 1 10W
St. Maries, U.S.A. 158 C5 47 19N 116 35W
St. Marks, U.S.A. 152 E5 30 9N 84 12W
St-Martin, W. Indies 165 C7 18 0N 63 0W
St-Martin, C., Martinique 164 c 14 52N 61 14W
St. Martin, L., Canada 143 C9 51 40N 98 30W
St-Martin-de-Crau, France 29 E8 43 38N 4 48 E
St-Martin-de-Ré, France 28 B2 46 12N 1 21W
St-Martin-d'Hères, France 29 C9 45 9N 5 45 E
St-Martin-Vésubie, France 29 D11 44 4N 7 15 E
St. Martins, Barbados 165 g 13 5N 59 28W
St-Martory, France 28 E4 43 9N 0 56 E
St. Mary, U.S.A. 156 G7 37 53N 89 57W
St. Mary, Mt., Papua N. G. 132 E4 8 8 S 147 2 E
St. Mary Is., India 95 H2 13 20N 74 35 E
St. Mary Pk., Australia 128 A3 31 32 S 138 34 E
St. Marys, Australia 127 G4 41 35 S 148 11 E
St. Marys, Canada 150 C3 43 20N 81 10W
St. Mary's, Corn., U.K. 21 H1 49 55N 6 18W
St. Mary's, Orkney, U.K. 22 C6 58 54N 2 54W
St. Mary's, Alaska, U.S.A. 144 E7 62 4N 163 10W
St. Marys, Ga., U.S.A. 152 E8 30 44N 81 33W
St. Marys, Ohio, U.S.A. 157 D12 40 33N 84 24W
St. Marys, Pa., U.S.A. 150 E6 41 26N 78 34W
St. Marys →, U.S.A. 152 E8 30 43N 81 27W
St. Mary's, C., Canada 141 C9 46 50N 54 12W
St. Mary's B., Canada 141 C9 46 50N 53 50W
St. Marys Bay, Canada 141 D6 44 25N 66 10W
St-Mathieu, Pte., France 26 D2 48 20N 4 45W
St. Matthew I., U.S.A. 144 F4 60 24N 172 42W
St. Matthews, Ky., U.S.A. 157 F11 38 15N 85 39W
St. Matthews, S.C., U.S.A. 152 B9 33 40N 80 46W
St. Matthews, I. = Zadetkyi Kyun, Burma 87 G1 10 0N 98 25 E
St. Matthias Group, Papua N. G. 132 A5 1 30 S 150 0 E
St-Maurice, Switz. 32 D4 46 13N 7 0 E
St-Maurice →, Canada 140 C5 46 21N 72 31W
St-Maximin-la-Ste-Baume, France 29 E9 43 27N 5 52 E
St-Médard-en-Jalles, France 28 D3 44 53N 0 43W
St-Méen-le-Grand, France 26 D4 48 11N 2 12W
St. Meinrad, U.S.A. 157 F10 38 10N 86 49W
St. Michael, U.S.A. 144 E7 63 29N 162 2W
St-Mihiel, France 27 D12 48 54N 5 32 E
St. Moritz, Switz. 31 J5 46 30N 9 51 E
St-Nazaire, France 26 E4 47 17N 2 12W
St. Neots, U.K. 21 E7 52 14N 0 15W
St-Nicolas-de-Port, France 27 D13 48 38N 6 18 E
St-Niklaas, Belgium 24 C4 51 10N 4 8 E
St. Niklaus, Switz. 32 D5 46 10N 7 49 E
St-Omer, France 27 B9 50 45N 2 15 E
St-Palais-sur-Mer, France 28 C2 45 38N 1 5W
St-Pamphile, Canada 141 C6 46 58N 69 48W
St-Pardoux-la-Rivière, France 28 C4 45 29N 0 45 E
St. Paris, U.S.A. 157 D13 40 8N 83 58W
St. Pascal, Canada 141 C6 47 32N 69 48W
St. Paul, Canada 142 C6 54 0N 111 17W
St-Paul, France 29 D10 44 31N 6 45 E
St-Paul, Réunion 121 c 20 59 S 55 17 E
St. Paul, Alaska, U.S.A. 144 H5 57 7N 170 17W
St. Paul, Ind., U.S.A. 157 E11 39 26N 85 38W
St. Paul, Minn., U.S.A. 154 C8 44 57N 93 6W
St. Paul, Nebr., U.S.A. 154 E5 41 13N 98 27W
St-Paul →, Canada 141 B8 51 27N 57 42W
St. Paul →, Liberia 112 D2 6 25N 10 48W
St. Paul, I., Ind. Oc. 121 H6 38 55 S 77 34 E
St-Paul-de-Fenouillet, France 28 F6 42 48N 2 30 E
St. Paul I., Canada 141 C7 47 12N 60 9W
St. Paul I., U.S.A. 144 H5 57 10N 170 15W
St-Paul-lès-Dax, France 28 E2 43 44N 1 3W
St. Paul's Bay, Malta 38 F7 35 57N 14 24 E
St-Péray, France 29 D8 44 57N 4 50 E
St. Peter, U.S.A. 154 C8 44 20N 93 57W
St. Peter-Ording, Germany 30 A4 54 20N 8 36 E
St. Peter Port, U.K. 21 H5 49 26N 2 33W
St. Peters, N.S., Canada 141 C7 45 40N 60 53W
St. Peters, P.E.I., Canada 141 C7 46 25N 62 35W
St. Petersburg = Sankt-Peterburg, Russia 58 C6 59 55N 30 20 E
St. Petersburg, U.S.A. 149 M4 27 46N 82 39W
St. Petersburg Beach, U.S.A. 153 H7 27 45N 82 45W
St-Philbert-de-Grand-Lieu, France 26 E5 47 2N 1 39W
St-Phillippe, Réunion 121 c 21 21 S 55 44 E
St-Pie, Canada 151 A12 45 30N 72 54W
St-Pierre, Martinique 164 c 14 45N 61 10W
St-Pierre, Réunion 121 c 21 19 S 55 28 E
St-Pierre, St- P. & M. 141 C8 46 46N 56 12W
St. Pierre, Seychelles 121 E3 9 20 S 46 0 E
St-Pierre, L., Canada 140 C5 46 12N 72 52W
St-Pierre-d'Oléron, France 28 C2 45 57N 1 19W
St-Pierre-en-Port, France 26 C7 49 48N 0 30 E
St-Pierre et Miquelon □, St- P. & M. 141 C8 46 55N 56 10W
St-Pierre-le-Moûtier, France 27 F10 46 47N 3 7 E
St-Pierre-sur-Dives, France 26 C6 49 2N 0 1W
St-Pol-de-Léon, France 26 D3 48 41N 4 0W
St-Pol-sur-Mer, France 27 A9 51 1N 2 20 E
St-Pol-sur-Ternoise, France 27 B9 50 23N 2 20 E
St-Pons, France 28 E6 43 30N 2 45 E
St-Pourçain-sur-Sioule, France 27 F10 46 18N 3 18 E
St-Priest, France 29 C8 45 42N 4 57 E
St-Quay-Portrieux, France 26 D4 48 39N 2 51W
St. Quentin, Canada 141 C6 47 30N 67 23W
St-Quentin, France 27 C10 49 50N 3 16 E
St-Rambert-d'Albon, France 29 C8 45 17N 4 49 E
St-Raphaël, France 29 E10 43 25N 6 46 E
St. Regis, U.S.A. 158 C6 47 18N 115 6W
St-Renan, France 26 D2 48 26N 4 37W
St. Robert, U.S.A. 156 G4 37 48N 92 9W
St-Saëns, France 26 C8 49 41N 1 16 E
St-Savin, France 28 B4 46 34N 0 53 E
St-Savinien, France 28 C3 45 53N 0 42W
St. Sebastien, Tanjon' i, Madag. 117 A8 12 26 S 48 44 E
St-Seine-l'Abbaye, France 27 E11 47 26N 4 47 E
St-Sernin-sur-Rance, France 28 E6 43 54N 2 35 E
St-Sever, France 28 E3 43 45N 0 35W
St-Siméon, Canada 141 C6 47 51N 69 54W
St. Simons I., U.S.A. 152 D8 31 12N 81 15W
St. Simons Island, U.S.A. 149 K5 31 9N 81 22W
St. Stephen, Canada 141 C6 45 16N 67 17W
St. Stephen, U.S.A. 152 B10 33 24N 79 55W
St-Sulpice, France 28 E5 43 46N 1 41 E
St-Sulpice-Laurière, France 28 B5 46 3N 1 29 E
St-Sulpice-les-Feuilles, France 28 B5 46 19N 1 21 E
St-Syprien = St-Cyprien, France 28 F7 42 37N 3 2 E
St-Thégonnec, France 26 D3 48 31N 3 57W
St. Thomas, Canada 140 D3 42 45N 81 10W
St. Thomas Bay, Malta 38 F8 35 51N 14 34 E
St. Thomas I., U.S. Virgin Is. 165 e 18 20N 64 55W
St-Tite, Canada 140 C5 46 45N 72 34W
St-Tropez, France 29 E10 43 17N 6 38 E
St. Troud = St. Truiden, Belgium 24 D5 50 48N 5 10 E
St. Truiden, Belgium 24 D5 50 48N 5 10 E
St-Vaast-la-Hougue, France 26 C5 49 35N 1 17W
St-Valery-en-Caux, France 26 C7 49 52N 0 43 E
St-Valéry-sur-Somme, France 27 B8 50 11N 1 38 E
St-Vallier, France 27 F11 46 38N 4 22 E
St-Vallier-de-Thiey, France 29 E10 43 42N 6 51 E
St-Varent, France 26 F6 46 53N 0 13W
St-Vaury, France 28 B5 46 12N 1 46 E
St. Vincent = São Vicente, C. Verde Is. 9 j 17 0N 25 0W
St. Vincent, Italy 44 C4 45 45N 7 39 E
St. Vincent, G., Australia 128 C3 35 0 S 138 0 E
St. Vincent & the Grenadines ■, W. Indies 165 D7 13 0N 61 10W
St-Vincent-de-Tyrosse, France 28 E2 43 39N 1 19W
St. Vincent Passage, W. Indies 165 D7 13 30N 61 0W
St-Vith, Belgium 24 D6 50 17N 6 9 E
St-Vivien-de-Médoc, France 28 C2 45 25N 1 2W
St. Walburg, Canada 143 C7 53 39N 109 12W
St-Yrieix-la-Perche, France 28 C5 45 31N 1 12 E
Saintala, India 94 D6 20 26N 83 20 E
Ste-Adresse, France 26 C7 49 31N 0 5 E
Ste-Agathe-des-Monts, Canada 140 C5 46 3N 74 17W
Ste-Anne, Guadeloupe 164 b 16 13N 61 24W
Ste. Anne, Seychelles 121 b 4 36 S 55 1 E
Ste-Anne, L., Canada 141 B6 50 0N 67 42W
Ste-Anne-des-Monts, Canada 141 C6 49 8N 66 30W
Ste-Croix, Switz. 32 C3 46 49N 6 34 E
Ste-Enimie, France 28 D7 44 22N 3 26 E
Ste-Foy-la-Grande, France 28 D4 44 50N 0 13 E
Ste. Genevieve, U.S.A. 156 G6 37 59N 90 2W
Ste-Hermine, France 28 B2 46 32N 1 4W
Ste-Livrade-sur-Lot, France 28 D4 44 24N 0 36 E
Ste-Marguerite →, Canada 141 B6 50 9N 66 36W
Ste. Marie, Gabon 114 C2 3 48 S 11 1 E
Ste-Marie, Martinique 164 c 14 48N 61 1W
Ste-Marie, Réunion 121 c 20 53 S 55 33 E
Ste-Marie-aux-Mines, France 27 D14 48 15N 7 12 E
Ste-Marie de la Madeleine, Canada 141 C5 46 26N 71 0W
Ste-Maure-de-Touraine, France 26 E7 47 7N 0 37 E
Ste-Maxime, France 29 E10 43 19N 6 39 E
Ste-Menehould, France 27 C11 49 5N 4 54 E
Ste-Mère-Église, France 26 C5 49 24N 1 19W
Ste-Rose, Guadeloupe 164 b 16 20N 61 45W
Ste-Rose, Réunion 121 c 21 8 S 55 45 E
Ste. Rose du Lac, Canada 143 C9 51 4N 99 30W
Ste-Savine, France 27 D11 48 18N 4 3 E
Ste-Sigolène, France 29 C8 45 15N 4 14 E
Saintes, France 28 C3 45 45N 0 37W
Saintes, I. des, Guadeloupe 164 b 15 50N 61 35W
Stes-Maries-de-la-Mer, France 29 E8 43 26N 4 26 E
Saintfield, U.K. 23 B6 54 28N 5 49W
Saintonge, France 28 C3 45 40N 0 50W
Saipan, Pac. Oc. 134 F6 15 12N 145 45 E
Sairang, India 90 D4 23 50N 92 45 E
Sairecábur, Cerro, Bolivia 174 A2 22 43 S 67 54W
Saitama □, Japan 73 A11 36 25N 139 30 E
Saiteli = Kadınhanı, Turkey 100 C5 38 14N 32 13 E
Saiţi, Moldova 53 D14 46 30N 29 24 E
Saito, Japan 72 E3 32 3N 131 24 E
Saiyid, Pakistan 92 C5 33 7N 73 2 E
Sajama, Bolivia 172 D4 18 7 S 69 0W
Sajama, Nevado, Bolivia 172 D4 18 6 S 68 54W
Sajan, Serbia, Yug. 52 E5 45 50N 20 20 E
Sajó →, Hungary 52 C6 47 56N 21 7 E
Sajószentpéter, Hungary 52 B5 48 12N 20 44 E
Sajum, India 93 C8 33 20N 79 0 E
Sak →, S. Africa 116 E3 30 52 S 20 25 E
Saka Kalat, Pakistan 91 D2 27 3N 65 3 E
Sakaba, Nigeria 113 C6 11 4N 5 35 E
Sakai, Japan 73 C7 34 30N 135 30 E
Sakaide, Japan 72 C5 34 19N 133 50 E
Sakaiminato, Japan 72 B5 35 38N 133 11 E
Sakākah, Si. Arabia 96 D4 30 0N 40 8 E
Sakakawea, L., U.S.A. 154 B4 47 30N 101 25W
Sakami →, Canada 140 B4 53 40N 76 40W
Sakami, L., Canada 140 B4 53 15N 77 0W
Sâkâne, 'Erg i-n, Mali 113 A4 20 30N 1 30W
Sakania, Dem. Rep. of the Congo 119 E2 12 43 S 28 30 E
Sakar I., Papua N. G. 132 C5 5 25 S 148 6 E
Sakaraha, Madag. 117 C7 22 55 S 44 32 E
Sakarya, Turkey 100 B4 40 48N 30 25 E
Sakarya →, Turkey 100 B4 41 7N 30 39 E
Sakashima-Guntō, Japan 71 M2 24 46N 124 0 E
Sakassou, Ivory C. 112 D3 7 29N 5 19W
Sakata, Japan 70 E9 38 55N 139 50 E
Sakawa, Japan 72 D5 33 28N 133 11 E
Sakchu, N. Korea 75 D13 40 23N 125 2 E
Sakeny →, Madag. 117 C8 20 0 S 45 25 E
Sakété, Benin 113 D5 6 40N 2 45 E
Sakha □, Russia 67 C13 66 0N 130 0 E
Sakhalin, Russia 67 D15 51 0N 143 0 E
Sakhalinskiy Zaliv, Russia 67 D15 54 0N 141 0 E
Sakhi Gopal, India 94 E7 19 58N 85 50 E
Şaki, Azerbaijan 61 K8 41 10N 47 5 E
Šakiai, Lithuania 15 J20 54 59N 23 2 E
Sakmara →, Russia 64 F5 51 46N 55 1 E
Sakoli, India 94 D4 21 5N 79 59 E
Sakon Nakhon, Thailand 86 D5 17 10N 104 9 E
Sakrand, Pakistan 92 F3 26 10N 68 15 E
Sakri, Maharashtra, India 93 F12 26 13N 86 5 E
Sakri, Maharashtra, India 94 D2 21 2N 74 20 E
Sakrivier, S. Africa 116 E3 30 54 S 20 28 E
Sakskøbing, Denmark 17 K5 54 49N 11 39 E
Sakti, India 93 H10 22 2N 82 58 E
Saku, Japan 73 A10 36 17N 138 31 E
Sakuma, Japan 73 B9 35 3N 137 49 E
Sakura, Japan 73 B12 35 43N 140 14 E
Sakurai, Japan 73 C7 34 30N 135 51 E
Saky, Ukraine 59 K7 45 9N 33 34 E
Sal →, Russia 61 G5 47 31N 40 45 E
Sal Rei, C. Verde Is. 9 j 16 11N 22 53W
Sala, Eritrea 107 D4 16 53N 37 36 E
Šal'a, Slovak Rep. 35 C10 48 10N 17 50 E
Sala, Sweden 16 E10 59 58N 16 35 E
Sala →, Eritrea 107 D4 16 53N 37 36 E
Sala, O. →, Chad 109 E4 17 0N 20 53 E
Sala Consilina, Italy 47 B8 40 23N 15 36 E
Sala-y-Gómez, Pac. Oc. 135 K17 26 28 S 105 28W
Salaberry-de-Valleyfield, Canada 140 C5 45 15N 74 8W
Saladas, Argentina 174 B4 28 15 S 58 40W
Saladillo, Argentina 174 D4 35 40 S 59 55W
Salado →, Buenos Aires, Argentina 174 D4 35 44 S 57 22W
Salado →, La Pampa, Argentina 176 A3 37 30 S 67 0W
Salado →, Río Negro, Argentina 176 B3 41 34 S 65 3W
Salado →, Santa Fe, Argentina 174 C3 31 40 S 60 41W
Salado →, Mexico 155 M5 26 52N 99 19W
Salaga, Ghana 113 D4 8 31N 0 31W
Sālah, Syria 103 C5 32 40N 36 45 E
Sălaj □, Romania 52 C8 47 15N 23 0 E
Sálakhos, Greece 38 E11 36 17N 27 57 E
Salal, Chad 109 F3 14 48N 17 12 E
Salala, Liberia 112 D2 6 42N 10 7W
Salala, Sudan 106 C4 21 17N 36 16 E
Salālah, Oman 99 C6 16 56N 53 59 E
Salamanca, Chile 174 C1 31 46 S 70 59W
Salamanca, Spain 42 E5 40 58N 5 39W
Salamanca, U.S.A. 150 D6 42 10N 78 43W
Salamanca □, Spain 42 E5 40 57N 5 40W
Salamat, Bahr →, Chad 109 G3 9 20N 18 0 E
Salāmatābād, Iran 96 C5 35 39N 47 50 E
Salamina, Colombia 168 B2 5 25N 75 29W
Salamis, Cyprus 39 E9 35 11N 33 54 E
Salamís, Greece 48 D5 37 56N 23 30 E
Salamonie L., U.S.A. 157 D11 40 46N 85 37W
Salaóra, Greece 39 A2 39 2N 20 52 E
Salar de Atacama, Chile 174 A2 23 30 S 68 25W
Salar de Uyuni, Bolivia 172 E4 20 30 S 67 45W
Sălard, Romania 52 C7 47 12N 22 3 E
Salas, Spain 42 B4 43 25N 6 15W
Salas de los Infantes, Spain 42 C7 42 2N 3 17W
Salatiga, Indonesia 85 D4 7 19 S 110 30 E
Salavat, Russia 64 E5 53 21N 55 55 E
Salaverry, Peru 172 B2 8 15 S 79 0W
Salawati, Indonesia 83 B4 1 7 S 130 52 E
Salay, Phil. 81 G5 8 52N 124 47 E
Salaya, India 92 H3 22 19N 69 35 E
Salayar, Indonesia 82 G6 6 7 S 120 30 E
Salazar →, Spain 40 C3 42 40N 1 20W
Salbris, France 27 E9 47 25N 2 3 E
Salcedo, Phil. 81 F5 11 9N 125 40 E
Salcia, Romania 53 G9 43 56N 24 55 E
Sălciua, Romania 53 D8 46 24N 23 26 E
Salcombe, U.K. 21 G4 50 14N 3 47W
Saldaña, Spain 42 C6 42 32N 4 48W
Saldanha, S. Africa 116 E2 33 0 S 17 58 E
Saldanha B., S. Africa 116 E2 33 6 S 18 0 E
Saldus, Latvia 15 H20 56 38N 22 30 E
Saldus □, Latvia 54 B9 56 35N 22 30 E
Sale, Australia 129 E7 38 6 S 147 6 E
Sale, Burma 90 E5 20 50N 94 45 E
Sale, Italy 44 D5 44 59N 8 48 E
Salé, Morocco 110 B3 34 3N 6 48W
Sale, U.K. 20 D5 53 26N 2 19W
Sale City, U.S.A. 152 D5 31 16N 84 1W
Salekhard, Russia 66 C7 66 30N 66 35 E
Salelologa, Samoa 133 W23 13 41 S 172 11W
Salem, India 95 J4 11 40N 78 11 E
Salem, Fla., U.S.A. 152 F6 29 53N 83 25W
Salem, Ill., U.S.A. 156 F8 38 38N 88 57W
Salem, Ind., U.S.A. 157 F10 38 36N 86 6W
Salem, Mass., U.S.A. 151 D14 42 31N 70 53W
Salem, Mo., U.S.A. 155 G9 37 39N 91 32W
Salem, N.H., U.S.A. 151 D13 42 45N 71 12W
Salem, N.J., U.S.A. 148 F8 39 34N 75 28W
Salem, N.Y., U.S.A. 151 C11 43 10N 73 20W
Salem, Ohio, U.S.A. 150 F4 40 54N 80 52W
Salem, Oreg., U.S.A. 158 D2 44 56N 123 2W
Salem, S. Dak., U.S.A. 154 D6 43 44N 97 23W
Salem, Va., U.S.A. 148 G5 37 18N 80 3W
Salemi, Italy 46 E5 37 49N 12 48 E
Sälen, Sweden 16 C7 61 15N 13 22 E
Salernes, France 29 E10 43 34N 6 15 E
Salerno, Italy 47 B7 40 41N 14 47 E
Salerno, G. di, Italy 47 B7 40 32N 14 42 E
Sales, Brazil 169 D5 4 2 S 63 40W
Salford, U.K. 20 D5 53 30N 2 18W
Salgir →, Ukraine 59 K8 45 38N 35 1 E
Salgótarján, Hungary 52 B4 48 5N 19 47 E
Salgueiro, Brazil 170 C4 8 4 S 39 6W
Salher, India 94 D1 20 40N 73 55 E
Salhus, Norway 18 D2 60 30N 5 15 E
Salibabu, Indonesia 79 D7 3 51N 126 40 E
Salibea, Trin. & Tob. 169 F9 10 43N 61 2W
Salida, U.S.A. 146 C5 38 32N 106 0W
Salies-de-Béarn, France 28 E3 43 28N 0 56W
Şalif, Yemen 98 D3 15 18N 42 41 E
Salihli, Turkey 100 C3 38 28N 28 8 E
Salihorsk, Belarus 59 F4 52 51N 27 27 E
Salin, Burma 90 E5 20 35N 94 40 E
Salina, Italy 47 D7 38 34N 14 50 E
Salina, Kans., U.S.A. 154 F6 38 50N 97 37W
Salina, Utah, U.S.A. 159 G8 38 58N 111 51W
Salina Cruz, Mexico 163 D5 16 10N 95 10W
Salinas, Brazil 171 E3 16 10 S 42 10W
Salinas, Chile 174 A2 23 31 S 69 29W
Salinas, Ecuador 168 D1 2 10 S 80 58W
Salinas, U.S.A. 160 J5 36 40N 121 39W
Salinas →, Guatemala 163 D6 16 28N 90 31W
Salinas →, U.S.A. 160 J5 36 45N 121 48W
Salinas, B. das, Angola 115 E2 14 11 S 12 21 E
Salinas, B. de, Nic. 164 D2 11 4N 85 45W
Salinas, Pampa de las, Argentina 174 C2 31 58 S 66 42W
Salinas Ambargasta, Argentina 174 B3 29 0 S 65 0W
Salinas de Hidalgo, Mexico 162 C4 22 30N 101 40W
Salinas Grandes, Argentina 174 C3 30 0 S 65 0W
Saline, U.S.A. 157 B13 42 10N 83 47W
Saline →, Ark., U.S.A. 155 J8 33 10N 92 8W
Saline →, Kans., U.S.A. 154 F6 38 52N 97 30W
Salines, C. de ses, Spain 38 B4 39 16N 3 4 E
Salinópolis, Brazil 170 B2 0 40 S 47 20W
Salins-les-Bains, France 27 F12 46 58N 5 52 E
Salir, Portugal 43 H2 37 14N 8 2W
Salisbury = Harare, Zimbabwe 119 F3 17 43 S 31 2 E
Salisbury, U.K. 21 F6 51 4N 1 47W
Salisbury, Md., U.S.A. 148 F8 38 22N 75 36W
Salisbury, Mo., U.S.A. 156 E4 39 25N 92 48W
Salisbury, N.C., U.S.A. 149 H5 35 40N 80 29W
Salisbury I., Canada 139 B12 63 30N 77 0W
Salisbury Plain, U.K. 21 F6 51 14N 1 55W
Săliște, Romania 53 E8 45 45N 23 56 E
Salitre →, Brazil 170 C3 9 29 S 40 39W
Salka, Nigeria 113 C5 10 20N 4 58 E
Salkehatchie →, U.S.A. 152 C9 32 37N 80 53W
Şalkhad, Syria 103 C5 32 29N 36 43 E
Salla, Finland 14 C23 66 50N 28 49 E
Sallanches, France 29 C10 45 55N 6 38 E
Sallent, Spain 40 D6 41 49N 1 54 E
Salles, France 28 D3 44 33N 0 52W
Salles-Curan, France 28 D6 44 11N 2 48 E
Salling, Denmark 17 H2 56 40N 8 55 E
Salliq, Canada 139 B11 64 8N 83 10W
Sallisaw, U.S.A. 155 H7 35 28N 94 47W
Sallom Junction, Sudan 106 D4 19 17N 37 6 E
Salluit, Canada 139 B12 62 14N 75 38W
Salmās, Iran 101 C11 38 11N 44 47 E
Salmerón, Spain 40 E2 40 33N 2 29W
Salmo, Canada 142 D5 49 10N 117 20W
Salmon, U.S.A. 158 D7 45 11N 113 54W
Salmon →, Canada 142 C4 54 3N 122 40W
Salmon →, U.S.A. 158 D5 45 51N 116 47W
Salmon Arm, Canada 142 C5 50 40N 119 15W
Salmon Gums, Australia 125 F3 32 59 S 121 38 E
Salmon River Mts., U.S.A. 158 D6 45 0N 114 30W
Salo, C.A.R. 114 B3 3 10N 16 8 E
Salo, Finland 15 F20 60 22N 23 10 E
Salò, Italy 44 C7 45 36N 10 31 E
Salobreña, Spain 43 J7 36 44N 3 35W
Salome, U.S.A. 161 M13 33 47N 113 37W
Salon, India 93 F9 26 2N 81 27 E
Salon-de-Provence, France 29 E9 43 39N 5 6 E
Salonga →, Dem. Rep. of the Congo 114 C4 0 10 S 19 50 E
Salonga-Nord, Parc Nat. de la, Dem. Rep. of the Congo 114 C4 1 55 S 21 45 E
Salonga-Sud, Parc Nat. de la, Dem. Rep. of the Congo 114 C4 2 25 S 21 0 E
Salonica = Thessaloníki, Greece 50 F6 40 38N 22 58 E
Salonta, Romania 52 D6 46 49N 21 42 E
Salor →, Spain 43 F3 39 39N 7 3W
Salou, Spain 40 D6 41 4N 1 8 E
Salou, C. de, Spain 40 D6 41 3N 1 10 E
Saloum →, Senegal 112 C1 13 50N 16 45W
Salpausselkä, Finland 15 F22 61 0N 27 0 E
Salsacate, Argentina 174 C2 31 20 S 65 5W
Salses, France 28 F6 42 50N 2 55 E
Salsette I., India 94 E1 19 5N 72 50 E
Salsk, Russia 61 G5 46 28N 41 30 E
Salso →, Italy 46 E6 37 6N 13 57 E
Salsomaggiore Terme, Italy 44 D6 44 49N 9 59 E
Salt, Spain 40 D7 41 59N 2 47 E
Salt →, Canada 142 B6 60 0N 112 25W
Salt →, Ariz., U.S.A. 159 K7 33 23N 112 19W
Salt →, Mo., U.S.A. 156 E5 39 28N 91 4W
Salt Cay, Bahamas 165 B5 21 20N 71 11W
Salt L., U.S.A. 145 K14 21 21N 157 55W
Salt Lake City, U.S.A. 158 F8 40 45N 111 53W
Salt Range, Pakistan 92 C5 32 30N 72 25 E
Salt Springs, U.S.A. 153 F8 29 21N 81 44W
Salta, Argentina 174 A2 24 57 S 65 25W
Salta □, Argentina 174 A2 24 48 S 65 30W
Saltara, Italy 45 E9 43 45N 12 50 E
Saltash, U.K. 21 G3 50 24N 4 14W
Saltburn by the Sea, U.K. 20 C7 54 35N 0 58W
Saltcoats, U.K. 22 F4 55 38N 4 47W
Saltee Is., Ireland 23 D5 52 7N 6 37W
Salters, U.S.A. 152 B10 33 36N 79 51W
Saltfjellet, Norway 14 C16 66 40N 15 15 E
Saltfjorden, Norway 14 C16 67 15N 14 10 E
Saltholm, Denmark 17 J6 55 38N 12 43 E
Salthólmavík, Iceland 11 B5 65 24N 21 57W
Saltillo, Mexico 162 B4 25 25N 101 0W
Salto, Argentina 174 C3 34 20 S 60 15W
Salto, Uruguay 174 C4 31 27 S 57 50W
Salto da Divisa, Brazil 171 E4 16 0 S 39 57W
Salto del Guaíra, Paraguay 175 A5 24 3 S 54 17W
Salton City, U.S.A. 161 M11 33 29N 115 51W
Salton Sea, U.S.A. 161 M11 33 15N 115 45W
Saltpond, Ghana 113 D4 5 15N 1 3W
Saltrød, Norway 18 F5 58 30N 8 49 E
Saltsburg, U.S.A. 150 F5 40 29N 79 27W
Saltsjöbaden, Sweden 16 E12 59 15N 18 20 E
Saluda, U.S.A. 152 A8 34 0N 81 46W
Saluda →, U.S.A. 149 J5 34 1N 81 4W
Salug, Phil. 81 G4 8 7N 122 47 E
Salûm, Egypt 106 A2 31 31N 25 7 E
Salûm, Khâlig el, Egypt 106 A2 31 35N 25 24 E
Salur, India 94 E6 18 27N 83 18 E
Salut, Is. du, Fr. Guiana 169 B7 5 15N 52 35W
Saluzzo, Italy 44 D4 44 39N 7 29 E
Salvación, B., Chile 176 D1 50 50 S 75 10W
Salvador, Brazil 171 D4 13 0 S 38 30W
Salvador, Canada 143 C7 52 10N 109 32W
Salvador, L., U.S.A. 155 L9 29 43N 90 15W
Salvaterra, Brazil 170 B2 0 46 S 48 31W
Salvaterra de Magos, Portugal 43 F2 39 1N 8 47W
Salvisa, U.S.A. 157 G12 37 54N 84 51W
Sálvora, I. de, Spain 42 C2 42 30N 8 58W
Salween →, Burma 90 G6 16 31N 97 37 E
Salyan, Azerbaijan 101 C13 39 33N 48 59 E
Salza →, Austria 34 D7 47 40N 14 43 E
Salzach →, Austria 34 C5 48 12N 12 56 E
Salzburg, Austria 34 D6 47 48N 13 2 E
Salzburg □, Austria 34 D6 47 15N 13 0 E
Salzgitter, Germany 30 C6 52 9N 10 19 E
Salzkotten, Germany 30 D4 51 40N 8 37 E
Salzwedel, Germany 30 C7 52 52N 11 10 E
Sam, Gabon 114 B2 0 58N 11 16 E

San Salvador, I., Ecuador 172 a 0 16 S 90 42W
San Salvador de Jujuy, Argentina 174 A3 24 10 S 64 48W
San Salvador I., Bahamas 165 B5 24 0N 74 40W
San Salvo, Italy 45 F11 42 3N 14 44 E
San Sebastián = Donostia-San Sebastián, Spain 40 B3 43 17N 1 58W
San Sebastián, Argentina 176 D3 53 10 S 68 30W
San Sebastian, Puerto Rico 165 d 18 20N 66 59W
San Sebastián de la Gomera, Canary Is. 9 e1 28 5N 17 7W
San Serra = Son Serra, Spain 38 B4 39 43N 3 13 E
San Serverino Marche, Italy 45 E10 43 13N 13 10 E
San Severo, Italy 45 G12 41 41N 15 23 E
San Simeon, U.S.A. 160 K5 35 39N 121 11W
San Simon, U.S.A. 159 K9 32 16N 109 14W
San Stéfano di Cadore, Italy 45 B9 46 34N 12 33 E
San Stino di Livenza, Italy 45 C9 45 44N 12 41 E
San Telmo = Sant Telm, Spain 38 B3 39 35N 2 21 E
San Telmo, Mexico 162 A1 30 58N 116 6W
San Teodoro, Phil. 80 E3 13 26N 121 1 E
San Tiburcio, Mexico 162 C4 24 8N 101 32W
San Valentin, Mte., Chile 176 C2 46 30 S 73 30W
San Vicente de Alcántara, Spain 43 F3 39 22N 7 8W
San Vicente de la Barquera, Spain 42 B6 43 23N 4 29W
San Vicente del Caguán, Colombia 168 C3 2 7N 74 46W
San Vincente del Raspeig, Spain 41 G4 38 24N 0 31W
San Vincenzo, Italy 44 E7 43 6N 10 32 E
San Vito, Costa Rica 164 E3 8 50N 82 58W
San Vito, Italy 46 C2 39 26N 9 32 E
San Vito, C., Italy 46 D5 38 11N 12 41 E
San Vito al Tagliamento, Italy 45 C9 45 54N 12 52 E
San Vito Chietino, Italy 45 F11 42 18N 14 27 E
San Vito dei Normanni, Italy 47 B10 40 39N 17 42 E
San Yanaro, Colombia 168 C4 2 47N 69 42W
Saña, Peru 172 B2 6 54 S 79 36W
Sana', Yemen 98 D4 15 27N 44 12 E
Sana →, Bos.-H. 45 C13 45 3N 16 23 E
Sanaba, Burkina Faso 112 C4 12 25N 3 47W
Şanāfīr, Si. Arabia 106 B3 27 56N 34 42 E
Sanaga →, Cameroon 113 E6 3 35N 9 38 E
Sanak I., U.S.A. 144 J7 54 25N 162 40W
Sanaloa, Presa, Mexico 162 C3 24 50N 107 20W
Sanām, Si. Arabia 98 B4 23 40N 44 45 E
Sanana, Indonesia 82 B3 2 4 S 125 58 E
Sanand, India 92 H5 22 59N 72 25 E
Sanandaj, Iran 101 E12 35 18N 47 1 E
Sanandita, Bolivia 174 A3 21 40 S 63 45W
Sanaroa I., Papua N. G. 132 E6 9 37 S 151 0 E
Sanary-sur-Mer, France 29 E9 43 7N 5 49 E
Sanāw, Yemen 99 C5 17 50N 51 5 E
Sanawad, India 92 H7 22 11N 76 5 E
Sanbe-San, Japan 72 B4 35 6N 132 38 E
Sancellas = Sencelles, Spain 38 B3 39 39N 2 54 E
Sancergues, France 27 E9 47 10N 2 54 E
Sancerre, France 27 E9 47 20N 2 50 E
Sancerrois, Collines du, France 27 E9 47 20N 2 40 E
Sancha He →, China 76 D6 26 48N 106 7 E
Sanchahe, China 75 B14 44 50N 126 2 E
Sanchakou, China 65 D9 39 47N 78 20 E
Sánchez, Dom. Rep. 165 C6 19 15N 69 36W
Sanchez-Mira, Phil. 80 B3 18 34N 121 14 E
Sanchor, India 92 G4 24 45N 71 55 E
Sanco Pt., Phil. 81 G6 8 15N 126 27 E
Sancoins, France 27 F9 46 47N 2 55 E
Sancti Spíritus, Cuba 164 B4 21 52N 79 33W
Sancy, Puy de, France 28 C6 45 32N 2 50 E
Sand, Norway 18 E3 59 29N 6 16 E
Sand →, S. Africa 117 C5 22 25 S 30 5 E
Sand Cr. →, U.S.A. 157 E11 39 3N 85 51W
Sand Hills, Guyana 169 B6 6 27N 58 19W
Sand Hills, U.S.A. 154 D4 42 10N 101 30W
Sand I., U.S.A. 145 K14 21 19N 157 53W
Sand Point, U.S.A. 144 J7 55 20N 160 30W
Sand Springs, U.S.A. 155 G6 36 9N 96 7W
Sanda, Japan 73 C7 34 53N 135 14 E
Sandakan, Malaysia 85 A5 5 53N 118 4 E
Sandalwood, Australia 128 C4 34 55 S 140 9 E
Sandan = Sambor, Cambodia 86 F6 12 46N 106 0 E
Sandane, Norway 18 C3 61 46N 6 13 E
Sandanski, Bulgaria 50 E7 41 35N 23 16 E
Sandaré, Mali 112 C2 14 40N 10 15W
Sandared, Sweden 17 G6 57 43N 12 47 E
Sandarne, Sweden 16 C11 61 16N 17 9 E
Sanday, U.K. 22 B6 59 16N 2 31W
Sande, Møre og Romsdal, Norway 18 B2 62 15N 5 27 E
Sande, Sogn og Fjordane, Norway 18 C2 61 20N 5 47 E
Sande, Vestfold, Norway 18 E7 59 36N 10 12 E
Sandefjord, Norway 18 E7 59 10N 10 15 E
Sandeid, Norway 18 E2 59 33N 5 52 E
Sanders, Ariz., U.S.A. 159 J9 35 13N 109 20W
Sanders, Ky., U.S.A. 157 F12 38 40N 84 56W
Sanderson, Fla., U.S.A. 152 E7 30 15N 82 16W
Sanderson, Tex., U.S.A. 155 K3 30 9N 102 24W
Sandersville, U.S.A. 152 C7 32 59N 82 48W
Sandfire Roadhouse, Australia 124 C3 19 45 S 121 15 E
Sandfloegga, Norway 18 E4 59 58N 7 10 E
Sandfly L., Canada 143 B7 55 43N 106 6W
Sandfontein, Namibia 116 C2 23 48 S 29 1 E
Sandhammaren, C., Sweden 17 J8 55 23N 14 14 E
Sandía, Peru 172 C4 14 10 S 69 30W
Sandıklı, Turkey 49 C12 38 28N 30 17 E
Sandila, India 93 F9 27 5N 80 31 E
Sandilands, Bahamas 9 b 25 3N 77 19W
Sandnes, Aust-Agder, Norway 18 F4 58 53N 7 45 E
Sandnes, Rogaland, Norway 15 G11 58 50N 5 45 E
Sandnessjøen, Norway 14 C15 66 2N 12 38 E
Sandoa, Dem. Rep. of the Congo 115 D4 9 41 S 23 0 E
Sandomierz, Poland 55 H8 50 40N 21 43 E
Sândominic, Romania 53 D10 46 35N 25 47 E
Sandona, Colombia 168 C2 1 17N 77 28W
Sandongo, Angola 115 F4 15 30 S 21 28 E
Sandoval, U.S.A. 156 F7 38 37N 89 7W
Sandover →, Australia 126 C2 21 43 S 136 32 E
Sandoway, Burma 90 F5 18 20N 94 30 E
Sandoy, Færoe Is. 14 F9 61 52N 6 46W
Sandpoint, U.S.A. 158 B5 48 17N 116 33W
Sandray, U.K. 22 E1 56 53N 7 31W
Sandringham, U.K. 20 E8 52 51N 0 31 E
Sandstone, Australia 125 E2 27 59 S 119 16 E
Sandu, China 76 E6 26 0N 107 52 E
Sandumba, Angola 115 E3 13 45 S 17 34 E
Sandur, India 95 F3 15 6N 76 33 E
Sandusky, Mich., U.S.A. 150 C2 43 25N 82 50W
Sandusky, Ohio, U.S.A. 150 E2 41 27N 82 42W
Sandusky →, U.S.A. 157 C14 41 27N 83 0W
Sandvig, Sweden 17 J8 55 18N 14 47 E
Sandvika, Norway 18 E7 59 54N 10 31 E
Sandviken, Sweden 16 D10 60 38N 16 46 E
Sandwich, U.S.A. 157 C8 41 39N 88 37W
Sandwich, C., Australia 126 B4 18 14 S 146 18 E
Sandwich B., Canada 141 B8 53 40N 57 15W
Sandwich B., Namibia 116 C1 23 25 S 14 20 E
Sandwip I., Bangla. 90 D3 22 30N 91 25 E
Sandy, Oreg., U.S.A. 160 E4 45 24N 122 16W
Sandy, Pa., U.S.A. 150 E6 41 6N 78 46W
Sandy, Utah, U.S.A. 158 F8 40 35N 111 50W
Sandy B., St. Helena 9 h 16 0 S 5 43W
Sandy Bay, Canada 143 B8 55 31N 102 19W
Sandy Bight, Australia 125 F3 33 50 S 123 20 E
Sandy C., Queens., Australia 126 C5 24 42 S 153 15 E
Sandy C., Tas., Australia 127 G3 41 25 S 144 45 E
Sandy Cay, Bahamas 165 B4 23 13N 75 18W
Sandy Cr. →, U.S.A. 158 F9 41 51N 109 47W
Sandy L., Canada 140 B1 53 2N 93 0W
Sandy Lake, Canada 140 B1 53 0N 93 15W
Sandy Point, India 95 J11 10 32N 92 22 E
Sandy Springs, U.S.A. 152 B5 33 56N 84 23W
Sandy Valley, U.S.A. 161 K11 35 49N 115 36W
Sanford, Fla., U.S.A. 149 L5 28 48N 81 16W
Sanford, Maine, U.S.A. 149 D10 43 27N 70 47W
Sanford, N.C., U.S.A. 149 H6 35 29N 79 10W
Sanford →, Australia 125 E2 27 22 S 115 53 E
Sanford, Mt., U.S.A. 144 E11 62 13N 144 8W
Sang-i-Masha, Afghan. 92 C2 33 8N 67 27 E
Sanga, Angola 115 E3 11 9 S 15 21 E
Sanga, Mozam. 119 E4 12 22 S 35 21 E
Sanga →, Congo 114 C3 1 5 S 17 0 E
Sangaie, Dem. Rep. of the Congo 115 D4 6 48 S 22 46 E
Sangamner, India 94 E2 19 37N 74 15 E
Sangamon →, U.S.A. 156 D6 40 7N 90 20W
Sanganeb Atoll Marine Nat. Park, Sudan 106 D4 19 33N 37 11 E
Sangar, Afghan. 92 C1 32 56N 65 30 E
Sangar, Russia 67 C13 64 2N 127 31 E
Sangar Sarai, Afghan. 92 B4 34 27N 70 35 E
Sangareddi, India 94 F4 17 38N 78 7 E
Sangaredi, Guinea 112 C2 11 7N 13 52W
Sangarh →, Pakistan 92 D4 30 43N 70 44 E
Sangasangadalam, Indonesia 85 C5 0 36 S 117 13 E
Sangasso, Mali 112 C3 12 5N 5 35W
Sangatte, France 27 B8 50 56N 1 44 E
Sangay, Ecuador 168 D2 2 0 S 78 20W
Sangchris L., U.S.A. 156 E7 39 35N 89 30W
Sange, Dem. Rep. of the Congo 118 D2 6 58 S 28 21 E
Sangeang, Indonesia 85 D5 8 12 S 119 6 E
Sângeorz-Băi, Romania 53 C9 47 22N 24 41 E
Sanger, U.S.A. 160 J7 36 42N 119 33W
Sângera, Moldova 53 D13 46 55N 28 58 E
Sangerhausen, Germany 30 D7 51 28N 11 18 E
Sanggan He →, China 74 E9 38 12N 117 15 E
Sanggau, Indonesia 85 B4 0 5N 110 30 E
Sanghar, Pakistan 92 F3 26 2N 68 57 E
Sangihe, Kepulauan, Indonesia 82 A3 3 0N 125 30 E
Sangihe, Pulau, Indonesia 82 A3 3 35N 125 30 E
Sangju, S. Korea 75 F15 36 25N 128 10 E
Sangkapura, Indonesia 85 D4 5 52 S 112 40 E
Sangkhla, Thailand 86 E2 14 57N 98 28 E
Sangkulirang, Indonesia 83 B5 0 59N 117 58 E
Sangla, Pakistan 92 D5 31 43N 73 23 E
Sangli, India 94 F2 16 55N 74 33 E
Sangmélima, Cameroon 113 E7 2 57N 12 1 E
Sango, Angola 115 D2 9 51 S 15 44 E
Sangod, India 92 G7 24 55N 76 17 E
Sangole, India 94 F2 17 26N 75 12 E
Sangpang Bum, Burma 90 B5 26 30N 95 50 E
Sangre de Cristo Mts., U.S.A. 155 G2 37 30N 105 20W
Sangre Grande, Trin. & Tob. 169 F9 10 35N 61 8W
Sangro →, Italy 45 F11 42 14N 14 32 E
Sangrur, India 92 D6 30 14N 75 50 E
Sangudo, Canada 142 C6 53 50N 114 54W
Sangue →, Brazil 173 C6 11 1 S 58 39W
Sangüesa, Spain 40 C3 42 37N 1 17W
Sanguinaires, Îs., France 29 G12 41 51N 8 36 E
Sangzhi, China 77 C8 29 25N 110 12 E
Sanhala, Ivory C. 112 C3 10 3N 6 51W
Sanibel, U.S.A. 149 M4 26 26N 82 1W
Sanibel I., U.S.A. 153 J7 26 26N 82 6W
Sanirajak, Canada 139 B11 68 46N 81 12W
Sanjawi, Pakistan 92 D3 30 17N 68 21 E
Sanje, Uganda 118 C3 0 49 S 31 30 E
Sanjiang, China 76 E7 25 48N 109 37 E
Sanjo, Japan 70 F9 37 37N 138 57 E
Sankarankovil, India 95 K3 9 10N 77 35 E
Sankeshwar, India 95 F2 16 23N 74 32 E
Sankh →, India 93 H11 22 15N 84 48 E
Sankosh →, India 90 B2 26 24N 89 47 E
Sankt Andrä, Austria 34 E7 46 46N 14 50 E
Sankt Antönien, Switz. 33 C9 46 58N 9 48 E
Sankt Augustin, Germany 30 E3 50 45N 7 10 E
Sankt Blasien, Germany 31 H4 47 47N 8 7 E
Sankt Gallen, Switz. 33 B8 47 26N 9 22 E
Sankt Gallen □, Switz. 33 B8 47 25N 9 22 E
Sankt Goar, Germany 31 E3 50 12N 7 43 E
Sankt Ingbert, Germany 31 F3 49 16N 7 6 E
Sankt Johann im Pongau, Austria 34 D6 47 22N 13 12 E
Sankt Johann in Tirol, Austria 34 D5 47 30N 12 25 E
Sankt Margrethen, Switz. 33 B9 47 28N 9 37 E
Sankt Moritz, Switz. 33 D9 46 30N 9 50 E
Sankt-Peterburg, Russia 58 C6 59 55N 30 20 E
Sankt Pölten, Austria 34 C8 48 12N 15 38 E
Sankt Ulrich = Ortisei, Italy 45 B8 46 34N 11 40 E
Sankt Valentin, Austria 34 C7 48 11N 14 33 E
Sankt Veit an der Glan, Austria 34 E7 46 47N 14 22 E
Sankt Wendel, Germany 31 F3 49 27N 7 9 E
Sankt Wolfgang, Austria 34 D6 47 43N 13 27 E
Sankuru →, Dem. Rep. of the Congo 115 C4 4 17 S 20 25 E
Sanliurfa, Turkey 101 D8 37 12N 38 50 E
Sanlúcar de Barrameda, Spain 43 J4 36 46N 6 21W
Sanluri, Italy 46 C1 39 34N 8 54 E
Sânmartin, Romania 53 D10 46 19N 25 58 E
Sanmen, China 77 C13 29 5N 121 35 E
Sanmenxia, China 74 G6 34 47N 111 12 E
Sanming, China 77 D11 26 15N 117 40 E
Sannan, Japan 73 B7 35 2N 135 1 E
Sannaspos, S. Africa 116 D4 29 6 S 26 34 E
Sannat, Malta 38 E6 36 1N 14 15 E
Sannicandro Gargánico, Italy 45 G12 41 50N 15 34 E
Sânnicolau Mare, Romania 52 D5 46 5N 20 39 E
Sannieshof, S. Africa 116 D4 26 30 S 25 47 E
Sannīn, J., Lebanon 103 B4 33 57N 35 52 E
Sanniquellie, Liberia 112 D3 7 19N 8 38W
Sannûr, W. →, Egypt 106 B3 28 59N 31 3 E
Sano, Japan 73 A11 36 19N 139 35 E
Sanok, Poland 55 J9 49 35N 22 10 E
Sanquhar, U.K. 22 F5 55 22N 3 54W
Sans Souci, Trin. & Tob. 169 F9 10 50N 61 0W
Sansanding, Mali 112 C3 13 48N 6 0W
Sansepolcro, Italy 45 E9 43 34N 12 8 E
Sansha, China 77 D13 26 58N 120 12 E
Sanshui, China 77 F9 23 10N 112 56 E
Sanski Most, Bos.-H. 45 D13 44 46N 16 40 E
Sansui, China 76 D7 26 58N 108 39 E
Sant Antoni Abat, Spain 38 D1 38 59N 1 19 E
Sant Boi de Llobregat, Spain 40 D7 41 21N 2 2 E
Sant Carles, Spain 38 C2 39 3N 1 34 E
Sant Carles de la Ràpita, Spain 40 E5 40 37N 0 35 E
Sant Celoni, Spain 40 D7 41 42N 2 30 E
Sant Feliu de Guíxols, Spain 40 D8 41 45N 3 1 E
Sant Feliu de Llobregat, Spain 40 D7 41 23N 2 2 E
Sant Ferran, Spain 38 D1 38 42N 1 28 E
Sant Francesc de Formentera, Spain 38 D1 38 42N 1 26 E
Sant Jaume, Spain 38 B5 39 54N 4 4 E
Sant Joan Baptista, Spain 38 C2 39 5N 1 31 E
Sant Jordi, Ibiza, Spain 38 D1 38 53N 1 24 E
Sant Jordi, Mallorca, Spain 38 B3 39 33N 2 46 E
Sant Jordi, G. de, Spain 40 E6 40 53N 1 2 E
Sant Llorenç de Morunys, Spain 40 C6 42 8N 1 35 E
Sant Llorenç des Cardassar, Spain 38 B4 39 37N 3 17 E
Sant Mateu, Baleares, Spain 38 C1 39 3N 1 23 E
Sant Mateu, Valencia, Spain 40 E5 40 28N 0 10 E
Sant Miquel, Spain 38 C1 39 3N 1 26 E
Sant Telm, Spain 38 B3 39 35N 2 21 E
Santa, Peru 172 B2 8 59 S 78 40W
Sant' Ágata Militello, Italy 47 D7 38 2N 14 8 E
Santa Agnés, Spain 38 C1 39 3N 1 21 E
Santa Ana, Beni, Bolivia 173 C4 13 50 S 65 40W
Santa Ana, La Paz, Bolivia 172 D4 15 31 S 67 30W
Santa Ana, Santa Cruz, Bolivia 173 D6 18 43 S 58 44W
Santa Ana, Santa Cruz, Bolivia 173 D5 16 37 S 60 43W
Santa Ana, Ecuador 168 D1 1 16 S 80 20W
Santa Ana, El Salv. 164 D2 14 0N 89 31W
Santa Ana, Mexico 162 A2 30 31N 111 8W
Santa Ana, Phil. 80 B4 18 28N 122 20 E
Santa Ana, Solomon Is. 133 N12 10 50 S 162 30 E
Santa Ana, U.S.A. 161 M9 33 46N 117 52W
Santa Ana →, Venezuela 168 B3 9 30N 71 57W
Sant' Ángelo Lodigiano, Italy 44 C6 45 14N 9 25 E
Sant' Antíoco, Italy 46 C1 39 4N 8 27 E
Santa Bárbara, Santa Maria, Azores 9 d4 36 59N 25 4W
Santa Bárbara, Terceira, Azores 9 d1 38 41N 27 20W
Santa Bárbara, Chile 174 D1 37 40 S 72 1W
Santa Bárbara, Colombia 168 B2 5 53N 75 35W
Santa Bárbara, Honduras 164 D2 14 53N 88 14W
Santa Bárbara, Mexico 162 B3 26 48N 105 50W
Santa Bárbara, Phil. 81 F4 10 50N 122 32 E
Santa Bárbara, Spain 40 E5 40 42N 0 29 E
Santa Barbara, U.S.A. 161 L7 34 25N 119 42W
Santa Bárbara, Amazonas, Venezuela 168 C4 3 57N 67 6W
Santa Bárbara, Barinas, Venezuela 168 B3 7 47N 71 10W
Santa Bárbara, Mt., Spain 41 H2 37 23N 2 50W
Santa Bárbara, Serra de, Azores 9 d1 38 44N 27 19W
Santa Barbara Channel, U.S.A. 161 L7 34 15N 120 0W
Santa Barbara I., U.S.A. 161 M7 33 29N 119 2W
Santa Catalina, Colombia 168 A2 10 36N 75 17W
Santa Catalina, Phil. 81 G4 9 20N 122 52 E
Santa Catalina, Solomon Is. 133 N12 10 53 S 162 29 E
Santa Catalina, Gulf of, U.S.A. 161 N9 33 10N 117 50W
Santa Catalina, I., Mexico 162 B2 25 40N 110 50W
Santa Catalina I., U.S.A. 161 M8 33 23N 118 25W
Santa Catarina □, Brazil 175 B6 27 25 S 48 30W
Santa Catarina, I. de, Brazil 175 B6 27 30 S 48 40W
Santa Caterina di Pittinuri, Italy 46 B1 40 6N 8 27 E
Santa Caterina Villarmosa, Italy 47 E7 37 35N 14 2 E
Santa Cecília, Brazil 175 B5 26 56 S 50 18W
Santa Clara, Cuba 164 B4 22 20N 80 0W
Santa Clara, Calif., U.S.A. 160 H5 37 21N 121 57W
Santa Clara, Utah, U.S.A. 159 H7 37 8N 113 39W
Santa Clara, El Golfo de, Mexico 162 A2 31 42N 114 30W
Santa Clara de Olimar, Uruguay 175 C5 32 50 S 54 54W
Santa Clarita, U.S.A. 161 L8 34 24N 118 30W
Santa Clotilde, Peru 168 D3 2 33 S 73 45W
Santa Coloma de Farners, Spain 40 D7 41 50N 2 39 E
Santa Coloma de Gramenet, Spain 40 D7 41 27N 2 13 E
Santa Comba, Spain 42 B2 43 2N 8 49W
Santa Croce Camerina, Italy 47 F7 36 50N 14 31 E
Santa Croce di Magliano, Italy 45 G11 41 42N 14 59 E
Santa Cruz, Argentina 176 D3 50 0 S 68 32W
Santa Cruz, Bolivia 173 D5 17 43 S 63 10W
Santa Cruz, Brazil 170 C4 6 13 S 36 1W
Santa Cruz, Chile 174 C1 34 38 S 71 27W
Santa Cruz, Costa Rica 164 D2 10 15N 85 35W
Santa Cruz, Madeira 9 c 32 42N 16 46W
Santa Cruz, Peru 172 B2 5 40 S 75 56W
Santa Cruz, Davao del S., Phil. 81 H5 6 50N 125 25 E
Santa Cruz, Laguna, Phil. 80 D3 14 20N 121 24 E
Santa Cruz, Marinduque, Phil. 80 E4 13 28N 122 2 E
Santa Cruz, Mind. Occ., Phil. 80 E3 13 4N 120 43 E
Santa Cruz, Zambales, Phil. 80 D2 15 46N 119 55 E
Santa Cruz, U.S.A. 160 J4 36 58N 122 1W
Santa Cruz, Venezuela 169 B5 8 3N 64 27W
Santa Cruz □, Argentina 176 C3 49 0 S 70 0W
Santa Cruz □, Bolivia 173 D5 17 43 S 63 10W
Santa Cruz →, Argentina 176 D3 50 10 S 68 20W
Santa Cruz, I., Ecuador 172 a 0 38 S 90 23W
Santa Cruz Cabrália, Brazil 171 E4 16 17 S 39 2W
Santa Cruz da Graciosa, Azores 9 d1 39 5N 28 1W
Santa Cruz das Flores, Azores 9 d2 39 27N 31 7W
Santa Cruz de la Palma, Canary Is. 9 e1 28 41N 17 46W
Santa Cruz de Mudela, Spain 43 G7 38 39N 3 28W
Santa Cruz de Tenerife, Canary Is. 9 e1 28 28N 16 15W
Santa Cruz del Norte, Cuba 164 B3 23 9N 81 55W
Santa Cruz del Retamar, Spain 42 E6 40 8N 4 14W
Santa Cruz del Sur, Cuba 164 B4 20 44N 78 0W
Santa Cruz do Rio Pardo, Brazil 175 A6 22 54 S 49 37W
Santa Cruz do Sul, Brazil 175 B5 29 42 S 52 25W
Santa Cruz I., U.S.A. 161 M7 34 1N 119 43W
Santa Cruz Is., Solomon Is. 134 J8 10 30 S 166 0 E
Santa Cruz Mts., Jamaica 164 a 17 58N 77 43W
Santa Domingo, Cay, Bahamas 164 B4 21 25N 75 15W
Sant' Egídio alla Vibrata, Italy 45 F10 42 49N 13 42 E
Santa Elena, Argentina 174 C4 30 58 S 59 47W
Santa Elena, Ecuador 168 D1 2 16 S 80 52W
Santa Elena, Phil. 80 D4 14 12N 122 24 E
Santa Elena, C., Costa Rica 164 D2 10 54N 85 56W
Sant' Eufémia, G. di, Italy 47 D9 38 51N 16 4 E
Santa Eulàlia des Riu, Spain 38 D2 38 59N 1 32 E
Santa Fe, Argentina 174 C3 31 35 S 60 41W
Santa Fe, Nueva Viscaya, Phil. 80 C3 16 10N 120 57 E
Santa Fe, Romblon, Phil. 80 E4 12 10N 122 0 E
Santa Fe, Spain 43 H7 37 11N 3 43W
Santa Fe, U.S.A. 159 J11 35 41N 105 57W
Santa Fé □, Argentina 174 C3 31 50 S 60 55W
Santa Fé, Canal de, Ecuador 172 a 0 48 S 89 55W
Santa Fé, I., Ecuador 172 a 0 49 S 90 5W
Santa Fé do Sul, Brazil 171 F1 20 13 S 50 56W
Santa Filomena, Brazil 170 C2 9 6 S 45 50W
Santa Fiora, Italy 45 F8 42 50N 11 35 E
Santa Gertrudis, Spain 38 C1 39 0N 1 26 E
Santa Giustina, Italy 45 B9 46 10N 12 5 E
Santa Helena, Brazil 170 B2 2 14 S 45 18W
Santa Helena de Goiás, Brazil 171 E1 17 53 S 50 35W
Santa Inês, Bahia, Brazil 171 D4 13 17 S 39 48W
Santa Inês, Maranhão, Brazil 170 B2 3 39 S 45 20W
Santa Inés, Spain 43 G5 38 32N 5 37W
Santa Inés, I., Chile 176 D2 54 0 S 73 0W
Santa Isabel = Rey Malabo, Eq. Guin. 113 E6 3 45N 8 50 E
Santa Isabel, Argentina 174 D2 36 10 S 66 54W
Santa Isabel, Solomon Is. 133 M10 8 0 S 159 0 E
Santa Isabel, Pico, Eq. Guin. 113 E6 3 36N 8 49 E
Santa Isabel do Araguaia, Brazil 170 C2 6 7 S 48 19W
Santa Isabel do Morro, Brazil 171 D1 11 34 S 50 40W
Santa Isabel do Río Negro, Brazil 169 D4 0 24 S 65 2W
Santa Lucía, Corrientes, Argentina 174 B4 28 58 S 59 5W
Santa Lucía, San Juan, Argentina 174 C2 31 30 S 68 30W
Santa Lucia, Phil. 80 C3 17 7N 120 27 E
Santa Lucía, Spain 41 H4 37 35N 0 58W
Santa Lucía, Uruguay 174 C4 34 27 S 56 24W
Santa Lucia Range, U.S.A. 160 K5 36 0N 121 20W
Santa Luzia, C. Verde Is. 9 j 16 50N 24 35W
Santa Magdalena, I., Mexico 162 C2 24 40N 112 15W
Santa Margarita, Argentina 174 D3 38 28 S 61 35W
Santa Margarita, Spain 38 B3 39 42N 3 6 E
Santa Margarita, U.S.A. 160 K6 35 23N 120 37W
Santa Margarita →, U.S.A. 161 M9 33 13N 117 23W
Santa Margarita, I., Mexico 162 C2 24 30N 111 50W
Santa Margherita, Italy 46 D1 38 58N 8 58 E
Santa Margherita Ligure, Italy 44 D6 44 20N 9 11 E
Santa María, Argentina 174 B2 26 40 S 66 0W
Santa Maria, Azores 9 d4 36 58N 25 6W
Santa Maria, Brazil 175 B5 29 40 S 53 48W
Santa Maria, C. Verde Is. 9 j 16 31N 22 53W
Santa Maria, Ilocos S., Phil. 80 C3 17 22N 120 29 E
Santa Maria, Isabela, Phil. 80 C3 17 28N 121 45 E
Santa Maria, Switz. 33 C10 46 36N 10 25 E
Santa Maria, U.S.A. 161 L6 34 57N 120 26W
Santa María →, Mexico 162 A3 31 0N 107 14W
Santa María, B. de, Mexico 162 B3 25 10N 108 40W
Santa Maria, C. de, Portugal 43 J3 36 58N 7 53W
Santa María, I., Ecuador 172 a 1 17 S 90 26W
Santa Maria Cápua Vétere, Italy 47 A7 41 5N 14 15 E
Santa Maria da Feira, Portugal 42 E2 40 55N 8 35W
Santa Maria da Vitória, Brazil 171 D3 13 24 S 44 12W
Santa María de Ipire, Venezuela 169 B4 8 49N 65 19W
Santa Maria del Camí, Spain 38 B3 39 38N 2 47 E
Santa Maria di Léuca, C., Italy 47 C11 39 47N 18 22 E
Santa Maria do Boiaçu, Brazil 169 D5 0 25 S 61 48W
Santa Maria do Suaçuí, Brazil 171 E3 18 12 S 42 25W
Santa Maria dos Marmelos, Brazil 173 B5 6 7 S 61 51W
Santa María la Real de Nieva, Spain 42 D6 41 4N 4 24W
Santa Marinella, Italy 45 F8 42 2N 11 52 E
Santa Marta, Colombia 168 A3 11 15N 74 13W
Santa Marta, Sierra Nevada de, Colombia 168 A3 10 55N 73 50W
Santa Marta de Tormes, Spain 42 E5 40 57N 5 38W
Santa Marta Grande, C., Brazil 175 B6 28 43 S 48 50W
Santa Marta Ortigueira, Ría de, Spain 42 B3 43 44N 7 45W
Santa Maura = Levkás, Greece 39 B2 38 40N 20 43 E
Santa Monica, U.S.A. 161 M8 34 1N 118 29W
Santa Olalla, Huelva, Spain 43 H4 37 54N 6 14W
Santa Olalla, Toledo, Spain 42 E6 40 2N 4 25W
Santa Paula, U.S.A. 161 L7 34 21N 119 4W
Santa Pola, Spain 41 G4 38 13N 0 35W
Santa Ponça, Spain 38 B3 39 30N 2 28 E
Santa Quitéria, Brazil 170 B3 4 20 S 40 10W
Santa Rita, Brazil 168 D4 3 29 S 69 19W
Santa Rita, Colombia 168 C4 4 53N 68 24W
Santa Rita, Phil. 81 F5 11 27N 124 56 E
Santa Rita, U.S.A. 159 K10 32 48N 108 4W
Santa Rita, Venezuela 168 A3 10 32N 71 32W
Santa Rita do Araquaia, Brazil 173 D7 17 20 S 53 12W
Santa Rosa, La Pampa, Argentina 174 D3 36 40 S 64 17W
Santa Rosa, San Luis, Argentina 174 C2 32 21 S 65 10W
Santa Rosa, Beni, Bolivia 172 C4 14 10 S 66 53W
Santa Rosa, Pando, Bolivia 172 C4 10 36 S 67 20W
Santa Rosa, Santa Cruz, Bolivia 173 D5 17 7 S 63 35W
Santa Rosa, Brazil 175 B5 27 52 S 54 29W
Santa Rosa, Colombia 168 C4 3 32N 69 48W
Santa Rosa, El Oro, Ecuador 168 D2 3 27 S 79 58W
Santa Rosa, Galápagos Is., Ecuador 172 a 0 40 S 90 25W
Santa Rosa, Puno, Peru 172 C3 14 30 S 70 50W
Santa Rosa, San Martin, Peru 172 B2 6 41 S 76 37W
Santa Rosa, Phil. 80 D3 15 25N 120 57 E
Santa Rosa, Calif., U.S.A. 160 G4 38 26N 122 43W
Santa Rosa, N. Mex., U.S.A. 155 H2 34 57N 104 41W
Santa Rosa, Venezuela 168 C4 1 29N 66 55W
Santa Rosa Beach, U.S.A. 152 E3 30 22N 86 14W
Santa Rosa de Amanadona, Venezuela 168 C4 1 29N 66 55W
Santa Rosa de Cabal, Colombia 168 C2 4 52N 75 38W
Santa Rosa de Copán, Honduras 164 D2 14 47N 88 46W
Santa Rosa de la Roca, Bolivia 173 D5 16 3 S 61 34W
Santa Rosa de Osos, Colombia 168 B2 6 39N 75 28W
Santa Rosa de Río Primero, Argentina 174 C3 31 8 S 63 20W
Santa Rosa de Viterbo, Colombia 168 B3 5 53N 72 59W
Santa Rosa del Palmar, Bolivia 173 D5 16 54 S 62 24W
Santa Rosa I., Calif., U.S.A. 161 M6 33 58N 120 6W
Santa Rosa I., Fla., U.S.A. 149 K2 30 20N 86 50W
Santa Rosa Range, U.S.A. 158 F5 41 45N 117 40W
Santa Rosalía, Mexico 162 B2 27 20N 112 20W
Santa Sylvina, Argentina 174 B3 27 50 S 61 10W
Santa Tecla = Nueva San Salvador, El Salv. 164 D2 13 40N 89 18W
Santa Teresa, Argentina 174 C3 33 25 S 60 47W
Santa Teresa, Australia 126 C1 24 8 S 134 22 E
Santa Teresa, Brazil 171 E3 19 55 S 40 36W
Santa Teresa, Mexico 163 B5 25 17N 97 51W
Santa Teresa, Venezuela 169 C5 4 43N 61 4W
Santa Teresa di Riva, Italy 47 E8 37 57N 15 22 E
Santa Teresa Gallura, Italy 46 A2 41 14N 9 11 E
Santa Teresinha, Brazil 170 D1 10 28 S 50 31W
Santa Uxía, Spain 42 C2 42 36N 8 58W
Santa Vitória, Brazil 171 E1 18 50 S 50 8W
Santa Vitória do Palmar, Brazil 175 C5 33 32 S 53 25W
Santa Ynez →, U.S.A. 161 L6 35 41N 120 36W
Santa Ynez Mts., U.S.A. 161 L6 34 30N 120 0W
Santa Ysabel, U.S.A. 161 M10 33 7N 116 40W
Santadi, Italy 46 C1 39 5N 8 43 E
Santaella, Spain 43 H6 37 34N 4 51W
Santahar, Bangla. 90 C2 24 48N 88 59 E
Santai, China 76 B5 31 5N 104 58 E
Santaluz, Brazil 170 D4 11 15 S 39 22W
Santana, Brazil 171 D3 13 2 S 44 5W
Santana, Madeira 9 c 32 48N 16 52W
Sântana, Romania 52 D6 46 20N 21 30 E
Santana, Coxilha de, Brazil 175 C4 30 50 S 55 35W
Santana do Ipanema, Brazil 170 C4 9 22 S 37 14W
Santana do Livramento, Brazil 175 C4 30 55 S 55 30W
Santander, Colombia 168 C2 3 1N 76 28W
Santander, Phil. 81 G4 9 25N 123 20 E
Santander, Spain 42 B7 43 27N 3 51W
Santander □, Colombia 168 B3 7 0N 73 15W
Santander Jiménez, Mexico 163 C5 24 11N 98 29W
Santanilla, Is., Honduras 164 C3 17 22N 83 57W
Santanyí, Spain 38 B4 39 20N 3 5 E
Santaquin, U.S.A. 158 G8 39 59N 111 47W
Santarcángelo di Romagna, Italy 45 D9 44 4N 12 26 E
Santarém, Brazil 169 D7 2 25 S 54 42W
Santarém, Portugal 43 F2 39 12N 8 42W
Santarém □, Portugal 43 F2 39 10N 8 40W
Santaren Channel, W. Indies 164 B4 24 0N 79 30W
Santee, U.S.A. 161 N10 32 50N 116 58W
Santee →, U.S.A. 149 J6 33 7N 79 17W
Santéramo in Colle, Italy 47 B9 40 49N 16 45 E
Santerno →, Italy 45 D8 44 34N 11 58 E
Santhià, Italy 44 C5 45 22N 8 10 E
Santi-Quaranta = Sarandë, Albania 38 B9 39 52N 19 55 E
Santiago = São Tiago, C. Verde Is. 9 j 15 0N 23 40W
Santiago, Bolivia 173 D6 18 19 S 59 34W
Santiago, Brazil 175 B5 29 11 S 54 52W
Santiago, Chile 174 C1 33 24 S 70 40W
Santiago, Panama 164 E3 8 0N 81 0W
Santiago, Peru 172 C2 14 11 S 75 43W
Santiago, Ilocos S., Phil. 80 C3 17 18N 120 27 E
Santiago, Isabela, Phil. 80 C3 16 41N 121 33 E
Santiago □, Chile 174 C1 33 30 S 70 50W
Santiago →, Mexico 136 G9 25 11N 105 26W
Santiago →, Peru 168 D2 4 27 S 77 38W
Santiago, C., Chile 176 D1 50 46 S 75 27W
Santiago, Punta de, Eq. Guin. 113 E6 3 12N 8 40 E
Santiago, Serranía de, Bolivia 173 D6 18 25 S 59 25W
Santiago de Chuco, Peru 172 B2 8 9 S 78 11W
Santiago de Compostela, Spain 42 C2 42 52N 8 37W
Santiago de Cuba, Cuba 164 C4 20 0N 75 49W
Santiago de los Cabelleros, Dom. Rep. 165 C5 19 30N 70 40W

Santiago del Estero, *Argentina* **174 B3** 27 50 S 64 15W
Santiago del Estero □, *Argentina* **174 B3** 27 40 S 63 15W
Santiago del Teide, *Canary Is.* **9 e1** 28 17N 16 48W
Santiago do Cacém, *Portugal* **43 G2** 38 1N 8 42W
Santiago Ixcuintla, *Mexico* **162 C3** 21 50N 105 11W
Santiago Papasquiaro, *Mexico* **162 C3** 25 0N 105 20W
Santiaguillo, L. de, *Mexico* **162 C4** 24 50N 104 50W
Santiguila, *Mali* **112 C3** 12 42N 7 25W
Santillana, *Spain* **42 B6** 43 24N 4 6W
Säntis, *Switz.* **33 B8** 47 15N 9 22 E
Santisteban del Puerto, *Spain* **43 G7** 38 17N 3 15W
Santo →, *Peru* **172 B2** 8 56 S 78 37W
Santo Amaro, *Brazil* **171 D4** 12 30 S 38 43W
Santo Anastácio, *Brazil* **175 A5** 21 58 S 51 39W
Santo André, *Brazil* **175 A6** 23 39 S 46 29W
Santo Ângelo, *Brazil* **175 B5** 28 15 S 54 15W
Santo Antão, *C. Verde Is.* **9 j** 16 52N 25 10W
Santo Antónia, *São Tomé & Principe* **115 G6** 1 37N 7 27 E
Santo Antonio, *Brazil* **169 D5** 2 24 S 60 58W
Santo Antônio de Jesus, *Brazil* **171 D4** 12 58 S 39 16W
Santo Antônio do Içá, *Brazil* **168 D4** 3 5 S 67 57W
Santo Antônio do Leverger, *Brazil* **173 D6** 15 52 S 56 5W
Santo Corazón, *Bolivia* **173 D6** 18 0 S 58 45W
Santo Domingo, *Dom. Rep.* **165 C6** 18 30N 69 59W
Santo Domingo, *Baja Calif., Mexico* **162 A1** 30 43N 116 2W
Santo Domingo, *Baja Calif. S., Mexico* **162 B2** 25 32N 112 2W
Santo Domingo, *Nic.* **164 D3** 12 14N 84 59W
Santo Domingo de la Calzada, *Spain* **40 C2** 42 26N 2 57W
Santo Domingo de los Colorados, *Ecuador* **168 D2** 0 15 S 79 9W
Santo Domingo Pueblo, *U.S.A.* **159 J10** 35 31N 106 22W
Santo Stéfano di Camastro, *Italy* **47 D7** 38 1N 14 22 E
Santo Tirso, *Portugal* **42 D2** 41 21N 8 28W
Santo Tomás, *Ecuador* **172 a** 0 51 S 91 2W
Santo Tomás, *Mexico* **162 A1** 31 33N 116 24W
Santo Tomás, *Peru* **172 C3** 14 26 S 72 8W
Santo Tomás, Volcán, *Ecuador* **172 a** 0 48 S 91 7W
Santo Tomé, *Argentina* **175 B4** 28 40 S 56 5W
Santo Tomé de Guayana = Ciudad Guayana, *Venezuela* **169 B5** 8 0N 62 30W
Santomera, *Spain* **41 G3** 38 4N 1 3W
Santoña, *Spain* **42 B7** 43 29N 3 27W
Santoríni = Thíra, *Greece* **49 E7** 36 23N 25 27 E
Santos, *Brazil* **175 A6** 24 0 S 46 20W
Santos, Sierra de los, *Spain* **43 G5** 38 7N 5 12W
Santos Dumont, *Brazil* **171 F3** 22 55 S 43 10W
Sanur, *Indonesia* **79 K18** 8 41 S 115 15 E
Sanwer, *India* **92 H6** 22 59N 75 50 E
Sanxenxo, *Spain* **42 C2** 42 24N 8 49W
Sanxiang, *China* **69 G9** 22 21N 113 25 E
San'yō, *Japan* **72 C3** 34 2N 131 5 E
Sanyuan, *China* **74 G5** 34 35N 108 58 E
Sanyuki-Sammyaku, *Japan* **72 C6** 34 5N 134 0 E
Sanza Pombo, *Angola* **115 D3** 7 18 S 15 56 E
São Bartolomeu de Messines, *Portugal* **43 H2** 37 15N 8 17W
São Benedito, *Brazil* **170 B3** 4 3 S 40 53W
São Benedito →, *Brazil* **173 B6** 9 11 S 57 2W
São Bento, *Brazil* **170 B3** 2 42 S 44 50W
São Bento do Norte, *Brazil* **170 C4** 5 4 S 36 2W
São Bernardo do Campo, *Brazil* **171 F2** 23 45 S 46 34W
São Borja, *Brazil* **175 B4** 28 39 S 56 0W
São Brás de Alportel, *Portugal* **43 H3** 37 8N 7 37W
São Braz, C. de, *Angola* **115 D2** 9 58 S 13 19 E
São Caitano, *Brazil* **170 C4** 8 21 S 36 6W
São Carlos, *Brazil* **175 A6** 22 0 S 47 50W
São Cristóvão, *Brazil* **170 D4** 11 1 S 37 15W
São Domingos, *Brazil* **171 D2** 13 25 S 46 19W
São Domingos, *Guinea-Biss.* **112 C1** 12 19N 16 13 E
São Domingos do Maranhão, *Brazil* **170 C3** 5 42 S 44 22W
São Félix, *Brazil* **171 D1** 11 36 S 50 39W
São Felix do Xingu, *Brazil* **173 B7** 6 38 S 51 59W
São Filipe, *C. Verde Is.* **9 j** 15 2N 24 30W
São Francisco, *Brazil* **171 E3** 16 0 S 44 50W
São Francisco →, *Brazil* **170 D4** 10 30 S 36 24W
São Francisco do Maranhão, *Brazil* **170 C3** 6 15 S 42 52W
São Francisco do Sul, *Brazil* **175 B6** 26 15 S 48 36W
São Gabriel, *Brazil* **175 C5** 30 20 S 54 20W
São Gabriel da Cachoeira, *Brazil* **168 D4** 0 8 S 67 5W
São Gabriel da Palha, *Brazil* **171 E3** 18 47 S 40 39W
São Gonçalo, *Brazil* **171 F3** 22 48 S 43 5W
São Gotardo, *Brazil* **171 E2** 19 19 S 46 3W
Sao Hill, *Tanzania* **119 D4** 8 20 S 35 12 E
São João, *Guinea-Biss.* **112 C1** 11 32N 15 25W
São João da Baliza, *Brazil* **169 C6** 0 52N 59 52W
São João da Boa Vista, *Brazil* **175 A6** 22 0 S 46 52W
São João da Madeira, *Portugal* **42 E2** 40 54N 8 30W
São João da Pesqueira, *Portugal* **42 D3** 41 8N 7 24W
São João da Ponte, *Brazil* **171 E3** 15 56 S 44 1W
São João del Rei, *Brazil* **171 F3** 21 8 S 44 15W
São João do Araguaia, *Brazil* **170 C2** 5 23 S 48 46W
São João do Paraíso, *Brazil* **171 E3** 15 19 S 42 1W
São João do Piauí, *Brazil* **170 C3** 8 21 S 42 15W
São João dos Patos, *Brazil* **170 C3** 6 30 S 43 42W
São Joaquim, *Amazonas, Brazil* **168 D4** 0 1 S 67 16W
São Joaquim, *Sta. Catarina, Brazil* **175 B6** 28 18 S 49 56W
São Joaquim da Barra, *Brazil* **171 F2** 20 35 S 47 53W
São Jorge, *Azores* **9 d1** 38 38N 28 3W
São Jorge, Canal de, *Azores* **9 d1** 38 30N 28 0W
São Jorge, Pta. de, *Azores* **9 d1** 38 42N 27 3W
São Jorge, Pta. de, *Madeira* **9 c** 32 50N 16 53W
São José, *Brazil* **175 B5** 27 38 S 48 39W
São José, B. de, *Brazil* **170 B3** 2 38 S 44 4W
São José da Laje, *Brazil* **170 C4** 9 1 S 36 3W
São José de Mipibu, *Brazil* **170 C4** 6 5 S 35 15W
São José do Norte, *Brazil* **175 C5** 32 1 S 52 3W
São José do Peixe, *Brazil* **170 C3** 7 24 S 42 34W
São José do Rio Prêto, *Brazil* **175 A6** 20 50 S 49 20W
São José dos Campos, *Brazil* **175 A6** 23 7 S 45 52W
São Leopoldo, *Brazil* **175 B5** 29 50 S 51 10W
São Lourenço, *Brazil* **171 F2** 22 7 S 45 3W
São Lourenço →, *Brazil* **173 D6** 17 53 S 57 27W
São Lourenço, Pantanal do, *Brazil* **173 D6** 17 30 S 56 20W
São Lourenço, Pta. de, *Madeira* **9 c** 32 44N 16 39W
São Lourenço do Sul, *Brazil* **175 C5** 31 22 S 51 58W
São Luís, *Brazil* **170 B3** 2 39 S 44 15W
São Luís do Curu, *Brazil* **170 B4** 3 40 S 39 14W
São Luís do Tapojós, *Brazil* **169 D6** 4 25 S 56 12W
São Luís Gonzaga, *Brazil* **175 B5** 28 25 S 55 0W
São Marcos →, *Brazil* **171 E2** 18 15 S 47 37W
São Marcos, B. de, *Brazil* **170 B3** 2 0 S 44 0W
São Martinho da Cortiça, *Portugal* **42 E2** 40 18N 8 8W
São Mateus, *Azores* **9 d1** 38 26N 28 27W
São Mateus, *Brazil* **171 E4** 18 44 S 39 50W
São Mateus →, *Brazil* **171 E4** 18 35 S 39 44W
São Mateus do Sul, *Brazil* **175 B5** 25 52 S 50 23W
São Miguel, *Azores* **9 d3** 37 47N 25 30W
São Miguel do Araguaia, *Brazil* **171 D1** 13 19 S 50 13W
São Miguel do Oeste, *Brazil* **175 B5** 26 45 S 53 34W
São Miguel dos Campos, *Brazil* **170 C4** 9 47 S 36 5W
São Nicolau, *C. Verde Is.* **9 j** 16 20N 24 20W
São Nicolau →, *Angola* **115 E2** 14 16 S 12 22 E
São Nicolau →, *Brazil* **170 C3** 5 45 S 42 2W
São Paulo, *Brazil* **175 A6** 23 32 S 46 37W
São Paulo □, *Brazil* **175 A6** 22 0 S 49 0W
São Paulo, I., *Atl. Oc.* **8 F9** 0 50N 31 40W
São Paulo de Olivença, *Brazil* **168 D4** 3 27 S 68 48W
São Pedro do Sul, *Portugal* **42 E2** 40 46N 8 4W
São Rafael, *Brazil* **170 C4** 5 47 S 36 55W
São Raimundo das Mangabeiras, *Brazil* **170 C2** 7 1 S 45 29W
São Raimundo Nonato, *Brazil* **170 C3** 9 1 S 42 42W
São Romão, *Brazil* **171 E2** 16 22 S 45 4W
São Roque, *Madeira* **9 c** 32 46N 16 48W
São Roque, C. de, *Brazil* **170 C4** 5 30 S 35 16W
São Roque do Pico, *Azores* **9 d1** 38 31N 28 19W
São Sebastião, *Azores* **9 d1** 38 39N 27 6W
São Sebastião, I. de, *Brazil* **175 A6** 23 50 S 45 18W
São Sebastião do Paraíso, *Brazil* **175 A6** 20 54 S 46 59W
São Simão, *Brazil* **171 E1** 18 56 S 50 30W
São Teotónio, *Portugal* **43 H2** 37 30N 8 42W
São Tiago, *C. Verde Is.* **9 j** 15 0N 23 40W
São Tomé, *Brazil* **170 C4** 5 58 S 36 4W
São Tomé, *São Tomé & Principe* **115 G6** 0 10N 6 39 E
São Tomé, C. de, *Brazil* **171 F3** 22 0 S 40 59W
São Tomé, Pico de, *São Tomé & Principe* **115 G6** 0 16N 6 33 E
São Tomé & Principe ■, *Africa* **115 G6** 0 12N 6 39 E
São Vicente, *Brazil* **175 A6** 23 57 S 46 23W
São Vicente, *C. Verde Is.* **9 j** 17 0N 25 0W
São Vicente, *Madeira* **9 c** 32 48N 17 3W
São Vicente, C. de, *Portugal* **43 H1** 37 0N 9 0W
Saona, I., *Dom. Rep.* **165 C6** 18 10N 68 40W
Saône →, *France* **27 G11** 45 44N 4 50 E
Saône-et-Loire □, *France* **27 F11** 46 30N 4 50 E
Saonek, *Indonesia* **83 B4** 0 22 S 130 55 E
Saoura, O. →, *Algeria* **111 C4** 29 0N 0 55W
Sápai, *Greece* **51 E9** 41 2N 25 43 E
Sapam, Ao, *Thailand* **87 a** 8 0N 98 26 E
Sapanca, *Turkey* **100 B4** 40 41N 30 16 E
Sapão →, *Brazil* **170 D2** 11 1 S 45 32W
Saparua, *Indonesia* **82 B3** 3 33 S 128 40 E
Sapé, *Brazil* **170 C4** 7 6 S 35 13W
Sape, *Indonesia* **85 D5** 8 34 S 118 59 E
Sapele, *Nigeria* **113 D6** 5 50N 5 40 E
Sapelo I., *U.S.A.* **152 D8** 31 25N 81 12W
Sapelo Sound, *U.S.A.* **152 D8** 31 30N 81 10W
Şaphane, *Turkey* **49 B11** 39 1N 29 13 E
Sapi Safari Area, *Zimbabwe* **119 F2** 15 48 S 29 42 E
Sapiéntza, *Greece* **48 E3** 36 45N 21 43 E
Sapindji, *Dem. Rep. of the Congo* **115 D4** 9 39 S 23 12 E
Sapo Nat. Park, *Liberia* **112 D3** 5 15N 8 30W
Sapone, *Burkina Faso* **113 C4** 12 3N 1 35W
Saposoa, *Peru* **172 B2** 6 55 S 76 45W
Sapouy, *Burkina Faso* **113 C4** 11 34N 1 44W
Sapozhok, *Russia* **60 D5** 53 59N 40 41 E
Sapphire, *Australia* **126 C4** 23 28 S 147 43 E
Sappho, *U.S.A.* **160 B2** 48 4N 124 16W
Sapporo, *Japan* **70 C10** 43 0N 141 21 E
Sapri, *Italy* **47 B8** 40 4N 15 38 E
Sapu, *Angola* **115 E3** 12 28 S 19 26 E
Sapudi, *Indonesia* **85 D4** 7 6 S 114 20 E
Sapulpa, *U.S.A.* **155 H6** 35 59N 96 5W
Saqqez, *Iran* **101 D12** 36 15N 46 20 E
Sar Dasht, *Iran* **97 C6** 32 32N 48 52 E
Sar-e Pol, *Afghan.* **91 A2** 36 10N 66 0 E
Sar-e Pol □, *Afghan.* **91 A2** 36 20N 65 50 E
Sar Gachīneh = Yāsūj, *Iran* **97 D6** 30 31N 51 31 E
Sar Planina, *Macedonia* **50 E4** 42 0N 21 0 E
Sara, *Burkina Faso* **112 C4** 11 40N 3 53W
Sara, *Niger* **109 D2** 20 46N 12 35 E
Sara, *Phil.* **81 F4** 11 16N 123 1 E
Sara Buri = Saraburi, *Thailand* **86 E3** 14 30N 100 55 E
Sarāb, *Iran* **101 D12** 37 55N 47 40 E
Sarabadi, *Iraq* **96 C5** 33 1N 44 48 E
Saraburi, *Thailand* **86 E3** 14 30N 100 55 E
Saradiya, *India* **92 J4** 21 34N 70 2 E
Saraféré, *Mali* **112 B4** 15 50N 3 40W
Saragossa = Zaragoza, *Spain* **40 D4** 41 39N 0 53W
Saraguro, *Ecuador* **168 D2** 3 35 S 79 16W
Sarai Naurang, *Pakistan* **92 C4** 32 50N 70 47 E
Saraikela, *India* **93 H11** 22 42N 85 56 E
Saraipali, *India* **94 D6** 21 20N 82 59 E
Saraiu, *Romania* **53 F13** 44 43N 28 10 E
Sarajevo, *Bos.-H.* **52 G3** 43 52N 18 26 E
Sarakhs, *Turkmenistan* **97 B9** 36 32N 61 13 E
Saraktash, *Russia* **64 F6** 51 47N 56 22 E
Saramacca →, *Surinam* **169 B6** 5 50N 55 55W
Saramati, *Burma* **90 C5** 25 44N 95 2 E
Saran, Gunung, *Indonesia* **85 C4** 0 30 S 111 25 E
Saranac, *U.S.A.* **157 B11** 42 56N 85 13W
Saranac L., *U.S.A.* **151 B10** 44 20N 74 10W
Saranac Lake, *U.S.A.* **151 B10** 44 20N 74 8W
Saranda, *Tanzania* **118 D3** 5 45 S 34 59 E
Sarandë, *Albania* **38 B9** 39 52N 19 55 E
Sarandí del Yi, *Uruguay* **175 C4** 33 18 S 55 38W
Sarandí Grande, *Uruguay* **174 C4** 33 44 S 56 20W
Sarangani □, *Phil.* **81 J5** 5 45N 125 20 E
Sarangani B., *Phil.* **81 J5** 6 0N 125 13 E
Sarangani Is., *Phil.* **81 J5** 5 25N 125 25 E
Sarangarh, *India* **94 D6** 21 30N 83 5 E
Saransk, *Russia* **60 C7** 54 10N 45 10 E
Sarapul, *Russia* **64 C4** 56 28N 53 48 E
Sarar Plain = Bannaanka Saraar, *Somali Rep.* **120 C3** 9 25N 46 17 E
Sarasota, *U.S.A.* **149 M4** 27 20N 82 32W
Saratoga, *Calif., U.S.A.* **160 H4** 37 16N 122 2W
Saratoga, *Wyo., U.S.A.* **158 F10** 41 27N 106 49W
Saratoga Springs, *U.S.A.* **151 C11** 43 5N 73 47W
Saratok, *Malaysia* **78 D4** 1 55N 111 17 E
Saratov, *Russia* **60 E7** 51 30N 46 2 E
Saravane, *Laos* **86 E6** 15 43N 106 25 E
Sarawak □, *Malaysia* **85 B4** 2 0N 113 0 E
Saray, *Tekirdağ, Turkey* **51 E11** 41 26N 27 55 E
Saray, *Van, Turkey* **101 C11** 38 38N 44 9 E
Saraya, *Guinea* **112 C2** 12 50N 11 45W
Saraya, *Senegal* **112 C2** 12 50N 11 45W
Saraycık, *Turkey* **49 B11** 39 1N 29 49 E
Sarayköy, *Turkey* **49 D10** 37 55N 28 54 E
Saraylar, *Turkey* **51 F11** 40 39N 27 40 E
Sarayönü, *Turkey* **100 C5** 38 16N 32 24 E
Sarbāz, *Iran* **97 E9** 26 38N 61 19 E
Sarbīsheh, *Iran* **97 C8** 32 30N 59 40 E
Sárbogárd, *Hungary* **52 D3** 46 50N 18 40 E
Sarca →, *Italy* **44 C7** 45 52N 10 52 E
Sarcelles, *France* **27 D9** 48 59N 2 23 E
Sardalas, *Libya* **108 C2** 25 50N 10 34 E
Sardarshahr, *India* **92 E6** 28 30N 74 29 E
Sardegna □, *Italy* **46 B1** 40 0N 9 0 E
Sardhana, *India* **92 E7** 29 9N 77 39 E
Sardina, Pta., *Canary Is.* **9 e1** 28 9N 15 44W
Sardinata, *Colombia* **168 B3** 8 5N 72 48W
Sardinia = Sardegna □, *Italy* **46 B1** 40 0N 9 0 E
Sardinia, *U.S.A.* **157 F13** 39 0N 83 49W
Sardis, *Turkey* **49 C10** 38 28N 28 2 E
Sardis, *U.S.A.* **152 C8** 32 58N 81 46W
Sārdūīyeh = Dar Mazār, *Iran* **97 D8** 29 14N 57 20 E
Saren, *Indonesia* **79 J18** 8 26 S 115 34 E
S'Arenal, *Spain* **38 B3** 39 30N 2 45 E
Sarentino, *Italy* **45 B8** 46 38N 11 21 E
Saréyamou, *Mali* **112 B4** 16 7N 3 10W
Sargans, *Switz.* **33 B8** 47 3N 9 15 E
Sargasso Sea, *Atl. Oc.* **8 D4** 27 0N 72 0W
Sargent, *U.S.A.* **152 B5** 33 26N 84 52W
Sargodha, *Pakistan* **91 B4** 32 10N 72 40 E
Sarh, *Chad* **109 G8** 9 5N 18 23 E
Sarhala, *Ivory C.* **112 D3** 8 22N 6 8W
Sarhro, Jebel, *Morocco* **110 B4** 31 6N 5 0W
Sārī, *Iran* **97 B7** 36 30N 53 4 E
Sari d'Orcino, *France* **29 F12** 42 3N 8 49 E
Sária, *Greece* **49 F9** 35 54N 27 17 E
Saria, *India* **93 J10** 21 38N 83 22 E
Sariab, *Pakistan* **92 D2** 30 6N 66 59 E
Sarıbeyler, *Turkey* **49 B9** 39 24N 27 35 E
Saricumbe, *Angola* **115 E3** 12 12 S 19 46 E
Sarıgöl, *Turkey* **100 C3** 38 14N 28 41 E
Sarikamiş, *Turkey* **101 B10** 40 22N 42 35 E
Sarıkaya, *Turkey* **100 C6** 39 29N 35 22 E
Sarikei, *Malaysia* **85 B4** 2 8N 111 30 E
Sarıköy, *Turkey* **51 F11** 40 12N 27 37 E
Sarila, *India* **93 G8** 25 46N 79 41 E
Sarina, *Australia* **126 C4** 21 22 S 149 13 E
Sariñena, *Spain* **40 D4** 41 47N 0 10W
Sariri, *Papua N. G.* **132 E5** 9 11 S 148 35 E
Sarita, *U.S.A.* **155 M6** 27 13N 97 47W
Sariwŏn, *N. Korea* **75 E13** 38 31N 125 46 E
Sariyar Barajı, *Turkey* **100 B4** 40 2N 31 33 E
Sariyer, *Turkey* **51 E13** 41 10N 29 3 E
Sarju →, *India* **93 F9** 27 21N 81 23 E
Sark, *U.K.* **21 H5** 49 25N 2 22W
Sarkad, *Hungary* **52 D6** 46 47N 21 23 E
Sarkari Tala, *India* **92 F4** 27 39N 70 52 E
Şarkışla, *Turkey* **100 C7** 39 21N 36 25 E
Şarköy, *Turkey* **51 F11** 40 36N 27 6 E
Sarlat-la-Canéda, *France* **28 D5** 44 54N 1 13 E
Sărmăşag, *Romania* **52 C7** 47 21N 22 50 E
Sărmaşu, *Romania* **53 D9** 46 45N 24 13 E
Sarmi, *Indonesia* **83 B5** 1 49 S 138 44 E
Sarmiento, *Argentina* **176 C3** 45 35 S 69 5W
Sarmizegetusa, *Romania* **52 E7** 45 31N 22 47 E
Särna, *Sweden* **16 C7** 61 41N 13 8 E
Sarnano, *Italy* **45 E10** 43 2N 13 18 E
Sarnen, *Switz.* **32 C6** 46 53N 8 13 E
Sarnia, *Canada* **140 D3** 42 58N 82 23W
Sarno, *Italy* **47 B7** 40 49N 14 37 E
Sarnthein = Sarentino, *Italy* **45 B8** 46 38N 11 21 E
Särö, *Sweden* **17 G5** 57 31N 11 57 E
Saroako, *Indonesia* **82 B2** 2 31 S 121 22 E
Sarolangun, *Indonesia* **84 C2** 2 19 S 102 42 E
Saronikós Kólpos, *Greece* **48 D5** 37 45N 23 45 E
Saronno, *Italy* **44 C6** 45 38N 9 2 E
Saros Körfezi, *Turkey* **51 F10** 40 30N 26 15 E
Sárospatak, *Hungary* **52 B6** 48 18N 21 33 E
Sarowbī, *Afghan.* **91 B3** 34 36N 69 44 E
Sarpsborg, *Norway* **15 G14** 59 16N 11 7 E
Sarracín, *Spain* **42 C7** 42 15N 3 45W
Sarralbe, *France* **27 D14** 49 0N 7 1 E
Sarrat, *Phil.* **80 B3** 18 9N 120 39 E
Sarre = Saar →, *Europe* **24 E6** 49 41N 6 32 E
Sarre, *Italy* **44 C4** 45 40N 7 15 E
Sarre-Union, *France* **27 D14** 48 57N 7 4 E
Sarrebourg, *France* **27 D14** 48 43N 7 3 E
Sarreguemines, *France* **27 C14** 49 5N 7 4 E
Sarria, *Spain* **42 C3** 42 49N 7 29W
Sarrión, *Spain* **40 E4** 40 9N 0 49W
Sarro, *Mali* **112 C3** 13 40N 5 15W
Sarstedt, *Germany* **30 C5** 52 14N 9 52 E
Sartène, *France* **29 G12** 41 38N 8 58 E
Sarthe □, *France* **26 D7** 48 10N 0 10 E
Sarthe →, *France* **26 E6** 47 33N 0 31W
Sartilly, *France* **26 D5** 48 45N 1 28W
Saruhanlı, *Turkey* **49 C9** 38 44N 27 36 E
Săruleşti, *Romania* **53 F11** 44 25N 26 39 E
Saruna →, *Pakistan* **92 F2** 26 31N 67 7 E
Sarupeta, *India* **90 B3** 26 30N 91 5 E
Saruwaged Ra., *Papua N. G.* **132 D4** 6 13 S 146 45 E
Sárvár, *Hungary* **52 C1** 47 15N 16 56 E
Sarvar, *India* **92 F6** 26 4N 75 0 E
Sarvestān, *Iran* **97 D7** 29 20N 53 10 E
Särvfjället, *Sweden* **16 B7** 62 42N 13 30 E
Sárviz →, *Hungary* **52 D3** 46 24N 18 41 E
Sary-Tash, *Kyrgyzstan* **66 F8** 39 44N 73 15 E
Saryaghash, *Kazakstan* **65 C4** 41 27N 69 9 E
Sarybulaq, *Kazakstan* **65 B5** 43 23N 71 29 E
Sarych, Mys, *Ukraine* **59 K7** 44 25N 33 45 E
Sarykemer, *Kazakstan* **65 B5** 43 0N 71 30 E
Sarykolskiy Khrebet, *Tajikistan* **65 D7** 38 30N 74 30 E
Saryözek, *Kazakstan* **65 A8** 44 22N 77 59 E
Saryshagan, *Kazakstan* **66 E8** 46 12N 73 38 E
Sarzana, *Italy* **44 D6** 44 7N 9 58 E
Sarzeau, *France* **26 E4** 47 31N 2 48W
Sasabeneh, *Ethiopia* **120 C2** 7 59N 44 43 E
Sasamungga, *Solomon Is.* **133 L9** 7 0 S 156 50 E
Sasan Gir, *India* **92 J4** 21 10N 70 36 E
Sasaram, *India* **93 G11** 24 57N 84 5 E
Sasari, Mt., *Solomon Is.* **133 M10** 8 10 S 159 30 E
Sasayama, *Japan* **73 B7** 35 4N 135 13 E
Sasebo, *Japan* **72 D1** 33 10N 129 43 E
Saser, *India* **93 B7** 34 50N 77 50 E
Saskatchewan □, *Canada* **143 C7** 54 40N 106 0W
Saskatchewan →, *Canada* **143 C8** 53 37N 100 40W
Saskatoon, *Canada* **143 C7** 52 10N 106 38W
Saskylakh, *Russia* **67 B12** 71 55N 114 1 E
Sasolburg, *S. Africa* **117 D4** 26 46 S 27 49 E
Sasovo, *Russia* **60 C5** 54 25N 41 55 E
Sassandra, *Ivory C.* **112 E3** 4 55N 6 8W
Sassandra →, *Ivory C.* **112 E3** 4 58N 6 5W
Sássari, *Italy* **46 B1** 40 43N 8 34 E
Sassnitz, *Germany* **30 A9** 54 29N 13 39 E
Sasso Marconi, *Italy* **45 D8** 44 24N 11 15 E
Sassocorvaro, *Italy* **45 E9** 43 47N 12 30 E
Sassoferrato, *Italy* **45 E9** 43 26N 12 51 E
Sasstown, *Liberia* **112 E3** 4 45N 8 27W
Sassuolo, *Italy* **44 D7** 44 33N 10 47 E
Sástago, *Spain* **40 D4** 41 19N 0 21W
Sastöbe, *Kazakstan* **65 B4** 42 33N 70 0 E
Sasumua Dam, *Kenya* **118 C4** 0 45 S 36 40 E
Sasvad, *India* **94 E2** 18 20N 74 2 E
Sasyk, Ozero, *Ukraine* **59 K5** 45 45N 29 20 E
Sata-Misaki, *Japan* **72 F2** 31 0N 130 40 E
Satadougou, *Mali* **112 C2** 12 25N 11 25W
Satakunta, *Finland* **15 F20** 61 45N 23 0 E
Satama-Soukoura, *Ivory C.* **112 D4** 7 55N 4 27W
Satara, *India* **94 F1** 17 44N 73 58 E
Satara, *S. Africa* **117 C5** 24 29 S 31 47 E
Satbarwa, *India* **93 H11** 23 55N 84 16 E
Satellite Beach, *U.S.A.* **153 G9** 28 10N 80 36W
Såtenäs, *Sweden* **17 F6** 58 27N 12 41 E
Säter, *Sweden* **16 D9** 60 21N 15 45 E
Satevó, *Mexico* **162 B3** 27 57N 106 7W
Satilla →, *U.S.A.* **152 E8** 30 59N 81 29W
Satipo, *Peru* **172 C3** 11 15 S 74 25W
Satka, *Russia* **64 D7** 55 3N 59 1 E
Satkania, *Bangla.* **90 D4** 22 4N 92 3 E
Satkhira, *Bangla.* **90 D2** 22 43N 89 8 E
Satmala Hills, *Andhra Pradesh, India* **94 E4** 19 45N 78 45 E
Satmala Hills, *Maharashtra, India* **94 D2** 20 15N 74 40 E
Satna, *India* **93 G9** 24 35N 80 50 E
Šator, *Bos.-H.* **45 D13** 44 11N 16 37 E
Sátoraljaújhely, *Hungary* **52 B6** 48 25N 21 41 E
Satpura Ra., *India* **94 D3** 21 25N 76 10 E
Satrup, *Germany* **30 A5** 54 41N 9 36 E
Satsuma-Hantō, *Japan* **72 F2** 31 25N 130 25 E
Satsuna-Shotō, *Japan* **71 K5** 30 0N 130 0 E
Sattahip, *Thailand* **86 F3** 12 41N 100 54 E
Sattenapalle, *India* **95 F5** 16 25N 80 6 E
Satu Mare, *Romania* **52 C7** 47 46N 22 55 E
Satu Mare □, *Romania* **52 C8** 47 45N 23 0 E
Satui, *Indonesia* **85 C5** 3 50 S 115 27 E
Satun, *Thailand* **87 J3** 6 43N 100 2 E
Satupa'itea, *Samoa* **133 W23** 13 45 S 172 18W
Saturnina →, *Brazil* **173 C6** 12 15 S 58 10W
Sauce, *Argentina* **174 C4** 30 5 S 58 46W
Sauceda, *Mexico* **162 B4** 25 55N 101 18W
Saucillo, *Mexico* **162 B3** 28 1N 105 17W
Sauda, *Norway* **15 G12** 59 40N 6 20 E
Saūdakent, *Kazakstan* **65 B4** 43 48N 69 58 E
Saudasjøen, *Norway* **18 E3** 59 38N 6 17 E
Saúde, *Brazil* **170 D3** 10 56 S 40 24W
Sauðarkrókur, *Iceland* **11 B7** 65 45N 19 40W
Saudi Arabia ■, *Asia* **96 B3** 26 0N 44 0 E
Sauerland, *Germany* **36 C4** 51 12N 7 59 E
Saugatuck, *U.S.A.* **157 B10** 42 40N 86 12W
Saugeen →, *Canada* **150 B3** 44 30N 81 22W
Saugerties, *U.S.A.* **151 D11** 42 5N 73 57W
Saugues, *France* **28 D7** 44 58N 3 32 E
Saugus, *U.S.A.* **161 L8** 34 25N 118 32W
Saujon, *France* **28 C3** 45 41N 0 55W
Sauk Centre, *U.S.A.* **154 C7** 45 44N 94 57W
Sauk City, *U.S.A.* **156 A7** 43 17N 89 43W
Sauk Rapids, *U.S.A.* **154 C7** 45 35N 94 10W
Saül, *Fr. Guiana* **169 C7** 3 37N 53 12W
Sauland, *Norway* **18 E5** 59 37N 8 56 E
Saulgau, *Germany* **31 G5** 48 1N 9 29 E
Saulieu, *France* **27 E11** 47 17N 4 14 E
Sault, *France* **29 D9** 44 6N 5 24 E
Sault Ste. Marie, *Canada* **140 C3** 46 30N 84 20W
Sault Ste. Marie, *U.S.A.* **139 D11** 46 30N 84 21W
Saumlaki, *Indonesia* **83 C4** 7 55 S 131 20 E
Saumur, *France* **26 E6** 47 15N 0 5W
Saundatti, *India* **95 G2** 15 47N 75 7 E
Saunders, C., *N.Z.* **131 F5** 45 53 S 170 45 E
Saunders I., *Antarctica* **7 B1** 57 48 S 26 28W
Saunders Point, *Australia* **125 E4** 27 52 S 125 38 E
Saunemin, *U.S.A.* **157 D8** 40 54N 88 24W
Saupite, *Angola* **115 E3** 13 54 S 17 43 E
Saurbær, *Borgarfjarðarsýsla, Iceland* **11 C5** 64 24N 21 35W
Saurbær, *Eyjafjarðarsýsla, Iceland* **11 B8** 65 27N 18 13W
Sauri, *Nigeria* **113 C6** 11 42N 6 44 E
Saurimo, *Angola* **115 D4** 9 40 S 20 12 E
Sausalito, *U.S.A.* **160 H4** 37 51N 122 29W
Sausapor, *Indonesia* **83 B4** 0 31 S 132 4 E
Sautatá, *Colombia* **168 B2** 7 50N 77 4W
Sauveterre-de-Béarn, *France* **28 E3** 43 24N 0 57W
Sauzé-Vaussais, *France* **28 B4** 46 8N 0 8 E
Savá, *Honduras* **164 C2** 15 32N 86 15W
Sava, *Italy* **47 B10** 40 24N 17 33 E
Sava →, *Serbia, Yug.* **52 F5** 44 50N 20 26 E
Savage, *U.S.A.* **154 B2** 47 27N 104 21W
Savage I. = Niue, *Cook Is.* **135 J11** 19 2 S 169 54W
Savage River, *Australia* **127 G4** 41 31 S 145 14 E
Savai'i, *Samoa* **133 W23** 13 28 S 172 24W
Savalou, *Benin* **113 D5** 7 57N 1 58 E
Savane, *Mozam.* **119 F4** 19 37 S 35 8 E
Savanna, *U.S.A.* **156 B6** 42 5N 90 8W
Savanna-la-Mar, *Jamaica* **164 a** 18 10N 78 10W
Savannah, *Ga., U.S.A.* **152 C8** 32 5N 81 6W
Savannah, *Mo., U.S.A.* **156 E2** 39 56N 94 50W
Savannah, *Tenn., U.S.A.* **149 H1** 35 14N 88 15W
Savannah →, *U.S.A.* **152 C9** 32 2N 80 53W
Savannah Beach = Tybee Island, *U.S.A.* **152 C9** 32 1N 80 51W
Savannakhet, *Laos* **86 D5** 16 30N 104 49 E
Savant L., *Canada* **140 B1** 50 16N 90 44W
Savant Lake, *Canada* **140 B1** 50 14N 90 40W
Savantvadi, *India* **95 G1** 15 55N 73 54 E
Savanur, *India* **95 G2** 14 59N 75 21 E
Săvârşin, *Romania* **52 D7** 46 1N 22 14 E
Savaştepe, *Turkey* **49 B9** 39 22N 27 42 E
Savda, *India* **94 D2** 21 9N 75 56 E
Savé, *Benin* **113 D5** 8 2N 2 29 E
Save →, *France* **28 E5** 43 47N 1 17 E
Save →, *Mozam.* **117 C5** 21 16 S 34 0 E
Sāveh, *Iran* **97 C6** 35 2N 50 20 E
Savelugu, *Ghana* **113 D4** 9 38N 0 54W
Savenay, *France* **26 E5** 47 20N 1 55W
Săveni, *Romania* **53 C11** 47 57N 26 52 E
Saverdun, *France* **28 E5** 43 14N 1 34 E
Saverne, *France* **27 D14** 48 43N 7 20 E
Savièse, *Switz.* **32 D4** 46 17N 7 22 E
Savigliano, *Italy* **44 D4** 44 38N 7 40 E
Savigny-sur-Braye, *France* **26 E7** 47 53N 0 49 E
Sávio →, *Italy* **45 D9** 44 19N 12 20 E
Šavnik, *Montenegro, Yug.* **50 D3** 42 59N 19 10 E
Savo, *Finland* **14 E22** 62 45N 27 30 E
Savo, *Solomon Is.* **133 M10** 9 8 S 159 48 E
Savognin, *Switz.* **33 C9** 46 36N 9 37 E
Savoie □, *France* **29 C10** 45 26N 6 25 E
Savona, *Italy* **44 D5** 44 17N 8 30 E
Savona, *U.S.A.* **150 D7** 42 17N 77 13W
Savonlinna, *Finland* **58 B5** 61 52N 28 53 E
Savoonga, *U.S.A.* **144 E5** 63 42N 170 29W
Savoy = Savoie □, *France* **29 C10** 45 26N 6 25 E
Şavşat, *Turkey* **101 B10** 41 15N 42 20 E
Sävsjö, *Sweden* **17 G8** 57 20N 14 40 E
Savur, *Turkey* **96 B4** 37 34N 40 53 E
Savusavu, *Fiji* **133 A2** 16 34 S 179 15 E
Savusavu B., *Fiji* **133 A2** 16 45 S 179 15 E
Sawahlunto, *Indonesia* **84 C2** 0 40 S 100 52 E
Sawai, *Indonesia* **83 B3** 3 0 S 129 5 E
Sawai Madhopur, *India* **92 G7** 26 0N 76 25 E
Sawaleke, *Fiji* **133 A2** 17 59 S 179 18 E
Sawang Daen Din, *Thailand* **86 D4** 17 28N 103 28 E
Sawankhalok, *Thailand* **86 D2** 17 19N 99 50 E
Sawara, *Japan* **73 B12** 35 55N 140 30 E
Sawatch Range, *U.S.A.* **159 G10** 38 30N 106 30W
Sawdā', Jabal as, *Libya* **108 C3** 28 51N 15 12 E
Sawel Mt., *U.K.* **23 B4** 54 50N 7 2W
Sawfajjin □, *Libya* **108 B3** 31 0N 15 0 E
Sawfajjin, W. →, *Libya* **108 B2** 31 41N 14 44 E
Sawi, *Thailand* **87 G2** 10 14N 99 5 E
Sawla, *Ghana* **112 D4** 9 17N 2 25W
Sawmills, *Zimbabwe* **119 F2** 19 30 S 28 2 E
Şawqirah, *Oman* **99 C7** 18 7N 56 32 E
Şawqirah, Ghubbat, *Oman* **99 C7** 18 35N 57 0 E
Sawtell, *Australia* **129 A10** 30 19 S 153 6 E
Sawtooth Range, *U.S.A.* **158 E6** 44 3N 114 58W
Sawu, *Indonesia* **82 C2** 10 35 S 121 50 E
Sawu Sea, *Indonesia* **82 C2** 9 30 S 121 50 E
Saxby →, *Australia* **126 B3** 18 25 S 140 53 E
Saxmundham, *U.K.* **21 E9** 52 13N 1 30 E
Saxon, *Switz.* **32 D4** 46 9N 7 11 E
Saxony = Sachsen □, *Germany* **30 E9** 50 55N 13 10 E
Saxony, Lower = Niedersachsen □, *Germany* **30 C4** 52 50N 9 0 E
Saxton, *U.S.A.* **150 F6** 40 13N 78 15W
Say, *Mali* **112 C4** 13 50N 4 57W
Say, *Niger* **113 C5** 13 8N 2 22 E
Saya, *Nigeria* **113 D5** 9 30N 3 18 E
Sayabec, *Canada* **141 C6** 48 35N 67 41W
Sayaboury, *Laos* **86 C3** 19 15N 101 45 E
Sayán, *Peru* **172 C2** 11 8 S 77 12W
Sayan, Vostochnyy, *Russia* **67 D10** 54 0N 96 0 E
Sayan, Zapadnyy, *Russia* **67 D10** 52 30N 94 0 E
Saydā, *Lebanon* **103 B4** 33 35N 35 25 E
Sayghān, *Afghan.* **91 B2** 35 10N 67 55 E
Sayhandulaan = Oldziyt, *Mongolia* **74 B5** 44 40N 109 1 E

Sayḩūt, *Yemen* **99 D5** 15 12N 51 10 E
Sayiádha, *Greece* **38 B10** 39 38N 20 12 E
Saykhin, *Kazakstan* **61 F8** 48 50N 46 47 E
Saylac = Zeila, *Somali Rep.* **120 B2** 11 21N 43 30 E
Saylorville L., *U.S.A.* **156 C3** 41 48N 93 46W
Saynshand, *Mongolia* **69 B6** 44 55N 110 11 E
Sayō, *Japan* **72 C6** 34 59N 134 22 E
Sayre, *Okla., U.S.A.* **155 H5** 35 18N 99 38W
Sayre, *Pa., U.S.A.* **151 E8** 41 59N 76 32W
Sayreville, *U.S.A.* **151 F10** 40 28N 74 22W
Sayula, *Mexico* **162 D4** 19 50N 103 40W
Sayward, *Canada* **142 C3** 50 21N 125 55W
Saywūn, *Yemen* **99 D5** 15 56N 48 47 E
Saza, *Japan* **72 D1** 33 14N 129 39 E
Sazanit, *Albania* **50 F3** 40 30N 19 20 E
Sázava →, *Czech Rep.* **34 B7** 49 53N 14 24 E
Sazin, *Pakistan* **93 B5** 35 35N 73 30 E
Sazlika →, *Bulgaria* **51 E9** 41 59N 25 50 E
Sbeïtla, *Tunisia* **108 A1** 35 12N 9 7 E
Scaër, *France* **26 D3** 48 2N 3 42W
Scafell Pike, *U.K.* **20 C4** 54 27N 3 14W
Scalea, *Italy* **47 C8** 39 49N 15 47 E
Scalloway, *U.K.* **22 A7** 60 9N 1 17W
Scalpay, *U.K.* **22 D3** 57 18N 6 0W
Scammon Bay, *U.S.A.* **144 F6** 61 51N 165 35W
Scandia, *Canada* **142 C6** 50 20N 112 0W
Scandiano, *Italy* **44 D7** 44 36N 10 43 E
Scandicci, *Italy* **45 E8** 43 45N 11 11 E
Scandinavia, *Europe* **14 E16** 64 0N 12 0 E
Scansano, *Italy* **45 F8** 42 41N 11 20 E
Scapa Flow, *U.K.* **22 C5** 58 53N 3 3W
Scappoose, *U.S.A.* **160 E4** 45 45N 122 53W
Scarámia, Capo, *Italy* **47 F7** 36 47N 14 29 E
Scarba, *U.K.* **22 E3** 56 11N 5 43W
Scarborough, *Trin. & Tob.* **165 D7** 11 11N 60 42W
Scarborough, *U.K.* **20 C7** 54 17N 0 24W
Scargill, *N.Z.* **131 C7** 42 56 S 172 58 E
Scariff I., *Ireland* **23 E1** 51 44N 10 15W
Scarp, *U.K.* **22 C1** 58 1N 7 8W
Scarsdale, *Australia* **128 D5** 37 41 S 143 39 E
Scebeli, Wabi →, *Somali Rep.* **120 D2** 2 0N 44 0 E
Šćedro, *Croatia* **45 E13** 43 6N 16 43 E
Schaal See, *Germany* **30 B6** 53 36N 10 55 E
Schaan, *Liech.* **33 B9** 47 10N 9 31 E
Schaffhausen, *Switz.* **33 A7** 47 42N 8 39 E
Schaffhausen □, *Switz.* **33 A7** 47 42N 8 36 E
Schagen, *Neths.* **24 B4** 52 49N 4 48 E
Schaghticoke, *U.S.A.* **151 D11** 42 54N 73 35W
Schangnau, *Switz.* **32 C5** 46 50N 7 47 E
Schänis, *Switz.* **33 B8** 47 10N 9 3 E
Schärding, *Austria* **34 C6** 48 27N 13 27 E
Scharhörn, *Germany* **30 B4** 53 57N 8 24 E
Scheessel, *Germany* **30 B5** 53 10N 9 29 E
Schefferville, *Canada* **141 B6** 54 48N 66 50W
Scheibbs, *Austria* **34 C8** 48 1N 15 9 E
Schelde →, *Belgium* **24 C4** 51 15N 4 16 E
Schell City, *U.S.A.* **156 F2** 38 1N 94 7W
Schell Creek Ra., *U.S.A.* **158 G6** 39 15N 114 30W
Schellsburg, *U.S.A.* **150 F6** 40 3N 78 39W
Schenectady, *U.S.A.* **151 D11** 42 49N 73 57W
Schenevus, *U.S.A.* **151 D10** 42 33N 74 50W
Scherfede, *Germany* **30 D5** 51 32N 9 2 E
Schesaplana, *Switz.* **33 B9** 47 5N 9 43 E
Schesslitz, *Germany* **31 F7** 49 58N 11 1 E
Schiedam, *Neths.* **24 C4** 51 55N 4 25 E
Schiermonnikoog, *Neths.* **24 A6** 53 30N 6 15 E
Schiers, *Switz.* **33 C9** 46 58N 9 41 E
Schiltigheim, *France* **27 D14** 48 35N 7 45 E
Schio, *Italy* **45 C8** 45 43N 11 21 E
Schladming, *Austria* **34 D6** 47 23N 13 41 E
Schlanders = Silandro, *Italy* **44 B7** 46 38N 10 46 E
Schlei →, *Germany* **30 A5** 54 40N 10 0 E
Schleiden, *Germany* **30 E2** 50 31N 6 28 E
Schleinitz Ra., *Papua N. G.* **132 B6** 3 0 S 151 30 E
Schleiz, *Germany* **30 E7** 50 35N 11 49 E
Schleswig, *Germany* **30 A5** 54 31N 9 34 E
Schleswig-Holstein □, *Germany* **30 A5** 54 30N 9 30 E
Schlieren, *Switz.* **33 B6** 47 26N 8 27 E
Schlüchtern, *Germany* **31 E5** 50 20N 9 32 E
Schmalkalden, *Germany* **30 E6** 50 44N 10 26 E
Schmölln, *Germany* **30 E8** 50 54N 12 19 E
Schneeberg, *Austria* **34 D8** 47 47N 15 48 E
Schneeberg, *Germany* **30 E8** 50 35N 12 38 E
Schneider, *U.S.A.* **157 C9** 41 13N 87 28W
Schneverdingen, *Germany* **30 B5** 53 7N 9 48 E
Schœlcher, *Martinique* **164 c** 14 36N 61 7W
Schoharie, *U.S.A.* **151 D10** 42 40N 74 19W
Schoharie →, *U.S.A.* **151 D10** 42 57N 74 18W
Scholls, *U.S.A.* **160 E4** 45 24N 122 56W
Schönberg, *Mecklenburg-Vorpommern, Germany* **30 B6** 53 52N 10 56 E
Schönberg, *Schleswig-Holstein, Germany* **30 A6** 54 23N 10 21 E
Schönebeck, *Germany* **30 C7** 52 2N 11 44 E
Schönenwerd, *Switz.* **32 B6** 47 23N 8 0 E
Schongau, *Germany* **31 H6** 47 47N 10 53 E
Schöningen, *Germany* **30 C6** 52 8N 10 56 E
Schoolcraft, *U.S.A.* **157 B11** 42 7N 85 38W
Schopfheim, *Germany* **31 H3** 47 38N 7 50 E
Schorndorf, *Germany* **31 G5** 48 47N 9 32 E
Schortens, *Germany* **30 B3** 53 31N 7 56 E
Schouten I., *Australia* **127 G4** 42 20 S 148 20 E
Schouten Is. = Supiori, *Indonesia* **83 B5** 1 0 S 136 0 E
Schouten Is., *Papua N. G.* **132 B3** 3 30 S 144 30 E
Schouwen, *Neths.* **24 C3** 51 43N 3 45 E
Schramberg, *Germany* **31 G4** 48 13N 8 22 E
Schrankogel, *Austria* **34 D4** 47 3N 11 7 E
Schreckhorn, *Switz.* **32 C6** 46 36N 8 7 E
Schreiber, *Canada* **140 C2** 48 45N 87 20W
Schrems, *Austria* **34 C8** 48 47N 15 4 E
Schrobenhausen, *Germany* **31 G7** 48 34N 11 16 E
Schröcken, *Austria* **33 B10** 47 17N 10 5 E
Schroffenstein, *Namibia* **116 D2** 27 11 S 18 42 E
Schroon Lake, *U.S.A.* **151 C11** 43 50N 73 46W
Schruns, *Austria* **34 D2** 47 5N 9 56 E
Schuler, *Canada* **143 C6** 50 20N 110 6W
Schuls, *Switz.* **33 C10** 46 48N 10 18 E
Schumacher, *Canada* **140 C3** 48 30N 81 16W
Schüpfen, *Switz.* **32 B4** 47 2N 7 24 E
Schüpfheim, *Switz.* **32 C6** 46 57N 8 2 E
Schurz, *U.S.A.* **158 G4** 38 57N 118 49W
Schuyler, *U.S.A.* **154 E6** 41 27N 97 4W
Schuylerville, *U.S.A.* **151 C11** 43 6N 73 35W
Schuylkill →, *U.S.A.* **151 G9** 39 53N 75 12W
Schuylkill Haven, *U.S.A.* **151 F8** 40 37N 76 11W
Schwabach, *Germany* **31 F7** 49 19N 11 2 E
Schwaben □, *Germany* **31 G6** 48 15N 10 30 E
Schwäbisch Gmünd, *Germany* **31 G5** 48 48N 9 47 E
Schwäbisch Hall, *Germany* **31 F5** 49 6N 9 44 E
Schwäbische Alb, *Germany* **31 G5** 48 20N 9 30 E
Schwabmünchen, *Germany* **31 G6** 48 10N 10 46 E
Schwalmstadt, *Germany* **30 E5** 50 55N 9 10 E
Schwanden, *Switz.* **33 C8** 46 58N 9 5 E
Schwandorf, *Germany* **31 F8** 49 20N 12 7 E
Schwaner, Pegunungan, *Indonesia* **85 C4** 1 0 S 112 30 E
Schwanewede, *Germany* **30 B4** 53 14N 8 35 E
Schwarmstedt, *Germany* **30 C5** 52 39N 9 38 E
Schwarze Elster →, *Germany* **30 D8** 51 48N 12 50 E
Schwarzenberg, *Germany* **30 E8** 50 32N 12 47 E
Schwarzenburg, *Switz.* **32 C4** 46 49N 7 20 E
Schwarzrand, *Namibia* **116 D2** 25 37 S 16 50 E
Schwarzwald, *Germany* **31 G4** 48 30N 8 20 E
Schwatka Mts., *U.S.A.* **144 C8** 67 20N 156 30W
Schwaz, *Austria* **34 D4** 47 20N 11 44 E
Schwechat, *Austria* **35 C9** 48 8N 16 28 E
Schwedt, *Germany* **30 B10** 53 3N 14 16 E
Schweinfurt, *Germany* **31 E6** 50 3N 10 14 E
Schweizer Mittelland, *Switz.* **32 C4** 47 0N 7 15 E
Schweizer-Reneke, *S. Africa* **116 D4** 27 11 S 25 18 E
Schwenningen = Villingen-Schwenningen, *Germany* **31 G4** 48 3N 8 26 E
Schwerin, *Germany* **30 B7** 53 36N 11 22 E
Schweriner See, *Germany* **30 B7** 53 43N 11 28 E
Schwetzingen, *Germany* **31 F4** 49 23N 8 35 E
Schwyz, *Switz.* **33 B7** 47 2N 8 39 E
Schwyz □, *Switz.* **33 B7** 47 2N 8 39 E
Sciacca, *Italy* **46 E6** 37 31N 13 3 E
Sciao, *Somali Rep.* **120 D3** 3 26N 45 21 E
Scicli, *Italy* **47 F7** 36 47N 14 42 E
Scilla, *Italy* **47 D8** 38 15N 15 43 E
Scilly, Isles of, *U.K.* **21 H1** 49 56N 6 22W
Ścinawa, *Poland* **55 G3** 51 25N 16 26 E
Scione, *Greece* **50 G7** 39 57N 23 36 E
Scioto →, *U.S.A.* **157 D13** 38 44N 83 1W
Scituate, *U.S.A.* **151 D14** 42 12N 70 44W
Scobey, *U.S.A.* **154 A2** 48 47N 105 25W
Scone, *Australia* **129 B9** 32 5 S 150 52 E
Scordia, *Italy* **47 E7** 37 18N 14 51 E
Scoresby Sund, *Greenland* **10 C8** 70 28N 21 46W
Scoresbysund = Ittoqqortoormiit, *Greenland* **10 C8** 70 20N 23 0W
Scorniceşti, *Romania* **53 F9** 44 34N 24 33 E
Scotia, *Calif., U.S.A.* **158 F1** 40 29N 124 6W
Scotia, *N.Y., U.S.A.* **151 D11** 42 50N 73 58W
Scotia Sea, *Antarctica* **7 B18** 56 5 S 56 0W
Scotland, *Canada* **150 C4** 43 1N 80 22W
Scotland □, *U.K.* **22 E5** 57 0N 4 0W
Scott, C., *Australia* **124 B4** 13 30 S 129 49 E
Scott City, *U.S.A.* **154 F4** 38 29N 100 54W
Scott Glacier, *Antarctica* **7 C8** 66 15 S 100 5 E
Scott I., *Antarctica* **7 C11** 67 0 S 179 0 E
Scott Is., *Canada* **142 C3** 50 48N 128 40W
Scott L., *Canada* **143 B7** 59 55N 106 18W
Scott Reef, *Australia* **124 B3** 14 0 S 121 50 E
Scottburgh, *S. Africa* **117 E5** 30 15 S 30 47 E
Scottdale, *U.S.A.* **150 F5** 40 6N 79 35W
Scottish Borders □, *U.K.* **22 F6** 55 35N 2 50W
Scotts Head, *Australia* **129 A10** 30 45 S 153 0 E
Scottsbluff, *U.S.A.* **154 E3** 41 52N 103 40W
Scottsboro, *U.S.A.* **149 H3** 34 40N 86 2W
Scottsburg, *U.S.A.* **157 F11** 38 41N 85 47W
Scottsdale, *Australia* **127 G4** 41 9 S 147 31 E
Scottsdale, *U.S.A.* **159 K7** 33 29N 111 56W
Scottsville, *Ky., U.S.A.* **149 G2** 36 45N 86 11W
Scottsville, *N.Y., U.S.A.* **150 C7** 43 2N 77 47W
Scottville, *U.S.A.* **148 D2** 43 58N 86 17W
Scranton, *U.S.A.* **151 E9** 41 25N 75 40W
Screven, *U.S.A.* **152 D7** 31 29N 82 1W
Scugog, L., *Canada* **150 B6** 44 10N 78 55W
Sculeni, *Moldova* **53 C12** 47 20N 27 37 E
Scunthorpe, *U.K.* **20 D7** 53 36N 0 39W
Scuol Schuls, *Switz.* **33 C10** 46 48N 10 17 E
Scusciuban, *Somali Rep.* **120 B4** 10 18N 50 12 E
Scutari = Shkodër, *Albania* **50 D3** 42 4N 19 32 E
Scutari = Üsküdar, *Turkey* **51 F13** 41 0N 29 5 E
Sea Lake, *Australia* **128 C5** 35 28 S 142 55 E
Seabra, *Brazil* **171 D3** 12 25 S 41 46W
Seabrook, L., *Australia* **125 F2** 30 55 S 119 40 E
Seaford, *U.K.* **21 G8** 50 47N 0 7 E
Seaford, *U.S.A.* **148 F8** 38 39N 75 37W
Seaforth, *Australia* **126 J6** 20 55 S 148 57 E
Seaforth, *Canada* **150 C3** 43 35N 81 25W
Seaforth, L., *U.K.* **22 D2** 57 52N 6 36W
Seagraves, *U.S.A.* **155 J3** 32 57N 102 34W
Seaham, *U.K.* **20 C6** 54 50N 1 20W
Seal →, *Canada* **143 B10** 59 4N 94 48W
Seal L., *Canada* **141 B7** 54 20N 61 30W
Seale, *U.S.A.* **152 C4** 32 18N 85 10W
Sealy, *U.S.A.* **155 L6** 29 47N 96 9W
Seaman, *U.S.A.* **157 F13** 38 57N 83 34W
Searchlight, *U.S.A.* **161 K12** 35 28N 114 55W
Searcy, *U.S.A.* **155 H9** 35 15N 91 44W
Searles L., *U.S.A.* **161 K9** 35 44N 117 21W
Seascale, *U.K.* **20 C4** 54 24N 3 29W
Seaside, *Calif., U.S.A.* **160 J5** 36 37N 121 50W
Seaside, *Oreg., U.S.A.* **160 E3** 46 0N 123 56W
Seaspray, *Australia* **129 E7** 38 25 S 147 15 E
Seattle, *U.S.A.* **160 C4** 47 36N 122 20W
Seaview Ra., *Australia* **126 B4** 18 40 S 145 45 E
Seaward Kaikoura Ra., *N.Z.* **131 C8** 42 10 S 173 44 E
Seba, *Indonesia* **82 D2** 10 29 S 121 50 E
Sebago L., *U.S.A.* **151 C14** 43 52N 70 34W
Sebago Lake, *U.S.A.* **151 C14** 43 51N 70 34W
Sebangka, *Indonesia* **84 B2** 0 7N 104 36 E
Sebastian, *U.S.A.* **153 H9** 27 49N 80 28W
Sebastián Vizcaíno, B., *Mexico* **162 B2** 28 0N 114 30W
Sebastopol = Sevastopol, *Ukraine* **59 K7** 44 35N 33 30 E
Sebastopol, *U.S.A.* **160 G4** 38 24N 122 49W
Sebba, *Burkina Faso* **113 C5** 13 35N 0 32 E
Sebderat, *Eritrea* **107 D4** 15 26N 36 42 E
Sebdou, *Algeria* **111 B4** 34 38N 1 19W
Sébé →, *Gabon* **114 C2** 1 2 S 13 6 E
Sébékoro, *Mali* **112 C3** 12 58N 9 0W
Seben, *Turkey* **100 B4** 40 24N 31 34 E
Sebeş, *Romania* **53 E8** 45 58N 23 34 E
Sebeşului, Munţii, *Romania* **53 E8** 45 36N 23 40 E
Sebewaing, *U.S.A.* **148 D4** 43 44N 83 27W
Sebezh, *Russia* **58 D5** 56 14N 28 22 E
Sebha = Sabhah, *Libya* **108 C2** 27 9N 14 29 E
Sébi, *Mali* **112 B4** 15 50N 4 12W
Şebinkarahisar, *Turkey* **101 B8** 40 22N 38 28 E
Sebiş, *Romania* **52 D7** 46 23N 22 13 E
Seblat, *Indonesia* **84 C2** 3 14 S 101 38 E
Sebnitz, *Germany* **30 E10** 50 58N 14 15 E
Sebou, Oued →, *Morocco* **110 B3** 34 16N 6 40W
Sebring, *Fla., U.S.A.* **149 M5** 27 30N 81 27W
Sebring, *Ohio, U.S.A.* **150 F3** 40 55N 81 2W
Sebringville, *Canada* **150 C3** 43 24N 81 4W
Sebta = Ceuta, *N. Afr.* **110 A3** 35 52N 5 18W
Sebuku, *Indonesia* **85 C5** 3 30 S 116 25 E
Sebuku, Teluk, *Malaysia* **85 B5** 4 0N 118 10 E
Sečanj, *Serbia, Yug.* **52 E5** 45 25N 20 47 E
Secchia →, *Italy* **44 C8** 45 4N 11 0 E
Sechelt, *Canada* **142 D4** 49 25N 123 42W
Sechura, *Peru* **172 B1** 5 39 S 80 50W
Sechura, Desierto de, *Peru* **172 B1** 6 0 S 80 30W
Seclin, *France* **27 B10** 50 33N 3 2 E
Secondigny, *France* **26 F6** 46 37N 0 26W
Sečovce, *Slovak Rep.* **35 C14** 48 42N 21 40 E
Secretary I., *N.Z.* **131 F1** 45 15 S 166 56 E
Secunderabad, *India* **94 F4** 17 28N 78 30 E
Sécure →, *Bolivia* **173 D5** 15 10 S 64 52W
Security-Widefield, *U.S.A.* **154 F2** 38 45N 104 45W
Sedalia, *U.S.A.* **156 F3** 38 42N 93 14W
Sedam, *India* **94 E3** 17 11N 77 17 E
Sedan, *Australia* **128 C3** 34 34 S 139 19 E
Sedan, *France* **27 C11** 49 43N 4 57 E
Sedan, *U.S.A.* **155 G6** 37 8N 96 11W
Sedano, *Spain* **42 C7** 42 43N 3 49W
Sedaw, *Burma* **90 D6** 22 19N 96 19 E
Seddon, *N.Z.* **131 B9** 41 40 S 174 7 E
Seddonville, *N.Z.* **131 B7** 41 33 S 172 1 E
Sedé Boqér, *Israel* **103 E3** 30 52N 34 47 E
Sedeh, *Fārs, Iran* **97 D7** 30 45N 52 11 E
Sedeh, *Khorāsān, Iran* **97 C8** 33 20N 59 14 E
Séderon, *France* **29 D9** 44 12N 5 32 E
Sederot, *Israel* **103 D3** 31 32N 34 37 E
Sédhiou, *Senegal* **112 C1** 12 44N 15 30W
Sedico, *Italy* **45 B9** 46 8N 12 6 E
Sedlčany, *Czech Rep.* **34 B7** 49 40N 14 25 E
Sedley, *Canada* **143 C8** 50 10N 104 0W
Sedona, *U.S.A.* **159 J8** 34 52N 111 46W
Sedova, Pik, *Russia* **66 B6** 73 29N 54 58 E
Sedrata, *Algeria* **111 A6** 36 7N 7 31 E
Sedro Woolley, *U.S.A.* **160 B4** 48 30N 122 14W
Sedrun, *Switz.* **33 C7** 46 36N 8 47 E
Šeduva, *Lithuania* **54 C10** 55 45N 23 45 E
Sędziszów, *Poland* **55 H7** 50 35N 20 4 E
Sędziszów Małapolski, *Poland* **55 H8** 50 5N 21 45 E
Seebad Ahlbeck, *Germany* **30 B10** 53 56N 14 10 E
Seefeld in Tirol, *Austria* **34 D4** 47 19N 11 13 E
Seehausen, *Germany* **30 C7** 52 54N 11 45 E
Seeheim, *Namibia* **116 D2** 26 50 S 17 45 E
Seeheim-Jugenheim, *Germany* **31 F4** 49 49N 8 40 E
Seeis, *Namibia* **116 C2** 22 29 S 17 39 E
Seekoei →, *S. Africa* **116 E4** 30 18 S 25 1 E
Seeley's Bay, *Canada* **151 B8** 44 29N 76 14W
Seelow, *Germany* **30 C10** 52 32N 14 23 E
Sées, *France* **26 D7** 48 38N 0 10 E
Seesen, *Germany* **30 D6** 51 54N 10 10 E
Seevetal, *Germany* **30 B6** 53 26N 10 1 E
Sefadu, *S. Leone* **112 D2** 8 35N 10 58W
Seferihisar, *Turkey* **49 C8** 38 10N 26 50 E
Séfeto, *Mali* **112 C3** 14 8N 9 49W
Sefrou, *Morocco* **110 B4** 33 52N 4 52W
Sefton, *N.Z.* **131 D7** 43 15 S 172 41 E
Sefuri-San, *Japan* **72 D2** 33 28N 130 18 E
Sefwi Bekwai, *Ghana* **112 D4** 6 10N 2 25W
Seg-ozero, *Russia* **56 B5** 63 20N 33 46 E
Segaf, Kepulauan, *Indonesia* **83 B4** 2 10 S 130 28 E
Segag, *Ethiopia* **120 C2** 7 39N 42 50 E
Segamat, *Malaysia* **87 L4** 2 30N 102 50 E
Şegarcea, *Romania* **53 F8** 44 6N 23 43 E
Ségbana, *Benin* **113 C5** 10 55N 3 42 E
Segbwema, *S. Leone* **112 D2** 8 0N 11 0W
Seget, *Indonesia* **83 B4** 1 24 S 130 58 E
Segezha, *Russia* **56 B5** 63 44N 34 19 E
Seggueur, O. →, *Algeria* **111 B5** 32 14N 1 48 E
Seghe, *Solomon Is.* **133 M9** 8 32 S 157 54 E
Segonzac, *France* **28 C3** 45 36N 0 14W
Segorbe, *Spain* **40 F4** 39 50N 0 30W
Ségou, *Mali* **112 C3** 13 30N 6 16W
Segovia = Coco →, *Cent. Amer.* **164 D3** 15 0N 83 8W
Segovia, *Colombia* **168 B3** 7 7N 74 42W
Segovia, *Spain* **42 E6** 40 57N 4 10W
Segovia □, *Spain* **42 E6** 40 55N 4 10W
Segré, *France* **26 E6** 47 40N 0 52W
Segre →, *Spain* **40 D5** 41 40N 0 43 E
Seguam I., *U.S.A.* **144 K4** 52 19N 172 30W
Seguam Pass, *U.S.A.* **144 L4** 52 0N 172 30W
Séguédine, *Niger* **109 D2** 20 9N 12 55 E
Séguéla, *Ivory C.* **112 D3** 7 55N 6 40W
Séguénéga, *Burkina Faso* **113 C4** 13 25N 1 58W
Seguin, *U.S.A.* **155 L6** 29 34N 97 58W
Segundo →, *Argentina* **174 C3** 30 53 S 62 44W
Segura →, *Spain* **41 G4** 38 3N 0 44W
Segura, Sierra de, *Spain* **41 G2** 38 5N 2 45W
Seh Konj, Kūh-e, *Iran* **97 D8** 30 6N 57 30 E
Seh Qal'eh, *Iran* **97 C8** 33 40N 58 24 E
Sehitwa, *Botswana* **116 C3** 20 30 S 22 30 E
Sehlabathebe Nat. Park, *Lesotho* **117 D4** 29 53 S 29 7 E
Sehore, *India* **92 H7** 23 10N 77 5 E
Sehulea, *Papua N. G.* **132 E6** 9 58 S 151 10 E
Sehwan, *Pakistan* **91 D2** 26 28N 67 53 E
Şeica Mare, *Romania* **53 D9** 46 1N 24 7 E
Seikpyu, *Burma* **90 E5** 20 54N 94 48 E
Seil, *U.K.* **22 E3** 56 18N 5 38W
Seiland, *Norway* **14 A20** 70 25N 23 15 E
Seilhac, *France* **28 C5** 45 22N 1 43 E
Seiling, *U.S.A.* **155 G5** 36 9N 98 56W
Seille →, *Moselle, France* **27 C13** 49 7N 6 11 E
Seille →, *Saône-et-Loire, France* **27 F11** 46 31N 4 57 E
Sein, Î. de, *France* **26 D2** 48 2N 4 52W
Seinäjoki, *Finland* **15 E20** 62 40N 22 51 E
Seine →, *France* **26 C7** 49 26N 0 26 E
Seine, B. de la, *France* **26 C6** 49 40N 0 40W
Seine-et-Marne □, *France* **27 D10** 48 45N 3 0 E
Seine-Maritime □, *France* **26 C7** 49 40N 1 0 E
Seine-St-Denis □, *France* **27 D9** 48 58N 2 24 E
Seini, *Romania* **53 C8** 47 44N 23 21 E
Seirijai, *Lithuania* **54 D10** 54 14N 23 49 E
Seistan = Sīstān, *Asia* **97 D9** 30 50N 61 0 E
Seistan, Daryācheh-ye = Sīstān, Daryācheh-ye, *Iran* **97 D9** 31 0N 61 0 E
Sejerø, *Denmark* **17 J5** 55 54N 11 9 E
Sejerø Bugt, *Denmark* **17 J5** 55 53N 11 15 E
Sejny, *Poland* **54 D10** 54 6N 23 21 E
Seka, *Ethiopia* **107 F4** 8 10N 36 52 E
Sekayu, *Indonesia* **84 C2** 2 51 S 103 51 E
Seke, *Tanzania* **118 C3** 3 20 S 33 31 E
Seke-Banza, *Dem. Rep. of the Congo* **115 D2** 5 20 S 13 16 E
Sekenke, *Tanzania* **118 C3** 4 18 S 34 11 E
Sekhira, *Tunisia* **108 B2** 34 20N 10 5 E
Seki, *Japan* **73 B8** 35 29N 136 55 E
Seki, *Turkey* **49 E11** 36 48N 29 33 E
Sekigahara, *Japan* **73 B8** 35 22N 136 28 E
Sekondi-Takoradi, *Ghana* **112 E4** 4 58N 1 45W
Sekota, *Ethiopia* **107 E4** 12 40N 39 2 E
Seksna, *Russia* **58 C10** 59 13N 38 30 E
Sekudai, *Malaysia* **87 d** 1 32N 103 39 E
Sekuma, *Botswana* **116 C3** 24 36 S 23 50 E
Selah, *U.S.A.* **158 C3** 46 39N 120 32W
Selama, *Malaysia* **87 K3** 5 12N 100 42 E
Selangor □, *Malaysia* **84 B2** 3 10N 101 30 E
Selárgius, *Italy* **46 C2** 39 16N 9 10 E
Selaru, *Indonesia* **83 C4** 8 9 S 131 0 E
Selatan, Selat, *Malaysia* **87 c** 5 15N 100 20 E
Selawik, *U.S.A.* **144 C8** 66 36N 160 0W
Selawik L., *U.S.A.* **144 C7** 66 30N 160 45W
Selb, *Germany* **31 E8** 50 10N 12 7 E
Selbusjøen, *Norway* **18 A7** 63 15N 10 50 E
Selby, *U.K.* **20 D6** 53 47N 1 5W
Selby, *U.S.A.* **154 C4** 45 31N 100 2W
Selca, *Croatia* **45 E13** 43 20N 16 50 E
Selçuk, *Turkey* **49 D9** 37 56N 27 22 E
Selden, *U.S.A.* **154 F4** 39 33N 100 34W
Seldovia, *U.S.A.* **144 G10** 59 26N 151 43W
Sele →, *Italy* **47 B7** 40 29N 14 56 E
Selebi-Pikwe, *Botswana* **117 C4** 21 58 S 27 48 E
Selemdzha →, *Russia* **67 D13** 51 42N 128 53 E
Selendi, *Manisa, Turkey* **49 C10** 38 43N 28 50 E
Selendi, *Manisa, Turkey* **49 C9** 38 46N 27 53 E
Selenga = Selenge Mörön →, *Asia* **68 A5** 52 16N 106 16 E
Selenge, *Dem. Rep. of the Congo* **114 C3** 1 58 S 18 11 E
Selenge Mörön →, *Asia* **68 A5** 52 16N 106 16 E
Selenicë, *Albania* **50 F3** 40 33N 19 39 E
Selenter See, *Germany* **30 A6** 54 18N 10 26 E
Sélestat, *France* **27 D14** 48 16N 7 26 E
Seletan, Tanjung, *Indonesia* **85 C4** 4 10 S 114 40 E
Selevac, *Serbia, Yug.* **50 B4** 44 28N 20 52 E
Selfoss, *Iceland* **11 D6** 63 56N 21 0W
Sélibabi, *Mauritania* **112 B2** 15 10N 12 15W
Seliger, Ozero, *Russia* **58 D7** 57 15N 33 0 E
Seligman, *U.S.A.* **159 J7** 35 20N 112 53W
Şelim, *Turkey* **101 B10** 40 30N 42 46 E
Selîma, El Wâhât el, *Sudan* **106 C2** 21 22N 29 19 E
Selimiye, *Turkey* **49 D9** 37 24N 27 40 E
Selinda Spillway →, *Botswana* **116 B3** 18 35 S 23 10 E
Selinoús, *Greece* **48 D3** 37 35N 21 37 E
Selinsgrove, *U.S.A.* **150 F8** 40 48N 76 52W
Selizharovo, *Russia* **58 D7** 56 51N 33 27 E
Selje, *Norway* **18 B2** 62 3N 5 22 E
Seljord, *Norway* **18 E5** 59 30N 8 40 E
Selkirk, *Canada* **143 C9** 50 10N 96 55W
Selkirk, *U.K.* **22 F6** 55 33N 2 50W
Selkirk I., *Canada* **143 C9** 53 20N 99 6W
Selkirk Mts., *Canada* **138 C8** 51 15N 117 40W
Sellama, *Sudan* **107 E2** 12 51N 29 46 E
Selliá, *Greece* **39 E5** 35 12N 24 23 E
Sellières, *France* **27 F12** 46 50N 5 32 E
Sells, *U.S.A.* **159 L8** 31 55N 111 53W
Sellye, *Hungary* **52 E2** 45 52N 17 51 E
Selma, *Ala., U.S.A.* **149 J2** 32 25N 87 1W
Selma, *Calif., U.S.A.* **160 J7** 36 34N 119 37W
Selma, *N.C., U.S.A.* **149 H6** 35 32N 78 17W
Selmer, *U.S.A.* **149 H1** 35 10N 88 36W
Selong, *Indonesia* **85 D5** 8 39 S 116 32 E
Selongey, *France* **27 E12** 47 36N 5 11 E
Selouane, *Morocco* **111 A4** 35 7N 2 57W
Selous Game Reserve, *Tanzania* **119 D4** 8 37 S 37 42 E
Selowandoma Falls, *Zimbabwe* **119 G3** 21 15 S 31 50 E
Selpele, *Indonesia* **83 B4** 0 1 S 130 5 E
Selsey Bill, *U.K.* **21 G7** 50 43N 0 47W
Seltso, *Russia* **58 F8** 53 22N 34 4 E
Seltz, *France* **27 D15** 48 54N 8 4 E
Selu, *Indonesia* **83 C4** 7 32 S 130 55 E
Sélune →, *France* **26 D5** 48 38N 1 22W
Selva = La Selva del Camp, *Spain* **40 D6** 41 13N 1 8 E
Selva, *Argentina* **174 B3** 29 50 S 62 0W
Selvagens, Ilhas, *Madeira* **110 B1** 30 5N 15 55W
Selvas, *Brazil* **172 B4** 6 30 S 67 0W
Selwyn L., *Canada* **143 B8** 60 0N 104 30W
Selwyn Mts., *Canada* **138 B6** 63 0N 130 0W
Selwyn Passage, *Vanuatu* **133 F6** 16 3 S 168 12 E
Selwyn Ra., *Australia* **126 C3** 21 10 S 140 0 E
Sem, *Norway* **18 E7** 59 14N 10 17 E
Seman →, *Albania* **50 F3** 40 47N 19 30 E
Semara, *W. Sahara* **110 C2** 26 48N 11 41W
Semarang, *Indonesia* **85 D4** 7 0 S 110 26 E
Sematan, *Malaysia* **85 B3** 1 48N 109 46 E
Semau, *Indonesia* **82 D2** 10 13 S 123 22 E
Sembabule, *Uganda* **118 C3** 0 4 S 31 25 E
Sembawang, *Singapore* **87 d** 1 27N 103 50 E
Sembé, *Congo* **114 B2** 1 39N 14 36 E
Sembung, *Indonesia* **79 J18** 8 28 S 115 11 E
Şemdinli, *Turkey* **101 D11** 37 18N 44 35 E
Sémé, *Senegal* **112 B2** 15 4N 13 41W
Semeih, *Sudan* **107 E3** 12 43N 30 53 E
Semenanjung Blambangan, *Indonesia* **79 K17** 8 42 S 114 29 E
Semendua, *Dem. Rep. of the Congo* **114 C3** 3 10 S 18 6 E
Semenov, *Russia* **60 B7** 56 43N 44 30 E
Semenovka, *Chernihiv, Ukraine* **59 F7** 52 8N 32 36 E
Semenovka, *Kremenchuk, Ukraine* **59 H7** 49 37N 33 10 E
Semeru, *Indonesia* **85 D4** 8 4 S 112 55 E
Semey, *Kazakstan* **66 D9** 50 30N 80 10 E
Semichi Is., *U.S.A.* **144 K1** 52 42N 174 0 E
Semikarakorskiy, *Russia* **61 G5** 47 31N 40 48 E
Semiluki, *Russia* **59 G10** 51 41N 39 2 E
Seminoe Reservoir, *U.S.A.* **158 F10** 42 9N 106 55W
Seminole, *Fla., U.S.A.* **153 H7** 27 50N 82 47W
Seminole, *Okla., U.S.A.* **155 H6** 35 14N 96 41W
Seminole, *Tex., U.S.A.* **155 J3** 32 43N 102 39W
Seminole, L., *U.S.A.* **152 E5** 30 43N 84 52W
Seminole Draw →, *U.S.A.* **155 J3** 32 27N 102 20W
Semipalatinsk = Semey, *Kazakstan* **66 D9** 50 30N 80 10 E
Semirara I., *Phil.* **80 E3** 12 4N 121 23 E
Semirara Is., *Phil.* **81 F3** 12 0N 121 20 E
Semisopochnoi I., *U.S.A.* **144 L2** 51 55N 179 36 E
Semitau, *Indonesia* **85 B4** 0 29N 111 57 E
Semiyarka, *Kazakstan* **66 D8** 50 55N 78 23 E
Semiyarskoye = Semiyarka, *Kazakstan* **66 D8** 50 55N 78 23 E
Semmering P., *Austria* **34 D8** 47 41N 15 45 E
Semnān, *Iran* **97 C7** 35 40N 53 23 E
Semnān □, *Iran* **97 C7** 36 0N 54 0 E
Sempang Mengayou, Tanjong, *Malaysia* **85 A5** 7 0N 116 40 E
Semporna, *Malaysia* **85 B5** 4 30N 118 33 E
Semuda, *Indonesia* **85 C4** 2 51 S 112 58 E
Semur-en-Auxois, *France* **27 E11** 47 30N 4 20 E
Sen →, *Cambodia* **78 B3** 13 45N 105 12 E
Sena, *Bolivia* **172 C4** 11 32 S 67 11W
Senā, *Iran* **97 D6** 28 27N 51 36 E
Sena, *Mozam.* **119 F4** 17 25 S 35 0 E
Sena →, *Bolivia* **172 C4** 11 31 S 67 11W
Sena Madureira, *Brazil* **172 B4** 9 5 S 68 45W
Senachwine L., *U.S.A.* **156 C7** 41 10N 89 18W
Senador José Porfírio, *Brazil* **169 D7** 2 35 S 51 55W
Senador Pompeu, *Brazil* **170 C4** 5 40 S 39 20W
Senaja, *Malaysia* **85 A5** 6 45N 117 3 E
Senaki, *Georgia* **61 J6** 42 15N 42 7 E
Senang, Pulau, *Singapore* **87 d** 1 10N 103 44 E
Senanga, *Zambia* **115 F4** 16 7 S 23 16 E
Senatobia, *U.S.A.* **155 H10** 34 37N 89 58W
Sencelles, *Spain* **38 B3** 39 39N 2 54 E
Sendafa, *Ethiopia* **107 F4** 9 11N 39 3 E
Sendai, *Kagoshima, Japan* **72 F2** 31 50N 130 20 E
Sendai, *Miyagi, Japan* **70 E10** 38 15N 140 53 E
Sendai-Wan, *Japan* **70 E10** 38 15N 141 0 E
Senden, *Bayern, Germany* **31 G6** 48 19N 10 4 E
Senden, *Nordrhein-Westfalen, Germany* **30 D3** 51 52N 7 22 E
Sendhwa, *India* **92 J6** 21 41N 75 6 E
Sendurjana, *India* **94 D4** 21 32N 78 17 E
Sene →, *Ghana* **113 D4** 7 30N 0 33W
Senec, *Slovak Rep.* **35 C10** 48 12N 17 23 E
Seneca, *Ill., U.S.A.* **157 C8** 41 19N 88 37W
Seneca, *S.C., U.S.A.* **149 H4** 34 41N 82 57W
Seneca Falls, *U.S.A.* **151 D8** 42 55N 76 48W
Seneca L., *U.S.A.* **150 D8** 42 40N 76 54W
Senecaville L., *U.S.A.* **150 G3** 39 55N 81 25W
Senegal ■, *W. Afr.* **112 C2** 14 30N 14 30W
Sénégal →, *W. Afr.* **112 B1** 15 48N 16 32W
Senegambia, *Africa* **104 E2** 12 45N 12 0W
Senekal, *S. Africa* **117 D4** 28 20 S 27 36 E
Senftenberg, *Germany* **30 D10** 51 32N 14 0 E
Senga Hill, *Zambia* **119 D3** 9 19 S 31 11 E
Senge Khambab = Indus →, *Pakistan* **91 D2** 24 20N 67 47 E
Sengiley, *Russia* **60 D9** 53 58N 48 46 E
Sengua →, *Zimbabwe* **119 F2** 17 7 S 28 5 E
Senguerr →, *Argentina* **176 C3** 45 35 S 68 50W
Senhor-do-Bonfim, *Brazil* **170 D3** 10 30 S 40 10W
Senica, *Slovak Rep.* **35 C10** 48 41N 17 25 E
Senigállia, *Italy* **45 E10** 43 43N 13 13 E
Seniku, *Burma* **90 C6** 25 32N 97 48 E
Senio →, *Italy* **45 D9** 44 35N 12 15 E
Senirkent, *Turkey* **49 C12** 38 6N 30 33 E
Senise, *Italy* **47 B9** 40 9N 16 17 E
Senj, *Croatia* **45 D11** 45 0N 14 58 E

Sheldon, *Mo., U.S.A.* 156 G2 37 40N 94 18W
Sheldon, *S.C., U.S.A.* 152 C9 32 36N 80 48W
Sheldon Point, *U.S.A.* 144 E6 62 32N 164 52W
Sheldrake, *Canada* 141 B7 50 20N 64 51W
Shelek, *Kazakstan* 65 B9 43 33N 78 17 E
Shelengo, Khawr →, *Sudan* 107 E2 10 33N 28 40 E
Shelikhova, Zaliv, *Russia* 67 D16 59 30N 157 0 E
Shelikof Strait, *U.S.A.* 144 H9 57 30N 155 0W
Shell Lakes, *Australia* 125 E4 29 20 S 127 30 E
Shellbrook, *Canada* 143 C7 53 13N 106 24W
Shellharbour, *Australia* 129 C9 34 31 S 150 51 E
Shellman, *U.S.A.* 152 D5 31 46N 84 37W
Shellsburg, *U.S.A.* 156 B5 42 6N 91 52W
Shelon →, *Russia* 58 C6 58 13N 30 47 E
Shelter I, *U.S.A.* 151 E12 41 5N 72 21W
Shelton, *Conn., U.S.A.* 151 E11 41 19N 73 5W
Shelton, *Wash., U.S.A.* 160 C3 47 13N 123 6W
Shemakha = Şamaxi, *Azerbaijan* 61 K9 40 38N 48 37 E
Shëmri, *Albania* 50 D4 42 7N 20 13 E
Shemsi, *Sudan* 106 D2 19 2N 29 57 E
Shen Xian, *China* 74 F8 36 15N 115 40 E
Shenandoah, *Iowa, U.S.A.* 154 E7 40 46N 95 22W
Shenandoah, *Pa., U.S.A.* 151 F8 40 49N 76 12W
Shenandoah, *Va., U.S.A.* 148 F6 38 29N 78 37W
Shenandoah →, *U.S.A.* 148 F7 39 19N 77 44W
Shenandoah Nat. Park, *U.S.A.* 148 F6 38 35N 78 22W
Shenchi, *China* 74 E7 39 8N 112 10 E
Shencottah, *India* 95 K3 8 59N 77 18 E
Shendam, *Nigeria* 113 D6 8 49N 9 30 E
Shendî, *Sudan* 107 D3 16 46N 33 22 E
Shendurni, *India* 94 D2 20 39N 75 36 E
Shenge, *S. Leone* 112 D2 7 54N 12 55W
Shengfang, *China* 74 E9 39 3N 116 42 E
Shenggeldi, *Kazakstan* 65 B8 43 59N 77 27 E
Shëngjergj, *Albania* 50 E4 41 17N 20 10 E
Shëngjin, *Albania* 50 E3 41 50N 19 35 E
Shengzhou, *China* 77 C13 29 35N 120 50 E
Shenjingzi, *China* 75 B13 44 40N 124 30 E
Shenmu, *China* 74 E6 38 50N 110 29 E
Shennongjia, *China* 77 B8 31 43N 110 44 E
Shenqiu, *China* 74 H8 33 25N 115 5 E
Shensi = Shaanxi □, *China* 74 G5 35 0N 109 0 E
Shenyang, *China* 75 D12 41 48N 123 27 E
Shenzhen, *China* 77 F10 22 32N 114 5 E
Shenzhen Shuiku, *China* 69 F11 22 34N 114 8 E
Shenzhen Wan, *China* 69 G10 22 27N 113 55 E
Sheo, *India* 92 F4 26 11N 71 15 E
Shepetivka, *Ukraine* 59 G4 50 10N 27 10 E
Shepetovka = Shepetivka, *Ukraine* 59 G4 50 10N 27 10 E
Shepherd Is., *Vanuatu* 133 F6 16 55 S 168 36 E
Shepherdsville, *U.S.A.* 157 G11 37 59N 85 43W
Shepparton, *Australia* 129 D6 36 23 S 145 26 E
Sheppey, I. of, *U.K.* 21 F8 51 25N 0 48 E
Shepton Mallet, *U.K.* 21 F5 51 11N 2 33W
Sheqi, *China* 74 H7 33 12N 112 57 E
Sher Khan Qala, *Afghan.* 91 C2 29 53N 66 13 E
Sher Qila, *Pakistan* 93 A6 36 7N 74 2 E
Sherab, *Sudan* 107 E1 10 44N 24 41 E
Sherabad, *Uzbekistan* 65 E3 37 40N 67 1 E
Sherborne, *U.K.* 21 G5 50 57N 2 31W
Sherbro →, *S. Leone* 112 D2 7 45N 12 55W
Sherbro I., *S. Leone* 112 D2 7 30N 12 40W
Sherbrooke, *N.S., Canada* 141 C7 45 8N 61 59W
Sherbrooke, *Qué., Canada* 141 C5 45 28N 71 57W
Sherburne, *U.S.A.* 151 D9 42 41N 75 30W
Sherburne Reef, *Papua N. G.* 132 B5 3 20 S 148 0 E
Sherda, *Chad* 109 D3 20 7N 16 46 E
Shereik, *Sudan* 106 D3 18 44N 33 47 E
Shergaon, *India* 90 B4 27 7N 92 16 E
Shergarh, *India* 92 F5 26 20N 72 18 E
Sherghati, *India* 93 G11 24 34N 84 47 E
Sheridan, *Ark., U.S.A.* 155 H8 34 19N 92 24W
Sheridan, *Ill., U.S.A.* 157 C8 41 32N 88 41W
Sheridan, *Ind., U.S.A.* 157 D10 40 8N 86 13W
Sheridan, *Wyo., U.S.A.* 158 D10 44 48N 106 58W
Sheringham, *U.K.* 20 E9 52 56N 1 13 E
Sherkin I., *Ireland* 23 E2 51 28N 9 26W
Sherkot, *India* 93 E8 29 22N 78 35 E
Sherman, *U.S.A.* 155 J6 33 40N 96 35W
Sherpur, *Bangla.* 90 C3 25 0N 90 0 E
Sherpur, *India* 93 G10 25 34N 83 47 E
Sherridon, *Canada* 143 B8 55 8N 101 5W
Sherwood, *U.S.A.* 157 C12 41 17N 84 33W
Sherwood Forest, *U.K.* 20 D6 53 6N 1 7W
Sherwood Park, *Canada* 142 C6 53 31N 113 19W
Sheslay →, *Canada* 142 B2 58 48N 132 5W
Shethanei L., *Canada* 143 B9 58 48N 97 50W
Shetland □, *U.K.* 22 A7 60 30N 1 30W
Shetland Is., *U.K.* 22 A7 60 30N 1 30W
Shetrunji →, *India* 92 J5 21 19N 72 7 E
Sheung Shui, *China* 69 F11 22 31N 114 7 E
Shevaroy Hills, *India* 95 J4 11 58N 78 12 E
Shevgaon, *India* 94 E2 19 21N 75 14 E
Shewa □, *Ethiopia* 107 F4 9 33N 38 10 E
Shewa Gimira, *Ethiopia* 107 F4 7 4N 35 51 E
Sheyenne →, *U.S.A.* 154 B6 47 2N 96 50W
Shibām, *Yemen* 99 D5 15 59N 48 36 E
Shibata, *Japan* 70 F9 37 57N 139 20 E
Shibecha, *Japan* 70 C12 43 17N 144 36 E
Shibetsu, *Japan* 70 B11 44 10N 142 23 E
Shibîn el Kôm, *Egypt* 106 H7 30 31N 30 55 E
Shibîn el Qanâtir, *Egypt* 106 H7 30 19N 31 19 E
Shibing, *China* 76 D7 27 2N 108 7 E
Shibogama L., *Canada* 140 B2 53 35N 88 15W
Shibukawa, *Japan* 73 A11 36 29N 139 0 E
Shibushi, *Japan* 72 F3 31 25N 131 8 E
Shibushi-Wan, *Japan* 72 F3 31 24N 131 8 E
Shicheng, *China* 77 D11 26 22N 116 20 E
Shickshinny, *U.S.A.* 151 E8 41 9N 76 9W
Shickshock Mts. = Chic-Chocs, Mts., *Canada* 141 C6 48 55N 66 0W
Shidād, *Si. Arabia* 98 B3 21 19N 40 3 E
Shidao, *China* 75 F12 36 50N 122 25 E
Shidian, *China* 76 E2 24 40N 99 5 E
Shido, *Japan* 72 C6 34 19N 134 10 E
Shiel, L., *U.K.* 22 E3 56 48N 5 34W
Shield, C., *Australia* 126 A2 13 20 S 136 20 E
Shīeli, *Kazakstan* 66 E7 44 20N 66 15 E
Shifang, *China* 76 B5 31 8N 104 10 E
Shiga □, *Japan* 73 B8 35 20N 136 0 E
Shigaib, *Sudan* 109 E4 15 5N 23 35 E
Shigu, *China* 76 D2 26 51N 99 56 E
Shiguaigou, *China* 74 D6 40 52N 110 15 E
Shihan, W. →, *Yemen* 99 C5 17 24N 51 26 E
Shihchiachuangi = Shijiazhuang, *China* 74 E8 38 2N 114 28 E
Shihezi, *China* 68 B3 44 15N 86 2 E
Shiiba, *Japan* 72 E3 32 29N 131 4 E
Shijak, *Albania* 50 E3 41 21N 19 33 E
Shijiazhuang, *China* 74 E8 38 2N 114 28 E
Shijiu Hu, *China* 77 B12 31 25N 118 50 E
Shikarpur, *India* 92 E8 28 17N 78 7 E
Shikarpur, *Pakistan* 91 D3 27 57N 68 39 E
Shikine-Jima, *Japan* 73 C11 34 19N 139 13 E
Shikohabad, *India* 93 F8 27 6N 78 36 E
Shikoku, *Japan* 72 D5 33 30N 133 30 E
Shikoku □, *Japan* 72 D5 33 30N 133 30 E
Shikoku-Sanchi, *Japan* 72 D5 33 30N 133 30 E
Shiliguri, *India* 90 B2 26 45N 88 25 E
Shilka, *Russia* 67 D12 52 0N 115 55 E
Shilka →, *Russia* 67 D13 53 20N 121 26 E
Shillelagh, *Ireland* 23 D5 52 45N 6 32W
Shillington, *U.S.A.* 151 F9 40 18N 75 58W
Shillong, *India* 90 C3 25 35N 91 53 E
Shilo, *West Bank* 103 C4 32 4N 35 18 E
Shilong, *China* 77 F9 23 5N 113 52 E
Shilou, *China* 74 F6 37 0N 110 48 E
Shilovo, *Russia* 60 C5 54 25N 40 57 E
Shima-Hantō, *Japan* 73 C8 34 22N 136 45 E
Shimabara, *Japan* 72 E2 32 48N 130 20 E
Shimada, *Japan* 73 C10 34 49N 138 10 E
Shimane □, *Japan* 72 C4 35 0N 132 30 E
Shimane-Hantō, *Japan* 72 B5 35 30N 133 0 E
Shimanovsk, *Russia* 67 D13 52 15N 127 30 E
Shimba Hills Nat. Reserve, *Kenya* 118 C4 4 14 S 39 25 E
Shimen, *China* 77 C8 29 35N 111 20 E
Shimenjie, *China* 77 C11 29 29N 116 48 E
Shimian, *China* 76 C4 29 17N 102 23 E
Shimizu, *Japan* 73 C10 35 0N 138 30 E
Shimo-Jima, *Japan* 72 E2 32 15N 130 7 E
Shimo-Koshiki-Jima, *Japan* 72 F1 31 40N 129 43 E
Shimoda, *Japan* 73 C10 34 40N 138 57 E
Shimodate, *Japan* 73 A11 36 20N 139 55 E
Shimoga, *India* 95 H2 13 57N 75 32 E
Shimoni, *Kenya* 118 C4 4 38 S 39 20 E
Shimonita, *Japan* 73 A10 36 13N 138 47 E
Shimonoseki, *Japan* 72 D2 33 58N 130 55 E
Shimotsuma, *Japan* 73 A11 36 11N 139 58 E
Shimpuru Rapids, *Namibia* 116 B2 17 45 S 19 55 E
Shimsha →, *India* 95 H3 13 15N 77 10 E
Shimsk, *Russia* 58 C6 58 15N 30 50 E
Shin, L., *U.K.* 22 C4 58 5N 4 30W
Shin-Nan'yō, *Japan* 72 C3 34 3N 131 49 E
Shin-Tone-Gawa →, *Japan* 73 B12 35 44N 140 51 E
Shinan, *China* 76 F7 22 44N 109 53 E
Shinano-Gawa →, *Japan* 71 F9 36 50N 138 30 E
Shināş, *Oman* 97 E8 24 46N 56 28 E
Shīndand, *Afghan.* 91 B1 33 12N 62 8 E
Shingbwiyang, *Burma* 90 B6 26 41N 96 13 E
Shinglehouse, *U.S.A.* 150 E6 41 58N 78 12W
Shingū, *Japan* 73 D7 33 40N 135 55 E
Shingwidzi, *S. Africa* 117 C5 23 5 S 31 25 E
Shinji, *Japan* 72 B4 35 24N 132 54 E
Shinji-Ko, *Japan* 72 B4 35 26N 132 57 E
Shinjō, *Japan* 70 E10 38 46N 140 18 E
Shinkafe, *Nigeria* 113 C6 13 8N 6 29 E
Shinminato, *Japan* 73 A9 36 47N 137 4 E
Shinshār, *Syria* 103 A5 34 36N 36 43 E
Shinshiro, *Japan* 73 C9 34 54N 137 30 E
Shintuya, *Peru* 172 C3 12 41 S 71 15W
Shinyanga, *Tanzania* 118 C3 3 45 S 33 27 E
Shinyanga □, *Tanzania* 118 C3 3 50 S 34 0 E
Shio-no-Misaki, *Japan* 73 D7 33 25N 135 45 E
Shiogama, *Japan* 70 E10 38 19N 141 1 E
Shiojiri, *Japan* 73 A9 36 6N 137 58 E
Shipchenski Prokhod, *Bulgaria* 51 D9 42 45N 25 15 E
Shiping, *China* 76 F4 23 45N 102 23 E
Shippegan, *Canada* 141 C7 47 45N 64 45W
Shippensburg, *U.S.A.* 150 F7 40 3N 77 31W
Shippenville, *U.S.A.* 150 E5 41 15N 79 28W
Shiprock, *U.S.A.* 159 H9 36 47N 108 41W
Shiqian, *China* 76 D7 27 32N 108 13 E
Shiqma, N. →, *Israel* 103 D3 31 37N 34 30 E
Shiquan, *China* 74 H5 33 5N 108 15 E
Shiquan He = Indus →, *Pakistan* 91 D2 24 20N 67 47 E
Shīr Khān, *Afghan.* 65 E4 37 11N 68 36 E
Shīr Kūh, *Iran* 97 D7 31 39N 54 3 E
Shirabad = Sherabad, *Uzbekistan* 65 E3 37 40N 67 1 E
Shiragami-Misaki, *Japan* 70 D10 41 24N 140 12 E
Shirahama, *Japan* 73 D7 33 41N 135 20 E
Shirakawa, *Fukushima, Japan* 71 F10 37 7N 140 13 E
Shirakawa, *Gifu, Japan* 73 A8 36 17N 136 56 E
Shirane-San, *Gumma, Japan* 73 A11 36 48N 139 22 E
Shirane-San, *Yamanashi, Japan* 73 B10 35 42N 138 9 E
Shiraoi, *Japan* 70 C10 42 33N 141 21 E
Shīrāz, *Iran* 97 D7 29 42N 52 30 E
Shirbîn, *Egypt* 106 H7 31 11N 31 32 E
Shire →, *Africa* 119 F4 17 42 S 35 19 E
Shiretoko-Misaki, *Japan* 70 B12 44 21N 145 20 E
Shirin, *Uzbekistan* 65 C4 40 14N 69 7 E
Shirinab →, *Pakistan* 92 D2 30 15N 66 28 E
Shiriya-Zaki, *Japan* 70 D10 41 25N 141 30 E
Shirley, *U.S.A.* 157 E11 39 53N 85 35W
Shiroishi, *Japan* 70 F10 38 0N 140 37 E
Shirol, *India* 94 F2 16 47N 74 41 E
Shirpur, *India* 94 D2 21 21N 74 57 E
Shīrvān, *Iran* 97 B8 37 30N 57 50 E
Shirwa, L. = Chilwa, L., *Malawi* 119 F4 15 15 S 35 40 E
Shishaldin Volcano, *U.S.A.* 144 J7 54 45N 163 58W
Shishi, *China* 77 E12 24 44N 118 37 E
Shishmaref, *U.S.A.* 144 C6 66 15N 166 4W
Shishou, *China* 77 C9 29 38N 112 22 E
Shitai, *China* 77 B11 30 12N 117 25 E
Shively, *U.S.A.* 157 F11 38 12N 85 49W
Shivpuri, *India* 92 G7 25 26N 77 42 E
Shixian, *China* 75 C15 43 5N 129 50 E
Shixing, *China* 77 E10 24 46N 114 5 E
Shiyan, *Guangdong, China* 69 F10 22 42N 113 56 E
Shiyan, *Hubei, China* 77 A8 32 35N 110 45 E
Shiyan Shuiku, *China* 69 F10 22 42N 113 54 E
Shiyata, *Egypt* 106 B2 29 25N 25 7 E
Shizhu, *China* 76 C7 29 58N 108 7 E
Shizong, *China* 76 E5 24 50N 104 0 E
Shizuishan, *China* 74 E4 39 15N 106 50 E
Shizuoka, *Japan* 73 C10 34 57N 138 24 E
Shizuoka □, *Japan* 73 B10 35 15N 138 40 E
Shklov = Shklow, *Belarus* 58 E6 54 16N 30 15 E
Shklow, *Belarus* 58 E6 54 16N 30 15 E
Shkodër, *Albania* 50 D3 42 4N 19 32 E
Shkumbini →, *Albania* 50 E3 41 2N 19 31 E
Shmidta, Ostrov, *Russia* 67 A10 81 0N 91 0 E
Shō-Gawa →, *Japan* 73 A9 36 47N 137 4 E
Shoal Cr. →, *U.S.A.* 156 E3 39 44N 93 32W
Shoal L., *Canada* 143 D9 49 33N 95 1W
Shoal Lake, *Canada* 143 C8 50 30N 100 35W
Shoalhaven →, *Australia* 129 C9 34 54 S 150 42 E
Shoals, *U.S.A.* 157 F10 38 40N 86 47W
Shōbara, *Japan* 72 C5 34 51N 133 1 E
Shōdo-Shima, *Japan* 72 C6 34 30N 134 15 E
Shokpar = Shoqpar, *Kazakstan* 65 B7 43 49N 74 21 E
Sholapur = Solapur, *India* 94 F2 17 43N 75 56 E
Sholaqqūrghan, *Kazakstan* 65 B4 43 46N 69 9 E
Shologontsy, *Russia* 67 C12 66 13N 114 0 E
Shōmrōn, *West Bank* 103 C4 32 15N 35 13 E
Shoqpar, *Kazakstan* 65 B7 43 49N 74 21 E
Shoranur, *India* 95 J3 10 46N 76 19 E
Shorapur, *India* 95 F3 16 31N 76 48 E
Shoreham by Sea, *U.K.* 21 G7 50 50N 0 16W
Shorewood, *U.S.A.* 157 A9 43 5N 87 54W
Shori →, *Pakistan* 92 E3 28 29N 69 44 E
Shorkot Road, *Pakistan* 92 D5 30 47N 72 15 E
Shornak, *Kazakstan* 65 B4 43 24N 68 2 E
Shorter, *U.S.A.* 152 C4 32 24N 85 57W
Shorterville, *U.S.A.* 152 D4 31 34N 85 6W
Shortland I., *Solomon Is.* 133 L8 7 0 S 155 45 E
Shortland Is., *Solomon Is.* 133 L8 7 0 S 155 45 E
Shortt's I., *India* 94 D8 20 47N 87 4 E
Shoshone, *Calif., U.S.A.* 161 K10 35 58N 116 16W
Shoshone, *Idaho, U.S.A.* 158 E6 42 56N 114 25W
Shoshone L., *U.S.A.* 158 D8 44 22N 110 43W
Shoshone Mts., *U.S.A.* 158 G5 39 20N 117 25W
Shoshong, *Botswana* 116 C4 22 56 S 26 31 E
Shoshoni, *U.S.A.* 158 E9 43 14N 108 7W
Shostka, *Ukraine* 59 G7 51 57N 33 32 E
Shotor Khūn, *Afghan.* 91 B2 34 19N 64 56 E
Shotover →, *N.Z.* 131 E3 44 59 S 168 41 E
Shou Xian, *China* 77 A11 32 37N 116 42 E
Shouchang, *China* 77 C12 29 18N 119 12 E
Shouguang, *China* 75 F10 37 52N 118 45 E
Shouning, *China* 77 D12 27 27N 119 31 E
Shouyang, *China* 74 F7 37 54N 113 8 E
Show Low, *U.S.A.* 159 J9 34 15N 110 2W
Showa, *Japan* 73 B10 35 36N 138 29 E
Shpola, *Ukraine* 59 H6 49 1N 31 30 E
Shreveport, *U.S.A.* 155 J8 32 31N 93 45W
Shrewsbury, *U.K.* 21 E5 52 43N 2 45W
Shri Mohangarh, *India* 92 F4 27 17N 71 18 E
Shrigonda, *India* 94 E2 18 37N 74 41 E
Shrirampur, *India* 93 H13 22 44N 88 21 E
Shropshire □, *U.K.* 21 E5 52 36N 2 45W
Shū, *Kazakstan* 66 E8 43 36N 73 42 E
Shū →, *Kazakstan* 65 A3 45 0N 67 44 E
Shuangbai, *China* 76 E3 24 42N 101 38 E
Shuangcheng, *China* 75 B14 45 20N 126 15 E
Shuangfeng, *China* 77 D9 27 29N 112 11 E
Shuanggou, *China* 75 G9 34 2N 117 30 E
Shuangjiang, *China* 76 F2 23 26N 99 58 E
Shuangliao, *China* 75 C12 43 29N 123 30 E
Shuangshanzi, *China* 75 D10 40 20N 119 8 E
Shuangyang, *China* 75 C13 43 28N 125 40 E
Shuangyashan, *China* 69 B8 46 28N 131 5 E
Shu'b, Ra's, *Yemen* 99 D6 12 30N 53 25 E
Shubra Khit, *Egypt* 106 H7 31 2N 30 42 E
Shucheng, *China* 77 B11 31 28N 116 57 E
Shufu, *China* 65 D7 39 27N 75 52 E
Shugozero, *Russia* 58 C8 59 54N 34 10 E
Shuguri Falls, *Tanzania* 119 D4 8 33 S 37 22 E
Shuḥayr, *Yemen* 99 D5 14 41N 49 23 E
Shuiji, *China* 77 D12 27 13N 118 20 E
Shuiye, *China* 74 F8 36 7N 114 8 E
Shujalpur, *India* 92 H7 23 18N 76 46 E
Shukpa Kunzang, *India* 93 B8 34 22N 78 22 E
Shulan, *China* 75 B14 44 28N 127 0 E
Shulaveri, *Georgia* 61 K7 41 22N 44 45 E
Shule, *China* 65 D8 39 25N 76 3 E
Shullsburg, *U.S.A.* 156 B6 42 35N 90 13W
Shumagin Is., *U.S.A.* 144 J8 55 7N 160 30W
Shumen, *Bulgaria* 51 C10 43 18N 26 55 E
Shumerlya, *Russia* 60 C8 55 30N 46 25 E
Shumikha, *Russia* 64 D9 55 10N 63 15 E
Shunchang, *China* 77 D11 26 54N 117 48 E
Shunde, *China* 77 F9 22 42N 113 14 E
Shungay, *Kazakstan* 61 F8 48 30N 46 45 E
Shungnak, *U.S.A.* 144 C8 66 52N 157 9W
Shuo Xian = Shuozhou, *China* 74 E7 39 20N 112 33 E
Shuozhou, *China* 74 E7 39 20N 112 33 E
Shūr →, *Fārs, Iran* 97 D7 28 30N 55 0 E
Shūr →, *Kermān, Iran* 97 D8 30 52N 57 37 E
Shūr →, *Yazd, Iran* 97 D7 31 45N 55 15 E
Shūr Āb, *Iran* 97 C6 34 23N 51 11 E
Shūr Gaz, *Iran* 97 D8 29 10N 59 20 E
Shūrāb, *Iran* 97 C8 33 43N 56 29 E
Shurab, *Tajikistan* 65 C5 40 3N 70 33 E
Shurchi, *Uzbekistan* 65 E3 37 59N 67 47 E
Shūrjestān, *Iran* 97 D7 31 24N 52 25 E
Shurkhua, *Burma* 90 D4 22 15N 93 38 E
Shurugwi, *Zimbabwe* 119 F3 19 40 S 30 0 E
Shūsf, *Iran* 97 D9 31 50N 60 5 E
Shūsh, *Iran* 101 F13 32 11N 48 15 E
Shūshtar, *Iran* 97 D6 32 0N 48 50 E
Shuswap L., *Canada* 142 C5 50 55N 119 3W
Shuya, *Russia* 60 B5 56 50N 41 28 E
Shuyak I., *U.S.A.* 144 G9 58 31N 152 30W
Shuyang, *China* 75 G10 34 10N 118 42 E
Shuzenji, *Japan* 73 C10 34 58N 138 56 E
Shūzū, *Iran* 97 D7 29 52N 54 30 E
Shwebo, *Burma* 90 D5 22 30N 95 45 E
Shwegu, *Burma* 90 C6 24 15N 96 26 E
Shwegun, *Burma* 90 G6 17 9N 97 39 E
Shwegyin, *Burma* 90 G6 17 55N 96 53 E
Shweli →, *Burma* 90 D6 23 45N 96 45 E
Shwenyaung, *Burma* 90 E6 20 46N 96 57 E
Shyamnagar, *India* 95 H11 13 21N 92 57 E
Shyghanaq, *Kazakstan* 65 A6 45 6N 73 59 E
Shyghanaq, *Kazakstan* 65 A5 44 49N 70 0 E
Shymkent, *Kazakstan* 66 E7 42 18N 69 36 E
Shyok, *India* 93 B8 34 13N 78 12 E
Shyok →, *Pakistan* 93 B6 35 13N 75 53 E
Si Chon, *Thailand* 87 H2 9 0N 99 54 E
Si Kiang = Xi Jiang →, *China* 77 F9 22 5N 113 20 E
Si-ngan = Xi'an, *China* 74 G5 34 15N 109 0 E
Si Prachan, *Thailand* 86 E3 14 37N 100 9 E
Si Racha, *Thailand* 86 F3 13 10N 100 48 E
Si Xian, *China* 75 H9 33 30N 117 50 E
Siachen Glacier, *Asia* 93 B7 35 20N 77 30 E
Siahaf →, *Pakistan* 92 E3 29 3N 68 57 E
Siahan Range, *Pakistan* 91 D2 27 30N 64 40 E
Siak →, *Indonesia* 84 B2 1 13N 102 9 E
Siaksriindrapura, *Indonesia* 84 B2 0 51N 102 0 E
Sialkot, *Pakistan* 91 B4 32 32N 74 30 E
Sialsuk, *India* 90 D4 23 24N 92 45 E
Sialum, *Papua N. G.* 132 D4 6 5 S 147 36 E
Siam = Thailand ■, *Asia* 86 E4 16 0N 102 0 E
Sian = Xi'an, *China* 74 G5 34 15N 109 0 E
Sianów, *Poland* 54 D3 54 13N 16 18 E
Siantan, *Indonesia* 84 B3 3 10N 106 15 E
Siàpo →, *Venezuela* 168 C4 2 7N 66 28W
Siāreh, *Iran* 97 D9 28 5N 60 14 E
Siargao I., *Phil.* 81 G6 9 52N 126 3 E
Siari, *Pakistan* 93 B7 34 55N 76 40 E
Siasi, *Phil.* 79 C6 5 34N 120 50 E
Siasi I., *Phil.* 81 J3 5 33N 120 51 E
Siassi, *Papua N. G.* 132 C4 5 40 S 147 51 E
Siátista, *Greece* 50 F5 40 15N 21 33 E
Siaton, *Phil.* 81 G4 9 4N 123 2 E
Siau, *Indonesia* 82 A3 2 50N 125 25 E
Šiauliai, *Lithuania* 15 J20 55 56N 23 15 E
Šiauliai □, *Lithuania* 54 C10 55 56N 23 19 E
Siazan = Siyäzän, *Azerbaijan* 61 K9 41 3N 49 10 E
Sibâi, Gebel el, *Egypt* 96 E2 25 45N 34 10 E
Sibang, *Gabon* 114 B1 0 25N 9 31 E
Sibang, *Indonesia* 79 K18 8 34 S 115 13 E
Sibay, *Russia* 64 E7 52 42N 58 39 E
Sibay I., *Phil.* 81 F3 11 51N 121 29 E
Sibayi, L., *S. Africa* 117 D5 27 20 S 32 45 E
Sibdu, *Sudan* 107 E2 10 57N 26 17 E
Šibenik, *Croatia* 45 E12 43 48N 15 54 E
Siberia, *Russia* 6 D13 60 0N 100 0 E
Siberut, *Indonesia* 84 C1 1 30 S 99 0 E
Sibi, *Pakistan* 91 C2 29 30N 67 54 E
Sibil = Oksibil, *Indonesia* 83 B6 4 59 S 140 35 E
Sibiloi Nat. Park, *Kenya* 118 B4 4 0N 36 20 E
Sibiti, *Congo* 114 C2 3 38 S 13 19 E
Sibiu, *Romania* 53 E9 45 45N 24 9 E
Sibiu □, *Romania* 53 E9 45 50N 24 15 E
Sibium Mts., *Papua N. G.* 132 E5 9 19 S 148 25 E
Sibley, *Ill., U.S.A.* 157 D8 40 35N 88 23W
Sibley, *Iowa, U.S.A.* 154 D7 43 24N 95 45W
Sibolga, *Indonesia* 84 B1 1 42N 98 45 E
Sibsagar, *India* 90 B5 27 0N 94 36 E
Sibu, *Malaysia* 85 B4 2 18N 111 49 E
Sibuco, *Phil.* 81 H4 7 20N 122 10 E
Sibuguey B., *Phil.* 81 H4 7 50N 122 45 E
Sibut, *C.A.R.* 114 A3 5 46N 19 10 E
Sibutu, *Phil.* 85 B5 4 45N 119 30 E
Sibutu Group, *Phil.* 81 J2 4 45N 119 20 E
Sibutu Passage, *E. Indies* 81 J3 4 50N 120 0 E
Sibuyan I., *Phil.* 80 E4 12 25N 122 40 E
Sibuyan Sea, *Phil.* 80 E4 12 30N 122 20 E
Sic, *Romania* 53 D8 46 56N 23 53 E
Sicamous, *Canada* 142 C5 50 49N 119 0W
Sicapoo, Mt., *Phil.* 80 B3 18 1N 120 56 E
Sicasica, *Bolivia* 172 D4 17 22 S 67 45W
Siccus →, *S. Austral., Australia* 127 E2 31 26 S 139 30 E
Siccus →, *S. Austral., Australia* 128 A3 31 55 S 139 17 E
Sichuan □, *China* 76 B5 30 30N 103 0 E
Sichuan Pendi, *China* 76 B5 31 0N 105 0 E
Sicilia, *Italy* 47 E7 37 30N 14 30 E
Sicily = Sicilia, *Italy* 47 E7 37 30N 14 30 E
Sicuani, *Peru* 172 C3 14 21 S 71 10W
Šid, *Serbia, Yug.* 52 E4 45 8N 19 14 E
Sidamo □, *Ethiopia* 107 G4 5 0N 37 50 E
Sidaouet, *Niger* 113 B6 18 34N 8 3 E
Sidári, *Greece* 38 B9 39 47N 19 41 E
Siddapur, *India* 95 G2 14 20N 74 53 E
Siddhapur, *India* 92 H5 23 56N 72 25 E
Siddipet, *India* 94 E4 18 5N 78 51 E
Sidensjö, *Sweden* 16 A12 63 18N 18 17 E
Sidéradougou, *Burkina Faso* 112 C4 10 42N 4 12W
Siderno, *Italy* 47 D9 38 16N 16 18 E
Sidhauli, *India* 93 F9 27 17N 80 50 E
Sídheros, Ákra, *Greece* 39 E7 35 19N 26 19 E
Sidhi, *India* 93 G9 24 25N 81 53 E
Sidhirókastron, *Greece* 50 E7 41 13N 23 24 E
Sîdi Abd el Rahmân, *Egypt* 106 A2 30 55N 29 44 E
Sidi Ahmed Rgueibi, *W. Sahara* 110 C2 27 32N 11 16W
Sîdi Barrâni, *Egypt* 106 A2 31 38N 25 58 E
Sidi-bel-Abbès, *Algeria* 111 A4 35 13N 0 39W
Sidi Bennour, *Morocco* 110 B3 32 40N 8 25W
Sîdi Haneish, *Egypt* 106 A2 31 10N 27 35 E
Sidi Ifni, *Morocco* 110 C2 29 29N 10 12W
Sidi Kacem, *Morocco* 110 B3 34 11N 5 49W
Sîdi Omar, *Egypt* 106 A1 31 24N 24 57 E
Sidi Slimane, *Morocco* 110 B3 34 16N 5 56W
Sidi Smaïl, *Morocco* 110 B3 32 50N 8 31W
Sīdi 'Uzayz, *Libya* 108 B4 31 41N 24 55 E
Sidlaw Hills, *U.K.* 22 E5 56 32N 3 2W
Sidley, Mt., *Antarctica* 7 D14 77 2 S 126 2W
Sidmouth, *U.K.* 21 G4 50 40N 3 15W
Sidmouth, C., *Australia* 126 A3 13 25 S 143 36 E
Sidney, *Canada* 142 D4 48 39N 123 24W
Sidney, *Mont., U.S.A.* 154 B2 47 43N 104 9W
Sidney, *N.Y., U.S.A.* 151 D9 42 19N 75 24W
Sidney, *Nebr., U.S.A.* 154 E3 41 8N 102 59W
Sidney, *Ohio, U.S.A.* 157 D12 40 17N 84 9W
Sidney Lanier, L., *U.S.A.* 152 A5 34 10N 84 4W
Sido, *Mali* 112 C3 11 37N 7 29W
Sidoarjo, *Indonesia* 85 D4 7 27 S 112 43 E
Sidoktaya, *Burma* 90 E5 20 27N 94 15 E
Sidon = Saydā, *Lebanon* 103 B4 33 35N 35 25 E
Sidra, G. of = Surt, Khalīj, *Libya* 108 B3 31 40N 18 30 E
Sidrolândia, *Brazil* 173 20 55 S 54 58W
Siedlce, *Poland* 55 F9 52 10N 22 20 E
Sieg →, *Germany* 30 E3 50 46N 7 6 E
Siegburg, *Germany* 30 E3 50 47N 7 12 E
Siegen, *Germany* 30 E4 50 51N 8 0 E
Siem Pang, *Cambodia* 86 E6 14 7N 106 23 E
Siem Reap = Siemreab, *Cambodia* 86 F4 13 20N 103 52 E
Siemiatycze, *Poland* 55 F9 52 27N 22 53 E
Siemreab, *Cambodia* 86 F4 13 20N 103 52 E
Siena, *Italy* 45 E8 43 19N 11 21 E
Sieniawa, *Poland* 55 H9 50 11N 22 38 E
Sieradz, *Poland* 55 G5 51 37N 18 41 E
Sieraków, *Poland* 55 F3 52 39N 16 2 E
Sierck-les-Bains, *France* 27 C13 49 26N 6 20 E
Sierning, *Austria* 34 C7 48 2N 14 18 E
Sierpc, *Poland* 55 F6 52 55N 19 43 E
Sierpe, Bocas de la, *Venezuela* 169 G9 10 0N 61 30W
Sierra Blanca, *U.S.A.* 159 L11 31 11N 105 22W
Sierra Blanca Peak, *U.S.A.* 159 K11 33 23N 105 49W
Sierra City, *U.S.A.* 160 F6 39 34N 120 38W
Sierra Colorada, *Argentina* 176 B3 40 35 S 67 50W
Sierra de Yeguas, *Spain* 43 H6 37 7N 4 52W
Sierra Gorda, *Chile* 174 A2 22 50 S 69 15W
Sierra Grande, *Argentina* 176 B3 41 36 S 65 22W
Sierra Leone ■, *W. Afr.* 112 D2 9 0N 12 0W
Sierra Madre, *Mexico* 163 D6 16 0N 93 0W
Sierra Mojada, *Mexico* 162 B4 27 19N 103 42W
Sierra Nevada, *Spain* 43 H7 37 3N 3 15W
Sierra Nevada, *U.S.A.* 160 H8 39 0N 120 30W
Sierra Vista, *U.S.A.* 159 L8 31 33N 110 18W
Sierraville, *U.S.A.* 160 F6 39 36N 120 22W
Sierre, *Switz.* 32 D5 46 17N 7 31 E
Sifani, *Ethiopia* 107 E5 12 18N 40 19 E
Sifié, *Ivory C.* 112 D3 7 59N 7 5W
Sífnos, *Greece* 48 E6 37 0N 24 45 E
Sifton, *Canada* 143 C8 51 21N 100 8W
Sifton Pass, *Canada* 142 B3 57 52N 126 15W
Sig, *Algeria* 111 A4 35 32N 0 12W
Sigaboy = Governor Generoso, *Phil.* 81 H6 6 39N 126 5 E
Sigatoka, *Fiji* 133 B1 18 8 S 177 32 E
Sigatoka, *Fiji* 133 B1 18 8 S 177 30 E
Sigdal, *Norway* 18 D6 60 3N 9 38 E
Sigean, *France* 28 E6 43 2N 2 58 E
Siggiewi, *Malta* 38 F7 35 51N 14 26 E
Sighetu-Marmaţiei, *Romania* 53 C8 47 57N 23 52 E
Sighişoara, *Romania* 53 D9 46 12N 24 50 E
Sigira, *Yemen* 99 D6 12 37N 54 20 E
Sigiriya, *Sri Lanka* 95 L5 7 57N 80 45 E
Sigli, *Indonesia* 84 A1 5 25N 96 0 E
Siglufjörður, *Iceland* 11 A8 66 12N 18 55W
Siglunes, *Iceland* 11 A8 66 12N 18 50W
Sigmaringen, *Germany* 31 G5 48 5N 9 12 E
Signa, *Italy* 44 E8 43 45N 11 10 E
Signakhi = Tsnori, *Georgia* 61 K7 41 40N 45 57 E
Signal, *U.S.A.* 161 L13 34 30N 113 38W
Signal Pk., *U.S.A.* 161 M12 33 20N 114 2W
Signau, *Switz.* 32 C5 46 56N 7 45 E
Signy-l'Abbaye, *France* 27 C11 49 40N 4 25 E
Sigourney, *U.S.A.* 156 C4 41 20N 92 12W
Sigsbee, *U.S.A.* 152 D6 31 16N 83 52W
Sigsig, *Ecuador* 168 D2 3 0 S 78 50W
Sigüenza, *Spain* 40 D2 41 3N 2 40W
Siguiri, *Guinea* 112 C3 11 31N 9 10W
Sigulda, *Latvia* 15 H21 57 10N 24 55 E
Sihanoukville = Kampong Saom, *Cambodia* 87 G4 10 38N 103 30 E
Sihaus, *Peru* 172 B2 8 40 S 77 40W
Sihawa, *India* 94 D5 20 19N 81 55 E
Sihora, *India* 93 H9 23 29N 80 6 E
Sihui, *China* 77 F9 23 20N 112 40 E
Siikajoki →, *Finland* 14 D21 64 50N 24 43 E
Siilinjärvi, *Finland* 14 E22 63 4N 27 39 E
Siirt, *Turkey* 101 D9 37 57N 41 55 E
Sijarira Ra. = Chizarira, *Zimbabwe* 119 F2 17 36 S 27 45 E
Sijungjung, *Indonesia* 84 C2 0 42 S 100 58 E
Sika, *India* 92 H3 22 26N 69 47 E
Sikao, *Thailand* 87 J2 7 34N 99 21 E
Sikar, *India* 92 F6 27 33N 75 10 E
Sikasso, *Mali* 112 C3 11 18N 5 35W
Sikelenge, *Zambia* 115 E4 14 53 S 24 14 E
Sikeston, *U.S.A.* 155 G10 36 53N 89 35W
Sikhote Alin, Khrebet, *Russia* 67 E14 45 0N 136 0 E

Skrwa →, *Poland* **55 F6** 52 35N 19 32 E
Skudeneshavn, *Norway* **18 E2** 59 10N 5 10 E
Skull, *Ireland* **23 E2** 51 32N 9 34W
Skultorp, *Sweden* **17 F7** 58 24N 13 51 E
Skultuna, *Sweden* **16 E10** 59 43N 16 25 E
Skunk →, *U.S.A.* **156 D5** 40 42N 91 7W
Skuodas, *Lithuania* **15 H19** 56 16N 21 33 E
Skurup, *Sweden* **17 J7** 55 28N 13 30 E
Skutskär, *Sweden* **16 D11** 60 37N 17 25 E
Skútustaðir, *Iceland* **11 B9** 65 34N 17 2W
Skvyra, *Ukraine* **59 H5** 49 44N 29 40 E
Skwierzyna, *Poland* **55 F2** 52 33N 15 30 E
Skye, *U.K.* **22 D2** 57 15N 6 10W
Skykomish, *U.S.A.* **158 C3** 47 42N 121 22W
Skyring, Seno, *Chile* **176 D3** 52 35 S 72 0W
Skyros = Skíros, *Greece* **48 C6** 38 55N 24 34 E
Skyttorp, *Sweden* **16 D11** 60 5N 17 44 E
Slade Pt., *Australia* **126 K7** 21 5 S 149 13 E
Slættaratindur, *Færoe Is.* **14 E9** 62 18N 7 1W
Slagelse, *Denmark* **17 J5** 55 23N 11 19 E
Slamet, *Indonesia* **85 D3** 7 16 S 109 8 E
Slaney →, *Ireland* **23 D5** 52 26N 6 33W
Slangberge, *S. Africa* **116 E3** 31 32 S 20 48 E
Slănic, *Romania* **53 E10** 45 14N 25 58 E
Slano, *Croatia* **50 D1** 42 48N 17 53 E
Slantsy, *Russia* **58 C5** 59 7N 28 5 E
Slaný, *Czech Rep.* **34 A7** 50 13N 14 6 E
Śląsk, *Poland* **36 C9** 51 0N 16 30 E
Śląskie □, *Poland* **55 H6** 50 30N 19 0 E
Slätbaken, *Sweden* **17 F10** 58 25N 16 45 E
Slate Is., *Canada* **140 C2** 48 40N 87 0W
Slater, *U.S.A.* **156 E3** 39 13N 93 4W
Slatina, *Croatia* **52 E2** 45 42N 17 45 E
Slatina, *Romania* **53 F9** 44 28N 24 22 E
Slatina Timiş, *Romania* **52 E7** 45 15N 22 17 E
Slatington, *U.S.A.* **151 F9** 40 45N 75 37W
Slaton, *U.S.A.* **155 J4** 33 26N 101 39W
Slave →, *Canada* **142 A6** 61 18N 113 39W
Slave Coast, *W. Afr.* **113 D5** 6 0N 2 30 E
Slave Lake, *Canada* **142 B6** 55 17N 114 43W
Slave Pt., *Canada* **142 A5** 61 11N 115 56W
Slavgorod, *Russia* **66 D8** 53 1N 78 37 E
Slavinja, *Serbia, Yug.* **50 C6** 43 9N 22 50 E
Slavkov u Brna, *Czech Rep.* **35 B9** 49 10N 16 52 E
Slavonija, *Europe* **52 E2** 45 20N 17 40 E
Slavonski Brod, *Croatia* **52 E3** 45 11N 18 1 E
Slavuta, *Ukraine* **59 G4** 50 15N 27 2 E
Slavyanka, *Russia* **70 C5** 42 53N 131 21 E
Slavyanovo, *Bulgaria* **51 C8** 43 28N 24 52 E
Slavyansk = Slovyansk, *Ukraine* **59 H9** 48 55N 37 36 E
Slavyansk-na-Kubani, *Russia* **59 K10** 45 15N 38 11 E
Sława, *Poland* **55 G3** 51 52N 16 2 E
Slawharad, *Belarus* **58 F6** 53 27N 31 0 E
Sławno, *Poland* **54 D3** 54 20N 16 41 E
Sławoborze, *Poland* **54 E2** 53 55N 15 42 E
Sleaford, *U.K.* **20 D7** 53 0N 0 24W
Sleaford B., *Australia* **127 E2** 34 55 S 135 45 E
Sleat, Sd. of, *U.K.* **22 D3** 57 5N 5 47W
Sleðbrjótur, *Iceland* **11 B12** 65 34N 14 30W
Sleeper Is., *Canada* **139 C11** 58 30N 81 0W
Sleepy Eye, *U.S.A.* **154 C7** 44 18N 94 43W
Sleetmute, *U.S.A.* **144 F8** 61 42N 157 10W
Sleman, *Indonesia* **85 D4** 7 40 S 110 20 E
Slemon L., *Canada* **142 A5** 63 13N 116 4W
Ślesin, *Poland* **55 F5** 52 22N 18 14 E
Slide Mt., *U.S.A.* **151 E10** 42 0N 74 25W
Slidell, *U.S.A.* **155 K10** 30 17N 89 47W
Sliema, *Malta* **38 F8** 35 55N 14 30 E
Slieve Aughty, *Ireland* **23 C3** 53 4N 8 30W
Slieve Bloom, *Ireland* **23 C4** 53 4N 7 40W
Slieve Donard, *U.K.* **23 B6** 54 11N 5 55W
Slieve Gamph, *Ireland* **23 B3** 54 6N 9 0W
Slieve Gullion, *U.K.* **23 B5** 54 7N 6 26W
Slieve Mish, *Ireland* **23 D2** 52 12N 9 50W
Slievenamon, *Ireland* **23 D4** 52 25N 7 34W
Sligeach = Sligo, *Ireland* **23 B3** 54 16N 8 28W
Sligo, *Ireland* **23 B3** 54 16N 8 28W
Sligo, *U.S.A.* **150 E5** 41 6N 79 29W
Sligo □, *Ireland* **23 B3** 54 8N 8 42W
Sligo B., *Ireland* **23 B3** 54 18N 8 40W
Slippery Rock, *U.S.A.* **150 E4** 41 3N 80 3W
Slite, *Sweden* **17 G12** 57 42N 18 48 E
Sliven, *Bulgaria* **51 D10** 42 42N 26 19 E
Slivnitsa, *Bulgaria* **50 D7** 42 50N 23 2 E
Sljeme, *Croatia* **45 C12** 45 57N 15 58 E
Sloan, *U.S.A.* **161 K11** 35 57N 115 13W
Sloansville, *U.S.A.* **151 D10** 42 45N 74 22W
Slobodskoy, *Russia* **64 B3** 58 40N 50 6 E
Slobozia, *Moldova* **53 D14** 46 45N 29 42 E
Slobozia, *Argeş, Romania* **53 F10** 44 30N 25 14 E
Slobozia, *Ialomiţa, Romania* **53 F12** 44 34N 27 23 E
Slocan, *Canada* **142 D5** 49 48N 117 28W
Slocomb, *U.S.A.* **152 D4** 31 7N 85 36W
Słomniki, *Poland* **55 H7** 50 16N 20 4 E
Slonim, *Belarus* **59 E3** 53 4N 25 19 E
Slough, *U.K.* **21 F7** 51 30N 0 36W
Slough □, *U.K.* **21 F7** 51 30N 0 36W
Sloughhouse, *U.S.A.* **160 G5** 38 26N 121 12W
Slovak Rep. ■, *Europe* **35 C13** 48 30N 20 0 E
Slovakia = Slovak Rep. ■, *Europe* **35 C13** 48 30N 20 0 E
Slovakian Ore Mts. = Slovenské Rudohorie, *Slovak Rep.* **35 C12** 48 45N 20 0 E
Slovenia ■, *Europe* **45 C11** 45 58N 14 30 E
Slovenija = Slovenia ■, *Europe* **45 C11** 45 58N 14 30 E
Slovenj Gradec, *Slovenia* **45 B12** 46 31N 15 5 E
Slovenska Bistrica, *Slovenia* **45 B12** 46 24N 15 35 E
Slovenske Konjice, *Slovenia* **45 B12** 46 20N 15 28 E
Slovenské Rudohorie, *Slovak Rep.* **35 C12** 48 45N 20 0 E
Slovyansk, *Ukraine* **59 H9** 48 55N 37 36 E
Słubice, *Poland* **55 F1** 52 22N 14 35 E
Sluch →, *Ukraine* **59 G4** 51 37N 26 38 E
Sluis, *Neths.* **24 C3** 51 18N 3 23 E
Slŭnchev Bryag, *Bulgaria* **51 D11** 42 40N 27 41 E
Slunj, *Croatia* **45 C12** 45 6N 15 33 E
Słupca, *Poland* **55 F4** 52 15N 17 52 E
Słupia →, *Poland* **54 D3** 54 35N 16 51 E
Słupsk, *Poland* **54 D4** 54 30N 17 3 E
Slurry, *S. Africa* **116 D4** 25 49 S 25 42 E
Slutsk, *Belarus* **59 F4** 53 2N 27 31 E
Slyne Hd., *Ireland* **23 C1** 53 25N 10 10W
Slyudyanka, *Russia* **67 D11** 51 40N 103 40 E
Småland, *Sweden* **17 G9** 57 15N 15 25 E
Smålandsfarvandet, *Denmark* **17 J5** 55 10N 11 20 E
Smålandsstenar, *Sweden* **17 G7** 57 10N 13 25 E
Smalltree L., *Canada* **143 A8** 61 0N 105 0W
Smallwood Res., *Canada* **141 B7** 54 0N 64 0W
Smarhon, *Belarus* **58 E4** 54 20N 26 24 E
Smarje, *Slovenia* **45 B12** 46 15N 15 34 E
Smartt Syndicate Dam, *S. Africa* **116 E3** 30 45 S 23 10 E
Smartville, *U.S.A.* **160 F5** 39 13N 121 18W
Smeaton, *Canada* **143 C8** 53 30N 104 49W
Smedby, *Sweden* **17 H10** 56 41N 16 13 E
Smederevo, *Serbia, Yug.* **50 B4** 44 40N 20 57 E
Smederevska Palanka, *Serbia, Yug.* **50 B4** 44 22N 20 58 E
Smedjebacken, *Sweden* **16 D9** 60 8N 15 25 E
Smela = Smila, *Ukraine* **59 H6** 49 15N 31 58 E
Smerwick Harbour, *Ireland* **23 D1** 52 12N 10 23W
Smethport, *U.S.A.* **150 E6** 41 49N 78 27W
Smidovich, *Russia* **67 E14** 48 36N 133 49 E
Śmigiel, *Poland* **55 F3** 52 1N 16 32 E
Smila, *Ukraine* **59 H6** 49 15N 31 58 E
Smilyan, *Bulgaria* **51 E8** 41 29N 24 46 E
Smith, *Canada* **142 B6** 55 10N 114 0W
Smith B., *U.S.A.* **144 A9** 70 30N 154 20W
Smith Center, *U.S.A.* **154 F5** 39 47N 98 47W
Smith I., *India* **95 H11** 13 20N 93 4 E
Smith Sund, *Greenland* **10 B3** 78 30N 74 0W
Smithburne →, *Australia* **126 B3** 17 3 S 140 57 E
Smithers, *Canada* **142 C3** 54 45N 127 10W
Smithfield, *S. Africa* **117 E4** 30 9 S 26 30 E
Smithfield, *N.C., U.S.A.* **149 H6** 35 31N 78 21W
Smithfield, *Utah, U.S.A.* **158 F8** 41 50N 111 50W
Smiths, *U.S.A.* **152 C4** 32 32N 85 6W
Smiths Falls, *Canada* **140 D4** 44 55N 76 0W
Smithton, *Australia* **127 G4** 40 53 S 145 6 E
Smithville, *Canada* **150 C5** 43 6N 79 33W
Smithville, *Ga., U.S.A.* **152 D5** 31 54N 84 15W
Smithville, *Mo., U.S.A.* **156 E2** 39 23N 94 35W
Smithville, *Tex., U.S.A.* **155 K6** 30 1N 97 10W
Smoky →, *Canada* **142 B5** 56 10N 117 21W
Smoky Bay, *Australia* **127 E1** 32 22 S 134 13 E
Smoky Hill →, *U.S.A.* **154 F6** 39 4N 96 48W
Smoky Hills, *U.S.A.* **154 F5** 39 15N 99 30W
Smoky Lake, *Canada* **142 C6** 54 10N 112 30W
Smøla, *Norway* **14 E13** 63 23N 8 3 E
Smolensk, *Russia* **58 E7** 54 45N 32 5 E
Smolikas, Óros, *Greece* **50 F4** 40 9N 20 58 E
Smolník, *Slovak Rep.* **35 C13** 48 43N 20 44 E
Smolyan, *Bulgaria* **51 E8** 41 36N 24 38 E
Smooth Rock Falls, *Canada* **140 C3** 49 17N 81 37W
Smoothstone L., *Canada* **143 C7** 54 40N 106 50W
Smorgon = Smarhon, *Belarus* **58 E4** 54 20N 26 24 E
Smulţi, *Romania* **53 E12** 45 57N 27 44 E
Smyadovo, *Bulgaria* **51 C11** 43 2N 27 1 E
Smygehamn, *Sweden* **17 J7** 55 21N 13 22 E
Smyrna = İzmir, *Turkey* **49 C9** 38 25N 27 8 E
Smyrna, *Del., U.S.A.* **148 F8** 39 18N 75 36W
Smyrna, *Ga., U.S.A.* **152 B5** 33 53N 84 31W
Snæfell, *Iceland* **11 C11** 64 48N 15 34W
Snaefell, *U.K.* **20 C3** 54 16N 4 27W
Snæfellsjökull, *Iceland* **11 C3** 64 49N 23 46W
Snæfellsnessýsla □, *Iceland* **11 C3** 65 0N 23 0W
Snake →, *U.S.A.* **158 C4** 46 12N 119 2W
Snake I., *Australia* **129 E7** 38 47 S 146 33 E
Snake Range, *U.S.A.* **158 G6** 39 0N 114 20W
Snake River Plain, *U.S.A.* **158 E7** 42 50N 114 0W
Snasahögarna, *Sweden* **16 A6** 63 13N 12 21 E
Snåsavatnet, *Norway* **14 D14** 64 12N 12 0 E
Snedsted, *Denmark* **17 H2** 56 55N 8 32 E
Sneek, *Neths.* **24 A5** 53 2N 5 40 E
Sneeuberge, *S. Africa* **116 E3** 31 46 S 24 20 E
Snejbjerg, *Denmark* **17 H2** 56 8N 8 54 E
Snelling, *Calif., U.S.A.* **160 H6** 37 31N 120 26W
Snelling, *S.C., U.S.A.* **152 B8** 33 15N 81 27W
Snells Beach, *N.Z.* **130 C3** 36 25 S 174 44 E
Snezhnoye, *Ukraine* **59 J10** 48 0N 38 58 E
Sněžka, *Europe* **36 C8** 50 41N 15 50 E
Snežnik, *Slovenia* **45 C11** 45 36N 14 35 E
Śniadowo, *Poland* **55 E8** 53 2N 22 0 E
Sniardwy, Jezioro, *Poland* **54 E8** 53 48N 21 50 E
Śnieżka, *Europe* **34 A8** 50 44N 15 44 E
Snigirevka = Snihurivka, *Ukraine* **59 J7** 47 2N 32 49 E
Snihurivka, *Ukraine* **59 J7** 47 2N 32 49 E
Snillfjord, *Norway* **18 A6** 63 24N 9 30 E
Snina, *Slovak Rep.* **35 C15** 48 58N 22 9 E
Snizort, L., *U.K.* **22 D2** 57 33N 6 28W
Snøhetta, *Norway* **15 E13** 62 19N 9 16 E
Snohomish, *U.S.A.* **160 C4** 47 55N 122 6W
Snønuten, *Norway* **18 E3** 59 31N 6 52 E
Snoul, *Cambodia* **87 F6** 12 4N 106 26 E
Snow Hill, *U.S.A.* **148 F8** 38 11N 75 24W
Snow Lake, *Canada* **143 C8** 54 52N 100 3W
Snow Mt., *Calif., U.S.A.* **160 F4** 39 23N 122 45W
Snow Mt., *Maine, U.S.A.* **151 A14** 45 18N 70 48W
Snow Shoe, *U.S.A.* **150 E7** 41 2N 77 57W
Snowbird L., *Canada* **143 A8** 60 45N 103 0W
Snowdon, *U.K.* **20 D3** 53 4N 4 5W
Snowdoun, *U.S.A.* **152 C3** 32 15N 86 18W
Snowdrift →, *Canada* **143 A6** 62 24N 110 44W
Snowflake, *U.S.A.* **159 J8** 34 30N 110 5W
Snowshoe Pk., *U.S.A.* **158 B6** 48 13N 115 41W
Snowtown, *Australia* **128 B3** 33 46 S 138 14 E
Snowville, *U.S.A.* **158 F7** 41 58N 112 43W
Snowy →, *Australia* **129 D8** 37 46 S 148 30 E
Snowy Mt., *U.S.A.* **151 C10** 43 42N 74 23W
Snowy Mts., *Australia* **129 D8** 36 30 S 148 20 E
Snowy River Nat. Park, *Australia* **129 D7** 37 15 S 147 29 E
Snug Corner, *Bahamas* **165 B5** 22 33N 73 52W
Snyatyn, *Ukraine* **59 H3** 48 27N 25 38 E
Snyder, *Okla., U.S.A.* **155 H5** 34 40N 98 57W
Snyder, *Tex., U.S.A.* **155 J4** 32 44N 100 55W
Soacha, *Colombia* **168 C3** 4 35N 74 13W
Soahanina, *Madag.* **117 B7** 18 42 S 44 13 E
Soalala, *Madag.* **117 B8** 16 6 S 45 20 E
Soaloka, *Madag.* **117 B8** 18 32 S 45 15 E
Soamanonga, *Madag.* **117 C7** 23 52 S 44 47 E
Soan →, *Pakistan* **92 C4** 33 1N 71 44 E
Soanierana-Ivongo, *Madag.* **117 B8** 16 55 S 49 35 E
Soanindraniny, *Madag.* **117 B8** 19 54 S 47 14 E
Şoarş, *Romania* **53 E9** 45 56N 24 55 E
Soasiu, *Indonesia* **82 A3** 0 40N 127 26 E
Soavina, *Madag.* **117 C8** 20 23 S 46 56 E
Soavinandriana, *Madag.* **117 B8** 19 9 S 46 45 E
Soba, *Nigeria* **113 C6** 10 58N 8 4 E
Sobat, Nahr →, *Sudan* **107 F3** 9 22N 31 33 E
Soběslav, *Czech Rep.* **34 B7** 49 16N 14 45 E
Sobger →, *Indonesia* **83 B6** 3 42 S 140 16 E
Sobhapur, *India* **92 H8** 22 47N 78 17 E
Sobinka, *Russia* **58 E11** 56 0N 40 0 E
Sobo-Yama, *Japan* **72 E3** 32 51N 131 22 E
Sobótka, *Poland* **55 H3** 50 54N 16 44 E
Sobra, *Croatia* **45 F14** 42 44N 17 34 E
Sobradinho, Represa de, *Brazil* **170 C3** 9 30 S 42 0 E
Sobral, *Brazil* **170 B3** 3 50 S 40 20W
Sobrance, *Slovak Rep.* **35 C15** 48 45N 22 11 E
Sobreira Formosa, *Portugal* **42 F3** 39 46N 7 51W
Soc Giang, *Vietnam* **76 F6** 22 54N 106 1 E
Soc Trang, *Vietnam* **87 H5** 9 37N 105 50 E
Soča →, *Europe* **44 B6** 46 20N 13 40 E
Socastee, *U.S.A.* **149 J6** 33 41N 79 1W
Sochaczew, *Poland* **55 F7** 52 15N 20 13 E
Soch'e = Shache, *China* **65 D8** 38 20N 77 10 E
Sochi, *Russia* **61 J4** 43 35N 39 40 E
Social Circle, *U.S.A.* **152 B5** 33 39N 83 43W
Société, Is. de la, *Pac. Oc.* **135 J12** 17 0 S 151 0W
Society Hill, *U.S.A.* **152 C4** 32 26N 85 27W
Society Is. = Société, Is. de la, *Pac. Oc.* **135 J12** 17 0 S 151 0W
Socompa, Portezuelo de, *Chile* **174 A2** 24 27 S 68 18W
Socorro, *Colombia* **168 B3** 6 29N 73 16W
Socorro, *Phil.* **81 G5** 9 37N 125 58 E
Socorro, *N. Mex., U.S.A.* **159 J10** 34 4N 106 54W
Socorro, *Tex., U.S.A.* **159 L10** 31 39N 106 18W
Socorro, I., *Mexico* **162 D2** 18 45N 110 58W
Socotra, *Yemen* **99 D6** 12 30N 54 0 E
Socovos, *Spain* **41 G3** 38 20N 1 58W
Socuéllamos, *Spain* **41 F2** 39 16N 2 47W
Soda L., *U.S.A.* **159 J5** 35 10N 116 4W
Soda Plains, *India* **93 B8** 35 30N 79 0 E
Soda Springs, *U.S.A.* **158 E8** 42 39N 111 36W
Sodankylä, *Finland* **14 C22** 67 29N 26 40 E
Soddy-Daisy, *U.S.A.* **149 H3** 35 17N 85 10W
Söderala, *Sweden* **16 C10** 61 17N 16 55 E
Söderbärke, *Sweden* **16 D9** 60 5N 15 33 E
Söderfors, *Sweden* **16 D11** 60 23N 17 25 E
Söderhamn, *Sweden* **16 C11** 61 18N 17 10 E
Söderköping, *Sweden* **17 F10** 58 31N 16 20 E
Södermanland, *Sweden* **15 G17** 58 56N 16 55 E
Södermanlands län □, *Sweden* **16 E10** 59 10N 16 30 E
Södertälje, *Sweden* **16 E11** 59 12N 17 39 E
Sodiri, *Sudan* **107 E2** 14 27N 29 0 E
Sodo, *Ethiopia* **107 F4** 7 0N 37 41 E
Södra Dellen, *Sweden* **16 C10** 61 48N 16 43 E
Södra Finnskoga, *Sweden* **16 D6** 60 42N 12 34 E
Södra Sandby, *Sweden* **17 J7** 55 43N 13 21 E
Södra Ulvön, *Sweden* **16 B12** 62 59N 18 38 E
Södra Vi, *Sweden* **17 G9** 57 45N 15 45 E
Sodražica, *Slovenia* **45 C11** 45 45N 14 39 E
Sodus, *U.S.A.* **150 C7** 43 14N 77 4W
Sodwana Bay Nat. Park, *S. Africa* **117 D5** 27 35 S 32 43 E
Soe, *Indonesia* **82 C2** 9 52 S 124 17 E
Soekmekaar, *S. Africa* **117 C4** 23 30 S 29 55 E
Soest, *Germany* **30 D4** 51 34N 8 7 E
Soest, *Neths.* **24 B5** 52 9N 5 19 E
Sofádhes, *Greece* **48 B4** 39 20N 22 4 E
Sofala □, *Mozam.* **117 B5** 19 30 S 34 30 E
Sofara, *Mali* **112 C4** 13 59N 4 9W
Sofia = Sofiya, *Bulgaria* **50 D7** 42 45N 23 20 E
Sofia →, *Madag.* **117 B8** 15 27 S 47 23 E
Sofievka, *Ukraine* **59 H7** 48 6N 33 55 E
Sofikón, *Greece* **48 D5** 37 47N 23 3 E
Sofiya, *Bulgaria* **50 D7** 42 45N 23 20 E
Sofiya □, *Bulgaria* **50 D7** 42 15N 23 20 E
Sōfu-Gan, *Japan* **71 K10** 29 49N 140 21 E
Sogakofe, *Ghana* **113 D5** 6 2N 0 39 E
Sogamoso, *Colombia* **168 B3** 5 43N 72 56W
Sogār, *Iran* **97 E8** 25 53N 58 6 E
Sögel, *Germany* **30 C3** 52 50N 7 31 E
Sogeri, *Papua N. G.* **132 E4** 9 26 S 147 35 E
Sogn og Fjordane □, *Norway* **18 C3** 61 40N 6 45 E
Sogndalsfjøra, *Norway* **15 F12** 61 14N 7 5 E
Søgne, *Norway* **15 G12** 58 5N 7 48 E
Sognefjorden, *Norway* **15 F11** 61 10N 5 50 E
Sogod, *Phil.* **81 F5** 10 28N 124 59 E
Söğüt, *Bilecik, Turkey* **49 A12** 40 2N 30 11 E
Söğüt, *Burdur, Turkey* **49 D11** 37 2N 29 50 E
Söğüt Dağı, *Turkey* **49 D11** 37 50N 29 55 E
Söğütköy, *Turkey* **49 E10** 36 40N 28 8 E
Sŏgwipo, *S. Korea* **75 H14** 33 13N 126 34 E
Soh, *Iran* **97 C6** 33 26N 51 27 E
Sohâg, *Egypt* **106 B3** 26 33N 31 43 E
Sohagpur, *India* **92 H8** 22 42N 78 12 E
Sohano, *Papua N. G.* **132 C8** 5 22 S 154 37 E
Sohela, *India* **94 D6** 21 18N 83 24 E
Sŏhori, *N. Korea* **75 D15** 40 7N 128 23 E
Soignies, *Belgium* **24 D4** 50 35N 4 5 E
Soin, *Burkina Faso* **112 C4** 12 47N 3 50W
Soira, *Eritrea* **107 E4** 14 45N 39 30 E
Soissons, *France* **27 C10** 49 25N 3 19 E
Sōja, *Japan* **72 C5** 34 40N 133 45 E
Sojat, *India* **92 G5** 25 55N 73 45 E
Sok →, *Russia* **60 D10** 53 24N 50 8 E
Sokal, *Ukraine* **59 G3** 50 31N 24 15 E
Söke, *Turkey* **49 D9** 37 48N 27 28 E
Sokelo, *Dem. Rep. of the Congo* **119 D1** 9 55 S 24 36 E
Sokh, *Uzbekistan* **65 D5** 39 56N 71 9 E
Sokhós, *Greece* **50 F7** 40 48N 23 22 E
Sokhumi, *Georgia* **61 J5** 43 0N 41 0 E
Sokki, Oued In →, *Algeria* **111 C5** 29 30N 3 42 E
Sokna, *Norway* **18 D6** 60 16N 9 58 E
Sokndal, *Norway* **18 B7** 62 57N 10 13 E
Soko Banja, *Serbia, Yug.* **50 C5** 43 40N 21 51 E
Soko Islands, *China* **69 G10** 22 10N 113 54 E
Sokodé, *Togo* **113 D5** 9 0N 1 11 E
Sokol, *Russia* **58 C11** 59 30N 40 5 E
Sokolac, *Bos.-H.* **52 G3** 43 56N 18 48 E
Sokółka, *Poland* **54 E10** 53 25N 23 30 E
Sokolo, *Ségou, Mali* **112 C3** 14 53N 6 8W
Sokolo, *Sikasso, Mali* **112 C3** 10 52N 6 59W
Sokolov, *Czech Rep.* **34 A5** 50 12N 12 40 E
Sokołów Małpolski, *Poland* **55 H9** 50 12N 22 7 E
Sokołów Podlaski, *Poland* **55 F9** 52 25N 22 15 E
Sokoły, *Poland* **55 F9** 52 59N 22 42 E
Sokoto, *Nigeria* **113 C6** 13 2N 5 16 E
Sokoto □, *Nigeria* **113 C6** 12 30N 6 0 E
Sokoto →, *Nigeria* **113 C5** 11 20N 4 10 E
Sokuluk, *Kyrgyzstan* **65 B7** 42 52N 74 18 E
Sol Iletsk, *Russia* **64 F5** 51 10N 55 0 E
Sola, *Norway* **18 F2** 58 53N 5 36 E
Sola, *Vanuatu* **133 C5** 13 51 S 167 33 E
Sola →, *Poland* **55 H6** 50 4N 19 15 E
Solai, *Kenya* **118 B4** 0 2N 36 12 E
Solan, *India* **92 D7** 30 55N 77 7 E
Solana, *Phil.* **80 C3** 17 39N 121 41 E
Solander I., *N.Z.* **131 G1** 46 34 S 166 54 E
Solano, *Phil.* **80 C3** 16 31N 121 15 E
Solapur, *India* **94 F2** 17 43N 75 56 E
Solca, *Romania* **53 C10** 47 40N 25 50 E
Solda Gölü, *Turkey* **49 D11** 37 33N 29 42 E
Soldăneşti, *Moldova* **53 C13** 47 49N 28 48 E
Soldotna, *U.S.A.* **144 F10** 60 29N 151 3W
Soléa, *Cyprus* **39 E9** 35 5N 33 4 E
Solec Kujawski, *Poland* **55 E5** 53 5N 18 14 E
Soledad, *Colombia* **168 A3** 10 55N 74 46W
Soledad, *U.S.A.* **160 J5** 36 26N 121 20W
Soledad, *Venezuela* **169 B5** 8 10N 63 34W
Sølen, *Norway* **18 C8** 61 53N 11 31 E
Solent, The, *U.K.* **21 G6** 50 45N 1 25W
Solenzara, *France* **29 G13** 41 53N 9 23 E
Solesmes, *France* **27 B10** 50 10N 3 30 E
Solfonn, *Norway* **15 F12** 60 2N 6 57 E
Solhan, *Turkey* **101 C9** 38 57N 41 3 E
Sølheim, *Norway* **18 D2** 60 53N 5 27 E
Soligalich, *Russia* **56 C7** 59 5N 42 10 E
Soligorsk = Salihorsk, *Belarus* **59 F4** 52 51N 27 27 E
Solihull, *U.K.* **21 E6** 52 26N 1 47W
Solikamsk, *Russia* **64 B6** 59 38N 56 50 E
Solila, *Madag.* **117 C8** 21 25 S 46 37 E
Solimões = Amazonas →, *S. Amer.* **169 D7** 0 5 S 50 0W
Solin, *Croatia* **45 E13** 43 33N 16 30 E
Solingen, *Germany* **30 D3** 51 10N 7 5 E
Sollebrunn, *Sweden* **17 F6** 58 8N 12 32 E
Sollefteå, *Sweden* **16 A11** 63 12N 17 20 E
Sollentuna, *Sweden* **16 E11** 59 26N 17 56 E
Sóller, *Spain* **38 B3** 39 46N 2 43 E
Sollerön, *Sweden* **16 D8** 60 55N 14 37 E
Solling, *Germany* **30 D5** 51 42N 9 38 E
Solnechnogorsk, *Russia* **58 D9** 56 10N 36 57 E
Solo →, *Indonesia* **79 G15** 6 47 S 112 22 E
Solofra, *Italy* **47 B7** 40 50N 14 51 E
Sologne, *France* **27 E8** 47 40N 1 45 E
Solok, *Indonesia* **84 C2** 0 45 S 100 40 E
Sololá, *Guatemala* **164 D1** 14 49N 91 10W
Solomon, N. Fork →, *U.S.A.* **154 F5** 39 29N 98 26W
Solomon, S. Fork →, *U.S.A.* **154 F5** 39 25N 99 12W
Solomon Is., *Papua N. G.* **132 D8** 6 0 S 155 0 E
Solomon Is. ■, *Pac. Oc.* **133 L8** 6 0 S 155 0 E
Solomon Sea, *Papua N. G.* **132 D6** 7 0 S 150 0 E
Solon, *China* **69 B7** 46 32N 121 10 E
Solon Springs, *U.S.A.* **154 B9** 46 22N 91 49W
Solonópole, *Brazil* **170 C4** 5 44 S 39 1W
Solor, *Indonesia* **82 C2** 8 27 S 123 0 E
Solotcha, *Russia* **58 E10** 54 48N 39 53 E
Solothurn, *Switz.* **32 B5** 47 13N 7 32 E
Solothurn □, *Switz.* **32 B5** 47 18N 7 40 E
Solsona, *Spain* **40 C6** 42 0N 1 31 E
Solsvik, *Norway* **18 D1** 60 26N 4 58 E
Solt, *Hungary* **52 D4** 46 45N 19 1 E
Šolta, *Croatia* **45 E13** 43 24N 16 15 E
Solṭānābād, *Khorāsān, Iran* **97 C8** 34 13N 59 58 E
Solṭānābād, *Khorāsān, Iran* **97 B8** 36 29N 58 5 E
Soltau, *Germany* **30 C5** 52 59N 9 50 E
Soltsy, *Russia* **58 C6** 58 10N 30 30 E
Solund, *Norway* **18 C1** 61 5N 4 50 E
Solunska Glava, *Macedonia* **50 E5** 41 44N 21 31 E
Solvang, *U.S.A.* **161 L6** 34 36N 120 8W
Solvay, *U.S.A.* **151 C8** 43 3N 76 13W
Sölvesborg, *Sweden* **17 H8** 56 5N 14 35 E
Solvychegodsk, *Russia* **56 B8** 61 21N 46 56 E
Solway Firth, *U.K.* **20 C4** 54 49N 3 35W
Solwezi, *Zambia* **119 E2** 12 11 S 26 21 E
Sōma, *Japan* **70 F10** 37 40N 140 50 E
Soma, *Turkey* **49 B9** 39 10N 27 35 E
Somabhula, *Zimbabwe* **117 B4** 19 42 S 29 40 E
Somali Pen., *Africa* **104 F8** 7 0N 46 0 E
Somali Rep. ■, *Africa* **120 C3** 7 0N 47 0 E
Somalia = Somali Rep. ■, *Africa* **120 C3** 7 0N 47 0 E
Sombe Dzong, *Bhutan* **90 B2** 27 13N 89 8 E
Sombernon, *France* **27 E11** 47 20N 4 40 E
Sombo, *Angola* **115 D4** 8 42 S 20 59 E
Sombor, *Serbia, Yug.* **52 E4** 45 46N 19 9 E
Sombra, *Canada* **150 D2** 42 43N 82 29W
Sombrerete, *Mexico* **162 C4** 23 40N 103 40W
Sombrero, *Anguilla* **165 C7** 18 37N 63 30W
Sombrero Channel, *India* **95 L11** 7 41N 93 35 E
Şomcuta Mare, *Romania* **53 C8** 47 31N 23 28 E
Somdari, *India* **92 G5** 25 47N 72 38 E
Somers, *U.S.A.* **158 B6** 48 5N 114 13W
Somerset, *Bermuda* **9 a** 32 17N 64 52W
Somerset, *Ky., U.S.A.* **148 G3** 37 5N 84 36W
Somerset, *Mass., U.S.A.* **151 E13** 41 47N 71 8W
Somerset, *Pa., U.S.A.* **150 F5** 40 1N 79 5W
Somerset □, *U.K.* **21 F5** 51 9N 3 0W
Somerset East, *S. Africa* **116 E4** 32 42 S 25 35 E
Somerset I., *Bermuda* **9 a** 32 17N 64 52W
Somerset I., *Canada* **138 A10** 73 30N 93 0W
Somerset West, *S. Africa* **116 E2** 34 8 S 18 50 E
Somersworth, *U.S.A.* **151 C14** 43 16N 70 52W
Somerton, *U.S.A.* **159 K6** 32 36N 114 43W
Somerville, *U.S.A.* **151 F10** 40 35N 74 38W
Someş →, *Romania* **52 C7** 47 49N 22 43 E
Someşul Mare →, *Romania* **53 C8** 47 9N 23 55 E
Somme □, *France* **27 C9** 49 57N 2 20 E
Somme →, *France* **27 B8** 50 11N 1 38 E
Somme, B. de la, *France* **26 B8** 50 14N 1 33 E
Sommen, *Jönköping, Sweden* **17 F8** 58 12N 14 58 E
Sommen, *Östergötland, Sweden* **17 F9** 58 0N 15 15 E
Sommepy-Tahure, *France* **27 C11** 49 15N 4 31 E
Sömmerda, *Germany* **30 D7** 51 9N 11 7 E
Sommesous, *France* **27 D11** 48 44N 4 12 E
Sommières, *France* **29 E8** 43 47N 4 6 E
Somnath, *India* **92 J4** 20 53N 70 22 E
Somogy □, *Hungary* **52 D2** 46 19N 17 30 E
Somogyszob, *Hungary* **52 D2** 46 18N 17 20 E
Somosomo, *Fiji* **133 A3** 16 47 S 179 58W
Somosomo Str., *Fiji* **133 A3** 16 0 S 180 0 E
Somoto, *Nic.* **164 D2** 13 28N 86 37W
Sompolno, *Poland* **55 F5** 52 26N 18 30 E
Somport, Puerto de, *Spain* **40 C4** 42 48N 0 31W
Somuncurá, Meseta de, *Argentina* **176 B3** 41 30 S 67 0W
Somvarpet, *India* **95 H2** 12 36N 75 52 E
Son, *Norway* **18 E7** 59 32N 10 42 E
Son →, *India* **93 G11** 25 42N 84 52 E
Son Ha, *Vietnam* **86 E7** 15 3N 108 34 E
Son Hoa, *Vietnam* **86 F7** 13 2N 108 58 E
Son La, *Vietnam* **76 G4** 21 20N 103 50 E
Son Serra, *Spain* **38 B4** 39 43N 3 13 E
Son Servera, *Spain* **38 B4** 39 37N 3 21 E
Son Tay, *Vietnam* **76 G5** 21 8N 105 30 E
Soná, *Panama* **164 E3** 8 0N 81 20W
Sonamarg, *India* **93 B6** 34 18N 75 21 E
Sonamukhi, *India* **93 H12** 23 18N 87 27 E
Sonamura, *India* **90 D3** 23 29N 91 15 E
Sonar →, *India* **93 G8** 24 24N 79 56 E
Sŏnch'ŏn, *N. Korea* **75 E13** 39 48N 124 55 E
Sondags →, *S. Africa* **116 E4** 33 44 S 25 51 E
Sóndalo, *Italy* **44 B7** 46 20N 10 19 E
Sondar, *India* **93 C6** 33 28N 75 56 E
Søndeled, *Norway* **18 F6** 58 46N 9 3 E
Sønder Felding, *Denmark* **17 J2** 55 57N 8 47 E
Sønder Omme, *Denmark* **17 J2** 55 50N 8 54 E
Sønderborg, *Denmark* **17 K3** 54 55N 9 49 E
Sønderjyllands Amtskommune □, *Denmark* **17 J3** 55 10N 9 10 E
Sondershausen, *Germany* **30 D6** 51 22N 10 51 E
Søndre Strømfjord = Kangerlussuaq, *Greenland* **10 D5** 66 59N 50 40W
Sóndrio, *Italy* **44 B6** 46 10N 9 52 E
Sondur →, *India* **94 D6** 20 40N 82 1 E
Sone, *Mozam.* **119 F3** 17 23 S 34 55 E
Sonepur, *India* **94 D6** 20 55N 83 50 E
Sonfim, *Brazil* **172 B4** 6 0 S 67 52W
Song, *Nigeria* **113 D7** 9 49N 12 39 E
Song, *Thailand* **86 C3** 18 28N 100 11 E
Song Cau, *Vietnam* **86 F7** 13 27N 109 18 E
Song-Köl, *Kyrgyzstan* **65 C7** 41 50N 75 12 E
Song Xian, *China* **74 G7** 34 12N 112 8 E
Songadh, *India* **94 D1** 21 9N 73 33 E
Songan, *Indonesia* **79 J18** 8 13 S 115 24 E
Songavatnet, *Norway* **18 E4** 59 52N 7 32 E
Songch'ŏn, *N. Korea* **75 E14** 39 12N 126 15 E
Songea, *Tanzania* **119 E4** 10 40 S 35 40 E
Songeons, *France* **27 C8** 49 32N 1 50 E
Songgang, *China* **69 F10** 22 46N 113 50 E
Songhua Hu, *China* **75 C14** 43 35N 126 50 E
Songhua Jiang →, *China* **69 B8** 47 45N 132 30 E
Songimvelo Game Reserve, *S. Africa* **117 D5** 25 50 S 31 2 E
Songjiang, *China* **77 B13** 31 1N 121 12 E
Songjin, *N. Korea* **75 D15** 40 40N 129 10 E
Songjŏng-ni, *S. Korea* **75 G14** 35 8N 126 47 E
Songkan, *China* **76 C6** 28 35N 106 52 E
Songkhla, *Thailand* **87 J3** 7 13N 100 37 E
Songming, *China* **76 E4** 25 12N 103 2 E
Songnim, *N. Korea* **75 E13** 38 45N 125 39 E
Songo, *Angola* **115 D2** 7 22 S 14 51 E
Songololo, *Dem. Rep. of the Congo* **115 D2** 5 42 S 14 2 E
Songpan, *China* **76 A4** 32 40N 103 30 E
Songtao, *China* **76 C7** 28 11N 109 10 E
Songwe, *Dem. Rep. of the Congo* **118 C2** 3 20 S 26 16 E
Songwe →, *Africa* **119 D3** 9 44 S 33 58 E
Songxi, *China* **77 D12** 27 31N 118 44 E
Songzi, *China* **77 B8** 30 12N 111 45 E
Sonhat, *India* **93 H10** 23 29N 82 31 E
Sonid Youqi, *China* **74 C7** 42 45N 112 48 E
Sonipat, *India* **92 E7** 29 0N 77 5 E
Sonkach, *India* **92 H7** 22 59N 76 21 E
Sonkovo, *Russia* **58 D9** 57 50N 37 5 E
Sonmiani, *Pakistan* **91 D2** 25 25N 66 40 E
Sonmiani B., *Pakistan* **92 G2** 25 15N 66 30 E
Sonnino, *Italy* **46 A6** 41 25N 13 14 E
Sono →, *Minas Gerais, Brazil* **171 E2** 17 2 S 45 32W

Stadlandet, *Norway* **18 B2** 62 10N 5 10 E
Stadskanaal, *Neths.* **24 A6** 53 4N 6 55 E
Stadtallendorf, *Germany* **30 E5** 50 48N 9 1 E
Stadthagen, *Germany* **30 C5** 52 19N 9 13 E
Stadtlohn, *Germany* **30 D2** 51 59N 6 55 E
Stadtroda, *Germany* **30 E7** 50 52N 11 44 E
Stäfa, *Switz.* **33 B7** 47 14N 8 45 E
Stafafell, *Iceland* **11 C12** 64 25N 14 52W
Staffa, *U.K.* **22 E2** 56 27N 6 21W
Staffanstorp, *Sweden* **17 J7** 55 39N 13 13 E
Stafford, *U.K.* **20 E5** 52 49N 2 7W
Stafford, *U.S.A.* **155 G5** 37 58N 98 36W
Stafford, L., *U.S.A.* **153 F7** 29 20N 82 29W
Stafford Springs, *U.S.A.* **151 E12** 41 57N 72 18W
Staffordshire □, *U.K.* **20 E5** 52 53N 2 10W
Stagnone, *Italy* **46 E5** 37 53N 12 26 E
Staines, *U.K.* **21 F7** 51 26N 0 29W
Stainz, *Austria* **34 E8** 46 53N 15 17 E
Stakhanov, *Ukraine* **59 H10** 48 35N 38 40 E
Stalać, *Serbia, Yug.* **50 C5** 43 43N 21 28 E
Stalden, *Switz.* **32 D5** 46 14N 7 52 E
Stalingrad = Volgograd, *Russia* **61 F7** 48 40N 44 25 E
Staliniri = Tskhinvali, *Georgia* **61 J7** 42 14N 44 1 E
Stalino = Donetsk, *Ukraine* **59 J9** 48 0N 37 45 E
Stalinogorsk = Novomoskovsk, *Russia* **58 E10** 54 5N 38 15 E
Stallarholmen, *Sweden* **16 E11** 59 22N 17 12 E
Ställdalen, *Sweden* **16 E8** 59 56N 14 56 E
Stalowa Wola, *Poland* **55 H9** 50 34N 22 3 E
Stalybridge, *U.K.* **20 D5** 53 28N 2 3W
Stamford, *Australia* **126 C3** 21 15 S 143 46 E
Stamford, *U.K.* **21 E7** 52 39N 0 29W
Stamford, *Conn., U.S.A.* **151 E11** 41 3N 73 32W
Stamford, *N.Y., U.S.A.* **151 D10** 42 25N 74 38W
Stamford, *Tex., U.S.A.* **155 J5** 32 57N 99 48W
Stamnes, *Norway* **18 D2** 60 40N 5 45 E
Stamping Ground, *U.S.A.* **157 F12** 38 16N 84 41W
Stampriet, *Namibia* **116 C2** 24 20 S 18 28 E
Stamps, *U.S.A.* **155 J8** 33 22N 93 30W
Stanberry, *U.S.A.* **156 D2** 40 13N 94 35W
Stančevo = Kalipetrovo, *Bulgaria* **51 B11** 44 5N 27 14 E
Standerton, *S. Africa* **117 D4** 26 55 S 29 7 E
Standish, *U.S.A.* **148 D4** 43 59N 83 57W
Stanford, *S. Africa* **116 E2** 34 26 S 19 29 E
Stanford, *U.S.A.* **158 C8** 47 9N 110 13W
Stånga, *Sweden* **17 G12** 57 17N 18 29 E
Stange, *Norway* **18 D8** 60 43N 11 5 E
Stanger, *S. Africa* **117 D5** 29 27 S 31 14 E
Stangvik, *Norway* **18 B5** 62 55N 8 28 E
Stanhope, *Australia* **129 D6** 36 27 S 144 59 E
Stanhope, *U.S.A.* **156 B3** 42 17N 93 48W
Stanišić, *Serbia, Yug.* **52 E4** 45 56N 19 10 E
Stanislaus →, *U.S.A.* **160 H5** 37 40N 121 14W
Stanislav = Ivano-Frankivsk, *Ukraine* **59 H3** 48 40N 24 40 E
Stanisławów, *Poland* **55 F8** 52 18N 21 33 E
Stanley, *Australia* **127 G4** 40 46 S 145 19 E
Stanley, *Canada* **143 B8** 55 24N 104 22W
Stanley, *China* **69 G11** 22 13N 114 12 E
Stanley, *Falk. Is.* **9 f** 51 40 S 59 51W
Stanley, *U.K.* **20 C6** 54 53N 1 41W
Stanley, *Idaho, U.S.A.* **158 D6** 44 13N 114 56W
Stanley, *N. Dak., U.S.A.* **154 A3** 48 19N 102 23W
Stanley, *N.Y., U.S.A.* **150 D7** 42 48N 77 6W
Stanley Res., *India* **95 J3** 11 50N 77 40 E
Stanovoy Khrebet, *Russia* **67 D13** 55 0N 130 0 E
Stanovoy Ra. = Stanovoy Khrebet, *Russia* **67 D13** 55 0N 130 0 E
Stans, *Switz.* **33 C6** 46 58N 8 21 E
Stansmore Ra., *Australia* **124 D4** 21 23 S 128 33 E
Stanthorpe, *Australia* **127 D5** 28 36 S 151 59 E
Stanton, *Ky., U.S.A.* **157 G13** 37 54N 83 52W
Stanton, *Tex., U.S.A.* **155 J4** 32 8N 101 48W
Stanwood, *U.S.A.* **160 B4** 48 15N 122 23W
Staples, *U.S.A.* **154 B7** 46 21N 94 48W
Stąporków, *Poland* **55 G7** 51 9N 20 31 E
Star City, *Canada* **143 C8** 52 50N 104 20W
Star Harbour, *Solomon Is.* **133 N12** 10 47 S 162 19 E
Star Lake, *U.S.A.* **151 B9** 44 10N 75 2W
Stará L'ubovňa, *Slovak Rep.* **35 B13** 49 18N 20 42 E
Stara Moravica, *Serbia, Yug.* **52 E4** 45 50N 19 30 E
Stara Pazova, *Serbia, Yug.* **52 F5** 44 58N 20 10 E
Stara Planina, *Bulgaria* **50 C7** 43 15N 23 0 E
Stará Turá, *Slovak Rep.* **35 C10** 48 47N 17 42 E
Stara Zagora, *Bulgaria* **51 D9** 42 26N 25 39 E
Starachowice, *Poland* **55 G8** 51 3N 21 2 E
Staraya Russa, *Russia* **58 D6** 57 58N 31 23 E
Starbuck I., *Kiribati* **135 H12** 5 37 S 155 55W
Starchiojd, *Romania* **53 E11** 45 19N 26 11 E
Starcke Nat. Park, *Australia* **126 A4** 14 56 S 145 2 E
Stargard Szczeciński, *Poland* **54 E2** 53 20N 15 0 E
Stårheim, *Norway* **18 C2** 61 56N 5 40 E
Stari Bar, *Montenegro, Yug.* **50 D3** 42 7N 19 10 E
Stari Trg, *Slovenia* **45 C12** 45 29N 15 7 E
Staritsa, *Russia* **58 D8** 56 33N 34 55 E
Starke, *U.S.A.* **152 F7** 29 57N 82 7W
Starnberg, *Germany* **31 H7** 48 0N 11 21 E
Starnberger See, *Germany* **31 H7** 47 54N 11 19 E
Starobilsk, *Ukraine* **59 H10** 49 16N 39 0 E
Starodub, *Russia* **59 F7** 52 30N 32 50 E
Starogard Gdański, *Poland* **54 E5** 53 59N 18 30 E
Starokonstantinov = Starokonstyantyniv, *Ukraine* **59 H4** 49 48N 27 10 E
Starokonstyantyniv, *Ukraine* **59 H4** 49 48N 27 10 E
Starominskaya, *Russia* **59 J10** 46 33N 39 0 E
Staroshcherbinovskaya, *Russia* **59 J10** 46 40N 38 53 E
Starrs Mill, *U.S.A.* **152 B5** 33 19N 84 31W
Start Pt., *U.K.* **21 G4** 50 13N 3 39W
Stary Sącz, *Poland* **55 J7** 49 33N 20 35 E
Staryy Biryuzyak, *Russia* **61 H8** 44 46N 46 50 E
Staryy Chartoriysk, *Ukraine* **59 G3** 51 15N 25 54 E
Staryy Krym, *Ukraine* **59 K8** 45 3N 35 8 E
Staryy Oskol, *Russia* **59 G9** 51 19N 37 55 E
Stassfurt, *Germany* **30 D7** 51 51N 11 35 E
Staszów, *Poland* **55 H8** 50 33N 21 10 E
State Center, *U.S.A.* **156 B3** 42 1N 93 10W
State College, *U.S.A.* **150 F7** 40 48N 77 52W
Stateline, *U.S.A.* **160 G7** 38 57N 119 56W
Staten, I. = Estados, I. de Los, *Argentina* **176 D4** 54 40 S 64 30W
Staten I., *U.S.A.* **151 F10** 40 35N 74 9W
Statenville, *U.S.A.* **152 E6** 30 42N 83 2W
Statesboro, *U.S.A.* **152 C8** 32 27N 81 47W
Statesville, *U.S.A.* **149 H5** 35 47N 80 53W
Statham, *U.S.A.* **152 B6** 33 58N 83 35W
Stathelle, *Norway* **18 E6** 59 3N 9 41 E
Stauffer, *U.S.A.* **161 L7** 34 45N 119 3W
Staunton, *Ill., U.S.A.* **156 F7** 39 1N 89 47W
Staunton, *Va., U.S.A.* **148 F6** 38 9N 79 4W
Stavanger, *Norway* **15 G11** 58 57N 5 40 E
Stavelot, *Belgium* **24 D5** 50 23N 5 55 E
Stavern, *Norway* **15 G14** 59 0N 10 1 E
Stavoren, *Neths.* **24 B5** 52 53N 5 22 E
Stavropol, *Russia* **61 H6** 45 5N 42 0 E
Stavros, *Cyprus* **39 E8** 35 1N 32 38 E
Stavrós, *Itháki, Greece* **39 C2** 38 27N 20 39 E
Stavrós, *Kríti, Greece* **39 E5** 35 12N 24 45 E
Stavrós, Ákra, *Greece* **39 E5** 35 26N 24 58 E
Stavroúpolis, *Greece* **51 E8** 41 12N 24 45 E
Stawell, *Australia* **128 D5** 37 5 S 142 47 E
Stawell →, *Australia* **126 C3** 20 20 S 142 55 E
Stawiski, *Poland* **54 E9** 53 22N 22 9 E
Stawiszyn, *Poland* **55 G5** 51 56N 18 4 E
Stayner, *Canada* **150 B4** 44 25N 80 5W
Stayton, *U.S.A.* **158 D2** 44 48N 122 48W
Steamboat Springs, *U.S.A.* **158 F10** 40 29N 106 50W
Steane, *Norway* **18 E5** 59 16N 8 33 E
Stebbins, *U.S.A.* **144 E7** 63 31N 162 17W
Steblevë, *Albania* **50 E4** 41 23N 20 33 E
Steckborn, *Switz.* **33 A7** 47 44N 8 59 E
Steele, *Ala., U.S.A.* **152 B3** 33 56N 86 12W
Steele, *N. Dak., U.S.A.* **154 B5** 46 51N 99 55W
Steelton, *U.S.A.* **150 F8** 40 14N 76 50W
Steelville, *U.S.A.* **156 G5** 37 58N 91 22W
Steen River, *Canada* **142 B5** 59 40N 117 12W
Steenkool = Bintuni, *Indonesia* **83 B4** 2 7 S 133 32 E
Steens Mt., *U.S.A.* **158 E4** 42 35N 118 40W
Steenstrup Gletscher, *Greenland* **10 B5** 75 15N 57 0W
Steenwijk, *Neths.* **24 B6** 52 47N 6 7 E
Steep Pt., *Australia* **125 E1** 26 8 S 113 8 E
Steep Rock, *Canada* **143 C9** 51 30N 98 48W
Ştefan Vodă, *Moldova* **53 D14** 46 27N 29 42 E
Ştefănesti, *Romania* **53 C12** 47 44N 27 15 E
Stefanie L. = Chew Bahir, *Ethiopia* **107 G4** 4 40N 36 50 E
Stefanie Nat. Park, *Ethiopia* **107 G4** 4 55N 36 55 E
Stefansson Bay, *Antarctica* **7 C5** 67 20 S 59 8 E
Steffisburg, *Switz.* **32 C5** 46 47N 7 38 E
Stege, *Denmark* **17 K6** 54 59N 12 18 E
Ştei, *Romania* **52 D7** 46 32N 22 27 E
Steiermark □, *Austria* **34 D8** 47 26N 15 0 E
Steigerwald, *Germany* **31 F6** 49 44N 10 26 E
Steilacoom, *U.S.A.* **160 C4** 47 10N 122 36W
Steilrandberge, *Namibia* **116 B1** 17 45 S 13 20 E
Stein am Rhein, *Switz.* **33 A7** 47 39N 8 51 E
Steinbach, *Canada* **143 D9** 49 32N 96 40W
Steinfurt, *Germany* **30 C3** 52 9N 7 20 E
Steinhatchee, *U.S.A.* **152 F6** 29 40N 83 23W
Steinhausen, *Namibia* **116 C2** 21 49 S 18 20 E
Steinheim, *Germany* **30 D5** 51 51N 9 5 E
Steinhuder Meer, *Germany* **30 C5** 52 29N 9 21 E
Steinkjer, *Norway* **14 D14** 64 1N 11 31 E
Steinkopf, *S. Africa* **116 D2** 29 18 S 17 43 E
Steinshamn, *Norway* **18 B3** 62 47N 6 28 E
Stellarton, *Canada* **141 C7** 45 32N 62 30W
Stellenbosch, *S. Africa* **116 E2** 33 58 S 18 50 E
Stelvio, Paso dello, *Italy* **33 C10** 46 32N 10 27 E
Stenay, *France* **27 C12** 49 29N 5 12 E
Stendal, *Germany* **30 C7** 52 36N 11 53 E
Stende, *Latvia* **54 A9** 57 11N 22 33 E
Stenhamra, *Sweden* **16 E11** 59 20N 17 41 E
Stenón Ithákis, *Greece* **39 C2** 38 22N 20 39 E
Stenón Kerkiras, *Greece* **38 B10** 39 36N 20 5 E
Stenstorp, *Sweden* **17 F7** 58 17N 13 45 E
Stenungsund, *Sweden* **17 F5** 58 6N 11 50 E
Steornabhaigh = Stornoway, *U.K.* **22 C2** 58 13N 6 23W
Stepanakert = Xankändi, *Azerbaijan* **101 C12** 39 52N 46 49 E
Stepanavan, *Armenia* **61 K7** 41 1N 44 23 E
Stephens, C., *N.Z.* **131 A8** 40 42 S 173 58 E
Stephens Creek, *Australia* **128 A4** 31 50 S 141 30 E
Stephens I., *Canada* **142 C2** 54 10N 130 45W
Stephens I., *N.Z.* **131 A9** 40 40 S 174 1 E
Stephens L., *Canada* **143 B9** 56 32N 95 0W
Stephenville, *Canada* **141 C8** 48 31N 58 35W
Stephenville, *U.S.A.* **155 J5** 32 13N 98 12W
Stepnica, *Poland* **54 E1** 53 38N 14 36 E
Stepnoi = Elista, *Russia* **61 G7** 46 16N 44 14 E
Stepnoye, *Russia* **64 D8** 54 4N 60 26 E
Steppe, *Asia* **62 D9** 50 0N 50 0 E
Stereá Ellas □, *Greece* **48 C4** 38 50N 23 0 E
Sterkstroom, *S. Africa* **116 E4** 31 32 S 26 32 E
Sterling, *Alaska, U.S.A.* **144 F10** 60 32N 150 46W
Sterling, *Colo., U.S.A.* **154 E3** 40 37N 103 13W
Sterling, *Ga., U.S.A.* **152 D8** 31 16N 81 34W
Sterling, *Ill., U.S.A.* **156 C7** 41 48N 89 42W
Sterling, *Kans., U.S.A.* **154 F5** 38 13N 98 12W
Sterling City, *U.S.A.* **155 K4** 31 51N 101 0W
Sterling Heights, *U.S.A.* **157 B13** 42 35N 83 0W
Sterling Run, *U.S.A.* **150 E6** 41 25N 78 12W
Sterlitamak, *Russia* **64 E6** 53 40N 56 0 E
Sternberg, *Germany* **30 B7** 53 42N 11 50 E
Šternberk, *Czech Rep.* **35 B10** 49 45N 17 15 E
Stérnes, *Greece* **39 E5** 35 30N 24 9 E
Sterzing = Vipiteno, *Italy* **45 B8** 46 54N 11 26 E
Stettin = Szczecin, *Poland* **54 E1** 53 27N 14 27 E
Stettiner Haff, *Germany* **30 B10** 53 47N 14 15 E
Stettler, *Canada* **142 C6** 52 19N 112 40W
Steubenville, *U.S.A.* **150 F4** 40 22N 80 37W
Stevenage, *U.K.* **21 F7** 51 55N 0 13W
Stevens Point, *U.S.A.* **154 C10** 44 31N 89 34W
Stevens Pottery, *U.S.A.* **152 C6** 32 57N 83 17W
Stevens Village, *U.S.A.* **144 C10** 66 1N 149 6W
Stevenson, *U.S.A.* **160 E5** 45 42N 121 53W
Stevenson L., *Canada* **143 C9** 53 55N 96 0W
Stevensville, *U.S.A.* **158 C6** 46 30N 114 5W
Stevns Klint, *Denmark* **17 J6** 55 17N 12 28 E
Steward, *U.S.A.* **156 C7** 41 51N 89 1W
Stewardson, *U.S.A.* **157 E8** 39 16N 88 38W
Stewart, *Canada* **142 B3** 55 56N 129 57W
Stewart, *Ga., U.S.A.* **152 B6** 33 25N 83 52W
Stewart, *Nev., U.S.A.* **160 F7** 39 5N 119 46W
Stewart →, *Canada* **138 B6** 63 19N 139 26W
Stewart, C., *Australia* **126 A1** 11 57 S 134 56 E
Stewart, I., *Chile* **176 D2** 54 50 S 71 15W
Stewart I., *N.Z.* **131 G2** 46 58 S 167 54 E
Stewarts Point, *U.S.A.* **160 G3** 38 39N 123 24W
Stewartsville, *U.S.A.* **156 E2** 39 45N 94 30W
Stewartville, *U.S.A.* **154 D8** 43 51N 92 29W
Stewiacke, *Canada* **141 C7** 45 9N 63 22W
Steynsburg, *S. Africa* **116 E4** 31 15 S 25 49 E
Steyr, *Austria* **34 C7** 48 3N 14 25 E
Steyr →, *Austria* **34 C7** 48 3N 14 25 E
Steytlerville, *S. Africa* **116 E3** 33 17 S 24 19 E
Stia, *Italy* **45 E8** 43 48N 11 42 E
Stigler, *U.S.A.* **155 H7** 35 15N 95 8W
Stigliano, *Italy* **47 B9** 40 24N 16 14 E
Stigtomta, *Sweden* **17 F10** 58 47N 16 48 E
Stikine →, *Canada* **142 B2** 56 40N 132 30W
Stilfontein, *S. Africa* **116 D4** 26 51 S 26 50 E
Stilís, *Greece* **48 C4** 38 55N 22 47 E
Stillmore, *U.S.A.* **152 C7** 32 27N 82 13W
Stillwater, *Minn., U.S.A.* **154 C8** 45 3N 92 49W
Stillwater, *N.Y., U.S.A.* **151 D11** 42 55N 73 41W
Stillwater, *Okla., U.S.A.* **155 G6** 36 7N 97 4W
Stillwater Range, *U.S.A.* **158 G4** 39 50N 118 5W
Stillwater Reservoir, *U.S.A.* **151 C9** 43 54N 75 3W
Stilo, Pta., *Italy* **47 D9** 38 25N 16 35 E
Stilwell, *U.S.A.* **155 H7** 35 49N 94 38W
Štip, *Macedonia* **50 E6** 41 42N 22 10 E
Stíra, *Greece* **48 C6** 38 9N 24 14 E
Stirling, *Canada* **150 B7** 44 18N 77 33W
Stirling, *N.Z.* **131 G4** 46 14 S 169 49 E
Stirling, *U.K.* **22 E5** 56 8N 3 57W
Stirling □, *U.K.* **22 E4** 56 12N 4 18W
Stirling Ra., *Australia* **125 F2** 34 23 S 118 0 E
Stirling Range Nat. Park, *Australia* **125 F2** 34 26 S 118 20 E
Stittsville, *Canada* **151 A9** 45 15N 75 55W
Stjernøya, *Norway* **14 A20** 70 20N 22 40 E
Stjørdalshalsen, *Norway* **14 E14** 63 29N 10 51 E
Stock Island, *U.S.A.* **153 L8** 24 32N 81 34W
Stockach, *Germany* **31 H5** 47 50N 9 1 E
Stockaryd, *Sweden* **17 G8** 57 19N 14 36 E
Stockbridge, *Ga., U.S.A.* **152 B5** 33 33N 84 14W
Stockbridge, *Mich., U.S.A.* **157 B12** 42 27N 84 11W
Stockerau, *Austria* **35 C9** 48 24N 16 12 E
Stockholm, *Sweden* **16 E12** 59 20N 18 3 E
Stockholms län □, *Sweden* **16 E12** 59 30N 18 20 E
Stockhorn, *Switz.* **32 C5** 46 42N 7 33 E
Stockport, *U.K.* **20 D5** 53 25N 2 9W
Stocksbridge, *U.K.* **20 D6** 53 29N 1 35W
Stockton, *Calif., U.S.A.* **160 H5** 37 58N 121 17W
Stockton, *Ill., U.S.A.* **156 B6** 42 21N 90 1W
Stockton, *Kans., U.S.A.* **154 F5** 39 26N 99 16W
Stockton, *Mo., U.S.A.* **155 G8** 37 42N 93 48W
Stockton-on-Tees, *U.K.* **20 C6** 54 35N 1 19W
Stockton-on-Tees □, *U.K.* **20 C6** 54 35N 1 19W
Stockton Plateau, *U.S.A.* **155 K3** 30 30N 102 30W
Stoczek Łukowski, *Poland* **55 G8** 51 58N 21 58 E
Stöde, *Sweden* **16 B10** 62 28N 16 35 E
Stoeng Treng, *Cambodia* **86 F5** 13 31N 105 58 E
Stoer, Pt. of, *U.K.* **22 C3** 58 16N 5 23W
Stogovo, *Macedonia* **50 E4** 41 31N 20 38 E
Stoholm, *Denmark* **17 H3** 56 30N 9 8 E
Stoke, *N.Z.* **131 B8** 41 19 S 173 14 E
Stoke-on-Trent, *U.K.* **20 D5** 53 1N 2 11W
Stoke-on-Trent □, *U.K.* **20 D5** 53 1N 2 11W
Stokes Nat. Park, *Australia* **125 E2** 29 55 S 115 6 E
Stokes Pt., *Australia* **127 G3** 40 10 S 143 56 E
Stokes Ra., *Australia* **124 C5** 15 50 S 130 50 E
Stokkseyri, *Iceland* **11 D5** 63 50N 21 2W
Stokksnes, *Iceland* **11 C12** 64 14N 14 58W
Stokmarknes, *Norway* **14 B16** 68 34N 14 54 E
Stolac, *Bos.-H.* **50 C1** 43 5N 17 59 E
Stolberg, *Germany* **30 E2** 50 47N 6 13 E
Stolbovoy, Ostrov, *Russia* **67 B14** 74 44N 135 14 E
Stolbtsy = Stowbtsy, *Belarus* **58 F4** 53 30N 26 43 E
Stolin, *Belarus* **59 G4** 51 53N 26 50 E
Stöllet, *Sweden* **16 D7** 60 26N 13 15 E
Stolnici, *Romania* **53 F9** 44 31N 24 48 E
Stomíon, *Greece* **39 E4** 35 21N 23 32 E
Ston, *Croatia* **45 F14** 42 51N 17 43 E
Stone, *U.K.* **20 E5** 52 55N 2 9W
Stone Mountain, *U.S.A.* **152 B5** 33 49N 84 10W
Stoneboro, *U.S.A.* **150 E4** 41 20N 80 7W
Stonehaven, *U.K.* **22 E6** 56 59N 2 12W
Stonehenge, *Australia* **126 C3** 24 22 S 143 17 E
Stonehenge, *U.K.* **21 F6** 51 9N 1 45W
Stonewall, *Canada* **143 C9** 50 10N 97 19W
Stongfjorden, *Norway* **18 C2** 61 26N 5 10 E
Stonington, *U.S.A.* **156 E7** 39 44N 89 12W
Stony L., *Man., Canada* **143 B9** 58 51N 98 40W
Stony L., *Ont., Canada* **150 B6** 44 30N 78 5W
Stony Point, *U.S.A.* **151 E11** 41 14N 73 59W
Stony Pt., *U.S.A.* **151 C8** 43 50N 76 18W
Stony Rapids, *Canada* **143 B7** 59 16N 105 50W
Stony River, *U.S.A.* **144 F8** 61 47N 156 35W
Stony Tunguska = Tunguska, Podkamennaya →, *Russia* **67 C10** 61 50N 90 13 E
Stonyford, *U.S.A.* **160 F4** 39 23N 122 33W
Stopnica, *Poland* **55 H7** 50 27N 20 57 E
Storå, *Sweden* **16 E9** 59 42N 15 6 E
Storå →, *Denmark* **17 H2** 56 20N 8 19 E
Stora Gla, *Sweden* **16 E6** 59 30N 12 30 E
Stora Le, *Sweden* **16 E5** 59 5N 11 55 E
Stora Lulevatten, *Sweden* **14 C18** 67 10N 19 30 E
Stóra-Vatnshorn, *Iceland* **11 B5** 65 4N 21 33W
Storavan, *Sweden* **14 D18** 65 45N 18 10 E
Stord, *Norway* **15 G11** 59 52N 5 23 E
Stordal, *Norway* **18 B4** 62 23N 7 0 E
Store Bælt, *Denmark* **17 J4** 55 20N 11 0 E
Store Heddinge, *Denmark* **17 J6** 55 18N 12 23 E
Store Jukleggi, *Norway* **18 C5** 61 3N 8 12 E
Store Koldewey, *Greenland* **10 B9** 76 30N 19 0W
Store Sølnkletten, *Norway* **18 C7** 61 59N 10 16 E
Store Sotra, *Norway* **18 D1** 60 18N 5 4 E
Storebro, *Sweden* **17 G9** 57 35N 15 52 E
Støren, *Norway* **18 A7** 63 3N 10 18 E
Storerikvollen, *Norway* **18 A8** 63 7N 11 58 E
Storfjellseter, *Norway* **18 C7** 61 40N 10 30 E
Storfjorden, *Møre og Romsdal, Norway* **18 B3** 62 8N 6 33 E
Storfjorden, *Møre og Romsdal, Norway* **18 B3** 62 28N 6 35 E
Storfors, *Sweden* **16 E8** 59 32N 14 17 E
Stóridalur, *Iceland* **11 D7** 63 38N 19 57W
Stórinúpur, *Iceland* **11 C6** 64 3N 20 10W
Storli, *Norway* **18 B6** 62 42N 9 5 E
Storlien, *Sweden* **16 A6** 63 20N 12 5 E
Storm B., *Australia* **127 G4** 43 10 S 147 30 E
Storm Lake, *U.S.A.* **154 D7** 42 39N 95 13W
Stormberge, *S. Africa* **116 E4** 31 16 S 26 17 E
Stormsrivier, *S. Africa* **116 E3** 33 59 S 23 52 E
Stornoway, *U.K.* **22 C2** 58 13N 6 23W
Storo, *Italy* **44 C7** 45 51N 10 35 E
Storozhinets = Storozhynets, *Ukraine* **59 H3** 48 14N 25 45 E
Storozhynets, *Ukraine* **59 H3** 48 14N 25 45 E
Storrs, *U.S.A.* **151 E12** 41 49N 72 15W
Storsjøen, *Hedmark, Norway* **18 D8** 60 20N 11 40 E
Storsjøen, *Hedmark, Norway* **18 C8** 61 30N 11 14 E
Storsjön, *Gävleborg, Sweden* **16 D10** 60 35N 16 45 E
Storsjön, *Jämtland, Sweden* **16 B7** 62 48N 13 7 E
Storsjön, *Jämtland, Sweden* **16 A8** 63 9N 14 30 E
Storstrøms Amtskommune □, *Denmark* **17 J5** 54 50N 11 45 E
Storuman, *Sweden* **14 D17** 65 5N 17 10 E
Storuman, sjö, *Sweden* **14 D17** 65 13N 16 50 E
Stóruvellir, *Iceland* **11 B9** 65 30N 17 29W
Storvätteshågna, *Sweden* **16 B6** 62 6N 12 30 E
Storvigelen, *Norway* **18 B9** 62 32N 12 2 E
Storvik, *Sweden* **16 D10** 60 35N 16 33 E
Storvreta, *Sweden* **16 E11** 59 58N 17 44 E
Story City, *U.S.A.* **156 B3** 42 11N 93 36W
Stouffville, *Canada* **150 C5** 43 58N 79 15W
Stoughton, *Canada* **143 D8** 49 40N 103 0W
Stoughton, *U.S.A.* **156 B8** 42 55N 89 13W
Stour →, *Dorset, U.K.* **21 G6** 50 43N 1 47W
Stour →, *Kent, U.K.* **21 F9** 51 18N 1 22 E
Stour →, *Suffolk, U.K.* **21 F9** 51 57N 1 4 E
Stourbridge, *U.K.* **21 E5** 52 28N 2 8W
Stout L., *Canada* **143 C10** 52 0N 94 40W
Stove Pipe Wells Village, *U.S.A.* **161 J9** 36 35N 117 11W
Støvring, *Denmark* **17 H3** 56 54N 9 50 E
Stow, *U.S.A.* **150 E3** 41 10N 81 27W
Stowbtsy, *Belarus* **58 F4** 53 30N 26 43 E
Stowmarket, *U.K.* **21 E9** 52 12N 1 0 E
Strabane, *U.K.* **23 B4** 54 50N 7 27W
Stracin, *Macedonia* **50 D6** 42 13N 22 2 E
Stradella, *Italy* **44 C6** 45 5N 9 18 E
Strahan, *Australia* **127 G4** 42 9 S 145 20 E
Strajitsa, *Bulgaria* **51 C9** 43 14N 25 58 E
Strakonice, *Czech Rep.* **34 B6** 49 15N 13 53 E
Straldzha, *Bulgaria* **51 D10** 42 35N 26 40 E
Stralsund, *Germany* **30 A9** 54 18N 13 4 E
Strand, *Norway* **18 C8** 61 17N 11 17 E
Strand, *S. Africa* **116 E2** 34 9 S 18 48 E
Stranda, *Møre og Romsdal, Norway* **15 E12** 62 19N 6 58 E
Stranda, *Nord-Trøndelag, Norway* **14 E14** 63 33N 10 14 E
Strandasýsla □, *Iceland* **11 B5** 65 45N 21 45W
Strandby, *Denmark* **17 G4** 57 30N 10 29 E
Strangford L., *U.K.* **23 B6** 54 30N 5 37W
Strängnäs, *Sweden* **16 E11** 59 23N 17 2 E
Stranraer, *U.K.* **22 G3** 54 54N 5 1W
Strasbourg, *Canada* **143 C8** 51 4N 104 55W
Strasbourg, *France* **27 D14** 48 35N 7 42 E
Strasburg, *Germany* **30 B9** 53 30N 13 43 E
Strășeni, *Moldova* **53 C13** 47 8N 28 36 E
Stråssa, *Sweden* **16 E9** 59 44N 15 12 E
Stratford, *N.S.W., Australia* **129 B9** 32 7 S 151 55 E
Stratford, *Vic., Australia* **129 D7** 37 59 S 147 7 E
Stratford, *Canada* **140 D3** 43 23N 81 0W
Stratford, *N.Z.* **130 F3** 39 20 S 174 19 E
Stratford, *Calif., U.S.A.* **160 J7** 36 11N 119 49W
Stratford, *Conn., U.S.A.* **151 E11** 41 12N 73 8W
Stratford, *Tex., U.S.A.* **155 G3** 36 20N 102 4W
Stratford-upon-Avon, *U.K.* **21 E6** 52 12N 1 42W
Strath Spey, *U.K.* **22 D5** 57 9N 3 49W
Strathalbyn, *Australia* **128 C3** 35 13 S 138 53 E
Strathaven, *U.K.* **22 F4** 55 40N 4 5W
Strathcona Prov. Park, *Canada* **142 D3** 49 38N 125 40W
Strathmore, *Canada* **142 C6** 51 5N 113 18W
Strathmore, *U.K.* **22 E5** 56 37N 3 7W
Strathmore, *U.S.A.* **160 J7** 36 9N 119 4W
Strathnaver, *Canada* **142 C4** 53 20N 122 33W
Strathpeffer, *U.K.* **22 D4** 57 35N 4 32W
Strathroy, *Canada* **140 D3** 42 58N 81 38W
Strathy Pt., *U.K.* **22 C4** 58 36N 4 1W
Strattanville, *U.S.A.* **150 E5** 41 12N 79 19W
Stratton, *U.S.A.* **151 A14** 45 8N 70 26W
Stratton Mt., *U.S.A.* **151 C12** 43 4N 72 55W
Straubing, *Germany* **31 G8** 48 52N 12 34 E
Straumnes, *Iceland* **11 A3** 66 26N 23 8W
Strausberg, *Germany* **30 C9** 52 35N 13 54 E
Strawberry →, *U.S.A.* **158 F8** 40 10N 110 24W
Strawberry Point, *U.S.A.* **156 B5** 42 41N 91 32W
Strážnice, *Czech Rep.* **35 C10** 48 54N 17 19 E
Streaky B., *Australia* **127 E1** 32 48 S 134 13 E
Streaky Bay, *Australia* **127 E1** 32 51 S 134 18 E
Streator, *U.S.A.* **154 E10** 41 8N 88 50W
Středočeský □, *Czech Rep.* **34 B7** 49 55N 14 30 E
Streetsboro, *U.S.A.* **150 E3** 41 14N 81 21W
Streetsville, *Canada* **150 C5** 43 35N 79 42W
Strehaia, *Romania* **53 F8** 44 37N 23 10 E
Strelcha, *Bulgaria* **51 D8** 42 25N 24 19 E
Strelka, *Russia* **67 D10** 58 5N 93 3 E
Streng →, *Cambodia* **86 F4** 13 12N 103 37 E
Stresa, *Italy* **44 C5** 45 52N 8 28 E
Streymoy, *Færoe Is.* **14 E9** 62 8N 7 5W
Strezhevoy, *Russia* **66 C8** 60 42N 77 34 E
Stříbro, *Czech Rep.* **34 A6** 49 44N 13 0 E
Strickland →, *Papua N. G.* **132 D1** 7 35 S 141 36 E
Strimón →, *Greece* **50 F7** 40 46N 23 51 E
Strimonikós Kólpos, *Greece* **50 F7** 40 33N 24 0 E
Stroeder, *Argentina* **176 B4** 40 12 S 62 37W
Strofádhes, *Greece* **48 D3** 37 15N 21 0 E
Stroma, *U.K.* **22 C5** 58 41N 3 7W
Strómboli, *Italy* **47 D8** 38 47N 15 13 E
Stromeferry, *U.K.* **22 D3** 57 21N 5 33W
Strømmen, *Norway* **18 E7** 59 58N 10 59 E
Stromness, *U.K.* **22 C5** 58 58N 3 17W
Strömsbruk, *Sweden* **16 C11** 61 52N 17 18 E
Stromsburg, *U.S.A.* **154 E6** 41 7N 97 36W
Strömsnäsbruk, *Sweden* **17 H7** 56 35N 13 45 E
Strömstad, *Sweden* **17 F5** 58 56N 11 10 E
Strömsund, *Sweden* **14 E16** 63 51N 15 33 E
Stronghurst, *U.S.A.* **156 D6** 40 45N 90 55W
Strongilí, *Greece* **49 E11** 36 6N 29 42 E
Stróngoli, *Italy* **47 C10** 39 16N 17 3 E
Strongsville, *U.S.A.* **150 E3** 41 19N 81 50W
Stronie Ślaskie, *Poland* **55 H3** 50 18N 16 53 E
Stronsay, *U.K.* **22 B6** 59 7N 2 35W
Stropkov, *Slovak Rep.* **35 B14** 49 13N 21 39 E
Stroud, *U.K.* **21 F5** 51 45N 2 13W
Stroud Road, *Australia* **129 B9** 32 18 S 151 57 E
Stroudsburg, *U.S.A.* **151 F9** 40 59N 75 12W
Stroumbi, *Cyprus* **39 F8** 34 53N 32 29 E
Struer, *Denmark* **17 H2** 56 30N 8 35 E
Struga, *Macedonia* **50 E4** 41 11N 20 44 E
Strugi Krasnyye, *Russia* **58 C5** 58 21N 29 1 E
Strumica, *Macedonia* **50 E6** 41 28N 22 41 E
Strumica →, *Europe* **50 E7** 41 20N 23 22 E
Struthers, *Canada* **140 C2** 48 41N 85 51W
Struthers, *U.S.A.* **150 E4** 41 4N 80 39W
Stryama, *Bulgaria* **51 D8** 42 16N 24 54 E
Stryker, *U.S.A.* **158 B6** 48 41N 114 46W
Stryków, *Poland* **55 G6** 51 55N 19 33 E
Stryn, *Norway* **18 C3** 61 54N 6 43 E
Stryy, *Ukraine* **59 H2** 49 16N 23 48 E
Strzegom, *Poland* **55 H3** 50 58N 16 20 E
Strzelce Krajeńskie, *Poland* **55 F2** 52 52N 15 33 E
Strzelce Opolskie, *Poland* **55 H5** 50 31N 18 18 E
Strzelecki Cr. →, *Australia* **127 D2** 29 37 S 139 59 E
Strzelin, *Poland* **55 H4** 50 46N 17 2 E
Strzelno, *Poland* **55 F5** 52 35N 18 9 E
Strzybnica, *Poland* **55 H5** 50 28N 18 48 E
Strzyżów, *Poland* **55 J8** 49 52N 21 47 E
Stuart, *Fla., U.S.A.* **149 M5** 27 12N 80 15W
Stuart, *Iowa, U.S.A.* **156 C2** 41 30N 94 19W
Stuart, *Nebr., U.S.A.* **154 D5** 42 36N 99 8W
Stuart →, *Canada* **142 C4** 54 0N 123 35W
Stuart Bluff Ra., *Australia* **124 D5** 22 50 S 131 52 E
Stuart I., *U.S.A.* **144 E7** 63 35N 162 30W
Stuart L., *Canada* **142 C4** 54 30N 124 30W
Stuart Mts., *N.Z.* **131 F2** 45 2 S 167 39 E
Stuart Ra., *Australia* **127 D1** 29 10 S 134 56 E
Stubbekøbing, *Denmark* **17 K6** 54 53N 12 9 E
Stuben, *Austria* **34 D3** 47 10N 10 8 E
Studen Kladenets, Yazovir, *Bulgaria* **51 E9** 41 37N 25 30 E
Studenka, *Czech Rep.* **35 B11** 49 44N 18 5 E
Studholme, *N.Z.* **131 E6** 44 42 S 171 9 E
Stugudal, *Norway* **18 B8** 62 53N 11 53 E
Stugun, *Sweden* **16 A9** 63 10N 15 40 E
Stühlingen, *Germany* **33 A6** 47 44N 8 26 E
Stuhr, *Germany* **30 B4** 53 5N 8 44 E
Stull L., *Canada* **140 B1** 54 24N 92 34W
Stung Treng = Stoeng Treng, *Cambodia* **86 F5** 13 31N 105 58 E
Stupart →, *Canada* **140 A1** 56 0N 93 25W
Stupava, *Slovak Rep.* **35 C10** 48 17N 17 2 E
Stupino, *Russia* **58 E10** 54 57N 38 2 E
Sturgeon B., *Canada* **143 C9** 52 0N 97 50W
Sturgeon Bay, *U.S.A.* **148 C2** 44 50N 87 23W
Sturgeon Falls, *Canada* **140 C4** 46 25N 79 57W
Sturgeon L., *Alta., Canada* **142 B5** 55 6N 117 32W
Sturgeon L., *Ont., Canada* **140 C1** 50 0N 90 45W
Sturgeon L., *Ont., Canada* **150 B6** 44 28N 78 43W
Sturgis, *Canada* **143 C8** 51 56N 102 36W
Sturgis, *Mich., U.S.A.* **157 C11** 41 48N 85 25W
Sturgis, *S. Dak., U.S.A.* **154 C3** 44 25N 103 31W
Sturkö, *Sweden* **17 H9** 56 5N 15 42 E
Štúrovo, *Slovak Rep.* **35 D11** 47 48N 18 41 E
Sturt Cr. →, *Australia* **124 C4** 19 8 S 127 50 E
Sturt Nat. Park, *Australia* **127 D3** 27 17 S 141 37 E
Sturts Meadows, *Australia* **128 A4** 31 18 S 141 42 E
Stutterheim, *S. Africa* **116 E4** 32 33 S 27 28 E
Stuttgart, *Germany* **31 G5** 48 48N 9 11 E
Stuttgart, *U.S.A.* **155 H9** 34 30N 91 33W
Stuyvesant, *U.S.A.* **151 D11** 42 23N 73 45W
Stykkishólmur, *Iceland* **11 B4** 65 2N 22 40W
Styria = Steiermark □, *Austria* **34 D8** 47 26N 15 0 E
Styrsö, *Sweden* **17 G5** 57 37N 11 46 E
Su-no-Saki, *Japan* **73 C11** 34 58N 139 45 E

Svetlaya, *Russia* **70 A9** 46 33N 138 18 E
Svetlogorsk = Svyetlahorsk, *Belarus* **59 F5** 52 38N 29 46 E
Svetlograd, *Russia* **61 H6** 45 25N 42 58 E
Svetlovodsk = Svitlovodsk, *Ukraine* **59 H7** 49 2N 33 13 E
Svetlyy, *Russia* **64 F8** 50 48N 60 51 E
Svidník, *Slovak Rep.* **35 B14** 49 20N 21 37 E
Svignaskarð, *Iceland* **11 C5** 64 40N 21 42W
Svilaja Planina, *Croatia* **45 E13** 43 49N 16 31 E
Svilajnac, *Serbia, Yug.* **50 B5** 44 15N 21 11 E
Svilengrad, *Bulgaria* **51 E10** 41 49N 26 12 E
Svinafell, *Iceland* **11 D10** 63 59N 16 51W
Svir →, *Russia* **58 B7** 60 30N 32 48 E
Sviritsa, *Russia* **58 B7** 60 29N 32 51 E
Svishtov, *Bulgaria* **51 C9** 43 36N 25 23 E
Svislach, *Belarus* **59 F3** 53 3N 24 2 E
Svitava →, *Czech Rep.* **35 B9** 49 11N 16 37 E
Svitavy, *Czech Rep.* **35 B9** 49 47N 16 28 E
Svitlovodsk, *Ukraine* **59 H7** 49 2N 33 13 E
Svobodnyy, *Russia* **67 D13** 51 20N 128 0 E
Svoge, *Bulgaria* **50 D7** 42 59N 23 23 E
Svolvær, *Norway* **14 B16** 68 15N 14 34 E
Svorkmo, *Norway* **18 A6** 63 10N 9 46 E
Svoronáta, *Greece* **39 C2** 38 7N 20 31 E
Svratka →, *Czech Rep.* **35 B9** 49 11N 16 38 E
Svrljig, *Serbia, Yug.* **50 C6** 43 25N 22 6 E
Svullrya, *Norway* **18 D9** 60 25N 12 23 E
Svyetlahorsk, *Belarus* **59 F5** 52 38N 29 46 E
Swa, *Burma* **90 F6** 19 15N 96 17 E
Swa Tende, *Dem. Rep. of the Congo* **115 D3** 7 9 S 17 7 E
Swabian Alps = Schwäbische Alb, *Germany* **31 G5** 48 20N 9 30 E
Swainsboro, *U.S.A.* **152 C7** 32 36N 82 20W
Swakop →, *Namibia* **116 C2** 22 38 S 14 36 E
Swakopmund, *Namibia* **116 C1** 22 37 S 14 30 E
Swale →, *U.K.* **20 C6** 54 5N 1 20W
Swamihalli, *India* **95 G3** 14 52N 76 38 E
Swan →, *Australia* **125 F2** 32 3 S 115 45 E
Swan →, *Canada* **143 C8** 52 30N 100 45W
Swan Hill, *Australia* **128 C5** 35 20 S 143 33 E
Swan Hills, *Canada* **142 C5** 54 43N 115 24W
Swan Is. = Santanilla, Is., *Honduras* **164 C3** 17 22N 83 57W
Swan L., *Canada* **143 C8** 52 30N 100 40W
Swan Peak, *U.S.A.* **158 C7** 47 43N 113 38W
Swan Ra., *U.S.A.* **158 C7** 48 0N 113 45W
Swan Reach, *Australia* **128 C3** 34 35 S 139 37 E
Swan River, *Canada* **143 C8** 52 10N 101 16W
Swanage, *U.K.* **21 G6** 50 36N 1 58W
Swansea, *N.S.W., Australia* **129 B9** 33 3 S 151 35 E
Swansea, *Tas., Australia* **127 G4** 42 8 S 148 4 E
Swansea, *Canada* **150 C5** 43 38N 79 28W
Swansea, *U.K.* **21 F4** 51 37N 3 57W
Swansea, *U.S.A.* **152 B8** 33 44N 81 6W
Swansea □, *U.K.* **21 F3** 51 38N 4 3W
Swanton, *U.S.A.* **157 C13** 41 33N 83 53W
Swar →, *Pakistan* **93 B5** 34 40N 72 5 E
Swartberge, *S. Africa* **116 E3** 33 20 S 22 0 E
Swartmodder, *S. Africa* **116 D3** 28 1 S 20 32 E
Swartnossob →, *Namibia* **116 C2** 23 8 S 18 42 E
Swartruggens, *S. Africa* **116 D4** 25 39 S 26 42 E
Swarzędz, *Poland* **55 F4** 52 25N 17 4 E
Swastika, *Canada* **140 C3** 48 7N 80 6W
Swatow = Shantou, *China* **77 F11** 23 18N 116 40 E
Swaziland ■, *Africa* **117 D5** 26 30 S 31 30 E
Sweden ■, *Europe* **15 G16** 57 0N 15 0 E
Swedru, *Ghana* **113 D4** 5 32N 0 41W
Sweet Home, *U.S.A.* **158 D2** 44 24N 122 44W
Sweet Springs, *U.S.A.* **156 F3** 38 58N 93 25W
Sweetgrass, *U.S.A.* **158 B8** 48 59N 111 58W
Sweetwater, *Nev., U.S.A.* **160 G7** 38 27N 119 9W
Sweetwater, *Tenn., U.S.A.* **149 H3** 35 36N 84 28W
Sweetwater, *Tex., U.S.A.* **155 J4** 32 28N 100 25W
Sweetwater →, *U.S.A.* **158 E10** 42 31N 107 2W
Swellendam, *S. Africa* **116 E3** 34 1 S 20 26 E
Swider →, *Poland* **55 F8** 52 6N 21 14 E
Świdnica, *Poland* **55 H3** 50 50N 16 30 E
Świdnik, *Poland* **55 G9** 51 13N 22 39 E
Świdwin, *Poland* **54 E2** 53 47N 15 49 E
Świebodzice, *Poland* **55 H3** 50 51N 16 20 E
Świebodzin, *Poland* **55 F2** 52 15N 15 31 E
Świecie, *Poland* **54 E5** 53 25N 18 30 E
Świerzawa, *Poland* **55 G2** 51 1N 15 54 E
Świętokrzyskie □, *Poland* **55 H7** 50 45N 20 45 E
Świętokrzyskie, Góry, *Poland* **55 H7** 51 0N 20 30 E
Swift Current, *Canada* **143 C7** 50 20N 107 45W
Swiftcurrent →, *Canada* **143 C7** 50 38N 107 44W
Swifts Creek, *Australia* **129 D7** 37 17 S 147 44 E
Swilly, L., *Ireland* **23 A4** 55 12N 7 33W
Swindon, *U.K.* **21 F6** 51 34N 1 46W
Swindon □, *U.K.* **21 F6** 51 34N 1 46W
Swinemünde = Świnoujście, *Poland* **54 E1** 53 54N 14 16 E
Swinford, *Ireland* **23 C3** 53 57N 8 58W
Świnoujście, *Poland* **54 E1** 53 54N 14 16 E
Switzerland ■, *Europe* **32 D6** 46 30N 8 0 E
Swords, *Ireland* **23 C5** 53 28N 6 13W
Swoyerville, *U.S.A.* **151 E9** 41 18N 75 53W
Syasstroy, *Russia* **58 B7** 60 9N 32 33 E
Sycamore, *Ill., U.S.A.* **157 C8** 41 59N 88 41W
Sycamore, *Ohio, U.S.A.* **157 D13** 40 57N 83 10W
Sychevka, *Russia* **58 E8** 55 59N 34 16 E
Syców, *Poland* **55 G4** 51 19N 17 40 E
Sydenham →, *Canada* **150 D2** 42 33N 82 25W
Sydney, *Australia* **129 B9** 33 53 S 151 10 E
Sydney, *Canada* **141 C7** 46 7N 60 7W
Sydney L., *Canada* **143 C10** 50 41N 94 25W
Sydney Mines, *Canada* **141 C7** 46 18N 60 15W
Sydprøven = Alluitsup Paa, *Greenland* **10 E6** 60 30N 45 35W
Sydra, G. of = Surt, Khalīj, *Libya* **108 B3** 31 40N 18 30 E
Syeverodonetsk, *Ukraine* **59 H10** 48 58N 38 35 E
Syfteland, *Norway* **18 D2** 60 14N 5 27 E
Syke, *Germany* **30 C4** 52 55N 8 50 E
Sykesville, *U.S.A.* **150 E6** 41 3N 78 50W
Sykkylven, *Norway* **18 B3** 62 23N 6 35 E
Syktyvkar, *Russia* **56 B9** 61 45N 50 40 E
Sylacauga, *U.S.A.* **152 B3** 33 10N 86 15W
Sylarna, *Sweden* **14 E15** 63 2N 12 13 E
Sylhet, *Bangla.* **90 C3** 24 54N 91 52 E
Sylt, *Germany* **30 A4** 54 54N 8 22 E
Sylte, *Norway* **18 B4** 62 18N 7 17 E
Sylva →, *Russia* **64 B6** 58 0N 56 54 E
Sylvan Beach, *U.S.A.* **151 C9** 43 12N 75 44W
Sylvan Lake, *Canada* **142 C6** 52 20N 114 3W
Sylvania, *Ga., U.S.A.* **152 C8** 32 45N 81 38W
Sylvania, *Ohio, U.S.A.* **157 C13** 41 43N 83 42W
Sylvester, *U.S.A.* **152 D6** 31 32N 83 50W
Sym, *Russia* **66 C9** 60 20N 88 18 E
Symón, *Mexico* **162 C4** 24 42N 102 35W
Synelnykove, *Ukraine* **59 H8** 48 25N 35 30 E
Synnfjell, *Norway* **18 C6** 61 5N 9 46 E
Synnott Ra., *Australia* **124 C4** 16 30 S 125 20 E
Syracuse, *Ind., U.S.A.* **157 C11** 41 26N 85 45W
Syracuse, *Kans., U.S.A.* **155 G4** 37 59N 101 45W
Syracuse, *N.Y., U.S.A.* **151 C8** 43 3N 76 9W
Syracuse, *Nebr., U.S.A.* **154 E6** 40 39N 96 11W
Syrdarya, *Uzbekistan* **65 C4** 40 50N 68 40 E
Syrdarya →, *Kazakstan* **66 E7** 46 3N 61 0 E
Syria ■, *Asia* **101 E8** 35 0N 38 0 E
Syriam, *Burma* **90 G6** 16 44N 96 19 E
Syrian Desert = Shām, Bādiyat ash, *Asia* **96 C3** 32 0N 40 0 E
Sysert, *Russia* **64 C8** 56 29N 60 49 E
Sysslebäck, *Sweden* **16 D6** 60 44N 12 52 E
Syvde, *Norway* **18 B2** 62 5N 5 44 E
Syzran, *Russia* **60 D9** 53 12N 48 30 E
Szabolcs-Szatmár-Bereg □, *Hungary* **52 B6** 48 2N 21 45 E
Szadek, *Poland* **55 G5** 51 41N 18 59 E
Szamocin, *Poland* **55 E4** 53 2N 17 7 E
Szamos →, *Hungary* **52 B7** 48 7N 22 20 E
Szamotuły, *Poland* **55 F3** 52 37N 16 33 E
Száraz →, *Hungary* **52 D6** 46 10N 21 15 E
Szarvas, *Hungary* **52 D5** 46 50N 20 38 E
Százhalombatta, *Hungary* **52 C3** 47 20N 18 58 E
Szczawnica, *Poland* **55 J7** 49 26N 20 30 E
Szczebrzeszyn, *Poland* **55 H9** 50 42N 22 59 E
Szczecin, *Poland* **54 E1** 53 27N 14 27 E
Szczecinek, *Poland* **54 E3** 53 43N 16 41 E
Szczeciński, Zalew = Stettiner Haff, *Germany* **30 B10** 53 47N 14 15 E
Szczekociny, *Poland* **55 H6** 50 38N 19 48 E
Szczucin, *Poland* **55 H8** 50 18N 21 4 E
Szczuczyn, *Poland* **54 E9** 53 36N 22 19 E
Szczyrk, *Poland* **55 J6** 49 43N 19 2 E
Szczytna, *Poland* **55 H3** 50 25N 16 28 E
Szczytno, *Poland* **54 E7** 53 33N 21 0 E
Szechwan = Sichuan □, *China* **76 B5** 30 30N 103 0 E
Szécsény, *Hungary* **52 B4** 48 7N 19 30 E
Szeged, *Hungary* **52 D5** 46 16N 20 10 E
Szeghalom, *Hungary* **52 C6** 47 1N 21 10 E
Székesfehérvár, *Hungary* **52 C3** 47 15N 18 25 E
Szekszárd, *Hungary* **52 D3** 46 22N 18 42 E
Szendrő, *Hungary* **52 B5** 48 24N 20 41 E
Szentendre, *Hungary* **52 C4** 47 39N 19 4 E
Szentes, *Hungary* **52 D5** 46 39N 20 21 E
Szentgotthárd, *Hungary* **52 D1** 46 58N 16 19 E
Szentlőrinc, *Hungary* **52 D3** 46 3N 18 1 E
Szerencs, *Hungary* **52 B6** 48 10N 21 12 E
Szigetszentmiklós, *Hungary* **52 C4** 47 21N 19 3 E
Szigetvár, *Hungary* **52 D2** 46 3N 17 46 E
Szikszó, *Hungary* **52 B5** 48 12N 20 56 E
Szklarska Poreba, *Poland* **55 H2** 50 50N 15 33 E
Szkwa →, *Poland* **55 E8** 53 11N 21 43 E
Szlichtyngowa, *Poland* **55 G3** 51 42N 16 15 E
Szob, *Hungary* **52 C3** 47 48N 18 53 E
Szolnok, *Hungary* **52 C5** 47 10N 20 15 E
Szombathely, *Hungary* **52 C1** 47 14N 16 38 E
Szprotawa, *Poland* **55 G2** 51 33N 15 35 E
Sztum, *Poland* **54 E6** 53 55N 19 1 E
Sztutowo, *Poland* **54 D6** 54 20N 19 15 E
Szubin, *Poland* **55 E4** 53 1N 17 45 E
Szydłowiec, *Poland* **55 G7** 51 15N 20 51 E
Szypliszki, *Poland* **54 D10** 54 17N 23 2 E

T

Ta Khli Khok, *Thailand* **86 E3** 15 18N 100 20 E
Ta Lai, *Vietnam* **87 G6** 11 24N 107 23 E
Tab, *Hungary* **52 D3** 46 44N 18 2 E
Tabacal, *Argentina* **174 A3** 23 15 S 64 15W
Tabaco, *Phil.* **80 E4** 13 22N 123 44 E
Tabagné, *Ivory C.* **112 D4** 7 59N 3 4W
Ţābah, *Si. Arabia* **96 E4** 26 55N 42 38 E
Tabajara, *Brazil* **173 B5** 8 56 S 62 8W
Tabalo, *Papua N. G.* **132 A5** 1 24 S 149 40 E
Tabalos, *Peru* **172 B2** 6 26 S 76 37W
Tabanan, *Indonesia* **79 K18** 8 32 S 115 8 E
Tabankort, *Niger* **113 B5** 17 44N 0 20 E
Tabar I., *Papua N. G.* **132 B7** 2 56 S 152 0 E
Tabar Is., *Papua N. G.* **132 B7** 2 50 S 152 0 E
Tabarka, *Tunisia* **108 A1** 36 56N 8 46 E
Ţabas, *Khorāsān, Iran* **97 C9** 32 48N 60 12 E
Ţabas, *Khorāsān, Iran* **97 C8** 33 35N 56 55 E
Tabasará, Serranía de, *Panama* **164 E3** 8 35N 81 40W
Tabasco □, *Mexico* **163 D6** 17 45N 93 30W
Tabāsīn, *Iran* **97 D8** 31 12N 57 54 E
Tabatinga, *Brazil* **172 A4** 4 16 S 69 56W
Tabatinga, Serra da, *Brazil* **170 D3** 10 30 S 44 0W
Tabayin, *Burma* **90 D5** 22 42N 95 20 E
Tabelbala, Kahal de, *Algeria* **111 C4** 28 47N 2 0W
Tabelembila, *Algeria* **111 D5** 24 43N 4 16 E
Taber, *Canada* **142 D6** 49 47N 112 8W
Taberg, *Sweden* **17 G8** 57 40N 14 6 E
Taberg, *U.S.A.* **151 C9** 43 18N 75 37W
Tabi, *Angola* **115 D2** 8 10 S 13 18 E
Tabira, *Brazil* **170 C4** 7 35 S 37 33W
Tabla, *Niger* **113 C5** 13 46N 3 1 E
Tablas I., *Phil.* **80 E4** 12 25N 122 2 E
Tablas Strait, *Phil.* **80 E3** 12 40N 121 48 E
Table, Pte. de la, *Réunion* **121 c** 21 14 S 55 48 E
Table B. = Tafelbaai, *S. Africa* **116 E2** 33 35 S 18 25 E
Table B., *Canada* **141 B8** 53 40N 56 25W
Table C., *N.Z.* **130 F7** 39 6 S 178 0 E
Table Grove, *U.S.A.* **156 D6** 40 20N 90 27W
Table I., *Burma* **95 G11** 14 12N 93 22 E
Table Mt., *S. Africa* **116 E2** 34 0 S 18 22 E
Table Rock L., *U.S.A.* **155 G8** 36 36N 93 19W
Tabletop, Mt., *Australia* **126 C4** 23 24 S 147 11 E
Tabocal, *Brazil* **169 D6** 2 42 S 57 40W
Tábor, *Czech Rep.* **34 B7** 49 25N 14 39 E
Tabora, *Tanzania* **118 D3** 5 2 S 32 50 E
Tabora □, *Tanzania* **118 D3** 5 0 S 33 0 E
Taboshar, *Tajikistan* **65 C4** 40 34N 69 38 E
Tabou, *Ivory C.* **112 E3** 4 30N 7 20W
Tabrīz, *Iran* **101 C12** 38 7N 46 20 E
Tabuaeran, *Kiribati* **135 G12** 3 51N 159 22W
Tabubil, *Papua N. G.* **132 C1** 5 20 S 141 15 E
Tabuenca, *Spain* **40 D3** 41 42N 1 33W
Tabuk, *Phil.* **80 C3** 17 24N 121 25 E
Tabūk, *Si. Arabia* **96 D3** 28 23N 36 36 E
Tabwemasana, Mt., *Vanuatu* **133 E4** 15 20 S 166 44 E
Täby, *Sweden* **16 E12** 59 28N 18 4 E
Tacámbaro de Codallos, *Mexico* **162 D4** 19 14N 101 28W
Tacarigua, Laguna de, *Venezuela* **168 A4** 10 15N 65 50W
Tacheng, *China* **68 B3** 46 40N 82 58 E
Tach'i, *Taiwan* **77 E13** 24 46N 121 0 E
Tachia, *Taiwan* **77 E13** 24 25N 120 28 E
Tachibana-Wan, *Japan* **72 E2** 32 45N 130 7 E
Tachikawa, *Japan* **73 B11** 35 42N 139 25 E
Tach'ing Shan = Daqing Shan, *China* **74 D6** 40 40N 111 0 E
Táchira □, *Venezuela* **168 B3** 8 7N 72 15W
Tachov, *Czech Rep.* **34 B5** 49 47N 12 39 E
Tácina →, *Italy* **47 D9** 38 57N 16 55 E
Tacloban, *Phil.* **81 F5** 11 15N 124 58 E
Tacna, *Peru* **172 D3** 18 0 S 70 20W
Tacna □, *Peru* **172 D3** 17 40 S 70 20W
Tacoma, *U.S.A.* **160 C4** 47 14N 122 26W
Tacuarembó, *Uruguay* **175 C4** 31 45 S 56 0W
Tacurong, *Phil.* **81 H5** 6 40N 124 41 E
Tacutu →, *Brazil* **169 C5** 3 1N 60 29W
Tada-u, *Burma* **90 E5** 21 49N 95 58 E
Tadahadi, *Solomon Is.* **133 N11** 10 18 S 161 35 E
Tademaït, Plateau du, *Algeria* **111 C5** 28 30N 2 30 E
Tadent, O. →, *Algeria* **111 D6** 22 25N 6 40 E
Tadéra, *Niger* **111 D6** 20 29N 8 18 E
Tadine, *N. Cal.* **133 U21** 21 33 S 167 52 E
Tadio, L., *Ivory C.* **112 D3** 5 10N 5 15W
Tadjerdjeri, O. →, *Algeria* **111 C6** 26 0N 8 0 E
Tadjerouna, *Algeria* **111 B5** 33 31N 2 3 E
Tadjettaret, O. →, *Algeria* **111 D6** 21 20N 7 22 E
Tadjmout, *Laghouat, Algeria* **111 B5** 33 52N 2 30 E
Tadjmout, *Saoura, Algeria* **111 C5** 25 37N 3 48 E
Tadjoura, *Djibouti* **107 E5** 11 50N 42 55 E
Tadjoura, Golfe de, *Djibouti* **107 E5** 11 50N 43 0 E
Tadmor, *N.Z.* **131 B7** 41 27 S 172 45 E
Tadotsu, *Japan* **72 C5** 34 16N 133 45 E
Tadoule, L., *Canada* **143 B9** 58 36N 98 20W
Tadoussac, *Canada* **141 C6** 48 11N 69 42W
Tadpatri, *India* **95 G4** 14 55N 78 1 E
Tadrés, Réserve Totale de Faune du, *Niger* **113 B6** 16 0N 7 10 E
Tadzhikistan = Tajikistan ■, *Asia* **66 F8** 38 30N 70 0 E
Taechŏn-ni, *S. Korea* **75 F14** 36 21N 126 36 E
Taegu, *S. Korea* **75 G15** 35 50N 128 37 E
Taegwan, *N. Korea* **75 D13** 40 13N 125 12 E
Taejŏn, *S. Korea* **75 F14** 36 20N 127 28 E
Taen, Ko, *Thailand* **87 b** 9 22N 99 57 E
Tafalla, *Spain* **40 C3** 42 30N 1 41W
Tafar, *Sudan* **107 F2** 6 52N 28 15 E
Tafassasset, O. →, *Algeria* **111 D6** 22 0N 9 57 E
Tafelbaai, *S. Africa* **116 E2** 33 35 S 18 25 E
Tafelney, C., *Morocco* **110 B3** 31 3N 9 51W
Tafermaar, *Indonesia* **83 C4** 6 47 S 134 10 E
Taffermit, *Morocco* **110 C3** 29 37N 9 15W
Tafí Viejo, *Argentina* **174 B2** 26 43 S 65 17W
Tafīhān, *Iran* **97 D7** 29 25N 52 39 E
Tafilalet, *Morocco* **110 B4** 31 20N 4 45W
Tafiré, *Ivory C.* **112 D3** 9 4N 5 4W
Tafjord, *Norway* **18 B4** 62 14N 7 24 E
Tafnidilt, *Morocco* **110 C2** 28 47N 10 58W
Tafo, *Ghana* **113 D4** 6 15N 0 20W
Tafraoute, *Morocco* **110 C3** 29 50N 8 58W
Tafresh, *Iran* **97 C6** 34 45N 49 57 E
Taft, *Iran* **97 D7** 31 45N 54 14 E
Taft, *Phil.* **81 F5** 11 57N 125 30 E
Taft, *U.S.A.* **161 K7** 35 8N 119 28W
Taftān, Kūh-e, *Iran* **97 D9** 28 40N 61 0 E
Tafwap, *India* **95 L11** 7 23N 93 43 E
Taga, *Samoa* **133 W23** 13 46 S 172 28W
Taga Dzong, *Bhutan* **90 B2** 27 5N 89 55 E
Tagana-an, *Phil.* **81 G5** 9 42N 125 35 E
Taganrog, *Russia* **59 J10** 47 12N 38 50 E
Taganrogskiy Zaliv, *Russia* **59 J10** 47 0N 38 30 E
Tagânt, *Mauritania* **112 B2** 18 20N 11 0W
Tagap Ga, *Burma* **90 B6** 26 56N 96 13 E
Tagatay, *Phil.* **80 D3** 14 6N 120 56 E
Tagauayan I., *Phil.* **81 F3** 10 58N 121 13 E
Tagaung, *Burma* **90 D6** 23 30N 96 2 E
Tagawa, *Japan* **72 D2** 33 38N 130 51 E
Tagbilaran, *Phil.* **81 G4** 9 39N 123 51 E
Tage, *Papua N. G.* **132 D2** 6 19 S 143 20 E
Tággia, *Italy* **44 E4** 43 52N 7 51 E
Taghzout, *Morocco* **110 B4** 33 30N 4 49W
Tagish, *Canada* **142 A2** 60 19N 134 16W
Tagish L., *Canada* **142 A2** 60 10N 134 20W
Tagkawayan, *Phil.* **80 E4** 13 58N 122 32 E
Tagliacozzo, *Italy* **45 F10** 42 4N 13 14 E
Tagliamento →, *Italy* **45 C10** 45 38N 13 6 E
Táglio di Po, *Italy* **45 D9** 45 0N 12 12 E
Tagna, *Colombia* **168 D3** 2 24 S 70 37W
Tago, *Phil.* **81 G6** 9 2N 126 13 E
Tago, Mt., *Phil.* **81 G5** 8 23N 125 5 E
Tagomago, *Spain* **38 C2** 39 2N 1 39 E
Tagourāret, *Mauritania* **112 B3** 17 45N 7 45W
Taguatinga, *Brazil* **171 D3** 12 16 S 42 26W
Tagudin, *Phil.* **80 C3** 16 56N 120 27 E
Taguenout Haggueret, *Mali* **111 D4** 21 14N 0 48W
Tagula, *Papua N. G.* **132 F7** 11 22 S 153 15 E
Tagula I., *Papua N. G.* **132 F7** 11 30 S 153 30 E
Tagum, *Phil.* **81 H5** 7 33N 125 53 E
Tagus = Tejo →, *Europe* **43 F2** 38 40N 9 24W
Tahakopa, *N.Z.* **131 G4** 46 30 S 169 23 E
Tahala, *Morocco* **110 B4** 34 0N 4 28W
Tahan, Gunong, *Malaysia* **87 K4** 4 34N 102 17 E
Tahānah-ye sūr Gol, *Afghan.* **91 C2** 31 43N 67 53 E
Tahara, *Japan* **73 C9** 34 40N 137 16 E
Tahat, *Algeria* **111 D6** 23 18N 5 33 E
Tāherī, *Iran* **97 E7** 27 43N 52 20 E
Tahiti, *Pac. Oc.* **133 S16** 17 37 S 149 27W
Tahlab →, *Pakistan* **91 C1** 28 9N 62 45 E
Tahlequah, *U.S.A.* **155 H7** 35 55N 94 58W
Tahoe, L., *U.S.A.* **160 G6** 39 6N 120 2W
Tahoe City, *U.S.A.* **160 F6** 39 10N 120 9W
Tahoka, *U.S.A.* **155 J4** 33 10N 101 48W
Taholah, *U.S.A.* **160 C2** 47 21N 124 17W
Tahora, *N.Z.* **130 F3** 39 2 S 174 49 E
Tahoua, *Niger* **113 C6** 14 57N 5 16 E
Tahrūd, *Iran* **97 D8** 29 26N 57 49 E
Tahsis, *Canada* **142 D3** 49 55N 126 40W
Tahta, *Egypt* **106 B3** 26 44N 31 32 E
Tahtaköprü, *Turkey* **51 G13** 39 57N 29 39 E
Tahtalı Dağları, *Turkey* **100 C7** 38 20N 36 0 E
Tahuamanu →, *Bolivia* **172 C4** 11 6 S 67 36W
Tahulandang, *Indonesia* **82 A3** 2 27N 125 23 E
Tahuna, *Indonesia* **82 A3** 3 38N 125 30 E
Taï, *Ivory C.* **112 D3** 5 55N 7 30W
Taï, Parc Nat. de, *Ivory C.* **112 D3** 5 25N 7 5W
Tai Au Mun, *China* **69 G11** 22 18N 114 17 E
Tai Hu, *China* **77 B12** 31 5N 120 10 E
Tai Mo Shan, *China* **69 G11** 22 25N 114 7 E
Tai O, *China* **69 G10** 22 15N 113 52 E
Tai Pang Wan, *H.K.* **69 F11** 22 33N 114 24 E
Tai Po, *China* **69 G11** 22 27N 114 10 E
Tai Shan, *China* **75 F9** 36 25N 117 20 E
Tai'an, *China* **75 F9** 36 12N 117 8 E
Taiarapu, Presq. de, *Tahiti* **133 S16** 17 47 S 149 14W
Taibei = T'aipei, *Taiwan* **77 E13** 25 2N 121 30 E
Taibique, *Canary Is.* **9 e1** 27 42N 17 58W
Taibus Qi, *China* **74 D8** 41 54N 115 22 E
Taicang, *China* **77 B13** 31 30N 121 5 E
T'aichung, *Taiwan* **77 E13** 24 9N 120 37 E
Taieri →, *N.Z.* **131 G5** 46 3 S 170 12 E
Taiga Madema, *Libya* **108 D3** 23 46N 15 25 E
Taigu, *China* **74 F7** 37 28N 112 30 E
Taihang Shan, *China* **74 G7** 36 0N 113 30 E
Taihape, *N.Z.* **130 F4** 39 41 S 175 48 E
Taihe, *Anhui, China* **74 H8** 33 20N 115 42 E
Taihe, *Jiangxi, China* **77 D10** 26 47N 114 52 E
Taihu, *China* **77 B11** 30 22N 116 20 E
Taijiang, *China* **76 D7** 26 39N 108 21 E
Taikang, *China* **74 G8** 34 5N 114 50 E
Taikkyi, *Burma* **90 G6** 17 20N 96 0 E
Tailem Bend, *Australia* **128 C3** 35 12 S 139 29 E
Tailfingen, *Germany* **31 G5** 48 15N 9 1 E
Tailuko, *Taiwan* **77 E13** 24 9N 121 37 E
Taimyr Peninsula = Taymyr, Poluostrov, *Russia* **67 B11** 75 0N 100 0 E
Tain, *U.K.* **22 D4** 57 49N 4 4W
T'ainan, *Taiwan* **77 F13** 23 0N 120 10 E
Taínaron, Ákra, *Greece* **48 E4** 36 22N 22 27 E
Tainggyo, *Burma* **90 G5** 17 49N 94 29 E
Taining, *China* **77 D11** 26 54N 117 9 E
Taiobeiras, *Brazil* **171 E3** 15 49 S 42 14W
Taipa, *China* **69 G10** 22 10N 113 35 E
T'aipei, *Taiwan* **77 E13** 25 2N 121 30 E
Taiping, *China* **77 B12** 30 15N 118 6 E
Taiping, *Malaysia* **87 K3** 4 51N 100 44 E
Taipingzhen, *China* **74 H6** 33 35N 111 42 E
Taipu, *Brazil* **170 C4** 5 37 S 35 36W
Tairbeart = Tarbert, *U.K.* **22 D2** 57 54N 6 49W
Tairenpokpi, *India* **90 C4** 24 39N 93 40 E
Tairua, *N.Z.* **130 D4** 37 0 S 175 51 E
Taisha, *Japan* **72 B4** 35 24N 132 40 E
Taishan, *China* **77 F9** 22 14N 112 41 E
Taishun, *China* **77 D12** 27 30N 119 42 E
Taita Hills, *Kenya* **118 C4** 3 25 S 38 15 E
Taitao, C., *Chile* **176 C1** 45 53 S 75 5W
Taitao, Pen. de, *Chile* **176 C2** 46 30 S 75 0W
T'aitung, *Taiwan* **77 F13** 22 43N 121 4 E
Taivalkoski, *Finland* **14 D23** 65 33N 28 12 E
Taiwan ■, *Asia* **77 F13** 23 30N 121 0 E
Taiwan Strait, *Asia* **77 E12** 24 40N 120 0 E
Taixing, *China* **77 A13** 32 11N 120 0 E
Taiyara, *Sudan* **107 E3** 13 12N 30 47 E
Taïyetos Óros, *Greece* **48 D4** 37 0N 22 23 E
Taiyiba, *Israel* **103 C4** 32 36N 35 27 E
Taiyuan, *China* **74 F7** 37 52N 112 33 E
Taizhong = T'aichung, *Taiwan* **77 E13** 24 9N 120 37 E
Taizhou, *China* **77 A12** 32 28N 119 55 E
Taizhou Liedao, *China* **77 C13** 28 30N 121 55 E
Ta'izz, *Yemen* **98 D4** 13 35N 44 2 E
Tājābād, *Iran* **97 D7** 30 2N 54 24 E
Tajapuru, Furo do, *Brazil* **170 B1** 1 50 S 50 25W
Tajarḥī, *Libya* **108 D2** 24 21N 14 28 E
Tajikistan ■, *Asia* **66 F8** 38 30N 70 0 E
Tajima, *Japan* **71 F9** 37 12N 139 46 E
Tajimi, *Japan* **73 B9** 35 19N 137 8 E
Tajo = Tejo →, *Europe* **43 F2** 38 40N 9 24W
Tajrīsh, *Iran* **97 C6** 35 48N 51 25 E
Tājūrā, *Libya* **108 B2** 32 51N 13 21 E
Tak, *Thailand* **86 D2** 16 52N 99 8 E
Takāb, *Iran* **101 D12** 36 24N 47 7 E
Takachiho, *Japan* **72 E3** 32 42N 131 18 E
Takachu, *Botswana* **116 C3** 22 37 S 21 58 E
Takada, *Japan* **71 F9** 37 7N 138 15 E
Takahagi, *Japan* **71 F10** 36 43N 140 45 E
Takahashi, *Japan* **72 C5** 34 51N 133 39 E
Takaka, *N.Z.* **131 A7** 40 51 S 172 50 E
Takamaka, *Seychelles* **121 b** 4 50 S 55 30 E
Takamatsu, *Japan* **72 C6** 34 20N 134 5 E
Takanabe, *Japan* **72 E3** 32 8N 131 30 E
Takaoka, *Japan* **73 A9** 36 47N 137 0 E
Takapau, *N.Z.* **130 G5** 40 2 S 176 21 E
Takapuna, *N.Z.* **130 C3** 36 47 S 174 47 E
Takasago, *Japan* **72 C6** 34 45N 134 48 E
Takasaki, *Japan* **73 A11** 36 20N 139 0 E
Takatsuki, *Japan* **73 C7** 34 51N 135 37 E
Takaungu, *Kenya* **118 C4** 3 38 S 39 52 E
Takayama, *Japan* **73 A9** 36 18N 137 11 E
Takayama-Bonchi, *Japan* **73 B9** 36 0N 137 18 E
Take-Shima, *Japan* **71 J5** 30 49N 130 26 E
Takefu, *Japan* **73 B8** 35 50N 136 10 E
Takehara, *Japan* **72 C4** 34 21N 132 55 E
Takeli, *Tajikistan* **65 C4** 40 29N 69 26 E
Takengon, *Indonesia* **84 B1** 4 45N 96 50 E
Takeo, *Japan* **72 D2** 33 12N 130 1 E
Tåkern, *Sweden* **17 F8** 58 22N 14 45 E
Tākestān, *Iran* **97 C6** 36 0N 49 40 E
Taketa, *Japan* **72 E3** 32 58N 131 24 E
Takev, *Cambodia* **87 G5** 10 59N 104 47 E
Takh, *India* **93 C7** 33 6N 77 32 E
Takhār □, *Afghan.* **91 A3** 36 40N 70 0 E
Takht-Sulaiman, *Pakistan* **92 D3** 31 40N 69 58 E
Taki, *Papua N. G.* **132 D8** 6 29 S 155 52 E
Takikawa, *Japan* **70 C10** 43 33N 141 54 E
Takla L., *Canada* **142 B3** 55 15N 125 45W
Takla Landing, *Canada* **142 B3** 55 30N 125 50W
Takla Makan = Taklamakan Shamo, *China* **68 C3** 38 0N 83 0 E
Taklamakan Shamo, *China* **68 C3** 38 0N 83 0 E
Takotna, *U.S.A.* **144 E8** 62 59N 156 4W
Taku, *Japan* **72 D2** 33 18N 130 3 E
Taku →, *Canada* **142 B2** 58 30N 133 50W
Takua Thung, *Thailand* **87 a** 8 24N 98 27 E
Takum, *India* **90 B4** 27 47N 93 37 E
Takum, *Nigeria* **113 D6** 7 18N 9 36 E
Takundi, *Dem. Rep. of the Congo* **115 C3** 4 45 S 16 34 E
Takutu →, *Guyana* **169 C5** 3 1N 60 29W
Tal Halāl, *Iran* **97 D7** 28 54N 55 1 E
Tala, *Uruguay* **175 C4** 34 21 S 55 46W
Talachyn, *Belarus* **58 E5** 54 25N 29 42 E
Talacogan, *Phil.* **81 G5** 8 32N 125 39 E
Talagang, *Pakistan* **92 C5** 32 55N 72 25 E
Talagante, *Chile* **174 C1** 33 40 S 70 50W
Talahouhait, *Algeria* **111 D5** 24 52N 1 5 E
Talaimannar, *Sri Lanka* **95 K4** 9 6N 79 43 E
Talaïnt, *Morocco* **110 C3** 29 41N 9 40W
Talak, *Niger* **113 B6** 18 0N 5 0 E
Talakag, *Phil.* **81 G5** 8 16N 124 37 E
Talamanca, Cordillera de, *Cent. Amer.* **164 E3** 9 20N 83 20W
Talant, *France* **27 E11** 47 19N 4 58 E
Talara, *Peru* **172 A1** 4 38 S 81 18W
Talas, *Kyrgyzstan* **66 E8** 42 30N 72 13 E
Talas, *Turkey* **100 C6** 38 41N 35 33 E
Talas →, *Kazakstan* **65 B5** 44 0N 70 20 E
Talas Ala Too, *Kyrgyzstan* **65 B6** 42 15N 72 0 E
Talasea, *Papua N. G.* **132 C6** 5 20 S 150 2 E
Talasskiy Alatau = Talas Ala Too, *Kyrgyzstan* **65 B6** 42 15N 72 0 E
Talâta, *Egypt* **103 E1** 30 36N 32 20 E
Talata Mafara, *Nigeria* **113 C6** 12 38N 6 4 E
Talaud, Kepulauan, *Indonesia* **82 A3** 4 30N 126 50 E
Talaud Is. = Talaud, Kepulauan, *Indonesia* **82 A3** 4 30N 126 50 E
Talavera de la Reina, *Spain* **42 F6** 39 55N 4 46W
Talavera la Real, *Spain* **43 G4** 38 53N 6 46W
Talawgyi, *Burma* **90 C6** 25 4N 97 19 E
Talayan, *Phil.* **81 H5** 6 52N 124 24 E
Talayuela, *Spain* **42 F5** 39 59N 5 36W
Talbandh, *India* **93 H12** 22 3N 86 20 E
Talbert, Sillon de, *France* **26 D3** 48 53N 3 5W
Talbot, *Australia* **128 D5** 37 10 S 143 44 E
Talbot, C., *Australia* **124 B4** 13 48 S 126 43 E
Talbotton, *U.S.A.* **152 C5** 32 41N 84 32W
Talbragar →, *Australia* **129 B8** 32 12 S 148 37 E
Talca, *Chile* **174 D1** 35 28 S 71 40W
Talcahuano, *Chile* **174 D1** 36 40 S 73 10W
Talcher, *India* **94 D7** 21 0N 85 18 E
Talcho, *Niger* **113 C5** 14 44N 3 28 E
Taldy Kurgan = Taldyqorghan, *Kazakstan* **66 E8** 45 10N 78 45 E
Taldy-Suu, *Kyrgyzstan* **65 B9** 42 48N 78 26 E
Taldyqorghan, *Kazakstan* **66 E8** 45 10N 78 45 E
Tālesh, *Iran* **97 B6** 37 58N 48 58 E
Tālesh, Kūhhā-ye, *Iran* **97 B6** 37 42N 48 55 E
Talgar = Talghar, *Kazakstan* **65 B8** 43 19N 77 15 E
Talgar, Pik, *Kazakstan* **65 B8** 43 5N 77 20 E
Talghar, *Kazakstan* **65 B8** 43 19N 77 15 E
Talguharai, *Sudan* **106 D4** 18 19N 35 56 E
Talguppa, *India* **95 G2** 14 13N 74 56 E
Tali Post, *Sudan* **107 F3** 5 55N 30 44 E
Taliabu, *Indonesia* **82 B2** 1 50 S 125 0 E
Talibon, *Phil.* **81 F5** 10 9N 124 20 E
Talibong, Ko, *Thailand* **87 J2** 7 15N 99 23 E
Talihina, *U.S.A.* **155 H7** 34 45N 95 3W
Talikota, *India* **95 F3** 16 29N 76 17 E

Tin Amzi, O. →, *Algeria* **111 D6** 18 20N 4 32 E
Tin Atanai, *Algeria* **111 C5** 25 52N 1 37 E
Tin Can Bay, *Australia* **127 D5** 25 56 S 153 0 E
Tin Ethisane, *Mali* **113 B4** 19 3N 0 52W
Tin Gornai, *Mali* **113 B4** 16 38N 0 38W
Tin Mt., *U.S.A.* **160 J9** 36 50N 117 10W
Tina →, *S. Africa* **117 E4** 31 18 S 29 13 E
Tîna, Khalîg el, *Egypt* **106 A3** 31 20N 32 42 E
Tinaca Pt., *Phil.* **81 J5** 5 30N 125 25 E
Tinaco, *Venezuela* **168 B4** 9 42N 68 26W
Tinafak, O. →, *Algeria* **111 C6** 27 10N 7 0 E
Tinajo, *Canary Is.* **9 e2** 29 4N 13 42W
Tinca, *Romania* **52 D6** 46 46N 21 58 E
Tindal, *Australia* **124 B5** 14 31 S 132 22 E
Tindivanam, *India* **95 H4** 12 15N 79 41 E
Tindouf, *Algeria* **110 C3** 27 42N 8 10W
Tinée →, *France* **29 E11** 43 55N 7 11 E
Tineo, *Spain* **42 B4** 43 21N 6 27W
Tinerhir, *Morocco* **110 B3** 31 29N 5 31W
Tinfouchi, *Algeria* **110 C3** 28 52N 5 49W
Ting Jiang →, *China* **77 E11** 24 45N 116 35 E
Tinggi, Pulau, *Malaysia* **87 L5** 2 18N 104 7 E
Tingkawk Sakan, *Burma* **90 B6** 26 4N 96 44 E
Tinglayan, *Phil.* **80 C3** 17 15N 121 9 E
Tinglev, *Denmark* **17 K3** 54 57N 9 13 E
Tingo Maria, *Peru* **172 B2** 9 10 S 75 54W
Tingrela, *Ivory C.* **112 C3** 10 27N 6 25W
Tingsryd, *Sweden* **17 H9** 56 31N 15 0 E
Tingstäde, *Sweden* **17 G12** 57 44N 18 37 E
Tingvoll, *Norway* **18 B5** 62 55N 8 12 E
Tingwon Group, *Papua N. G.* **132 B5** 2 37 S 149 42 E
Tinh Bien, *Vietnam* **87 G5** 10 36N 104 57 E
Tinharé, I. de, *Brazil* **171 D4** 13 30 S 38 58W
Tiniguiban, *Phil.* **81 F2** 11 22N 119 30 E
Tinjar →, *Malaysia* **85 B4** 4 4N 114 18 E
Tinn = Atrå, *Norway* **18 E5** 59 59N 8 45 E
Tinnevelly = Tirunelveli, *India* **95 K3** 8 45N 77 45 E
Tinnoset, *Norway* **18 E6** 59 43N 9 3 E
Tinnsjø, *Norway* **18 E5** 59 55N 8 54 E
Tinogasta, *Argentina* **174 B2** 28 5 S 67 32W
Tínos, *Greece* **49 D7** 37 33N 25 8 E
Tiñoso, C., *Spain* **41 H3** 37 32N 1 6W
Tinpahar, *India* **93 G12** 24 59N 87 44 E
Tinputz, *Papua N. G.* **132 C8** 5 33 S 155 0 E
Tinsukia, *India* **90 B5** 27 29N 95 20 E
Tinta, *Peru* **172 C3** 14 3 S 71 20W
Tintina, *Argentina* **174 B3** 27 2 S 62 45W
Tintinara, *Australia* **128 C4** 35 48 S 140 2 E
Tintioulé, *Guinea* **112 C3** 10 13N 9 12W
Tinto →, *Spain* **43 H4** 37 12N 6 55W
Tinui, *N.Z.* **130 G5** 40 52 S 176 5 E
Tinwald, *N.Z.* **131 D6** 43 55 S 171 43 E
Tioga, *N. Dak., U.S.A.* **154 A3** 48 23N 102 56W
Tioga, *Pa., U.S.A.* **150 E7** 41 55N 77 8W
Tioman, Pulau, *Malaysia* **87 L5** 2 50N 104 10 E
Tione di Trento, *Italy* **44 B7** 46 2N 10 43 E
Tionesta, *U.S.A.* **150 E5** 41 30N 79 28W
Tior, *Sudan* **107 F3** 6 26N 31 11 E
Tioulilin, *Algeria* **111 C4** 27 1N 0 2W
Tipp City, *U.S.A.* **157 E12** 39 58N 84 11W
Tippecanoe →, *U.S.A.* **157 D10** 40 30N 86 45W
Tipperary, *Ireland* **23 D3** 52 28N 8 10W
Tipperary □, *Ireland* **23 D4** 52 37N 7 55W
Tipton, *Calif., U.S.A.* **160 J7** 36 4N 119 19W
Tipton, *Ind., U.S.A.* **157 D10** 40 17N 86 2W
Tipton, *Iowa, U.S.A.* **156 C5** 41 46N 91 8W
Tipton, *Mo., U.S.A.* **156 F4** 38 39N 92 47W
Tipton Mt., *U.S.A.* **161 K12** 35 32N 114 12W
Tiptonville, *U.S.A.* **155 G10** 36 23N 89 29W
Tiptur, *India* **95 H3** 13 15N 76 26 E
Tiquié →, *Brazil* **168 C4** 0 5N 68 25W
Tiracambu, Serra do, *Brazil* **170 B2** 3 15 S 46 30W
Tirahart, O. →, *Algeria* **111 D5** 23 45N 3 10 E
Tīrān, *Iran* **97 C6** 32 45N 51 8 E
Tīrān, *Si. Arabia* **106 B3** 27 57N 34 32 E
Tiranë, *Albania* **50 E3** 41 18N 19 49 E
Tirano, *Italy* **44 B7** 46 13N 10 10 E
Tiraspol, *Moldova* **53 D14** 46 55N 29 35 E
Tiratimine, *Algeria* **111 C5** 25 56N 3 37 E
Tirau, *N.Z.* **130 D4** 37 58 S 175 46 E
Tirdout, *Mali* **113 B4** 16 7N 1 5W
Tire, *Turkey* **49 C9** 38 5N 27 45 E
Tirebolu, *Turkey* **101 B8** 40 58N 38 45 E
Tiree, *U.K.* **22 E2** 56 31N 6 55W
Tiree, Passage of, *U.K.* **22 E2** 56 30N 6 30W
Tîrgovişte = Târgovişte, *Romania* **53 F10** 44 55N 25 27 E
Tîrgu-Jiu = Târgu-Jiu, *Romania* **53 E8** 45 5N 23 19 E
Tîrgu Mureş = Târgu Mureş, *Romania* **53 D9** 46 31N 24 38 E
Tirich Mir, *Pakistan* **91 A3** 36 15N 71 55 E
Tiriolo, *Italy* **47 D9** 38 57N 16 30 E
Tiririca, Serra da, *Brazil* **171 E2** 17 6 S 47 6W
Tiriro, *Guinea* **112 C3** 10 27N 8 40W
Tiris, *W. Sahara* **110 D2** 23 10N 13 20W
Tirlyanskiy, *Russia* **64 D7** 54 14N 58 35 E
Tirna →, *India* **94 E3** 18 4N 76 57 E
Tírnavos, *Greece* **48 B4** 39 45N 22 18 E
Tirodi, *India* **94 D4** 21 40N 79 44 E
Tirol □, *Austria* **34 D3** 47 3N 10 43 E
Tiros, *Brazil* **171 E2** 19 0 S 45 58W
Tirrukkovil, *Sri Lanka* **95 L5** 7 7N 81 51 E
Tirschenreuth, *Germany* **31 F8** 49 53N 12 19 E
Tirso →, *Italy* **46 C1** 39 53N 8 32 E
Tirstrup, *Denmark* **17 H4** 56 18N 10 42 E
Tirthahalli, *India* **95 H2** 13 42N 75 14 E
Tirua Pt., *N.Z.* **130 E3** 38 25 S 174 40 E
Tiruchchendur, *India* **95 K4** 8 30N 78 11 E
Tiruchchirappalli, *India* **95 J4** 10 45N 78 45 E
Tirukkoyilur, *India* **95 J4** 11 57N 79 12 E
Tirumangalam, *India* **95 K3** 9 49N 77 58 E
Tirumayam, *India* **95 J4** 10 14N 78 45 E
Tirunelveli, *India* **95 K3** 8 45N 77 45 E
Tirupati, *India* **95 H4** 13 39N 79 25 E
Tiruppattur, *Tamil Nadu, India* **95 J4** 10 8N 78 37 E
Tiruppattur, *Tamil Nadu, India* **95 H4** 12 30N 78 30 E
Tiruppur, *India* **95 J3** 11 5N 77 22 E
Tirur, *India* **95 J2** 10 54N 75 55 E
Tiruttani, *India* **95 H4** 13 11N 79 58 E
Tirutturaippundi, *India* **95 J4** 10 32N 79 41 E
Tiruvadaimarudur, *India* **95 J4** 11 2N 79 27 E
Tiruvalla, *India* **95 K3** 9 23N 76 34 E
Tiruvallar, *India* **95 H4** 13 9N 79 57 E
Tiruvannamalai, *India* **95 H4** 12 15N 79 5 E
Tiruvettipuram, *India* **95 H4** 12 39N 79 33 E
Tiruvottiyur, *India* **95 H5** 13 10N 80 22 E
Tisa, *India* **92 C7** 32 50N 76 9 E
Tisa →, *Serbia, Yug.* **52 E5** 45 15N 20 17 E
Tisdale, *Canada* **143 C8** 52 50N 104 0W
Tishomingo, *U.S.A.* **155 H6** 34 14N 96 41W
Tisjön, *Sweden* **16 D7** 60 56N 13 0 E
Tisnaren, *Sweden* **17 F9** 58 58N 15 56 E
Tišnov, *Czech Rep.* **35 B9** 49 21N 16 25 E
Tisovec, *Slovak Rep.* **35 C12** 48 41N 19 56 E
Tissamaharama, *Sri Lanka* **95 L5** 6 17N 81 17 E
Tissemsilt, *Algeria* **111 A5** 35 35N 1 50 E
Tissint, *Morocco* **110 C3** 29 57N 7 16W
Tista →, *India* **90 C2** 25 23N 89 43 E
Tistedal, *Norway* **18 E8** 59 8N 11 27 E
Tisza = Tisa →, *Serbia, Yug.* **52 E5** 45 15N 20 17 E
Tiszaföldvár, *Hungary* **52 D5** 46 58N 20 14 E
Tiszafüred, *Hungary* **52 C5** 47 38N 20 50 E
Tiszalök, *Hungary* **52 B6** 48 1N 21 20 E
Tiszavasvári, *Hungary* **52 C6** 47 58N 21 18 E
Tit, *Ahaggar, Algeria* **111 D6** 23 0N 5 10 E
Tit, *Tademait, Algeria* **111 C5** 27 0N 1 29 E
Tit-Ary, *Russia* **67 B13** 71 55N 127 2 E
Titabar, *India* **90 B5** 26 36N 94 12 E
Titaguas, *Spain* **40 F3** 39 53N 1 6W
Titao, *Burkina Faso* **113 C4** 13 45N 2 5W
Titel, *Serbia, Yug.* **52 E5** 45 10N 20 18 E
Tithwal, *Pakistan* **93 B5** 34 21N 73 50 E
Titicaca, L., *S. Amer.* **172 D4** 15 30 S 69 30W
Titisee, *Germany* **31 H4** 47 54N 8 10 E
Tititira Hd., *N.Z.* **131 D4** 43 36 S 169 25 E
Titiut, *Burma* **90 F5** 18 54N 95 16 E
Titiwa, *Nigeria* **113 C7** 12 14N 12 53 E
Titlagarh, *India* **94 D6** 20 15N 83 11 E
Titlis, *Switz.* **33 C6** 46 46N 8 27 E
Tito, *Italy* **47 B8** 40 35N 15 40 E
Titograd = Podgorica, *Montenegro, Yug.* **50 D3** 42 30N 19 19 E
Titova Korenica, *Croatia* **45 D12** 44 45N 15 41 E
Titu, *Romania* **53 F10** 44 39N 25 32 E
Titule, *Dem. Rep. of the Congo* **118 B2** 3 15N 25 31 E
Titusville, *Fla., U.S.A.* **149 L5** 28 37N 80 49W
Titusville, *Pa., U.S.A.* **150 E5** 41 38N 79 41W
Tivaouane, *Senegal* **112 C1** 14 56N 16 45W
Tivat, *Montenegro, Yug.* **50 D2** 42 28N 18 43 E
Tiverton, *U.K.* **21 G4** 50 54N 3 29W
Tívoli, *Italy* **45 G9** 41 58N 12 45 E
Tiwī, *Oman* **99 B7** 22 45N 59 12 E
Tiyo, *Eritrea* **107 E5** 14 41N 40 15 E
Tiyo, Peg., *Indonesia* **83 B5** 4 0 S 135 30 E
Tizga, *Morocco* **110 B3** 32 1N 5 9W
Ti'zi N'Isli, *Morocco* **110 B3** 32 28N 5 47W
Tizi-Ouzou, *Algeria* **111 A5** 36 42N 4 3 E
Tizimín, *Mexico* **163 C7** 21 0N 88 1W
Tiznados →, *Venezuela* **168 B4** 8 16N 67 47W
Tiznap He →, *China* **65 D8** 38 23N 77 24 E
Tiznit, *Morocco* **110 C3** 29 48N 9 45W
Tjæreborg, *Denmark* **17 J2** 55 28N 8 36 E
Tjällmo, *Sweden* **17 F9** 58 43N 15 21 E
Tjeggelvas, *Sweden* **14 C17** 66 37N 17 45 E
Tjirebon = Cirebon, *Indonesia* **85 D3** 6 45 S 108 32 E
Tjluring, *Indonesia* **79 J17** 8 25 S 114 13 E
Tjøme, *Norway* **18 E7** 59 8N 10 26 E
Tjörn, *Sweden* **17 F5** 58 0N 11 35 E
Tkibuli = Tqibuli, *Georgia* **61 J6** 42 26N 43 0 E
Tkvarcheli = Tqvarcheli, *Georgia* **61 J5** 42 47N 41 42 E
Tlacotalpan, *Mexico* **163 D5** 18 37N 95 40W
Tlahualilo, *Mexico* **162 B4** 26 20N 103 30W
Tlaquepaque, *Mexico* **162 C4** 20 39N 103 19W
Tlaxcala, *Mexico* **163 D5** 19 20N 98 14W
Tlaxcala □, *Mexico* **163 D5** 19 30N 98 20W
Tlaxiaco, *Mexico* **163 D5** 17 18N 97 40W
Tlemcen, *Algeria* **111 B4** 34 52N 1 21W
Tleta Sidi Bouguedra, *Morocco* **110 B3** 32 16N 9 59W
Tłuszcz, *Poland* **55 F8** 52 25N 21 25 E
Tlyarata, *Russia* **61 J8** 42 9N 46 26 E
Tmassah, *Libya* **108 C3** 26 19N 15 51 E
Tnine d'Anglou, *Morocco* **110 C3** 29 50N 9 50W
To Bong, *Vietnam* **86 F7** 12 45N 109 16 E
To-Shima, *Japan* **73 C11** 34 31N 139 17 E
Toa Payoh, *Singapore* **87 d** 1 20N 103 51 E
Toad →, *Canada* **142 B4** 59 25N 124 57W
Toad River, *Canada* **142 B3** 58 51N 125 14W
Toamasina, *Madag.* **117 B8** 18 10 S 49 25 E
Toamasina □, *Madag.* **117 B8** 18 0 S 49 0 E
Toay, *Argentina* **174 D3** 36 43 S 64 38W
Toba, *China* **76 B1** 31 19N 97 42 E
Toba, *Japan* **73 C8** 34 30N 136 51 E
Toba, Danau, *Indonesia* **84 B1** 2 30N 97 30 E
Toba Kakar, *Pakistan* **91 C3** 31 30N 69 0 E
Toba Tek Singh, *Pakistan* **92 D5** 30 55N 72 25 E
Tobago, *Trin. & Tob.* **165 D7** 11 10N 60 30W
Tobarra, *Spain* **41 G3** 38 37N 1 44W
Tobelo, *Indonesia* **82 A3** 1 45N 127 56 E
Tobermory, *Canada* **140 C3** 45 12N 81 40W
Tobermory, *U.K.* **22 E2** 56 38N 6 5W
Tobi, *Pac. Oc.* **83 A4** 2 40N 131 10 E
Tobias Fornier, *Phil.* **81 F3** 10 30N 121 57 E
Tobin, *U.S.A.* **160 F5** 39 55N 121 19W
Tobin, L., *Australia* **124 D4** 21 45 S 125 49 E
Tobin L., *Canada* **143 C8** 53 35N 103 30W
Toblach = Dobbiaco, *Italy* **45 B9** 46 44N 12 14 E
Toboali, *Indonesia* **84 C3** 3 0 S 106 25 E
Tobol, *Kazakstan* **64 E9** 52 40N 62 39 E
Tobol →, *Russia* **66 D7** 58 10N 68 12 E
Toboli, *Indonesia* **82 B2** 0 38 S 120 5 E
Tobolsk, *Russia* **66 D7** 58 15N 68 10 E
Tobor, *Senegal* **112 C1** 12 40N 16 15W
Toboso, *Phil.* **81 F4** 10 43N 123 31 E
Tobruk = Tubruq, *Libya* **108 B4** 32 7N 23 55 E
Tobyhanna, *U.S.A.* **151 E9** 41 11N 75 25W
Tobyl = Tobol →, *Russia* **66 D7** 58 10N 68 12 E
Tocache Nuevo, *Peru* **172 B2** 8 9 S 76 26W
Tocantínia, *Brazil* **170 C2** 9 33 S 48 22W
Tocantinópolis, *Brazil* **170 C2** 6 20 S 47 25W
Tocantins □, *Brazil* **170 D2** 10 0 S 48 0W
Tocantins →, *Brazil* **170 B2** 1 45 S 49 10W
Toccoa, *U.S.A.* **149 H4** 34 35N 83 19W
Toce →, *Italy* **44 C5** 45 56N 8 29 E
Tochi →, *Pakistan* **92 C4** 32 49N 70 41 E
Tochigi, *Japan* **73 A11** 36 25N 139 45 E
Tochigi □, *Japan* **73 A11** 36 45N 139 45 E
Tocina, *Spain* **43 H5** 37 37N 5 44W
Töcksfors, *Sweden* **16 E5** 59 31N 11 52 E
Toco, *Chile* **172 E4** 22 5 S 69 35W
Toco, *Trin. & Tob.* **169 F10** 10 50N 60 4W
Toconao, *Chile* **174 A2** 23 11 S 68 1W
Tocopilla, *Chile* **174 A1** 22 5 S 70 10W
Tocumwal, *Australia* **129 C6** 35 51 S 145 31 E
Tocuyo →, *Venezuela* **168 A4** 11 3N 68 23W
Tocuyo de la Costa, *Venezuela* **168 A4** 11 2N 68 23W
Todal, *Norway* **18 B5** 62 49N 8 44 E
Todd →, *Australia* **126 C2** 24 52 S 135 48 E
Todeli, *Indonesia* **82 B2** 1 40 S 124 29 E
Todenyang, *Kenya* **118 B4** 4 35N 35 56 E
Todgarh, *India* **92 G5** 25 42N 73 58 E
Todi, *Italy* **45 F9** 42 47N 12 24 E
Tödi, *Switz.* **33 C7** 46 48N 8 55 E
Todos os Santos, B. de, *Brazil* **171 D4** 12 48 S 38 38W
Todos Santos, *Mexico* **162 C2** 23 27N 110 13W
Todtnau, *Germany* **31 H3** 47 49N 7 56 E
Toe Hd., *U.K.* **22 D1** 57 50N 7 8W
Toecé, *Burkina Faso* **113 C4** 11 50N 1 16W
Toetoes B., *N.Z.* **131 G3** 46 42 S 168 41 E
Tofield, *Canada* **142 C6** 53 25N 112 40W
Tofino, *Canada* **142 D3** 49 11N 125 55W
Tofte, *Norway* **18 E7** 59 33N 10 34 E
Tofua, *Tonga* **133 P13** 19 45 S 175 5W
Toga, *Vanuatu* **133 C4** 13 26 S 166 42 E
Tōgane, *Japan* **73 B12** 35 33N 140 22 E
Togba, *Mauritania* **112 B2** 17 26N 10 12W
Togbo, *C.A.R.* **114 A3** 6 0N 17 27 E
Toggenburg, *Switz.* **33 B8** 47 16N 9 9 E
Togiak, *U.S.A.* **144 G7** 59 4N 160 24W
Togian, Kepulauan, *Indonesia* **82 B2** 0 20 S 121 50 E
Togliatti, *Russia* **60 D9** 53 32N 49 24 E
Togo ■, *W. Afr.* **113 D5** 8 30N 1 35 E
Togtoh, *China* **74 D6** 40 15N 111 10 E
Toguzak →, *Kazakstan* **64 D9** 54 3N 62 44 E
Tohma →, *Turkey* **100 C7** 38 29N 38 23 E
Tōhoku □, *Japan* **70 E10** 39 50N 141 45 E
Töhöm, *Mongolia* **74 B5** 44 27N 108 2 E
Tohopekaliga, L., *U.S.A.* **153 G8** 28 12N 81 24W
Toi, *Japan* **73 C10** 34 54N 138 47 E
Toibalewe, *India* **95 J11** 10 32N 92 30 E
Toili, *Indonesia* **82 B2** 1 24 S 122 26 E
Toinya, *Sudan* **107 F2** 6 17N 29 46 E
Toiyabe Range, *U.S.A.* **158 G5** 39 30N 117 0W
Tojikiston = Tajikistan ■, *Asia* **66 F8** 38 30N 70 0 E
Tojo, *Indonesia* **82 B2** 1 20 S 121 15 E
Tōjō, *Japan* **72 C5** 34 53N 133 16 E
Tok, *U.S.A.* **144 E12** 63 20N 142 59W
Tok →, *Russia* **64 E4** 52 46N 52 22 E
Tok-do, *Japan* **71 F5** 37 15N 131 52 E
Toka, *Guyana* **169 C6** 3 58N 59 17W
Tokaanu, *N.Z.* **130 E4** 38 58 S 175 46 E
Tokachi-Dake, *Japan* **70 C11** 43 17N 142 5 E
Tokachi-Gawa →, *Japan* **70 C11** 42 44N 143 42 E
Tokai, *Japan* **73 B8** 35 2N 136 55 E
Tokaj, *Hungary* **52 B6** 48 8N 21 27 E
Tokala, *Indonesia* **82 B2** 1 30 S 121 40 E
Tōkamachi, *Japan* **71 F9** 37 8N 138 43 E
Tokanui, *N.Z.* **131 G3** 46 34 S 168 56 E
Tokar, *Sudan* **106 D4** 18 27N 37 56 E
Tokara-Rettō, *Japan* **71 K4** 29 37N 129 43 E
Tokarahi, *N.Z.* **131 E5** 44 56 S 170 39 E
Tokashiki-Shima, *Japan* **71 L3** 26 11N 127 21 E
Tokat, *Turkey* **100 B7** 40 22N 36 35 E
Tokat □, *Turkey* **57 F6** 40 15N 36 30 E
Tŏkch'ŏn, *N. Korea* **75 E14** 39 45N 126 18 E
Tokeland, *U.S.A.* **160 D3** 46 42N 123 59W
Tokelau Is., *Pac. Oc.* **134 H10** 9 0 S 171 45W
Toki, *Japan* **73 B9** 35 18N 137 8 E
Tokmak, *Kyrgyzstan* **66 E8** 42 49N 75 15 E
Tokmak, *Ukraine* **59 J8** 47 16N 35 42 E
Toko Ra., *Australia* **126 C2** 23 5 S 138 20 E
Tokomaru Bay, *N.Z.* **130 E7** 38 8 S 178 22 E
Tokoname, *Japan* **73 C8** 34 53N 136 51 E
Tokoro-Gawa →, *Japan* **70 B12** 44 7N 144 5 E
Tokoroa, *N.Z.* **130 E4** 38 13 S 175 50 E
Tokorozawa, *Japan* **73 B11** 35 47N 139 28 E
Toksook Bay, *U.S.A.* **144 F6** 60 32N 165 0W
Toktogul, *Kyrgyzstan* **65 C6** 41 50N 72 50 E
Toktogul Suu Saktagychy, *Kyrgyzstan* **65 C6** 41 48N 72 51 E
Toku, *Tonga* **133 P13** 18 10 S 174 11W
Tokuji, *Japan* **72 C3** 34 11N 131 42 E
Tokuno-Shima, *Japan* **71 L4** 27 56N 128 55 E
Tokushima, *Japan* **72 C6** 34 4N 134 34 E
Tokushima □, *Japan* **72 D6** 33 55N 134 0 E
Tokuyama, *Japan* **72 C3** 34 3N 131 50 E
Tōkyō, *Japan* **73 B11** 35 45N 139 45 E
Tōkyō □, *Japan* **73 B11** 35 40N 139 30 E
Tōkyō-Wan, *Japan* **73 B11** 35 25N 139 47 E
Tokzār, *Afghan.* **91 B2** 35 52N 66 26 E
Tolaga Bay, *N.Z.* **130 E7** 38 21 S 178 20 E
Tolbukhin = Dobrich, *Bulgaria* **51 C11** 43 37N 27 49 E
Tolé, *C.A.R.* **114 A3** 6 34N 16 1 E
Töle Bī, *Kazakstan* **65 B6** 43 42N 73 46 E
Toledo, *Brazil* **175 A5** 24 44 S 53 45W
Toledo, *Phil.* **81 F4** 10 23N 123 38 E
Toledo, *Spain* **42 F6** 39 50N 4 2W
Toledo, *Ill., U.S.A.* **157 E8** 39 16N 88 15W
Toledo, *Iowa, U.S.A.* **156 C4** 42 0N 92 35W
Toledo, *Ohio, U.S.A.* **157 C13** 41 39N 83 33W
Toledo, *Oreg., U.S.A.* **158 D2** 44 37N 123 56W
Toledo, *Wash., U.S.A.* **158 C2** 46 26N 122 51W
Toledo, Montes de, *Spain* **43 F6** 39 33N 4 20W
Toledo Bend Reservoir, *U.S.A.* **155 K8** 31 11N 93 34W
Tolentino, *Italy* **45 E10** 43 12N 13 17 E
Tolfa, *Italy* **45 F8** 42 9N 11 56 E
Tolga, *Algeria* **111 B6** 34 40N 5 22 E
Tolga, *Australia* **126 B4** 17 15 S 145 29 E
Tolga, *Norway* **18 B8** 62 26N 11 1 E
Toliara, *Madag.* **117 C7** 23 21 S 43 40 E
Toliara □, *Madag.* **117 C8** 21 0 S 45 0 E
Tolima, *Colombia* **168 C2** 4 40N 75 19W
Tolima □, *Colombia* **168 C2** 3 45N 75 15W
Tolitoli, *Indonesia* **82 A2** 1 5N 120 50 E
Tolkmicko, *Poland* **54 D6** 54 19N 19 31 E
Tollarp, *Sweden* **17 J7** 55 55N 13 58 E
Tollensesee, *Germany* **30 B9** 53 30N 13 13 E
Tollhouse, *U.S.A.* **160 H7** 37 1N 119 24W
Tolmachevo, *Russia* **58 C5** 58 56N 29 51 E
Tolmezzo, *Italy* **45 B10** 46 24N 13 1 E
Tolmin, *Slovenia* **45 B10** 46 11N 13 45 E
Tolna, *Hungary* **52 D3** 46 25N 18 48 E
Tolna □, *Hungary* **52 D3** 46 30N 18 30 E
Tolo, *Dem. Rep. of the Congo* **114 C3** 2 55 S 18 34 E
Tolo, Teluk, *Indonesia* **82 B2** 2 20 S 122 10 E
Tolo Harbour, *China* **69 G11** 22 27N 114 12 E
Tolochin = Talachyn, *Belarus* **58 E5** 54 25N 29 42 E
Tolokiwa I., *Papua N. G.* **132 C4** 5 19 S 147 37 E
Tolong Bay, *Phil.* **81 G4** 9 20N 122 49 E
Tolono, *U.S.A.* **157 E8** 39 59N 88 16W
Tolosa, *Spain* **40 B2** 43 8N 2 5W
Tolox, *Spain* **43 J6** 36 41N 4 54W
Toltén, *Chile* **176 A2** 39 13 S 74 14W
Toluca, *Mexico* **163 D5** 19 20N 99 40W
Toluca, *U.S.A.* **156 C7** 41 0N 89 9W
Tolybay, *Kazakstan* **64 F9** 50 31N 62 19 E
Tom Burke, *S. Africa* **117 C4** 23 5 S 28 0 E
Tom Price, *Australia* **124 D2** 22 40 S 117 48 E
Toma, *Burkina Faso* **112 C4** 12 45N 2 53W
Tomah, *U.S.A.* **154 D9** 43 59N 90 30W
Tomahawk, *U.S.A.* **154 C10** 45 28N 89 44W
Tomai, *Moldova* **53 D13** 46 34N 28 19 E
Tomakomai, *Japan* **70 C10** 42 38N 141 36 E
Tomales, *U.S.A.* **160 G4** 38 15N 122 53W
Tomales B., *U.S.A.* **160 G3** 38 15N 123 58W
Tomanlivi, *Fiji* **133 A2** 17 37 S 178 1 E
Tomar, *Portugal* **43 F2** 39 36N 8 25W
Tómaros, Óros, *Greece* **48 B2** 39 29N 20 48 E
Tomarza, *Turkey* **100 C6** 38 27N 35 48 E
Tomás Barrón, *Bolivia* **172 D4** 17 35 S 67 31W
Tomaszów Lubelski, *Poland* **55 H10** 50 27N 23 25 E
Tomaszów Mazowiecki, *Poland* **55 G7** 51 30N 20 2 E
Tomatlán, *Mexico* **162 D3** 19 56N 105 15W
Tombadonkéa, *Guinea* **112 C2** 11 0N 14 25W
Tombador, Serra do, *Brazil* **173 C6** 12 0 S 58 0W
Tombe, *Sudan* **107 F3** 5 53N 31 40 E
Tombel, *Cameroon* **114 B1** 4 45N 9 40 E
Tombigbee →, *U.S.A.* **149 K2** 31 8N 87 57W
Tombôco, *Angola* **115 D2** 6 48 S 13 18 E
Tombouctou, *Mali* **112 B4** 16 50N 3 0W
Tombstone, *U.S.A.* **159 L8** 31 43N 110 4W
Tombua, *Angola* **116 B1** 15 55 S 11 55 E
Tomé, *Chile* **174 D1** 36 36 S 72 57W
Tomé-Açu, *Brazil* **170 B2** 2 25 S 48 9W
Tomelilla, *Sweden* **17 J7** 55 33N 13 58 E
Tomelloso, *Spain* **43 F7** 39 10N 3 2W
Tömenaryk, *Kazakstan* **65 A3** 44 2N 67 1 E
Tomingley, *Australia* **129 B8** 32 26 S 148 16 E
Tomini, *Indonesia* **82 A2** 0 30N 120 30 E
Tomini, Teluk, *Indonesia* **82 B2** 0 10 S 121 0 E
Tominian, *Mali* **112 C4** 13 17N 4 35W
Tomiño, *Spain* **42 D2** 41 59N 8 46W
Tomintoul, *U.K.* **22 D5** 57 15N 3 23W
Tomioka, *Japan* **73 A10** 36 15N 138 54 E
Tomislavgrad, *Bos.-H.* **52 G2** 43 42N 17 13 E
Tomkinson Ranges, *Australia* **125 E4** 26 11 S 129 5 E
Tommot, *Russia* **67 D13** 59 4N 126 20 E
Tomnop Ta Suos, *Cambodia* **87 G5** 11 20N 104 15 E
Tomo, *Colombia* **168 C4** 2 38N 67 32W
Tomo →, *Colombia* **168 B4** 5 20N 67 48W
Tomobe, *Japan* **73 A12** 36 20N 140 20 E
Tomra, *Norway* **18 B3** 62 34N 6 56 E
Toms Place, *U.S.A.* **160 H8** 37 34N 118 41W
Toms River, *U.S.A.* **151 G10** 39 58N 74 12W
Tomsk, *Russia* **66 D9** 56 30N 85 5 E
Tomtabacken, *Sweden* **17 G8** 57 30N 14 30 E
Tona, *Spain* **40 D7** 41 51N 2 14 E
Tonalá, *Mexico* **163 D6** 16 8N 93 41W
Tonale, Passo del, *Italy* **44 B7** 46 16N 10 35 E
Tonami, *Japan* **73 A8** 36 40N 136 58 E
Tonantins, *Brazil* **168 D4** 2 45 S 67 45W
Tonasket, *U.S.A.* **158 B4** 48 42N 119 26W
Tonate, *Fr. Guiana* **169 C7** 5 0N 52 28W
Tonawanda, *U.S.A.* **150 D6** 43 1N 78 53W
Tonbo, *Burma* **90 F5** 18 31N 95 5 E
Tonbridge, *U.K.* **21 F8** 51 11N 0 17 E
Tonda, *Papua N. G.* **132 E1** 8 55 S 141 34 E
Tondabayashi, *Japan* **73 C7** 34 30N 135 36 E
Tondano, *Indonesia* **82 A2** 1 35N 124 54 E
Tondela, *Portugal* **42 E2** 40 31N 8 5W
Tønder, *Denmark* **17 K2** 54 58N 8 50 E
Tondi, *India* **95 K4** 9 45N 79 4 E
Tondi Kiwindi, *Niger* **113 C5** 14 28N 2 2 E
Tondibi, *Mali* **113 B4** 16 39N 0 14W
Tondoro, *Namibia* **116 B2** 17 45 S 18 50 E
Tone →, *Australia* **125 F2** 34 25 S 116 25 E
Tone-Gawa →, *Japan* **73 B12** 35 44N 140 51 E
Tonekābon, *Iran* **97 B6** 36 45N 51 12 E
Tong I., *Papua N. G.* **132 B4** 2 2 S 147 47 E
Tong Xian, *China* **74 E9** 39 55N 116 35 E
Tôngâ, *Sudan* **107 F3** 9 28N 31 3 E
Tonga ■, *Pac. Oc.* **133 P13** 19 50 S 174 30W
Tonga Trench, *Pac. Oc.* **134 J10** 18 0 S 173 0W
Tongaat, *S. Africa* **117 D5** 29 33 S 31 9 E
Tongala, *Australia* **129 D6** 36 14 S 144 56 E
Tong'an, *China* **77 E12** 24 37N 118 8 E
Tongareva, *Cook Is.* **135 H12** 9 0 S 158 0W
Tongariro Nat. Park, *N.Z.* **130 F4** 39 8 S 175 33 E
Tongass Nat. Forest, *U.S.A.* **144 H14** 56 30N 134 0W
Tongatapu, *Tonga* **133 Q14** 21 10 S 174 0W
Tongatapu Group, *Tonga* **133 Q13** 21 0 S 175 0W
Tongbai, *China* **77 A9** 32 20N 113 23 E
Tongcheng, *Anhui, China* **77 B11** 31 4N 116 56 E
Tongcheng, *Hubei, China* **77 C9** 29 15N 113 50 E
Tongchŏn-ni, *N. Korea* **75 E14** 39 50N 127 25 E
Tongchuan, *China* **74 G5** 35 6N 109 3 E
Tongdao, *China* **76 D7** 26 10N 109 42 E
Tongeren, *Belgium* **24 D5** 50 47N 5 28 E
Tonggu, *China* **77 C10** 28 31N 114 20 E
Tonggu Jiao, *China* **69 G10** 22 22N 113 37 E
Tongguan, *China* **74 G6** 34 40N 110 25 E
Tonghai, *China* **76 E4** 24 10N 102 53 E
Tonghua, *China* **75 D13** 41 42N 125 58 E
Tongjiang, *China* **76 B6** 31 58N 107 11 E
Tongjosŏn Man, *N. Korea* **75 E15** 39 30N 128 0 E
Tongkil, *Phil.* **81 H3** 6 4N 121 48 E
Tongking, G. of = Tonkin, G. of, *Asia* **68 E5** 20 0N 108 0 E
Tongliang, *China* **76 C6** 29 50N 106 3 E
Tongliao, *China* **75 C12** 43 38N 122 18 E
Tongling, *China* **77 B11** 30 55N 117 48 E
Tonglu, *China* **77 C12** 29 45N 119 37 E
Tongnae, *S. Korea* **75 G15** 35 12N 129 5 E
Tongnan = Anyue, *China* **76 B5** 30 9N 105 50 E
Tongoa, *Vanuatu* **133 F6** 16 54 S 168 34 E
Tongobory, *Madag.* **117 C7** 23 32 S 44 20 E
Tongoy, *Chile* **174 C1** 30 16 S 71 31W
Tongquil I., *Phil.* **81 H3** 6 2N 121 51 E
Tongren, *China* **76 D7** 27 43N 109 11 E
Tongres = Tongeren, *Belgium* **24 D5** 50 47N 5 28 E
Tongsa Dzong, *Bhutan* **90 B3** 27 31N 90 31 E
Tongue, *U.K.* **22 C4** 58 29N 4 25W
Tongue →, *U.S.A.* **154 B2** 46 25N 105 52W
Tongwei, *China* **74 G3** 35 0N 105 5 E
Tongxiang, *China* **77 B13** 30 39N 120 34 E
Tongxin, *China* **74 F3** 36 59N 105 58 E
Tongyang, *N. Korea* **75 E14** 39 9N 126 53 E
Tongyu, *China* **75 B12** 44 45N 123 4 E
Tongzi, *China* **76 C6** 28 9N 106 49 E
Tonica, *U.S.A.* **156 C7** 41 13N 89 4W
Tonj, *Sudan* **107 F2** 7 20N 28 44 E
Tonj →, *Sudan* **107 F2** 7 31N 28 55 E
Tonk, *India* **92 F6** 26 6N 75 54 E
Tonkawa, *U.S.A.* **155 G6** 36 41N 97 18W
Tonkin = Bac Phan, *Vietnam* **86 B5** 22 0N 105 0 E
Tonkin, G. of, *Asia* **68 E5** 20 0N 108 0 E
Tonle Sap, *Cambodia* **86 F4** 13 0N 104 0 E
Tonnay-Charente, *France* **28 C3** 45 56N 0 55W
Tonneins, *France* **28 D4** 44 23N 0 19 E
Tonnerre, *France* **27 E10** 47 51N 3 59 E
Tönning, *Germany* **30 A4** 54 19N 8 56 E
Tono, *Japan* **70 E10** 39 19N 141 32 E
Tonopah, *U.S.A.* **159 G5** 38 4N 117 14W
Tonoshō, *Japan* **72 C6** 34 29N 134 11 E
Tonosí, *Panama* **164 E3** 7 20N 80 20W
Tons →, *Haryana, India* **92 D7** 30 30N 77 39 E
Tons →, *Ut. P., India* **93 F10** 26 1N 83 33 E
Tønsberg, *Norway* **15 G14** 59 19N 10 25 E
Tonsina, *U.S.A.* **144 F11** 61 39N 145 11W
Tonstad, *Norway* **18 F3** 58 40N 6 45 E
Tonumea, *Tonga* **133 Q13** 20 30 S 174 30W
Tonya, *Turkey* **101 B8** 40 53N 39 16 E
Tonzang, *Burma* **90 D4** 23 36N 93 42 E
Tonzi, *Burma* **90 C5** 24 39N 94 57 E
Toobanna, *Australia* **126 B4** 18 42 S 146 9 E
Toodyay, *Australia* **125 F2** 31 34 S 116 28 E
Tooele, *U.S.A.* **158 F7** 40 32N 112 18W
Toompine, *Australia* **127 D3** 27 15 S 144 19 E
Toomsboro, *U.S.A.* **152 C6** 32 50N 83 5W
Toora, *Australia* **129 E7** 38 39 S 146 23 E
Toora-Khem, *Russia* **67 D10** 52 28N 96 17 E
Toowoomba, *Australia* **127 D5** 27 32 S 151 56 E
Top-ozero, *Russia* **56 A5** 65 35N 32 0 E
Top Springs, *Australia* **124 C5** 16 37 S 131 51 E
Topalu, *Romania* **53 F13** 44 31N 28 3 E
Topaz, *U.S.A.* **160 G7** 38 41N 119 30W
Topeka, *U.S.A.* **154 F7** 39 3N 95 40W
Topl'a →, *Slovak Rep.* **35 C14** 48 45N 21 45 E
Topley, *Canada* **142 C3** 54 49N 126 18W
Toplica →, *Serbia, Yug.* **50 C5** 43 15N 21 49 E
Toplița, *Romania* **53 D10** 46 55N 25 20 E
Topo, *Azores* **9 d1** 38 33N 27 45W
Topo, Pta. do, *Azores* **9 d1** 38 33N 27 46W
Topocalma, Pta., *Chile* **174 C1** 34 10 S 72 2W
Topock, *U.S.A.* **161 L12** 34 46N 114 29W
Topola, *Serbia, Yug.* **50 B4** 44 17N 20 41 E
Topolčani, *Macedonia* **50 E5** 41 14N 21 25 E
Topol'čany, *Slovak Rep.* **35 C11** 48 35N 18 12 E
Topolnitsa →, *Bulgaria* **51 D8** 42 11N 24 18 E
Topolobampo, *Mexico* **162 B3** 25 40N 109 4W
Topoloveni, *Romania* **53 F10** 44 49N 25 5 E
Topolovgrad, *Bulgaria* **51 D10** 42 5N 26 20 E
Topolvățu Mare, *Romania* **52 E6** 45 46N 21 41 E
Toppenish, *U.S.A.* **158 C3** 46 23N 120 19W
Topraisar, *Romania* **53 F13** 44 1N 28 27 E
Topusko, *Croatia* **45 C12** 45 18N 15 59 E

U

Urgench = Urganch, *Uzbekistan* **66 E7** 41 40N 60 41 E
Ürgüp, *Turkey* **96 B2** 38 38N 34 56 E
Urgut, *Uzbekistan* **65 D3** 39 23N 67 15 E
Uri, *India* **93 B6** 34 8N 74 2 E
Uri □, *Switz.* **33 C7** 46 43N 8 35 E
Uribante →, *Venezuela* **168 B3** 7 25N 71 50W
Uribe, *Colombia* **168 C3** 3 13N 74 24W
Uribia, *Colombia* **168 A3** 11 43N 72 16W
Uricani, *Romania* **52 E8** 45 20N 23 9 E
Urimba, *Angola* **115 E3** 10 56 S 16 32 E
Uriondo, *Bolivia* **174 A3** 21 41 S 64 41W
Urique, *Mexico* **162 B3** 27 13N 107 55W
Urique →, *Mexico* **162 B3** 26 29N 107 58W
Urirotstock, *Switz.* **33 C7** 46 52N 8 32 E
Urk, *Neths.* **24 B5** 52 39N 5 36 E
Urla, *Turkey* **49 C8** 38 20N 26 47 E
Urlaţi, *Romania* **53 F11** 44 59N 26 15 E
Urmia = Orūmīyeh, *Iran* **101 D11** 37 40N 45 0 E
Urmia, L. = Orūmīyeh, Daryācheh-ye, *Iran* **101 D11** 37 50N 45 30 E
Urnäsch, *Switz.* **33 B8** 47 19N 9 17 E
Urner Alpen, *Switz.* **33 C7** 46 45N 8 45 E
Uroševac, *Kosovo, Yug.* **50 D5** 42 23N 21 10 E
Uroteppa, *Tajikistan* **65 D4** 39 55N 69 1 E
Uroyan, Montanas de, *Puerto Rico* **165 d** 18 12N 67 0W
Urrao, *Colombia* **168 B2** 6 20N 76 11W
Urshult, *Sweden* **17 H8** 56 31N 14 50 E
Uruaçu, *Brazil* **171 D2** 14 30 S 49 10W
Uruana, *Brazil* **171 E2** 15 30 S 49 41W
Uruapan, *Mexico* **162 D4** 19 30N 102 0W
Uruará, *Brazil* **169 D7** 3 42 S 53 51W
Uruará →, *Brazil* **169 D7** 2 6 S 53 38W
Urubamba, *Peru* **172 C3** 13 20 S 72 10W
Urubamba →, *Peru* **172 C3** 10 43 S 73 48W
Urubaxi →, *Brazil* **169 D5** 0 31 S 64 50W
Urubu →, *Brazil* **169 D6** 2 55 S 58 25W
Uruçara, *Brazil* **169 D6** 2 32 S 57 45W
Uruçuí, *Brazil* **170 C3** 7 20 S 44 28W
Uruçuí, Serra do, *Brazil* **170 C3** 9 0 S 44 45W
Uruçuí Prêto →, *Brazil* **170 C3** 7 20 S 44 38W
Urucuia →, *Brazil* **171 E2** 16 8 S 45 5W
Urucurituba, *Brazil* **169 D6** 2 41 S 57 40W
Uruguai →, *Brazil* **175 B5** 26 0 S 53 30W
Uruguaiana, *Brazil* **174 B4** 29 50 S 57 0W
Uruguay ■, *S. Amer.* **174 C4** 32 30 S 56 30W
Uruguay →, *S. Amer.* **174 C4** 34 12 S 58 18W
Urumchi = Ürümqi, *China* **66 E9** 43 45N 87 45 E
Ürümqi, *China* **66 E9** 43 45N 87 45 E
Urup →, *Russia* **61 H5** 45 0N 41 10 E
Urup, Ostrov, *Russia* **67 E16** 46 0N 151 0 E
Urutaí, *Brazil* **171 E2** 17 28 S 48 12W
Uryupinsk, *Russia* **60 E5** 50 45N 41 58 E
Urzhum, *Russia* **60 B9** 57 10N 49 56 E
Urziceni, *Romania* **53 F11** 44 40N 26 42 E
Usa, *Japan* **72 D3** 33 31N 131 21 E
Usa →, *Russia* **56 A10** 66 16N 59 49 E
Uşak, *Turkey* **49 C11** 38 43N 29 28 E
Uşak □, *Turkey* **49 C11** 38 30N 29 0 E
Usakos, *Namibia* **116 C2** 21 54 S 15 31 E
Usborne, Mt., *Falk. Is.* **9 f** 51 40 S 59 55W
Ušće, *Serbia, Yug.* **50 C4** 43 30N 20 39 E
Usedom, *Germany* **30 B10** 53 55N 14 2 E
Useless Loop, *Australia* **125 E1** 26 8 S 113 23 E
'Usfān, *Si. Arabia* **98 B2** 21 58N 39 27 E
Ush-Tobe, *Kazakstan* **66 E8** 45 16N 78 0 E
Ushakova, Ostrov, *Russia* **6 A12** 82 0N 80 0 E
Ushant = Ouessant, Î. d', *France* **26 D1** 48 28N 5 6W
Usharal, *Kazakstan* **65 B5** 43 53N 70 31 E
Ushashi, *Tanzania* **118 C3** 1 59 S 33 57 E
Ushat, *Sudan* **107 F2** 7 59N 29 28 E
'Ushayrah, *Si. Arabia* **106 C5** 21 46N 40 42 E
Ushibuka, *Japan* **72 E2** 32 11N 130 1 E
Ushuaia, *Argentina* **176 D3** 54 50 S 68 23W
Ushumun, *Russia* **67 D13** 52 47N 126 32 E
Usino, *Papua N. G.* **132 C3** 5 32 S 145 23 E
Usk, *Canada* **142 C3** 54 38N 128 26W
Usk →, *U.K.* **21 F5** 51 33N 2 58W
Uska, *India* **93 F10** 27 12N 83 7 E
Uskedal, *Norway* **18 E2** 59 56N 5 53 E
Üsküdar, *Turkey* **51 F13** 41 0N 29 5 E
Uslar, *Germany* **30 D5** 51 39N 9 38 E
Usman, *Russia* **59 F10** 52 5N 39 48 E
Usmat, *Uzbekistan* **65 D3** 39 45N 67 38 E
Usoke, *Tanzania* **118 D3** 5 8 S 32 24 E
Usolye, *Russia* **64 B6** 59 28N 56 31 E
Usolye Sibirskoye, *Russia* **67 D11** 52 48N 103 40 E
Usoro, *Nigeria* **113 D6** 5 33N 6 11 E
Uspallata, P. de, *Argentina* **174 C2** 32 37 S 69 22W
Uspenskiy, *Kazakstan* **66 E8** 48 41N 72 43 E
Ussel, *France* **28 C6** 45 32N 2 18 E
Usson-du-Poitou, *France* **28 B4** 46 16N 0 31 E
Ussuri →, *Asia* **70 A7** 48 27N 135 0 E
Ussuriysk, *Russia* **67 E14** 43 48N 131 59 E
Ussurka, *Russia* **70 B6** 45 12N 133 31 E
Ust-Aldan = Batamay, *Russia* **67 C13** 63 30N 129 15 E
Ust-Amginskoye = Khandyga, *Russia* **67 C14** 62 42N 135 35 E
Ust-Bolsheretsk, *Russia* **67 D16** 52 50N 156 15 E
Ust-Buzulukskaya, *Russia* **60 E6** 50 8N 42 11 E
Ust-Chaun, *Russia* **67 C18** 68 47N 170 30 E
Ust-Donetskiy, *Russia* **61 G5** 47 35N 40 55 E
Ust-Ilimpeya = Yukta, *Russia* **67 C11** 63 26N 105 42 E
Ust-Ilimsk, *Russia* **67 D11** 58 3N 102 39 E
Ust-Ishim, *Russia* **66 D8** 57 45N 71 10 E
Ust-Kamchatsk, *Russia* **67 D17** 56 10N 162 28 E
Ust-Kamenogorsk = Öskemen, *Kazakstan* **66 E9** 50 0N 82 36 E
Ust-Khayryuzovo, *Russia* **67 D16** 57 15N 156 45 E
Ust-Kut, *Russia* **67 D11** 56 50N 105 42 E
Ust-Kuyga, *Russia* **67 B14** 70 1N 135 43 E
Ust-Labinsk, *Russia* **61 H4** 45 15N 39 41 E
Ust-Luga, *Russia* **58 C5** 59 35N 28 20 E
Ust-Maya, *Russia* **67 C14** 60 30N 134 28 E
Ust-Mil, *Russia* **67 D14** 59 40N 133 11 E
Ust-Nera, *Russia* **67 C15** 64 35N 143 15 E
Ust-Nyukzha, *Russia* **67 D13** 56 34N 121 37 E
Ust-Olenek, *Russia* **67 B12** 73 0N 120 5 E
Ust-Omchug, *Russia* **67 C15** 61 9N 149 38 E
Ust-Port, *Russia* **66 C9** 69 40N 84 26 E
Ust-Tsilma, *Russia* **56 A9** 65 28N 52 11 E
Ust Urt = Ustyurt Plateau, *Asia* **66 E6** 44 0N 55 0 E
Ust-Usa, *Russia* **56 A10** 66 2N 56 57 E
Ust-Vorkuta, *Russia* **56 A11** 67 24N 64 0 E
Ustaoset, *Norway* **18 D5** 60 30N 8 2 E
Ustaritz, *France* **28 E2** 43 24N 1 27W
Uster, *Switz.* **33 B7** 47 22N 8 43 E
Ústí nad Labem, *Czech Rep.* **34 A7** 50 41N 14 3 E
Ústí nad Orlicí, *Czech Rep.* **35 B9** 49 58N 16 24 E
Ústica, *Italy* **46 D6** 38 42N 13 11 E
Ustinov = Izhevsk, *Russia* **64 C4** 56 51N 53 14 E
Ustka, *Poland* **54 D3** 54 35N 16 55 E
Ustroń, *Poland* **55 J5** 49 43N 18 48 E
Ustrzyki Dolne, *Poland* **55 J9** 49 27N 22 40 E
Ustupo, *Panama* **168 B2** 9 27N 78 34W
Ustyurt Plateau, *Asia* **66 E6** 44 0N 55 0 E
Ustyuzhna, *Russia* **58 C9** 58 50N 36 32 E
Usu, *China* **68 B3** 44 27N 84 40 E
Usuki, *Japan* **72 D3** 33 8N 131 49 E
Usulután, *El Salv.* **164 D2** 13 25N 88 28W
Usumacinta →, *Mexico* **163 D6** 17 0N 91 0W
Usumbura = Bujumbura, *Burundi* **118 C2** 3 16 S 29 18 E
Usure, *Tanzania* **118 C3** 4 40 S 34 22 E
Usutuo →, *Mozam.* **117 D5** 26 48 S 32 7 E
Usva, *Russia* **64 B6** 58 41N 57 37 E
Uta, *Indonesia* **83 B5** 4 33 S 136 0 E
Utah □, *U.S.A.* **158 G8** 39 20N 111 30W
Utah L., *U.S.A.* **158 F8** 40 10N 111 58W
Utansjö, *Sweden* **16 B11** 62 46N 17 55 E
Utara, Selat, *Malaysia* **87 c** 5 28N 100 20 E
Utarni, *India* **92 F4** 26 5N 71 58 E
Utatlan, *Guatemala* **164 C1** 15 2N 91 11W
Ute Creek →, *U.S.A.* **155 H3** 35 21N 103 50W
Utebo, *Spain* **40 D3** 41 43N 1 0W
Utemurat, *Uzbekistan* **65 B2** 42 6N 65 42 E
Utena, *Lithuania* **15 J21** 55 27N 25 40 E
Utete, *Tanzania* **118 D4** 8 0 S 38 45 E
Uthai Thani, *Thailand* **86 E3** 15 22N 100 3 E
Uthal, *Pakistan* **92 G2** 25 44N 66 40 E
Utiariti, *Brazil* **173 C6** 13 0 S 58 10W
Utica, *N.Y., U.S.A.* **151 C9** 43 6N 75 14W
Utica, *Ohio, U.S.A.* **150 F2** 40 14N 82 27W
Utiel, *Spain* **41 F3** 39 37N 1 11W
Utikuma L., *Canada* **142 B5** 55 50N 115 30W
Utinga, *Brazil* **171 D3** 12 6 S 41 5W
Utkela, *India* **94 D6** 20 6N 83 10 E
Utne, *Norway* **18 D3** 60 25N 6 37 E
Utnur, *India* **94 E4** 19 22N 78 46 E
Uto, *Japan* **72 E2** 32 41N 130 40 E
Utö, *Sweden* **16 F12** 58 56N 18 16 E
Utopia, *Australia* **126 C1** 22 14 S 134 33 E
Utraula, *India* **93 F10** 27 19N 82 25 E
Utrecht, *Neths.* **24 B5** 52 5N 5 8 E
Utrecht, *S. Africa* **117 D5** 27 38 S 30 20 E
Utrecht □, *Neths.* **24 B5** 52 6N 5 7 E
Utrera, *Spain* **43 H5** 37 12N 5 48W
Utsira, *Norway* **18 E1** 59 19N 4 53 E
Utsjoki, *Finland* **14 B22** 69 51N 26 59 E
Utsunomiya, *Japan* **73 A11** 36 30N 139 50 E
Uttar Pradesh □, *India* **93 F9** 27 0N 80 0 E
Uttaradit, *Thailand* **86 D3** 17 36N 100 5 E
Uttaranchal □, *India* **93 D8** 30 0N 79 30 E
Uttoxeter, *U.K.* **20 E6** 52 54N 1 52W
Utuado, *Puerto Rico* **165 d** 18 16N 66 42W
Utva →, *Kazakstan* **64 F4** 51 28N 52 40 E
Uummannaq, *Greenland* **10 B4** 77 0N 69 0W
Uummannarsuaq = Nunap Isua, *Greenland* **10 F6** 59 48N 43 55W
Uusikaarlepyy, *Finland* **14 E20** 63 32N 22 31 E
Uusikaupunki, *Finland* **15 F19** 60 47N 21 25 E
Uva, *Russia* **60 B11** 56 59N 52 13 E
Uvá →, *Colombia* **168 C3** 3 41N 70 3W
Uvac →, *Serbia, Yug.* **50 C3** 43 35N 19 30 E
Uvalda, *U.S.A.* **152 C7** 32 2N 82 31W
Uvalde, *U.S.A.* **155 L5** 29 13N 99 47W
Uvarovo, *Russia* **60 E6** 51 59N 42 14 E
Uvat, *Russia* **66 D7** 59 5N 68 50 E
Uvdal, *Norway* **18 D5** 60 17N 8 48 E
Uvelskiy, *Russia* **64 D8** 54 26N 61 22 E
Uvinza, *Tanzania* **118 D3** 5 5 S 30 24 E
Uvira, *Dem. Rep. of the Congo* **118 C2** 3 22 S 29 3 E
Uvs Nuur, *Mongolia* **68 A4** 50 20N 92 30 E
Uwa, *Japan* **72 D4** 33 22N 132 31 E
'Uwairidh, Ḩarrat al, *Si. Arabia* **96 E3** 26 50N 38 0 E
Uwajima, *Japan* **72 D4** 33 10N 132 35 E
Uwanda Game Reserve, *Tanzania* **118 D3** 7 46 S 32 0 E
Uweinat, Jebel, *Sudan* **106 C1** 21 54N 24 58 E
Uwekuli, *Indonesia* **82 B2** 1 25 S 121 6 E
Uxbridge, *Canada* **150 B5** 44 6N 79 7W
Uxin Qi, *China* **74 E5** 38 50N 109 5 E
Uxmal, *Mexico* **163 C7** 20 22N 89 46W
Uyak, *U.S.A.* **144 H9** 57 38N 154 0W
Üydzin, *Mongolia* **74 B4** 44 9N 107 0 E
Uyo, *Nigeria* **113 D6** 5 1N 7 53 E
Uyu →, *Burma* **90 C5** 24 51N 94 57 E
Uyuk = Oyyq, *Kazakstan* **65 B5** 43 36N 71 16 E
Üyüklü Tepe, *Turkey* **49 D9** 37 5N 27 21 E
Uyûn Mûsa, *Egypt* **103 F1** 29 53N 32 40 E
Uyuni, *Bolivia* **172 E4** 20 28 S 66 47W
Uzbekistan ■, *Asia* **66 E7** 41 30N 65 0 E
Uzen, *Kazakstan* **57 F9** 43 29N 52 54 E
Uzen, Bolshoi →, *Kazakstan* **61 F9** 49 6N 49 56 E
Uzen, Mal →, *Kazakstan* **61 F9** 49 4N 49 44 E
Uzerche, *France* **28 C5** 45 25N 1 34 E
Uzès, *France* **29 D8** 44 1N 4 26 E
Uzgen = Özgön, *Kyrgyzstan* **65 C6** 40 46N 73 18 E
Uzh →, *Ukraine* **59 G6** 51 15N 30 12 E
Uzhgorod = Uzhhorod, *Ukraine* **59 H2** 48 36N 22 18 E
Uzhhorod, *Ukraine* **59 H2** 48 36N 22 18 E
Užice, *Serbia, Yug.* **50 C3** 43 55N 19 50 E
Uzlovaya, *Russia* **58 F10** 54 0N 38 5 E
Üzümlü, *Turkey* **49 E11** 36 44N 29 14 E
Uzunköprü, *Turkey* **51 E10** 41 16N 26 43 E
Uzunkuyu, *Turkey* **49 C8** 38 17N 26 33 E
Uzwil, *Switz.* **33 B8** 47 26N 9 9 E
Uzynaghash, *Kazakstan* **65 B8** 43 35N 76 20 E
Uzynaghash, *Kazakstan* **65 B8** 43 13N 76 19 E

V

Vaal →, *S. Africa* **116 D3** 29 4 S 23 38 E
Vaal Dam, *S. Africa* **117 D4** 27 0 S 28 14 E
Vaalbos Nat. Park, *S. Africa* **116 D3** 28 22 S 24 20 E
Vaalwater, *S. Africa* **117 C4** 24 15 S 28 8 E
Vaasa, *Finland* **14 E19** 63 6N 21 38 E
Vabkent, *Uzbekistan* **65 C2** 40 1N 64 30 E
Vabre, *France* **28 E6** 43 42N 2 24 E
Vác, *Hungary* **52 C4** 47 49N 19 10 E
Vacaria, *Brazil* **175 B5** 28 31 S 50 52W
Vacata, *Fiji* **133 A3** 17 15 S 179 31W
Vacaville, *U.S.A.* **160 G5** 38 21N 121 59W
Vaccarès, Étang de, *France* **29 E8** 43 32N 4 34 E
Vach = Vakh →, *Russia* **66 C8** 60 45N 76 45 E
Vache, Î. à, *Haiti* **165 C5** 18 2N 73 35W
Väckelsång, *Sweden* **17 H8** 56 37N 14 58 E
Vacoas, *Mauritius* **121 d** 20 18 S 57 29 E
Vada, *India* **94 E1** 19 39N 73 8 E
Väddö, *Sweden* **16 D12** 60 0N 18 50 E
Väderstad, *Sweden* **17 F8** 58 19N 14 55 E
Vadheim, *Norway* **18 C2** 61 13N 5 49 E
Vadnagar, *India* **92 H5** 23 47N 72 40 E
Vado Lígure, *Italy* **44 D5** 44 17N 8 26 E
Vadodara, *India* **92 H5** 22 20N 73 10 E
Vadret, Piz, *Switz.* **33 C9** 46 51N 9 58 E
Vadsø, *Norway* **14 A23** 70 3N 29 50 E
Vadstena, *Sweden* **17 F8** 58 28N 14 54 E
Vaduj, *India* **94 F2** 17 36N 74 27 E
Vaduz, *Liech.* **33 B9** 47 8N 9 31 E
Værlandet, *Norway* **18 C1** 61 18N 4 44 E
Værøy, *Norway* **14 C15** 67 40N 12 40 E
Vagalat, *Albania* **38 B10** 39 44N 20 8 E
Vågåmo, *Norway* **18 C6** 61 52N 9 6 E
Vágar, *Færoe Is.* **14 E9** 62 5N 7 15W
Vaggeryd, *Sweden* **17 G8** 57 30N 14 10 E
Vaghena, *Solomon Is.* **133 L9** 7 25 S 157 45 E
Vagney, *France* **27 D13** 48 1N 6 43 E
Vagnhärad, *Sweden* **17 F11** 58 57N 17 33 E
Vagos, *Portugal* **42 E2** 40 33N 8 42W
Vågsfjorden, *Norway* **14 B17** 68 50N 16 50 E
Váh →, *Slovak Rep.* **35 D11** 47 43N 18 7 E
Vahsel B., *Antarctica* **7 D1** 75 0 S 35 0W
Váï, *Greece* **39 E7** 35 15N 26 18 E
Vaigach, *Russia* **66 B6** 70 10N 59 0 E
Vaigai →, *India* **95 K4** 9 15N 79 10 E
Vaiges, *France* **26 D6** 48 2N 0 30W
Vaihingen, *Germany* **31 G4** 48 54N 8 57 E
Vaijapur, *India* **94 E2** 19 58N 74 45 E
Vaikam, *India* **95 K3** 9 45N 76 25 E
Vail, *U.S.A.* **146 C5** 39 40N 106 20W
Vailala →, *Papua N. G.* **132 D3** 7 57 S 145 25 E
Vailly-sur-Aisne, *France* **27 C10** 49 24N 3 31 E
Vaippar →, *India* **95 K4** 9 0N 78 25 E
Vaisali →, *India* **93 F8** 26 28N 78 53 E
Vaison-la-Romaine, *France* **29 D9** 44 14N 5 4 E
Vaitogi, *Amer. Samoa* **133 X24** 14 24 S 170 44W
Vajpur, *India* **94 D1** 21 24N 73 17 E
Vakaga →, *C.A.R.* **114 A4** 9 48N 21 32 E
Vakarai, *Sri Lanka* **95 K5** 8 8N 81 26 E
Vakarel, *Bulgaria* **50 D7** 42 35N 23 40 E
Vakfikebir, *Turkey* **101 B8** 41 2N 39 17 E
Vakh →, *Russia* **66 C8** 60 45N 76 45 E
Vakhsh, *Tajikistan* **65 E4** 37 43N 68 50 E
Vakhsh →, *Tajikistan* **65 E4** 37 6N 68 18 E
Vakhtan, *Russia* **60 B8** 57 53N 46 47 E
Vaksdal, *Norway* **18 D2** 60 29N 5 45 E
Vakuta I., *Papua N. G.* **132 E6** 8 51 S 151 10 E
Vál, *Hungary* **52 C3** 47 22N 18 40 E
Val-de-Marne □, *France* **27 D9** 48 45N 2 28 E
Val-d'Isère, *France* **29 C10** 45 27N 6 59 E
Val-d'Oise □, *France* **27 C9** 49 5N 2 10 E
Val-d'Or, *Canada* **140 C4** 48 7N 77 47W
Val Marie, *Canada* **143 D7** 49 15N 107 45W
Valaam, *Russia* **58 B6** 61 22N 30 57 E
Valadares, *Portugal* **42 D2** 41 5N 8 38W
Valahia, *Romania* **53 F9** 44 35N 25 0 E
Valaichenai, *Sri Lanka* **95 L5** 7 54N 81 32 E
Valais □, *Switz.* **32 D5** 46 12N 7 45 E
Valais, Alpes du, *Switz.* **32 D5** 46 5N 7 35 E
Valandovo, *Macedonia* **50 E6** 41 19N 22 34 E
Valašské Meziříčí, *Czech Rep.* **35 B10** 49 29N 17 59 E
Valáxa, *Greece* **48 C6** 38 50N 24 29 E
Vålberg, *Sweden* **16 E7** 59 23N 13 11 E
Valbo, *Sweden* **16 D10** 60 40N 17 0 E
Valbondione, *Italy* **44 B7** 46 2N 10 1 E
Vălcani, *Romania* **52 D5** 46 0N 20 26 E
Vâlcea □, *Romania* **53 F9** 45 0N 24 10 E
Valcheta, *Argentina* **176 B3** 40 40 S 66 8W
Valdagno, *Italy* **45 C8** 45 39N 11 18 E
Valdahon, *France* **27 E13** 47 8N 6 21 E
Valday, *Russia* **58 D7** 57 58N 33 9 E
Valdayskaya Vozvyshennost, *Russia* **58 D7** 57 0N 33 30 E
Valdeazogues →, *Spain* **43 G6** 38 45N 4 55W
Valdecañas, Embalse de, *Spain* **42 F5** 39 45N 5 25W
Valdemarsvik, *Sweden* **17 F10** 58 14N 16 40 E
Valdemoro, *Spain* **42 E7** 40 12N 3 40W
Valdepeñas, *Spain* **43 G7** 38 43N 3 25W
Valderaduey →, *Spain* **42 D5** 41 31N 5 42W
Valdérice, *Italy* **46 D5** 38 4N 12 37 E
Valderrobres, *Spain* **40 E5** 40 53N 0 9 E
Valdés, Pen., *Argentina* **176 B4** 42 30 S 63 45W
Valdez, *Ecuador* **168 C2** 1 15N 79 0W
Valdez, *U.S.A.* **144 F11** 61 7N 146 16W
Valdivia, *Chile* **176 A2** 39 50 S 73 14W
Valdivia, *Colombia* **168 B2** 7 11N 75 27W
Valdobbiádene, *Italy* **45 C8** 45 54N 12 0 E
Valdosta, *U.S.A.* **152 E6** 30 50N 83 17W
Valdoviño, *Spain* **42 B2** 43 36N 8 8W
Valdres, *Norway* **15 F13** 61 5N 9 5 E
Vale, *Georgia* **61 K6** 41 30N 42 58 E
Vale, *U.S.A.* **158 E5** 43 59N 117 15W
Vale of Glamorgan □, *U.K.* **21 F4** 51 28N 3 25W
Valea lui Mihai, *Romania* **52 C7** 47 32N 22 11 E
Valea Mărului, *Romania* **53 E12** 45 49N 27 42 E
Valemount, *Canada* **142 C5** 52 50N 119 15W
Valença, *Brazil* **171 D4** 13 20 S 39 5W
Valença, *Portugal* **42 C2** 42 1N 8 34W
Valença do Piauí, *Brazil* **170 C3** 6 20 S 41 45W
Valençay, *France* **27 E8** 47 9N 1 34 E
Valence = Valence d'Agen, *France* **28 D4** 44 6N 0 53 E
Valence, *France* **29 D8** 44 57N 4 54 E
Valence d'Agen, *France* **28 D4** 44 6N 0 53 E
Valencia, *Phil.* **81 H5** 7 57N 125 3 E
Valencia, *Spain* **41 F4** 39 27N 0 23W
Valencia, *Trin. & Tob.* **169 F9** 10 39N 61 11W
Valencia, *U.S.A.* **159 J10** 34 48N 106 43W
Valencia, *Venezuela* **168 A4** 10 11N 68 0W
Valencia □, *Spain* **41 F4** 39 20N 0 40W
Valencia, G. de, *Spain* **41 F5** 39 30N 0 20 E
Valencia de Alcántara, *Spain* **43 F3** 39 25N 7 14W
Valencia de Don Juan, *Spain* **42 C5** 42 17N 5 31W
Valencia I., *Ireland* **23 E1** 51 54N 10 22W
Valenciennes, *France* **27 B10** 50 20N 3 34 E
Văleni, *Romania* **53 F9** 44 15N 24 45 E
Vălenii de Munte, *Romania* **53 E11** 45 11N 26 2 E
Valensole, *France* **29 E9** 43 50N 5 59 E
Valentigney, *France* **27 E13** 47 27N 6 51 E
Valentim, Sa. do, *Brazil* **170 C3** 6 0 S 43 30W
Valentin, *Russia* **70 C7** 43 8N 134 17 E
Valentine, *U.S.A.* **155 K2** 30 35N 104 30W
Valenza, *Italy* **44 C5** 45 1N 8 38 E
Våler, *Hedmark, Norway* **18 D8** 60 41N 11 50 E
Våler, *Østfold, Norway* **18 E7** 59 29N 10 51 E
Valera, *Venezuela* **168 B3** 9 19N 70 37W
Valesdir, *Vanuatu* **133 F6** 16 47 S 168 10 E
Valestrand, *Norway* **18 E2** 59 40N 5 26 E
Valga, *Estonia* **15 H22** 57 47N 26 2 E
Valguarnera Caropepe, *Italy* **47 E7** 37 30N 14 23 E
Valier, *U.S.A.* **158 B7** 48 18N 112 16W
Valinco, G. de, *France* **29 G12** 41 40N 8 52 E
Valjevo, *Serbia, Yug.* **50 B3** 44 18N 19 53 E
Valka, *Latvia* **15 H21** 57 42N 25 57 E
Valkeakoski, *Finland* **15 F20** 61 16N 24 2 E
Valkenswaard, *Neths.* **24 C5** 51 21N 5 29 E
Vall de Uxó = La Vall d'Uixó, *Spain* **40 F4** 39 49N 0 15W
Valla, *Sweden* **16 E10** 59 2N 16 20 E
Valladolid, *Mexico* **163 C7** 20 40N 88 11W
Valladolid, *Spain* **42 D6** 41 38N 4 43W
Valladolid □, *Spain* **42 D6** 41 38N 4 43W
Vallata, *Italy* **47 A8** 41 2N 15 15 E
Valldemossa, *Spain* **38 B3** 39 43N 2 37 E
Valle, *Norway* **18 E4** 59 13N 7 33 E
Valle d'Aosta □, *Italy* **44 C4** 45 45N 7 15 E
Valle de Arán, *Spain* **40 C5** 42 50N 0 55 E
Valle de la Pascua, *Venezuela* **168 B4** 9 13N 66 0W
Valle de las Palmas, *Mexico* **161 N10** 32 20N 116 43W
Valle de Santiago, *Mexico* **162 C4** 20 25N 101 15W
Valle de Suchil, *Mexico* **162 C4** 23 38N 103 55W
Valle de Zaragoza, *Mexico* **162 B3** 27 28N 105 49W
Valle del Cauca □, *Colombia* **168 C2** 3 45N 76 30W
Valle Fértil, Sierra del, *Argentina* **174 C2** 30 20 S 68 0W
Valle Hermoso, *Mexico* **163 B5** 25 35N 97 40W
Valledupar, *Colombia* **168 A3** 10 29N 73 15W
Vallehermoso, *Canary Is.* **9 e1** 28 10N 17 15W
Vallejo, *U.S.A.* **160 G4** 38 7N 122 14W
Vallenar, *Chile* **174 B1** 28 30 S 70 50W
Vallentuna, *Sweden* **16 E12** 59 32N 18 5 E
Valleraugue, *France* **28 D7** 44 6N 3 39 E
Vallet, *France* **26 E5** 47 10N 1 15W
Valletta, *Malta* **38 F8** 35 54N 14 31 E
Valley Center, *U.S.A.* **161 M9** 33 13N 117 2W
Valley City, *U.S.A.* **154 B6** 46 55N 98 0W
Valley Falls, *Oreg., U.S.A.* **158 E3** 42 29N 120 17W
Valley Falls, *R.I., U.S.A.* **151 E13** 41 54N 71 24W
Valley of the Kings, *Egypt* **110 B3** 25 41N 32 34 E
Valley Springs, *U.S.A.* **160 G6** 38 12N 120 50W
Valley Station, *U.S.A.* **157 F11** 38 6N 85 52W
Valley View, *U.S.A.* **151 F8** 40 39N 76 33W
Valley Wells, *U.S.A.* **161 K11** 35 27N 115 46W
Valleyview, *Canada* **142 B5** 55 5N 117 17W
Valli di Comácchio, *Italy* **45 D9** 44 40N 12 15 E
Vallimanca, Arroyo, *Argentina* **174 D4** 35 40 S 59 10W
Vallo della Lucánia, *Italy* **47 B8** 40 14N 15 16 E
Vallon-Pont-d'Arc, *France* **29 D8** 44 24N 4 24 E
Vallorbe, *Switz.* **32 C2** 46 42N 6 20 E
Valls, *Spain* **40 D6** 41 18N 1 15 E
Valmaseda = Balmaseda, *Spain* **40 B1** 43 11N 3 12W
Valmeyer, *U.S.A.* **156 F6** 38 18N 90 19W
Valmiera, *Latvia* **15 H21** 57 37N 25 29 E
Valnera, *Spain* **42 B7** 43 9N 3 40W
Valognes, *France* **26 C5** 49 30N 1 28W
Valona = Vlorë, *Albania* **50 F3** 40 32N 19 28 E
Valongo, *Portugal* **42 D2** 41 8N 8 30W
Valozhyn, *Belarus* **58 E4** 54 3N 26 30 E
Valpaços, *Portugal* **42 D3** 41 36N 7 17W
Valparai, *India* **95 J3** 10 22N 76 58 E
Valparaíso, *Chile* **174 C1** 33 2 S 71 40W
Valparaíso, *Mexico* **162 C4** 22 50N 103 32W
Valparaiso, *Fla., U.S.A.* **153 E3** 30 29N 86 30W
Valparaiso, *Ind., U.S.A.* **157 C9** 41 28N 87 4W
Valparaíso □, *Chile* **174 C1** 33 2 S 71 40W
Valpovo, *Croatia* **52 E3** 45 39N 18 25 E
Valpoy, *India* **95 G2** 15 32N 74 8 E
Valréas, *France* **29 D9** 44 24N 5 0 E
Vals, *Switz.* **33 C8** 46 39N 9 11 E
Vals →, *S. Africa* **116 D4** 27 23 S 26 30 E
Vals, Tanjung, *Indonesia* **83 C5** 8 26 S 137 25 E
Vals-les-Bains, *France* **29 D8** 44 42N 4 24 E
Valsad, *India* **94 D1** 20 40N 72 58 E
Valsamáta, *Greece* **39 C2** 38 10N 20 36 E
Valtellina, *Italy* **44 B6** 46 11N 9 55 E
Valþjofsstaður, *Iceland* **11 B12** 65 1N 14 59W
Valtí, *Greece* **39 C3** 38 27N 21 7 E
Valuyki, *Russia* **59 G10** 50 10N 38 5 E
Valverde, *Canary Is.* **9 e1** 27 48N 17 55W
Valverde del Camino, *Spain* **43 H4** 37 35N 6 47W
Valverde del Fresno, *Spain* **42 E4** 40 15N 6 51W
Vama, *Romania* **53 C10** 47 34N 25 42 E
Vambori, *India* **94 E2** 19 17N 74 44 E
Vamdrup, *Denmark* **17 J3** 55 25N 9 17 E
Våmhus, *Sweden* **16 C8** 61 7N 14 29 E
Vammala, *Finland* **15 F20** 61 20N 22 54 E
Vámos, *Greece* **39 E5** 35 24N 24 13 E
Vamsadhara →, *India* **94 E7** 18 21N 84 8 E
Van, *Turkey* **101 C10** 38 30N 43 20 E
Van, L. = Van Gölü, *Turkey* **101 C10** 38 30N 43 0 E
Van Alstyne, *U.S.A.* **155 J6** 33 25N 96 35W
Van Blommestein Meer, *Surinam* **169 C6** 4 45N 55 5W
Van Buren, *Canada* **141 C6** 47 10N 67 55W
Van Buren, *Ark., U.S.A.* **155 H7** 35 26N 94 21W
Van Buren, *Maine, U.S.A.* **149 B11** 47 10N 67 58W
Van Buren, *Mo., U.S.A.* **155 G9** 37 0N 91 1W
Van Canh, *Vietnam* **86 F7** 13 37N 109 0 E
Van Diemen, C., *N. Terr., Australia* **124 B5** 11 9 S 130 24 E
Van Diemen, C., *Queens., Australia* **126 B2** 16 30 S 139 46 E
Van Diemen G., *Australia* **124 B5** 11 45 S 132 0 E
Van Gölü, *Turkey* **101 C10** 38 30N 43 0 E
Van Horn, *U.S.A.* **155 K2** 31 3N 104 50W
Van Horne, *U.S.A.* **156 B4** 42 1N 92 4W
Van Meter, *U.S.A.* **156 C3** 41 32N 93 57W
Van Ninh, *Vietnam* **86 F7** 12 42N 109 14 E
Van Rees, Pegunungan, *Indonesia* **83 B5** 2 35 S 138 15 E
Van Tivu, *India* **95 K4** 8 51N 78 15 E
Van Wert, *U.S.A.* **157 D12** 40 52N 84 35W
Van Yen, *Vietnam* **76 G5** 21 4N 104 42 E
Vanadzor, *Armenia* **61 K7** 40 48N 44 30 E
Vanavara, *Russia* **67 C11** 60 22N 102 16 E
Vanceburg, *U.S.A.* **157 F13** 38 36N 83 19W
Vancouver, *Canada* **142 D4** 49 15N 123 10W
Vancouver, *U.S.A.* **160 E4** 45 38N 122 40W
Vancouver, C., *Australia* **125 G2** 35 2 S 118 11 E
Vancouver, Mt., *U.S.A.* **144 F13** 60 20N 139 41W
Vancouver I., *Canada* **142 D3** 49 50N 126 0W
Vandalia, *Ill., U.S.A.* **156 F7** 38 58N 89 6W
Vandalia, *Mo., U.S.A.* **156 E5** 39 19N 91 29W
Vandalia, *Ohio, U.S.A.* **157 E12** 39 54N 84 12W
Vandavasi, *India* **95 H4** 12 30N 79 30 E
Vandeloos B., *Sri Lanka* **95 L5** 8 0N 81 45 E
Vandenburg, *U.S.A.* **161 L6** 34 35N 120 33W
Vanderbijlpark, *S. Africa* **117 D4** 26 42 S 27 54 E
Vandergrift, *U.S.A.* **150 F5** 40 36N 79 34W
Vanderhoof, *Canada* **142 C4** 54 0N 124 0W
Vanderkloof Dam, *S. Africa* **116 E3** 30 4 S 24 40 E
Vanderlin I., *Australia* **126 B2** 15 44 S 137 2 E
Vänern, *Sweden* **17 F7** 58 47N 13 30 E
Vänersborg, *Sweden* **17 F6** 58 26N 12 19 E
Vang, *Norway* **18 C5** 61 7N 8 34 E
Vang Vieng, *Laos* **86 C4** 18 58N 102 32 E
Vanga, *Kenya* **118 C4** 4 35 S 39 12 E
Vangaindrano, *Madag.* **117 C8** 23 21 S 47 36 E
Vangsnes, *Norway* **18 C3** 61 9N 6 39 E
Vanguard, *Canada* **143 D7** 49 55N 107 20W
Vangunu, *Solomon Is.* **133 M10** 8 40 S 158 5 E
Vanimo, *Papua N. G.* **83 B6** 2 42 S 141 21 E
Vanino, *Russia* **67 E15** 48 50N 140 5 E
Vanivilasa Sagara, *India* **95 H3** 13 45N 76 30 E
Vaniyambadi, *India* **95 H4** 12 46N 78 44 E
Vanj, *Tajikistan* **65 D5** 38 22N 71 27 E
Vânju Mare, *Romania* **52 F7** 44 25N 22 52 E
Vanna, *Norway* **14 A18** 70 6N 19 50 E
Vännäs, *Sweden* **14 E18** 63 58N 19 48 E
Vannes, *France* **26 E4** 47 40N 2 47W
Vanoise, *France* **29 C10** 45 25N 6 40 E
Vanrhynsdorp, *S. Africa* **116 E2** 31 36 S 18 44 E
Vansada, *India* **94 D1** 20 47N 73 25 E
Vansbro, *Sweden* **16 D8** 60 32N 14 15 E
Vanse, *Norway* **18 F3** 58 6N 6 41 E
Vansittart B., *Australia* **124 B4** 14 3 S 126 17 E
Vantaa, *Finland* **15 F21** 60 18N 24 58 E
Vanua Balavu, *Fiji* **133 A3** 17 12 S 178 55W
Vanua Lava, *Vanuatu* **133 C5** 13 50 S 167 30 E
Vanua Levu, *Fiji* **133 A2** 16 33 S 179 15 E
Vanua Vatu, *Fiji* **133 B3** 18 22 S 179 15W
Vanuatu ■, *Pac. Oc.* **133 E6** 15 0 S 168 0 E
Vanwyksvlei, *S. Africa* **116 E3** 30 18 S 21 49 E
Vanzylsrus, *S. Africa* **116 D3** 26 52 S 22 4 E
Vapnyarka, *Ukraine* **59 H5** 48 32N 28 45 E
Var □, *France* **29 E10** 43 27N 6 18 E
Var →, *France* **29 E11** 43 39N 7 12 E
Vara, *Sweden* **17 F6** 58 16N 12 55 E
Vara, Pico da, *Azores* **9 d3** 37 48N 25 13W
Varada →, *India* **95 G2** 15 0N 75 40 E
Varades, *France* **26 E5** 47 25N 1 1W
Varáita →, *Italy* **44 D4** 44 9N 7 53 E
Varaldsøy, *Norway* **18 D2** 60 6N 5 59 E
Varallo, *Italy* **44 C5** 45 49N 8 15 E
Varanasi, *India* **93 G10** 25 22N 83 0 E
Varangerfjorden, *Norway* **14 A23** 70 3N 29 25 E
Varangerhalvøya, *Norway* **14 A23** 70 25N 29 30 E
Varano, Lago di, *Italy* **45 G12** 41 53N 15 45 E

W

Wanganella, *Australia* 129 C6 35 6 S 144 49 E
Wanganui, *N.Z.* 130 F4 39 56 S 175 3 E
Wanganui →, *W. Coast, N.Z.* 131 D5 43 3 S 170 26 E
Wanganui →, *Wanganui-Manawatu, N.Z.* 130 F4 39 55 S 175 4 E
Wangaratta, *Australia* 129 D7 36 21 S 146 19 E
Wangary, *Australia* 127 E2 34 35 S 135 29 E
Wangcang, *China* 76 A6 32 18N 106 20 E
Wangcheng, *China* 77 C9 28 22N 112 49 E
Wangdu, *China* 74 E8 38 40N 115 7 E
Wangdu Phodrang, *Bhutan* 90 B2 27 28N 89 54 E
Wangen, *Germany* 31 H5 47 41N 9 50 E
Wangerooge, *Germany* 30 B3 53 47N 7 54 E
Wangi, *Kenya* 118 C5 1 58 S 40 58 E
Wängi, *Switz.* 33 B7 47 30N 8 57 E
Wangiwangi, *Indonesia* 82 C2 5 22 S 123 37 E
Wangjiang, *China* 77 B11 30 10N 116 42 E
Wangmo, *China* 76 E6 25 11N 106 5 E
Wangolodougou, *Ivory C.* 112 D3 9 55N 5 10W
Wangqing, *China* 75 C15 43 12N 129 42 E
Wani, *India* 94 D4 20 5N 78 55 E
Wanigela, *Papua N. G.* 132 E5 9 21 S 149 9 E
Wankaner, *India* 92 H4 22 35N 71 0 E
Wanlaweyne = Uanle Uen, *Somali Rep.* 120 D2 2 37N 44 54 E
Wanless, *Canada* 143 C8 54 11N 101 21W
Wannian, *China* 77 C11 28 42N 117 4 E
Wanning, *China* 86 C8 18 48N 110 22 E
Wanon Niwat, *Thailand* 86 D4 17 38N 103 46 E
Wanqinsha, *China* 69 F10 22 43N 113 33 E
Wanquan, *China* 74 D8 40 50N 114 40 E
Wanrong, *China* 74 G6 35 25N 110 50 E
Wanshan, *China* 76 D7 27 30N 109 12 E
Wanshan Qundao, *China* 69 G10 21 57N 113 45 E
Wanshengchang, *China* 76 C6 28 57N 106 53 E
Wanstead, *N.Z.* 130 G5 40 8 S 176 30 E
Wantage, *U.K.* 21 F6 51 35N 1 25W
Wanyin, *Burma* 90 E6 20 23N 97 15 E
Wanyuan, *China* 76 A7 32 4N 108 3 E
Wanzai, *Guangdong, China* 69 G10 22 12N 113 31 E
Wanzai, *Jiangxi, China* 77 C10 28 7N 114 30 E
Wapakoneta, *U.S.A.* 157 D12 40 34N 84 12W
Wapato, *U.S.A.* 158 C3 46 27N 120 25W
Wapawekka L., *Canada* 143 C8 54 55N 104 40W
Wapello, *U.S.A.* 156 C5 41 11N 91 11W
Wapikopa L., *Canada* 140 B2 52 56N 87 53W
Wapinda, *Dem. Rep. of the Congo* 114 B4 3 41N 22 48 E
Wapiti →, *Canada* 142 B5 55 5N 118 18W
Wappingers Falls, *U.S.A.* 151 E11 41 36N 73 55W
Wapsipinicon →, *U.S.A.* 156 C6 41 44N 90 19W
Warab □, *Sudan* 107 F2 7 30N 28 30 E
Warabi, *Japan* 73 B11 35 49N 139 41 E
Warangal, *India* 94 F4 17 58N 79 35 E
Waraseoni, *India* 93 J9 21 45N 80 2 E
Waratah, *Australia* 127 G4 41 30 S 145 30 E
Waratah B., *Australia* 129 E7 38 54 S 146 5 E
Warburg, *Germany* 30 D5 51 28N 9 11 E
Warburton, *Vic., Australia* 129 D6 37 47 S 145 42 E
Warburton, *W. Austral., Australia* 125 E4 26 8 S 126 35 E
Warburton Ra., *Australia* 125 E4 25 55 S 126 28 E
Ward, *N.Z.* 131 B9 41 49 S 174 11 E
Ward →, *Australia* 127 D4 26 28 S 146 6 E
Ward Hunt, C., *Papua N. G.* 132 E5 8 2 S 148 10 E
Ward Hunt Str., *Papua N. G.* 132 E6 9 30 S 150 0 E
Ward Mt., *U.S.A.* 160 H8 37 12N 118 54W
Wardang I., *Australia* 128 C2 34 30 S 137 20 E
Warden, *S. Africa* 117 D4 27 50 S 29 0 E
Wardha, *India* 94 D4 20 45N 78 39 E
Wardija Point, *Malta* 38 E6 36 2N 14 11 E
Wardo, *Indonesia* 83 B5 1 2 S 135 50 E
Ware, *Canada* 142 B3 57 26N 125 41W
Ware, *U.S.A.* 151 D12 42 16N 72 14W
Waregem, *Belgium* 24 D3 50 53N 3 27 E
Wareham, *U.S.A.* 151 E14 41 46N 70 43W
Waremme, *Belgium* 24 D5 50 43N 5 15 E
Waren, *Germany* 30 B8 53 31N 12 40 E
Waren, *Indonesia* 83 B5 2 16 S 136 20 E
Warendorf, *Germany* 30 D4 51 57N 8 1 E
Waresboro, *U.S.A.* 152 D7 31 15N 82 29W
Waria →, *Papua N. G.* 132 D4 7 49 S 147 41 E
Warialda, *Australia* 127 D5 29 29 S 150 33 E
Wariap, *Indonesia* 83 B4 1 30 S 134 5 E
Warin Chamrap, *Thailand* 86 E5 15 12N 104 53 E
Warka, *Poland* 55 G8 51 47N 21 12 E
Warkopi, *Indonesia* 83 B4 1 12 S 134 9 E
Warkworth, *N.Z.* 130 C3 36 24 S 174 41 E
Warm Springs, *Ga., U.S.A.* 152 C5 32 53N 84 41W
Warm Springs, *Nev., U.S.A.* 159 G5 38 10N 116 20W
Warman, *Canada* 143 C7 52 19N 106 30W
Warmandi, *Indonesia* 83 B4 0 22 S 132 39 E
Warmbad, *Namibia* 116 D2 28 25 S 18 42 E
Warmbad, *S. Africa* 117 C4 24 51 S 28 19 E
Warmińsko-Mazurskie □, *Poland* 54 D8 54 0N 21 0 E
Warminster, *U.K.* 21 F5 51 12N 2 10W
Warminster, *U.S.A.* 151 F9 40 12N 75 6W
Warnemünde, *Germany* 30 A8 54 10N 12 4 E
Warner Mts., *U.S.A.* 158 F3 41 40N 120 15W
Warner Robins, *U.S.A.* 152 C6 32 37N 83 36W
Warnes, *Bolivia* 173 D5 17 30 S 63 10W
Warnow →, *Germany* 30 A8 54 6N 12 9 E
Waroona, *Australia* 125 F2 32 50 S 115 58 E
Warora, *India* 94 D4 20 14N 79 1 E
Warracknabeal, *Australia* 128 D5 36 9 S 142 26 E
Warragul, *Australia* 129 E6 38 10 S 145 58 E
Warrego →, *Australia* 127 E4 30 24 S 145 21 E
Warrego Ra., *Australia* 126 C4 24 58 S 146 0 E
Warren, *Australia* 129 A7 31 42 S 147 51 E
Warren, *Ark., U.S.A.* 155 J8 33 37N 92 4W
Warren, *Ill., U.S.A.* 156 B7 42 29N 90 0W
Warren, *Ind., U.S.A.* 157 D11 40 41N 85 26W
Warren, *Mich., U.S.A.* 157 B13 42 30N 83 0W
Warren, *Minn., U.S.A.* 154 A6 48 12N 96 46W
Warren, *Ohio, U.S.A.* 150 E4 41 14N 80 49W
Warren, *Pa., U.S.A.* 150 E5 41 51N 79 9W
Warrenpoint, *U.K.* 23 B5 54 6N 6 15W
Warrensburg, *Ill., U.S.A.* 156 E7 39 56N 89 4W
Warrensburg, *Mo., U.S.A.* 156 F3 38 46N 93 44W
Warrensburg, *N.Y., U.S.A.* 151 C11 43 29N 73 46W
Warrenton, *S. Africa* 116 D3 28 9 S 24 47 E
Warrenton, *Ga., U.S.A.* 152 B7 33 24N 82 40W
Warrenton, *Mo., U.S.A.* 156 F5 38 49N 91 9W
Warrenton, *Oreg., U.S.A.* 160 D3 46 10N 123 56W
Warrenville = Gloverville, *U.S.A.* 152 B8 33 32N 81 48W
Warri, *Nigeria* 113 D6 5 30N 5 41 E
Warrina, *Australia* 127 D2 28 12 S 135 50 E
Warrington, *N.Z.* 131 F5 45 43 S 170 35 E
Warrington, *U.K.* 20 D5 53 24N 2 35W
Warrington, *U.S.A.* 149 K2 30 23N 87 17W
Warrington □, *U.K.* 20 D5 53 24N 2 35W
Warrnambool, *Australia* 128 E5 38 25 S 142 30 E
Warroad, *U.S.A.* 154 A7 48 54N 95 19W
Warrumbungle Nat. Park, *Australia* 129 A8 31 18 S 149 1 E
Warruwi, *Australia* 126 A1 11 36 S 133 20 E
Warsa, *Indonesia* 83 B5 0 47 S 135 55 E
Warsak Dam, *Pakistan* 92 B4 34 11N 71 19 E
Warsaw = Warszawa, *Poland* 55 F8 52 13N 21 0 E
Warsaw, *Ill., U.S.A.* 156 D5 40 22N 91 26W
Warsaw, *Ind., U.S.A.* 157 C11 41 14N 85 51W
Warsaw, *Ky., U.S.A.* 157 F12 38 47N 84 54W
Warsaw, *Mo., U.S.A.* 156 F3 38 15N 93 23W
Warsaw, *N.Y., U.S.A.* 150 D6 42 45N 78 8W
Warsaw, *Ohio, U.S.A.* 150 F3 40 20N 82 0W
Warstein, *Germany* 30 D4 51 26N 8 22 E
Warszawa, *Poland* 55 F8 52 13N 21 0 E
Warta, *Poland* 55 G5 51 43N 18 38 E
Warta →, *Poland* 55 F1 52 35N 14 39 E
Warth, *Austria* 33 B10 47 15N 10 11 E
Warthe = Warta →, *Poland* 55 F1 52 35N 14 39 E
Warthen, *U.S.A.* 152 B7 33 6N 82 48W
Waru, *Indonesia* 83 B4 3 30 S 130 36 E
Warud, *India* 94 D4 21 30N 78 16 E
Warwick, *Australia* 127 D5 28 10 S 152 1 E
Warwick, *U.K.* 21 E6 52 18N 1 35W
Warwick, *Ga., U.S.A.* 152 D6 31 50N 83 57W
Warwick, *N.Y., U.S.A.* 151 E10 41 16N 74 22W
Warwick, *R.I., U.S.A.* 151 E13 41 42N 71 28W
Warwickshire □, *U.K.* 21 E6 52 14N 1 38W
Wasaga Beach, *Canada* 150 B4 44 31N 80 1W
Wasagaming, *Canada* 143 C9 50 39N 99 58W
Wasatch Ra., *U.S.A.* 158 F8 40 30N 111 15W
Wasbank, *S. Africa* 117 D5 28 15 S 30 9 E
Wasco, *Calif., U.S.A.* 161 K7 35 36N 119 20W
Wasco, *Oreg., U.S.A.* 158 D3 45 36N 120 42W
Wase, *Nigeria* 113 D6 9 4N 9 54 E
Waseca, *U.S.A.* 154 C8 44 5N 93 30W
Wasekamio L., *Canada* 143 B7 56 45N 108 45W
Wash, The, *U.K.* 20 E8 52 58N 0 20 E
Washago, *Canada* 150 B5 44 45N 79 20W
Washburn, *Ill., U.S.A.* 156 D7 40 55N 89 17W
Washburn, *N. Dak., U.S.A.* 154 B4 47 17N 101 2W
Washburn, *Wis., U.S.A.* 154 B9 46 40N 90 54W
Washim, *India* 94 D3 20 3N 77 0 E
Washington, *U.K.* 20 C6 54 55N 1 30W
Washington, *D.C., U.S.A.* 148 F7 38 54N 77 2W
Washington, *Ga., U.S.A.* 152 B7 33 44N 82 44W
Washington, *Ill., U.S.A.* 156 D7 40 42N 89 24W
Washington, *Ind., U.S.A.* 157 F9 38 40N 87 10W
Washington, *Iowa, U.S.A.* 156 C5 41 18N 91 42W
Washington, *Mo., U.S.A.* 156 F5 38 33N 91 1W
Washington, *N.C., U.S.A.* 149 H7 35 33N 77 3W
Washington, *N.J., U.S.A.* 151 F10 40 46N 74 59W
Washington, *Pa., U.S.A.* 150 F4 40 10N 80 15W
Washington, *Utah, U.S.A.* 159 H7 37 8N 113 31W
Washington □, *U.S.A.* 158 C3 47 30N 120 30W
Washington, Mt., *U.S.A.* 151 B13 44 16N 71 18W
Washington Court House, *U.S.A.* 157 E13 39 32N 83 26W
Washington I., *U.S.A.* 148 C2 45 23N 86 54W
Washington Land, *Greenland* 10 A4 80 30N 66 0W
Washougal, *U.S.A.* 160 E4 45 35N 122 21W
Washpool Nat. Park, *Australia* 127 D5 29 22 S 152 20 E
Washuk, *Pakistan* 91 D2 27 42N 64 45 E
Wasian, *Indonesia* 83 B4 1 47 S 133 19 E
Wasilków, *Poland* 55 E10 53 12N 23 13 E
Wasilla, *U.S.A.* 144 F10 61 35N 149 26W
Wasior, *Indonesia* 83 B4 2 43 S 134 30 E
Waskaganish, *Canada* 140 B4 51 30N 78 40W
Waskaiowaka, L., *Canada* 143 B9 56 33N 96 23W
Waskesiu Lake, *Canada* 143 C7 53 55N 106 5W
Wassaw I., *U.S.A.* 152 D9 31 53N 80 58W
Wassaw Sd., *U.S.A.* 152 D9 31 55N 80 55W
Wassen, *Switz.* 33 C7 46 42N 8 36 E
Wasserauen, *Switz.* 33 B8 47 17N 9 26 E
Wasserburg, *Germany* 31 G8 48 3N 12 14 E
Wasserkuppe, *Germany* 30 E5 50 29N 9 55 E
Wassy, *France* 27 D11 48 30N 4 58 E
Wasu, *Papua N. G.* 132 C4 5 58 S 147 12 E
Wasua, *Papua N. G.* 132 E2 8 18 S 142 52 E
Waswanipi, *Canada* 140 C4 49 40N 76 29W
Waswanipi, L., *Canada* 140 C4 49 35N 76 40W
Watam, *Papua N. G.* 132 B3 3 55 S 144 33 E
Watampone, *Indonesia* 82 B2 4 29 S 120 25 E
Watamu, *Kenya* 118 C5 3 23 S 40 0 E
Watansoppeng, *Indonesia* 82 B1 4 10 S 119 56 E
Watarrka Nat. Park, *Australia* 124 D5 24 20 S 131 30 E
Watee, *Solomon Is.* 133 N12 10 30 S 162 2 E
Water Park Pt., *Australia* 126 C5 22 56 S 150 47 E
Water Valley, *U.S.A.* 155 H10 34 10N 89 38W
Waterberg Plateau Park, *Namibia* 116 C2 20 25 S 17 18 E
Waterberge, *S. Africa* 117 C4 24 10 S 28 0 E
Waterbury, *Conn., U.S.A.* 151 E11 41 33N 73 3W
Waterbury, *Vt., U.S.A.* 151 B12 44 20N 72 46W
Waterbury L., *Canada* 143 B8 58 10N 104 22W
Waterdown, *Canada* 150 C5 43 20N 79 53W
Wateree →, *U.S.A.* 152 B9 33 45N 80 37W
Waterford, *Canada* 150 D4 42 56N 80 17W
Waterford, *Ireland* 23 D4 52 15N 7 8W
Waterford, *Calif., U.S.A.* 160 H6 37 38N 120 46W
Waterford, *Mich., U.S.A.* 157 B13 42 45N 83 32W
Waterford, *Pa., U.S.A.* 150 E5 41 57N 79 59W
Waterford, *Wis., U.S.A.* 157 B8 42 46N 88 13W
Waterford □, *Ireland* 23 D4 52 10N 7 40W
Waterford Harbour, *Ireland* 23 D5 52 8N 6 58W
Waterhen L., *Canada* 143 C9 52 10N 99 40W
Waterloo, *Belgium* 24 D4 50 43N 4 25 E
Waterloo, *Ont., Canada* 140 D3 43 30N 80 32W
Waterloo, *Qué., Canada* 151 A12 45 22N 72 32W
Waterloo, *S. Leone* 112 D2 8 26N 13 8W
Waterloo, *Ill., U.S.A.* 156 F6 38 20N 90 9W
Waterloo, *Ind., U.S.A.* 157 C11 41 26N 85 1W
Waterloo, *Iowa, U.S.A.* 156 B4 42 30N 92 21W
Waterloo, *N.Y., U.S.A.* 150 D8 42 54N 76 52W
Waterloo, *Wis., U.S.A.* 156 A8 43 11N 88 59W
Waterman, *U.S.A.* 157 C8 41 46N 88 47W
Watersmeet, *U.S.A.* 154 B10 46 16N 89 11W
Waterton Lakes Nat. Park, *U.S.A.* 158 B7 48 45N 115 0W
Watertown, *Conn., U.S.A.* 151 E11 41 36N 73 7W
Watertown, *Fla., U.S.A.* 152 E7 30 11N 82 36W
Watertown, *N.Y., U.S.A.* 151 C9 43 59N 75 55W
Watertown, *S. Dak., U.S.A.* 154 C6 44 54N 97 7W
Watertown, *Wis., U.S.A.* 154 D10 43 12N 88 43W
Waterval-Boven, *S. Africa* 117 D5 25 40 S 30 18 E
Waterville, *Canada* 151 A13 45 16N 71 54W
Waterville, *Maine, U.S.A.* 149 C11 44 33N 69 38W
Waterville, *N.Y., U.S.A.* 151 D9 42 56N 75 23W
Waterville, *Pa., U.S.A.* 150 E7 41 19N 77 21W
Waterville, *Wash., U.S.A.* 158 C3 47 39N 120 4W
Watervliet, *Mich., U.S.A.* 157 B10 42 11N 86 18W
Watervliet, *N.Y., U.S.A.* 151 D11 42 44N 73 42W
Wates, *Indonesia* 85 D4 7 51 S 110 10 E
Watford, *Canada* 150 D3 42 57N 81 53W
Watford, *U.K.* 21 F7 51 40N 0 24W
Watford City, *U.S.A.* 154 B3 47 48N 103 17W
Wathaman →, *Canada* 143 B8 57 16N 102 59W
Wathaman L., *Canada* 143 B8 56 58N 103 44W
Watheroo, *Australia* 125 F2 30 15 S 116 0 E
Watheroo Nat. Park, *Australia* 125 F2 30 19 S 115 48 E
Wating, *China* 74 G4 35 40N 106 38 E
Watkins Glen, *U.S.A.* 150 D8 42 23N 76 52W
Watkinsville, *U.S.A.* 152 B6 33 52N 83 25W
Watling I. = San Salvador I., *Bahamas* 165 B5 24 0N 74 40W
Watmuri, *Indonesia* 83 C4 7 25 S 131 42 E
Watom I., *Papua N. G.* 132 C7 4 7 S 152 4 E
Watonga, *U.S.A.* 155 H5 35 51N 98 25W
Watrous, *Canada* 143 C7 51 40N 105 25W
Watrous, *U.S.A.* 155 H2 35 48N 104 59W
Watsa, *Dem. Rep. of the Congo* 118 B2 3 4N 29 30 E
Watseka, *U.S.A.* 157 D9 40 47N 87 44W
Watsi Kenga, *Dem. Rep. of the Congo* 114 C4 0 49 S 20 34 E
Watson, *Australia* 125 F5 30 29 S 131 31 E
Watson, *Canada* 143 C8 52 10N 104 30W
Watson Lake, *Canada* 142 A3 60 6N 128 49W
Watsontown, *U.S.A.* 150 E8 41 5N 76 52W
Watsonville, *U.S.A.* 160 J5 36 55N 121 45W
Wattenwil, *Switz.* 32 C5 46 46N 7 31 E
Wattiwarriganna Cr. →, *Australia* 127 D2 28 57 S 136 10 E
Wattwil, *Switz.* 33 B8 47 18N 9 6 E
Watu, *Dem. Rep. of the Congo* 114 C4 3 18 S 20 3 E
Watuata = Batuata, *Indonesia* 82 C2 6 12 S 122 42 E
Watubela, Kepulauan, *Indonesia* 83 B4 4 28 S 131 35 E
Watubela Is. = Watubela, Kepulauan, *Indonesia* 83 B4 4 28 S 131 35 E
Wau = Wâw, *Sudan* 107 F2 7 45N 28 1 E
Wau, *Papua N. G.* 132 D4 7 21 S 146 47 E
Waubamik, *Canada* 150 A4 45 27N 80 1W
Waubay, *U.S.A.* 154 C6 45 20N 97 18W
Waubra, *Australia* 128 D5 37 21 S 143 39 E
Wauchope, *N.S.W., Australia* 129 A10 31 28 S 152 45 E
Wauchope, *N. Terr., Australia* 126 C1 20 36 S 134 15 E
Wauchula, *U.S.A.* 149 M5 27 33N 81 49W
Waukarlycarly, L., *Australia* 124 D3 21 18 S 121 56 E
Waukeenah, *U.S.A.* 152 E6 30 25N 83 57W
Waukegan, *U.S.A.* 157 B9 42 22N 87 50W
Waukesha, *U.S.A.* 154 D10 43 1N 88 14W
Waukon, *U.S.A.* 154 D9 43 16N 91 29W
Waupaca, *U.S.A.* 154 C10 44 21N 89 5W
Waupun, *U.S.A.* 154 D10 43 38N 88 44W
Waurika, *U.S.A.* 155 H6 34 10N 98 0W
Wausau, *Fla., U.S.A.* 152 E4 30 38N 85 35W
Wausau, *Wis., U.S.A.* 154 C10 44 58N 89 38W
Wauseon, *U.S.A.* 157 C12 41 33N 84 8W
Wautoma, *U.S.A.* 154 C10 44 4N 89 18W
Wauwatosa, *U.S.A.* 157 A9 43 3N 88 0W
Waveland, *U.S.A.* 157 E9 39 53N 87 3W
Waveney →, *U.K.* 21 E9 52 35N 1 39 E
Waverley, *N.Z.* 130 F3 39 46 S 174 37 E
Waverley Hall, *U.S.A.* 152 C5 32 41N 84 44W
Waverly, *Ala., U.S.A.* 152 C4 32 44N 85 35W
Waverly, *Fla., U.S.A.* 153 H8 27 59N 81 37W
Waverly, *Ga., U.S.A.* 152 D8 31 6N 81 43W
Waverly, *Ill., U.S.A.* 156 E7 39 36N 89 57W
Waverly, *Iowa, U.S.A.* 156 B4 42 44N 92 29W
Waverly, *Mo., U.S.A.* 156 E3 39 13N 93 31W
Waverly, *N.Y., U.S.A.* 151 E8 42 1N 76 32W
Wavre, *Belgium* 24 D4 50 43N 4 38 E
Waw, *Burma* 90 G6 17 28N 96 41 E
Wâw, *Sudan* 107 F2 7 45N 28 1 E
Wāw al Kabīr, *Libya* 108 C3 25 20N 16 43 E
Wāw an Nāmūs, *Libya* 108 D3 24 55N 17 46 E
Wawa, *Canada* 140 C3 47 59N 84 47W
Wawa, *Nigeria* 113 D5 9 54N 4 27 E
Wawa, *Sudan* 106 C3 20 30N 30 22 E
Wawanesa, *Canada* 143 D9 49 36N 99 40W
Wawasee, L., *U.S.A.* 157 C11 41 24N 85 42W
Wawoi →, *Papua N. G.* 132 D2 7 48 S 143 16 E
Wawona, *U.S.A.* 160 H7 37 32N 119 39W
Waxahachie, *U.S.A.* 155 J6 32 24N 96 51W
Way, L., *Australia* 125 E3 26 45 S 120 16 E
Waya, *Fiji* 133 A1 17 19 S 177 10 E
Wayabula, *Indonesia* 82 A3 2 29N 128 17 E
Waycross, *U.S.A.* 152 D7 31 13N 82 21W
Wayi, *Sudan* 107 F3 5 8N 30 10 E
Wayland, *Mich., U.S.A.* 157 B11 42 40N 85 39W
Wayland, *N.Y., U.S.A.* 150 D7 42 34N 77 35W
Wayne, *Nebr., U.S.A.* 154 D6 42 14N 97 1W
Wayne, *W. Va., U.S.A.* 148 F4 38 13N 82 27W
Wayne City, *U.S.A.* 157 F8 38 21N 88 35W
Wayne Lakes, *U.S.A.* 157 D12 40 1N 84 40W
Waynesboro, *Ga., U.S.A.* 152 B7 33 6N 82 1W
Waynesboro, *Miss., U.S.A.* 149 K1 31 40N 88 39W
Waynesboro, *Pa., U.S.A.* 148 F7 39 45N 77 35W
Waynesboro, *Va., U.S.A.* 148 F6 38 4N 78 53W
Waynesburg, *U.S.A.* 148 F5 39 54N 80 11W
Waynesville, *Mo., U.S.A.* 156 G4 37 50N 92 12W
Waynesville, *N.C., U.S.A.* 149 H4 35 28N 82 58W
Waynesville, *Ohio, U.S.A.* 157 E12 39 32N 84 5W
Waynoka, *U.S.A.* 155 G5 36 35N 98 53W
Wayside, *U.S.A.* 152 B6 33 4N 83 37W
Waza, *Afghan.* 91 B3 33 22N 69 26 E
Waza, Parc Nat. de, *Cameroon* 109 F2 11 15N 14 38 E
Wazirkhwah, *Afghan.* 91 B3 32 11N 68 21 E
Wāzin, *Libya* 108 B2 31 58N 10 40 E
Wazirabad, *Pakistan* 92 C6 32 30N 74 8 E
Wda →, *Poland* 54 E5 53 25N 18 29 E
We, *Indonesia* 84 A1 5 51N 95 18 E
Wé, *N. Cal.* 133 K5 20 55 S 167 16 E
Weald, The, *U.K.* 21 F8 51 4N 0 20 E
Weam, *Papua N. G.* 132 E1 8 37 S 141 8 E
Wear →, *U.K.* 20 C6 54 55N 1 23W
Weatherford, *Okla., U.S.A.* 155 H5 35 32N 98 43W
Weatherford, *Tex., U.S.A.* 155 J6 32 46N 97 48W
Weaubleau, *U.S.A.* 156 G3 37 54N 93 32W
Weaverville, *U.S.A.* 158 F2 40 44N 122 56W
Webb City, *U.S.A.* 155 G7 37 9N 94 28W
Webequie, *Canada* 140 B2 52 59N 87 21W
Weber, *N.Z.* 130 G5 40 24 S 176 20 E
Webo = Nyaake, *Liberia* 112 E3 4 52N 7 37W
Webster, *Mass., U.S.A.* 151 D13 42 3N 71 53W
Webster, *N.Y., U.S.A.* 150 C7 43 13N 77 26W
Webster, *S. Dak., U.S.A.* 154 C6 45 20N 97 31W
Webster City, *U.S.A.* 156 B3 42 28N 93 49W
Webster Springs, *U.S.A.* 148 F5 38 29N 80 25W
Weda, *Indonesia* 79 D7 0 21N 127 50 E
Weda, Teluk, *Indonesia* 82 A3 0 20N 128 0 E
Weddell I., *Falk. Is.* 9 f 51 50 S 61 0W
Weddell Sea, *Antarctica* 7 D1 72 30 S 40 0W
Wedderburn, *Australia* 128 D5 36 26 S 143 33 E
Weddin Mountains Nat. Park, *Australia* 129 C8 33 59 S 148 0 E
Wedel, *Germany* 30 B5 53 34N 9 42 E
Wedemark, *Germany* 30 C5 52 32N 9 43 E
Wedgeport, *Canada* 141 D6 43 44N 65 59W
Wednesday I., *Australia* 132 F2 10 31 S 142 16 E
Wedowee, *U.S.A.* 152 B4 33 19N 85 29W
Wedza, *Zimbabwe* 119 F3 18 40 S 31 33 E
Wee Waa, *Australia* 127 E4 30 11 S 149 26 E
Weed, *U.S.A.* 158 F2 41 25N 122 23W
Weed Heights, *U.S.A.* 160 G7 38 59N 119 13W
Weedsport, *U.S.A.* 151 C8 43 3N 76 35W
Weedville, *U.S.A.* 150 E6 41 17N 78 30W
Weenen, *S. Africa* 117 D5 28 48 S 30 7 E
Weener, *Germany* 30 B3 53 9N 7 20 E
Weert, *Neths.* 24 C5 51 15N 5 43 E
Weggis, *Switz.* 33 B6 47 2N 8 26 E
Węgierska-Górka, *Poland* 55 J6 49 36N 19 7 E
Węgliniec, *Poland* 55 G2 51 18N 15 10 E
Węgorzewo, *Poland* 54 D8 54 13N 21 43 E
Węgorzyno, *Poland* 54 E2 53 32N 15 33 E
Węgrów, *Poland* 55 F9 52 24N 22 0 E
Wehda □, *Sudan* 107 F3 8 30N 30 0 E
Wei He →, *Hebei, China* 74 F8 36 10N 115 45 E
Wei He →, *Shaanxi, China* 74 G6 34 38N 110 15 E
Weichang, *China* 75 D9 41 58N 117 49 E
Weichuan, *China* 74 G7 34 20N 113 59 E
Weida, *Germany* 30 E8 50 46N 12 2 E
Weiden, *Germany* 31 F8 49 41N 12 10 E
Weifang, *China* 75 F10 36 44N 119 7 E
Weihai, *China* 75 F12 37 30N 122 6 E
Weil, *Germany* 31 H3 47 35N 7 37 E
Weilburg, *Germany* 30 E4 50 28N 8 17 E
Weilheim, *Germany* 31 H7 47 50N 11 9 E
Weimar, *Germany* 30 E7 50 58N 11 19 E
Weinan, *China* 74 G5 34 31N 109 29 E
Weinfelden, *Switz.* 33 A8 47 34N 9 6 E
Weingarten, *Germany* 31 F4 49 3N 8 31 E
Weinheim, *Germany* 31 F4 49 32N 8 39 E
Weining, *China* 76 D5 26 50N 104 17 E
Weipa, *Australia* 126 A3 12 40 S 141 50 E
Weir →, *Australia* 127 D4 28 20 S 149 50 E
Weir →, *Canada* 143 B10 56 54N 93 21W
Weir, L., *U.S.A.* 153 F8 29 0N 81 57W
Weir River, *Canada* 143 B10 56 49N 94 6W
Weirsdale, *U.S.A.* 153 G8 28 59N 81 55W
Weirton, *U.S.A.* 150 F4 40 24N 80 35W
Weiser, *U.S.A.* 158 D5 44 10N 117 0W
Weishan, *Shandong, China* 75 G9 34 47N 117 5 E
Weishan, *Yunnan, China* 76 E3 25 12N 100 20 E
Weissenbach, *Austria* 33 B11 47 26N 10 39 E
Weissenburg, *Germany* 31 F6 49 2N 10 58 E
Weissenfels, *Germany* 30 D7 51 11N 12 0 E
Weisshorn, *Switz.* 32 D5 46 7N 7 43 E
Weisskugel, *Austria* 33 C11 46 48N 10 44 E
Weissmies, *Switz.* 32 D6 46 8N 8 1 E
Weisstannen, *Switz.* 33 C8 46 59N 9 22 E
Weisswasser, *Germany* 30 D10 51 30N 14 36 E
Weitra, *Austria* 34 C7 48 41N 14 54 E
Weixi, *China* 76 D2 27 10N 99 10 E
Weixin, *China* 76 D5 27 48N 105 3 E
Weiyuan, *China* 74 G3 35 7N 104 10 E
Weiz, *Austria* 34 D8 47 13N 15 39 E
Weizhou Dao, *China* 76 G7 21 0N 109 5 E
Wejherowo, *Poland* 54 D5 54 35N 18 12 E
Wekusko L., *Canada* 143 C9 54 40N 99 50W
Welch, *U.S.A.* 148 G5 37 26N 81 35W
Weldya, *Ethiopia* 107 E4 11 50N 39 34 E
Welega □, *Ethiopia* 107 F3 9 25N 34 20 E
Welford Nat. Park, *Australia* 126 D3 25 5 S 143 16 E
Weligama, *Sri Lanka* 95 M5 5 58N 80 25 E
Welkite, *Ethiopia* 107 F4 8 15N 37 42 E
Welkom, *S. Africa* 116 D4 28 0 S 26 46 E
Welland, *Canada* 140 D4 43 0N 79 15W
Welland →, *U.K.* 21 E7 52 51N 0 5W
Wellawaya, *Sri Lanka* 95 L5 6 44N 81 6 E
Wellesley Is., *Australia* 126 B2 16 42 S 139 30 E
Wellingborough, *U.K.* 21 E7 52 19N 0 41W
Wellington, *Australia* 129 B8 32 35 S 148 59 E
Wellington, *Canada* 150 C7 43 57N 77 20W
Wellington, *N.Z.* 130 H3 41 19 S 174 46 E
Wellington, *S. Africa* 116 E2 33 38 S 19 1 E
Wellington, *Somst., U.K.* 21 G4 50 58N 3 13W
Wellington, *Telford & Wrekin, U.K.* 21 E5 52 42N 2 30W
Wellington, *Colo., U.S.A.* 154 E2 40 42N 105 0W
Wellington, *Kans., U.S.A.* 155 G6 37 16N 97 24W
Wellington, *Mo., U.S.A.* 156 E3 39 8N 93 59W
Wellington, *Nev., U.S.A.* 160 G7 38 45N 119 23W
Wellington, *Ohio, U.S.A.* 150 E2 41 10N 82 13W
Wellington, *Tex., U.S.A.* 155 H4 34 51N 100 13W
Wellington □, *N.Z.* 130 G4 41 0 S 175 30 E
Wellington, I., *Chile* 176 C2 49 30 S 75 0W
Wellington, L., *Australia* 129 E7 38 6 S 147 20 E
Wellman, *U.S.A.* 156 C5 41 28N 91 50W
Wells, *U.K.* 21 F5 51 13N 2 39W
Wells, *Maine, U.S.A.* 151 C14 43 20N 70 35W
Wells, *N.Y., U.S.A.* 151 C10 43 24N 74 17W
Wells, *Nev., U.S.A.* 158 F6 41 7N 114 58W
Wells, L., *Australia* 125 E3 26 44 S 123 15 E
Wells, Mt., *Australia* 124 C4 17 25 S 127 8 E
Wells Gray Prov. Park, *Canada* 142 C4 52 30N 120 15W
Wells-next-the-Sea, *U.K.* 20 E8 52 57N 0 51 E
Wells River, *U.S.A.* 151 B12 44 9N 72 4W
Wellsboro, *U.S.A.* 150 E7 41 45N 77 18W
Wellsburg, *U.S.A.* 150 F4 40 16N 80 37W
Wellsford, *N.Z.* 130 C3 36 16 S 174 32 E
Wellsville, *Mo., U.S.A.* 156 E5 39 4N 91 34W
Wellsville, *N.Y., U.S.A.* 150 D7 42 7N 77 57W
Wellsville, *Ohio, U.S.A.* 150 F4 40 36N 80 39W
Wellsville, *Utah, U.S.A.* 158 F8 41 38N 111 56W
Wellton, *U.S.A.* 159 K6 32 40N 114 8W
Welmel, Wabi →, *Ethiopia* 107 F5 5 38N 40 47 E
Welo, *Somali Rep.* 120 C3 9 25N 48 55 E
Welo □, *Ethiopia* 107 E4 11 50N 39 48 E
Wels, *Austria* 34 C7 48 9N 14 1 E
Welshpool, *Australia* 129 E7 38 42 S 146 26 E
Welshpool, *U.K.* 21 E4 52 39N 3 8W
Welwyn Garden City, *U.K.* 21 F7 51 48N 0 12W
Wem, *U.K.* 20 E5 52 52N 2 44W
Wembere →, *Tanzania* 118 C3 4 10 S 34 15 E
Wemindji, *Canada* 140 B4 53 0N 78 49W
Wen Xian, *China* 74 G7 34 55N 113 5 E
Wenatchee, *U.S.A.* 158 C3 47 25N 120 19W
Wenchang, *China* 86 C8 19 38N 110 42 E
Wencheng, *China* 77 D13 27 46N 120 4 E
Wenchi, *Ghana* 112 D4 7 46N 2 8W
Wenchow = Wenzhou, *China* 77 D13 28 0N 120 38 E
Wenchuan, *China* 76 B4 31 22N 103 35 E
Wenden, *U.S.A.* 161 M13 33 49N 113 33W
Wendeng, *China* 75 F12 37 15N 122 5 E
Wendesi, *Indonesia* 83 B4 2 30 S 134 17 E
Wendo, *Ethiopia* 107 F4 6 40N 38 27 E
Wendover, *U.S.A.* 158 F6 40 44N 114 2W
Weng'an, *China* 76 D6 27 5N 107 25 E
Wengcheng, *China* 77 E9 24 22N 113 50 E
Wengen, *Switz.* 32 C5 46 37N 7 55 E
Wengyuan, *China* 77 E10 24 20N 114 9 E
Wenjiang, *China* 76 B4 30 44N 103 55 E
Wenling, *China* 77 C13 28 21N 121 20 E
Wenlock →, *Australia* 126 A3 12 2 S 141 55 E
Wenona, *U.S.A.* 156 C7 41 3N 89 3W
Wenshan, *China* 76 F5 23 20N 104 18 E
Wenshang, *China* 74 G9 35 45N 116 30 E
Wenshui, *China* 74 F7 37 26N 112 1 E
Wensleydale, *U.K.* 20 C6 54 17N 2 0W
Wensu, *China* 68 B3 41 15N 80 10 E
Wensum →, *U.K.* 20 E8 52 40N 1 15 E
Wentworth, *Australia* 128 C4 34 2 S 141 54 E
Wentzel L., *Canada* 142 B6 59 2N 114 28W
Wentzville, *U.S.A.* 156 F6 38 49N 90 51W
Wenut, *Indonesia* 83 B4 3 11 S 133 19 E
Wenxi, *China* 74 G6 35 20N 111 10 E
Wenxian, *China* 74 H3 32 43N 104 36 E
Wenzhou, *China* 77 D13 28 0N 120 38 E
Weott, *U.S.A.* 158 F2 40 20N 123 55W
Wepener, *S. Africa* 116 D4 29 42 S 27 3 E
Werda, *Botswana* 116 D3 25 24 S 23 15 E
Werdau, *Germany* 30 E8 50 44N 12 22 E
Werder, *Ethiopia* 120 C3 6 58N 45 1 E
Werder, *Germany* 30 C8 52 23N 12 55 E
Werdohl, *Germany* 30 D3 51 15N 7 46 E
Wereilu, *Ethiopia* 107 E4 10 40N 39 28 E
Weri, *Indonesia* 83 B4 3 10 S 132 38 E
Werneck, *Germany* 31 F6 49 58N 10 5 E
Wernigerode, *Germany* 30 D6 51 50N 10 47 E
Werra →, *Germany* 30 D5 51 24N 9 39 E
Werribee, *Australia* 128 D6 37 54 S 144 40 E
Werrikimbee Nat. Park, *Australia* 129 A10 31 11 S 152 15 E
Werrimull, *Australia* 128 C4 34 25 S 141 38 E
Werris Creek, *Australia* 129 A9 31 18 S 150 38 E
Wertach →, *Germany* 31 G6 48 22N 10 54 E

X

Xiliao He →, *China* **75 C12** 43 32N 123 35 E
Xilin, *China* **76 E5** 24 30N 105 6 E
Xilókastron, *Greece* **48 C4** 38 5N 22 38 E
Ximana, *Mozam.* **119 F3** 19 24 S 33 58 E
Xime, *Guinea-Biss.* **112 C2** 11 59N 14 57W
Ximeng, *China* **76 F2** 22 50N 99 27 E
Xin Jiang →, *China* **77 C11** 28 45N 116 35 E
Xin Xian = Xinzhou, *China* **74 E7** 38 22N 112 46 E
Xinavane, *Mozam.* **117 D5** 25 2 S 32 47 E
Xinbin, *China* **75 D13** 41 40N 125 2 E
Xincai, *China* **77 A10** 32 43N 114 58 E
Xinchang, *China* **77 C13** 29 28N 120 52 E
Xincheng, *Guangxi Zhuangzu, China* **76 E7** 24 5N 108 39 E
Xincheng, *Jiangxi, China* **77 D10** 26 48N 114 6 E
Xindu, *China* **76 B5** 30 50N 104 10 E
Xinfeng, *Guangdong, China* **77 E10** 24 5N 114 16 E
Xinfeng, *Jiangxi, China* **77 D11** 27 7N 116 11 E
Xinfeng, *Jiangxi, China* **77 E10** 25 27N 114 58 E
Xinfengjiang Skuiku, *China* **77 F10** 23 52N 114 30 E
Xing Xian, *China* **74 E6** 38 27N 111 7 E
Xing'an, *Guangxi Zhuangzu, China* **77 E8** 25 38N 110 40 E
Xingan, *Jiangxi, China* **77 D10** 27 46N 115 20 E
Xingcheng, *China* **75 D11** 40 40N 120 45 E
Xingguo, *China* **77 D10** 26 21N 115 21 E
Xinghe, *China* **74 D7** 40 55N 113 55 E
Xinghua, *China* **75 H10** 32 58N 119 48 E
Xinghua Wan, *China* **77 E12** 25 15N 119 20 E
Xinglong, *China* **75 D9** 40 25N 117 30 E
Xingning, *China* **77 E10** 24 3N 115 42 E
Xingping, *China* **74 G5** 34 20N 108 28 E
Xingren, *China* **76 E5** 25 24N 105 11 E
Xingshan, *China* **77 B8** 31 15N 110 45 E
Xingtai, *China* **74 F8** 37 3N 114 32 E
Xingu →, *Brazil* **169 D7** 1 30 S 51 53W
Xingwen, *China* **76 C5** 28 22N 104 50 E
Xingyang, *China* **74 G7** 34 45N 112 52 E
Xinhe, *China* **74 F8** 37 30N 115 15 E
Xinhua, *China* **77 D8** 27 42N 111 13 E
Xinhuang, *China* **76 D7** 27 21N 109 12 E
Xinhui, *China* **77 F9** 22 25N 113 0 E
Xining, *China* **68 C5** 36 34N 101 40 E
Xinjian, *China* **77 C10** 28 37N 115 46 E
Xinjiang, *China* **74 G6** 35 34N 111 11 E
Xinjiang Uygur Zizhiqu □, *China* **68 C3** 42 0N 86 0 E
Xinjie, *China* **76 D3** 26 48N 101 15 E
Xinjin = Pulandian, *China* **75 E11** 39 25N 121 58 E
Xinjin, *China* **76 B4** 30 24N 103 47 E
Xinkai He →, *China* **75 C12** 43 32N 123 35 E
Xinken, *China* **69 F10** 22 39N 113 36 E
Xinle, *China* **74 E8** 38 25N 114 40 E
Xinlitun, *China* **75 D12** 42 0N 122 8 E
Xinlong, *China* **76 B3** 30 57N 100 12 E
Xinmin, *China* **75 D12** 41 59N 122 50 E
Xinning, *China* **77 D8** 26 28N 110 50 E
Xinping, *China* **76 E3** 24 5N 101 59 E
Xinshao, *China* **77 D8** 27 21N 111 26 E
Xintai, *China* **75 G9** 35 55N 117 45 E
Xintian, *China* **77 E9** 25 55N 112 13 E
Xinwan, *China* **69 F10** 22 47N 113 40 E
Xinxian, *China* **77 B10** 31 36N 113 51 E
Xinxiang, *China* **74 G7** 35 18N 113 50 E
Xinxing, *China* **77 F9** 22 35N 112 15 E
Xinyang, *China* **77 A10** 32 6N 114 3 E
Xinye, *China* **77 A9** 32 30N 112 21 E
Xinyi, *China* **77 F8** 22 25N 111 0 E
Xinyu, *China* **77 D10** 27 49N 114 58 E
Xinzhan, *China* **75 C14** 43 50N 127 18 E
Xinzheng, *China* **74 G7** 34 20N 113 45 E
Xinzhou, *Hubei, China* **77 B10** 30 50N 114 48 E
Xinzhou, *Shanxi, China* **74 E7** 38 22N 112 46 E
Xinzo de Limia, *Spain* **42 C3** 42 3N 7 47W
Xiongyuecheng, *China* **75 D12** 40 12N 122 5 E
Xiping, *Henan, China* **74 H8** 33 22N 114 5 E
Xiping, *Henan, China* **74 H6** 33 25N 111 8 E
Xiping, *Zhejiang, China* **77 C12** 28 16N 119 29 E
Xique-Xique, *Brazil* **170 D3** 10 50 S 42 40W
Xiruá →, *Brazil* **172 B4** 6 3 S 67 50W
Xisha Qundao = Paracel Is., *S. China Sea* **78 A4** 15 50N 112 0 E
Xishui, *Guizhou, China* **76 C6** 28 19N 106 9 E
Xishui, *Hubei, China* **77 B10** 30 30N 115 15 E
Xitole, *Guinea-Biss.* **112 C2** 11 43N 14 50W
Xiu Shui →, *China* **77 C10** 29 13N 116 0 E
Xiuning, *China* **77 C12** 29 45N 118 10 E
Xiuren, *China* **77 E8** 24 27N 110 12 E
Xiushan, *China* **76 C7** 28 25N 108 57 E
Xiushui, *China* **77 C10** 29 2N 114 33 E
Xiuwen, *China* **76 D6** 26 49N 106 32 E
Xiuyan, *China* **75 D12** 40 18N 123 11 E
Xixia, *China* **74 H6** 33 25N 111 29 E
Xixiang, *China* **74 H4** 33 0N 107 44 E
Xiyang, *China* **74 F7** 37 38N 113 38 E
Xizang Zizhiqu □, *China* **68 C3** 32 0N 88 0 E
Xlendi, *Malta* **38 E6** 36 2N 14 13 E
Xu Jiang →, *China* **77 D11** 28 0N 116 25 E
Xuan Loc, *Vietnam* **87 G6** 10 56N 107 14 E
Xuan'en, *China* **76 C7** 30 0N 109 30 E
Xuanhan, *China* **76 B6** 31 18N 107 38 E
Xuanhua, *China* **74 D8** 40 40N 115 2 E
Xuanwei, *China* **76 C5** 26 15N 103 59 E
Xuanzhou, *China* **77 B12** 30 56N 118 43 E
Xuchang, *China* **74 G7** 34 2N 113 48 E
Xudat, *Azerbaijan* **61 K9** 41 38N 48 41 E
Xuddur = Oddur, *Somali Rep.* **120 D2** 4 11N 43 52 E
Xuefeng Shan, *China* **77 D8** 27 5N 110 35 E
Xuejiaping, *China* **77 B8** 31 39N 110 16 E
Xun Jiang →, *China* **77 F8** 23 35N 111 30 E
Xun Xian, *China* **74 G8** 35 42N 114 33 E
Xundian, *China* **76 E4** 25 36N 103 15 E
Xunwu, *China* **77 E10** 24 54N 115 37 E
Xunyang, *China* **74 H5** 32 48N 109 22 E
Xunyi, *China* **74 G5** 35 8N 108 20 E
Xupu, *China* **77 D8** 27 53N 110 32 E
Xúquer →, *Spain* **41 F4** 39 5N 0 10W
Xushui, *China* **74 E8** 39 2N 115 40 E
Xuwen, *China* **77 G8** 20 20N 110 10 E
Xuyen Moc, *Vietnam* **87 G6** 10 34N 107 25 E
Xuyong, *China* **76 C5** 28 10N 105 22 E
Xuzhou, *China* **75 G9** 34 18N 117 10 E
Xylophagou, *Cyprus* **39 F9** 34 54N 33 51 E

Y

Ya Xian, *China* **86 C7** 18 14N 109 29 E
Yaamba, *Australia* **126 C5** 23 8 S 150 22 E
Ya'an, *China* **76 C4** 29 58N 103 5 E
Yaapeet, *Australia* **128 C5** 35 45 S 142 3 E
Yabassi, *Cameroon* **113 E6** 4 30N 9 57 E
Yabelo, *Ethiopia* **107 G4** 4 50N 38 8 E
Yabelo Wildlife Reserve, *Ethiopia* **107 F4** 6 0N 37 50 E
Yablanitsa, *Bulgaria* **51 C8** 43 2N 24 5 E
Yablonovy Ra. = Yablonovyy Khrebet, *Russia* **67 D12** 53 0N 114 0 E
Yablonovyy Khrebet, *Russia* **67 D12** 53 0N 114 0 E
Yabrai Shan, *China* **74 E2** 39 40N 103 0 E
Yabrūd, *Syria* **103 B5** 33 58N 36 39 E
Yabucoa, *Puerto Rico* **165 d** 18 3N 65 53W
Yacheng, *China* **69 E5** 18 22N 109 6 E
Yackandandah, *Australia* **129 D7** 36 18 S 146 52 E
Yacuiba, *Bolivia* **174 A3** 22 0 S 63 43W
Yacuma →, *Bolivia* **173 C4** 13 38 S 65 23W
Yadgir, *India* **94 F3** 16 45N 77 5 E
Yadkin →, *U.S.A.* **149 H5** 35 29N 80 9W
Yadrin, *Russia* **60 C8** 55 57N 46 12 E
Yadua, *Fiji* **133 A2** 16 49 S 178 18 E
Yaeyama-Rettō, *Japan* **71 M1** 24 30N 123 40 E
Yafran, *Libya* **108 B2** 32 4N 12 31 E
Yafran □, *Libya* **108 B2** 32 0N 12 20 E
Yagaba, *Ghana* **113 C4** 10 14N 1 20W
Yagasa Cluster, *Fiji* **133 B3** 18 57 S 178 28W
Yağcılar, *Turkey* **49 B10** 39 25N 28 23 E
Yagodnoye, *Russia* **67 C15** 62 33N 149 40 E
Yagoua, *Cameroon* **109 F3** 10 20N 15 13 E
Yaguas →, *Peru* **168 D3** 2 45 S 70 10W
Yahila, *Orientale, Dem. Rep. of the Congo* **114 B4** 1 48N 23 37 E
Yahila, *Orientale, Dem. Rep. of the Congo* **118 B1** 0 13N 24 28 E
Yahk, *Canada* **142 D5** 49 6N 116 10W
Yahotyn, *Ukraine* **59 G6** 50 17N 31 46 E
Yahuma, *Dem. Rep. of the Congo* **114 B4** 1 0N 23 10 E
Yahyalı, *Turkey* **100 C6** 38 5N 35 2 E
Yaita, *Japan* **71 F9** 36 48N 139 56 E
Yaiza, *Canary Is.* **9 e2** 28 57N 13 46W
Yaizu, *Japan* **73 C10** 34 52N 138 20 E
Yajiang, *China* **76 B3** 30 2N 100 57 E
Yajua, *Nigeria* **113 C7** 11 27N 12 49 E
Yakage, *Japan* **72 C5** 34 37N 133 35 E
Yakamba, *Dem. Rep. of the Congo* **114 B3** 2 42N 19 38 E
Yakima, *U.S.A.* **158 C3** 46 36N 120 31W
Yakima →, *U.S.A.* **158 C3** 47 0N 120 30W
Yakkabag, *Uzbekistan* **65 D3** 38 55N 66 51 E
Yako, *Burkina Faso* **112 C4** 12 59N 2 15W
Yakobi I., *U.S.A.* **142 B1** 58 0N 136 30W
Yakoma, *Dem. Rep. of the Congo* **114 B4** 4 5N 22 27 E
Yakoruda, *Bulgaria* **50 D7** 42 1N 23 39 E
Yakossi, *C.A.R.* **114 A4** 5 37N 23 19 E
Yakovlevka, *Russia* **70 B6** 44 26N 133 28 E
Yakshur Bodya, *Russia* **64 C4** 57 11N 53 7 E
Yaku-Shima, *Japan* **71 J5** 30 20N 130 30 E
Yakumo, *Japan* **70 C10** 42 15N 140 16 E
Yakutat, *U.S.A.* **144 G13** 59 33N 139 44W
Yakutat B., *U.S.A.* **144 G12** 59 45N 140 45W
Yakutia = Sakha □, *Russia* **67 C13** 66 0N 130 0 E
Yakutsk, *Russia* **67 C13** 62 5N 129 50 E
Yala, *Thailand* **87 J3** 6 33N 101 18 E
Yalboroo, *Australia* **126 J6** 20 50 S 148 40 E
Yale, *U.S.A.* **150 C2** 43 8N 82 48W
Yalgoo, *Australia* **125 E2** 28 16 S 116 39 E
Yalgorup Nat. Park, *Australia* **125 D2** 24 34 S 115 2 E
Yali, *Dem. Rep. of the Congo* **114 B4** 0 4N 21 3 E
Yaligimba, *Dem. Rep. of the Congo* **114 B4** 2 13N 22 56 E
Yalikanda, *Dem. Rep. of the Congo* **114 B4** 0 23N 24 47 E
Yalinga, *C.A.R.* **114 A4** 6 33N 23 10 E
Yalkubul, Punta, *Mexico* **163 C7** 21 32N 88 37W
Yalleroi, *Australia* **126 C4** 24 3 S 145 42 E
Yalobusha →, *U.S.A.* **155 J9** 33 33N 90 10W
Yaloké, *C.A.R.* **114 A3** 5 19N 17 5 E
Yalong Jiang →, *China* **76 D3** 26 40N 101 55 E
Yalova, *Turkey* **51 F13** 40 41N 29 15 E
Yalta, *Ukraine* **59 K8** 44 30N 34 10 E
Yalu Jiang →, *China* **75 E13** 40 0N 124 22 E
Yalvaç, *Turkey* **100 C4** 38 17N 31 10 E
Yam Ha Melaḥ = Dead Sea, *Asia* **103 D4** 31 30N 35 30 E
Yam Kinneret, *Israel* **103 C4** 32 45N 35 35 E
Yamada, *Japan* **72 D2** 33 33N 130 49 E
Yamaga, *Japan* **72 D2** 33 1N 130 41 E
Yamagata, *Japan* **70 E10** 38 15N 140 15 E
Yamagata □, *Japan* **70 E10** 38 30N 140 0 E
Yamagawa, *Japan* **72 F2** 31 12N 130 39 E
Yamaguchi, *Japan* **72 C3** 34 10N 131 32 E
Yamaguchi □, *Japan* **72 C3** 34 20N 131 40 E
Yamal, Poluostrov, *Russia* **66 B8** 71 0N 70 0 E
Yamal Pen. = Yamal, Poluostrov, *Russia* **66 B8** 71 0N 70 0 E
Yamanaka, *Japan* **73 A8** 36 15N 136 22 E
Yamanashi, *Japan* **73 B10** 35 41N 138 40 E
Yamanashi □, *Japan* **73 B10** 35 40N 138 40 E
Yamanie Falls Nat. Park, *Australia* **126 B4** 18 29 S 146 9 E
Yamantau, Gora, *Russia* **64 D7** 54 15N 58 6 E
Yamasaki, *Japan* **72 C6** 35 0N 134 32 E
Yamato, *Japan* **73 B11** 35 27N 139 25 E
Yamatotakada, *Japan* **73 C7** 34 31N 135 45 E
Yamba, *Australia* **127 D5** 29 26 S 153 23 E
Yambarran Ra., *Australia* **124 C5** 15 10 S 130 25 E
Yambata, *Dem. Rep. of the Congo* **114 B4** 2 26N 21 58 E
Yambéring, *Guinea* **112 C2** 11 50N 12 18 E
Yâmbiô, *Sudan* **107 G2** 4 35N 28 16 E
Yambol, *Bulgaria* **51 D10** 42 30N 26 30 E
Yamboyo, *Dem. Rep. of the Congo* **114 B4** 0 40N 22 18 E
Yambuya, *Dem. Rep. of the Congo* **114 B4** 1 17N 24 34 E
Yamdena, *Indonesia* **83 C4** 7 45 S 131 20 E
Yame, *Japan* **72 D2** 33 13N 130 35 E
Yamethin, *Burma* **90 E6** 20 29N 96 18 E
Yamma-Yamma, L., *Australia* **127 D3** 26 16 S 141 20 E
Yamoussoukro, *Ivory C.* **112 D3** 6 49N 5 17W
Yampa →, *U.S.A.* **158 F9** 40 32N 108 59W
Yampi Sd., *Australia* **124 C3** 16 8 S 123 38 E
Yampil, *Moldova* **59 H5** 48 15N 28 15 E
Yampol = Yampil, *Moldova* **59 H5** 48 15N 28 15 E
Yamrat, *Nigeria* **113 C6** 10 11N 9 55 E
Yamrukchal = Botev, *Bulgaria* **51 D8** 42 44N 24 52 E
Yamuna →, *India* **93 G9** 25 30N 81 53 E
Yamunanagar, *India* **92 D7** 30 7N 77 17 E
Yamzho Yumco, *China* **68 D4** 28 48N 90 35 E
Yan, *Nigeria* **113 C7** 10 5N 12 11 E
Yan Oya →, *Sri Lanka* **95 K5** 9 0N 81 10 E
Yana →, *Russia* **67 B14** 71 30N 136 0 E
Yanagawa, *Japan* **72 D2** 33 10N 130 24 E
Yanahara, *Japan* **72 C6** 34 58N 134 2 E
Yanai, *Japan* **72 D4** 33 58N 132 7 E
Yan'an, *China* **74 F5** 36 35N 109 26 E
Yanaul, *Russia* **64 C5** 56 25N 55 0 E
Yanbian, *China* **76 D3** 26 47N 101 31 E
Yanbu 'al Baḩr, *Si. Arabia* **96 F3** 24 0N 38 5 E
Yanchang, *China* **74 F6** 36 43N 110 1 E
Yancheng, *Henan, China* **74 H8** 33 35N 114 0 E
Yancheng, *Jiangsu, China* **75 H11** 33 23N 120 8 E
Yanchep Beach, *Australia* **125 F2** 31 33 S 115 37 E
Yanchi, *China* **74 F4** 37 48N 107 20 E
Yanchuan, *China* **74 F6** 36 51N 110 10 E
Yanco, *Australia* **129 C7** 34 38 S 146 27 E
Yanco Cr. →, *Australia* **129 C6** 35 14 S 145 35 E
Yandé, Î., *N. Cal.* **133 T17** 20 3 S 163 49 E
Yandina, *Solomon Is.* **133 M10** 9 7 S 159 13 E
Yandja, *Dem. Rep. of the Congo* **114 C3** 1 41 S 17 43 E
Yandongi, *Dem. Rep. of the Congo* **114 B4** 2 51N 22 16 E
Yandoon, *Burma* **90 G5** 17 0N 95 40 E
Yanfeng, *China* **76 E3** 25 52N 101 8 E
Yanfolila, *Mali* **112 C3** 11 11N 8 9W
Yang Xian, *China* **74 H4** 33 15N 107 30 E
Yang-Yang, *Senegal* **112 B1** 15 30N 15 20W
Yangambi, *Dem. Rep. of the Congo* **118 B1** 0 47N 24 24 E
Yangbi, *China* **76 E2** 25 41N 99 58 E
Yangcheng, *China* **74 G7** 35 28N 112 22 E
Yangch'ü = Taiyuan, *China* **74 F7** 37 52N 112 33 E
Yangchun, *China* **77 F8** 22 11N 111 48 E
Yanggao, *China* **74 D7** 40 21N 113 55 E
Yanggu, *China* **74 F8** 36 8N 115 43 E
Yangi-Nishan, *Uzbekistan* **65 D2** 38 49N 65 47 E
Yangiabad, *Uzbekistan* **65 C5** 41 7N 70 6 E
Yangikishlak, *Uzbekistan* **65 C3** 40 25N 67 10 E
Yangirabad, *Uzbekistan* **65 C2** 40 2N 65 58 E
Yangiyer, *Uzbekistan* **65 C4** 40 16N 68 49 E
Yangiyul, *Uzbekistan* **65 C4** 41 0N 69 3 E
Yangjiang, *China* **77 G8** 21 50N 111 59 E
Yangliuqing, *China* **75 E9** 39 2N 117 5 E
Yangon = Rangoon, *Burma* **90 G6** 16 45N 96 20 E
Yangonde, *Dem. Rep. of the Congo* **114 B4** 0 3N 22 43 E
Yangping, *China* **77 B8** 31 12N 111 25 E
Yangpingguan, *China* **74 H4** 32 58N 106 5 E
Yangquan, *China* **74 F7** 37 58N 113 31 E
Yangshan, *China* **77 E9** 24 30N 112 40 E
Yangshuo, *China* **77 E8** 24 48N 110 29 E
Yangtse = Chang Jiang →, *China* **77 B13** 31 48N 121 10 E
Yangtze Kiang = Chang Jiang →, *China* **77 B13** 31 48N 121 10 E
Yangudi Rassa Nat. Park, *Ethiopia* **107 E5** 10 50N 40 42 E
Yangxin, *China* **77 C10** 29 50N 115 12 E
Yangyang, *S. Korea* **75 E15** 38 4N 128 38 E
Yangyuan, *China* **74 D8** 40 1N 114 10 E
Yangzhong, *China* **77 A12** 32 22N 119 22 E
Yangzhou, *China* **77 A12** 32 21N 119 26 E
Yanhe, *China* **76 C7** 28 31N 108 29 E
Yanji, *China* **75 C15** 42 59N 129 30 E
Yanjin, *China* **76 C5** 28 5N 104 18 E
Yanjing, *China* **76 C2** 29 7N 98 33 E
Yankari Nat. Park, *Nigeria* **113 D7** 9 50N 10 28 E
Yankton, *U.S.A.* **154 D6** 42 53N 97 23W
Yanonge, *Dem. Rep. of the Congo* **118 B1** 0 35N 24 38 E
Yanqi, *China* **68 B3** 42 5N 86 35 E
Yanqing, *China* **74 D8** 40 30N 115 58 E
Yanshan, *Hebei, China* **75 E9** 38 4N 117 22 E
Yanshan, *Jiangxi, China* **77 C11** 28 15N 117 41 E
Yanshan, *Yunnan, China* **76 F5** 23 35N 104 20 E
Yanshou, *China* **75 B15** 45 28N 128 22 E
Yantabulla, *Australia* **127 D4** 29 21 S 145 0 E
Yantai, *China* **75 F11** 37 34N 121 22 E
Yantian, *China* **69 F11** 22 35N 114 16 E
Yanting, *China* **76 B5** 31 11N 105 24 E
Yantra →, *Bulgaria* **51 C9** 43 40N 25 37 E
Yanuca, *Fiji* **133 B1** 18 24 S 178 0 E
Yanwa, *China* **76 D2** 27 35N 98 55 E
Yanykurgan = Zhangaqŭrghan, *Kazakstan* **65 B4** 43 50N 68 48 E
Yanyuan, *China* **76 D3** 27 25N 101 30 E
Yanzhou, *China* **74 G9** 35 35N 116 49 E
Yao, *Chad* **109 F3** 12 56N 17 33 E
Yao, *Japan* **73 C7** 34 32N 135 36 E
Yao Noi, Ko, *Thailand* **87 a** 8 7N 98 37 E
Yao Xian, *China* **74 G5** 34 55N 108 59 E
Yao Yai, Ko, *Thailand* **87 a** 8 0N 98 35 E
Yao'an, *China* **76 E3** 25 31N 101 18 E
Yaodu, *China* **76 A5** 32 45N 105 22 E
Yaoundé, *Cameroon* **113 E7** 3 50N 11 35 E
Yaowan, *China* **75 G10** 34 15N 118 3 E
Yap I., *Pac. Oc.* **134 G5** 9 30N 138 10 E
Yapehe, *Dem. Rep. of the Congo* **114 C4** 0 13 S 24 28 E
Yapen, *Indonesia* **83 B5** 1 50 S 136 0 E
Yapen, Selat, *Indonesia* **83 B5** 1 20 S 136 10 E
Yapero, *Indonesia* **83 B5** 4 59 S 137 11 E
Yappar →, *Australia* **126 B3** 18 22 S 141 16 E
Yaqaga, *Fiji* **133 A2** 16 35 S 178 36 E
Yaqui →, *Mexico* **162 B2** 27 37N 110 39W
Yar, *Russia* **64 B4** 58 14N 52 5 E
Yar-Sale, *Russia* **66 C8** 66 50N 70 50 E
Yaracuy □, *Venezuela* **168 A4** 10 20N 68 45W
Yaracuy →, *Venezuela* **168 A4** 10 33N 68 15W
Yaraka, *Australia* **126 C3** 24 53 S 144 3 E
Yaransk, *Russia* **60 B8** 57 22N 47 49 E
Yarbasan, *Turkey* **49 C10** 38 59N 28 49 E
Yardımcı Burnu, *Turkey* **49 E12** 36 13N 30 25 E
Yare →, *U.K.* **21 E9** 52 35N 1 38 E
Yaremcha, *Ukraine* **59 H3** 48 27N 24 33 E
Yarensk, *Russia* **56 B8** 62 11N 49 15 E
Yarfa, *Si. Arabia* **106 C4** 24 37N 38 35 E
Yarí →, *Colombia* **168 D3** 0 20 S 72 20W
Yarīm, *Yemen* **98 D4** 14 20N 44 22 E
Yaritagua, *Venezuela* **168 A4** 10 5N 69 8W
Yarkand = Shache, *China* **65 D8** 38 20N 77 10 E
Yarker, *Canada* **151 B8** 44 23N 76 46W
Yarkhun →, *Pakistan* **93 A5** 36 17N 72 30 E
Yarmouth, *Canada* **141 D6** 43 50N 66 7W
Yarmūk →, *Syria* **103 C4** 32 42N 35 40 E
Yaroslavl, *Russia* **58 D10** 57 35N 39 55 E
Yarqa, W. →, *Egypt* **103 F2** 30 0N 33 49 E
Yarra Ranges Nat. Park, *Australia* **129 D7** 37 40 S 146 3 E
Yarra Yarra Lakes, *Australia* **125 E2** 29 40 S 115 45 E
Yarram, *Australia* **129 E7** 38 29 S 146 39 E
Yarraman, *Australia* **127 D5** 26 50 S 152 0 E
Yarras, *Australia* **129 A10** 31 25 S 152 20 E
Yarrawonga, *Australia* **129 D7** 36 0 S 146 0 E
Yartsevo, *Sib., Russia* **67 C10** 60 20N 90 0 E
Yartsevo, *Smolensk, Russia* **58 E7** 55 6N 32 43 E
Yarumal, *Colombia* **168 B2** 6 58N 75 24W
Yasa, *Dem. Rep. of the Congo* **114 C4** 3 50 S 21 25 E
Yasawa, *Fiji* **133 A1** 16 47 S 177 31 E
Yasawa Group, *Fiji* **133 A1** 17 0 S 177 23 E
Yaselda, *Belarus* **59 F4** 52 7N 26 28 E
Yashbum, *Yemen* **98 D4** 14 19N 46 56 E
Yashi, *Nigeria* **113 C6** 12 23N 7 54 E
Yashikera, *Nigeria* **113 D5** 9 44N 3 29 E
Yashiro-Jima, *Japan* **72 D4** 33 55N 132 15 E
Yashkul, *Russia* **61 G7** 46 11N 45 21 E
Yasin, *Pakistan* **93 A5** 36 24N 73 23 E
Yasinovataya, *Ukraine* **59 H9** 48 7N 37 57 E
Yasinski, L., *Canada* **140 B4** 53 16N 77 35W
Yasinya, *Ukraine* **59 H3** 48 16N 24 21 E
Yasnyy, *Russia* **64 F7** 51 1N 59 58 E
Yasothon, *Thailand* **86 E5** 15 50N 104 10 E
Yass, *Australia* **129 C8** 34 49 S 148 54 E
Yasugi, *Japan* **72 B5** 35 26N 133 15 E
Yāsūj, *Iran* **97 D6** 30 31N 51 31 E
Yat, *Niger* **109 D2** 20 28N 13 27 E
Yata →, *Bolivia* **173 C4** 10 29 S 65 26W
Yata →, *C.A.R.* **114 A4** 10 23N 22 45 E
Yata-Ngaya, Réserve de Faune de la, *C.A.R.* **114 A4** 9 15N 23 25 E
Yatağan, *Turkey* **49 D10** 37 20N 28 10 E
Yatakala, *Niger* **113 C5** 14 50N 0 22 E
Yaté, *N. Cal.* **133 V20** 22 9 S 166 57 E
Yates Center, *U.S.A.* **155 G7** 37 53N 95 44W
Yates Pt., *N.Z.* **131 E2** 44 29 S 167 49 E
Yathkyed L., *Canada* **143 A9** 62 40N 98 0W
Yathong, *Australia* **129 B6** 32 37 S 145 33 E
Yatolemu, *Dem. Rep. of the Congo* **114 B4** 0 25N 24 35 E
Yatsuo, *Japan* **73 A9** 36 34N 137 8 E
Yatsushiro, *Japan* **72 E2** 32 30N 130 40 E
Yatsushiro-Kai, *Japan* **72 E2** 32 30N 130 25 E
Yatta Plateau, *Kenya* **118 C4** 2 0 S 38 0 E
Yatua →, *Venezuela* **168 C4** 1 30N 66 30W
Yauca, *Peru* **172 D3** 15 39 S 74 35W
Yauco, *Puerto Rico* **165 d** 18 2N 66 51W
Yauri, *Peru* **172 C3** 14 47 S 71 25W
Yauya, *Peru* **172 B2** 8 59 S 77 17W
Yauyos, *Peru* **172 C2** 12 19 S 75 50W
Yaval, *India* **94 D2** 21 10N 75 42 E
Yavan, *Tajikistan* **65 D4** 38 19N 69 2 E
Yavari →, *Peru* **172 A3** 4 21 S 70 2W
Yávaros, *Mexico* **162 B3** 26 42N 109 31W
Yavatmal, *India* **94 D4** 20 20N 78 15 E
Yavero →, *Peru* **172 C3** 12 6 S 72 57W
Yavne, *Israel* **103 D3** 31 52N 34 45 E
Yavoriv, *Ukraine* **59 H2** 49 55N 23 20 E
Yavorov = Yavoriv, *Ukraine* **59 H2** 49 55N 23 20 E
Yavuzeli, *Turkey* **100 D7** 37 18N 37 24 E
Yawatahama, *Japan* **72 D4** 33 27N 132 24 E
Yawnghwe, *Burma* **90 E6** 20 39N 96 56 E
Yawri B., *S. Leone* **112 D2** 8 22N 13 0W
Yaxi, *China* **76 D6** 27 33N 106 41 E
Yazagyo, *Burma* **90 D5** 23 30N 94 6 E
Yazd, *Iran* **97 D7** 31 55N 54 27 E
Yazd □, *Iran* **97 D7** 32 0N 55 0 E
Yazd-e Khvāst, *Iran* **97 D7** 31 31N 52 7 E
Yazdān, *Iran* **91 B1** 33 30N 60 50 E
Yazıköy, *Turkey* **49 E9** 36 40N 27 20 E
Yazman, *Pakistan* **92 E4** 29 8N 71 45 E
Yazoo →, *U.S.A.* **155 J9** 32 22N 90 54W
Yazoo City, *U.S.A.* **155 J9** 32 51N 90 25W
Ybbs, *Austria* **34 C8** 48 12N 15 4 E
Yding Skovhøj, *Denmark* **17 J3** 55 59N 9 46 E
Ye-ngan, *Burma* **90 E6** 21 9N 96 27 E
Ye-u, *Burma* **90 D5** 22 46N 95 26 E
Ye Xian = Laizhou, *China* **75 F10** 37 8N 119 57 E
Ye Xian, *China* **74 H7** 33 35N 113 25 E
Yea, *Australia* **129 D6** 37 14 S 145 26 E
Yebawmi, *Burma* **90 C5** 25 15N 95 45 E
Yebbi-Souma, *Chad* **109 D3** 21 7N 17 54 E
Yebyu, *Burma* **86 E2** 14 15N 98 13 E
Yecheng, *China* **65 E8** 37 54N 77 26 E
Yechŏn, *S. Korea* **75 F15** 36 39N 128 27 E
Yecla, *Spain* **41 G3** 38 35N 1 5W
Yécora, *Mexico* **162 B3** 28 20N 108 58W
Yedashe, *Burma* **90 F6** 19 10N 96 20 E
Yedintsy = Edineţ, *Moldova* **53 B12** 48 9N 27 18 E
Yedri, *Chad* **109 D3** 22 25N 17 30 E
Yedseram →, *Nigeria* **113 C7** 12 30N 14 5 E
Yefremov, *Russia* **58 F10** 53 8N 38 3 E
Yegguéba, *Niger* **109 E2** 19 59N 12 52 E
Yeghegnadzor, *Armenia* **101 C11** 39 44N 45 19 E
Yegorlyk →, *Russia* **61 G5** 46 35N 41 57 E
Yegorlykskaya, *Russia* **61 G5** 46 35N 40 35 E
Yegoryevsk, *Russia* **58 E10** 55 27N 38 55 E
Yegros, *Paraguay* **174 B4** 26 20 S 56 25W
Yehbuah, *Indonesia* **79 J17** 8 23 S 114 45 E
Yehuda, Midbar, *Israel* **103 D4** 31 35N 35 15 E
Yei, *Sudan* **107 G3** 4 9N 30 40 E
Yei, Nahr →, *Sudan* **107 F3** 6 15N 30 13 E
Yejmiadzin, *Armenia* **61 K7** 40 12N 44 19 E
Yekaterinburg, *Russia* **64 C8** 56 50N 60 30 E
Yekaterinodar = Krasnodar, *Russia* **61 H4** 45 5N 39 0 E
Yekumbe, *Dem. Rep. of the Congo* **114 C4** 1 2 S 23 27 E
Yelabuga, *Russia* **60 C11** 55 45N 52 4 E
Yelan, *Russia* **60 E6** 50 55N 43 43 E
Yelandur, *India* **95 H3** 12 6N 77 0 E
Yelarbon, *Australia* **127 D5** 28 33 S 150 38 E
Yelatma, *Russia* **60 C5** 55 0N 41 45 E
Yelcho, L., *Chile* **176 B2** 43 18 S 72 18W
Yelets, *Russia* **59 F10** 52 40N 38 30 E
Yélimané, *Mali* **112 B2** 15 9N 10 34W
Yelizavetgrad = Kirovohrad, *Ukraine* **59 H7** 48 35N 32 20 E
Yelizavetinka, *Russia* **64 F7** 51 46N 59 45 E
Yell, *U.K.* **22 A7** 60 35N 1 5W
Yell Sd., *U.K.* **22 A7** 60 33N 1 15W
Yellamanchilli = Elamanchili, *India* **94 F6** 17 33N 82 50 E
Yellandu, *India* **94 F5** 17 39N 80 23 E
Yellapur, *India* **95 G2** 14 58N 74 43 E
Yellareddi, *India* **94 E4** 18 12N 78 2 E
Yellow →, *U.S.A.* **153 E3** 30 30N 87 0W
Yellow Sea, *China* **75 G12** 35 0N 123 0 E
Yellowhead Pass, *Canada* **142 C5** 52 53N 118 25W
Yellowknife, *Canada* **142 A6** 62 27N 114 29W
Yellowknife →, *Canada* **142 A6** 62 31N 114 19W
Yellowstone →, *U.S.A.* **154 B3** 47 59N 103 59W
Yellowstone L., *U.S.A.* **158 D8** 44 27N 110 22W
Yellowstone Nat. Park, *U.S.A.* **158 D9** 44 40N 110 30W
Yelnya, *Russia* **58 E7** 54 35N 33 15 E
Yelsk, *Belarus* **59 G5** 51 50N 29 10 E
Yelwa, *Nigeria* **113 C5** 10 49N 4 41 E
Yemanzhelinsk, *Russia* **64 D8** 54 58N 61 18 E
Yemassee, *U.S.A.* **152 C9** 32 41N 80 51W
Yembongo, *Dem. Rep. of the Congo* **114 B3** 3 12N 19 2 E
Yemen ■, *Asia* **98 D4** 15 0N 44 0 E
Yen Bai, *Vietnam* **76 G5** 21 42N 104 52 E
Yenagoa, *Nigeria* **113 E6** 4 58N 6 16 E
Yenakiyeve, *Ukraine* **59 H10** 48 15N 38 15 E
Yenakiyevo = Yenakiyeve, *Ukraine* **59 H10** 48 15N 38 15 E
Yenangyat, *Burma* **90 E5** 21 6N 94 48 E
Yenangyaung, *Burma* **90 E5** 20 30N 95 0 E
Yenanma, *Burma* **90 F5** 19 46N 94 49 E
Yenbo = Yanbu 'al Baḩr, *Si. Arabia* **96 F3** 24 0N 38 5 E
Yenda, *Australia* **129 C7** 34 13 S 146 14 E
Yende Millimou, *Guinea* **112 D2** 8 55N 10 10W
Yendéré, *Burkina Faso* **112 C4** 10 12N 4 59W
Yendi, *Ghana* **113 D4** 9 29N 0 1W
Yengisar, *China* **65 D8** 38 56N 76 9 E
Yengo, *Congo* **114 B3** 0 22N 15 29 E
Yengo Nat. Park, *Australia* **129 B9** 33 0 S 150 55 E
Yéni, *Niger* **113 C5** 13 30N 3 1 E
Yenice, *Ankara, Turkey* **100 C5** 39 14N 32 42 E
Yenice, *Aydın, Turkey* **49 D10** 37 49N 28 35 E
Yenice, *Çanakkale, Turkey* **49 B9** 39 55N 27 17 E
Yenice, *Edirne, Turkey* **51 F10** 40 42N 26 9 E
Yenice →, *Turkey* **100 D6** 37 37N 35 33 E
Yenifoça, *Turkey* **49 C8** 38 44N 26 51 E
Yenihisar, *Turkey* **49 D9** 37 22N 27 16 E
Yeniköy, *Bursa, Turkey* **51 F13** 40 31N 29 22 E
Yeniköy, *Çanakkale, Turkey* **49 B8** 39 55N 26 10 E
Yeniköy, *Kütahya, Turkey* **49 C11** 38 52N 29 17 E
Yenipazar, *Turkey* **49 D10** 37 49N 28 11 E
Yenisaía, *Greece* **51 E8** 41 1N 24 57 E
Yenişehir, *Turkey* **51 F13** 40 16N 29 38 E
Yenisey →, *Russia* **66 B9** 71 50N 82 40 E
Yeniseysk, *Russia* **67 D10** 58 27N 92 13 E
Yeniseyskiy Zaliv, *Russia* **66 B9** 72 20N 81 0 E
Yennádhi, *Greece* **38 E11** 36 2N 27 56 E
Yenne, *France* **29 C9** 45 43N 5 44 E
Yenotayevka, *Russia* **61 G8** 47 15N 47 0 E
Yenyuka, *Russia* **67 D13** 57 57N 121 15 E
Yeo →, *U.K.* **21 G5** 51 2N 2 49W
Yeo, L., *Australia* **125 E3** 28 0 S 124 30 E
Yeo I., *Canada* **150 A3** 45 24N 81 48W

Yeola, *India* 94 D2 20 2N 74 30 E
Yeoryioúpolis, *Greece* 39 E5 35 20N 24 15 E
Yeovil, *U.K.* 21 G5 50 57N 2 38W
Yepes, *Spain* 42 F7 39 55N 3 39W
Yeppoon, *Australia* 126 C5 23 5 S 150 47 E
Yérakas, Ákra, *Greece* 39 D2 37 42N 20 59 E
Yeráki, *Greece* 48 D4 37 0N 22 42 E
Yerbent, *Turkmenistan* 66 F6 39 30N 58 50 E
Yerbogachen, *Russia* 67 C11 61 16N 108 0 E
Yerevan, *Armenia* 61 K7 40 10N 44 31 E
Yerington, *U.S.A.* 158 G4 38 59N 119 10W
Yerkesik, *Turkey* 49 D10 37 7N 28 19 E
Yerköy, *Turkey* 100 C6 39 38N 34 28 E
Yerla →, *India* 94 F2 16 50N 74 30 E
Yermak, *Kazakstan* 66 D8 52 2N 76 55 E
Yermo, *U.S.A.* 161 L10 34 54N 116 50W
Yerólakkos, *Cyprus* 39 E9 35 11N 33 15 E
Yeropol, *Russia* 67 C17 65 15N 168 40 E
Yeropótamos →, *Greece* 39 E5 35 3N 24 50 E
Yeroskipos, *Cyprus* 39 F8 34 46N 32 28 E
Yershov, *Russia* 60 E9 51 23N 48 27 E
Yerupaja, Cerro, *Peru* 172 C2 10 16 S 76 55W
Yerushalayim = Jerusalem, *Israel* 103 D4 31 47N 35 10 E
Yerville, *France* 26 C7 49 40N 0 53 E
Yes Tor, *U.K.* 21 G4 50 41N 4 0W
Yesagyo, *Burma* 90 E5 21 38N 95 14 E
Yesan, *S. Korea* 75 F14 36 41N 126 51 E
Yeshin, *Burma* 90 D5 23 43N 95 6 E
Yeşilhisar, *Turkey* 100 C6 38 20N 35 5 E
Yeşilırmak →, *Turkey* 100 B7 41 22N 36 37 E
Yeşilkent, *Turkey* 100 D7 36 57N 36 12 E
Yeşilköy, *Turkey* 51 F12 40 57N 28 49 E
Yeşilova, *Turkey* 49 D11 37 31N 29 46 E
Yeşilyurt, *Manisa, Turkey* 49 C10 38 22N 28 40 E
Yeşilyurt, *Muğla, Turkey* 49 D10 37 10N 28 20 E
Yesnogorsk, *Russia* 58 E9 54 32N 37 38 E
Yeso, *U.S.A.* 155 H2 34 26N 104 37W
Yessentuki, *Russia* 61 H6 44 5N 42 53 E
Yessey, *Russia* 67 C11 68 29N 102 10 E
Yeste, *Spain* 41 G2 38 22N 2 19W
Yetman, *Australia* 127 D5 28 56 S 150 48 E
Yetti, *Mauritania* 110 C3 26 10N 7 50W
Yeu, Î. d', *France* 26 F4 46 42N 2 20W
Yevlakh = Yevlax, *Azerbaijan* 61 K8 40 39N 47 7 E
Yevlax, *Azerbaijan* 61 K8 40 39N 47 7 E
Yevpatoriya, *Ukraine* 59 K7 45 15N 33 20 E
Yeya →, *Russia* 59 J10 46 40N 38 40 E
Yeysk, *Russia* 59 J10 46 40N 38 12 E
Yezd = Yazd, *Iran* 97 D7 31 55N 54 27 E
Yezerishche, *Belarus* 58 E5 55 50N 29 59 E
Yhati, *Paraguay* 174 B4 25 45 S 56 35W
Yhú, *Paraguay* 175 B4 25 0 S 56 0W
Yi →, *Uruguay* 174 C4 33 7 S 57 8W
Yi 'Allaq, G., *Egypt* 103 E2 30 22N 33 32 E
Yi He →, *China* 75 G10 34 10N 118 8 E
Yi Xian, *Anhui, China* 77 C11 29 55N 117 57 E
Yi Xian, *Hebei, China* 74 E8 39 20N 115 30 E
Yi Xian, *Liaoning, China* 75 D11 41 30N 121 22 E
Yialí, *Greece* 49 E9 36 41N 27 11 E
Yialiás →, *Cyprus* 39 E9 35 9N 33 44 E
Yi'allaq, G., *Egypt* 106 A3 30 21N 33 31 E
Yialousa, *Cyprus* 39 E10 35 32N 34 10 E
Yiáltra, *Greece* 48 C4 38 51N 22 59 E
Yianisádhes, *Greece* 39 E7 35 20N 26 10 E
Yiannitsa, *Greece* 50 F6 40 46N 22 24 E
Yibin, *China* 76 C5 28 45N 104 32 E
Yichang, *China* 77 B8 30 40N 111 20 E
Yicheng, *Henan, China* 77 B9 31 41N 112 12 E
Yicheng, *Shanxi, China* 74 G6 35 42N 111 40 E
Yichuan, *China* 74 F6 36 2N 110 10 E
Yichun, *Heilongjiang, China* 69 B7 47 44N 128 52 E
Yichun, *Jiangxi, China* 77 D10 27 48N 114 22 E
Yidu, *China* 75 F10 36 43N 118 28 E
Yidun, *China* 76 B2 30 22N 99 21 E
Yifag, *Ethiopia* 107 E4 12 4N 37 46 E
Yifeng, *China* 77 C10 28 22N 114 45 E
Yihuang, *China* 77 D11 27 30N 116 12 E
Yijun, *China* 74 G5 35 28N 109 8 E
Yıldız Dağları, *Turkey* 51 E11 41 48N 27 36 E
Yıldızeli, *Turkey* 100 C7 39 51N 36 36 E
Yilehuli Shan, *China* 69 A7 51 20N 124 20 E
Yiliang, *Yunnan, China* 76 D5 27 38N 104 2 E
Yiliang, *Yunnan, China* 76 E4 24 56N 103 11 E
Yilong, *China* 76 B6 31 34N 106 23 E
Yimen, *China* 76 E4 24 40N 102 10 E
Yimianpo, *China* 75 B15 45 7N 128 2 E
Yinchuan, *China* 74 E4 38 30N 106 15 E
Yindaik, *Burma* 90 D5 23 35N 95 22 E
Yindarlgooda, L., *Australia* 125 F3 30 40 S 121 52 E
Ying He →, *China* 74 H9 32 30N 116 30 E
Ying Xian, *China* 74 E7 39 32N 113 10 E
Yingcheng, *China* 77 B9 30 56N 113 35 E
Yingde, *China* 77 E9 24 10N 113 25 E
Yingjiang, *China* 76 E1 24 41N 97 55 E
Yingjing, *China* 76 C4 29 41N 102 52 E
Yingkou, *China* 75 D12 40 37N 122 18 E
Yingshan, *Henan, China* 77 B9 31 35N 113 50 E
Yingshan, *Hubei, China* 77 B10 30 41N 115 32 E
Yingshan, *Sichuan, China* 76 B6 31 4N 106 35 E
Yingshang, *China* 77 A11 32 38N 116 12 E
Yingtan, *China* 77 C11 28 12N 117 0 E
Yining, *China* 66 E9 43 58N 81 10 E
Yinjiang, *China* 76 C7 28 1N 108 21 E
Yinmabin, *Burma* 90 D5 22 10N 94 55 E
Yiofiros →, *Greece* 39 E6 35 20N 25 6 E
Yioúra, *Nótios Aiyaíon, Greece* 48 D6 37 32N 24 40 E
Yioúra, *Thessalía, Greece* 48 B6 39 23N 24 10 E
Yipinglang, *China* 76 E3 25 10N 101 52 E
Yirápetra, Ákra, *Greece* 39 B2 38 51N 20 41 E
Yirba Muda, *Ethiopia* 107 F4 6 12N 38 42 E
Yirga Alem, *Ethiopia* 107 F4 6 48N 38 22 E
Yirol, *Sudan* 107 F3 6 33N 30 30 E
Yirrkala, *Australia* 126 A2 12 14 S 136 56 E
Yishan, *China* 76 E7 24 28N 108 38 E
Yishui, *China* 75 G10 35 47N 118 30 E
Yishun, *Singapore* 87 d 1 26N 103 50 E
Yíthion, *Greece* 48 E4 36 46N 22 34 E
Yitong, *China* 75 C13 43 13N 125 20 E
Yiwu, *China* 77 C13 29 20N 120 3 E
Yixing, *China* 77 B12 31 21N 119 48 E
Yiyang, *Henan, China* 74 G7 34 27N 112 10 E
Yiyang, *Hunan, China* 77 C9 28 35N 112 18 E
Yiyang, *Jiangxi, China* 77 C11 28 22N 117 20 E
Yizhang, *China* 77 E9 25 27N 112 57 E
Yizheng, *China* 77 A12 32 18N 119 10 E
Yli-Kitka, *Finland* 14 C23 66 8N 28 30 E
Ylitornio, *Finland* 14 C20 66 19N 23 39 E
Ylivieska, *Finland* 14 D21 64 4N 24 28 E
Yngaren, *Sweden* 17 F10 58 50N 16 35 E
Yoakum, *U.S.A.* 155 L6 29 17N 97 9W
Yob Wildlife Reserve, *Eritrea* 107 D4 17 15N 37 50 E
Yobe □, *Nigeria* 113 C7 12 0N 11 30 E
Yobuko, *Japan* 72 D1 33 32N 129 54 E
Yog Pt., *Phil.* 80 D5 14 6N 124 12 E
Yogan, *Togo* 113 D5 6 23N 1 30 E
Yoğuntaş, *Turkey* 51 E11 41 50N 27 4 E
Yogyakarta, *Indonesia* 85 D4 7 49 S 110 22 E
Yogyakarta □, *Indonesia* 85 D4 7 48 S 110 22 E
Yoho Nat. Park, *Canada* 142 C5 51 25N 116 30W
Yojoa, L. de, *Honduras* 164 D2 14 53N 88 0W
Yŏju, *S. Korea* 75 F14 37 20N 127 35 E
Yokadouma, *Cameroon* 114 B2 3 26N 14 55 E
Yōkaichi, *Japan* 73 B8 35 6N 136 12 E
Yōkaichiba, *Japan* 73 B12 35 42N 140 33 E
Yokkaichi, *Japan* 73 C8 34 55N 136 38 E
Yoko, *Cameroon* 113 D7 5 32N 12 20 E
Yokohama, *Japan* 73 B11 35 27N 139 28 E
Yokosuka, *Japan* 73 B11 35 20N 139 40 E
Yokote, *Japan* 70 E10 39 20N 140 30 E
Yola, *Nigeria* 113 D7 9 10N 12 29 E
Yolaina, Cordillera de, *Nic.* 164 D3 11 30N 84 0W
Yolombo, *Dem. Rep. of the Congo* 114 C4 1 36 S 23 12 E
Yoloten, *Turkmenistan* 97 B9 37 18N 62 21 E
Yom →, *Thailand* 78 A2 15 35N 100 1 E
Yombi, *Gabon* 114 C2 1 26 S 10 37 E
Yonago, *Japan* 72 B5 35 25N 133 19 E
Yonaguni-Jima, *Japan* 71 M1 24 27N 123 0 E
Yŏnan, *N. Korea* 75 F14 37 55N 126 11 E
Yonezawa, *Japan* 70 F10 37 57N 140 4 E
Yong Peng, *Malaysia* 87 L4 2 0N 103 3 E
Yong Sata, *Thailand* 87 J2 7 8N 99 41 E
Yongama, *Dem. Rep. of the Congo* 114 B4 0 2N 24 35 E
Yongamp'o, *N. Korea* 75 E13 39 56N 124 23 E
Yong'an, *China* 77 E11 25 59N 117 25 E
Yongcheng, *China* 74 H9 33 55N 116 20 E
Yŏngch'ŏn, *S. Korea* 75 G15 35 58N 128 56 E
Yongchuan, *China* 76 C5 29 17N 105 55 E
Yongchun, *China* 77 E12 25 16N 118 20 E
Yongde, *China* 76 E2 24 5N 99 25 E
Yongdeng, *China* 74 F2 36 38N 103 25 E
Yongding, *China* 77 E11 24 43N 116 45 E
Yŏngdŏk, *S. Korea* 75 F15 36 24N 129 22 E
Yŏngdŭngpo, *S. Korea* 75 F14 37 31N 126 54 E
Yongfeng, *China* 77 D10 27 20N 115 22 E
Yongfu, *China* 76 E7 24 59N 109 59 E
Yonggyap Pass, *India* 90 A5 29 17N 95 37 E
Yonghe, *China* 74 F6 36 46N 110 38 E
Yonghong, *India* 90 B5 26 28N 94 58 E
Yŏnghŭng, *N. Korea* 75 E14 39 31N 127 18 E
Yongji, *China* 74 G6 34 52N 110 28 E
Yongjia, *China* 77 C13 28 10N 120 45 E
Yŏngju, *S. Korea* 75 F15 36 50N 128 40 E
Yongkang, *Yunnan, China* 76 E2 24 9N 99 20 E
Yongkang, *Zhejiang, China* 77 C13 28 55N 120 2 E
Yongnian, *China* 74 F8 36 47N 114 29 E
Yongning, *Guangxi Zhuangzu, China* 76 F7 22 44N 108 28 E
Yongning, *Ningxia Huizu, China* 74 E4 38 15N 106 14 E
Yongping, *China* 76 E2 25 27N 99 38 E
Yongqing, *China* 74 E9 39 25N 116 28 E
Yongren, *China* 76 D3 26 4N 101 40 E
Yongshan, *China* 76 C4 28 11N 103 35 E
Yongsheng, *China* 76 D3 26 38N 100 46 E
Yongshun, *China* 76 C7 29 2N 109 51 E
Yongtai, *China* 77 E12 25 49N 118 58 E
Yŏngwŏl, *S. Korea* 75 F15 37 11N 128 28 E
Yongxin = Jinggangshan, *China* 77 D10 26 58N 114 15 E
Yongxing, *China* 77 D9 26 9N 113 8 E
Yongxiu, *China* 77 C10 29 2N 115 42 E
Yongzhou, *China* 77 D8 26 17N 111 37 E
Yonibana, *S. Leone* 112 D2 8 30N 12 19W
Yonkers, *U.S.A.* 151 F11 40 56N 73 54W
Yonne □, *France* 27 E10 47 50N 3 40 E
Yonne →, *France* 27 D9 48 23N 2 58 E
Yopal, *Colombia* 168 B3 5 21N 72 23W
Yopurga, *China* 65 D8 39 15N 76 45 E
York, *Australia* 125 F2 31 52 S 116 47 E
York, *U.K.* 20 D6 53 58N 1 6W
York, *Ala., U.S.A.* 155 J10 32 29N 88 18W
York, *Nebr., U.S.A.* 154 E6 40 52N 97 36W
York, *Pa., U.S.A.* 148 F7 39 58N 76 44W
York, C., *Australia* 126 A3 10 42 S 142 31 E
York, City of □, *U.K.* 20 D6 53 58N 1 6W
York, Kap, *Greenland* 10 B4 75 55N 66 25W
York, Vale of, *U.K.* 20 C6 54 15N 1 25W
York Haven, *U.S.A.* 150 F8 40 7N 76 46W
York Sd., *Australia* 124 C4 15 0 S 125 5 E
Yorke Pen., *Australia* 128 C2 34 50 S 137 40 E
Yorketown, *Australia* 128 C2 35 0 S 137 33 E
Yorkshire Wolds, *U.K.* 20 C7 54 8N 0 31W
Yorkton, *Canada* 143 C8 51 11N 102 28W
Yorkville, *Calif., U.S.A.* 160 G3 38 52N 123 13W
Yorkville, *Ga., U.S.A.* 152 B5 33 55N 84 58W
Yorkville, *Ill., U.S.A.* 157 C8 41 38N 88 27W
Yoro, *Honduras* 164 C2 15 9N 87 7W
Yoron-Jima, *Japan* 71 L4 27 2N 128 26 E
Yorosso, *Mali* 112 C4 12 17N 4 55W
Yos Sudarso, Pulau = Dolak, Pulau, *Indonesia* 83 C5 8 0 S 138 30 E
Yos Sudarso, Teluk, *Indonesia* 83 B6 2 35 S 140 45 E
Yosemite Nat. Park, *U.S.A.* 160 H7 37 45N 119 40W
Yosemite Village, *U.S.A.* 160 H7 37 45N 119 35W
Yoshida, *Japan* 72 C4 34 40N 132 42 E
Yoshimatsu, *Japan* 72 F2 32 0N 130 47 E
Yoshkar Ola, *Russia* 60 B8 56 38N 47 55 E
Yŏsu, *S. Korea* 75 G14 34 47N 127 45 E
Yotala, *Bolivia* 173 D4 19 10 S 65 17W
Yotvata, *Israel* 103 F4 29 55N 35 2 E
You Jiang →, *China* 76 F6 22 50N 108 6 E
You Xian, *China* 77 D9 27 1N 113 17 E
Youbou, *Canada* 160 B2 48 53N 124 13W
Youghal, *Ireland* 23 E4 51 56N 7 52W
Youghal B., *Ireland* 23 E4 51 55N 7 49W
Youkounkoun, *Guinea* 112 C2 12 35N 13 11W
Young, *Australia* 129 C8 34 19 S 148 18 E
Young, *Canada* 143 C7 51 47N 105 45W
Young, *Uruguay* 174 C4 32 44 S 57 36W
Young Ra., *N.Z.* 131 E4 44 10 S 169 30 E
Younghusband, L., *Australia* 128 A2 30 50 S 136 5 E
Younghusband Pen., *Australia* 128 D3 36 0 S 139 25 E
Youngstown, *Canada* 143 C6 51 35N 111 10W
Youngstown, *Fla., U.S.A.* 153 E4 30 22N 85 26W
Youngstown, *N.Y., U.S.A.* 150 C5 43 15N 79 3W
Youngstown, *Ohio, U.S.A.* 150 E4 41 6N 80 39W
Youngsville, *U.S.A.* 150 E5 41 51N 79 19W
Youngwood, *U.S.A.* 150 F5 40 14N 79 34W
Youssoufia, *Morocco* 110 B3 32 16N 8 31W
Youxi, *China* 77 D12 26 10N 118 13 E
Youyang, *China* 76 C7 28 47N 108 42 E
Youyu, *China* 74 D7 40 10N 112 20 E
Yozgat, *Turkey* 100 C6 39 51N 34 47 E
Ypané →, *Paraguay* 174 A4 23 29 S 57 19W
Yport, *France* 26 C7 49 45N 0 15 E
Ypres = Ieper, *Belgium* 24 D2 50 51N 2 53 E
Ypsilanti, *U.S.A.* 157 B13 42 14N 83 37W
Yreka, *U.S.A.* 158 F2 41 44N 122 38W
Ysabel Chan., *Papua N. G.* 132 B5 2 0 S 150 0 E
Yssingeaux, *France* 29 C8 45 9N 4 8 E
Ystabø, *Norway* 18 E2 59 3N 5 23 E
Ystad, *Sweden* 17 J7 55 26N 13 50 E
Ysyk-Köl = Balykchy, *Kyrgyzstan* 65 B8 42 26N 76 12 E
Ysyk-Köl, *Kyrgyzstan* 66 E8 42 25N 77 15 E
Ythan →, *U.K.* 22 D7 57 19N 1 59W
Ytre Arna, *Norway* 18 D2 60 27N 5 25 E
Ytre Enebakk, *Norway* 18 E8 59 44N 11 0 E
Ytre Rendal, *Norway* 18 C8 61 46N 11 8 E
Ytterhogdal, *Sweden* 16 B8 62 12N 14 56 E
Ytyk-Kyuyel, *Russia* 67 C14 62 30N 133 45 E
Yu Jiang →, *China* 76 F7 23 22N 110 3 E
Yu Shan, *Taiwan* 77 F13 23 30N 120 58 E
Yu Xian = Yuzhou, *China* 74 G7 34 10N 113 28 E
Yu Xian, *Hebei, China* 74 E8 39 50N 114 35 E
Yu Xian, *Shanxi, China* 74 E7 38 5N 113 20 E
Yuan Jiang →, *Hunan, China* 77 C8 28 55N 111 50 E
Yuan Jiang →, *Yunnan, China* 76 F4 22 20N 103 59 E
Yuan'an, *China* 77 B8 31 3N 111 34 E
Yuanjiang, *Hunan, China* 77 C9 28 47N 112 21 E
Yuanjiang, *Yunnan, China* 76 F4 23 32N 102 0 E
Yüanli, *Taiwan* 77 E13 24 27N 120 39 E
Yüanlin, *Taiwan* 77 F13 23 58N 120 30 E
Yuanling, *China* 77 C8 28 29N 110 22 E
Yuanmou, *China* 76 E3 25 42N 101 53 E
Yuanqu, *China* 74 G6 35 18N 111 40 E
Yuanyang, *Henan, China* 74 G7 35 3N 113 58 E
Yuanyang, *Yunnan, China* 76 F4 23 10N 102 43 E
Yuat →, *Papua N. G.* 132 C2 4 10 S 143 52 E
Yuba →, *U.S.A.* 160 F5 39 8N 121 36W
Yuba City, *U.S.A.* 160 F5 39 8N 121 37W
Yūbari, *Japan* 70 C10 43 4N 141 59 E
Yubdo, *Ethiopia* 107 F4 8 58N 35 24 E
Yūbetsu, *Japan* 70 B11 44 13N 143 50 E
Yubo, *Sudan* 107 F2 5 23N 27 25 E
Yucatán □, *Mexico* 163 C7 21 30N 86 30W
Yucatán, Canal de, *Caribbean* 164 B2 22 0N 86 30W
Yucatán, Península de, *Mexico* 136 H11 19 30N 89 0W
Yucatán Basin, *Cent. Amer.* 136 H11 19 0N 86 0W
Yucatan Channel = Yucatán, Canal de, *Caribbean* 164 B2 22 0N 86 30W
Yucca, *U.S.A.* 161 L12 34 52N 114 9W
Yucca Valley, *U.S.A.* 161 L10 34 8N 116 27W
Yucheng, *China* 74 F9 36 55N 116 32 E
Yuci, *China* 74 F7 37 42N 112 46 E
Yudu, *China* 77 E10 25 59N 115 30 E
Yuechi, *China* 76 B6 30 34N 106 25 E
Yuen Long, *China* 69 G11 22 26N 114 2 E
Yuendumu, *Australia* 124 D5 22 16 S 131 49 E
Yueqing, *China* 77 C13 28 9N 120 59 E
Yueqing Wan, *China* 77 D13 28 5N 121 20 E
Yuexi, *Anhui, China* 77 B11 30 50N 116 20 E
Yuexi, *Sichuan, China* 76 C4 28 37N 102 26 E
Yueyang, *China* 77 C9 29 21N 113 5 E
Yufu-Dake, *Japan* 72 D3 33 17N 131 33 E
Yugan, *China* 77 C11 28 43N 116 37 E
Yugoslavia ■, *Europe* 50 C4 43 20N 20 0 E
Yuhuan, *China* 77 C13 28 9N 121 12 E
Yühuan Dao, *China* 77 C13 28 5N 121 15 E
Yujiang, *China* 77 C11 28 10N 116 43 E
Yukhnov, *Russia* 58 E8 54 44N 35 15 E
Yūki, *Japan* 73 A11 36 18N 139 53 E
Yukon →, *U.S.A.* 144 E7 62 32N 163 54W
Yukon Territory □, *Canada* 138 B6 63 0N 135 0W
Yüksekova, *Turkey* 101 D11 37 34N 44 16 E
Yukta, *Russia* 67 C11 63 26N 105 42 E
Yukuhashi, *Japan* 72 D2 33 44N 130 59 E
Yulara, *Australia* 125 E5 25 10 S 130 55 E
Yule →, *Australia* 124 D2 20 41 S 118 17 E
Yuleba, *Australia* 127 D4 26 37 S 149 24 E
Yulee, *U.S.A.* 152 E8 30 38N 81 36W
Yuli, *Nigeria* 113 D7 9 44N 10 12 E
Yuli, *Taiwan* 77 F13 23 20N 121 18 E
Yulin, *Guangxi Zhuangzu, China* 77 F8 22 40N 110 8 E
Yülin, *Hainan, China* 87 C7 18 10N 109 31 E
Yulin, *Shaanxi, China* 74 E5 38 20N 109 30 E
Yuma, *Ariz., U.S.A.* 161 N12 32 43N 114 37W
Yuma, *Colo., U.S.A.* 154 E3 40 8N 102 43W
Yuma, B. de, *Dom. Rep.* 165 C6 18 20N 68 35W
Yumali, *Australia* 128 C3 35 32 S 139 45 E
Yumbe, *Uganda* 118 B3 3 28N 31 15 E
Yumbi, *Équateur, Dem. Rep. of the Congo* 114 C3 1 53 S 16 34 E
Yumbi, *Maniema, Dem. Rep. of the Congo* 118 C2 1 12 S 26 15 E
Yumbo, *Colombia* 168 C2 3 35N 76 28W
Yumen, *China* 68 C4 39 50N 97 30 E
Yumurtalık, *Turkey* 100 D6 36 45N 35 43 E
Yun Gui Gaoyuan, *China* 76 E3 26 0N 104 0 E
Yun Ho →, *China* 75 E9 39 10N 117 10 E
Yun Ling, *China* 76 D2 27 0N 99 20 E
Yun Xian, *Hubei, China* 77 A8 32 50N 110 46 E
Yun Xian, *Yunnan, China* 76 E3 24 27N 100 8 E
Yuna, *Australia* 125 E2 28 20 S 115 0 E
Yunak, *Turkey* 100 C4 38 49N 31 43 E
Yunan, *China* 77 F8 23 12N 111 30 E
Yunaska I., *U.S.A.* 144 K5 52 38N 170 40W
Yuncheng, *Henan, China* 74 G8 35 36N 115 57 E
Yuncheng, *Shanxi, China* 74 G6 35 2N 111 0 E
Yunfu, *China* 77 F9 22 50N 112 5 E
Yungas, *Bolivia* 173 D4 17 0 S 66 0W
Yungay, *Chile* 174 D1 37 10 S 72 5W
Yungay, *Peru* 172 B2 9 2 S 77 45W
Yunhe, *China* 77 C12 28 8N 119 33 E
Yunkai Dashan, *China* 77 F8 22 30N 111 0 E
Yunlin, *Taiwan* 77 F13 23 42N 120 30 E
Yunlong, *China* 76 E2 25 57N 99 13 E
Yunmeng, *China* 77 B9 31 2N 113 43 E
Yunnan □, *China* 76 E4 25 0N 102 0 E
Yunotsu, *Japan* 72 B4 35 5N 132 21 E
Yunquera de Henares, *Spain* 40 E1 40 47N 3 11W
Yunt Dağı, *Turkey* 49 C9 38 56N 27 13 E
Yunta, *Australia* 128 B3 32 34 S 139 36 E
Yunxi, *China* 74 H6 33 0N 110 22 E
Yunxiao, *China* 77 F11 23 59N 117 18 E
Yuping, *China* 76 D7 27 13N 108 56 E
Yupukarri, *Guyana* 169 C6 3 45N 59 20W
Yupyongdong, *N. Korea* 75 D15 41 49N 128 53 E
Yuqing, *China* 76 D6 27 13N 107 53 E
Yuraygir Nat. Park, *Australia* 127 D5 29 45 S 153 15 E
Yurga, *Russia* 66 D9 55 42N 84 51 E
Yurimaguas, *Peru* 172 B2 5 55 S 76 7W
Yurla, *Russia* 64 B5 59 22N 54 10 E
Yurya, *Russia* 64 B2 59 1N 49 13 E
Yuryev-Polskiy, *Russia* 58 D10 56 30N 39 40 E
Yuryevets, *Russia* 60 B6 57 25N 43 2 E
Yuryuzan, *Russia* 64 D7 54 57N 58 28 E
Yuscarán, *Honduras* 164 D2 13 58N 86 45W
Yūsef, Bahr →, *Egypt* 106 B3 28 25N 30 35 E
Yushan, *China* 77 C12 28 42N 118 10 E
Yushanzhen, *China* 76 C7 29 28N 108 22 E
Yushe, *China* 74 F7 37 4N 112 58 E
Yushu, *Jilin, China* 75 B14 44 43N 126 38 E
Yushu, *Qinghai, China* 68 C4 33 5N 96 55 E
Yusufeli, *Turkey* 101 B9 40 50N 41 33 E
Yutai, *China* 74 G9 35 0N 116 45 E
Yutian, *China* 75 E9 39 53N 117 45 E
Yuxarı Qarabağ = Nagorno-Karabakh, *Azerbaijan* 101 C12 39 55N 46 45 E
Yuxi, *China* 76 E4 24 30N 102 35 E
Yuyao, *China* 77 B13 30 3N 121 10 E
Yuzawa, *Japan* 70 E10 39 10N 140 30 E
Yuzha, *Russia* 60 B6 56 34N 42 1 E
Yuzhno-Sakhalinsk, *Russia* 67 E15 46 58N 142 45 E
Yuzhnouralsk, *Russia* 64 D8 54 26N 61 15 E
Yuzhou, *China* 74 G7 34 10N 113 28 E
Yvelines □, *France* 27 D8 48 40N 1 45 E
Yverdon-les-Bains, *Switz.* 32 C3 46 47N 6 38 E
Yvetot, *France* 26 C7 49 37N 0 44 E
Yvonand, *Switz.* 32 C3 46 48N 6 44 E
Yzeure, *France* 27 F10 46 33N 3 22 E

Z

Zaalayskiy Khrebet, *Tajikistan* 65 D6 39 20N 73 0 E
Zaanstad, *Neths.* 24 B4 52 27N 4 50 E
Zab, Monts du, *Algeria* 111 B6 34 55N 5 0 E
Zāb al Kabīr →, *Iraq* 101 D10 36 1N 43 24 E
Zāb aş Şagīr →, *Iraq* 101 E10 35 17N 43 29 E
Žabalj, *Serbia, Yug.* 52 E5 45 21N 20 5 E
Žabari, *Serbia, Yug.* 50 B5 44 22N 21 15 E
Zabarjad, *Egypt* 106 C4 23 40N 36 12 E
Zabaykalsk, *Russia* 67 E12 49 40N 117 25 E
Zabbar, *Malta* 38 F8 35 53N 14 32 E
Zabīd, *Yemen* 98 D3 14 0N 43 10 E
Zabīd, W. →, *Yemen* 98 D3 14 7N 43 6 E
Zabki, *Poland* 55 F8 52 17N 21 7 E
Ząbkowice Śląskie, *Poland* 55 H3 50 35N 16 50 E
Žabljak, *Montenegro, Yug.* 50 C3 43 18N 19 5 E
Zabłudów, *Poland* 55 F9 53 0N 23 19 E
Żabno, *Poland* 55 H7 50 9N 20 53 E
Zābol, *Iran* 97 D9 31 0N 61 32 E
Zābol □, *Afghan.* 91 B2 32 0N 67 0 E
Zābolī, *Iran* 97 E9 27 10N 61 35 E
Zabré, *Burkina Faso* 113 C4 11 12N 0 36W
Zábřeh, *Czech Rep.* 35 B9 49 53N 16 52 E
Zabrze, *Poland* 55 H5 50 18N 18 50 E
Zabzuga, *Ghana* 113 D5 9 20N 0 30 E
Zacapa, *Guatemala* 164 D2 14 59N 89 31W
Zacapu, *Mexico* 162 D4 19 50N 101 43W
Zacatecas, *Mexico* 162 C4 22 49N 102 34W
Zacatecas □, *Mexico* 162 C4 23 30N 103 0W
Zacatecoluca, *El Salv.* 164 D2 13 29N 88 51W
Zachary, *U.S.A.* 155 K9 30 39N 91 9W
Zachodnio-Pomorskie □, *Poland* 54 E2 53 40N 15 50 E
Zacoalco, *Mexico* 162 C4 20 14N 103 33W
Zacualtipán, *Mexico* 163 C5 20 39N 98 36W
Zadar, *Croatia* 45 D12 44 8N 15 14 E
Zadawa, *Nigeria* 113 C7 11 33N 10 19 E
Zadetkyi Kyun, *Burma* 87 G1 10 0N 98 25 E
Zadonsk, *Russia* 59 F10 52 25N 38 56 E
Zafarqand, *Iran* 97 C7 33 11N 52 29 E
Zafora, *Greece* 49 E8 36 5N 26 24 E
Zafra, *Spain* 43 G4 38 26N 6 30W
Żagań, *Poland* 55 G2 51 39N 15 22 E
Žagarė, *Lithuania* 54 B10 56 21N 23 15 E
Zagaoua, *Chad* 109 E4 15 30N 22 24 E
Zagazig, *Egypt* 106 H7 30 40N 31 30 E
Zāgheh, *Iran* 97 C6 33 30N 48 42 E
Zaghouan, *Tunisia* 108 A2 36 23N 10 10 E
Zaglivérion, *Greece* 50 F7 40 36N 23 15 E
Zaglou, *Algeria* 111 C4 27 17N 0 3W
Zagnanado, *Benin* 113 D5 7 18N 2 28 E
Zagorá, *Greece* 48 B5 39 27N 23 6 E
Zagora, *Morocco* 110 B3 30 22N 5 51W
Zagorje, *Slovenia* 45 B11 46 8N 15 0 E
Zagórów, *Poland* 55 F4 52 10N 17 54 E
Zagorsk = Sergiyev Posad, *Russia* 58 D10 56 20N 38 10 E
Zagórz, *Poland* 55 J9 49 30N 22 14 E
Zagreb, *Croatia* 45 C12 45 50N 15 58 E
Zāgros, Kūhhā-ye, *Iran* 97 C6 33 45N 48 5 E
Zagros Mts. = Zāgros, Kūhhā-ye, *Iran* 97 C6 33 45N 48 5 E
Žagubica, *Serbia, Yug.* 50 B5 44 15N 21 47 E
Zaguinaso, *Ivory C.* 112 C3 10 1N 6 14W
Zagyva →, *Hungary* 52 C5 47 5N 20 4 E
Zahamena, Réserve Naturelle Intégrale de, *Madag.* 117 B8 17 37 S 48 49 E
Zāhedān, *Fārs, Iran* 97 D7 28 46N 53 52 E
Zāhedān, *Sīstān va Balūchestān, Iran* 97 D9 29 30N 60 50 E
Zahirabad, *India* 94 F3 17 43N 77 37 E
Zahlah, *Lebanon* 103 B4 33 52N 35 50 E
Zahna, *Germany* 30 D8 51 55N 12 49 E
Záhony, *Hungary* 52 B7 48 25N 22 11 E
Zahrān, *Si. Arabia* 98 C3 17 40N 43 30 E
Zainsk, *Russia* 60 C11 55 18N 52 4 E
Zaïre = Congo →, *Africa* 115 D2 6 4 S 12 24 E
Zaire □, *Angola* 115 D2 7 0 S 14 0 E
Zaječar, *Serbia, Yug.* 50 C6 43 53N 22 18 E
Zaka, *Zimbabwe* 117 C5 20 20 S 31 29 E
Zakamensk, *Russia* 67 D11 50 23N 103 17 E
Zakani, *Dem. Rep. of the Congo* 114 B4 2 33N 23 16 E
Zakataly = Zaqatala, *Azerbaijan* 61 K8 41 38N 46 35 E
Zakbayemé, *Cameroon* 114 B2 4 2N 10 34 E
Zakháro, *Greece* 48 D3 37 29N 21 40 E
Zakhodnaya Dzvina = Daugava →, *Latvia* 15 H21 57 4N 24 3 E
Zākhū, *Iraq* 101 D10 37 10N 42 50 E
Zákinthos, *Greece* 39 D2 37 47N 20 54 E
Zákinthos □, *Greece* 48 D2 37 47N 20 57 E
Zakopane, *Poland* 55 J6 49 18N 19 57 E
Zakouma, *Chad* 109 F3 10 54N 19 49 E
Zakouma, Parc Nat. de, *Chad* 109 F3 10 52N 19 45 E
Zakroczym, *Poland* 55 F7 52 26N 20 38 E
Zákros, *Greece* 39 E7 35 6N 26 10 E
Zala, *Angola* 115 D2 7 52 S 13 42 E
Zala, *Ethiopia* 107 F4 6 28N 37 13 E
Zala □, *Hungary* 52 D1 46 42N 16 50 E
Zala →, *Hungary* 52 D2 46 43N 17 16 E
Zalaegerszeg, *Hungary* 52 D1 46 53N 16 47 E
Zalakomár, *Hungary* 52 D2 46 33N 17 10 E
Zalalövő, *Hungary* 52 D1 46 51N 16 35 E
Zalamea de la Serena, *Spain* 43 G5 38 40N 5 38W
Zalamea la Real, *Spain* 43 H4 37 41N 6 38W
Zalău, *Romania* 52 C8 47 12N 23 3 E
Zalazna, *Russia* 64 B4 58 39N 52 31 E
Žalec, *Slovenia* 45 B12 46 16N 15 10 E
Zaleshchiki = Zalishchyky, *Ukraine* 59 H3 48 45N 25 45 E
Zalew Wiślany, *Poland* 54 D6 54 20N 19 50 E
Zalewo, *Poland* 54 E6 53 50N 19 41 E
Zalim, *Si. Arabia* 98 B3 22 43N 42 10 E
Zalingei, *Sudan* 109 F4 12 51N 23 29 E
Zalishchyky, *Ukraine* 59 H3 48 45N 25 45 E
Zaltan, *Ajdābiyā, Libya* 108 C3 28 51N 19 52 E
Zaltan, *Zuwārah, Libya* 108 B2 32 57N 11 52 E
Zaltan, Jabal, *Libya* 108 C3 28 46N 19 45 E
Zalun, *Burma* 90 G5 17 29N 95 34 E
Zama L., *Canada* 142 B5 58 45N 119 5W
Zambales □, *Phil.* 80 D3 15 20N 120 10 E
Zambales Mts., *Phil.* 80 D3 15 45N 120 5 E
Zambeke, *Dem. Rep. of the Congo* 118 B2 2 8N 25 17 E
Zambeze →, *Africa* 119 F4 18 35 S 36 20 E
Zambezi = Zambeze →, *Africa* 119 F4 18 35 S 36 20 E
Zambezi, *Zambia* 115 E4 13 30 S 23 15 E
Zambezi Nat. Park, *Zimbabwe* 119 F2 17 54 S 25 41 E
Zambezia □, *Mozam.* 119 F4 16 15 S 37 30 E
Zambia ■, *Africa* 119 F2 15 0 S 28 0 E
Zamboanga, *Phil.* 81 H4 6 59N 122 3 E
Zamboanga del Norte □, *Phil.* 81 H4 8 0N 123 0 E
Zamboanga del Sur □, *Phil.* 81 H4 7 35N 123 0 E
Zambrano, *Colombia* 168 B3 9 45N 74 49W
Zambrów, *Poland* 55 F9 52 59N 22 14 E
Zametchino, *Russia* 60 D6 53 30N 42 30 E
Zamfara □, *Nigeria* 113 C6 12 10N 6 0 E
Zamfara →, *Nigeria* 113 C5 12 5N 4 2 E
Zamora, *Ecuador* 168 D2 4 4 S 78 58W
Zamora, *Mexico* 162 D4 20 0N 102 21W
Zamora, *Spain* 42 D5 41 30N 5 45W
Zamora □, *Spain* 42 D5 41 30N 5 46W
Zamora →, *Ecuador* 168 D2 2 59N 78 13W

Zamora-Chinchipe □, *Ecuador* **168 D2** 4 15 S 78 50W
Zamość, *Poland* **55 H10** 50 43N 23 15 E
Zams, *Austria* **33 B11** 47 9N 10 35 E
Zamtang, *China* **76 A3** 32 26N 101 6 E
Zamuro, Sierra del, *Venezuela* **169 C5** 4 0N 62 30W
Zamzam, W. →, *Libya* **108 B2** 30 58N 14 48 E
Zan, *Ghana* **113 D4** 9 26N 0 17W
Zanaga, *Congo* **114 C2** 2 48 S 13 48 E
Záncara →, *Spain* **41 F1** 39 18N 3 18W
Zanderij, *Surinam* **169 B6** 5 20N 55 16W
Zandu, *Dem. Rep. of the Congo* **115 D3** 5 11 S 18 16 E
Zandvoort, *Neths.* **24 B4** 52 22N 4 32 E
Zanesville, *U.S.A.* **150 G2** 39 56N 82 1W
Zangābād, *Iran* **96 B5** 38 26N 46 44 E
Zangue →, *Mozam.* **119 F4** 17 50 S 35 21 E
Zanjān, *Iran* **97 B6** 36 40N 48 35 E
Zanjān □, *Iran* **97 B6** 37 20N 49 30 E
Zanjān →, *Iran* **97 B6** 37 8N 47 47 E
Zannone, *Italy* **46 B6** 40 58N 13 3 E
Zante = Zákinthos, *Greece* **39 D2** 37 47N 20 54 E
Zanthus, *Australia* **125 F3** 31 2 S 123 34 E
Zanzibar, *Tanzania* **118 D4** 6 12 S 39 12 E
Zanzūr, *Libya* **108 B2** 32 55N 13 1 E
Zaouatallaz, *Algeria* **111 D6** 24 52N 8 30 E
Zaouiet El-Kala = Bordj Omar Driss, *Algeria* **111 C6** 28 10N 6 40 E
Zaouiet Reggâne, *Algeria* **111 C5** 26 32N 0 3 E
Zaoyang, *China* **77 A9** 32 10N 112 45 E
Zaozhuang, *China* **75 G9** 34 50N 117 35 E
Zap Suyu = Zāb al Kabīr →, *Iraq* **101 D10** 36 1N 43 24 E
Zapadna Morava →, *Serbia, Yug.* **50 C5** 43 38N 21 30 E
Zapadnaya Dvina = Daugava →, *Latvia* **15 H21** 57 4N 24 3 E
Zapadnaya Dvina, *Russia* **58 D7** 56 15N 32 3 E
Západné Beskydy, *Europe* **35 B12** 49 30N 19 0 E
Zapadni Rodopi, *Bulgaria* **50 E7** 41 50N 24 0 E
Západočeský □, *Czech Rep.* **34 B6** 49 35N 13 0 E
Zapala, *Argentina* **176 A2** 39 0 S 70 5W
Zapaleri, Cerro, *Bolivia* **174 A2** 22 49 S 67 11W
Zapata, *U.S.A.* **155 M5** 26 55N 99 16W
Zapatón →, *Spain* **43 F4** 39 0N 6 49W
Zapiga, *Chile* **172 D4** 19 40 S 69 55W
Zapolyarnyy, *Russia* **56 A5** 69 26N 30 51 E
Zaporizhzhya, *Ukraine* **59 J8** 47 50N 35 10 E
Zaporozhye = Zaporizhzhya, *Ukraine* **59 J8** 47 50N 35 10 E
Zaqatala, *Azerbaijan* **61 K8** 41 38N 46 35 E
Zara, *Turkey* **100 C7** 39 58N 37 43 E
Zarafshon, *Uzbekistan* **65 C2** 41 34N 64 12 E
Zaragoza, *Colombia* **168 B3** 7 30N 74 52W
Zaragoza, *Coahuila, Mexico* **162 B4** 28 30N 101 0W
Zaragoza, *Nuevo León, Mexico* **163 C5** 24 0N 99 46W
Zaragoza, *Spain* **40 D4** 41 39N 0 53W
Zaragoza □, *Spain* **40 D4** 41 35N 1 0W
Zarand, *Kermān, Iran* **97 D8** 30 46N 56 34 E
Zarand, *Markazī, Iran* **97 C6** 35 18N 50 25 E
Zărandului, Munţii, *Romania* **52 D7** 46 14N 22 7 E
Zaranj, *Afghan.* **91 C1** 30 55N 61 55 E
Zarasai, *Lithuania* **15 J22** 55 40N 26 20 E
Zárate, *Argentina* **174 C4** 34 7 S 59 0W
Zarautz, *Spain* **40 B2** 43 17N 2 10W
Zaraysk, *Russia* **58 E10** 54 48N 38 53 E
Zaraza, *Venezuela* **169 B4** 9 21N 65 19W
Zarbdar, *Uzbekistan* **65 C4** 40 3N 68 10 E
Zard, Kūh-e, *Iran* **97 C6** 32 22N 50 4 E
Zāreh, *Iran* **97 C6** 35 7N 49 9 E
Zari, *Nigeria* **113 C7** 13 4N 12 45 E
Zaria, *Nigeria* **113 C6** 11 0N 7 40 E
Żarki, *Poland* **55 H6** 50 38N 19 23 E
Zárkon, *Greece* **48 B4** 39 38N 22 6 E
Zarneh, *Iran* **96 C5** 33 55N 46 10 E
Zărneşti, *Romania* **53 E10** 45 33N 25 18 E
Zarós, *Greece* **39 E5** 35 8N 24 54 E
Żarów, *Poland* **55 H3** 50 56N 16 29 E
Zarqā', Nahr az →, *Jordan* **103 C4** 32 10N 35 37 E
Zarrīn, *Iran* **97 C7** 32 46N 54 37 E
Zaruma, *Ecuador* **168 D2** 3 40 S 79 38W
Żary, *Poland* **55 G2** 51 37N 15 10 E
Zarza de Granadilla, *Spain* **42 E4** 40 14N 6 3W
Zarzaîtine, *Algeria* **111 C6** 28 15N 9 34 E
Zarzal, *Colombia* **168 C2** 4 24N 76 4W
Zarzis, *Tunisia* **108 B2** 33 31N 11 2 E
Zas, *Spain* **42 B2** 43 4N 8 53W
Zaskar →, *India* **93 B7** 34 13N 77 20 E
Zaskar Mts., *India* **93 C7** 33 15N 77 30 E
Zastron, *S. Africa* **116 E4** 30 18 S 27 7 E
Žatec, *Czech Rep.* **34 A6** 50 20N 13 32 E
Zaterechnyy, *Russia* **61 H7** 44 48N 45 11 E
Zator, *Poland* **55 J6** 49 59N 19 28 E
Zavala, *Bos.-H.* **50 D1** 42 50N 17 59 E
Zavāreh, *Iran* **97 C7** 33 29N 52 28 E
Zave, *Zimbabwe* **117 B5** 17 6 S 30 1 E
Zavérdhas, Kólpos, *Greece* **39 B2** 38 47N 20 51 E
Zavetnoye, *Russia* **61 G6** 47 13N 43 50 E
Zavidovići, *Bos.-H.* **52 F3** 44 27N 18 10 E
Zavitinsk, *Russia* **67 D13** 50 10N 129 20 E
Zavodovski, I., *Antarctica* **7 B1** 56 0 S 27 45W
Zavolzhsk, *Russia* **60 B6** 57 30N 42 0 E
Zavolzhye, *Russia* **60 B6** 56 37N 43 26 E
Zawadzkie, *Poland* **55 H5** 50 37N 18 28 E
Zawichost, *Poland* **55 H8** 50 48N 21 51 E
Zawidów, *Poland* **55 G2** 51 1N 15 1 E
Zawiercie, *Poland* **55 H6** 50 30N 19 24 E
Zāwiyat al Bayḑā = Al Bayḑā, *Libya* **108 B4** 32 50N 21 44 E
Zāwiyat Masūs, *Libya* **108 B4** 31 35N 21 1 E
Zâwyet Shammas, *Egypt* **106 A2** 31 30N 26 37 E
Zâwyet Um el Rakham, *Egypt* **106 A2** 31 18N 27 1 E
Zâwyet Ungeîla, *Egypt* **106 A2** 31 23N 26 42 E
Zāyā, *Iraq* **96 C5** 33 33N 44 13 E
Zāyandeh →, *Iran* **97 C7** 32 35N 52 0 E
Zaymah, *Si. Arabia* **98 B3** 21 37N 40 6 E
Zaysan, *Kazakstan* **66 E9** 47 28N 84 52 E
Zaysan, Oz., *Kazakstan* **66 E9** 48 0N 83 0 E
Zayü, *China* **76 C1** 28 48N 97 27 E
Zazafotsy, *Madag.* **117 C8** 21 11 S 46 21 E
Zāzamt, W. →, *Libya* **108 B2** 30 29N 14 30 E
Zazir, O. →, *Algeria* **111 D6** 22 0N 5 40 E
Zázrivá, *Slovak Rep.* **35 B12** 49 16N 19 7 E
Zbarazh, *Ukraine* **59 H3** 49 43N 25 44 E
Zbąszyń, *Poland* **55 F2** 52 14N 15 56 E
Zbąszynek, *Poland* **55 F2** 52 16N 15 51 E
Zblewo, *Poland* **54 E5** 53 56N 18 19 E
Žďár nad Sázavov, *Czech Rep.* **34 B8** 49 34N 15 57 E
Zdolbuniv, *Ukraine* **59 G4** 50 30N 26 15 E
Ždrelo, *Serbia, Yug.* **50 B5** 44 16N 21 28 E
Zduńska Wola, *Poland* **55 G5** 51 37N 18 59 E
Zduny, *Poland* **55 G4** 51 39N 17 21 E
Zearing, *U.S.A.* **156 B3** 42 10N 93 18W
Zēbāk, *Afghan.* **65 E5** 36 31N 71 20 E
Zeballos, *Canada* **142 D3** 49 59N 126 50W
Zebbug, *Malta* **38 F7** 35 52N 14 26 E
Zebbug, *Gozo, Malta* **38 E6** 36 4N 14 14 E
Zebediela, *S. Africa* **117 C4** 24 20 S 29 17 E
Zebila, *Ghana* **113 C4** 10 55N 0 30W
Zebulon, *U.S.A.* **152 B5** 33 6N 84 21W
Zeebrugge, *Belgium* **24 C3** 51 19N 3 12 E
Zeehan, *Australia* **127 G4** 41 52 S 145 25 E
Zeeland, *U.S.A.* **157 B10** 42 49N 86 1W
Zeeland □, *Neths.* **24 C3** 51 30N 3 50 E
Zeerust, *S. Africa* **116 D4** 25 31 S 26 4 E
Z̨efat, *Israel* **103 C4** 32 58N 35 29 E
Zegdou, *Algeria* **110 C4** 29 51N 4 45W
Zege, *Ethiopia* **107 E4** 11 43N 37 18 E
Zeggerene, Iracher, *Mali* **113 B5** 16 49N 2 16 E
Zégoua, *Mali* **112 C3** 10 32N 5 35W
Zehdenick, *Germany* **30 C9** 52 58N 13 20 E
Zeigler, *U.S.A.* **156 G7** 37 54N 89 3W
Zeil, Mt., *Australia* **124 D5** 23 30 S 132 23 E
Zeila, *Somali Rep.* **120 B2** 11 21N 43 30 E
Zeist, *Neths.* **24 B5** 52 5N 5 15 E
Zeitz, *Germany* **30 D8** 51 2N 12 7 E
Zejtun, *Malta* **38 F8** 35 51N 14 32 E
Żelechów, *Poland* **55 G8** 51 49N 21 54 E
Zelengora, *Bos.-H.* **50 C2** 43 22N 18 30 E
Zelenodolsk, *Russia* **60 C9** 55 55N 48 30 E
Zelenogorsk, *Russia* **58 B5** 60 12N 29 43 E
Zelenograd, *Russia* **58 D9** 56 1N 37 12 E
Zelenogradsk, *Russia* **15 J19** 54 53N 20 29 E
Zelenokumsk, *Russia* **61 H6** 44 24N 44 0 E
Železná Ruda, *Czech Rep.* **34 B6** 49 8N 13 15 E
Železnik, *Serbia, Yug.* **50 B4** 44 43N 20 23 E
Zelfana, *Algeria* **111 B5** 32 27N 4 15 E
Zelienople, *U.S.A.* **150 F4** 40 48N 80 8W
Želiezovce, *Slovak Rep.* **35 C11** 48 3N 18 40 E
Zelina, *Croatia* **45 C13** 45 57N 16 16 E
Zell, *Baden-W., Germany* **31 H3** 47 42N 7 52 E
Zell, *Rhld-Pfz., Germany* **31 E3** 50 1N 7 10 E
Zell am See, *Austria* **34 D5** 47 19N 12 47 E
Zella-Mehlis, *Germany* **30 E6** 50 39N 10 40 E
Zelów, *Poland* **55 G6** 51 28N 19 14 E
Zeltweg, *Austria* **34 D7** 47 11N 14 45 E
Zembra, I., *Tunisia* **108 A2** 37 5N 10 56 E
Zémio, *C.A.R.* **118 A2** 5 2N 25 5 E
Zemmora, *Algeria* **111 A5** 35 44N 0 51 E
Zemmur, *W. Sahara* **110 C2** 25 5N 12 0W
Zemongo, Réserve de Faune de, *C.A.R.* **114 A5** 6 45N 25 5 E
Zemoul, O. →, *Algeria* **110 C3** 29 15N 7 0W
Zempléni-hegység, *Hungary* **52 B6** 48 25N 21 25 E
Zemplínska šírava, *Slovak Rep.* **35 C15** 48 48N 22 0 E
Zemun, *Serbia, Yug.* **50 B4** 44 51N 20 25 E
Zendeh Jān, *Afghan.* **91 B1** 34 21N 61 45 E
Zengbé, *Cameroon* **113 D7** 5 46N 13 4 E
Zengcheng, *China* **77 F9** 23 13N 113 52 E
Zenica, *Bos.-H.* **52 F2** 44 10N 17 57 E
Zentsūji, *Japan* **72 C5** 34 14N 133 47 E
Zenza →, *Angola* **115 D2** 8 45 S 13 24 E
Zenza do Itombe, *Angola* **115 D2** 9 16 S 14 13 E
Žepče, *Bos.-H.* **52 F3** 44 28N 18 2 E
Zephyrhills, *U.S.A.* **153 G7** 28 14N 82 11W
Zepu, *China* **65 D8** 38 12N 77 18 E
Zeraf, Bahr ez →, *Sudan* **107 F3** 9 42N 30 52 E
Zeravshan, *Tajikistan* **65 D4** 39 10N 68 39 E
Zeravshan →, *Asia* **65 D1** 39 22N 63 45 E
Zeravshanskiy Khrebet, *Tajikistan* **65 D4** 39 20N 69 0 E
Zerbst, *Germany* **30 D8** 51 58N 12 5 E
Żerków, *Poland* **55 F4** 52 4N 17 32 E
Zermatt, *Switz.* **32 D5** 46 2N 7 46 E
Zernez, *Switz.* **33 C10** 46 42N 10 7 E
Zernograd, *Russia* **61 G5** 46 52N 40 19 E
Zerqan, *Albania* **50 E4** 41 27N 20 20 E
Zestaponi, *Georgia* **61 J6** 42 6N 43 0 E
Zetel, *Germany* **30 B3** 53 25N 7 58 E
Zeulenroda, *Germany* **30 E7** 50 39N 11 59 E
Zeven, *Germany* **30 B5** 53 17N 9 16 E
Zevenaar, *Neths.* **24 C6** 51 56N 6 5 E
Zévio, *Italy* **44 C8** 45 22N 11 8 E
Zeya, *Russia* **67 D13** 53 48N 127 14 E
Zeya →, *Russia* **67 D13** 51 42N 128 53 E
Zeytinbaği, *Turkey* **51 F12** 40 24N 28 47 E
Zeytindağ, *Turkey* **49 C9** 38 58N 27 4 E
Zghartā, *Lebanon* **103 A4** 34 21N 35 53 E
Zgierz, *Poland* **55 G6** 51 50N 19 27 E
Zgorzelec, *Poland* **55 G2** 51 10N 15 0 E
Zguriţa, *Moldova* **53 B13** 48 8N 28 1 E
Zhabasak, *Kazakstan* **64 F8** 50 22N 61 41 E
Zhabinka, *Belarus* **59 F3** 52 13N 24 2 E
Zhailma, *Kazakstan* **64 F8** 51 37N 61 33 E
Zhalanash, *Kazakstan* **65 B9** 43 3N 78 38 E
Zhambyl = Taraz, *Kazakstan* **66 E8** 42 54N 71 22 E
Zhanatas, *Kazakstan* **65 B4** 43 35N 69 35 E
Zhangaly, *Kazakstan* **61 G10** 47 1N 50 37 E
Zhangaqazaly, *Kazakstan* **66 E7** 45 48N 62 6 E
Zhangaqŭrghan, *Kazakstan* **65 B4** 43 50N 68 48 E
Zhangatas = Zhanatas, *Kazakstan* **65 B4** 43 35N 69 35 E
Zhangbei, *China* **74 D8** 41 10N 114 45 E
Zhangguangcai Ling, *China* **75 B15** 45 0N 129 0 E
Zhangjiabian, *China* **69 F9** 22 33N 113 28 E
Zhangjiakou, *China* **74 D8** 40 48N 114 55 E
Zhangping, *China* **77 E11** 25 17N 117 23 E
Zhangpu, *China* **77 E11** 24 8N 117 35 E
Zhangshu, *China* **77 C10** 28 4N 115 29 E
Zhangwu, *China* **75 C12** 42 43N 123 52 E
Zhangye, *China* **68 C5** 38 50N 100 23 E
Zhangzhou, *China* **77 E11** 24 30N 117 35 E
Zhanhua, *China* **75 F10** 37 40N 118 8 E
Zhanjiang, *China* **77 G8** 21 15N 110 20 E
Zhannetty, Ostrov, *Russia* **67 B16** 76 43N 158 0 E
Zhanyi, *China* **76 E4** 25 38N 103 48 E
Zhanyu, *China* **75 B12** 44 30N 122 30 E
Zhao Xian, *China* **74 F8** 37 43N 114 45 E
Zhao'an, *China* **77 F11** 23 41N 117 10 E
Zhaocheng, *China* **74 F6** 36 22N 111 38 E
Zhaojue, *China* **76 C4** 28 1N 102 49 E
Zhaoping, *China* **77 E8** 24 11N 110 48 E
Zhaoqing, *China* **77 F9** 23 0N 112 20 E
Zhaotong, *China* **76 D4** 27 20N 103 44 E
Zhaoyuan, *Heilongjiang, China* **75 B13** 45 27N 125 0 E
Zhaoyuan, *Shandong, China* **75 F11** 37 20N 120 23 E
Zharkovskiy, *Russia* **58 E7** 55 56N 32 19 E
Zhashkiv, *Ukraine* **59 H6** 49 15N 30 5 E
Zhashui, *China* **74 H5** 33 40N 109 8 E
Zhayyq →, *Kazakstan* **57 E9** 47 0N 51 48 E
Zhdanov = Mariupol, *Ukraine* **59 J9** 47 5N 37 31 E
Zhdanovo, *Kazakstan* **65 B5** 43 40N 71 6 E
Zhecheng, *China* **74 G8** 34 7N 115 20 E
Zhegao, *China* **77 B11** 31 46N 117 45 E
Zhejiang □, *China* **77 C13** 29 0N 120 0 E
Zheleznodorozhnyy, *Russia* **56 B9** 62 35N 50 55 E
Zheleznogorsk, *Russia* **59 F8** 52 22N 35 23 E
Zheleznogorsk-Ilimskiy, *Russia* **67 D11** 56 34N 104 8 E
Zheltyye Vody = Zhovti Vody, *Ukraine* **59 H7** 48 21N 33 31 E
Zhen'an, *China* **74 H5** 33 27N 109 9 E
Zhenba, *China* **76 A6** 32 34N 107 58 E
Zhenfeng, *China* **76 E5** 25 22N 105 40 E
Zheng'an, *China* **76 C6** 28 32N 107 27 E
Zhengding, *China* **74 E8** 38 8N 114 32 E
Zhenghe, *China* **77 D12** 27 20N 118 50 E
Zhengyang, *China* **77 A10** 32 37N 114 22 E
Zhengyangguan, *China* **77 A11** 32 30N 116 29 E
Zhengzhou, *China* **74 G7** 34 45N 113 34 E
Zhenhai, *China* **77 C13** 29 59N 121 42 E
Zhenjiang, *China* **77 A12** 32 11N 119 26 E
Zhenkang, *China* **76 F2** 23 58N 99 0 E
Zhenlai, *China* **75 B12** 45 50N 123 5 E
Zhenning, *China* **76 D5** 26 4N 105 45 E
Zhenping, *Henan, China* **74 H7** 33 10N 112 16 E
Zhenping, *Shaanxi, China* **76 B7** 31 59N 109 31 E
Zhenxiong, *China* **76 D5** 27 27N 104 50 E
Zhenyuan, *Gansu, China* **74 G4** 35 35N 107 30 E
Zhenyuan, *Guizhou, China* **76 D7** 27 4N 108 21 E
Zherdevka, *Russia* **60 E5** 51 56N 41 29 E
Zherong, *China* **77 D12** 27 15N 119 52 E
Zhetigen, *Kazakstan* **65 B8** 43 40N 77 6 E
Zhetiqara, *Kazakstan* **64 E8** 52 11N 61 12 E
Zhetisay, *Kazakstan* **65 C4** 40 46N 68 19 E
Zhezqazghan, *Kazakstan* **66 E7** 47 44N 67 40 E
Zhicheng, *China* **77 B8** 30 25N 111 27 E
Zhidan, *China* **74 F5** 36 48N 108 48 E
Zhigansk, *Russia* **67 C13** 66 48N 123 27 E
Zhigulevsk, *Russia* **60 D9** 53 28N 49 30 E
Zhijiang, *Hubei, China* **77 B8** 30 28N 111 45 E
Zhijiang, *Hunan, China* **76 D7** 27 27N 109 42 E
Zhijin, *China* **76 D5** 26 37N 105 45 E
Zhilinda, *Russia* **67 C12** 70 0N 114 20 E
Zhirnovsk, *Russia* **60 E7** 50 57N 44 49 E
Zhitomir = Zhytomyr, *Ukraine* **59 G5** 50 20N 28 40 E
Zhizdra, *Russia* **58 F8** 53 45N 34 40 E
Zhlobin, *Belarus* **59 F6** 52 55N 30 0 E
Zhmerinka = Zhmerynka, *Ukraine* **59 H5** 49 2N 28 2 E
Zhmerynka, *Ukraine* **59 H5** 49 2N 28 2 E
Zhob, *Pakistan* **91 C3** 31 20N 69 31 E
Zhob →, *Pakistan* **92 C3** 32 4N 69 50 E
Zhodino = Zhodzina, *Belarus* **58 E5** 54 5N 28 17 E
Zhodzina, *Belarus* **58 E5** 54 5N 28 17 E
Zhokhova, Ostrov, *Russia* **67 B16** 76 4N 152 40 E
Zhongdian, *China* **76 D2** 27 48N 99 42 E
Zhongdong, *China* **76 F6** 22 48N 107 47 E
Zhongdu, *China* **76 E7** 24 40N 109 40 E
Zhongning, *China* **74 F3** 37 29N 105 40 E
Zhongshan, *Guangdong, China* **77 F9** 22 26N 113 20 E
Zhongshan, *Guangxi Zhuangzu, China* **77 E8** 24 29N 111 18 E
Zhongshankong, *China* **69 F9** 22 35N 113 29 E
Zhongtiao Shan, *China* **74 G6** 35 0N 111 10 E
Zhongwei, *China* **74 F3** 37 30N 105 12 E
Zhongxiang, *China* **77 B9** 31 12N 112 34 E
Zhongyang, *China* **74 F6** 37 20N 111 11 E
Zhoucun, *China* **75 F9** 36 47N 117 48 E
Zhouning, *China* **77 D12** 27 12N 119 20 E
Zhoushan, *China* **77 B14** 30 1N 122 6 E
Zhoushan Dao, *China* **77 C14** 30 5N 122 10 E
Zhouzhi, *China* **74 G5** 34 10N 108 12 E
Zhovti Vody, *Ukraine* **59 H7** 48 21N 33 31 E
Zhovtneve, *Ukraine* **59 J7** 46 54N 32 3 E
Zhovtnevoye = Zhovtneve, *Ukraine* **59 J7** 46 54N 32 3 E
Zhu Jiang →, *China* **77 F9** 22 45N 113 37 E
Zhuanghe, *China* **75 E12** 39 40N 123 0 E
Zhūantöbe, *Kazakstan* **65 A4** 44 46N 68 49 E
Zhucheng, *China* **75 G10** 36 0N 119 27 E
Zhugqu, *China* **74 H3** 33 40N 104 30 E
Zhuhai, *China* **77 F9** 22 17N 113 34 E
Zhuji, *China* **77 C13** 29 40N 120 10 E
Zhujiang Kou, *China* **69 G10** 22 20N 113 45 E
Zhukovka, *Russia* **58 F7** 53 35N 33 50 E
Zhumadian, *China* **74 H8** 32 59N 114 2 E
Zhuo Xian = Zhuozhou, *China* **74 E8** 39 28N 115 58 E
Zhuolu, *China* **74 D8** 40 20N 115 12 E
Zhuozhou, *China* **74 E8** 39 28N 115 58 E
Zhuozi, *China* **74 D7** 41 0N 112 25 E
Zhushan, *China* **77 A8** 32 15N 110 13 E
Zhuxi, *China* **76 A7** 32 25N 109 40 E
Zhuzhou, *China* **77 D9** 27 49N 113 12 E
Zhytomyr, *Ukraine* **59 G5** 50 20N 28 40 E
Zi Shui →, *China* **77 C9** 28 40N 112 40 E
Žiar nad Hronom, *Slovak Rep.* **35 C11** 48 35N 18 53 E
Zīārān, *Iran* **97 B6** 36 7N 50 32 E
Ziarat, *Pakistan* **92 D2** 30 25N 67 49 E
Zibo, *China* **75 F10** 36 47N 118 3 E
Zichang, *China* **74 F5** 37 18N 109 40 E
Zidarovo, *Bulgaria* **51 D11** 42 20N 27 24 E
Ziębice, *Poland* **55 H4** 50 37N 17 2 E
Zielona Góra, *Poland* **55 G2** 51 57N 15 31 E
Zierikzee, *Neths.* **24 C3** 51 40N 3 55 E
Ziesar, *Germany* **30 C8** 52 16N 12 17 E
Zifta, *Egypt* **106 H7** 30 43N 31 14 E
Zigey, *Chad* **109 F3** 14 43N 15 50 E
Zigon, *Burma* **90 F5** 18 20N 95 37 E
Zigong, *China* **76 C5** 29 15N 104 48 E
Ziguinchor, *Senegal* **112 C1** 12 35N 16 20W
Zihuatanejo, *Mexico* **162 D4** 17 38N 101 33W
Zijin, *China* **77 F10** 23 33N 115 8 E
Zile, *Turkey* **100 B6** 40 15N 35 52 E
Žilina, *Slovak Rep.* **35 B11** 49 12N 18 42 E
Žilinský □, *Slovak Rep.* **35 B12** 49 10N 19 0 E
Zillah, *Libya* **108 C3** 28 30N 17 33 E
Zillertaler Alpen, *Austria* **34 D4** 47 6N 11 45 E
Zima, *Russia* **67 D11** 54 0N 102 5 E
Zimane, Adrar in, *Algeria* **111 D5** 22 10N 4 30 E
Zimapán, *Mexico* **163 C5** 20 54N 99 20W
Zimba, *Zambia* **119 F2** 17 20 S 26 11 E
Zimbabwe, *Zimbabwe* **119 G3** 20 16 S 30 54 E
Zimbabwe ■, *Africa* **119 F3** 19 0 S 30 0 E
Zimi, *S. Leone* **112 D2** 7 20N 11 20W
Zimnicea, *Romania* **53 G10** 43 40N 25 22 E
Zimovniki, *Russia* **61 G6** 47 10N 42 25 E
Zina, *Cent. Amer.* **109 F2** 11 19N 14 54 E
Zinal, *Switz.* **32 D5** 46 8N 7 38 E
Zinave, Parque Nacional de, *Mozam.* **117 C5** 21 35 S 33 40 E
Zinder, *Niger* **113 C6** 13 48N 9 0 E
Zinga, *C.A.R.* **114 B3** 3 49N 18 34 E
Zinga, *Tanzania* **119 D4** 9 16 S 38 49 E
Zingst, *Germany* **30 A8** 54 26N 12 39 E
Ziniaré, *Burkina Faso* **113 C4** 12 35N 1 18W
Zinnowitz, *Germany* **30 A9** 54 4N 13 54 E
Zion, *U.S.A.* **157 B9** 42 27N 87 50W
Zion Nat. Park, *U.S.A.* **159 H7** 37 15N 113 5W
Zionsville, *U.S.A.* **157 E10** 39 57N 86 16W
Zipaquirá, *Colombia* **168 C3** 5 0N 74 0W
Zirbitzkogel, *Austria* **34 D7** 47 4N 14 34 E
Zirc, *Hungary* **52 C2** 47 17N 17 52 E
Žiri, *Slovenia* **45 B11** 46 5N 14 5 E
Žirje, *Croatia* **45 E12** 43 39N 15 42 E
Zirl, *Austria* **34 D4** 47 17N 11 14 E
Zirndorf, *Germany* **31 F6** 49 27N 10 57 E
Ziros, *Greece* **39 E7** 35 5N 26 8 E
Zirreh, Gowd-e, *Afghan.* **91 C1** 29 45N 62 0 E
Zisterdorf, *Austria* **35 C9** 48 33N 16 45 E
Zitácuaro, *Mexico* **162 D4** 19 28N 100 21W
Žitava →, *Slovak Rep.* **35 C11** 48 14N 18 21 E
Žitište, *Serbia, Yug.* **52 E5** 45 30N 20 32 E
Zitong, *China* **76 B5** 31 37N 105 10 E
Zítsa, *Greece* **48 B2** 39 47N 20 40 E
Zittau, *Germany* **30 E10** 50 53N 14 48 E
Zitundo, *Mozam.* **117 D5** 26 48 S 32 47 E
Živinice, *Bos.-H.* **52 F3** 44 27N 18 36 E
Ziwa Maghariba □, *Tanzania* **118 C3** 2 0 S 31 30 E
Ziway, L., *Ethiopia* **107 F4** 8 0N 38 50 E
Zixi, *China* **77 D11** 27 45N 117 4 E
Zixing, *China* **77 E9** 25 59N 113 21 E
Ziyang, *Shaanxi, China* **74 H5** 32 32N 108 31 E
Ziyang, *Sichuan, China* **76 B5** 30 6N 104 40 E
Ziyuan, *China* **77 D8** 26 2N 110 40 E
Ziyun, *China* **76 E6** 25 45N 106 5 E
Ziz, Oued →, *Morocco* **110 B4** 31 40N 4 15W
Zizhong, *China* **76 C5** 29 48N 104 47 E
Zlarin, *Croatia* **45 E12** 43 42N 15 49 E
Zlatar, *Croatia* **45 B13** 46 5N 16 3 E
Zlatar, *Serbia, Yug.* **50 C3** 43 25N 19 47 E
Zlataritsa, *Bulgaria* **51 C9** 43 2N 25 55 E
Zlaté Moravce, *Slovak Rep.* **35 C11** 48 23N 18 24 E
Zlatibor, *Serbia, Yug.* **50 C3** 43 45N 19 43 E
Zlatitsa, *Bulgaria* **51 D8** 42 41N 24 7 E
Zlatna, *Romania* **53 D8** 46 8N 23 11 E
Zlatna Panega, *Bulgaria* **51 C8** 43 5N 24 9 E
Zlatni Pyasŭtsi, *Bulgaria* **51 C12** 43 17N 28 3 E
Zlatograd, *Bulgaria* **51 E9** 41 22N 25 7 E
Zlatoust, *Russia* **64 D7** 55 10N 59 40 E
Zletovo, *Macedonia* **50 E6** 41 59N 22 17 E
Zlín, *Czech Rep.* **35 B10** 49 14N 17 40 E
Z̨līṭan, *Libya* **108 B2** 32 32N 14 35 E
Złocieniec, *Poland* **54 E3** 53 30N 16 1 E
Złoczew, *Poland* **55 G5** 51 24N 18 35 E
Zlot, *Serbia, Yug.* **50 B5** 44 1N 21 58 E
Złotoryja, *Poland* **55 G2** 51 8N 15 55 E
Złotów, *Poland* **54 E4** 53 22N 17 2 E
Zmeinogorsk, *Kazakstan* **66 D9** 51 10N 82 13 E
Żmigród, *Poland* **55 G3** 51 28N 16 53 E
Zmiyev, *Ukraine* **59 H9** 49 39N 36 27 E
Znamenka = Znamyanka, *Ukraine* **59 H7** 48 45N 32 30 E
Znamyanka, *Ukraine* **59 H7** 48 45N 32 30 E
Żnin, *Poland* **55 F4** 52 51N 17 44 E
Znojmo, *Czech Rep.* **34 C9** 48 50N 16 2 E
Zobeyrī, *Iran* **96 C5** 34 10N 46 40 E
Zobia, *Dem. Rep. of the Congo* **118 B2** 3 0N 25 59 E
Zoetermeer, *Neths.* **24 B4** 52 3N 4 30 E
Zofingen, *Switz.* **32 B5** 47 17N 7 56 E
Zogang, *China* **76 C1** 29 55N 97 42 E
Zogno, *Italy* **44 C6** 45 48N 9 40 E
Zogqên, *China* **76 A2** 32 13N 98 47 E
Zolfo Springs, *U.S.A.* **153 H8** 27 30N 81 48W
Zollikofen, *Switz.* **32 C4** 47 0N 7 28 E
Zollikon, *Switz.* **33 B7** 47 21N 8 34 E
Zolochev = Zolochiv, *Ukraine* **59 H3** 49 45N 24 51 E
Zolochiv, *Ukraine* **59 H3** 49 45N 24 51 E
Zolotonosha, *Ukraine* **59 H7** 49 39N 32 5 E
Zomba, *Malawi* **119 F4** 15 22 S 35 19 E
Zongo, *Dem. Rep. of the Congo* **114 B3** 4 20N 18 35 E
Zonguldak, *Turkey* **100 B4** 41 28N 31 50 E
Zongyang, *China* **77 B11** 30 42N 117 12 E
Zonqor Pt., *Malta* **38 F8** 35 52N 14 34 E
Zonza, *France* **29 G13** 41 45N 9 11 E
Zoo Baba, *Niger* **109 E2** 18 13N 13 2 E
Zorgo, *Burkina Faso* **113 C4** 12 15N 0 35W
Zorita, *Spain* **43 F5** 39 17N 5 39W
Zorleni, *Romania* **53 D12** 46 14N 27 44 E
Zornitsa, *Bulgaria* **51 D10** 42 23N 26 58 E
Zorritos, *Peru* **172 A1** 3 43 S 80 40W
Żory, *Poland* **55 H5** 50 3N 18 44 E
Zorzor, *Liberia* **112 D3** 7 46N 9 28W
Zossen, *Germany* **30 C9** 52 13N 13 27 E
Zou Xiang, *China* **74 G9** 35 30N 116 58 E
Zouan-Hounien, *Ivory C.* **112 D3** 6 55N 8 15W
Zouar, *Chad* **109 D3** 20 30N 16 32 E
Zouérate = Zouîrât, *Mauritania* **110 D2** 22 44N 12 21W
Zouîrât, *Mauritania* **110 D2** 22 44N 12 21W
Zouri, *Gabon* **114 C1** 1 1 S 8 53 E
Zourika, *Niger* **113 B6** 19 16N 7 52 E
Zourma, *Burkina Faso* **113 C4** 11 20N 0 50W
Zousfana, O. →, *Algeria* **111 B4** 31 28N 2 17W
Zoutkamp, *Neths.* **24 A6** 53 20N 6 18 E
Zrenjanin, *Serbia, Yug.* **52 E5** 45 22N 20 23 E
Zuarungu, *Ghana* **113 C4** 10 49N 0 46W
Zuba, *Nigeria* **113 D6** 9 11N 7 12 E
Zubayr, *Yemen* **98 D3** 15 3N 42 10 E
Zubtsov, *Russia* **58 D8** 56 10N 34 34 E
Zudáñez, *Bolivia* **173 D5** 19 6 S 64 44W
Zuénoula, *Ivory C.* **112 D3** 7 34N 6 3W
Zuera, *Spain* **40 D4** 41 51N 0 49W
Zuetina = Az Zuwaytīnah, *Libya* **108 B4** 30 58N 20 7 E
Z̨ufār, *Oman* **99 C6** 17 40N 54 0 E
Zug, *Switz.* **33 B7** 47 10N 8 31 E
Zug, *W. Sahara* **110 D2** 21 36N 14 9W
Zug □, *Switz.* **33 B7** 47 9N 8 35 E
Zugdidi, *Georgia* **61 J5** 42 30N 41 55 E
Zugersee, *Switz.* **33 B7** 47 7N 8 35 E
Zugspitze, *Germany* **31 H6** 47 25N 10 59 E
Zuid-Holland □, *Neths.* **24 C4** 52 0N 4 35 E
Zuidbeveland, *Neths.* **24 C3** 51 30N 3 50 E
Zuidhorn, *Neths.* **24 A6** 53 15N 6 23 E
Zújar, *Spain* **43 H8** 37 34N 2 50W
Zújar →, *Spain* **43 G5** 39 1N 5 47W
Żukowo, *Poland* **54 D5** 54 21N 18 22 E
Zula, *Eritrea* **107 D4** 15 17N 39 40 E
Zulia □, *Venezuela* **168 B3** 10 0N 72 10W
Zülpich, *Germany* **30 E2** 50 41N 6 39 E
Zumaia, *Spain* **40 B2** 43 19N 2 15W
Zumárraga, *Spain* **40 B2** 43 5N 2 19W
Zumbo, *Mozam.* **119 F3** 15 35 S 30 26 E
Zummo, *Nigeria* **113 D7** 9 51N 12 59 E
Zumpango, *Mexico* **163 D5** 19 48N 99 6W
Zundi, *Angola* **115 E3** 10 28 S 16 48 E
Zungeru, *Nigeria* **113 D6** 9 48N 6 8 E
Zunhua, *China* **75 D9** 40 18N 117 58 E
Zuni, *U.S.A.* **159 J9** 35 4N 108 51W
Zunyi, *China* **76 D6** 27 42N 106 53 E
Zuo Jiang →, *China* **76 F6** 22 50N 108 6 E
Zuozhou, *China* **76 F6** 22 42N 107 27 E
Županja, *Croatia* **52 E3** 45 4N 18 43 E
Žur, *Kosovo, Yug.* **50 D4** 42 13N 20 34 E
Zura, *Russia* **64 C4** 57 36N 53 24 E
Zurbātīyah, *Iraq* **101 F12** 33 9N 46 3 E
Zürich, *Switz.* **33 B7** 47 22N 8 32 E
Zürich □, *Switz.* **33 B7** 47 26N 8 40 E
Zürichsee, *Switz.* **33 B7** 47 18N 8 40 E
Żuromin, *Poland* **55 E6** 53 4N 19 51 E
Zurrieq, *Malta* **38 F7** 35 50N 14 28 E
Zurzach, *Switz.* **33 A6** 47 35N 8 18 E
Žut, *Croatia* **45 E12** 43 52N 15 17 E
Zutphen, *Neths.* **24 B6** 52 9N 6 12 E
Zuurberg Nat. Park, *S. Africa* **116 E4** 33 12 S 25 32 E
Zuwārah, *Libya* **108 B2** 32 58N 12 1 E
Zuyevka, *Russia* **64 B3** 58 27N 51 10 E
Zūzan, *Iran* **97 C8** 34 22N 59 53 E
Žužemberk, *Slovenia* **45 C11** 45 52N 14 56 E
Zvenigorodka = Zvenyhorodka, *Ukraine* **59 H6** 49 4N 30 56 E
Zvenyhorodka, *Ukraine* **59 H6** 49 4N 30 56 E
Zverinogolovskoye, *Russia* **66 D7** 54 26N 64 50 E
Zvezdets, *Bulgaria* **51 D11** 42 6N 27 26 E
Zvishavane, *Zimbabwe* **119 G3** 20 17 S 30 2 E
Zvolen, *Slovak Rep.* **35 C12** 48 33N 19 10 E
Zvonce, *Serbia, Yug.* **50 D6** 42 57N 22 34 E
Zvornik, *Bos.-H.* **52 F4** 44 26N 19 5 E
Zwedru = Tchien, *Liberia* **112 D3** 5 59N 8 15W
Zweibrücken, *Germany* **31 F3** 49 15N 7 21 E
Zweisimmen, *Switz.* **32 C4** 46 33N 7 22 E
Zwenkau, *Germany* **30 D8** 51 13N 12 20 E
Zwettl, *Austria* **34 C8** 48 35N 15 9 E
Zwickau, *Germany* **30 E8** 50 44N 12 30 E
Zwierzyniec, *Poland* **55 H9** 50 36N 22 58 E
Zwiesel, *Germany* **31 F9** 49 1N 13 13 E
Zwoleń, *Poland* **55 G8** 51 21N 21 36 E
Zwolle, *Neths.* **24 B6** 52 31N 6 6 E
Zwolle, *U.S.A.* **155 K8** 31 38N 93 39W
Żychlin, *Poland* **55 F6** 52 15N 19 37 E
Żyrardów, *Poland* **55 F7** 52 3N 20 28 E
Zyryan, *Kazakstan* **66 E9** 49 43N 84 20 E
Zyryanka, *Russia* **67 C16** 65 45N 150 51 E
Zyryanovsk = Zyryan, *Kazakstan* **66 E9** 49 43N 84 20 E
Żywiec, *Poland* **55 J6** 49 42N 19 10 E

KEY TO EUROPEAN MAP PAGES

Large scale maps (>1:3 900 000)
Medium scale maps (1:4 000 000 – 1:9 900 000)
Small scale maps (<1:10 000 000)

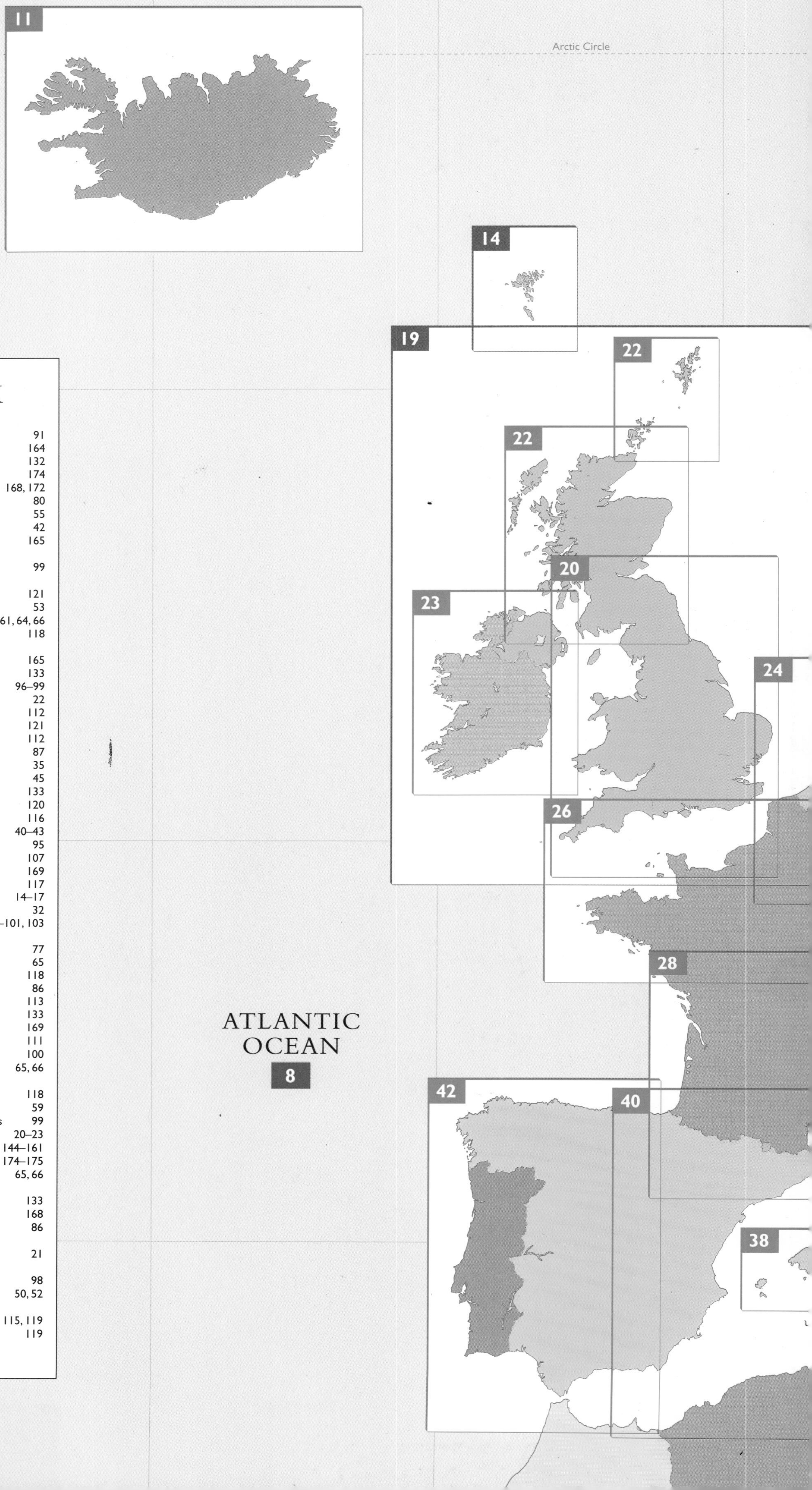

11
Arctic Circle
14
19
22
22
20
23
24
26
28
ATLANTIC OCEAN
8
42
40
38

World Country Index